ISBN 978-0-428-63158-1
PIBN 11252519

CHAMBERS'S

EDINBURGH JOURNAL.

NEW SERIES.

CONDUCTED BY

WILLIAM AND ROBERT CHAMBERS,

EDITORS OF 'CHAMBERS'S EDUCATIONAL COURSE,' 'INFORMATION FOR THE PEOPLE,' &c.

VOLUME III.

Nos. 53 TO 78. JANUARY—JUNE, 1845.

WILLIAM AND ROBERT CHAMBERS, EDINBURGH;
AND Wm. S. ORR, LONDON.

MDCCCXLV.

LONDON:
BRADBURY AND EVANS, PRINTERS, WHITEFRIARS.

INDEX.

FAMILIAR SKETCHES AND MORAL ESSAYS.

POETRY.

TALES.

BIOGRAPHIC SKETCHES.

MISCELLANEOUS ARTICLES OF INSTRUCTION AND ENTERTAINMENT.

ANECDOTES AND PARAGRAPHS.

CONDUCTED BY WILLIAM AND ROBERT CHAMBERS, EDITORS OF 'CHAMBERS'S INFORMATION FOR THE PEOPLE,' 'CHAMBERS'S EDUCATIONAL COURSE,' &c.

No. 53. New Series. SATURDAY, JANUARY 4, 1845. Price 1½d.

A FEW WORDS TO OUR READERS.

It is nine years since we addressed our readers in a formal manner about ourselves. Will they have patience with an egotism which observes such a long silence? We presume they will, and shall therefore proceed to say a few words about our position and prospects.

The Journal is now entering upon its fourteenth year. We begin to get letters from lady subscribers, who tell us they commenced reading it when they were little girls, and now have two babies rapidly rising to strike in as readers too. In fact, it is becoming a somewhat venerable publication. Well, we trust it is not the worse for that, but somewhat the better. We are at least assured that its acceptance with the public is not less than it ever was, for its sale—raised one-half by the change of size—is not much under ninety thousand copies. The most popular magazines circulate, we believe, from six to nine thousand; but the sale of the Journal in its magazine shape alone (the monthly part being strictly a magazine) is about forty thousand. During the currency of this work, we have brought out several others: a series of books designed to aid in the realisation of an improved education;* a kind of encyclopædia for the middle and working-classes;† a history of English literature, chiefly intended to introduce the young to the Pantheon of our national authors.‡ And all of these works have met with success hardly less marked than that of the Journal. Indeed, that of the Information for the People has been considerably more, for the average sale of the numbers of that publication has been about a hundred and thirty thousand—a fact, we believe, unprecedented in the same department of literature. More recently we have commenced another work, a series of Tracts designed for the instruction and entertainment of a still humbler class of readers;§ and already it would appear as if the ordinary sale of this work is to be greatly beyond that of any other, the impressions required of the first few numbers (all yet prepared) having been in no case less than a hundred and fifty thousand, and in some instances nearly two hundred thousand, copies. Verily, it must be admitted, there is here a vast diffusion of literature, of whatever kind it may be. Or may we not rather say that these things mark an entirely new era in literature, something which throws all the former efforts of the press into the shade?

Let us just look for a moment into the details of this phenomenon. We write at present in a huge building of four storeys, flanked by a powerful steam-engine, and with the noise of ten printing machines continually sounding in our ears. Several of these are engaged in working off impressions, the production of which at a common hand-press, such as formed the sole means of typography a few years ago, would have required nearly the time then requisite for a voyage to India and back. A hundred and twenty persons are required for all the duties which proceed in this large structure, though these have exclusively a regard to works edited by ourselves. Upwards of a quarter of a million of printed sheets leave the house each week, being as many as the whole newspaper press of Scotland issued in a month about the year 1833. Our publications, which at first were expected by the booksellers to be the ruin of their business, do not yield them less than fifteen thousand pounds a-year of profit; while yet the number of ordinary books published each year, instead of being diminished, is considerably increased. These are some of the material details; but who shall say what are the particulars of the moral results of this enormous contagion of paper and print! We willingly allow each man to judge from what he observes in his own familiar circle. We have, for our part, a general and all-sufficient faith.

Friends to whom we chance to mention some of these matters, often say to us, 'What a power for good or evil you possess!' There could not be a greater mistake. It is not a power for evil at all. This has been tried, and fully proved, by other editors. Similar works without number have been presented to the public, but, because they pandered to the meaner feelings of our nature, they invariably failed. We have ever felt, that, whatever might be our own inclinations, we must aim at the pure, the elevating, and good, if we would wish our publications to acquire any permanent hold of the public mind. It is a common notion, we believe, among the clever fellows, that the public is to be gulled, tickled, addressed as a child, and that, the lower the tone assumed, they will be the more pleased. Our experience says quite the reverse. We have, and always have had, an unfeigned respect for both the intellectual and moral character of the public. We sincerely believe that the higher sentiments rule its general procedure, and that the grosser souls are in all ordinary circumstances powerless. We therefore never doubted that, in earnestly seeking to give good counsel and innocent entertainment, we were taking the course which common prudence would have dictated, all the sophistications of all the Jenkinsons notwithstanding; and it is thus that we feel assured of our publications being attended with good effects upon the community. They only have a large sale because they address and meet responses in the better feelings of the mass of our countrymen.

When the publications of Mr Knight and others are

* Educational Course—37 volumes published.

† Information for the People, 2 vols. royal 8vo.

‡ Cyclopædia of English Literature, 2 vols. royal 8vo.

§ Miscellany of Useful and Entertaining Tracts, appearing in weekly numbers at a penny and halfpenny each.

taken into account, it will be seen that the amount of literature now diffused among the people must be something very different from what it was a few years ago. On a moderate calculation, we cannot doubt that our own publications are fully doubled by the other works of a respectable kind now issued weekly; that is to say, there are not fewer than half a million of cheap sheets published every week. Add to these the very considerable number of cheap book-publications, copyright and otherwise, and it must be apparent that there is a moral agency at work in this country such as has never been formerly known, except in the most feeble form. Is it not now, indeed, for the first time, that the powers of the printing-press have been turned to their right account? And yet, after all, it is highly questionable if anything like full advantage has been taken of the powers of this marvellous engine. There is no default in its own mechanism, but the mechanism for the diffusion of its productions is still far from being what is desirable. The system of bookselling in this country has not undergone an improvement at all comparable to that which we have seen in the paper-making and typographical departments. No fault is it in the members of that excellent fraternity. But books such as we refer to ought to be sold by many others besides ordinary booksellers. Why should it be that tea, tobacco, and even less approvable articles demanded by the people, should be purchasable in the smallest quantities in every village in the empire, and not that literature which has become, in one form or another, almost as much a necessary of life as any? Surely, in many of the little establishments where the needs and cravings of the frail body are supplied, those of the immortal spirit might also be gratified; and that without necessarily diminishing the trade of the ordinary booksellers? One fact will illustrate this. In a little village, where at one time none of our publications were sold, a philanthropic gentleman induced a female dealer in small wares to commence selling the 'Tracts.' She quickly found regular customers for forty copies. Here were forty copies sold where formerly the work was unheard of; and we cannot doubt that thousands of places are in the like predicament. There must certainly be some improvement in the bookselling system of the country; we must have this kind of wares presented in many quarters where it formerly was unthought of, ere we can say that the system of cheap publication is complete, or has 'gathered all its fame.' A benevolent friend has suggested that persons verging upon pauperism might often help themselves in some degree to a livelihood, if individuals taking a kindly interest in them were to furnish them with a first stock of such wares. We have had the plan tried in several instances, and have found it effectual.* Perhaps by such means, in addition to all others, the extreme limits of the diffusibility of popular literature might in time be reached.

When this point is attained, and great effects begin to become apparent to those who watch the signs of nations, it is not unlikely that the humble services of the individuals now addressing the public will be remembered and inquired into. It will perhaps be recollected that Chambers's Journal was the first periodical work which aimed at giving respectable literature at a price which made it accessible to every class of persons really desirous of reading, and that in that and several other publications, without the slightest extraneous support, its editors arrived at and maintained for several years an extraordinary degree of success. May it not then be asked, what was the cause of this success? To what are we to attribute the existence of that vast ten-machine printing-house? Will it be worth while to listen for a moment to the impressions which were entertained on that subject by ourselves? Presuming that there may be some curiosity on such a point, we will here mention that we attribute it not to any peculiar literary talent; we attribute it not to any extraordinary intellectual gifts; neither do we think fortune had anything whatever to do with it. It arose solely from the view we took of the duties resting upon those who make a profession of the pen. We felt, in the first place, that foresight, punctuality, and other homely and prudential virtues, were necessary even for the purpose of enabling us to possess our minds in peace—that peace without which no studious life can be conducted to any good results. And it was but a corollary from that view, that we should have a publishing system under our own command, as by no other means could the requisite unity of movement, and procedure have been attained. On this point we would observe incidentally, that we trust yet to make out a problem of no small consequence to men of letters—that is to say, we trust to establish, that to employ a printing and bookselling system to work out his purposes, is a much more eligible position for the literary labourer, than to come with all his powers of thought, and the aspirations attending them, and subordinate these to a man of trade. We think it will be found that the first position, which is ours, is that by far the best fitted to secure independence of action, and even that elevation of mind which is supposed to rest apart from trade, as well as exemption from those degrading cares which are so hostile to the exercise of the higher faculties, and have been the shipwreck of so many votaries of letters. We further felt that the tasks assumed by us were of a very different character from what their external features indicated to the shallower class of minds. Even to speak of materialities alone, the aggregate vastness of a cheap publication was calculated to impress a strong sense of the importance of such a work. What came before the eyes of individuals as a single sheet at an infinitesimal price, presented itself to our sense in colossal piles of paper and print, and large commercial transactions. At the fountain-head, its respectability, in the common sense of the word, could not be matter of doubt, whatever it might in the remote rills of diffusion. But, remarking the great appetency of the middle and humbler classes for the reading of such works, it was impossible not to advance to far higher considerations, and see, in the establishment of such a miscellany as the Journal, the attainment of a predicatorial position hardly paralleled in the country. It fully appeared that such a work, if conducted in a right spirit, might enable its editors weekly to address an audience of unexampled numbers. We felt that by this means a vast amount of unequivocal good might be effected amongst the humbler classes in particular. Coming before them with no stamp of authority to raise prejudice, but as the undoubted friend of all, it could convey counsel and instruction where more august missionaries might fail. Gaining the heart of the poor man, always inclined to jealousy, it might, by dint of its absolute transparent well-meaning, force reproofs and maxims upon him which he would take from no other hand. By such a work the young might be, even in the receipt of amusement, actuated to industrious and honourable courses. Everywhere, by presenting entertainment of a pure nature, and of superior attractiveness, that which was reprehensible might be superseded. Nor might it be impossible, even in so small a work, to present papers of an original kind in the departments of fancy and humour, as well as of observation and re-

* A mendicant, applying for alms at our office in Glasgow, was furnished with two copies of a tract, that he might endeavour to sell them in the streets, and thus make money by a more legitimate mode. He disposed of them in ten minutes, and came back with the money to purchase more. Having sold these also, he returned for a new supply, and, in short, his transactions in four hours reached six shillings, leaving himself a clear gain of one and sixpence. He was to have come back to renew his efforts next morning; but, unfortunately, from whatever cause, he never re-appeared.

flection, such as might be expected to cultivate the higher powers of the popular intellect. While, then, many superficial persons scoffed at the course we had entered upon, we saw in it the means of a large usefulness, and gave ourselves to it with cordial good-will. Determining first upon a few leading principles—particularly that political and theological controversy should never receive a moment's attention; animated by sincere and earnest wishes to promote whatever was clearly calculated to be beneficial to our fellow-creatures in the mass; despising all trivial and petty objects, and aiming ever to confer a dignity upon our own pursuits—we advanced in our course, and persevered in it year after year; never once doubting that the issue would justify and illustrate our first resolutions. The result, we may surely say, is to some extent determined, and that in a manner favourable to the soundness of our views; for how otherwise could it be that (to look no higher for proof) there is at this time no literary *system* in the country which approaches ours in magnitude? How else should it be that, while all other literary operations are conducted with more or less jarring between associated interests, and while most have to resort to extraneous expedients for success, we scatter the matter of hundreds of thousands of volumes annually over the land, without experiencing the slightest disturbance from sordid details, or ever having to look a moment beyond the intrinsic value of the article itself for a means of arresting public attention.

We would, in conclusion, express our humble trust that the ordinary readers of the Journal can be under no risk of misunderstanding the nature of these remarks. We have spoken in the language of earnestness and of truth, on a subject on which we are conscious of entertaining other besides feelings of self-love, and where public interests are, we think, as much concerned as our own. This kind of language usually meets with sympathy, and we humbly hope that on the present occasion there will be no exception from the rule.

SHORT NOTES ON THE WEST INDIES.

BY A LATE RESIDENT.

FIRST ARTICLE.

There are three things which forcibly attract the eye of a European upon entering a town in one of the West India islands, and these are, the houses, the streets, and the colour of the people. The houses are rendered remarkable from various circumstances. Built chiefly of wood, they are shingled, and not tiled, and are generally painted white, with green Venetian blinds terminating the upper part of the front of each storey. In towns, the streets of which lie on a declivity, it is not unusual to observe the houses perched high above the streets, their elevation being occasioned by the gradual washing away of the soil by the heavy rains which fall at certain seasons. The advantage of such a location is, a slight freedom from the dust which three-fourths of the year flies about in clouds; but perhaps this is counterbalanced by the necessity for more frequently repairing the foundations of the houses, and of adding occasionally to the flights of steps by which they are approached, lest communication with the inhabitants should be entirely cut off. One striking peculiarity of a West India house is the circumstance of its being incapable of almost any species of privacy. The apartments all open into each other, and are so situated, that a stranger on his first entrance has, for the most part, a panoramic view of every one, from the piazza to the kitchen. One of the reasons assigned for the adoption of this style of building is, that it produces a free circulation of air; another, that it enabled the master or mistress, during the periods of slavery, to keep a watchful eye over the proceedings of the slaves. But whatever the cause, to a European so complete an exposure of the whole economy of a domestic establishment is far from pleasing.

I have spoken of the piazza. This every one knows to be an apartment of, or adjunct to, the house—half-promenade, half-sitting room. Around this are the Venetian windows placed, and in it the family sit in the cool of the evening, to receive the full benefit of the 'land-wind,' to enjoy social converse, observe the passers-by, or pass the time in other equally important occupations.

The houses have no bells, and knockers are not universal; the knuckles, a walking-stick, or an umbrella handle frequently supplying their place. Carpets are unknown, but oil-cloths are sometimes used in their stead, being cooler. The floors are, however, more frequently polished, as in France; with this difference, that the hands and knees are employed in the one case, and in the other the feet. Stoves and grates are of course unnecessary, and the chimney-tops which adorn the roofs of houses in European towns are absent.

There are few moneyed builders, or speculations in building, in the West Indies. It therefore follows that there is little uniformity in the situations of the houses, and that a house which requires to be propped up, frequently stands adjacent to one newly erected. This gives the towns an exceedingly irregular and unsightly appearance, notwithstanding that the streets run generally at right angles. The irregular appearance is increased by a want of uniformity in the erection of the approaches to the houses, or flights of steps, and sometimes the absence of any such convenience. The carriage ways are not paved, and I may add, that causeways or flag-pavements for foot-passengers are seldom to be met with. In the rainy seasons, the water accumulates in these streets in floods, and foundations—sometimes old houses—are washed away. It is no uninteresting sight to observe the 'rivers' rushing down the principal streets during a heavy shower of rain, and the circumstances which usually accompany such an event. On come the floods, foaming and frothing at every bound; now eddying deep in a hollow of the street, now whirling round some immoveable obstacle. Away go steps, stones, palings, fences, trees, &c. till one is disposed to think half the town in danger of removal.

The streets being usually in straight lines, one is enabled generally to see their whole length: and when the mountains terminate the view at one end and the sea at the other, the effect is beautiful, and compensates in some degree for minor irregularities, bad repairs, or heavy sand. At any rate, while admiring the beauty and grandeur of the distant mountains, or the majesty of the somewhat nearer sea, all remembrance of unsightly defects, even to the droves of hungry pigs which rove in all the dignity of filth and independence about the streets, is lost. But perhaps the different hues observable in the visages of the population, present to the stranger a more interesting, because more extraordinary appearance. There are few shades of human complexion, from the sickly white of the Albino to the deep black of the Mandingo, which may not be observed in one of the towns of the West Indies. To the stranger full of the memory of the roseate complexions of Europe, the sallow tint which pervades most countenances conveys the impression of illness; and a dread of miasma, fever, &c. is apt to come across his mind. In bodily health, however, there are few among those whom he observes inferior to the heartiest peasant in England; and 'Johnny Newcome' would perhaps be startled to learn, as is asserted on good authority, that he must part with a portion of his florid and robust health before he becomes acclimated, and beyond the probable reach of that terror to Europeans—yellow fever.

The Negro Dialect.—When the negro addresses a stranger with 'Huddie, massa,' a little reflection may enable the latter to discover the meaning, 'How do you do, master?' When he says 'Gar-a mightie bless you,' a little further reflection may lead to the discovery, that he intends to exclaim, 'God Almighty bless you.' When, however, rolling his tongue, and giving a peculiar broadness to his words, he perhaps inquires, 'An da warra fa, sa, you bin com ya?' the stranger will most probably be fairly puzzled. Nor will he readily learn to comprehend the language of the old Africans. The Creole negro, however, prides himself on his English, and these the stranger may soon very readily understand, although the dialect which is spoken by the Creole is still but of a mongrel description.

From hearing the negro dialect so commonly spoken, the younger branches of respectable families insensibly fall into the habit of speaking it. Hence, when children from England arrive in the West Indies, the purity of their language and pronunciation is a subject of general admiration. And, indeed, pure English will always command attention; for even the heads of respectable families are often themselves not free from a 'touch of the negro brogue,' and many, particularly in country districts, acquire a drawling tone by no means agreeable.

It has been charged against the slave proprietors of the West India colonies, that they invented the negro dialect for the purpose of degrading that class of persons, and keeping them in ignorance. This seems rather a far-fetched charge. The most natural mode of accounting for the dialect seems to be, to regard the pronunciation as originally African, and the jumble of words sometimes used, as a natural admixture of the several dialects of the African tongue with the English, Scotch, Irish, French, and Spanish languages. As the African slave happened to be settled on the property, or attached to the establishment of an Englishman, Scotchman, Irishman, Frenchman, or Spaniard, he would learn a portion of the language and accent of each, which would be communicated to his fellow-countrymen, receiving in return a similar communication of what the others had learned; and the whole being uttered according to the best of their ability—but still with a strong infusion of the African accent—the dialect now under consideration might readily have been formed. Assuredly it would be impossible to invent it; while the master or mistress, so far from entertaining an idea of intended degradation as attached to it, very frequently uses it in a kind or playful mood, when not required to resort to it for the purpose of rendering him or herself intelligible.

An inquiry into the properties of the negro dialect might prove interesting to the philologist. If attempted, among its chief characteristics would be found a frequent elision of terminal consonants, and a fondness for terminal vowels—a constant change in the sound of vowels, most usually from a fine to a broad sound—a brevity of expression, and contraction and union of words—a predilection for the letter r—a substitution of d for th—and probably a collocation of words in a sentence not far removed from classical—the whole forming, as might be expected, a most uncouth and unmusical mode of communicating ideas.

The Mixtures.—'These mixtures will be the death of us,' observed a lady at the elegant supper-table at a 'ball' given by Sir ——. 'Which?' said a wag; 'the sweets or the company?' The lady meant the company; but as more than fair justice had been done to the dainties and delicacies of the table, there was some point in the inquiry.

It is some years since those high in authority in the colonies overstepped the barriers which prejudice had interposed between the social mingling of the several classes, and extended their hospitality to respectable parties, of whatever colour they might be. But no levelling of distinctions gives satisfaction, and consequently ebullitions of feeling similar to the above occasionally take place. They are, however, chiefly confined to a class of persons whose day went by with the fall of slavery; and a new order of things is quickly springing up, and a new class of persons arising, who all seem willing to admit that respectability of education, occupation, and character, are the only just criteria by which to judge of claims for admission into the first circles of society.

The 1st of August.—The day of universal freedom in the colonies rose brightly and happily for that numerous class of individuals who, first as slaves and subsequently as apprentices, spent their lives in thankless and unrequited toil. It rose serenely and calmly; no noise or bustle, no commotion or disturbance was heard; and as the soft voice of prayer and thanksgiving went abroad upon the breath of morning, a stillness as of the holy Sabbath told that the day would be kept as one of solemn fast. The public offices remained closed, and private individuals did honour to the occasion, in abstaining from pursuing their accustomed daily avocations. At the usual hour of public prayer might be observed thousands proceeding to the several places of worship—chiefly, however, those for whose benefit the great boon had been given. The occasion will induce us to believe that their prayers were fervent, and their thanksgivings sincere. The service over, the emancipated greeted each other with heartfelt congratulations at the arrival of the day which many among them had never expected to behold, but which as a body they had so ardently desired. Their countenances were lighted up with joy, the laugh went round, and each seemed supremely happy.

Were there, however, no melancholy hearts on this great day of rejoicing? were all faces lighted up with smiles? or were there not heavy hearts and weeping eyes? There were. The master had been deprived of his 'property.' He could not sympathise in the general joy. True, compensation in part had been awarded him; yet the certainty with which he could previously look forward to the cultivation of his land had been taken away, and to him the future was now a blank. His heart then was heavy. The great number of persons dependent on the prosperity of the master partook of his doubts and fears. Their hearts were also heavy. A number of females depended for subsistence on the weekly wages which they received for the services of one, two, or three slaves. When the compensation which they had received had been expended, what resource had they left? None, probably, save the parish. Their hearts then were also heavy. Indeed, on this great day of the mighty triumph of justice and benevolence over wrong and despotic principles, it is difficult to say whether the amount of sorrow and suffering which was felt exceeded or fell short of the amount of joy which seemed so universally to pervade at least one portion of society.

Domestic Pets.—In England, the mistress of an establishment pets a parrot or canary bird. In the West Indies, she sometimes also pets a little black or coloured boy or girl, who in the end turns out of course to be entirely useless either to him or herself, or any one else. My next-door neighbour, an old maid, who had apparently passed the grand climacteric, had a little black boy, and although the only servant on her premises, he was converted into a pet. The little fellow, at all times obstinate and remarkably insolent, would sometimes prove refractory, whereupon his mistress would strap him. At length, when matters were about resolving themselves into an appeal to the whip, he would climb up a neighbouring tree, and there, occasionally laughing at the old spinster, he would remain till her rage was over, or he was required to perform some domestic office, when, a truce being agreed on, he would leisurely descend. Parties who convert their young servants into pets are not probably aware of the pernicious effect of their intended kindness, or rather perhaps of the gratification of their own feelings. It is impossible to prevent the individuals petted from forming an erroneous idea of their position, and imbibing notions quite incompatible with future service. With these notions they are frequently at the death of their mistresses left unfriended, or, becoming too old to be made pets of, they are cast off, and thus society is burdened with an idle, discontented, ignorant, puffed-up, and ultimately demoralised race. I have every reason to think that most of the profligate women in the West Indies, as well as most of the idle and dissolute of the lower classes, have commenced their career as household pets, and that they have, for their unfortunate and degraded condition, chiefly to thank the injudiciousness of those with whom their periods of infancy and youth were passed.

Acuteness of the Negro.—The acuteness of the negro (and it may be necessary to observe that the term 'negro' is used by me simply in a distinctive sense) has become proverbial. Few, it is known, will overreach him in a bargain where ample discretion has been allowed; and his penetration of character is remarkable. In no mode, however, perhaps, is his shrewdness more apparent than in the converting of his philosophical and moral deductions (if I may be permitted so to speak) into proverbs. There are not many occurrences of a moral or immoral tendency, and yet fewer states of being from which a useful lesson may be derived, for which the negro has not some appropriate adage or proverb. If a negro wish forcibly to express that he has been treated with ingratitude, he says, in his most quiet and resigned manner, 'Good me do, tènkee me get.' If he wish to mark the neglect with which the memory of the departed often meets, he exclaims, 'Man dead, grass grow da him door.' If he wish to express the restraint under which he lies in the expression of his sentiments, he will tell you, 'No say fe want a tongue, mèk cow no talk.' When he would point out how mean and insignificant some men appear when overtaken by misfortune, who are otherwise bold and obtrusive in their demeanour and conversation, he will say, 'When trouble ketch man, buoy britches fit him;' and when he would express how much superior is natural ability without education to education without ability, he exclaims, 'Cunny better dan edication.' 'When trouble day da bush, no bring him in da house,' is one of the adages by which he inculcates caution; and 'Any cry will do fe berrin,' a proverb in which he very satirically expresses the insincerity which too frequently attends the tears of parties at the funeral of a deceased person. I have no doubt a volume might be filled with similar pithy sentences, all in common use among the negroes, and tending to show that this class of persons possess a great deal of acuteness, and are neither deficient in observation nor in judgment. The language in which their ideas are expressed is uncouth, nay, if you will, vulgar, but we know that the diamond is valuable even though unpolished.

Superstitions.—Belief in ghosts is about the most common superstition that can be found in any nation; and there are few of the old unenlightened Creoles of the West Indies who do not pretend to have seen, heard, or felt innumerable ghosts. The enlightened portion of society, as in Europe, either believe or disbelieve these supernatural appearances, according as their love of the marvellous or their moral idiosyncracy directs. I have heard well-informed persons of both places contend for the existence of ghosts, and quote Scripture in support of their views. I knew a talented lady in the West Indies who laboured under the firm conviction that a deceased brother had returned to earth, and spoken to her; and that her deceased husband had entered her bedroom at night while she lay in bed, and played with her feet. Superstitions of this nature are, to say the worst of them, idle. There are others, however, which bespeak weakness of intellect, depravity of heart, and gross mental obscurity and demoralisation. Among the first may be classed certain ceremonies which even at this day accompany the event of death in the families of many old black and coloured persons, who should certainly know better. As soon as a death takes place in such families, every particle of water in the house at the time is thrown away; for death cools his dart in the water as he departs, and it would be improper, if not injurious, to drink it. All the mirrors and looking-glasses in the house are covered, or turned to the walls, lest, forsooth, the spirit of the departed should be reflected in them; while, immediately after the removal of the corpse, the bed on which it was laid is made up, a jar of water placed in the room, and a light kept burning for nine nights; for on these nine nights the deceased returns to his room, when he would require a light to guide his footsteps, and water to quench his thirst. These superstitious practices are only surpassed in folly by the feasts which were formerly held over the graves of the dead African or other party, and the libations offered up at such graves. They prevail in nine-tenths of the old coloured and black families, although it is but justice to say that the younger and more enlightened branches regard them with contempt.

One of the superstitions of a more serious nature, yet equally ludicrous, is the belief that the devil sometimes comes for the soul of the departed who has spent his life in this world as the wicked often do. I am not aware that his Satanic majesty is ever seen; but as he comes at night, and is supposed to be black, his invisibility may be accounted for. However, the rattling of the chains which he brings for the soul of the deceased is distinctly heard, and not by one or two persons, but by a whole neighbourhood; and the traces of his cloven feet along the sand of the street in which the deceased resided are next morning clearly seen. I could name a case in which it is believed by a great many persons, many of them leaders in churches, that all these circumstances occurred; that the rattling of the chains was heard; that just previous to the departure of life, a seeming internal struggle was observed to take place in the body of the deceased; that a whole neighbourhood was disturbed by the clanking noise of the chains; and that crowds of persons went early the succeeding morning to view the marks of the devil's cloven feet!

One of a rather curious description of supernatural appearances of which I have heard, was a peculiar kind of apparition, which nobody seems to have seen. Its proximity was denoted by the rattling of chains (a usual accompaniment on all similar occasions), which, grating horribly on the ear, struck terror into the hearts of all believers. Its name was the 'rolling calf.' Another was a sow and ten pigs. These nocturnal visitors had the credit of viciously pursuing every person they saw in the streets after a certain hour; and hence, after such hour, very few servants could be induced to go out—a good preventive to idle gossiping and gadding about, and probably originally invented as such.

When an infant or young child is to be bathed, a tub of water is frequently placed in the sun, in order that the chill might be taken off; and this is usually done about mid-day. At twelve o'clock, however, day as well as night, 'duppies' (a negro term for ghosts) are permitted to perambulate the earth. How, then, shall they be prevented playing about, or probably bathing in the water? The sign of the cross comes to the aid of the anxious nurse or other domestic; and straightway two sticks are placed across the tub which contains the water, to scare away the duppies. Duppies are also apt to disturb children in the night-time. A Bible placed under their pillow will prove a sufficient protection; and Maunder's Treasury, in mistake for the holy book, has not unfrequently been devoted to the accomplishment of this object.

One may smile at these idle fancies. For the sake of human nature, however, he cannot but lament that they do not stop here; and that in the superstitions connected with Obeahism and Myalism, there is everything to be found that is gross, demoralising, and senseless. Obeahism seems to be but another name for witchcraft, and its practice is accompanied by many of the uncouth ceremonies which usually attended the practice of its European prototype. Like the ingredients of the witches' caldron in Macbeth, the instruments of which the Obeah man makes use for the accomplishment of his nefarious ends are a combination of many strange and ominous things. Earth gathered from a grave, human blood, a piece of wood fashioned in the shape of a coffin, the feathers of the carrion-crow, a white cock, a live serpent, a snake or alligator's tooth, and pieces of eggshell, are among the most common. Resort is had to Obeahism as a means of detecting crime, of influencing the affections or passions, of terrifying the timid, and of obtaining revenge. In the last light, it seems to be deducible into little less than an expert system of poisoning; and deaths innumerable have been attributed to the result of draughts administered under the directions of the Obeah man. Myalism, as far as I understand it, seems a system of counter-witchcraft, equally demoralising, and, I believe, equally pernicious; and it is but a short time since I read an account of a meeting of Myalists for the purpose of 'freeing the shadow' of one of the disciples. Laws against both Myalism and Obeahism are severe; but the enlightenment and religious instruction of the people seem alone calculated to eradicate such practices. An Obeah man sometimes makes confession on his deathbed. His confessions, it is said, often implicate parties who had previously borne respectable characters in their own sphere.

THE AFRANCESADO.*

AN EPISODE OF THE PENINSULAR WAR.

The Levante, or south-east wind, had been blowing strongly for twenty-four hours, and the inhabitants of Cadiz had, as is usual during its prevalence, kept their windows closed, in order to screen themselves from its baneful effects; the Alameda was deserted, the Plaza de San Antonio equally so; and not a single lounger was to be seen in the gay Calle Ancha, the Bond Street of Cadiz.

The bay, too, was bereft of its accustomed animation. Generally, towards sunset, a little fleet of fishing-boats, with their large latteen sails, was to be seen returning to port; but the Levante had now confined them to the mole. The only object that met the eye in the offing was a large boat pulling across from the direction of Rota. As it approached, a horse was perceptible standing in the centre; a man was by his side; and there were four rowers; a fifth individual steered, and seemed at the same time to be keeping watch over some object lying in the stern-sheets. Suddenly the sail was hoisted, and the boat ran up the bay of Cadiz. On nearing the mole, she was hailed enthusiastically by the fishermen and others assembled there. The crew were habited like the generality of Spanish boatmen, in jackets and trousers of coarse brown cloth; wide red worsted sashes encircled their loins; and their heads were covered with woollen caps of the same colour. Their bark was similar to the larger class of passage-boats plying between Cadiz and the Isla de Leon.

The man who seemed to be the owner of the horse was of middle height, and well made; his complexion very dark, and features regular; his eyes were jet black, and piercing, and he had an enormous pair of whiskers. Under an ample brown cloth cloak, which hung gracefully on one shoulder, could be perceived his ordinary dress, consisting of a jacket, open at the bosom, but fitting closely to his athletic arms, and having several rows of silver buttons at the sides and wrists. Underneath was a cloth vest, and strapped round his waist a canana, or flexible leathern cartridge-case. He wore velveteen breeches, of a dark colour, the outer seams being adorned with curiously-wrought silver buttons. On his legs were leathern gaiters, reaching to the knees, but open at the calf. His hat, or sombrero, was of coarse beaver, very low in the crown, and broad in the brim. A black silken net, with small tassels at the end, fell from underneath this hat upon his shoulders; and he carried a long lance in his right hand.

The horse was full sixteen hands high, and of the true Andalusian breed; his small ears, fiery eyes, and glowing nostrils, were sure indications of strength and courage.

Leaning his elbow on the saddle, the guerrilléro—for such he was—looked anxiously towards the landing-place, and then turning to the steersman, said in an under voice, 'Remember your charge; be firm and collected.'

At this moment the prow of the boat struck the mole; this was succeeded by a shriek, and the head of an old man emerged from the bundle at the steersman's feet. 'Misericordia! misericordia!' cried the wretched prisoner. The sailor laid his hand on the old man's mouth, forced him to lie down again, and covered him with a shabby blanket.

The guerrilléro landed with the horse's bridal over his arm. The sagacious animal watched its master; and when he said, 'Venga amigo, venga!' (Come friend, come!) he sprang on shore, then shook himself, neighed, and having rubbed his mouth against his master's face, erected his crest, and seemed to invite the guerrilléro to mount.

By this time a knot of persons had collected at the landing-place, some of whom attempted to get into the boat, and enter into conversation with those on board; but this the guerrilléro positively forbade, making a sign at the same moment to one of the crew, who came on shore and went towards the guard-house at the Puerta del Mar, or sea-gate.

'Ho! Diego!' cried a rough-looking fellow, addressing one of the boatmen, 'what freight have you brought from Rota?'

'Nothing worth speaking of,' was the reply.

'But you have a little live stock, for we heard a pig squeak.'

'Ay, ay,' roared several voices; 'a French pig!—a French pig!—we saw its snout!'

The guerrilléro was, at this juncture, preparing to light his cigar; turning to the bystanders, he said quietly, 'Is there any crime in bringing over a French pig?'

'No crime—no crime; but we know that you did not go to Seville merely to carry off a hog.'

'Diego,' cried the man who had spoken first, 'is the *puerco* of the real French breed, or only an Afrancesado?—if the latter, here is wherewithal to cut its throat?'—and he drew forth a knife, about a foot in length, ground to a point, and sharpened at both edges.

The guerrilléro drew a pistol from his belt. 'My friends,' he said, 'whatever is in that boat—man or beast—is under my protection; and the first person who shall attempt to interfere is a dead man.'

The tramp of soldiers' footsteps interrupted this dialogue. There were, however, but six men, commanded by a corporal. This little guard was ranged on either side of the steps; and, on a signal from the guerrilléro, two of the boat's crew lifted up the unhappy being who lay trembling at their feet, and brought him on shore. No sooner were they on the mole than a terrific howl burst from the crowd, and fifty long knives were brandished in the air.

'Down with the French hog! Death to the Afrancesado!' cried the mob.

Instantly the old man was placed between the soldiers, who marched onward. The guerrilléro sprang upon his horse, and brought up the rear. Frequently was he obliged to turn round, and make a sort of charge upon the crowd, who were burning with rage, and panted to take summary vengeance on the Afrancesado, for such they now knew the culprit to be. He was, however, safely lodged in the guard-house, into which the guerrilléro also entered, leaving his horse in charge of a soldier.

The appearance of the prisoner was most singular

* The author of this paper accompanies it with a letter, from which the following is an extract:—

'—— I was in Cadiz when the transactions described took place, and I have endeavoured to render the narrative as characteristic of the period as possible. Unfortunate Spain is now apparently on the eve of a sanguinary reaction in consequence of the proceedings of the modern Afrancesados, towards whom the same feeling of animosity on the part of the majority of the Spanish people still exists, as was displayed during the memorable Peninsular war.'

He was rather under the middle size, and seemed to be about sixty years of age. He was dressed in a full suit of black, with silk stockings, and rich buckles in his shoes; but his whole costume was so covered with dust and mud, that he had somewhat the air of one of those itinerant mountebanks who are to be seen in France at country fairs. The lace frill was torn and dirty; his gray hair fell in scanty meshes about his ears; and he endeavoured to conceal his face with his right hand, on the fore-finger of which shone a valuable diamond ring.

The officer on guard had been previously informed by the boatman who the prisoner was; and he now communed apart with the guerrilléro as to the most eligible mode of getting him conveyed to the jail, which is situated at a considerable distance from the sea-gate. It was by this time quite dark, and the officer expressed his apprehensions lest the populace should gain possession of the captive, and sacrifice him.

'Senor,' said the guerrilléro, 'I alone brought the old sinner all the way from Seville; and, aided by half a dozen soldiers, I will engage to lodge him securely in the prison.'

'Be it so,' replied the officer; 'sergeant, take six of your best men, and accompany this brave fellow and his prisoner: let no one approach them.'

The old man now fell on his knees before the officer: 'Misericordia! misericordia!' he cried; 'for the love of God and of the blessed Virgin, save me from the fury of the rabble!—let me remain here!'

The appeal was fruitless; the officer bade him rise, but the poor creature seemed incapable of doing so. The guerrilléro lifted him up, and carried him, in almost a state of insensibility, to the door of the guard-house; the escort was in readiness, and in the twinkling of an eye the bold horseman placed the little old man on the saddle-bow, and mounted himself afterwards. Encircling his prisoner with his left arm so as to be able also to hold the bridle, he seized the lance with his right hand. The sergeant and two men were placed before the horse, a soldier on either side, and two others behind.

No sooner had this singular cortège appeared, than a fearful murmur issued from the market-place, close to the sea-gate, and where a considerable crowd had assembled. As the party advanced, it was so strongly pressed upon by the infuriated mob, that the soldiers had much difficulty in opening a passage.

The old man's head fell upon his breast, and he trembled so violently under the muscular arm of the guerrilléro, that the latter was obliged to press him still closer to his body, in order not to lose his equilibrium.

'Maldito Afrancesado!' shrieked the crowd.

'Yes; accursed be the old monster!' bawled an athletic butcher, brandishing a hatchet with a short iron handle; 'down with him! Hark'ee, Senor Guerrilléro, deliver up your prisoner, or we'll force him from you.'

'Never!' replied the brave horseman. 'Sergeant, I rely on you and on your men to keep off the mob.'

At this moment a rush was made by several men, armed with large knives. The soldiers in vain offered resistance; their muskets were wrested from their hands before they had time to make use of them.

The guerrilléro now wheeled round; then making his horse plunge, and wielding his lance like a knight of the olden time, he succeeded in clearing a space before him. Galloping across the market-place, he reached the narrow street leading to the prison, which is within a stone's-throw of the barracks; but he had not advanced far before his passage was barred by another mob, whilst his former antagonists closed again on his rear.

'Amigos,' cried the guerrilléro, 'I would not willingly harm any of ye, nor do I think you would wish to injure me; however, not a hair of my prisoner's head shall be touched by you whilst I exist. I have brought this infamous culprit at the risk of my life from the very head-quarters of the enemies of our country; he will be tried by the law of the land, and assuredly will not escape the punishment due to his crimes, *but he must not be assassinated.*'

There was a short pause after this address. During the momentary calm the horseman managed to advance a few paces, and had reached the corner of a short street leading to an open space near the jail, when a shriek of 'Vengeance! vengeance!' issued from the crowd, and a woman rushed forth.

''Tis the mother of Antonio,' said a ferocious-looking fellow; 'Antonio, who was sentenced to death by this infamous Afrancesado, and was executed at Seville. Blood for blood! Come, Senor Guerrilléro, give up your prisoner quietly; we are resolved to have him.'

'Misericordia! misericordia!' cried the terrified old man.

'No mercy! no quarter! we'll tear thee limb from limb!'

'Vengeance! vengeance! the blood of my murdered child cries for vengeance!' screamed the woman.

The guerrilléro now let his lance swing loosely from the strap to which it was attached to his arm, and drew a pistol from his breast. A lamp that was burning before the image of a saint at the corner of the street shed a faint light upon his figure, and enabled the mob to see his actions. Pointing the pistol at the person nearest him, he repeated his former manœuvre, cleared the way by means of his horse, and though still closely beset by the mob, was making some progress towards a more open spot, when he was once more hemmed in.

At this crisis, a lad of about twelve years old crept under the horse and cut the saddle-girths; this startled the noble animal, who bounded forwards; the movement caused the saddle to turn round, and the rider, with his trembling burden, fell to the ground.

At the commencement of the turmoil, a respectable individual who happened to be on the spot ran to the barracks hard by, and described the perilous situation of the guerrilléro to the officer on duty, who, at the head of a few soldiers, hastened to the point indicated by the stranger. They arrived just as the guerrilléro fell from his horse, and forcing their way through the crowd, succeeded in rescuing him and his prisoner, and escorted them to the jail, where the latter was safely lodged.

Don Cayetano ——, the son of a rich merchant of Cadiz, had been educated for the law, and rose to the dignity of a judge, which position he occupied with perfect credit to himself, when the royal family of Spain were inveigled away by the intrigues and hardihood of Napoleon, and a puppet king, in the person of the brother of the French emperor, was sent to take their place at Madrid. When that revolution was brought about, a few Spaniards, some of whom were actuated by mistaken political views, others by a regard to their own interests, professed adherence to the French interest, or became, in the language of the country, Afrancesadoes: the bulk of the nation, I need scarcely say, beheld the French and the intruso-king with deep-seated indignation, insomuch that even in Cadiz, under the protection of a British garrison, it would have been dangerous for any one to be heard speaking a French word.

Among the military officers and courtiers who came with Joseph to Madrid, were two whom Don Cayetano had known many years before, when he visited Paris, and appeared at the court of Louis XVI. The old companions met, and, after the usual remarks on the changes which had taken place in their personal appearance since they had last seen each other, they naturally began to talk of politics. Don Cayetano did not hesitate to express his detestation of the unjustifiable part which Napoleon had played, and his conviction that his influence would ultimately be extinguished in Spain. The two French functionaries smiled at his 'prejudices,' and endeavoured very mildly to argue him out of them. Other meetings took place. The ex-judge—for such he had been since Joseph's arrival—kept aloof from court; but he did not deem it necessary to avoid the society of his old friends. In time, they found his weak side, a desire of reforming the laws. They also discovered that he was not without a little vanity. The man, therefore, whom wealth unlimited could not have induced to do a dishonourable action, was overcome when the prospect was held out to him of acquiring a name as the regenerator of the civil and criminal jurisprudence. He consented to accept a place on the bench under Joseph, and thus became—fatal word—an Afrancesado.

The head-quarters of the French army of Andalusia were at this time at Seville, and a strong division under Marshal Victor was besieging Cadiz. Serious interruptions to the operations of the French were constantly occasioned by the guerrillas, whilst conspiracies of various kinds were on foot at Seville and its vicinity to free the country from the iron yoke of the invaders. The severest measures were adopted by them to counteract these plots; and Don Cayetano, after swearing fidelity to King Joseph, was directed to proceed to Seville in his judicial capacity.

Great confidence was inspired by his well-known energy and penetration; and, as is usual in such cases, the renegade became remarkable for his severity. Numbers of Spaniards were condemned to death by the Afrancesado judge, and his name was execrated throughout Andalusia. He became completely infatuated with the French, probably because he knew that his existence depended on their success; and it appeared as though he endeavoured to lull the pangs of remorse by plunging into the vortex of gay society. He attended all the grand parties given by the French authorities, and, in his turn, invited them to splendid entertainments. An observant eye might, however, have discovered in the countenance of the Afrancesado evident marks of deep anxiety, and the wearing effects of a smiting conscience.

A short time before the scene we attempted to describe at the commencement of this tale, he had condemned to death a brother of our guerrilléro, whose only offence was, that, having quarrelled with a French subordinate civil officer, he had, in the heat of passion, cried out, 'Viva Fernando Septimo! muéra José!' He was thereupon seized by the police, dragged before the judge, who passed sentence of death on him, as having been guilty of *treason;* and the unfortunate young man was forthwith executed.

When this sad intelligence reached the brother, he vowed vengeance against the Afrancesado judge. His method of attaining his object was singular and characteristic. 'I will not soil my hands with the blood of the base murderer,' said he; 'but I will carry him off in the blaze of his infamous splendour, and take him to Cadiz, his birthplace, and the seat of the regency governing in the name of Ferdinand the Seventh. *There* he cannot fail of being condemned to death, after being judged as justly as he has judged others unjustly.'

The guerrilléro was at this time in the mountains of Ronda, where he did his part, in common with others, in harassing the French. He had a thorough knowledge of all the by-paths in Andalusia, and had frequently gone over to Cadiz with despatches to the Spanish regency from the guerrilla chiefs. He was acquainted with some fishermen who lived near a little creek in the vicinity of Rota, and who had more than once taken him over, keeping his horse for him until his return. He now made the best of his way to their humble dwelling, and obtained a passage to Cadiz, where he had some relatives, who were market boatmen, and upon whose hearty co-operation in avenging his brother's death he well knew he could reckon.

The plan was soon agreed upon. His three kinsmen and two others were to go in their large market boat, on the following night, to the little creek near Rota, and there await the arrival of the guerrilléro; who, immediately after this arrangement was made, returned with the fishermen to the other side of the bay. Mounting his gallant steed, he took the road to Seville, where he arrived on the evening of the second day. He could have reached that city in a less space of time, but he was anxious to keep his horse fresh, well knowing that he must soon tax his strength to the uttermost. Having carefully examined his pistols, he entered the city after dark, and rode up to the judge's house. It was brilliantly lighted up; for Don Cayetano gave a grand entertainment that evening to the French general-in-chief, his staff, and a numerous party of Afrancesadoes.

The guerrilléro held in his hand what appeared to be an official despatch, sealed up, as usual, in an envelope of large dimensions. He dismounted, and knocked loudly at the handsome gateway. A servant, in rich livery, quickly appeared, and demanded his business.

'I have a despatch for his excellency the judge.'

'Very well,' said the domestic; 'give it to me, and it shall be handed to him immediately.'

'My orders are to deliver the packet into the judge's own hands.'

'He is just now engaged with a large party, and I dare not disturb his excellency.'

'Then *I* will,' said the guerrilléro, 'for the despatch has been forwarded with the utmost speed from Madrid; and when it was handed to me by the governor of Carmona, he commanded me not to give it to any one but the judge himself.'

The guerrilléro then made a movement to penetrate into the courtyard; but the servant, convinced by the earnestness of his manner, and by the mention of the governor of Carmona's name, undertook to speak to his master.

'Make haste,' cried the guerrilléro, 'for I am tired, and so is my horse. Tell his excellency that if he will just step out, 'twill only be the affair of an instant. All I want is to accomplish my mission, and make the best of my way back.'

Whilst this scene was passing outside the mansion, the guests, who were assembled in its superb apartments, were diverting themselves in various ways. In one saloon dancing was kept up with spirit; the French officers displayed their accustomed elegance in the ball-room, the Spanish senoritas, graceful and enchanting as they are at all times, being peculiarly animated; and many tender conversations were held between the youthful French gallants and the lovely Andalusian damsels. In another room gambling was carried on with great avidity. Around the *monte* table were seated several grave-looking Spanish gentlemen and ladies beyond the meridian of life, all intent upon the game. Behind them were numbers of French officers, among whom were mingled several of the beautiful girls from the ball-room, playing in partnership with the warriors; and it was painful to observe the intensity with which those fair creatures watched the chances, gloried in their winnings, or deplored their losses.

In a spacious and splendid saloon were assembled the French general-in-chief, and a number of his superior staff officers, the Spanish authorities acting under the French *regime*, various other Spaniards, and their hospitable host, the Afrancesado judge. They were in full conversation when the servant entered, and in an under tone informed his master that a horseman was at the gate bearing a despatch from the governor of Carmona, which he was ordered to deliver into the judge's own hands. The old man at first desired that the messenger might be sent up stairs; but the servant having told him that he did not seem to like to leave his horse, the judge quitted the saloon, descended the grand staircase, crossed the courtyard, and advanced to the gate. There stood the guerrilléro with the packet in his hand: as the old man held out his to receive it, the guerrilléro grasped his arm, dragged him over the threshold, lifted him in a second on to the pommel of his saddle, then vaulting into it himself, galloped off at full speed, covering the judge's mouth with one hand to prevent him from crying out, and was clear of the city before the alarm could be given; for the servant who had accompanied his master to the gate was so astounded by what he had witnessed, that he did not recover his faculties till several minutes afterwards.

As soon as the French general was informed of what had taken place, parties of cavalry were despatched in pursuit of the guerrilléro, but without effect; he had leaped his noble horse over a broken wall, distant from the sentinels, and had struck at once into paths unknown to the French cavalry, and where they would hardly have ventured to follow him, had he been seen to enter them. Rapidly, and without obstacle, did the guerrilléro return to the little creek near the Guadalquiver; he found his faithful companions on the alert, embarked in the long market boat, having first deposited his trembling charge in the stern, and placed his horse amid-ships. His arrival at Cadiz has been already described.

The proofs of Don Cayetano's guilt were too numerous and too notorious to require any lengthened process—he was condemned to be strangled.

At that period the monks and friars still possessed great influence in Spain; and the relatives of Don Cayetano, who were in Cadiz, used every exertion to obtain a prolongation of the customary time between the sentence and its execution, in the hope of effecting his escape by means of great pecuniary sacrifices, and through the instrumentality of the priesthood. The superior of one of the convents was accordingly applied to, on the plea, in the first instance, of obtaining the spiritual services of one or more of his community for the condemned judge. By degrees, and with caution, it was afterwards intimated to the superior that a very large sum would be at the disposal of whomsoever might insure his escape. The hint was at first but slightly attended to: shortly afterwards, however, the friends of Don Cayetano were informed that, for the moment, all that could be done was to retard the execution of the sentence, on the ground that the guilty man's mind required a lengthened pious preparation and repentance, before that absolution could be granted to him which was necessary for the future welfare of his immortal soul. To obtain this respite a large sum was required—it was instantly paid.

Nearly two months passed away in anxiety on the part of the captive and his friends, and in promises and demands for more money on that of the superior of the convent, who declared that he was paving the way for the judge's escape. How he managed to induce the authorities to sanction the delay is beyond our knowledge. Certain it is, that at length every pecuniary resource within the reach of Don Cayetano's connexions became exhausted; and the monks at the very same time evinced a mysterious doubtfulness as to the issue of their negotiations. In their visits to the prisoner, they dwelt solely on religious matters, admonishing him, above all things, to prepare for the worst, and returning vague replies to his anxious questions relative to his escape or pardon; the same manner and language were observed towards his now empty-handed friends during their interviews with the holy fathers.

Murmurings faintly arose about this time among the lower classes, like the distant moanings of the ocean preparatory to a violent storm. Gloomy and uncouth men, and fearful-looking women, hovered about the fishermen after they had moored their boats in the evenings; and the name of Cayetano, the French hog, as they termed him, was pronounced with vengeful tone and gesture. Night after night these symptoms of popular fury were exhibited, augmenting hourly in intensity. By what means the irritation of the lower classes, as described at the commencement of our narrative, had been so long repressed, was a matter of surprise to all who reflected on the circumstance; the mother and brother of the deceased Antonio were still in Cadiz, and it could not be doubted that they continued to be animated by the most ardent desire for vengeance on the judge.

The fact, however, was, that the monks had, up to this time, exercised their powerful influence over the minds of the people, who, at their bidding, had remained tranquil; but the object having now been obtained—the possession of the property of the aged culprit, and of all the available resources of his friends—they had no further inducement to inculcate forbearance; at least this was strongly suspected to be the case. The pent-up passions of the mob were therefore allowed to burst forth with redoubled force, and carried all before them. In front of the jail, before the houses of the magistrates, at the military barracks, crowds assembled continually, preceded by Antonio's mother and brother, demanding the execution of the sentence passed upon the hated Cayetano. The Spanish soldiers also sympathised in this fiery wrath against an Afrancesado: his execution, therefore, became inevitable.

The civil authorities now applied to the superior of the convent to report upon the spiritual condition of the prisoner. He no longer hesitated, but declared that he was in a penitent and edifying frame of mind, fit for absolution, and that this was a favourable moment for the condemned judge to pay the penalty of his worldly offences. The warrant for carrying the sentence into execution in thirty-six hours was accordingly signed.

* * *

The wretched Cayetano, seated in a corner of his cell, was pondering over his awful situation, and overwhelmed with dire presentiments occasioned by the altered manner of his reverend attendants, when the massive bolts were slowly withdrawn, and the usher of the criminal tribunal entered. He was rather a portly personage, dressed in a full suit of black. In his left hand he held a scroll of parchment; and advancing with noiseless step towards the prisoner, who regarded him with piercing eyes, bowed ceremoniously, and said, 'God guard you, senor!'—and slowly unrolling the parchment, thus addressed the careworn culprit:—'In pursuance of the decree of the competent authorities, I am about to perform the painful duty of reading to you the warrant for the fulfilment of the sentence of death pronounced against you.

The prisoner neither spoke nor moved.

The usher having read the warrant, retired. In a few minutes the jailer entered, followed by two assistants, and conducted the captive to the place where he was to pass the few remaining hours of his existence.

During the period that a condemned criminal is in *capilla*, as it is termed, he is not only attended by a priest, or priests, for the purpose of affording him spiritual consolation, but every bodily comfort is placed at his disposal. Of neither of these advantages, however, could the old judge be persuaded to avail himself. He remained seated on the little bed, his head drooping on his chest, and totally regardless of the orisons and exhortations of the two monks by whom he was constantly attended. In this state he remained until the hour appointed for his execution.

* * *

It was a fine spring morning; the vivifying rays of the sun enlivened and beautified the face of nature; but this very brilliancy produced a melancholy feeling, for it was also a morning on which a human being was to perish on the scaffold. At dawn, a small table, covered with black cloth, was to be seen at the gate of every church in Cadiz. On this table were placed a crucifix, and a wooden box with a chink in the lid. At each end of the table stood a member of one of the Hermandades, or religious societies, covered with a silken cloak, the colour whereof designated the Hermandad, or brotherhood, to which he belonged, soliciting alms from the passers-by. This appeal was complied with even by the very humblest, the product being destined to pay for masses for the repose of the malefactor's soul.

The hour fixed for the execution was noon—the spot a rising ground on the *campo*, not far from the jail. A platform about six feet from the ground had been erected; it was reached by a few steps formed of rough planks. From the centre of the platform rose a post, jutting out from which was a narrow fixed seat; a groove or slit was perceptible in the middle of the post. From an early hour crowds of persons emerged from every street, and hastened to this spot, which was guarded by a body of troops; the people were ranged on the rising ground, as in an amphitheatre, a space being kept clear by the soldiers between the spectators and the platform, as well as a passage thence to the jail. As the appointed hour approached, the crowd became tremendous; for, independently of the anxiety that is common in every part of the world to obtain good places at those spectacles which justice presents gratis to the people, the inhabitants of Cadiz were on the present occasion animated by a most ferocious curiosity, and by a determination to be able to certify—after ocular proof—to the ignominious death of the Afrancesado judge: they would even have revolted against the government had an attempt been made to deprive them of their prey. Grievous and appalling it was to see this compact mass of infuriated people waiting impatiently to gloat over the moral and physical agony of a fellow-creature!

In the midst of this horrible excitement, when all were speaking and gesticulating in that expressive and energetic manner peculiar to Spaniards, the bells of all the churches began to toll: the effect was most extraordinary. Instantaneously there was dead silence; every man bared his head, and the whole multitude noiselessly, but with moving lips and downcast eyes, appeared absorbed in prayer. This lasted for a minute or two, and then the shouts, and cries, and gestures became more violent than ever.

Precisely at noon the gates of the jail were thrown open: the bell of the prison-chapel tolled, and the lugubrious sounds were echoed from all the church-towers. The melancholy procession now emerged from the prison gate. First came a penitent, masked, and wearing a long loose robe of coarse brown cloth, tightened at the waist by a broad leathern belt; his head was overshadowed by a cowl: he carried a moderate-sized bell in his right hand, and sounded it three times at each tenth step; it had a cracked and sickening tone. He was followed by another man in a similar costume, bearing a large silver cross, and attended on each side by an acolyte, carrying a yellow torch; afterwards came six masked penitents, two and two.

The judge now appeared; and a howl, the horrible effect of which it would be in vain to attempt to describe, issued from the excited mob. The poor creature was bare-headed, and wore a long loose brown greatcoat; his hands were tied with cords. His head was bent towards the ground, and it was with difficulty that he could be prevented from sinking. On one side of him was a priest, who frequently held a crucifix close to his withered face, and seemed to be exhorting him to repentance: another priest recited the prayers for the dying. The procession was closed by several members of the different Hermandades, or religious associations, and mounted alguazils, protected by the military.

The executioner had been for some little time on the platform with an assistant. He was a tall spare man, wearing a close-fitting black vest, breeches of the same colour, white cotton stockings, and dress shoes; the cuffs of his vest were turned up. He had been fixing an iron collar on the post at the back of the seat, and behind the same was a spindle, like that of a vice, made of polished iron. A few cords were lying at this man's feet; and as the procession advanced, he was amusing himself by twirling round the bright spindle, to ascertain, apparently, whether it would work glibly.

On reaching the foot of the platform, the aged and sinking culprit stood for some minutes at the bottom of the steps; the priest seemed to be earnestly exhorting him, but the poor man took no notice. He was then helped up the steps, backwards, by the executioner's assistant, the priests following, and holding the crucifix close to his face. Soon he was seated across the stool; the iron collar was slipped over his head; the executioner twirled the spindle, screwed it twice, and all was over.

The crowd rapidly dispersed, a few soldiers being left to guard the body, which remained in the sitting posture just described until about sunset, when the members of one of the Hermandades, accompanied by a priest, performed, as usual, the pious office of placing it in a coffin, the priest repeating the prayers for the dead. The coffin having been placed in a black covered cart, drawn by a sorry mule, the modest procession proceeded slowly to the Campo Santo, or public cemetery, at a short distance outside the walls of Cadiz, where the remains of the Afrancesado judge were deposited in a humble grave.

PERIPHRASIS.

'PLEASE, papa,' inquired Robert, taking his eyes from a book he was studying, 'what is periphrasis?'

It is well known that there is nothing so difficult as off-hand definition, and my son's question placed me in rather an awkward predicament: I did not choose to risk a random explanation of the word, for fear of misleading him; while to remain silent would cause him to suppose me ignorant of that which I well knew, though not able to define it at a moment's warning. This is one of the little difficulties in which children sometimes place us. I tried to get out of the present dilemma by delay; I went on writing, in which I appeared too much absorbed to hear what he had said; but was all the time mentally framing an answer to his question. After watching anxiously till I came to a full stop, he hoped I would not be angry for disturbing me, adding, 'But what, papa, *is* periphrasis?'

Still, I was not quite ready with a proper reply; and after slowly laying down my pen, and gaining an instant or two by a sort of hecking cough, I found myself quite at a loss to invent another instant's delay, and plunged desperately into the subject. 'Periphrasis, Robert, is—that is to say, it comes from two Greek words, *peri*, about, and *phrasis*, speech.'

'Yes, but what does it mean, papa?'

'Why, it signifies a figure of speech much in use among orators, poets, newspaper-writers, and indeed, now I think of it, more or less by everybody in common conversation, to express, in a great many words, what they could say in one. For instance, I use the figure of periphrasis when, instead of speaking of you as "Robert," I say "my youngest son."'

'Then I suppose,' remarked the observant little rogue, after a little reflection, 'when mamma, in alluding to Mr Ammerton who comes here so regularly, calls him a "certain young gentleman," it is periphrasis that makes sister Clotilda blush so?'

'Perhaps it is,' I remarked, trying to look grave.

'Yes, but why *does* mamma call him so? why does she not say Mr Ammerton at once? I want to know, papa, what is the *use* of periphrasis?'

I explained as well as I could the uses of that figure in poetry and in rhetoric; but when the persevering young gentleman would know the various uses to which it is put in ordinary conversation and everyday life, I told him he might go and bowl his hoop; for though the question suggested a long train of thought, my reflections were of a nature not to benefit his inexperienced mind. Perhaps older readers may, however, be amused by them.

Of all the graces of rhetoric, none is so largely, or perhaps so usefully employed, in every grade of society, from the cottage to the crown, as periphrasis. In literature, it is said to sweeten and ornament a discourse carried on in propriety of language: so in our personal intercourse with mankind, its judicious employment softens asperities, dilutes expressions when they are becoming too strong, and blunts the edge of personality when it is going to be too pointed. But there is, alas! no use without its abuse; and unfortunately this elegant trope is occasionally turned to very bad account. The fact is, when pressed into the service of scandal, it is a tremendous engine.

While discussing the subject in my own mind in its domestic relations, it was natural that my son's allusion to my excellent partner (I use *this* periphrasis in all sincerity; for, despite a few peculiarities, a better wife, a better mother, or a better housekeeper than Mrs Parkinson nowhere exists) should remind me of the constant use *she* makes of the branch of rhetoric we are considering. If she has anything in the least degree unfavourable to communicate of any person, it is extremely difficult to draw from her actual names: her favourite periphrastic substitutes being either 'some folks' or 'certain parties.' 'Some folks,' she remarked the other day, 'should, I think, be a little more circumspect regarding their daughters, especially being parsonage folks. Certain parties, who shall be nameless, were seen yesterday walking with certain other parties—alone—when, too, it was nearly dusk. To be sure people who have, poor things, only one daughter married out of four, can be forgiven a little latitude in that respect.' Now, by this round-about method of communication, Mrs Parkinson made herself unintelligible to our guest from London, who happened to be present; while I was as perfectly in possession of her meaning as if she had said outright that the Goodsons, mother and daughter, were alluded to. In like manner, I can always tell on what terms my wife happens to be with them, or indeed with any of our neighbours, by her different modes of designating them. When a little 'tiff' has happened, the Reverend Mr Goodson and family are designated 'the people at the end of the village.' Should, however, Mrs Parkinson be speaking in praise of them—detailing, for example, any of Mrs Goodson's numerous acts of charity—she calls her 'that dear woman at the parsonage.' In short, Mrs Parkinson—like many others whom my readers will be able to point out amidst their own respective circles—is afflicted with a very great dread of 'mentioning names,' for fear, as she diplomatically observes, of 'compromising herself.'

I am, however, inclined to think that domestic life is not the soil in which our favourite flower of rhetoric flourishes best. To see it in its highest perfection, we must take a glance at the learned professions and the legislature. I select my first instance from the pulpit, because it happened to furnish me with a bit of judicious periphrasis, which had a most beneficial effect on Mrs Parkinson. To say the truth, her prevailing foible is love of dress, and I almost blush to add that she used to select the least appropriate day in the week for indulging it; consequently she and Clotilda seldom entered church till after all the rest of the congregation had assembled, to their manifest disturbance. The Reverend Mr Goodson had already complained to me of the annoyance, and I had communicated my views on the subject to my wife in terms much too strong to admit of any periphrasis whatever. Still, Mrs Parkinson would not be warned, and continued to arrive in the midst of the service. As a last resource, therefore, our reverend pastor made a pointed allusion from the pulpit. The subject was, lukewarm Christians considered as more effectual enemies to Christianity than confirmed sceptics. The accomplished preacher pointed out the various descriptions of this character, till at last he came to the class in which I felt sure my wife was included. 'Of these, my brethren,' continued the preacher, 'there are some who, when all is silent save the voice of the pastor, announce their presence by the rustling of silks and the streaming of ribbons.' Nobody could mistake to whom this periphrasis applied; for the preacher cast a side-glance at my wife, which acted as a conductor to the eyes of the whole congregation, and they were concentrated on the same focus. Mrs Parkinson blushed as pink as her bonnet, and from that day never entered late, or otherwise than plainly attired.

Passing the learned professions, in some of which periphrasis is carried to an extent more tedious than amusing, I must invite my readers to seats in the Houses of Parliament, for there periphrasis reigns in all its glory. In these great assemblies, to refer to persons by their actual designations is strictly forbidden. 'The honourable member for Bumbleborough,' or 'the honourable and gallant member,' or 'honourable and learned gentleman,' according as a military or legal senator is indicated, must serve in the Commons for all more precise appellatives. This does tolerably well; but, in the Lords, where men, as members, have no local habitation any more than they have a name, much more difficulty is experienced. This is best illustrated in a 'reply.' After a certain peer has made a motion, the other lords deliver their opinions for and against it; and when all have spoken, it is usual for the mover to reply to the several arguments. The periphrastic shifts he is put to in designating the various orators are sometimes really distressing. If two bishops have spoken, one is the 'right reverend prelate who took an early part in the debate,' and the other, 'the right reverend prelate who usually votes with the ministry;' then comes a bit of logic for 'the noble and learned baron on the cross-bench,' succeeded by an exposure of the fallacies of 'a noble viscount on the opposite side of the house;' with a cordial eulogy on the clear-sighted views propounded by 'the noble lord on the woolsack.' The further the orator proceeds, the poorer he naturally gets in his periphrases, till towards the end he is reduced to 'the noble lord who preceded the last speaker,' or 'the noble and gallant duke who addressed to their lordships a few pithy sentences previous to the noble lord who preceded the last speaker.' Finally, he comes to the oft-mentioned last speaker himself, who is designated either as 'the noble lord who has just sat down,' or as 'the noble lord who was last on his legs.' It is obvious, that exactly as Mrs Parkinson's bit of scandal was quite unintelligible to our stranger guest, so the debates in the House of Lords would be almost Greek to the public if they appeared in the newspapers exactly as they are conducted. The reporters, however, render them intelligible by inserting within parentheses the actual names of the peers so mysteriously and circuitously alluded to. A few periphrases are common to both houses; the most striking being the circumspection with which the name of the sovereign is avoided. She is hinted at as the throne, the crown, or an illustrious personage; and when some bold debater wishes to be very personal indeed, he speaks of 'the highest personage in the realm.' I do really believe that the utterance of these widely-cherished words, 'Queen Victoria,' in the House of Commons, would cause as extraordinary a sensation as was created by the Irish reporter who amidst the gravest silence called on the speaker 'for a song.'

It seems also to be held as highly improper for any person to talk of the 'House of Lords' in the one place, or of the 'House of Commons' in the other; each assembly being delicately shadowed forth as 'another place.' Nay, this etiquette is carried to an almost boundless extent; for, in mentioning an occurrence which may have happened anywhere else than in either of the 'other places,' or Houses of Parliament, the expression to be used is 'out of doors.' Thus the legislative wisdom of this country divides the terrestrial globe into two sections: that which is comprised 'within doors,' and that which exists 'out of doors.'

'The gentlemen of the press'—a pleasing periphrasis for reporters—luxuriate in the figure even more than orators. I am tempted to believe that this arises from the fiscal arrangements of newspaper proprietors, who remunerate a certain class of writers at so much per line. It is obviously, therefore, the interest of the reporter to convey a single fact in as many words and lines as possible: hence he adopts the circumlocutory or periphrastic style of composition, in order to blend elegant diction with pecuniary profit. Supposing, for example, he hears that old Lord Stalkington has proposed marriage to Alderman Crumpet's youngest daughter; that information, conveyed in so many words, would not only prove extremely uninteresting to his readers, but very unprofitable to himself. He therefore spreads out this inch of fact into a foot of paragraph, somewhat after the following fashion:—

'APPROACHING MARRIAGE IN HIGH LIFE.—It is rumoured in the fashionable circles, that an earl of recent creation—whose laurels as a general officer were won in the Peninsula, and who held office under a late administration, but resigned on the breaking up of that cabinet—is about to lead to the hymeneal altar the lovely and accomplished daughter of an opulent city alderman, who not long since passed the civic chair with the marked approbation of his fellow citizens. Though the noble lover has passed the grand climacteric, and the fair intended is in the early bloom of womanhood, yet the alliance is said to be purely one of affection on both sides. The dower of the future countess is said to be immense.'

Upon this principle it is seldom that, in newspapers, things or persons are called by their ordinary names. Fire is the destructive element; dancing, tripping it on the light fantastic toe; drowning, finding a watery grave; eating, the pleasures of the table; drinking, sacrificing at the shrine of Bacchus. Barristers are gentlemen of the long robe; actors, votaries of Thespis; shoemakers, sons of St Crispin; tailors, knights of the thimble; doctors, disciples of Esculapius. Soldiers are all gallant sons of Mars; and every sailor is a son of Neptune.

By the time I had written thus far, Robert rushed into the room with the intelligence that poor Clotilda had been seized with another fit of periphrasis; for a 'certain gentleman' had just arrived, bringing with him his father and lawyer. 'Bless me,' I exclaimed, wiping my spectacles, and ringing for my dress-coat, 'I had forgotten all about Ammerton and the marriage settlement.' This effectually awoke me from my reflections; for if there is anything calculated to end a reverie concerning periphrasis, it is a law-deed.

BOYD'S HISTORY OF LITERATURE—ORIGIN OF TIME RECKONINGS.

Two volumes out of four have appeared, of a 'History of Literature, or the Progress of Language, Writing, and Letters, from the Earliest ages of Antiquity to the Present Time; with a View of the State of Science and the Fine Arts;' the author being Sir William Boyd, M.D. The second volume terminates with the Augustan age of Rome. Without pretension to any brilliant originality, this work appears to us to present a very fair and judicious view of the progress of letters amongst mankind; the biographies of writers, and criticisms on their writings, are generally spirited, and the specimens of classic productions of celebrity are for the most part ably translated. For youthful study, we do not know a book upon the same subject calculated to be equally useful.

On a perusal of the work, it has appeared to us that none of the purely literary notices could be so appropriate for quotation in this place as the brief view which the author gives of the origin of time reckonings, a subject which comes under his attention in treating of the history of astronomy among the ancients. 'Days, years, months, the sky, the constellations, &c. are,' he says, 'ideas which common and uncultivated minds possess; nevertheless these are the elements of astronomy. The notion of a day is obviously and constantly impressed upon man in every condition in which he is placed. The recurrence of light and darkness, of warmth and cold, of noise and silence, of activity and repose, makes the notion of a day necessarily occur. A year is a notion formed in a similar manner, implying the idea of recurring facts, with the faculty of arranging them in time, and of appreciating their recurrence. The notion, however, of a year, though obvious, is, on many accounts, less so than that of a day. The repetition of similar circumstances at equal intervals is far less manifest, and the intervals being much longer, an exertion of memory becomes requisite in order that the recurrence may be perceived. Nations generally have marked this portion of time by some word having a reference to the returning circle of the seasons. The Latin *annus* signifies a ring, and the Greek term *eniautos*, means something which returns into itself. To make the term year imply a fixed number of days, it is necessary to know how many days the cycle of the seasons occupies, a degree of knowledge beyond what has been already alluded to; and men cannot reckon as far as any number approaching that of days in a year, without possessing a system of numerical terms, and methods of practical numeration, on which such a system is founded. Among the Greeks the seasons were at first only summer and winter; the latter included the wet and cold portion of the year.

'The sun goes through his cycle of positions in the same period that the stars go through a cycle of appearances belonging to them: and it appears that the latter were also carefully observed to determine the exact length of the year. Several of the groups of fixed stars are readily recognised, as exhibiting always the same configuration, and stars particularly bright become more prominently objects of attention. These are observed at particular seasons to appear in the west after sunset; it is remarked, however, that when they do this, they are found nearer and nearer to the sun every successive evening, till they become invisible by his light; it is also observed, that at certain intervals after this, they rise before the dawn of day renders them imperceptible, and afterwards they rise at a longer interval before the sun. The risings and settings of the stars under the above circumstances were, in countries where the sky is usually clear, a great help in marking the various seasons. Thus, the rising of the Pleiades in the evening was an emblem of the approach of winter; the rising of the waters of the Nile coincided with the heliacal rising of Sirius: even without an artificial division of time, it was not impossible to carry observations of this kind to such a degree of accuracy, as to learn from them the number of days which compose a year, and to fix the season from the appearance of the stars. By such means it is said to have been determined that the year consisted at least of nearly 365 days. We are told by Herodotus that the Egyptians claimed the honour of this discovery; and the priests informed him that they were the first who divided it into twelve equal parts, or months, consisting of thirty days each, and that they added five days more* at the end of the year, and thus the circle of the seasons came round. It appears that the Jews at an early period had a similar method of reckoning time; for the deluge is stated to have continued 150 days,† from the 17th day of the second‡ month, to the 17th day of the seventh§ month; that is, five months of thirty days. A year thus settled as a period of a certain number of days, is called a civil year, and is one of the institutions of states possessing any degree of civilisation; and one of the earliest portions of systematical knowledge is the finding out the length of the civil year, so that it may agree with the natural year of the seasons. By such a mode of reckoning, however, the circle of the seasons would not come round exactly; the actual length of the year is very nearly 365 days and a quarter; so that if a year of 365 days were used, in four years the year would commence a day too soon, when considered with reference to the sun and stars; and in sixty years it would begin fifteen days too soon, a number perceptible to even a loose share of attention. Various contrivances were used to keep the year correct. The method which we employ, consisting in counting an additional day at the end of February every fourth, or leap year, is an

* Syncellus says that, according to the legend, it was King Aseth who first added the five additional days to 360 for the year, about 1800 B. C.

† Genesis, c. vii., v. 24. ‡ Genesis, c. vii., v. 11.

§ Genesis, c. viii., v. 4.

example of the principle of intercalation, by which the correction was more usually made. Methods of intercalation for the above purpose were found to exist in the new world; the Mexicans added thirteen days at the end of fifty-two years. The plan of the Greeks was more complex, by means of a cycle of eight years, which had the additional object of accommodating itself to the motions of the moon. The Egyptians, on the other hand, knowingly permitted their civil year to deviate at least so far as their religious ceremonies were concerned. According to Geminus, they did not wish the same sacrifices to be made always at the same time, but that they should go through the various seasons, in order that the same feast might happen in summer and winter, in spring and autumn. There were other nations that did not regulate their civil year by intercalation at short intervals, but rectified it at long periods when considered necessary. The Persians are said to have added a month of thirty days every 120 years. The Roman calendar, at first rude in its structure, was reformed by Numa, and was directed to be kept in order by the constant interposition of the augurs. This, however, was from various causes neglected, and the reckoning fell into complete disorder, in which state it was found by Julius Cæsar. By the advice of Sosigenes the astronomer, who came from Alexandria to correct the calendar, he adopted the mode of intercalation of one day in four years, which we still retain; and to amend the derangement which had been produced, he added ninety days to a year of the usual length, which consequently became what was called the year of confusion. The Julian calendar thus corrected came into use January 1, 45 B. C.

'The circle of changes through which the moon passes in about thirty days, was marked in the earliest stages of languages by the word *month*, as the circle of changes of the seasons was designated by that of *year*. The lunar changes are much more obvious to the senses than the annual. When the sun has set, the moon is the great natural object which attracts our notice. Her changes of form and place are marked and definite to all; and the duration of her cycle is so short, as to require little effort of memory to embrace it. It was therefore more easy, and, in the earlier stages of civilisation, more common to reckon time by moons than by years. The month is not an exact number of days, being more than twenty-nine, and less than thirty; the latter was first tried as possessing the advantage of regularity; it existed for a long period in many countries. A few months of thirty days, however, would suffice to derange the agreement between the days of the month and the moon's appearance; but a further trial of twenty-nine and thirty days alternately, would preserve for a considerable period the agreement. The Greeks adopted this calendar, and considered the days of their month as representing the changes of the moon; the last day of the month was styled the old and new, as belonging to both the waning and the reappearing moon; and their festivals and sacrifices, as determined by this mode of reckoning, were considered to be connected with the same periods of the cycles of the sun and moon. According to Geminus, "Their laws and oracle directed that they should in sacrifices observe three things: and months, days, and years were so understood." With such a persuasion, a correct system became a religious duty. The rule of alternate months of twenty-nine and thirty days, supposes the length of the lunar month to be twenty-nine days and a half, which is not exact. Accordingly, the months and the moon became at variance;* the correction of this inaccuracy, however, was not pursued singly; it was combined with another object, that of securing an exact correspondence between the lunar and solar years, the chief purpose of the early cycles.

'According to the above rule, 12 lunations in a year would make 354 days, leaving about 11¼ days of difference between such a lunar and a solar year. The first cycle, which produced a near correspondence between the reckoning of the moon and the sun, was the Greek octaeteris, or period of 8 years; 8 years of 354 days, together with 3 months of 30 days each, made up 2922 days, which is the amount of 8 years of 365¼ days each. The usual method, it is said, was to add a month at the end of the third, fifth, and eighth year of the cycle. It is not known with certainty at what period, or by whom this method was introduced; probably about the sixth century before the Christian era. This cycle was imperfect, and was corrected by others of 16 and 160 years, which were suggested when the length of the solar and lunar periods became known with accuracy. At length a more exact cycle was introduced by Meton of Athens, 431 B. C. This cycle consisted of 19 years, and is so correct and convenient, that it continues in use among ourselves; the time occupied by 19 years, and by 235 lunations, is about the same; the former being less than 6940 days by 9½ hours, the latter by 7⅓; hence, if the 19 years be divided into 235 months, so as to agree with the changes of the moon at the end of that period, the same succession may begin again with much exactness. The coincidence of the solar and lunar period in this cycle was certainly an important discovery; indeed it is so exact, that it is still used in calculating the new moon for the time of Easter; and what is called the golden number by the moderns in stating such rules, is the number of this cycle corresponding to the current year.* Meton's cycle was made still more exact by Calippus 100 years later, 330 B. C.; he discovered the error of it by observing an eclipse of the moon six years before the death of Alexander the Great; he calculated a period of four cycles of 19 years, and left out a day at the end of 76 years, to make an allowance for the hours by which, as already mentioned, 6940 days are greater than 19 years, and 235 lunations. * *

'The planets doubtless attracted the notice of men while they were becoming acquainted with the fixed stars. Venus, owing to her brightness, and her accompanying the sun at no great distance, and so appearing as the morning and evening star, was conspicuous; Pythagoras is said to have been the first who maintained that the evening and morning star are the same body. Jupiter and Mars, sometimes brighter than Venus, were also very observable; Saturn and Mercury, less so, would, in a clear climate, still be detected, with their motions, by persons who studied the aspect of the heavens. To reduce to rules the movements of these luminaries, must have taken time and thought; a remarkable evidence of their antiquity is to be found in the structure of one of our most familiar objects of time, the week, which comes down to us, according to the Jewish scriptures, from the commencement of the existence of mankind on earth. The same usage is found all over the East; it existed among the Assyrians, Egyptians, and Arabians. The week is found in India among the Brahmins; it has there also its day marked by those of the heavenly bodies. The idea which led to the usual designations of the days of the week is not easily discovered; the order in which the names are assigned, beginning with Saturday, is, Saturn, the Sun, the Moon, Mars, Mercury, Jupiter, and Venus. Various accounts are given of the manner in which the above order was derived from a previous one; all the methods proceeded on arithmetical processes connected with astrological views. Laplace considers the week as the most ancient

* Aristophanes, in 'The Clouds,' makes the moon complain of this disorder in the calendar—

'The moon by us to you her greeting sends,
But bids us say that she's an ill-used moon,
And takes it much amiss that you will still
Shuffle her days, and turn them topsy-turvy:
So that when gods, who know their feast days well,
By your false count are sent home supperless,
They scold and storm at her for your neglect.'

* The same cycle of nineteen years has been used by the Chinese for a vast length of time; their civil year consisting, like that of the Greeks, of months of twenty-nine and thirty days. The Siamese also use the same period.

monument of astronomical knowledge. This period has gone on without interruption from the earliest recorded times to our own days, surviving the extent of ages and the revolutions of empires.'

BENEFICIAL CO-OPERATION OF THE WORKING-CLASSES.

Among the various schemes which have been tried of late years for the improvement of the labouring classes, we know none more efficient than those that induce and enable them to assist themselves. In the hope of stimulating others to follow in this track, we give the case of a benefit scheme which has been in operation for the last nine months among the workmen of the lighting and cleaning departments of the police of Edinburgh, and which may, we believe, be taken as a specimen of what can be done among a class of men employed at a low rate of wages, and without any advantages or facilities beyond what are common to the whole labouring population.

The scheme, we understand, originated in the benevolent exertions of Mr Ramsay, the superintendent of these departments, to alleviate the distress which befell the workmen under his care when death occurred in their families, being stimulated thereto by witnessing the privations which were submitted to by the men in the establishment when a wife or child died. It frequently happened that the parties were altogether destitute of the means to bury their dead; and hence, as a matter of necessity, that duty was devolved upon the parish. In other cases, the expenses of the funeral hung like a millstone about the neck of many an honest and industrious man, and the debts then incurred were sometimes the commencement of the ruin of a whole family. From the want of ready money, the most indispensable articles were procured at a cost sometimes amounting to double or even triple their value; the only choice left to the poor man being, not where he was to buy cheapest, but where he could obtain credit. Then followed the usual train of evils which break the heart or ruin the health—children in rags, clamorous for food—the father insufficiently clad to resist the cold and rain to which his avocations constantly expose him—with bad shoes on his feet, he is laid up by a cold, which terminates in rapid consumption. His children are then beggars; and a blessed deathbed is his if they become nothing worse.

To obviate or lighten some of these evils, a scheme was organised, under which each person in these departments was taxed to the extent of 6d. on the death of a husband or wife, and 3d. for that of a child, to defray the cost of the funeral; the sums realised varying, in the former case, from L.3 to L.4 and upwards, and, in the latter, to the half of these sums. This scheme existed for thirteen years, in the course of which time nearly L.300 of funeral money was collected and expended. The mere extent of relief afforded was no doubt great; but it was held of far more importance to form habits of self-reliance, and altogether to repudiate even the idea of assistance from public charity. One condition, therefore, was, that no part of the funeral expenses was to be defrayed by the parish. The practical working of this scheme, though on the whole beneficial, was found to be imperfect, inasmuch as it afforded relief from one source only of the casualties to which the men were exposed; and its success suggested the idea of extending the system of self-reliance and mutual assistance, so as to preclude the necessity of pecuniary relief from public charity, or of any dependence upon gratuitous medical aid.

For this purpose Mr Ramsay devised a plan, by means of which all persons employed under him were bound to contribute from their pay 6d. a week, in return for which the following benefits were secured to them:—*First*, Aliment, during sickness, at the rate of 9d. per day, or 5s. 3d. per week, for the first thirteen weeks; 3s. 6d. per week for the next thirteen weeks; and 2s. 6d. per week for the next twenty-six weeks. *Second*, Funeral money at the rate of L.4 for a man, L.3 for a wife, and 15s. for a child. *Third*, Medicine and medical attendance for the men and their whole families, however numerous, or whatever the nature of the illness under which they might labour. The balance remaining, after defraying these sources of expense, to be divided twice in the year, in the rates of their respective contributions.

The scheme, and the data on which it was founded, were submitted at the outset to the board of police, who after mature consideration, gave it their sanction. It has now been in operation for nine months; and we have just received the state of the accounts for the six months ending the 15th November, which was submitted to the police board at one of their late meetings. From this statement it appears that the working of the scheme has been most successful, and is full of instruction as to one important means of improving the condition of the class for whose benefit it was intended. It appears that the subscriptions received from 152 men, during the six months, amounted to L.99, 14s. 6d.; out of which there has been paid for aliment to thirteen men, whose united periods of sickness amounted to ninety-one days, the sum of L.3, 8s. 9½d.; for the funeral money of one man, one wife, and seven children, L.12, 5s.; while the salary paid to the surgeon, which we may mention is fixed at the rate of 2d. per man per week, amounted to L.33, 2s., and the allowance to a clerk of L.2, 12s. The whole expenditure, therefore, amounted to L.51, 7s., 7½d., being about the rate of 1d. per week for aliment and funeral money, or 3d. per week, including the allowance to the medical officer. The surplus, therefore, which amounted to about half the sum contributed, has been returned to the men, and has afforded a dividend of 6s. 6d. to each man employed in these departments. No doubt the amount of sickness has been, during the last half year, smaller than can be calculated upon at an average; but even in the most unhealthy seasons, the sum required from such a large body of workmen to insure the same amount of benefits as is allowed on this scheme is so small, in comparison with the advantages to be derived, as to form no burden even upon the lowest rate of wages: while the conscious feeling of independence enjoyed by the men, from their having secured to them, at so trifling an amount of expense, a provision in the event of sickness, and a small fund in the case of death, together with medicine and medical attendance for themselves and their families, are of the utmost value in elevating them in their own estimation, and relieving them from the degrading necessity of application to the ordinary sources of charity.

In connexion with this scheme, a contract was entered into with a respectable undertaker for the supply of coffins at fixed prices, varying according to size, from the smallest, 18 inches long, which costs 2s. 9d., to that of 6 feet 6 inches, at a cost of 16s. 11½d. The coffins are covered with cloth, and mounted with lace, and delivered in a decent and proper manner at the houses of any of the men who may require them.

Still farther to improve the condition of the men under his care, Mr Ramsay has added to the benefit scheme a plan partaking of the benefits of a co-operative society, under which such of the workmen as choose to join in it are supplied with bread, oatmeal, potatoes, and coal, at an expense considerably below the ordinary retail prices. This is done by entering into a contract for the supply of the articles required, which, from the number of the men, is necessarily on a large scale; and, consequently, the articles are furnished at the lowest wholesale prices, and dealt out to the men in such quantities as suits their convenience.

To show the working of this part of the scheme, we may state what is brought out in the abstract before us, that there have been supplied within the last six months 5981 loaves, 2250 pecks of oatmeal, 158 bolls of potatoes, and 180 tons of coal; the aggregate cost of which is L.376, 6s. 8d. This of course is an expenditure altogether separate from the benefit scheme, and, unlike which, it is entirely optional for the men to enter into it or not, though the money saved by this mode of purchasing provisions and other necessary articles greatly more than repays the cost of the benefit scheme, to say nothing of the additional comfort and thrift of obtaining coal in tons, and potatoes in bushels, and other articles in proportional quantities, compared with the wretched system, so common among the poor, of purchasing their necessaries in the smallest quantities, and, as a consequence, at the highest price, though of inferior quality. It is probable that much of the success of this scheme may arise from the unintermitting watchfulness of Mr Ramsay, under whose superintendence it has been got up, and who has always taken a deep interest in its management. There is, however, a committee appointed by the men themselves, under whose inspection the contracts are made, who take charge of the collection and disbursements of the money, and whose duty it is to see that the contracts are properly fulfilled. This is an important feature in the scheme identifying the men with its

ing, and interesting them in its success. A scheme of this kind can be carried out to its full measure of success only where there is a considerable body of workmen; but wherever men are permanently employed, even a small number may, with great advantage, make arrangements to secure a part, if not the whole of the benefits enjoyed by the plan of co-operation we have described, and for the maturing of which Mr Ramsay deserves the thanks of the community.

REMARKABLE BOOKS.

There are few subjects so barren as not to afford matter of delight, and even of instruction, if ingeniously treated. Montaigne has written an essay on *Coaches*, and another on *Thumbs*. Lyonnet has written a large work on the goat-moth caterpillar; and Straus-Durckeim another big volume on the cockchafer. Evelyn wrote a discourse on sallads, entitled *Acetaria*, which has been admired and commended by the best judges of literature. In 1669 Mr Steadman published a book called *Campanologia, or the Art of Ringing*, which reached three editions in the course of a few years. Another work on the same subject was published by Mr Shipway, in three parts, in 1816. A curious little treatise on sneezing, entitled *Mart: Schookii de Sternutatione tractatus copiosus, omnia ad illam pertinentia*, &c. was published at Amsterdam in 1664. Tobias Swinden, an English clergyman, wrote an *Inquiry into the Nature and Place of Hell*, and a second edition of his work appeared in 1727, with an illustrative plate. In this singular work the reverend gentleman endeavours to prove that the sun is Tartarus! Chevreau has written *A History of the World*, in which he tells us that it was created a little after four o'clock in the afternoon of Friday, September 6!—a very precise bit of information. The rare edition of the *Biblia Germanica*, in two folio volumes, published in 1487, contains many coloured woodcuts, remarkable for the singularity of their designs; for instance, Bathsheba is represented washing her feet in a small tub of water, and Elias ascending to heaven in a four-wheeled wagon. H. Maurice's *Impartial Account of Mr John Mason of Water Stratford*, 1695, informs us that Mr Mason, who is supposed to have been the founder of the gymnastic sect of Jumpers, preached a sermon announcing that our Saviour's reign of a thousand years upon earth was about to commence on the very spot where he was standing, which was received with so much favour, that a great concourse of people, for many miles round, took up their habitations there in expectation of the event—truly an excellent stratagem for increasing a congregation.

An edition of the *Classics*, published on the Continent, has a curious frontispiece representing on one side a divine personage, and on the other a figure of the author, from whose mouth issues a label with these words:—'Lord, lovest thou me?' which question is answered by another label affixed to the mouth of the sacred figure, with these words:—'Highly-famed, excellent, and most learned rector of Seger, imperial poet, and well-deserving master of the school at Wirtemberg, yes, thou knowest I love thee!' The interesting and enthusiastic letters of the Prince of Mirandola were so highly admired and prized by his contemporaries, that some of the earlier editions are entitled *The Golden Epistles of the most learned, most noble, and most eloquent of Mortals.* One of the rarest of privately-printed works is a curious folio volume entitled *Pauli Cortesii Protonotarii Apostolici, de Cardinalata, libri iii.*, 1510. The author of this book, tired of the vicissitudes and troubles of public life, retired to the town of Montana Villa, two miles from St Germain, in France, and determined to devote the remainder of his life to literary pursuits. In this seclusion, a short time before his decease, he established a printing-press, whence issued only the above work. Clavell's *Recantation of an Ill-led Life, or a Discoverie of the High-way Law, with vehement Dissuasions to all in that kind Offenders, with Instructions how to know, shun, and apprehend a Thief, most necessary for all Travellers*, 1634, is a scarce book in verse by a celebrated highwayman, and contains also a poetical address to the author's uncle, Sir W. Clavell, and others to the Lord Chief Justice, &c. A rare little book, *The Academy of Pleasure*, 1656, contains a portrait, supposed to represent its author, in the dress of a book-chapman.

Some books are remarkable on account of certain events and anecdotes which they have given rise to. Thus, the Marchioness of Lambert's excellent works (Paris, 1761) are additionally interesting, from the circumstance that it was upon seeing the Empress Elizabeth reading them that Peter the Great lamented his want of education. Brewer's play of *Lingua, or the Combat of the Tongue and the Five Senses for Superioritie*, 1632, is more esteemed, owing to Winstanley's statement, that when it was performed at Cambridge, Oliver Cromwell acted the part of Tactus in it, from which he imbibed his sentiments of ambition. The second edition of Woolaston's *Religion of Nature*, is valued from the fact of Benjamin Franklin having assisted in the printing of it. 'I was employed,' he says, 'at Palmer's on the second edition of that work. Some of Woolaston's arguments appearing to me not to be well-founded, I wrote a small metaphysical treatise, animadverting on those passages. It was called *A Dissertation on Liberty and Necessity, Pleasure and Pain*, of which I printed only a few copies.' A little book, entitled *Epistolæ Obscurorum Virorum ad Dn M. Ortuinum Gratium*, 1643, is interesting, at first sight, from the story of Erasmus having laughed so heartily on reading it, that he broke an imposthume of which he lay dangerously ill, and in consequence recovered without undergoing any operation. The rare Latin commentary on the Marquis of Montrose's military exploits, written under the signature of T. G. by the Rev. George Wishart, a Scotch prelate, and published at Paris in 1648, is remarkable from a historical anecdote thus related by Hume:—'As the Marquis of Montrose was led forth to his execution, they made yet one effort more to insult him in this last and melancholy scene: the executioner brought that book which had been published in elegant Latin concerning his great military actions, and tied it by a cord about his neck.' Father Auchfer's *Armenian and English Grammar* (Venice, 1819) is prized from the statement that Lord Byron contributed the English portion. William Fowler's *Engravings of Mosaic Pavements, Stained Glass*, &c. in two large folio volumes, are highly interesting from the fact of their author having been originally a journeyman carpenter, of patient and persevering habits, and who had to encounter almost insurmountable difficulties in executing this work, which is scrupulously correct in all its details, and is entirely his own: the drawing, the engraving, the preparation of the colours, and even the making of the paper (for he could get no paper-maker to undertake it), and the binding, are all the work of his own hands. As not more than forty copies were ever completed, it is now an extremely rare and valuable work.

Certain books are rendered precious by their containing personal sketches and notices nowhere else recorded. This is the case with Robert Armin's *Nest of Ninnies*, 1608, which contains anecdotes, in verse and prose, of various celebrated fools and jesters. In Casio's *Libro Intitulato Bellona*, 1525, an extremely rare book, are numerous notices of Ariosto and the contemporary poets. A rare and neglected work, entitled *Horanyi Memoria Hungarorum et Provincialium Scriptis editis Notorum*, in three volumes, published at Vienna in 1777, contains the lives of several authors, and bibliographical information not to be found elsewhere. A little book, entitled *Th: Spizelii Infelix Literatus, Labyrinthis et Miseriis suis cura posteriori ereptus, et ad Supremæ Salutis Domicilium deductus, sive de Vita et Moribus Literatorum*, 1680, contains an abundance of 'Calamities of Authors,' unnoticed by D'Israeli and all others who have written on that very encouraging subject.

A MODEL FRENCH FARM KITCHEN.

Perhaps a more gratifying sight does not exist than the interior of a large farm kitchen prepared for the evening meal, especially during the winter season. Its bright wood fire, the long table covered with the savoury, smoking dishes, the huge tankards of foaming beer or cider, with the happy countenances scattered round, speak of peaceful labour and healthful industry. The farm kitchen of Bouqueval was a fine exemplification of this remark. Its immense open chimney, about six feet high and eight feet wide, resembled the yawning mouth of some huge oven. On the hearth blazed and sparkled enormous logs of beech or oak; and from this prodigious brazier there issued forth such a body of light, as well as heat, that the large lamp suspended from the centre beam sunk into insignificance, and was rendered nearly useless. Every variety of culinary utensils, sparkling in all the brightness of the most elaborate cleanliness, and composed invariably of copper, brass, and tin, glowed in the bright radiance of the winter fire, as they stood ranged with the utmost nicety and effect on their appropriate shelves. An old-fashioned cistern of elaborately-polished copper showed its bright face, polished as a mirror; and close beside stood a highly-polished bread-trough and cover, composed of walnut-tree wood, rubbed by the hand of housewifery till you could see your face in it, and from which issued a most tempting smell of hot bread. A long and substantial table occupied the centre of the kitchen; a table-cloth, which, though coarse in texture, vied with the falling snow for whiteness, covered its entire length; while for each expected guest was placed an earthenware plate, brown without, but white within, and by its side a knife, fork, and spoon, lustrous as silver itself. In the midst of the table, an immense tureen of vegetable soup smoked like the crater of a volcano, and diffused its savoury vapours over a dish of ham and greens, flanked by a most formidable array of mutton, most relishly stewed with onions and potatoes. Below was placed a large joint of roast veal, followed by two great plates of winter salad, supported by a couple of baskets of apples; and a similar number of cheeses completed the arrangements of the table. Three or four stone pitchers, filled with sparkling cider, and a like quantity of loaves of brown bread, equal in size to the stones of a windmill, were placed at the discretionary use of the supping party.—*Eugene Sue.*

LAWS OF NATURE.

If the laws of nature, on the one hand, are invincible opponents, on the other they are irresistible auxiliaries; and it will not be amiss if we regard them in each of these characters, and consider the great importance of them to mankind. 1. In showing us how to avoid attempting impossibilities. 2. In securing us from important mistakes in attempting what is in itself possible, by means either inadequate, or actually opposed to the ends in view. 3. In enabling us to accomplish our ends in the easiest, shortest, most economical, and most effectual manner. 4. In inducing us to attempt, and enabling us to accomplish objects, which, but for such knowledge, we should never have thought of undertaking.—*Herschel.*

DOGS' SCENT FOR GAME.

There is a notion that dogs lose their scent or smell for game-birds during the season of incubation. That, however, says a correspondent of the Gardeners' Chronicle, I consider to be wrong. I think it is more likely that the birds lose, or rather do not emit, scent or smell during the time in question; hence the notion. I mentioned this to a gentleman well acquainted with dogs and game, and he told me the following in favour of what I have advanced. He was once aware of a partridge's nest that was 'hard set upon' near where a party of gipsies had fixed their abode, and although they had three dogs with them, yet the wary bird led off her brood three days afterwards. There must be some truth in what I have stated, otherwise the smell from the bird on the nest would have led the prowling dogs upon her. If my views on this subject are correct, it shows a wise provision of Nature to protect birds from harm during incubation; for if it were not so, they must often fall a prey to canine enemies. It may be asked, how does it happen that birds do not emit smell while sitting on eggs? That may be owing to the habits or conditions of birds being changed; for during the time of incubation, they lose in a great measure all thought of self-preservation.

FORCE OF PERIODIC VIBRATIONS.

Many curious instances might be mentioned of the great effects produced by periodic vibrations: one of the most familiar, perhaps, is the well-known result of marching a company of soldiers over a suspension-bridge, when the latter, responsive to the measured step, begins to rise and fall with excessive violence, and, if the marching be still continued, most probably separate in two parts. More than one accident has occurred in this way, and has led to the order (we believe) that soldiers, in passing these bridges, must not march, but simply walk out of time. Another curious effect of vibration in destroying the cohesion of bodies, is the rupture of drinking-glasses by certain musical sounds. It is well known that most glass vessels of capacity, when struck, resound with a beautifully clear musical note of invariable and definite pitch, which may be called the peculiar note of the vessel. Now, if a violin or other musical instrument be made to sound in the same note, it soon begins to respond, is thrown into vibrations, the note grows louder and louder, and eventually may break. In order to insure the success of this experiment, the glass should not be perfectly annealed; however, the *tendency* to break is invariably the same.—*Polytechnic Magazine.*

WHERE ARE THEY?

BY S. W. PARTRIDGE.

Where are they—the companions of our games,
With whom in youth we gambolled on the sod;
The gray-haired fathers and the gentle dames,
Whose hospitable thresholds erst we trod;
The beauteous forms that taught our hearts to love,
And woke our hopes and fears with magic spell;
The cheerful friends with whom we wont to rove,
Whose tales around the hearth we loved so well—
Where are they?

Where are they—the gay train of laughing hours,
Youth's longed-for morrows and glad yesterdays,
That joyous season of hope's budding flowers,
That fairy portal to life's thorny maze;
The pregnant sunny seed-months of life's year,
The calm bright moments of its April sky,
Ere stormy passion and beclouding care
Had vexed and marred its blue serenity—
Where are they?

Where are they—the fond dreams of buoyant youth,
Trusting to-morrow, scornful of to-day,
As, yet undoubting the fair syren's truth,
Slumbering in hope's soft lap entranced we lay?
Where are the glowing visions that arose
Before our eyes like purpling clouds of eve,
Of beauty, fortune, honour, and repose,
And all the witcheries hope alone can weave—
Where are they?

Where are they—the resolves of life's young morn,
The resolutions firm to be and do,
When, weakness, difficulty laughed to scorn,
Sage plans for future years we fondly drew;
The deep devotedness to love and truth,
The manly purpose and the sacred vow,
That clustered, big with promise, in our youth,
Like opening spring-buds, blushing on the bough—
Where are they?

MISS MARTINEAU'S CASE.

'Few medical men of any experience will have the slightest difficulty in perfectly comprehending the state so graphically described by the sufferer. It is seen every day in women at the turn of life; and the grand mistake that is ever committed in regard to it, is to look on mere functional derangement, accompanied by pain and excessive discharge, as organic disease.'—*Medical Gazette.* There is no theorist like your opposer of theories. In these and a few more like sentences the Medical Gazette disposes of Miss Martineau's illness and her so-called cure by mesmerism, the mere supposition of a person unconnected with the case being presented as sufficient to overpower all that was patiently observed and cautiously said by others on the spot, including the patient herself. Whatever be the real character of Miss Martineau's case, one cannot but be amused to see extremes thus return upon themselves, and scepticism pretend to an oracular power far beyond the ordinary stretch of the grossest superstition.

BELIEF.

Were we to believe nothing but what we could perfectly comprehend, not only our stock of knowledge in all the branches of learning would be shrunk up to nothing, but even the affairs of common life could not be carried on.—*Tucker.*

*** Complete sets of the Journal, *First Series*, in twelve volumes, and also odd numbers to complete sets, may be had from the publishers or their agents. A Stamped Edition issued for transmission, post free, price Twopence halfpenny.

Printed by William Bradbury, of No. 6, York Place, and Frederick Mullett Evans, of No. 7, Church Row, both of Stoke Newington, in the county of Middlesex, printers, at their office, Lombard Street, in the precinct of Whitefriars, and city of London; and Published by WILLIAM SOMERVILLE ORR, of 2, Amen Corner, at No. 2, AMEN CORNER, both in the parish of Christchurch, and in the city of London.—Saturday, January 4, 1845.

CONDUCTED BY WILLIAM AND ROBERT CHAMBERS, EDITORS OF 'CHAMBERS'S INFORMATION FOR THE PEOPLE,' 'CHAMBERS'S EDUCATIONAL COURSE,' &c.

No. 54. New Series. SATURDAY, JANUARY 11, 1845. Price 1½d.

'AN APOLOGY

The appearance of sincere penitence is perhaps the most touching of all things. Anger at the offence vanishes; the error is forgiven; and the offender, so far from being degraded by his confession, runs a good chance of being exalted. There is something which makes these results among the most certain of all mental phenomena. We all feel the weakness of our nature, and, like an Irish cotter helping a beggar, because he does not know but he may be a beggar next year himself, we sympathise with acknowledged transgression, because we never can be sure that we are not to be very speedily in the confessional too. Therefore it is that men in general melt at the sight of penitence, even in those who may have been aiming at their own hurt, or wounding their own self-esteem. They might be full of the bitterest indignation while the offence was still in the course of being given, or while the offender remained incontrite; but the moment that error or obduracy was exchanged for a humble sense of the wrong done, however faintly that might be expressed, all anger must vanish; and it is the direct and simple tendency of man's nature, when unprevented by other feelings, to receive his errant brother back again to his heart, and be the same to him as ever.

It is, however, very unlucky that some persons either never can see that they do wrong, or will not, on any compulsion, acknowledge it. To impute to them an error of any kind, to complain of an injury or insult having been offered by them, only rouses their self-love, and throws them into a paroxysm of obstinacy, during which they will dispute the clearest reasoning that may be brought against them, and even deny their own acts, if these tend to their condemnation. The no-wrong-doers and always-in-the-right-men are a very considerable class in point of numbers, and it is sometimes not a little amusing to observe that thorough conviction of their own entire innocence which bears them up against charge and challenge of every kind. Some take an imputation very tartly, however justly made. Some fall sulkily upon their self-esteem, and simply refuse to admit anything so derogatory. Others coolly pity the absurd people who think they have been mistreated, and wonder that any one could be so foolish as to imagine that *they* COULD BE in the wrong. Perhaps there is still another sub-class who merely act from false system or bad habit, and only refuse to own their error because they never have been taught to see that to do so handsomely and readily is, and can be, no disgrace to a human being, but, on the contrary, is a virtue. Much harm of course follows from this indisposition to own error; for if the guilty will not make concession, much less is it to be expected that the innocent and injured parties are to do so; and therefore alienation, and all its train of evils—if not positive and active hostility—are sure to take place. Many a time must the doggedness of a moment have made those enemies who, otherwise, would have continued friends, and embittered whole lives which otherwise might have been happy. One moment will suffice for such an effect; for this little space of time is often the determining point of all future conduct. Had *that moment* been graced by the beauty and holiness of repentance, instead of being signalised by a spasm of wicked and selfish obstinacy, all might have been well. But it was not so, and misery came of course. The no-wrong-doers maintain their self-esteem in high mettle no doubt; they may cherish a pride somewhat like that of a fortress which never surrendered or was taken; but they have a small chance of being happy. They will necessarily be on bad terms with many persons, which is always a great inconvenience. They will, in a vast number of cases, only be tolerated, instead of being liked, and thus lose all the benefit of that general goodwill which often acts like a favouring gale to blow the vessel of a man's fortunes into port. In short, the injury they do to society by their shortsighted and selfish policy will powerfully react against them, and that which is only a temporary cause of irritation to those whom they aggrieve or injure, may prove something little, if at all short, of their own permanent ruin.

To be ready, on the other hand, to acknowledge and ask forgiveness of an error or offence, tending as it does to the general comfort, by preserving the sweetness of mutual relations in society, ought to, and ever does, favour the happiness of the individual. We must, from the constitution of our nature, occasionally speak or act amiss: this must be submitted to as unavoidable. There is but one remedy for it—that he who does either the one or the other, should take the earliest opportunity of manifesting regret for the error. To be thus penitent —thus to give obedience to what appears as a great law in our being—entitles us to forgiveness; for it is all that the providential arrangements of our nature admit of being done to repair the wrong we have committed. We have a right thereafter to be made the same as if we had never done wrong, for we have fulfilled the great law upon the subject. Political institutions, for reasons of their own, do not act upon this maxim with their offenders; but the greatest criminal will, upon a perfect repentance, obtain forgiveness from men as individuals. And those refusing to forgive a minor offence against themselves, when it has been thoroughly repented of, are sure to be condemned by public opinion. When any one, then, has done wrong, and expresses penitence, he is not to be considered as humiliating himself to a poor fellow-creature no better than himself. He is obeying a great natural institution, and thereby yielding obedience to a power far above that of mortals. All men do not see the matter in this its true light—they do not know the fact philosophically; but they *feel* that it is so, and act accordingly. We instinctively recognise the beauty and virtue of a handsome apology.

Apologies, expressions of regret for light offences given, intreaties for forgiveness of those of graver moment, thus take a place among high things, however familiarly we may from habit regard them. Heaven's face shines on every word of this kind spoken in sincerity and for peace-sake. Error may be great—alas! how great may our errors be!—but no error can be so great but penitence may be greater, and absolution must then be granted by the wronged party, or to him that moment is the whole guilt transferred. Let no one, then, ever grudge to confess himself in the wrong, or pridefully refuse to ask remission of his offence. He can never suffer for taking this course in any eyes but his own, and that will never be but at the moment. The next instant, if his repentance has been sincere and unreserved, he must experience the comfort of that peace which attends every truly good action.

There is but one danger on the other side. It is necessary to guard against being lulled into a too great dependence upon the apologetic principle. Error, when it becomes habitual, and frequent of occurrence, ceases to have any rightful claim to forgiveness upon the mere expression of regret, because, if that regret were true, it might be presumed to have the effect of forbidding such a recurrence of error. Hence we all feel, when a transgression is repeated for the fiftieth time, and is instantly followed by the customary expression of penitence, that the latter is a mockery, adding to, rather than extenuating the evil, seeing that, besides the original offence, a thing in its proper character sacred has been perverted to a wrong purpose. The young, after their first experiences of the benefit of an apology, are particularly apt to rely overmuch upon it. This, however, is an error calling for its own check, and that check, we should think, it can never be difficult to impose. And it is hardly necessary to remark, that no abuse to which penitence is liable can ever take from the absolute value of penitence itself—the blessed medicating principle in our nature, the preserver of peace among men, the talisman that promises us more than aught that earth has ever given, or ever can give.

THE ROYAL OBSERVATORY AT GREENWICH.

It is fair to suppose that but few persons in this country are ignorant of the existence of the institution whose name stands at the head of these columns. Some, during a visit to London, and while sauntering in Greenwich Park, may have seen its exterior. Others, again, have read of it in books of voyages, or seen the words printed in the margin of maps, as the point from which longitude is reckoned. But very few possess any definite idea as to the nature of the operations carried on within it; of the patient watching, amounting to severe labour, in conducting the extensive, various, and delicate observations for which it has long been celebrated; or of their high importance in a scientific and commercial point of view.

These points are, however, ably elucidated in the annual report for the present year of G. B. Airy, Esq. the astronomer royal, which, while it explains the satisfactory state of the scientific proceedings, contains also some general notices that may enable the great body of readers to comprehend the more than national value of such an establishment.

It would not be out of place to give, before proceeding farther, a brief history of the building, which is erected on the top of a gravelly hill in Greenwich Park, on the site of the ancient tower built by Duke Humphrey in the reign of Henry VI., commanding a fine and impressive view over the smoke-shrouded city, the flowing river alive with vessels, and the fertile plains of Essex. It was built by order of Charles II., who, with all his levity, seems to have been aware of the importance of science: the first stone was laid by Flamsteed, who had been appointed astronomer royal in August 1675, and no delay took place in its completion and furnishing it with accurate instruments. By the words of Flamsteed's commission, he was directed 'to apply himself with the utmost care and diligence to the rectifying the tables of the motions of the heavens, and the places of the fixed stars, in order to find the so-much desired longitude at sea, for perfecting the art of navigation.' With what success this has been done, may be inferred from the remarkable words of Delambre, who, writing on the four volumes of observations by Maskelyne, astronomer royal at the commencement of the present century, observes, 'that if, by a great revolution, the sciences should be lost, and that this collection only were saved, there would be found in it materials sufficient to rear almost an entire new edifice of modern astronomy.'

The whole establishment comprehends two principal buildings, one the observatory, the other the dwelling-house; the former is a low oblong erection, placed east and west, with four principal apartments on the ground-floor, in which the most important observations are carried on; in one of these, which has a double sloping roof fitted with sliding shutters, for convenience in observing transits, is the transit instrument, eight feet in length, resting on two stone pillars, and interesting from having been used by the astronomers royal from the days of Halley. In an adjacent apartment is the magnificent mural circle by Troughton, which was placed on its stone pier in 1812, and although it has a diameter of nearly eight feet, such is the accuracy with which it has been constructed, that its position may be ascertained to the tenth of a second. In the other rooms are other circles, and a variety of astronomical instruments, as well as a library containing many scarce scientific books.

It is, however, beyond our province to attempt a description of the splendid and complicated instruments contained within the observatory, which we should scarcely succeed in making intelligible to the general reader; suffice it to say, that the establishment is supported at the expense of government, and is under the direction of the lords of the admiralty.

Astronomical time is not divided, like civil time, into two periods of twelve hours, but is counted regularly from one to twenty-four. Now, it is one of the most important objects in the duties of the observatory to find the *true time*; this is ascertained at Greenwich by accurate determination of the places of various stars, and their transit over the meridian. From these observations the mean solar time is computed; and this once known, the finding of the longitude of any place is comparatively easy. A knowledge of the true time being of the highest importance in keeping the reckoning of a ship on a voyage, the lords of the admiralty determined, about ten years since, on a means for making known daily the hour of one o'clock. Such is the skill displayed in the observations, that this hour is now ascertained with the utmost nicety, and from the summit of the building has been made known with the greatest regularity from the time the plan was first adopted.

Every day, at five minutes to one, the captains of vessels in the river, within sight of the observatory, may be seen directing their telescopes towards a black ball slowly rising on a pole fixed on the roof of its north-western angle; they then prepare their chronometers, and keeping their attention fixed on the ball, which has become stationary at the top of the pole, they note the instant when it begins to descend; at that instant it is one o'clock; and it will be obvious that the mariner has then the opportunity of knowing whether his chronometer is fast or slow; he may set it to the true time, and, by daily observation of the descent of the ball, ascertain its rate of going.

There is an apartment in the building appropriated to chronometers. It is the custom with makers of those instruments to send them to the observatory for correction and trial. Their daily rate is then observed, and noted down for the use of the owners; the same course is followed with the chronometers of ships lying in port. Visitors to Greenwich Park may frequently see a captain descending the hill with his time-keeper in a handkerchief under his arm. The present number of chronometers on trial exceeds one hundred, many of them being from government ships paid off, and thirty in preparation for the determination of the longitude of Valentia in Ireland.

Another very important object in the institution and maintenance of the observatory, is the observations of the moon, and the determination of the places of fixed stars necessary for ascertaining instrumental errors arising in those observations. In the early history of the building, these were regarded merely as secondary, but they appear to have been followed up with the greatest regularity, even when all others were neglected. The effect of this regularity is most honourable to the institution; for the existing theories and tables of the moon are everywhere founded on the observations at Greenwich, which is looked to as that from which alone adequate observations can be expected; and it is fair to predict that, while the duties are as efficiently performed as at present, lunar tables will always be founded on the same authority. To seafaring men lunar tables are of little less importance than true time; relying on their correctness, they sail away into the broad ocean, over which the calculations made thousands of miles distant serve as finger-posts. In order to render this branch of the observations still more efficient, an additional building is being erected, in which the moon may be observed through her entire passage. Owing to the construction of the portion of the building at present devoted to this purpose, one half of her course is very imperfectly observed, and one fourth is quite lost. When the new part is completed, it is anticipated that the observations on our satellite may be made almost every night; at present, from the cause above alluded to, they do not exceed one hundred in the year. Some idea of the patience necessary on the part of the observer, may be inferred from the fact of his being required to watch from moonrise to an hour or more after sunrise, or from an hour before sunset to moonsetting.

Of late years, in addition to the astronomical, a series of magnetic and meteorological observations have been conducted at the observatory. For the observation of the magnetic dip, and some other points which could not be carried on near the great magnets, or other disturbing influences, a small outbuilding has been raised of wood, the greatest care being taken that no particle of iron should be used in the construction. Such is the extreme delicacy and susceptibility of some of the instruments in this apartment, that they are suspended by skeins of fibrous silk, enclosed, in some instances, within tubes of glass. These skeins are prepared at Manchester expressly for the purpose; the fibres consist of seven or eight threads, as when reeled off in readiness for spinning: the slightest twist would render them unfit for use; and it is essential that they should be of uniform thickness.

There are three magnetometers, the magnets for which were made at Göttingen; they are of polished steel, each two feet in length, one inch and a half in width, and one quarter of an inch in thickness. In reading off the results, allowance is made for the presence of iron in the apparatus which supports them, or in other parts of the room. These instruments, with the barometer, and the wet and dry thermometers, are observed every two hours, day and night (except on Sundays); the dew point four times every day; the magnetic dip is observed on the forenoon and afternoon of each of two days in every week; on one particular day in every month, previously determined for the observatories in various parts of the world, and known as a term day, magnetic observations are made at every five minutes; on one day in each month, hourly observations of the barometer are made; observations with the actinometer, an instrument for ascertaining the radiation of solar rays, are made when circumstances are favourable; electrical and extraordinary observations of any kind, when circumstances require them. The indications of the self-registering instruments are regularly preserved or read off; the rain gauges, &c. which are cumulative, but not self-registering, are read, some once in a day, some once in a week.

In addition to these instruments, there are an atmospheric electrometer, a galvanometer, and an anemometer. The last registers of itself the force, direction, and duration of winds. There are also self-registering thermometers, which are suspended from the side of the Dreadnought hospital ship, for ascertaining the temperature of the water of the Thames, with the object of assisting the registrar-general in the meteorological report affixed to his weekly sanitary report.

In astronomical science, everything depends on the precision with which the longitude of a place is determined as regards any other fixed place: by the transmission of chronometers from one point to the other, this may be ascertained. An operation of this nature is now in progress to determine the difference of longitude between Greenwich and Pulkowa, in Russia. As it is necessary that the observers as well as the instruments should be interchanged, M. Struve, astronomer at the latter place, has come over to make his observations from this point, for which purpose a transit instrument has been placed at his disposal.

The Nautical Almanac is generally printed three years in advance, for the benefit of those who go long voyages: the volume for the year 1847 is now published. The list of stars for this work has a first claim in the astronomical observations; and it is a rule that each star shall be observed at least twenty times in every three years. Besides these, there are observations of stars for refraction; of those selected for the moon-culminating list of the almanac; of those compared with comets, and others observed in trigonometrical survey. The sun, moon, and planets are observed at every practicable opportunity, the latter through all hours of the night (except on Sundays), when the moon only, with accompanying stars, is observed. Occultations, diameters, and the eclipses and movements of Jupiter's satellites, complete a catalogue which, for scope and detail, reflects the highest credit on those concerned in its execution.

The electrical apparatus is attached to a pole 80 feet high, fixed in the garden; a wire connected with this is led into one of the rooms of the building, where pith balls, suspended near a bell, are attached to it. When the apparatus is excited by the electric state of the atmosphere, the balls become violently agitated, and, striking against the bell, cause a ringing, which immediately attracts the attention of the attendant.

In Flamsteed's time, a well was sunk in this garden 100 feet in depth, with steps leading to the bottom, for the purpose of observing the stars in the daytime; but this has long since been arched over, as the improvements in the construction of telescopes render it unnecessary.

The whole mass of observations, both meteorological and astronomical, is regularly printed, a quarto volume of some thousand pages appearing once in the year. Most of these are distributed amongst the observatories all over the world, with a view to assist the cause of science, and to facilitate the great series of observations, undertaken at the expense of government, which have now been carried on for four or five years, and are expected to be brought to a conclusion in the present year. In order to have some security that the assistants, of whom there are nine regularly on the establishment, are in attendance to take their observations at the time appointed, a clock, commonly termed 'the watchman's clock,' is fixed in the anteroom; it has no hands, but a series of knobs, to which cords are attached on the dial-plate, which turns round; this is secured by a door with a lock and key, so that the only external communication is by the cords, one of which being pulled by the assistant when he leaves, a knob is displaced, the dial-plate turns round, and thus a complete check is kept upon the attendance of the subordinate officers.

Among the extraordinary scientific operations to which the observatory has contributed its aid, was that of instructing the officers of the corps of Royal Engineers, who were appointed to trace the Canadian boundary; one portion of which, a straight line of a distance of 70 miles, was to connect two defined points. The country through which this line was to pass is described as surpassing in its difficulties the conception of any European. It consists of impervious forests, steep ravines, and dismal swamps. A survey of the line was impossible; a plan was therefore arranged by the astronomer royal, founded on a determination of the absolute latitude and difference of longitude of the two extremities. The difference of longitude was determined by the transfer of chronometers, by a very circuitous route, from one end to the other; after which the necessary computations were made, and marks laid off for starting with the line from both extremities. One party, after cutting more than 42 miles through the woods, were agreeably surprised on the brow of a hill at seeing before them a gap in the woods on the next line of hill, which opened gradually, and proved to be the line of the opposite party. On continuing the lines till they were abreast of each other, their distance was found to be 341 feet, a difference which arose in an error of only a quarter of a second of time in the difference of longitude. The performance of this operation reflects the highest honour on the officers engaged. Transits were observed, and observations made, on whose delicacy everything depended, when the thermometer was lower than 19 degrees below zero, and when the native assistants, though paid highly, deserted on account of the severity of the weather.

Such is a brief outline of an establishment which, whether we consider the nature and utility of its operations, or the comparatively small expense at which they are conducted, has great claims on our respect. We trust that our necessarily brief sketch will tend to diminish the stupid wonder with which the unpretending structure is regarded by thousands who climb the hill on which it stands. Let them think over its historical associations, and its importance not merely nationally, but in connexion with the whole world.

SHORT NOTES ON THE WEST INDIES.

BY A LATE RESIDENT

SECOND ARTICLE.

Travelling.—Travelling was at one time in the West Indies, it is said, so comfortable as to cost nothing. For instance, all that a respectable party had to do who desired to travel from one end of the island of Jamaica to the other, was to call in at the several estates on his way, when his horses would be cared for, himself provided with bed and board, and every attention paid him that he could require. These certainly must have been palmy days. I have heard of nothing like them at the present time: 'the more's the pity;' for the public inns are miserable, and their fare worse. I have frequently been unable to get a dinner at one of them, while it has been necessary to turn my horse out on the sides of the highway to feed, or to send my servant miles away to procure a blade of grass. Fried ham and eggs form in some places a standing dish; and the traveller considers himself fortunate if his host is enabled to present him with a chicken broiled, which little biped he had seen not half an hour before sporting in the fields, the same having been first hunted off its legs to be caught, and then hurriedly cooked.

The greatest pleasure connected with travelling in the West Indies is certainly derived from the magnificent scenery which bursts upon the view at every step. Cloud-capped hills, rugged rocks, lofty heights, deep precipices, broad savannahs, meandering streams, rushing rivers, verdant shades, outstretched seas, embosomed bays, blue-tinted skies, and all the ingredients which poetic imagery might require to present an enchanting prospect to the imagination, are visible by day, while the literally 'spangled firmament,' the clear bright moon, the countless lights proceeding from innumerable fire-flies, themselves invisible, and the lights appearing like a fairy illumination of a densely-populated fairy country—all render a journey delightful by night; and if the traveller be a stranger, they will probably lead him on to rapture. There are drawbacks, however, in travelling in the West Indies, which in some degree counterbalance all these pleasant sights, or which at any rate will in a short time diminish the amount of rapture which might have been occasioned. Rutty roads, narrow dangerous tracks, sandy beds, rugged 'gullies,' swollen rivers, rapid fordings, unwholesome lagoons, muddy ways, trackless waters, burning suns, and feverish airs, are sufficient, probably, to check any moderate person's excessive admiration. Still, however, there is little doubt that the balance is in favour of the pleasurable, as well as the healthy side of travelling, as far as nature is concerned. I cannot say as much for the conveniences dependent on man. Hotels, or rather inns, as I have already observed, are abominably bad, besides being scattered as widely apart as plums in schoolboys' pudding. Livery vehicles are of the most disgraceful kind, awkward, old, and shabby, while the cost of travelling, to those who do not journey in their own conveyances, and with their own horses, is sufficiently high. Not caring to use my own horse, I have often paid twenty-four shillings for a horse and chaise to go thirteen miles, besides expense of tollage, feed of horses, and gratuity to the boy. The traveller may, however, thank his stars if he have no more than these things to complain of. Should an accident happen to his horse or vehicle on the way, he would call 'spirits from the vasty deep' with as much success as a farrier from a forge, or a mender of chaises from a workshop. He would have no resource but to complete his journey on foot (unless some stray traveller, with a seat to spare, should pass by), leaving his vehicle and horse upon the road in charge of his servant.

The Militia.—Our colonists are inordinately fond of 'playing at soldiers;' and the truth is, where the mode of life is as monotonous as in the colonies, it is not very surprising that much devotion should be paid to that which, if it does nothing more, creates a little stir and excitement. And the morning of 'muster' is indeed a period of excitement to most militiamen, from the colonel-in-chief to the merest 'private.' Old stagers there are—men who have 'grown old in the service'—whom it would be as difficult to move out of their steady track as to stem the torrent of a hurricane: the great portion, however, yield to the excitement. As early, probably, as three o'clock on the morning of 'muster' a preparatory roll of the drum is heard, whereupon the young soldier starts from bed, strikes a light, puts on his 'accoutrements,' and, lest he should not be in time, rushes off to the parade with the utmost haste. There he takes his dark and solitary walk, pluming himself on his zeal, while the initiated, 'turning his sides and his heavy head,' snoozes on till five o'clock, when the drum is again beat, but on this occasion apparently more peremptorily. He then gets up, dresses leisurely, fortifies himself against a long drill with a cup of coffee, and quietly takes his march to the field. When he arrives, he probably finds that the rolls have been called.

He reports himself, however, to the serjeant of his company, who notes him 'present.' In consequence of these tardy arrivals, an hour after the appointed time probably elapses ere the companies are formed, which being done, the business of the morning commences. First, the serjeants under the direction of the commanding-officers of the companies see that the recruits have arranged the belts properly; that the men cover each other; that they are arranged according to gradations in height, &c. The commander of each company then puts his men through certain manœuvres; and, if he be a young officer, there is no reluctance on the part of the men to offer suggestions, nor on his to receive them. In fact, the most cordial understanding usually exists between the officers and men, holding the same rank as civilians which they very often do, and *faux-pas* on either side are leniently dealt with.

When the men have been formed into line, and have presented arms, &c. they generally pass in review, when the little inconsistencies of dress and inefficiencies of duty scarcely escape the detection and censure of the reviewing officer. 'What are you doing on that pivot, sir?' 'Good ——, where is that company going to?' are exclamations which fall, like tropic rain, 'thick and fast.' Should the morning be devoted to the practice of firing, among other exercises, the circumstance adds much to the excitement, not simply of the soldier, but of the crowd of persons, particularly the young raggamuffins collected on the ground. The soldier is excited lest his whiskers should be carried away by the contents of his neighbour's gun, the crowd lest some accident should happen, and the raggamuffins from the hope of finding a cartridge or two of powder, dropped from the nervous hands of some of the soldiers, or scattered by stealth among the youngsters. On the subject of accidents—a soldier in haste, on charging his gun, once left his ramrod in it. A boy was shot through the body at the next discharge.

The men having been baked in the sun for three or four hours, a close column of companies is formed, and they are dismissed—very frequently to the stirring tune of 'Oh, be joyful.' Now, however, comes the reward of the young officer for the arduous toil he has undergone, and the uncomfortable position in which he has been placed. 'Tis then that, with span new coat, golden epaulettes, shining sword, stately step, and warlike glance, he struts on foot, or careers on horseback, through the town, acknowledging the encouraging smiles of fair friends, or, as he goes, exciting the admiration of the multitude. To return, however, to 'head-quarters.'

The 'colonel-in-chief,' or 'colonel,' of militia, as it may happen to be, is, as I have said, no unimportant personage. Each individual in the several communities being called upon after a certain age to do militia duty, and each being fined for non-attendance under the warrant of the colonel, or liable to be tried by court-martial for breach of duty, all feel it in some degree their interest to pay him proper respect, and many great deference. The promotions from the ranks, also, being made by the executive, at the suggestion or recommendation of the colonels, a mighty engine of power is at their command. No one who hopes for promotion must offend the colonel, and consequently the influence which he exercises in every department, whether military (militiary), civil, or mercantile, is overpoweringly great. And it may readily be believed that this influence is not always exercised in a fair, judicious, or disinterested spirit; and that, in the days of oppression, it was very often used as an engine to check the rising ambition, if not to crush the daring and independent spirit, of the coloured or black man. At the same time neither the public nor private character of many who held the rank of colonel would bear scrutiny on the point of honesty, sobriety, intelligence, or wealth. Since the abolition of slavery, a feeling has gone abroad against the militia, which will most probably end in the utter disbandonment of the force.

The Coloured Clerk.—I have every reason to believe that there are few classes in the West Indies—that land where oppression has been until late years the rule, and justice the exception—who have been more hardly dealt with than the coloured clerks. Descendants of Africa, as their name implies, yet often for generations freed from the bodily thraldom to which those were subject to whom they were so closely allied, they seemed fated, like them, to be the victims of a cruel prejudice and hopeless toil. Untiring and faithful labourers for their masters' interests, yet were they doomed to move in one ceaseless round of unthankful and pitiless servitude. The coloured clerk probably found his way at twelve or fourteen years of age into a merchant's office in this manner. His parents, or relatives, or friends, hearing of a vacancy in a particular counting-house, and having resolved that it was quite time the child should learn to do something for himself, would apply on his behalf for the situation. 'Salary being no object'—that is, the amount required being small, or probably nothing demanded for the first year—the probabilities were that the tender of the boy's services would be accepted. At the appointed time, therefore, he would enter the counting-house, and find perhaps half a dozen other clerks employed. Like their employers, they would be white, and as an amalgamation of the several classes was not even thought of, his situation would at once promise to be uncomfortable. He knew by intuition that the several views of 'matters and things' entertained by his fellow-clerks differed widely from his own, and the odds being against him, he would mentally anticipate many a hard struggle. However, it was a fine thing to be a merchant, and he had come to learn to be one. Courage, therefore, and, in despite of any trifling unpleasantness, diligence and attention would no doubt bring him to the goal. Without one positively gloomy apprehension, then, he would occupy the desk which had been assigned him, and enter upon his duties. Young as he was, however, he would speedily discover that his brother clerks courted neither his company nor his conversation. No familiar intercourse passed between them; and on retiring from business, it would happen daily that occasion called them in a separate direction from that which he intended to pursue. The result was, that very little communication passed between them beyond matters of mere business, and when they met in the streets, a nod of recognition was very often omitted. Thus would years pass on, and probably find the coloured clerk in the same counting-house, toiling amongst those with whom no bond of fellowship existed. He would probably have now no desire that it should exist, content, as it would appear, thus to work on until his period of promotion should arrive. He had hopes of promotion—that is, of being promoted to a share of his master's business. Rare as had been the occurrence when a coloured clerk was so promoted, he still hoped on; for he had spent the best days of his youth and manhood in the employment of the same master; and who knew what a day might bring forth? True it was that others had been, times out of number, placed above him in less important departments; that the last opening in the firm had been filled by one many years his junior: yet justice was not always blind, nor was the wheel of fortune always stationary. His turn must come some day, and then he would be content. Forlorn hope! The turn of the coloured clerk for promotion to a share in the business of his white master never came. Still, however, he hoped on. The paltry pittance which at length, as head clerk, he received, might have told a despairing tale; but he would hear nothing, see nothing, that would tend to deprive him of this hope—this one hope of his weary life. When hope ultimately deserted him, he not unfrequently sought consolation in the bottle, and sank prematurely to the grave. The community placed the termination of his hapless career to the account of dissipated habits; but a nearer insight into the matter would have shown that it was the result of that 'hope,' which, 'long deferred, maketh the heart sick.' The evil here depicted, though not so glaring at the present day, is still a marked feature of the colonial system.

Negro Amusements.—Passing over many which are not different from the amusements indulged in by their white brethren, I come at once to the favourite dancing associations of the negroes, known under the odd names of *Setts* and *John Canoes.* The John Canoe parties, composed exclusively of men, are marked by frequent tumults, sometimes leading even to bloodshed. The Setts, which are composed of women, bear also marks of a barbarous origin, the leader or mistress being furnished with a whip with which to flog any inactive member. There is a description of John Canoe termed 'the actors,' who do not dance, but recite portions of plays in a pompous and mouthing manner. Like the Setts, they claim the privilege of entering houses, and must therefore be placed in the first rank. The other John Canoes, of which many kinds perambulate the streets, dance to the sound of drums, fifes, &c. They all wear masks, either beautiful or ludicrous, as occasion calls for. The Setts, composed of probably a dozen women, are accompanied by a violin and tambourine, and occasionally a 'Jack in the green,' which constantly revolves to the sound of music; while the 'girls,' with parasols in their hands, their dresses floating in circles in the air, whirl round with inconceivable rapidity as they traverse the streets, singing in a most clamorous key some unintelligible ditty composed for the occasion; such as

'Good mornin', sista Sue,
And how is Breda Chalis?
Go, tell sista Quabna,
Fe put on de peppa pot.
Sing debe, debe, doo,
Sing glory to Hallelu.'

Or the following, called 'Monkey loss him tail, hold him:'—

'You worry me, you tease me,
You make my dandy leab me;
Jackass wid de lang tail,
And de bigue a cocoa coming down.'

John Canoeing and Sett Dancing—in the days of slavery much patronised by masters and mistresses—usually take place, where still kept up, at Christmas. Independently of affording amusement to the lower classes, they are systems of levying money which frequently prove very successful. No John Canoe or Sett will dance unless payment is given; and in addition to money, they are often presented with wine, &c. What is the origin of their separation into parties I have never heard; but there is always a blue and a red party, which vie with each other in the magnificence of their dress; and a certain day being appointed, a judge declares which party has excelled the other in splendour or taste. A blue and red John Canoe of any importance never meet without a conflict; but the struggle which takes place on each side is rather to destroy each other's dress than to damage each other's person. The like occurrence takes place among the Setts, which are also divided into reds and blues; and as its women are very expert at the matter, a very few seconds sometimes suffice to make every shred of finery disappear. Why the demon of destructiveness should enter so completely into the character of these representations, it is difficult to conceive. The dresses on either side, although sometimes tawdry, are expensive, and large sums must be lost by them.

One might be led to conceive, that amid all the noise and license which naturally attend these amusements, many scenes of rioting and drunkenness occur. The contrary is the case; for, with the exception of the squabbles between the 'reds and blues'—sufficiently unseemly however—nothing of the kind occurs. The negroes are by no means addicted to strong liquors—the chief incentive to broils and bloodshed. A great evil attendant on these amusements, however, is, that many unprincipled dancers resort to thieving about the approach of Christmas, in order to be enabled to dress with sufficient splendour. This and other objections which may be readily conceived, have given rise to much opposition to the amusements; and in a few years they will be more properly numbered among the things that were. In part, they have been already put down; not, however, without the shedding of blood.

A Watering-Place.—I would take you with me in imagination to the shore, or rather to the beach, which hems in one of the largest and most commodious harbours in the West Indies. The sea plays in tiny ripples at our feet, by turns displacing and replacing the shells and shingle which lie scattered around. A slight breath fans our cheek; but looking seaward, we perceive a white foam cresting the tiny waves, and know that this slight breath is but the precursor of the coming 'sea-breeze.' Nearer and nearer it comes; the undulating motion of the waters increase; and each wave seems to rise in order more fully to catch the influence of the stirring blast. The ripples no longer play modestly at our feet, but becoming bolder and bolder, seem offering to gird us round. Here, then, we may no longer remain. We come to gaze on the hills and sky, and deep blue waters, and not to bathe our frame in those waters, however grateful and reviving. Yonder is a projection, stretching some three hundred feet into the harbour, along which water from the adjacent springs issues at stated times for the supply of less favoured places. There we may gaze, undisturbed, at the combination of enchanting objects which lie spread before us. Let us take our stand, then, and note the soft beauty of the distant hills, the bright serenity of the azure sky, and the broad expanse of the clear water, with the things upon and beneath it. The water comes in undulating swells, and with a gentle rushing noise beats against the supports of the projection on which we stand, and, breaking, flows onwards towards the shore. Around the supports is seen a host of the finny tribe gamboling in the clear element, now diving downwards, then glancing nimbly through each other's ranks, occasionally rising to the surface. Seaward appears a long arid strip of land, connected with the main on the left, that is, to the east, and stretching on to the right till lost to view. That strip of arid land—but two hundred odd feet across in certain parts, and not twice the number in any one from the broad bosom of the Caribbean sea to the waters of the harbour—has withstood the tempests of five thousand years, and the surging of a myriad of billows. A town, the relict of that which existed previous to a vast upheaving of the earth, and an awful conflagration, occupies its extreme point. Beyond, till lost in the haze of distance, the harbour stretches apparently in interminable length, and in the intermediate space are seen canoes and boats of varied rig and form, their white sails swelling with the breeze, and themselves dancing with a light careering motion over the ruffled surface of the dark-blue water. Now turn we to the land. On the main, to the right, lies a fort of no formidable front or impregnable build. Its whitened turrets and sea-girt walls give it, however, a sufficiently imposing appearance. To the right, as far as the eye can reach—beyond, as far as the gaze may scan—to the left, as far as it may pierce, rise in unspeakable and varied simplicity, dignity, and grandeur, one hundred hills, capped with snow-white clouds, or clad in garb of mingled green and russet, in either case reflected to the eye with the softness of richest velvet. At no great distance from the shore-end of the projection on which we stand lies the public highway, thronged with passengers on foot, in carriages, and on horseback. Here rolls the carriage of the rich, there the gig of the less aspiring; here a horseman spurs his mettled charger, there a negro trudges it on foot, urging on his ass, laden with provisions, he himself bearing a basket-load on his head; while women, with petticoats tucked up, ankles, calves, and knees bare, haste on, heedless of shoes or stockings, with burdens on their heads and young children on their backs. A small stream crosses the road on the left. Up the stream is observed a host of half-dressed chattering women, engaged in no very romantic occupation. A strange banging noise is heard —the women are beating the clothes given them to wash—that being the process usually employed to cleanse them. No mercy have they on the owners' pockets, no consideration for their garments. Leaving them, however, we observe still farther to the left a pleasantly situated little house, somewhat retired from the road. We find no difficulty in ascertaining its character; there, then, when we have satisfied our gaze with the prospect which surrounds us, we will resort and seek refreshment, satisfied if we obtain it but in the shape of 'so-so' water.*

Negro Appellations.—The negroes in the West Indies are much in the habit of giving such names to the animals which belong to them, or the small properties which they possess, as shall denote some particular event, or record some particular fact. I have been told of a pig that was named 'Good me do, tankee me get,' being the words of one of the negro proverbs, and intended no doubt to perpetuate some act of ingratitude towards the owner of the pig. Another was named 'Try, see;' that is, 'make a trial,' probably a trial whether the breeding of pigs would not be profitable. Within late years, the source from whence the negroes obtained the means wherewith they purchased their small properties, is sometimes pointed out by the name given to the settlement, as 'Carting.' Sometimes the opportunity of carrying on the culture is indicated by the appellation 'Occasion Hall;' and sometimes 'the spirit which led them to clear the wilderness, and to plant there a garden,' is shown in the name 'Endeavour' and 'Freeman's Hut.' In their appellations, also, the shrewdness of the negro, mingled with the quaintness observable in the above examples, shows itself. A certain woman of that class had a violent husband, who quarrelled with her upon every possible opportunity. Too timid to take any direct means to procure peace, the woman recurred to an appellation for her dog. The dog was styled 'Begin;' and thus, whenever she perceived the approach of an outbreak of her husband's temper, she would cry out, apparently addressing the dog, but in reality her husband, 'Begin, Begin, Begin;' till at length her boisterous mate became ashamed to 'begin,' and was thus cured of his quarrelsome propensity. This story is good enough, but not equal to that which describes a forlorn damsel as giving her dog the appellation of 'Little did I thought that man was so deceitful.'

The Way to Rise.—It is unnecessary to state that innumerable instances occur in the colonies where parties who left this country in the most subordinate situations, or walking in the humblest ranks of life, have risen to the highest offices, and become possessors of the greatest wealth. Needy footmen have become large traders, and sons of the needle presidents of council. Far be it from me to reflect dishonour where no dishonour is. Too many cases occur, however, where the men who have so risen have not been *sans reproche*, and were an inquiry instituted only into the item of the administration of bygone executorships, I fear that a tale would be told of orphans plundered, widows ruined, and property usurped or unaccounted for, that would pass the present limits of our credulity. On the other hand, self-denial and unswerving integrity have been occasionally used, and successfully so, as a means of advancement to wealth and importance. In the West Indies, as in other countries, the Scotch very often prove more cautious, provident, and enterprising than other Europeans; and, ever extending a helping hand to each other, they seldom fail to 'get on in the world.' I know not whether to regard it as creditable or discreditable to that people, that in some parts of the West Indies a tall, leafless, barren trunk of the majestic cotton tree—ascended from its base by a small creeping plant, which, increasing in vigour and size as it grows, saps the juices of the fostering tree till it ultimately rears its triumphant head above the barren trunk—is shown to the passing traveller as 'the Scotchman hugging the Creole.'

* 'So-so' water means pure water, in contradistinction to spirits and water.

PEPPER AND MUSTARD.

Human life, though a great and momentous affair, is the sum and result of many little and apparently insignificant arrangements. Who, without experience, could think that pepper and mustard could materially influence our enjoyments—could affect, even in a moral point of view, either the head or the heart? Yet so it is—'these little things are great to little men.' Suppose that we are set down to dinner, and that we have been helped to some hot and savoury soup; we take up the pepper-box, but find it either empty, or half filled with large particles which will not pass through; or if it contains a supply of good pepper, the holes are so stuffed up that not a particle can make its escape; or, what is still worse than all, the lid has been so carelessly put on, that the moment we begin to use it, off it tumbles, and the whole contents of the cruet fall into our plate at once. Or, on the other hand, suppose that we have been presented with a plate of beef; the mustard-pot is empty, or it is partially filled with the rancid remains of a former day, dirtily clogged around the sides and top of it; or it may be filled with a thin tasteless fluid, the result of a hasty dash of water put into the half-empty vessel before dinner. It may not even be found on the table at all; and, after several times calling for it, and during the time lost in going for it or searching it out, you are obliged silently to eat your beef without the aid of its stimulating flavour. If, on the contrary, you are resolved to wait its appearance, your patience and temper undergo a severe trial, and your keen appetite is lost in the anxiety of hope deferred, while the tedious process is gone through of procuring a fresh supply. First of all, the keys have to be found; or, it may be, the key which opens the work-basket which contains the key which opens the closet which contains the shelf where, huddled among a dozen heterogeneous packages, the paper containing the mustard powder is to be found. Then this powder, which has lost more than half its pungency by being kept in paper instead of a stone jar, has to be hurriedly mixed up with water, and is brought at last, after a world of delay, with large knots of dry powder interspersed among the half-liquid mass. If, under the same auspices, you should dine day after day at the same table, it is ten to one but the same neglects are repeated. If you should ask for pickles to your beefsteak, they also will have to be waited for in the same manner; or if on the table, they will in all probability contain a metallic spoon, the action of the acid on which producing a poisonous mixture, will effectually deter you from partaking of them. In short, these little arrangements are an index of the mind of the presiding mistress. It may sometimes be the fault of the servants; but the omissions of servants, unless they are incorrigible, more frequently depend on the guiding spirit of the house than on their own peculiar faults. When one sees the arrangements of the table perfect, even including the well-filled, clean, and inviting mustard-pot, he may be assured that all the other most important departments of domestic management are in their proper order. 'My dear,' says Mrs Slovenloof, 'why should you vex and fret yourself so about such a trifle as the omission of the mustard? How often do you tell *me* not to fret myself about trifles! Besides, I do not think either pepper or mustard agrees with you; and I have been reading lately that too much of such things is unwholesome.' 'Yes, *too much* of anything is unwholesome; but what do you say to too little, or none at all?' 'I have read, my dear,' retorts Mrs Slovenloof, 'that man in a state of nature requires none of these things; that half-broiled beef or venison, of which *you* so often complain, is devoured by the savage without salt, or pepper, or anything else, and reckoned a most savoury meal; and I do think, that all the niceties of cookery are very useless, and I am sure they are very, very troublesome!' 'The savage,' replies the husband, 'takes his food thus because his squaw knows no better; but depend upon it, did she present him with a well-cooked and well-seasoned mess, he would eat it with a double relish, and thrive under it too, in a way quite different from what he does under his ill-cooked fare. But even your instance of the savage is an unfortunate one. Your "man of nature" is just as fond of aromatics and other stimulants as a civilised man. Witness his avidity for salt, for aromatic and bitter roots and herbs, for the intoxicating cava, for beer, for tobacco. Nay, if we stoop to the analogy of the lower animals—whose appetites you will allow are under the guidance of unerring instinct—we shall find that they, too, are equally incited by appetite to take along with their food stimulants, such as salt and aromatic herbs and roots.' Mrs Slovenloof, however, was unwilling to be convinced. There are none more fertile in evasive excuses than the really indolent and negligent; and she spun out the argument for two hours after dinner, advancing, however, nothing but commonplaces in support of her theory, till at last she unconsciously gave it a practical deathblow, by partaking freely of both tea and coffee in the evening; both of which, according to her view of the question, were equally unnecessary as pepper and mustard.

BIOGRAPHIC SKETCHES.

DR ARNOLD.

The profession, avocations, and retirement-loving temperament of the late Dr Arnold, have prevented his name from being so widely known as that of many a less worthy candidate for public honours. It may be, therefore, necessary to inform our readers that he was a doctor of divinity, head master of Rugby school, and professor of modern history at the university of Oxford. His literary fame chiefly rests upon his History of Rome, his edition of the historian Thucydides, his Lectures on Modern History, and seven volumes of Sermons. It is, however, in the character of a schoolmaster that his name will be most revered and respected by posterity; for to him we are indebted for great improvements in the management of the public schools of England.

Thomas Arnold was a native of West Cowes, in the Isle of Wight, of which port his father was for many years collector of customs. He was born on the 13th of June 1795, and at an early age was sent to Warminster, in Wiltshire, to school; thence he went to Winchester. In 1811, when only sixteen, he was elected a scholar of Corpus Christi College, Oxford; and when only twenty, became a fellow of Oriel College. Though he was ordained a deacon, he did not obtain a living in the church, but settled at Laleham, in Berkshire, and marrying soon after Miss Mary Penrose, the sister of a college companion, received into his house nine young gentlemen to prepare them for the universities. Upon these pupils he commenced that improved system of moral and intellectual culture which he so successfully practised at Rugby. He constantly instilled into them the wholesome principle, that good honest work is, after all, the only respectable calling. At the close of 1827, the head-mastership of Rugby school becoming vacant, he was elected to the office solely from the weight of the testimonials in his favour. The event proved that few men were better qualified for the office. It was, in fact, remarkably suited to his natural tastes. Tuition was always to him a labour of love; and this love grew so strongly upon him, that he sometimes declared he could hardly live without some such employment.*

Rugby—situated on the classic river Avon in Warwickshire—is one of the principal foundation schools selected by the aristocracy for the education of their boys. It was founded in 1567 by Laurence Sheriffe, citizen of London, a native of the neighbourhood. Any person who has resided during two years in, or within ten miles of, the town, may send his sons to be educated, free of expense; in other words, he may place them 'on the foundation.' Other pupils pay a fee, and are obliged to lodge at some of the boarding-houses in the town, or with one of the masters, of whom, besides the chief, there are eight classical tutors, with subordinate teachers of writing, French, and the mathematics. The number of pupils in Dr Arnold's time may have been about three hundred, sixty or seventy of whom were on the foundation.

On entering upon his duties, Dr Arnold found the school 'quite enough to employ any man's love of reform.' The boarding-house system, withdrawing as it did the boys from the supervision of the masters, was fraught with evils. We may here state, that this disadvantage still exists to a great extent at other public schools we refrain from naming, and cannot be too strongly reprehended. Boys of from thirteen to fifteen are supplied by their wealthy friends with incomes infinitely larger than they can spend wholesomely either for body or mind.† When out of school, they are nearly bereft of control, assume the manners and habits of men, and ape their vices; amongst which it is painful to state, that drunkenness and gaming are not unfrequently predominant.

Such practices were found to exist at Rugby when Dr Arnold was called to preside over the school. They naturally shocked and alarmed him; and he determined to strike at the root of the evil by insisting that all the masters should take boarders, so that at all times the pupils might be under their supervision, and that the irresponsible boarding-houses should 'die a natural death.' He also introduced an elaborate system of private tuition, by means of which he established a pastoral and friendly intercourse between the masters and the boys under their care. He had another terrible evil to combat with, which was a marked abuse of the 'fagging system' instituted in all the public schools of England. The merits or demerits of this system have long formed a subject of controversy, into which, however, it is no business of ours to enter. It mainly consists in rewarding boys who have attained proficiency in learning—who are, in fact, the head pupils of the school—by giving them certain powers over the junior boys, who are bound to obey them in everything—in whatever, even, may be extra scholastic. It is manifest that these powers, placed in hands guided by young heads and impulsive hearts, are liable to great abuse. Dr Arnold did not attempt to alter the system, neither did he wish to do so.‡ 'Another,' he said, 'may be better in itself; but I am placed in this system, and am bound to try what I can make of it.' In other words, he determined to use, and to improve to the utmost, the existing machinery of the sixth form and of fagging; understanding, by the sixth form, the thirty boys who composed the highest class—'those,' he would say, 'who, having risen to the highest form in the school, will probably be at once the oldest, and the strongest, and the cleverest; and, if the school be well ordered, the most respectable in application and general character.' How he set about the well ordering of the school by

* Life and Correspondence of Thomas Arnold, D.D., by Rev. A. P. Stanley, fellow and tutor of University College, Oxford. 2 vols. London: Fellowes. 1844.

† We know an instance of two Eton boys who were allowed by their family eight hundred a-year between them!

‡ Dr Arnold was in favour of fagging as a system, and drew down a vast amount of public censure by his advocacy of it. His views on the subject may be seen in the ninth volume of the Journal of Education. They were replied to in the succeeding number by the editor of that work.

means of the præposters or pupils composing the sixth form, furnishes one of the most interesting chapters in his life. In the first place, he continually impressed upon these thirty young gentlemen the notion, that they were as much his and his fellow-teachers' coadjutors in the government of the school as pupils. 'You should feel,' he once remarked, 'like officers in the army or navy, whose want of moral courage would indeed be thought cowardice.' He tried every means in his power to attract their affections and confidence rather than to excite their awe. He would, for instance, never seem to doubt what any one of them asserted. 'If you say so, that is quite enough—*of course* I believe your word;' and there grew up in consequence a general feeling that 'it was a shame to tell Arnold a lie—he always believes one.' He wished to lead rather than to drive his pupils into the ways of morality and learning. 'Is this a Christian school?' he indignantly asked at the end of one of those addresses in which he had spoken of an extensive display of bad feeling amongst the boys, and then added, 'I cannot remain here if all is to be carried on by constraint and force; if I am to be here as a jailer, I will resign my office.' When any boy was found to be confirmed in wicked habits, he expelled him at once. 'It is *not* necessary,' he told the assembled scholars on one such painful occasion, 'that this should be a school of three hundred, or one hundred, or of fifty boys; but it *is* necessary that it should be a school of Christian gentlemen.' In fact, his main principle, after expostulation and kindness, was the separation of the bad from the good. He had no liking for mere cleverness, however great the talents of a troublesome and vicious boy might be; while to a naturally dull but persevering pupil he gave every encouragement. At Laleham he had once got out of patience, and spoken sharply to a pupil of this kind, when the pupil looked up in his face, and said, 'Why do you speak angrily, sir? indeed I am doing the best that I can.' Years afterwards he used to tell the story to his children, and said, 'I never felt so much ashamed in my life—that look and that speech I have never forgotten.' And though it would of course happen that clever boys, from a greater sympathy with his understanding, would be brought into closer intercourse with him, this did not affect his feeling, not only of respect, but of reverence to those who, without ability, were distinguished for high principle and industry. 'If,' he observed on one occasion 'there be one thing on earth which is truly admirable, it is to see God's wisdom blessing an inferiority of natural powers, where they have been honestly, truly, and zealously cultivated.' In speaking of a pupil of this character, he once said, 'I would stand to that man *hat in hand*.' In those who did their work 'with a will,' and kept the straight line of moral conduct pretty evenly, he took an interest which lasted far longer than their Rugby pupilage. 'To any pupil,' remarks his classical and elegant biographer, 'who ever showed any desire to continue his connexion with him, his house was always open, and his advice and sympathy ready. No half year, after the four first years of his stay at Rugby, passed without a visit from his former scholars: some of them would come three or four times a-year; some would stay in his house for weeks. He would offer to prepare them for their university examinations by previous examinations of his own; he never shrunk from adding any of them to his already numerous correspondents, encouraging them to write to him in all perplexities. To any who were in narrow circumstances, not in one case, but in several, he would at once offer assistance, sometimes making them large presents of books on their entrance at the university, sometimes tendering them large pecuniary aid, and urging to them that his power of doing so was exactly one of those advantages of his position which he was most bound to use. In writing for the world at large, they were in his thoughts, "in whose welfare," he said, "I naturally have the deepest interest, and in whom old impressions may be supposed to have still so much force, that I may claim from them at least a patient hearing." And when annoyed by distractions from within the school, or opposition from without, he turned, he used to say, to their visits as "to one of the freshest springs of his life."'

Though, upon a principle he had formed for himself in school government, and from inclination arising from a sympathy with the intellectual and the good, Dr Arnold's chief and most unwearied cares were bestowed on the head boys, yet he was not unmindful of the juniors. Though a severe and firm disciplinarian, 'the liveliness and simplicity of his whole behaviour must always have divested his earnestness of any appearance of moroseness and affectation. "He calls us *fellows*," was the astonished expression of the boys when, soon after his first coming, they heard him speak of them by the familiar name in use amongst themselves; and in his later years they observed with pleasure the unaffected interest with which, in the long autumn afternoons, he would stand in the school field, and watch the issue of their favourite games of football.—With the very little boys, indeed, his manner partook of that playful kindness and tenderness which always marked his intercourse with children; in examining them in the lower forms, he would sometimes take them on his knee, and go through picture-books of the Bible or of English history, covering the text of the narrative with his hand, and making them explain to him the subject of the several prints.'

The life and correspondence of Dr Arnold show us that no man ever studied so constantly, or knew so completely, every corner of the mind of boys. He seemed to know well the thoughts and characters of every pupil in the school—those of his favourite præposters thoroughly. The searchingness of his practical insight into boys was such, that, in the words of one of his scholars, 'when his eye was upon you, he looked into your inmost heart.' This, then, was precisely the man to carry a thorough reform into a public school. Looking, therefore, at Dr Arnold in his true character, namely, that of a schoolmaster, it is one of the most complete and perfect in the range of biography; and the public owe much to his friend and pupil Stanley for presenting it in so clear, so impartial, so true a light.

But Arnold was something more than a schoolmaster. A man of extensive sympathies, he promoted, by every means in his power, whatever would generalise education amongst the people. His writings and sermons abound with pictures of the distresses of the poor, and urgent appeals to his auditors and readers for their relief. As a literary man, his tastes were decidedly for geography and history. His edition of Thucydides, and his History of Rome, in which—sometimes following Niebuhr, and sometimes striking out a new and bright light of his own, across the 'dim vista of antiquity'—he separates the fabulous from the really historical, have already established him in the highest rank of historians. His sermons are manifestly the offspring of a practical Christianity which would do good to all men. His piety was not a mere sentiment; it was an active philanthropy, which would have embraced all men within its influence, so as to lead *them* as well as himself 'upward.'

The mere incidents in such a life as that of Dr Arnold are too few and tame to be interesting, and are only enlivened by occasional excursions abroad; for he was passionately fond of travelling. In 1825 he visited Italy, and in 1827 explored every corner of Rome, to which his historical tastes and knowledge gave a peculiar charm. His latest tour was in France in 1841. In the same year he was offered the professorship of modern history at Oxford—the great triumph of his life. Dr Arnold had in former years been extensively unpopular amongst the Oxford authorities for certain principles concerning church matters, which he vehemently advocated; again, from the laity he had received every species of censure for his unflinching defence of the 'fagging system' in public schools. His unpopularity melted away before the overwhelming balance of good which existed in his character, both as a divine and as a preceptor: the Oxford authorities made him one of their professors, and the public have since acknowledged this his *practised* school system was the true one, despite his strong, but purely *theoretical* advocacy of fagging; and 'the services which he rendered both to Rugby, and to the cause of public education generally, are now fully acknowledged, and cannot probably be too highly estimated. Not so much among his own pupils, nor in the actual scene of his labours, as in every public school throughout England, is to be sought the chief and enduring monument of Dr Arnold's head-mastership at Rugby.'

The year after he became an Oxford professor, and the fourteenth of his Rugby mastership, was, alas! his last. The story of his death is thus affectingly told. On Sunday morning, June 1842, Dr Arnold, who had been previously no more than slightly indisposed, 'awoke with a sharp pain across his chest, which he mentioned to his wife, on her asking whether he felt well, adding, that he had felt it slightly on the preceding day, before and after bathing. He then again composed himself to sleep; but her watchful care, always anxious, even to nervousness, at the least indication of illness, was at once awakened; and on finding from him that the pain increased, and that it seemed to pass from his chest to his left arm, her alarm was so much roused from a remembrance of having heard of this in connexion with angina pectoris, and its fatal consequences, that, in spite of his remonstrances, she rose and called up an old servant, whom they usually consulted in cases of illness. She observed him, as she was dressing herself, lying still, but with his hands clasped, his lips moving, and his eyes raised upwards, as if engaged in prayer, when all at once he repeated, firmly and earnestly, "And Jesus said unto him, Thomas, because thou hast seen thou hast believed; blessed are they who have not seen, and yet have believed;" and soon afterwards, with a solemnity of manner and depth of utterance which spoke more than the words themselves, "But if ye be without chastisement, whereof all are partakers, then are ye bastards and not sons." From time to time he seemed to be in severe suffering; but to his wife he uttered no expressions of acute pain, dwelling only on the moments of comparative ease, and observing that he did not know what it was. But the more than usual earnestness which marked his tone and manner, especially in repeating the verses from scripture, had again aroused her worst fears; and she ordered messengers to be sent for medical assistance, which he had at first requested her not to do, from not liking to disturb at that early hour the usual medical attendant, who had been suffering from indisposition. She then took up the prayer book, and was looking for a psalm to read to him, when he said quickly, "The fifty-first," which she accordingly read by his bedside, reminding him, at the seventh verse, that it was the favourite verse of one of the old almswomen whom he was in the habit of visiting.' Of the physician who was called in, Dr Arnold calmly inquired, 'Is it (the disease) generally suddenly fatal?' 'Generally.' On being asked whether he had any pain, he replied that he had none but from the mustard plaster on his chest, with a remark on the severity of the spasms in comparison with this outward pain; and then, a few moments afterwards, inquired what medicine was to be given; and on being told, answered, 'Ah, very well.' The physician, who was dropping the laudanum into a glass, turned round, and saw him looking quite calm, but with his eyes shut. In another minute he heard a rattle in the throat, and a convulsive struggle—flew to the bed, caught his head upon his shoulder, and called to one of the servants to fetch Mrs Arnold. She had but just left the room before his last conversation with the physician, in order to acquaint her son with his father's danger, of which he was still unconscious, when she heard herself called from above. She rushed up stairs, told her son to bring the rest of the children, and with her own hands applied the remedies that were brought, in the hope of reviving animation, though herself feeling, from the moment that she saw him, that he had already passed away. He was indeed no longer conscious. The sobs and cries of his children, as they entered and saw their father's state, made no impression upon him—the eyes were fixed—the countenance was unmoved: there was a heaving of the chest—deep gasps escaped at prolonged intervals; and just as the usual medical attendant arrived, and as the old school-house servant, in an agony of grief, rushed with the others into the room, in the hope of seeing his master once more—he breathed his last.

'It must have been shortly before eight A.M. that he expired, though it was naturally impossible for those who were present to adjust their recollections of what passed with precise exactness of time or place. So short and sudden had been the seizure, that hardly any one out of the household itself had heard of his illness before its fatal close. His guest, and former pupil (who had slept in a remote part of the house), was coming down to breakfast as usual, thinking of questions to which the conversation of the preceding night had given rise, and which, by the great kindness of his manner, he felt doubly encouraged to ask him, when he was met on the staircase by the announcement of his death. The masters knew nothing till the moment when, almost at the same time at the different boarding-houses, the fatal message was delivered, in all its startling abruptness, "that Dr Arnold was dead." What that Sunday was in Rugby it is hard fully to represent: the incredulity—the bewilderment—the agitating inquiries for every detail—the blank, more awful than sorrow, that prevailed through the vacant services of that long and dreary day—the feeling as if the very place had passed away with him who had so emphatically been in every sense its head—the sympathy which hardly dared to contemplate, and which yet could not but fix the thoughts and looks of all on the desolate house where the fatherless family were gathered round the chamber of death.'

'THE CLAIMS OF LABOUR.'

'THE Claims of Labour' is 'an essay on the duties of the employers to the employed,' recently published in a small volume [Pickering, London] by a gentleman who withholds his name, but who has already attracted some notice by a book of beautiful and pleasant thought, entitled 'Essays Written in the Intervals of Business.' The present volume has rather too much of a dilettante air; yet it is evidently, too, the production of one who has given his mind earnestly to the subject, and writes not unadvisedly. Starting with the fact, now becoming so generally acknowledged, that the condition of the working-classes in this country presents many features of a distressing kind, he asks, 'Is this the inevitable order of things?' He answers, Pagans might believe so. 'But we cannot doubt that the conditions of labour, under which man tills the earth, express the mercy and goodness, no [illegible] than the judgment of God.' He does not, however, believe that merely increase of employment and better wages would put things quite right. There is requisite 'an earnest and practical application, on the part of the employing class, of thought and labour for the welfare of those whom they employ.' A foreign enemy hanging on our shores, would concentrate all our energies in their defence; why should not the same zeal be displayed in meeting the 'domestic evils' which stand as threateningly around us? 'It seems to me,' he says, 'a thing far more to be dreaded, that any considerable part of our population should be growing up in a state of absolute ignorance, than would be the danger, not new to us, of the combined hostility of the civilised world.'

He appeals not, however, to 'a man's apprehension of personal loss or suffering, but his fear of neglecting a sacred duty.' 'It will be found,' he adds, and here we cordially concur with him, 'that the highest motives are those of the most sustained efficiency.' He calls on the Masters of Thought—namely, the literary men of England—to ascend above frivolous pursuits, and look to the great interests of Man as their noblest field. He demands of the government at least the appointment of men of suitable ability for all offices bearing upon popular interests, and the selection for honours of men who prove of service in this matter. Let the rich not be looked to alone for effort or sacrifice. I take, says he, 'some member of that large class of persons who are not rich, nor great employers of labour, nor in any station of peculiar influence. He shudders as he reads those startling instances of suffering or crime in which the distress and ignorance of the labouring population will occasionally break out into the notice of the world. "What can I do?" he exclaims. "I feel with intensity the horrors I read of: but what can one man do?" I only ask him to study what he feels. He is a citizen. He cannot be such an isolated being as to have no influence. The conclusions which he comes to, after mature reflection, will not be without their weight. If individual citizens were anxious to form their opinions with care, on those questions respecting which they will have to vote and to act, there would be little need of organised bodies of men to carry great measures into effect. If those who have actively to distribute the labour of the world knew that you, the great mass of private men, regarded them not for their money, but for their conduct to those in their employ, not for the portion which they may contrive to get for themselves, but for the wellbeing which they may give rise to, and regulate, amongst others; why, then, your thoughts would be motives to them, urging them on in the right path.' Your own treatment of any one dependent on you may also tell. And here even more considerateness may be required. 'It is a sad thing for a man to pass the working part of his day with an exacting, unkind master: but still, if the workman returns at evening to a home that is his own, there is a sense of coming joy and freedom which may support him throughout the weary hours of labour. But think what it must be to share one's home with one's oppressor; to have no recurring time when one is certain to be free from those harsh words, and unjust censures, which are almost more than blows, ay, even to those natures we are apt to fancy so hardened to rebuke. Imagine the deadness of heart that must prevail in that poor wretch who never hears the sweet words of praise or of encouragement. Many masters of families, men living in the rapid current of the world, who are subject to a variety of impressions which, in their busy minds, are made and effaced even in the course of a single day, can with difficulty estimate the force of unkind words upon those whose monotonous life leaves few opportunities of effacing any unwelcome impression. There is nothing in which the aid of imagination, that handmaid of charity, may be more advantageously employed, than in considering the condition of domestic servants. Let a man endeavour to realise it to himself, let him think of its narrow sphere, of its unvarying nature, and he will be careful not to throw in, unnecessarily, the trouble even of a single harsh word, which may make so large a disturbance in the shallow current of a domestic's hopes and joys.' These are just and laudable sentiments, beautifully expressed.

The great employers of labour—'would that they all saw the greatness of their position. Strange as it may sound, they are the successors of the feudal barons; they it is who lead thousands to peaceful conquests, and upon whom, in great measure, depends the happiness of large masses of mankind. Can a man, who has this destiny intrusted to him, imagine that his vocation consists merely in getting together a large lump of gold, and then being off with it, to enjoy it, as he fancies, in some other place: as if that, which is but a small part of his business in life, were all in all to him; as if, indeed, the parable of the talents were to be taken literally, and that a man should think that he has done his part when he has made much gold and silver out of little.' Something more is required—a benevolent superintendence of the interests of the employed, where from any cause it is needed, or may be found desirable. The author urges the duty of not working for worldly success alone, in some sentences truly eloquent. 'Consider the prospect which each unveiled night affords us, telling of wonders such as we have hardly the units of measurement to estimate; and then think how strange it is that we should ever allow our petty personal possessions of to-day to render us blind to the duties, which, alone, are the great realities of life. There was some excuse, perhaps, for the men of olden time, who looked upon this earth, the birthplace of their gods, as no mean territory. That they should dote upon terrestrial things, was not to be wondered at. But what is to be said for us who know that this small planet is but a speck, as it were, from which we look out upon the profusion of immensity? To think that a man who knows this, should nevertheless not hesitate to soil his soul, lying here, cringing there, pursuing tortuous schemes of most corrupt policy; or that he should ever suffer himself to be immersed, innocently, if it may be so, in selfish, worldly pursuits, forgetful of all else; when, at the best, it is but to win some acres of this transitory earth, or to be noted as one who has been successful for himself. The folly of the gambling savage, who stakes his liberty against a handful of cowrie shells, is nothing to it.'

Patience is necessary, and a resolution to battle with disappointment. 'For similar reasons, I would have you take care that you do not adopt mere rules, and seek to impress them rigidly upon others, as if they were general principles, which must at once be suitable to all mankind. Do not imagine that your individual threads of experience form a woven garment of prudence, capable of fitting with exactness any member of the whole human family.' * * 'There is nothing which a wise employer will have more at heart than to gain the confidence of those under him. The essential requisites on his part are truth and kindness. These qualities may, however, belong in a high degree to persons who fail to gain the confidence of their dependents. In domestic life, confidence may be prevented by fits of capricious passion on the part of the ruling powers; and a man who, in all important matters, acts justly and kindly towards his family, may be deprived of their confidence by his weakness of temper in little things. For instance, you meet with persons who fall into a violent way of talking about all that offends them in their dependents, and who express themselves with as much anger about trivial inadvertencies as about serious moral offences. In the course of the same day that they have given way to some outbreak of temper, they may act with great self-denial and watchful kindness; but they can hardly expect their subordinates to be at ease with them. Another defect which prevents confidence, is a certain sterility of character, which does not allow of sympathy with other people's fancies and pursuits. A man of this character does not understand any likings but his own. He will be kind to you, if you will be happy in his way; but he has nothing but ridicule or coldness for anything which does not suit him. This imperfection of sympathy, which prevents an equal from becoming a friend, may easily make a superior into a despot. Indeed, I almost doubt whether the head of a family does not do more mischief if he is unsympathetic, than even if he were unjust. The triumph of domestic rule is for the master's presence not to be felt as a restraint.'

The author proceeds to point out matters for the care of the employers, and after speaking of all due attention to the health of the men in the workshop and factory, the education of their children, and their recreations, he comes to the most important point of all—home. 'That the workman should have a home, which, however humble it may be, should yet afford room and scope for the decencies, if not for some of the comforts and refinements of civilised life, is manifestly essential, if we wish to preserve the great body of the people from a state of savageness. There is an important and original remark on this subject in the Hand-loom Weavers' Report of 1842:—

"The man who dines for 6d., and clothes himself during the year for L.5, is probably as healthily fed, and as healthily clad, as if his dinner cost two guineas a-day, and his dress L.200 a-year. But this is not the case with respect to habitation. Every increase of accommodation, from the corner of a cellar to a mansion, renders the dwelling more healthy, and, to a considerable extent, the size and goodness of the dwelling tends to render its inmates more civilised."

'Indeed, if civilisation does not show itself in a man's home, where else is it likely to take much root with him? Make his home comfortable, and you do more towards making him a steady and careful citizen than you could by any other means. Now, only look around and see how entirely this has been neglected, at least until within a recent date. Our workers are toiling all day long, or, if they have leisure, it is mostly accompanied by pecuniary distress; and can you expect in either case that they will busy themselves about those primary structural arrangements without which it is scarcely possible to have a comfortable home? Many of the things, too, which are needful for this end, require capital, or at least such conjoint enterprise as can hardly be expected from the poor. Take any individual workman. Suppose there is defective drainage in his street, or, as often happens, no drainage at all, what can one such man do, even if at all alive to the evil? When you consider the dependent condition of the labouring classes, and how little time they have for domestic arrangements of any kind, does it not behove the employer of labour to endeavour that his workmen should have opportunities of getting places to live in fit for human beings in a civilised country? I use the phrase "employer of labour" in its widest sense; and at once say, that there are many things bearing upon the comfort of the habitations of the poor, which both the local authorities and the imperial government ought to look to.

'There is at present in the metropolis,' continues our author, 'a society for "improving the dwellings of the industrious classes;" but what is one society? This is a matter which ought to interest the owners of property and the employers of labour throughout the country. Such a society as the one named may do great good by building model houses, making scientific investigations, and frequently laying before the public information on the subject. But the proper division of labour, as it seems to me, would be that the state should give every legislative facility for contemplated improvements in the way of building, should encourage all researches into the subject, and be ready to enforce by law such regulations as, without any great intrusion upon private property, might secure for small houses those primary requisites without which it cannot be expected that they will be anything but nests of disease. In fact, the state might eventually so order the matter, that builders should not merely build such houses as the poor would take—for there is nothing in the way of a shelter which they will refuse to occupy—but such as ought to be let to them, with due care at least for the public health. The local authorities should take upon themselves the lighting, cleansing, paving, supplying with water, and the like. For private individuals there remains the most important part of the task, namely, the building of an improved class of small houses. In this good work the employers of labour may be expected to come prominently forward. Many a man will speculate in all kinds of remote undertakings; and it will never occur to him that one of the most admirable uses to which he might put his spare capital, would be to provide fit dwelling-places for the labouring population around him. In the present state of things, the rents of small houses are disproportionately high, because of the difficulty and uncertainty of collecting the rents for them; but by any improvement you introduce into the habits of the occupiers of such houses, you make this difficulty and uncertainty less, and thereby diminish rents. And thus in this case, as in many others, physical and moral improvement go on acting and reacting upon each other. It is likely, too, that these poor people will pay with readiness and punctuality even a higher rent, if it be for a really good tenement, than a small one for a place which they must inhabit in the midst of filth, discomfort, and disease, and therefore with carelessness and penury. Besides, the rents they pay now will be found, I believe, sufficient to reimburse the capitalist for any outlay which would suffice to build tenements of a superior description to the present ones.

'I do not mean to say that the beginners of such a system of employing capital might not have a great deal to contend with; and it is to their benevolence, and not to any money motives, that I would mainly appeal. The devout feeling which in former days raised august cathedrals throughout the land, might find an employment to the full as religious in building a humble row of cottages, if they tell of honour to the great Creator, in care for those whom he has bidden us to care for, and are thus silently dedicated, as it were, to His name.'

After pointing to many other matters, in which it behoves the master class to be stirring, the benevolent writer gives them a final admonition to keep in mind that simple rule long known as the golden. 'Oh,' he says, 'if we could but begin by believing and acting upon some of the veriest commonplaces! But it is with pain and grief that we come to understand our first copy-book sentences.' * * 'We say that kings are God's vicegerents upon earth; but almost every human being has, at one time or other of his life, a portion of the happiness of those around him in his power, which might make him tremble if he did but see it in all its fulness. But at any rate, the relation of master and man is a matter of manifest and large importance. It pervades all societies, and affects the growth and security of states in the most remarkable and pregnant manner; it requires the nicest care; gives exercise to the highest moral qualities; has a large part in civil life; a larger part in domestic life; and our conduct in it will surely be no mean portion of the account which we shall have to render in the life that is to come.'

We take leave of our author in a friendly and sympathising spirit; but yet feel it a duty to warn all such as he against taking one-sided views on this great question. Much as we are disposed in our own humble sphere to act upon his requirements, we cannot but feel that looking for a correction of existing and acknowledged evils solely to the kindly impulses of one class, and that one which is manifestly much engrossed in their own proper labours, can hardly end otherwise than unsatisfactorily. We must take human nature as it is, and we must mainly take social arrangements as they are too, and endeavour out of the principles there involved to work out some practical improvements. Public opinion, and advancing knowledge in all the parties concerned, will probably in a little time suggest and accomplish the necessary measures. Meanwhile, we would respectfully enter a caveat against both the urging of unjust charges against employers as a class, and the demanding from them of exertions and sacrifices beyond what they can fairly be expected to make. To assume that the whole employed class is to sit still, while the class of employers is to set about doing some great things for them, is manifestly calculated to do harm on all hands, instead of any good.

Beneficial changes are certainly on the way—the exposure of the evil makes this certain—but they must not be expected from too exclusive a source.

THE LOST GLOVES, OR WE SHALL SEE.

A STORY FOR LITTLE GIRLS.

On a fine afternoon in autumn, Mrs Merton was sitting in her library at Bayswater, with her bonnet and cloak on, and her parasol in her hand, apparently ready to take a walk. She was evidently waiting for some one, and not very patiently, for several times she looked at her watch, and then she rose and went to the window, and then sat down again. At last she rose, apparently quite tired out, and rang the bell, on which a servant appeared.

'Tell Miss Louisa, if she does not come directly, I shall go without her.' The servant vanished, and in five minutes Louisa came rushing down stairs.

'Oh, my dear mamma!' cried she, 'I am so sorry to have kept you waiting; but I could not find my gloves.'

'You never can find them when they are wanted,' said Mrs Merton; 'but surely you have more pairs than one?'

'Yes, mamma, I had; but you know I lost one of my silk gloves at the Chinese exhibition, and one of my kid gloves fell into the water when I was feeding the ducks in Kensington Gardens, and——'

'It is of little use telling me the history of all your lost gloves now; it is clear you have none to put on; and as you cannot go to town with me without gloves, we must buy another pair at the shop in Black Lion Lane.'

'But that will delay us so much.'

'It can't be helped; but I do hope, Louisa, that you will be more careful in future. After Christmas, I shall allow you two guineas a-year to find yourself in gloves and shoes, and whenever you have not any fit to go out, you shall stay at home.'

'Two guineas! Surely my gloves and shoes do not cost two guineas a-year?'

Mrs Merton smiled, and said, 'During the last year they have cost nearly double that sum.

Louisa thought this impossible; but of course she did not say so; and by this time they had reached the shop. A pair of kid gloves was bought, which were so exactly what Louisa liked, that she could not help saying, as she put them on, 'You may depend upon it, mamma, I will take care of these gloves.'

We shall see,' said Mrs Merton.

Now, if there was any one set of words that Louisa could not bear to hear her mamma utter, it was that phrase, 'we shall see.' Louisa loved her mamma dearly; very few little girls could love a mamma better; but when Mrs Merton said 'we shall see,' with that peculiar look and tone, Louisa felt so provoked, that she thought she did not love her mamma at all. Mrs Merton had indeed an incredulous way of speaking that was very provoking, particularly when Louisa, who was rather sanguine, thought the case so clear that it was impossible any one could doubt it: and there was nothing that Louisa felt to mortify her so much, as when a case of this kind had occurred, and circumstances had proved that the mamma was right, and the little girl was wrong. Louisa was very fond of making good resolutions, and she liked to be praised when she told her mamma that she had done so; but her mamma thought it was quite time enough to praise her when the resolutions were carried into effect; and then the dreadful phrase, 'we shall see,' came like cold water on all Louisa's glowing feelings, and chilled her more than I can express.

We left Louisa putting on her gloves, which fitted beautifully; and even after they left the shop, Louisa kept putting the fingers of one hand through those of the other, so as to push on the gloves the better; and as the leather was soft and flexible, it expanded so as to admit her fingers properly without a single tear, or even a crack; and Louisa. as she looked at her gloves again and again, thought there was little danger of such gloves as those being lost for want of care.

When Louisa and her mamma reached the house of Mrs Merton's friend, they found they were too late, and that, after waiting for them for some time, she had been obliged to leave town without seeing them. Louisa was very much vexed at this, as she knew it would be of importance to her mamma, and her conscience told her she was in fault; and when they walked away from the door, she stammered a few words of apology for having kept her mamma so long while she was looking for her gloves. Mrs Merton, however, was evidently very much displeased. 'Say no more now, Louisa,' said she, 'but let what has happened to-day be a lesson to you another time.'

My readers may easily suppose, that after all this Louisa took the greatest care of her gloves when she reached home; and indeed for several days she always wrapped them up one within the other, and put them in the wardrobe before she took off her bonnet and cloak. Indeed I do think that the gloves would have been kept till they were quite worn out, if an unfortunate accident had not happened to them. One day some ladies called on Mrs Merton, and they were talking of worsted work, and Berlin patterns, and wool, and other things of that kind, when one of the ladies said she had heard of a manner of working in worsted on cloth that was practised abroad, but was not common in England.

'I am so anxious to see it,' said she, 'that I should think it almost worth taking a journey to Germany for that purpose alone.'

'I can gratify your curiosity, I believe,' said Mrs Merton, 'without your taking so much trouble. Go up stairs, Louisa, and fetch the cap your aunt worked in Poland.'

The cap in question was very beautifully worked in the manner the lady had described; and Louisa was very anxious it should be shown; but she remembered with dismay that she had borrowed it of her mamma to take the pattern of the work; and she remembered also that her mamma had been unwilling to lend it; and that Louisa had promised again and again to take the greatest care of it; and that her mamma had said 'we shall see;' and, worse than all, that she, Louisa, had not now the slightest recollection of what she had done with the cap, or where it was. All this rushed through her mind as she ran up stairs, and searched first in her own little sitting-room, then in the nursery, and then in the chiffonnier in the drawing-room, as the ladies were luckily in the parlour; and a sort of dim recollection glanced across her mind that she had been in the drawing-room when she began to draw the pattern. A half-drawn pattern was indeed in the chiffonnier, but no cap, and Louisa stood quite in despair, when suddenly the idea struck her that she had put it in the wardrobe in her bed-room, and she darted there like lightning. My readers may suppose the hurry and agitation with which she searched the wardrobe, which, I am sorry to say, was not in the very neatest order. A shawl or two tumbled out, but Louisa was too much absorbed to pick them up, when, oh joy of joys, she dragged out the much-wished-for cap! It is not possible to describe Louisa's delight. She never stopped to pick up the fallen shawls—she could not wait to shut the doors of the wardrobe, or even that of her bed-room, but flew down stairs, triumphantly holding the cap on her fingers; and she had the pleasure of hearing the ladies admire it even more than she expected. It was just what had been described, and Louisa's heart beat with joy and pride: she heard the ladies repeatedly say how glad they were to have seen it, and that they did not think there was another of the kind in England. Mrs Merton also seemed very much pleased, and after the ladies were gone, she told Louisa that she was very glad to find she had been mistaken; for, she added, 'I really was afraid that some accident had happened to it, when I found you stay so long before you returned.'

Louisa felt more proud and elated than she had ever done before as she skipped gaily up stairs; but, as she passed the door of her bed-room, which still stood wide open, she saw the shawls that had fallen out of the wardrobe lying upon the floor, and her little dog Fairstar lying upon them, apparently very busy eating something. At first Louisa thought it was a bone, and was frightened lest it should have tumbled the shawls; but oh how much worse was the truth! It was her gloves! her darling gloves that Fairstar was eating! they had fallen from the wardrobe with the shawls, and Fairstar, which, like all other puppies, was very fond of gnawing everything that came in his way, had found them, unwrapped them, and having gnawed off the end of one of the thumbs, was now very composedly proceeding to the fingers. Louisa stood for some moments quite overwhelmed with the extent of this misfortune; but she was soon roused from her stupor by her mamma's voice telling her to put on her things to go out. This was the climax. She darted forward, and giving poor Fairstar a violent blow, snatched up the gloves. But, alas! the mischief was already done, and both gloves had been so gnawed and wet, that it was impossible to put them on. Luckily, some fresh visitors came to see Mrs Merton, and they stayed till it was too late to go out, so Louisa escaped for that day; but the next, she knew her mamma was sure to go out, and she racked her brain to think what she could do, as she was quite ashamed to tell her mamma what had happened. It was but little more than a week since the gloves had been bought, and this was the result of the care she had promised; and then she looked at the gloves again, and tried to smooth them out; but it would not do; the thumb of one was quite gone, and Louisa, when she looked at them, absolutely cried with vexation. When she went to bed, it was a long time before she could sleep; and in the morning when she woke, she felt as if some dreadful misfortune had happened, before she could recollect what it was. All day long poor Louisa was thinking about the gloves, and never had she said her lessons so badly, or made so many mistakes in what she was desired to do. Never had any morning appeared so long, and yet she dreaded luncheon time coming, as she knew her mamma would probably go out as soon as it was over. This time, however, did come, and the words, 'Go up stairs, Louisa, and put your bonnet on,' had been said: no delay was therefore to be thought of, and though Louisa crawled up stairs as slowly as possible, she dared not be long in putting on her things; but how could she tell her mamma about the gloves? How she wished she had but courage to run down stairs and tell her mamma at once; but false shame kept her back. She thought of her mamma's dreadful 'we shall see;' and she felt she really could not bear to own just then how much in the right she found her mamma had been. Again she looked at the gloves, but they were even worse now than they had been the night before, for they had become hard and dry since they had been crumpled up. Then she thought of keeping her hands under her cloak, and she was just taking out her cloak to try how she could manage it, when her muff fell to the ground. Louisa caught it up with great delight—'This is the very thing,' thought she; 'mamma likes me to walk with both my hands in my muff, and as the day is cold, I can wear it quite well; besides, as we are going along, perhaps something will occur, so that I may be able to tell her about the gloves more easily than I could do now.'

And so Louisa, feeling quite rejoiced to have put off the evil day, tripped down stairs with both hands hidden in her muff. It happened that a lady was with Mrs Merton when Louisa came down stairs, and I am afraid that the little girl was glad when she found that this lady was going to walk out with them, as it would put off still longer the explanation about the gloves; for, though Louisa heartily wished it over, she dreaded the beginning so much that she was very glad to have a further respite. When Louisa reached the parlour, Mrs Merton was talking too earnestly to her friend Miss Hutchins to notice her daughter's muff; but the little girl was horror-struck when her mamma rose and said, 'Open the door, Louisa;' for how could she open the door, and yet keep both hands concealed? Luckily, however, the door was a little ajar, and Louisa contrived to push it open with her foot; but her heart beat violently at the narrow escape she had had, and she trembled lest her mamma should tell her to open the hall door, or to unlock the gate, if the servant, whose duty it was to perform these offices, should happen not to be ready in time; and it is impossible to describe the relief Louisa felt when she found herself safely in the open road. It was fortunate that Mrs Merton had a companion, for Louisa could think of nothing but her gloves, and yet of those she felt every moment more and more reluctant to speak. As they passed the end of Black Lion Lane, she could not help shuddering when she thought of the shop where the gloves were bought, and her exultation at the thought of keeping them carefully only five short days before; and where were they now? As they entered the door leading into Kensington Gardens, Mrs Merton saw a beautiful little bit of granite lying on the road, and pointed it out to her daughter, as she knew Louisa was making a little grotto for her cousin's birthday with all the pretty bits of stone she could find. The granite sparkled beautifully in the sun, and it was just the size and shape that Louisa wanted; but as it could not be picked up without taking her hands out of her muff, poor Louisa was obliged only to shake her head and pass it by. They now entered the gardens, and while they were walking under the trees, Louisa saw on the grass a beautiful caterpillar of the sphinx moth. Now, it had been Louisa's ardent desire for several months to meet with one of these creatures. She had seen one in Devonshire the summer before, and, on her return, had described it to her cousin Harriet, when Charlotte, one of Harriet's friends, who was present, and who was a most disagreeable girl, had laughed scornfully, and said she did not believe a word of it, adding, with a sneer, that travellers told strange tales. Now, there was nothing in the world that was so painful to Louisa as to have it supposed that she did not tell the truth, as she had a horror of falsehood, and had never told one in her whole life. She was therefore most anxious to find a sphinx caterpillar to show her cousin that she had not even exaggerated its description; and there one lay as beautiful as possible, with its bands of shaded green and lilac on a cream-coloured ground, and its curious horn even longer than the one Louisa saw in the country; and yet there she was obliged to let it lie, for how could she pick it up, and, above all, carry it home uninjured, without taking her hands out of her muff: the thing was impossible, and so Louisa walked on with tears in her eyes, and looking back every moment, till her mamma, looking at her attentively, asked why she was lingering, and Louisa's guilty conscience made her hurry on. They had now reached the pond, and the ducks crowded round Louisa, some of the most impudent pulling her cloak, as though they were asking her to give them something. Mrs Merton felt in her reticule, and finding a bit of bun, held it out to Louisa, that she might have the pleasure of feeding her old favourites. Louisa's heart beat—the moment for discovery was now surely come—for how could she avoid taking the bun; when, luckily, the large swan stretched out his long neck, and snatched the piece out of Mrs Merton's hand. Mrs Merton laughed, and telling Louisa that she must be quicker another time, turned away.

They now quitted the gardens, and went to call on a lady who lived at Kensington. Here some cakes were produced, and Louisa pressed to take one, which she would have been very glad to do if she could have contrived any means of getting it into her mouth without using her hands; but as there was not, she was obliged to decline. The lady of the house was very partial to Louisa; and seeing her sit so silent, with both her hands in her muff, and seeming so very uncomfortable, she very kindly proposed to Mrs Merton to let her little girl take a run round the garden behind the house. Louisa, terrified at this, for she felt she could not run without her hands being at liberty, hastily declined; and Mrs Merton, fearing that her poor little girl was ill, rose to return home. Another terror seized Louisa when she found that Miss Hutchins might possibly remain behind, as then she knew her mamma would be sure to take her hand; but Miss Hutchins came back with them almost as far as their own home; and thus they passed through Kensington Gardens without the dreaded discovery being made. A new fear, however, had taken possession of Louisa's mind, which haunted her through the gardens; and this was, that when they reached their own gate, how could she avoid ringing the bell, which she had always been used to do, to save her mamma the trouble: but even this danger was escaped, for the gate happened to stand open. They were now at home; and Louisa had thought several times during her painful walk, that if she could but reach home without discovery, she would be quite happy. And was she happy? Alas, no! she was more miserable than ever; and she felt more unable than ever to confess the truth. They were now ascending the stone steps leading to the hall door, when Mrs Merton, who had been looking behind her, trod on a bit of apple-paring, and, her foot slipping, she would have fallen, had not Louisa extended her hand. In the agitation of the moment the gloves were quite forgotten, and the muff fell to the ground. Mrs Merton's eyes met those of Louisa, and then glanced at her ungloved hands. The whole truth was now revealed; and in a very few minutes Mrs Merton was sitting in the parlour, and Louisa kneeling and hiding her face in her mother's lap. 'Oh, mamma,' cried the weeping girl, 'I will never, never do anything that I must conceal from you again. If you knew what I have suffered during this dreadful morning. Every time you looked at me I trembled all over, and felt as cold as death; and when I tried to speak, I was almost choked. I wonder that people do not die with fright when they have done anything wrong, and are taken up by a policeman. What a dreadful thing it is to have a secret! What I have suffered to-day will be a lesson to me as long as I live. I do not mean about the gloves, though I will try to take as much care as I can of the next pair you are so kind as to give me; but I mean I will never be so confident again, and that I will never again boast so conceitedly of what I will do. And, more than all, if I should do wrong, that I will have the courage to come and tell you at once, and to submit to any punishment you may think proper; for I am sure no punishment you would inflict upon me could ever make me feel one-tenth part of the pain I have endured this morning.'

STATE OF SCOTLAND A CENTURY AGO.

The following letter, descriptive of the condition of our country a century ago, was written by Mr John Maxwell of Munches, to Mr Herries of Spottes, both in the stewartry of Kirkcudbright, in the year 1811, when the venerable writer was above ninety. It has been several times printed, but nevertheless is sufficiently curious to merit the extended circulation which the Journal can give it.

'I was born at Buittle, in this parish, which in old times was the fortress and residence of John Baliol, on the 7th day of February, old style, 1720, and do distinctly remember several circumstances that happened in the years 1723 and 1724. Of these particulars, the falling of the bridge of Buittle, which was built by John Frew in 1722, and fell in the succeeding summer, while I was in Buittle garden, seeing my father's servants gathering nettles. That same year many of the proprietors enclosed their grounds to stock them with black cattle; and by that means turned out a vast number of tenants at the term of Whitsunday 1723, whereby numbers of them became destitute, and, in consequence, rose in a mob, when, with pitchforks, gavellocks, and spades, they levelled the park-dikes of Barncailzie and Munches at Dalbeaty, which I saw with my own eyes. The mob passed by Dalbeaty and Buittle, and did the same on the estates of Netherlaw, Dunrod, &c. and the laird of Murdoch, then proprietor of Kilwhaneday, who turned out sixteen families at that term. The proprietors rose with their servants and dependants to quell this mob, but were not of sufficient force to do it, and were obliged to send for two troops of dragoons from Edinburgh, who, upon their appearing, the mob dispersed. After that, warrants were granted for apprehending many of the tenants and persons concerned in the said mob; several of them were tried, those who had any funds were fined, some were banished to the plantations, whilst others were imprisoned; and it brought great distress on this part of the country. At that period justice was not very properly administered; for a respectable man of the name of M'Clacherty, who lived in Balmaghie parish, was concerned in the mob, and, on his being brought to trial, one of the justices admired a handsome Galloway which he rode, and the justice told him if he would give him the Galloway he would effect his acquittal, which he accordingly did. This misfortune, with what happened the Mississippi Company in the year 1720, did most generally distress this quarter of the kingdom. It is not pleasant to represent the wretched state of individuals as times then went in Scotland. The tenants in general lived very meanly, on kail, groats, milk, graddon ground in querns, turned by the hand, and the grain dried in a pot, together with a crock ewe now and then about Martinmas. They were clothed very plainly, and their habitations were most uncomfortable. Their general wear was of cloth, made of waulked plaiding, black and white wool mixed, very coarse, and the cloth rarely dyed. Their hose were made of white plaiding cloth sewed together, with single-soled shoes, and a black or blue bonnet, none having hats but the lairds, who thought themselves very well dressed for going to church on Sunday with a black kelt-coat of their wives' making. It is not proper for me here to narrate the distresses and poverty that were felt in the country during these times, which continued till about the year 1735. In 1725 potatoes were first introduced into this stewartry by William Hyland, from Ireland, who carried them on horses' backs to Edinburgh, where he sold them by pounds and ounces. During these times, when potatoes were not generally raised in the country, there was for the most part a great scarcity of food, bordering on famine; for in the stewartry of Kirkcudbright and county of Dumfries there was not as much victual produced as was necessary for supplying the inhabitants; and the chief part of what was required for that purpose was brought from the Sandbeds of Esk in tumbling cars, on the Wednesdays, to Dumfries; and when the waters were high by reason of spates, and there being no bridges, so that these cars could not come with the meal, I have seen the tradesmen's wives in the streets of Dumfries crying because there was none to be got. At that period there was only one baker in Dumfries, and he made bawbee baps of coarse flour, chiefly bran, which he occasionally carried in creels to the fairs of Urr and Kirkpatrick. The produce of the country in general was gray corn; and you might have travelled from Dumfries to Kirkcudbright, which is twenty-seven miles, without seeing any other grain except in a gentleman's croft, which, in general, produced bere or big for one-third part, another third in white oats, and the remaining third in gray oats. At that period there was no wheat raised in the country; what was used was brought from Teviot; and it was believed that the soil would not produce wheat. In the year 1735 there was no mill in the country for grinding that sort of grain; and the first flour-mill that was constructed within these bounds was built by old Heron, at Clouden, in the parish of Irongray, some years after that date.

In these times cattle were also very low. I remember being present at the Bridge-end of Dumfries in 1736, when Anthony M'Kie, of Netherlaw, sold five score of five-year-old Galloway cattle, in good condition, to an Englishman, at L.2, 12s. 6d. each; and old Robert Halliday, who was tenant of a great part of the Preston estate, told me that he reckoned he could graze his cattle on his farms for 2s. 6d. a-head; that is to say, that his rent corresponded to that sum.

At this period few of the proprietors gave themselves any concern anent the articles of husbandry, their chief one being about black cattle. William Craik, Esq. of Arbigland's father died in 1735, and his son was a man of uncommon accomplishments, who, in his younger days, employed his time in grazing of cattle, and studying the shapes of the best kinds, his father having given him the farm of Maxwelltown to live upon. The estate of Arbigland was then in its natural state, very much covered with whins and broom, and yielding little rent, being only about 3000 merks a-year.* That young gentleman was among the first that undertook to improve the soil; and the practice of husbandry which he pursued, together with the care and trouble he took in ameliorating his farm, was very great. Some of it he brought to such perfection, by clearing off all weeds and stones, and pulverised it so completely, that I, on walking over the surface, sunk as if I had trodden on new-fallen snow.

The estate of Arbigland was bought by his grandfather, in 1722, from the Earl of Southesk, for 22,000 merks.

In 1735 there were only two carts for hire in the town of Dumfries, and one belonging to a private gentleman.

About the years 1737 and 1738 there was almost no lime used for building in Dumfries, except a little shell-lime, made of cockle-shells, burned at Colvend, and brought to Dumfries in bags, a distance of twenty miles; and in 1740, when Provost Bell built his house, the under storey was built with clay, and the upper storeys with lime, brought from Whitehaven in dry-ware casks. There was then no lime used for improving the land. In 1749 I had day-labourers at 6d. per day, and the best masons 1s. This was at the building of Mollance House, the walls of which cost L.49 sterling.

* Eighteen merks make L.1 sterling, or L.12 Scots.

DOMESTIC RELATIONS IN ITALY.

The duties of husband and wife are in England observed with even more sanctity than they obtain credit for. But in how many instances do our affections and duties begin and end there, with the exception of those exercised by the parents towards their *very young* children. We all know that when a son or daughter marries, they literally fulfil the dictum of Adam, 'therefore shall a man leave his father and mother, and cleave unto his wife.' Our family affections centre in the small focus of the married pair, and few and ineffectual are the radii that escape and go beyond. Now, it must be acknowledged that, however endearing at the outset, however necessary and proper to a certain extent such a state of things may be, it often degenerates after a little time into the most sordid selfishness. The Italians are deficient in this self-dedication to one; but they have wider extended family attachment, of a very warm and faithful description. We consider it a necessity of life to have a *ménage* to ourselves; each couple in its nest cannot understand the harmony and affection nourished in a little republic, often consisting of grandfather and grandmother, who may be said to have abdicated power, and live in revered retirement—their days not counted and grudged, as with us is too frequently the case; then come father and mother respected and loved, and then brothers and sisters. If a sister marries, she becomes a part of another family, and goes away. The son brings his wife under his father's roof; but the size of their houses renders them independent in their daily life. The younger sons are not apt to marry, because, in addition to their want of fortune, too many women, essentially strangers, would thus be brought under one roof, and would be the occasion of discord. We know how readily the human heart yields to a law which it looks on as irrefragable: submitting to single life, uncles learn to love their nephews and nieces, as if they were their own offspring, and a strong family chain is thus formed. A question may arise as to how much of family tyranny turns these links into heavy fetters. In the first place, their families are seldom as numerous as with us. The necessities of their position fall lightly on the males. All over the world, younger sons seldom marry, or only do so to exchange luxury for straitened circumstances; and younger sons who continue to grow old under the paternal roof, sharing by right the luxuries to which they were born, and in which they were educated, are better off than our younger sons, who are often thrust forth from the luxurious home of their youth, to live on a bare pittance in a wretched lodging. Unmarried women all over the continent have so much the worst of it, that few remain single. How they contrive to dispose of their girls, now convents are in disuse, I cannot tell; but, as I have said, there are not so many as with us, and they usually contrive to marry. At times you may find a maiden aunt, given up to devotion, who sheds a gentle and kindly influence over the house. It does not strike me that, as regards daughters who survive their parents, things are better managed with us. This family affection nurtures many virtues, and renders the manners more malleable, more courteous and deferential. For the rest, though I cannot pretend to be behind the scenes—and though, as I have said, their morality is confessedly not ours—I am sure there is much both to respect as well as love among the Italians.—*Mrs Shelley's Rambles.*

A MONEY-MAKER.

About twelve years ago, a poor Frenchwoman, residing at Buenos Ayres, being exceedingly perplexed with regard to the 'ways and means,' set her inventive genius to work, and hit upon the following expedient:—Observing a vast quantity of bones and animal offal thrown away from the slaughter-houses with which Buenos Ayres abounds, a thought struck her that she might turn this waste to a profitable account. Having procured a large iron pot, and collected a quantity of bones, &c. she commenced operations by boiling them, and skimming off the fat, which she sold at the stores in Buenos Ayres. Finding the proceeds of her industry amply reward her labour, she persevered, advancing from a pot to a boiler, and from a boiler to a steaming-vat, until she possessed a magnificent apparatus capable of reducing a hundred head of cattle to tallow at one steaming. Four years ago she sold her manufactory, retired from business, and now rolls through the streets in one of the handsomest carriages in Buenos Ayres. There is now scarcely a respectable merchant in that place, or in Monte Video, but is in some way connected with cattle-steaming.—*Cape Frontier Times.*

ELEGANT HABITS OF BEES.

Did any one ever sufficiently admire—did he, indeed, ever notice—the *entire elegance* of the habits and pursuits of bees? their extraction of nothing but the quintessence of the flowers; their preference of those that have the finest and least adulterated odour; their avoidance of everything squalid (so unlike flies); their eager ejection or exclusion of it from the hive, as in the instance of carcases of intruders, which, if they cannot drag away, they cover up and entomb; their love of clean, quiet, and delicate neighbourhoods—thymy places with brooks; their singularly clean management of so liquid and adhesive a thing as honey, from which they issue forth to their work as if they had nothing to do with it; their combination with honey-making of the elegant manufacture of wax, of which they make their apartments, and which is used by mankind for none but patrician or other choice purposes; their orderly policy; their delight in sunshine; their attention to one another; their apparent indifference to anything purely regarding themselves, apart from the common good. * * In the morning, the bee is honey; in the evening, the waxen taper; in the summer noon, a voice in the garden, or in the window; in the winter, and at all other times, a meeter of us in books. She talks Greek to us in Sophocles and Theocritus; Virgil's very best Latin in his Georgics; we have just heard her in Italian; and besides all her charming associations with the poets in general, one of the Elizabethan men has made a whole play out of her, a play in which the whole *dramatis personæ* are bees!—*Ainsworth's Magazine.*

BONNY BONALY.

Bonny Bonaly's wee fairy-led stream
Murmurs and sobs, like a child in a dream,
Falling where silver light gleams on its breast,
Gliding through nooks where the dark shadows rest,
Flooding with music its own tiny valley—
Dances in gladness the stream of Bonaly.

Proudly Bonaly's gray-browed castle towers,
Bounded by mountains, and bedded in flowers;
Here bends the blue-bell, and there springs the broom,
Nurtured by Art, choicest garden flowers bloom;
Heather and whin scent the breezes that dally,
To play 'mid the green knolls of bonny Bonaly.

Pentland's high hills raise their heather-crowned crest,
Peerless Edina expands her white breast;
Beauty and grandeur are blent in the scene,
Bonny Bonaly lies smiling between;
Nature and Art hand-in-hand wander gaily—
Friendship and Love dwell in bonny Bonaly.

—*From 'The Gaberlunzie's Wallet,' by James Ballantyne.*

MANGOLD-WURZEL.

A French newspaper tells the following story of the introduction of this root into cultivation in Flanders:—When Napoleon was endeavouring to protect himself against the inconveniences felt from the impossibility of obtaining colonial produce, in consequence of the activity of the English cruisers, an order was given that measures should be taken to induce the Flemings to grow beet, for sugar-making. The prefect of the department of Jemappes, accordingly, invited all the farmers of his district to set about the cultivation of the root, and distributed seed among them. The Flemish farmers hit upon its management immediately, and the first season gave them a large crop. But when the roots were ready, nobody knew what to do with them; so the farmers resolved to cart them to the prefecture. And accordingly, one fine morning, the prefect was surprised by the arrival of heavy carts, bringing him some hundred thousand kilogrammes of beet. Having no means of taking it in—for the buildings in which it was to be manufactured had not been thought of—he had no resource but to pay for the crop, and get the country people to cart it away again. This led them to consider whether cattle could not be fed upon it; and the result we all know.

GENTLENESS.

Gentleness which belongs to virtue, is to be carefully distinguished from the mean spirit of cowards and the fawning assent of sycophants. It removes no just right from fear; it gives up no important truth from flattery; it is, indeed, not only consistent with a firm mind, but it necessarily requires a manly spirit and a fixed principle in order to give it any real value.—*Blair.*

** Complete sets of the Journal, *First Series*, in twelve volumes, and also odd numbers to complete sets, may be had from the publishers or their agents. A Stamped Edition issued for transmission, post free, price Twopence halfpenny.

Printed by William Bradbury, of No. 6, York Place, and Frederick Mullett Evans, of No. 7, Church Row, both of Stoke Newington, in the county of Middlesex, printers, at their office, Lombard Street, in the precinct of Whitefriars, and city of London) and Published (with permission of the Proprietors, W. and R. CHAMBERS,) by WILLIAM SOMERVILLE ORR, Publisher, of 2, Amen Corner, at No. 2, AMEN CORNER, both in the parish of Christchurch, and in the city of London.—Saturday, January 11, 1845.

CONDUCTED BY WILLIAM AND ROBERT CHAMBERS, EDITORS OF 'CHAMBERS'S INFORMATION FOR THE PEOPLE,' 'CHAMBERS'S EDUCATIONAL COURSE,' &c.

No. 55. New Series. SATURDAY, JANUARY 18, 1845. Price 1½d.

THE NEWSPAPER PRESS IN AMERICA.

In no other country in the world, perhaps, is the newspaper press so powerful an engine as in the United States. Nowhere else is it so omnipresent in its action, so omnipotent in its influence. It addresses itself not to a class or a section of the people, but universally to the nation. In the social structure of America, there is no great class devoid of the first elements of education. In the northern states especially, the ability to read and write is universal. In a state of society which converts every man into an active politician, the species of information most in demand, and most greedily devoured, may be readily surmised. The constant yearning for political intelligence is incredible to any but an eye-witness. The newspaper offices may be said to be, to the Americans generally, what the gin-palaces are to a section of the London population—the grand source whence they derive the pabulum of excitement. Such being the case, it is no wonder that journals should multiply amongst them. Almost every shade of opinion, political, social, or religious, has now its representative organ or organs. The press in America speaks to every one, and of every one. Its voice is heard in every cabin in the land; its representatives are found thickly scattered over every settlement; it is a power irresistible, and which must be conciliated; making itself felt in every public department, and at the same time exercising a tremendous influence over private life.

In England, the daily papers are confined to the metropolis. In America, the daily press may be said to be the rule, the semi-weekly and weekly the exception. The newspaper is an essential feature in almost every American village. Towns, such as in England would have no newspaper of their own, have in America their daily journals. It is seldom that a population as low as two thousand is to be found without them, battling for the great factions which agitate every corner of the country. They take a pride in having their local organs, and enterprise soon avails itself of this feeling. The reader may better judge of their multiplicity from a single instance. I select a town which stands on the borders of Lake Ontario, and which contains about 20,000 inhabitants. In that town there are at this moment three daily papers; two of them appearing in the morning, the other being an evening paper. They are all independent of each other, and none of them neutral. The evening paper takes a strong party stand with one of its morning contemporaries; and although these represent the opinions of the minority both in the town and county, there is yet sufficient room for them both: they are, indeed, all flourishing. Besides these, a weekly paper is issued from their respective establishments, which is widely circulated in the county amongst those who cannot afford the luxury of one daily; but with each of them, the number of daily impressions despatched into the surrounding townships is fully equal to that of the weekly editions. They are all to be met with in the bar-rooms of taverns, and in private houses, according to the political bias of the inmates; and there are few houses, amongst the farmers especially, which are not thus provided. The inhabitants of this town have also a weekly medical paper, a weekly paper exclusively agricultural, another exclusively literary, and another of a satirical character. All these have existed for years, and keep their ground well. Superadded to these, hundreds of daily papers, issued from Albany or New York, arrive by post for subscribers resident in the town—the latter being taken principally for the more authentic information, and the better comments they contain upon matters of general policy, which their readers are thus in possession of before the local papers can copy them.

The universal interest taken in politics is not the only means of accounting for the astonishing variety and number of American newspapers. The cheap rate at which they can be obtained, and the extensively available channel which they open for advertising, contribute materially to the increase of their number. A daily paper of the first class can be procured for eight dollars annually—less than two pounds sterling. Many are furnished for six dollars; and some respectable daily prints are published in New York as low as three. A daily English paper costs more than three times the price of the highest of these, or from six to seven pounds. Some are sold in the streets of New York at the rate of a cent a number—that is, a fraction more than an English halfpenny. The character of the American papers, their general tone and literary ability, in comparison with those of England, are not at present under consideration. With all the trashy and pernicious stuff which the majority of them diffuse throughout the community, they circulate a vast mass of useful and solid information, creating a degree of intellectual activity which cannot but be beneficial to a people.

As an advertising medium, the public journals of America are used to an extent unparalleled in this country. With a white population amounting to little more than half that of Great Britain, and with a commerce scarcely equalling in extent one-third of that of this country, the number of advertisements published in America within the last seven years, as compared with the number published during the same period in this country, was in greater proportion than six to one. This difference is created by the absence of all advertisement duties, by the general cheapness in the rate of advertising, and by the extensive circulation of the different papers—a circulation, as already shown, large, from the enormous political appetite of the public, but greatly increased by the universality of the practice of advertising. In general, even the remotest inland papers lay out three-fourths of their space for advertisements. The rate of insertion is exceedingly moderate, and their profits arise from the species of wholesale advertising business which they carry on. Many papers adopt the system of letting as much of their space as will let for a specified time, the lessee selecting his own part of the paper as he would his pew in a church, or his family burying-ground in a cemetery, and paying for it by its square measurement. To secure permanent customers of this sort, the rate is lowered to a kind of wholesale price; and sometimes a year's advertising, not exceeding from thirty to forty lines each day, can be thus procured as low as seventeen dollars. During the period to which a bargain of this kind extends, the control of the advertiser over the spot selected by him is in a manner absolute, and his announcements are to be found in all shapes and positions—upside down, in the form of a pyramid or cross, diagonal, vertical, or Chinese fashion. Almost every one advertises, for every one is busy. In the northern states there are no idlers; every man has his vocation; and from the lawyer to the chimney-sweep, their services are offered to the public through the medium of the newspaper. Indeed it is common for the former functionaries, especially in the interior, to have standing cards in their local papers, informing the public both of their place and hours of business. Its advertising columns are frequently the most amusing, though sometimes a very disgusting part of a paper: every trick is resorted to to arrest attention; each page is illuminated with hats, houses, boots, umbrellas, barrels, cattle of all descriptions, every item of male attire, locomotives, steamboats, canal boats, 'fast-sailing schooners,' and a multitude of other objects which enter into the multifarious business of mankind; and the smile which this occasions is often prolonged by the mode of announcement in the letter-press. Announcements such as follow are selected from a thousand others equally absurd and bombastic:—'North, south, east, and west, your interests are in danger;' and when one eagerly reads on to learn the source of alarm, he finds it to consist perhaps of the additional cent per yard which all but the advertiser charge on some flaunting calico pattern. 'Shopping a luxury,' 'money no object,' 'competition floored,' 'stern defiance,' 'to arms, to arms, to arms! the body politic in danger from—Jack Frost,' &c.; and these are sometimes surmounted by grotesque designs, in some of which the advertiser is seen engaged in a race of speed with his neighbours and competitors, and outstripping them all. A shrewd observer of human nature was the Alabama sheriff, who headed an advertisement of a land sale with—'Don't read this.'

If there be one thing more than another which marks an American newspaper, it is the violence of its political disquisitions. On the subject of politics, a transatlantic journal is unacquainted with moderation; and of the thousands published daily and weekly, there are few that begin by being, and fewer still that continue to be, neutral. Into the political vortex they are all drawn, there to be tossed to and fro, in a delirious round; on one side or another, in the strife of party, they are all ranged. On the eve of an election, their political complexion is discerned at a glance by the 'ticket' which heads their editorial columns, the 'ticket' consisting of the names, in large type, of the candidates whose election they advocate. This is done in their election both for state and for federal offices. The 'ticket' is called [illegible] Henry Clay, of Mr Polk, or of Martin Van Buren, as the case may be. As soon as a nomination, by the different parties, of candidates takes place, all the papers are committed; and some are bold enough, even before a nomination, to hoist at once its own favourite flag, although, as soon as the nomination takes place—such is their devotion to party—these are invariably hauled down to make way for the 'ticket' of the fortunate nominees. The asperity with which they conduct the political battle under their respective ensigns is a great blemish on their character. They take and they give no quarter. On the approach of an election, a stranger would anticipate, from perusing their columns, that every polling-place in the country must inevitably become the scene of a diabolical carnage; and yet, in the main, the business of polling in America is a very peaceable affair. In 1840, upwards of two millions of votes were recorded for the contending claimants to the presidency, and yet not a drop of blood was spilt throughout the length and breadth of the land. The wrath of the people effervesces in their party organs; and that bitterness and vituperation which are the creations of their printing-presses, seldom lead to any desperate personal collision. The worst feature of the journals is, unquestionably, their gross and disgusting personality. To serve a party purpose, they invade, without scruple, the sanctity of private life. Daily, in some quarter or other, is one of their prominent senators reminded of some trifling peccadillo, of which he is alleged to have been guilty at school, when about eleven years old; and Ex-Governor Marcy of New York will be reminded by the Whig press to his dying day that he charged the treasury two shillings and ninepence for mending his breeches, which were accidentally damaged during an official tour through the state. The party names and epithets which they bestow upon each other are amusing, though sometimes degrading enough; 'Loco Focos,' 'Blue Lights,' and 'Hoco Pocos,' being sufficient as samples of their political Billingsgate. They have no idea of receiving an electioneering triumph with quiet satisfaction. The exultation of the successful party is unbounded; and they like to try the temper of their crest-fallen opponents, by making it as ostentatious as possible. They celebrate their victory by illuminating their houses, while their organs illuminate their pages. Sometimes a cock is perched at the head of the editorial columns, and being in the attitude of crowing, there can be no mistake of the object for which he is thus placed. In 1838 and 1840, when the Whigs triumphed in New York, a leading journal in Albany, the capital of the state, devoted one whole side to an enormous eagle, which was represented with outstretched wings flying over the country with the 'glorious intelligence.'

The same rivalry in seeking to obtain early or exclusive news which distinguishes the London press, is also a marked feature in the conduct of American journals. To be the first to furnish the public with a president's message—with some great speech in Congress, which has been eagerly looked forward to—with any minor or secret intelligence concerning the cabinet and its doings—with the fate of any important measure in the legislature—or with European intelligence, is, particularly with the New York and Philadelphia papers, sufficient to induce them to incur a lavish expenditure. In some instances a whole edition of a New York paper has been printed in Washington, on the opening of the legislative session, so that the train from the capital, [illegible] from which they might publish for themselves, has brought their more alert contemporary in full sheet, which realised an enormous sale in the streets before its rivals could make their appearance. Many of the New York papers have their regular couriers in Boston, who start with the European files the moment the packet arrives, arranging the news for their different offices on the road; and some of them, as soon as a vessel from Europe is telegraphed in 'the Narrows,' hire a steamboat with which to meet her, so that the news which she bears is hawked about the streets long before she reaches the Battery.

In a literary point of view, nine-tenths of the American journals are at Zero in the scale of respectability. Their editors are more frequently rather men of bustling enterprise than of talent and education. In the main, the business of editing in America is destructive of everything like delicacy or refinement. What is required is tantamount to a pair of good fists in physical scuffling—to give good blows, and have a hard head to receive them in return. In many cases the editors are, simultaneously with the conduct of the paper, engaged in other pursuits—mechanical, mercantile, or professional—a part of their time only being devoted to their editorial duties. When it is recollected that this is the case even in the management of a daily paper, its slovenly appearance and inferior general character are in part accounted for. There is seldom the requisite degree of unity in their management to make even a tolerable paper. When there are several proprietors, it is not unfrequent to find them—although they have a nominal editor—all acting as editors, and sending paragraphs to the compositor without the slightest consultation with the responsible party. This gives rise of course to many serious incongruities, and involves them in many awkward inconsistencies. The editor is seldom called upon to write; his position is more that of a receiver of paragraphs than a writer. He draws far more frequently upon the editor's box than upon his own brain; he seldom ventures on what may be called a leading article, trusting for general political intelligence to his more ably conducted metropolitan contemporaries. Instead of this, the original matter of these papers often consists of a host of letters from young and ambitious politicians, each of whom, aspiring to the presidency, is anxious to make himself known to fame as speedily as possible. These effusions are all characterised by what seem essential ingredients in American polemics—gross abuse, and acrimonious invective. They are eagerly read, especially when the object or party attacked is of a local character or standing. The columns of the journals are likewise freely open to the essayist, from whose prolific pen they often insert long dull and vapid nothings. A poet's corner is an almost invariable appendage; and, judging from its constant occupation, the muse is most extensively, if not very successfully, cultivated in America. The vast majority of poetic contributors are sentimental young ladies. Is there a child born into the world?—its parents are sure to have some poetic friend, in the shape of a young lady, who indites an ode to its advent; is it baptised?—another ode, commemorative of the event, is inflicted upon the public. Is there a marriage?—some one is sure to torture into being a hymeneal hymn for the occasion. Is there a death?—it is no easy matter for an editor to select from the bundle of elegies he receives. Is there a shipwreck or any great national event?—and the poor beworried *nine* are called upon to inspire a thousand pens, and to direct a thousand very errant fancies. When a young lady marries, however poetically inclined she may have been before, she rapidly subsides into the prosaic mass, finding, when she has babies of her own, that she has more urgent duties to attend to than to write poems about them. The newspaper literature of America is of enormous bulk, but of no elevation. It is one great dead sea of stagnant water, with no flashing wave to break its dull surface—no phosphorescence to illuminate its depths.

The editor of an American newspaper, writing but little, is in almost every other sense a working-man. In general, the control of every department in the establishment is vested in him alone: he keeps the books, receives and pays out money, takes the advertisements, and, on an emergency, can sometimes turn compositor. When he enters with zeal into his task, his labours are of the most multifarious description. He must attend all political meetings of his own party, and must be found in the van of practical out-door politicians. He is always expected to be an orator, and is generally an oracle. At party meetings he must pander well to the peculiar tastes of his hearers; and, consequently, he who on such occasions surpasses all others in the measure of his language and the fury of his gestures, is in most cases—the editor. His field extends also to the committee-room and the secret 'Caucus.' He is always installed in the most laborious post, and generally fulfils his duty to the satisfaction of his constituents. In England, the paper is everything, the editor nothing. In America, the editor is invariably identified with his paper. It is he who is the recipient of contemporary abuse; it is on his shoulders that fall all the odium and acrimony of the opposite faction. This is universally so. In New York, in Albany, in Boston, and in other leading towns, the editors are all known, and assailed respectively by one another. In the interior, this system is of course carried to a greater and more revolting extent than in the capitals. From each paper might be culled the complete biography of the editor of its opponent. The moment a new editor makes his appearance in any place, the opposition paper opens upon him; and everything to which malicious ingenuity can impart an equivocal character is evoked from the past, and presented as a series of delicious morsels to the palate of faction. In self-defence the outraged stranger must retort, and a host of recriminations ensue, to the great gratification of all who are out of the ring, and, if possible, more scurrilous in their character than were the bulls and invectives which for seventy years, during the great western schism, were fulminated between Avignon and Rome. To the leading party-journals much is frequently owing in the issue of an election. But even then it is the editor who is lauded and rewarded. The party is not satisfied with the expression of a vague gratitude to an establishment; it seizes upon the editor as a more tangible object, and on him lavishes its praises, and sometimes proves its appreciation of his services by presenting him, as was done to the editor of the Albany Evening Journal in 1840, with—a cloak. Known as they are, it is seldom, as is the case in France, that they are raised to any political eminence. They are hard-working party hacks; their influence in the political world chiefly arising from their party services. Their power is the reverse of that which emanates from intellectual and moral dignity.

Frequently as the law is infringed, it is seldom that an American newspaper is brought in contact with a civil court. The law of libel is clearly defined in the statute-books; but American juries have tastes not very consistent with a too rigid administration of it. It is seldom, therefore, that the libelled individual looks beyond his walking-stick, his riding-whip, his pistol, or his bowie knife, for redress. The case of the novelist Cooper is an exception to this assertion. He brought several actions for libel against different papers, in some of which he adroitly pleaded his own cause, and in many of which he was successful. The libels of which he complained, arising as they did from literary criticisms, were not such as generally instruct and amuse the public. Had they been of a strong personal cast, it is questionable if he would have got a verdict sufficient even to carry costs. This, it must be allowed, indicates a low tone of public morals.

The foregoing sketch is applicable to the great majority of American newspapers. Very few can be named as exceptions to the general description. Some of these, it must be admitted, do honour to themselves, and credit to their country. Their political writing is characterised by temper, judgment, and ability; and the literary department of some of them is conducted in a style, and marked with a spirit, which would do no discredit to the most respectable journals of the old world. The great bulk of their contemporaries are, on the whole, more prejudicial than advantageous to the public morals and tastes. It is a pity to see so powerful an engine so wofully misdirected. If its energies emanated from proper principles—were the zeal which directs its efforts a zeal for man's intellectual and moral good—the press in America, from its increased and increasing power, might undo in a very short time much of the mischief which its vicious direction has entailed upon the country, and work a great social cure where it is now creating nothing but social disorders.

THE BARGAIN.

'MAY I trouble you to show me that dress-cap with blue trimmings in the window?' said a lady-like person as she entered a fashionable lace-shop.

The proprietor, with a polite bow, handed the lady a chair, and producing the cap alluded to, recommended it in the usual set phrases.

'Pray, what is the price?' inquired Mrs Mowbray with a dissatisfied air, after viewing it in every imaginable position, and scrutinising its materials and workmanship with the most patient minuteness.

'The price is seven shillings, madam,' answered the shopkeeper, rubbing his hands.

'Seven shillings!' exclaimed Mrs Mowbray; 'why, I have seen them marked up at a score of places for six, and at the bazaars they are cheaper still.'

'Excuse me, madam,' replied the shopkeeper, 'not such a cap as that, I think. Observe the fine quality of the materials, and the neatness of the workmanship. It is a first-rate article.'

'Oh yes, I see,' rejoined Mrs Mowbray; 'but the caps to which I allude are quite equal to it in every respect. The fact is, I do not particularly want it; but if *six* shillings will do, I will take it.'

The shopkeeper hesitated. 'I suppose you must have it then, madam,' said he with a saddened countenance, 'but really I get no profit by it at that price.'

'Oh,' said Mrs Mowbray with a bantering air, 'you shopkeepers never get any profit, if we are to believe you. You mean to say you do not pocket quite fifty per cent. by it.'

The shopkeeper, with a faint effort to smile, shook his head as he neatly folded and wrapped up the delicate article, and Mrs Mowbray having counted out the six shillings, he politely thanked her, opened the shop-door, and bade her good-day.

'There, Jane,' said Mrs Mowbray as she entered the parlour on her arrival at home, 'what do you think of my purchase?' holding up her new acquisition. 'Is it not a love of a cap? Guess what I gave for it.'

Jane examined it minutely, and guessed the price to be seven or eight shillings, the materials and work being, as she remarked, so very good.

'Only *six* shillings,' said Mrs Mowbray triumphantly; 'the shopkeeper asked seven, but I succeeded in getting it for six; and (putting it on, and walking up to the looking-glass) I assure you I am not a little pleased with my bargain.'

'Well,' said Jane, 'it is a wonder they can afford to sell such a cap for the money; the materials alone, I should think, would cost as much as that.'

'It *is* a wonder,' replied Mrs Mowbray indifferently, as she turned herself round before the looking-glass, and inquired of her sister how it suited her face, and whether the colour of the ribbon were adapted to her complexion.

A loud double knock at this moment was heard at the door, and Mrs Mowbray, taking off the cap in the greatest trepidation, remarked that she would not for the world that her husband should know of her purchase, as her last month's millinery bill had been very heavy, and Edward would be displeased at what he would term her extravagance.

The cap was safely deposited before Edward had entered the room; who, throwing himself on the sofa, declared he was fatigued, and should be glad of a cup of tea.

'You are late, my dear, this evening, are you not?' inquired Mrs Mowbray.

'I *am* later than usual,' answered Mr Mowbray; 'I have been attending a committee-meeting of our benevolent society, which detained me some time.'

'Your benevolent society is always detaining you I think,' said Mrs Mowbray somewhat reproachfully; 'benevolent societies are very good things no doubt, but I think *you* have quite sufficient to do, both with your time and your money, without attending to any such things. What can *we* do for the poor? It is very well for those who have nothing to do, and plenty of money to spare; but I cannot see how persons with so limited an income as ours have any business with benevolent societies.'

'Well, my dear,' replied Edward, 'I have thought on the subject sufficiently to entitle me to a decided opinion; and I am sure if you had been with us to-day, and had heard the instances of the good we have already effected, you would not hold so lightly the exertions of even such humble individuals as we. I hope I am neither neglecting my business nor my home in these efforts, and I am confident you will rejoice with me when I tell you that we have good reason to hope that we are making some impression, however little, upon the vice and ignorance which have so long made those lanes and alleys at the back of our house a nuisance to the neighbourhood.'

'Of course, my dear,' said Mrs Mowbray, 'I wish always to sympathise with you in any of your efforts to do good.'

'We have some funds in hand,' remarked Mr Mowbray, 'and I have promised our committee to visit the poor families myself to-morrow, to ascertain their individual circumstances, and the best means of serving them. Let me add, my dear,' said he coaxingly, 'that I hope you will accompany me, and share with me the pleasure of inquiring into their necessities, and endeavouring to alleviate their distress.'

Mrs Mowbray would willingly have conceded to her husband the monopoly of this pleasure; but, after making a host of objections and excuses, which were successfully combated by him, was at last brought to acquiesce in his wish, and promised to be in readiness on the following afternoon to accompany him on what she nevertheless deemed a Quixotic expedition.

The next day Mrs Mowbray was reluctantly ready on her husband's return from business, and, roughly attired for the occasion, they started on their exploratory tour.

Leaving the main thoroughfare, with its genteel dwelling-houses and glittering shops, they turned down a little by-street, at the end of which they found themselves in the midst of a huge nest, as it were, of courts and alleys, which presented a striking contrast with the gaudy street they had just left. Mrs Mowbray was so shocked at the sight of such wretchedness, that she hesitated to proceed, till reassured by her husband, who well knew the locality, and had often visited the poor families there before.

The appearance of the spot was indeed deplorable, and not a little startling to one whose walks had been confined to the public thoroughfares. It was a lovely afternoon, yet even the sun's piercing beams could scarcely penetrate some of these cheerless gloomy nooks. Here were clusters of pestiferous hovels, some without doors, crowded with human beings, though unfit even for the habitation of the most valueless animal. In many, the old window-panes were almost all broken, while in others they were so dirty, and patched with paper or stuffed with rags, that they but very partially admitted the light of day. Ragged and vicious boys were gambling in groups, and barefooted children were playing about in the slimy mud, some squalid and puny in consequence of bad air and insufficient food, and others whose chubby features displayed, in spite of dirt and privation, a robustness of health that would have done credit to the nursery of a nobleman. Here were gaunt men, with dull meaningless countenances, sitting on their comfortless thresholds, and bony haggard women screeching for their strayed children, while the scarcely-concealed forms of some of the younger females might have served as models for the painter or sculptor. Yet even here were traces of human sympathies of the purest kind. Girls were nursing their baby sisters with the most patient devotedness. The playful innocent-faced kitten, a universal favourite, frolicked about in the dirty window-sill; the social dog seemed quite at home with the children, as they shared with him their pittance of bread; and from many a superannuated saucepan and spoutless tea-pot, at the upper windows, grew the fragrant bergamot and the blushing geranium with strange luxuriance.

The appearance in such a neighbourhood of two well-dressed persons soon caused an unusual excitement, especially as Mr Mowbray was known among the poor inhabitants; and whenever he appeared there, it might be safely calculated there was something to be given away. Children, after a hasty glance at the intruders, left their playfellows and ran to their homes; heads were thrust out at the windows; some shuffled to their own rooms, that they might be ready if called on; others obtruded themselves in the way with an obsequious curtsey; some came to their doors with their little ones peeping from behind their aprons; and all around were on the tiptoe of expectation.

As they climbed the creaking stairs, and explored the naked garrets of the various houses, it was singular to mark the dissimilarity in character and circumstances of the various inmates—alike only in their poverty. Even in form and feature the contrast was striking. In the countenances of some might be unmistakeably read the sensual and the brutish; while in the lineaments of others might be traced, notwithstanding dirt and rags, the predominance of the gentle, and even the refined. Here was the round-cheeked boor, who fattened amid the filth that seemed natural to him; and here the angular-featured man of thought and of observation, whom more favourable circumstances might have placed in a far different sphere. The student of human character could not have desired a finer field for the prosecution of his studies than such a one as this; and the more so, as character was here so forcibly developed for good or evil, unweakened by any of the influences which affect civilised life. Mrs Mowbray, as she joined her husband in kind conversation with the various families they visited, soon began to feel a deep interest in them, soothingly advised with them, and relieved some of their more pressing wants.

They had completed their intended round of visits, and were just leaving the court to return homeward, when a young woman, carrying in her hand a milliner's basket, crossed before them. She was very meanly clad, and her appearance bespoke deep poverty, yet there was an air of respectability about her that could not be mistaken. She evidently shrunk from observation; but as she looked up with a surprised air at the unusual sight of two respectably-dressed persons in such a place, her sad countenance, beaming with intelligence, so forcibly impressed Mr Mowbray, that he stopped her, and asking her where she lived, expressed a wish to pay her a visit.

The young woman curtseyed, and led the way to a house superior to most of those they had just left, but scarcely less wretched and ruinous. It was a large building, and had perhaps once been tenanted by the wealthy; but it had long since fallen into decay, and its lofty capacious rooms had been divided into a number of small ones, each of which now contained a family, large or small as the case might be. Mr and Mrs Mowbray followed the young woman up the wide staircase to the top of the house, and then turning into a long gallery, their guide stopped at length at a door, and, lifting the latch, with a curtsey and an apology for the untidiness of the humble room, ushered them into her apartment, and dusting the chair (there was but one), invited Mrs Mowbray to take a seat.

The room was spacious, and appeared the larger in consequence of being so scantily furnished. Some half-dozen old books lay in the window, a few articles of crockery-ware were arranged on a box in the corner of the room, and these, with a little table, a chair, and a box which seemed to serve occasionally as a seat, comprised nearly all the articles visible in the room. Everything, however, was clean and tidy, and there was an air of decency and respectability about the room which pleasingly contrasted with those they had just left.

'Do you live here alone, pray?' inquired Mr. Mowbray.

'No, sir,' replied the young woman feebly, 'my aged mother lives with me; but (pointing to a bed at the further end of the room, and which the gathering shadows of evening had prevented them from before observing) she is ill, and has been confined to her bed for the last month.'

'Have you no father?' inquired Mr Mowbray.

The young woman was silent for a moment as her tongue struggled to articulate an answer, while a tear trickled down her cheek.

'My father is dead, sir,' she replied: 'he died about six months ago after a short illness, and we were in consequence compelled to leave our former nice home, and take this room.'

'And pray how do you support yourself and your mother?' asked Mr Mowbray, glancing at the table, which was strewed with pieces of lace, ribbon, &c.

'I make caps and collars, sir,' said the young female, 'when I can get work to do; but it is very precarious, and so badly paid for, that I have been obliged to pawn nearly all our furniture to keep out of debt. I am unwilling that my poor mother should be chargeable to the parish; but my hardest exertions are insufficient to supply us even with bread.'

'Pray, whom do you work for?' inquired Mrs Mowbray, looking curiously at an unfinished cap which lay on the table.

'I work principally, madam,' replied the young woman, 'for the large lace-shop in the street close by. That cap, madam, will only bring me 5s. when it is finished, and I have already spent nearly a day in making it, and the materials cost me 4s. 6d. Even this poor profit is to be reduced, for my employer told me last night he could not afford to give me so much for them, as ladies refuse to give him his price.'

'*Ladies*, indeed!' exclaimed Mr. Mowbray indignantly. 'They little think, when they are so mercilessly hunting for bargains, how sadly they are diminishing the wages of the poor.'

Mrs. Mowbray turned her head aside and blushed deeply, for she recognised in the cap before her the counterpart of the one she had bought the preceding day, and in the employer of this poor young woman the laceman of whom she had bought it.

Mr. Mowbray made some further inquiries, and leaving the poor cap-maker a trifle, promised to send a doctor to visit her mother, and to call on her again; and Mrs Mowbray, before leaving, gave her an order, with an assurance that she would endeavour to interest her friends on her behalf.

Mrs Mowbray, though ashamed and self-convicted, returned home pleased with her novel tour, and henceforward was the frequent companion of her husband on such occasions. Bargain-hunting had been in her case the result rather of thoughtlessness than of an unfeeling disposition; and from this time she was more liberal in her purchases, and never felt disposed to depreciate the value of an article without thinking of the poor capmaker. She came to the wise conclusion, that an unnecessary or bad article can never be cheap, and that a good article is always worth a fair price. A bargain was ever afterwards associated in her mind with depreciated wages and the misery of the poor; and the charm which it had once possessed in her eyes was entirely dispelled by the recollection of the sorrow and oppression which were so often involved in its production.

POPULAR INFORMATION ON SCIENCE.

INFLUENCE OF LIGHT ON PLANTS AND ANIMALS.

Most persons are aware how indispensable air, heat, and moisture are to the development of vegetable and animal life; but it is not so generally known how intimately the agency of light is connected with the same operation. By light, we mean the diffusion of solar rays which are always less or more illuminating the earth's surface, and without which the vision of animals would be a useless and unnecessary gift. The emanation of rays from the sun is attended with two very obvious and well-known results, namely, heat and light; it also effects such a chemical change in the properties of bodies, as is exemplified in the Daguerreotype and other similar processes. Whether these three effects—light, heat, and chemical change—be different manifestations of one grand principle, or whether solar radiation be composed of three distinct principles, science has not yet determined; though, as far as experiments have gone, the latter seems to be the true conclusion. It is possible, for instance, by a simple contrivance, to receive the heat and reflect or throw back the light, or to admit the light and obstruct the heat; and it is equally possible to produce chemical effects which neither light nor heat of themselves could accomplish. The chemical influence of the sunbeams, or *actinism*, as it has been appropriately termed,* may act on substances which remain unaffected by heat or light; and light may perform its functions as in the matter of vision, where heating and chemical rays, were they to be active, might be positively deleterious. Presuming, therefore, that solar radiation is made up of three different sets of rays, we shall endeavour to point out some of the more obvious effects of light and actinism in the development of vegetable and animal life, distinguishing between their effects where we can, and speaking of them as one principle only where science has not yet been able to draw the line of demarcation.

The germination of vegetable seed is the change of the inert and apparent lifeless embryo into a living plant; and this is effected by the presence of heat, air, and moisture. The influence of light is destructive to this process; and it is only in darkness that a vigorous germination can be induced. But while the light-yielding rays of the sun retard the vivification of the vegetable embryo, the actinic rays have been found to forward the process in a remarkable degree. The same principle seems to operate widely in the development of animal life; and when experiments have become more accurate and numerous, it will be found that actinism is as necessary to the vivification of the ova of many animals as it is to that of the vegetable embryo. Where the sunbeam spreads its genial influence, there life in all its myriad forms is found; where the sun-rays cannot penetrate, there space is a lifeless blank. At the surface of the ocean, and around its shores, marine animals and plants, varied in form and beautiful in colour, are found abundantly. As we descend, we find life gradually sinking in the scale of organisation; and below a certain depth, varying probably in different latitudes, no creature stirs the ever-silent sea. As in the ocean, so on land. The southern slopes of our hills and mountain ranges are always clothed with a more elaborated and more developed race of plants than the northern slopes; and this depends wholly upon the greater degree of light which the former enjoy. The northern side may sometimes be as verdant, but it never will be so flowery as the southern exposure; and the attentive observer may detect new tribes on either side almost as soon as he has passed the summit. The myriads of minute forms which are called into life under the tropical sun, seem to depend upon the same influence for their vivification — a vivification which, under simple light and heat, it has been found impossible to induce. It would seem, therefore, that actinism is a more subtle force than air, or heat, or light, or even electricity; that it brings us as it were to the confines of vital energy; and though not of itself a *vis creatrix*, yet indispensable to the manifestations of vitality.

It has been remarked, that a sunbeam cannot pass over a plate of iron without leaving indications of its path; so active, yet subtle, is the chemical principle of actinism. As with inanimate substances, so also with organic tissues: a sunbeam cannot fall on the leaf of a plant, or on the skin of our hand, without inducing a change which is manifested by an alteration of colour. The green hue which is universal in healthy vegetation, depends immediately and directly upon the influence of light. Every one must have seen the white and sickly stem of a potato grown in a dark cellar; and must have observed how it was attracted towards any feeble ray of light that did enter, as if in search of the element so necessary to its perfect development. The stem may have grown for months, shooting to the length of six or eight feet, and yet no trace of anything like the green colour of its perfect health will be discernible till it has come within the influence of solar light, and then a few days or even hours will suffice to clothe it in its natural hue. Mr Ellis states, in the Gardeners' Magazine, that 'in North America the operation of light in colouring the leaves of plants is sometimes exhibited on a grand scale and in a striking manner. Over the vast forests of that country clouds sometimes spread, and continue for many days, so as almost entirely to intercept the rays of the sun. In one instance, just about the period of vernation, the sun had not shone for twenty days, during which time the leaves of the trees had reached nearly their full size, but were of a pale and whitish colour. One forenoon the sun broke through in full brightness, and the colour of the leaves changed so fast, that by the middle of the afternoon the whole forest for many miles in length exhibited its usual summer's dress.'

The effects of light upon animal tissues is not less remarkable. In man, for example, it is well known that his complexion changes from fair to brown, and

* See a paper on Actino-Chemistry in No. 38 of our current series.

from brown to an almost sooty colour, by simple removal from a temperate to a tropical region; and though this may in some measure depend on original constitutional variation, yet in most cases the effects of strong solar light are too obvious to be doubted. The negro, with his sooty complexion and woolly hair, may be a different variety of the human species from the European; but there is also every reason to believe that the same pigmental apparatus which gives the dark hue to the skin of the former, is also present under the skin of the latter, and that it only requires an excess of solar light to bring it into full excreting operation. Even under the comparatively feeble light of our own latitude, the summer's sun will in a few hours convert the pale face of the sedentary student into a tawny brown—an action as purely actinic as the colouring of the leaves of the American forest. Heat and light cannot have anything to do with this change, otherwise the artificial fires and lustres of our apartments would produce some complexional alteration; but such is not the case; and since artificial and natural heat manifest themselves similarly, and since the eye is affected in the same manner by the beams of the sun and the rays of a gas lustre, this change of colour, caused by solar radiation, must depend upon some principle peculiar to sunlight—in a word, on actinism.

Production of colour is perhaps the most obvious of the changes produced in organic bodies by the influence of light; but there are others equally general and important. Vegetable growth is directly and immediately dependent upon it. It has been proved that the carbon or woody structure of plants is derived from the decomposition of carbonic acid, which they principally absorb by their leaves from the atmosphere; and that this decomposition of carbonic acid gas proceeds only when the plant is under the influence of solar light. Remove the plant from that influence to a dark cellar, or let the sun sink beneath the horizon, and the operation ceases. Solar light may therefore be said to be the prime promoter of vegetable growth; that influence by which the assimilation of carbon is effected and colour produced, and that power by which the circulation of their sap, if not wholly caused, is at least greatly facilitated. This last operation was tested by De Candolle. 'If you select,' says he, 'three plants in leaf, of the same species, of the same size, and of the same strength, and place them in close vessels, one in total darkness, the other in the diffused light of day, and the third in sunshine, it will be found that the first pumps up very little water, the second much more, and the third a great deal more than either. These results vary according to species and circumstances; but it uniformly happens that plants in the sun absorb more than those in diffused light, and the latter more than those in darkness; the last, however, pumping up something.' It is nevertheless worthy of remark, that although the direct solar rays are necessary for the decomposition of carbonic acid, the production of colour, and the promotion of circulation, yet the most feeble diffused light of day is sufficient to produce these results less or more in a natural state. Thus we find that plants growing in wells, on the north side of high walls, and in rooms partially darkened, become green, and often perform all their functions without much apparent inconvenience. Yet De Candolle found the purest daylight, the brightest lamplight, insufficient to bring about the decomposition of carbonic acid in an obvious manner. From this, therefore, we must infer, that it is neither heat-giving nor light-giving rays to which these results can be ascribed; but that they are directly owing to the actinic or chemical principle of solar radiation.

The influence of light or actinism is not concerned in the matter of growth alone, it is equally indispensable to the elaboration of the various vegetable secretions, and to the perfection or maturation of the seeds by which plants are propagated. 'We see in practice,' says the author of the article Botany, in the Library of Useful Knowledge, 'that the more plants are exposed to light when growing naturally, the deeper is their green, the more robust their appearance, and the greater the abundance of their odours or resins; and we know that all the products to which these appearances are owing are highly carbonised. On the contrary, the less a plant is exposed to sunlight, the paler are its colours, the laxer its tissue, the fainter its smell, and the less its flavour. Hence it is that the most odoriferous herbs are found in the greatest perfection in places or countries in which the light is strongest; as sweet herbs in Barbary and Palestine, tobacco in Persia, and hemp in the bright plains of extra-tropical Asia. The peach, the vine, and the melon also, nowhere acquire such a flavour as under the brilliant sun of Cashmere, Persia, Italy, and Spain. This is not, however, a mere question of luxury, as odour or flavour may be considered. The fixing of carbon by the action of light contributes in an eminent degree to the quality of timber—a point of no small importance to all countries. Isolated oak trees, fully exposed to the influence of light, form a tougher and more durable timber than the same species growing in dense forests; in the former case, its tissue is solidified by the greater quantity of carbon fixed in the system during its growth. Thus we have every reason to believe that the brittle wainscot oak of the Black Forest is produced by the very same species as produces the tough and solid naval timber of Great Britain. Starch, again, in which carbon forms so large a proportion, and which in the potato, cassava, corn, and other plants, ministers so largely to the nutriment of man, depends for its abundance essentially upon the presence of light. For this reason, potatoes grown in darkness are, as we say, watery, in consequence of no starch being developed in them; and the quantity of nutritious or amylaceous matter they contain, is in direct proportion to the quantity of light to which they are exposed.'

The germination, colouring, growth, and maturation of plants may be considered as the great operations in which light or actinism is directly active; but there are other minor phenomena in the vegetable kingdom seemingly dependent upon the same influence. Thus the expansion and closing of the leaves and blossoms, the motions of the leaves, the twining of tendrils, and the like, all have regard to the presence or absence of solar radiation, and seem to receive its impressions as rapidly and certainly as does the photogenic paper of the artist. A passing cloud will interrupt the process of the Daguerreotype and calotype, and though we have not yet learned to mark such transient impressions on the leaves and blossoms of plants, yet certain we are that they must be affected by these interruptions. The white marigold closes its flowers on the approach of a rain-cloud; and many plants were observed to fold their leaves and blossoms during the solar eclipse of 1836. When a mere temporary absence or presence of sunlight thus affects vegetation, it is no wonder that its continued intensity should produce such results as we find in warm and cloudless climates. At the Cape of Good Hope, Herschel found by his actinometer (an instrument for measuring the intensity of solar radiation) that the force of sunshine was 48¾, while ordinary good sunshine in England is only from 25 to 30; and from this we can easily account for the brilliancy of many of the Cape flowers, which we in vain attempt to rear in their native perfection in our stoves and conservatories. The gardener can readily furnish heat to any amount; but science has not yet discovered how to produce the subtle principle of solar radiation.

Turning now to the animal economy, we find growth, health, and development also curiously affected by the absence or presence of the solar influence. Dr Edwards has shown that if tadpoles be nourished with proper food, and are exposed to the constantly-renewed action of water (so that their bronchial respiration may be maintained), but are entirely deprived of light, their growth continues, but their metamorphosis into air-breathing animals is arrested, and they remain in the form of large tadpoles. He also observes that persons who live in caves and cellars, or in very dark and narrow streets, are apt to produce deformed children; and that men who work in mines are liable to disease and deformity beyond what the simple closeness of the atmosphere would be likely to produce. It has been stated, on the authority of Sir A. Wylie, that the cases of disease on the dark side of an extensive barrack at St Petersburg, have been uniformly for many years in the proportion of three to one on the side exposed to strong light. Further, Dupuytren relates the case of a lady whose maladies had baffled the skill of several eminent practitioners. This lady resided in a dark room (on which the sun never shone) in one of the narrow streets of Paris. After a careful examination, Dupuytren was led to refer her complaints to the absence of light, and recommended her removal to a more exposed situation. This change was followed by the most beneficial results; all her complaints vanished. The more, therefore, that animals are exposed to the influence of light, the more freedom in ordinary circumstances do they find from irregular action and deformity. Humboldt has remarked that among several nations of South America, who wear very little clothing, he never saw an individual with a natural deformity; and Linnæus, in his account of his tour through Lapland, enumerates constant exposure to solar light as one of the causes which render a summer's journey through high northern latitudes so peculiarly healthful and invigorating.

It is not to be supposed, however, that exposure to continued solar light is a normal condition of existence; on the contrary, it seems that plants and animals, as well as inanimate nature, require a period of repose from that activity and motion of their elements which actinism so unerringly excites. A taper will no doubt burn brighter in a medium of oxygen gas than in common air, but it just consumes so much the more quickly. So it may be with bodies exposed to perpetual light. The vegetation of our own latitude springs, grows, and ripens slowly, requiring for its perfect development a period of several months; the plants of the arctic regions, under continual daylight, start suddenly into life, and perform their circle of being in a few weeks. In this particular, organic life seems strictly analogous to physical force: we cannot gain power unless at the expense of time, or gain time unless by the exertion of superior power. 'If,' says Dr Lindley, 'changes in their condition be requisite to the wellbeing of plants, so in like manner are the diurnal changes of light and darkness. If plants were kept incessantly growing in light, they would be perpetually decomposing carbonic acid, and would, in consequence, become so stunted, that there would be no such thing as a tree, as is actually the case in the polar regions. If, on the contrary, they grow in constant darkness, their tissue becomes excessively lengthened and weak, no decomposition of carbonic acid takes place, none of the parts acquire solidity and vigour, and consequently they perish. But under natural circumstances, plants which in the day become exhausted by the decomposition of carbonic acid, and by the emptying of their tissue by evaporation, repair their forces at night by inhaling oxygen copiously, and so forming a new supply of carbonic acid, and by absorbing moisture from the earth and air without the loss of any portion of it.'

It would appear, then, from what we have stated, that actinism, as distinct from mere visual light, is one of the most important and universal agencies in nature. We see its power everywhere around us, alike on animate and inanimate objects. Like the lyre of Memnon under the rays of the rising sun, organic life is thrown into motion by its influence; vitality is as it were revivified, and even inert matter changes its hues and properties. As yet, its operations constitute an imperfectly-interpreted chapter in the history of creation; but the subject has interest and value sufficient to excite to its perfect explanation. Chemical action, magnetism, electricity, are subtle agents, and science has already subjected them in a thousand ways to the purposes of human life: need we therefore despair of obtaining in time a like control over this ethereal principle of solar radiation?

DEGENERATE DAYS.

A very common phrase in the mouths of those who speak by rote, and who repeat from others, without any very distinct perception of its meaning, any sentence that to a limited understanding appears true or half-true, is, that 'the present are degenerate days.' These people—who are generally old, and have lost the capacity of all enjoyments except those of grumbling and argumentation—not only imagine that the world has been growing worse ever since the flood, but that a very great difference, to the world's disadvantage, has taken place since they were young. The weather is not so fine, the men are not so strong, and the women are not so beautiful, as when they were juveniles. They will not even allow a storm of these days to be equal to the storms of the past. The very thunder does not roar so grandly as it used to do, and the lightning is pale and feeble in comparison with the flashes that they have known. The wine of life they imagine is in the lees, and the fire of nature growing cold.

It is in vain to tell them that the fault is in themselves; that they have lost the power of enjoyment; that they have no longer the keen appreciation of the beautiful which they had in their young days; that their palates are dulled, and that, therefore, they consider the fine pine-apple to be no better than a pippin, and the golden pippin itself to be no better than the harsh uncultivated crab. No; they maintain that the fault is not in them, but in the age; and they could weep for its degeneracy, had they not too much philosophy to weep for anything.

We once knew a very fine specimen of this class of prosers. Our friend was about seventy-eight years of age, still tolerably hale and hearty, and in possession of a snug sum in the three-and-a-half per cents. He was the oracle of the chief inn of the village, in the parlour of which he was nightly to be seen occupying the large arm-chair, and laying down the law, like a Solon, to the juniors who surrounded him. Scrupulously neat and clean was he, well powdered was his scanty hair, carefully brushed were his black coat and gray nether garments, white as snow was his neckcloth, and brilliant were his shoes as the best blacking could make them. Remnant of ancient days, his queue hung over the collar of his coat, and scattered over it the floating powder in a silvery spray. Decently and comfortably had he passed this life; his character was unexceptionable; and a great man was he in his native village, and for five miles round it, and a mighty potentate in the parlour of the Red Lion. So great was the estimation in which he was held, that his portrait had been painted at the expense of the landlord, and hung up in a broad gilt frame over the mantelpiece, to fire the young with emulation, and keep him in the remembrance of those who might come after him.

This worthy soul had a word to say upon every subject; he was a 'dictionary of dates and universal reference;' and if he did not know any matter that might be in dispute, he pretended to know; and to the majority of those with whom he came in contact, this was the same thing. He swore that there was no eloquence in modern parliaments—no public spirit in modern ministers; that the abolition of the rotten boroughs had destroyed the nation; and that the sun of Great Britain had set for ever, unless we should return to the old system, increase sinecures and taxation, and go to war with the whole world, as we did in the days of the French Revolution.

In literature, his notions were equally antique. The latest novel he had read was Sir Charles Grandison, and the most modern poet, with whom he deigned to acknowledge acquaintance, was Pope. He had heard of Scott and his wonderful genius, but would not read his works. When advised to do so, he inquired if he were equal to Shakspeare, and when answered in the negative, he tossed his head with a disdainful smile, and pitied the degeneracy of the age, which, with all the boasted march of intellect, and the discoveries of science, could not produce another Shakspeare. 'And then your modern poets,' he exclaimed, 'your Byrons, your Moores, your Campbells, your Southeys; glorious John Dryden is worth them all—and Pope worth a thousand of them. Talk of poetry, indeed,' said he; '"An honest man's the noblest work of God;" and all your Childe Harolds, and Irish Melodies, and Pleasures of Hope, and Pleasures of Memory, and Ancient Mariners, and Christabels, and Thalabas, can never equal that one line; that line is indeed fine, and good poetry, and cannot be disputed.'

'But no poetry can be good, in the first degree of goodness, that is not true, and I maintain that that line is not true.'

'How?' said he, starting from his chair, and grasping his silver-headed staff in a paroxysm of astonishment and indignation as we spoke; 'not true?'

'An honest man may be a fool—a dolt, without ideas, enterprise, energy, or talent of any kind, beyond the talent of making a profit upon a yard of tape; and would he be as noble a work as Isaac Newton or Francis Bacon?'

'Sir, you have no taste or judgment,' said the stickler for degeneracy, 'or you would not speak thus. The world has degenerated, indeed, if one of this generation fails to appreciate that sublimest passage of our greatest poet. But I will not argue with you; you are no judge of poetry.'

'Well, perhaps not. But, leaving such matters of taste and opinion, you will allow that in one respect this age is much in advance of any other—the wonderful discoveries of science and art?'

'Ay, ay,' said he with a smile of triumph, 'you are coming to steam, I see, and railroads! Now, I maintain that steam is a curse, and not a blessing to society. Talk of your steamboats; give me the good ship, with all her sails swelling to the breeze, and skimming merrily over the waters, without a monstrous boiler in her inside, in danger of bursting every moment, and blowing every soul on board of her to destruction! And as for your railroads, give me the old highway I say. I never travelled by a railroad, and I never will. I love the old ways, the neat inns by the road-side, the civil coachman, the swift horses, and the merry bugle of the guard. No; railroads are the bane of all enjoyment in travelling; and, to say nothing of the danger of collisions, which may send the heads and limbs of five hundred passengers flying in the air in a moment, you cannot even enjoy a sight of the fields, and trees, and hills, and all the beauties of the country, if once you intrust yourself in the train. No, no; there can never come any good out of steam.'

'But,' said we, wishing to draw him out, and without the slightest hope that he would agree with us, 'suppose we concede that steam travelling is not so pleasant as it might be, you must at least allow that by means of steam we bring nations together—that we gain a victory over time and space, and aid the great cause of human civilisation by carrying our arts, our productions, our knowledge, and our religion, to remote regions—that, but for steam, and the impetus it has given to the intellect of man, we would not have enjoyed these blessings for ages yet to come. You will allow that?'

'Sir, I will not allow that any good is done by that. True, we carry what we call our civilisation into savage lands, but we carry our vices and our diseases along with it; and I am not sure that the savages are not better without us than with us. They are free, they are strong, they are healthy, and have few wants; and the utmost we do for them is to instil wants into them, which, when they cannot supply, they become miserable. No; they are better without us; we only make them as degenerate as ourselves.'

Our friend has long since been gathered to his fathers, but there are many more like him to be met with daily. The secret of their dogmatism is easily discovered, and it is vanity. If the world has degenerated, the greater their merit not to have degenerated with it. They fancy that they have remained bright when all has been growing dark, and they are pleased with themselves accordingly. It is fortunate that their fancies are harmless, and that the world can get on without them.

HEALTH OF TOWNS COMMISSION.

The first volume of the Report of the Health of Towns Commission, which we noticed in a recent number of the Journal, contains the evidence on the 'causes of disease, and means of prevention;' the second, the more bulky of the two, comprises that bearing on the supply of water to towns, drainage, surveys, &c. We purpose, in the present article, to call attention to the fearful details of the former, which opens with an explanatory report by the commission, stating their object to have been the institution of inquiries 'into the present state of large towns and populous districts in England and Wales, with reference to the causes of disease amongst the inhabitants; the best means of promoting and securing the public health; the drainage of lands; the erection, drainage, and ventilation of buildings; and the supply of water in such towns and districts, whether for purposes of health, or for the better protection of property from fire; and how far the public health, and the condition of the poorer classes of the people of this realm, and the salubrity and safety of their dwellings, may be promoted by the amendment of the laws, regulations, and usages at present prevailing with regard to those matters.'

The whole of the evidence adduced on these points goes to establish that, 'defective drainage, neglect of house and street cleansing, ventilation, and imperfect supplies of water, contribute to produce atmospheric impurities which affect the general health and physical condition of the population, generating acute, chronic, and ultimately organic disease, especially scrofulous affections and consumption, in addition to fevers, and other forms of disease.' The startling facts brought forward as to the *creation*, we may call it, of scrofulous affections by impure air, are new, and present some of the gloomiest features of the volume, inasmuch as they prove the fatal effects of the pernicious influences complained of, in the existence of a deteriorating population, diseased in themselves, and bequeathing disease to a still more wretched posterity. Joseph Toynbee, Esq. one of the witnesses examined, appears to have devoted special attention to this part of the subject: on being asked as to his observation of 'the effect of defective ventilation,' he replies—'The defective ventilation appears to me to be the principal cause of the scrofulous affections, which abound to an enormous extent amongst our patients. When I have had a scrofulous patient come before me, I have always been able to trace this as one of the agents.' He cites the work of a French physician, M. Baudeloque, in which it is stated 'that the repeated respiration of the same atmosphere is the cause of scrofula; that if there be entirely pure air, there may be bad food, bad clothing, and want of personal cleanliness, but that scrofulous disease cannot exist.' The following facts are further quoted:—'The development of scrofula is constantly preceded by the sojourn, more or less prolonged, in air which is not sufficiently freshened. It is impossible to deny that hereditary disposition, the lymphatic temperament, uncleanliness, want of clothing, bad food, cold and humid air, are of themselves circumstances non-effective for the production of scrofula.

'When it is seen, on the other hand, that this disease never attacks persons who pass their lives in the open air, and manifests itself always when they abide in an air which is unrenewed, and this whatever may be the extent of other causes, it appears evident that the non-renewal of the air is a necessary condition in the production of scrofula. Invariably, it will be found on examination, that a truly scrofulous disease is caused by a vitiated air, and it is not always necessary that there should have been a prolonged stay in such an atmosphere. Often a few hours each day is sufficient; and it is thus that persons may live in the most healthy country, pass the greater part of the day in the open air, and yet become scrofulous, because of sleeping in a confined place, where the air has not been renewed. This is the case with many shepherds. It is usual to attribute scrofula, in their case, to exposure to storms, and atmospheric changes, and to humidity. But attention has not been paid to the circumstance, that they pass the night in a confined hut, which they transport from place to place, and which protects them from wet; this hut has only a small door, which is closed when they enter, and remains closed also during the day; six or eight hours passed daily in a vitiated air, and which no draught ever renews, is the true cause of their disease. I have spoken of the bad habit of sleeping with the head under the clothes, and the insalubrity of the *classes* where a number of children are assembled together.'

An instance is adduced in corroboration: 'At three leagues from Amiens lies the village of Oresmeaux; it is situated in a vast plain, open on every side, and elevated more than 100 feet above the neighbouring valleys. About sixty years ago, most of the houses were built of clay, and had no windows; they were lighted by one or two panes of glass fixed in the wall; none of the floors, sometimes many feet below the level of the street, were paved. The ceilings were low; the greater part of the inhabitants were engaged in weaving. A few holes in the wall, and which were closed at will by means of a plank, scarcely permitted the air and light to penetrate into the workshop. Humidity was thought necessary to keep the threads fresh. Nearly all the inhabitants were seized with scrofula, and many families, continually ravaged by that malady, became extinct; their last members, as they write me, died *rotten with scrofula.*

'A fire destroyed nearly a third of the village; the houses were rebuilt in a more salubrious manner, and by degrees scrofula became less common, and disappeared from that part.' Other facts are brought forward, all tending to prove the fatal effects of vitiated air, and the beneficial results of a constantly pure atmosphere, not only on the health, but on the morals of the people. Other authorities—Dr Blacke, Dr Blakely Brown, Dr Duncan, and Professor Alison—fully confirm these statements, in addition to which, we are informed that 'defective ventilation may be considered one great cause of all the diseases of the joints which we so frequently meet with, as well as of the diseases of the eye and skin—shingles, lepra, and *porrigo*, or ringworm. Besides the eye, the ear is injuriously affected by vitiated air, which thus becomes the cause of many cases of deafness. It is a fact, that at least two times more of the children of the labouring-classes are affected by earache and deafness, than of children of the rich and better-conditioned classes, less exposed to the like influences.'

The report in continuation states, that fifty towns were selected by the commission, 'where the rate of mortality appeared, by the returns of the registers of deaths, with a few exceptions, to be the highest.' These included the largest manufacturing towns and principal ports after London, comprehending a population of more than three millions of persons. Each of these towns was visited by the commissioners, who examined into their condition on the spot, particularly of the most crowded and the most unhealthy districts, making personal inquiries of the inhabitants, and hearing such statements as were made by them, or respecting them, by medical and other officers.

In the evidence of Dr Duncan, physician to the Liverpool dispensary, we are made aware of the great extent of mortality arising from defective drainage, cleansing, ventilation, scanty supplies of water, and other causes.

This witness brings forward two tables, showing the difference of mortality in town and country districts; in an area of the latter, equal to 17,254 square miles, the number of inhabitants to each square mile being 205, the annual mortality was as 1 in 54·91; while in town districts, comprising an area of 747 square miles, the inhabitants to each mile being 5045, the rate of mortality for the same period was 1 in 38·16.

More than one cause may be assigned for this marked difference in the two districts; but the one great cause, which in its operation seems to absorb all others, is the vitiation of the atmosphere of towns; to effect which many agencies are constantly at work. By the mere action of the lungs of the inhabitants of Liverpool, for instance, a stratum of air sufficient to cover the entire surface of the town, to the depth of three feet, is daily rendered unfit for the purposes of respiration. Add to this the exhalations from forges, furnaces, and other fires, the enormous combustion of gas, oil, and candles, nightly consumed in large towns, with the escape of gaseous effluvia from manufactories, and we shall have some idea of the vitiation of the air of towns.

It has been estimated, from the census of 1841, that the number of the working-classes of Liverpool is 160,000, who are distributed as follows:—

In 1982 courts, containing 10,692 houses, the inhabitants are	55,534
In 6294 cellars, ...	20,168
In 621 do.	2,000

thus showing that one-half only of the industrious population live in rooms or houses facing the street, or in a comparatively pure atmosphere. The courts consist usually of two rows of houses placed opposite to each other, with an intervening space of from 9 to 15 feet, which communicates with the street by a passage or archway about 3 feet wide, often built up overhead, and the farther end closed by a wall, or other building. Such an arrangement almost bids defiance to the entrance and circulation of air. Of these courts, 629 are closed at both ends, 875 are closed at one end, and 478 only are open at both ends.

If the courts are, as described, the noisome sinks of impurity, the cellars are still more horrible; 'they are generally 10 or 12 feet square, and flagged; but frequently have only the bare earth for a floor, and sometimes less than six feet in height. There is often no window, so that light and air can enter only by the door, the top of which, in numerous instances, is not higher than the level of the street. They are of course dark, and, from the defective drainage, are also very generally damp. Some of them have a back-cellar, used as a sleeping apartment, having no direct communication with the external air, which, with its supply of light, must be derived solely from the front room.'

Can it be matter of surprise that disease and depravity exist to such an alarming extent in these dens, when we know that in 26 streets inhabited by the working-classes, two-thirds of the houses were without yard, ash-pit, or other convenience. The consequence is, that the surface of the ground is covered with putrescent and offensive matter, which, when sufficiently fluid, sometimes 'oozes through into the neighbouring cellars, filling them with pestilential vapours, and rendering it necessary to dig wells to receive it, in order to prevent the inhabitants being inundated. One of these wells, four feet deep, filled with this stinking fluid, was found in one cellar under the bed where the family slept.'

These cellars are often used as lodging-houses, chiefly for the migratory Irish; 'the floors, sometimes the bare earth, are covered at night with straw; and there the lodgers—all who can afford to pay a penny for the accommodation—arrange themselves as best they may, until scarcely a single available inch of space is left unoccupied. In this way as many as thirty human beings or more are sometimes packed together underground, each inhaling the poison which his neighbour generates, and presenting a picture in some degree of the Black Hole of Calcutta. Each individual, in the course of the night vitiates about 300 cubic feet of atmospheric air; and if we suppose 30 pair of lungs engaged in this process, we shall have 9000 cubic feet of air rendered noxious during the period of sleep. But as the cubical atmospheric contents of the cellars do not exceed 2100 feet, the thirty individuals are consequently furnished with a supply of air sufficient only for the wants of *seven*.'

We have dwelt at some length on this part of the evidence, from a conviction that the evils of imperfect ventilation are almost universally disregarded. To what other cause can be attributed the reluctance to open a window for the admission of air, which so many persons exhibit; the absurd custom also of closing bedrooms during the night against the entrance of air. Not only are doors locked, and windows fastened against the pure circulation, but it is still further impeded by the close curtains of the bed; the consequence is, that the atmosphere of a bedroom in the morning smells more like that of a charnel-house than an apartment fit for the repose of human beings. With one more extract from the doctor's evidence, bearing on the deadly effects of foul air, we must leave this part of the subject. 'It will be proper to say a few words as to the nature of the effluvia arising from cess-pools, and other offensive sources. The principal gas given out from these deposits is sulphuretted hydrogen, the most deadly of the gaseous poisons, two or three cubic inches causing instant death when injected into a vein, or into the chest, or beneath the skin of animals. A rabbit died in ten minutes after being enclosed in a bag containing sulphuretted hydrogen, although its head was left free so as to allow it to breathe the pure atmosphere. Nine quarts injected into the intestines of a horse killed it in a minute; a dog was killed by being made to breathe a mixture of one part of this gas with 800 parts of common air; and air containing only 1·1500th part of sulphuretted hydrogen proves speedily fatal to small birds. Although these effluvia are breathed by the inhabitants of our courts and back-streets in a state, of course, of extreme dilution, we cannot suppose that they are on that account entirely harmless. What, in a concentrated form, is so very deadly, must, in a diluted state, be injurious to health.'

It is sickening to contemplate the physical evils here described; these, however, sink into comparative insignificance when compared with the moral degradation that necessarily ensues. Mr Toynbee, in reply to a question as to the over-crowding of rooms, observes that, 'in respect to morals, as well as health, it is terrible. I am now attending one family, where the father, about fifty, the mother about the same age, a grown-up son, about twenty, in a consumption, and a daughter, about seventeen, who has scrofulous affection of the jaw and throat, for which I am attending her, and a child—all sleep in the same bed, in a room where the father and three or four other men work during the day as tailors, and they frequently work there late at night with candles. I am also treating, at the present time, a woman with paralysis of the lower extremities, whose eldest son, the son by a former wife, and a girl of eleven or twelve years of age, all sleep in the same bed.' Mr Aldis, physician to the London dispensary, states, that he has 'found grown-up young men sleeping in the same bed with a middle-aged or young mother; brothers and sisters, above the age of puberty, lying in the same bed. But the moral effects only come to our knowledge accidentally.' Mr Hawksley, of Nottingham, says, that 'rooms of eleven feet square often contain families of four, five, or six individuals, consisting not unfrequently of nearly-related adults of different sexes, who live and sleep promiscuously.'

We gladly turn from the perusal of these cases of depravity, induced, in a great measure, by local circumstances, to the promise of amelioration—to the prospect of convenient and healthful dwellings for the busy multitudes—to the constant and abundant supply of pure and wholesome water—to the erection of baths and wash-houses, furnishing the means of cleanliness at an almost nominal price; and in their effect rendering the working-man's home a scene of pleasure and hope, where the practice of cleanliness shall pave the way for other and equally exalting virtues.

The publication of a report such as the one under consideration, is in itself an encouraging and unmistakeable sign of the times; it proves that right feelings are making progress; that they who have begun the good work are earnest in persevering. The commissioners say, in concluding their report, 'We have especially turned our attention to the means for improving the worst and the most crowded districts in large towns, a subject of great importance, and very great difficulty. It may appear to be a comparatively easy task to provide against the occurrence in new districts of the evils which at present prevail in parts of old towns; but in the heart, and even in the immediate suburbs of towns, not only of ancient but also of modern date, where these evils chiefly abound, the value of the property, the intricacy and variety of the interests involved, and the occupations and callings of the inhabitants, increase in a great degree the difficulty of devising measures which we may with confidence be able to recommend as effectual, and at the same time as capable of enforcement. In order to admit of the recommendation of systematic and comprehensive measures, adequate to the magnitude of the subject, many practical details are involved, which must be minutely examined and viewed equally in respect to accuracy of principle, economy of execution, and adequate provision for regulating and defraying the necessary expenses. This subject is still engaging our most anxious attention.'

We intend to return to this subject in a future number, in which we shall consider the remedial measures to be gathered from the evidence of the second volume. Meanwhile, much remains to be done. The announcement of difficulties should be a spur to exertion; much may be done individually in anticipation of the good that may be expected to result from the institution of inquiries like the present. The many important facts elicited are worthy of the most serious attention: the cause is one which enlists our highest sympathies—one in which all are concerned—and to which all, if they will, may contribute their assistance.

PERIODICAL WORK CONDUCTED BY LUNATICS.

Lunatics, who, fifty years ago, were dungeoned and whipped, are now treated to balls and soirées, they conduct farms, and are admitted to public worship. A new feature has been developed in their treatment at the Crichton Institution, Dumfries: they there club their wits to prepare and issue a monthly periodical sheet. The first number of *The New Moon, or Crichton Royal Institution Literary Register*, appeared on the 3d of December, in the form of a double leaf in quarto. It is sold to the public, but we are not informed at what price. In the prospectus, the fact of the exclusive management of the work by inmates is asserted; and the object is stated to be, a humble endeavour to lead persons of that class 'to think aright on the chief subjects which should occupy their attention under present circumstances, so that they may leave the institution wiser and better men and women than they entered it.'

Not only is the literary matter sane in its general tone, and rhetorically correct, but there is positive merit in several of the little articles. For example, a gentleman signing himself Sigma, thus addresses Dr Browne, the superior of the establishment (and we would ask if many men under Thomas Moore could write in the same style more smartly):—

'I am sorry to learn you have got rheumatism,
Which is, I am told, a corporeal schism
Not very unlike what is called Puseyism.
If you take my advice, my kind friend, you wont follow
The cold-water cure of that Pluvius Apollo,

Who at Graefenberg cures old and young of the dumps,
By the magical aid of a couple of pumps.
Old Pindar, 'tis true, as you very well know,
In the choicest of Greek has proclaimed long ago,
"*Ariston men hudor*;" but, then, what of that?
The man was a pagan—so, *verbum sap. sat.*
Your *kids*, you will learn with much pleasure, I know,
Are all as you left them, and in *statu quo*.
(This same is a classical phrase, else, ecod!
I would break Priscian's head, and write *statu* QUOD;
Some mad as March hares, but a few like the Dane,
With a slight touch north-east, yet otherwise sane. * *
Mr Sacre, that sage transcendental philosopher,
(I wonder if ever he read Alexander Ross over?)
As his use and wont is, has been blowing the balmy,
And looks, as a smoker should, really quite palmy.
He swears the debates are detestable stuff—
Not worth a cigar, or a pinch of Scotch snuff;
And, faith, I believe that for once, *entre nous*,
He's not very far wrong—I'm blowed if I do.
At billiards to-day I gave him a maul;
And wasn't he savage? ho, no! not at all:
He fumed and he fretted—"The cues were a scandal,
And really unfit for a gemman to handle;"
Then concluded by saying, he would give me thrice six
Out of twenty-four points, and beat me to sticks!' * *

'J. C.,' who from his style seems of clerical education, preaches to the following effect, and however trite the ideas, assuredly their arrangement here is as good as could be expected from any other quarter whatever:—'Although it is a proper, natural, and laudable wish to be splendidly and extensively useful, yet as every man is most delighted with the esteem, and interested in the good conduct and happiness of his domestics and friends, he ought to be the more careful to "walk before his house with a perfect heart." That such instruct their families and lead them in the ways of righteousness, is what is required of them. This is the province of which the care has been assigned to, and of which the improvement will be required at their hands; and he who exerteth himself in this his station and sphere of action, however low or limited, is as meritorious in the sight of God, and likely to be as happy in himself, as he who, disengaging himself from all domestic ties and duties, gives a wider but more contingent range to his zeal and philanthropy, and encompasses sea and land to promote the improvement, reformation, and happiness of his fellow-men. But, above all, it certainly deeply concerns parents to set a good example before their children. This is equally beneficial to the public and to themselves; and the neglect equally fatal to both. If ever any real and substantial reformation of society is to be effected, this is the source from which it must flow; the sure foundation must be laid in the instruction, education, and moral training of youth.'

We conclude with a short lyrical poem, which has, we think, absolute merits sufficient to entitle it to notice, apart from all consideration of the interest arising from the condition and circumstances of the writer:—

'The harp so loved awakes no more,
Its chords are mute, its charms are gone;
The mind may joy not in its lore,
Where hope and happiness are flown.

For though it soothed in other days,
It cannot reach a wo so deep
As that which o'er this bosom strays,
To wake the pangs that never sleep.

The wind blows cold o'er glen and hill,
And nature all is worn and wan;
But nature's bosom bears no ill,
Like that which haunts the heart of man.

What though the torrents dash the steep,
And frosts her flaunting flowers deform,
And bid her lift her voice and weep,
In thunder, strife, and winter's storm;

The life remains that genial spring
Can still to wonted state restore,
And cause her wide her glories fling
O'er all that lay so waste before.

The wild bee hums around the flower
That opes so brightly on the brae;
The bird sings from the budding bower,
And cheers the wanderer on his way.

And far upon the moorland gray,
The plover seeks its summer home;
And sunshine crowns the scene of day,
As far as foot or eye can roam.

And thus are nature's charms replaced,
As if they had been ever new;
Her garlands blooming on her breast,
Her ringlets beaded with the dew.

But when, amid life's devious track,
Draws on the darkness of decay,
Oh, what to man shall ere bring back
The charms that time hath swept away!

And if the young must oft deplore
The ills that curb their early glee,
Oh, what again shall joy restore
To my loved mountain harp and me!—J. R.'

It might be asked, Supposing the writers of these extracts had been at liberty, and had been guilty of some capital outrage, would not such compositions have proved as strong proofs of their sanity, and consequent liability to punishment, as any that have been adduced in cases where punishment has been suffered, or, at best, narrowly missed (that of Macnaughton, for instance)? and yet these persons are deemed fit inmates for a lunatic asylum, and actually are in such an asylum at this moment.

SHORT NOTES ON THE WEST INDIES.

BY A LATE RESIDENT.

THIRD ARTICLE.

The Economy of Estates.—The negroes in Jamaica have a song, the burden of which is 'Massa, me no dead yet; car' him along.' The following is given as its origin. About forty years ago, the owner of a certain property was in the habit, when any of his slaves became old and useless, of directing them to be carried to a 'gully' on his estate, and there left to whatever fate should befall them—such fate being to be devoured by the crows before life became extinct. The object of this proceeding was, that the monster of a master should be saved the cost of keeping the old slave in his last days; and in order that he might lose as little as possible even by this transaction, he always directed that the dying man should be stripped naked, and his clothes brought back, together with the board which had been used to convey him to his miserable destiny. It happened that on one occasion a poor wretch, who was being so disposed of, collected sufficient courage and strength to exclaim, 'Massa, me no dead yet,' at the same time imploring to be saved from the horrible death which apparently awaited him. His brutal master, however, was deaf to his intreaties; and the bearers of the sick man hesitating, as one naturally supposes, whether they should proceed with their burden, the master sternly cried out, 'Carry him along.' This was the origin of the song—now for the sequel of the story. The poor man was taken to the gully, and there stripped and left, as directed by his master. In the night, however, came some of his friends, who, finding him still alive, took him to their homes, and, unknown to their master, bestowed such care upon him, that in course of time he recovered, and gained sufficient strength to leave the property. One unlucky day the poor fellow encountered his master in the streets of Kingston. The latter was thunderstruck. He had, however, sufficient presence of mind not to lose sight of his interest. At once claiming the 'dead-alive' as his slave, he ordered his attendants to take him into custody, and conduct him home. But the old man had no idea of undergoing a second exposure to the crows. He justly thought he had a fair claim to the free disposal of the few remaining days of his life. Accordingly he made such resistance, and uttered such cries, as speedily collected a crowd about him. His tale was soon told—the people were shocked and infuriated at the horrid recital, and, had his master not decamped, they would most probably have immolated him upon the spot.

This short narrative will give a forcible idea of the slave system as it once existed. Happily for the state of society in the colonies—nay, happily for the African race—that system has gone by never to return, and men have now not only safe custody of their lives, but of their property and persons. With this change it is evident a corresponding alteration must have taken place in the economy of estates and plantations. Apparent, if not heartfelt kindness, must have succeeded to brutality; and honourable inducements have thrust aside coercion and the scourge. Were it otherwise, matters would not go on at all. The fact is, where attorneys once sought overseers of a stern, unbending, nay, cruel temper, they now seek for those of kind, conciliating, yet firm dispositions; and I have reason to believe that not a few attorneys have been shorn of their honours, who found it impossible to accommodate themselves to the new spirit of things.

Attorneys, overseers, bookkeepers, and, in the olden times, drivers, are the chief animal machinery by which an estate is managed. The condition of a bookkeeper is little removed in comfort from the meanest labourer. His title implies a sort of clerk, who keeps the books of the estate, but he has as little to do with them as with the proceeds of the crop. His department is that of a general drudge, and his position that of an upper servant. He is barely tolerated at the table of the overseer, particularly if the attorney be present; and must be satisfied with such fare as is given him. The neck of a fowl is generally considered as his peculiar perquisite, and is known under the title of 'the bookkeeper's wing.'

In course of time the bookkeeper rises to the grade of overseer—a functionary who, in the absence of the attorney, rules paramount upon an estate. The dissolute life led by this class of persons had, under the old system, become proverbial. Much must be laid, however, to the system itself, and to the circumstances in which the overseers were placed. As bookkeepers, their days were spent in the fields; and, having no better society, and but slight moral culture, their nights were devoted to the company of dissolute women on the estates. As overseers, they had more time on their hands, and more liberty to devote it to some good purpose. Ere this, however, their habits were formed, and little disposition would be felt to improve it. If we add to all this, that the tenure by which the overseer held his office was the will or caprice of the attorney, and that he might be thrust from his situation without a day's notice, we see at once that his habits could not have been otherwise than dissolute. Many overseers, by dint of economy and 'perquisites,' ultimately became owners of estates. The next most probable step, however, upwards, was that of attorney; and as the overseer was, as it were, the king of bookkeepers, so was the attorney the king of overseers. He stood, in fact, *in loco* proprietor, and matters went on smoothly or not, according to his supreme will. A triton among the minnows, a Jupiter among the gods, was this same attorney, and marvellous the deference which was paid him—great the fear in which he was held. Pleased or chafed—

'He speaks, and awful bends his sable brows,
Shakes his ambrosial curls, and gives the nod,
The stamp of fate, and semblance of a god—
Poor Busha, with trembling the dread signal takes,
And every blackie to his centre quakes.'

Like Jupiter, however, the attorney now finds himself less mighty than of yore; the proprietor occasionally handling the thunderbolts, which, like another Vulcan, he alone had forged. To quit metaphor. Proprietors, in a few instances, I have heard, now take charge of their own estates, and it is hoped and anticipated that their example will be followed by many others.

The buildings on an estate or plantation generally consist of the 'great house'—place of residence for the proprietor, or the attorney, whenever he happens to visit the estate; the overseer's house—the 'works,' or buildings where the several operations in the manufacture of sugar, or curing of coffee, are carried on; and the 'negro houses,' or, as they have been sometimes of late years termed, 'villages,' generally removed away from the view of the great house, or overseer's house. The cattle chiefly used on estates are oxen and mules; and the motive power otherwise resorted to, when steam is not employed, is water.

Grades of Society.—A 'merchant' is a term of somewhat wider signification in the West Indies than in England. Nearly every person in business, whatever the extent of his dealings, or the nature of them, is called a merchant. The party who sells a small quantity of spirits, or a single ham, is called a 'provision and spirit merchant;' and he who will sell a single piece of linen, or a yard of ribbon, a 'dry-good merchant.' Many, however, deal at the same time largely in these several departments; but even these would not in England be entitled to the term. The merchant, including in the term the several grades referred to, seems to take about the first rank in colonial society; for although professional men, on stated occasions, take a higher stand, yet their far smaller number throws them comparatively in the shade. The title is, in fact, regarded as a universal passport—a sort of 'open sesame' into society. Few public undertakings succeed which are not patronised by the merchants; and the merchant's clerk thinks himself entitled of right to a commission in the militia, so soon as he writes himself down partner or master.

Probably the planter takes the next stand. I should find myself in doubt whether he ought not to be placed first, were it not that he is for the most part dependent on the merchant for the means of carrying on the cultivation of his estate. This at once settles the question. To place the dependent before him on whom he depends would be a solecism in manners most unpardonable. Let the planter, therefore, occupy the second place.

There is some difficulty in filling up the third grade. Two classes, of seeming equal pretensions, put in their claim, and leave me in doubt. Merchants' clerks and customhouse officers, lawyers' hacks and tide-waiters, contest the palm. We will leave them to settle precedence.

Those classes of persons called sometimes fancy storekeepers and shopkeepers, undoubtedly come next. The former are a description of milliners and haberdashers, and the latter a mixture of publicans, bakers, grocers, cheesemongers, Italian warehouse-keepers, &c. The fancy storekeepers, in honour of the ladies, should perhaps come first, the others next.

Then follows a heterogeneous mass of tradesmen—builders, carpenters, joiners, cabinetmakers, bricklayers, pediars, servants, &c. &c. all respectable or not, in colonial parlance, according as they may be black or white.

Editors of newspapers seem, as in England, to take rank according to the individual character of the party. Sometimes they are among the most respectable and influential classes, sometimes of the lowest characters, properly estimated.

For the most part, the two first classes above referred to 'rule the roast' in the West Indies. Since the levelling of all social distinctions, however, and the extension of the franchise, considerable approaches to a balance of power has been effected.

Two great requisites, to render society in the colonies what it should be, may be here mentioned. These are, a steady working-class, with no foolish aspirations upwards; and a wealthy and thoroughly independent body of men, above the paltry airs and local prejudices which are occasionally put on by many who now ape wealth and assume independence. Until these are obtained, society in the colonies must remain as disjointed as a human body without a head and but half a trunk.

Negro Riddles.—'Ma riddle, ma riddle; guess the riddle; p'rhaps not. What is that which goes up black and comes down white? you give it up? Milk.' 'Ma riddle, ma riddle, &c. Pretty Miss Nancy was going up stairs, when she tore her fine yellow gown, and not a sempstress in the town could mend it; you give it up? A plantain.' 'Ma riddle, ma riddle, &c. Up chim-cherry, down chim-cherry, nobody can catch chim-cherry; you give it up? Smoke.' It is to be observed that the asker is always as anxious to tell the solution of the riddle as the seekers to discover it. Thus the latter have frequently no time allowed them to 'give it up,' ere out it comes.

A Nancy Story.—Once upon a time there lived two sisters very happily together. At length, however, one of them fell ill and died, leaving a little daughter to the care of her sister. This sister was very cruel, and treated her niece very badly, making her a drudge to herself and daughter. One day the child having broken a water-jar, was turned out of the house, and ordered not to return till she could bring back as good a one. As she was going along weeping, she came to a large cotton tree, under which was sitting a woman without a head. The old woman immediately inquired of her, 'Well, my pickaninny, wha' you see?' 'Oh, grandee,' answered the child, 'me no see nuttin.' 'Good pickaninny,' cried the old woman, 'and good will come to you.' Not far distant was a cocoa-nut tree, and here was another old woman, also without a head. The same question was asked her, and she failed not to give the same answer, which had already met with so good a reception. Still she travelled forward, and at length began to feel faint through want of food, when, under a mahogany tree, she not only saw a third old woman, but one who had at length got a head. She stopped and made her best curtsey. 'How d'ye, grandee?' (grandee, or grandmother, is always a term of respect given to an old woman) said the girl. 'How d'ye, my pickaninny, wha's maka you no look well.' 'Grandee, me berry hungry.' 'My pickaninny, you see dat hut yander; go da, an' you wi' find some rice in one pot; nyam it; but if you see one black puss, mind you give him him share.' The child hastened to profit by the permission; the 'black puss' made its appearance, and was served first to its portion of rice, after which it departed; and the child had but just finished her meal, when the mistress of the hut entered, and told her that she might help herself to three eggs out of the fowl-house, but that she must not take any of the talking ones; perhaps, too, she might find the black puss there also, but if she did, she was to take no notice of him. The girl then entered the fowl-house, but she had no sooner done so, than a great many eggs commenced crying out, 'take *me*, take *me*.' However, she was implicit in her obedience; and although the talkative eggs were large and fine, she searched about till she had collected three dirty-looking eggs, which did not talk. The old woman now dismissed her guest, bidding her return home without fear, but not to forget to break one of the eggs under each of the three trees near which she had seen an old woman in the morning. The girl did as she was told, and breaking the first egg, it produced a water-jug exactly similar to that which she had broken; out of the second came a large sugar estate; and out of the third a splendid equipage, in which she returned to her aunt, delivered up the jug, related that a strange grandee had made her as grand as she was, and then departed in triumph to her sugar estate. Stung by envy, the aunt lost no time in sending her own daughter to search for the same good fortune which had befallen her cousin. She found the cotton tree and the headless old woman, and had the same question addressed to her; but instead of returning the same answer, 'Wha' me see?' said she, 'Me see one old woman widout head.' 'Bad girl,' replied the old woman, 'and bad will come to you.' Matters were no better managed near the cocoa tree, and when she came to the mahogany tree, she scarce deigned to salute the old woman at all. However, she received permission to eat rice at the cottage, coupled with the injunction of giving a share to the black puss, an injunction, however, which she totally disregarded, although she scrupled not to assure her hostess that she had suffered puss to eat till it could eat no more. The old lady then despatched her to the fowl-house for three eggs as she had before done her cousin; but having in a similar manner been cautioned against taking the talkative eggs, she conceived that these must needs be the most valuable, and made a point of selecting those which talked the most. Then, lest their chattering should betray her disobedience, she thought it best not to return into the hut, and accordingly set forward on her way home. She had not, however, yet reached the mahogany tree, when curiosity induced her to break one of the eggs. To her infinite disappointment it proved to be empty. In a rage she dashed the second on the ground, when out came a large yellow snake, which flew at her with dreadful hissings. Away ran the girl; a fallen bamboo lay in her path; she stumbled over it and fell. In her fall, the third egg was broken, when out came a huge tiger, which straightway slew and devoured her, as a warning to all rude, disobedient, and lying children.

Nancy stories are a kind of nursery and legendary tales with which the negroes amuse each other, and the young children of their masters or mistresses' family. A principal ingredient in them is the marvellous and startling, and they have also always a moral. The moral in that which I have just related is good, while the points of satire occasionally developed are excellent. Their effect on children, however, is far from salutary, as it renders them superstitious and fearful of being alone, particularly in the night-time. Accompanied with wild or mournful chants, as the occasion requires, they are at times rendered very impressive, and have all the influence of ghost stories, with far more ingenuity. I need not say that the art of telling a Nancy story, or inventing one, is not possessed by every negro, and that it is consequently much thought of among them, particularly among the 'old tune' negroes. To be capable of inventing one of these tales certainly displays some literary talent, which, if cultivated, might have produced greater things. Many negroes require to be paid before they will unfold their tales, asking sometimes as much as threepence for each story. The practice, however, is discouraged by the elder portion of families, in consequence of the pernicious effects produced on the minds of children.

THE INDIAN MAIL.

In a former volume we furnished a detailed account of the route through France, the Mediterranean, Egypt, the Red Sea, and Indian Ocean, to Hindustan.* We are now enabled to add a few more interesting particulars regarding the detailed operations of the means by which mails and passengers are conveyed.

The time ordinarily occupied for performing the whole distance is thirty days, thus distributed. From London to Paris occupies one day, Paris to Marseilles three days, Marseilles to Malta four days—thence to Alexandria four days. From Alexandria, by way of Cairo, to Suez, three days, and from Suez to Bombay fifteen days; except during the raging of the monsoon, when the voyage takes ten days longer. When the railways through France are completed, even this short time will be abbreviated at least two days.

Every month, a vessel belonging to the Oriental and Peninsular Steam Navigation Company leaves Southampton for Gibraltar direct, with mails and passengers; thence reaching Malta, she takes in a second mail and party of passengers, which have left London five days later, having been conveyed, by way of Calais, to Marseilles by diligence, and from Marseilles to Malta by steamboat. The Oriental Navigation Company's vessel then sails for Alexandria with her double freight. The passengers and mails then descend the canal

* Vol. xi. p. 413.

of Mahomedeh to Atfeh, where it joins the Nile, which they ascend to Bulac, the port of Cairo. They have then to cross the desert to Suez, which is accomplished in the following manner:—An association, sanctioned and protected by the pasha of Egypt, has recently been formed. Under the name of the Egyptian Transit Company, it bought up the transit establishments of Messrs Hill and Waghorn. They provide carriages on two wheels, each drawn by four horses, and the eighty miles of desert is crossed in twenty-four hours, or more than double the time which a stage-coach on an English road would take to perform a similar journey; but the sandy and stony nature of the road opposes difficulties which sufficiently account for delays. The tents from the Eglintoun tournament, which we mentioned in our former article as having been set up at various stages along the route, have been struck, and regular stables for the horses, and inns for the passengers, since erected. There are seven of these structures, which are designated simply by the numbers they bear. Nos. 1, 3, 5, and 7, are nothing more than stables, in which relays (consisting of from twelve to sixteen horses) are kept. Nos. 2 and 6 contain, besides stables, only bare accommodations for refreshment—dining-rooms and kitchens. Here the passengers stop to partake of breakfast, dinner, or supper, according to the hour of their arrival. No. 4 is the only building which has all the accommodations of a hotel, and in that, sleeping apartments, besides every other convenience required by the traveller, is provided. Between all these station-houses a line of telegraphs has been established, by means of which the persons in charge of them receive notice of the approach of travellers, for whom they are enabled to provide.

This establishment is necessarily expensive to keep up. Water being a very scarce article in these latitudes, every drop required for the horses and travellers is obliged to be conveyed from the Nile to the various stables and refreshment stations on the backs of camels, together with food and fodder. This renders the journey rather an expensive one; twelve pounds being the fare for each passenger; but that includes provisions. In that inhospitable district, it cannot be expected that accommodations can be very complete either on the road or at the stations. The carriages, in particular, are complained of for the extreme inflexibility of their springs, and the consequent joltings inflicted on the passengers. Consequently this eighty miles is reckoned by far the most fatiguing part of the whole route to India; and many plans have been proposed to obviate it. We have already adverted (at page 94 of our latest volume) to the scheme of cutting a canal across the isthmus of Suez; but attention has since been directed to the formation of a railway between Grand Cairo and the town of Suez. Considered mechanically, few difficulties appear to stand in the way of such an undertaking. Four-fifths of the ground over which the present road passes is firm and solid, whilst the other fifth would require but little engineering to adapt it for the successful laying of rails. Difficulties, however, more formidable than those opposed by nature stand in the way of the enterprise. Foreign states look with a jealous eye upon the scheme, seeing in it a supposed desire of our country to acquire the sole means of overland transit to the East. A French newspaper now before us regards it as a sort of attempted invasion, and declares in all seriousness that England has changed her mode of conquest; that she has turned her sword into a 'rail,' and intends aggrandising her power in future by means of locomotives! Alarmed, therefore, by the railway plan, the continental journals are advocating the canal expedient; to be executed, however, 'by all, for all;' that is to say, by a union of the resources and skill of all Europe. We sincerely trust that their proposition may be carried out; for travellers to and from India, whatever be their nation, will care very little by what country the work is performed, so it be done by somebody. For our own part, we should like to see a canal and a railroad besides, if the transit trade prove sufficient to support both undertakings.

We return from this digression to Suez, whence the mail and passengers are embarked for Bombay. The steam-vessels employed in this service belong to the East India Company. In their way, they call at our newly-acquired territory of Aden to take in coals, arriving in Bombay, on an average, in fifteen days. It occupies seven days more to get to Madras, eight to Pondicherry, and thirteen to Calcutta.

THE ORIGIN OF VARIOUS BOOKS.

The motives and suggestions for writing books are sometimes as curious and interesting as their contents. Thus, Newton's *Principia* originated in his philosophical contemplations on the fall of an apple. Milton's *Comus* was suggested by the incident of Lady Egerton losing her way in a wood; and his *Paradise Regained* is attributable to his having been asked by Elwood, the quaker, what he could say on that subject. The author of that popular romance, *The Castle of Otranto*, states, in a letter to Mr Cole, now in the British Museum, that it was suggested to him by a dream, in which he thought himself in an ancient castle, and that he saw a gigantic hand in armour on the uppermost banister of the great staircase. We are indebted for a fine ode by Prior to the circumstance of the poet having incurred the writing of it as a punishment from his tutor, for neglecting to be present one morning at chapel service at Westminster.

Gower's *Confessio Amantis* was written at the suggestion of King Richard II., who, accidentally meeting with the poet on the Thames, called him into the royal barge, and requested him 'to booke some new thing.' Perefixe's *Life of Henry IV.* was written at the command of Louis XIV., to whom he was preceptor, and contains a better account of the monarch than Daniell's larger history of him. At the age of forty-five, Cowper was induced by Mrs Unwin to begin writing a poem, that lady giving him for a subject *The Progress of Error*, the first important offspring of his muse. Dr Beddoes's curious and privately printed poem, entitled *Alexander's Expedition down the Hydaspes and the Indus to the Ocean*, originated in a conversation at the table of Mr W. Reynolds, in which it was contended that the poetical effusions of Darwin could not be imitated. Dr Beddoes some time after produced the manuscript of the above poem as from his friend Darwin, and completely succeeded in the deception. When Wilkie and Washington Irving were rambling together through the old cities of Spain, the painter urged his companion 'to write something about them, in the Haroun Alraschid style,' with a dash of that Arabian spice which pervades everything Spanish. Irving set about the task with enthusiasm, while lodging with Wilkie in the Alhambra; the result was two volumes of *Tales*.

Lord Monboddo tells us that his work on the *Origin and Progress of Language* was suggested by a perusal of Sagard's extremely rare *Dictionnaire de la Langue Huronne* (Paris, 1632). From this curious book we learn that the language of the Hurons is so defective, that it has neither tense, persons, numbers, nor genders; the deficiency being supplied by accents only, by means of which different significations are imparted to the same word. There can be no doubt that Sterne derived the idea of his *Tristram Shandy* from a perusal of Bouchet's very rare little volumes, entitled *Les Serées*, 1598, containing many very laughable, and some very serious anecdotes. Sterne's mind seems, however, to have been chiefly impressed with the most ludicrous and extravagant parts of the book. Defoe is supposed to have had the idea of his celebrated novel, *Robinson Crusoe*, suggested to him by reading Captain Rogers's *Account of Alexander Selkirk in Juan Fernandez*, 1718. Hogarth, according to Granger, derived the idea of his *Analysis of Beauty* from Haydock's translation of *Lomatius's Tracte, containing the Artes of Curious Painting, Carving, and Building*, 1598. Milton's *Paradise Lost* seems to have been suggested to him by more than one work, perused during his classical and theological studies. Its origin has been ascribed by one writer to the poet having read Giovani Battista Andreini's very rare drama, entitled *L'Adamo Sacra Representatione*, Milan, 1633; by another, to his perusal of Jacob von Theramo's *Das Buch Belial*, &c. 1472, a rare folio volume. Dunster, in his treatise on the early reading of Milton, says that the prima stamina of *Paradise Lost* is to be found in Sylvester's translation of Du Bartas's *Divine Weekes and Workes*, 1633. M. Guizot thinks that our bard's immortal poem was suggested by an attentive perusal of a Latin one on the same subject, written by a French bishop at the beginning of the sixth, and published at the commencement of the sixteenth century, and several passages in which are very similar to some of Milton's. It is said that Milton himself confessed that he owed much of his work to Phineas Fletcher's rare and valuable poem, entitled *Locusts or Apollyonists*, 1627.

Many books have been written for the praiseworthy purpose of appropriating their proceeds to the assistance of distressed persons, and to add to the funds of benevolent institutions. It was for the object of contributing to the fund for the propagation of the gospel in foreign parts that Young wrote his tragedy of *The Brothers*. Marmontel wrote some of his celebrated tales to assist his friend Boissy, then intrusted with the editorship of the well-known journal, *Le Mercure de France*. In order to benefit Gretry, the musical composer, Marmontel worked up several little stories into comic operas, all of which were acted with great success. *The Tribute*, a volume of poems by various living authors, and edited by Lord Northampton, originated from a benevolent wish to appropriate its profits to the assistance of the Rev. C. Smedly, editor of the *Encyclopædia Metropolitana*, who, through hard study, had contracted a severe disorder of the eyes, which disabled him from further literary labour. Dr Johnson wrote his *Rasselas* to enable him to pay the expenses of his mother's funeral. Walter Scott's chief object in publishing *Marmion*, was to procure the necessary funds to relieve his brother from certain difficulties into which he had fallen while practising as a writer to the signet. In a letter to Crabbe, Scott says, 'It is curious enough that you should have republished *The Village* for the purpose of sending your young men to college, and I should have written *The Lay of the Last Minstrel* to buy a new horse for the Volunteer Cavalry.'

FIRST JUDGMENTS ON NEW DISCOVERIES.

However void of practical utility any discovery may at first appear, it is impossible to tell to what important results it may eventually lead. Who could have foreseen an acquaintance with the minutest wonders of the heavens from the child of a spectacle-maker amusing itself with convex glasses—the marvellous results of steam machinery from the steam issuing from a kettle—or the illumination of our towns from burning a piece of coal in the bowl of a tobacco pipe? One ingenious contriver of a steam-ship was advised by a former president of the Royal Society to employ his time on some practicable scheme, and not on a visionary speculation; and thus it is that the suspicion and distrust with which any novelty is commonly received, has tended to damp inquiry and retard science. I have been assured by that eminent geologist, the Rev. W. D. Conybeare, that his early investigation of the more recent strata of this kingdom, and especially of the Portland oolite, &c. was treated as an idle occupation of time, and as leading to no useful purpose; whereas the progress of geology, since that time, has shown that the stability of our great public edifices depends on a proper selection from the rocks best adapted for building; and Mr William Smith, who shared in the obloquy of following such useless pursuits in the infancy of the science, was in his old age employed by government, in conjunction with Mr De la Beche and others, to examine the various strata of the United Kingdom, with a view to selecting the best stone for building the new houses of parliament.—*T. Sopwith on Glaciers in Great Britain.* Leeds: 1842.

TUFT-HUNTERS AT OXFORD.

Now, the dean's father was—I beg his pardon, had been—a linen-draper; neither well educated nor well behaved; in short, an unmitigated linen-draper. Consequently the dean's adoration of the aristocracy was excessive. There are few such thorough tuft-hunters as your genuine Oxford Don; the man who, without family or station in society, often without any further general education and knowledge of the world than is to be found at a country grammar-school, is suddenly, upon the strength of some acquaintance with Latin and Greek, or quite as often from having first seen the light in some fortunately-endowed county, elevated to the dignity of a fellowship, and permitted to take rank with gentlemen. The 'high table' in hall, the Turkey carpet and violet-cushioned chair in the common room, the obsequious attention of college servants, and the more unwilling 'capping' of the under-graduates, to such a man are real luxuries, and the relish with which he enjoys them is deep and strong. And if he have but the luck to immortalise himself by holding some university office, to strut through his year of misrule as proctor, or even as his humble 'pro,' then does he at once emerge from the obscurity of the family annals a being of a higher sphere. And when there comes up to commemoration a waddling old lady, and two thin sticks of virginity, who horrify the college butler by calling the vice-principal 'Dick,' no wonder that they return to the select society of their native town with an impression, that though Oxford was a very fine place, and they had real champagne, and wax candles, and everything quite genteel, and dear Richard was very kind, still they did think he was grown rather proud, as he never once asked after his old acquaintances the Smiths, and didn't like to be teased about his old flame Mary. No wonder that in the visits, few and far between, which, during the long vacation, the pompous B.D. pays to his humble relations in the country (when he has exhausted the invitations and the patience of his more aristocratic friends), they do not find a trace remaining of the vulgar boy who, some twelve years ago, quitted the seat of the provincial muses to push his fortunes in the university of Oxford.—*Blackwood's Magazine.* [This is a sad picture of character; but can we expect linen-drapers' sons to be quite exempt from such foibles while there is such a thing as rank to exercise its peculiar influence over them? It seems to us that rank is everywhere worshipped in this manner in England, precisely in proportion to the immediateness of its presence. Linen-drapers' sons at Oxford must, we should think, be so peculiarly exposed, that their escape is not to be expected. Satire and ridicule are useful, but they should be rightly directed. Here, we think, the direction is wrong, the persons ridiculed being only the victims of a system against which not a word is said. And we often hear persons of rank praised for their apparent indifference on the subject—so different from the fussy veneration paid to it by *parvenus*. How absurd! It would only be surprising if men were to appear anxious about what all the ordinary world is so prone to acknowledge.]

ELIZABETH AND VICTORIA.

People seem to think it flattering to the young Victoria to be likened to the ancient Elizabeth; but it is by no means so certain that the advantage was so far on the side of the Virgin Monarch. The illustrious old lady could talk Latin, but it was confessedly 'rusty:' her taste was so low in some things, that she could not comprehend shadow in pictures: her dancing must have been ludicrous gymnastics: she was a musician—such as virginals could form: she ever hankered after what she had not the courage to take to herself—a husband: and she died in a thicket of self-disappointment and remorse, 'no sons of hers succeeding.' Victoria is an artist, an accomplished musician, a happy wife, a proud mother. If the statesmen and authors of Elizabeth's time were greater, Victoria's country is greater a hundredfold—her possessions outrun the dreams of Elizabeth. The youthful queen may feel a satisfaction in historical associations, but there is little flattery in the comparison. Shakspeare graced Elizabeth's day, but Victoria's day is more worthy of Shakspeare.—*Spectator.*

GENIUS.

It is interesting to notice how some minds seem almost to create themselves, springing up under every disadvantage, and working their solitary but irresistible way through a thousand obstacles. Nature seems to delight in disappointing the assiduities of art, with which it would rear dulness to maturity; and to glory in the vigour and luxuriance of her chance productions. She scatters the seeds of genius to the winds, and though some may perish among the stony places of the world, and some may be choked by the thorns and brambles of early adversity, yet others will now and then strike root even in the clefts of the rock, struggle bravely up into sunshine, and spread over their sterile birthplace all the beauties of vegetation.—*Irving.*

Printed by William Bradbury, of No. 6, York Place, and Frederick Mullett Evans, of No. 7, Church Row, both of Stoke Newington, in the county of Middlesex, printers, at their office, Lombard Street, in the precinct of Whitefriars, and city of London; and Published (with permission of the Proprietors, W. and R. CHAMBERS,) by WILLIAM SOMERVILLE ORR, Publisher, of 2, Amen Corner, at No. 2, AMEN CORNER, both in the parish of Christchurch, and in the city of London.—Saturday, January 18, 1845.

CONDUCTED BY WILLIAM AND ROBERT CHAMBERS, EDITORS OF 'CHAMBERS'S INFORMATION FOR THE PEOPLE,' 'CHAMBERS'S EDUCATIONAL COURSE,' &c.

No. 56. New Series. SATURDAY, JANUARY 25, 1845. Price 1½d.

ANTAGONISM.

Few seem to be aware, or if aware, seem to estimate how much mankind are swayed by feelings of opposition or antagonism. I do not allude to that petty querulousness and obstinacy of temper which delight in keeping their own victim and every one else around them in a state of disquietude and misery; but to that broader principle of resistance in human nature which, when once awakened, gives development to character of a kind often the least expected. Three months ago, John Smith was a plain unnoticed shoemaker, who, had he been let alone, might have cobbled to the end of his being without attracting a glance of notice from any save his customers: but now Mr Smith is chief orator at burgh meetings; his name figures in the newspapers; in fact, he is a martyr to fame; and all this because his antagonism was aroused by the imposition of some local tax, which he has resisted to imprisonment. As with John Smith so with a thousand others; we know nothing of them, hear nothing of them, till they are provoked into notice through the operation of this principle, and then we know them for something very different from what they had heretofore been suspected. Thus antagonism may be the means of developing talents and feelings which hitherto lay dormant; of binding the most heterogeneous dispositions into a compact brotherhood; and of giving birth to opinions which at one time were as much derided and opposed as they are now fondly cherished. Though generally invested with the attributes of evil, the feeling may nevertheless be employed as an instrument for good; and though commendable actions arising from such a source are apt to be clouded with suspicion, yet the principle might be used with effect in the development of character, when appeals to apparently more amiable feelings would be in vain. Let us take, by way of example, a few of its operations; and if we cannot commend their origin, we shall at least find that other feelings than antagonism not unfrequently reap the merit of their results.

An acquaintance in holy orders was, five years ago, one of the most ordinary members of the brotherhood. There was nothing in his appearance, manners, or ministrations, to attract the notice of any one; or, if notice was accidentally drawn towards him, it was merely to mark how unremarkable he was, and then to forget him. *Now*, this individual is one of the most eloquent, active, and energetic members of the church; and this all from being, on one occasion, and in the ordinary course of business, placed in opposition to a fellow-member with whom he was not, in private, on the best of terms. Had it not been for this incident, he might have slumbered on to the end of his days in his quiet, commonplace obscurity. Hitherto, he may have done his duty; but that consisted in a negative observance of what he ought not to do, rather than in a positive fulfilment of what was required. Something seemed wanting to stimulate him to exertion, and induce him to apply the talent that was in him; in fact, his mind could only be stirred up through the medium of antagonism; hence the result. Nor was this new development of character merely temporary; for it has long survived the feeling that gave rise to it, seemingly sustained by love of approbation, or some other equally powerful incentive. It might be more charitable in such a case as this, to ascribe the change to 'awakened sense of duty,' or some other equally amiable cause; but the truth is, antagonism was directly and perceptibly the impelling principle. The propensity may have more commendable counterparts; but why should a feeling, which has been given us to resist unwarrantable encroachments, when kept within its proper limits, not receive the credit which is due to it?

Take another case. A landed proprietor living in all the ease and unexcitement of the country, and in absolute horror of anything like social or political change, all at once becomes a public orator and reforming patriot. From the blissful ignorance of everything relating to public life, he plunges at once into its vortex; advocates changes which he lately deprecated; and familiarly associates with those who, but a few years ago, were severed from him by an ocean of antipathies. And why all this change? Simply because his lordly neighbour on the other side of the river, and who takes quite an opposite course, has managed by certain acts to excite his antagonism. What arose from the smallest of beginnings was nursed to its present strength partly by popular applause, and partly by the opposition which was offered by his original opponent. As he proceeded, his knowledge of men and things increased; he saw the world in a different light from that in which he was accustomed to view it; and now, when every source of antagonism is removed and forgotten, the ideas which were implanted during its operation continue to be the governing principles of his life. As with this individual, so with thousands; it is not love of popular applause, nor is it patriotism, nor hatred of oppression, which gives the impetus to their public career. The prime mover is antagonism—an opposition to men around them. Ten to one they have been compelled to resist, and, resisting, have felt their own power: gratified by their success, and stimulated by the approbation of others, they hold on in their new course; and when all these incentives have died away, they persevere merely because habit has created for their feelings a channel, removal from which would be to them absolute misery. When the world ascribes the conduct of such men to antagonism, it is at once right and wrong—right in as far as the origin of the change is concerned, but wrong in supposing that mere combative feelings continue to sustain them in their career. And when, on the other hand, it lands the whole as 'patriotism' and 'innate love of justice,' it is equally mistaken; though, to be sure, it errs in a charitable direction. The beginning of such changes is in many cases as I have recorded; the after-growth is nurtured by different feelings, and ought to be estimated accordingly.

Again; let us take an individual who, up to a certain period, to my knowledge, never did a charitable act, and in whose heart there was apparently as much sympathy for the distressed as there is in the heart of a brick-bat. This person, through the operation of antagonism, now lavishes hundreds on schemes of charity and benevolence. He who would have grudged a fivepenny loaf to keep a poor decayed brother from starvation, will now more readily write down fifty pounds, and rejoice in the deed. Nor has vanity or love of display anything to do with such acts; for no one could be more insensible to these feelings than the individual alluded to. Antagonism alone is at the root of the matter, produced and sustained by some peculiar notions respecting poor-laws and poor-law discipline, when these came to be locally agitated. Some may question the benevolence which proceeds from such a source, and, for my own part, I can scarcely commend it; all that I do is merely to exhibit the influence which antagonism so frequently exercises on human conduct. However stimulated into activity, the act of charity, long practised, must, like all other acts, in time become a habit, and then continue to diffuse blessings around it long after every trace of its questionable origin has been obliterated. Indeed it would scarcely do to analyse upon this principle even many of the best of human actions; or if we were, ten to one we should find that few could boast of that ideal purity demanded by the moralist. A little of pride, or vanity, or love of approbation, or spite, or antagonism, mingles too frequently with our better intentions; and perhaps necessarily so; for man, it seems, is so constituted, that he is impelled more by direct incentives than by the result of abstract reflections.

Such are some of the greater workings of antagonism; but there are a thousand cases where it shows itself in provoking and malicious littleness. The petty critic, who sees nothing but barrenness and blunder in every page that does not emanate from his own pen, is not more disagreeable than contemptible. When Mrs Smith subscribes five guineas more than her husband's means will allow to the Blanket Society, merely 'to spite' Mrs Brown—with whom she has waged warfare for the last six years in the field of millinery—then Mrs Smith does an act equally silly and sinful. Or when Mrs Jones, who has really a handsome income at her command, dresses her daughters in drugget, because the Pantons over the way, who are miserably poor, affect the most expensive finery, then Mrs Jones does what is very foolish, and at the same time commits an injury on her children. A man may not be always sunny and cheerful in society; but when he argues with one, dissents from another, and does the very reverse of other men, merely from the impulses of antagonism, then he renders himself not only disagreeable, but is guilty of an unwarrantable infringement on the happiness of others. Again, when a person who held a certain opinion yesterday controverts it to-day, merely because he has learned that his rival entertains the same sentiment, then does that individual not only falsify himself, but weaken the reverence for truth among those who, by their relations, may depend on him for moral guidance. Or when antagonism prevents a native of one country from seeing anything of virtue, or talent, or bravery in the natives of that which is separated from his own by the mere breadth of a streamlet, and urges him to treat them in a derisive and derogatory spirit, then does that man, notwithstanding all his wit and illustration, nay, notwithstanding what may be true in his remarks, demean himself from the standard of sense and perception to the pettiness of illiberalism and prejudice. Such ebullitions of antagonism are unworthy and hateful, and differ widely from that broader principle of resistance which has been alluded to as frequently giving development to human character in new and valuable directions, and which might therefore be employed as a corrective, while other more commendable methods prove unavailing.

Be this as it may, no one, I think, will deny that antagonism operates powerfully in swaying mankind; and that changes in disposition and character, often ascribed to other causes, are its direct and immediate results. It is well to know this fact, and award to it its proper value in our estimation of conduct. If we are endowed with combative or resistive faculties to ward off unwarranted encroachments, and if we employ these in praiseworthy emulation with others, why may we not, within proper limits, allow them to have a share in the direction of general conduct, and in the formation of character? The philosophy that would exclude such inferior feelings, as they are called, from the direction of conduct, is about as wise as that economy which would exclude fire from the purposes of life, merely because, when not properly regulated, it is a dangerous and destructive element.

THE ROSE.

Among flowering plants, the rose is a universal favourite; the ornament and charm both of the palace and cottage. It is symbolical of love, and beauty, and innocence, and has furnished lovers and poets with more comparisons and imagery than all other flowers taken together. For unknown ages it has been admired, sung of, and cultivated in Europe and Asia; nor does time seem to weaken man's love for his favourite, or to lessen his devices for rearing it in perfection. It may interest the reader, therefore, to know something of the history and properties of the rose, and to learn the origin of some of those allusions to it with which our literature abounds.

Botanically, the rose is the type of the large natural order *Rosaceæ*, which embraces all those plants that more or less agree with the common wild rose in the construction of their flowers. By this test the reader will discover a very striking resemblance between the flower of the wild rose and those of the hawthorn, bramble, raspberry, mountain ash, apple, pear, plum, peach, cherry, &c. all of which are of course included under this order. It is evident, however, that very marked differences exist not only between the fruits, leaves, and stems of these plants, but also between their habits and properties; and therefore, for the purposes of detail, botanists have found it necessary to subdivide the order into six tribes. The first or typical tribe comprehends the *Roseæ*, or roses proper, all less or more esteemed for the beauty and fragrance of their flowers, which have originally only five slightly-indented petals, of a red, white, or yellow colour, with numerous yellow anthered stamens; but which, by culture, can be made to assume a mixture of colours, and to repeat their petals a hundredfold. The fruit of the rose is a hip, or false pericarp, enclosing numerous bony carpels, each enveloped in a hairy covering. The leaves are pinnate, consisting of two or more leaflets, and ending with an odd one; each set being furnished with very large stipules. The stems have numerous prickles, which differ from thorns in being articulated; that is, they may be taken off the stem on which they grow, only leaving the scar or mark of their articulation. The leaves of some of the species, as the sweetbrier, are replete with small glands filled with a fragrant oil, which is always less or more evaporating; hence their delightful perfume. By rubbing such leaves between the fingers, the thin cuticle which covers the glands is broken, the fluid escapes more copiously, and the fragrance is increased.

Until the beginning of the present century, few sorts

of roses appear to have been cultivated in Europe; but since then, a great number of beautiful varieties have been raised from seed on the continent, chiefly in France. Upwards of 300 new varieties have been raised in Britain, principally from the Scotch rose (*R. spinosissima*), thus swelling up the gardener's catalogue to upwards of 1000 names. Many individuals in this vast catalogue so nearly resemble each other, that they can scarcely be considered as distinct varieties, but as merely exhibiting temporary and accidental variations, according to the situation, soil, &c. in which they are grown. This is particularly the case with many of the French roses; and the best judges have come to the conclusion that there do not exist many more than 500 distinct varieties of the genus Rose. Whatever the number of varieties, it is clear that none save a professed botanist can hope ever to remember them all; and therefore, for the purposes of ordinary readers, it is best to arrange them into divisions according to their natural habits. By doing so, five groups comprehend the whole, which then become more easily treated, both in point of science and culture. The first group embraces all those which, like the Scotch rose, have slender shoots, small and numerous thorns, and fibrous roots spreading near the surface of the ground, and which naturally grow on heaths and other shallow soils. Being generally surrounded by plants of a low stature, they are much exposed to the browsing of cattle, and have therefore the power of speedily renewing themselves by the creeping nature of their roots. The second group are those which, like the French and cabbage roses, are strong-growing perennial plants, though somewhat shallow-rooted like the preceding. They furnish us with the most beautiful in the flower garden, and seem in their native habitats to be continually shifting their places by sending out suckers, which in turn grow up into new plants at the expense of the original tree, which becomes exhausted and decays. The third, those which, like the common dog-rose, are strong deep-rooted plants, growing naturally among other shrubs and trees, and therefore more elevated in their growth, and taking worse with artificial pruning and training than any other sort. The fourth division comprehends those which, like the evergreen-rose, naturally trail along the ground, or support themselves by bushes growing near them. Under culture they require to be trained along a wall or trellis, and do not, like the three preceding groups, grow up into independent tree-like shrubs. The fifth group includes our monthly, China, and dwarf roses. 'The sudden and rapid way,' says a writer in the Magazine of Botany, 'in which these roses send forth their shoots immediately on a change from cold to heat, points them out as growing in their wild state on mountains covered with snow a part of the year, and, like other natives of such places, with rapidity taking advantage of an interval of warmth to grow, bloom, and ripen their seeds.' Under culture they are generally grown in pots or trained against sheltered walls. It will be seen that though this arrangement has little to do with specific nomenclature, it is sufficiently distinctive to render the habits and characters of the different roses perfectly intelligible.

The rose, in a wild state, always exhibits single flowers in the north of Europe; but in the southern parts, particularly Italy, Greece, and Spain, it is not uncommon to find roses with double flowers growing spontaneously in the fields and woods. It is to culture, however, and to the devices of the gardener, that we owe our present stock of exuberant and variegated blossoms; and this brings us to speak of the history of the rose, which we shall principally glean from the extended account in Loudon's Arboretum. The rose is mentioned by the earliest writers of antiquity as an object of culture. Herodotus speaks of the double rose, and Solomon of the rose of Sharon, and of the plantations of roses at Jericho. Theophrastus tells us that the hundred-leaved rose grew in his time on Mount Pangæus; and it appears that the Isle of Rhodes (Isle of Roses) received its name from the culture of roses carried on there. Pliny mentions several sorts of roses which were known to the Romans, and which modern authors consider as the same with the Damascus, French, and cabbage roses. The ancients do not appear to have known either the yellow or the white rose, unless we except those which Pliny calls the roses of Alabanda, in Caria, which had the petals whitish. Roses were more highly prized than any other flowers by the Romans, who had even attained the luxury of forcing them. Under the reign of Domitian, the Egyptians thought of offering to the emperor's court, as a magnificent present, roses in winter; but this the Romans smiled at, so abundant were roses in Rome at that season. In every street, says Martial, the odour of spring is breathed, and garlands of flowers, freshly gathered, are displayed. 'Send us corn, Egyptians, and we will send *you* roses.' Roses were employed, both by the Greeks and Romans, to decorate tombs; and instances are given of rose-gardens being bequeathed by their proprietors, for the purpose of furnishing flowers to cover their graves.

Of the history of the rose from the time of the Romans till the days of Tournefort, when botany became a science, very little is known; but there can be no doubt that, in the dark ages, they were held in esteem by all who could procure them. When Saladin took Jerusalem in 1128, he would not enter the shrine of the temple, then converted into a church by the Christians, till the walls had been thoroughly washed and purified with rose-water. Voltaire says, that, after the taking of Constantinople by Mahomet II. in 1453, the church of Sophia was washed with rose-water in a similar manner before it was converted into a mosque. We read in the 'History of the Mogul Empire,' by Father Catron, that the celebrated Princess Nourmahal filled an entire canal with rose-water, upon which she was in the habit of sailing with the Great Mogul. The heat of the sun disengaged the essential oil from the rose-water: this was observed floating upon the surface: and thus was made the discovery of the essence, otto, or attar of roses. In 1503 Ludovico Verthema, who had travelled in the East, observes that Taessa was particularly celebrated for roses, and that he saw a great quantity of these flowers at Calicut. Sir John Chardin, in 1686, found the gardens of the Persians filled with roses: and all modern travellers bear testimony of the esteem in which the flower is held in Persia, Syria, and Egypt. Sir W. Ouseley says that he was perfectly overwhelmed with roses in the garden of the castle of Fassa; Jackson speaks of mattresses being made of the roses of the Nile for men of rank to recline on; and Buckingham mentions the rose plantations of Syria as occupying many acres in extent. At marriages and other festivities in the middle ages, the guests were adorned with this flower; and it was customary to carry large vessels of rose-water to baptisms. Indeed, the fondness of our ancestors for this fragrant and elegant flower, explains the feudal custom of vassals being required to pay so many bushels of roses to their lords.

In Britain one of the earliest notices of the rose occurs in Chaucer, who wrote early in the thirteenth century; and in the beginning of the fifteenth century, there is evidence of the rose having been cultivated for commercial purposes, and of the water distilled from it being used to give a flavour to a variety of dishes, and to wash the hands at meals—a custom still preserved in some of our colleges, and also in many of the public halls within the city of London. Among the New-Year's gifts presented to Queen Mary in 1556, was 'a bottle of roose-water;' and among the items of a dinner of Lord Leycester, when he was chancellor of Oxford university, in 1570, is mentioned three ounces of the same liquid. In 1576 the tenant of Ely House covenants to pay the bishop on midsummer day a red rose for the gate-house and garden; and for the ground (fourteen acres) ten loads of hay, and £10 per annum; the bishop reserving to himself and successors free access through the gate-house, for walking in the gardens and gathering twenty bushels of roses yearly. Gerard, in 1597, speaks of the damask-rose, and the cinnamon-rose, as common in English gardens; but as roses in the middle ages were used in the festivals of the church, it is likely that they were generally introduced into the gardens of priories and abbeys long before Gerard's time. The musk-rose is said to have been brought from Italy into England in 1592, the single yellow rose from Syria in 1629, and the moss-rose from Holland early in the eighteenth century. One of the most valuable roses, the China rose, was introduced in 1789; and it may be said to have created a revolution in the culture of roses, by the innumerable varieties which have been raised between it and the European roses.

The great use of the cultivated rose, in all countries where it is grown, is as a floriferous shrub; but it is nevertheless cultivated for the uses to which its flowers are applied in medicine and domestic economy in different parts of Europe, in the north of Africa, and more especially in Asia. In Syria it has been cultivated from time immemorial; and indeed the aboriginal name of that country, *Suristan*, is said to signify the land of roses. The rose plantations of Damascus, those of Cashmere, of the Barbary coast, and of Fayoum in Upper Egypt, are cultivated solely for the making of the attar, or essence of roses. In France, the rose de Provins is extensively cultivated in the neighbourhood of the town of that name, about sixty miles south-east of Paris, and also at Fontenay aux Roses, for products of a similar nature. In Britain, in the neighbourhood of London, Edinburgh, and other large towns, and in many private gardens, the flowers are gathered for making rose-water, or drying as perfumes. The various preparations from the flowers are the preserved petals, rose-water, vinegar of roses, spirit of roses, conserve of roses, honey of roses, oil of roses, and attar or otto of roses. In Syria the natives sometimes convert the leaves and flowers into cakes and tarts—the latter, according to modern British travellers, are very delicious; and at Damascus, the young shoots of the rose-trees are gathered and eaten as vegetables. There are other minor uses to which the flowers and leaves of the rose are applied, such as the communicating flavour to wines, &c. but to these we need not further advert.

The poetical, mythological, and legendary allusions to the rose are exceedingly numerous in every country in which it is known. It was dedicated by the Greeks to Aurora as an emblem of youth, from its freshness and reviving fragrance; to Venus as an emblem of love and beauty, from the elegance of its flowers; and to Cupid as an emblem of fugacity and danger, from the fleeting nature of its charms, and the wounds inflicted by its thorns. Anacreon makes its birth coeval with those of Venus and Minerva:—

> Then, then, in strange eventful hour,
> The earth produced an infant flower,
> Which sprang with blushing tinctures drest,
> And wantoned o'er its parent breast.
> The gods beheld this brilliant birth,
> And hailed the rose—the boon of earth.

A beetle is often represented on antique gems as expiring surrounded by roses; and this is supposed to be an emblem of a man enervated by luxury—the beetle being said to have such an antipathy to roses, that the smell of them will cause its death. The Romans, like the Greeks, were also excessively fond of roses; and, while they adopted the same legends, they made use of the flowers in a more practical manner. At feasts they garnished their dishes with them, floated them in their Falernian wine, perfumed their baths with rose-water, sculptured wreaths of them on the shields of their victorious generals, and strewed them on the tombs of their departed friends. In the East the rose has always been a favourite with the poets, and volumes of fable and allusion might be gathered from their works. The most beautiful, undoubtedly, is that of the nightingale and rose, in which the former is represented as wooing his favourite flower by his inimitable song.

The rose was also celebrated in the Catholic church. A golden rose was considered so honourable a present, that none but crowned heads were thought worthy either to give or to receive it. Roses of this kind were sometimes consecrated on Good Friday, and given to such potentates as it was desirable to conciliate. The custom of blessing the rose is still preserved in Rome, and the day in which the ceremony is performed is called *Dominica in Rosâ*. The rose was always considered as a mystical emblem by the church; and, as Schlegel observes, it enters into the composition of all the ornaments of Catholic churches in combination with the cross. The rosary used in devotional exercise is generally made of beads, manufactured in the following manner. Rose leaves contain certain acids which act on iron, and advantage is taken of this property by beating the petals of the flowers with cloves and other spices in an iron mortar, till a thick black paste is formed, which hardens on exposure to the air, and is then polished or turned, so as to form the perfumed beads of the rosary. In 530 St Mèdard, bishop of Noyon, instituted a festival at Salency for adjudging annually the prize of a crown of roses to the girl who should be acknowledged by all her competitors to be the most amiable, modest, and dutiful in the village. This custom was continued to the time of Madame de Genlis, who has written a beautiful little drama, entitled *La Rosière de Salency*, on the subject. In the middle ages, the knights at a tournament wore a rose embroidered on their sleeves, as an emblem that gentleness should accompany courage, and that beauty was the reward of valour. The French parliament had formerly a day of ceremony called Baillee de Roses, because a great quantity of roses were then distributed, or rather because the nobles were then accustomed to receive from their vassals their annual tribute of roses, and then to interchange and make presents of them to one another.

The rose is the national badge of England; but the origin of its assumption is not explained by any of our antiquaries. Shakspeare, who no doubt followed some old legend or chronicle, derives the assumption of the *red* and *white* roses by the rival houses of York and Lancaster from a quarrel in the Temple gardens between Richard Plantagenet, Duke of York, and the Earl of Somerset, the partisan of Henry of Lancaster. Finding that their voices were getting too loud, Plantagenet proposes that they shall

> In dumb significance proclaim their thoughts;

adding—

> Let him who is a true born gentleman,
> And stands upon the honour of his birth,
> If he supposes I have pleaded truth,
> From off this brier pluck a *white* rose with me.

To which Somerset replies—

> Let him who is no coward, nor no flatterer,
> But dare maintain the party of the truth,
> Pluck a *red* rose from off this thorn with me.

Their respective followers gathered the different-coloured roses; hence tradition says these flowers were adopted as the badges of the houses of York and Lancaster. Camden assigns a different and earlier origin to these badges; namely, that as it was then customary to assume badges, Edmund Crouchback and Edmund of Langley respectively assumed the red and white roses as theirs, not from any hostile feeling, but as mere marks of distinction. Be this as it may, the red and white roses were subsequently employed as Shakspeare relates; and the York and Lancaster rose, which has one-half of the flower red and the other white, was named in commemoration of the union of the two houses by the marriage of Henry VII. of Lancaster with Elizabeth of York.

'The expression "under the rose" took its origin,' says Jenoway, 'from the wars between the houses of York and Lancaster. The parties respectively swore by the *red* or the *white* rose; and these opposite emblems were displayed as the *signs of two taverns*, one of which was by the side of, and the other opposite to, the parliament house in Old Palace Yard, Westminster. Here the retainers and servants of the noblemen attached to the Duke of York and Henry VI. used to meet. Here also, as disturbances were frequent, measures either of defence or annoyance were taken, and every transaction was said to be done *under the rose;* by which expression the most profound secrecy was implied.' According to others, this term originated in the fable of Cupid giving the rose to Harpocrates, the god of silence, as a bribe to prevent him from betraying the amours of Venus, and was hence adopted as the emblem of silence. The rose was for this reason frequently sculptured on the ceilings of drinking and feasting rooms, as a warning to the guests that what was said in moments of conviviality should not be repeated; from which what was intended to be kept secret was said to be held 'under the rose.'

THE ROCK FAMILY; OR A NIGHT'S SPORT IN TEXAS.*

BY PERCY B. ST JOHN.

'Down jib, Mr Goodall; stand by your main and foresheets; look out for a jibe; hard-a-lee; let go your sheets; unspreet the sails;'—such were my orders to my crew, composed of two old men-of-wars-men, a pert young midshipman, and our captain's clerk, as, one beautiful afternoon last spring, we reached a halting-place on Dickenson's bayou. These orders having been obeyed, my cutter glided gently into a little indentation under the bank of one of those numerous and singular streams which intersect in every direction the prairie and woods of Texas, and which give promise, when its day has come, of great facilities of commerce to the young republic.

We had halted at a house some twenty miles from any other habitation, not so much to seek shelter for the night, for any dry spot would have served our purpose, as to become acquainted with the inmates of this dwelling, concerning whom I had heard a great deal. Before, however, we walk up to the mansion, let us observe its position, and give the reader some idea of the domain of a family of leatherstockings. About twelve miles from the mouth of the river, which pursued its winding course up to this spot uninterruptedly through the bare prairie—not a tree, not a bush checking the wind, the tall brown grass alone occupying its banks—the forest began to make its appearance; and here was situated the house of the settlers. The stream was here about twenty yards wide, with scarcely any perceptible current, or, if any showed itself, it was up the bayou, as the tide had been coming in the whole afternoon. The banks of the river were in no place two feet above the level of the water, and even when standing upright on the thwarts, the prairie on both sides was so flat as to appear to descend and gain a level far inferior to that of the water, so smooth, unbroken, and sea-like was the surface of the savannah. Higher up, the bank became more bluff, and was soon thickly skirted with trees of various descriptions, so as to be rendered certainly more picturesque, but perhaps less grand, than the endless plains below.

The house was built upon an eminence, rising gradually from the little harbour to the height of about seven or eight feet, and covered in all parts by short stunted grass. It was the most solitary, wild, and unpromising location of all the many unpromising spots which I had yet seen within the confines of Texas, and this is saying not a little. There was a frame-house, with veranda in front, the whole built upon piles, of elegant design, and which doubtless had once looked very social and pleasant; but, alas! what a falling off was here! The structure, as well as the numerous outhouses and sheds for negroes, had evidently been erected several years before by some rich settler; but now the roof was falling in; the planks which formed the walls were in many places torn down; while weeds and herbage grew around the door. Not a domestic animal was to be seen, not even the universal pig; and I began to wonder what could induce any civilised person to dwell in so extraordinary a place. My curiosity had been long excited with regard to its inmates, and what I saw was not likely to decrease it.

Our approach, as I afterwards learned, had been for some time noticed; which was not to be wondered at, since the front of the house faced the wide plain across which we appeared to have been sailing, a man-of-war's pennant at our peak, and the Texan ensign at the masthead. So winding was the course of the river, it was not surprising that we had been for more than an hour in sight of the house. We had, therefore, scarcely entered the creek, when there issued from the door the gaunt figure of an aged man, some six feet high, habited in buckskin trousers, mocassins, a huge thick blanket-coat, and the never-failing American rifle on his shoulder. Having taken a very quiet survey of us from the veranda, he advanced towards the water's edge, where we were busily engaged stowing our sails, and putting our craft in order.

'How does it progress with you, Mr Rock?' said Mr Midshipman Goodall, who had seen him before; 'I guess you're well? You'll reckon we're up here hunting, and you wont be much out; we intend camping in the dry timber to-morrow; but we've progressed pretty considerable to-day, I reckon, and we'd better stop here to-night. So Mr —— had agreed to it.'

'Mr —— is welcome,' replied Mr Rock, turning to me, and raising his antiquated beaver. 'Whatever accommodation we have is at your service; for, I say, captain, it's God's truth we don't often have our threshold darkened by a stranger; no, by St Patrick.'

Oh, oh, sweet Tipperary, thought I, how are you? Here was a surprise. Some ten thousand miles from the green isle, in a wild uncivilised district but a few years back inhabited solely by the wolf, the deer, the panther, or perhaps the red man, I had arrived at a house, expecting to encounter at all events some huge Kentuckian or Virginian hunter; but no—Paddy all the world over.

'I reckon you don't see such strangers every day?' replied Goodall, ere I could open my mouth; 'strangers with a considerable supply of 'bacca and sartchle flip: if we don't slant your perpendicular, it's a caution, Mr Rock.'

'Mr Goodall is right,' said I, leaping ashore, and addressing the old man, whose eyes glistened at the unwonted intelligence; 'we have some brandy and tobacco at your service; but I am sure this will not be required to induce you to give hospitality to one from the old country?'

This time the old man's eye grew dim, as, seizing my hand, and almost crushing it in his iron grasp, he exclaimed—'Welcome to Texas, welcome; it is long since I have seen one direct from home.'

'Oh,' I continued, calling the captain's clerk to me, 'here is Mr Doyle, a countryman in earnest, while I am an Englishman.'

'I know him, sir,' replied Captain Rock, his popular name; 'but, excuse me, you have not long been in the navy?'

'A very short time.'

'But I am keeping you standing, Mr ——; perhaps you will come up to the house, such as it is.'

Shouldering my gun, and having furnished my pockets with a bottle and tobacco, I followed Rock up to the house, where I was introduced to the whole of the family, with the exception of Jim Rock, who was out hunting. By this occupation the industrious young leatherstocking almost wholly supported the family. By constant practice, as well as by the force of necessity, he had become a dead shot, invariably bringing in a

* In the Journal No. 13, new series, I gave some account of the Rock family, under the title of 'The Wedding.' Considerable curiosity having been excited by the facts narrated in connexion with these backwood settlers, I have examined my journal, and now extract my first impressions in regard to these personages.

buck, a doe, or half-a-dozen brace of ducks. The apartment in which we were received by the rest of the family was unique. It had been once carefully boarded; but, with an economy peculiar to backwoodsmen, the planks had been torn down for firewood, and their place supplied with deer-skins, which hung over the apertures. In one corner of the room stood a raised platform, which we afterwards found to be a bed; in the centre was an old iron cauldron suspended from the roof over a fire of chips of greenwood, and attended by Mrs Rock, a quiet reserved little old woman. I was next introduced to the daughters, Miss Mary and Miss Betty, of whom I almost despair of giving a faithful delineation. Mary was nineteen, and Betty twenty-one, both as perfect specimens of Dutch Venuses as ever emanated from the fertile pencils of Rubens or Houdekoetter, with cheeks of that rosy hue,

'Whose blush would thaw the consecrated snow
On Dian's lap.'

Never in the whole course of my existence, in my European or transatlantic peregrinations, had I seen females at their age so inordinately large. Their faces were perfect full moons, round, fat, with sparkling blue eyes, pert noses, and well-shaped mouths. Their forms were, I have said, huge, but were not misshapen, speaking volumes for the salubrity of the wilderness around them, and the wild fare of a Texan prairie. Their dress was original. Covering for their heads they had none; but their bust was cased in a coarsely-made body of deer-skin, lacing in front, and disclosing an under-garment of red flannel. Their petticoats were of blanket stuff, and composed of so many pieces, that my arithmetic fairly shrunk from the enumeration. They wore gaiters and mocassins; and were, in fact, altogether the most original pair I had ever beheld.

They were 'young, fresh, loved, though scarcely delicate;' yet two more delightful girls I never met. Ignorant they certainly were, but it was pure, simple, unsophisticated ignorance; that is to say, they could not read, they could not write, they knew absolutely nothing of civilised life. How should they have done so? They had entered Texas with the first colonists under General Austin in the year 1832, and before that, had been vegetating at the foot of the Alleghany mountains. But then they could hunt, fish, and row an oar; they could tell you all about the neighbourhood, its characteristics, its beauties; they were true children of nature; and never having associated with low or vulgar persons, they were neither low nor vulgar themselves; and then their father and mother had seen better days, were very correct in their mode of speaking, and the children followed them. Betty, I soon found, was engaged to a neighbour (living some thirty miles off) named Luke, and accordingly Mary, by an inexplicable law of nature, became my favourite. But I soon won the good graces of both, especially when I set to work with great gusto to aid them in preparing our evening meal. It was varied in character. I provided beef, biscuit, and coffee, besides a supply of fine oysters, taken in at the mouth of the river; they brought forth Indian corn cakes, hot and tempting, deer's meat, salt and fresh, and a pumpkin pie. A Yankee would have luxuriated upon this last delicacy, taken from a very paradise of pumpkins about half a mile from the house, and which in itself was a curiosity, so numerous and large was the produce. A field once planted with this vegetable, seldom needs planting again; the scattered seeds sow themselves, and the plants are cultivated with the corn; they often reach so large a growth, that one is as much as a man can lift, and have a sweet and very palatable flavour.

Supper concluded, we took to coffee and pipes, and the conversation turned upon various matters. Among other topics which were brought upon the *tapis*, or rather upon the mud floor, old Rock alluded to an island formed by the river branching off into two streams, and meeting again about a mile below, which was much frequented by aquatic birds, as also by mustangs or wild horses; of the latter, however, I was told but a few remained.

'I should like very much to spend a few hours upon this island, Mr Rock, as my principal object in visiting this part of the country is to see all its peculiarities.'

'And why not go at once?' said Mary, starting from her seat on a huge pine log; 'by moonlight is the time to see the horses, and then on our way back we may perhaps catch a red fish.'

'You are right, Mary,' said Captain Rock, 'and it is a great pity Jim is from home, who knows every hole and corner; but you two girls can go and show it to Mr ——; that is, if you, sir, are not too fatigued?'

I protested of course against any such supposition, and accordingly rose for the purpose of starting immediately. I summoned Mr Goodall and Mr Doyle to accompany me; but as I saw they were not disposed to 'dare the vile contagion of the night,' and appeared to prefer coffee and tobacco to moonlight and romance, I did not insist; especially knowing that a pert young Yankee midshipman, even though with his superior officer, was not likely to enhance the pleasure of the expedition. My fair companions took each a fowling-piece, and also some fishing-tackle, and trotted down to the water's edge, whither I followed them. The very sound of their merry clear voices, as they laughingly essayed to trip down the path—a very unsuccessful attempt—was enough to cheer the spirits and encourage one to proceed. I found, on reaching the bank, that the young ladies intended making the voyage in an Indian canoe, which occasioned in me some qualms of conscience, since a piroque is at all times a ticklish concern; but with three persons in it, and two of them no sylphs, it appeared a very serious undertaking. I ventured a very polite observation on the subject, when my companions burst out laughing, and pointed peremptorily to the frail bark.

'Enter, enter,' said Mary, 'or else, taking offence at your very rude insinuation about our weight, we shall give up the journey.'

There was no resisting such an appeal; accordingly I stepped gently into the canoe, and sat down in the middle, 'submitting me unto the perilous night' with a full expectation of being ducked for my temerity. Nor was I without fear for the young ladies themselves, who, in case of a capsize, I dare swear had gone to the bottom before they could have said an *Ave*. Betty sat in the stern, and Mary in the bow, and away we went, the canoe urged along by Betty's paddle, which she managed with much dexterity.

The night was lovely; the moon, lately risen, poured a rich flood of light upon the rippling waters of the river, over which we glided almost noiselessly. Far off on the prairie we could hear the distant howl of the jackal, as, hurrying to some feast, he gave notice of his presence; sometimes a stray duck or goose would go quacking over our heads, or perhaps a buzzard or a sand-hill crane. Having proceeded about a quarter of a mile, during the journey over which we did not spare the jest, a few trees began to border the river's bank, casting their trembling shadows upon us as we passed, and affording a delightful contrast to the sea of molten silver over which we were gliding. The trees gradually becoming more thickly spread, we soon swept along down a gloomy avenue of foliage, which wrapped the river in darkness, and the eye refused to penetrate the depths of the long vista which presented itself to my gaze. Nor was the course of the river entirely free from fallen timber and snags, rendering our progress very cautious and slow, and forcing Miss Mary to keep a sharp look-out. A few minutes again elapsed, after entering within the sombre domains of the 'big timber,' when the canoe glided gently between the overhanging boughs of a thick bush, and presently stood still. We had reached the island, but of course to me it presented the appearance of being the right bank of the river. Mary Rock, having warned me to stoop my head as low as possible, impelled the canoe forward a few yards more by means of the branches above, and we entered a small creek, before perfectly concealed by the bush we had passed.

Silence was now strongly recommended me by my fair associates, and we left the canoe, taking with us our arms, not without surprise on my part at finding myself in so solitary a spot, from which there appeared no visible means of exit. No sooner, however, did we stand on terra firma, than I was led by a circuitous path through a dense thicket, and thence to the foot of a rising bank, on which stood a grove of lofty pine trees, through which the wind gently murmured, and whose tops were silvered by the light of the moon. Betty whispered me to be very circumspect, and to make no noise, but advance along the grove to the edge of the rising bank, and look out cautiously upon the open but small prairie. She then disappeared most mysteriously in the thicket, leaving Mary to be my guide; and so stealthy was her mode of proceeding, that, though I stood and listened carefully, yet I could not catch a sound of her footsteps. Following Mary with 'solemn steps and slow,' I soon gained the desired spot, where an opportune log being pointed out, I sat down beside my interesting guide, and threw my glances around the little plain. The atmosphere was impregnated with perfumes sweet and exquisite, most refreshing after the tropical heat of the day; in fact, when I gazed upon the scene around me, and gave way to the emotions it created, I thought I had never looked upon anything in the shape of scenery so beautiful, or which more forcibly impressed itself upon my imagination. I was silent during many minutes, having risen from the log and leant myself upon my gun; and, amid the universal stillness, drank my fill of all that was sublime in the time, the place, and the associations it conveyed. Presently, turning to my companion, I thanked her most warmly for the pleasure her considerate kindness had afforded me.

'Nonsense,' said she; then seizing my arm, she added, 'hush, and look yonder!' pointing to an opening in the forest on our left, whence a crowd of animated bodies were moving. Crack went a gun, and the whole group of wild horses—for such they were—came rushing and scampering in our direction across the plain. In number they were about twenty, and led by a beautiful white horse; they pawed the ground as, in long Indian file, they rushed past us, snorting, neighing, furious at being disturbed in their peculiar haunts. I could plainly distinguish them in the brilliant light of the moon, and thought I had never seen anything more admirably proportioned. In fact, if fine delicate heads, wide nostrils, thin tapering and clean limbs, small and hard hoof, and an Arabian symmetry of form, constitute a beautiful horse, there are abundant of beautiful horses in the Texan prairie. Those who judge of these wild animals from the mustangs which are commonly brought to market, are misled if they underrate the animal, since the most inferior are generally caught, while the more noble escape the *lazo*, itself enough to ruin the finest beast.

My gun was levelled at them by a natural instinct as they passed; but it was allowed to remain undischarged, as I reflected how useless, and even sacrilegious a waste of life it would be to bring down one of these noble animals. It was lucky I did so, since a much fitter object for bringing into play the murderous propensities of a Texan novice was at hand: a few minutes after, we heard the loud cry of the caiotoe in the distance, in chase of some animal, and as the hunt was evidently approaching our way, we prepared ourselves.

'Hush!' said Mary Rock, kneeling down behind a bush, and motioning me to follow her example; 'it is the prairie wolves after a deer; and I am sure the beast will take to the water, and seek refuge on the island, so be perfectly quiet, and we shall perhaps carry home an unexpected prize.'

I did not answer, as the loudly-repeated howl of the vicious animals in chase, the splashing sound of the frightened victim taking to the river, the rush of his pursuers after him, warned us to be on the alert; and, in another instant, a fine buck flew by us on the plain, at the distance of about fifty yards, followed by some dozen wolves in full chorus. As our various positions allowed us no choice, Mary Rock fired at the deer, I at the wolves, giving them both barrels; which was not their only infliction, since the echoes of my volleys had scarcely died away, and the terrified animals had not gained the wood, when a sheet of flame poured out from an opposite thicket; our Betty's ambuscade sent them back howling toward us. Mary now gave them her remaining barrel, and we rose to follow the buck; he was, it appeared, only wounded, though severely, and we could plainly discern him dragging himself slowly along amid the tall grass.

'Who'll catch him,' said Mary, laughing and pointing to Betty, who was hurrying across the prairie in his direction: 'I really think you mean to let us do every thing to-night.'

I made some gallant reply or other, and loading my gun as I moved along in company with Mary, we soon came up with our prize without being under the necessity of again firing, as the animal was dead ere we reached it. After some little conversation with Betty relative to the scene around, and the effect produced on my mind by the horses, we proceeded to prepare the deer for carrying to the boat; and had severed the head, &c. when the sharp crack of a rifle in the distance startled me.

'Brother Jim, for a dollar,' said Mary laughing; 'he has heard our firing, and will be home, doubtless, before us, unless we make haste.'

Satisfied with this explanation, I continued to assist my female Nimrods in their task, which completed, and a suitable pole being found, I and Betty slung the deer upon it, and raised it on our shoulders, while Mary carried the guns, and led the way to the canoe. Suddenly, as if a brilliant idea had struck me, I halted.

'Miss Rock, you will excuse me,' said I with the utmost gravity of voice and countenance, 'but do you intend adding this unfortunate brute to the former load of the canoe?'

Peals of laughter followed this insinuation concerning the ponderosity of my jocund companions, and we continued our journey to the piroque, not without experiencing considerable difficulty in making our way, loaded as we were, through the thicket above alluded to. Fortunately, neither silks nor satins were here to be destroyed; my companions were no

'Jeunes damoiseaux
Plus emplumés que des oiseaux;'

and it was a matter of very great indifference to them how many rents there were in their petticoats when they returned home, since what easier than to mend them. The canoe gained, a council was held as to our future proceedings. Betty, the *fiancée*, and of course the most prudent of my companions, hinted at a return, but without throwing much warmth into her arguments; and finding that I was not trespassing upon the kindness of my guides, I proposed we should at all events try our luck with the fishing-tackle.

'Certainly,' said Mary, who would hardly let me finish my speech—'certainly, and we are sure to catch some such a night as this. Have you ever tasted any red fish?'

'Never, my charming friend, though I have long desired to do so.'

'Never! then you shall have some for breakfast to-morrow morning, if I stay out all night to catch them. What say you, sister? Besides, you know we don't have such company every day.'

I acknowledged the frank compliment, for such I felt it to be, from this child of nature; and Betty agreeing, we pushed once more into the stream, and paddling gently towards home, put up in a little bight of water half way to Rockville, as the habitation of the family was familiarly called. Three lines were now produced, and the hooks were baited with mullet, with a supply of which they had provided themselves on leaving home; and standing some ten yards apart upon the bank, we threw in our tackle, and sitting down, awaited with patience the result. It is to me no wonder that angling proves so fascinating an amusement as it is known to be, when it incites us to linger round such exquisite and unrivalled scenery as the teeming rivers of every clime abound in; but though, I confess, I ever loved the sport, and had followed it in-less rustic guise on the banks of the Thames, in the Rhone's muddy waters, on Leman's translucent lake, and on the vine-bordered streams of the Cote d'Or, I do not think I ever angled under such romantic influences as crowded upon me on that night.

'I have got one, I have got one,' exclaimed my friend Mary in loud and merry accents, as, running back from the water's edge, she drew on shore a large fish, which splashed the water in its impotent endeavours to escape, and when drawn on terra firma, struggled most furiously to regain its native element. It was a red fish, considerably upwards of twenty pounds; no joke of a fellow for a young lady of nineteen to handle in the manner in which Miss Mary pulled him ashore. She had but just baited her hook a second time, when we were summoned by Betty, this time most anxiously, as she appeared to fear her prize would prove too much for her; and no wonder, for when all three of us laid hold of the cord, which was a treble red fish line, it was with the utmost difficulty our united force could cope with the monster of the deep, which had by some error of judgment, I opine, swallowed our barbed hook. Certainly, be he what he might, he did not like his position, for he darted here and there with furious perseverance; now up, now down, splashing the waters about with his tail, then sinking to the bottom. But despite his angry gambols we were not disposed to let him off, and accordingly held on with might and main; and presently having fastened a stake to the line, and fixed one end in the ground, it was not difficult to prevent his gaining upon us. My curiosity, much excited, and the young ladies protesting their ability to hold on, I went close to the water's edge, and watched the struggles of the furious animal. I could plainly see that in size he was no trifle; he appeared indeed many yards in length, and I verily believe, if the line had broken, I should until this day have imagined it to be a crocodile; but his force was beginning to be expended, blood tinged the clear surface of the waters, and uniting our combined forces, we drew him on shore.

'I thought so,' said Betty pettishly; 'a nasty useless alligator gar.'

Mary laughed outright, and exclaimed against having worked so hard for nothing, while I smiled, but expressed my thanks to Betty for procuring me a sight of a fish I had never before seen. This immediately reconciled the young lady to her capture, though Mary did not spare her jokes for all that. An alligator gar is a huge fish—this was three yards long—with an enormous snout, a back covered with scales, and in fact very similar in general appearance to an alligator, for which it is often mistaken when in the water. Nothing daunted, however, we pursued our sport with various success for another half hour, when the paddles of a canoe, or dug-out, fell on our ears, and presently brother Jim, in the smallest and most elegant Indian canoe I had ever seen, joined us. He was a slim small made lad about sixteen, very quiet and sedate, who expressed no surprise whatever on seeing a stranger, but invited us to return with him. We did so, taking with us our game, to which was now added a doe and fawn, the result of Jim's hunt.

My crew were all sleeping off the whisky, as well as old Rock and his wife, and we did not think fit to disturb their slumbers, but occupied ourselves in preparing some fresh coffee, while Mary broiled some steaks of red fish, which proved as delicious as salmon, though less rich, and we made a most excellent supper, enlivened by the merriest and most delightful conversation. Our meal concluded, my friends, 'fair and fat,' but, united, only 'forty,' wished me good night, warning me at the same time that they should be up early in the morning to take me to a duck pond about a mile off, and then went to rest. I and Jim, whom I found very intelligent, and quite communicative on such points as he knew anything about, smoked a pipe, drank a tumbler of brandy and water, and then followed the example of those around us.

> 'Soon as Aurora heaved her orient head
> Above the waves that blushed with early red,'

I was on foot, and armed for the conflict, which, though not likely to be dangerous, was yet most likely to be sanguinary. Mary and Betty were again my only companions, since the rest still slept soundly, as I afterwards found, in consequence of heavier potations than they were accustomed to. Our walk was through the savannah. It was not long, or at all events it appeared not so to my merry jocund friends, ere we reached the pond we were in search of, skirted by a few low bushes, which enabled us to take a survey without alarming the wild fowl which covered it. I had long ceased to be astonished at the myriads of ducks, geese, and swans, as well as teal, snipes, &c. which are everywhere, and at all times, to be met with in this country; but still, upon this occasion my surprise was renewed; the pond was literally black with them; and as we shouted and let fly six barrels among the affrighted masses, they appeared a dark cloud obscuring the light of heaven.

'What do you think of that now?' said Mary; 'was it not worth getting up for?'

I protested that the agreeable walk was worth ten early risings, especially when honoured with such company; and compliments being thus passed, we picked up our game, not without considerable laughter from all parties, the Miss Rocks having, to catch their quota, to enter the water until it reached above their knees. The number we collected was nineteen, very respectable materials for a breakfast; an appetite for which meal being by this time obtained, we returned towards the house. On approaching, we observed the whole party, save Mrs Rock, congregated down by the water's edge, and, preparatory to joining them, we entered the house by the back door to deposit our game.

In the apartment in which we had been the previous evening was Mrs Rock, her sleeves tucked up above her elbows, holding in one hand the handle of a frying-pan, which was placed over a hot but slow fire, and with her other, in which a ladle was held, stirring slowly and deliberately the contents of that very useful cooking utensil. She was turned from us, and did not notice our approach, until a loud scream from my fair friends aroused her, as, throwing down their game, guns, everything about them, they scampered off to a respectable distance from the house. What could be the meaning of all this? Were the suspicions which arose in my mind the previous day, and which I had not ventured to put into shape, about to be verified? Had I travelled all this distance to come across, not a Lancashire, but a Texan witch? And what was the result? But Mrs Rock did not leave me long in doubt.

'Retire, sir, for your life; my daughters will explain,' said she, emptying at the same time the contents of the frying-pan into an old newspaper in the corner of the room. What on earth were those round seed-like globules which fell with such clatter on the old *New Orleans Picayune*? I waited to see the result, though, in obedience to her directions, I had moved off a little.

'Oh, sir, come away; are you mad?' at this juncture cried Mary in so frantic a tone of voice, that I immediately joined her; 'my mother is certainly mad if you are not. How she frightened me! I shan't get over it for a month.'

'What in the name of heaven is she at?' inquired I, my curiosity roused more than ever.

'Do you not know? Did you never hear about my mother? Oh, if it is new to you, follow me and you shall see.'

Saying this, Mary—Betty was sitting, hardly yet recovered from her fright, on a log—led the way once more to the back of the house, to where, by standing on an old table, I could through a window survey the operations. Imagine my astonishment when, just as I rose, I saw Mrs Rock deliberately take up a tin canister of fine gunpowder, which on the previous day I had given Rock, but which had got damp, and pour out a quantity of it into the frying-pan. Then raising that culinary utensil, she as calmly as before placed it over the fire, and began to stir it round with the old wooden ladle. I turned to Mary and exclaimed against such infatuation; she replied that it certainly was so, but that, though for years her mother had been thus in the habit of drying gunpowder, no accident had ever happened. Whenever it was done, she added, in order that the whole risk might rest on her own shoulders, she cleared the house of all its inmates, and carried on her extraordinary operation alone. Despite the fool-hardiness of the old Irishwoman, I could not but admire her great courage, as also the care with which she removed all danger from her family.

'Well, Mary,' said I, 'you have surprised me indeed; but come, let us join your father.'

We accordingly did so, and old Rock was loud in his praises of our industry, both of the previous night and the morning, and appeared also somewhat ashamed of his anti-teetotal exhibition, but still did not refuse very shortly afterwards a pretty stiff morning, when offered him by the Yankee middie, who, I verily believe, had plied him with liquor out of mere mischief the night before; and when I afterwards expostulated with him on the impropriety of his conduct, he tried to look grave, and said—'Well, sir, the old man warn't used to it, and sartainly was pretty extensively chawed up; but then, sir, it ain't often he takes a slanting perpendicular, and you can't blame me for not putting a bowie knife between the old man and the bottle.'

We were shortly summoned to breakfast, after which, having received an affectionate embrace from both my fair friends, and not without much regret visible on both sides, we departed, and pulled up the river to the 'big timber,' accompanied by young Rock, who was to serve as our cicerone. In accordance with solemn promises given on my part, I more than once again visited Rockville, and the reader has already had some account of one of my peregrinations.

ITALIAN PRIESTS IN PEKIN.

Such of our readers as perused the notices on the Chinese which have from time to time appeared in this Journal, will be fully aware of the obstacles which oppose every foreigner who endeavours to travel amongst that jealous people. Hence the personal narrative of any European who has penetrated into China, and who has resided there for a series of years, is valuable in proportion to the extreme dearth of such narratives. We feel, therefore, the more gratification in introducing to our readers a book of this nature, which has been recently issued by Mr Murray as one of that cheap and excellent series of works called 'The Home and Colonial Library.' It is entitled 'The Memoirs of Father Ripa, during Thirteen Years' Residence at the Court of Pekin, in the Service of the Emperor of China.'*

After all that is known of the rigid caution with which the Chinese exclude foreigners from their country, it may puzzle our readers to imagine how an Italian missionary was allowed to live in the very heart of the empire for so many years. This we deem it necessary to explain:—By the sixteenth century, that powerful community of Roman Catholics known as 'Jesuits' had caused their missionaries to penetrate into Africa and Asia; but China was still closed against them. In 1579, however, Miguel Ruggiero, an Italian Jesuit, reached Canton, where he was allowed to take up an insecure and precarious residence. In a few years he was joined by his compatriot, Matthew Ricci, a man of great genius and unquenchable religious enthusiasm. The principles which guided the Jesuits in their missionary efforts were such as could only succeed in China. Their well-known practice was to appear to succumb to every prejudice, to engage in every sort of experiment which was not actually sinful that would aid to the consummation of making converts. Their leading motto was, 'the end justifies the means.' Guided by such principles, Ricci actually pretended to be converted to Budhism, and assumed the garb of a Bonze, or priest of that persuasion! This course he soon found inexpedient, and speedily abandoned it, taking upon himself the character of one of the Chinese literati. For this he was fully qualified. Already a man of profound learning and great scientific acquirement, he increased his stock of knowledge by mastering the Chinese language, and much of its literature. After employing about seventeen years in these pursuits, his fame reached Pekin, where he was received with great favour by the emperor. He soon invited other Jesuits to join him: the court was delighted with the scientific experiments and knowledge of their guests, who—gradually introducing the principles of Christianity—along with astronomical, chemical, and other sciences, in time gained the ear of the emperor. The native literati praised such Christian precepts as coincided with those of Confucius; but the doctrine of monogamy, and several tenets opposed to their own, they repudiated. Ricci and his coadjutors, however, were so successful, that permission was given them to build two churches; and they would in all probability have gone on prosperously, had they not been opposed by missionaries belonging to different 'orders' of the Catholic church, who disapproved of the means they used to introduce Christianity, and went to Pekin expressly to oppose it. Squabbles ensued of a nature to give the Chinese a mistrust not only of the professors of Christianity, but of its doctrines; and although they were not expelled the kingdom (being found extremely useful in the mechanical and fine arts), they were sometimes imprisoned, and always mistrusted. Such was the state of the Catholic missions soon after the death of Ricci, and up to the year 1692, when things took a favourable turn. Kang-hi, one of the most enlightened of the emperors, issued a decree permitting the exercise of the Christian religion. From the writings of the missionaries who from time to time resided in China, all that was ever known in Europe regarding China was made known.

We are now prepared to take up the interesting story before us. The subject of it, Matteo Ripa, commences his narrative by the following striking passage:—'In the year 1700, as I was strolling one day about the streets of Naples in search of amusement, I came to the open space before the viceregal palace, just at the moment when a Franciscan friar, mounted on a bench, began to address the people. I was only eighteen; but, though so young, I was then leading a life which I could scarcely describe without shocking the reader. Amid all my vices, however, it was fortunate for me that I always listened with pleasure to religious discourses, not indeed with a view to derive any profit or instruction from them, but merely out of curiosity. The preacher took for his text these words of the prophet Amos, "For three transgressions of Damascus, and for four, I will not turn away the punishment thereof;" and he proved that there were a certain number of sins which God would forgive, but that beyond that number there is no salvation for any one. From the proofs, he passed to the morality of the doctrine, and here he brought in the beautiful illustration of the scales, which, when equally balanced, the smallest addition will weigh down. "Thus," said the worthy father, "if, when our sins are equal to our counterpoise, we commit one more offence, the beam on which our lot is weighed will turn and fix our eternal perdition; and as we do not know when our scales are balanced, if we transgress at the risk of such a punishment, we deserve condemnation." This was not to me

* Selected and translated from the Italian by Fortunato Prandi.

a mere figurative illustration, it was a gleam of heavenly light by which I perceived the dangerous path I was treading; and methought I saw God himself menacing me from above, while below the torments of hell lay ready to receive me. On recovering from the horror I felt at the sight of the danger to which I had so long thoughtlessly exposed myself, I ardently thanked the Almighty for thus recalling me to himself, and, full of repentance, I resolved to devote the remainder of my life entirely to his service. When the Franciscan had finished his impressive sermon, to strengthen my purpose I proceeded at once to the church of the great apostle of India, St Francis Xavier, which was close by; and there having found a Jesuit who, by the will of God, was preaching on the same subject in the presence of the Host, I had the most favourable opportunity of fulfilling my object.'

Ripa lost no time in qualifying himself for the priesthood, and was in due time ordained. Feeling an irrepressible desire to spread the gospel in foreign parts, he was accredited by the Propaganda (the head-quarters of Catholic missions in Rome) to China. Starting for England, he obtained a passage in one of the East India Company's ships, and arrived at Canton in the early part of 1710. True to the principles which actuated the early Romish missionaries, Ripa kept his real object in the back-ground, and employed himself as a painter, having acquired a proficiency in the arts. In this quality he had the good fortune to be engaged by the emperor; set off for Pekin, and arrived there on the 5th January. Of this city the worthy father affords some curious particulars, which, although relating to it as it existed a century and a-half ago, applies in the main features to the present time; for the Chinese are such 'incurable conservatives,' that their modes of life never alter, and their cities present exactly the same general appearance now as they did thousands of years ago. The only difference is, that with the increase of population they have increased in size. 'The city of Pekin,' as Ripa correctly explains, 'was once called Se-yun-tien-fu; but it received its present appellation when the emperors of China removed the government from Nankin to the north of the empire, in order to oppose the incursions of the Tartars. As Nankin means south royal residence, thus Pekin signifies north royal residence; the word *nan* meaning south, *pe* north, and *king* royal residence. It lies in a plain which stretches to the south for more than ten days' journey without interruption, whilst at no great distance towards the north it is bounded by very numerous mountains. Owing to this extensive plain on the south, and this multitude of mountains on the north, Pekin is exposed to deadly heat in summer, and severe cold in winter. The transition from one extreme to the other, however, is slow and gradual, so that the Chinese of the upper classes go on changing their clothes all the year round. In summer they wear a cotton shirt, a waistcoat of light ko-poo, linen, a loose gown of the same material, called ppow-zoo, and over this a light silk spencer, called why-ttao. When the heat begins to decrease, they exchange the ko-poo for a sort of crape called sha, and this again for satin; and, as the weather gets cool, they wear the ppow-zoo lined, and the why-ttao wadded, then both these garments wadded, after which they adopt the furs of ermine, sable, and fox, in the same gradation. In the depth of winter, besides having both the ppow-zoo and why-ttao lined with fox-skin, they wear an under waistcoat of lamb-skin, and the loose gown over it wadded; and when it snows, they put on a long cloak covered over with seal-skin. In spite of all this, they still shiver with cold; and Count Ismailof, the Russian ambassador, told me that he and all his suite had been obliged to add garments to those they had been accustomed to wear, as the cold was far more intense here than at Moscow. During the period of frost, that is, from October till March, Northern Tartary sends to the capital an enormous quantity of game, consisting chiefly of stags, hares, wild boars, pheasants, and partridges; whilst Southern Tartary furnishes a great abundance of excellent sturgeon, and other fish, all of which being frozen, can easily be kept during the whole winter. At the close of the old year, and the beginning of the new, huge heaps of game and fish are exposed for sale in the streets, and it is surprising to see how cheap they are sold. For seven or eight silver tchens, which are equivalent to four shillings, one may buy a stag; for a trifle more, a wild boar; for five halfpence, a pheasant; and so on in the same proportion. During the winter, it never rains at Pekin, and it snows but seldom and sparingly. From March to June there are occasional showers; but in July and August it rains copiously.' It is not a little singular that so vast a difference of climate should exist between Ripa's native city, Naples, and that of Pekin; for there is scarcely one degree difference of latitude between the two places; yet 'in Pekin, from September till March, the cold increases in uniform gradation, and from March to September decreases in the same manner, while at Naples the weather passes from one extreme to another in the course of the same day, owing to the prevailing siroccos,' or violent south-east winds.

'Pekin,' continues the missionary, 'is composed of two distinct cities, one being called the Tartar city, the other the Chinese. The Tartar city is so named because it is inhabited by Tartars, and by those who, though not Tartars, are enrolled in the Ki-hiu-ti, or eight bands which constitute the Tartar troops. The Chinese city is inhabited by Chinese alone. It may be proper to observe, that the district now called the Tartar city was in former times inhabited by the eunuchs in waiting, who amounted to ten thousand; but under the present dynasty, it is inhabited, as I have said, by Tartars and Chinese of the Ki-hiu-ti. The eunuchs, now about six thousand in number, live entirely within the walls of the palace. The Tartar city is square, and encircled by a yellow wall. It is within this yellow wall that the imperial palace is situated; but it is surrounded again by another wall, more lofty than that of the city, and of vast extent. The inhabitants within amount to a great multitude; for, besides the six thousand eunuchs, there is in the seraglio a vast assembly of women, of whom the emperor alone knows the number. There is also within the imperial residence a great number of Tartars who are in the service of the emperor's sons, each of whom has his separate court; so that this palace may be very well considered as a third division, and Pekin described as containing three distinct cities. The Tartar city has nine gates, and each side of it is three miles in length. The Chinese city, which is also walled, joins the northern wall, which separates it from the Tartars. It is of the same size, but of a different form, being longer from east to west than from north to south; and it is more densely peopled with the middle and lower classes than the other city. In its four sides there are seven gates; and thus Pekin has in all sixteen gates, and outside every gate there is a large suburb. The two cities together are twenty-one miles in circuit, according to a measurement made by the command of the emperor. If to the circumference of twenty-one miles be added the suburbs and environs, which are also very populous, particularly those towards the west, through which nearly the whole commercial traffic of the Chinese capital passes, some idea may be formed of the vast size of this city. The palace, standing in the midst of the Tartar city, as already stated, has a southern aspect, and is in shape an oblong square, two miles in length, one in breadth, and six in circumference. The walls are enclosed and protected by a broad and deep ditch. There are three gates on each side, that in the centre being opened for the emperor only, that towards the south for the heir-apparent, and the third for general use. These gates are guarded night and day by soldiers. Within and above these defences rises another wall, forming as it were an inner palace, in which reside the emperor, his ladies, the women in waiting, the eunuchs, and the imperial family. There is also a spacious garden, into which no one is admitted without an express permission from the sovereign. Those thus favoured, upon entering, write down their names, and upon leaving it blot them out. The splendour of the palace is equal to its extent; and though constructed according to the singular architecture of the Chinese, which resembles no other, except perhaps, in a slight degree, the Gothic, yet the whole is pleasing, and contains much that is excellent and even wonderful.'

It is well known that the emperor of China very seldom exhibits the light of his august countenance to his subjects. When he has occasion to stir abroad, he is 'always preceded by a great number of horsemen, who clear the streets entirely, causing all the houses and shops to be shut, and a canvass to be drawn before every opening, so that no one might see him. The same precautions are taken when the emperor's ladies, or those of his sons, are about to pass. His majesty generally comes forth on horseback, and the ladies are always conveyed in close carriages.' Upon, however, the celebration of Kang-hi's sixtieth birth-day, which was a great day of rejoicing,* his celestial majesty condescended to show himself to his admiring people. 'The openings of the cross streets were not stopped, nor the doors shut, nor were the people driven away. The streets and roads were now crowded with countless multitudes desirous of beholding their sovereign. He rode on horseback, wearing a robe covered with dragons, magnificently embroidered in gold, and having five claws, the five-clawed dragon being exclusively worn by the imperial family. He was preceded by about two thousand horse soldiers, in splendid array, and immediately followed by the princes of the blood, who were succeeded by a great number of mandarins. After these came a large body of soldiers, marching in a promiscuous mass, without observing any order. We Europeans were disposed in a rank near a bridge at no great distance from the palace, where we awaited the arrival of his majesty upon our knees. On passing by, he paid particular attention to each of us, and smilingly inquired which were those employed in drawing the map. A vast number of aged but healthy men had been sent to Pekin from all the provinces. They were in companies, bearing the banner of their respective provinces. They also carried various other symbols and trophies, and being symmetrically drawn up along the streets through which the emperor was to pass, they presented a very beautiful and uncommon appearance. Every one of these old men brought a present of some kind to the emperor, which generally consisted of vases and other articles in bronze. His majesty gave to each of them twelve silver tahel, a coin worth about five shillings, together with a gown of yellow silk, which is the imperial colour. They afterwards assembled all together in a place where the emperor went to see them: and it was found that this venerable company amounted to four thousand in number. His majesty was highly gratified with this spectacle; he inquired the age of many, and treated them all with the greatest affability and condescension. He even invited them all to a banquet, at which he made them sit in his presence, and commanded his sons and grandsons to serve them with drink. After this, with his own hand, he presented every one of them with something; to one who was the most aged of the whole assembly, being nearly a hundred and eleven years old, he gave a mandarin's suit complete, together with a staff, an inkstand, and other things. Many compositions in verse and prose were produced on this auspicious occasion; and some of our missionaries humbly petitioned his majesty for a copy of the collection to send to Europe, which he granted, commanding Father Bovet to translate them. In these poems divine titles and honours were given to Kang-hi, who was indeed held in such veneration throughout China, that he often received the appellation of *Fo*, a national deity universally adored both by Tartars and Chinese. I myself very frequently heard him designated as the living *Fo*.' To show the extreme reverence in which the emperor is held, and the extraordinary restraints imposed on those who are near his person, we need only quote the following anecdote. His celestial majesty was on a hunting excursion:—'Although,' says Ripa, 'our party amounted to about thirty thousand persons—a number which, under all circumstances, must produce great noise and confusion—yet when the emperor was encamped, and the sun had set, the silence enforced was perfectly astonishing. One day Pedrini and myself having returned to the encampment after sunset, my friend ordered a servant to call our conductor, to whom he wanted to speak. The poor fellow resisted for some time, but being pressed by his master, he at last obeyed; and scarcely had he opened his mouth, before he was seized by the soldiers of the guard, and very severely bastinadoed.'

* In China, sixty years is reckoned as a century.

Some of Father Ripa's personal experiences were extremely curious, and prove very instructive as to the habits and manners of the Chinese. We have never met with a more graphic instance of that filial piety for which the Chinese are proverbial, than that which he relates. 'One day as I was talking in my own house with a mandarin who had come to pay me a visit, his son arrived from a distant part of the empire upon some business relating to the family. When he came in we were seated, but he immediately went down upon one knee before his father, and in this position continued to speak for about a quarter of an hour. I did not move from my chair till, by the course of conversation, I discovered who the person was, when I suddenly arose, protesting to the mandarin that I would stand unless he allowed his son to sit down also. A lengthened contest ensued, the father saying that he would quit his seat if I continued to stand; I myself declaring that it was impossible for me to sit while his son was kneeling; and the son protesting that before his father he must remain on his knees. At last, however, I overcame every scruple, and the mandarin signified to his son by a sign that he might be seated. He instantly obeyed, but retreated to a corner of the room, where he timidly seated himself upon the edge of a chest. A year after this, the son again came to visit me, having now become a mandarin himself. I offered him the seat of honour which was due to him, but he refused it, saying that it did not become him to take the same seat which, as I might remember, his father had occupied the year before. Accordingly, when an emperor dies, his son never sits upon the same throne, but upon that which had been used by his grandfather.'

Having acquired a proficiency in the Chinese language, Ripa was appointed interpreter, especially to a co-missionary who was intrusted with the care of the emperor's innumerable clocks and watches. While serving in this capacity his patron, Kang-hi, died, and this event turned the father's thoughts towards home. While that monarch lived, departure would have been impossible, because every person, on entering the imperial employment, takes a solemn oath that he will serve the emperor 'even unto death.' As it was, the object could not be easily attained; and the manner in which it was effected at once illustrates the official punctiliousness of the Chinese, and the extent to which the elastic consciences of the class of missionaries to which Father Ripa belonged will stretch. As the new emperor, Young Chin, 'was still sorrowing for his father's death, and as great indulgence is generally shown in China to persons recently bereft of their parents, I hoped to succeed by *alleging a similar loss*'—in other words, by telling a downright fib. 'Accordingly, I applied to the emperor's sixteenth brother, who expressed himself well inclined in my favour, and advised me to petition the Too-yoo-soo. This board referred me to his majesty's thirteenth brother, who had the charge of the collection of clocks and watches, and was consequently my immediate superior. The prince kept me a long time in suspense, with a profusion of gracious smiles and words; sometimes he even turned aside as he passed, and pretended not to see me whilst I waited for him on my knees. At length I discovered that, in spite of all his promises, he was opposed to my departure; and knowing the magic power of gifts in China, I took all the European curiosities I still had in my possession, and sent them to his residence. They were all accepted, which was a good omen; and soon after, the joyful announcement was sent me that the emperor, in consideration of the services I had rendered to his father, had been pleased to grant my petition, ordering, moreover, that I should receive some valuable farewell gifts of silk and porcelain.'

After a voyage full of miseries and vicissitudes, Father Ripa arrived in England, and met with a brilliant reception from George I. and his court. He then proceeded to Naples, and having brought with him three Chinese youths and an adult convert, he founded a college in Naples for the reception and education (for missionary purposes) of a limited number of Chinese. From this college Lord Macartney, when he undertook an embassy to China in 1793, selected his interpreters. It still exists, and contains eight pupils, six of whom are natives of China. Father Ripa, while living in the college as its chief, composed his autobiography, from which the work now before us is selected and translated. He died on the 22d of November 1745.

BLUNDERS OF FRENCH TRANSLATORS.

There are no translators so persevering and fearless in blundering as the French. It is notorious that, as a rule, English, Spanish, and German words, whenever they occur in French print, are spelled wrong; correctness being only a rare exception. Doubtless the French words, with which it has become fashionable of late amongst certain authors to sprinkle our own language, are not always correctly printed; but, in the case of proper nouns, we do not at least perpetuate error. Now, the French appear to make a point of misspelling every name of a place or individual which they find in a foreign tongue. It is a peculiarity as old as the days of Froissart, who calls Edinburgh *L'Islesbourg*, and Dalkeith *D'Alquest*, and makes similar errors all through his book, as if he had regarded it as of some importance thus to transmogrify our language. To this day, this disposition to misrepresent English names is as rife amongst our neighbours as ever. We have an example before us in a French newspaper a few weeks old, where there is a list of the guests entertained by an English gentleman at Cannes, in Normandy, who are said to be amongst the most celebrated people in this country; from the manner in which their names are given, it is quite impossible to know who they may be.

The story is well known of the French translator, who came to a passage in which Swift says that the Duke of Marlborough *broke* an officer, and who, not knowing that the expression meant dismissing a person from the army, rendered the passage by the word *roué*, by which it was conveyed that Marlborough broke the poor man on the wheel. Another Frenchman gives a not very delicate notion of Cibber's comedy of 'Love's Last Shift,' by calling it *La Dernière Chemise de l'Amour*. In like manner, a writer of Congreve's life, missing a letter in the tragedy of the 'Mourning Bride,' translated it *l'Epouse du Matin*, 'The Bride of Morning.' But the most singular mistaking of a book-title is that mentioned by D'Israeli, who declares that a modern French bibliopole placed Edgeworth's 'Essay on Irish Bulls' in a catalogue of works on natural history, as if it had been a treatise on horned cattle.

A series of blunders have been committed through a more pardonable ignorance of English idioms. An early French editor of Shakspeare's plays, not approving of his predecessor Le Tourneur's paraphrastical version, boasted of giving a more faithful one. As one proof of his capabilities for the task, he conveyed a most ridiculous notion of the following couplet in the Earl of Northumberland's celebrated speech in Henry IV.—

> 'Even such a man, so faint, so spiritless,
> So dull, so dead in look, *so woe-begone*.'

The last words were paraphrased thus:—*ainsi, douleur! va-t'en!* which, re-translated into English, signifies—'So, grief—be off with you!' In one of Sir Walter Scott's novels, that favourite supper-dish, 'a Welsh rabbit,' is mentioned. The French translator renders it literally by the words *un lapin du pays de Galles:* adding, in a note, that the wild rabbits of the Welsh mountains have a peculiarly fine flavour, which makes them to be uncommonly relished throughout Great Britain.

It is, however, in the works of French travellers that we shall find the most amusing mistakes, arising from a very natural ignorance of our idioms and customs. One gentleman, perceiving that an inn in London was called 'The Green Man and Still,' assured his readers that the sign meant the 'Green and Quiet Man,' by translating it *l'Homme Vert et Tranquille*. A large amount of diversion is to be gleaned from the work of a certain M. de Grosley, which purports to give an account of English customs. Amongst other things, he is very learned on what he is pleased to call 'the Boxk,' by which he means boxing. 'Everybody,' he remarks, 'knows the passion of all classes and conditions of the English for the boxk;' adding, that the boxk is an indispensable part of an English gentleman's education. Fathers *and mothers* make their children fight in their presence. From an utter confounding of the term 'professor,' he mistakes the now almost extinct class of professors of boxing for the professors at the universities; which induces him with amusing earnestness to lead his readers to suppose that the grave and reverend professors 'in all the schools and colleges' encourage, like the fathers and mothers, their pupils to fight. There is an irresistible comicality in the idea of an Oxford professor of divinity, or the Edinburgh professor of moral philosophy, demanding 'a ring' at the close of his lecture, and selecting a couple of favourite pupils for a pugilistic contest, for the edification of the junior students. The same writer explains the etymology of 'black-leg,' by declaring that all English cheats and sharpers wear boots, 'which they never take off.' A more diverting, because a more elaborated blunder, occurred some weeks since in a daily French newspaper. An English journal, in giving an account of a horse-race, declared that a number of persons belonging to Birmingham had lost large sums on the issue; but, in the phraseology generally adopted in reference to such matters, announced that the 'Birmingham school' had suffered severely. To this paragraph the French editor added the following edifying commentary:—'Thus, we perceive, that in England to such a pitch has the passion for betting arrived, that there exist all over the country schools and seminaries for teaching the young how to lay wagers.' But this is even less amusing than the felicitous accuracy of another travelling journalist, who translated 'The Independent Whig,' a now deceased English newspaper, by the words *La Perruque Independante*. A tourist, wishing to give accurately the origin of the above term, used to denote a particular political party, says they take their name from the Isle of *Wighh;* but not content with this blunder, he ends the same sentence by confounding the

Isle of Wight with Gretna Green; 'it is there,' he adds, 'that all runaway matches are made.' It would seem that many French translators prefer imagination to inquiry in supplying information to their readers.

VIEWS OF CANADA AND THE COLONISTS.

This is the title of a little volume, which we hail with much satisfaction as a fresh and trustworthy informant on the most important of our colonies.* The author has been induced by modesty to withhold his name from the title-page; but we can vouch that he is known in our city as a highly respectable person, free from all connexions which could produce a bias in his mind in favour of either the colony generally, or any of its particular districts. Sent thither on a business mission, he was induced to remain for a few years in the London district in the upper province, and he has only returned temporarily, from considerations as to his health. The volume contains—first, ample information of a minute and faithful character respecting the beautiful and prosperous district in which the author resided; second, a series of chapters of general intelligence respecting Canada, with instructions for those desirous of emigrating. Much of this intelligence is from official sources, and the whole has the advantage of being recent—a point of considerable consequence, where a country is concerned upon which every two or three years works a material change.

Mr Brown, for this is the author's name, is generally favourable to Canada. He speaks of the comfort of the farming class, with their 'own free farms, light taxes, and plenty of beef, bread, and wool;' also the appearance of abundance at their tables; yet admits discomforts of a physical and social nature, which may not be easily put up with by certain persons. One fact is apt to strike an inhabitant of our own country with peculiar surprise, that in the London district, amongst a population of 30,000, 'the number of persons subsisting on alms is *ten!*—one for every 3000; the paupers of England being, we believe, one in every twelve. 'And even this amount of pauperism,' says Mr Brown, 'is perhaps not real; at least I should say it is of a different nature, arising from other causes than yours—chiefly from four causes, I should suppose; first, extreme intemperate habits; old age distant from relations; physical disability in like circumstances; and, lastly, it may be a depraved choice, attended sometimes by some one or more of the three other causes. But this is a good deal conjecture, owing to the subject engaging so little attention, and in the humiliating forms in which you have it, being almost excluded from observation. During the four years I have been in Western Canada, I have scarcely met a case of the low beggary which is so pitifully prominent with you. Of cases which I can call to mind, I will tell you two which occurred this last winter. One cold morning, a woman poorly clad, with a sickly-looking child in her arms, entered a shop and begged assistance. She had lost her husband, she said, and was travelling in search of him, and her child was ill and in want of food. The shopkeeper on the instant told the case to a few of the neighbours, and the result was a contribution of a little money, an article or two of clothing, and a supply of food. In about an hour or so after this, the woman was observed in the open street, half-sitting, half-lying upon the ground, in a state of intoxication, and with her poor sick babe uncared for, and the loaves of bread she had received scattered on the road. The other case was that of a man who represented himself as a weaver from Paisley, who had come to Canada the previous season with his family, and had been unable to procure employment; and that his wife, whom he had lodged some miles distant, was confined, and in want of several necessaries. The man's appearance and story being trusted, he received on the spot some few articles necessary in the circumstances he had represented; and, by being recommended for further assistance, a trifle of money was collected for him. Perhaps you have anticipated the result—it was afterwards believed to have been so—a case of deception. In this country, you perceive, there is this so different from yours, we are apt to be more liberal, and doubt less when assistance is asked—indications certainly favourable of the state of society.'

Speaking of the *township* of London—'In 1817, there were only two families living in this township, and now the population may be stated at nearly 7000—having 90,000 acres of land, 17,000 of which are cultivated. The first regular settlement was commenced in 1818, under Mr Talbot, a gentleman from Ireland, accompanied by several of his countrymen, for whom he obtained from government free grants of land, and a free passage to Montreal. In 1829, seven years after settlement, the township contained a population of 2415, with 5941 acres of cleared land; in 1834, it had increased to 5051, with 12,841 cleared acres; and in 1841, it was 6257. These two last-mentioned periods include the town; but in 1841, the township alone had a population of over 4000. A son of the founder, writing in 1834 respecting this township, gave this account of the colonists who emigrated with his father:—"Scarcely an individual who accompanied Mr Talbot to this country was possessed of more than L.100, and many on their arrival in this township had not more than L.50; yet of all those persons there is scarcely one that is not now wholly independent, in the possession of fine farms, of an abundance of stock, and in the enjoyment of all the comforts, and many of the luxuries of life."' The *town* of London, which enjoys a central situation amidst the lakes Ontario, Erie, and Huron, and which can be *approached in five directions by mail coaches*, is laid out 'on the plan of several main streets running parallel with each other, east and west, and cross ones intersecting at right angles. There are five of what we call the main, and four of the cross streets, which have as yet been much built upon; and on the west point of the town, overlooking the river, an open space in the form of a square is left, on which the district court-house and jail is built, and which from this receives the name of Court-house Square. This public building has a rather striking appearance from its castellated style, and being built of brick coated with mortar, to resemble stone. The internal accommodations, however, have been found too inconvenient and limited for the increasing population of the district, and a considerable addition is contemplated during this summer. At one of the corners of this square is the district school, a respectable-looking two-storey wooden-frame building. Next to the school is another two-storey building, but much larger, with pediment and portico, and intended to be finished with columns. This is the hall of the Mechanics' Institute. A stranger may well be astonished at the evidence in this stately-looking and capacious building, of the zeal for knowledge and enterprise in a town like this, which had no existence seventeen years ago. London, I believe, in the spirit with which this institute is supported, is an example to the whole province. I am not aware of another instance in Canada—not even in the comparatively polished and most English-like town, Toronto—where a building has been erected for a popular institute. The hall of the London institute was opened last winter, and contains on the ground-floor rooms for a day and evening school, for a drawing and modelling class, a library, museum, a room for chemical and other apparatus, and apartments for a teacher or keeper, and the whole of the floor above is occupied as a spacious lecture-hall. During the winter evenings, the inhabitants are enlivened by lectures upon scientific and general topics, delivered by ordinary and honorary members resident in the town and neighbourhood. One of the best lectures delivered last winter was by the warden of the district, John Wilson, Esq. a barrister of talent and eminence, who is greatly respected here. The subject

* Views of Canada and the Colonists. By a Four Years' Resident. Edinburgh: A. and C. Black. 1844. 18mo. Pp. 268.

was optics, and was so ably handled and illustrated by drawings and apparatus, that, altogether, I do not think, even had the lecture been in your own Modern Athens, you could have desired to have been more gratified. James Corbett, Esq. a gentleman connected with the department of royal engineers, also delivered before the institute lectures on geology; and several others, including members of the clergy, contributed their services: such is generally the good feeling and understanding among all classes. The lectures are remarkably well attended, aided much by the enlivening presence of the ladies. There is a tolerably good library, rapidly increasing, in connexion with the institution; the fees of membership are 3s. a-quarter, and 4s. at entry; and members are restricted to no class of the community. You may perceive from this, that, with a circulating library, and reading-room besides, kept by one of the three booksellers in town, we are not quite in the wild woods here shut out from all knowledge. Two-thirds and more of our books are supplied through the United States, by means of the astonishingly cheap reprints, of which you will have heard. Think of Allison's Europe for 16s., and Blackwood's Magazine for 9d.! Besides Blackwood, we have the Dublin University, Bentley, the New Monthly, and all the Quarterlies, reprinted regularly with wonderful rapidity by one publishing house in New York soon after arrival, and the whole of them speedily circulated at low rates all over Canada. The Penny Magazine and Chambers's Journal have also large circulations.'

'Entering the streets,' continues our author, 'one is most struck by the irregular appearance of the wooden buildings, each owner of a lot or site having built in such a manner as suited his convenience, and according to his taste or fancy. There are several large three-storey buildings, one or two of brick, a number of two storeys, and the greater proportion of dwelling-houses are neat and comfortable-looking cottages; though there are a good many, too, of small cheap temporary houses scattered throughout, chiefly in parts farthest off the main streets. The breadth of the streets strikes one neither as spacious nor narrow, being about sixty feet, though in an extension of the bounds of the town the width is considerably increased. The principal street, towards the west end near the square, is occupied by the shops, of which there is no want, for the supply of every comfort and luxury usually to be had in most of your own provincial towns. There is the respectable grocer's, where you may have good coffee fresh ground every morning at 1s. per pound, young hyson tea from 3s. to 4s., and black cheaper; good brown sugar at 5d., loaf at 7d.; then there are dried fruits, oranges, and lemons; and the good housewives need not fear for starch, blues, Day and Martin's and Warren's blacking, Bath brick, and all such et ceteras. In short, these shops are just much like your own, and in the prices of the staple articles, as I have shown you above, much more moderate than those you get so highly taxed at home. The province imports tea, coffee, sugar, and other groceries at moderate duties, from whatever country it can cheapest: we get a great part from the United States and the West Indies. Such articles as London porter and Edinburgh ale, Lochfine herrings, Glo'ster cheese, Elizabeth Lazenby's pickles, and Harvey's sauce, which are all commonly to be had, you do, indeed, pay a good deal higher for than in England. The drapers' shops, called here dry-good stores, are decked out about as gaily with silks, velvets, costly shawls, ribbons, laces, &c. as your own shops, and contain, as the rival advertisements say, which we have here too, large and varied stocks. With the keen competition that exists generally over Canada among the merchants and storekeepers, all descriptions of British manufactures are sold exceedingly low.'

The venerable originator of this settlement lives in a rural mansion, which Mr Brown describes very pleasingly. 'It was a delightful summer day on which I visited it; and entering by a prepossessing gateway leading off the good main road, I found myself in a spacious noble-looking avenue. As far as I could see, there was the wide road with its grassy margin, and overhanging and bordering each side was the luxuriant and shady recesses of the tall, deep, old forest. I dropped the reins on my pony's neck, and the exquisite imagery of some of those rich portions of Spencer's Faëry Queen flowing on my recollection, translated this far western spot of young Canada into a scene of hallowed old English ground:—

> "A shady grove * * *
> Whose lofty trees, 'yclad with summer's pride,
> Did spread so broad, that heaven's light did hide."

Here, methought, might have been the fair Una, when

> "One day, nigh weary of the irksome way,
> From her unhasty beast she did alight;
> And on the grass her dainty limbs did lay,
> In secret shadow, far from all men's sight;
> From her fair hair her fillet she undight,
> And laid her stole aside: her angel's face,
> As the great eye of heaven, shined bright,
> And made a sunshine in the shady place;
> Did never mortal eye behold such heavenly grace."

Having reached a winding of the avenue, I was led by a gentle ascent and crescent-sweep to a view of the open grounds, where sheep and horned cattle were grazing in numbers. Descending into a flat grassy vale, through which a stream flowed, I crossed a bridge; and on gaining the top of the opposite bank, a range of a fine park presented itself, and at its extremity, overlooking the lake, I perceived the dwelling of the old colonel. I was struck by the grand view of the lake here: in a little I found myself standing on the edge of the lofty and steep bank overlooking the expanse of waters, without speck or ruffle, as they were that day, and a light haze bounding the farthest view. The slight motion of the lake laving the foot of the bank was all—as I stood some moments entranced by the scene with its calm stillness—that fell upon the ear. While turning towards the humble hermit-dwelling of the man with bold heart and nerve who had subdued a mighty wilderness, and saw growing up around him the beginnings of a new country he had aided so to plant—the flitting fancies of an imagination winging into the far future, presented, instead of the homely cottage, a magnificent mansion, and all detail in keeping with the noble-looking grounds and the grandeur of the expanded lake. I thought I could conceive, too, looking along its shores, the distant rising of smoke, as if from a mighty city. But the views vanished, and the regret came instead—who has not had such a regret?—that one could not live to see the full growth of those beginnings; he could only, when having to part with them for ever, witness the early healthful promises.'

An older township—that of Delaware—was settled in 1795, under circumstances partaking of the romantic. 'Upper Canada,' says our author, 'first began to be peopled in 1784; the whole of it then was one vast forest. Niagara, situated on that finely salubrious neck of land between the head of Lake Ontario and the foot of Lake Erie, was one of the first settlements, as was also a similarly favoured tract of country some little way up Lake Erie, included now in the Talbot district, and familiarly called Long Point country. These two places were among the first foot-holds of the early settlers. The next steppings forth into the interior were directed to the spot where now stands the pleasantly situated village of Ancaster, seven miles west of Hamilton, at the head of Lake Ontario. Soon after this first settlement of Ancaster, some members of the families who had removed there, pushing young men, conceived an expedition still farther into the country. The love of adventure, and the novelty of exploring a new country, would readily favour the idea of a trading speculation with the Indians; and off on this errand set the party westward, with some stores of tobacco, whisky, calicoes, knives, and trinkets. Having reached so far as Oxford, on one of the branches of the river Thames, east of London, they determined proceeding down the river in a canoe; and so loosening their well-laden little bark to the current, away went the adventurers adown the winding and rapid Thames, beautifully wooded along its banks, the tangling brushwood and graceful sweeping willow overhanging its many bends and pleasant nooks. Steering around many a lengthened curve, and by the small, low, wooded islands—some like clumps of trees alone rising from the water—now between banks, with their bold steeps of rich black and clayey loam, crowned by the luxuriant forest; next would open the fertile flats of meadow-land, more thinly wooded with the stately and widely-branching sycamore, and here and there willows and bushes of alder, with the wild vine twining about them, then bending over and dipping into the margin of the clear lively stream. Tired of the watchful steering and tending of their course down a rapid stream, without opportunity sufficient to mark the wild and stately luxuriance of the scenery, telling them of a wondrously rich soil, the adventurers naturally thought of halting for rest. So, fastening their canoe by the bank, the next moment they stood upon the threshold of the stately and shady olden woods—the towering forest—its far sombre and stilly depths, vaulted by the thick intertwining branches high above, seeming like some mighty temple, the rays of sunlight here and there flickering on the lower leaves of the less and bushier trees, or shooting in narrow streams down some massy trunk. Our tired adventurers seated themselves most likely upon one of the many old fallen trees scattered like benches about, as if inviting to rest and contemplation within the shady temple; some newly fallen, others mouldering, so that touching them, like a friable clod, they scatter into powder; others again—and those the forest wanderer loves much—with their thick elastic coatings of dry green moss, offering an easy seat across a clear cool spring—sometimes so small as nearly to be hidden—gurgling and playing lively through its miniature course of fallen leaves, and at times having even sand and pebbles for its diminutive bed. Upon one of these old mossy trunks our wanderers may have rested, the wild flowers around them appearing from amid the thickly-strewn leaves and long thin grass. Who would not have delighted to rest in such a place? The pillared, vaulted, and sombre forest, with its streaks of light and masses of shade—its carpet of leaves, and grass, and varied wild flowers—its mossy seats and purling streams—a scene awakening sensations at once pleasing and grand. You are charmed by the attractive novelty; you love the flowers, the streams, and the grandeur of the whole rising around you, and far overhead, in its vast and calm solitariness, imposes the mind with profoundest awe. Our wanderers, accustomed to such scenes, were most likely simply to experience (besides impressions of the richness of the soil) a grateful rest, and, it might be also, sensations of their solitariness in such a place, where for miles and miles around them all was forest—deep solitary forest—without a white footstep. Continuing their course, they would pass many a spot now enlivened by dwellings and cleared farms, and the din of mill-machinery; among others, the rising tableland on which now stands the town of London; unthinking it might be, as they looked upon the high banks, crowned and covered all backward by heavy forest—that here some of them would live to see, as they did, this spot the site of churches, shops, and a thousand or two busy inhabitants. Having reached the *Forks* (as the locality was long called before a house of the town was built, and even since, by old settlers, from the two branches of the river joining under the high west bank), they would then glide more smoothly upon the fuller stream, and keeping on their way till, fifteen or twenty miles further down, they made a halt. It was at one of the loveliest river nooks one could wish to linger by. It was the site of the present village of Delaware, admired by all for the beauty of its situation. The traveller along the main road from London westward, at once meets the river in a curving open valley; the opposite side high and wooded, and spreading from the foot of this rising bank are flats of meadow-land, with scatterings of willows, poplars, and thorns; then the river in the midst, almost close beneath the village on the near side, flowing gently, full, and clear, with its shining unbroken glassy surface. Such was the spot the adventurers chose as a sort of head-quarters in their Indian traffic. Finding it convenient for profitable trade in disposing of manufactured stores in exchange for furs, and doubtless influenced, too, by the natural attractions of the place for a settlement, the result was an invitation to their friends, the older folks at Ancaster, who soon joined them, and so commenced the settlement of Delaware.'

Referring to the volume itself for a great and varied range of information, we only deem it necessary to add, that Mr Brown inculcates caution to those who think of casting their lot in this colony. He endeavours to sober the views of artisans with regard to the remuneration of their labours, and plainly tells the bad workman, the intemperate, and the feeble, that Canada will not improve their circumstances. The following remarks seem to us highly judicious, and eminently deserving of attention at home. 'I would first observe, as a fundamental principle, that colonies appear to be as much, and of necessity, governed by the laws of demand and supply in regard to the amounts of the various descriptions of population required, as are individuals, companies, or communities in their ordinary transactions; and any departure from those laws inflict injury as much in the one case as in the other. Grand schemes of emigration, conducted in the present state of our information with regard to our colonies, it is believed, would most probably present similar disheartening results, which grand schemes of other shipments would which had not been "ordered," or had been sent without full acquaintance with the particular necessities or demands of the country. The paupers "shovelled" out from England, and thrown under the rock of Quebec in ignorance or disregard of the wants of the colony, or fitness of the individuals to be proper colonists; the hand-loom weavers of the west of Scotland, unfitted, the majority of them, to supply the wants of Canada, yet flocking out in ship-loads to Quebec, and forwarded to the upper country at government expense—in many instances only to experience disappointment, and to be obliged to swell the public factories of the neighbouring republic—these are cases illustrative of the evils connected with even a very limited emigration, conducted without regard to the principles of demand and supply; and which, if extended as proposed, so as to allow a freer communication with our colonies, would only aggravate evils. The great error lies in supposing that the classes of persons who are overabundant at home, and consequently least wanted, are exactly those most needed by the colony. Broken-spirited paupers, hand-loom weavers, and other persons unaccustomed, and frequently quite unfit, for the kinds of labour in demand by the colony; as also a description of Irish labourers who either cannot, or will not work, except upon canals, and who flock out to the United States and to Canada, and are the cause of serious disturbances on account of their large numbers.'

AGRICULTURAL AND HORTICULTURAL SOCIETIES.

It is a very desirable matter that the aristocracy of any locality should take a deep and practical interest in agricultural and horticultural occupations. The sports of the field, though possibly necessary for the health and recreation of idle country gentlemen, and certainly great inducements to their residence on their rural estates, are often interrupted by unpropitious weather; and the extravagant amusements of the *turf*, or of the silly and cruel steeple-chase, are at best but brief periodical excitements, which are often seriously depressing in their consequences to the over-worked mind, and exhausting to the purse, while they tend to render the human heart as callous as the whip or spurs in which the jockey glories. The individual whose horse is to run for the high stakes of a celebrated race, has nervous sensations unfelt by him whose cattle quietly contend in the ploughing-match; and surely, in point of utility, there is no room for disputation as to the comparative advantages of the different pursuits. Then, as to gardening—where can there be found more innocent or interesting employment of the active kind, or which tends more, when scientifically conducted, to elevate and expand the mind? What relaxation for the saddened or fatigued spirit can be named, that is more calculated to soothe and relieve it than occupation in the greenhouse or open garden? And if idleness oppress—if the miserable sensation of want of something to do renders the fine lady or fine gentleman listless, where can a more pleasing excitement to thought and gentle exercise be found than in the garden and shrubbery? Nor is this pleasure occasional and evanescent—it may be enjoyed at all times; and the most delicate female can never be without inducement to inhale the free air of heaven—so essential to the preservation of her health and beauty—while she has her flower-garden and conservatory to visit and arrange. In short, the possession and management of a well-ordered farm and garden is a point of attraction to our gentry; and if they can support the expense of maintaining first-rate bailiffs and gardeners, who can win prizes in their respective departments, they not only encourage a class of men whose occupations are pre-eminently useful and pleasing, but they become the means of imparting to the inferior grades of rural occupiers that desire for acquiring good skill and taste in the management of their humble allotments which so decidedly tends to advance their condition. Although there may be occasional ground for dissatisfaction at the supposed ignorance or partiality of judges in the distribution of prizes, and that feeling of jealous rivalry which near minds so frequently entertain, with or without reason, still the principle of competition is useful. People of sense not only bear disappointments with good grace, but feel a generous pleasure in seeing displays of finer plants than they themselves possess, and, instead of grumbling at everything which has not been exactly in accordance with their own views and caprices, determine to persevere steadily in their efforts, being quite content to witness the progress of the art which they admire, without experiencing any mortification at their own failures, and very happy to see rich and poor assembled together for the enjoyment of a pure and rational pleasure.—*Martin Doyle.*

A HUMBLE READING-ROOM.

The following lately appeared in the *Glasgow Citizen* newspaper:—'How little do people know of what is passing daily around them! Until the other evening, we had not the remotest idea that, on being conducted up the first stair of a dingy low-roofed close in Saltmarket (No. 115), we should observe, painted in white letters on a door, the words "Reading-Room." Was it possible that in such a locality—in the midst of vice and wretchedness—surrounded, as it were, by the very dregs of our dense population, there existed an institution devoted to mental culture and self-improvement? By what strange accident had a ray of light from the upper levels of society descended to this obscure alley? On entering, we passed a small kitchen to the right, with a fire burning briskly, and a shelf along the wall, supporting some half-dozen coffee-cups, with three or four bottles of lemonade. Before us were two rooms with tables and forms, and sufficiently lighted with gas, although, on the whole, rather scantily furnished. In one of these apartments were a few workmen—for aught we know, common labourers—with hard bushy heads, greedily devouring the news; while in the other, there was some one reading aloud to two or three gaping listeners, whose education had been more neglected. On inquiry, we learned that the subscription to the rooms, which were pretty well furnished with newspapers and cheap periodicals—such as *Chambers's Journal* and *Miscellany*—was only *one shilling a-quarter*; and that among the subscribers there were no fewer *than eleven who could not read!* It was the first time we had heard of men ignorant of the alphabet subscribing to a news-room! This interesting establishment, which was started upwards of eight months ago, through the praiseworthy exertions of a person named Mr James Partridge, is denominated "The City Teetotal Reading-Room," and affords a curious instance of the good that is sometimes doing by private individuals in obscure places, and under circumstances apparently the most adverse. The funds, we understand, are at a low ebb; but a few subscriptions might easily be obtained in support of so laudable an object.'

THE CONVICT SHIP.

BY THOMAS K. HERVEY.

Morn on the waters!—and, purple and bright,
Burst on the billows the flushing of light!
O'er the glad waves, like a child of the sun,
See the tall vessel goes gallantly on;
Full to the breeze she unbosoms her sail,
And her pennant streams onward, like hope, in the gale!
The winds come around her, in murmur and song,
And the surges rejoice, as they bear her along!
See! she looks up to the golden-edged clouds,
And the sailor sings gaily aloft in the shrouds;
Onward she glides, amid ripple and spray,
Over the waters—away, and away!
Bright as the visions of youth, ere they part,
Passing away, like a dream of the heart!
Who, as the beautiful pageant goes by,
Music around her, and sunshine on high,
Pauses to think, amid glitter and glow,
Oh! there be hearts that are breaking below?

Night on the waves!—and the moon is on high,
Hung, like a gem, on the brow of the sky;
Treading its depths, in the power of her might,
And turning the clouds, as they pass her, to light!
Look to the waters!—asleep on their breast,
Seems not the ship like an island of rest?
Bright and alone on the shadowy main,
Like a heart-cherished home on some desolate plain!
Who—as she smiles in the silvery light,
Spreading her wings on the bosom of night,
Alone on the deep!—as the moon in the sky—
A phantom of beauty!—could deem, with a sigh,
That so lovely a thing is the mansion of sin,
And souls that are smitten lie bursting within?
Who, as he watches her silently gliding,
Remembers that wave after wave is dividing
Bosoms that sorrow and guilt could not sever,
Hearts that are parted and broken for ever?
Or deems that he watches, afloat on the wave,
The deathbed of hope, or the young spirit's grave?

'Tis thus with our life, while it passes along,
Like a vessel at sea, amid sunshine and song!
Gaily we glide, in the gaze of the world,
With streamers afloat, and with canvass unfurled;
All gladness and glory to wandering eyes,
Yet chartered by sorrow, and freighted with sighs;
Fading and false is the aspect it wears,
As the smiles we put on, just to cover our tears;
And the withering thoughts which the world cannot know,
Like heart-broken exiles, lie burning below;
While the vessel drives on to that desolate shore
Where the dreams of our childhood are vanished and o'er!

—*From a Scrap-book.*

SEA-SICKNESS.

There is now in the collection of useful inventions in the gallery of the Royal Polytechnic Institution, London, a model of a swing sofa, invented by a Mr Joseph Brown, for the purpose of preventing that dreaded malady, sea-sickness. Mr Brown's invention is at once simple and ingenious, applying itself to the cause, and not to any empirical cure of the disease when once engendered. Sofas, beds, couches, cots, or chairs, are so suspended on springs, that however a vessel may roll and pitch, the sofa or chair, as the case may be, is preserved on a perfectly horizontal equilibrium, and all oscillation effectually prevented. The motion of the ship, even during the most tempestuous weather, being thus counteracted, those who recline or sit on the sofas and chairs are as perfectly steadied against any lurch, as if they were sitting or reclining on land. A number of the higher class passenger ships, it is said, have adopted Mr Brown's invention; and there can be no doubt that, if it effectually overcomes the motion, it will avert the disease.

COMMON SENSE.

Fine sense, and exalted sense, are not half so valuable as common sense. There are forty men of wit for one man of sense; and he that will carry nothing about him but gold, will be every day at a loss for ready change.—*Browne.*

⁎ Complete sets of the Journal, *First Series*, in twelve volumes, and also odd numbers to complete sets, may be had from the publishers or their agents. A Stamped Edition issued for transmission, post free, price Twopence halfpenny

Printed by William Bradbury, of No. 6, York Place, and Frederick Mullett Evans, of No. 7, Church Row, both of Stoke Newington, in the county of Middlesex, printers, at their office, Lombard Street, in the precinct of Whitefriars, and city of London; and Published (with permission of the Proprietors, W and R. CHAMBERS,) by WILLIAM SOMERVILLE ORR, Publisher, of 2, Amen Corner, at No 2, AMEN CORNER, both in the parish of Christchurch, and in the city of London.—Saturday, January 25, 1845.

CONDUCTED BY WILLIAM AND ROBERT CHAMBERS, EDITORS OF 'CHAMBERS'S INFORMATION FOR THE PEOPLE,' 'CHAMBERS'S EDUCATIONAL COURSE,' &c.

No. 57. NEW SERIES. SATURDAY, FEBRUARY 1, 1845. PRICE 1½d.

PENNY-A-LINERS.

PENNY-A-LINERS are the stragglers of the London press—the foragers for stray news—the narrators of fires, street accidents, suicides, murders, police cases, and all the odds and ends that fill up the columns of newspapers in default of political opinions, debates, and foreign intelligence. They have no engagement with the press. They are often wholly unknown, except by name, to its conductors. Their plan of life is simply to contribute, to all journals alike, whatever scraps of news they may be able to collect. For this purpose they hang about hospitals, fire-offices, and coroners' courts; besiege police-officers, churchwardens, overseers, and magistrates: and are perpetually going about in watch for what the chapter of accidents may throw in their way. They are paid by the line for their contributions, and hence their designation; although, of late years, they have so far advanced in the world as to receive three-halfpence per line, instead of one penny, as formerly. They have of course an inducement to tell their stories at as great length as possible; and one of the chief miseries of London editors and sub-editors is to prune their exuberance—'cut them down,' as it is technically termed—by weeding their phraseology of all their superabundant epithets and needless circumlocutions. There may be about sixty men known as having this off-and-on connexion with the press, besides perhaps as many more who pretend to the same connexion, and live by the frauds they commit under that assumption.

The penny-a-liner, humble and unknown as he is—gaining a precarious and generally miserable existence; having £10 in his pocket one week, the proceeds of some interesting murder, and starving the next, because people are too moral or too fortunate to afford him, for the time, anything to write about—passes a life, we seriously believe, by no means deficient of enjoyment. Amidst all the occasional distresses of his situation, he must have some satisfaction in seeing the extensive circulation given, by the press at home and abroad, to his homely lucubrations: And his very duty or business involves a variety of scene and pursuit that cannot be otherwise than agreeable.

Delightful to him must be the first rumour of one of the grander class of murders. He scents the affair afar off. The slightest hint gives him a clue to 'further particulars;' and with a zeal, an energy, and an acuteness that are seldom equalled, he will scour the country for miles around the metropolis in search of all kinds of collateral information. He manages also to excite the curiosity that he is afterwards to feed, and which is to feed him. For the sake of his little fee, he will attach himself to a great criminal from his first commission of the deed of blood until his life pays the penalty of his crime—tracking him by surmises when he is at large—attending his examination before magistrate or coroner when apprehended: he narrates his behaviour in prison, who visits him, what he eats and drinks, what books he reads, what conversations he has with his jailers or visitors, what coloured coat and nether garments he wears, and how he behaves when brought upon the scaffold. The penny-a-liner never ceases to take an interest in him while he lives; and even when he dies, he continues to gain a few days' subsistence by the after-anecdotes he rakes up about him, or his friends or connexions.—Cases of romantic suicides are also great helps to the penny-a-liner; steamboat collisions are strokes of fortune to him; the fall of railway stations gives him a lift; fires where great damage is done make the fire on his own hearth burn brighter; a great robbery gives him coin to count; and misfortunes and iniquities make him happy and prosperous.

Some penny-a-liners have circuits as extensive as the judges, and traverse periodically a certain district, narrating, in default of crimes and misfortunes, the details of parish squabbles, local elections, the appearance of the crops—anything that appears to them of sufficient public interest to warrant a paragraph. In some districts, the travelling penny-a-liner passes for a very great man, and receives no small attention, with good fare and free quarters, from inn and hotel keepers, from the hope that some day, in the Times or the Morning Chronicle, he will say a good word for the excellence of his accommodation, and the urbanity and good wines of the host—an expectation which the obscure penny-a-liner but rarely has an opportunity of fulfilling. He is also a person of some consequence with police-inspectors, whom he may have occasion in some future paragraph to designate as 'zealous and active officers.' Nor is his consideration less with parish orators; for if he cannot repeat their eloquence in full, he can manage to say in print that they delivered 'able speeches,' and that they were 'loudly and repeatedly cheered.' If the penny-a-liner of this kind have any faults besides his verbosity, it is his impudence. He has no scruples. A private house is not private to him; he lives by narrating incidents, and incidents he will have, at whatever sacrifice. It has happened ere this that the penny-a-liner has been ducked under a pump for his impertinent prying; that he has been left on a mud-bank by the indignant boatmen, for obtruding himself on the privacy of distinguished or royal personages in their own barge; and suffered various other like mishaps and indignities in the 'pursuit of knowledge under difficulties.' Nay, the penny-a-liner has been known to suffer indignity with a willing mind, and even with delight, if it would aid him to write a report for the morning journals which no rival penny-a-liner could have the opportunity of supplying. He has been known to put on the livery of a great family, and wait upon the guests at table, napkin in hand, like any other footman, that he might gather the names of the distinguished guests, and describe their rich banquet next morning in the columns of all the journals. And when he could not do this by the connivance of the great man himself, he has bribed the butler, and been admitted as an extra hand for the extraordinary occasion. It is not often, however, that he is reduced to shifts like these; for the great man who gives a feast, or his great lady, is generally but too happy to have his or her magnificence duly emblazoned in the newspapers; and the confidential butler is instructed to treat the penny-a-liner well, give him all the particulars he desires, with meat and drink, and a fee into the bargain.

This class of penny-a-liners has been somewhat fattened of late by the progresses of her majesty to Scotland, and to the mansions of her nobility. Travelling in the wake, as it were, of the regularly accredited reporter of each journal, they described with painful minuteness every inch of her journey, giving facts, however small, wherever they could get them, and substituting surmises when facts were not to be obtained. No respect had they for royal privacy; and the colour of the royal gown or bonnet, or of the royal spouse's hat and hat-band, and shooting-jacket, were carefully noted from day to day—always with a view to the three-halfpences that were thus to be acquired. Every place that her majesty passed, or obtained even a glimpse of in passing, became of consequence immediately in their eyes; and its past history was raked up from county-books and other sources, and its present appearance described with all the minuteness of an auctioneer's inventory. All the deeds of all the ancestors of all the noblemen visited have also been detailed for the gratification of idle readers, and to the enrichment of the penny-a-liners, whose loyalty is ever most active when her majesty is active, and who love the queen the more she travels.

There is, however, a far larger class of penny-a-liners, who never move for business out of the limits of the metropolis, and who, enjoying there a beat of their own, might chance to meet with unpleasant resistance if they were to set a foot professionally in any suburban or provincial walk which a brother of the trade had, from use and wont, appropriated to himself. It is curious to note how, without authority, and solely by the prescriptive right of prior occupation and long usage, men of this kind have contrived to parcel out the metropolis amongst them, each man reigning supreme penny-a-liner and representative of the press in his own district, and taking charge of its news to the exclusion of every competitor. Some of these districts are very large, and some comparatively small. A few of them, in the neighbourhood of the Strand and Westminster more especially, are quite overrun with these literary prowlers. Each police-office has several hangers-on; every coroner is literally hunted by them from place to place; and every hospital is periodically visited by a shabby man, with a note-book and a pencil, to know who has been admitted with a broken leg. Every clerk of every parish is similarly favoured with a visitor, to know when the poor-law will next be discussed in the vestry—when the church-rate is to be proposed and opposed—or when the rector or the churchwarden is to have a new squabble with the parishioners. Generally speaking, the penny-a-liners of London may be divided into the following varieties:—the police-reporter, the fashionable reporter, the fireman, the accident and murder man, the inquest man, and the vestry man; with now and then a mingling of these various functions in the person of some more active and intelligent member of the fraternity.

The police penny-a-liner, by dint of perseverance in attending one particular police court, and furnishing to the morning papers accurate and well-written reports of the cases heard, contrives to establish himself in it, after a certain time, and becomes ultimately a person of some note in his little sphere. It must in justice be said of this class of London reporters, that by far the greater number of them discharge their functions with great ability, and report very accurately all the cases of importance that are heard. With the sole exception of the wordiness, which is a consequence of the plan of payment adopted towards them [which may be deplored, but not easily remedied], they give no ground of complaint to any person of the manner in which they comport themselves. Sometimes, when an onslaught between the Munster and Connaught men, or any other Irish 'row' occurs, or a case involving any ludicrous incidents is heard, the penny-a-liner relates it with a talent and humour not surpassed by our best novel-writers; and police-reports are not unfrequently seen from the Mansion House of London, or from the Marlborough Street court, which would have excited universal admiration for their wit and style, and raised a reputation for their author, if they had appeared as part of a tale in three volumes. To their honour it should also be stated, that they are no flatterers of the powers that be. The magistrate, high and mighty as he is in his own court, has no authority over them; his nod inspires them with no awe; and if he is a man who gives arbitrary, contradictory, or foolish decisions, or utters absurdities, which is but too often the case, the penny-a-liner shows him no mercy. Without writing one sentence of his own, but merely by an over faithful kind of reporting, he contrives to hold up the peccant dignitary to the ridicule of the public. To the persevering exertions of one penny-a-liner of this independent class was solely owing, some years ago, the public outcry raised against a magistrate whose decisions were at variance with common sense, and whose tyrannical behaviour outraged all decency. Though his means of livelihood were at stake, though the magistrate was powerful, and though every means were employed to cajole or intimidate him, he held firm; and ultimately the lord chancellor sent the magistrate a gentle hint, that resignation was better than dismissal; and the hint was taken.

Another magistrate took offence at a penny-a-liner, who was constantly on the watch for the absurdities he might utter, and directed one of his officers to expel the offender by force. He miscalculated his own powers. A police court is an open one, and no magistrate has a right to expel any person who does not misbehave himself, or obstruct the administration of justice. The penny-a-liner, besides holding up this stretch of authority to the animadversion of the public, commenced an action of assault against the usher by whom he was thrust out; and the magistrate was ultimately but too happy to compromise the matter, and again give the penny-a-liner free ingress and egress to report what he thought proper. The latter, on his part, made no compromise, and continued the offensive reports; the most annoying part of the business to the aggrieved magistrate being, that it was impossible to say that they were inaccurate in any particular, however trifling; while they very dexterously made him appear ridiculous, by words which he could not deny that he had uttered.

In some of the remote police courts, where cases of no great importance are heard, the penny-a-liner finds it difficult to live on the proceeds of the few cases of interest that are worth insertion in the newspapers; and if he has a rival in the same court, his position becomes doubly precarious. He has, however, another source of income, less honourable, but by which it is well known that very considerable sums have been made. Mr Jones, or Mr Smith, or Mr Tomkins, for instance, has been brought before the magistrate for a street row, or a drunken frolic; and Mr Jones, Mr Smith, and Mr Tomkins, though persons of no consequence at all to the world, imagine that their disgrace will create a great sensation, if published, in all circles of society the following morning, and laid on the breakfast-tables of fifty thousand people. What is to be done? The penny-a-liner, as the representative of the press, is appealed to; and his promise of not reporting the delinquencies of the aforesaid Jones or Tomkins, is rewarded by such a fee as the fears or the generosity of Jones or Tomkins will bestow. It may, however, happen that a case will occur which, from the peculiarity or importance of the circumstances, cannot be suppressed, and in which the penny-a-liner would lose more by not reporting for the newspaper than he would gain by the fee for suppression. How to please both parties is the problem which an ingenious penny-a-liner finds little difficulty in solving. Mr Brown of King Street, for instance, is the unlucky gentleman who is in the dilemma; and, for a consideration, Brown is transformed into Green or Black, and his abode is shifted from King Street into Queen Street; and thus all parties are satisfied: the public has the details of the scandal it so dearly loves; the penny-a-liner has his extra fee, and the feelings of the delinquent's friends, as well as his own, are spared by the mistake, which, after all, say they who are not in the secret, is a thing not to be wondered at in the hurry of reporting. The income of an established penny-a-liner of his class ranges, according to his ability, and the opposition from rivals of his own calling that he has to encounter, from L.100 to L.300 per annum.

The coroner's inquest man is a penny-a-liner of an inferior grade; though there are some able, honest, and intellectual men, worthy of better things, who are but too glad to resort to the coroners' courts for the means of subsistence. Generally speaking, however, they are men of little character, and of no attainments: some of them are not only ignorant of grammar, but even of orthography, and pass their time alternately in the workhouse, the gin-shop, and the jury-room. We have seen men of this class poorly clad, and the very pictures of misery and destitution, running behind a coroner's gig or carriage, through the storm and the plashing rain, to track him to the public-house where he was to hold his inquest; and keeping up with him too, in spite of the efforts of the driver to get in advance of them. At other times, a more respectable member of the fraternity has been honoured with a seat alongside of the coroner, who is in general happy when he can find a person of good attainments and decent character to record his proceedings. Besides penny-a-liners, who are merely discreditable from ignorance and low habits, there are vultures professedly of this class, who are in fact not penny-a-liners at all, and who never wrote a line for a newspaper in their lives, nor could do so even if they tried, but who haunt the purlieus of every place where an inquest is about to be held, lured, like other vultures, by a dead body, and anxious to prey upon it by plundering the relatives and survivors. Wherever a suicide has been committed, there they swarm—numerous as midges over a pool, or as crows over carrion. A few instances, in which we shall not mention any names, though our facts shall defy contradiction, will suffice to show the mode in which their vile trade is carried on, and put the public on their guard as to their malpractices in future. It happened not very long ago that a gentleman of some eminence in his profession committed suicide in a fit of insanity. His partner in business was exceedingly anxious that the case should not be published, as it would hurt his own feelings, and the feelings of others who were dear to the deceased, and might, besides, do injury to his professional prospects. Then was the harvest of these harpies. They gathered round his house one after another, clamouring for money as the price of the suppression; and every applicant received his fee, for which he wrote a receipt, to convey to the mind of him who paid the money the impression that the transaction was fair and legitimate, and all in the regular way of business. They were cunning enough, however, in this case, as they generally are, to write the receipts in disguised handwritings, and in false names, to avoid the evil consequences that might ensue if the conductors of the morning journals ever heard of the circumstance, or thought it necessary to trace the scoundrels, who, by falsely representing themselves as connected with the press, had brought this disgrace upon it. The case was published after all. * *

Still more cruel cases have occurred repeatedly: widows whose husbands have been lying dead in their houses, just after the commission of the last deed of insanity, have been visited by these prowlers, and money has been extorted from them in the very midst of their misery, as the price of the suppression of the details. The anguish of mind of a survivor is enough in these unhappy cases, without the additional pang that the promulgation of all the details for the satisfaction of a vulgar and prurient curiosity is sure to cause; and the self-called penny-a-liners of this class know the fact but too well, and trade upon it. It has been stated, upon undoubted authority, and we personally know the fact, that, to satisfy a demand of this nature, a heart-broken woman has taken the ring from her finger and the gold chain from her neck; and that the recipient having got his own share of plunder, has sent a companion as vile and as desperate as himself to try his fortune in extorting something else. Many similar or worse instances might be cited, if need were; for they occur every day, and the system has many ramifications; but enough has been said to enlighten many who were once ignorant, and perhaps to prevent much extortion for the future. While upon this part of the subject, it should be stated that the same persons, when inquests fail to supply them with the means of living, resort to the courts of excise, where publicans are fined for adulterating their beer, where they contrive sometimes to gain as large a fee as the Crown does a fine, upon condition of not publishing the name of the delinquent. Tradesmen who are fined for using short weights also swell the revenues of these pests of literature; but as the latter class of victims, however much they may be fleeced, excite little or no sympathy, no more need be said on this score.

Another class of penny-a-liners are the fire reporters, who generally undertake the accidents also; gleaning all their information of the first, that they have not themselves been able to attend, from firemen and insurance offices, and of the latter from the secretaries and surgeons of the hospitals. An active penny-a-liner of this class takes measures to be aroused from his bed at the first alarm of fire in any part of London, as effectually as the superintendent of a fire-engine station himself. Wherever there is a great fire, there is he in the thickest of the throng, gathering his materials for the next morning's paragraph; telling how 'the neighbourhood' of such and such a place 'was thrown into the utmost alarm and consternation by the discovery of an awful fire;' how 'the devouring element' raged in spite of the efforts of the firemen to extinguish it with the 'copious floods of water discharged upon it;' how the 'whole atmosphere was illuminated by the flames;' and how 'the inmates escaped almost in a state of nudity to the adjoining house.' Neither does he forget to state at the very outset of his story which engine of what office 'arrived first at the scene of conflagration,' and by what other engines 'it was speedily followed.' These are great points—in fact, essential points—on which rests the favour of the reporter with the insurance company—and some portion of his profits too, or common rumour has fallen into an error. Often will the adventurous penny-a-liner ride upon the engine with the firemen in its headlong course through the streets of the metropolis, and often travel twenty miles and back with them in search of the fire that throws a light upon the distant horizon; and all for a paragraph for the morning papers. In all weathers, frost, hail, sleet, or strong wind, he is to be seen with the moving multitudes of London; either with the firemen, or alone, riding or trudging on foot to the place of devastation; and gaining his honest and hard-won bread in the exercise of his useful though very humble function. Were all the penny-a-liners as honest as those who report the fires and the accidents, there would be no room to say anything against their character, whatever might be said of their style or attainments.

We have now to speak of a more clever and ingenious branch of the fraternity—the pure inventors, the romance writers of the daily press, who palm off their romances as truths, and cheat the public of their sympathy for horrors that never occurred, and excite their admiration for remarkable events that have no other existence than in their own fancy. This is, however, a dangerous trade, and great caution and cunning, as well as imagination, are displayed by those who embark in it. Whenever an imposition of this kind is to be practised upon an editor, and through him upon the public, the penny-a-liner calculates his time. The papers generally pay on Saturday morning, and a fabrication of this kind, to be successful, must be sent round on Friday night; and if the editor is not on the alert, and confides in the accuracy of the very precise and circumstantial report of the awful catastrophe, or atrocious murder, that is sent to him, it is inserted in the paper of Saturday morning, and paid for a few hours afterwards, before any one has time to send a contradiction. Of course the fraud is discovered; but the penny-a-liner, who had written under a false name, cares nothing for that. He has received his three-halfpences, and when he has another invention of the kind to send, will send it in another name, and in a different handwriting; and, to allay the suspicion of the editors, will get one or two accomplices to write accounts of the same imaginary occurrence in other words, and with other signatures; and this being considered corroborative evidence of its truth, the false report is not unfrequently again inserted. Murders, duels, elopements, explosions, and romantic suicides, are the staple commodities of this kind of swindlers; and the very minute manner in which they relate their false stories, their mention of dates, names, and places, so very precisely and particularly, is calculated to disarm suspicion. It must not, however, be supposed that they have invention enough to carry on this game long. No: the annual register, and the files of newspapers fifteen or twenty years old, supply them with abundant materials; and an old murder of the times of our boyhood frequently comes before us again as a murder of yesterday, with merely the change of names and localities, but with all the original circumstances identically the same as before. Antiquated accidents are brought into the light of modern days by the same industrious and unscrupulous grubbers; explosions a quarter of a century old terrify us once more in a new burst of horror; and the romantic love tragedies of the days of our grandfathers and grandmothers are repeated —the scene being laid in Whitechapel perhaps, and the time shifted to the day before yesterday. There was a few years ago a penny-a-liner who was the most remarkable specimen of this class of men, who pursued his calling in the most open and unblushing manner, weaving original stories, so interesting, but so indefinite as to time, place, and name, as to defy contradiction; and so framed, that if they once got into a newspaper, they gave him no trouble to defend their authenticity.

There are some other divisions and subdivisions of the penny-a-line fraternity; such as those who attend boat-races, yacht-matches, cricket-matches, pugilistic encounters, and other real or miscalled sports. Formerly the horse-races used to be supplied by members of the same corps; but of late years this system has been altered, and there is a regular turf reporter, who supplies all the newspapers with sporting intelligence, and against whom all penny-a-line opposition would be fruitless. There are also penny-a-liners who loiter about at railway meetings, to pick up scraps of news, or interesting facts of any kind, to be woven into paragraphs, and who sometimes contrive to be of considerable service to the speculators in the line, by a short but judicious statement forwarded to all the editors, who are quick enough at detecting a puff in a paragraph of which insertion is requested as a favour, but who are slow to suspect it in the contributions of the regular purveyors of small news, to be paid for by the line.

It may be stated, in conclusion, that the five morning journals of London pay on the average about L.1000 a-year each for penny-a-line reports; and that, with the smaller payments made by the evening and Sunday journals, the penny-a-liners share among them about L.7000 per annum. What the dishonest members of the fraternity draw from the public by their extortions and frauds, cannot be so easily calculated; but from the repeated instances that occur in which large sums are paid for suppressions, the whole amount must be very considerable.

In this slight description, it is trusted that, although many things have been omitted, enough has been said to throw light upon the means of livelihood of a singular and important class of the community, whose numbers are few, but whose influence is great. The talent of some of them, and the usefulness of most, have been freely acknowledged; and if the veil has been lifted to expose the roguery of others, it has not been done for the satisfaction of mere curiosity, but to clear the high-minded and independent press of London from the aspersions that the malpractices of these false pretenders to a connexion with it have too often brought upon its character.

RESEARCHES IN ANIMAL ELECTRICITY.

Among the more prominent of modern scientific discoveries, stand the researches of Signor Matteucci of Pisa into the philosophy of animal electricity. His labours have gained deserved praises from men in the highest ranks of science throughout Europe. The Royal Society, the first of the learned societies of England, have awarded him their gold Copley medal, to mark their esteem of his contributions to the progress of philosophical knowledge. Signor Matteucci has verified and extended the experiments and discoveries of Galvani, first made known towards the end of the last century; and he has laid a foundation on which other philosophers may raise with safety a new superstructure of theory and investigation.

We shall endeavour to present to our readers, in as clear a form as the subject will admit, a brief review of the history and present state of the science, as contained in the work by the professor and his coadjutor, M. Paul Savi, recently published in Paris.

It appears that the celebrated Swammerdam was aware of the fact of the contraction of the muscular fibre when acted on by the influence of two metals, copper and silver; he performed the experiment before the Grand Duke of Tuscany in 1678, or nearly a century before Galvani announced his discoveries. To the latter, however, belongs the honour of developing principles; and as he was ignorant of the fact above cited, his reputation as a discoverer is in no degree diminished. It has been said that Galvani first noticed the contraction of the muscles by electricity in some frogs which had been prepared for cooking, and were lying on the table near the machine with which he was operating. Be this as it may, we find that, from the time of his first experiments in 1780, he waited eleven years in patient research before he gave them to the world—a distrust of his own achievements ever found associated with a high degree of genius.

The first phenomenon described by Galvani was the contractions in the limbs of a frog, prepared in the ordinary manner: as often as it was brought into communication with the earth and a conducting body, a spark was drawn from the machine in proportion to the distance of the frog from the conductor. In continuing this experiment, he subjected a prepared frog to the passage of the electricity of the atmosphere, when he discovered that this little animal is the most sensitive of electroscopes. It is with a feeling of dread that we read of his grasping between his hands the isolated column of an atmospheric conductor at the instant of the discharge of lightning from the clouds, in order to try the effect of the atmospheric current on his own person. Galvani ascertained that the contractions took place when the extremities of a circle, formed of two different metals united together, were applied, one point to the nerve, and the other to the muscle of the frog: from this and other experiments he deduced the existence of an animal electricity, or a nervo-electric fluid, which he supposed to reside condensed in the interior of the muscle. According to his theory, the nerve was but the conducting medium for the discharge of two kinds of electricity contained in the muscle; the direction of the current being from the latter to the former. He found also, on further research, that on touching the nerves of a prepared frog at two different points with a piece of muscular substance taken from a living animal, the same contractions were excited as when a metallic agent was employed.

This philosopher was followed in his inquiries by Volta, who, in pursuit of the same subject, first discovered, in 1796, the electricity developed in the contact of two metals; from which arose the discovery of the Voltaic pile, a discovery whose influence on other sciences has only been equalled by the rapidity of its spread. The famous Humboldt, among others, directed his attention to this science; and to him are we indebted for the discovery of the action of the electric current in the pulsation of the heart, and the natural movement of the intestines: he also, with the courage of a devotee of science, removed several portions of his skin, by means of blisters, in order to carry out his experiments on parts beneath the surface. The philosopher Valli, in the course of his experiments on the same subject, observed that, on tying the artery of one of the limbs of a living frog, the power of contraction was soon after destroyed, and that the nerves are less sensitive at their roots than at their extremities.

Later research has not changed the results of the earlier investigators, but has confirmed, in most instances, their views and experience. Professor Matteucci has cleared up many of the doubts under which this science was obscured, and established the laws of muscular contraction. He has constructed a 'pile' or 'battery' of the hind quarters of frogs placed alternately in line on a board; and found, by the indications of his galvanometer, that the force of the current rests on no uncertainty, but depends entirely on the number and vivacity of the frogs killed for the occasion, the direction of the current being invariably from the interior to the surface. The same effects were produced with portions of an eel, from which the skin had been stripped, when properly disposed on the board. Living tenches were taken, and after being skinned, slices were cut from the muscle down the whole length of the back of the fish; these slices, when cut into pieces, and arranged as in the preceding examples, were found to cause a similar disturbance in the galvanometer, while the direction of the current was precisely the same from the interior to the surface. The results were identical when the experiments were tried on warm-blooded animals; with the muscles of the legs and the hearts of pigeons, of fowls, sheep, and oxen. These experiments constitute a fundamental result, that, without exception, whenever the interior of the muscle of any animal recently killed is brought into contact with its surface, an electric current is found to pass from the former to the latter, varying in intensity in different animals, proportionately with the number of muscular elements disposed as a pile, and ceasing entirely in a short period after death. The higher we go in the scale of creation, the feebler are the developments of the electric current. Of three piles composed of an equal number of limbs of frogs, pigeons, and rabbits, the power of the first was as 22 to 14 for the second, and 8 for the third. In an hour after, all indications of electricity had totally disappeared in the rabbit pile, while that of the pigeons was as 3 to 10 for the frogs, which, even after the lapse of twenty-four hours, still gave some signs of contractility. Subsequent experiments, however, led the professor to infer that the intensity of the muscular current in animals increases in proportion to their rank in the system of nature.

It appears that there is no change in the force or direction of the muscular current even when the integrity of the nervous system is destroyed. Signor Matteucci verified this by a very cruel experiment: he passed a red-hot wire into the spinal marrow of six frogs, exactly at the lower vertebræ; the frogs immediately lost all movement and sensation in their hinder extremities: they were then replaced in a vessel of water with six other frogs in their natural vigour, and after four days the whole were killed, and two piles prepared. On trying the respective piles by the galvanometer, it was ascertained that the greatest force was derived from the frogs whose limbs had been paralysed by the heated wire; a result attributed to the consequent inflamed state of the muscles, but which proves the electric action to be independent of the nerve. In order to ascertain the effect of the electric current on central portions of the nervous system, the skull of a rabbit was trepanned, so as to expose the brain: the first contact was then made on the two cerebral hemispheres, but without any movement on the part of the animal: the same result was obtained when the current was passed through the cerebellum: but when the two poles of the pile were applied to the base of the brain, the rabbit uttered loud cries, and was seized with violent contractions of the whole body.

These results, as Matteucci observes, are far from proving the existence of *free* electricity in living animals. It is equally well proved that the signs of the current found in muscular masses exist independently of the integrity of the nervous system, and even after this system has ceased, although irritated, to excite contractions. For the production of this current, the organic arrangement, which constitutes living muscular fibre, is as necessary as the action which maintains it in that condition. Is it not natural to suppose that the nutrition, such as is proved to take place in the muscle, and in all parts of living bodies, develops electricity? It would be difficult not to admit it. In fact, it is well known at the present day that the action of the oxygen of arterial blood is felt in every part of the living body, that the whole organised system is constantly renewed, and that a species of combustion always accompanies this renewal, with a development of carbonic acid, and a loss of heat. Is it right to suppose that such a chemical action takes place without the production of electricity? Muscular fibre may represent a plate of metal, and arterial blood the acidulated liquid. The surface of the muscle, or any other conducting body which is *not* muscular fibre, may represent a second metallic plate, serving to complete the circuit. The natural direction of the muscular current is such as would arise in the muscle under a chemical action as here described.

The sum of the series of experiments proves that the electric current alone has the power, according to the direction of its action on a nerve, of exciting separately contractions or sensations. When this current is long-continued, no effect is produced; but it may be again excited on passing the current in a contrary direction; and this current is that which possesses the power of arousing the excitability of a nerve, however weak it may be, above all other stimulating agents. These conclusions in turn prove that the mode of action of the electric current on the nerves is in some degree analogous to the unknown force which calls the nervous system into play.

The circulation of electricity in the nerves cannot be admitted, without supposing such an arrangement in the structure of the nervous system as would be necessary to form a complete circuit. The labours, however, of the German anatomists, remarkable as they are, are far from proving satisfactorily the existence of such an arrangement, especially in its ramifications among the muscles. In all the experiments made on the nerves of living animals, even when the whole extent of the nerve has been brought to the test, no evidence of native electricity could be produced.

The electric muscular current is a phenomenon, as has been shown, which may owe its origin to the chemical action constituting the nutrition of the muscle. It has also been established that this current, strictly analogous to that produced by the combination of two bodies, exists only in the molecules, and never circulates in those media but in particular cases, which were realised in the experiments only by experience. The nerves have no direct influence in the existence of this current, and have no other power than that of a bad conducting body communicating with certain portions of the muscle.

What is, then, this mysterious moving power? According to the hypothesis of Professor Matteucci, it is identical with that which appears in heat, light, and natural electricity. There exists in animals such a structure, or disposition of certain parts of their organisation, that, by the act of the unknown force of the nervous system, electricity is set free. Ether exists in diffusion in every portion of the nervous system, as in all the matter of the universe, which in this system may have a particular arrangement. When the organic molecules of a nerve are disturbed by any cause, the ether, or more properly the nervous fluid, is brought into a certain movement, which, if directed from the extremities towards the brain, produces a sensation; but, on the contrary, excites a contraction when the direction is from the brain to the extremities. Philosophy is advancing daily towards a greater simplification of its hypotheses, or, more properly, towards a single hypothesis, which will explain all the phenomena of heat, light, and electricity. What hypothesis, indeed, is more worthy of the rank to which efforts are being made to elevate it, than on a matter which is susceptible of so great a number of different movements, capable of transforming one into the other, and thereby representing very various phenomena. The most essential characteristics of this matter, such as the immense rapidity of the propagation of its movements, a certain intangible materiality, its transformations, belong to the unknown power of the nervous system, as well as to electricity, light, and heat. The relation between these operations of the ether become much more intimate when not only one can be transformed into the other, but when this, in its turn, can be transformed into the first.

The great object of Signor Matteucci, through the whole course of his experiments, appears to have been the relief of human suffering, and we shall now notice his observations on electricity as a therapeutic or curative agent, which he tells us has been applied by practitioners with a blind confidence, or treated with discouragements equally inconsiderate. Instantaneous or general cures were not to be expected; and this means should not have been employed empirically, or without proper study and knowledge of electro-physiology. It is certain that electricity may be wisely applied in nervous affections, and in cases of total or partial paralysis; and, acting on the results before noticed, as a paralysed limb is in the condition of one which has lost its powers by the passage of a continued electric current, the current must be passed in the contrary direction; regard being had, however, as to whether the paralysis be of motion or sensibility: the former requires the inverse current, the latter the direct: but in a case of complete paralysis, there is no reason why the direction of the current should not always be direct. Another rule to be observed in this application is, that the passage of the current should not be maintained for too long a period, as the risk of increasing the malady would, in such a case, be incurred. The more intense the current, the shorter should be the time of its duration. The intensity should vary with the degree of the disease, and the currents be passed for two or three minutes, at intervals of a few seconds; after these two or three minutes, during which twenty or thirty shocks may have been given, the patient should be left to repose before repeating the treatment.

A Voltaic pile of 100 pairs, or an electro-magnetic machine, may be employed in these remedies, which it would be desirable to accompany with puncturation by needles, in order to carry the current as near as possible to the paralysed nerve. Great patience is required in this mode of treatment; in some of the cures effected by Marianini, the applications were continued through several months: in two cases the cure was only complete after 2500 electric shocks had been given to the paralysed member. Among other cures are several by the celebrated Magendie of Paris: and at Pisa, the professor was a witness of the cure of a man, whose lower limbs were completely paralysed, in the hospital of that city, effected entirely by means of electricity and acu-puncturation. These results, though few in number, will perhaps suffice to induce physicians to make a serious study of electro-physiological phenomena; and to succeed by persevering efforts, which science will enlighten, in the employment of a curative method, peculiarly adapted to the removal of a class of complaints which unfortunately too often resist all other remedies.

Another affection for which the application of electricity has been proposed, is tetanus, on which, in the human subject, Signor Matteucci has been the first to make a trial. He noticed that frogs suffering under the effects of narcotic poisons, such as opium, nux vomica, &c. were at first stupified, then over-excited, and, shortly before death, were seized with violent tetanic convulsions. If, while in this latter condition, an electric current of a certain continuous strength was passed through these animals, the rigidity of their members and the spasms were seen to disappear. The frogs died from the effect of the poison, but without exhibiting any signs of tetanus. The trial was made on a man suffering from an attack of this malady, in consequence of an injury of the muscles of the leg, and during the passage of the current the severe spasms abated: he was able to open and shut his mouth; and the course of the circulation and the perspiration seemed to be re-established. Although this first experiment was not successful in saving the man's life, it has brought to light a means of mitigating the severity of a very painful affection.

The patience and perseverance of Professor Matteucci have been proportionate to the great objects of his pursuit: he tells us that he has published no statement which has not been verified by repeated and scrupulous experiment. His work is written in an easy and unassuming style, and its clearness is such, that every person may, to use his own words, 'place themselves in a condition to repeat and add to the experiments.'

Science is a severe mistress, and they who devote themselves to her cause must divest themselves of some of their finer sensibilities. It is impossible to read of the destruction of thousands of frogs, besides other animals, without a shudder. This forms a serious drawback to the interest excited by Matteucci's experiments. Humanity to 'those that creep and those that crawl' is oftentimes too little thought of; yet without it, genius loses half its lustre. In the present case, however, the end may be said, in some degree, to justify the means; and if human suffering can be alleviated, we may overlook the cruelty in the compensation.

HEART.

There are some persons in the world who are special favourites among all who know them, who find or make friends everywhere, whose company every one enjoys, and from whom every one is loath to separate. Their frank and easy manners inspire confidence at first sight, and one numbers them as friends almost as soon as one has made their acquaintance. No one is ever 'not at home' to them; their visit is anticipated as a pleasure, and no one feels disposed to part with them without the cordial inquiry, 'When shall we see you again?' There is an exuberance of pleasurable life about them which seems to diffuse itself among all around, and their presence is felt to be an addition to the general amount of happiness in the circle privileged with their company. In selecting a party of friends, their name always suggests itself first, and the absence of any two others would be a less disappointment than theirs. Every one seeks their side at the dinner-table, and he deems himself fortunate whose chair in the social circle is next to theirs. Innocent childhood loves to sit on their knee and prattle its earnest nonsense in their ear; impetuous youth finds in them cordial companions; and old age values them as pleasant and estimable friends. And yet it is not to their personal comeliness that they are indebted for this popularity, for their exterior is often far from prepossessing; nor to their intellect, for even their best admirers do not imagine them Byrons, nor do they themselves turn down their shirt-collars to be thought such. They have no remarkable vein of humour to boast of, never made a pun, perhaps, in their lives, scarcely know what an epigram is, are quite incapable of setting the table in a roar, and are distinguished neither for their fine clothes nor their long purses. One quality, however, they possess, which proves an over-match for every other distinction, namely, a transparent kindly nature, a desire to promote the happiness of all around them, a generous warmth of feeling, a frank cordial bearing, a universal sympathy—in one word, 'heart.'

It is refreshing, amidst the cold conventionalisms of the world, to meet with these men of 'heart,' or to see in any one developments of naturalness. He must be a misanthrope, indeed, who can witness without pleasure the hearty shake of the hand of two friends at an unexpected meeting after a long absence. What a mutual pouring out of soul, as it were, is there on both sides! What an infectious gladness is that which beams on their countenances! Who has not, with a fine chubby little fellow seated on his knee, listened with delight to his enthusiastic narration of some trivial incident which has been engrossing his interest? How his meaning sparkles in his full eyes, and struggles for utterance in his speaking features! What clumsy dull things words seem, to express those intense feelings which are welling up in his heaving bosom! What a charming development of 'heart' is there in that lisping eloquence! Who, again, has not felt charmed at the sight of an aged man romping with a child, and entering heartily into the sports and feelings of youth? Who has not admired the verdant old age of such a one, his feelings, unchilled by the freezing influences of threescore years and ten, still fresh and glowing as in his childhood; who has neither become so falsely wise nor so sourly proud as to disdain the sports and pleasures of his youth; and who, while he has learned to think as a man, has not forgotten to feel as a child? Who has not been gladdened, amid the monotony of the crowded street, with some manifestation of 'heart' in the sincere though perhaps awkward gallantry of some rough impetuous Irishman, in his efforts to succour helpless childhood or timid womanhood; or the powerful expression of natural feeling in some unsophisticated tar, vulgar perhaps in the estimation of ordinary beholders, but pleasant and refreshing to those who value the unrestrained utterings of nature beyond the mere tinsel affectation of art? Even among the lower animals, it is also observable that those in whom this quality is most apparent are our greatest favourites. The peacock, with his rainbow hues, and his magnificent train, excites in us but very cold emotions compared with those we experience at the sight of a robin on the hedge-top, or even the sober-suited sparrow in the garden. There seems to be a 'heart' about them of which the vain fop is destitute; the one we cannot refuse to admire, but the others we cannot do less than love.

This quality of 'heart' commends itself so powerfully to every one's best feelings, that its development is pleasing even to the most stoical, and needs only to be seen to be imitated. It is singular to observe sometimes the changed behaviour of the sons of pride and fashion in the presence of a man of 'heart.' How strangely will fashion forget its effeminate lispings, and blush for its own squeamishness, ready to forego the applause even of its butterfly circle, to hang upon the lips, and bask in the glad honest countenance, of one who is a disciple of nature! How out of love will it seem with its own sickly insipidity, how desirous to emancipate itself from the iron tyranny of its bondage, as it contemplates the moral robustness of one who dares to be natural! How uneasy often is bloated pride at its own fancied superiority, and how insensible, in spite of itself, will it change its freezing loftiness into affability in the presence of one whose manly independence of character and bold naturalness contrast so advantageously with its own hollow arrogance! How forcibly does every look, every expression, mirror forth to the proud man the unnaturalness of that character which he has unhappily assumed, and render him more pleased with the society of his warm-hearted companion of the hour than with that of his ordinary frivolous and heartless associates.

It is to be regretted that, in the education of the young, so much is done towards discouraging the natural manifestations of 'heart.' No sooner is the child able to understand, than it is taught not to make free with the servants; it must not associate with other children unless they are very 'respectable;' it must not laugh above a certain standard of loudness; and must obey a thousand other conventional laws which tend only to destroy naturalness in character, and substitute cunning, hypocrisy, pride, and a host of other hateful pests to private peace and social harmony. As the boy grows older he becomes still more artificial, frightened, as it were, at the shadow of his own feeling; he is taught to despise whatever is common, to hate what is vulgar; and that self-respect which, judiciously encouraged and wisely directed, might have been of the greatest use in inducing a becoming spirit and preserving from debasing pursuits, is pampered up into an arrogant and offensive pride. The public school completes the vicious education; the manly is forgotten in the 'gentlemanly;' honour, morality, duty, are words only used as texts for witless jokes; the stream becomes more contaminated as it recedes from the source; the youth grows older only to grow worse, and the dew-drops that gemmed the morning of life are

'Parched and dried up in manhood's noon.'

The confiding trust, the truthfulness, and the uncalculating generosity of youth, soon merge into the cold suspicious selfishness of manhood; the head is disciplined at the expense of the heart; and the boasted wisdom of age is but a poor substitute for that freshness of feeling which it was unhappily the first effort of education to discourage and eradicate.

To the manifestation of this quality some of our most favourite authors and poets chiefly owe their almost universal popularity. This has made them writers and poets for the mass, and rendered their thoughts and words familiar with all who read and think. Shakspeare, Goldsmith, Cowper, and Burns, stand conspicuous for the development of 'heart' in their writings—and whose writings are read more extensively, or retain more powerfully their hold on our affections and memory? Others, with acknowledged genius and undoubted learning, have a while glared, meteor-like, upon their wondering fellows, but they only dazzled the blinded eye for the passing hour; their light was rather the cold and lifeless radiance of the moon, than the warm life-giving brightness of the sun, and they have consequently been unsuccessful in gaining the affections or even the prolonged attention of the mass. To this cause, also, must be mainly ascribed the popularity of some of our musicians and ballad composers. Here consists the principal charm of Dibdin's songs—there is so much 'heart' in them; they vibrate upon the feelings, not of this or that conventional class of persons, but in the breast of common humanity. They are grounded upon the broad base of human nature, and consequently retain their hold on the affections of the people, while productions fully equal to them in musical and poetical merit have long since been forgotten. Here is the secret of the great influence which some preachers and senators have exerted over their hearers, and to the want of this quality must be mainly ascribed the little impression often produced by even the most laborious harangues. This is the leverage so powerful in the hands of the singer, and especially of the actor, and by which they call forth the smiles and tears of their audience at will.

In the female character, this quality of 'heart' is often seen developed to admiration, and where it exists, is more charming, and frequently proves more attractive to the other sex, than either beauty of countenance or symmetry of form. Though coupled with plain features, how often do we see those who possess this quality pair off into the matrimonial list before the handsome and the accomplished! How often, even when the rubicon of the 'teens' has been long passed, do we see one of these agreeable women, with her pleasure-diffusing smiles and animated manner, contrast with the greatest advantage with the lifeless insipidity and the haughty pretension of the merely beautiful and intellectual around her! And even when ruthless Time has bleached her flowing locks, and paled her roseate cheek, yet a woman with 'heart' is always a delightful companion, to be loved and honoured; there is still an atmosphere of joyous love around her; *her* years are undated; we miss not youth and beauty; we see no defects; the *tout ensemble* is loving and loveable; and young and old are alike charmed by her. Her cheerful smile, her sympathising look, her thousand kind offices—too minute to be described, but not too minute to be appreciated—so gentle, so unobtrusive, are all developments of 'heart' which insinuate themselves around our purest affections, and commend themselves to the affectionate admiration and reciprocation of the sterner sex.

LEGEND OF A FRENCH COOK.

A TALE OF THE FIFTEENTH CENTURY.

History supplies us with a rule to which there are very few exceptions. Both ancient and modern annals show that the eldest sons of kings reverse the order of nature, and are, very generally, their parents' opponents. Such was the case with Charles VI. of France, who, though so much beloved by his subjects as to be called *Le Bien Aimé*, had, in his eldest born, a rebel and a traitor. This undutiful son, however, on coming himself to the throne, was destined to feel a full measure of retribution. After having regained his kingdom—which the English, partly by his early treasons against his sire, had contrived to acquire—and settled down to enjoy his conquest in quiet, he found in *his* eldest son so bitter an enemy, that there was no crime which he believed the dauphin would not be guilty of to get rid of him. Hence the latter years of Charles VII. were spent in a constant dread of his son's machinations. The dauphin, knowing this terror to exist in his father's mind, took full advantage of it, and originated an unfounded report that his majesty's life was menaced. These rumours, artfully spread, were at first vague and indefinite. Presently they gained strength, and were conveyed to the ears of the king through so many different channels, and accompanied by so many apparent corroborations, that the unhappy monarch lived under the horrible expectation of being made the victim of certain slow but deadly poisons.

In proportion as the terrors of the king were manifested, so the insidious rumours gained strength and probability, until the majesty of France was brought to a state of existence like that of Tantalus; for, though surrounded by profusion, he dared not satisfy the cravings of hunger for fear of poison. His mind was a prey to suspicion. He looked on those courtiers whose duties brought them near to his person as a set of conspirators, sworn to put an end to his existence, and wondered each day which of them it was who had been selected to introduce the terrible drugs into his food; for, amidst all this misery, he was blessed with one gleam of satisfaction—the court cooks were incorruptible, and he knew that his death would never be compassed in the kitchen. But he dreaded his upper servants with an intensity that was likely to bring about the unusual catastrophe of a powerful king dying of want. After, however, some consideration, he hit upon a plan for obtaining his meals, which the unimpeachable fidelity of his cooks rendered practicable. There were four of them—the brothers Taillevent—descendants of an illustrious line of cooks, who had roasted, boiled, and fried for the royal family of France for three generations. These he distributed in his four domestic establishments at the palaces of Fontainbleau, Compiegne, Vincennes, and Beauté-sur-Marne. To one of these confidential cuisiniers he daily sent, by a trusty and secret messenger, a head of living game—but to *which* of them, was kept a profound secret from his court. The destined food was always accompanied with a letter of instructions as to how and when it was to be cooked. So scrupulous was he, that the royal epistle was sealed and directed (by the superannuated minister Tanneguy Ducâtel) in the writer's presence. By this contrivance no one ever knew where or when his majesty was going to dine—not even the selected cook himself—till a few hours before the king appeared to partake of his meal.

While his majesty was suffering from the tormenting dread of poison, the whole of Picardy rang with the miracles said to have been performed upon the sick by the medical skill of a monk named Didier, by his preaching, and by certain relics of St Bernadin, of which he was the fortunate possessor. During the Lent of 1454, this wonderful preacher was seen at Péronne, followed by twenty thousand proselytes, ten thousand of whom were cripples, and performed their discipleship on crutches. The grand object which he professed was, to reform the order of St Francis, by introducing the rules or 'observances' bequeathed by St Bernadin of Sienna (a recently canonised saint), and with the alms he collected from the sick and the pious, to found, build, and endow several new convents. Notwithstanding, however, all his popularity, and the potency of the relics he carried about, he was unable to collect sufficient funds for his purpose, and determined to apply to the king for assistance. Accordingly, on one of the earliest days of July, in the year of grace 1461, the monk, being in the neighbourhood of Fontainbleau, determined to look in upon his majesty, and endeavour to excite in him a holy zeal for his project. It happened that the king had dined there the day before; and brother Didier was fortunate enough to be granted an interview. The monk's fame for extraordinary sanctity had already reached the monarch's ears, and he was anxious to see a person whose object was to spread the rigid discipline and observances of the rigorous St Bernadin.

When Didier was announced, the half-starved monarch thought to have beheld a figure emaciated with penance and wan with fasting, who would be able to sympathise with him on the subject of abstinence. The monk entered, and the king almost started from his seat to behold a portly, plump, rosy-cheeked individual, who bore all the outward signs of an indulgence in the good things of this life, which his patron saint so strictly prohibited, and against which he himself so vehemently preached. Having, to give himself the greater ease, loosened the cord which confined his robe around his ample person, brother Didier, with a degree of self-possession much at variance with the humility imposed by the famous 'observances,' explained in detail all his plans regarding the new religious houses. His conversation was insinuating, and he plentifully mingled with it the sign of the cross. 'My dread sire,' he said, 'permit me to remind you that my most holy and blessed master, Bernadin of Sienna, having been by the papal court appointed vicar of the observance of St Francis to the Italian States, introduced his reform into three hundred religious establishments of that order during his lifetime. May the saint and your august majesty aid me in introducing the same reform into the twelve or fourteen monasteries and convents it is my sacred wish to found.'

The politeness of Charles the Victorious induced him to listen to the long-winded harangue, which was concluded as above; but it was quite evident he was thinking of something else. This was proved by the irrelevancy of his answer. 'You have, holy brother,' he remarked, 'made yourself famous for your skill in pharmacy. Pray, amongst your collections of drugs and simples, have you any antidotes?'

'Against what, an it please your illustrious majesty?'

'Poison,' replied the king with a shudder.

The gray eye of the monk twinkled beneath his bushy and downcast brows. He saw in this question a promising perspective of patronage and alms. 'My beloved seigneur,' he replied, 'I have preventives and antidotes for the most deadly poison that ever sprung through the earth from the lower regions (from which may Heaven in its mercy exempt your supreme highness), provided those who need them be filled with faith; and,' continued the wily monk, casting his eyes on a schedule of his monastic plans which he had placed before the king—'and provided they liberally engage in good works.'

The quick comprehension of Charles immediately saw the drift of the suppliant. The price of the antidote was to be a liberal contribution of cash and patronage; and from that moment he condescended to enter with warmth and zeal into a discussion of brother Didier's building schemes. In return for this, Didier promised his majesty a valuable relic, consisting of a bit of St Bernadin's robe, 'which,' said the monk, 'will protect your grace from the deadliest of poisons.'

The king accepted the promise with eager delight, and it was with some difficulty that Didier could get the conversation brought back to the patronage and alms. At length he succeeded.

'And as to the proposed monastery, it shall be established under our royal sanction as soon as may be. To-morrow,' continued the king, 'I——' here he suddenly checked himself, and, looking steadfastly at the monk, asked if he could trust him. 'With your life, sire,' was the loyal answer. 'Then,' said his majesty, 'I will confide to thee a secret.'

'It shall be kept as sacredly as the holy relics of St Bernadin,' replied the monk.

Charles looked round to see that no intruders were there, and said, speaking in the monk's ear, 'To-morrow I dine at my palace of Beauté!' It was some time before Didier could discover that *this* was the important secret; but when he was assured of it, he made fresh protestations of fidelity. 'Thither,' continued the king, 'do thou repair, and we will confer more fully on thy projects. Meantime I will furnish you with a letter to my father confessor. Wait here till it be brought.'

Charles retired to an inner room, occupied by his confidant and secretary, Ducâtel. As he had to despatch his dinner for the morrow to his cook, he sat down to write to Taillevent, with, as was usual, his own hand. The second letter to the father confessor at Beauté (Jean D'Aussy, almoner of France, and bishop of Langres), which Didier was to take, being of far less importance, he merely dictated to Ducâtel. The epistle to the cook ran thus:—

'Master Taillevent, on pain of death, be secret! It is my royal will that to-morrow—which will be Thursday, the day of St Loup—I shall sup at my chateau of Beauté. To this end I send you the accompanying live game; and you will kill it about an hour after sunrise. In the dressing and serving thereof, you will eschew the use of rose-water, verjuice, milk, ginger-wine, marjoram-sauce, salt, butter, or other things which may have been adulterated out of the kitchen; for I know that the wicked poisoners are again conspiring against me. Such is our royal will: whereof fail not. CHARLES.'

Didier's letter of introduction to the royal almoner, then staying at Beauté, was as follows:—

'Messire Jean D'Aussy, I send you a holy person whom I love and esteem; do not be surprised. I desire that he be hospitably entertained by you in my chateau of Beauté with all honour and the greatest secrecy. I have high and mighty designs in reference to this noble bird, who seeks to build a holy nest for the faithful. May Heaven preserve thee in health. CHARLES.'

His majesty's haste to despatch Didier, and to ratify the bargain for the relic, was very great, and the old secretary was so flurried, that he sent an equerry with a caged bittern to the bishop of Langres, and accredited the monk to Monsieur Taillevent, the cook.

The right reverend the father Jean D'Aussy, bishop of Langres, and confessor to Charles the Victorious, was seated at his studies in an apartment of the chapel-ward of the palace of Beauté-sur-Marne, when the equerry appeared bearing in one hand a letter, and in another a cage. On seeing that the letter was sealed with the *fleur-de-lis*, which no hand but that of his majesty was allowed to impress, the confessor hastened to open it, and to devour its contents, in which, however, he was much interrupted by the fluttering, screaming, scratching, and biting of the prisoned bittern. He could scarcely believe his eyes; he looked at the letter, and then at the occupant of the cage, and asked the equerry if he were sure no human being accompanied him. The reply was, that his only companion was in the cage, and an extremely troublesome one he had proved. 'Was this the holy person? Impossible!'

A little reflection, however, brought an inference into the priest's mind, which he feared would be disloyally expressed in his countenance, and telling the messenger to set down the bird, he bade him retire. Jean D'Aussy then re-read the missive, in the hope of proving to himself that his royal master was *not* insane, and began a series of erudite reflections concerning the sanctification of animals. He remembered the bird Ziz, spoken of by the Rabbs Bar Bar Channa in the Talmudic legends, and also the sacred cock, which is said to have saved the life of the prophet Akeba; but as these were, he verily believed, traditions of most suspicious origin, he rejected them as evidence in favour of the holiness of the winged wretch before him. He carefully turned over in his capacious memory the writings of all the Christian fathers, but could not find any warrant for the sanctification of either eagles, cocks, or bitterns; at length he could resist the unpleasant inference no longer, and came to the painful conclusion, that continued fasting had turned the king's brain. Still he dared not disobey the will of his liege lord, and proceeded to entertain the 'holy bird' hospitably, by thrusting from time to time some crumbs of bread between the bars of the cage, at the imminent risk of his fingers.

The eve of the festival of St Loup, in the year 1461, was excessively hot, and while Father D'Aussy was suffering from this perplexity, the illustrious* Taillevent, who had the honour of presiding over the kitchen of Beauté-sur-Marne, paced up and down his dominion, wearied of having nothing to do, and so thirsty that he was obliged to recruit exhausted nature occasionally with huge draughts of hypocràs and spiced wine. Ever and anon he reviewed the shining pots and pans, ranged in rows along the walls, with the pride of a general sur-

* We use this term advisedly, for the head cook to Charles VII. is a historical personage; and as the history of cookery forms a part of the history of France, several notices have been preserved of him. He is most celebrated for being the earliest author on the subject of his art since the invention of printing. Several years after the events recorded in the above historiette, he gave to the world a concise and learned treatise, entitled 'Viandier pour appareiller toutes mannières de viands, que Taillevent, queux de roy notre sire fist, tout pour habillier, est appareiller boully rousty,' &c. (The way of dressing all manner of meats, as practised by Taillevent, cook to our sovereign the king, &c. &c.) This was one of the earliest works which was printed from metal types in France.

veying his forces, and with something of his regret in times of peace, when no use could be made of so fine an army. 'By the feasts of St Boniface,' exclaimed the corpulent kitchen-man, 'things were not thus in the time of Charles V. of blessed memory. In his day the royal hearths *never* cooled—not even in ember weeks or vigils. But now our chicken-hearted king, his grandson, fasts like a hermit! And when he does eat, it is something hardly worthy of a beggar's wallet; some tough crane or old bittern, or anything his gamekeepers choose to send him alive. Possibly to-morrow he will send me a wild boar, or a rhinoceros, to be served up for the royal digestion.'

While he was thus soliloquising in the dusk, something nearly as large as the animals he had mentioned entered the apartment. On perceiving the apparition, the cook's first instinct was to seize the cutlass-like knife which was stuck into his girdle, to exercise his office on the beast, which, by some supernatural agency, had, he imagined, seconded his thoughts. As, however, he perceived, on closer inspection, that it stood upon two legs instead of four, and that it could speak, he was convinced that he had made a mistake.

'Are you Master Taillevent?' inquired our friend the Franciscan monk, reading the superscription of the epistle.

'I am,' replied the cook, sheathing the knife. 'What is your will?'

'Read this and you will learn,' returned Didier, surprised that the king should have commended him to a man of such humble station. As the cook read the royal missive, the monk watched his large, dull, inexpressive features, endeavouring to glean from them some clue to the mystery. 'Well,' asked Taillevent, folding up the letter, and tucking it inside his belt, 'where is the game—the bird?'

The monk's surprise increased, and observing a twinkle in the cook's eye, he thought he could perceive the germ of a practical joke which was being played upon him. 'A bird?' he echoed. 'Hark ye, Master Saucemaker, if any one presumes to shoot jests at me, let him understand it will be jeering the head of the church, seeing that I am the representative of his holiness.'

At these words a thought entered Taillevent's head which somewhat troubled him: he re-opened the letter—read it carefully again. 'By the crock of St Andouillard,' he muttered to himself, 'am I to be degraded from the office of master-cook to that of butcher or executioner? Yet the command is as plain and express as it is terrible. Tell me, reverend father,' he inquired aloud, to make himself quite sure, 'have you really brought no animal or bird, wild or tame, for me to cook?'

'Forsooth no, Sir Jester; I bring nothing but your royal master's command to treat me with all hospitable courtesy; forasmuch as in me you behold the patron of the order of the observance, and possessor of the relics of Monsieur St Bernadin of Sienna.'

The small eyes of Monsieur Taillevent were turned towards the speaker, and he gazed on Didier with the critical scrutiny he usually employed on surveying a fatted ox or pig. 'Alas, alas!' he exclaimed, slowly shaking his ponderous head, 'my holy victim, say your paternosters—make your private supplications—you have only till an hour after daybreak to-morrow for this world. This way if you please!' The cook, with a doleful countenance, conducted Father Didier into a buttery with nearly the same feelings that would have possessed him on driving a fat ox into the stall of a shambles. The monk entered willingly enough, when he perceived in the small apartment two things which comforted his inner man—a couch, and a rich collection of eatables; for he was both tired and hungry. The strange words and manner of his host, however, gave him some very uncomfortable presentiments, and these were much increased when the door was closed, and the key turned upon him. 'A person—a servant of the church, too—under the king's protection,' he exclaimed, 'and a prisoner! Can it be?' In his perplexity he kicked at the door, and shouted, insisting, with threats, on being let out. But he might as well have called for help in the cave of St Anthony. No one answered him. At length, tired of this exercise, he surveyed the viands so temptingly arrayed on the table and shelves of the buttery, and felt there would be no difficulty in passing away the time. He immediately set to work. He began with a caviar (or pie made of sturgeon's roe), and having devoured about half of it, he directed his attention to an ample bowl of *coscoton*, or beef-soup, thickened with flour. Feeling this to be hardly solid enough, he passed on to a leg of mutton with onion-sauce; then filled up the crevices with a few pickings of stewed pigeons *à l'eau bénite*, and a larded quail; finishing the meal with a quince tart, and a cream *au miel*. When he had washed down this well-selected snack with a flask of Brétagne, and some half-dozen bumpers of Malmsey, a blast of the warder's horn announced it was midnight, and he was delighted to find that he had beguiled away five hours of his imprisonment pleasantly enough. Upon this he dozed off into a digestive sleep.

Meanwhile, Taillevent kept widely, wretchedly, painfully awake. He did not attempt to retire to his couch, for he knew he could not sleep. Though a cook who had been obliged to do a little butchering of late, in consequence of his royal master's whim of having the killing and dressing of his food performed on the same day, yet he was not devoid of sensibility. A plump partridge, or even a well-fed swine, would have been more in his way; but a monk!—he really was not equal to it. Besides, it would be flat sacrilege.

Thus perplexed and agitated, the unhappy artist read and re-read his instructions; but, after hours spent thus, he could only put the worst construction on his sovereign's letter. 'It must be so,' he muttered; 'this sleek churchman has been found out in some diabolical design against the crown of France—has in all probability made some desperate attempt on my beloved master's life. Still, my sovereign aforesaid hath put my love and devotion to a terrible test. But as it is my duty, I must obey him. This ill-favoured animal must pay the forfeit of his misdeeds. Parblieu!' These reflections were interrupted by loud snores from the buttery, and the pity of the cook was awakened anew. The whole of that night he was a prey to contending passions. According as they agitated him, he wept for or denounced the monk; so that sometimes he sighed, and sometimes he whetted his knife.

By daylight he had fully convinced himself that it was his duty to become the executioner of his guest; and with agitated steps, eyes still wet with weeping, and a cutlass exquisitely sharpened, he softly unlocked the door of the buttery. Its occupant did not notice him, for he was busily breakfasting off the remains of his last night's supper. The cook, who was really an enthusiast, paused on the threshold, feeling it impossible to interrupt a man who was doing such honour to his art. As he surveyed the extraordinary satisfaction with which Didier smacked his lips, his former indecision returned; and when, after taking a first taste of a *croquille de veau panné*, the epicure patted his stomach, and uttered an elongated and intensely-approving 'Ha-a!' the naked weapon fell from Taillevent's hand. The noise of its descent on the floor attracted Didier's attention, and arrested his jaws just as they were going to close upon the tiddest of bits: open-mouthed, he stared first at the cook, and then at the cutlass; he trembled violently, and nearly choked himself by attempting to swallow a whole snipe at a mouthful.

'No,' thought Taillevent, 'it cannot be. There must be some mistake. A man who is blessed with so great a relish for good cheer, and who has so fine a taste for the cook's art, cannot be a traitor. The king must have been deceived: besides, if he suspect him, why did he not have him regularly tried by his court of parliament? Let me again recollect what is due to my office, a-master-cook. Shall I disgrace it by assassinating one of the best eaters in Christendom? Never!'

After Didier had managed to swallow the snipe, he watched his companion's countenance, and eyed the naked cutlass with great anxiety. The cook determined to end the perplexity by showing the monk the king's letter. He was horror-stricken! He had heard much of the duplicity of princes, but in this case it had reached its acmé. He was, moreover, horribly afraid: his nerves were so shaken by the disclosure, that he trembled like a jelly. In a paroxysm of dread he fell down before the cook on his knees, and intreated him to be so obliging as not to kill him just then.

'By the chitterlings of Troyes!' exclaimed Taillevent, assisting the good father to rise, 'I will neither kill thee nor prepare thee for the spit, albeit I am commanded by my august master to do so, on pain of death. But shall the sovereign of France turn cannibal, and eat monk's flesh? Not, by St Dunstan, while I rule the roast at Beauté-sur-Marne.' These words were scarcely out of the cook's mouth, before the monk attempted to embrace him, and was only prevented by his own and his companion's corpulency.

'But,' asked Taillevent, 'how am I to save my own neck for this disobedience of the king's orders?' This was a poser, and the monk, to clear his ideas, took a long draught of the Madeira. After a moment's musing, he joyfully patted Taillevent on the back, declaring he had 'hit it;' and forthwith began to propose a scheme by which Charles VII.'s orders might be partly executed without the unpleasant alternative of bloodshed.

By five o'clock that evening the monk and the cook had entered into a compact of the warmest friendship. Indeed, it may be remarked in passing, that there has existed from the earliest ages a very close alliance between these two fraternities. The execution of Didier's scheme was completed just as the blast of distant horns announced the approach of his majesty.

When the king arrived, he appeared sad and dejected—no wonder, for he had been afraid to eat since the preceding mid-day. He ordered his dinner to be instantly served, and while he was going into the *tinnel*, or eating-room, he encountered the bishop, his confessor. He drew his ear closely to him, and asked, 'Well, what of the holy person I sent thee?'

'He is, in truth, a noble bird, my lord,' answered the priest; 'but if I may be so bold as to ask, *hath* he really given any special proofs of sanctity?'

'Assuredly. Hast thou never heard of the ten thousand cripples who followed him into Péronne? Return, holy father, and bring him to me, that the sanctity of St Bernadin's relics may be near me during my repast.' The wondering bishop retired to do the king's bidding.

On entering the dining-hall, Charles started with a sort of affright at beholding an enormous pie, which formed the centre-piece of the repast. Turning to the trembling Taillevent, he exclaimed, 'How now, sir cook; have I, think you, a hundred English troopers in my train to attack this enormous pie? Say, sirrah, has the bittern which I sent thee from Fontainbleau been duly dressed?'

'Alack, dread seigneur, I did the best I could with the game you wot of; I never dressed the like dish before.'

While the king was breaking the seal of some bread (for every article brought to table was sealed by Taillevent, for fear of poison being introduced into it), a terrible screaming was heard, and presently the holy Father D'Aussy appeared with the bittern—which had somehow escaped from the cage—hanging on his arm by its bill, which it had dug deeply into the unfortunate almoner's flesh. 'See, see, my lord,' he exclaimed in his agony, 'how the sacred brute bites!'

'What means this?' asked the sovereign, suspecting treason, and turning to the cook. 'An the bittern be still alive, what is in the pie?'

Presently the crust of the huge pasty rose, and a man's head made its appearance, then his shoulders, lastly his whole body. It was brother Didier, who, seeing the fright he had caused the king, fell on his knees in the middle of the pie, like a saint in a niche, and presented the majesty of France with two reeking dishes. This unexpected occurrence drew forth peals of laughter from those who saw the unexpected turn the adventure had taken. The king himself condescended to conceal the intense fright he was in, by joining in the hilarity of his court. Taillevent fell on his knees, and, presenting the letter Didier had brought him, implored forgiveness for the freak; the whole blame and concoction of which he threw upon the friar. Charles extended the royal pardon; but, on learning that the good old Ducatel had been the cause of the blunder, presented him on the spot with a handsome superannuation pension.

Would we could end our story with this ludicrous adventure; but history has willed it otherwise. Not even the relic of St Bernadin, which Charles obtained from the monk, not the fidelity of the brothers Taillevent, nor common sense, could banish the dread which Charles VII. had imbibed of poison, and he died a very short time after (namely, on the 22d July 1461) at Meun-sur-Yevre, in the province of Berri, from debility and exhaustion, brought on by overmuch abstinence. When this event happened, he was fifty-nine years old.

As to Father Didier, he went about collecting alms for years afterwards, though, whether he ever applied the proceeds to a monastic foundation, history does not state. Taillevent lived, as we have before noted, to become an author, and one of the celebrities of the fifteenth century.

HEALTH OF TOWNS.

AIR, VENTILATION, WATER, DRAINAGE.

In a former article on the report of the Health of Towns Commission, we proposed to notice some of the measures which might, and doubtless will be adopted as remedies for the existing evils. We hear that the commission is likely to publish another volume, in which these remedies will be distinctly explained; meanwhile, the matter before us affords ample material for a brief discussion of the evidence, which in no instance is more precise or positive than on the points involving due supplies of water and air. We are accustomed, superficially speaking, to consider our national progress as something far beyond all that has preceded it of a similar nature. But when we come to look beneath the surface—to turn aside from the polished street or the broad highway—and inquire into the condition of the swarming millions who toil, and know no respite from their earliest breath to their latest sigh—we are rebuked and abashed. We there find the existence of evils which have long been regarded as inseparable from civil progress: they are, like the air we breathe, everywhere; and as common objects excite but little attention, they have not been thought worthy—if thought of at all—the trouble of investigation. The slight remove from a state of barbarism, as regards the nation at large, cannot be better illustrated than in the imperfect arrangements existing for the distribution of water, for ventilation, and drainage. Water is regarded, and justly, as one of nature's cheap and simple, yet highly efficacious agents in the maintenance of health: most persons regard water as a very useful liquid: we require it for cleanliness, economy, and morality. A dirty population—they who cannot, if they would, remove the impurities from their persons or their garments—will always be found depraved and immoral. The report gives us several instances of families leaving the open country, the green fields, and leafy lanes, driven by want of work and food to settle down in some dark and polluted alley in London. At first they clean and sweep their houses and doorways with laudable perseverance; but the ceaseless accumulation of filth, the unwholesome influences around them, soon break down their energies; their rosy cheeks become pale; and at last they sink into the common mass of the haggard and the wretched. Their pure and healthful excitement being gone, they seek to renew it by gin-drinking, to which their poverty is often attributed, when, in many cases, it is the result, and not the cause. 'A people may exhibit qualifications for which mere outward cleanliness of habit would be a poor exchange; but in that minor virtue there is always one great advantage, that its existence checks the career of degradation at a certain point. Religion, morality, education, have their higher spheres of protection; but when none of these is at hand, in this despised virtue there is a check before the utmost stage is reached.'* Mr Cubitt, in his evidence, says that 'the more cleanly the people become, the more anxious are they to get rid of offensive accumulations; and it appears to me that people become, by living in a very dirty place, very much degraded; and, on the other hand, they improve if the place is kept clean about them.'

All the evidence bearing on the supply of water to towns goes to prove the extreme cheapness with which it may be afforded. Mr Robert Thom states, that, in small towns, a family of five individuals may be supplied for about 1s. 4d. per annum. In Greenock and Paisley, where the pipes are kept constantly full, the charges are 2s. 6d. and 2s. 9d. respectively, for the same period. And here a fact is elicited, to which attention should be drawn, and that is, the economy and advantage of keeping the pipes, including the branches to every house, constantly full at the proper pressure. The effect of the economy does not benefit the landlord and tenant alone, but the water company also. Where alternate supplies are delivered, and the system of fixing tanks, ball-cocks, &c. in the houses is carried out, an expenditure of capital on the part of the landlord and tenant is involved, altogether unnecessary, and equal in some cases to that of the company. In addition to this, there is the saving of room occupied by the tank. 'In many houses, where there is no convenience for a tank in the upper part of the house, it is placed in a lower apartment, and the water must be borne up stairs for use; the labour incurred necessarily restricts the free employment of the water for many purposes to which it might be beneficially and healthfully employed. Another, and a very serious inconvenience, affecting the habits and sanitary condition of the population, attendant on the system of partial or occasional supply is, that it creates an inconvenience and an obstacle to the use of baths. With a constant supply of water at sufficient pressure, baths might be supplied in private houses with little difficulty or expense, so little, indeed, that I believe it to be practicable, and hope yet to see baths introduced into the houses of labouring men for the use of themselves and families.'† In poor districts, among a working population, but little time is devoted to the cleansing of their butts or cisterns; they are often altogether neglected; and being uncovered, are exposed to many sources of impurity, which render the water unfit for use: the loss of time in cleansing, and the deterioration of the water, would be immediately and effectually prevented by the arrangement of keeping the pipes constantly full. 'One experienced man, and one boy of about eighteen years of age, are, on the system of constant supply, quite sufficient to manage the distribution of the supply to about 8000 tenements, and keep all the works of distribution in perfect repair.'‡ The charge for a small house is stated to amount to about 1d. per week: rather more than 5000 tenements are supplied on these terms, no restrictions being made as to the quantity the occupiers shall consume. Before the water was laid on in Nottingham, the poorer classes were compelled to purchase water at the rate of ¼d., and sometimes ½d. per bucketful. If they chose to fetch water for themselves, instead of buying it, the necessary labour, at the rate of three journeys a-day, would be worth 3d. per week; 'but the company carries into every house 79 gallons for a farthing; and delivers water night and day, at every instant of time that it is wanted, at a charge twenty-six times less than the old delivery by hand.' The increase of personal cleanliness in the town, when the water was first laid on, is described as 'very marked indeed; it was obvious in the streets. The medical men reported that the increase of cleanliness was very great in the houses, and that there was less disease. There was also an advantage in the removal of the assemblages round the public pumps.' The observation, that it would be difficult to persuade the poor to pay for a supply of water, is thus replied to:—'When the company introduced the uninterrupted supply at Nottingham, the poorest tenants required it of their landlords; the landlords then said, "If you will consent to pay an additional penny per week of rent, we will try to arrange it with the company." This was the case in thousands of instances. The charge was in these cases made upon the landlord, and he put it upon his rent, and the tenant most cheerfully paid it.'

Mr Liddle states, that where the water is not led into the house, it is vain to expect that any extra trouble will be taken, on the part of the inmates, to fetch a proper supply. 'It is only done for the most urgent purposes; cleanliness is entirely neglected, and their persons and clothes remain in a most dirty state. The smell of their linen, when they give me a towel, which they tell me is quite clean, is most offensive. Their clothes are pressed through dirty water, to avoid the trouble of going out to fetch water. If proper measures were carried out for the removal of cesspools, and abundant supplies of pure water carried into the houses to every floor, and, if required, to every room, I see no reason to doubt that the health of the labouring classes might be made quite as good as that of the better classes, and that it is practicable to do so. Drainage, supplies of water, and ventilation, would extensively diminish existing mortality.' In this gentleman's evidence, we have a further illustration of the advantages of cleanliness; he quotes an instance of a filthy court, never free from disease, that was paved and supplied with the means of being kept constantly clean; there were 41 cases of sickness in the court in the seven months previous to the improvement, while in five subsequent months the cases of sickness were but two. The rent is at the same time better paid; and the landlord finds that he has benefited himself by the outlay, in addition to the improvement in the health of his tenants.

It appears that the low charge for water, already mentioned, might be very materially reduced by the substitution of pipes made of fire-clay for those of iron in ordinary use; these, which have been proved to resist a pressure equal to a perpendicular column of water of 900 feet, may be laid down at one-half of the usual expense; while they possess the advantage of being fit for immediate use, which is not the case with iron, owing to the rust and tarred yarn used in making the joints.

We come now to the suggestions for the adoption of water-closets in all classes of houses, in place of the ordinary receptacles, which are particularly prejudicial to health, as they sap and destroy the foundations of houses, permeate the earth in every direction, rendering the water of wells offensive and injurious, besides poisoning the atmosphere with noxious exhalations. The expense of a glazed earthen soil-pan connected with the house-drain and the sewer, fitted with a tap and the necessary apparatus in a cheap form, supposing the water to be constantly on, would not be more than 2½d. weekly; one half of the charge incurred by the use and emptying of cesspools, and utterly insignificant when compared with

* Tait's Magazine; December 1841.
† T. Hawksley, Esq. ‡ Ibid.

the amelioration of health that would accrue from their use. It is stated that the new apparatus has been introduced in Glasgow and other manufacturing towns, and in London into the dwellings of the working-classes, who express their satisfaction with the arrangement, and are eager to avail themselves of it.

With such facts as these before them, it can hardly be supposed that the authorities will hesitate to recommend the immediate application of the obvious remedies: the evidence is too conclusive as to the fearful sacrifice of life, mind, and body, under the existing evils, to suffer from contradiction: it is of no use attempting to deny or disguise the facts; there they are: how long they shall remain, depends on the nation at large.

The effluvia created by imperfect drainage not only operate prejudicially on the public health, but tend also to deteriorate the value of property; rows of convenient houses are built, but being situated near stagnant ditches, or open drains, no respectable tenants will remain in them. 'My tenants have repeatedly complained of the open sewer not only as a nuisance, but of serious illness occasioned by the stench arising from it. Were it not for the sewer, I could get a better class of tenants for these houses than the present occupants; as it is, I am obliged to let the houses to poor families who depend upon lodgers for the payment of their rent, and those lodgers are continually leaving from illness. Only ten days ago one of my tenants said to me, "Sir, it is impossible to let my best rooms; every person who lives in them is taken ill." This is not a solitary case; in the neighbourhood of Bethnal Green there are many open ditches which serve as sewers, the exhalations from which affect the surrounding houses with typhus fever. Whatever may be left undone, such nuisances should not be suffered to exist an hour.'* Sewers and drains are, however, useless without a proper supply of water. 'The finest formed sewers, and the best arrangement of them, would be of no use without an adequate supply of water. The drains but furnish the ways or vehicles for transportation; the water is the moving power or carrier, and it is the cheapest that can be procured. In fact, the supply of water to a town, and the discharge of the refuse, are two branches of the same subject, and unless the water be abundant enough, and distributed enough to cleanse the drains, these last would be more offensive than useful.'†

The importance of water as an element of health will justify the space we have given to the discussion of the arrangements into which it enters. there are, however, many other points of the evidence worthy of notice, to which we can give no more than a hasty glance: one of the most striking is, 'the desultory manner in which new streets are planned, which prevents sufficient drains being made. No houses ought to be built within or near a populous town, until a proper approach thereto has been made by a street or road, paved or macadamised. This arrangement would lessen the cost of building by the facility of conveying materials, and tenants would prefer houses with good approach and sufficient drainage.'‡ 'Experience has amply proved that the necessary precaution for health, comfort, and cleanliness, has been, and will be, neglected by the public. Ignorance of the requisite preventives, and the interference of conflicting local interests, which, after the London fire, prevented the adoption of Sir Christopher Wren's admirable scheme, have always since that time, and will further continue to prevail in baffling the efforts made towards improvement by the enlightened minority. There seems every reason to believe that, unless public provision be made to obtain efficient drainage, the same effects will continue to depress the health and deteriorate the property of all classes, pressing particularly heavy on the poorer classes, who cannot protect themselves. In the canvassing of the respective merits of various plans, ventilation of the streets and buildings, and the reservation of public walks and open spaces, should hold a most important place. It is really surprising to witness with what complete disregard of these considerations new districts, built for working men and manufacturing classes, are designed. While the public concur to a man in lamenting the past neglect on this point, it seems that for all, except the habitations of the wealthy, its importance is yet completely disregarded in practice. To secure ventilation, the streets should be straight, and should radiate from a centre; they will then open directly on the surrounding country; thereby the air will be most readily and continuously changed, and the pure atmosphere of the fields will rush directly through the town, attenuating the noxious gases, and revivifying the used air.'*

We shall conclude this article with a few observations on ventilation, an operation which yields to none in importance or beneficial results. A very simple and economical ventilation is described by Mr Toynbee, which 'consists of a plate of zinc, very finely perforated with two hundred and twenty holes to an inch. Their size varies from four to twelve inches square, according to the size and construction of the room. They are generally introduced in the uppermost portion of the window, and in the corner pane the farthest from the fireplace. These fine orifices prevent the air coming in with a rush, which would occasion discomfort, and tend to diffuse the air equally and gently throughout the apartment. The expense of these ventilators, with the fixing, is about 2s. The general observation of those who have tried them is, that the room is much more comfortable and airy; they have frequently said that they have been in much better spirits since they have had these ventilators, and have always been most grateful for them. In one house I have put ten ventilators on the stairs and landing, and the whole of the people there express a very high sense of the comfort they have experienced. In one of the rooms the smell was so bad that I could not enter into or remain in it, unless the windows were opened. I can now go there without annoyance.

Two thousand years ago, Hippocrates wrote on the importance of pure air; and all the observations made since that time, have confirmed the views of the early philosopher. We cannot see the air we breathe, and are not, in consequence, sufficiently alive to the condition in which we breathe it. Dr Harwood observes, that 'the want of wholesome air does not manifest itself on the system so unequivocally or imperatively; no urgent sensation being produced like that of hunger; and hence the greater danger of mistaking its indications. The effects of its absence are only slowly and insidiously produced, and thus too frequently are overlooked, until the constitution is generally impaired, and the body equally enfeebled.' Dr James Johnson, speaking of the effects of impure air, says, 'that ague and fever, two of the most prominent features of the malarious influence, are as *a drop of water in the ocean*, when compared with the other less obtrusive but more dangerous maladies that silently disorganise the vital structure of the human fabric, under the influence of this deleterious and invisible poison.'

There is one fact relating to ventilation which distinguishes it from the question of supply of water, drainage, &c.; it may be, without delay, made serviceable to all: let those who are suffering from stagnant air and confined rooms simply open the door and window occasionally to allow a current of air to pass through, and they will find the good effects in the improvement of their health and spirits. 'The renewal of the air is not so light a matter as is supposed. To effect it, a *simple communication is not sufficient*—a mere contact of the external and internal air. It is necessary that one or more currents exist to multiply that contact, and cause the pure air to pervade that which is vitiated.'

Legislative enactments are sometimes good; but self-

* W. E. Hickson, Esq. † Captain Vetch, R. E.
‡ Mr Sopwith.

* Butler Williams, Esq.

dependence and exertion are still better. Let every one exert himself to remove the evils within his own sphere, and the task of the government will be comparatively easy.

SHORT NOTES ON THE WEST INDIES.

BY A LATE RESIDENT.

FOURTH ARTICLE.

Houses of Assembly.—Until that apple of discord, the emancipation question, was thrown into the Houses of Assembly, the work of legislation, I have been informed, assumed the simplest form possible. Some leading man, conceiving a particular evil required a particular remedy, would proceed to the house with a bill in his pocket, and there propound it. It would be passed, probably without amendment—at any rate without anything approaching to discussion or debate. It was left for modern times to elicit the spark of oratory which lay smothered within the bosoms of our colonial orators. There is now as much talking in the Houses of Assembly as there is any occasion for, and sometimes more than is consistent with a proper discharge of the public business. On all occasions, however, strict adherence to parliamentary usage is maintained, and 'Hatsel' quoted as a work of standing authority.

I have been present at the bar of a House of Assembly for many consecutive nights, and for many succeeding sessions, but I do not recollect an occasion, where a question arose peculiarly affecting the *people* and a strong *contest* of party ensued, that the liberal (that is, the anti-slavery) portion of the house came off victorious. Some doubt may naturally exist whether there is, in the West Indies, a fair, that is, an equal, representation. I have also stood at the bar of a House of Assembly, and observed the individual interests of the members swaying their deliberations, as a current of wind would the waters of a standing pool. The planter has wished for this, the grazier has sought for that, the merchant has desired the other, and then, as the force of a rising public opinion, or the expressed or obvious wish of the government has been brought to bear upon the discussion, those individual interests have been all forced to merge in some measure calculated for the general good. I will not say that this has often occurred, but this I have seen. The newly emancipated have not yet had a full opportunity of showing what description of representatives they would return; but they anticipate it will soon occur, as the termination of the first septennial parliament of the present reign is near.

The squabbles which were once so common between the Houses of Assembly and the representatives of majesty have gradually diminished within the last few years; occasionally, we have some account of a rupture, and of members being sent to their constituents. When this happens, however, the style in which each party addresses the other is no longer indecent, insulting, or outrageous.

Home.—The word 'home' is as expressive in the colonies as it is in England; but unfortunately for the former, all its force is centered in the mother country. 'Home,' in fact, is the word used expressly to designate Great Britain. The merchant will say that he receives his consignments from 'home;' the planter that he ships his produce 'home;' the young Creole that he expects to take a trip 'home;' and thus it goes on to the last person who may have occasion to refer to the mother country—often to those who never expect to see it—very frequently to those who have no friends or connexions residing there. This I take to arise, with reference to one class of persons, from the fact, that they contemplate going or returning to the mother country so soon as they have attained a competency, and, with reference to another, that there is little in the colonies to excite in their minds the idea of the endearing ties attached to the word 'home'—many of them having either heard of or experienced the immense moral, civil, and social advantages possessed by Great Britain. Their affections become thus engaged, and they give the most endearing name to that place to which those affections cling. Others, again, use the expression from custom, from fashion, or otherwise; but from whatever cause, among all classes it is common. This may enable us to form some idea of the nature of the estimation in which the mother country is held, and of the interest which is taken in all proceedings there, whether political or otherwise. With reference to politics, the colonies are generally as much affected by the success or defeat of a ministry, as if their own existence depended upon either. This may appear natural enough, but it is really not so; for, whatever the ministry, the government of the colonies usually remains the same, probably for this reason, that they have no voice at home, or but a very feeble one. Once only, as far as I am aware, was this estimation in which the mother country is held somewhat shaken, and that was when the discussion of the slave question reached its climax. It was then gravely canvassed in certain circles whether the colonies should not be put under the protection of America. Such a measure would have been opposed to the death by the coloured and black classes, who hate the Americans; but it shows that the good feeling which had prevailed with reference to the mother country was somewhat lessened; whether justly so or not, we will not stay to inquire.

Many good results no doubt arise from this engrossing affection towards the mother country; but one evil effect induced is, that no general attempt is made by the inhabitants of the colonies to improve their institutions, or to increase their moral, social, or intellectual resources. Few good works originate with them, or, if originated, are brought to completion, because parties do not contemplate the enjoyment of any improvement that might be made. Hence again the absence of all public spirit. It is not thus in the French West India colonies, which are universally admitted as taking a higher stand than the British in moral, social, and intellectual advancement. When the Frenchman leaves his native country for the colonies, he makes the latter his 'home;' and casting few lingering regrets to the old world, he endeavours to render the new as comfortable as his means will allow. As the attempt is half the victory, he seldom fails. I fear little improvement in the respect here commented on will take place with us, until the 'old things shall have become new,' and the now rising generation shall have made some further progress in the attainment of knowledge, of conscious importance, and wealth. Not that I would have them hereafter to regard the mother country with less affection, but the colonies, the place of their birth, with the greater.

Negro Preaching.—There are negro 'preachers' or parsons in the West Indies of the dissenting persuasion, who attract large congregations of their own class; but I am not in a situation to form an opinion on the extent of their theological learning, or the general nature of their discourses. Passing one of their conventicles on one occasion, I stayed for about two minutes to listen to the preacher who was then delivering his sermon. He was in the act of comparing the Bible to a mirror, in which every individual may view himself reflected, and I thought he discharged himself creditably of his task. One original character I have heard of, who seems to give some verity to the caricatures we sometimes see in the print-shops of London on the subject of negro sermons. He had been, and probably continued to be, a fisherman, and would illustrate his discourses by circumstances or ideas connected with his calling. Dilating on the nature and extent of Job's patience, he would say, 'My bredren, you been yerry 'bout Job. Berry well. You want pe yerry what da Job-pashance? Me will tell you. Fisherman go out all night—him fish—fish—fish—tä daybroke, and no mo ketch so, so tree prat. Him come home—him put him tree prat 'pon top-a-house fe dry. Jan-Cro' come, tèk one—berry well—Jan-Cro' come, tèk nada—him come tird time, take tarra. De prat all gone—but fisherman no say "—— —— Jan-Cro'!" Dat da Job-pashance!'

Climate.—Most Europeans entertain dreadful ideas relative to the climate of the West Indies; but I am inclined to think that the climate has not only to bear the burden of its own sins, but also that of the sins of those who resort to it. Great mortality is found to exist in the army and navy stationed in the West Indies: the climate is at once adduced as the cause. Young men sent out as planters, or merchants' clerks, die in a short time: the climate is blamed. Parties do not reflect, or probably do not know, that soldiers and sailors are the most debauched classes in the West Indies; while parents do not bear in mind that the wildest and most hair-brained of their children was selected as he who should be shipped off; or who probably went of his own accord. I don't mean to infer that, to a European, the climate is as salubrious as that of his native country. Extreme changes are always dangerous, whether to the native of a temperate, or to the native of a torrid zone. But I would be understood to say, that a vast majority of the deaths which are attributed to climate should be set down to unsteadiness and intemperance. However strange it may appear, many Europeans, respectably and delicately nurtured, no sooner reach the colonies than they throw off all restraint, and pursue such courses of life as would at home procure them the character of reprobates. These die off, of course; but it is unreasonable to charge the climate with their death. Perhaps one of the most forcible arguments which may be used in favour of the view, that the climate is not as unhealthy as supposed, is the fact—I believe it is a fact—that European females do not fall sick and die in the same proportion with the males. They are not exposed, say some. Not so: they are temperate, and this secures them from the pernicious effects of the climate, as it secures males who are temperate also. A goodly number of European missionaries visit the West India colonies; but I have never heard it remarked that deaths among them are numerous. They are as much exposed to the effects of the climate as any body of men whose occupation is not that of manual labour in the fields, yet do they not die away as men in the army and navy. The secret undoubtedly is—they are temperate. Labour in the fields, under a burning sun, would certainly tell fearfully on the constitution of Europeans: again, however, there are certain localities which are not unfavourable to European labour,* the only difficulty being to confine Europeans to the spot. It was found impossible so to confine them; hence, with dissolute habits, the dreadful mortality which ensued. In the absence of anything which I can regard as correct data of the general unhealthiness of the climate—the circumstance that less care is necessary, and less actually taken, in the West Indies with relation to diet and clothing—that less fears are entertained relative to the approach of illness, so that, probably, not one tenth part of the medicines are taken which are taken in England—may lead to the presumption, that the natural causes of disease at anyrate are not so formidable as many suppose. The yellow fever seems to be the 'death's-head and bloody bones' of the colonies; for my own part, I think 'consumption' as fruitful a cause of death in England as the yellow fever has ever proved in the colonies: consumption, too, affects Europeans, while the yellow fever seldom visits the natives of the tropics.

Homage.—One of the natural results of slavery in the West Indies is a morbid love of homage and personal deference, which not only pervades the upper classes, but, by a process of imitation, even those who were the subjects of slavery. Respectable children are usually taught, or suffered by their parents, when called, to reply 'ma'am' and 'sir,' instead of the endearing appellations of 'mother' and 'father;' and wo would it have been to the poor slave who heedlessly forgot those first titles of respect. On the other hand, a young negro must not address an old one without adding the title of 'uncle' or 'anty,' 'goddie' or 'grandee,' 'daddy' or 'mammy,' unless he wishes to offend in the grossest manner possible. It is no doubt this feeling which leads many of them to be excessively annoyed when addressed with an opprobrious or slighting epithet. Hence the police-offices are generally deluged with complaints of abuse or assaults, originating in such trifling expressions as, 'Look how him tan,' 'Him face tan like a baboon,' &c. This thin-skinnedness, however, is not confined to the lower classes. I once saw an apparently respectable lady at a peace office complaining of a negro, who had said that she was a 'John-Crow flying from the four quarters of the world, to come to pitch and grow fat upon the property.'

Prejudices.—The prejudices of caste, which once took such firm hold of parties in the West Indies, are, as I have already said, fast disappearing. They are too intimately connected with the history of the colonies, however, to be passed by without some further remark. The object of those prejudices was of course to uphold the authority of the dominant class; and as the colour of that class was white, white became the standard of perfection, and the sole claim to consideration and advancement. The free man who was not white was not permitted to have an interest in the free institutions of his country, and he could neither elect nor be elected, however great his wealth or talent. Like others, he paid his contributions to the exigences of the public, but he received no benefit from the funds collected; he was a subject, and was yet denied the benefit of the laws; he was punished when he offended against them, yet could not obtain redress when offended; he was insulted, yet he could not retaliate; beaten, but he could not strike. His family was often outraged, yet he had no relief; his limbs maimed, yet the courts of justice would not receive his evidence of the injury. He was an heir, yet he could not always inherit; a husband, and could not protect. By and by, however, individuals saw the iniquity of the system; a sense of intense injustice disseminated itself; the oppressed became strong; they petitioned for equal rights; many swore to obtain them or die in the attempt; and at length we saw granted to expediency that which was denied to justice. Such, I believe, has been the history of despotism in every quarter of the globe —rampant when it may safely be so, but crumbling powerless to the earth when its victims feel their strength and use it.

Christian Names.—Many of the Christian names among the lower classes are scriptural, others classical; others, again, simply pretty, according to the whim of the masters or mistresses, relatives or friends, who gave them. The most common are Daniel, David, Patience, Prudence, Charity, Hope, Faith, Phœbe, Hebe, Homer, Cato, Cæsar, Diana, Duke, and Prince. The surnames used generally to be those of the masters and mistresses.

THE OLIVE TREE.

About twenty different kinds of olives are known in this country at the present day, some of which are esteemed for their fragrance, as *Olea fragrans*, and others for their fruit, as *O. Europæa* and its varieties. This last species has been known and cultivated for many ages, and from very ancient custom, the olive branch has been used as an emblem of peace. It is a native of the south of Europe and the north of Africa, where it is very generally and extensively cultivated. It is supposed to have been carried from Egypt into Attica about 1556 before the Christian era. It

---

* In the blue book for the West Indies, 1841, vol. ii. p. 5, is an account of the settlement of 'Freeman's Hall,' in the interior of Trelawney, Jamaica, by fifty English and German emigrants. At that date it had been successful, not a death having occurred. In the blue book for 1844, on emigration to the West Indies, p. 11, will be found another account. These go to show that, under certain circumstances, European emigration will succeed: the great majority of cases is, however, the other way.

was first planted in Italy in the thirteenth year of the reign of Servius Tullius, the sixth king of Rome. The Romans appear to have paid great attention to its culture, and considered it next in value to the vine. According to the best authenticated accounts, the olive was introduced into England in 1570; and although it has been so long an inhabitant of this country, it is cultivated in but few places, and in these few it is generally known in the greenhouse as an ornamental plant. In its native country, the olive is extensively cultivated for the sake of the oil extracted from the berries; but the variableness of our climate renders the probability of crops of the fruit very precarious out of doors, and they are not of sufficient value to grow extensively under glass. The oil of olives is contained in the pulp only, and not in the nut or kernel, as in most other fruits. It is obtained by simple pressure: the olives are first bruised by a millstone, and then put into bags, after which the liquor is pressed out by means of a press. The bags are either made of linen, hemp, or rushes, and occasionally woollen ones are used; but as these are apt to become dirty and rancid, they are not in much repute. Those of linen or rushes are reckoned the best. Olive oil is the main support of commerce in some provinces in Italy. The quantity imported into Britain in the course of a year is upwards of 2,000,000 gallons, the duty on which amounts to about L.75,000. The most valuable is imported from the south of France. Besides the extraction of oil, olives are used for pickling and preserving; and Gerard, in his 'Historie of Plants,' enumerates many medicinal properties which they possess. It is stated that two glass jars of olives, and olive oil, have been dug out of the ruins of Pompeii, both of which were fit for use.—*Magazine of Botany.*

MUTUAL BENEFICENCE.

Nothing is more unpleasing than to find that offence has been received when none was intended, and that pain has been given to those who were not guilty of any provocation. As the great end of society is mutual beneficence, a good man is always uneasy when he finds himself acting in opposition to the purposes of life; because, though his conscience may easily acquit him of *malice prepense*, of settled hatred, or contrivances of mischief, yet he seldom can be certain that he has not failed by negligence or indolence, that he has not been hindered from consulting the common interest by too much regard to his own ease, or too much indifference to the happiness of others.—*Rambler.*

'BUT.'

'But' is to me a more detestable combination of letters than 'no' itself. *No* is a surly honest fellow, speaks his mind at once. *But* is a sneaking, evasive, half-bred, exceptious sort of a conjunction, which comes to pull away the cup when it is at your lips—

It does allay
The good preceded; fie upon '*but yet.*
But yet is a jailer to bring forth
Some monstrous malefactor.—*Sir Walter Scott.*

PEACE WITH THE WORLD.

The arms by which the ill dispositions of the world are to be combated, and the qualities by which it is to be reconciled to us, and we reconciled to it, are moderation, gentleness, a little indulgence to others, and a great deal of distrust of ourselves, which are not qualities of a mean spirit, as some may possibly think them, but virtues of a great and noble kind, and such as dignify our nature as much as they contribute to our repose and fortune; for nothing can be so unworthy of a well-composed soul as to pass away life in bickerings and litigations, in snarling and scuffling with every one around us. We must be at peace with our species, if not for their sakes, yet very much for our own.—*Burke.*

AIMING AT PERFECTION.

There is no manner of inconvenience in having a pattern propounded to us of so great perfection as is above our reach to attain to; and there may be great advantages in it. The way to excel in any kind, is to propose the brightest and most perfect examples to our imitation. No man can write after too perfect and good a copy; and though he can never reach the perfection of it, yet he is likely to learn more than by one less perfect. He that aims at the heavens, which yet he is sure to come short of, is like to shoot higher than he that aims at a mark within his reach.—*Tillotson.*

TO MY WIFE.

BY JOHN BOLTON ROGERSON.

Thy cheek is pale with many cares,
Thy brow is overcast,
And thy fair face a shadow wears,
That tells of sorrows past.
But music hath thy tongue for me;
How dark soe'er my lot may be,
I turn for comfort, love, to thee,
My beautiful, my wife!

Thy gentle eyes are not so bright
As when I wooed thee first;
Yet still they have the same sweet light,
Which long my heart hath nurst:
They have the same enchanting beam,
Which charmed me in love's early dream,
And still with joy on me they stream,
My beautiful, my wife!

When all without looks dark and cold,
And voices change their tone,
Nor greet me as they did of old,
I feel I am not lone;
For thou, my love, art aye the same,
And looks and deeds thy faith proclaim:
Though all should scorn, thou wouldst not blame,
My beautiful, my wife!

A shadow comes across my heart,
And overclouds my fate,
Whene'er I think thou mayst depart,
And leave me desolate;
For, as the wretch who treads alone
Some gloomy path in wilds unknown,
Such would I be if thou wert gone,
My beautiful, my wife!

If thou wert dead, the flowers might spring,
But I should heed them not;
The merry birds might soar and sing—
They could not cheer my lot.
Before me dark despair would rise,
And spread a pall o'er earth and skies,
If shone no more thy loving eyes,
My beautiful, my wife!

And those dear eyes have shone through tears,
But never looked unkind;
For shattered hopes and troubled years,
Still closer seem to bind
Thy pure and trusting heart to mine.
Not for thyself didst thou repine,
But all thy husband's grief was thine,
My beautiful, my wife!

When, at the eventide, I see
My children throng around,
And know the love of them and thee,
My spirit still is bound
To earth, despite of every care:
I feel my soul can do and dare,
So long as thou my lot dost share,
My beautiful, my wife!

[The above piece is copied directly from an American newspaper; but its author is a poet of English growth—residing, we believe, in Manchester—who has published several volumes of his effusions, from one of which probably the above is extracted.]

DISAPPOINTMENT.

Men are very seldom disappointed, except when their desires are immoderate, or when they suffer their passions to overpower their reason, and dwell upon delightful scenes of future honours, power, or riches, till they mistake probabilities for certainties, or wild wishes for rational expectations. If such men, when they awake from these voluntary dreams, find the pleasing phantom vanish away, what can they blame but their own folly?—*Dr Johnson.*

A HINT TO LECTURERS.

I have seen many Chartist and Anti-Bread Tax lectures advertised in the manufacturing districts, but I never heard of any lectures given with a view to convey correct information to the people on the influences that regulate the natural price of labour, and yet of all information there is none which it is of more importance for the poor workmen to receive.—*Kohl's England.*

Printed by William Bradbury, of No. 6, York Place, and Frederick Mullett Evans, of No. 7, Church Row, both of Stoke Newington, in the county of Middlesex, printers, at their office, Lombard Street, in the precinct of Whitefriars, and city of London; and Published (with permission of the Proprietors, W. and R. CHAMBERS,) by WILLIAM SOMERVILLE ORR, Publisher, of 2, Amen Corner, at No. 2 AMEN CORNER, both in the parish of Christchurch, and in the city of London.—Saturday, February 1, 1845.

CONDUCTED BY WILLIAM AND ROBERT CHAMBERS, EDITORS OF 'CHAMBERS'S INFORMATION FOR THE PEOPLE,' 'CHAMBERS'S EDUCATIONAL COURSE,' &c.

No. 58. New Series. SATURDAY, FEBRUARY 8, 1845. Price 1½d.

MORNINGS WITH THOMAS CAMPBELL.

It was on a fine morning in May 1840, that I first called on Mr Campbell. He then lived in chambers, No. 61, Lincoln's Inn Fields, up two pairs of stairs. He had offered to act as cicerone, and show me the lions of London; and it was with no small pride and pleasure that I repaired to the spot, where he was so often to be seen pacing up and down in solitary meditation. He was always a great walker, and this habit continued with him to the last. I found on the outer door of his rooms, below the brass knocker, a slip of paper on which was written, in his neat classical-like hand, this curious announcement—'Mr Campbell is particularly engaged, and cannot be seen till past two o'clock.' As he had expressly mentioned that I should call between nine and ten o'clock, I concluded that this prohibition could not be meant to be universal, and resolved to hazard an application. He received me with great kindness, and explained that the announcement on his door was intended to scare away a *bore*, who had been annoying him with some manuscripts, and would neither take a refusal nor brook delay. The poet was breakfasting in his sitting-room, which was filled with books, and had rather a showy appearance. The carpet and tables were *littered* with stray volumes, letters, and papers; whence I inferred that his housemaid was forbidden to interfere with the arrangements of his sanctum. At this time he was, like Charles Lamb, a worshipper of the 'great plant,' and tobacco pipes were mingled with the miscellaneous literary wares. A large print of the queen hung near the fireplace, the gilded frame of which was covered with lawn paper. He drew my attention to the picture, and said it had been presented to him by her majesty. He valued it highly: 'money could not buy it from me,' he remarked. In another part of the room was a painting of a little country girl, with a coarse shawl of network pulled over her head and shoulders. The girl was represented as looking out below the shawl with a peculiarly arch and merry expression, something like Sir Joshua Reynolds's Puck. He seemed to dote upon this picture, praised the arch looks of the 'sly little minx,' and showed me some lines which he had written upon her. These he afterwards published; but as they are comparatively little known, and are not unworthy of his genius, I subjoin them:—

'ON GETTING HOME THE PORTRAIT OF A FEMALE CHILD, SIX YEARS OLD, PAINTED BY EUGENIO LATILLA.

Type of the cherubim above,
Come, live with me, and be my love!
Smile from my wall, dear roguish sprite,
By sunshine and by candle-light;
For both look sweetly on thy traits;
Or, were the Lady Moon to gaze,
She'd welcome thee with lustre bland,
Like some young fay from fairy-land.
Cast in simplicity's own mould,
How canst thou be so manifold
In sportively-distracting charms?
Thy lips—thine eyes—thy little arms
That wrap thy shoulders and thy head,
In homeliest shawl of netted thread,
Brown woollen network; yet it seeks
Accordance with thy lovely cheeks,
And more becomes thy beauty's bloom
Than any shawl from Cashmere's loom.
Thou hast not to adorn thee, girl,
Flower, link of gold, or gem, or pearl—
I would not let a ruby speck
The peeping whiteness of thy neck:
Thou need'st no casket, witching elf,
No gaud—thy toilet is thyself;
Not even a rosebud from the bower,
Thyself a magnet, gem, and flower.
My arch and playful little creature,
Thou hast a mind in every feature;
Thy brow with its disparted locks,
Speaks language that translation mocks;
Thy lucid eyes so beam with soul,
They on the canvass seem to roll—
Instructing both my head and heart
To idolise the painter's art.
He marshals minds to Beauty's feast—
He is Humanity's high priest,
Who proves by heavenly forms on earth,
How much this world of ours is worth.
Inspire me, child, with visions fair!
For children, in creation, are
The only things that could be given
Back, and alive—unchanged—to Heaven.'

The verses were written on folio paper, the lines wide apart, to leave room for correction—for Campbell, it is well known, was a laborious and fastidious corrector. The passion for children which he here evinces, led some time afterwards to a ludicrous circumstance. He saw a fine child, about four years old, one day walking with her nurse in the Park; and on his return home, he could not rest for thinking of his 'child sweetheart,' as he called her, and actually sent an advertisement to the *Morning Chronicle*, making inquiries after his juvenile fascinator, giving his own address, and stating his age to be sixty-two! The incident illustrates the intensity of his affections, as well as the liveliness of his fancy—for, alas! the poet had no home-object to dwell upon, to concentrate his hopes and his admiration. Several hoaxes were played off on the susceptible poet in consequence of this singular advertisement. One letter directed him to the house of an old maid, by whom he was received very cavalierly. He told his story—but 'the *wretch*,' as he used to say, with a sort of peevish humour, 'had never heard either of him or his poetry!'

When I had read the lines, Mr Campbell retired for a few minutes. 'You can look over the books,' he said, 'till I return.' Who has not felt the pleasure of looking over the shelves of a library, with all their varied and interesting associations? The library of a man of genius, too, has peculiar attraction, for it seems to admit us to his familiar thoughts, tastes, and studies. Campbell's library was not very extensive. There were some good old editions of the classics, a set of the *Biographie Universelle*, some of the French, Italian, and German authors, the Edinburgh Encyclopædia (to which he had been a large contributor), and several standard English works, none very modern. He did not care much to keep up with the literature of the day; and his chief delight was—when not occupied with any task—to lounge, in his careless indolent way, over some old favourite author that came recommended to him by early recollections. He occasionally made marginal notes on the books he read. I happened to take down the first volume of 'The Beauties of English Poesy, selected by Oliver Goldsmith,' 1767. On the blank leaf of this unfortunate compilation Campbell had written the fact, that 'poor Goldy' had inserted among his 'Beauties,' *designed for young readers*, Prior's stories of Hans Carvel and the Ladle. 'The circumstance,' he added, 'is as good as the tales, besides having the advantage of being true.' I may here remark, that Mr Campbell could scarcely ever read Goldsmith's poetry without shedding tears.

The poet soon returned from his dressing-room. He was generally careful as to dress, and had none of Dr Johnson's indifference to fine linen. His wigs (of which he had a great number) were always nicely adjusted, and scarcely distinguishable from natural hair; while about an inch of whisker on the cheek was coloured with some dark powder, to correspond with the wig. His appearance was interesting and handsome. Though rather below the middle size, he did not seem little; and his large dark eye and countenance altogether bespoke great sensibility and acuteness. His thin quivering lip and delicate nostril were highly expressive. When he spoke, as Leigh Hunt has remarked, dimples played about his mouth, 'which nevertheless had something restrained and close in it, as if some gentle Puritan had crossed the breed, and left a stamp on his face, such as we often see in the female Scotch face rather than the male.' He had, like Milton, a 'delicate tunable voice,' its high notes being somewhat sharp and painful. When a youth, Campbell was singularly beautiful, which, added to the premature development of his taste and genius, made him an object of great interest. A few literary persons still survive (Joanna Baillie among the number) who knew him at this period, and remember him, like a vision of youth, with great enthusiasm. He was early in flower—the fruit, perhaps, scarcely corresponding (at least in quantity) with the richness of the blossom. Campbell was quite sensible of his interesting appearance, and was by no means disposed to become *venerable*. He cared little for the artist who copied nature exactly. Lawrence painted and Baily sculptured him *en beau*. Late in life he sat to Park, the sculptor, but he would not take off his wig; and the bust (a true and vigorous one) was no especial favourite because of its extreme fidelity. In personal neatness and fastidiousness, no less than in genius and taste, Campbell, in his best days, resembled Gray. Each was distinguished by the same careful finish in composition, the same classical predilections and lyrical fire, rarely but strikingly displayed. In ordinary life they were both somewhat finical, yet with great freedom and idiomatic plainness in their unreserved communications; Gray's being evinced in his letters, and Campbell's in conversation. Gray was more studious of his dignity; Campbell often acted rashly from the impulse of the moment, careless of consequences. When the late Mr Telford, the engineer, remonstrated with him on the inexpediency of contracting an early marriage, he said gaily, 'When shall I be better off? I have fifty pounds, and six months' work at the Encyclopædia!' To these personal *nugæ* I may add, that his Scottish accent was not strongly marked, and did not detract from his point and elegance either as a lecturer or converser.

We shortly sallied out. Mr Campbell was rather nervous, and hesitated at the street crossings. I said the noise of London was intolerable, but that long usage must reconcile people to it. 'Never with some,' said he; 'I have been used to it for nearly forty years, and am not yet reconciled to it.' He certainly seemed uneasy when within the full sound of the great Babel and her interminable roar. When we got to a quiet alley or court, he breathed more freely, and talked of literature. He expressed his regret at having edited Shakspeare, or rather written his life for a popular edition of the dramas, as he had done it hurriedly, though with the right feeling. 'What a glorious fellow Shakspeare must have been,' said he; 'Walter Scott was fine, but had a worldly *twist*. Shakspeare must have been just the man to live with.' He spoke with affection and high respect of Lord Jeffrey. 'Jeffrey,' said he, 'will be quite happy now. As a judge, he has nothing to do but seek and follow truth. As an advocate, he must often have had to support cases at which his moral nature revolted.' Talking of Jeffrey's criticism, I instanced his review of Campbell's Specimens of the Poets, which is copious, eloquent, and discriminating. 'You must have taken great pains with some of the lives,' I said. 'I did,' he replied, '*yet they say I am lazy*. There is a washy, wordy style of criticism, and of telling facts, which looks specious, and imposes on many: I wanted, above all things, to avoid that.' 'You might perhaps have added to your Specimens with advantage. Part of Thomson's Seasons, for example, might have been given, as well as the first canto of the Castle of Indolence.' 'The Castle of Indolence is a glorious poem,' was his only answer. It must be admitted that in his selections from the poets Mr Campbell sometimes betrays the waywardness and caprice of a man of genius; but his criticism is invariably sound, and his style of narrative picturesque and graceful. 'Spenser,' he continued, 'is too prolix—his allegory too protracted. Here Thomson, from the nature of his subject, had the advantage. What a fine picture is that of Spenser reading the Fairy Queen to Raleigh on the green beside his Irish castle! Raleigh such a noble fellow, and Spenser so sweet a poet; and the country so savage, with its Irish kernes and wild Desmonds, with their saffron-coloured kilts and flowing hair!' And the kindling poet quoted some of Spenser's lines—

> 'I sat, as was my trade,
> Under the foot of Mole, that mountain hoar,
> Keeping my sheep amongst the coolly shade
> Of the green alders by the Mulla's shore.'

'The *Mole*,' said Campbell, 'is the Balligowra hills, and the *Mulla* is the Awbeg river: they should change the names, making Spenser godfather. With equal poetical grace Spenser calls Raleigh the "Shepherd of the Ocean," and the "Summer's Nightingale," both fine characteristic appellations. I like the last particularly, for Raleigh was really a poet, and he planted all about his house at Youghal with myrtles and sweet-smelling plants. Spenser's place, Kilcolman Castle, was only a few miles from Youghal, and no doubt they saw many sunsets together.' Campbell was here on a congenial theme, and I am tempted to quote what he has said so eloquently and picturesquely on the same subject in his Specimens:—

'When we conceive Spenser reciting his compositions to Raleigh in a scene so beautifully appropriate, the mind casts a pleasing retrospect over that influence which the enterprise of the discoverer of Virginia, and the genius of the author of the Fairy Queen, have respectively produced on the fortune and language of England. The fancy might even be pardoned for a momentary superstition, that the genius of their country hovered, unseen, over their meeting, casting her first look of regard on the poet that was destined to inspire her future Milton, and the other on the maritime hero who paved the way for colonising distant regions of the earth, where the language of England was to be spoken, and the poetry of Spenser to be admired.'

This would form a fine painting in the hands of Maclise, or some other post-spirited artist. Only a few fragments of Spenser's castle remain, matted with ivy; but the situation is still lonely and beautiful—undefaced by any incongruous images or associations. Some of Raleigh's myrtles have also been preserved, and his house still stands. The melancholy fate of both these great men deepens the interest with which we regard their residences. The poet, as is well known, was driven from Kilcolman by a furious band of rebels, who set fire to the castle, burning an infant child in the ruins, and causing, within a few months, from melancholy and despair, the death of the gifted Spenser. Raleigh was sacrificed to the cruelty and cupidity of James I. Let us drop a tear over their sad and chequered history, and thank God that genius, taste, and enterprise, now flourish under milder suns and happier influences!

Campbell was keenly alive to such impressions, and loved to tread as it were in the footsteps of the departed great. He regretted that only one of Milton's London houses should be left—one occupied by him when Latin secretary in Westminster. This house looks into St James's Park, and is situated in York Street (No. 18), in a poor and squalid neighbourhood; but it was then 'a pretty garden-house, next door to the Lord Scudamore's.' Milton occupied it eight years—from 1651 to 1659. We went also to Dryden's last residence, in Gerrard Street, Soho. Here 'glorious John' wrote his magnificent Ode and his Fables, and here he died on May morning 1700. The house is a respectable old-fashioned dwelling. It was formerly occupied by a comely dame—a Wife of Bath—who dealt in contraband laces, gloves, &c. The late Lord Holland often called to see the interior; but the cautious mistress, presuming that his portly and comfortable presence was that of a custom-house officer or other government functionary, kept the door in her hand, and steadily rejected the solicitations of the peer. Windmill Street, where Sir Richard Steele ran off on seeing the bailiff, is in the close vicinity, and the incidents are, in character and keeping, not unlike each other. There was also Congreve's house at Surrey Street, in the Strand; Johnson's famous residence in Bolt Court, Fleet Street (now profaned, as he would deem it, by its conversion into a printing-office for a dissenters' newspaper), and poor Goldsmith's chambers in the Temple, No. 2, Brick Court. His rooms were on the right hand ascending the staircase (as the faithful Mr Prior relates in his Memoir), and consisted of three apartments. These are now occupied by a solicitor, who pens law papers in the room where Goldy wrote his plays, or watched the rooks cawing about the time-honoured court and garden.

'I have,' he says in his Animated Nature, 'often amused myself with observing their plan of policy from my window in the Temple, that looks upon a grove where they have made a colony in the midst of the city. At the commencement of spring, the rookery, which during the continuance of winter seemed to have been deserted, or only guarded by about five or six, like old soldiers in a garrison, now begins to be once more frequented; and in a short time all the bustle and hurry of business is fairly commenced.'

And there they still bustle and hurry in spring, while Goldsmith sleeps without a stone in the Temple burying-ground. The poet's apartments were looked upon as airy and even splendid in their day. The walls are wainscotted, but have now a dingy appearance. Their occupant was thought to have spent an unnecessarily large sum (L.400) in furnishing them, yet the sale catalogue (printed by Prior) shows only one department of profuse expenditure—one highly characteristic of the poet's principal foible, personal vanity. He had only one bed, one sofa, and a moderate complement of necessaries, but he had 'two oval glasses, gilt frames,' 'two ditto, two light girandoles,' '*a very large dressing-glass*, mahogany frame,' and 'a three-plate bordered chimney-glass, gilt frame.' In this multiplicity of mirrors the poet could dress and admire his little undignified person, arrayed in his bloom-coloured coat and blue silk breeches. Goldsmith, though contemned and laughed at in his day, and held far inferior to his illustrious friend Johnson, now overtops the whole of that brilliant circle in real popularity and genuine fame. 'The wonder is,' as Campbell remarked, 'how one leading so strange a life from his youth upwards, could have stored his mind with so much fine knowledge, taste, and imagery. His essays are full of thought, and overflow with choice and beautiful illustration.'

'Have you been to Windsor?' asked Mr Campbell. I replied that I had, and spoke of the magnificence of the palace and the parks. 'Ay,' said he, 'the old oaks—the noble old oaks. Did you notice how they spread out their gnarled roots and branches, laying hold of the earth with their talons?' and he put out his clenched hand to help the expression of his vigorous and poetical image. All Scotchmen visiting London in spring should go, he said, a night or two to Windsor, Kew, or Richmond, to hear the nightingale. It was also heard in full voice in the grove around Sion House, the seat of the Duke of Northumberland. He thought Milton's description of the nightingale's note correct as well as rich—

> The Attic bird
> *Trills* her *thick-warbled* notes the summer long.

He maintained, also, with Chaucer and Charles James Fox (a singular juxtaposition), that the nightingale's note was a *merry* one, and 'though Theocritus mentions nightingales six or seven times, he never mentions their note as plaintive or melancholy.' Because it is heard in the silence of night, generally when we are alone, and amidst the gloom of thick woods, we attach melancholy associations to it. 'For pure English nature, feeling, and expression, read Dryden. He is the best informer and expositor.' We must understand this as applicable to Dryden's late productions—not his rhyming tragedies and stiff quatrains, which are anything but natural or pleasing.—*To be continued.*

NOTES OF A NATURALIST.

Plants.—In watching the development of plants, one is sometimes almost inclined to believe that their movements are the result of premeditation and thought, so nearly do they approach to the actions of animals.

A few plants of sweet pea, dug up when very young, were placed upon a table with their small springing rootlets turned half way round from a wet sponge placed within two inches of the seed lobes. In two days the rootlets had twisted completely round till their extremities touched the sponge, from which they could derive the moisture necessary for their growth. In another experiment a potato which had begun to germinate was placed in a dark box, in which was a small hole exposed to the sun. The potato was placed two feet from this hole, and at a little interval two stones were placed in a line between the potato and the hole. At the end of two weeks the white slender stem of the potato had crawled forward, but, meeting with the opposing stone, it made a bend round one side of it, and again grew out in nearly a straight direction, till, coming again in contact with the second stone, which still obstructed the light, it made a similar bend round it, but more in an upward direction, so as to reach the opening and the desired light.

On the same principle of seeking nourishment, strawberry plants set on the border of a gravel walk will send the whole of their roots into the garden soil, and not into the dry gravel. These movements may be all explained by supposing a strong attraction to subsist between the fibres of the plants and the moist soil by which they are drawn together; and, in the case of the potato, of all plants for the light of the sun. But the well authenticated instance of the shrub planted on the top of a stone wall, as related by Sir E. Smith, is of a more complicated nature.

An ash tree was observed to grow from a scanty portion of soil lodged in a crevice on the top of a garden wall. The stem advanced to a certain height, when, apparently from want of due nourishment, it made a stop. Soon after this pause in its growth a rootlet was seen growing out from the plant, which continued rapidly to shoot downwards, till at last it reached the soil at the bottom of the wall: no sooner had this taken firm possession in the ground, than the main stem again commenced growing with renewed vigour. Now, this was apparently as near a resemblance to the deliberative acts of animal instinct as it is possible to conceive.

There is an aquatic plant, the spiral valisneria, which is common in the ditches of Italy. This plant has the male and female flowers growing on different stalks, and at the period of seeding, it is singular to mark the means by which fructification is produced. The greater part of the plant grows below the surface of the water, and the female flower is produced on the extremity of a long slender stem, twisted round and compressed like a screw or coiled-up piece of wire. When these flowers are ready to blow, the compressed and twisted stem suddenly relaxes, and is consequently lengthened, so that the blossom mounts up and floats on the surface. At the same time the male blossoms are evolved from other plants; they also mount to the surface, but immediately break off from the stem. The slightest breeze then floats them along, until they reach the female blossoms, around which they are seen to cluster in great numbers. The spiral stems afterwards shrink, and the female buds return under water, there to mature their seeds.

The ground nut of South America (*arachis hypogea*) has a very singular mode of planting its seeds. It is an annual plant, with long trailing stalks, furnished with winged leaves composed of four hairy lobes. The flowers grow singly in long stalks, and are of the pea family. They produce oval pods, containing two or three oblong seeds. As the flowers fall off, the young pods are forced into the ground by a particular motion of the stalks, and are thus buried to a considerable depth in the soil.

When great drought prevails for a considerable time, all plants hasten onwards to fructification. They immediately cease to throw out new leaves or branches; but summoning, as it were, all their remaining vigour, they push out the seed-stalk and the fructifying organs, in order to secure a succession of offspring before they die. There is a beautiful palm, the taliput, or Palmyra palm, a native of Ceylon, which does not produce flowers till its eightieth year, the last also of its existence. At this period, when it has attained its full growth, the flower-spike, which is then as white as ivory, bursts with a loud report. In the course of fifteen or twenty months it showers down its abundance of nuts. This effort to provide a numerous succession proves fatal to the parent. Thus it presents the singular phenomena of a long-lived plant only blossoming once during its existence, when it dies, and, in dying, like the fabled Phenix, sheds the seeds of a future generation around it. Mr Bennet mentions that the flower is occasionally thirty feet in length: this gentleman witnessed several of the singular explosions of these palms in the forests of Ceylon. The broad leaves of this tree are used by the natives as fans; and all their books are written upon thin laminæ of the leaves. Tents are also constructed of them; and the pith of the trunk furnishes a substance like sago, which is used for food.

Animals.—Much has been written on the instincts or mental gifts of animals, but much is still required to throw light upon this curious subject. Authentic anecdotes of the habits and actions of brutes are always interesting: the more of these that can be collected, the more are we likely to know of what may be called the *psychology* or history of the mind of the inferior animals.

It appears to me that, in the general manifestations of the animal mind, some one of the senses is employed in preference to the others; that sense, for instance, which is most acute and perfect in the animal. In the dog, for example, the sense of smell predominates, and we accordingly find that, through the medium of this sense, his mental faculties are most commonly exercised. A gentleman had a favourite spaniel, which for a long time was in the practice of accompanying him in all his walks, and became his attached companion. This gentleman had occasion to leave home, and was absent for more than a year, during which time he had never seen the dog. On his return along with a friend, while yet at a little distance from the house, they perceived the spaniel lying beside the gate. The gentleman thought that this would be a good opportunity of testing the memory of his favourite, and accordingly arranged with his companion, who was quite unknown to the spaniel, that they should both walk up to the animal, and express no signs of recognition. As they both approached nearer, the dog started up, and gazed at them attentively, but he discovered no signs of recognition even at their near approach. At last he came up to the stranger, put his nose close to his clothes, and smelt him, without any signs of emotion: he then did the same to his old master, but no sooner had he smelt him than recognition instantly took place; he leaped up to his face repeatedly, and showed symptoms of the most extravagant joy. He followed him into the house, and watched his every movement, and could by no means be diverted from his person. Now, here was an instance of deficient memory through the organs of sight, but an accurate recollection through the organs of smell.

I have been more than once surprised, during the sunny days of summer, and in the smoke and din of the city, to find my box of fragrant mignionette visited by the hive bee. I could not but admire this laborious creature as I saw it alight and diligently explore every expanded blossom, collect the treasured sweets, and then, without loss of time, wend its way again through the smoky atmosphere, bearing its treasure to its distant rural hive. What could have led it into such a Babel of stone and lime, and smoke and hubbub, but its exquisite sense of smell, which could even at a great distance discriminate the odour of a flower from the other noisome scents with which it must have been mingled? To our obtuse sensations, such a refinement of smell is almost inconceivable. Yet such powers are manifested by many other animals.

The story which Dr Franklin tells of the ants and cup of treacle is well known; but I suspect the doctor's deductions are erroneous. Finding a number of ants eating up a quantity of treacle in a cup, he took and suspended it by a thread to the roof of the room, in order to isolate it completely. One end of the thread, however, he inadvertently left communicating with the floor, and with the pin in the ceiling. A single ant, which had been left in the cup, found its way along the cord to the ceiling, and from thence, by the continuation of the string, to the ground. In a few minutes hundreds of the other ants were seen ascending by this string, and descending to the cup; from whence the doctor concludes that the single ant had made some communication of the circumstance to its companions, by some natural signs analogous to language. Now, I would rather suggest that the ant, in making its escape by the cord, had thus left all along it an odour of treacle, and that this being quickly perceived by its companions, was the immediate and sensual means of the communication; and that, guided solely by smell, they retraced the path of their companion. Mr James, in his account of Travels to the Rocky Mountains, mentions that the smell of the bison is so acute, that when their party advanced within two or three miles to windward of flocks of those animals, even though they were not yet in sight of each other, the wild cattle immediately took the alarm, and were to be seen in great numbers taking a circuitous route to escape them—cows, bulls, and young calves running along with great swiftness.

In the horse, the sense of vision predominates. He has a large and beautiful eye, well adapted for vision during the day, but, from the form of the retina, peculiarly suited for night. A horse, if his rider give him a free rein, will pick his way in a dark night with astonishing precision, and will safely reach home through pitchy darkness, in which his rider can discover no object whatever.

The lion, the cat, and other night-preying animals, have also vision in a very perfect degree at that season, though, during the glare of sunshine, this faculty is so inapplicable as to render them stupid and timid in the extreme. Birds of prey have very acute vision, and the following anecdote illustrates this in the case of the vulture. In the year 1778, Mr Baber and several other gentlemen were on a hunting party in the island of Cassembuzar, in Bengal. They killed a wild hog of uncommon size, and left it on the ground near the tent. An hour after, walking near the spot where it lay, the sky being perfectly clear, a dark spot in the air at a great distance attracted their attention. It appeared to increase in size, and move directly towards them: as it advanced, it proved to be a vulture flying in a direct line to the dead hog. In an hour, seventy others came in all directions, which induced Mr Baber to remark that this cannot be smell. Dr Russel remembers to have observed at Aleppo, in the most severe weather, when not a speck was to be seen in the sky, if any dead animal was left behind by hunting parties, in the space of a few minutes it was surrounded by birds, although just before none were visible. In the very lowest animals, where only two, or at most three of the five senses are present, we find even here some one of surpassing acuteness.

We are sometimes surprised and puzzled with actions in our domestic animals, which can, however, be often traced to their original instincts. Thus every one has observed how the dog, before he lies down to sleep, turns two or three times round, whether he be going to make his bed on the ground, on a bare floor, or on the hearth-rug. If you ask the reason of this, you will perhaps be jocularly told that it is because he does not know the head of his bed from the foot. It has been suggested, as the true explanation, that in a wild state he takes up his night's quarters in a field of tall withered grass, or among reeds or rushes, and thus wheeling round, he separates the rushes in the spot where he is to lie, so that he forms a bed with overhanging curtains all round for his protection and warmth. The natural instincts may also be strangely altered or modified, as illustrated by the following anecdote of the dog, related by Mr Charles Darwin in his very interesting travels in South America:—

'When riding, it is a common thing to meet a large flock of sheep, guarded by one or two dogs, at the distance of some miles from any house or man. I often wondered how so firm a friendship had been established. The method of education consists in separating the puppy, while very young, from the bitch, and in accustoming it to its future companions. A ewe is held three or four times a-day for the little thing to suck, and a nest of wool is made for it in the sheep pen. At no time is it allowed to associate with other dogs, or with the children of the family. From this education, it has no wish to leave the flock; and just as another dog will defend its master, man, so will these the sheep. It is amusing to observe, when approaching a flock, how the dog immediately advances barking, and the sheep all close in his rear, as if round the oldest ram. These dogs are also easily taught to bring home the flock at a certain hour in the evening. Their most troublesome fault, when young, is their desire of playing with the sheep; for, in their sport, they sometimes gallop their poor subjects most unmercifully. The shepherd dog comes to the house every day for some meat, and immediately it is given him, he skulks away as if ashamed of himself. On these occasions the house dogs are very tyrannical, and the least of them will attack and pursue the stranger. The minute, however, the latter has reached the flock, he turns round and begins to bark, and then all the house dogs take very quickly to their heels. In a similar manner, a whole pack of hungry wild dogs will scarcely ever (I was told by some never) venture to attack a flock guarded even by one of these faithful shepherds. The whole account appears to me a curious instance of the pliability of the affections in the dog race. F. Cuvier has observed, that all animals that readily enter into domestication consider man as a member of their society, and thus fulfil their instinct of association. In the above case, the shepherd dogs rank the sheep as their fellow brethren; and the wild dogs, though knowing that the individual sheep are not dogs, but are good to eat, yet partly consent to this view, when seeing them in a flock, with a shepherd dog at their head.'

The same author gives a curious instance of the adaptations of an animal's instinct to its peculiar situation. A crab, closely allied to, or identical with the *burgos latro*, inhabits Keeling's island, in the South Seas; it feeds on cocoa nuts, and grows to a monstrous size. It has its great pair of legs terminated by very strong and heavy pincers, and the last pair by others which are narrow and weak. It would at first be thought quite impossible for a crab to open a strong cocoa nut covered with the husk; but M. Leisk, resident in the island, assured Mr Darwin that he has seen the operation frequently performed. The crab begins by tearing the husk fibre by fibre, and always from that end under which the three eye holes are situated. When this is completed, the crab commences hammering with its heavy claws on one of these eye holes till an opening is made, then, turning round its body by the aid of its posterior and narrow pair of pincers, it extracts the white albuminous substance. 'I think,' adds Mr Darwin, 'this is as curious a case of instinct as ever I heard of, and likewise of adaptation in structure, between two objects apparently so remote from each other, in the scheme of nature, as a crab and a cocoa-nut tree.' The burgos is dormant in its habits; but every night it is said to pay a visit to the sea, no doubt for the purpose of moistening its branchiæ.

THE ALIBI.

Some twenty years ago (before steam and railroads had annihilated distances, and made 'going to London' the everyday affair it now is from all parts of the kingdom), I awoke, on a beautiful April morning, from the uneasy slumbers of a mail-coach passenger, just in time to drink in, at eye, ear, and nose, the brilliant sparkle, refreshing sound, and reviving odour of my native waves, as they leaped up to kiss, as if in fondness, the rocky barrier which our eastern coast opposes to the not always placid German Ocean. I was, ere long, to pass a barrier of a different description (now happily a nominal one) between two sister nations; or, in plain English, to enter the town of Berwick-on-Tweed, a few miles beyond which, on the southern side of the border, business obliged me to proceed.

At the inn door where we stopped to change horses, in this capital of 'no man's land'—whose inhabitants assert their anomalous independence by speaking a dialect which they take care shall be neither Scotch nor English—*I* also exchanged, for the brief remainder of my journey, a taciturn, commonplace sort of a fellow-passenger—from whose physiognomy I never dreamed of auguring anything—for one of a very different description, from whose modest, yet speaking countenance, and the evident interest she excited in the few who were astir at that early hour, it was impossible to avoid auguring a great deal.

The coach door was opened, and with swimming eye, flushed cheek, and silver hair blowing about in the morning wind, a venerable-looking man took leave with even more than parental tenderness of a simply-dressed, yet genteel-looking young woman; who, returning his tremulous 'God bless and reward you!' with an almost filial farewell, drew down over her face a thick black veil, and stepped in opposite to me. I now felt more inclined, and at the same time more at a loss, to open a conversation. To intrude on female sorrow seemed unjustifiable, to treat it with callous indifference impossible. That of my new companion appeared to be of a gentle, subdued sort, arising more from sympathy with others than from personal causes; and ere long, putting back her veil with the reviving cheerfulness of one whose heart is lightened of an unmerited burden, she looked calmly out on the fresh aspect of nature, so in unison with her own pure and innocent countenance, and said, in the tone of one breathing after release from the pressure of painful feelings, 'How beautiful everything does look this fine spring morning.'

'It does indeed,' said I, struck with the confiding *naiveté* of this involuntary remark; 'and I suppose you are the more sensible of it from being a young traveller?' Her only answer was one of those quiet smiles which admit of various translations, and which, coupled with her air of rural simplicity, I chose to construe as assent. Coupling the remark with the circumstance of her only luggage being a small bandbox, I set her down for a farmer's daughter of the neighbourhood, and said, 'I suppose, like myself, you are not going far?'

'I am going to London, sir,' said she in a tone of calm self-possession, as if such a journey had been to her an everyday occurrence: and so indeed had been, not metaphorically, but literally the case.

'To London!' repeated I, with more surprise than I could well account for; 'were you ever there before?'

'Oh yes!' was the reply, rendered more *piquant* by its singular composure; 'I came from seventy miles beyond it the day before yesterday.'

It would be quite superfluous to say that my curiosity was greatly excited by this singular occurrence, and I daresay my readers will set me down as a very stupid fellow (for a lawyer especially), for not having the dexterity to gratify it.

But my companion, as if ashamed of having so far committed herself to a stranger, now sat back in the coach, and answered one or two indifferent questions with that laconic gentleness which is infinitely more discouraging than sullen silence. I felt that I had not the smallest right to ask directly, 'My dear, what *could* make you undertake so long a journey for the sake of one day?' and as I saw she had not the least mind to tell me, I must plead guilty to being ashamed to use the advantage my years and knowledge of the world gave me, to worm out a secret which, from another quiet tear which I saw trickling down behind her veil, I guessed must be fraught with pain rather than pleasure.

The struggle was well nigh over, when the arrival of the coach at my friend's gate gave to my better feelings no very meritorious triumph. Now that all idea of intrusion was at an end, I could venture on kindness; and I said (I am sure in honest sincerity), 'The thought of your going such a long journey by yourself, or with chance company, grieves me. Can I be of any use in recommending you to the protection of the guard, or otherwise?'

'Thank you, sir, a thousand times,' said she, raising for the first time a pair of mild innocent eyes to my face; 'but He who put it in my mind to come, and blessed the purpose of my journey, can carry me safe back again; and I should be silly indeed to mind going a few hundred miles by land, when I am about to sail to the other end of the world. I am much obliged to you, sir, though,' said she, 'all the same for thinking of it; and if we had time——'

Time, however, at all times despotic, is inexorable when armed with a mail-coach horn. I could only shake hands with the gentle being I left behind me, slip a crown into the guard's hand to look well after her (which I was glad to see he took as a tacit affront), and turn my thoughts, by a strong effort, to my Northumbrian friend's affairs.

These occupied me fully and disagreeably all the morning; and early in the afternoon, I was reluctantly obliged to forego the good gentleman's old claret and old stories (for I had shot snipes on his lands with my first gun some twenty years before), to fulfil an engagement in Edinburgh the following morning. I compounded for this outrage on my friend's hospitality by accepting his carriage to convey me back to Berwick in time for a coach which I knew would start thence for the north in the evening.

No sooner did I find myself once more at the door of the King's Arms, than the circumstance brought full on my memory the romantic occurrence which had been for the last few hours eclipsed behind a mass of dusty law-papers, and the portly persons of a brace of hard-favoured and harsh-toned Northumbrian attorneys.

I found myself a few minutes too early; and as I stood shivering on the steps in the cold evening air, and pondering on the vicissitudes of an April day, I could not help asking the landlord, a civil old-fashioned Boniface—'Pray, sir, do you know anything about the history of that nice young woman who started with me for London from your house this morning?'

'Know, sir!' said he, as if in compassion for my ignorance, 'ay, that I do, and so does all Berwick; and it would be well if all England and Scotland knew it too! If ever there was a kind heart and a pretty face in Berwick bounds, it's surely Mary Fenwick's. But it's rather a long story, sir, and the horses are just coming round. However, I'm thinking there's one going with you as far as Haddington that wont want pressing to give you the outs and ins on't.' So saying, he pointed to a stout grazier-looking personage in a thick greatcoat and worsted comforter, who, by his open countenance and manly yeoman-like bearing, might have been own brother to Dandie Dinmont himself.

'This gentleman,' said the landlord, with a respectful glance at myself and a familiar nod to the borderer, 'wishes to hear all about Mary Fenwick. You've known her from the egg (we've a great trade in eggs here, sir), and besides, were in court all the time of the trial; so you'll be able to give it him, chapter and verse, from the beginning.'

Reserving his breath for the narrative, which his assenting nod to the landlord led me to hope for, my ponderous *vis à vis* adjusted himself in the coach, his broad open honest face inviting question, as much as the poor girl's downcast retiring one had checked it. Having explained, for the sake of propriety, that my interest in the damsel arose from the singular circumstance of one so young and apparently unprotected travelling above six hundred miles to pass one day in Berwick, he civilly begged my pardon, and assured me that no one there felt the least uneasiness as to the success of Mary's journey. 'There's a blessing on her and her errand, sir; and that the very stones on the road know; and besides, she's so staid and so sensible, and has so much dignity about her, that she's as fit to go through the world alone as her grandmother.'

To all this I assented the more readily, that this very dignity had made me forego all inquiry into what I wished so much to know; and even now I listened with all the more satisfaction for the hint she had thrown out, as if of regret for not being able to tell me herself.

'Does she belong to this place,' asked I, 'that you seem to know her so well?'

'Yes, sir, born and bred in Berwick bounds. She was a farmer's daughter, a mile out of town, and just what a farmer's daughter ought to be. Her mother, a clever notable woman, taught her to bake and brew, and knit and sew; in short, everything that many girls in her station are now too fine to do. They think these good old-fashioned things make them ungenteel; but they never made Mary Fenwick so; for I'm sure, sir, but for her suitable dress and simple manner you might have taken her for a lady.

'Well, Mary came often in her father's little cart to market, to sell her butter and eggs (you heard landlord say there's a most o' them go from here to London), and somehow or other she met with a young man of our town, a journeyman saddler, who was taken with her good looks, and cared for very little else. His old father, however (the old man who put Mary in the coach this morning), made many inquiries about his son's sweetheart; and, as he heard nothing but good of her, had the sense to see that though she was one of a large hard-working family, she would be the very wife to reclaim his gay, idle, thoughtless son, if anything would.

'And very idle and extravagant he was, sir. The only son of people well to do in the world, and a good deal spoilt from a child, he neglected his business whenever he could, and loved dress and company, and horse-racing, and all that, far too well. But he really loved Mary Fenwick; and no sooner saw that she would not so much as listen to him while all this went on, than he quite left off all his wild courses, and became a new man to gain her favour.

'It was not done in a hurry; for Mary had been brought up very piously, and had a horror for everything evil. But Dick Marshall was very clever as well as handsome, and, when he pleased, could make one believe anything; and, to give him his due, as long as he had any doubts of Mary's love, no saint could behave better. At last, however, he fairly gained her innocent heart; though, I believe, it was as much by the aid of his good father and mother's constant praise of him, and doting fondness for Mary, as by his own winning ways.

'When he saw she loved him—and it was not by halves, though in her own gentle way—he wanted to marry her immediately; and Mary's father would have consented, for it was a capital match for his portionless girl. But Mary said, "Richard, you have kept free of cards, and dice, and folly one six months, to gain your own wish; let me see you do it another to make *my* mind easy, and then I'll trust you till death divides us."

'Dick stormed, and got into a passion, and swore she did not love him; but she answered, "It is just because I do that I wish to give you a habit of goodness before you are your own master and mine. Surely it is no hardship to be for six months what you mean to be all the rest of your life!"

'Richard was forced to submit, and for three of the six months behaved better than ever. But habit, as Mary said, is everything, and his had for years sat the wrong way. With the summer came fairs, and idleness, and pleasure parties, and, worst of all, races, into the neighbourhood. Dick first stayed away with a bad grace; then went, just to show how well he could behave; and ended by losing his money, and getting into scrapes, just as bad as ever. For a time he was much ashamed, and felt real sorrow, and feared Mary would never forgive him. But when she did so, sweet gentle soul! several times—though her pale sad face was reproach enough to any man—he began to get hardened, and to laugh at what he called her silly preciseness.

'Mary was twenty times near giving him up; but his parents hung about her, and told her she only could save him from perdition. And, in truth, she thought so herself; and those who love from the heart, know how much it can bear before it lets go. That thought, joined to the love for him, which was the deeper for its slow growth, made her still ready to risk her own welfare for his.

'It is not to be told what she bore of idleness, extravagance, and folly (for guilt was never as yet laid to his door), in the hopes that, when these wild oats were sown, Richard would settle again into a sober working man. At last, however, to crown all, there came players to the town, and Dick was not to be kept from either before or behind the curtain. He fell in with a gay madam of an actress, who persuaded him that to marry a poor farmer's daughter was quite beneath him, and to be kept in awe by her more contemptible still.

'In short, sir, to make an end of a long story, Dick, after trying in vain to force his poor heart-broken Mary to give him up, that he might lay his ruin at her door, had the cruelty to tell her one night, as he met her going home to her father's from nursing *his* sick mother, "that he saw she was not a fit match for him either in birth or manners, and that if ever he married, it should be a wife of more liberal ways of thinking."

'He had been drinking a good deal, it is true, and was put up to this base conduct by his new stage favourite; but when he found that, instead of a storm of reproaches, or even a flood of tears, poor Mary only stood pale and shaking, and kept saying, "Poor Richard! oh, poor Richard!" without once bestowing a thought on his behaviour to herself, he grew sobered, and would fain have softened matters a little. But she summoned all her strength, and ran as fast as she was able, till she came to her father's garden; and two days after, when the old Marshalls drove out in a postchaise to try and make it all up, and get their son put once more on his trial, Mary was off, her parents would not tell whither.'

'And where did she go?' said I, for the first time venturing to interrupt the borderer's *con amore* narrative.

'It came out, sir, afterwards, that, before her marriage was agreed on, an uncle in London had invited her to come up and visit him; and as she had another sister now quite ready to take her place at home, she told her parents it would save her much misery to leave home for a while, and even go to service to keep out of the way till Dick Marshall should be married. "Or hanged!" said her father (in his passion, as he afterwards acknowledged), "which is more likely," little thinking how near it was being the case. There was a salmon smack lying in the harbour just then, whose master was Mary's cousin; so she slipped quietly on board, and got safe to London.'

'How long was this ago?' asked I.

'Oh, about four or five months perhaps,' answered my *vis à vis*. 'Let me see; it was October, and this is April. Well, sir, Mary stayed but a few days with her uncle, as idleness was a thing she never liked; but through his wife, who had been housekeeper to a nobleman, she got a delightful place in the same family as upper nursery-maid; which her gentle manners, and steady temper, and long experience in her father's house among small children, made her every way fit for.

'She had not been long with them when Lord S—— was appointed to a government in India, and as he resolved to take out his family, nothing would serve Lady S—— but Mary must go out with them. They were grown so fond of her, that her services on the voyage would be invaluable; and then her staid, sober, dignified manners, it seems, made her a perfect treasure in a country where, I understand, girls' heads are apt to be turned. Lady S—— knew her story, and thought it recommendation enough. So the parents were written to—half of Mary's ample wages secured to them by her desire; and Mary went down to the sea-side with the family, to be in the way to embark at the last moment when all the tedious outfit for a great man's voyage should be complete.'

'So,' said I, 'that explains a hint she threw out about the world's end. Then she is going to India?'

'Yes, sir; and would have been half way there by this time, if it had not pleased God to send a contrary wind to save Dick Marshall's life.'

'His life, poor wretch!' said I. 'Did he take to worse courses still?'

'Pretty bad, sir; but not quite so bad as he got credit for. I'll tell you as short as I can. There came about Berwick now and then a scamp of a fellow, whom everybody knew to be a gambler and a cheat, and whom none but such idle dogs as Dick Marshall would keep company with. This man, sir, was known to be in or about town last autumn, and to have won money both on the turf and at the card-table. He and his worthless comrades had a row about it it seems, high words, and even a scuffle; but few knew or cared, and Jack Osborne went away as he came, with none the wiser.

'However, about six weeks or two months ago, it began to be whispered that he had been missed of late from his old haunts, and that Berwick was the last place where he had been seen; and good-for-nothing as he was, he had decent relations, who thought it worth while to inquire into it. The last person in whose company he had been observed in our town was certainly Dick Marshall, who, when asked about him, denied all knowledge of his old companion. But Dick's own character was by this time grown very notorious; and though no one here, from respect to his family, would have breathed such a notion, Jack Osborne's stranger uncle felt no scruple in saying that his nephew had met with foul play, and insisted on an investigation. In the course of this, a very suspicious circumstance came out. A pair of pistols, well known to be Osborne's, was found in Dick's possession; and a story of his having received them in part payment of a gambling debt was of course very little if at all believed.

'There were plenty of people who could depone that, on the 23d of October, at a tavern dinner, the two fit associates had quarrelled, and had high words; though they were afterwards seen to go out separately, but apparently good friends. The next step in evidence was two people having returned late that evening, and, on passing a little stunted thicket about half a mile from town, having heard something like groans and cries, which, however, they paid little attention to, being in a great hurry. This caused the place to be searched; and in an old sand-pit near the spot, to the surprise and horror of all, were found the remains of poor Jack Osborne, whose clothes, from the dry nature of the place, were in good preservation.

'Things began now to put on an aspect terribly serious for Dick Marshall; especially as another man now came forward to say (people should be very cautious, sir, how they trust to likenesses) that he had met Dick, or some one so like him that he had no doubt it was he, on the road to that very spot just before the hour when the groans were heard; though, on being addressed by his name, he passed on and took no notice.

'Between the quarrel, and the pistols, and the groans, and the dead body, and, above all, the evidence of this man, a complete case was made out for a jury; and there were a great many circumstances besides to give it a colour: especially poor Dick's now reckless and profligate habits, and his evident confusion and agitation when first asked where he had been and what he had been doing on the evening of the 23d of October.

'To those who saw his face on that occasion, his conscience-stricken looks when taken by surprise, and his angry defiance afterwards, when aware of the drift of the question, there was no doubt of his guilt. Dick was committed for trial; and, oh sir, it was a sad day for all who knew his worthy parents, and had seen the creature himself grow up before them a pretty curly haired child, and then a manly spirited boy.

'His behaviour in prison was chiefly dogged and sullen. He seemed to scorn even denying the fact to those who could suppose him guilty; as most did, except his poor father, who never could credit it; urging him to think, for the sake of his gray hairs, whether some means or other of averting this sad fate might not yet be found.

'He at length said, though it seemed extorted from him by his parents' distress, "There's one person on earth who could clear me of this horrible charge; but even if she were angel enough to do it, I suppose she's left England—and that's poor Mary Fenwick! This is a judgment on me, father, for my usage of that girl!"

'The agonised parents, from what they gathered further, lost not a moment in writing Mary the most pathetic letter ever broken hearts dictated. They feared she would have sailed; but it pleased God to order otherwise; and instead of the former uncertain delay from contrary winds (which had now set in fair), there was now a fixed detention of one week, for some official reasons.

'Mary carried the letter to her good mistress, and told her all the circumstances; and she readily obtained leave for the journey, and was offered the escort of a fellow-servant; but she was steadfast in declining it. "I would wish no unnecessary witnesses of poor Richard's shame and his parents' sorrow, my lady," said she; "and God will protect one that is going to return good for evil."

'There was not a moment to be lost to let Mary appear at the assizes yesterday, and get back to Portsmouth in time for the ship; so into the mail she stepped, and got here as soon as a letter would have done. When they saw her, the poor old Marshalls almost fainted for joy. They kissed, and wept over her, as they had done many a time when their son's wildness grieved her gentle spirit; but they soon came to look up to her as a guardian angel come to shield their gray hairs from disgrace and despair. They would have proposed to her to see and comfort Richard, but she said mildly, "We have both need of our strength for to-morrow. Tell him I forgive him, and bless God for bringing me to save him, and pray that it may not be from danger in this world alone."

'She was quite worn out with fatigue, it may be supposed, and glad to lay down her head once more to sleep in her mother's room, in the bed where she was born, and where she had hardly expected ever to lay it again. She rose quite refreshed, and able for the hard trial of appearing in court before her whole townspeople on so melancholy an occasion.

'She was indulged with a chair, and sat as much out of sight as possible, surrounded by kind friends, till she should be called on. The case for the prosecution was gone into, and a chain of circumstantial evidence made out so very conclusive against poor Dick, that the counsel against him, a rather flippant young man, remarked, "that nothing short of an alibi could bring the prisoner off."

"And that shall be proved directly, my lord," replied very unexpectedly some of the prisoner's friends. "We have a witness here come more than three hundred miles for the purpose;" and Mary, shaking like a leaf, and deadly pale, was placed in the box.

'The counsel had nothing for it but to examine her. I should be sorry to say he wished to find her testimony false; but really, sir, lawyers have a frightful degree of pride in showing their own ingenuity, and he did not quite like his case to be overturned. At all events, his manner was anything rather than encouraging to a poor frightened girl; but he little knew that Mary, timid as she was by nature, could be firm as a rock when duty was concerned.

'On being desired to say what she knew of this business, Mary simply asserted, in as few words as possible, that Richard Marshall could not have been in Overton wood at the hour mentioned for the murder of John Osborne, as he was at that very time with her on the road to B—— farm, in an exactly opposite direction.

"Very pleasantly engaged, I daresay, my dear," said the counsel flippantly; "but I am afraid the court will not be the more disposed to admit your evidence for what passed on that occasion."

"I am sure they ought," said Mary in a tone of deep and solemn sincerity.

"And pray what reason may you have for remembering so particularly that it was the 23d of October, and no other day, that Richard Marshall met you at nine in the evening?" said he, recovering himself. "Richard Marshall met you, you say, on the road to B—— at a little after nine on a certain evening. Pray what reason can you give for remembering the hour?"

"Because I had stayed to give his mother her nine o'clock draught before I left; and because, just as I got to my father's gate, the church clock struck ten."

"Very accurate! and pray what led you to be so very positive as to the day?"

"Because the very next morning I sailed for London in a smack, whose sailing day is always on Friday, and Thursday was the 23d."

"Very good and logical indeed. And now, my dear, to come more to the point, how came you to remember this meeting itself so particularly? It was not the first, I daresay?"

"No, sir," said Mary, with wonderful self-possession, "but it was the last! I remember it, because we were engaged to be married; and on that very night, and I bless God it was no other, Richard Marshall told me, and not very kindly either, I was not a fit wife for him, and that all that had been going on between us so long was for ever at an end. I've a right to remember this, sir, I think."

'Mary had made, to preserve her utterance in this testimony, all the exertion nature permitted. She fell back fainting into her father's arms, and a murmur of admiration ran round the court.

"This is an alibi with a witness," said the old shrewd senior crown council. "'Tis not likely a discarded sweetheart would travel six hundred miles to perjure herself for a scoundrel like this!"

'In corroboration of Mary's simple testimony, should any be required, there was handed to the jury a "housewife," whose few leaves of rude memoranda contained, evidently inserted at the moment, and blotted by a still discernible tear, "This day parted for ever with poor Richard Marshall in this world. God grant we may meet in the next!"'

'And did they meet again in this world, sir?' said I, when my honest friend had got rid of something troublesome in his eyes.

'No, sir; Mary thought it was better otherwise, and no one durst press it upon her. She wrote him a letter though, which no one else saw; and I hear he says his life was hardly worth saving since he has lost Mary. Poor wretch! we'll see if this great escape will sober him.'

Little more passed between me and my friend, as the lights of Haddington were now in view. I have since been in Berwick, and find Richard lives with his parents, a sadder and wiser man; and Mary is married in India to a young chaplain, to whom Lord S—— has promised a living in the north on his return to England.

OCCASIONAL NOTES.

NEW GRAPHIC WONDERS.

Since the invention of M. Daguerre, by which nature becomes her own copyist, and imprints by means of her own light the fac-simile of any opaque object on metal surfaces, various new discoveries have been made, and improvements effected, in that extraordinary principle, each more surprising than the former. The latest of these seems to be the climax; for surely nothing can go beyond what we are about to describe.

The January number of the Art-Union contains an account of a process by means of which any sort of engraving, printing, or writing, can be so exactly imitated, that it is next to impossible for the most critical eye to distinguish the original from the copy. Moreover, the transcript is made not on paper, but on a steel plate, and when printed, the impression exactly resembles the original proof or print from which the plate was taken. In short, when once a subject has been engraved, it may be multiplied to infinity.

The nature of the invention enforces that it should remain a secret. 'All we know of it,' says the editor of the Art-Union, 'may be briefly told. Some months ago we stated that a discovery had been made by which, in a few days, a large and elaborate line engraving might be so accurately copied, that there should be no perceptible difference between the original and the copy; that an engraving on steel or copper might be produced from an impression of the print—the original plate never having been seen by the copyist; and that such plate should be warranted to yield from 10,000 to 20,000 impressions. We stated, also, that it was stated to us that the producer would undertake to supply a Bank of England note so exactly copied, that the person who signed and issued it should not be able to swear which was the original and which the copy.'

In proof of the correctness of this statement, the impression of a plate, produced as above described, is stitched into the Art-Union. It is the head of our Saviour, engraved in the line manner by the well-known French engraver M. Blanchard, from a painting by Delaroche. Having procured an original impression of this plate from the publishers, the editor of the Art-Union handed it to a gentleman who undertook to be the agent of communication, and by whom it was passed to the inventor, who chooses, perhaps wisely, to remain behind the scenes for the present. The promise was, that within a fortnight a plate should be produced capable of yielding impressions which should be the exact counterpart of the pattern print. In seven days an impression was sent to the conductor of the Art-Union, which, in the technical language of engravers, is called 'a proof in progress;' in other words, an impression of the copy-engraving in an unfinished state. In seven days more the plate itself and a 'finished' proof were forwarded; together with the original print, *exactly in the same state in which it was sent*, which, so far from having been destroyed, or even injured, had not a speck upon it. From the plate between four and five thousand impressions were struck off, to be presented to the subscribers, without any perceptible wearing of the plate. Thus the lines and indentations made by the new process appear to be as deep and durable as those of the graver. In short, the copied plate answers the purpose of the original one in *every* respect.

'As soon,' continues the editor, 'as the plate was placed in our hands finished, we submitted it to several artists—painters and engravers; at the same time we laid before them impressions from the plate, and a proof of the original plate, taken, of course, in Paris. The opinion at which they arrived was, that although it was not difficult to distinguish the original from the copy, they were so thoroughly alike, that any person of practised eye might suppose the two to be from the same plate, the one being merely taken with greater care than the other; that they were precisely the same, line for line and "touch for touch;" and that this example completely established the principle: they considered the invention to be the most wonderful and the most unaccountable that had been made in modern times in connexion with art.'

Upon this evidence, therefore, we must come to the conclusion that the inventor of this process has at his command a power for good of the greatest magnitude: by it he is enabled to multiply the best works of art so rapidly and infinitely, that they will be quite accessible to the humbler orders of people, to spread amongst them the humanising influences of a refined intellectual taste. Nor will the injury to artists and engravers, by this augmented means of production, be so great as they may at first imagine; for, of course, before a copy can be taken, an original must be provided. The engraving must be first made, and as the public taste for prints will naturally increase with the cheap rate at which they will be procured, a far greater demand for originals is to be reasonably expected than exists at present. Thus artists generally will, in all probability, be benefited by the new invention instead of injured. But there is a reverse to these bright considerations. The inventor, besides an influence for good, wields a vast power for evil; for it is clear that he has means of committing forgery to any amount! And not only himself; for so simple is the process—so easy of performance—that he cannot even take out a patent for his invention, as the specification itself would place it in the power of any person to infringe the patent without a chance of being detected. Nor is it likely that such a secret can be very long retained; it will no doubt be soon universally known, and extensively acted upon.

Innumerable have been the conjectures which have been made, by artists quite competent to form them, as to the process. *We* have at once set it down to a new and improved application of the Daguerreotype process. Our reason is twofold: first, it is the most obvious mode of accounting for the graphic phenomenon; and next, very good evidence is supplied by the inventor himself. The specimen given in the Art-Union, wonderful as it seems to our unprofessional eye, has, it seems, some minute faults, which are thus accounted for. 'The inventor,' remarks the editor, 'has produced our example under serious disadvantages—being in ill health, having had to work *in dark and frosty weather*, and having been far too much hurried by us, in consequence of our desire to issue our copies with our January part. Moreover, the steel was not prepared expressly for the purpose, and was by no means fortunate for work.' Now, unless light and the atmosphere were the main agents in producing the plate, the excuse of the dark and frosty weather would not have been made.

But even with this startling novelty, the wonders of graphic art are not exhausted. Another gentleman, whose name is no secret, Mr Joseph Woods, of Bucklersbury, London, is the inventor of a process called Anastatic printing. It is the reproduction of any form of letterpress, or any quality of print, drawing, engraving, or lithograph, in unlimited quantity, in an inconceivably brief space of time. Any journal—say for instance the Times—might in twenty minutes be prepared for reprinting merely from a single number, and worked off with the ordinary rapidity of the steam-press. In less than a quarter of an hour from the time of receiving the sketch, the printer will present to the artist proofs of his work, which shall resemble the original as perfectly as if it had been reflected on the paper touch for touch. We shall not be far wrong, perhaps, in attributing this invention to a more perfect process of electrotyping than has hitherto been attained.

In contemplating the effect of these astonishing inventions, it is impossible to foresee their results upon the ordinary transactions of life. If any deed, negotiable security, or other legal instrument, can be so imitated that the writer of, and subscriber to it, cannot distinguish his own handwriting from that which is forged, new legislative enactments must be made, and new modes of representing money, and securing property by documentary record, must be resorted to. A paper currency and copyhold securities will be utterly useless, because they will no longer fulfil the objects for which they, and instruments of a like nature, are employed. Again, the law of copyright as respects literary property will have to be thoroughly revised. Let us, for an instant, view the case in reference to 'The Times' newspaper. Suppose an early copy of that powerful journal to be some morning procured, and anastatyped in a quarter of an hour. The pirated pages may be subjected to printing machinery, and worked off at the rate of 4000 copies in each succeeding hour, and sold to the public, to the ruinous injury of the proprietors. The government newspaper stamp would be no protection, for of course that could be imitated as unerringly as the rest. This, too, is an extreme case against the imitators; for a newspaper would have to be done in a great hurry. Books, maps, prints, and music, could be pirated wholesale, and at leisure.

Let us not be understood to apply any of these remarks to the inventors, as presuming for an instant, or by the remotest hint or inference, that *they* would be guilty of unworthy conduct. We merely state what is, we fear, inevitable when their inventions become public property, which, according to our information, from their extreme simplicity, is likely very soon to be the case.

'OLD CRUSTED PORT.'

If the lovers of 'old crusted port' were aware of the manner in which their much admired crust is frequently produced, they would certainly be less disposed to take so fallacious a standard as a test of excellence. The tricks of the trade are vividly exposed in the following notice—taken from the proceedings of the London Chemical Society—respecting the composition of certain kinds of green or bottle glass:—Some green glass bottles had been submitted to Mr Warrington of Apothecaries' Hall for examination on the ground of their having imparted a bad flavour to the wine contained in them. On inspection, they were found to have the inner surface rough and opaque, and to be readily acted upon by tartaric acid. A comparative analysis of the glass of these bottles with other green glass, showed that a large preponderance of bases, especially lime, had been employed in their fabrication. A few of the objectionable bottles were then filled with dilute sulphuric acid, and placed aside. After the lapse of a fortnight the bottles cracked, and the fluid escaped; and upon examination they were found to be incrusted over the whole of their inner surface with sulphate of lime, to the thickness of a copper penny-piece—the liberated silica being partly washed away in a gelatinous form, and partly enclosed in the crystalline mass. Mr Warrington stated that a considerable quantity of wine had been bottled in this glass, one merchant alone having, to his knowledge, bottled three hundred dozen, the manufacturer alleging that in these 'improved' bottles the crust of port wine would form earlier, and adhere firmer to the glass than in ordinary bottles.—In the remarks that followed on Mr Warrington's paper, it was stated, that so imperfectly fabricated were some kinds of green glass, that even a little free acetic acid in porter was known to have acted upon them. It was further mentioned that barytes was occasionally used in the manufacture of green glass, an excess of which, forming a soluble silicate, would be most deleterious; and, indeed, that almost all the glass of this sort now fabricated in Britain contained some soluble silicate.

This is certainly no very flattering account of our manufactures; but your connoisseurs in wine are much to blame for it. Mr Jones must have his 'old crusted port;' but Mr Smith the wine merchant, however anxious to oblige, cannot produce age at pleasure. He applies in his difficulty to Mr Brown the glassblower, and he with a few bushels of lime settles the matter in a twinkling. Of course Mr Brown, in his anxiety to produce a ripe old age on 'the shortest possible notice,' is very liable to overstep the exact per centage of lime; and thus Mr Smith occasionally pays his three hundred dozen as the penalty of fraud and dissimulation. Lucky are all such cases for poor Mr Jones, who, in his love for 'crust,' might otherwise have had his stomach absolutely lined with plaster of Paris, besides being ballasted with calculi to an indefinite amount.

A SUGGESTION TO MARINERS.

Very great inconvenience arising at all times, but particularly in bad weather, from the want of light in the ordinary mode of lighting vessels—binnacles not casting a sufficient light on the compasses, which, in fact, are often thrown into a shadow by the vessel rolling or pitching heavily—the attention of the maritime public is called to the following simple and cheap expedient for completely obviating the evil.

In all binnacles fitted in the ordinary mode—that is, with a light placed between two compasses—if small mirrors are placed, one on each side of the binnacle, opposite the light, taking care to fix them in the angle that fully reflects the light on the cards, the light being also a fixture, then, however much the vessel may labour, the cards will always be well illumined, and when the vessel is comparatively easy, the cards will receive a very great increase of light.

We present this note at the suggestion of Lieutenant

Cox, commander of her majesty's revenue cutter Lapwing, whose mind was directed to the expedient in consequence of his own vessel's very quick motion, and who found it to answer to his complete satisfaction. The required mirrors cost about two shillings, and the result is equal to that of an apparatus which cannot be obtained under eight or nine pounds.

LOITERINGS IN FRANCE—1844.

BEAUCAIRE—ARLES.

We were left in a broiling heat at Avignon, our only chance for fresh and somewhat cool air being a walk at dusk upon the long suspension-bridge which here crosses the left branch of the Rhone. On the third day, finding no vessel descending the river at a convenient hour, we departed from this ancient city by means of a voiture for Tarascon, another town about eighteen miles further down the Rhone.

The journey was destitute of general interest, and to us only amusing from the nature of the road. Having at two or three miles' distance from Avignon crossed the Durance by a long temporary bridge, the principal suspension one having been destroyed by a torrent some time before, we got into a tract of country apparently resting on limestone, of which the road was composed. The stones, ground by heavy roulage, formed a fine whitish-brown dust several inches deep, and this, raised by a breeze which had arisen, swept in clouds over the face of nature. Hedgerows, trees, fields, houses, were universally covered, as if under a snow storm. The drift drove in the faces of men and horses, shrouding them with its odious particles. Suffering the melting heats of summer, we appeared to be wandering in a dreary waste in the heart of winter. Never till now did we feel the force of the observation made by travellers, that in the southern parts of Europe there are, practically, two winters in the year—the winter of winter, and the winter of summer, in either of which work out of doors is unpleasant or impossible.

In due time we got into Tarascon, a poor old town, whence we crossed the Rhone, by a suspension-bridge of magnificent proportions, to Beaucaire, another town equally old and dull, but now the scene of an annual fair, the largest of its kind in Europe, which we proposed to see before going further. This, however, we soon discovered to be no easy matter. Embosomed still more in the limestone district of the south, the town was at present retired from public observation. It lay concealed in a cloud of the everlasting dust, and to get into its streets, one required to walk backwards and sideways with his face carefully buried in his handkerchief, feeling his way all the time with his feet. By dint of edging ourselves along in this curious fashion, we were enabled to reach a point on the quay, where numerous booths and tents were pitched for the accommodation of tradesmen with their goods. Here, from the general shelter afforded by these erections, as well as the concourse of people, the dust had comparatively little scope for its vagaries, and we were now permitted to look about us.

From the boulevard or quay adjoining the Rhone, we wandered into the heart of the town, everywhere finding the streets and lanes choked with people and merchandise. The scene was striking, and unlike anything we had seen before. Across the narrow streets were stretched gaudy sign-*boards* of yellow, red, and blue cotton, forming a brilliant perspective of colours, while above, from the tops of the houses, coverings of white linen were placed, to shelter the passengers and goods beneath, alike from the sun and the dust blown from the environs. Much of the merchandise was out of doors, ranged along the walls; and the fronts of the shops being quite open, like booths, everything was exposed to view. From flaunting signs overhead, we perceived that there were merchants from places in France hundreds of miles distant—cutlers from Thiers, jewellers from Paris, wine dealers from Bourdeaux, drapers and haberdashers from Lyons, booksellers from Limoges, gunmakers from St Etienne, and so on; tradesmen bringing their wares from the most remote localities. There were also not a few foreigners—Turks, Spaniards, Italians, Swiss, Greeks, Armenians—but not, as far as we could see, a single Englishman. Some streets were apparently devoted to wholesale dealings, and there carts were loading and unloading, and porters busy packing and carrying goods to and fro. Others were laid out for retail, and classified according to trades. One booth contained nothing but small spinning-wheels, such as were used by our thrifty grandmothers before factory spinning unsettled and uprooted domestic manufactures. It was interesting to observe, from the exhibition, that the housewives and maidens of the south of France were only beginning to use that which had been forty years ago thrown aside in the greater part of Scotland. To these good dames and demoiselles the spinning-wheel, antiquated as we are disposed to think it, is an engine greatly in advance of what it supersedes—the distaff—which, till the present moment, is as common in France as it was two hundred years ago in England. The spectacle of a country girl carrying home a spinning-wheel from a fair would now be considered an oddity in our own country.

The fair of Beaucaire is of great antiquity, and keeps its ground among many declining usages. Yet it is considered to be falling off, like other assemblages of the kind. Commencing on the 1st of July, it lasts the whole of the month, and attracts a hundred thousand persons from all surrounding and many distant places to make purchases. The heaviest part of the business is transacted, I was told, two or three days before the fair commences. The day of our visit was almost at the close, yet the bustle was considerable, and without any external appearance of soon abating. When finished, and all trace of the concourse removed, the town subsides into little else than a city of shut and empty houses; and were its fair extinguished, it would speedily fall into a state of neglect and ruin. The advantageous situation of Beaucaire for this great annual market, on the lower part of the Rhone, has been improved by the opening of a canal which leads from the Rhone immediately below the town across the country to the Garonne. On the banks of the canal and of the river, the traffic of barges, from the glance we had of it, seemed to be on an extensive scale.

It being useless to attempt remaining in a town during such a paroxysm of trade, our party gladly took advantage of a steamboat whose boiler was hissing at the quay, and by it we were carried rapidly down the Rhone towards Arles, which we designed should be our quarters for the night.

In descending the river from Beaucaire, the country on both sides begins to assume the character of a flat and marshy delta. The stream, hitherto impetuous, slackens in its speed, and winds through a region destitute of any object of interest, and in some places the view from the steamer is shut in by clusters of willows which flourish on the banks of the river, and on large flat islands round which the vessel toils its way. At the distance of about twenty-five miles from Beaucaire the river parts in two, a lesser branch going off on the right, called the Petit Rhone, while the larger keeps on its way to Arles, now near at hand. Our approach to the venerable city is indicated by the emerging of certain old gray buildings from behind the willowy bank on our left, and amidst which is observed rearing its gigantic form the ancient Roman amphitheatre for which Arles has obtained such distinction. The town generally being situated on a low rocky protuberance, near the summit of which the amphitheatre is placed, the approach from the river is favourable for taking a comprehensive view of the place.

Arles, once the Roman capital of Gaul, and afterwards the chief city of Trans-Jurane Burgundy, is now a poor old provincial town of France; but, possessing an abundance of magnificent ruins, the spectral relics of former glories, it is still impressive in its decay, and commands our respect as well as our commiseration. While Avignon is alone distinguished for the degenerate remains of middle-age architecture, Arles exhibits some of the grandest specimens of the best ages of Rome—magnificent and more perfect than almost anything of the kind in Rome itself.

We spent a day at Arles roaming amidst its ruins; but an antiquary, who did not mind modern discomforts, might well spend a month. The thing which attracts one the moment he arrives is the amphitheatre. Wending our way through some narrow and crooked alleys, in a direction eastwards from the central Place of the town, we came upon this remarkable edifice, which, by some recent alterations, has been liberated from contiguous and mean buildings, and now stands aloof, surrounded by an iron railing. It is difficult to know how to describe such a vast and curiously constructed mass. Exteriorly, we have before us a gray sandstone structure, oval in form, consisting of two storeys of pilasters, with windows or openings, the whole rising from the ground a height of seventy to eighty feet. The lower storey is Doric, and the upper of the Corinthian order, and being mostly composed of large blocks of stone, the surface is wonderfully entire. Where time or violence has seriously damaged the pilasters or arched openings, the French government, greatly to its credit, has effected repairs by the introduction of new stones. Neither the large arched openings in the lower storey, anciently used as the vomitoires or outlets, nor the openings above, point inwards in a direction parallel with each other. It is remarked, that all the arches are concentric; that is, proceed towards the centre of the oval; an arrangement which must have been accomplished with much additional trouble to the planner and builders. Although now liberated, as I have said, from clusters of parasitic edifices, the building is not approachable on every point, for one side rests on an elevated part of the rocky knoll, which mars the general unity of the exterior wall.

The only entrance now in use is at the western extremity, and by this we were admitted through a lofty arched passage to the interior of the structure. Walking forward, we are in the middle of a flat space, the original though partially broken floor of the arena, and around us, from the top of the podium or bounding parapet, to the summit of the outer wall, are seen gradually ascending rows of stone seats. The rows, however, are greatly broken in some places, and in others they are entirely gone, showing the ghastly fragments of arches which once supported them. The whole interior area, including the space covered by seats, measures an oval of 459 feet in length, and 338 in breadth, and accommodated 25,000 spectators. There never was any roof. All is open to the sky; but, from poles fixed in the upper part of the outer wall, awnings were drawn across to shelter the spectators from the sun.

The ascent to the seats was by stone stairs leading from different entrances, and several stairs still remain. The visitor of the ruin, however, gains the top by arched doorways in the podium opening on the arena, through which the wild beasts were wont to be ushered from dens in the interior of the building. We were conducted into these dismal recesses, where were pointed out the dingy vaults in which these ferocious beasts, and also the unfortunate beings whose doom it was to encounter them in the arena, were separately confined. From these gloomy passages we ascended by one of the stairs to a part of the amphitheatre the least decayed. Here, sitting down, we could estimate the imposing scene which the place must have presented when filled with spectators. From the front, or lowest, to the topmost seat, we reckoned, as nearly as possible, thirty rows of stone benches, each from sixteen to eighteen inches broad, by about the same in depth; by which means, every block or bench, while serving as a seat for one party, accommodated the feet of the party immediately behind. What seemed a little puzzling, no two rows were alike in dimensions, though quite regular in general aspect. Probably the accommodation was suited in some degree to the different ranks of spectators.

The spot on which we had seated ourselves was in the southern side of the oval, midway from the front to the upper extremity. Here the seats seemed most entire, and we were able to count at least twenty rows together in a nearly undamaged condition. So huge are the square blocks of stone forming the seats, that great violence must have been employed to uplift and destroy them. In all probability, they were abstracted as building materials for the numerous churches and convents which were erected in the town during the middle ages, or for the walls and towers raised in defence of the place.

At present, all cumbrous rubbish being removed, leaving the ruin clear, we are enabled to note with perfect accuracy the internal organisation of the structure. Except, indeed, that large patches of the seats are gone, exposing the tops of the arches which bore them up, everything is much in the state in which it was left by the Romans, although fifteen hundred years have elapsed since they set their foot within it.

It is only, I imagine, by a visit to such a place that one can fully realise an idea of the barbaric amusements of the Roman people. Here the thing is before us, an undoubted substantiality. The stories of gladiators fighting against each other in the arena—of unhappy Christian captives being set upon by savage beasts of prey—of slaves and malefactors condemned to wrestle in deadly struggle, all for popular amusement, are felt to have been no fictions, but sad realities. From the bench whence we now looked down on the arena, doubtless, had been shouted the horrid *hoc habet* which signalised the death-wound of the unfortunate combatant, accompanied by the ominous turning downwards of the thumbs, which bade the conqueror despatch his victim. Realising, by a small stretch of fancy, the spectacle of such barbaric amusements, a visit to the amphitheatre of Arles likewise affords a vivid notion of the greatness of the Roman people in works of art. Although much smaller than the Coliseum at Rome, the edifice we are now visiting is nevertheless on a stupendous scale, and the cost of its erection must have been enormous. It affords a lively illustration of the importance in the Roman state of that privileged class, usually called 'the people,' but in reality a burghal aristocracy. Amphitheatres were erected for the amusement of this class in Nismes, and other places comparatively of a provincial character, and all the entertainments were provided at the public cost. The only restriction consisted in taking the seat which was assigned, and this was regulated by rank and other circumstances. In the front, next the podium, were placed the senators, ambassadors of foreign nations, and also, in a particular seat, the emperor, or his representative the prefect. Next were seats assigned to the judges and ordinary magistrates; these, as well as the seats in front, being provided with cushions. The next higher rows, styled the *popularia*, were of right taken by 'the people.' And the uppermost and most distant benches, like the galleries of modern theatres, were appointed to the inferior orders and slaves.

Not to dwell unnecessarily on these slight illustrations, we may now quit the spot where we have been a few minutes ruminating, and ascend the sloping rows of steps to the top of the building. Here a more commanding view is obtained: but we may go still higher, and look without as well as within the amphitheatre. Conducted by our guide, we were led up a narrow stair to the top of a massive square tower on the outer wall. This tower, which is a comparatively modern excrescence, is matched by another on the opposite side. Both are understood to have been erected about a thousand years ago, when the building was used as a fort either by the Saracenic intruders in this part of France, or by the native powers who expelled them. Other two similar towers—four having been erected—are now gone.

From the lofty situation we had gained, we had a wide and uninterrupted view over the town immediately below us, and of the great marshy plain beyond, which stretched southwards to the Mediterranean, and through which the branches of the Rhone were threading their way amidst groves of willows—the whole a dreary flat, whence the heat of the sun was raising an unwholesome mist. On descending to the arena, we looked round for some kind of inscription, but were not more successful in the search than hosts of antiquaries who had gone before us. Faint traces of characters are alone visible on the broken marble slabs which face the podium. It is understood that the building was erected in the reign of the Emperor Titus, nearly eighteen hundred years ago.

Our next visit was to a singularly beautiful relic of art, which has lately been exposed to view at a short distance from the amphitheatre, on ground a little more elevated. This is the fragment of a Roman theatre, which had for centuries been partly buried in rubbish, and partly engrossed in some mean domestic structures. The principal objects now standing exposed in the midst of the excavation are two marble columns of the Corinthian order, surmounted by a portion of elegant entablature. These had formed pillars of the scene, others for a similar purpose being destroyed, and lying in pieces on the ground. Part of the flight of stone seats for the audience is also entire, with some portions of walls used for the orchestra and the support of the stage.

Throughout the town there are other antiquities worth visiting, and a museum of relics formed in a disused church; but any notice of these would not afford matter of interest to the reader, whom I therefore invite to follow us in our next move in quest of the picturesque. This was no less than a voyage by steam back to Beaucaire, where, having once more groped our way through a whirlwind of limestone dust, we were so fortunate as to find seats in a railway train ready to set off for Nismes. This was a journey of more than twenty miles, but was rapidly performed, and the only discomfort attending it was the blowing of one of those strange gusty winds which haunt the borders of the Mediterranean, and whirl not only dust, but small stones and other light objects into the atmosphere.

BENEFICIAL CO-OPERATION OF THE WORKING-CLASSES.

We have had a vast number of inquiries regarding the article which under this head appeared in the Journal on the 4th of the past month; and with a view to supply such further information as may enable bodies of workmen to enter into arrangements similar to those existing amongst the men employed by Mr Ramsay in the lighting and cleaning departments of the Edinburgh police, we lay this article before our readers. With those who, like ourselves, take an interest in everything which concerns that great mass of our countrymen who earn their bread by bodily labour, any measure tending, in however small a degree, to ameliorate the hardships and distresses incident to their condition in life, will always be viewed with a high degree of interest and favour; and if there be any considerable number of persons who entertain the opinion that the working-classes themselves are disposed to look with apathy and indifference on schemes of this character, we have only to refer to the multitude of inquiries produced by our notice of the scheme in operation amongst Mr Ramsay's men, as a conclusive and satisfactory reply. It is indeed pleasing to find large bodies of workmen in every district of the kingdom eager and anxious for information as to the means of emancipating themselves from the thraldom and degradation of dependence on charity, and entering with earnestness and avidity into the consideration of a scheme which repudiates eleemosynary aid, and trusts only to that relief and assistance which it purchases and pays for, and which, for a given consideration, it is entitled to demand.

Mr Ramsay's scheme is of a twofold nature, and although its two branches are substantially separate, they admit of easy and beneficial combination; or, where their junction may be unnecessary, may be carried on separately. As stated in our previous article on this subject, the first is a benefit scheme, in the usual and proper sense of the word, securing an alimentary allowance, and medicine and medical attendance for the sick and hurt; an allowance for funerals; and finally, the division of the whole funds in hand at Martinmas and Whitsunday in each year, in exact proportion to the contributions. This branch of the scheme is compulsory, and contributions at the rate of 6d. per man per week is one of the conditions of obtaining employment in the establishment. The contributions are retained from the wages, and placed in bank weekly as collected. Nothing can be simpler, more efficient, or more easily worked than this important branch. A card, with the designation of the scheme printed upon it, is put into the hands of each of the men, and on these cards each man legibly and accurately writes his address, and when illness occurs in his family, sends it to the medical officer, who, on receiving it, immediately visits and redelivers the card, that it may be in readiness for the next occasion. If it happen to be the man himself who is taken ill, he sends notice also, on the first day of his illness, to his overseer, or to a member of the visiting committee, and on pay-day (Wednesday) presents an application, upon a printed form which is furnished to him, for aliment; and, on this being subscribed by the medical officer, he receives his allowance of 9d. per day. Aliment, however, is not allowed to any one who has been less than fourteen days on the establishment from the date of his last appointment, nor whose illness has been brought on by his own misconduct. Those receiving aliment are not permitted to be out of their dwellings after eight o'clock in the evening, on pain of being struck off the roll of the establishment, and deprived of all further benefit; and *no aliment is allowed to those in receipt of any public charity*. Funeral money is paid on a certificate of death by the medical officer, and of interment by a member of the visiting committee; and if a coffin be required from the undertaker having the contract for furnishing them, the price is retained out of the funeral money. If the funeral money shall not be claimed till the second termly division after the death of the party, it is then to be distributed as a part of the free dividend; *but no funeral money is allowed in any case where the expenses of the funeral are defrayed in whole or in part by the parish or other public charity*; and the committee, if they see cause, may withhold payment till a receipt for payment of the churchyard dues is presented to them.

In so far as a mere benefit scheme goes, these arrangements seem at once simple, judicious, and comprehensive, and afford in a limited degree nearly all the advantages which can be derived from any similar design. The allowances both for sickness and funerals are no doubt small, but then the wages of the men are not such as enable them to afford a high rate of contribution. This, however, is the less necessary, as they are all strongly urged to enter at least one other benefit society, and thus to a certain extent to protect themselves against one of the worst evils of sickness in the house of the working-man—that of poverty—a recommendation which, almost without exception, has been acted on. The cost of these advantages is incredibly small. The whole expenditure for the half year ended 15th November last, for aliment, at 5s. 3d. per week, being only L.3, 8s. 7½d.; and for funeral money, at the rate of L.4, L.3, and 15s., for a man, a wife, and child respectively, only L.12, 5s., the strength of the establishment during that period averaging 152 men. The average cost to each man for aliment, therefore, is only a fraction more than 5½d. for the half year, or eight-tenths of a farthing per man per week. In like manner, the cost to each man for funerals is a fraction more than 1s. 7½d. in the half year, or almost exactly three farthings per man per week. The conjoined expense of these two important items is only L.15, 13s. 7½d., and the aggregate cost per man 2s. 1d., or rather less than 1d. per man per week. These, added to the fixed allowance of 2d. per man per week to the surgeon, amount to a total expense of 3d. per man per week nearly, being rather under the one-half of the sums retained as contributions, and enabling the committee to return 6s. 6d. to each man out of 13s. contributed within the half year. The past season, to be sure, has been a remarkably healthy one; but the wages must be miserable indeed which cannot afford so small a sum wherewith to purchase so many advantages.

From an elaborate table of statistics, prepared by Mr Ramsay, applicable to a period of five years, and laid before the commissioners of police, when the benefit scheme was under their consideration, it appears, that in a number of yearly societies, where a similar amount of benefit is rendered as in that of the police, comprising an annual aggregate of 1828 members of all ages—from 15 to 60—the average cost for aliment was three farthings per member per week; and for funeral money, a sum represented by a decimal of ·98, or something less than a penny. This is higher than the police scheme has yet cost; but as many of the members of which these societies are composed are persons by no means in robust health, the avocations of another portion sedentary and unhealthy, and the ages of a considerable section unfavourable, Mr Ramsay's scheme, making a slight allowance for the circumstance of an unusually healthy season, and also for the accounts being applicable only to the summer half year, which is known to be healthier than the winter, may be taken as a close approximation to the expense of maintaining a society where all the members are able-bodied workmen engaged in out-door employment. When a higher rate of benefit is required, or where circumstances exist unfavourable to the health of the members, an increased rate of contribution is of course necessary.

It is proper to notice a circumstance which has in some measure no doubt beneficially affected the results of the police benefit scheme, and that is, that, as a body, they are probably not excelled for sobriety by any similar number of men of their own rank in the empire; a remarkable and gratifying proof of which is to be found in the fact, that during the whole of the holidays at the end of 1843 and the commencement of 1844, out of 180 men then employed, not one was known to have been in the slightest degree under the influence of liquor.

Arising out of the benefit scheme, and closely connected with it, came a co-operative scheme, scarcely second in importance and advantage even to the former. The purpose of this was to procure certain necessary articles for the use of the men at the lowest wholesale prices. The idea, we believe, was suggested by an article which appeared in the Journal on the 11th of May last, and adopted immediately thereafter. It was then proposed to enter into a contract for bread; and when it is stated that, as soon as the matter became known, although the committee limited their applications for offers to a small number of bakers of the first respectability, known to sell only bread of the first quality, they had offers from several persons to furnish it at 16 per cent. discount from the ordinary selling price. These the committee rejected, and contented themselves with a much lower rate of discount, on the ground that they wished the contractor to realise a fair profit, and furnish an unexceptionable article both as to weight and quality. The value of this contract may be conceived, when it is stated that several of the men required *seven* loaves a week each for their families; and for a considerable period after the contract was entered on, the consumpt varied from 350 to 420 loaves weekly.

The next article contracted for was the best oatmeal, delivered in quantities of not less than a firlot (35 lbs). This is furnished at the lowest wholesale price, being generally upwards of a penny a peck under the retail price. A peck is seven pounds.

A contract for coal was then entered into from a particular pit, where the coal was known to be of excellent quality. A fixed price at the pit was agreed to, and a person engaged to deliver coal in quantities of not less than half a ton as required. The price, including cartage, was only 8s. per ton, and as the article is of very superior quality, it has given great satisfaction. Nearly all the men were in the practice of purchasing coal in single hundredweights, for which they paid from 7d. to 8d., being from 11s. 8d. to 13s. 4d. per ton, and of a quality greatly inferior. The comfort and economy of thus obtaining coal in cart-loads at a low rate is of great value, and has been fully appreciated.

In October, the committee bought several hundred bolls (4 cwt. to a boll) of potatoes from a farmer, upwards of 300 bolls of which are already delivered; they are furnished in quantities of not less than half a boll. Some of the men use six or seven bolls in the season, the average being from three to four.

The purchase of other articles has been contemplated; but as yet it has been limited to those we have enumerated. One obstacle in the way of extending these contracts will readily present itself, in the difficulty of thoroughly specifying and defining the quality of the articles required. The principle adopted by Mr Ramsay on this point, is to contract only for such articles as admit of easy comparison with a sample, or which may be specified with so much precision as to quality, conditions of delivery, &c. as not to admit of dispute. Where one or other of these rules cannot be applied, the trust must be in the mutual understanding and good faith of the parties.

When the co-operative branch of the scheme was suggested, the first obstacle arose from the want of funds. In order to form a small capital, it was agreed that the surplus cash belonging to the benefit scheme should be applied to this new purpose; and to augment this stock, as well as to establish the individual credit of the men, each of them subscribed such small sums as their means could afford, and as their requirements as to the articles contracted for rendered necessary. In this way each man became possessed of an immediate interest in the fund to the extent of the value of his share of the surplus of the benefit scheme, and of the capital he paid in added together, and to the amount of these at least he was entitled to be supplied with such articles as were contracted for by the committee. Many of the men, besides, found it a most useful place of deposit for such little savings as they could from time to time spare from their wages. Deposits, varying from sixpence to three and four shillings a-week, were accordingly made; and as these might at all times be got up on demand, under deduction only of what might be owing to the scheme, sums were accumulated for the purchase of shoes, or clothes, or the payment of rents, and other necessary purposes, which, in some instances at least, would probably have been squandered on less important articles.

The wages of each man being paid with the utmost regularity, it was laid down at the outset, as a fixed rule, that, supposing a man were supplied with bread, meal, coal, or potatoes, from the scheme, he should make a weekly payment equal to the extent of his weekly consumption of the articles furnished. A man, for example, who required four loaves of bread in the week, a firlot of meal in a fortnight, a boll of potatoes in a month, and a ton of coal in three months, paid for the whole of the bread, the half of the meal, the fourth of the potatoes, and the twelfth of the coal, every week. In this way they paid exactly for what they got, at the same rate per week as if the articles had been served out of a shop in weekly quantities; with this important difference, that articles of the very best quality were supplied to them at the very lowest wholesale prices.

It happened frequently—indeed almost constantly—that men with large families required to order articles probably to twice or thrice the amount of their interest in the fund; and in order to accommodate them, and at the same time to protect the committee, whose services in the whole business are purely gratuitous, a printed form of application for the articles was prepared, authorising the committee, in the event of the applicant leaving the establishment while any part of the articles were unpaid, to uplift whatever money might be due to him either on account of the benefit scheme, the co-operative fund, or for wages, and to apply it in liquidation of any claim against him for articles furnished. A printed form in similar terms is also, in such cases, required to be subscribed by two persons on the establishment as cautioners, so that the committee are, on the whole, tolerably well protected against loss by bad debts.

The clerk for the benefit scheme is also clerk for this branch, and no goods of any description are furnished to any one except on his order.

The benefits arising from these conjoined schemes are probably more numerous and important than may at first sight appear. The first and most obvious are clearly the providing a means of relief when the men are laid off work by sickness, and the payment of a sum on the death of any member of the family, for the purpose of defraying the funeral charges. Next to these in importance is the arrangement for providing medical attendance and medicine to the men and their families. The surgeon being elected by a committee appointed for that purpose by the men themselves, the utmost confidence is placed in his professional skill, while the right to demand his services in any emergency, and the consciousness that these services are paid for, elevates them in their own estimation, and places them in a position in all respects superior to those who are under the necessity of begging medical relief as a charity, and of submitting, as sometimes happens, to be treated by persons in whose skill they have not the confidence usually inspired by previous personal acquaintance. The division of the surplus funds at Martinmas and Whitsunday becomes an important contribution towards the payment of the house-rent falling due at these terms; and to those who do not require it for that purpose, it comes opportunely either for the purchase of articles of dress, or as a nucleus to which further savings may be added. Amongst its negative merits, it may be mentioned that its meetings are never held in taverns, and that it is conducted without expense. But benefits of a higher, more ennobling, and more important character than those which pertain to the mere saving of money arise from this scheme, from the feeling of independence which it inspires and fosters, and from the boldness and manliness with which it trusts to its own efforts alone in its discarding of all reliance on extrinsic aid. That feeling, also, which is the very bane of the working-classes—want of confidence in each other—is here practically subdued; their interests inseparably united; and individual wants and afflictions felt as matters in which all are concerned. We had almost added, that their sympathy for each other was promoted; but the writer of this article well knows the generous and kindly hearts of that portion of his brethren whose hands are hardened with daily toil; and if there be any class of his countrymen whose charities towards each other never fail, it is that of the humblest, the hardest worked, and the worst paid among them. He could tell of patient endurance, of self-denial, of exalted generosity, all calmly and unostentatiously exercised, and all unheard of by that mass of persons who call themselves the world, which would make the ears of the coldest tingle, and the proudest hang down their heads.

It is perhaps scarcely necessary to add that any body of men, consisting of a dozen or upwards, may enter into the whole or any part of these schemes. If the benefit scheme only be adopted, and if the number be very small, the benefits might either be longer deferred, or money borrowed to meet such contingencies as require a larger sum than may be on hand at the time. A better way, perhaps, is to make no division of the funds for the first year, except in the case of members who may leave, and to retain the amount acquired as a sort of standing capital. A year's contributions would thus always be on hand to cover any demands that might occur.

LONDON FOGS.

Fogs, says Mr Main, are more dense about London, and probably all other great cities, than elsewhere, because the vast quantity of fuliginous matter floating over such places mingles with the vapour, and renders the whole so thick, that a noonday darkness is sometimes produced, rendering candles and gas-lights necessary for the transaction of the ordinary business of the shops and public offices. Such circumstances happen frequently during winter; but on some occasions (as about two o'clock P.M. on the 27th December 1831) this darkness is truly awful. This extraordinary appearance is, however, caused by a very ordinary accident, namely, a change of winds, and which may be accounted for as follows:—The west wind carries the smoke of the city to the eastward, in a long train, extending to the distance of twenty or thirty miles, as may be seen in a clear day by any person on an eminence, as, for instance, at Harrow-on-the-Hill. In this case, suppose the wind to change suddenly to the east, the great body of the smoke will be brought back in an accumulated mass, and as this repasses the city, augmented by the clouds of smoke from every fire therein, it causes the murky darkness alluded to. This effect of the smoke being thrown back on its source may be easily conceived; indeed it may be seen, under favourable circumstances, first reverted, and gradually accumulating, till it is dispersed on the opposite side; but wherever the accumulation is, in its progress backwards there will be an unusual degree of darkness. It is to be observed, that the cause of fogs is also the cause of the smoke floating near the earth; and, of course, where there is so much of the latter, the former is doubly dense. Besides fogs, we have also mist or haze, usually accompanying east winds, especially in the spring months. In the counties to the westward of the metropolis, this is called London smoke; but as it is seen to the eastward as well as westward of the city, the appellation is improper. The most natural idea we can form of this hazy appearance is, its being caused by the constitutional coldness of the east wind, which, checking the ascent of vapour raised by the sun, carries it horizontally along the lowest stratum of the air; hence its visibility. A lurid gloom is also sometimes produced by clouds of snow, when the water floating in the air becomes frozen into spicula, and congregating into flakes, contrary currents of wind wheel them into irregular masses, which obstruct the light from the sky, so as to wrap every object immediately below in a deep yellow light. This latter circumstance almost always precedes, and is a certain sign of, a fall of snow.—*Magazine of Natural History.*

CULTURE OF RICE IN CHINA.

The Chinese conduct this cultivation with great care, endeavouring in this, as in all the offices of husbandry in which they engage, to draw from the soil the greatest possible produce. The care of the cultivator begins before the seeds are placed in the earth. The grains destined for that purpose are put in baskets, and immersed in water, in which situation they remain for some days; this softens them, and tends to hasten their germination. The land which is to be sown with this crop is previously saturated with water, until the surface is like soft mud. In this state it is stirred up with a plough of very simple construction, to which is yoked a single buffalo. A rude kind of hurdle, drawn also by one buffalo, succeeds the plough, the driver sitting upon the hurdle to increase its weight, by which means the clods are broken down, and the ground made smooth. All stones are carefully removed; and as far as possible, every weed is extirpated. Water is then again let in upon the land, in just sufficient quantity to cover its surface, and a harrow, with several rows of great iron teeth, still further smooths and completes the preparation of the ground. Only those grains which have sprouted in the water are selected for sowing, since, as they have begun to germinate, their goodness is ascertained; all the rest are rejected. The seed is sown thickly and evenly on only part of the ground; this serving as a nursery for the rest. A day after the seeds have been sown, the points of the plants appear above the surface of the ground. As soon as the plants have acquired a little strength, they are sprinkled with lime-water, for the purpose of destroying insects, which might otherwise prey upon the young shoots. This operation is performed with a small basket, attached to a long handle, the basket being filled by immersion from another vessel; it is moved over the plants, and the fluid runs through, and is thus equally distributed over them. When the young plants appear in thick vegetation, they are thinned; the superfluous plants being carefully taken up with their rootlets, and transplanted in a quincunx order in the unoccupied portion of the land which has been prepared for their reception. No delay must take place in this work, so that the plants may be as short time as possible out of the ground; a calm day is usually selected for the purpose. As soon as planting is completed, the water is admitted to overflow the plants. For the advantage of irrigation, the rice fields are usually situated near to a rivulet, pond, or other water, from which they are separated only by a bank, and through this a communication is readily made. Sometimes, however, it happens that the water is below the level of the fields; in this dilemma, the moisture so essential to the success of the crop is supplied by means of buckets, which is a most tedious and laborious operation. The grounds are kept perfectly clean from weeds, which are taken up by the root with the hand, although the soil is in such a swampy state that the labourers employed in this task cannot step upon the ground without sinking knee deep. The maturity of the grain is known by its turning yellow in the same manner as wheat; it is then cut with a sickle, tied in sheaves, and conveyed into sheds or barns, where it is thrashed with flails very similar to those used in England.—*Porter, in the Oriental Agriculturist.*

AN ACCOMPLISHED YOUNG LADY.

Her edication is slicked off complete; a mantymaker gets her up well, and she is sent back to home with the Tower stamp on her, 'edicated at a boardin'-school.' She astonishes the natives round about where the old folks live, and makes 'em stare agin, she is so improved. She plays beautiful on the piano two pieces; they were crack pieces, larned onder the eye and ear of the master; but there is a secret nobody knows but her—she can't play nothin' else. She sings two or three songs, the last lessons larnt to school, and the last she ever will larn. She has two or three beautiful drawin's; but there is a secret here too—the master finished 'em; and she can't do another. She speaks French beautiful; but it's fortunate she ain't in France now, so that secret is safe. She is a very agreeable gal, and talks very pleasantly, for she has seen the world. She was to London for a few weeks; saw the last play, and knows a great deal about the theatre. She has been to the opera onc't, and has seen Celeste and Fanny Essler, and heard Lablache and Grisi, and is a judge of dancin' and singin'. She saw the queen a horseback in the Park, and is a judge of ridin'; and was at a party at Lady Syllabub's, and knows London life. This varnish lasts a whole year. The two new pieces wear out, and the songs get old, and the drawin's everybody has seed, and the London millinery wants renewin', and the queen has another princess, and there is another singer at the opera, and all is gone but the credit, 'she was edicated at a boardin'-school.'—*Sam Slick in England.*

THE STURGEON FISHERY.

The river Volga, especially near its mouth, is the principal scene of this fishery. When the fish enter the river, which they do, like many others, at stated seasons, for the purpose of depositing their spawn, large enclosures of strong stakes are set across the current, to intercept and prevent their return; the enclosures narrow up the river, and the animal getting into these confined places, is easily speared. This fish (*Accipenser sturo*), of which there are several species, breeds in the Caspian in such numbers, as to fill the rivers flowing into that sea. Fifteen thousand sturgeons are sometimes taken in one day with the hook, at the station of Sallian on the Persian coast; and upwards of 700,000 were taken in the year 1829 in the Russian dominions off the coast of the Caspian. The *flesh* of the sturgeon is salted and dried for consumption during the numerous fasts enjoined by the Greek church; but the two most valuable products are *isinglass* and *caviare*. The former is prepared from the air-bladder, and large quantities of it are annually imported into England from St Petersburg. Caviare is a preparation from the roe, of a strong, oily, but agreeable flavour; and is increasing in estimation here, if we may judge by the increased importation of it: a great deal is also consumed in Italy.

THE ROSE AND THE LILY.

[FROM THE GERMAN OF DEUERN.]

A LOVELY Rose and Lily growing
In a garden, side by side,
The Rose, with love's own radiance glowing,
Turned and said, in beauty's pride:
'Wherefore raise thy head so high,
Since not half so fair as I?

Sure all the magic charms that hover
O'er the lips of maiden fair,
In my bosom's depths the lover,
Fondly seeking, findeth there:
On her dewy lips repose
All the glories of the Rose!'

The Lily turned to speak, soft smiling
With a proud yet gentle grace,
For well she knew the charm beguiling
Of her pure and virgin face:
'The whiteness of the maiden's breast,
Of beauty is the surest test.'

That moment, through the garden bounding,
Comes the treasure of my life;
As light they hear her footfall sounding,
Ceased each angry word of strife.
The lovely flowers she stands before,
And they are sisters evermore!

Her fair young cheek, where lilies, roses,
In fast friendship ever bloom,
To the rival flowers discloses,
In beauty's garden both have room:
Each declares, from envy free,
None so beautiful as she!

Jan. 1845. R. L.

ARSENIC.

M. Grimaud, a chemist of Poictiers, proposes the following mode of rendering poisoning by arsenic more difficult. He recommends that this article shall be sold only when mixed with a certain quantity of sulphate of iron and cyanure of potash. About one per cent. of each substance would, he alleges, be sufficient. The arsenic, thus qualified, shows itself either by colour or smell, when used in the various aliments fit for man. Thus, arsenic prepared this way, and thrown into warm meat soup, gives immediately a green bronze colour; into hot milk, an opal; into red wine, a violet; into bread, a deep blue; and so on for twenty mixtures on which M. Grimaud has made experiments.

PREPARATION OF COFFEE.

It is a fact well known in Prague, that the water of the wells in that town is better adapted for use in making coffee than the river water; comparative analyses of the water indicate that this depends on the carbonate of soda contained in the former. Pleischl found this opinion corroborated by the fact, that a small quantity of the salt added to coffee improves its flavour, and advises consequently the addition of 43 grains of the pure carbonate to each pound of roasted coffee, as an improvement to the flavour, and also to the curative effect of this beverage, as it neutralises the acid contained in the infusion.—*Pharmaceutical Journal.*

*** Complete sets of the Journal, *First Series*, in twelve volumes, and also odd numbers to complete sets, may be had from the publishers or their agents. A Stamped Edition issued for transmission, post free, price Twopence halfpenny.

Printed by William Bradbury, of No. 6, York Place, and Frederick Mullett Evans, of No. 7, Church Row, both of Stoke Newington, in the county of Middlesex, printers, at their office, Lombard Street, in the precinct of Whitefriars, and city of London; and Published (with permission of the Proprietors, W. and R. CHAMBERS,) by WILLIAM SOMERVILLE ORR, Publisher, of 2, Amen Corner, at No. 2 AMEN CORNER, both in the parish of Christchurch, and in the city of London.—Saturday, February 8, 1845.

CONDUCTED BY WILLIAM AND ROBERT CHAMBERS, EDITORS OF 'CHAMBERS'S INFORMATION FOR THE PEOPLE,' 'CHAMBERS'S EDUCATIONAL COURSE,' &c.

No. 59. New Series. SATURDAY, FEBRUARY 15, 1845. Price 1½d.

THE WILL AND THE WAY.

The old saying, that where there is a will there is a way, might be called an extreme proposition; yet it is so often found true, that proverbial wisdom is amply justified in adopting it. The roads which we incline not to travel are all sadly beset with specimens of the feline tribe; and when a gentleman is asked for money by a companion often in need of it, he is extremely apt to have a large and exhausting payment to make at the end of the week. But when he is really determined to push his way along the road, opposing lions have usually little terror for him, and, if anxious to oblige his friend, he will almost certainly be able to do so without the breach of any of his own engagements. So, also, I observe that my son Tom is very liable at ordinary times to a prejudice as to his power of mastering the lessons set to him by his master; but I seldom hear of any difficulty when a half holiday is made to depend on his being fully accomplished in them. In fact, the most wonderful feats are sometimes performed under the influence of a powerful impulse operating upon the will. When the Texan prisoners of the Santa Fé expedition were told, for instance, by their brutal conductor, that any who should prove unable to walk would be shot, many who had up to that moment seemed at the last gasp of exhaustion, plucked up and set off at a stout pace, which they kept up all day. Quentin Matsys thought he could not paint, till his master told him his daughter's hand depended on his producing a picture of merit within six months; and then he painted the well-known 'Misers,' now preserved in Windsor Castle.

Even in scientific matters this proverb is found applicable. An ingenious man, whose mind runs before its age, discovers some unexpected principles, and repeats the experiments by which they were ascertained over and over again to his entire satisfaction. Being inconsistent with some of the many preconceptions which ignorance or slight knowledge has fixed in the public mind, they are received with distrust, and the usual anxiety is shown by all the associates of the discoverer to find him out to be a base impostor, or at the best a pitiable dreamer. Some therefore go over the experiments, or think they do so, and, as they anticipated, can find no such results. And they really do not find the results. It is the common case. And all the world sits quietly down, saying, 'Oh, of course it was a mere delusion.' And then, if the discoverer is a modest timid man, there is an end of the matter perhaps for twenty years, when at length the principle is discovered again, and forced into notice by other persons. Now, what is the explanation of this? Simply, that the second experimenters came to the trial with sceptical distrustful minds, much more willing to see the hypothesis disproved than to find it true. All such experiments require to have a number of minutiæ, which are almost inexpressible in writing, carefully attended to; for example, the strength or freshness of a particular ingredient may be of material consequence. Thus, although the experiment may have been to appearance fully and fairly made, some little points, *such as a person otherwise disposed would have been sure to attend to,* are neglected; and for this reason the results are a failure. Such circumstances are continually taking place in the scientific world. The failure is often the result of no feeling so decided as ill-will, but merely of indifference or carelessness. Microscopic accuracies necessary for the success of the experiment will only be fully attended to by the person who feels a heart interest in that success, and is disposed to take any trouble or make any sacrifice to attain it. Besides the actual discoverer, there is no such person, or, if there be, it is a rare case.

The kind of men called great are usually remarkable for powerful will. Cæsar, Cromwell, Frederick, Napoleon, Wellington — see in them all this efficacious principle towering over almost every other, and rendering opposing circumstances as nothing in their path. They resolve, and the thing is done. The secret of this success is here. Such men first affect their lieutenants, and officers immediately around them. These persons, finding all hesitation unacceptable, and no difficulties acknowledged, are inspired to make great efforts. They again affect the mass, and thus the spirit of one man impresses and energises all. The word impossible becomes a lost term in such hosts. Great talents of any kind without this one central principle would not serve. What is required to animate and conquer is WILL; a principle only connected with intellect, but not intellect itself — far from it; a thing essentially selfish, yet a needful aid in the whole procedure of our nature. Men remarkably endowed with will are not always either just, or kind, or judicious. Often, finding it serve them well in some instances, and hearing men whisper flattering remarks upon it, they begin to make it an object of worship. They do not will that they may do; but they act because they take a pleasure in Willing. Obstinate, harsh, pestilent they often are to their fellow-creatures; not unfrequently great martyrs to their own dogged irrational determinations. Yet there is a sublimity in powerful will, which compels all men to venerate. It is the *sine-qua-non* of all mastership and command. He who lacks it may be amiable, ingenious, upright, wise beyond the wisest, but never will fix decided esteem in the multitude, or come to anything great.

It is extremely puzzling to say how far the common notion, that men might in general act better if they would, is true. We see one man act well, and it is natural to think that another might do the same, if he chose, particularly as we often see an impulse or motive applied to a man which induces him to exert himself as he never did before. But the perplexing point is, where are we to get, in all cases, the adequate external impulse? The will is a natural endowment as well as the moral faculties themselves. Young persons, and many who continue to be always of mediocre character, have generally little of it. The want of it is often the first, and continues to be the leading feature of insanity. When we see a man acting in a certain way from no want of judgment or good intention, but defect of will to do rightly, can we say that the case is different, either essentially or in its relations, from a case in which there was neither judgment nor good intention? As bad to want will as to want anything. Indeed, most persons who have had occasion to endeavour to operate upon the moral nature of their fellow-creatures, will be prepared to acknowledge that there was no class of cases so apt to appear to them utterly hopeless as those in which there was, while other features of an estimable kind were present, an utter want of will. The passive resistance presented by such natures is felt as a more deadly obstacle than the most perverse actual tendencies. Yet here we should remember our own maxim, where there is a will there is a way, and not be too ready to abandon those who are little ready to reflect upon us the lustre of success. After the many instances which we know of a thorough change of human conduct under the application of right and fitting means, it would surely be unjust to conclude that there is any fellow-creature beyond being set up in moral beauty, if we only could bring the right agency to bear upon the part of his mind which is fitted to yield to it.

It is in regarding it as a star of hope to all under difficulties and disasters, that the maxim is presented to us in its most interesting light. The youth who feels what a hard task he has before him ere he can say that he has attained his proper place in life, knows this golden sentence, and girds his loins up cheerily for that long probation which at once tests his virtue and wins his fortune. The unfortunate on whom the clouds of evil seem closing all round, and who fears that he must be overwhelmed by them, recalls the animating adage, and because he wills, *does* break through all. In short, hardly any difficulty could be cited to which this philosophy is not applicable; and every one will find, if he tries, that, be it through the brakes of entangling and bewildering passions, be it over the wide and unmarked moor of uncertainty, be it through the slough of despond itself, WHERE THERE IS A WILL THERE WILL BE A WAY.

MORNINGS WITH THOMAS CAMPBELL.

SECOND ARTICLE.

In the course of our ramble we called on the poet's namesake, Mr Thomas Campbell the sculptor. In looking through the studio, I had occasion to notice the excessive admiration with which he regarded beauty of form and expression. A female bust absolutely entranced him. There was no tearing him away from it. The fascination was as complete as in the instance of the 'Child Sweetheart.' This did not seem to be equally the case with pictures. We were afterwards in the National Gallery, and I did not notice any peculiar susceptibility to the beauties of the few very fine pictures in the collection. The charm of the rounded contour, and the effect of the lucid marble, in works of sculpture, no doubt formed part of the spell. In his Life of Mrs Siddons, Campbell has recorded his impressions on first seeing the Apollo Belvidere in the Louvre; and as the passage is one of the few really worthy of him in that memoir, and illustrates the peculiarity alluded to, I shall extract it:—

'From the farthest end of the spacious room, the god seemed to look down like a president on the chosen assembly of sculptured forms; and his glowing marble, unstained by time, appeared to my imagination as if he had stepped freshly from the sun. I had seen casts of the glorious statue with scarcely any admiration; and I must undoubtedly impute that circumstance in part to my inexperience in art, and to my taste having till then lain torpid. But still I prize the recollected impressions of that day too dearly to call them fanciful. They seemed to give my mind a new sense of the harmony of art—a new visual power of enjoying beauty. Nor is it mere fancy that makes the difference between the Apollo himself and his plaster casts. The dead whiteness of the stucco copies is glaringly monotonous, whilst the diaphanous surface of the original seems to soften the light which it reflects. Every particular feeling of that hour is written indelibly on my memory. I remember entering the Louvre with a latent suspicion on my mind that a good deal of the rapture expressed at the sight of superlative sculptures was exaggerated or affected; but as we passed through the passage of the hall, there was a Greek figure, I think that of Pericles, with a chlamys and helmet, which John Kemble desired me to notice; and it instantly struck me with wonder at the gentlemanlike grace which art could give to a human form with so simple a vesture. It was not, however, until we reached the grand saloon that the first sight of the god overawed my incredulity. Every step of approach to his presence added to my sensations, and all recollections of his name in classic poetry swarmed on my mind as spontaneously as the associations that are conjured up by the sweetest music.'

We next went to the British Museum. I had previously seen the Elgin marbles and other works of art, and Mr Campbell proposed that we should just glance at the library. He sent in his card to Sir Henry Ellis, who came and conducted us through the rooms. The poet was warm in his admiration of the large room. Sir Henry said there were about 300,000 volumes in the library. The Louvre contains 700,000 or 800,000; but single pamphlets or thin volumes are counted separately; not bound together, several in a volume, as in our national institution. The Cambridge University library consists of about 150,000 volumes—the Bodleian, I should suppose, considerably more; and the rate of increase is about 5000 a-year. It is scarcely possible for a bookish man, new from the solitude of the country, to survey these princely collections without echoing the sentiment of James I.—'If it were so that I must be a prisoner, I would have no other prison than such a library, and be chained together with all these goodly authors!'

From the museum we proceeded to the house of Mr Rogers in St James's Place. The venerable author of 'The Pleasures of Memory' gave his brother bard a courteous and kind reception. He seemed delighted to see him. 'Mr Rogers,' said the younger of the poets, 'I have taken the liberty to bring a friend from the country to see your house, as I was anxious he should not leave London without this gratification.' Mr Rogers shook me cordially by the hand, and said every friend of Mr Campbell's was welcome. 'But, Campbell,' added he, 'I must teach you to speak English properly.' [Here the sensitive poet stared and reined up a little.] 'You must not abuse that excellent word *liberty*, as you have done on this occasion.' We now looked over the pictures and works of art—a marvellous collection for so small a depository! Mrs Jameson, Miss Sedgwick, and others, have described the classic mansion in St James's Place. The hospitality of Rogers is proverbial—his breakfasts are famous. Indeed the poet has the credit of establishing the breakfast-party as a link in London society. He 'refined it first, and showed its use.' Mornings in St James's Place are scarcely inferior to the 'delicious lobster nights' of Pope. With the poet of memory, manners the most bland and courteous are, even to strangers, united to the fullest and freest communication of thought and opinion. His delicacy of feeling and expression, and his refined taste, are indeed remarkable; but, in place of rendering him miserable, as

Byron has surmised, I should say they contributed to his happiness and enjoyment. His life has been long and prosperous, and his relish of it seems unabated: he has had a 'latter spring,' lusty and vigorous.

No person perhaps possesses so many literary relics and curiosities as Mr Rogers. The beautiful manuscripts of Gray, written with a crow-quill pen, are among his treasures. In his library—framed and glazed—is the celebrated agreement between Milton and his publisher for the copyright of Paradise Lost. The great poet's signature, though he was then old and blind, 'fallen upon evil days,' is singularly neat and distinct. He has also a bust of Pope, the clay model by Roubiliac. 'My father,' said Mr Rogers, 'stood by the side of Pope when Roubiliac was modelling that part of the drapery.' A bust of Pope, enriched by such associations, is indeed valuable. The features are larger than the common prints represent. I had seen an original painting of him, taken when he was ten or twelve years younger, by Jervas, but it is greatly inferior in expression. Here we had Pope calm, thoughtful, penetrating, somewhat wasted by age, disease, and study, but still the clear fine thinker and man of genius. Mr Rogers showed us also an original sketch by Raphael, for which, if we recollect right, he said the Marquis of Westminster had offered him as much land as would serve for a villa! Autograph letters, 'rich and rare,' abound in Mr Rogers's repositories, with scarce books almost as valuable. On one of the tables lay a large piece of amber enclosing a fly, entire in 'joint and limb.' Mr Campbell mentioned that Sidney Smith, who has always some original or humorous remark to make on every object, taking up this piece of amber one day, said, 'Perhaps that fly buzzed in Adam's ear.' After a couple of hours delightfully spent among the books and pictures, Mr Rogers invited us to breakfast next morning. When we got to the door, Campbell broke out—'Well, now, there is a happy and enviable poet! He is about eighty, yet he is in the full enjoyment of life and all its best pleasures. He has several thousands per annum, and I am sure he gives away fifteen hundred in charity.'

Next morning Mr Campbell called at the Tavistock hotel, where he had kindly agreed to meet me, that we might go together to St James's Place. On the way, I mentioned that I had been reading Leigh Hunt's book about Lord Byron, which I had purchased at a stall. 'There is a great deal of truth in it,' said he; 'but it is a pity Hunt wrote it.' He thought Byron would have been a better man if he had continued to live in England: 'the open light of English society and English manners would have kept him more generally right.' We found at Mr Rogers's two other guests—Major Burns, second son of the poet, and the Honourable Charles Murray. Neither of these gentlemen had seen Campbell before, and they appeared highly gratified at the meeting. In the conversation that passed, I shall of course only glance at literary or public topics, not casual or hasty remarks. Captain Murray informed the poet of the present state of Wyoming in Pennsylvania, which has lost, if it ever possessed, that romantic seclusion and primitive manners drawn so beautifully by Campbell: it is now the scene of extensive iron and coal works. The conversation then turned on Captain Murray's adventures among the American Indians. He was several months without seeing a white man. He said he fully believed the stories told in narratives of shipwrecks, of men becoming wolfish and unnatural from excessive hunger. He was at one time nearly two days without food, though undergoing severe exercise on horseback. At the close of the second day he got a piece of raw buffalo flesh, which he devoured greedily; and had it been a piece of human flesh, he was almost convinced he could not have refrained from eating it. Major Burns instanced Byron's vivid description of the shipwreck in Don Juan, which was founded on fact. 'Yes,' said Campbell, 'Byron read carefully for materials for his poems.' The manner in which Byron introduces the cannibalism of the famished seamen—their first dark hints on the subject of murdering one of their number for food—is certainly a very powerful piece of painting. As the cant phrase is—it is like a sketch by Rembrandt.

The presence of Major Burns naturally led to remarks on his father's genius. Campbell got quite animated. He said Burns was the Shakspeare of Scotland—a lesser diamond, but still a genuine one. Tam O'Shanter was his masterpiece, and he (Campbell) could still repeat it all by heart. It reminded him of a certain class of sculpture—the second or Alexandrian class—in which the figures were cast, not hewn or worked out by patient labour. Tam O'Shanter appeared to have been produced in a similar manner, cast out of the poet's glowing fancy, perfect at once. The actual circumstances attending the composition of Tam O'Shanter are not unlike this, as may be seen from the interesting account given by Mr Lockhart. As Johnson loved to *gird* at David Garrick, but would allow no one else to censure him, Campbell liked occasionally to have a hit at his countrymen, on the score of their alleged Pharisaical moderation and prudence. Burns, he maintained, had none of the *pawkiness* characteristic of his country—he was the most unScotsmanlike Scotsman that ever existed. Some of us demurred to this sally, and attempted to show that Burns had the national character strongly impressed upon him, and that this was one of the main sources of his strength. His nationality was a font of inspiration. Mr Rogers said nothing. Campbell then went on to censure the Scotch for their worship of the great. Even Scott was not exempt from the failing. 'I was once,' said he, 'in company with Walter Scott, where there were many of us, all exceedingly merry. He was delightful—we were charmed with him; when suddenly *a lord* was announced. The lord was so obscure, that I had never heard of him, and cannot recollect his name. In a moment Scott's whole manner and bearing were changed. He was no longer the easy, delightful, independent good fellow, but the timid, distant, respectful worshipper of the great man. I was astonished: and, after all, you might have made a score of dukes and lords out of Walter Scott, and scarcely missed what was taken away.' Mr Rogers said, if he had a son who wished to have a confidential friend, he would recommend him to choose a Scotsman. He would do so in the spirit of the old maxim, that a man will be found the best friend to another who is the best friend to himself. A Scotsman will always look to himself as well as to his friend, and will do nothing to disgrace either. Thus, in his friend, my son would have a good example as well as a safe adviser.

Mr Campbell said he had, when a young man, an interview with Charles James Fox, which gave him a very high idea of him as a man. It was too bad, he added, in Sir Walter Scott, even in those bad times, to write of Fox as he did in his political song on Lord Melville's acquittal, Fox being at the time on his deathbed. Mr Rogers explained that Sir Walter had in that room expressed his deep regret at the circumstance: he said he would sooner have cut off his hand than written the lines if he had known the state in which Fox then was. 'This,' added Rogers, 'Scott told me with tears in his eyes.' I mentioned having seen some unpublished letters of Sir Walter, addressed to Lady Hood (now Mrs Stewart Mackenzie of Seaforth), in which he also expressed regret on account of his unlucky political song, for which he had been blamed by Lady Hood and the then Marchioness of Stafford.

The poets talked of Shakspeare. Rogers said playfully that Shakspeare's defects of style and expression were so incorporated with his beauties, and we were so blinded by admiration, that we did not discover them. He instanced the construction of the fine passage—

> 'And the poor beetle that we tread upon,
> In corporal sufferance finds a pang as great
> As when a giant dies.'

'The beetle feels nothing when a giant dies, but of course the poet meant that it felt at its own death a pang as great as a giant feels when he dies. Naturalists will not concede this; but I speak only of the construction of the lines; such slovenly and elliptical expression would not be tolerated in an inferior poet.' 'We are all taught from youth to idolise Shakspeare,' said Campbell. 'Yes,' rejoined Rogers, 'we are brought up in the worship of Shakspeare, as some foreigner remarked.' The sonnets of Shakspeare were then adverted to, Mr Rogers expressing a doubt of their genuineness, from their inferiority to the dramas. The quaint expression, and elaborate, exaggerated style of these remarkable productions would not, however, appear so singular in the time of Elizabeth. Poets are generally more formal and stiff in youth than in riper years, and in the plays of Shakspeare we see the gradual formation of his taste and his acquisition of power. It is worthy of remark, however, as Mr Campbell mentioned, that the Venus and Adonis (a truly fine Shakspearian poem) was written before the sonnets, as the poet, in his dedication to Lord Southampton, calls it 'the first heir of his invention.'

I took occasion to ask Campbell if it was true that Sir Walter Scott had got the whole of the Pleasures of Hope by heart after a few readings of the manuscript one evening. 'No,' said he; 'I had not met Scott when the Pleasures of Hope was in manuscript; but he got Lochiel's Warning by heart after reading it once, and hearing it read another time: it was a wonderful instance of memory.' He corrected me for pronouncing 'Lochiel' as a dissyllable. 'It is Loch-ee-il,' said he; 'such is the pronunciation of the country; and the verse requires it.' Rogers laughed heartily at the anecdote told by Moore, that Scott had never seen Melrose by moonlight, notwithstanding his poetical injunction—

'If thou would'st view Melrose aright,
Go visit it by the pale moonlight,' &c.

'He had seen other ruins by moonlight, and knew the picturesque effect, or he could very easily imagine it.' Major Burns said that Scott admitted the same to him on the only occasion he had ever met the great minstrel; and Jonny Bower, the sexton, confirmed the statement, adding, 'He never got the key from me at night, and if he had got in, he must have *speeled the wa's*.' Campbell was greatly amused at this.

Some observations were made on the English style of Scotch authors. It was acknowledged by both the poets that Beattie wrote the purest and most idiomatic English of any Scotch author, not even excepting those who had been long resident in England. The exquisite style of Hume was warmly praised. 'He was substantially honest too,' said Campbell. 'He was, from principle and constitution, a Tory historian, but he makes large and liberal admissions on the other side. When I find him conceding to his opponents, I feel a certainty in the main truth of his narrative. Now, Malcolm Laing is always carping at his opponents, and appears often in the light of a special pleader.' 'Hume has one sentence in his history,' said Mr Rogers, 'which all authors should consider an excellent specimen of his style;' and the venerable poet, with great alacrity, went up to the library, and brought down a volume of Hume. He opened it at the account of the reign of James I., and read aloud with a smile of satisfaction—'Such a superiority do the pursuits of literature possess above every other occupation, that even he who attains but a mediocrity in them, merits the pre-eminence above those that excel the most in the common and vulgar professions.' 'Dr Chalmers,' continued Mr Rogers, 'went farther than this. In one of his sermons here, which all the world went to hear, he remarked, when speaking of the Christian character, that it was above that of the warrior, the statesman, the philosopher, and *even the poet*—thus placing you, Campbell, above the Duke of Wellington.' 'Very good,' said Campbell laughing, 'I would place *his* father (looking to Major Burns) above any of them.' It was impossible not to think of Campbell's own lines in his Ode to the Memory of Burns:—

'O deem not 'midst this worldly strife
An idle art the poet brings;
Let high philosophy control,
And sages calm the stream of life,
'Tis he refines its fountain-springs,
The nobler passions of the soul.'

The only instance of Mr Rogers's *severity* which I noticed in the course of the forenoon, was a remark concerning a literary foreigner who had been on a visit to London, and left an unfavourable impression on his English admirers. 'He made himself one evening,' said he, 'so disagreeable, that I had a mind to be *very severe*. I intended to have inquired in the tenderest tone how his wife was?' The gentleman alluded to and his wife had, it appears, separated a few days after their marriage from incompatibility of temper. The conversation now turned to the subject of marriage. Mr Rogers said he thought men had judged too harshly of Swift for his conduct towards Stella and Vanessa. Swift might have the strongest affection for both, yet hesitate to enter upon marriage with either. Marriage is an awful step (a genuine old bachelor conclusion!), and Johnson said truly, that to enter upon it required great moral courage. 'Upon my word,' said Campbell, 'in nine cases out of ten it looks like madness.' This led to some raillery and laughter, and we shortly afterwards took our leave. Captain Murray had been compelled to leave early, and we were thus deprived of his lively and varied conversation. Four hours had sped away to my infinite delight. The poets parted with many affectionate words and congratulations, promising 'oft to meet again.' I walked with Mr Campbell to the Clarence Club, and on quitting him there, he said, 'Be sure to go to Dulwich in the afternoon and see the pictures: you can easily get there, and in the evening roll back to London in that chariot of fire, the railway train.'

I did so, and also attempted to Boswellise our morning's talk—my first and only attempt of the kind. Let any one make a similar effort to recall and write down a four hours' conversation, and he will rise with a higher idea of Boswell than he ever previously entertained!

I had afterwards frequent opportunities of meeting the poet. He was seen to most advantage in the mornings, when a walk out of doors, in the sunshine, seldom failed to put him in spirits. He had a strong wish to 'make a book' on Greek literature, taking his lectures in the New Monthly Magazine for his groundwork. Sometimes I found him poring over Clarke's Homer, or a copy of Euripides, on which occasions he would lay down the volume, take off his spectacles, and say, with pride, 'I was at this by seven o'clock in the morning.' Early rising was a favourite theme with him, though latterly he was, like Thomson, more eager to inculcate than to adopt the practice. 'Gertrude of Wyoming' was a daylight production, written during his residence at Sydenham, near London—his first home after marriage, and the scene of his brightest and happiest days. Mr Campbell spoke with animation one morning of a breakfast he had just had at Mr Hallam's. 'It was the breakfast of the poets,' said he, 'for Moore, Rogers, Wordsworth, and Mr Milman were there. We had a delightful talk.' Campbell had very little regard for the 'Lake Poets,' as they were called, but he held Wordsworth to be greatly superior to the others. He admired Coleridge's criticism, but maintained that he got some of his best ideas from Schlegel. 'He was such an inveterate dreamer,' said he, 'that I daresay he did not know whether his ideas were original or borrowed.' Yet Campbell used to ridicule most of the charges brought against authors of direct plagiarism. One day the late John Mayne, the Scottish poet, accused him of appropriating a line from an old ballad—

'Adown the glen rode armed men.'

'Pooh,' said he, 'the old ballad-writer had it first—that

was all.' Two well-known images in the Pleasures of Hope are taken, it will be recollected, one from Blair's Grave, and the other from Sterne. A poet, in the hour of composition, waiting for the *right word*, or the closing image, he once compared to a gardener or florist waiting for the summer shower that was to put all his flower-beds into life and beauty. In his own moments of inspiration, however, Campbell was no such calm expectant. He used to be much excited—walking about—and even throwing himself down. In the island of Mull, where he first felt the force of his rapidly-awakening powers, his friends, at such times, used to think him crazed. But to return to our memoranda. Moore, according to Campbell, had the most sparkling and brilliant fancy of any modern poet. 'He is a most wonderful creature—a fire-fly from heaven—yet, as Lady Holland said, what a pity we cannot make him bigger!' Scott, he said, had wonderful art in extracting and treasuring up old legends and characteristic traits of character and manners. 'In his poems there is a great deal about the Highlands, yet he made only passing visits to the country. After his Lord of the Isles came out, a friend said to me, "Where can Walter Scott have got all those stories about the West Highlands? I was six weeks there, making inquiries, yet heard nothing of them." "It is his peculiar talent—his genius," I replied; for I was nearly six years there, and knew nothing of them either. Crabbe was a pear of a different tree. What work he would have made among the Highland bothies! His *musa severior* would have shown them up. No romance—no legends—but appalling scenes of sordid misery and suffering. Crabbe was an amazingly shrewd man, yet mild and quiet in his manners. One day at Holland-house they were all lauding his simplicity—how gentle he is! how simple! I was tempted to exclaim, "Yes, simplicity that could buy and sell the whole of you!"'

The early struggles and ill-requited literary drudgery which Campbell had to submit to for years, gave a tinge of severity to some of his opinions and judgments both of men and things. These splenetic ebullitions, however, never interfered with his practical charity and kindness. He loved to do good, and he held fast by old friends and old opinions. Like Burns, he worshipped 'firm resolve,'

> That stalk of carl-hemp in man.

Among the literary opinions of Mr Campbell, was one which he was fond of maintaining—the superiority of Smollett as a novelist, compared with Fielding. This is mentioned in the Life of Crabbe; and I asked in what points he considered the superiority to consist? 'In the vigour and rapidity of his narrative,' he said, 'no less than in the humour of his incidents and characters. He had more imagination and pathos. Fielding has no scene like that in the robber's hut in Count Fathom: he had no poetry, and little tenderness in his nature.' Yet the real life and knowledge of human nature evinced by Fielding, his wit, and the unrivalled construction of his plots, seem to place him above his great associate in English fiction. Neither was remarkable for delicacy; but Smollett was incomparably the coarser of the two. Certainly, like good wines, Fielding improves with age, and the racy flavour of his scenes and characters has a mellow ripeness that never cloys on the taste. Mr Campbell, as already hinted, had a roving adventurous fancy, that loved a quick succession of scenes and changes, and this predilection might have swayed him in favour of Smollett. *Some things* Smollett may have done better than Fielding, but not *entire novels*.

After an interval of two years, I again met Mr Campbell in London. He was then much changed—feeble and delicate in health, but at times rallying wonderfully. I have a very vivid recollection of a pleasant day spent with him at Dr Beattie's cottage at Hampstead. We walked over the heath, moralising on the great city looming in the distance, begirt with villas—

> Like a swarth Indian with his belt of beads.

At Beattie's he was quite at home. The kind physician knew him well, and had great influence over him. Mr Campbell at this time resided at Pimlico. A young Scottish niece acted as his housekeeper, and to this lady he left the whole of his little property.

His letters from Boulogne were few and short, mostly complaining of the cold weather. In a note dated 17th November 1843, we find him remarking—'The climate here is naturally severer than in England. Joy to you in Scotland, whom Jove treats more mildly! I suppose the cold of the north has been ordered to march all to the south, and that it is to be long billeted upon us!' One cause of the poet's residence in Boulogne was the promotion of his niece's education. Mr Hamilton, the English consul, was, as usual, kind and attentive; but though Campbell now and then looked in upon a ball-room or festive party, he seldom stayed longer than an hour. Dr Beattie generously went to succour him in his last illness, and the poet had the Church of England service for the sick read to him by the Protestant clergyman of Boulogne. He died calmly and resignedly—his energies completely exhausted. He used to say he was of a long-lived race. Sixty-seven, however, is no very prolonged span of life; yet his two favourite poets, whom he resembled in genius, died much earlier. Gray, at the period of his death, was fifty-five, and Goldsmith only forty-five. Campbell's magnificent funeral in Westminster Abbey is matter of history. *Requiescat in pace!*

THE FESTIVAL AND ITS CONSEQUENCES.

A SCENE IN NAVARRE.

It was a fine afternoon in the spring of 1834; the birds were cheerfully singing on the trees, the flocks and herds contentedly cropped the young herbage, and the air was perfumed with odours. Not only did the face of nature brightly smile, but some festive ceremony was evidently about to be performed in the village of ——, in Navarre. Numbers of young girls were seated at the cottage doors, weaving garlands of spring flowers, whilst several youths looked on and encouraged them. Here and there an old man, wrapped in a rusty-brown cloak almost as ancient as himself, stood observing the juvenile groups; and on the threshold of a miserable hovel sat an aged woman singing a wild air, accompanied by uncouth gestures; but whether they betokened joy, grief, or anger, it would have been difficult for a stranger to determine.

At length the damsels rose, each bearing in her hand the blooming wreath she had entwined, and the whole party proceeded to a small *plaza*, or square, in front of the church, where, waving their chaplets gracefully, they danced to the sound of a large tambourine and the mountain-pipe, called the *gaeta*, the tones of which strongly resemble those of the bagpipes. Nor was the human voice wanting: the harsh and discordant chant of the beldame was again heard; and by her side a lean rickety boy, of about fourteen, with wiry flaxen hair, imbecile look, and unmeaning grin, beat time by clapping his hands. The dancers became more and more animated every moment; the fine hair of the young women, which had hitherto been plaited and arranged with natural good taste, was, by some sudden process, allowed to fall loosely on their shoulders; and at the same moment each maiden placed a chaplet on her head, the young men slinging larger garlands across their breasts, like the broad ribbons of chivalric orders.

At the conclusion of the dance, the great gates of the church were thrown open; at the eastern end the altar, resplendent from the effect of numerous large wax candles, had an imposing appearance. The cura, or priest, habited in richly-embroidered vestments, stood under the portico, and spreading forth his hands, bestowed a blessing on the people, who knelt reverentially to receive it.

While this act of devotion was in progress, a loud

creaking sound was heard, and presently a small body of men appeared advancing along the road which runs close by the square. Their heads were covered with the flat cap called La Boina; they wore coarse brown cloth jackets, and loose white linen trousers, their waists being encircled with broad red woollen sashes, below which, and in front, were strapped their cananas, or cartridge-pouches: instead of shoes they had alpargatas, or hempen sandals: they were armed with muskets; and bayonets without scabbards were stuck in their belts. This vanguard was followed by four wains, each drawn by two oxen, guided by a peasant bearing a long staff, with a goad at one end. The oxen moved very slowly, the creaking sound being produced by the evolutions of the heavy wooden axle-trees of the wains, which were followed by a much larger party, clothed and armed in the same manner as that in advance, the whole being commanded by an officer in uniform. Three of the bullock-cars contained each a new bronze mortar of moderate size; the fourth was laden with ammunition-boxes. On their arrival in the plaza, the escort uncovered their heads, knelt, and received the priest's benediction. The assemblage then rose; the tambourine and mountain-pipe struck up; the old woman resumed her discordant song; the half-witted urchin clapped his lean hands more vehemently than ever; the young men and maidens moved towards the wains with a solemn dancing step; and, finally, the girls decorated the horns and necks of the oxen with the wreaths they had been gracefully waving during the dance; whilst the youths encircled the mortars with the larger garlands; the whole ceremony being performed with the utmost enthusiasm.

Meanwhile, the priest had retired to the interior of the church; but when all the arrangements were completed—the oxen adorned with their glowing honours, standing patiently in the sun, and the murderous bronze artillery decked with sweet and peaceful flowers—he again came forth, preceded by a youthful acolyte carrying a large silver cross, elevated on a staff apparently of the same metal. By his side was another boy wearing a scarlet cassock, over which was a white muslin tunic: he bore a silver censer, which, when this little procession had reached the wains, he threw up into the air, and then drew it back again by its silver chain, making the white smoke of the incense cloud over the mortars, and around the heads of the oxen, after which the priest sprinkled them with holy water. The instant this ceremony was completed, there was a general shouting of '*Viva Carlos Quinto! Viva la Religion!* Success to the new mortars! Death to the Christinos!' Amidst these fervent cheers the bullock-cars moved on, escorted as before; the young men accompanying them as a guard of honour a little way beyond the limits of the village. On parting, the soldiers cried —'To Elizondo! to Elizondo!' and soon entering a mountain gorge, they disappeared.

The day after this scene there was considerable agitation in the village. Several fathers of families, who had been absent acting as scouts attached to Don Carlos's army, or otherwise connected with it, returned. They brought accounts of the retreat of the Carlist chief, Zumalacarreguy, from before Elizondo; and it was whispered that the mortars which had passed through on the previous day, and had been welcomed with so much pomp, were on their way back. The confusion occasioned by these reports was at its height when a stranger, covered with dust, rushed into the plaza with breathless haste. He was a fine well-made man of about thirty; his features, though handsome, bore a strong stamp of cunning; and the expression of his large gray eyes, set in a face the colour of which was only a shade removed from black, was so peculiar, as to render it painful to meet their gaze. The stranger's costume was unlike that of the Navarrese peasants. He wore a jacket of dark-blue velveteen, open, displaying a waistcoat of the same material, adorned with three rows of large open-worked silver buttons, hanging loosely; his breeches were of coarse dark cloth, with silver buttons down the outer seams; he also wore a blue worsted sash, and hempen sandals. Round his head was a cotton handkerchief of bright and variegated colours, tied behind, with two long ends hanging down; above the handkerchief appeared a cone-shaped black beaver hat, with a narrow brim turned up all round; the front of the hat was ornamented with three tarnished tinsel stars—green, ruby, and yellow—stuck on a strip of rusty black velvet. His thick neck was bare, and, from constant exposure to the sun and weather, as dark as his face. He was a *gitano*, or gipsy.

'I am sent by Zumalacarreguy,' said this man, 'to tell you that the mortars are on their way back, and that they must be concealed in this neighbourhood; all, therefore, must unite in conveying them to a place of safety. The general's orders are, that every man proceed instantly to meet them: they must not re-enter the village: your privileges, your lives even, depend on promptitude and energy: the *holy* guns must be placed in security.'

This appeal met with a ready echo in the breast of every hearer; for the whole population of the village had identified themselves with the fate of the consecrated artillery. All the men immediately sallied forth with Zumalacarreguy's messenger. They had not proceeded far along the road, before the well-known creaking of the bullock-cars indicated that the objects they had set forth to meet were approaching: they soon appeared, bereft, however, of their gay adornments.

The gitano immediately addressed himself to the officer in command of the escort: and after a brief parley, three of the village elders were summoned to join in the consultation. Much animated discourse ensued, accompanied by that lively gesticulation by which the Spaniards are characterised. The result was, that the wains were drawn along a by-road to a field, under the guidance of the villagers, the gipsy and the escort following. On arriving at the centre of the field, the oxen were taken out of the wains, which, being tilted up, the mortars glided easily to the ground. The peasants had brought with them the large hoes used by the husbandmen of Navarre, and having dug trenches of about three feet deep, the mortars, which only the day before were adorned with garlands, and sent with shouts and vivas to be employed against the Christinos, were now buried in the earth in solemn silence.

The oxen were again yoked to the wains, and led to the high road, whence they departed in an opposite direction: the escort took the shortest route to the mountains, and the villagers hastened to regain their homes. The gipsy proceeded to the residence of the cura, with whom he was closeted for some time: he then went to the small venta, or village inn. After his departure, the alcalde was summoned to attend the cura: they held a long conference, at the conclusion whereof the alcalde visited every house, and made a communication of solemn import to its inmates.

Towards evening several little groups were assembled in the plaza, and before the house doors. They conversed energetically, and, on separating at nightfall, their countenances and manner indicated that a definitive and decided resolution had been universally adopted upon some highly interesting and important matter.

The following morning, just as the mists were clearing away from the summits of the neighbouring mountains, General Mina entered the village, having marched during the greater part of the night. He had previously caused the place to be surrounded by his troops, in order to prevent the escape of any of the inhabitants. Attended by his staff, he rode to the plaza, whither the whole population were summoned by the crazy drum and drawling voice of the prégonéro, or public crier.

The people, who only two days before had hastened to the same spot with dancing step and exulting eye, cheered by the tambourine and mountain-pipe, now crept one by one out of their dwellings with fearfully-anxious looks, and wended their unwilling way towards the plaza.

Mina eyed them sharply as they emerged from the narrow avenues; but his weather-beaten face did not betray any inward emotion. By his side stood the cura, dressed in a rusty-black cassock, holding between both hands his oblong shovel-hat, and pressing its sides within the smallest possible compass. His countenance was ghastly, and his small jet-black eyes peered from beneath their half-closed lids, first at the villagers as they glided into the plaza, and then askance at the general, who had already questioned him closely with regard to the mortars, which he had been assured the villagers had voluntarily assisted in attempting to convey to Elizondo—then in possession of the queen's forces, and fortified—for the purpose of bombarding it. He had also heard of the ceremony of decorating and rejoicing over the mortars, and of their subsequent concealment, with the connivance and aid of the cura's parishioners.

The priest, however, pretended to be totally ignorant of the matter. 'Senor General,' he said, 'the cura of —— will never sanction rebellion against his rightful sovereign.'

As soon as there words had escaped his lips, a loud clapping of hands was heard immediately behind him. Upon turning round, the cura perceived the idiot lad, who laughed in his face, and trailed his half-dislocated legs along, in grotesque imitation of dancing. The cura looked affrighted; the muscles of his visage became suddenly contracted; and his eyes flashed fire upon the urchin whose noisy movements seemed to strike terror into his soul.

The plaza was now crowded with men, women, and children; shortly afterwards an aid-de-camp appeared, followed by an officer's guard. The former approached the general, and reported that, in pursuance of his orders, every house had been searched, and that, to the best of his knowledge, all the male inhabitants who remained in the village were now present.

'Let them be separated from the women and children,' said the general.

This order was promptly executed, the men being drawn up in a line before Mina. It was a strange, an anxious scene: the elderly men stood, like ancient Romans, with their cloaks thrown about them in every variety of picturesque drapery; some of their younger companions were dressed in brown woollen jackets, their snow-white shirt collars falling on their shoulders; others in short blue smock-frocks, confined round the waist by broad girdles of bright mixed colours. All wore the picturesque boina, but of varied hues—blue, white, or red.

The women and children formed a gloomy back-ground to this singular picture: they were far more numerous than the men, one or more of every family having joined the Carlist party. The young girls, who only forty-eight hours before had been weaving chaplets with so much glee and energy, now stood motionless, some looking fixedly on Mina; others, their hands clasped, and their beautiful eyes raised towards heaven, appeared absorbed in prayer. The old woman, crouched on the ground, plied her knitting-needles with great diligence; her lips moved rapidly, but no sound escaped from them; and she had so placed herself as to be able to peer through the slight separation between two of the men who stood before her.

Mina now advanced a few paces in front of his staff-officers, and thus addressed the villagers:—

'I know that, two days ago, three mortars passed through your village on their way to Elizondo, and that, yesterday, they were brought back. I also know that they have been concealed in this vicinity with the knowledge of the inhabitants: where are they?'

Not a syllable was uttered in reply

'Where are the guns?' cried Mina with a loud voice and irritated manner—'the mortars you decorated with garlands, because you supposed they were shortly to be used against the queen's forces?'

The people continued silent.

Whilst this was going on—the eyes of the staff-officers and the troops being all fixed on the general and the villagers—the cura had managed to glide into a narrow alley by the side of the church (at the back of which, by a strange oversight, no sentinel had been placed), then darting down a lane, he crossed a rivulet at the end, and plunged into a dell covered with brushwood: thence, through paths well known to him, he bent his course towards a small town about a league off, where he knew there was a Carlist garrison.

Mina, finding he could not make any impression on the determined people before him, turned sharply round with the intention of commanding the cura to use his influence to induce them to give him the information he required; not seeing him, he said, 'Where is the cura? Search the church!—search his house!'

In the former there was not a living being; and at the latter only the ama, or housekeeper, a good-looking young woman, who declared that she had not seen his reverence since he was summoned to the general's presence early in the morning.

This being reported to Mina, he shrugged his shoulders, and proceeded once more to harangue the multitude:—'Well,' he said, 'you appear resolved to refuse giving me the information I ask for: now, listen to the voice of Mina, who never promises nor threatens in vain. If, in one quarter of an hour by this watch (drawing it from his pocket), the place where the Carlist mortars are hidden be not divulged, I will decimate the men now before me. Every tenth man shall be instantly shot: decide for yourselves.'

It was a fearful quarter of an hour. Each man was joined by a female—a mother, wife, sister, or one to whom his heart was devoted: the only individual unnoticed by any of the women was the gipsy. He was a stranger in the village, and belonged to a race for which there was no sympathy on the part of the Navarrese, although its members were at that early period of the civil war employed on important missions by the Carlist chieftains. He stood alone with his arms folded, and was apparently in a state of abstraction.

The drum was beat—the quarter of an hour had elapsed: the soldiers again began to separate the men from the women. In the confusion, the idiot boy crept up to the gipsy, and roused him from his reverie by saying in a half-whisper, 'Ho, Senor Gitano! stand last on the line, and you are safe.'

The stranger looked intently for an instant at the lad, who rubbed the palms of his hands together, and glanced confidently towards the extremity of the line of men now almost formed. The gipsy contrived to place himself the last.

Silence having been commanded and obtained, Mina said, 'This is the last moment—confession or decimation.' No answer, no sign.

'Sergeant, do your duty,' said the general.

Immediately a non-commissioned officer began counting along the line. On arriving at the tenth man, he was made to stand forth. The sergeant then went on reckoning in like manner. Four more were thus selected. The sergeant recommenced counting. There were but nine left, the gipsy being the ninth. The rank was closed up again, and the five men were left standing about a yard in front of the others. An officer and eight soldiers now marched into the centre of the plaza; and the villager, who had the unenviable precedency in this mournful selection, was led to the general, who thus addressed him: 'Reveal the hiding-place, and you are safe. I should rejoice if your life could be spared.'

'Senor,' replied the prisoner, a fine young man, 'I know it not.'

Mina rode to the front of the line of villagers and said, 'Will any of you confess, and save this youth?'

'The mortars did not pass through the village on their return,' cried the men.

Mina then rode to the rear, and questioned the women.

'General, general,' they all shrieked together, 'we know nothing of the mortars. Spare him, spare him; be merciful, for the love of God!'

This reply—this appeal for mercy—had scarcely been sent forth, ere a young and beautiful woman rushed from the group, and falling on her knees before Mina, exclaimed in imploring accents, 'Spare, oh spare my brother! He was all yesterday in the mountains cutting wood, and did not return till after nightfall.'

'There is no remedy,' replied Mina, 'unless the secret be disclosed.'

Five minutes after Mina's return to the spot where his staff were assembled, the young man was led to the wall of a house fronting the plaza; his arms were pinioned, and a handkerchief was tied over his face. He was then shot dead by four soldiers, who all fired at one and the same instant. Three more shared a similar fate, after every endeavour to induce them or the other villagers to give information concerning the mortars. They all met their fate with heroic calmness and dignity. The fifth was an old man. His anxious eyes had followed each of his fellow-captives to the death-station. His own turn was now at hand. There lay the bleeding corpses of his young companions, and he was interrogated as they had been previously to their execution. 'I call God to witness,' cried the aged man, 'that I know nothing of the matter. I confess to having been present when the mortars passed through on their way to Elizondo, but I was not here when they were brought back.'

''Tis true, 'tis true,' shouted the people, forgetting, in the fearful excitement of the moment, that they were condemning themselves by this declaration.

'Then save his life by confessing,' answered Mina.

'We have nought to confess; Francisco is innocent,' was the universal reply, to which succeeded a sepulchral silence.

As the old man was being conducted towards the wall where lay the four dead bodies, he passed close to Mina's horse; and at the moment when his arms were about to be tied behind him by two soldiers, he broke from them, and casting himself on his knees, clasped the general's thigh with both his shrivelled hands, crying, 'For the love of the Holy Virgin, spare me, spare me! Oh! by the affection you bore your own father, save the life of an aged parent! I never saw the mortars after they left the village the first day.'

Mina moved not; his face appeared as though it had been chiselled out of a block of brown stone. The two soldiers in vain endeavoured to loosen the poor old man's hands from Mina's thigh: he clung to, and grasped it with all the strength of desperation. At length, however, by dint of repeated efforts, he was removed, and having been taken in a state of exhaustion to the fatal wall, he speedily fell, pierced by the deadly bullets.

After this awful execution, Mina said, in a loud voice, 'Now let the last man in the line be brought forward.'

Mina had observed, immediately after the old villager had been shot, that an interchange of glances full of meaning took place between the gipsy and the half-witted boy; and surmised, all at once, that the stranger might be influenced by the fear of death to divulge the secret.

On hearing the order for his being brought forward, the gitano's swarthy complexion assumed a deep yellow tinge, and he trembled from head to foot. 'You have but five minutes to live unless the mortars be found,' said Mina, addressing the gitano.

The moral construction of the gipsy was of a very different nature to that of the peasantry of the northern provinces of Spain, although he had been a zealous hired agent of the Carlist junta in stirring up the people to the pitch of enthusiasm to which the Navarrese had been wrought at that period, under the idea that all their rights, privileges, and religious observances were at stake, and could only be secured by the annihilation of the Christinos. He had expected to escape by means of the position in which he had contrived to place himself on the line of villagers, and had therefore remained silent during the previous interrogations; but now, finding that the very manœuvres he had put in practice to save his life had, on the contrary, brought him to the verge of destruction, he lost all command over himself. In tremulous accents he begged permission to speak privately to the general. He was led, tottering from fright, to the side of his horse. Mina was obliged to stoop to listen to his almost inaudible whisper, rendered doubly indistinct by the chattering of his teeth. 'Senor Mina, my general,' he muttered, 'if I divulge the secret, will you take me with you? Will you protect me from the vengeance of these villagers?'

'I will,' answered Mina.

'Then—send a party of soldiers, with some pioneers, down the lane to the left of the church, and when they arrive at a spot where there are three evergreen oaks, let them turn into a field to the right; in the centre of it they will see a heap of manure; let that be removed; then let them dig about three feet deep, and they will find the mortars.'

Mina instantly gave orders to the above effect; and during the absence of the party—about half an hour—a solemn silence reigned in the plaza. The gitano stood close to Mina's horse with downcast eyes, though occasionally he glanced furtively at the villagers, who all regarded him with menacing gravity.

At length a sergeant arrived from the exploring party, and informed Mina that the mortars had been found. 'Your life is spared,' said the general to the trembling gipsy, 'and your person shall be respected—you march with us.'

It took the greater part of the day to get the mortars exhumed and placed in bullock-cars pressed from the inhabitants, who were also compelled to dig up the guns and hoist them into the wains, the owners of which were forced to guide the oxen, under a strong guard.

* * *

The foregoing narrative, the leading features of which are traced from facts, displays the indomitable spirit of the Navarrese peasantry. Heart-rending it is to reflect upon the frightful evils of civil war, which none can fully conceive but those who have been eye-witnesses of them.

LIFE IN THE SEWERS.

Few who walk along the streets of London, and see mile on mile of carriage-way and foot-pavement stretching out before them, and branching off on every side, reflect upon the vast and wonderful scheme of sewerage that extends underneath. From the remotest district of London to the river, small sewers flow into larger ones; and these again, after a long course and many windings, into the Thames. Were a map executed of these subterranean currents, so intricate, yet so regular, like the large veins and arteries of the body, it would convey a grander idea of the civilisation of the capital than even the magnificent streets, filled with the productions of the world, that extend above ground. Formed of substantial brick-work, well arched and secure, they represent a sunken capital which has been variously estimated at the enormous sum of from one million and a half to two millions sterling. It is an interesting sight when any one of the main sewers is under repair in a principal thoroughfare, to see how deep the excavation is, and how many lines of gas and fresh water pipes have to be traversed before the strong current of foul water, running in its capacious brick channel, is reached by the workmen. Several of these main sewers were open streams, meandering through the fields, before London became so gigantic as it is now; and among the number may be cited the Fleet, running from beyond Islington, through Bagnigge Wells, Clerkenwell, Fieldham, Holborn, and Farringdon Street, into the Thames, once capable, it appears, of bearing merchant vessels as far as Holborn; the Walbrook, running from Moorfields past the Mansion-House, and by the church of St Stephen, Walbrook, and by Dowgate, into the Thames; and the Lang or Long Bourne, which still gives name to one of the wards of London.

Any one who has walked over Blackfriars or Waterloo Bridge when the tide is down, may have observed men and boys, and occasionally women, walking upon the shores of the river, knee deep in the slime, with baskets upon their backs, or slung over their arms, picking up pieces of wood that have been left behind by the tide, or bits of coal that have fallen from the numerous coal barges that come up laden from the Pool, where the collier vessels are moored, to discharge their cargoes at the wharfs further to the west. These 'mud-larks,' as they are sometimes called, bear generally a bad character, being accused of not contenting themselves with the prizes they find on the shore, but of robbing the coal barges or other vessels, on board of which they can creep at nightfall without detection. However this may be, their functions do not end with the shore, but in the sewer. With torch in hand, to preserve them from the attacks of numerous large and ferocious rats, they wade, sometimes almost up to the middle, through the stream of foul water, in search of stray articles that may have been thrown down the sinks of houses, or dropped through the loop-holes in the streets. They will at times travel for two or three miles in this way—by the light of their torches, aided occasionally by a gleam of sunshine from the grating by the wayside—far under the busy thoroughfares of Cornhill, Cheapside, the Strand, and Holborn, very seldom able to walk upright in the confined and dangerous vault, and often obliged to crawl on all fours like the rats, which are their greatest enemies. The articles they mostly find are potatoes and turnips, or bones, washed down the sinks by careless scullery-maids; pence and halfpence, and silver coins; occasionally a silver spoon or fork, the loss of which may have caused considerable distress and ill-will in some house above; and not unfrequently more valuable articles, which thieves, for fear of detection, have thrown down when they have been hard pressed by the officers of justice. It might be thought that a life amid the vilest filth, and amid so much danger and unpleasantness of every kind, would allure but few; but the hope of the great prizes sometimes discovered in this miserable way deprives it of its terrors, and all the principal sewers that branch into the Thames have their regular frequenters. Were it not that the tide gives them too little time for that purpose, they would extend their researches to the extremities of London; but two or three miles inland is the utmost bound of their peregrinations. Those who value their lives will not be tempted to extend their researches further, lest they should be drowned by the rising waters of the river.

About two years ago, these and some other particulars of their mode of life were first elicited in consequence of the following circumstance:—An old man who had long pursued this calling was suddenly missed. Every search was made for him by the few to whom he was known; and his wife and family, not without many fears that he had lost his way in the sewers, or had been surprised by the tide, and drowned in his efforts to escape, made anxious inquiries at every police office in London; but without receiving any tidings of his fate. Months elapsed, and his name was passing from the remembrance of all but those who had lost their husband and father by his disappearance, when a young man, passing with his torch up the Fleet, at nearly a mile distant from the place where it discharges itself into the Thames, was startled at seeing the figure of a man amid the darkness sitting at the junction of a smaller sewer with the main current of the Fleet. He shouted, but received no answer, and heard nothing but the rolling of the black and fetid water, and the splash or squeak of the numerous rats which he had alarmed. Advancing nearer, he held the light to the face of the silent figure, and beheld the ghastly countenance of a skeleton. He was not a man of strong mind, and losing his self-possession in his horror, he stumbled against it and fell. His light was extinguished. His situation was now sufficiently awful; but the added horror of the total darkness recalled his startled faculties instead of scattering them entirely. He knew his way by the number of iron gratings at intervals above, and groped along cautiously, shouting as loudly as he could, to keep up his own courage, and to startle the rats from his path, lest he should tread upon one which would turn upon him and fasten on his flesh. Grating after grating was thus passed, and he heard the carriages rattling above whenever he came near, and at times the conversation of people. Once he stopped under a grating, by the side of which an old woman sat at her apple-stall, and overheard her discourse with her customers, and was tempted to give the alarm, that he might be drawn up. This, however, would have been a work of time, and he therefore decided to go on. He proceeded accordingly, and arrived at the Thames without accident, and immediately informed his companions of the discovery he had made. It was surmised at once that the skeleton was that of the man who had been so long missing. Information was given to the police, and a constable was despatched to see the issue. He would not, however, venture up the sewer, but remained by the river side to await the return of the three 'mud-larks' who went up with torches and a basket to bring out the remains of the dead man. They found, on reaching the spot, that the discoverer, in his fright, by falling against the skeleton, had overturned it from its sitting position. A skull, a mass of bones, with a few buttons, and a portion of his shoes, alone remained—his flesh and his attire having been devoured piecemeal by the rats. The remains were collected and brought out without accident. A coroner's inquest was held on the following day, and the identity was established by the buttons, the only means by which it could be proved. Of course it could never be known to a certainty how the life of this unfortunate being had been lost; but the general supposition was, either that he had been suffocated by foul air, or that he had been seized with a fit of apoplexy in that darksome sewer. The simple verdict 'found dead' was returned by the jury.

Such is the romance of common things; and such is one of the many marvels that lie around us and beneath us, observable only by those who are disposed to study the manners, the habits, and the struggles of the poor.

THE RETREAT OF THE TEN THOUSAND.

There are certain facts in ancient history to which popular attention is, at intervals, pointedly directed, because they bear a resemblance to some passing occurrence of the present time. Thus, the recent disastrous retreat of British troops from Cabul, in the heart of Asia, has caused much to be said of late, by way of comparison, of a like military evolution performed some two thousand years ago, under nearly similar circumstances, but with far more fortunate results. The historian to whom we are indebted for the details of this military expedition was Xenophon, a Greek philosopher and soldier who accompanied it. His simple and circumstantial narrative—called the Anabasis (literally, 'The going up')—is one of the most interesting specimens of literature which has been snatched from the wreck of time. A modern, and therefore to us a double interest has been infused into it by an indefatigable and learned eastern traveller, who, having lately passed over four-fifths of the route, has been able, from personal inspection, to identify the sites of most of the places mentioned by Xenophon, and thus to place the minute fidelity of his history beyond all question.* The small portion of the

* Travels in the Track of the Ten Thousand Greeks; being a geographical and descriptive account of the expedition of Cyrus, and of the retreat of the ten thousand Greeks, as related by Xenophon. By William F. Ainsworth, F.G.S., &c. surgeon to the late Euphrates expedition; author of Travels in Asia Minor, &c.

track which this writer did not visit, has fortunately been inspected by Major Rennel, and by Mr Hamilton Junior. From these various authors, ancient and modern, we propose furnishing our readers with a sketch of the renowned expedition under Cyrus; chiefly, however, in reference to its most celebrated events—the battle, and the retreat of the Greeks.

In the year 404 before Christ, the seat of the Persian empire was Babylon, and its sovereign Darius II. He had two sons, Artaxerxes Mnemon and Cyrus; the latter being satrap or viceroy over a large district of Asia Minor. In the same year Darius died, and Artaxerxes succeeded him. Cyrus conspired against his brother, in order to obtain the throne: his treason was discovered by Tissaphernes, satrap of another province, who happened to be in the capital, and it was only the intercession of his mother (Parysatis) which saved him from the death of a traitor. He was, moreover, restored to his government, and returned to it with a mind exasperated by disgrace, and meditating a revengeful return for his brother's clemency.

No sooner did Cyrus return than he collected a vast army of the Asiatics belonging to his own principality, secretly intending to march to Babylon against his brother. It happened at this time that Clearchus, a Spartan general, had landed from Greece to subdue the Byzantines, or inhabitants of modern Turkey; but, instead of obeying the orders of his superiors, had taken part with the people he had been sent to fight against. A second army of his own countrymen was shipped off against him, by whom he was defeated. In this terrible emergency he offered himself and his whole army to Cyrus, who received him with open arms, and paid him a large sum of money. Thus, despite the classical interest which Xenophon has thrown around this famous expedition, it was, in reality, composed entirely of rebels and traitors.

Having collected a sufficient number of men, Cyrus assembled the whole army at Sardes, in Lydia, which is now Sarte in the Turkish province of Anadolia. Cyrus deceived his army into the belief that he only intended to invade the country of the Psidians, none but the Greek general, Clearchus, being in the secret. Tissaphernes, however, on hearing of the vast equipment, suspected the truth, and posted off to the Persian king to put him on his guard. Thus Cyrus's main object, secrecy, was defeated.

It was here—at Sardes—that Xenophon joined the expedition; for he was not amongst the army of Clearchus when it first hired itself to the Persian. Being at Athens, Xenophon received a letter from Proxenus, a friend of his at Sardes, to come and he would introduce him to Cyrus. Xenophon, having consulted both the Delphian oracle and his master, Socrates, accepted the invitation. Curiosity to behold, rather than join so vast an army, appears chiefly to have prompted him. On arriving at Sardes, however, he volunteered into the service of Cyrus, under Clearchus.

Everything being ready, Cyrus commenced his undertaking, which was to march with his vast army 1505 geographic miles,* and then to fight his way to the throne of the most powerful empire then extant. On the 7th of February, in the year 401 B.C., three years after his father's death, and about two subsequent to the beginning of his preparations, Cyrus and his immense military train commenced their eastward march. Except the shifts to which he was occasionally put to conceal his real object from the soldiery, and the danger of desertion which impended when he was obliged at length to make it publicly known, nothing very startling occurred, till—arrived at a spot on the banks of the Euphrates within about 108 miles of Babylon—there appeared the foot-prints and dung of horses, which were judged to amount to about two thousand in number. In the onward progress of the army, it was perceived that this cavalry had burned all the forage, and laid waste the country which lay in the line of march, so as to deprive the invaders of provisions. Thus Cyrus, to his surprise and mortification, perceived that all his plans were known, and that his brother was fully prepared for his reception.

At about 72 miles north-west of Babylon Cyrus halted, and held a review at midnight; for he expected Artaxerxes would appear next morning at the head of his army to give him battle. This took place between the 1st and 9th of September (B.C. 401), eight months after setting out from Sardes. At the review, it was ascertained that the effective force consisted of 10,400 heavy-armed Greeks, and 2400 targeteers of the same nation; and that of the native Asiatics from his viceroyalty (always called by Xenophon 'Barbarians'), there were 100,000 men, with about twenty chariots armed with scythes.

The next day Cyrus commanded his army to march in order of battle. They had only proceeded four miles and a half, when they came upon a trench, five fathoms broad, three deep, and thirty-six miles long, which had been dug across their route, between the Euphrates and Tigris, by way of fortification. This the invaders were allowed to pass unmolested, probably to throw them off their guard; an effect, indeed, it seems to have had, for they concluded that the Persians had given over all thoughts of fighting. Hence Cyrus marched with less circumspection; and the third day rode in his car, very few marching before him in their ranks; and great part of the soldiers observed no order, their arms being carried in wagons and upon sumpter-horses.

'It was approaching,' as Xenophon expresses it, 'about the time of day when the market is usually crowded, the army being near the place where they proposed to encamp, when Patagyas, a Persian, one of those whom Cyrus most confided in, was seen riding towards them at full speed, his horse all in a sweat, and calling to every one he met, both in his own language and in Greek, that the king was at hand with a vast army, marching in order of battle; which occasioned a general confusion among the Greeks, all expecting he would charge them before they had put themselves in order: but Cyrus, leaping from his car, put on his corslet, then mounting his horse, took his javelin in his hand, ordered all the rest to arm, and every man to take his post; by virtue of which command the entire army was skilfully disposed by the various generals in battle array.' This happened in the plain of Cunaxa, on the Euphrates, called at present Imseyab. 'It was now,' says Xenophon, 'the middle of the day, and no enemy was yet to be seen; but in the afternoon there appeared a dust like a white cloud, which not long after spread itself like a darkness over the plain! When they drew nearer, the brazen armour flashed, and their spears and ranks appeared, having on their left a body of horse armed in white corslets (said to be commanded by Tissaphernes), and followed by those with Persian bucklers, besides heavy-armed men with wooden shields reaching down to their feet (said to be Egyptians), and other horse and archers, all which marched according to their respective countries, each nation being drawn up in a solid oblong square; and before them were disposed, at a considerable distance from one another, chariots armed with scythes fixed aslant at the axletrees, with others under the body of the chariot, pointing downwards, that so they might cut asunder everything they encountered, by driving them among the ranks of the Greeks, to break them.

'The Persians came regularly on; the Greek army standing on the same ground, the ranks being formed as the men came up: in the meantime, Cyrus, riding at a small distance before the ranks, surveying both the enemy's army and his own, was observed by Xenophon, who rode up to him and asked whether he had anything to command? Cyrus, stopping his horse, or-

Parker, London: 1844. The entire space travelled over by the Grecian army was 3465 geographical miles, only 600 of which Mr Ainsworth left untraversed.

* Such being the distance from Sardes to Babylon by the line of march he afterwards followed.

dered him to let all know that the sacrifices* and victims promised success. While he was saying this, upon hearing a voice running through the ranks, he asked him what it meant? Xenophon answered that the word was now giving for the second time. Cyrus, wondering who should give it, asked him what the word was; the other replied, "Jupiter the preserver, and victory." Cyrus replied, "I accept it; let that be the word."' We stop for an instant to remark that these war-cries have descended down to modern times. The signal, 'England expects every man to do his duty,' given by Nelson at the battle of Trafalgar, is the last of these battle-mottoes on record. Cyrus 'immediately returned to his post, and the two armies being now within three or four stadia of each other, the Greeks sung the Pæan, and began to advance against the enemy; but the motion occasioning a slight break in the line of battle, those who were left behind hastened their march, and at once gave a general shout, as their custom is when they invoke the god of war; and all ran forward, striking their shields with their pikes, as some say, to frighten the enemy's horses; so that the Persians, before coming within reach of their darts, turned their horses and fled; but the Greeks pursued them as fast as they could, calling out to one another not to run, but to follow in their ranks. Some of the chariots were borne through their own people without their charioteers; others through the Greeks, some of whom seeing them coming divided, while others being amazed, were taken unawares; but even these were reported to have received no harm; neither was there any other Greek hurt in the action, except one upon the left wing, who was said to have been wounded by an arrow.

'Cyrus, seeing the Greeks victorious on their side, rejoiced in pursuit of the enemy, and was already worshipped as king by those about him. He was not so far transported as to leave his post, and join in the pursuit. He charged with his horse, but was unsuccessful. However, upon discovering Artaxerxes properly attended, he exclaimed, "I see the man!" and ran furiously at him, and striking him on the breast, wounded him through his corslet, as Ctesias the physician says, who affirms that he cured the hurt. While Cyrus was giving the blow, he received a wound under the eye from somebody who threw a javelin at him with great force. The king and Cyrus still engaged hand to hand.' In this encounter Cyrus was slain. The whole of the Asiatics, or 'Barbarians,' were signally defeated by that division of the Persian army immediately commanded by Artaxerxes. The head and right hand of Cyrus were cut off on the spot where he was slain, and the king's army broke into and plundered his camp.

Meanwhile the Greeks pursued that division of the Persian forces they had previously routed to a village near to the trench before mentioned. 'Hereupon,' says Xenophon, 'the Greeks halted (it being near sunset), and, lying under their arms, rested themselves; in the meantime wondering that neither Cyrus appeared, nor any one from him; not knowing he was dead, but imagined that he was either led away by the pursuit, or had rode forward to possess himself of some post. However, they consulted among themselves whether they should stay where they were, and send for their baggage, or return to their camp. Resolving upon the latter course, and arriving at their tents about supper-time, they found the greatest part of their baggage plundered, with all the provisions, besides the carriages, which, as it was said, amounted to four hundred, full of flour and wine, which Cyrus had prepared, in order to distribute them among the Greeks, lest at any time his army should labour under the want of necessaries; but they were all so rifled by the king's troops, that the greatest part of the Greeks had no supper: neither had they eaten any dinner; for before the army could halt in order to dine, the king appeared. And in this manner they passed the night.'

* It was the custom of the ancients to make sacrifice to the warrior-deities before a battle. From the agonies of the victims when dying, they drew favourable or unfavourable auguries.

The next morning Clearchus and the Greeks were made to see the full extent of the danger in which they were placed. They found themselves nearly two thousand miles from home, in the midst of the territories of an enemy at whose mercy they were. They were, in fact, surrounded on all sides. In the evening heralds arrived from Artaxerxes ordering the Greeks to deliver up their arms. After some consultation amongst the Greek generals, they sent the following answer to the Persian king:—'If it is proposed we should be friends to the king, we shall be more valuable friends by preserving our arms than by parting with them; and if we are to go to war with him, we shall make war with greater advantage by keeping our arms than by delivering them!' To this it was replied, that if the Greeks attempted to retreat, Artaxerxes would attack them. Afterwards, however, he consented to a truce.

Ariæus, Cyrus's lieutenant-general, now offered to guide the Greeks through the country, if they decided upon forcing a retreat. This guidance Clearchus accepted, and about the 16th of September (B.C. 401) the Greeks commenced the retreat, which proved one of the most famous events in ancient history.

They had not marched far, when they had reason to suspect that Ariæus and his Asiatic followers had been tampered with by the Persians. This suspicion was strengthened when it was found that Tissaphernes was also hovering around their track with a second army, under pretence of returning to the seat of his viceroyalty. However, no actual hostile movement was made till after the Ten Thousand had crossed the Tigris, which they did between the 11th and the 29th of October. Arrived on the northern bank of the Zabatus (now the 'Zab,' a feeder of the Tigris), the Greeks entered into a friendly conference with Tissaphernes, who invited Clearchus to a conference in his quarters. After some debate amongst the Greeks, their chief consented to accept the invitation, but with the precaution of being accompanied by five generals, twenty captains, and about two hundred soldiers, who went under pretence of buying provisions. 'When they came to the door of Tissaphernes, the generals, Proxenus, a Bœotian, Menon, a Thessalian, Agias, an Arcadian, Clearchus, a Lacedæmonian, and Socrates, an Achaian, were called in; the captains stayed without. Not long after, at a given signal, those who were within were apprehended, and those without cut to pieces. After this, some of the Barbarian horse, scouring the plain, killed all the Greeks they met with, both freemen and slaves. The Greeks, from their camp, seeing these excursions of the horse, were surprised, and in doubt of what they were doing, till Nicarchus, an Arcadian, came flying from them, being wounded in the belly, and bearing his bowels in his hands, and informed them of all that had passed. Upon this the Greeks were amazed, and expecting they would immediately come and attack their camp, ran to their arms. But they did not all come; only Ariæus, and ten other generals. 'When within hearing, Ariæus said, "Clearchus, O Greeks! having been found guilty of a violation both of his oath and of the article of peace, is justly punished with death. Of you the king demands your arms, for he says they are his, as having belonged to Cyrus, who was his subject." The snare here tendered was too palpable, and the Greeks answered indignantly, upbraiding Ariæus, whom they termed the most wicked of men.'

This treachery nerved the Greeks in their despair: they determined more firmly than ever to cut their way out of the country, or to die by the way; and proceeded to choose new generals, amongst whom was Xenophon, to whom was intrusted the command of the rear-guard. At this point the historian first appears as a prominent actor in his own narrative. Of the perfidy exhibited by Ariæus and Tissaphernes, Mr Ainsworth justly remarks, that it leaves 'an indelible stain on the Oriental character, somewhat similar to that which belongs to our own era, after the lapse of twenty-two centuries, in the conduct of Akbar Khan and his Afghans to the retreating Britons.' It was under pretence of guiding the British troops from Cabul that Akbar Khan caused it to be cut to pieces in the fatal Khoord-Cabul pass. The massacre of the Greek generals in Tissaphernes's camp took place, according to Major Rennel's computation (which we have followed throughout), on the 29th of October, 401 years B.C.

With a very slender knowledge of the country, and with no other guide than the sun, the Greeks recommenced their northward retreat towards the Euxine or Black Sea, surrounded by enemies always hovering around their track. After many skirmishes and difficulties, marching near Nineveh, they came to an eminence that commanded the road, on which the Persians having got before them in the night, had obtained a position. This pass it was determined to force. 'On which occasion,' says the historian, 'there was a great shout raised, both by the Greek army and that of Tissaphernes, each encouraging their own men. Xenophon, riding by the side of his troops, called out to them, "Soldiers! think you are this minute contending to return to Greece—this minute to see your wives and children: after this momentary labour, we shall go on without any further opposition." Upon this a discontented soldier, whose name is preserved by the historian, Soteridas the Sicyonian, said, "We are not upon equal terms, O Xenophon! for you are on horseback, while I am greatly fatigued with carrying my shield." Xenophon, hearing this, leaped from his horse, and thrust him out of the ranks, and taking his shield, marched on as fast as he could. He had, however, on him a horseman's corslet, which impeded his progress, and the rest of the soldiers beat and abused Soteridas, and threw stones at him, till he was glad to retake his shield and go on. Xenophon then remounted, and led them on horseback as far as the way would allow; and when it became impassable for his horse, he hastened forward on foot. At last they gained the top of the mountain, and turned the position of the enemy, who then fled, every one as he could, leaving the Greeks masters of the eminence. Tissaphernes and Ariæus with their men turned out of the road, and went another way, while Cheirisophus (commander of the Greek vanguard) with his forces marched down into the plain, and encamped in a village abounding in everything. There were also many other villages in this plain, near the Tigris, full of all sorts of provisions.' The plain here alluded to, remarks Ainsworth, 'is evidently the district around the modern Jezireh ibn 'Omar, the Bezabde of the Romans, and Zozarta of the Chaldeans.'

'When they came to their tents, the soldiers employed themselves in getting provisions, and the generals and captains assembled, and were in great perplexity; for on one side of them were exceeding high mountains, and on the other a river so deep, that when they sounded it with their pikes, the ends of them did not even appear above the water. While they were in this perplexity, a certain Rhodian came to them and said, "Gentlemen, I will undertake to carry over 4000 heavy-armed men at a time, if you will supply me with what I want, and give me a talent for my pains." Being asked what he wanted, "I shall want," says he, "two thousand leather bags. I see here great numbers of sheep, goats, oxen, and asses: if these are flayed, and their skins blown, we may easily pass the river with them. I shall also want the girths belonging to the sumpter-horses: with these," adds he, "I will fasten the bags to one another, and, hanging stones to them, let them down into the water instead of anchors, then tie up the bags at both ends, and when they are upon the water, lay fascines upon them, and cover them with earth. I will make you presently sensible," continues he, "that you cannot sink, for every bag will bear up two men, and the fascines and the earth will prevent them from slipping."' This proposition affords one amongst a hundred proofs furnished by modern travellers of the minute fidelity of Xenophon's narrative. Ainsworth states, that at about thirty miles from the junction of the Zab (on the banks of which the massacre of the Greek generals took place) with the Tigris, the 'actual ferry over the river, performed by means of rafts supported on inflated skins, exists in the present day at a place called Kelek I'zedi, or the ferry of the Izedis or Yezidis.' The Rhodian's ingenuity was not, however, put to the test, for the Greeks decided on continuing their march along the eastern bank of the Tigris, and to enter Karduchia (Kurdistan). By a masterly manœuvre, they managed to pass the mountains, and enter Kurdistan without molestation from the enemy. The spot they passed over was part of a remarkable district, it being 'the point,' says Ainsworth, 'where the lofty mountain chain, now designated as Jébel Júdi, and the same, according to Chaldean, Syriac, and Arabian traditions, as that on which the ark rested, comes down to the very flood of the Tigris, which it encloses in an almost impassable barrier of rock.' After this we hear nothing more of Tissaphernes and Ariæus. The diligence and skill of the generals, and the indomitable perseverance of their followers, had completely baffled them. The retreat was, however, constantly impeded by new enemies, consisting of the various people through whose territories they passed in their northward course to the shores of the Euxine.

Arrived in the country of the Scythians (at present partly occupied by the Turkish province of Armenia), they reached a holy mountain called Theches (Kop Tagh), whence, to their inexpressible delight, the sea was visible. 'As soon as the men who were in the vanguard ascended the mountain, and saw the sea, they gave a great shout, which, when Xenophon and those in the rear heard, they concluded that some other enemies attacked them in front; for the people belonging to the country they had burned followed their rear, some of whom those who had charge of it had killed, and taken others prisoners in an ambuscade. The noise still increasing as they came nearer, and the men, as fast as they came up, running to those who still continued shouting, their cries swelled with their numbers, so that Xenophon, thinking something more than ordinary had happened, mounted on horseback, and, taking with him Lysius and his horse, rode up to their assistance; and presently they heard the soldiers calling out, "the sea! the sea!" and cheering one another. At this they all set a-running, the rear-guard as well as the rest, and the beasts of burden and horses were driven forward. When they were all come up to the top of the mountain they embraced one another, and also their generals and captains, with tears in their eyes; and immediately the men, by whose order it is not known, bringing together a great many stones, made a large mount, upon which they placed a great quantity of shields made of raw ox-hides, staves, and bucklers taken from the enemy.' 'Xenophon's description,' says Rennel, speaking of this scene, on the arrival of the vanguard of the army on mount Theches, when they caught the first glimpse of the sea, 'is highly pathetic. No one, we presume (and indeed hope), can read it without emotion. What a number of tender ideas must have crowded at once into their minds! The thoughts of home, wives, children, friends—thoughts which they had scarcely ventured to indulge before that moment! In a word, it was a prospect of deliverance; like an opening view of heaven to departing souls.'

Many of the towns on the southern shores of the Euxine having been originally Greek colonies, the retreating army were, with few exceptions, allowed to pass unmolested. As they were originally traitors to the republic of Athens, they of course made no attempt to return thither; but most of them settled in the Byzantine territories. The whole of the way, both of the expedition and of the retreat, comprised 215 days' march of 1155 parasangs, or leagues, and of 34,650 stadia, or 3465 geographic miles; and the time employed in both was a year and three months.

The first news Xenophon heard was that of his having been publicly banished from Athens for the part he had taken in the expedition of Cyrus, and having now become a general, he gave his services to Agesilaus in his Asiatic wars. Here he acquired both fame and riches. He afterwards retired to Scellus, a small Spartan town, where he wrote his Anabasis and the other works which have made his name revered by posterity. The rest of his time was employed in rural pursuits and amusements. Having been driven from his retreat to Corinth, he died there, 359 years before the Christian era, in the 90th year of his age.

THE CHAPLAIN'S REPORT ON THE PRESTON HOUSE OF CORRECTION.

Not the least satisfactory among the evidences of the moral progress of society—of the tendency, though slow and imperfect, to a better state of life and action than at present prevail—is the care bestowed on the moral and physical condition of criminals. Ventilation, cleanliness, order, and cheerfulness, are now found in those places which formerly were the most noisome dens of dirt, depravity, and despair; in which ignorance grew to villany, and lax principle to confirmed vice. In the treatment of the culprit at the present day, an object is aimed at beyond that even of the devoted Howard. Punishment is no longer regarded as the sole end of imprisonment; the reclamation of the offender, and his restoration to a steady course of life, now constitute the chief object of criminal discipline.

The publication of prison reports, while affording matter for congratulation, enables us to compare the statistics of former years with the actual amelioration. We have before us one of these reports, of a highly interesting nature, by the Rev. J. Clay, chaplain to the Preston House of Correction. In reading the statements which it gives as to the character of some of the prisoners, we cannot avoid noticing the apparently narrow boundary between a life of hope and usefulness, and one of crime and disgrace. All the facts which prison reports bring to light corroborate what has been so much insisted on in the evidence on the recent sanitary inquiries, that where the population is physically most wretched, there will be the greatest amount of crime. A miserable home, a dirty neighbourhood, have been the primary causes of ruin to many who, in a more favourable position, might have become respected members of society. The little hope that can be entertained for the cultivation of virtuous feelings, the fostering of good motives, amid surrounding depravity, has been frequently adverted to: the obvious inference is, that the deteriorating influences must be mitigated or removed, before we shall see the genuine fruits of the inculcation of sound morality. A gentleman, well known from his connexion with a leading London journal, has said, in reply to the remarks of his friends on this subject, 'You may talk about the effect of education on your labourers and workpeople as long as you please; but morality cannot exist on an empty stomach. I will take care that those on my estate shall be well clothed, housed, and fed, and will not shrink from any comparison with others.' This, though an extreme assertion, has nevertheless some foundation in truth.

The report now quoted sets out with stating that the improvement which has taken place in trade during the past year has had a material effect in diminishing the number of committals to the house of correction. In the year 1842–3 they amounted to 2050, while in the corresponding period of 1843–4 they were 1549. Foremost among the offences stand 'assaults on the police.' 'This offence always arises from intoxication—a vice which unfortunately becomes prominent as a cause of offence in proportion as increased wages permit increased indulgence in it.' We find the number of larcenies of 'exposed articles' serves as a sort of index of the seasons when work is abundant or scarce. 'During a long period of embarrassment and distress, coal, clothing hung out to dry, and other unprotected property, tempted into crime the idle and the poor. In the last year, when all persons willing to take work could readily find it, offences of this description were less numerous by half than in the previous years.'

On referring to the table annexed to the report, it appears that the greater proportion of the petty larcenies are committed by the young; and the difficulty is pointed out 'of reforming a child who has been born and reared amidst poverty, neglect, and ill example. The evil which has grown with his growth and strengthened with his strength, cannot be remedied by the discipline proper to a jail. The first offence of a young criminal is generally followed by a sentence intended to check and to warn. This check and warning, where there have been some previous religious training, and where parents have been willing to assist in the reformation of their child, are found effectual—at least in preventing a relapse into crime.' When these conditions are wanting, the prospect of reformation seems all but hopeless, so great is the amount of labour and watchfulness required to produce it. From a boy in these circumstances, 'every injurious influence should be kept away; the powers of his mind should be roused; his affections should be cultivated; religious knowledge and religious principle should be engrafted, not merely as something to be occasionally referred to, but as the ever-present guide through the hours of his life. All this, it is manifest, cannot be accomplished in a prison. It may be said that an education is here contemplated for the little outcast felon attainable at present by few children belonging to a less degraded class. I can only reply, that such an education *ought* to be given, and when the country has a clearer perception of its duty and interests, *will* be given to all children, and especially to those who, without it, are sure to grow up in brutality and crime, miserable and degraded in themselves, a disgrace and peril to the community.'

The case of nine boys is then given, of whom 'six scarcely possessed a feeling or an idea which could be made available for good. They were ignorant of the alphabet, incapable of uttering a prayer, and unacquainted with even the name of the Saviour.' It is obvious that, on such offenders as those enumerated, the ordinary discipline of a prison will have but little effect. Solitary confinement, unaccompanied by any incentives to a better course of life, is undergone with a feeling in which repentance has no share. It is not regarded as remedial, but as a punishment; and in this view, in nine cases out of ten, the heart is hardened, and vicious habits confirmed. It is to be hoped that the light now thrown on the moral and physical condition of the lower orders of society, will have the effect of promoting the adoption of precautionary and preventive measures, whereby not only the injurers, but the injured will be gainers; for 'when the young criminal, liberated from the punishment of his first discovered offence, runs again into crime, and again stands convicted at the bar, the community demands the infliction upon him of a sentence rendered necessary by its own neglect; and pays a hundred pounds for the removal from the country of a dangerous pest, who, for one-tenth part of the money, might have been educated to fulfil, happily and creditably, the duties of the station for which Providence designed him.'

One of the tables illustrates the connexion between occupation and crime, which involves some important considerations. It will hardly be contended that any trade is in itself vicious; 'but if one demands more attention than another, leaving the person less exposed to the temptations of idleness; or if, on the contrary, an uneducated man's occupation be such as to allow a visit to the alehouse whenever he may be inclined, the probability is greater that, in the latter case, bad habits will be formed and criminal acts committed. It appears that the tendency to crime in the trades enumerated—beginning with the one most productive of offence—is in the following series:—1, grooms, coachmen, postboys, &c.; 2, bricklayers; 3, colliers; 4, plasterers and slaters, &c.; 6, painters, plumbers, &c.; 7, machine-makers; 8, weavers; 9, carters, &c.; 10, joiners; 11, butchers; 12, blacksmiths; 13, calico printers; 14, factory hands; 15, sawyers; 16, masons; 17, tailors; 18, shoemakers; 19, domestics (females); 20, factory hands (females). The first name and occupation on the list clearly shows the moral evils attendant on irregular employ.' The 'colliers' appear to have been more remarkable for vice than for ignorance; and 'weavers' are less to be depended on than factory hands, because 'the ceaseless activity which must be exerted by every person in a cotton-mill affords, there is no doubt, a wholesome preventive to crime. In such places, where every one is under the eye of a vigilant director, there is no leisure for either planning or executing a scheme of plunder. But the case is widely different in regard to weavers; who, working at their own homes, are, with respect to the appropriation of their time, their own masters. Uncontrolled by the fear of losing a good situation, they can leave their employment at any moment, and for any length of time; and, under such circumstances, it is not surprising that temptation should find more victims among them than among the inmates of a well-regulated factory.' The class exhibiting the lowest number of offences is that of tailors and shoemakers; which may probably be accounted for by the fact of many in these trades having a stake in society, by carrying on a small business of their own: this requires a certain degree of attention, and excites a habit of reflection, which may induce the individual, even without the exercise of any high moral motive, to prefer the small but certain gain of his business, to the greater booty, which may be followed by detection, disgrace, and punishment.

We come next to the details given as to the treatment of prisoners: 'Every one, on his arrival, is taken to the reception ward, and an officer, appointed to the duty, enters in a book a minute description of his person, including his age, height, weight, &c. He is then placed in a warm bath, and, after undergoing a thorough cleansing, he is clothed in the dress appropriated to the class to which he may belong. His own clothing is washed and fumigated, and laid up in a well-arranged store-room, until he may require it again on his discharge.' If a prisoner be awaiting trial at the sessions, he has the choice allowed of passing his time in the work-room and yard, or of being placed in a new cell by himself. 'Wherever any sentiment of self-respect remains, wherever sorrow, or a sense of disgrace is weighing on the mind, the offer of separation is gladly embraced. A prisoner under summary conviction is generally, but not always, taken to the work-room. Should he be of any trade—that of a tailor, for instance—which can be exercised in the room or in a cell, he is employed accordingly; if otherwise, he is usually set to picking cotton. In the work-room the strictest silence is maintained, except when, the allotted tasks being completed, a prisoner reads aloud, for the benefit of his fellows, some proper book furnished for the purpose. From the moment of a prisoner's committal, he is informed of the rule forbidding communication by word, look, or gesture; he sees it operating in full force on all his fellow-prisoners; and should he for a moment imagine that, as a new comer, he may venture to violate it, after an admonition on his first offence, the stoppage of a meal, which follows his second experiment in disobedience, assures him that the prison authorities are in earnest.'

Some of the convictions are followed by a sentence of solitary confinement, in which case the meals are taken in the cells, and a discretionary power is exercised in giving work to the prisoner: the term, however, of this species of punishment never exceeds twenty-eight days. 'The seclusion tends to arouse beneficial workings of the mind: the memory, the conscience, and the feelings, seem to develop some of their latent powers, and to derive great moral benefit in their exercise. "Everything that ever I did since I was a child has come back to me; and I see things now different to whatever I did before." Such remarks as this are often heard; and under the most unfavourable circumstances of ignorance, hardness, or levity, the irksome solitude may, and certainly does, fix in the mind a dread of the liability to such punishment again.

'All the prisoners attend the chapel every morning, and twice on the Sunday; a Bible and prayer-book are placed in their cells; they are allowed a due proportion of exercise, and the illiterate have the opportunity of joining the classes under the superintendence of the schoolmaster.'

A comparison is next drawn between the county of Lancaster and some of the agricultural counties, in which the result as regards moral progress comes out favourably for the former: we then meet with personal histories of some of the prisoners, which relieve occasionally the general darkness of criminal statistics; 'and perhaps the pursuit of mere knowledge under difficulties has seldom been illustrated more singularly than in the narrative of one of them sentenced to two months' imprisonment—"I am forty-four years old. I worked at the print-works at A—— for 11s. a-week. I have a wife and seven children. I went first to a Baptist, and then to a Swedenborgian Sunday school until I was sixteen. I learned to read and write. I married when I was twenty-one. I was always fond of reading. I read all Swedenborg's works before I married. Afterwards I read Goldsmith, Hume, and Smollett. For thirteen or fourteen years I earned from 20s. to 30s. a-week, and I spent all I could spare in books, although I drank a little occasionally. My books altogether cost me between L.50 and L.60. In botany alone I spent more than L.10. After I read Hume and Smollett, I tried to master Guthrie's geography; then I read Goldsmith's Greece and Rome; then Rollin's Ancient History; then I bought Goldsmith's Natural History, edited by Brown. I joined a chemical society at A——, and bought Murray's Elementary Chemistry, and Ure's Chemical Dictionary. I afterwards bought Sheridan's, Walker's, and Bailey's Dictionaries. I took 20s. worth of Dr Adam Clarke's New Testament. When I took to botany, the Swedenborgian minister said a little Greek would assist me, and he made me a present of a Greek Testament; after that I got one of Bagster's editions, Greek and English; and I also bought two Greek Lexicons. The minister lent me Frey's Hebrew Lexicon, and I made some way in it, so that, when reading theology, I could make out any Hebrew words. I made most labour of botany, and got so far as to understand the cryptogamous plants. I only studied the system of Linnæus; though Smith's Grammar contained both his system and Jussieu's. I continued reading these things until I came here. My children went to the Sunday school; but my wife was very fond of drink, and we had a wretched home. I have often had to carry her home like a log of wood. Her bad conduct spoiled the children." This man's dialect is the broad Lancashire, and would often be unintelligible to those who are not familiar with it.' A slight test of his chemical knowledge was made, by asking him to describe the process of respiration, which he did, according to the general views of it. He translated also several verses from the Greek gospel, though his acquaintance with the grammar and pronunciation was imperfect. Had this man been mated with a good wife, he would have had a cheerful home, well-conducted children, and all the happiness which a love of literature, in connexion with domestic comforts, seldom fails to induce.

We finish our notice of this excellent report with the concluding words of its author, who urges, as an apology for unusual length, 'the anxiety I feel to interest all who have wealth or influence not so much for a few prisoners, as for the thousands whom those prisoners in many respects represent: thousands who, if ignorant, have had no means of learning; if vicious, never saw or understood the beauty of virtue. Breathing the same air, daily in our sight, we know them little better than we know the people of the opposite hemisphere. In my intercourse with them, few things have struck me more forcibly than the evidences of their complete non-intercourse with persons of superior intelligence and station. Yet this estrangement cherishes prejudices in each against the other, alike unfounded and mischievous; and for the interest and happiness of all, no efforts should be spared for their removal, and for the promotion of mutual confidence and respect.

MORNING.

The morn is the birth-time of the new day, come to lend fresh light to enable us to renew our labours. It should be welcomed with joy and gladness, as the offer of another chance to us for the fulfilment of our hopes, and the accomplishment of our designs. He who feels that he has a load to bear, and much to do, should regard the first peep of day as a signal to be up and stirring in the battle with opposing circumstances. Early rising, which is nothing more than availing one's self of as much of the daylight as we can, has been a distinguishing habit in the character of most men who have achieved greatness in their professions, trades, and studies. In the middle of the day, we incessantly hear the anxious inquiry, 'What's o'clock?' and it is generally followed by the exclamation, 'Dear me, is it really so late! What shall I do?' It would sound more to the credit of such busy people to hear them asking, 'At what time will it be light to-morrow morning?' and arranging matters overnight so as to be up at the exact hour. We have no doubt that in Britain there are thousands of young men (ah! and young women too) who have never beheld the beautiful spectacle of sunrise and the gradual opening of day. All the operas and plays that were ever performed we would have foregone, rather than they should have prevented us from attending the rising of the sun—a sight which cannot fail to impress the contemplative beholder with lessons of hope, endless diligence, and silent good-doing. The indefatigable, cheerful, kind old sun—who, it has been remarked, is almost the only thing that is the same to us in old age as in youth—rises early to inspect the world, and we ought to be up at his grand review. Do not disobey the summons of so exemplary a general, but let your eyelids

'open to his rising ray,
And close when Nature bids at close of day.'

Our ancestors did wisely in acting their plays at such seasonable hours of the day as would not interfere with people's retiring to bed at such time as would allow of their rising next morning with the lark. Late amusements and late suppers are evils that call loudly for reform. The next day's business suffers from them. The old admonitory song of

'Early to bed, and early to rise,
Makes a man healthy, wealthy, and wise,'

ought to be written in large letters on the walls of every ball-room, supper-room, and bed-chamber. Good useful maxims like that would be much more agreeable than the fantastic and unmeaning patterns of the paper-stainer. If argument be not sufficient with men who have the inclination to get up betimes, but want the courage to do so, let them imitate the example of Buffon. 'In my youth,' says he, 'I was very fond of my bed, but my old servant Joseph greatly assisted me to conquer that propensity; for I promised to reward him every time that he aroused me at six. The first few mornings I repulsed him, and treated his calls with ill humour, which was making him give way to me again; and then I begged of him not to mind my temper, but insist on my rising, and so earn his reward according to promise. "If you let me sleep, Joseph, you will gain nothing, and I shall lose my time; so think only of my promise, and do not listen to my threats." The next morning, and ever after, he forced me, in spite of my anger, to rise at six; and when I was thoroughly dressed, and perfectly refreshed, I thanked and rewarded him. To poor Joseph's perseverance in waking me at six, I attribute ten or twelve volumes of my works.' The industrious and accomplished young naturalist Kühl, used to fee the watchman to give an early pull at a string hung out of a window, and fastened to his toe while in bed. On this being pulled, the youth used to rise immediately and commence his arduous studies, wherein he made such progress, that he astonished the oldest professors who conversed with him. Linnæus used, in summer, to go to bed at ten, and rise at three; in winter, he went to bed at nine, and rose at seven. A young nobleman, who visited Apsley House, was shown the truckle-bed in which the Duke of Wellington sleeps, and being astonished at its narrow dimensions, said, 'Why, there isn't room to turn in it!' 'Turn in it!' exclaimed his Grace; 'when once a man begins to turn in his bed, it is time to turn out.'

Late rising is not the habit of the very highest classes, for royalty itself sets the contrary example; and we have met, before now, princes taking their ride before breakfast at six o'clock. The present king of Hanover we have repeatedly seen out at that time. We have known Lord Brougham, when chancellor, make appointments on matters of business at his private residence for eight o'clock in the morning; his own time of rising being four in summer, and half-past six in winter. Supposing that a man rises at six, instead of eight, every morning of his life, he will save, in the course of forty years, twenty-nine thousand hours, which is a great accession of available time for study or business despatch; being, in fact, a gaining of three years, four months, two weeks, and six days. To any person of foresight, calculation, and industry, this fact will prove a sufficient temptation to practise the healthy and useful habit of early rising.

CALLING OF THE SEA.

As the foreknowledge of approaching changes in the weather is of importance, especially to fishermen and agriculturists, I invite attention to a very common, but not generally known, indication of such changes. In Mount's Bay, and probably in all places similarly situated, there is often heard inland, at a distance from the shore, a peculiar hollow, murmuring sound, locally termed 'the calling of the sea,' which, if proceeding from a direction different from the wind at the time, is almost always followed by a change of wind, generally within twelve, but sometimes not until a lapse of twenty-four or even thirty hours. It is heard sometimes at the distance of several miles, although on the shore from which it proceeds the sea may not be louder than usual; and yet at other times, even when the sea on the shore is louder than usual, and in apparently equally favourable states of the atmosphere, it cannot be heard at the distance of a mile. When the sound, in fine weather, proceeds from the coves or cliffs on the west or south of the observer, it is followed by a wind from about west or south, accompanied generally with rain. When it comes from the east or north of the observer, a land-wind from about east or north succeeds, attended with fine weather in summer, and often with frost in winter. All my own observations during the last twelve months confirm the above statement; indeed none of those of whom I have inquired, and who have for many years been accustomed to observe these indications, can recollect a single instance of their failure. This sound must not be confounded with that arising from a 'ground sea,' which is the well-known agitation along the shore occasioned by a distant storm, and which may likewise often proceed from the direction subsequently taken by the wind; for this latter noise propagates itself in every direction, and chiefly in that of the wind; whereas the 'calling' is heard only from one direction, and usually contrary to the wind. Besides, if this 'calling' come from the north-eastern or inmost shore of the bay, and the wind afterwards change to that quarter, it could not possibly arise from a 'ground sea' produced by a distant storm from that direction. Hence it appears that the 'calling' of the sea depends not on the condition of the sea, but on that of the atmosphere. I am informed, too, that previously to a change of weather, all distant sounds are heard loudest in the direction which the wind subsequently takes.—*Report of the Polytechnic Society of Cornwall.*

MY MOTHER.

I HEAR the evening winds among
The hoary forest trees,
As falling leaf and bending twig
Are rustling in the breeze:
But, oh! the music of the leaves—
Leaves meetly strewn and sear—
Reminds me of thy sweet, sweet voice,
Long silent, mother dear!

It brings to never-dying mind
Those oft-remembered hours,
When I, a thoughtless child, with thee
Would wander 'mong the flowers,
And pu' their fairest, while ye smiled
Mair sweet than tongue can tell:
The gowan aye was thine, and mine
The bonnie heather-bell.

And how ye twined them in a wreath,
To place them on my brow—
To tell me that a pretty king
Of flowers ye crowned me now;
Then how my happy heart would beat
With love for all, and thee;
And loud I laughed, and danced, and sang,
In childhood's harmless glee.

Then all was spring, for new-blown joys
Sprung on each passing hour;
Or summer, for they ne'er would die,
But ever freshly flower:
Ah! dark clouds dimmed that sunny sky—
Now winter chills the year,
For thou wert summer's gentle queen,
My long-lost mother dear!

Still, when the bright, the summer sun,
Shines lovely from above,
And pours on every hill and dale
A golden tide of love,
I wander to those early haunts,
And think full long of thee,
And ponder if thy spirit keeps
A loving ward o'er me.

For when thy dark eye ceased to shine,
Thy kind-toned voice to speak,
And when thy gentle hand no more
Could pat me on the cheek,
No eye there was to watch o'er me,
No voice to whisper mild,
No hand to lead, no heart to cheer,
A weary little child.

Yet still, in sunny dreams, betimes,
I see thee by my side,
And, if I've done aught wrong, methinks
I hear thee gently chide;
While sadly in thy downcast eye
Appears the briny tear,
To guide my frail, though willing steps,
In truth, my mother dear!

But when I walk in wisdom's ways,
And let my words be mild,
Methinks I hear thy praising voice
In every woodnote wild:
And thus, oh mother! lead my steps
Through every changing year—
My heart to God, my lips to truth,
As thou wouldst, mother dear!

—*Poems by J. C. Paterson.* Ayr: 1845.

THE IMMENSITY OF THE UNIVERSE.

The space in which the systems composing the universe move is illimitable. Were we to attempt to assign its limits, what could we imagine to be beyond? The number of worlds is infinitely great; it is inexpressible, indeed, by numbers. A ray of light traverses 180,000 miles in a second of time. A year comprises millions of seconds, yet there are fixed stars so immeasurably distant, that their light would require billions of years to reach our eyes. We are acquainted with animals possessing teeth, and organs of motion and digestion, which are wholly invisible to the naked eye. Other animals exist, which, if measurable, would be found many thousands of times smaller, which, nevertheless, possess the same apparatus. These creatures, in the same manner as the larger animals, take nourishment, and are propagated by means of ova, which must, consequently, be again many hundreds of times smaller than their own bodies. It is only because our organs of vision are imperfect, that we do not perceive creatures a million times smaller than these. What variety and what infinite gradations do the constituents of our globe present to us in their properties and their conditions! There are bodies which are twenty times heavier than an equal volume of water; there are others which are ten thousand times lighter, the ultimate particles of which cannot be known by the most powerful microscopes. Finally, we have starlight—that wonderful messenger which brings us daily intelligence of the continued existence of numberless worlds, the expression of an immaterial essence which no longer obeys the laws of gravitation, and yet manifests itself to our senses by innumerable effects. Even the light of the sun—with the arrival of which upon the earth inanimate nature receives life and motion—we cleave asunder into rays, which, without any power of illumination, produce the most important alterations and decompositions in organic nature. We separate from light certain rays, which exhibit among themselves a diversity as great as exists amongst colours. But nowhere do we observe either a beginning or an end.—*Liebig's Letters on Chemistry (Second Series).*

INFANT TUITION.

Pour in knowledge gently. Plato observed that the minds of children were like bottles with very narrow mouths; if you attempted to fill them too rapidly, much knowledge was wasted, and little received; whereas with a small stream, they were easily filled. Those who would make young children prodigies, act as wisely as if they would pour a pail of water into a pint measure.—*Educational Magazine.*

*** Complete sets of the Journal, *First Series*, in twelve volumes, and also odd numbers to complete sets, may be had from the publishers or their agents. A Stamped Edition issued for transmission, post free, price Twopence halfpenny.

Printed by William Bradbury, of No. 6, York Place, and Frederick Mullett Evans, of No. 7, Church Row, both of Stoke Newington, in the county of Middlesex, printers, at their office, Lombard Street, in the precinct of Whitefriars, and city of London, and Published (with permission of the Proprietors, W. and R. CHAMBERS,) by WILLIAM SOMERVILLE ORR, Publisher, of 2, Amen Corner, at No. 2, AMEN CORNER, both in the parish of Christchurch, and in the city of London.—Saturday, February 15, 1845.

CONDUCTED BY WILLIAM AND ROBERT CHAMBERS, EDITORS OF 'CHAMBERS'S INFORMATION FOR THE PEOPLE,' 'CHAMBERS'S EDUCATIONAL COURSE,' &c.

No. 60. New Series. SATURDAY, FEBRUARY 22, 1845. Price 1½d.

'BONA FIDE.'

It would be of great importance if any philosophical writer could lay down something like a rule as to the extent to which the tendency to feign and deceive exists in our race. At present, all is vagueness and uncertainty on this point. We see tremendous cases of imposture, and know that insincerity prevails throughout the whole of artificial life. But there is much truth and candour also, and often hollowness is suspected and attributed where in reality no such thing exists. Perplexities thus arise, and it becomes unavoidable that, where a question is to be argued upon the mere probability or improbability of there being good faith in the persons concerned, we are left each to his own accidental sense of the secretive power of human nature, or the charity which he may feel with regard either to his fellow-creatures in general, or to the particular individuals for the time under judgment. Were there, on the contrary, some fixed ideas respecting the capability of, and tendency to, deception in the human breast, we might expect to see many things pronounced upon much more clearly and promptly than at present, and a vast amount of unprofitable disputation spared. Perhaps, in the necessary absence of an authoritative rule on this subject, I may be allowed to make a few remarks on points connected with it, thus helping a little towards the desired end.

There are perhaps few things more astounding to the public than to find one of its members, after a long course of fair seeming, accompanied by unusually strong moral professions, all at once prove to have been, during the whole time, deeply dyed with some gross vice, or engaged in a professional course tending to the betrayal of all who confided their interests to his care. The common explanation is—he was a hypocrite all the time; that is, the real character operated in the concealed transgressions, and the outward appearances were entirely assumed for the purpose of cloaking the corruption underneath. This is a ready and plausible way of solving the mystery; but there is certainly much room to doubt if it be the right one. It proceeds upon the supposition, manifestly untenable, that there can be no opposite dispositions in human nature. We know, on the contrary, from daily experience in our own consciousness, if from no other source, that human nature is—as it has been proclaimed in all ages—full of inconsistencies. The simple truth is, that this nature comprehends many *pairs* of tendencies (as pride and veneration, selfishness and benevolence, &c.) which are directly opposed to each other; and though most persons have the one or the other predominating, so as to produce, so far, a certain consistency of conduct, there are many who have them in such equipoise, as to be liable to act under the influence of each alternately, or at least to be, in this respect, the mere puppets of circumstances. It is, then, not impossible that such mysterious delinquents were all along as sincere in their good professions as they were culpable in their acts, bating only the disturbance which a consciousness of error must occasion in some degree to a mind possessing also dispositions towards good; and this, after all, might be but a slight subtraction, seeing how wonderfully accommodating our minds generally are to inconsistent opinions and feelings of all kinds. It only remains to be considered whether there is most likelihood in the idea of a designed deception, or in the reverse.

Here I will admit at once the wonderful power which individuals have shown of imposing upon their fellow-creatures. The annals of malingering are sufficient in themselves to establish the vast extent of this power even in minds of a humble class. But I think it will generally be found, in cases of proved imposture, that the deception was for a limited time. It might be for a month—for six months—or a year. But cases where imposture was proved to have been sustained quite perfectly for a large portion of a lifetime, are comparatively rare, and usually in such cases there was no object beyond the mere love of deceiving—the pleasure of masquerade—or whatever else we may choose to call it. Nor is all this wonderful; for there is nothing more difficult than to sustain a fictitious part for even a moderate space of time. Observe—the real nature continually tends to break out; there must, in such a case, be a constant restraint—one of the most unpleasant of all things. Then every tittle of the assumed character must be in keeping: we have, therefore, to presume such a degree of ingenuity in device, as well as of vigilance in maintaining guard over the behaviour, as would form a painful task to the ablest men even for a brief period. In short, there are so many difficulties to be presumed in the case of a life-long hypocrisy, that, though the idea is conceivable to all, hardly the most skilled tactician in reasoning could verify it. I therefore see little room for hesitating to affirm that the outward professions of the delinquents in question are much more likely to have been sincere than the contrary. Taking, for delicacy's sake, a historical instance by way of illustration, I would say that the ordinary idea entertained of Cromwell's character by his contemporaries of the opposite party, namely, that he was a bad ambitious man, who used pious professions as a means of imposing upon his countrymen and gaining his ends, is totally insupportable. The ability of any human being to go through such a career of twenty years, without a particle of faith on his own part in the religious ideas which he daily and hourly breathed, must be entirely denied. The real fact seems to be, that such men are in the first place self-deceived. They impose upon themselves, and then undesigningly impose upon others. Perhaps we are not nearly yet aware of all the various influences which operate in swaying a certain class of minds towards a course which looks to cold reason like imposture, or the assumption of extraordinary gifts. But even taking such persons upon the grounds of what we know, their self-deceivableness is only too plain.

In the struggles of party, it is remarkable that each side invariably denies sincerity to the other. Each sees so clearly the truth of its own views, that it cannot imagine anything like an earnest conviction in the opposite. Each is so sensible of its own disinterestedness in its particular class of sentiments, that it cannot suppose a similar feeling being entertained respecting sentiments of a different kind. Hence it is that we so frequently hear from partisans that their opponents are entirely animated by love of power or pelf—that they make patriotism but a pretext for the advancement of their personal interests—that they affect a veneration for institutions merely for the sake of preserving what they have unjustly acquired—and many other allegations to a like purport. Even when the conduct of a party is, to all ordinary perceptions, marked by a denial of sordid interests, the spirit of opposition will find grounds for attributing it to motives different from those professed. And this spirit always becomes the more extreme in its judgments the more hotly that civil contentions are carried on; till, finally, in revolutions, we have men voting their opponents to death, not so much as a punishment for their acts, as from a horror at the false motives under which they are believed to have acted. This incapacity to see sincerity in opponents makes party-spirit one of the basest feelings which beset us. It is base, because it is so utterly destitute of magnanimity—because it treats candour as an impossibility—because it scoffs at faith, and continually libels human nature.

It is not difficult to see the causes of these false judgments in party men. Unwilling to allow that their opponents can be in any degree right, unable to conceive how any man can seriously think differently from themselves, they eagerly embrace the alternative, that all is false on that other side, and thus at once cut through the difficulty. Such errors are not a whit the less wild than are those which we make in deciding upon individual cases of presumed hypocrisy. A third and unconcerned party, looking coolly on, knows that there must be earnestness alike on both sides, even to produce that mutual charge of dishonesty in which they both take refuge. Great bodies of men may, no doubt, make a hollow show, or a deceptious move, occasionally; but to suppose that a multitude can truly conspire for anything, and particularly for the purpose of affecting a continuous strain of conduct not based upon or connected with their actual sentiments, is to suppose something of which we have not, in the whole range of human experience, one proved instance. It may be safely denied upon the mere incapacity of human nature to such an effect. The sceptical and distrustful have, it is true, a very practical and worldly air when they attribute extensive hypocrisies and deceits; it looks safest to argue for human wickedness; but in reality such persons are the greatest dreamers, seeing that their surmises are, in degree at least, utterly irreconcilable with what we know of the laws of mind; while it is not less true that, in erroneously attributing or suspecting deception, an evil is incurred which may be not less than the actual fact of being deceived—a consideration too little regarded when we assume a distrustful line of conduct.

The illustrations here presented tend, it will be admitted, to lessen the presumption as to the power and inclination of men to put on deceptious appearances. Their purport is to leave human nature under a lighter charge of guilt in this respect than is usually assigned to it. Perhaps I may assert with some confidence, that we may safely attribute good faith, or at least deny its one set of sentiments for the greater part of a lifetime, or find one strain of feeling and opinion pervading, for long or short spaces of time, any large body of men. The fact seems to be, that the true cause of the frequent deception which we experience from our fellow-creatures, is the liability on their part to self-deception and to misinterpretation of appearances. The erroneousness of their perceptions and judgments, the delusions arising from their feelings and wishes, are infinite; their power of actively and designingly deceiving is extremely small. In a word, the verb *deceive* is chiefly known in the passive voice. We are continually taking deceptions—almost tempting others to deceive us—putting a premium, as it were, upon imposture; but the disposition deliberately to set about plans for passing off tricks and impostures upon our fellow-creatures is actually or truly seen in but rare and limited instances. If this be sound philosophy, it becomes evident that what we are chiefly called upon to guard against in our dealings with men, is, not their bad faith, but their defective understanding and judgment. Human testimony is to be received as generally well meant, but liable to great error through the imperfection of the human intellect; and we are to judge of those who propose to be our leaders, or from whom we are called upon to take instruction, not so much with a jealousy as to their inclination to impose upon us, as with a caution lest they have been in the first place deceived themselves.

SOPHIA ROBARTES'S FLIRTATIONS.

On a cold frosty winter's morning, Mrs Robartes and her daughters sat in their luxurious morning room, engaged in various female occupations. There had been a silence of some minutes, which was broken by Harriet, the youngest of the three sisters, exclaiming, 'Really, Julia and Sophia, you are excessively entertaining this morning, almost as cheering as the weather. Have you nothing to tell us of Mrs Mackenzie's party?—was nobody either delightfully entertaining or charmingly absurd?'

'No,' replied Julia, 'it was too stupid even to laugh at afterwards; I never was more completely ennuyée in my life. I cannot imagine how it is, but it seems as if the very air of the place had the effect of destroying the power of being agreeable; for people who are really most charming elsewhere, are always dull at Mrs Mackenzie's.'

'Even the charming Miss Robartes; eh, Julia?' said Harriet; 'but I can explain the enigma. It is because the—the what shall I call it?—the assembly is presided over by the goddess of dulness herself in the shape of Mrs Mackenzie; and, you know, "What mortal can resist the yawn of gods."'

'Come, come, Harriet,' said Sophia; 'Mrs Mackenzie does her best to make her house agreeable, and we should be grateful for her good intentions.'

'No, Sophia, it is just a case in which good intentions only aggravate the offence. It is high treason against pleasure for any one to give evening parties who is so utterly devoid of all qualifications, natural or acquired, for such an undertaking as Mrs Mackenzie. Such persons deserve no mercy.'

'For my part,' said Sophia, 'I must say I have been at more stupid parties than the one last night.'

'Well, certainly,' remarked Julia, 'I was wrong to say that everybody lost the power of being agreeable; I ought to have excepted Mr Lowe. By the by, Sophia, he is remarkably attentive.'

Sophia blushed slightly, and Harriet laughingly remarked, 'Oh, a solitary exception serves only to estab-

evidence cannot be admitted, as it appears you were not in circumstances to form a correct judgment.'

At this moment a servant entered with a letter for Sophia. She broke the seal, and after reading the first few lines, glanced her eye at the signature, whilst the colour rose to her temples. She then silently placed the letter before her mother, who, as she folded it up after reading it, said, 'Well, my dear, I am not surprised; nor are you, I daresay. From Mr Lowe's manner, I have rather expected this for some time. All you can do, my dear, is to write as kind and polite a note as possible, expressive of your great esteem, and so on, and regretting that it is not in your power to return the sentiments he expresses for you. Certainly he is an excellent young man; one whose person, manners, and character, are, as far as I know anything of him, unobjectionable; and your father tells me few young men are doing so well in business; still, your forming such a connexion is not to be thought of, he has so many relations all low people, and residing in the town too. Not one of them but is quite unpresentable in anything like society. I pity him extremely; it really is a great misfortune for a rising young man to have such a host of vulgar relations.'

'But, mamma,' suggested Sophia, 'it surely is not necessary that Mr Lowe should be intimate with all his relations?'

'Certainly not; but it unfortunately happens that the very worst amongst them, the most vulgar and disagreeable, are the most nearly related; his brothers and sisters, for instance.'

'Besides,' added Julia, 'you know his opinions on that subject. Remember the severe remarks he made upon the conduct of Mr Seaton to his sister, who made that low match.'

'And,' said Harriet, laughing heartily, 'only fancy Sophia, with her refined taste and love for the intellectual, condemned to pass a long day with Mrs Jeremiah Lowe, in her fine house, where a book or an engraving is never to be seen from the first day of January to the last of December: but never mind, Sophia, I daresay she would entertain you charmingly with the cost of her tables and chairs, and the wonderful escape the splendid mirror in her drawing-room had during the last frost.'

'Yes,' chimed in Julia; 'and then there is Miss Tamar Lowe, who keeps your admirer's house (by the way, what very peculiar names they have in that family); what should you do with her, Sophia? Oh, retain her in your house to detail all the transgressions of the servants; how Patty threw a whole potato into the tub for the pigs, and John ruins all the edges of the knives.'

'And do not forget Mr and Mrs Pratt,' said Harriet, 'with their tribe of rough, ill-bred children, who must come and see Aunt Charles. Mind, Sophia, you always give us warning when you expect a visitation from the Pratts.'

'What nonsense you do talk,' said Sophia, with something very like a forced laugh.

'Nonsense do you call it?' replied Harriet; 'I call it very good sense; but remember, Sophia, I shall not be your bride's-maid in conjunction with Miss Tamar; that would be a sacrifice quite beyond my sisterly affection to make.'

'You need not concern yourself, Harriet,' said Mrs Robartes; 'I am sure Sophia has no idea of putting your affection to such a test.'

'Oh, indeed, mamma, I am not so sure of that,' returned Harriet, looking archly at her sister; 'what do you say, Sophia; is it quite impossible to get over the legion of relatives?'

'Yes, Harriet,' said her sister in a decided but low tone of voice; 'yes, I think, quite impossible.' But the words were followed by a sigh; for Sophia Robartes had never seen any young man she thought so agreeable as Charles Lowe.

Dr Robartes was a physician in good practice, residing in a populous town. He had been brought up to the profession of medicine, with the view of practising as a surgeon; but having early in life married a lady of considerable property, he had, at her earnest and repeated solicitations, obtained a physician's diploma. Mrs Robartes was a handsome woman, and had what all her own particular acquaintances called most delightful manners. To these recommendations she united an intimate acquaintance with all the forms and refinements of polished society; but out of that particular division of the human race amongst whom she had all her life lived and moved, she knew little, and cared less. Like the insect in the magic circle, she moved round and round, incapable of penetrating beyond her own little sphere. She had, of course, as every well-bred woman has, a great horror of vice, and admiration of virtue; but she could better tolerate the one if veiled under a specious refinement and polished manner, than endure the other if accompanied by an awkward carriage and ignorance of the usages of polite life. As she often said to her daughters in the course of their education, 'I can do with anything but vulgarity;' meaning by vulgarity not coarseness of mind, but of manner. Brought up under such a mother, it will of course be concluded that the Misses Robartes were perfect in all the graces and accomplishments which, though they do not form a good foundation, are, it must be admitted, a very agreeable addition to female acquirements. Nor were they deficient in more solid and intellectual attainments, especially the two youngest; for Dr Robartes was a man of considerable and varied information, and by no means so great a slave to conventionalism as his wife; so that his company and conversation exercised a beneficial influence on the minds of his daughters. Sophia especially bore a striking resemblance to her father, which fact may perhaps account for Mr Charles Lowe's opinion, that Dr Robartes was a man of a high order, the only wonder to him being, how he ever came to marry so foolish and heartless a woman as his wife. Charles might be forgiven for entertaining a decidedly mean opinion of Mrs Robartes's penetration; for it was very evident that she did not properly appreciate him. He was in some measure aware of the obstacles which his numerous and not very refined relations presented to his forming such a matrimonial connexion as he wished; and though he believed it a prejudice, which a closer acquaintance with their many estimable qualities would do much to dissipate, yet this knowledge had for some time acted as a shield against the arrows of the little god. At length, however, the citadel had surrendered to the charms of Miss Sophia Robartes; and gathering hope from the young lady's encouraging manner, and her father's evident approbation, he ventured to address to her the letter which gave rise to the foregoing conversation.

We shall not attempt to describe the feelings of our hero on receiving Miss Sophia's letter expressive of regret and esteem; for never having been in the situation of a rejected lover ourselves, we might totally fail, which would be anything but pleasant. Or, supposing that, by a happy effort of genius, or an immense exertion of the imaginative faculties, we succeeded in faithfully portraying the effect of such a catastrophe on a mind such as his, to others of a more placid and resigned disposition it might seem over-coloured, whilst those of a still more ardent temperament would pronounce it tame and passionless. This much only we shall say, that Charles Lowe's feelings on first reading that properly-worded epistle were not unmixed with indignation, for he did think that he had not been well used. Miss Sophia Robartes had certainly given him tacit encouragement; and the more he reflected on the matter, the more he felt convinced, by many little signs which a man in love well knows how to interpret, that she was not indifferent to him. Believing that his rejection was solely owing to Mrs Robartes, and that this difficulty might be overcome, he made many efforts, but without success, to bring the young lady to some more decided expression of her sentiments. In this manner months dragged on, until summer, bright, cheering, glowing summer made its appearance. Now, the Robarteses were in the habit of going from home during the summer months to visit some fashionable watering-place. This had become a practice chiefly for amusement, and to distinguish themselves from the unfortunate vulgar who always vegetate in one spot. But this year Mrs Robartes had found herself compelled to acknowledge the humiliating fact, that she was afflicted with that very *common* complaint, the rheumatism, and consequently Dr Robartes issued his command that the summer's excursion must be to Buxton. Accordingly, in the brilliant month of July, thither did the family repair, the young ladies consoling themselves with the reflection, that though Buxton was not the place of all others they would have chosen, yet when the 12th of August came, numbers of young sportsmen would make it their headquarters. Now, fate had decreed that Miss Tamar Lowe should, from her youth up, have been a martyr to this same complaint; and Dr Robartes, good easy man, thinking that what was good for Mrs Robartes might be beneficial to Miss Tamar, and, with the perversity common to husbands, forgetting how far from agreeable it would be to his wife to acknowledge her in the presence of her genteel acquaintances, recommended his old patient to Buxton too. Charles Lowe was most affectionately urgent with his sister to follow Dr Robartes's advice; and offered, would she consent, to make such arrangements in his business as should enable him to accompany her; for though he certainly, had the choice been given him, would not have selected his sister as his companion at a watering-place, still, as he was sadly in want of a pretext for going himself, and as no better seemed likely to offer, he availed himself of it. Miss Tamar, quite flattered, agreed to go, 'though she knew things would be ruined at home, for want of somebody to look after them.'

We must now transport our readers to Buxton, a place in itself wonderful, and surrounded by some of nature's most beautiful and glorious scenes. It was a fiercely hot August morning (too hot for any place but Buxton, where there is always a fresh breeze), and the fashionable hour for promenading. Numerous gay groups were walking on the terraces, and amongst these none so distinguished for their elegance as the Robarteses. Mrs Robartes, in graceful and becoming invalid costume, was leaning upon the arm of her eldest son, Mr Percy Robartes, a young man just called to the bar, and remarkably gentleman-like, if dress and any conceivable amount of assumption give a claim to that title. The young ladies, blooming in youth, and radiant with gratified vanity, were accompanied by several of those desirable young sportsmen, whose company had been so anticipated. 'Miss Sophia,' exclaimed one of these young men, 'do look, I beg, at that most extraordinary old young lady just descending from that britska. Positively that is a gentlemanly-looking fellow, though, assisting the old quiz. One would think he must have expectations in that quarter.' Miss Sophia looked, and was dismayed; for she beheld her lover, Charles Lowe. And, alas! his companion was Miss Tamar: and, was ever anything more provoking, they chose that hotel for their resting-place at which she, her mamma, and sisters were staying. Mr Smythe, the gentleman who had addressed her, wondered why Miss Sophia made no reply to his remark; and was astonished at, though he could not but admire, the beautiful colour which rose indignantly as she pondered over the assurance of Mr Lowe in following her to Buxton. Yes, there they were. Miss Tamar, hot though it was, mindful of her rheumatism, looking not very unlike a bale of woollen goods; and persisting, despite her brother's unwillingness, in seeing all her packages safely deposited in the hotel. At last, satisfied that all was right, she disappeared; the carriage drove round to the stables; and Mr Lowe, after casting a hasty glance round, entered the house. When the ladies retired to dress for dinner, a cabinet council was held in Mrs Robartes's room. 'Well, mamma, what is to be done now,' exclaimed Harriet; 'here is Charles Lowe come after Sophia, and has brought Miss Tamar with him, by way of fascinating her, I suppose?'

'Do not rattle so, Harriet,' interrupted her eldest sister; 'I do not see what there is to laugh at; for it really is too provoking that they should come here now to annoy us with their vulgar ways, when we have just become so intimate with the Churchills; and they so refined and exclusive, what must they think when they see us claimed as acquaintances by that odiously vulgar woman?'

'Yes,' said Sophia, 'though we really know little of her, she will always be so very intimate.'

'Well, my dears,' replied their mother, 'it certainly is a very unfortunate circumstance, but it cannot be helped now. We must make the best of it. Be lady-like, but as distant as possible in your manners; and, if she has not the sense to see that we do not wish for her acquaintance, surely her brother will, and endeavour to do something to keep his most extraordinary sister quiet.'

'Well, I hope he may succeed,' exclaimed Harriet, 'but for my part I do not think it possible; however, we shall see. Come, Sophia; never mind; arm yourself for fresh conquests. Mr Smythe is dazzled already. You wicked girl, I do not know how it is you manage to fascinate all the gentlemen, but I conclude it is the gentle timidity of your manners that flatters their lordly sense of superiority. Oh, commend me to a gentle, modest coquette; and now to dress, and then to dinner with what appetite the arrival of our evil genius in the shape of Miss Tamar has left us.'

When Charles Lowe entered the dining-room of the hotel with his sister on his arm, the first persons on whom his eye fell were the Robarteses, seated at the upper end of the table. He had previously ascertained that they were staying at this hotel, so that he was not entirely taken by surprise; but he certainly had not calculated upon the very cool return made to his bow of recognition. Mrs Robartes even put up her eye-glass; but at anything she might do, he could not be surprised. As last arrivals, he and his sister took their seats at the lower end of the table; and Miss Tamar, who really was short-sighted, did not at first discover her acquaintances. As soon, however, as she had settled herself comfortably, guarded her handsome silk dress from any chance spots of gravy, weighed the merits of the various dishes before her, and determined upon which to try, she began to look round upon the company.

'Why, Charles,' exclaimed she, 'there are the Robarteses. Well, how very lucky.' Then, stretching past her neighbour as far up the table as possible, she said, in a tone of voice sufficiently loud to arrest the attention of all present, 'How d'ye do, Mrs Robartes; I hope your rheumatism is better? As I've been saying to Charles, we're quite lucky to meet with you so soon, though the doctor told us we should find you here. And Miss Robartes, and Miss Sophia, and Miss Harriet (nodding to each as she named them), all looking as rosy as when they left Hilderston. Well, to be sure, what a pleasure it is to meet with friends.'

Alas! the persons she addressed could not echo this sentiment under the present circumstances; and they were painfully conscious that, whatever the fact might have been previously, it was most certainly true that they looked very rosy indeed at that moment. As for Miss Tamar, totally unconscious of the sensation she had excited, she with great equanimity commenced an attack upon a plate of boiled chicken and asparagus with which her brother had supplied her, so that her mouth was stopped for a time; but his feelings may be better imagined than described at this inauspicious opening of his Buxton campaign. At the head of the table sat an elderly gentleman of prepossessing appearance, and at his left hand a young lady, whose resemblance to the gentleman at once announced that she was his daughter. She was not handsome; but hers was a countenance that could not have been passed unnoticed by the most indifferent observer. The open intellectual fore-head, the eye at once soft and arch, the frank and good-humoured mouth, all bespoke a cultivated mind, a well-regulated temper, united with a kind and social disposition. To this young lady did Mrs Robartes now address herself.

'What a misfortune it is, Miss Churchill, to be the wife of a physician. People think that you must be intimate with all your husband's patients. Oh, my dear,' added she affectedly, 'never marry a professional man: if you wish only for the society of the *refined few*, be assured that you will be pounced upon by the *vulgar many*.'

'Indeed,' said the young lady very gravely; 'and you think that is the case in all the professions, do you?'

This was rather an embarrassing question to Mrs Robartes, for Mr Percy had been, much to his mother's satisfaction, paying Miss Churchill considerable attention: so, after a minute's silence, during which time the young lady appeared to wait anxiously for an answer, she said, 'No; perhaps not to all. I daresay it may be different in some; but what I have said certainly applies to the medical profession. Now,' continued she, 'that person who just addressed me in so vulgar a manner is, as you would gather, one of Dr Robartes's patients. They are nouveaux riches; and the young man is really very well informed and agreeable. We have occasionally met him; but of the sister I know absolutely nothing, and yet you see how she claims me for an acquaintance. Of course she is a person I could never associate with, as she is thoroughly vulgar in all her ideas.'

Miss Churchill made no answer to this tirade except by a bow; but she thought if that benevolent countenance was the index of a thoroughly ill-bred mind, she would give up all belief in physiognomy. During the rest of dinner, Miss Tamar was so well occupied with the contents of her plate, and the conversation of an old gentleman, her neighbour, who related to her some most miraculous hydropathic cures for rheumatism, that she had not leisure to make any further attacks upon her friends the Robarteses.

Mr Churchill, a country gentleman of moderate fortune and good family, was a man of enlarged and cultivated mind, and truly liberal spirit; for he could appreciate talent, revere virtue, and esteem integrity of character and high principle wherever and amongst whomsoever found. Brought up with such principles, his daughter Helen was prepared to find ability and worth amongst all ranks, and to esteem them highly. The Robarteses called her exclusive. True, she was so in the best sense of the term; for she always wished excluded from her society the vulgar in mind and mean in character.

Mrs Churchill, a confirmed invalid, was now at Buxton for her health. When Helen entered her mother's room after dinner, she as usual related all the amusing occurrences of the day, and after describing Miss Tamar, her speech, and Mrs Robartes's horror, she said, 'Mamma, do you know I think that must be the very Miss Lowe Edward used to be so fond of when he was at school near Hilderston. If you remember, there was a Charles Lowe, whom he liked better than any of his schoolfellows; and Miss Lowe used to send them cakes and all sorts of good things; and sometimes he went to see her, and she was very kind and good-humoured, and so indulgent. Do you think it is the same, mamma? I shall go directly and inquire from Mrs Robartes. Edward would be so delighted to see his old friend again, she was such an especial favourite of his.'

'Do so, my dear,' replied her mother; 'and should you prove right in your conjecture, say from me that I shall be happy to see and thank her for her kindness to your brother.' To fulfil her intention, Miss Churchill made her appearance in the public drawing-room; but she had no occasion to make any inquiries. Miss Tamar had heard the name Churchill mentioned at the dinner-table. She had a retentive memory for the names of those she had loved, or to whom she had ever had it in her power to render a kindness; and she was not long in ascertaining that this was the same family of Churchills whose son had shared with her young brother in all her kind attentions and indulgences. Miss Tamar never stood upon punctilio; she knew little, and cared less for etiquette. No sooner, then, did she see Miss Churchill's beaming countenance than she exclaimed, 'Yes, it is the very same; she is the image of her brother. My dear young lady, you'll excuse me, I am sure; but I want so much to hear of that brother of yours. How is he, and where is he? Dear me, how I should like to see him again. Charles, Charles, this is Miss Churchill, sister to your friend Edward Churchill.' Thus called upon, Charles, in some confusion, turned to acknowledge this singular introduction; but his embarrassment was immediately relieved by the well-bred cordiality with which Helen received her brother's friend. Great was the astonishment of the Robarteses when they found the acquaintance of the Lowes sought by such *very genteel* people; but from the conversation which passed, they learned one important fact—young Mr Churchill was expected. Here was an opportunity not to be neglected. The prudent mamma recommended her daughters to adopt a more courteous manner towards their Hilderston acquaintance, since they were likely to be intimate in that quarter. In the course of a few days Edward Churchill arrived, and he heartily renewed his intimacy with his old schoolfellow. Frank, gay, and light-hearted, Edward entered with great zest into all the pleasures and amusements of the place. He sang, danced, and flirted incomparably better than any gentleman there, and was, withal, so clever and good-humoured, that he soon became the life of the circle. For some time it appeared doubtful which of the ladies excited his especial admiration, so equally were his attentions and compliments bestowed from Miss Robartes to Miss Tamar Lowe; but at length his wavering choice fixed upon Miss Sophia, who from that time abandoned Mr Smythe to his fate—her mamma having assured her that he was not a marrying man. Nothing could be more agreeable to the Robarteses than the prospect of such an alliance, uniting the two great advantages of good property and unexceptionable family connexions; and Miss Sophia spared no pains to secure the captive she flattered herself she had made. One thing did rather puzzle her; she could not be quite sure what were his real sentiments towards the Lowes: but after some consideration, she decided that he was willing, for the amusement they afforded him, to renew an acquaintance at a watering-place with persons whose society nearer home he would not consider quite so desirable. It may perhaps excite some surprise that Edward should voluntarily place himself in rivalry with Charles; but the truth was, that, with the keen eye which young men often possess in such cases, he had from the first suspected how matters stood; and it was not long before he heard the whole history from his friend. But, said Charles in conclusion, 'I now see plainly that Sophia Robartes would not suit me. She is entirely a slave to appearances, and, with her views and feelings, nothing but family disunion could be expected. She looks with contempt on my relations, who, though deficient in that polish of manner which is to be obtained only early in life, possess intrinsic merit, which those who have the good sense and courage to penetrate beyond the mere outside, must discover and esteem.'

'Well, my dear fellow,' said Edward, 'in my opinion you have had a happy escape; but I think I must teach Miss Sophia a lesson on her folly. To be tied to a woman who lives in constant dread of the sneers of miscalled refined society, would be wretched indeed; so congratulate yourself.' And Charles did congratulate himself; for, his eyes being now completely opened to the motives and opinions of his former fair one, he could not but be struck by the contrast between her and Miss Churchill. He saw Sophia Robartes lovely and accomplished, with a cultivated understanding, and a mind capable of appreciating everything good and noble, devoting all her charms, calling up all her fascinations, and bending all her energies to the task of securing such a connexion as should raise her in the scale of society; willingly lending herself to the exaggerated expression of admiration from a man of whose character, habits, and principles, she was almost totally ignorant, merely because he was what is called a good match. On the other hand, he saw Helen untainted by coquetry or affectation, courteous and obliging to all, unmindful of herself, intent on promoting the comfort and happiness of those dear to her, and as ready to produce her accomplishments for the gratification and amusement of Miss Tamar, as for those better able to appreciate them. He saw, and wondered how he could possibly have imagined himself in love with one whose character now appeared to him so contemptible. He did not, however, at first so plainly perceive where his wonderings and reflections were leading him. His acquaintance with her brother had placed him in a position of intimacy with Miss Churchill which none of the other gentlemen enjoyed. She liked his manners, admired his talents, and sympathised with the noble and generous sentiments he expressed, and with the benevolent and enlightened view he took of the advantages and opportunities afforded by his situation in life, as an extensive manufacturer, of benefiting his fellow-creatures. Her esteem for his character was much increased by his conduct towards his sister, and by the manner in which, when occasion required, he spoke of the rest of his family, whose peculiarities she had heard described and ridiculed by the Misses Robartes. When a young lady and gentleman begin with mutual esteem and admiration, it is not difficult for lookers-on to see where it is most probable they will end. But Charles had not yet dared to hope, nor had a thought of him as a lover ever crossed Helen's mind; and the time fixed for their leaving Buxton was fast approaching. It had been settled that, previous to their departure, the Robarteses, Churchills, and, by Edward's express desire, the Lowes, together with several young ladies and gentlemen staying at the same hotel, should make an excursion to Castleton to view the many wonders of the Peak. Various emotions were brought into play by the prospect of this trip. Edward Churchill, true to his determination of teaching Sophia that if she would be a female flirt, she must expect to meet with masculine jilts, had paid her such attention as might fairly permit the inference that he admired her exceedingly, and that more unlikely things had happened than that he should wish to make her his wife.

So Sophia attired herself most becomingly, and thought that, wandering amidst the romantic scenery of the Peak, the anticipated offer surely must be made: whilst Edward soliloquised—'Now for the finale; I must bid Miss Sophia a polite adieu. Pity I cannot write a letter of esteem and proffered friendship.' In pursuance of his plan, Edward selected Miss Tamar as the object of his assiduous and most devoted attentions on their drive, conducted her with the utmost gallantry through the vaulted passages and widely-arched chambers of the cavern of the Peak, would allow no one to make the passage of the Styx with her but himself, and finished by giving her his arm in walking back to the inn. Here Miss Tamar declared her inability to proceed any farther in search of wonders and prospects, and made known her determination to give herself a 'comfortable rest and warm,' whilst they mounted the hill where stand the ruins of the once proud castle of the Peak.

'Really, Mr Edward,' said one of the young ladies when they were some little distance from the inn, 'how absent you are; don't you see Miss Sophia Robartes walking alone?'

'Indeed! Miss Sophia,' exclaimed he, 'I beg your

Deeply mortified though she was, she judged it better to pass over his neglect quietly; but as she accepted his proffered assistance, she remarked—'You seem to have enjoyed yourself much, Mr Edward?'

There was a touch of reproach in the tone of her voice; but his heart was callous, and he answered gaily, 'Oh yes, very much; I never was more interested and amused.'

'Ah,' said the lady, smiling affectedly, 'you are such a quiz.'

'A quiz,' he replied; 'excuse me for repeating your words so rudely, but I do not understand what you mean.'

'Oh, Mr Edward,' said Sophia, 'you know very well you have been quizzing; that is, laughing at Miss Tamar Lowe.'

'Indeed you are mistaken,' replied he. 'Of course I see Miss Tamar's eccentricities, and think them amusing; but to draw her out for the purpose of ridiculing her myself, or affording mirth to others, is an act of which I hope and believe I am incapable. I respect and esteem her highly: no one can help doing so who is acquainted as I am with her many excellences; and if no other motive restrained me, as the sister of my friend she is safe from any such attempt on my part.'

Sophia saw that she had got wrong, and to change the subject began to talk of leaving Buxton; of how much she had enjoyed herself, and wondered when the same party would meet again.

'Some of us, I hope, soon,' said Edward; 'Lowe is going with me to Oaklands, and after that I intend to renew my acquaintance with Hilderston. I suppose he has got a charming bachelor establishment; but if I am not very much mistaken, he would rather have a complete establishment for *two*. What do you think, Miss Sophia?'

Completely thrown off her guard by the concluding part of this speech, imagining that she must have been mistaken in Edward's motives, and that his intention the whole time had been to interest her for his friend, and not for himself, she replied, 'I believe you are quite correct: to my knowledge he has made some attempts in that way; but he is too ambitious. Mr Lowe must look for a wife in his own class, for no woman accustomed to good society could put up with his host of vulgar relations.'

'Do you think so,' said Edward coolly; 'I scarcely thought to have heard such an objection advanced in these days, when almost every one has vulgar relations of one kind or another; but I cannot say I agree with you. I think Charles has every chance of success in his present pursuit; for the lady, I know, never did trouble herself much about such subjects, having, I presume, sufficient self-esteem to keep on good terms with herself, despite her share of the small annoyances to which the happiest state in this life is liable.'

Poor Sophia! The blow was almost too much even for her well-tutored, self-possessed manners. She felt sick and giddy as the truth flashed across her mind that she had lost her old lover, and, far from gaining another, was actually an object of amusement, if not of contempt, to the man she had considered her captive. Bitterly was she mortified: yet so much are we the slaves of habit, and so difficult is it to free the mind from long-indulged prejudices, that she felt only aggrieved and wronged by the turn affairs had taken. Her attention once awakened, however, she was too acute an observer not to be convinced of the truth of Edward Churchill's hints; and after several hours passed in vain efforts to assume gaiety of manner, she found herself alone, and at liberty to give vent to her long-suppressed feelings by bitter tears of mortified vanity and wounded self-love. Of all the family of Robarteses, none were more rejoiced at the termination of their Buxton campaign than Sophia; who, ill at ease, and wanting the sustaining influence of self-respect, imagined herself deeply injured both by the Lowes and Churchills, and tried to

be to regain the ease and contentment she had lost. When, however, some months had passed away, and calm reflection succeeded to this tumult of feeling, Sophia Robartes became wiser and happier for her experience. Influenced by the sole desire of securing a good establishment, she had been for a time mortified by the failure of her projects; but she had too much good sense not to draw a useful lesson from the past. From the time of her visit to Buxton, the character of Sophia underwent a gradual change. Having once had the courage to find herself in the wrong, to look her errors in the face, and acknowledge them as such, she acquired strength to forsake them. Thoroughly ashamed of her heartless conduct towards Charles, she endeavoured, by respectful attention to his family when thrown into their society, to atone for her past hauteur. Perhaps nothing tended more to confirm and strengthen Sophia's altered views than witnessing the domestic happiness experienced by her former lover and his charming wife. In Helen she observed the rare union of true dignity and firmness with an unusually conciliating address; and she found it both instructive and amusing to observe the tact with which she contrived to steer clear of undue familiarity on the one hand, and an assumption of superiority on the other. With her husband's relatives the young wife was a universal favourite; whilst the qualities of her mind, and simple lady-like manners, caused her society to be courted by the truly estimable and refined. With such a standard, it is no wonder that Sophia Robartes became as superior in character as she had ever been in personal and mental qualifications; nor is it matter of great surprise that Edward Churchill should, when again thrown into her society, find her a charming girl; as unlike as possible to his Buxton belle. As the chosen friend of his sister, Edward had many opportunities of familiar intercourse with Sophia; and he did not deem it her least attraction that she bore him no ill-will for his former gallantry and subsequent neglect. With the cordial approbation of all his friends, Edward at length made Sophia an offer of his hand and heart, which offer being considered by the young lady's friends every way eligible, and by none more so than by Sophia herself, was duly and formally accepted. The good doctor rejoiced in the happiness of his favourite child; Mrs Robartes congratulated herself on the proper settlement of one of her daughters; and the sisters were well pleased with the anticipated bustle and eclât of a wedding, and the visits to the bride seen in the distance.

'Pray, Sophia, if I may venture upon such delicate ground,' asked Edward on the eve of his marriage, 'what have you done with your prejudices against Lowe's relations? Has it never occurred to you that there is certainly a fatality in these affairs, which dooms you, after all, to become a relative of Miss Tamar's?'

'With such an example before me of the power of affection to conquer prejudice and overcome aversion, I have not found it difficult to submit to my fate,' returned she archly.

'What do you mean?' asked Edward, colouring slightly, and with a touch of embarrassment in his manner.

'My dear Edward,' said Sophia, 'you once thought me very foolish, proud, and prejudiced; and so I was; but if my pride took one direction, have I been wrong in supposing that yours took another, and that the peculiarities of Miss Tamar were not more offensive to me than what you considered the assumption of myself and family to you?'

'Well, I confess, my dear little Sophia, that I did think there was "much ado about nothing;" but "all is well that ends well;" and we may thank Miss Tamar for our happiness. Dear old lady, if it had not been for her, I do believe you would have accepted Charles, and then what would have become of poor unhappy me, to say nothing of Helen?' With this confession she was fain to rest content; but, years after her marriage, Sophia Churchill was heard to say that she owed much of her happiness as a wife to the severe but salutary lesson which taught her the meanness and folly of Sophia Robartes's flirtations.

THE ZOLLVEREIN.

This word, which frequently occurs in the commercial articles of newspapers, signifies 'customs-confederation' (*zoll*, toll or custom, and *verein*, union or confederation), and applies to an agreement which has of late years been entered into by the governments of various German states to exact a uniform rate of duty upon imported goods, and to vest the management and collection of such dues in a central establishment. An explanation and short account of this union may be useful to some, and interesting to most of our readers.

Every tourist in Germany used to complain with very good reason of the inconvenient frequency with which he was made to stop on the road to get his passport examined. In the heart of Germany—which is made up of a cluster of petty states—he could scarcely travel a stage without having himself and his passport scrupulously examined by a policeman; for, as many of the ducal territories are not larger than a good-sized English estate, their frontiers lie pretty closely together. If, then, the mere pleasure tourist had to complain of this state of things, how much more reason had the merchants of the country to be dissatisfied, when they could not send the smallest packet of goods a few hundred miles without having it subjected to some half-dozen custom-house examinations, and having to pay upon it the same number of rates of duty? each little territory having a tariff of its own. By the time, therefore, a small parcel reached its destination, an amount of rates and duties had been accumulated upon it which perhaps exceeded its value. Moreover, it took a very good arithmetician to calculate the amount of the sum-total of dues which it had incurred; for every state had not only a separate tariff, but a distinct coinage and monetary system, all of which had to be assimilated on the bill of parcels by the merchant to whom the parcel was consigned. Hence in Germany commerce—which it is necessary to encourage by every possible facility of transit—was as complicated a business as can well be imagined.

Such enormous hindrances to trade could not, in the nature of things, be continued without some efforts towards amendment; and Prussia being the largest and most powerful of the German states, was therefore the best able to set reform on foot; which she did immediately after the battle of Waterloo had diffused the blessings of peace throughout Europe. Before, however, beginning to correct the fiscal faults of her neighbours, she commenced amending her own. A law was promulgated on the 26th May 1818, by which the old commercial restrictions, which excluded certain foreign articles from the Prussian market altogether, were removed, and foreign productions, whether natural or fabricated, were allowed to be freely imported, consumed, and conveyed throughout the whole breadth and length of the monarchy; whilst all home produce, whether raw or manufactured, was to be exported with equal freedom. Bounded, however, as Prussia is to a great extent by other territories, the new law would have been a dead letter, as regarded the land-carriage of goods to and from other countries, without the concurrence of neighbouring rulers, across one or other of whose boundaries merchandise destined for Prussia would have to pass, and to be subjected to *their* customs laws. The Prussian government therefore sought to induce them to join in this scheme; but so many obstacles supervened, by complexity of interests and jealousy of rights, that it was not till after several years of incessant negotiation that the object could be accomplished. Threats, intreaties, and concessions, however, prevailed, and at length the Prussian government was joined in its commercial scheme by the princes of Schwarzbourg, Sondershausen, and Schwarzbourg-Rudolstadt, the Grand Duke of Saxe-Weimar, the Duke of Anhalt-Bernbourg, the Grand Duke of Mecklenbourg-Schwerin, and the Duke of Anhalt-Dessau. Though none of their principalities are by any means extensive, yet the government of Prussia had more trouble and difficulty in negotiating and haggling with these petty rulers, than with all the more important states which afterwards joined the union.

Prussia, and the small territories which hang on her skirts, formed then a nucleus from which to spread the Zollverein further over the German continent. The Prussian government persevered, and, by 1826, had included in the union all those countries which extend on the north, east, and west, from Memel in the northernmost seaport of Prussia to Aix-la-Chapelle in Westphalia; and those from north to south, which lie between Stralsund and the Austrian frontier, behind Munich in Bavaria. The boundaries of the confederation are as follow: on the east, Russia and Poland; on the south, Austria and Switzerland; on the west, France; on the north-west, Belgium and Holland; and finally, on the north, Hanover and the other states which have hitherto declined to join this useful and vast commercial union. At present, it takes in about 8392 square miles, upon which reside a population equal to that of Great Britain and Ireland, being about twenty-seven millions. By the year 1831, the operations of the league were fully developed.

The leading effect of the Zollverein was to render that portion of Germany which we have indicated above, as one country. Throughout its entire extent a uniform rate of duty is charged in (happily for clerks and book-keepers) one sum at either of the boundaries we have mentioned, after which the goods thus taxed may be sent from one end of the united territories to another—from Aix-la-Chapelle to Tilsit, and from Stettin and Dantzic to the frontiers of Switzerland and Bohemia, without let or hindrance. The whole of the dues are collected and sent to a common and central treasury. The sum thus collected is periodically divided amongst the various governments which form the Zollverein.

In the early progress of the union, the difficulty of making the division equitably and fairly, opposed a great obstacle to the fulfilment of the scheme. After much deliberation, the following plan was resorted to, and appears to work to the satisfaction of all parties:—A basis of the calculation for apportioning the gross amount of dues is formed by the amount of the population of each territory, in proportion to the amount of which the revenues are, in the main, allotted to each state; but this calculation is wisely checked by the respective accounts kept in the line of customhouses established upon the frontiers within which the confederation exists. These calculations and payments are made once in every three years, when each government sends to the centre of management in Berlin an envoy or deputy to assist at the settlement of the accounts, and to propose such modifications or alteration in commercial taxation as time or change of circumstances may have rendered necessary in his particular district.

It is now necessary to say a word on the nature and amount of the duties levied by the Zollverein. In the first place, instead of publishing a cumbrous and inconvenient list of the scarcely numerable subjects of commerce, the framers of the Prussian tariff went on more comprehensive principles: they divided all articles of trade into five grand sections, ranging in each such things as had a similar origin or use. The first division includes foreign materials, which cannot be produced within the countries of the Zollverein; the second, foreign produce, which *is* produced within the union; the third, articles necessary to industry and manufactures; the fourth, manufactured goods; and the fifth, small wares. Upon the articles included in each of these sections a uniform duty is levied; but every three years those rates are altered—if possible, diminished. The tariff now in force having been settled on the 1st January 1843, expires with the present year. The list of prohibited articles of import, which, previous to the union, was very great, is now reduced to two—salt and playing cards.

The liberal commercial principles which guided and were carried into effect by the Zollverein, have given a great impetus to German industry and commercial prosperity. Amongst other reforms, this useful league has swept away all tolls and other impediments which formerly obstructed the free navigation of the Rhine and the Elbe; and many mischievous monopolies held by companies and city guilds no longer obstruct the healthy working of competition.

The Zollverein has concluded treaties of commerce and navigation with every power in the world with whom a trading intercourse is worth having, and its flag is already flying in all the most important ports throughout the globe. Since 1834, the amount of dues collected has trebled. In 1843, the duties paid into the common treasury amounted to 23,121,324 thalers, equal to nearly L.3,500,000 sterling. The commercial power which increasing prosperity gives, will in all probability force those states who have not yet joined the confederation to form a part of it, and at no distant day we may expect to find the union extending throughout the whole of the Germanic empire.

THE CURLERS' ANNUAL.

OUR English friends are, we believe, altogether unacquainted with a game practised amongst us under the name of *curling*. It is comparatively local even amongst ourselves, for in many districts of Scotland it has never been introduced: it may be said to reign chiefly in the south-west and central provinces, namely, the counties of Dumfries, Peebles, Edinburgh, Fife, and Perth. Comprehensively, it is *bowls played upon ice*, but with stones which slide instead of rolling, each being fitted with a handle whereby it is impelled. Depending as it does upon frost of some continuance, it is a game which no one ever gets time to tire of. Played upon the surfaces of ponds in gentlemen's parks, or upon rivers and lakes bosomed high amidst beautiful scenery, while the air is clear and sharp, and every shred of vegetation hung with nature's sparkling jewellery—while men know, too, that they are only allowed by our inconstant Jove to snatch a fearful joy—no sport can be more thoroughly delighted in by its votaries than curling. The ice of rank thaws before the sunny face of this game: priests, lawyers, country gentlemen, may be seen joining in it with the village shopkeeper and blacksmith—and this as no Young England novelty, but a matter of course that has been known in Scotland from all time, and seems likely to know no end. In fact, curling appears to have the power of bringing all men back to the common starting level of mere children; it fuses all hearts into one mass. And such bouncing and running, such sweeping and roaring—what shouts at great shots, what derision at failures! while the stones are every minute heard cracking against each other, filling the glen as with peals of thunder. Curlers, it may well be imagined, are all enthusiasts in their sports. The present writer met an elderly gentleman one morning on his way to a *rink* amidst the Braid Hills, near Edinburgh. 'Well,' said he, 'this is my sixtieth winter as a curler, for I first handled the stones in the '83.' Looking on, one day, at a match played upon that same rink, I observed a gentleman sink to the bottom of the pond with one leg. One of his partners was just throwing off his stone: it was a shot of deep importance. He had been for a few moments fixed in an attitude of absorbed attention. The accident to the leg was therefore unregarded till the fate of the stone was decided at the upper end of the pond, when he deliberately pulled out his dripping limb as if nothing had been the matter. Such little traits will convey, even to the unfortunate denizens of mild climates, some faint idea of the glory and the joy (*tantus amor... atque gloria*) of curling.

The Annual of the Royal Caledonian Curling Club for 1845* makes us aware that that club is now the common tie or head of 120 local or district clubs throughout the country, numbering in all about 5000 members. We learn from it that curling has an evidenced antiquity of above two centuries, but is supposed to be of much older standing; and that there are local clubs which have had peculiar ceremonies of initiation, not much unlike those of free-masonry, from time immemorial. The rules of the central fraternity, and lists of the office-bearers of many of the local establishments, are given, together with accounts of matches and social meetings, and specimens of the original poetry produced on those occasions. The good-humoured enthusiasm of the volume is highly amusing. Mr Durham Weir, for instance, toasting 'Scotland's ain game of curling' at the dinner of the Royal club, January 23, 1844, delivers himself as follows:—'It is almost unnecessary for me to tell you, fellow-curlers, that of the various amusements that have attracted the attention of mankind, there is none of them worthy of being compared with that noble and manly recreation which has this evening been the happy means of assembling so many around these festive boards. Well may the game of curling be designated the Game of Games; for whilst it invigorates our bodies, it at the same time imparts a delightful and indescribable buoyancy to our spirits. In proof of this, I need only quote the authority of the poet Pennycuick, who flourished about a century and a half ago, and whose poetical effusions must speak to the heart of every true curler:—

> To curl on the ice doth greatly please,
> Being a manly exercise;
> It clears the brain—stirs up the native heat—
> And *gives a gallant appetite for meat.*

Of all scenes upon earth, fellow-curlers, there is none more interesting, none more fascinating, none more animating, than on a fine still frosty morning, when the sun is shining upon the snow-fleeced ice, the diamond-bespangled ground and the silver-tasselled trees, to behold groups of old Scotia's sturdy sons hastening to the field of contest—the glassy bosom of some sequestered glen or romantic lake—with their hearts beating high in the expectation of carrying away victory's well-contested palm.

> Even aged men,
> Smit with the eagerness of youth, are there;
> While love of conquest lights their beamless eyes,
> New nerves their arms, and makes them young once more.

All are in motion; all are upon the tiptoe of expectation. See how they vie with each other in the friendly and exhilarating competition! Behold the keen glistening of their eyes while they survey the ponderous curling-stones as they go booming down the icy rinks. Curling not only enlivens our spirits and braces our nerves, but strengthens and enlarges the sphere of social intercourse, by bringing into contact many a kindred spirit who, but for such occasions as the present, would in all probability never have met on this side the grave. It is likewise the means of renewing friendships with those whom we had almost forgotten, and with whom, in our thoughtless and giddy boyhood, we had spent many of our happiest days, "paidling in the burn, or running about the braes, pouing the gowans fine."'

A short essay 'On the Moral Effects of Curling' digresses into a few remarks on those of a more tangible character. 'We have heard recorded, as amongst the rarest sights in nature, a dead donkey, and a tinker's funeral (we mean no offence by the illustration); but who *ever heard of a sick curler?* Let a man be wincing under the twitches of rheumatism, or roaring with the agonies of its superlative, gout, or pining under any of the nine hundred and ninety-nine maladies which prey upon the internal constitution.

> Get stanes and a broom, tak' a season o' curling,
> And the pains o' disease in a giffy will flee.'

Amongst the social meetings recorded is one of a curious nature, which took place in the latter part of July, '44, on the top of the hills overlooking the Carse of Gowrie. The Fingask Curling Club there entertained their president, Sir Peter M. Threipland, Bart. as a mark of gratitude for his having prepared a pond for their amusement. The festivity took place in a gay pavilion perched on a spot seven hundred feet above the level of the sea, and from which the hills of a dozen surrounding and distant counties could be seen. The affair seems to have been one of those kindly conventions of gentlemen and commoners which have fortunately never been discontinued in Scotland, and which take place there, not under any notion of such meetings being desirable for ulterior objects, but simply because the rural people of all orders in that country feel, as they have ever felt, the most cordial dispositions towards each other. The facetious chairman of this occasion seems to have had a peculiar knack of turning everything to account in favour of the game. In toasting Prince Albert, for example, he alluded to a pair of curling stones which had been presented to him when at Scone palace in September 1842. 'The last time I heard of these stones,' said he, 'they formed a part of the valuable articles which adorn one of the galleries in Windsor palace. At that time some of the English nobility and gentry, on observing them, wondered greatly what they were, and expressed great anxiety to know what was the use of them. The palace at Windsor may, for anything I know, be a very good curling house, but I would ten times rather have heard of them being in a wee housie on the banks of the Serpentine, which would have shown that the prince was a chip of the right block, and a true son of the broom!' The Prince of Wales was thus adverted to: 'He has scarcely begun his education, but you will all agree with me in maintaining, that if, in the progress of that education, he is not made a "keen, keen curler"—if he is not thoroughly initiated into all the mysteries of that health-restoring, strength-renovating, nerve-bracing game of curling—his education will be entirely bungled.' Presenting the stones to the guest of the evening, he said, 'Let one of these stones be always placed on the tee, a perfect *pat lid*. The other, a few feet behind, a complete *guard*; at any rate, put them always over the *hog score*, and you may rest assured that, if there is broom or heather on the Sidlaw Hills, we will sweep them to the *tee-head*.' Finally came some jocundity respecting the propagandism of the game. 'The curlers are a set of the most benevolent fellows on the face of the earth—their benevolence is of a very diffusive description; and I am going to carry your benevolence across the wide Atlantic to our brethren in Canada, where you will find the

* Printed for the R. C. C. Club, by W. Forrester, 6 St Andrew Square, Edinburgh.

besom, and across the German Ocean, up to Petersburg, where you will find the channelstane. The Scotch games are beginning to spread far and wide over the face of the earth. The other week, when I was at Montrose, Davidson the club-maker was busy preparing to export golf-clubs and balls to the Mauritius, the Cape of Good Hope, and to Bombay. It is true that the noble game of curling cannot, in ordinary circumstances, be practised in these warmer regions; but last night I met with two young gentlemen who had the other day skated on artificial ice in Liverpool, which answered the purpose remarkably well. It seems that this artificial ice is composed of rosin and salts. From this a very good rink could be formed, and might be introduced into the East Indies with great effect. But should this be found not to answer the purpose, there is still another method by which curling might be enjoyed in that country. In the northern regions of India, our old friend John Frost possesses a large territory, and I am sure he would be delighted to afford some splendid rinks among the Himalaya mountains. The distance is trifling—only 1500 miles from Bombay. I hope we shall, by and by, see in the *Bengal Hurkaru*, or in some of the East India papers, a paragraph to the following effect:—"This morning a number of elephants, laden with curling stones, left Bombay for the Himalaya mountains, to which place a large party of Scottish gentlemen are to proceed for the purpose of enjoying for a few weeks their favourite game of curling." (Laughter and cheers.)'

Enough of this good-natured nonsense, which we do not half understand even in point of language, exclaims some testy southern. By no means—you must first listen to, and endeavour if possible to comprehend, Walter Watson of Chryston's song on curling:—

'When snell o'er our snaw tappet mountains,
The breath o' the north taks a flight,
And seals up our lochs and our fountains
Wi' something like magical sleight,
Syne on the clear surface we venture,
Wi' a' our equipments in tune,
To join in the sports o' the Winter,
Wi' skates and weel tacketed shoon.
Brods and crampets and a',
Stanes and besoms and a',
How social the sport, and how manly,
Wi' stanes and besoms and a'.

Our forehand now ready for action,
Is metin' the lead wi' his e'e,
And hearin' his usual direction,
Has clappet his hand on his knee.
Stand back at the hog wi' a besom,
Soop, soop, for the ice is but new;
He's back, but we'll hae to excuse him,
We ken what our leader can do.
Leadin' and drawin' and a',
Guardin' and strikin' and a',
How social the sport, &c.

Our watchfu' opponents in motion,
Direct to draw up by a side;
Ye'll come to my cowe, I've a notion—
Keep close, for ye maunna flee wide.
Weel done, sir—up hands—he's a' roarin'—.
It's lost if it passes the ring;
That shot's rather strong for a forehand,
Yet no very far frae the thing—
Soopin' and scrapin' and a',
Shakin' o' besoms and a',
How social the sport, &c.

Now, stane after stane in rotation,
Ilk wishin' to do as he's bid,
Till some in the brough get a station,
And ane's termed a vera pat lid.
Now, John, do you see a' the winner,
If no, tak' this wick at my cowe;
Then til't he comes roarin' like thunner,
And spreads them like sheep on a knowe—
This way and that way and a',
Out o' the ring and awa',
How social the sport, &c.

Fine ports has been entered and blocket,
Guid stanes has been laid on ilk side;
Yet though we've been equally yoket,
Now vict'ry maun come and decide.
Our hinhand unrivalled at drawin',
Sends up a tee-shot to a hair—
Game, game, wi' loud cheers and huzzain',
While besoms play sough in the air!
Thankin' and roosing and a',
Powin' o' bottles and a',
Then hey for a beef and green dinner,
Wi' jaws o' guid toddie and a'.'

SHORT NOTES ON THE WEST INDIES.

BY A LATE RESIDENT.

FIFTH AND LAST ARTICLE.

Style and Cost of Living.—The style of living of the upper classes in the West Indies differs, I think, not so much from that of the middle classes in England as is generally supposed. Made dishes and soups are certainly more frequent, and wine and spirits are more used. Otherwise, with the exception of the addition of colonial vegetables and fruits, I have found no difference. Roast and boiled beef, roast and boiled mutton (very often goat mutton), poultry, fish, &c. are all as generally eaten in the West Indies, although a like degree of justice is certainly not done to them, as in England. Many dainties are procurable in the colonies not to be had in England; on the other hand, many delicacies are to be had in England which are not procurable in the colonies. The variety in fish is endless, and many of them are much esteemed. The calapaver, the mountain mullet, the June or Jew fish, and the mud fish, are among those which are found most delicious. Turtle, being no rarity, is very little prized, and is about the cheapest dish that can be procured. Ortolans, commonly called 'pinks,' from their cry, are, in season (about October), much sought after. A great many kinds of beans and peas are to be met with, which are converted into delicious soups, although not introduced at table on set occasions. Alongside the far-famed 'pepper-pot,' which is very delicious, there is used at family dinners a sort of paste termed 'moossean,' which is not masticated, but gulped, lest it should adhere to the teeth and gums. Few like the process at first, but it becomes by no means unpleasant after a little practice. Rice boiled dry is a very common dish, and is among the class of provisions termed 'bread-kind.' Among vegetables, the yams, plantains, cocoas, ackies, avocado pears, chochos, &c. are exclusively colonial. Oysters, crabs, lobsters, crayfish, shrimp, &c. are to be had as in England—the two first, however, of a smaller, and, it is thought, of a more delicate description. Among the fruits, the shaddock, pine apple, orange, forbidden fruit, star apple, nesberry, and Grenadella, rank the first. A mixture of the star apple and orange is excellent, and not unlike strawberries and cream. The preserves are well known. Confectionary is by no means equal to what may be procured in England. Among the lower classes is found an interminable variety of 'country pots,' which it would be impossible to give a fair idea of on paper.

Proceeding downwards to the lower classes, it is possible that living is with them much less expensive than with the same grade in England. The agricultural population raise nearly all the provisions and vegetables brought to market. They may therefore procure them at little cost. They do not, however, live solely on such provisions. Salted pork, salted cod, herrings, shad, and mackerel, form chief ingredients of their daily fare; and these, although not dearer, are not cheaper than food in England.

Without reference to the expense of 'living,' there are items which render the 'keeping up of appearances in the colonies much more costly than in England. Few persons of any pretensions to respectability deny themselves the pleasure of keeping an equipage, or a horse, which brings other incidental expenses. In fact, so general is the practice of keeping a horse, that a labourer who toils every day in the week in the fields may be seen riding on Sunday to prayers. Nay, more; the bankrupt, probably for the tenth time, will, a day after the declaration of his insolvency, be seen as usual in his carriage. One observation must be made in behalf of those who keep vehicles or horses they may fairly call their own. The heat of the climate renders it a necessary rather than a luxury of life, and it is about the only rational resource they have by way of recreation or change from the monotonous life which is generally led in the colonies.

Hospitality and Benevolence.—I would consider any series of observations on the West Indies as incomplete which did not include a few remarks on the benevolence of the several classes; and as I have observed no particular connexion in my notes, the remarks which I have to make under this head may as well be inserted here as elsewhere. To whatever cause it may be owing—whether to the genial nature of the climate, which warms the heart as well as the body, or any other—it is no doubt true that the inhabitants of the West Indies are an hospitable and benevolent set of persons. Introductions to parties there are not mere matters of form, as they are, generally speaking, in England. The stranger at once finds himself treated as an old friend, and no little attention is omitted which seems calculated to render his stay, whether for a short or for a long period, comfortable. He receives more invitations than he can conveniently accept; the equipages of his new acquaintances are at his command; and the chances are, that, if his introductions are good, and he intends remaining in the West Indies, a road to a comfortable livelihood, if not a competence, is at once opened to his industry. The item of benevolence may perhaps best be elucidated by the circumstance, that a case of starvation, arising from positive inability to obtain food, is unknown. It is not to be denied that in the West Indies hospitality and benevolence frequently lapse into abuse; that is, the hospitality becomes lavish profusion, and the benevolence weakness. Of the evils of want and profusion, or niggardliness and indiscriminateness, however, I would choose in either case the latter—it being better that man should have in abundance than be in need.

Kindness and attention to the sick is also a marked feature of the West Indian character, particularly that of the female; and the middle class of coloured women are known as the most skilful and considerate nurses in the world. Their knowledge of the several diseases of the climate frequently surpasses that of the medical man, and the latter is not too proud to acknowledge, or too opinionated to take advantage of it. If the stranger be attacked by fever, by all means let him obtain the services of one of these nurses. Their presence is really very nearly a pledge of recovery, while their charges are reasonable, and as often as not they make no charge. Children's nurses are also a most affectionate set; and the attachment they entertain for the infants whom they have tended is to be broken only by death. I have 'a case in point.' On leaving the West Indies, an old black woman, whom I had not seen for many years, but whom I knew as the nurse of a person that had left some time back for England, came to me, and requested that if I saw her 'young massa,' I would tell him 'how d'ye,' and say that she often thought of him. I promised to do so; but am sorry to say that I forgot to perform my promise, although the opportunity to do so has often been afforded me.

A Governor's Ball.—The governor being the representative of majesty, a ball given by that functionary answers of course to the drawing-room of her majesty in England, and the one occasions in a small way as much excitement as the other. For days before the invitations are issued, a fever of anxiety prevails to ascertain who are to be the invited parties; and as the invitations are sent through the post-office, we must suppose the clerks of that establishment have the benefit of the first cooling draught which is administered, they having the opportunity of first gratifying their curiosity. The whole island has, however, no sooner been quieted on this point, than another excitement ensues. The governor has issued invitations of very questionable propriety in the eyes of would-be lords and lady patronesses, who accordingly feel for the time seriously afflicted. Mantua-makers and milliners, haberdashers and merchant tailors, are ere this in requisition. Prices are given which, strange to say, are never received, and bills run up that are never suffered to run down. Ladies and gentlemen are, however, finally equipped, and at length the happy moment approaches. The carriages are in waiting, the clock probably strikes ten, in jump the parties, smack go the whips, and away the vehicles roll to government house. A line of the rabble occupies each available position near the building; but the immediate vicinity of the representative of majesty, wonderment at the scene, and the police, awe them into quiet. The carriages approach the door with no obstruction or delay beyond that of the driver's overshooting the steps, and the parties emerge. 'Your names,' inquires a footman in waiting: they are furnished, and straight resound through the hall of introduction or ball-room, according as the host may have placed himself. If in the ball-room, the ceremony of introduction or obeisance is probably for the moment postponed; for to edge one's way at once through the dense concourse of persons who have quickly assembled to the upper end of the room, where perhaps the governor and his lady—should he have one—sit enthroned on a dais, is a work of some difficulty. The parties who have arrived late, therefore, either take seats on the couches and chairs arranged throughout the apartment, or fall into the quadrilles, if they can succeed in squeezing out places for themselves, partners, and *vis-à-vis*. The quadrilles over, the setts proceed *en promenade* round the room, making their obeisances to the representative of majesty (and spouse, if in being, and present), as they pass the spot occupied by them. This is the moment for such introductions as are yet to be made. He, however, who has no friend at court, must be content to introduce himself, or humbly worship at a distance in the revolving crowd. Popular governors make it a point of traversing the room occasionally, for the purpose of shaking the hand of every guest. The other, however, being the most dignified, is, I believe, the most usual practice. After this the band (usually a military one) probably strikes up a waltz, whereupon the floor is cleared, and away start off a dozen couples whisking round the room like double-pegged tops, and chasing each other as though the object were to be first at the end of the circle. The windows are all thrown open, and a pleasant current of air enters the apartment; but waltzing is warm work, and pearly drops now follow each other down the dancers' cheeks. At length the band becomes fatigued (the waltzers never are), and the music ceases. The ladies then cast themselves listlessly on couches, and the gentlemen agitate their partners' fans, bestowing on themselves as great a share of the reviving current of air produced as decency will permit. In a few minutes they are all ready for the next quadrille. A circular promenade had been formed at the termination of the waltz by the lookers-on, but with the sound of the music it is converted into large quadrille setts, and dancing again commences. This, with an occasional visit to the refreshment tables—where gentlemen consume large quantities of 'sangaree' and 'mixed hock,' while ladies modestly imbibe 'iced lemonade' and 'capillaire'—is the routine until supper time. When that hour arrives, the host leads one of his most distinguished guests—probably the chief-justice's lady, or the lady of the president of the council—to the table in another apartment, and is followed by as many couples as can obtain places. Probably the ladies are all accommodated, and the good things gradually disappear. At length the governor's health is proposed and drank with nine times nine, and his excellency returns thanks in a most gracious speech; he then retires, as do the ladies, with a sprinkling of gentlemen: most of the latter remain to do yet greater justice to the hospitality of the host, in which they seldom fail. After this period many ludicrous, if not indecorous occurrences transpire. Among the former, I recollect the case of a gallant colonel of militia, who, discovering that he was unable to reach with dignity or safety beyond the middle of the stairs leading from the supper to the ball-room, very judiciously sat himself down. The ladies tittered, and the gentlemen laughed; but the colonel's friends coming to his assistance, he was speedily marched off the field, like many a gallant veteran, in a worse plight than when he entered it. With the disappearance of supper, little of interest remains for the elder portion of the guests. These therefore shortly after depart, while the younger portion keep up the dance until his excellency rises to retire. This is the signal for all to take their leave and disperse, which they do, wondering whether his excellency will give another entertainment shortly, or whether those who have enjoyed his hospitality on the present occasion will subscribe and give his excellency a ball in return, that being the mode in which parties are usually reciprocated.

State of Society.—Enough has been said in the course of these notes to lead the reader to conclude that society in the West Indies has not as yet assumed its most attractive garb, although in a very advanced stage of improvement. Whatever might have been its condition previous to the era of slavery, we have sufficient evidence for believing that that degrading system speedily engulfed, in its horrid and vicious practices, such humanising influences as had existed. By and by, however, as the communication with the mother country became more frequent, a ray of light would, as it were, intrude itself into the darkness, showing the desolation which prevailed. Young 'creoles,' sent home for their education, would return bringing 'more light.' A better infusion from Europe, too, would prevail; representations of the state of the colonies would induce missionaries to go out, for the purpose of communicating instruction to the people; and the several sparks of improvement thus elicited, once permitted to ignite, soon spread into a flame, which began, and has continued to consume the wide-spreading branches of the moral upas tree which overshadowed every corner of colonial society. To continue the simile, although probably at the expense of my narrative, the old tree, though not yet dead, has been so scorched as to leave us certain that it will never again shoot out vigorous branches; and we may now entertain every reasonable hope that the colonies will by and by present a happy illustration of the effects of moral contact and instruction. This event, however, is still in perspective, as has been said. A contempt for the matrimonial rite, taking so prominent a stand in the history of the colonies, though greatly lessened, has not yet ceased; and what is technically called 'hard living' among certain classes, has diminished, but still often occurs. Education among the lower orders advances probably with as great strides as it has ever done in any country where it has been but recently introduced; and attendance on public worship among all classes is more general, if not more sincere, than it once was.

The Press.—The press is as influential in the colonies as in other quarters of the globe. But as until late years its voice was never elevated in the defence of liberty, and it dared not, for the sake of its own existence, paint vice in the nakedness of its deformity, we must conclude its influence was rather for evil than for good. When it assumed the censorship of morals, and advocated the equal rights of all classes, its influence was evidently of a beneficial kind, although much evil attended its practices in detail. In order to hold up vice to public reprobation, it was necessary to describe its most hidden features; hence arose a necessity for laying bare the private affairs of individuals. In order to further the interests of freedom, it was necessary to decry those who upheld slavery; hence attacks on individual character. Thus, while slavery lasted, the colonial press was a repertory for all that was scandalous and libellous; the one party resorting to this use of it as a means—though it cannot be denied as an evil one—of obtaining a good end; the other, by way of retaliation, and support of a favourite but falling system. There was, however, a portion of the colonial press which with the new order of things at once put on a new aspect; and the cause for which it had battled having been gained, threw down its ancient weapons of war, appearing as a mediator between the two parties who seemed disposed still to carry on the contest; the one on the ground that the labourer, though free, required protection; the other on the plea that the planter had been ruined through the instrumentality of their opponents, and also required an advocate. This moderate set of papers has succeeded in lulling the resentment which prejudices and causes of dispute had occasioned, and bringing the colonies nearer to that period when complete union will prevail. I have reason to believe that the effort which enabled the conductors of this portion of the press to pursue the course which they did was great. Popular influence was before them, and a community of injuries goaded them on; but a paramount sense of public duty prevailed over personal considerations, and good has been the result. With respect to the scurrility and party spirit of the colonial press, it may be as well to observe that they were at one period so great, as to induce the government at home to direct that no editor of a newspaper in the colonies should be included in a new magisterial commission. This was certainly an interference with the freedom of public discussion which nothing but a great exigency could warrant. The restriction has, however, now been removed.

The Future.—We cannot penetrate into futurity, and therefore are not in a situation to predict the destiny of the colonies. We may, however, point out what appears necessary to be attained, and what to be avoided, ere that destiny can possibly be a happy one. Passing over the two items—want of labour and deficient agriculture—we may point to capital as a great desideratum in the colonies. I have been told of cases where the labourer would have at least six weeks' wages due him, and have heard of others where tickets are presented him in payment of labour—such tickets to be redeemed at some future time. These are not incentives to industry in older free countries than the colonies, and cannot prove so in the latter. Economy in every department is another requisite. By way of commencing at the fountain-head: there seems no reason why the office of attorney should not be abolished; the overseer, who is now often also attorney, being competent to the discharge of the duties of the estate. Absenteeism must also be modified. If proprietors cannot make it convenient to reside in the colonies, at least let them rent their properties to parties who can. The aid of government must be obtained in creating for the colonies an interest in the bosoms of those who are destined to spend their lives there—that is to say, offices of emolument must not be confined, as hitherto, to the *protegés* of government supporters at home, but distributed among the deserving in the colonies. These are amongst the chief desiderata. Among the items to be avoided, are a distrust of or contempt for the natural labourers of the colonies—of the labourers who, though coerced to it, made the colonies what they were and are. It cannot be expected that they will labour cheerfully for those who mistrust or despise them. They must also be regarded as entitled to as much consideration and as much pay as imported labourers. He will feel that an unjust distinction is made when additional 'comforts' are given to the latter which are denied him. Lastly, there must be union among all classes; for we are told, on the highest authority, that 'a house divided against itself shall not stand.'

RECREATIONS WITH THE MAGNIFYING MIRROR.

A SKETCH FOR YOUNG PEOPLE.

Even the sunniest days of summer are like life's pleasures—not always to be calculated upon. We had proposed for to-day a visit to the woodlands to study nature in the fields and open air; but the morning lowered, and to a dense drizzling fog succeeded a continued rain, which steeped everything in moisture. There is no time that one feels a disappointment from the weather more than in the long and bright days of summer, and especially when some out-door excursion is in view. The young people felt it much, and looking out upon the green shrubbery, every leaf of which was now weighed down with the dripping moisture, and on the prostrate roses with compressed and soiled petals, and then, giving many an anxious gaze up to the dense and sombre heavens, they could not help contrasting the sunny smiles of yesterday, and their out-of-door gambols, with the dreary solitude of this.

Under these circumstances, other amusement was to be sought for within doors; so, making some arrangements beforehand with the magnifying mirror, the young people were called in. 'Look here, Henry, and as your observations are generally pretty accurate, tell us what you see.' 'I see a green park with shrubbery; in the distance a handsome lodge, and in the foreground several trunks of trees lying about as if newly felled.' After a short pause—'Oh! I see on one of the prostrate trees a creature, a beautiful animal. I declare it moves; it climbs up over the fallen trunk, and now it stands on the upper side of it. How beautiful and majestic it looks! It has a dark-brown or olive body, with numerous fair yellow spots, a finely-shaped neck, small head, two horns, and soft and beautiful eyes. It moves again; it must be alive: it stalks along like a deer, or the pictures we have seen of a chamois. Tell me, is it really a living animal or a deception?' 'It is indeed,' said I, 'a living creature.' 'I thought so,' replied Henry, 'for its movements could not be but those of life and nature. How slender and elegant is its make—its limbs how pliant, and adapted for quick and easy motion! It now moves again down the sloping trunk of the tree, and along the side of another.' It was Anna's turn to view it next. 'I do see the creature, but it is half concealed among the branches: nothing now is seen but its beautiful head with its slender tapering horns and soft intelligent eyes. It is gone; I wish it would appear again. Oh! here comes from the other side another, and another, and another. What beautiful creatures! They move on with all the calmness and majesty of tame roes: they stand, look round, move their horns, and then wheel off, succeeded by others. Oh! here is a little one, a young creature, of a bright yellow, with a body so transparent that you may almost see through it.' Elizabeth, who had given place to the younger children, now had her curiosity raised. She now viewed the mimic scene, peopled with really living creatures, with some amazement. 'They are indeed like a troop of deer,' she says; 'but this is impossible; and, let me see, they have six feet instead of four.' 'Six feet!' cried Henry, somewhat piqued at his failing to observe this; 'are you sure of that? let me look again.' It was found that they had six feet, and, therefore, that they could not be quadrupeds. I then inquired what class of animals had six feet, and they all answered me, 'Insects generally.' They were, however, loath all at once to bring down their fine troop of deer, or, at the least, chamois, to insects; but as the investigation of truth should at all times be made the paramount object, the mimic show was dissolved, and the trunks of trees in the foreground proved to be some slips of our favourite myrtle, which I had discovered to be infested with the *aphis*, or plant louse. While reading near the window, one of these animals crawled across my book, and I was so struck with the beauty and elegance of its form, that after ascertaining from whence it came, and that it had left there numerous companions, I resolved on showing it on a magnified scale; and, by arranging a coloured landscape of a park and trees in the way mentioned, I succeeded in inducing in the children the association of deer in a park.

Our attention was now directed to the myrtle, and to its stock of living inhabitants, which it had, unfortunately for its health and vigour, acquired. The question now was, where had these insects come from? The myrtle had hitherto been perfectly free from them, and as the species of aphis appeared to be that generally found on the willow, I conjectured that the colony had come from the willows on the outskirts of the shrubbery. But how could they come from such a distance, over walls and through hedgerows? How? what is to hinder an animal which you compared to a deer from bounding over all these obstacles? But look here, some of these insects are winged, while others, and the great majority, are wingless. This is a singular difference in animals of exactly the same species: but so it is; some are furnished with wings, in order that they may flee away and produce new colonies, while the remainder, creeping along from plant to plant, leave none in their neighbourhood untenanted. They are perhaps the most numerous of all insects, and the most prolific. One parent will bring forth from ninety to a hundred young; in five or six weeks as many generations will have sprung from each of these ninety, so that, in the course of a short season, not less than six thousand millions will have sprung from a single parent. You see these clusters of minute brown spots on the under side of the leaf? these are the eggs from which young will be hatched in a few days. Towards the close of the season, eggs are always produced and deposited in crevices of the green bark; these eggs endure the cold of winter, and insure a brood in spring, thus affording a careful provision by which nature secures the preservation of the species.

'And what part of the plant do these animals feed on?' inquired Elizabeth. 'They extract the juice by a proboscis, the end of which pierces the leaf or tender stem. If you gently turn up one of these myrtle leaves, you will find a group of the insects on the under side, and with this glass we shall probably see some of them feeding. They are always found on the under side of the leaf, and thus are protected from the weather and from their enemies.' 'Here,' cries Henry, 'is one busy at work; I see his proboscis distinctly; it is not unlike that of the elephant.' 'And here is another on this side,' said Elizabeth, 'just unfolding its proboscis, and we shall watch it piercing the leaf. How quickly and easily is this operation performed. But do they not injure the leaves by this process?' 'Very much,' I replied: 'you see how many of the leaves of yon myrtle are curled up and shrivelled and sickly from the operations of these creatures; in a very short time the whole plant would suffer from the abstraction of its due nourishment. In this way these animals are very destructive to all plants on which they settle, and especially to tender and succulent ones, which they prefer. You see, too, on many of the leaves a clammy whitish fluid; this is what is called honey dew; in reality a kind of sugar or honey which drops from the animal, and is the refuse of its digestion. This is what gives the clammy feel to the stems and leaves of many plants, which you have often remarked, and which is found covering them, as the beech and hop, like a hoar frost. Some have supposed that this dew exuded or sweated from the pores of the plant itself, from the state of the weather, but there can be no doubt that it is caused by the aphis, for it is only found on those parts of the plant where they are domiciled. Other insects are very fond of, and feed on this honey dew, and it is much more common in some seasons than in others—those years of *blight*, which, by repressing and retarding the vigorous growth of plants, favour the propagation of the aphis.'

'You make me displeased with the aphis now, which I formerly admired,' said Elizabeth; 'how shall we rid our dear myrtle of these pests?' 'The rascally vermin!' cries Henry; 'we shall utterly exterminate them, not only from the myrtle, but from the willows and the garden too.' 'Moderate your wrath a little, my dears,' I said; 'they have enemies enough, as you shall presently hear; besides, they perform their parts in the great chain of existence, and would be as much missed by many hungry stomachs, as our sheep or our poultry would be by us.' 'Let us hear of some of their enemies,' they all exclaimed. 'In the first place, they are preyed upon incessantly by many of the larger flies, which pounce upon them, and suck up all the juices of their bodies. Among these is the ichneumon fly—a brown fly with a long piercer attached to its body, which I have formerly shown you. This fly pitches upon a poor aphis, pierces its little body, and then deposits its egg in the hole which it has made. In a few days the egg becomes a little grub, having such a voracious appetite that it soon devours every particle of the creature into whose body it had been so curiously inserted, except its skin, when, piercing a hole in this, it creeps out, and leaves the dry skin hanging on the leaf like a drop of dew. Myriads of them fall in this manner. And the well-known insect, the lady-bird you have often seen creeping among the bushes, many a dinner does it make on a fattened aphis. But they have more enemies still. You see that blue tomtit there busy among the leafy bushes; even in this rainy day he must have his dinner. See how he perches with his back downwards, and picks, picks incessantly at the backs of the leaves; every pick indicates the death of an aphis: not fewer are made than one hundred in the minute, so that in half an hour, for his share alone, he has bagged three thousand head. And no doubt many other species of the soft-billed birds are making similar dinners in various other corners.'

'I relent against the poor aphis,' cries Anna, 'and must again pity it: no wonder that they have fled from the willows and the cruel ichneumons, and have come to take shelter in our myrtle: we must not kill them: yet if they would only be content with cabbages, and not destroy our beautiful myrtle, I would feed them myself daily.' Here followed a sharp discussion on the propriety or impropriety of their destruction. Henry was firm in the determination that, as they had unlawfully entered the house, and taken possession of the plant, they should be exterminated without compunction. The others hesitated much, on the plea that the creatures were innocent, and had sought their protection; and proposed that the plant should be taken out into the lawn and washed with water till freed of them. I stated that this plan would be ineffectual, for water was found not to kill them, and the most minute washing would not eradicate them; that in all greenhouses, and other similar places where their rapid increase could not be checked by the operations of their lawful enemies, man had no hesitation in exterminating them by his art. I then explained the means by which I intended to preserve the myrtle from their further ravages, which was to place it within a large box, and apply over it the fumes of tobacco; this, or sprinkling the leaves with tobacco juice, being generally approved of as the best means of getting quit of such destructive creatures. I then turned to the pages of our favourite poet of 'The Seasons,' and desired Henry to read the passage referring to these insects.

'For oft, engendered by the hazy north,
Myriads on myriads, insect armies waft
Keen in the poisoned breeze, and wasteful eat,
Through buds and bark, into the blackened core
Their eager way. A feeble race! yet oft
The sacred sons of vengeance, on whose course
Corrosive famine waits, and kills the year.
To check this plague the skilful farmer chaff
And blazing straw before his orchard burns;
Till, all involved in smoke, the latent foe
From every cranny suffocated falls;
Or scatters o'er the blooms the pungent dust
Of pepper, fatal to the frosty tribe;
Or, when the envenomed leaf begins to curl,
With sprinkled water drowns them in their nest;
Nor, while they pick them up with busy bill,
The little trooping birds unwisely scares.'

'The author, you see, here describes concisely and elegantly what I have been telling you.'

'He is at fault, however,' said Henry, 'with regard to the remedy of water as a destroyer of them.'

'And he omits,' added Anna, 'all mention of the cruel ichneumon.'

'Still here, as indeed throughout his whole poem, he paints his sketches not only with the eye of a poet, but of an accurate naturalist.'

PERSECUTED POETS.

Happily such a being as a persecuted poet has no existence in this country. No court censor wields his pen to score out, from his manuscript, a bard's finest thoughts, because they may, in the cold unsympathising opinion of the official, be construed by the public into something having a political tendency opposed to the powers that be.

But abroad—especially in Germany and Italy—the case is different: nothing can be done in imaginative art without the sanction of the government. To show how rigidly this rule is enforced, we may cite a curious instance of the small despotism which the heads of a great empire will sometimes exercise over half-a-dozen simple words. A few months since, a noble Florentine, Count Masetti, anxious to save it from the ravages of time and the vandalism of speculators, purchased the house, on the Lung' Arno, in which Alfieri lived and died, and placed over the gate, on a white marble slab, the following inscription:—'Vittorio Alfieri, Principe dell' Italiana Tragedia, per la gloria e regenerazione d' Italia qui detto e qui mori'—('Here Victor Alfieri, the Prince of Italian Tragedy, for the glory and regeneration of Italy wrote and died.') There was nothing very alarming in this monumental record; the local censorship gave its *visa*, and the prefect of police his *exequatur*. The inscription had been open to public view for several days, when, all at once, the Austrian chargé d'affaires at Florence took exception to it, in the name of his imperial master. At first it was naturally believed by the Tuscan government that he could not be serious; but despatches from Vienna came which fully proved that the chargé d'affaires perfectly represented the notions as well as the power of the Austrian emperor. Protest, lampoon, pasquinade, and epigram, were all in vain. The Florentine authorities were obliged to yield, and the inscription was removed in the name of Austria.

If, it will be asked, this sort of vigilance be exercised over mere poetical inscriptions, what must be its effect upon poets and poems themselves? The reply will appear in the few facts we are about to narrate. They do not, it is true, apply to Austria, but to other parts of Germany, where the jealousy of literary censorship is equally rigid and oppressive. So much so, that the youthful continental poet has to struggle not only against want of patronage and the other evils which unknown genius is heir to in every clime, but runs the risk—even when his fondest hopes are accomplished in finding his verses in print—of being punished for some perhaps accidental, perhaps designed eulogy on a forbidden subject—such, for instance, as 'freedom.' Many instances of this have occurred in Germany in former times, without exciting our especial wonder. But now, the spread of knowledge and a more ripened political experience would, one would think, diminish the number of persecuted poets. This, however, does not appear to be the case. Our readers may recollect an account, in our twelfth volume, of the case of George Herwegh, who was banished from the Prussian dominions as an incorrigible votary of ideas inconsistent with the existing political system. In the last number of the Foreign Quarterly Review we find some interesting particulars respecting an equally able poet, and apparently more amiable man, Ferdinand Freiligrath, who has been recently banished for publishing a song we shall presently quote, and for translating Burns's noble ditty, 'A man's a man for a' that!' From the above source we learn that Ferdinand Freiligrath was born at Detmold, in Westphalia, where his father was a teacher in the burgher school, and early destined for the pursuit of commerce. He is said to have given proofs, even in childhood, of a poetic temperament, and, at the age of seven, to have delighted his father by the production of his first copy of verses. At an early age he was removed to the care of an uncle at Soest, in Munster. This relation, a man of ample means and liberal sentiments, allowed his poetic nephew to follow the bent of his inclinations. Much to the credit of Ferdinand, he took the best possible advantage of his uncle's kindness; for during the six years he remained with him, he acquired the English, French, and Italian languages. 'His mind,' says our authority, 'had already taken its decided bent, and not all the prosaic details of the wharf and the counting-house could smother the fire of genius within him: on the contrary, his vigorous imagination throve well upon such food as would have killed a weaker one of indigestion. Invoices of sugar and whale-oil are not, perhaps, the sort of reading best fitted, in all instances, to nourish and develop the poetic faculty; but in every tub of oil Freiligrath had bodily before him the life of the hardy whaler, its perils, hardships, and bursts of intense joyous excitement; every cask of sugar spoke to him of tropic skies and tropic vegetation, of tornadoes and earthquakes, of pirates and slavers, and negroes toiling under the white man's lash, who, in their own wild land, had fought victoriously with the lion and rhinoceros for their spoils. The sights and sounds of the sea, which the great bulk of his countrymen know only by report, became for him visible and audible realities; he mingled with travellers and seafaring men, for his muse was not of that squeamish sort that "loves not the savour of tar and pitch;" and many a band of emigrants, from his own Germany, did he see departing for the new world, and he talked with them of the untried homes they were seeking, and of that dear land they were never again to visit but in dreams. Thus his mind accumulated a vast store of images, not isolated or partial, but concrete and entire; he could say of himself,

"My eyes make pictures when they're shut"—

pictures which he projected into his verses, glowing with the vivid colours of the most intense life.'

His poems, which he began to publish in 1830, in various periodicals, were first issued in a collected form in 1838, and they have now, in six years, reached as many editions. In 1839, encouraged by the enthusiasm with which his first volume was received, Freiligrath withdrew from commercial pursuits. His means, which were probably not large, were increased, in 1842, by a small pension spontaneously bestowed on him by the king of Prussia. On New-Year's day 1844, however, Freiligrath thought it advisable to resign his pension, and shortly after published a poem, of which the following is a translation:—

'FREEDOM AND RIGHT.

O say not, believe not, the gloom of the grave
  For ever has closed upon Freedom's glad light,
For that sealed are the lips of the honest and brave,
  And the scorners of baseness are robbed of their right.
Though the true to their oaths into exile are driven,
Or, weary of wrong, with their own hands have given
Their blood to their jailers, their spirits to Heaven—
  Yet immortal is Freedom, immortal is Right.
Freedom and Right!

Let us not be by partial defeats disconcerted;
  They will make the grand triumph more signal and bright;
Thus whetted, our zeal will be doubly exerted,
  And the cry be raised louder of Freedom and Right!
For these two are one, and they mock all endeavour
Of despots their holy alliance to sever;
Where there's Right, be ye sure there are freemen, and ever
  Where freemen are found, will God prosper the right.
Freedom and Right!

And let this thought, too, cheer us—more proudly defiant
  The twins never bore them in fight after fight,
Never breathed forth a spirit more joyous and buoyant,
  Making heroes of dastards in nature's despite.
Round the wide earth they're marching; their message they've spoken,
And nations leap up at the heart-thrilling token;
For the serf and the slave they have battled, and broken
  The fetters that hung upon black limbs and white.
Freedom and Right!

And battle they still, where the voice of earth's sorrow
  Tells of wrongs to avenge, of oppressors to smite;
And, conquerors this day, or conquered to-morrow,
  Fear ye not, in the end they will conquer outright.
Oh! to see the bright wreath round their victor brows shining,
All the leaves that are dear to the nations combining,
Erin's shamrock, the olive of Hellas entwining,
  With the oak-leaf, proud emblem of Germany's might.
Freedom and Right!

There are sore aching bosoms and dim eyes of weepers
  Will be gathered to rest ere that day see the light;
But ye too will hallow the graves of the sleepers;
  O ye blest ones, we owe to them Freedom and Right!
Fill your glasses meanwhile. To the hearts that were true, boys,
To the cause that they loved when the storm fiercest blew, boys,
Who had wrong for their portion, but won right for you, boys,
  Drink to them, to the Right, and to Freedom through Right!
Freedom through Right!"

These lines, and a translation of 'A man's a man for a' that,' which appeared about the same time, were absolutely prohibited, and as our readers would perhaps like to see a specimen of official criticism from the pen of a continental censor, we produce the following from the chief of the Upper Court of Censorship of Berlin:—'The fundamental notions from which both poems proceed are, in their clear and pure conception and application, perfectly true, and may even be uttered and extolled in a poetical form. But such a turn and import is given them in the said poems, that a provocative appeal is thereby made to the tendencies in conflict with the existing social and political order of things; the first poem, namely, addressing itself to false ideas of freedom, the second to the mutually hostile opposition of the several ranks of society; wherefore these poems are manifestly at variance with the principles of the censorship, as laid down in the fourth article of the Instructions.'

The practical operation of these prohibitions is graphically described by a correspondent to the League newspaper. 'Standing,' he says, 'in a bookseller's shop (in Frankfort), where I had called to inquire for a new work, I saw a man enter with a sheet of paper in his hand, which he handed to the bookseller. After reading part of its contents, the bookseller wrote his name in the paper, and returned it. He turned then to me, and said, smiling, "A notice from the magistracy that Freiligrath's new poems are prohibited, and liable to confiscation." "Why," replied I, "that would make a poet's fortune in England." "Here, too," said he, "the only person who is not dissatisfied with the order is the publisher." He then handed me the volume to look at. * * * The verses are good, and the expression conceived in such general terms, that none but a Prussian, or some one well versed in the domestic policy of Germany, would think of applying them to Berlin. The most explicit piece the book contains is a translation of Campbell's "Ode to the Germans," in comparison with which the others are gentle complaints. Freiligrath has a remarkable tact in translating from the English, and has even been able to give his countrymen a taste of the beauties of Burns. In the preface, he declares his envy of the land in which it was possible to publish "A man's a man for a' that," without every verse being applied to Alnwick, Apsley House, or Buckingham

Palace, and the authors being thus brought into conflict with the pillars of the state. Burns would assuredly, in Germany, have been exchequered, instead of sharing, even in a humble capacity, the profit of the excise office; and his danger would have been of course the greater in a land where the state professes to have but one pillar, which will not bear shaking.'

Before Freiligrath could venture to publish any more poems, he was compelled to put himself out of the reach of the royal censor, and now resides in exile at Brussels.

The above account of Freiligrath, with the translated poem, is from the last number of the *Foreign Quarterly Review*, a work now of long standing, and which we are happy to see kept up with unabated spirit. There is perhaps no department of intellectual culture more neglected in England than the study of continental literature.

POLYTECHNIC SOCIETY OF NEWCASTLE.

An institution called the 'Tyne Polytechnic Society' was established in the above town in the early part of September last. There were a Literary and Philosophical Society, a Natural History Society, and a Mechanics' Institution, previously in existence; but the terms of the Literary and Philosophical Society (two guineas per year) are too high for the limited income of the majority of the working classes. The Mechanics' Institution has hitherto confined its funds to the formation of a library and purchasing philosophical apparatus; and all classes which have been established under its auspices have been charged extra to the students attending them. A branch of the Government School of Design is also established at Newcastle, and affords an excellent opportunity for instruction in the art of design, as applied to manufactures. But there was still something wanted to complete the education of the great majority of the artisans in that populous and important town. Impressed with this idea, a few individuals met at a private house, and resolved to establish a society for the purpose of affording mutual instruction in the several departments of science, until their funds should allow of payment to lecturers. And such has been the success of the measure, that, in the short space of four months, upwards of eighty members have joined the society, and numbers are daily being admitted. Classes for the study of mathematics, chemistry, English grammar, the French language, and drawing, are now in active operation; and others for the Latin language, elocution, music, and modelling, will be added as soon as the necessary arrangements for their establishment are completed. The pupils already number amongst their teachers professional men, who have handsomely offered their services gratuitously. They have purchased furniture for the room, and also the requisite books, out of the quarterly subscriptions (3s. per quarter above the age of eighteen years, and 1s. 6d. below that age); aided only by a donation from the mayor of the town, A. L. Potter, Esq. It is intended to form a library of scientific works; but the books will not be allowed to circulate, the want of success of the classes attached to some Mechanics' Institutions having been traced to the inducement afforded by their libraries for members to remain at home, instead of attending the classes. The committee of the society take in rotation the duty of attending every week, and thus save the salary of an attendant or librarian. We have entered somewhat minutely into detail, for the purpose of showing the advantages likely to result from the formation of similar institutions in other towns. So far as this institution has been carried on, no expense whatever has been incurred for the teachers of the various classes. Ultimately, however, it is the intention of the members to engage feed teachers and lecturers when their finances will permit.

WOMAN'S MISSION.

As the vine which has long twined its graceful foliage about the oak, and been lifted by it in sunshine, will, when the hardy plant is rifted by the thunderbolt, cling around it with its caressing tendrils, and bind up its shattered boughs, so is it beautifully ordered by Providence that woman, who is the mere dependent and ornament of man in his happier hours, should be his stay and solace when smitten with sudden calamity—winding herself into the rugged recesses of his nature, tenderly supporting the drooping head, and binding up the broken heart.—*Washington Irving.*

WE ARE GROWING OLD.

We are growing old—how the thought will rise
When a glance is backward cast
On some long remembered spot that lies
In the silence of the past:
It may be the shrine of our early vows,
Or the tomb of early tears;
But it seems like a far-off isle to us,
In the stormy sea of years.
Oh; wide and wild are the waves that part
Our steps from its greenness now,
And we miss the joy of many a heart,
And the light of many a brow;
For deep o'er many a stately bark
Have the whelming billows rolled,
That steered with us from that early mark—
Oh, friends, we are growing old.

Old in the dimness and the dust
Of our daily toils and cares,
Old in the wrecks of love and trust
Which our burdened memory bears.
Each form may wear to the passing gaze
The bloom of life's freshness yet,
And beams may brighten our latter days,
Which the morning never met.
But oh the changes we have seen,
In the far and winding way;
The graves in our path that have grown green,
And the locks that have grown gray!
The winters still on our own may spare
The sable or the gold;
But we saw their snows upon brighter hair—
And, friends, we are growing old.

We have gained the world's cold wisdom now,
We have learned to pause and fear;
But where are the living founts whose flow
Was a joy of heart to hear?
We have won the wealth of many a clime,
And the lore of many a page;
But where is the hope that saw in time
But its boundless heritage?
Will it come again when the violet wakes,
And the woods their youth renew?
We have stood in the light of sunny brakes,
Where the bloom was deep and blue;
And our souls might joy in the spring-time then,
But the joy was faint and cold,
For it ne'er could give us the youth again
Of hearts that are growing old.

Stranorlar. FRANCES BROWNE.

THE KAMPTULICON.

Such is the name given to a new life-boat invented and constructed by the Elastic Pavement Company of London, whose applications of caoutchouc to a number of economical purposes we noticed in No. 33 of our present series. The 'Kamptulicon,' so called from the elastic nature of its materials, is composed principally of cork and India-rubber, the gunwale, keel, seats, and fittings, being of wood. She is 34 feet long and 12 feet wide, and is 4 feet deep in the midships from gunwale to keel; she is fitted with four victualling-boxes, and ten air-boxes, covering an area of about 19 feet by 10 feet, which may be fitted up at will either with air or water—with air, of course, when increased buoyancy is required, and with water when extra ballast is wanted. She is capable of holding about fifty persons; and though an open boat, with no sails or rigging of any description, little doubt is entertained of her capability to live in the roughest sea, the specific gravity of the material of which she is composed being so small, that she would not sink if full of water. She weighs about two tons, and draws fifteen inches of water when her crew and passengers are on board.

*** Complete sets of the Journal, *First Series*, in twelve volumes, and also odd numbers to complete sets, may be had from the publishers or their agents. A Stamped Edition issued for transmission, post free, price Twopence halfpenny.

Printed by William Bradbury, of No. 6, York Place, and Frederick Mullett Evans, of No. 7, Church Row, both of Stoke Newington, in the county of Middlesex, printers, at their office, Lombard Street, in the precinct of Whitefriars, and city of London; and Published (with permission of the Proprietors, W. and R. CHAMBERS,) by WILLIAM SOMERVILLE ORR, Publisher, of 2, Amen Corner, at No. 2, AMEN CORNER, both in the parish of Christchurch, and in the city of London.—Saturday, February 22, 1845.

CONDUCTED BY WILLIAM AND ROBERT CHAMBERS, EDITORS OF 'CHAMBERS'S INFORMATION FOR THE PEOPLE,' 'CHAMBERS'S EDUCATIONAL COURSE,' &c.

No. 61. NEW SERIES. SATURDAY, MARCH 1, 1845. PRICE 1½d.

SEVENTEEN FORTY-FIVE AND EIGHTEEN FORTY-FIVE.

THE arrival of the year forty-five in this century has produced a slight sensation—in Scotland particularly—over and above what the commencement of a new year generally occasions. We are all set a-thinking of that former forty-five in which such a remarkable series of domestic occurrences took place, deciding the fate of a dynasty with which an obsolete system of government and of faith was connected, and determining the current of public affairs and of social progress into a channel which it has never since left. We also recollect the extraordinary character of the transactions of the last forty-five, so highly calculated to take hold of the imagination and feelings; a piece of mediæval romance, as it were, which had by chance wandered into the age of whiggery and hoop-petticoats; sounding, amidst hosts of the commonplaces by which we are still surrounded, the expiring trumpet notes of chivalry. That great round in the markings of time, a century—impressive because it is just the first grand period which living man must all but despair of seeing accomplished in his own life—has now been completed since a disinherited prince, tartanned, targetted, pedestrian, but an Apollo of youthful grace and natural dignity, trailed his cloud of self-devoted Highlanders through Lowland Scotland and Central England, to regain the crown of a hundred ancestors (the faith made it a reality), or die in the attempt. How much was there concentrated in that strange pageant! —divine right breaking its head in madness against the impregnable walls of popular privileges—the Celt, in his dress and arms older than Romulus or Pericles, perishing in a last attack upon the overwhelming force of the higher-endowed Goth—generous feelings, eagerness to redress what were thought personal wrongs, unselfish worship of an ancient idea almost identified with religion, meeting a murderous rebuke from the cannon-mouth and the scaffold, and, in the inexorable sternness of human contendings, ridiculed as folly and condemned as crime! Since all this happened, a hundred years have passed, and laid everything but a memory beneath the sod. 'It will be all the same a hundred years hence,' some rustic philosopher might have said at the time, as he heard the shouts of strife and the wailings of wo; and behold those hundred years have passed, and it *is* the same in the sense he meant it. We are only a few historical chapters the richer.

But the recurrence of a 'forty-five' is not to awaken these romantic associations alone. We are also called upon as a nation to reflect with grateful feelings upon the progress which has been made by our country since the last of our civil wars, showing, as the retrospect powerfully does, the benefits which flow from intestine peace. The England, and still more particularly the Scotland, of 1745, how different from those of 1845! Hardly in any one particular is there not an improvement; while, taking the whole together, and considering it either by itself absolutely or relatively towards other states, an advance of a most remarkable nature is apparent. In that time Great Britain has acquired India, and planted far more colonies than are required to make up for the few New England states of 1745, which she has since lost. She has bound Ireland to her in incorporating union, making a United Kingdom, which probably contains not less than three times the population which existed on the same space in 1745. The national debt of 1745 has indeed increased from fifty, to be now not less than eight hundred millions; a somewhat alarming fact at first sight; and yet it cannot be doubted, considering the relative population and wealth, that the debt of a hundred years ago was a heavier burden than that of the present day. David Hume prophesied that when the national obligations came to a hundred millions, England must be ruined; but that sum has been multiplied by eight without insolvency, and no one would now expect that an advance to a thousand millions would be fatal to our national fortunes. The annual expenditure is now somewhat above the whole amount of the debt in 1745—a fact which may be partly to be deplored; but does it not indicate also a vast increase in the national resources? Since 1745, the productive powers of the soil, especially in the northern section of the island, have been more than doubled, in consequence of improved methods of agriculture and husbandry; but the improvement in this respect is small compared with that which has taken place in other branches of industry. The cotton manufacture has been created since 1745, and all the other great manufactures have been prodigiously increased. The shipping of the country has gone on in equal paces. See the best exponents of these facts in the rise of Manchester, Liverpool, Leeds, Birmingham, Glasgow, from the small towns which they were in 1745 to what they now are. Liverpool was not so important a town in 1745 as to have a newspaper. Manchester had only one. There were but twenty-eight in all provincial England, two in Scotland, and four in Ireland (in the two last cases, confined to the respective capitals). London was then a town of under half a million of population—about one and a half of the present Manchester. Edinburgh had forty, and Glasgow twenty thousand: now the latter is computed to have 311,000. Lancashire has since then added just about one million to her population! The whole annual revenue of the country from customs in 1745 (about a million and a half) was not a *third* of what is now drawn on that account in Liverpool port alone. The entire annual revenue of the empire during the reign of George II. (about eight millions on the average of thirty-three years), is now considerably exceeded by the amount of customs received in the port of London. Since 1745, England and Scotland have been overspread with canals and railways, immensely facilitating the transit of merchandise. Enormous sums have also been spent on the construction of roads; and the principal public buildings of the three kingdoms have been reared in that time.

The advance has been much greater in North than in South Britain; and indeed we might affirm, with little chance of contradiction, that no country out of America has made a greater progress within the last century, or ever in one century made a greater progress, than Scotland has done in that time. In 1745, this ancient kingdom, at the distance of forty years, had not forgotten an unpopular union. There was a large party, including a considerable proportion of the gentry, decidedly disaffected to the reigning family. Some old sores, such as the Glencoe massacre and Darien expedition, still rankled in the Scottish bosom. Thus the spirit of the nation was distracted. It was impossible, in such circumstances, that there could be any hearty application to courses of industry, or to enterprises promising general advantage. But when the claims of the Stuarts were finally quelled on Culloden moor, a new era seemed to commence, and from that time the pursuits of peace acquired a decided ascendant. Scottish historians usually conclude their narratives in 1707, saying that after that time their country has no history: a most surprising blunder indeed; the fact being, that our history before that period is merely curious and romantic—hardly in any degree instructive—while the subsequent period would possess for the political philosopher the highest value. A history of the country from that time to the present would be the history of human energies applied to their best purposes, and achieving the most admirable results. Most interesting is it, truly, to see this little nation, with their sterile mountains and moors, and only patches of good land between, setting themselves to overcome all difficulties, and, by dint of pure mental force—a perseverance which knows no tire, a sagacity hardly ever at a loss, ingenuity not to be baffled, prudence never to be lulled asleep—working out what we now see, a land made blithe with plough and harrow, firths whitened with merchant fleets, streams persuaded, since they are making falls at any rate, to fall for the benefit of huge mills planted upon their banks, and splendid cities rising where once there were only little towns. The agriculture of Scotland was, in 1745, but the agriculture of cotters, embracing not one mode calculated to favour the powers of simple nature. Now its farming is an economical and scientific application of principles; not yet what it may be, but in the meantime a notable example to all other portions of the empire. Manufactures worthy of the name did not exist in 1745. Look now to the busy banks of the Clyde and Tay, not to speak of many other minor scenes of industry. In 1839, there were 676 'factories' in Scotland. Of the commerce of the country in 1745, we have an idea from the fact that Leith, the principal port, then had shipping under two thousand aggregate tonnage. The amount in 1840 was 19,954 tons. At Dundee, the writer of these pages played at whist two years ago with a hale elderly gentleman, who said he had once farmed the shore dues of that port at L.300: they had reached, in 1839, the large sum of sixteen thousand pounds! This town has risen from a population of 5302 in 1746, to 62,794 in 1841. A story is told that the mail bag from London arrived one day in Edinburgh, a short time after the year 1745, *with one letter*, being a missive addressed to the British Linen Company. It is hardly necessary to remark how huge the mail bags now are each day. The revenue of Scotland was at the Union L.110,694; in 1788, it was L.1,099,148: that collected last year was above five millions, being about what the revenue of the whole state was in the reign of George I. It may also be mentioned that the Scottish coin, when called in at the Union, was found to amount to little more than eight hundred thousand pounds. An old lady worth exactly *double that sum of money* died in Edinburgh about three years ago! There is perhaps nothing which more emphatically marks the national progress than the history of its banks. Of these establishments, there were two on the joint-stock principle in Edinburgh in 1745, and one private establishment in Glasgow; none at Aberdeen, Dundee, Perth, or any other town. The Bank of Scotland had, it seems, tried a branch at Aberdeen, but it failed to obtain sufficient business to make it worth while, and the money was quickly withdrawn, being brought, it is said, to Edinburgh on the backs of horses, the only mode of carriage which was then practised. At the present time, there are twenty-three joint-stock banks in Scotland, having three hundred and thirty branch establishments. The aggregate capital employed by the two Edinburgh banks in 1745 was L.200,000: that now employed in joint-stock banks somewhat exceeds eleven millions. And here it may safely be remarked, that no banking concerns in the world have ever been managed with better success than those of Scotland—a fact mainly attributable to the caution which forms so conspicuous a feature of the national character. There has not been, within the memory of the living generation, a declaration of insolvency from more than four banks, and three of these were comparatively small provincial concerns; and the public, as distinguished from the shareholders, did not lose one farthing by them.

The progress of the capital forms a good criterion of that of the country, and no city assuredly could well show a greater change in a century than Edinburgh has done during that time. This city was, in 1745, one of 40,000 inhabitants—antique and inconvenient in structure, and pent up within walls capable of being defended against an enemy unprovided with artillery. The accommodations possessed by families of good figure were generally limited to three or four rooms, not more than one of which would be unprovided with a bed. Of the middle ranks, most lived in bedrooms. Arrangements now deemed indispensable for cleanliness and delicacy were unknown. There was much homely comfort, but little elegance. It is entirely since 1767 that Edinburgh has burst from the limits of the Old Town, and spread herself in matchless beauty over the adjacent fields. Now we see the streets, which are devoted to the domestic accommodation of the middle and upper ranks, almost uniformly elegant, and houses occupied by shopkeepers which a judge or a landed gentleman could not have obtained eighty years ago. And the whole habits of life of these parties are equally improved. It is common to hear old people praising the easy good-humoured life of their young days; but it was in reality full of inconveniences, which either must have been constantly giving vexation, or were overlooked solely because of the low state of mind of those exposed to them. We learn from Sir Walter Scott's memoirs, that his parents lost all their children in infancy while they lived in the Old Town, and that he only escaped by being sent to the country. Another literary man born in Edinburgh, Mr Kerr, editor of a well-known collection of voyages and travels, was the eighth or tenth child of his parents. All his predecessors had perished in consequence of the narrowness of the domestic accommodations, and his preservation was owing to the same cause as Scott's. Can we wonder at such results when we learn that Mr Bruce of Kennet, a gentleman of estate, who, being in the law, became a judge of the supreme court, occupied with his family, about the beginning of the reign of George III., a house of one floor, rented at fifteen pounds, and containing three rooms, one of which was employed partly as his study, and partly as a bedroom for his children? When we know such things, we can hardly be surprised at Mr Creech telling us, about 1790, that a French teacher left, for want of accommodation, the house which thirty years before sufficed for Lord Drummore. There cannot be a doubt that, built as Edinburgh now is, many a man of income exempt from property-tax is lodged better than men of rank and fortune were in 1745.

Since that period, the changes in the moral and intellectual character of the people, in their manners, customs, and language, have been equally great. Farmers then sat at the same table with their servants. It looks an amiable custom; but the sole cause was, that the farmers had no education or taste superior to their servants, and were in reality labouring people themselves. Gentlemen and ladies spoke broad Scotch; the former swore a good deal; the latter snuffed. Their meetings were rare, and without refinement. Female accomplishments, by which such a charm is now given to home, were then unknown. Few women could even write a letter; fewer still spell one correctly. The savagery still surviving in the national mind, even in cities, is shown strikingly in the execution of *Lynch law* upon Captain Porteous in 1736. The bigotry is shown in the Catholic riots of thirty years later. We have to go back but twenty-three years from 1745, to come to the last burning of a witch in Scotland. Then the state of public sentiment respecting the natural liberty and dignity of man, what an idea do we get of it from such facts as this—that, in 1755, while a press was going on for the Seven Years' War, a man who had been committed to the guard-house in Edinburgh 'for swearing,' was sent on board the tender, and, though earnest petitions were presented to the Court of Session to procure his liberation, the lords refused to interfere—or this, that, on the 30th of August 1766, the Edinburgh Courant advertised a female negro slave for sale. At the latter fact we need hardly be surprised, when we recollect that, for thirty years after 1745, the whole class of colliers and salters in Scotland were bondmen. We hear more now of the miseries among the humbler classes than our forefathers did in 1745; but this is not to prove that miseries were then unknown in that class. Groan as the poor might formerly, their voice was never heard; no inquiry was ever made into their condition. In the very fact of the groans being now heard, and their causes zealously sought for with a view to redress, it might be argued that we see something in favour of the present time. The spirit of the Scottish representatives of the former period was most abject. Their gross servility to the minister of the day was perhaps what mainly depreciated the national character in the eyes of the English, and produced the satires of Foote and Churchill. In reality, they were not a representation of the people of Scotland; but this our southern neighbours had no reason to suppose. Now, the Scottish members are fully as independent as any equal number taken at random out of the parliamentary lists; and, if we are not much misinformed, their election is conducted with an exemption from corrupting influences which is not paralleled in any other part of the United Kingdom. That the Scottish people, amidst all their changes, have not in any degree lost the peculiar religious spirit which distinguished them of old, recent events have fully shown. On a subject of some delicacy, it is not necessary to say more; but what is said is much.

Upon the whole, it appears to us that the British empire has made an advance in all the prime elements of greatness during the last hundred years, such as cannot be found paralleled on the same scale in any history. If we look into the past, we nowhere see such a bound forward made by any country; so that we may fairly say that here is a new exemplification of the power of a naturally well-endowed race to advance in national greatness when circumstances of a greatly unfavourable kind, such as war, are not allowed a strong operation. It is very clear that no person living in 1645, and looking abroad upon *his* past and present, could have seen grounds for supposing that a century later was to commence such a period as we now see closing. Does not that period argue a degree of *national improvability* to which it might be difficult to set limits? Does it not show that, if no worse catastrophe than has marked the past century shall mark the future career of this empire, the condition at which it shall have arrived in 1945, in physical and moral greatness, must be something of which we would vainly at present endeavour to imagine the particulars? Why, this great and still increasing London may in 1945 be a town of eight millions of inhabitants—a phenomenon which the world has not heretofore witnessed. A vast amount of the waste and barbarous parts of the earth—perhaps all Asia, excepting that belonging to Russia—shall have then yielded to a British sway, and begun to adopt the manners, language, and moral ideas of this people. To how many of the distresses of the sons of earth will remedies have then been applied! How many great questions in physical science and ethics will then have been solved! How sweetly will the wheels of the social machine, as well as the current of individual life, then move! Alas, why have we been condemned to live in the early part of this darkling century, streaked but with the dawnings of so much glory! How enviable those who shall be born unto our children's children!

CHECK-MATED—A TALE.

'Oh yes, revenge is pleasing, let moralists contend as they will,' said a young man whom we will name Mackisson, while in conversation with another. 'Nay more, there is something of ecstacy in the pleasure which we feel when we have it in our power to repay with interest the injury or insult which we have undergone.'

'Say not so, Mackisson,' replied the other, whom we will call Vincent; 'the pleasure is rather that of a demon exulting in his own bad passions, than of a human being possessed of rational and moral qualities. My creed is that of our celebrated philosopher Bacon. "In taking revenge," he remarks, "a man is but even with his enemy, but in passing it over, he is superior." Again, "That which is past and gone is irrecoverable, and wise men have enough to do with things present and to come; therefore they do but trifle with themselves that labour in past matters."'

'Mere theory, I assure you, if not something bordering on hypocrisy,' retorted the other. 'Bacon himself was not celebrated for too strict an adherence to the principles which he taught.'

'Some of those principles, however,' replied Vincent, 'among which I number that respecting revenge, are of themselves immortal and incontrovertible.'

'Nonsense; why should we not avenge the injury we have received?'

'One reason is, that we gain no ultimate good; on the contrary, we insure to ourselves evil.'

'I should like much to hear how you make that out.'

'Willingly. Society is so constituted, that we can never be said to be independent of each other. If we revenge every injury, whether intentional or not, which we receive, we place ourselves without the pale of sympathy or assistance, when probably we stand most in need of it.'

'That would apply equally to the original offence.'

'Which would not weaken its application to the revenge.'

'But then the pleasure of making our adversary feel something of the pain that we have felt!'

'If pleasure there be, it is of too diabolical a kind to be taken into the account.'

'Then you would permit your enemy, and one who had deeply aggrieved you, to go scatheless?'

'I would.'

'So would not I; and there ends the matter. Good-bye.'

Such was the conversation of the two young men on the occasion of this interview; and little did they think how soon they would be led each to put his principles into practice.

Their principles being diametrically opposed, it is not surprising that their dispositions were equally so. Mackisson was conceited, passionate, ambitious, and vain; consequently jealous. Vincent modest, good-tempered, yet reserved; unobtrusive, yet firm. The one was affected by every trifling occurrence; the other thought few occurrences were of sufficient importance to be permitted to disturb the equanimity of his temper. Mackisson was aspiring, but not always observant of the proper means; Vincent was not indifferent to distinction, but thought it procured at too great a price if at the sacrifice of honour.

It is not an easy task to explain the precise degree of estimation in which each was held in the circles in which they moved. Mackisson, always accessible, easily led to enter into the spirit of every passing event or topic of conversation, not deficient in humour, seemed a general favourite, and was usually surrounded by a host of persons. Vincent, modest and retiring, not easily led to attach importance to that which seemed to him not worthy of consideration, not always conversable, yet able to take no mean part in conversation when moved to do so, seemed at times neglected when in the company of his more brilliant associate. There was, however, always this distinction between the small circle which sought his conversation, and that large one which thronged around his companion—the one was remarkable for its frivolity and boisterous hilarity, the other for its quiet yet cheerful gravity. An occasional intermingling would of course take place between these circles; but soon again the members of each would, by a sort of antagonism, resume their former places; like two uncombining fluids which, agitated, will assume a temporary intermixture of parts, yet resort each to its original state as soon as the external force which caused them to intermingle is withdrawn.

Between the parties themselves there had long existed an acquaintance; but the probability of a perfect intimacy had become daily lessened as the force of their natural characters developed itself. Mackisson thought Vincent too 'soft,' as he would term it; and Vincent thought Mackisson too boisterous and assuming. The one would prolong a debate after every point had been conceded; the other detested useless discussion. The one would wrangle for a straw's end; the other rather abandon the straw *in toto*. Yet were they no equal match in force and strength of intellect, as Mackisson's wounded vanity was frequently compelled to admit.

Discussions similar to that just narrated, and ending similarly in favour of Vincent, were not calculated to narrow the natural antipathy, if I may so term it, of their characters. In fact, at every fresh defeat—and the occasions were many, for Mackisson's vanity and ambition led him to enter upon every discussion, however unacquainted with the subject—the extent of that antipathy became greater; and as Mackisson's principles fairly developed themselves, Vincent saw the necessity of having as little in common with his companion as possible. Matters were in this state when another discussion, attended with the mortifying circumstance of publicity, gave a fresh impetus to this mutually opposing principle. Mackisson and Vincent were present on an occasion in which an argument arose on the subject of party spirit, and its effects on society. As usual, Mackisson took a prominent part, and, addressing himself frequently to Vincent, ultimately involved him in the discussion. As it became warm, however, the latter proposed that it should cease, there being no necessity for permitting it to proceed to the extent which it promised to do.

'I'll allow it to cease,' said Mackisson, 'if you admit yourself vanquished?'

'By no means,' replied the other; 'yet I am no longer disposed to continue the argument.' Those, however, who entertained opinions similar to Vincent's, and had in a degree abandoned their cause to his advocacy, were not desirous that the discussion should terminate in so unsatisfactory a manner. At their solicitations, then, he again replied to the positions which had been assumed by Mackisson, and the argument approached a climax. 'You say,' continued Vincent, 'that party spirit is beneficial to society, by reason of the force which it engenders, and that that force being in a right direction, good must result. How if it be in a wrong?'

'We must prevent it from being so.'

'How will you prevent it?'

'By inculcating correct opinions.'

'But does not the existence of party spirit imply the existence of two factions at least?'

'It does.'

'Well, then, can both of them be in the right?'

'Certainly not.'

'Can it be for the good of society that any body of men should be in the wrong?'

'Of course not.'

'And yet *this* is party spirit!' A laugh from his opponents, Vincent's supporters, annoyed Mackisson exceedingly; and already at a loss, he floundered on in the discussion.

'No, no, you do not understand me,' he continued, after a short but embarrassing pause. 'I do not intend that any body of men should entertain erroneous opinions. I would have all mankind advocating correct principles.'

'Well, then, suppose they were?'

'If they were, we should have the benefit of their united force tending in the right direction.'

'Where, then, would be the party spirit for which you contend? If all were unanimous in advocating correct principles, how could party spirit possibly exist? and if good resulted from this unanimity, how would you charge it as the result of that spirit?'

'Vanquished, by all that's good,' exclaimed Vincent's supporters. 'Mackisson, go hide your diminished head.'

'I will not—I am not conquered—I will not be conquered by him,' cried Mackisson, much excited.

'Oh, good, good!' echoed the others.

'A man convinced against his will,
Is of the same opinion still—

but every one knows he has lost the game.'

'I tell you I've not,' he replied, stamping his feet on the ground, 'and I'll prove it out of that fellow's own text-book.' Vincent reddened at the term, but remained calm.

'He pins his faith,' continued Mackisson, 'on every word that falls from the pen of that old peculator Bacon. Now, Bacon himself says, that "it is good to side one's self to a faction."' The misapplication of this quotation was so glaring, that it was followed by a simultaneous burst of laughter, at which Mackisson, unable to control his anger, or to bear the point of their sarcasms, abruptly left the room.

Here, as elsewhere, the vast superiority of temper over passion was amply manifest. Vincent, as I have already observed, was not a general favourite; but the mode in which he had conducted himself throughout the discussion, won considerably upon the esteem of his companions. Above all, the moderation under provocation which he had shown, far from detracting from the good opinion, tended rather to enhance it. Thus will forbearance usually receive its due homage, although we may not at all times be enabled to emulate it.

Mackisson, on the other hand, lost much of the good opinion of his own supporters; and, the victim of a scene which he himself had tended to create, retired to his home possessed of the most outrageous feelings of jealousy—of all passions the most permanent and the most corroding. Anger may evaporate with the passing of the occasion which induces it, hatred may give way to a sense of the unworthiness of its object, but jealousy ever nourishes and prolongs the cause which excites it; and the very self-esteem which, in the case of hatred, contributes to allay the passion, here, by a depreciating comparison, perpetuates it. Had Mackisson been simply angry, a few hours would have sufficed to allay the feeling; but being also jealous, we find him days subsequently nourishing his resentment, and seeking to avenge himself in a manner peculiarly characteristic.

inferiority, and the publicity which had accompanied the last manifestation of it, were the causes of Mackisson's jealousy. It therefore became his object to lessen its degree in any possible shape, accompanied with equal publicity. How, he reflected, could that object be attained? All contest with Vincent in debate or general acquirement, he was reluctantly compelled to admit, was vain. Vincent was too far in advance, and too industrious himself, to permit a fair chance of speedy equality. Would games of skill effect the object? It seemed unlikely. Vincent was no admirer of, and seldom played them. Little credit was therefore to be procured by excelling him at them. But there was one game, superior to them all, confessedly a game of mind, of which Vincent was devotedly fond, and at which he possessed the reputation of being an expert player. Was it possible to contend with him at this game—to vanquish him with his own weapons? Oh what triumph for him, Mackisson! what humiliation for his opponent if it were! And it should be possible! Nights and days would he devote to all the intricacies of the game, to all the mysteries of the several moves; and then, when he had rendered himself master of them, then he would challenge and conquer his opponent, under circumstances that should obliterate the memory of all past discomfitures.

Mackisson had energy and perseverance, and some talent, although of a second grade. To resolve to prosecute the study of the game, was to do so. Every spare moment was devoted to it—all mere pleasure sacrificed to it. Every move was patiently investigated, and a variety of combinations committed to heart over and over again; and then, when he thought himself sufficiently proficient, he requested Vincent to pass an evening with him, transmitting at the same time invitations to all their mutual acquaintances to be there. Vincent went, and found to his surprise many persons assembled. The feeling, however, soon wore off. Mackisson was unusually gay, and somewhat marked in his attentions to Vincent. The latter, regarding this conduct as the result of a desire to atone for the occurrence of the last meeting, responded with cordiality. At length Mackisson proposed to Vincent that they should play a game of chess. 'I suppose,' he added, 'there is very little probability of my being conqueror, having but within the last few weeks acquired a knowledge of the game.' The truth at once occurred to Vincent; Mackisson had learned the game to compete with him, and the guests had been assembled to witness what he undoubtedly expected would be his triumph. 'Mackisson,' observed Vincent, giving utterance to his suspicions, 'I perceive this is a preconcerted challenge?' 'I candidly confess it,' said Mackisson, 'and these gentlemen will bear witness of my intention to win back the many laurels I have lost.' 'A challenge, a challenge!' cried the guests; 'let's have the game; five to one on Mackisson; four to one on Vincent,' &c. 'I accept the challenge,' replied Vincent, inwardly determined, if possible, to allay for ever that restless vanity on the part of his companion, which was continually engaging himself and others in hostile contests.

Vincent played white, and Mackisson red, and for some time the game was maintained with equal skill. At length Vincent made what Mackisson regarded as an exceedingly bad move. 'Your game is gone,' he cried exultingly to Vincent. 'Say you so?' replied the other; 'we shall see.' 'I am magnanimous enough to inform you,' continued Mackisson, 'that unless you use exceeding skill, the game is mine.' 'Well, then, if you will be so positive,' said Vincent, 'let me in my turn inform you that you shall be check-mated in my four next moves.' 'Pooh, pooh!' exclaimed Mackisson, 'you dream: I've moved; 'tis your turn to play.' 'Well, then, check to your king with my castle.' 'Ha, ha! a most awkward blunder—I take your castle with my king.' 'Be it so; check with my other castle.' 'Well, I move out of check; that makes two moves.' 'Check with my castle again.' 'Ha, ha, ha! really, this is too good; I take your castle once more with my king.' 'So you do, but I check-mate you with my queen!'* ''Tis false!' exclaimed Mackisson—''tis false! I'm *not* check-mated!' and then, a moment after, seeing that the game *was* lost, he swore a terrible oath, and flung the board and men to the extreme end of the apartment. There was an end to the hilarity of the remainder of the evening, and the guests soon after separated.

From simple jealousy, Mackisson's feeling towards Vincent was now converted into hatred. The pit which he had dug for another he had fallen into himself, and he now regarded that other with the bitterest feelings of animosity. No means were left unexplored which he thought could injure—no devices untried which appeared calculated to wreak his revenge. One of the most important attempts of this nature occurred but a few weeks subsequent to the date of the scene just described.

'Do you know young Vincent?' inquired a gentleman at the house of a third party, on an occasion when Mackisson was present. 'Very slightly,' they replied; 'what of him?' 'Nothing of moment,' rejoined the inquirer; 'but I have some reason for learning the character he bears.' 'By the by,' observed one of the company, 'Mackisson may be in a situation to afford you the necessary information: apply to him.' The party addressed himself to Mackisson. 'I know Vincent well,' replied the latter; 'very well indeed.' 'Let me hear something of him.' 'Why, he is as good as the generality of us; but——' and he made a significant pause. 'Pray, go on,' urged the other, who seemed much interested. 'The fact is,' added Mackisson, appearing suddenly to recollect himself, 'I should not like to report anything to Vincent's discredit.' 'Discredit!' ejaculated the other, 'I have been led to believe him a very exemplary young man.' 'I make use of the term discredit,' continued Mackisson; 'but I perceive I have already said too much.' 'For heaven's sake explain yourself!' exclaimed the party; 'I am free to confess to you that Vincent is much interested in the result of my inquiries respecting him.' 'Then is it the more necessary that I should hold my peace,' said Mackisson. To further solicitation, he replied, 'I beg to assure you, sir, that I *know* (with much emphasis on the word) nothing calculated to affect our good opinions of Vincent's character.' 'Can you not tell me something of this young man which may dissipate these doubts?' said the inquirer, addressing himself generally to those present. 'We know nothing of him,' they replied, 'except that he is very reserved, and is not a general favourite.' One other attempt did the party make to obtain some explicit information from Mackisson, but the reply added the more to his perplexity. 'It does not become me,' said Mackisson, 'to repeat that which might, after all, be but the result of unfounded suspicions.' Mackisson was aware that a vague allegation ofttimes more surely blights the character of an individual than any definite charge. The mind has in the former case the entire circle of offences through which to wander: in the latter, but a solitary segment of the circle.

We should not understand Mackisson's character aright, were we to suppose that he avoided the society of Vincent while thus calumniating him. On the contrary, he sought his presence, and manifested an apparent deference and respect towards him which he had never before exhibited. It is the part of low and revengeful cunning to wear the mask of friendship, that it may the more securely wound.

Vincent had returned home one evening from his day's occupation, when a letter left for him during his absence was placed in his hands. Its contents were calculated greatly to surprise him. A distant relative, possessed of considerable wealth, had died, leaving him his heir; and the letter requested that Vincent would,

* The curious may see a game played in this manner in the Illustrated London News of 4th January 1845.

at his earliest convenience, favour the writer with an interview. Vincent, therefore, immediately repaired to the address of the party (an attorney), from whom he learned all the particulars of his good fortune. There is but one portion of the conversation held on the occasion to which it is necessary to refer. 'You see, my dear sir,' said the attorney, 'what friends we have in the world. Had I placed implicit confidence in the character furnished me of you by your friend, you never would have inherited the splendid fortune now at your command.' 'This is not the only favour of the kind which I have to place to his account, as he shall some day know,' said Vincent: and having made certain arrangements with the attorney, he returned home.

Our hero was now, like all his prototypes, in possession of a large income; and although generally as retiring and reserved as heretofore, he was admitted to be, by some species of magic perfectly familiar to men of the world, a very fine fellow. His entertainments were not sufficiently frequent; but there was something so chaste about those which he gave, that every allowance was to be made. His conversation was not racy, but then his wine was of the first vintage; and so on. It was evident that Vincent, wealthy and independent, was a much more important personage, and had far more extensive privileges allowed him, than Vincent, a clerk and dependent.

Well, at one of these chaste entertainments given by our hero were assembled many guests, among whom were Mackisson and other acquaintances of early days. The cloth had been removed, and wine brought on. During a temporary cessation in the conversation, Vincent remarked, addressing himself to his guests, 'By the by, gentlemen, let me tell you, I have recently discovered so atrocious a combination of hypocrisy, malice, and ingratitude, that I am assured, when I relate to you the circumstances, and name the party, known to you all, you will unanimously eject him from your society.' 'Who is he? who is he?' echoed from all sides; and Mackisson's voice was heard among the loudest, although he experienced a feeling amounting to suffocation. 'I'll name him presently;' and then producing some papers, Vincent continued—'this individual and I have been on terms of intimacy from our earliest years, and never on one occasion, I am assured, have I given him just cause for an angry feeling. Of me he has always exhibited a degree of jealousy that was unaccountable; but I have ever striven to allay it. He has insulted me, but I have passed by his insults unnoticed. He has endeavoured to blight my character and to wreck my fortune, but I have forgiven it all. On a particular occasion, he had so planned as to render me, but for a happy chance, the ridicule of our mutual friends; but I fortunately escaped the toils he had set for me. From that moment his every sentiment has seemed ingulfed in one of revenge, and he has resorted to every device which he thought calculated to effect my ruin. The more adroitly, however, to veil his schemes, he professed a reviving attachment to me. While he secretly undermined, or attempted to undermine, my reputation, he openly exhibited his apparent friendship; while he stealthily sought to mar my prospects, he outwardly courted my society; while he strove to wreck my happiness, he seemed only anxious to promote it.' A pause enabled the guests to express in the strongest terms the unpardonable ignominy of such conduct. Mackisson's situation may be conceived, but not expressed. Vincent continued—'I do not, gentlemen, speak unadvisedly, or without authority. The fortune I now possess had been lost, had his report of my character been received. I can produce an attorney on whose credulity he played successfully for a time. My hopes of domestic felicity were basely threatened. Here is a letter infamously maligning my conduct to a lady whom I have the honour to esteem, and which letter I am enabled to trace as emanating from his hands. He has carried his hostility and his envenomed feelings, for aught I know, up to this very moment of time; for here is another letter dated to-day, addressed to one of my most intimate friends, scandalously, yet secretly as he imagined, misrepresenting circumstances which transpired between us.' Vincent again paused, and glancing his eyes slowly around the table, permitted them to rest fixedly for a moment, but only for a moment, on Mackisson. The latter was exceedingly pale. 'What think you, gentlemen,' he again continued, 'should be the punishment of such a wretch?' 'It is impossible to suggest one too ignominious,' observed a guest. 'He should be scourged beyond the limits of respectable society,' said another. 'He should be publicly whipped,' cried a third. Mackisson's agony was intense as he contemplated the probable accumulation of all this wrath on his own head. 'Name him!' shouted a fourth. He started. This indeed was what he dreaded: this indeed would be the acmé of shame and humiliation. To be pointed at as a hypocrite, an ingrate, a liar! Oh how bitterly he repented having given way to an unprincipled jealousy and a feeling of malicious revenge! He would have given much to have crept out silently and unobserved. The overwhelming sentence of social excommunication would then pass over comparatively unheeded. But escape was impossible. One faint hope presented itself. Would Vincent relent? Oh no!—there was no compassion in that indignant voice—no mercy in that determined look. 'Name him!' shouted the voice; 'name him! (Mackisson felt a sickening sensation at heart; his brain reeled)—name him, that we may brand him as an unprincipled wretch and base defamer.' 'I will not name him,' said Vincent calmly; 'he knows the obloquy which he has incurred, and will appreciate my present forbearance and forgiveness.' Mackisson at that moment felt that he could die to serve the man whom he had hitherto bent every energy to embarrass and defame.

The following morning he addressed a penitential letter to Vincent, acknowledging the unworthy nature of his conduct, and pledging himself ever to remember Vincent's forbearance with gratitude. It is pleasing to remark that he added, 'I can now appreciate the divine nature of forgiveness, and the consequent diabolical character of revenge. Had you pursued the course which I should have done, you would have rendered my hatred implacable. You forgave me, and have awakened my esteem. I hope hereafter to prove to you my affection.'

THE JOURNAL OF A NEGRO PROPRIETOR.

MATTHEW GREGORY LEWIS—whose 'Journal of a West India Proprietor' has been lately republished in Murray's Colonial Library*—was, during the beginning of the present century, a shining literary star, especially amongst the higher circles of society. Indeed he was the fashionable author of the day; but though his fame was extensive while he lived, of such an ephemeral and indeed objectionable cast were some of his writings, that it would in all probability have died with him, had he not left behind the above journal, one of the most graphic and amusing specimens of its class in the English language. The father of Lewis was, at the time of his birth, in 1775, the deputy-secretary at war, and otherwise a man of large fortune, which was derived chiefly from two extensive sugar estates in Jamaica. Matthew was put through the routine of education common to the sons of opulent parents—Westminster school, Oxford, and the usual continental tour. On his return to England, after the production of his first novel, he found himself courted by the highest circles; than which nothing could have been more agreeable to his taste; for his leading foible was a love of great people. 'He had always dukes and duchesses in his mouth,' remarks Sir Walter Scott in a note appended to Byron's

* Under the title of 'M. G. Lewis's Negro Life in the West Indies.'

Diary,* 'and was pathetically fond of any one that had a title.' In corroboration of this, Byron, in his Detached Thoughts, relates that at Oatlands Lewis 'was observed one morning to have his eyes red, and his air sentimental. Being asked why; he replied, that when people said anything kind to him, it affected him deeply, "and just now the Duchess (of York) has said something so kind to me, that——" here tears began to flow. "Never mind, Lewis," said Colonel Armstrong to him; "never mind—don't cry—*she could not mean it.*"'

In 1802 Matthew Lewis succeeded the celebrated author of 'Vathek,' and owner of Fonthill Abbey (Mr Beckford), as M. P. for Hindon, in Wiltshire; but only sat in parliament during one session, determined to devote himself in future to literary pursuits. Not only his fame, but his range of noble and fashionable acquaintanceships was enlarged by his dramatic, or rather melo-dramatic productions; the most popular of which were 'The Castle Spectre,' 'The Bravo of Venice,' 'The Captive,' 'Blue Beard,' and 'Timour the Tartar.' In 1815 his father died, and left him the sole command of a large fortune, in which the two Jamaica estates were included. Amidst all the foibles which are inseparable from a petted author, and a haunter of the nobility's saloons, Matthew Lewis had always shown himself a man of the warmest benevolence. At that time the horrors of negro slavery were constantly depicted both in and out of parliament by the abolitionists, with Wilberforce at their head. Lewis had now become a proprietor of slaves, and although in the zenith of his popularity, the associate of princes, and the proudest names of rank and genius of which this country could boast, he determined to leave all the luxuries and allurements of the sort of existence he best loved, to make perhaps a perilous, certainly an uncomfortable voyage to his estates in Jamaica.

We are now prepared to open the journal of Lewis's experiences of 'negro life in the West Indies.' On the 11th of November 1815, he started from Gravesend in the good ship 'Sir Godfrey Webster;' and, after a stormy voyage, some of the incidents of which he describes with the most felicitous humour, the ship 'squeezed herself into the champagne bottle of a bay,' formed by the estuary of Black river. On New-Year's day 1816, he arrived at Savannah-la-Mar, and he was met by the 'trustee' or agent of his estates, who conducted him to that called Cornwall. His enthusiastic reception at this property he thus describes:—'As soon as the carriage entered my gates, the uproar and confusion which ensued sets all description at defiance. The works were instantly all abandoned: everything that had life came flocking to the house from all quarters; and not only the men, and the women, and the children, but, "by a bland assimilation," the hogs, and the dogs, and the geese, and the fowls, and the turkeys, all came hurrying along by instinct, to see what could possibly be the matter, and seemed to be afraid of arriving too late. Whether the pleasure of the negroes was sincere, may be doubted, but certainly it was the loudest that I ever witnessed; they all talked together, sang, danced, shouted, and, in the violence of their gesticulations, tumbled over each other, and rolled about upon the ground. Twenty voices at once inquired after uncles, and aunts, and grandfathers, and great-grandmothers of mine, who had been buried long before I was in existence, and whom, I verily believe, most of them only knew by tradition. One woman held up her little naked black child to me, grinning from ear to ear—"Look massa, look here! him nice lilly neger for massa!" Another complained—"So long since none come see we, massa; good-massa come at last." As for the old people, they were all in one and the same story—now they had lived once to see massa, they were ready for dying to-morrow; "them no care." The shouts, the gaiety, the wild laughter, the strange and sudden bursts of singing and dancing, and several old women, wrapped up in large cloaks, their heads bound round with different-coloured handkerchiefs, leaning on a staff, and standing motionless in the middle of the hubbub, with their eyes fixed upon the portico which I occupied, formed an exact counterpart of the festivity of the witches in Macbeth. Nothing could be more odd or more novel than the whole scene; and yet there was something in it by which I could not help being affected —perhaps it was the consciousness that all these human beings were my *slaves*: to be sure, I never saw people look more happy in my life, and I believe their condition to be much more comfortable than that of the labourers of Great Britain: and, after all, slavery, in *their* case, is but another name for servitude, now that no more negroes can be forcibly carried away from Africa, and subjected to the horrors of the voyage, and the seasoning after their arrival: but still I had already experienced that Juliet was wrong in saying, "What's in a name?" for soon after my reaching the lodging-house at Savannah-la-Mar, a remarkably clean-looking negro lad presented himself with some water and a towel. I concluded him to belong to the inn; and on my returning the towel, as he found that I took no notice of him, he at length ventured to introduce himself by saying, "Massa not know me; *me your slave!*"—and really the sound made me feel a pang at the heart. The lad appeared all gaiety and good humour, and his whole countenance expressed anxiety to recommend himself to my notice; but the word "slave" seemed to imply that, although he did feel pleasure then in serving me, if he had detested me, he must have served me still. I really felt quite humiliated at the moment, and was tempted to tell him, "Do not say that again; say that you are my negro, but do not call yourself my slave." Altogether, they shouted and sang me into a violent headache. It is now one in the morning, and I hear them still shouting and singing. I gave them a holiday for Saturday next, and told them that I had brought them all presents from England; and so, I believe, we parted very good friends.' The joy which 'massa's' presence caused spread even beyond the boundary of his estate. 'Many manumitted negroes also came from other parts of the country to this festival on hearing of my arrival; because, as they said, "if they did not come to see massa, they were afraid that it would look ungrateful, and as if they cared no longer about him and Cornwall, now that they were free." So they stayed two or three days on the estate, coming up to the house for their dinners, and going to sleep at night among their friends in their own former habitations, the negro huts; and when they went away, they assured me that nothing should prevent their coming back to bid me farewell before I left the island. All this may be palaver; but certainly they at least play their parts with such an air of truth, and warmth, and enthusiasm, that after the cold hearts and repulsive manners of England, the contrast is infinitely agreeable.'

The first thing which shocked the feelings of the humane proprietor was the revolting use made of the cart-whip, and he at once abolished it. 'I am indeed assured by every one about me, that to manage a West Indian estate without the occasional use of the cart-whip, however rarely, is impossible; and they insist upon it, that it is absurd in me to call my slaves ill-treated because, when they act grossly wrong, they are treated like English soldiers and sailors. All this may be very true; but there is something to me so shocking in the idea of this execrable cart-whip, that I have positively forbidden the use of it on Cornwall; and if the estate must go to rack and ruin without its use, to rack and ruin the estate must go.' The effect of his lenient measures was very much as had been anticipated. Deprived abruptly of what had been their only incentive to labour, and as yet unprovided with any of a superior nature, while all the arrangements were of course unfitted to maintain the new system in any degree of efficiency, the negroes became idlers and

* Life and Works of Byron, vol. vii.

skulkers to a distressing degree, and even felt so indifferent to their master's interests, that, when the cattle got among the canes by night, they would not take the trouble to drive them out again. 'They rejoice sincerely,' says Lewis, 'at being very well off, but think it unnecessary to make the slightest return to massa for making them so.' Still, he persevered in his good designs; and the strongest step he could be induced to take before quitting the island, was to draw up a code of laws for the guidance of the trustees on his estates, and admitting of punishments only under many humane restrictions.

On the 31st of March he prepared to return to England, and thus describes the leave-taking:—'With their usual levity the negroes were laughing and talking as gaily as ever till the very moment of my departure; but when they saw my curricle actually at the door to convey me away, then their faces grew very long indeed. In particular, the women called me by every endearing name they could think of. "My son! my love! my husband! my father!" "You no my massa, you my tata!" said one old woman; and when I came down the steps to depart, they crowded about me, kissing my feet and clasping my knees, so that it was with difficulty that I could get into the carriage. And this was done with such marks of truth and feeling, that I cannot believe the whole to be mere acting and mummery.' The really pathetic farewell which he received from a beautiful female slave inspired her master with the following pretty verses:—

YARRA.

Poor Yarra comes to bid farewell,
But Yarra's lips can never say it;
Her swimming eyes, her bosom's swell—
The debt she owes you, these must pay it.
She ne'er can speak, though tears can start,
Her grief that fate so soon removes you;
But One there is who reads the heart,
And well He knows how Yarra loves you.

See, massa, see this sable boy:
When chill disease had nipped his flower,
You came and spoke the word of joy,
And poured the juice of healing power.
To visit far Jamaica's shore,
Had no kind angel deigned to move you,
These laughing eyes had laughed no more,
Nor Yarra lived to thank and love you.

Then grieve not, massa, that to view
Our isle you left your English pleasures;
One tear, which falls in grateful dew,
Is worth the best of Britain's treasures.
And sure the thought will bring relief,
Whate'er your fate, wherever rove you,
Your wealth's not gained through pain and grief,
But given by hands and hearts that love you.

May He who bade you cross the wave,
Through care for Afric's sons and daughters,
When round your bark the billows rave,
In safety guide you through the waters!
By all you love with smiles be met;
Through life each good man's tongue approve you;
And though far distant, don't forget,
While Yarra lives, she'll live to love you!

After another rough passage, Mr Lewis landed at Gravesend on the 1st June 1816. He made but a short stay in London, and started for Italy, meeting at Geneva his friends Lord Byron and the unfortunate Shelly. By the advice and assistance of these poets Lewis made a codicil to his will, which bore exclusive reference to the comfort of his slaves. 'Having convinced myself,' he testifies, 'that the negroes cannot with certainty be protected in their rights and comforts if they are left entirely to the care of an attorney, and never visited by their proprietor, I wish to prevent this from ever happening again, to the very utmost of that power which the law allows me. I therefore order that whoever shall, after my death, be in possession of my estate of Cornwall, shall (if a man) pass three whole calendar months in Jamaica every third year, either in person, or by deputing one of his sons, or one of his brothers. If a woman, she must perform this condition either in her own person, or by deputing her husband, or one of her sons, or one of her brothers.' To this codicil the illustrious names of Byron and Percy Bysshe Shelly, with the less known one of John Polidori, are appended as witnesses to the testator's signature.

The interest which Lewis took in his Jamaica negroes would not allow him to rest in England, and, unwilling to impose a condition on his successors which he shrunk from fulfilling himself, he embarked for a second visit to his estates in the following year, arriving at Cornwall on the 25th January 1818. All his dependents were, he writes to his mother, 'delighted to see me; but all said that everything during my absence had gone on just as if I had never left them; that all their superintendents were kind to them, treated them well, and they were quite easy and contented. Many have come to tell me how sick they were, and likely to die, if they had not been so well nursed in the hospital; others have been to say, that they had formerly complained to me of such and such things, but now they were so well treated, that they begged to withdraw their complaints, and assured me that they were ready to do *anything* that might be thought necessary for my service. On the other hand, my attorneys declare themselves well satisfied with the general conduct of my negroes. One of them (who is also attorney for Lord Holland's estate, adjoining mine) owns that he finds it much more troublesome to manage Lord H.'s negroes than mine, and that mine work much better. In particular, they have already dug one hundred acres of cane-holes, without any hired assistance, for next year's planting, while Lord H.'s have not dug one acre, although he has forty negroes more, and pays nearly L.400 a-year for hired labour besides. If all this had been *written* to me, I should not have believed a word of it. But I see it with my own eyes, and shall leave the island with a heart a thousand pounds lighter, for having acquired the certainty that I leave my poor negroes in hands that will treat them kindly.'* In his journal he states, under the 14th February, 'Although I have now at least seen every one of them, and have conversed with numbers, I have not yet been able to find one person who had so much as even an imaginary grievance to lay before me. Yet I find that it has been found necessary to punish with the lash, although only in a very few instances; but then this only took place on the commission of absolute *crimes*, and in cases where its necessity and justice were so universally felt not only by others, but by the sufferers themselves, that instead of complaining, they seem only to be afraid of their offence coming to my knowledge; to prevent which, they affect to be more satisfied and happy than all the rest; and now, when I see a mouth grinning from ear to ear with a more than ordinary expansion of jaw, I never fail to find, on inquiry, that its proprietor is one of those who have been punished during my absence. I then take care to give them an opportunity of making a complaint, if they should have any to make; but none is uttered; "everything has gone on perfectly well, and just as it ought to have done." Upon this I drop a slight hint of the offence in question, and instantly away goes the grin, and down falls the negro to kiss my feet, confess his fault, and "beg massa forgib, and them never do so bad thing more to fret massa, and them beg massa pardon, hard, quite hard!" But not one of them has denied the justice of his punishment, or complained of undue severity on the part of his superintendents.'

One chief inducement for Mr Lewis's second trip was to visit his other estate, which was situated near the northernmost extremity of the island, and called Hordley. The extraordinary condition in which he found this plantation is thus detailed:—'Report had assured me that Hordley was the best-managed estate in the island; and, as far as the soil was concerned, report appeared to have said true: but my trustee had also assured me that my negroes were the most contented

* Life and Correspondence, vol. ii.

and best-disposed, and here there was a lamentable incorrectness in the account. I found them in a perfect uproar; complaints of all kinds stunned me from all quarters; all the blacks accused all the whites, and all the whites accused all the blacks; and, as far as I could make out, both parties were extremely in the right. There was no attachment to the soil to be found *here;* the negroes declared, one and all, that if I went away, and left them to groan under the same system of oppression, without appeal or hope of redress, they would follow my carriage and establish themselves at Cornwall. * * * I had been assured that, in order to produce any sort of tranquillity upon the estate, I must begin by displacing the trustee, the physician, the four white book-keepers, and the four black governors. What with the general clamour, the assertions and denials, the tears and the passion, the odious falsehoods, and the still more odious truths, and (worst of all to me) my own vexation and disappointment at finding things so different from my expectations, my brain was nearly turned, and I felt strongly tempted to set off as fast as I could, and leave all these black and white devils to tear one another to pieces—an amusement in which they appeared to be perfectly ready to indulge themselves. It was, however, considerable relief to me to find, upon examination, that no act of personal ill-treatment was alleged against the trustee himself, who was allowed to be sufficiently humane in his own nature, and was only complained of for allowing the negroes to be maltreated by the book-keepers, and other inferior agents, with absolute impunity. Being an excellent planter, he confined his attention entirely to the cultivation of the soil, and when the negroes came to complain of some act of cruelty or oppression committed by the book-keepers or the black governors, he refused to listen to them, and left their complaints uninquired into, and consequently unredressed. The result was, that the negroes were worse off than if he had been a cruel man himself; for his cruelty would have given them only one tyrant, whereas his indolence left them at the mercy of eight. Still, they said that they would be well contented to have him continue their trustee, provided that I would appoint some protector, to whom they might appeal in cases of injustice and ill usage.' A protector being appointed, and some of the inferior officers superseded, 'I read to them my regulations for allowing them new holidays, additional allowances of salt, fish, rum, and sugar, with a variety of other indulgences and measures taken for protection, &c. All which, assisted by a couple of dances, and distribution of money on the day of my departure, had such an effect upon their tempers, that I left them in as good humour, apparently, as I found them in bad.' A little kindness and judicious treatment effected a complete reform throughout the whole estate, and its proprietor returned to Cornwall.

The good which Mr Lewis's presence and benevolent management effected, may be inferred from the closing paragraph in his journal. 'What other negroes may be, I will not pretend to guess; but I am certain that there cannot be more tractable or better disposed persons (take them for all in all) than my negroes of Cornwall. I only wish that, in my future dealings with white persons, whether in Jamaica or out of it, I could but meet with half so much gratitude, affection, and goodwill.' On the 4th May 1818 Lewis embarked on his homeward voyage. He was in excellent health at this time; but some days after, the dreaded yellow fever made itself apparent on board. More from fright than real illness, Mr Lewis took to bed; and feeling one night extremely discomposed, he had the ship's steward called up, and demanded a dose of an emetic. Remonstrance was useless: in the hurry of the moment, to comply with his impatience, a strong emetic was imprudently administered by the steward, who had the care of the medicine chest; and on the 14th May our amiable journalist breathed his last. His remains were on the same day committed to the deep. Such was the untimely end of one in whom were strangely blended some of the most frivolous and most respectable of human qualities—a fashionable novelist, a butterfly of fashion, yet at bottom a right-hearted and conscientious man. 'I would,' says Byron—

> 'I would give many a sugar-cane
> Mat. Lewis were alive again.'

DISCOVERIES IN PRINTING.

Under the head of 'New Graphic Wonders,' we described in our 58th number an invention by which the finest engraving on steel can be transferred to other plates, so as to multiply impressions to infinity. We also adverted to a second process by which the same advantage can be obtained for letterpress, by means of what the patentees designate Anastatic Printing. The means by which this is to be accomplished has been fully developed in the February number of the Art-Union. 'Let us suppose a newspaper about to be reprinted by this means. The sheet is first moistened with dilute acid, and placed between sheets of blotting-paper, in order that the superfluous moisture may be absorbed. The ink neutralises the acid, which is pressed out from the blank spaces only, and etches them away. In all cases where the letterpress is of recent date, or not perhaps older than half a year, a few minutes suffice for this purpose. The paper is then carefully placed upon the plate with which the letterpress to be transferred is in immediate contact, and the whole passed under a press, on removal from which, and on carefully disengaging the paper, the letters are found in reverse on the plate, which is then rubbed with a preparation of gum, after which the letters receive an addition of ink, which is immediately incorporated with that by which they are already formed. These operations are effected in a few minutes. The surface of the plate round the letters is bitten in a very slight degree by the acid, and on the application of the ink it is rejected by the zinc, and received only by the letters, which are charged with the ink by the common roller used in hand-printing. Each letter comes from the press as clear as if it had been imprinted by type metal; and the copies are fac-similes which cannot be distinguished from the original sheet.

'Thus far it may be necessary to describe the process, that it may be understood by those of our readers who are not versant with lithographic manipulation; those who are, will recognise some similarity in the methods of preparing the stone and the zinc, as far as regards the gum, &c. The practicability of transferring letterpress, especially prepared or quite recent, to stone or zinc, has long been known. A main advantage, however, and a most important one, possessed by the zinc over the stone, as a mere material to work from, is its portability, and being easily formed into a cylinder; for, although we have only spoken of a plate of zinc in relation with the results we have witnessed, it is to be understood that in extensive operations cylinders will be employed.' Thus it will be seen that the new process produces all the effects of stereotyping, with the advantage of taking the duplicate from a printed *impression*, instead of from the metal types themselves. So far, however, as we can ascertain, one disadvantage attaches to the new process, which is, that in working off impressions from the zinc plates, a kind of press must be used different from that employed for types—one partaking somewhat of the nature of a lithographic press. Till, therefore, the inventors proceed with their improvements so far as to cause the acid to corrode the interstices of the letters sufficiently deep into the plate, as to make them stand relief of equal height with types, we do not anticipate that, as a substitute for stereotyping, it will be so extensively used as they anticipate. It may also be remarked that the economy of this invention will chiefly be seen in works of limited sale. In such as the present, the typographical arrangements sink into a bagatelle beside the enormous outlay for paper, an abolition of the duty on which would be of more use to such works than an invention doing away with every other expense whatsoever.

In another department of relief printing, there is no question that the anastatic process will cause a complete revolution, and that very speedily; namely, in illustrative and ornamental printing. Wood-engraving will be entirely superseded, for no intermediate process will now be necessary between the draughtsman and the printing of his design. It is generally known that at present the artist draws in pencil his design on the boxwood, and that the engraver, with sharp instruments, cuts away all the white parts or interstices, so as to cause the objects previously figured to stand in relief, that they only may receive the ink passed over them in printing. Unfortunately, many wood-engravers, from want of skill in drawing, do not render the intentions of the designer with fidelity. Now, however, all the draughtsman will have to do will be to make his drawing on paper, and *that*, line for line, will be transferred to the zinc, and produce, when printed, exactly the same effect as his original draught. A pen is recommended for this purpose, which may be used 'on any paper free from hairs or filaments, and well sized. The requisite ink is a preparation made for the purpose, and may be mixed to any degree of thickness in pure distilled water, and should be used fresh and slightly warm when fine effect is to be given. In making or copying a design, pencil may be used, but the marks must be left on the paper, and by no means rubbed with India-rubber or bread. The paper should be kept quite clean, and free from rubbing, and should not be touched by the fingers, inasmuch as it will retain marks of very slight touches.' A drawing thus produced can be readily transferred to the zinc in the manner above described for typography.

Two pages of the Art-Union are printed upon the new plan. Besides the letterpress, from which we derive our present information, are five printed drawings and an illuminated letter. 'The letterpress,' says the editor, 'was first set in type by the ordinary printer of the Art-Union, leaving spaces for the drawn or engraved illustrations, which having been set into their respective places on a proof of the letterpress, the whole was cast on to a zinc plate, and so printed off.' Neither is it to printing of recent date only that the invention is applicable; transfers from books a century old have already been made. 'Rare editions' and 'unique copies' will in a few years vanish from the counter of the book-sale and the shelves of the bibliomaniac. Now it is ascertained how exactly they may be counterfeited, not even Doctor Dibdin himself will be able to venture to pronounce upon a 'genuine black-letter.'

AN AUTUMN DAY AT BADEN-BADEN.

I HAD for the whole summer beaten about from one German bath to another, with perhaps as little defined a purpose as Captain Absolute enjoyed in his celebrated journey to Bath. I had taken the *Kurbrunnen* at Homburg, and witnessed the *petit jeu* of the players by profession, who, now exiled from Paris, fix their quarters there for the whole year. I had listened to the long catalogue of complaints for which our countrymen and women flow in shoals to Wiesbaden. I had climbed the hill at Schlangenbad, to read the inscription upon the column placed by a newly-married count, in commemoration of his wedding trip, and the happy hours passed at this retreat with his 'Fanny.' I had seen the great lion of Schwalbach, the Fenner von Fenneberg, who still retails the same phrases, rendered immortal by his old Bubble historian. Last of all, I had met with Russians and Mexicans, Norwegians and Spaniards, at the *table d'hôte* at Ems, and had elbowed at the *Kranchen* princes and princesses, dukes and duchesses ... from every principality in Germany. At each of these places had I been assailed with the inquiry—'Have you not yet seen Baden?' 'No.' 'Then you have as yet seen nothing. The view from the Alte Schloss exceeds everything that is to be witnessed hereabouts,' said a chance-thrown companion at Ems. 'Oh, how miserably dull and wretched is this place!' exclaimed in one voice a newly-married pair, the first of my acquaintances I saw at Schwalbach. 'Dear Baden-Baden, how gay, how charming last year!—the conversation-house, the music, the promenades, the rides, the drives!' sighed forth the bride, blushing in her orange blossoms. 'The *Gros jeu*, the restaurant, the *Gallerie des fumeurs*,' chimed in the bridegroom in the base tones of his voice. 'Oh, my dear fellow, if you have not yet been to Baden-Baden, either go there at once, or cease to speak of Nassau.'

'Upon my word,' thought I, as I left them with their commendations ringing in my ears, 'I must be off to Baden.' So, walking meditatively back to my hotel, I immediately ordered my *rechnung*, and, what is more, paid it. I made up pack and baggage. I had thus passed the Rubicon of many a previous hesitation. Preferring, on account of the warm weather, the old beaten track up the Rhine to the Eilwagen with dusty roads, Frankfort, and the picturesque Bergstrasse, I took the steamboat at Coblentz to Manheim.

In few places, perhaps, does the sun at its setting present a more beautiful appearance than when seen upon this river. Owing to the mountainous nature of the country, one has but little of the intermediate light, the gradual sinking and dying away witnessed in flat lands. The sun, long before its actual disappearance from the horizon, vests in but little less than its noonday splendour upon some tall peak, throws a last farewell upon the violet-coloured hills, and then is lost. He departs like a man in the pride and prime of life, evincing none of the glimmerings and decrepitudes of decline; and as such, he remains upon the memory. Accident very much heightened the effect; for I do not imagine myself illustrious traveller enough to suppose that the scene was got up for my especial gratification, at the expense of a village. It was a lovely clear night, when, in the distance, one of those occurrences so frequent in Germany took place—a fire burst out: it issued first from a chimney, it then blazed through a long range of windows, and, to judge from the heightening flames, its work of devastation was complete, when a turn in the river, and our arrival at Manheim, hid it from sight.

Two years ago it was a somewhat lengthy journey from Manheim to Baden-Baden; but now four hours by railroad accomplish it. 'Not a soul in Baden—quite deserted this year—given up—fashion gone by,' was my first greeting at the station at Oos, from an acquaintance upon the point of leaving.

'What! with a list of twenty-seven thousand visitors?' said I quietly, making use of a piece of information I had obtained.

'No matter—very dull—last year thirty thousand;' and he hurried off, discontented with really a paradise, like a thousand other tourists, because the Smiths, the Joneses, and the Snooks of his peculiar set had not been there. In how many cases does man absurdly reverse the telescope of his perception, and receive impressions through the narrowest medium.

I must confess that I entered Baden with that self-same curiosity, if not awe, which one invariably feels in

always been held up to me as a very great one, my feelings of expectation were proportionate. And I was not disappointed; it is indeed the very king, queen, and whole royal family to boot, of German spas. It was September; the season was drawing towards its conclusion. Still, sufficient people were remaining to give a perfect notion of its attractions when the season is at its height. As some inducement to us later birds of passage to prolong our stay, if not to offer us some compensation for the past glories we had lost, what were we promised?—a boar hunt—a real German boar hunt!

From the hunting of the Caledonian boar, down to these our times, there has been for me a certain excitement in the very name: it speaks of danger, of the thick and noble forest, of the jager's horn, of the baying of hounds, of foaming steeds, of stirring strife, of green, and gold, and buff. And here I was to have the reality of many a wishful dream.

At seven o'clock of Saturday, 21st September, all was in motion.

> There was a hurrying to and fro.

The merry horn and cavalcade started me from my coffee, and hastily drawing on a huge pair of postilions' boots, borrowed for the nonce, and taking a thick whip, my only arms, I threw myself with three others into an open light calèche, and off we set. I had taken the precaution of sending on a stout Wurtemburg hack an hour or so earlier, to be ready for the chase.

At starting, the morning was fresh and lovely, clear as in the spring, and on we dashed through forest glade and village. A mile or two out of Baden, one of those changes of weather to which the neighbourhood of the Rhine is liable in the autumn, enveloped us in a thick fog, and we drove on in almost worse than a Scotch mist; but, sticking closely to our pipes, we defied the cold; and by keeping up a dense cloud of smoke, we managed to make our immediate atmosphere warm and dry enough. The *rendezvous de chasse* was some three pipes, one cigar and a half, German reckoning, distant; that is, about a two hours' drive. Our cavalcade having upon the road become somewhat disorganised, we halted at a village a quarter of an hour this side of the scene of action. All the stragglers came in by twos and threes, some on horse, some on foot, but the greater number in that most comprehensive of all terms, and teams, a wagen, as it embraces every denomination, from a four-in-hand to a go-cart. If not so lordly a scene, it was much more picturesque, because more unsophisticated, than the meet of the queen's hounds at Windsor. The good villagers were crowded at every door, and from every window peeped out the head of some village beauty. We took possession of the whole place, and, the mist clearing off, giving way to a splendid sun, ladies and huntsmen, in every variety of costume, horses, dogs, and carriages, pipes, cigars, tobacco smoke, whip-smacking and horn-blowing, stood out in bold relief, and in most laudable rivalry in chattering and noise.

Having at last taken order, we proceeded to the forest in excellent style. A soul-stirring fa fa led us on. At a short distance within the wood was a large open space, just in the rear of which were the boars—

> Cabined, cribbed, confined.

Four had been procured from the neighbourhood of Carlsruhe, and were penned up in a wooden enclosure, with a trap-door to turn them out at. The whole meet was capitally marshalled in the open space, men on foot being foremost, horsemen next, and carriages in the back-ground. A short half hour sufficed for preparation and necessary directions, during which time breathless expectation and excitement appeared upon every face. About ten couples of hounds had been brought to the rear of the enclosure, just near enough to catch a good sight of the savage inmates, and sufficiently far away to allow a fair start. The ground now assumed a stirring aspect: the hounds bayed; the boars, roused to fury, roared; the horsemen ranged themselves in two semicircles, and the men on foot completed a serried avenue, forcing upon the boar no choice as to his course when turned out upon the world.

'Sound the fa fa,' shouted Monsieur Haug; and a merry clang rang through the forest. 'Turn out the boar,' shouted Haug again.

'Turn out the boar,' echoed a hundred voices in German, French, and English, with every variation of native and foreign accent.

And out he was turned; and away he started amidst shouts and bayings, neighings, and shrill notes from the bipeds and quadrupeds behind him; horse, and foot, and hounds, all pell-mell. He was a fine fellow, rather beyond the middle size, with long tusks. He took gallantly across the small plain, the hounds following close at his heels, and we were soon almost lost to each other in the wood. Here and there a horseman might be spied through the trees. The most of *jeune France* returned quickly back to the rendezvous, thinking it better to display their *caracoles*, and high boots, and ornamented *couteaux de chasse* to

> The sweet eyes of a ladye fayre,
> Than rouse the wylde boar from his layre.

On, on we hurried, as fast as the nature of our hunting-ground would allow, sometimes close upon our prey, oftener at fault, as he better knew the dodges than the hounds, which were unfortunately novices. We at length got on the right scent; and after a long and well-managed attack and defence through almost every bit of underwood, without coming actually to close quarters, we succeeded in getting him quite at bay on the confines of the forest. Escape seemed impossible; but, worried to the uttermost by the bellowing hounds and shouting horsemen, our friend made a desperate rush, and fairly broke through. Off he took himself to a wide plain beyond, running as hard as he could. We pushed on out of the wood in full pursuit. A large pond stood a quarter of a mile off; at it he dashed, and in he rushed, and slaking his thirst, quietly swam about, as unconcerned as though he were in his native fastness feeding amongst his companions. Our hounds at this juncture fairly showed the white feather. One or two jumped in, but kept at a respectful distance. The remainder did their worst, which began and ended with a bark. A shot here at the boar might easily have finished the sport; but all disdained to take advantage of so brave a foe. Having amused himself to his own contentment, he swam out, and, like a giant refreshed, bid us fair defiance. The hounds were become mere playthings for him, and we gave him all the chances of the game. Could he but reach a forest opposite, we should be again at fault: the hounds, dead beat, were not at all inclined to come to close quarters. One by one the pursuers were dropping off, and the boar was very nearly having the honours of the day entirely to himself. At length, thinking the chase had lasted long enough, and not very desirous of having our work to do over again, we made head, and came up to our antagonist. There were but two stanch fellows, Germans, and myself at the mort, and no hounds to receive their curée. The boar, nothing daunted, turned round, halted, grunted defiance, and waited the attack. The young and chivalrous Lieutenant Baron de H——, eager for distinction, pressed bravely on. The poor boar was still undaunted, and 'nothing in his life would have become him like his leaving it;' when, in the very moment of the baron's assumed triumph—his arm nerved like iron, his eye and hand steady as a marble Actæon—his foot unfortunately slipped, and the sword missed its aim. The boar, slightly wounded, rushed towards him, and caught in his ugly fangs the baron's left hand as he was falling, and bit it through. And now, goaded by fury, and thirsting for more blood, he threatened to make sad work of our handsome friend, and undoubtedly would have done so but for our rescue. Pressing sorely on the enraged animal, we succeeded in diverting him from his victim. He turned fiercely on the nearest horseman, the Baron K——, tore off the heel of his heavy boot, and left us nothing to hope for from him in the shape of kindness. K—— thought it high time to turn the tables; so, presenting his sword, our adversary ran upon it, and next instant fell dead without a struggle. We returned in triumph to the shady glade, and the hero of the chase deposited his spoil at the feet of a Russian princess.

Thus ended the boar hunt, but not so our entertainment. It was to our no less satisfaction than surprise that we found, upon our return, as if by magic, dinner-tables spread under the green trees. Where but two or three hours earlier we had left nothing but the sylvan sward, stood all the appliances of Haug's restaurant. What could be better? Fires were blazing in all directions, soups boiling, cutlets broiling, coffee sending forth its delicious aroma, kellners hieing everywhere, Bourdeaux wine, *premier crue*, covering the tables, which were decked with cloths white as the fleecy clouds above us, and the ladies, with the *sans ceremonie* of a pic-nic, were seated around them. The Distin family, with their horn band, kept up a lively strain, and nothing could exceed the hilarity of the party. The agreeable surprise, the beauty of the scenery, and the lovely weather, carried the mind back to those delightful descriptions of Boccaccio, so much read and dwelt upon, but so seldom realised. I think, had every one present been canvassed, life in the woods would have been for the time the unanimous choice.

The fact was, upon the road, early in the morning, we had overtaken a huge tumbril wagon, which the practised eye of a sailor would have set down for a most rakish and suspicious-looking craft. It was strongly guarded by six stout fellows, armed to the teeth, who, in default of a more intimate acquaintance, might well have been imagined to guard some state prisoner. The team dragged slowly and heavily on through the ruts of a cross road, and nothing could induce the drivers to pull up to let us pass; 'ja, ja,' and a cloud of smoke, was the only answer we could get to our remonstrances. The sturdy troop of guardians prevented of course an appeal to arms. At the time, the whole thing seemed a mystery, one of those Quixotic appearances that, to any other but ourselves, so well versed in the good realities of German life, would have been something too ideal for an adventure.

We at last got on, and the circumstance passed from our minds. A little patience not only cures most evils, but solves many a mystery; so it was with us. In one corner of the enclosure quietly stood our tumbril of the morning, disemburthened of its hidden contents in the shape of the good cheer surrounding us on all sides. The guards were transformed into bustling kellners, whose guns were peaceably laid aside for their after share in the day's fun. The truth is, that it was one of the annual offerings that the liberality of the millionaire Benazet makes to the visitors of Baden-Baden, a sort of wind-up to the season for those who are leaving, and an opening of the sports to those who remain during the winter.

No sooner had every eatable and drinkable been fairly disposed of—when it really became a matter of difficulty to wind one's way through the straggling squares and streets and lanes of empty bottles everywhere formed upon the ground—than a clearance was made for the third act of this exciting drama. A mark was set up, and we were presently engaged in a scene beating hollow in its picturesqueness everything seen, heard, and known of the trial-shot in Freischutz. The Germans are excellent marksmen, and fond of the amusement. At every shot arose a shout of triumph from the friends of the man who had fired. The music continued inspiring and woodland notes, and the approach of evening alone put an end to the sports. We were then marshalled into the same order as upon our coming, and, preceded by the piqueurs, who bore in a car the second hero of the day in triumph, and with the merry fa fa all the way, we returned to Baden, where again and again we have since hunted the boar over many a flasch of markgrafer.

'THE TRADE.'

FIRST ARTICLE.

BOOKSELLING BEFORE THE INVENTION OF THE PRESS.

It has long been acknowledged that the bookselling business, from its very nature, requires a greater amount of intelligence to be successfully carried on than any other branch of trade. Authors—who must be considered good judges of the matter—have, as a body, testified in favour of this view of bookselling; and although disappointed writers occasionally show an aptitude to decry 'the trade' and its professors, yet the most eminent authors have seldom joined in such a condemnation. Dr Johnson speaks of them only too highly, for he designates them 'the patrons of literature,' whilst in truth they are only the agents of its real patrons, the public. D'Israeli the elder remarks, that 'eminent booksellers, in their constant intercourse with the most enlightened class of the community—that is, the best authors and the best readers—partake of the intelligence around them.' Booksellers are inseparably identified with literary history. Whoever, therefore, takes an interest in that progress of civilisation which has been helped on so materially by letters, will find much to instruct and entertain him in tracing back, through the records of past time, the rise and vicissitudes of the book-trade, and by finally looking round on the present condition of things, and following its progress up to the state in which it now exists. With this view we have busied ourselves in collecting various historical notices and anecdotes concerning booksellers and their craft from the earliest down to the present time.

Before the invention of printing, the articles in which the booksellers dealt were manuscripts. These were inscribed on some flexible material, manufactured either from the inner bark of trees (hence the Latin word *liber*, and the German buche or book), from the leaves of the papyrus plant, or from leather or parchment. In one of the earliest forms of books, only one side of the material was written on, and one sheet was joined to the end of another till the work, or one section of it, was finished, when it was rolled up on a cylinder, or staff. The leaves composing such books were designated paginæ, from which we derive our term 'page;' the sticks upon which they were rolled were *cylindri*, at each end of which was a knob for evolving the scroll. These balls were called *umbilici*, or *cornua*, 'horns,' of which they were often made, though sometimes composed of bone, wood, or metal, either elaborately carved, or richly inlaid with gold, silver, or precious stones; the edges of the scroll were called *frontes*. On the outside of each scroll was written its title.* In the earlier manuscripts, the writing was not divided into words, but joined in continuous lines. The Greeks read from right to left, and from left to right alternately, the reader commencing the one line immediately under the termination of the line above. This was a highly necessary arrangement for the guidance of the reader, who, by adopting the modern plan, would have been very apt to 'lose his place' on account of the extreme length of the lines; for those ancient volumes were much larger than we at the present day have any notion of.† The scroll,

* The ancients seldom numbered the divisions of their works as we do, but named them after some deity or patron. Thus the books of Herodotus respectively bear the names of the Muses.

† The implements used by a Grecian or Roman scribe were as follow:—'A reed cut like our pens; inks of different colours, but chiefly black; a sponge to cleanse the reed, and to rub out such letters as were written by mistake; a knife for mending the reed; pumice for a similar purpose, or to smooth the parchment; compasses for measuring the distances of the lines; scissors for cut-

when rolled up, was often a yard and a half long, and the lines of manuscript consequently very little short of that, across. When extended, each volume was sometimes fifty yards long. A roll of calico, such as is seen standing at linen-drapers' shop windows, will give the reader some idea of the external form of an ancient book, without its umbilicus or roller. Each scroll was usually washed in cedar-oil, or strewn between each wrap with cedar or citron-chips, to prevent it from rotting or being eaten by insects. Ancient books did not exclusively consist of scrolls. The Romans had also books of papyrus, or vellum, folded in square leaves like ours. These they called *codices*.

Such were the articles which formed the stock in trade of a Grecian bookseller. The trader was also the manufacturer, keeping a number of transcribers to make copies of the works he sold. Diogenes Laertius mentions that there were at Athens public book-shops called Bibliopoleia; nor were these libraries solely devoted to the copying and selling manuscript books, for it was the custom among the learned to meet in the shops to discuss the literary gossip of the day, to criticise, possibly, a new comedy by Aristophanes, the tragedy of the last feast of Bacchus, or to dispute on the latest philosophic theory. In those times when, from the extreme labour of producing them, books were both dear and scarce, the shopkeeper sometimes hired a qualified person to read a new manuscript to his learned customers, and to give an exposition or lecture concerning it. This must have been an important branch of his business; for, from the high price of books, the sale of copies must have been upon a very limited scale. The works of Plato appear to have had an unusually large circulation, for concerning them history records one of the earliest instances of literary piracy: Hermodorus the Sicilian, a disciple of that philosopher, having turned his attention to bookselling, extended the sale of his master's works not only throughout Greece, but as far as Sicily. This was done, however, without the consent of the author.

When literature, in its onward course, left the shores of Greece and fixed itself for a time at Alexandria, under the fostering encouragement of the Ptolemies, the bookselling business had become of so important a character, that a regular market was established for the sale of manuscripts. 'The trade' was chiefly composed of emigrant Greeks, who had by that period acquired a character all over the civilised world for cunning and knavery. Hence we find Strabo bitterly complaining that most of the volumes at the Alexandrian market were 'copied only for sale;' in other words, hastily, and without revision or comparison with the originals. He also laments that the impertinence of the transcribers introduced matter which the author never penned. This scanty information is all which exists concerning the booksellers of the old world. When, however, literature forsook the east, and, travelling westward, set up a long rest in Rome, more ample details concerning their mode of doing business are at our disposal.

The first mention of Latin books, as forming regular articles of commerce, is made by several writers who existed during the time of the Roman emperors. It is to be inferred that, previous to that time, people of distinction borrowed works from their authors, and caused copies to be made either by professed scribes (*librarii*), or by their own slaves. Gradually, however, the demand for books made it worth while for certain individuals to devote time and capital to their purchase, and these tradesmen were designated, after their Grecian brethren, bibliopolæ. Their shops were in public places: in, for instance, the well-frequented streets near the Forum, the Palladium, the Sigilarii, the Argilletum, and the Temple of Peace; but principally, according to Gellius, in the Via Sandalinaria. These shops being, as at Athens, much resorted to by men of letters, were the chief sources of literary information; they formed what modern newspapers call an 'excellent advertising medium:' announcements of new works were constantly exhibited not only outside the shops, but upon the pillars of the interior. Depôts for the sale of manuscripts were also to be met with in the provincial towns. Amongst the Roman booksellers originated the practice of purchasing copyrights, and it has been clearly ascertained that several of the most celebrated Latin works were the exclusive property of certain bibliopolæ. The names of several of these booksellers have been handed down to posterity, chiefly on account of their excellent mode of doing business, and for the care which they took in insuring the correctness of the manuscripts they sold; frequently going to the additional expense of employing the authors themselves to examine and compare the copies made from their works. The Tonsons, Longmans, Cadells, and Murrays of the times of Horace, Cicero, Martial, and Catullus (who mention them), were the 'speculative' Tryphon, the 'prudent' Atrectus, Tul. Lucensis 'the freed man,' the brothers Sosius, Q. P. Valerianus Dicius, and Ulpius. We are informed by Galenus that less respectable book-dealers took dishonest advantage of the fair fame of these magnates in the 'trade,' by forging the imprints of those celebrated publishers upon imperfect and ill-written copies.*

With the fall of the Roman empire the bookselling business not only declined, but was for a time swept away from the list of trades. Literature and science, ingulfed in the monastic system, were hidden in the cloister. The monks became the transcribers of books, and in this laborious occupation the learned Benedictines are known to have particularly excelled. The works produced by these religious men were almost exclusively missals, or books of devotion; copies of the Scriptures were also produced by them, though to a less extent. There was, however, at this period, a great difficulty in procuring material on which to write books, and the device, more ingenious than commendable, was resorted to of deterging the writing of old classics, and then using the cleaned parchment for the works required. This practice is understood to have caused the loss to the world of several classic authors. Occasionally, in old collections of manuscript books, a missal or copy of the Gospels is to be seen inscribed on vellum, on which shines faintly the not-altogether obliterated work of an ancient writer. We lately saw, in the Bibliothèque Royale, or great public library in Paris, a copy of the Gospels as old as the ninth century, which had thus been written on the cleaned pages of a classic author. Whether on new or old vellum, a great number of books were copied and collected in England during the eighth century; the monks of that period having been exceedingly emulous of attaining skill in writing and illuminating; and at a later period, this was enumerated as one of the accomplishments even of so great a man as St Dunstan. They abandoned the system of writing on scrolls, adopting the form in which books are now printed. Yet posterity had little benefit from these great assemblages of books; for, during the numerous inroads of the Danes from the ninth to the eleventh century, many of the richest libraries were committed to the flames, along with the monasteries which contained them.† In the thirteenth century, books were, from these destructions, extremely scarce, and the few that existed were exclusively in the hands of the monks; for they were almost the only persons who could read them. 'Great authors, says D'Israeli, 'occasionally composed a book in Latin, which none but other great authors cared for, and which

ting the paper; a pumober to point out the beginning and end of each line; a rule to draw lines and divide the sheets into columns; a glass containing sand, and another glass filled with water, probably to mix with the ink.'—*Manual of Classical Literature: from the German of J. J. Eschenburg.*

* History of the Book-Trade and the Art of Book-Printing. By Frederick Metz. Darmstadt: 1834.

† Biographia Britannica Literaria, pp. 35 and 107.

the people could not read.' For these reasons, the small amount of bookselling which took place in the middle ages was solely conducted by monks; and works, being scarce, fetched prices which would astonish the modern bibliomaniac. It is well authenticated that the homilies of Bede, and St Austin's psalter, were sold in 1174 by the monks of Dorchester (Oxfordshire) to Walter, prior of St Swithin's (Winchester), for twelve measures of barley and a splendid pall, embroidered in silver with historical representations of St Birinus converting a Saxon king. At a later period, a copy of John of Meun's 'Romance of the Rose' was sold before the palace gate at Paris for 40 crowns, or L.33, 6s. 8d. A learned lady, the Countess of Anjou, gave for the homilies of Haimon, bishop of Halberstadt, the unheard-of exchange of two hundred sheep, five quarters of wheat, and the same quantity of rye and millet. Among these instances of the high prices sometimes set on unprinted books, we cannot exclude mention of an extraordinary work, which was executed in a singular manner. It consists of the finest vellum, the text cut out of, instead of inscribed on each leaf, and being interleaved with blue paper, it is as easily read as print. The title involves one of the paradoxes in which authors of that age so much delighted: it is 'Liber passionis Domini Nostri Jesu Christi, cum figuris and characteribus nulla materia compositis'—(The book of the passion of our Lord Jesus Christ, with figures and characters composed of nothing). For this singular curiosity the Emperor Rodolph II. of Germany offered 11,000 ducats. As the book bears the royal arms of this country, it is thought to have been executed by some ingenious and patient English monk. We mention the work to account in some measure for the high prices adverted to, which Robertson, in his history of Charles V., adduces as a proof of the *scarcity* of manuscripts. The truth is, that some copies were intrinsically valuable for the beauty and richness of the binding; and a few others were rendered almost beyond price, from having the relics of saints inserted in them. At a visitation of the treasury of St Paul's cathedral, in the year 1295, by Ralph de Baldock (afterwards bishop of London), there were found twelve copies of the Gospels, all adorned with silver, some with gilding, pearls and gems, and one with eleven relics, which were ingeniously let in to the plates of precious metal that surrounded each page.*

We cannot find that bookselling awoke from its monastic torpor till the establishment of universities in various parts of the continent. But in 1259, sellers of manuscripts, chiefly on theological subjects, became so numerous in Paris, that special regulations were instituted regarding them. Pierre de Blois mentions that they were called librarii or stationarii. The former were brokers or agents for the sale and loan of manuscripts. By stationarii (so called from having stations in various parts of cities and at markets) were meant sellers and copiers of manuscripts, like their Roman prototypes. It appears that at the time the above laws were made, there were in Paris twenty-nine booksellers and book-brokers, two of whom were females. The enormous prices they demanded for their books became a public scandal, and one object of the new law was to regulate their charges. *Taxatores Librorum*, or book-taxers, were employed to determine the price which every manuscript should be charged, that, on the one hand, the stationarii should have a reasonable profit, and that, on the other, the purchaser should not pay too dear.† But the most profitable branch of the trade appears to have been lending books, which were generally so valuable, that for their safe return security was taken. When Louis XI. borrowed the works of Rhases, the Arabian physician, he not only deposited, by way of pledge, a large quantity of plate, but was obliged to find a nobleman to join him as surety in a deed binding him under a great penalty to restore the book unharmed. Some books were so highly prized, that they were conveyed or pledged as security for loans, as estates are mortgaged. It is recorded that one Geoffrey de St Lieges deposited the *Speculum Historiale in Consuetudines Parisienses* (Historical Mirror of the Customs of the Parisians) with Gerrard de Montagu, king's advocate, as security for a sum equal to about L.10.

From these facts, it would appear that bookselling was in Paris—then the chief seat of learning—a profitable calling between the twelfth and fifteenth centuries. They were not, however, the only members of the trade existing in Europe. Wherever universities were established, booksellers also resided, especially in Vienna, Palermo, Padua, and Salamanca. Gradually, 'the trade' spread itself over less learned places; and by the time printing was invented, both librarii and stationarii exercised their vocations in most of the larger European towns.

Such was the condition of the trade up to the year 1440, when it felt the effects of a revolution which shook far more important professions and institutions to their base. About the year 1430 it was whispered in Mayence that one John Guttenberg had invented a process by which he and an assistant could produce more copies in one day than two hundred and fifty of the most expert penmen. The learned were incredulous; but a few years afterwards their doubts were silenced by the appearance of a Bible in Latin—*printed* from metal types. This wonder was effected by a machine which has since done more for the advance of civilisation than all the other expedients of ingenious man to save his labour, or to promote his welfare—THE PRESS.

* Dugdale's Monasticon, iii. p. 309-324.

† Annals of Parisian Typography. By the Rev. Parr Greswell. London: 1833.

MISCELLANEA.

Dr Watt's Abstract of the Glasgow Mortality Bill for 1844 is marked by the usual abundance of valuable statistical information. The population is now estimated at 311,000. The year 1842 was one of extreme commercial depression; but, from the mildness of seasons, and the regulated dispensation of subsistence to the poorest class, exhibited a lower mortality than usual. Commercial prosperity, reviving in 1843, has been at an unusual height in 1844. These preliminary facts will enable the reader to appreciate the results of Dr Watt's inquiries.

It appears that the total burials of 1844 (8092) is a decrease of no less than 2268, or more than a fourth upon the amount of 1843. The baptisms of 1844 are 217 above 1843; the increase of marriages is 398. In 1842, the year of greatest commercial depression, the proportion of marriages to population had sunk to 1 in (nearly) 150. In the improving year, 1843, the proportion rose to 1 in 144 (omitting fractions); in the best year, 1844, it was 1 in 126; showing that, upon the whole population of Glasgow, there is a coincidence between prosperity and the disposition to a matrimonial union. It has been ascertained, however, that the diminution of marriages in bad, and their increase in good times, chiefly obtains in those districts of the city which are the residence of the middle and upper classes. The humbler population marry with less regard for circumstances—a rule, we believe, universal, and the causes of which are not difficult to understand.

The Glasgow bill shows that the amelioration of public health in 1844 chiefly affects the humbler classes. One-half of the decrease of burials is in that class which take place at the expense of the public. During the few by-past years, the humbler people have been in the same circumstances as usual as to their dwellings, the drainage and cleaning of their streets, ventilation, &c. The change has been in the abundance of their means of subsistence. Dr Watt therefore remarks that, while he attaches due importance to the measures in contemplation for improving the health of towns, he is at the same time convinced of the still more pressing importance of measures 'for relieving the wants of the poor and destitute, more especially during times of commercial distress, to prevent disease and death from increasing and spreading with unmitigated violence among them. One inference,' he says, 'to be drawn from the facts before us is, that when these wants are supplied, human life, like vegetation, assumes a more vigorous and healthy condition during dry and favourable seasons than in others, in defiance of defective drainage.'

A system which goes against nature—can such be right in any circumstances; and is not its being against nature its sufficient condemnation? A royal personage of this country has his wife provided for him by the state, and the blessings of heaven are invoked upon a union where the most obvious dictates of heaven are disregarded. Let the reader say if we here speak too strongly, after reading the following account of the first interview between the Prince of Wales (afterwards George IV.) and the lady who had been brought from her foreign home to be married to him. It is from the Diary of the Earl of Malmesbury, who had conducted the princess to England:—'I immediately notified the arrival to the king and Prince of Wales; the last came immediately. I, according to the established etiquette, introduced (no one else being in the room) the Princess Caroline to him. She very properly, in consequence of my saying to her it was the right mode of proceeding, attempted to kneel to him. He raised her (gracefully enough), and embraced her; said barely one word, turned round, retired to a distant part of the apartment, and calling me to him, said, "Harris, I am not well; pray get me a glass of brandy." I said, "Sir, had you not better have a glass of water?" Upon which he, much out of humour, said, with an oath, "*No;* I will go directly to the queen;" and away he went. The princess, left during this short moment alone, was in a state of astonishment; and, on my joining her, said, "*Mon Dieu! est ce que le prince est toujours comme cela? Je le trouve très gros, et nullement aussi beau que son portrait.*" [Is the prince always thus? I find him, too, very fat, and not at all so good-looking as his portrait.] I said his royal highness was naturally a good deal affected and flurried at this first interview, but she certainly would find him different at dinner. She was disposed to further criticisms on this occasion, which would have embarrassed me very much to answer, if luckily the king had not ordered me to attend him. The drawing-room was just over. His majesty's conversation turned wholly on Prussian and French politics; and the only question about the princess was, "Is she good-humoured?" I said, and very truly, that in very trying moments I had never seen her otherwise. The king said, "I am glad of it;" and it was manifest from his silence he had seen the queen since she had seen the prince, and that the prince had made a very unfavourable report of the princess to her. At dinner, at which all those who attended the princess from Greenwich assisted, and the honours of which were done by Lord Stopford, as vice-chamberlain, I was far from satisfied with the princess's behaviour: it was flippant, rattling, affecting raillery and wit. The prince was evidently disgusted: and this unfortunate dinner fixed his dislike; which, when left to herself, the princess had not the talent to remove, but, by still observing the same giddy manners, and attempts at cleverness, and coarse sarcasm, increased it till it became positive hatred. From this time, though I dined frequently during the first three weeks after the marriage at Carlton House, nothing material occurred; but the sum of what I saw there led me to draw the inferences I have just expressed. After one of these dinners, where the Prince of Orange was present, and at which the princess had behaved very lightly, and even improperly, the prince took me into his closet, and asked me how I liked this sort of manners: I could not conceal my disapprobation of them, and took this opportunity of repeating to him the substance of what the Duke of Brunswick had so often said to me, that she had been brought up very strictly, and if she was not strictly kept, would, from high spirits and little thought, certainly emancipate too much. To this the prince said, "I see but too plainly: but why, Harris, did you not tell me so before, or write it to me from Brunswick?" I replied that I did not consider what the duke (a severe father himself towards his children) said of sufficient consequence; that it affected neither the princess's moral character nor conduct, and was intended solely as an intimation, which I conceived it only proper to notice to his royal highness at a proper occasion—at such a one as now had offered; and that I humbly hoped his royal highness would not consider it as casting any *real* slur or aspersion on the princess; that as to not writing to his royal highness from Brunswick, I begged him to recollect that I was not sent on a *discretionary* commission, but with the *most positive commands to ask the Princess Caroline in marriage, and nothing more;* that to this sole point respecting the marriage, and no other, those commands went; any reflection or remarks that I had presumed to make would (whether in praise of, or injurious to her royal highness) have been a direct and positive deviation from those his majesty's commands. They were as *limited* as they were *imperative.* That still, had I discovered notorious or glaring defects, such as were of a nature to render the union unseemly, I should have felt it as a bounden duty to have stated them; but it must have been *directly to the king,* and to no one else. To this the prince appeared to acquiesce; but I saw it did not please, and left a *rankle* in his mind.'

Fog in a Large City—with what fancy, yet truth, is it described in the following newspaper paragraph! 'It has been satisfactorily demonstrated that snow serves to keep the earth warm: and although a fog is not very easily seen through, it appears to us that it is a kind of nightcap which the earth puts on during the day, when the weather happens to be unusually cold. At the moment we write, there are neither ends to the streets nor tops to the houses. Steeples, and monuments, and towers, and chimney-stalks, have gone off in smoke. The sun at noonday is no longer a type of clearness. Everything is a blank. In the centre of the thronged thoroughfares, we are as much out of sight of land as a vessel in mid-ocean. But what strange shapes flit and loom about us! On every side there is a series of dissolving views in continual process of exhibition. Beef-eating compounds of undeniable flesh and blood are threading the mist-like phantoms. We are revelling in a dance of shadows. Whichever way we turn, individuals appear and vanish like witches on a blasted heath. What a phantasmagoria of dim and vapoury forms! What a universal game at blind-man's buff! Strange freak of nature!—a populous city partially stricken with blindness—men's visions contracted to an ell's length—every street a dark passage—everybody cautious and groping. Who's there? No answer. Perhaps a lamp-post—perhaps a pump. What frosted lights are these? Is that a house, a shop, a square, a bridge, or a river? Where are we? Which direction is south, and which north? Is this a man or a minibus? The largest objects are only to be scanned by the touch, as a near-sighted person reads small print with his nose on the paper. Lights, links, and lanterns!—we shall be in the canal! It is plain that man is an imperfect animal, and wants tentacula [it should be *antennæ*]. There's a horse's head in our neck. We are in the heart of a cloud that, seen afar off, would be sufficiently alarming. What a cover for a retreating army! Stop thief! "That handkerchief did an Egyptian to my mother give!" The thief and the handkerchief, however, are both gone. Two strides, in fact, constitute an *alibi.* Charity is almost at a stand-still, for so dense is the fog, that it is impossible for the left hand to see what the right is doing. We have also been informed of an individual who had been suddenly prosperous in the world, passing through some of the principal streets without recognising a single old acquaintance.'—*Glasgow Citizen.*

To vulgar and commonplace minds all things are vulgar and commonplace. Sunbeams strained through them would come out woollen threads. See how this is verified in the following extract from Kohl's Travels in Scotland:—'I was much annoyed that circumstances would not allow me to pay a visit to Abbotsford. "You may make yourself easy about that, sir!" began one of our inside passengers, addressing me, after he had taken off his right leg for greater convenience, and placed it behind him in a corner of the coach—he had a wooden leg, to wit—"make yourself easy about that, sir! There are prettier seats in Scotland than this Abbotsford; and if you have seen Taymouth Castle, Dunkeld, and Dalkeith, you may travel past this comfortably enough. Walter Scott, as I know myself, purchased this house when it was a little farm, upon which at first he built only a very confined and small mansion. The greater his means became, the more he extended his habitation, until it became at length the irregular and wonderful little seat you now see before you. Besides, the house is no longer in the condition in which the Great Unknown, or rather the Great Well-known, left it. More than this; I cannot comprehend how people can be so incredibly curious about *souvenirs* and memorials of Sir Walter Scott. Believe me, sir, people have exaggerated the fame and praises of Sir Walter Scott, as they have exaggerated the fame of other celebrated persons, in an inconceivable manner. Who, then, was Sir Walter Scott? He was clerk to the writers to the signet. Haven't I seen him myself, every other morning, coming out of the Parliament House, or over the hills there? He had nothing of the English gentleman about him—nothing so fine and distinguished. On the contrary, he had a very plain, common, old Scotch face, little eyes, round, big, thick nose, that always looked as if it were a little swollen. And then he did not look quite so clever as people represent him. His broad, somewhat hanging lips, gave him rather a somewhat stupid appearance. He had, besides, very clumsy feet, and walked a little lame. If any one accosted him, he usually returned a blunt Scottish good-day. 'How d'ye do, sir?' was his usual mode of salutation, uttered in a gruff tone, and laying the stress of the accent on the 'do,' just like the common people. He could not pronounce the 'r' properly, and made something like a 'ch' of it, while he emitted the sound from the back part of his mouth. When he wished to say 'rock,' it sounded almost like 'cock.' In a word, if the good man did not happen to be dead, and could you see him there, walking towards you as I have described him, in his coarse, green old greatcoat, with large metal buttons, which he used to wear at Abbotsford, you would fancy that you were looking at a farmer rather than a poet." '

Heroic versus Industrious Policy, is well exhibited in the following remarks from the *Spectator*:—'French statesmen seek to extend the manufactures and commerce of their country, and increase its wealth, with a view to increase its naval and military power. English statesmen seek to render the defensive establishments of their country by sea and land more perfect, in order to protect its manufactures and commerce. The statesmen of both countries direct their attention to the same objects; but what is the means with the one is the end with the other. An interesting paper on the mining statistics of France, by Mr Porter of the Board of Trade, which has just been published in the journal of the Statistical Society, affords an opportunity of contrasting the results of what may be called the direct and indirect processes for increasing national power. A strong steam navy has become an object desirable in both countries. The most important material elements of a steam navy are coal and iron. The French government has set itself with energy to construct war-steamers; and has laboured strenuously, by a system of artificial protection, to increase the internal production of coal and iron, in order that, in the event of war, it might be independent of foreign supplies. The protection afforded to the iron trade of France has been prompted less by a desire to increase the national wealth, than to obtain a home supply of materials for war. Meanwhile the English government, though not inattentive to augmenting its force of war-steamers, has pursued, with respect to the coal and iron trades, a course of policy which had in view solely the general development of the national resources, regardless of their bearing upon our means of defence. While the French government has been hedging its iron trade round with fiscal protection, the English government has gradually been stripping its iron trade of every vestige of protection. The French government, with an eye to contingent wars, has been labouring to insure a stock of warlike materials: the English government, with an eye to turning peace to the best account, has left the day of war to care for itself. The result has been, that in 1841 the quantity of coal raised in this country was at least ten times the quantity raised in France; and that in the same year four tons of iron were made in this country for every ton made in France. The coal consumed in the iron works alone of Great Britain rather more than doubled the whole quantity of coal raised in France. In Great Britain, the average quantity of coal raised within the year by each person employed in coal mines was 253 tons; in France it was only 116 tons. In France, 47,800 persons were employed in producing one-fourth the quantity of iron produced in Great Britain by 42,400. The prices of iron to the consumer in France are from 200 to 250 per cent. higher than in England. France has not even succeeded in making herself independent of foreign supplies: the quantity of coal imported in 1841 was within a trifle of half the quantity raised; and nearly 50,000 tons of British iron were imported, pig-iron being subject to a duty of L.3, 2s. 6d., and plates, bars, and rods, to a duty varying from L.8, 7s. 4d. to L.16, 14s. 9d. Britain, in whose policy war has been scarcely taken into account at all, possesses at this moment a more abundant and cheap supply of materials for its steam navy than France, which, by the artificial encouragement given to its iron manufacture, has diverted industry and capital from other branches of trade, voluntarily sacrificing wealth to increase its warlike force. France has, in consequence, only its royal steam navy to rely upon; while the steam navy of our wealthier traders could, at a short notice, supply a formidable body of war-steamers. If French statesmen would take a leaf out of the British book, and adopt a commercial policy really and sincerely intended to promote their country's commercial prosperity, without any *arrière pensée* of war, they would find this indirect way of increasing the national strength by far the most certain.'

YEARNING FOR WONDERLAND.

[FROM THE GERMAN OF SCHILLER.]

AH! that I could wing my way
  Through earth's valley—deep and dreary—
Ah! that I could float all day,
  Pinions never tired or weary,
O'er the everlasting hills,
And the ever-gushing rills,
Where come blight and sorrow never,
Ever green, and youthful ever!

Where Heaven's harmonies resound,
  Holy Peace for ever singing;
Where light Zephyr sports around,
  Odours from the flower-buds wringing;
Through the trees' dark foliage dancing—
O'er the fruit all golden glancing—
By no wintry blast affrighted—
Kissing the soft flowers delighted;
  Flowers that never lose the sun,
    Never close the laughing eye;
  With existence never done;
    Know not what it is to die!

Wo is me! what rolls between?
  'Tis a rapid river rushing—
'Tis the stream of Death, I ween,
  Wildly tossing, hoarsely gushing;
While my very heartstrings quiver
At the roar of that dread river!

But I see a little boat
  The rough waters gently riding;
How can she so fearless float?
  For I see no pilot guiding.
Courage!—on!—there's no retreating:
Sails are spread in friendly greeting.
On then, on!—in love we must,
Without pledge or warrant, trust!
The white-armed sails a message bear:
'There are wonders everywhere!
The wondrous faith wherein you stand
Must bear you to the Wonderland!'

January 11, 1845. E. L.

A NOBLE TASK FOR THE TRUE POET.

And whom shall we look to first but the masters of thought? Surely the true poet will do something to lift the burden of his own age. What is the use of wondrous gifts of language, if they are employed to enervate, and not to ennoble their hearers? What avails it to trim the lights of history, if they are made to throw no brightness on the present, or open no track into the future? And to employ imagination only in the service of vanity or gain, is as if an astronomer were to use his telescope to magnify the pot-herbs in his kitchen garden. Think what a glorious power is that of expression, and what responsibility follows the man who possesses it. That grace of language which can make even commonplace things beautiful, throwing robes of the purest texture into forms of all-attractive loveliness: why does it not expend its genius on materials that would be worthy of the artist? The great interests of man are before it, are crying for it, can absorb all its endeavour, are indeed the noblest field for it. Think of this; then think what a waste of high intellectual endowments there has been in all ages from the meanest of motives. But what wise man would not rather have the harmless fame which youths on a holiday scratch for themselves upon the leaden roof of some cathedral tower, than enjoy the undeniable renown of those who, with whatever power, have written, from slight or unworthy motives, what may prove a hindrance to the wellbeing of their fellowmen?—*The Claims of Labour.*

Printed by William Bradbury, of No. 6, York Place, and Frederick Mullett Evans, of No. 7, Church Row, both of Stoke Newington, in the county of Middlesex, printers, at their office, Lombard Street, in the precinct of Whitefriars, and city of London; and Published (with permission of the Proprietors, W. and R. CHAMBERS,) by WILLIAM SOMERVILLE ORR, Publisher, of 2, Amen Corner, at No. 2, AMEN CORNER, both in the parish of Christchurch, and in the city of London.—Saturday, March 1, 1845.

CONDUCTED BY WILLIAM AND ROBERT CHAMBERS, EDITORS OF 'CHAMBERS'S INFORMATION FOR THE PEOPLE,' 'CHAMBERS'S EDUCATIONAL COURSE,' &c.

No. 62. New Series. SATURDAY, MARCH 8, 1845. Price 1½d.

A FEW DAYS IN A FRENCH CHATEAU.

BY A LADY.

I often wonder at what has been a thousand times wondered at already—the remarkable resemblance between the course of events in English and French history. A king possessing many good qualities, falling on evil times, is carried by his people to the scaffold. Next follows a pretended republic, which merges in a military despotism. This ends, and then comes back the old reigning family. But this family not conducting itself properly, loses the popular affection, is turned adrift, and a far-off cousin is elected king. To make the parallel pretty nearly complete, the family of the dethroned monarch lives in a distant land, hoping for better times, and retains a hold on the loyalty and compassion of certain old families of distinction, whose feelings cannot brook an unhesitating submission to the powers that be. One thing more, indeed, as respects France is still wanting to render the resemblance complete—an insurrection led on by these old-fashioned loyalists, and fruitless in everything but utter ruin to their expiring cause.

No such mad freak having yet occurred, the legitimists of France, as they are pleased to term themselves, occupy a position parallel with the Jacobites in Scotland and the Cavaliers in England, a short time before their annihilation as a party by the rebellion of 1745. In the same manner that these sturdy Jacobites and Cavaliers used to shun the court of George I. and II., and live in grumbling retirement in their old castles and halls, so do the legitimists of France eschew the court of Louis-Philippe, and shutting themselves up in their chateaux or their town mansions, live but for their families, and dream only of a second restoration. James III. was 'the king over the water,' who, the Cavalier party declared, should one day 'enjoy his own again;' the young Duke of Bourdeaux (nominally Henri V.) is the object of veneration among the saddened adherents of the Bourbons.

Visionary as everybody now allows the projects of the Cavaliers and Jacobites to have been, nothing can make me disbelieve them to have been a noble set of men—gentlemen of high principle, brave, generous; their very misfortunes making one almost love them in spite of their manifold errors. Had I lived a hundred years ago, I daresay I should have attended the ball of 'the prince' in Holyrood, at least if so gallant a personage as Fergus M'Ivor had asked me. I am certain I should have wept the fate of Lords Kilmarnock and Balmerino and Charles Ratcliffe; and even now I have a degree of tender regard for the 'bonny white rose,' the emblem of the unfortunate house of Stuart. Of such poetical inclinations, it will not be thought surprising that, on a late visit to Paris, with a party of friends, I should have wished to see and know something of the old loyalist families who still cling to the *fleur-de-lis*—the De Sullys, the De Montmorencies, the De Choiseuls, and other remnants of the shattered noblesse.

In ordinary circumstances it is no easy matter to become acquainted with these families; for they do not mingle much in general society. The few who dwell in Paris reside in the Fauxbourg St Germain, a *quartier* which has now become synonymous with their party, and the inhabitants of which are associated in the mind with the brilliant court of Louis XIV. The loyalists who have retained their fortunes display their taste for magnificence only in the sumptuous adornment of their palace-like houses, and in the splendour of their equipages. The brilliant *toilette*, so dear to all other Frenchwomen, is by the ladies of these families discarded, and replaced by the neatest and most simple attire. Their manners partake of the same simple character; they are frank, and at the same time polite; merry without being boisterous, and never exacting; for they have been schooled by that best of teachers—adversity.

A previous acquaintance in London with certain members of one of these ancient and noble families, was now fortunately instrumental in bringing us an invitation to spend a few days with them and their venerable relative at their seat in the country; and as life in a French chateau can be but little known in England, I propose—adopting, as may be supposed, fictitious titles—to attempt a sketch of what fell under our observation at the chateau of our new but valued friend.

The Comte de Beaulieu, one of the sons-in-law of the nobleman to whose country house we had been so hospitably invited, offered to come to Paris to escort us to Linière; but this stretch of politeness we positively declined, and only would consent to meet him at Versailles, where we intended to remain for a few days previous to quitting France. Behold our party, then, at Versailles, where on the appointed day the comte made his appearance; and after an interesting stroll with him through some of the private apartments of the palace, to which he had special access, we set off for Linière early in the afternoon, and under as bright a sun as ever shone on la belle France, being preceded by the comte, who drove an elegant open carriage, built from a design of his own, and drawn by a pair of fine English bay horses. The excursion was short and delightful. Passing through a district of country tolerably wooded, we had here and there a glimpse of an old chateau, whose white walls contrasted finely with the bright green of the trees which surrounded it, and were thus prepared for what we might expect at the conclusion of our drive. On we went, and in about two hours arrived at the park gates of Linière. At the head of an avenue of trees stood the mansion, a fine pile of building, with a spacious flight of steps in the middle, from the top of which, on each side, branched off a terrace with a balustrade of stone running across the front of the chateau. The steps at both sides were flanked by quantities of geranium and other fragrant plants in full bloom, which imparted an air of elegance to the scene.

At our near approach, the venerable master of the house, the Marquis de Tourville, accompanied by another of his sons-in-law, the Vicomte de Saint Prosper, descended the steps where they had been waiting some time. The truly hospitable and kind manner in which we were thus welcomed, could only be equalled by that which we experienced from the ladies, when a few moments after we arrived at the vestibule, where they reiterated the same kind expressions in the most engaging manner. We then walked through the antechamber and billiard-room into the drawing-room, where we chatted for a short time, and then adjourned up stairs, preceded by the Marchioness and the Countess de Beaulieu, who pointed out our individual apartments, and quickly retired, warning us that we had not much time before dinner for the duties of the toilet. In a short time the great dinner bell rung, and when the ladies tapped at our door to conduct us to the drawing-room, we were not quite prepared to descend. When we made our appearance in the drawing-room, we found all the family assembled; therefore, whilst waiting for the announcement of dinner, let me describe our host, hostess, and family. The marquis numbers more than seventy years, although he does not appear so old: from his military bearing, no portion of his height is lost, and this, combined with an aquiline nose and eagle eye, give him such an imposing presence, that one cannot approach him without feeling a degree of awe. From infancy he had been in attendance upon Marie Antoinette, as his family was one of those who enjoyed the intimate acquaintance of that unfortunate queen.

The marquis in early life joined the allied army, and is linked in the dearest bonds of friendship with some of our brave old generals with whom he had served. After the Restoration, he was reinstated in his former rank and position, and succeeded in regaining a great part of his fortune. When Charles X. ascended the throne, he was intrusted with a high and responsible command of great honour, which he filled up to the moment of the Revolution. He has ever since lived apart from the court, and never takes his seat in the Chamber of Peers unless some question involving the vital interests of his country is to be agitated. The marchioness is the descendant of one of the most renowned families in France: her mother and grandmother both perished under the guillotine. She has passed middle life, is peculiarly graceful both in person and manner, has a sweet but sad expression of countenance, and in youth must have been beautiful. She dresses to perfection; never tries, by any youthful denudings, to take one year off her age; and wears her own nice gray hair. Her family consists of three daughters, who are all married. The eldest, the Countess de Beaulieu, always resides with her parents; she is an elegant, self-possessed, intelligent woman, with a very engaging expression, and excels in music and painting. She has six children. The comte, who is the heir of a house as ancient as that of his wife, is a handsome, dark-complexioned man, and highly accomplished. The youngest daughter, who was staying here, resembles a lovely young Englishwoman: she is a beautiful blonde, and is married to the Vicomte de Saint Prosper, eldest son to the Duke de Saint Prosper, with whom they reside nine months every year, the other three being passed at Linière. The vicomte is a tall, handsome, fair-complexioned man, and so much like a John Bull, that he has frequently been mistaken for an Englishman. They have also six children.

On dinner being announced, the marquis politely offered one of us his arm, with the air of an old cavalier, and the rest of the company followed. According to French custom, the host and hostess sat at opposite sides of the table, on which the display was simple and tasteful, the eye being feasted as well as the palate. I was particularly struck with a large and handsome basket occupying the middle of the table, and filled with the most beautiful flowers. As soon as the soups were despatched, and the covers removed, an immense joint of roasted beef, as a compliment to us, stood revealed, towering over all the delicate dishes. After three courses, which would have done credit to Ude himself, the table, with the cloth still on, was replenished with the most delicious fruits, sweetmeats, and iced creams.

The conversation during dinner, which lasted about two hours, was lively and entertaining. A number of merry stories were related of the mistakes made by English people in France, and *vice versa*; indeed the Comtesse de Beaulieu told some very laughable anecdotes of her own experience in London. After finger-glasses were handed round, we were all escorted back again in the same order to the drawing-room. On the way, we saw eight lovely little girls, all dressed alike, playing in the billiard-room. They accompanied us into the drawing-room, and as soon as coffee was dispensed, the party quickly broke into little social knots. Music, conversation, and looking at the gentlemen playing billiards in the adjoining apartment, made the evening pass most agreeably. When the drawing-room was lighting up, a new contrivance struck us as having a pretty effect. Two brilliant lamps were placed in superb china vases on each side of the mantel-piece, throwing down a light upon a pyramidal stand of flowers, which entirely concealed the fireplace. Tea was served at a late hour. The marquis told us that, although they always had this beverage in Paris, they had not yet habituated themselves to it in the country. Tea, indeed, is still a rare luxury among the French.

We had been so long accustomed to the narrow and uncomfortable beds in French hotels, that when, on having retired for the night, we sunk in capacious down couches, with linen akin to cambric, and pillows trimmed with fine lace, we could scarcely credit our senses that we were really in France. We arose early to enjoy the delightful view from our windows. The beautiful park, studded with lofty clumps of trees, reminded us of merry England. At eight o'clock the waiting-maid of the marchioness brought in a large tray covered with a napkin, upon which were placed tea, coffee, hot rolls, butter in curious devices covered with pieces of ice, and sundry kinds of cakes quite hot. The cups and saucers were each ornamented by a marquis's coronet, and were of the finest Sèvres china. The entire establishment being conducted by men-servants, with the exception of the respective waiting-maids and nursery attendants, was the reason that the marchioness, in consideration of our English prejudices, was so kind as to let her own maid bring in our breakfast; which we enjoyed very much.

Fain would we now have rambled about the grounds, but, knowing that it is customary for the ladies to stay in their own rooms until the bell for the *grand déjeuner*, or general breakfast, summons all the family, we constrained ourselves to conform to the rules of the house. By adhering to this plan, each separate family is enabled to make their own private arrangements, and give their orders for the day, the remainder of which they spend together free from household cares. The ladies have each a cup of coffee at eight o'clock, or earlier, and the gentlemen also when they are indisposed, but not otherwise. Prevented from going out, we took the opportunity of taking a look round the apartments allotted for our use. Our bedrooms were very large, carpetted all over, and superbly furnished with footstools, arm and small chairs, sofas, marble-topped cabinets, chests of drawers, dressing-tables, and last, but certainly not least in our estimation, capacious mahogany bedsteads, terminating at each end in Greek scrolls, and provided with two sets of curtains, appended to a gilt coronet fastened into the wall, the outside hangings light-coloured silk, to match the window-curtains, the inside ones fine clear white muslin. In the centre of each bedroom stood a library table, furnished with writing materials, matches, wafers, almanacs, wherein the saints' days were peculiarly notified; and these articles complete the list, with the addition of hanging pin-cushions at each side of the large looking-glass which stood on the mantel-piece. Attached to each sleeping apartment was a handsome dressing-room, leading to another small apartment designed for a waiting-maid, from which there is an exit to the corridor. Each visitor therefore may be said to have a cluster of two or three private apartments. The other parts of the mansion are on the same princely scale. It was built in the reign of Louis XIII., and consists of a centre two storeys high, with a wing at each side of the same height. Staircases lead to the long corridors, which run from one end of the chateau to the other, and from which all the bedrooms are entered. The lower corridor is hung with family portraits—knights and belles of 'high degree'—and is lighted by the windows which form part of the façade. The lower floor of one of the wings contains the suite of rooms appropriated to the marchioness, the other those of the marquis, and the entire upper part of each is occupied by the children, their servants, and English governesses. The drawing, billiard, and dining-rooms are noble apartments, and, with antechambers, run the entire length and breadth of the chateau. In one of the drawing-rooms is placed a marble bust of the Duke de Bordeaux, in a most conspicuous position. It is valuable both as a likeness, and as a fine work of art. Luxury and comfort are singularly combined in this charming room, from which the grounds can be entered by means of a flight of steps.

The ladies had the kindness again to call at our door, to convey us down stairs as soon as the bell rang for the usual breakfast. We found all the family assembled in the drawing-room. Some of the gentlemen had been walking in the grounds, others in the village, and the intellectual comte had been giving his accustomed German lessons to his daughters. We were all conducted in the same order to the dining-room as we had been the preceding evening. We found the beautiful polished table covered by a delicious melange of poultry, joints of roasted meat, bread, cakes, potatoes in divers forms, and most recherché made dishes. Tea, coffee, and chocolate were poured out from silver pots by servants at each person's desire, the cups and saucers alone being placed on the table. Eggs, poached and dressed in oil, were found to be delicious: they were, however, served only in small earthenware pipkins with handles, which certainly appeared rather incongruous amongst such a brilliant display of plate. Sweetmeats of the rarest and most curious description, strawberries, cherries, and various fruits, some of them iced, were also present; likewise wines and liqueurs—the whole reminding me of the far-famed breakfasts of the Scotch. The absence of the table-cloth, however, gave a foreign air to the repast. Finger-glasses, as at dinner, was the signal for rising from table, when we were again marshalled to the drawing-room, where all the children were assembled, preparatory to their walking out. They breakfast at half-past seven o'clock, and have all their lessons over by twelve, after which they take exercise and dine. Music, drawing, and different kinds of needlework occupy them till five o'clock, when they take some light supper, and appear in the drawing-room, after their parents' dinner, for about an hour—a custom which is infinitely preferable to the English habit of admitting a troop of children into the dining-room during the dessert.

Having settled ourselves in the drawing-room, some of the party sat down to embroidery, and others to reading, the table being covered with newspapers just arrived from Paris; whilst we visited by invitation the apartments of the marchioness, which, as before observed, occupy all the ground-floor of the left wing. We entered her library from a door in the drawing-room leading into it, and were much pleased to find such a choice collection of French translations of English works, as madame cannot read them in the original. Sir Walter Scott's works occupied a large space. We were much amused, on opening one of his novels, by seeing an attempt at a translation of Edie Ochiltree's Scotch; and a very queer attempt it was. In a recess stood a handsome bedstead, draped with pale blue *gros de Naples*, covered by the most beautiful and delicate lace-work of that species called *application*. The coverlet and toilet-cover were likewise of the same material; the former was flounced round in a corresponding pattern. All these elegant specimens of needlecraft have been the result of the marchioness's own industry. In the middle of a large bow-window stood the toilet-table, covered by a profusion of silver, gold, china, Venice glass, and coloured stone dressing utensils. Near the fireplace is hung a rosary, in a glass-case, which was pointed out to us with pride and veneration, as it is believed to contain a piece of the true cross. The beads are formed from precious stones. This interesting object was presented to an ancestor of the marchioness by the celebrated Père Joseph, the friend and agent of Richelieu.

The gentlemen and the marchioness having proposed a walk through the grounds, in order to show them to us, we readily assented, and were greatly pleased with the excursion. The walks were diversified, and so well laid out, that from different points of the higher grounds we had charming prospects of the country around, including the old village and church of Linière. Finally, we visited the orangerie and hothouses, and were then conducted by the marchioness to her favourite spot, laid out to resemble, and called an English garden. She showed us a small parterre of pretty Scotch roses, which had been sent her as a present from the venerable Lord Lynedoch, a brother in arms of the marquis. We had scarcely returned to the house, when we were told to prepare for a drive, as they wished us to see some of the neighbouring chateaux. When we were ready, three handsome equipages drove up—a caleche, Brougham, and the Comte de Beaulieu's favourite, each drawn by a pair of fine English horses. We visited two chateaux. One of these contained a rare collection of paintings by the old masters, hung in a gallery evidently copied from the Louvre. The luxury of everything there was regal. Precious bronzes and antique marble busts were distributed through the apartments. The dining-room was worthy of Lucullus. The house had belonged to one of the ancient noblesse, whose widow, after his decapitation, had been obliged to sell it for a trifle to a citizen. This man had a daughter, in whom all his wealth centered; she married a young member of the old aristocracy, and is now a widow with two children. Some years back, her husband was sent as ambassador to England by Louis XVIII. We were particularly struck by the sofas with awnings dispersed through the grounds, and by an octagon room, some of the windows of which opened upon the lawn; they had also awnings over them, and at each side of the steps flowers in vases. A beautiful ornamented cottage in the grounds was most tastefully furnished, and would make a charming summer abode. The riding-house and some of the stables are built with the stones which once formed a part of the celebrated convent, the 'Port Royal,' where the virtuous Arnaulds flourished so long, both as reformers and as the great supporters of Jansenism. At the other chateau the garden pleased us most. The noble duke who is the proprietor seldom visits it; therefore it presented a very different appearance from the one we had just quitted. On our return we entered a very ancient church, with most exquisitely painted windows. Madame de Beaulieu was much pleased at her eldest daughter, nine years old, being able to recognise and narrate the different Scripture histories set forth thereon. As soon as we arrived within sight of the great altar, all our friends, gentlemen as well as ladies, dropped upon their knees, and appeared for some minutes to be lost in devotion. After a delightful drive, we returned to Linière just in time to dress for dinner.

As I have now detailed our proceedings for one day, it would be only a vain repetition to continue to do so, as nearly every hour was spent much in the same manner, with some exceptions; as, for instance, when the day was wet, we each took our work and had some interesting conversation. The marchioness was engaged upon the finest piece of needlework we ever saw, which is intended as a cover for the great altar in her own church at Linière. Every day, after our first breakfast, we read until the general one, always over night providing ourselves with the books which we desired to peruse. During a morning excursion we visited the ruins of one of the strongholds of the bold Jean de Montford, Duke of Brittany, celebrated in one of the ruthless wars of the fourteenth century.

During our stay we had many animated discussions relative to the difference both in manners and customs of our respective countries; but they all ended, as such conversations generally do, by leaving each individual wedded to the opinion expressed at first. One part of French chateau life had for some years puzzled us, but we think we understand it *now;* I allude to the harmonious manner in which many branches of one family reside under the same roof. The Marquis de Tourville, one day when speaking on this subject, said he rejoiced to entertain us at his chateau, that we might witness the patriarchal manner in which he lived with his daughters and their husbands and children, among whom never a jar occurred. I am inclined to ascribe this felicity to the strict etiquette and habitual politeness of the French. Although all relations, and living together in one house, each branch keeps itself to itself, and no one takes undue liberties with another. I observed that the two sons-in-law of the marchioness always addressed her as *maman*, or *ma chère maman.* One tolerably obvious reason for this clubbing together of families is narrowness of fortune. It will also be recollected that, by the new law of inheritance in France, properties are divided equally among the children, and all seem to maintain an equal hold on the paternal feelings. While acknowledging that this practice of equal division seems the most reasonable and just, I have, after all, doubts of its general efficacy. It no doubt appears scandalous, that, by our law of primogeniture, while the elder son gets all, the younger sons get nothing; yet it causes universal exertion, and is probably best for the nation at large. Few things are more striking to a stranger in France than the hosts of genteel idlers everywhere—men waiting for slices of their fathers' fortune; and it would not, I think, improve society in England to fill it with such a class of persons. I am, however, no politician, and speak diffidently on a question of such moment.

At the chateau, a German gentleman had been invited to meet us, and to remain for some days, as he had the reputation of speaking English fluently. When this worthy man, however, was placed next one of our party at dinner, not a word could he muster in our language; and he appeared to discover for the first time that reading and speaking a foreign tongue are two separate things. He, however, conversed fluently in French; and being a very well informed man, we considered him a great addition to our little society. He bore the jokes passed upon his failure of English with much good humour. The perfect harmony which prevailed in this family was delightful to witness. The venerable marquis was considered by the children as common property during the hour they remained in the drawing-room after dinner. One beautiful urchin climbed his knee; a little girl seated herself on the other; one pulled his hair; another mounted on his back: in fact, he resembled Gulliver when the Lilliputians covered him all over. The parents were likewise besieged; but the instant the time for going to bed arrived, there was no hankering, no shuffling, to gain half an hour. Strict obedience was demanded, and, I must say, cheerfully paid. The Comtesse de Beaulieu's two eldest daughters played the piano remarkably well. The second, who is only eight years old, is quite a musical genius. Both conduct themselves like women. They asked us such intelligent questions relative to our country, which they are most anxious to see, that it was a pleasure to answer them. They both speak and write our language correctly. The young vicomtesse has two lovely little boys who were beginning to lisp English; and from what I saw and heard here and elsewhere, I should imagine the time is not far distant when every one among the higher classes in France will be able to speak English as well as ourselves. The constant intercourse with England and America is forcing on this result.

I am now brought to the conclusion of my visit. The day of our departure from this charming mansion arrived, and we were obliged to bid adieu to our friends, whom we quitted with much regret, mingled with gratitude, for the very kind and hospitable manner in which we had been treated during our stay in the chateau.

'THE TRADE.'

SECOND ARTICLE.

BOOKSELLING AFTER THE INVENTION OF PRINTING.

Some time between the years 1430 and 1445, there lived in Mayence a rich goldsmith, whose name was John Fust or Faust, the first man who sold a printed book. His name has always been associated with that of Guttenberg and Schoeffer as one of the *inventors* of printing; but, as is reasonably to be inferred, erroneously; for in all the evidence with which the annals of typography supply us, he appears as the capitalist by whose pecuniary advances Guttenberg was able to bring his art into practical operation. Having vainly endeavoured to produce good print in Strasburg, after expending a fortune, Guttenberg returned to his native town, Mayence, and opened his mind to Faust. The goldsmith—manifestly a shrewd man of business—saw, from the progress his fellow-citizen had made in his new method of producing books, that the thing was likely to turn out a good speculation, and warmly embarked in it. A partnership was speedily entered into, and in 1445 a printing-press was set up in Mayence, for taking impressions from the wooden blocks with which Guttenberg commenced his art. The goldsmith and his associate worked in secret, and for some time without success; till Peter Schoeffer, an illuminator of manuscripts, and a confidential person in their employ, hit upon the expedient of making moveable metal types by means of punches and matrices. Faust was so delighted with Schoeffer for his ingenuity, that he not only took him into partnership, but gave him his daughter in marriage. This happened in 1452. Much patience and capital were expended even after this advance in the art made by Peter Schoeffer. The first book they tried the new system on was the Latin bible, and before twelve sheets of it had been printed, Guttenberg and Faust had expended upwards of 4000 florins. Still they persevered, and after three years of laborious exertion, the bible was completed.* A good number of this—the first of all first editions—having been struck off ready for the market, the next thing was to devise means for disposing of them, and it was determined that Faust should travel with copies, *calling them manuscripts.* 'It is certain,' says Lambinet, 'that Faust, Schoeffer, and their partners, sold or exchanged in Germany, Italy, France, and the most celebrated universities, the books

* This bible—the first perfect printed book which ever was issued—was a folio, in two volumes, consisting of 637 leaves, printed in large Gothic or German characters. It has no date, and is known by bibliopolists as the 'Mazarine bible,' a copy of it having been discovered, long after it was printed, in the library of Cardinal Mazarine, in the *College des Quartre Nations.* Several other copies have since turned up. It is executed with wonderful accuracy and neatness, considering it was the first specimen of the press.

which they had printed.'* This was a matter of very great difficulty and delicacy. The process by which the books were produced was a secret, which every person whom Guttenberg or Faust took into their employ was bound by oath not to divulge; to say that the bibles were produced otherwise than by the usual plan, would have partly divulged the secret, and it was for that reason that the whole of their work was executed in exact imitation of writing. The bible was printed on parchment, the capital letters illuminated with blue, purple, and gold, after the manner of ancient manuscripts, and they were sold as such at manuscript price—namely, sixty crowns.

About the year 1463, Faust set out on a bookselling expedition through Italy, Germany, and finally to Paris, with a stock in trade, consisting chiefly of bibles and psalters. In each place there is every reason to believe he not only busied himself in selling his bibles and psalters, but organised agencies for the sale of his wares in his own absence. Having disposed of as many of his folios as he could to the Parisians at sixty crowns, he — unwisely perhaps — reduced their price, first to forty, and then to twenty crowns. This naturally excited the apprehension and the ire of the *libraires* and scribes, of whom Paris was at that period the head quarters, there being no fewer than six thousand persons who subsisted by copying and illuminating manuscripts. It was not in nature that this large and important body—who held their privileges under the university—should sit tamely by and see a man selling for twenty crowns what they got from sixty to a hundred for. The rapidity with which Faust produced his pseudo-manuscripts, so as to supply the constant demands which his low charges produced on his stock, gave rise to a suspicion that he dealt with the Evil One. This suspicion was strengthened when the transcribers—who were principally monks—set about comparing the various copies of Faust's bibles. They found a degree of resemblance in each of the books—even to the minutest dot—which they concluded could only have been produced by supernatural means. The enmity of the scribes against Faust as an underselling bookseller now threatened to become a religious persecution. The fraud once discovered, however, Faust's case was taken up by the civil power, and he was obliged to fly from Paris, to escape the officers of justice. He returned to Mayence, but found no rest there; wherever he had sold his books, he had of course practised deception, and the agents of justice were equally clamorous for him in his native town. He withdrew to Strasburg.

In the meanwhile, Mayence was taken by storm by Adolphus of Nassau. By this event Faust and Schoeffer's journeymen were dispersed, and deeming themselves absolved from their oath of secrecy, they carried the invention into various parts of Europe, many of them setting up presses of their own. Then, and not till then, Faust made a merit of necessity, and wrote and circulated a work in which he described the whole process by which his books were executed. That there should be no further doubt or ambiguity as to whether the productions of himself and partners were manuscripts or print, he placed at the end of his little book the following colophon or inscription:—'This present work, with all its embellishments, was done, not with the pen and ink, but by a newly invented art of casting letters, printing, &c. by me, John Faust, and my son-in-law, Peter Schoeffer, in the famous city of Mentz upon the Rhine.' In this, as in every other instance, honesty proved to be the best policy; for now that Faust had cleared up the mystery, he was no longer pursued as an impostor; and ultimately we find him in 1466 in Paris, making arrangements for establishing a permanent agency for the sale of the productions of his own and his son-in-law's press. This, as we shall presently see, he effected. In the midst of his labours, however, death overtook him. In that year the plague raged in the French capital, and John Faust fell a victim to it, far away from his home and his friends.

Such is a bare outline of the career of one of the parents of printing, and the sole father of modern bookselling. John Faust (otherwise John *Hand*) was the very reverse of such a necromancer and personal friend of the Evil One as tradition and error have succeeded in picturing him. The truth is, he is often confounded with Jean-Frederic Faust, a charlatan and almanac-maker, who lived about a century after the goldsmith's death, and upon whose history Goëthe, the German poet, constructed his celebrated play. Nothing could be more opposite than the characters of the two men: the one a plodding, yet withal liberal and far-sighted tradesman; the other a quack, but one, we may mention, not quite unconnected with the mysteries of the book-trade. To insure his almanacs a large sale, he advertised them as having been annually dictated to him by Beelzebub. The confounding of the two men took its rise most likely from the cunning of the monks, after the Reformation; of which, there is no question, the diffusion of the bible, by means of the press, was the primary cause. They therefore owed John Faust no good-will for the part he unwittingly took in destroying their system, and tried to defame his memory by mixing up his life with that of a mountebank.

The venerable goldsmith, printer, and bookseller, did not depart this life till he had placed the Paris agency on a secure footing. The name of the agent he employed was Herman de Statten, and the agency was carried on at the house of one John Guymier, as we learn from a curious document found in a copy of Faust and Schoeffer's edition of the Latin bible. It is a deed of sale of the book to Tourneville, bishop of Angiers, and runs thus:—'I, Herman, a German, workman of the honest and discreet John Guymier, sworn bookseller of the university of Paris, acknowledge to have sold to the illustrious and learned master William, of Tourneville, archbishop and canon of Angiers, my most respectable lord and master, a bible, printed at Mentz (Mayence) upon vellum, in two volumes, for the price and sum of forty crowns, which I have absolutely received, which also I ratify by these presents, promising to abide by the same, and guaranteeing my lord, purchaser of the said bible, against any one who would dispossess him. In ratification of which I have hereunto affixed my seal, this 5th day of the month of April, in the year of our Lord M.CCCCLXX. Herman.'* By this we perceive that since they first came into Paris, the printed bibles were elevated in price.

It happened, unfortunately, that Herman of Statten failed to obtain any legal instrument of naturalisation in France; and when he died—which he did a few years after his master Faust—his effects were confiscated as the property of a foreigner. The books intrusted to him by Schoeffer, and amounting in value to 1100 francs, were included in the confiscation. Schoeffer, however, obtained restitution through the liberality of Louis XI. It is a striking illustration of the value and scarcity of money at that period, that the king of France found it inconvenient to pay the sum—equal only to L.45, 6s. 8d.—at once; but did so in two yearly instalments!

The distribution of Faust, Schoeffer, and Company's workmen at the siege of Mayence in 1462, began by this time (1470) to operate throughout Europe, by supplying printers to various continental cities. At this early time most printers sold their own books; and if we state the different periods at which printing was introduced into various countries, we shall show also when books of print began to be sold in each place. The first introduction of this invention into Italy was at Subbiaco, in 1465; into Paris, in 1469; into England (Westminster), in 1474; into Spain (Barcelona), in 1475; into Abyssinia, in 1521; into Mexico, in 1550; into the East Indies (Goa), in 1577; into Peru (Lima), in 1586;

* '*Recherches sur l'Origine de l'Imprimerie*'—(Researches on the Origin of Printing).

* Dr Dibdin's Bibliotheca Spenceria, vol. i. page 16, note.

into North America (Cambridge, Boston, and Philadelphia), in 1640. One of the most active of the German printers and booksellers, between 1473 and 1513, was Ant. Kober, at Nuremberg, who had 24 presses, and nearly 100 workmen in his employ, and kept open shops at Frankfort, Leipsic, Amsterdam, and Venice, all conducted with the greatest regularity and order. He had on sale not only works of his own publication, but also works of other publishers. At Ulm and Basle there were likewise several booksellers carrying on an extensive trade. The many pilgrimages (Wallfahrten) to holy places in the interior of Germany—which were then as much frequented as the sacred shrines in India, and are so still in some Roman Catholic countries—offered them good opportunities for disposing of their books, particularly of those having a religious tendency, which were printed on cheap linen-paper, instead of the expensive parchment formerly in use.

Wherever we turn, we shall find that, once introduced into a country, the press was kept in extraordinary activity, and books were spread in all directions. There were in England, from the time of Caxton to 1600, no fewer than three hundred and fifty printers. Ames and Herbert have recorded the titles of ten thousand different works printed here in the same interval; the yearly average number of distinct works issued and sold in the hundred and thirty years was seventy-five. The number of copies of each was, however, in all probability small, for the early booksellers were cautious. Even Grafton only printed 500 copies of his complete edition of the Scriptures (that of 1540); and yet so great was the demand for the English bible, that there are still extant copies of 326 editions of it which were printed between 1526 and 1600.

In Italy the works of the old classic Roman authors were rapidly printed, when means for doing so were introduced. In Switzerland, especially at Geneva and Basle, a great number of books, chiefly of a religious character, were printed and sold immediately after presses were set up. Indeed the trading talent of the Swiss manifested itself in the beginning of the sixteenth century very prominently in reference to books, for they supplied booksellers even to Germany — to which we must now return.

In the dawn of literary commerce, wholesale trade, in whatever article, was chiefly conducted at fairs, which took place once, twice, or thrice a-year. To these great meetings manufacturers and agriculturists brought such produce as was not of a perishable character, and which was purchased by retailers, who either came from different parts of the country, or employed local agents to purchase on their account. Amongst other manufacturers, the printers brought their goods, which were bought by retailers, and distributed by them throughout the country. At first the greatest quantity of booksellers' stalls was assembled at the Frankfort fairs, where multitudes of strangers and merchants met. Ant. Kober of Nuremberg, Ch. Plantin of Antwerp, and Stephanus (Etienne) of Paris, are recorded as booksellers visiting the Frankfort fair as early as the year 1473. From this period Frankfort gradually became the great book-mart. In 1526 Christopher Froschauer, from Basle, wrote to his principal, Ulrich Zwingli, informing him of the rapid and profitable sale of his books at Frankfort, to persons who had sent for them from all parts. In 1549 Operin of Basle, publisher of the classics, visited Frankfort, and made a profitable speculation. At this period appeared Luther, the great champion of the Protestant world, protesting loudly and openly, both in speech and in writing, against the many abuses that had crept into the church of Rome; and the great cause of the Reformation, while it derived great assistance from the printing-press, repaid this benefit by contributing largely to its development and extension. Saxony, with its enlightened universities (Wittenberg and Leipsic), now became the seat and central point of free theological discussion and investigation, and the booksellers soon found it worth their while to visit also the Leipsic fair. Besides, the literary intercourse in that country was free and unfettered, whilst at Frankfort it had to contend, in later years, with several difficulties, arising from the peculiar situation of a smaller state, and the restrictions and vexations of an Imperial Board of Control (Kaiserliche Bücher Commission) established by the German emperor, through the influence of the Catholic clergy. Archbishop Berthold of Mayence had previously (in 1486) established a similar censorship in his dominions. The chief object of that board was to watch and visit the book-shops—which, in Frankfort, were all situated in one street, still called the Buchgasse—seizing forbidden books, claiming the seven privilege copies ordered by law to be presented to the universities, and, in fact, exercising the power of a most troublesome police. Against this the booksellers often remonstrated, but without success.* At length the principal part of the book-trade withdrew to Leipsic, where general fairs were held thrice every year, and where—next to Frankfort—the greatest number of books was sold.

The earliest accurate information obtained respecting the sale of books at Leipsic fair refers to 1545, when we find the printers Steiger and Boskopf, both of Nuremberg, repairing thither with their 'wares.' A few years later, the fame of this market as a place of sale for books spread over the rest of the continent, and in 1556 it was visited by the Paris bookseller Clement, and in 1560 by Pietro Valgrisi from Venice. From the accidental mention of these visits and names in the annals of the Leipsic fair, we may infer that booksellers from other parts of the world also frequented it habitually, although no record of their presence has been made. The different languages which they spoke had little effect upon the sale of their books, the greater part of which, wherever printed, was in Latin. In 1589, the number of *new* works brought to Leipsic was 362, of which 246, or 68 per cent., were in the Latin language. The literary tastes of that time may be guessed from the fact, that of the whole number of these literary novelties, 200 were on theological subjects, 48 on law and jurisprudence, and 45 on philosophy and philology.

The trade in books carried on in Leipsic increased so rapidly, that it banished traffic in other articles from the fair. No fewer than fourteen printers and booksellers had, by 1616, taken up their residence in the city. The names of these individuals have become dear to the modern bibliomaniac, from the rarity of the works bearing their respective imprints.† These 'publishers' (for by this period the wholesale bookseller was distinguished from the retailer by that expression) brought to the Easter fair of 1616 no less than 153 new works, the productions of their own presses. Of other publishers in various parts of Germany, eight resided at Frankfort-on-the-Maine, seven belonged to Nuremberg, four to Jena, three to Ulm, and the same number to Hamburg; Wittenberg, Strasburg,‡ Gotha, Cologne, Breslau, had each two, and Lübeck, Goslar, Heidelberg, Rostock, and Luneburg, one.

The Easter fair held at Leipsic was now exclusively devoted to books. The booksellers had already organised a system, by which they were enabled to print a catalogue of every new work that was to be sold at the fair, so that purchasers had no difficulty in making their selection; and Leipsic Eastor fair became the great book-mart for the whole continent.

Having brought our notices of 'the trade' in Germany down to that great era in its existence, the establishment of the Leipsic book-fair, and in England to the unhappy time when our country was torn by civil war, and the book, with all other trades, was in a struggling and depressed condition, we shall, in succeed-

* Quarterly Journal of the Statistical Society, vol. ii. page 164.

† The chief amongst them were—James Apel, Joh: Boerner, Elias Rehfeld, Joh: Ryering, Christ: Ellinger, Henning Grosse and his father, Abr: Lamberg, Caspar Kloseman, Bartholomew Voigt, and John Perfect.

‡ Strasburg and all Alsace belonged at that time to Germany.

ing articles, offer some interesting facts concerning the modern system of bookselling, as practised in various countries where any very considerable literary commerce is carried on.

THE LOST NEW-YEAR'S GIFT.

BY FRANCES BROWNE.

It was the last day of the year—the last dress of Lady Fitzalbert's costly mourning had just been finished, and the working girls of one of the largest millinery establishments in London were dismissed to seek their distant homes at three o'clock on a December morning. The frost was clear and keen, and the wind, which swept through the now silent and deserted streets, sent a chill to the hearts of that worn-out company, as on they passed by many a noble mansion, and many an ample warehouse. None spoke, for they had talked themselves out in the workroom; none looked up, though the London sky was for once without a cloud, and the stars were shining there as they shone when London was a forest. But heart, and brain, and eye had been exhausted by two days of continued labour, and they thought of nothing but hurrying home to sleep. One after another parted from the group with a murmured good night, as they reached their respective dwellings, till at last none was left but Lucy Lever, whose home happened to be the most distant of all.

Lucy was a young and beautiful girl of eighteen, whose bright blue eyes, golden hair, and fair transparent complexion, might have graced a prouder station. She was the daughter of a poor country tradesman, who had some years before removed to London with his family, in hopes of bettering their fortunes, but died soon after of one of those fatal epidemics which so often visit the poorer habitations of our large towns. The mother had struggled on, through poverty and toil, to have her eldest girl instructed in needlework, and to maintain two younger daughters; but a severe attack of rheumatism, which at length became chronic, had totally unfitted her for her laborious employment as a washerwoman, and the whole burthen of the family support fell upon Lucy, whose small earnings were barely sufficient to keep them from absolute want.

They had one friend in London, the sister of Lucy's mother, who was married to a small shopkeeper, accounted rich among his class; but, like too many of the rich in every class, possessed of a griping and covetous disposition. They had no family, and the man's affections turned so much on saving, that it was only by stealth his wife could afford any little assistance to the pinched and poverty-stricken household of her sister. This, however, she did at times, particularly to Lucy; for the childless woman was much attached to her beautiful niece, and had lately given her the present of a crown to buy what she liked best as a New-Year's gift.

Lucy had not seen so much money to call her own for many a day, as the pressing wants of the family required every penny as soon as it was earned. The crown was therefore carried home, and shown in triumph to her mother, who agreed it would be very useful, but advised Lucy to take it in her pocket to the workroom, that the girls might see she could have money about her as well as other people. She had done so; and now, cold and weary as she was, the young girl could not help taking out her prize to look at it, and thinking how much it would buy, to beguile the way. Ah! blessed power in the heart of youth, to draw streams of joy and comfort from the first mossy rock it can find in the desert of life! Time may have bright things in store for those who outlive the early darkness of their destiny, but never can bring back the dews of that clouded morning, or the greenness of those blighted springs.

Lucy Lever was but a poor dressmaker's girl; yet she found more pleasure in contemplating that crown than many a monarch can gain from his, as she thought how, after purchasing a cheap shawl for her mother, and pinafores a-piece to the little girls, something might be saved to buy a watch-ribbon, or peradventure a pocket-handkerchief, for William Seymour, a young man of her own station, who had given her a pair of gloves last New-Year's day. They had been long acquainted, and report said there was a promise between them; but William had a mother and little sisters to support as well as Lucy, and marriage could not be thought of till better days.

Lucy paused, and put up her crown, for she had now reached the narrow, close, and steep staircase which led to their single room. She knew her mother would be waiting for her, and hastily mounted the steps, but started as the light of an opposite street lamp, which shone into the narrow entrance, fell full on the face and figure of a woman, who rose at the moment from her very feet. She was young as Lucy herself, but much taller, and strikingly handsome, though her face was ghastly pale; and there was in the large dark eyes an expression of great inward suffering; but it seemed past. Lucy was much struck with her appearance, and her wretched clothing for such a night. It consisted of nothing but a soiled muslin cap, an old worn-out calico gown, and shoes for which the lowest pawnbroker would not give a penny.

'Why do you stand looking at me, girl?' demanded the stranger in a low and husky voice, but with a manner commanding and stern. 'Have you never seen a woman in poverty before? But perhaps,' she added in a milder tone, 'you also wish for a seat on the steps?'

'Oh no,' said Lucy; 'I am going home.'

'You have a home, then,' rejoined the woman quickly; 'and so had I once, but never will again.'

'Yes,' said Lucy, alarmed at what she considered symptoms of insanity. 'We live here, and I am a dressmaker's girl.'

'I was a merchant's daughter,' said the woman. 'I had a father and mother, ay, and sisters too.'

'And why are you so poor and lonely now?' said Lucy, who, in spite of her weariness, felt interested in the desolate condition and singular conversation of the stranger.

'I have fallen from my first estate, girl. It is a common story. I loved and trusted, and was betrayed, and now all is past. I have lost one place in life, and have sought for another in vain. But two choices still remain to me, and I am sitting here to deliberate which I shall take.'

'And what are they?' earnestly inquired Lucy.

'The Thames or the streets, girl,' said the woman sullenly, as she once more took her seat on the cold and frosty stones.

Lucy's heart grew sick within her. 'Oh, don't think of the like,' she said. 'Remember the precepts you must have been taught in better days. Would you destroy yourself both in this world and the next?'

'There is no other choice, girl. I'm starving. For the last week I have sought employment in vain. I have pledged every article on which I could raise anything; and my long black hair, that was braided for many a ball, I have cut it off and sold it for bread. Oh, well may the miser value money,' continued the stranger with energy; 'for half the price of one of the handkerchiefs I used to have would now save me from destruction.'

Lucy stood still, for she could not go. She feared what her mother would say if she ventured to ask the stranger in under such circumstances; but she could not leave the desolate woman there.

'Girl,' said the stranger, after a minute's pause, 'you are the first that has cast a friendly look on me; and will you now, for the sake of charity, if you have it, lend me a few shillings, or one, even one—for one would save me?

Lucy hesitated. She knew that the dressmaker owed her one-and-sixpence, which she could not get that night, because her mistress had no change. She felt her aunt's New-Year's gift in her pocket; but how could she part with it? Oh, if it were morning, for it would be impossible to get change at that hour; but where would the woman be in the morning?

'Lend it to me if you can,' continued the stranger; for Lucy's hand was already in her pocket. 'I will pay you, if ever it is in my power, a thousandfold.'

Lucy thought of her mother and her little sisters, and then of her aunt, and what she might say; but the woman's dark imploring eye was upon her, and, without another word, she took out the treasured coin, dropped it into her lap, and darted up the steps like one pursued by an enemy. Reader, in the days of the old world's faith, when charity was said to be the key of heaven, that single act might have purchased a passport through many sins, and secured the right of entrance for ever. But Lucy had no such thoughts. When she cast her bread upon those troubled waters, it was with no expectation of finding it again, either in time or eternity. She gave freely from her own heart's impulse, and fled for fear of thanks. When Lucy reached her mother's door she found it closed, but not fastened, and entered without noise. Her two little sisters slept on their low bed in the corner; but they moaned and trembled at times through their sleep, for the cold was too great for their scanty covering. The mother sat still by the hearth, where now only a few embers were flickering. Before her was a table, with a turned-down candle, and some humble preparation for Lucy's supper; but, worn out with watching, the poor woman had dropped the little frock she had been mending, leant her head upon the table, and had fallen fast asleep.

'Oh, mother dear, it's late,' said Lucy, gently waking her.

'It is, child; but why did you stay so long? I thought you would never come. But there's some coal here still, and I'll get something warm for you in a minute.'

'Oh, never mind, mother. I'm very sleepy, and will go to bed. But you know,' continued Lucy, 'Lady Fitzalbert wanted her mourning to appear in to-morrow; and as she didn't know which of the dresses she should choose to wear, we had to finish them all.'

'Then, if I were a great lady, I would pay poor girls something over for a hurry.'

'Ay, mother, but there's many a thing great ladies ought to do that they wont,' said Lucy, as she laid aside the last of her garments; and in a few minutes more the over-wrought girl and her mother were both fast asleep.

'It is well you have not to go early to work to-day, Lucy,' said her mother, as the family assembled round their humble breakfast-table at a rather advanced hour in the morning. 'But we have very little bread,' continued she. 'Did you get the one-and-sixpence, dear, you were speaking of?'

'No, mother,' said Lucy; 'Mrs Simson had no change last night.'

'If you would change that crown your aunt gave you, we might take the price of a loaf out of it and make it up again,' said her mother.

'Oh yes, Lucy,' cried the two little girls, speaking together, 'and tell us what you will buy with it, for to-morrow's the day, you know.'

This was a great trial to Lucy. She knew not what to say; for her mother was looking to her for the price of a loaf, and she feared to tell her what had been done with the crown. 'I'll go myself, mother,' said she, taking down her well-worn cloak and bonnet. 'Eat you and the children what is in the house till I come back; it wont be long; and be sure I'll not come without a loaf.'

Lucy was down the stairs before her mother could reply, and lost no time in hastening to the dressmaker's, from whom she hoped to obtain at least as much as would supply the present necessity.

'You're just come in time,' said Miss Lacy the forewoman, in answer to Lucy's good morning; 'for we have got a very large order, and I was about to send for you.'

'Thank you, ma'am,' said Lucy (who, as may have been observed, was one of the living-out girls, as those are called who take their meals at home); thank you, ma'am; but I have not got any breakfast yet.'

'No breakfast yet,' said Miss Lacy, who thought herself privileged to make what remarks she pleased on inferiors. 'Bless me, what an idle set you must have at home.'

'My mother's neither idle nor lazy, said Lucy, while her cheek crimsoned. The last word, inadvertently used by her, was particularly obnoxious to the forewoman, because a thoughtless young lady, whose dress was not finished in time, once, in the hearing of the girls, applied it to her instead of her own name, which in sound it much resembled.

'No lady cares about you or your mother, miss,' said the queen of the workroom, while her eye flashed fire; 'but since you are clever enough to be pert this morning, what is your business here?'

Lucy was young, and though a dressmaker's girl, her spirit was still unbroken; and not knowing how she had offended Miss Lacy, she could not help feeling angry at what she considered unprovoked insolence. She therefore answered rather proudly that she did not come to quarrel with Miss Lacy, but to inquire if it were convenient for Mrs Simson to give her the trifle she had earned, adding that she would not trouble her but to supply the necessities of the family. The latter part of her speech was unheard by any but the girls in the workroom, for Miss Lacy had flounced out in a great passion, but returning in a few minutes, she gave Lucy the money, saying, 'There's all Mrs Simson owes you, and you need not come here again, for she does not like impertinent people.'

Poor Lucy felt that any remonstrance would be in vain. Though insulted, and probably misrepresented to her employer, she had no redress, and therefore taking the paltry recompense of many a weary hour, which was now the only dependence of the family, she went forth to traverse the crowded streets of London in search of employment. Her heart would indeed have found relief in pouring out its painful feelings to her mother; but fearing the old woman's thoughts might again revert to the crown, she determined, if possible, not to go home without at least the prospect of another situation. The promised loaf, and all that remained of the money, were accordingly sent home by an acquaintance who was going that way, and Lucy requested her to tell her mother she had something to do, and would not get home till the evening.

The winter day wore on; street after street was traversed, milliner after milliner applied to, but all without success. One had as many girls as she could employ, another had all her work done by apprentices, and a third never employed any girl whose character she did not know. Many a question of low curiosity, many an insulting look and censorious remark, were borne by that young searcher 'for leave to toil,' till at length she discovered an establishment where her services were acceptable; but they did only inferior work, and allowed scarcely half the usual remuneration. 'I will come if I can do no better,' said Lucy on hearing the terms.

'Oh do,' answered her proposed mistress, a rather coarse and plain-spoken woman; 'people who can do no better just answer us; and while there are so many depending on the needle, we are always sure to have plenty of them; but remember you must come to-morrow.'

Lucy promised she would; and, through the fast closing night, and a heavy shower of snow, worn out and dispirited she returned home.

'Oh Lucy, child, you are frozen,' cried her mother; 'but did you hear the news?'

'No, mother; what is it?'

'Why, about the Seymours. William was here today himself, and told us all. Their rich old aunt in Plymouth is dead, and has left them her fine shop and furnished house, and I can't tell you how much money in the bank; besides, they have got ten pounds—whole ten pounds, Lucy, to pay their expenses, and take them down decently.'

'It's a great deal of money,' said Lucy; 'but is it long since William was here?'

'Oh no, just an hour ago; and he inquired for you, and said he would call again to-morrow, and bring you a New-Year's gift,' said Sarah, the eldest of the children. 'But have you laid out the crown yet? Ah, Lucy, tell us what did you buy?' Lucy was spared the trouble of answering by her mother's inquiring—'Where have you been, child, all day; for Mary Jenking told me that she heard you dismissed from Mrs Simson's.' Bad news travels fast, and Lucy was now obliged to explain to her mother the transactions of the day, and also the situation she had at last obtained. The mother listened with that silent patience which many trials had taught her; but when Lucy mentioned the miserable payment, the natural pride of the old woman rose. 'You wont work for that, Lucy,' cried she; 'indeed you wont, and you such a capital needlewoman: they ought to give you something more than a common girl.'

'Mother, they do only common work, and would give no more to any one.'

'We'll wait for a day or two, and look out for a better place. Sure you have your aunt's crown; and if the worst should come, we could live ever so long on that.'

'I lost it, mother; I lost it,' said Lucy; but the words nearly stuck in her throat; yet the old woman caught the sound, and springing from her seat with an agility which only the excitement of the moment could give her, she cried, 'Lost, Lucy; did you say you lost your aunt's crown—the whole crown, Lucy? Where did you lose it? Tell me, tell me fast, and I'll ask everybody; perhaps Thomas the postman might see it, for he finds everything.'

Small things are great to the poor, and Lucy's mother was hurrying to the door to raise a general alarm about the lost crown among her neighbours, who were known to be generally honest and industrious people, when Lucy stopped her. It was the first deceit she had ever practised, and sore were the stings within, between her unwillingness to deceive her mother and her fear to tell her the truth. Yet it was not a storm of angry reproaches which she dreaded; it was the reproving look of that sad patient face—it was the sight of her little sisters pinched and pining from day to day on her now reduced earnings, whilst they knew that she had given away what might have purchased so many comforts for them all. Her aunt, too, kind as she was, was a woman of most violent temper, and should the story come to her ears, it might have bad consequences for the family. These terrors prevailed, and grasping the old woman's skirt, she cried, 'Stay, mother, stay; the money is lost, and will never be found; there is no use in making a noise about it.'

'You're not sure of that, child; some of the neighbours might find it. Do let me go and tell them.'

'Oh no, mother; I didn't lose it in the neighbourhood.'

'And where, then, child? Do you know the place?'

'I do not, mother; I do not,' said Lucy, drawing her hand across her brow, which now ached and burned between the fatigues of the day and the suffering of the moment; 'but don't mention it to my aunt, and we will try to live without it.' But the mother and little sisters were not so easily satisfied. Question followed question regarding the time, the place, and the manner of her loss. Many were the schemes suggested for its recovery; many an ill contrived falsehood and clumsy excuse had poor Lucy to make in her endeavours to quiet them, and conceal the real cause of the crown's disappearance. At length the mother agreed that it was best not to mention their loss to her neighbours, lest her sister might hear of it, who, she well knew, could never forgive what she would consider Lucy's carelessness of her present. But the old woman kept it as a subject of secret conversation and wonder for herself and the children; and many a search they had in the streets and corners, in the vain hope of discovering the lost treasure. Next morning, when ladies were receiving gifts, and gentlemen presenting them, when friends were wishing each other happy New-Years, and people preparing for parties, Lucy was preparing to enter on her new employment with the same worn cloak and broken bonnet.

There was a quick tap at the door, and a tall good-looking young man, dressed in an unmistakeably new suit, stepped into the room: it was William Seymour. 'A happy New-Year, Lucy,' said he: 'it is well I came in time.'

'A happier year to you, William, with all your good fortune,' said Lucy, as her pale face brightened up; for Lucy had grown pale and thin of late. 'But sit down, and tell me is it all true?'

'It is indeed, Lucy,' said William; and he repeated what her mother had told her the evening before, adding some hints 'that one could now please one's self, and a man was never settled in life till fairly married. But we must go,' said he, 'by the Plymouth stage, and I only came to bid you farewell. Farewell, darlings;' and William, as he kissed the children, put something into the hand of each.

'A whole sixpence,' cried little Susan, running to her mother.

'And I have got one too,' echoed her sister.

'Oh, William, why do you waste your money with the children?' said Lucy; for the Levers were still a little proud.

But William would not hear that: he shook hands with the mother, hoped her rheumatism would be better when he came back, paused, thrust his hand into his pocket, and seemed as if he would say something more, but got ashamed; and at last asked Lucy if she would see him down stairs. Many a time those same stairs had been their meeting-place. Smile not, reader; for, whether amid mountain heath or city smoke, holy are the spots hallowed by our young affections: the exile revisits them in dreams, the old man's memory wanders back to them through many changes, and, it may be, over many graves.

William and Lucy talked long together, with many a promise of letters, and many a hope for the future. William vowed to come back with the ring as soon as he could get things settled; and then Lucy would never have to work, nor her mother and little sisters want again. 'They'll all live with us, Lucy,' said he. 'But the times are hard now, and perhaps you can't earn much.' The young man drew out some money as he spoke.

'Oh no, William,' said Lucy, whose womanly pride would not allow her to accept any assistance from him; 'we don't want for anything, and I have got a new situation. Besides, you will have need of all you have to go decently to Plymouth, among such great friends as I know you have there.' William felt half-offended; but he reiterated his promise of returning soon, gave Lucy a new handkerchief to wear for his sake, and a seal with 'Forget-me-not' on it, which she promised to use on all her letters. In return, poor Lucy had nothing to present him with but a braid of her own bright hair tied with a morsel of blue ribbon, for constancy, which William promised to keep as long as he lived; and so they parted.

Days passed on, as winter days are wont to pass in London, with frost, and fog, and sleet, and rain, and sometimes snow by way of variety. The festivities of the season went on, the fashions came and went, and Lucy Lever toiled on, day after day, and often night after night, for a pittance which scarcely supplied the little family with the necessaries of life. Often did she deprive herself of bread that they might have enough; often did she practise those stratagems which necessity teaches the poor, to make the shortest means go the longest way: but all her exertions would fail at times; and then, like a dagger to Lucy's heart, came her poor mother's repinings for that lost crown. She did not speak of it before Lucy, for she knew the subject was painful; but often, when most pressed by want, she would talk in her sleep like one who searched for something she could not find, and exclaim, 'Oh, if I could come upon poor Lucy's crown.' As the season advanced, coal grew dearer, the clothes of the family were wearing out, and there was no fund to replace them. Their aunt could now afford them no assistance, as her husband had discovered some transactions of the kind, and kept a stricter eye upon her than ever.

But amid all these trials, Lucy had still one source of comfort in the letters of William. Pleasant it was to hear the postman's knock when she chanced to be at home, pleasant to hear her mother's announcement, when she returned late from her weary work, 'Lucy, there is a letter for you to-day.' At first these letters came frequently and regularly, full of true love and vows of unchanging constancy; but by degrees they became less frequent, and spoke more of his own wealth and grandeur, and the fine acquaintances he had found in Plymouth.

Alas! the men of the earth are not the men of our early imaginations. But spring came at last, and London sent forth its thousands to meet her by the broad rivers and the heathy hills, and the tokens of her far-off reign came like the breath of a distant blessing to the crowded homes of the city poor. The wants of winter were no longer felt; the children went out to play in the retired streets and lanes, and complained no more of their scanty clothing: Lucy had longer days to work, and the walk to her place of labour was more pleasant, for the cold mornings and stormy nights were gone; but to her sleep there came dreams of the green sunny slope where their old cottage stood, and strange yearnings came over her at times to see once more the violet bed at the foot of the green old mossy tree where she had played in childhood; but it was far away in the country, and Lucy must sew for bread. Summer came with its dewy mornings, its glorious days and long lovely twilights, rich with the breath of roses from greenwood dingle and cottage wall; autumn with its wealth of corn, its gorgeous woods, and the pride of its laden orchards; but the seasons brought no change to Lucy, save that her cheek had grown paler, and her step less light. William's letters had grown fewer and colder too, and at length they ceased altogether. Winter returned, and with it came the news that he had married a rich shopkeeper's daughter with good connexions, red hair, five hundred pounds, and a piano.

Lucy heard it and said nothing; but her acquaintances observed that from that time she grew more silent and thoughtful, and never wore a handsome handkerchief which they had always remarked on her neck before. 'Don't go to work to-day, Lucy,' said her mother on a winter morning whose dim light was scarcely visible through one continuous torrent of sleet and rain. 'Don't go to work to-day; you know we have threepence in the house. Oh, child, you're growing pale and thin, and cough so much at night, it breaks my heart to hear you.'

'It's only a cold, mother, and will soon be over.'

'Ay, Lucy, but you don't laugh and talk as you used to do when things were as bad with us.'

'I'm growing old, mother, and maybe wiser,' said Lucy as she stepped out, for her employer had warned her to come, as there was a great deal of work in haste to be finished; for common people can be in haste as well as ladies.

'Old,' said the mother to herself; 'God help the girl, and she not nineteen yet!'

Oh, it is a weary thing to feel the grayness of life's twilight coming down upon the heart before we have reached its noon; to see the morning of our days pass from us unenjoyed, and know that it can never return. The evening came, but Lucy didn't arrive; the mother sat up, for she could not sleep: but the night wore away; and when the gray light was breaking, her low knock was heard at the door.

'Come to the fire, Lucy, child; you're wet to the skin.'

'Oh no, mother, let me go to bed; I never was so tired; but this will buy something for to-morrow,' said Lucy, as she put a shilling into her mother's hand.

That shilling was the last of this world's coin that Lucy ever earned. All day they kept the house quiet, that she might sleep; and so she did, except when disturbed by a deep hollow cough which came at short intervals. Next morning Lucy talked of going to work, and tried to rise, but could not. Another day passed, another, and another, till a long week rolled away, and still Lucy grew worse. Meantime the funds of the family were completely exhausted, and the few articles left from better days had been sold to raise money sufficient for the rent.

It was another night of December, clear and cold like that on which our story commenced, and almost as far advanced in the season. There was no light in the Levers' room; the fire had died for want of coals; the children had crept together in a corner, for they had no bed now; the mother sat on the floor, with her head leaning on her knees, close by the bed where Lucy lay as usual without complaint or moan. The old woman slept, and talked to herself in her sleep about the lost crown, which still haunted her memory as a golden one might that of a dethroned monarch. 'There it's—there it's,' said she; 'that's poor Lucy's crown; she lost it this time last year.'

'Mother, mother,' said the girl; for she was wide awake, and the cry was loud enough to waken the mother also. 'Mother, dear, I cannot die and deceive you. Forgive me that one falsehood—I did not lose the coin, but gave it to a starving woman I met on the stairs.'

'Oh, the wicked woman, where is she?' cried the mother, starting up in the darkness, as if her vision of regaining the crown had been realised; but at that moment a loud impatient knock came to the door.

'Open the door, mother; that's the knock of the postman.'

The old woman mechanically did so, and the postman indeed presented himself; for Lucy knew his voice as he called loudly, 'Have you no light here? Here is a letter for Miss Lucy Lever, and a shilling on it.'

'A shilling!' said the mother; 'we have no money.'

'Well, there's money enough in it,' said the postman.

'Money!' said the mother. 'Is it God that's sending money to us?'

'What's that, mother,' said Lucy, raising herself by a great effort in her bed.

'It's money!' cried the mother, rushing to her child; 'it's money, and you'll be saved yet!'

'God be praised, mother!' said the girl, falling back, the old woman thought heavily, upon her breast; 'and take it with thankfulness, for it is the payment of my lost New-Year's gift.'

The postman, who was in some degree acquainted with the family, had by this time procured a light, which he gave with the letter to one of the astonished children, saying he would call for the postage some other time. But some minutes after a wild piercing cry startled the neighbourhood. It came from the Levers' room—and those who rushed in to see what was the matter, found the mother still holding Lucy in her arms; but the girl was dead, and an open letter containing a bank bill for ten pounds lying before her on the floor—the relief had come too late.

By whom it was sent was never known, for the letter merely stated that the money came from one who owed it to Lucy. The mother survived her loss as she had done so many trials; but the hand of poverty never again pressed on her or hers. Further supplies were sent from time to time; and in the following season, the passage of the family to America was paid by the same unknown hand. There, it is said, the mother has at last found a grave, and Sarah and Susan have grown up almost as handsome as their lost sister, and expect to be provided for by the lady who has brought them up, a respectable milliner of New York, who is said to have been the daughter of a London merchant, and the same who received Lucy's Lost New-Year's gift.

SCRAWLERS.

There is a class of persons, who, owing to some deficiency in their early education, or an absorbing attention to other pursuits, have unfortunately so far neglected the valuable attainment of a plain and unmistakeable handwriting, as, however great their talents or genius, to deserve the appellation of scrawlers. The mysterious hieroglyphics which they use in expressing their thoughts are a constant source of puzzling vexation: an uncertainty rests upon the minds of the most experienced decipherers of their enigmatical characters, and a probable guess is all that the uninitiated can attain to.

Various and amusing are the peculiarities of handwriting in these people. Some join one word with another along the whole breadth of the paper, so as to resemble a very uneven line. Others ingeniously, with a tortuous pen, make those parts of their letters thin which should be thick, and *vice versa*. Some, of still more original genius, form their letters perpendicularly, or the reverse of the usual angle, their characters resembling music rather than writing. Others are so impatient, that they cannot afford time to finish their words, and this adds very amusingly to the perplexity of the reader, rendering it almost necessary that the writer should append a key to his system of shorthand. Some, as if still more to mystify their epistles, use neither points nor attempt to form sentences, so that the ambiguities afford a pleasing exercise for the reader's patience and ingenuity. Such is a glimpse at the vagaries of this vexatious class of persons.

Great is the trouble and annoyance, and many are the mistakes, which such people cause in social and commercial life. Many a letter is handed about at the post-office, from one clerk to another, in the vain hope of puzzling out the direction, and, after the most sagacious have shrugged up their shoulders in despair, has been consigned to the mouldy repositories of the 'dead-letter office.' Many a postman travels needless miles, worries the inmates of unknowing houses, and brings the servant maids down from their 'two pair,' all in vain, because the direction on his letter is written in such vague characters. Many a friendly epistle is turned over from one member of a family to another, and despairingly dismissed with a 'Well, we can guess what he means;' and the pleasure of receiving a letter from such a correspondent is thus sadly lessened by the difficulty of deciphering it. The meaning of many a business letter is provokingly mistaken, confusion created, and loss sustained, because the order or the directions for executing it were so obscurely written; and many a pleasant appointment irrevocably lost. Nay, so foolishly affected are many people in the style of their own signatures, that these are utterly illegible save by those to whom habit has rendered them familiar. We have known instances where the personal property of travellers was lost simply because no one could be found to decipher the autograph of the owner; and we venture to assert, that for two ordinary individuals who can make out the names of the cashiers and secretaries on our Scottish bank-notes, there will be found twenty to whom the curves and blotches of ink called characters will remain an inextricable mystery.

Of all scrawlers, those are the most annoying who affect bad writing as fashionable, and deem a scrawl one of the indications of a gentleman. Of all silly distinctions, none can be more childish than this, or argue less for the sense of those who affect it. To wear one's coat inside out would be a distinction certainly, but such a distinction as any one of the least sense or sanity would avoid. Whatever is worth doing at all is worth doing well; and to write badly and illegibly, is surely indicative of pitiable incompetence, or blameable carelessness, or, worse than either, a despicable affectation. A laboured schoolboy's squareness of every letter is certainly not desirable; but writing may surely be legible without being puerile, and easy and business-like without appearing as if scrawled with a skewer.

To those who are accustomed to write for the press, a plain handwriting is of great importance, though literary men are often sadly deficient in this respect. We have known instances, indeed, of authors being utterly unable to read parts of their own manuscript, and who have been compelled to erase whole sentences, and substitute something else. Authors whose manuscript is very bad have to pay an additional charge for the extra trouble they give to the printer, besides what they have unavoidably to pay for the many corrections which works printed from such writings almost invariably require. The process of printing, necessarily slow, and always liable to error, is still more retarded, and the chances of error fearfully increased by an author's obscure manuscript. The compositor—the person who arranges the type—is generally too intent upon the mechanical process of picking up the letters, to bestow much pains in deciphering his vexatious 'copy;' and even the sleepless vigilance of the corrector of the press, or 'reader,' as he is termed, may sometimes inadvertently pass over an error where there is so much to puzzle and perplex. When it is remembered how many millions of letters are used in the pages of a very thin book, it is wonderful that even ordinary correctness is attained. When it is considered, also, how important is the transposition of even a single letter, several hundreds of which are used in every page, the difficulty of final correctness, even under the most favourable circumstances, must be apparent, and certainly need not be increased. A most important and ludicrous mistake may be occasioned by the transposition or omission of a single letter. The word 'hops' for 'hopes,' 'tailors for 'sailors,' 'voracity' for 'veracity,' 'cows' for 'vows,' 'cats' for 'oats,' 'tongs' for 'songs,' 'posts' for 'poets,' 'dairies' for 'diaries,' and a thousand others, though they might seem to an ordinary reader sufficiently stupid mistakes, yet might all be produced by the error—omission or transposition of one letter. Surely, where correctness is so desirable, and error so easy, an author cannot well be too careful in preparing his manuscript for the press.

If authors who write illegibly could see their works in an incipient state as they leave the hands of the compositor, they would tremble, and not without reason, for the final correctness of their tropes and metaphors, as they beheld their pathos whimsically transformed into bathos, and their sublimest figures into figures of fun. When such ludicrous errors (to mention only two out of a host we could adduce as having actually happened within our own knowledge) as 'gaiters and garters' for 'gaieties and gravities,' and 'primroses and pears' for '*primores et pares*,' are made, well may the author tremble for the inaccuracy of a work the manuscript of which is obscure. Fewer would be the 'errors of the press' if the manuscript of the author were as unmistakeably plain as manuscript written to be printed ought to be.

But the schoolmaster is abroad, education is being settled upon a more intelligent basis, and the time, we may hope, is fast approaching when the tribe of scrawlers will be extinct, and when no one will be allowed to arrive at maturity without being taught the valuable art of making known his thoughts in characters not only to be understood, but not to be misunderstood. Men will see the absurdity of wholly devoting their time to the attainment of Greek and Latin, while incapable of writing their own language in an understandable manner. In proportion, also, as a healthy common sense prevails, the fashionable affectation of scrawling will pass away, and will no more be esteemed a desirable distinction than an impediment in the speech which should prevent the speaker from being understood.

THE ROMANS IN NORTH BRITAIN.

AN able and highly *readable* volume has just appeared on the transactions of the Romans in Scotland, and the remains they have left behind them in that part of the island.* It has been remarked that the Roman occupation of Britain was of far more consequence than is generally supposed, extending as it did over a tract of time as great as from the reign of Henry V. to the present day. It forms also a peculiarly interesting portion of our history, as it presents an example of a rude nation brought under the influences of civilisation through the efficacy of human passions. The occupation of lowland Scotland by the Romans commenced in the year 80, under Agricola. That energetic people formed roads, camps, and even towns. Few who now live in Mid-Lothian bethink them that Roman citizenship and luxuries once flourished on the hill of Inveresk, or that 'Jove the most excellent and the greatest' had an altar smoking to him at Cramond. Yet the baths and wine-cellars of the former place were found only about sixty years ago, and Jove's Cramond altar now stands in the Advocates' Library. In the year 140, while Antoninus Pius was emperor, the army formed that singular monument of their country's grandeur—a fortified wall across the island, the object of which was to shut out the annoying tribes who dwelt in the Highlands. From this they were, seventy years afterwards, obliged to recede to the Tyne, where a second and similar bulwark was formed; but at a still later period (A. D. 367) the northern wall was re-established by the general Theodosius, and such continued to be the limit of the empire as long as the Romans remained in Britain, which was till about the year 422. In the latter part of the Roman sway, the south of Scotland formed a regular province of the empire, under the name of Valentia.

The little that is known of the acts of the Romans in Scotland, and of the state of the people in that age, is stated by Mr Stuart in a graceful and flowing narrative, in which (upon the supposition that he is a young man) we are inclined to trace the augury of future distinction in literature. The view which he gives of the country, at the time when it was yet a sylvan wilderness, occupied by tribes not much different from those of Missouri and Araucania, is like a chapter in some beautiful romance. The roads and camps are all traced carefully, even unto Ptoroton and Bona (Burgh-head and Loch Ness), and an ample chapter at the end is devoted to the wall of Antoninus. The author modestly acknowledges that his first design was to give only what has been discovered or learned respecting these antiquities since the publication of the works of Horsley, Gordon, and Roy in the last century; but he was ultimately induced to present a view of the whole subject, from a consideration that those works had long been extremely scarce. His volume is thus to be regarded as partly a compilation, and partly a work of original observation: in both characters we esteem it as far above respectability. The scholar has here a satisfactory account of the Roman antiquities of Scotland, illustrated by numerous draughts (in lithography); while the general reader is presented with a work which he may peruse for the sake of its information, without ever feeling it in the least dull.

Taking up the latter part of the work first—the great wall of Antoninus, extending (as our present author thinks) from Carriden near Borrowstowness on the Forth, to West Kilpatrick on the Clyde, and thus measuring about twenty-seven miles, was formed upon the basis of a line of prætenturæ, or military stations, previously erected by Agricola, but subsequently reconstructed by Antonine's general, Lollius Urbicus. Not only is the island here narrowest, but there is a sort of valley stretching across nearly the whole way, the south side of which presented some natural advantages in point of fortification. The work was performed by the soldiers of two legions, the sixth and the twentieth, and is believed to have been executed in a much shorter space of time than might be supposed; probably not more than a year. It 'consisted, in the first place, of an immense fosse or ditch—averaging about forty feet in width by some twenty in depth—which extended over hill and plain, in one unbroken line, from sea to sea. Behind this ditch, on its southern side, and within a few feet of its edge, was raised a rampart of intermingled stone and earth, strengthened by sods of turf; which measured, it is supposed, about twenty feet in height, and twenty-four in thickness at the base. This rampart or *agger* was surmounted by a parapet, behind which ran a level platform, for the accommodation of its defenders. To the southward of the whole was situated the Military Way—a regular causewayed road, about twenty feet wide—which kept by the course of the wall at irregular distances, approaching in some places to within a few yards, and in others receding to a considerable extent. Along the entire line, from West Kilpatrick to Carriden, there were established, it is believed, nineteen principal stations or forts; we cannot be quite certain of the number, because, towards the east end of the wall, the traces of their existence have, for two centuries at least, been either very indistinct or entirely obliterated. Calculating by those whose remains have been plainly perceptible, the mean distance between each may be stated at rather more than two English miles. Along these intervals were placed many smaller *castella*, or watch-towers, of which only some two or three could be observed in the year 1755. While the continuous rampart seems to have been little more than a well-formed earthen mound, it is probable that many, if not all of the stations, were either rivetted with stone, or entirely built of that material. In some places it would even appear that the *vallum* itself had been raised upon a stone foundation—probably in situations where the ground was low and marshy, and where it was necessary to form drains beneath the works, to prevent the accumulation of water on their interior side.'

The stations along the line were of various size and appearance, some being small and slightly fortified, while others were defended by a succession of ramparts and ditches, and seem to have had towns connected with them. These stations, in all instances but one, were within or to the *south* of the wall, thus having the benefit of its protection. In most places the vestiges of the whole work have been obliterated by modern cultivation; but in a few moorland districts, and in the pleasure-grounds of Callander and Bantaskin, it is still possible to trace the ditch, accompanied by a slight mound; of the stations, Kirkintilloch alone has left any remains. In the course, however, of the last century and a half, a great number of stones containing inscriptions and devices, as also stone altars bearing the names of deities and their votaries, have been dug up at various stations: there have also been found remains of tombs, of baths, of granaries, and other buildings, the whole of which, being faithfully delineated and described in this book, bring forcibly before us the *reality* of Roman cohorts posted in Stirling and Dumbartonshires, with all their various ideas in religion and polity so different from our own. Here we see bodies of these soldiers erecting tablets in honour of their purpled Cæsar amidst the wilds of Duntocher and Kilsyth; modestly adding that they had accomplished the construction of so much of the wall. There we find Quintus Pisentius Justus dedicating a similar stone to the Eternal Field Deities, 'his vow being most willingly performed.' At

* Caledonia Romana; a Descriptive Account of the Roman Antiquities of Scotland, &c. Edinburgh: Bell and Bradfute. London: Pickering. 1845. 4to, pp. 304. [The dedication is signed by Robert Stuart.]

a place called Auchindavy, Marcus Cocceius Firmus leaves, huddled into a hole under-ground, four altars which he had himself dedicated—one to Jove, a second to Mars, Minerva, and the Field Deities, another to Diana and Apollo, and the last (*Genio Terræ Britannicæ*) to the genius of the British soil. Shirva, near the same place, exhumes for us the monument which Salmanes raised 'to the shade [*dis manibus*] of Salmanes, who died at the age of fifteen;' a father's tribute, doubtless, to a lost son. Castlecary, in like manner, presents an altar inscribed—'To the God Mercury, the soldiers of the Sixth Legion, the Victorious, the Pious, the Faithful—Natives of Sicily, Italy, and Noricum: their vow being most willingly fulfilled.' Men from the Upper Danube, from the plains of Megara and Agrigentum, as well as from Italy, had come to spend their lives as stipendiaries of Rome amidst these Caledonian deserts; where now, such is the change which fifteen centuries will bring, we see the bustle of a 'station' of the Edinburgh and Glasgow Railway! A votive altar found at Nether Croy is inscribed by the vexillation (or soldiers of the standard) of the sixth legion to the Nymphs or Genii of the woods and streams, the deities most apt to occur to their minds in such a situation. 'The inscription,' says Mr Stuart, 'is well executed, and seems to belong to the second century. The fairy spirits to whom it was dedicated were no doubt supposed to trip, with invisible steps, the thickets around—pleased with the votive offerings of military devotion, and not unmindful of their worshippers amid the dangers of the service. It mattered not where the ancient Roman might be placed, as the thousand guardian deities of his prolific religious system were ever around him. Among the forests of Britain, as in the desert plains of Africa, he addressed himself to the *genii locorum* in perfect confidence of spirit, satisfied that the Immortals were of no particular clime, but alike open to his aspirations in every quarter of the world.' A more curious discovery than any of these took place at Castlecary in 1771; namely, a large hollow in a rock, containing nearly a hundred quarters of wheat, 'quite hard and black, and mixed with numerous pieces of charred wood, as if the whole had been exposed to the action of fire. It was scattered about the ground, and some of it lay exposed for many years: a few particles, indeed, may still be seen about the spot, by turning aside the tufts of grass under which they are concealed. So large a quantity of grain would never have been thus abandoned, unless by the hasty and final departure of those who were alone acquainted with the secret of its existence; hence the common opinion which supposes it to have formed part of the stores of the Roman garrison.'

It is surely matter of more than antiquarian interest—matter that touches some of the deepest springs of our moral nature—thus to find such clear-speaking memorials of a people who passed off the field of existence so many ages ago—voices, as it were, left by the long dead to tell us that they once had living feelings and thoughts like ourselves. And these people, too, the countrymen of Tacitus and of Seneca, dwelt for ages upon the very grounds now daily ploughed by our simple Scottish swains, the whole *system* to which they belonged having vanished into the sepulchres of history for above a thousand years.

It would ill suit, we fear, with our light pages, to go more minutely into Mr Stuart's account of the Roman antiquities; but a short extract from his supposed journey of a stranger into Scotland before the days of the Roman invasion, may not be reckoned superfluous. Trusting to the unpurchased faith of a simple people, the visitor might have leisure, he presumes, to observe the natural productions of the country. 'The oak, the fir, and the graceful birch, would rise by his side, or hang above him from the rocky cliffs; the hazel and matted bramble would obstruct his way as he laboured through the thickets; and, when resting by some sheltered stream, he might, if so disposed, have gathered a variety of the same wild fruits as may yet be found in autumn within the silent coppices of our Highland glens. Wherever, in an open district, any considerable grove appeared, there in all likelihood would he find the rude tent-like habitations of the people, clustered for shelter and safety within the margin of the wood. Around these villages browsed their tame cattle, protected by the vicinity of the owners, whose places of abode were in general strongly fortified; while far away, in the deepest glades of the forest, reposed the wild herds of the island—quick of ear to catch the most distant sound, and to start in flight while the tread of the hunter was yet far off. One prominent feature of the scenery, peculiarly calculated to strike his attention, would be the symmetrical clusters of oak which were held sacred to the rites of religion. These were numerous throughout the country, and wherever found, must have proved objects of much curiosity to the stranger. The profound mystery which ever hung over them, the jealous care which guarded their precincts from his approach, the reverential awe with which the Briton regarded it, as he pointed to the spot where stood the monuments of his faith, all would conspire to throw over the Druid's secluded temple an interest greater perhaps than ever extended to the marble fanes of Rome's time-honoured gods, the "blue-eyed Pallas and the Olympian Jove." Within these groves may also have been situated the houses of the priests—probably the only ones in the land arranged with any pretensions to comfort, in our idea of the term; but, as their owners courted mystery and seclusion, the passing wayfarer could have no opportunity, we may suppose, of becoming either a guest of the priesthood, or at all acquainted with the arcana of their domestic arrangements. Beyond the isthmus of the Forth and Clyde lay the great forest of *Celyddon*, which gave, in the Celtic dialect, its name to the Western Highlands, and which, when altered by the Romans to "Caledonia," became the designation of the whole country situated to the north of the wall of Antoninus. From the district of Athol, in Perthshire, it spread over the mountainous interior as far as the county of Sutherland, descending on the west coast to the peninsula of Cantire, and thence stretching eastward to the banks of Loch Lomond. If the country through which he had already passed had been too bountifully supplied with its "leafy mantle-green," and somewhat difficult to penetrate, here the troubles or dangers of the traveller must have been greatly increased. The respected Camden, indeed, on the faith of more ancient authors, endows the Caledonian forest with so many terrors, that we may believe our tourist to have been brought to a stand upon its verge, as even a Roman nerve might have shrunk from the task of entering that gloomy stronghold of the *horribiles ultimosque Britannos*. Impervious from the thick growth of trees and underwood, it was, we are told, infested with wolves, wild bulls, and boars; and, according to some accounts, the grizzly bear had even been known to revel within its dark recesses. Bleak craggy mountains, and dismal swamps of great extent, may have afforded some variety to the landscape, although they added nothing to its attractions. Within those forbidding wilds, however, a considerable population seems to have existed in early times; and, from the many Druidical remains discovered in that part of the country, it appears evident that its inhabitants were not entirely savages, and not quite such unapproachable monsters as the poet Claudian declares them to have been; for it is well known that, wherever the Druids had power, they introduced many customs which tended to humanise and otherwise improve the character of the people; and however selfish may have been the hidden objects of their implied theocracy, their system of religious rule certainly did much to smooth down the salient angles of original barbarism.

'In a region, however, such as this, the population was doubtless small when compared with the extent of their gloomy possessions. Unlike the tribes of the Lowlands, the inhabitants of the forest did not probably apply themselves in any great degree to the rearing of cattle, but subsisted chiefly on the produce of the chase, or on the attractive, if not most creditable amusement, of plundering their wealthier neighbours. Within their own inaccessible bounds roamed the wild white cattle, a race not yet extinct, and of which a considerable number now find shelter in the noble woods at Hamilton Palace. The red deer and boar were also plentiful in this district, with the wolf, the hare, and many smaller animals which nature threw in his way, to supply the Caledonian of old with food and raiment. Brought up from childhood as a hunter, he became, in a high degree, nimble, expert, and daring—in any situation an enemy of no mean repute, but on his native hills, it may be said, invincible; and, such as it was, his native forest—the stronghold of many tribes—required no fabled terrors to render it the best defence possessed by our primitive ancestors against the oft-recurring encroachments of foreign ambition. Within its recesses were foiled the exertions of the best troops the world could then produce. On one occasion only was it traversed by the Roman legions. At their approach, its spreading oaks were levelled, its morasses drained, its mountain torrents made passable, and the heart of the wilderness was gained; but only to be again abandoned with immense loss—the frequent attacks of the natives, and the extreme hardships to which the soldiery were exposed, in struggling through so difficult a country, having annihilated the greatest part of the invading army.

'Leaving on his left this region—to him another dread retreat of Cimmerian gloom—the lone adventurer, whose course we follow, may be supposed to have proceeded by Strathearn to the Tay, and thence along the eastern sea-coast towards the extremity of the island. Throughout the first part of his progress, the way was probably beset, as usual, with many difficulties; the rich alluvial valley drained by the Earn being then in all likelihood widely covered with woods and thickets: but whenever he approached the sea, beyond what are now the boundaries of Perthshire, the scene would materially change, and the hitherto abundant vegetation give place to a long extent of open moorland country; for such appears to have been the general aspect of that part of Scotland, from the mouth of the Tay as far as the Moray Firth—an extensive track, naturally bleak and sterile, from its exposure to the keen blasts which swept the German Ocean. Wandering by those shores where beat the angry waves which, he might imagine, were rolling on to bury themselves amid the sluggish waters of "Thule," the solitary traveller would at length find himself on the coast of Nairn or Banff, where we shall suppose him to have brought his journeyings to a close. Little more was open to his curiosity in this remote corner of the world. The northern part of the island, Sutherland and Caithness, was, in ancient times, nothing but an immense morass, here and there covered with trees. It was, besides, much infested by wolves; and, take it all in all, it must have been a region of the most forbidden character, from which the wearied stranger might gladly turn away.'

ADVENTURES OF A FOOT-SERGEANT.*

MR T. MORRIS appears to be the son of respectable parents, residing in the very heart of Cockaigne, and near to that redoubtable garrison the Tower of London. He acquired a thirst for military renown at the time of Napoleon's threatened invasion, when the brave shopkeepers of Great Britain flew to arms, and enrolled themselves in various regiments of volunteers in defence of their hearths and liberties. Volunteering, though eminently useful in deterring the enemy, produced many odd associations and ludicrous incidents. A vast majority of the male population above sixteen in years, and five feet two in height, appeared at least once a-week in regimentals. The current talk in every town was that of the mess and barrack-room. Marching, counter-marching, and every species of manœuvring and stratagetic, were discussed from the squire's drawing-room to his stable—from the mayor and corporation in the town-hall to the gossips at the tea-table. Ladies had their drapery measured to them by majors on the staff, and gentlemen were frequently indebted to bombardiers of artillery for the fashion and make of their coats.* Nor was all this military ardour a mere empty and vainglorious ebullition of patriotism. Hundreds died in defence of British liberty; not, it is true, by the sword of an enemy, but from severe colds caught during inclement field-days, when military discipline forbade the use of greatcoats, or even of umbrellas. Despite, however, all such dangers, the enthusiasm was intense while it lasted, and amongst others whom it inspired was Mr T. Morris.

At the earliest possible age—sixteen—and in the year 1812, this aspirant became a volunteer; 'and oh!' he exclaims, 'how proud did I feel when, having gone through my course of drill, I was permitted to join the ranks. Even now, I often think of the delightful sensation I experienced on our forming on the regimental parade-ground, and marching from thence to the Tenter-ground, in Goodman's Fields—at that time a most convenient place for the exercise of troops, and where our evolutions and martial exercises excited the admiration and wonder of crowds of nursery-maids and children, who invariably attended on such occasions. Then, how delightful, on our return home, to parade the streets in our splendid uniform, exhibiting ourselves as the brave defenders of our country, should the Corsican attempt to carry into effect his threatened invasion of England.' But these, after all, were but insipid raptures compared with those experienced in 'a grand sham fight between us and the Ratcliffe [Highway?] Volunteers! The ground selected for the event was where Fairlop Fair is held [in Epping Forest], and on the day appointed we left town at six A. M., in the midst of the greatest excitement, accompanied by a great number of our friends, as also by sundry wagons for the conveyance of the sick or wounded, together with some covered carts and a brewer's dray, containing abundance of ham, beef, and bread, as well as a plentiful supply of ale and porter; which good things, it was understood, were for distribution among us, if we should perform our duty manfully in the encounter. How exhilarating, on our road to the scene of action, to be saluted by the cheers of the crowd, the waving of handkerchiefs, the shouting of boys, the thrilling tones of the bugle, and the merry fife and drum. On our arrival at the ground, we found our antagonists had already taken up their position. We were allowed some half-hour's breathing-time, during which the band of the Tower Hamlet's Militia—whose services had been specially retained—enlivened us by the performance of some martial airs calculated to inflame our minds with that enthusiasm so necessary to constitute the character of the soldier. At length the time for action arrived. We fell in, and commenced the duties of the day, which consisted in marching and counter-marching, attacking and retreating, forming squares to repulse imaginary attacks of cavalry, and firing some thirty pounds of blank cartridges at each other. At last the moment came which was to close our operations by a grand charge with fixed bayonets. The two regiments faced each other in line, and after each firing a volley, the men being directed to fire low, that their shots might be more effectual, the

* Recollections of Military Service in 1813, 1814, and 1815, through Germany, Holland, and France; including some details of the battles of Quatre Bras and Waterloo. By Thomas Morris, late Sergeant of the 2d Battalion of the 73d Regiment of Foot. London: James Madden and Co. 1845.

* The Royal Artillery Company of London was incorporated by Henry VIII., and has always been considered the most distinguished of militia corps. It is still a highly effective force. Its members are, with very few exceptions, tailors.

lines advanced, the word "Charge!" was given, "Forward, forward!" and on we went with the desperate determination of men resolved to conquer or die. When we had arrived within about twenty paces of each other, our commanding officers, fully satisfied of our coolness and bravery, and unwilling to expose us to unnecessary danger, gave the word "Halt!" and thereby relieved the apprehension of those who thought a collision unavoidable. Having performed our evolution to the satisfaction of our commanding officer, we were permitted to retire beneath the ample foliage of the forest trees, there to enjoy ourselves with the good things provided for us; and there being no restriction in the serving out as to quantity, we were able to invite those of our friends who had accompanied us from town: and after doing ample justice to the stock of provisions, we formed into parties, and indulged in the merry song and dance. When it was thought we had sufficiently enjoyed ourselves, we were ordered to prepare for the march home; but whether it was the effects of the weather, or the potency of the ale or porter, truth compels me to admit that our return was not of the orderly soldier-like description of our journey outwards in the morning; and many of the men were compelled to avail themselves of the conveyance of the wagons. However, we returned in safety, deposited our colours at the major's residence, and retired to our respective homes, much satisfied with our trip.'

Whether from an augmented love of glory, communicated by this inspiriting sham-fight, or satisfactory reminiscences of the admirable commissariat arrangements of the brewer's dray, Mr Morris, on returning to the purlieus of the Tower, determined to *play* at soldiers no longer, but to become a warrior in earnest. With this view he enlisted in his majesty's 73d, a Highland foot regiment. Having been properly drilled at the depôt at Colchester, Morris was 'passed' as fit to join the service companies, then about to embark for the Peninsula from Yarmouth. Arrived at Stralsund, the 73d was afterwards ordered to co-operate, under the command of General Gibbs, with a body of German troops led by Count Walmoden. On the plains of Gordo, near Danenberg, Morris had the first opportunity of comparing a real with a sham battle. The gallant 73d met with the French, whom they helped to defeat. After the fight, Morris doubtless sighed for the covered wagons and bottled stout of Epping Forest; for the hungry soldiers had to sleep on the bare ground drenched with rain. As this was his first 'affair,' the worthy sergeant evidently thinks it was of as much importance to the operations of the war as it was to himself; for he complains that historians have been so unkind as not to take the smallest notice of it.

From Germany the 73d passed into Holland, seeing occasionally very severe service. At length (in 1815) the Anglo-Prussian army, commanded by the Duke of Wellington and Blucher, was concentrated in Belgium, and Morris was quartered with his comrades at 'a sweet village three miles from the town of Soignes. On the 15th of June, some of the officers and men were playing at ball against the gable-end of a house in the village, when an orderly dragoon brought despatches from General Halket, who commanded a brigade, ordering us to fall in immediately, and proceed to the town of Soignes. The men were scattered about, variously engaged; but they soon understood, from the roll of the drums and the tones of the bugles, that their attendance in marching order was immediately necessary. About four o'clock the order came, and by six we had fallen in and were off. On our arrival at Soignes we found the town filling fast with troops. There was evidently something extraordinary in this sudden movement, but no one knew the cause. About nine o'clock that night we had one day's provision served out, and as the meat was raw, we thought it advisable to cook it, not knowing how we might be situated next day. At twelve o'clock at night we fell in, and in another hour had left the town behind us, and soon entered what is very appropriately called the "dark wood of Soignes."' In fact, they were on their way to commence that series of actions by which the peace of Europe was to be secured. Urged forward with the utmost celerity, they at length reached the scene of strife, at Quatre Bras, and took part in the action, as a portion of Sir Colin Halket's brigade. During the fight, a circumstance occurred which plainly shows that, from the intensity of the excitement, a man may be wounded unconsciously. It affords, moreover, a pretty little episode. 'Ensign Deacon, of our regiment, was on my right, close to me, when we were charging the enemy, and a private on my left being killed by a musket-ball through the temple, the officer said, "Who is that, Morris?" I replied, "Sam Shortly;" and pointing to the officer's arm, where a musket-ball had passed through, taking with it a portion of the shirt sleeve, I said, "You are wounded, sir." "God bless me! so I am," said he, and dropping his sword, made the best of his way to the rear. After getting his wound dressed, he went in search of his wife, whom, with her three children, he had left with the baggage guard. During the whole night he sought her in vain; and the exertion he used was more than he could bear, and he was conveyed by the baggage-train to Brussels. The poor wife, in the meantime, who had heard from some of the men that her husband was wounded, passed the whole night in searching for him among the wounded as they passed. At length she was informed that he had been conveyed to Brussels, and her chief anxiety then was how to get there. Conveyances there were none to be got; but, encouraged by the hope of finding her husband, she made the best of her way on foot, with her children, exposed to the violence of the terrific storm of thunder, lightning, and rain, which continued unabated for about ten hours. Faint, exhausted, and wet to the skin, having no other clothes than a black silk dress and light shawl, yet she happily surmounted all these difficulties, reached Brussels on the morning of the 18th, and found her husband in very comfortable quarters, where she also was accommodated.'

Early on the morning of the 17th, the British army retreated upon Waterloo. 'As soon as the troops reached that part of the Brussels road nearest to the farmhouse of La Haye-Sainte, the different brigades filed off to the right or left, to take up their respective positions; and it was now understood that this was to be our battle-field, if the enemy should think proper to engage us. Our brigade was placed about midway between La Haye-Sainte and Hugamont; the footguards were on our right; the whole of the ground was covered with corn, and the soil of so loose a nature, that, owing to the heavy rain which continued to fall, we were literally knee deep in mud. We could perceive the enemy taking up their position opposite to us, at the distance of about a mile and a half. Their artillery began to play on us, and did some, but not much damage. One of their large shot killed two of our light company; it struck one of them on the cheek, and the other was killed with the wind of the passing ball, as effectually as if he had been struck by it. As the storm continued, without any signs of abatement, and the night was setting in, orders were given to pile arms, but no man was on any account to quit his position. Under such circumstances, our prospect of a night's lodging was anything but cheering, the only provision we had being the remnant of the salt meat served out on the 16th. Having disposed of that, we began to consider in what way to pass the night; to lie down was out of the question, and to stand up all night was almost equally so. We endeavoured to light some fires, but the rain soon put them out, and the only plan we could adopt was to gather armsful of the standing corn, and, rolling it together, make a sort of mat, on which we placed the knapsack; and sitting on that, each man holding his blanket over his head to keep off the rain, which was almost needless, as we were so thoroughly drenched: however, this was the plan generally adopted and maintained during the night.' Such was the condition in which thousands of candidates for 'glory' passed the eve of the memorable 18th of June 1815. By six o'clock the next morning, however, the storm had cleared away, and under the cheering influence of a powerful sun, the 73d began to clean their muskets for the coming strife. Morris narrates—with a degree of naïveté only to be appreciated when we reflect he was on the eve of a battle which all knew would be a tremendous struggle, and that he was up to his knees in mud—that, having *shaved himself and put on a clean shirt*, he felt *tolerably comfortable*.

The 30th and 73d regiments of foot formed together one of those solid squares by which it is well known the battle was won. Three times in the course of the day did Napoleon's terrible cuirassiers charge this indomitable square of human beings without success. At the fourth, says our sergeant, 'they deliberately walked their horses up to the bayonet's point, and one of them, leaning over his horse, made a thrust at me with his sword. I could not avoid it, and involuntarily closed my eyes. When I opened them again, my enemy was lying just in front of me, within reach, in the act of thrusting at me. He had been wounded by one of my rear-rank men; and whether it was the anguish of the wound, or the chagrin of being defeated, I know not, but he endeavoured to terminate his existence with his own sword; but that being too long for his purpose, he took one of our bayonets which was lying on the ground, and raising himself up with one hand, he placed the point of the bayonet under his cuirass, and fell on it.' Presently the French infantry were brought against them, and the two regiments were ordered to retire. While doing so, 'Sergeant Mure of the grenadiers, a very brave and good soldier, in turning round to have a look at the enemy, received a musket-ball in the forehead, and fell on his back a corpse. A cousin of his, named Morrison, on hearing of his death, ran back, in the face of a most destructive fire, to where his cousin lay, kissed his cheek, let fall a tear or two, and then joined us again.'

When the battle was won, the British troops marched towards Paris. During the occupation of that city by the allies, Morris, while quartered in the neighbourhood, was promoted to the rank of sergeant. About the middle of December the 73d received the route for England, and they arrived in the regimental depôt at Colchester before the end of the year. Some time after, the company to which Sergeant Morris belonged was ordered to Wolverhampton, and the reception they met with in that town shows the enthusiasm felt respecting the recent services of the army. 'The people at Wolverhampton were all excitement when they heard that part of a Waterloo regiment was coming among them; and as soon as I had announced myself to the constable whose duty it was to prepare the billets, he gave me one on the "Eagle and Child," a decent public-house near the old churchyard; and when the news circulated that one of the Waterloo-men was actually there, people flocked in in such numbers, that the house could not accommodate them. Hundreds of them shook hands with me, and if I could have eaten and drank gold, I might have had it. The house was kept open very late that night, and I was obliged to remain, explaining the nature and circumstances of the battle; and was not sorry when the house closed, and I was suffered to go to bed. The next morning the house of the constable was beset by publicans, who, instead of striving, as they do in London, to shift the burden from them, were anxious to have men billeted on them, finding that it would for a time bring "grist to the mill."'

In 1819 Sergeant Morris's allotted term of seven years' service having expired, he quitted the army, and 'soon, unassisted, attained a respectable rank in civil society.' We congratulate him on the change, and offer our best commendations on the successful manner in which he has 'fought his battles o'er again' in the volume which we are now closing.

GOODNESS OF HEART.

There was a great master among the Jews who bade his scholars consider and tell him what was the best way wherein a man should always keep. One came and said that there was nothing better than a *good eye*, which means in their language a liberal and contented mind; another said a *good companion* was the best thing in the world; a third said a *good neighbour* was the best thing he could desire; and a fourth preferred a man that could foresee things to come, that is, a *wise person*. But at last came in one Eleazer, and he said a *good heart* was better than them all. True, said the master; thou hast comprehended in two words all that the rest have said; for he that hath a good heart will be both contented, and a good companion, and a good neighbour, and will easily see what is fit to be done by him. Let every man then seriously labour to find in himself a sincerity and uprightness of heart at all times, and that will save him abundance of other labour.—*Bishop Patrick.*

THE ITALIAN BOY—A SONNET.

BY S. W. PARTRIDGE.

CHILD of the South, I love thy smiling face,
Serene and glowing as thy native sky,
Nor sourly would thy tinkling airs decry.
Gentlest and soberest of the nomadic race,
Not uselessly thou saunterest through life's maze,
For, poor dispenser of cheap luxury,
Thy notes still soothe exhausted Labour's sigh,
And Sorrow's wrinkles for awhile erase.
Amid the scuffle dire for place and gain,
With noiseless steps thou track'st thy placid way;
And, though the child of insult and disdain,
Plod'st mirthfully, among the gayest gay.
Here, Luxury, health, with scanty fare behold;
Here, Avarice, here contentment without gold.

ANECDOTE OF THE ANT.

Mr Kirkby, in his Bridgewater Treatise, relates, on the authority of Colonel Sykes, the following anecdote of an Indian species of ant, instancing in a wonderful manner their perseverance in attaining a favourite object:—When resident at Poonah, our dessert, consisting of fruits, cakes, and various preserves, always remained upon a small side-table in a verandah of the drawing-room. To guard against inroads, the legs of the table were immersed in four basins filled with water: it was removed an inch from the wall, and, to keep off dust through open windows, was covered with a table-cloth. At first the ants did not attempt to cross the water, but as the strait was very narrow—from an inch to an inch and a half—and the sweets very tempting, they appear at length to have braved all risks, to have committed themselves to the deep, to have scrambled across the channels, and to have reached the objects of their desires; for hundreds were found every morning revelling in enjoyment. Daily, vengeance was executed upon them, without lessening their numbers; at last the legs of the table were smeared, just above the water, with a circle of turpentine. This at first seemed to prove an effectual barrier, and for some days the sweets were unmolested, after which they were again attacked by these resolute plunderers. How they got at them seemed totally unaccountable, till Colonel Sykes, who often passed the table, was surprised to see an ant drop from the wall, about a foot from the table, upon the cloth that covered it; another and another succeeded. Thus, though the turpentine and the distance from the wall appeared effectual barriers, still the resources of the animal, when determined to carry its point, were not exhausted, and by ascending the wall to a certain height, with a slight effort against it, in falling, it managed to land upon the table in safety.

NOTE.

We have pleasure in stating, upon the authority of a correspondent, that the poem entitled 'The Wife to her Husband,' lately reprinted in the Miscellany of Tracts, and formerly in the Journal, is by Mrs Gillies, formerly Mrs Lemar Grimstone, author of *Cleone*, *Character*, and other novels of acknowledged merit.

Printed by William Bradbury, of No. 6, York Place, and Frederick Mullett Evans, of No. 7, Church Row, both of Stoke Newington, in the county of Middlesex, printers, at their office, Lombard Street, in the precinct of Whitefriars, and city of London; and Published (with permission of the Proprietors, W. and R. CHAMBERS,) by WILLIAM SOMERVILLE ORR, Publisher, of 2, Amen Corner, at No. 2, AMEN CORNER, both in the parish of Christchurch, and in the city of London.—Saturday, March 8, 1845.

CONDUCTED BY WILLIAM AND ROBERT CHAMBERS, EDITORS OF 'CHAMBERS'S INFORMATION FOR THE PEOPLE,' 'CHAMBERS'S EDUCATIONAL COURSE,' &c.

No. 63. New Series. SATURDAY, MARCH 15, 1845. Price 1½d.

PRIDE—OFFENSIVE AND DEFENSIVE.

The French have two words to express pride, *La Fierté*, and *L'Orgueil*. A lady being asked to define the difference, replied very promptly and happily that the first was 'defensive,' and the second 'offensive pride.' The distinction is important. Of the first, it is impossible to have too much; of the second, it is equally impossible to have too little. Defensive pride is that proper self-respect which will not allow its possessor to commit an unworthy, a base, or a mean action. It is that which keeps us from making friends and companions of the vicious, the dishonest, and the disreputable. It is that which urges us to distinguish ourselves above the crowd of the idle, the ignorant, the dilatory, and the variable, by our industry, our wisdom, our perseverance, and our constancy; and which prompts us to win the applause of our fellows by our goodness, and consequent greatness. Defensive pride is the shield with which we keep off the assaults of those who, openly or insidiously, would bring us down to a lower moral level than our judgment and our conscience inform us we ought to hold: it is the amulet with which we preserve ourselves from the machinations of evil, and the perfume by aid of which we may walk amid the haunts of vice without contamination. Without a due proportion of pride like this, in some one of its various developments, no man yet has ever arrived at distinction, or left behind him a name which the world holds in honour. It is the nurse of emulation and ambition, and, like the antagonism of which we spoke in a previous article, becomes, when properly or opportunely excited, the spur to urge the timid or the sluggish to do the good which another has left undone; the steel upon some flinty nature, eliciting heat and light which might otherwise have remained latent for ever. Pride of this kind sits as well upon the humblest as upon the loftiest. It is the pride of a man independent of his rank, his wealth, or his station; the pride of the gold, and not of the stamp upon it. Pride of this kind has found its most poetical, and at the same time its best and truest utterance in the song of Robert Burns, 'A man's a man for a' that.' Every one who feels his heart glow at the sentiments expressed in that glorious lyric, feels defensive pride; and if he continues to feel it, and makes it the guide of his life, he becomes—though he toil all day, and far into the night, for hard and scanty bread; though he 'wear hodden gray,' and dwell in a hut scarcely sheltered from the winds and rains of heaven—an ornament to his kind, and a blessing to himself.

Offensive pride, on the other hand, shows the little mind, as defensive pride exhibits the great one. It is the pride of externals, as defensive pride is that of internals; the pride of the adventitious circumstances in which a man is placed, and not of the qualities of the man himself. Offensive pride assumes various forms, and is in all of them equally a proof of ignorance, presumption, and heartlessness. To the man of sense, it is always ridiculous; and wherever it does not excite the anger, it is sure to excite the contempt of the well-minded. When we see a man proud of his high lineage, and expecting that we shall do homage to him for the virtues of his ancestors, although he have none of his own, we despise him all the more for the highness of his name: his pride and his lordly airs gall us, if we are of stern nature; and provoke us to laughter, if we are of the number of those who can find amusement in the contemplation of human folly. Proud men of this class have been happily compared to turnips and potatoes; all the best part of them is under ground.

Equally, if not more offensive, is the pride of wealth. This pride is the parent of every meanness. We may be quite sure, when we see a man proud of his money, that he has gained it in a dirty manner, and that he makes really, though not perhaps visibly to all men's eyes, a dirty use of it. If he have a large house, it is not for use but for ostentation. If he have fine carriages, valuable horses, and footmen in gay liveries, it is that he may excite more attention from the frivolous and unthinking, than some one else who has hitherto rivalled him. If he give splendid entertainments, it is that he may make the earls or the barons who condescend, or the poor dependents who fawn and cringe, to appear at them, envious of the wealth which their own can never equal. If he give charity, it is that it may be blazoned abroad; for he will refuse five guineas to a deserving object if the donation is to remain secret, when he would give a hundred to a less deserving one if the fact could be trumpeted in the newspapers. Such a man pays for the publication of his charitable deeds; and not only does not hide from his left hand what his right hand does, but fees the common crier of the streets to promulgate it with embellishments. Such a man is not proud of being charitable, but of being thought so—not thankful for wealth, because it enables him to do good, but proud of it, because it gives him the means of attracting more worldly attention than better men, and enables him to ride and drink wine when superior merit walks and can only afford small beer.

There is also a pride of beauty, a pride of strength, a pride of skill, and a pride of talent, which all become offensive if they are loudly expressed, and are unsupported by other qualities which it is the province of a defensive pride to foster in the mind. When a woman is proud of her beauty, and has neither wit, nor sense, nor good nature, nor any charm of mind that will endure when beauty fades, her pride is offensive. When a man is proud of his physical strength, and acts the giant, and has no mental strength, nor thinks it worth the cultivation, his pride is offensive. When another vaunts his skill in any particular pursuit—a skill which may be undoubted—and thrusts it inopportunely and pertinaciously forward, his pride is offensive: and when a man who has gained some credit for talent is always fearful that he will lose it, unless he daily and hourly impresses the recollection of it upon those with whom he may be brought in contact, his pride is offensive, and is that of a little talent only, and not of a great one. Combined, on the contrary, with defensive, and not with offensive pride, beauty, strength, skill, and talent become enhanced in our eyes. Beauty then knows and acts upon the knowledge that goodness will lend her additional charms; physical strength learns not to be proud merely of that which it has in common with the brutes, but to be strong in mind; and skill and talent, conscious that self-praise is no recommendation to the world, resolve to win the world's applause by future good deeds, and not by boasting vaingloriously of the deeds that are past.

There is another great difference between defensive and offensive pride; which is, that while the one invariably keeps its thoughts to itself, the other as invariably shouts them into all men's ears. Defensive pride never makes a boast; but offensive pride is never easy but when the boast is on its tongue. The one is silent, the other is loquacious. Defensive pride is retiring; offensive pride is forward; and the one lives upon the rewards of conscience, while the other only exists upon the babble of the crowd.

There are other kinds of pride which are as offensive as those already mentioned. We would cite, especially, 'sensitive pride,' and the 'pride that apes humility.' Sensitive pride is founded not upon a proper self-respect, but upon inordinate vanity, linked with some degree of cowardice. If it has taken root in the breast of a poor man, or one of inferior station in society, it leads him to imagine insults from the rich and the lofty which are not intended, and to suppose that all the world are thinking how they can show him disrespect, when, in fact, the world is not giving itself the slightest concern about him. But this truth never enters into his mind; for if it did, he would be still more miserable. His consolation is, that the world hates him, and tries to trample him down, and he flies to that rather than to the thought, annihilating to his vanity and self-conceit, that the world most likely does not even know of his existence. In a rich or powerful man, this pride generally springs from some defect, physical or moral, but most often from the former, as in the case of Lord Byron and his lameness. Upon this point his pride was ridiculously sensitive and offensive, and laid bare the weaknesses of his mental constitution—a vanity pained to be conscious of a physical deformity, which rendered him less perfect than the most perfect of his fellow-creatures, and a cowardice that prevented him from rising superior to the possible sneers of the thoughtless or unfeeling.

Of the 'pride that apes humility,' it may be truly said that it is, of all kinds of pride, the most offensive. In addition to the bad qualities inherent in a false and unfounded estimate of self, it possesses that of hypocrisy; and no junction can be more odious than that of hypocrisy and pride. Foolish pride may offend, but hypocritical pride offends and disgusts us. The pride of wealth, of rank, of power, of beauty, or of talent, though they may be unjustifiable, at least lean upon something that exists, or is supposed to exist; but the pride that apes humility leans upon a lie, which it knows to be a lie. It unites the bad qualities of every other kind of pride, and is, in a manner, the concentrated essence of offensiveness.

GARDEN FAVOURITES.

'One does not now hear,' says Bosc, 'of 20,000 francs being given for a tulip; of a florist depriving himself of his food, in order to increase the number and variety of his anemones, or passing entire days in admiring the colours of a ranunculus, the grandeur of a hyacinth, or trembling lest the breath of an over-curious admirer should hurt the bloom of an auricula.' Certainly not; but cool and calculating as we of the nineteenth century are, it may at least be matter of curiosity to glance at the history of some of these favourites, and to learn the extravagant prices which they frequently brought during the period of their ascendancy. And first of the hyacinth, whose fibrous-rooted bulb and delicate blossoms are now adorning the crystal vases of our parlours and drawing-rooms.

The Hyacinth, which belongs to the same natural order as the lily and tulip, is a native of the Levant; but has been cultivated in Britain for nearly three hundred years. It is in Holland, however, that the plant is reared in perfection, the florists of that country carrying on a regular trade in the bulb, and using every effort and device to increase the varieties. Mr Knight, who travelled in the bulb district in 1830, saw more than a hundred acres of hyacinths in bloom between Leyden and Haarlem; and some of these bloomestries had been established for upwards of a century. At first, only single hyacinths were cultivated, but about the middle of last century attention was paid to double flowers; and some of the earliest of these varieties brought the high price of 1000 florins, or L.100 per bulb. As the art of cultivation improved, so rose the mania to possess rare varieties, and as much as L.200 has been known to be given for a single root. The passion for this, as well as for many of our older favourites, has long since declined: other exotic novelties have taken their place; and it is now rarely that we hear of more than L.8 or L.10 being given for the finest hyacinth. The ordinary price for good bulbs is indeed seldom beyond eight or ten shillings; and what are called common mixtures may be had, as imported, for L.2 or L.3 per hundred. The criterion of a fine double hyacinth, according to the Botanical Magazine, is as follows:—The stem should be strong, tall, and erect, supporting numerous large bells, each suspended by a short and strong peduncle, or footstalk, in a horizontal position, so that the whole may have a compact pyramidal form, with the crown or uppermost part perfectly erect. The flowers should be large, and perfectly double; that is, well filled with broad bold petals, appearing to the eye rather convex than flat or hollow; they should occupy about one half the stem. The colours should be clear and bright, whether plain red, white, or blue, or variously intermixed and diversified in the eye; the latter, it must be confessed, gives additional lustre and elegance to this beautiful flower. Strong bright colours are in general preferred to such as are pale.

Tulips.—These fine showy plants are considered to be natives of the Levant, and are very common in Syria and Persia, where they are known by the name of *thoulyban*, from which our word is evidently derived. The Persian word also signifies a turban, and was probably applied to the tulip on account of the resemblance between the form of the flower and that article of dress.

It was first brought into Europe in 1554 by Busbequius; and Conrad Gesner describes it as blooming in gardens at Augsburg in 1559. The period of its introduction into England is uncertain; but Gerarde, in his Herbal, 1597, speaks of it in the following manner:—'My loving friend, Mr James Garret, a curious searcher of simples, and learned apothecary in London, hath undertaken to find out, if it were possible, the infinite sorts by diligent sowing of their seeds, and by planting those of his own propagation, and by others received from his friends beyond the seas for the space of twenty years, not being yet able to attain to the end of his travail, for that each new year bringeth forth new plants of sundry colours not before seen; all which, to describe particularly, were to roll Sisyphus' stone, or number the sands.' Though the tulip was somewhat earlier cultivated on the continent, it was not till about the middle of the seventeenth century that it reached the meridian of public favour; and then, what had hitherto been an object of legitimate regard among gardeners and amateurs, became in the Netherlands a source of extensive gaming and mad speculation. To such a height did the passion for tulips arrive in 1637, that at a public auction which took place at Alkmaar, one hundred and twenty bulbs were sold for L.7875; and one sort alone, the viceroy, was exchanged for articles valued at 2500 florins—L.190! Beckmann, in his 'History of Inventions,' gives an account of this tulipomania, during which tulip bulbs were sold and re-sold after the manner of stocks on the stock exchange of our own country. 'The species *Semper Augustus*,' says he, 'has been often sold for 2000 florins; and it once happened that there were only two roots of it to be had, the one at Amsterdam, the other at Haarlem. For a root of this species one agreed to give 4600 florins, together with a new carriage, two gray horses, and a complete harness. Another agreed to give twelve acres of land for a root. Those who had not ready money, promised their moveable and immoveable goods, house and lands, cattle and clothes. The trade, in which 60,000 florins were sometimes cleared in one month, was followed not only by mercantile people, but also by the first noblemen, citizens of every description, mechanics, seamen, farmers, turf-diggers, chimney-sweeps, footmen, maid-servants, and old clothes women. At first every one won, and no one lost. Some of the poorest people gained in a few months houses, coaches and horses, and figured away like the first characters in the land. In every town some tavern was selected, which served as a 'Change, where high and low traded in flowers, and confirmed their bargains with the most sumptuous entertainments. They formed laws for themselves, and had notaries and clerks.'

The object of these speculations, however, had nothing to do with the desire to possess or cultivate the plant; it was a mere gaming for money, and totally unconnected with the feelings which prompted the first purchasers. It was a theme which drove the grave, the prudent, the ponderous Dutchman as wild as ever did the South-Sea Bubble his more excitable and less calculating brother, John Bull. 'A speculator,' continues our authority, 'often offered and paid large sums for a root which he never received, and never wished to receive. Another sold roots which he never possessed or delivered. Oft did a nobleman purchase of a chimney-sweep tulips to the amount of 2000 florins, and sold them at the same time to a farmer; and neither the nobleman, chimney-sweep, nor farmer, had roots in their possession, or wished to possess them. Before the tulip season was over, more roots were sold and purchased, bespoke and promised to be delivered, than in all probability were to be found in the gardens of Holland; and when Semper Augustus was not to be had, which happened twice, no species was oftener purchased and sold. In the space of three years, more than 10,000,000 florins were expended in this trade in only one town in Holland.' The bubble, however, burst at last: the ultimate purchasers failed to meet the demands made upon them, and as many were then ruined as had previously made fortunes. The Dutch government interfered, and a decree was passed, ordering that every seller should produce and offer his bulbs to the purchaser, and in the event of the latter refusing to receive them, the vender had it in his power to retain his tulips, and sue for damages. This laid the axe to the root of the tulipomania of the Netherlands; but the passion for the flower from which the mania arose still continues to influence the floriculturists of that country, who are, without doubt, the best bulb-growers in the world. The taste for tulips in England appears to have arrived at its climax about the end of the seventeenth and beginning of the eighteenth centuries; and they still remain flowers of considerable value among florists; for, according to Mr Hogg, a moderate collection of choice bulbs cannot now be purchased for a sum much less than L.1000, at the usual prices.

In its habit and structure, the tulip is closely allied to the lily, and is therefore ranked under the natural order *Liliaceæ;* by some botanists it is itself regarded as the type of the order, which is then known by the name of *Tulipaceæ*. In cultivation, tulips are classified according to the character of their perianths or floral portions thus:—1. *Byblœmens*, such as have a white ground variegated with purple, the edges well feathered, the leaflets of the perianth erect—the whole forming a well-shaped cup; 2. *Bizzdres*, having a yellow ground, variegated with scarlet, purple, rose, or velvet, and well feathered round the edge; 3. *Roses* with white ground, variegated with rose colour, scarlet, or crimson; and, 4. *Selfs*, or plain-coloured tulips of a white or yellow ground, without any marks. As it is solely for ornament that the tulip is reared in our gardens, the great object of florists, for nearly three centuries, has been variety, rarity and delicacy of pencilling, and perfection of form. For these ends tulips seem to possess a peculiar adaptation; and thus at the present moment we have, by carefully selecting and crossing, a variety and exuberance of colouring which is almost inconceivable. Nor is it to be presumed that this Protean power in the tulip is exhausted: we know as little of the limits of vegetable adaptation as we know of the cause which determines the form of the leaf or the colour of the blossom.

Dahlias.—'These splendid plants,' says Maund, 'are natives of Spanish America, and though noticed by the Spaniards about the middle of the seventeenth century, did not attract much attention till they had flowered at Madrid in 1790, when Cavanilles described them in the first volume of his Icones. In 1802 he sent plants to Paris, where they were successfully cultivated by M. Thouin, who shortly afterwards published coloured figures, and a description of them. The first introduction of the dahlia into England was by the Marchioness of Bute in 1789; but the plants, it may be presumed, were soon lost. In 1802 and 1803 others were sent from Paris, and in 1804 seeds from Madrid; yet for several years they were scarcely heard of amongst us. Their habits being unknown, their increase was slow, whilst on the continent innumerable and splendid varieties were produced; so that, after the peace in 1814, they were poured upon us in all the variety of their present tints; exciting the astonishment of every beholder, and the joy of those who could number such beauties amongst their own collections. Since that time they have been rapidly increased and improved, and England can now boast of varieties as superb as any in the world.' The dahlia takes its name from Andrew Dahl, a Swedish botanist, and ought to be pronounced with the *a* open, as in far, to distinguish it from a very different genus, *dālea*, called after our own countryman, Dale. It belongs to the natural order *Compositæ*, and is now so common, that anything like minute description is unnecessary. 'In form and stature,' says a recent writer, 'it is a Proteus; in tints it is a vegetable prism. Neither are the form nor colours constant in the same individual. The first flowers will be single and of one colour, and the last double and of another hue; and such is the versatility of the self-colour of a parent, that its seedlings will be edged, or striped, or blotched, and altogether as unlike the mother as change of colour can make them.' We are not aware of a blue variety having been reared; and according to De Candolle, the production of such a hue in the dahlia is impossible.

Ranunculuses and *Anemones*, which have long been favourites in our gardens, both belong to the same natural order, *Ranunculaceæ*, of which the common yellow crowfoot of our meadows is the type and representative. The garden ranunculus belongs originally to the milder climates of the Mediterranean, but has been cultivated in England for nearly three centuries. Gerarde reared them in 1594; Parkinson, in 1629, enumerates eight varieties; and Ray, in 1665, increases the list to twenty-five. It was not, however, till between the middle and end of last century that ranunculuses reached their meridian in England, when hosts of new sorts were reared, and florists, as Bosc informs us, became absolute idolaters of the beauty and variety of their colouring. The anemone is a native of the same region as the ranunculus, and was brought into England from Italy about the end of the sixteenth century. Like most other plants, the anemone, in its wild state, has its flowers single; but the corolla can be multiplied almost indefinitely by the conversion of its stamens and pistils into petals, under a judicious system of culture. Both the Dutch and English florists have excelled in this course, the former indeed having sometimes reared varieties with stems half a yard in height, and with blossoms six inches across. The anemone derives its name from a Greek word signifying wind-flower, an appellation actually bestowed upon it by our ancestors, from the circumstance of its naturally growing on open plains or exposed situations, where its feathery grains produce a singular shining appearance when waved by the breeze. The single-leaved varieties are generally known as *poppy anemones*, and the double sorts as the garden, star, or broad-leaved anemones. When first introduced, there were only a few species, but now art has so increased the varieties of this light and graceful favourite, that florists have ceased to distinguish them by individual names. The colours of the ranunculus and anemone are clear, rich, and brilliant, partaking of almost every hue—are either in single uniform tints, or mottled with stripes and patches.

The *Auricula* belongs to the *Primulaceæ* or Primrose tribe, and is found wild on the Swiss and Tyrolese Alps, and on the Caucasian and other mountain ranges of Southern Europe. It was early cultivated in Britain under the name of bears' ears or mountain cowslips; and even in 1768 a gardener near Colchester is said to have reared them in such perfection, that he could boast of not fewer than 133 flowers on a single stem. England, indeed, seems to have carried the palm for the cultivation of auriculas; for about a hundred years ago we used to supply the Dutch florists, though they at an after period re-supplied us with the progeny of our own flowers. The plant is certainly worthy of all the care that has been bestowed upon it; and the more so, that it is as often found gladdening the tiny front-plot or window-sill of the artisan, as the flower garden of the rich and great. The colours of the flower, in its wild state, are yellow, purple, and variegated; but these can be broken by cultivation into a vast variety of hues—yellow, purple, red, scarlet, and blush coloured, with edgings of gray, green, or white. The delicate velvety texture, which adds so much to the beauty of the auricula, is easily tarnished by wind and rain; hence the great care necessary to protect them from stormy weather, and yet afford them that full exposure to light and sun upon which their perfection so much depends. It may strike the uninitiated as an anomaly, that a native of Alpine regions should require so much care and shelter when brought to the less exposed plains of England. The explanation is thus given by Dr Lindley:—'In Alpine districts, it might be supposed that it experiences intense cold in winter; but this is probably not the fact; for it is covered early in the winter with a thick coat of snow, under which it lies buried till the return of spring, protected from the severest cold, and screened from the stimulating effect of light. When the snow melts, it begins to feel the excitement of brilliant light, and to unfold beneath a pure and equable atmosphere, perpetually refreshed by the breezes that blow over it, and rooting into rich vegetable mould, which is kept continually damp by the melting snow; but never becomes wet, on account of the steepness of the situations in which the plant delights to dwell. Under the same circumstances they flower and perfect their seeds: the drier weather of summer arriving, they cease to grow with vigour, and in autumn have reached a state of complete torpidity.' To imitate these conditions, the cultivator in the plains must have recourse to artificial means; the snow blanket he provides by a frame of glass and ashes, sheltered by mats; the perpetual moisture he supplies by his watering pan; the moistened soil he imitates by a compound of rich mould laid on broken pottery; the light and sunshine he affords them at the proper season, so often as our unstable climate will permit. Even with all this trouble, the care of the florist is not ended. 'The auricula,' says one of the first cultivators, 'must be bred as high as a race-horse, by a corresponding attention to pedigree; and it is for want of this attention to high breeding that so many persons fail to obtain a single good variety from a thousand seedlings.'

Hollyhocks.—These magnificent plants are natives of most eastern countries, being found in China, India, Africa, and even Siberia. At what period they were introduced into England is unknown. Dr Turner speaks of them as familiar plants in 1564; and Gerarde, in 1597, observes that they were then sown in gardens almost everywhere. There can be no doubt that they were very early cultivated, their majestic height and splendid flowers rendering them special objects of attention. In a wild state, their corollas are generally single, and of a red, white, or yellow colour; but by transference to more fertile soil, and to a favourable situation, their flowers can be doubled to any extent, and, by care on the part of the cultivator, brought into almost every hue. 'We have but few flowers,' says Phillips in his Flora Historica, 'that contribute more to the embellishment of large gardens than the hollyhock, although its hardy nature and easy propagation has rendered it so common, that it is much less regarded by the generality of florists than it deserves. It yields to no flower for the grandeur and beauty of its appearance, as well as for the great variety of its colours, which embraces all the shades of the rose, from the palest blush to the deepest carmine; from a pure white the yellows are equally numerous, until they reach to the richest orange, from which the colour is carried on to a dark chestnut. Others are dyed of a pale reddish purple, running up to a black. The noble stalks which these plants send up, like so many floral banners garnished with roses, render the hollyhock particularly desirable for ornamenting the borders of plantations, and for giving gaiety to the shrubbery in the latter season of the year, since it generally continues its succession of flowers until the time of frost.' Botanically, the hollyhock belongs to the order *Columniferæ*, and to the genus *Alcea*, which takes its name from the Greek word *alké*, on account of its supposed medicinal value in dysentery, &c. The English name is derived from the Saxon hollyoak or holihec—a term, the appropriateness of which is not very perceptible. Besides their floral beauty, hollyhocks are of great utility to bees, as they flower at a season when most other blossoms have faded. The fibrous bark of the flower-stalks furnishes no mean substitute for hemp; and a blue dye, little inferior in beauty and permanence to indigo, can be obtained from the whole plant.

Such is the history of some of our commonest garden pets—such the care, and toil, and anxiety which a few comparatively valueless objects of ornament may cost.

when vanity, ambition, or emulation is concerned in their production. The above, however, is a mere glimpse at an almost inexhaustible record, from which we may hereafter glean another chapter.

THE ROMANCE OF AN AUTHORESS'S CHILDHOOD.

I SHALL here relate a simple story, not so much to show the heart of a young child, as those little quaint pictures of life and nature in which a child's heart found faith and strength: to teach anew, in a story divested of all its intermingled pain, that the very strength acquired by us through circumstance, does but increase the debt of usefulness we owe to society; and that our faculties, our opportunities, and our industry, bind us only the more to turn them to account by increasing the happiness of those we may influence.

I was born in the west of England, and am an only daughter. The circumstances of my birth were those of tribulation and sorrow—a time of commercial distress, that pressed heavily upon the middle classes of society; the failure of my father's only brother, a merchant till then of prosperous fortunes, who had held in his hands the savings of my father's more fortunate and early years; and my father's entrance upon a new scene of professional labour, with all its cares and anxieties.

I was sickly from my birth, but I had a tender nurse in my eldest brother. He taught me to walk, to talk; even before I could understand him, he used to place me in a corner and tell me tales. But before this time, we had left the town where I was born, for another in an adjacent county, and, for a season, more prosperous events had come about. I slept in a little closet adjoining my brothers' room, and could hear them beginning to talk at break of day. I knew the eldest was entertaining the others with some long story, and I used to sit down outside their room door and hear what I could. There were two standard tales, the Black Dwarf, and Robinson Crusoe; but the latter was the favourite. When it was put up to vote which tale should be told, it was always 'Robinson Crusoe, and don't forget the footstep in the sand.' Morning after morning this same thing was said; yet when I knew the 'footstep in the sand' was coming, I grew breathless, and would creep nearer and nearer the door. The 'footstep' was an incident that never could grow old. At length I was found one morning. From that time I became one of the licensed auditory.

The country in which we lived is one of pre-eminent beauty of scenery. Its grand features are mountain and woodland. The 'sedgy' Severn flows swiftly through it, skirting the town in which we lived, and flowing onward through vales and pastures as silent and lonely as the untrodden valleys of the far-west. All the hours my brother could spare from school were devoted to angling. He was an indefatigable fly fisher. I was mostly his companion in his long rambles; for he would carry me miles in his arms, with his creel swung across his back. No ford was too deep to wade, no rock amidst the waters too inaccessible, no little island too overshadowed for our retreat. Solitude and silence became accustomed things; for I have sat whole hours watching the fly upon the dancing waters, only pressing my brother's hand, or looking up into his face, when it would sink far down the stream, and drawing the line swiftly from the reel, make me sure that another fish was ready for the basket. The newly-taken fish often made us our dinner, broiled in true fisherman style across a fire made from the dried sticks shaken by the winter's winds from the very tree that then afforded us shade from the summer's sun. A little ale, from such a road-side inn as Nasmyth painted, was our drink, or a cup of milk from some farm upon the uplands. Bright days were these: at the distance of years the heart grows young again, and the spirit gains an accession of elasticity and joyousness, by the mere memory of that green and unforgotten past.

I believe it was upon a little island in the Severn that I first learned to read. My spelling-book was a thumbed copy of Cowley, not trimly decked in morocco, but smelling of the fresh-plucked grass and oozy trout, with here and there, tucked between the leaves, a hackle, or a wing of some bright-coloured bird. Often during the heat of the mid-day sun, whilst my brother prepared his Greek or Latin lesson for the next school-day, I, too, had some task to learn—generally a verse of poetry—till, soothed by the sound of the falling waters, I would nestle to his side, and sink into the sleep of childhood. One of these noonday lessons was, I well remember, a little hymn by Kirke White, beginning, 'When marshalled on the nightly plains;' another, Wordsworth's 'We are seven.' I was thus, as it were, insensibly taught to read and love poetry together. From such a summer's life by stream, and in the far-off woods, lessons from the great book of nature were learnt and understood. Birds, fishes, flowers, the change of the seasons, the colour of the waters, the tints of the sky, the hue of the woodlands, the clustering fruits of autumn, were so many glorious things, that in their freshness and beauty spoke to the child of the love and divinity of God.

In these rambles we often met with adventure and characters. Sometimes in the braken, where no human foot seemed near, we would find some worthy brother of the angle. There seems a kind of freemasonry among the craft. The little courtesy of a borrowed line or float would often lead to a conversation that might have delighted Cotton or his worthy father Walton. From habit, I was quite expert at judging the difference between a May fly or a June fly, a gnat that suited the shallow ford, or a worm for the deep waters. Many a thank these worthy brothers of the angle would bestow on me; and I still remember that tinted dragon-fly, and that passage of Cowley, which brought me kind words from one illustrious as a philosopher. To the dialogues that often arose from these fishing adventures, I was always a silent listener, till the moon, rising in the heavens, would cast upon the trickling waters its silver light, or the nightingale, raising its clear notes in the upland coppice, would warn us that home was far away. Surely in the glory of such an hour, when peace had fallen upon the earth, and nature herself seemed to worship the great Spirit of the universe, the heart of the young child must have prayed too. The visible presence of thanksgiving in the rippling stream and nightingale's voice, might well make father Walton sing, 'Lord, what music hast thou prepared for thy saints in heaven, when thou affordest men such music upon earth!'

Old water-mills, with dripping slimy wheel, the foaming waters in the mill-dam, the gutted cottage standing half-way in the stream, the coppice lane, the silent wood, the hewn timber, or the loaded wain, were to me so many things of natural delight!

My brother and I several times narrowly escaped with our lives, by fording the river at flood times. Once by being pursued by an infuriated bull. Roaring and pawing the earth, it had pursued us across several fields, from a shallow rivulet by which we had been sitting. My brother flung aside his rod and creel, and seizing me in his arms, fled with naked feet (for he had been wading) for his life. The bull gained upon us field by field, till his very horns were within a foot of us, when my brother, still holding me tightly, plunged at one bound from the steep bank into the deep waters below, and gained in safety the other side of the river.

Amongst the many that my father's profession made him acquainted with, was a family with whom I became a favourite. There were a father and mother, a brother and two sisters. Their happy home, their love and union, their wise and rational piety, are remembered by me to this hour. The son was a large bookseller, the father agent for the publishing house of Childs of Bungay. In this happy home of theirs six days of the week were often spent. As soon as I could read, I used to creep into the shop, and carrying with me the old lady's footstool, find a quiet unseen corner, where, with a lapful of books, the hours passed by unregarded. As every book was found replaced, I was privileged and allowed to pick and choose at will. My little unseen corner became a sacred spot, from which no inducement of pleasure could win me. At night, there was the cheerfullest hearth to sit by I ever knew. The high-piled fire roared merrily up the quaint wide chimney, and twinkling with ruddy glow across the polished floor, took even from the oaken press and ancient chairs their look of dark-brown age. The supper would be spread, the sisters side by side, the mother in her ancient chair, the father gravely meditating over his evening pipe, whilst within the glow of the hearth stood the tankard of winter ale, its creamy top half hidden by the crisp brown toast. Then after supper would come dropping in, perhaps, the minister, or some grave man, who had been out upon the hills with monthly copies of devout books and holy bibles, who, travel-worn, had yet come to give first greeting to the 'master.' The scatterer of holy Bunyans, large-typed Doddridges, or Divine Meditations, never lapsed into a smile, but ever bore about with him the conscious dignity of his calling: wisely, too, and not unworthily. For the dissemination of a truth is next to its creation; and the apostle of knowledge, like the apostle of old, bore not the burden of truth without consciousness of its holiness.

In a distant part of the house was a very large and ancient room, filled all round from the floor to the ceiling with the grave literature I have spoken of. At times I took my little stool there. I know not how it was, but in that room I rather thought than read, going round the walls, counting the many shelves, and wondering how, and when, and why, men had written so much.

I must now speak of my father; for, as I grew up, I became his companion. I scarcely ever went to school, but rather picked up the rudiments of learning from overhearing my brothers at their lessons, and from an unceasing and unchecked love of reading. To modify a natural feebleness of body, I enjoyed much out-door exercise, and became the chosen companion of my father in many rambles about the country during his spare professional hours. Sometimes from home, sometimes from the houses of country friends, we would visit particular spots remarkable for their scenery, or for the historical or antiquarian events associated with them. All our walks had a pursuit annexed to them. Perhaps a book in the vestry of some ancient church among the hills, perhaps some spot alluded to in Tacitus or Cæsar, or some legend in a county manuscript, might be the object of attraction. One summer we visited Offa's Dyke, not on one day, but on many, seeing and tracing it from many points. This dyke was the boundary of the great Mercian kingdom on its western side. It extended from Flintshire into Herefordshire, and was a defence against the incursions of the Welsh into the kingdom of the Saxon heptarchy. The parts which are yet entire consist of a trench and mound, carried over hills and through almost inaccessible morasses.* The ditch is invariably on the Welsh side; and in many places it yet serves as a boundary line. The mound is seen stretching for miles across the border hills. Many an evening on its lofty height I have sat and listened to its history and origin. With the illimitable distance stretched out to view, the river glinting across the plains like silver threads, the woodlands casting broad shadows over the green-clad valleys, whilst far away the sinking sun shed its last glory on the mountain tops, with no sound of human voice, I have sat and listened till my heart has grown courageous, and my hand strong, as if, in truth, I were the daughter of ancient border chieftain.

Another summer, when I had grown older, we made excursions to Wroxeter, now a mean village, but once the site of Uriconium, the celebrated western city of the Romans during their dominion in Britain. This

* Hartshorn's Salopia Antiqua.

was once so extensive, that it covered from three to four hundred acres.* No vestige of it is now left, except the ruins of a gigantic wall, some twenty yards in length. But the buried relics of the city were many. Often has the ploughshare thrown out into the darkened furrows coins, bones, fragments of pottery, and pieces of glass, after their burial of sixteen or seventeen hundred years. Over the streets of this once great city, where temples had stood, where human ambition and human care had toiled, rich harvests of wheat now grow, richer and more luxuriant than common harvests,† because fed by the very ashes of the buried city from household hearths, market-places, sepulchres, and altars. From the distant uplands we have in spring-time traced the outlines of the buried city by the darker fallow and the deeper green of the springing wheat or grass.

Old Roman encampments were often found. Passing through the ferny brake, crushing the young primrose or violet, we would toil up the steep ascent, and resting at last in the inner vallum, drop pebbles down the well, that, still entire, with an old mountain-ash now growing from its side, once supplied the Roman camp with water.

Upon recovering from a severe illness when I was about eight years of age, I was sent for change of air to a relation's in a distant part of England. Every comfort that money or the providing hand of love could procure, was heaped upon me; and, under the care of a friend, I left home one fine morning in May. I spent a whole week with this friend in London, at the house of a city merchant in Crutched Friars. I well remember the old, gloomy, oak-panelled rooms, with staircases and galleries wide enough to have held a coach-and-six. The very number of the stairs, the very patterns of the carpets, the dusty mirrors, the figures on the old Dutch clock in the gallery, are as fresh before me as if I had seen them yesterday.

I was received by my relations with an overwhelming show of kindness, which, as a prodigy, lasted for a whole week. At the end of that time things changed; and the Eden that was to be, proved a wilderness of bitterness. I was weak in health and emaciated in body. At the end of the one week I was stripped of what I wore and what I brought, starved, beaten, and driven from the house, from early dawn till night, to some fields in the rear of the house, with nothing but a hollow pit of sand to hide myself in, or the peas or carrots from the field for food. I, too, who had been reared with all a father's love, who had thoughts so far beyond those who oppressed me, that, hiding them in my own heart, secretly and proudly, like precious jewels, I laughed to myself, and said, 'These ye cannot touch, oppress as ye best may.' I sometimes look back upon those eleven dreary months, and wonder how I lived: yet what were they to what the future was to be! It was soon found out that I was clever at the needle. From thenceforth many days, from early dawn till night, were passed at it, executing narrow embroidery; so that when I did get a day in the fields or the barren heath beyond, it was a coveted luxury. When I would creep back at night, I generally found my day's food thrust upon the step of the staircase; for I was forbidden to return to the house within stated hours. With this I would steal to the garret where I slept. It was the topmost room in the house, with a shelving roof, a narrow window, partly without glass, an old oaken bedstead, a wide chest, and one chair. Often, as I lay sleepless, a large bat, which, during the day, had lodged in the worm-eaten curtains of the bed, would crawl forth, and whizzing past to the window, which it knew would never shut, leave me in a state of terror it were impossible to describe. Sometimes, when the moon was bright, and the night fine, I would draw the chair to the window, where, leaning out upon the roof, I could watch the stars, to wonder perhaps why misery or oppression was on earth, when all above in heaven

* Hartshorn's Salopia Antiqua.
† Plymley's Report on Agriculture before the House of Commons.

bespoke peace and uniformity. What wonder was it, then, that I thought, and afterwards wrote, what I then conceived to be poetry? It was a secret which, for years after, I guarded as my life. But I must tell upon what I wrote.

Adjoining to the house where I lived were a Catholic chapel and some cottages, where the officiating priests dwelt. An extensive garden, belonging to the priests, ran parallel for a considerable way to the fields I frequented, and was divided only by a ditch and hedge. Everything, to one so solitary, was soon a matter of observance. I found that, at certain hours of the day, an aged priest came to a little green plot that, shaded in by bushy shrubs, lay at the extremity of the garden nearest the heath. This place was a sodded hollow, in which was a sun-dial, and beds of the rarest carnations. To these the old man attended with assiduous care, watering and pruning, propping and pressing up their bursting flowers with round pieces of card and paper. As these flowers died, the card or paper was taken off. That they might not litter this little dainty plot of ground, they were placed in a corner of the rustic seat upon which the priest daily sat to read. When he had tended his flowers, he usually read a book he brought, mostly aloud, and always in the Latin tongue. I have since thought that that old man might have written on his sun-dial what the monk of old did, *Horas non numero nisi serenas*—'We only count the hours that are serene.' One day, after a storm of wind, I found the pile of card and paper scattered and blown by the wind over the thick hawthorn fence. These little papers seemed like a providential gift. I gathered them, and carefully concealed them in my bosom. That night, in the bright moonlight, with the window-ledge for my table, and a burnt skewer for my pen, I first wrote down my thoughts. My nights were no longer unhappy, or the hours long. The moon was to me like the face of a dear friend in the far-heavens. How to hide these papers became a matter of grave thought. If they were found, I should be beaten; if I hid them on the heath or in the fields, the rain might destroy them: my room contained no hiding-place. At length I found the strangest one in the world: no comic romance could have devised a stranger: it was a worm-eaten hollow in the leg of the bedstead. To me it was the rarest cabinet ever devised; for it safely held all my worldly treasures.

The life I led is too terrible to describe. No Oliver Twist in a workhouse had a worse. I was without friends, without sympathy, without books. I knew my heart was breaking. At length, without warning, one bitter day in March I was hurried to the nearest town, and on to a coach. With a begging letter and half-a-crown I commenced my journey of three hundred miles. My half-crown proved to me an inexpressible torment; my whole thoughts were how to divide it. Every time I saw a guard or coachman dismount, I thought of the necessary shilling. To do the best I could, I changed it for five sixpences: when the coach stopped in the night, the coachman came for his gratuity; I put a sixpence into his hand, and burst into tears. 'I am very poor,' I said; ''tis all I can give.' He pressed back the sixpence, held up a lantern to my face, left me, and returned in five minutes with a steaming glass of weak brandy and water, and a plate of sandwiches. I had had no food since early morning. He made me eat and drink, thrust the remnant of the sandwiches into my lap, bade me a cheerful good night, and shouting out to the guard, 'I say, Joe, be good to this little 'un, as the Lord loves you,' disappeared within the tavern door. About three o'clock in a drizzling March morning the coach reached the metropolis; I alighted, and had to sit upon my box on the pavement in Oxford Street, whilst the merits of the letter I carried were discussed within the coach-office. At last, after a weary time, I was placed in a hackney-coach with an intoxicated man; my terror was indescribable. One of my sixpences was called for to pay a turnpike gate. At length the western coach was overtaken, and my journey continued. I had for my companion an aged Jew. As dawn broke, he viewed me very attentively, and vowing that I was like his dead daughter Rachel, invited me to partake of his breakfast, consisting of hard eggs and brown bread. This I declined; but I was an attentive listener to his story—as pathetic, if not so poetical, as that of Jephtha's daughter.

The early morning of another day found me in a large town some few miles from my own. One of my memorable shillings had been divided between two obliging coachmen. I sat with the last in my hand upon a settle within the bar of the inn where the coach stopped. The landlord came to ask me if I would not have breakfast? I resolutely said no. I had then a habit, as I have now, of unconsciously talking aloud. I debated the expenditure of the shilling; I was overheard; the fat landlord reappeared; he took me by the hand, led me to his own breakfast-table, watched whilst the landlady sweetened my tea well, told me some long story about his own boyish travels, and considered my outspoken comment upon the shilling as an amazing joke. I reached the end of my journey with *that* shilling unbroken.

They did not know me when I reached home. My father wept over me like a child—I was so altered—so broken-hearted. I became insensible from excess of joy. If, like the ancient king, I counted up the number of my happy days, that day of return would be one of them.

THE STREETS OF LONDON.

NO. I.—MONMOUTH STREET.

Among the many streets of London that have a peculiar character, and are inhabited by a peculiar people, one of the most remarkable in all respects is Monmouth Street. It is a somewhat broad thoroughfare, taking a semicircular bend from the top of High Street, St Giles's, south-west towards the intricate regions of Seven Dials on the one side, and of Soho on the other. It is the main thoroughfare of that crowded district, and is crowded and wretched enough in itself; but different in the kind of crowd, and the degree and description of wretchedness, from all that surrounds it. The most careless observer cannot enter it without being struck by the singularity of its appearance. It abounds with dealers in second-hand articles, chiefly of apparel, and is the grand entrepôt for old clothes for the west end, just as Petticoat Lane and Rag Fair are for the eastern quarters of the metropolis. The stranger, on passing through it, is struck with the unhealthiness depicted on the pallid faces of the children, with which it absolutely teems; and with the strange disagreeable musty smell that arises from its overcrowded cellars, and pervades the houses to the very chimney-pots. To those who do know it, and who wish to study human life and character, there is no spot in the whole metropolis that offers a more fruitful subject for observation.

It takes its name from the unfortunate son of Charles II., who was executed for rebellion in the year 1685. Soho Square, in the immediate vicinity, which was built about the same time, was originally called Monmouth Square, in honour of the same personage; but after his execution, its name was changed to that which it now bears. The street retains its first appellation. At that period the neighbourhood was fashionable; but fashion gradually travelled to the west and north, to Gerrard Street and Dean Street, and then upwards to Tyburn; and the whole place, south and east of Soho Square, about eighty or ninety years ago, was left to the lowest of the population of London. At what time the Jews first took possession of Monmouth Street is not exactly known. Gay, in his amusing poem of 'Trivia, or the Art of Walking the Streets of London,' mentions Monmouth Street as famous for 'old suits' in the year 1712; so that generation after generation of the same race of people, and the same peculiar class of traders, have continued, through all the chances and changes of time and fashion, to make it their dwelling-place. It numbers about fifty houses on each side of the way; and on the right-hand side, on entering from High Street, forty-five at least out of the fifty are shops occupied by dealers in old clothes, chiefly Jews; the remainder being chandlers' shops, to supply the hourly wants of the inhabitants. The other side is not quite so full of Jews; but at least one-half of the shops even there are occupied by them, and the other half by dealers in the cast-off apparel of ladies. Their wares are spread out to the best advantage, and cover the windows to such a degree, that very little light can penetrate into the shops. The doors are also half blocked up by strings of garments, which dangle in the impure atmosphere, and shut out by that inlet also the light which might otherwise enter. In fact, the whole stock in trade of one of these shops is sometimes displayed in front of it; for when you enter, little else is to be seen besides a deal counter, and a beggarly account of empty shelves. Jews have for the most part this striking peculiarity—they love not only to do business, but to enjoy pleasure as much as possible out of doors. Enter the street when the tide of business has most strongly set in, and you will be sure to see before some of the shops the process of a bargain and sale enacted in its minutest details. The actors in the scene are usually the shopkeeper as buyer, and one of his peripatetic brethren—of whom so many perambulate the streets with long bags and incessant inquiries after 'Old Clo'—as vender. Observe the 'diamond cut diamond' fashion with which the negotiation is carried on—'When Jew meets Jew, then comes the tug of war.' It is curious to witness the searching scrutiny with which the purchaser examines the garment. It is a coat. First of all, it is held in outstretched arms against the light, that any transparencies in the texture may be detected in the back and skirts. Then the sleeves are turned up, and the elbows carefully examined as to the number of threads which wear has rendered visible, or the quantity of grease they have imbibed—sure indices of the amount of service the garment has seen. Then comes the important question of price, concerning which a warm discussion takes place. Again the coat is examined, the number of 'thin' places and the quantity of grease about the collar and cuffs carefully estimated. Presently the storm subsides; the coat and a half-crown or two change owners, and the parties separate.

In a day or two that same coat makes its appearance amongst the rest of the stock in front of the shop, and none but an experienced hand would know it again. When it was bought, it was rusty, dirty, and threadbare; now it is to be sold, it is glossy, black, and with a very respectable appearance of nap. It has in fact undergone a mysterious process called 'duffing.' By the aid of soap and turpentine the grease has been removed; a wire clothes-brush has scratched up a nap from the bare threads, whilst a sort of pigment, which partakes partly of the nature of dye, partly of that of blacking, has been rubbed into it; 'and,' exclaims the Jew as he hangs it up exultingly for sale, 'who's to tell it from a new one?'

With baits of this kind, the Monmouth Street shopkeepers have no mean power in attracting and fixing the fancies of many persons who have little to spare for the adornment of the outward man. It is a maxim with the fraternity, that whoever appears in the street is a customer; or if not, that he ought to be. Consequently, nothing is wanting on their part to draw him into a 'transaction.' They pace up and down before their shops, and inquire of every passenger 'if he wants anything in their way?' The answer is generally in the negative: whereupon the adroit tradesman steps up beside the stranger, and in a confidential manner whispers into his ear, 'Have you anything to sell, sir?' This sort of importunity is not, however, nearly so characteristic of Monmouth Street as of the more eastern depôts of cast-off garments near the Strand or Whitechapel. The truth is, Monmouth Street has a spice of aristocracy attached to it. It is one of the principal media by which the cast-off clothes of the nobility reach, through their servants and valets, the middle and poorer classes. In fact, fortunes have been made in Monmouth Street; its denizens, therefore, are in some small degree more civilised than their brethren of the east.

While it is a rule in Monmouth Street that the old-clothes dealers have the shops, and all the houses above them, the cellars are inhabited by a different race. They are almost invariably appropriated to the sale of old boots and shoes; and the passenger who walks along, and looks down as he goes, will see at the foot of every dirty stair leading from the street an industrious cobbler busily at work. Upon one side up the stairs, boots and shoes of all ages and sizes, rubbed thickly over with wax to hide their manifold deficiencies, are neatly arranged, while the other side is set apart for apples or sweetmeats, or now and then for cheap crockery, to be exchanged for old shoes with those who come to sell and not to buy. These wretched cellars, which receive no other light than the feeble glimmer that penetrates down the stair, are let at the enormous rentals of four, five, or six shillings a-week, unfurnished; and in these a family of eight or ten persons are cooped up, working, eating, and sleeping within the same dark, damp, unwholesome walls. If there is a father to the family, he is generally a cobbler, while the mother plies the mangle; and so 'cribbed and confined' are they of necessity, that the mangle not unfrequently does service for a table at dinner-time, and is made a bed for the younger branches of the family at night. Fresh air there is little or none. The floor is mostly of earth; and when it is not, the dirt has been known to accumulate until it became three inches thick upon the boards; and the whole so damp, that mushrooms have grown in the corners, and mosses in every scanty hole that was not trodden upon by the feet of its superabundant inhabitants. Any one who enters must stoop and walk backwards, like one who descends into the hold of a ship; and if he be not well acquainted with the ways of the place, he runs a risk of overthrowing some hundreds of pairs of old shoes, and—worse mishap still—as many pieces of crockery. Besides these, however, Monmouth Street has its more extensive firms in the second-hand boot and shoe line. There are several respectable people who, under pretence of corns and bunions, declare they cannot wear *new* leather, because it 'draws the feet.' These are the customers of the larger shops. Amongst the above-ground depôts, both for boots and clothes, there are some proprietors well known for their wealth, and who are talked respectfully of 'in the city:' the capital they have accumulated in doctoring up boots, they largely employ in discounting bills.

The trade in cast-off ladies' clothes, largely carried on in Monmouth Street, is a mysterious subject, which, it must be honestly confessed, we are unable to fathom. What becomes of the faded satin gowns and crushed bonnets displayed at the door-posts; who may be the consumers of the second-hand artificial flowers, the mock jewellery, the cast-off hair-combs, the dilapidated fans, the broken feathers, the mended kid gloves, the darned lace, and the dirty packs of cards, which are displayed in the windows—we are at a loss to conjecture. The only clue to the mystery which we know of, is presented in the costume of the ladies who perform the fashionable characters at the minor theatres.

Monmouth Street puts on its best face on the Jews' and Christians' Sabbaths. The Hebrews, as we before hinted, have a great liking for the open air; consequently, on fine holiday evenings, some of them are to be seen seated in chairs on the pavement before their shops, the men smoking pipes, and the women joining in moderate potations of porter; a pewter quart of which stands just inside the door on a little round table. Children are playing about. The whole group is well, perhaps elegantly dressed. Most of the Monmouth Street denizens are Jews, and that race are remarkably fond of fine clothes, disdaining shabby or second-hand articles for their own holiday use, as they love them for 'the sake of the profits' at other times.

In spite of a few cases of affluence, the general effect of the street upon strangers is far from inviting. It smells of old age and squalidness; its atmosphere seems as if no breath of heaven ever stirred it; the very loaves in the chandlers' shops look dirty and musty. The herrings that dangle from the windows of the same receptacles appear as old and dried, and out of date, as the garments; the butter has a jaundiced and unclean look; and the eggs are of a yellow as dingy as the thickest fogs of London.

Altogether, Monmouth Street presents features which make it one of the most curious thoroughfares in London. It has been the receptacle of the crumbs and offals of fashion for nearly a century and a half; and a true history of its shops would be a correct history of British costume during that long period. Neither is it without its uses and benefits to the public. It helps to exemplify Mr Fisher Murray's axiom, that 'in London you can get anything you want at the moment you want it.' A man of limited means, having a sudden call for a suit of clothes, for instance, can obtain them at his own price in Monmouth Street at five minutes' warning. It is, we must admit, a dangerous market to deal in; for the Jews invariably ask you double the price which a thing is worth, or what they will, if hard pressed, consent to take. Lately, their trade in cast-off garments has suffered greatly from the introduction of cheap new clothing; some of which is manufactured by a process little better than 'duffing.' Rotten cloth rags, oakum, and other materials of an equally worthless kind, are reduced by machinery to a state which is called (we quote a well-known M.P.) 'devils' dust.' By dint of a vast deal of pressure, and a very little weaving of the fibrous material, a sort of cloth is produced, which, though it has a good outside appearance, possesses very little stability. Garments made of this description of stuff are so cheap that they have withdrawn much business from Monmouth Street.

'THE TRADE.'

THIRD ARTICLE.—BOOKSELLING ABROAD.

In treating of any subject respecting books, it is difficult to get away from Germany. There modern literature first took root, and, nurtured by the press, branched off into the 'uttermost corners of the earth.' There also literary commerce has been reduced to a system more complete and effectual than in any other country in which 'the trade' flourishes. It is to Germany, therefore, that our present notices of the book-trade must be for a while confined.

Piracy and fraud are as old as bookselling itself. The ingenious devices of the dishonest kept pace with the extensive development of the book-trade by the printer's art; and as soon as a publisher became famous for the correctness and legible neatness of his editions, his name and 'marks' were fraudulently forged by inferior typographers, to insure a readier sale for works than their own merits would have procured. We must here digress for a moment, to say a word concerning the symbols adopted by the old booksellers, who were (and by the book-fancier still are) so well known by the devices they placed on their title-pages, that neither their name nor place of residence was necessary. Of these marks, the best known are as follows:—The anchor, the sign adopted by Raphelengius of Leyden; an anchor, with a dolphin twisted round it, was the symbol of the Mavutti of Venice and Rome. The Stephenses of Paris and Geneva put forth the olive-tree; and the Elzevirs of Amsterdam adopted the same symbol. The signs of the Zodiac were likewise appropriated as marks by some publishers; while others constructed rebuses. Thus, Richard Harrison, an English printer, who died in 1562, printed on his title-pages a *hare*, a sheaf of *rye*, and a representation of the *sun*. William Norton, who, besides a bookseller, was treasurer of Christ's Hospital (1593), had a 'sweet *William*' growing out of a *tun*, inscribed with the word *nor*. Others equally puerile might be cited. The literary pirates who forged the marks of the best booksellers chiefly resided in Geneva and Vienna. In the last-named city, one J. Thomas Edler Von Trattner made himself as famous in the book-trade by the daring boldness of his piracies, as the Sallee rovers did amongst the shipping interests of the civilised world. No sooner had a printer put forth a carefully-prepared edition of some valued classic, than these forgers set their presses to work, and produced an exact imitation of it at a much lower price. This system had risen by the year 1765 to a pitch so ruinous to the regular trade, that the German publishers entered into a confederacy to put a stop to it. Erasmus Reich, one of the partners in the Weidmannsche Buchhandlung (an extensive publishing concern), called a meeting at Frankfort, and proposed certain laws and regulations, the chief object of which was to tie down the booksellers of Germany not to sell any copies of the spurious editions. To this agreement fifty-nine booksellers subscribed. By the year 1797, the association spread its influence throughout the country, and ever since the latter year, no person can sell a book without being a member of the German booksellers' association (Deutschen Buchhandlers Verein) of Leipsic, to which place the book-trade has since been concentrated. By means of this concentration, improvements have gradually been made in the organisation of the book-trade, until formed into the system it is at present—an explanation of which will be found interesting.

The book-trade of Germany is divided into three distinct branches—1st, That of the publisher (Verlagsgeschäft); 2d, The booksellers' business (Sortimentshandel); 3d, The agencies (Commissionsgeschäft). The first two branches are frequently united, and often all three are carried on together. The business of the publisher needs little description. He buys the manuscript from the author, and gets it printed, either by his own presses, or by other parties for his account, and sends copies to such booksellers as he thinks likely to sell the work. The invoice is fastened on the outside of the parcel, half folded up, so that only the head, bearing the name of the bookseller to whom it is directed, and the name of the publisher from whom it comes, is to be seen. The parcels are all put in one bale, and sent to the publisher's agent in Leipsic, who distributes them to the different agents in that town. Every respectable bookseller of Germany employs an agent in Leipsic. Such copies of new works are called 'Nova;' on the invoice is put 'pr. Nov.' (*pro Novitate*). They are sent 'on condition' (*à condition*), that is, with the option to keep them or to send them back. The returned books are properly called *remittiren*, though more frequently and jocosely krebse (crabs). By such conditional consignments, private persons have the advantage of being able to look into the merit of a work before they are called upon to buy it, whereby new publications get to all parts of the country, and at the same price as at the place of publication—a system which is quite peculiar to the German book-trade, and which has certainly contributed much to the diffusion of knowledge in Germany. The prices are put down either at the shop price or net price. On the shop price (ordinair) a discount of one-third, or thirty-three and one-third per cent., is usually allowed by the publishers to 'the trade' for books, and for prints and journals one-fourth, or twenty-five per cent. Books which have been published for some time are seldom sent out 'on condition,' but must be ordered, which is done by sending a small slip of paper (Verlangszettel)—containing the name of the publisher, the name of the bookseller who orders, and the title of the work—to the agent of the publisher, who transmits the work by the first opportunity, and, if quickly wanted, by post. Every publisher of note sends some copies of his publications to his agent in Leipsic, in order that he may execute without delay any orders which may come in; so that the shortest and cheapest way of procuring a work is generally by sending to Leipsic for it.

At the New Year, at Easter, and at Michaelmas, the fairs before alluded to* are held at Leipsic, exclusively devoted to the sale of books. Of the three, however, the grand concentration of the trade takes place at Easter (Jubilatemesse); for that is the time when all accounts are, or should be, closed between the booksellers of various parts of Germany, who either attend the fair personally for that purpose, or send some confidential clerk.

Although the book-trade of Germany is centralised in Leipsic, yet it must not be supposed that it is exclusively conducted at the fairs. New publications, though usually first issued at them, are occasionally forwarded for general distribution in the monthly parcels, of which many thousand bales annually arrive, and are sent away. Thus, wherever a book may be printed, it is invariably published or issued in Leipsic; where every local *Sortimentshandler* has his *commissionär*, or agent. Instead, therefore, of applying directly to the local publisher for a new work, he sends to this commissioner in Leipsic, and through him the order reaches its destination. If a bookseller of Berlin, for instance, has ordered books from Vienna, Strasburg, Munich, Stuttgard, and a dozen other places, they are all transmitted to his Leipsic agent, who then forwards them in one mass much more cheaply than if each portion had been sent separately and directly to Berlin.

The censorship of the press, which is exercised in every state belonging to the German confederation, opposes a great and important hindrance to the prosperity of literature, especially in a commercial point of view. Each journal and publication under twenty sheets, whatever be the subject of which it treats—politics, literature, arts, or science—must be sent in manuscript to the censor, who strikes out what he thinks proper before the printing of it is allowed. The delay, and frequently arbitrary or capricious interference arising from this system, are evident; nor can it be denied that much bad feeling and discontent are thereby created. Moreover, not only all German books published in the country are subject to this censorship, but in some of the states all books imported from other states belonging to the German confederation are similarly treated. In Austria, for instance, all books coming from Prussia, or from the minor states of Germany, are considered as foreign books, and are subject to a second censorship in that country. They are either admitted free by the word 'Admittitur,' or admitted with the restriction not to be advertised ('Transeat'); sometimes they are to be delivered only to certain persons to whom the censorship has given special leave to receive them ('Erga schedam'); or they are totally prohibited ('Damnatur'). In Prussia, all books printed out of Germany in the German language must be laid before the College of Upper Censorship (Ober Censur Collegium) before the sale of them is allowed. These separate interests and separate laws prove very efficacious in encouraging piracy. In Germany, neither author nor publisher has much chance of making a fortune; each state of the confederation having its own law of copyright, and the protection it affords of course only extends over the territory itself; hence, no sooner does a work of merit appear in one state than it is pirated by the next, and as the same language is common to the whole confederation, nothing more is wanted than a mere reprint. This practice affords an explanation of several peculiarities which attach to German bookselling. The most prominent of which are, firstly, the cheapness of literary labour; for a publisher cannot be expected to give much for a work which, if it be bad, has no sale, and if good, is forthwith stolen. Secondly, the frequency of publications by subscription; for there is no other method by which even authors of the greatest genius can secure a reasonable profit. Thirdly, the coarseness of paper and types for which German books are distinguished; for the publisher has no chance of competing with the pirate except by making his own edition too cheap to be undersold.

Despite these hindrances, however, 'the trade' flourishes. The number of German booksellers has so much increased within the last twenty years, that many of those who have been long established are complaining of underselling and other irregularities; but in that respect the older members of the trade may be said to suffer no more than their compeers in other branches of commerce, whose profits and modes of doing business are interfered with from competition set up through the demands of an augmenting population. The number of booksellers in Leipsic in 1839 was 116; the total number in Germany was 1283, who resided in 337 towns. Besides these, were 49 booksellers belonging to German-Switzerland, and 99 foreigners who regularly do business at the Leipsic fairs.* Since 1839, however, the number of foreign houses in connexion with Leipsic has increased, especially those of Great Britain. Several firms, both in London and Edinburgh, regularly attend at least one of the fairs yearly.

Having disposed of the book-trade of Germany, we now proceed to glance at that of Russia. Here the dawning of literature began with Peter the Great. The first book ever printed in the country was struck off at St Petersburg in 1713, and the first newspaper in the year following. Now there are 25 booksellers and printers at St Petersburg, besides several others at Moscow, Riga, Dorpat, Reval, Warsaw, and Wilna. Among the number are many German establishments, which supply that part of the population who speak the German language, and such of the natives as are fond of German literature, who are pretty numerous. In 1837, the number of new works published in Russia was 866, of which 740 were original, and 122 translated works. There were also 48 periodicals treating of politics and literature. The censorship of the press is extremely rigid.

Of the book-trade carried on in the more southern portions of Europe, Paris is the head quarters: we shall therefore treat of French bookselling in this place. In France there is no such organisation of the book-trade as in Germany. Paris is the great central point where almost all works of any renown are printed, and where the most distinguished men of letters, artists, and authors, are to be found. The booksellers of the departments, it is true, have also their agents in Paris, but they do not maintain such a regular and constant intercourse as those in Germany. Besides, the publishers (*Editeurs Libraires*) seldom send their publications '*à condition*;' the booksellers (*Marchands Libraires*) must order, and generally pay for them in cash. Sometimes, however, a credit of three, four, or six months is granted. The trade allowances are regulated not as in other countries, by the sale price, but by the subjects of the works. The discount on historical, critical, and elementary books, is twenty-five per cent.; that on mathematical and

* See p. 150 of our last number.

* See the Quarterly Journal of the Statistical Society, vol. iii.

strictly scientific works, is from ten to fifteen per cent.; while upon romances, tales, and literature of the lighter order, it is often as high as fifty per cent. Literary censorship was early introduced into France, and exercised most severely. Charles IX. published an edict in 1563, by which he forbade printers to issue unauthorised works 'under pain of hanging or strangulation.' The censorship continued to be enforced down to the reign of Charles X., whose unfortunate ordonnance of the 27th July 1830, by which he would have further circumscribed the liberty of the press, produced the last French revolution. From that time the censorship was abolished; but a sort of substitute for it remains, in the very stringent laws against libel. In the year 1830, there were in France 620 printers, residing in 283 towns, and 1124 booksellers and stationers; all of whom are obliged to be *brevetés*, that is, licensed, and sworn to abide by certain prescribed rules. A Paris paper states that their press had produced within the last year as many as 6377 works in the dead and living languages, 1388 prints and engravings, 100 musical works, 54 maps and charts; whilst the copies of newspapers struck off amounted in number to 34,750,000.

In Italy there is no regular intercourse whatever among booksellers. It is only with the greatest trouble and expense that a work published in any part of Italy can be procured in a remote town not belonging to the same government. The counterfeiting of books is so prevalent, that one printed at Milan is counterfeited at Florence, and *vice versa*. The censorship also presses heavily on all kinds of publications, much more so than in Germany. The customs' duty on foreign works is so enormous, that it is cheaper to pirate popular books than to import them. In the kingdom of the Two Sicilies, each octavo volume has to pay 3 carlini, or 1s. entrance duty; a quarto volume 6 carlini; and a volume in folio 10 carlini, or 3s. 4d.

In Holland, the chief seat of the book-trade is Amsterdam, which boasts of 80 booksellers, who have adopted the German system in dealing with their provincial brethren, of whom there are 101. In 1828 there were published in Holland 770 new books. In Belgium, Brussels is almost the only town where works of any note are published. They consist principally of re-publications of French and English works, which are much in demand, on account of their neatness and cheapness. There are several extensive printing establishments at Brussels, and also a joint company of publishers, whose open and avowed aim is the counterfeiting of good French and English works, published often at the same time as the original edition, or very soon after. By the constitution of 25th February 1831, Belgium enjoys an extensive freedom of the press. In the year 1838, there appeared in Belgium 84 periodicals, of which 40 were published at Brussels.* In other continental countries, the trade carried on in books is almost nominal.

Before we glance at the book-trade at home—which we shall do in a concluding article—we must notice the increasing demand for foreign books which has recently taken place in Great Britain. From the continental peace, which, happily, has not been disturbed since 1815, the importation into this country of foreign works has steadily augmented. Free commercial intercourse once established with our continental brethren, intellectual and literary intercommunion followed; and to render this the more effectual, the French, German, and Italian languages have been of late extensively studied. Books in those languages (especially in the two former) have therefore been eagerly read, and a demand for them increases daily. Five-and-twenty years ago, there was no English bookseller who confined his trade exclusively to foreign books; now, there are at least fifty German, French, and Italian booksellers in London alone. In Edinburgh, there are three of 'the trade' who make the sale of foreign works a prominent feature in their business. During the last ten years, an average of L.8000 has been annually paid for duties on foreign works imported into Great Britain.* The value of such books imported in 1843 was L.132,019.

* See the Quarterly Journal of the Statistical Society, vol. iii.

* This duty was, on books printed previous to 1801, L.1 per cwt.; on those printed after, L.5. By the new tariff of 1843, the latter item is reduced to L.2. 10s. per cwt.

DEER-STALKING IN GLENARTNEY.

[Extracted, with permission, from Sir T. D. Lauder's beautiful volume descriptive of the Queen's Visit to Scotland in 1842. Printed by T. Constable, Edinburgh, 1844.]

Clear and beautiful was the dawn of morning on Monday, the 12th of September, betokening weather perfectly delightful for carrying into effect the deer-stalking expedition to the forest of Glenartney, which Lord Willoughby de Eresby had planned for the amusement of his royal guest, Prince Albert.

Glenartney has been already alluded to when passing down Stratherne, by Comrie, the river Ruchill there joining the Erne, having its origin in the forest. Let not the Cockney suppose that the word forest necessarily implies a district covered with noble oaks, chestnuts, or trees of any other description. The first meaning of the word may have been that of a wooded country, but in our old times it was applied to a large extent of surface, whether wooded or not, set apart by royal edict for the wild beasts and fowls of chase, certain laws being established within its precincts. A forest, as the word was strictly taken in early times, could not be in the hands of any one but the king; but, in later periods, forests have become the property of subjects, or have been created by them, though without being protected by forest laws. The royal forest in the Isle of Wight, in which there is not a tree, is not the only English example still remaining of the view here taken of this old meaning of the word. Where the soil was rich, such a tract of country, so appropriated, naturally became woodland, and in this way the original meaning of the word may have again become applicable. From this cause, the forests long appropriated in Scotland as a range for red-deer, may have some woods about their lower outskirts, as that of Braemar and some others; but, in general, they are altogether devoid of trees, or even bushes, the defences of the stag consisting in the wild nature of the ground—its bareness, which allows him to see strange objects at the distance of several miles from the spot where he and his hinds may be feeding—and in the strongholds of the steep and lofty mountains, in the seamed parts of which are found those large hollows sloping outwards, surrounded on three sides by high and frequently inaccessible and often shivered precipices, called, in deer-stalking language, by their Gaelic name of corries, in which the deer delight to dwell, and from which they issue to bound upwards to the breezy ridges of the mountains for better outlook, or to follow the rills that issue from them downwards to better pasture below. He who, in painting an ideal picture of a Highland forest, therefore, should select a portion of the noble oak scenery of the New Forest, or of Windsor, for his study from nature, would commit a most lamentable error.

The forest of Glenartney has, on its north and western borders, the high mountains of Stuck-a-chroan, Benvoirlich, and their associates, rising out of the southern side of Locherne. The deer have it thus in their power to occupy some lofty positions, and the intricacies produced by the lower supports of these mountains are such as to give them great advantages. The forest abounds in streams, having rich vegetation on their banks, and its whole surface is naturally good deer pasture. In the words of old Donald Cameron, Lord Willoughby's head forester, who has now been in Glenartney upwards of forty years, 'The nature of the ground is good and healthy, interspersed with heath and *rashes*, and natural grass, and it is beautiful to the eye of a traveller'—that is, to the eye of a traveller who, like Donald, has all his life been looking after deer—or to the eye of the enthusiastic traveller, who loves to look upon nature in some of her wildest forms; but for the eye that loves the deep repose of nature, beneath the giant limbs of oaks, whose thick-set tops, spreading over roods of ground, produce an ever-enduring shade throughout the whole of the grand aisles of that leafy edifice, supported by their huge and knotted stems, save where a transient sunbeam may break through some accidental opening above to chequer the solemn ground—such a scene as Glenartney would be absolute barrenness.

It had been announced by Lord Willoughby that Mr Campbell of Monzie, one of the most active deer-stalkers in Scotland, and one who is well acquainted with every foot of the forest of Glenartney, should accompany Prince Albert to the forest, for the purpose of taking him up to a deer. The prince and Lord Willoughby set out in an open carriage and four for the lodge of Dalclathick, at six o'clock in the morning, attended by his royal highness's jäger. The distance to the lodge is ten miles; and, on reaching it at seven o'clock, they found Mr Campbell of Monzie, and Donald Cameron, faithful to *tryst*.

The moment the open carriage stopped, the prince laid his hand on its side, and vaulted lightly out upon the ground. Advancing towards Monzie with the utmost affability, he said, 'Mr Campbell, I understand you are to show me the forest, and how to kill a deer?' Monzie replied he had been informed that he was to have that honour. He trusted that the prince would excuse that free-masonry which was essential in deer-stalking, as it was hopeless to attempt to succeed without it, and that for himself he was not one of the court, courtly, and would require the indulgence of his royal highness. The prince assured him that he would place himself entirely under his guidance, and that he would follow it implicitly. He then put some questions about the weather—asked whether it was favourable for the sport, and inquired whether his dress, which was a gray Glengarry bonnet, with a shooting-coat and trousers of the same colour, would do for deer-stalking; and on Monzie assuring him that it was in all respects perfect, he proposed starting immediately for the mountains of the forest, which were seen rising in huge and lofty masses at some miles' distance towards the north. A Highland pony was in readiness, which he mounted. Lord Willoughby and Mr Campbell both offered to carry his rifle, but this he would by no means allow, and he instantly slung it over his own back, saying, 'I am riding, and you are walking;' and from thenceforward the prince continued to carry it himself during the whole day. Lord Willoughby had arranged that the party should include no one but the individuals already mentioned, as nothing is more destructive to deer-stalking than being followed by '*a tail*.' It happened, from some accident, that Monzie did not bring any hounds with him.

The party now went rapidly up the side of the forest burn, and after a considerable walk, Monzie discovered a large herd of deer on the brow of Coir'-eangain, or the Hindsback-corry. The prince's eye glistened with delight; and certainly never were deer beheld to greater advantage, for the morning sun now shone fully upon them; and there is no position in which those antlered denizens of the mountains appear so gloriously as when thus seen on a breezy brow, high above the hunter's eye, with their coats glistening under as bright a sun as then shone upon them, and with so clear a sky behind—all these circumstances tending to make them look as aërial as those not very deeply learned in the mysteries of deer-stalking frequently find them to be.

As it was manifestly impossible to stalk these deer directly from hence, they hastened up the march burn, with the intention of getting to a pass to the northward of the base of Coir'-eangain, with the hope that they might move thither. But they were so wild, and the ground so smooth, that they changed their position, and went too high up the hill to enable the deer-stalkers to effect their object as at first planned. They were now, therefore, compelled to change their stratégie, and to make a hasty detour by Leathad-na-Sgéith, or the Wing Brae, so as to endeavour to meet the herd as they were in the act of crossing from Coir'-eangain into Coir'-gairian. To effect this, they had to go round the foot of Coir'-eangain, and then to climb to the summit of the highest ridge of mountains extending round the forest. This involved the necessity of a smart and arduous walk of an hour.

After they had gone about half-way up the mountain, the prince dismounted for the day. The party then moved on in Indian files, and in deep silence, though at a very rapid pace, towards the brow of the hill above Coir'-coinean (Coir'-coin-fhirm, White Hound Corry). The deer made a slight check there, and appeared disposed to break at another part of the hill; but finally, they set their heads straight for Coir'-coinean. It then became a race whether deer or deer-stalkers should get thither first; and after a great deal of toil and fatigue, it terminated considerably in favour of the deer; for just as the prince got to the point whence the shot is usually obtained, the hindmost of the herd were dropping out of sight into Coir'-coinean. But Prince Albert seized his rifle, and though the deer nearest to him could not have been at a less distance than 150 yards, and bounding at full speed, he fired and wounded it. It was afterwards found within a few hundred yards of the place where the shot was fired; but at that moment circumstances were too exciting to allow them to look for it, as they expected that some of those in advance would hear the report, and move. The prince, indeed, not aware that his shot had been fatal, was doomed, whilst his rifle was reloading, to experience that feeling of mingled delight and regret to which every deer-stalker is exposed when beholding the glorious spectacle of a noble herd sweeping rapidly into the gloomy shadow of the glen below, the serenity of his passing thoughts being at the same time disturbed by the consciousness that one of them 'hath ta'en a hurt;' and that, after all, his hope of getting him is but small indeed; for every one who has followed this princely sport must know full well that nothing short of *instant* death, which is but rarely produced, can secure the immediate possession of a deer. The view from the summit above Leathad-na-Sgéith is one of the grandest in the whole forest; for, at the foot of the deep Coir'-coinean, the yet more profound and much more rugged Glen-Coinean opens to the eye, and carries it on through a long perspective of barren wildness and magnificence, one huge form succeeding another, till the flight of human vision rests on the snow-clad summit of Benvoirlich. The contemplation of this wild Highland scene, with the dusky deer darting away far off in the glen, called forth a burst of admiration from the prince worthy of the most enthusiastic mountaineer, and which would have gratified any true Highland heart.

Again the party proceeded with great expedition, in the hope of meeting some deer which they saw before them near Stuc-na-càbaig, or the Cheese Cliff. When they had almost reached the top of the Stron, it became necessary to advance more leisurely, and with some degree of caution, and having got to a place a little way from the brow of the hill, they began to move forward on their knees, as there was reason to hope that the deer were at no great distance. As it was absolutely essential that silence should be preserved, Monzie whispered to the old forester, 'Hold the prince back, Donald, whilst I creep to the brow to see where the deer are.' 'Hoo am I to do that?' replied Donald Cameron. 'Just lay hold of his arm if the deer come forward, until it is time to fire.' 'Haud the prince!' said Donald, with a degree of astonishment which, forty years' deer-stalker as he was, had nearly deprived him of his presence of mind—'haud the prince! I'll no do that. Ye maun just grip him yoursel, Monzie, and *I'll* look owre the broo.' Monzie was obliged to consent to old Donald's arrangement, and, to insure success, was compelled to take the necessary liberty with the prince's arm. The herd did not come forward, but turned back round the hill. Indeed the wind was so unsteady, and shifted so often during that day, that the deer were wilder, and much more difficult to approach, than Monzie, or even old Donald himself, had ever before seen them. But throughout all the vicissitudes of the sport to which the prince was exposed, whilst he was quite as eager as any other young deer-stalker, he exhibited a patience and good-humour under disappointment which few old ones have ever possessed; and well indeed were these qualities tried during that day. Shortly after this they descried a single deer standing by himself on a brow considerably in advance, and somewhat below them. The prince had by this time shown so much promptly-acquired knowledge of the work, that his conductor was anxious he should stalk this deer by himself, and his royal highness was equally desirous to make the attempt. Off he set, therefore, entirely alone, creeping and wading on his hands and knees through a long succession of wet moss hags, sinking deep into their black chaos, now unseen, and then again appearing, until at length, when he had been for some time out of sight, the smoke of his rifle curled up from behind a knoll, its smart crack was heard, and although it turned out that the deer had gone off, it was afterwards retrieved.

The party then proceeded to the Stron-nam-breidhleag, or Cranberry Snout. Just before reaching it, the prince fired at a deer and broke its leg. It has already been said that they had no deer-hounds with them; but one of the under foresters having joined them a little before this, they left him to look after and watch the movements of the wounded animal, and hurried forward to the brow of a hill at the back of the Stron, as they saw a herd making for a pass in a small rocky burn before them. They were pushing on in Indian files, and in double quick time, through some deep moss hags, the prince walking as if he had been a native of these mountains, when Monzie suddenly descried the points of a horn appearing over a brow below. Thus immediately perceiving that the herd had changed its course, he had just time to seize the prince's arm with his left hand, and to reach the nearest part of old Donald's ancient person with the toe of his right foot—such liberties being considered as quite complimentary in deer-stalking, and at all times extremely gratifying, as conveying the pleasing intelligence that there are deer in sight. The prince and Monzie squatted like hares in their forms, and down went Donald on his back, partly from the kick, and partly from instinctive feeling; but it was this last that twitched up his features into that exquisite grin of happiness with which his countenance was moved as he lay on his back among the heather. All three were thus concealed from the deer, and the herd continued to draw slowly over the brow where they first appeared, and passed round the hill. Now came that glorious and exciting moment in deer-stalking, when the prospect of having your most sanguine hopes crowned with success is immediate, and where, at the same time, the smallest untoward accident may altogether blast them. The prince eagerly demanded, 'What am I to do?' 'Up! up!' cried Monzie. 'Nothing for it now but a rush down that moss hag; never mind the wet!' But he might have spared the latter advice; for before the words were well uttered, the prince was deep in the mysteries of that sable compound of vegetable matter, to explain the nature of which so many large volumes have been written both by philosophical and practical men. Down, down they sped, sometimes running in that most painful of all positions, with the legs straight, and the back bent till the face almost touches the ground, and sometimes ploughing through the black bog on hands and knees, utterly regardless of future personal appearance, as well as of those awkward salutations which their limbs met with from knaggy roots of antediluvian trees deeply concealed in the soft and sinking matter. The deer was all they thought of. And they just succeeded; for, by thus slanting the hill, they were enabled to arrive at a point precisely as the herd was crossing their line of advance at some little distance below them. The prince had only time to discharge one barrel before the herd disappeared from his sight. By that peculiar sound which is so gratifying to the ear of a deer-stalker, it was known that the ball had told, and some hair was observed to be *dusted* out of the point of the shoulder. His royal highness thought he had missed, and seemed somewhat incredulous when Monzie told him where he had seen the ball hit. But all doubt upon the question was speedily removed; for, while they were reloading the rifle, Donald trotted onwards a few hundred yards and came to a sudden stop, and with his eyes fixed on the ground like a pointer on game, began to fumble for his skian-dhu. 'Ha!' exclaimed the prince, 'he stops—he takes out his knife—it is dead!' And dead indeed it was; for on going up to it, there it lay with a hole through the point of the shoulder just as Monzie had said. 'Ah!' exclaimed the prince, 'it is a hind. I am so sorry that it is not a stag, for I promised the teeth of the first I killed to the queen.' The teeth, which are considered by the superstitious as a charm against the evil eye, are likewise preserved as trophies by deer-stalkers, and various little ornaments are made of them, such as beautiful studs or buttons. It must be observed that this was the first deer that had dropped to hand, though those previously fired at were afterwards retrieved.

They now fell back round the hill into Coir'-dhu, where much time was lost in waiting in vain for deer. Although every 'dodge' was tried, there was no getting them to move towards the pass. 'Have you killed many deer,' demanded the prince of Monzie, 'for I hear you are a great deer-stalker?' Monzie replied that he had shot about forty last year. 'Ah!' said the prince jocularly, 'that is the reason they will not come to me, for they know you are with me.' They did come at last, however, but so irregularly, and they rattled so rapidly down a hill, that his chance was a very poor one. He fired notwithstanding, and again that short deafened sound, which it is as impossible for an experienced hunter to mistake as it is to describe, announced that the deer was hit, and he was accordingly found some hundred yards below.

The day being considerably advanced, they now turned their faces homeward, as Prince Albert was most anxious to accompany her majesty in her drive. In their way, they tried for another deer at the back of Leathad-na-Sgèith; but the herd having been previously disturbed, they found it impossible either to stalk or to drive them, as they are wont to do on such occasions; the animals kept continually wheeling round and round in a constant succession of evolutions, such as deer alone can accomplish. Every effort was made by the deer-stalkers, but without success, as, in spite of all their exertions, the herd broke away through a pass leading over the very summit of the mountain, and as the prince was stationed at the bottom of the hill, he was disappointed of a shot; and thus ended the chase.

Prince Albert would not wait for the pony to be brought to him, but proceeded on foot to the lodge at Dalclathick, where luncheon was prepared. His royal highness pressed Lord Willoughby and Mr Campbell to sit down with him, and on their declining to do so, he filled three glasses of champagne, and presenting one to each, drank the third himself to their healths, thanking them at the same time for the excellent sport he had enjoyed. Though Lord Willoughby de Eresby did not always go with the prince directly up to the places where he expected to have shots, yet he followed his royal highness the whole day with a rifle in his hand. The prince and Lord Willoughby got into the carriage, and drove off to Drummond Castle, which they reached by three o'clock. This day's slaughter produced two stags and three hinds, the trophies of which were all collected and sent to Windsor.

MADEMOISELLE LENORMAND.

The French have been accused of incredulity and want of faith in matters of high and weighty import. How far this may be true we are not now about to inquire; but the sum of 500,000 francs, amassed by Mademoiselle Lenormand, the celebrated fortune-teller, testifies strongly to the credulity of the nation in subjects on which a want of faith might justly be defended. And that credulity, strange to say, was manifested at a time when what were called the fetters of ancient superstition were cast aside by a large portion of society. Moreover, in the character of this far-famed prophetess there does not seem to have been any remarkable elevation, or any great display of intellect. A few fortunate coincidences, an unbounded self-confidence, and considerable shrewdness, were the groundwork of her fortunes, and served to call forth, in a singularly striking form, the weakness of many of the most celebrated characters of the last half century; though it must be acknowledged that her own countrymen alone were not the dupes of her imposture.

The father of Mademoiselle Lenormand was of Falaise; but having married a Mademoiselle Guilbert of Alençon, he established himself in the latter city, where the celebrated fortune-teller was born, besides a younger sister, and a brother who entered the military service. M. Lenormand died young, and his widow, who re-married, did not long survive her second nuptials. The second husband also soon consoled himself for his loss, and took another wife; by which event Mademoiselle Lenormand, her brother and sister, became dependent on the care of a father and mother-in-law; who, to be quit of a young family which did not belong to them, placed the daughters in a convent of Benedictine nuns in the town; from whence, when they had learned all that the good sisters could teach, they were removed to that of the Visitation; and so on through all the convents of Alençon in their turn, after which the future prophetess was apprenticed to a milliner. It was in the house of the Benedictines that Mademoiselle commenced her vocation, by predicting that the superior would soon be deprived of her office; for which ill-boding the young lady was subjected to punishment, and underwent a penance; but the event soon justified the prediction. She continued the career she had begun by announcing the name, age, and various other particulars respecting the successor of the deprived abbess. There were at the time many candidates for the office, and the ultimate decision remained in doubt and abeyance. Verifying at length the truth of the oracle, it confirmed the pretensions of the damsel to a supernatural power of revealing the events of futurity. But the town of Alençon was too confined a theatre for her aspiring disposition, and the needle too ignoble an instrument for one who aspired to wield the wand of prophecy. She persuaded her mother-in-law to send her to Paris, where her stepfather was then residing; and at fourteen years of age Mademoiselle Lenormand started for the metropolis, with no other worldly possessions than the clothes on her back, and a piece of six francs in her pocket, given to her by her maternal guardian.

Arrived in the great city, her father-in-law obtained for the young adventuress a place in a shop, where she soon gained the good-will of her employers, and *la grosse Normande* became a universal favourite. One of the clerks undertook to instruct her in arithmetic and book-keeping, and gave her some knowledge also of mathematics. Pursuing her studies with great industry, she soon surpassed her instructor, and resolved, after a time, to gain the means of subsistence by her own exertions, and in a manner congenial to her habits and inclinations. To this end she established in the Rue de Tournon a *bureau d'ecriture*, which succeeded well, and where she continued to exercise her vocation as a prophetess till the time of her death in 1843. Her success enabled her, after a time, to get her sister married as she desired, and to promote her brother in his military career. It was towards the end of the reign of Louis XVI. that Mademoiselle Lenormand commenced practice. She found the troubles of the times, which unhinged the minds of all around her, and filled them with alarm and anxiety, very propitious to her views. The unfortunate Princess de Lamballe, whose untimely fate she predicted, was one of her frequent visitors; and she possessed a letter from Mirabeau, written from his prison at Vincennes, in which he intreated her to tell him when his captivity would cease. The Revolution followed, and applicants for the benefit of her oracular powers increased. Alarmed at the rapid progress of events, and rendered superstitious by their fears, crowds of anxious inquirers flocked to the Rue de Tournon under various disguises, which it required no great shrewdness or talent to discover. It was at this time that two French guards who had joined the crowd in the attack on the Bastile visited the celebrated reader of futurity: to one she predicted a short but glorious military career, and an early death by poison; to the other the baton of a marechal of France. The former was afterwards General Hoche, whose untimely fate fulfilled the augury; the other the celebrated Lefebvre. The Comte de Provence (afterwards Louis XVIII.), on the night of his flight from Paris, sent to consult the sybil of the Rue de Tournon, 'en qualité de voisine,' previous to his departure.

During the Reign of Terror, Mademoiselle Lenormand continued for some time undisturbed in the exercise of her divination, and was visited one evening by three men, who demanded with smiles of evident incredulity to learn their future destiny. On examining their hands attentively, she became greatly agitated, probably knowing the parties she had to deal with; they encouraged her, however, to speak without fear, as they were ready, they said, to hear whatever doom she should pronounce. For some time she remained silent, and continued to examine the cards apparently with great attention, but evidently under considerable excitement; yielding at length to their encouragement, she foretold their destiny, and, tragic as it was, her visitors received the prophecy with shouts of incredulous laughter. 'The oracle has failed for once,' observed one of them; 'if we are destined to destruction, we shall at least fall at the same time; it cannot be that I should be the first victim, and receive such splendid honours after death, whilst the people shall heap your last moments with every possible insult.' 'She slanders the citizens, and should answer for it at the tribunal,' observed the youngest of the party. 'Bah!' replied the third; 'the dreams of prophecy are never worth regarding.' The death of Marat, one of the inquirers, soon after, confirmed the first part of the prediction; and the completion of the second alone saved the prophetess from destruction, she being incarcerated when Robespierre and St Just, the other two visitors, met the destiny she had foretold them. How it chanced that the science of Mademoiselle did not guard her against the danger in which she was involved, is nowhere recorded. Occupied, we must suppose, with the destiny of others, she seems to have neglected to read her own, and fell into perils she might otherwise have avoided by examining the lines in her own fair palm, or dealing out the cards for once for her own information and instruction. Yet that she really had faith in her own power of divination, seems to be proved by her conduct with regard to her brother, who, as has been stated, was in the army. Receiving intelligence that he was severely wounded in an engagement, she never ceased seeking, by means of the cards, to know the state of his health; and at length, after having passed a night in various cabalistic researches, she was found in the morning by her attendant bathed in tears, and gave orders for mourning, having ascertained, she said, that her brother was dead; which was soon afterwards confirmed by the arrival of letters.

After the Reign of Terror, the celebrity of the prophetess continued to increase. Barrère was one of her constant visitors. Madame Tallien seldom allowed a week to pass without availing herself of her supernatural powers. Barras frequently sent for her to the Luxembourg. From the access she had to the leaders of all parties, it required no great skill in divination to predict many of the events which took place at that time. The empire was, however, the season of her richest harvest. Josephine, as is generally known, was a firm believer in auguries and prophetic intimations. The early prediction of her future greatness, and its termination, has been so frequently repeated, without receiving any contradiction, that it is become a fact which no one questions, and would easily account for the firm faith she reposed in the oracles of Mademoiselle Lenormand, to whom she constantly sent to ask, amidst other questions, explanations respecting the dreams of Napoleon; and when the latter projected any new enterprise, the empress never failed to consult the reader of futurity as to its results. The disasters of the Russian campaign, it is said, were clearly predicted by Mademoiselle Lenormand; and it was from her also that Josephine received the first intimations of the divorce which was in contemplation, which premature revelation, unfortunately for the authoress, procured for her an interview with Fouché, who, on her being introduced, inquired, in a tone of raillery, if the cards had informed her of the arrest which awaited her? 'No,' she replied; 'I thought I was summoned here for a consultation, and have brought them with me;' at the same time dealing them out upon the table of the minister of police without any apparent embarrassment. Without mentioning the divorce, Fouché began to reproach her with many of the prophecies she had lately uttered; and which, notwithstanding the kindness she had received from the empress, had been employed to flatter the hopes of the royalists in the Faubourg St Germain. Mademoiselle Lenormand continued to deal the cards, repeating to herself in an under tone, 'The knave of clubs! again the knave of clubs!' Fouché continued his reprimands, and informed her that, however lightly she might be disposed to regard the matter, he was about to send her to prison, where she would probably remain for a considerable time.

'How do you know that?' asked the prophetess. 'Here is the knave of clubs again, who will set me free sooner than you expect.'

'Ah, the knave of clubs will have the credit of it, will he?'

'Yes, the knave of clubs represents your successor in office—the Duc de Rovigo.'

The fall of Napoleon brought fresh credit and honour to Mademoiselle Lenormand. She had foretold the restoration of the Bourbons, and received the rewards of divination. The Emperor Alexander visited and consulted her; and her old patron, Louis XVIII., again availed himself of her science and advice. But it was not the monarchs of Europe alone that gave their support to this singular woman. Prince Talleyrand, with all his incredulity, and with all his knowledge of man, and Madame de Staël, with all her boasted talents and wisdom, both were carried away in the general delusion.

It was during the consulate, when Madame de Staël returned to Paris, after a lengthened absence, that she allowed herself to be persuaded to make a visit to the Rue de Tournon. In the course of conversation, Mademoiselle Lenormand observed, 'You are anxious about some event which will probably take place to-morrow, but from which you will receive very little satisfaction.' On the succeeding day, Madame de Staël was to have an audience of the first consul, who well knew her pretensions, and was but little disposed to yield to them. Madame, however, flattered herself that the power of her genius, and the charms of her conversation, would overcome the prejudice she was aware he had conceived against her. The lady was received in the midst of a numerous circle, and fully expected to produce a brilliant effect upon Bonaparte, and all who surrounded him. On her being introduced, the consul abruptly asked, 'Have you seen *la pie voleuse*, which is so much in fashion?'* Surprised at the unexpected question, Madame de Staël hesitated a moment for a reply. 'On dit,' he added; 'we are soon to have *la pie séditieuse* also.' The second observation completed the lady's confusion; and the first consul, not wishing to increase it, turned and entered into conversation with some more favoured visitor. After this memorable audience, Madame de Staël called to mind the observation of Mademoiselle Lenormand, and from that time had great confidence in her skill, paying her many subsequent visits.

The residence of the prophetess for forty years was at the extremity of a court (No. 5, Rue de Tournon), and over the door was inscribed, 'Mademoiselle Lenormand, Libraire.' The profession of a prophetess not being recognised by the code, she took a 'patente de libraire,' to receive her visitors and exercise her vocation, without giving offence to the prefect de police or his agents; and, under the title of librarian, her name is inscribed in the royal and national almanac. On ringing at the door of the oracular abode, a servant appeared, and you were introduced into an apartment in which there was nothing extraordinary. So well was the character of Mademoiselle established, that no additional means of imposture were requisite to support it. Some thirty or forty volumes were arranged on shelves against the wall, chiefly consisting of the works of the lady herself—'Les Souvenirs Prophétiques,' 'La Réponse à Mon. Hoffman, journaliste,' 'Les Memoires Historiques,' and five or six other works chiefly on cabalistic subjects. Mademoiselle soon made her appearance—a short fat little woman, with a ruddy face, overshadowed by the abundant curls of a flaxen wig, and surmounted by a semi-oriental turban, the rest of her attire being much in the style of a butter-woman.

'What is your pleasure?' she demanded of her visitor.

'Mademoiselle, I come to consult you.'

'Well, sit down; what course of inquiries do you wish to make? I have them at all prices; from six, to ten, twenty, or four hundred francs.'

'I wish for information to the amount of a louis-d'or.'

'Very well; come to this table; sit down, and give me your left hand.' Then followed several queries—'What is your age? What is your favourite flower? To what animal have you the greatest repugnance?' During the course of her questions she continued shuffling the cards; and at length presenting them, desired you to cut them with your left hand. She then dealt them out upon the table one by one, at the same time proclaiming your future fate with a volubility that rendered it very difficult to follow up all she said, and as if she were reading with great rapidity from a printed book. In this torrent of words, sometimes quite unintelligible, occasionally occurred something which particularly struck the inquirer, whose character, tastes, and habits, she sometimes described very accurately, probably in part from phrenological observation. Very often she mentioned remarkable circumstances in their past life with great correctness, at the same time predicting future events, which many of her visitors found to be afterwards realised. Of the failures, probably innumerable, nothing was heard. In justice to the lady, it must however be observed, that her natural shrewdness and observation frequently enabled her to give advice which was of considerable advantage to the inquirer.

Mademoiselle Lenormand, notwithstanding the favours she received from the emperor and Josephine, was a steady and devoted adherent to the elder branch of the Bourbons; and, after the revolution of July, retired very much from her usual business, both in consequence of her age, and from the diminution of her visitors; passing much of her time at Alençon, where she purchased lands and houses, and built herself a residence which she called 'La petite maison de Socrate.' Remembering the little honour a prophet receives in his own country, she refused to exercise her vocation in her native town, saying that she came to Alençon to forget that she was a 'devineresse,' and only calculated horoscopes at Paris.

How far she believed in her own skill, cannot be exactly ascertained; but from the fact relative to her brother's death, she seems decidedly to have had some faith in the revelations she drew from cards. Another instance is recorded in which she acted from some principle analogous to those from which her conclusions were sometimes drawn. At the time of the first invasion by the allies, Mademoiselle Lenormand had beside her a considerable sum of money, and many articles of value, which she was anxious to intrust to some one in whom she could place confidence. The only person who presented himself at the time was not much known to her, but at the moment there was no one else to whom she chose to address herself. 'To what animal,' she asked in her usual routine, 'have you the most repugnance?' 'To rats,' was the reply. 'It is the sign of a good conscience,' she observed. 'And to which do you give the preference?' 'Oh, I prefer dogs far beyond all others.' Mademoiselle, without hesitation, committed the important charge to his care, as one in whom she could place entire confidence.

The prophetess was in person excessively fat and ugly; but her eyes even in age preserved their brightness and vivacity, and the good citizens of Alençon were wont to say, 'Que ses yeux flamboyants leur faisaient peur.' It was never understood that Mademoiselle Lenormand showed the smallest inclination to marriage, nor was there ever a question on the subject; but she was well known to have a great aversion to young children. Besides a large funded property, and her houses and lands at Alençon, she possessed a very handsome house in the Rue de la Santé at Paris; a chateau at Poissy, eight leagues from the metropolis; and a large collection of very good pictures, principally representing the acts and deeds of members of the house of Bourbon; also a vast collection of very curious notes respecting the events of which she was either a spectatress or an actress, all written in her own hand, which, by the by, is a most cabalistic-looking scrawl. She had also autographic and confidential letters from most of the sove-

* The Thieving Magpie, a play so called; the same, we presume, as that called in English the Maid and the Magpie.

reigns of Europe, and was in fact a remarkable proof of the credulity of the nineteenth century, and of an imposture which, for its long and continued success, has had few rivals in any age of the world.

Of the two children of her sister, which she adopted after their mother's death, the daughter died young of consumption, and the son is now an officer of rank. On the decease of his aunt during the last year, he inherited all her property.

[The above article is communicated by an English gentleman residing in France. We would be understood as not pledging ourselves for the literal correctness of all its statements, though neither have we any reason to doubt that it has been prepared from the best sources of information which may be available in the case.—*Ed.*]

READING WORKS OF FICTION.

There has been considerable difference of opinion in regard to the effects produced upon the mind by fictitious narratives. Without entering minutely upon the merits of this controversy, I think that it may be contended that two evils are likely to arise from much indulgence in works of fiction. The one is a tendency to give way to the wild play of the imagination—a practice most deleterious both to the intellectual and moral habits. The other is a disruption of the harmony that ought to exist between the moral emotions and the conduct—a principle of extensive and important influence. In the healthy state of the moral feelings, for example, the emotion of sympathy excited by a tale of sorrow ought to be followed by some efforts for the relief of the sufferer. When such relations in real life are listened to from time to time without any such efforts, the emotion gradually becomes weakened, and that moral condition is produced which we call selfishness or darkness of heart. Fictitious tales of sorrow appear to have a similar tendency—the emotion is produced without the corresponding conduct; and when this habit has been much indulged, the result seems to be, that a cold and barren sentimentalism is produced, instead of the habit of active benevolence. If fictitious narratives be employed for depicting scenes of vice, another evil of the greatest magnitude is likely to result from them, even though the conduct exhibited should be shown to end in remorse and misery; for, by the mere familiarity with vice, an injury is done to the youthful mind, which is in no degree compensated by the moral at the close. Imagination, therefore, is a mental power of extensive influence, and capable of being turned to important purposes in the cultivation of individual character. But to be so, it must be kept under the strict control of reason and virtue. If it be allowed to wander at discretion through scenes of imagined wealth, ambition, frivolity, or pleasure, it tends to draw the mind from the important pursuits of life, to weaken the habits of attention, and to impair the judgment. It tends in a most material manner to prevent the due exercise of those nobler powers which are directed to the cultivation both of science and virtue.—*Dr Abercrombie.*

LIEBIG WHEN A BOY.

Liebig was distinguished at school as 'booby,' the only talent then cultivated in German schools being verbal memory. On one occasion, being sneeringly asked by the master what he proposed to become, since he was so bad a scholar, and answering that he would be a chemist, the whole school burst into a laugh of derision. Not long ago, Liebig saw his old schoolmaster, who feelingly lamented his own former blindness. The only boy in the same school who ever disputed with Liebig the station of 'booby' was one who never could learn his lesson by heart, but was continually composing music, and writing it down by stealth in school. This same individual Liebig lately found at Vienna, distinguished as a composer, and conductor of the Imperial Opera-House. I think his name is Reuling. It is to be hoped that a more rational system of school instruction is now gaining ground. Can anything be more absurd or detestable than a system which made Walter Scott and Justus Liebig 'boobies' at school, and so effectually concealed their natural talents, that, for example, Liebig was often lectured before the whole school on his being sure to cause misery and broken hearts to his parents, while he was all the time conscious, as the above anecdote proves, of the possession of talents similar in kind to those he has since displayed.—*Dr Gregory on the Head and Character of Liebig, in the Phrenological Journal.*

THOMAS CAMPBELL'S 'ADVERTISEMENT.'

A correspondent points out that the writer of Mornings with Thomas Campbell, published in the Journal a few weeks ago (No. 58), has somewhat misunderstood the poet's account of his fancy for the beautiful child whom he met in St James's Park. What the author of the Pleasures of Hope sent to the newspapers was the following jeu d'esprit:—

LINES ON HIS NEW CHILD-SWEETHEART,

BY THOMAS CAMPBELL.

I hold it a religious duty,
To love and worship children's beauty;
They've least the taint of earthly clod—
They're freshest from the hand of God.
With heavenly looks, they make us sure
The Heaven that made them must be pure:
We love them not in earthly fashion,
But with a beatific passion.

I chanced to, yesterday, behold
A maiden child of beauty's mould;
'Twas near—more sacred was the scene—
The palace of our patriot queen:
The little charmer, to my view,
Was sculpture brought to life anew.
Her eyes had a poetic glow,
Her pouting mouth was Cupid's bow;
And through her frock I could descry
Her neck and shoulders' symmetry;
'Twas obvious, from her walk and gait,
Her limbs were beautifully straight.
I stopped the enchantress, and was told,
Though tall, she was but four years old.
Her guide so grave an aspect bore,
I could not ask a question more;
But followed her. The little one
Threw backward ever and anon
Her lovely neck, as if to say,
'I know you love me, *Mister Grey*;'
For by its instinct childhood's eye
Is shrewd in physiognomy;
They well distinguish fawning art
From sterling fondness of the heart.

And so she flirted, like a true
Good woman, till we bade adieu!
'Twas then I with regret grew wild—
Oh! beauteous, interesting child!
Why asked I not thy home and name?
My courage failed me—more's the shame.

But where abides this jewel rare?
Oh! ye that own her, tell me where!
For sad it makes my heart and sore,
To think I ne'er may meet her more.

Our correspondent adds, that the lines were answered in a poetical address by a member of the young lady's family, who fully appreciated the honour he had done them.

SANITARY OR SANATORY.

We hear much now-a-days of sanatory inquiries, the sanatory state of towns and districts, and so forth. At a time when the word is so much used, it may not be amiss to devote ten lines to denote the fact, that the proper word in these cases is *sanitary*. Sanatory, from the supine of *sano*, I heal, would imply something connected with medicaments or medical practice. Sanitary, from *sanitas*, health, obviously is applicable, and alone is so, to that which concerns the condition of a people or place in respect of what has well been called the greatest of earthly blessings. We observe that the error has even crept into state documents.

CHARITY.

It is an old saying, that 'charity begins at home;' but this is no reason it should not go abroad. A man should live with the world as a citizen of the world; he may have a preference for the particular quarter or square, or even alley in which he lives, but he should have a generous feeling for the whole.—*Cumberland.*

Printed by William Bradbury, of No. 6, York Place, and Frederick Mullett Evans, of No. 7, Church Row, both of Stoke Newington, in the county of Middlesex, printers, at their office, Lombard Street, in the precinct of Whitefriars, and city of London; and Published (with permission of the Proprietors, W. and R. CHAMBERS,) by WILLIAM SOMERVILLE ORR, Publisher, of 2, Amen Corner, at No. 2, AMEN CORNER, both in the parish of Christchurch, and in the city of London.—Saturday, March 15, 1845.

CONDUCTED BY WILLIAM AND ROBERT CHAMBERS, EDITORS OF 'CHAMBERS'S INFORMATION FOR THE PEOPLE,' 'CHAMBERS'S EDUCATIONAL COURSE,' &c.

No. 64. New Series. SATURDAY, MARCH 22, 1845. Price 1½d.

RAILWAY LITERATURE.

Amongst the very great alterations in our social system which railway extension over the breadth and length of Great Britain has produced, the effect it has had upon literature should not be overlooked. Railways have created a new class of publications exclusively devoted to their interests. They have called into existence not merely a new branch of literature, but a whole literature of their own, with each department definitely marked and industriously filled. They have their useful, serious, business books and periodicals for the public to consult, as it does the Ready-Reckoner or the Times newspaper. They have also their light and graceful belles lettres, which the fashionable world is beginning to prefer to commonplace poetry and blasé fiction. A glance at this new and comprehensive literature will assuredly be instructive of the ever-advancing progress of this country.

In the useful department, pre-eminence must be given to a neat waistcoat-pocket compendium, which is as portable as the tiniest Ready-Reckoner, and quite as necessary to the man of business. It may be with truth designated the traveller's best companion, although its real title is 'Bradshaw's Railway Guide.' It consists of a set of tables, interspersed with distinctly engraved maps. The tables tell us the respective distances, the times of starting from and arriving at *every* railway station in Great Britain; to which is added a list of the fares for each distance. Supposing, therefore, a man to be lounging in the neighbourhood of John o' Groat's a few years hence (when all the railways in this island shall have been complete), and he possess a copy of Mr Bradshaw's miniature time-book, he will only have to make one or two references to it to be able to inform himself of the hour, nay, of the precise minute, at which he would arrive at the Land's End in Cornwall. Even by the aid of the edition now before us, a traveller being in Newcastle-upon-Tyne, may very safely order by post a dinner for the next day at Mr Wynn's excellent hotel in Falmouth at a certain number of minutes before or after any particular hour; and start with the assurance that, though he will have to go over some four hundred and sixty miles—not of ground exactly, but of iron rail—he will be nearly sure of finding himself seated at table just as the Falmouth cook is dishing up the pilchards. He can also, before setting out, calculate from the lists of fares the exact amount of money the excursion will cost him, and know, by consulting the maps, through what counties, towns, and villages he will pass. All this information, and much more about steamboats, coaches, and carriers, is compressed into the smallest possible compass, and bound up in a neat cloth cover.

Next in utility, though perhaps far above Mr Bradshaw's little work in point of importance, come several newspapers, which are exclusively devoted to railway affairs. Those already existing are the Railway Journal, the Railway Times, the Railway Record, and the Irish Railway Gazette, published weekly, and the Railway Register, issued monthly. All these periodicals are conducted by scientific men, with a high degree of respectability and independence; the last, a most essential qualification; for their conductors are manifestly more open to temptations of partiality and favouritism than any other class of editors. Hence there resides much influence in these journals for good or for evil. Being looked up to by the public as authorities on the subject to which they are devoted, they have the power either to puff off unstable schemes, which are never intended to be carried further than the share market; or, by dint of cautious inquiry and fearless exposure, to guard capitalists against them. As vehicles for the publication of various transactions connected with old as well as new lines, they put their readers in possession of data upon which to form correct opinions concerning the actual condition and progress not only of particular companies, but of the aggregate of the new but gigantic interest which is now centered in this mode of conveyance. To the honour of all the important companies be it spoken, open unconcealed trading appears to be their rule of conduct, and each publishes a weekly account of the amount of business done during every eight days. Under the head of 'Official railway traffic returns,' there appears in the railway newspapers a table setting forth the money received for the transit of passengers and goods. That every means of calculation and deduction may be afforded to the interested reader, beside this item is placed the amount of receipts of the corresponding weeks in as many previous years as the line has been in operation; also the authorised capital of every company, the amount of its periodical expenses, and the dividend per cent. received by each shareholder at the last division of profits. Thus, by the aid of the railway journals, a person who wishes to invest money may know the exact value of the shares he would purchase on the very day he desires to buy them; and, moreover, be able to form a tolerably correct notion as to whether the property is likely to improve, or to become deteriorated in value. Thanks, therefore, to the exertions of 'railway editors,' there is no species of property which a capitalist can purchase with his eyes so widely open as railway property; for if he wishes to invest his money in houses, he must depend greatly upon the opinion of his builder, or upon the interested report he gets regarding the character and responsibility of the tenants. If, again, he desires land property, he is almost entirely in the hands of his surveyor; but, in buying railway shares, he has only to consult the railway newspapers, and he may judge unerringly for himself. To assist him in such cases, the 'Railway Record' attaches to its weekly account 'Notes on the traffic table,' in which is set forth a short statement of the condition (whether finished or not) of the line, or any specialty in the monetary affairs of each company.

There is one peculiarity belonging to these newspapers which, so far as we recollect, no others possess. They are entirely and unmixedly devoted to their one subject, to the exclusion of every other description of matter whatever. The military and naval journals contain short accounts of what is going on in the civil world; the doings of laymen are recorded in the religious papers; and, in short, most of the publications addressed to special classes show some little sympathy with the ordinary affairs of life by some brief chronicle of them. Not so with the papers under consideration. We have one before us, for instance, containing twenty-four pages of close print, and not one single word relative to anything besides railways. So inflexible do the conductors appear in this respect, that they even exclude the flourishing eloquence of puffing advertisers. Out of ten pages of advertisements, not one but has direct or indirect reference to railways. Besides several of the official advertisements of the various companies, they consist of announcements of patent inventions for particular parts of railway machinery, of the names and addresses of share-brokers, and other announcements only relating to railways. The news is equally exclusive. Reports of meetings of companies, letters from aggrieved travellers or disappointed shareholders, information concerning foreign railways, railway police reports, with a leading article, and an essay or two on locomotive topics, form the sum of contents in a railway newspaper.

From the researches we have made from time to time in these very exclusive vehicles of railway information, we may conscientiously say that—considering the temptations we have before hinted at which lie in their way to diverge from the straight line of honesty and truth—a better conducted class of newspapers does not exist. Some, of course, are better than others; but it would be as invidious as unnecessary here to make distinctions.

A few of the temptations to which railway editors are exposed, may be mentioned in the second section of our little treatise on the useful department of railway literature. The readers of general newspapers may have observed that almost every one of these organs, whether provincial or metropolitan, devotes a column or so to 'Railway Intelligence,' in which all the several haps that the railway is heir to are duly chronicled. Where, in the case of a provincial paper, a line is projected or in progress through the district in which it is published, that of course forms the subject for the exercise of the editor's pen — the pivot on which to turn the graces of rhetoric in his leaders. When rival lines are proposed, rival newspapers naturally take a stand in their favour, and a fierce pen and ink war ensues; which introduces us to the controversial department of railway literature. Without hinting a breath of disrespect against provincial editors as a body, we may now produce our instances of the temptations to tergiversation to which they are exposed. We learn from one of the parliamentary reports, that in a certain district a warfare between two rival companies ran so high, and was so energetically supported, that the older of the projecting companies thought it expedient to 'buy off' the opposition of their vigorous opponent, and he was soon able to present an exception to a very general rule; namely, that of a literary man retiring upon a fortune! In his case railway literature had proved a golden egg, though he managed to hatch it under very discreditable circumstances. Another even stronger example of the height to which literary warfare has been carried, is mentioned on good authority. In a midland county, an editor wielded his facts and his logic so manfully, that, in the opinion of the opposed company, he created an effect upon the minds of his readers far too serious not to damage, perhaps to overthrow, their project. Against bribes—unlike his above-mentioned brother journalist—he was proof. A new paper was started in opposition, but the leaders were weak and ineffective compared with his. Every scheme was tried that ingenuity could invent, or cash execute, to silence him; but the more this was attempted, the stronger he wrote, and the more fiercely he denounced the scheme. At length one of the directors hit upon an expedient worthy of Machiavel. He got himself cautiously introduced to the proprietor of the journal, professed a desire to risk a few thousands in a newspaper property, and by the dazzling offers he made, actually induced the unconscious proprietor, unknown to his editor (who would perhaps have told him better), to sell the property. The moment the bargain was concluded, it was discovered too late that the railway company had, through the wily director, possessed themselves of the copyright of the paper, of the printing-office, and of the services of the editor. He, however, nobly refused to change his railway politics, and was accordingly dismissed, taking with him the respect both of friends and enemies. This case will readily be credited when we state that in one of the reports adverted to, it is stated that the cost of a certain railway in 'buying off' opposition from land proprietors as well as editors, and in law, amounted to L.1800 per mile; and that before a single rail was laid, or a spade put into the ground.

Before dismissing the four well-conducted special railway journals, and the regular stand which railway intelligence and controversy has taken in the columns of the press in general, we must not forget that the London Gazette has of late become almost a railway newspaper. By a recent act of parliament, not only notices of every projected line must be set forth, but the decisions of the government railway board concerning their expediency promulgated in that official publication. During the present session of parliament, notices for no fewer than 248 new branches or new lines have been issued, and it is no uncommon thing to see the Gazette nearly filled with them.

But of the vast masses of printing called into existence by railways, there is nothing to equal in quantity the reports of parliamentary committees—those enormous folio 'blue-books,' so dreadful to the visions of busy editors, but so dear to the eyes of enthusiastic statisticians. Whenever a dispute occurs concerning the expediency of having more than one line laid down between the same places, or when certain interested parties deem any railway whatever inexpedient, the controversy is referred to a 'select committee of the House of Commons.' These committees consist of some eight or ten members of parliament, who hear evidence on both sides, and give their decision in 'reports.' It often happens that weeks are employed in merely taking evidence; every word of which is accurately noted in short-hand, afterwards printed, and stitched into the well-known blue covers. Besides this, there is a report of the committee printed separately, as well as addenda, appendices, &c. Now, it happened that, in the course of the last session of parliament, between forty and fifty of these committees sat, heard evidence, reported, and — printed. Consequently, at the very least five-and-forty blue-books were issued, with their equally blue satellites, in the shape of reports, additions, and appendices. Supposing we give to each of these twelve hundred and fifty pages (a moderate average), we may calculate that in one year railway speculation and railway opposition called into existence upwards of sixty thousand folio pages of print! And this is not all. These reports give rise to countless pamphlets, written either in reply to some of the witnesses, or for the advocacy of particular views. As regards the utility or instructiveness of the blue-book branch of railway literature, we can only say that its chief fault is its extreme bulkiness; for much honey is to be extracted from it. Amongst the witnesses are the most eminent engineers, who furnish valuable information in answer to questions put to them; practical men of business supply lessons of sound wisdom; whilst non-professional witnesses sometimes relieve the tedium of scientific detail by the quaintness or jocularity of their replies.

From the statistical, periodical, and controversial writings which the all-powerful locomotive has created, we now turn to its historical literature. Upon this subject much has been written, and a short summary of what has already appeared we now propose to give. Railways being still in their infancy, of course their history is short.

The mere notion of lessening the draught of wheeled carriages by running them on the smooth surface of wooden or iron rails, is by no means new; such rails, in the form of grooves or ruts, for the reception of the edges of wheels, and called trams, were in use quite two centuries ago in the English collieries. Roger North, in describing the 'way-leaves' granted for the privilege of laying down such roads, and of transit over them at Newcastle, says, 'When men have pieces of ground between the colliery and the river, they sell *leave* to lead coals over their ground, and so dear, that the owner of a rood of ground will expect L.20 per annum for this leave. The manner of the carriage is by laying rails of timber from the colliery down to the river exactly straight and parallel, and bulky carts are made with four rowlets fitting these rails, whereby the carriage is so easy, that one horse will draw down four or five chaldrons of coals, and is an immense benefit to the coal-merchants.'*

This practice was somewhat older than 1676, when the above passage was written. By the middle, however, of the last century, the iron works of Shropshire and Staffordshire had become sufficiently extensive to enable the Northumberland coal proprietors to substitute iron for wooden trams, and to attract the system southward. In 1760, iron plates were first laid down upon wooden rails in Colebrook Dale, Shropshire, and were speedily adopted in all the English and Welsh mines and collieries; so that by 1811 there were, in South Wales alone, above 150 miles of this description of railway. Still, the power of steam remained unapplied till the year 1813, when Mr George Stephenson constructed the first locomotive engine. Mere theorists thought him crazed; for it was never supposed that the smooth wheels of a steam-carriage would adhere sufficiently to the equally smooth rails, so as to produce locomotion. It was thought that the wheels would run, or rather slip, round without moving the carriage; that, in short, 'they would not *bite*.' But George Stephenson determined to try by actual experiment. 'The first locomotive which I made,' said that gentleman, at a dinner given to him late last year in Newcastle, 'was at Killingworth colliery, and with Lord Ravensworth's money. Yes! Lord Ravensworth and Co. were the first parties that would intrust me with money to make a locomotive engine. That engine was made 32 years ago, and we called it "My Lord." I said to my friends that there was no limit to the speed of such an engine, provided the works could be made to stand.' A partial failure on the Stockton and Darlington line—on which Stephenson's locomotive was tried, and which was opened in 1825, for conveying passengers by means of horse-draught — led to a temporary prejudice against his sanguine views as to amount of speed. One writer, who professed himself a friend of locomotive engines, delivered himself as follows: — 'It is far from my wish to promulgate to the world that the ridiculous expectations, or rather professions, of the enthusiastic speculatist will be realised, and that we shall see engines travelling at the rate of twelve, sixteen, eighteen, twenty miles an hour. Nothing could do more harm towards their general adoption and improvement than the promulgation of such *nonsense!*'

Still Stephenson, who knew well what he was about, persisted in asserting the above 'nonsense;' but it was so little heeded even by experienced men, that when, in 1828, the promoters of the Liverpool and Manchester railway employed him, and he was summoned as a witness before a committee of the House of Commons, they intreated him not to shock the common sense of the members by stating his expectations of higher speed than ten miles an hour. 'When,' said Mr Stephenson, in the above-quoted speech, 'I went to Liverpool to plan a line to Manchester, I pledged myself to attain a speed of ten miles an hour. I said I had no doubt the locomotive might be made to go much faster, but we had better be moderate at the beginning. The directors said I was quite right; for if, when they went to parliament, I talked of going at a greater rate than ten miles an hour, I would put a cross on the concern. It was not an easy task for me to keep the engine down to ten miles an hour; but it must be done, and I did my best. I had to place myself in that most unpleasant of all positions—the witness-box of a parliamentary committee. I was not long in it, I assure you, before I began to wish for a hole to creep out at. I could not find words to satisfy either the committee or myself. Some one inquired if I were a foreigner, and another hinted that I was mad. But I put up with every rebuff, and went on with my plans, determined not to be put down. Assistance gradually increased — improvements were made every day—and to-day a train, which started from London in the morning, has brought me in the afternoon to my native soil, and enabled me to take my place in this room, and see around me many faces which I have great pleasure in looking upon.' Thanks to the indomitable perseverance of Stephenson in persisting in his 'nonsense,' there are at present nearly a hundred lines in Great Britain in full operation, on not one of which is the average rate of speed less than twenty miles per hour. So much for the 'ridiculous expectations of enthusiastic speculatists.' From this scrap of railway history, we turn to a consideration of its light literature.

We cannot conscientiously recommend so strongly as the railway newspapers, certain other periodicals professing to be devoted to the lighter matters which float about railways, because they seem in a great measure to hoist false colours. On looking into them, we cannot perceive that they are anything more than repertories of general facts and stray witticisms, illustrated with wood engravings. We must therefore dismiss them at once, to consider the effects which railways are gradually spreading over the current literature of the day.

Composed as a railway train is of mechanical details, and connected as it is with utilitarian maxims and doings, it possesses, we believe, some of the elements of poetry. Sink details—remove it to a distance where we only witness its force and speed, and, even as a sight, it becomes sublime. Regard it further as a recent product of man's restless ingenuity—a surprising application of physical principles to the convenience of our race, and the sublimity becomes moral. Here there surely is poetry. *Against* railways, indeed, the voice of a distinguished English poet has lately been raised. But his effusion was promptly answered by other sonnetteers, who adopted the views we are now advocating. And why should it not be? The ship, with all its attributes and accessories, has for ages furnished similes for poets: who can say that, when Time has sufficiently hallowed such objects, steamers and locomotives will not be equally prolific in tropes? To the novelist, a railway train is invaluable; for where can he bring his characters so unexpectedly, yet so probably together as in a double-seated carriage? His elopements may be managed with far more celerity — hence with far more excitement—by rail than by the slow-going posters of the old north road; and then for a catastrophe, what would satisfy poetical justice and a melo-dramatic author so abundantly, as to crush up all his bad characters by a railway collision? We perceive that one writer

* Life of Lord Keeper Guilford, vol. i. p. 265.

has taken to the rail for his plots in right earnest. In recent numbers of the Dublin University Magazine appears a series entitled 'Tales of the Trains, being some chapters of Railroad Romance.

We take leave of the subject by mentioning one very gratifying fact which is intimately connected with it. Some of the liberal minded amongst the railway directories have provided for their engineers, stokers, and other employées, small and compact libraries for their amusement or instruction during the many intervals of leisure which necessarily occur. These collections of books, enclosed in a case so as to be easily removed from one station to another, form libraries always at the command of the companies' servants at the hours they most need them. Some time ago we had the pleasure of selecting such a collection at the request of the authorities of a railway near Edinburgh.

THE ENGLISH PEASANTRY IN THE MIDDLE AGES.

The rural population forms a very large proportion of the inhabitants of the British islands: on them we are dependent for much of our domestic comfort and national prosperity; for all those agricultural ameliorations which have changed the barren heath into a fertile field, and converted the unwholesome swamp into the verdant meadow; and yet how few have ever troubled themselves to inquire into the origin and history of the tillers of the soil. A little information on this subject may be of service to those well-intentioned individuals who take pleasure in improving the condition of their dependents. The past is a mighty teacher, and the great lessons it sets before us are not to be lightly regarded.

We learn that the progress of the class whose history we are about to consider has ever been, though slow and often checked, upwards, onwards. Starting from the lowest point to which humanity can descend, they have bravely, and to a great degree successfully, contended against the disheartening impediments thrown in their way—a result which certainly entitles them to our respect, and one that should lead us to look upon their lack of education, and rudeness of manners, with a little more charity than is our wont.

Those who have journeyed much over the pleasant roads of England, who have stepped aside from the highway to the green and leafy lanes, cannot fail to have remarked the peculiarities of appearance, manners, and speech, which the peasantry of that country exhibit; characteristics that vary with every change of county, showing most of them marked traces of the original extraction of the race who have gone on ploughing and sowing from the days of the Heptarchy to the present time, little thought of in the strife of interests, the exactions, privations, and sufferings, which so materially affected their own position, and retarded their advance towards those changes which, releasing them from bondage to the soil, has left them in the circumstances presented by our own day.

We shall avail ourselves of the publication of an interesting paper in the thirtieth volume of the Archæologia, to throw light on the physical history of this little-heeded race, which it appears sprang originally from a class of *slaves*, and is quite distinct from the pure Anglo-Saxon stock. For the source of this state of things, we must go back to the days when the Teutonic tribes existed in all their warlike ferocity over the whole of Germany: when flocks and herds were held in more esteem than tillage; and when attachment to chiefs, and councils held in the open air, were the chief characteristics of their nomadic or wandering life. Society was then divided into two great classes—the masters and the slaves; the latter most probably having been brought into that condition by conquest, while their numbers were maintained undiminished by captives taken in predatory expeditions, or by others sold or condemned to slavery. A similar state of things exists in Russia even in the present day; there the serfs, or lowest portion of the agricultural population, occupy the same place as did the slaves of the Germanic nations.

The first code of laws affecting the condition of the Anglo-Saxon serf was made under the influence of St Augustine in the sixth century: our knowledge of the previous ages is very uncertain. When the Angles and Saxons first came to settle in this island, which happened soon after the departure of the Romans (the fifth century), we are told by old chroniclers that they came in such great numbers as to depopulate their own countries: they must consequently have brought with them a numerous servile class of settlers, who would be employed in cultivating their new possessions, already occupied by the people subjugated and abandoned by Rome. From this intermixture may be traced the peculiar characteristics of the rural population. The earlier kingdoms of the Anglo-Saxons were Kent, under the dominion of Ethelbert, the patron of St Augustine; Essex; Wessex, under King Ina, which would naturally contain the greater part of the foreign race of agriculturists; while in Mercia, the remoter parts of Northumberland, governed by Edwin, and the western districts of the island, the majority must have consisted of the older British population.

The common name of the serf under the Anglo-Saxons was *theow*, a bondman. The term for a female was *wylor*. Of these the unmarried portion had no recognised protection from the outrages of their lords. Marriages could not take place between those residing on two different estates, as such a connexion would involve division of families, and lead to disputes between the proprietors. Marriages of theows were looked upon as legitimate; but if one party obtained freedom without being able to free the other, the marriage was no longer binding, and the liberated slave was at liberty to choose another partner. The master had the power of life and death over the theows, for whom there was no appeal: and although they were not prevented from acquiring property, it was never safe in their possession; and it appears that the only punishment ever thought of for those who defrauded them of their gains, was that of penance under the ecclesiastical law, of which we find different degrees enjoined against those who stole from the theows the money they had lawfully earned; or those who slay them without judgment or cause; or a lady who beats her wylor, so that she die within three days; or a free man who, by order of his lord, killed a theow. According to the laws of King Ina of Wessex, if a theow worked on the Sunday by his lord's command, the lord lost all right over him, and he became free; but if he worked without his master's consent, he was to 'suffer in his hide,' or be flogged.

During the whole of the Anglo-Saxon period, the number of the theows was continually changing by manumission and the condemnation of free men to slavery—a punishment equivalent to that of a modern sentence to the hulks or galleys. If a freeman worked on the Sunday by his own choice, he incurred the penalty of servitude, or a fine of sixty shillings. If he struck one of the royal foresters on duty, or killed one of the king's deer, he was equally deprived of freedom. 'If he stole himself,' or ran away, he was to be hanged. In times of distress many persons voluntarily sold themselves to *theowdom*, with the object of securing protection and a livelihood. A father might sell his own children before they reached their seventh year; after that age he could not do so without the child's consent. It does not appear that the theows paid any direct tax to the king, though a toll was exacted for their sale. We learn from a passage in the Coloquium of Alfric, published early in the eleventh century, a few particulars as to the nature of the service they rendered to their lords. A ploughman is examined concerning his occupations:—'"What sayest thou, ploughman; how dost thou perform thy work?" The answer is, "My lord, I labour excessively. I go out at dawn of day, driving my oxen to the field, and yoke them to the plough. There is no weather so severe that I dare rest at home, for fear of my lord; but having yoked my oxen, and fastened the share and coulter to the plough, every day I must plough a whole field (acre?) or more." The teacher continues, "Hast thou any companion?" "I have a boy who urges the oxen with a goad, and who is now hoarse with cold and shouting." "What more doest thou in the day?" "Truly, still I do more: I must fill the mangers of the oxen with hay, and water them, and carry out their dung." "Oh! oh! it is great tribulation." "Yea, it is great tribulation, *because I am not free.*"'* The concluding words of this examination contain the key to that sullen spirit of opposition too often encountered among the humbler classes of society in all ages of the world, while the remark of the teacher shows that the serfs were kindly and compassionately regarded by the Anglo-Saxon clergy, who encouraged the practice of gratuitous manumission as an action highly meritorious in the eyes of the church. We are informed that Athelstan Mannessone set free thirteen men in every thirty, choosing them by lot, through all his lands, for the salvation of his soul; 'that being placed in the open road, they were at liberty to go whither they would.' It sometimes happened that a man who had no theows of his own, bought one, in order to emancipate him, an instance of which is recorded in the case of Alfric, canon of Exeter, 'who redeemed Reinold of Heberdii and his children and all their offspring for two shillings, and Alfric proclaimed him free and sac-less in town and out of town, for the love of God.' The theows sometimes saved sufficient money to purchase their own freedom and that of their families. At Exeter, Huscarl liberated himself for forty pennies. Leofwine, son of Feala, bought 'himself and his offspring, to be at liberty to choose themselves masters where they would,' for half a pound.

This was the condition of the great mass of the population during the long period embracing the Saxon and Danish lines of rulers; but when the Normans, under William the Conqueror, invaded and subjugated the country, they viewed their dependents in a less favourable light than their Anglo-Saxon masters had done. The cruelties and exactions of the new oppressors, in their own country, had goaded the peasantry into frequent insurrections; in which the latter were defeated by their lords with the most contemptuous and horrible cruelties. In England, they enforced the laws which strengthened their own power with the greatest severity, while they disregarded or rejected those which favoured the suffering theows. They even degraded the free and wealthy occupiers to a level with the poorest, diminishing at the same time the security of personal property. They also introduced the Norman term, *villani*, for the theows. We have several striking pictures of the condition to which the peasants were reduced under the feudal barons. They were loaded with taxes; and when fines were levied by the king on their masters, these were always wrung from the poor villans, who complained that 'their lords do nothing but persecute them. They cannot have their goods safe, nor their earnings, nor the fruits of their labour. They pass their days in tribulation, with great pain and labour. Every year is worse than that which preceded. Every day their beasts are taken from them for aid and services; there are so many claims brought against them, and taxes old and new. There are so many reeves, and beadles, and bailiffs, that they cannot have one hour's peace; they can have no security either against the lord or against his sergeant, who keep no covenant with them, and some even apply to them opprobrious epithets.' Most of the services required of the villans were galling and degrading in the extreme. They could not marry without paying a tax to their lord. In fact, they were looked on as no better than cattle: a contempt which at times cost their masters dear; for to the brutality of the tax-gatherers of Richard II. to the daughters of the peasantry, we may look as among the immediate causes of the insurrection under Wat Tyler.

We may gain a pretty accurate idea of the condition of the oppressed serf from one of the metrical romances or ballads which were so popular during the thirteenth century. 'There was a poor villan who had a wife and children, whom he supported by cutting wood in an adjoining forest. One day, whilst thus employed, and bemoaning his miserable condition, he heard a voice which issued from the root of a tree, and which offered to raise him from his poverty if he would promise to be pious and charitable when he became rich. The spirit then told him that his name was Merlin; that when he returned home, if he dug in a certain spot in his garden he would find a great treasure; and that at the end of a year he might return to the tree and intimate his further wishes. At the end of the year the villan returned, and humbly and respectfully made known his desire to become provost of the town. This wish was immediately granted: but the villan, elected provost, became cruel and oppressive to all his inferiors. At the end of another year the villan returned again to the wood, and addressed the spirit familiarly, and with somewhat less respect than before. "What is your will now?" said Merlin. "I desire that my son, *who is a clerc*, may become a bishop." Within a few weeks a bishopric fell vacant, and the villan's son was elected. At the end of a third year the villan, still less respectfully, required that his daughter might be married to "the grand provost of Aquileia," which also soon afterwards came to pass. The villan had now arrived at the summit of his wishes; and, at the end of the fourth year, it was only at the request of his wife that he would condescend to return to the wood, and rudely say farewell to his benefactor. The spirit reproached him with his ingratitude, and threatened him with punishment. Within a short time his daughter (the grand provost's wife) and his son, the bishop, died; and, which was still worse, "*his lord*," soon after engaging in war with a powerful neighbour, was in want of money to carry on his hostilities, and demanded of the rich villan a thousand pounds; the villan pleaded that he could not raise the money, and refused to pay it, and then the lord, in revenge, seized all his property, and left him only enough to buy an axe, to enable him to resume his old trade of a woodcutter.

This tale not only conveys a beautiful moral, but proves that the sons of the serfs were not debarred from learning. In the example above, we see mention is made

* It is remarkable how correctly this description applies to the labours of a Scottish (perhaps also English) ploughman of the present day. In our country, it is his practice everywhere to commence work at daybreak all the year over, and to go on through the day performing exactly the duties above described; the severity of which, it is strongly to be suspected, tells heavily upon the constitutions of these men, scantily provided as they are with the main necessaries of life: hence our farm-labourers—a quiet and generally well-behaved class—become for the most part prematurely old about five-and-forty.—Ed.

of the *clerc* rising to a bishopric. At the same time it is evident that, with the acquisition of riches and honours, the villan had not ceased to be a slave. His case furnishes an illustration of the impunity with which the class were frequently plundered by their lords, who were strangers to them both in blood and language. The villans were virtually outlaws; they could not legally inherit lordship, bring any action, or give testimony in a court of law. A poet of that day disdains the idea of teaching villans and making them priests. 'I see,' he says, 'many places dishonoured by them; there are plenty of gentlemen; and he did a great sin who ever introduced a villan among them.' The poets and minstrels of the age, by their songs, increased the contempt of their lords for the peasantry: they delighted in drawing pictures of the hatred with which the villan regarded all of gentle birth: 'the doggish villan is he who sits before his door on Sundays and holidays, and mocks all who pass; and if he see pass a gentleman with a hawk on his fist, he will cry out, "Ha! that kite there will eat to-night a hen, which would be sufficient to fill all my children."' Some of the writers inquire, 'Why should villans eat beef or any dainty food? They ought to eat, for their Sunday diet, nettles, reeds, briers, and straw; while pea-shells are good enough for their every-day food. They ought to go forth naked on four feet in the meadows, to eat grass with the horned oxen.' A villan was declared to be incapable of telling the truth, or of feeling gratitude. Another writer says, 'God, who hast sent the multitude of rustics for the service of clerks and knights, and who hast sowed discord between us and them; grant us, we beseech thee, to live upon their labours, and to rejoice in their mortification.'

But the English minstrels, they who wandered among the populace, told a different story. Their songs abound with stirring recitals of the wrongs, of the injustice and oppression endured by the peasantry, who at length were driven to appeal to the king. The time had come when the slaves were to be heard; and the decline of the feudal system accelerated the movements which broke out vigorously in the fourteenth century.

It appears that at an early period there were villans possessed of sufficient courage to speak in court in defence of their fellows. This generosity was, however, turned into ridicule; they were called 'prince villans, who go to plead before the bailiff for the gain of one hundred sols.' Many persons, also, skilled in the laws, aided the villans in their pleadings against their oppressors; these were paid by subscriptions raised among the serfs themselves; and it appears that at this period they met in great numbers, and swore to stand by each other in defence of their rights.

In the reign of Henry II., a law was passed to forbid the seizure of the property of the villans in payment of the debts of their lords; and boroughs were then first incorporated, from which the freemen derived great privileges and protection from the power of the barons. The next reign saw the great charter wrung from the tyrannical John: one article related to the villans—when fines were inflicted on them, they were to be permitted to retain their tools; a proof of the wretchedness of their condition, when this was regarded as a measure of justice. It is, however, from the time of the third Henry that the commons date their importance, being then first admitted to parliament, and privileges granted to them which were afterwards confirmed. Great truths began to be perceptible; the preaching of Wickliffe awakened the minds of the peasantry; a new light broke upon them; the democratic precepts of the Bible pleased them: it was said that at the 'beginning of the world there were no slaves;' and the villans, finding their appeal to the laws productive of little or no benefit, resolved on striking a great blow for their freedom. They assembled to the number of 100,000, and marched, 'with arms in their hands, to lay their grievances before the king. They hastened towards London from the eastern and south-eastern counties, where the reforming spirit was generally strongest, on account of their frequent communication with the agitators on the continent. On the way, they would not let slip the opportunity of trying if "villans' blows were as hard as lords' blows;" and a few acts of violence showed that they were but too willing "to destroy all gentility." Their leaders, indeed, preached to them that in the days of Adam there were no gentlemen. They obtained for a moment possession of London; and if their leaders had been steady and skilful, it is impossible to say what might have been the result. They had come together with a variety of complaints, which, however, at last merged into one great grievance; and when the king had consented to give general charters of enfranchisement, they returned willingly to their homes. But when they had laid down their arms, the charters of enfranchisement were withdrawn, and the villans were not only reduced to their old condition again, but hundreds of executions evinced the vengeance and hatred of their masters. Another age of slavery followed before the wretched peasantry were allowed to be considered in the light of men. The change was gradual, and has left fewer traces in history than might have been expected. The shadow of the old state of things is still preserved in many of our old manorial customs; and the memory of the old feeling of the lords towards their dependents has been perpetuated in the signification now attached to the word villain.'

We will now take a long step in advance, and look at the condition of the labourers at a later period—the reign of Edward VI. In the interval, the great increase and spread of commerce and manufactures, and the suppression of monastic institutions, had entirely changed the social relations. The peasantry no longer formed part of the value of the estate on which they had been born; they could go where they pleased, and, consequently, were no longer fed or cared for by the lords: they endured many privations, which were in a great measure relieved by the benevolence of the church; their daily necessities had been relieved at the gates of the monasteries throughout the land. But the despoiling of these establishments in the preceding reign had cut off the source of ecclesiastical charity, and thrown a great burden of indigence and misery upon the community at large: it was then found necessary to devise measures of relief, and at the same time to provide employment and stimulate industry. A statute for the *punishment of idleness* was the consequence: severity was regarded as the first remedy. *Sloth*, when detected, subjected the offender to *two years of slavery* either to his parish, or to those who captured him. The law further recommended that the individuals thus captured should be punished by the severest of labour, with scanty food; from which, if the poor wretch attempted to escape, he became the property of his master *for life*, and was stamped on the breast with a red-hot iron with the letter S for *slave*. A second attempt to run away was punished by hanging. Idle children were legally recognised as the slaves of any one who would be at the trouble of catching them—boys until the age of twenty-four, and girls to twenty-one—and might be confined with rings or chains at the discretion of their captors. It is easy to imagine what must have been the intolerable abuses of such a law. It was repealed before the end of the reign, and two collectors were appointed in every parish to receive money, the payment of which, for the relief of the starving peasantry, was enforced by a law, which continued in operation down to the time of Elizabeth, when the price of labour was fixed, and those who had no ostensible occupation were compelled to resort to agricultural labour, or other specified employments. The period of notice on quitting service, as well as the regulations for the apprenticeship of children, was also fixed. Houses of correction were established, and overseers appointed. All of these measures were finally embodied in the act maintained, with little alteration, until the late change from which the 'unions' date their origin.

We have thus given a slight outline, extending over a long period of history, and embracing many phases in the progress of a race who require, above all, a spur to independent and honourable exertion—the constant support of an elevating motive.

TRAVELS BY A SCOTTISH CLERGYMAN.

THE REV. WILLIAM ROBERTSON,* minister of the New Grayfriars Church, Edinburgh, was in 1841 commissioned by the Colonial Committee of the General Assembly to proceed to Gibraltar, for the purpose of arranging the appointment of a Presbyterian chaplain for the troops. Besides executing his mission, he visited, in going, Vigo, Lisbon, and Cadiz; and while at Gibraltar, made excursions to such places of note as were within the reach of the time and means at his command: amongst these were Seville, Malaga, and Granada. He also crossed the Strait of Gibraltar, and visited Tangier, which recent events have brought into much notice. Since his return, he has presented his observations in a volume marked by much more sprightliness than was to have been expected from his profession or his mission. We propose glancing over this work, and showing a few specimens of the metal it is made of.

TANGIER.

The town of Tangier, built at the eastern mouth of the Gibraltar Straits, is surrounded by a Gothic wall, flanked at short distances with small towers. A fosse not more than three or four feet deep surrounds the base of the wall in its entire extent, which is about two thousand and a half yards. This ditch is either in ruins or planted with vegetables. In front of the port, and at its entrance, many batteries arise, of two storeys, armed in all with about sixty pieces of ordnance. Tangier being the residence of the foreign consuls, and of a large number of Christians as well as Jews, is called by strict Mussulmen the town of infidels. The number of inhabitants has been variously estimated at from six to twelve thousand.

Under the guidance of an intelligent and well-dressed cicerone, Mr Robertson, and two gentlemen who accompanied him from Gibraltar, surveyed the town. 'Town,' he continues, 'I presume it must be called; but so unlike is it to anything that bears that name in Europe, that were it not for the houses of the consuls, it bears about as much resemblance to a town as a city of ant-hills. The houses are so small, that one might believe them to be inhabited by a race of pigmies, were it not for the tall, brawny, muscular fellows who are seen going in and out. The houses never exceed two storeys in height, and these very low. The entrance is low and narrow. Each house has an open court like the Spanish patio in the middle, in which there is invariably to be found a fig, vine, or olive tree; so that in this happy land every man reposes "under his own vine, and under his own fig-tree." These interior courts or quadrangles are, like the apartments of the house, of very small dimensions; but they serve to keep the rooms cool and airy, as they all enter from them. The roofs are perfectly flat, and covered with *terras*, a composition of lime and small stones beaten smooth with wooden mallets. In the better class of houses, there are pipes which conduct the rain-water from the roof to cisterns under ground. But in general there is no such provision; and the cement being quite insufficient to exclude the wet, in the rainy season the rain penetrates both roof and walls, and keeps the whole house in a miserable state. All the apartments are on the veriest pigmy scale. If the Moor has room to squat, he wants no more. The furniture is common and simple; and almost the only ornament in their rooms is a rich and beautiful piece of Morocco needlework, wrought on coarse muslin, of various patterns and the most brilliant colours, occasionally hung as drapery round a small looking-glass on the wall, or in front of the bed. The streets are rarely wider than is absolutely necessary to allow two donkeys to pass each other; and if both are laden, they may sometimes find the passage narrow enough. They are littered with all kinds of refuse. Very few of the houses have any windows to the street; so that one appears to be walking in narrow lanes betwixt two dead walls, in place of in the streets of a populous town.'

Of the castle of Tangier, which lately received such rough treatment from the guns of the French, our traveller says, 'It stands on an eminence overhanging the town, and commands a magnificent view over the town and bay. The hill on which it stands had once been extensively fortified, but the works are now entirely dismantled, and almost in ruins. The castle itself externally appears almost as ruinous as the fortification, but is nevertheless still used as the residence of the governor when at Tangier. On entering, we were astonished to find the apartments in such good repair, belying their outward promise. One is astounded, after scrambling over broken walls, and through heaps of lime and rubbish, to be conducted into elegant and tasteful apartments, adorned with all the beautiful and fantastic ornaments peculiar to Moorish architecture. In the centre of the building there is, as usual, a large open quadrangle, surrounded by an elegant colonnade of white marble. The pillars are of the slender and graceful proportions so much admired in Moorish buildings, and their capitals fantastic and varied, but all bearing a resemblance to the Corinthian. The apartments on both storeys are small, but a great portion of their gaudy and glittering, but most tasteful decorations, is entire. The vaulted roofs, richly ornamented and embossed, and painted in various brilliant colours, are in perfect preservation. Much of the ancient party-coloured glazed tiling also remains, and the delicate tracery of the lacework on the walls is uninjured, except by whitewash. In fact, the castle of Tangier, in the style of its decorations, is the counterpart of the Alcazar of Seville; perhaps more perfect in respect of the ornamental part, but possessing no such elegantly proportioned apartments, and especially nothing at all comparable to the noble Hall of the Ambassadors. At present, it looks desolate and empty. There is not a single stick of furniture in any of the rooms; and the governor, when he visits Tangier, brings his furniture along with him.'

Of the personal exterior of the Moors, Mr Robertson gives a glowing description. 'The Moor, especially when somewhat advanced in life, is a magnificent lion-like creature. He is rather above the middle size, stout-built, large of limb, with great display of muscle; noble features approaching to the Roman, an ample brow, a dark eye, and (in jockey phraseology) uncommonly fine action; lifts high, steps out well, and sets down his foot with a firmness of tread peculiar to himself. With turbaned head, his loins girt with a red sash, wide white trousers, and naked limbs, as he moves along with his free, unfettered stride, he presents a remarkable contrast to the close-buttoned European, with his artificial manner and confined garb—

"That sewed-up race—that buttoned nation,
Who, while they boast their laws so free,
Leave not one limb at liberty;
But live, with all their lordly speeches,
The slaves of buttons and tight breeches."

The striking peculiarity of the Moor is his lion-like appearance. Often have I stood and gazed with admiration on a group of these swarthy turbaned children of the sun, squatted cross-legged, pipe in mouth, solemn and silent, under shelter of the parapet wall of the king's bastion, and wondered at the singular resemblance which their grave countenance, strongly-marked features, and air of savage dignity, gave them to the lord of the desert in repose. Place them under a palm-tree beside the

* Journal of a Clergyman During a Visit to the Peninsula in the Summer and Autumn of 1841. Edinburgh: Blackwood and Sons.

Diamond of the Desert, and Rubens would glory in the picture.'

Having gratified his curiosity at Tangier, Mr Robertson returned to Gibraltar. His next excursion was to

GRANADA.

The most remarkable object in this ruined capital of ancient Moorish power and splendour is the Alhambra. 'The external appearance of this renowned palace is as remarkable for meanness and deformity as its internal structure is for richness and grace. It is precisely what Swinburne describes—"a heap of as ugly buildings as can well be seen, all huddled together, seemingly without the least intention of forming one habitation out of them." The roof is covered with deeply-channeled tile. The walls are built in a slovenly manner, and coarsely plastered. There is not the slightest attempt at external ornament—no symptom of regularity of design; so that the whole mass looks like a confused heap of coarsely-finished barns or granaries. I know not whether the external ugliness of Moorish palaces is the result of design, and in order to increase the effect by contrast of the taste, beauty, richness, and symmetry within. Certainly the effect thus produced is absolutely startling, and the surprise one experiences on entering literally bewildering. The suddenness of the change appears like enchantment. By an obscure and rudely-finished door, and through a dead wall, the construction of which would discredit a farm-yard, we are ushered into a palace which might rival the most brilliant descriptions of eastern romance. I shall not attempt to describe this singular edifice. No description, indeed, can convey the slightest idea of the building, either in the arrangement of its apartments or in its decorations. They are altogether unlike anything with which the eye is familiarised in European architecture; and the very names by which we should be forced to distinguish the different compartments, would necessarily convey a false impression of their appearance. To describe the ornaments and decorations of this fairy palace would especially be a hopeless task. The exquisite symmetry of the various courts and halls, the singular lightness and elegance of the slender marble pillars, with their fanciful capitals and richly ornamented arches, the gorgeous colouring on roof and cupola, the tasteful minuteness of the stucco lacework on walls and ceilings, the pleasing variety of mosaic patterns, the singular airy loveliness and most graceful richness of the whole, are things of which neither pen nor pencil can convey any correct idea. The fresh loveliness of the brilliant decorations of the Alhambra seems to mock the faded glories of its ancient lords. The perfect symmetry of the apartments, and the exquisite harmony of their decorations, detract much from their apparent size. But though actually of larger dimensions than they appear, they are by no means of great size. Beauty, and not grandeur, is the object aimed at by the Moorish architect; and the dimensions of the various apartments are admirably proportioned to the peculiar style of decoration. The light and elegant pillars, with their endless variety of capital; the finical yet most graceful minuteness of the fretwork which adorns the walls; the beautiful, rich, but fanciful ornaments of the arches and ceilings; the carving and inlaying, and brilliant vermilion and azure colouring of the alcoves—would, in apartments of great size, be regarded as frippery and gingerbread. Here they are in perfect harmony, and accord so exquisitely with the style, dimensions, and proportions of each apartment, as to produce a whole of unrivalled grace and beauty. The Court of the Myrtles, by which we enter the palace, is the plainest, and has suffered much in its ornaments; but were it not for its proximity to the celebrated Court of the Lions, would be exceedingly admired. This last is a most exquisite specimen of that peculiarity in Moorish architecture—the open court—from which, doubtless, the Spaniards have derived their patio. The elegant and oft-described Fountain of the Lions still shoots up its crystal jet in the centre of this splendid court. It consists of a double marble basin, one rising on a pedestal from the centre of the other; and from the centre of this upper basin the water is projected through a marble tube or pillar. The jet falls into the upper basin, from whence the water overflows into the lower, and is discharged from the mouths of the twelve lions which support it. The lions are grotesque, misshapen, ugly brutes. The basins are of very elegant shape and workmanship, ornamented with sculptured festoons and Arabic inscriptions. It is said to have been constructed professedly in imitation of Solomon's molten sea; to the description of which, in 1st Kings, it bears no small resemblance. "It stood upon twelve oxen, three looking toward the north, and three looking toward the west, and three looking toward the south, and three looking toward the east; and the sea was set above them, and all their hinder parts were inward. And it was an hand-breadth thick, and the brim thereof was wrought like the brim of a cup, *with flowers of lilies*." The oxen of the molten sea supported the basin in the same manner as the lions in the fountain of the Alhambra. The Court of the Lions probably presents the most finished specimen of architectural beauty and elegance in the world. According to Swinburne's measurement, it is one hundred feet in length and fifty in breadth. It is surrounded by an open corridor of indescribable lightness and elegance, the roof of which rests on richly-ornamented arches, supported by one hundred and sixty-four slender marble columns, curiously sculptured, and with such a variety of capitals, that no two appear to be alike. The ceiling of the corridors is of carved wood, originally gorgeously painted in azure, vermilion, and gold, and inlaid with ivory; but only enough remains of these rich decorations to prove their ancient magnificence. Three noble and gorgeously-ornamented halls open from this corridor, namely, the Sala de los Abencerrages, or "Hall of the Abencerrages," on the south; the Sala de las Dos Hermanas, or "Hall of the Two Sisters," on the north; and the Sala de Justicia, or "Hall of Justice," on the east.'

Besides mere descriptions of interesting localities, Mr Robertson's pages are interspersed with anecdotes and remarks strongly illustrative of the various people amongst whom he travelled. We select the following:—

PATRIOTIC SEAMEN.

'Captain Marryatt takes notice of the fact, that the American navy is in great part manned by British sailors, and speculates on what line of conduct they might adopt in case of a war betwixt the two countries. An interesting circumstance in point occurred lately in the Bay of Gibraltar. It was at the time when great apprehensions of hostilities were entertained, owing to M'Leod's imprisonment. Two men-of-war, of nearly equal force, one British and one American, were lying opposite each other in the bay, and no one could tell but that the next post might bring tidings which should convert them into mortal enemies. In this state of matters, a considerable number of the crew of the American being British born, held a consultation together, and agreed to send a deputation to the quarterdeck to inform their captain that, in the event of a rupture betwixt the two countries, he must not depend on them, for that they would not fight against their countrymen. This is an honourable trait in the character of poor Jack, which ought not to be forgotten.'

A ROBBER EXPLOIT.

'A few weeks ago a well-dressed and gentlemanly person called at one of the principal schools of Granada, and represented himself to the teacher as a near relative of two of his young pupils. The boys were sons of a wealthy merchant of the city. The teacher, entertaining no suspicions of the purpose of his visitor, suffered him to take the boys along with him, under pretence of purchasing some little present for them. Though they did not return so soon as was expected, little uneasiness was felt on their account, until the parents received a note informing them that their children were safe and well, and that they need entertain no apprehensions regarding them, but demanding a considerable sum of money as the condition of their being restored. The money has not yet been paid; all search has proved ineffectual; and the children are still in the hands of the thieves.'

Mr Robertson having put the chaplainship of the Presbyterian troops at Gibraltar on a better footing than hitherto, returned to his native country. His work is interspersed with many grave remarks concerning the morality of the British soldiers and sailors, to which attention cannot be too earnestly recommended, especially to those in power, who have the ability to cause the very great improvement which appears to be necessary in this respect. To all classes of readers, however, Mr Robertson's work will be found instructive and entertaining.

BIOGRAPHIC SKETCHES.

JOHN JOACHIM WINCKELMANN.

John Joachim Winckelmann, the celebrated historian of ancient art, was born on the 9th of December 1717, at Stendal, a town of Prussia, about eighty miles from Berlin. His father belonged to almost the lowest rank of life, being in fact a cobbler, struggling not only with poverty but with disease, which, at an early period of Winckelmann's life, forced him to take refuge in an hospital. As the boy grew up, he showed great anxiety to go to school; but his parents were unwilling to lose even his trifling services, and it was not without much difficulty that he at last persuaded them to send him to the burgh seminary. Once there, the rector, Esaias Wilhelm Tappert, a very worthy man, was struck with his dawning genius and earnest perseverance. He offered to instruct him for less than the usual fee, and by procuring him at the same time admission into the choir, enabled him, without drawing on his father's scanty resources, to remain at school. Young Winckelmann proved the most apt and diligent of scholars; he seldom joined in the sports of his companions: generally, when they were playing, he might be seen conning some difficult passage of a classic, or learning by heart from a manuscript before him long lists of Greek and Latin words. With his industry and fine faculties he made such progress, that Tappert promoted him, while quite a stripling, to the rank of usher; some also of the Stendal burghers employed him in giving private lessons to their children; and with the trifling gains thus acquired, Winckelmann began to find himself contributing to the support of his parents.

In time, a closer intimacy sprang up between the rector and his young protegé. Tappert lost his eyesight, and the other became his daily visitor, read to him, wrote for him, and tried in a thousand ways to cheer his solitary hours. The chief want of Winckelmann, as of every poor student, that of books, was now supplied. He had free access to his patron's well-chosen library, and he read with avidity Homer, the Greek dramatists, and works on archæology and history. Meanwhile he was giving indications of something rarer than even an industrious and affectionate disposition. He wished to travel, he used to say, when quite a child; above all, he longed to visit Egypt, that he might behold the pyramids. His innate love for objects of art began also to display itself, as well as it could in a place so sequestered as Stendal. Long after, when the poor cobbler's son had become a famous man, his companions remembered how he incited them, by the hope of some petty reward, to search the surrounding country for antiquarian remains; and, so recently as 1821, two Roman urns were to be seen in the library of the Stendal school, which were exhibited with pride as the product of one of these excursions.

When he had reached his seventeenth year, the kind Tappert despatched him to Berlin, with a letter of introduction to the rector of a gymnasium there, under whose roof he remained for a twelvemonth, alternately instructing and instructed. He was then recalled to Stendal, where his friend the rector placed him at the head of the choir. He spent the next four years in unremitting study, endeavouring at the same time to support himself and assist his family by teaching in public and in private. We have no detailed account of his life during this period. One anecdote only remains, which relates to his residence in Berlin, and deserves to be repeated as a pleasing illustration of his youthful enthusiasm. He had heard, it is said, that the library of the celebrated Fabricius was about to be sold at Hamburgh, and he determined to proceed there on foot and be present at the sale. He set out accordingly, asking charity (a common practice with poor German students in their rambles, and not considered disgraceful) of the clergymen whose houses he passed on the road; and having collected in this way a little sum, he purchased on his arrival some of his darling poets, and returned to Berlin overjoyed with his success.

Winckelmann was now twenty-one, and it was quite time for him to choose a profession. His Stendal friends thought him fitted for the church, and they sent him to obtain the necessary qualifications at the university of Halle. He had no special inclination towards theology, but he obeyed in silence, and applied himself to it with his usual ardour. At Halle he had access to public libraries, and his studies seem to have been of the most miscellaneous kind, ranging from Homer and the higher mathematics, to medicine and the ponderous tomes of the feudal lawyers. At the end of two years he abandoned theology, probably because the help from home began to fail him. He remained at Halle for six months longer, arranging the library of one of the academic authorities; and then, with the small sum that he received for this, found himself thrown friendless upon the world. He was too poor to enter any profession, and a thousand vague wishes began to agitate his breast. His love of study had been confirmed into a habit: the magnificent gallery at Dresden, to which, on the occasion of some festivities, he had paid a flying visit, was ever before his eyes, and he resolved to devote his life to literature and art. Meanwhile his early passion for wandering revived, and he now put in execution a scheme which savours of less wisdom than might have been expected from a youth of twenty-three, who had seen something of the world. Fascinated with a fresh perusal of Cæsar's Commentaries, he began, in the summer of 1740, a pedestrian journey to France, solely, his biographers assure us, to visit the scene of the great Roman's military exploits. As is usual in such cases, his funds were speedily exhausted; and when near Frankfort-on-the-Maine, he was compelled to retrace his steps. The most laughable part of the story remains to be told. Arriving at the bridge of Fulda, he remarked his own dishevelled, travel-stained appearance, and fancying no one near, resolved to remedy it. He had pulled out a razor, and was about to operate on his chin, when he heard a noise, and turning round, perceived a party of ladies, who, thinking him on the point of committing suicide, were shouting for help. The truth, however, was speedily explained, and the fair intruders, it is added, generously forced on his acceptance a gift of money sufficient for him to pursue his retreat in comfort.

Poor Winckelmann now discovered that life was made of sterner stuff than such romantic dreams. He went to Jena, and there, besides mastering Italian and English, struggled hard to complete his knowledge of medicine, with a view to making it a profession. But this scheme also, after a few months, poverty compelled him to forego. He became tutor in a family at Heimersleben, and during the year and a half which he spent there, devoted his leisure to historical studies, reading, we are informed, Bayle's dictionary twice through. At last the conrectorship of the school at Seehausen was offered him, with a yearly salary of 250 thalers, little more than L.35. Small as this was, it was a larger income than he had ever enjoyed: it enabled him to send something to his infirm and aged parents; accordingly he accepted the post with joy, and in the autumn of 1743 we find him installed at Seehausen.

During no period of his life does Winckelmann appear more deserving of our regard than in the years of obscure drudgery which he passed at Seehausen. He found, on his arrival, none of his scholars acquainted with more than the first rudiments of Latin and Greek; many were ignorant of their ABC; and the poorer ones could obtain no money from their parents for the purchase of the necessary school-books. Thus, in spite of his title of conrector, Winckelmann had little scope for the display of his fine genius and deep erudition. But nothing daunted, nothing discouraged him. He made, with his own hand, copies of such passages in the classical authors as his scholars became qualified to read, and these he distributed among them. He laboured and laboured, until at last things began to wear a flourishing aspect. Beyond the sphere, too, of his immediate duties, he found time both for his own intellectual improvement and for the indulgence of his kindly disposition. After school, he gave a few private lessons. In the evening, a favourite pupil, whom he instructed in philosophy and mathematics, remained till ten. Then Winckelmann belonged to himself. Seizing his Sophocles (a favourite author, of whom he was projecting a new edition), he read and annotated till midnight. When twelve struck, he never dreamt of going to bed, but, wrapping himself closely in an old fur cloak, leant back in his chair, and slept among his books till four. He then renewed his own studies for two hours more; at six the favourite pupil returned, and stayed until it was time to open school. Few scholars of Winckelmann's eminence have had, during the early portion of their career, so little leisure for private study; none ever turned that little to better account.

Five years of this laborious existence did not impair Winckelmann's health of body or cheerfulness of mind. He was modest and wise enough to be content with his situation, and might have remained all his life at Seehausen, had not some vexatious interference on the part of the school-inspector forced him reluctantly to leave it. After resolving on this step, he made several unsuccessful attempts to procure employment, and had finally made up his mind to betake himself to London, where, with his knowledge of languages, he hoped easily to obtain a situation as corrector of the press. Happily, during a brief visit to Dresden, in the June of 1748, he heard some one mention the vast collection of books which the Count Von Bünau, at his estate of Nöthenitz, near Dresden, was then amassing and arranging. He penned immediately a modest letter to that nobleman, imploring the most trifling literary engagement. The count inquired into his character and accomplishments, was pleased with both, and offered his petitioner a subordinate post in his library, with a yearly salary of L.12! Winckelmann accepted the offer, received the money for his travelling expenses, hurried to Stendal, taking with him all the books he had through life painfully collected, commissioned a friend to sell them, and apply the proceeds in a weekly allowance to his father, to whom he bade farewell, and then proceeded, light of heart, to Nöthenitz.

The count was engaged in the composition of a history of the German empire, and Winckelmann's principal employment at Nöthenitz was to make such copies of, and extracts from, old documents as were to find a place in that work. He acquitted himself altogether to the satisfaction of his employer; nay, at first he laboured with such assiduity that his hair became gray: we do not find, however, that he received any more solid encouragement from his excellency than praises and kind words. Nevertheless, with board and lodging provided him, and a little leisure on his hands, Winckelmann was for some time tolerably happy. He had a noble library at his command; from time to time he made excursions to Dresden, where he could converse with such men as Hagedorn and Oeser; and, still better, range at will through its picture-gallery and collection of antiquities. At last, what with the laborious fulfilment of his duties and the intensity of his private studies, even his Herculean strength gave way; his health grew daily worse; his drooping gait and emaciated frame betokened the approach of death; and his friends advised him, if he wished to live, at once to seek a warmer climate. Meanwhile (in the spring of 1751) Archinto, the papal nuncio at Dresden, came to Nöthenitz, and made, during his stay there, Winckelmann's acquaintance. He was charmed with his learning and exquisite taste, and, observing his debility, strongly recommended him to go to Italy. 'That,' cried Winckelmann, 'is the goal of all my wishes.' The nuncio begged him to pay him a visit at Dresden. There he introduced him to Father Rauch, the confessor of the king; and both hinted, among other things, that Winckelmann, by becoming a Catholic, might obtain a pension from the court of Dresden, and thus repair to Italy. Hints soon became persuasions: after long wavering, in an evil hour Winckelmann consented, and on the 11th of July 1754, abjured Lutheranism to enter the pale of the Romish church. Such changes, when they proceed from conviction, can never deserve to be visited with reprobation; but in this case, the most friendly of Winckelmann's biographers admit far other motives were at work. We learn with pleasure, that at the moment he was severely punished by the estrangement of his very dearest friends. At the same time, the Count Von Bünau must not escape uncensured. Even the tolerant and aristocratic Goethe is indignant at his niggardly neglect: the acquisition of a book-rarity the less, nay, a simple application from a minister of his influence to the court of Dresden, would have furnished the slender aid which Winckelmann purchased at so dear a rate.

His excellency contented himself with being very angry, and Winckelmann was soon of course forced to quit Nöthenitz. He repaired to Dresden; and here he found himself moneyless as ever: Archinto was in Italy, and Rauch, though very polite, kept his hand closed. Meanwhile, Winckelmann (narrowly escaping starvation) projected, drew, wrote, and studied—the last generally in the Brühl library, where Heyne was then employed. 'It is a curious fact,' remarks Mr Carlyle, in his notice of the latter,* 'that these two men, so singularly correspondent in their early sufferings, subsequent distinction, line of study, and rugged enthusiasm of character, were at one time, while both as yet were under the horizon, brought into partial contact. "An acquaintance of another sort," says Heeren, "the young Heyne was to make in the Brühl library, with a person whose importance he could not then anticipate. One frequent visitor of this establishment was a certain almost wholly unknown man, whose visits could not be specially desirable for the librarians, such endless labour did he cost them. He seemed insatiable in reading, and called for so many books, that his reception there grew rather of the coolest. It was John Winckelmann. Meditating his journey for Italy, he was then laying in preparations for it. Thus did these two men become, if not confidential, yet acquainted; who at that time, both still in darkness and poverty, could little suppose that in a few years they were to be the teachers of cultivated Europe, and the ornaments of their nation."' For Winckelmann, both the 'darkness' and the 'poverty' were soon to be at an end. He found means, in the May of 1755, to publish his first book, the 'Reflections on Imitation of the Greeks in Painting and Statuary,' which was dedicated to the king, and brought its author high and sudden fame. A month or two afterwards, he received the promise of an annual pension of L.30; Rauch sent eighty ducats for travelling ex-

* Miscellanies, vol. ii. pp. 49-8.

penses; and in the following October Winckelmann, now about to enter his thirty-ninth year, found himself at last in Rome.

It is not our intention to detail with the same minuteness the remaining thirteen years of Winckelmann's life, years of almost uninterrupted happiness. In Rome his health was completely restored; he needed little for the supply of his bodily wants, and that little he always obtained without difficulty. When his pension ceased, on the death, in 1759, of his patron Archinto, the Cardinal Albani invited him to become keeper of his collections, with an ample salary, and merely nominal duties. He was appointed by the Pope, in 1763, Antiquario della Camera Apostolica, or Superintendent of the Antiquities of Rome, an honourable post, congenial to his tastes. He lived on a familiar footing with the great and opulent; the most eminent of the artists resident in Rome were his daily companions; he had free access to the noblest collections of art in the world; and in the purest intellectual enjoyment and effort, he speedily forgot his past sufferings and struggles. Every foreigner of distinction who visited the Eternal City was proud to have Winckelmann for a cicerone: he himself delighted, when he found rank and genuine taste combined, to act in that capacity, and his conversation on such occasions was of the most brilliant and fascinating kind. The thoughts and emotions which were excited in him by the beautiful remains of antiquity, found moreover enduring expression in a long series of masterly writings. The principal of these, his History of Ancient Art, was begun in the second year of his residence at Rome, and published at Dresden in 1764.

The publication of this work raised him to the pinnacle of European celebrity, and more than one German potentate (the great Frederick among the rest) endeavoured, without success, to tempt Winckelmann to his court. His friends in Germany, however, prevailed upon him, in 1768, to pay them a visit; and, in the company of a Roman sculptor named Cavaceppi, he set out for his native country in the April of that year. But as the distance increased between him and his beloved Rome, he sank into a deep melancholy: when they were crossing the Tyrolean Alps, he pointed to the gloomy sky overhead, and exclaimed, 'Torniamo a Roma' (Let us return to Rome). Cavaceppi persuaded him to continue his journey, and they reached Ratisbon, where the Empress-Queen, Maria Theresa, was then residing. Winckelmann now resolved to go no further. The Austrian prime minister, Kaunitz, himself joined his expostulations to those of Cavaceppi in vain. He remained at Ratisbon till the end of May, and having been presented to the empress, who bestowed on him some costly medals in proof of her regard, proceeded to Trieste, where (preserving, we know not why, a strict incognito) he took an apartment in a hotel, purposing to sail to Italy in the first ship bound for Ancona.

He met at the common dining-table of the hotel an Italian stranger named Francesco Arcangeli, who, it afterwards appeared, had been banished for theft from the Austrian dominions. This scoundrel easily gained his confidence, by introducing him to the captain of a ship bound for Ancona, and by an agreeable and winning manner. The unsuspecting Winckelmann told him everything about himself except his name, and showed him the presents of the empress; these excited the Italian's cupidity. On Wednesday the 8th of June Arcangeli left the hotel early in the morning, and having made some purchases, returned to his room, where he remained for some time, and then (as he was daily in the habit of doing) paid a visit to Winckelmann in his apartment. The latter was sitting, without neckcloth or upper garment, at his writing-table, on which, as it chanced, there lay unfinished his literary testament. He rose to greet his guest, and they walked together up and down the room till ten, talking of his approaching departure. Winckelmann was in the gayest humour, spoke with enthusiasm of his patron Albani's splendid villa, and begged the other to come and visit him at Rome. Suddenly, Arcangeli asked him to show the company at dinner that day the empress's medals. He refused. 'Will you tell me, then, what your name is?' 'No; I do not wish to be recognised,' was Winckelmann's reply; and, offended with the abruptness of the questions, he sat down, with his back towards the Italian, and began to write. Arcangeli immediately took from his pocket, and threw over Winckelmann's head, a knotted cord, which, as he started up, tightened round his throat. They closed, and had struggled together for a short time, when Arcangeli drew a knife and plunged it into his victim. At this moment a servant, hearing the noise, rushed up and opened the door, through which Arcangeli escaped unpursued. It is needless to protract the catastrophe. Physicians were summoned; but all was vain; and at four in the afternoon Winckelmann expired. The assassin was some weeks afterwards captured, tried, and executed.

The news of this unexpected, mysterious, and melancholy death, was received with regret throughout all Europe, especially in Germany, where many of his admirers (the youthful Goethe among the number) were ignorant of Winckelmann's abrupt return towards Italy, and were preparing to welcome him with enthusiasm. We have left ourselves no room to speak of his works: his biography is now before the reader. We wish that Winckelmann, by avoiding the fatal error of apostacy, had allowed us to say that his was a life altogether worthy of a scholar and a man.

EVENINGS WITH THE OLD STORY-TELLERS.

We can confidently recommend to young persons, and to the attention of all who have charge of them, a small and cheap, but elegant volume, entitled '*Evenings with the Old Story-Tellers*,' being a member of a series entitled *Burns's Fireside Library*, in which we find many excellent reprints and adaptations prepared with remarkable taste, and even elegance, notwithstanding the small prices at which they are published. The particular volume here referred to contains a connected series of examples of the stories popular in the middle ages, chiefly from the well-known collection called the Gesta Romanorum; the translations being only executed by the editor where there did not exist happier versions by authors of established reputation. These stories, with their unscrupulous supernaturality, their allegorically-religious characters, and primitive ideas with regard to the course of nature and providence, are a curious and interesting study; nutritive of the imagination and feelings, at the same time that they have a historical value as exponents of European opinion in past ages. They are here very pleasantly strung upon a series of conversations represented as taking place in one of the Oxford colleges. The following may serve as a specimen of the collection:—

JOVINIAN THE PROUD EMPEROR.

In the days of old, when the empire of the world was in the hands of the lord of Rome, Jovinian was emperor. Oft as he lay on his couch, and mused upon his power and his wealth, his heart was elated beyond measure, and he said within himself, 'Verily, there is no other god than me.'

It happened one morning after he had thus said unto himself, that the emperor arose, and summoning his huntsmen and his friends, hastened to chase the wild deer of the forest. The chase was long and swift, and the sun was high in the heavens when Jovinian reined up his horse on the bank of a clear bright stream that ran through the fertile country on which his palace stood. Allured by the refreshing appearance of the stream, he bade his attendants abide still, whilst he sought a secluded pool beneath some willows, where he might bathe unseen.

The emperor hastened to the pool, cast off his garments, and revelled in the refreshing coolness of the waters. But whilst he thus bathed, a person like to him in form, in feature, and in voice, approached the river's bank, arrayed himself unperceived in the imperial garments, and then sprang on Jovinian's horse, and rode to meet the huntsmen, who, deceived by the likeness and the dress, obeyed his commands, and followed their new emperor to the palace gates.

Jovinian at length quitted the water, and sought in every direction for his apparel and his horse, but could not find them. He called aloud upon his attendants, but they heard him not, being already in attendance on the false emperor. And Jovinian regarded his nakedness, and said, 'Miserable man that I am! to what a state am I reduced! Whither shall I go? Who will receive me in this plight? I bethink me, there is a knight hereabout whom I have advanced to great honour; I will seek him, and with his assistance regain my palace, and punish the person who has done me this wrong.'

Naked and ashamed, Jovinian sought the gate of the knight's castle, and knocked loudly at the wicket.

'Who art thou, and what dost thou seek?' asked the porter, without unclosing the gate.

'Open, open, sirrah!' replied the emperor, with redoubled knocks on the wicket.

'In the name of wonder, friend, who art thou?' said the old porter as he opened the gate, and saw the strange figure of the emperor before the threshold.

'Who am I, askest thou, sirrah? I am thy emperor. Go, tell thy master Jovinian is at his gate, and bid him bring forth a horse and some garments, to supply those that I have been deprived of.'

'Rascal,' rejoined the porter—'thou the emperor! Why, the emperor but just now rode up to the castle with all his attendants, and honoured my master by sitting with him at meat in the great hall. Thou the emperor! a very pretty emperor indeed. Faugh; I'll tell my master what you say, and he will soon find out whether you are mad, drunk, or a thief.'

The porter, greatly enraged, went and told his lord how that a naked fellow stood at the gate calling himself the emperor, and demanding clothes and a good steed.

'Bring the fellow in,' said the knight.

So they brought in Jovinian, and he stood before the lord of the castle, and again declared himself to be the emperor Jovinian. Loud laughed the knight to the emperor.

'What, thou my lord the emperor! Art mad, good fellow? Come, give him my old cloak, it will keep him from the flies.'

'Yes, sir knight,' replied Jovinian, 'I am thy emperor, who advanced thee to great honour and wealth, and will shortly punish thee for thy present conduct.'

'Scoundrel!' said the knight, now enraged beyond all bounds; 'traitor! Thou the emperor! ay, of beggars and fools. Why, did not my lord but lately sit with me in my hall, and taste of my poor cheer? And did not he bid me ride with him to his palace gate, whence I am but now returned? Fool, I pitied thee before, now I see thy villany. Go, turn the fellow out, and flog him from the castle ditch to the river side.'

And the people did as the knight commanded them. So when they ceased from flogging the emperor, he sat him down on the grass, and covered him with the tattered robe, and communed on his own wretchedness.

'Oh, my God!' said Jovinian—for he now thought of other gods beside himself—'is it possible that I have come to such a state of misery, and that through the ingratitude of one whom I have raised so high?' And as he thus spake, he thought not of his own ingratitude to his God, through whom alone all princes reign and live. And now he brooded over vengeance. 'Ay,' said he, as he felt the sore weals on his back from the scourging—'ay, I will be avenged. When he next sees me, he shall know that he who gives can also take away. Come, I will seek the good duke, my ablest counsellor; he will know his sovereign, and gladly aid him in his calamity.' And with these thoughts he wrapped his cloak round him, and sought the house of the good duke.

Jovinian knocked at the gate of the duke's palace, and the porter opened the wicket, and seeing a half-naked man, asked him why he knocked, and who he was.

'Friend,' replied the emperor, 'I am Jovinian. I have been robbed of my clothes whilst bathing, and am now with no apparel, save this ragged cloak; and no horse; so tell the duke the emperor is here.'

The porter, more and more astonished at the emperor's words, sought his master, and delivered Jovinian's message to him.

'Bring in the poor man,' said the duke; 'peradventure he is mad.'

So they brought Jovinian into the duke's great hall, and the duke looked on him, but knew him not. And when Jovinian reiterated his story, and spoke angrily unto the duke, he pitied him. 'Poor mad fellow,' said the good duke, 'I have but just now returned from the palace, where I left the very emperor thou assumest to be. Take him to the guard-house. Perhaps a few days' close confinement on bread and water may cool his heated brain. Go, poor fellow; I pity thee!'

So the servants did as their lord commanded, and they fed Jovinian on bread and water, and after a time turned him out of the castle; for he still said he was the emperor. Sorely and bitterly did the emperor weep and bewail his miserable fate when the servants drove him from the castle gate. 'Alas, alas!' he exclaimed in his misery, 'what shall I do, and whither shall I resort? Even the good duke knew me not, but regarded me as a poor madman. Come, I will seek my own palace, and discover myself to my wife. Surely she will know me at least.'

'Who art thou, poor man?' asked the king's porter of him when he stood before the palace gate, and would have entered in.

'Thou oughtest to know me,' replied Jovinian, 'seeing thou hast served me these fifteen years.'

'Served you, you dirty fellow,' rejoined the porter. 'I serve the emperor. Serve you, indeed!'

'I am the emperor. Dost thou not know me? Come, my good fellow, seek the empress, and bid her, by the sign of the three moles on the emperor's breast, send me hither the imperial robes, which some fellow stole whilst I was bathing.'

'Ha, ha, fellow! Well, you are royally mad. Why, the emperor is at dinner with his wife. Well, well, I'll do thy bidding, if it be but to have the whipping of thee afterwards for an impudent madman. Three moles on the emperor's breast! How royally thou shalt be beaten, my friend.'

When the porter told the empress what the poor madman at the gate had said, she held down her head, and said with a sorrowful voice unto her lord, 'My good lord and king, here is a fellow at the palace gate that hath sent unto me, and bids me, by those secret signs known only to thou and me, to send him the imperial robes, and welcome him as my husband and my sovereign.'

When the fictitious emperor heard this, he bade the attendants bring in Jovinian. And lo! as he entered the hall, the great wolf-hound, that had slept at his feet for years, sprang from his lair, and would have pulled him down, had not the attendants prevented him; whilst the falcon, that had sat on his wrist in many a fair day's hawking, broke her jesses, and flew out of the hall—so changed was Jovinian the emperor.

'Nobles and friends,' said the new emperor, 'hear ye what I will ask of this man.'

And the nobles bowed assent, whilst the emperor asked of Jovinian his name, and his business with the empress.

'Askest thou me who I am, and wherefore I am come?' rejoined Jovinian. 'Am not I thy emperor, and the lord of this house and this realm?'

'These our nobles shall decide,' replied the new king. 'Tell me now, which of us twain is your emperor?'

And the nobles answered with one accord, 'Thou dost trifle with us, sire. Can we doubt that thou art our emperor, whom we have known from his childhood? As for this base fellow, we know not who he is.'

And with one accord the people cried out against Jovinian that he should be punished.

On this the usurper turned to the empress of Jovinian—'Tell me,' said he, 'on thy true faith, knowest thou this man, who calls himself emperor of this realm?'

And the empress answered, 'Good, my lord; have not thirty years passed since I first knew thee, and became the mother of our children? Why askest thou me of this fellow? And yet it doth surprise me how he should know what none save you and I can know.'

Then the usurper turned to Jovinian, and with a harsh countenance rebuked his presumption, and ordered the executioners to drag him by the feet by horses until he died. This said he before all his court; but he sent his servant to the jailer, and commanded him to scourge Jovinian, and for this once to set him free.

The deposed emperor desired death. 'Why,' said he to himself, 'should I now live? My friends, my dependents, yea, even the partner of my bed, shun me, and I am desolate among those whom my bounties have raised. Come, I will seek the good priest, to whom I so often have laid open my most secret faults: of a surety he will remember me.'

Now the good priest lived in a small cell nigh to a chapel about a stone's cast from the palace gate; and when Jovinian knocked, the priest being engaged in reading, answered from within, 'Who's there? Why troublest thou me?'

'I am the Emperor Jovinian; open the window; I would speak to thee,' replied the fugitive.

Immediately the narrow window of the cell was opened, and the priest, looking out, saw no one save the poor half-clothed Jovinian. 'Depart from me, thou accursed thing,' cried the priest; 'thou art not our good lord the emperor, but the foul fiend himself, the great tempter.'

'Alas, alas!' cried Jovinian, 'to what fate am I reserved, that even my own good priest despises me? Ah me! I bethink me; in the arrogance of my heart I called myself a god. The weight of my sin is grievous unto me. Father, good father, hear the sins of a miserable penitent.'

Gladly did the priest listen to Jovinian; and when he had told him all his sins, the good priest comforted the penitent, and assured him of God's mercy if his repentance was sincere. And so it happened that on this a cloud seemed to fall from before the eyes of the priest; and when he again looked on Jovinian, he knew him to be the emperor, and he pitied him, clothing him with such poor garments as he had, and went with him to the palace gate.

The porter stood in the gateway, and as Jovinian and the priest drew near, he made a lowly obeisance, and opened the gate for the emperor. 'Dost thou know me?' asked the emperor.

'Very well, my lord,' replied the servant; 'but I wish that you had not left the palace.'

So Jovinian passed on to the hall of his palace; and as he went, all the nobles rose and bowed to the emperor; for the usurper was in another apartment, and the nobles knew again the face of Jovinian.

But a certain knight passed into the presence of the false emperor. 'My lord,' said he, 'there is one in the great hall to whom all men bow; for he so much resembleth you, that we know not which is the emperor.'

Then said the usurper to the empress, 'Go and see if you know this man.'

'Oh, my good lord,' said the empress, when she returned from the hall, 'whom can I believe? Are there, then, two Jovinians?'

'I will myself go and determine,' rejoined the usurper, as he took the empress by the hand, and, leading her into the great hall, placed her on the throne beside himself. 'Kinsfolk and nobles,' said the usurper, 'by the oaths ye have sworn, determine between me and this man.'

And the empress answered, 'Let me, as in duty bound, speak first. Heaven be my witness, I know not which is my lord and husband.'

And all the nobles said the same.

Thereupon the feigned Jovinian rose and spake: 'Nobles and friends, hearken! That man is your emperor and your master; hear ye him! Know that he did exalt himself above that which was right, and made himself equal unto God. Verily he hath been rewarded. He hath suffered much indignity and wrong; and, of God's will, ye knew him not. He hath repented him of his grievous sin, and the scourge is now removed. He has made such satisfaction as man can make. Hear ye him, know him, obey him.'

As the feigned emperor thus addressed the astonished nobles, his features seemed illumed with a fair and spiritual light, his imperial robes fell from off him, and he stood confessed before the assembly an angel of God, clothed in white raiment. And as he ended his speech, he bowed his head, and vanished from their sight.

Jovinian returned to his throne, and for three years reigned with so much mercy and justice, that his subjects had no cause to regret the change of their emperor. And it came to pass, after the space of three years, the same angel appeared to him in a dream, and warned him of his death. So Jovinian dictated his troublous life to his secretaries, that it might remain as a warning unto all men against worldly pride, and an incitement to the performance of our religious duties. And when he had so done, he meekly resigned himself, and fell asleep in death.

The moral of the story is thus given:—'Jovinian was but the picture of the proud, worldly-minded man, entirely given up to vanity and folly. The first knight whose castle he visited was True Wisdom, ever disdainful of the pomps and vanities of the world. The next knight was Conscience. The dog that turned against his old master was the lusts of the flesh, our own evil desires, which will ever in the end turn against those who have pampered them. The falcon is God's grace; the empress, man's soul; and the clothes in which the good priest clothed the half-frozen emperor are those kingly virtues which he had thrown off when he gave loose to the vanities of the world.

SAVINGS' BANKS IN FRANCE.

The establishment of savings' banks, recognised as they now are by government, is a measure calculated to benefit the humbler classes of society. The advantages they offer are twofold—safe custody, and 'improvement' by interest. The poor man cannot command the same facilities with his scanty savings as the rich man with his large accumulations; he does not find it easy to meet with fit persons who will take charge of it; and if he retains it in his own possession he makes no profit, and is exposed to the chance of being plundered. Here, then, the savings' banks afford him the opportunity of making a secure deposit, whether for present or for future use. Once in the safe keeping of the bank, the sum may become a nucleus of accumulation, and is beyond the risk of improvident emergencies. The greatest difficulty with working men is to lead them to acquire the *first* habits of order, foresight, and economy. Induce a labourer or an artisan to deposit even the smallest saving, week by week, until the entire sum shall amount to L.5, and it is certain that, before arriving at that period, he will become sensible of the propriety and the necessity for saving. He will appear a new individual; one who no longer regards himself as an outcast, without a future, but who will take and maintain his standing among the producers and preservers of national wealth. His conduct will become more regular, his habits more moral; he will be a better workman, better husband, father, and citizen.

From a little work written on this subject by Baron Charles Dupin,* we learn that savings' banks were introduced into France soon after their legal establishment in England. A model bank, presided over by the duke of Larochefoucauld-Liancourt, was started in Paris in the year 1818, from which date up to the year 1830, only twelve others were instituted, and those were all in the departments; that is, the country. In 1831, a year remarkably fatal to the interests of the working population, no new bank was founded; but in 1832, when the effects of the Revolution of July began to be felt in popular institutions, four others were established; in 1833, nine; forty-eight in 1834; and at the present day, France contains four hundred and fifty savings' banks, showing a remarkable and rapid progress, which impressively illustrates the blessings and advantages of peace.†

In 1830, the year of the Revolution, the deposits in the savings' banks in France amounted to L.207,824, and the sums drawn out to L.150,276, being L.100,000 more than in the previous year. In 1831—a year characterised by riots at Lyons and Paris, and great commercial distress, when the poor were excited against the rich, and civil war showed its head for a moment—

* Histoire, Constitution, et Avenir des Caisses d'Epargne de France. Paris: 1844.

† The first savings' bank in England was started, but unsuccessfully, in the year 1798. The idea was adopted with better success in Scotland in 1807 by the minister of the parish of West Calder, who instituted a bank for his parishioners; and afterwards, in 1810, by Henry Duncan, minister of Ruthwell, in Dumfriesshire. The latter took the care of the administration of the establishment upon himself, and published the result in a well written pamphlet, in which he explained the system and its advantages, and succeeded in drawing public attention to the enterprise. In 1813, Sir William Forbes established the bank of Edinburgh upon a plan which served as a model to all that succeeded it. From the additional experience gained by the experiments in Scotland, the original bank was founded in London within a year or two afterwards, under the management of Mr Baring.

the sums withdrawn were less by L.60,000 than in 1830. In 1832—when France, in common with other countries, was visited by the cholera, when the deaths in Paris increased from their usual average of 25,000 to 48,000—the deposits were L.125,808, and the sums withdrawn L.122,668. The statistics of the succeeding years are not given; but in 1842, it appears that the deposits amounted to L.3,800,000; a proof, as Baron Dupin observes, that the people have begun to appreciate the peaceful tendencies of the age.

In 1815, an attempt was made to unite the savings' banks of Paris with the *Monts Piétés*, or pawnbrokers' institutions. This plan had been adopted in other parts of the kingdom, but was successfully resisted in the capital. One of the strongest objections urged against it was the check it would give to depositors, from the repugnance that many would feel to enter an establishment in which it might be supposed they placed pledges rather than deposits. Baron Dupin avails himself of the statistics of the Monts Piétés to draw a few conclusions as to the physical condition of the people at certain periods. He takes the first quarters of the years 1837, 1838, and 1839 respectively, and finds that 1838 presents the most favourable indications, and 1839 the most unfavourable; while the amount of pledges, for the three quarters taken together, exceeded that of objects redeemed by L.117,480. There is one other point of view which these returns present of the condition of the community, relating to their means of recreation. The Easter festivities are regarded by the working population of Paris with especial favour: they make every exertion to redeem their wearing apparel, in order to take part in the general holiday. The tables show, that in 1837 the amount for articles withdrawn exceeded that of pledges by L.1604; in 1838, by L.1408; but in 1839, a year of distress, the pledges were in excess to the amount of L.15.

These facts are interesting, although not strictly connected with the subject under consideration. We have introduced them, to show the wide views taken by Baron Dupin in his inquiries, which are those of a philosopher earnest for the truth. He goes on to draw a comparison between the banks of Paris and those of London during a period of eighteen years, when, making allowance for the difference of population, the balance, as regards the number of depositors, is in favour of the former city by more than half; but when the counties of England are compared with the departments of France, the returns of the former are as 12 to 1 of the latter. The comparison is then extended to various cities and towns of France, the result of which is shown in a table giving the number of depositors to every 1000 inhabitants; and here it is justly observed, that the savings' banks may be taken as a moral index of the state of the population. In Metz, the chief town of the department of the Moselle, the proportion of depositors is 71 to each 1000 inhabitants; while in the commercial city of Lyons it is only 3 to the 1000: in the department of the Rhone, in which the latter city is situated, each 1000 of the population contributes L.322 annually to the lotteries; in the Moselle, for the same number, the contribution is L.20. This is public gaming; but in private the result is still worse. For the same numbers, the duty on playing cards, in the Rhone department, is L.5; the Moselle, eight shillings. The actual state of the respective localities confirms these conclusions. In Metz, many excellent schools of popular instruction have been established by men eminent for their zeal and disinterestedness, which comprehend the teaching of adults, and the application of science to the arts and to the business of daily life. There reason, prudence, and virtue are held up as honourable to the career of the working man, at the same time that he is improved in his knowledge of his peculiar occupation: but at Lyons everything remains to be done: the higher classes have yet to learn 'the pleasure of succouring the weak; and the latter, the happy experience of gratitude for enjoyed benefits.'

With regard to the moral progress of the population of Paris, we are informed that, a quarter of a century ago, they threw L.1,160,000 annually into the lotteries; but now not a sixpence is expended in this way: formerly, L.240,000 to L.360,000 were lost in other fatal games of chance, now unknown. Gaming-houses, scandalously tolerated or authorised, devoured alike the abundance of the rich and the last sou of the poor: they are now abolished by the laws. Then, the practice of economy was unknown or neglected among the working-classes, now they save L.1,440,000 annually; and the number of depositors, of which *bona fide* workmen constitute three-fourths, increases from 12,000 to 14,000 every year. The proportion of paupers, as well as of illegitimate births, is also diminishing, but with deplorable slowness. At the commencement of the era, 205 in every 1000 births were abandoned; now only 120; which, observes Baron Dupin, 'are 120 too many.' The streets and public places do not present the same aspect of debauchery and unmitigated license as before. Thus far the results are favourable and gratifying; but we learn that, on the other hand, one third of the population is, at the present time, living in a state of concubinage, one third of the children is illegitimate, one third of the deaths takes place in the pauper wards of the hospitals, uncared for or unwept by the surviving relatives; such are the morals of Paris—Paris ameliorated. Baron Dupin endeavours to account for this state of things by the fact, that two thirds of the population have not yet come forward as depositors in the savings' banks, and of those who do so, many do not deposit their savings oftener than once in six months; while others grow indifferent, and cease to deposit at the end of five or six years. The savings' bank in such a case, instead of being the perpetual treasury of the people, is in reality, for the mass, only the magic lantern of transient economy.

At the present day, savings' banks are to be found in 450 cities and towns of France, in which places 600,000 families, the élite of the working-classes, have confided to the treasury of the state more than L.1,360,000, saved penny by penny, the fruits of their self-denying industry. Soldiers and seamen, to the number of 40,000, are possessors of L.1,240,000, which, every year, at the expiration of their term of service, enables them to buy a small portion of land, or the tools of a trade, in order to live honourably and actively after having served their country. Of the 80,000 national guards, one half are depositors; and, taking the whole kingdom, there are 35,000 clerks in public or private establishments whose deposits amount to L.1,400,000. A similar sum is held by 96,000 orphans and 46,000 widows; two classes who are thus sheltered from the privations usually attendant on their bereaved condition. The number of workmen and domestic servants enrolled as depositors is 250,000; the amount of their deposits is not stated; but the number is continually increasing. Last on the list appear 140,000 labourers, the owners of L.400,000.*

Baron Dupin concludes with an appeal to the good sense of the working-classes. 'Our commercial laws are free: all may rise: an iron barrier no longer excludes the workman: the only conditions required are, that he be active, intelligent, and industrious. Many names might be cited, now associated with honour and splendour, whose owners were originally workmen, who began by depositing a shilling in the bank.' He then indulges in a little national feeling, and anticipates the time when the present monarch of France may say, 'I found L.240,000 in the people's banks, and leave therein L.40,000,000.'

We close this article with a few lines from Mr Tidd Pratt's work on savings' banks. 'Every person who has vested his savings in the public funds has a stake in the security of the country, proportioned not merely

* The present number of depositors in the savings' banks of the United Kingdom exceeds 950,000; the amount of deposits is nearly L.27,000,000 and a half.

to the sum total of those savings, but to the value of that sum to himself, and will be deterred from compassing the disturbance of his native land by a personal motive, added to the influence of duty. He will feel the importance of public peace and public credit with that strong conviction which individual interest never fails to inspire; and, in answer to the objections of those who would be jealous of the support thus obtained to the ruling powers, it should be observed, that he who possesses property in a country is not interested in the stability of the administration for the time being, but in the perpetual stability of universal order and good government.'

RURAL NOTES—ALGÆ, OR SEA-WEEDS.

[This little paper is abridged from the *Inverness Courier* newspaper. It is interesting as a fair specimen of the compositions of the numerous reflecting and observant men scattered over our country in the capacity of land-agents; and we have no doubt that its thoughtful reference to nature at large will, with most of our readers, be sufficient to excuse the local application of some of its details.]

We have a great and growing antipathy at the term *weed*, and cannot help coming to the belief that Dr Johnson was not following his *own* nose when he defined weed as an herb 'noxious or useless,' as we apprehend such an anomaly as a weed, in the sense entertained by the doctor, has no place in nature. The doctor, if he had exercised his own judgment in the matter, would, we are convinced, have come to a different conclusion, and would, or at least should, have defined it 'an herb, the use of which is not *yet* understood.' With all due deference to the great lexicographer, and as the term is probably too firmly fixed in our language ever to be eradicated, we would define weed as an agent for gathering, arranging, and storing up matter below the reach of, and intangible to, animal and the higher grades of vegetable life; thus fulfilling a great and mighty end in the scheme of creation—the gathering together of the stray substances which, amid nature's varied manufactures, has as it were slipped through her fingers, and would have run to waste, and converting them, by sure and certain processes, into tangible and useful compounds.

In the article of the algæ, or sea-weeds, we are particularly struck with the economy of nature in so singularly adapting the means to the end. The office of these plants is to collect the stray substances held in solution by the salt water, particularly the alkalies and phosphates; and as these have to be extracted from the water, and not from the earth beneath it, the plants have no roots, properly speaking, but simply processes for clinging to the hard and flinty rocks, as points of attachment; while, at the same time, in place of a firm and erect stem to keep the branches and leaves expanded, as in terrestrial plants, and which would be cumbrous and unhandy for plants which change their medium as often and as regularly as the tides, they are furnished with innumerable air-bags or vessels for accomplishing this purpose, so that the branches and leaves of the plant may come in contact with the greatest possible quantity of water consistent with its size—these air-vessels serving the double purpose of furthering the plant in its destined office, and when this is accomplished, floating it to our shores and beaches to be applied to useful purposes. * *

In sailing or steaming round our west and northern coasts in the months of April and May, one is struck with the number of boats and men, and horses and carts, and women and boys, and creels, all busily employed at ebb tide in cutting and carrying away sea-weed from the shores, for the purpose of manuring the fields; and when we think of the immense quantities of potatoes raised almost exclusively by this manure, and the number of people who live upon them not only in the country, but in the towns to which they are exported, we must come to the conclusion that the algæ, or sea-weeds, are a tribe of plants of vast importance to a large section of the population of Scotland at least; and, when taken in conjunction with the peaty and waste soils round our coasts, almost invaluable, as no species of manure reduces a rough peaty soil so quickly to a state fit for the production of human food. There is no need of waiting for the 'meliorating effects of the atmosphere' where there is plenty of sea-weed. The lotter, with sea-weed at command, commences his spring labour at the middle of April, and by the middle of May, if the weather be propitious, will have planted potatoes sufficient to serve a numerous family all the year round; and that on the most forbidding peaty soils, never before touched by the spade of man, and of the value, in its natural state, of some three-halfpence or twopence per Scotch acre. This is always done on what is called the lazy-bed system, which, in spite of the name, is perhaps the best system for 'bringing in' all rough, deep, peaty soils, as the lotter can always calculate on a crop the first season by this mode—an immense affair to a person whose capital or stock in trade consists merely of his 'thews and sinews.' * *

If we may judge from the scramble there is for sea-ware all over the thickly-peopled parts of our sea-coasts in March, April, and May, there is evidently a very great demand and want of sea-ware for agricultural purposes; as, besides the great breadths annually cut from the shores at spring tides, hundreds of boats and men are yearly employed dragging it from the bottom with grappling irons—and a most laborious and tedious operation it is—to eke out the scanty supply, and which supply will become yearly more scanty as population increases and waste lands are being taken in. With these views, I need not say that I believe an increase of the sea-ware round our coasts would be a very great blessing and advantage, and would form a permanent source of subsistence to thousands yet unborn; and I am gratified to say that this can be accomplished to a very great extent in a great many situations, and at an expense not likely to prove a barrier in this age of overflowing capital. It is well known that sea-weed prevails most on our rocky coasts; and the reason of this simply is, that the weed requires a point of attachment—something tangible and steadfast to hold by—that it may spread its branches and leaves to catch the stray matter held in solution by the water. With this point of attachment, nothing further is required to constitute a perennial field of algæ; nature does all the rest. And hence there need be no dread of greedy and slothful tenants over-cropping the land, dissipating the phosphates, and allowing the drains to choke up, and forgetting to pay the per centage on the capital you had invested in them. This is a bargain you are making with nature, and she never repudiates. Here, for once, that wise old saw of that wise old cock, Franklin—namely, that always taking out of the meal tub, and never putting in, soon runs to the bottom—is rendered null. There is nothing but cut and come again with the sea-weed: it is, in fact, a modern exemplification of the widow's cruise and the barrel of meal on a gigantic scale. In walking along the sea-coast at ebb tide, we see that, wherever a beetling cliff projects into the sea, and, as a consequence, the shattered rocks that tumble down from time to time are strewed along the beach, here it is that the sea-weeds are most luxuriant. Now, what nature does in this case we can do artificially, and that to our advantage, as, from the laws that govern falling bodies, the beach must have a certain inclination before the shattered rocks can roll into, and remain in, the zone where the algæ naturally grow. Now, the inclination required to be so great where stones roll in by their own gravity, that the breadth of this zone is consequently greatly narrowed, and instead of having a breadth of sea-weed—as we may have artificially—of a half, or even a whole mile, we have frequently only a few yards.

All that is necessary to constitute a field of sea-weed, is to strew the shore under high-water mark with rough boulders from the nearest cliff; and in order that the shores may be regularly planted, the stones should be regularly laid down at the rate of about one in every yard square. This 'planting' of the shores is not at all a new thing, but has been practised on a small scale in various parts of the Highlands, and, in every instance that I have heard of, with the very best success. I lately visited a small patch that had been thus artificially done, some twenty or twenty-five years since, and was quite pleased with the result, as it looked better than any natural piece of sea-ware within miles of it. The piece consisted of about one-third of a Scotch acre, and was done by a small lotter in liquidation of arrears of rent. He, the lotter, I believe, still enjoys the sea-ware of this piece, which he and a neighbour of his assured me could be easily disposed of at 24s. every two years, or 12s. yearly, being at the rate of 36s. yearly per Scotch acre. I could not so easily ascertain the expense the job had actually cost, as your genuine Celt has an innate caution about him in all matters relative to pounds, shillings, and pence, and has as much dread of breaking through or establishing any precedent that may hereafter infringe his interests, as any lawyer who ever sat at the Queen's Bench. I, however, understood that the job had been the 'dernier resort' of the landlord, and probably cost twice as much as it would have done under ordinary circumstances.

In looking at the job, I had no doubt that it could have been done in the present day at about L.8 or L.10 per Scotch acre. Supposing, then, the value of an acre of sea-weed at 30s., and the expense of creating it L.10, the investment would be something about a seven years' purchase—no bad 'spec,' one should think, in the present state of the money market; and in *stock* as permanent as the earth itself.

In carrying out improvements of this kind, little engineering skill is required. The only thing to be considered is the nature of the rock or stone to be laid down; and, contrary to what one would expect, land stones are greatly superior to stones taken from either salt or fresh water, and in all cases give, and continue to give, a much superior crop. The reason of this seems simply to be, the smoothness of the surface of rolled or water-worn stones not permitting the seeds of the plant, in the first instance, to form a lodgment; and, in the second place, being too smooth for the fibrous attaching apparatus of the plant to keep a permanent hold of. In regard to the size of the stones, little nicety is required; large stones will do equally as well as small; but it is evident they will be much more expensive in first laying down. Stones of from twenty to forty pounds would be a very handy size, and such as carry a close covering of lichens, and break with a rough granular fracture, will probably answer best. When too small, they are apt to be carried out to sea, or cast upon the beach when under a full crop of buoyant sea-weed. The conveniency and accessibility of the situation will naturally influence the planter; as also the risk of the new-laid stones being lifted or sanded up; but this is easily guarded against. When we look at the miles and miles on end of barren gravel and sand on some of our sea-coasts, without one vestige of vegetation, and our eye at last rests on some rocky corner abounding in marine vegetable life, we are struck with the difference, but merely imagine that this corner, somehow or other, is favourable to the growth of sea-weed. We do not advert to the fact, that the sea is imbued with the same qualities and influences on the barren and gravelly beach as in the rocky and weedy corner; nevertheless it is the same. The rent and shattered rocks precipitated into the sea from the cliffs above is the work of nature in her incessant career of building up and pulling down. This operation we can happily imitate, to the extent at least of strewing our shores with the fragments of our mountains; while nature at the same time 'bears a hand,' and clothes these fragments with perpetual verdure.

BRIEF LIFE OF THE 'ITALIAN BOYS.'

The following affecting passage occurs in the recently published 'Address' of a society formed for the protection and education of these wanderers, of whose history and mode of life a sketch was given in No. 622 of our former series:—Of the poor Italian boys who have so long enlivened our streets with almost the only music which could be had out of the concert or drawing-room, hundreds are the victims of a set of men who periodically visit Italy, and convert the face of that lovely land into a slave-market, selecting chiefly from the mountains the little creatures whom we see daily around us, making an agreement with the parents to house, feed, and clothe them for a term of years, and at the end of that time to set them free with a certain sum—seldom or never paid. The boys arrive here, and then what is their condition? Day after day, early and late, in the hottest time of summer, in the stormiest and most inclement of winter, are these poor fellows forced to drag along their heavy organs from street to street; they have to live as they best can on the casual charity of passers-by; they are expected to bring home a certain sum daily; and also frequently towards nightfall—not daring to meet their masters without the stipulated amount—they may be seen begging piteously. Their clothes are filthy rags; their lodging is of the most miserable description. They are huddled together in one of the most unhealthy, the most crowded, the lowest localities of London, in small, ill-ventilated rooms, many in a room, worse housed than animals, badly as slaves ever were. From being so many hours a-day under the weight of a heavy organ (to say nothing of their long exposure, ill-clad and ill-fed, to our fickle climate), they contract fearful disorders, such as hernia, varicose veins, diseases of the spine, &c.; and it has been calculated by a medical man, one of their own countrymen, that the average duration of time during which they can continue such occupation is about *eight years*, by which time their constitutions are utterly broken down. 'We know,' says a public journal, commenting upon this passage, 'of but one cure for this species of importation, and that is, a universal public agreement never to give these beggars *any money to carry to their masters*. Let them once learn that the trade is unprofitable, and it will assuredly cease.

THE MAIDEN AND THE LOOKING-GLASS.

FROM THE GERMAN OF HEINRICH DOERING.

MAIDEN.

Hateful Mirror! prithee say,
Why torment me every day?
Why to shatter thee provoke me?
Spiteful thing! I here invoke thee;
Why detect each summer stain?
Ever glad to give me pain?
Every spot malicious show,
Though unseen by any beau?

MIRROR.

Maiden! wherefore thus complaining?
'Tis unjust. I love not paining
Thee, nor any other beauty;
To each and all I do my duty.
To praise or blame I'm always ready—
Fearless—faithful—honest—steady:
To tell the truth to every creature,
Is part of my transparent nature!

MAIDEN.

Hence! I hate thee! get away!
More unsufferable each day
Thine unfeeling bluntness grows,
Blemishing each charm that glows
O'er a form—a face so fair,
All my lovers say, and swear,
Angels in their forms divine,
Scarce in brighter beauty shine!

MIRROR.

Maiden, maiden! blustering youth,
Hectoring over sense and truth,
Who such shameless flatteries lavish,
Would thy sober senses ravish!
Coming years each grace will banish,
And these false ones all shall vanish:
Say—shall thy true friend be broken?
Be it so—the words are spoken.
I am ready for the worst.
Strike!—but thou must promise first,
Heartless fops that fawn and flatter,
With indignant scorn to scatter
From thy presence, like a haze
Of stinging gnats in summer days;
Trust me, then, thy woman's heart
From thy true friend will not part.
Anger for a time controls
Vanity's misguided souls.
Thou'rt all too noble, and too pure,
Long such thraldom to endure.
Nor would'st thou break this heart of mine:
Thou wilt but firmer intertwine
Our bonds of love!—since now thou'rt 'ware
Of vanity's perfidious snare.

London, Feb. 1845. E. L.

DUTY.

Duty is far more than love. It is the upholding law through which the weakest become strong, without which all strength is unstable as water. No character, however harmoniously framed and gloriously gifted, can be complete without this abiding principle: it is the cement which binds the whole moral edifice together, without which all power, goodness, intellect, truth, happiness, love itself, can have no permanence; but all the fabric of existence crumbles away from under us, and leaves us at last sitting in the midst of ruin, astonished at our own desolation.—*Mrs Jameson.*

Printed by William Bradbury, of No. 6, York Place, and Frederick Mullett Evans, of No. 7, Church Row, both of Stoke Newington, in the county of Middlesex, printers, at their office, Lombard Street, in the precinct of Whitefriars, and city of London; and Published (with permission of the Proprietors, W. and R. CHAMBERS,) by WILLIAM SOMERVILLE ORR, Publisher, of 3, Amen Corner, at No. 2, AMEN CORNER, both in the parish of Christchurch, and in the city of London.—Saturday, March 22, 1845.

CONDUCTED BY WILLIAM AND ROBERT CHAMBERS, EDITORS OF 'CHAMBERS'S INFORMATION FOR THE PEOPLE,' 'CHAMBERS'S EDUCATIONAL COURSE,' &c.

No. 65. NEW SERIES. SATURDAY, MARCH 29, 1845. PRICE 1½d.

UPRIGHT, DOWNRIGHT, AND STRAIGHTFORWARD.

It is very common to say of such a man that he is 'upright,' it is not less common to say of such another that he is 'downright,' or of a third that he is 'straightforward.' Occasionally, the same person is said to be both upright and downright, and even straightforward, all at the same time; and we now and then hear a man called upright one day, downright another, and straightforward on the next. It would thus seem that the words are to some extent synonymous. It will be found, however, on examination, that they have a moral meaning as distinct and definable as their more obvious and physical significations. Popular usage, in fact, required three words to express three distinct varieties of character, and adopted these, all of good Saxon descent, to supply the want. Thus a downright man, although he may be an upright one, is not necessarily so, and *vice versa;* and the straightforward man may possess qualities which are not inherent to, and of necessity existing in, the character of either.

Mr Smith, for instance, is an upright man. He acts with fairness in all his dealings. He would wrong no man of a farthing. He would not injure his neighbour by word or deed. His fame is pure before the world. His word was never broken; and his promise is as good in the market as another man's bond. He holds up his head, is not ashamed to look anybody in the face, and walking erect in the dignity of conscious honesty, is called upright accordingly.

Mr Brown, again, is a downright man. He may or may not exhibit the moral rectitude of Mr Smith. He may not, strictly speaking, be an upright man; but he does not thereby forfeit his title to be classed among the downright. The phrase implies not so much a moral quality, as a manner and a peculiarity. The upright man may hold his tongue; but the downright man will speak out, loudly and boldly, without fear of the consequences. Mr Brown always allows his indignation to find vent. He speaks his mind; and if he combines both uprightness and downrightness, calls a rogue a rogue, and a lie a lie, and cares not whom he offends by so doing. A great conqueror is, with him, a great murderer; a duellist, an assassin; a fraudulent bankrupt, a robber. He condemns in plain terms what he does not approve, and never deals in inuendos, 'or hints his doubts.' Neither will he indulge in courtesies when his mind is full of bitter meanings, and call him an 'honourable gentleman' whom he imagines to be the very reverse, nor designate another as his 'noble friend' whom in his heart he considers his very ignoble enemy. He has no patience with, or toleration for, any kind of terms which tend to gloss over error. Even where no deception is attempted, he does battle on behalf of plain speaking. When people talk of operatives, he talks of workmen; the endearing word 'wife' is not banished from his vocabulary for that of 'lady;' and 'man' is a word of dignity and significance with him, instead of being degraded to imply something the opposite of a gentleman. If a man who is not habitually downright were to say a tithe of the strong things that Mr Brown may say with impunity, he would get knocked down for his frankness; but the very audacity of the downright man takes the world by surprise, and forces it into admiration. It forgives the insolence for the sake of the courage, and the harshness for love of the sincerity. Mr Brown, moreover, has a clear head for detecting a sophism, and a knack of getting at the gist of a dispute, though it may be swathed about in redundancies and circumlocutions. He clenches an argument with homely common sense, and drives a truth into the mind of an antagonist with as much force and as little ceremony as a carpenter drives a nail into a block. He is a man, to use a very common phrase, who will 'stand no nonsense,' and would rather a thousand times be thought rude, boorish, and disagreeable (which he very generally is), than call a spade other than a spade, compromise an opinion, or abandon a prejudice that he had once defended.

In every condition of life, in the very extremity of distress and poverty, a man may be upright, and will be the better for it; but to be downright is not overprudent in him who has his fortune to make, or any worldly advantages to expect from his fellows. If a man be rich, his downrightness is not much in his way. It may even become ornamental to him, and pass for caustic wit and interesting eccentricity. The worst that will be said of him is, that his ill-nature is extremely piquant and original. If he be poor, it will receive no such honourable appreciation, but be universally condemned as unjustifiable misanthropy. It is rather a dangerous weapon in any one's hands, but doubly dangerous in the grasp of those who have not high birth or station, or the right of rich revenues, to privilege them to wield it.

Mr Jones, the straightforward man, has the candour of the downright man without his incivility. He uses clear and intelligible language on all occasions, but does not hold himself bound to select the harshest phrases which can be found. Integrity also belongs to his character; but, being more conspicuously marked by straightforwardness, no one thinks of speaking of his uprightness. The notable points in the straightforward man are the directness and openness with which he acts in his intercourse with the world. He takes the broad highway, and not the crooked path. His objects may partake of the usual business character of selfishness, but he does not make them worse by attempts to disguise them. No; he says, I am here a man of business, and pursue my interests, leaving others to do so too, as they have a right to do. Thus everybody knows at once 'what he would be at;' and arrangements are made and bargains struck with half the trouble which they would cost in other hands. Sometimes this straightforwardness is felt as a little out of taste; but all are sensible of its being extremely convenient, and generally acknowledge in the long-run that Mr Jones's mode of doing business is the best. It is amusing to see a quirky or circumambient man come into dealings with Mr Jones. He is apt to be confounded by the very transparency of the other's mind. It puts him out. He could manage admirably with one who took cunning ways too, however much he might be upon his guard; but straightforwardness is a new mode of fence, and he sinks under it. It is the same way with the sophist, and the man who has a bad cause to defend by clever arguments. The arrow-flight directness of Mr Jones's common sense overthrows him at the first encounter.

Straightforwardness is not always combined with wisdom; but when it is, it becomes a masterful power. Even by itself it can hardly fail to elevate its possessor in the esteem of mankind. As a rogue is defined to be 'a fool with a circumbendibus,' so may one who has no bad designs and no circumbendibus about him be said to possess a kind of wisdom. In Don Quixote, we see straightforwardness united with hallucinations; and it is interesting to reflect how that one good quality—the good faith, simplicity, and thorough honesty of the poor hidalgo—makes him respectable amidst all his absurdities. Generally, however, the straightforward man is no fool, but one in whom all the elements are well combined, with a keen eye, a clear head, a good heart, a passionate love of truth, and an unfaltering determination to pursue it.

We trust, as the world gets older, upright and straightforward men will increase amongst us, and downright men become more scarce. The first qualities are unquestionably virtues; but the last is at the best an unpleasant characteristic. Downright men do not see things quite in their true light. They are oddities in our social scene. The soft words which they deprecate, and which they never will consent to use, what are they but the result of an improved civilisation? In a ruder age, when bad actions were more frequent and of a grosser nature than now, it would have been cowardice and baseness in any who could see the evil to speak of it mildly. But now, when a tolerably equable standard of good conduct exists in all classes aiming at being called respectable, and when a vast tribunal instantly condemns any occasional aberration, softer terms are sufficient; and merely to express surprise at any little delinquency, conveys, in these days, a severer reproof than would have been borne two hundred years ago by a violent public declamation.

SUPERSTITIONS AND CUSTOMS OF TOURAINE.

[The following article has been prepared at our request by an English gentleman who has lived several years in Touraine, and acquired a thorough knowledge of the manners and customs of the people. Our object was to ascertain in what degree the popular fancies and habits of that province in central France resembled those of our own country, as detailed in Ellis's edition of Brand's Antiquities, and outlined three years ago in a series of papers in this Journal, entitled 'English Popular Festivals.' We trust, therefore, that the present paper will be found to possess a value beyond that arising from its power of amusing a passing hour.]

Like the fossils in the strata of the earth, marking the several epochs in which families of living beings have had their existence, the superstitions and customs which prevail in the rural districts and communes of Touraine mark the various periods when the Druid, the Roman, and the Frank, were lords of the soil. Time has not worn out, nor the mingling of various races obliterated the strong impress left by religious creeds and observances which have been long lost in the oblivion of centuries gone by, since they were the rule and guide of those who were then lords of the soil, and formed the population of ancient Gaul. The observation of the 1st of January, in nearly all the communes of the arrondissement of Loches, is evidently a Druidical ceremony. It is called Aguillauneu, or Aguillonés. All the peasants, and more particularly the younger ones, on that day go from house to house wishing their neighbours a happy New-Year, and crying for les aguillauneu, or aguillonés, upon which they generally receive some small present. In the towns, 'les étrennes' are given and received; but in the country, the aguillauneu has descended from the time when the Druids cut the sacred guy, or mistletoe from the oak, which was done with a golden knife, and the plant received in a white linen sheet, and distributed to the people, crying 'à guy l'an neuf,' whence the word aguillauneu. This plant was considered as a specific against various diseases and infirmities, as epilepsy, sterility, poisons, &c. and is still held in high estimation, more particularly when cut from the oak. There is, however, strong reason to believe that what is found as a parasite upon that tree is not the common mistletoe, but an allied plant (perhaps Loranthus Europæus, which is abundant on the oak in some parts of Europe, and much resembles the common mistletoe). La Bis Bergère, another ancient fête, is held on quinquagesima Sunday, Le Dimanche Gras: all the shepherds of each hamlet assemble, when the weather will permit, in the open air after vespers, each bringing with him provisions of bread, wine, bacon, and, above all, eggs, the frying of which is an essential part of the ceremony. All the domestics and young people from the neighbouring farms attend, and great part of the night is spent in songs and dances.

Le Dimanche des Brandons.—On the evening of the first Sunday in Lent, as soon as it grows dark, all the lads and lasses of the neighbourhood spread themselves over the fields sown with corn, with a flaming torch or brandon in their hands. In Berri they carry poles, on the tops of which are bundles of flaming straw; in some places the torch is made of the dried stems of the mullein, covered with tar. The object of their search is the 'nielle,' or corn cockle, which they consider as very injurious to the crop. The search continues about an hour, after which they repair to the respective farms, where a feast is prepared, one of the chief dainties of which consists of 'pancakes,' which are distributed to the young people in proportion to the quantity of nielle they have collected. This fête is considered the same as that celebrated amongst the ancients in honour of Cybele or Ceres, the first teacher of husbandry.

Christmas Eve.—On the night preceding Christmas Day, the largest log which can be found is placed on the hearth; this is called 'Le Souche de No,' or 'Ferefeu.' The head of the family then mounts on the block, and cries three times with a loud voice, 'No, no, no, que ce jour est serio par le bon Dieu et la bonne Vierge, le ferefeu est au feu; on se mit à genoux.' They then say a paternoster and an ave, and sing carols till it is time to attend the midnight mass; but, before the family departs, food is given to the cattle, after which great care is taken that no one goes near the stable till the mass is concluded; for on this night the beasts are able to converse, and wo be to him who listens to their conversation. A terrible tale of the punishment inflicted on a listener has descended from generation to generation, and is fully credited by the peasantry of the district. The master of a house, once upon a time, had great curiosity to know what his oxen had to say, and to that purpose hid himself in the stable. As soon as midnight sounded, he heard one of the oxen say to another in a very terrible voice, 'What shall we do to-morrow?' 'Drag our master to his grave,' bellowed his companion. A horrible shudder passed through the frame of the terrified farmer, who was scarcely able to crawl to his bed, where he very soon expired, and was buried according to the prediction. This dreadful example has effectually prevented any listeners ever since. As to the fire which has been kindled, it is not so much for the purpose of warming the family when they return from church—for every one attends the mass, except the sick and aged who are confined to their beds—but during their absence the Virgin is supposed to come and warm herself, to spin, or swathe the infant Jesus. The block or 'souche de no' continues to burn during the three fêtes of Christmas, after which the ashes are collected, and pieces of charcoal suspended from the ceiling, and over the bed; the remainder is carefully preserved as a very fine thing for cows when they calve, to whom the powder is administered mingled with their drink.

Le Gâteau des Rois, or Twelfth-Night Cake.—The master of the family cuts up the cake, which is an enormous flat piece of pie-crust, and in which a bean is concealed: he then places the youngest child upon the table, addressing her by the name of 'Phœbe.' She replies by the word 'Domine,' and he then asks to which of the party such and such a morsel of the cake shall be given. The child names each guest without distinction of rank or precedency, all the domestics being present; in whosoever's portion the bean is found, the holder becomes king for the night, and the revels take place after the manner of the Roman Saturnalia, to which nation the use of the words 'Phœbe' and 'Domine' evidently refers the manner of the celebration.

La Joineé.—On the eve of St John, June 24, in every village and hamlet, and in the faubourgs of every town, in the department of Indre et Loire, fires are kindled at night, which are called La Joineé, or Johanneé. As soon as it grows dark, men, women, and children assemble, and the fire is kindled by the oldest or principal person, who marches at the head of the party thrice round the flaming pile, praying aloud; when the wood previously provided is nearly consumed, branches of juniper and other aromatic plants are thrown on the heap, and a thick smoke produced, when all the cattle in the neighbourhood are brought forth and driven thrice round the fire, after which the young people dance rondes, singing and shouting until midnight; and any one who rises before daybreak, and searches carefully amongst the ashes, will, it is said, find some of St John's hair. The ashes themselves are thought to possess various peculiar and marvellous properties.

Fairies.—The belief in these spirits is much the same as in other lands; they are considered as heavenly beings, dwarf in size, living in caves during the day, or in clefts of rocks, and particularly near solitary fountains, where they wash their robes very frequently: they are considered as generally well-disposed; but sometimes ride horses during the night, and tie knots in their manes to form stirrups, leaving the horse gear in great disorder. They are fond of moonlight dances, and you may easily trace the place of their assembly by the dark rings in the grass. My informants all agree that they are by no means so common as in former times; and some assure me, that they have understood that about 800 years ago the greater number of these spirits were driven from France into a very distant country, the name of which they did not know, but that they were doomed to remain in banishment 1000 years; so that in two centuries more they will return to their former haunts. In the fosse of the chateau at Loches are two pillars which supported a drawbridge, erected to facilitate the evasion of Mary of Medicis from the pursuit of Cardinal Richelieu: these are shown as the work of fairy hands, and said to have been erected in one night. One species of fairy, called 'La Bête Havette,' is of rather a malignant description: she lives in wells and fountains, and is very fond of children, sometimes pulling them into the water and drowning them.

La Milloraine, or Demoiselle, is a white phantom, chiefly seen in Normandy, of enormous size, appearing in lonely places, but with no distinct form or features; grows larger and larger as you approach nearer; but when you arrive at the precise spot, she vanishes over the trees, making a noise like a hurricane amongst the leaves. Another species of goblin haunts houses, and plays very troublesome and mischievous tricks, knocking at the doors, or on empty casks, moving the furniture, whispering words,' heard indistinctly, sighing, groaning, and pulling off the bed-clothes, making ugly faces at the children, &c. One in particular is very obnoxious, and is called 'La Bête de St Germain.' Apparitions of black rams vomiting flames, black cats with eyes of fire, red bulls with enormous horns, and black dogs which stand immoveable where treasure lies buried, are by no means rare; but, above all, white rabbits are very dangerous at night.

Le Chasse del Chien, or St Hubert's Hunt, is frequently heard in the air at night, and consists of the barking of dogs, rattling of chains, and doleful cries, supposed to proceed from demons who are carrying away condemned souls to a place of punishment: this is also called 'Le Chasse Briquet,' or 'Chasse à Ribaud;' and there are very few peasants who have not heard it—proceeding, no doubt, from flocks of wild geese or other migratory birds.

Sorciers.—Tales of sorcerers are very common, and of the grand assemblies they have been seen to hold. Many of these histories probably arose from the meetings of the Huguenots and other persecuted sectaries in former times. They are now considered as a very evil race, and are said to anoint themselves with the fat of unbaptised babies before they attend their grand assemblies. Magicians differ considerably from sorcerers, and do not go to these abominable meetings; they are the masters, and not the servants of the devil. They have great power over men and animals, causing madness in the former, and various diseases in the latter; dry up cows' milk, and make horses restive and inclined to run away. They are frequently known to throw a powder into the air at fairs and markets, which drives the beasts wild, and causes a great commotion. They also stop vehicles on the highway, put out fires, make philtres, and have the power of rendering themselves invisible, or taking the forms of divers animals. Their secrets are written in a book called 'Grimoire,' and much studied by Italians, Jews, a people called philosophers, and by a good many priests. No one is more to be feared in a canton: their power extends over the health of man and beast: any one who displeases them is attacked by a disease of which he languishes and dies: sometimes the enchantment is confined to the cattle, and the whole stock upon a farm perishes. The curés in the country, by means of their 'Grimoire,' have great power over storms, and can, if they will, direct them away from their own parish, preserving the crops from hail and other accidents; but if they are angry, and their will is not obeyed, they are able to lay waste the whole district. Not long ago a terrible storm devastated the arrondissement of Loches, on which occasion two priests, whose names are well known in the district, were seen on the borders of a pond at Louroux; one, carrying his 'Grimoire' in his hand, seated himself near the edge of the water, which the other beat with his staff till it arose in the form of a trumpet, and caused the hail which devastated the lands. Several persons vouched for the truth of this tale, in which they evidently fully believed.

In many of the cottages you will find two things suspended from the ceiling; namely, a plant of house-leek (sempervivum tectorum), which shows, by immediately withering away, when a sorcerer enters the house; and on the arrival of a stranger, an anxious eye is often turned to the house-leek. The other is a small loaf (pain de noël), which is made and baked on Christmas night, and possesses the singular property of curing mad dogs; a morsel also taken every day is very good for the health. Small cakes made on the eve of all the grand fêtes, and baked under the ashes, have the virtue of saving the soul from purgatory, and are called 'sauve ame.' Also behind the door you will generally find a branch of box, which was blessed on Palm Sunday, and which has the property of protecting the house from lightning and from fire. Sometimes every room is thus protected; and in case of a violent storm, the master or mistress of the house has recourse to the 'buis beni,' dips it in holy water, sprinkling the room and all the parties present, after which they all kneel in prayer. Fortune-tellers and gipsies find out thieves and stolen goods, and are believed to read futurity by chiromancy and cards; a belief by no means extraordinary amongst the peasants, when we consider the large fortune accumulated by Mademoiselle Lenormand through the credulity of the highest ranks in Paris.

Hidden Treasure.—It is universally believed, that during the various civil wars and revolutions which have desolated France, vast treasures have been buried or concealed in caves and ruins. The peasantry of Touraine believe that these hoards of wealth are guarded by black dogs, which, if they come to your house, and are well-treated, will sometimes guide you to the spot where they are deposited. To obtain them, you must fast for some days, and then dig a trench about the place, so as to turn up a large mass of soil, without which precaution the devil, to whom all these treasures belong, will carry it off. Having begun your work, you must on no account desist till it is completed; and as the first living creature which raises the treasure will die within the year, you should provide yourself with an old horse of no value, who will then become the property of the devil instead of the treasure you have gained. In a valley in the forest of Loches are the remains of a house built by Charles VII., as a 'rendezvous de chasse' for himself and his court; beneath it is a cave, in which a prodigious treasure is deposited, guarded by a dragon, which I am assured any one may see if he has the courage to visit the spot at midnight quite alone, the animal then lying at the entrance of the cave, and guarding the treasure in a wicker basket. This valley is called 'Or Sous,' and the name perhaps gives rise to the tale. No one has ever ventured to test the truth of this universally-believed legend.

Charms and Amulets.—Throughout the arrondissement, and particularly in the faubourgs of Loches, if an infant is seized with convulsions, either from dentition or worms, it is said to have 'Le mal d'Exive.' Physicians are in vain; and a journey to Exive is the only remedy. This place, on the banks of the Cher, near Montrichard, possesses a holy spring, whence its ancient name Aique Vive, or Aquæ Vivæ. Probably its sanctity is of Druidical origin, and was afterwards preserved by an abbey of the order of St Augustin, founded on the spot; but the abbey is now in ruins, and the curé of Montrichard directs the necessary rites and observances, and receives the fees, which are not inconsiderable, and formerly were part of the revenue of the abbey. During the prevalence of any epidemic or contagious disease, a well-known preventive is to take the young shoots of a fig-tree and cut them into pieces about half an inch long; these are strung in the manner of a chaplet, and taken to a priest, who says certain prayers over them, gives them his blessing, and places them in contact with a statue of St Rock, after which the person wears them for nine days, during which prayers should be said for him, and he is safe from the disease, or speedily cured in case of an attack from it.

Many married women wear two amulets to procure them safety during childbirth, the one called a 'crapaudine,' which consists of a ring worn round the neck or on the finger, which has set in it a crapaudine, or petrified tooth of a shark; the other is a ribbon of white silk, which has touched the veritable ceinture of the blessed Virgin, and is precisely of the same length, namely, two metres five centimetres. Upon it are printed these words—'Mesure de la veritable ceinture de la très Saint Vierge, conservée dans l'Eglise du chateau royal de Loches, à moi N..., servante de Dieu je vous salue Marie.' This ribbon is first worn by young girls when they make their first communion, and again on their wedding-day; some wear it under their garments all their lives. The girdle itself was given to the church of Loches by Geoffrey Grise Gonelle, Count of Anjou, who was living in 958, and received it as a present from a queen of France. It was originally brought from Constantinople by Lothaire.

On a death taking place in a house, the water in the bucket, any wine or liquid in the drinking vessels, is immediately thrown out, lest the soul of the departed should receive any damage by falling into them. If it is the master of the house who is dead, some one runs immediately to the bee-hives, knocks gently on each, and says, 'My little friends, be quiet; you have lost your master, but do not leave us; we will take the same care of you, and be kind to you.' They also attach a morsel of black stuff to each hive, that they may wear mourning like the rest of the family. It is also considered as a well-known fact, that if the master of the house is violent, and swears or quarrels, the bees never thrive so well as in a family which lives in concord and harmony. It is also considered very wrong to count the number of hives; and in purchasing bees, it is particularly necessary that the money be very honestly gained, or the bees will never thrive; whence it is not uncommon to say of any sum gained with considerable labour—'Ho! cet argent est bien bon pour achêter des abeilles.'

Les Coquards, or cocks' eggs.—The dwarf eggs laid by hens are believed to be produced by the cock, particularly by old cocks; and if submitted to incubation, and allowed to be hatched, they produce that very formidable animal called a basilisk, which is a species of winged dragon, whose eyes by a single glance are able to destroy the unfortunate person who comes within their influence: if, however, a man is able to fix his eye first upon the basilisk, the latter dies immediately. The same superstition prevails in Bretagne, where I was shown a well in which I was told there existed not long ago a crocodile which possessed the same destructive powers as the basilisk of Touraine, but which was at length fortunately destroyed by the powerful eye of some beholder, who was beforehand with the dreadful animal.

Les Loups Garous, or men who for some time have been excommunicated—or misers who have sold themselves to the Evil One, and are compelled to assume the shape of wolves, though an article of faith, are not supposed to exist at present in Touraine, wolves themselves being rare; but a belief in 'Brous' is nearly universal, and I was referred to those who had been witnesses of their existence.

Les Brous probably derive their name from the old Armorican 'brous,' a thicket, because these creatures are supposed to gallop all night over the forests and thickets. I received the following testimony from men who were not particularly credulous in other matters:—Joseph Guebin, a small landholder and jobber in cattle, who has no fear of ghosts or fairies, sorcerers or magicians, knows two brous, who have been in the habit of scouring the country at night; they are near neighbours of his at Ferriere Larçan. One is a mason about sixty years of age, who was long suspected of being a brou, from the circumstance of his never being at home at night; and after his day's work, of course he would not have spent his time in racing over the forest, had he not been a decided brou; which was at length clearly proved by a neighbour of the present writer, who was returning late at night from the market at Ligeuil, when he found a very beautiful sheep on the route. Thinking it had strayed from some flock in the vicinity, he took it on his shoulders, carried it home, and locked it up in the stable with his donkey; when, next morning, on opening the stable door, the sheep had vanished, and in its place was the mason in the act of placing some straw in his sabots: of course he was a brou; and the reason was, that in his youth he had been a thief and a very wild young man. The second instance was a young man, who, having stolen some cloth, became a brou, and ran over the country at night, killing and devouring dogs, poultry, and other animals; but he afterwards confessed himself to a priest, was absolved, and never *galloped* again. The writer has frequently seen the remains of dogs which have been destroyed and half devoured by brous, especially their paws.

Louis Manceau, a merchant of cattle, about thirty-six years of age, and by no means *bête* in general affairs, an inhabitant of the town of Loches, and accustomed to travel over the country in his vocation, informed me that he had seen and known several brous, but that they are not so numerous as they were some few years ago, because the priests are forbidden to act as they used to do. Some fifteen years ago, if you were robbed, you went to a priest and gave him a louis-d'or, for which he read some prayers out of a book, and then placed two loaves of bread upon the altar, which, after a short time, became quite black; and if the person who had stolen the property did not restore it, he was destined to become a brou, and to gallop the country from the time the angelus sounded in the evening till it rang again in the morning. The curé of La Selle, in the commune of Ligeuil, was very celebrated for making brous, till the priests were forbidden such practices.

A young man, named Charles Robin, a small farmer, assured me that a few years ago, on going into his garden one fine moonlight night, he saw a small sheep walking slowly up one of the paths, and on attempting to lay hold of it, it bounded over a high wall, and ran off to the forest, uttering the most unearthly shouts of laughter. He called his uncle, who was in the house, and who ran into the garden, and also heard the laughing, which was quite supernatural. The uncle confirmed this statement; and, moreover, informed me that he knows a woman whose husband was suspected of being a brou, and of galloping the country at night. In order to detect him, she took a needle and thread to bed with her, and sewed his shirt to her chemise. The neighbours saw him gallop, notwithstanding something still remained in bed with the wife, either a lifeless body, or something which had taken the form of the suspected person. Sometimes this credulity has had very fatal effects. Some twelve years ago a man was shot at St Hippolyte, near Loches, by one of his neighbours, and killed upon the spot, upon suspicion of being a brou, and his family was so persecuted that they left the village, and took up their residence at Loches, where they still remain.

There are also female brous. A domestic residing in a family at Loches declares that she knows a married female with a family, in the village of Liege, who galloped in the form of a sheep also, and was found by a man passing along the road to St Quentin late at night, who took the animal on his shoulders, and soon after found the weight of his burden very much increased; and when he got near his own door, was astonished at the sheep asking in a human voice where he was carrying her. He was dreadfully alarmed, and threw down his load, which instantly became a woman, and fled away, leaping prodigiously high, and uttering loud laughter. This same informant has often heard the 'chasse à briquet,' and believes it to be caused by hunting in the air. Certainly it is not from birds; for you may distinctly hear the barking, for all the world like a common dog. She also knows that if a coquard is hatched, it will produce a basilisk; and one of her relatives lost several children by the mal d'Exive.

There are also many other superstitions existing in the department, and presages believed in, some of which are common to many other countries. For instance, the aurora borealis is considered a sign of war and tumults. White moons in July and August are signs of evil. The sun is believed to dance three times on the horizon when he rises on St John's day. The screaming of owls forebodes death. A branch of sweet-brier suspended over the door of a house protects the inmates from fever.

Some babies, as soon as they are born, run about the house, get under the bed, and make horrible grimaces at the persons present: it is necessary to drive away such unnatural monsters with pitchforks. On no account wash your linen 'entre les deux chasses;' that is to say, on the eight days between the Fête Dieu and the day of its octave, when 'les chasses,' containing the relics of various saints, are carried from Loches to the adjoining town of Beaulieu, and from Beaulieu to Loches; if you neglect this, you are sure to wash your winding-sheet. Take care not to bake on rogation days, otherwise your bread will be bad all the year. Never spin on the Thursday or Friday in holy week, or your cows will have 'le fourchet;' that is, an ulcer between their hoofs, which lames them. If you wish for good success in rearing poultry, you should dance on the dunghill in the farmyard on Shrove Tuesday. After the corn is sown, you must abstain from eating toasted bread, or you will have a bad harvest. It is very dangerous to hear the cuckoo for the first time fasting, and invariably brings fever. The moths which fly to the candles at night are the wandering souls of the dead; take great care that they do not burn themselves. Many persons, when they take their meals, leave a small portion of meat on their plate for the Evil One. This sort of offering renders him less malicious: there is no knowing what may happen—'il est bon d'avoir des amis partout.' Crickets bring good luck to a house, and must not be disturbed. 'La chere-année,' or cockroach, is an insect of bad omen, and forebodes a bad harvest and dear bread; hence its name. The cobwebs floating in the air in August are produced by the holy Virgin, who is then spinning robes for the angels. Great care is requisite in placing a bedstead so that it be parallel with the beams of the chamber; if placed at right angles, it will cause serious evils to the person who sleeps on it. Never begin a journey on a Friday; some mischief will befall you if you neglect this precaution. If a hare crosses your path, your journey will be unfortunate. Marriages made on Friday are sure to be unlucky: Monday and Tuesday are the most propitious days. Thirteen at table a fatal number: spilling the salt, or crossing your knife and fork, to be carefully avoided. If you see a woman with her head bare in the morning, some misfortune will happen during the day. Small spiders spin small sums of money, large ones bring more considerable profit. A spark flying from the chimney presages a visit from a stranger. If, at washing-time, the chaldron be left empty, it is a sign of death in the family. A magpie scattering the horse-dung in the road, shows that a funeral will soon pass the spot. The wren is a sacred bird, in consequence of her having brought fire from heaven; in doing which she burnt her feathers, on which accident all the other birds gave her one, except the owl, who on that account is hooted whenever he is seen. If you eat an egg, be sure to crush the shell, for fear some enemy should fill it with dew, and stick it upon a white thorn; for as the sun dries up the dew, the person who has eaten the egg dries up and dies also.

Similar superstitions exist in other provinces. In Normandy, for example, they tell that a gentleman living near the embouchure of the Saire had a son who was a monk. A farmer came one day to pay his rent, and not finding the father at home, gave the money to the son, who afterwards denied the fact, and wished, if he had taken it, the devil might carry him into the sea; which took place immediately. The monk, however, was not drowned, but is often heard screaming near the shore, and has been seen in his monk's frock and cowl; indeed one man played at cards with him one fine night, and lost every sou he possessed.

At Gildo, on the coast of Bretagne, the ghosts of those who have been drowned in crossing the ferry scream dreadfully before bad weather. At the fountain of Bodilis, in Finisterre, lovers try the virtue of their mistresses by floating a pin taken from their corslet: fortunately, in that primitive district the ladies fasten their attire with sharpened pieces of wood. In the department of Loire Inferieure, an enormous phantom, called Louis Courtois, is believed to pass over the heaths at night, uttering direful cries, which cause the death of the hearers. A grain of consecrated wheat is believed, in Bretagne, to be a certain cure for sore eyes.

A LECTURE BY MR FARADAY AT THE ROYAL INSTITUTION.

Although the dweller in the monster city—smoky, foggy London—labours under many disadvantages as to sources of recreation, when compared with the pure open-air enjoyments of the inhabitant of the country, he yet possesses many advantages to which the provincial is a stranger; and these are found in the numerous scientific institutions which London, notwithstanding her noise, bustle, and mercantile abstraction, encourages and supports. One of the first, if not the most important, is the Royal Institution of Great Britain in Albemarle Street, founded in the year 1800, 'for diffusing the knowledge, and facilitating the general introduction of useful mechanical inventions and improvements, and for teaching, by courses of philosophical lectures and experiments, the application of science to the common purposes of life.' How far this promise of the prospectus has been carried out, may be judged of by the eminent support which the institution receives, and by the numerous audiences which crowd the theatre at the weekly lectures; the privilege of hearing which, with the other advantages presented by the establishment, being secured by an annual subscription of two guineas. A reference to some of the names connected with the history of the institution will be sufficient to show the high character of the advantages offered by it. We find at the earlier period those of Count Rumford, Sir Joseph Banks, the Duke of Bridgewater, and Sir Humphry Davy, followed by the present professors Brande and Faraday, who ably sustain the distinction earned by their predecessors. The latter, as is well known, originally a bookbinder, was appointed as one of Davy's assistants in the laboratory of the institution, and now, by the force of genius, the servant succeeds the master, and ranks among the first of modern chemists.

A few weeks since, the writer of the present article had the pleasure of hearing him deliver a highly interesting lecture on the Liquefaction and Solidification of Substances usually considered Gaseous, a subject which, for a long period, has occupied the attention of scientific men, who have considered that the origin or basis of gases, the lightest known substances, would be found in solid matter, although, with few exceptions, the attempts made to solidify them have proved unsuccessful. Mr Faraday commenced his lecture by stating that he had been constantly engaged in researches on this subject for six months; and traced briefly the history of the labours of other philosophers.

The first trials were made in 1761 by John Canton, who succeeded in compressing, with the force of two or three atmospheres, the air in which a thermometer filled with water, and open at one end, was introduced. The investigations were afterwards continued by Perkins, and Oersted of Copenhagen; and still later, the French Academy awarded a prize to Messieurs Sturm and Colladon for their researches. Subsequent to these were the experiments of M. Aimé, who caused the gases to be sunk to a great depth in the sea, thinking to solidify them by the enormous pressure. But as it was impossible to see the gases while in this state of compression, and as they were exposed only to ordinary temperatures, the results could be of no value or authority. M. Cagniard-Latour, in his experiments upon ether, discovered that, at a certain temperature, liquids are transformed into vapour without any diminution of volume; and Thilorier found that a very low temperature could be obtained by employing a bath of carbonic acid combined with ether: but an unfortunate explosion, by which several persons were killed, interrupted his researches; he, however, employed his bath only in the ordinary temperature, while Mr Faraday, as will be seen, used it *in vacuo*.

The lecturer then went on to observe, that he had investigated the subject in a strictly philosophical point of view, aiming at certain effects by philosophical induction and research, of which, as a striking example, he adduced the safety-lamp of his predecessor Davy. He then read an extract from a letter written by Professor Liebig, in which that celebrated philosopher observed, that Germany and England pursued opposite courses with regard to science; in the latter, the practical was too much thought of, while, in the former, the theoretical and philosophical were alone considered as worthy attention; but that, in his opinion, the golden mean would be the wiser course for both countries. Mr Faraday next observed, that the failure of the experiments of so many eminent chemists in the solidification of gases, arose from the attempts having been made under ordinary temperatures; but if the point of liquefaction be, as it appears to be, in the lowest degree possible with the lightest and most volatile bodies existing as gases, there would be scarcely any hope of liquefying such substances as hydrogen, oxygen, or azote at any pressure while in an ordinary temperature, or even of a temperature very much below the ordinary. These observations furnish the key to the whole of the lecturer's method of operating. He brought forward a cylindrical vessel of iron, about two feet in length and a few inches in diameter, fitted with a moveable tube, and a stop-cock at the upper end: in this carbonic acid gas was condensed in the form of water. On turning the cock, this liquid rushed out with so great a velocity through the tube into a close round box, that farther condensation was produced; and, on opening the box, the gas appeared in the beautiful form of snow. This was taken out, and the box refilled, until a sufficient quantity was obtained, when the whole was deposited in a glass jar, and preserved from evaporation by being placed within other jars, protected by numerous folds of flannel. From this store of freezing power several lumps were taken and placed in a shallow saucer, for the purpose of making the 'cold bath.' Although sufficiently cold to freeze mercury, they were taken in the hand without inconvenience, owing to the rapid evaporation which forms a stratum of gas between the solid mass and the hand. Something is yet required to produce contact without affecting the low temperature. This is effected by moistening the lumps with ether, after which it would be dangerous to touch them with the finger, as vitality would be as certainly destroyed as by the most intense heat. A small quantity of mercury was then poured into the bath, where it became immediately frozen, and was lifted out, hanging to a wire, in a perfectly solid state. This low degree of cold was, however, not yet low enough to produce the solidification of the gases, and the lecturer explained his further process by a very simple illustration: he took a kettle of water, which was brought in boiling at the commencement of the lecture, but which, for half an hour, had been standing on the floor, and poured a small quantity into a flask, when, on being placed under the exhausted receiver of the air-pump, it boiled violently, proving that the diminution of the pressure had the effect of extracting the heat from the water; a fact which was confirmed by pouring a few drops of the contents of the flask and of the kettle respectively over a piece of phosphorus: with the former, this inflammable substance was not affected, but the heat yet remaining in the latter set it immediately on fire. The same process was gone through with the carbonic acid bath. On being placed under the receiver, and the air exhausted, the ebullition was as violent as with the warm water in the former experiment: the result was a degree of cold of which we can form but little conception, being equivalent in some instances to a hundred degrees below zero. But cold of itself is not the only agent required; there must be pressure; and it became of importance to find a material which would show the results, and at the same time bear a pressure varying from twenty to two hundred atmospheres. Flint-glass tubes were tried, but proved to be unfit for the purpose, as they flew into atoms under a comparatively slight degree of compression: tubes of green or bottle glass were then thought of, and found to answer admirably; and such was Mr Faraday's satisfaction with the service he had obtained from them, that he dwelt at some length upon the qualities and properties of various kinds of glass. He made use of these tubes fitted with stop-cocks, and in some cases connected with small tubes of copper in such a manner, that with two condensing pumps, the gas which was the subject of experiment could be forced into them, and compressed with the requisite power, and at the same time exposed to the intense cold obtained under the receiver, where the effects of the compression could be seen. The low temperature, and the pressure together, produce effects which remain undeveloped under a single influence. To these combined powers is Mr Faraday indebted for the important results he has already obtained, as shown by the following specification:—

Olefiant gas, when condensed, appears as a beautifully transparent, colourless liquid: it is not solidified; and will dissolve oily, resinous, and bituminous bodies. Pure hydriodic acid may be obtained either in a solid or liquid state. When solid, it is very clear, colourless, and transparent, generally traversed by fissures through the whole mass, which bears great resemblance to common ice. Hydrobromic acid can also be obtained as a clear and transparent solid body, or as a limpid and colourless liquid. Fluosilicic acid has been condensed to the liquid state; but in this experiment it was found necessary to perform the operation at the very lowest temperature: the result is extremely fluid, and as easily disturbed as warm ether. No positive effect has yet been witnessed with phosphoretted hydrogen and fluoboric acid; both have, however, presented some results of solidification. Hydrochloric acid liquefies readily at a pressure of one atmosphere, but does not solidify; sulphurous acid, on the contrary, becomes immediately solid, as might be expected. Sulphuretted hydrogen appears as a white, transparent, crystalline mass, resembling congealed nitrate of ammonia or camphor. Euchlorine shows itself as a reddish orange crystal, very friable, but presenting no indications of explosive power. The protoxide of azote had been made the subject of experiment in France by M. Natterer, who obtained it in the liquid state. It now solidified in the cold bath, but evaporated rapidly, producing so low a degree of cold, that on placing the vase containing it in the bath of carbonic acid, the latter, in which mercury froze instantaneously, operated as a heated liquid, and caused the protoxide of azote to boil violently: in the solid state, it is crystalline and colourless. Cyanogen and ammonia pass into the solid state: the latter, when pure and dry, forms a substance similar to that produced from sulphuretted hydrogen. Arseniuretted hydrogen and chlorine become liquid; but have hitherto baffled all attempts to solidify them. Alcohol submitted to the pressure, presents the thick appearance of cold oil, but does not solidify: the same result is seen in caoutchine, camphine, and oil of turpentine, which all become extremely viscous. The binoxide of azote, and the oxide of carbon, offer no sign of liquefaction, even with the lowest temperature which it was possible to produce, and with a pressure of thirty to thirty-five atmospheres. Carbonic acid, in passing from the liquid to the solid state, and prevented from dispersing itself as snow, forms a beautiful substance, whose transparency is such, that for some time the operator was uncertain if the tube were full or empty, and was obliged to melt one end in order to assure himself of the fact.

Many results have been obtained relative to the point of fusion of these various gases, and their tension under certain degrees of temperature. The gas prepared for the evening's experiment was olefiant, contained in a glass vessel connected by a tube with a condensing pump of one-inch bore; this, in turn, communicated with a smaller pump of half an inch bore, from which the gas was driven along a metallic tube to the glass tube in the receiver of the air-pump, where, after a few strokes of the pumps, it was distinctly visible, compressed in the form of liquid. The lecturer concluded, amid well-earned plaudits, by observing that he had hoped to make oxygen the subject of the experiment, but from some as yet undetected cause, it had baffled his attempts at solidification; possibly some oversight in the manipulation. He had, however, great reason to believe, from certain indications which he had met with, that his efforts would be eventually successful in solidifying not only oxygen, but azote and hydrogen. He is inclined to believe, with M. Dumas of Paris, that the latter will show itself in a metallic form. Time and experience will determine whether these views are correct—whether the lightest and most volatile of all known bodies be in its origin akin to the most dense and heavy.

Not the least charm of Mr Faraday's lectures is his agreeable manner and ready and easy utterance. He is a perfect master of his subject, and seizes on illustrative examples with happy facility; and as his experiments always succeed, his audience is not wearied with idle delays. In listening to him, the writer recognised the truth, that the best lecturers are always the simplest; they make no display of turgid or mysterious phraseology, but appeal directly to the reason and common sense of their hearers.

ADVERTISEMENTS OF THE TIMES.

In the whole range of periodical literature, there is no greater curiosity than the columns daily devoted to advertisements in the Times newspaper. From those ponderous pages the future historian will be able to glean ample and correct information relative to the social habits, wants, and peculiarities of this empire. How we travel, by land or sea—how we live, and move, and have our being—is fully set forth in the different announcements which appear in a single copy of that journal. The means of gratifying the most boundless desires, or the most fastidious taste, are placed within the knowledge of any one who chooses to consult its crowded columns. Should a man wish to make an excursion to any part of the globe between Cape Horn and the North Pole, to any port in India, to Australia, to Africa, or to China, he can, by the aid of one number of the Times, make his arrangements over his breakfast. In the first column he will find which 'A. 1. fine, fast-sailing, copper-bottomed' vessel is ready to take him to any of these distant ports. Or, should his travelling aspirations be of a less extended nature, he can inform himself of the names, size, horse-power, times of starting, and fares, of numberless steamers which ply within the limits of British seas. Whether, in short, he wishes to be conveyed five miles—from London to Greenwich—or three thousand—from Liverpool to New York—information equally conclusive is afforded him.

The head of the second, or sometimes the third column, is interesting to a more extensive range of readers—namely, to the curious; for it is generally devoted to what may be called the romance of advertising. The advertisements which appear in that place are mysterious as melodramas, and puzzling as rebuses. Some of them are worded after the following fashion:—

'To Charles.—Be at the pastry-cook's at the corner of S—— Street, at two. Jemima is well.—Alice.'

Out of such an advertisement, a novelist of ordinary tact might construct a whole plot. 'Charles' is a lover;

the course of whose love has been crossed by some inquisitive papa or guardian; he has been forbidden the house of his adored Jemima. Correspondence by post is also impracticable; so the lovers advertise one another in the Times. Happily, the lady has a confidante, to whom is intrusted the advertising department of the affair. The above is an assignation concocted by her ingenuity, and signed with her name.

Perhaps a week after, another announcement in the same column will furnish the novelist with the catastrophe. It runs thus:—

'To THE YOUNG LADY WHO WAS LAST SEEN at the pastry-cook's at the corner of S—— Street. You are implored to return home immediately, and all will be forgiven.'

The fact is, Jemima met Charles punctually, and eloped with him from the bun-shop. Her father has relented; and as no further advertisements can be detected from the same parties, it is fair to infer that their little family differences have been made up; that Charles and Jemima are married, and are as happy as they deserve to be. Occasionally, however, we find this interesting column occupied with notices which force upon us more painful inferences. A young man has defrauded his employers, and absconded; and his parents invoke him, by the initials of his name, to disclose the amount of his defalcations. In other instances, a cowardly bankrupt has run away from his creditors, and left his wife to bear the brunt of their importunities. She implores him, through the Times, to return and help her through the difficulty.

Beneath such brief tales of mystery are usually advertised articles which have been lost or stolen. These vary in style, from the coarse and mercenary offer of 'One sovereign reward,' to the delicate hint that 'If the lady who took the ermine cloak away *by mistake* from the Marchioness of Crampton's rout on Thursday evening will send the same to the owner, her own camlet wrapper will be returned to her.' One of the most refined of this class actually appeared in its proper place a few months since. As a superfine appeal to the susceptible sentiments of a couple of pickpockets, it has no equal in the history of advertising:—

'IF the clever artists, male and female, who combined to relieve an elderly gentleman of his letter-case and purse on Friday evening last will return the former, with the papers it contained, they will oblige. The case and papers are of no use to them.'

Succeeding the 'Lost and Stolen,' it is usual to find one or two of those heart-stirring appeals to the benevolent which—despite the efforts of the Mendicity Society—have maintained many an impostor in idleness for years together. Like Puff, in Sheridan's 'Critic,' these advertisers support themselves upon their (assumed) misfortunes, by means of the proceeds of addresses 'to the charitable and humane,' or 'to those whom Providence has blessed with affluence.' The account which Puff gives of his fictitious misfortunes so little exaggerates the advertisements which appear occasionally in the Times, that we quote it. 'I suppose,' he boasts, 'never man went through such a series of calamities in the same space of time. I was five times made a bankrupt, and reduced from a state of affluence by a train of unavoidable misfortunes. Then, though a very industrious tradesman, I was twice burnt out, and lost my little all both times. I lived upon those fires a month. I soon after was confined by a most excruciating disorder, and lost the use of my limbs. That told very well; for I had the case strongly attested, and went about to collect the subscriptions myself! Afterwards, I was a close prisoner in the Marshalsea for a debt benevolently contracted to serve a friend. I was then reduced to—oh no—then I became a widow with six helpless children. Well, at last, what with bankruptcies, fires, gouts, dropsies, imprisonments, and other valuable calamities, having got together a pretty handsome sum, I determined to quit a business which had always gone rather against my conscience.' The police reports testify that pathetic advertisements, equally unfounded, find their way into the third column of the Times, despite the utmost vigilance of the clerks. Some, on the other hand, are manifestly from objects worthy both of credit and of relief. Of the latter, we select one which appeared on the 7th of February 1844, and which bears evident marks of genuineness. Addressing the sympathies of the benevolent by the borrowed aid of a popular fiction was a happy thought:—

'To THE BROTHERS CHEERYBLE, or any who have hearts like theirs. A clergyman, who will gladly communicate his name and address, desires to introduce the case of a gentleman, equal at least to Nickleby in birth, worthy, like him, for refinement of character, even of the best descent; like him, of spotless integrity, and powerfully beloved by friends who cannot help him, but no longer, like Nickleby, sustained by the warm buoyancy of youthful blood. The widowed father of young children, he has spent his all in the struggles of an unsuccessful but honourable business, and has now for eighteen months been vainly seeking some stipendiary employment. To all who have ever known him he can refer for commendation. Being well versed in accounts, though possessed of education, talents, and experience, which would render him invaluable as a private secretary, he would accept with gratitude even a clerk's stool and daily bread. Any communication addressed to the Rev. B. C., post-office, Cambridge, will procure full particulars, ample references, and the introduction of the party, who is now in town, and ignorant of this attempt to serve him.'

The succeeding couple of columns in the first page of the Times usually display the multifarious 'wants' which an endless variety of desiderators are anxious to get satisfied. Situations by far outnumber the other wants. A governess, a gardener, an editor, a schoolmaster, a tailor, a clerk, or a shopman, who is in want of employment, seeks it through the pages of the Times newspaper. The accomplished, intellectual, honest, moral, in short, 'unexceptionable' characters, who thus paint their own portraits, give to the fourth and fifth column of the leading journal the semblance of a catalogue of spotless worthies.

Some, again, try to gain employment by eccentric appeals. Foremost among these we place the annexed little autobiography from a person who advertised himself on the 22d of last February as

'A CHARACTER.—The noblemen and gentlemen of England are respectfully informed that the advertiser is a self-taught man—a "genius." He has travelled (chiefly on foot) through the United Kingdom of Great Britain and Ireland, in Holland, Germany, Switzerland, Belgium, France, and Italy. He has conducted a popular periodical, written a work of fiction in three vols., published a system of theology, composed a drama, studied Hamlet, been a political lecturer, a preacher, a village schoolmaster, a pawnbroker, a general shopkeeper; has been acquainted with more than one founder of a sect, and is now (he thanks Providence) in good health. spirits, and character, out of debt, and living in charity with all mankind. During the remainder of his life he thinks he would feel quite at home as secretary, amanuensis, or companion to any nobleman or gentleman who will engage a once erratic but now sedate being, whose chief delight consists in seeing and making those around him cheerful and happy. Address A. Z., at Mr P——'s, B—— Street, Regent's Park.'

It would appear that the self-praise thus published sometimes requires a little help; hence, besides 'undoubted ability' and 'unexceptionable references,' a *douceur* is occasionally offered 'to any one who will procure the advertiser a respectable situation.' This 'sweetener' we have known to vary from five to five thousand pounds, 'according to the emoluments.' Despite, however, all eccentricities, deception, and other evils, there can be no question that through the advertising columns of the Times many a servant has procured a good situation, and many a master has been indebted for a valuable servant. As a specimen of the appeals, the truth of which it is difficult to doubt, we print the following. The fickleness of fortune is strongly exemplified by the fact of a gentleman of 'high rank' seeking the humblest employment:—

'It would be a noble act of humanity if any generous and kind-hearted individual would procure or grant employment to a suffering individual, in whose behalf this appeal is made. He is of high rank, education, and manners, and in every point of view fit to fill any situation. He is without influential friends, and, from complicated frauds and misfortunes, is unable to continue the education of eight lovely children. He seeks nothing for himself, except to be so placed, giving to the hands of his kind benefactor all he receives for his children's present and future support. This will save him from a broken heart. Any situation that will enable him to effect this object will be received with heartfelt gratitude, and filled with honour, assiduity, and fidelity. Most respectable reference, &c. N. B. No pecuniary assistance can be received.'

The 'want' which usually succeeds that for situations is common at some time or other of his life to every living being. The bottom of the fifth column of the Times generally contains some half-dozen announcements that X. Y. or A. B. wants money. In a modern comedy, one of the characters, with a view to borrowing, tells a rich friend 'that he is terribly in want of a thousand pounds.' The other, with a comprehensive experience of the world, replies, 'I have no doubt of it; for you may take it as a rule that *every* man wants a thousand pounds.'* Of this vast multitude of mankind, there are, it appears, only a few superlatively sanguine individuals who hope to obtain the required cash by advertising. 'Ample security' or usurious interest is generally the bait held forth to lenders; but we are able to produce one remarkable instance in which the advertiser expresses a wish for the loan of a bagatelle of four thousand pounds without security, and which he proposes to repay, not with interest, but with gratitude:—

'A man of rank, holding a distinguished public office, moving in the highest society, and with brilliant prospects, has been suddenly called upon to pay some thousands of pounds, owing to the default of a friend for whom he had become guarantee. As his present means are unequal to meet this demand, and he can offer no adequate security for a loan, the consequence must be ruin to himself and his family, unless some individual of wealth and munificence will step forward to avert this calamity, by applying L.4000 to his rescue. For this he frankly avows that he can, in present circumstances, offer no other return than his gratitude. A personal interview, however painful, will be readily granted, in the confidence that the generosity of his benefactor will be the best guarantee for his delicate observance of secrecy. He hopes his distressing condition will protect him from the prying of heartless curiosity; and to prevent the approaches of money-lenders, he begs to repeat that he can give no security. Address to "Anxious," General Post-office, London.' This 'anxious' man of rank made known his trifling want in the Times of January 1844.

The sixth and last column of the first page of the Times is invariably devoted to equestrian and vehicular advertisements. Any gentleman who may want a clever hack, a quiet cob, a powerful horse of splendid action, warranted to ride or drive; or any tradesman requiring a team of superior young cart-horses, has only to consult his newspaper.

Over leaf, on the second page of the Times, persons in want of 'apartments' or lodgings, 'with or without board,' will find many places to choose from. Announcements of public companies which are of a more general interest come next. Amongst them sometimes appear singular effusions, chiefly consisting of the schemes of enthusiastic patriots and headlong politicians, who invent plans for setting everything to rights in this complicated community, as fast as the horses, announced for sale in a previous column, can gallop. One, which was published about twelve months since, we have carefully preserved. It is by a political regenerator who dates from Cheapside:—

'To the Ministers of State, Nobility, and Community at large.—A Remedy for the Distresses of England.—Every considerate person admits the present condition of society to be perfectly anomalous. A remedy has at length been discovered—a remedy which would effectually arrest the progress of pauperism, confer incalculable benefits upon the industrial community, and diffuse joy and gladness throughout the length and breadth of the land, making England (without exaggeration) the envy of surrounding nations, and the admiration of the world. The plan possesses the peculiar merit of being practicable, and easy of application, without in the slightest degree infringing the rights of property as by law established, or in any way disturbing the present relations of society. The advertiser will communicate his discovery either to the ministers of state, nobility, or those who may take an interest in the wellbeing of society, on condition of his receiving (if his plans are approved, and made available for the purposes contemplated) L.100,000. "If the nation be saved, it is not to be saved by the ordinary operations of statesmanship."—Lord Ashley.' The modesty of the advertiser prevents him from adding in words what he evidently wishes the reader to conclude; namely, that the nation is only to be saved by E. S., of No. 142 Cheapside.

The rest of the columns of the Times usually occupied by advertisements are filled with announcements of new works, either just out, or in preparation; patent medicines, and sales by auction. One department is benevolently set aside for the insertion of short applications for places from domestic servants. These advertisements are received at a price which little more than covers the duty, and expense of composing.

Lastly come the rhetorical advertisements. These flow from the fervent pens of imaginative auctioneers, 'who'—to quote Mr Puff once more—'crowd their announcements with panegyrical superlatives, each rising above the other, like the bidders in their own auction-rooms;' inlaying 'their phraseology with variegated chips of exotic metaphor.' The skill with which their descriptions of houses or of lands magnify excellences and conceal defects without making an entire sacrifice of truth, is on some occasions wonderful. When a mansion is dilapidated, that is described as a lucky circumstance, for, 'with a trifling outlay, the fortunate purchaser will be afforded a fine opportunity of exercising his taste in restoration, alteration, and decoration.' Sometimes the auctioneer is 'happy' to announce that a large portion of the estate now for sale is in a completely uncultivated state, so that the possessor will have a fine field for the introduction of those wonderful improvements in draining and agricultural chemistry which are now at his disposal. We must admit, however, that these wordy announcements are less frequent in the Times than in other newspapers, although the above expressions are copied from its pages. The truth is, the graces of rhetoric are not exempted from the high charges of that densely filled journal, but cost as much per line as the veriest cheesemonger's puff. Economy therefore obliges the verbose auctioneer to be sparing of adjectives, and to cut out his most exalted superlatives. It is only when the magnitude of the transaction enables him—*heureusement*—to puff off the property 'regardless of expense,' that he is able to take a high flight in a long advertisement.

We have now reviewed the various announcements which, taking the average, daily appear in the Times newspaper. By an orderly arrangement of the printer, the different kinds we have adverted to appear as nearly

* Bubbles of the Day, by Douglas Jerrold.

as possible in the portions of the vast sheet which we have described, so that a practised reader can tell, within a column or so, where to pitch upon the sort of announcement he may wish to peruse. No one possessed of a spice of philosophy can glance over those broad sheets, without extracting a deep meaning from the mass, and without getting a strong insight into human nature from many of the individual advertisements. Had the *Acta Diurna* of the Romans contained similar announcements, we should have learned more of their private life and habits from one of its numbers, than from all the classical works which have been handed down to us.

LUKE HUSLER.

A TALE OF AMERICAN LIFE, BY PERCY B. ST JOHN.

There are many characters in whom the good predominates very much over the evil, and yet who, from the mere fact of their being unable to say 'no,' when asked to join either in the execution of wise or foolish plans, or to do that which their native genius prompts them to declare an error, have fallen from the place in which their fortune and their personal endowments had placed them, and become members of the great body of the outcast. There are two forms of this weakness. With some, it is the effect of constitutional feebleness of mind; with others, it arises solely from want of that moral courage which prompts the firm man never to deviate from the right path to please the fancies of others. 'I did not like to say no,' is a phrase with which the half of mankind, particularly young men, excuse those faults which are at the same time their own bane and that of all around them.

In a small village in a remote county of the state of New York, there lived, some short time before my visit to the republic of Texas, a young man of the name of Luke Husler. From his own confession to me at a later period, the characteristic, which I have above slightly sketched, was peculiarly his. To proceed, however, chronologically. The village to which I allude was small, and very picturesquely situated. Like every similar locality in America, it possessed a church, or rather chapel, and a schoolhouse. But though it had a considerable number of inhabitants, it did not boast—a rare circumstance in the United States—either a newspaper or a grog-shop. One reason for the absence of a local organ, was the population being divided pretty equally among English, German, and French, all speaking of course their own languages. Why the public-house existed not, was a fact which often puzzled the heads of even the oldest inhabitants. But as every one in the village had already a distinct business, and all were thriving, no one thought proper to take upon himself the responsibility of setting on foot so serious an undertaking.

Little York, as the village was called, possessed the usual variety of 'characters;' but the purpose of my narrative only demands that I should allude to a few. In the first place, Luke Husler was no mean person, either in his own opinion or in that of those around him. At three-and-twenty owner of a fancy store, where articles of both male and female clothing were to be had perfectly new at a moment's notice, and possessed of a handsome countenance and prepossessing manner, young Luke, as he stood with his hands in his pockets, chewing an unlit cigar, in the front of his store, could nod and bow to every inhabitant in Little York, and yet by no means be thought to make himself too familiar. The neatness of his store in some measure conduced to his popularity. Built of pine boards, on a raised platform of piles, one storey in height, with conical roof, the whole carefully whitewashed, with a flight of wooden steps leading to the door, it was a very model of order and cleanliness. Behind its two plain but neat counters were rows of shelves, containing the articles in which he dealt, while at the rear of the premises was the 'snuggery,' where the owner took his meals, and which also served the purpose of a sleeping chamber. An aged female, black as Erebus, was his charwoman, with whose hired assistance everything was kept in that particular style of order which is familiarly though strangely enough known as 'apple-pie.'

'Luke Husler, Dry Store,' were the words which appeared in large letters over the door, while exactly opposite, a small private house, with white curtains, green blinds, and whitewashed boards, like the store, exhibited on a scroll in small letters the words, 'Martha Dalton, Milliner.' To this house Luke's eyes were directed oftener than to any other in the neighbourhood, which may in part be explained by its situation. But a pair of blue eyes, a fair and gentle face, and auburn ringlets, were continually to be seen near the little open window; and whether the house or the lady formed the peculiar attraction, is a matter which I leave to be decided by the acute and discerning reader. Martha Dalton was a widow; but Martha Dalton was not the object of Luke Husler's solicitude, but her daughter. An Englishwoman by birth, as was her daughter, they had lost their only male relative some years before. Their income, the interest of a few thousand dollars, being small, they had retreated to this retired locality, and, more to occupy their time, and give themselves a settled position, than from any other reason, had opened the business which I have already designated. Mary Dalton and Luke Husler, at the time I now speak of, were engaged in marriage, and a very short time was to ensue ere they were to be united for ever.

When business was over, as it is ever at a very early hour in American villages, Luke would make himself smart, and, with a regularity as great as that of the clock which guided his movements, spend his evening in company with his beloved. They were very happy; no untoward occurrence ever chequered their quiet life. With the young man, business was regular and profitable; with Mary and her mother, it was as good as they had any wish for it to be. Few American villages were so quiet and well conducted as Little York. There was just enough of sociality to give zest to existence; while there were no dissipations of any kind to tempt the sober citizens from their steady and uneventful life.

One morning in the spring of 1839, the inhabitants of Little York were surprised, on rising from their peaceful couches, to hear the loud clamour of men engaged in building. Hammers were being used at a most rapid rate by some half-dozen men, saws were heard grating, and the loud voice of one in authority directing the proceedings. A general rush took place into the streets—street I should say—and in a very short time the whole male population were congregated at the western extremity of the village. Here, at early dawn, a large frame-house had been marked out, and ere the primitive inhabitants of Little York had risen from their beds, the whole of the supporting beams had been firmly planted. Cart-loads of planks, shingle, logs, &c. were heaped up, and a dozen men busily employed in giving shape and form to the rude materials. Hard by, standing upon a heap of wood, was a small thin man, who in a shrill but very loud voice was giving his orders right and left. Despite the crowd which had collected, he paid not the slightest attention to them, continuing the rapid enunciation of his command. The Little Yorkites were thunderstricken. What could he be about? The house was manifestly of too large dimensions for a private residence. Its frame, too, divided into apartments large and small, showed it not to be a church.

After some deliberation, Luke, who was, as I have already stated, a popular man, advanced toward the little individual above mentioned, and in a very polite manner 'reckoned' he was a stranger. The little man very drily 'guessed' he was. Luke, not at all abashed, 'concluded' he was building 'a pretty considerable tall' house; the little man had a 'notion' it *was* 'smart.' Luke 'calculated' it would cost a few dollars; the little man 'supposed' it would. It was evident that 'slanting,' as the Americans call it, was of no use; a point blank question could alone elicit the truth. Luke therefore at length very gravely and seriously inquired the stranger's object. 'Well, friend,' replied the other, 'I a'n't exactly availed what I'll do yet, and that's a fact. About four o'clock I reckon to have made up my mind.'

Luke withdrew at once from the contest; and the hour of breakfast approaching, the crowd rapidly dispersed. Great was the excitement in the minds of all; and so much were they moved, that even some regular down-east Yankees were heard to express an opinion between the rapid mouthfuls in which Americans usually silently indulge. The morning passed; noon came; and under the industrious hands of numerous workmen, the huge wooden house was approaching rapidly towards completion. Before four o'clock it was finished, and the white-washers were hard at work on the outside, while the 'hands' were busily engaged in unloading from a covered wagon the owner's goods and chattels, amongst which I may perhaps be allowed to include a buxom dame, who appeared to be his wife, and a pretty girl, who was without doubt his daughter. Still the mystery was unsolved, as to the view with which the house was erected. This mystery, however, was not long to continue; for the wagon being at length unloaded, the men drew from beneath a long narrow piece of wood, on which, in red letters on a white ground, were written the fatal words, 'Silas Hoit—The General Jackson Liquor Store, Nine-pin Alley.' The patriarchs groaned audibly: the peace, virtue, and happiness of Little York, they felt, had departed with the erection of what was clearly nothing more nor less than a grog-shop. The young men were silent: the thing had come upon them so unexpectedly, they knew scarcely what to make of it. The crowd dispersed, and each little group departed to discuss the occurrence over their own fireside. That evening many a sigh emanated from the bosom of wives and mothers: all felt as if a moral revolution had taken place, and the genius of riot and disorder had triumphed over peace and domestic happiness. Mary Dalton, her mother, and Luke Husler were as usual together, when the subject was brought up. Luke firmly protested against the innovation in no measured terms, the more that the cutting manners of the host still rankled within his bosom. Mary was delighted, as well as her mother, and the conversation glided into other channels.

No matter how small the number of any community, there are sure to be within its circle some one or more dissolutely-disposed members. Almost before the shelves were erected on which the liquor bottles were to be displayed, a small knot of men had congregated round the bar of the General Jackson, and on the second evening of its existence, a card table was in full play. Several, who dropped in merely to pass an hour in the Nine-pin Alley, were tempted to take a glass at the bar. One followed another, until, excited by the seducing power of the great current poison of the earth, they also stopped; and, just 'to pass the time,' games of gucca, rounce, and loo, were proposed and voted by acclamation.

Amid the general infection, which in two months spread with fatal virulence, Luke remained uncorrupted, and on no one occasion did he set his foot within the doors of the lazar-house of Little York. Mary was delighted, while every grieved father and mother whose son had been drawn into the vortex pointed him out as a model. It was Luke's habit—strolling with one's future wife not being etiquette in certain parts of America—to take a walk every evening ere he visited the Daltons. These walks always took him by the door of the General Jackson, which doubtless made the merit of his abstinence the greater. On one occasion Luke was returning from his stroll, or 'slouch,' as he was wont to call it, when, as he neared the mansion owned by Silas Hoit, two friends rushed forth from the door and saluted him. 'Come, Luke,' said one, 'we must drink a glass to your health.' 'And welcome,' replied he, tendering a quarter dollar. 'Mr Husler,' exclaimed the pair in unison, both the worse for whisky, 'when we liquor at a friend's expense, we do so with him.' 'Come to my store then.' 'Here's the Gin'ral, a deal handier.' 'I never enter grog-shops,' replied Luke. 'Nonsense! it's all that girl. Well, I wouldn't be tied to a pair of apron strings after that fashion, nohow you can fix it.' 'Sir!' exclaimed Luke scornfully, 'you are beneath my notice, or I'd chastise your insolence;' and he walked away.

The following evening the two friends again waylaid him, this time sober, and with many apologies excused their rudeness of the previous day. Luke good-humouredly forgave them; and when they proposed to cement their reconciliation over a glass, hesitated. Their sneers about the influence of Mary Dalton over him had told—he was vexed to be publicly ridiculed for what he felt inwardly to be an influence for good. The proverb about hesitation is well known. Luke entered the General Jackson, and drank at the bar. The whole conclave crowded round to be treated. Luke could not avoid drinking with all. That evening Mary Dalton spent alone. It was very late ere she retired to rest, in the faint hope of her lover at length making his appearance.

Morning found Luke in a fever both of mind and body. He was heartily ashamed of himself, while the prospect of an explanation in the evening with his fair betrothed tended nowise to tranquillise his thoughts. Stay in his store all day he could not; his ideas were too unsettled for business; and accordingly, leaving his female attendant in charge of his affairs, he stole out by the back way, and, just to pass the time until the hour for his visit to Mary came round, joined the idlers who now ever thronged the bar-room of the grog-shop. Society alone was not a sufficient distraction, and cards were resorted to. Again Mary Dalton spent her evening without seeing her lover, until, after watching past midnight, she perceived him reel home in a state of senseless intoxication. Mary sighed, and went to bed.

Before Luke was up, a message was brought him from Mrs Dalton, inquiring most kindly after his health, and gently reproaching him with his absence; she further requested his company to breakfast. He went, and was received without a word of reproach; until Mary sweetly, and with a tear in her eye, shook her head, and observed—'We thought, Luke, you were not coming to see us again.' The young man could not withstand this; but speaking with extreme volubility, confessed his error, and made a strong promise of amendment. During the progress of his speech he let fall the words—'I did not like to say no, and that is the real truth.' Both Mary and her mother started, and were silent for a moment. At length Mrs Dalton roused herself and spoke: 'Those words of yours have raised within me very sad remembrances. My husband, Luke, was a well-disposed and honest man, but he was weak—he could not say no. Drink was poison to him, but he had not the heart to refuse to join a friend in a glass. A hundred times, when ill and feverish from a slight over-indulgence, has he said, "Martha, I know I have done wrong, but I didn't like to say no." For Heaven's sake, my dear Luke, let this be a warning to you. This easy disposition in Richard Dalton made me a widow; let it not deprive me of a son-in-law.' The young man blushed deeply, and promised to exert more firmness of mind. After some further conversation he took his leave.

Luke was neither badly-disposed nor more weak-minded than usual, but he was very young, and naturally fond of excitement. It was some time, however, before he again visited the scene of temptation; but visit it again he did; until at length, drawn into a complete vortex of dissipation, the habit grew upon him, and became confirmed. For some time his dereliction from the path of rectitude was kept secret from Mary, though his altered manners and mien gave sufficient token of the company he now kept.

Six months passed, and Luke Husler was a ruined man: his business had fallen to decay, his capital was exhausted, and his credit gone. His folly burst upon Mary like a thunder-clap, and firmly, but kindly, she upbraided him with his deception, and then added—'And now, Luke, all is ended between you and me. Your poverty would be no bar to our union. With an honest, industrious, steady man, it would not cause a moment's thought, much more a regret. But your ruin has been the effect of your own folly, and I have nothing but your promise to give me hope of your future wisdom. You vow industry, frugality, and an abandonment of those evil habits and companions for which you have forfeited your own good opinion and that of your friends; but, Luke, how often have you secretly broken your word to me? Can I put faith in him who during six months has systematically deceived me? No; the man I wed I must honour and respect as well as love.'

The lover's eloquence was all in vain. They parted. Mary remained with her mother, and Luke Husler went to Texas, the last refuge of all who have failed, from misfortune or wickedness, in the United States. To Luke, misfortune was no useless monitor. He sold the wreck of his business; and when he landed in Galveston, the seaport of Texas, had in his possession one hundred dollars. He had firmly made up his mind; he had thrown off the yoke of his folly; and, despite the very natural doubts of Mary Dalton, was a new man.

Some eighty miles up the Trinity River, Luke was informed that there existed a small log-house, a little clearing, and a field of sweet potatoes, utterly deserted, the proprietor having been killed in a brawl when on a visit to Galveston: heirs there were none. Luke, delighted at so good an opportunity of settling himself, took his departure in a boat bound for up Trinity. A gun, an axe, powder and shot, were all he carried with him, save his box of clothes; and in this manner he was set ashore alone upon the banks of the river, with directions how to find the much-desired place of refuge. In the centre of a thick wood, beside a sluggish stream, and on the summit of a sloping bank, Luke found the hut. It was neat and strong, though small, with a rude bedstead, stools, a table, and, above all, a certain amount of clearing. Luke was delighted.

From that hour he applied himself most assiduously to labour: he cultivated his little field; he sowed vegetables of various kinds; he hunted, and deer-skins were piled rapidly within his little home. Luke was not alone in thus finding an uninhabited house without expense. The wars which have desolated Texas, added to Indian surprises and fevers, have rendered deserted huts far too numerous. In his case, however, the circumstance was taken advantage of with courage and ability: and at the expiration of a twelvemonth, the change which the patient, resigned industry of this solitary man had brought about was wonderful. It was then I saw him. While hunting on the Trinity, I came suddenly upon his hut. I found it neat, clean, and orderly; the potato house was piled up, a dozen pigs roamed about, while fowls were numerous, fat, and thriving. His story interested me. I saw that he intended to claim Mary Dalton still. I pressed him to do so at once; told him the Neptune steamboat was about to start for New York; offered him a passage down in my boat, and my interest for a cheap berth on board the packet. I even volunteered a joking certificate of his industry and perseverance. Luke, with a laugh—which was, however, to hide a tear—said to these propositions he really could not say 'no.'

We started for Galveston on the second evening after my arrival at his hut, and in twenty-four hours more he was on his way to New York, bearing the promised certificate from myself, in the shape of a very long and eloquent letter in his favour. For three months I heard no more of him, when I was surprised to receive a letter addressed to myself, sealed with black. Luke Husler's initials were in the corner, and the post-mark was New York. I opened it with much anxiety, for Luke had deeply interested me. Martha Dalton was dead; while Mary, as soon as a reasonable period of mourning had elapsed, was about to become the wife of Luke; my epistle, according to his view of the matter, having done wonders with the English girl. At length they came—a happy couple, their joy clouded somewhat by the death of their almost common parent, but with youth and courage to meet the arduous life of the Texan backwoods. Luke wisely preserved the capital of his wife's income, and continued to receive the dividends, which, with his little farm, that soon was his by right of purchase, enabled himself and wife to live in peace, contentment, and happiness.

The above narrative, true in its details, is related with a double view. Had Luke possessed the power to say 'no' when temptation offered, he would not have been driven into ignominious exile; in his native land he would have been spared the dangers and difficulties of a forest life; his position would have been an assured one; while his folly, though it did not utterly ruin, threw him at least ten years behind in the race of fortune. His subsequent success further proves, that whatever may be the errors of earlier youth, it is, as the old proverb has it, 'never too late to mend.' The change of manners and life entailed by the introduction of a 'grog-shop' into a village, before without a similar resort, has occurred in more than one locality in the American Union.

'THE TRADE.'

CONCLUDING ARTICLE.—BOOKSELLING IN GREAT BRITAIN.

The glimpses—slight as they are—which our former articles have afforded of the early English trade in books, allows us to resume the subject at a period when bookselling took a firm commercial stand; which it did about the beginning of the last century. This has been called the Augustan age of literature, when Dryden, Steele, Addison, Swift, Pope, with a lesser host of geniuses, flourished.

At that period the mode of selling books was widely different to that which now prevails. Readers were fewer, and the means of making known the merits of a book far more limited. The only prospect an author had of profitable remuneration for his labours was to issue his book by subscription. To obtain a sufficiently large number of subscribers, it was necessary that he should secure the patronage of some man of rank and influence; if possible, a nobleman whose opinion on literary matters was held in respect, or whose more solid influence over dependents or friends gave to his expressed wish that they should subscribe, the nature of a command. The patron who took a genius by the hand in this way made it his business to praise him in every society—at court, at balls, masquerades, parties, and in the numerous London coffee-houses where the wits of the day were wont to assemble. To assist him in this sort of canvass, his protegé provided him with a sort of prospectus of the forthcoming work, in which was set forth its scope and nature. These 'proposals' he industriously distributed along with his verbal puffs of the author's talents. When, by these means, a sufficient number of subscribers was obtained to render it a safe speculation to incur the expense of printing, the obliged author was expected to make some return to the patron for his exertions. This always consisted of a panegyrical 'dedication' conspicuously placed at the commencement of the volume. Some of these fulsome and extravagant lucubrations are sufficient evidence of the debasing influence which this system of publication must have exercised over literature. In most of them, truth was glaringly sacrificed, and notorious falsehoods promulgated, by motives manifestly interested. The nobility were the real though indirect publishers; and without their aid, to print even a good book would have been a certain loss, whilst hundreds of bad ones were foisted by this system on the world.

The author seldom went to the printer direct, but applied to the bookseller (of whom many eminent ones were in business at the time we refer to), taking with him his manuscript and his subscription list. In the eyes of the publisher, the merits or demerits of the book were of less consequence than the number of subscribers. He carefully weighed one with the other: he considered the probabilities of a chance demand for the book over and above the sale assured from subscriptions; and offered the author a certain sum to be allowed to take the whole thing off his hands. In the case of a writer of established reputation, competition occasionally occurred amongst 'the trade' for the bargain. Some of the intricacies of these transactions may be learned from Dr Johnson's account of the manner in which Pope's Homer's Iliad was brought out. The poet, in his 'proposals,' offered the work—in six volumes quarto—for six guineas. 'The greatness of the design,' says the elegantly verbose doctor, 'the popularity of the author, and the attention of the literary world, naturally raised such expectations of the future sale, that the booksellers made their offers with great eagerness; but the highest bidder was Bernard Lintot, who became proprietor on condition of supplying at his own expense all the copies which were to be delivered to subscribers or presented to friends, and paying two hundred pounds for every volume. Of the quartos, it was, I believe, stipulated that none should be printed but for the author, that the subscription might not be depreciated; but Lintot impressed the same pages upon a small folio, and paper perhaps a little thinner; and sold exactly at half the price, for half a guinea each volume, books so little inferior to the quartos, that, by a fraud of trade, those folios, being afterwards shortened by cutting away the top and bottom, were sold as copies printed for the subscribers. Lintot printed two hundred and fifty on royal paper in folio, for two guineas a volume; of the small folio, having printed seventeen hundred and fifty copies of the first volume, he reduced the number in the other volumes to a thousand. It is unpleasant to relate that the bookseller, after all his hopes and all his liberality, was, by a very unjust and illegal action, defrauded of his profit. An edition of the English "Iliad" was printed in Holland in duodecimo, and imported clandestinely for the gratification of those who were impatient to read what they could not yet afford to buy. This fraud could only be counteracted by an edition equally cheap and more commodious; and Lintot was compelled to contract his folio at once into a duodecimo, and lose the advantage of an intermediate gradation. The notes, which in the Dutch copies were placed at the end of each book, as they had been in the large volumes, were now subjoined to the text in the same page, and are therefore more easily consulted. Of this edition two thousand five hundred were first printed, and five thousand a few weeks afterwards; but indeed great numbers were necessary to produce considerable profit.'

Sometimes publishers employed authors to write books for small sums; and having sufficient interest to procure the services of that very necessary person, a noble patron, obtained subscriptions on their own account in the name of the author. By this proceeding large profits were sometimes realised. Indeed, despite all drawbacks arising from piracy and other causes, some of the booksellers of this period made large fortunes. The Lintots (of whom there were four in the trade), the Tonsons, Curll, Cave, and other contemporary publishers, realised large sums of money by their speculations.

While, however, the patron and subscription system of bookselling was in full operation, a small and silently-working influence was gradually gaining strength to overthrow it; and this was periodical literature. By 1709, several newspapers had been established in London; but these had little or no effect upon 'the trade,' compared with such periodicals as the Tatler, Spectator, and Guardian. Not many years afterwards (1731), Mr Cave conceived the idea of collecting the principal original papers from the newspapers into a monthly repository, to which the name of magazine should be applied. Hence the 'Gentleman's Magazine,' which began in that year, and still exists, the venerable parent of a host of lighter-headed children. Its success was so great, that rivals soon started up. The 'London,' the 'Monthly Review,' and the 'Critical,' were the most remarkable: these works in time changed the whole system of bookselling. They became channels of information on literary subjects, and by their aid an author's merits were made known to the public without the intervention of a titled patron. They took the patronage of men of letters out of the hands of the great and fashionable, and transferred it to the people. Literature becoming no longer a matter of mere fashion but of intellectual taste and art, booksellers began to buy manuscripts from authors at their own risk, and to address them directly to the reading public, without the aid of previous subscribers. By this change the trade was conducted on a more solid and independent basis. That a riddance of the thraldom which literature had hitherto endured was beneficial to it, is proved from the fact, that in proportion as the subscribing plan was abandoned (for it is not wholly given up even at present), so the number of published works increased. From 1700 to 1756, only about 5280 new works (exclusive of tracts and pamphlets) were issued—or about ninety-three per annum; whilst from the latter year to 1803, this average of new works increased nearly ninety-three per cent.*

From the more independent system of publishing, must be dated the footing upon which the English trade now stands. The London booksellers who were rich enough to buy manuscripts, and to get them printed on their own responsibility, formed themselves into a class, who sold wholesale, and got the title of 'publishers;' whilst those who retailed the works remained booksellers. It was during the latter part of the career of such men as Johnson, Goldsmith, Smollett, Fielding, Richardson, &c. that this division took place. The publishers—who chiefly resided in London or in Edinburgh—few in number, exhibited less rivalry than is usually seen in other trades. When an author presented himself whose great reputation warranted him in demanding a large price for his manuscript, the publishers united to purchase the copyright. Hence, one half of the title-pages of many works published at the end of the last century is occupied by a list of the publishers who took shares in the risk. By this sort of combination, an expensive book was 'pushed' amongst the connexion of each shareholder, and had a better chance of success than if undertaken by one individual.

This sort of unanimity amongst 'the trade' was very injurious to the public. It kept the price of books so high, that none but persons of fortune could afford to buy them; and the only method by which a man of moderate means could get access to them was by joining a book-club, or by borrowing from circulating libraries. But the cause of the high price of books must not be solely attributed to publishers. Paper-making and printing were at that time slow and expensive processes, and that of itself rendered books dear.

At the end of the last century, a new era dawned on the career of the book-trade. A shrewd, intelligent, but humble journeyman printer saw that the publishers of his day, by the price at which they kept their works, exclusively addressed a single class instead of the whole public. He could not, it is true—from the expense of materials—devise any plan to reduce the cost of books; but he invented a mode of issue by which they were rendered accessible to the humbler classes. As this was the earliest attempt at *popular* bookselling, we shall dwell a little upon it, and upon its originator.

Henry Fisher, the individual alluded to, while yet a journeyman in the employment of Mr Jonas Nuttall, the founder of the 'Caxton press' in Liverpool, conceived the happy notion, that if expensive works were supplied to poorer customers in cheap parts, and perio-

* Penny Magazine, vol. vi. p. 506.

dically till complete, a vast number of persons would become eager purchasers, who regarded books as an unattainable luxury. This plan, however, had its obstacles. The easy, almost sleepy manner in which bookselling was conducted by the metropolitan publishers and their provincial agents, forbade a hope that the regular trade would second it. When, for instance, they sold a bible, it was one transaction, which cost little trouble; but to have that bible divided into twenty parts, and disposed of by twenty instalments, of course entailed twenty times the trouble. Such an increase of business, without the prospect of an accession of profit, was not to be thought of. Again, if even the general trade *had* fallen in with Fisher's views, it was quite unlikely that they could have carried them out. *Their* customers were few, and essentially a *class;* the market was limited, and something was necessary to be done to extend it. Young Fisher therefore proposed to Nuttall that he should not only print standard works in cheap numbers, but sell them upon an entirely new plan. This consisted in establishing depôts in every principal town. To each of these was attached a staff of hawkers, who branched off all over the district, going from door to door, leaving prospectuses, and offering the numbers for sale. By such means books found their way into remote places, and into houses in which they were never before seen. Though only twenty years old, Fisher was intrusted with the establishment and management of the depôt at Bristol. Amongst the first books printed for sale in this manner were the Family Bible, Bunyan's Pilgrim's Progress, Josephus, and several standard devotional works. The bible was issued in forty parts, at a shilling each. The hawker, when he made his call, displayed the first part as a temptation. If he could not succeed in securing a customer at once, he requested permission to leave it for a week, and generally found at his second visit that a decision had been come to in favour of keeping that number, and of periodically purchasing the succeeding ones. Thus, persons who could easily afford the disbursement of a shilling a-week for the gradual purchase of a book, but would have passed their lives without entertaining the thought of giving two pounds for a bible in one sum, became in time the possessors of a little but select library.

As a pecuniary speculation, this 'number system,' as it was called, succeeded beyond its projector's hopes. Fisher was employed at Bristol for three years with so much benefit to his employer and credit to himself, that Mr Nuttall recalled him to Liverpool, took him into partnership, and allowed him, besides his share of the business, L.900 a-year for managing it. The plan was adopted by others, and by none without enabling them to realise large fortunes. Several old and respectable publishers in London, Edinburgh, and Glasgow, date their origin from their founders commencing as 'canvassers' in the employ of Nuttall and Fisher.

Singularly confirmative of Fisher's views was the fact that, after his plan had been extensively carried out for several years, it was found that it had wrought but little change on the regular trade, despite strong anticipations that so active a competition would have very much damaged it. The truth was, the market created for the 'numbers' was entirely new; the people who purchased them never did buy, and never would have bought, the expensive works of the more aristocratic branches of 'the trade,' who, despite the vast spread of books in the substrata of society, still retained their old customers at the old prices. The great metropolitan publishers went on realising large profits upon a limited amount of business as heretofore, till the invention of steam-printing caused them to bestir themselves a little more actively.

It was about this time (1825) that Archibald Constable of Edinburgh propounded to Sir Walter Scott and Mr Lockhart a plan for revolutionising the entire trade by the aid of steam and cheap printing. 'Literary genius,' he exclaimed, 'may or may not have done its best; but printing and bookselling, as instruments for enlightening mankind, and of course for making money, are as yet in mere infancy. Yes, the trade are in their cradle.' He then shadowed forth his outline:—'A three shilling or half-crown volume every month, which must and shall sell, not by thousands, or tens of thousands, but by hundreds of thousands—ay by millions! Twelve volumes in the year, a halfpenny of profit upon every copy of which will make me richer than the possession of all the copyrights of all the quartos that ever were, or will be hot-pressed!—twelve volumes so good, that millions must wish to have them; and so cheap, that every butcher's callant may have them, if he pleases to let me tax him sixpence a-week!'* Bright, and not extravagant visions; but, alas! it was destined that others should realise them. In the following year Constable was a bankrupt. When his affairs were wound up, he commenced his Miscellany, but with crippled means and a crushed spirit, which soon after was quelled in death. By his successors, the series was managed with little success, and after a few years it was discontinued. Still, however, the plan did not sink. Murray in his 'Family Library,' Longman and Co. in their 'Cabinet Cyclopædia' and other such series, Colburn and Bentley in their 'National Library,' carried it out for several years with more or less success; and at that time it appeared as if no books other than monthly volumes at five or six shillings would sell.

Meanwhile, the Society for the Diffusion of Useful Knowledge had commenced a series of sixpenny publications, embracing the principal sciences, and thus were showing the way to still further declensions in the cost of literature. It was remarked, however, that even these comparatively cheap issues were absorbed, not by the working-classes, to whom they were professedly addressed, but by the middle ranks. And thus it has ever been with books of all kinds: direct them to one class, and they hit the next above. It became necessary, in order to reach the great bulk of the people, that cheaper works still should be presented. It was with some such views that the publishers of the present work commenced it on the 4th of February 1832. Weekly sheets, composed of matter chiefly compiled, and aiming at no literary distinction, had previously been by no means rare; nor were they unsuccessful. But this, we believe, was the first attempt to furnish original literary matter of merit through such a medium. It was followed, almost immediately, by the well-known Penny Magazine, the Saturday Magazine, and other similar series, most of which attained, like the Journal, a circulation of many thousands. This mode of publication, followed as it has been by that of cheap editions of books in and out of copyright, has produced a great change in the trade. The warehouses of the great publishers are much less scenes of quiet and ease than they were; trouble is multiplied, and profit diminished, but the trade is enormously extended. The number of retailers of books, especially in suburban situations, has been vastly increased through the same cause. In short, a revolution has taken place, and if the bookseller now feels himself somewhat less stately and at ease than he used to be, he may have the satisfaction of feeling that his usefulness as a member of society has been greatly extended.

It is now time to give a short summary of the internal arrangements by which bookselling is carried on; for, unlike some other trades, it has few 'secrets.' The first step which a publisher usually takes when he has printed a new book, is to send it round to his brethren to have it 'subscribed;' that is, to learn from each house how many copies they will venture to take; and, to induce them to speculate, the copies thus subscribed for are delivered at a certain per centage less than the regular trade price. The copies thus supplied to the wholesale metropolitan houses are then distributed throughout the retail trade, both in town and country; for every provincial bookseller selects a London or Edinburgh pub-

* Lockhart's Life of Scott.

lishing house as his agent, for the supply of whatever works he may order. Such books are purchased by the agent from the publisher; and when they have accumulated sufficiently to cover the expense of carriage, they are made up into a parcel, and sent to the retailer. This generally happened, up to about ten years ago, on the last day of a month, when the magazines are published; for of them alone the general demand is so great, that they form a bulky parcel for each bookseller. In 1837, one of 'the trade,' many years conversant with the great literary hive of London on 'Magazine Day,' made the following computations: The periodical works sold on the last day of the month amounted to 500,000 copies. The amount of cash expended in the purchase of these was L.25,000. The parcels despatched into the country per month were 2000. These parcels, it must be remembered, not only contained magazines, but all the works ordered during the preceding part of the month.

Since then, however, the vast increase of weekly publications, the opening of railroads, the extension of steam navigation, and other causes, have in a great measure withdrawn the bulk of books from the monthly to weekly parcels, one of which every respectable provincial bookseller now regularly receives. To estimate the contents or number of these would be impossible; but we have no hesitation in saying that they more than double the above computation in all its calculations.

We learn by the abstract of occupations from the last census, that in Great Britain there are 13,355 booksellers, publishers, and bookbinders, 5499 of whom reside in London. In Scotland, there are 2547 persons following the same trades. In Edinburgh alone, there are 786 individuals connected with 'the trade.'

MISCELLANEA.

Amusements for the Insane are commented upon in an interesting manner in Dr Browne's last report on the Crichton Institution of Dumfries. 'The great and engrossing business of the life of the insane is,' he says, 'to support sorrow, to contend with intense emotion, or to be bound and deadened by delusion or fatuity. However numerous and varied the fancies and feelings in some of these states may appear to be, the characteristic of all is sameness, monotony, insipidity. The mind dwells upon a single idea, it excludes all collateral associations, or it bends all its powers or stores into this focus; or the same train of thought returns day after day, hour after hour, attracting and converting every new impression into the main current; or it is a desert, a void, a chaos. In alleviating these conditions, mirth and recreation become endowed with higher attributes—they cease to be frivolous diversions, and assume the rank of instruments of cure. They suggest and supply new and delightful sources of reflection to the barren and inactive mind; they supplant more debased and more painful impressions; they seduce and deceive the sorrowful and dejected into temporary composure, and diffuse that tone of gentle hilarity which is so conducive to health and peace.' Dr Browne then proceeds to describe the measures resorted to in his institution for supplying this needful mental medicine and sustenance. 'Wherever it was possible,' he says, 'such entertainments were selected as seemed calculated to yield higher and purer gratification than mere mirth, such as, if failing "to point a moral," might impart some truth, recall some natural affection or sympathy, arrest attention, stimulate reflection. In strict accordance with this view, a successful attempt was made to introduce lectures upon natural science, as a mode of communicating a class of ideas totally new and unexciting, and of demonstrating by experiment and explanation the actual simplicity of many facts and phenomena and natural processes apparently as mysterious and inexplicable as the hallucinations which prevailed among the audience. Notwithstanding the incompleteness of the machinery, several evenings were most usefully and pleasantly occupied in lectures by Mr Aitken of Dumfries on the physical, and Mr Balfour on the chemical, properties of the atmosphere. Fifty-five patients attended these exhibitions. Their deportment indicated deep interest and curiosity; and although wonder was perhaps the predominating feeling, it was rather the wonder of newly-awakened intelligence than of awe or ignorance. Subsequent inquiries, discussions, and criticisms, proved that much information had been acquired or revived, and that the principles of the pump or syphon, and the analysis of water, had neither been misconstrued nor forgotten. In situations where the splendours of chemistry may be exhibited while its truths are taught, inexhaustible means will always exist to amuse and improve the insane.

'Theatrical representation, as a mean of cure and pleasure to the insane, is not now confined to the Crichton Institution. Melo-dramas have been acted before the inmates of asylums in this country; and Tartufe has been produced by the patients in Saltpetriere with the same sort of poetical justice which suggested the selection of Redgauntlet by the company in this asylum. Three pieces were brought out during last season; of these the Mock Doctor was the favourite. It contains some ludicrous allusions to asylums and their governors; and the shouts of laughter and triumph with which the exposure of the savage practices formerly pursued in these places was received, indicated how keenly some portion of the audience understood the point and truth of the satire, and how cordially they rejoiced at the revolution which had established the gentler rule under which they then were. Eleven patients participated in some degree or other in the representation. Four of these have since left the institution; and a fifth, who is undoubtedly indebted to the exercise of memory, in acquiring his part, for a resuscitation of intellect, will soon obtain liberty. But the company will survive such losses, even the desertion of our active stage-manager. In one case only, either among the actors or the auditors, could excitement be attributed to the effects of the amusements. A plain prosaic, but perhaps vain artisan was raised to the rank of lord of the bedchamber, and although all that was required in the part was to stand still and look steadily at a particular point during a mimic pageant, the assumption of dignity, the novelty of the position, or the constraint necessary, destroyed the equanimity which had been previously established, and retarded convalescence. But this event was the consequence of injudicious selection, of a sanguine estimate of the stability of reason, not of the ordeal to which the mind was subjected, and might have followed an incautious appeal to vanity, or the liberation of the patient. After an experience of two successive years, and when about to commence a third season, and after a dispassionate examination of the effect which the stage, when well directed, is capable of exerting by the exposure and correction of follies, by the discipline, consecutive intellectual training, and the concentration imposed upon the performers, and by the gaiety and good humour excited in the spectators, this conclusion appears to be inevitable—that no human mean as yet employed has, at so little risk, and with so little trouble and expense, communicated so much rational happiness to so many of the insane at the same time, or so completely placed them in circumstances so closely allied to those of sane beings, or so calculated either to remove the burden of mental disease, or to render it more bearable. The attempt is no longer an experiment. It is a great fact in moral science, and must be accepted and acted upon.

'Parties of patients have attended all the public concerts which have taken place. They derived exquisite pleasure from these entertainments, and have rarely disturbed the pleasure of others. A lady who had not left the precincts of an asylum, or mingled in the society of the sane for twelve years, was one of Mr Wilson's auditors. She was at the same time in an intermediate state between fury and fatuity, when her mind is more clear and vivacious than during health. The immediate effect, partly of her reunion with her own species, partly of melodies to which she was familiar in other times, was deep and impassioned interest: the ultimate effect was the revival of a taste for music, which enlarges the sphere of her enjoyments, if it does not elevate their nature and tendency. The kindness of amateurs, and the opportune visits of glee singers, have enabled us to vary our ordinary routine of recreation by vocal concerts. A recent arrangement with a respectable instrumental band places a monthly musical soirée at our command; and as the choice of pieces ranges from the efforts of the first masters to simple national airs, the plan provides for all tastes, and is exceedingly popular. It would be preposterous to claim for music any special power over either the savage or insane breast; but those who have joined our festivities will be inclined to yield to it considerable influence in tranquillising agitation, in assuaging sorrow, and in subduing passion.

'These have been the staple and most novel pastimes; but others have been resorted to with equal success. The great festivities of burning the Christmas Log, Twelfth Night, Hallowe'en, have diffused the cheerfulness of these seasons, and have refreshed and revived early and healthy associations. Balls and meetings for music and dancing have been numerous, and form epochs in the calendar. Legerdemain, phantasmagoria, have been exhibited and explained, that the illusions might be attributed to their legitimate sources, and not regarded as realities. Amusement has been sought abroad when the resources in the asylum failed. Public lectures have been attended: the theatre, the circus, the menageries, the races—even the cattle-shows—have obtained patrons and admirers. Fifty-nine patients have visited these places. Excursions have been made to those spots which present objects of interest either in natural beauty, or as remains of antiquity. The addition of a new, and handsome, and commodious omnibus to the establishment, which is capable of containing fourteen or eighteen persons, divided into three parties, will render these journeys more agreeable, and accessible to a greater number. Patients have partaken of the hospitality of friends and strangers; and, which is more extraordinary, they have revisited the homes of their youth, still inhabited by their relatives, and returned to the home of their altered position with alacrity and gladness. In one or other of these amusements generally, or only upon certain occasions, have one hundred and six patients, of both sexes, joined freely, voluntarily, or by advice.'

The Monthly Satellite, a temperance journal published at Banff, contains the following paragraph, written in the earnestness of a most laudable enthusiasm, yet irresistibly amusing:—

SNUFF SACRIFICES.

A, had been a snuffer for thirty years—used to spend on an average fully one shilling per week, or the price of a suit of clothes per annum—has lately given it up.

B, a fifteen-year-old snuffer—has also given it up about two months ago.

C, a thirteen-years' proficient—has laid aside his box, and, with the price of keeping it full, takes out Chambers's Journal, and saves threepence weekly

D, ten years—has also given it up.

Reader! if a snuffer, go thou and do likewise.

THE MOON.

Among the natives of the East, a belief in the hurtful effect of the moon's rays, especially on the head and eyes, is universal. This belief, the result of experience, ought not to be altogether slighted, even by those who think themselves wiser. It is very common to regard this as a mere superstition, and to deny the possibility of the moon's rays producing any effect of the kind. A mere theoretical opinion, however, is not to be depended on, when opposed to the result of experience and observation. It is a fact that the moonbeams in certain countries have a pernicious influence. It is known that in Bengal, for example, meat which has been exposed to the moonlight cannot be afterwards salted or cured, but will speedily go to corruption; whereas the same kind of meat, if sheltered from the moon, may be cured and preserved. Not only is this idea of the dangerous influence of the moon entertained by the semi-barbarous tribes of the East, but European shipmasters trading to the Mediterranean are firmly impressed with the same conviction; and they are cautioned against exposing themselves to the danger by their Sailing Guides, published in England. On one occasion, many years ago, I was on board a Maltese schooner commanded by an Englishman. We were off the coast of Africa; it was spring, and the weather delicious. It was a brilliant moonlight night, and I lay down to sleep near the poop, wrapped in my cloak. I was soon after awoke by a sense of suffocation, and found the cape of my cloak drawn close over my face. I removed it, and again fell asleep. The same thing occurred a second time, and again I rid myself of the encumbrance, when the captain of the vessel cautioned me against sleeping in the moonlight with my face uncovered. I laughed at what I considered his simplicity; but, to confirm his opinion, he mentioned several instances in which the neglect of this precaution had been followed by very injurious consequences, and appealed to his Sailing Guide as authority. There I found the caution very strongly urged; and blindness, and even (if I mistake not) derangement, stated as the too frequent consequence of the moonbeams being allowed to beat for any length of time on the head and eyes during sleep. I returned to my couch on deck, but took the precaution of fastening a handkerchief over my face.—*Journal of the Rev. W. Robertson.*

WIND AND RAIN GAUGE, ROYAL EXCHANGE.

This ingenious apparatus, which the inventor, Mr Follett Osler, calls an anemometer, consists of a vertical fan or fly, such as is used in the construction of the modern mill, which keeps the pressure-plate always in a direct line with the wind. The pressure-plate acts on four springs of varied degrees of strength; a slight breeze presses only on the first and weakest spring, a stronger wind brings the second into play, and so on to the third and fourth—the whole four being more than equal to any force of wind which can be expected in this country. The pressure-plate works a rod, at the extremity of which is a pencil acting on a cylinder of tracing paper in the subscription room. As the pressure-plate is forced back by the wind, the pencil is proportionately pushed down on the cylinder, and thus the *intensity* of the wind is accurately self-registered. The direction of the wind is shown on the dials in the various parts of the building, by the usual system of rods and bevel wheels: it is also registered on the cylinder, by the agency of a perpetual screw working up and down the indicating pencil. A rain gauge is also attached to the anemometer. The rain that falls into the gauge descends into a receiver at the bottom of the anemometer; and this being suspended, in connexion with a delicate indicating rod and pencil, as it sinks, the rod falls; and thus the smallest quantity of rain is at once self-registered. The registration is effected on a cylinder, covered with graduated paper, which is made to turn round once in ninety-six hours. The clock-work is so constructed as to produce uniformity of motion. On this paper the vertical lines indicate time, while the pencils mark the pressure and velocity of the wind, and the amount of rain that falls. At the end of every ninety-six hours the paper is changed, and the register carefully preserved for reference.—*Athenæum.*

WHY DO THEY DIE?

BY WILLIAM FORSYTH.

In the fresh glow of beauty, the first flush of light,
Should the day-dawn be swathed in the shadows of night,
And the star of the morning pass fruitless away,
And break to the fair earth its promise of day?
Ah no! Then why fade thus the loveliest flowers?
Oh why do the young and the beautiful die,
Ere they drink of the rapture of summer's sweet hours,
Ere the brow hath a cloud or the bosom a sigh?

They spring like young fountains—as pure and as free,
To freshen the earth where their pathways may be;
They lighten the cot, and they gladden the hall,
In every land beaming—the loved ones of all.
But, alas! there are gems on the night-shrouded earth,
Only lit by the stars of yon ambient sky;
The gathering cloud quenches their light at its birth,
And like those do the young and the beautiful die.

With holy love gazing through summer-lit eyes,
The free falcon-glance where no faithlessness lies,
The glad tones of laughter, the song, and the smile,
And low gentle voice that each care can beguile;
They come in the beauty of shadowless truth,
Bringing flowers to the green tree, and leaves to the bare;
They circle their brows with the bright dreams of youth,
Like the garlanded dreamers, as fleeting as fair.

Oh, could not earth foster such flowers where they grew,
With its love like the sunshine, and tears like the dew;
Oh, could not hope strengthen, nor watchfulness bind,
Nor the shadows of sorrow that brooded behind,
Detain them—the loved ones? Ah no! Day by day,
We list for some footfall in vain at the door;
Their voices of joy from some hearth pass away,
And the woodlands re-echo their laughter no more.

Be hushed! They are happy who die in their youth,
With their bosoms untainted, unspotted their truth,
Ere they feel the rude burden of earth's many ills,
Where misery saddens, and heartlessness chills.
Though, like heaven's own visions, they come and depart,
And leave not a trace to the lovingest eye,
In the faith, and the love, and the hope of the heart,
Eternally dwelling, they never can die.

—*Aberdeen Herald.*

Printed by William Bradbury, of No. 6, York Place, and Frederick Mullett Evans, of No. 7, Church Row, both of Stoke Newington, in the county of Middlesex, printers, at their office, Lombard Street, in the precinct of Whitefriars, and city of London; and Published (with permission of the Proprietors, W. and R. CHAMBERS,) by WILLIAM SOMERVILLE ORR, Publisher, of 2, Amen Corner, at No. 2, AMEN CORNER, both in the parish of Christ-

CONDUCTED BY WILLIAM AND ROBERT CHAMBERS, EDITORS OF 'CHAMBERS'S INFORMATION FOR THE PEOPLE,' 'CHAMBERS'S EDUCATIONAL COURSE,' &c.

No. 66. New Series. SATURDAY, APRIL 5, 1845. Price 1½d.

BUCKSHEESH.

The word 'bucksheesh,' or 'bickshash,' though strange in our latitude, is but too familiar to all who have visited the East. The traveller, often wholly at the mercy of his desert guides, is compelled to endure their unreasonable exactions. Every little service has its price, and the sordid attendant seems quite incapable of assisting with one hand, without expecting in the other his customary gratuity, or bucksheesh.

Though the word is little known among us, the thing is unfortunately too common. In a thousand ways do we meet with this unwelcome manifestation of the 'itching palm.' So intimately, indeed, is bucksheesh woven into our social system, that it has been remarked by foreigners that all England might be traversed with little inconvenience, by any one who knew enough of the English language to pronounce the phrase 'How much?'

The salaries of waiters, waitresses, &c. are often, as is well known, wholly made up of bucksheesh, in the shape of little voluntary acknowledgments for civility; and in some favourable circumstances, indeed, so great is the aggregate of these small sums, that the custom of the master paying the servant is reversed, and the servant pays his employer for permission to fill the situation. The leaving servants to be thus remunerated by customers must of course be regarded as a confession that their civil attendance is not to be secured in any other way; it implies that no influence which the master possesses is regarded as sufficient to enforce upon his servants the propriety of their performing carefully the duties intrusted to them. What a confession to make respecting so large a portion of the community! And accordingly, it certainly is within the observation of most persons, that the neatly-dressed, hair-curled youth, or the smart demoiselle, with her florid cap and apron, who, as the case may be, serves up your beef-steak, will have little regard for the comfort of the man who neglects the proper modicum of bucksheesh. Failing this, your chop will be apt to vacillate between the extremes of the raw and the carbonised condition, and your plate to be sent in unwarmed. Surely arrangements fairer towards all parties might be made.

Not a little annoyance is experienced by tradesmen in the more fashionable localities at the rapacious demands of gentlemen's servants for bucksheesh, for the privilege of serving the establishments of their masters. Stewards, butlers, housekeepers, &c. have much of this patronage at their disposal, and the 'good-will' is thus put up to the highest bidder, and the tradesman who can bid most, or, in other words, fee most liberally, obtains the orders. This, however, falls heavily upon tradesmen, especially those of slender means, and practices are too often resorted to, not very honourable or even honest, to enable them to pay the demands of their patrons of the kitchen. Christmas bills are elongated with strange items, astonished masters are cajoled by shrewd stewards, and the bucksheesh of the servant is too often secured at the sacrifice of candour, and even of honesty and truth.

The general adoption of the railway system of locomotion has rendered nearly obsolete in many parts of the country a very offensive branch of bucksheesh. This 'black-mail' of civilised life was by none more pertinaciously levied than by the coachman and guard of the old school. How often have we indignantly seen the bronzed triple-coated son of the whip, who drove his own horses, and who owned a snug little 'box' on the line of road, appeal in no very gentle manner to a poor widow, whose friends had clubbed together to procure her a comfortless outside place, and who had forgotten to add to the regular fare the exactions of three coachmen and a guard! And with what unutterable contempt would Capes look at the proffered coin, if deemed less than the 'regular' gratuity! How sour-visaged was that rosy son of the road if disappointed in his previous calculations, even though poverty stared at him in the threadbare garments and scantily-clad form of the passenger! Not that we blame him, and his brother of the horn behind, as having less of the milk of human kindness than other men. It was a part of the system, the staple of their salary, and the system we blame rather than the men. The infection, too, was contagious among all in the atmosphere of coaches. The ostler who brought the ladder for the convenience of the female 'outsider,' touched his cap significantly before he took it away; and the porter, with a similar movement, forgot not to thrust his head into the coach to inform you that he had safely deposited your carpet-bag in the boot. Without a gratuity, not a cup of cold water, not a wisp of straw in a soaking rain, could be had: the commonest civility had its price: and he who would not quietly submit to pay the accustomed fees, was unceremoniously dubbed 'no gentleman.' Something similar, on a more elegant scale, was practised at the inns on the road upon those who ventured upon the costly experiment of alighting for refreshment. The decoys, the allurements, the display, the stentorian voice of the guard summoning you at the first mouthful, and the shameless bill which concluded your fifteen minutes' refreshment, are well known, though rapidly becoming features of the past.

Perhaps the most offensive manner in which bucksheesh is levied among us is in connexion with our sacred edifices—the cathedral, the church, and the chapel. That so many of those glorious piles of masonry, so interesting from their associations with bygone times, great men, and stirring incidents, containing so much calculated to elevate and improve the mind and heart, should be closed to the mass, is to be deeply lamented. The pompous verger, with his massive keys, admits none but the buckshesh-payer within his privileged domain: no vulgar foot must enter, no peasant eye must feast upon the fretted roofs, the long perspectives, and all the magic 'blossomings of stone.' Even when a part of the building is necessarily thrown open gratuitously (hated word to him!) to the public, for the purposes of public worship, he prevents as much as possible the stragglers from wandering, and urges the lingerers to move on, with the most commendable consideration for decency and decorum, grudging you the momentary glimpse of beauties, from the more leisurely seeing of which he makes so snug a revenue. In our humbler places of worship, the buckshesh of the pew is not less offensive, and the more so from its incongruity with the solemn associations which such places should suggest. The pew-opener, accustomed to look upon the frequenters of the place as her customers, renders to each his appropriate attention and sitting, according to the amount of the accustomed gratuity. The seats and the sitters are graduated according to this standard; and under her guidance the liberal donor is ushered with all due formality into the reserved seats, and the empty-handed is consigned to the free sittings or some back unfurnished pew, where, in the shadow of an obstructing pillar, he is left to lament that sight and hearing are alike impossible. The sixpenny, shilling, and half-crown donor each finds his appropriate seat, and the sagacious pew-opener can, from long experience, tell at a glance under which head to class a stranger. The gentleman buckshesh-payer sprawls on the luxurious cushions of the half-filled pew, while the delicate female who cannot afford the fee is left standing in the aisle unnoticed and uncared for.

There is one variety of buckshesh which we ought not to omit noticing in terms of serious reprobation; namely, the buckshesh of the workshop and the factory. Among the higher classes, this species of buckshesh is levied in the shape of 'fees,' which in some cases are so exorbitant, as to be almost ruinous to those who are ambitious of honours or preferment. Among workmen, however, it is known by the term 'paying footing,' and is often levied in the most heartless manner. It is the more unreasonable, inasmuch as it has not for its plea past services, but merely a promise of future ones, or rather of non-hostility. Strange that mechanics and artisans, who are generally so sensitive of anything like oppression on the part of their employers, do not see the injustice and the tyranny of this practice. Surely, among all the right-thinking and right-feeling, especially among those whom poverty and toil has associated together, kindness and good-will should be mutually extended without the intervention of a paltry bribe or a cruel exaction. Let us hope that the day is not far distant when the buckshesh of the workshop will be numbered among the things of the past.

In England, perhaps the most singular mode of levying buckshesh is that practised at Eton during the 'montem,' which is held triennially, on which occasion the 'captain' for the year, assisted by his staff, hands round his bag to the company for the accustomed 'salt,' as it is termed, and which usually amounts to about a thousand pounds, which, with certain deductions, is appropriated to his own use. Of the thousands of the nobility and gentry and old Etonians who flock thither on such occasions to grace the spectacle, not one escapes being compelled to 'stand and deliver.' The captain, with the due admixture of the *suaviter in modo* and *fortiter in re*, unceremoniously opens the door of every carriage, and with gentlemanly audacity bags the buckshesh, and in return gives a ticket indemnifying the donors from future exactions. The ceremony altogether, the origin of which is enveloped in obscurity, is a strange relic of barbarous times, which would doubtless long since have passed into oblivion, had it not been found so profitable to ask on the one hand, and so ungracious or unsafe to deny on the other.

At fashionable watering-places, however, the buckshesh system is in its fullest glory, and its ingenious developments at these places are not a little amusing. No sooner do you step outside your door with your carpet-bag, to spend a few days at the sea-side during the season, than you find all about you conspiring, as it were, to lighten your purse. Unless you clutch your portmanteau with decision, it will to a certainty be snatched from your hand by some kind porter insisting on carrying it for you. On board the steamer, not only is your fare expected, but one of the sailors invariably introduces to your notice a box, the contents of which vaguely profess to be 'for the benefit of the ship's company.' On landing, the buckshesh plot seems to thicken. You cannot be allowed to carry your carpet-bag off the boat yourself, however light it may be; a fellow snatches it up in your very teeth, for which of course you have to pay. You are fortunate if there is no pierage, and very unfortunate if you imprudently make it known that you are in search of lodgings. If you only look round inquiringly, the cards of a dozen touters are immediately thrust into your hand, while agents of the baker, butcher, milkman, &c. skirmish in the background, waiting to see where you will settle down, in order to pounce upon a new customer. Then there is the bath-room, the subscription concert, the excursion, the raffle, and a thousand other genteel ramifications of buckshesh, none of which, if you have any pretensions to respectability, can you avoid. Cards innumerable follow immediately you have chosen a lodging. Asses' milk, baths, donkeys, home-made bread, guides, circulating libraries, are all obtruded upon your notice with a pertinacity that seems determined you *shall* want them, whether you do or not. You *must* subscribe to the library, because all the gentlemen go there to read the newspapers: you *must* have a copy of the 'guide' to the curiosities of the place; namely, waterfalls without water, and hosts of other marvellous nothings. Then you must visit the bazaar, and, fascinated by the blandishments of the fair proprietress (oh the refinement of buckshesh!) add your name to the raffle paper, and be too happy to purchase what she chooses to sell you at whatever price she chooses to ask. The poor Italian boy travels down hither from the great metropolis, as a locality likely to suit his purpose, or rather that of his tyrannical employer; and even the little urchins in the neighbourhood are on the *qui vive* as well as their elders, obtruding on your attention specimens of 'silver ore' found in the neighbourhood, offering to be your 'guide' to any neighbouring curiosity, or looking expectation while they hold open the gate for you to pass through. If you only whisper a word about an excursion, a dozen fly-boys, intent upon securing the job, collect round the door, noisily urging the pre-eminent merits of the establishment with which they are connected. In short, at fashionable watering-places, whether you eat, or drink, or sleep, or ride, or walk, or sail, or bathe, buckshesh will haunt you as your shadow; and if, before setting out on your expedition, you put in your purse double the sum necessary for your reasonable expenses, you will be a fortunate man if you bring anything back.

Can the prevalence of buckshesh be owing to anything in the social arrangements of England, not existing in other countries? Not unlikely. The American 'humbler classes' are proudly unconscious of the custom, and a servant there would regard as an insult the offer of one of those gratuities the withholding of which would here be so much resented. Even in Scotland, if we keep away from certain tourist-frequented parts of the Highlands, there is little of that constant out-looking for money gratuities which we always feel to be so annoying when we happen to travel southward. Perhaps the tendency of English institutions is to put the humbler classes too much on a stipendiary footing, and thus accustom them to be constantly looking for money from everybody who appears with a good coat upon his back. Nor is this corruption so limited, for an idea is evidently prevalent amongst the middle and higher classes that money is the measure of all the desirables of life. We see it in the outcry made about every kind of merit if it happens to be connected with poverty, as if the first duty towards a more than usually deserving person were to cram money into his hand. Can we doubt for a moment that all such views and practices must tend to sink and extinguish in the breasts of a people, that self-respect which is the first principle of nearly all virtue?

BIOGRAPHIC SKETCHES.

JOHN DALTON.

There are some men whose lives form eras in history—points from which we date the onward progress of mankind in science and civilisation. Among these may be justly numbered John Dalton, the author and expounder of the Atomic Theory, by which chemical investigation has assumed the certainty of mathematical demonstration, and the determination of its results the simplicity of an arithmetical problem. The life of such a man, though in a great measure devoid of those incidents and adventures which commonly give zest to biography, cannot fail to be of interest to that public which reaps so directly the fruits of his labours; and for this reason we propose to draw from certain sources at our command* a brief sketch of his personal history, adverting, as we proceed, to the nature and value of his discoveries.

John Dalton was born at Eaglesfield, near Cockermouth, in Cumberland, on the 5th of September 1766. His father, Joseph Dalton, was originally a person of no property; but after the death of an elder brother, he became possessed of a small copyhold estate, which he farmed with the assistance of his sons. He had six children, of whom only three survived to maturity—Jonathan, John, and Mary. The first-named of these obtained the estate on the decease of his father, and retained it till his own death, in 1835, when it became the property of John. Though straitened in circumstances, old Dalton strove to give his family the best education within his reach, and the subject of our memoir attended a school conducted by a member of the Society of Friends, until he had attained his twelfth year. We have no means of knowing the nature or amount of the instruction which he received at this school—the only one he ever attended—but he is said 'to have made very considerable progress in knowledge;' and he always spoke with respect of his early preceptor.

That Dalton did make the progress here spoken of, and that he gave early proof of rare energy and natural capability, may be gathered from the fact, that at the age of thirteen he commenced a school in his native village, and persevered in teaching during two winters. So modest, unassuming, and conscientious a man as he proved himself in after life to be, must have been well assured, even at that early age, of the possession both of knowledge and of the power to impart it, or he would not have undertaken so difficult a task. How he prospered in this vocation we are not told; but probably not greatly, for we learn that a considerable portion of his time was spent in assisting his father in the works of the farm. At this period his principal study was mathematics, in which he was joined by a youth in the service of a Mr Robinson, who, along with his lady, an accomplished woman, was instrumental in directing the pursuits of the young philosophers. An anecdote is told of the boy-teacher, which, though homely, exhibits the early possession of that confidence and self-reliance which in after years were prominent traits of Dalton's character. The correctness of one of his solutions being questioned, he promptly persisted in its accuracy, backing his opinion with a bet—the result of which was a supply of candles through the winter for his little school.

In 1781, at the age of fifteen, Dalton removed to Kendal, to officiate as usher in the boarding-school of his cousin George Bewley. Here he resided till 1792, actively engaged in learning and teaching mathematics and the physical sciences. During his residence in that town, he attracted the attention of Mr Gough, a blind gentleman, who, in spite of his misfortune, was devoted to the study of physics and natural history. This individual had an excellent library, and some apparatus, which he placed freely at the disposal of Dalton, who soon became his assistant and companion. The service required was of a light and pleasant description, and the blind philosopher, who was possessed of excellent natural abilities, and a liberal education, appears to have acted the kindest part towards his young friend, who, in return, was never weary of expressing his sense of obligation. When he published his Meteorological Essays, he said, in reference to Mr Gough—'If there be anything new, and of importance to science, embraced in this work, it is owing in great part to my having had the advantage of his instructions and example in philosophical examinations.' And although we may believe that Dalton's modesty led him somewhat to over-estimate his obligation to Mr Gough, there can be no doubt that one whose early education had been comparatively so neglected, must have derived the greatest benefit from intercourse with such a person as the latter is described to have been. During his residence at Kendal, and for some time after, we find Dalton frequently contributing answers to mathematical and philosophical questions which appeared in 'The Gentleman's and Lady's Diary,' a periodical then of some celebrity, but now little remembered. In 1788 he commenced his meteorological observations, which led directly or indirectly to all his great discoveries, and which were continued without intermission till the day before his death.

In 1793 Dalton gave to the public his first work, entitled 'Meteorological Observations and Essays,' to which more particular reference will be made hereafter. Some time previous to the appearance of that publication, he had thought of qualifying as a physician or a lawyer, and corresponded with a friend in London on the subject. But his views were changed in consequence of the receipt of a letter, by his friend Mr Gough, from Dr Barnes, making inquiry for a gentleman to fill the situation of professor of mathematics and natural philosophy in the New College, Mosley Street, Manchester. Dalton's offer to undertake the duties was accepted, and he removed in 1793 to Manchester, where he spent the remainder of his days. The year after settling in that town, he joined a society which had been established for some time, under the title of the Manchester Literary and Philosophical Society. To the transactions of this body—the most celebrated of all our provincial scientific associations—he contributed a series of papers containing the results of original researches of the highest value. These, along with a few others on kindred subjects, have

---

* The sources to which we refer are a manuscript original memoir, obligingly confided to us by its author, and an able and ingenious article on the Life and Discoveries of Dalton, in the opening number of the British Quarterly Review. This article—of which our sketch may generally be regarded as an abridgment—is from the pen of Dr George Wilson of Edinburgh, and is, in point of method and perspicuity, one of the most successful efforts in scientific biography which we ever had the pleasure to peruse.

onferred on the society's periodical publications, best nown as the 'Manchester Memoirs,' a celebrity which as extended beyond the nations of Europe. Dalton reided for about six years within the Mosley Street Intitution, and continued to officiate there till the college vas removed to York in 1799, when he began to teach athematics and natural philosophy privately, at the harge, it is said, of eighteenpence an hour. In this umble occupation he was engaged when, in 1804, he nfolded and expounded the laws which he had discoered to regulate the proportions in which substances ombine chemically with each other, along with the ypothesis by means of which he accounted for their xistence. The laws and hypothesis are generally, hough erroneously, taken together, and included under he single title of his *Atomic Theory*.

Up to this period Dalton must be considered as a athematician and meteorologist, rather than in the ght of a chemical inquirer: his studies, however, ere fast tending in the latter direction. He taught athematics, and solved philosophical problems, sucessfully as regards abilities, but with little pecuniary rofit. Indeed the appearance of an English gramar from his pen, in 1801, indicates rather necessitous ircumstances; for, to judge from his general characer, such a book is the last he would have composed s a matter of choice. This little work, which is now ll but unknown, is not without marks of a peculiar rder and definiteness of expression, that exhibit the vorkings of an acute mathematical and mechanical mind. We do his intellectual powers no injustice when we thus haracterise them, for he was almost totally devoid of iterary tastes, and was one of the most limited readers, inding his pleasure in original physical observation and nquiry, and not in the discoveries and thoughts of thers, however brilliant and enticing. As a meteoroogist, his progress had been more successful: and this eed not be wondered at, seeing that his mind was so eculiarly adapted for the frequency and regularity of hat observation which the science of the atmosphere requires. For more than fifty years of his life, he was in the habit of taking about a dozen observations daily, registering in all upwards of two hundred thousand independent notices; and it would have been remarkable if from this enormous field he had not deduced many laws practically as well as theoretically important. Of these discoveries, either published independently or in the Manchester Society's Memoirs, we can only give the merest abstract, extending as they do over a space of twelve or fourteen years—and those among the most active and vigorous of his existence.

His observations on the weight of the atmosphere led him to the discovery of the fact, that the rise and fall of the barometer depends upon the amount of watery vapour floating in the air; every grain of water, when dissolved in that medium, becoming an elastic vapour capable of sustaining 1-24th of an inch of mercury. He connected the aurora borealis with magnetic phenomena, and explained the cause of the trade-winds, without being aware of the explanations of others on these points. From 1794 to 1803, he was busily engaged with experiments and observations on such subjects as the fall of rain, the deposition of dew, the origin of springs, the power of fluids to conduct heat, the constitution of mixed gases, the force of steam, evaporation, and the expansion of gases by heat; all the while conducting his meteorological observations with the utmost regularity and minuteness. In this wide range of investigation his studies were chiefly physical, yet treading on the confines of chemistry, and leading him insensibly to connect chemical views with his mechanical hypotheses. In using a diagram of the atmosphere, for example, the particles of oxygen are represented by small diamonds, those of nitrogen by dots, those of carbonic acid by triangles, and those of aqueous vapour by asterisks; thus showing that, two years before he announced his Atomic Theory, Dalton had accustomed himself to look upon bodies as composed of molecules, ultimate particles, or *atoms*, as he afterwards called them, and to consider the properties of the masses as dependent upon the manner in which their ultimate particles comported themselves to one another. In 1803 he published an essay 'On the Tendency of Elastic Fluids to Diffusion through each other,' and another 'On the Absorption of Gases by Water and other Liquids.' The latter contains the first announcement of his discovery of the laws of combining proportion, and the germ of his celebrated hypothesis. In discussing this matter, he employs his usual mode of illustration; namely, representing the particles of the liquids by one kind of dot, and the particles of the gases by another kind—thus showing the hold which a belief in the atomic constitution of matter had taken of his mind, and the use which he made of it in discussing purely physical problems, before he had occasion to apply it to chemical questions at all. It is needless to state that he took a mechanical view of the absorption of the gases by liquids. But if this mingling were a mechanical and not a chemical action, how does it happen that water dissolves its own bulk of one gas, carbonic acid, and only three per cent. of its own volume of another, such as oxygen? Dalton saw the difficulty, and devised a hypothesis to overcome it, which we give in his own words:—'Why does water not admit its bulk of every gas alike? This question I have duly considered, and though I am not yet able to satisfy myself completely, I am nearly persuaded that the circumstance depends upon the weight and number of the ultimate particles of the several gases; those whose particles are lightest and single being least absorbable, and the others more, according as they increase in weight and complexity.' To this there is a foot-note—'Subsequent experience renders this less probable:' and the text is followed by a passage which we put in italics. '*An inquiry into the relative weights of the ultimate particles of bodies is a subject, so far as I know, entirely new: I have been prosecuting the inquiry with remarkable success.*' On the succeeding page is a table of the relative weights of the ultimate particles of gaseous and other bodies. This was the first attempt at a table of *atomic weights*; and though every one of them was wrong, with the exception of hydrogen, which he assumed as unity, one cannot regard it otherwise than with respect. Such, we believe, were the steps by which Dalton was conducted to the discovery of the laws which regulate the combining proportions of different bodies. He was testing by experiment the truth of a hypothesis as to the cause of the specific solubility of gases in water, which proved in the end quite untenable; but, like Columbus, who missed an Eldorado, but found an America, he discovered something better.

And what is this Atomic Theory? This is not the place to answer such a question in detail; but we may state shortly its nature and bearings. It supposes every known substance to be composed of indefinitely small particles or ultimate atoms, each atom being endowed with the weight, solidity, fluidity, colour, and other sensible properties of the mass to which it belongs. These atoms may or may not be in absolute contact, but may each be surrounded by an atmosphere of heat, electricity, &c.; they may be of different shapes and sizes, and must necessarily be of different weights or densities, according to the nature of the body of which they are the constituents. We do not know what may be the *absolute* weight of an atom of any elementary body, whether it be the millionth or the ten-millionth part of a grain; all that the chemist knows and proceeds upon is the *relative* weights, assuming some one as a standard. Dalton took as his standard the atom of hydrogen, which is the lightest known body: this he called 1; and as a given weight of hydrogen always requires eight times as much of oxygen to form water, he drew the certain inference, that the atom of oxygen was to the atom of hydrogen as 8 to 1. Again, olefiant gas consists of hydrogen and carbon; namely, one part of the former to six of the latter: therefore the carbon atom must be represented by 6. Proceeding upon this method, the relative weights of all the known elements were determined—hydrogen 1, oxygen 8, carbon 6, nitrogen 14, silver 108, gold 199, &c.—and a table constructed, in which these proportions were set down for future guidance. According to Dalton's hypothesis, then, the proportions in which bodies combine with each other are supposed to depend upon the weights of the atoms that make them up, and to be identical with them. By this view, when bodies combine together, their ultimate particles do not interpenetrate, or become fused together, so that the individuality or identity of any is lost. The atoms only come in close proximity, and lie side by side, or above and below each other; and when the compound they form is decomposed, they separate and reappear with all their original properties. The smallest possible quantity of water is in this way conceived to consist of one atom of hydrogen and one of oxygen, bound together without loss of the individuality of either, by the unknown and invisible tie which we term chemical affinity. We shall see how aptly the atomic hypothesis explains all the laws of combining proportion, on which the science of chemistry depends.

The *first* great law is, that the same compound consists invariably of the same components. Water, for example, always consists of oxygen and hydrogen; common salt of chlorine and sodium; vermilion of sulphur and mercury. Indeed this is a fundamental law of nature, and one upon which the other chemical laws are based. The *second* teaches that the elements which form a chemical compound are always united in the same proportion by weight. Water not only consists invariably of oxygen and hydrogen, but the weight of oxygen present is always eight times greater than that of hydrogen. It is the same with every compound: common salt always contains 35 parts of chlorine to 22 of sodium; vermilion 16 of sulphur to 101 of mercury. The *third* law enforces the remarkable truth, that when one body combines with another in several proportions, the higher proportions are multiples of the first or lowest. Thus 8 of oxygen and 1 of hydrogen form water; and 16 of oxygen and 1 of hydrogen a substance called the peroxide of hydrogen. Here the 16 is twice 8, or a multiple of the first or atomic weight of oxygen. Again, oxygen is found to unite with nitrogen in 5 different compositions, each union forming a different substance. These proportions are 8, 16, 24, 32, and 40, to 14 of nitrogen. Here also we have not 8½, or 16¼, or 19, but a regular multiple of 8, or the lowest atomic weight of oxygen; and necessarily so, since atoms are regarded as the ultimate units or entireties of matter. We can conceive 2, or 16 atoms of oxygen, uniting with 1 atom, or 14 of nitrogen; but not of 2½, otherwise there were no faith to be placed in the theory of atoms being the *ultimate* particles of matter. The *fourth* law is to the effect, that if two bodies combine in certain proportions with a third, they combine in the very same proportion with each other. Thus 16 parts of sulphur combine with 8 of oxygen, and 27 parts of iron combine with 8 of oxygen; therefore 16 parts of sulphur must be the quantity that combines with 27 of iron, as may be verified by experiment. This law is of the utmost practical value to the chemist; but for its existence, his labours as an analyst would be endless, and the work of a lifetime would go but a short way in ascertaining the combining proportions of a single substance. As it is, however, if the proportion be ascertained in which one body combines with any other, the proportion in which it will combine with every other may be ascertained, not by analysis, but by simple calculation. The *fifth* law is that which teaches that the combining proportion of a compound body is the sum of the combining proportions of its components. The combining proportion of water, for example, is found to be 9, or a multiple of 9; but this number is the sum of its constituents, 8 oxygen and 1 hydrogen. So with every other. The equivalent of carbonic acid is 22, which is just the sum of 16 oxygen and 6 carbon of which it is composed.

Such are the laws which regulate the deductions of the chemist, and which are all beautifully and intelligibly explained by the hypothesis of Dalton. We have only to gain a perfect conception of the atomic constitution of nature, and the innumerable combinations, separations, and recombinations of matter appear before us in naked and unalterable simplicity. It is true that some of these laws were known and acted upon by chemists before the time of John Dalton; but he may be justly said to have discovered all of them for himself; and even if he had not, he had at least the merit of lighting them up anew, and concentrating their energies to the elevation of chemistry, from the state of an empirical art to that of an inductive science.

The first glimpse of the Atomic Theory, as has been stated, was obtained by Dalton in 1803. In 1804 he touched upon it in his lectures in Manchester, and at the Royal Institution of London; and in the same year he explained it to Dr Thomson of Glasgow, who spent a day or two with him in Manchester. By the latter chemist, and not by Dalton himself, it was first explicitly made known to the world, in 1807, in the third edition of his 'System of Chemistry.' In the same year Dalton explained his views in the course of lectures which he delivered in Edinburgh and Glasgow; but it was not till 1808 that he fully expounded them in his well-known work entitled, 'New System of Chemical Philosophy.' Between the years 1803 and 1810, Dalton was chiefly occupied in the prosecution of analyses to verify his theory, in teaching mathematics, and in delivering lectures before the mechanics' institutions of the principal towns. He was not a fluent speaker, nor had he any great talent for teaching. He declined, however, all the offers made by his friends to provide him with a competency, so that he might devote his undivided attention to scientific pursuits. To such overtures he replied, 'that teaching was a kind of recreation, and that, if richer, he would not probably spend more time in investigation than he was accustomed to do.' For many years he had the usual fate of the prophet, and received 'no honour in his own country.' He had always around him in Manchester, however, a small circle of appreciating friends, who did all they could to extend his fame. In 1814 they had his portrait taken by Allen, and an engraving made from it for distribution. In 1817 they conferred on him a further mark of their esteem, by electing him president of the Literary and Philosophical Society, of which he had long been the most distinguished member; and he had the honour of being re-elected every year till his death. In 1822 he visited Paris, and during his sojourn there was introduced to La Place, and to all the more distinguished French philosophers; invited to attend the meetings of the institute; and treated both in public and private as one whom all delighted to honour. The generous appreciation of his merits shown by the French, as contrasted with the indifference exhibited by all but his personal friends, and a few men of science at home, made a strong impression on Dalton. Although a man of few words, little given to betray his feelings, and very indifferent to applause, he was so moved by his reception, as to say when he returned home—'If any Englishman has reason to be proud of his reception in France, I am that one.'

At length his countrymen became more alive to his merits; and for the last ten years of his life Dalton was the object of universal esteem. In 1826, the council of the Royal Society of London unanimously awarded to him the royal gold medal of fifty guineas' value, placed at their disposal by George IV. It is to the British Association for the Advancement of Science, however, that Dalton was indebted for the respect in which latterly he was held. He attended its earliest meeting at York in 1831, where he was seen for the first time by many who had long esteemed him at a distance, and now rejoiced in an opportunity of vying with each other in showing him respect. At the next meeting of the association, held at Oxford in the following year, the university conferred upon him the title of Doctor of Civil Law. In 1833, when the association met at Cambridge, the president, Professor Sedgwick, took a public opportunity of expressing his regret that the university could not honour herself, as the sister one had done, by conferring upon Dalton an honorary degree, as these cannot be granted without royal mandamus. At the close of his speech, he announced 'that his majesty, King William IV., wishing to manifest his attachment to science, and his regard for a character like that of Dr Dalton, had graciously conferred on him, out of the funds of the civil list, a substantial mark of his royal favour.' This 'substantial mark' was a pension of L.150, which was raised to L.300 in 1836.

In the same year, 1833, a number of his friends subscribed the sum of L.2000, and employed Chantrey to execute a full-length statue of him in marble, which is now erected in the entrance hall of the Royal Manchester Institution. While in London giving the requisite sittings for his bust, he was most cordially welcomed by men of science; and through the influence of Mr Babbage the mathematician, of Lord Brougham, who was then chancellor, he was introduced to his late majesty, William IV. In 1834 he attended the meeting of the British Association at Edinburgh, where every sort of kindness and new honours awaited him. The university conferred upon him the degree of LL.D., the royal society elected him a member, and the town council presented him with the freedom of the city. In 1835 he was present at the Dublin meeting of the association, where all parties, from the lord-lieutenant downwards, vied with each other in extending to him the marks of their esteem.

'We have now,' says Dr Wilson, 'reached the 70th year of his laborious career, and it will not surprise the reader that the silver cord should be beginning to be loosed, the golden bowl to be broken at the fountain. In 1837, when in his 71st year, he suffered from a severe attack of paralysis, which left his right side powerless, and also deprived him of speech. He experienced a second slight attack on the 21st of the same month, and for some time both his mental and bodily faculties appeared to be much affected. After an illness of some months, however, his health improved, and his mind began to evince something of its former vigour, though his articulation always remained less distinct than before. On the 17th of May 1844 he had a third paralytic stroke, which partially deprived him of the use of his right side, and increased the indistinctness of his utterance. He recovered in some degree from this attack also, and on the 19th of July 1844, was present at a meeting of the council of the Manchester Literary and Philosophical Society, where he received an engrossed copy in vellum of a resolution of that society, passed at its annual meeting, recording "their admiration of the zeal and perseverance with which he has deduced the mean pressure and temperature of the atmosphere, and the quantity of rain for each month and for the whole year; with the prevailing direction and force of the wind at different seasons in this neighbourhood, from a series of more than two hundred thousand observations, from the end of the year 1793 to the beginning of 1844, being a period of half a century." Dalton received the resolution sitting, and being unable to articulate a reply, handed a written one, which was read by his old and attached friend, Peter Clare, Esq. This was the 19th of the month—on the 27th Dalton was no more!

'The news of Dalton's death, although it must have been looked for by many, was heard with sorrow throughout the whole length and breadth of the land. His townsmen, anxious to express their sense of the irreparable loss they had sustained, resolved to give him a public funeral, which accordingly took place, attended by thousands, on the 12th of August. His remains were interred in the cemetery at Ardwick Green.

'In stature, Dalton was about the middle size, of strong rather than of elegant proportions. The likeness between his head and face and those of Newton was often observed during his lifetime, and is said to have become more striking after death. Till his seventieth year, he enjoyed robust health; and he was all his lifetime fond of exercise in the open air. He made a yearly journey to his native mountains of Cumberland and Westmoreland, and climbed Helvellyn, and often also Skiddaw. He was very methodical and regular in his habits. The afternoon of every Thursday he spent at a bowling-green, where he could join with some congenial associates in a turn at the old English game of bowls. He was equally regular in attending the meetings of the Society of Friends, at which he was present twice every Sunday. On the same day he was in the habit, for more than forty years, of dining at a friend's house; and even when the family were absent, he paid his accustomed visit.

'In endeavouring to form a conception of his mental peculiarities, we shall be assisted by comparing him with some of his great fellow-chemists. The labourers to whom chemistry has been indebted for its greatest advances, admit of a natural division into two great classes. The one of these, and by far the smaller, contains men possessed of enthusiastic, imaginative, poetical temperaments, of sanguine, hopeful spirits, and great rapidity, subtlety, and comprehensiveness of mind. Such pre-eminently was Davy; such is the great living chemist Liebig; and if we accept a very subtle fancy instead of a far-stretching imagination, such, too, was Priestley. The other and larger class consists of men in whom the poetical element was at a minimum, who were characterised by great patience, self-concentration, and perseverance in thinking; for whom the working motto was, "Non vi sed sæpe cadendo:" and in whom great self-possession and self-reliance were strongly developed, producing indifference to the opinion of others, and, in extreme cases, an almost repulsive hardness, sternness, and severity of character. To this class belong Black, Cavendish, Wollaston, Bergman, Scheele, Lavoisier, Dalton, and, if we include the living, and confine ourselves to our own country, Faraday, Graham, and Thomson. Thinkers of both these classes have done, and will yet do, excellent service to chemistry. We sum up their peculiarities in a word, if we say, with the late Dr Henry, that the great object of the first class is to discover truth; of the second, to avoid error.

'Such was Dalton; a simple, frugal, strictly honest, and truthful man. For the independence, gravity, and reserve of his character, he was doubtless much indebted to his birth as a Cumberland yeoman, and his long connexion with the Society of Friends. The individuality of his nature showed itself in his great mathematical capacity, his thorough self-reliance and power of patient, persevering work, the native clearness of his intellectual perception, and the extraordinary power of fearless generalisation which he brought to bear upon what nature unfolded to him. In the latter quality, in particular, he excelled every one of his scientific contemporaries.

'The inhabitants of Manchester have announced their intention of erecting a monument to Dalton's memory. We trust that the proposition of founding a chair of chemistry, especially for the exposition of chemical atomics, will take the precedence of every other, as the best means of carrying out that intention. Every one, we think, must feel that bronze statues, or other costly erections, would be altogether out of keeping with the character of the plain Quaker man of science. A "Dalton" chair of chemistry, on the other hand, would be a fitting memorial, and in conformity with the wishes of him* whom it is intended to honour. We offer these suggestions with all deference to those who seek, by some befitting token, to keep before us the memory of Dalton, because we should grieve to

* Dalton, it is well known, left the sum of L.2000 to endow such a chair at Oxford; but revoked it before his death, with the view, it is believed, of giving the money to friends who had assisted him in his early days.

think that a great sum of money had been spent for this purpose in vain. So far as he himself is concerned, we have no fear. Dalton will never be forgotten. He is the second Newton of English physics, and will go down to posterity along with the first.'

DUTY—A TALE.

TRANSLATED FROM THE FRENCH.

DISPLEASURE was strongly marked on the habitually placid features of Monsieur Dormans. His wife was busily engaged in some household duty, but he neither noticed her, nor made any of his usual inquiries or remarks concerning the events of the past day. Victoire, his daughter, and Louise, his niece, were each embroidering a black lace veil by the light of a small lamp. Victoire's eyes were often raised to the lamp, as if intreating it to give more light: Louise was less engrossed by her work; she seemed to be anxiously expecting some one, for whenever a step was heard on the stairs, she turned eagerly towards the door, and as the steps passed on, stole an uneasy glance at her uncle's troubled countenance.

This scene was passing at Lyons, in the Rue des Augustins. The clock of St Louis's church struck nine. M. Dormans wound up his watch, paced the room impatiently for some minutes, and then asked if supper was ready. On Madame Dormans observing that it would be served in a quarter of an hour, he replied, 'Say rather we must wait a quarter of an hour longer for Mr Edward; where can he be at this hour?'

'Promise me not to be angry with him?' said the mother imploringly, as she approached her husband.

'I shall promise nothing,' he replied sternly; 'why is he not at home?'

'You are too severe upon him, my dear; young men will naturally seek amusement. He is gone to the theatre to see——'

The steady piercing look of the father so disconcerted the poor mother, that she was forced to apply to Louise for the name of the piece: it was the Huguenots.

'And where does he find means to pursue these pleasures, he who gains nothing?' asked M. Dormans sternly. 'Who has supplied him with money to go to the theatre? Doubtless his sister or his cousin, from their little earnings?'

'His pleasures are so few,' urged the mother.

'Are mine more numerous?'

The father's displeasure threw a gloom over the supper; it was eaten in silence; and all but M. Dormans retired soon after. Edward came in at eleven.

'I have been waiting for you, sir,' said his father.

The young man endeavoured to excuse himself.

'Your employers are dissatisfied with you; they have complained to me to-day of your negligence and incapacity.'

'I have no taste for measuring cloth all day long,' said Edward sullenly.

'Desjardins is my intimate friend, and your mother's relative; he will promote you. As soon as you have proved yourself competent and trustworthy, he has promised to give you a situation worth from two to three thousand francs a-year.'

'I have an unconquerable dislike to trade. For the last twelvemonth I have been learning to manufacture cloth, and during the whole of that time have been a prey to sorrow and disgust.'

'That is to say, you would rather be idle?'

'I should like to work at my own time and pleasure; to be at liberty to walk out when the weather invites me, and to be no longer a slave.'

'For forty and six years,' said the old man gravely, 'have I reckoned figures before a grated window, into which the sun never shines, and I have never asked for a more agreeable occupation.'

'You were perhaps fond of arithmetic, father?'

M. Dormans looked at his son with ill-suppressed anger as he replied bitterly, 'I also loved pleasant walks and sunshine; but duty forbade the indulgence of these relaxations, and I obeyed. It was not by enjoying the fresh air, and lounging under the trees through the warm summer days, that I was enabled to keep you at school so long. Your mother wished you to have a better education than your father, and what is the result? The ignorant father must toil for the learned son. Absurd vanity! What is the use of your knowledge, if it cannot teach you to maintain your place in society? I am sixty-five years old, and for fifty-five of those years I have been indebted solely to my own exertions for support. When about ten years of age, on returning from school one day, I found my mother weeping bitterly. She had made up a small parcel of some of her wearing apparel, and was going out to sell it. "Do not sell it, mother," I cried; "but tell me what I can do for our support." "Alas! my child, you are too young," she said. "I love you," was my reply; and the following day I obtained employment, and gained more than any other boy of my age.'

'But, father,' said Edward, somewhat abashed, 'I do not dislike work; I only ask a profession that I can like.'

'And what would you wish to be?'

'An artist, father. I have painted in secret for a long time, and my endeavours were favourably received at the last exhibition. That is the path of life to which I am destined; I can apply to nothing else.'

'You wish to be admired and spoken of,' said M. Dormans severely; 'and you mistake your foolish vanity for genius. You neither possess the perseverance nor the ardour requisite to make a good painter, and never, with my consent, shall you embrace that profession.'

These discussions were often renewed, but neither would yield to the other. The father remained inflexible, and the young man continued to neglect his commercial duties for the indulgence of his favourite pursuit. This struggle between father and son threw a shade of sadness over the little household; but none felt it so acutely as Louise, Edward's cousin. They had been brought up together; and Madame Dormans, in conversation with the young girl, had often alluded to the probability of a union between them, so that Louise had gradually accustomed herself to look upon Edward as her future husband. She became of age, and M. Dormans, with his accustomed scrupulous exactitude, gave his accounts into her hands, and placed her little fortune of thirty thousand francs at her own disposal. The same evening Edward found the entire sum in his desk, with the following note:—

'This sum will enable you to go to Paris to complete your studies as an artist, and take the place to which your talents entitle you. Accept it as a loan from a friend, and make her happy by seeing you so.'

Edward was at no loss to discover from whom the money and note had come. He loved Louise sincerely, and it was his dearest wish to be one day united to her; but the uncertainty of his present position had hitherto forced him to be silent on that subject. Now, however, he hastened to the parlour, where he found the young girl alone; and tenderly embracing her, exclaimed, 'I accept it, Louise, on the condition that you will accompany your *husband* to Paris!'

A month afterwards the young couple arrived at the great metropolis, where Edward hoped to follow his chosen profession with success, having now no one to oppose his inclinations. Landscapes and flowers were the branches of the art to which he had specially devoted his attention, and he began to work with ardour, in hopes of proving to his father, by prompt and brilliant success, the injustice of his opposition, and the failure of his predictions.

But, alas! success did not come so rapidly as his sanguine aspirations had led him to expect: his ardour soon began to abate, and ere long he had returned to his former careless and indolent habits. Louise vainly endeavoured to discover the cause of the alteration in her husband. If she hazarded a gentle remark on his inactivity, he found fault with his colours, with the light, with the noise from the street; with everything, in fact, but the only true fault—his inconstant and yielding nature. The freshest flowers faded in the water in which he had placed them, before he had even sketched their outlines, and then he murmured at the evanescent nature of his models. His easels were always covered with bedaubed canvass; for no sooner was a painting begun, than he abandoned it for something new; and it was seldom that he finished anything. His fondness for walks and amusement soon returned: he spent whole days lounging about the public galleries and gardens; dreaming of fame, but too indolent to pursue the road which led to it. This unprofitable manner of spending his time gave him occasionally some remorse; but he had not sufficient moral courage to keep his resolutions of amendment. He retired to rest at the close of each day regretting the ill use he had made of it, and wishing and intending to do something on the morrow. But when it came, he was as little disposed to work as before: his head was heavy; his mind void of enthusiasm; he 'wanted inspiration,' he said; and, as usual, went to seek it in the streets of the metropolis, or in its beautiful environs. The fruitful inspiration did not come, and another day was spent as vainly as the last. The search for a fine subject absorbed his attention for a long time; and when at length he thought he had succeeded in finding one, he took up his pencils and began to work with some degree of enthusiasm. But the exhibition was at hand; he became frightened at the few days that remained; the painting, well begun, became a task, and his conceptions of the beautiful and sublime were swallowed up in the absolute necessity of haste.

'It was thus the great Rubens painted,' said he, by way of comforting himself, and reassuring his wife. 'A patient execution, and an exquisite finish, are only for inferior minds. Genius prompts a rapid flight with daring sublimity.'

With these sentiments the painting advanced rapidly, and was finished in time. The first day the Louvre was opened to the public, Edward hastened thither, expecting to see his picture in one of the most conspicuous places. But he sought it in vain; his grand production had been refused! Some artists of merit had met with the same affront through prejudice, and Edward, numbering himself among these distinguished victims, consoled himself with the reflection, that it was frequently the fate of genius to be unappreciated. It was, nevertheless, a severe blow, and discouraged him not a little. Unfortunately, he attributed his failure partly to the comparative obscurity of his life, and resolved to visit more, and to form acquaintance with artists of note. This was a new mode of dissipation; and as Louise had become a mother, and could not leave her child, he soon acquired the habit of leaving her alone. The affectionate and inexperienced young wife could not think her husband to blame. She never complained of his long and frequent absence, for fear of grieving him; and then he was so kind and gentle towards her, so attentive to all her wants; he apologised for leaving her so much alone with such apparent sorrow, representing to her how necessary it was that he should use all his endeavours to succeed in his profession, Louise had not the heart to chide, or even to think herself unhappy.

Three years passed away. Another infant had come to increase the expenses of the little household: the greater part of Louise's little fortune was spent: she began to think of the future with dread, and communicated her anxiety to her husband.

'You are in the right, Louise,' said he. 'I really must do something. I have wasted time enough in unprofitable visits and amusements; but a painter's life, you know, cannot resemble that of a clerk; it is a life of passion and irregularity. An artist may be months without touching the pencil, but a few weeks' work will often amply atone. And, after all, I cannot think I have been altogether idle; I have a dozen subjects in my head that only want working out. I muse upon them in the crowd; I dream of them at night.' Produce them, then, Louise might have said; but she was silent. 'I only ask,' continued Edward, 'a few more days of relaxation and enjoyment before I shut myself in my study, and devote my whole time and attention to these great subjects.'

Three weeks from that time he felt the absolute necessity of a pleasure tour. 'Nature called him,' he said; 'he was weary of the world, of noise and bustle. He wanted to see the ocean, and seek inspiration in its grandeur and sublimity.' Louise bent her head over her baby's face to conceal a tear.

When Edward returned, his wife requested to see his sketches and studies from nature. He had nothing to show: one day the fine weather, and another the rain, had prevented him from doing anything.

'I have produced nothing apparent, it is true,' said he in some confusion, 'but I have done a great deal interiorly; my head and imagination are stored. We artists, even in our repose, are progressing towards fame; but pray do not torment me with your puerile fears, or all the inspirations of genius will vanish.' Louise said nothing, but her eyes were opened; and when her husband delayed the commencement of a painting till *to-morrow*, she sighed or smiled sorrowfully. At the same time, she did all in her power to retard the poverty he was preparing for them. She discharged her maid, under the pretence that she did not suit her; and did all the household work herself, besides attending to her little ones. She sat sewing beside them during the long winter evenings, until the night was far advanced, with one candle and no fire; and ere long, these watchings and anxieties produced their usual effect—her cheek paled, and her eye lost its brightness; she daily became more weak and languid, until at length she herself began to be frightened at her condition.

And Edward still continued to trifle away his time among companions as idle and thoughtless as himself, and was only roused from his indifference by the intelligence that a very small sum remained of Louise's money. This startled him. He shut himself determinedly in his study, and finished two or three paintings, that were not refused this time. His wife had witnessed the change with joy; and ill as she was, resolved upon accompanying him to the Louvre, to view his productions, and enjoy the admiration he expected they would excite. But, alas! they were obscurely placed, and all the notice they attracted was a cursory glance. Near the best of them, however, the young couple saw with delight two gentlemen, one of whom was a noted artist, and the other a well-known connoisseur, whose word was law. They stopped to examine the painting, and Edward and his wife approached to hear their opinion and judgment. 'Only look,' said the connoisseur, 'at the slovenliness and incorrectness of that piece. It is not a picture; it can hardly be called a sketch; everything is wanting but presumption.'

'What is chiefly wanting,' observed the painter, 'is the creative power. The painter is evidently one of those young upstarts who can talk a great deal, but is incapable of performing anything, and who has nothing of the artist but his aspirations. His hundredth piece will be like this—it will be a crude idea, but never a picture. He was not born for an artist.'

'That is evident,' returned the connoisseur, and they passed on.

Edward remained pale and motionless. 'They are mistaken, love,' whispered Louise.

'I fear not,' said he, humbled and despairing; 'all they have said is true, quite true: I see it now. That painting is cold, senseless. I could trample it under my feet!'

'Edward,' said Louise imploringly, 'be calm, I intreat you, and if you have been mistaken, remember we are still with you—I and your children.'

The conversation at the Louvre was for Edward a ray of light. He began to doubt his talent for painting; but, alas! this was only another motive for inaction. Incapable of acting with resolution, and seeking the end of life, not in the fulfilment of duty, but in self-gratification, he abandoned himself to discouragement and despair. Louise's health continued to decline, and resolving to know the worst, she sent for a noted physician, at a time when she knew her husband would be absent. She explained every symptom, answered all his questions, and then, looking earnestly at him, intreated him to tell her candidly if it was possible for her to recover.

'It is possible, madam,' coldly replied the physician; 'your disorder has not reached the last stage; but you must obey my directions implicitly.'

'What are they?'

'Absolute rest, no watching, and, above all, no painful emotions.'

Louise burst into tears, and exclaimed, 'My children must then be orphans, for none of this is permitted or possible.'

The physician bowed gravely, and withdrew. As the door closed upon him, that of the study opened, and Edward entered in tears.

'No, dearest, our children shall not be orphans,' he said, tenderly embracing his wife; 'I was there and heard all. Can you forgive me, Louise? I have been an egotist and a coward!'

Louise started.

'Yes, a coward,' he continued; 'for I have done nothing to maintain mine own. I have not had the virtue of the meanest journeyman of our street. But tranquilise yourself, love; from this day I have found my true place, and shall, I hope, keep it;' and again embracing his wife, he went out.

Louise was glad to see a change in her husband, but uneasy about his present projects. She, however, waited patiently for him till the evening was far advanced. Still he did not return, and she began to be terrified lest some evil should have befallen him. The night was dark and stormy; heavy drops of rain began to fall; the dark waters of the Seine rolled sullenly along. A kind of delirium seemed to have seized upon the young wife. Overcome by her undefined apprehensions, she went from her sleeping children to the window, and from the window to her children, her hands joined in supplication, and asking nothing but her husband's return. At length she fancied she saw him coming along the dark street, and, without waiting to hear him knock, flew to the door, opened it, and exclaiming, 'Thank God, you are safe!' fell fainting into his arms. She soon, however, returned to consciousness; and her husband, after soothing her over-excited feelings, told her that, having heard that M. Duteuil, the rich manufacturer of Lyons, was in Paris, he had gone to seek him. Louise's eyes asked the reason. 'See,' said Edward, showing her a paper, 'this is the contract by which I have engaged myself as designer in his establishment.'

'Ah, now I am convinced that you love me!' exclaimed Louise, embracing her husband.

'My dreams of fame are over,' continued the young man; 'I understand at length that the law for each is to make inclination yield to duty and circumstances; and you, Louise, shall not fall a victim to your husband's unpardonable indolence.'

Edward returned to Lyons, fulfilled the duties of his new situation diligently, and made his wife happy.

CURIOSITIES OF HERALDRY.

MR M. A. LOWER, whose treatise on surnames we formerly introduced to the reader's notice (vol. xi. p. 283), has published a new work under the above title,* which we find to be not less curious and amusing in its details. His panegyric on heraldry we entirely pass over: enough for us is the fact, that the most refined portion of the European community have, during several ages, found in this science a solace for their best aspirations, and that it has consequently become a portion of the history of civilisation. The custom of expressing characters and pretensions emblematically in fashions of clothes and arms, and figures borne upon both, seems to have taken its rise in Germany during the century preceding the conquest of England by William of Normandy. It assumed a fixed character in England about the reign of Richard I., who appears on his great seal of date 1189, with two lions combatant on his shield. The Crusades added to its stock of emblems; and by the time of Edward I., 'we find that all great commanders had adopted arms, which were at that date really *coats*, the tinctures and charges of the banner and shield being applied to the surcoat or mantle, which was worn over the armour, while the trappings of horses were decorated in a similar manner.' 'In the succeeding reigns,' says Mr Lower, 'the science rapidly increased in importance and utility. The king and his chief nobility began to have heralds attached to their establishments. These officials, at a later date, took their names from some badge or cognizance of the family whom they served, such as Falcon, Rouge Dragon; or from their master's title, as Hereford, Huntingdon, &c. They were, in many instances, old servants or retainers who had borne the brunt of war, and who, in their official capacity, attending tournaments and battlefields, had great opportunities of making collections of arms, and gathering genealogical particulars. It is to them, as men devoid of general literature and historical knowledge, Mr Montagu ascribes the fabulous and romantic stories connected with ancient heraldry; and certainly they had great temptations to falsify facts, and give scope to invention, when a championship for the dignity and antiquity of the families upon whom they attended was at once a labour of love and an essential duty of their office.'

In time, armorial bearings and devices spread far beyond men of the sword. Every peaceful bourgeois corporation had its 'arms:' even monasteries and ladies were thus decked out. We have ourselves recollections of shopkeepers' signs in country towns adorned with the emblems thus spoken of by our author:—'Persons of the middle class, not entitled to coat-armour, invented certain arbitrary signs called MERCHANTS' MARKS, and these often occur in the stonework and windows of old buildings, and upon tombs. Piers Plowman, who wrote in the reign of Henry III., speaks of "merchauntes' markes ymedeled" in glass. Sometimes these marks were impaled with the paternal arms of aristocratic merchants, as in the case of John Halle, a wealthy woolstapler of Salisbury, rendered immortal by the Rev. Edward Duke in his "Prolusiones Historicæ." The early printers and painters likewise adopted similar marks, which are to be seen on their respective works. A rude monogram seems to have been attempted, and it was generally accompanied with a cross, and occasionally a hint at the inventor's peculiar pursuit. The heralds objected to such marks being placed upon a shield; for, says the writer of Harl. manuscript, 2252

* London: John Russell Smith. 1845. 8vo. pp. 320.

(fol. 10), "THEYS BE NONE ARMYS, for every man may take hym a marke, but not armys without a herawde or purcyvaunte;" and in "The duty and office of an herald," by F. Thynne, Lancaster Herald, 1605, the officer is directed "to prohibit merchants and others to put their names, marks, or devices in escutcheons or shields, which belong to gentlemen bearing arms, and none others."'

We have from Mr Lower a long chapter on heraldric charges, enumerating the many various objects thus employed. Among them are both reptiles and insects, not excluding the toad and gadfly. 'Such was the taste for allusive arms, that the Botreuxes of Cornwall relinquished a simple ancient coat in favour of one containing three toads, because the word "botru" in the Cornish language signified a toad.' Another chapter enumerates the many chimerical animals, as the unicorn, dragon, griffin, cockatrice, wyvern, which figured upon coats armorial, and as supporters. 'The unicorn of antiquity was regarded as the emblem of strength and the guardian of chastity. His horn was a test of poison, and in virtue of this peculiarity the other beasts of the forest invested him with the office of water-"conner," never daring to taste the contents of any pool or fountain until the unicorn had stirred the waters with his horn, to ascertain if any wily serpent or dragon had deposited his venom therein. Upton and Leigh detail the "wonderful art" by which the unicorn is captured. "A mayde is set where he haunteth, and she openeth her lappe, to whome the Vnicorne, as seeking rescue from the force of the hunter, yeldeth his head, and leaneth all his fierceness, and resting himself vnder her protection, sleapeth vntyll the is taken and slayne!" The Hebrew *reem* being rendered in our version of the Bible unicorn, has confirmed the vulgar notion that the animal intended was the cloven-hoofed and single-horned figure of heraldry. But there is nothing in the word sanctioning the idea that the animal was single-horned; and on referring to the passages in which the term is introduced, the only one which is quite distinct on this point seems clearly to intimate that the animal had *two* horns. That passage is Deut. xxxiii. 17. "His horns are like the *horns* of the reem:" the word here is singular, not plural, and should have been "unicorn," not "unicorns," in our version. It has lately been attempted to prove that the reem of Scripture was the animal now known as the nhyl-gau. Leigh declares the unicorn of our science to be a mortal foe to elephants, and such, according to zoologists, is the character of the rhinoceros. These two are, however, the only points of resemblance; for, while the unicorn of heraldry is of light and elegant symmetry, the rhinoceros of the African deserts is an animal so clumsy and ponderous, that it has been known to require eight men to lift the head of one into a cart.'

Allusive arms are elaborately treated by our author. He gives lists of the most curious—as *Wolseley*, a wolf's head; *Foulis*, three leaves (feuilles, Fr.); Fraser, three strawberry leaves (fraises, Fr.); *Wylie*, a fox; *Trotter*, a horse, &c. He then comes to crests and badges, on which he is most learned. 'Badges are a kind of subsidiary arms used to commemorate family alliances, or some territorial rights or pretensions. Sometimes, also, and perhaps more generally, they serve as trophies of some remarkable exploit achieved by an ancestor of the bearer. In the feudal ages, most baronial families had their peculiar badges, and their dependents were recognised by having them embroidered upon their sleeves or breasts. They were generally placed upon a ground tinctured of the livery colours of the family. Something analogous to this fashion is retained in the crest which adorns the buttons of our domestic servants, and still more so in the badges by which the firemen and watermen of London are distinguished. Badges were also employed in various other ways; as, for example, on the furniture of houses, on robes of state, on the caparisons of horses, on seals, and in the details of Gothic edifices. An instance of the various applications of the badge of one noble family has been familiar to me from childhood—the Buckle; the badge assumed by Sir John de Pelham in commemoration of his having been principally concerned in the capture of John, king of France, at the battle of Poictiers. This trophy occurs as an appendage to the family arms, into which it is also introduced as a quartering; on the ecclesiastical buildings, of which the family were founders, or to which they were benefactors; on the architectural ornaments of their mansions at Laughton, Halland, &c.; on ancient seals; as the sign of an inn near their estate at Bishopstone, &c.; and among the humbler uses to which the buckle has been applied, may be mentioned the decoration of the cast-iron chimney-backs in the farmhouses on the estate, the embellishment of milestones, and even the marking of sheep. Throughout the whole of that part of eastern Sussex over which the Pelham influence extends, there is no "household word" more familiar than the PELHAM BUCKLE.'

It is uncertain as to mottoes whether they arose from the pious expressions placed in ancient times upon tombs, as DREDE GOD, JESU MERCY, LADY HELPE, or from war-cries used for mutual encouragement at the moment of onset, of which the following are specimens:—The king of France, 'Montjoye St Denis!' The king of Scots, 'St Andrew!' The emperor of Germany, 'A dextre et a sinistre!' They are classed as enigmatical, sentimental, and emblematical. According to Mr Lower, 'The enigmatical are those whose origin is involved in mystery, as that of the Duke of Bedford, "Che sara, sara"—What will be, will be; and that of the Duke of Bridgewater, "Sic donec"—Thus until ——! A late barrister used "Non bos in lingua"—I have no bull upon my tongue; alluding to the Grecian didrachm, a coin impressed with that animal, and expressive, probably, of the bearer's determination not to accept a bribe. The motto of the Lords Gray was, "Anchor, fast anchor;" and that of the Dakynses of Derbyshire, "STRIKE DAKYNS; THE DEVIL'S IN THE HEMPE"—enigmatical enough certainly.

'Sentimental mottoes are very numerous. A multitude of them are of a religious character; as "Spes mea in Deo"—My hope is in God; "In Deo salutem"—In God I have salvation; "Sola virtus invicta"—Virtue alone is invincible; "Non mihi, sed Christo"—Not to myself, but to Christ; "Sub cruce"—Under the cross. Many are loyal and patriotic; as "Vincit amor patriæ"—Love of country conquers; "Non sibi, sed patriæ"—Not for himself, but for his country; "Patria cara, carior libertas"—My country is dear, but my liberty is dearer. Others are philanthropic; as "Homo sum"—I am a man; "Non sibi solum"—Not for himself alone. Treffry of Cornwall used "WHYLE GOD WYLLE," and Cornwall of the same county, "WHYLE LYFF LASTETH."

'But the most curious class of mottoes are the emblematical, some of which allude to the charges in the arms, and others to the surname, involving a pun. Of those allusive to the arms or crest, the following are examples:—That of the Earl of Cholmondeley is "Cassis tutissima virtus"—Virtue the safest helmet; alluding to the helmets in his arms: and that of the Egertons, "Leoni, non sagittis fido"—I trust to the lion, not to my arrows; the arms being a lion between three pheons, or arrow-heads. The crest of the Martins of Dorsetshire was an ape, and their motto, HE. WHO. LOOKS. AT. MARTIN'S. APE, MARTIN'S. APE. SHALL. LOOK. AT. HIM.!' In a long miscellaneous list which follows, we find many which consist of puns. D'Oyle of Norfolk bears, 'Do no YLL, quoth D'Oyle!' Fairfax, 'Fare fac!' Speak, do—A word and a blow. Dixie of Leicestershire, 'Quod dixi dixi'—What I've said I have said. Fitton, *Fight on, quoth Fitton*. For Mr Lower's benefit, we take leave to introduce one which we lately saw in connexion with the arms of Menzies of Menzies, over the door of the old church of Weem in Perthshire, and which excels all we know in pith and brevity—'VIL GOD, I SAL.' Let any one try, by any other arrangement of ten letters, to say as much. The date of the stone is 1600.

Some curious anecdotes appear under the head 'Historical Arms; Augmentations.' For example—'Bulstrode of Bulstrode, co. Bucks, bore, as a crest, A bull's head, erased gules, attired argent, between two wings of the same. When William the Conqueror subdued this kingdom, he gave the estate of this family to one of his own followers, and lent him a thousand men for the purpose of taking possession, *vi et armis*. The rightful owner calling in the aid of some neighbouring gentlemen (among others, the ancestors of the Penns and the Hampdens), gallantly resisted the invader, intrenching himself with an earthwork, which is still pointed out as evidence of the truth of the story. It seems that the besieged party, wanting horses, mounted themselves upon *bulls*, and, sallying out of their camp, so affrighted the Normans, that many of the latter were slain, and the rest put to flight. The king, hearing of this strange affair, and not wishing to push matters to an imprudent extent, sent for the valiant Saxon, with a promise of safe conduct to and from his court. The Saxon paid the Conqueror a visit, riding upon a *bull*, accompanied by his seven sons similarly mounted. The result of the interview was, that he was allowed to retain his estate. In commemoration of these events, he assumed the crest above described, together with the name of *Bulstrode!* The whole narration exhibits strong characteristics of that peculiar genus of history known as "Cock and *Bull* stories;" although it is probably quite as true as a distich preserved in the family, that

WHEN WILLIAM CONQUERED ENGLISH GROUND,
BULSTRODE HAD PER ANNUM THREE HUNDRED POUND.'

Another—'Sir Richard Waller was at the battle of Agincourt, where he took prisoner Charles, Duke of Orleans, father of Charles XII. (afterwards king of France.) This personage was brought to England by his captor, who held him in "honourable restraint" at his own mansion, at Groombridge, co. Kent, during the long period of twenty-four years, at the termination of which he paid 400,000 crowns for his ransom. In accordance with the chivalrous spirit of that age, the captor and captive lived together on terms of the strictest friendship. This appears from the fact, that the duke, at his own expense, rebuilt for Sir Richard the family house at Groombridge. He was also a benefactor "to his parish church of Spelhurst, where his arms remain in stonework over the porch." Previously to this event, the family arms had been the punning device of "Sable, on a bend voided argent, three *walnut* leaves or;" and the crest, "A *walnut* tree fructed proper." To one of the lower boughs of this tree was now appended a shield, charged with the arms of France—"Azure, three fleurs-de-lis or, differenced with a label of three points;" an augmentation which continues to be borne by the descendants of Sir Richard Waller to this day.'

Some arms bore reference to the situation of the family mansion. Thus Wallop, Earl of Portsmouth, has 'argent, a bend wavy sable,' alluding to a *well* springing from a hillside or *hope* near the family house in Hampshire; the name being derived from this local circumstance. 'Hume of Nine Wells, the family of the great historian, bore, "Vert, a lion rampant argent within a bordure or, charged with *nine wells* or springs barry-wavy azure and argent." "The estate of Nine Wells is so named from a cluster of springs of that number. Their situation is picturesque; they burst forth from a gentle declivity in front of the mansion, which has on each side a semicircular rising bank, covered with fine timber, and fall, after a short course, into the bed of the river Whitewater, which forms a boundary in the front. These springs, as descriptive of their property, were assigned to the Humes of this place as a difference in arms from the chief of their house."'

'Here,' says Mr Lower, 'we may be allowed to digress, to say a few words on the origin of *inn signs*, which are generally of a heraldric character. In early times, the town residences of the nobility and great ecclesiastics were called inns, and in front of them the family arms were displayed. In many cases these inns were afterwards appropriated to the purposes of the modern hotel, affording temporary accommodation to all comers. The armorial decorations were retained, and under the names of signs, directed the public to these places of rest and refreshment. On calling to mind the signs by which the inns of any particular town are designated, a very great majority of them will be recognised as regular heraldric charges. In addition to the full armorials of great families, as the Gordon Arms, the Pelham Arms, the Dorset Arms, we find such signs as the Golden Lion, Red Lion, White Lion, Black Lion, White Hart, Blue Boar, Golden Cross, Dragon, Swan, Spread Eagle, Dolphin, Rose and Crown, Catherine-Wheel, Cross-Keys, *cum multis aliis*, abundant everywhere. These were originally, in most cases, the properly emblazoned armories of families possessing influence in the locality; and frequently the inns themselves were established by old domestics of such families. But owing to the negligence of mine host, or the unskilfulness of the common painter who from time to time renovated his sign, the latter often lost much of its heraldric character; the shield and its tinctures were dropped, and the charges only remained; while, by a still further departure from the original intention, three black lions, or five spread eagles, were reduced to one. A house in the town of Lewes was formerly known as the "Three Pelicans," the fact of those charges constituting the arms of Pelham having been lost sight of. Another is still called "The Cats," and few are aware that the arms of the Dorset family are intended. In villages, innumerable instances occur of signs taken from the arms or crests of existing families, and very commonly the sign is changed as some neighbouring domain passes into other hands. There is a kind of patron and client feeling about this—feudality some may be disposed to call it—which a lover of old England is pleased to contemplate.'

The work is elegantly printed, and contains many illustrative wood-engravings.

BIRTHS, MARRIAGES, AND DEATHS IN ENGLAND.

ONE of the most ponderous presents which her majesty has commanded to be made to both houses of parliament for some time, is an immense blue-book, some five inches thick, containing the annual report of the Registrar-General for births, deaths, and marriages.* It is compiled from the registers of the year 1842, and presents a mass of statistical information not only important in a legislative point of view, but highly interesting to the general reader.

From the complication of facts collected concerning BIRTHS, we learn that during the year 1842 there were born in England 517,739 children. Comparing this number with the amount of births which respectively took place in the three previous years, we find further corroboration of the uniformity with which nature operates in dealing with large masses of facts of every description:—In 1839 there were 492,574 children born; in the following year, 502,303; in 1842, the increase of population by births was 517,739. Thus the increase was gradual and uniform. The Registrar-General proves that, during the four years 1839–42, about 6¼ per cent. of the whole female population were mothers; that is to say, out of every hundred women who lived in England during that period, one in every sixteen produced a baby. The proportion for the respective years were, in 1839, of every hundred women, 6·211 was a mother; in 1840 the per centage was 6·250; in 1841 it was 6·289; and in 1842, 6·273. The most

* The Sixth Annual Report of the Registrar-General of Births, Deaths, and Marriages registered in England during the year 1842. Presented to both Houses of Parliament by command of her Majesty.

prolific parts of England were Lancashire and Cheshire, where the number of births in proportion to the population was 3·599 per cent. The least prolific were the south-eastern districts, in which the per centage was 2·887.

Concerning the next great event in human existence —MATRIMONY—the Registrar-General has accumulated a mass of statistics quite commensurate with the importance of the subject. In 1842 there were wedded in England 118,825 couples. Of these, 26,198 had been previously married; namely, 15,619 widowers, and 10,579 widows. By striking an average of the gross number of marriages which occurred in the four years 1839-42, the result appears that there was one marriage in each year to every 130 individuals living. In 1842 there were fewer persons married by from three to four thousand than during any of the three previous years, which the Registrar accounts for by the commercial depression of that year. But this surmise (which he calls a 'fair inference') is quite at variance with the opinions and facts produced by M. Quetelet and Mr Rickman, who found that when distress most prevailed, marriages were most largely resorted to as a ready but improvident solace for misery. Besides, the Registrar's inference is far from a 'fair' one: for what is the fact? The 'great depression of trade, and stagnation of commerce,' which he adverts to, were far more severe in the three years previous than in 1842, when the dawn of prosperity began. Now, in 1839 there were 4341 more marriages, and in 1841, 3671 more than in 1842; so that the fairest inference is, that Quetelet's and Rickman's deductions in reference to the effect of national distress on matrimony are correct, and that not commercial stagnation, but that prudence which invariably accompanies a gleam of prosperity, was the cause of the decrease of marriages during 1842. That greater prudence prevailed, from whatever cause, is proved by another fact. By a reference to the ages of the persons wedded in 1842, we perceive there was a decrease of youthful, and therefore of rash and imprudent marriages. The minors married in 1841 were 21,647; in 1842, 21,390, or about 1 per cent. less than the former number; whilst the diminution in the number of persons of full age married was 7085 in 223,345, or 3 per cent.—facts which seem to be favourable to the future wellbeing of the population, who must inevitably suffer more or less by an increased number of (too often improvident) marriages. In the south and east of England, the proportion of marriages to the population was either stationary or only slightly increased; while in other parts of the country, and in the metropolis, they decreased. This supplies us with another corroboration of an important and singular natural law, which statists have discovered; namely, that the greater the number of marriages in a community (up to a certain point), the fewer the births. The south-eastern districts of England (see above) were the least prolific by about 1 per cent., while in nearly the same counties the proportion of marriages to the population was if anything increased.

We now come to the statistics of MORTALITY. In 1842 the number of deaths amounted to 349,519, or nearly 1 in every 46 of the then population: the average annual rate of mortality for the five years 1838-42 was 1 in 45 persons. The mortality in Cheshire, Lancashire, Yorkshire, the metropolis, and the northern and midland divisions, remained below the average; whereas in the southern divisions of the island the mortality was higher than in 1841, and higher than the average of those divisions for 1838-42, which, nevertheless, had in the five years fewer deaths in comparison to their population than any other tracts of country of equal extent from which returns had been obtained. In 1842, the mortality under five years of age was somewhat lower—of persons at more advanced ages a little higher—than in the preceding year. The rate of mortality in England appears to be lower than in France, Prussia, Austria, and Russia.

From a comparison of the births with the deaths which occurred in the years 1839-42, we discover that, as the gross amount of the former was 2,024,774, and of the latter 1,391,979, the excess of births was in that period 632,795; so that the mean annual increase of population was about 158,199. Supposing this rate of augmentation to be quite uniform, and remembering that the last census gave the population of England, on the 1st July 1841, at 15,927,867, its probable increase by the 1st of July of the present year from births alone will raise it to nearly 16,600,000.

Some interesting but at the same time painful facts are disclosed relative to unexpected and violent deaths. Many remarkable cases were given, showing what slight causes are sufficient to terminate life, either through ignorance, inadvertence, or the want of proper precaution. Amongst others, we find a case of tetanus produced by a stick thrust up the nose, choking by a string, suffocation by substances intruding themselves into the windpipe, choking from a bullace, convulsions from eating hard peas, explosion of fireworks in the pocket, a knitting-needle piercing the hand, eating yew-berries, taking poisons by accident, an over-dose of tartar emetic, cantharides, oil of bitter almonds, incautious use of mercury, drinking aquafortis, eating berries of the dulcamara, inhaling the fumes of whitelead, drinking spirits and spirits of wine, the bite of a pig, &c.

The tables contained in this enormous folio will doubtless supply bases for important legislative enactments. A revision of the mortality tables, upon which assurance-offices charge their usually too high premiums, will, we trust, be an early effect of this voluminous report.

A WORKING MAN'S MEMOIRS.

THE thirty-fourth issue of Mr Knight's 'Weekly Volume for all Readers' consists of the autobiography of a journeyman tailor, which, without offering much to interest general readers in point of incident, furnishes an instructive lesson of patient perseverance and honest industry. The hero mentions neither his own name nor that of his native town—an unnecessary delicacy, for which no reason is given, but which deprives the reader of a main source of interest. The memoirs—which are written in plain, homely, but good English—are not the first attempts of their author in literature, for, amongst other productions, he previously wrote The Manual for the Apprentices to Tailors, which formed one of the Guides to Trade published by Knight and Co.

It appears that from the beginning this working-man was doomed to misfortune, and that his existence was only prolonged from the hour of his birth by an accident. 'I was born,' he narrates, 'on July 5, 1792, but in so feeble a state, as to be thought dead. After having been put aside for some little time, a neighbour in attendance upon my mother observed that I showed symptoms of being alive, on which she took me in hand, and thus saved me from a premature death. But although it was given me to live, I proved to be of a feeble constitution, which in subsequent years brought upon me many infirmities and inconveniences. I am indeed unable to apprehend fully the pleasurable sensations attendant upon robust and unbroken health, having never enjoyed that invaluable blessing; but I suppose them to be very delightful, and cannot but wish that all who possess what is called "good health" were duly sensible of its value.' Still, he grew up in an ailing state, and when about five or six years old, was taught to read by his mother, who kept a dame's school, and at ten became a candidate for admission into a Protestant dissenter's charity school. It was required that applicants for admission should present themselves to the managing committee, to prove their capabilities by reading in the New Testament. The autobiographer proceeds to draw a graphic picture of the class of people who, half a century ago, were the patrons of educational establishments. It will amuse the modern reader. 'I well remember the subdued feelings with which I wended my way to the place of trial. It was on a winter's evening, when the dreary aspect of everything around me was in keeping with the solemnity of the business in which I was engaged. It was well for me that my good mother took me under her wing, as otherwise I should certainly have been confounded when I came before my examiners. These worthy, but to me awful, personages were assembled in a large upper room of an ancient inn. They were seated around a fire that was blazing cheerfully, and almost eclipsing the light of the candles, which of themselves would have but just sufficed to make "darkness visible." I was too much abashed to allow of my surveying the room very closely; what I saw of it, therefore, was only by occasional and hasty glances. I observed, however, that the table was well furnished with bottles and glasses, pipes and tobacco, indicating that the company present thought it wise to relieve the cares of business by a little of that which tends to make the heart glad. I cannot now remember all who were present, but have a clear recollection of several, among whom was the minister of the congregation, an aged, venerable-looking man, whose close-fitting, neatly-curled wig, and somewhat antiquated dress, accorded well with his age and character. There was also a worthy gentleman, one of the deacons, whose portly figure, powdered head, and commanding aspect, filled me with profound awe. He was, however, a kind-hearted and affable man. I could have spoken without much perturbation to either of these good men, had I met him alone and casually; but to see them all at once in a strange place, and invested with authority to question me, was too much for one so timid as I then was. A novitiate monk in the august presence of his holiness, and a full conclave of cardinals, or a presumed heretic at the tribunal of the Inquisition, could hardly feel more discomposed than I did when directed to read aloud in the hearing of my assembled judges. I obeyed this dread mandate with much trepidation, but was enabled to do it so as to escape censure. My mother gave such further information about me as was required: upon which I was unanimously elected, with some expressions of approbation.

'Thus ended my much dreaded trial, to my no small relief and satisfaction: I had passed through the ordeal unscathed, although much frightened, and I could not but rejoice at my success. I was well satisfied with the treatment I had met with from my examiners; but, as a faithful chronicler, I am bound to state that I was not a little puzzled at a part of their proceedings. They were smoking; and as I had been accustomed to regard this practice as indicative of intemperate or loose habits, I was greatly surprised at seeing "grave and reverend" men like these wielding the ominous tobacco-pipe. Even the minister was thus employed: this was the most inexplicable circumstance of all. I afterwards learned that he was an inveterate smoker, which intelligence further increased my perplexity. I feared that all was not right, but I was too poor a casuist to grapple with so knotty a question; I was therefore compelled to leave it until I should be more equal to the task.'

While at school, the future working-man describes his habits as having been studious. He was very fond of reading, and made great sacrifices to obtain books, and to get leisure to read them. When only thirteen years old, he obtained a situation as an errand boy to a tailor and woollen-draper. His duties were neither light nor pleasant, for he was constantly at the beck of no fewer than twenty-one persons; namely, 'his master and mistress, five children, two maid-servants, a shopman, two apprentices, a foreman, and eight journeymen.' In this very large family, however, he found a friend in his master's son, who, amongst other favours, gave him access to a library which consisted of 'Enfield's Speaker, Goldsmith's Geography, an abridged History of Rome, a History of England, Thomson's Seasons, the Citizen of the World, the Vicar of Wakefield,' and a few others. To be able to read these books, says our hero, 'I arose earlier from bed, read while walking or eating, and took care not to waste the spare minutes which sometimes fell to my lot in the course of my working-hours. By these means I saved more time in the aggregate than I had previously thought to be possible. It was indeed made up of fragments, yet I contrived to make it answer my purposes.' With praiseworthy perseverance, he also learnt to become an expert tailor in the few spare hours which fell to his share; and the manner in which this sickly but persevering youth economised his time, fully realises the adage, that 'where there is a will there is a way.' 'Instead of cleaning the tailor's shop, preparing fuel, and getting the furnace ready in the morning, I did these and other needful things at night, after the men had left off work; by this plan I secured an hour, in the best part of the day, for learning to sew. In addition to this contrivance, I also rose yet earlier than before, in order to help one of the workmen who lived close at hand. I worked with him until it was time to go to the shop, and by this means got both instruction and a little money—sometimes as much as eightpence or tenpence at the week's end—which was no unimportant addition to the contents of my private purse. Besides these plans, I adopted that of working at home whenever an opportunity offered for so doing. Nor did I always allow myself to make a holiday of even the few red-letter days that fell to my lot; for I well remember having worked on a Good Friday, a beautifully fine day, which seemed almost audibly to invite me into the green and delightful fields. On that day I also contrived to amuse myself by committing to memory a large portion of Gray's beautiful Ode on Vicissitude. I further remember to have worked on other holidays—especially on that which, in 1809, was kept in commemoration of the king having entered upon the fiftieth year of his reign. By dint of persevering industry and attention, aided by the good offices of several of the workmen, I soon got such an insight into the business as enabled me to be very useful upon the board. Ere long my master saw that my services there were more profitable to him than they could be elsewhere; and therefore he consented to hire another, but a younger boy, to do the greater part of the work which previously had chiefly employed my time.' This welcome promotion materially diminished the labours, and increased the comforts and emoluments of the persevering youth, who, when he had arrived at man's estate, had acquired not only a proficiency in his trade, but a valuable stock of literary information; for he still went on reading whenever a moment of leisure presented itself.

The working-man, finding himself a competent tailor, determined to try his fortune in London, and travelled thither in 1810. The information conveyed in the following passage is curious:—'On the day after my arrival in London, I went out in quest of employment. This I did in the way which at that time was the most in favour with my fellow-craftsmen, as being thought both more respectable and more profitable than that of waiting upon masters to ask for work. This was by causing my name to be entered in the call-book of a tailors' trade-club, which was held, as all such clubs then were, at a public-house, thence denominated a "house of call." To these houses the masters applied when they wanted workmen. They could here procure, if needful, a fresh supply of men three times per day; namely, at six o'clock in the morning, then at nine o'clock, and again at one o'clock in the afternoon. The master had the power of discharging a workman at his pleasure, after having given him three hours' work or wages. Thus the men could have as many as three masters in the course of one day.

'I was called to work during the very day on which I had my name entered on the call-book; but it was merely for the remainder of that day, as my master was himself a journeyman, who wanted a little help about an occasional job of master-work. Here I was in due form invested with all the shop-board rights and privileges of the craft, by paying what was technically called my "footing;" that is, in plain English, by treating my workfellows to a fair allowance of porter—a practice which I subsequently set my face against, and with much success. At night I was discharged, and again repaired to the "house of call," where I received orders to go to work at six o'clock in the following morning for a master residing in Hatton Garden. I now felt myself at ease. I had fairly launched my tiny bark upon the broad expanse of life's ocean, and I was resolved, if possible, to make a profitable voyage. With this view I applied myself to work with all practicable diligence. It required my utmost efforts to get through the allotted amount of a day's work within the appointed time—for the time, as well as the amount of work, was strictly regulated. This daily task was considerably too much for any one but a clever and very quick hand; but then, as it was fixed by the workmen themselves, there was neither room for complaining of the masters, nor any good end to be answered by grumbling to the men. I therefore took the matter quietly, and did my best. This task was, in shop-board phrase, called "the log;" and a very appropriate name it truly was, for the task was indeed a heavy one. Yet, as it showed the equitable principles upon which our trade-unions were founded—in providing that the largest possible amount of labour should be given in exchange for the good wages demanded—it was generally approved of even by such as, like myself, were not fully equal to the labour it imposed. When I received my first week's wages, amounting to thirty-three shillings, I was not a little pleased. I felt that I had fairly performed the part of a man, and my self-love prompted me to look upon so meritorious a personage as myself with more respectful feelings than heretofore. My week's wages was a larger sum than I ever before could at one time call my own; I was therefore comparatively a rich man. Yet, after all, I would gladly have taken three shillings per week less in wages, if thereby I could have escaped from the pressure of that incessant, and, to me, exhausting toil which I was compelled to undergo, in order to keep up to "the log." My strength, like that of many others, was not equal to this toil, especially in so hot and otherwise unhealthy a place as is a tailor's workshop, in which I was confined for full twelve hours per day, the hours of working being from six o'clock in the morning until seven o'clock in the evening, one hour only being subtracted for dinner. As to time for breakfast, or any other refreshment, there was not allowed even a moment.'

In this way he went on, sometimes overwhelmed with employment, at others with nothing to do, but on the whole maintaining himself creditably, till he resolved to take unto himself a wife—in the person of a young woman he had long known. His wedding-day is thus described:—'About the end of May 1819, we were married at St Paul's, Covent Garden, which was my parish church. We spent a part of our wedding-day in looking at the royal artists' exhibition of paintings at Somerset House, in which we found much that gave us very pleasant entertainment. Afterwards, as the day was beautifully clear and serene, we indulged ourselves with a short excursion, in a westerly direction, upon the broad and gently-flowing Thames.' In a few days he returned to his native town, where he commenced business on his own account.

Years passed on, the working-man being gradually surrounded with a large family, whom he brought up in a praiseworthy manner, living respectably and respected amidst the companions of his youth; but constitutional ill health, increased by his energetic exertions to support his family with credit, demanded change. His physician assured him, he remarks, 'that nothing more could be done for me in the way of medicine while I continued to breathe the somewhat keen air of my native town. I therefore resolved to try whether that of London would be more favourable. I had, as I have already observed, been effectually relieved by it when a younger man, and I hoped it might prove useful to me again, although I did not expect it would be so to the same extent as formerly.' Accordingly, the working-man again changed the scene of his labours, and indeed the nature of them; for having published a volume of lectures previously delivered by himself in his native town, and obtained, through that, other literary engagements, he divided his time between the pen and the needle. This is, it appears, his present mode of livelihood, and he concludes his memoirs in these words:—'Except when wholly overborne by bodily pain or infirmity, I am *rarely* unemployed, either in the day-time or in the sleepless hours of the night, of which I have not a few. I aim to be useful, and am occasionally encouraged to believe that I am not wholly unsuccessful. Not unfrequently a cheering ray breaks through the clouds that rest upon the future, and shows me some glimpses of a brighter world and a happier state of being. Thus I pursue my course with tolerable equanimity of feeling. There is much attainable good wherewith to compensate the inevitable evils of my lot. I aim to secure the first, and would fain extract some good from the second. Unceasing occupation of the mind upon some given subject, and with a view to the happiness of others, is one of the best means of drawing off the attention from personal sufferings, and of preventing the affections from becoming either chilled or selfish. The work of writing these memoirs has many a time raised me above the depressing influence of great bodily disorder. I should grieve that my task is done, but that I have already resolved to begin another.'

The want of uncommon incidents is well supplied in this little story of a good and well-spent life, by the indomitable self-reliance which the author exemplifies in every page. It is considered creditable for a man of robust constitution to fight through the world unscathed, and to bring up a family respectably amidst the strife; but for one who from his cradle was borne down with sickness—occasionally prostrating him for weeks, undoing all which care and industry had previously done—to arrive towards the close of existence so well as our author has done, is assuredly a sort of heroism. We take leave of the working-man, wishing him all success in his future career.

APOLOGY FOR THE NERVES.

Sir George Lefevre, M.D., has published a clever volume under this somewhat eccentric title, which by no means expresses the miscellaneous character of the work, though justified in some degree by the author's theory as to the concern of the nervous system in the production of various diseases. We have been particularly struck by Sir George's speculations on the Cholera Morbus, which came strongly under his attention at St Petersburg. Here, especially, he insists on the important part played by the nervous system; but the main impression left on the mind is, that the Asiatic scourge of 1832-3 arose primarily from meteorological causes.

'I had,' says he, 'during my residence in St Petersburg, some opportunities of seeing this disease in its most murderous form; for the deaths in the city averaged more than a thousand daily at its onset. I published the results of some of my experience, and now, after a lapse of fourteen years, I must subscribe to the truth of Dr Holland's assertion, as expressed, page 568, in his Notes and Observations:—"That strange pestilence of our time, which, while affrighting every part of the world by its ravages, has seemed to put at nought all speculations as to its causes, or the laws which govern its course—a disease, nevertheless, which, by the mystery of its first appearance, its suddenness, inequality, and fatality, and the failure hitherto of every method of treatment, may well excite the inquiry of all who are zealous for the extension of medical science." The idea of its originating in insect life was adopted by several German professors very soon after its first appearance. The eccentric movements of the malady, its zig-zag direction, quitting the broad line of route, flying off at a tangent to appear in a widely distant point, would all argue certain atmospheric currents wafting their poisonous contents in regions beyond our powers of arrest.* Dr Prout's observations, proving that there was a constant increase in the weight of the atmosphere, deserve much attention in our future investigations, for this may not have been a casual coincidence; its constancy during the whole prevalency of the disease militates against this opinion. Freely confessing that what we professed to know about this plague, when in the heat of the battle, was but mere presumption, we still pertinaciously adhere to the belief of its non-contagious character; and we repeat, in the words of our former little treatise, "As far as my practice is concerned, both in the quarter allotted me, and also in private houses in different parts of the town, I have no proof whatever that the disease is contagious. In one case I attended a carpenter in a large room, where there were at least thirty other workmen, who all slept upon the floor among the shavings; and though this was a very severe and fatal case, no other instance occurred among his companions. In private practice, and amongst those in easy circumstances, I have known the wife attend the husband, the husband the wife, parents their children, children their parents, and in fatal cases too, where, from long attendance and anxiety of mind, we might conceive the influence of predisposition to operate, yet in no instance have I found the disease communicated to the attendants; . . . so that, as far as proof can be drawn from my own limited experience, I have none to offer in favour of contagion." In the history of its prevalence in St Petersburg, it is certain that the anti-contagionists did increase with the increase of the disease; and its spread over Europe has considerably increased their ranks, and the number of those has much diminished who contributed at one time to excite so much alarm among the people.

'This is, perhaps, all the knowledge we have gained upon the subject, and the evidence has been sufficient to convince most that the disease has nothing in its form or features, nor in its mode of propagation, which can entitle it to rank amongst those of a positively contagious character. Even negative evidence may become positive in certain circumstances, and of this the town of Odessa has furnished convincing proofs at two separate periods since the retreat of the cholera from Europe. It was found that the strictest military cordons did not, in any country whatever, arrest its progress. It stole its way through them, dodged the sentries—defied the point of the sword and bayonet.

'It is said to have reached Sunderland by a ship which left Hamburg before it was recognised to exist in that city, where its appearance some days afterwards was sufficient, with some logicians, to prove that it was imported from thence. It must be recollected that none of the crew were attacked by it on the voyage; and here we may quote Dr Holland:—"Nor will previous communication, though certainly concerned in part in the transmission of the disorder, resolve these singularities." It was not human contagion that operated in this instance. Still, this distinguished physician observes, "Man becomes an agent in the diffusion," p. 577; and again, in his hypothesis of insect life as a cause of this disease, he observes, "But also possessing the power of reproducing itself, so as to spread the disorder by fresh creation of the virus which originally produced it."—P. 574.

'To return to the Hamburg brig, which discharged her cholera cargo at Sunderland, and might then, as far as her crew was concerned, have got a clean bill of health, it is still an anomaly that she should transport a disease from a town where it did not exist when she left the port, when so many more ships could not effect this which left infected ports. This was the case with Elsinore, where upwards of five hundred vessels touched, all chartered in the port of Cronstadt, where the cholera raged furiously. We do not know that up to the present day this town was visited by a single case, although its *vis a vis* across the Sound, the Swedish town, where no vessels touched, suffered severely. This is one of the inexplicable frolics of this disease.

'Now, with respect to the negative evidence, which becomes positive. The plague has twice been imported into Odessa from Turkey within the last few years, and several have died of it; but by means of rigid quarantines and cordons, and the energy which Count Woronzoff displayed in arresting its progress, such as hanging a Jew who was about to violate the laws established, not a single death occurred without the city; the plague never got out of the gates.

'Why should not the same observances and precautions, for they were the same, have succeeded in both cases? The cholera has never been arrested by human means in its progress—the plague often.

'When the former has located itself in a country, it will be easy enough for those so disposed to find evidence of its human communication and propagation from one town to another. A man may take it by railroad from Liverpool to Manchester, at least be supposed to do so; but have we evidence of its first invasion in this way wherever it has appeared? Has any landsman, any sailor, made his appearance in any place with the disease upon him, and first communicated it to the inhabitants of town or village? It was not so propagated in Sunderland. It was not so in St Petersburg. Hundreds came into the latter city from Moscow, where it raged eight months previously: not a soul was affected on the whole line of route. When it did appear, the same anomaly was presented as in the Hamburg ship. It was said to be brought down by the tallow barks from the frontiers of Siberia, though not a single bargeman had been affected during the long transit. The man who was said to be first affected was not so till after his arrival in St Petersburg. In three days every quarter of that wide spreading city was grievously punished by the disease. The man died in the suburbs of the town amongst the lowest class of the inhabitants, none of whom could, directly or indirectly, have communicated with the higher orders. Many locked themselves up in their rooms as soon as the disease was announced, and died isolated from human communication. There was no more proof that the bargeman brought it than that he found it at St Petersburg. It is the argument *ad absurdum* to say that it should take a tortuous route of three thousand miles to arrive there, when it was raging for seven months at Moscow, a distance of five hundred only, and with which there were all the time daily communications.

'A fact well worthy of note is the circumstance, that of the eleven medical men who fell a sacrifice to it in St Petersburg, they were almost all practitioners who had the least to do with it—men practising in private, and not those who were attached to the great hospitals, of whom I do not recollect that more than one perished; and precisely the same observation was made by one of our colleagues who practised in Dantzic.

'As regards the nature of the disease, Dr Wilson has observed—"Epidemic cholera is the result of an atmospheric poison, or other vice in the blood." I had two opportunities of seeing its attack—of recognising the first symptoms of its presence.

'I observed a labourer who was walking in the street stagger, reel, put his hand to his head, and fall down. I thought he was in liquor, and overcome by the heat of a burning sun. Upon approaching him, I found him attacked by cholera. He was removed to the nearest hospital. I do not know his fate. A director of one of the cholera hospitals was presiding at a committee where I was present. In discussing some matter with one of the physicians, he suddenly put his hand to his forehead, and complained of a shooting pain through his head, which he attributed to having taken a pinch of strong snuff. It increased, however, in the evening. It was the commencement of the disease, which carried him off on the fifth day. In these two cases it would appear that the brain was first attacked. In some few instances it hardly deserved the name of spasmodic, to judge from the outward manifestation of spasm. I have known it kill in six hours, without much pain in the muscular fibre, but here the injury done to the nerves was more manifest. The derangement of all those functions under their control—as the loss of animal heat, suspension of secretions, conversion of insensible perspiration into clammy sweat, the almost involuntary pouring out of the contents of the stomach, all proved how much the great vital power was paralysed. Of the offence to the blood there can be no doubt, and of the reaction of this diseased fluid again upon the nerves; but it is questionable if the poison first creep in through the blood. Supposing the poison to be in the blood, the spasm and cramp are in the muscles, and this in a ratio with the virulence of the poison.

'As regards the use of opium, it was found, as Dr Wilson has stated, to be followed by very deleterious effects. Low nervous fever was the result of its employment in repeated

* This would equally apply to malaria, which is transportable in this way, as proved by Dr Macculloch.

doses; and if the disease were thoroughly formed, it was never arrested by the use of this drug: but I must add, that for those uneasy symptoms which threatened a commencement, a dose of laudanum, combined with an antispasmodic, stood me in much service in my practice. In many, probably in most cases, there was no other disease to combat than the effects of fear, where this antidote proved useful. The patient, attentive to every little pain and ache, was rendered more susceptible of the malady, and the immediate relief afforded him by this diffusible stimulus dispelled his fears of future consequences. John Brown, one of the brightest but most eccentric meteors that ever illumined the medical horizon, has observed, that no man, however disposed he might be to commit suicide previously, would ever think of doing so after a dose of laudanum, at least while under its intoxicating influence. He ranked it amongst the most powerful stimulants. I therefore put all who were in the habit of consulting me in possession of a "sovereign remedy," in case of need, and I had no reason to repent of so doing.'

Amongst other subjects treated by Sir George are the Blood, Sympathy, Dreams, Headaches, Fevers, Homœopathy, and Mesmerism. An observation which he makes in the last mentioned chapter—that, if some of the alleged facts be true, they are miracles—seems to us eminently unphilosophical: they would only show, we apprehend, that our ordinary views of the compass of nature are too limited. The following anecdotes are new to us, and very striking:—'As long as nervous excitement can be kept up, the resistance of cold is very great. General Piroffsky informed me, that in the expedition to Khiva, notwithstanding the intenseness of the cold, the soldiers marched along singing, with the breasts of their coats open, but only as long as they were flushed with the hopes of success. Where there is nothing to excite, and where exposure to cold takes place under the common routine of parade, its depressing effects are lamentably felt by those long exposed to it. In the time of the Grand Duke Constantine, a regiment of horse was marched from Strelna to St Petersburg, a distance of twelve miles and upwards. He marched at their head at a foot-pace all the way. He had well wadded himself, and smeared his face over with oil. It was the gratification of a whim to expose the soldiers to a great degree of cold. They arrived at the square before the palace, and were dismissed to their barracks. The following day one-third of the regiment was in the hospital, attacked by nervous fever, of which many died. There was no stimulus of necessity in this case, but the moral feeling aggravated the physical suffering.'

COMPANY.

There is a certain magic or charm in company, for it will assimilate and make you like to them by much conversation with them. If they be good company, it is a great means to make you good, or confirm you in goodness; but if they be bad, it is twenty to one but they will corrupt and infect you. Therefore be wary and shy in choosing and entertaining, or frequenting any company or companions; be not too hasty in committing yourself to them; stand off awhile till you have acquired of some (that you know by experience to be faithful) what they are; observe what company they keep; be not too easy to gain acquaintance, but stand off and keep a distance yet awhile, till you have observed and learned touching them. Men or women that are greedy of acquaintance, or hasty in it, are oftentimes snared in ill company before they are aware, and entangled so that they cannot easily get loose from it after when they would.—*Sir Matthew Hale.*

CURIOUS EFFECTS OF EARTHQUAKES.

The St George's Chronicle—island of Grenada, West Indies—mentions the following remarkable fact: namely, that on the occurrence of the earthquake there on the 19th of January 1844, those clocks of which the pendulums oscillated from east to west were almost all stopped, while those whose pendulums vibrated north and south were not affected. It is also mentioned that the needles of the compasses on board the Thames steamer, which was then among these islands, revolved on their centres with great rapidity during the convulsion.

THE PAINTER'S LOVE.

The summer day had reached its calm decline
When the young painter's chosen task was done,
At a low lattice, wreathed with rose and vine,
And open to the bright descending sun,
And ancient Alps, whose everlasting snows
And forests round that lonely valley rose.
Yet lovely was the brow and bright the hair
His pencil pictured; for an Alpine maid,
In blooming beauty, sat before him there;
And well had the young artist's hand portrayed
The daughter of the south, whose youthful prime
Was bright as noontide in her native clime.
Perchance the maiden dreamt not that amid
The changeful fortune of his after days
That early-treasured image should abide,
The only landmark left for memory's gaze.
Perchance the wanderer deemed his path too dim
And cold for such bright eyes to shine on him;
For silently he went his lonely way,
And, like the currents of far-parted streams,
Their years flowed on; but many a night and day
The same green valley rose upon their dreams—
To *him* with her young smile and presence bright,
To *her* with the old home, fires, love, and light:
For she, too, wandered from its pleasant bowers,
To share a prouder home and nobler name
In a far land. And on his after hours
The golden glow of art's bright honours came;
And time rolled on, but found him still alone,
And true to the first love his heart had known.
At length, within a proud and pictured hall,
He stood amid a noble throng, and gazed
Upon one lovely form, which seemed of all
Most loved of sages, and by poets praised
In many a song; but to the painter's view
It had a spell of power they never knew;
For many an eye of light and form of grace
Had claimed his magic pencil since its skill
To canvass gave the beauty of that face.
But in his memory it was brightest still;
And he had given life's wealth to meet again
The sunny smile that shone upon him then.
There came a noble matron to his side,
With mourning robes and darkly flowing veil,
Yet much of the world's splendour and its pride,
Around long silvered hair and visage pale;
But at one glance, though changed and dim that eye,
Lit up the deserts of his memory.
It brought before his sight the vale of vines,
The rose-wreathed lattice, and the sunset sky,
Far gleaming through the old majestic pines
That clothed the Alpine steeps so gloriously.
And oh! was this the face his art portrayed,
Long, long ago beneath their peaceful shade!
The star his soul had worshipped through the past,
With all the fervour of unuttered truth—
His early loved and longed for, who at last
Gazed on that glorious shadow of her youth!
And youth had perished from her; but there stayed
With it a changeless bloom that could not fade.
The winters had not breathed upon its prime,
For life's first roses hung around it now,
Unblanched by all the waves and storms of time,
That swept such beauty from the living brow;
And withering age, and deeply cankering care,
Had left no traces of their footsteps there.
The loved one and the lover both were changed,
Far changed in fortune, and perchance in soul;
And they whose footsteps fate so far estranged,
At length were guided to the same bright goal
Of early hopes; but oh to be once more
As they had been in that sweet vale of yore!
They cast upon each other one long look;
And hers was sad; it might be with regret
For all the true love lost; but his partook
Of wo, whose wordless depth was darker yet;
For life had lost its beacon, and that brow
Could be no more his star of promise now.
And once again the artist silently
Passed from her presence; but from that sad hour,
As though he feared its fading heart and eye,
Forsook all mortal beauty for the power
Of deathless art. By far and fabled streams
He sought the sculptured forms of classic dreams,
And pictured glories of Italian lore,
But looked on living beauty never more.

FRANCES BROWNE.

Stranorlar, Jan. 1845.

Printed by William Bradbury, of No. 6, York Place, and Frederick Mullett Evans, of No. 7, Church Row, both of Stoke Newington, in the county of Middlesex, printers, at their office, Lombard Street, in the precinct of Whitefriars, and city of London; and Published (with permission of the Proprietors, W. and R. CHAMBERS,) by WILLIAM SOMERVILLE ORR, Publisher, of 2, Amen Corner, at No. 2, AMEN CORNER, both in the parish of Christchurch, and in the city of London.—Saturday, April 5, 1845.

CONDUCTED BY WILLIAM AND ROBERT CHAMBERS, EDITORS OF 'CHAMBERS'S INFORMATION FOR THE PEOPLE,' 'CHAMBERS'S EDUCATIONAL COURSE,' &c.

No. 67. NEW SERIES. SATURDAY, APRIL 12, 1845. PRICE 1½d.

ARCHÆOLOGY OF THE WORD COCKNEY.

THE attributes of a 'Cockney'—a term exclusively applied to a native of London—are fast passing away. His chief characteristics arose from his being always confined within the walls of 'The City;' for, seldom ranging beyond them, he had the credit of being ignorant of rural affairs, and indeed of everything which did not exist within the bounds of London. Now, however, every day lessens the number of Londoners to whom such circumscribed notions can be fairly attributed. The spread of knowledge has dispelled his prejudices, and the locomotive advantages of steam have enlarged his sphere of actual observation. The Cockney is fast becoming a character of past time, and Cockneyism a matter of history.

As it is always pleasant to preserve fading traditions, we purpose saying a word or two on the origin of the term Cockney, and on the peculiarities of the almost extinct class to whom it is applied.

A Cockney is a denizen of Cockaigne, a nick-name for the overgrown capital which William Cobbett called 'The Great Wen,' and which has also received the titles of the 'Great Metropolis,' the 'Modern Babylon,' and many other less apt but equally humorous designations. Etymologists, in tracing the origin of the term Cockaigne, have pushed their persevering and erudite researches as far back as the annals of classical Greece. It means a land of plenty; and Pherecratus, a comic author of Athens, who was contemporary with Plato, furnished the earliest idea on record of the country which afterwards got the name of the land of Cockaigne. The first description of a place actually so called was given in the thirteenth century, in a French poem entitled 'The Land of Cockaigne.' To save our readers trouble in endeavouring to ascertain the whereabouts of this favoured country, we must premise, that reference to the usual sources of geographical information will assuredly fail; for, like the Happy Valley of Rasselas, and the Territories of Oberon and Titania, it only existed in the pages of a story-book. The poem commences by stating that its author having made a pilgrimage to Rome, to obtain absolution for his sins, the pope inflicted penance by banishment. On arriving at the scene of exile, he was agreeably surprised to find that, instead of its being a place of pains and penalties, it was the head-quarters of luxurious ease—

> 'For in this country—called Cockaigne—
> The more I sleep, the more I gain.'

It was a perfect larder of good living; the walls of the city were made of divers comestibles, the rafters of immense sausages, the roofs of lard, and the laths of barley-sugar. In the streets were tables liberally supplied with eatables, of which everybody was invited to partake; and there were shops from which goods were to be had without money. A river ran through the city, which consisted on one side of red wine, and on the other of white, whilst three times every week it rained hot custards. Concerts and balls were perpetually given; and no such thing as disagreement or war was known, for people had everything in common. All the females were young and engaging; because in this delightful country existed the fountain of youth, so that whenever a lady began to look old, she had only to drink of the waters, and she felt and looked young again. This glowing description differs but little from the similar one by Pherecratus. Another Greek author, Felecidus supplied a few even more luscious traits to the absurd picture, which the French writer failed to copy. He declared that delicious sweet cakes disputed with equally nice bread which should enter the mouth of the visitor first, and the fish came into the houses ready fried. The Romans added ('Festival of Tremalum'), that tempting little pigs ran about the streets ready roasted. From these materials the author of the Land of Cockaigne formed his picture; and since his time, Cockaigne, adopted probably from the Latin word *coquino*, to cook, has always been used to express a land of plenty.

Festivals in honour of this fanciful territory were held all over Europe till a recent period. The latest account of one we find in Keysler's Travels in Italy, published in 1778. 'Among the public entertainments at Naples,' he says, 'one of the most remarkable is the procession with four triumphal cars on the four Sundays immediately preceding Lent; the first loaded with bread, the second with flesh, the third with vegetables, and the fourth with fish. These provisions are piled up very high, with musicians placed at the top, and guarded by armed men, till they are given up to be pillaged by the populace. But that which draws the greatest concourse at Naples is the *Cocagna* or Castle, built according to the rules of fortification, and faced all over with pieces of beef, bacon, hams, geese, turkeys, and other provisions, with which the imaginary country of Cocagna is said to abound; where the very trunks or branches of trees are supposed to be Bologna sausages. This welcome spectacle is exhibited once a-year; and on each side of the castle is a fountain running with wine during the whole day. A party of soldiers is posted to restrain the ardour of the populace till the viceroy appears in the balcony, which is the signal for the assault.'

Having shown that the 'Cockney Country' meant, ever since the thirteenth century, a land of good cheer, we proceed to state how London came to be distinguished by that flattering appellation. Hicks, in his Anglo-Saxon grammar (vol. i. p. 254), explains the connexion by remarking that the nick-name Cockney, or inhabitant of Cockaigne, was used by the French in early times to designate an ease-loving, gluttonous individual. This term was generally applied by the rural population to the inhabitants of towns and large cities, because—devoted to sedentary employments—they were supposed to obtain the means of a more luxurious life by little exertion. When, therefore, London rose to importance, it was looked upon as a city overflowing with wealth and luxury—a sort of Utopia. This idea took its rise, not unreasonably, from the extraordinary privileges which the citizens exacted from the earliest kings of England in return for the loans of money which they constantly made to the crown. Indeed, up to the protectorate of Cromwell, to be a burgess of the city of London was to possess privileges and immunities of real pecuniary and social value. It is no wonder, then, that the less favoured part of the population should give to the metropolis attributes not very dissimilar to those of the imaginary country of Cockaigne, and should thence call its citizens 'Cockneys.'

We learn from Dugdale that this nick-name was applied to Londoners at a very early period. The lawyers of the Temple had a feast held on Candlemas-day (28th December), over which a character called king of the Cockneys presided. It would appear, from orders issued by Henry VIII. in 1517, that this rival majesty had taken unto himself a few not very proper privileges, and that his subjects had occasionally exceeded the bounds of good order, for the bluff monarch enjoins that 'the *king of Cockneys*, on *Childermas-day*, should sit and have due service; and that he and all his officers should use honest manner and good order, without any waste or destruction making in wine, brawn, chely, or other vitails; and also that he, and his marshal, butler, and constable marshal, should have their lawful and honest commandments by delivery of the officers of Christmas, and that the said king of Cockneys, ne none of his officers medyl neither in the buttery, nor in the Stuard of Christmass his office, upon pain of forty shillings for every such medling.' This custom seems to have been discontinued after the great rebellion.

To be a true Cockney, a person must be born within the sound of the bells of Bow Church, which, being situated in the centre of the city, could be heard in every part of it. For in those quiet times, when this condition to the title of Cockney was impósed, there were few carriages in the streets to drown the peal, locomotion being performed either by means of the river Thames, or by horses on soft unpaved streets. In other words, then, a Cockney must be born within the walls of the city.

That an unusual love of good eating and drinking, and the ability to indulge in the pleasures of the table, has perpetuated the designation to the Londoners, is scarcely to be doubted. The capital of England has always been the metropolis of good fare. The lord mayor's feasts have been celebrated for their profusion from the days of William the Conqueror. We have seen the bill of fare of a regal banquet given to the court of Edward III., on the occasion of a tournament held in Cheapside, which would excite the longings of a modern alderman. Nor has the lustre of these celebrated feasts been dimmed by the lapse of four centuries: on the contrary, all the refinements of the foreign *cuisine* have been added to the substantial roast beef of old England; of which several 'barons' were prepared alike for the royal appetite of the third Edward, and for illustrious visitors who graced his lordship's tables on the 9th of November last past; that substantial 'piece de resistance' having been from the earliest ages as necessary to a Guildhall dinner, as the mace to the induction of a new lord mayor, or the regalia to a coronation.

High feeding being so intimately connected with the office of chief magistrate, it is no wonder that it should extend its influence over the lesser functionaries and inhabitants of the city. This influence is so potent, that even to this day—when the salient characteristics of the genus Cockney are worn down and rounded off by the attrition of travel and extended intercourse—the main peculiarity of the Londoner is his extraordinary solicitude to keep his digestive organs in action. The blessings and evils of this life are referred by him to food. By the capability a man possesses of giving good dinners, he judges of his affluence; and in the lower ranks of Cockney life, a neighbour's private circumstances are invariably judged of by the nature and quality of his Sunday dinners. The beggar who appeals to the true Cockney by an assurance that he is hungry, or that he has a wife and seven *starving* children, is sure of relief; for of all the endless variety of forms which human suffering takes, none is so shocking to his sympathies as starvation. Some years ago, during the banishment of Napoleon Bonaparte to St Helena, a gentleman connected with one of the London journals happened to draw, in the presence of a Cockney, an over-wrought picture of the ex-emperor's sufferings: he mentioned his sudden reversal from boundless regal splendour to the narrow conveniences of a remote island—torn from all those he held dear in his own country—pining in obscurity, neglected and forlorn. Here the sympathising listener supplied from his own imagination a finishing touch. 'And then, poor fellow,' he exclaimed, 'perhaps *he's short of victuals too!*' Beyond this

'The force of misery could no further go,'

and the kind soul was visibly affected.

Of lesser Cockney characteristics few traces remain. The Londoner of twenty years ago having every hour of his time fully occupied in the great business of existence, had little leisure for comparing his own knowledge or ideas with more extensively-informed men; and as his intercourse lay chiefly with fellow-Cockneys, his notions were bounded, as it were, by the bills of mortality. London being acknowledged by everybody to be the greatest of cities, its inhabitants, he reasoned, must be the greatest people in the world. Hence Cockneys constituted themselves and their city a standard by which to judge of everything else in nature. Whenever they had to make a simile, one member of the comparison was sure to be something belonging to themselves or to their native Babylon. A Cockney who, by some extraordinary train of events, found himself at the summit of one of the Alps, would be less struck with the stupendous grandeur of the scenery, than with the glorious exaltation of finding himself

'Ninety-nine times as high as St Paul's.'

Place him in the Polar regions, and he would measure the thickness of the ice not in inches, but by its being so much thicker than the ice in the Serpentine or in the London Docks. It is characteristic of a Londoner, also, that his comparisons will be always in favour of London and its attributes. 'The best of everything,' he tells you, 'exists in London.' A city shopman, having been pressed into the sea-service, and captured by the French, described in a letter to his friends the horrors of his prison, mentioning that it was overrun with rats: 'but they are lean, half-starved wretches,' he added; 'and nothing to compare to our London rats.'

This pardonable prejudice in favour of the great metropolis abated, the Londoner is generally acknowledged to be far above the ordinary run of mankind in shrewdness. Constantly moving amidst the most bustling of life's scenes—revolving in a whirl of occupation—he knows the value of time, and makes the most of it. Hence he is quick in his observations, in his motions, in his speech. He sees at a glance what others dawdle and ponder over. He begins and finishes a transaction while a provincial rival is 'turning the matter over in his mind.' His questions are categorical, and his replies direct and decisive. In trade, he loses but little time in buying and selling. 'That's my price,' he will say, if he be a purchaser; 'take it or leave it:' and according to the reply, so he buys or not; but the affair must be settled in a minute. He eats, walks, and even takes pleasure in a hurry. These habits render the Londoner rather pert and authoritative in his manner to strangers; but without his meaning to be so, for it is natural to him. To contradict him is to excite, instead of anger, pity at the dissenter's ignorance; for it is his comfortable creed, that all who disagree with him are in the wrong.

As the rustics retain their local dialects, so uneducated Londoners (amongst which class real Cockneys are now only to be found) cling, with a fondness which no intercommunication can subdue, to their peculiarities of speech. They have a great aversion to the aspirate *h*, and so obstinately substitute the *v* for the *w*, that where the *u* gets a double sound, they put themselves to the trouble of inserting the *v*, even if it be in the middle of a word. Thus they prefer saying *kvaurter* to quarter, and *kveer* to queer. Present participles are not considered complete without a prefixed *a*: hence they are invariably a-coming or a-going. It is in London, also, amongst the lowest orders, that the basest of coined words—slang, is most used.

As we have before remarked, Cockneyism is fast wearing away. Facilities of intercourse with the provinces and with foreign countries,

> 'Modestly discover
> That of themselves which yet they knew not of,'

and have thus taken from Cockneys their self, or rather city esteem. Still, they retain the quality from which they derived their appellation; for now, as ever, the best dinners and the best feeders in the empire are to be found within a radius of two miles of the Royal Exchange.

THE FIRST LADY OF LORETTO.

BY FRANCES BROWNE.

'Never have I seen the carnival so joyously celebrated, nor the devotions of this holy day so carelessly attended,' said Cardinal Montalto to his faithful servant Ludivico, as they stood together on the evening of the first day of Lent under the vast and now silent dome of the great St Peter's.

Cardinal Montalto was one to whom even the conclave looked up with reverence; his great learning—for he was esteemed one of the best theologians of his time, and skilled in the most abstruse questions of controversy—was equalled only by his zealous and somewhat ascetic piety, which eminently qualified him for his office of consultor of the Inquisition, and peculiarly recommended him to the favour of the reigning pontiff, Gregory XIII. His life was without reproach, and his orthodoxy above suspicion; yet it seemed that there was less of love than fear in the deference with which the cardinal was almost universally regarded. He had wrought his way up, it was said, from a very humble origin, through the austerities and labours of the Franciscans, whose vows he had taken while yet a child, but had ever been looked on less as a brother than a censor of the order; and now, though their vicar-general and controversial champion, of whom the brethren might well be proud, they loved him as little as they had done twenty years before, when, as Fra Felix Peretti, he had been driven from their convent in Venice for his censorious sanctity. It was even supposed that the honours which his holiness showered upon him were rather bestowed for the good of the church than the love of the man; for the easy and cheerful character of the old pope formed a strange contrast with the zeal and austerity of the cardinal, whose piety belonged rather to the iron than the golden age of religion. Yet there was one individual of all Montalto had ever known, and of all who had ever known him, though many they were, of high and low estate, and only one who loved him, and whom, if he did not love—for there seemed no room for the gentler affections in his strong nature—at least he trusted, and that individual was his servant Ludivico. How long he had been in the cardinal's service, none in Rome could tell, for his master and he had grown gray together, and years had made them friends; but, saving that both were natives of the March of Picena, there seemed no other bond of union between them, for Ludivico had no share in either his master's zeal or piety, but was still an honest and faithful peasant, as he had been born; more strict, indeed, in the performance of his devotional duties than most peasants of the period; but that was by command of his master, and Ludivico knew no other law.

The last tinge of sunset was fading from the modern palaces and old eternal ruins of Rome, and the gray of the deepening twilight filled the vast but deserted temple in which they stood. The cardinal had that day officiated as the pope's own substitute (for such tasks of late had often devolved on him, as the increasing age and infirmity of Gregory seemed strangely augmented since the last intimation he received of the weakness of the pontificate in the celebrated bandit Marianazzo's refusal to accept a pardon from his hand); but the last of the worshippers had departed, and nothing remained in the great church but the lamp still burning on the altar, and the cardinal, with Ludivico behind him, his tall figure slightly bent as he leant upon his staff, and his dark immoveable countenance turned with an earnest look of old recollection to a beautiful picture of the virgin that hung immediately above the shrine. Many an eye, indeed, had turned with admiration to that picture as well as that of the cardinal, but none with the same gaze of memory; and never did he enter the church of St Peter, whether as a preacher or a hearer, but his first look was there; and never did he leave the holy place, no matter in what haste, without lingering to bestow a farewell glance on the picture of Picena, for so it was called, and said to be the work of an obscure and unknown artist, who had sent it as a pious present to the church, in the same year that Montalto was made cardinal.

'It is growing late, my lord,' said Ludivico, who had often glanced at the door, and hemmed, in the vain hope of breaking up his master's reverie, which seemed on this occasion to be deeper than usual—'it is growing late, my lord: were it not well to return to the palace?'

'Thou art right, Ludivico,' said the old cardinal starting; 'it is indeed late, and we are left alone here. Not a single votary lingers to pray at the holy shrine; nay, not even a priest remains to refresh his spirit by pious contemplation in this most holy place. Oh, Ludivico, it is a degenerate age; the zeal and sincerity of the early times are departed; and even at this sacred season, men give themselves up to the world, as if it were not dust. Not such were they, the men who built this temple, or planned it, before there was a schism in the church, or heresy in Europe. Minds were mighty and sleepless in those days. Look around thee, Ludivico; was there not a shadow of eternity on his soul who planned this glorious building? But the world is growing weak, and we have no Angelos now.'

'Truly no, your eminence; they're all gone astray, doubtless, with the rest of the heretics; and this is a very nice church, and a very great church. But oh, my lord, it is growing late.'

The cardinal looked at him with a compassionate gaze, and said, 'Ludivico, how long hast thou served me?'

'Thirty-five years, your eminence—thirty-five years exactly, all but the three weeks two days and four hours which I served the Marchese de Colonna, when your highness cast me off for forgetting to fast on Good Friday.'

'True, true, Ludivico, that was a grievous sin; but thou hast repented.'

'I have indeed, my lord; but will your eminence return to the palace?'

'In a moment, Ludivico; but look for me at this picture, and tell me, on thy true love and faith, if thou hast ever seen face or form of mortal mould that resembled it?'

Ludivico gazed long and steadfastly at the picture, though he had done so often enough to know every hair upon the virgin's brow; but implicit obedience had become a second nature to him, and he answered, 'As I am a Christian, my lord, I know not any whom this picture resembles excepting, with great humility to the virgin and your eminence, the bandit Marianazzo.'

'What!' said the cardinal with astonishment, which was not often expressed on that calm and stern face, 'he who hath lately insulted the most holy chair of St Peter by refusing pardon from his holiness? Well hath the Scripture said, "cast not your pearls before swine;" and truly the states of the church are now infested by swine, worse than the possessed herd which ran into the sea. It becomes not us to speak lightly of our holy father the pope; but were I in his place,' said the cardinal, as his voice sunk low and he swept the darkening church with an anxious and hurried glance—'were I in his place, no bandit should be offered pardon. Verily, I would use the sword of St Peter to root them out, together with all heretics and infidels; and then would the church prosper. But I am an old man hastening to the grave, and the burden of such a mighty trust is more than ought to be desired.' Montalto spoke the last words in a louder tone; but there was something in his eye that belied them, and Ludivico answered,

'My lord, I have heard your eminence called Fra Felix Peretti, then bishop of St Agatha, next Vicar-General of the Franciscans, now Cardinal Montalto; and in my soul I believe I will live to hear them say your holiness yet.'

'These are vain thoughts,' replied the cardinal; 'yet my father had a dream, and I also have dreamt; but all things are in the hand of God. But, Ludivico, where hast thou seen the bandit Marianazzo?'

'When I served the Marchese de Colonna, he travelled with his daughter, the fair Donna Alonzina, to Naples with a strong escort, and I was one of the train; but the robbers surrounded us on the road, and all our armed men fled, for none could stand before the bandit of Picena. Marianazzo himself was there. But the virgin preserved us doubtless for the piety of the fair flower of Colonna, for so I have heard the donna called; for the bandit took nothing of all the marchese's wealth but a small gold ring from the fair lady's finger; and none but the virgin could turn the heart of a robber from so much riches. Truly, it is sad to think that Marianazzo is a bandit, for he is stately in form and noble in bearing, and his face is so wondrous fair. Oh, your eminence, it is mighty like that picture! But to go on with my story. The bandit left us with many fair speeches and graceful bows to the Donna Alonzina and her father, and, better than that, three good handfuls of gold, which he cast to us poor servants with the air of an anointed sovereign. And we proceeded safely to Naples, from whence your eminence graciously recalled me. But I have heard them say that Donna Alonzina never recovered the fright of that day, and has refused to wed a most noble husband, because of her earnest desire to take the veil. Indeed your eminence may remark her great devotion, for all day long her eyes were never from that picture, and she often comes hither to pray before it.'

'Well she may,' said the cardinal, with a vehemence which he seldom displayed—'well she may, for it hath a most glorious brow: and yet, Ludivico, I saw one of which it is but the shadow. Listen; thou hast served me well and faithfully ever since the days of my poverty, when I was but a friar; but thou knowest not the darkness of my earlier days, when I watched the swine in the fields and the fruit in the gardens of Fermo. My father was a poor Dalmatian exile, to whom Heaven had given only a heritage of hope for his son. He dreamt, Ludivico, of more than the purple for me; but poverty was upon him, and the old man pined night and day, because he could not spare the five bajocchi* demanded monthly by our village teacher; and I, to whom time promised so much, sat by the fountain at the wayside, and learned my first lessons from boys who passed to school. Not far from that fountain, in the garden which I watched, there stood the broken columns of an ancient temple, where the old unforgotten race had worshipped one of the demons that in early times had power over the heathen. But its altar was broken down; for time had made it desolate, and vine and ivy had twined around the columns, and summer covered them with a veil of flowers. I had heard the peasants tell of ancient treasures hidden in those pagan temples; and with a childish hope of finding something to relieve our poverty, I once went there alone early before sunrise. The dew was on the tangled weeds and wild flowers that covered what once had been its marble pavement; but my thoughts were full of the hidden treasure, and stooping at a spot which sounded hollow, I began to dig with my father's spade, when a sound of rustling came faintly through the vines. I looked up with fear—for there are strange voices and shadows that pass yet over these unhallowed places—but a mortal woman stood before me. Ludivico, I have looked on many a face and many a strange scene since, but the memory of that stranger, seen so long ago, is with me yet fresher than them all, and it rises at times upon my dreams, bringing back through many parching years the morning breath of my childhood, that seems like a far-off land of spring, whose light lies behind me for ever. I have prayed—for it seemed to me there was sin in the thought, for it ever came with a longing to see that face once more—and at last it did depart from me; but that picture has brought it back upon mine age. Yet, Ludivico, it is not a dream of sinful vanity. But would that, ere the grave closed over me, I could learn that some blessing had repaid the hand that relieved my first cravings, for I have never been able to trace out her habitation, and long ere this she must be gathered to her place.'

'But, your eminence,' said Ludivico, 'what good work did the stranger do, for no doubt it will be remembered to her in judgment; and with the aid of your eminence's prayers, she may have reached heaven ere this?'

The cardinal groaned deeply, as he answered, 'Have I not taught thee that the good works of heretics and infidels avail not, and no prayers can avail for them? but thou art ignorant.'

'Truly I am, my lord,' as a beast. But what did the stranger do?' answered Ludivico, whose absolute submission to the will of his lord was in this instance equalled by his curiosity, and horror too; for he added in the same breath, 'Holy Virgin, preserve me! I knew not that she was a heretic.'

'Thou didst not, good Ludivico,' said the cardinal in a more kindly tone; 'but listen—the lady smiled on me, for I was then a child, and inquired what I came to dig for there, and in my simplicity I told her all my father's poverty, and my own wish to learn. She was not rich, Ludivico, as I afterwards discovered; but while I spoke, she drew out a little purse, and gave me from it five silver florins—I am sure it was the half of all it contained—and oh what treasures mine eyes have looked on since. And I have had dreams, Ludivico, great dreams, of gathering heaps of gold for the service of the holy church; but nought of all I have ever dreamt of or possessed could give me such gladness now as the sight of those five florins did then. I could not speak for very joy, and strange visions of hope came thronging upon me, bright but indefinite; and the lady seemed to guess my thoughts, for she said something in her own strange language, and walked away. When I came to myself, indeed, I tried to overtake and thank her, but could not, for she was gone from my sight, and I hurried home with the florins to my father. There was great joy in our cottage that day, and next morning I went

* See the history of Sixtus V. in Ranke's Lives of the Popes.

to school. At noon the scholars went home, and I returned by the way of the ruined temple—the lady was there standing in the same spot beside the broken altar. I hastened to her and poured out my thanks, and in my young heart's gratitude—for, Ludivico, I was young then—I promised I know not what return to her goodness in future years. The lady bade me cease; for she was not then alone, but held an infant boy by the hand, like herself, and wondrous beautiful. Young peasant, she said, I know that thou wilt come to great power and fortune; and shouldst thou meet this boy in after days, for his stars are not so prosperous as thine, remember then the kindness of his mother, and know him by this sign. As she spoke, she drew up the sleeve of the child's tunic, and showed me upon his right arm the picture of a serpent in many coils of dark blue, painted, as it were, into the very flesh. No wave, she said, could wash out that strange picture, for it was painted in her native land by one who knew the early arts of Greece; for I have learned she was a Grecian lady of most noble birth, and niece of the patriarch of Constantinople; but she wedded a Jew, and renounced her Christian faith, and the heavy curse of the eastern church was upon her. Why she came to Italy I never knew. Perhaps it was to avoid the wrath of the eastern Christians: but her Jewish husband had died of the plague, and she was alone with her child and an ancient Greek servant, who had followed her from her father's house. The peasants had strange tales of her at Fermo; for it was said she had turned not to Judaism, but the old idolatry, and therefore frequented that ruined temple. Our bishop began to inquire concerning her, and then she left the place and went to Venice.'

'Perhaps the holy Inquisition converted her, my lord?' broke in Ludivico.

'No, no,' cried the cardinal; 'I have been consultor these fifteen years; but they told me she had gone to Spain, and sailed from thence to the far west in a ship of the Conquisador's; but a great tempest met them on the sea, and the ship went down with all that it contained near the coast of Barbary. But many a thought I have had, Ludivico, concerning that strange woman; and would that I knew the painter's name whose hand hath given the church that glorious picture, for assuredly it is but a copy of her face, and the sight was pleasant to me; for I have thought, perchance it was but a delusion, that it betokened grace to her son: but thou sayest it also resembles the bandit Marianazzo?'

'On my salvation it does, my lord, if mine eyes were not deceived,' said Ludivico.

'It may be so, it may be so,' rejoined the cardinal; 'this earth hath strange resemblances: yet I could wish thou hadst not spoken of the thing, for hitherto I have looked upon that picture with much of memory and something of hope; but henceforth it shall seem to my spirit like an altar overturned and a sanctuary profaned.'

'Oh, my lord, it is my greatest grief to have spoken aught that may offend your eminence; yet, believe me, it is true.'

'No doubt, no doubt, good Ludivico,' was the cardinal's reply to the humble remonstrance of his servant. 'But it grows late: let us return home: and, Ludivico, see that you mention nothing of what I have spoken.'

'Not a word, my lord,' said Ludivico; who, though simple as a child in all other matters, was known to be a most impenetrable secret keeper from all but his master.

'But sure,' he continued, as the cardinal glanced sadly back, 'when your eminence comes to be pope, your commands will be sufficient to have this virgin taken down and another fairer one painted in her stead.'

'Who told thee, Ludivico,' said Montalto—but there was pleasure in his look in spite of the stern tone—'who told thee that I should be pope?'

'Craving your eminence's pardon, I humbly confess it was a Bohemian fortune-teller at Fermo many years ago.'

'The Bohemians are heretics, and no Christian should consult them,' cried the cardinal with real anger.

'Oh, my lord, I fasted three days, and said three hundred aves for it. But nevertheless I am sure it is true; and would that I were as near a cardinal's hat as my master is to the triple crown of St Peter.'

'When I am pope thou shalt be cardinal, my good Ludivico. Meantime, see that thou keep thine own secrets, and watch over thy soul;' and with these words the cardinal and his servant passed together from the portal of St Peter's.

* * *

Five years had passed away, and they had left strange traces on both the faces and fortunes of Ludivico and his master, when they stood together again at the close of another day. But the last gleams of the twilight now shone through the high-arched windows and stately old chambers of the Vatican upon Pope Sixtus V. and Cardinal Gallo. The day had been one long to be remembered in the annals of Catholic Rome, for in it the dream of many a pope had been accomplished, when, amid the music of the Roman choirs, the thunder of cannon, and the shouts of Italy, the old Egyptian obelisk, raised from its resting-place, where the memory of the Cæsars had hung around it for fifteen hundred years, was placed, as an offering to its faith, in front of the great temple of the Christian world. All was over, and the hush of coming night had fallen upon the eternal city: the people were gone to their homes, and the princes to their palaces; but the wearer of the triple crown still stood, like one whose work was yet unfinished, near the window of a great hall, whose high old shelves and long closed cases rose to the height of the ceiling, piled up with ponderous volumes and manuscripts gathered from the libraries of nations whose very capitals were dust. It was the library of the Vatican; and the pope who stood there had more to think of at that hour than books.

'Ludivico,' said he, addressing his companion by the name of former days—for elevation had wrought little change in their intercourse, though Sixtus had kept his promise to his servant, even in spite of the eloquence of Francis Toledo,* and Ludivico was now his eminence—'Ludivico, much yet remains to do. With help, I have put down the bandits. No heretics dare show themselves in the states of the church; and the Catholic princes will soon take up the sword against the Lutherans. The treasure also in the vaults of St Angelo grows apace, and the new city of Loretto hath risen to glorify the virgin; but, Ludivico, the matchless image which I intend for the church of the blessed Madona, hath it been brought to Rome?'

'It is come, my lord your holiness,' replied the newmade cardinal, who never could recollect in time the more exalted title of his former master.

'It is well,' said Sixtus: 'and hast thou conveyed it, as I desired, to the treasure-vault of St Angelo, that no man may open the case or look upon it save ourselves? For if it excel not all the statues of the Capitol, which, thanks be to God, are now removed, to pollute our holy city no more with the remembrance of pagan idolatry—I say, if this image excel them not, it shall never have a place in the church of our lady of Loretto.'

'Doubt not, my lord—I mean your holiness—that the image is a most excellent virgin, seeing the sculptor hath pledged his life upon the work, and sent it expressly from Florence for your holiness's inspection.

'Would it may be so, Ludivico,' continued Sixtus; 'and may the virgin accept my great works in her honour. And now the promise of my father's dream has been fulfilled: I am pope; and thou, too, in spite of the Jesuits, art a cardinal: but, Ludivico, I am old; yet would that I might live to behold the great cupola of St Peter's finished, and see the head of that wicked one, Jazino Marianazzo, set up on a pole at the gate of

* This Jesuit preached a sermon against Pope Sixtus V. for having elevated his servant to the rank of cardinal.

the Vatican. Ludivico, hast thou heard anything of that accursed one of all the bandits? He is the last who defies our power, and the one, above all others, whom we long to bring to justice; but no doubt God will destroy him. Yet would I might see the church delivered from all her enemies. But now is the time: give me my cloak, Ludivico;' and the cardinal mechanically obeyed with all the alacrity of his servant days. 'Now, let us go,' continued Sixtus; 'this key will allow us to pass by the secret door to avoid observation.'

As the pope spoke, he drew out a small and singularly-formed key, which seemed rather for ornament than use, for it was made of gold. But golden keys have been powerful at all times; and, applying it to what seemed a small chink in the door of one of the book-cases, it opened without a sound, disclosing a narrow passage, through which Sixtus and the cardinal passed together. At the end of it was an iron grate, which the pope opened by touching a secret spring concealed in one of the bars, and then they descended a flight of steps, and passed on through another passage, so long and dark, that Ludivico thought they would never reach the end of it. At length, the light of the lamp which Gallo carried fell on what seemed to him a thick wall; but Sixtus, after a moment's pause, in which he looked anxiously behind him, once more applied his golden key to an almost invisible chink, and then, without a sound, a small narrow door opened, and they descended together down a few steps, and Gallo found himself in the treasure-vault of St Angelo. The holy fortress, as it was called, was at that time the repository of the pope's wealth; and the subterraneous passage which extended from it to the Vatican, was said to be often trodden by the successor of St Peter, who constantly kept the key, with as tenacious a grasp as the mystic ones of his office.

There was a wild brightness in the old man's eyes as he gazed on the great iron chest, dedicated to the Holy Virgin by an inscription deeply cut on its ponderous lid; for it contained more than three millions of golden scudi. Besides that coffer, there was no furniture in the chamber, nor any article but the long wooden case containing the image destined for the church of Loretto, which had been conveyed hither for the pope's private inspection. After satisfying himself that all was safe in that impenetrable chamber, Sixtus turned to his cardinal, who stood astonished at all he saw.

'Come, Ludivico,' said the pope, 'let us open this,' and he handed him the key, which as usual had been in his own safe keeping. Gallo placed the lamp on the floor, and applied the key; but the lock was deranged, and he could not get it opened; and Sixtus, who, with all his piety, had never been remarkable for the virtue of patience, pushed him away, exclaiming testily, 'I cannot endure thy awkward delay. I will open it myself.' As the old pope spoke, he gave the key one vigorous turn, and at the same moment the lid flew up, and a man dressed in the usual style of a bandit leader, and fully armed with sword and pistol, bounded from the case, and rushed to the door.

Sixtus called loudly to the Virgin, and Gallo stood petrified; but the moment he recovered his speech, the poor cardinal exclaimed, 'Call louder, my lord your holiness, for as I am a living man it is Jasino Marianazzo.' The bandit had by this time firmly closed the door, and planted himself against it; and Sixtus, who was the first to regain his presence of mind, was struck by his singular beauty. He was a tall dark young man, with long and rich black hair; but when the old pope raised the lamp, and the light of it fell full upon his face, the fear and the astonishment seemed to pass away before some deep dream of memory which that countenance recalled. Gallo shouted, 'Oh, my lord, did I not tell you true; does he not resemble the virgin of Picena? But, for the holy Madona's sake, great signor bandit, do spare our lives.' And Gallo cast himself on his knees at the bandit's feet.

The proscribed leader looked down and almost smiled, but motioned him to rise; and then turning to Sixtus, who still stood gazing upon him with that earnest look of recognition, 'Holy father,' said he, 'fifty long years ago, a Grecian lady, of whom I am the only living heir, bestowed upon your holiness the sum of five silver florins, which you promised to repay if ever it should be in your power; and now, in your treasure-chamber in the castle of St Angelo, I come to demand payment not only of the sum lent, not only of the interest it has borne in your hands, but also of the free good-will with which it was given—of the generous charity that gave its mite when there was only a mite remaining. This is the only inheritance bequeathed to our family, and I am its last descendant. Behold the sign!' At the instant the bandit exhibited his bare right arm, on which the figure of a serpent was represented in a dark blue circle, as if twisted round the limb.

'And art thou, then, the child that stood by the altar?' inquired Sixtus earnestly; 'and tell me where is she?'

'My grandame—rest her soul—sleeps on the desert coast of Barbary, where she and her son were shipwrecked many years ago; and I am that son's child, brought up among the Jews of Fez, amongst whom my mother, a Roman lady of the noble house of Ghishin, found refuge from slavery, to which she was brought by a corsair of Algiers; and I have been a bandit in my mother's land. What other portion was there for me? My father died fighting for the cause of Christian Spain; and my mother sleeps in her own land, though not in the vaults of her family. But I was an outcast, for whom there was no place in the path of honour. And now, holy father, make good your promise, and pay me, if thou canst, all that I demand.'

'Oh, my lord, your holiness, pay him—pay him!' vociferated Gallo. 'Is there not gold enough in the chest?'

'Peace, profane wretch!' cried Sixtus, for the master chord was touched. 'I cannot touch the treasures of the Holy Virgin.'

'Pope,' said the young bandit, 'gold I want not: there is gold enough in this world for the winning.'

'What, then, dost thou ask?' demanded Sixtus.

'Two things,' said Marianazzo: 'first, a free and unconditional pardon for myself and all my followers; and secondly, a line or two from your holiness to the abbess of St Theresa, regarding the novice Donna Alonzina Colonna, that she may depart unquestioned from the convent with the bearer. This is all I at present require; and whatsoever your holiness is pleased to add in your sovereign liberality, shall be gratefully received.'

'Holy virgin,' said the pope, 'thou hast been a grievous enemy to the church; nevertheless'—and the old man paused, and looked again long on the bandit's face—'there is a beauty on thy brow which hath hung long about my memory; and for the mite that had the wealth of my life's hope in it, and for the joy it gave my childhood, which no wealth can give my age, and, more than all, for the long-remembered one who gave it, I grant thy request. But, alas, alas! I fear it is a grievous sin.'

That night, it was said, the pope and his favourite cardinal kept vigil in the chapel of the Vatican, and the nuns of St Theresa were roused before the break of day by a loud knock, and a solemn mandate from the pontiff for the novice Alonzina Colonna instantly to repair to Rome. Great was the amazement of the convent: but the lady went with the messenger, who brought a noble escort of well-armed and mounted cavaliers; and many a day the abbess waited to hear tidings of her novice; and news came at last, which said that the noble maiden had been married to an unknown stranger, in the chapel of the Vatican, by the Cardinal Gallo. There was great gossip in Rome; but they talked of it in whispers; for no one cared to speak aloud of things which the stern pontiff chose to consider secret. But from that night the bandit Jasino Marianazzo was never seen, but there was a brave Italian knight, who did good service in the war against the Huguenots in France, whose lady was said to be the fairest in Christendom, and sprung from the noble house of Colonna.

There was great rejoicing among the pious inhabitants of the new city of Loretto, when Sixtus V., with all his train of cardinals and bishops, came to consecrate the great church, and set up the image of the Virgin, which had been found one morning at the gate of the Vatican; though the Florentine sculptor declared, on his salvation, he had sent it in a case to Rome with a special escort, and secretly, as his holiness commanded. But the pope had made no inquiry into the affair, and the populace thought the Virgin had a right to come as she pleased. And Cardinal Gallo whispered to his confidential servant, 'Pray Heaven we may see no more images as troublesome as the First Lady of Loretto.'

GLASS.

The new financial arrangements of the legislature, by which the price of glass will be greatly reduced, afford us a fit occasion for presenting our readers with some of the many interesting facts connected with that important and beautiful article.

Glass is formed by mixing together some sort of silicious earth, such as fine sand or pounded flint, with an alkali (soda or potash), and subjecting them to a strong heat. Concerning its origin, an interesting anecdote is narrated by Pliny, which, without much examination as to its probability, has been taken for granted, and copied into all the encyclopædias and treatises on glass that have been written for ages. We give it in the quaint words of an early English translator.* 'The common voice and fame runneth, that there arrived sometime certaine marchants in a ship laden with nitre, in the mouth of the river Belus, in Phœnicia, and being landed, minded to seeth their victuals upon the shore and the very sands; but for that they wanted other stones to serve as trevets to beare up their pans and cauldrons over the fire, they made shift with certaine pieces of sal nitre (saltpetre) out of the ship to support the said pans, and so made fire underneath; which being once afire among the sand and gravell of the shore, they might perceive a certaine clear liquor run from under the fire in very streams, and hereupon they say came the first invention of making glasse.' From the context, it is deduced that the time of this accidental discovery of glass was supposed by Pliny to be about the Christian era. The recent discoveries of Sir Gardner Wilkinson, however, in the tombs of Thebes, make it certain that the Egyptians were in full possession of the various modes of glass manufacture upwards of 3500 years ago. The process of glass-blowing is represented on the paintings of tombs of the time of Osirtasen I. and his successors, and repeated in various parts of Egypt in tombs of various epochs. 'But,' continues Wilkinson,† 'if the sceptic should feel disposed to withhold his belief on the authority of a painted representation, and deny that the use of glass could be proved on such evidence, it may be well to remind him that images of glazed pottery were common at the same period, that the vitrified substance with which they are covered is of the same quality as glass, and that, therefore, the mode of fusing, and the proper proportions of the ingredients for making glass, were already known to them; and we can positively state, that 200 years after, or about 1500 B.C., they made ornaments of glass; a bead bearing a king's name who lived at that period having been found at Thebes by my friend Captain Henvey, R.N., the specific gravity of which, 25 degrees 23 minutes, is precisely the same as of crown glass now manufactured in England.' Many glass bottles and objects of various forms have been met with in the tombs of Upper and Lower Egypt, some unquestionably of very remote antiquity, though not readily ascribed to any fixed epoch, owing to the absence of royal names, indicative of their date; and glass vases, if we may trust to the representations in the Theban paintings, are frequently shown to have been used for holding wine, at least as early as the Exodus, 1490 years before our era. Such, too, was the skill of the Egyptians in the manufacture of glass, and in the mode of staining it of various hues, that they successfully counterfeited the amethyst and other precious stones, and even arrived at an excellence in the art which their successors have failed to retain, and which our European workmen, in spite of their improvements in other branches of this manufacture, are still unable to imitate; for not only do the colours of some Egyptian opaque glass offer the most varied devices on the exterior, distributed with the regularity of a studied design, but the same hue and the same device pass in right lines directly through the substance; so that, in whatever part it is broken, or wherever a section may chance to be made of it, the same appearance, the same colours, and the same device present themselves, without being found ever to deviate from the direction of a straight line, from the external surface to the interior.

In later times—when Egypt was under Roman dominion—there existed an extensive manufactory of glass in Alexandria, from which the whole of the western world was supplied. According to the eminent German antiquary Wincklemann, it was used for a greater variety of articles by the ancients than by the moderns. Glass was not only made into beads, bottles, cups, and other household utensils, but was used for mosaic work, for sacred emblems, and even for coffins.* Of this material was made the Barberini, or, as it was usually called, the Portland, vase, which was some months since so wantonly destroyed by a visitor to the British Museum.

From Pliny it is ascertained that glass was made extensively in Rome long before the days of Nero (who died A.D. 68); for that tyrant is said to have given the enormous sum of L.50,000 (6000 sesterces) for a couple of two-handled glass cups. They are said to have been of immense size and exquisite workmanship.

The art of making glass was introduced into England, it is supposed, as early as the year A.D. 663. Benedict, the abbot of Wearmouth, procured men from France who not only glazed the windows of his church and monastery, but, we are assured, instructed the Anglo-Saxons in the making and painting of glass. The first regular window-glass manufactory of which we have an authentic account appears, however, to have been commenced in Crutched Friars, London, A.D. 1557. Soon afterwards, five articles of flint glass were made in Savoy House, Strand. In 1635 great improvements were introduced by Sir Robert Mansell, by the use of coal instead of wood. The first sheets of blown glass for looking-glasses and coach windows were made in 1663, at Lambeth, by Venetian artists, employed under the patronage of the Duke of Buckingham. The casting of mirror-plates began in France about the year 1688, by A. Thevart. They were soon rivalled in excellence and cheapness by the English. Still, it was long before glass was used for windows; and though it cannot be a matter of surprise that the ancient inhabitants of warm climates should never have adopted glass windows, yet there were seasons even in Rome when her inhabitants were glad to shut out the too keen air without being deprived of light. The Romans were contented with the cheaper article of *talc* instead of glass for that purpose. But we naturally are disposed to wonder why, in a climate such as our own, glazed windows were not introduced earlier than they were. So essential a comfort are they in our present estimation, that most of the ideas of luxury with which the nations of antiquity are associated, vanish from our minds when

* Holland's Plinie, book 36, chap. 26.

† Manners and Customs of the Ancient Egyptians, vol. iii.

* The body of Alexander the Great is said to have been enclosed in a glass coffin at Alexandria.

we reflect that in cold weather they could only exclude air at the expense of light. There is no authentic evidence of glass being used in windows previously to the third or fourth century; and then, and for long after, it was employed only in churches and other public buildings. In this country, even so late as the latter part of the sixteenth century, glass was very rarely met with. In a survey of Alnwick Castle, the patrimony of the Dukes of Northumberland, made in 1573, it is stated—'And, because throwe extreme winds, the glasse of the windowes of this and other my lord's castles and houses here in the country dooth decay and waste, yt were good the whole leights of everie windowe, at the departure of his lordshippe from lyinge at any of his said castels and houses, and dowring the tyme of his lordship's absence, or others lyinge in them, were taken doune and lade up in safety. And at sooche time as ather his lordshippe or anie other sholde lye at anie of the said places, the same might then be set uppe of newe, with smale charges, whereas now the decaye thereof shall be verie costlie and chargeable to be repayred.' Sir F. M. Eden thinks it probable that glass windows were not introduced into farmhouses in England much before the reign of James I. They are mentioned in a lease in 1615, in a parish in Suffolk. In Scotland, however, as late as 1661, the windows of ordinary country houses were not glazed; and only the upper parts of even those in the king's palaces had glass; the lower ones having two wooden shutters, to open at pleasure, and admit the fresh air.* From a passage in Harrison's Description of England, it may be inferred that glass was introduced into country houses in the reign of Henry VIII. He says, 'Of old time' (meaning, probably, the beginning of the century), 'our countrie houses, instead of glasse, did use much lattise, and that made either of wicker or fine rifts of oke in checkerwise. I read also that some of the better sort, in and before the time of the Saxons, did make panels of horne instead of glasse, and fix them in wooden calmes (casements); but as horne in windowes is now (1584) quite laid downe in everie place, so our lattises are also growne into disuse, because glasse is come to be so plentiful, and within verie little so good, cheape, if not better than the other.'

Even, therefore, in respect of the single article of windows, the 'good' old times will not bear comparison with the present. Without glass, it is easy to understand how, in this cold and damp climate, history supplies us with so many deaths occasioned by 'agues'—a disease invariably owing to humidity and cold, but which is now scarcely ever heard of. To impress the reader with the importance of the article, we present a few of the fine euphonious periods of Dr Samuel Johnson. 'Who, when he saw the first sand or ashes by a casual intenseness of heat melted into a metalline form, rugged with excrescences, and clouded with impurities, would have imagined that in this shapeless lump lay concealed so many conveniences of life, as would in time constitute a great part of the happiness of the world? Yet by some such fortuitous liquefaction was mankind taught to procure a body at once in a high degree solid and transparent, which might admit the light of the sun, and exclude the violence of the wind; which might extend the sight of the philosopher to new ranges of existence, and charm him at one time with the unbounded extent of material creation, and at another with the endless subordination of animal life; and, what is yet of more importance, might supply the decays of nature, and succour old age with subsidiary sight. Thus was the first artificer in glass employed, though without his own knowledge or expectation. He was facilitating and prolonging the enjoyment of light, enlarging the avenues of science, and conferring the highest and most lasting pleasures; he was enabling the student to contemplate nature, and the beauty to behold herself.'*

That an article capable of a greater variety of useful application than perhaps any other in existence, except wood, should be of easy access to the public, is a matter of the highest importance. The duties exacted upon glass are, it seems, from 200 to 300 per cent. on its actual value!† Firstly, makers of glass were obliged to take out a license, which cost L.20 a-year for each glass-house; secondly, such raw materials as are obtained from abroad are subject to a custom's duty; and thirdly, the materials, when in the melting-pot, are assessed at 3d. per pound, or, when taken out of the pot, at 6d. per pound (for the material gains 100 per cent. when shaped), at the discretion of the excise officer. We mention these things to show the disadvantages under which glass is at present produced, and to point out the small encouragement existing for a capitalist to embark in the manufacture. In the latest act of parliament respecting these duties, there are no fewer than thirty-two regulations, prohibitions, and penalties, under which glass can alone be made. An exciseman is frequently on the premises to enforce and exact them; and the glass-maker is cramped and tied by his supervision. This being the case, it is readily to be inferred that the number of glass-works is limited. In 1833 there were only 126 in the whole country—namely, 106 in England, 10 in Ireland, and 10 in Scotland.

Now, however, the whole of these restrictions are to be taken off, and it is impossible to foresee to what useful purposes glass will be put, and how cheaply it will be possible to obtain it. It is not merely a release from the sums paid for excise duties, but relief from the vexatious regulations imposed on its manufacture, which will bring down the price. An elasticity will be given to the trade, and new enterprisers will embark in it. There will be competition, of which at present none may be said to exist, and competition not only as regards price, but in quality, beauty of form, and workmanship. Glass-houses will multiply, and, with them, articles furnished in glass which now are made of less convenient materials.

We need only refer to our article 'On the Influence of Light on Plants and Animals,'‡ to point out the advantages of living in plenty of light; in other words, of having plenty of windows; and although by another description of tax, still exacted, the latter advantage is not to be obtained without expense, yet cheapness of glass is one step towards such a desirable convenience. It is impossible to foresee the advantages of cheap glass which will be reaped by horticulturists. Conservatory frames and other glazed implements of their art are so serious an item of expense, that recent insurance companies have thought it worth their while to afford insurances against hail—a severe storm of which has been known to ruin many a struggling gardener. Private individuals also will be able to have conservatories; and we hope to see the majority of town residences adorned with cases for containing plants. A new impulse will also be given to chemistry. The expense of retorts, tubes, and other glass articles of apparatus, makes a chemist less bold and confident in his experiments than if he did not act under the fear of breakage, and consequently under a dread of incurring inconvenient expenses. We might indeed go to a tedious enumeration of trades and professions by which this important change in our fiscal laws will be benefited. It will be better, however, to mention a few of the novel uses to which glass will be in all probability put.

The coarse 'bottle glass' will make better, clearer, and more durable pipes than the iron ones which are at present used for subterranean conveyance of water to the inhabitants of towns. They will be more durable,

* Several windows of this form are still to be seen in the old parts of Edinburgh, and probably in other towns.—Ed.

* Rambler, No. 9.

† Speech by Sir Robert Peel in the House of Commons.

‡ See p. 36 of the present volume.

because not liable to rust; and more wholesome, because the fluid will not be impregnated with oxide. If they supersede the smaller leaden pipes, there will be no danger of our drinking sugar of lead with our daily meals. Tiles will also, it is expected, be fashioned out of a more transparent glass; and the light denied to more than six windows at the side of a house by the other tax, may be received into the top rooms from the roof. The number of household utensils which will be fashioned out of the coarser qualities of glass, such as green, clouded, and other semi-transparent sorts, are infinitely too numerous to allow of our mentioning more than a few; such as milk-pans, ewers, cups and saucers, and various other kinds of crockery; slabs for tables, side-shelves, &c. which might be made varied by the mixture of several coloured glasses.

Of the finer sorts for ornamental purposes, a great scope for taste and ingenuity will be afforded. Vases, standishes, and many other such articles we shall see in new forms and brilliant colours. Looking-glasses, the best of all ornaments to a room, and useful too for reflecting and retaining light entering from windows, will also be found in more habitations than at present. It is always gratifying to see in the houses of the poor this emblem of self-respect and tidiness. It is, we know, adopted by the poets as the emblem of vanity; but the use of a mirror generally proceeds from a pardonable, respectable vanity.

The removal of duty from glass is universally regarded by those best able to judge as one of the most important fiscal regulations which has been made for many years, chiefly from the influence it will have in increasing the comforts of the poor. The only persons who seem to object to it are the few glass-makers, who, knowing the old excise regulations are an effectual barrier to new speculators entering into competition with them, dread the throwing open of the trade by their removal.

BIOGRAPHIC SKETCHES.

THE REV. SYDNEY SMITH.

There are two characters which, when combined in the same individual, seldom obtain the undivided esteem of the public, namely, a wit and a clergyman. Those who admire him as a wit, wish that the dangerous gift existed apart from the sacred office; whilst those who experience edification from the preacher, would, if possible, banish from their minds that he is a wit.

Such is the exact predicament in which the subject of the present memoir was placed during at least fifty years of a long and active life. For him, however, it may be said that no man ever united the two characters with less offence than he. Although a party and controversial writer, he never forgot, while launching the shafts of satire, that he was a Christian, and seldom overstept the bounds of charity, even while dealing with his most bitter opponents. His private life also conformed much better to what is expected from a minister of the gospel, than with what is looked for in a maker of jests.

The parents of Sydney Smith resided at Lydiard, near Taunton, in Somersetshire, though it happened that he was born, in the year 1768, at Woodford in Essex. After having been instructed in the rudiments of education, he was sent to Winchester School, that ancient seat of knowledge, founded by William of Wykeham, at which so many of the most celebrated English scholars have drank their first draughts of knowledge. His progress was so distinguished, that at a very early age he was elected a scholar of New College, Oxford, of which, at the age of twenty-two, he became a fellow. It was not, however, till he had attained the age of thirty that he took a degree—that of master of arts. Both at school and college he associated with many men who afterwards attained the highest distinction and celebrity—amongst others the present primate of all England. 'I was at school and college,' he says in one of his amusing letters to Archdeacon Singleton, 'with the archbishop of Canterbury; fifty-three years ago he knocked me down with a chess-board for checkmating him.'

Except his academical acquirements, he had no influence to obtain a living, and was glad to get a curacy of fifty pounds per annum. 'When I first went into the church,' are the first words of the preface to his collected works, 'I had a curacy in the middle of Salisbury Plain.' The parish was Netheravon, near Amesbury. 'The squire of the parish took a fancy to me,' he continues; and after serving for two years, 'the squire'—who was Mr Hicks Beach, M.P. for Cirencester—engaged him as tutor to his son; and it was arranged that Mr Smith and his pupil should proceed to the university of Weimar, in Saxony. They set out; but before reaching their destination, Germany was disturbed by war, and, says the facetious divine, 'in stress of politics we put in to Edinburgh.' Amongst the earliest acquaintances which Mr Smith made in this city were Mr (now Lord) Brougham, and Mr Jeffrey, who now graces the bench of the Scottish judicature; an acquaintance which afterwards led to important results. Meanwhile Sydney, besides attending to his pupil, officiated at the Episcopal chapel in Carrubber's Close during most of the time he remained in Edinburgh, which was five years. One day, towards the end of his residence here, he, Brougham, and Jeffrey 'happened to meet'—we quote his own words—'in the eighth or ninth storey or flat [probably second or third] in Buccleuch Place, the elevated residence of the then Mr Jeffrey. I proposed that we should set up a review; this was acceded to with acclamation. I was appointed editor, and remained long enough in Edinburgh to edit the first number of the Edinburgh Review. The motto I proposed for the Review was—

Tenui musam meditamur avena.

"We cultivate literature upon a little oatmeal."

But this was too near the truth to be admitted, and so we took our present grave motto from *Publius Syrus*, of whom none of us had, I am sure, ever read a single line;* and so began what has since turned out to be a very important and able journal. When I left Edinburgh, it fell into the stronger hands of Lord Jeffrey and Lord Brougham, and reached the highest point of popularity and success.'

The first number of the Edinburgh Review was published in October 1802, and to it Sydney Smith contributed four articles, all of them written with a remarkable combination of humour and logic. In the notice of Dr Parr, he reviewed that sententious scholar's wig, of 'boundless convexity of frizz,' along with his sermons, and contrived in the first paragraph a parallel as close as it was startling and ludicrous. His broadest hit was, however, levelled at Dr Langford's 'Anniversary Sermon of the Royal Humane Society.' It consists of the following sentences, which, with an extract, and two lines of comment, make up the entire review:—'An accident, which happened to the gentleman engaged in reviewing this sermon, proves in the most striking manner the importance of this charity for restoring to life persons in whom the vital power is suspended. He was discovered, with Dr Langford's discourse lying open before him, in a state of the most profound sleep, from which he could not by any means be awakened for a great length of time. By attending, however, to the rules prescribed by the Humane Society, flinging in the smoke of tobacco, applying hot flannels, and carefully removing the discourse itself to a great distance, the critic was restored to his disconsolate brothers.'

Though the Review had hardly commenced when Mr Smith left Edinburgh, he continued to support it for many years afterwards. His early contributions gave him a rapid and widely-spread celebrity; and in the year

* Judex damnatur cùm nocens absolvitur—"The judge is condemned when the criminal is acquitted."

1803 he removed to London, to commence a new career; namely, that of a 'fashionable preacher.' In the metropolis, and a few other large towns, besides the usual and well-known places of worship, there is one class, the internal management of which is, we apprehend, not so generally nor so well understood: these are called 'proprietary chapels'—that is to say, they are the exclusive property of one or more individuals, to whom they are sources of pecuniary profit, in proportion as they are well attended. To obtain large congregations, every allurement is held out. A fine organ is set up, and a skilful organist engaged, together with a professional choir. But of course the chief aim is to procure the services of a popular preacher—such a person as Sydney Smith was likely to be. Accordingly he was, to copy a word from a periodical of that day, 'engaged' to preach at the Berkeley and Fitzroy chapels, and also at the Foundling Hospital. No sooner had he entered on this sphere, than he proved himself a 'star' of the first attraction. His sermons were pointed and elaborate without the appearance of art, natural without any affectation of ease, and spirited without one flagrant breach of ecclesiastical propriety. What he said of Sir James Mackintosh may with truth be applied to his sermons:—'New and sudden relations of ideas flashed across them in reasoning, and produced the same effect as wit, and would have been called wit, if a sense of their utility and importance had not often overpowered the admiration of novelty, and entitled them to the higher name of wisdom.' There was nothing of levity either in his sermons or in his manner of delivering them. His language was argumentative and convincing, and his delivery earnest, though never impassioned: he could convince the reason, though he seldom reached the heart. The chapels in which Mr Smith preached in London were crowded with the wealthy, the dignified, and even with the learned inhabitants of that great city, a circumstance which naturally attracted the attention of those gentlemen who manage the affairs of the Royal Institution, and they solicited his services as a lecturer. The subject he chose was the *belles lettres;* and never was the lecture theatre of the Royal Institution so crowded with 'overflowing audiences' as during the delivery of this course. While enjoying the sweets of fashionable popularity, Mr Smith fell in love. The object of his affection was Miss Pybus, a banker's daughter, whom he married. This important event took place when he had attained the mature age of thirty-five. The result was nothing but happiness until death dissolved the union.

All this while Sydney Smith kept up a running fire of articles in the Edinburgh Review, chiefly on church politics. Like Dean Swift, he seldom wrote for mere hire or fame, but only when stirred up by inward principle to advocate some great cause. His uncompromising honesty, therefore, his keen satire, and invulnerable logic, incited as it was by justice and enthusiasm, took tremendous effect; less, however, in advancing his own principles than in damaging those of his adversaries, amongst whom were arrayed the most powerful people in the realm. At that time (the early years of the present century) the expression of public opinion was scarcely free, as it is now. 'It was an awful period,' says Sydney in his preface, 'for those who had the misfortune to entertain liberal opinions, and who were too honest to sell them for the ermine of the judge or the lawn of the prelate: and not only was there no pay, but there were many stripes. It is always considered as a piece of impertinence in England, if a man of less than two or three thousand a-year has any opinions at all upon important subjects.' In 1806, however, the aspect of the political world changed, and the parson's political friends obtained a short ascendancy. One of the first uses they made of it was to present their witty advocate to the living of Frostonin, in Yorkshire, value L.500 per annum.

He was scarcely settled in his living, when his patrons, wishing to remove the disabilities under which our Catholic fellow-subjects then laboured, were driven from their places by needless alarms of the consequences such a concession would produce. It was then that the celebrated 'Letters of Peter Plymley to his Brother Abraham in the Country, on the Subject of the Catholics,' appeared. Its extraordinary humour and vigorous arguments procured for the pamphlet a prodigious success. The new government 'took great pains,' says Mr Smith, 'to find the author. All they *could* find was, that they were brought to Mr Budd the publisher by the Earl of Lauderdale. Somehow or other it came to be conjectured that he was the author. * * They had an immense circulation at the time, and I think above 20,000 copies were sold.' The art with which wit and argument are combined in every page of these humorous letters could hardly be surpassed. At the time concession was denied to the Irish Catholics, Napoleon was in the full career of his military successes, and England was in want of soldiers. 'I want,' says Peter Plymley, 'soldiers and sailors for the state; I want to make a greater use than I now can do of a poor country full of men; I want to render the military service popular among the Irish; to check the power of France; to make every possible exertion for the safety of Europe, which in twenty years' time will be nothing but a mass of French slaves: and then you, and ten thousand other such boobies as you, call out—"For God's sake do not think of raising cavalry and infantry in Ireland! . . . They interpret the Epistle to Timothy in a different manner from what we do!" . . . What! when Turk, Jew, heretic, infidel, Catholic, Protestant, are all combined against this country; when men of every religious persuasion, and no religious persuasion; when the population of half the globe is up in arms against us, are we to stand examining our generals and armies as a bishop examines a candidate for holy orders, and to suffer no one to bleed for England who does not agree with you about the 2d of Timothy? You talk about the Catholics! If you and your brotherhood have been able to persuade the country into a continuation of this grossest of all absurdities, you have ten times the power which the Catholic clergy ever had in their best days.'

Mr Smith continued to discharge the duties of a parish clergyman at Frostonin with great credit to himself till the year 1829. In the interval, he laid aside the pen of the political partisan, and occupied himself solely (except, indeed, an occasional contribution to the Edinburgh Review) with the care of his flock. He was then presented to the more lucrative living of Combe Flory, in Somersetshire; and in 1831 became canon-residentiary of St Paul's cathedral. His habits of life, while ministering the clerical office, were ever those of a respectable, frugal, well-conducted clergyman. 'Till thirty years of age,' he says in one of his letters to Archdeacon Singleton, 'I never received a farthing from the church; then L.50 per annum for two years; then nothing for ten years; then L.500 per annum, increased for two or three years to L.800; till, in my grand climacteric, I was made canon of St Paul's; and before that period I had built a parsonage house, with farm offices for a large farm, which cost me L.4000, and had reclaimed another from ruins at the expense of L.2000.' It may be remarked, that he enjoyed great popularity amongst his flock. His kindly manners, and the practical benefit they derived from his medical assistance—for he had studied medicine at Edinburgh with this express view—conduced, with his spiritual services, to bring about this effect.

While canon-residentiary of St Paul's, his keen controversial spirit was roused by certain proposed interferences with the revenues of the English church, and he put forth his opinions on the subject in three letters to an imaginary archdeacon, whom he called 'Singleton.' It was proposed by a commission to take from the higher sinecure incomes, in order to improve the stipends of the humbler clergy; a measure patronised by several members of the Episcopal bench, and which we, in our ignorance, would suppose to have been a rational and laudable one; but not so thought our wit. It was his opinion that 'large prizes,' in the form of a few goodly incomes, were calculated to do more good than a monotony of moderate stipends. Adverting, in a commentary on one of the ecclesiastical commissioners' reports, to the general question, he says, 'A picture is drawn of a clergyman with L.130 per annum, who combines all moral, physical, and intellectual advantages—a learned man, dedicating himself intensely to the care of his parish, of charming manners and dignified deportment, six feet two inches high, beautifully proportioned, with a magnificent countenance, expressive of all the cardinal virtues and the ten commandments; and it is asked with an air of triumph if such a man as this will fall into contempt on account of his poverty? But substitute for him an average, ordinary, uninteresting minister—obese, dumpy—neither ill-natured nor good-natured—neither learned nor ignorant—striding over the stiles to church, with a second-rate wife, dusty and deliquescent, and four parochial children, full of catechism and bread and butter: or let him be seen in one of those Shem-Ham-and-Japhet buggies—made on Mount Ararat soon after the subsidence of the waters—driving in the High Street of Edmonton among all his pecuniary, saponaceous, oleaginous parishioners. Can any man of common sense say that all these outward circumstances of the ministers of religion have no bearing on religion itself!' A picture which he draws of the commissioners in the character of paymasters of these small stipends is broadly humorous:—'There is some safety in dignity. A church is in danger when it is degraded. It costs mankind much less to destroy it when an institution is associated with mean, and not with elevated ideas. I should like to see the subject in the hands of H. B. I would entitle the print—"The Bishops' Saturday Night; or Lord —— —— at the Pay-table." The bishops should be standing before the pay-table, and receiving their weekly allowance; Lord —— and —— —— counting, ringing, and biting the sovereigns, and the bishop of E—— insisting that the chancellor of the exchequer has given him one which was not weight. Viscount ——, in high chuckle, should be standing with his hat on and his back to the fire, delighted with the contest; and the deans and canons should be in the background, waiting till their turn came, and the bishops were paid; and among them a canon, of large composition, urging them on not to give way too much to the bench. Perhaps I should add the president of the Board of Trade, recommending the truck principle to the bishops, and offering to pay them in hassocks, cassocks, aprons, shovel-hats, sermon-cases, and such-like ecclesiastical gear.'

The latest of Mr Smith's literary productions concerned the non-payment of the interest of the Pennsylvanian loan, by which it is understood that he was himself a heavy sufferer. He first petitioned the American legislature on the injustice of the defalcation; and then, when he found that produced no effect, wrote a letter to a London newspaper in his usual irresistible style. 'I never,' he declares, 'meet a Pennsylvanian at a London dinner without feeling a disposition to seize and divide him—to allot his beaver to one sufferer and his coat to another—to appropriate his pocket-handkerchief to the orphan, and to comfort the widow with his silver watch, Broadway rings, and the London Guide, which he always carries in his pocket. How such a man can set himself down at an English table, without feeling that he owes two or three pounds to every man in company, I am at a loss to conceive; he has no more right to eat with honest men than a leper has to eat with clean men. If he has a particle of honour in his composition, he should shut himself up, and say, "I cannot mingle with you; I belong to a degraded people; I must hide myself—I am a plunderer from Pennsylvania." Figure to yourself a Pennsylvanian receiving foreigners in his own country, walking over the public works with them, and showing them Larcenous Lake, Swindling Swamp, Crafty Canal, and Rogues' Railway, and other dishonest works. "This swamp we gained (says the patriotic borrower) by the repudiated loan of 1828; our canal robbery was in 1830; we pocketed your good people's money for the railroad only last year." All this may seem very smart to the Americans; but if I had the misfortune to be born among such a people, the land of my fathers should not retain me a single moment after the act of repudiation.'

During his residence in London, Sydney Smith was the delight of the society in which he mingled, till almost the end of his days. He was, to use a phrase of his own, a diner-out of the first lustre. The good things which he dropped in the course of conversation were, unlike Sheridan's, unpremeditated. He never hoarded or polished jokes, that they might be brought forward in their highest state of finish before an audience sufficiently large or sufficiently brilliant to yield him satisfactory applause. They came from the fulness of his lively and cheerful nature, as much to amuse himself as others. He used to say that he had reason to thank Heaven for bestowing upon him a mind which was to himself an exhaustless fund of amusement. Yet he had occasionally his melancholy days, like all intensely nervous men, and now and then he became so abstracted as to appear grave. Even then, droll ideas would arise and be delivered, and he would join in the hearty laugh they were sure to occasion. Many of his happy expressions and phrases have entered into the current intellectual language of our time; as his celebrated definition of orthodoxy and heterodoxy, his speaking of a gentleman with 'a very landed manner,' and his wishing for 'a forty-parson power of conversation.' His wit in favour of the Catholics undoubtedly had political importance, and the Reform Bill was sensibly helped forward by his comparison of the opposition to Mrs Partington vainly trying to mop out the Atlantic. Of his many table witticisms and humours, hundreds will be remembered in London society beyond the present generation; as, for example, his answering that he had not read such a book—he would wait a month, in hopes it would blow over; or his telling his brethren of the chapter, when they were debating about wooden pavement for St Paul's churchyard, that they had only to lay their *heads* together, and the thing was done. There was a logic and a soundness of sense in almost all his witticisms, that gave them one half their effect. At the same time there was no spice of ill-nature in any of them. Annoyed one evening at a young gentleman, who, though a new acquaintance, was encouraged by his jocular reputation to address him by his surname alone, and hearing him tell that he had to go that evening to the house of the Archbishop of Canterbury for the first time, he pathetically said, 'Don't call him Howley.' Some one remarking that the marriage of a young relation of his had been introduced in rather flaming terms into the Morning Post, he said, 'Very absurd indeed—mistaking us for fashionable people—why, we pay our bills.' It would be stupid to give a mere series of his good things, and we shall not attempt it. After all, his estimate with posterity will rest on higher grounds. In the words of a contemporary writer—'In everything which he attempted he appears to have been eminently successful. At college he graduated with honour, and obtained a fellowship. He projected and contributed to a review which has enjoyed the highest degree of prosperity; he attempted an ambitious style of preaching, with a vigour of talent which distanced all rivalry; he became a public lecturer, and the whole world of Mayfair flocked to Albemarle Street to enjoy his humour, and become enlightened by his researches; he published political works, which have gone through editions so numerous, that as many as 20,000 copies of some have been sold; he lived long enough to enjoy his reputation, and to attain to a greater age than falls to the lot of ordinary mortals; and yet those who appreciate wit, who can admire learning, and who honour the man that used both for the good of his species, will be disposed to think that, old as Sydney Smith was, he died too soon.' The melancholy event took place on the 22d of February last, at his residence in Green Street, Grosvenor Square.

LOITERINGS IN FRANCE—1844.

NISMES—PONT DU GARD—RETURN HOME.

We arrived in Nismes from Beaucaire in an open railway train, and involved in one of those remarkably gusty winds which haunt this southern region of France. Lying at the extremity of the hilly range which extends from the centre of France to this quarter, Nismes occupies a pleasant situation, sheltered from the north, and with a sunny exposure towards the flat tract of country bordering on the Mediterranean. Anciently an important seat of the Roman power in Gaul, we find it in modern times a populous and more than usually neat French provincial town, abounding in objects which attract the curiosity of travellers interested in ancient history or art. To see some of these was the sole object of our visit.

After settling ourselves at a hotel, we strolled along a handsome street, resembling the Boulevards of Paris, the thoroughfare being lined with trees, and the resort of a well-dressed lounging population. At the western extremity of this fine street stands the principal object of antiquity in Nismes—a Roman amphitheatre, gray, massive, and in a wonderfully good state of preservation. Fresh from viewing the amphitheatre at Arles, the novelty of such a sight was worn off; but in this there was something likewise to interest us. Although somewhat smaller than that at Arles, it is fully more striking at first sight, from standing in the midst of an open Place, and on perfectly level ground. Walking freely all round it, we are able to form an estimate of every external feature, and deliberate on its probable appearance some two thousand years ago, when it formed the place of amusement of a barbarous populace.

Abused and damaged in various ways during the middle ages, and subsequently neglected, this massive structure has in recent times been carefully restored where most injured, at the expense of the French government. The architecture, resembling that of the amphitheatre at Arles, has in numerous places been repaired, whole arches and pilasters, with commendable taste, being built in the original style. By these means, and with occasional mendings, the structure will in all probability survive much in its present condition till the fortieth or fiftieth century, if not till a far longer stretch into futurity. Surely the preservation of such interesting memorials of a past state of things is one of the most praiseworthy acts of an enlightened administration.

By an entrance on the west we gained access to the interior, which we found to consist of a cleared arena, oval in form, and environed by flights of stone benches to the top of the bounding wall. Some portions of the seats are entirely gone, showing the broken arches on which they had rested, and this gives a generally ragged and spectral appearance to the scene. We were able, however, to clamber up the ascent, from bench to bench, and gaining the summit, to look down on the now deserted and silent arena, which had once resounded to the yells of wild beasts and their miserable victims. On the top of the bounding wall are the holes, formed in projecting stones, which had received the poles that supported the velaria or awnings, drawn across to shelter the spectators from the sun. According to the best measurement, the amphitheatre is an oval of 437 feet in length by 332 in breath, and, with 30 or 32 rows of seats, it could accommodate about 20,000 spectators. This was doubtless, as at Arles, a greater number than the whole population of the town; but provision was made for hosts of soldiery, and also for the people of the country around.

Besides *Les Arènes*, as the amphitheatre is now called, the town possesses a singularly beautiful Roman structure, termed the *Maison Carrée* (square house). This is situated nearly opposite the modern theatre, in a boulevard going northward from Les Arènes, and consists of a temple of Corinthian architecture of elegant proportions. Twenty pillars are connected with the sides of the structure, and ten are detached in front, forming the portico, to which there is a flight of steps giving access to the interior. For ages in a neglected condition, and damaged in some places by vulgar violence, it has been latterly restored, and put into the best possible state. Lighted from the roof, it forms a gallery of pictures open to the public. Our visit being on a holiday, we found it crowded with townsfolk of all classes. By the archæologist of taste, this building will be viewed with much pleasurable emotion. It is, I believe, the most perfect ancient edifice in the pure Grecian now in existence, and on account of it alone, Nismes is well worthy of a visit.

At the distance of about half a mile in a westerly direction, and on the outskirts of the town, we found other objects attractive from their antiquity. Pursuing our way along the banks of a canal, under the cool shade of a line of lofty trees, we are led to the source of this water-course in a public garden sloping from the base of a steep hill. In this spot nature has sent forth a powerful spring, which the Romans had embellished with architecture, and laid out as baths on an extensive scale. The buildings, renovated in comparatively modern times, still remain, with the water flowing through them towards the canal in the lower grounds. Adjoining the baths, and situated within the enclosure of a paltry cabaret, are shown the remains of a temple of elegant architecture, in the best Grecian taste. It is apparent, from these and other relics, that the garden was anciently a scene of more than usual splendour. Not satisfied with the amount of water delivered by the fountain, the Roman builders of the city had augmented it by a supply brought by an aqueduct from a distance of many miles—an effort at supplying a population with one of the prime necessaries of life, which no one can justly estimate who has not visited this very interesting spot.

The termination of this stupendous work of art had been at, or near, the fountain in the garden; the water, according to all accounts, being conducted down the declivity of the hill behind, so as to form a cataract at the base, in the midst of a rural scene, in which handsome edifices, clusters of leafy trees, and the glitter of falling water, all conspired to form an enchanting piece of suburban scenery. In the present day, no appearances of the aqueduct or its outlet are visible on the face or sides of the hill, which is laid out as a shrubbery, with public promenades; and by one of these winding and ascending pathways we proceeded to the summit, a height of perhaps five hundred feet. Having gained the top of the ascent, we were rewarded by a magnificent prospect of the town beneath and its environs; but to gain a still better view, we climbed the summit of a lofty tower which crowns the rocky shoulder of the hill. This tower is a curiosity and a puzzle to everybody. Its antiquity baffles research. Its style is nondescript, and its uses unintelligible. It is a clumsy mass of masonry, tapering to the top, not unlike a glass-house. The walls are several feet thick; and it does not appear to have had originally any windows. The most feasible conjecture is, that *La Tourmagne*, as it is called, was a mausoleum of some great personage. That it was of a date prior to the intrusion of the Romans into Gaul, seems certain; for they incorporated it with the walls of Nismes, and made it serve the purpose of a watch-tower. In England, such a curious old structure would of course have been left to go to decay; but it is the policy of the French government, as I have already said, to afford a trifle towards the preservation of works of art, and La Tourmagne has accordingly not been forgotten. Not many years ago it was carefully repaired; and, admitted by a door, we find that a spiral stone stair has been raised from the centre of the floor to the top of the bell-shaped roof. On ascending, we were landed on a bartisan at the apex of the tower; and here the prospect embraced a vast range of country, from the hills of Provence to the borders of Spain. Looking southwards, we had on our left the Rhone and Arles; in front was a large flat plain, dotted over with olive trees, to the shore of the Mediterranean, whose waters could be dimly recognised through the mists which glimmered in the heated atmosphere; towards the right, the country rose into a hilly tract, over the top of which, like a pyramid piercing the sky, was seen the Pic du Midi, one of the loftiest of the Pyrenees.

In catching a glimpse of this far-distant region, our satisfaction was damped by the consideration that we must, at least for the meanwhile, postpone paying it a visit. It had been our design to proceed from Nismes by Toulouse to Pau and the Pyrenees; but symptoms of an alarming complaint, brought on by the excessive heats, admonished me not to attempt such a journey, and with the best philosophy we could assume, we resolved on turning our faces homewards. After a short stay in Nismes, therefore, we proceeded in the direction of Avignon, in order to reach Lyons by the Rhone, the easiest channel of conveyance. In performing this short journey across the country, it was gratifying to have an opportunity of loitering an hour or two over one more object of interest—the aqueduct which had supplied the fountain of Nismes with water in the days of its Roman greatness.

The distance from Nismes to Avignon is about twenty miles, the road stretching across a hilly piece of country, bare, and not very interesting. About half way we arrive at a valley which, by contrast with the brown uplands, may be called pretty, and through it is seen meandering a refreshing little river, the Gardon. Turning by the road up the right bank of the stream, it was with a degree of breathless anxiety that we watched every turn in the banks, to catch a sight of the Pont du Gard, such being the modern name of the object we were in quest of.

'There it is at last,' we exclaimed. 'How grand!—how stupendous! Stop, let us dismount; we must have a thorough inspection of this wonderful work of art.'

We accordingly dismounted from our vehicle, and approaching at an open part of the valley, had the best opportunity of seeing the Pont du Gard, clear and relieved from the connecting banks, with a back ground of open blue sky. The spectacle presented was that of a bridge composed of three ranges of arches, one above another, and extending across a valley of upwards of 800 feet in breadth. As the caleche moved on, and left us to ponder in silence on the object before us, we felt that we were looking on one of the grandest memorials of Roman greatness. In the silence and seclusion of a picturesque scene, did this vast piece of masonry stand proudly before us, and nearly in the same state of preservation as it had been left by the workmen two thousand years ago. Yet it is only a fragment of a line of aqueduct which extended twenty-five miles in length; here spanning a valley, there creeping along a hill-side, or crossing a heathy upland, but always keeping on one level, or slightly inclining from the source to the point of outlet.

We took a long look of the mass at this distance, so as to fix its appearance well in the memory, and then advanced to view it more closely. The arches are as entire as if built yesterday, although constructed of not a particularly hard sandstone. The three ranges of arches differ in size and number. The lowest row, resting partly in the river, are six in number, and of a fine semicircular span; the second or central row consists of eleven arches, and are nearly half the size of those beneath; in the uppermost row are as many as thirty-five, and these are of very diminished proportions. A few of the uppermost which had rested on the north bank are broken away, leaving this extremity in ruin, and unapproachable. About a century ago, the states of Languedoc placed a row of arches alongside the lower range, to form a bridge to carry the road across the valley, and this in some degree impairs the antique character of the aqueduct. It is justice, however, to say that this addition is made in strict keeping with the older parts, and cannot be detected till on a near approach. While our vehicle turned slowly on its way by this modern bridge, we remained on the right or southern bank of the stream, determined to gain a sight of the top of the structure where it is alone accessible. This we were able to do by means of a zig-zag footpath recently cut in the shrubby bank. Having got to the point where the upper row of arches reaches the hill, we found this portion of the building as solid and entire as that beneath. The duct for conveying the water consists of a channel now open to intrusion, but covered with flag-stones through its whole length, except where a fragment of stone has been here and there dislodged; and by the crevices so formed, the beams of the sun penetrate and light up the passage. I must here observe, what no one else has thought fit to notice, that the duct is not straight, neither is it of equal dimensions throughout, and consequently the opening on the north can scarcely be seen from the southern entrance. My own impression is, with respect to the present and other relics of Roman art which I have described, that either the architects did not study to be very exact in their plans, or the masons were allowed to go on by a species of guess-work in their operations. Perhaps the great length of time occupied in these enormous works of art, and the defectiveness of means, caused a laxity in their execution, it being deemed quite sufficient if the structures were completed any way. From whatever cause, the Pont du Gard is far from uniform in point of detail. Several arches in the same row vary in size, and the duct on the top, following the general and apparently needless bend, is by no means straight. The total length of the upper row of arches is 873 feet, and the height of the top from the river 188 feet. The breadth of the structure diminishes as it rises. Underneath, the piers of the arches measure about eighteen feet; the middle arcade is narrower; and at top the breadth is not more than five or six feet.

The pathway by which we ascended the bank leading us direct to the mouth of the duct, we did not scruple to enter to investigate its character. The shape was that of a conduit, about four feet and a half high, and varying from twenty to twenty-four inches wide. The roof was of flat stones; but the sides and bottom were lined with a firm dark-coloured cement, and water-tight. The space being sufficient for our walking through it in a stooping posture, we proceeded to its further extremity, where we observed that preparations were making for building a stone stair to connect it with the adjacent bank. At this end, however, we had an opportunity of seeing it, after we had descended, crossed the bridge, and mounted the left bank of the river; and here also we traced the clusters of low broken arches for some distance through the vineyards which partially covered the higher grounds. In pursuing this search, the sun glared with the heat of a furnace, and rendered the walk scarcely endurable; but the novelty of the scene, and the quantity of sweet-scented herbs which perfumed the atmosphere, tempted us onward. We could observe fragmentary masses, varying in height from ten to fifty feet, extended in an irregular course over a wide tract of country; the whole duct, in its original state, having gathered and brought along the water of two rivulets, the Airan and Ure, situated at a distance of twenty-five miles from Nismes.

In taking a final glance at the Pont du Gard, the most imposing fragment of this ancient aqueduct, we did not feel less impressed with its grandeur than when it first burst into view. It was evident that the Romans, who constructed it, must have been animated with the strongest disposition to supply their cities with pure water on the largest scale consistent with their means. Yet, after all—and is there not an 'after all' in everything?—when one reflects on the comparatively small results achieved by this stupendous mass of masonry, how much are we struck with the great waste of labour! The compass of the stream of water desired to be carried such a distance from its fountain, was not greater than could be contained in an iron tube of two feet in diameter; and if a tube of this dimension had been employed, following in its course all the sinuosities of the ground, how moderate would have been the scale of engineering—how comparatively insignificant would have been the expenditure of time, money, and other requisites! It is highly probable that the severest part of the labour in constructing the aqueduct was performed by slaves—captives taken in battle—many of whom perished under the oppressions to which they were exposed; and, what is almost a matter of certainty, the money expended on the works would be tribute extorted from conquered nations. And yet, though erected by the plunder of the world, how inferior in point of magnitude is this great work; how little did the Romans actually do, in comparison with what is now effected by the voluntary union of honestly-accumulated capital—railways hundreds of miles in length, bridges and viaducts of much grander proportions than the Pont du Gard in all its glory!

These random gossippings on what fell under our notice in the course of a tour in France in 1844 are now, to the relief of the reader, concluded. In a few days after our visit to Nismes, we had ascended the Rhone, proceeded from Lyons to Paris, and landed in our own dear country, glad once more to breathe the exhilarating air of the north, after our sufferings under the heats of a southern summer.

STUDIES ON THE SEA-SHORE.

ADDRESSED TO YOUNG PERSONS.

There are few young people who have been brought up in an inland district, to whom their first visit to the ocean does not form a remarkable era in their juvenile life. The scene is so perfectly new, everything is so strange, the shores abound with so many glittering pleasures, while the prospect of the vast expanse does at the same time inspire a kind of solemn awe, that the youthful mind is filled and impressed with recollections that never afterwards fade. A long-promised visit to the sea-coast was at last accomplished, and a beautiful autumn evening found us for the second time wandering on the smooth white sands of the shore. The receding tide had left dry the far-sloping beach; the sea was still and placid, with now and then a slight ripple glittering in the sun; a few boats and distant ships glided with their white sails on the deep, nearly as like things of life as the agile sea-birds that dipped and sported in the shallow water. The hearts of the young people bounded with an exquisite and new joy; and after skipping about for some time in many circles over the sands, they returned to me to give words to their novel delight.

'How lovely is everything to-night!' said Elizabeth. 'I have now got familiar with the great ocean. I confess my mind yesterday was filled with a strange dread; those noisy and foaming breakers seemed so angry like; the waves came one after the other, rolling up to us like so many coiling serpents; and my heart shuddered as I looked far, far onward, and saw nothing but one dim expanse of green water; but now the waves, instead of menacing us, have retired far out. All is lulled and quiet, and such a beautiful beach is left us, that I shall never tire wandering over it, and exploring its curious productions.'

'We have been fortunate, my dears, in this our first and short visit, to witness the ocean in its two extreme phases. Yesterday was indeed a storm; less, however, in its violence in this locality than it must have been seaward; for the swelling waves and high surf extending in that vast circular line which you witnessed with such astonishment, indicated that a high wind at a distance had raised the commotion.'

'I had many strange dreams last night,' said Henry, 'about vessels foundering, and the cries of sailors clinging to the broken masts, or dashed among the rocks, and dying without any to help them. Nor shall I forget the appearance of last night's sun, as it set redly amid dark purple-looking clouds, which came in huge masses careering with the wind, while the frothy spray dashed up among the hollow rocks. Beautiful as the scene before us now is, I almost regret that it is so changed. I hope we shall have another storm before we go; for I delight to watch the turmoil of the waters, the screaming of the sea-birds, and the roar of the surf against the rocks. What, after all, is our lake, and hills, and green fields at home, compared to this magnificent scene? I long to launch upon those waters, and explore them to their uttermost boundaries.'

'So Henry is become a sailor at once, cries Mary; 'but he shall never speak ill of our loved home; and instead of sailing over the seas, let us go and collect beautiful shells and pebbles to carry home with us.'

'Mary is right,' we exclaimed; 'instead of speculating about untried enjoyments, let us improve those which the present time presents. The storm of yesterday has been at work for our gratification; the beach is strewed with the treasures of the deep; marine plants have been torn up and drifted along the shore; shells and marine animals have been scooped from their caves and hiding-places; and all are now exposed to view, and await our inspection. You see those piles of sea-wrack?—that is the vegetation of the deep; and though differing greatly in form and appearance from land plants, yet they are not without their importance, nor are they without their admirers.'

'Do trees, then, grow in the sea?' inquired Mary.

'Not exactly trees,' I replied, 'but a kind of simple plants called *fuci*, having stems and broad leaves of a soft leathery structure, nearly resembling the lichens which I have shown you on our rocks, and bearing seeds of a very simple kind like them. You see they are of all sizes, from this small delicate-tufted plant to those large-leaved tangles of many feet in length. Indeed many parts of the ocean, to the depth of several hundred feet, are clothed with a vegetation as luxuriant as that on land, the tangled stems and leaves of which form the abiding places of myriads of fishes and marine animals of various kinds. We shall now pause at this spot, and examine a few of the plants. That long cord-like specimen which Henry draws out to the length of ten or twelve feet, is very common in the northern seas: in Orkney it is called sea-catgut, with us sea-lace. It grows in large patches, just like long grass in a meadow, attaining a length of from 20 to 30 feet. This other plant, with the tall round stem, terminated by a broad and long leaf, is a very common one, called the *laminaria*, or sea-tangle, of which there are several species, those of warm seas growing to the height of 25 feet, with a stem as thick as that of a small-sized tree. The gigantic fucus of South America attains a height much greater than this, but with a diameter of stem not more than an inch. Captain Cook describes these fuci as attaining the astonishing length of 360 feet. They flourish in immense groves throughout the southern ocean, and are all alive with innumerable animals, that take shelter among and derive their sustenance from them.'

'The sea, then,' said Henry, 'can boast of taller vegetables than the land; for, if I recollect rightly, the tallest palms do not exceed 150 feet, and the araucaria of New Holland is not above 60 feet more.'

'You are quite correct, Henry; and I may mention another sea-plant, which is said to reach 500 to 1500 feet in length. It is a slender weed, called *macrocystes*. the leaves are long and narrow, and at the base of each is placed a vesicle, which is filled with air, and which serves to buoy up and float the plant near the surface of the water, otherwise, from its weight, it would sink to the bottom.'

'And what is the use of all these plants?' inquired Elizabeth.

'Like land vegetation, they fulfil the important office of affording food and shelter for the myriads of animals with which the sea, like the land, is peopled. They are also not without their uses to man. These heaps of drifted weed form the best of manures for the soil. In some countries sea-weed is collected and burnt, and the ash, which is called *kelp*, produces soda. Several kinds are also capable of being boiled down into a sort of glue; and here is the little rock-weed, which is erroneously termed Irish moss, but which is in fact a sea-plant (*chondrus crispus*). This plant, when well washed, so as to free it of its salt, and then slowly boiled in water, forms a light and nutritious jelly, of which I think you have often partaken when made up with milk and sugar.'

'But look here,' said I, pointing to a small object lying under the heap of wrack which we had just been examining; 'what do you take that to be?' They all pronounced it to be a small marine plant just like many of the others strewed around. 'Now, scrutinise it particularly,' said I. Henry took it up with his hand, and laid it on a piece of paper prepared to receive some other plants. To their surprise the object made several movements: it again moved, and again was still: they watched it with some eagerness, and not without some dread. At last I picked off two or three of the branches of the apparent plant; a claw of an animal now was visible: I continued to pick off more; a head of a crab-like creature was displayed; and finally, clearing off the whole, a small but complete and living creature of the crustaceous family was exhibited to their wondering gaze. A flood of questions now assailed me. 'This little crab (*macropodia phalangium*) is an inhabitant of our sea-shores, and is remarkable for its instinctive propensity of adopting the disguise of a vegetable. It, in short, lives a continued life of masquerade. For this purpose it selects the branches of a small fucus just about its own size, and sticks them so artfully over its limbs and body, that the whole is masked, so as to represent exactly the plant which it has selected. Whether the pieces of plant adhere by their own glutinous juices, or whether the animal spreads over its body a juice peculiar to itself, I cannot tell, but certain it is the animal is found always thus dressed; and it would appear to change its coat whenever it becomes old, for the leaves are always fresh and unshrivelled. The reason of this disguise is evidently concealment—either to conceal itself from its own foes, or to enable it the better to pursue its prey, or perhaps for both these purposes. At all events, the instinct is a very singular one. There is another crustacean, and a better known one than the other—the hermit crab. This fellow likes a good comfortable house, but he will not build one for himself, so he looks about for the first empty shell that will fit him, and in he walks back foremost. You see how he looks out at his door, and now how he scampers off with his house upon his back. To convince you that the creature takes up its abode in a chance shell, here are several more of them, and all the shells you see are of different forms. As the young animal increases in bulk, it leaves its first small shell and takes to a larger. You see this well exemplified in the various sizes of the animals before us.'

Mary had now got hold of a large shell, the waved buccinum, and had applied it to her ear, listening to the hollow sound which it thus emitted. She had been prompted to this from having practised the same thing with shells at home, and I now asked Henry if he recollected Landor's verses in allusion to this circumstance. He promptly called to mind those shells

> 'Of pearly hue
> Within, for they that lustre have imbibed
> In the sun's palace porch, where, when unyoked,
> His chariot-wheel stands midway in the wave.
> Shake one, and it awakens—then apply
> Its polished lips to your attentive ear,
> And it remembers its august abodes,
> And murmurs as the ocean murmurs there.'

'Sure enough it murmurs,' cries Mary; 'but if we carry it away with us, will it still preserve this mysterious union with the ocean?'

'It will still continue to sound when applied to your ear wherever you carry it; but so will any other hollow thing—a tin box, a cup, an empty tumbler, or any such—and yet I am sorry thus to dissipate with plain matter of fact the beautiful fancy of the poet.'

'What is the real matter of fact, then?' inquired Henry.

'It is simply that the concave sides of the shell reverberate the current of warm air which is always passing off and upwards from the surface of our bodies, its place being as constantly taken by a fresh supply from the surrounding atmosphere. The hollow murmuring is the slight sound produced by the air-current striking against the sides of the shell, and being echoed, as it were, from every point, and returned again to the ear.'

'I am almost vexed you have explained this to me,' said Mary; 'for at home I have often pleased myself with the thoughts that the shell roared or murmured when the tides of its parent ocean flowed in, and that it was silent until the time of the flowing tide returned. So bewitching is fancy! And yet, after all, I believe I shall be more satisfied with truth. I shall carry this shell home with me, however; and when I wish to recall the dashing of the sea-waves and the roar of the surf along the sands, and up among the rocks, I will have only to apply this talisman to my ear. In this respect it will be to me still the shell of the poet.'

As we continued our walk, several little tracks in the sand attracted our attention. Henry determined to follow up one of them, in order to ascertain their cause: he continued to trace one for more than ten yards, and at last stopped almost at the brink of the water. We hastened to the spot, and perceived that the trail was made by the common cockle. It was curious to mark the creature pushing out its single foot from between its two-valved shell, and pressing it against the soft sand, thus pushing itself onward step by step. It had thus travelled at least ten to fifteen yards in the few hours since it had been left on the beach at high water, and now it seemed to be returning to the sea to feed. A little onwards we came to two other well-known edible shell animals, the oyster and mussel. Unlike the cockle, both these were stationary animals. They were securely anchored to stones, and we spent some time in examining the fine silken fibres (the *byssus*) which proceeded from their bodies, and were fixed by the other end to the rocks, thus forming a secure cable.

The frequent lash of the returning tide, and the rapidly descending sun, now warned us that it was time to return home. We did so reluctantly, and paused for a moment to take a look at the descending luminary. How different was the sunset from last evening. The sky was one sea of soft mellow light, curtained above by stripes of filmy clouds of the brightest hues. The sun was just dipping its orb into the deep, and sent a long line of flickering rays athwart the glassy mirror, even reaching to our feet. Sea-birds were speeding along on swift wing to the shores; one or two little boats were seen gliding homewards; but the distant ships steadily held on their way, now almost lost in the misty distance—night and day pursuing their course over the vast deep. As we ascended the sloping beach, we were recalled from our visions of the sea by objects reminding us of the land. The cattle from the neighbouring fields had wandered down to the beach, and their dark massive forms were seen between us and the sky, as they straggled along the shore. 'I think these cattle are actually feeding on the sea-weed,' cried Henry; 'I am sure I see one cow busily chewing a piece of sea-tangle.'

'That is the very object,' I replied, which has made

them wander here. Why should not cows and oxen love the sea-side as well as we? All graminivorous animals are exceedingly fond of salt, and of every substance which contains it. Hence they chew with avidity the sea-weed and lick the salt incrusted on the rocks. Nay, they will also feed with avidity on fish.

"At the western extremity of the island of Lismore, on the Argyleshire coast," says Dr Macculloch, "are some rocks separated at low water, where the cattle may be daily observed resorting, quitting the fertile pastures to feed on the sea-weed. It has erroneously been supposed that this practice, as well as the eating of fish, was the result of hunger. It appears, on the contrary, to be the effects of choice, in cattle as well as in sheep, that have once found access to this diet. The accuracy with which they attend to the diurnal variations of the tide is very remarkable, calculating the times of the ebb with such nicety, that they are seldom mistaken even when they have some miles to walk to the beach. In the same way, they always secure their retreat from these chosen spots in such a manner as never to be surprised and drowned by the returning tide. With respect to fish, it is equally certain that they often prefer it to their best pastures. It is not less remarkable that the horses of Shetland eat dried fish from choice, and that the dogs brought up on these shores continue to prefer it to all other diet, even after a long absence."

'Herodotus mentions that the inhabitants in the vicinity of the lake Prasias were in the practice of feeding their horses and cattle on fish. The Icelanders and Faroese do the same, both with fish and dried whales' flesh, which they generally serve up as a soup, with a small quantity of fodder. "In the northern parts of the state of Michigan," says Captain Marryat in his Diary in America, "hay is very scarce, and in winter the inhabitants are obliged to feed their cattle on fish. You will see," says he, "the horses and cows dispute for the offal; and our landlord told me that he has often witnessed a particular horse wait very quietly while they were landing the fish from the canoes, watch his opportunity, dart in, steal one, and run away with it in his mouth."'

'This surprises me,' said Elizabeth, 'I thought animals, if left to their own choice, would always confine their tastes to the particular kind of food to which they were destined by their structure.'

'As a general rule, this holds true; few carnivorous animals, I believe, would be disposed to exchange their beef for greens; but then, again, those who live on greens seem to have a hankering now and then after a piece of beef. I daresay you may have observed at home how pertinaciously a cow will keep chewing at a bone a whole day, to the utter neglect of her grass, and to the no small dismay of the dairy-maid in the evening, when the cow returns without a drop of milk?'

'I have observed it frequently,' cried Henry, 'and I have been taught to creep close to said cows when so employed, and throw into their mouth a handful of sand and small pebbles; this, by mixing with their favourite morsel, spoils the whole, and they then reluctantly throw the mouthful out and take to their grass.'

Darker and darker now grew the evening shadows as we slowly took our way landwards. The waving sand-hills at last shut out all view of the ocean, and its hollow murmurs only reached our ears. We bade it a last adieu, after having spent two delightful days admiring its wonders, and having brought away with us numerous trophies, to remind us of our studies on the sea-shore.

ELECTRIC CLOCKS.

The following extract, from a letter from Mr Finlaison of Loughton Hall, appears in a recent number of the Polytechnic Review:—Mr Bain has succeeded to admiration in working electric clocks by the currents of the earth. On the 28th of August 1844 he set up a small clock in my drawing-room, the pendulum of which is in the hall, and both instruments in a voltaic circle as follows:—On the north-east side of my house two zinc plates, a foot square, are sunk in a hole, and suspended by a wire, which is passed through the house to the pendulum first, and then to the clock. On the south side of the house, at a distance of about forty yards, a hole was dug four feet deep, and two sacks of common coke buried in it; among the coke another wire was secured, and passed in at the drawing-room window, and joined to the former wire at the clock. The ball of the pendulum weighs nine pounds; but it was moved energetically, and has ever since continued to do so with the self-same energy. The time is to perfection; and the cost of the motive powers was only seven shillings and sixpence. There are but three little wheels in the clock, and neither weights nor spring; so there is nothing to be wound up.

RESPECT FOR GENIUS.

Genius, strictly speaking, is only entitled to respect when it promotes the peace, and improves the happiness and comfort of mankind. What should we think of the gardener who planted his flower-bed with henbane and deadly nightshade? What should we think of the general who, being intrusted with an army, and a plentiful supply of military stores, applied these powers to degrading and enslaving his own country? He should be visited with scorn, and punished as a traitor. And why should the man who directs the artillery of his genius, delegated to him for high and holy purposes, to shaking those foundations on which the happiness of his species rests, and who applies the divine spark within him to the kindling of low and debasing passions, be allowed to hear his plaudits swelled in proportion as his powers of doing mischief become apparent? Talent is always accompanied with the responsibility of using it rightly; and the neglect or pity of the virtuous is the penalty which the child of genius pays, or ought to pay, for its abuse. However splendid talents may compel our admiration, they have no right to claim the general esteem of mankind when their possessor exercises them without regard of what is due to the wellbeing of society and himself.—*Literary Gazette.*

A SONG FOR MARCH.

[FROM THE GERMAN OF GANDENES VON SALIS.]

See the tender grass up-springing,
Where the snow and ice have been;
Rosy buds from lime-twigs swinging,
Sport the sprouting leaves between;
While the breath of renovation,
Through the air fresh seedlets winging,
Wafts new life o'er all the scene.

All adown the meadow rivers,
The veiled violet of the field
'Neath its tender foliage quivers,
Bursting through its leafy shield,
To meet the primrose paley-gold;
While the naked crocus shivers,
Though a sand-bank shelter yield.

All renewed life are feeling;
Falcons on the gnarled oaks
Perch aloft; while warbling, wheeling,
Larks sweep high in airy flocks
Through the gladsome glorious heaven;
And young lambs are gently stealing
Through the vale—beneath the rocks.

See, the uprisen bees are swarming
Round the fragrant almond tree;
Joyous children, all unharming,
Sporting in their circled glee
Round their *hoarded eggs* of Easter,
While the aged men are warming
In the sun's rays joyously!

Blossoms, that fresh life are feeling,
Burst your bonds! Soft flowers, that bloom,
Through the tender mosses stealing,
That in pity deck the tomb—
Come ye forth, and tell your mission!
Types to holiest hopes appealing,
Emblems of our happy doom!
Truth's sublime in everything
Waked to life by breath of spring.
Thus shalt thou awaken me—
Breath of immortality!

London, March 1845. R. L.

Printed by William Bradbury, of No. 6, York Place, and Frederick Mullett Evans, of No. 7, Church Row, both of Stoke Newington, in the county of Middlesex, printers, at their office, Lombard Street, in the precinct of Whitefriars, and city of London; and Published (with permission of the Proprietors, W. and R. CHAMBERS,) by WILLIAM SOMERVILLE ORR, Publisher, of 2, Amen Corner, at No. 2, AMEN CORNER, both in the parish of Christchurch, and in the city of London.—Saturday, April 12, 1845.

CONDUCTED BY WILLIAM AND ROBERT CHAMBERS, EDITORS OF 'CHAMBERS'S INFORMATION FOR THE PEOPLE,' 'CHAMBERS'S EDUCATIONAL COURSE,' &c.

No. 68. New Series. SATURDAY, APRIL 19, 1845. Price 1½d.

A WORD ON THE ROADS.

Until about the year 1555, the highways and byways of England were under no law, and the making and maintaining of them was left to any parties who felt interested in preserving a communication between one place and another—a state of things not very creditable to the nation; for the Romans, fifteen hundred years before, had set an example of making and keeping up great leading thoroughfares from one end of the kingdom to the other. A law at length passed on the subject in the reign of Philip and Mary laid down no general principles for road-making, further than that each parish should maintain its own roads, by means of forced labour, at the order of surveyors annually chosen by the inhabitants. Till the present day, all the parish and cross-roads are made and supported in terms of this primitive code, the forced labour, however, being generally commuted for certain exactions in cash on the lands and houses in the parish. The road rates are a kind of taxes too well known to need any particular explanation of their character.

Half a century had not elapsed from the passing of the act in the reign of Philip and Mary, when the plan of supporting all the roads on the parish system was found to be inadequate for the general accommodation. Some parishes would have the road running this way, some that way; some did not care about having roads at all; a few kept the roads in good repair; and many let them remain in the worst possible condition. Instead of utterly overthrowing this complex and clumsy arrangement, a plan was introduced for maintaining, on something like a uniform and efficient principle, certain great roads through the country. The era of this improvement was the year 1641, when the notable expedient was adopted of throwing barriers across the roads at regulated distances. For the device of turnpike gates, as they are now termed, we have therefore to thank the parliamentary wisdom of the reign of Charles I. The English by no means relished this novel method of maintaining the chief thoroughfares: it was quite opposed to all their ideas of freedom, and was so very unpopular, that for more than a century it was not adopted for any other channel of communication than that called by travellers the Great North Road, which passed through Hertfordshire, Cambridgeshire, and Huntingdonshire. The roads, generally, remained in a disgracefully bad condition till past the middle of the eighteenth century. Even in the neighbourhood of the metropolis, they were at certain seasons scarcely passable. In 1703, when Prince George, husband of Queen Anne, went from Windsor to Petworth, to visit Charles III. of Spain, the distance being about forty miles, he required fourteen hours for the journey, the last nine taking six. The writer who records this fact says, with much simplicity, that the long time was the more surprising, as, except when overturned, or when sunk fast in the mire, his royal highness made no stop during the journey!

In 1763 turnpike gates were established in all parts of England, and since that period they have been the grand engine for supporting the principal thoroughfares, the parish and cross-roads remaining under their own local management. The history of the roads in Scotland is the same as that for England, only that the compulsory or statute labour, and also the toll system, were of later introduction. Turnpike gates did not make their appearance in Scotland for half a century after their general introduction into the neighbouring country. The first set up were also equally unpopular, and it required all the powers of the law to preserve them from destruction. By the united efforts of parish and other rates, commutation of statute labour, and revenue from tolls, the roads generally throughout Great Britain, from Cornwall to the furthest limits of Scotland, are now in excellent condition, though far from what they might be under a more rational process of management. According to returns to parliament, the length of the turnpike roads in England and Wales in 1829 was 19,798 miles, and in Scotland 3666; making a total of 23,464 miles. At the same period, the length of all the other roads was 116,000 miles; making the entire length of the public highways and byways at least 139,000 miles. In England and Wales, the number of turnpike gates was 4871; the debts on the roads amounted to L.7,304,803; and the current expenditure on all the roads for one year was L.1,455,291. In Scotland, the debts were L.1,495,082, and the expenditure L.181,028.

Such are a few of the more prominent statistics respecting the financial affairs of roads; but one still more worthy of note is the number of bodies who take on themselves the management of this vast machine. There are ten thousand parishes in England; but as many are small, and unite for road business with adjoining parishes, it is believed that there are not more than seven thousand boards of management, each with proper functionaries paid for attending to the condition of the highways. To this seven thousand are to be added the trusts appointed by the legislature to manage the turnpikes. Of this class, in 1829, there were 1119, and the number of the acts of parliament, which inspired them with life and vigour, was 3783. To keep the 19,798 miles of great roads in repair, required, we say, the apparatus of 1119 distinct trusts, 4871 toll-bars, and 3783 acts of parliament. According to this rate, a trust is required for every 17¾ miles, and an act of parliament for every 5 and a fraction miles. As an act of parliament generally costs L.500, the turnpike roads of England and Wales may be said to have cost L.100 per mile for legislation. The ratio is somewhat different in Scotland.

In that country, a trust seems to be required for every 9¼ miles, and an act of parliament for every 19 and a fraction miles; which is at the rate of little more than L.26 per mile for legislation. Not bad this, however, for Scotland, considering that a number of the Highland roads are supported by government, and do not require much doctoring in the way of special acts of parliament.

Placed in this broad and grotesque light, the whole road system of Great Britain, with its eight or nine thousand managements, its endless exactions, and its universal network of toll-bars, is, without exception, the most awkward and absurd institution on the face of the earth. Laying aside altogether the loss of time, and the personal trouble and expenses of the individuals composing the trusts, the cost incurred for making and maintaining the roads is enormously disproportionate to the ends attained. No plan could have been invented to act so ruinously on the funds, as that of levying money at turnpike-gates from travellers; for the cost of a turnpike-house and gate every five or six miles, and the cost of supporting a keeper, must all fall to be deducted from the proceeds. Were it possible to institute a rigorous examination, it would probably be found that, what with charges for acts of parliament, charges for toll-houses, gates, and tariff boards, profits of lessees of gates, and support of keepers, with heavy miscellaneous charges, not more than from fifty to sixty per cent. of all the money collected is at the disposal of the trustees for behoof of the roads. In other words, from two to three pence, out of every sixpence handed to the turnpike-men, are absorbed by managerial expenses.

In a work recently published, to which we have pleasure in referring—'Road Reform,' by Mr William Pagan, a Scotch country solicitor*—the ratio of managerial expenses for toll-bars is stated at nearly what we have here supposed it to be. Speaking of the counties of Fife and Kinross, the writer describes them as containing 394 miles of parish or statute-labour roads, and 461⅞ of turnpike roads; total 855⅞ miles. The annual average amount of all levies whatsoever for these roads is L.33,547, 7s. Of this sum, less than one-half, or only L.16,110, 17s. 7d. is expended on the ordinary repair of roads and bridges; L.7061 is disposed of for management; and the remainder goes to pay the interest, and to reduce the principal of the road debts. But this, he says, does not include the cost of local road legislation, law expenses incurred between lessees and private parties in questions of tolls, and the loss arising from the unproductive nature of toll-houses and gardens. Nine acts of parliament are at present in operation on the roads of the two counties, and the cost of these has been L.3532, 10s. 9½d. One of them, procured in 1842, cost as much as L.575, 7s. 3d. At the renewal of the acts, equally heavy expenses will have to be incurred. Mr Pagan calculates that the annual burden for local road acts on the two counties is L.207, 6s. 1d.—a large sum for a district of country not larger than Hertfordshire. With respect to the loss incurred in erecting toll-houses, he tells us that there are within the district 78 of these establishments, independently of a large number of small lodges and collection boxes; the whole together, along with 69 steelyards, or cart-weighing machines, having cost the road funds not less than L.10,000.

Enough has now been said to show how ineconomical—or rather how positively wasteful—is the present mode of maintaining the roads of Great Britain. But the direct pecuniary loss, bad as it is, is perhaps less grievous than the universal dissatisfaction which tolls create, their impediment to free intercourse, their injurious effects on manufactures and commerce, and their prevention of agricultural improvement. 'The whole working of turnpike tolls,' observes Mr Pagan, 'has been again and again condemned—we may almost say by the universal voice of the country—and a spirit of dissatisfaction has been roused against it, which, in South Wales particularly, very recently attempted to put down the system by physical force. In that part of the kingdom, as will be well remembered, multitudes of people met, night after night, under the leadership of Rebecca—sometimes at one point and sometimes at another—and, despite all the local authorities, straightway destroyed toll-gate after toll-gate, razing, at the same time, the toll-houses to their very foundations. In short, for a time the Rebeccaites held undoubted sway in South Wales, to the dismay of that portion of the empire, and, indeed, to the uneasiness of the government and the country at large. The military had to be called in from a distance; the London police had to locate themselves in the disturbed districts; a few, but very few, of the numerous persons concerned in the riots and in the bloodshed—for some unoffending toll-keepers suffered—were brought to justice; and it was only after measures of energy and conciliation on the part of the executive, that the disaffected were overcome and the districts restored to peace. These proceedings occasioned enormous expense.

'In South Wales, as elsewhere, turnpike gates had been oppressively numerous, and the rates correspondingly severe. Farmers were met by tolls in every movement of their produce; they could not drive any distance after paying a toll, till, at probably the next turn, they came upon what some act of parliament had constituted a separate trust, and where they found it necessary, before going farther, to pull up and pay a second toll. A little farther on, by some other legal arrangement, there would be another trust and another toll, and so on. And, while the farmers were in the first instance the sufferers, their customers—the public at large—had to share the cost with them, the price of their produce being necessarily increased to enable them to carry on their business. Their grievances were proved before a special commission, which was appointed with a view to discover the cause of the toll-bar riots, and the remedy, and their report (6th March, 1844) forms a thick folio volume of the parliamentary papers.' The result of the inquiry was a thorough reform of the South Wales toll system. Riot, it is sad to say, procured that which peaceful remonstrance failed to accomplish. By a consolidation of trusts, and a reduction of the number of turnpike-gates to one in every seven miles, her majesty's Welsh subjects have been happily pacified.

That the Scotch have not broken out into such excesses as happened in Wales, is ascribable more to the long-suffering character of our countrymen, and their commendable respect for the law, than to the mildness or equity of their toll-bar system. Edinburgh is surrounded with a mesh of thirty-five toll-bars and checks, several indecently placed within the streets of the town, and the greater number in the immediate environs. Cupar, the county town of Fife, is surrounded by thirteen toll-bars within a circuit of three miles of the market-cross, and seven of them close to the town, preventing intercourse with the adjoining fields. The author before us, however, gives even a worse case than this. Speaking of a road between Leven and Kirkaldy, 'this

* Edinburgh: Blackwood and Sons. 1845.

presents to the world the *beau ideal* of the toll-bar system, for there the trustees have done their work so well in the matter of toll-gates, that it is acknowledged to be quite impracticable to set foot upon the road at all without being caught by some one or other of their gates. The length of the road is just 7¾ miles, and we find upon it exactly 7 gates—that is, one for every mile—five of them upon the line of road, and two of them by way of supporters or cheek-bars. On entering this road from the east (after having paid at Lundinmill toll-gate, in the St Andrews district, only two miles back), we are taxed at Scoonie toll-gate, where we may be asked whether we are to stop at Leven, or how far we are going? and not being disposed to afford this information to our inquisitor, we ask him in turn what is the lowest sum at which he will permit us to pass his gate? He then explains that his is what is called a half toll, and, gig and all, we get through for threepence. Half a mile forward we are upon the lively town of Leven and its excellent new bridge, where we find a pontage-gate, and there both biped and quadruped must make their bow to Charon, and submit to his toll exaction. A short distance further we are upon Methil-hill toll-gate and its check, where we must pay sixpence, which clears the remaining bars on this road, as the toll-ticket thrust into our hand informs us. Armed with this passport, we get through the Percival and Bowhouse gates without further payment, and make our way to Kirkaldy—before entering which, however, we come upon the barrier of the trustees of that district—the East Bridge toll-gate—where we have to pay our ninepence.'

The prevalence of so many barriers to free intercourse, as is well known, leads to evasion in every imaginable way, it being thought quite fair to trick the toll-keeper out of his dues. A knowledge of this proneness to deception of course renders the 'pikeman churlish, and he not infrequently goes beyond the bounds of his commission. The truth is, toll-keepers give a very wide interpretation to the statute; they do not readily observe that there are no rules without exceptions. Hence a world of small litigation. Mr Pagan relates a case of a 'pikeman attempting to take toll a second time in one day for the same cart, on the plea that it was a different loading. The carter having resisted, the 'pikeman seized his horse and cart; and thence a litigation ensued. After being battled through several courts, the case was quashed, each party paying his own expenses, which amounted to L.54, 17s. for the 'pikeman, and L.124, 18s. 10d. for the carter. Besides incurring this damage, the unfortunate recusant lost his horse, which, having been put to livery by the tollman, was sold, after incurring a bill of L.18 for his keep. Both parties appear to have been the victims of an ambiguity in the act of parliament. In the following case, embracing a mixture of the dolorous with the grotesque, we are reminded of the famous litigation of Bullum *versus* Boatum. A Dumbartonshire tollman brought a passenger before a justice of peace court for attempting to cheat him of ninepence, and the charge being substantiated the passenger was fined L.2, with L.3 of expenses. But the 'pikeman had better let the case drop; for the passenger prosecuted him for an assault, and showed that he had been beat and cut at the time he attempted the evasion. The sheriff before whom this grave charge came for trial, decreed for L.14 of damages and L.2 of fine; but this not satisfying the prosecutor, he carried the case to the court of Justiciary, which increased the damages to L.100, and L.5 of fine, with expenses. The 'pikeman was doubtless left L.200 out of pocket by the transaction.

When we speak of 'pikemen suffering such awful losses, we perhaps fall into an error; for in most instances they are only servants of tacksmen, or lessees. Anciently, it was customary for poor men with wooden legs, or some other infirmity, to take a toll-bar, and on the free proceeds they were able to rear a family in something like respectability. Capital, which has spread its paws over everything, has not made an exception in favour of this humble means of livelihood. The old wooden-leg men are now generally driven far a-field. When the day for auctioning the toll-bars of a trust arrives, capitalists, who know all about the roads and their capabilities, attend and swamp the small bidders. One man will thus take a dozen bars all round a neighbourhood, and, by employing sharp and trustworthy keepers, on whom he keeps an eye, will contrive to make a little fortune in the course of a few years. If a wooden-leg man be now anywhere seen at a toll-bar, it is only as a servant to some great master 'pikeman, or on some remote and little-frequented road.

In this way the keeping of toll-bars has been pretty generally monopolised by clusters of capitalists. Any new capitalist, not of the 'pike corporation, is well known to have no chance as a competitor; because, if a toll be knocked down to him, the enemy will drive him from the road. We have heard it confidently asserted, that any new man taking a toll-bar near London, will be ruined by those who look upon him as an intruder. They will entice all kinds of public conveyances to come by other bars; so that in the end the luckless wight is glad to give up his bargain, and retire to some new field of enterprise. These monopolists of the road are, it seems, not less sensitive on the score of intrusion by the trustees. Occasionally, trustees feel aggrieved by perceiving how profitable the toll-bars are to their lessees, and they determine to take the gates into their own hands, only employing servants as collectors. In almost every instance this turns out a false move. No such toll-bar ever pays: it is impossible it should pay: the employé, a very decent man, cannot tell how it is, but there is no money taking. Sixpence only passed yesterday, and eighteenpence the day before. The thing evidently wont do. Seeing that the world has resolved against travelling so long as they keep the toll-bar in their own hands, the trustees prudently put it up once more to auction, glad to rid themselves of the incumbrance.

We have said so much of road mismanagement under the barbarous toll-bar system, and of the loss it causes to the country, that what we have to offer by way of reform must be stated very briefly. The whole scheme, however, may be contained in a nut-shell. Abolish the parochial or cross-road managements; abolish every kind of road-rate and statute-labour assessment; and abolish the toll-bars as one of the greatest nuisances that ever afflicted a free country. In lieu of this complicated machinery, the author of 'Road Reform' proposes to consolidate the road trusts, each to embrace a whole county, or at least a considerable district; the trusts at the same time to be somewhat more popularly constituted than they are at present. His method of raising funds to maintain all the roads and bridges in the kingdom, to pay the interest and principal of the road debts, and to liquidate every necessary expense, consists in laying a tax of 30s. annually on every horse; and to prove how well this plan would work, he enters into a calculation of what would be produced in the counties of Fife and Kinross. In that district there are 12,000 horses, by which, at 30s. per head, the sum of L.18,000 would be raised; such, as already shown, being the amount required to maintain all roads and bridges in the two shires. According to this simple plan of operation, there would, in comparison with the present absurd process of exaction, be an annual saving of L.15,000, that being the sum at present thrown away on 'pikemen and other engines of collection. To be exact, the difference between the two plans is expressed by the comparison of L.18,055, 16s. 8d. with L.33,547, 7s. What would hold good for two agricultural and populous Scotch counties, may be supposed to be answerable for Great Britain at large; and if so, then is the problem of road reform at once settled; we need not say how much to the relief of travellers, coach proprietors, agriculturalists, and the public generally. Our own ideas of road reformation would have pointed to the public revenue for the means, and to government for the management; but, on consideration, Mr Pagan's proposal is so simple, so likely to be generally popular, besides being efficient in minor details, that we give it the preference. At all events, throwing down the subject, we leave it to fructify in the minds of our readers.

BE JUST BEFORE YOU ARE GENEROUS.

A TALE, BY MISS ANNA MARIA SARGEANT.

'HERE'S a gentleman wants to know the rent of our first floor, mother,' cried little Frank Ashton, running, as he spoke, into the back parlour, where a quiet-looking young woman sat engaged with her needle. Mrs Ashton arose in haste, that she might answer the interrogation of the stranger, wondering at the same time whether her son had dignified him by the appellation of gentleman from courtesy, and thinking that if such were not the case, her accommodations would not be sufficiently good.

The question put to the child was repeated to the mother by a tall middle-aged man, whose manner and bearing bespoke him to be something above the class of persons inhabiting the little street in which he was now seeking for a home; and Mrs Ashton having answered it, led the way up the narrow but clean staircase, to tempt the stranger by the sight of her plain neatly furnished apartments. A brief survey was sufficient; and the terms being agreed upon, he begged permission to take possession of them immediately, as all the luggage he had, he said, was a portmanteau, which was at a neighbouring inn. The hesitating manner with which this request was received caused a flush to mount to his before pale cheeks. 'You require a reference, ma'am,' he quickly said; 'and it is right perhaps that you should do so of a stranger; but I have none to give. I am unknown in London, having but recently arrived from America, in which country I have spent the principal part of my life. All I can do,' he added, 'is to offer a few weeks' rent in advance.'

This reasonable apology for the want of the usual credentials satisfied the unsuspecting mind of the worthy matron, and she readily acceded to the terms, at the same time politely offering that her little handmaid should fetch his luggage. He declined smilingly, replying that he was not above carrying it himself; and adding, that he would, with her permission, employ her during his absence in lighting him a fire, and preparing the comfortable beverage of tea. 'I shall soon be quite at home here, I see,' he pursued, looking at a group of lovely children who had stolen one by one up the stair, and were now clustered at the door to get a peep at the 'strange gentleman;' and he familiarly patted the cheek of one, and stroked the glossy curls of another, as he passed.

'Oh, father, we have got such a nice new lodger,' exclaimed the three younger children in a breath as they clung about Robert Ashton's knees, 'the envied kiss to share,' on his arrival at the wonted evening hour.

'A new lodger!' he repeated in some surprise, and he looked at his wife for an explanation.

Mrs Ashton in a few words related the circumstances under which she had taken in a fresh occupant for her floor, and concluded by saying that she hoped her husband would not think she had acted imprudently.

'You have acted just as I should have done had I been at home, my love,' was his reply.

'But I am not quite certain that it was exactly prudent notwithstanding,' she gaily rejoined; 'we were so unfortunate with our last lodgers.'

The conversation was broken in upon by the arrival of two young men, one of whom had been long acquainted with the family. 'Ah, Ashton, my dear fellow,' he exclaimed, as he shook him heartily by the hand; 'I knew I should find you here, like a good Benedict, by the side of your wife in your own home.'

'This is my world, Morris,' Ashton returned, as he smiled complacently on the dear ones around him.

'And a happy world it is,' rejoined his friend. 'I never leave your fireside without a determination to marry, and have such a home of my own. But to proceed to the subject which brought us hither to-night: I am come to make an appeal to your benevolence.'

'I am sorry for that, Morris,' cried Ashton, 'since my resources are pretty well exhausted. However, I am not so destitute as to be without a few shillings for a fellow-creature in need. Pray, tell me the case.'

'My good friend here is raising a subscription for the widows of the poor men who were drowned last week,' Morris made answer.

'And have you been at all successful in your errand of charity?' Ashton asked, addressing his visitor.

'Far from it,' was the reply; 'people cry out so much at the badness of the times: they have scarcely enough to enable them to be just, much less to be generous, they say.'

'That is a paltry excuse,' cried Ashton contemptuously; 'an excuse made by the niggardly to apologise for their parsimony. Alice, my love,' he added, 'draw us a jug of ale, and let us drink success to this gentleman's undertaking; meanwhile, I will subscribe my mite;' and as he spoke he placed a piece of gold in the hand of the young man.

'Oh, sir, were all the world like you, there would be no misery arising from want,' was the exclamation of his visitor, as he gazed in surprise at the liberal donation from one whose apparent circumstances scarcely warranted the hope of a fourth of the sum. 'I assure you,' he added, 'that I have talked for half an hour to men who revel in riches, and, after all, could with difficulty wring from them a small piece of silver.'

'Alas! this is a selfish world,' responded Ashton with a sigh.

'I told you that I would answer for your success there,' exclaimed Morris, when he and his companion had left the door. 'There is not a more generous fellow breathing than Bob Ashton, and yet I am afraid he is but indifferently off. I hear he is much in debt.'

'In debt!' repeated his friend in astonishment and concern. 'I wish,' he added, 'that you had informed me of that circumstance before, for I certainly would not then have made the application.'

'Why not?' interrogated Morris. 'Is a man never to give away a penny because he owes a pound?'

'His just debts have undoubtedly the first claim,' was the reply.

Whilst this conversation passed between the two friends without, a dialogue of a somewhat similar nature was carried on within. 'Mother,' cried little Frank, as with his brothers and sister he knelt at Mrs Ashton's feet to offer up their evening devotions; 'mother, tell me, if you please, which is the greatest virtue, generosity or justice.'

'Justice, my child,' was the mother's unhesitating reply.

'I thought so,' pursued the little inquirer; 'but I was not quite sure.'

'I am glad that you asked me, then, my dear boy,' she tenderly returned, bending to kiss his glowing cheek as she spoke; 'I am very glad that you asked me, because I wish you to bear that in mind through life. Generosity,' she pursued, 'is a brilliant quality, which attracts general admiration; but it may be possessed by persons wanting in almost every other virtue. Men who have set at nought every moral, social, and divine law, have been frequently known to be eminent for generosity; whereas justice is of so solid a character, that it can scarcely dwell in a soil which has not some other excellences.'

'But we may admire generosity if it be in a robber, may we not?' asked the child, looking earnestly in his mother's face.

Mrs Ashton smiled. 'We can scarcely do otherwise than admire that which is in itself lovely, be it found where it may,' she made answer; 'but we must never, my dear Frank, let our admiration get the better of our judgment, or we may be led to imitate the vices and failings of an individual, because there is some shining quality about them. The generosity of some persons,' she pursued, 'is an impulse, producing that indiscriminating charity which frequently encourages vice, and does more evil than good; and that benevolence is only worthy of admiration which flows from a sense of duty to God and our fellow-creatures.'

'Dear mother,' resumed the child, encouraged by her gentle tones to proceed, 'I think it must have been a struggle between generosity and justice that I felt this morning, when I was coming back from the toy-shops after buying my humming-top. I met a poor blind man looking so hungry and cold, that I could not help wishing I had seen him in my way there, that I might have given him the money instead of laying it out for a toy; and whilst I was thinking so, a gentleman near me dropped a shilling from his purse without noticing it. This shilling, thought I, would buy the poor beggar man two or three meals, and the gentleman looks as if it could be no object to him to lose it.'

'And what did you do, my dear?' Mrs Ashton with eagerness inquired, seeing the boy hesitate whether to proceed.

'Why, mother,' he returned, 'I must confess that I was strongly tempted to conceal the money, and afterwards give it to the beggar; but that little voice which you have told me was conscience, softly whispered that it would be a theft, as much as if I had taken it out of the gentleman's purse with my own hands, and that I had no right to be generous with that which was not my own; so I gave the gentleman his shilling, and left the poor blind man without. Did I do right, mother?'

'Quite right, my dear boy,' Mrs Ashton exclaimed, folding him in her maternal embrace; 'we certainly ought never to do evil that good may come, and I trust this little incident will be a lesson to you through life, never to sacrifice what you know to be right to gratify even such an honourable feeling as benevolence, or in any way compromise justice for the sake of indulging in generosity.'

'Alice, my love,' cried Ashton, when Bessie had taken the children to their chamber, and they were left alone, 'I thought you praised the probity of our dear little boy to the exclusion of his warmer feelings; surely some word of commendation was due to the kind wish which would have given up the humming-top he has so long been setting aside his pocket money to purchase, for the sake of affording a meal to a fellow-creature in want?'

'Your experience in the world must have led you to observe how often such impulses end where they began—in *wishes*,' she smilingly returned. 'The benevolence which I deem most worthy of commendation is *active*. In the case of our little Frank, however, I believe it to have been sincere,' she added; 'and the only fear is, of its becoming too exuberant.'

'Too exuberant! Do you deem it possible for it to be too exuberant? Can we be too self-sacrificing for the good of others, Alice?'

'Nay, my dear Robert,' she gently returned; 'we cannot, I think, be too *self*-sacrificing; but we may sacrifice one duty in order to practise another; and it was the triumph of right over false reasoning that I thought the most worthy of notice in the little transaction which our dear boy was relating.'

'We differ a little, Alice, in our ideas of generosity,' Ashton interposed; 'and yet,' he quickly added, 'it is only with your theory that I quarrel—with your practice, my love, I find no fault.'

'It were better to be defective in theory than in practice,' she gaily returned; 'but I only contend that, to be really valuable, generosity must be united with other moral virtues, and with justice in particular, otherwise its lustre fades into comparative nothingness.'

Ashton sat musing, but did not reply; and the entrance of Bessie with the supper put a period to the conversation.

Week after week passed away, and Mrs Ashton had no cause to be dissatisfied with her new lodger, who was found to possess those two virtues which are of the highest esteem in the opinion of the lodging-house keeper—quietness, and regularity in the payment of rent. Meanwhile, the strange gentleman (for such he was still denominated) made rapid progress in the favour of every member of the family. Frank was delighted with his glowing accounts of the wild scenery of America—the younger children with his willingness to share in their gambols. Ashton felt interested in him from the very fact of his being apparently friendless and unfortunate, and Alice from a combination of all.

'Oh, father, the strange gentleman is gone,' was the simultaneous exclamation of the little group one evening as Robert Ashton entered his home.

'Gone!' he repeated in surprise. 'Is this information true, my love?' he interrogated, addressing his wife.

'Too true,' she returned, whilst a tear stole down her cheek in spite of her efforts to repress it. 'He is gone, my dear Robert, under circumstances of a most painful nature.'

'Yes, father, the men took him away; and mother says they will not let him come back again to play with us,' pursued the little prattlers.

Ashton turned to the mother for an explanation. 'The poor man was arrested this morning, and carried off to the Fleet prison,' she said; 'but I believe, from a few words which were dropped, that there is some injustice in the transaction. It appears to be for the expenses of a lawsuit which he has been urged to engage in on false grounds by the very person who has now arrested him.' Ashton uttered an ejaculation of indignant feeling, and was adding a somewhat illiberal and sweeping remark upon the legal profession, when his wife interrupted him by observing that the best way to show his sympathy would be for him to offer his services to the stranger in such a time of need, which, she doubted not, would be most acceptable, as he appeared not to have a friend in London.

'You are right, my love,' he returned; 'I may perhaps procure his enlargement by becoming bail for him.'

'Do nothing precipitately, dear Robert,' exclaimed his wife; 'you know nothing of his character, and his name has only this day become known to us.'

'Yes, we found out his name, poor gentleman, through the bailiffs,' cried Bessie, who was in the parlour busily employed preparing tea. 'They asked for Mr Paul Logan, and when I said I didn't know such a person, but that I would ask the gentleman on our first floor if that was his name, they followed me up the stairs.'

'Logan, did you say—Paul Logan?' Ashton exclaimed.

'Yes, sir, I know it was that, for I thought it a strange outlandish name.'

'Do you *know* the name, Robert?' Alice asked in surprise, for she could not but notice that it had awakened some unpleasant feelings in the breast of her husband.

'Yes—that is, I once knew a family of the name of Logan,' was his reply. 'But are you sure it was *Paul* Logan?' he further interrogated; and Bessie, nothing loath to be a speaker, proceeded to attest the truth of her assertion by saying that she heard the bailiffs call him by that name several times.

'Are you ill, dear Robert?' cried Mrs Ashton in alarm, perceiving with the quick eye of love that a sudden paleness had overspread her husband's cheek.

'I am not quite well,' he faintly replied, leaning his head upon his arm as he spoke.

Alice flew to offer him a cup of the refreshing beverage she had just prepared. 'I shall not be able to go out to-night, my love,' he said; 'I will retire to bed; perhaps a night's rest may restore me to myself.' Alice urged that medical advice should be procured; but he positively refused to permit it, requesting only her assistance in ascending the stairs to his chamber.

The duties of the mother called Mrs Ashton from the

side of her husband, but her thoughts wandered as she gathered her little ones around her. The sudden indisposition of Ashton had obviously arisen from the associations connected with Mr Logan's name; and yet, strange to say, she had never heard him mention it before. A vague foreboding of evil came over her; though she called into exercise that strength of mind which was natural to her character, and strove to repel it.

Ashton attempted to dissipate the fears of his wife, by making light of his indisposition; but perceiving that he was really ill, she positively refused to retire to rest, and taking up her needlework, she seated herself quietly by his bedside, assuring him with a smile of affection that a night thus spent would do her no injury. Finding her resolute in her determination, he resisted no longer, and strove to compose himself for sleep; but vain was the attempt. 'Tired nature's sweet restorer' fled from his pillow, and he lay tossing from side to side in a state of feverish excitement, which called forth the worst fears in his anxious partner. 'You must allow me to send for medical aid as soon as it is light,' she tenderly said, as she took his burning hand within hers, and counted the quick throbbings of his pulse.

Ashton shook his head.

'Nay, I must act without your concurrence for once, then,' she returned, 'for I deem it my duty to do so; you are not in a state to attend to your business as usual.'

'Medicine cannot minister to a *mind* diseased, dearest Alice,' he made answer.

'A *mind* diseased!' she repeated. 'Oh! my beloved husband, if your malady is of the mind, why not confide in the faithful breast of one who would sympathise in all your sorrows, and do her utmost to alleviate them?'

'I shrunk from telling you the cause of my distress, my own Alice,' he passionately returned, 'because I could not endure the thought of sinking in your esteem; but now I feel that I can bear this torturing concealment no longer; and though it lead you to despise me, I must tell you all.'

'Despise you, dear Robert!' the wife exclaimed, while her mild eyes filled with tears; 'surely you cannot have been guilty of anything so heinous as to call forth such feelings from *me?* Speak freely, my husband; open your whole heart to me, and no word of reproof shall, I promise you, escape me.'

'It is not your reproaches I fear, dearest Alice,' he made answer. 'I know you are too kind to inflict further torture; but your nice sense of justice will recoil from the conduct of your erring husband, though he may not have acted as the world in general would censure. No, it is not your words of condemnation I shrink from, but the verdict of your upright heart.'

'The pangs of self-reproach are far more bitter to endure than any other,' the wife interposed; 'and these,' she added, 'may perhaps be removed. If you have, as your words seem to indicate, committed an act of injustice, is there no way of making reparation?'

'None, none,' was his reply, and he buried his face in his hands in an agony of grief.

'Say not so, my husband,' she soothingly rejoined; 'let me hear the circumstances, and we will together see if reparation be impossible; perchance it is not quite so difficult as you imagine.'

'It can only be accomplished by reducing you, my Alice, and our children to beggary,' he exclaimed bitterly.

'And do you think that I would shrink from sharing poverty with you?' she asked.

'You might not, my dearest Alice; your firm mind would, I feel assured, meet any exigence; but I must be the basest of men to put you to the trial. No, let me suffer alone.'

'You cannot suffer alone,' pleaded the wife; 'every throb of your heart is responded by mine, and with tenfold acuteness. But I must hear your confession, and we will then decide upon the right course to be pursued.'

Ashton raised himself on his pillow: never had he felt so truly humbled as at this moment. So full of self-love is the human heart, that it not unfrequently feels less compunction in committing error than in acknowledging it.

'You have often heard me speak of my father,' he began, 'as a man proverbial for his integrity; indeed so much so, that his word was deemed of more value than the bond of most men. But this character for probity has unfortunately been the means of throwing temptation in the path of his less high-principled son. Amongst his acquaintances was a person of the name of Logan. This gentleman was far his superior in birth and education, yet a warm friendship existed between them, which was only terminated by death. Mr Logan died in the prime of life, leaving my father his executor and guardian to his children, who were handsomely provided for; but a fit of apoplexy shortly after carried him also to the grave. It was not till after my parent's decease that I became aware of the extent of the trust reposed in him by his friend; and this intelligence was communicated to me through the medium of a letter I found amongst his papers, which was addressed to me, in case of any accidents befalling him. He began by informing me that Mr Logan had a son by a former marriage, who had left his home, and (it was supposed) embarked for America, owing to the unkind treatment he had received from his stepmother. Of this youth no tidings had ever after been heard; yet the father cherished the hope that he lived, and would some day return to his family. With this impression on his mind, he lodged the sum of five hundred pounds in the hands of his friend, trusting to his known integrity for its being safely delivered to his unfortunate son, should he ever appear; for so entirely had he been governed by his second wife, that he dared not make any provision for him in his will; thus the transaction was only known to themselves.' Ashton here paused to wipe the cold damps from his brow; then looking earnestly at his wife, hurriedly added, 'You surmise the rest, dear Alice; you see the brink upon which I stood. My father adjured me to preserve the sum, and permit the interest to accumulate, with the same scrupulous integrity as he himself would have done, and on no account to appropriate any part of it to my own use. But I was young, and almost unprovided for, my love—for you also had its share in making the temptation stronger. I knew that your parents would object to my suit had I nothing to commence the world with, and I purchased the furniture of our house, and the business in which I am engaged, with Paul Logan's property, and now retributive justice has brought the man I have injured to my very home.' As the unhappy young man spoke, he clasped his hands in an agony of grief, and sunk exhausted upon the pillow from which he had raised himself.

No burst of anguish, however, escaped the lips of his firm-minded wife. She sat a few moments in silence; and that brief time was sufficient to show her the course which her husband ought to pursue. 'Give not way to unavailing sorrow, dearest Robert,' she tenderly said; 'the past, though lamentable, cannot be recalled; the present only is our own, and it calls but for promptitude and strength of mind. The line of duty is straight and obvious, and however repugnant to our feelings, must be adhered to.'

'Alice, would you have me make you and our children beggars to enrich a stranger?' he almost fiercely asked.

'No, my husband,' she gently replied; 'it will not be to enrich a stranger, but to perform an act of justice; nor shall we, I trust, be reduced quite so low as you represent.'

'I see no alternative but absolute ruin if I attempt to refund the money,' he cried, 'and that is too serious a matter to be decided upon rashly.'

'I do not advocate rashness,' returned the wife, 'but the course which alone can restore your self-respect, and consequently your peace of mind. Oh, my husband,' she energetically added, as she sunk on her knees beside his bed, 'make, I intreat you, no compromise with your conscience. It has, I feel assured, already pointed out the right path for your pursuit; and however humiliating, however detrimental to your interests, or even to the interests of those whom I know you love dearer than yourself, I beseech you swerve not from it.'

'Alice,' cried Ashton, whilst his voice became almost choked by strong emotion, 'have you taken into consideration that to make up this sum I must dispose of my business, which is our only means of support; that we must part with the furniture of our house; and, what is even worse, I must be myself liable to become an inhabitant of a prison for debts it will then be out of my power to liquidate?'

'Debts!' the wife repeated, with surprise and concern; 'I was not aware, Robert, that you were in debt. I understood that, having commenced business with a small capital, you had avoided contracting any, and I thought that our expenditure was rather within our income.'

'It was so till within the last twelve months,' Ashton in some confusion returned, 'when,' he added, 'I was what you, Alice, will perhaps call *foolish* enough to do a generous action. To serve my old friend Johnson, I accepted some bills to a larger amount than was perhaps consistent with prudence, and the result was, I was obliged to pay them.'

Alice sighed deeply. 'And why,' she gently asked, 'did you not name this to me before? I would have made any sacrifices at home rather than that you should be involved in difficulties in your business.'

'I should soon have recovered these slight embarrassments, my love,' he rejoined, 'and I could not bear that you should be made unhappy by them; but now, if I follow your counsel, and part with all to refund this five hundred pounds, and the interest, my creditors will of course come upon me for the debts, and I must become insolvent.'

This was a fresh blow to the feelings of the unhappy wife, and she sat for some time in silent thoughtfulness. Meanwhile Ashton, who shrunk still more from the acknowledgment of his breach of trust to the world than he did from the poverty it would involve, was planning some compromise. 'Alice,' he at length exclaimed, 'I have come to the determination of seeing Mr Logan in the morning, and gaining from him if possible an account of the distresses under which he labours. I may be able to serve him without utterly ruining myself and family.'

Alice forbore to say more at present; she saw that his health was already seriously impaired by the excitement of his mind, and she resolved to await the result of his visit to the prison, ere she urged a course which she still saw to be the only right one, however great the sacrifice might be.

The temporary relief Ashton found in the plan he had proposed so far tranquillised him, as to enable him to arise and put it into execution. Mr Logan was overwhelmed with astonishment and gratitude at what he deemed the generous interest taken in his affairs by a stranger, and consequently became as communicative as he had hitherto been reserved. The world, he said, had, from his very boyhood, used him so roughly, that he scarcely believed in the existence of disinterested kindness; and then followed the tale of his early life, which was too well known to his auditor. He further stated, that after spending more than twenty years in America, during which time he had met with misfortunes of various kinds, he had accidentally heard of the death of his father, and supposing that some of his property had been bequeathed to him in common with his other children, he had come over to England for the express purpose of examining the will. This examination, he said, had proved unsatisfactory, his name not being included; but having reason to suspect, from the circumstance of his relatives affecting to disbelieve in his identity, that a forgery had been practised, he had consulted an attorney, who, as appeared from his subsequent conduct, basely encouraged him to engage in a lawsuit for the purpose of involving him in expenses; when, upon discovering that he was unable to pay but in the event of success, he had not only stopped the proceedings, but arrested him for the sum already due, which amounted to forty pounds.

The feelings of the self-condemned Ashton may be more easily imagined than described, as he was compelled to express indignation at injustice which he could not but own was not more worthy of censure than that he had himself been guilty of, and to listen to protestations of gratitude from the man whom he had in reality so deeply injured. The sum of forty pounds, though more than his present means could command, might, he thought, be without difficulty borrowed of those friends whom he had so often served; and he consequently ventured to promise it, making his anxiety to get the matter settled a pretext for hurrying away.

Mr Logan had implied that it was now his desire to return to America as soon as he could obtain his enlargement, from whence he hoped to remit the sum which Mr Ashton had so generously proffered, though, he said, he should ever deem himself his debtor. This intelligence Ashton joyfully communicated to his wife, whom he found awaiting his return with the most intense solicitude: but she, to his disappointment, felt no satisfaction at the prospect. He thought that time would enable him to repair the injustice he had committed without having any definite plan in view. But the conscience of Alice was not so easily silenced: she saw that justice demanded immediate reparation, and she would have cheerfully submitted to the sacrifices it would necessarily involve—nay, she had already formed projects by which her personal exertions were to assist her husband in the maintenance of the family, and dwelt with pleasure on the peace of mind they should experience in the midst of privation arising from the performance of a right action.

Ashton found the task of borrowing forty pounds less easy than he had at first imagined. After spending the day in going from house to house with little success, he was compelled to raise the greater part of the sum by pledging his watch and some other articles of value; and this done, he lost no time in procuring the release of his lodger. Mr Logan's return was hailed with delight by all save Alice, who, under any other circumstances, would have been the first to 'rejoice with those that do rejoice:' but her oppressed heart could feel no satisfaction whilst her husband's integrity was at stake. She listened with a sickening spirit to the warm eulogiums bestowed upon him by the man whom he had injured, and the singularity of her manner led her lodger to suspect that she had disapproved of the exertions Ashton had made in his behalf; yet this supposition was so opposed to the general tenor of her conduct, that he found it difficult to comprehend the apparent anomaly.

Ere Mr Logan quitted England, he obtained the advice of an eminent professor of the law upon the probable issue of the suit he had before taken in hand, and received information that it was hopeless. Ashton knew too well the circumstances of the case, and the illegality of the claim; but he dared not hint at his knowledge, and was even fearful of offering the advice he would have otherwise given, lest it should betray his secret. 'It is somewhat singular,' Logan observed, as he returned from his last examination of the will at Doctor's Commons—'it is very singular; but it was, I find, a person of your name, a Mr Robert Ashton, who was made my father's executor; and but for the high character he bore in the neighbourhood for integrity, I should have suspected him of collusion with my family.'

Ashton endeavoured to imply surprise by a sudden ejaculation; but his lips moved in vain—his tongue could not articulate a syllable.

'He died of apoplexy twelve months after my father, I heard,' Logan pursued, 'and his son married, and came to reside in London; but no one could give me any further intelligence concerning him. I don't know that it would avail me anything,' he added, 'but I should like to have seen the young man before I left England; he might have thrown some light upon the matter.'

'Possibly so,' Ashton, with a strong effort at composure, remarked; 'but London is a wide place, and the name is a very common one.'

'My circumstances will not admit of further delay,' Logan rejoined. 'The situation I gave up in order to inquire into this affair may yet be vacant, and I am anxious to return, if it were only in order to repay the sum you have so generously raised for me; but perhaps you will bear it in mind, and, when you can do so without any inconvenience or loss of time, make inquiry for me. I know not another person in London that I could ask.'

This last remark caused Ashton to breathe a little more freely, and he with apparent readiness promised to comply with the request. This discovery of the name was a fresh source of disquiet to the self-condemned young man; for he could feel no security whilst his lodger yet remained in England; but, fortunately for him, Mr Logan was, though from different motives, equally anxious for his departure. Many tears were shed by the little ones when he bade them adieu; and even Bessie Brown lamented him, and readily forgave the concealment of his name, which she now saw arose not from any disgrace attached to it, but the false pride men of birth and education are apt to feel when in reduced circumstances.

Month after month passed away, and the family of the Ashtons were, to the eyes of their neighbours and friends, equally prosperous and happy as before; but there was a canker in the bosom of the elder members of which the world knew nothing. Alice was still the same gentle affectionate being, ever studying the comfort of those around her; but her society was less attractive to her husband, from the knowledge that he had sunk in her esteem. She, from regard to his feelings, seldom alluded to the affair, or even mentioned the name of their late lodger; but he could not but see that it was constantly in her thoughts, and that she ceased to enjoy the comforts of her home, because they were purchased at the sacrifice of duty.

Mr Logan was punctual in the performance of his engagement to refund the forty pounds; but Ashton could feel no pleasure in receiving it, but was rather pained by an act of justice in one from whom he felt he did not deserve it.

It was nearly twelve months subsequent to the departure of Mr Logan for America, that Alice was called upon to fulfil the melancholy duty of attending the deathbed of her only remaining parent. Mr Crosby was a man who had been esteemed prudent even to parsimony; but he had brought up a numerous family in respectability, and realised sufficient in trade to enable him to retire and spend the residue of his days free from the cares of business. It was generally supposed that he would have but little to leave at his death; but to the great surprise of his daughter Alice, who was the youngest, and had always been his favourite, he with his dying breath revealed to her that he had set aside for her the sum of four thousand pounds, adding that he had settled it exclusively upon herself, that it might not be touched by her husband. Alice listened to this information with feelings far from pleasureable. 'Oh, my father,' she exclaimed, 'let not your last act be one of injustice. I have no right to the whole of this sum. An equal distribution would be much more agreeable to my feelings, and the few hundred pounds which would be my rightful share would make me'—very happy she was about to add, for her thoughts were full of the idea of releasing her beloved husband from the weight on his conscience, but the melancholy spectacle before her repressed the ebullition of joy. The dying man could not but admire his daughter's noble act; but it was too late for him to legally repair the injury he had done his other children. She assured him, however, that she would scrupulously divide the property, and not only so, but make known that such was his latest wish.

The grief of Alice Ashton upon the occasion of her parent's death was much softened by the happy circumstances attending it. She had a double opportunity of exercising that justice she had ever extolled, and the purity of her motives was displayed in the manner in which it was accomplished. The fact of the money having been designed for herself was kept a profound secret, excepting to those persons from whom it could not be concealed; and as she placed her own share in the hands of her husband, and begged him to use it for repairing the breach of trust which had caused them so much pain, she felt a tranquillity of spirit it was long since she had enjoyed.

Ashton saw too clearly how much happiness the payment of the sum would cause his inestimable wife, to make any scruples about depriving her of it. But the next subject for consideration was the manner in which it was to be done. He still shrunk from the exposure of his unfaithfulness to the trust reposed in him, and proposed availing himself of the opportunity given by Mr Logan's commission to discover the son of the executor. It would be easy, he said, to inform him that he had been so fortunate as to meet with the young man, and that he had through his medium conveyed to him the sum, with interest, left in the care of the deceased Mr Robert Ashton. The distance at which Mr Logan resided would, he thought, prevent all further knowledge of the matter, and he should be spared the humiliation of confession. Alice consented to, without approving of the plan, and it was immediately put into execution.

Ashton was in daily and somewhat anxious expectation of an answer to his communication to Logan, when, to the surprise of both husband and wife, that gentleman made his appearance at their door. His hearty greeting met with a restrained reception on their part, which excited his surprise; but attributing it to the circumstance of his sudden and unexpected arrival, he proceeded to inform them that it was his wish to again engage their apartments, if vacant, as he had business which would detain him in London for a few weeks. After thanking them in the warmest terms for the share they had taken in restoring to him his right, Mr Logan expressed a wish to see the noble young man who had so faithfully fulfilled the trust reposed in him.

'You behold him before you—I am he,' Ashton exclaimed, seeing all further concealment would be impossible; 'but I am not,' he bitterly added, 'the noble young man you suppose. So far from faithfully fulfilling, I have basely betrayed the confidence placed in my integrity, and, but for this excellent woman, should never have made the reparation I have done.'

Logan stood paralysed with astonishment, and Alice burst into tears.

'I was too cowardly to reveal the truth even when I had the means of doing justice,' Ashton resumed, whilst the changes in his countenance evinced the strong workings of his soul; 'but retribution follows, and I am not allowed to escape the humiliation of confession. Let your contempt, however, fall on me alone, for I alone deserve it. My angel wife was not a sharer in the crime; but she it was who, by a noble self-sacrifice, made the restitution.'

'You will not—you are too generous to treat my unhappy husband with contempt,' pleaded Alice, now coming forward. 'The temptation to use the property was strong, when your long absence gave grounds for belief in your death; and when he, by the discovery of your name, ascertained the injury he had done you, the reparation would have effected the ruin of his own family. These considerations will, I am sure, soften your resentment, Mr Logan,' she pursued. 'My husband may have been culpable, but he is not so base as intentionally to wrong any one.'

It was some time before Logan could recover his astonishment sufficiently to speak; but when he did so, it was not to upbraid, but to soothe the self-condemned young man and his weeping partner. Grateful for this delicate consideration for his feelings, Ashton now frankly related every circumstance connected with the transaction, to which his auditor listened with mingled sensations of pleasure and pain. His admiration of the conduct of Alice amounted almost to veneration, and for her sake alone he could have overlooked the tardy justice of her husband. But there was in his character also something to admire, though much to lament. So deep was his contrition for the error he had committed, that there is little probability of its recurrence, even should a similar temptation assail him; and he now sees the necessity of enforcing upon his children the truth he once deemed a fallacy, that impulsive generosity is frequently accompanied by weakness of character, and that it is only when it becomes ennobled by being associated with justice, that it is really estimable in itself, or extensively beneficial in its results.

PROPOSALS FOR A NEW ORDER OF MERIT.

There was once such a thing as the Golden Age. I am persuaded one of its chief constituent features must have been there being no authors in it. Men were then innocent of all crimes, writing books included. Delightful age, too good by far to last! Error and writing came together, and the Golden Age was no more. It is remarkable how soon the world came to be marked by this dismal propensity to scribbling. Look we in upon it three thousand years ago, we find the Jewish sage declaring that of writing of books there was no end. Glance at it two thousand years ago, we see Horace bewailing how, learned and unlearned, all were writing. At the present time, the evil has reached a magnitude which seriously threatens all domestic comfort. The difficulty is now to find a man or woman who does not write. A gentleman proposed to us one day to compile a dictionary of living authors. 'It is done already, sir,' said we; 'have you ever seen a book called Pigot's Directory?' There is a story told of a gentleman who, having a great detestation of authorship and authorcraft, but at the same time liking men of sense and ability, went about for some years in search of such a person who should not have written a book. There was no appearance of success, till one night, travelling from Selkirk to Edinburgh by the coach, he found in one of his travelling companions all the requisites of intelligence and pleasant manners, without the smallest trace of any connection with the press. He felt sure he had at length found the proper person, and longed for morning light to enable him to behold the man whom he was to take to his heart of hearts. The coach stopped at its destination while it was still dark; the stranger came out into the lamplight. The friend-seeker rushed to examine him, when, behold, the chatty, agreeable, and apparently non-literary stranger proved to be no other than Walter Scott, by that time the author of a century of volumes. The story concludes by representing the inquirer as vanishing in an agony of despair.

And well he might, for evidently there is hardly any such person now living. I have a faint recollection of meeting just one man in very early life, who was clever and agreeable, and yet was *said* not to have written anything; but I cannot be quite sure of his innocence. Perhaps, if rigid inquiry were made, he might be found to have produced a dozen condemned plays, or a score of still-born volumes. Not the daylight lantern of Diogenes, not the offer of a premium of fifty guineas in the Times, could now elicit the happy individual who has not at some time tormented his fellow-creatures with pen and ink. It is a terrible case. We used to have strong edicts long ago in our nursery against that state of things when all speak and nobody hears; but what is that to a grown up world in which everybody writes and no one reads?

Clearly, something ought to be done—but what? An association binding the members to buy no new books—that would be of no avail, for the want of sale has evidently no terrors for the literary tribe. A Society for the Suppression of Superfluous Literature by positive means—that would only do harm, for everybody would fly to see the books which had been proscribed by such a grave and reverend body. Might the interference of the legislature be looked for? Or would it be of avail? Doubtless, the British legislature would do anything in reason for the discouragement of authors. See already that well meant, though, after all, but little effectual measure, the taxing of paper equally which sells over the booksellers' counter, and which goes to the trunkmaker. But I fear that the legislature has done its best already; it has exhausted its means of repressing the literary trade. Fiscal measures evidently wont do. Suppose a bill to fine publishers for every bad book they brought out? Alas! the publishers already do their very utmost to keep bad books from appearing. One half their time is occupied in declining offered manuscripts, and battling off print-determined poets and sages. Murray has had to refuse a volume of poems regularly once a fortnight ever since he ceased to publish for Byron. Should there be a tax, then, on all books? No use. They would be printed on the continent, and smuggled in. No, nothing of that kind will do. What, what, then, should be done?

We must look to the human nature of the case, and address ourselves to that. The literary mania mainly arises from an activity of the organ of love of approbation. Could we turn this to operate for the abandonment instead of the taking up of the pen, the object would be attained. Here, unquestionably, lies the key of the question. But how could men and how could women—how, in short, could the men, women, and children who write—be tempted through their love of approbation not to write? Easily enough. This is a matter calling for the interference of the fountain of honour. Establish an order of merit for the positive reward of such persons as resist the temptations of the pen. If it were understood that, on proof being afforded of twenty years having been spent in public life without any connexion with the press, one were entitled to be a claimant for the star of some kind of legion, certainly a vast influence would be exerted for keeping men unspotted by ink. They would deliberate thus with themselves: 'If I print, I perhaps acquire celebrity, perhaps not. But, if I don't print, I am sure of being a Knight of the Order of the Inverted Ink-bottle. Of course, I shan't print.' There might be difficulty in the details, particularly as to the authentication of the proper qualifications. A man might have published anonymously, and it might be difficult to convict him. But even though doubtful cases might thus arise, there would still be enough of certain ones to operate in inducing men to keep out of print. Let it be understood that the faintest ground of suspicion had a condemnatory effect, and you would see few suspicious cases. There should of course be various degrees of honour, bearing some proportion to the degrees of self-denial exercised. Those who only could say, We received a good education, and have been careful not to abuse it by becoming authors, would constitute the great first rank. A simple riband would serve to distinguish them. When any one had it to say, 'I made a tour on the continent, and never put pen to paper on the subject,' or, 'I once preached a funeral sermon, which the friends asked me to print, and I refused.' then that man should have some higher honour. The intimate friend of a great man who abstained from writing his life in two octavo volumes after his death, would deserve one of considerable distinction. And when it could be fully and satisfactorily established of any otherwise qualified man, that he had passed the age of twenty-one, in love, and yet abstained from printing a volume of poems, he should be made a knight-commander at the least. What I calculate on is this, that, by such means, all the finer spirits would be diverted from the walks of literature, and the blacking of paper be left only to a few abandoned persons, whose characters would soon bring it into such odium, that books would become duly rare, and only appear under the pressure of exigent occasions.

The proposed arrangement would undoubtedly serve for all those cases in which the moving cause was of an amateur character. But what to do with the vast class where the impulse comes from the desire of making a livelihood? Here I would suggest a humane extension of the poor-law act. To take away all excuse from those who profess to scribble for bread, there might be a department in the union workhouses for their reception, provided with stones to be broken for roads, and old ropes to be teased into oakum, or employed in any other way that might be thought advantageous. The application of such a test to the scribbleomania would, I apprehend, be effectual. It would then be seen, when any one continued to pester the public with his books, that not bread but notoriety was the object, and, cut off by unrelenting booksellers, and a pocket-buttoned public, he would be compelled to give up his pursuit, and become a useful, or at least not a troublesome member of the community.

Thus, by one means and another, it might be hoped that society would be restored to a healthy tone, and human genius turned to good and serviceable courses, instead of being misexpended as at present. I can imagine the gradual operation of such measures—here a gentleman amateur converted from a tendency to print, there a poor-devil author rescued from literature, and set to an honest trade, like the appearance of hill-top after hill-top on the subsidence of the Flood. Perhaps, in the course of ten years, we should be finding it possible to pass a day without being asked if we have read such a book, or to enter a drawing-room where we should not have to stand in instinctive horror of two authoresses. Oh, Saturnian time! shall we ever see thee thus return?

AN ENGLISHWOMAN IN EGYPT.

Thirty years ago 'the land of Egypt' was looked upon with awe. Its gigantic temples, whose origin dates beyond the records of history; its mysterious pyramids and puzzling sphinxes; its gorgeous tombs, and its mummies preserved for more than two thousand years, with the names, residences, and professions of the defunct as accurately inscribed in hieroglyphics as the epitaph on a tomb-stone cut yesterday*—naturally excited feelings of veneration, that were consecrated in the mind by the biblical associations with which the mysterious banks of the Nile are connected.

Now, however, the powers of steam and the march of inquiry are fast dispelling the clouds of mystery in which Egypt was wrapt. It is no longer a rarity to meet with a traveller who has mounted the pyramid of Cheops, or stood in the halls of Karnac. Rapid and easy communication with Europe has covered the country with a varnish of utter moderness. European merchants set up their shops under the very eye of Cleopatra's needle: the harbour which was ploughed by the argosies of Mark Antony, is now hourly agitated by the paddles of steamboats: and in the city founded by Alexander the Great, Italian operas are performed at least once in every week 'during the season.' Huge cotton mills rear their ugly fronts not far from some of the grandest architecture in the world: and to crown all, the track of the exodo of the Israelites has been recently surveyed by that eminent engineer Mr Galloway, with a view to a railway between Grand Cairo and that part of the Red Sea in which Pharaoh and all his hosts were drowned.

Over these innovations and commonplace novelties the antiquary and reader of Herodotus sincerely mourns; but we cannot wholly sympathise with his lamentations. The means by which this amalgamation of the old with the new has been effected is also the means of extended intercourse with our eastern brethren, which has immense advantages. It breaks down the barriers of prejudice, across which each party steps to mingle and to fraternise. The Mussulman no longer insults the Christian by the name of 'dog;' and we, on our part, cease to regard Mahommedanism as the sensual, immoral creed which it was formerly believed to be. The people of the East, and those of the West, are daily coming to an improved understanding, and to regard each other with a charity which increases in degree on further acquaintance. By means of this feeling, the blessings of knowledge are spread, and commercial communication—the mainspring of social comfort between whatever countries it exists in—is augmented. These are far more substantial advantages than can be derived from a dreamy admiration of the monuments of antiquity, or from the ultra-conservative efforts of those who, to preserve traces of the past, would damage the prospects of the future. Still, to such enthusiasts the union of the modern with the ancient, which the outward and visible signs of Egypt present, are extremely distressing. Five-and-twenty years ago, an amateur of the antique happened to see a lady's-maid in a pink spencer amongst the ruins of Thebes. This so shocked his notions, that he made the best of his way back to France. 'Having,' he says, 'no longer any desire to look at anything, I departed that very night.' What would he say now, when with every Indian mail dozens of English damsels pass through Lower Egypt; when a European female is by no means a rarity in the streets of Alexandria; and when there is a lady who is now actually residing in Grand Cairo? It is to introduce this lady to our readers that the foregoing remarks have been made.

One effect steam communication seems to have had, is to extinguish in the European fair sex all dread of trusting themselves in the land of harems. Till the authoress of 'The Englishwoman in Egypt,'* whose work we have just perused, none had been bold enough to choose that country as her abode. This lady—Mrs Poole, sister of Mr Edward Lane, the author of that minutely curious and interesting work, 'The Manners and Customs of the Modern Egyptians'—determined to leave the pleasing vicinity of Kensington, to accompany her brother to the crowded, hot, and uncomfortable city to which the natives give the grandiloquent name of Al-Kahirah, 'The Victorious.'

After a short voyage, the fair traveller and her family arrived at Alexandria, and proceeding through the canal of Mahmoodiyeh, thence into the Nile, were speedily steamed up that renowned river to Bulac, the port of, and two miles distant from, Cairo. The sole means of conveyance for this short journey is on the back of an ass; and it was thus that Mrs Poole made her entrance into Cairo. This mode of conveyance, which is thought somewhat disrespectfully of in England, is by no means so derogatory in Egypt; the donkey of that country being as far superior to other donkeys as the Arabian charger is to the Suffolk punch. 'The ass of Cairo,' says the lively author of Scenes and Impressions in Egypt, 'even the hired ass, is a lineal descendant of the *Sprightly* of the Arabian Nights; a fine-sized animal with a parti-coloured pack-saddle, having a high pommel covered with red leather, on which you may lounge, lean your hand, or suffer your hands to lie. He is provided with stirrups and

* The mummies in the Egyptian room of the British Museum are inscribed with hieroglyphics, which—translated in the catalogue—give the minute particulars above adverted to.

* Being Letters from Cairo during 1842-4, with E. W. Lane, Esq., author of the Modern Egyptians; by his sister (Mrs Poole). In two volumes. Charles Knight and Co.

bridle, half European.' These animals are such favourites, that upwards of forty thousand of them were said to have been in use in Grand Cairo alone.

Mrs Poole's first impressions of the city are thus described:—'It has the appearance of having been deserted for perhaps a century, and suddenly re-peopled by persons who had been unable, from poverty or some other cause, to repair it, and clear away its antiquated cobwebs. I never saw such cobwebs as hung in many apertures, in gloomy dark festoons, leading me to consider the unmolested condition of their tenants. I wish I could say that I do not fear these creatures; but surely in the insect world there is nothing so savage-looking as a black thick-legged spider. After passing through several of the streets, into which it appeared as though the dwellings had turned out nearly all their inhabitants, we arrived at an agreeable house, situated in the midst of gardens, in which we are to take up our temporary abode. Graceful palm-trees, loaded with their fruit, meet our eyes in every direction, while acacias, bananas, orange and lemon trees, pomegranate trees, and vines, form a splendid variety; and but for one essential drawback, the coup-d'œil would be charming; this drawback is the want of refreshing showers. The foliage on which we look is perfectly covered with dust, and the soil of the gardens is watered by a wheel worked by a patient bullock, who pursues his round-about with little intermission, and thrives in his persevering labour. The plan of the gardens is very curious; they are divided by long parallel walks, with gutters on either side, and subdivided into little square compartments, each about two yards wide, by ridges of earth about half a foot high, and the water is admitted into these squares one after another. When I looked upon the little ditches and squares of water, remaining for some time without absorption, I could not but remember our bright pretty gardens in England, and how carefully, in watering our flowers, we avoided saturating the mould, both because it would be injurious to them, and displeasing to the eye; and these recollections almost brought me to the conclusion, that a garden in Egypt is not worth the trouble of cultivation. So much for national prejudice and love of home scenes.'

The writer's first necessity was of course to procure a house, and, after having searched for a month without success, she at length succeeded in finding one to her mind, which she thus describes:—'On the ground-floor is a court, open to the sky, round which the apartments extend, gallery above gallery. Round the court are five rooms; one large room (a mandarah), intended for the reception of male guests, with a fountain in the centre; a winter room; a small sleeping-room for any male guest; a kitchen and a coffee-room for servants. On the right hand, immediately on entering the street-door, is the door of the harem, or the entrance to the stairs leading to the ladies' apartments; the whole of the house, excepting the apartments of the ground-floor, being considered as the "harem." On the first floor is a marble-paved chamber, with a roof open towards the north, and sloping upwards, conveying into the chamber generally a delightful breeze. There are also five other rooms on the first floor; and in each of the two principal apartments, the greater portion of the floor, forming about three-fourths, is raised from five to six inches, the depressed portion being paved with marble. The reason for thus laying the floors is, that the outer slippers are left on the depressed portion, and the raised part, which is matted, is not to be defiled with anything which is unclean. The feet are covered, in addition to the stockings, with a kind of inner slippers, the soles of which, as well as the upper leathers, are of yellow morocco; they are called mezz; and the outer slippers, which are without heels, are styled báboog. The latter, by the way, I am often losing, and I fear I shall continue to do so, for I despair of learning to shuffle like the ladies of the country. When wearing the riding or walking dress, the mezz are exchanged for a pair of high morocco socks, and the báboog are worn as usual. They are always pale yellow. The walls throughout are white-washed, and the ceilings composed of fancifully-carved woodwork, in some instances extremely tastefully arranged. Besides the rooms I have mentioned, there are three small marble-paved apartments, forming, *en suite*, an antechamber, a reclining chamber, and a bath. We little thought, when we congratulated ourselves on this luxury, that it would become the most abominable part of the house. Above are four rooms, the principal one opening to a delightful terrace, which is considerably above most of the surrounding houses; and on this we enjoy our breakfast and supper under the clearest sky in the world; but we always remember that the sweet air which comforts us in the mornings and evenings of our sultry days blows from the direction of our own dear country; and the thought renders it the more welcome.' This description applies to all the better sort of houses in Cairo. The rent paid for this mansion was only L.12 per year. Indeed, on turning to Mr Lane's minute work on the Modern Egyptians, we perceive, from an account of household expenses in the appendix, that living is remarkably cheap in Egypt. It appears that a man may live like a gentleman for some L.26 (2600 piastres) per annum, exclusive of house rent and servants.

After Mrs Poole had resided in the city some time, she made several acquaintances amongst the Caireen ladies, and in her visits to them obtained a more minute insight into the economy and manners of an eastern harem than has, to our knowledge, been ever yet furnished. One of her visits to the household of a person of rank we quote in an abridged form:—'When we arrived at the house of Habeeb Eféndee, and had passed the outer entrance, I found that the harem apartments, as in other houses of the great in this country, are not confined to the first and upper floors, but form a separate and complete house, distinct from that of the men. Having passed a spacious hall, paved with marble, we were met at the door of the first apartment by the elder daughter of Habeeb Eféndee, who gave me the usual eastern salutation, touching her lips and forehead with her right hand, and then insisted on removing my riding-dress herself, although surrounded by slaves. This was a mark of extraordinary condescension, as you will presently see. In the houses of the middle classes, the ladies generally honour their visitors by disrobing them of their riding-dress; but in the high harems this office is generally performed by slaves; and only by a member of the family when a guest is especially distinguished. When the lady I have mentioned had removed my surtout apparel, a slave in attendance received them in an exquisite pink kerchief of cashmere, richly embroidered with gold. The kerchiefs of this kind, in the harems of the wealthy, are generally very elegant, but that was the most perfect specimen I have seen of correct and tasteful embroidery. The riding-dress was immediately taken into another room, according to a common custom, which is observed for the purpose of creating a short delay, giving an opportunity to offer some additional refreshment when the guest has proposed to take her leave. My new acquaintance then conducted me to the divan, and placed me next to the seat of honour, which was reserved for her mother, the first cousin of the late Sultan Mahmoud, who soon entered the room, and gave me a cordial welcome, assigning to me the most distinguished seat on her right hand, the same to which her daughter had conducted me, while the grandmother of Abbas Pasha sat on her left. She was soon followed by her second daughter, who greeted me with much politeness, and in a very elegant manner assured me that I was welcome. A number of white slaves formed a large semicircle before us, and received from others, who waited in the ante-chamber, silver trays, containing glass dishes of sweet-meats. There were three spoons in each dish, and two pieces of sweetmeat in each spoon. These were immediately succeeded by coffee, which was also brought on silver trays; the small china cups being, as usual, in stands shaped like egg-cups; but these were not, as in ordinary houses, simply of silver filigree, or plain, but decorated with diamonds. They were certainly elegant, but more costly than beautiful. The coffee is never handed on the tray, but gracefully presented by the attendant, holding the little stand between the thumb and finger of the right hand. After these refreshments a short time elapsed, when two slaves brought in sherbet on silver waiters, in exceedingly elegant cut-glass cups, with saucers and covers. Each tray was covered with a round pink richly-embroidered cover, which the slave removed as she approached us. To receive our cups, of the contents of which, according to custom, we drank about two-thirds, another slave approached, with a large white embroidered kerchief, ostensibly for the purpose of wiping the mouth; but any lady would be thought quite a novice who did more than touch it with her lips. In the course of conversation I expressed my admiration of the Turkish language; and, to my surprise, the elder of the young ladies gave me a general invitation, and proposed to become my instructress. I thanked her for her very polite offer, but made no promise that I would become her pupil; foreseeing that it would lead to a very considerable waste of time. In all the harems I have visited, Arabic is understood and spoken; so I do not expect any advantage from a knowledge of Turkish, unless I could devote to its study considerable attention.

'The perfect good humour and cheerfulness which pervaded this family circle is well worthy of remark, and much engaged my thoughts during the morning of my visit. All that I observed of the manners of the eastern women at Habeeb Eféndee's and elsewhere, leads me to consider the perfect contrast which the customs of eastern life present to the whole construction of European society.

'Before our departure, it was proposed that I should see their house; and the elder daughter threw her arm round my neck, and thus led me through a magnificent room which was surrounded by divans; the elevated portion of the floor was covered with India matting; and in the middle of the depressed portion was the most tasteful fountain I have seen in Egypt, exquisitely inlaid with black, red, and white marble. The ceiling was a beautiful specimen of highly-wrought arabesque work, and the walls, as usual, whitewashed, and perfectly plain, with the exception of the lower portions, which, to the height of about six feet, were cased with Dutch tiles. I was conducted up stairs in the same manner, and I could not help feeling exceedingly amused at my situation; and considering that these ladies are of the royal family of Turkey, you will see that I was most remarkably honoured. When we approached the bath, we entered the reclining-room, which was furnished with divans, and presented a most comfortable appearance; but the heat and vapour were so extremely oppressive in the region of the bath, that we merely looked into it, and gladly returned to the cool gallery. I am not surprised that you are curious on the subject of the bath, and the eastern manner of using it; and I hope to devote a future letter to a description of the operation (for such indeed it may be styled), and the place in which that operation is performed. On our reaching the stairs, the second daughter of Habeeb Eféndee took her sister's place; and with her arm round my neck, we descended the stairs, and re-entered the room where I had received so kind a reception. When we rose to take our leave, the elder daughter received my riding-dress from a slave, and was about to attire me, when her sister said, "You took them off; it is for me to put them on." The elder lady partly consented, retaining the habarah, and thus they dressed me together. Then, after giving me the usual salutation, they each cordially pressed my hand, and kissed my cheek. We then descended into the court, attended by the ladies and a crowd of white slaves. Having crossed the court, we [illegible] at the great gate, through which I had before [illegible] which was only closed by a large mat suspended before it, forming the curtain of the harem. This mat was raised by black eunuchs, who poured from a passage without, and immediately after the ladies bade us farewell, and returned, followed by their slaves. The principal eunuch ascended first the mounting platform, and placed me on the donkey, while two others arranged my feet in the stirrups; our own servants being kept in the background. A few days after this visit I received a second invitation from this harem, with the polite assurance that they intended making a festival and fantasia for my amusement.'

Mrs Poole gives in her second volume a minute account of her visit to the apartments of the wives of no less a person than Mohammed Ali, the great pasha. Assuredly this is a curious subject for contemplation. Here we have an English lady paying morning visits to a Turkish harem, in which she is received on the most liberal and friendly footing. This is a simple fact to be regarded as a sign of the times by no means unimportant. It augurs the beginning of a friendly intercourse between the most distant nations, and a charitable toleration of opposite prejudices, which will in time produce the most beneficial results in every quarter of the globe where the same degree of intercommunion has been established.

We must not take leave of Mrs Poole without recommending her interesting work to general perusal. It is full of interesting facts, well and simply told.

SKETCHES IN NATURAL HISTORY.

THE CACTUS FAMILY.

'The monster cactus at Kew,' which has been the vegetable wonder of the newspapers for the last three months, has sent us a rambling—not exactly among the hills and ravines of tropical America with tin-case and root-hook — but amid histories, systems, and monographs, to glean something respecting the nature of this most curious and interesting family.

The majority of our readers must have some idea of the outward characters of the cacti; for they are now extensively cultivated in conservatories and on domestic flower-stands, either for the beauty of their evanescent blossoms, or for the singularity of their structures. To those who are not familiar with the physiognomy of the tribe, we would say—Go to the nearest botanic garden or private hothouse, and study for half an hour the aspect of the melon-cactus, with its globular spiny stem and woolly crest; of the old-man cactus, with its round oblong stalk so profusely covered with long white hairs, and so like the silvered head of age; of the opuntia, with its spiny tongue-shaped stems and branches springing from each other, and jointed together in more than Siamese brotherhood; of the creeping cereus, with its whip-like stems hanging down from the pot in which it is generally suspended—do this, and we guarantee the fixture in your mind's eye of an image not readily to be effaced, with the conviction at the same time that the cacti constitute one of the most singular and interesting orders of the vegetable kingdom. They are unique in their forms and habits, and meet with but very distant allies in any other of the fleshy-leaved orders. The aloe, house-leek, and pine-apple tribes, are also characterised by thick fleshy members; but in them these members are true leaves, performing the regular functions of that organ. The little yellow flower of the house-leek is elevated on its own independent stem; and the flower-stalk of the Agavè Americana rises from fifteen to thirty feet above the leaves which give it birth. Not so with the cacti: their leaves are either so rudimentary that they are scarcely discernible, or fall off from the young shoots almost as soon as they expand; their place being supplied by spines either solitary or in the form of star-like tufts and bunches. As plants, they are all stem and branch, appearing above ground as spiny tubercles; as globular masses, branching tongue-shaped bodies, creeping snake-like stems dangling from the arid rock, angular zig-zag stalks of considerable height, as leaf upon leaf, or in other forms the most irregular and grotesque. Nor is this form stationary in the same individual; for as the stem consists chiefly of cellular tissue, with little woody fibre, it is peculiarly liable to sudden expansions and developments, so that however angular or compressed the branches of a plant may originally have been, the trunks become in time either perfectly cylindrical or with scarcely any visible angles. The flowers, which are white, scarlet, or purple, and often showy and attractive, spring in some species from the woolly crests of the stems, in some from the tufts of spines, and in others from the angular edges and clefts, as if the order was endowed with a reproductive power at every point of the surface. The fruit, like the flower, adheres to the stem, and might be taken for one of the fleshy lobes, were it not for its scarlet or purple colour; so concentrated and huddled together in this family are the stem, branches, leaves, flower, and fruit—organs which in most tribes are separate and well-defined. So much for the general characteristics of the cactaceæ; let us now glance at their distribution and habits, at their individual peculiarities, and economical uses.

All the species of cacti are said to be natives of tropical America; only a few having escaped to the southern states of North America, and to the highlands of Chili and Mendoza. This is rather a circumscribed range; for although the opuntias which cover the volcanic soil of Sicily may be justly regarded as exotics, we can scarcely consider the opuntias, rhipsales, and other cactaceous plants which are found in Central and Southern Africa as other than true natives. Be this as it may, the cacti grow chiefly on hot dry rocks or plains, where the commoner forms of vegetation could not exist, and may be considered as one of the means which nature has provided for the support of animals in regions where neither food nor water can be procured—their stems being filled with an abundant insipid wholesome juice, and their fruit being succulent, and of an agreeable acidulous flavour. To enable them to endure the excessive drought to which they are exposed, they are furnished with an unusually tough leathery skin, which has few, if any, evaporating pores. This envelope prevents the escape of what moisture their long penetrating roots may collect from the soil; and thus during the hotest season they are turgid with juice, while during the rainy season their turgidity breaks forth into new branches, buds, and flowers. No adaptation, indeed, could be more perfect than that of the cactus to the soil and seasonal influences of its native habitat. During the brief period of rain, it puts forth its shoots and blossoms with astonishing rapidity, the flowers of some species, as the *Cereus grandiflorus*, actually opening during night, and fading before the morning. On the return of the drought, the plant concentrates its vital energies, and becomes dormant; its pores are closed, and its skin toughens and thickens, to protect the nutritive juices from waste or injury. And here the cultivator of exotics may learn a useful lesson: were he to attempt to force such plants as the cactaceæ into a perpetual growth, he would speedily impair or exhaust their vitality; but by imitating the conditions under which they naturally grow—by keeping away the stimulant of combined heat and moisture, and by allowing them a season of dormancy and rest, he may preserve them in perfect health for generations.

Plants thus rooting themselves among fissured rocks and on arid shingle, or suspending their whip-like stems from the clefts of decayed trunks, may readily be supposed to be endowed with various means of reproduction, since the chances of soil and moisture are against them. Such, indeed, is the case. The cacti are propagated not only by their seed, but with amazing facility by their buds and branches. Take, for example, the branch or joint of an opuntia, dry it a little, place it in a hot damp place, no matter how scanty the soil, and it strikes root immediately. A jointed plant thus broken asunder by the tread of a foot or the fall of a branch, is actually increased by the very accident which would be certain destruction to plants of a different order. Nay, each tuft of spines is a bud, and if the top of the plant be cut down or injured, every tuft swells and becomes a bud; every bud a branch, which, when detached, will strike root, and spring up into a new individual. Many hundreds, and even thousands of tufts, have been counted on a single gigantic cactus; so that, with a power of increase so enormous, we can readily account for the frequency and distribution of the order among the rocks and plains of Central America, notwithstanding the numerous severities of soil and climate to which they are subjected. Naturalists have descanted on the uses of the mosses and lichens in clothing the naked rock with soil; the cacti are also not without their importance in this respect, though operating in a somewhat different manner. De Candolle, in speaking of the opuntia, remarks, that it is employed to good purpose in fertilising the old lavas at the foot of Mount Ætna. 'As soon as a fissure is perceived, a branch or joint of an opuntia is stuck in; the latter pushes out roots, which are nourished by the rain that collects round them, or by whatever dust or remains of organic matter may have collected into a soil; these roots once developed, insinuate themselves into the most minute crevices, expand, and finally break up the lava into mere fragments. These fragments suffer further decomposition by exposure to the atmosphere and human culture, and so in time constitute the basis of a fertile soil.'

Regarding the peculiarities of the respective genera, little need be said, as these depend rather upon difference of form than on any essential distinction of habit or property. The order is usually divided by botanists into two sections—*Opuntiaceæ* and *Rhipsalidæ*—on account of a minute difference in the manner in which the seed is arranged within the fruit. That this distinction is unimportant in a general point of view, may be learned from the fact, that the first section comprehends all the genera save one—the solitary *Rhipsalis*, on which the second section is founded. The described genera are—*Cactus*, *Melocactus*, *Opuntia*, *Cereus*, *Mamillaria*, *Echinocactus*, *Epiphyllum*, and *Pereskia*, of which we may particularise the following:—The mamillaria, so called from the pap-like tubercles which cover its sub-cylindrical stem, is a common form in our conservatories. Each tubercle is covered with a little tuft of radiating spines, and the flowers which sit close to the stem are ranged in a kind of zone round the plant, giving it rather an elegant appearance. The melon-cactus, or Turk's cap, one of the most singularly formed, has a globose melon-shaped stem, covered with alternate furrows and ridges, the latter being armed with spiny tufts, which effectually guard the succulent parts from the depredations of animals. The stem is crowned by a woolly tuft—the tassel of the fancied cap—which bears the flowers and fruit. This genus delights in the most arid plains of America, and is often the only vegetable that gladdens the waste. It is found of all ages, and from the size of a hand-ball to that of the largest bomb. The wild horses are said to seek its refreshing juice when every vestige of external moisture has failed, striking asunder its succulent trunk with repeated blows of the forefoot—an operation which, from the dangerous nature of its spines, requires considerable address. The echinocactus, or hedgehog thistle, has also a globose stem, but wants the woolly head, and has its flowers springing from the tufts of spines which arm its ridges. It is to this genus that the 'monster at Kew' belongs, of whose history and dimensions we learn the following particulars from a recent number of the Gardeners' Chronicle:—

The gigantic cacti in the royal gardens—for it seems there are two—are the gift of Frederick Staines, Esq., of San Luis, Potosi, in compliment to whom one of them has been named *Echinocactus Stainesii*; and the other *E. Visnaga*, from a native word signifying twice pointed, in allusion to the character of its prickles. The former was received towards the end of 1844, and the latter, which has been designated 'the monster,' par excellence, so recently as February 1845. Mr Staines made the discovery of this Titan in 1843, and thus announced his intention of sending him to England. 'I mean to have him deposited in a strong box, sending the box first to the mountain where the monster grows, and placing it on the springs of a carriage, which I shall despatch for that purpose, and so forward it to Vera Cruz. My monster friend cannot travel any other way, from his stupendous size and immense ponderosity, which cannot be accurately calculated here, where the largest machine for conveying weights does not pass 400 pounds. This enormous plant will require twenty men at least to place it upon the vehicle, with the aid of such levers as our Indians can invent upon the occasion. Should this huge specimen reach Kew, what must be your admiration on seeing it, when you express such delight on receiving the former one. The viznaga grows in the deep ravines of our loftiest mountains, amongst huge stones: the finest plants are inaccessible to wheeled vehicles, and even on horseback it is difficult to reach them. Still, I shall use my utmost endeavours to get a large one, and shall cause the palm-mats to be sewed most carefully round his huge and thorny circumference, before applying to his roots the crowbars destined to wrench him from his resting-place of unknown centuries. He will have to travel 300 leagues; and happy shall I be if I hear that the carriage has not broken down between this city and Mexico, through which capital he must pass on his way to Vera Cruz. These monsters are of a dark green colour, with formidable black spines, 3 inches long.' After various trials and difficulties—the breaking down of the carriage, and the impossibility of getting a proper box constructed for his reception—the cactus was brought down to Vera Cruz, packed as a bale, and shipped for England. 'It was on Saturday, February 15, 1845, that the viznaga, together with five large boxes filled with other individuals of the same tribe, and rarities of different kinds, reached the Botanic Gardens in a condition of security and vigour which were quite remarkable, considering their bulk and weight, the vast overland journey, mainly performed through a country of high mountains and perilous roads, and their arrival in our island during one of the severest frosts that had been experienced for many winters. This degree of safety can only be attributed to the extreme care that had been bestowed upon the packing, and the materials with which the specimens were surrounded. The large cactus was first surrounded with a dense clothing of the Spanish moss (*Tillandsia usneoides*), and well corded. Fifteen mats, each as large and as thick as an ordinary door-mat, and composed of the fibres of a palm sewn together, formed the exterior envelope. Freed from these incumbrances, the monster viznaga was seen as perfect, as green, and as uninjured, as if it had been that morning removed from its native rocks, the very long flagelliform roots arranged in coils like the cable of a ship. Ten of our strongest men with difficulty placed it in scales, to ascertain its precise weight; and afterwards, with still greater difficulty, transferred it perfectly unharmed to a tub prepared with suitable soil.' The net weight was 713 pounds; height from the surface of the earth, 4½ feet; measured over the top from the ground, on each side, 10½ feet; circumference at one foot from the ground, 8 feet 7 inches; number of ridges or costæ, 44; each ridge had 50 tufts of spines; and as in each tuft there are four spines, the total number must be 8800—no insignificant armature, when we remember that each spine is not less than 3 inches long. Compared with the ordinary growth of the globular cacti, the viznaga is a Titan indeed; the dimensions of the majority varying within the limits we have already mentioned.

Following out our detail, the next in order is the *Pilocereus*, or old-man cactus, so called from its resemblance, when of small size, to an old man's head, being covered with long white hairs, which hang down like hoary locks. In our hothouses it is generally of small size; but in its native country it is said to attain the height of 12 or 15 feet, thereby losing its likeness to the object from which it has received its most familiar name. The Peruvian torch thistles (*Cereus Peruvianus* and *hexagonus*) are still more gigantic plants, often attaining a height of 40 feet, though their stems be not much thicker than a man's arm. The creeping cereus (*C. flagelliformis*) is well known from its long snake-like stems, which hang down from the sides of the suspended pots in which it is usually grown; and the night-flowering cereus (*C. grandiflorus*), the blossoms of which open during night, and fade before morning, has been long an object of attraction. It has an angular, branched, and clambering stem, which throws out roots at every joint, and has a magnificent flower; the rays of the calyx of a bright yellow when open, and the petals of the most delicate white. The flower-bud begins to open at seven or eight o'clock in the evening, is fully blown by eleven, and by three or four in the morning is faded and withered. The *Opuntias*, which are numerous and useful, are distinguished by their oblong, flat, leaf-like branches, united together by joints, and for the most part covered by spines. In Europe, the height they attain is insignificant; but in warmer regions they sometimes rise to 10 or 15 feet above the arid soil that supports them. In South Africa, Mr Backhouse saw an opuntia 10 feet high, with numerous branches, and covered with splendid yellow blossoms. Compared with the genera of the first section, the *Rhipsalis* is an insignificant plant, having a slender-jointed stem, not unlike the common rock samphire.

The economical value of the cactaceæ is not the least important feature in their history. Many of the species yield an esculent fruit, which partakes of that acidulous flavour so much esteemed in the gooseberry and currant family. The pulpy berry of the Opuntia tuna, which resembles in shape and size the fig of Europe, has gained for it the name of 'Indian fig'—a term by which the whole family is sometimes designated. This fruit forms a very refreshing repast in Spanish America and the West Indies; and that gathered from the common opuntia of Ætna is sold for a similar purpose in all the towns of Sicily. The fruit of the different species is known by such names as Indian fig, prickly pear, strawberry pear, &c.—the latter being the produce of a cereus, and the most highly-prized for its flavour and cooling properties. In Brazil, the opuntias are much planted round houses, as a fence which neither man nor animals can easily break through—a use to which we believe they are also applied in the south of Europe. When the island of St Christopher (St Kitts) was to be divided between the British and French, three rows of the *O. tuna* were planted by common consent to form the boundary. The chief importance of the cacti and opuntias, however, consists in their being the natural food of the cochineal insect—*coccus cacti*—so valuable in the arts. This insect, which is not unlike the mealbug of our gardens, has the substance of the body coloured of a rich scarlet throughout; the richness of the dye depending upon the nature of the plant on which it feeds. The species in greatest repute is the *Opuntia coccifera*, or spineless cochineal fig, of which there are extensive plantations in Mexico and the West Indies, for the purpose of preparing cochineal. The male insect is winged; the female alone is used as a dye. There are two kinds of cochineal, which are reputed to feed on different species of cacti. One of these, the wild or common cochineal, is covered with a silky envelope, and is not so valuable as the cultivated sort, which has a powdery or mealy covering. The female insects, after feeding on the cacti for three or four months, are brushed off by means of a squirrel's tail, and are then killed by exposure either to the sun or to the vapour of hot water. When dried, they are exported in large quantities; and the colouring matter is easily extracted by water and alcohol, or hartshorn. It is stated that 800,000 pounds of cochineal are annually brought to Europe; each pound containing about 70,000 insects. The annual consumption in Great Britain alone is estimated at upwards of 150,000 pounds; about L.300,000 sterling. So valuable to man is an insect which ignorance would be apt to regard as mean and insignificant.

It is a curious consideration that two such important substances as silk and cochineal—the one adding beauty to the other's utility—should be the produce of small and apparently insignificant insects. The silkworm obtains its food from the mulberry; the cochineal insect feeds on the cactus. The *materiel* of silk and cochineal must exist in the vegetable structure; yet man, with all his boasted skill in chemical science, can neither imitate the fibre of the one nor the dye of the other. The animal chemistry of the tiny insect outstrips the most ambitious effort of the laboratory, as far as the works of nature will ever surpass the efforts of human art. The insect, however—and here lies the consoling distinction—in producing its finest fabric, merely obeys a law of nature which it cannot avoid; with man, every product is the result of intellectual skill and responsible reason.

From the preceding sketch, the reader may form some idea of this singular order of vegetation, and be enabled more fully to appreciate the merits of the giant visnaga at Kew. To gaze at an object without some knowledge of its relations, properties, and uses, is mere senseless wonderment: we can only admire where we are sufficiently informed.

WRITING HISTORY FOR THE PEOPLE.

We have not for a long time met anything more entirely accordant with our own views upon a speculative subject, than certain remarks which the Athenæum quotes in a late number from a brief essay of M. de Lamartine, *On the Manner of Writing History for the People.* With thanks to our periodical brother for bringing these remarks under our attention, we transfer them entire to our own columns. Let our readers of every rank deeply ponder upon them.

'I have often said to myself what you say with so much good sense to your readers in the introduction to your useful book, "After having equalised rights, we must equalise as nearly as possible intellects. The task of our times is to raise the masses to the conditions of civilisation; of that relative leisure and ease which may permit them to instruct themselves. A popular encyclopædia would be a peaceful revolution." * * But in what spirit will you and your friends write a history for the use of the people? Popular writers have hitherto grossly flattered the people—a proof that they had no great esteem for them; for we flatter only those whom we seek to seduce. Why were they flattered? Because they were made an instrument, and not an end. Such writers said to themselves, The force is there: we want it to upset governments which constrain us, or to absorb countries which we covet: let us invite the people; let us intoxicate them with their own praises; let us tell them that right resides with numbers, that their will is justice, that God is on the side of great armies, that all means are good to secure the success of the popular cause, and that even crime is effaced by the grandeur and the sanctity of results. They will believe us, follow us, and lend us the physical force we need; and when, by the aid of their arms, their blood, and even their crimes, we shall have overthrown a despotism, and convulsed Europe, we will dismiss them, and tell them in our turn, Be silent, work, and obey. This is the way in which they have hitherto been addressed; thus have the vices of courts been transported into the streets, and the people been inoculated with such a love of adulation, and such a craving for obsequiousness and caresses, that, like certain sovereigns of the Lower Empire, they would only be spoken to kneeling.

This is not the course to be pursued. We must speak to them erect, on a level, face to face. The people are neither better nor worse than the other elements of the nation; numbers are nothing. Take each of the individuals [illegible] find? The same ignorances, the same errors, the same passions, often the same vices, as elsewhere. Are these men before whom to kneel? No. Multiply all these ignorances, vices, passions, miserable weaknesses, by as many millions as you will, you will not change their nature. Let us leave talking of numbers, and respect only truth.

In writing history for the people, you must consider truth alone. And do not think that you will be less listened to, or less popular on that account: the people have indeed acquired a depraved taste for adulation and falsehood; but their natural tastes are for truth and courage. They respect those who dare to brave them, and despise those who fear them.

This being the case, what point of view will you select for writing your people's history? There are three principal views which you may take—that of glory, that of patriotism, and that of civilisation, or of the morality of the acts you are about to relate. If you consider an act under the aspect of glory, you will delight a warlike nation, which has been dazzled long before it has been enlightened, and which this false glitter has so often blinded as to the true value of the men and things which appeared in its horizon. If you place yourself in the exclusive point of view of its patriotism, you will excite all the enthusiasm of a people which pleads the excuse of its safety and its greatness for its lofty egotism, and which, in the feeling of its greatness and its strength, has sometimes forgotten that it was not alone in Europe. But neither of these points of view will give you the real truth—that is, the general truth; they will give you only the French truth. But French truth is true only at Paris; cross the frontier, and it is a lie. It is not this truth, circumscribed within the limits of a nation, that you wish to inculcate; it is not to this that you would bring down the intelligence of the people. What, then, remains? The universal and permanent point of view; that is to say, the point of view of the morality of the actions of the individuals or of the nations which you have to describe. All other aspects of the subject are enlightened by false or partial gleams: this alone stands in the full and divine light of day: this alone can guide the infirmity of human judgments through the labyrinth of personal or national prejudices, opinions, passions, interests, and enable a people to say—this is right; this is wrong; this is great or noble. In a word, if you wish to form the judgment of the masses, to rescue them from the immoral doctrine of success, do what has never been done yet—*give a conscience to history.* This is the work demanded for our age, and worthy of our people. By treating history thus, you will perhaps have less immediate popularity; you will not strike the passionate imagination of the masses; but you will render a thousand times better service to their cause, their interests, and their reason.

To give an example: one of the great events of the age—one of those days which divide for a length of time the fate of a revolution, of a nation, or of an empire—was the 18th Brumaire. You would doubtless have to relate it: how would you contemplate it? Should it be under the aspect of glory? That is dazzling; it glitters like a drawn sword in the sun; it whirls like the dust raised by a squadron of horse galloping by, filling the ear with noise and the eye with *éclat!* Here is a man coming from distant camps, preceded by his name, strong in his renown, accustomed to military discipline, weary of the tardiness, the resistance, and the inconvenient noise of a government of discussion; who, impatient of the slow and collective work of establishing liberty, takes advantage of a momentary discouragement of the public mind, mounts his horse at the head of a few grenadiers, breaks all this republican machine with his sword, and says, "Give me the empire; you can only talk, I will act." He succeeds; the revolution falls into his hands; he transforms it at his will: incapable of constituting the disordered elements into a nation, he forms them into an army, launches it against the world, intoxicates it with victories, and seizes the crown it tenders him. This is very fine. Make this glitter in the eyes of the masses—they will be dazzled by it: will you have instructed them?

Or will you contemplate the same event in the patriotic point of view? It is the universal monarchy of the French flag; the people sees itself everywhere under the image of its victorious armies; French patriotism appears vast as the continent of Europe, and exclaims, "L'Europe c'est moi;" it deifies itself. By presenting the fact thus, you will excite the people to enthusiasm for an event which has robbed them of all the fruits of the revolution before they were ripe, and of all the moral conquests of the eighteenth century. Will you have elevated their character?

Lastly, will you view this same event under the aspect of the morality of the act and of its influence on true civilisation? It completely changes. There is a man to whom the free government of his country has intrusted an army for its defence against factions, and who converts that army into a military faction against that government. Here is an anarchical and bloody revolution, which by the sheer force of the public mind, and the spontaneous course of civil reactions, had traversed the most deplorable crises, and washed its hands with shame of the blood odiously shed; and whose violent oscillations daily became more temperate, and showed a tendency to confine themselves within the limits of a vital but regular motion. This man comes and stops the revolutionary movement exactly at the point where it ceased to be convulsive, and began to be creative. He arms himself with all the repentances, the resentments, the apostacies, which a revolution always leaves in its train; he reconstitutes an *ancien régime* with names and things of yesterday; he imposes a censorship on the press, and silence on the tribune; creates a nobility of plebeians, and converts religion into a tool of government. He stifles throughout Europe all sympathy with French ideas, under the hatred inspired by violence and conquest. What is the result of this drama with one actor? You see. A name the more in history; but France twice invaded, and her boundaries narrowed from without and from within—reason, liberty, and the improvement of the masses indefinitely retarded by this episode of glory, and condemned, perhaps, to pass a century in recovering what it lost in a day. Such is the 18th Brumaire under its three aspects. Need I tell you which is mine?

You may treat every incident of the French Revolution in the same manner: you will, in every case, find these three aspects: the purely individual—glory; the exclusively national—patriotism; and the moral—civilisation. And if you follow out the consequences logically, you will invariably arrive at this result, that glory and patriotism, severed from general morality, are sterile for a particular nation as well as for humanity at large.

To teach the people by facts, by events, by the hidden meaning of those great historic dramas of which men see only the scenes and the actors, but whose plot is contrived by an invisible hand; to teach them to know, to judge, to moderate themselves; to make them capable of distinguishing those who serve from those who mislead them, those who dazzle from those who enlighten; to point to every great man or great event of their own history, and say, Weigh them yourselves, not with the false weights of your passions of a day—your prejudices, your anger, your national vanity, your narrow patriotism—but with the just weights of the universal conscience of the human race, and the utility of the act to the cause of civilisation; to convince them that every nation has its post, its part assigned to it, every class of society its relative importance in the sight of God; to teach the people hence to respect themselves, and to participate religiously, and with full consciousness of what they are doing, in the progressive accomplishment of the great designs of Providence; in a word, to create in them a moral sense, and to exercise that moral sense on great events and men of their history, and on themselves; I venture to say that this were to give the people much more than empire, power, or government: it were to give them conscience; the judgment and the sovereignty of themselves: it were to place them above all governments; for, indeed, the very day on which they are fit to reign, they will reign—it signifies little under what form or what name. It is the people that must be modified; governments will modify themselves after its image; for be assured, as is the people, so is the government; and when a people complains of its own, it is because it is unworthy to have another. This was the opinion of Tacitus in his days, and it is equally true in our own.

OATMEAL MORE NUTRITIOUS THAN WHEAT.

The following playful comparison between the relative alimentary powers of oatmeal and wheaten flour, is copied from a useful article on Practical Agriculture in Blackwood's Magazine for March:—Professor Johnston, in the recent edition of his Elements of Agricultural Chemistry and Geology, tells us that, from experiments made in the laboratory of the Agricultural Chemistry Association of Scotland, it turns out that oats are far richer in muscular matter, fat, and starch, than the best wheat flour grown in any part of England—that they contain eighteen or twenty per cent. of that which forms muscle, five to eight of fat, and sixty-five of starch. The account, therefore, between shelled oats (groats) and fine wheaten flour stands thus. One hundred pounds of each contain—

	Wheat.	Oats.
Muscular matter, ...	10 lbs.	18 lbs.
Fat, ...	3 ...	6 ...
Starch, ...	50 ...	65 ...
	63 lbs.	89 lbs.

What do you say to these numbers, Mr Cockney? You wont pity us, Scotch oatmeal-eaters, any more, we guess. Experience and science are both on our side. What makes your race-horses the best in the world, may be expected to make our peasantry the best too. We offer you, therefore, a fair bet. You shall take ten English ploughmen, and feed them upon two pounds and a half of wheaten flour a-day, and we shall take as many Scotch ploughmen, and feed them upon the same weight of oatmeal a-day—if they can eat so much, for that is doubtful—and we shall back our men against yours for any sum you like. They shall walk, run, work—or fight you, if you like it—and they shall thrash you to your heart's content. We should like to convince you that Scotch parritch has some real solid metal in it. We back the oatcake and the porridge against all the wheaten messes in the world. We defy your home-made bread, your bakers' bread, your household bread, your leaven bread, and your brown Georges—your fancy bread and your raisin bread—your baps, rolls, scones, muffins, crumpets, and cookies—your bricks, biscuits, bakes, and rusks—your Bath buns and your Sally Luns—your tea-cakes, and saffron-cakes, and slim-cakes, and plank-cakes, and pan-cakes, and soda-cakes, and currant-cakes, and sponge-cakes, and seed-cakes, and girdle-cakes, and singing-hinnies—your shortbread and your currant-buns—and if there be any other names by which you designate your wheaten abominations, we defy and detest them all. We swear by the oatcake and the porridge, the substantial bannock and the brose—long may Scotland produce them, and Scotchmen live and fight upon them!

PURSUIT OF KNOWLEDGE.

He that enlarges his curiosity after the works of nature, demonstrably multiplies the inlets to happiness; therefore we should cherish ardour in the pursuit of useful knowledge, and remember that a blighted spring makes a barren year, and that the vernal flowers, however beautiful and gay, are only intended by nature as preparatives to autumnal fruits.—*Johnson.*

SONNET.

BY S. W. PARTRIDGE.

Urging with queenly grace her upward way
Through the blue lonely sky, night's mateless queen
Lights up the landscape with her silver sheen,
And gladdens all around with softened ray.
On the cold pearly ground the shadows play;
The dusky trees in gloomy grandeur lean
O'er the gray moveless stream in sleep serene;
And all things dream the silent hours away.
Vision of beauty, my poor senses reel,
Intoxicated with thy witchery:
My heart o'erbrims with joy; and yet I sigh,
Such hushing melancholy awe I feel!
Alas that drowsy sleep should o'er me steal,
And to thy charms seal up my ravished eye.

We are occasionally asked by correspondents why they cannot obtain title-pages and tables of contents for the volumes of our Miscellany of Useful and Entertaining Tracts. In reply to these inquiries, we beg to say that titles and contents at the price of a number can always be had from the booksellers. Any bookseller who has not got them, can be supplied on demand.

Printed by William Bradbury, of No. 6, York Place, and Frederick Mullett Evans, of No. 7, Church Row, both of Stoke Newington, in the county of Middlesex, printers, at their office, Lombard Street, in the precinct of Whitefriars, and city of London; and Published (with permission of the Proprietors, W. and R. CHAMBERS,) by WILLIAM SOMERVILLE ORR, Publisher, of 3, Amen Corner, at No. 2, AMEN CORNER, both in the parish of Christchurch, and in the city of London.—Saturday, April 15, 1843.

CONDUCTED BY WILLIAM AND ROBERT CHAMBERS, EDITORS OF 'CHAMBERS'S INFORMATION FOR THE PEOPLE,' 'CHAMBERS'S EDUCATIONAL COURSE,' &c.

No. 69. New Series. SATURDAY, APRIL 26, 1845. Price 1½d.

THE VISITATION OF RICHES.

A very alarming consideration has lately been presented to the people of England, who once dreamt not of ever suffering from such a cause—namely, that they are getting too rich. The true source of the manifold evils of our state is at length discovered to be, that we have far too much money. Individuals have too much money, and are greatly the worse of it. The community, as a community, has too much money, and daily suffers unheard-of misery in consequence. It is a terrible business. Charles Lamb, when reminded by his sister of the days when they were poor, and capable of enjoying every little treat with the keenest relish, so different from these days when they were rich, stately, and dull, said, 'Well, Bridget, since we are in easy circumstances, we must just endeavour to put up with it.' But, I fear, no such maxims of resignation will now avail in either the particular or the general case. It is not ennui which has come with affluence—no; somehow, this abundance of capital is now found to be attended with a vast amount of positive mischief. Political writers declaim day by day on the dismal effects of wealth upon the poor, and professors of light literature find themselves weighed down with a sense of the turpitude of all rich men. Men are compelled to work, because there is money to be had for it—a thing heretofore unheard of in this world. Every man that has anything, necessarily becomes depraved in himself, and a tyrant over others. And, unfortunately, so prevalent has wealth become, that if you would seek for any vestige of the virtues in England, you have to look for it in persons who used to be thought almost too humble and obscure for notice long ago; such as ultra-ragged street-porters, and that selection of the rural population who take to poaching. In short, England, once the envy of surrounding nations on political grounds, is rapidly becoming an object fit only for their pity and contempt through the efficacy of this disease of wealth. Powerful remedies are required, and if such be not speedily applied, it is to be feared that all will soon go to wreck, and the sun of British glory, as the newspapers have it, set for ever.

In these terrible circumstances, it becomes all who wish well to their country to exert themselves to the utmost in its behalf. So feeling, I am anxious here to set down a few observations upon the subject, which I think may just possibly be found of some service. I am a plain man, who always go straight to the point when I can; and it therefore occurs to me, as the first expedient, to set forth to my countrymen a strong warning on the sin and danger of getting rich. They must for the future avoid this error, if they would see their country rescued from impending ruin, or themselves saved from being altogether demoralised. It might form a strong inducement to them to abstain from money-making, if they would only consider that, so long as they remain poor, and of no account in the world, they will be held poetically entitled to possess every excellence; whereas, if they add to their store of goods, they are sure to become cold-blooded, heartless wretches, fit for nothing but to be impaled in the anatomical museum of modern fiction. Indeed, were things properly understood, we should be seeing the comfortable millionaires of the city—going about, I was going to say, like the characters in the play of the Bottle Imp, endeavouring to get others to take upon them the burden of their wealth; but this, I now reflect, were a vain endeavour, seeing that no one could, in such circumstances, be induced to relieve them of the load—trying, then, to destroy this wealth so effectually, that it should be hurtful to no other men. We should see nobles and country gentlemen surrendering their possessions to be employed as commons, and well-beneficed clergymen returning to a state of apostolical simplicity. Such a thing as a rich old bachelor uncle should not be known upon earth: all they have should, with full consent of nephews and nieces, be thrown into the sea. In short, there should be a universal retrogression to that beautiful and happy state in which our painted forefathers were about two thousand years ago. This is taking a somewhat strong view, and perhaps, constituted as the public mind now is, it cannot be hoped that any but those who are in the last extreme of poverty already will go so far. We must take men as we find them, and be content to get them along with us on a right course as far as they will go. I can see nothing, however, to prevent us from putting a stop to the further acquisition of wealth, seeing that all are agreed that depravity is the certain fate of those who have much more than themselves. Everybody will naturally see it to be right that he should stop short in that career in which he finds all who have got before himself to be marked by the most detestable qualities that belong to human nature.

It is an awkward thing to ask of an Englishman; but yet, let it be ever so awkward, I must ask it, for it is indispensable. Henceforth let them pause at every thing which appears before them in the form of an 'opening.' An Englishman naturally likes an opening. It is his grand temptation. But let him look through the opening, and see what is beyond. He will there behold a number of persons who, having gone into it, are now affluent, but at the same time extremely bad. Perhaps they are 'guardians,' who of course grind the poor; perhaps justices, who condemn vagrants possessed of more honourable feelings than themselves; perhaps patrons of charities, who are necessarily mere bags of the wind of vanity, using the objects of their beneficence only as instruments for promoting their own honour and glory, and not possessing a single particle of the true spirit of good deeds. Think how dreadful it would be to rise into such conditions as these—think, pause; remain content where you are. You could take the state, and resist its temptations! Ay, so all think before they enter on the fatal road; but yet they invariably become the hardened selfish vain wretches which you see; and how can you suppose that it is to be otherwise with you? No, no, my friends. Lay no such flattering unction to your souls. Depend upon it, the moment you step beyond the state of immaculate indigence in which a kind Providence has placed you, you become changed men. Every trace of goodness forsakes you, and you stand, in the eyes of contemporary moralists, as only so much dross.

So much for private measures; but surely, if the evils in question be so clear, we may expect ere long to see them brought under the sage notice of parliament. This body has always shown a remarkable anxiety to take away the peccant matter of the disease, and undoubtedly it would exert itself to greater purpose than ever for the depletion of the nation's system, if necessary. A country, indeed, with such a government as ours, ought never to be at any loss, one would say, for phlebotomy, and I therefore believe that the petitions required to bring the attention of parliament to this point, would be much fewer than is customary. Having once heard the national will upon the subject, the senate would doubtless quickly pass an act enforcing voluntary impoverishment all over the empire; another for preventing any man from making more than what he can fairly consume in meat and drink day by day. All just and proper quarrels with bread and butter, such as strikes, short work, and the laying aside of female labour, would at the same time be legislatively encouraged to the uttermost, and, in short, everything done to maintain the righteous cause of poverty against all contrary influences and tendencies. The first effect would undoubtedly be to reduce the population of the country to something like what it was in the days of King Vortigern; but what of that? A short though sharp evil would be well worth encountering, where the ultimate results were of so promising a kind. A fair start in a new national career, free from the accursed presence of gold, would be worth purchasing at any expense. Only let us take care, both as individuals and as a nation, never to grow rich any more.

But can we expect that the people are to call upon the legislature for any such measures? There is the point. With a few popular authors at the head of the movement, setting an example by consenting to abjure all profits from their works beyond what might have sustained an ancient Spartan, I would not despair. Are my suggestions pronounced impracticable, and are we still to see the ideas, Englishman and wealth, in unholy conjunction; are the Crœsuses of the Exchange and the factories still to be ogres of our maturer childhood; and must we never hope to see the days of primeval simplicity restored? Be it so. If the evil must be, let us endeavour, in the spirit of Charles Lamb, to put up with it; the more so that we are not without something to compensate it on the other side. For it is a beautiful feature of our present condition, that, just as there is an extreme of society who are corrupted by wealth, so is there another which derives the highest lustre from poverty. Not the poverty which our fathers used to speak of as respectable; namely, that of honest men toiling for their daily bread, and eating it in independence, but the poverty which is attended by a practical contempt for such mean virtues as prudence, and is at constant war with the detestable house of Have. Seeing things thus balanced, we may yet hope that England will at least be able to rub on for a few more generations. She will have many sons who, spite of everything, will continue to make money, and contrive to abide by its lamentable consequences; she will see these men withholding the least share of their abundance from workhouses, hospitals, and other modes of succouring the poor, in practice among less wealth-corrupted nations. Her Bowleys, her Cutes, and her Filers, will be base, besotted wretches, disgracing her name. But then she will have a great fund of excellence among those classes who, in other countries, are usually held as vile, and the honour of the British name, which once lay in her high-spirited gentlemen and her honourable burghers, will be upheld by her mendicants and malefactors.

POPULAR INFORMATION ON SCIENCE.

MORPHOLOGY.

One of the most curious doctrines connected with vegetable life, is that which affirms that all the parts of a plant—stem, branches, flower, fruit, and seed—are but various modifications of one common organ; namely, the leaf. This view was first broached by Linnæus, improved upon by Wolff, and subsequently expounded by the German poet Goethe. It is to the latter that we are mainly indebted for the exposition of the doctrine: he it was that clothed it with a poetic mystery, and sung in glowing language the series of developments which takes place between the germination of the seed and the ripening of the fruit. His reasoning proceeds upon the basis, that if one organ can be transformed into another, there is an identity in their origin and nature. If, for example, leaves are sometimes converted into bracts, bracts into a calyx, and the calyx into a corolla, then it is almost self-evident that the corolla, calyx, and bracts, have the same origin as the leaves. Let us glance at the facts by which this doctrine is sought to be established.

Varied as are the forms and properties of plants, the plan upon which their development proceeds is simple in the extreme. Growth is but a modification of one kind of tissue, and one kind of external organ. Every plant in the embryo or seed state consists of minute spherical cells possessing vitality—these constitute its elementary tissue. If the seed be planted under favourable conditions of soil, heat, and moisture, the cells will be excited to growth; that is, they will give birth to new cells, these again to other cellules, and so on, till the principle of vitality be exhausted. In this process the cells develope themselves variously—some by their elongation giving rise to woody fibre, some by the manner of their arrangement to spiral vessels, and others merely to cells like themselves—thus forming the different vessels, fibres, &c. of which the substance of the plant is composed, and through which its sap is conveyed and disseminated. So far as the mere elementary tissue is concerned, there might or might not have been any external organs; that is, parts assuming a definite form, and having a definite function assigned them; and such is the case with many of the lower fungi and lichens, which are mere irregular aggregations of spherical cells. In the higher orders of vegetation—and it is of these that we are now speaking—nature has decreed otherwise. A plant must respire, must receive nourishment from the air as well as from the soil, and must accordingly have a structure fitted to perform these functions. At the dawn of its development, therefore, the elementary tissue expands into a certain form or structure, which we regard as primary. This form we designate *a leaf*: it is that which first presents itself on the germination of a seed: it is the first effort of the elementary tissue; and all subsequent efforts are but special modifications of the original. Such is the simple plan upon which vegetable development takes place. The whole substance of a plant is modified cellular tissue; all its external organs of branch, flower, and fruit, but modifications of one organ—the leaf. Indeed the growth of all living matter, whether vegetable or animal, is based upon cellular development; and we find also in the higher animals that their various external organs are but metamorphosed forms of one common type. Take, for example, the fore-leg or arm of the vertebrata, assuming that of man as the type, and observe how differently it is formed in the monkey, the bear, the horse, the cow, the bat, and the wing of the pigeon.

skeleton of the pigeon's wing and the leg of the bear are nevertheless formed upon the same plan as the arm of man, each being but modifications of the same organ, according to the destined habits of the animal. Skilful anatomists can detect the corresponding bones in each, can say where development is directed from the normal type, can tell what parts are atrophied, and what peculiarly expanded. So it is with the botanist; he can detect the leaf-type in all the members of a plant, be these spines, bracts, petals, stamens, or pistils.

The first protrusion of the seed-germ is leaf-like; subsequently true leaves are developed; and the elementary tissue, in its effort to produce a succession of these, forms the stem. The branches of the stem take their origin from leaf-buds, and these again are clothed with branchlets and leaves by the same process as the main stem. As a branch proceeds towards the point of fructification, the leaves assume the form of bracts; these again are succeeded by the leaf-like sepals of the calyx; and next by the petals of the corolla or blossom. Within the petals are the stamens, which sometimes assume a leafy form; next the pistil, which is often leafy; and ultimately the seed-vessels, which almost always bear internal evidence of their being composed of peculiarly altered leaves. Even the seeds are but leaves in another form, embalmed and preserved for the production of another plant; and in many, such as the beech-mast, the leaflets of the embryo may be distinctly seen, folded and imbedded in their future nutriment.

> 'Here root, and leaf, and bud, enfolded lie
> Enshrined within their husky tenement
> Incipient foretypes of the coming plant:
> In silent life, half-formed and colourless;
> But soon again, replete with earth-given moisture,
> The leaf expands above surrounding night,
> And breathes the incense of the open day.'

Thus the growth and reproduction of plants may be regarded as a circle of leaf-like changes, the leaf, or some modification of it, being in all cases the organ which administers to the functions of vitality. The great object of a plant's life is to preserve, during all the phases of its growth, a leaf, or an assemblage of leaves, for the purpose of reproduction. A growing branch terminates in a leaf-bud; that is, in a number of embryo leaves folded over the vital point, and carefully covered with scales or gummy matter, to protect them from the inclemency of the winter: a branch in which development is exhausted terminates in flower and seed. And mark how beautifully the latter is produced! The branch that had hitherto luxuriantly given birth to leaves, suddenly ceases to prolong itself; the leaves are developed more closely to each other; and gradually they lose the form of true leaves, and become bracts; the bracts are succeeded by the little leaf-like sepals of the calyx, which are set together still more closely, and in a circular form; the leafy petals of the corolla succeed, and are followed by the stamens and pistil, all of which circle inwards to a common centre, that centre being the ovary and seed. The seed is the ultimate effort in this case, just as the leaf-bud was in the other, and is merely a leaf, or couple of leaves curiously folded, imbedded in proper nutriment, and protected by a husk, a nut, a stony drupe, or some other covering, as safely and tenderly as a mother would her infant. The leaf-bud and seed differ only in the latter being a more concentrated form of vitality. The bud can only exist in connexion with a living plant; the seed, when matured, will endure for centuries. In the leaf-bud, the energies of the plant are more directed to the increase of the individual; in the seed they are directed towards the propagation of the species.

We have further proof of the truth of morphology in the fact, that all the organs—leaves, sepals, petals, stamens, &c.—are often found assuming the forms and functions of one another. Thus in some roses the bracts are exactly similar to the leaves, while in the tulip they frequently partake both of the colour and texture of the sepals, as well as of the texture of the leaf. Again, that [illegible]re is no essential difference between the sepals of the [illegible]yx and the petals of the corolla, is evident from the sepals being frequently coloured, and forming the most beautiful portion of the blossom. In the monkshood, the blue part which forms the flower is botanically the calyx, the petals being entirely concealed under the hood. In the fuchsia, the bright scarlet part is the calyx, and the small purple petals within, the corolla; while in the tulip and crocus the sepals and petals are all coloured alike, so that it would be impossible to distinguish one from the other, did not the sepals grow a little lower on the stem. In some plants the petals and sepals are identical in colour, texture, and odour; and when the perianth is single, these parts seem to be combined. In like manner there is no physiological difference between the petals and leaves. Both have a framework of veins, the interstices of which are filled up with cellular tissue; and both have an epidermis furnished with pores for absorption and respiration. The absolute change of leaves into sepals, and thence into petals, may be occasionally seen in the tulip, the bracts or floral leaves of which are sometimes partially coloured like the proper petals of the flower; or, conversely, the sepals may be often seen presenting the appearance of true leaves; as in the rose, which has sometimes a ring of leaves instead of sepals; or in the polyanthus, whose brown corolla is often surrounded by common leaves. The construction and arrangement of the stamens also point to the same leafy origin. These have occasionally their filaments dilated and leaf-like, as in the white water-lily; and in many cases—such as the double roses, anemones, and ranunculuses—a transition is observable from the outer petals of the corolla to the true stamens; the petals gradually becoming smaller, and ultimately assuming the colour and form of the latter. The pistil and ovary seem formed in the same way by the metamorphosis and union of leaves. Many pistils have a laminated or blade-like shape, and the stigma of some, such as the iris, is leafy. The leafy origin of the seed-vessel is still more perceptible—a follicle or legume, as the pea, being evidently composed of two leaves folded and adhering at the edges. These pods, indeed, sometimes reassume the leafy form, and, instead of seeds, produce along their edges a number of expanded lobes. Even the fleshy apple is but a number of leaves metamorphosed by an increase of cellular tissue, and united so as to form one continuous mass. The leafy origin of fleshy fruits is often very distinct when newly formed, or when by some accident they are rendered abortive at this stage. Nor does this leaf-like circle end with the seed-vessel. Let any one carefully dissect an apple, and he will find that it is not only composed of five leaves united and enlarged by increase of cellular tissue, but that it has in the axil of these leaves a seed or seeds, each composed of two lobes or cotyledons, prepared to commence the circle anew when the season of growth returns.

What are called monstrosities in flowers, furnish another evidence that the floral appendages are merely modifications of the leaf, or at least that the same structure is common to both. These monstrosities generally arise from some accidental circumstance operating, so as to change the flower-bud into a leaf-bud during the germination of the flower. Thus, if a plant be supplied with abundance of moisture and warmth, but with little sunlight, the growing point will be developed into a bud in the centre of the flower, and sometimes a second blossom will be produced at the extremity. A further confirmation of the common origin of the flower and leaf is afforded by the fact, that fuchsias are sometimes found with the flowers half leaves, and the leaves half flowers. One of the properties of the leaf is to produce branches from its axil, or angle which it forms with the stem. The same property is often observable in the sepals, and not unfrequently in the petals, as, for example, in the common pimpernel. In the Gardeners' Chronicle for May 1844, a flower of this plant is figured with two of the petals producing young shoots, in no way distinguishable from the shoots which proceed from the axils of the true leaves. We have thus, without direct evidence, every cause for suspecting that the petals are nothing but modified leaves. We also know that removing a wild plant, as the dog-rose, into a garden, has a tendency to make the flowers double, because enough of cellular tissue is produced to convert the stamens into petals. Leaves and branches are frequently transformed into spines and thorns. Indeed thorns are regarded as leaf-buds which have been rendered abortive by some accidental stoppage of the sap, which prevents the addition of cellular tissue to form perfect leaves. Branches which also take their origin from leaf-buds may be arrested at a certain stage of their growth, so as to form spines instead of perfect branches; and such spines not unfrequently give birth to new leaf-buds and leaves, as may be seen in the common hedge-thorn. 'We see, therefore,' says Dr Lindley, in winding up this curious subject, 'that there is not only a continuous uninterrupted passage from the leaves to the bracts, from bracts to calyx, from calyx to corolla, from corolla to stamens, and from stamens to pistil—from which circumstance alone the origin of all these organs might have been referred to the leaves—but there is also a continuous tendency to revert to the form of the leaf.'

The preceding is a rapid glance at the leading principles of morphology, which, when thoroughly understood, exhibit the whole plan of vegetable growth in the utmost simplicity and uniformity. Increase of substance, in whatever part, is but cellular development; multiplicity of form and organisation, mere modification of the leaf. Or we may regard the leaf as the individual, and the entire plant as an assemblage of individuals—each set being modified according to the functions they have to perform. There is certainly nothing more incredible in the statement of these modifications, than there is in the well-known morphosis of the frog from the tadpole, or of the butterfly from the successive stages of caterpillar and chrysalis. The drone, working-bee, and queen-bee, differ in structure according to the functions they are destined to execute; yet they can be transformed into each other, proving that they are but modifications of one common form. So it is with the leaves of plants; one set administers to the process of growth, another to defence, and a third to the functions of reproduction—each assuming a form suitable to its appointed office. Nature is never prodigal of her resources: by the slightest modifications of one great design, she can produce a thousand different results; and thus it is that in creation we find the greatest variety with the utmost simplicity, and in time the most gigantic results from movements all but imperceptible.

EL COLL DE BALAGUER.

A MODERN CATALONIAN STORY.

THE road from Barcelona to Valencia passes over the skirt of a cordillera, or mountain ridge, known by the name of El Coll de Balaguer. This road is edged by the sea on one side and the Coll on the other; and at one point especially, where there is an elbow or short turn, there are several enormous blocks of stone, which appear to have become detached from the main rock, and to have lodged in situations exactly suitable for the concealment of banditti, and affording facilities for pouncing upon the unsuspecting traveller from the narrow passages by which they are separated.

Between the years 1828 and 1831, several robberies and assassinations had been perpetrated close to this spot; and six rude crosses, erected within a very short distance of each other, were sad mementos of the fact. All these murders had been accompanied by circumstances marked by a singular similarity. The first victim who perished in this dreaded neighbourhood was a rich merchant, who was travelling from Lérida to Tortosa. It was supposed that, having had occasion to transact business in places out of the direct road, he had branched off, and had joined the Barcelona route near the Coll de Balaguer. He was seen one afternoon riding along on his mule in that direction, and early on the following morning a mendicant friar found his dead body, bathed in blood. A bullet had struck him in the forehead, just between the eyes. His money and other light valuables were gone; but the assassin appeared to have disdained to take any other part of his property, for his mule was quietly cropping the scanty grass a short distance off, and the little portmanteau was still strapped on the crupper pad. A remarkable as well as unaccountable circumstance attending this catastrophe was, that a roughly-fashioned wooden cross had been placed in the clasped hands of the murdered merchant. The most prompt and diligent steps were taken, under the direction of the authorities, for the discovery of the assassin, but without effect.

Seven months afterwards, on the eve of the festival of San Hilarion, in the month of October, a dealer—who had been to Barcelona to dispose of a large quantity of Segovia wool, and who was on his way to Murcia with a considerable sum of money in his possession—was robbed and murdered near the Coll de Balaguer; and about the middle of the following year, Don Andres Escoriasa, a manufacturer of firearms, was found dead at the same place.

In February 1830, a pedlar named Zoannofer, who had been selling his wares in different parts of the country, commencing his traffic in Navarre and ending in Catalonia, when on his road from Barcelona to Tortosa, in order to return to the north by one of the passage-boats which ascend the Ebro, was also killed by a bullet near the fatal spot; and eight days before the festival of Todos los Santos, or All-Saints, in the same year, Antonio P. Dirba, a contrabandista, and also a great sportsman, who had that very morning succeeded in smuggling a cargo of French tobacco on that part of the coast, was assassinated, evidently without having had an opportunity of defending himself; for the *trabuco* or blunderbuss, with which he was armed, was still loaded, and lying beside his corpse.

In January 1831, the dead body of a person named Nervas y Alaves, who had been selling a lot of liquorice juice at Tortosa, was discovered at El Coll de Balaguer.

These six victims had all been rifled of their money alone, and all had been mortally struck with equal good aim by a single bullet. Moreover, each was found with a rough wooden cross fixed in his lifeless hands.

The Coll de Balaguer became, as may naturally be supposed, the terror of travellers, as well as of the surrounding country, in consequence of these murderous waylayings; and few persons had the hardihood to travel by that route, unless they were numerously and stoutly accompanied. Many whose affairs called them from Barcelona to Tortosa and Valencia, diverged from the high road, and willingly encountered the toil and inconvenience of making a circuit of several leagues over rugged paths, regaining that high road at a safe distance from the dreaded Coll de Balaguer.

Some goat-herds, who had occasionally conducted their flocks to browse upon the mountain herbage near the spot, declared that they had found some faded flowers which had been deposited by an unknown hand at the foot of each of the six wooden crosses which marked the burial places of the murdered travellers, and they went so far as to add, that at sunset they had more than once descried a tall figure enveloped in a cloak gliding along until it arrived close to the crosses, when it sank on its knees, and appeared absorbed in prayer; but that upon their approach, it suddenly vanished. They also imagined that they had occasionally heard doleful groans and sobs, apparently proceeding from some person in grief or suffering, at the foot of the Coll. Under these mysterious circumstances, he would have been a bold man who would venture to pass that spot alone after nightfall.

A few years antecedent to these startling events, a person named Venceslas Uriarte took up his residence in the environs of Tortosa. He was not a Catalonian, and his previous history was unknown in those parts. It was rumoured, however, that before the revolution of 1822, when the Inquisition was abolished, he had been *alcáyde*, or jailer, in some prison belonging to that dread tribunal. According to his own account, he had served in what was called the Army of the Faith, a body of implacable fanatics, who hesitated at no means, however astute or cruel, to endeavour to perpetuate a system which had been for ages the bane of domestic felicity, the curb to rising intelligence, and the fosterer of the most evil passions.

That baleful system having at length been resisted in the most determined manner by the mass of the Spanish people, the majority of its agents and abettors had either fallen in the various encounters between the constitutional forces and those of the Army of the Faith, or had emigrated to France, Italy, and other countries, whilst considerable numbers dispersed themselves in various parts of Spain, where they were generally regarded with suspicion and hatred, not unmingled with fear, in spite of their prostrate position; for they bore the indelible stamp of beings who had been in the habit of perpetrating crimes of the very deepest dye, either in the dungeons of the Inquisition, where none but the monsters in human form who tortured their victims in secret could hear their shrieks for mercy; or in districts which the Army of the Faith had held under its domination, persecuting and castigating those whose words, actions, or even looks, could be so distorted or misinterpreted as to be made the groundwork of a suspicion.

This Venceslas Uriarte's habits were expensive; but the source whence he drew his pecuniary supplies was unknown; and although he practised all the outward forms of religion with scrupulous exactitude, and had, on that account, gained a certain reputation for piety in some quarters, he was generally looked upon as a dangerous person. Strange and ominous expressions, fearfully indicating that he was familiar with crime, escaped his lips in unguarded moments; and he gave way occasionally to the most furious bursts of passion in altercations with his associates, his vengeful glances causing the bystanders to tremble lest he should put an end to the dispute in some violent and tragical manner. Nor were their fears groundless, although the fatal blow might not be struck in their presence. The following instances are characteristic of the man:—

Some one having asked him how it was that, being so excellent a shot, he so seldom went out for a day's sport, his reply was—'To find a hare, it is necessary to undergo fatigue. Then, if you shoot it, you must run some little distance to pick it up; and you must afterwards walk a long way if you wish to sell it. 'Tis much better to wait for a man; he comes of his own accord; and when you have killed him, all you have to do is to ransack his *alforjas*' [saddle-bags.]

One day, however, he went to shoot wild-fowl in company with Antonio P. Dirba, the contrabandista, to Los Alfaques, which are a cluster of small islands or banks near the mouth of the Ebro, thickly overgrown with tall reeds, and which afford shelter to great numbers of wild ducks and flamingoes. At the close of their day's sport, they entered a fisherman's hut in search of refreshment; but all they could obtain was a salad, cut into very small pieces, and, as is the custom in Catalonia, swimming in a profusion of liquid called *caldo*, composed of water, oil, and vinegar.

Antonio, in helping his companion to some caldo, used rather clumsily the roughly-fashioned wooden spoon which the fisherman had produced; for though he seemed to be ladling out the caldo, he in reality transferred scarcely any to his companion's plate; and Venceslas insisted that he had turned the spoon the wrong way upwards, and that he was stupidly trying to take up the caldo with the convex side of the spoon. Antonio maintained that he was using the hollow part, and out of this trifling matter a most violent quarrel arose. And yet, as is the case with regard to many other serious quarrels, the origin thereof was not only insignificant, but groundless; for a person who accidentally came into the fisherman's hut, and to whom the matter was referred, declared, on the first glance at the object in dispute, that both sides of the spoon were alike; that is, nearly flat.

Three days after this absurd contention between Venceslas Uriarte and poor Antonio P. Dirba, the latter was found lying dead, with a rude wooden cross in his stiffened hands, near the Coll de Balaguer.

During Lent, in the year 1832, a troop of strolling players had been performing with great success at Tarragona one of those *Autos Sacramentales*, or sacred plays, which excite great interest among the Spanish people; inasmuch as they are living representations, displayed with great exactness, aided by scenic illusions, of some of the most remarkable and exciting events recorded in the sacred writings; the martyrdom of saints being frequently represented on the stage apparently in all their horrible reality. The auto sacramental which the company had enacted with so much éclat at Tarragona was, The Beheading of St John the Baptist; and in the hope of meeting with equal good fortune at Tortosa, they departed early one morning from Tarragona by the high road which passes by the Coll de Balaguer.

The baggage, wardrobe, and other theatrical equipments of the company, were laden upon several mules; but the actor, one Fernando Garcia, who performed the part of St John, preferred to carry one part of his costume himself.

Fernando Garcia was a short man, which was a main point for the effective representation of the principal character in the auto sacramental; for, in order to give an appearance of reality to the scene of the beheading of St John the Baptist, a *bonetillo*, or leathern skull-cap, was placed on the head of the actor of low stature, and upon the said skull-cap there was fixed, by means of a spring, a false head imitating nature; and the actor's dress or raiment was so arranged as to reach above, and cover his own head, leaving visible only the false one, which being struck off by the executioner on the stage, and placed apparently bleeding on a dish, or charger, produced a startling and exciting effect upon the spectators.

Now, Fernando Garcia could not make up his mind to confide this precious *cabeza*, or head, which was so essential an instrument of his theatrical success, to the care of a muleteer; for it was not merely well modelled, light in point of materials—the features being painted so as to imitate nature to perfection, with real hair parted over the forehead, and hanging gracefully over the back part of the neck—but it had glass eyes, which were constantly in motion by means of an internal spring, which was acted upon by the pressure of the said imitation-head on the skull-cap surmounting the actor's real one.

So little Fernando thought that the safer way of conveying this all-important piece of mechanism was to make himself a head taller on his journey, by ingrafting it on his own pate, as he was wont to do on the stage; and accordingly, in this guise, and mounted on a hired horse, he wended his way towards Tortosa, with the rest of the company.

Towards evening, however, he found himself alone. He had loitered on the road, and, like all loiterers, he was exposed to inconvenience. The weather was chilly, and in order to ward off its uncomfortable effects, he covered his face, and even his eyes, with his *capa*, or cloak; and trusting to the intelligence and sure-footedness of his horse, he beguiled the time by thinking of the plaudits which would be showered down upon him at Tortosa, when he should personate to the life the saint whose counterfeit head overtopped his own, without feeling any ill effects from the cold against which he had so snugly sheltered himself from top to toe. Suddenly—just at the turn of the road at the Coll de Balaguer, that fatal spot where so many mysterious murders and robberies had been committed—a shot was fired from behind one of the enormous blocks of stone already described. The actor's horse reared, and threw his double-headed and muffled-up rider, who, whilst struggling to disencumber himself from the folds of his cloak, was terrified beyond measure at seeing a man with a carbine in his hand in the act of pouncing upon him.

Fernando, however, was not wanting in courage, and, having luckily just on that moment got free from the *capa*, he leaped upon his legs, and drawing forth a poniard, prepared for resistance.

Venceslas Uriarte—for he it was who was rushing upon his supposed victim—astounded at having for the first time missed his aim, was about to take to flight; but he lost all command over himself, and became riveted to the spot upon beholding a being with two heads; the upper one—that of St John the Baptist—rolling its eyes in the most horrible manner, whilst the menacing orbs of little Fernando Garcia were flashing on him from their sockets in his own living head underneath, and the glistening poniard was elevated, ready to be plunged into his breast.

The robber's guilty conscience raised up the most fearful imaginings; his countenance became livid, his mouth gaped widely, his parched tongue clove to the palate, and he gazed wildly on the horrible apparition. In a minute or two, however, he made another desperate effort to escape; but, although accustomed to all the rugged paths, and agile in surmounting every obstacle when pursuing his prey, or in rapid flight with his booty, such was his trepidation, that his *alpargatas*, or hempen sandals, got entangled among the briers, and threw him down several times. He tried to climb at once up to the higher part of the Coll, and for that purpose caught at a shrub which was growing out of a crevice; but the force of his desperate grasp, and the weight of his convulsed body, drew it out by the root, and he fell again at the feet of the double-headed comedian, who had hotly pursued him.

'Avaunt, Satan! Touch me not, demonio!' cried the assassin, making the sign of the cross. But his exorcisms had no effect upon the bold Fernando Garcia, or upon St John the Baptist's head; for the former stood over him with the drawn dagger, crying out stoutly at the same time for his comrades by the odd names which actors are apt to adopt, and which no doubt sounded to the prostrate robber like calls for a host of demons to carry him to the realms of eternal torment; and the latter kept rolling its eyes frightfully.

The rest of the company hastened to the relief of Fernando on hearing his cries, and found the murderer helpless from the effect of fright and a smiting conscience. He was bound and taken to the nearest town, where he was searched in presence of the proper authorities. He wore a coarse haircloth shirt; and there were found upon him a rosary, a little book of prayers, and a sort of locket, containing—according to a memorandum on the piece of parchment in which it was wrapped—some of the hair of St Dominic. But he carried also concealed a poniard of highly-tempered steel; and in a pouch were four bullets, each wrapped in a small piece of greased linen, and fitting his carbine. There were also a few charges of fine gunpowder in a flat powder-horn.

This hypocritical and cruel malefactor was reduced to a state of abject cowardice by what he considered to have been a supernatural interposition, and confessed that he was the assassin of El Coll de Balaguer.

'But,' said the magistrate, 'how could you dare to place the cross in the hands of your victims?'

'It is no great matter,' replied the reckless murderer, 'to kill the body; but to destroy the soul is an abominable crime! I adorned their tombs with flowers, and I prayed fervently that they might be spared some days of purgatory. I placed in their hands, immediately after their death, crosses upon which I had previously procured a blessing, in order that, if they were not in a state of grace, they might at all events repulse the devil! But *there* he is! I see him! I see him now!' he cried, on perceiving little Fernando Garcia advancing with his two heads, in order to show the magistrate how it was that his life had been saved.

'There he is! Avaunt, Satanos! avaunt!' muttered the wretched assassin, and fell into a swoon, after some violent contortions.

He was tried by the proper tribunal, sentenced to death, and executed; and the brave little comedian had reason to rejoice for the remainder of his days at the practical proof which had been exhibited in his own person of the truth of the old saying, that two heads are better than one.

It is almost needless to add, that the auto sacramental was witnessed at Tortosa, and other places, with increased interest by the thousands who flocked to the theatre when it was represented, in consequence of the important part the head had performed in the drama at the Coll de Balaguer, and in bringing to justice the notorious Venceslas Uriarte.

BIOGRAPHIC SKETCHES.

M. GUIZOT.

M. Guizot, the present prime minister of France, seems to us, in more than one respect, a singular and interesting personage. Previously to the revolution of July, his literary productions had acquired him a European fame; and these now entitle him, in the opinion of competent judges, to be considered the founder of that new historical school to which we owe the brilliant writings of Michelet and Thierry. With the memorable convulsion of 1830, he leaped at one bound into high official rank; and he is now beyond all dispute acknowledged to be the leading statesman of France. This double success in literature and in life, so rare, though not unexampled in our time, was of itself sufficient to command attention and excite curiosity. But our surprise at Guizot's political triumphs is heightened when we reflect on the circumstances under which they have been achieved. He has reached and maintained himself on his present elevation, although a man of obscure birth and no fortune; nor can he be said to have displayed, or to possess, the peculiar qualities with which, in stormy times, those who have forced their way into power have, for the most part, been gifted. Guizot's chief characteristics are a clear logical understanding, and a certain cold philosophical composure: he has nothing about him of the Chatham or the Mirabeau.

For these reasons, a minute narrative of Guizot's personal and political career could not fail, we think, in the hands of a well-informed writer, to prove in a high degree pleasing and instructive. Such a task we have no intention of attempting; the materials, were it nothing else, are, and may for long be wanting: meanwhile, however, some few and scanty facts which, in the field of French contemporary biography, we have been able to glean respecting this remarkable man, may perhaps be acceptable to a large class of our readers.

Francis Peter William Guizot was born at Nismes, a town in the department of Gard, and province of Languedoc, on the 4th of October 1787. His family had long been settled in the south of France as respectable citizens of the middle rank, and in communion with the reformed church, of which Guizot himself is, and has always been a member. His father was an advocate of Nismes, a man of talent and eminence in his profession, and, as the anecdote we are about to quote will show, of humane and heroic temper. Like his brother Protestants, he had welcomed with joy the revolution of 1789, which relieved the French dissenters from all restrictions on the public exercise of their religion. After the execution of the king, however, his zeal, with that of so many others, began to cool. When the Reign of Terror was nearly at its height, he saw himself one of the 'suspected,' and was forced to conceal himself, to avoid imprisonment and death. 'He was found,' says a trustworthy biographer of his son, 'in his hiding-place by a gendarme; but this person regretting to have discovered him, and unwilling to have any share in his destruction, offered to let him escape. M. Guizot perceived that, to save his own life, he must compromise that of his merciful captor, and did not hesitate for an instant before relinquishing his only chance of preservation.' He was guillotined at Nismes on the 8th of April 1794, a few days after the execution at Paris of Danton and Camille Desmoulins. The young Guizot was then seven years of age. The sad spectacle of his father's death, as may be well supposed, produced a deep impression on his mind. We learn that it has never forsaken him; and perhaps it may in part account for that hatred of anything like revolutionary anarchy which he has manifested through life.

Immediately after this fatal event, Madame Guizot removed with her two sons to Geneva, where her own relatives resided. She has been described as an excellent woman of the old school; religious, true-hearted, and energetic; bound up in the welfare and right education of her children. She was one day, we have somewhere read, found by a visitor with Guizot on her knee, to whom she was repeating stories from the lives of the great reformers. 'I am trying,' she said, 'to make my Frank a resolute and diligent boy.' At the age of twelve, Guizot was sent to the public school of Geneva; and here he proved that his mother's efforts had not been thrown away. Indeed so absorbing was the vigour with which he applied himself to whatever he had in hand, that he became the butt of his more mercurial companions, who delighted in teasing with all sorts of practical jokes the abstracted little student. Aided by perseverance, his talents produced, in four years only, results that seem almost incredible: at sixteen, we are told Guizot could read and enjoy, in the originals, 'Thucydides and Demosthenes, Cicero and Tacitus, Dante and Alfieri, Schiller and Goethe, Gibbon and Shakspeare.' The two succeeding years were devoted to metaphysical studies, from which his mind, so eminently reflective, drew nourishment even more appropriate than that which it had found in the masterpieces of poetry and history. Finally, when he had gained the highest academical honours, it was thought by his mother and her friends that he could not but succeed in his father's profession. For a young man, too, of his gifts and accomplishments, they decided Paris was the only fitting sphere. Accordingly, towards the end of 1804, Madame Guizot returned once more to Nismes, whence, after a brief stay, Guizot himself proceeded, full of hope and ambition, to study law and push his fortunes in the French metropolis.

It was in 1805, the year after Napoleon's elevation to the imperial throne, that Guizot arrived in Paris. 'Poor and proud, austere and ambitious,' he saw himself in the midst of a brilliant, frivolous, and intriguing society, unfurnished, by his strict Genevese education, with the means of shining in such a world, and disinclined by nature to make the attempt. The Revolution, moreover, had destroyed, with so much else, the Paris law school, and Guizot was left, without a teacher, or any aid but that of books, to sound as he best might the mysterious depths of jurisprudence. The first twelvemonth of his stay in Paris was spent in solitary study; happily, during the next, he made the acquaintance of a M. Stopfer, the former representative of the Swiss republics, and, with the connexion which sprang out of it, Guizot seems to have abandoned all thoughts of law as a profession. This gentleman was a person of worth and learning, deeply versed in German metaphysics, a subject on which he had more than once appeared before the world as an author. Beneath his roof, as preceptor to his children, Guizot resided during the years 1807-8. In Stopfer he found not only an employer, but a paternal friend: under his guidance he was enabled to master the philosophy of Kant, and he had leisure enough still remaining to recommence the study, and perfect his knowledge of the classical authors. Besides this, he procured him admission to the society he most coveted—that of literary men. Among those of this class to whom he introduced him, one was M. Suard: at his house Guizot became a constant and grateful visitor: here, on a footing of perfect equality, he met the most distinguished members both of the old school and the new one, already beginning to displace it. In Suard's saloon might be seen in friendly converse Chateaubriand and the Abbé Moullet, Madame de Fontane and the Chevalier de Boufflers.

Guizot, though at this time a silent and reserved young man, made such use of these opportunities, that when, in 1809, he ceased to reside with M. Stopfer, he could with safety—so far at least as regarded the certainty of employment—enter on the perilous career of the author by profession, who trusts to his pen alone for his support. He became a contributor to a number of the graver periodicals of the day. His first book appeared in 1809 itself; it was a 'Dictionary of French Synonymes,' and in part a compilation; but he prefixed to it an original treatise on the philosophical character of the French language, 'that displayed already,' says a critic, 'that genius for precision and method which to-day distinguishes M. Guizot.' This was followed in 1811 by a translation of Rehfus' work on Spain, and by an essay on the state of the fine arts in France, and the Paris art-exhibition of 1810. The same year he was appointed conductor of the 'Annals of Education,' a valuable periodical, which continued till 1815 to appear under his editorship. Guizot was beginning to rise in public estimation. Literature, indeed, could not then be said, even with less justice than at present, to be a source of wealth to its cultivators; but it brought him enough for his simple wants. Powerful friends were promising him their aid for the future; so prudence itself, he thought, no longer forbade him to complete his union with the gifted lady (first seen by him in the literary circle assembled at Suard's) to whom for several years he had been attached and engaged. The way in which their intimacy originated is probably known to but few of our readers: it is one of those romances of real life more surprising than any fiction. In this case the romance is not the less interesting to us from its being one of real *literary* life.

Pauline de Meulan was born in Paris in the year 1773, fourteen years earlier than her future husband. Her father, after having enjoyed for the greater part of his life the possession of a considerable fortune, saw it swept away by the Revolution, and dying in 1790, the year after its loss, left a widow and large family almost wholly unprovided for. Some time after Mademoiselle de Meulan had reached womanhood, it flitted one day across her mind that she too might perhaps possess some literary talent, and in this way contribute to the support of those she loved. The thought was immediately put into action: she began a novel, and, chaining herself to her desk for several weeks, at last saw it duly completed. Some old friends of her father found her a publisher. The book was successful; and, thus enlisted in the corps of authors, she became one of its most industrious members. A year or two afterwards, M. Suard established a journal called the Publicist. Mademoiselle de Meulan, now a practised writer, was appointed contributor-in-chief, and her light graceful female pen soon made the work exceedingly popular. At last, in the first months of 1807, she was seized with a dangerous illness, brought on or hastened by over-exertion. The malady was of such a kind that she could not continue her labours; yet for years the produce of her essays in the Publicist had been the sole resource of her mother and herself. In this painful situation she received one day by post an article written in happy imitation of her style and manner: it was accompanied by an anonymous letter, in which she was requested to set her mind at rest, as, until her health should be restored, a similar article would be forwarded to her for each future number of the Publicist. The offer was tacitly accepted, and the articles came with the utmost regularity. On her recovery, she mentioned the circumstance in M. Suard's saloon, little thinking that the pale taciturn young philosopher, who was listening calmly to her story, held the key of the mystery. Unable to discover her benefactor, she at last, in the Publicist itself, requested him to disclose his name.

Guizot now acknowledged himself to be the unknown friend, and five years afterwards Mademoiselle de Meulan became his wife. They were married in the April of 1812; and though the lady was, as we have seen, fourteen years older than her husband, their union was the happiest possible. Madame Guizot is said, from the purity and severity of her moral nature, to have exerted a powerful influence on her husband's spiritual culture. In a humbler way than this too she was of great assistance to him. Thus, the translation of Gibbon,* which, during the first year of their marriage, appeared under his auspices, and with his valuable notes, was revised and corrected by her; and she relieved him likewise in great part from the labour of editing the 'Annals of Education.'

The year 1812 was altogether a remarkable one in Guizot's hitherto tranquil career. In the course of it, his friends Baron Pasquier and M. de Fontanes attempted to introduce him to political life by soliciting for him the post of auditor to the imperial council of state. Muret, Duke of Bassans, to whom the application was made, directed him to draw up a state-paper as a specimen of his ability. The subject was to be an exchange, then talked of by Napoleon, between Great Britain and France of their respective prisoners of war. But the emperor, it was well known, was insincere in making the proposal, as he deemed the support of the French prisoners a burden to Great Britain, while he himself was, at the time, in no want of soldiers. A suspicion of this insincerity was too prominent in Guizot's performance: he did not seem a fit man for ministerial purposes, and the application remained without effect. M. de Fontanes procured him, however, the professorship of modern history in the Paris Faculty of Letters, afterwards the scene of some of his noblest triumphs. This situation brought him into contact with his colleague Royer-Collard, the well-known professor of philosophy, to whom Guizot in every way owes much. They formed a friendship which promised to be lasting, and indeed it did last for a long period. Unhappily, after the revolution of July, it was dissolved by political differences.

In 1813 he was occupied with the duties of his chair: he published also his 'Lives of the French Poets during the age of Louis XIV.,' a first volume only, which has had no successor. In 1814, after so protracted a separation, he paid a visit to his mother at Nismes, and while there, the first restoration of the Bourbons occurred, an event with which Guizot's entry into public life begins. On returning to Paris, he was recommended by his friend Royer-Collard to the minister of the interior, the Abbé de Montesquiou, who appointed him his chief secretary, a subordinate, but, in Guizot's hands, an influential post. Along with Royer-Collard, he framed the severe law against the press, which was presented by M. de Montesquiou to the Chamber of 1814, and he was made one of the royal censors. When Napoleon came back from Elba, Guizot did not resign his situation; but he was, however, dismissed by Carnot, the new minister of the interior. This was in May 1815. A few days afterwards, when it was perceived that the great European powers would not treat with Napoleon, whose fall, sooner or later, was therefore inevitable, Guizot was despatched by the constitutional royalists to Ghent, where Louis XVIII. then resided, to plead with that monarch the cause of the charter, and point out the necessity of removing from his council M. de Blacas, the leader of the stiff-necked unyielding royalists of the old régime. His expedition was a successful one. On his return to France, after the battle of Waterloo, Louis XVIII. dismissed M. de Blacas, and promised, in the proclamation of Cambrai, a more faithful adherence to the charter. This is the origin of the epithet, 'Man of Ghent,' applied to Guizot by his political opponents, and with which every reader of newspapers is familiar.

During the first five years of the second restoration, Guizot filled, with little intermission, various semi-official posts of respectability indeed, but of slender importance. Such influence as he possessed (and though not a deputy, it was considerable), he exerted to liberalise the successive ministries under which he served. It was during this period that the small knot of thoughtful politicians of which Royer-Collard, Camille Jordan, and Guizot were the heads, received the nickname of 'Doctrinaires.' The meaning of the word 'doctrinaire,' in its present extensive application, it would be difficult or impossible to explain; but its origin, as a party designation, may be stated for the benefit of those of our readers who have heard the term used without being able to attach to it any idea. The 'doctrinaires' were, before the revolution of '89, a French Catholic community, which had various colleges for the instruction of young persons. Royer-Collard had been educated in one of these. This philosopher's speeches in the Chamber of Deputies were for the most part of an abstract and rather pedantic kind, teeming with phrases more suited to the schools than to that political arena. One of his favourite expressions was 'doctrine,' and as this word dropped from him one day, an ultra-royalist wag seized the opportunity to exclaim, 'Ah! there go the doctrinaires.'

In the February of 1820, the assassination of the Duke de Berri produced an anti-liberal reaction. The Decazes ministry was forced to resign, and with its fall Guizot lost the situation which had been created for him in the preceding year, of 'Director of the Municipal Administrations of France.' He now resumed the duties of his chair, which had meanwhile, we suppose, been performed by deputy, and endeavoured to make up for the loss of his official income by renewed and strenuous literary labour. 'After the fall of M. Decazes,' says a writer in the Revue des Deux Mondes, 'the interior of M. Guizot's house long presented a curious spectacle. His brother-in-law, M. Devaines, prefect of the Nievre, had been, like himself, deprived of his situation, and he returned to Paris with his wife and two nieces, one of whom M. Guizot afterwards married. On one side you saw Madame Guizot and her nieces slitting up, re-making, and annotating Le Tourneur's translation of Shakspeare; on the other, M. Guizot was busied with his researches into the history of France; further on, a few young men, docile pupils of the master, were ferreting, with the aid of a lexicon, in the barbarous Latin of Ordericus Vitalis; others were translating the Memoirs of Clarendon or the Eikon-Basilike of Charles I., laboriously erecting, stone by stone, that great edifice, the Collection of Memoirs relating to the English Revolution, which bears on its front the signature of M. Guizot.' An interesting peep into a literary workshop.

The fruits of this industry were speedily given to the world. In 1821 appeared a new edition of Rollin and Le Tourneur's now amended and annotated translation of Shakspeare; in both of which enterprises, though Guizot bore away the honour, his wife had the principal share. The researches mentioned in the passage just quoted, were for his lectures on the history of representative government in France, delivered during the winter of 1821–2. In 1822, an event took place which made him more dependent than ever on his literary exertions. He had found time, in the course of 1821, for the composition of a long political pamphlet, in which his favourite doctrine of liberty, in alliance with order, was powerfully and elaborately developed. The new ministry disliked his love of freedom, although it was united with a respect for established institutions. They feared, above all, his influence as a teacher on the rising generation, and accordingly suspended him from the functions of his professorship.

For several years after this occurrence Guizot remained a stranger to politics. His sensible and far-seeing turn of mind kept him from lending his aid to any of

* By the way, few persons (even though professed bibliographers) are aware that a considerable portion of this translation was executed by Louis XVI. when dauphin. It was completed 'by various hands;' and being the French version of Gibbon in general use, has had a number of editors, from Monsieur (or rather Madame) Guizot downwards.

the thousand-and-one (sometimes very extensive) conspiracies which, while the Villèle ministry remained in power, every day brought forth, though only to be crushed. He calmly waited till the time should come when he might with safety, and some prospect of success, take a part in public affairs. Meanwhile, historical studies, and the preparation of historical works, kept him constantly employed. In 1823 appeared his Essays on the History of France, and the first volumes of two grand collections of memoirs, one relating to the great English revolution, the other to the early history of France: these, as they were published serially, demanded his almost undivided attention for a considerable period. Yet his industry did not altogether hinder him from enjoying social life; and though he was poor, his visitors were not solely—strange as it may seem to an Englishman—from the ranks of the indigent and obscure. It is of the Guizot of that period that a writer in Fraser's Magazine thus speaks:—'Small were his apartments—far, far too small to admit the crowds of literati who sought to claim the honour of his acquaintance, or who, having made, were not willing to lose it. On his reception-nights, the small street at the back of the Madeleine in which he resided was crowded with carriages, as well as all the contiguous streets; and his visitors moved more quickly from one little room to another than they otherwise would have done, because they felt that they owed this act of courtesy to those who came pressing after them. If it had been the drawing-room of a young and beautiful queen, or the levee of a popular and distinguished cabinet minister, no anxiety to be admitted, to speak, to exchange looks, could have been more closely and strongly marked than on these occasions. Madame Guizot, and one or two female friends—often the late Duchess de Broglie, the Lady Peel of France—presided at a tea-table, where the simplest fare was distributed by pretty taper fingers, which even vied with bright eyes and enchanting smiles. Yet were those entertainments sumptuous with wit, with poetry, with philosophy, and with the best life of good society and of the élite of Paris. But death here also has intruded too frequently to permit me to think upon those once happy reunions; and the dear little house in the Rue de l'Evesque has witnessed tears and sobs, and agonies of grief, which none can portray, and which even few can feel.' This allusion is to Guizot's loss of the beloved companion both of his toils and his enjoyments, not long before that of their only child. Madame Guizot had been unwell during a considerable portion of 1826. With the new year, it was evident that she was slowly sinking. On the 30th July 1827, she perceived that her end was at hand: she summoned her son and her friends to her side, and bade them farewell—the former was soon to follow her to the tomb. On the morning of the next day she asked her husband to read to her; he took down a volume of Bossuet, and began the funeral oration of Henrietta Maria of England; when he had finished, he looked towards her, and saw that she was no more. We must now hurry on.

The year which was marked by this domestic calamity was also that of Guizot's return to politics. Perhaps his chief motive for this is to be found in the fact, that he was now forty years of age, and therefore qualified to enter the Chamber of Deputies. In 1828 he established the Revue Française, as an organ for the expression of his opinions, and he became an active member of the Aide-toi* Society, then just formed, the objects and procedure of which were quite in accordance with his views. It was founded to protect the electoral system from the assaults of the Villèle ministry. Nothing could be less revolutionary than the mode in which it sought its end, by appealing, namely, but with the cumulative force which is the great result of association, whenever the law was infringed, to the authorised legal tribunals.

* In full—Aide-toi, le ciel t'aidera—'Help thyself, and Heaven will help thee.'

In the January of 1828, the liberal ministry of M. de Martignac displaced that of Villèle, and one of its first acts was to restore Guizot his chair. It was now, amid the enthusiastic plaudits of a brilliant audience, that he began his well-known lectures on the History of Modern Civilisation in Europe. With the August of 1829, the Polignac ministry came into office; its subsequent history is familiar to our readers. Guizot threw himself energetically into opposition, attacking with his vigorous pen, in the columns of the Temps, and the Journal des Débats, the policy of that too famous administration. Chosen deputy by the electoral college of Lisieux in the January of 1830, he was among the protesting 221. He returned from Nismes to Paris on the 26th of July, to learn the publication of those ordinances which cost Charles X. a throne. On the 27th, at the meeting of deputies held at Casimir Périer's house, the protest drawn up by Guizot was the one agreed on to be signed. He was the author also of the address in which, on the 28th, the Duke of Orleans was invited to undertake the office of lieutenant-general of the kingdom. On the last of the Three Days, it was Guizot that proposed the appointment of a commission to secure the maintenance of order. On the 30th, he was named by it provisional minister of public instruction; and at the accession of Louis-Philippe, he accepted the most important and difficult post of all, that of minister of the interior.

Guizot's career since the revolution of 1830 belongs not to biography but to history. Yet we must not conclude without at least alluding to the benefits which, as minister of public instruction, he has conferred on his country. Perhaps we cannot better close this slight sketch than by quoting, from his circular to the instructors of youth then under his jurisdiction, the following noble passage:—'There is no fortune to be made, scarcely any reputation, in the round of those laborious duties which the teacher performs. Destined to behold his life glide on in monotonous toil, sometimes to meet with, in those around him, the injustice or the ingratitude of ignorance, he would often mourn, and perhaps despair, if his strength and courage were brought from no other source than the calculation of his immediate and purely selfish interest. A deep feeling of the moral importance of his labours must sustain and inspire him. In the austere pleasure of serving men, and contributing in secret to the public weal, let him find his worthiest recompense, one which only his conscience gives him. His glory is to aspire to nothing beyond the sphere of his obscure and laborious avocations; to exhaust himself in sacrifices little heeded by those who profit by them; in fine, to toil for men, and look for his reward to Heaven alone.'

WEST INDIA MAIL.

Having, in a late number of the Journal, given an account of the East India mail, we now proceed to detail a few particulars respecting the mail to and from the West Indies, which, it is hoped, will prove interesting to all, and possibly new to many, of our readers.

The mails for these important colonial possessions and foreign places are made up in London on the 2d and 17th of every month. Letters posted in London up till eight o'clock on either of these mornings are in time for the packet. The mails are conveyed by the South-Western Railway to Southampton, where they arrive about mid-day, and are transferred, without delay, by means of a small steamer, to one of the splendid steam ships belonging to the Royal Mail Steam-Packet Company; which transatlantic steamer, having her steam up, and all in readiness, at once proceeds on her voyage.

A gigantic undertaking is this line of West India steam-packets. There are eighteen vessels, the largest of which are about 2000 tons burthen, gross measurement. Fitted up in the most handsome and comfortable manner, a West India mail-packet is capable of carrying about 100 passengers, to each of whom a separate sleeping berth is allowed. What a contrast to the old pent-up sailing packets! Besides the amount of passage-money now being less, and the time occupied only about one half, the great comfort and ease with which a passenger can 'stretch his legs' on board the steamers, can only be truly felt by an old *voyageur* in one of the late sailing craft.

Each out-steamer, after leaving Southampton, proceeds to Funchal in Madeira. The run to this place, 1287 miles, occupies seven days. Mails and passengers are landed here in a few hours; and fresh meat, eggs, and fruit having been obtained, the steamer directs her course across the Atlantic.

The island of Madeira has lately become a great resort of invalids from England; and no wonder, seeing what different residents at that place state as to the nature of the climate. One writer in the Monthly Repository of 1834 says, 'People ought to be happy here.' The author of Six Months in the West Indies observes, 'I should think the situation of Madeira the most enviable in the world. It insures almost every European comfort, with almost every tropical luxury. Any degree of temperature may be enjoyed. The seasons are the youth, maturity, and old age of a never-ending, still-beginning spring.' Sir James Clark, in his valuable work on the Sanative Influence of Climate, writes as follows:—'Madeira has been long held in high estimation for the mildness and equability of its climate; and we shall find, on comparing this with the climate of the most favoured situations on the continent of Europe, that the character is well founded.' Dr Heneikin says, 'Could I enjoy, for a few years, a perpetual Madeira summer, I should confidently anticipate the most beneficial results.'

The Guide to the West Indies, &c. thus contrasts the approach of the steamer to Barbadoes with that of the intrepid Columbus:—'Onward ploughs the giant ship. What to her are the winds? She heeds them not! The waves? They are but her highway! Onward she goes; untiring, unresting, with steady purpose. What to us in this noble ship were the fears, the superstitions, the terrors of those who accompanied that man who first sought, through these waters, the new world?—who, with firm faith, on that eventful 3d of August 1492, pushed off his three small ships—one only of which was completely decked—to seek that new world which had for years existed in his thought, and flourished in his imagination. We are not to be terrified by fancied shrieks in the wind, or of hostile armies imaged in the clouds. The change in the direction of the compass does not fill us with dread; nor do we suppose that the masses of sea-weed that may encircle us are sent by spirits of evil to bar our approach! To us these things are as idle dreams; but they were strong and fearful realities to those lone men in their little vessels who first entered those seas. They were realities to all but him whose firmness, decision, and indomitable will led them on, in firm trust in that God whose religion he sought to establish in a world unknown. What must have been his thoughts and feelings when, after many years of contest and delay, he stood among his superstitious crew, in the middle of night, on his vessel's deck, and for the first time saw a moving light on shore:

> Pedro, Rodrigo! there methought it shone!
> *There*, in the west; and now, alas! 'tis gone.
> 'Twas all a dream—we gaze and gaze in vain!
> But mark, and speak not—*there* it comes again:
> It *moves!* What form unseen, what being there,
> With torch-like lustre, fires the murky air?
> His instincts, passions, say, how like our own;
> Oh! when will day reveal a world unknown?'—*Rogers.*

The island of *Barbadoes** is the first place in the West Indies where the steamers call. The voyage from Madeira occupies fourteen days. Having stopped one day for home-mails, the steamer proceeds to *Grenada*, which she reaches in about fifteen hours. The total distance from Southampton to Grenada, called route No. 1, is 4037 nautical miles, and is performed in twenty-three days, including the stoppages.

Grenada is the principal place where the mail-packets meet to exchange the different mails, replenish coal, water, and other stores, and refit after long voyages. These objects being all accomplished, and all in readiness, before the packet arrives from England a delay of not more than twelve hours occurs in the transfer to the respective branch packets.* All the mail-steamers described in the subjoined note work in together, keeping up one grand combination, affording to all places mentioned opportunities, some twice, others once a month, of receiving letters both from Europe and inter-insularly, of transmitting replies thereto, and of transit to travellers going in any direction. *Now* we can calculate almost to an hour when advices will reach us—a circumstance of the highest importance to the commercial world: *regularity*, rather than fits and starts of celerity, being the great desideratum.

Letters can be despatched on the 2d and 17th from London for Barbadoes, Grenada, St Thomas, and Bermuda, and answers will be received back in fifty days; (despatched 17th) New Grenada and Guatemala, in

---

* At those places marked in italics, the packets meet to exchange outward, homeward, and inter-colonial mails.

* The dispersion takes place in the following order:—On route 2, a packet starts fortnightly from *Barbadoes*, with out-mails for Tobago and Demerara, where she stops a week; then returns with home-mails to Tobago, *Grenada* (where the home-mails are deposited), and *Barbadoes*.

On route 3, one starts fortnightly from *Grenada* with the out-mails for Trinidad, where she remains nine days; then returns with home-mails to *Grenada*.

On route 4, one starts fortnightly from *Grenada* with the out-mails for St Vincent, St Lucia, Martinique (French), Dominica, Guadaloupe (French), Antigua, Montserrat, Nevis, St Kitt's, Tortolla, *St Thomas* (Danish), and Puerto Rico (Spanish). At this latter place the stoppage of the steamer is only a few hours, after which she returns to *St Thomas* to coal; afterwards calling at each island already mentioned, on her way back to *Grenada*.

On route 5, one starts fortnightly from *Grenada* with the out-mails for Jacmel (Haytien), *Jamaica*, and St Jago de Cuba (Spanish). Here the stop is two days, when she returns to *Jamaica* to coal; and after having allowed this island eight days from the first arrival there, for receiving replies from the interior, she returns to Jacmel; thence proceeds to Puerto Rico and *St Thomas*.

On route 6, one starts monthly from *Jamaica* with the out-mails for *Havannah* (Spanish), where she coals, Vera Cruz, and Tampico (both Mexican); at this place she remains from five to ten days, according as shipments can be effected, which are often almost impracticable, the bar at the entrance, outside of which the steamer anchors, being often impassable, especially when one of the violent and dreaded 'northers' sets in. At this place, and also Vera Cruz, very large shipments of specie take place, there being sometimes an amount exceeding two and a half million dollars sent on board—coming from the mines in the interior for England—at one time. After waiting off Tampico long enough, the packet returns to Vera Cruz and *Havannah*. Here she re-coals, then proceeds to Nassau and *Bermuda*, where she coals up for the Atlantic voyage; then proceeds direct to Southampton, arriving there on the 7th of each month.

On route 7, one starts monthly from *St Thomas* with the out, as well as home-mails, for *Bermuda*. Here she lands the out-mails, and delivers the home-mails to the last-mentioned ship, going (as in route 5) to England; then coals, and proceeds to Nassau, *Havannah*, and *Jamaica*.

On route 8, one starts monthly from *St Thomas* with all the collected home-mails, proceeding *via* Fayal to Southampton, arriving there on the 22d of each month.

On route 9, one starts monthly from *Grenada* with the out-mails for La Guayra and Puerto Cabello, stops there two days, and returns to La Guayra; then to *St Thomas* and *Grenada*.

On route 10, one starts monthly from *Jamaica* with the out-mails for Santa Martha, Carthagena, Chagres, and San Juan de Nicaragua, in the newly-acquired British territory on the Mosquito shore. This latter has been taken possession of by our government, to secure to this country a means of crossing to the Pacific, by way of the San Juan river, independent of any adverse state. Although done without noise, this is nevertheless a most important step to this country; one which shows that our rulers have their eyes open to the future political as well as commercial benefits that will result from the possession of this *key* to the Pacific! But to return to No. 10 steamer: she proceeds, after a day's stop at San Juan, to *Jamaica* with mails for England, calling at each place already mentioned on the backward route.

On route 11, one starts monthly with out-mails from *Havannah* for Belize in Honduras; stops a few days; thence returns to *Havannah*.

eighty days; (despatched 2d) Mexico and Honduras, in ninety-five days; (despatched 2d and 17th) all other places in sixty-five days.

The fare to Madeira is L.22, or L.30; to Barbadoes L.32, or L.42; to Jamaica L.40, or L.50; and to other places in proportion to the distance. These certainly are very moderate rates for travelling such long distances. To Mexico, the country farthest away, an expanse of sea exceeding 7000 miles has to be traversed. It appears, however, that for upwards of the three years these steam-ships have been constantly at sea (during which time 154 voyages have been performed out and home, only a few of which occupied more than the time now allowed), many of them have run over a space of 115,000 miles respectively—more than four times round the world—yet in no instance has the least mishap to a single pin of their gigantic machinery occurred. This certainly goes to prove the superior construction of the ships and engines, and correctness of the officers in command. The very *Atlantic* may now be said to be *timed*, as by a railway!

THE GREEK STAGE.

The novel and successful attempt which has been recently made in London to excite sympathy amongst an English audience for one of the lofty tragedies of Greece, may perhaps render acceptable a short sketch of the stage performances of the ancients. The same play has met with a gratifying reception in the capitals of France and Prussia; and it is stated that, under royal command, another Greek drama is shortly to be performed. Wonderful is it that plays produced considerably more than two thousand years ago, should, in spite of time, retain a power to delight in an eminent degree people of other lands and other languages. But our wonder will abate if we consider for a moment that it is one of the main attributes of genius to be ever fresh and inviting. We cannot glance round our libraries without perceiving that genius had contracted divine aspirations after the future, and, looking earnestly forwards, had written as much for posterity as for the present. Hitherto, the Greek plays have been conned as tasks in dusky studies, or enjoyed by the learned few; but it has now been shown that they contain matter fitted to delight the minds of the many. It may now be seen that Greek keeps concealed in its crabbed characters a peculiar manifestation of interest which we may look for in vain elsewhere, and even when adequately expressed through the medium of a translation. What has our own Milton said in praise of the Greek tragic writers?

'Thence what the lofty grave tragedians taught
In Chorus and Iambic, teachers best
Of moral prudence, with delight received,
In brief sententious precepts, while they treat
Of Fate and Chance and change in human life;
High actions and high passions best describing.'

But this was not all that Milton was pleased to say upon this topic. 'Tragedy' (we transcribe from the proem to Samson Agonistes, a drama written after the old models)—'Tragedy, as it was anciently composed, hath been ever held the gravest, moralest, and most profitable of all other poems; therefore said by Aristotle to be of power, by raising pity and fear, or terror, to purge the mind of these and such-like passions; that is, to temper and reduce them to just measure, with a kind of delight, stirred up by reading or seeing those passions well imitated. Hence philosophers and other gravest writers, as Cicero, Plutarch, and others, frequently cite out of tragic poets, both to adorn and illustrate their discourse. This is mentioned to vindicate tragedy from the small esteem, or rather infamy, which, in the account of many, it undergoes at this day, with other common interludes.'

They who assign to the drama no higher part in Grecian life than it plays in ours, are most grievously at fault. Inasmuch as amongst the Greeks the drama held a conspicuous position in their *religious* economy, it excited a far more serious attention in its performance, and a far deeper interest in its production, than can possibly arise in a land where the religion neither admits nor requires such assistance. Its effects were more deeply improved, and were more extensively diffused amongst the masses, as well by reason of their religious character, as that the theatre was almost the only place in which the people could obtain an audience of the intellectually great. A natural consequence was, that the government felt called upon not only to contribute large sums to the support of the theatre, but to interfere very frequently (and often injudiciously) in its actual management. Thus the price of admission at Athens was for a long time one drachma, a silver coin weighing about nine grains; but by the influence of Pericles, a decree was passed reducing the fee to a third, namely, two oboli; which sum, if beyond the means of any citizen, he could obtain from the magistrates. The perpetuity of this law was secured by an enactment which imposed the penalty of death upon those who unsuccessfully attempted to repeal it. The public treasures were thus foolishly squandered; and even the eloquence of Demosthenes was unable to convince the Athenians of the sin of this law. The legislature also took upon itself to regulate the number of the chorus in each drama. The services of a chorus were so frequently required in the solemnities at Athens, that each tribe was compelled to provide a choregus—an officer who, amongst the poorer tribes, was maintained by the state. His duties were to supply a band of vocal and instrumental performers, to provide them with embroidered clothing for festivals, and to appoint a chorus master. Upon holidays, he appeared at the head of his band wearing a gilt crown and rich robe. The watchful eye with which everything appertaining to the stage was regarded, may be gathered from an incident mentioned by Herodotus. The capture of Miletus by the Persians, an affair dishonourable alike to the arms and councils of Athens, was made the subject of a tragedy by Phrynichus; and such was the power with which it was treated, that the audience were moved to tears. The poet was mulcted in a thousand drachmæ for dramatising this calamitous occurrence, and the repetition of the piece was forbidden. Another anecdote, related on good authority, shows the fascination which theatrical amusements exercised over the Athenian mind. During the representation of a tragi-comedy, written by Hegemon near the close of the Peloponnesian war, the news of the total defeat of their fleet and army before Syracuse was communicated to the spectators. Almost every person in the house had lost a relation, and the performance was stopped by a burst of grief which the disastrous intelligence inevitably called forth. Nevertheless, as soon as the first paroxysm of sorrow was quelled, the audience reseated themselves, and covering their faces with their mantles, the play was ordered to proceed to its conclusion.

The theatres of the Greeks were not intended, as ours are, for performances during several consecutive months, but were open only for a short time at the seasons appointed for religious festivals, when the capitals were crowded with a population gathered from a wide circuit. The word 'theatre' is associated in our minds with night, and gas-light, and heated houses; but the acting of a play in Greece took place under very different circumstances. The performance was invariably by day, and their theatres had no roof, so that the spectators sat beneath the open sky. It was thought improper for women to appear on the stage, and female characters were therefore personated by men, as they were in England in the time of our early dramatists. A great concourse of people was the natural consequence of the particular period, and of the shortness of the time during which the theatres were open, and thus it was necessary to build them on a vast scale. Some were large enough to hold fifteen or sixteen thousand people. In this fact we may discover some justification for certain peculiarities of costume that would not be tolerated amongst ourselves, because they would remove one source of pleasure with which theatrical amusements are witnessed. The actors were raised above the ordinary height by means of the cothurnus, or buskin, and their faces were concealed by carved and painted masks. From the great size of the building, the spectators were too far removed from the stage to enable them to read on the actor's countenance that language of feeling and passion which speaks so powerfully, even when the tongue is silent. 'And how did Garrick speak the soliloquy last night?' 'O, against all rule, my lord; most ungrammatically! Betwixt the substantive and the adjective, which should agree together in number, case, and gender, he made a breach thus—— stopping as if the point wanted settling; and between the nominative case, which your lordship knows should govern the verb, he suspended his voice in the epilogue a dozen times, three seconds, and three fifths, by a stop-watch each time.' 'Admirable grammarian! But, in suspending his voice, was the sense suspended likewise? Did no expression of attitude or countenance fill up the chasm? Was the eye silent? Did you narrowly look?' 'I looked only at the stop-watch, my lord.' 'Excellent observer!' The critic's conduct, at which Sterne rightly dealt his sarcasm, would not have been so egregiously out of place in a Greek theatre. The masks were so fashioned as to indicate with more or less distinctness the person represented; and if they concealed the workings of emotion, the contrasting differences and nice transitions of expression, they helped to idealise the actor, and so far carried out the Greek notion of tragedy. In some lines addressed to an accomplished actress, Charles Lamb felicitously says,

'Your smiles are winds, whose ways we cannot trace,
That vanish and return we know not how.'

This is merely one example; but even the reader who never entered a theatre may conceive that the occasions are innumerable in which an actor, by his countenance, can add a most expressive commentary to his words, and at another time can hint a thousand words when he does not utter one. Yet all this kind of acting, and the pleasure derived from its successful accomplishment, the Greeks deliberately denied themselves by the use of masks. At the same time, it should not be forgotten that they were contrived with a view to increase the power of the voice, and that they were embellished to a high degree by the united efforts of the first sculptors and painters.

A Greek theatre was of a semicircular or horse-shoe shape. Tiers of seats for the audience were placed round that part of the interior which was curved, whilst the stage was formed by a platform in front. Magistrates and persons of quality were placed on the lower tiers, the middle seats were appropriated to the common people; and if females attended the theatre, which has been doubted, they occupied the highest range. The seats were reached by staircases, which mounted from tier to tier at equal distances from each other. What the French call the *parterre*, and we the pit, was not given up to spectators, but was occupied by the chorus, whose duty it was to sing or recite the lyrical pieces which formed a large portion of every play. In the middle of this space, then termed the orchestra, there was an elevated altar, on which sacrifice was offered before the drama commenced, and steps surrounded it, upon which the performers making the chorus stood when they were engaged in dialogue by the mouth of their *coryphæus* with the actors on the stage. This band of performers personated, just as the ends of the drama were best answered, aged men or venerable matrons, young men or priests. They were divided into two companies, who danced in time to the music whilst they recited the words assigned to them. When repeating the strophe they moved from right to left, then during the antistrophe from left to right; but when the epode was chanting, they looked full upon the audience. The style of the dance was of course regulated by the character of the music, and that again by the nature of the poetry which it accompanied. Great skill was frequently displayed by the dancers in adapting their gestures to the subject of the drama, and even to represent the course of the action. The name of one performer has been given whose movements were supposed to express very distinctly the events of the Seven Chiefs of Thebes, by Æschylus. The music introduced during the performance was probably not more than sufficient to guide the dances, and to assist the voices of the singers, without putting forward any claim to attention on its own account. The lyre, the flute, and the pipe, swelled with their blended sweetness, without overwhelming the vocal harmonies of the chorus; and although these simple instruments were manifestly incapable of producing the grand musical effects of modern orchestras, we may well believe that, acutely alive as the Grecians were in all matters of taste, they succeeded in forming an exquisite combination of voice and instrument.

That part of the stage on which the actors stood when speaking was termed the logeum; it was narrow in proportion to its length, covered with awning, and moveable. Behind, a wall rose to the height of the loftiest tier of seats, and between this wall and the logeum were placed the proscenium and the decorations. A palace or temple was usually represented in the back-ground, and views of distant scenery were given at the sides. It seems probable that in some cases the open country was permitted to be seen. It is noticeable that situations of great beauty were selected for the theatres: thus the theatre of Taurominium, in Sicily, was so constructed that the audience had Mount Ætna in prospect. The theatre at Athens commanded Mount Hymettus, the Saronic Gulf, and the three ports of Piræus. Immediately above it stood the Parthenon on its Acropolis. 'The beautiful situation,' says an intelligent writer, 'occupied by the remains of many of the ancient theatres, justifies the supposition that they were studiously placed so as to command and to incorporate with their own architectural features the finest objects of the adjacent country. The majestic mountains and luxuriant plains, the groves and gardens, the land-locked and open sea, in the neighbourhood of many of the principal cities of Greece, presented the finest materials which taste could suggest or desire for such combinations. But the charm of southern landscape depends not solely on the romantic or beautiful features which enter into its composition. In that land of the sun, the purity of the atmosphere, the rich and magical lines of colour, the soft loveliness of the aërial perspective, the powerful relief of light and shadow, produce impressions of pleasure rarely equalled, even in our finest days, in these northern regions.'

The machinery of the stage was very simple, and it was concealed from view as much as possible; for the Greeks were desirous that their representations should rely as little as need be upon stage artifices. There were various entrances for the performers. The chorus came in at a door in the orchestra, which it seldom quitted for the stage. There was also an entrance in the orchestra for characters who were supposed to come from a distance, and they attained the logeum by a staircase. On the logeum itself there was another entrance, and by this the inhabitants of the town found their way. Again, there were three points of ingress in the back wall of the scene; through the main one the great characters came before the audience, whilst the side ones served for subordinate persons. The scene was generally adorned with columns and statues in rich variety; and we are told that vases and hollow vessels were distributed here and in other parts of the theatre, for the purpose of aiding the diffusion of sound.

We may now allude to the appearance of the actors on the stage. The Grecian eye, acquainted with formal grace in all its shapes, demanded not only that every action should be conducted with submission to their severe rules of taste, but that the arrangements of all persons on the stage should be governed by the same rules. The actors were taught to fall into exquisite groups, and to feast the eye with the beauty of symmetry and proportion, whilst the ear was delighted with the sound of the most musical of languages. Thus the theatre was a place which the artist and the poet might frequent with equal instruction. The narrowness of the stage would throw the figures into strong relief, its length would bestow a frieze-like appearance on the whole disposition, and the mechanical aids that were called in for the regulation of light would materially increase the statuesque effect. Æschylus derived part of his celebrity from his improving the costume of his characters. The deities he placed on the stage were clothed in imitation of the finest and most appropriate statues; and the drapery of all his performers was arranged with such elegance, that the priests were furnished with hints for a more finished style of dress in themselves. In the same way Romney the painter is said to have reformed the fantastic method of arranging the hair of ladies, prevalent at the close of the last century, by showing in some of his pictures the superior effect of a more natural manner.

MISCELLANEA.

The Scuir of Eigg is a magnificent pillar of basalt that rises in one of the Western Islands, above a stratum of oolite rock, containing fossil remains of a peculiar pine of that era, when the earth contained no animals superior to birds and reptiles. In the *Witness* (Edinburgh newspaper), there is at present in progress a series of chapters descriptive of a visit paid last summer to these islands by the editor, Mr Hugh Miller, whose speculations on the old red sandstone have made his name well known to geologists. The extraction of some specimens of the *Pinites Eiggensis*, as it is called, from the oolitic bed underneath the Scuir, forms the occasion of some curious remarks in the third chapter.

After speaking of the oolite stratum as formed in the sea, and afterwards upheaved by volcanic agency with the mass of basalt over it, the writer thus proceeds:—'The annual rings of the wood, which are quite as small as in a slow-growing Baltic pine, are distinctly visible in all the better pieces I this day transferred to my bag. In one fragment I reckon sixteen rings in half an inch, and fifteen in the same space in another. The trees to which they belonged seem to have grown on some exposed hill-side, where, in the course of half a century, little more than from two to three inches were added to their diameter. Viewed through the microscope in transparent slips, longitudinal and transverse, it presents, within the space of a few lines, objects fitted to fill the mind with wonder. We find the minutest cells, glands, fibres, of the original wood preserved uninjured; there still are those medullary rays entire that communicated between the pith and the outside; there still the ring of thickened cells that indicated the yearly check which the growth received when winter came on; there the polygonal reticulations of the cross section, without a single broken mesh; there, too, the elongated cells in the longitudinal one, each filled with minute glands that take the form of double circles; there, also, of larger size and less regular form, the lacunæ in which the turpentine lay; every nicely-organised speck, invisible to the naked eye, we find in as perfect a state of keeping in the incalculably ancient pile-work on which the gigantic Scuir is founded, as in the living pines that flourish green on our hill-sides. A net-work, compared with which that of the finest lace ever worn by the fair reader would seem a net-work of cable, has preserved entire, for untold ages, the most delicate peculiarities of its pattern. There is not a mesh broken, nor a circular dot away!'

From facts plainly placed before our eyes, 'we now know,' says Mr Miller, 'that the ancient Eigg pine, to which the detached fragment picked up at the base of the Scuir belonged—a pine alike different from those of the earlier carboniferous period and those which exist cotemporary with ourselves—was, some three creations ago, an exceedingly common tree in the country now called Scotland; as much so, perhaps, as the Scotch fir is at the present day. The fossil trees found in such abundance in the neighbourhood of Helmsdale, that they are burnt for lime—the fossil wood of Eathie, in Cromartyshire, and that of Shandwick, in Ross—all belong to the *Pinites Eiggensis*. It seems to have been a straight and stately tree, in most instances, as in the Eigg specimens, of slow growth. One of the trunks I saw near Navidale measured two feet in diameter, but a full century had passed ere it attained to a bulk so considerable; and a splendid specimen in my collection from the same locality, which measures twenty-one inches, exhibits even more than a hundred annual rings. In one of my specimens, and one only, the rings are of great breadth. They differ from those of all the others in the proportion in which I have seen the annual rings of a young vigorous fir that had sprung up in some rich moist hollow, differ from the annual rings of trees of the same species that had grown in the shallow hard soil of exposed hill-sides. And this one specimen furnishes curious evidence that the often-marked but little understood law, which gives us our better and worse seasons in alternate groups, various in number and uncertain in their time of recurrence, obtained as early as the age of the oolite. The rings follow each other in groups of lesser and larger breadth. One group of four rings measures an inch and a quarter across, while an adjoining group of five rings measures only five-eighth parts; and in a breadth of six inches there occur five of these alternate groups. For some four or five years together, when this pine was a living tree, the springs were late and cold, and the summers cloudy and chill, as in that group of seasons which intervened between 1835 and 1841; and then for four or five years more springs were early and summers genial, as in the after group of 1842, 1843, and 1844. An arrangement in nature—first observed, as we learn from Bacon, by the people of the Low Countries, and which has since formed the basis of meteoric tables, and of predictions, and elaborate cycles of the weather—bound together the twelvemonths of the oolitic period in alternate bundles of better and worse: vegetation throve vigorously during the summers of one group, and languished in those of another in a state of partial development.'

Captain Osborne, in his work entitled The Court and Camp of Runjeet Sing, gives an account of a Fakir who professed to have an extraordinary power of suspending animation in his body for a great length of time, during which he allowed himself to be kept in a burial vault, apart from all supply of air and food. 'The monotony of our camp life,' he says, 'was broken this morning by the arrival of a very celebrated character in the Punjaub, a person wo had all expressed great anxiety to see, and whom the Maha-Rajah had ordered over from Umrutser on purpose. He is a fakir by name, and is held in extraordinary respect by the Sikhs, from his alleged capacity of being able to bury himself alive for any period of time. So many stories were current on the subject, and so many respectable individuals maintained the truth of these stories, that we all felt curious to see him. He professes to have been following this trade, if so it may be called, for some years, and a considerable time ago several extracts from the letters of individuals who had seen the man in the Upper Provinces, appeared in the Calcutta papers, giving some account of his extraordinary powers, which were at the time, naturally enough, looked upon as mere attempts at a hoax upon the inhabitants of Calcutta. Captain Wade, political agent at Ludhiana, told me that he was present at his resurrection after an interment of some months; General Ventura having buried him in the presence of the Maha-Rajah and many of his principal sirdars; and, as far as I can recollect, these were the particulars as witnessed by General Ventura:—After going through a regular course of preparation, which occupied him seven days, and the details of which are too disgusting to dilate upon, the fakir reported himself ready for interment in a vault which had been prepared for the purpose by order of the Maha-Rajah. On the appearance of Runjeet and his court, he proceeded to the final preparations that were necessary in their presence, and after stopping with wax his ears and nostrils, he was stripped and placed in a linen bag; and the last preparation concluded by turning his tongue forwards, and thus closing the gullet, he immediately died away in a kind of lethargy. The bag was then closed, and sealed with Runjeet's seal, and afterwards placed in a small deal box, which was also locked and sealed. The box was then placed in a vault, the earth thrown in and trod down, and a crop of barley sown over the spot, and sentries placed round it. The Maha-Rajah was, however, very sceptical on the subject, and twice in the course of the ten months he remained under ground, sent people to dig him up, when he was found to be in exactly the same position, and in a state of perfectly suspended animation. At the termination of the ten months, Captain Wade accompanied the Maha-Rajah to see him disinterred, and states that he examined him personally and minutely, and was convinced that all animation was perfectly suspended. He saw the locks opened and the seals broken by the Maha-Raja, and the box brought into the open air. The man was then taken out, and on feeling his wrist and heart, not the slightest pulsation was perceptible. The first thing towards restoring him to life was the forcing his tongue back to its proper position, which was done with some little difficulty by a person inserting his finger and forcibly pulling it back, and continuing to hold it until it gradually resumed its natural place. Captain Wade described the top of his head to have been considerably heated; but all other parts of the body cool and healthy in appearance. Pouring a quantity of warm water upon him constitutes the only further measures for his restoration, and in two hours' time he is as well as ever.

'On my return to Simla, accident placed in my hands the appendix to a medical topography of Ludhiana by Dr Macgregor of the horse artillery, by whose permission I have extracted the following account of the former interments and resurrections of the fakir:—A fakir who arrived at Lahore engaged to bury himself for any length of time, shut up in a box, and without either food or drink. Runjeet naturally disbelieved the man's assertions, and was determined to put them to the test. For this purpose the fakir was shut up in a wooden box, which was placed in a small apartment below the middle of the ground: there was a folding door to his box, which was secured by a lock and key. Surrounding this apartment, there was the garden-house, the door of which was likewise locked, and outside the whole a high wall, having its doorway built up with bricks and mud. In order to prevent any one from approaching the place, a line of sentries was placed and relieved at regular intervals. The strictest watch was kept up for the space of forty days and forty nights, at the expiration of which period the Maha-Raja, attended by his grandson and several of his sirdars, as well as General Ventura, Captain Wade, and myself, proceeded to disinter the fakir. The bricks and mud were removed from the outer doorway; the door of the garden-house was next unlocked; and lastly, that of the wooden box containing the fakir: the latter was found covered with a white sheet, on removing which the figure of the man presented itself in a sitting posture; his legs and arms were pressed to his sides, his legs and thighs crossed. The first step of the operation of resuscitation consisted in pouring over his head a quantity of warm water; after this a hot cake of otta (wheat flour) was placed on the crown of his head; a plug of wax was next removed from one of his nostrils, and on this being done, the man breathed strongly through it. The mouth was now opened, and the tongue, which had been closely applied to the roof of the mouth, brought forward, and both it and the lips anointed with ghee (clarified butter). During this part of the proceeding, I could not feel any pulsation at the wrist, though the temperature of the body was much above the natural standard of health. The legs and arms being extended, and the eyelids raised, the former were well rubbed, and a little ghee was applied to the latter; the eyeballs presented a dim suffused appearance, like those of a corpse. The man now evinced signs of returning animation; the pulse became perceptible at the wrist, whilst the unnatural temperature of the body rapidly diminished. He made several ineffectual efforts to speak, and at length uttered a few words, but in a tone so low and feeble as to render them inaudible. By and by his speech was re-established, and he recognised some of the bystanders, and addressed the Maha-Raja, who was seated opposite to him watching all his movements. When the fakir was able to converse, the completion of the feat was announced by the discharge of guns and other demonstrations of joy. A rich chain of gold was placed round his neck by Runjeet, and ear-rings, baubles, and shawls were presented to him. However extraordinary this fact may appear, both to the Europeans and natives, it is difficult, if not impossible, to explain it on physiological principles. The man not only denied his having tasted food or drink, but even maintained that he had stopped the function of respiration during a period of forty days and nights. To all appearance this long fasting had not been productive of its usual effects, as the man seemed to be in rude health, so that digestion and assimilation had apparently proceeded in the usual manner; but this he likewise denied, and piously asserted, that during the whole time he had enjoyed a most delightful trance. It is well known that the natives of Hindoostan, by constant practice, can bring themselves to exist on the smallest portion of food for several days; and it is equally true that, by long training, the same people are able to retain the air in their lungs for some minutes; but how the functions of digestion and respiration could be arrested for such a length of time, appears unaccountable. The concealment of the fakir during the performance of his feat, so far from rendering the latter more wonderful, serves but to hide the means he employs for its accomplishment, and until he can be persuaded to undergo the confinement in a place where his actions may be observed, it is needless to form any conjectures regarding them.'

THE FEARLESS DE COURCY.

[The following is a specimen of *Lays and Ballads from Old English History* (*London, James Burns*, 1845), a beautifully embellished little volume of original poetry, professedly 'by S. M.,' and dedicated 'to seven dear children, for whose amusement the verses were originally written.' Generally speaking, history in a versified shape is miserable trash; but here we have something very different; and we shall be much surprised if this volume does not long maintain a place amongst the parlour-window favourites of the young. The ballads are not only charmingly written, as far as mere literary art is concerned, but have, besides, a life-like spirit, and a tone of high imaginative feeling, which are peculiarly their own.]

The fame of the fearless De Courcy
Is boundless as the air;
With his own right hand he won the land
Of Ulster, green and fair!
But he lieth low in a dungeon now,
Powerless, in proud despair;
For false King John hath cast him in,
And closely chained him there.

The noble knight was weary
At morn, and eve, and noon;
For chilly bright seemed dawn's soft light,
And icily shone the moon;
No gleaming mail gave back the rays
Of the dim unfriendly sky,
And the proud free stars disdained to gaze
Through his lattice, barred and high.

But when the trumpet-note of war
Rang through his narrow room,
Telling of banners streaming far,
Of knight, and steed, and plume;
Of the wild *mêlée*, and the sabre's clash,
How would his spirit bound!
Yet ever after the lightning's flash,
Night closeth darker round.

Down would he sink on the floor again,
Like the pilgrim who sinks on some desert plain,
Even while his thirsting ear can trace
The hum of distant streams;
Or the maimèd hound, who hears the chase
Sweep past him in his dreams.

The false king sate on his throne of state,
'Mid knights and nobles free;
'Who is there,' he cried, 'who will cross the tide,
And do battle in France for me?
There is cast on mine honour a fearful stain,
The death of the boy who ruled Bretagne;*
And the monarch of France, my bold suzerain,
Hath bidden a champion for me appear,
My fame from this darkening blot to clear.
Speak—is your silence the silence of fear,
My knights and my nobles? Frowning and pale
Your faces grow as I tell my tale!
Is there not one of this knightly ring,
Who dares do battle for his king?'

The warriors they heard, but they spake not a word;
The earth some gazed upon;
And some did raise a steadfast gaze
To the face of false King John.
Think ye they feared? They were Englishmen all,
Though mutely they sate in their monarch's hall;
The heroes of many a well-fought day,
Who loved the sound of a gathering fray,
Even as the lonely shepherd loves
The herds' soft bell in the mountain-groves.
Why were they silent? There was not one
Who could trust the word of false King John;
And their cheeks grew pallid as they thought
On the deed of blood by his base hand wrought;
Pale, with a brave heart's generous fear,
When forced a tale of shame to hear.

'Twas a coward whiteness then did chase
The glow of shame from the false king's face;
And he turned aside, in bootless pride,
That witness of his guilt to hide;
Yet every heart around him there,
Witness against him more strongly bare!

* Prince Arthur of Brittany, whose melancholy fate has been too often the theme of song and story to require notice here.

Oh, out then spake the beauteous queen;*
'A captive lord I know,
Whose loyal heart hath ever been
Eager to meet the foe;
Were true De Courcy here this day,
Freed from his galling chain,
Never, oh never should scoffers say,
That amid all England's rank and might,
Their king had sought him a loyal knight,
And sought such knight in vain!'
Up started the monarch, and cleared his brow,
And bade them summon De Courcy now.
Swiftly his messengers hasted away,
And sought the cell where the hero lay;
They bade him arise at his master's call,
And follow their steps to the stately hall.

He is brought before the council—
There are chains upon his hands;
With his silver hair, that aged knight,
Like a rock o'erhung with foam-wreaths white,
Proudly and calmly stands.
He gazes on the monarch
With stern and star-like eye;
And the company muse and marvel much,
That the light of the old man's eye is such,
After long captivity.
His fetters hang upon him
Like an unheeded thing;
Or like a robe of purple worn
With graceful and indifferent scorn
By some great-hearted king.
And strange it was to witness
How the false king looked aside;
For he dared not meet his captive's eye!
Thus ever the spirit's royalty
Is greater than pomp and pride!

The false king spake to his squires around,
And his lifted voice had an angry sound:
'Strike ye the chains from each knightly limb!
Who was so bold as to fetter him?
Warrior, believe me, no hest of mine
Bade them fetter a form like thine;
Thy sovereign knoweth thy fame too well.'
He paused, and a cloud on his dark brow fell;
For the knight still gazed upon him,
And his eye was like a star;
And the words on the lips of the false king died,
Like the murmuring sounds of an ebbing tide
By the traveller heard afar.

From the warrior's form they loosed the chain;
His face was lighted with calm disdain;
Nor cheek, nor lip, nor eye gave token
E'en that he knew his chains were broken.
He spake—no music, loud or clear,
Was in the voice of the gray-haired knight;
But a low stern sound, like that ye hear
In the march of a mail-clad host by night.
'Brother of Cœur de Lion,' said he,
'These chains have not dishonoured me!'
There was crushing scorn in each simple word,
Mightier than battle-axe or sword.

Not long did the heart of the false king thrill
To the touch of passing shame,
For it was hard, and mean, and chill;
As breezes sweep o'er a frozen rill,
Leaving it cold and unbroken still,
That feeling went and came;
And now to the knight he made reply,
Pleading his cause right craftily;
Skilled was his tongue in specious use
Of promise fair and of feigned excuse,
Blended with words of strong appeal
To love of fame and to loyal zeal.
At length he ceased; and every eye
Gazed on De Courcy wistfully.
'Speak!' cried the king in that fearful pause;
'Wilt thou not champion thy monarch's cause?'

The old knight struck his foot on the ground,
Like a war-horse hearing the trumpet sound;
And he spake with a voice of thunder,
Solemn and fierce in tone,
Waving his hand to the stately band
Who stood by the monarch's throne,
As a warrior might wave his flashing glaive
When cheering his squadrons on:
'I will fight for the honour of England,
Though not for false King John!'

He turned and strode from the lofty hall,
Nor seemed to hear the sudden cheer
Which burst, as he spake, from the lips of all.

* Isabella of Angoulême, wife to King John, celebrated for her beauty and high spirit.

And when he stood in the air without,
He paused as if in joyful doubt;
To the forests green and the wide blue sky
Stretching his arms embracingly,
With stately tread and uplifted head,
As a good steed tosses back his mane
When they loose his neck from the servile rein;
Ye know not, ye who are always free,
How precious a thing is liberty.
'O world!' he cried; 'sky, river, hill,
Ye wear the garments of beauty still;
How have ye kept your youth so fair,*
While age has whitened this hoary hair?'
But when the squire, who watched his lord,
Gave to his hand his ancient sword,
The hilt he pressed to his eager breast,
Like one who a long-lost friend hath met;
And joyously said, as he kissed the blade,
'Methinks there is youth in my spirit yet.
For France! for France! o'er the waters blue;
False king—dear land—adieu, adieu!'

He hath crossed the booming ocean,
On the shore he plants his lance;
And he sends his daring challenge
Into the heart of France:
'Lo, here I stand for England,
Queen of the silver main!
To guard her fame and to cleanse her name
From slander's darkening stain!
Advance, advance! ye knights of France,
Give answer to my call;
Lo! here I stand for England,
And I defy ye all!'

From the east and the north came champions forth—
They came in a knightly crowd;
From the south and the west each generous breast
Throbbed at that summons proud.
But though brave was each lord, and keen each sword,
No warrior could withstand
The strength of the hero-spirit
Which nerved that old man's hand.
He is conqueror in the battle—
He hath won the wreath of bay;
To the shining crown of his fair renown
He hath added another ray;
He hath drawn his sword for England;
He hath fought for her spotless name;
And the isle resounds to her farthest bounds
With her gray-haired hero's fame.
In the ears of the craven monarch,
Oft must this burthen ring—
'Though the crown be thine and the royal line,
He is in heart thy king!'

So they gave this graceful honour
To the bold De Courcy's race,
That they ever should dare their helms to wear
Before the king's own face:
And the sons of that line of heroes
To this day their right assume;
For, when every head is unbonneted,†
They walk in cap and plume!

ZINC RINGS FOR RHEUMATISM.

We find the following sensible note in a recent number of the Agricultural Gazette:—Galvanic rings are not of any more ascertained efficacy than metallic tractors, horse-shoe magnets, and the thousand-and-one humbugs that profess to afford relief to suffering humanity. The galvanic rings consist merely of a copper and zinc plate formed into a ring. The galvanic action of these metals, when the circle is completed by means of the moist skin, must be exceedingly small, and certainly not enough to produce an effect upon the diseased tissues of the body. In some cases they may have afforded relief, by diverting the attention of the patient from his disease to the remedy. It is, however, most probable, when persons get well after wearing them, that, like the king's touch for the evil, the cure was rather a coincidence than a consequence. The sellers of them assert that they can do no harm if they do no good. This is not altogether true. A medical friend of ours was called in the other day to a poor man who had worn one of these rings for rheumatism, and found his finger swollen and inflamed; so that in this case much unnecessary pain—and the loss of a week's wages we presume—was the result of the experiment.

* The reader of German will here recognise an exquisite stanza from Uhland, very inadequately rendered.

† The present representative of the house of De Courcy is Lord Kinsale.

TUNNELLING BY THE ROMANS.

The following extraordinary account is set forth in a letter from Marseilles in the Débats:—There has been long known, or believed to exist at Marseilles, a tunnel or submarine passage passing from the ancient abbey of St Victoire, running under the arm of the sea, which is covered with ships, and coming out under a tower of Fort Saint-Nicolas. Many projects for exploring this passage have been entertained, but hitherto no one has been found sufficiently bold to persevere in it. M. Joyland, of the Ponts-et-Chaussées, and M. Matayras, an architect, have, however, not only undertaken, but accomplished this task. Accompanied by some friends and a number of labourers, they went a few days ago to the abbey, and descended the numerous steps that lead to the entrance of the passage. Here they were the first day stopped by heaps of the ruins of the abbey. Two days afterwards, however, they were able to clear their way to the other end, and came out at Fort Saint-Nicolas, after working two hours and twenty minutes. The structure, which is considered to be Roman, is in such excellent condition, that in order to put it into complete repair, a cost of no more than 500,000 francs will be required; but a much larger outlay will be wanted to render it serviceable for modern purposes. This tunnel is deemed much finer than that of London, being formed of one single vault of sixty feet span, and one-fourth longer.

A FACT FOR TEMPERANCE ADVOCATES.

One vulgar argument in favour of spirituous liquor is, that in winter it 'keeps out the cold.' That it creates for a short time an excitement productive of heat, there is no doubt; but when its short-lived influence has passed away, a reaction takes place, which causes the drinker to be infinitely colder than he would have been without it. In proof that people can get on without spirits in the most frigid parts of the world, we may instance a case mentioned in the third volume of Lord Monboddo's Ancient Metaphysics:—A gentleman named Andrew Graham, set out from Severn River (latitude 56° 10′ north), in Hudson's Bay, in the depth of the winter of 1773, and travelled to Churchill River—a distance of 350 miles—without tasting spirits or sleeping under a roof. He was accompanied by three Europeans, six native Americans, and four Newfoundland dogs, who pulled in a sledge their luggage, consisting of beaver and blanket coverings, biscuit, bacon, flour, but *no* wine, beer, or other spirituous liquors; which Mr Graham did not choose to carry with him, because he knew his attendants would never be quiet till he had drank them all. Their drink was melted snow. They all arrived—after twenty days' exposure to the most severely cold climate in the world—at the end of their journey in perfect health; and Mr Graham says he never enjoyed his food nor ever slept better in his life. This anecdote is fatal to the supposition that alcohol is necessary to cold climates, as many suppose.

A SCOTCH MUSSULMAN.

Osman's history is a curious one. He was a Scotchman born, and when very young, being then a drummer-boy, he landed in Egypt with Mackenzie Fraser's force. He was taken prisoner, and, according to Mohammedan custom, the alternative of death or the Koran was offered to him. He did not choose death, and therefore went through the ceremonies which were necessary for turning him into a good Mohammedan. But what amused me most in his history was this, that, very soon after having embraced Islam, he was obliged in practice to become curious and discriminating in his new faith, to make war upon Mohammedan dissenters, and follow the orthodox standard of the prophet in fierce campaigns against the Wahabees, who are the Unitarians of the Mussulman world. The Wahabees were crushed, and Osman, returning home in triumph from his holy wars, began to flourish in the world: he acquired property, and became effendi, or gentleman. At the time of my visit to Cairo, he seemed to be much respected by his brother Mohammedans, and gave pledge of his sincere alienation from Christianity by keeping a couple of wives. He affected the same sort of reserve in mentioning them as is generally shown by Orientals. He invited me, indeed, to see his harem, but he made both his wives bundle out before I was admitted. He felt, as it seemed to me, that neither of them would bear criticism; and I think that this idea, rather than any motive of sincere jealousy, induced him to keep them out of sight. The rooms of the harem reminded me of an English nursery rather than of a Mohammedan paradise. One is apt to judge of a woman, before one sees her, by the air of elegance or coarseness with which she surrounds her house. I judged Osman's wives by this test, and condemned them both. But the strangest feature in Osman's character was his inextinguishable nationality. In vain they had brought him over the seas in early boyhood; in vain had he suffered captivity and conversion; in vain they had passed him through fire in their Arabian campaigns; they could not cut away or burn out poor Osman's inborn love of all that was Scotch; in vain men called him effendi; in vain he swept along in eastern robes; in vain the rival wives adorned his harem. The joy of his heart still plainly lay in this, that he had three shelves of books, and that the books were thorough-bred Scotch—the Edinburgh this, the Edinburgh that; and, above all, I recollect he prided himself upon the 'Edinburgh Cabinet Library.'—*Traces of Travel.*

RESULTS OF A LITTLE NEGLECT.

I was once, in the country, a witness of the numberless minute losses that negligence in household regulation entails. For want of a trumpery latch, the gate of the poultry yard was for ever open; there being no means of closing it externally, 'twas on the swing every time a person went out, and many of the poultry were lost in consequence. One day a fine young porker made his escape into the wood, and the whole family, gardener, cook, milkmaid, &c. presently turned out in quest of the fugitive. The gardener was the first to discover the object of pursuit, and, in leaping a ditch to cut off his further escape, got a sprain that confined him to his bed for the next fortnight; the cook found the linen burnt that she had left hung up before the fire to dry; and the milkmaid having forgotten in her haste to tie up the cattle properly in the cow-house, one of the loose cows had broken the leg of a colt that happened to be kept in the same shed. The linen burnt and the gardener's work lost were worth full twenty crowns, and the colt about as much more; so that here was a loss in a few minutes of forty crowns, purely for want of a latch that might have cost a few halfpence at the utmost; and this in a household where the strictest economy was necessary; to say nothing of the poor man, or the anxiety and other troublesome incidents. The misfortune was, to be sure, not very serious, nor the loss very heavy; yet when it is considered that similar neglect was the occasion of repeated disasters of the same kind, and ultimately the ruin of a worthy family, 'twas deserving of some little attention.—*From the French.*

PERSEVERANCE.

All the performances of human art, at which we look with praise or wonder, are instances of the resistless force of perseverance: it is by this that the quarry becomes a pyramid, and that distant countries are united by canals. If a man was to compare the effect of a single stroke of a pick-axe, or of one impression of the spade, with the general design and last result, he would be overwhelmed by the sense of their disproportion; yet those petty operations, incessantly continued, in time surmount the greatest difficulties, and mountains are levelled, and oceans bounded, by the slender force of human beings.—*Dr Johnson.*

HUMANITY.

True humanity consists not in a squeamish ear; it consists not in starting or shrinking at tales of misery, but in a disposition of heart to relieve it. True humanity appertains rather to the mind than to the nerves, and prompts men to use real and active measures to execute the actions which it suggests.—*Charles James Fox.*

RICHES.

If men were content to grow rich somewhat more slowly, they would grow rich much more surely. If they would use their capital within reasonable limits, and transact with it only so much business as it could fairly control, they would be far less liable to lose it. Excessive profits always involve the liability of great risks, as in a lottery, in which, if there *are* high prizes, there must be a great proportion of blanks.—*Wayland.*

Printed by William Bradbury, of No. 6, York Place, and Frederick Mullett Evans, of No. 7, Church Row, both of Stoke Newington, in the county of Middlesex, printers, at their office, Lombard Street, in the precinct of Whitefriars, and city of London; and Published (with permission of the Proprietors, W. and R. CHAMBERS,) by WILLIAM SOMERVILLE ORR, Publisher, of 2, Amen Corner, at No. 2, AMEN CORNER, both in the parish of Christ-church, and in the city of London.—Saturday, April 26, 1845.

CONDUCTED BY WILLIAM AND ROBERT CHAMBERS, EDITORS OF 'CHAMBERS'S INFORMATION FOR THE PEOPLE,' 'CHAMBERS'S EDUCATIONAL COURSE,' &c.

No. 70. New Series. SATURDAY, MAY 3, 1845. Price 1½d.

CAPABILITIES.

It has often been a question whether great men are the producers or the produced of great crises. We see a Cromwell live for forty years a quiet country-town life, till at length a national convulsion arising, he, being strongly interested in the views of one of the parties, dashes forward, and, before passing fifty, has all but the crown of England upon his head. Again, we see a French sous-lieutenant of artillery plunging into his country's history at a time of similar confusion, and making himself the most formidable sovereign upon earth before he is thirty-five. If we were to limit our regard to such facts as these, we should be disposed at once to conclude, that a man of powerful character is nothing, unless an opportunity arise for his entering upon a grand career. But, on the other hand, we often see a powerful mind arise in times comparatively tranquil, and work great marvels, apparently by its own inherent energies. We see at times what seem to be occasions for the coming forward of great men upon the stage, and yet they do not come. We then begin to think that perhaps a Cromwell or a Bonaparte contributes to some great, though indefinable extent, in producing the events to which his appearance at first seemed subordinate. We suspect that the civil wars of England, and the French Revolution, would not have taken the turn they did, but for the potent and overmastering influence of these individual actors. Thus we are prevented from coming to a decision on the point. And, in fact, this is a question which stands unsettled amongst thinking men until the present hour.

The question, as it appears to me, can never be definitely settled on one side or the other; for neither view is wholly true. But I believe that the truth preponderates in favour of the argument which considers men as requiring circumstances to evoke their mental powers. Strong, active, and original minds will ever tell to some degree upon their circumstances, be these as impassible as they may; but they cannot tell to a great degree, unless at a time when the social elements are in some confusion. And this is simply because, let a single mind be ever so powerful, the fabric of society and its conventionalities is, in ordinary circumstances, stronger still, so that no one can do more than merely modify it in some slight degree, or prepare the way for future operations whereby it may be affected. If the matter be narrowly examined, it will always be found that, where an occasion for the appearance of a great leader passed over without any one coming forward, the necessary stir of the social elements was wanting. The *vis inertiæ* of the mass is what all single minds find fatal to them, when they attempt to do great things with their fellow-creatures. Hence a Luther, rising in the twelfth century, when the Romish church was at its highest pitch of power, would have only broken his head against its walls. As an obscure heretic, his name would have been forgotten in a few years. Such minds as his must, in the course of nature, have arisen at various periods among the conventual brotherhoods; but they would never become distinguished for more than a somewhat latitudinarian way of dealing with the authority of the prior, or perhaps an occasional fractiousness at the elections of sacristans. It is like the wind-sown seed, much of which comes to nothing because it lights in stony places, while only what chances to fall on good ground fructifies. And there is another thing to be considered. The most powerful minds are more or less dependent upon things external to them, in order to be roused into due activity. Such a mind droops like the banner by the flag-staff, till the wind of occasion unfurls it. It may pine, and chafe, and wear itself out in vain regrets and ennui, like the prisoned huntsman, or, in the desperation of forced idleness, or unworthy occupation, waste itself upon frivolities idler than idleness itself. But still it will be for the most part a lost mind, unless circumstances shall arise capable of raising it to its full force, and eliciting all its powers. Here a consideration occurs, calling for some collateral remark. We are apt, at a tranquil period, to pity the men who have to fight through civil broils such as those in which Spain has for some years been engaged. In reality, these men are happier than we think them. They have the pleasure of feeling their faculties continually at the full stretch. Victorious or defeated, hunting or hunted, they are thoroughly engrossed in the passing day; not a moment for the torture of excessive ease. Providence is kind to the men who undertake dangerous enterprises. Even when death comes to them—no matter how dreadful his shape—he is met in a paroxysm of mental activity, which entirely disarms him of his terrors.

It follows from these considerations, that there must, at all but extraordinary times, be a vast amount of latent capability in society. Gray's musings on the Cromwells and Miltons of the village are a truth, though extremely stated. Men of all conditions do grow and die in obscurity, who, in suitable circumstances, might have attained to the temple which shines afar. The hearts of Roman mothers beat an unnoted lifetime in dim parlours. Souls of fire miss their hour, and languish into ashes. Is not this conformable to what all men feel in their own case? Who is there that has not thought, over and over again, what else he could have done, what else he could have been? Vanity, indeed, may fool us here, and self-tenderness be too ready to look upon the misspending of years as anything but our own fault. Let us look, then, to each other. Does almost any one that we know appear to do or to be all that he might? How far from it! Regard for a moment the manner in which a vast proportion of those who, from independency of fortune and from education, are able to do most good in the world, spend their time, and say if there be not an immense proportion of the capability of mankind undeveloped. The fact is, the bond of union among men is also the bond of restraint. We are committed not to alarm or distress each other by extraordinary displays of intellect or emotion. There are more hostages to fortune that we shall not do anything great, than those which having children constitutes. Many struggle for a while against the repressive influences, but at length yield to the powerful temptations to nonentity. The social despotism presents the fêtes with which it seeks to solace and beguile its victims; and he who began to put on his armour for the righting of many wrongs, is soon content to smile with those who smile. Thus daily do generations ripe and rot, life unenjoyed, the great mission unperformed. Do angels ever weep? If they do, what a subject for their tears in the multitude of young souls who come in the first faith of nature to grapple at the good, the true, the beautiful, but are instantly thrown back, helpless and mute, into the limbo of Commonplace. Oh Conventionality, quiet may be thy fireside hours, smooth thy pillowed thoughts; but at what a sacrifice of the right and the generous, of the best that breathes and pants in our nature, is thy peace purchased!

Is not one great cause of the dissatisfaction which rests on the close of most lives just this sense of having all the time made no right or full use of the faculties bestowed upon us? The inner and the true man pent up, concealed from every eye, or only giving occasional glimpses of itself in whimsical tastes and oddities—uneasy movements of undeveloped tendency—we walk through a masque called life, acting up to a character which we have adopted, or which has been imposed upon us, doing nothing from the heart, 'goring' our best thoughts to make them lie still. Pitiable parade! The end comes, and finds us despairing over precious years lost beyond recovery, and which, were they recovered, we would again lose. And, if such be a common case, can we wonder at the slow advance of public or national improvement? There must be a design with regard to highly-endowed natures, that they are to bear upon all around them with such intellectual and moral force as they possess, and thus be continually working on for the general good. This we might consider as a sort of pabulum requisite for the public health—something analogous to air or food with respect to the bodily system. But is this moral necessary of life diffused as it ought to be? Let the endless misdirections and repressions of human capability answer the question.

HISTORY OF THE FIREPLACE.

During the last few years, public attention has been laudably directed to the defective means which still exist for warming and ventilating houses. Although we have arrived at a high state of civilisation in some respects, yet the method still in use for producing an artificial climate in modern habitations, is perhaps more primitive and defective than any of our domestic contrivances. We burn coal in a vessel or stove which is no whit better in principle than the ancient fire-basket. Whilst the chimney-wall in each room is often heated like an oven, those opposite and at the sides are but a few degrees above the temperature of the atmosphere. In this respect the ancients evinced much greater ingenuity than we do; and many of the so-called inventions of modern date were, it appears, in general use hundreds and thousands of years ago. By the research of a recent author, many curious and interesting facts concerning warming and ventilation have been brought to light;* and as in this country all ideas of comfort and sociality are centered around the hearth, we doubt not that a historical sketch of the 'fireplace,' chiefly drawn from the above source, will prove interesting.

The history of the fireside may be said to commence in the dark ages; for it reaches back to a time when man was unacquainted with the existence of fire. The early records of nearly all nations refer to a time when that element was unknown. Indeed instances of such ignorance have been met with in comparatively modern times. When Magellan visited the Marian Islands in 1521, the natives believed themselves to be the only people in the world. They were without everything which we regard as necessaries, and in total ignorance of fire. Several of their huts being consumed, they at first considered the flame to be a kind of animal that attached itself to the wood, and fed upon it. Some who approached too near, being scorched, communicated their terror to the rest, who durst only look upon it at a distance. They were afraid, they said, that the terrible animal would bite them, or wound them with its violent breathing. They speedily learned to use fire with as much address as Europeans. Few historical facts, therefore, are less doubtful than that man was once without means of artificial heat. A Phœnician tradition attributed its discovery to a hunter observing a conflagration that had been excited in a forest by the attrition of some trees during a storm. Another tradition varies the account: in the winter season, Vulcan the king, coming to a tree on the mountains that had been fired by a thunderbolt, was cheered by its heat; and adding more wood to preserve it, he invited his companions to share in his pleasure, and thereupon claimed to be the inventor of flame. Fire once discovered, the primeval savages, though at first alarmed, gradually felt its blessed influence; and it is thus that tradition gives us an account of the earliest fireside; for around the embers of the burning trees men first learned to herd; 'and as the intercourse continued under the bond of the common enjoyment, the incoherent sounds by which they expressed their emotions were by degrees roughly cast into the elements of speech; thus the discovery of fire gave rise to the first social meeting of mankind, to the formation of language, to their ultimate union, and to all the wonders of subsequent civilisation.'* The Chinese historians attribute the earliest power of producing fire at will, by the friction of two pieces of dried wood, to Souigine, one of their first kings. This power once known, the nomadic races in all countries ever availed themselves of it; though a fire made of dried wood or grass in the open air, or in a rude tent, was their sole provision against cold for many ages.

Increased intelligence induced mankind to seek for greater warmth under substantial cover, and the first houses they took to were ready built, being chiefly caves. In the middle of these they made fires, in spite of the smoke, for which there was no other outlet than the hole by which the inhabitants came in and out. The same rude method was continued even when men learnt to build houses, and to congregate in cities; only they made a hole in the roof to let the smoke out, exactly like the Laplanders and some of the Irish at the present day.

The parents of western civilisation, the Egyptians, although they built themselves excellent houses, and were scrupulously nice in their domestic arrangements, either made their fires (for it is cold enough even in that warm climate to need them occasionally) on a central hearth, or used pans of live charcoal to carry about from one room to another. To them is ascribed the invention of bellows to concentrate the energy of fire. The reader will see in the second volume of Wilkinson's Manners and Customs of the Ancient Egyptians, copies of that instrument taken from paintings on tombs, at least three thousand years old. During the exode and wanderings of the Jews, their fireplaces were precisely like those

* On the History and Art of Warming and Ventilating Rooms and Buildings, &c. By Walter Bernan, Civil Engineer. 2 vols. Bell: London.

* Vitruvius, b. ii. c. i.

both of the primitive races and of the modern Arabs—small bonfires in conical tents, with a hole in the apex of the cone to let out the smoke; but after their establishment in Canaan, their houses, it has been inferred, resembled those of the Egyptians, 'wide, thorough aired with windows, and large chambers ceiled with cedar, and painted with vermilion;'* and, judging from the terms they had to mark the position, size, and manner of closing the apertures, they must have paid great attention to domestic accommodation. The winter in Palestine being cold and long, and wood abundant, particular apartments were appropriated to the season when fires were wanted, to avoid the nuisance of smoke pervading the house, and soiling its furniture and ornaments. About the latter end of November, king Jehoiakim was sitting in his 'winter house,' when he threw the roll of Baruch 'into the fire that was burning on the hearth before him.' The prophet Amos alluded to the same custom, when he declared that the 'winter house, with the summer house,' would be destroyed. From the hearths and braziers in these brumal apartments, the smoke was emitted at a hole in the roof, or by the *arubbah;* for, notwithstanding what some rabbis have written about the Jews being so scrupulous to preserve the purity of the Holy City, that they would not permit the erection of a chimney in Jerusalem, they were, perhaps, as ignorant as the Egyptians of that contrivance. The great improvement that chimneys would have made on Mount Sion itself, is graphically described by Baruch, when he notices 'the faces that were blacked by the smoke that cometh out of the temple.'

The method of using fuel among the Greeks was the same as among the Hebrews, but perhaps without their care for ventilation. Homer describes his princes undressing themselves in the palace, to kill with their own hands the sheep, oxen, and swine they were to eat at dinner; roasting the entrails, and during the entertainment handing them to each other as delicacies. The repast being finished, he shows them sitting for their pleasure on the piled skins of the animals they had slain and devoured, and playing at games of chance, and one of them taking a pastern bone out of a basket in which it was lying, and throwing it at the head of a beggar, but on missing its aim, making a grease spot where it fell on the opposite wall. From this picture of the grossness of ancient manners, it may be concluded that when the poet says, Penelope's maids threw the glowing embers out of the braziers upon the floor, and heaped fresh wood upon them, he did not mean to depict his immortal barbarians burning odoriferous fuel on purpose to sweeten what must have been a vitiated atmosphere. The fire that was quickly to blaze on the hearth, had to diffuse the comforts of light as well as warmth; and the fragrant logs were known to abound with the resinous material of illumination. In the heroic age, they had oil and tallow in abundance, but were ignorant of the method of burning them in lamps; and the only use they appear to have made of wax, was to put it in the ear to shut out sound. Burning fuel was carried into the apartment where light was required, and sometimes placed on altars for the same purpose; and long thin pieces of lighted wood were carried in the hand when they moved from one place to another in the night.

Coal, it has been thought, was known to the Greek naturalists. Theophrastus speaks of fossil substances found in Liguria, and in Elis, in the way to Olympia, and used by smiths, that when broken for use are earthy, and that kindled and burned like wood-coal. The general fuel was green wood; and where that was unattainable, other vegetable and even excrementitious substances were used on the hearth for combustibles. On days of ceremony, it was also customary to burn fragrant substances. When Alexander the Great was at an entertainment, given in the winter by one of his friends, 'a brazier was brought into the apartment to warm it. The day being cold, and the king observing the small quantity of fuel that had been provided, jeeringly desired his host,' says Plutarch, 'to bring more wood or incense.' The supply of the precious firing appeared to the king too scanty for producing the required warmth; and if it arose from his host being niggardly of the costly fuel, he hinted that some even of the common sort would be acceptable.

The Romans made vast strides of improvement in fireplaces, although they were quite unable to rid themselves of the smoke nuisance. Vitruvius, in his work on architecture, directs that the walls of rooms 'in which fires or many lights are burned, should be finished above the *podium* with polished panels of a *black* colour, having red or yellow margins round them; and he advises that delicate ornaments should not be introduced into the cornices, because they are spoiled, not only by the smoke of the house, but also by that from the neighbouring buildings.' The principal fireplace in a Roman house of the best kind was built in the bath, chiefly to heat the *caldarium* or sweating-room of a bath. It was a sort of furnace, and called a *hypocaust,* and served also to heat the walls of the whole habitation; quite upon the principle of the hot-air system which has recently been introduced as a modern invention. 'The hypocaust being constructed in the under storey of a building, in the manner described by Vitruvius, several pipes of baked clay were then built into the walls, having their lower ends left open to the hypocaust. These pipes were carried to the height of the first or second storey, and had their upper orifices made to open into the chamber that was to be heated. They were closed by moveable covers. While green wood was burning in the furnace, and the hypocaust filled with its acrid smoke, the covers were not removed from the caliducts; but as soon as the wood was charred, the upper orifices of the pipes were opened, and the hot vapour from the hypocaust then flowed into the chamber.' It is singular, that although these hot-air ducts would have answered to carry off smoke, the Romans never hit upon the expedient of applying them to that purpose.

The excavations of Pompeii have revealed to us the family hearths of the Romans, such as were used in rooms not sufficiently heated by the hypocaust. The general method of procuring a warm in-door climate, was by burning charcoal in a brazier on the pavement in the middle of the room, and allowing the vapour to exude at the door and window. These braziers and tripods, formed of all sizes, in iron and bronze, occasionally displayed great elegance of design and neatness of workmanship, and sometimes were contrived to heat water. One of this description, in the museum at Naples, is 28 inches square, and has four towers, one at each angle, fitted with a lid that can be raised by a ring. The fire-hearth is placed in the square part in the middle, which is lined with iron, as in the common braziers. The fluid to be heated was contained in the towers. Another use of these cup-like towers reminds us once more that there is nothing new under the sun. When Dr Arnott's stove was introduced, it was found to have an injuriously drying effect upon the air, consequently a vase of water was added, to supply the necessary humidity by evaporation. Now, what says Mr Bernan on the use of these foculari? 'The cold dry air of an Italian winter and spring was desiccated to a high degree after being expanded by the heat of a hypocaust, or a fire of charcoal; and these braziers appear a very elegant method of diffusing that quantity of moisture in the air of an apartment that was necessary to make it agreeable and salubrious. Perhaps the evaporation was partially regulated by shutting or opening the lids of the water vessels.'

When the Romans landed in Britain, they found our savage forefathers living either in detached wigwams of wicker-work, in huts of loose stones without chimney or window, or in excavated caves, like the Germans, surrounded by their winter provisions, and stifled with smoke. The following fireside picture is drawn from the Welsh historian Gyraldus:—'Families inhabit a large hut or house, which, having a fire in the midst,

* Jerem. xxii. 14.

serves to warm them by day and to sleep round by night; and he describes the bands of young men who followed no profession but arms, visiting families to whom they were always welcome, and passing the day with the most animated cheerfulness. At length, sunk into repose on a thin covering of dried reeds, spread round the great fire placed in the middle, they lay down promiscuously, covered only by a coarse-made cloth called *brychan*, and kept one another warm by lying close together; and when one side lost its genial heat, they turned about, and gave the chilly side to the fire. The great men endeavoured to improve on this custom during the day. A Welsh prince had an officer in his court called a foot-bearer, whose duty it was, at meal-times, when his master was seated at table, to sit with his back to the fire, and keep the princely feet warm and comfortable by cherishing them in his bosom.' In the later feudal times, the spacious lofty hall, left open to the roof, had its windows placed high from the floor, and filled with oiled linen or louver boards, or occasionally with painted glass. The floor of stone or earth had a part at one end raised a little above the general level, and laid with planks. On this platform or dais stood a massive table, and ponderous benches or forms, and a high-backed seat for the master under a canopy. On the hearth, in the middle of the hall, were placed the andirons for supporting the ends of the brands, that were arranged by means of a heavy two-pronged fork, the type and predecessor of the modern poker. On the roof over the hearth was a turret or louver, filled with boards arranged so as to exclude rain and wind, and permit the escape of smoke; and this was sometimes an object of considerable architectural beauty in the external aspect of the building. In this gaunt and aguish apartment, heated by a single fire, the company were in a position not much different from what they would be in the open air: not a particle of heated air could add to their comfort, for as fast as produced, it escaped through the louver: light was the only solace the greater number could derive from the blazing fuel; and the few who were in a situation to feel the radiant heat, were incommoded by the current of cold air sweeping like a hurricane along the floor towards the fire. From the height of the louver, and low temperature of the smoke, few of the buoyant flakes of charcoal found their way into the atmosphere; and the larger the bonfire the thicker was the layer of soot deposited on each individual. Boisterous weather also brought its annoyance. Had the fire been made in an open field, they might have moved to the windward of the smoke, but in the hall, where could they flee to from its miseries? The country houses of inferior landholders and farmers were generally one storey high. If they were built with two storeys, the roof was so deep as to reach to the ceiling of the lower room. The hall and kitchen forming one apartment, and roughly plastered, was open to the timbers of the roof, and sometimes had a louver, and a window that could be closed with a shutter:

> 'Barre we the gates,
> Cheke we and cheyne we and eche chine stoppe,
> That no light leopen yn at lover ne at loupe.' *

When these houses had a room to sleep in, old and young reposed in the same apartment, and several in one bed; servants made their beds on the floor in the kitchen.

Cottages had neither louver nor loupe, and their inmates lay round the fire. Longlande describes one of a vagrant group:—

> 'Suten at even by the hote coles,
> Unlouk his legges abrod other lygge at hus ese,
> Rest hym and roste hym and his ryg turn,
> Drynke drue and deepe, and draw hym than to bedde.'

In lodging-houses, the same packing system was followed, and when a person had a bed to himself, it was a mark of distinction, and recorded accordingly. In the magnificent strongholds, built near the time of the Conquest, a central hearth is seldom found. Having several storeys in height, and their roofs being used as a terrace for defence, an exit in the common form for the smoke, even from the uppermost chambers, would have been impracticable. A huge recess, therefore, was built at one side of the hall, and on its hearth fuel was burnt, the smoke finding egress by a contrivance which may be regarded as a chimney in its infancy. Over the hearth was a sort of huge funnel, or hole in the wall, which sloped up through its thickness, till it reached daylight in the outer side of the wall.

Wood, turf, and furze were almost the only fuel. The first legal mention of coal was made in 1239, when Henry III. granted a charter to the inhabitants of Newcastle to dig for it; but so great was the prejudice against it, from an erroneous notion that it was injurious to the health, that it was not in general use till the seventeenth century. Meanwhile, the funnel-like smoke-duct of the feudal castle became gradually improved into a chimney. Leland says in his Itinerary, speaking of Bolton Castle, 'One thynge I muche notyd in the hawle of Bolton, how chimeneys were conveyed by tunnells made on the syds of the walls betwyxt the lights in the hawle, and by this means, and by no covers, is the smoke of the harthe in the hawle wonder *strangely* conveyed.' *

Chimneys were afterwards generally adopted. To old buildings they were added, whilst new ones were never constructed without what a wordy author calls 'the elegant and commodious tube now known by the name of a chimney.' By its help the fireside was greatly improved.

The following description applies to the firesides of the end of Henry VIII.'s reign, by which time chimneys or flues had become universal:—'The windows had curtains, and were glazed in the manner described by Erasmus; but in inferior dwellings, such as those of copyholders and the like, the light-holes were filled with linen, or with a shutter. The hearth-recess was generally wide, high, and deep, and had a large flue. The hearth, usually raised a few inches above the floor, had sometimes a halpas or dais made before it, as in the king's and queen's chambers in the Tower. Before the hearth-recess, or on the halpas, when there was one, a piece of green cloth or tapestry was spread, as a substitute for the rushes that covered the lower part of the floor. On this were placed a very high-backed chair or two, and footstools, that sometimes had cushions, and, above all, high-backed forms and screens—both most admirable inventions for neutralising draughts of cold air in these dank and chilling apartments. Andirons, fire-forks, fire-pans, and tongs, were the implements to supply and arrange the fuel. Hearth-recesses with flues were common in the principal chambers of houses of persons of condition; and were superseding what Aubrey calls flues, like louver holes, in the habitations of all classes. The adage, that "one good fire heats the whole house," was found true only in the humbler dwellings; for in palace and mansion, though great fires blazed in the presence chamber, or hall, or parlour, the domestics were literally famishing with cold. This discomfort did not, however, proceed from selfish or stingy housekeeping, but rather from an affectation of hardihood, particularly among the lower classes, when effeminacy was reckoned a reproach. Besides, few could know what comfort really was; but those who did, valued it highly. Sanders relates that Henry VIII. gave the revenues of a convent, which he had confiscated, to a person who placed a chair for him commodiously before the fire, and out of all draughts.'

* Ritson. Metrical Romances.

* Though many authors antecedent to Leland use the term 'chimney,' yet they mean by that word simply 'fireplace,' or 'hearth-recess;' and the verbal equivalent to the word in the Reformer's Testament is 'furnace.' Leland himself, in using the word, almost defines it by saying, 'that the chimeneys were conveyed by tunnells;' or, in other words, the fireplace was continued by a tunnel to the top of the building.

This description of an English fireside is accurate, even applied to a much later period—to indeed all the intervening space between the time of Queen Mary and that of William, Prince of Orange; for it was not till the latter reign that coal became the staple fuel. The prejudice against it, which we have before adverted to, was as strong as it was unaccountable. As an instance of it, we may mention, in passing, that when first introduced, the Commons petitioned the crown in 1306 to prohibit burning the 'noxious' fuel. A 'royal proclamation having failed to abate the growing nuisance, a commission was issued to ascertain who burned sea-coal within the city and in its neighbourhood, and to punish them by fine for the first offence, and by demolition of their furnaces if they persisted in transgression; and more vigorous measures had to be resorted to. A law was passed making it a capital offence to burn sea-coal within the city of London, and only permitting it to be used in forges in the neighbourhood. Among the records in the Tower, Mr Astle found a document, importing that in the time of Edward I., a man had been tried, convicted, and executed, for the crime of burning sea-coal in London.' It took, then, three centuries to efface this prejudice; but when once coal was adopted, the whole aspect of the fireside was changed. For the capacious hearth, was substituted the narrower, less social, though compact and tidy one now in use. Chimney-pieces were introduced at first elaborately carved in wood, and afterwards of marble. The fire—held in a grate or stove—was smaller and more concentrated to one part of the room. Despite the hosts of inventions which have for more than a century been in use to improve the grate, it still remains in principle and general utility the same as it did from the first day coal was generally burned. And despite the patents of Polignac, Bernhard, Evelyn, Rumford, for open grates, and those of Arnott and others for closed ones, our family circles still draw around a fireplace differing in no very essential particular from that which warmed our grandfathers and grandmothers. So little good have all modern contrivances really effected, that we of the present hour suffer the same inconveniences as the occupants of the Welsh fireside in the dark ages: when we remain near the fire, the part of our bodies nearest to it is liable to be roasted, whilst our back feels freezing, so that we are obliged, when 'one side has lost its genial heat, to turn about and give the chilly side to the fire.' No invention has as yet enabled us to preserve a uniform and genial artificial climate in every part of our dwellings—an art in which even the Romans excelled us. Yet this is the age of ingenuity and luxury.

SOPHIA OF WOLFENBUTTEL.*

Carolina Christina Sophia of Wolfenbuttel, sister of the wife of the emperor Charles VI., was united in marriage to the Prince Alexis, son and presumptive heir of Peter the Great, czar of Muscovy. In her were mingled the fairest gifts of nature and education: lovely, graceful, with a penetrating and cultivated mind, and a soul tempered and governed by virtue; yet with all these rare gifts, which softened and won every other heart, she was nevertheless an object of aversion to Alexis, the most brutal of mankind. More than once the unfortunate wife was indebted for her life to the use of antidotes to counteract the insidious poisons administered to her by her husband. At length the barbarity of the prince arrived at its climax: by an inhuman blow, he reduced her to so wretched a state, that she was left for dead. He himself fully believed that which he so ardently desired, and tranquilly departed for one of his villas, calmly ordering the funeral rites to be duly celebrated.

But the days of the unfortunate princess were not yet terminated. Under the devoted care of the countess of Konigsmark, her lady of honour, who had been present at the horrible event, she slowly regained health and strength, while her fictitious obsequies were magnificently performed and honoured throughout Muscovy, and nearly all the European courts assumed mourning for the departed princess. This wise and noble countess of Konigsmark, renowned as the mother of the brave marshal of Saxony, perceived that, by not seconding the fortunate deceit of the Prince Alexis, and the nation in general, and by proclaiming her recovery, the unhappy Princess Carolina, already the sport of such cruel fate, would expose herself to perish sooner or later by a more certain blow. She therefore persuaded her wretched mistress, who had scarcely strength to undertake the journey, to seek refuge in Paris, under the escort of an old man, a German domestic. Having collected as much money and jewellery as she was able, the princess set out, with her faithful servant, who remained with her in the character of father, which he sustained during his life; and truly he possessed the feelings and tenderness, as well as the semblance, of a parent.

The tumult and noise of Paris, however, rendered it a place of sojourn ill adapted to the mind of Carolina, and to her desire of concealment. Her small establishment having been increased by a single maid-servant, she accordingly embarked for Louisiana, where the French, who were then in possession of this lovely portion of South America, had formed extensive colonies. Scarcely was the young and beautiful stranger arrived at New Orleans, than she attracted the attention of every one. There was in that place a young man, named Moldask, who held an office in the colony; he had travelled much in Russia, and believed that he recognised the fair stranger; but he knew not how to persuade himself that the daughter-in-law of the Czar Peter could in reality be reduced to so lowly a condition, and he dared not betray to any one his suspicions of her identity. He offered his friendship and assistance to her supposed father; and soon his attentive and pleasing manners rendered him so acceptable to both, that a mutual intimacy induced them to join their fortunes, and establish themselves in the same habitation.

It was not long before the news of the death of Alexis reached them through the public journals. Then Moldask could no longer conceal his doubts of the true condition of Carolina, and finding that he was not deceived, he offered with respectful generosity to abandon his pursuits, and to sacrifice his private fortune, that he might reconduct her to Moscow. But the princess, whose bitterest moments had been there passed, preferred, after her adventurous flight, to live far from the dazzling splendour of the court in tranquillity and honourable obscurity. She thanked the noble-hearted Moldask; but implored him, instead of such splendid offers, to preserve her secret inviolable, so that nothing might trouble her present felicity. He promised, and he kept his promise: his heart ardently desired her happiness, in which his own felicity was involved. Living under the same roof, in daily communion, their equal age and ardent feelings kindled in the young man's soul a livelier flame than mere friendship; but respect controlled it, and he concealed his love in his own bosom.

At length the old domestic, who, in the character of father, had shielded the princess, died, and was followed to the tomb by the sincere grief of his grateful mistress—a just recompense for such fidelity. Propriety forbade that Moldask and Carolina should inhabit together the same dwelling after this event. He loved her truly, but loved her good fame more, and explained to her, not without grief, that it was necessary he should seek another abode, unless she, who had already renounced all thought of pride and rank, were content to assume a name dearer and more sacred still than that of friend. He gave her no reason to doubt that vanity, instead of love, was the origin of this pro-

* This extraordinary, but, we believe, true story, is translated from the *Novelle Morali* of Francesco Soave.

posal, since the princess herself was firm in her desire to remain happy in private life. With all delicacy he sought to assure her that he could not but remember, in case of a refusal, that it was scarcely undeserved. Nor could he ever forget how much was exacted from him, by the almost regal birth of her to whose hand he thus dared aspire.

Love, and her desolate and defenceless condition, induced the princess willingly to consent; and, in constituting his felicity, she increased her own. Heaven blessed so happy a union; and in due time an infant bound still closer the marriage tie. Thus the Princess Carolina, born of noble blood, destined to enjoy grandeur, homage, even a throne, having abandoned the magnificence of her former state, in private life fulfilled all the duties of nature and of society.

Years passed happily on, until Moldask was attacked with disease, which required the aid of a skilful surgeon. Carolina was unwilling to confide a life so precious and beloved to the care of surgeons of doubtful skill, and therefore resolved to visit Paris. She persuaded her husband to sell all their possessions, and to embark. The winds were propitious to this pilgrimage; and the medical skill of Paris restored Moldask to health. Being now perfectly cured, the husband sought to obtain employment on the island of Bourbon; and was successful.

Meanwhile, the wife was one day walking with her graceful little girl in a public garden, as was her wont. She sat down on a green bank, and conversed with her child in German, when the marshal of Saxony passing by, was struck with the German accent, and stayed to observe them. She recognised him immediately, and, fearing the same from him, bent her eyes to the ground. Her blushes and confusion convinced the marshal that he was not mistaken; and he cried out, 'How, madame? What do I see? Is it possible?' Carolina suffered him not to proceed, but drawing him aside, she declared herself, praying him to keep sacred the needful secret, and to return with her to her dwelling, where she might with greater care and security explain her situation. The marshal was faithful to his promise; visited the princess many times, though with all due precaution, and heard and admired her history. He wished to inform the king of France, that this august lady might be restored to her rightful honours and rank, and that he himself might thus complete the good work begun by his mother the countess of Konigsmark. But Carolina wished neither to consent, nor openly to oppose his generous design. She asked him to defer his project, until certain plans now pending were accomplished, the termination of which could not be long delayed. Thus she, too happy in being united to a wise and virtuous consort, and contented to live in happy obscurity, kept the marquis at bay.

Near the end of the specified time he again visited her, and learned that, two days previous, she had departed with her husband for the isle of Bourbon. He quickly informed the king of all, who gave orders, through the governor of the island, that Moldask and his wife should be treated with the greatest consideration. Afterward he treated with the Empress Maria Theresa in what way her august aunt should be restored to the splendour due to her rank. The haughty wife, and mother of the czar, knew how to please the most Christian king, and not less generously sent letters to Carolina, in which she invited her to Vienna, promising to overwhelm her with distinctions. But Carolina, foreseeing that a return to her pristine rank at this regal court would debar her from fulfilling the sweet duties of wife and mother, in which all her felicity consisted, refused this offer courageously, but without haughtiness. 'I am so used,' she said to the officer who proposed to reconduct her to the court—'I am so used to this domestic and private life, that I will never change it. Neither to be near a throne, nor to receive the greatest homage, nor to enjoy riches, nor even to possess the universe, would give me the shadow of the pleasure and delight I feel at this moment.' So saying, she tenderly embraced the one and the other of her dear family.

She lived long with her husband and daughter, serene and contented, dividing her cares and occupations between assisting and amusing the one, and educating the mind and heart of the other. Death snatched from her, within a short interval, these two beloved ones, who had filled her heart with such sweet emotions; and for a long time that heart was a prey to one only sentiment of the deepest grief. Yet not even this sorrow affected her so much, but that she believed the unhappiness of grandeur to be still greater. She constantly refused the repeated invitations to Vienna; and, accepting only a small pension from the liberality of the empress, she retired to Vitry, near Paris, where she wished still to pass under the name of Madame Moldask; but it was impossible longer to conceal her high birth and illustrious ancestry. Notwithstanding this, she never abandoned her accustomed simplicity and retirement of life, in which alone she had begun to find, and found to the last, true felicity.

THE ADVENTURES OF A HOUSE.

A HOUSE being usually a fixed object, it may be difficult at first to understand how it should be capable of adventures. Some, indeed, have *wings*, and might therefore be supposed to have volatile propensities. We talk also of the *foot* of the stairs. But these are mere phrases, you will say. I grant that a house may be *stable* to all intents and purposes except one, and yet somehow it does not seem to me impossible that it may have its adventures. Cutting short discussion, let me endeavour to bring you to my views by an instance.

The subject of this memoir is a small villa, of which I have a full view from my study window. It is situated in the parish of Podgington, at a convenient distance from London, and belongs to Mr George Burroughs, the eminent wholesale druggist of Camomile Street. It is built at the foot of the hill upon which my own house stands, and was, I must confess, always an eyesore to me; though its owner ever regarded it, I have reason to believe, as one of the most tasteful and elegant structures within twenty miles of the metropolis. When I have described it as it appeared before its adventures began, the reader shall judge whether I am justified in my dislike for the house, or whether Mr Burroughs is to be commended for his taste. It was a square building of faced brick, with a sloping roof of slate. Though it had been built for more than seven years, its glaring newness of outer coating made it a most offensive object in the landscape. The bricks were stuccoed over to imitate stone; and the proprietor had it punctually 'pointed' (as masons call it) every spring, lest it should seem to beholders spoiled and dirty. The style of architecture was of that miscellaneous nature which the learned call composite. When the end of the house happened first to meet your view, you would have pronounced it Gothic, from the pointed arch over the solitary window, and the three tufted towers which started stiffly up from the top and two ends of the roof. The chimneys were florid Tudor of party-coloured bricks. Before the principal entrance was an uncommonly white flight of steps, adorned on each side with a couple of Grecian figures in plaster of Paris. The great dining-room window was an Elizabethan bow.

The lawn was of the finest turf, and kept in such trim order, that I noticed in fine weather the housemaid swept it every morning, as if it were a carpet. The garden walls were of fine red brick, interlined with streaks of mortar dazzlingly white, and against them fruit trees were nailed with the most formal neatness. It was evident that the character of the owner was that of a rich, rigid, discipline-enforcing, ease-loving citizen, with a taste for architecture and landscape-gardening by no means refined.

It was, I think, as near as possible this time two

years that the first inkling of adventure took place. I was looking abstractedly at the landscape, being in the agonies of a very difficult sentence which I could not arrange to my satisfaction, when a couple of men made their appearance, and descended the hill towards the house, which, I ought to say was named, in compliment to the street in which Mr Burroughs had made his fortune, 'Camomile Villa.' One of the men was dressed in a velveteen shooting-jacket, and carried a small brass telescope, while his attendant's burthen showed me at once that he was a surveyor. The latter bore in his hand two or three staves, with small flags at the end; and on his shoulder, that instrument of torture to conservative country gentlemen, called a theodolite. I augured from this that the doubts, and hopes, and fears which had agitated the parish for the last six months were to be set at rest, and that the eastern branch of the southern railroad was really to pass through Podgington. The surveyor was not long in commencing operations. He planted his flag directly opposite one corner of the Camomile Villa garden, and, after a few telescopic movements, went up to the house and knocked at the door, with a view, as I supposed, of asking permission to enter the grounds. Presently out came Burroughs without his hat, evidently in a terrible passion; now striding about, now pointing to his garden-wall, then at the flag in the field, and finally concluding by retreating back into the villa, and shutting the door in the intruder's face. However, the man had a duty to perform, and did it. He coolly went into the garden by a side gate, and having called to his man, they knocked out a few bricks so as to make a couple of peep holes through each opposite wall. Having taken the necessary levels, they proceeded to an adjoining meadow, and were soon out of sight. This was the first adventure.

The second took place about a fortnight afterwards. On getting up one morning, I found a host of excavators digging the ground within fifty yards of Camomile Villa, and carting the earth against its garden-wall. Again Mr Burroughs appeared without his hat, and began gesticulating to, and stamping at the workmen, who went on shovelling away without taking the smallest notice of his complaints. In explanation of these violent gestures, I learned from a neighbour that Burroughs and the railway company were at open war: but it was manifest from what was going on, that the latter were getting much the best of the contest. It had been decided that Camomile Villa was to be razed, in terms of the act of parliament in the case of that railway specially made and provided. Mr Burroughs, on the other hand, had determined that his house should *not* be pulled down, and thereupon the parties joined issue. Burroughs declared that he would remain in his 'willa' while one brick stood upon another, and indignantly refused compensation for its destruction. But it was evident to me, a casual disinterested looker-on, that poor Burroughs would be turned out of house and hold in the end. In fact, the next morning the work of demolition began. The sharpest, acutest, and best 'pointed' corner of his garden-wall was actually pulled down in spite of threats and remonstrances; and an entire tulip-bed was destroyed by the first layers of a huge embankment which was to fill up the hollow in which the house stood. 'Surely,' I said to my wife, 'the man will not be mad enough to continue to live in the house after so significant a notice to quit?'

But he did; although every day a huge piece was nibbled away from the garden walls, and fresh heaps of earth piled upon the flower-beds, till some of the crumbs of the miniature mountain must have actually intruded themselves into the kitchen window. The rooms on the ground floor were evidently darkened by the mass; for, on passing the villa one day, I saw Mr Burroughs dining by candle-light during a hot sunshine. Still there he was; although the house which contained him could stand another week only by a miracle, for the line of the embankment would—when completed—actually cut off one end of the building.

That week passed away; the works went on; a new and most disastrous adventure had befallen the devoted house; yet it was still its owner's castle, for in it he continued to reside. One morning, Mr Burroughs was awakened by a thundering noise at the fore door, as if it were being fired at by a company of fusileers. Presently there was a grand crash, and the noise intruded itself into the hall. The obstinate inhabitant got up, and found his passage filled with earth, brick-bats, and rubbish. The truth was, the embankment had been, during the morning's work, widened so as to cover the nice clean door-steps; and, by pressure against the door, had burst it open, and forced its way into Camomile Villa; though not, as I have said, without first knocking very loudly, as each truck of earth was unloaded against it. 'Never mind!' exclaimed the stoic to the contractor, whom he hailed out of a first-floor window; 'the back door is still open to me!'

This contractor was evidently a very good sort of man, and a humorist; for I asked him one day why he did not pull down the house at once without further ceremony. 'Pull it down!' he repeated laughing; 'why, I would not do such a thing for the world, till needs must. It is not much in the way as yet, and I love to see the old fellow hold out as he does. Why, all his servants have left, except an old crone, who cannot get another place, and she lives in nightly terror of being swallowed up in an earthquake. However,' he continued, looking towards the Gothic window, 'I *must* take a shaving off this corner of the house to-morrow, for the embankment is to be completed in a fortnight.'

Sure enough, a day or two afterwards, the threatened 'shaving' *was* taken off. It consisted of a great portion of the Gothic end, with a small strip of the front wall. This adventure was decidedly the most serious which had befallen the house, and its effects were strangely grotesque. One bedroom, with its furniture properly arranged for a comfortable night's rest, was, by the removal of the walls, completely exposed to the public gaze, and to the sport of the elements. I could plainly discern with the naked eye, from my study window, the washing-stand and ewer flanked by a couple of clean towels on an airing horse. The glazed earthenware glistened in the sun, and the bed curtains sported about in the wind. What had become of the toilet table, on which Burroughs's shaving and dressing tackle was wont, I had been told, to be ostentatiously arranged, the rough 'navigators' who pulled down the wall against which it stood could only tell. It is certain that one of these burly operatives was seen some days after scraping his shovel with an ivory-handled boot-hook, while another was caught in the act of greasing his wheelbarrow out of a pot of *pommade divine.* What the delvers had spared in the devoted bedroom, the wind destroyed. I was witness myself to its causing the bed-curtain sweep the adjacent mantel shelf of its profusion of ornaments, the whole of which fell with a crash upon the floor. About the middle of the day it rained; new disasters were the consequence. The carpet changed colour, the mahogany drawers lost their polish, and the mirror was speckled all over like a frosted scene in a fairy drama. The bed was soon so completely soaked, that it became admirably adapted for an invalid experimenting in the cold water cure.

The general aspect of the room, seen as it was from such an unusual point of view, was curious. Never before had the privacies of the domestic hearth been revealed by means of such a section. I tried to compare it with the descriptions in 'The Devil on Two Sticks;' but the comparison failed; for Asmodeus showed Don Cleophas what was going on within doors by lifting off the roofs. *He* exhibited a bird's-eye view of private life; mine was a view from its side-scenes.

But did the residence of the sturdy citizen survive this heavy blow? It did; and he continued to hold his own at the other end of the house, to all appearance 'a prosperous gentleman;' which indeed he was, in more senses than one. The proverb says, 'When things come to the worst they will mend;' and so it happened to him and his house. This destruction of one of its sides was the crisis, for a gleam of prosperity now began to dawn.

A few days after the exposure of the bedroom to the vulgar gaze of the parishioners of Podgington, the works of the railway were stopped. There was something wrong at head-quarters; either the engineer was at fault, or the treasurer had gone away to see how the railways got on in America, or Mr Burroughs had succeeded in his litigations; for I forgot to mention that he had brought some eighteen or twenty actions respectively against the directors, surveyors, engineers, contractors, and excavators of the company, on various pleas, and for the recovery of divers amounts of damages. These actions were either for assault and battery—a shovelful of dirt having been somehow thrown over him on one occasion, while he was haranguing the labourers from his door-step—or for trespass and defamation of character, one of the clerks of works having given out that he was mad. At all events, from whatever cause, the works were suddenly put to a stand-still, and remained exactly in the same state as they were left when the men went away on the night of the cessation. The hall of Camomile Villa was still choked up with dirt; the bed-curtains still wantoned amidst the furniture: the end of the carpet, which hung over the hole in the floor, where it had joined the departed wall, still flapped about in the breeze.

I was looking out of my window about this time, when I saw—'could it be a dream?'—an extensive company of bricklayers busily employed in rebuilding the ruined gable of the house, and once more enclosing the exposed dormitory. To be quite certain that this was no optical illusion, I went out to inspect this extraordinary proceeding. I was not mistaken. The new wall had already half hidden from view the housekeeper's room on the ground-floor. On extending my survey to the front of the house, I was forcibly reminded of the celebrated Mrs Partington, who endeavoured to oppose the progress of the encroaching Atlantic from her parlour with a mop; for some men were engaged in *excavating* the choked-up hall, and penetrating into the base of the embankment to dig out the steps; though as fast as one step was brought to light, its next neighbour got re-engulfed. I could not understand the meaning of all this; but at length learnt that Mr Burroughs had met with a temporary success in his lawsuit against the directors, and was rebuilding on the strength of it. He was only waiting, I understood, to receive the amount of the swinging damages he expected to recover, to undo all which had been done, and to restore Camomile Villa to its original amenity.

Thus, then, despite the imminent dangers to which the house had been subjected, it still remained firm on its foundations; and although hardly in such good condition as at first, was in a fair way of recovery. The repairs were completed in a short time, and, in spite of the embankment before the front windows, his family and servants returned, and Burroughs was left in quiet and triumphant possession of his much-loved 'willa.'

The winter came on: and although the druggist had hitherto invariably left his country residence to spend his time in his town-house at that season, yet on the present occasion he altered his plans. To have, as he said, 'beaten the railway company,' was a glorious achievement, and he was determined to live and die in his beloved cottage ornée, in commemoration of the fact. It must be owned, however, that it was a poor monument of his perseverance. Its recovery from the loss of its side left it in a very unsightly condition. The quite new and very white gable contrasted unpleasantly with the huge ugly long brown mound of earth, the removal of which was found a much more difficult process than its deposition. Then the other walls were spattered with clay; and the most industrious housemaid and the whitest Bath-stone were unequal to keeping the door-steps in that snow-like purity which they used to exhibit; for the rain constantly brought down a detritus of dirty rubbish to dim their lustre. Still, in spite of all, the house had come out of its troubles with surprising stamina, and promised to last quite as long as its owner.

Months went by: the winter set in severely, and nothing happened to the house; in which a merry Christmas was spent by the Burroughses. But, alas! such is the uncertainty of railway speculations, and of the law, that whoever or whatever is so much under their influence as Camomile Villa happened to be, cannot rest long undisturbed. The shareholders had settled their squabbles, and the lord chief justice of the common pleas had, with the full concurrence of twelve jurymen, finally decided against Mr Burroughs's claim for damages. As I laid down the newspaper containing this news, I exclaimed to my wife 'Surely Camomile Villa cannot last much longer now.'

A few days more, and my conjecture seemed in full course of fulfilment. The works of the line were resumed with more vigour than ever; all that part of the embankment which Burroughs had been months in removing, was replaced in one morning, and his family and servants were once more obliged to make use of the back door in their escape to London. But the head of the establishment, despite the heavy discouragements he had received, was still inflexibly determined to remain master of his own house, and to keep possession, in spite of law, railway contractors, and blocked-up doors and windows. Like a second Rienzi, he would cling with a despairing firmness even to the ruins of his capitol.

The workpeople soon gave him an opportunity of indulging in this piece of Romanesque heroism; for the next adventure which befell the house was the removal of its roof, an operation which was adroitly performed on one of the frostiest mornings of the season. How long after this the druggist held out I never heard; but this I know, that a week later, a couple of wagons passed our road laden with the villa furniture. I could not help being affected by the sight, as the carts wound slowly up the hill. It looked like a funeral procession, headed by Burroughs in his buggy, who seemed to act as chief mourner; then came the old housekeeper in cloak and hood, walking silently and sorrowfully, and looking for all the world like a mute. The furniture came next. Peace to Borroughs's mahogany! I trust it has found a less mutable asylum than that which it left.

Of course it was ridiculous giving myself any more thought about the house, for its doom was evidently sealed. The repaired Gothic side soon disappeared, and it was not likely that, by the end of a week, one brick would be left standing on another. Consequently, I seldom removed myself from my study fire to look out of my window in that direction. When, therefore, I once more turned my eyes that way, I expected to find that Camomile Villa's last adventure had been consummated, and that it was swept from the face of the parish; but conceive my astonishment when I beheld, instead, a company of slaters replacing the roof! The tenacity of existence which this house showed was really marvellous. No effort of destruction seemed capable of turning it into a ruin. Its roof, like the heads of Hydra, was no sooner taken off than it reappeared. Well had it been named 'Camomile' Villa; for, like that obstinate flower, the more despitefully it was used, the more it prospered.

In course of time the railway was finished; yet, though hardly credible, it is nevertheless true that, despite all its adventures, a part of the house still stands where it did! The roof replaced, and the ugly Gothic side removed, it was turned into the Podgington station; the drawing-room—now level with the rails—being a ticket-office. I have only one other adventure to record. Last Thursday night a locomotive ran away with a luggage train, and got off the line just in time to take a second 'shaving' off the front entrance. At this moment workmen are busily repairing the damage; which was not so great as might have been expected.

Thus end for the present the adventures of the house—for of course you will acknowledge that the phrase is applicable. The career of Camomile Villa may not even yet be closed. But let us hope that, having taken its stand as a decent railway station, it may rest in peace for some years to come.

BIOGRAPHIC SKETCHES.

DR EDWARD JENNER.

This celebrated man, the discoverer of the art of vaccination, was born in the vicarage of Berkeley, in Gloucestershire, on the 17th of May 1749. He was the third son of the vicar, and his mother was descended from an ancient and respectable family in the neighbourhood. Losing his father at an early age, he was indebted for his education to the care and solicitude of an elder brother. Young Jenner chose the profession of medicine, and after acquiring the elements of the art at Sodbury, near Bristol, he went to London, and became a pupil and inmate of the celebrated John Hunter. From this enthusiastic and successful cultivator of the science of life Jenner caught the true art of philosophic investigation. They instantly became friends, and this friendship continued during life. Having finished his preliminary studies, he now returned to his native village to practise his profession. Other offers were then and subsequently held out to him, but his love of the country made him proof against them all. He was indeed a true lover of nature. With an inquiring and ever active mind, which prompted him to the investigation of nature's works, he had also that deep feeling of the beautiful and fair which accompanies a poetic temperament. His professional journeys through the district were lightened and diversified by scientific pursuits, and many of his leisure hours devoted to discoveries in natural history. His remarks on the singular and anomalous habits of the cuckoo excited the attention of the members of the Royal Society, and found a place in their printed transactions.

But one subject took possession of his mind, and engrossed his chief attention even from his earliest youth. In the great dairy county of Gloucestershire, where his inclination, and, it may be said, his destiny had placed him for a great purpose, it was a prevalent opinion that a disease was communicated from the teats of the cows to the hands of their milkers, by which the latter were ever afterwards protected from small-pox. While Jenner was a student at Sodbury, a young country woman came to seek advice. The subject of small-pox was mentioned in her presence: she immediately observed, 'I cannot take that disease, for I have had cow-pox.' This incident rivetted the attention of Jenner, and the impression then made took full possession of his mind, and was never effaced. He communicated his views some time afterwards to John Hunter, who, although he had not turned his mind to the subject, was far from stifling any inquiry of the kind, and who, in his characteristic way, replied to the young philosopher, 'Don't think, but try; be patient, be accurate.' From his professional friends in the country, however, his theory met with nothing but discouragement: they, too, as well as Jenner, had heard the vulgar reports of the country people; but the circumstance was so out of the common routine, that they gave it no credit, and never thought of putting it to the test of experiment. In vain did Jenner urge on the discussion of the subject at their professional meetings—they refused to listen, and even laughed him to scorn. But Jenner, though he was thus compelled to fall back upon his own solitary thoughts, was not the character thus to be persuaded from his pursuit; like every man destined to achieve great things, he was firm of purpose. For twenty years he brooded over the subject, collected facts, and made experiments; till at last, being fully convinced in his own mind that he had compassed the whole bearings of the subject, he came to the resolution of presenting the great discovery as a gift to mankind. The conclusions to which he arrived were as follows:—

The disease called *variola*, or small-pox, is common to man, and to several of our domestic animals, as the cow, horse, goat, &c.; but while in man it presents a severe and virulent disease, in passing through the system of brutes it becomes a mild and innocent affection.

The heels of horses are often affected with this disease, which, though frequently accompanied by what is called grease, is not identical with this latter. If a portion of the matter from the *vesicles* or little blisters on the heel of the horse be taken and applied to the nipples of the cow, the peculiar disease is communicated to the cow; or, on the other hand, the horse may be infected from the cow. Matter taken from the vesicle of the horse or the cow, and inserted below the skin of the human subject, produces there a similar vesicle of a peculiar nature, which, running its course, protects the individual from an attack of the small-pox.

In order to insure complete success in this operation, certain cautions are necessary. The lymph must be taken before the expiry of a certain number of days, and the person to be vaccinated must be free from any other disease of the skin. Unless these conditions are attended to, a true vaccine disease will not be produced, and consequently no protection will follow.

In the true small-pox, it is a well-ascertained fact, that occasionally there are cases where persons who have gone through the disease regularly have again been seized with a second attack.

The same thing holds true with cow-pox. Although the great majority of those vaccinated are for ever afterwards protected from the disease, yet cases occur where, after vaccination, an attack of small-pox has followed.

Vaccination, then, though not an absolute and universal protection, is as much so as small-pox is from a second attack of the same; with this important recommendation, that it substitutes a mild and harmless affection, or rather, it may be called, a remedy, for a violent and dangerous disease.

Even in those rare cases where small-pox occurs after the most careful vaccination, the disease is always mitigated, and very rarely proves fatal.

Such are briefly the conclusions to which Jenner had arrived at this early period of his investigations; and as a proof of his superior sagacity and accuracy of observation, it may be stated that little more has ever been added to his great discovery, and that subsequent experience has only illustrated the truth of his opinions and the efficacy of his practice.

The first 'Inquiry into the Nature of Cow-Pox,' published by Jenner, was a calm, philosophical, and extremely modest statement of his discoveries; and perhaps on this account it was received with the greater favour by the reflecting portion of the public. Some writers have hinted that he too sanguinely maintained the efficacy of cow-pox, and its future power of totally extirpating small-pox. Some degree of enthusiasm might be pardoned in the original discoverer of such a remedy; but on candidly comparing Jenner's conclusion with the facts which have subsequently occurred, there seems nothing overstrained, and little that can be deducted from his statements.

In the spring of 1780, while riding in company with one of his earliest and dearest friends, his mind being full of the subject, he ventured to unbosom himself of his cherished hopes and anticipations; and after a detail of his opinions—'Gardner,' said he, 'I have intrusted a most important matter to you, which I firmly believe will prove of essential benefit to the human race. I know you, and should not wish what I have stated to be brought into conversation; for should anything untoward turn up in my experiments, I should be made, particularly by my medical brethren, the subject of ridicule, for I am the mark they all shoot at.'

It was not, however, till 1796, on the 14th day of May, that the first attempt was made to convey, by artificial means, the vaccine virus from one person to another. On that day Jenner took some matter from the hand of Sarah Nelones, who had been infected by her master's cows, and inserted it by two slight scratches of a lancet into the arms of James Phipps, a healthy boy of eight years of age. The disease took effect, and went through its stages in the most regular and satisfactory manner. But now the most agitating part of the experiment remained: it was necessary to ascertain whether this boy was secured from the infection of small-pox. In the following July, variolous matter was carefully inserted into his skin by various incisions, and to the delight and satisfaction of Jenner no disease followed—the protection was complete. He now pursued his experiments with redoubled ardour: the goal of all his ardent hopes was seen close at hand. It was his custom at this time to meditate much as he rambled in the meadows under the castle of Berkeley. He has left us a picture of his feelings at this period full of interest:—'While the vaccine discovery was progressive, the joy I felt at the prospect before me of being the instrument destined to take away from the world one of its greatest calamities, blended with the fond hope of enjoying independence and domestic peace and happiness, was often so excessive, that, in pursuing my favourite subject among the meadows, I have sometimes found myself in a kind of reverie. It is pleasant to me to recollect that these reflections always ended in devout acknowledgments to that Being from whom this and all other mercies flow.'*

It was in 1798 that Jenner's discovery was first published. His intention was, that it should have appeared in the Transactions of the Royal Society; but the subject was so strange, so novel, and, withal, so improbable, that some of the learned members hinted in a friendly manner that he should be cautious not to diminish, by any other doubtful discovery, the partial fame which his account of the cuckoo had already gained him. Such facts as these impart some idea of the difficulties his discovery was doomed to encounter. On the publication of his 'Inquiry,' he proceeded to London in person, in order to exhibit to the profession there his process of vaccination, and the success attending it. But—will it be believed?—he remained two months there, and at last returned home without getting any medical man to make trial of it, or any patient to submit voluntarily to the simple and harmless process. That process, which in a few years afterwards millions of individuals eagerly availed themselves of, could not be exhibited, even for a bribe, in a single being. It was only after his return home that Mr Cline, the surgeon, almost clandestinely inserted the matter into a patient, by way of an issue for a diseased joint! Yet it is a wise provision of affairs in this world, that truth will at last and infallibly prevail. The subject of vaccination began to engross public attention; and although many were incredulous, and scoffed at the matter, as is ever the case with what is new and uncommon, yet many, on the other hand, had faith to make trial of it; and finding success attend their experiments, the practice of vaccination extended on all hands. But there never was a discoverer yet who has not in a greater or less degree suffered martyrdom—the ignorant, the envious, the narrow-minded, the purely malicious, for ever hang on the footsteps of the discoverer, irritating and obstructing his progress, and raising a clamour in which they hope the sober and subdued voice of truth will be drowned. Poor Jenner passed many harassing days and sleepless nights, less fearful about the wreck of his own honest fame, than for the success of his great and darling project. He had to answer every blunderer, who, in spite of the plainest directions, was sure always to go wrong in the most essential points—every failure of every careless experimenter was laid to his door—he was caricatured as a magician, who by and by would turn the human race into cows; and, baser than all, some of those who at one time scoffed at his theories, and despised his attempts to put them into practice, now endeavoured to avert the discovery from Jenner entirely, if not to appropriate it to themselves. Yet time and circumstances, and his own tact and perseverance, seconded by his unyielding confidence in his opinions, brought him many friends and supporters. 'The drop of pearl upon a rose-bud,' as he poetically described the vaccine vesicle to the great statesman Fox, was such a simple, and easy, and beautiful substitute for the loathsome and dreaded blotches of small-pox, that the public at large, and more particularly the female part of it, became the warm and active propagators of the limpid virus. From Britain the practice extended rapidly to the continent. In America, the early cases were most successful: and at last the remotest countries in the world began to share its benefits, till there was not a corner of the peopled globe where the name of Jenner did not become familiar, and where his life-preserving process was not eagerly adopted. Among the many honours and acknowledgments which now and afterwards continued to be poured in upon him, not the least interesting was a document from a race of the North American Indians, authenticated by the symbolical signatures of their chiefs.

The discovery of vaccination now evidently appeared as a manifest boon to mankind. In several countries on the continent of Europe, where the nature of the government allowed of a free control over the habits of the people, the practice of vaccination was so systematically pursued, that small-pox was almost entirely eradicated. In the British navy and army, under a similar surveillance, small-pox was also unknown; but though in the British dominions several vaccinating boards were instituted, yet from the habits of the people, and the absence of a compulsory law, vaccination was not there, and never yet has been, so complete and universal as to banish entirely the lurking malady of small-pox from our shores.

Considering, however, what devotion Jenner had bestowed on the subject, both theoretically and practically; considering the generous and disinterested manner in which, the moment that he became acquainted with its perfect efficacy, he hastened to lay his discovery before the world, his claim to a national compensation and reward could no longer be denied. In 1802 a committee of parliament was appointed to investigate his discovery, and decide on a remuneration. Of the many claimants on national bounty, few ever came forward with better pretensions than Jenner. Yet much caution was employed; and, in the first instance, a grant of only L.10,000 was voted, subject to the delays and deductions of fees with which such grants are too often encumbered. This, as Jenner and his friends affirmed, was barely equal to the expenses he incurred, considering his multifarious correspondence, as well as his relinquishment of private practice, and the actual toil of responding to the querists from every region of the globe. Yet it is not to be wondered at if parliament had a wary suspicion of the reports of cures of any kind; for who does not hear of wonderful cures accomplished every day, and well-authenticated also, and yet experience, or further inquiry, proves them all ultimately fallacious; nor could it be forgotten that half a century had not elapsed since the same parliament voted its thousands for a nostrum which was utterly worthless. Happily for the fame of the legislature, however, and for the honour of the country in all future times, in the present instance it judged aright: even its caution was commendable: and allowing an interval of five more years, a further grant of L.20,000 redeemed their sense of the progressive importance and continued efficacy of the vaccine discovery. In the meantime, Jenner had taken up his residence in London, with a view to the better furtherance of the interests of vaccination, and

* Baron.

with an idea of establishing himself in practice in the metropolis. But his was not a character fitted for the artificial bustle of the vast city, or the jarring conflicts of professional interests; his mind sickened amid the smoke, as one of his own meadow cowslips would have done, and he hastened back to his fields and his pure country air, and never left his beloved village again.

But he did not return to apathy or indolence. In London some finessing on the part of his professional brethren prevented him from acting as director of the national vaccine board, to which he had been in the first instance appointed; but now, in his own words, he retired to be 'Director-General to the World.' In addition to this, the country people from all the districts around flocked to him for the benefits of vaccination, and his time and skill were ever at the service of the poor. He now, too, enjoyed his favourite pursuits of the study of nature, and shared his leisure hours among his fossils, his birds, his flowers, and the society of his family and his friends. Of every man who has achieved great things, we have a desire to know something not only of his thoughts and habits, but of his personal appearance. An early sketch of Jenner is thus given by his friend Gardner.

'His height was rather under the middle size; his person was robust but active, and well formed. In his dress he was peculiarly neat, and everything about him showed the man intent and serious, and well prepared to meet the duties of his calling. When I first saw him, it was on Frampton Green. I was somewhat his junior in years, and had heard so much of Jenner of Berkeley, that I had no small curiosity to see him. He was dressed in a blue coat and yellow buttons, buckskins, well-polished jockey boots, with handsome silver spurs, and he carried a smart whip with a silver handle. His hair, after the fashion of the times, was done up in a club; and he wore a broad-brimmed hat. We were introduced on that occasion, and I was delighted and astonished. I was prepared to find an accomplished man, and all the country spoke of him as a skilful surgeon and a great naturalist; but I did not expect to find him so much at home in other matters. I, who had been spending my time in cultivating my judgment by abstract study, and smit from my childhood with the love of song, had sought my amusement in the rosy fields of imagination, was not less surprised than gratified to find that the ancient affinity between Apollo and Æsculapius was so well maintained in his person.' At a later period, his biographer, Dr Barron, then a young man, thus gives an account of a first interview with him. 'He was living at Fladong's hotel, Oxford Street, in the summer of 1808, making arrangements for the national vaccine establishment. The greatness of his fame, his exalted talents, and the honours heaped upon him by all the most distinguished public bodies of the civilised world, while they made me desirous of offering my tribute of respect to him, forbade the expectation of more than such an acknowledgment as a youth circumstanced as I was might have expected. I soon, however, perceived that I had to do with an individual who did not square his manners by the cold formality of the world. He condescended as to an equal. The restraint and embarrassment that might naturally have been felt in the presence of one so eminent, vanished in an instant. The simple dignity of his aspect, the kind and familiar tone of his language, and the perfect sincerity and good faith manifested in all he said and did, could not fail to win the heart of any one not insensible to such qualities. He was dressed in a blue coat, white waistcoat, and nankeens. All the tables in his apartment were covered with letters and papers on the subject of vaccination. He spoke with great good humour of the conduct of the anti-vaccinists, and gave me some pamphlets illustrative of the controversy then carrying on. The day before I saw him, he had had an interview with the Princess of Wales, and he showed me a watch which her royal highness had presented to him on that occasion.' The same friend, at a much later period of their acquaintance, again remarks—'Dr Jenner's personal appearance to a stranger at first sight was not very striking; but it was impossible to observe him, even for a few moments, without discovering those peculiarities which distinguished him from all others. The first things that a stranger would remark were the gentleness, the simplicity, the artlessness of his manner. There was a total absence of all ostentation or display, so much so, that in the ordinary intercourse of society he appeared as a person who had no claims to notice. He was perfectly unreserved, and free from all guile. He carried his heart and his mind so openly, so undisguisedly, that all might read them. His professional avocations, and the nature of his pursuits, obliged him to conduct his inquiries in a desultory way. At no period of his life could he give himself up to continued or protracted attention to one object: there was, nevertheless, a steadiness in working out his researches amid all the breaks and interruptions which he met with, that can only belong to minds constituted as his was.'

With all the simple and genial qualities of an unsophisticated heart, Jenner had, when the occasion required, all the firmness and dignity becoming a man conscious of the possession of talent. On one occasion, in the drawing-room of St James's, he chanced to overhear a noble lord mention his name, and repeat the idle calumny which had got abroad, that he himself had not really confidence in vaccination. He with much promptitude refuted the charge, and stepping up to the noble lord, to whom he was unknown, calmly observed, 'I am Dr Jenner.' Any unpleasant recollection of this circumstance was most likely, on the part of Jenner, soon dissipated; but not so with the noble statesman; his remarks some time afterwards, in his place in parliament, when Jenner's claims came to be discussed, showed that he had not forgotten it.

When the continental sovereigns visited London in 1814, Jenner was presented to the Emperor Alexander of Russia by his sister, the grand duchess of Oldenburg. In describing this interview, he says, 'I was very graciously received, and was probably the first man who had ever dared to contradict the autocrat. He said, "Dr Jenner, your feelings must be delightful. The consciousness of having so much benefited your race must be a never-failing source of pleasure, and I am happy to think that you have received the thanks, the applause, and the gratitude of the world." I replied to his majesty that my feelings were such as he described, and that I had received the thanks and the applause, but not the gratitude of the world. His face flushed; he said no more; but my daring seemed to give displeasure. In a short time, however, he forgot it, and gave me a trait of character which showed both great goodness of heart and knowledge of human nature. My inquiries respecting disease of the lungs had reached the ears of the grand duchess, the most interesting being that I had ever met with in a station so elevated. She was present, and requested me to tell to her brother, the emperor, what I had formerly said to her imperial highness. In the course of my remarks I became embarrassed. She observed this, and so did the emperor: "Dr Jenner," said she, "you do not tell my brother what you have to say so accurately as you told me." I excused myself by saying that I was not accustomed to speak in such a presence. His majesty grasped me by the hand, and held on for some time, not quitting me till my confidence was restored by this warm-hearted and kind expression of his consideration.'

As his life was an active and benevolent, so, on the whole, may it be termed a prosperous and a comparatively happy one. Latterly, he had domestic afflictions, which to a sensitive heart are the heaviest of sorrows. He lost his favourite son, his newly-married daughter, and at last his amiable wife, whose delicate constitution he had tended with all the assiduity which deep affection and respect could dictate. He reached a good old age, with his general health and mental powers unimpaired to the last. On the 26th January 1823, he died suddenly of apoplexy, in the 74th year of his age. He lies buried in the chancel of the church at Berkeley, where a monument has been erected to his memory by his professional brethren.

It is now almost half a century since the first introduction of vaccination, and at least forty years since its general adoption—a sufficient time, one would think, to test its efficacy, and yet there are several circumstances relating to it which have not yet been definitely determined. In the first place, it cannot be denied that on the whole it has been a successful remedy, and that it has produced a remarkable effect on the general population. Small-pox, if it has not been entirely eradicated, has been disarmed of most of its terrors; and notwithstanding the cases of failure of protection from its ravages which occasionally occur, yet the general confidence never has been withdrawn from the practice of vaccination.

Both before and since the death of Dr Jenner, it became known that cases sometimes occurred where persons who had been vaccinated were seized with small-pox. At first, it was supposed that those cases were instances where vaccination had not taken proper effect, either from an imperfect quality of the virus used in vaccination, or from a peculiar habit of the person vaccinated. But it was afterwards ascertained that persons in whom the process had been practised with the utmost care, and in whom the disease appeared to go through its course in the most favourable manner, were yet not protected from small-pox. It is true, in all these cases of seizure the affection was of a much milder kind than even the inoculated small-pox, and in a very small proportion indeed did death occur, perhaps not one case in several thousands; yet there could be no doubt but that the disease was in reality true small-pox, under a mild and modified form.

It became evident, then, that there were exceptions to the universal protection against small-pox, and that this disease might occur after vaccination, just as an individual might be seized with a second attack of small-pox. This was a fact known to Dr Jenner even before he gave his discovery to the world. In his early pursuit of the inquiry he was much staggered by it, but further experience enabled him to perceive that it was only an exception to a general rule; and all experience since, both in public vaccine institutions and in private practice, has only tended to confirm it.

Seeing, then, that such exceptions from time to time continued to occur, and as they multiplied in number by time and the general diffusion of vaccination, another question began to be agitated—whether the vaccine matter, by passing through innumerable human beings, had not lost its character and consequent efficacy; and whether it would not be necessary again to have recourse to the cow?

The most experienced vaccinators seem to give no countenance to this opinion. They affirm that the character of the vaccine vesicle is exactly the same, and its development, in all its stages, as regular and complete as it was when first discovered; and that, when compared with vesicles produced by matter directly from the cow, there is no difference; that even in the early stages of the employment of vaccination, failures, as already stated, began to appear; and that these failures are probably not more in proportion now than they were then.

A suggestion of another kind has been advanced—that probably the protection of the vaccine matter is only of a temporary nature, and that it becomes exhausted in the course of time, and thus leaves the constitution open to an attack of small-pox. If this had been the case, then in the course of the last forty-five years all those persons vaccinated should have by this time successively had attacks of small-pox when exposed to infection. This, however, has by no means happened; so that the fact cannot be true as a general rule, though, as we shall afterwards state, it may hold in some respects as regards individuals at different periods of life; and thus the propriety of a second vaccination about the age when the individual is entering on the period of manhood has been frequently suggested.

Taking all these exceptions into account, there can be no doubt but that the practice of vaccination, with its partial drawbacks, has been an inestimable boon to mankind. It has been ascertained that every fourteenth child born was cut off by small-pox; and that in most cases where adults were infected, a death occurred out of every seven. If to this we add the other fatal diseases called into action by this malady, the influence on the increase of population by the check it has received from vaccination must be held to be very considerable. We accordingly find that, previous to 1780, the annual mortality in England and Wales was rated at one in forty; whereas at the present time it is one in forty-six. No doubt other causes have combined to improve the general health, but that the preventive power of vaccination has been mainly instrumental, appears, even from the diminished deaths from small-pox, sufficiently evident. Indeed we have only to call to mind the scarred and pitted faces, marred features, and opaque and sightless eyeballs of former days, to be convinced of the essential service which has been rendered to the community.

'TALES OF THE COLONIES.'

Eighteen months ago, we noticed a work under the above title, of which it would be difficult to say whether it abounded more in the spirit-stirring scenes usually found in fiction, or in sound views respecting emigration to, and settlement in, perhaps the finest of the Australian colonies—Van Diemen's Land. As to a great extent the adventures of a settler—an English farmer—in that distant colony, who, after undergoing many mishaps, while the country was still in a crude condition, had lived to reap the reward of his perseverance, such a work could not fail to be very generally acceptable; and we are glad to know that it has been so much so as to pass already into a third edition. Desirous of rendering his work more extensively available, the author has judiciously issued it in a single volume;* and as a copy of this cheap edition has been placed under our notice, we take leave to bring it once more before our readers.

Having on the former occasion described the contents of the book at considerable length, it is now unnecessary to say more on that subject. Being desirous, however, of conveying an idea of the author's powers of narration, we may offer the following extract, which refers to a state of society in the colony, now, we believe, gone.

THE BUSHRANGER.

In crossing the country one day, and at a distance from any habitation, Mr Thornley, the settler, to his surprise and fear beheld at a short distance approaching him a noted bushranger, known by the name of 'the Gipsy,' who had latterly, with a band of associates, become the dread of the colony. He was a tall well-made man, one apparently above the ordinary character of convicts, and whom it was distressing to see in such a situation. The parties approached each other with mutual distrust. Thornley knew he had a desperate character to deal with, and pointed his gun at him: but the bushranger seemed desirous of a parley, and after a few words, says the writer, 'he laid his gun quietly on the grass, and then passed round me, and sat down at a few yards' distance, so that I was between him and his weapon. "Well, Mr Thornley," said he, "will that do? You see I am now unarmed. I don't ask you to do the same, because I cannot expect you to trust to me; but the truth is, I want to have a little talk with you. I have something on my mind which weighs heavy on

* London: Smith. Elder. and Co. 1845.

me, and whom to speak to I do not know. I know your character, and that you have never been hard on your government men, as some are. At any rate, speak to some one I must. Are you inclined to listen to me?"

'I was exceedingly moved at this unexpected appeal to me at such a time and in such a place. There was no sound, and no object save ourselves, to disturb the vast solitude of the wilderness. Below us flowed the Clyde, beneath an abrupt precipice; around were undulating hills, almost bare of trees; in the distance towered the snowy mountain which formed the boundary to the landscape. I looked at my companion doubtfully; for I had heard so many stories of the treachery of the bushrangers, that I feared for a moment that this acting might only be a trick to throw me off my guard. Besides, this was the very man whom I knew to have been at the head of the party of bushrangers who had been captured at the Great Lake.

'He observed the doubt and hesitation which were expressed in my looks, and pointed to his gun, which was on the other side of me.

"What more can I do," said he, "to convince you that I meditate neither violence nor treachery against you? Indeed, when you know my purpose, you will see that they would defeat my own object."

"What is your purpose, then? Tell me at once—are you one of the late party of bushrangers who have done such mischief in the island?"

"I am: and more than that, I am—or rather was—their leader. I planned the escape from Macquarie harbour; and it was I who kept them together, and made them understand their strength, and how to use it. But that's nothing now. I do not want to talk to you about that. But I tell you who and what I am, that you may see I have no disguise with you; because I have a great favour—a very great favour—to ask of you; and if I can obtain it from you on no other terms, I am almost inclined to say, take me to Camp as your prisoner, and let the capture of the Gipsy——ah! I see you know that name, and the terror it has given to the merciless wretches who pursue me——I say, let the capture of the Gipsy, and his death, if you will—for it must come to that at last—be the price of the favour that I have to beg of you!"

"Speak on, my man," I said; "you have done some ill deeds, but this is not the time to taunt you with them. What do you want of me? and if it is anything that an honest man can do, I promise you beforehand that I will do it."

"You will!—but you do not know it yet. Now listen to me. Perhaps you do not know that I have been in the colony for ten years. I was a lifer. It's bad that; better hang a man at once than punish him for life: there ought to be a prospect of an end to suffering; then the man can look forward to something; he would have hope left. But never mind that. I only speak of it because I believe it was the feeling of despair that first led me wrong, and drove me from bad to worse. Shortly after my landing I was assigned to a very good master. There were not many settlers then, and we did not know so much of the country as we do now. As I was handy in many things, and able to earn money, I soon got my liberty on the old condition; that is, of paying so much a-week to my master. That trick is not played now, but it was then, and by some of the big ones too. However, all I cared for was my liberty, and I was glad enough to get that for seven shillings a-week. But still I was a government prisoner, and that galled me; for I knew I was liable to lose my license at the caprice of my master, and to be called into government employ. Besides, I got acquainted with a young woman, and married her, and then I felt the bitterness of slavery worse than ever; for I was attached to her sincerely, and I could not contemplate the chance of parting from her without pain. So about three years after I had been in this way, I made an attempt to escape with her in a vessel that was sailing for England. It was a mad scheme, I know; but what will not a man risk for his liberty?"

"What led you to think of going back to England? What were you sent out for?"

"I have no reason to care for telling the truth. I was one of a gang of poachers in Herefordshire, and on a certain night we were surprised by the keepers, and somehow, I don't know how, we came to blows; and the long and the short of it is, one of the keepers was killed; and there's the truth of it."

"And you were tried for the murder?" "I and two others were; and one was hanged, and I and my mate were transported for life." "Well, the less that's said about that the better; now go on with your story; but let me know what it is you would have me do for you."

"I'll come to that presently; but I must tell you something about my story, or you will not understand me. I was discovered in the vessel, concealed among the casks, by the searching party, and brought on shore with my wife; and you know, I suppose, that the punishment is death. But Colonel Davey—he was governor then—let me off: but I was condemned to work in chains in government employ. This was a horrid life, and I determined not to stand it. There were one or two others in the chain-gang all ready for a start into the bush, if they had any one to plan for them. I was always a good one at head-work, and it was not long before I contrived one night to get rid of our fetters. There were three others besides myself. We got on the top of the wall very cleverly, and first one dropped down (it was as dark as pitch, and we could not see what became of him), then another dropped, and then the third. Not a word was spoken. I was the last, and glad enough was I when I felt myself sliding down the rope outside the yard. But I had to grin on the other side of my mouth when I came to the bottom. One of the sneaks whom I had trusted had betrayed us, and I found myself in the arms of two constables, who grasped me tightly. I gave one of them a sickener, and could have easily managed the other, but he gave the alarm, and then lots of others sprang up, and lights and soldiers appeared. I was overpowered by so many. They bound my arms, and then I was tried for the attempt to escape, and the assault on the constable, and condemned to Macquarie harbour for life.

"I have not told you that my wife brought me a child. It is now seven years old. I loved that child, Mr Thornley, more than a parent usually loves his child. It was all in all to me. It was the only bright thing that I had to look upon. When I was sentenced to Macquarie harbour for life, it would have been a mercy to put me to death. I should have put myself to death, if it had not been for the thought of that little girl. Well, sir, I will not say more about that. When a man takes to the bush, and has done what I have done, he is thought to be a monster without feeling or affection. But people don't understand us. There is no man, sir, depend upon it, so bad that he has not some good in him; and I have had some experience: for I have seen the worst of us—the very worst—in the most miserable of all conditions—for that Macquarie harbour is a real hell upon earth! There is no time to tell you about the hardships and the miseries which the prisoners suffer in that horrible place—it soon kills them. But my greatest misery was being deprived of my little girl—my plaything—my darling—my life! I had not been at Macquarie harbour a month, before news came that my wife was dead. I'll tell you the truth, sir: attached to her as I was, I was rather glad than sorry for it. I could not bear the thought of her falling into anybody else's hands; and as our separation was now absolutely and hopelessly for ever—it is the truth—I was rather glad than sorry when I heard of her death. But my poor little child! I thought of her night and day, wondering and thinking what would become of her! I could think of nothing else. At last my thoughts began to turn to the possibility of escaping from Macquarie harbour, desperate as the attempt appeared; for, to cross the bush without arms, and without provisions, exposed to the attacks of the natives, seemed all but an impossibility. But almost anything may be done by resolution and patience, and watching your opportunity."

[The escape having been effected,] "We scrambled away as well as we could, till we got a little distance off, and out of hearing, and then we set to with a will, and rid ourselves of our fetters, all except three, and these were too tightly fitted to be got off on a sudden without better tools. We got the three chained men along with us, however, as well as we could, for we would not leave them; so we helped them on by turns; and the next day, when we were more easy, we contrived to rid them of their incumbrances. We hastened on all night. I ought to tell you that we heard the bell rung and the alarm given; but we had gained an hour good, and the ungagging of the sentinels and the overseers, and hearing their story, took up some time no doubt. Besides, it is not easy to hit on a track in the dusk, and as there were fourteen of us, armed with two muskets, our pursuers would not proceed so briskly as they otherwise might, and would not scatter themselves to look after us. We were without provisions; but we did not care about that; and not being used to long walks, we were soon knocked up. But the desire of liberty kept us up, and we struck right across the country in as straight a line as we could guess. The second day we were all very sick and faint, and the night before was very cold, and we were cramped and unfit to travel. The second night we all crept into a cave, which was sandy inside, where we lay pretty warm, but we were ravenously hungry. We might have shot more than one kangaroo that day, but it was agreed that we should not fire, lest the report of our gun should betray our resting-place to our pursuers. As we lay huddled together, we heard the opossums squeeling in the trees about, and two of us, who were least tired, tried to get some of them. When we climbed up the trees, they sprang away like squirrels, and we had no chance with them that way; besides, it was dark, and we could distinguish them only faintly and obscurely. We did contrive, however, to kill five by pelting them on a long overhanging bough; but they remained suspended by their tails, and did not drop, although dead. To hungry men a dead opossum is something; so one of us contrived to climb to them and get them down; and then we lighted a fire in the cave, quite at the extremity inside, to prevent the flame from being seen, and roasted them as the natives do. They were horrid rank things to eat, and almost made us sick, hungry as we were; but I don't think a hair of them was left among us. The next day we shot a kangaroo; but we feared to light a fire because of the smoke, so we ate it raw.

"We first struck on the outskirts of New Norfolk, and we debated what we should do. Some were for attacking the settlement, and getting arms; but I persuaded them that it would be better for us to endeavour to seize some small vessel, and escape altogether from the colony; and in the meantime to keep ourselves close, and not give any alarm. My companions agreed to this, and we struck across the country to Brighton Plains, and so to Pitt Water, where we expected to find some large boats, or perhaps some small vessel, by means of which we might get away."

"And how was it that you did not follow that plan?"

"We did follow it: we got to Pitt Water, and lay snug there for a while: but we were obliged to rob a settler's house of provisions for food, and that first gave the alarm. We made a dash at a boat, but it was too late; precautions had been taken, and the soldiers were out after us. We were then obliged to retreat from Pitt Water, intending to get into the neighbourhood of the lakes, and go farther westward if necessary, and retreat to the coast, where we judged we should be too far off to be molested."

"You did a great deal of mischief at Pitt Water before you left it, if all the stories are true?"

"We did, Mr Thornley, I own it: but my men were determined to have arms, and the settlers of course resisted, and some of my men got wounded, and that made them savage."

"And afterwards you attacked poor Moss's cottage?"

"My men had been told that he had a large sum in dollars at his hut—I am surprised that settlers can be so foolish as to take valuables into the bush—that was all they wanted."

"But why did you take poor Moss along with you?"

"I was obliged to do it to save his life. Some of my men would have knocked him on the head if I had not prevented them. It's true, Mr Thornley, it is indeed—I saved his life."

"Well, that's something in your favour. And now, as the sun is sinking fast, and as the dusk will come on us presently, tell me at once what you would have me do for you."

"Mr Thornley," said the bushranger, "I have told you of my little girl. I have seen her since the dispersion of my party at the Great Lake. You know that I and another escaped. Since then I have ventured in disguise into Hobart Town itself, and have there seen my child. The sight of her, and her embraces, have produced in me a strange feeling. I would willingly sacrifice my life to do her good; and I cannot conceal from myself that the chances are that I must be taken at last; and that if I do not perish miserably in the bush, I shall be betrayed, and shot or hanged."

"And what can I do to prevent it?"

"You can do nothing to prevent that end, for I know that I am too deep in for it to be pardoned. If I were to give myself up, the government would be obliged to hang me for example's sake. No, no; I know my own condition, and I foresee my own fate. It is not of myself that I am thinking, but of my child. Mr Thornley, will you do this for me—will you do an act of kindness and charity to a wretched man, who has only one thing to care for in this world? I know it is much to ask, and that I ought not to be disappointed if you refuse it. Will you keep an eye on my poor child, and, so far as you can, protect her? I cannot ask you to provide for her; but be her protector, and let her little innocent heart know that there is some one in the wide world to whom she may look up for advice—for assistance, perhaps, in difficulty; at all events, for kindness and sympathy: this is my request. Will you have so much compassion on the poor, blasted, and hunted bushranger, as to promise to do for me this act of kindness?"

'I gazed with astonishment, and, I must add, not without visible concern, on the passionate appeal of this desperate man in behalf of his child. I saw he was in earnest: there is no mistaking a man under such circumstances. I rapidly contemplated all the inconveniences of such an awkward charge as a hanged bushranger's orphan. As these thoughts passed through my mind, I caught the eye of the father. There was an expression in it of such utter abandonment of everything but the fate of his little daughter, which seemed to depend on my answer, that I was fairly overcome, and could not refuse him. "I will look after her," I said; "but there must be no more blood on your hands: you must promise me that. She shall be cared for; and now that I have said it, that's enough—I never break my word."

"Enough," said he, "and more than I expected. I thank you for this, Mr Thornley, and could thank you on my knees. But what is that? Look there! A man on horseback, and more on foot. I must be on my guard."

'As he spoke, the horseman galloped swiftly towards us. The men on foot came on in a body, and I perceived they were a party of soldiers. The Gipsy regarded them earnestly for a moment, and then ran to his gun, but in his eagerness he tripped and fell. The horseman, who was one of the constables from Hobart Town, was too quick for him. Before he could recover himself and seize his gun, the horseman was upon him. "Surrender, you desperate villain, or I'll shoot you."

'The Gipsy clutched the horse's bridle, which reared and plunged, throwing the constable from his seat. He was a powerful and active man, and catching hold of the Gipsy in his descent, he grappled with him, and tried to pinion his arms. He failed in this, and a fearful struggle took place between them. "Come on," cried the constable to the soldiers; "let us take him alive."

'The soldiers came on at a run. In the meantime, the constable had got the Gipsy down, and the soldiers were close at hand, when suddenly, and with a convulsive effort, the Gipsy got his arms round the body of his captor, and with desperate efforts rolled himself round and round, with the constable interlaced in his arms, to the edge of the precipice. "For God's sake!" cried the constable with a shriek of agony, "help, help! We shall be over!" But it was too late. The soldiers were in the act of grasping the wretched man's clothes, when the bushranger, with a last convulsive struggle, whirled the body of his antagonist over the dreadful precipice, himself accompanying him in his fall. We gazed over the edge, and beheld the bodies of the two clasped fast together, turning over and over in the air, till they came with a terrible shock to the ground, smashed and lifeless. As the precipice overhung the river, the bodies had not far to roll before they splashed into the water, and we saw them no more.'

The reader may be interested to know that Mr Thornley was better than his word. He sought the daughter of the unfortunate man, took her home to his house, and afterwards sent her to England.

MODEL CHEAP LODGING-HOUSE.

The lodging-houses resorted to by occasional residents of the humbler classes in large cities, are generally of a wretched kind. The persons who keep them necessarily seek to make a profit on tenants at the rate of about threepence a-night, for which they furnish, besides bed-accommodation, the use of a fire for cooking, and, in some cases, the means of cleaning or blacking shoes. Situated in the meanest neighbourhoods, often wretchedly furnished and ill-kept, unprovided with direct supplies of water, or the conveniences necessary for the preservation of delicacy, these houses are not, in general, either healthy, comfortable, or favourable to the morals of their occupants. It is indeed one of the most affecting of the many forms of hardship incidental to the poor man's life, that it forbids him on many occasions to dispose himself amongst things which are pure and of good report, or which any good taste he may possess would incline him to select. It often happens, we understand, from the indiscriminate manner in which lodgers are received in these houses, that an honest labouring man is robbed between night and morning of the scanty earnings which he had realised at harvest or otherwise, and on which he was depending for the fulfilment of the most important objects when he should have reached his home. Such houses, too, having no regulations against the introduction of liquors, it necessarily follows that the sober are exposed to temptation, or at least to the disgust with which they must unavoidably behold intemperate indulgences.

Not overlooking the fact, that many houses of this kind are managed by decent and well-disposed persons, but believing that the majority are otherwise, and that it is desirable that an example of superior management should be set before them, a society of charitable persons lately resolved to attempt such an establishment in Edinburgh. In the humble street called the West Port, remarkable for the proportion of poor Irish in its population, there is a tall modern tenement, consisting, besides a floor of shops on the level of the street, of one sunk floor and three upper storeys. The whole of this house, exclusive of the shops, was obtained at a rent of twenty-five pounds, and it was immediately furnished in a plain but cleanly and substantial style, each room containing one or more beds, while, in the lower floor, there is a kitchen for general resort and for cooking, besides a wash-house and scullery. On each floor there is a water-pipe with sink: other needful conveniences are not overlooked. This large mansion was put under the care of a veteran sergeant and his wife—persons of select character—who, with a servant, keep the whole in order.

The Victoria Lodging-house, as it is called, has been in operation since September of last year, and seems likely to thrive. We visited it lately, and found that scarcely a night passes without seeing it nearly full. It is a pattern of cleanliness, and the whole of the arrangements seem to be excellent. At present, the number of lodgers receivable is limited to about thirty-eight; but, finding the number of applicants often exceeding their complement, the managers contemplate furnishing an additional floor, and will then be able to accommodate fully fifty. There may be a curiosity as to the style of the rooms and furniture. The former are plain whitewashed well-lighted apartments, such as those usually devoted to servants in genteel houses: it strikes us that we have occupied inferior rooms in hotels at half-a-crown a-night, when we chanced to be among the last of many arrivals. The chief article of furniture in each is an iron bedstead, provided with a flock-bed, blankets, and sheets. We were particular in turning down the clothes, and were pleasingly surprised to find the article last-mentioned clean and comfortable, albeit of the homeliest texture. The kitchen, or rather hall for general resort, is a comfortable place, provided with a good fire, oven, and boiler for continual hot water. Here the inmates attend to their own cuisine, for it is a rule of the establishment not to go beyond its proper line of offering simple domestic accommodation.

The daily charge for an individual is threepence. For this sum he has the use of a furnished house the whole day, and of a bed at night. Here, moreover, he is sure that discrimination is, as far as possible, exercised with respect to those who are to be his associates, and that he is safe from all connexion with intemperate revels and their tissue of disgusting consequences—for *no liquor can on any account be introduced into the house.* The privilege thus placed within the reach of the poor man we hold to be of infinitely more importance than clean rooms and comfortable furnishings, although these are also to be estimated highly. In particular cases, a group of people connected with each other—as, for instance, a detachment of Highland reapers—are allowed to have a separate room. Last year, such a band actually were accommodated in this manner over a Sunday, and thus were enabled to have scriptural readings and devotions in the language and fashion of the mountains, without troubling or being troubled by others. It is remarkable how much the generality of the inmates are disposed to observe and support the rules of the house. The New Year might have been supposed to be a trying time for these poor people, accustomed as most of them must have been to usher it in with conviviality; but on that occasion not one of the twenty or thirty inmates attempted to introduce a single gill of liquor.

If this establishment were designed, by the employment of charitable funds, to supersede the exertions of poor persons in a humble line of business, who, having to live by their trade, could not pretend to compete with such rivalry, it would not be entitled to public sympathy. But the object of the founders is of no such nature. They aim at making the establishment support itself; in which case—as the salary of the superintendent and his wife would be a profit to a humble couple carrying on the business on their own account—it would be shown that the usual daily outlay of the labouring man for lodging ought to obtain for him, at the hands of private enterprise, better accommodation than at present, with exemption from much that is disgusting and corrupting, as well as immediately dangerous, in such resorts. If the Victoria Lodging-house shall serve as merely a stimulus to the partial improvement of private establishments of the same kind, no one can doubt that it will have done an unequivocal good.

THE MIRROR OF THE DANUBE.

BY FRANCES BROWN.

On forests bright with fading leaves,
On hills of misty blue,
And on the gathered gold of sheaves
That by the Danube grew,
The setting sun of autumn shed
A mellow radiance rich and red,
As ever dyed the storied flood,
Since Roman blent with Dacian blood.
But Rome and Dacia both were gone,
Yet the old river still rolled on;
And now upon its sands, apart,
A peasant mother stood,
With beaming eye and bounding heart,
Marking the fearless mood
Of her young children's mirth that rang
Where late the joyous reaper sang.
She blessed each yet unsaddened voice,
Each head of golden hair,
Her rosy girl, her blooming boys,
And their young sire: for there
Was gathered all that meek heart's store·
The earth for her contained no more.
Yet with the love of that long gaze,
Were blent far dreams of future days;
And oh to learn what time's swift wing
To her life's blossoms yet might bring.
Then came a sound like passing wind
O'er the old river's breast,
And that young mother turned to find,
Upon the wave impressed,
The mirrored semblance of a scene
That never on its banks had been.
It seemed a pillared fane that rose
For justice far away,
In some old city at the close
Of a long trial day;
When hope and doubt alike were past,
And bright the midnight torches cast
Their splendour on a breathless crowd,
Dense as the summer's thunder cloud;
E'er the first lightning breaks its gloom,
Waiting the words of death and doom.
But far amid that living sea
Of faces dark and strange,
One visage claimed her memory;
In spite of time and change,
And all that fortune's hand had done,
The mother knew her first-born son.
Sternly he sat in judgment there;
But who were they that stood
Before him at that fatal bar?
Was he—the unsubdued
In heart and eye, though more than age
Had written on his brow's broad page
The fiery thoughts of restless years,
Whose griefs had never fallen in tears;
Unblanched by guilt, untouched by scorn,
Her beautiful, her youngest born,
And he upon whose hair and heart,
Alike had fallen the snows
Of winters that no more depart;
The worn of many woes
And hopeless years—was he in truth
The loved, the chosen of her youth?
She knew not what of wo and crime
Had seared each form and soul,
Nor how the tides of fate and time
Had borne them to that goal;
So much unlike that peaceful scene
Of stream, and corn, and sunset sheen:
And they, oh how unlike to those
Whose fearless joy around her rose!
And yet through sorrow, guilt, and shame,
She knew they were the very same.
Their judge, perchance, he knew them not;
For o'er his brow there passed
No troubled shade of haunting thought
From childhood's roof-tree cast;
Save that his glance, so coldly bright,
Fell with a strange unquiet light
Upon a face that still was fair,
Though early worn and wan.
Yet lines of loftier thought were there;
The spirit's wealth, that ran
To waste, for sin bore darkly down
What might have worn an angel's crown.
And o'er that mother's eye, which yet
Beheld, and wept not till it met
The gaze of her lost girl, there came
A sudden gush of sorrow's stream,
As though the drop that overflowed
Its urn had fallen there.
But when it passed that darkening cloud,
And she looked forth again
On the old river, vanished all
Were city, crowd, and judgment-hall.
The autumn night, with sudden gloom,
Came down on sea and shore,
And silently her cottage home
She sought; but never more
Gazed on the Danube's slumbering wave,
Nor wept above an early grave;
Or cast one look of pride and joy
On rosy girl or blooming boy;
And even from their haunts of play
Her glance was sadly turned away;
But deep in dreamless slumber sealed
Her eyes from all the tears
Whose coming that bright eve revealed.
And well the after years
Kept the dark promise of that hour.
And had the earth's old rivers power
To mirror the far clouds that lie
So darkly in life's distant sky,
How many a loving heart would turn,
Like hers, for comfort to the urn.

INTRUSIONS ON LITERARY MEN.

An author's time is generally his sole estate, a fact forgotten by a class of loungers who are continually honouring authors with their visits, or rather their visitations, and thus sadly interrupting the culture of the said literary estate. Thus, to humour one man, an author is frequently compelled to lay down the pen with which he was going to amuse and instruct thousands, and is also hindered in the attempt to earn his bread. Locke has justly remarked, 'If we are idle, and disturb the industrious in their business, we shall ruin the faster.'

The elder Aldus, the famous Venetian printer, placed an inscription over his door, saying, 'No leisure for gossiping, and those only are admitted who come upon business, which they are especially requested to despatch in as few words as possible.' In the same way, but more gently, a learned Italian wrote over his study door that no one could be allowed to remain with him unless able to co-operate in his labours. The illustrious Robert Boyle found it necessary to advertise in the newspapers that he could not receive visits on certain days, that he might have leisure to finish some of his works. Boileau used to be visited by an idle and ignorant person, who complained to him that he never returned his visits. 'Sir,' replied the wit, 'we are not upon equal terms; you call upon me merely to get rid of your time—when I call upon you, I lose mine.' The amiable scholar, Melancthon, uttered no reproach on such occasions, but coolly noted down the time he had expended, that by greater industry he might make up for the lost time. Evelyn was obliged to study during great part of the night, to redeem the continual loss of time through the calls of morning visitors. 'We are afraid,' said some of those visitors to Baxter, 'that we break in upon your time?' 'To be sure you do,' was the sharp and frank reply. Montesquieu, complaining of one of these bores, says, 'The favour he confers by often passing his mornings with me, occasions great damage to my work, as well by his impure French, as the length of his details.' The biographer of Sir Walter Scott states that the great novelist was always at home to everybody, man or woman, rich or poor, 'and he never seemed discomposed when intruded on, but always good-humoured and kind. Many a time have I been sorry for him; for I have remained in his study in Castle Street, in hopes to get a quiet word with him, and witnessed the admission of ten intruders besides myself. Noblemen, gentlemen, painters, players, and poets, all crowded to Sir Walter. At Abbotsford, his house was almost constantly filled with company, and it was impossible not to be sorry for the time of such a man thus broken in upon.'

AFFECTATION.

Affectation in any part of our carriage, is lighting up a candle to our defect, and never fails to make us be taken notice of, either as wanting sense or as wanting sincerity.—*Locke.*

Printed by William Bradbury, of No. 6, York Place, and Frederick Mullett Evans, of No. 7, Church Row, both of Stoke Newington, in the county of Middlesex, printers, at their office, Lombard Street, in the precinct of Whitefriars, and city of London; and Published (with permission of the Proprietors, W. and R. CHAMBERS,) by WILLIAM SOMERVILLE ORR, Publisher, of 2 Amen Corner, at No. 2 AMEN CORNER, both in the parish of Christchurch, and in the city of London.—Saturday, May 3, 1845.

CONDUCTED BY WILLIAM AND ROBERT CHAMBERS, EDITORS OF 'CHAMBERS'S INFORMATION FOR THE PEOPLE,' 'CHAMBERS'S EDUCATIONAL COURSE, &c.

No. 71. New Series. SATURDAY, MAY 10, 1845. Price 1½d.

MOTIVES.

The knowledge that we are rational beings, and that as such we should ever well consider ere we determine to act, seems to have induced the general belief that action, or the omitting to act, is always preceded by some immediate impelling motive. Accordingly, the imputing of motives is one of the most common occurrences in life. No matter what the nature of the subject—be it great or small, important or non-important—straightway is it believed to have had its origin in some motive. If a party give the right, instead of the left side of the way, he is supposed to be actuated by some preconsideration; if he address you as dear sir, instead of my dear sir, there is no doubt about it; if he subscribe himself yours obediently, instead of yours faithfully, it is equally certain; if he omit to take wine with you, the whole affair is as clear as the light of day. Now, nothing can be more incorrect than this view—nothing more true than that on ordinary occasions we all act independently of any motive whatever. In going home from the city, for example, we perhaps invariably walk on one side of the way, although we may have no motive for doing so—not even that of convenience. Perhaps we are occasionally taciturn, and not disposed at all times to be conversible; and yet it may be that for such silence we have not a single discoverable motive. Every or anything else but motive may have an influence in producing the particular state or occurrence complained of or remarked on. Habit, peculiar temperament, accident, thoughtlessness, unavoidable circumstances, may each occasion its portion of the results usually attributed to this otherwise certainly important cause of men's actions; but they are all overlooked in an account of the matter. One party will become exceedingly suspicious at the non-answering of a letter, another very angry at the omission to acknowledge a bow or other compliment. The correspondent in the one case had simply forgotten the letter of his friend—a great offence no doubt, but still not so important as that imputed—and the offending party in the other had omitted to return the bow or other compliment from mere inadvertence. Now, had anything but a motive been thought of, or rather had no motive been assigned, all would have been right. But no: we are, as I have observed, reasonable beings, and therefore must be supposed to act at all times with a view to results and consequences.

Motives are of course divisible into good and evil; and a good motive, if imputed, cannot well be productive of unpleasantness or inconvenience. The misfortune, however, is, that we are more prone to attribute the evil than the good. This unfortunate propensity is occasionally productive of serious consequences. On the occasion of the non-answering of a letter requiring an answer, as on that of the non-return of a compliment, if a motive be imputed at all, it cannot be a favourable one; hence coolness, severance of friendship, quarrels. In that of simple taciturnity, we have all the evils resulting from a false conviction of pride, ill-feeling, desire of concealing some important circumstance, as influencing the party disposed to hold his peace. How much more good feeling would there be in the world, and how much more friendly communion among those inhabiting it, were it but possible to eradicate this erroneous practice!

One great reason why it should be eradicated is, that the evil or injustice remains not against the party improperly suspected, but reflects in an equal degree upon ourselves. It is a veritable principle in moral as in physical science, that like begets like. Let us attribute improper motives, and we shall find that the same will be attributed to us; nay, we shall perhaps also discover that the other party begins to suspect that there was good reason for that which possibly arose from accident or inadvertence. On the other hand, let us impute those which are good; and if there be one single spark of feeling or principle in the composition of the party to whom we attribute them, we shall find that he will reciprocate; and whether he have good feeling or not, that he will give us credit for having deserved a good opinion, or at any rate will not conclude that we merited the neglect which had been exhibited towards us. These principles are in daily operation. Apart from the subject of motive, which perhaps implies some circumstance with which we are individually connected, let us unjustly accuse an individual of a desire to act unfairly, and we shall discover that he repels the charge with indignation. Let us give him credit, equally unjustly, for a desire to do that which is honourable, and we perceive that he endeavours to deserve it. Our feeling and passions seem so constituted, as reciprocally to act on their like when excited. Thus benevolence acts on benevolence, anger on anger, pride on pride, and self-esteem on self-esteem. Every one knows how the principle operates with respect to the education of children; and it is only to be regretted that it is not more generally regarded in riper life.

It may be true that to impute good motives at all times would be ridiculous. There are certain circumstances under which they cannot be presumed to exist, and which of course are not included in these remarks. It may be also true that in imputing them, we sometimes throw our own conduct open to misconstruction. This can only be, however, when we act without due regard to a principle, and when we impute good motives at one period and bad at another, just according as our whim and caprice dictate. It cannot happen where we make it the rule always to adopt the former course, until we are certain that we are wrong in doing so. In imputing a good motive, we may occasionally find that we have been mistaken; but the mistake will be on the better side; and it will never occur that we have committed an injustice, or that we have unnecessarily and foolishly lost a friend.

PLANTS YIELDING FOOD.

Whether we look upon the vegetable kingdom with the eye of the poet, the naturalist, or economist, we find it alike replete with matter for reflection. To the latter, indeed, it presents a twofold interest; he can at once admire the beauty and multiplicity of its forms, and the value of its products. For the perfect comprehension of its importance, however, it is necessary that he know it botanically; that is, that he be acquainted with the various orders of plants, and their relations to soil, climate, and other conditions; for, without such knowledge, he can never obtain from vegetation the full amount of its utility. Nor is it to any one section that the economist must direct his attention; for, from the lowest members—the *fungi*, to which belong the mushroom and truffle; and the *algæ*, which yield the carageen or Iceland moss—up to the higher forms that produce our grains and fruits, every member of the vegetable kingdom has its interest and value. It is somewhat wonderful, therefore, considering this fact, that we have no general treatise on the *Natural History of Plants Yielding Food;* but that the ordinary reader, to obtain any information on this point, must search amid systems of botany, of materia medica, dictionaries of commerce, books of travel, &c. and even after all reap but little from his toilsome pursuit. This desideratum may arise partly from the present imperfect state of our botanical knowledge, and partly from the undecided hypotheses respecting animal nutrition; but chiefly, we presume, from the reluctance which men of science absurdly feel in condescending to inform the common mind. In this particular we believe them grievously mistaken: there can be no degradation in attempting to elevate the knowledge of the masses, and they know little of the true condition of our population if they suppose that there are not among them hundreds of thousands capable of appreciating the facts of any of the sciences, if expounded in plain and perspicuous language.

It would seem, however, that this void in popular instruction is already in course of being supplied, for we perceive that several of our popular institutes have been favoured with lectures on the very subject in question. The Manchester Royal Institution, for example, has recently had a series of lectures by Dr Edwin Lankester, on the Natural History of Plants Yielding Food—a published synopsis* of which has led us into the preceding reflections. This outline, brief as it is, abounds with valuable information, and presents the subject in a light so attractive, that no one who sits down to its perusal, but will regret with us that the author should not have extended it to five hundred instead of to fifty pages. As specimens of the style and manner, we select one or two of the commonest subjects—again premising that Dr Lankester's remarks are merely in outline, not in finished lectures.

'*Coffee*, which is consumed by man in considerable quantities, is the produce of the *Coffea Arabica*, so named from its growing spontaneously near the town of Caffa, in Arabia. Recourse has been had to the use of coffee much more recently than to that of tea. We have no earlier notice of it than 1554, when it was used at Constantinople as a common drink; but it was forbidden, in consequence of its supposed intoxicating properties; and it would seem as if there were no way more likely to make people fond of anything than to interdict it. In 1580, Prosper Alpinus, a traveller, brought it to Venice, and described the means of raising it. In 1610, it was grown by the Dutch in the West Indies; and in 1652, coffee-houses were established in London. The people of England got passionately fond of this beverage; and in 1675 it was supposed to have an injurious effect on the constitution, and all coffee-houses were therefore suppressed. But another reason was probably this, that people assembled together for the purpose of drinking coffee, and there laid plots supposed to be dangerous to the state. The native countries of coffee at present are Ethiopia and Arabia Felix. It there reaches from 14 to 15 feet in height; is an elegant shrub with white flowers, and has all the characteristics of the class *exogens*. The fruit is a red berry, and in this red berry is contained a little seed, covered with an envelope, botanically called parchment. These seeds vary in different districts and various parts of the world.

'On a chemical analysis, coffee gives a large number of constituents. It gives two or three parts of caffeic and gallic acids, and a narcotic oil mentioned by several writers, but denied by others. However, there was no doubt that it did possess a narcotic oil, even in its raw state. It had also an alkaloid, named *caffein;* and it is very remarkable that the composition of this is identical with that of *thein* (derived from tea); they were, in fact, one and the same thing, obtained from two different plants. This is very remarkable:—500,000,000 pounds of tea are consumed annually; next, 300,000,000 pounds of coffee are consumed annually in the world, the matter of both beverages containing the same salt. This does seem to point out that there must be something in this salt; that it was not mere accident that led mankind to use two things which undoubtedly act in the same way. Coffee acts in the same manner as tea upon the system, and we use it precisely under the same circumstances: one might be substituted for the other: the only difference is that of flavour: those who like coffee may take it, and those who like tea may take it, with precisely the same effect. However, the preparation of coffee, and the changes which take place in it, will produce some change in its constituents. The coffee is not eaten in the state of the raw berry, but is roasted, during which certain changes take place; an empyreumatic oil is developed, in conjunction with the acids spoken of, and this renders coffee, in some points of view, a different thing from tea. This empyreumatic oil, like all other oils, has the power of arresting decay; and if, as Professor Liebig and Dr Playfair maintain, the action of digestion is very similar to that of decay, and this resembles the process of fermentation, then, as the empyreumatic oil will stop this process out of the body, in all probability it will do the same in the body; and thus we can account for the injurious effects of taking coffee immediately after taking large quantities of food. We arrest the process of digestion; and, instead of assimilating the food, we stop its assimilation, and a large mass is thus kept in the stomach a longer period than usual; the consequence of which is, that a feeling of heaviness and indigestion takes place. Thus we see there is a limit to the use of coffee, which we cannot put to the use of tea, which may be taken after meals, and used so far as the narcotic oil is concerned; but it is only right to observe, that large quantities of any fluid after heavy meals are altogether incompatible with facilitating the process of digestion.

'There has been lately some attention paid to an article which was formerly introduced into France as a substitute for coffee, namely, *chicory*. This plant grows in the greatest abundance in the south of Europe, and is also indigenous to Great Britain. It is found in abundance in the long magnesian limestone tracts of Nottingham, Yorkshire, and Durham. The root of this plant has been actually used as a substitute for coffee. He had on the table some of the dried roots, in the state in which it was employed. The decoction was coloured very much like coffee; but, when boiled alone with water, had a much less agreeable flavour. Why had it not been used alone? Because in chicory we have no alkaloid; we have no

* Report of Lectures on the Natural History of Plants Yielding Food, with incidental remarks on the Functions and Disorders of the Digestive Organs. Delivered by Edwin Lankester, M.D., F.L.S., &c. Churchill, London: 1845.

oil; we have a quantity of resinous matter; a certain quantity of a matter closely resembling *lactucarium* (a narcotic substance obtained from the common lettuce), and which is the only constituent for which chicory can be used. All chicoraceous plants possess a milky juice, in which resides a narcotic element. Chicory, then, he believed, could not in any way be used as a substitute for coffee. It had not been examined carefully, and therefore he did not pledge himself to the examination of that particular; but it had been proposed as an addition to coffee, and used extensively as an adulteration to coffee. He wished to draw the distinction between the addition of chicory to coffee, and the adulteration of coffee with chicory. In France, where they use more coffee than we do, chicory is added in small quantities, and persons will not drink coffee without it. It has been used in this country by the fraudulent seller to adulterate coffee; but he had no hesitation in stating that coffee, prepared with small quantities of chicory, was much more pleasant to the taste, and less liable to interfere with the process of digestion, than when taken without chicory. He was not prepared to explain how this was; but still we might find something in chicory which combines with the oil of coffee, so as to render it comparatively less injurious. Thus chicory was added throughout France and the coffee-drinking part of Germany, to prevent these supposed ill effects of coffee. Persons in this country, when not aware that the coffee is adulterated with chicory, or that it has chicory in it, prefer it with this addition. He knew a respectable coffee dealer who conscientiously objected to put it in. He kept on selling his coffee, but lost gradually almost all his customers for that article. He was not able to account for it at all; but an old lady, who had long been his customer, at length said, "You don't sell such good coffee as your neighbour." He examined his neighbour's coffee, and found chicory in it, which might easily be detected by throwing some of it into water, when the chicory will float. The next coffee he sold to her he added some chicory, and she said, "Now your coffee is very good." He added some to his commonest coffee, for his own use, and his wife exclaimed, "My dear, you have been giving us some of your best coffee." Then he added a little to the coffee of his stock; and soon he did not send out a pound of coffee without chicory, and his coffee trade is now larger than ever. There was this to be said too; at one time it was the law that a person adding chicory to coffee was liable to a penalty for adulteration; but government had now legalised the addition of chicory to coffee, and it might be legally added. He would say to those who were in the habit of grinding their own coffee, that they really would find it an agreeable addition to purchase chicory, and add a little to it. They would then be sure that the dealer did not add too much chicory, which was in fact the real danger; chicory being a much cheaper article than coffee.'

In the same pleasant manner Dr Lankester treats of tea and its proposed substitutes; of Paraguay tea; of potatoes, arrowroot, tapioca; of wheat, rice, maize, and the other grains; of vegetable oils, of cocoa, and the edible nuts; of acid fruits, as the orange, lemon, apple, &c.; of sugar and the sugar cane; of the grape; and of the numerous products of fermentation, as wine, beer, and spirits. From this inviting field we select another common example, once more recommending the whole to the best attention of our readers:—

'*Wheat*, so extensively used as an article of food, is the produce of a plant called *Triticum hybernum*, belonging to the natural order *Graminaceæ*, or grain-bearing plants, which, although so apparently insignificant as to contain all the common grasses that prove such pests in our gardens, also included wheat, barley, oats, rye, millet, maize, and the sugar-cane. We were lost in attempting to trace the origin of the use of wheat amongst mankind. It seems to have been used from time immemorial, and there is no question that the earliest records in the Bible refer to this form of wheat. He showed stalks in ear of wheat, barley, and oats, and observed that the grain was merely the fruit of the plant. In preparing the grain for food, the pericarp or covering of the seed was separated in the form of bran, and all that was used was the interior, which was really the seed. Wheat is cultivated extensively throughout Europe and several other parts of the world, and forms the great basis of European food; and the importance of attention to its cultivation had become much more apparent from the investigations of modern chemists. Wheat contained certain principles which we could supply from without. Previously to our knowledge of this fact, we were in some difficulty as to the proper way to supply food to this plant, so as to obtain from it the greatest quantity of nutritious matter; but the investigations of chemists had led us to see what were really the elements of which wheat consists. The principal components of wheat are starch, gluten or fibrin (protein), and a certain number of inorganic constituents, and these were found not to be unimportant in wheat. Although we had starch maintaining the heat of the body, and protein building up its fabric, we had still these other ingredients hitherto regarded as unimportant; and one of these was phosphate of lime, of which the bones of animals were composed; so that these particles in the wheat were taken into the system to build up the bony fabric of the body; and had we not this small portion of phosphate of lime, our bones would not acquire that hardness necessary to maintain the muscular fabric laid upon them.

'One of the simplest modes of preparing flour was that of which he had specimens on the table, in the form of a vermicelli and maccaroni; which substances were prepared by moistening flour and passing it through moulds, so as to give the substance its form. This wheat contained a different kind of starch from that of ordinary European wheat, or it would not be able to assume that form. The subject had not been sufficiently investigated how it was the Italian wheat assumed this form so much more readily than other European wheat. Maccaroni was used in puddings, pies, &c. and, as well as vermicelli, was introduced into soups, and was an exceedingly agreeable article of diet. Another preparation of wheat flour was called "farinaceous food." It was a secret preparation, and was sold by persons to be used as food for children, being merely flour submitted to heat; and, so far as he was aware, he believed nothing of an injurious kind was added to it. The advantage of submitting flour to heat, previously to preparing it, was, that the little cells of starch were thus burst, and the starch was then more readily acted upon by the stomach. This pointed out the necessity of cooking, so as to burst the cells; for, when used as food without previous cooking, the starch was not so easily digestible. This would account for the fact, that many fruits eaten raw were not easily digestible. Many fruits contain considerable quantities of starchy matter, and subserve the purpose of respiration on that account; and these fruits, such as apples, pears, &c. would be much more easily digested in the stomach, if previously heated. Bread was the principal form in which flour was cooked; and there were two modes of making it—fermented and unfermented. The advantage of fermenting the flour was, that, thus prepared, it was lighter and more easily digestible than the unfermented bread, such as captains' and sea biscuits. In the process of cooking, a fermentation went on very analogous to that in sugar for the purpose of forming alcohol, and it was well known that considerable quantities of alcohol were given off from bread during the period of its being baked. This fermentation had been called the panary, in order to distinguish it from the vinous and the acetous fermentation; but it was questionable whether it was different from the vinous. At one time, in London, a company was established for the purpose of baking bread, and they had an apparatus for condensing the spirit from the bread, and thus carried on the two different trades of bakers and distillers. However, the poor people got to know that the spirit was abstracted from their loaves, and they were prejudiced against the company—a prejudice of which the bakers availed themselves, by putting bills in their windows, "Bread sold here with the gin in it."

'Bread was exposed to considerable adulterations, the most common of which, in London, was the use of alum, which acts as an astringent upon the system, though not a poison. It might easily be detected by the application of the usual tests for alum, and it should be carefully avoided. Of all the forms in which bread could be used, that which was most wholesome and best adapted for the system was that of brown bread, in which form the flour contained a small portion of the bran. Its advantages were, that the brown particles, or outside pericarp of the seed, contain a volatile oil, which acts as a stimulant, and assists digestion; there is also a mechanical action of the particles of bran; and many persons were much relieved from indigestion and its consequences by eating brown instead of white bread. There was a new mode of preparing bread without fermentation, and yet not unleavened like rusks or biscuits. This consists in preparing the flour with carbonate of soda, adding to it a small quantity of hydrochloric or muriatic acid, which sets free the carbonic acid, and during the process of baking, the carbonic acid acts in the same manner as in fermentation, and throws up the bread into that vesicular form which makes it light and easy of digestion. It ought to be mentioned, that starch had one peculiar property—that of entering readily into combination with oil, forming a peculiar chemical compound, exceedingly indigestible; but which was not formed at a low temperature, so that the starch in ordinary bread and butter would not combine with the butter, but it would so combine with oleaginous matter in baking or boiling; and this was why pie-crust and other matters were so exceedingly indigestible. Plumcake, plumpudding, pancakes, &c. ought to be interdicted altogether as articles of diet, by those who wish to retain their digestive powers in all their original integrity

THE DISAPPOINTED SETTLER.

We lately noticed the lively account of a Van Diemen's Land settler's experience in the bush, and how, after a number of years of toil and anxiety, he was able to look around with satisfaction on the extent of his possessions. Here is a work of quite a different stamp—Mr Richard Howitt's account of his attempted settlement in Australia,* the vexations he encountered, and the reasons which ultimately induced him to throw up the whole affair in disgust, and return to old England. While in the one case perhaps too little was said of the troubles to be encountered in the bush, in the other they are brought forward and dwelt upon to an extent which leads one to fear they are overdrawn. Making every allowance, however, for feelings of chagrin and disappointment, we believe that Mr Howitt's revelations of what is necessarily to be endured for several years in any of these colonies are in the main correct, and their publication may be of no little service to persons who are contemplating emigration. Gathered from a number of irrelevant matters, including scraps of poetry, with which the volume is crowded, the following is the substance of his story.

On the 30th of August 1839, he embarked at Gravesend, along with a brother and nephew, for Port Philip, which was reached, after a short stay at Van Diemen's Land in passing, on the 5th of the ensuing April. Arriving in the Port Philip district when the land mania was at its height, it was difficult to procure a location at a reasonable price, and after seeing many dear lots, and much bad land, an allotment of ninety-five acres on the south side of the river Yarra was purchased The situation looked delicious, the soil was tolerably rich, the slopes most graceful, the windings of the Yarra, near and far off, were beautiful; white cockatoos were sitting on the old gum trees, and parrots were flitting about gorgeously numerous. In this promising little paradise the emigrants planted themselves on the 2d of October, and set about getting a weather-boarded cottage from Melbourne. This proved a difficult matter. At that time the district was at the height of its prosperity; all was activity; all the drays and the workmen were fully employed. A carter, with a horse and dray, considered it poor work to get only six pounds per week. After a fortnight's search in quest of one of these gentlemen, one was found who obligingly carted the cottage to its future station for six pounds. All things considered, this was poor payment. There were no roads; the face of the country was covered with growing trees, or with partly burnt timber, boughs, and rank grass, to say nothing of the bed of a torrent, full of rough stones, and partially flooded, which required to be crossed. However, by dodging backward and forward, the dray finally brought the cottage to its location; the only accident which occurred being an unfeeling jolt among the rocks, which threw a basket of glass and tea-things to the ground in irretrievable ruin.

There was now, proceeds Mr Howitt, 'employment enough before us in the wilderness. Our house was in about a week erected. The first night that we slept in it, it was but partially roofed, and the bats made free to flit about over our heads, and the moon and stars to peep in; the one with bland smiles, the others apparently regarding us with prying eyes.

'When our wood-work was completed, there also wanted brick-work—a chimney to make our abode convenient and comfortable. Here again was a new difficulty. I ran here and there to persuade people for good money to bring us the required number of bricks. It was worth nobody's while: nobody would do it. Well, we had been woodmen, house-carpenters; we grew weary of begging to have that done for which we must also pay handsomely. We set ourselves industriously to find clay, and found it too; yes, and made a brick-mould and bricks. Yes, and we burnt them too. Pretty figures we were both during the making and the burning of the bricks; and many a hearty laugh we had at ourselves, saying, "What would our English friends say if they saw us?" But the bricks were good bricks; and my nephew, one of the most ingenious as well as industrious men in the world—and considerate too—had not neglected to bring a bricklayer's trowel with him; and, like a good Jack-of-all-trades, he built the chimney, and did it so cleverly, that it passed muster with the world's other chimneys.

'This carpentering and brickmaking, this house-building, was done after all somewhat grudgingly, for the gardening season was passing by. Nevertheless, we dug up the ground for a garden between whiles, planting fruit trees, setting potatoes, peas, &c. Then and after we made a large and useful garden, only it was not fenced in, for we had no time to do that. We trusted that our vigilance, and that of our two faithful dogs, would be a fence for it until we could make one. Then we had to begin land-clearing. The steep fronting the Yarra had many large stones in it, and to get out these, and also in many parts of the garden, was the labour of weeks. Then to cut down the timber, gum, box, she-oak, and wattle-trees, was a Herculean task.

'Day after day, it was no slight army of trees against which we had to do battle; we had to fight hard with them to gain possession of the soil, for the trees in those days were giants. I then felt thankful, knowing well how to appreciate my advantages, that having been born and brought up on an English farm, all kinds of tools, agricultural and others, were at home in my hands. There was

* Impressions of Australia Felix, by Richard Howitt. London: 1845.

a world of work, digging to lay bare the roots, felling, and then cutting the boles and boughs up with the saw and axe. Such of the boles as were good for anything we cut into proper lengths for posts; splitting and mortising them for that purpose. Rails also we had to get when there were any boughs straight enough. Some of the trees were of unconscionable girth, six or eight yards in circumference. Immense was the space of ground that had to be dug away to lay bare the roots. And then, what roots! They were too large to be cut through with the axe; we were compelled to saw them in two with the cross-cut saw. One of these monsters of the wild was fifteen days burning, burning night and day, and was a regular ox-roasting fire all the time. We entirely routed the quiet of that old primeval forest solitude, rousing the echo of ages on the other side of the river, that shouted back to us the stroke of the axe, and the groan and crash of falling gum trees. Night never came too soon, and we slept without rocking. Then what curious and novel creatures—bandicoots, flying squirrels, opossums, bats, snakes, guanas, and lizards—we disturbed, bringing down with dust and thunder their old domiciles about their ears. Sometimes, also, we found nests of young birds and of young wild cats; pretty black creatures, spotted with white. The wild denizens looked at us wildly, thinking probably that we were rough reformers, desperate radicals, and had no respect for immemorial and vested rights. It was unnatural work, and cruel; especially when, pile after pile, we added to our other ravages the torment and innovation of vast fires. The horrid gaps and blank openings in the grand old woods seemed, I felt at times, to reproach us. It was reckless waste, in a coalless country, to commit so much fuel to the flames. Timber, too, hard in its grain as iron almost, yet ruddy and more beautiful than mahogany. No matter, we could not eat wood; we must do violence to our sense of the beautiful, and to nature's sanctities; we must have corn-land; and we, with immense labour, cleared seventeen acres. On one occasion I was laid up for a fortnight, keeping my bed part of the time, having been struck by a falling tree. I had to change almost immediately my linen; wringing wet with the perspiration of that blow's agony. Still, the most vexatious circumstance of that misery was the lost time.'

The troubles of woodcutting being for the present over, new vexations arise. A garden which had been made and planted was beautiful; but one night the cabbages were devoured by a stray bullock, and this led to a long spell of fencing. This being done, other sorrows turned up. A dray with four bullocks being indispensable, they were bought; but the vehicle requiring to be strengthened at the blacksmith's, a week was spent in the operation; and when all was ready, it was discovered that one of the bullocks had escaped. Days and days are spent in searching for the vagrant animal, and at length he is found; but in the meantime he has been caught and sold, and it is a long ravelled business recovering him. He is brought home just as the wet weather sets in.

'Wet as the weather was, we commenced bringing down our fencing materials. And through what a kind of country we had to bring them! Along the sides of sloping hills, and through marshes, and deep break-neck ravines. Our first attempt was unfortunate: something about the pole of the cart broke, and off the bullocks set in a gallop—crash went the wheels against a tree, and the cart was broken, the team all at liberty. The bullock-driver declared it to be useless trying again, for not one of the four bullocks were leaders. Two more bullocks were bought, after nearly a week's inquiry, and a dray was borrowed. Again and again, when the weather would permit us, a load was got down. I walked up the ten miles and home again, that if any accident happened, I might be at hand to render any assistance. Day after day I went: for if I did not go, I had no rest at home through apprehension. Sometimes at the gulleys or ravines we had to unload the cart for it to get over, and, when over, to re-load it. On some occasions we had the bullocks down; and then there was danger of their necks being broken; it was a time of great uneasiness, and great anxiety. Once we had decided for John, with the team, to go up one day, stay all night with the splitter, and so return the next. Days passed over, and no John returned to allay our anxiety: the bullocks in the forest got constantly lost; again we had recurrence to our old plan; again there was delay, the splitter was ordered to shift from his place to another, the land there being sold. This done, and the weather still finer I began to think fortune would favour us now, and that we should progress more satisfactorily. So thinking, John and I went up with the team towards the new splitting location. Before we reached it, a man came running nearly breathless, exclaiming, "Thank God you're come; poor Ellen, Mrs Smith's companion, is burnt to death!" So it proved, at least partly so. The poor young woman was burnt dreadfully. Standing by the out-door fire, the breeze had blown her apron into the flames, and, running in her fright, she had helped it on most fatally. In our cart, leaving our post and rail, she had to be taken into the town, where she died. This lost us three more days. Wearied out, we hired the carriage of the rest, and had L.9 to pay for their conveyance. So days, and weeks, and months had passed away vexatiously. Then, when all the materials were carefully got over the river, came a flood and swept a great portion of them into it.'

This brings the settlers to May 1841, and now terrible anxieties are felt about ploughing, fencing, and sowing. The fencing was the grand standing annoyance. While about it, the sowing season went by, and the corn having been put too late into the ground, the crops were worthless. 'Thus one year's labour, outlay, and seed, were thrown away. Still, there remained to us hope: we did not relax our endeavours. Other seasons there would be, and, by fencing and clearing other portions of the farm, we prepared ourselves to take advantage of them. On still we progressed—field after field was cleared and enclosed. Land and produce came down in value every day; we were toiling against hope—"We were not at rest, and trouble came." It was now time to plough again; but three of our bullocks had strayed away, and were nowhere to be found; to buy others would have been madness, in the every-day depreciation of all kinds of property. Search everywhere, and offered rewards of L.1 each in the newspapers, were tried in vain. A year and a half elapsed before anything was heard of them, and then only of two. The second season was lost, or nearly so. Our garden was tolerably productive, and on the land, without any seed or labour, there was an immense though coarse crop of oaten hay. These second, and even third crops, there being no winter to kill them, are under some circumstances advantageous; they also prove a curse, growing where and when they are not wanted. Three, four, or five times the land must be ploughed to get rid of the old plants of corn, potatoes,' &c.

The nephew now gets disgusted with the farm, and joins a friend of his recently arrived from England at cow-keeping. 'They purchased three cows and calves with them, and a few dairy articles, for L.30. My nephew and his partner kept their cattle in the open bush sometimes, and sometimes in our paddocks. Part of the milk they sold at home to the labourers employed by government on the Heidelburg road, and the rest in Melbourne. This, after a fair trial, proved to be like most other colonial undertakings. It seemed well to realise twenty pounds in about six months; but the cattle began to give less milk, squatters near Melbourne began to undersell them, and cows daily lessened in value. There was nothing so certain as that every week would add to their loss. At length, after keeping them a year, the concern was disposed of for, cattle and all, L.16; leaving a few shillings per week net profit. So much for Australian cow-keeping.'

One day unexpected visitors appear—'Being alone in the house, I heard the most melancholy noise in the-bush, not far off: I thought some one had met with a serious accident, and ran out terrified. It proved to be the forerunning announcement of three coming black fellows. Two women, one with a piccaniny at her back, had turned down to the ford below. Three men came forward. One of them had on a short white sailor's frock, and common black wool hat. The others had brown blankets wrapped round them loosely. Their hair was ornamented with white cockatoo feathers, and profusely with kangaroo teeth. Their object was to beg white money. When I turned one of my pockets out to show them I had nothing, they laughed in their loud manner, and felt at the other. So away they went dissatisfied; and they, with the women and child, busied themselves in crossing the ford. Soon they disappeared in the bush on the other side of the river. The men were armed with spears and waddies.'

About Christmas 1841, the disconsolate settlers have great yearnings to return to England, which they begin to think not such a bad country to live in after all. However, at the beginning of 1842, they courageously set to work to clear and improve a meadow of three acres. Trees, stumps, and boughs, are got rid of by enormous toil. 'If ever a bit of ground was earned by the labour bestowed upon it, that was. The rising sun found us felling trees, severing with our saw the trunks, and grubbing up roots; under the burning noonday sun we were often roasting ourselves by huge fires; and the sun dipped down in the western waves, leaving us, thankful for the short cool twilight, still at our labour. What was the result? We made the plot of land like a garden, fenced it with the post and rail split by ourselves out of the timber we had felled; planted it with potatoes; and, just as the rows were looking green and beautiful, there came a flood, destroyed the crop, and we had to plant it again. Nor was that the only loss: there were two splitters located near us, and these men I had engaged to get for me, as they had a license to split timber on the crown lands, a quantity of posts on the opposite side of the river; these, for which I had paid nearly six pounds, were carried away also.'

This was the finishing blow. All the poetry of Australian farming had now evaporated. The farm was let in February 1843 to the nephew, who got everything into first-rate order. Wheat, oats, barley, potatoes, cabbages, turnips, onions, all in their rich luxuriant greenness, how well they looked. No man in Australia, however, should reckon his crops before they are housed. The fine-looking crop of potatoes was destroyed by a flood. Fresh potatoes were sown, but as soon as they came up in goodly rows, the tops were attacked by myriads of flies, and what escaped the flies was devoured by clouds of grasshoppers, before which everything green disappeared. Rows of full-grown cabbages were hollowed like egg-cups; not a particle of vegetation escaped destruction. This was a grand consummation—the fly, flood, and grasshopper year! At the beginning of 1844, the nephew gave up the farm, which was re-let, and it was now unanimously resolved to quit the country. The party of unfortunates accordingly return to England, which they are delighted once more to behold. 'And here,' says Mr Howitt, concluding his narrative, 'I was again in England, where our forefathers, sleeping, generation after generation, in the bosom of their green and beautiful land, where they age after age not only fashioned for themselves, by their industry, comfortable homes of rural enjoyment and rest, but bequeathed it to their descendants better cultivated, a more wealthy and habitable country. The labour, affection, and cares of its myriads of sleeping benefactors, who toiled, adorned, and fought for it, have made it what it is—conspicuously the glory of all nations, a paradise of love, and joy, and liberty. Not, alas! wholly exempt from crime, and wo, and want, and disease; but animated by a quick spirit of Christian philanthropy, every day rendering the sum of these less and less. Full of these sentiments, and strongly impressed by the sense of our national greatness, and unwearied activity in the diffusion of universal good, I blessed the land in my heart; and was satisfied that the most singularly earthly good fortune, the greatest honour that could fall to the lot of mortal man, was to have been born in England; and the truest earthly wisdom, to endeavour to live in it!'

So ends the history of a disappointed settler; and now for the moral, if there be one. It appears to us that Mr Howitt, like hundreds of others, had expected too much in his adopted country—was perhaps heedless in buying land before he became fully acquainted with the district and its climate—imprudent in some of his undertakings—and wanted that cool patience which every settler should possess. Emigration is a step which no one ought to take without being able and willing to endure the greatest hardships and anxieties, in many instances to submit to privations scarcely felt by even the most abject of our population—all with the reasonable prospect of ultimate advantage. We would, in plain terms, put every intending emigrant through the following catechism, not bating him a single iota:—Will you be contented to lie for a time on the bare ground, or at all events in a miserable turf hut, no better than a pig-stye? No. Then you must on no account go to Australia. Can you submit to live for years on mutton, damper, and tea? No. Then don't think of going to Australia. Can you go unshaved, and never entertain the notion of having your shoes brushed? No. Then we would recommend you not to go to Australia. Can you submit to be tormented and half eaten up with insects? No. Then it is out of the question your going to Australia. Can you milk a cow? No; but I will try. Then our advice is, if you want a genteel and easy profession, lay out your money in cow-keeping, and *stay at home*.

THE STREETS OF LONDON.

NO. II.—THE SEVEN DIALS.

In the midst of the populous district that extends between Monmouth Street on the west, Drury Lane on the east, High Street St Giles on the north, and Long Acre on the south, is situated the small congregation of streets long known by the name of the Seven Dials. The place was originally built about the year 1694, as may be seen from an entry in Evelyn's Diary under date of the 5th of October in that year; in which he says, 'I went to see the building beginning near St Giles's, where seven streets make a star from a Doric pillar, placed in the middle of a circular area, said to be built by Mr Neale, introducer of the late lotteries in imitation of those at Venice.' Gay, in his Trivia, canto ii., thus describes it:—

> 'Where famed St Giles's ancient limits spread,
> An inrailed column rears its lofty head;
> Here, too, seven streets, seven dials count the day,
> And from each other catch the circling ray.'

The place wears a different aspect now. The 'inrailed column' has long since disappeared, and the original seven dials with it. Of late years an attempt has been made to restore the 'dials' in another shape. The seven streets have escaped amid the improvements that are being effected all around them, and run into the same small area as heretofore. When we last passed through it, not many months ago, four out of the seven houses that form the angles between the different streets were occupied as gin-shops, or 'palaces, and each of these had a large clock with an illuminated dial in its uppermost storey. These dials, with the houses to which they belong, form the most remarkable characteristics of the place. All around are poverty and wretchedness: the streets and alleys are rank with the filth of half a century: the windows are half of them broken and patched with rags or paper; and, when whole, are begrimed with dirt and smoke: little brokers' shops abound, filled with lumber, the odour of which taints even that tainted atmosphere; and the pavement and carriage-way swarm with pigs, poultry, and ragged children. These are the objects that meet the gaze of the stranger on every side, as, from the midst of the dials, he looks down either of the seven thoroughfares that have their confluence in it. But in the space called the Dials itself, the scene is far different. There at least rise splendid buildings, with stuccoed fronts and richly-ornamented balustrades; windows of valuable plate glass, and mahogany doors revolving on easy hinges, and ever half open to afford the passer-by a glimpse of the spacious, handsome, and well-stocked apartment within. These are the gin-palaces for which the spot is celebrated, the very Brocken of the fiends of intemperance, that here meet to hold high saturnalia. From six in the morning until midnight, the liquid poison is dispensed, at three-halfpence per glass, to crowds of idle, debauched, and vicious men, and squalid and dissipated women; and in no other place in London can the intemperance of the London populace be seen to more advantage or disadvantage than in this. A description of one of these houses will suffice for all, as, in their principal features, both external and internal, each bears a strong likeness to the other.

It is always a great matter to appeal to the eye and the imagination of the multitude, and the keepers of London gin-palaces know it full well. They exhibit to their customers a magnificence which they may not only admire from a distance, but which they may share—which is, in fact, their own, and has been created for them. The beggar in his rags, the street-sweeper bespattered with the mire of the crossings, the meanest and the most miserable of man or womankind may look, it is true, at the wealth displayed in the windows of the jewellers and linen-drapers of London, but they may not enter; they may admire, but they may not touch; and this admiration not unfrequently leads to envy and jealousy, and sometimes to a still fiercer feeling. The splendour of the gin-palace, which is often superior to that of the goldsmith or the dealer in the finest products of the loom, has, on the contrary, been raised for the especial enjoyment of those who are dirty, wretched, and vicious, if they can but command the small sum of three-halfpence. With this they can enter a large and warm room brilliantly illuminated with gas, and adorned with handsome mirrors, in which, behind a counter or 'bar' of finely-polished or carved wood, stands an obsequious and obliging person, male or female, to supply their wants, and hand them the clear draught of intoxication with smiles of welcome. All around are arranged huge vats, or the semblance of them, on which are inscribed the tempting words, 'Cream of the valley,' 'The milk of life,' or 'Old Tom,' while large printed placards state that 'millions' of gallons are in stock; flattering the imagination of the poor with the notion of the inexhaustible stores of the cellars beneath. The legislature has forbidden the owners of these establishments to provide seats for their customers, under the heavy penalty of the forfeiture of their licenses. Notwithstanding this discomfort, which was invented with the view of discouraging drunkenness, but which is very far from answering its intent, the gin-palaces are far more crowded than the old public-houses ever were, although the latter provided seats and every other requisite accommodation. Their 'bars' are besieged by eager clamants, who would forego not only a seat, but even bed and board, sooner than their 'cream of the valley.' Hither husbands bring their wives, and wives (most horrible!) their children. Here they crowd, not only for the sight of more wealth and luxury than their own hovels or scantily-furnished attics can afford them, but for the warmth, the light, the conversation, and the excitement with which the place supplies them at so cheap a rate. In some of these shops, though fortunately not in many, it has been known that a small stool or pair of steps has formed a part of the usual furniture, for young children to stand upon, so that their heads might appear above the counter when they swallowed their small glassful. The most melancholy truth of all remains to be told, which is, that it is not from mere thoughtlessness or misjudging kindness that wretched women act thus towards their offspring, but from a calculation and the working out of the dire problem which misery and vice have set them—the problem how to kill without murdering the helpless beings that depend on them for subsistence. A woman, haggard and ragged, with sallow face and sunken eyes, and with a sickly and melancholy-looking child of six years of age, to whom she was administering gin, was asked how she could be so thoughtless. Her reply told a dreadful secret. She said that she gave the child gin because it satisfied a craving, and destroyed the appetite; and because, in a word, it was cheaper sustenance than bread. Nor was hers by any means a solitary case. The same fearful story has been told repeatedly before magistrates and judges; and the hapless victims of so cruel a sacrifice have long crowded the three houses which are always open for the devotees of gin—the workhouse, the hospital, and the prison.

The Seven Dials is a place which should be seen between the hours of eight and twelve on a Saturday night, by him who desires to witness the intemperance of a London populace at its full height. Though the scene cannot but fill the friend of humanity with mournful feelings for the self-abasement of his kind, it is not without animation. It has its ludicrous as well as its melancholy side; its fierce excitement, its reckless merriment, and its striking contrasts of the maddest mirth with the most squalid misery. Let the reader imagine the small space we have described glowing with gas-lights and crowded with people. From four or perhaps five large gin-palaces—crammed almost to suffocation with men and women, girls and boys, people of all ages—arises a confused hubbub of voices, intermingled now and then with shrill screams, loud laughter, or hoarse imprecations. When a door opens for the ingress or egress of one of the drinkers, the Babel of voices sounds louder and louder into the street, and drowns for the time the faint imploring cry of the numerous beggars who are stationed without, to catch the charity of those whose sympathies are most excitable when they are most inebriated. It is difficult to pass through the street for the multitude of people, composed of match-venders, children with weak thin voices selling tapes and pins, hoary-headed old men, looking as feeble and ill as if they had risen from the bed of death to mingle once more in the tide of human existence ere they sink beneath it for ever, singing love-songs with tremulous and scarcely audible voices; apple-women and fish-women selling their wares; and, noisiest of the throng, the ballad-sellers with stentorian lungs calling out the names of the last new songs, often in strange and startling combinations enough, and offering them at the rate of a halfpenny per yard. Ever and anon there is a rush of many feet, as some obstreperous drunkard is forcibly expelled for his noisiness or quarrelsomeness; and the crowd gather round him to cheer him on to further excesses, and take pleasure in the sight of his degradation, as he clamours fiercely for readmission, and threatens with fearful oaths to break all the windows in the house if he is refused. If it be a woman who has created the disturbance, the uproar is louder and more prolonged. The shrill voice rises high above the din; and if she threatens to smash the windows or do other damage, she fulfils her threat, and sends volleys of stones through large squares of glass, amid the ironical cheering of the delighted crowd. The drunken man is led off to durance by the police with comparative ease, but the drunken woman is more difficult to manage. She will not be led off by the police; she scorns to walk, and will either go in a coach to the station-house, or be carried. She throws herself upon the ground or into the gutter. She kicks and screams and scratches, and with horrid oaths, and a volubility of curses—which sound doubly odious from woman's lips—declares her good-will and pleasure to tear out the eyes of the first person who approaches her. She is ultimately carried off by four men, two at her head and two at her heels, followed by a crowd, who abuse the police instead of sympathising with their most unpleasant duty, and call them harsh names for their cruelty to a woman. By her removal comparative quiet is for a while restored; the ordinary hubbub alone resounds; except that perhaps some strolling band of musicians strike up their merriest tunes to increase the uproar, and win their share of the copper coins that workmen and their wives have to spare from the gin-shop. As it approaches towards midnight, the venders refuse to supply more liquor, the lights are extinguished, the shutters are closed, and the uproar gradually begins to subside. Those who are still able to guide themselves find their way home; some sit down upon door-steps and sleep till morn, in utter unconsciousness that they are not in bed; while others roam through the town in a more active state of intoxication, and disturb many a peaceful neighbourhood, till the strong arm of authority removes them to the lock-up. This is the ordinary scene in Seven Dials on a Saturday night; and the same drama is enacted, with but slight variations, in scores of the most populous thoroughfares in London—in Whitechapel, in Lambeth, in Somers Town, in east, west, north, and south—and not on Saturday night only, but every night of the week. Though many thousands of the working-classes of the metropolis have taken the pledge of total abstinence, and kept it, there is no visible diminution of the evils of intemperance. The stream of vice seems full to overflowing, and always to be replenished, whatever drains may be made from it by the great apostles of social improvement.

We have dwelt so long upon the drunkenness which is the outward and visible sign of the Seven Dials, as to have left ourselves but little space to give an account of its literature. for which it is even more celebrated. The Seven Dials has long been known as the great mart of songs and street ballads; and the press of Catnach has acquired a wide-spread renown for its humble but apparently inexhaustible stores of broadsides. There are two other printers of the same class, who provide ballads for the hawkers, to be retailed at a halfpenny per yard. They find their chief customers in servant-girls and footmen, and more especially among those just raw from the country, to whom the excessive cheapness is not the least of the novelty or the temptation. These are the real songs and ballads of the English people, and generally include that universal favourite, 'Black Eyed Susan,' or 'Sally in our alley,' 'All round my hat;' or that famous poaching ditty, 'It's my delight, on a shiny night, in the season of the year;' or the more modern effusions of 'Some love to roam,' 'The sea, the sea,' 'Jim along Josey,' 'Jim Crow,' 'Meet me by moonlight alone,' 'We met—'twas in a crowd,' 'The soldier's tear,' &c. All these and a score or two more are often included in the halfpenny yard; with the addition of illustrative woodcuts, the which, if by any rare and singular chance they should alone survive to future ages, would convey the impression that art was in its first rude dawning in England in the year of grace 1845. Here also are not only imprinted, but written, the last dying speeches of notorious criminals—all composed upon the Tyburn model of the age that has passed away—and the rude ballads in which the incidents of the murder are chanted for an admiring populace to the old airs of Derry down or Malbrook, with a chorus fully as long as the stanza. We well remember buying the ballads in which the deeds of Greenacre and Daniel Good were all set forth in the minutest particular, and in the most uncouth rhyme and most villanous grammar. They had both the mark of the Seven Dials upon them; but appearing, as they did, in the light as it were of a new work, of which the copyright was of additional value, there was but one ballad for the halfpenny, and not the yard with a half-hundred, which could have been afforded had this been old as the few above named. Upon some future occasion we may perhaps give the details of a visit we once made to a Seven Dials' poet, the concocter of these and various other popular effusions of a like calibre; but in the meanwhile we conclude by mentioning that vast quantities of ballads and dying speeches are exported from the Seven Dials into all the rural districts of England; together with cheap 'Dream-Books,' and 'Oracles of Fate,' and other trumpery of the same class, which all find in the provinces a much readier market than in the capital.

SHIPWRECK OF THE DELPHINE.

TRANSLATED FROM THE FRENCH.

[The subjoined, though perhaps less characterised by startling occurrences than many other narratives of a similar nature, may yet possess some claims to our attention from the successful issue of the persevering efforts adopted for the safety of the isolated victims of calamity. The painful interest attaching to events of this nature, is increased in the present instance from its having taken place in the same region as the shipwreck of the Wager, one of Anson's squadron, of whose wreck so interesting an account has been left by the ancestor of the poet Byron. The peninsula of Tres Montes, mentioned in the following translation, is the same over which, it may be remembered, Byron and his companions passed with their Indian guides. All the travellers who have visited that part of America agree in their description of the climate, which is bad in the extreme. Everything is always wet: there are scarcely ten days in a year on which snow or rain does not fall; and not more than thirty on which it does not blow with the greatest violence. The island of Chiloe is situated in a great bay at the southern extremity of Chili, and is the largest of a group the number of which, comprehending those of Chonos, is eighty-two. With these remarks, which were necessary for the proper understanding of what is to follow, we proceed at once to the narration.]

We sailed from Havre for Valparaiso on the 30th March 1840, in the ship Delphine, Captain Coisy, with a crew of sixteen sailors and four passengers. In three days we were clear of the channel, and, the wind being favourable, saw the Canaries and Cape de Verd Islands, and soon after crossed the line. In short, at the expiration of thirty days from the time of our departure, we had reached the latitude of Rio Janeiro. The wind then became contrary, and, forcing us to lie to, so retarded our progress, that we did not arrive in the latitude of the Falkland Islands until the 28th May. On the 30th we saw Staten Island, and on the 9th June Cape Horn and Terra del Fuego. In spite of the usual stormy weather of this region, and the enormous masses of floating ice which we encountered in all directions, we doubled the Diego Islands on the 11th. The bad weather still continued: but on the next day a short interval of brightness enabled us to take an observation, for the last time, as it proved, on board the Delphine. The wind then veered round to the south, and we believed ourselves sure of a speedy termination to the voyage, when, without any warning, it chopped round to the north-east, bringing its attendant fog. We were steering our course by computation, when in the night of the 19th, a few hours before daylight, we were suddenly awoke by the frightful grinding of the ship's keel upon the rocks. 'Land, land!' cried out the second mate; and in an instant every one, crew and passengers, was on the deck. On all sides the vessel was surrounded by rocks and breakers, while through the gloom the outline of high land was visible at a distance, exaggerated by the obscurity, and adding to the terrors of the moment, which it would be difficult to describe. The ship was yet afloat, but the shock had been too severe to leave any hope that she would continue to swim: every instant we feared she was sinking under us. The passengers ran to the pumps, and the crew, by orders of the captain, flew to the rigging. The pumps were soon dry, when, on hastening to the tiller, we found to our consternation that the rudder had been carried away. The ship struck again. We braced the yards round, to allow her to drift off the land, and cut the lashings which held the long-boat and yawl to the deck, during which time the grinding of the keel on the rocks became more violent than before, threatening the entire destruction of the vessel. We let go the best bower, in the hope of keeping her from drifting farther in; but the anchor dragged over the smooth rocky bottom. The water gained on us so fast, that we hastened to get the long-boat overboard; a work of great difficulty, as it dashed against the bulwarks with every roll of the ship, and endangered the lives of the men. At length we succeeded in getting her afloat; and, throwing in some provisions, we all jumped in, followed by the captain, who was the last to leave the deck. It was then five o'clock, and we waited for daylight among the rocks and sea-wrack, watching the ship, which at last struck on some rocks surrounding a small island. At daybreak we perceived a bay, towards which we rowed, and landed ourselves and the provisions on a sandy beach. The captain, with the sailors, returned immediately to the ship, to save, if possible, a greater quantity of provisions, and other matters necessary to our existence. They found her quite fast about half a mile from the place of our landing; all the between decks full of water, with the exception of the stern. They returned to the shore three hours afterwards, bringing the yawl, both boats laden with everything they could lay their hands on. A temporary tent was hastily set up, in the centre of which a great fire was lighted; round this we spread some sail-cloth saved from the cargo, which served us for beds during the night. The two following days were passed in saving more provisions from the wreck, while a party who remained on shore got up another tent with the fore-sail, that had been brought for the purpose. A few days afterwards, a violent squall drove the long-boat on the rocks and staved her in, which obliged us to haul her on shore, to prevent her entire loss.

A fortnight passed in this manner, the yawl replacing the long-boat in our visits to the ship, when the weather would permit. The captain took an observation, from which we learned that our position was in 49 degrees south latitude, upon an island two leagues in length, separated by a narrow channel from the great island of Campana, as we ascertained from the English chart which the captain had taken the precaution to save, with his sextant and two compasses, on the first day of the wreck. Everything conspired, unfortunately, to render a long abode in this dreary region inevitable—the winter just commenced, the continued northerly winds of the season, and the distance which separated us from any settlement of Europeans. We calculated that our stock of biscuits and flour would last nearly four months, and determined that our wisest course would be to wait until the bad season was over, before venturing to seek for assistance in the long-boat, which by that time, as was proposed, would be repaired and decked in.

The captain did not forget that, in our present circumstances, the preservation of the health of the men from the inclemency of the climate was the first duty. Another tent was built with the mainsail, of greater dimensions than the former, in which the beds were so arranged as to be at some distance above the surface of the ground. The spot fixed on for the erection was the entrance of a wood which overlooked the whole bay, and in the first days of July* we took possession. The old tent was left standing, in which, although the materials at our disposal were very scanty, we managed to build an oven.

Certain unequivocal indications had led us to believe that the island was occasionally visited by savages. We had seen in different places a rude kind of hut, constructed of branches of trees, in which we found the remains of shell-fish and the bones of animals. Shortly after we entered on our new habitation, the captain's dog, which had been saved along with us, growled all night in spite of our efforts to pacify him. We were all on the alert the next morning on learning that the prints of naked feet had been seen on the sand: none of our party went barefoot, and the traces were those of persons running from the wood where our tent was situated. This circumstance led us to suspect that we were watched; and indeed, on the 9th July, while our party had gone on the usual salvage trip to the wreck, one of the passengers who had wandered to a distance returned hastily, telling us he had seen the savages. We armed ourselves immediately with all the offensive weapons within reach; and the captain, having advanced with a few men, soon came in sight of what he was in search of. There were nine of them, unarmed, their only clothing being the skin of a seal hanging over their back. At first they hesitated to move; but seeing that we approached with friendly demonstrations, they became familiar. We gave them some presents; but prevented their going to our tent, which they seemed greatly to desire. After staying a short time they left us, but soon repeated their visit, bringing with them their wives, whose clothing did not differ from that of the men. Subsequently, we permitted them to enter our tent, and went several times to visit them upon the different islands to which they transport themselves in canoes. Their huts were similar to those we had seen in our island, but were covered with skins. These savages are generally of middling height, strong, and well formed. They are evidently the same race as the Indians of Chiloe, and are always accompanied by great packs of dogs, which they use for hunting seals, on whose flesh, with occasional supplies of shell-fish, they principally subsist. This food, however, often fails them in rough weather, when their canoes cannot put to sea. In their visits to us they were always asking for food, which was most probably their principal object; at the same time they often stole some of our things without being detected. In short, they appeared to us to be very miserable, and lazy to excess. The wreck of the Delphine was a fortunate event for them, as they picked up many articles floating about among the rocks.

During the earlier period of our residence on the island our time passed in a very uniform manner. The shore party provided wood for the fire, of which the consumption was indispensably great, on account of the continued rainy weather, and for the prevention of sickness. Another party was regularly employed with the yawl in saving things from the wreck. Our young lieutenant, Lepine, took charge of this laborious duty, and, by his zeal and activity, sustained the courage of the sailors both on the ship or among the islands after she was broken up. Meantime the month of September drew on. The carpenter had finished the repairs of the long-boat, which was covered with a deck, and rigged as a schooner, as well as was possible in our state of privation. Although the weather remained unseasonable, we always hoped it would change for the better. The captain, however, resolved on putting his project into immediate execution—to sail with a few men for San Carlos of Chiloe, to seek the means of rescuing the whole party from their perilous situation. The necessary preparations were made in consequence, and on Tuesday the 3d September our little vessel was launched, in order to be ready for the first favourable wind. But what was our disappointment when we saw that she filled with water before our eyes. We tried at first to stop the leaks while she was afloat; but this being impossible, we were compelled to haul her again on shore, where we took away a portion of the lining, and carefully examined the seams, and then caulked and stopped every chink by which it was possible the water could enter; and on Saturday evening, at high water, she was again launched. The next day we found her again half full of water; for her timbers were old and crazy. The captain, however, persisted in his resolution, and gave orders for her to be baled out—replying to those who expressed uneasiness that the wood would swell up in the water. A quantity of sail-cloth was used for ballast, which at the same time served for beds, although, in order to prevent their complete soaking, the baling was kept up incessantly. The provisions, calculated for eight days, with wine and spirits, were put on board; and a generous allowance of wine was given at dinner to the master and four men who were selected to accompany the captain and Lieutenant Lepine. At two in the afternoon they set sail, with fine weather and a stiff breeze from the south.

Seven of our number had left us; thirteen remained behind. We watched for a long time, from the top of the cliffs and rocks, the departure of our companions in misfortune, on whom our fate depended. The day was far advanced when we lost sight of them, and we returned to our tent with a feeling of sadness, justified by our actual position; for, leaving out of sight the probability of the loss of those who had gone away—an event but too possible—how much was there, in our own position on the island, to give cause for uneasiness. Was it not to be feared that the savages, who, until then, had been inoffensive, would become emboldened on seeing our diminished number; and that their greediness, or possibly want alone, might lead them to attack us, and take by force our little remaining provisions, as well as other things in our possession which had excited their cupidity? These reflections, however, were soon banished by the majority of our little band. Those who

* A winter month answering to the January of Europe.

had drunk farewell to their companions in a pitcher of wine, were not sorry to drink a few more bumpers to their prosperous voyage: conviviality, in short, was the prevailing feature of the moment, when an unexpected incident drew us all out of the tent. A small hut, built of wood and moss by one of the sailors and a passenger, not far from our tent, had taken fire, and was nearly consumed, with all its contents, before we could succeed in putting it out. This event finished the day, and each one threw himself, dispirited and melancholy, on what was called his bed.

Next day, nothing else was thought of but what was best for us to do under our present circumstances. Just before the departure of the long-boat, the daily ration for each man was eight ounces of biscuit. At this rate our stock would not last more than three weeks, and we could not expect to be released at least before a month. We therefore reduced our allowance to six ounces, and of wine one quart a-day. We had a great quantity of spirits, and were thus enabled to continue the usual allowance to the sailors. In this way we hoped to go on for more than a month. The savages came to visit us as before, and soon saw our diminished strength; but their demeanour towards us did not alter. The first thing they did whenever they landed was to come and warm themselves at our fire, so that we were careful to leave some one to keep guard when we went out to fish.

The month of September went by; our biscuit diminished rapidly; we reduced the ration to four ounces a-day. Towards the middle of the first week of October we began to feel uneasy. We remembered that, on the third day after our companions sailed, a heavy gale had set in. Was it not to be feared that they had perished? And, without taking the worst view, it was still possible that the captain might not find the expected succour at Chiloe. In this case, as our abode on the island would be lengthened, we decided on another reduction of our ration of biscuit to two ounces; just sufficient for a little daily sop. We succeeded in making the savages understand that, if they brought us food, we would repay them with the things they most desired; from which time they began to bring us the eggs of sea-fowl. Thus we went on until the middle of October, the sixth week since the long-boat sailed. Our anxieties now augmented, and many of us began to think of the means for our own rescue.

We had already, as a precautionary measure, collected the planks and pieces of wood of the shattered vessel. The idea occurred to us of constructing a boat capable of carrying the whole party, and we recommended to those who went out fishing to bring in the masts, yards, planks, or other portions of the wreck which they might find floating. By this means a great quantity of materials was collected; and the carpenter began to work upon the keel, which was thirty feet long.

On the 15th October our little ration of two ounces of biscuit failed us entirely, and we were reduced to the indifferent shell-fish, and the eggs—which were almost always addled when the savages brought them to us—and to some birds which we occasionally killed. We wished the natives to bring us some of the flesh of the sea-wolf, which we had seen them eat; but whether the season was unfavourable, or they caught no more than sufficient for themselves, we could never obtain any. They gave us some dogs, and appeared greatly astonished when they saw that we had eaten them; for, notwithstanding the repugnance of some among us to eat dogs' flesh, our hunger was so great that we devoured them all. At the end of October we had ceased to hope, except in ourselves. Some of us were always occupied in seeking for wood or food; while the others were as persevering in their labours on the vessel, which went on very slowly, as much from the weakness to which our privations had reduced us, as from the bad weather which often prevented our working, and the want of proper tools. Thus the time wore away until the middle of November, all of the party suffering more or less from attacks of dysentery: still, in spite of the continual rain and prevailing humidity, and the want of shoes, no one was so ill as to be detained in the tent. The hope of eventually succeeding in our efforts to escape from this dreary life supported our courage. We could see that, although slowly, our vessel approached completion: the slips, with the necessary inclination for the launch, were securely placed; the head and stern-posts were fixed on the keel; the greater portion of the ribs were made, and we cut others every day in the woods, to complete the number.

If we were deceived in the hope of saving ourselves, and in the means for its prosecution, the resolution of attempting it never failed us. Such was our situation when, on the morning of the 12th November, we heard a sailor who had just left the tent cry 'Sail, ho! sail, ho!' with all his might. Although this same sailor, deceived by a false appearance, had raised the same cry a month previously, we all ran precipitately towards the shore. This time the report was not false; we saw a vessel anchored in the bay. A heavy shower prevented our seeing distinctly, but we thought she belonged to some ship of war. The yawl was afloat in a moment, and a few men jumping in, were soon on board, not the boat of a man-of-war, but a *lanche* of San Carlos. Those on board of her were not strangers; they were Captain Coisy, Lieutenant Lepine, our sailors and companions, who came to deliver us and bring us provisions. It would be useless to dwell on the universal joy that prevailed, and the eagerness with which both parties inquired about what had transpired.

The long-boat had left the island on the 6th September in so leaky a condition, that two men were constantly engaged in baling; during the first night the sea broke over her repeatedly, threatening to carry all to the bottom. On the fifth day they passed Cape Taitachaoun, and intended to double the island lying to the north of it, but were prevented by a gale, which obliged them to lie to for better weather. After some days, alarmed by the diminution of their provisions, they made sail, keeping as near their course as the wind would permit, and two days afterwards entered the great channel which separates the Chonos Archipelago from the Cordilleras. Thus they continued, with alternations of fair and foul weather, sometimes rowing, at others driven back, or landing to collect shell-fish for food, for twelve days, when one afternoon they saw smoke at a distance, to which they immediately directed their course, taking precaution to look to their arms, for fear of savages. The smoke was found to rise from a fisherman's fire, who, as soon as he understood their critical situation, set off to fetch provisions from his *casa*, three leagues distant, while they waited his return. After this they crossed to the islands of the Chiloe group, at one of which, marked Valasco Port, they were detained nine days by stress of weather, and were driven back in another attempt to cross the channel: but on the 3d October they again set sail, and on the 4th happily arrived at Chiloe, where they landed, for the purpose of procuring provisions at the first inhabited spot they saw. On the 10th, thirty-five days after their departure from our island, they reached San Carlos, having had incessantly rainy weather during the whole of this perilous voyage.

The captain lost no time in his endeavours after his principal object; the consular agent gave him all the assistance in his power; but, unfortunately, no ship of war or merchant vessel was lying in the port; there were only the miserable *lanchés* of the country, quite unfit for such a voyage as that to the place of our detention. Everything in the shape of a vessel was examined, in the hope that one might prove serviceable, but in vain. The captain then heard of a large and commodious *lanche* at a place twenty-five leagues higher up the channel, and, without a moment's delay, he took a whale-boat and started for the settlement indicated; but what was his disappointment to find, on arrival, that the vessel was yet on the stocks, and only half completed.

He returned immediately to San Carlos, and determined, as nothing better was to be had, to hire a *lanche* in good condition which had arrived during his absence. This kind of vessel, which is used only for the transport of wood or potatoes from one island to the other, is not decked, and a deck for the voyage to the open sea was indispensable. In spite of all the diligence that could be used, it was the end of October before she was ready. Provisions for two months, in the meantime, had been collected, with the consul's assistance; and on the 30th, the captain, with the lieutenant and four men, sailed from San Carlos in the *lanche*, which had been rigged as a lugger. The master was left behind, as fatigue and privation had rendered him incapable of undertaking the return voyage: the others embarked, confiding in the generous hope of saving their companions. They took a whale-boat in tow, for convenience in landing; but, after beating about among the islands for some time, when they reached the open sea it laboured so much that the seams opened, and they were compelled reluctantly to cut it adrift. Finally, after repeated delays, vexations, and dangers, they recognised the approaches to our island, and at seven in the morning of the 12th November, as already described, they were at anchor in the bay.

The unexpected return of the captain, after seventy-three days' absence, when we thought him lost, placed us immediately in a state of abundance as regarded provisions; but we were not the less desirous of quitting a place where we had been so long detained in spite of ourselves. It was impossible, however, to go off in the teeth of the north wind, and we were obliged to wait three weeks for a favourable change. On Thursday the 3d December we sailed at three in the afternoon, towing our yawl, whose preservation had cost us so much labour. We did not keep it long, for when off Cape Taitachaoun it broke loose, and drifted away in a squall. This was a serious misfortune, as it deprived us of the means of going on shore to cook our provisions, and of the chance of escape in case of wreck. The squall was the precursor of a furious gale, from which we incurred the greatest danger; the waves breaking over us from stem to stern, and pouring down into the confined space below, where we were crowded one on the other. Our situation was indeed a terrible one. We had given up all hope of safety, and resigned ourselves to the worst, when the storm began to moderate. We were quite uncertain as to our position, and steered for some land that was in sight: but what was our astonishment to find, when we drew near, that it was the island from which we had so recently sailed. We must have drifted sixty leagues during the four days that the gale continued. In our present circumstances, we were glad to re-enter a place we had so much desired to quit eight days previously. Having lost the yawl, we were forced to make a raft, which we drew from the shore to the *lanche*. The savages had not, as we feared, destroyed our tent; it was still standing. The miserable creatures had dug up the potatoes which we planted, with the view of leaving them a resource in the article of food. We divided our party: one half went every night to sleep on board the *lanche*, as a measure of precaution. The weather seemed to grow worse as the season advanced. We were covered with vermin, and dreaded that we should again be without provisions. On the 2d January 1841, the weather moderating, we were enabled once more to put to sea. No sooner had we cleared the bay than a heavy sea broke our rudder, and forced us to lie to. We secured it as well as possible with lashings, which quickly wore out and snapped. We then cut a few fathoms off our small chain, with which we secured the rudder from further danger. The weather continued stormy; but as the wind was in our favour, we shortly after passed the peninsula of Tres Montes; and once among the islands, we looked upon ourselves as saved.

After this we had fine weather. On the 14th, we landed for fresh provisions, of which we were in great need; and on the 20th, to our great joy, we arrived at San Carlos, eighteen days after our last departure from the island, and seven months and one day from the date of the wreck. We had great reason to congratulate ourselves that, during this long period of privation, suffering, and danger, not one of the party was lost. The captain had neglected nothing in his power to prevent such a misfortune, not only while we were on the island, but in moments of danger, never hesitating to expose himself the first to whatever might happen. To his courage and perseverance must be attributed the success of his great object—the safety of all.

On our arrival at San Carlos, the French consul, M. Fauché, who had so generously assisted the captain on his former visit, hastened to supply our wants. To him were we indebted for the means of pursuing our voyage, and eventually returning to our native country.

OLD MONUMENTAL FIGURES IN CHURCHES.

In old churches, particularly those in country parishes, may often be seen figures in stone or marble, reclining on monumental sarcophagi. Sometimes the figures represent females—old ladies in ruffs and farthingales—but more frequently males, and generally chieftains, in some kind of armour. Ordinary observers are for the most part puzzled with respect to the degree of antiquity of these figures, but the archæologist is acquainted with certain marks and appearances which guide him pretty surely to the era of their execution. There are few persons who do not feel an emotion of pleasure at beholding an object of art which has existed for ages; and that pleasure is increased tenfold when he is able to ascertain some circumstance connected with it—such as the time at which the monument was raised, the station or degree of the person whom it is meant to commemorate—when the record of such facts has been obliterated by time. To guide the lingerer in old churches to this sort of knowledge, we request his attention to the following facts.

Antiquaries have ascertained that monuments of the earliest date are stone sarcophagi, the top formed prism-shaped, like the sloping roof of a house, for the purpose of allowing wet to run freely off; for they were always placed in the open air. Such very ancient monuments are without inscriptions, their form being the only guide to their probable date. It appears that it was not till the year 1160 of the Christian era that these stone coffins with prismatic roofs began to be ornamented. From that period, carvings, chiefly of a grotesque character, but occasionally of armorial bearings (adopted at the beginning of the twelfth century), appear on them. These are the earliest specimens of sculpture; but they rise in excellence, completeness, and beauty, as the dates advance. The sloping roofs gradually disappear with the progress of sculptured emblems. Not content with merely carving the cover of the monument itself, figures were cut separate therefrom, and the roof flattened for them to be laid on it. This state of art seems not to have been arrived at till the thirteenth century, so that the spectator may be sure that a monument with a flat top is not of greater antiquity than that period, whether supporting an effigy or not. Of figures, there are various kinds. Those which have their hands laid on their breasts, with chalices in them, denote that the person commemorated was a priest. Prelates are always represented with their insignia—pontificals, croziers, or mitres. Knights, again, are to be known by their armour. Most of them are lying flat on their backs, and several with their legs crossed. In this case they have been either crusaders (from *crux*, a cross) or married men; beside the latter, a statue of the wife is sometimes laid. The various descriptions of armour by which the effigies of ancient military men are covered, are sure guides to the era of their existence. Warlike figures of the earliest date are found in tegulated or scale armour, like that of William Longspeè, Earl of Salisbury (son of Henry II. by Fair Rosamond), in Salisbury cathedral, who died in 1227. Chain armour, or mail composed of small iron rings, is seen on figures of later date, extending from the reigns of Richard Cœur de Lion to that of Henry III. A specimen of this kind of armour may be observed in Hitchendon church, Buckinghamshire. Plate armour seldom appears on knightly effigies more ancient than the latter reign. Female figures adorned with a mantle and a large ring, though they afford no clue to a date, denote that the deceased had taken the vow of chastity. Armorial *quarterings* of arms annexed to tombs show them to have been raised subsequently to the fourteenth century; while supporters were not adopted till Richard II.'s time.

At a later period, arches were raised over sepulchres, to protect them from the weather; but gradually, sepulchral monuments were removed within doors, and built in churches. In process of time, it was found that these arched monuments took up too much room, even in the most spacious cathedral. To lessen this evil, a plan was devised which gave rise to the practice of annexing chapels to the churches, expressly for containing such mausoleums. These chapels are in many instances only separated from the main body of the building by iron rails, and are entered by doors from the side aisles. This practice was not commenced till the fifteenth century.

Even figures in the ordinary sculpture, or half-relief, multiplied so much that a less elaborate mode was at an early period adopted as mementos of individuals. This was by simply engraving or incising the effigy on slabs or on brass plates. Amongst the earliest recorded instances in England may be mentioned the tomb of Jocelin, Bishop of Wells, placed by him during his lifetime in the middle of the choir, and described by Godwin as formerly adorned with a figure of brass. He died in 1242. The date of the earliest existing specimen is about 1290; it is the figure of Sir Roger de Trumpington, who accompanied Prince Edward in the holy wars, and is represented with his legs crossed. An interesting addition, hitherto unnoticed, has recently been made to the small list of sepulchral brasses of this early period, which represent knights in the cross-legged attitude; it is preserved in the church of Pebmarsh, near Halstead, in Essex.*

Although recumbent effigies continued to be either sculptured or engraved on tombs till the seventeenth century, yet other devices were meantime adopted. Immediately after the Gothic ages of chivalry, more solemn emblems of mortality were employed than effigies—whether knights or priests—attired in 'their habits as they lived.' Skeletons in shrouds began to be used in the fifteenth century; and these were succeeded by corpses (generally portraits) in shrouds, with the head bound up, and the feet tied. Sometimes images of children were placed at the feet; and cherubim figured at the corners of the tomb. The most remarkable of these tombs have, as it were, two storeys; in the upper one lies the shrouded corpse, whilst the lower compartment contains a skeleton or emaciated human body. Such sepulchral devices, always unpleasing, even when well executed, were chiefly adopted for ecclesiastics.

Besides the different effigies, and the clothing they are represented in, together with the other various ornaments carved upon tombs, the antiquary is guided to the date of their erection, and to the status of the person they were designed to commemorate, by the situations in which they are found. The most important class of sepulchres were those of saints, and other holy persons, who, on account of the great veneration in which they were held, were 'enshrined,' the shrines being usually placed on the east of the altar, though, when numerous, in any convenient part of the church. According to the sanctity of the deceased, so were his remains elevated above the ground. The bodies of unsainted men, of exemplary piety and mortification, were placed on a level with the surface of the earth; the coffins of saints of the second class rested on the flooring of the edifice; whilst the remains of martyrs were elevated. Effigies of saints, usually carved in wood, are placed above the shrine, to excite devotion. Monuments built up within the substance of walls are chiefly those of the founders of the chapel, or else of persons who had rebuilt that part of the edifice in which such mementos are found. Tablets or figures fixed *against* the walls, or let into the pillars of churches, did not come into use till after the Reformation. The actual burial-place of the founders of churches or chapels was the porch; for it was formerly the custom for worshippers, on entering the sacred edifice, to pray for the souls of its founders and benefactors. Thus Leofric, Earl of Mercia, and his celebrated countess, Godiva, were buried in the porch of the Abbey-church, Coventry, which they had founded. The heads of the religious houses were generally interred in their chapter-houses, or their cloisters; and rectors or vicars in the close vicinity of the altar, or in the chancel of the church to which they belonged. Lords of manors and patrons were often interred in the chancel, and sometimes within the rails.

The most obvious guides to the date of tombs are of course inscriptions. As, however, many of these exist without giving any information regarding the time at which they were cut, consisting simply of an epitaph, the following facts, taken in connexion with other evidences presented on the tomb itself, will lead to a near conjecture as to its age. During the first twelve centuries, churchyard epitaphs were all written in Latin; and the first inscribed funeral monuments are those bearing the names of Romanised Britons in Cornwall or Wales. These are written in capital letters; but a small hand was introduced about the seventh century. Lombardic capitals became general on tomb-stones in the thirteenth century, when epitaphs in the French language began to appear; which continued to be used till the middle of the fourteenth century, generally in German-text letters. From that period vernacular English and Roman print have been commonly employed for monumental inscriptions; though the clergy and learned have, as might be expected, always preferred the Latin.

* Archæological Journal, No. 3.

THE WISE THOUGHT.

[From Sketches of Irish Character, by Mrs S. C. Hall.]

She was sitting under the shadow of a fragrant lime tree that overhung a very ancient well; and, as the water fell into her pitcher, she was mingling with its music the tones of her 'Jew's harp,' the only instrument upon which Norah Clary had learned to play. She was a merry maiden of 'sweet seventeen;' a rustic belle, as well as a rustic beauty, and a 'terrible coquette;' and as she had what in Scotland they call a 'tocher,' in England a 'dowry,' and in Ireland a 'pretty penny o money,' it is scarcely necessary to state, in addition, that she had—a bachelor. Whether the tune—which was certainly given *in alto*—was or was not designed as a summons to her lover, I cannot take upon myself to say; but her lips and fingers had not been long occupied, before her lover was at her side.

'We may as well give it up, Morris Donovan,' she said somewhat abruptly; 'look, 'twould be as easy to twist the top off the great hill of Howth, as make father and mother agree about any one thing. They've been playing the rule of contrary these twenty years, and it's not likely they'll take a turn now.'

It's mighty hard, so it is,' replied handsome Morris, 'that married people can't draw together. Norah, darlint! that wouldn't be the way with us. It's *one* we'd be in heart and sowl, and an example of love and——'

'Folly,' interrupted the maiden, laughing. 'Morris, Morris, we've quarrelled a score o' times already; and a bit of a breeze makes life all the pleasanter. Shall I talk about the merry jig I danced with Phil Kennedy, or repeat what Mark Doolen said of me to Mary Grey? —eh, Morris?'

'Leave joking, now, Norry; God only knows how I love you,' he said, in a voice broken by emotion: 'I'm yer equal as far as money goes; and no young farmer in the country can tell a better stock to his share than mine; yet I don't pretend to deserve *you* for all that; only, I can't help saying that, when we love each other (now, don't go to contradict me, Norry, because ye've as good as owned it over and over again), and yer father agreeable, and all, to think that yer mother, just out of *divilment*, should be putting betwixt us for no reason upon earth, only to "spite" her lawful husband, is what sets me mad entirely, and shows her to be a good-for——'

'Stop, Mister Morris,' exclaimed Norah, laying her hand upon his mouth, so as effectually to prevent a sound escaping; 'it's *my* mother ye're talking of, and it would be ill-blood, as well as ill-bred, to hear a word said against an own parent. Is that the pattern of yer manners, sir; or did ye ever hear me turn my tongue against one belonging to you?'

'I ask yer pardon, my own Norah,' he replied meekly, as in duty bound; 'for the sake of the lamb, we spare the sheep. Why not? and I'm not going to gainsay, but yer mother——'

'The least said's the soonest mended!' again interrupted the impatient girl. 'Good even, Morris, and God bless you; they'll be after missing me within, and it's little mother thinks where I am.

'Norah, above all the girls at wake or pattern, I've been true to you. We have grown together, and since ye were the height of a rose-bush, ye have been dearer to me than anything else on earth. Do, Norah, for the sake of our young hearts' love, do think if there's no way to win yer mother over. If ye'd take me without her leave, sure it's nothing I'd care for the loss of thousands, let alone what ye've got. Dearest Norah, think; since you'll do nothing without her consent, do think—for once be serious, and don't laugh.

'I'm not going to laugh, Morris, replied the little maid at last, after a very long pause; 'I've got a wise thought in my head for once. His reverence, your uncle, you say, spoke to father—to speak to mother about it? I wonder (and he a priest) that he hadn't more sense! Sure, mother was the man; but I've got a wise thought. Good night, dear Morris; good night.'

The lass sprang lightly over the fence into her own garden, leaving her lover *perdu* at the other side, without possessing an idea of what her 'wise thought' might be. When she entered the kitchen, matters were going on as usual—her mother bustling in style, and as cross 'as a bag of weasels.'

'Jack Clary,' said she, addressing herself to her husband, who sat quietly in the chimney-corner smoking his *doodeen*, 'it's well ye've got a wife who knows what's what! God help me! I've little good of a husband, *barring* the name! Are ye sure Black Nell's in the stable?' The *sposo* nodded. 'The cow and the calf, had they fresh straw?' Another nod. 'Bad cess to ye, can't ye use yer tongue, and answer a civil question?' continued the lady.

'My dear,' he replied, 'sure one like you has enough talk for ten.'

This very just observation was, like most truths, so disagreeable, that a severe storm would have followed, had not Norah stepped up to her father and whispered in his ear, 'I don't think the stable door *is* fastened.' Mrs Clary caught the sound, and in no gentle terms ordered her husband to attend to the comforts of Black Nell. 'I'll go with father myself and see,' said Norah. 'That's like my own child, always careful,' observed the mother, as the father and daughter closed the door.

'Dear father,' began Norah, 'it isn't altogether about the stable I wanted ye, but—but—the priest said something to you to-day about—Morris Donovan.

'Yes, darling, and about yerself, my sweet Norry.'

'Did ye speak to mother about it?'

'No, darling, she's been so cross all day. Sure I go through a dale for peace and quietness. If I was like other men, and got drunk and wasted, it might be in rason; but—— As to Morris, she was very fond of the boy till she found that *I* liked him; and then, my jewel, she turned like sour milk all in a minute. I'm afraid even the priest 'll get no good of her.'

'Father, dear father,' said Norah, 'suppose ye were to say nothing about it, good or bad, and just pretend to take a sudden dislike to Morris, and let the priest speak to her himself, she'd come round.'

'Out of opposition to me, eh?'

'Yes.'

'And let her gain the day then?—that would be cowardly,' replied the farmer, drawing himself up. No, I wont.'

'Father, dear, you don't understand,' said the cunning lass; 'sure ye're for Morris; and when we are—that is, if—I mean—suppose—father, you know what I mean,' she continued, and luckily the twilight concealed her blushes—'if that took place, it's *you* that would have yer own way.'

'True for ye, Norry, my girl, true for ye; I never thought of that before!' and, pleased with the idea of 'tricking' his wife, the old man fairly capered for joy. 'But stay a while—stay; aisy, aisy!' he recommenced; 'how am I to manage? Sure the priest himself will be here to-morrow morning early; and he's out upon a station now, so there's no speaking with him; he's no way quick either; we'll be bothered entirely if he comes in on a *suddent*.'

'Leave it to me, dear father—leave it all to me!' exclaimed the animated girl; only pluck up a spirit, and whenever Morris's name is mentioned, abuse him—but not with all yer *heart*, father—only from the teeth out.'

When they re-entered, the fresh-boiled potatoes sent a warm curling steam to the very rafters of the lofty kitchen; they were poured out into a large wicker kish, and on the top of the pile rested a plate of coarse white salt; noggins of butter milk were filled on the dresser; and on a small round table a cloth was spread, and some delf plates awaited the more delicate repast which the farmer's wife was herself preparing.

'What's for supper, mother?' inquired Norah, as she drew her wheel towards her, and employed her fairy foot in whirling it round.

'Plaguy *snipeens*,' she replied: 'bits o' bog chickens, that you've always such a fancy for; Barney Leary kilt them himself.'

'So I did,' said Barney, grinning; 'and that stick wid a hook, of Morris Donovan's, is the finest thing in the world for knocking 'em down.'

'If Morris Donovan's stick touched them, they shan't come here,' said the farmer, striking the poor little table such a blow with his clenched hand, as made not only it, but Mrs Clary jump.

'And why so, pray?' asked the dame.

'Because nothing belonging to Morris, let alone Morris himself, shall come into this house,' replied Clary; 'he's not to my liking anyhow, and there's no good in his bothering here after what he wont get.'

'Excellent!' thought Norah.

'Lord save us!' ejaculated Mrs Clary, as she placed the grilled snipes on the table, 'what's come to the man?' Without heeding his resolution, she was proceeding to distribute the savoury 'birdeens,' when, to her astonishment, her usually tame husband threw the dish and its contents into the flames; the good woman absolutely stood for a moment aghast. The calm, however, was not of long duration. She soon rallied, and commenced hostilities: 'How dare you, ye spalpeen, throw away any of God's mate after that fashion, and I to the fore? What do you mane, I say?'

'I mane, that nothing touched by Morris Donovan shall come under this roof; and if I catch that girl of mine looking at the same side o' the road he walks on, I'll tear the eyes out of her head, and send her to a nunnery!'

'You will! And dare you to say that to my face, to a child o' mine! You will, will ye?—we'll see, my boy! I'll tell ye what, if *I* like, Morris Donovan *shall* come into this house, and, what's more, be master of this house; and that's what *you* never had the heart to be yet, ye poor ould snail!' So saying, Mrs Clary endeavoured to rescue from the fire the hissing remains of the burning snipes. Norah attempted to assist her mother; but Clary, lifting her up, somewhat after the fashion of an eagle raising a golden wren with its claw, fairly put her out of the kitchen. This was the signal for fresh hostilities. Mrs Clary stormed and stamped; and Mr Clary persisted in abusing not only Morris, but Morris's uncle, Father Donovan, until at last the farmer's helpmate *swore*, ay, and roundly too, by cross and saint, that, before the next sunset, Norah Clary should be Norah Donovan. I wish you could have seen Norry's eye, dancing with joy and exultation, as it peeped through the latch-hole; it sparkled more brightly than the richest diamond in our monarch's crown, for it was filled with hope and love

The next morning, before the sun was fully up, he was throwing his early beams over the glowing cheek of Norah Clary; for her 'wise thought' had prospered, and she was hastening to the trysting tree, where, 'by chance,' either morning or evening, she generally met Morris Donovan. I don't know how it is, but the moment the course of true love 'runs smooth,' it becomes very uninteresting, except to the parties concerned. So it is now left for me only to say, that the maiden, after a due and proper time consumed in teazing and tantalising her intended, told him her saucy plan, and its result. And the lover hastened, upon the wings of love (which I beg my readers clearly to understand are swifter and stronger in Ireland than in any other country), to apprise the priest of the arrangement, well knowing that his reverence loved his nephew, and niece that was to be (to say nothing of the wedding supper, and the profits arising therefrom), too well, not to aid their merry jest.

What bustle, what preparation, what feasting, what dancing, gave the country folk enough to talk about during the happy Christmas holidays, I cannot now describe. The bride of course looked lovely, and 'sheepish;' and the bridegroom—but bridegrooms are always uninteresting. One fact, however, is worth recording. When Father Donovan concluded the ceremony, before the bridal kiss had passed, Farmer Clary, without any reason that his wife could discover, most indecorously sprang up, seized a shilelah of stout oak, and, whirling it rapidly over his head, shouted, 'Carry me out! by the powers she's beat! we've won the day!—ould Ireland for ever! Success, boys!—she's beat, she's beat!' The priest, too, seemed vastly to enjoy this extemporaneous effusion, and even the bride laughed outright. Whether the good wife discovered the plot or not, I never heard; but of this I am certain, that the joyous Norah never had reason to repent her 'wise thought.'

LIBERATED CRIMINALS—WHAT SHOULD BE DONE WITH THEM?

A CORRESPONDENT of the Glasgow Herald newspaper calls public attention to the distressing fact, that short confinements of young criminals, even under a good system of prison discipline, are of little or no avail, and that, generally speaking, they do not stop in their career till transported. After mentioning six cases in particular, he proceeds:—'Here are the cases of six young persons (the number might as easily have been sixty), little more than children, every one of whom had undergone various terms of imprisonment prior to the committal of the last offence for which they have all been transported. In two cases, the ages are respectively thirteen and fourteen, and the periods of imprisonment that these children have undergone are twenty-four months and twenty-nine months, so that they could not be more than eleven years of age, if so much, when they were first convicted. In addition to other and shorter periods of confinement, each had been imprisoned for one term of eighteen months, and being very young, everything was in favour of their being so far improved by prison discipline, as to resort to some honest means of livelihood on their liberation; instead, however, of this being the case, we find them again pursuing a career of crime, and being at last transported, though but thirteen and fourteen years of age.

"'At first sight, one is almost inclined to draw the conclusion that prison discipline is of no avail, and that the hopes of the benevolent, who have laboured so long and so effectually in the amelioration of the condition of criminals, can never be realised. A little reflection, and an examination of the cases given above, will show that such an inference is not altogether warranted, and that the requisite opportunities have not yet been afforded for the full development of the results of the mild and humane treatment at present being pursued in our prisons. It will be observed that, in every case, shorter terms of imprisonment have been awarded before the criminals have been sentenced to such a lengthy period of confinement as would warrant hopes of reformation, and the necessary consequence of these repeated short imprisonments is so to habituate the prisoner to a life of confinement, as to deprive imprisonment of its chief power as a means of punishment; whilst the frequent liberation of a criminal unreformed, his reunion with his former associates, and his recurrence to a course of crime, all tend to deaden any trifling sense of morality that might have remained; make him more and more callous to remonstrance, and remove, almost beyond the bounds of probability, the hope of effectual reformation. Short imprisonments, as means of reformation, are worse than useless; they are positively injurious, as they deprive the unfortunate offender of any little chance he might have had of personal amelioration, whilst they cause him to be regarded with the same abhorrence as a longer term of confinement.

'Another, and perhaps not less powerful prevention of the good looked for from the present educational and moral treatment in prisons, is the necessity that liberated criminals are under of returning to their former places of residence, in search of employment, if willing to work, or in some other way to obtain a livelihood. So long as no means are provided for removing prisoners, after a long imprisonment, from the places where they are well known, where many of their former companions still reside, and where persons are always ready to re-entice them into a criminal course, and to profit by their turpitude, so long will it be next to hopeless to look for any extensive good from prison discipline, however excellent; and so long will our calendars of crime be swelled by the same persons again and again, and judges be called upon to perform their solemn duties upon criminals formerly sentenced by them. In fact, the necessity for some additional means of reformation is becoming every day more and more evident, and either more prisons must be built for the punishment of offenders, or other institutions must be erected for rendering their reformation permanent.

'Two measures appear to us as imperatively necessary in order that crime may be prevented, and criminals reformed. The precise means of accomplishing these measures, we, of course, leave to others better able to carry such plans into operation. We think that, instead of committing juvenile offenders to a prison for a short term of imprisonment, where their characters will be for ever blasted, and the hopes of reclamation almost destroyed, that magistrates should have the power, with the concurrence of the natural guardians, to send such young offenders to a house of refuge for a long term, say two or three years, where the knowledge of some useful occupation may be acquired without the taint of a prison attaching to the character; and, as many of these juvenile offenders become criminal through destitution, means should be employed to educate them, and train them in industrious pursuits, which could also be done in a house of refuge, taking care to classify the merely destitute and criminal inmates. The expense of such an institution should not devolve upon one locality, as the good would be general; nor do we think that, ultimately, the charge would be so great as all the cost of imprisonment and transportation to which most of these become subject at last. The other great measure that we think the present state of things calls for is, the adoption of some plan by which criminals, after a long term of imprisonment, who may have evinced a desire to change their former mode of life, may be preserved from the necessity of returning to the scene of their former crime and shame.'

In these humane and considerate observations we cordially concur. It should be the object of the magistracy to seize upon, retain, and thoroughly discipline the whole criminal population—the number of which is not great in each locality—and thus rid society of their presence. But this will not be enough. Society, we fear, will be baffled in every scheme to prevent the recurrence of crime in juvenile offenders, till it puts these offenders in the way of earning an honest livelihood on leaving the place of their confinement, whether that confinement be long or short, harsh or kind, good, bad, or indifferent. A plan having, to a certain extent, such an object in view, has been lately proposed by a benevolent gentleman in Birmingham. The scheme consists in each master engaging to receive back into his employment juvenile offenders who have undergone a term of correct prison discipline. We can only wish the measures which are adopted all the success they deserve.

TOBACCO MANUFACTORY OF SEVILLE.

Not the least among the curiosities of Seville is the tobacco manufactory. Tobacco is one of the royal monopolies, and it is manufactured in a palace. A very cursory glance at this singular establishment, will afford some idea of the great value of this monopoly. It is a noble and stately edifice, of a quadrangular form, 600 feet in length by 480 broad. It is surrounded by a moat, and approached by a drawbridge, like a regular fortification. Soldiers are continually on duty at the entrance and in the courts; all the workpeople are carefully searched every night on leaving the establishment, and no cloaks are permitted within its precincts—all precautions against the abstraction of the precious weed. It employs no fewer than 5000 hands. Of these, 3000 are women; almost all of whom are employed in twisting cigars. Of the 2000 men, a great proportion are similarly occupied; while a considerable number are employed in the manufacture of all the different articles and implements which are required in the establishment. Women are preferred for the manufacture of cigars, as lightness and delicacy of touch are of importance in this branch of the business. Two immense halls are set apart for the cigar-twisters, one for the men and the other for the women. The largest of these, in which 3000 women are seated, busily engaged in rolling up the fragrant leaf, each with a little basket of bread and fruit beside her for dinner, presents a very extraordinary spectacle. The work is performed with amazing rapidity, and a single individual will roll up from 500 to 600 cigars per day. The time of labour is from 7 o'clock A.M. to 4 P.M. One part of the process is sufficiently disgusting, but out of consideration for the lovers of cigars, we refrain from mentioning it. We saw the whole process of manufacturing snuff. The tobacco-leaves are first steeped in a decoction of Brazilian tobacco, plums, walnuts, lemon-peel, &c.; the heart-stalks are then removed, and the leaves twisted into ropes, and coiled up in tight packages. These are pressed by a machine, not unlike a large cheese-press, and are then stored up for six or eight months to ferment. Afterwards they are uncoiled, and chopped into small pieces by a very clumsy set of hammers worked by mules. When chopped sufficiently, the tobacco is conveyed to the mill and ground into snuff. The stems and heart-stalks are, I believe, manufactured into a coarser article. When the wind blows in a particular direction, it is said that this establishment may be nosed at a league distant. There are five royal tobacco manufactories in Spain, of which this at Seville is the largest. The quantity of cigars consumed by this nation of cigar-smokers is prodigious. Spaniards are decidedly the greatest smokers in Europe. All Spaniards smoke, and all smoke cigars. The pipe is comparatively unknown. The cigar gleams betwixt the lips of the haughty noble and the poor muleteer. Like death, it levels all distinctions; all are alike subjected to its sway. It overpowers the odour of garlic in the poor man's hut, and mingles with the rich perfumes of the halls of the wealthy. Europe is indebted to America for tobacco and the potato, but tobacco has far outstripped her compatriot; and while the humble and nutritious root which brings plenty to the poor man's home is only gradually, and by dint of much pains and patronage, forcing its way in the world, the nauseous and unwholesome weed is chewed, and smoked, and snuffed in almost every part of the known world, and that too in defiance of much opposition. The king of England wrote a book against it; the pope issued his bull against it; the magistrates of Transylvania punished its culture with confiscation; the king of Persia forbade it under pain of death; and the grand-duke of Moscow, under penalty of the loss of the nose! The last appears the most appropriate punishment. The progress of tobacco is, in fact, a singular phenomenon in the history of the human race; and proves how mankind will prefer the most disgusting and nauseous drug, provided it exert a narcotic or stimulating influence over the nerves, to the most nutritious and wholesome food, though as palatable as valuable. The history of tobacco, opium, and ardent spirits, is not very flattering to the dignity of human nature.—*Journal of a Clergyman, by the Rev. W. Robertson of Edinburgh.*

THE FORGET-ME-NOT.

[FROM THE GERMAN OF MÜCHLER.]

SILENT o'er the fountain gleaming,
In the silvery moonlight hour,
Bright and beauteous in its seeming,
Waves a friendly fragile flower.
Never let it be mistaken;
Blue—as heaven's own blessed eye,
By no envious clouds o'ertaken
When it laughs through all the sky.
Flower of heaven's divinest hue!
Symbol of affection true!
Whisper to the poor heart-broken
Consolation—heaven-spoken!

Loved one!—like the star of morning
Are thine eyes—so mild and fair—
Innocence with light adorning
Their pure radiance everywhere!
Maiden mine! attend my lay:
Be this flow'ret ne'er forgot—
Whispering through the far-away,
'Oh, forget—forget me not.'

Duty stern may bid us sever,
Tears bedew our parted lot;
Yet these flowers shall murmur ever,
'Ah, forget—forget me not!'

List, beloved! what it sayeth;
List each blossom's whispered sound!
As its lowly head it layeth
On the dew-besprinkled ground.
Bethink! each dewdrop is a tear,
That brims its dark blue eyes;
Remember—when you wander near—
'Forget me not' it sighs!

[The exquisite German legend of the origin of this humble flower's touching name, is known to many—perhaps not to all. A lover and his mistress were walking on the steep banks of a rapid river: the lady was struck by the beauty of a little flower, new to her, and growing on the sharpest declivity of the almost perpendicular bank. The veronica, according to some, the mouse-ear, as others say, was the plant, to obtain which for his beloved, the young man immediately sprang down the cliff to secure the treasure. At the moment when the prize was won, the earth gave way under the lover's tread, who, in the act of falling, threw the flower towards his mistress, uttering the words, 'Forget me not,' and was precipitated into the foaming current, which bore him many miles from the spot of the catastrophe. The body being found, was followed and borne to the grave by his affianced bride and her companions, arrayed in white, and scattering flowers of the 'forget-me-not' along their mournful path. This flower is a favourite subject among German poets.]—E. L.

THE EMPEROR OF RUSSIA'S FAMILY.

The lovely family of the Emperor Nicholas, consisting of four sons and three daughters, were brought up from the cradle by English nurses and governesses, under the superintendence of an old Scotchwoman, who was under-nurse to the present emperor in his infancy. This individual held the rank of a general officer (for everything in Russia is measured by a military scale), and had been decorated with the order of St Andrew, ennobled, and enriched. This woman, nevertheless, came as a servant girl to Russia, some five-and-fifty years ago, with a Scotch trader's family, who turned her adrift in St Petersburg. A lucky chance procured her the situation of under-nursery-maid in the Emperor Paul's family, when she was placed about the person of the present emperor, to teach him to speak English! His attachment to her was so great, that when he married, he placed her at the head of his nursery establishment, where she has honourably gone through all the military gradations of rank to her present one of general.—*Newspaper paragraph.*

Column for Young People.

You are fond of hearing your mamma tell stories; I will tell you a little story of two chickens that may perhaps amuse you. I live with my family in a large house in the country, at a good distance from any market-town, and therefore cannot on all occasions send out to buy things, as you are accustomed to see your parents do. Sometimes we are supplied with chickens by women who go about selling them, and as I like to see poor people honestly employed, I generally buy a chicken or two from them, even when we are not in immediate need of them.

Some time ago, a little girl neatly dressed came to the hall-door with a basket on her arm, in which were two chickens she wanted to sell. Her mother, she said, was in poor circumstances; she wanted money to buy some things that she stood in need of, and she had no way of procuring the money but by selling these chickens. I desired her to go round to the kitchen, and that, if the cook were pleased with them, they should be purchased. The poor girl replied that she had already been there, but that the cook had sent her away. On inquiry, I found that the chickens were considered not at all fit for the larder; being so very thin, that they were not worth the trouble of fattening. I suggested that they might be put in a coop, but the cook said they would die of cold; and when I hinted that they might run about the yard, she declared that the dogs would chase them and kill them. The cook had clearly set her face against having anything to do with the unfortunate chickens.

The poor chicken merchant was not altogether disconcerted with these resolutions. She eloquently pleaded the merits of the animals, and as a last resource, tried to enlist the children in her cause. Here she had no such critical judge to deal with as the cook. They were delighted with the appearance of the creatures. 'Oh, mamma!' cried Emily, 'there is one of the most beautiful chickens ever was seen: see what a fine tuft one of them has got. You know you promised me a hen, and I will keep this for one, to lay eggs, if you will buy it for me. Oh, do mamma; pray do.' There was no resisting this appeal, particularly as I had the best of the bargain; so I looked at the little despised fowls, and saw that one of them was of the golden pheasant breed, with a crown of feathers on its head nearly as large as its body. The other was of the common kind of poultry, and not a very handsome specimen either; but it was settled that the ugly one was to be bought to keep the handsome one company, as we had no other chickens at that season of the year. So the bargain was made, the girl paid, and the chickens changed mistresses, apparently to the satisfaction of all parties; and the cook consented to keep Miss Emily's chickens in the kitchen, at least for a few days, to see how they behaved themselves; for I assure you there is a great difference in the dispositions of chickens as well as children. They proved to be very well-conducted for their age, were very tame, and never flew up on the dresser to break the jugs and plates; so the cook placed a little stick near the fire for them to roost on; and they picked about the kitchen all day, and in the evening the cook put a chair under the perch, and they jumped up, first on the seat, then on the back of the chair, and then made a fly to their roost, where they slept quietly side by side all night; and in the morning, when daylight came, they flew down, and just went on as the day before. They were indeed very good chickens, and soon won the regard not only of Emily, who was predisposed to love them, but of the cross old cook, with whom they became most particular favourites and companions. In short, in a few weeks you would not have known them to be the poor miserable little orphans that they were before Emily adopted, and the cook nursed them; and well they showed the cook's care, for they were fat and well-feathered, and comfortable to look upon.

I have now told you how fond Emily and the cook were of them, and the ugly one was just liked as much as the pretty one, although they called one 'the Beauty,' and the other 'the Waiting-maid,' for distinction. But now I have to tell you of the affection they had for each other; they, it appeared by the following account, made no distinction of rank or beauty either:—

One evening Beauty was on the perch alone; and so, after waiting for some time to see if the Waiting-maid would come in herself—for by this time they had extended their excursions to wherever they chose—the cook commenced looking for her, and, after trying the yard and out-houses in vain, she inquired of every one if she had been seen lately by them. The only tidings she could obtain were, that the men who were thrashing had seen them both that day in the barn. The cook was in great tribulation, and so was Emily, as they both came to the conclusion that the dogs had chased and killed her; but just as the cook was putting the kitchen in order for the night, she discovered the poor little Waiting-maid sitting or rather lying in a corner, under the large table, quite unable to move. We supposed that she had been touched by a flail when in the barn, for she had no limbs broken, but she had lost the use of them, as if her back had got a hurt: we never could find out how she had contrived to come into the house afterwards. She was taken up tenderly, and placed on the roost. The next morning Beauty went forth alone. The Waiting-maid was quite helpless, and had to be waited on herself. Although the cook's friendship was difficult to obtain, yet, when once gained, it was very sincere, and to be depended on, which she proved in this instance; for she removed the invalid to her own room, which was boarded, and put her on the floor, with some hay to lie on, where she would not be annoyed by dogs, cats, or poultry, but could be perfectly quiet, perhaps too quiet; for, indeed, loneliness was all that she had any reason to complain of. But now a strange sight commenced; for Beauty—contrary to the usual customs of birds and beasts in general, which dislike those of their species who are sick or wounded, and often kill them—every morning, after she had taken a walk in the yard, came in, and making her way to the cook's room, sat down beside the Waiting-maid, where she remained all day; so that, one day happening to see them, I asked if Beauty was lame too; for she had her feet tucked up under her like the other, and sat there all day without stirring, until evening again, when she went out to air herself; and the moment the kitchen-door was opened for her, she ran to her sick companion, and sat beside her all night too, forsaking the perch altogether. For six weeks she tended her with the greatest diligence and care, invariably regular, and untired by the duty she had imposed upon herself. The good effects of sympathy and friendship soon appeared. The Waiting-maid began to look more cheerful and to pick a little after Beauty shared her sorrows; and she had the satisfaction in a short time to see her take a step or two along with her, and after that to go a little way into the yard with her. Invigorated by the fresh air, and a return to her natural habits, the Waiting-maid was in a week or two able to run about pretty smartly, and finally she had the power to fly up to her old perch in the kitchen. In these movements Beauty always attended the Waiting-maid as if delighted to see her well and happy. Now, they go on together as if no accident had occurred, reposing every night on the perch, to the great delight of Emily and the cook; and I suppose when Beauty lays her first egg, there will be as much rejoicing over her as there was over Barney Brady's goose.

Now, from the conduct of these little chickens two lessons may be learned. In the first place, their good conduct and civil deportment procured them kind friends, who aided them in their necessities. For it is not when we are in need of friends that we must *make* them; no, that is the time to prove the sincerity of their friendship. The second lesson is to be taken from the example of little Beauty, who was not only so affectionate and kind a nurse to her companion, but also never got tired of her occupation all the time that it was necessary. Now, I know that young people are not fond of being with those who are sick, and soon grow tired of attending them, and think it very wearisome to stay in a sick room. I would wish to know, when it is their turn to be sick, how they would like all their playfellows to go from them, and never come near or stop with them. They should remember to do as they would wish to be done by; and not only for a selfish reason would I wish them to consider their conduct, but, as their heavenly Father is merciful and good to them every day and every hour, they should also try to do all in their power to relieve the wants, and alleviate the sufferings of their fellow-creatures; and if they are neglecting their duty in this respect, I would admonish them to remember Beauty.

⁎ Complete sets of the *Journal*, *First Series*, in twelve volumes, and also odd numbers to complete sets, may be had from the publishers or their agents. A Stamped Edition issued for transmission, post free, price Twopence halfpenny.

Printed by William Bradbury, of No. 6, York Place, and Frederick Mullett Evans, of No. 7, Church Row, both of Stoke Newington, in the county of Middlesex, printers, at their office, Lombard Street, in the precinct of Whitefriars, and city of London; and Published (with permission of the Proprietors, W. and R. CHAMBERS,) by WILLIAM SOMERVILLE ORR, Publisher, of 2, Amen Corner, at No. 2, AMEN CORNER, both in the parish of Christ church, and in the city of London.—Saturday, May 10, 1845.

CONDUCTED BY WILLIAM AND ROBERT CHAMBERS, EDITORS OF 'CHAMBERS'S INFORMATION FOR THE PEOPLE,' 'CHAMBERS'S EDUCATIONAL COURSE,' &c.

No. 72. NEW SERIES. SATURDAY, MAY 17, 1845. PRICE 1½d.

A VISIT TO BIRKENHEAD.

A TIME of vast mechanical means like the present has its sublimities as well as the earlier ages of the world. A Liverpool millionaire said one day not long ago to a meeting of Perthshire proprietors, 'Unless you do so and so, *I'll take my railway* by the east of Fife.' Consider what a railway is, and say if Wolsey's 'Ego et Rex' was a grander thing for a subject to speak than this? About the same time, another great railway hero—a man who a few years since was a shopkeeper in York—was commissioned by a set of brother directors to accomplish a particular object for the general interest, and *two millions* were placed at his disposal for the purpose. 'Take that sum,' they told him, 'and make the best of it.' Alexander's passage of the Granicus with a handful of hardy Greeks was no doubt a fine thing; but there is as much of the grand, in its own way, in what many English merchants are doing every day. Talk of utility as having overpowered the poetical with us! On the contrary, the world has never seen or known a poetry like what a right spirit can trace in hundreds of the *facts* by which we are now surrounded.

One of the facts of this kind which have most deeply impressed us lately, is the sudden rise of a new city in England. A city we are accustomed to consider as the growth of centuries, for cities have heretofore always taken centuries to build. But now, such is the hugeness of the power created by the industry and wealth of this country, there is at least one city which will undoubtedly have risen within the brief space between the boyhood and manhood of its first inhabitants. We allude to Birkenhead on the Mersey, near Liverpool. By far the greater number of our readers will have never heard of this place even by name; yet it is one of the greatest wonders of the age, and indeed one of those by which the character of our age is most strongly expressed. We visited it lately, in order to ascertain how far the reports about it were true, and we now propose conveying to the public some idea of what we saw and learned on the spot.

The Mersey at Liverpool is a river or estuary, two-thirds of a mile in breadth. The ground opposite to the great emporium of commerce was, till a recent period, either altogether waste, or occupied by farms and hamlets. One of the latter, named Birkenhead, had risen in connexion with a priory of the eleventh century. Steam navigation at length facilitating the intercourse between the two sides of the river, the sloping banks opposite Liverpool had become crested by a few ranges of neat mansions for the merchants of that town, and thus things went on till four or five years ago. A few enterprising persons then became aware of the suitableness of a creek in the river at Birkenhead for commercial purposes, and proposed converting it into a set of docks supplementary to the mighty range covering six square miles in connexion with their own town. The corporation of Liverpool had bought the land surrounding Wallasy Pool, as this creek was called, for L.180,000, and now they were not unwilling to transfer their purchase. It was bought, and parliament applied to for permission to lay out L.400,000 in the formation of the proposed docks. This requisite being obtained, the Birkenhead docks were commenced last year, and are now in rapid progress. At the same time, a city capable of containing a hundred thousand inhabitants is rising close by, which our posterity will yet know as familiarly as we now do Liverpool itself, or any of the other large towns of Britain.

Our visit to Birkenhead took place on a sunny April morning of the present year. Landing from one of the steamers which cross the Mersey every half hour, we walked into this City of the Future with expectations which the reality by no means disappointed. When we had passed a mere frontier of short streets overlooking the river, we were at once launched into a mile's breadth of street-building, where unfinished houses, unmade roadways, brickfields, scaffoldings, heaps of mortar, loaded wains, and troops of busy workmen met the eye in every direction. It was like the scene which Virgil describes when he introduces Æneas and his companion into Carthage, but like nothing which had ever met our eyes in real life. Where houses were occupied, or shops opened, they had all a peculiarly fresh sparkling look, like furniture in an upholsterer's wareroom as compared with that in private dwellings. The very children playing or walking in the streets looked old beside them. In some streets, traceable as such by buildings posted here and there along a line, the substratum of the roadway was only in the course of being formed; in others, the process had advanced as far as the superficies of macadamised trap; but hardly anywhere was a beaten and smoothed road to be seen. You entered a piece of street with a particular name, and half an hour after, walking in quite a different part of the country—for country it still is in some measure—you fall into another piece of street bearing the same name. You wonder at first; but presently it appears that they are various extremities of one street; only there is a wide wilderness of brickfields between. You ask for the public buildings, and find they are all in the masons' hands, excepting a few churches. There is to be a capital town-hall—a capital market—a capital everything. We looked into the market, and found the walls and ceiling formed; a vast hall (430 by 131 feet), supported by light iron pillars, and lighted from the roof. The business going on while we were there was the laying down of the gas-pipes. Near by is the grand square of Birkenhead—a subject of pride with the inhabitants, as it happens there is nothing approaching it in spaciousness or elegance in Liverpool. But, probably from being spoilt by the beauties of our own fair city, we thought Hamilton Square no more than passable; nor did the interior of the houses make up, in elegance or comfort, for a somewhat poor kind of architecture. It is in Edinburgh alone that the mass of the middle ranks live in palaces.

Making a detour towards the east, we found a beautiful slope rising above the nascent town, and occupied by a fine range of villas scattered throughout its space. This is Clifton Park, and it comprehends an arrangement which we have often thought might be followed with advantage in every large town in the empire. The principle is, that the place is an ornamented piece of ground, which both generally and in its parts has the usual recommendations of pleasure-ground, while houses are only scattered over it, each having the command of a certain space without interfering with general arrangements for walks, or with the general effect from a distance. Thus each family may be said to have the advantage of neighbourhood combined with the *délices* of a fine rural situation.

After a considerable walk, we reached a part of the environs which is calculated to make a greater impression than perhaps any other thing connected with the town. The misfortune of all ordinary large towns is, that they have to struggle with the difficulties imposed by former centuries—narrow streets, the nuisance of cemeteries, the want of right sewerage and of places of recreation for the inhabitants. Here Birkenhead, being a town building from the foundation in an enlightened age, has a great advantage. Its sewerage may be perfect if the managers choose; and it will be their eternal disgrace if this essential point be overlooked or inadequately attended to. They need have no lanes, no cul-de-sacs, no courts, none of the architectural curses of Liverpool. Finally, they have it in their power to reserve part of the ground at their command for recreation. We feel the greatest pleasure in stating that, following the improved sanitary views of the last few years, they have made it one of their first cares to establish a 'park'—meaning thereby an open piece of ornamented ground—for the future inhabitants of their city. We found it in the course of being formed under the direction of the well-known Mr Paxton of Chatsworth; and, to judge from what we saw of it in rather unfavourable circumstances, it promises to be a fine place. The space to be operated upon was a hundred and eighty acres. Sixty being set apart for building purposes, there remain a hundred and twenty to be laid out in shrubberies, walks, and drives, for the free enjoyment of the public for ever. Remembering what has been made of the eleven acres given by Mr Strutt to the people of Derby, we cannot doubt that a quantity eleven times greater will fulfil the objects of the managers most amply. Already the required undulations of the ground have been effected; vast quantities of trees and flowers have been planted; two sheets of water are formed; several lodges are built; and though the act for purchasing the ground dates only from September last, we may be said to have the first sketch of a park presented to our eyes. The whole is expected to be complete and at the service of the public next September. We were delighted with what we saw here; but the satisfaction of the eye is nothing in such a case; the point really to be rejoiced in is that the ideas of men are now so far advanced with respect to the essentials of public health and conveniency, that, in preparing a new city, a park for the use of the inhabitants should have been among the first things legislated for. To the same advancement is it to be attributed that the ground set apart for burying the future inhabitants of Birkenhead is at a spot called Flaybrick Hill, which also will be out of town. Here excavations are in progress for the construction of sepulchral vaults and catacombs, the removed stone being used—for the managers, like Mrs Gilpin, are of a frugal mind—in the formation of the docks. The slaughter-houses are also out of town—a suite of buildings properly enclosed, and supplied with every requisite for the preservation of cleanliness and order. Birkenhead will teach many useful lessons to older towns, and this is one of them.

We came at last to the docks, which are formed by the simple process of sluicing the water of the Wallasy Pool, and building quays along its banks. The inner dock will be of 150 acres in extent, with 19 feet depth of water; and there will be an outer or low-water harbour of 37 acres, with quay space of 300 feet in breadth (reclaimed from the sea) on each side. A range of warehouses will front the wet dock on the side towards the town. Besides these accommodations for shipping, there will be a small dock of 3 acres, and a tidal basin of 16, with beaching ground for coasting vessels. There will thus be provided, on the Cheshire side of the Mersey, a range of docks containing an area of 206 acres. Such a work, undertaken and produced at once, may safely be pronounced without parallel in this country. Around the site of the proposed docks are already various important works. There is a large establishment belonging to Mr Laird for the construction of iron vessels, and at which many have been built. There are also copper mills, a varnish manufactory, an iron foundry, gun works, a patent slip for repairing vessels, and a boiler yard.

We found three ferries between various points of Liverpool and Birkenhead, the fare twopence. It is not unworthy of notice that the receipts are higher at that small rate than when they were double the sum. It is designed ere long to have steamers plying between the two shores every five minutes, which will certainly be making a near approach to the conveniency of a bridge. From one landing-place on the Birkenhead side, a railway starts for Chester, where it is continued by another line to a point on the Grand Junction, and thus brought in union with the principal ways of this kind in the kingdom. The mails from London to Dublin are conveyed by this route, and it is commonly used by parties passing between the Irish and English capitals. The steamer passes from Kingston near Dublin to Birkenhead in about ten hours, and from thence a mail-train will convey passengers to London in about the same time. It is also contemplated to have a railway to Manchester, a ship canal to connect the Mersey and the Dee, and various other great works.

It may be inquired how far Birkenhead is a built and inhabited town, and the answer is, that the actual population a few months ago was found to be about fifteen thousand. In 1823, it was a few hundreds, and probably in ten years it will be approaching a hundred thousand. Land, which a few years ago hardly possessed a value, is now selling at L.6 a square yard, and by good speculations in that line, large fortunes have been acquired. Amongst the last particulars we have heard of the place is, that houses for the working-classes are in preparation on such a scale, that the company will divide eight per cent. on their outlay, although giving a dwelling of three apartments with gas and water at L.5 of rent. We most earnestly trust they will see that these houses are arranged outwardly and inwardly in the manner most conducive to health. We now take leave of the subject, with best wishes for the success of Birkenhead. Of the probabilities of that success we say not a word; but we feel assured that, if the contemplated works shall be duly completed, the banks of the Mersey will present the grandest monument which the nineteenth century has erected to the genius of Commerce and Peace.

THE MISHAPS OF A YOUNG GERMAN.

A TRUE STORY.

In the year 1790, Alexander Facqz, Viscount de Honig, a young and enthusiastic German, determined to see the world, and acquire in the course of a few months a quantity of knowledge sufficient to last him the rest of his life. Leaving his mother's house in Suabia, he repaired first to Paris, for the purpose of getting some insight, if possible, into the French Revolution, which was then going on; but chancing shortly after his arrival to meet with a commercial friend who was on the point of setting out for London, he resolved to accompany him to that capital. The great metropolis afforded him occupation for some time; but at length beginning to think that he had exhausted London, and having heard much about the sister island, he resolved to pay a visit to Dublin. An essential preliminary to his trip was the receipt of a remittance from his mother. This having been written for and procured, the month of March 1791 found him walking idly up and down the streets of Dublin, looking at Irish sights with German eyes, and forming from all that he saw the most German conclusions. Somehow or other, however, his money wore away much faster than he wished; and he soon found it necessary to send another letter to his mother, requesting the too-indulgent lady to forward him a second remittance.

Living in lodgings in expectation of money is at no time a very agreeable predicament, whether in Dublin or anywhere else; and in the year 1791, the transmission of letters, and especially of money letters, between this country and the continent, was attended with even greater risk than in these days of more correct management. Our young German waited and waited on, but the money never came. He told his landlord the true state of the case, and for a while his gentlemanly manners, his young honest-like face, and his interesting foreign accent, operated in his favour. The landlady would not allow the landlord to use him ill. Still, landladies are but human beings, and there are limits to the power of a lodger's face in attesting his promises of payment; and at length, after the bill had run up to a considerable amount, the landlady went over to her husband's way of thinking, and our young German was arrested for the debt, and thrown into prison.

'A situation more dreadful can scarcely be conceived,' a novelist would say; and, without going quite so far as this, we can well believe that, for a young German of birth and education, who had left his country to acquire a knowledge of men and manners, thus to find himself locked up in a Dublin prison, was somewhat unexpected, and certainly anything but pleasant.

A Dublin prison of the old school was quite a different thing from its modern representative. There was no obligation by law to support prisoners for debt; and there were cases in which such prisoners were supposed to have died of want, and many more in which deaths from want would have occurred, but for the charity of fellow-prisoners. Our hero's only hope lay in the expected arrival of his mother's long-delayed remittance. Alas! the remittance had miscarried. The viscount had made no secret of his expectation of a money letter; and when a bill drawn on a house in Dublin was addressed to him from London, some evil-disposed persons had managed to get possession of it, and feloniously converted it into cash. It was not till a month after, that the viscount received another letter, apprising him that the money had been sent. Why he did not pursue the parties for forgery, or at least compel the payers of the bill to do so, and by that means recover the amount, is not stated. The circumstance of being a stranger, and poor, may perhaps explain what is otherwise so unaccountable. Be this as it may, this unfortunate, and, as we must pronounce him, heedless young man, would have perished for want in prison but for the compassion of his fellow-captives. His case was so peculiar, and his appearance so unusually interesting, that a prepossession was soon established in his favour, so strong, indeed, that they not only supported him by their charity in prison, but even set on foot a subscription for the purpose of discharging his small debt, and setting him at liberty. But here was another difficulty. What was he to do when he got out of prison, without any money in his pocket? Any ordinary person, with hands accustomed to work and a mind used to buffet the world, would have found no difficulty whatever; would have launched out of prison and exerted himself nobly; but to our languid and lugubrious German, with his white hands and inactive disposition, there seemed no resource whatever. He thought himself positively the most wretched man on the face of the earth; and when he looked out at the prison window, it was with the sickly feeling of a man who, never having had to rely upon himself, could not conceive how locomotion was possible in this world without money, nor how money was procurable in any other way than by asking one's mother for it. Accordingly, a letter was despatched to his mother acquainting her with his situation, and begging an immediate remittance; and in the meantime he remained in prison, and shared the bounty of Mr Fawcet and Monsieur Lafontaine, two debt prisoners who had taken a particular fancy to the unhappy foreigner.

Sunk pretty nearly to the verge of despair, in an evil hour temptation triumphed over the integrity of the weakly young man. About this time considerable sums were raised in England and Ireland by benevolent persons for the benefit of the French refugees; and it was suggested to Facqz, that, by representing himself to be a French refugee, he might obtain a sum of money sufficient to maintain him for some time, and so put an end to all his difficulties. It would be only a sort of loan; he could repay the money afterwards. So spake necessity; and our young hero had too yielding a constitution to resist the temptation. Having procured the money under the false pretence of being a French refugee, he prepared to leave prison and go in search of a lodging. It so happened that two men, who had been in the habit of visiting a friend in the Marshalsea, and who had become acquainted with Facqz, offered to accompany him, and find out a cheap and suitable lodging. Their names were James Jones and Thomas Neville. Seeking a lodging is a sore trial to anybody: greater men than our hero have sunk under it. It is an art only to be acquired by long practice; and it was with no small delight that Facqz accepted the kind offer of his two acquaintances to put him on the right track. Away went the three friends to seek lodgings. This street and that street were tried; this knocker knocked, and that bell rung; here a little slattern girl came to the door with a thin squeaking voice, there a huge dirty landlady; still the right place was not found. At last they came to a house with Mr James P—— on the door-plate. Here surely was a respectable house; quite the thing that was wanted.

Mr Jones, who seems to have been the obliging spokesman of the party, said they would be obliged to Mrs P—— for a sight of the rooms up stairs. By all means, said the lady; and so Jones and Facqz proceeded on their exploratory tour of the apartments. Neville declined to ascend. He was very much fatigued, and begged to be allowed to take a seat in the parlour till his friends came down. This arrangement being quite agreeable to all parties, Mr Neville seated himself in the room below, and before the return of

Jones and Facqz, he contrived with little difficulty to appropriate a watch which hung over the mantelpiece. Something was wrong about the lodgings, and the party left the house; but hardly had they proceeded twenty paces when an alarm was raised. They were pursued and captured, and the watch found on Neville's person. On the 5th of October 1791, they were tried before the recorder and magistrates of Dublin. Facqz, of course, protested his innocence, and no doubt he was innocent. But he had been in the company of two notorious swindlers, and to all appearance a coadjutor in the crime; and to crown his misfortune, it was now shown that he was a German, and not a Frenchman, as he had formerly declared himself to be. No man, it was argued, could be an honest man, who had committed such a deliberate falsehood. Influenced by these considerations, the jury included Facqz in the guilt of watch-stealing, and along with his two acquaintances he received sentence of transportation.

Behold our poor languid hero again in prison, and this time not for debt, but for felony, and waiting transportation. The mere imprisonment in such a place would have been punishment enough for the greatest crimes. There was then no established system of prison discipline; the prisoners were left to the tender mercies of the turnkeys; and those who could not bribe them, suffered the harshest treatment. Facqz had no money, and he became one of the victims.

In these dark days Mr Samuel Rosborough was the Howard of Ireland. The poor forgotten prisoners were his peculiar charge. For twenty years he had been accustomed to visit the prisons, rendering assistance to those who had no other friend. Facqz had heard of his name and character; and in the depths of his despair sent him the following letter:—

'Sir—From the many acts of generous kindness done by you to the unfortunate in this prison, I am induced to hope you will suffer my present melancholy tale to be heard by you, and interfere in my behalf.

'I am under the dreadful sentence of transportation, charged with committing a crime at which my nature revolts. To enter, however, upon any justification of myself at this time is not my object. From the 7th of this month, I have been lying in a cell, loaded with irons, which have been put on by Mr Walsh the turnkey, when he knew I had no money to give him. Well knowing you will not suffer me to remain any longer in this loathsome place without your merciful interference, I shall look with anxious expectation for you.

'During these five last days, my mind has enjoyed a calm by attentively listening to the prayers of an unfortunate man in the next cell, who, I hear, is shortly to suffer death. Oh that I were so near that period, for then I would be released from my sufferings!

'Excuse this freedom, and permit me, in addition to my fervent prayers for your welfare, to subscribe myself—Your most obedient and devoted servant,

October 26, 1791. Alexr. Facqz.'

Mr Rosborough immediately visited him; and his interference had the effect of procuring him better treatment. The poor prisoner began to hope that the same benevolence might be of use in procuring his release; and accordingly he sent many letters to Mr Rosborough, giving an account of himself, his previous mishaps in Dublin, and the manner in which he had been brought into his present situation. A person possessed of more sense would have told his story in a plain, straightforward, matter-of-fact way; but our young German's letters to Mr Rosborough were so fanciful, so sentimental, and so full of ohs, and ahs, and adjectives, that the good philanthropist read them with considerable distrust. At length, however, owing to the considerate interposition of Mr Lafontaine, who had now left prison, and who had procured some knowledge of the viscount's family, Mr Rosborough was induced to listen to what Facqz told him, and to attribute the sentimentalism of his letters to their right cause—namely, to his being a German, and one of weak character. 'From me,' wrote Facqz to him, 'you dissipate every gloom, and cheer and vivify my whole soul. May you long live to enjoy that ennobling virtue which alone gives dignity. May every instance of benevolence and humanity shown by you in this and every other place, be blessed with success; and when the hoar-frost of winter's age shall besprinkle your head, and the divine lamp of life yield its last gleam, may you enjoy that felicity which is the portion allotted by him who said "I was in prison and ye visited me." I have requested Mr Lafontaine to call on you. He will tell you who I am. If not redeemed from this horrible place, I shall perish. Mine eyes can scarce see what I have written; they are sore with weeping; my head aches for want of rest, and mine ears are tormented with hearing blasphemies. Oh that I had never been born, then should I be a stranger to such a place as this!'

Moved by these wailings, and by his own innate benevolence, Mr Rosborough did make some interest with the recorder in the young man's behalf. But the sad fact of his having passed himself off as a French refugee, and obtained money on false pretences, again rose up against him; for the recorder himself had been connected with the management of the refugee fund. Nothing could be done for such a person, and again Mr Rosborough gave him up. Oh that terrible falsehood!

Meanwhile, poor Facqz had been thinking of another way of effecting his escape. He had heard that money could do it, and he had written pressingly to Germany for money. Many wonderful escapes had been effected from the prison about this time, the mode of which was not discovered till afterwards. The principal agent in these escapes was the head-turnkey's wife. She had offered to give Facqz his liberty for forty pounds, and the following was to be the plan adopted. She was to administer to him draughts of tobacco water, and other narcotics, report him ill, and have him transferred to the hospital, where he was to grow gradually worse and die. When he was fairly dead, he was to be let out of prison; a corpse having been procured to be laid in his bed, for the satisfaction of the doctor. The plan may appear doubtful to our readers; but it had succeeded before, and Facqz hoped it might succeed in his case. But the forty pounds were still wanting; and the beginning of the year 1792 found him still languishing in jail.

Letter after letter he sent to Mr Rosborough, beseeching him to reconsider his case; and at length the good gentleman began to get a notion of the real simplicity of our hero's character. He interested himself again in his behalf, and represented the affair as well as he could to the recorder. Here was a young German, he said, of good family, who had got into a scrape, whether owing to folly or criminality, he would not say; but would it not serve all the purposes of banishment to send him home to his friends in Germany, instead of incurring the expense of sending him to Botany Bay? The recorder was induced to use his influence with the lord-lieutenant, and the consequence was, that Facqz received a free pardon. The rapture of Facqz on this announcement being made to him, threw him into a fever, from which he did not recover without difficulty. On his recovery, he pled his majesty's pardon in court, and was set at liberty, as will be seen from the following copy of a certificate, the original of which may be inspected by any one who chooses to consult the records of the clerk of the crown's office in Dublin:—'*Certificate*—"At an adjournment of sessions on the 31st of May 1792, Alexander Facqz de Honig pleaded his majesty's free pardon, which was allowed by the court, and he was thereupon discharged."—Extracted from the crown books—Allen and Greene, Clerks of the Peace.'

Our hero's mishaps were not yet over. Taking leave of his kind friends, Mr Rosborough and Mr Lafontaine, he proceeded to Liverpool with a little money in his pocket, supplied by them. 'I had scarcely landed in Liverpool,' he says in the account which he afterwards wrote to Mr Rosborough of his adventures, 'when I narrowly escaped breaking my leg in consequence of the absence of enclosures for the cellars in that filthy town. Into one of these holes I fell, and stripped thereby the bone of my leg completely of the flesh from the ankle to the knee.' Detained in Liverpool for a long time by this injury, his money was again all expended; and we hardly know by what means he arrived at York, whither it appears he had gone, with a view of proceeding thence to Hull, where he hoped to procure a passage to Hamburg. 'I arrived at York,' he says, 'about five o'clock in the evening, with fourpence in my pocket, my shoes worn to pieces, the big toe of my right foot projecting out.' Strolling into York minster, he attracted the notice of a benevolent and venerable clergyman, who entered into conversation with him, and after hearing his story, and putting its truth to the test by asking him questions which none but an educated man could answer, showed him much kindness, and not only paid his coach fare to Hull, but gave him a letter of introduction, which secured his passage to Hamburg. At length, after several ups and downs more, he reached his home in Suabia, and was clasped in the arms of his own dear remittance-sending mother. One of his first cares, after reaching home, was to write to his friends, enclosing the amount of money he had borrowed from them.

Our hero had probably obtained more wisdom and business talent in the course of his Irish misfortunes, than he would have obtained by any other mode of training; for the remainder of his life exhibits more sense and sedateness than might have been expected. Having procured a commission in the Russian army, he proceeded to St Petersburg, where the only drawback to the pleasure he took in his military duties was, that it was very cold. His abilities and accomplishments appear, however, to have succeeded in gaining him good friends; for, after serving in some inferior diplomatic situations, he was sent by the Empress Catherine on a mission to the English cabinet in the year 1796. He embraced the opportunity of doing two things, both of which were characteristic; in the first place, he bought a splendid carriage in London, with which he said he meant 'to cut a dash in St Petersburg;' and in the second place, he revisited his friends in Ireland. 'One morning,' says Mr Rosborough in narrating the story, 'I received a message from the Kildare Street hotel, informing me that a gentleman just arrived there wished to see me immediately. On repairing thither, I was received by a servant in gorgeous livery, who spoke with a foreign accent, and introduced me into a room, in which, to my unspeakable astonishment, I saw Viscount Facqz and Mr Lafontaine seated at breakfast.'

The three friends spent several happy days together. Unluckily, however, during our hero's visit, Mr Lafontaine, whose circumstances were still embarrassed, was again arrested for debt; and it bespeaks the true character of our hero, that, though he had bought a splendid carriage, and was living in a princely style, he yet had no other means of extricating his friend out of his difficulty than by pledging his watch. After staying a week in Dublin, during which he visited his old prison, he returned to London, and thence to St Petersburg, from which he kept up a constant correspondence with his two friends. In one of his letters, he tells them that he had recovered his estate of Honig, which had been taken possession of by the Carmagnoles; and he expresses his anxious wish that they were all three together living upon it, where he says 'he would nurse and cherish them, and make them so happy, that they should be like *diamonds in cotton*.' It was not till 1803, however, that, after having seen some hard service, and been completely shattered in health, he was able to retire to the Chateau de Honig. His last letter to his Irish friends is dated February 1803, and in it he is as sentimental as ever. He appears to have died in the same year.

And now, what was this Alexander Facqz, Viscount de Honig? He was a specimen of what we often see in the world—an accomplished, amiable, interesting young man, with a tolerably good head, a very affectionate heart, and a weak, languid, unmuscular character, that always began crying when a difficulty came in the way.

Like Æsop of old, we may conclude our tale with a moral, which it may be well for all young persons, including gentlemen under the age of twenty-five, to bear in mind. Let nothing tempt you to tell a falsehood; take care of the company you keep; labour honourably for your bread; and try to depend as little as possible on remittances from your mother.

THE SERVIANS AND THEIR SONGS.

The just and natural curiosity respecting Russia and its inhabitants, which during the last few years has been aroused in the English mind, will in all probability be increased rather than diminished in the course of this and the immediately succeeding generations. Nor will it ever, we are inclined to think, be finally satisfied with anything less than a thorough comprehension, not of the Russians only, but of the other interesting nations and tribes who, along with them, compose the great Slavonian family. Their growing political and commercial importance can escape the glance of no one; but, apart from such considerations, these fifty-five millions of Slavonians deserve attention on purely intellectual grounds; and even we, the countrymen of Shakspeare, of Milton, and of Burns, may find our account in the study of their literature and their languages. It was but the other day we heard a friend predict, that in thirty years a knowledge of Russian would be as common an accomplishment among us as a knowledge of German is at present. And strange as it may appear to many of our readers, we believe the prediction to be a correct one. From what we can learn respecting the contemporary literature of the Slavonians, it would seem that while in the west, as on all hands is admitted, the genius of poetry pauses in her career, in the east she is quickening her step, and perhaps about to pass us in the race. But however this may be, in one important department, the poetry of the people, the Slavonians have already immeasurably outstripped us; and by competent judges it is decided that the collective minstrelsy of all other countries must yield, both in wealth and in beauty, to that of the nations of Slavonian origin. There is, further, in this respect, a curious and interesting distinction between western and eastern Europe. Our accumulated stores of popular poetry seem closed to all accessions save from a somewhat distant past; but with the Slavonians, this very present, as it flies, its joys, its sorrows, all its varied emotions, are being changed into melody and song: here the stream has formed itself into a lake; yonder, receiving new tributaries, it still flows onward, widening and gathering strength as it proceeds.

Russian, Servian, Bohemian, Polish, at once the most cultivated and extensively-diffused of Slavonian dialects, while a strong family-likeness pervades the four, fall naturally into two divisions, one of which comprises Russian and Servian, the other Bohemian and Polish. Among these the language of the Servians stands pre-eminent for power, flexibility, and music; nay, we have even seen somewhere quoted an opinion of the historian Niebuhr, to the effect that theirs is altogether the noblest of European languages. The superiority of their popular poetry we cannot so confidently affirm, though we believe it to be on the whole pretty generally admitted. It was by a lady that the wonderful excellence of the Servian minstrelsy was first made known at all extensively in the west. Theresa von Iakol, the daughter of a German professor in one of the Russian universities, on her return to her fatherland, published in 1825 a translation of many of the Servian songs, and to the beauty of these, even in their foreign garb, the attention of Germany was decisively called by the greatest of recent poets and judges of poetry, Goëthe. From the few English translations executed by this lady (since her marriage with Professor Robinson, the well-known author of 'Biblical Researches in Palestine'), and from Dr Bowring's 'Specimens of Servian Poetry,' we propose to present some selections to the reader, with a slight preliminary sketch of the singular nation and country among and in which the songs themselves have arisen.*

Servia proper lies to the south of the Save and of the Danube, on either side of the river Morava, separated on the west from Bosnia by the Drina, on the east by the Timok from Bulgaria; and on the south from Macedonia and Albania by the heights that form a westward continuation of the great Balkan chain. It is a country with about a million of inhabitants, and of some four hundred square miles in extent, traversed and intersected by innumerable streams and mountains. Its mountains, as well as the large plains that stretch along the banks of the Danube and of the Morava, are covered with forests of oak on all sides towards the interior, of almost impenetrable thickness; and among these, here and there in the many valleys which the hill ranges compose, the brawling torrents collect themselves into peaceful lakes. South-eastwards, a road has been cut through the forests, which extends almost from the capital, Belgrade, to the border-fortress of Nyssa; and as it forms an important section of the route from Vienna to Constantinople, it is often traversed by lovers of the picturesque.

Compared, however, with the tracts once occupied by Servian tribes, Servia proper appears an inconsiderable speck, and its extent gives no idea of the territory even at this day inhabited by Servians in everything but name. Tributary to Austria or Turkey, some Christians, and others Mohammedans, they form a varied race, but still possess a strong national resemblance. Since the Servian revolution of 1817, the inhabitants of Servia proper, although paying a small tribute to the sultan, and having a pacha with 500 Turks to garrison Belgrade, have formed a kind of independent people. They have even, it would seem, a constitutional government, with the usual apparatus of a hereditary prince and a representative assembly; the latter, to the great joy of Lamartine, holding its meetings as in the patriarchal times, in the open air, beneath the shade of lofty trees!

The Servian houses are so constructed, and lie so far apart from each other, that a village of forty or fifty dwellings often occupies as much ground as a city like Vienna. In its first stage, the Servian house consists of a large square mud-built apartment, strewn with hay or dried moss and the bark of the lime tree, and in its centre the one fireplace of the family, from which the smoke ascends to escape through an opening in the roof. Here the father and mother sleep: round this, as a nucleus, stretch far and wide the sleeping-chambers of the other inmates, married and single; for in Servia the son, when he weds, remains with his bride under his parents' roof; nor even on the father's death is the family broken up, but the brothers select the strongest and skilfullest among themselves to rule in his stead. All the many inmates compose a single household; all labour and take their meals together; and in the winter evenings assemble round the common hearth. Living in this secluded fashion, the Servians have retained the simple and kindly manners of primitive times. As soon as a stranger approaches one of their dwellings, the master hastens to the door to greet him, and tell him he is welcome. As he crosses the threshold, the women and children kiss his hand. The largest table is straightway covered with the best the house affords; the men sit down to feast with the stranger, while the females stand round to wait upon his call. When the hour of rest approaches, a servant enters with a basin of water, and the hostess kneels to wash the feet of her wearied guest. In the morning again, he must not depart until he has partaken of a hearty repast, nor then without a cordial and respectful blessing.

Over communities such as we have described, the influence of the clergy might well be expected to be supreme. But in Servia, the bishops, all foreigners, and chosen by the patriarch of Constantinople, reside in the towns, and have no intercourse with their flocks. The papas, or priests, on the other hand, can scarcely be called a separate class; they are obliged to labour with their hands for their support, and their functions seem confined to reading from the liturgy at baptisms, marriages, and deaths. Thus the Servians have been allowed to retain, from the most remote ages of paganism, a number of usages, which, stripped perhaps of all that may have stood in direct hostility to the Christian faith, and sometimes indeed wonderfully blended with its results, seem to indicate, according to Professor Ranke, the mysterious connexion which the simple husbandman believes to exist between himself and nature. On these singular rites, adapted to the changeful phenomena of the natural year, an essay might be written. It need here only be observed, that song enters into all the strange half-symbolical ceremonies of the Servians. But with them it is not merely the solemn accompaniment of festivals, or an occasional holiday amusement. They do not love to listen to their inexhaustible lays only when chanted by a single performer; to the monotonous music of their simple one-stringed harp, the Guslè, at merry-makings, or by the fireside in the long winter evenings. A nation of singers, poetry is the natural organ of their spiritual life, prose but the medium of business-communications. Song enhances and reflects all their occupations and enjoyments; its choral melody rises not less frequent and loud from the herdsmen on the mountains, the plains where the reapers ply the sickle, than in the hall where the women sit spinning round the hearth, or from the square where the village youths and maidens assemble to dance the Kolo. We find in Servia no separate class of minstrels, whether composers or singers. By name the Servians know not, and do not care to know, the authors of their beautiful lays, which an unnoticeable bounty, like that of nature in her gifts, appears to have been for ever evolving from the dance of the Hours. In quick and striking alternation you hear them sing the ballad that narrates some heroic passage of their recent revolution, and that in which an ancient worthy has commemorated the mournful defeat of Kossova. The songs of yesterday are simple, touching, and peculiar as those of centuries ago—all appear fragments of one great work. It seems as if a national mind had been expressing, through varying generations, its unchanging thought and emotion, as if there had only been wanted some man of more than common susceptibility and skill to weave these unconnected utterances into a series of harmonious epics, that might rival—with reverence be it spoken—the unapproachable Homeric poems themselves.

Goëthe has well remarked, that the compositions of which we speak can be rightly enjoyed only in a collected form; yet, though our few specimens can give the reader but an imperfect notion of this collection, he will be enabled to form from them a clearer judgment of the spirit of the whole, than from many pages of disquisition. In conclusion, we may say that cheerfulness—a serene and cheerful transparency—is the principal characteristic of the Servian poetry. The pathetic incident is presented to the hearer or reader with a simple truthfulness beyond the reach of the most consummate art; but no complaint is heard from the singer; he stands altogether above his subject. And as the Servian

* Mr Lockhart also has printed for private circulation 'Translations from the Servian Minstrelsy,' but these are *not* 'in the metre of the original,' of which (in this case, we may say), consequently, they give no idea.

ballads want the deep melancholy, so also they want both the frequent obscurity, and, as has been justly observed, the dramatic vivacity of the Scottish and other northern lays. In the former, from the longest narrative to the tiniest love-song, everything is, in epic fashion, told, described, made distinctly visible. Nor are the actors to whom these songs introduce us invested with anything of an ideal greatness; their heroism and love are such as belong to the uncultivated, sometimes half-savage, children of nature. We are not raised into a purer and loftier region; yet, it must be added, on the reality in which we find ourselves the sun of true poesy shines, and in its ethereal light the trivial and repulsive disappear. Again, in these songs we are but sparingly introduced to the supernatural beings with whom the western and northern imagination has peopled in such profusion the waste and solitary places; almost the only personages of this kind in whom the Servians put faith being the female appearances, named Vilas—a fine creation of the fancy.

Our first specimen shall be the poem which narrates the death of the hero Marko, one belonging to the second earliest cycle of the Servian songs. Through 160 years the invulnerable Marko has survived, along with his horse Shâras, the strangest vicissitudes and adventures, and now, wildly mysterious as his life has been, so also is his death. Surely something of the matchless simplicity and pathos for which the original is famed is discernible in the translation.

DEATH OF KRALEVICH MARKO—(*Dr Bowring*).*

At the dawn of day, the noble Marko
Rode in sunlight on the Sabbath morning,
By the sea, along the Urvinian mountain.
Towards the mountain top as he ascended,
Suddenly his trusty Sharas stumbled;
Sharas stumbled, and began to weep there.
Sad it fell upon the heart of Marko,
And he thus addressed his favourite Sharas:—
'Ah! my faithful friend, my trusty Sharas,
We have dwelt a hundred years and sixty,
Dwelt together as beloved companions,
And till now have never never stumbled:
Thou hast stumbled now, my trusty Sharas;
Thou hast stumbled, and thine eyes are weeping.
God alone can tell what fate awaits me;
One of us is surely doomed to perish,
And my life or thine is now in peril.'

[While Marko apostrophises his trusty horse, the 'white Vila' announces to him that he is doomed to die, which enrages the hero, but the phantom continues—]

—'If thou wouldst doubt the mountain Vila,
Hasten to the summit of the mountain;
Look to right and look to left around thee.
Thou wilt see two tall and slender fir trees,
Fir trees towering o'er the mountain forests;
They with verdant leaves are covered over;
And between the fir trees is a fountain;
Look, and afterwards rein back thy Sharas;
Then alight, and bind him to the fir tree:
Bend thee down, and look into the fountain;
Look—as if the fountain were a mirror—
Look, and thou shalt see when death awaits thee.'

Marko did as counselled by the Vila.
When he came upon the mountain summit,
To the right and left he looked around him;
Then he saw two tall and slender fir trees,
Fir trees towering high above the forest,
Covered all with verdant leaves and branches.
Then he reined his faithful Sharas backward,
Then dismounted, tied him to the fir tree,
Bent him down, and looked into the fountain;
Saw his face upon the water mirrored,
Saw his death-day written on the water.

Tears rushed down the visage of the hero;
'O, thou faithless world! thou lovely flow'ret!
Thou wert lovely—a short pilgrim's journey—

[And so, for a considerable number of lines, Marko laments his fate; after which he breaks his sabre and lance, and flings away his weapons. He now drew]

From his breast a golden tablet;
From his pocket drew unwritten paper,
And the princely Marko thus inscribed it:—
'He who visits the Urvina mountain,
He who seeks the fountain 'neath the fir trees,
And there finds the hero Marko's body,
Let him know that Marko is departed.
When he died, he had three well-filled purses:
How well filled? well filled with golden ducats.
One shall be his portion, and my blessing,
Who shall dig a grave for Marko's body:
Let the second be the church's portion;
Let the third be given to blind and maimed ones,
That the blind through earth in peace may wander,
And with hymns laud Marko's deeds of glory.'

And when Marko had inscribed the letter,
Lo! he stuck it on the fir tree's branches,
That it might be seen by passing travellers.
In the fount he threw his golden tablets,
Doffed his vest of green, and spread it calmly
On the grass, beneath a sheltering fir tree;
O'er his eyes he drew his Samar-kâlpak,*
Laid him down—yes! laid him down for ever.

By the fountain lay the clay-cold Marko
Day and night; a long long week he lay there.
Many travellers passed, and saw the hero,
Saw him lying by the public pathway;
And while passing, said, 'The hero slumbers!'
Then they kept a more than common distance,
Fearing that they might disturb the hero.

[At length Vaso, a pious churchman from Vilindari, passes with his young attendant Isaja: attracted by what he considered the sleeping hero, and looking in anxious terror round him, he]

Saw the letter on the fir tree branches;
Read it from a distance; as he trembled,
Read that Marko had in death departed.
From his horse the astonished monk alighted,
Seized the hand of Marko; Marko moved not!
Long he had been dead—long since departed!

Tears rushed swiftly from the eye of Vaso,
Marko's fate filled all his thoughts with sorrow.
From the girdle, then, he took the purses,
Which he hid beneath his own white girdle:
Round and round inquired Iguman Vaso,
Where he should entomb the hero Marko;
Round and round he looked in fond inquiry.
On his horse he flung the hero's body,
Brought it safely to the ocean's borders,
Thence he shipped it for the Holy Mountain,
Near the white church, Vilindari, landed;
To that white church he conveyed the body;
And, as wont, upon the hero's body
Funeral hymns were sung; and he was buried
In the white church aisle—the very centre;
There the old man placed the hero's body.
But no monument he raised above him,
Lest when foes should mark the hero's grave-stone,
Theirs should be the joy, and theirs the triumph.

None of the Servian poems are more attractive than those which relate to love. But, alas! in Servia marriages are settled entirely by the parents, so that the forced termination of a long-cherished mutual affection forms there, as here, the theme of many a mournful ditty. Take, however, the following beautiful picture of two betrothed and happy lovers, which has an almost Chinese purity and clearness, along with an impassioned tenderness, to which the Chinese are strangers:—

MAY IT LAST.—(*Mrs Robinson.*)

Cross the field a breeze it bore the roses,
Bore them far into the tent of Jovo;
In the tent were Jovo and Maria—
Jovo writing, and Maria 'broidering.
Used has Jovo all his ink and paper,
Used Maria all her burnished gold thread.

Thus accosted Jovo then Maria:
'O sweet love, my dearest soul, Maria,
Tell me, is my soul, then, dear unto thee;
Or my hand, findst thou it hard to rest on?'

Then with gentle voice replied Maria:
'O, in faith, my heart and soul, my Jovo!
Dearer is to me thy soul, O dearest,
Than my brothers, all the four together.
Softer is thy hand to me to rest on,
Than four cushions, softest of the soft ones.

Here, as we have seen, the gentleman is assured that his beloved prefers him even to her 'brothers, all the four together,' a compliment which a British wooer would not very highly prize.

The reader will be struck with the likeness between

* All the versions given in this article are in the rhymeless, tensyllabled, trochaic metre of the original.

* 'Sable-cap.'

our next extract and Sir Walter's 'Young Lochinvar.' He may compare the description, in the opening lines, of a high-born Servian lady with that of a Scottish maiden in Burns's song, 'On Cessnock banks there lives a lass.'

AJKUNA'S MARRIAGE.—(*Dr Bowring.*)

Never, since the world had its beginning,
Never did a lovelier flow'ret blossom
Than the flow'ret we ourselves saw blooming
In the white court of the Bey Liubovich.
High above the level Nevesina
Towered the fascinating maid Ajkuna;
She, the Bey Liubovich's lovely sister.

She was lovely, nothing e'er was lovelier;
She was tall and slender as the pine tree;
White her cheeks, but tinged with rosy blushes,
As if morning's beam had shone upon them,
Till that beam had reached its high meridian;
And her eyes, they were two precious jewels;
And her eyebrows, leeches from the ocean;
And her eyelids, they were wings of swallows;
Silken tufts the maiden's flaxen ringlets;
And her sweet mouth was a sugar-casket;
And her teeth were pearls arrayed in order;
White her bosom, like two snowy dovelets;
And her voice was like the dovelet's cooing;
And her smiles were like the glowing sunshine;
And the fame, the story of her beauty,
Spread through Bosnia and through Herzgovina.

Such a peerless maiden has, as may be supposed, no lack of suitors. To only two of these are we introduced; one is 'the gray-headed Mustaph Aga'—gray-headed indeed; but then he 'proffers a thousand golden coins' in hard cash, not to mention a 'golden drinking vessel' of unspeakable magnificence and value: the other, Suko, may be young, and dwell 'upon the country's border, as a falcon dwells among the breezes;' but, alas! if we except his 'sabre and his steed so trusty,' all his wealth is ten ducats—surely a very inadequate sum! In spite of this, however, the candid 'Bey Liubovich' makes the fascinating maid, 'Ajkuna,' acquainted with both offers, and thus far merits our praise: like a confiding and dutiful sister, she bids him decide for her. The prudent nobleman, when the bridal party is met, of course points to the wealthy old man in the distance, which discomposing the lady, she asks who is that young man 'on the white horse seated?'

'It is the hero, Suko of Urbinia,
He who for thee with thy brother struggled,
Struggled well indeed, but could not win thee.'
When the lovely maiden heard the leader,
On the black, black earth, anon she fainted.
All to raise her, hastening, gather round her,
And the last of all came Mustaph Aga:
None could lift her from the ground, till Suko
Sticks into the earth his waving banner,
Stretches out his right hand to the maiden.
See her! see her! from the ground upspringing,
Swift she vaults upon his steed behind him;
Rapidly he guides the courser onwards,
Swift they speed across the open desert,
Swift as ever star across the heaven.

When the old man saw it, Mustaph Aga,
Loud he screamed with voice of troubled anger—
'Look to this, ye bidden to the wedding!
He, the robber! bears away my maiden:
See her, see her borne away for ever!'

But one answer met the old man's wailings:
'Let the hawk bear off the quail in safety.
Bear in safety—she was born to wed him;
Thou, retire thee to thy own white dwelling
Blossoms not for thee so fair a maiden.'

And so the curtain drops. We hope that in the long-run all parties, even the ill-used Mustaph Aga, were pleased.

We close our quotations with the following sweet and simple lines, entitled

THOUGHTS OF A MOTHER.—(*Dr Bowring.*)

Lo! a fir tree towers o'er Sarajevo,
Spreads o'er half the face of Sarajevo,
Rises up to heaven from Sarajevo;
Brothers and half-sisters there were seated;
And the brother cuts a silken garment,
Which he holds, and questions thus his sister:
'Brother's wife! thou sweet and lovely dovelet!
Wherefore art thou looking at the fir tree?
Art thou rather dreaming of the poplar;
Or art thinking of my absent brother?'

To her brother thus the lady answered:
'Golden ring of mine! my husband's brother!
Not about the fir tree was I dreaming,
Nor the noble stem of lofty poplar;
Neither was I dreaming of thy brother;
I was thinking of my only mother.

She with sugar and with honey reared me;
She for me the red wine poured at even,
And at midnight gave the sweet metheglin;
In the morning milk, with spirit chastened,
So to give me cheeks of rose and lily;
And with gentle messages she waked me,
That her child might grow both tall and slender.'

A SOCIETY OF LAND IMPROVERS.

The subject of the allotment and improvement of waste lands is one which has at various times deservedly claimed a share of public attention. Numerous reports have been published descriptive of the beneficial results which have followed the application of the system in different localities: in some, the success has been complete; in others, the experiment has partially failed, owing to the incompetence of the parties on whom the management devolved, or to the unwillingness of the labourers to undergo the requisite exertion. Ireland is a country possessing, as is generally allowed, peculiar claims upon active philanthropy; and among the schemes suggested or undertaken for her improvement, none have met with so favourable a reception as that for the reclamation of the neglected and uncultivated portions of her soil, conducted by an institution called the Irish Waste Land Improvement Society.

This society, it appears, with the Earl of Devon at its head, was formed in 1836, and being incorporated by act of parliament, it obtained the possession of many thousands of acres of waste land—mountain, and peat moss or bog—on leases of 99 years at a very low rent, averaging about 1s. 10d. per statute acre. The plan of the company was not to speculate in farming themselves, but to re-let the whole in small farms of 15 to 25 acres, on leases of 31 years, at a rent varying from 4s. to 10s. per acre, undertaking at the same time to make all the roads, main drains, and fences, at their own cost. In the present day, when almost every town has its improvement society, which does little else than talk, it is cheering to find that there is at least one institution, which actually works—really tries to accomplish what others only are contented with projecting.

Nor has this improvement society acted rashly in its operations; great caution has been employed in every step of its progress. The first purchase was a small mountain tract in Galway; the second, in the county of Limerick; the third, in Sligo; and lastly, a wild district in Connemara, comprising more than 7000 acres, was taken about three years since. It is a favourable feature of the proceedings, that the calls upon the shareholders have been made at long intervals: no more than L.8 per share has been paid up to the present time. The aggregate amount received, about L.25,000, has enabled the society to place the four estates, comprehending 10,000 acres, in a forward state of cultivation. The estate of Gleneask, in the county of Sligo, consists of 5699 statute acres, and is beautifully situated on the south-eastern slope of the Slievh Gauff mountains, commonly known as the Lurgan hills. Their height is about 1000 feet above the level of the sea, and they overlook a valley nearly seven miles in length, watered by numerous mountain streams. The soil is described as 'pure unmitigated *peat bog*, from two to eight feet in depth, with a substratum of clay or gravel.' A portion of the upper slopes is laid out in pasture, well adapted for rearing the Highland breed of cattle, of which the society possesses a thriving herd. The steward of the estate, Mr Lermont, is an industrious North Briton. With his wife and two daughters, he occupies the house adjoining the model farm, where, upon a piece of bog reclaimed within two years, were growing as fine Swedish turnips as could be found in the fertile barony of Cork. Near the entrance gate, standing on the society's land, are several whitewashed buildings; these are, a police station-house, porter's lodge, chapel, and national school. Proceeding onwards along a fine wide gravelled road, the plan of the allotments becomes visible, marked out by open drains, and green banks of sod, crowned by clipped hedges of furze. The dwellings of the servants are built facing the road, with which they communicate by narrow walks, bordered with the alder and Lombardy poplar. The houses of the tenants are 30 feet long, 13 feet wide, and 8 feet high; they are built of stone, and divided into two rooms, thatched and glazed; the cost of each to the society being L.16, 5s. This expense is greater than it otherwise would be, owing to the great depth to which it is necessary to dig for the foundation, which must be carried through the bog. The company do not, however, build for every tenant; they prefer to induce the settler to build for himself, giving him assistance from their supply of timber. This plan has been found to attach the occupant to the soil more securely than if he had been provided with a dwelling, while at the same time it serves to quicken and stimulate his exertions for the improvement of the property. The society offers powerful inducements in furtherance of this object: it gives a prize of L.2 for every acre of reclaimed land, which is equal to four years' rent at the higher rate. This plan is found to succeed, as, by the improved system of drainage, the unproductive bog soon becomes a flourishing field.

On every farm held by the smaller occupiers, turnips and clover were growing, and in many instances rape and vetches. The potatoes—lumpers, Peelers, and Americans—were everywhere excellent, and the presence of two or three head of cattle on each holding showed that the accumulation of manure was certain. The main drains are made from 4 to 6 feet wide at top, 2½ to 3½ at bottom, and from 3 to 5 feet in depth; the thorough drains are 2 feet wide at top and bottom, with a small channel in the centre from 6 to 8 inches in width, covered closely by a sod turned the green side downwards. The firmness of the soil is such, that the drains require no lining except in the clayey ground, where they are filled with stones. After draining, the surface is burned and limed, when two successive crops of potatoes are taken, then a crop of Aberdeen turnips, followed by oats laid down in clover. Recent analysis by Professor Kane has shown a rich bed of marl in the neighbourhood to contain some of the most important elements which can be applied to the fertilisation of peat. In some cases turnips have been raised as a *first* crop, thus proving the productive nature of the land. It is, however, recommended, in preference to this method, to follow the plan of culture above described. Much difficulty was experienced in persuading the ignorant Irish cotter to take the necessary steps to insure a good crop of turnips. Mr Lermont says, 'When I insisted on the plants being thinned out to nine inches' distance, and showed them the distance by pulling up a few myself, it was like pulling the hair out of their heads: some actually cried!'

The indispensable necessity of cleanliness, and the absence of all extraneous lumber in the dairy, to say nothing of the filthiness of keeping animals in the dwelling-house, are points strongly impressed upon the minds of the tenants by the managing director and the ever-watchful steward. Those who prove refractory are debarred from participating in the prizes which 'are given annually for draining, green crops, cattle, cleanliness, &c. Great emulation is excited among the tenantry by these premiums, of which the agricultural are paid in money, the household in kind; and a gown or shawl to the "good-wife" is found more effective than the purchase-money, where shops are so distant. The personal appearance and costume of the female peasantry in this mountain district contrast strikingly with those of Munster: small regular features are much more frequent; and the slovenly flounced cap is never seen but on married women and the aged: spinsters wear their hair exposed, and in neat order. The Sunday appearance of both males and females is not only respectable, but picturesque, reminding one of the Alpine Sabbath in more favoured lands. Scarlet and bright blue are the favourite colours of the females.

'Father Mathew has not overlooked Gleneask: nearly all the tenants are "teetotallers;" and illicit distillation, once so prevalent in the district, is now of rare occurrence.

'The unavoidable difficulties of a new settler during the first year are most considerately met by the admirable system of Colonel Robinson, the director, which provides him with the means of subsistence by employment in making the main drains and fences of his own allotment, thus rendering him independent of the land, until it is made, by his own labour, to produce a crop. The rate of wages is 8d. per day: 10d. per perch is paid for the fences; 4d. per perch for the larger main drains, and 2d. for the smaller. Some good attempts at a dairy have been made by several of the small holders, and Miss Lermont is indefatigable in her efforts to instruct them in the making of cheese, storage for which is provided at the farmery.'

The want of capital is often talked of as the cause of defective farming among the occupying tenants in Ireland; but what would capital avail them without the knowledge of its application? whereas personal instruction and encouragement would make their present capital—their labour—produce fourfold. Agricultural societies may do much for those who are able to read, and are otherwise more enlightened than their neighbours: but what have they effected, comparatively, for the cotter tenant, unable to read—perhaps, like some of the Gleneask tenants, unable to understand English? He may doubtless see the *results* of good farming at the annual shows, and, if he can afford it, hear the speeches and dissertations at the agricultural dinners; but will this induce him to thorough drain, subsoil plough, or sow turnips? or, if he were willing to learn, instruct him how the work should be done? Practical, sound instruction, is the only mode suited to the small farmer. It is not only necessary to tell him, but to show him how the work is to be done: the stimulants of precept and reward are insufficient—personal instruction, encouragement, and superintendence, are wanting. To supply those wants is one of the main objects of the Irish Waste Land Improvement Society. Colonel Robinson is not satisfied with the ordinary statement of rent and arrears, but examines personally every cottage, goes over every acre of reclaimed land, directs, corrects, and encourages. A cheerful recognition, a good-humoured reproof, a friendly jest or encouraging remark, play upon the surface of a well-considered system of moral and physical improvement. Human nature, in whatever grade, requires some stimulant for the development of her faculties; and whether it be wealth or power, praise or honour, or even the lowly stimulant of the poor Irish cotter—mere subsistence—where the pressure is not felt, the machinery becomes inert, and the 'time enough' and 'well enough' assume the places of labour and activity.

This no doubt involves labour and agricultural knowledge on the part of those intrusted with the management of estates; but men qualified to undertake such duties are not wanting; and how gratifying must be the sensations of that landlord who can point to a large tract of reclaimed mountain or a recent moor teeming with profitable vegetation, and say—'These once sterile acres afford now food and shelter to a thriving peasantry, blessing, like the quality of mercy—

Both him that gives, and him that takes.'

DREAM REVELATIONS.

An article published in the Journal last summer, treating dreams on what we thought philosophical grounds, has brought to our hands a number of communications, detailing instances of what may be called dream revelations, most of them narrated by the individuals to whom they occurred. It is of course inconsistent with our ordinary ideas of nature, that any one can acquire a knowledge, while asleep, of events that are afterwards to take place; and it is desirable that our ideas of natural procedure should not be in any degree confounded by a propensity to vulgar marvels. At the same time, no one can be quite sure that such things are out of the range of nature; and even Dr Abercrombie has thought it not improper to introduce several of them into his 'Intellectual Philosophy,' apparently in the hope that they may yet be explained on some principle connected with recognised laws. For this reason, but chiefly because we think they will harmlessly entertain our readers, we make a selection from the communications in question. The first is from a lady, resident in a remote and insulated region of Britain, whose sprightly talents have already been repeatedly evidenced in these pages.

'Though happily, both by constitution and education, more free from all superstitious influences than most people, I have been often led to make remarks on the subject of dreams; so often, that I am inclined to believe, if all were to contribute their stock of personal experience on this point, it would be found that there are *not* more things in earth and heaven than are dreamt of in our philosophy. I merely here intend to put down, at random almost, a very few of what I remember of my own experiences in the way of dreaming. In most of the instances when my dreams have been almost literally fulfilled, the recollection of them has only occurred to me on their fulfilment, which generally happens very speedily. On one occasion last winter, I imagined I was in church in the front seat of the side gallery, and while engaged in prayer, I saw some persons carry in a plain coffin into the lower area. The silence that ensued was breathless; and I was saying to myself, as I supposed each one was doing, "Is this for me?" when the coffin-bearers looked at me, and said solemnly, and in tears, "It is for ——," naming me. I awoke immediately. I was then in perfect health; but only the second day thereafter, I was most unexpectedly and dangerously taken ill, and for three months was frequently very near death; so that I never before had such a close view of an eternal world. It was not till I had nearly quite recovered, that my dream was recalled to my remembrance, by being told that a certain neighbour—none other than the chief coffin-bearer—had wept abundantly while my life was considered in danger.

'Earlier in life, I once dreamt I was bathing, and was dragged beyond my depth, near to drowning, by a particular friend; and was only rescued by my husband wading in with his clothes on, and seizing me as I was sinking. Within a week I was brought into an affecting dilemma by that same friend, and only relieved by the instrumentality of the same protecting hand.

'What led me at first to put down these remarks was, that the night, or rather morning before last, I had a very distressing dream of one of my little girls, four years old, being killed by the falling of the peat-stalk upon her; and last evening I was sitting alone, reading the article in Chambers's Journal on dreams, when I was startled by the most extraordinary rumbling noise and screams. On running to see what was the matter, I found the little girl alluded to had tumbled down the whole stair with a straw basket full of peats, which she had succeeded, with the love of enterprise so common in children, in dragging up stairs to take to the nursery fire. The dear child, and the peats together, rambling down a long wooden stair, were sufficiently alarming; but, happily, she was only frightened. The straw basket had preserved her at the foot uninjured, and I could soon laugh heartily at the incident, which I hope will stand for the fulfilment of my dream.

'With respect to presentiment, my experience has not been great; but has any person besides myself ever felt, in particular societies, or circumstances, or scenery, as if the scene were not new to him, but only the exact repetition of circumstances, conversation, and other particulars which he had been present at on some former occasion, though undoubtedly he actually never had? Often have I felt this, and it always appears as if I were remembering what had taken place in a dream.'

Our fair correspondent may rest assured that she is not singular in the latter class of experiences. They are very general amongst persons of a nervous organisation. One theory about them, more interesting than convincing, is that they are the reminiscences of an earlier state of existence.

The following anecdote is from a gentleman residing at Douglas, in the Isle of Man:—'My brother, ——, was in the Bush Hotel, in Bristol, one day in 183-, when the Welsh mail arrived, and a gentleman named J——, with whom he was acquainted, walked into the coffeeroom. As they sat in conversation, the melancholy news arrived of the loss of the Frolic steamer upon the Nass, with all on board. Hereupon Mr J—— assumed a look of unusual seriousness, and seemed deeply affected. My brother inquiring the reason, he said he felt as if he had been just rescued from a violent death. He had designed two mornings before to leave Haverfordwest by that steamer, but was prevented by the intreaty of his wife, who had awoke during the night from a terrible dream, in which she had seen the loss of the vessel during a heavy gale. Merely to calm her mind, he had put off his journey for a day, and travelled by the mail instead; by which means his life undoubtedly had been saved.' It may be remarked, that there might be nothing here beyond simple coincidence. The weather might be threatening, and the lady's dream produced by previous waking fears.

The following instances are more curious. They come from a gentleman engaged in legal business at a town in the south of Scotland:—

'Most of the writers,' he says, 'on the subject of dreams, deal with those which have reference to past events. To this extent I could readily accede to their reasoning. It is easy to conceive that impressions may and do remain on the mind, and that control being suspended by sleep, these impressions may present themselves in a confused and undefined mass. We frequently find remote events curiously blended with those of recent occurrence. We find places we may have visited strangely associated with those which we have read about, or heard described. We meet with relatives long since dead, and have the full conviction that we are engaged with them as in former days; or it may be that we believe them to be dead, and yet we feel no surprise that we are conversing with them. We are sometimes breathlessly ascending a steep, and at other times suffocating in water. We are conscious of fear, joy, pain, &c. All these, and a thousand other vagaries, though sufficiently mysterious, we are ready to account for on the ground that they all have some reference to, or connexion with, what the mind has already been engaged in, and that, composed of these remnant impressions, the most vivid of them present themselves when uncontrolled by the senses. I would even go a little further with this theory. Suppose a person labouring under great anxiety for the recovery of a sick relative, or for the favourable issue of some undertaking in which he is deeply interested, it often happens that, in a dream, the death of the former, and the failure of the latter, take place by anticipation. It would not be held that there was any preternatural communication of these events, because they were actually realised. Anxiety implies a dread of these results, and it is not to be wondered at that that impression should assume the appearance of an occurrence actually realised. This theory is, however, greatly unhinged and dissipated when we come to deal with cases—unquestionable and well-authenticated cases—where events are distinctly and minutely portrayed, of which it is utterly impossible the mind could have any anticipation, and which, even after awaking from the dream, there is no reasonable ground for supposing likely to be realised. Moreover, when even dates are condescended on, and the realisation comes exactly to correspond with the dates and representation in the dream, then the difficulty, not yet overcome, presents itself. It is not easy in such cases to assent to the abandonment of the mind to its own uncontrolled vagaries, as if it were a mere wheel of a vast machine left to go at random, while all the rest is still. Its random effusions are conceivable until we come to this point—events anticipated or foretold, if I may use the expression. It is said that these are the exceptions, not the rule—that striking dreams of future events do happen, and by chance may turn out to be realised; but that there can be no connexion between the dream and the event; and that in ninety cases out of a hundred, events may be dreamt of which never do take place. I shall not venture to grapple with the question, but shall briefly state what has occurred in my own experience.

'In the autumn of 1835, I dreamt that a near relative of my own, who died two years before, came to my bedside. I felt fully conscious of being in my own bed, and of raising myself on my elbow when my friend approached. I was also fully sensible that he was dead; and though in his morning gown, his countenance bore the impress of death. He mentioned my name, and presented to me a coffin-plate bearing the name, age, and date of the death of a lady—the latter was 25th December 1835. I said, "Where have you got that? Mrs —— is still in life; and besides, the date there has not yet arrived." He answered, "Take it, and keep it for her; she will require it." This lady was no relative of mine; I was only slightly acquainted with her. She was married, and had gone to a distance a considerable time before, and I had never seen nor heard of her since. When at breakfast, I in a casual way mentioned my dream, when some one jocosely remarked that I must have been thinking of her, and that to dream of deaths was always a marriage, and that my dream must have reference to her marriage. We thought no more of the matter, nor did it particularly attract the attention of any of us, until, in the course of the day, a lady happened to call, and in course of conversation asked if we had heard of the distressing illness of Mrs ——. We all declared we had not; when the lady stated that she passed through a neighbouring town yesterday on her way to her father's house, from the north, and that she was so ill, that she was obliged to remain some time at a friend's house before she could proceed. This was so far an association with the dream, that it struck all of us as a remarkable coincidence. The more extraordinary part remains to be told. On 31st December 1835 I attended her funeral, and the coffin-plate, with age and date as distinctly delineated in the dream, presented themselves to my gaze. It is needless to observe, that the impression on my mind was of a very peculiar kind, and equally so on the minds of those who some months before had heard the narrative of the dream.

'Another striking, though less interesting case, occurred of a more recent date. I dreamt that, on going into my office in the morning, I found seated at his usual desk a clerk who had left me a twelvemonth or more previously, and had since been in Edinburgh, where I had little or no communication with him. I said, "Mr D., how do you happen to be here; where in the world have you come from?" I had the most distinct answer, that he had come to the country for a few days, and, with my leave, would wish for a day to enjoy the reminiscence of his former happy feelings at that desk. I replied—"Certainly; I am glad to see you. Write that deed, and then take your dinner with me." Such was the dream; and though apparently of no importance, I happened to observe at the breakfast table that I had dreamt my old clerk D. had returned to my office. After having walked out half an hour, I directed my steps to the office, and my surprise was not a little excited when I found Mr D. seated exactly as had been represented in the dream. It might be supposed that, following out the dream, I put the question which it had suggested; but I am sure it was on the spur of the moment, and without reference to the dream, that I put that question, and my astonishment was doubly aroused when his answer corresponded almost verbatim with what I have stated. I immediately returned and stated the circumstance to my friends, who would only be satisfied of the fact by my calling Mr D. into their presence.

'I shall just notice one further instance, out of many equally striking, in my experience. My wife and I, with our only child—a girl of about a year old—were at a friend's house some miles from home. The child was then in perfect health. I dreamt that, on going to my room, I found my wife walking about with the child in her arms, closely wrapt in a shawl. I had the impression that she was in health. I opened the shawl to take the child in my arms, and what was my horror to see only a withered branch in place of my blooming child. It was but a dream; but so painful was the impression, that I could not help saying to a friend in the morning that I dreaded we were to lose our child, I had had so unpleasant a presentiment from my dream. He ridiculed the idea; but within one short month the darling branch gradually withered, and was consigned to an early tomb. This is one of those cases which is not wrapt in so much mystery, as it may be conceived that a parent's anxiety, even about a healthy child, might present itself in a dream in some distorted form. Still, it is an illustration of the mystery attending the mind when the senses are prostrated.

'I shall just mention one case which was told to me by an advocate. He had arranged to accompany a friend to Newhaven to bathe, and they were to set out at six o'clock in the morning. Immediately before getting out of bed, he dreamt that he was struggling in the water to save a young man from drowning. Within little more than an hour of the dream, he was in reality engaged in saving the life of a boy. He had just reached the sea-side, when he saw the boy beyond his depth, and without fully undressing, he rushed in and saved him.

'I could not have the slightest hesitation in giving you the names of every one to whom I have referred in these observations, though I should neither like their names nor my own to be made public.'

STATUE OF PETER THE GREAT, ST PETERSBURG.

The rapid change which Russia underwent during the reign of Peter the Great, her extraordinary advances under this sage legislator, are among the most important events of which history preserves the record. Proud of his glory, the nation wished to erect a monument in commemoration of his great actions, which in his own city should be a distinctive object to all posterity. In the then young state of their art, some deliberation took place before the design of the structure was decided on: during this the hero died, and the erection of the monument was consequently reserved for the reign of the empress Catherine II. The first step to be taken was the appointment of an artist capable of undertaking such a work. The choice fell upon M. Falconet, who, in his conception of an equestrian statue, determined that the subordinate parts should bear an equal impress of genius. He found that the pedestals in general use have no distinctive feature, and adapt themselves equally well to any subject; and being of so universal application, they produce no new or elevated feeling in the mind of the spectator. He wished to make the czar appear in his principal character—the father and legislator of his people; great and extraordinary in all; undertaking and completing that which others were unable to imagine. To carry out this conception, a precipitous rock was fixed on for the pedestal, on which the statue should appear with characteristics distinguishing it from those erected to other sovereigns.

The first idea was to form this pedestal of six masses of rock, bound together with bars of copper or iron; but the objection was urged, that the natural decay of the bands would cause a disruption of the various parts, and present a ruinous aspect, while it would be difficult to insure perfect uniformity in the quality and appearance of the different blocks. The next proposal was to form it of one whole rock; but this appeared impossible; and in a report to the senate, it was stated the expense would be so enormous, as almost to justify the abandonment of the undertaking; and even if made of six pieces, as first proposed, the outlay would be excessive. At length it was determined to transport to the city the largest rock that could be found, and add other portions to it as might be judged necessary. Still, great misgivings prevailed as to the possibility of removing the contemplated mass. The search was then begun, but with less success than had been anticipated, as the country around St Petersburg is flat and marshy, affording no traces of stone, while the nearest mountains are in the province of Finland. A whole summer was passed in exploration; and the idea of forming the pedestal of several smaller portions was again entertained, when a large stone was discovered near Cronstadt, which it was determined to apply as the principal mass; and the task of its removal was confided to the Admiralty, who, however, as well as many other mechanicians applied to in turn, refused to undertake it. The search for the smaller blocks was nevertheless continued, although no one appeared to have any definite notion of the use to be made of them in the event of their discovery.

Under these unexpected difficulties, the formation of the pedestal was intrusted to an officer of the corps of cadets, who had already given proofs of his mechanical skill. A native of Cephalonia, he had been compelled, for an offence against the laws, to seek refuge in Russia, where he lived under the assumed name of Lascary. He had strenuously recommended the adoption of the original design; and a few days after his appointment, he received information from a peasant of a large rock lying in a marsh near a bay in the Gulf of Finland, about twenty miles from the city by water. An examination was immediately instituted: the stone was found covered with moss; and on sounding around it, the base was fortunately ascertained to be flat. Its form was that of a parallelopipedon, 42 feet in length, 27 feet in width, and 21 feet in height—dimensions sufficiently extensive to realise the conceptions of M. Falconet, the sculptor. But when the authorities, under whose direction the work was placed, saw the prodigious size of the rock, they again hesitated, and recommended its division into smaller portions. The fear of accidents, however, and the hardness of the stone, caused them to yield to the representations of the engineer, who was now favoured by the support and encouragement of the minister Betzky; and the intelligence of the empress being superior to the senseless clamour raised by the envious and the ignorant, she gave orders for the commencement of the work.

A working model of the machinery with which it was proposed to remove the rock from its situation was first made. M. Lascary resolved on effecting this removal without the use of rollers, as these not only present a long surface, which increases the friction, but are not easily made of the great diameter that would have been required, owing to the soft and yielding nature of the ground on which the work was to be performed. Spherical bodies, revolving in a metallic groove, were then chosen as the means of transport. These offered many advantages. Their motion is more prompt than that of rollers, with a less degree of friction, as they present but small points of contact. Stout beams of wood, 33 feet in length, and 1 foot square, were then prepared. One side was hollowed in the form of a gutter, and lined, the sides being convex, to the thickness of two inches, with a compound metal of copper and tin. Balls of the same metal, five inches in diameter, were then made, to bear only on the bottom of the groove. These beams were intended to be placed on the ground in a line, in front of the stone, while upon them were reversed two other beams, prepared in a similar manner, each 42 feet long, and 1½ feet square, connected as a frame by stretchers and bars of iron 14 feet in length, carefully secured by nuts, screws, and bolts. A load of 3000 lbs., when placed on the working model, was found to move with the greatest facility; and the inventor hoped to satisfy the minister as well as the mechanicians by its public exhibition. The former was well pleased with the experiment, and expressed his belief in the possibility of removing the stone; while the latter raised absurd objections, with the cry of 'the mountain upon eggs.'

The first thing to be done, as the rock lay in a wild and deserted part of the country, was to build barracks capable of accommodating 400 labourers, artisans, and other persons required, who, with M. Lascary, were all lodged on the spot, as the readiest means of forwarding the work. A line of road was then cleared from the rock to the river Niva, a distance of six versts,* to a width of 120 feet, in order to gain space for the various operations, and to give a free circulation of air, so essential to the health of the workmen in a marshy district, as well as to the drying and freezing of the ground—a point of much importance, when the enormous weight to be removed is considered. In the month of December, when the influence of the frosts began to be felt, the operation of disinterring the rock from the earth, in which it was imbedded to the depth of 15 feet, was commenced: the excavation required to be of great width—84 feet all round—to admit of turning the stone, which did not lie in the most favourable position for removal. An inclined plane, 600 feet in length, was afterwards made, by means of which, when the stone was turned, it might be drawn up to the level surface.

Among the objections urged against the possibility of removing the rock, was the anticipated insurmountable difficulty of placing it upon the machine destined for its transportation. But the engineer was confident, and wisely preferring simplicity to complication, resolved on employing ordinary levers, known technically as levers of the first order; these were made of three masts, each 65 feet in length, and 1½ feet in diameter at the larger end, firmly bound together. To diminish the difficulty of moving these heavy instruments, triangles 30 feet high were erected, with windlasses attached near the base, from which a cord, passing through a pulley at the top, was fastened to the smaller end of the lever, which, being drawn up to the top of the triangle, was ready for the operation of turning: each of these levers was calculated to raise a weight of 200,000 lbs. A row of piles had been driven into the ground at the proper distance from the stone on one side, to serve as a fulcrum; and on the other a series of piles were disposed as a platform, to prevent the sinking of the mass on its descent. Twelve levers, with three men to each, were stationed at the side to be lifted, and the lower extremities being placed under the mass, the upper ends were drawn downwards by the united action of the twelve windlasses. When the stone rose to the height of a foot, beams and wedges were then driven underneath, to maintain it in that position, while the levers were arranged

* A verst is 3500 English feet.

for a second lift. To assist the action of the levers, large iron rings were soldered into the upper corner of the rock, from which small cables were passed to four capstans, each turned by 36 men, thus maintaining a steady strain; while the stone was prevented from returning to its original position when the levers were shifted. These operations were repeated until the rock was raised nearly to an equipoise, when cables from six other capstans were attached to the opposite side, to guard against a too sudden descent; and as a further precaution against fracture, a bed, six feet in thickness, of hay and moss intermingled, was placed to receive the rock, on which it was happily laid at the end of March 1769. As it was of great importance that all the workmen should act at one and the same time, two drummers were stationed on the top of the stone, who, at a sign from the engineer, gave the necessary signals on their drums, and secured the certainty of order and precision in the various operations.

Meantime the machinery for the removal had been made. Of the lower grooved beams already described, six pairs were prepared, so that when the rock had advanced over one pair, they might be drawn forward and placed in a line in advance of the foremost, without interrupting the movements. The balls were laid in the grooves 2 feet apart; the upper frame, intended as the bed for the rock, placed above: the mass, weighing in its original form 4,000,000 lbs., was then raised by means of powerful screws, and deposited on the frame, when it was drawn up the inclined plane by the united force of six capstans. The road did not proceed in a direct line to the river, owing to the soft state of portions of the marsh: in many places it was impossible to reach a firm foundation with piles 50 feet in length. This naturally added to the difficulties of the transport, as the direction of the draught was frequently to be changed. Piles were driven along the whole line on both sides, at distances of 300 feet apart: to these the cables were made fast, while the capstans revolved; two of which were found sufficient to draw the stone on a level surface, while on unequal ground four were required. The rate of motion was from 500 to 1200 feet daily, which, when regard is had to the short winter days of five hours in that high latitude, may be considered as rapid. So interesting was the spectacle of the enormous mass when moving, with the two drummers at their posts, the forge erected on it continually at work, and forty workmen constantly employed in reducing it to a regular form, that the empress and the court visited the spot to see the novel sight; and, notwithstanding the rigour of the season, crowds of persons of all ranks went out every day as spectators. Small flat sledges were attached to each side of the stone by ropes, on which were seated men provided with iron levers, whose duty it was to prevent the balls, of which fifteen on a side were used, from striking against each other, and thus impeding the motion. The tool-house was also attached, and moved with the stone, in order that everything might be ready to hand when required. Experiments were tried with balls and grooves of cast-iron; but this material crumbled into fragments as readily as if made of clay. No metal was found to bear the weight so well as the mixture of copper and tin; and even with this the balls were sometimes flattened, and the grooves curled up, when the pressure by any accident became unequal. The utility of rollers was also tried; but with double the number of capstans and power, the cables broke, while the stone did not advance an inch.

The work went on favourably, when it was suddenly checked by the sinking of the stone to a depth of 18 inches in the road, to the great chagrin of the engineer, who was suffering under a severe attack of marsh fever. He was not, however, disheartened, and speedily remedied the accident, spite of the idle clamours of the multitude; and in six weeks from the time of first drawing the stone from its bed, he had the satisfaction of seeing it safely deposited on the temporary wharf built for the purpose of embarkation on the banks of the river, when the charge fell into the hands of the Admiralty, who had undertaken the transport by water to the city.

A vessel or barge 180 feet in length, 66 feet in width, and 17 feet from deck to keel, had been built with every appliance that skill could suggest, to render it capable of supporting the enormous burden. Great precautions were now necessary to prevent the possibility of the falling of the rock into the stream: water was let into the vessel until she sunk to the bottom of the river, which brought her deck on a level with the wharf; the rock was then drawn on board by means of two capstans placed on the deck of another vessel, anchored at some distance from the shore. Pumps and buckets were now brought into use to clear the barge of the water with which she had been filled; but to the surprise and consternation of those engaged, she did not rise equally: the centre, bearing most of the weight, remained at the bottom, while the head and stern, springing up, gave to the whole the form of a sharp curve: the timbers gave way, and the seams opening, the water re-entered rapidly: 400 men were then set to bale, in order that every part might be simultaneously cleared; but the curve became greater in proportion to the diminution of the internal volume of water.

M. Lascary, who, from the time the rock had been placed on the deck of the vessel, had been a simple spectator of these operations, which occupied two weeks, now received orders to draw it again upon the wharf. He immediately applied himself to remedy the error—which had been committed in not distributing the weight equally—without removing the stone. He first caused the head and stern of the barge to be loaded with large stones, until they sank to a level with the centre; the rock was then raised by means of screws and beams of timber, diverging to every part of the vessel, placed under and against it; and on the removal of the screws, the pressure being equal in every part, she regained her original form. The water was next pumped out, the stones removed from the head and stern, a ship lashed on each side of the barge, which, on the 22d September, arrived opposite the quay where it was intended to erect the statue.

Not the least difficult part of the work, the debarkation, remained to be done. As the river was here of a greater depth than at the place of embarkation, rows of piles had been driven into the bottom alongside the quay, and cut off level at a distance of eight feet below the surface: on these the barge was rested; and, to prevent the recurrence of the rising of the head and stern when the supports should be removed, three masts, lashed together, crossing the deck at each extremity, were secured to the surface of the quay. It was then feared that, as the rock approached the shore, the vessel might heel and precipitate it into the river. This was obviated by fixing six other masts to the quay, which projected across the whole breadth of the deck, and were made fast to a vessel moored outside; thus presenting a counterpoise to the weight of the stone. The grooved beams were laid ready, the cables secured, and at the moment of removing the last support, the drummers beat the signal: the men at the capstans ran round with a cheer; the barge heeled slightly, which accelerated the movement; and in an instant the rock was safely landed on the quay.

Such was the successful result of an undertaking, extraordinary in its nature and the circumstances in opposition to it.* An example is here afforded to those who may have to struggle with difficulties in mechanical art, that will stimulate them to attempt what may appear impossible to the timid and unreflecting. He who contends successfully with the adverse opinions of men of learning, and the blind prejudices of the multitude, achieves a moral as well as a physical triumph, deserving of high praise and imitation.

* The whole expense of the removal did not exceed 70,000 roubles, or L.14,000; while the materials which remained were worth two-thirds of the sum.

It is to be regretted that the effect of this unrivalled pedestal was marred by the diminution of its size. Under the directions of the artist who had so successfully formed the statue, it was pared and chiseled, until the weight was reduced to 3,000,000 lbs.; and the outline, instead of being left bold and broken, as best suited the character of the group, was made smooth and uniform. It forms, however, one of the chief attractions of St Petersburg, standing 'in the square opposite the Isaac Bridge, at the western extremity of the Admiralty. Here the colossal equestrian statue of the founder of this magnificent city, placed on a granite rock, seems to command the undivided attention of the stranger. On approaching nearer, the simple inscription fixed on it, in bronze letters, "Petro Primo, Catharina Secunda, MDCCLXXXII," meets the eye. The same inscription in the Russian language appears on the opposite side. The area is enclosed within a handsome railing, placed between granite pillars. The idea of Falconet, the French architect, commissioned to erect an equestrian statue to the extraordinary man at whose command a few scattered huts of fishermen were converted into palaces, was to represent the hero as conquering, by enterprise and personal courage, difficulties almost insurmountable. This the artist imagined might be properly represented by placing Peter on a fiery steed, which he is supposed to have taught, by skill, management, and perseverance, to rush up a steep and precipitous rock, to the very brink of a precipice, over which the animal and the imperial rider pause without fear, and in an attitude of triumph. The horse rears with his fore-feet in the air, and seems to be impatient of restraint, while the sovereign, turned towards the island, surveys with calm and serene countenance his capital rising out of the waters, over which he extends the hand of protection. The bold manner in which the group has been made to rest on the hind legs of the horse only, is not more surprising than the skill with which advantage has been taken of the allegorical figure of the serpent of envy spurned by the horse, to assist in upholding so gigantic a mass. This monument of bronze is said to have been cast at a single jet. The height of the figure of the emperor is 11 feet, that of the horse 17 feet. The bronze is, in the thinnest parts, only the fourth of an inch, and one inch in the thickest part; the general weight of metal in the group is equal to 36,636 English lbs.'*

* Granville's Travels to St Petersburg.

MISCELLANEA.

A justifiable pride is felt in the beautiful public buildings of our cities, and the handsome residences of the higher classes in both town and country. But, as some one has remarked about the magnificent ceremonial religion of the middle ages, that it co-existed with barbarism in the people, so may it be observed of our fine buildings, that they—disgracefully to us as a community—stand side by side with dwellings for the humbler classes, which are hardly advanced from those of the most primitive state of society. Read on this subject the following remarks by Professor Low, in his recent work on the Management of Landed Property:—

'The subject of the dwellings of the rural population, whether they exist as detached cottages, or as groups of houses, in the form of hamlets or villages, merits more regard than has hitherto been paid to it. They who have been used to see only the decent habitations of the peasantry of many parts of England, can have but a faint conception of the state of the same class of dwellings over the larger part of the British islands. If we shall pass into Ireland, we shall find the country covered from end to end with huts and cabins of mud, even more wretched within than their ragged exterior indicates. The damp earth generally forms the floor, a hole in the roof allows the smoke to escape, the windows are holes usually stuffed with rags, and wood is wanting in every part. One wretched chamber contains the inmates, without distinction of age or sex; some huddled in filthy pallets, or on rude benches of planks, nay, on straw or heath spread on the ground. The fire of turf on the ground fills the shed with dust and smoke; while the refuse of wretched repasts, heaps of rags, nay, the filth of pigs and fowls, poison the air within. In such dens as these, fitter for the abodes of beasts than of men, dwell millions of peasants who have known no better lot. Can we wonder that, under such a condition of life, gross habits should prevail, and men be rude and reckless! * *

'Scotland, with respect to the habits of the peasantry, is in a somewhat different condition, although the dwellings of this class are in many cases as mean and wretched as those of the sister country. In Scotland, two very distinct races of peasants exist, the one of mixed lineage, but chiefly of Teutonic blood, inhabiting the lowland countries, and the other of Celtic descent, possessing the countries of the higher mountains. The lowland peasants are generally labourers employed upon the farms. In the southern counties, as well as in the north-eastern part of England, the principal servants of the farm are married persons, who engage their services for a specified time, almost always twelve months, and who receive wages partly in money, but chiefly in the produce of the farm, together with the use of cottages, small gardens, cows kept upon the farm, and other conveniences. The persons thus treated form the best class of farm-labourers of the British islands. They are hard worked from an early age, but they have all been educated, thoroughly understand the duties of their condition, and lead a life more tranquil and contented than the same class of labourers in any other part of the country. To the establishment of this admirable system of farm-economy, is due that practice of steady and regular labour by which the works of the farm are conducted with order throughout the year. The system prevails more or less throughout all the lowlands of Scotland, although with far less regularity in the northern than in the southern counties, where it has been the established practice of the farms time out of mind.

'But the existence of the system has led to certain peculiarities, and great defects, with respect to the construction of the dwellings possessed by the labourers. For carrying it into effect, it has sufficed that the cottagers should receive merely a rude room, sometimes with, but oftener without, a loft above. The labourers themselves possess a simple kind of furniture, which they call plenishing, consisting of large box-beds with sliding doors, chests for clothes, and shelves for plates and dishes. This furniture, with the common utensils of the household, as blankets and coarse linen, constitute, together with the cow, which is to supply the family with a great part of their food, the little stock or capital of the inmates. Until this can be obtained, the young peasant is not regarded as in a condition to enter into the state of matrimony and begin housekeeping; and this simple check, itself an inducement to habits of frugality, does more to prevent reckless unions than many moral lessons could effect. By the possession of their homely furniture, the married pair are enabled to fit up their rude room in a manner more consistent with humble comfort and decency than could be imagined. The closed box-beds are so large, that they serve in part for dressing and wardrobes. They are usually disposed in such a manner across the room, that it can be divided into two, and in this manner the separation of the members of the family is better promoted than, from the smallness of the apartments, would seem to be attainable. Yet the houses are exceedingly mean, ill fitted up, and comfortless. The floor is generally unpaved, consisting of an imperfect composition, or often merely of earth rammed hard. The fire is, for the most part, on the hearth, underneath a large chimney, too wide for allowing the apartment to be warmed, or even for carrying up the smoke. The windows are ill-constructed either for ventilation or warmth, and the doors are hung in such a manner as to allow the cold winds to penetrate the little chamber; and often the roofs are so ill formed or decayed as to admit the rain. Since the commencement of the present century, however, considerable attention has been paid to the improvement of this class of buildings, and almost always when the old ones have been taken down, new ones have been substituted, superior with respect to size, materials, and fitting up. Nevertheless, there are great numbers of the old buildings still in existence, and of the new ones, the greater number have received nothing like the improvement of which, by a slight pecuniary sacrifice, they are susceptible. The general defects of these new cottages are the want of proper flooring and lofting. If the practice before recommended were adopted, of raising the side walls, so that space for sleeping were to be given above, a great degree of additional accommodation could be afforded, and it may be said all the humble desires of the inmates, with respect to their dwellings, would be fulfilled. When we consider the high importance of preserving, to the peasantry of Scotland, the system of household economy which has been so happily established amongst them, the owners of estates should not begrudge the little sacrifice required of them to render this class of buildings suited to the modest wants of their possessors.

While the system of married labourers residing in their separate cottages, is beyond all question that which is the best adapted for maintaining the character which has hitherto distinguished the lowland peasantry of Scotland, it is to be regretted that considerations of ungenerous economy have, in many parts of the same country, introduced a different system, which has had the effect of destroying the older hamlets and farm-cottages, without providing a substitute. Under this system, the married labourers are as much as possible dispensed with, and lads only are taken, for whom a single cottage is built, termed a boothie or bothy. In this the poor youths are placed, free from all the restraints which should surround them in early life, mixed together, of every character, obliged to prepare their own food, and attend to their own wretched household. What can be expected under such a system but contamination of the youthful habits, and the neglect of all those decencies which may become the charm of the humblest cottage? There is a little saving in wages to the farmer, but the real gain is to the landlord, who avoids the erection of the necessary buildings. If there were suitable cottages, the young lads could board themselves in them as members of the family; or why should the decent, farmer-like, and honest practice be abolished, so general in England, of allowing the young labourers to live in the farm-house? But whatever be the course pursued, it will be scandalous to the landed proprietors of Scotland to permit the youthful peasants of their country to be corrupted by the want of a few decent cottages upon the farms.'

The two following anecdotes were found literally following each other, apparently by accident, in a newspaper:—

NAPOLEON CROSSING THE ALPS.—Artists have delineated him crossing the Alpine heights mounted on a fiery steed. The plain truth is, that he ascended the St Bernard in the gray surtout which he usually wore upon a mule, led by a guide belonging to the country, evincing, even in the difficult passes, the abstraction of a mind occupied elsewhere, conversing with the officers scattered on the road, and then, at intervals, questioning the guide who attended him, making him relate the particulars of his life, his pleasures, his pains, like an idle traveller who has nothing better to do. This guide, who was quite young, gave him a simple recital of the details of his obscure existence, and especially the vexation he felt because, for want of a little money, he could not marry one of the girls of his valley. The first consul, sometimes listening, sometimes questioning the passengers with whom the mountain was covered, arrived at the Hospice, where the worthy monks gave him a warm reception. No sooner had he alighted from his mule than he wrote a note, which he handed to his guide, desiring him to be sure and deliver it to the quarter-master of the army, who had been left on the other side of the St Bernard. In the evening, the young man, on returning to St Pierre, learned with surprise what powerful traveller it was whom he had guided in the morning, and that General Bonaparte had ordered that a house and a piece of ground should be given to him immediately, and that he should be supplied, in short, with the means requisite for marrying, and for realising all the dreams of his modest ambition. This mountaineer died not long since in his own country, the owner of land given to him by the ruler of the world. This singular act of beneficence, at a moment when his mind was engaged by such mighty interests, is worthy of attention. If there were nothing in it but a mere conqueror's caprice, dispensing at random good or evil, alternately overthrowing empires or rearing a cottage, it may be useful to record such caprices, if only to tempt the masters of the earth to imitation. But such an act reveals something more. The human soul, in those moments when it is filled with ardent desires, is disposed to kindness; it does good by way of meriting that which it is soliciting of Providence. —*Thiers' History of the Consulate and Empire.*

NELSON'S KINDNESS OF HEART.—Nelson's kindness of heart exhibits itself everywhere. Scarcely can a page of his correspondence be opened without some evidence of his affectionate disposition. Habitually, he treated all under his command, down to the very powder-monkey, as his children; and they had for him a love as for a father. In a private letter to his brother, speaking of his midshipmen, he calls them by the very name—'all my *children* are well,' he says. A letter from Lady Hughes, describing a scene on board the Boreas, in which she was a passenger, is beautiful:—'I was too much affected when we met at Bath to say every particular in which was always displayed the infinite cleverness and goodness of heart of our beloved hero. As a woman, I can only be a judge of those things which I could comprehend—such as his attention to the young gentlemen who had the happiness of being on his quarter-deck. It may reasonably be supposed that, among the number of thirty, there must be timid as well as bold; the timid he never rebuked, but always wished to show them he desired nothing of them that he would not instantly do himself; and I have known him say, "Well, sir, I am going a race to the mast-head, and beg I may meet you there." No denial could be given to such a wish, and the poor fellow instantly began his march. His lordship never took the least notice with what alacrity it was done; but, when he met in top, instantly began speaking in the most cheerful manner, and saying how much a person was to be pitied that could fancy there was any danger, or even anything disagreeable, in the attempt. After this excellent example, I have seen the timid youth lead another, and rehearse his captain's words. How wise and kind was such a proceeding! In like manner he every day went into the school-room, and saw them at their nautical business; and at twelve o'clock he was first upon deck with his quadrant. No one there could be behind-hand in their business when their captain set them so good an example. One other circumstance I must mention, which will close the subject, which was the day we landed at Barbadoes. We were to dine at the governor's. Our dear captain said, "You must permit me, Lady Hughes, to carry one of my aides-de-camp with me;" and, when he presented him to the governor, he said, "Your excellency must excuse me for bringing one of my midshipmen, as I make it a rule to introduce them to all the good company I can, as they have few to look up to besides myself during the time they are at sea." This kindness and attention made the young people adore him; and even his wishes, could they have been known, would have been instantly complied with.'—*Despatches and Letters of Admiral Lord Nelson.*

How curious thus to learn at length of traits of simple kind feeling in two men of whom, in our youth, while they were living, we used to hear only of their powers as agents of destruction among their fellow-creatures! Much less could these two 'heroes,' while pitted against each other like savage animals, conceive that in each other's bosoms there beat, after all, hearts that responded to the voice of social and domestic kindness. Above all, how sad to reflect that circumstances should ever be such, that men know each other only as deadly enemies, and devote their whole faculties to do each other injury, who, under happier auspices, would doubtless have gladly joined hands and hearts, and done what they could to promote each other's happiness, and that of all in whom they respectively felt interested!

BAD BREAD.

At a recent meeting of the members of the Devon and Cornwall Natural History Society, Dr Tripe read a paper on 'ropy bread,' in the course of which he stated that the state of bread termed 'ropy' was generally admitted to depend on the presence of fungi. Recent writers on the subject agreed in attributing the ropy state of bread to the presence of fungi. And they all accounted for the presence of fungi on the ground of the quality of the flour; but he thought it might in all probability originate from three causes—that of atmosphere, from yeast, which he thought the main cause, and from the flour. With respect to yeast, he said it appeared, from a microscopic examination of a mass of yeast, that it consists of minute disconnected vesicles, that appear to constitute one of the simplest forms of vegetation. These, like seeds, may remain for any length of time in an inactive condition without losing their vitality; but when placed in a fluid in which any kind of sugary matter is contained, they commence vegetating actively, provided the temperature be sufficiently high, and they assist in producing that change in the composition of the fluid which is known under the name of fermentation. Having referred to several opinions on fermentation, the learned gentleman went on to say, that if a small portion of the fermenting fluid be examined at intervals with a powerful microscope, it is observed that each of the little vesicles at first contained in it puts forth one or more prolongations, which in time become new vesicles like their parents. These organs perform the same office, so that in a few hours the single vesicles have developed themselves into rows of five or six. This is not the only way, however, in which they multiply; for sometimes the vesicles burst, and emit a number of minute granules, which are the germs of new plants, and which soon develop themselves into additional cells. By the time that five or six vesicles are formed in each group, the fermentation is sufficiently far advanced for the purposes to which it is to be applied, and measures are then taken to check it, by which the vegetation of the yeast plant is checked. If they could suppose any circumstance to arise by which the vegetation of the yeast was not suspended, or after it was checked and the yeast amalgamated with the flour, for the vegetation again to be active, they would have a sufficient cause for the origin of fungi in bread. The progress of the disease, as it may be called, in bakehouses, from one lot of bread to another, was elaborately gone into and pointed out, and instances were cited in which its ravages had prevailed to the extent of even ruining the bakers. As a remedy, he suggested ventilation, fumigation with chlorine, and the application of cold instead of hot washing. At the conclusion of the reading of the paper, a committee was appointed to inquire and report upon the subject.—*Plymouth Times.*

THE QUEEN'S PAPER AND INK.

Under this title certain new inventions have been patented, which combine in a remarkable degree utility with elegance. The ink is a limpid and colourless liquid, and not distinguishable by the eye from pure water. The paper is of two kinds, both like common writing-paper in appearance, and the ink is used with a quill or metallic pen in the ordinary way. If the one species of paper is employed, the writing executed with the colourless liquid is of a tint approaching to *black;* if the other species of paper is employed, it is a clear *blue.* The liquid has the farther advantage, that it does not stain the fingers, or anything with which it comes in contact. Having tried the mode of writing with these articles, we can bear testimony to its cleanliness and elegance, and we are not surprised that her majesty, after using them, permitted them to be styled 'her majesty's paper and ink.' The same ingenious person has invented an 'indelible ink' for records, which promises to be very valuable. Other inks so named only profess to protect the writing from obliteration by long exposure to the elements, but the ink we are now speaking of resists even chemical agents.—*Newspaper paragraph.*

ARTIFICIAL LIMBS.

At the Academy of Sciences in Paris lately, M. Magendie read, in the name of the committee of the academy, composed of MM. Gambey, Rayer, Velpeau, and himself, a report on an artificial arm, the invention of M. Van Petersen, a Dutch sculptor, and presented by him to the academy. The report was highly favourable to the ingenious and benevolent inventor. The members of the committee state that they had seen the apparatus tried upon five mutilated persons, and that it answered in every case admirably. One of these persons was an invalid who, in the wars of the empire, lost both arms, retaining only the mere stumps. With the aid of two of these artificial arms, he was able to perform many of the functions which had hitherto been performed for him by others. In presence of the committee, he raised, with one of the artificial hands, a full glass to his mouth, drank its contents without spilling a drop, and then replaced the glass on the table from which he had taken it. He also picked up a pin, a sheet of paper, &c. These facts are conclusive as to the mechanical skill evinced by M. Van Petersen, and which is particularly shown in the lightness of his apparatus, each arm and hand, with all its articulations, weighing less than a pound. The mode in which the motion is imparted to the articulations of the apparatus is exceedingly ingenious. A sort of stays is fixed round the breast of the person, and from this are cords made of catgut, which act upon the articulations according to the motion given to the natural stump of the arm. The invention fails only when the member that is wanting has been entirely removed from the socket, which is of comparatively rare occurrence. The report ends by stating that M. Van Petersen's invention is superior to any substitute for the natural arm hitherto made, and expresses a hope that he will be able to get his artificial arms manufactured at so low a cost as to be accessible to poor persons and mutilated soldiers.—*From a French newspaper.*

ADVANTAGES OF A BOOK.

Of all the amusements which can possibly be imagined for a hard-working man, after his daily toil, or in its intervals, there is nothing like reading an entertaining book—supposing him to have a taste for it, and supposing him to have a book to read. It calls for no bodily exertion, of which he has had enough, or too much. It relieves his home of its dulness and sameness, which, in nine cases out of ten, is what drives him out to the alehouse, to his own ruin and his family's. It transports him into a livelier and gayer and more diversified and interesting scene; and while he enjoys himself there, he may forget the evils of the present moment fully as much as if he were ever so drunk, with the great advantage of finding himself the next day with his money in his pocket, or at least laid out in real necessaries and comforts for himself and his family, and without a headache. Nay, it accompanies him to his next day's work, and if the book he has been reading be anything above the very idlest and lightest, gives him something to think of besides the mere mechanical drudgery of his every-day occupation—something he can enjoy while absent, and look forward with pleasure to return to. But supposing him to have been fortunate in the choice of his book, and to have alighted upon one really good and of a good class, what a source of domestic enjoyment is laid open! what a bond of family union! He may read it aloud, or make his wife read it, or his eldest boy or girl, or pass it round from hand to hand. All have the benefit of it—all contribute to the gratification of the rest, and a feeling of common interest and pleasure is excited. Nothing unites people like companionship in intellectual enjoyment. It does more, it gives them mutual respect, and to each among them self-respect—that corner-stone of all virtue. It furnishes to each the master-key by which he may avail himself of his privilege as an intellectual being, to

> Enter the sacred temple of his breast,
> And gaze and wander there a ravished guest—
> Wander through all the glories of the mind,
> Gaze upon all the treasures he shall find.

And while thus leading him to look within his own bosom for the ultimate sources of his happiness, warns him at the same time to be cautious how he defiles and desecrates that inward and most glorious of temples.—*Sir John Herschel.*

MENTAL CONTROL.

When we turn our serious attention to the economy of the mind, we perceive that it is capable of a variety of processes of the most remarkable and most important nature. We find also that we can exert a voluntary power over these processes, by which we control, direct, and regulate them at our will; and that when we do not exert this power, the mind is left to the influence of external impression, or casual trains of association, often unprofitable, and often frivolous. We thus discover that the mind is the subject of culture and discipline, which, when duly exercised, must produce the most important results on our condition as rational and moral beings; and that the exercise of them involves a responsibility of the most solemn kind, which no man can possibly put away from him.—*Abercrombie.*

CENSURE.

Censure, says an ingenious author, is the tax a man pays to the public for being eminent. It is folly for an eminent man to think of escaping it, and a weakness to be affected with it. All the illustrious persons of antiquity, and indeed of every age in the world, have passed through this fiery persecution. There is no defence against reproach but obscurity; it is a kind of concomitant to greatness, as satires and invectives were an essential part of a Roman triumph.—*Addison.*

Printed by William Bradbury, of No. 6, York Place, and Frederick Mullett Evans, of No. 7, Church Row, both of Stoke Newington, in the county of Middlesex, printers, at their office, Lombard Street, in the precinct of Whitefriars, and city of London; and Published (with permission of the Proprietors, W. and R. CHAMBERS) by WILLIAM SOMERVILLE ORR, Publisher, of 2, Amen Corner, at No. 2, AMEN CORNER, both in the parish of Christchurch, and in the city of London.—Saturday, May 17, 1845.

CONDUCTED BY WILLIAM AND ROBERT CHAMBERS, EDITORS OF 'CHAMBERS'S INFORMATION FOR THE PEOPLE,' 'CHAMBERS'S EDUCATIONAL COURSE,' &c.

No. 73. New Series. SATURDAY, MAY 24, 1845. Price 1½d.

STYLE.

What is worth doing at all, is allowed to be worth doing well; and so fully is this maxim recognised in life, that the performance of anything in an inferior or *shabby* manner is always supposed to be indicative of a certain meanness of mind. In English ethics, therefore, shabbiness bears a very contemptuous interpretation, while its opposite—a disposition to do things handsomely, or in style—commands universal applause. Nor can there be anything unreasonable in this view of matters, looking at appearances as the exponent of internal convictions. It may be generally observed, that the man who performs an act in a handsome manner, is also the most generous and estimable. No man was ever truly great who attempted to do things by halves.

So inextricably interwoven with the framework of our ideas is this estimate of *manner*, that the doing of a thing 'in style' has become, in common speech, synonymous with excellence itself. My friend Jackson is so thoroughly imbued with this notion of style, that with him it has become a ruling principle of life. He has faith in style, and would as soon forego belief in the thing itself, as in the potency of the manner in which it appears. He keeps house in style, and certainly a more elegant or more comfortable mansion does not exist. Dwellings there may be more gaudy and expensive, but none, we are confident, in which there are more substantiality and taste, without any attempt at lacquering, or effort in getting up. To crown the whole, there is a certain style about his beautiful wife and children which makes one almost feel envious; and envious we would most decidedly be, did not we know in our hearts that they belong to a man most perfectly deserving of such a treasury of happiness. As with his house, so with his establishment in the city; for my friend is not above the necessity of applying his head to business. This place is a model of elegance and strength: the grounds are laid out in green-sward and shrubbery, and gravelled walks, albeit they lead to a four-storeyed factory. Enter this cotton palace, and the entire arrangements, the aspect of the machinery, and the conduct of the men and women, strike you at once that the whole is under the presiding genius of one who is fully determined 'to do things in style.' Follow his employés to the streets and to their homes, and you will find alike from their demeanour, their dress, and their residences, that they have caught, as it were by inoculation, the spirit of their master, and are equally actuated by the principles of style. If there are fewer tattered garments and filthy apartments among them than among any other equal number of the population, rest assured that style is at the bottom of the reformation; so true is it that like begets like, and that there is no surer mode of raising a man's moral nature than by cultivating his perception of the chaste and beautiful. It is not, however, in what may be considered mere economical arrangements that Jackson's faith in manner predominates; he is equally guided by it in feeling and conduct. If he be called upon to subscribe for a distressed family, let him only be assured of their deserving necessity, and he hands his cheque for ten pounds with a willingness and sincerity of feeling that makes the gift doubly valuable. There is no hankering, no grumbling about the frequency of calls of this nature, no complaint of bad times, no prying inquisitiveness into circumstances, no railing at the improvidence of the poor; none, in short, of those obstacles which overwhelm the generosity of little souls, who have no notion whatever of the beauty of doing things in style. Again, let him be called upon in public meeting to subscribe for some city improvement, and his name goes down at once for one hundred or two hundred guineas, as the case may be; he hands the paper to his neighbours without boast or comment, leaving them to the conviction that, as usual, Jackson has done the thing in style. Nor is there any vanity in all this. To say that there is no pride, would be to talk absurdity; for a just and honourable pride must ever be at the foundation of self-respect; and it is self-respect that raises us above all that is mean, and heartless, and contaminating.

The public usually show a keen appreciation of style, and their verdict on this point is decisive for or against the individual who aspires to their favour. Let the premier come forward with a measure in which some great principle is involved—no matter what it be—if he present it boldly and frankly, without any equivocation or reserve, without any frittering or chopping which can lead to the suspicion of insincerity, then he is sure to be hailed with the merit of having done it in style. Be it a boon to be granted, or a necessity to be met, John Bull is equally indifferent, provided the thing be given or taken in a gentlemanly way. It is not the matter so much as the manner that puts him out of humour; he naturally hates all meanness and snivelling, but gloriously delights in affairs that are managed in style. The same standard he carries with him into private life. The heir who recently came to his estate, who keeps a fine equipage, converses with his tenants, improves his lands, and employs the peasantry, is applauded for living in style. The spendthrift or cheat may keep as gay an equipage, may have as many dogs and hunters; but the populace are not led to a false judgment by such appearances. We may hear of such a one living in 'grand style,' or in 'gay style;' but we never catch an echo of the satisfactory verdict that the spendthrift 'does it in style.' So it is with every other phase of conduct: a 'stylish' man is sure to be an elegant well-dressed person of gentlemanly demeanour; as far removed above foppery and tinsel as he is above rags and vulgarity; and a man of this stamp, if requested to confer a favour, would rather frankly decline doing it at all, than be suspected of the meanness of not doing it in style. To be sure we occasionally hear of this or that person being 'quite in style,' or of certain things being 'rather stylish;' but these are mere satirical applications of the term, intended to ridicule that aping vanity which would take upon itself the airs, and dress, and qualities of a rank incompatible with its situation.

We are now called on to observe, that this idea of style relates to something deeper than externals. It is indeed a principle—a reality in mind, and a characteristic of things as essential to their excellence as the substance of which they are composed. The stones and blocks which constitute a house are still the same materials, whether they are piled as taken from the quarry, or chiselled and arranged with reference to form and symmetry; but no one will hold for a moment that they are quite as good and apt in the one case as they are in the other. View them in the humblest light, as merely affording shelter from wind and rain, the blocks that are compactly and symmetrically arranged will answer that purpose infinitely better than those which are rudely thrown together. But, besides the elements of simple utility, we have an eye to be pleased, and a sense of beauty and form to be gratified. To withhold from these the legitimate objects of their desires, is to degrade man to the level of the brute, or at all events to prevent him from rising above the lowest state of savage existence. The acquirement of styles and modes of form is but the cultivation of intellectual tastes; and as these are elevated, so rise men in civilisation and refinement. The cultivation of refined tastes may not be virtue itself, but it is undoubtedly one of her most potent allies: beauty, rectitude, and chastity of mind, can expand nowhere so freely as when surrounded by beauty, and rectitude, and chastity of external forms. The acquirement of mere materials cannot therefore be the ultimate object of our pursuit; we ought only to rest satisfied when we have adjusted and arranged them in proper form; in other words, when we feel that, according to the popular phrase, we have done what we designed to do, in style. So also it is with matters of conduct. Men do not estimate actions solely by their intrinsic or abstract value; *manner* at all times constitutes a notable proportion of the estimate. Thus, though the ten pounds given willingly, frankly, and kindly in charity, is worth no more at the banker's than the ten pounds given grudgingly, sourly, and upbraidingly, yet in the wide world of humanity is it doubly and trebly valuable. Think you that the example of the man who acts handsomely and kindly is lost upon his fellow-men? Are we not creatures of imitation, prone not only to admire, but to follow a generous line of conduct? Even when some unworthy feeling creeps across the mind, how instantaneously is it dispelled by the sunshine of better example. It is thus that a Jackson's ten pounds may produce a hundred, stimulating the thoughtless to consideration, and shaming the niggard into liberality. But beyond this pecuniary view, there is a higher still. The object of our charity has thoughts and feelings keen as our own, and our respect for these is as imperative as our charity. We are commanded not only to bind the wound, but to drop the balm of consolation; not only to act justly, but to love mercy; and it is thus that the widow's mite becomes as valuable as the rich man's talent. So it is with all other doings—friendly, hospitable, charitable; with demeanour personal and with demeanour public: it is not enough that we say, and give, and do; if we wish to reap the respect of others, and enjoy satisfaction, we must be equally careful that these things be said, and given, and done in style.

Such an estimate and appreciation of style could not take place among any save a refined and civilised people, and to such a character—with all our faults—we may safely be allowed to lay claim. Were we less elevated, we would be less swayed by this idea; the 'doing of things in style' would never have become synonymous with excellence itself. But, independent of the high standard of value to which the phrase points, there is something exhilarating in its very tone. Let me only hear of a man who 'does things in style,' and I invariably ascribe to him a certain goodness of heart, affability of manner, and manliness of nature, which is quite delightful. I feel that everything connected with him must be first-rate of its kind; and I know, too, that if required to do an act of kindness or charity, that act would be done in a liberal and genial spirit. Nor is the doing of things in style confined to any rank or class: the man of L.40 a-year may act within his own sphere equally well with him who has L.4000. If he cannot afford Brussels carpet, he can at least keep his floor well polished and clean; if he cannot drink out of silver, he can at least have elegant delf; and though his coat be less costly, it may at least be clean, and neatly put on. It is taste, in fact, that regulates the whole matter; and that attribute of mind may be more exalted, purer, chaster, in a poor mechanic than in a pampered lordling.

HEALTH OF TOWNS IN LANCASHIRE.

The Health of Towns' Commission has issued another of its reports on the sanitary condition of the large towns in Lancashire, consisting of a return laid by Dr Lyon Playfair before this useful board of inquiry. So much has now been accumulated and published on this subject by different bodies of commissioners, that it may appear needless to collect any more facts, or draw any new conclusions. Parliament, it may be said, ought now to be thoroughly indoctrinated with the necessity for legislating on the health of towns: and this is true; but the public at large are still very ignorant of what is required; a prejudice in favour of all sorts of abominations—burial within towns, and even within chapels, slaughter-houses in the midst of a dense population, disregard of ventilation and cleanliness—is almost universal; and we can only hope, by a more general enlightenment, to prepare the way for that species of legislation which is so very desirable. To aid this good cause, we offer a few gleanings from Dr Playfair's report.

The places which the doctor selects as illustrative of the general state of large towns in Lancashire, are Liverpool, Manchester, Preston, Bolton, Wigan, Ashton-under-Lyne, Bury, and Rochdale, all with a large population engaged chiefly in manufactures and trade. In these places, and some others, there is much defective drainage and sewerage, seriously affecting the public health. Yet not a little has lately been done in various towns to effect improvements in these respects. In Manchester, since 1830, more than thirty-two miles of sewers have been constructed, and some hundreds of small streets paved and rendered approachable. Wherever such improvements have been effected, the medical examiners 'express their astonishment at the better appearance of the inhabitants and of the physical condition of these districts.' In Liverpool, the commissioners of sewers have expended above L.100,000 in new sewers and paving during the last few years; but very much remains to be done. 'There are thousands of houses,' says a witness examined in Liverpool, 'and hundreds of courts in this town, without a single drain of any description; and I never hail anything with greater delight than I do a violent tempest or a terrific thunder storm, accompanied by a heavy rain; for these are the only scavengers that thousands have had to cleanse away the impurities and filth in which they live, or rather exist.'

While most of the towns have very defective underground drainage, few if any can be said to be properly swept. It may be laid down as a principle, that every large town should be swept once a day; but few enjoy this advantage. Dr Playfair presents tables showing the comparative extent of scavengering in different towns in Lancashire and Scotland. Liverpool has 65 scavengers; its chief streets are swept once a-week; the cost of scavengering is L.4820; the amount obtained per annum for refuse is L.1150. Manchester has 78 scavengers; its streets are also swept weekly; the annual cost is L.5600; the amount obtained per annum for refuse is L.800. Edinburgh has 115 scavengers; its streets are swept every day; the annual cost is L12,000; the amount obtained for refuse is L.10,000. Glasgow has 64 scavengers; the principal streets only are swept daily, the others less frequently; the annual cost is L.2759; the amount obtained per annum for refuse is L.1100. Aberdeen has 51 scavengers, and is swept daily. Saving off this branch of civic economy is far from wise. 'In the preservation of streets and roads, frequent scavengering proves a positive and direct economy of public money, and in the prevention of disease, an evident, though no less certain, saving of public burdens.'

Some very conclusive evidence is presented respecting the uncleanly habits of the poorer classes. 'Asses, hens, and pigs, are not unfrequently kept in dwellings, and I have seen them even in the sitting-rooms of the poor. Fever is induced by the filthy state of the interior of the house, and being communicated to other persons in the vicinity, becomes an extensive source of general disease and misery. One house is depopulated by fever, or the head of the family being cut off, the remainder remove: new tenants enter the infected house; they also become victims, make way for more, and thus fever becomes extended and perpetuated, because the authorities do not possess the powers contained in the Metropolitan and Liverpool acts—powers, however, not sufficiently summary—for cleansing the interiors of private houses.' We may add, that it is the opinion of Mr Ramsay, late of the Edinburgh police, that it would be a wise expenditure of public money to lime-wash every year all the houses under L.4 rental which might require it; the number he estimates at three-fifths, and the utmost expense for the whole tenement would only be 7d.

By laying out a precautionary 7d. annually on every dwelling of the poor, thousands of lives would be saved, and consequently much public and private distress prevented. It is not believed that this cleansing process would be resisted by those to whose houses it was applied; the bulk of the humbler classes having no objection to be made objects of solicitude without cost to themselves. When nuisances, such as obstructions to drainage, or injurious manufactures, involve private interests, they cannot be so easily dealt with. The following may be cited as an example:—'Opposite the Manchester Royal Infirmary, and within the grounds attached to it, is situated a deep excavation, now filled with water. Formerly, erysipelas in an aggravated form, nearly allied to hospital gangrene, prevailed to a great extent amongst the patients in the infirmary. This excited the attention of the medical officers of that institution, who instituted an inquiry into the cause, and after mature deliberation, recommended that the stagnant pond alluded to should be kept constantly filled with water, to be renewed at stated periods. Since the introduction of this plan, and that of dry rubbing the floors of the building, the erysipelas has much abated, but has not yet disappeared. The pond could easily be filled up, but in this case the lord of the manor, and another party, might claim the ground, and, by building on it, encroach on the proper space for the infirmary.' This, we think, is a pretty broad hint to those who suffer stagnant water near their dwellings.

The smoke nuisance is cited as another instance of the opposition of individual interest to public benefit; 'and here, it is to be remarked,' says Dr Playfair, 'that those who occasion the nuisance, do so in ignorance of the benefits to be derived to themselves from a consumption of smoke. It has been clearly demonstrated by every well-conducted experiment on smoke-burning, that there is a saving of fuel varying from 5 to 20 per cent., and in some cases even more.' Serious vitiation of the air, injurious to health, is caused by the smoke of large towns; the smoke nuisance also causes much needless expense to the inhabitants. 'The pecuniary annual loss to the community of Manchester for the excess of washing rendered necessary by its smoke, is above L.60,000; for it has been found that a penny weekly per head of the population forms a very low estimate of the increased expense, when contrasted with the average expense of washing in towns free from smoke. By introducing into the calculation the excessive expense of renewed painting and whitewashing, it appears, by very low estimates, that the annual loss to Manchester by its smoke is double the amount of its poor rates.'

So much has been said of the dwellings in cellars and confined courts in Liverpool, that we need not here recur to the subject, but pass on to some observations on the motives for selecting such abodes. We are told that it would be an error to suppose that poverty was the sole cause of the selection. 'I know numerous instances of families,' says Dr Playfair, 'whose united wages amount to 40s. or 50s. a-week, yet possessing only one sleeping room.' Several cases of this kind are mentioned, but they cannot be extracted. The natural consequences of such overcrowding are great moral depravity, disease, and premature death. Dreadful as are the scenes observable in many private dwellings, they fall short of what are occurring in the lodging-houses for strangers, which all medical men concur in representing as the foci of malignant disease. The only remedy would be to place such houses under the cognisance of a medical police, with power to enforce sanitary regulations.

Strangely enough, bad ventilation is found in much higher establishments than lodging-houses for the poor and dissolute. The public schools of Lancashire are described as too frequently defective in this respect, the architects of such edifices having considered it quite sufficient to provide a certain number of doors and windows, without also furnishing atmospheric purity. Of 75 schools examined in Manchester, 35 were badly ventilated. When the pupils come from houses of a respectable order, the injury they sustain in school is not very observable; but those who live in cellars, or other badly ventilated dwellings, suffer prodigiously from the bad ventilation in their schools. In one school in Manchester, 70 per cent. of the infants living in cellars are always absent from sickness. In another, 27 per cent. of the cellar occupants are absent from sickness, while only 3$\frac{4}{8}$ per cent. of those who live in houses are absent from the same cause. In all the schools the average allowance of space to each child is about 5·9 cubic feet; 'and when it is considered that nearly double this amount of air passes through the lungs of a child, and is vitiated every hour, it cannot be considered surprising that the inmates of public schools, thus deprived of an adequate supply of fresh air, should suffer such a large amount of sickness, or that they should exhibit in their outward appearance the signs of a weakly and puny childhood. It is quite amazing to observe the difference in the appearance of children attending a well-ventilated and well-regulated school, and of those who attend schools of an opposite description, especially such as are usually denominated cottage schools. The sanitary disadvantages under which children labour in most of our schools, are so much opposed to their mental progress, that nothing would be more conducive to the rapid advance of education than attention to structural arrangements.'

With respect to the supply of water in the Lancashire towns, we have some useful observations. In Manchester, Liverpool, Bolton, and Wigan, the supply is intermittent; in Preston, Ashton, Oldham, Bury, and Rochdale it is continual. Intermittence of supply arises from a deficiency of water, and causes the parties receiving it to erect cisterns in their houses; the cost of a cistern and apparatus connected with it being from L.2 to L.4. When the supply is abundant, no cisterns are required; the water is continually on, and nothing more is wanting than a turn-cock on the pipe. In consequence of the expense of erecting and keeping cisterns in order, the charges of landlords on tenants in Liverpool for a stinted and intermittent supply of water are nearly double those charged for a constant and unlimited supply in Nottingham, Ashton, and some other towns. It ought to be a matter of first importance to give such an abundant supply of water to a town that no cisterns will be necessary, not only for the purpose of saving expense, but because water is more cool, pleasant, and healthful when taken from pipes than from any kind of in-door tank. We cordially agree with the following observations:—'There ought to be no limit put to the supply of water for domestic purposes, but on the contrary every facility should be afforded for its unsparing use. I have spent many days in visiting the houses of artisans in towns, both well and ill supplied with water, and I can state as an invariable rule, that there is a marked difference both in the moral tone and in the physical condition of the inhabitants of those towns; and this difference is even perceptible, though in a less degree, in the houses of the same town, according as they are or are not freely supplied with water.' It is mentioned, that in consequence of the water supplied to Manchester being somewhat hard, the inhabitants are put to an additional expense for soap; their loss in this way is estimated at L.49,363 annually, a sum nearly double the present gross water rental. So much for not procuring a perfectly soft water.

Dr Playfair presents a distressing body of facts illustrative of the havoc committed on infant life by the administration of opiates. But this subject we reserve for a separate paper.

We are furnished with some remarkable evidence on the general ratio of sickness and mortality in the county; the result given by a number of tables is, 'that there are every year in Lancashire 14,000 deaths and 398,000 cases of sickness which might be prevented; and that 11,000 of the deaths consist of adults engaged in productive labour. It further shows that every individual in Lancashire loses 19 years, or nearly one-half of the proper term of his life, and that every adult loses more than 10 years of life, and from premature old age and sickness, much more than that period of working ability. Without taking into consideration the diminution of the physical and mental energies of the survivors from sickness and other depressing causes; without estimating the loss from the substitution of young and inexperienced labour for that which is skilful and productive; without including the heavy burdens incident to the large amount of preventible widowhood and orphanage; without calculating the loss from the excess of births, resulting from the excess of deaths, or the cost of the maintenance of an infantile population, nearly one-half of which is swept off before it attains two years of age, and about 59 per cent. of which never become adult productive labourers; and with data in every case much below the truth, I estimate the actual pecuniary burdens borne by the community in the support of removable disease and death in Lancashire alone at the annual sum of five millions of pounds sterling.

THE INDIAN FARM.

BY PERCY B. ST JOHN.

Edward Wilson was the son of a substantial farmer in the west of England, who had nurtured him with the greatest kindness, and set him out in the world under as advantageous circumstances as possible. Having afterwards failed in health and in wealth, the old man came to reside with his son, who then endeavoured to repay his paternal care by using every effort and making every sacrifice for the promotion of his comfort. Edward was a very small farmer, and his farm was upon an ungenial soil. But he was hardy and persevering to an uncommon degree, and early and late he strove to make amends for the natural difficulties under which he laboured. The desire of success in life, and a wish to smooth the few remaining years of his much revered parent, were powerful incentives to action; but perhaps the hope of one day seeing pretty Amy Walcot the inmate of his humble dwelling acted as a more powerful stimulus.

Amy was the daughter of one in exactly the same station of life as himself, but who, in equally moderate circumstances, and with much exertion keeping from debt and embarrassment, had the disadvantage of being so at a later period of life. Edward Wilson was young, with a fair prospect of many days before him; but Walcot was a more than middle-aged widower, with one only child Amy. The young people had known each other from early youth, and to know with them was to love; their affection, at first that of children, had grown with their growth and strengthened with their strength, until, taking the character of warm and earnest love, their union was delayed only until the clouds of doubt and difficulty should cease to dim their horizon. Like many others, Amy and Edward waited for better days. But the times, instead of mending, seemed to grow more adverse: the crops were one season unusually scant, and Edward for a time grew moody and sad.

Walcot's farm—of which he was a freeholder—was situated on the verge of the great highway to London, just opposite to where a green lane opened upon the dusty road. It was an evening towards the latter end of September; the toils of the hot day were over, and Amy and her father stood in the gentle warmth of the setting sun, looking out upon the scene before them. It was a still quiet English landscape; a road lined by green hedges, with here an opening and there a clump of trees, over which in the distance rose the spire of a humble village church, while all around at intervals wreathed columns of smoke denoted the presence of the scattered homesteads of the people. At length the sun set in a bank of blood-red vapour, just as a figure was sharply relieved against the sky in the act of crossing the unusually high stile that terminated the lane which led from Farmer Wilson's abode. Standing in the very centre of the dying glory of day, it looked like some fantastic creation of the brain.

It was Edward himself.

The young man was received, as usual, with a hearty welcome, and entered the quiet tenement where dwelt his betrothed, to spend the evening with the father and daughter. His own father retired to rest at twilight Edward Wilson's visits were always matter of congratulation. Walcot had an affection for him quite paternal, while Amy loved him with a truth and sincerity which she was at no pains to conceal. Upon the present occasion, however, their neighbour was moody and silent; some weight seemed to hang upon his spirit, while he was loath, it seemed, to get rid of the burden.

'Why, lad, what is the matter with thee?' at length said Walcot; 'thee's most uncommon silent to-night.'

'I have good cause for being so,' replied the more polished and better educated Edward, glancing with uneasiness at the wondering Amy.

'Why, lad, thee's got nothing new, I hope,' continued the elder farmer; 'times is dreadful bad already.'

'So bad, Farmer Walcot,' exclaimed Edward Wilson, 'that I have solemnly resolved upon selling off all I have, farm and all, and leaving old England for ever.'

A dead silence followed this announcement. Amy turned pale, and seemed ready to burst into tears: it was not the first time she had heard of it. Walcot looked astonished; but giving time for neither of them to speak, Wilson opened his views at length to his friends, informing them that the United States of America was the country he intended to be that of his adoption. He explained how land was to be had there in hundreds of acres, well wooded and watered, for a mere trifle; expounded every advantage which might or could accrue from the change; and, growing eloquent, painted the land of promise in all the colours in which emigrants view the spot they are about to select for a home. He spoke for more than an hour in warm and glowing language, neither Amy nor her father interrupting him save by an occasional question.

'Well!' said Walcot, when he at length paused, 'if thee's quite made up thy mind to go, Edward, why I and Amy must just do likewise, since I fancy that's what thee's driving at. Things is dreadful bad, and they can't be worse over yonder, and mayhap they'll be better.'

Amy's countenance brightened up; a temporary shade was effaced from that of Edward; and during the rest of the evening their future arrangements were discussed with zest and animation.

About eight months after the conversation between Walcot and Edward Wilson, a cavalcade entered one of the dense forests of the most northern part of Kentucky. It was composed of several wagons, and owned by a young man and his smiling wife, and two males of a more mature age. Four young farm-labourers with two of their wives from the old country accompanied the emigrants, while a kind of half-witted boy, who hung about the extreme border town, served as guide to the land of which the new settlers had become the owners by right of purchase. Edward and Amy were now man and wife, and they were entering upon the dangers and difficulties of their forest life with good hopes, but at the same time with a firm resolution to shrink from none which were at all surmountable.

The journey through the wilderness was trying in the extreme to man and beast. No road existed, and the wagons of the emigrants were dragged through the forest over fallen logs, through brush and brier, at the rate of from three to five miles a-day. Now a huge tree had to be removed from their path, then a dense mass of thicket had to be cut through, and next a deep hole would force them to make a long and fatiguing circuit. Two of the oxen died in the struggle, and the settlers had an early specimen of the difficulties to be overcome in a new country. At length, however, their five hundred acre lot was reached, and the whole was found to be covered with the same heavy growth of timber they had all along contended against.

Wilson, however, was not of a nature to be discouraged. Unyoking his oxen, the wagons were left upon the side of the sloping hill where the emigrant had decided upon pitching his tent, not figuratively, but in reality, until a more substantial dwelling could be erected. This done, he returned to the frontier town, and hired two of those well-known workmen, who, with the American axe in hand, will lay low acres of forest in one-tenth the time that the European would take to do so. Their wages were high, but, as do all Yankees when once employed, they did their duty; and before the winter came on, a space of about eight acres was cleared, a house built, and the refuse of the timber, all but the solid logs, burnt to ashes. The space gained from the forest was small and unsightly—the trees which had been removed having been cut away two feet from the ground, and the stumps encumbering the fields—but it was still fields, and in due season they were filled with Indian corn, sweet potatoes, pumpkins, and all the usual agricultural produce of an American farm. Game, however, was the principal food of the settlers, who, despite the rudeness of their life and accommodation, were yet full of hope and energy.

The first discouraging symptom was manifest in the rainy season. The house was built half way down the slope of a hill, and nothing at first could be devised to keep it from being overflowed with water. A ditch, however, above the house, and trending away on each side, at length obviated this inconvenience. The spring came, and with it a trying time for the emigrants. The warmth of the weather, and the dense vegetation of the surrounding forest, brought sickness, and old Wilson died of the seasoning fever, while the young wife, who was about to make Edward a father, was within a hair-breadth of following the old man's example. One of the women lost her child; and to crown all, from inexperience in the practice of American agriculture, and from a sudden flood, their crops were utterly unproductive. The cattle, too, were sickly, and even some perished in consequence of the want of open pasture-ground.

From the anguish of mind and disappointment consequent on this series of calamities, Edward Wilson was awakened by the birth of a son. Still nothing seemed to prosper with him, and the second winter approached with little sign of amendment. The capital of both Edward and Walcot, the produce of the sale of their farms, was broken in upon more and more to supply the wants which disease and bad crops created. Neither of them, however, relaxed his efforts, and several additional acres were taken from the surrounding wilderness.

One evening, nearly two years after the first time when the several characters in this simple chronicle were introduced to our readers, the whole family were collected within the spacious log-hut, which, divided into several subdivisions, was the sleeping apartment of all. Wilson sat on one side of the huge and blazing fire, Walcot on the other, while Amy was near her husband, occupied in certain feminine offices respecting her babe, that slept in a wicker cradle at her feet. The labourers were fashioning rude handles for various farm implements, and the women were equally busy in sewing together the skins that with all served the purpose of outer garments. Edward was reading aloud from a newspaper, which had penetrated to this distant settlement, such scraps of news as were likely to prove interesting to his listeners.

While yet he read, a low knocking was heard at the door; the latch was then raised, and an unarmed Indian stood before them, panting for breath, and bleeding from many and fresh wounds. It was an aged Penobscot, but utterly unknown to all present.

'Indian wounded—faint—hungry—Sioux thirst for blood. Will white man give him meat and sleep?'

Wilson hesitated, Walcot half shook his head; but Amy at once settled any doubts which might have risen in the mind of her husband.

'Come to the fire, Indian,' said she kindly; 'and as soon as you have eaten, let us know what you have to say of the Sioux. Methinks if they be in the woods, we must look to ourselves;' and Amy gave a terrified glance at her sleeping babe.

'One, two, three,' said the Indian, gazing at the woman gratefully; 'ten, twenty bad Indian in woods. But squaw very good tell Indian welcome. Will white chief say so too?'

'Ay, that I will,' exclaimed Wilson warmly, his generous nature at once asserting its empire; 'eat, drink, and be glad, and then let us hear all that is needful to guard us against the enemy.

'Guard first, eat after,' said the Penobscot with dignity. 'Sioux close at hand, chase Wan-ti-mo through woods all day. Wan-ti-mo kill two,' added he, exhibiting the usual trophies of victory, 'but can't kill twenty.'

The old chief then left the hut, returning next moment with his rifle, tomahawk, and powder-horn, which he shook mournfully, exhibiting its empty condition. No sooner was he once more within the walls of the hut than he told Wilson to bar the door, and make every other preparation for defence against the Sioux. Edward complied, and with speed all the arms they could muster were brought out and prepared for use, while one of the labourers, who was considered unusually sharp, ascended a ladder leading to a hole in the roof, and blocking himself against the chimney, watched all around that the Sioux approached not unawares.

Meanwhile Amy busied herself bathing and dressing the wounds of the Penobscot, who also ate eagerly and drank sparingly from a flask of brandy which was placed at his disposal; so sparingly indeed as to cause Edward to press it upon him.

'When sick,' replied the Indian, 'fire-water good, little so much,' pouring a small quantity into the palm of his hand; 'but much take away head—man no fight then—like hog.'

Amy smiled, temperance views being unfortunately little in vogue in those days, and Edward and Walcot, though moderate men, sometimes indulging so far as to be slightly elevated. They, too, smiled, but no longer attempted to press the liquor upon the Penobscot, who now intimated his intention of taking up the position occupied by the young labourer. Ascending the ladder, he glided beside him, and then sent him below.

The white men were now left alone; the house was prepared for defence; the doors and windows were carefully and securely barred; the lights, by the Indian's suggestion, extinguished; and the fire nearly smothered. Then certain loopholes, previously stopped up, were opened in several parts of the hut. This duty had scarcely been performed, when the Indian came stealthily down the ladder with a finger upon his lips. As soon as he was on the earthen floor of the hut he seized his rifle, and motioning to the others to do so likewise, pointed it through one of the loopholes, and as soon as the others were ready, fired. A loud wailing cry followed a fierce whoop, and then all was still.

'Indian,' said Amy fervently, while she pressed her babe to her breast, 'you have saved my child, my husband, my all; ask me for what you will that is mine, and you shall have it.'

'White squaw give Indian welcome—that enough,' replied the Penobscot proudly.

A conference was now held, after which Wan-ti-mo returned to his post above, accompanied by Edward. Peering cautiously around, the white man and the red skin strove both to penetrate the deep darkness of the night. Before them lay the forest, and between a field, the fair surface of which was much deformed by the presence of the black stumps above alluded to. Habit had made Edward aware both of the number and situation of these, and his eye at once detected the appearance of what seemed several additional ones.

'Hist!' said he to the Indian; 'in yonder field are fourteen blackened stumps where this morning these eyes saw but six. This is some device of the Sioux.'

'Good,' said the Penobscot, in a tone of deep satisfaction. 'White man got sharp eyes'—and the two took simultaneous aim—'make good scout.'

The red skin and his companion fired both at the same time: a yell of rage and pain followed, and then there were but six of the unsightly objects which had before crowded so thick in the little field. From that moment all sign of the presence of an enemy disappeared, and the settlers reposed within their little castle, under the watch of the Penobscot, who, despite his wounds and fatigue, appeared yet the most active of the party. Day was just about to dawn when the Sioux again made their appearance, whooping and yelling like demons, upon the skirt of the wood. In numbers they were about forty, dividing which body into two, they boldly charged the hut. They were, however, met warmly, and repulsed; upon which they retired within the deep and sombre shelter of the forest, and all sank into a silence as deep as that which had prevailed before the white man laid bare a portion of its space to the light.

That the Indians had departed no one believed; and all therefore looked forward with horror to the protracted siege which it was evident they had determined on, and which, if conducted with any of the usual patience and energy exhibited by the savage, could not but terminate in his victory. No attack was made during the day, which passed to all wearily and slowly. Amy was sick at heart: the horrid fate which menaced her husband and child was ever before her eyes; while Wilson's more stern nature was also deeply moved. The Indian meanwhile laid him down and slept until the shades of evening again fell upon the scene, when he once more ascended the ladder, which enabled him to command a view of all around.

With the darkness came all these undefinable apprehensions which present themselves in such circumstances even to the strongest minds. For some time not a sound was heard, until one of the watchers at the loops announced the approach of the enemy. A straggling fire at once commenced, which lasted some time, the Penobscot's rifle being all the time silent. Edward was puzzled at the red skin's inaction, and leaving the rest to conduct the defence, ascended the ladder to question Wan-ti-mo. He was gone! This was a new source of fear and apprehension. Their assailants were proportionably stronger as they were weakened, though certainly the presence of a traitor was far from being desirable.

Edward descended with a heavy heart, and communicated his intelligence, which was heard by all with alarm, though Amy strongly asserted that, while they might have had a friend, she was sure they had not found an enemy. Edward replied not, but once more took up his post as commander of the little garrison. For hours the contest continued with small success on the part of the enemy, who, at length exasperated at the obstinacy of the defence, brought a new element to bear upon the besieged. The first intimation they received of this dreadful danger was the flight of a burning arrow which fell upon the dry and inflammatory corn-houses and barns, and instantly wrapt them in flames. A loud yell proclaimed the delight of the savages—a groan the anguish of the owners of the habitation.

As soon as Edward recovered from the astonishment into which this terrible event threw him, he commanded the men to grasp their arms and prepare for a more deadly struggle than had yet taken place, as well as to neutralise the object of the Indians. At a short distance from the house was the pile of logs which served for fuel, three heaps, forming three sides of a square. To this the women and children went, and while two men kept watch lest the Indians should rush upon them, the others were occupied in removing their valuables from the house into the open air. The burning, meanwhile, extended in force, and presently cast so brilliant a light that the white men were forced within their rude breastwork. Dawn broke upon them in this position, and then the Indians came whooping and yelling on, as if determined to take them by storm. Each man clutched his weapon, and as the foe neared them, rose and fired. The Indians paused, when the deadly discharge of twenty rifles in their rear, and the shadow of a dark line of men bursting over the fields headed by the Penobscot, sent them flying with their utmost speed over the expanse which lay between them and the forest, in whose recesses they concealed themselves.

Three hours after, Edward Wilson and his family stood gazing upon the ruins of his new home as it lay smouldering before him, in utter dejection of spirit. The allies from around whom the Penobscot had collected had plunged into the woods in chase of the Sioux. Silent and sad the emigrant leaned against the wood pile, his wife nursing her babe at his feet, and Walcot looking on sternly and gloomily. At this moment Wan-ti-mo and the white men returned, the latter at once offering to aid in the reconstruction of their neighbour's home. The Penobscot, however, now approached Edward while the others ate, and called him and his wife aside. Amy followed with her child in her arms. As soon as Wan-ti-mo had led them out of sight he turned to Edward.

'White man good to Indian—Indian got heart—heart feel,' said he; 'white man no think it, but Wan-ti-mo make him much happy. Follow Indian,' continued the Penobscot, pointing to the woods.

'No, Wan-ti-mo,' said Edward, 'I must look to the reconstruction of my home. I have not a moment to waste.'

The Indian was puzzled, though he would not own it; he was unable to express his intentions in English, still he urged Edward to follow him, but Wilson was inflexible. At length his eloquence being exhausted without avail, Wan-ti-mo turned towards Amy, and seizing the child with as much gentleness as possible, leaped away laughing to a distance from the astonished and alarmed parents. As soon as the Penobscot had gained a position about twenty yards from them, he halted, and holding up the child, motioned them to follow. This done, he turned round, and now Edward and his wife, treading forcibly in his footsteps, walked away through the forest at a slow pace. The path he followed was rude in the extreme, and one the difficulties of which had always deterred those connected with the farm from attempting it.

In about half an hour Wan-ti-mo halted and allowed Edward and his wife to reach his side, while he pointed exultingly to an open space beyond. It was a lonely forest glade of some thousand acres, an interior prairie, which by some accident had never, though fertile in the extreme, been overrun by the dense growth which prevailed around. Edward at once understood the Indian's motive in bringing them to this spot, which was perhaps the very best locality for a settlement of any within twenty miles.

'White man's farm gone—Sioux dog burn up,' said Wan-ti-mo, placing the child in its mother's arms; 'that bad down there—too much tree—too much wet—too hard work; here tree plenty—land plenty—this *Indian farm!*'

Wilson clutched the hand of the Penobscot, and thanking him warmly, intimated his resolve to remove at once. They returned to their ruined home, and Edward signifying his intention, those who had so opportunely saved him from destruction now joined in aiding his plans for renovating his position. The removal was effected, but not without much arduous toil and difficulty. It proved, however, a happy and most fortunate change, and from that hour all prospered with the emigrants. They had fertile fields and grazing land in abundance, with wood in equal plenty. A congregation of log-houses arose. The capital of the settlers enabled them to improve their location, and to purchase it. A village ere long occupied the space round what had once been Wilson's solitary hut. The Penobscot became a hired hunter, and when age came upon him was well cared for, Amy ever rejoicing, when she gazed upon her many prosperous and happy children, that she had protected the poor fugitive. She had saved him from his enemies, and all her subsequent happiness, and the success of those she loved, took its origin in the INDIAN'S GRATITUDE!

COUNTRY LIFE FOR LADIES.

IT is a remark we believe of Joseph Lancaster's, that if you wish boys educated speedily and pleasantly, set boys to teach them. The same remark may with equal justice be applied to 'children of a larger growth.' If, for instance, you want ladies instructed in any science or accomplishment—whether it comes immediately within their own sphere of duty, or belongs rather to that of the other sex—by all means set a lady to teach them. Should the requirement come under the latter category, its masculine aspect will in a great measure be softened down by the treatment of a female mind; and should it come under the former, then who so well qualified both by feeling and habit to discharge a duty strictly feminine? The subject that might be treated by man in a severe, concise, and generalising spirit, would be managed by a woman's pen fluently and diffusely, and, with a regard to particulars, in a manner especially enticing to the fairer sex. Woman possesses a keener perception of the lovely and delicate, a nicer handling of minor topics, and discovers the inroads to her sisters' attention with a tact peculiarly her own. On such a theme as Country Life, where the management of the house, the garden, domestic animals, and the like are assigned to the ladies, no one could be more expert, or more likely to be successful than a lady instructor. She has studied and practised these duties as exclusively her own, and man, were he to attempt the task, would make but a very sorry preceptor in comparison.

Among the many treatises on rural subjects written expressly for ladies, those of Mrs Loudon take a high position, alike for the variety and accuracy of their matter. Her works on Botany, on Gardening, &c. are already well known, and we are gratified to find another recently addressed to the fair sisterhood, which is still more directly applicable to their country duties and avocations.* 'This work,' says the author, 'is intended principally for the use of ladies who have been brought up in a town, but who from circumstances have been induced to reside in the country. Persons so situated are generally at first delighted with the change; but they soon become full of complaints of the inconveniences of a country life, particularly of the difficulty they have in getting what they want, without sending to a great distance. This last inconvenience, however, is easily obviated by a little forethought and management; and dulness and monotony will only be felt by those who take no interest in country pursuits. Having lived in the country myself, I know both the inconveniences and the enjoyments of a country life; and in the following pages I have endeavoured to save my readers the pain of buying their own experience, by giving them the advantage of mine.' Such is the intention of the 'Lady's Country Companion;' and after a perusal of its pages, we are led to the conclusion that Mrs Loudon has left few subjects untouched which relate either to the duties or recreation of the lady of the manor. The work is composed of a series of letters, addressed to an acquaintance who has been recently married to a country gentleman of ancient family—the author assuring us 'that Annie is not an imaginary being, but a young lady I have known from her birth, and to whom I am sincerely attached.'

These letters embrace a wide field of duty; but before

* The Lady's Country Companion; or How to Enjoy a Country Life Rationally. By Mrs Loudon, author of 'Gardening for Ladies,' &c. London: Longman and Co. 1845.

entering upon minutiæ, some salutary advice of a general nature is tendered. Thus, there is nothing more natural than that a person accustomed to the town should, on removing to the country, begin to experience a certain dulness and monotony; and, compared with the gaiety and bustle they have left, there is no doubt cause for the complaint. But if circumstances have cast one's lot in the country, it is obvious weakness in that individual—whether lady or gentleman—if he does not endeavour to find employment and amusement whereby not only to fill up his own time, but to make others happy around him. Thrown apart, to a certain extent, from society, we must look to ourselves and to surrounding objects for our pleasure; and on this point Mrs Loudon tenders her young friend some excellent advice:—'Happiness, I suspect, in most cases depends more upon ourselves than we are generally willing to allow; and I am quite sure that young married people who are attached to each other, and have a competency, may be happy if they will, particularly in the country, where their principal amusements must all centre in home. You will, perhaps, be surprised to find that I think this a cause of happiness, but you will find in time that I am right; and that our chances of being happy decrease in proportion as we depend upon others for our enjoyments. I cannot conceive a more miserable life than that of a beauty who has no pleasure but in being admired; and who, consequently, must pass her time in fits of alternate depression and excitement. It would give me the greatest pain to see you plunge into this species of mental intoxication, and I rejoice that you are placed in a situation where you will not be exposed to the temptations arising from bad example. In this respect your present abode seems to be everything I could wish; as, from the description you have given me of the difficulties attending visiting your neighbours, they seem to be enough to cure the most ardent lover of dissipation; and, unless the neighbours be more than commonly agreeable, I think you will not feel inclined,

——"Frequent visits to make
Through ten miles of mud for formality's sake,
With the coachman in drink and the moon in a fog,
And no thought in your head but a ditch or a bog."

Do not suppose from this that I think you should be unsociable; on the contrary, I think it a duty to mix occasionally with the world, as, unless we do so, we should soon learn to set a false value upon ourselves and upon everything around us. The society of persons in our own rank in life is, therefore, essential to teach us our true level; and I have no doubt you will find some agreeable persons among your neighbours when you know them better, whose friendship you will think worth cultivating.'

Having thus counselled her friend, the author proceeds to the more practical duties of the House and Kitchen. These, as every one well knows, are numerous and varied, and here they are spoken of sensibly, and just as one lady should discourse of them to another. Fires, ventilation, furniture, harmony of colours, ornaments, and so on, are separately discussed as belonging to the house: the making of wines and liqueurs, baking and cooking, with their numerous recipes, rank under the kitchen. We are at all times averse to trench on the prerogative of the ladies, and therefore dismiss this section with an expression of our belief, that Mrs Loudon's instructions, if followed, will produce not only an elegant and comfortable house, but a substantial and delicious dinner table. The Larder and Dairy are also very cleverly treated; and what little heterodoxy may appear under the latter head, is not to be wondered at. The author is not infallible more than any other person; and many of higher pretensions than she, are on this matter still widely at variance. After all, it signifies very little; for during the whole of our acquaintance with the country, we have never found a couple of ladies agreed on the subject of the dairy, nor did we ever know one who did not think her own method the best. Passing from these topics, the author takes up the Garden, the Greenhouse, the Park and Lawn; and here, as the widow of one of the first botanists and landscape gardeners of the age, she is perfectly at home. This is undoubtedly the most delightful, as it is the most instructive, section of the book; it is not a mere dry calendar of operations, but an essay full of good taste and sound judgment. Any lady who will attend to these directions—and they are given in plain and familiar language—may, in a few years, establish one of the finest gardens; and may also, now that the glass duties are abolished, rear the most delicate exotics at very little cost.

On the subject of the pleasure-grounds, Mrs Loudon's remarks strike us as in admirable taste; and as country ladies must spend so much of their time in and around their mansions, we cannot see how this department should not be almost exclusively intrusted to their care. 'An ancient mansion,' says she, 'embosomed in tall trees, with a fine broad terrace at the back, having a piece of still water lying like a liquid mirror below it, and a large park beyond overgrown with majestic trees, whose lower branches repose upon the turf beneath them, form a scene which sounds exceedingly well in description, but is very wearying to the eye which is destined continually to rest upon it. It is also not very healthy, as chilly vapours are sure to rise from the water, while the mass of trees beyond will obstruct the free current of air. You must not suppose from this that I admire a house in an open exposed situation, as I think nothing can have a more bleak and naked appearance. Besides, a house entirely unsheltered by trees is sure to be a very uncomfortable residence, from its exposure to the heat in summer and the cold in winter. It is, therefore, most desirable to have a sufficient quantity of trees near the house to shelter it, and yet to have numerous openings through those trees to admit distant prospects, and a free current of air. If a few openings could therefore be made in the plantations near your dwelling, I do not think there would be any danger in leaving the water in its present position; as, from your description, the house is elevated very much above it, and as, notwithstanding its appearance of stillness, there is a current through it. As to your house being on the ridge of a hill, I do not think that is any objection, as the rise is not very great on either side, and it is a proof that the prospect would be good if you would only cut down a sufficient number of trees to show it. Houses quite in a valley are frequently damp, and if on the summit of a high hill they are apt to be bleak; so that the side of a hill, or the ridge of a knoll, is in fact the best situation that can be imagined. Our ancestors, indeed, rarely went wrong on this subject; and it is quite an extraordinary case to find an old house badly placed. In the old times the country gentry lived in their mansions all the year, and only visited London occasionally, so that they were more anxious to make their homes comfortable than persons of the same rank at the present day, who live in London and only visit the seats of their ancestors as they would a watering-place.'

Again, in combating the young lady's objections to the 'monotony of foliage,' Mrs Loudon explains how the surrounding woods must have vistas and glades cut in them so as to open up distant prospects; and also shows that the sameness arises from the want of variety among the trees already planted. Woodland scenery can never be monotonous where there are different kinds of trees; for every genus has its own colours, and shapes, and styles of growth, presenting to the eye, when well arranged, a beauty and complication which is truly enchanting. Observe how charmingly this topic is handled. 'Forest scenery is extremely beautiful in itself, and principally from the great variety it presents in the same objects. A fine tree, even when bare of leaves in winter, is beautiful from the delicate tracery presented by its branches, which look like the masts and rigging of a large ship, intricate, yet without confusion. In snow, trees assume a new character; the weight sustained by the branches makes them droop, and a thousand graceful and elegant forms take the place of what was before a stern and rigid outline. In hoarfrost, trees glisten with a thousand gems, reflecting the rays of light in so many different colours, that they remind one of the description of Aladdin's magic garden. In spring they present vivid ideas of youth and fertility, and all nature appears awaking into new and vigorous life: the buds swell, their coverings burst, and the young leaves display their tender and delicate green; at first only half-unfolding their beautiful forms, and reminding one of a young and timid girl half-wishing and half-fearing to make her first appearance in the busy world. Trees now begin to assume each a new and decided character of its own. The leaves of no two trees are alike: those of the beech are of clear dark green, and so thin that they are almost transparent, and yet they are deeply marked with a strongly indented feather-like set of veins. The bark of the beech is clear and smooth, as though nature had intended it for the use to which it has so often been applied by lovers—to carve on it a fair one's name. The leaves of the elm are of a thick coarse texture, rugged and distorted, wrinkled, and of a dingy green; and the bark of the tree is cut into a thousand furrows. The leaves of the ash are light and pendulous, and cut into numerous leaflets; those of the oak are deeply indented, and generally grow in tufts. The palmate drooping leaves of the horse-chestnut contrast with the long, slender, and nearly erect leaves of the white willow; and those of the black poplar, which present a smooth outline, with those of the sweet chestnut, which are remarkable for their finely indented edges. In short, the leaves of every tree have beauties peculiar to themselves, in form as well as in colour. In autumn these colours become more decided: the lime trees take a yellowish tint, and the oak a reddish brown; the liquidambar becomes of a rich purplish crimson, and the maples and American oaks show a thousand varied dyes. Yes, my dear Annie, I repeat, the fault is not in the trees, for they are beautiful; you dislike them only because they are so crowded that you cannot see their beauties.'

The consideration of the Domestic Animals next engages attention, and under this section ponies, cows, pigs, poultry, and bees are treated in a style that will gladden the heart of the most ardent housewife. Nor is it all utilitarianism, for deer, pheasants, partridges, and other wild animals which are the ornaments of woods and pleasure-grounds, come in for an ample share of the country ladies' attention. The natural history of Rural Walks is also descanted upon, and the lady shown how every object around her may become one of interest and instruction. But, it may be asked after a perusal of all this immensity of cares and duties, is the country life of ladies to be one only of toil and business? By no means; for, although it might be shown that there is enough of recreation, ay and amusement too, combined with the above avocations, yet Mrs Loudon has a keener appreciation of her sisters' wants than deny them the enjoyment of lighter amusements. Archery, sketching in the open air, swinging, pleasure-boats, skating, sporting, &c. are the subjects of a special chapter; recreations to which we only wish that our towns' beauties had readier and more frequent access.

Much as there may be in all that precedes to occupy the attention of a lady's country life, still is there something of paramount importance to follow. We live not only for ourselves but for those around us, and it is a poor and miserable spirit—all the more miserable that it has the means—which does not systematically endeavour to contribute to the welfare of others. This is particularly the case with the wife of a landed proprietor, whom circumstances place both as the patroness of, and the model to, the surrounding peasantry. On this topic Mrs Loudon's exhortations are given in good taste, and in a feeling and benevolent spirit:—'I have now, my dear Annie, a few words to say on a more important subject than those I have yet touched upon; I mean the duties which are imposed upon you by your residence in the country. As your husband is the last descendant of an ancient family, it is particularly incumbent upon him, and of course also upon you, to keep up as much as possible the kindly feeling which existed in the olden time between the lords of the soil and its cultivators, but which has, of late years, been too much neglected. The proprietor of a large estate ought to be regarded by the labouring cottagers in the light of a protector, to whom they can look up for advice and assistance in their troubles; and as a friend upon whose kindness they may confidently rely, and who they know will be interested in their welfare. When this is the case, the tenantry of a country gentleman will form his best body-guard; and, instead of ever attempting to injure his property, they will do all in their power to protect it.

'I think it highly desirable that you should be personally acquainted with the poor people in the vicinity of your husband's mansion, that you may know how to afford them the most acceptable assistance, and who are most deserving of it. For this reason I think you should occasionally walk through the village, instead of confining your rambles exclusively to the park, and call frequently on your poorer neighbours; not with the apparent wish of dictating to them how they should live and how they should manage their families, but with the ostensible appearance of employing them in some little work, and in reality to see how you can best be serviceable to them, and how you can do them the most positive good. It is the blessed privilege of wealth and rank that they give us the power of making our fellow-creatures happy, with very trifling inconvenience to ourselves. A word or a kind look from the rich to the poor speaks volumes, and carries with it encouragement and pleasure, which no efforts of persons in their own rank in life can give. It is, however, difficult for the rich to know how to be of real service to the poor, as giving alms seldom does good except in cases of sudden and unforeseen distress. The best charity is first to teach the poor how to maintain themselves, and next to give them employment; and when they have this, they have a better chance of happiness than any riches could bestow combined with idleness. Perhaps, indeed, there is no state of existence more happy than that of a person who is usefully and profitably employed, and whose employment is of such a nature as to exercise moderately the faculties both of the body and the mind.

'Establishing schools is an important duty which the rich owe to the poor. Every girl ought to be able to sew neatly and well, and to read, write, and keep accounts. I think also it would be a great advantage if all the girls who have attained the age of fourteen were to receive a few lessons in dress-making, and making waistcoats and boys' clothes, from the regular mantua-maker and tailor of the village; or you might pay for this out of your own pocket, and make it a reward for good conduct. It is particularly useful to the wife of a labouring man to know how to cut out and make or alter clothes, as work of this kind can be taken up and laid down while the mother is nursing her children, or watching the boiling of a pot, or some similar kind of simple cookery.'

Mrs Loudon also advises teaching the daughters of the peasantry the best modes of cooking suitable to their rank in life—a subject at present very much neglected, and which, to the poor, is of great importance both dietetically and economically. She again diverges into the matter of employment, exhorting her young friend to teach the doctrines of self-reliance, and to help in furnishing the poor with something to do for their own permanent support, rather than to aid by mere temporary donations. 'In cases of illness,' she continues, 'I am sure you will be happy to assist your poor neighbours in every way in your power. When poor people are ill, their means of support are stopped, and they have not only to labour through the pains of illness, but they are also exposed to the greatest privations for the want of food at the very moment when food of a more nourishing nature than usual is required for them. Then it is that the helping hand of the rich is of the greatest value to the poor, and that charity takes its most graceful form.

'Many ladies in the country employ a portion of their time in making clothes for the poor; but with the exception of permitting young people to make baby-linen, I question whether it is advisable that much should be done in this way. The feelings of the poor are often hurt by having it dictated to them what they are to wear, and they are apt to look upon the clothes thus given to them, and which are probably quite different from what they would have purchased for themselves, almost as a badge of slavery which they are compelled to wear to please their patrons, but of which they hate the very sight.'

Such is an outline of the 'Lady's Country Companion,' which, upon the whole, is the best of its kind we have perused. The matter is exactly of the nature required for a young lady passing from a town to a country life. Of faults, we can only find inclination to denote those of diffuseness and occasional carelessness of expression. While the former may be a merit, as some subjects, like certain liquors, are rendered more palatable by a little dilution, we are altogether at a loss to invent an excuse for the latter in an author of Mrs Loudon's standing.

MRS STONE'S CHRONICLES OF FASHION.*

This book seems entitled to a respectable place among the lounging productions of the day. It assembles from all sources, accessible and otherwise, and strings up in a pleasant style, traits and anecdotes illustrative of the 'Cynthia of the minute,' in eating, dressing, and amusements, during the last two centuries. It is essentially a chronicle of that small body of people who, since Elizabeth's time, have been accustomed to assemble in London for a portion of the year, and there live in each others' eyes a life of vanity and vacuity, seeking in mere frivolous amusement, and in the cultivation of fine external appearances, that excitement which affluent circumstances deny their finding in any of the common pursuits of the world. We cannot say that this is a subject much concerning any rational person, or of any absolute dignity or importance: were we inclined to speak strongly, we might say something to the contrary purpose, besides remarking on the indecencies which some of its chapters necessarily involve. But the real object is only to amuse, and we take the book as we find it.

A chapter on Banquets and Food, with which the work opens, runs rapidly along from the coarse revels of James I.'s court to the luxurious but still inelegant entertainments of the second Charles, and thence to more refined table affairs of the eighteenth century, introducing tea and coffee by the way. One reference to a peculiarly idealised kind of banquet, given by the Duke of Buckingham about 1626, we cannot overlook. 'Ballets, accompanied by beautiful music, were performed between the courses; and indeed the arrangements seem to have been so managed, that the very matter-of-fact services of moving and replacing dishes were poetised by being done by attendants in fancy dresses, made to assimilate in appearance, and possibly in some degree to tally in action, with the subject and scene of the ballet. After dinner, they proceeded to the hall by a kind of turning door, which, admitting only one at a time, prevented all confusion, and another ballet was exhibited. To this succeeded dancing, and afterwards a supper of "five different collations" was served in beautiful vaulted apartments.' It may interest the reader to know the origin of the word toast, as implying the object of a health drinking. 'It happened that on a public day [at Bath in the reign of Charles II.] a celebrated beauty of those times was in the cross-bath, and one of the crowd of her admirers took a glass of the water in which the fair one stood and drank her health to the company. There was in the place a gay fellow, half fuddled, who offered to jump in, and swore, though he liked not the liquor, he would have the toast. He was opposed in his resolution; yet this whim gave foundation to the present honour which is done to the lady we mention in our liquors, who has ever since been called a toast.

The next chapter, on Manners, gives a distressing view of the coarseness and essential vulgarity which have marked the 'fashionable' class in this country almost to our own time. Next follow chapters on Habitations and Carriages. Amusements, as might be expected, fill a large space, including theatricals, balls, masquerades, Vauxhall and Ranelagh, &c. The impression everywhere conveyed is, that an improvement, both in morality and in taste, has taken place since the days of our fathers. It will surprise many who think that our ancestors surpassed us at least in religion, to know that almost to the close of the last century the court received company, and fashionable people in London had card parties, on Sunday. Even Queen Anne, that stanch friend of the church, 'was in the habit of having prayers read in an outer room while she dressed in an inner one. On one occasion the door was ordered to be shut whilst the queen changed some linen, and the chaplain ceased to read; on Anne expressing surprise at this, he had spirit enough to say that "he would not whistle the word of God through a key-hole."' It appears from the Spectator, that fashionables always saluted each other, and often interchanged words and snuff-boxes, in church.

'Almack's' took its rise at the close of the Seven Years' war, in consequence of the reduced state in which many of the upper classes were left by that contest, and to keep off the citizen class, who at the same time had been making rapid advances. Being no longer able to maintain their peculiar ground by expensive entertainments, they were obliged to resort to the expedient of a rigid exclusivism. At that time, and down till the close of the century, the minuet was a favourite dance—a slow and stately exhibition of a single pair in the midst of a circle of onlookers. 'At Bath,' we are told, 'each gentleman was expected to dance two minuets, and on the conclusion of the first, the master of the ceremonies led the lady to her seat, and conducted another fair one to the expecting gentleman, who stood awaiting her in *statu quo*, with his opera hat and his "dancing feet" in the most perfect position which the skill of his dancing-master or his own good taste enabled him to assume. Rather a nervous situation this, one should think; certainly quite enough to make a young man not thoroughly seasoned to the exhibition feel "rather all-overish." The young ladies of that day, too, must have had considerable nerves to brave the slow ordeal of a minuet with the eyes of a whole assembly of scrutinising dowagers, jealous-eyed young ladies, and quizzical men fixed upon them. But if to dance a minuet well required a degree of self-possession not always found in very young persons, it also entailed inevitably the cultivation of some degree of grace and dignity in manner and in movement—circumstances which, as every one knows, are by no means indispensable to the performance of the modern quadrille, or to the mazurka, or to the gallopade, or to the polka. No, it must surely be in the performance of the stately and graceful minuet—a descendant of the *pavan* of the knights and dames of chivalrous times—it must certainly be in the performance of the minuet that a woman dancing may claim the epithet which has been bestowed upon her—"a brandished torch of beauty."

* Chronicles of Fashion; from the time of Elizabeth to the early part of the nineteenth century, in Manners, Amusements, Banquets, Costume, &c. By Mrs Stone, authoress of 'The Art of Needlework,' &c. 2 vols. 8vo. London: Bentley. 1845.

In the time of the minuet, a circle was the form which company always took in a drawing-room when not employed at cards or in dances where many couples were engaged. This was a dull and chilling mode, and seems to have been felt as an intolerable tyranny by at least the gentlemen. The custom was first broken through by a Mrs Vesey, than whom none was better qualified to venture on such a revolution, as she is said to have been 'the charm of every society.' The means adopted consisted in simply throwing the chairs into little dispersed groups throughout the room. 'Mrs Vesey's parties have been thus described:—"Mrs Vesey had the almost magic art of putting all her company at their ease without the least appearance of design. Here was no formal circle to petrify an unfortunate stranger on his entrance—no rules of conversation to observe—no holding forth of one to his own distress and the stupifying of his audience—no reading of his works by the author. The company naturally broke into little groups, perpetually varying and changing; they talked or were silent, sat or walked about, just as they pleased. Nor was it absolutely necessary even to talk sense. Here was no bar to harmless mirth and gaiety; and while perhaps Dr Johnson in one corner held forth on the moral duties, in another two or three young people might be talking of the fashions and the opera, and in a third Lord Orford (then Mr Horace Walpole) might be amusing a little group around him with his lively wit and intelligent conversation. In these parties were to be met with occasionally most of the persons of note and eminence, in different ways, who were in London either for the whole or part of the winter. Bishops and wits, noblemen and authors, politicians and scholars—

'Chiefs out of war, and statesmen out of place—

all met there without ceremony, and mixed in easy conversation."'

We would here venture to remark, for the benefit of persons of mediocre rank who occasionally see company, that much more lies in the arrangement of the mere upholstery than they may be dreaming of. Two rows of sofas and chairs proceeding from the respective sides of a fireplace form too often the leading arrangement, the consequence of which is, that the company sits down in two still formal lines, where no one can speak to any but his next neighbours. And as changes in such a situation draw attention, it generally happens that each person is condemned to the society of two others only, for the whole evening. The case becomes worse when, as is often seen, the ladies are preferred to the seats on the sofas by themselves; for then they exchange not one word with a person of the opposite sex for the whole evening. Let our friends of the middle classes adopt and act upon Mrs Vesey's ideas about furniture, and they will find their parties increase amazingly in popularity.

Stars of fashion, eminent beaux, and fashionable watering-places, fill up a few chapters agreeably, and finally we come to an elaborate section on costume. Here a few passages may be selected almost at random, as the whole is amusing. After an account of etui-cases, our authoress thus proceeds:—

'It was in vain that Mr Isaac Bickerstaff intimates that he compelled or persuaded his sister, Mrs Jenny, to "resign her snuff-box for ever," on her marriage;* for all men and women, high and low, young and old, were inveterate snuff-takers during the last century; and indeed this dirty habit has only lately subsided, being upheld in the highest fashion by the practice and example of Queen Charlotte, and her son King George IV. At one time the same necessity which led to the adoption of strong perfumes might justify the use of snuff, otherwise fashion itself would hardly seem to account for its very general and excessive consumption. Of course the form and garniture of the snuff-box itself became a point of importance to the critically-dressed leader of ton, and on nothing has a greater profusion of taste, fancy, expense, and skill been lavished, than on the snuff-box. They became an article of virtù, critically assorted by collectors, and a choice and recherché offering of compliment in every possible way, as much so as the Spanish embroidered gloves of Elizabeth's day. The freedom of cities was given in a snuff-box, the donations of the charitable were handed in a snuff-box, the portrait of majesty was bestowed on a snuff-box, and the right hand of fellowship was extended with a snuff-box. A snuff-box, erstwhile, has been a fatal gift.

'The fair one who was proof against a jewelled necklace could not resist a diamond snuff-box; nor could a patriot resist the conviction which flashed before his eyes on opening for nasal refreshment the "slight token of regard" which bore his royal master's portrait enamelled and jewelled on the lid.

'Edward Wortley Montagu, the eccentric son of Lady Mary, is said to have possessed more snuff-boxes than would suffice a Chinese idol with a hundred noses—a collection which perhaps was never equalled unless by that of King George IV., who was not less extravagant and recherché in snuff and snuff-boxes than in other things.

'Frederick the Great of Prussia had a magnificent collection of snuff-boxes; he carried one of enormous size, and took it not by pinches but by handfuls. It was difficult to approach him without sneezing; and it was said that the perquisites that came to the valets-de-chambre from the snuff they got from drying his handkerchiefs were considerable.

'Beau Brummell had a remarkable collection of snuff-boxes. He and his royal patron were both remarkable for a peculiar and graceful manner of opening the snuff-box with one hand only—the left. Probably in these latter days, when perfect repose and quietude are the essence of good breeding, any display with the snuff-box farther than a very slight "illustration" of the jewelled finger in raising the lid of the box might be considered as *trop prononcé* for elegance; but such was not the idea of our great-great-grandmothers and grandfathers. They seem to have displayed it most actively and elaborately, if we may judge from a satirical advertisement which appeared in the Spectator.

'"The exercise of the snuff-box, according to the most fashionable airs and motions, in opposition to the exercise of the fan, will be taught with the best plain or perfumed snuff at Charles Lillie's, perfumer, at the corner of Beaufort Buildings, in the Strand; and attendance given for the benefit of the young merchants about the Exchange for two hours every day at noon, except Saturdays, at a toyshop near Garraway's coffee-house. There will be likewise taught the ceremony of the snuff-box, or rules for offering snuff to a stranger, a friend, or a mistress, according to the degrees of familiarity or distance; with an explanation of the careless, the scornful, the politic, and the surly pinch, and the gestures proper to each of them.

'"N.B.—The undertaker does not question but in a short time to have formed a body of regular snuff-boxes ready to meet and make head against all the regiment of fans which have been lately disciplined, and are now in motion."*

'A marvellous and spirit-stirring sight our grandmothers must have presented, with the fans which are represented as doing so much execution, and which were of a size to do execution, being often not less than a yard wide. The Spectator informs us, that "women are armed with fans as men with swords;" and we almost think it must have been so too, from the accounts we read of the various exercises and evolutions they performed with them, and the execution dire that was sometimes perpetrated by their means. The most effective exercise of the fan, as well as the most difficult to learn, for, according to the Spectator, its acquisition

* Tatler, No. 79.

* Spectator, No. 138.

took three months, was the flutter of the fan—as this flutter was capable of expressing any emotion which might agitate the bosom of the fair holder at the moment. There was "the angry flutter, the modest flutter, the timorous flutter, the confused flutter, the merry flutter, and the amorous flutter." Nay, the Spectator declares that he could tell by merely seeing the fan of a disciplined landlady, whether she were laughing, frowning, or blushing at the moment. It was in truth "a wondrous engine," and well might the careful guardian

"his lonely charge remind
Lest they forgetful leave their fans behind;
Lay not, ye fair, the pretty toy aside,
A toy at once displayed for use and pride,
A wondrous engine, that by magic charms
Cools your own breast, and every other's warms.
What daring bard shall e'er attempt to tell
The powers that in this little weapon dwell?
What verse can e'er explain its various parts,
Its numerous uses, motions, charms, and arts;
Its painted folds, that oft extended wide,
The afflicted fair one's blubbered beauties hide,
When secret sorrows her sad bosom fill,
If Strephon is unkind, or Shock is ill:
Its sticks, on which her eyes dejected pore,
And pointing fingers number o'er and o'er,
When the kind virgin burns with secret shame,
Dies to consent, yet fears to own her flame;
Its shake triumphant, its victorious clap,
Its angry flutter, and its wanton tap?"

'Very different were the fans of this day from the wavering group of feathers, with its jewelled handle, which Queen Elizabeth and her fair attendants fluttered. The Duchess of Portsmouth, King Charles's French mistress, wore a fan not unlike those of later times in shape. Madame de Maintenon had a most interesting one, on which her own apartment was represented to the life. The king appeared employed at his desk, Madame de Maintenon spinning, the Duchess of Burgundy at play, Mademoiselle d'Aubigny, niece to Madame de Maintenon, at her collation. Those of the Spectator's day were large, substantial, elaborate affairs, and, like some fashionable claptraps of the present time, quite "pictorial." At the time of Sacheverell's trial, nothing was seen on the fans of the high-church ladies but "pictorial" representations of Westminster Hall at the time of trial, with the meek and interesting "victim" at the bar. When Gulliver's Travels appeared, all the fans at the church and the opera testified the delight of the fashionable world in that production. One was sent as a present from a great person here to Lady Bolingbroke, with all the principal scenes from that celebrated work painted on both sides of the fan. When the Beggars' Opera was the rage, all the favourite songs in it were painted on the ladies' fans.

'Political emblems were so rife in those belligerent days, that a lady's opinions were known as well by her fan as by her patches. Fashionable women never appeared without their fans. They would as soon, perhaps sooner, have gone without their gowns. From the time of their rising in the morning to that of their retiring at night, at church or at market, in the crowded assembly or the solitary sick-room—everywhere, suspended from her wrist, the fashionable woman carried her fan.

'It need hardly be said that fan-making was, in the last century, an extensive and important business, and called into requisition the talents of the highest painters and the first-rate mechanicians. If they yielded in grace and elegance to those of Elizabeth's day, they did not in richness and magnificence. The handles were often splendidly mounted in diamonds, and inlaid with jewels; the fans exquisitely painted by first-rate artists. Many celebrated artists of fifty years since began life as fan painters. Miss Burney mentions several beautiful fans which she saw at Sir Joshua Reynolds's, painted on leather by Poggi, from designs of West, Reynolds, Cipriani, and others, which she says "were more delightful than can well be imagined." One was bespoken by the Duchess of Devonshire, as a gift to be sent abroad. This is by no means a solitary instance of fans of English manufacture being sent abroad as presents, yet it often appears that the Parisian ones were preferred in England. Walpole frequently writes to friends abroad, and when on the continent himself, is usually commissioned to procure fans for his friends. The Duchess of York, soon after her arrival in this country, displayed a splendid fan, "entirely of diamonds, with an ivory mounting, the sticks pierced and set with brilliants in a mosaic pattern; but the outside ones were set with a single row of diamonds, while very large brilliants fastened the fan at the bottom."

'The fan, though dwindled immeasurably from the magnificence of its predecessors, dwarfed in size, and

Fallen, fallen, fallen, fallen,
Fallen from its high estate

as an accredited instrument of coquetry—the fan, "all that remained of it," as Curran said of himself when obliged to plead without his wig—the fan, such as it was, was used, not elaborately, not conspicuously, not *avec prétension* as in the good old times—but still sleepily and languidly it was used even in this century. For many years it has been extinct, but appears now to be reviving. Some very beautiful ones have of late been exhibited by our caterers in virtù, and they are beginning to peep between the folds of satin and of the intricacies of lace in some of our aristocratic shops. What may this portend? Should the fan revive, may we hope that a new Spectator will arise phœnix-like to teach us its exercise!'

There is, we believe, no part of the human person which has been so much the sport of fashion as the head. On this subject we have a few pleasant gossipries:—'It now only remains,' says Mrs Stone, 'to notice that twin abomination of the last century,

"The pride of the topping, delight of all eyes!
That *tête* which attempted to rival the skies;
Whence Cupid, the god, and destroyer of hearts,
With rancour clancing the keenest of darts,
Sat smiling in ambush."

The tête indeed was a fitting accompaniment to the hoop; in fact, the one required the other. At the time when the hoop attained its greatest magnitude, a head the natural size would have appeared inconsistent, too minute for the enormous figure; and, *vice versa*, when headdresses, with their superstructures of feathers, flowers, gauze, &c. not to mention the still more absurd ornaments of bunches of vegetables, became so large that women of fashion were compelled to ride with their heads out of their carriage-windows, or kneel down in the carriage to accommodate them within, why, then, the most expanding hoop seemed to be only in fit proportion to the astonishing head.

'We have mentioned in our first volume, that in the time of Charles II. the falling and graceful ringlets of the "beauties" were exchanged for stiff frizzled tiers of curls, which, becoming still stiffer, more elaborate, and more artificial, were at length manufactured into the tower or commode of 1687. Why the term commode has been applied to all sorts of *in*conveniences, we cannot imagine; but nothing could be more appropriate than the word *tower* to the style of headdress which it represents. By the aid of true and false hair, of cushions and rolls, and other supporting scaffolds, crowned by gauze and ribbons, a piece of architecture was achieved, which was piled—to speak classically—like a Pelion on Ossa on the heads of the fair fashionables of the times of Mary and Anne. This made fine hair a very valuable and saleable commodity. Malcolm gives an anecdote of a young country girl coming to London, and selling her hair for fifty pounds, thereby realising the fortune which her lover's flinty-hearted father required, ere he would consent to their marriage. At a later period, the celebrated Mrs Howard (Lady Suffolk) sold her own beautiful hair in order to enable her husband (then in very narrow circumstances) to give a dinner of policy to a great man.

'The Duchess of Marlborough was noted for her beautiful hair, which, fortunately, she was not compelled to sell; though the circumstance of her cutting it off to spite the husband, who was affectionate and gallant enough greatly to admire it, is well known. Her daughter, Lady Sunderland, had equally beautiful hair, and was equally well aware of the circumstance; but, instead of parting with it in a fit of ill-temper, she tenderly cherished it, and was most peculiarly assiduous in combing, curling, and decorating it in the presence of those gentlemen whose political influence she wished to gain, and who were always courteously welcomed at her toilet.

'The Spectator says, "Sempronia is at present the most professed admirer of the French nation, but is so modest as to admit her visitants no farther than her toilet. It is a very odd sight that beautiful creature makes, when she is talking politics with her tresses flowing about her shoulders, and examining that face in the glass which does such execution upon all the male standers by. How prettily does she divide her discourse between her woman and her visitants! What sprightly transitions does she make from an opera or a sermon to an ivory comb or a pincushion! How have I been pleased to see her interrupted in an account of her travels by a message to her footman! and holding her tongue in the midst of a moral reflection, by applying the tip of it to a patch!"

'To return to the towers. Queen Anne's good taste led her after a while to discontinue them, and to resume a more simple and natural coiffure. The Spectator thus alludes to the change:—"There is not so variable a thing in nature as a lady's headdress; within my own memory I have known it rise and fall within thirty degrees. About ten years ago it shot up to a very great height, insomuch that the female part of our species were much taller than the men. The women were of such an enormous stature, that *we appeared as grasshoppers before them*. At present the whole sex is in a manner dwarfed, and shrunk into a race of beauties that seem almost another species. I remember several ladies who were once very near seven feet high, that at present want some inches of five. How they came to be thus curtailed I cannot learn; whether the whole sex be at present under any penance which we know nothing of, or whether they have cast their headdresses in order to surprise us with something in that kind which shall be entirely new; or whether some of the tallest of the sex, being too cunning for the rest, have contrived this method to make themselves appear sizeable, is still a secret; though I find most are of opinion, they are at present like trees new lopped and pruned, that will certainly sprout up and flourish with greater heads than before. For my own part, as I do not love to be insulted by women who are taller than myself, I admire the sex much more in their present humiliation, which has reduced them to their natural dimensions, than when they had extended their persons and lengthened themselves out into formidable and gigantic figures. I am not for adding to the beautiful edifices of nature, nor for raising any whimsical superstructure upon her plans: I must therefore repeat it, that I am highly pleased with the coiffure now in fashion, and think it shows the good sense which at present very much reigns among the valuable part of the sex. One may observe that women in all ages have taken more pains than men to adorn the outside of their heads; and indeed I very much admire that those female architects, who raise such wonderful structures out of ribbons, lace, and wire, have not been recorded for their respective inventions. It is certain there have been as many orders in these kinds of building as in those which have been made of marble: sometimes they rise in the shape of a pyramid, sometimes like a tower, and sometimes like a steeple."

'The gentlemen's wigs had all this time been enormous. Queen Anne was quite a patroness of full-bottomed wigs; and when the "Ramiliestie" came into fashion, by which the long waving curl, or to speak more accurately, the monstrous tail or fleece was gathered together by a ribbon behind, and one of her officers appeared at court in it, she said to a lady in waiting, "I suppose that presently gentlemen will come to court in their jack-boots."

'The large wigs were enormously expensive, costing as much, some of them, as forty guineas each. Of course they were as much in request amongst light-fingered gentry as a gentleman's watch; and incredible as it may appear, gentlemen were almost as easily deprived of them. We read in the Weekly Journal for March 30, 1717, that the thieves have got such a villanous way now of robbing gentlemen, that they cut holes through the backs of hackney-coaches, and take away their wigs, or the fine headdresses of gentlewomen. So a gentleman was served last Sunday in Tooley Street, and another but last Tuesday in Fenchurch Street; wherefore this may serve for a caution to gentlemen or gentlewomen that ride single in the night-time, to sit on the fore-seat, which will prevent that way of robbing. A most ingenious mode was for a thief to carry on his head a sharp boy in a covered basket, who, in passing through a crowd, would dexterously seize and conceal the most attractive-looking periwig.'

The 'Chronicles of Fashion' are embellished with many portraits, and the book is altogether a handsome, as it is a decidedly entertaining one.

POPULAR LIBRARIES.

The formation of libraries in parishes and other limited districts, which began in our country about sixty years ago, is now in the course of being extended over the whole empire. Libraries are also planted in hospitals, workhouses, and jails; in factories, war-vessels, and regiments. Indeed there is now hardly a group of persons of the humbler class which is not provided, or about to be so, with regular means of intellectual nourishment. Private persons, too, of no exalted rank or affluence, are enabled, in this age of cheap literature, to grace their homes with a goodly range of favourite authors, and thus add in a most important way to their rational enjoyments. While such is the case, we become sensible from applications repeatedly made to us that there is a great lack of right information with regard to the proper materials of popular libraries, both as respects the character of the books and what may be called the *bibliography* of the question; that is to say, the proper editions, and the prices at which they are to be purchased. It has occurred to us that in such circumstances we may, without incurring any charge of officiousness, come forward with an ideal catalogue of books suitable for the masses.

In doing so, we have of course as individuals been thrown much upon our own judgment. And our choice of books, like that of every other individual, being more or less peculiar, it follows that the present catalogue may not be, in all its particulars, what any one of those who peruse it would approve. Let it, however, be taken as a selection made to the best of our judgment and taste, and which we consider as liable to all kinds of modifications according to the peculiar views of those to whom it is offered. Many faults of both omission and commission will be found in it: a few interlineations will remedy the one, and a few dashes the other. We must at the same time state that, in forming the list, we have been guided to a considerable extent, both by hints from persons in the management of libraries, and by considerations as to the prices of books. Many classic works we omit, because they are found to be little called for in popular libraries; many others appear not here, simply because no moderately priced editions of them exist. The list, indeed, has been designed rather to comprehend the best of the cheap editions of contemporary publishers—the books fabricated expressly for the masses—than a perfect summary of the choicest productions of British intellect. It is only necessary further to remark, that the whole class of religious books is unavoidably left to the special judgment of our various readers, as, seeing that we address all sects throughout the United Kingdom, any selection we had made would have been useless, excepting for a more or less limited party.

[The books marked with an asterisk are considered as the most eligible. The initials express the names of the publishers—thus: Bal. Baldwin; Bent. Bentley; Bl. Blackwood and Sons; Bu. James Burns; C. and H. Chapman and Hall; Cad. Cadell; Ch. W. and R. Chambers; Cl. Clark; Col. Colburn; For. Fordyce, Newcastle; H. and D. Harvey and Darton; Kn. Knight; L. Longman and Co; Mox. Moxon; M. Murray; O. and B. Oliver and Boyd; Par. Parker; R. T. S. Religious Tract Society; S. and M. Simpkin and Marshall; Sm. Smith; T. Tegg; Wh. Whittaker and Co. The prices stated are for the most part the full nominal prices of the books, in boards or sewed, liable to a discount for ready money varying from five to ten per cent. In a few cases, a dagger is affixed, indicating that the price has been broken, and that the book is, by special care, to be had at a considerably lower rate.]

HISTORY AND BIOGRAPHY.

Barrow's Life of Sir Francis Drake. 1 vol. 2s. 6d. M.—Bastile and its Principal Captives, by R. A. Davenport. 1 vol. 5s. T.†—Bell's Life of Mary Queen of Scots. 1 vol. 3s. 6d. Wh.—Carrick's Life of Sir William Wallace. 1 vol. 3s. Wh.—Cortez and Pizarro. 2 books, each 3s. Bal.—D'Aubigne's History of the Reformation. 3 vols. 10s. 6d. Wh.—Exemplary and Instructive Biography. 1 vol. 2s. 9d. Ch.—History of the Rebellion in Scotland in 1745, by R. Chambers. 1 vol. 2s. 6d. Ch.—Life of Colonel Hutchinson, by his Widow. 1 vol. 2s. 6d. Sm.—Life of General Washington. 1s. 6d. Wogan, Dublin.—Life of Luther. 1 vol. 3s.—* Life of Napoleon Bonaparte. 2 vols. 10s. T.†—* Life of W. Hutton. 1s. 6d. Kn.—Lives of Individuals who have Raised Themselves. 3s. T.—Memoirs of Felix Neff, J. F. Oberlin, and Bernhard Overberg. 1 vol. 1s. 6d.—* Mignet's History of the French Revolution. 2 vols. 7s.—Ranke's History of the Popes. 3 parts. 12s. Wh.—* Scott's Tales of a Grandfather. 3 vols. 15s. Cad.—* Southey's Life of Nelson. 1 vol. 5s. T.†—Stories from English History. 2s. M.—Sketches of a Soldier's Life. 3s. Tait.—Thierry's History of the Conquest of England by the Normans. 1 vol. 7s. Wh.—Tytler's Life of Sir Walter Raleigh. 1 vol. 5s. O. and B.†

VOYAGES AND TRAVELS.

Anson's Voyage Round the World. 1 vol. 2s. 6d. Sm.—* Cook's Voyages. 1 vol. 2s. 6d. Par.—* Hall's Voyage to Loo Choo. 1 vol. 2s. 6d. Sm.; Travels in South America. 1 vol. 5s. Sm.; Fragments of Voyages and Travels. 1 vol. 12s. Mox.—Incidents of Travel in Egypt, Arabia, Petræa, and the Holy Land; in Greece, Russia, and Poland. 2 books in 1. 3s. 8d. Ch. (2s. 4d. For.)—Inglis's Journey through Switzerland, South of France, and the Pyrenees. 1 vol. 3s.; Solitary Walks through many Lands. 1 vol. 2s. 6d. Wh.—Journey to Lattakoo, by Rev. J. Campbell. 1 vol. 1s. 6d. R. T. S.—* Life and Travels of Mungo Park. 1 vol. 1s. 4d. Ch. (2s. 6d. Par.)—Morocco and the Moors, by Drummond Hay. 1 vol. 2s. 6d. M.—Narrative of a Residence in South Africa, by Thomas Pringle. 1 vol. 3s. 6d. Sm.—Pardoe's City of the Sultan. 3 vols. 6s. Cl.—Tour in Holland, the Countries on the Rhine, and Belgium, in 1838. Do. in Switzerland, in 1841. By William Chambers. 2 books in 1 vol. 3s. Ch.—Tour through Sicily and Malta, by Brydone. 1 vol. 1s. 4d. Ch.—Travels in South Africa, by Rev. J. Campbell. 1 vol. 1s. 6d. R. T. S.—Travels in the East, by De Lamartine. 1 vol. 3s. 9d. Ch.—* Travels of Humboldt in South America. 1 vol. 2s. 6d. Par. (5s. T.†)—* Voyages of Columbus. 1 vol. 2s. 6d. Par. (5s. T.†)

WORKS OF FICTION.

* Arabian Nights Entertainments. 6s. 6d. Dove.—Austen's (Miss) Pride and Prejudice. 2 vols. 3s. 6d.; Sense and Sensibility. 2 vols. 3s. 6d. Cl.—Brambletye House, by Horace Smith. 1 vol. 6s. Col.—Bremer's (Miss) Home. 2 vols. 4s.; H—— Family. 1 vol. 2s.; Strife and Peace. 1 vol. 1s. 6d.; President's Daughter. 1 vol. 2s. Cl.—* Bulwer's Last Days of Pompeii. 1 vol. 6s. Col.—Canterbury Tales. 2 vols. 12s. Col.—Carleton's Traits and Stories of the Irish Peasantry. 2 vols. 26s. Curry.—Croker's Fairy Legends of the South of Ireland. 1 vol. 5s. T.†—Cooper's Pilot; * Prairie; Last of Mohicans; Pioneers; and Borderers. 5 books. 6s. each. Col.—Diary of a Late Physician. 2 vols. 12s. Bl.—Dickens's Pickwick Papers. 1 vol. 21s.; Oliver Twist. 3 vols. 25s.; Nicholas Nickleby. 1 vol. 21s. C. and H.—Don Quixote (Roscoe's edition). 3 vols. 15s.—Edgeworth's Popular Tales. 2 vols. 10s.; Moral Tales. 2 vols. 10s.†; Parents' Assistant. 4 vols. 10s. Bal.—Evenings with the Old Story-Tellers. 1 vol. 1s. 6d. Bu.—Fables and Parables, from the German. 1 vol. 8d. Bu.—* Ferrier's Marriage; Inheritance. 2 books. 5s. each. Bl.—Florence Macarthy, by Lady Morgan. 1 vol. 6s. Col.—Galt's * Annals of the Parish and Ayrshire Legatees; Entail; and Lawrie Todd. 3 books. 5s. each. Bl.—Hajji Baba of Ispahan. 1 vol. S. N. 6s. Col.—* Hook's Gilbert Gurney. 1 vol. 6s. Col.—James's Richlieu; Darnley. 2 books. 6s. each. Col.—Lights and Shadows of Scottish Life. 1 vol. 2s. 6d. Bl.—Mansie Waugh. 1 vol. 2s. 6d. Bl.—Martineau's (Harriet) Deerbrook, and Hour and the Man. 2 books. 6s. each. Mox.; Rioters, the Strike, Hill and Valley, Feats of the Fiord. 4 books. 1s. each.—Paul and Virginia; The Indian Cottage; Elizabeth, or the Exiles of Siberia. 1 vol. 1s. 6d. Sm.—Peacock's Novels—Headlong Hall; Nightmare Abbey; &c. 1 vol. 6s. Col.—Reginald Dalton. 1 vol. 5s. Bl.—* Robinson Crusoe. 1 vol. 1s. 8d. Ch.—Rose of Tistelön, by Emilie Carlen. 2 vols. 4s. Cl.—Sandford and Merton. 1 vol. 3s. Lacy.—* Scott's Novels—Waverley; Guy Mannering; Antiquary; Rob Roy; Old Mortality; Heart of Mid-Lothian; Black Dwarf, and Legend of Montrose; Bride of Lammermoor; Ivanhoe; Kenilworth; Fortunes of Nigel; Pirate; Quentin Durward. 13 books. 4s. each. Cad.—Sedgwick's (Miss) Home. 1 vol. 1s. 3d. S. and M.—Rich Poor Man and Poor Rich Man. 1 vol. 2s. T.—* Stories of the Irish Peasantry, by Mrs Hall. 1 vol. 1s. 9d. Ch.—Thaddeus of Warsaw. 1 vol. 6s. Col.—* Tom Cringle's Log. 1 vol. 5s. Bl.—Two Old Men's Tales. 1 vol. 6s. Col.—* Vicar of Wakefield; Cottagers of Glenburnie. 2 vols. in 1. 1s. 4d. Ch.—Widow Barnaby, by Mrs Trollope. 1 vol. 6s. Col.

POETRY.

Baillie's (Joanna) Fugitive Verses. 1 vol. 1s. Sm.—* Ballads and Metrical Tales, selected from Percy, Ritson, &c. 1 vol. 2s. Bu.—* Burns's Poems. 1 vol. 2s. Ch.—* Campbell's Poetical Works. 2s. 6d. Mox.; Specimens of the British Poets. 1 vol. 15s. M.—Coleridge's Ancient Mariner and other Poems. 1 vol. 1s. Cl.—Cowper's Poems. 3s. 6d. Johnson.—Crabbe's Parish Register and other Poems. 1 vol. 6d. Ch.; Borough and Tales. 2 vols. in 1. 3s. 4d. Sm.—Hemans's Domestic Affections and other Poems. 1 vol. 1s. Cl.—Hogg's Queen's Wake. 1 vol. 8d. Ch.—Keats, Poetical Works of. 1 vol. 2s. Sm.—Kirke White's Poems. 1 vol. 1s. Sm.—Milton's Paradise Lost. 1 vol. 1s. 10d. Sm.—Poetical Works of Leigh Hunt. 1 vol. 2s. 6d. Mox.—Pope's Poetical Works. 1 vol. 5s.; Translation of the Iliad. 1 vol. 3s. Sm.—Readings in Poetry. 1 vol. 4s. 6d. Par.—* Select Poems of Byron—Childe Harold. 2s. 6d.; Giaour, Bride of Abydos, Corsair, Lara, Siege of Corinth, Parasina, Prisoner of Chillon. 1 vol. 3s. 6d. M.—* Select Poems of Scott—Last Minstrel, Marmion, Lady of the Lake. 3 vols. in 1. 2s. 2d. Ch.—Shakspeare's Plays, by Campbell. 1 vol. 16s. Mox.; Each play, 6d. Kn.—Thomson's Seasons, and Castle of Indolence. 1 vol. 1s. Sm.—Wordsworth, Select Poems of. 1 vol. 7s. 6d. Bu.

AMUSING AND INSTRUCTIVE BOOKS.

* Barbauld's Evenings at Home. 1 vol. 6s. 6d. (1s. 6d. For.): another edition. 2s. 9d.—Brown's (Capt. T.) Anecdotes of the Dog; of the Horse. 2 books.—Bubbles from the Brunnens of Nassau. 1 vol. 5s. M.†—Country Boy's Book, by W. Howitt. 4s. L.—Defoe's History of the Plague. 1 vol. 5s. T.†—Essays Moral and Humorous of Joseph Addison. 1 vol. 3s. 3d. Ch.—Gleig's Subaltern. 1 vol. 5s. Bl.—* Hundred Romances of Real Life, by Leigh Hunt. 1 vol. 3s. 6d. Wh.—Irving's Sketch-Book. 2 vols. 10s. T.†; History of New York. 1 vol. 2s. 3d. Sm.—Julian, or Adventures in Judea; Palmyra; Rome and the Early Christians. 3 books. 1s. 10d. each. Ch.—Letters from the Baltic, by Miss Rigby. 1 vol. 2s. 6d. M.—Letters on Natural Magic, by Sir David Brewster. 1 vol. 5s. T.†—Mutiny of the Bounty. 1 vol. 1s. 4d. Sm.

—Pursuit of Knowledge Under Difficulties. 2 vols. 8s. Kn.—The Amber Witch. 1 vol. 2s. Cl. (2s. 6d. M.)—* The Bible in Spain, by G. Borrow. 2 vols. in 1. 5s. M.—The Sea: Narratives of Adventure and Shipwreck; Tales and Sketches Illustrative of Life on the Ocean. 1 vol. 2s. 6d. Ch.—* Two Years before the Mast: a Personal Narrative of Life at Sea. 1 vol. 2s. 6d. Sm.—Traditions of Chelsea Hospital. 1 vol. 6s. Bent.—Wild Sports of the West, by Maxwell. 1 vol. 6s. Bent.—Willis's Pencillings by the Way. 1 vol. 6s. Col.

MISCELLANEOUS.

* Combe's (Dr Andrew) Physiology. 1 vol. 2s. 6d. Maclachlan and Stewart, Edinburgh.—Bertha's Journal. 4s. M.—Bird Architecture, by Rennie. 1 vol. 4s.—Boy's Country Book, by William Howitt. 1 vol. 8s. L.—Bunyan's Pilgrim's Progress. 1 vol. 10d. For.—Butler's Analogy of Natural and Revealed Religion. 1s. 2d. Ch.—Chambers's Information for the People. 2 vols. 16s. Ch.—Conversations on Political Economy, by Mrs Marcet. 1 vol. 7s. 6d. M.—Cottage Evenings. 1 vol. 1s. Kn.—Cyclopædia of English Literature, edited by R. Chambers. 2 vols. 18s. 6d. Ch.—Franklin's Life and Miscellaneous Writings. 1 vol. 1s. 4d. Ch.—* Fraser's Scientific Wanderings. 1 vol. 5s. Bell and Bradfute.—Hack's Lectures at Home. 3s. 6d.; Hack's Winter Evenings. 6s. 6d. H. and D.—Howitt's (Mrs) Work and Wages; Strive and Thrive. 2 books. 1s. 6d. each. T.—Jesse's Gleanings in Natural History. 1 vol. 6s. 6d. M.—Lapland and its Reindeer. 1s. H. and D.—Mrs Leicester's School. 2s. G.—Nichol's Architecture of the Heavens. 1 vol. 10s. 6d. Tait.—Paley's Natural Theology. 1 vol. 1s. 2d. Ch.—Philosophy in Sport Made Science in Earnest. 7s. L.—Practical Economy, by J. and A. Bethune. 1 vol. 4s. Blacks.—* Readings in Science. 1 vol. 5s. Par.—Swainson on the Habits and Instincts of Animals. 1 vol. 6s. L.—Wade's History and Political Economy of the Middle and Working Classes. 1 vol. 3s. 3d. Ch.

ADEN.

Aden is a station on the Arabian side of the Red Sea, established only a few years ago for the accommodation of steamers passing to and from Suez and Bombay. The following concise account of it was lately given at a meeting of the Asiatic Society, by assistant-surgeon Malcolmson, who had been a permanent resident there ever since the place was taken possession of by the British Indian government:—Mr Malcolmson states that the town is built in the centre of an extinct submarine volcano, whose activity must have surpassed any idea we can form in judging from the operations of existing volcanoes: that after a season of repose, which may have lasted myriads of years, it became active again, and formed a second crater on the north-western side of the valley. He places the second eruption at a period long anterior to the existence of animal life. With the exception of one peak, the whole of the peninsula is composed of rocks unfit for building purposes, as they peel off in thin laminæ when exposed to the air. The peak excepted is a basalt, projecting from the edge of the precipice, down the sides of which the masses required for building are thrown by the blast which detaches them into the valley below, where they are shaped for use. The writer is of opinion that Aden was once an island; and that the isthmus now connecting it with the continent, which is nowhere above six feet in height, or three quarters of a mile in breadth, was formed by the tides from each side meeting in the middle.

The animals of Aden are a few timid monkeys—believed by the Arabs to be the people of the tribe of Ad, transformed in consequence of their wickedness—some hyenas, many very beautiful foxes, and an immense number of rats. The reptiles are snakes, lizards, and scorpions of two kinds—one very large, reaching to eight inches in length, but whose sting is not dangerous; the other smaller, said to be very venomous. The plants are chiefly pretty flowers, growing in the hills; and there were some acacias of considerable size, and other trees, at the coming of the English; but these have been all cut down for fuel. The climate may be divided into two seasons, the hot and cold: in the hot season, the thermometer ranges as high as 104 degrees in the shade; but the heat is by no means unbearable; in fact, the difference between the sensible temperature and that shown by the thermometer is always very remarkable. This great heat does not produce sickness: and although the troops suffered dreadfully at first, from want of accommodation and proper food, from the great fatigue and watching to which they were exposed, and from the dreadful filth of the place, now that these causes are removed, the writer feels warranted in stating, that a more healthy station does not exist in any British colony.

When the place was first occupied by the British, the population consisted of about 1000 half-naked and half-starved inhabitants: there are now at least 20,000 residents, well clothed and well fed; besides the troops, amounting to 3500, and a fluctuating population of 1500 souls. The water is very superior, and obtained from wells, in which it remains at the same level at all seasons. It is not, unfortunately, sufficiently attainable for irrigation, and there is but little rain to supply its place: were it not for this impediment, the success of the government garden proves that the soil would be highly productive. There are remains of large tanks on the peninsula, which the writer thinks were abandoned when the wells were dug; but in all probability they were used for irrigation, and, if restored, might be again available for that purpose. The dwellings are principally composed of wooden uprights, whose intervals are filled with reeds, and lined with matting formed of leaves of the date tree: they are cool and comfortable; and better adapted to the climate than more costly edifices. The chief objection to them is, their liability to fire; of which an instance was seen in the whole of the lines of the 10th regiment having been destroyed in two hours. The place is now healthy; the troops and their families cheerful and happy: they have good quarters and excellent food, and are on good terms with the inhabitants. The town is improving; ruins have almost disappeared; many stone-houses have been built, and others are building; the streets are now well levelled and regular; and the revenue has doubled every year. Mr Malcolmson is decidedly of opinion that Aden is destined to be one of the most important posts belonging to England; as there is every indication that the intercourse with India will be restored, at least in part, to its ancient route.

MONUMENTAL RECORDS OF THE DEAD.

In our public monuments, persistent interest has been too much forgotten. Beauty and grandeur of form have been sought for; useful beauty has been neglected. Mankind have reared a statue, with sometimes elaborate decorations and accompaniments, at an immense cost; but beyond a chef-d'œuvre of art, little has been achieved; the enduring form appeals to the age, and the influence stops. The highest range of art is to combine the useful with the beautiful, to render the memorial subservient to the purposes of public good, and thus continue through all time, not alone the name and figure of the now unbreathing great man, but continue as it were the nobler part of him—his mind, his heart, with all its man-loving aspirations; thus enabling posterity not only to read his name and see his similitude, but to feel his influences in the good they at the same moment enjoy, and thus, 'he being dead, yet speaketh.' One of the noblest monuments in this country records the name of a humble, strong-minded man, Thomas Hobson, carrier, of Cambridge. It is on a plain stone building, which supports four spouts of a conduit, which conveys a stream of the most brilliant water, brought at the expense of Mr Hobson from the Chalk hills, near Cambridge, into the town. A young lady, a governess, some time ago died at or near Ockley, in Surrey, the poor inhabitants of which were but ill supplied with wholesome water. This lady left some four or five hundred pounds to be expended in digging a well and constructing a pump; and beneath a very appropriate and elegant rustic covering stands the pump, on which is inscribed—

'The benevolent bequest of Jane Scott, MDCCCXXXVII.'

The pump, constructed for the good of poor people, who must be content often to get but good water, by means of the intelligent kindness of the beneficent lady, Jane Scott, will cause her name to be read by many a passer-by with eye-glistening emotion. This Jane Scott must have been a good woman. The carrier and the governess have struck a new and most truly poetic style of monumental trophies. It is to be hoped the idea suggested by these examples may be followed out generally. Ockley is a beautiful village at the foot of Leith Hill, on one road to Worthing from London. The houses are stretched along an immense quadrangle, which forms a common, a delicious open green—everybody's park—and may it long be kept sacred from the enclosing edge. In the middle of this stands Jane Scott's pump. She also left funds for a school. There is an elegant school-house which bears her name.—*Historical Register.*

RISING IN THE WORLD.

You should bear constantly in mind that nine-tenths of us are, from the very nature and necessities of the world, born to gain our livelihood by the sweat of the brow. What reason have we then to presume that our children are not to do the same? If they be, as now and then one will be, endowed with extraordinary powers of mind, those powers may have an opportunity of developing themselves; and if they never have that opportunity, the harm is not very great to us or to them. Nor does it hence follow that the descendants of labourers are *always* to be labourers. The path upwards is steep and long to be sure. Industry, care, skill, excellence, in the present parent, lay the foundation of *a rise*, under more favourable circumstances, for the children. The children of these take *another rise*; and by and by the descendants of the present labourer become gentlemen. This is the natural progress. It is by attempting to reach the top at a *single leap* that so much misery is produced in the world; and the propensity to make such attempt has been cherished and encouraged by the strange projects that we have witnessed of late years for making the labourers *virtuous* and *happy* by giving them what is called *education*. The education which I speak of consists in bringing children up to labour with *steadiness*, with *care*, and with *skill*; to show them how to do as many useful things as possible; to teach them to do them all in the best manner; to set them an example in industry, sobriety, cleanliness, and neatness; to make all these habitual to them, so that they never shall be liable to fall into the contrary; to let them always see a good living proceeding from labour, and thus to remove from them the temptation to get at the goods of others by violent or fraudulent means, and to keep far from their minds all the inducements to hypocrisy and deceit.—*William Cobbett.*

SPEECH-MAKING.

Who has not known a pleasant party utterly done for—every element of its pleasantness extinguished by the demon of speech-making throwing its wet blanket over it. The interesting conversation, the smartly-maintained argument, the quick repartee, the good-humoured badinage—all paralysed in a moment by some unhappy speech-maker, who rises from his chair, like a ghost through a trap-door, and in an unfaltering stolid voice asks permission to propose a toast. It is granted of course. You know that all is over—the blow has been struck—enjoyment is lying sprawling under the table, dying or dead. You may as well take your hat and go home disconsolately in the rain: you know what will follow. You know that the wretch is going to propose your host's health—you know all that a creature of the kind says—he is always sure the toast he is about to give requires no comment—that its object requires no eulogium from him to make them all do that toast due honour. They all know their friend—their excellent, their valued friend—and that, as surely as he is known, he is esteemed—that they all can and do appreciate those many excellent qualities which have so generally endeared him, either as a husband, a father, or a friend. Knowing this, and feeling this, he did believe himself called upon to, &c. &c. &c. All the commonplace cant of compliment is duly gone through; and the mischief is, that the matter don't end here. The toastee (there is no law against coining words as against coining half-crowns) is in duty bound to return thanks, which process he performs by disclaiming *seriatim* all the flattery lavished upon him, and too often winding up by plastering it more upon another, who in his turn repeats the interesting operation. And so it goes round: the mania is as catching as the small-pox. Everybody proposes everybody else's health. It would be an insult given to leave out anybody—received, to be left out by everybody. Conversation, amusing or instructive, gives place to a vapid round of compliments, neither instructive, nor amusing, nor sincere. You no more mean what you say when you make an ordinary buttering after-dinner speech, than you do what you write when you finish a letter with 'your most obedient servant,' and address it to a fellow whom you mean to kick the first time you can catch him.—*New Monthly Magazine.*

CHILDREN.

[From 'The Child of the Islands,' by the Hon. Mrs Norton, newly published.]

Yes, deem her mad! for holy is the sway
Of that mysterious sense which bids us bend
Toward the young souls new clothed in helpless clay—
Fragile beginnings of a mighty end—
Angels unwinged—which human care must tend
Till they can tread the world's rough path alone,
Serve for themselves, or in themselves offend.
But God o'erlooketh all from his high throne,
And sees, with eyes benign, their weakness—and our own!

Therefore we pray for them, when sunset brings
Rest to the joyous heart and shining head;
When flowers are closed, and birds fold up their wings,
And watchful mothers pass each cradle-bed
With hushed soft steps, and earnest eyes that shed
Tears far more glad than smiling! Yes, all day
We bless them; while, by guileless pleasure led,
Their voices echo in their gleesome play,
And their whole careless souls are making holiday.

And if, by Heaven's inscrutable decree,
Death calls, and human skill is vain to save;
If the bright child that clambered to our knee,
Cold and inactive, fills the silent grave;
Then with what wild lament we moan and rave!
What passionate tears fall down in ceaseless showers!
There lies Perfection!—there, of all life gave—
The bud that would have proved the sweetest flower
That ever woke to bloom within an earthly bower!

For in *this* hope our intellects abjure
All reason—all experience—and forego
Belief in that which only is secure,
Our natural chance and share of human wo.
The father pitieth David's heart-struck blow,
But for himself, such augury defies:
No future Absalom *his* love can know;
No pride, no passion, no rebellion lies
In the unsullied depth of those delightful eyes!

Their innocent faces open like a book,
Full of sweet prophecies of coming good;
And we who pore thereon with loving look,
Read what we most desire, not what we should;
Even that which suits our own ambition's mood.
The scholar sees distinction promised there—
The soldier, laurels in the field of blood—
The merchant, venturous skill and trading fair—
None read of broken hope—of failure—of despair!

Nor ever can a parent's gaze behold
Defect of nature, as a stranger doth;
For these (with judgment true, severe, and cold)
Mark the ungainly step of heavy sloth—
Coarseness of features—tempers easy wroth;
But those, with dazzled hearts such errors spy,
(A halo of indulgence circling both:)
The plainest child a stranger passes by,
Shows lovely to the sight of some enamoured eye!

The mother looketh from her latticed pane—
Her children's voices echoing sweet and clear:
With merry leap and bound her side they gain,
Offering their wild field-flow'rets: all are dear,
Yet still she listens with an absent ear:
For, while the strong and lovely round her press,
A halt uneven step sounds drawing near:
And all she leaves, that crippled child to bless,
Folding him to her heart with cherishing caress.

Yea, where the soul denies illumined grace
(The last, the worst, the fatallest defect),
SHE, gazing earnest in that idiot face,
Thinks she perceives a dawn of intellect:
And, year by year, continues to expect
What time shall never bring, ere life be flown:
Still loving, hoping—patient, though deject,
Watching those eyes that answer not her own—
Near him—and yet how far! with him—but still alone!

Want of attraction *this* love cannot mar;
Years of rebellion cannot blot it out:
The prodigal, returning from afar,
Still finds a welcome, given with song and shout!
The father's hand, without reproach or doubt,
Clasps his—who caused them all such bitter fears:
The mother's arms encircle him about:
That long dark course of alienated years,
Marked only by a burst of reconciling tears!

Printed by William Bradbury, of No. 6, York Place, and Frederick Mullett Evans, of No. 7, Church Row, both of Stoke Newington, in the county of Middlesex, printers, at their office, Lombard Street, in the precinct of Whitefriars, and city of London; and Published (with permission of the Proprietors, W. and R. CHAMBERS,) by WILLIAM SOMERVILLE ORR, Publisher, of 2, Amen Corner, at No. 2, AMEN CORNER, both in the parish of Christchurch, and in the city of London.—Saturday, May 24, 1845.

CONDUCTED BY WILLIAM AND ROBERT CHAMBERS, EDITORS OF 'CHAMBERS'S INFORMATION FOR THE PEOPLE,' 'CHAMBERS'S EDUCATIONAL COURSE,' &c.

No. 74. New Series. SATURDAY, MAY 31, 1845. Price 1½d.

METAPHYSICS OF BUSINESS.

We hear much of various circumstances affecting business in this busy country, but few ever dream of its being liable to one influence, greater perhaps than all the rest put together—the workings of human nature.

A curious fact has been remarked, that the funds—all ordinary affecting circumstances being fully allowed for—always incline to be somewhat higher in spring than in autumn. There cannot, we think, be a doubt that this is owing to the various conditions of men's minds in the two seasons. In the opening of the year, there is an excitement of the hopeful and cheerful sentiments, under which we are more disposed to speculation and adventure. The decline of the year, on the contrary, raises melancholy and timorous sentiments; we then feel inclined to draw into our shells and wait for brighter days: speculation has no charms for us. In the one case we are under the influence of hope; in the other, of cautiousness. It would almost indeed appear as if we were, in this respect, subject to laws similar to those which affect birds and other lower animals, causing them to exhibit no active industry except in spring. It is only when we have a future bright before us, that our energies are fully roused.

The same feelings are seen exercising a most potent control over the state of markets, and in all adventurous kinds of business. These things are notedly oscillatory; and this is simply because hope and cautiousness take command over us in an alternating manner. The natural procedure of the two feelings is this: for a time after an experience of evil or a threat of danger, cautiousness is predominant. Gradually, after a cessation of these experiences, we forget them. Cautiousness is lulled; hope and confidence again awaken; and these go on in increasing activity, till danger and evil once more supervene, and then they give way in a moment to revived cautiousness. Thus it is that, for some years after such a 'crash' as that of 1825, joint-stock speculations are held in universal dread; so that even a really promising one would be shunned. But by and by the sufferings and losses are forgotten. Men begin to touch and taste, and finding no immediate harm, they at length take whole mouthfuls. Hope gets into full commission, *vice* cautiousness retired, and then we see the most visionary schemes eagerly embraced, where recently the most plausible and prudent would have been repudiated. A 'crash,' with its distressing consequences in the ruin of individuals, and embarrassment of general business, finally lays hope once more so completely prostrate, that for years men cannot be induced to venture even on the fairest chances. The rise or fall of prices in all affairs admitting of the least speculation, is governed by the same principle. A little rise from just causes excites hope, under whose influence a further and unwarranted rise takes place. While the progress in this direction remains unchecked by any external cause, all is sanguine expectation in the mercantile mind. No one seems to have the least conception of a possible reverse. Everybody wishes to buy from everybody. Reason has nothing to do with it: it is a mere sentiment which is at work. But let the slightest prognostic of a *turn* come into view, and in an instant the hopeful feeling sinks like a punctured wind-bag. A panic supervenes, and things never rest till they are as much below the fair and reasonable point as they were formerly above it.

Have we not here, also, nearly the whole philosophy of what are called 'gluts' and 'bad times?' Manufacturers go on for a while producing a particular article with the greatest diligence, as if they believed that mankind were in danger of some tremendous inconvenience for want of it. This enthusiasm in (we shall say) trouser stuffs finds at length a slight check. In an instant the manufacture ceases, the works are stopped, the workmen are thrown idle. For months there seems to reign over the district a dreary conviction that mankind are never to require trousers any more. Now it was neither true at first that mankind were in any pressing need of nether-garments, nor that they have now abjured all further use of them. They use such integuments in a regular monotonous manner, and will evermore do so. The irregularity is in the mental impulses of the producers of trousers. These men happen to regard their wares with alternative paroxysms of hope and despair. The consequence is that at one time a factory is put to top speed, and the workmen are tempted by high wages to exceed the proper hours of labour, in order to produce a good deal more cloth than the public has immediate use for, while at another the whole system is laid utterly idle, because men somehow feel a heavy market as an indication that the world is at an end. Hence arise most important results in our social economy. A Leeds, a Manchester, a Sheffield, is every now and then a famine city, because business affairs are regulated, not by the sense and judgment of mankind, but by mere sentiments not necessarily connected with reflection. How absurd to suppose business men to be prosaic and over-sober of mind! They are the greatest sentimentalists that breathe.

We must now consider another portion of our subject.

Accustomed as we are in this country to see almost every person engaged in some kind of business or craft, we are apt to suppose it the natural and ordinary state of things. A twelve hours' bill seems the general fate of man. But in reality constant working is the exception from the rule. There are very few nations which pursue regular callings continually. Some that are by no means uncivilised work extremely little.

The Turks, for example, are an indolent people. Powerless, handless, they spend the whole day in perfect vacuity, apparently never giving themselves the least concern about the means of subsistence. And yet, somehow, the Turks live. All the people along the south of Europe are comparatively inert. The *Dolce Far Niente* is the prevalent taste of the Mediterranean nations. The striking distinction of the Englishman in this respect seems to be in a certain anxiety about the welfare of himself and his family. He starts in life with an awful sense of the necessity of getting on in the world. He will, with the greatest coolness, commence a business which he knows will require his being a daily and nightly slave for thirty years, undreaming that he is making any extraordinary sacrifice. He sees ages of bill-troubles before him, but looks upon it all as a matter of relentless destiny. Even when the first claims of his sense of duty have been fulfilled, and he knows he is safe from poverty for life, he works on for the love of working, rather than walk into a system of idleness which would present to him no enjoyable advantages. Now, who ever heard, in the literature or history of any nations away from central Europe and the United States of America, of such a thought predominating among them as the necessity of getting on in the world? They are not, in general, altogether idle. They till, and weave, and fabricate in a way which seems to be sufficient for their wants; but they are totally unacquainted with that system of close and incessant moiling after increase of goods, which appears to be the first law of existence amongst us. It must also be remembered that we know of the world having existed for centuries upon centuries, before it exhibited *anywhere* an example of this passionate attachment to workshop, counter, and desk. There was no shopkeeping worth speaking of in ancient Greece or Rome. Factories existed not among the Ptolemies. While the crusades swept across Europe, there were few men calling themselves merchants in London, Paris, or Venice. It is entirely since the close of the middle ages that men have raised into vogue the idea that business is the sheet-anchor of individuals and of nations. There is thus a great difference from past time to present, as well as from other nations to us. This shows fully, we think, that business is not a thing necessary or unavoidable to our human nature. It can be no special result of certain faculties which have no other purpose or mode of action. Yet this is what we might suppose, if we were to see nothing in business but the gratification of the working or fabricating faculty, and of the love of gain. It therefore appears that the love of action and of excitement, or what Dr Darwin would have called 'an accumulation of sensorial power,' is what chiefly animates the hard-working nations, being the same impulse which once gratified men in war and in the chase, and still leads the born wealthy to the turf and the gaming-club. It is but the phase in which the mass of manly power and endowment appears in modern civilised nations. And accordingly trade has its heroes and conquerors as well as history. We shall find on many an 'exchange' combinations and calculations profounder than any that ever emerged in St James's or Versailles; and it would not be difficult for any one acquainted with such towns as Glasgow or Liverpool to point out men between whom and a Napoleon it is not easy to see any distinguishing qualities besides their superior worth.

The view which we are disposed to take respecting the benevolence of business accords with this idea as to their main ends being, after all, but the gratification of certain mental faculties. To appearance there is nothing but selfishness regarded in business, and if the pursuit of his own end by each individual conduces, as Adam Smith endeavours to show, to the general weal, it is no praise to the motives of particular parties. But the worship of fortune in reality involves no necessary subjection of the heart to selfishness. The fact is, that where business exists on a considerable scale, its votaries act under two opposite and apparently irreconcilable principles: in purely business matters, they are keen and inflexible, ever disposed to exact the whole of their rights; in domestic and social matters, they may be at the same time bountiful and conceding to a surprising degree. Meet them upon a bargain, and you would think them stern, and wrapped up in views of their own interest. See them next day in private, and you discover that they use their wealth with a generosity that shows they are far from loving it for its own sake. We have here a consideration which seems to take much from the force of those writings which hold up the present as an age of Mammon-worship. The following of Mammon is a fact in itself; but it ought to be taken in connexion with other circumstances, by which its effects are much modified. Our ruling competitive principle unquestionably calls out emulation and worse passions; but these are softened by the humanity and largeness of soul which are conspicuous features of the mercantile mind in all above the struggling classes. We are not, let it be fully understood, inclined to believe that the present plan is the best conceivable for the subsistence of nations. We thoroughly believe that, in time, such great bodies of people will feel and act more as only a large kind of families, and enjoy almost, if not altogether, in common the fruits of the general industry, finding that thereby they realise greater enjoyments than are to be obtained by each standing upon his individual acquisitiveness. All this may be unhesitatingly admitted, and yet we will say that the present system is far less selfish than is generally supposed, seeing that selfishness is the rule only in a certain routine of transactions so monotonous as almost to be a complete abstraction, while the kindly social affections in reality prevail over, and give character to the ordinary demonstrations of the individual.

We have here merely broken ground in a subject which appears to us to possess great interest. We willingly leave to others to investigate it more deeply, and place the matter in all the various lights in which it may be contemplated. Meanwhile, some of these speculations may be brought home to men's bosoms. It is very obvious that the interests of a vast body of people—of that class generally who live by labour—are involved to a serious extent in the briskness and dulness of business. It is of importance for them to be aware that, so long as the competitive mode endures, the amount of their incomes, and even the question whether they shall have an income at all or not, depend upon the extent to which the faculty of hope is active in the brains of the employing class. So long as employers are sanguine as to markets and results of mercantile combinations, the horde of the industrious are safe; let the tide turn—and its ebb is as sure as its flow—and a large proportion of this huge multitude must cease to be employed. The fact of hundreds of thousands of our people being thus withheld at any time from a penury verging upon and often trenching upon pauperism, only by the afflatus of an accidental sentiment in the minds of another portion of the community, is one of those great problems of modern times at which the wisest are the most apt to stand aghast. It is surely by no means creditable to our national sagacity, that we should contentedly see times of prosperity thus go on to the inevitable break-down, when thousands upon thousands are sure to be thrown into misery, and yet believe it all to be in the fair and proper course of things. No provision by the industrious themselves for the day of certain evil; no arrangement by the sage and politic for softening the blow when it comes; no lesson for the future taken from the past; and, above all, no whispered alarm into any mind as to the soundness of the social plans which involve such tremendous calamities. Verily, we are yet children acting upon our first instincts, and the manhood of man—the time of reason and true brotherly kindness—seems yet far off.

HISTORY OF A NEGRO PLOT.

MANKIND always fear those whom they oppress, and desirous of finding an excuse for their oppression, they are never slack in accusing the injured of a disposition to conspire and revolt. History abounds in instances of this species of injustice. Every country in Europe has had its *plots*, not one in a hundred of which rested on any other foundation than the real or pretended fears of the oppressing party. So also have all slave-holding countries their plots—mere figments of the imagination, but which are nevertheless made the plausible ground for renewed restrictions on the unhappy objects of oppression.

We propose to shame human nature with an account of one of these fabulous plots, and the cruelties of which it was made the pretence.

Slavery was a legal institution in the North American colonies previous to their declaration of independence; no one either at home or abroad thinking there was anything wrong in dealing in negroes as articles of merchandise, or in subjecting them to perpetual bondage. From the government in Britain the colonial governors had strict injunctions to cultivate the African trade, as it was called, and to take care that the negroes who were imported should be properly watched, lest they should commit the odious and ungrateful crime of seeking to emancipate themselves by violence. It was not necessary to give any such injunctions, for the colonists were so much alive to the necessity for checking an inclination to revolt, that, like all oppressors, they were continually imagining outbreaks, and taking the sharpest measures to prevent their occurrence. In the year 1741, a panic cry of negro revolt was raised in New York, which threw the inhabitants of that city into a state of great excitement and alarm; the rumour being that the negro population designed to burn the town and massacre every white inhabitant. This insane idea originated in the following circumstances.

A Spanish vessel had been brought into port as a prize, and a number of its sailors being men of colour, they were not treated as prisoners of war, but condemned as slaves in the court of admiralty, and accordingly sold to the highest bidder. These unfortunate men grumbled at this treatment. They declared they were freemen, who had hired themselves as mariners, and that it was grossly unjust to make them slaves. Of course these arguments went for nothing: the men had black or tawny skins, and by the colonial law they were liable to confiscation. One of these men was bought by a person whose house shortly after went on fire; immediately two or three other fires occurred in the city, including one in the government house, which was burnt with some adjoining buildings. Whether these fires were accidental, or the work of incendiaries, could not be discovered; but the cry was raised among the people, 'It is the Spanish negroes!—take up the Spanish negroes!' They were immediately incarcerated, and a fire occurring in the afternoon of the same day, the rumour became general that the slaves in a body were concerned in these wicked attempts to burn the city. The military was turned out, and the sentries were posted in every part of the town, while there was a general search of the houses, and an examination of suspicious persons. The lieutenant-governor, at the request of the city authorities, offered a reward of L.100 and a full pardon to any free white person who should discover the persons concerned in these incendiary acts, and freedom, with a reward of L.20, to any slave who should make the same discovery.

The offer of so tempting a reward induced a woman named Mary Burton to assume the office of informer. Some time before the outbreak of the fires, Mary had been a servant with a person named John Hughson, who kept a low tavern where negroes were in the habit of resorting. This man had been concerned in receiving some articles of which a house had been robbed, and in consequence of information given by his servant, he was seized and put in prison for this delinquency. Peggy Carey, a woman of infamous character, was also implicated in the robbery, and likewise committed to prison. It now seems to have occurred to Mary Burton that nothing would be more feasible than to attach the crime of incendiarism and insurrection to her late master, Hughson, and the woman Carey, along with three negroes, Cæsar, Prince, and Cuffee; and she emitted a declaration to that effect. She stated that she had heard these two white and three black persons conspiring to burn the town and massacre the inhabitants. The governor, the lawyers, and all the people were aghast with horror. The plot was atrocious, and demanded the most careful inquiry, the most signal punishment.

Many examinations ensued, and among others that of the wretched woman Peggy Carey. Peggy was bad enough, but she had never entertained half so magnificent a project as that of burning New York, and denied all knowledge of the plot and its abettors. On second thoughts, however, as she saw she was in a scrape for having received stolen goods, it appeared to her that she might escape punishment by trumping up what was so much in demand—a little knowledge of the plot. She now made a voluntary confession, in which she laid the scene of the plot in the house of John Romme, a shoemaker, and keeper of a tavern frequented by several negroes, to whom Romme administered an oath. She said they were to attempt to burn the city; but if they did not succeed, they were to steal all they could, and he was to carry them to a strange country and give them their liberty. All the slaves mentioned by her were immediately arrested. Romme absconded, but was afterwards taken.

The narrative of what now took place may be best gathered from the 'American Criminal Trials,' by P. W. Chandler, a work of much interest, recently published.

'On the 29th of May 1741, the negro slaves, Quack and Cuffee, were brought to trial before the supreme court, on a charge of a conspiracy to murder the inhabitants of the city of New York. The principal evidence against them came from Mary Burton. There was also some evidence against them from negroes. The prisoners had no counsel, while the attorney-general, assisted by two members of the bar, appeared against them. The evidence had little consistency, and was extremely loose and general. The arguments of the lawyers were chiefly declamatory respecting the horrible plot, of the existence of which, however, no sufficient evidence was introduced. "The monstrous ingratitude of this black tribe," was the language of one of them, in addressing the jury, "is what exceedingly aggravates their guilt. Their slavery among us is generally softened with great indulgence. They live without care; and are commonly better clothed and fed, and put to less labour, than the poor of most Christian countries. But notwithstanding all the kindness and tenderness with which they have been treated amongst us, yet this is the second attempt of the same kind that this brutish and bloody species of mankind have made within one age." The prisoners were immediately convicted, and were sentenced by one of the court, in an address singularly indicative of the general excitement on the subject, to be burnt to death. "You that were for destroying us without mercy," he said, "you abject wretches, the outcasts of the nations of the earth, are treated here with tenderness and humanity; and I wish I could not say with too great indulgence, for you have grown wanton with excess of liberty, and your idleness has proved your ruin, having given you the opportunities of forming this villanous and detestable conspiracy. What hopes can you have of mercy in the other world, for shall not the judge of all the earth do right?" and he urged them to confess, as affording the only hope of mercy.

'The prisoners protested their innocence, and utterly denied any knowledge of any plot whatever; but when they were taken out to execution, the poor creatures were much terrified; the officers again endeavoured to persuade them to confess, and after they were chained to the stake, and the executioner was ready to apply the torch, they admitted all that was required of them. An attempt was then made to procure a reprieve, but a great multitude had assembled to witness the executions, and the excitement was so great that it was considered impossible to return the prisoners to jail. They were accordingly burned at the stake. Although Hughson and his wife had already been tried, and were under sentence of death for the felony of receiving stolen goods, it was determined to bring them to another trial for being concerned in the conspiracy. Accordingly, on the 4th of June 1741, Hughson, his wife, his daughter, and Peggy Carey, were placed at the bar for trial. Mary Burton was at hand with her tales, and Arthur Price, a thief and an infamous character, who had been employed by the magistrates to go to Sarah Hughson and endeavour to make her accuse her father and mother, related a conversation he pretended to have had with her. The prisoners had no counsel, and almost every member of the bar appeared against them. The attorney-general made an address to the jury, which was full of outrageous invectives against Hughson. "Such a monster," he said, "will this Hughson appear before you, that, for the sake of the plunder he expected by setting in flames the king's house, and this whole city, he—remorseless he! counselled and encouraged the committing of all these most astonishing deeds of darkness, cruelty, and inhumanity — infamous Hughson! Gentlemen, this is that Hughson, whose name and most detestable conspiracies will no doubt be had in everlasting remembrance, to his eternal reproach, and stand recorded to the latest posterity. This is the man!—this, that grand incendiary!—that arch rebel against God, his king, and his country!—that devil incarnate, and chief agent of the Abaddon of the infernal pit and regions of darkness!"

'The prisoners severally and solemnly protested their innocence, declared that what the witnesses had said against them was false, and called upon God to witness their asseverations. They were all found guilty, and were sentenced to be hanged. "Good God!" exclaimed the judge in pronouncing sentence, "when I reflect on the disorders, confusion, desolation, and havoc which the effect of your most wicked, most detestable, and diabolical counsels might have produced, had not the hand of our great and good God interposed, it shocks me; and you, who would have burnt and destroyed without mercy, ought to be served in a like manner."

'The daughter of Hughson confessed and was saved. Peggy Carey had confessed, but retracted, and said that what she had confessed was a gross prevarication, and that she had sworn falsely against those she accused. She was accordingly executed. On the evening before her death, she sent for one of the judges, and reiterated to him her statement that she had forsworn herself in regard to the plot. Hughson and his wife asserted their innocence to the last, but were executed. When the three came to die, Hughson seemed to expect a rescue; his wife was senseless; and Peggy Carey met her fate with less composure than either of the others.

'Meanwhile, the trials were prosecuted with all possible vigour. On the 8th of June, six negroes were condemned to be chained to a stake and burned. On the 10th of June four more negroes were tried, convicted, and subsequently received the same sentence; one of them immediately made a confession in court, implicating a large number of negroes. On the 13th of June five more were convicted, and on the 15th of the same month were sentenced to death. On the 17th of June five of the Spanish negroes were brought to trial. By a law of the province, the testimony of slaves could only be used against each other, and it was used in the present instance; but the prisoners complained bitterly of the injustice done them, insisting that they were freemen in their own country. The court decided, however, that they were slaves, and the evidence of slaves was properly used against them; they were all condemned. On the 19th of June the lieutenant-governor offered a full pardon to all who would make confession before the 1st of July. The poor negroes, being extremely terrified, were anxious to take the only avenue of safety that was offered, and each strove to tell a story as ingenious and horrible as he could manufacture. "Now," says the historian of the plot, "many negroes began to squeak, in order to lay hold of the benefit of the proclamation. Some who had been apprehended, but not indicted, and many who had been indicted and arraigned, who had pleaded not guilty, were disposed to retract their pleas and plead guilty, and throw themselves on the mercy of the court." In one week after the proclamation there were thirty additional slaves accused, and before the 15th of July forty-six negroes, on their arraignment at different times, pleaded guilty. Suspected slaves were daily arrested, until at length the prison became so full that there was danger of disease, and the court again called in the assistance of the members of the bar, who agreed to bear their respective shares in the fatigue of the several prosecutions.'

While things were at this crisis, the cry of a negro plot became strangely mingled with a notion that the conspiracy was somehow fomented by the Roman Catholics—a Negro and Popish plot rolled into one—and this greatly aggravated the panic. Mary Burton, and William Kane, a soldier, who had himself been suspected, and escaped by confession, accused a nonjuring clergyman, named John Ury, who was living obscurely in New York, of meeting and conspiring with negroes. Nothing was too wild for belief. This poor gentleman, whose life appears to have been irreproachable, was brought to trial for the double offence of being a conspirator and a Roman Catholic priest. He pointedly denied both charges. He declared he was not a Roman Catholic, and we are led to infer from his defence, that he was one of those Scottish Episcopal clergymen, who, from conscientious motives, would not subscribe to the revolution settlement. The court, however, would give no credence to this acknowledgment: it held, contrary to all evidence, that he was a Roman Catholic priest; and according to the logic of the day, that was enough in itself to condemn him. When brought to the scaffold, he delivered a most affecting and pious address, solemnly denying all knowledge of the plot, and that he was even acquainted with Hughson, his wife, or the creature who was hanged with them. After the execution of this unfortunate man, a day of thanksgiving to Almighty God was observed by public command, 'for the deliverance of his majesty's subjects here from the destruction wherewith they were so generally threatened by the late execrable conspiracy.' The delusion continued a short time longer, and there was one more execution; but the public vengeance had been pretty well satiated, and prosecutions became unpopular, more especially as Mary Burton, the common informer, began to give out intimations against people of consequence in the city. The last act of the tragedy was the payment of this perjured creature by the city authorities of the reward of L.100, originally offered to any one who would disclose the plot.

To sum up the cruelties perpetrated during the excitement: the number of persons taken into custody on suspicion was upwards of one hundred and fifty. Of these, four white persons were hanged; eleven negroes were burnt; eighteen were hanged; and fifty were transported and sold, principally in the West Indies. Several persons who were suspected made their escape out of the colony. And all this, to the disgrace of the age, on no other ground than an idle public clamour. The whole, from first to last, had been an imposture and delusion.

POPULAR INFORMATION ON SCIENCE.

REPRODUCTION OF PLANTS.

The main object of a plant during growth seems to be the reproduction of its kind. Whether the term of its existence be limited by a day, by a year, or by centuries, its sole effort—as it proceeds from leaf to stem, from stem to branch, and from branch to flower and fruit—is the multiplication of itself. This is effected variously: by seeds, by spores or germs, by tubers, by runners, which put forth shoots as they elongate, by branches which send down roots, by slips or detached branches, or even by single leaves. We shall notice the more remarkable of these modes, as exhibiting at once the perfection of design, and the inexhaustible contrivances which nature has ever at her adoption for the accomplishment of the end in view.

Increase by seed is the most familiar mode of reproduction, being common to all flowering plants. Seeds are merely leaves preserved in peculiar cerements till the return of the season of growth. And here it may be remarked, that wherever we have a healthy-growing leaf, or number of leaves, there is no difficulty in rearing an independent plant, since, according to the doctrines of morphology, the leaf is the primary organ from which all other parts take their form and development. A numerous class of vegetables have their seeds composed of two leaves or lobes, as may be seen in the bean and apple; in another class, as the oat and cocoa-nut, they consist of a single lobe. But whether they have one or two lobes, in all of them the function of reproduction is of the most perfect description. To produce a fertile seed, the pollen or dusty granules which tip the stigmas must be conveyed to the pistil, and through the pistil to the embryo in the ovary. For this purpose a thousand beautiful adaptations have been called into existence. These precious granules, liable to be swept away by every breeze and shower, are protected by the sheltering calyx and corolla, which turn their backs to the wind, or droop like a pent-house to ward off the rain. And even should the pollen be scattered by accident, the pistil is covered with a fine mucilage, which intercepts and retains it in spite of every antagonist force. Some plants have the stamens and pistils in one and the same flower; in others the stigmas are in one flower and the pistil in another; while in not a few the male and female flowers are produced on separate stems—yet in all, the means of fertilisation are seldom rendered nugatory. If the male and female flowers are near, they are placed so as to be brought in contact by the slightest waving of a branch; or if distant, the passing breeze and the limbs of the wandering bee are the agents by which the pollen is carried to the destined receptacle. When properly matured, a seed must be provided, first, with the means of dispersion and preservation, and secondly, with a sufficiency of internal nourishment for the embryo plant, till its roots have struck into the soil, and its leaves have expanded in the atmosphere. Accordingly, some seeds are farinaceous, others albuminous, and many oleaginous—all of those products being converted, during germination, into those elements which enter into the structure of a growing plant. For the conversion of these products, a certain amount of heat and moisture is necessary; but too much heat would parch them, and too much cold or moisture would destroy their vitality. To provide against such contingencies, nature has conferred on the seeds of plants the most ingenious and perfect coverings. The cocoa has a tough fibrous coir and woody nut, impervious alike to drought and rain; the chestnut has a compact leathery envelope; the plum a hard stony drupe; the apple a fleshy pome, enclosing leathery cells; the rose a fleshy hip, packed with down; the pea and bean a pod of parchment; and seeds apparently naked have either a coriaceous membrane, or have the exterior tissue so condensed, that they look as if they had come from the hand of the japanner. Thus, the protection against cold, drought, moisture, and other destructive agencies is so complete, that seeds which have been buried for centuries have, on being brought to the surface, sprung up into healthy plants; even a crop of wheat has been reared from grain found in the case of an Egyptian mummy more than three thousand years old.

Equally perfect with this protection is the means for their dispersion over the surface of the globe. What could be better adapted for floating from island to island than the cocoa-nut, with its light, waterproof, fibrous coir and woody shell? What more easily caught up by the slightest breath of air than the seeds of the thistle or dandelion, with their little parachutes of down? Or what more aptly fitted for attachment to the coats of wandering animals than the hooked heads of the teasel and burrdock? Nor does contrivance end here. Many, when ripe, are ejected from the vessels which contain them with considerable force by means of elastic valves and springs. The cardamine impatiens throws its ripe seed to a considerable distance on being touched; so does the squirting cucumber, the geranium, the common broom, and others, as if they were endowed with vitality, and had a care for their embryo progeny. Some do not even part with their seeds till these have struck root as independent plants. Thus the mangrove, which flourishes amid the mud of tropical deltas and creeks, retains its berries till they have sent down long thread-like radicles into the silt below, as if it felt that the water and slime by which it was surrounded were elements too unstable to be intrusted with its offspring.

Plants that reproduce themselves by spores or germs belong to the cryptogamic or flowerless class of vegetation, as the ferns, sea-weeds, mosses, and mushrooms. In many of these the reproductive spores are so minute, that they float in the air unseen; and not a dried mushroom or puff-ball that is struck by the wandering foot, but disperses thousands of its kind around it. The little brown specks on the leaf of the fern, the snuff-like powder of the puff-ball, or the dust arising from the mould of a decayed cheese, are all alike the germs of future plants; and when we consider how minute each individual is, how liable to be borne about by winds, by water, and by the coverings of animals, to which they may adhere, we shall cease to wonder at the fact, that there is not a portion of surface, organic or inorganic, that may not be covered with their growth. The spores of the fuci or sea-weeds, which are always surrounded by water, are covered with a mucilage that enables them to adhere to whatever solid body they touch; and, what is peculiar in this adhesive substance, it is insoluble in water. 'Let chemistry,' says Macculloch, in his Illustrations of the Attributes of a God, 'name another mucilage, another substance, which water cannot dissolve, though apparently already in solution with water, and then ask if this extraordinary secretion was not designed for the special end attained? and whether, also, it does not afford an example of that Power which has only to will that it may produce what it desires, even by means the most improbable?'

Many plants, as the potato, reproduce themselves both by seeds and tubers. Both modes, however, do not take place with equal exuberance at one and the same time. In its native region of South America, where the climate is better adapted for blossom and maturation of seed, the potato flowers luxuriantly, but yields an insignificant crop of small acrid tubers; in our unstable climate, on the other hand, the underground progeny is the more abundant and prolific. Acting upon the knowledge of this principle, the farmer in Europe cuts off the flower-buds of the potato-plant to increase his crop of tubers; just as the tulip or hyacinth-fancier prevents his plants from flowering, in order to increase the stock of his bulbs, which throw out a number of offsets from their bases. There is, it would seem, a certain amount of vital force in every plant, and if that force be expended on flowering, tubers will not be produced, and if on the production of an underground progeny, the seed will not be matured, as is the case with the horse-radish and Jerusalem artichoke. Here, however, it must be remarked, that tubers are not roots in the botanical sense of the word; they are true underground stems, which, instead of terminating in fruit and seed, terminate in nodes full of eyes or leaf-buds, and supplied with a quantity of farinaceous matter for the support of the young buds, till they have struck their roots in the soil sufficient to elaborate their own sustenance. Let any one anearth a potato plant with care, and he will at once perceive the difference between the true roots spreading out into minute fibres, and the underground stems terminating in tubers. The former are tough and fibrous, diverging into minute radicles, each tipped with its little sucking point or spongiole; the latter are soft and succulent, undivided, and ending in a mass of farinaceous matter studded with young buds. Each of these buds, if detached with a portion of the tuber, and placed in proper soil, will spring up into a perfect plant—the farinaceous fragment supplying it with food, until roots and leaves are formed.

The manner in which plants reproduce themselves *viviparously* differs according to the constitutional character of the individual. Some, as the elm and poplar, have their roots furnished with buds, which sooner or later sprout forth into offsets and suckers, as they are called, and these annually increase in bulk and height—ultimately becoming, under proper conditions, perfect trees. Others, as the greater number of bulbs and tubers, multiply themselves by sending out runners, each of which produce several young plants; and herbaceous perennials extend themselves in the same way, either by runners under ground, as the couch-grass, or above ground, as the strawberry. Most people must have observed the continual efforts of the latter plant to extend itself in this way; and so it is with many others—the propensity being most powerful where there is the least opportunity of bringing forth seed. It is often highly interesting to watch the progress of these runners. Where the soil is soft and favourable throughout, the young shoots are developed at about equal distances; but where the soil is hard, or covered with stones, the runner pushes its way over these obstructions, refusing to put forth a single bud until the proper conditions for its maintenance be reached. We have often seen a gravel-walk thus crossed by a strawberry runner, the runner being as budless as a piece of copper wire, until it had arrived at the soil on the other side, where it immediately put forth its young progeny in abundance. Instances of this kind are often ascribed to vegetable instinct; and were it not for the essential differences which evidently exist between vegetables and animals, one would be almost tempted to assign to it a higher designation. Some plants produce living seeds in the vessels where the ordinary seed is matured, as may be seen in certain species of the onion family—known as tree and apple onions; and others, like some of the lilies, yield little perfect bulbs in the axils of the stem leaves.

Another manner in which trees multiply themselves is by their branches bending downwards till they touch the ground with the growing points, which then take root and spring up into independent stems. This frequently happens among trailing shrubs, as the bramble and honeysuckle, and may also be witnessed among our garden roses and gooseberries. A somewhat similar mode of extension is presented by the banyan, which becomes enlarged without the assistance of either seeds or suckers. Roots are produced by the under-side of the lower branches: these hang dangling in the air for months before they reach the ground; this at last they penetrate, and become stems to a new head of branches. An old tree of this kind presents a most magnificent object, forming concentric corridors over a great extent of surface. Acting upon the principles here pointed out by nature, gardeners propagate many of their favourites by layers; that is, by bending a branch or shoot till a portion of it be buried in the soil, where it throws out roots, and establishes itself as an independent plant. This being done, it is removed from the parent stock and placed in another situation.

Trees are also propagated by slips; that is, by detached young shoots being thrust into the soil, where they usually throw out roots, and grow up into healthy individuals. All plants of course cannot be slipped with the same facility; but, generally speaking, where there are well-developed leaf-buds in the axils of the perfect leaves, and where there is true wood formed, the slip will be found to take root and grow. Budding is another artificial mode of propagation: it is, in fact, merely slipping at an earlier stage of growth. In the one case there are many leaf-buds on a common stem, in the other there is only a single bud. The operation is performed by taking the leaf-bud from one tree, and neatly inserting it under the cuticle of another, where, fed by the necessary juices, it extends into a new bough or arm.

Perhaps the most curious mode of natural reproduction is that by the leaf. It is well known that many leaves, [as those of the echeveria, malaxis, gloxinia, orange, and others, when fallen to the ground in a young and growing state, put forth roots and become perfect plants. This fact is at present exciting much attention; and since all parts of a plant are but special developments of this single organ, it is argued that there is nothing to prevent the propagation of any species of vegetation by this simple means. Considering the truth and universality of the doctrines of morphology, we cannot see why there should; and feel justified in the hope, that, once gardeners have arrived at a knowledge of the proper times and modes, they shall be enabled to rear any form of vegetation from this universal organ.

What a curious view of vegetable life do the principles of reproduction unfold! namely, that all parts of a plant—whether root, tuber, bulb, stem, branch, leaf, or seed—will, under certain conditions, grow up into a perfect individual, similar to the parent from which it has sprung. All modes do not take place at one and the same time, for nature is never prodigally wasteful of her resources; but where climate or other conditions interrupt production by one source, another is developed more exuberantly than usual to supply its place. If we have not conditions to mature fruit and seed, there will be tubers, or suckers, or runners instead: and just as the chances of failure are great, so are the modes of reproduction proportionally increased. There is nothing corresponding to this in the animal kingdom, unless among the very lowest forms, as the polyps and sponges, which also increase by division. Lop away a branch from a tree, and its place may be supplied by another; break off the limb of a crab or insect, and another limb will shortly take its place; but while the detached branch will spring up into a tree similar to its parent, all vitality has fled from the separated limb of the crustacean. Higher animals than insects and crustaceans have no power to reproduce lost parts; but while devoid of this vegetative-like power, they have a more exalted sentient development; and if denied the power to reproduce a lost limb, they are endowed with faculties which can better protect them.

MADAME DE MIRAMION.

A ROMANCE OF REAL LIFE.

ROGER DE BUSSY, Comte de Rabutin, having only daughters by his first wife, was desirous of contracting a second marriage, in the hope of obtaining an heir to his name, and his parents were equally anxious on the subject. He wished to meet with a wife who united fortune with youth and beauty, considering this essential to support his rank at court, and to enable him to satisfy his inclination for pleasure, and his other expensive tastes.

He frequently discussed the matter with his uncle, who was prior at the Temple, and with whom he lodged when he came to Paris. At the residence of that personage, he became acquainted with an old citizen called Le Bocage, the proprietor of a considerable domain in the neighbourhood of the district of which Bussy had the command. Invited by his nephew, the prior often made that place his residence during the summer months, and there the two relatives would sometimes live for weeks together. It was in this neighbourhood that Le Bocage, Christopher de Rabutin, and the Comte de Bussy became intimate. Made acquainted with the wishes of the last to form a wealthy connexion, Le Bocage proposed to him a young and beautiful widow, equally remarkable for her piety, the sweetness of her temper, and the possession of a large fortune. Le Bocage did not know her personally, but he had a friend in whom, as her confessor and spiritual adviser, the lady placed great confidence. He was a father of the Order of Mercy, called Father Clement, but a monk of corrupt morals, willing to engage in any profligate scheme for a pecuniary consideration. With this man Bussy had a conference, and by his connivance he managed to obtain a sight of the young widow on two occasions at church. He was enraptured with her person, but was not able either to address or to approach her. Father Clement assured him, however, that he had made a favourable impression, stating, at the same time, that she could do nothing without the consent of her family, who were bent on her marrying some one of the legal profession. He advised Bussy not to run any risks, and to allow him to act for him, and he would undertake to communicate with some of her more influential relations, and induce them to consent to the marriage. In case of their refusal, he agreed to persuade the widow to avail herself of her right to dispose of herself. To forward his plan, he obtained money from Bussy, under the pretext of bribing her domestics; and the latter, completely his dupe, made over to him at different times sums to the amount of 2000 crowns. As the period approached for the opening of the military campaign, the monk persuaded Bussy not to delay his departure for the army. He set off on the 6th of May 1648, having obtained a promise from his negotiator to inform him of his proceedings.

Three weeks after his departure, he received a letter telling him that the relations of the widow were adverse to the match, and that she had not the resolution to resist them; but that she was desirous that Bussy should, by an apparent act of violence, obtain the consent she was ready to give. But the true version of the tale was as follows:—The perfidious monk had not succeeded in his plan. The moment she was aware of his object, Madame de Miramion had dismissed him, and taken another confessor. In revenge, he was determined to avail himself of the credulity and audacity of Bussy. Pretending that, as confessor, he still possessed the confidence of the widow, he induced Bussy to believe that she regarded him so favourably, that, if he carried her off by force, she would gladly take him as her husband. The young nobleman, thus deceived, determined on following his suggestions. A royal commission had been established by Cardinal Richelieu to oppose the encroachments and license of the nobles, who looked upon the placing themselves above the law as a privilege of caste. This new authority had not been so long formed as to enable them, in every instance, to prevent or punish the abuses they had undertaken to oppose; and the civil wars of La Fronde, whilst they weakened the government, had enabled the nobility to return to their previous habits of license and oppression—the more endeared to them as evidence of their former independence.

During these times of confusion, the cases of aggression on the part of those in power towards women of inferior rank, or those who, from belonging to the mercantile class, were without family support or connexion at court, were the more frequent, because they remained almost always unpunished.

As Bussy enjoyed the favour and protection of the Prince de Condé, he related to him the whole affair. The proposed adventure pleased the young prince, who offered to give his friend a commission at Paris, and even to make over to him the command of Bellegarde, one of his own places in Burgundy, in order to facilitate his plans. Bussy expressed his gratitude, and accepted the commission, but refused the offer with regard to Bellegarde; all he required was the means of transferring his beautiful prisoner to Launay, where was an ancient castle, surrounded by thick walls, and only to be entered by drawbridges. No sooner, therefore, had he fulfilled the commission given to him by the prince, than he went to his coadjutor, who confirmed all he had previously written, and encouraged him in his scheme; not doubting, he said, that once separated from her family, Madame de Miramion would consent to marry him without difficulty.

Nothing could have been easier than for Bussy to have satisfied himself of the real state of the lady's feelings before adopting so desperate a measure; but whether his own self-conceit did not allow him to doubt of his success, or from shame of having been so duped, he declares in his own memoirs that his agent had no interest in it, beyond the wish to gratify a friend, and he could not therefore doubt the sincerity of Clement. It must be allowed also that the profession to which the father belonged, and the nature of his connexion with the young widow, were sufficient of themselves to allay suspicion; so that, whilst this innocent victim was totally ignorant of the pretensions of the comte, or even of his wish to marry her, no one having given a hint on the subject, Bussy was firmly persuaded that she had not only given her consent, but had long since been made acquainted with his intentions.

Madame de Miramion was the daughter of a rich burgess of Orleans. A child of precocious understanding, she doted on her mother with an energy beyond her years; and when, at scarcely nine years of age, she was deprived by death of this beloved parent, the event made a deep and lasting impression on her sensitive nature, which seemed to resist every effort made to dispel it. One of her aunts, who had the charge of her education, though the sister of a bishop, considered that religious fervour was taking too strong a hold on the mind of her young pupil; and in some measure to counteract it, she drew her into society, and took her to balls and to the theatre. Wherever she went, the beauty of her person, more than her wealth, attracted universal admiration, and many were the suitors for her hand. In 1645 she married Jean Jacques de Beauharnois, lord of Miramion, counsellor of the parliament of Paris, whose fortune equalled her own. He was only twenty-seven years of age, handsome, with a commanding figure, and of a most amiable disposition. By her husband she was not restrained, as by her aunt, in her pious exercises. So well assorted a union made her feel a happiness to which she had been a stranger from childhood. She loved and was beloved. She had but one wish, by the strict discharge of every duty not to allow her prospect of future welfare to be endangered by the prosperity and happiness she enjoyed in this life. Only six months passed in the enjoyment of this happiness: at the end of that period her husband was taken from her by a pulmonary attack. Soon after, she gave birth to a daughter, so weak and sickly that it was with the utmost difficulty her life could be preserved. Religion and maternal tenderness prevented Madame de Miramion from sinking in despair; she passed the two first years of her widowhood in the closest seclusion, alternately at the foot of the altar, and by the cradle of her child.

Born in 1629, she was little more than sixteen when she became a widow and a mother. Her relations, who were tenderly attached to her, feared she would take the veil. They wished to keep her amongst them, and flattered themselves, from her extreme youth, that she might in time be induced to form a second connexion; and having allowed her a long period for the indulgence of her grief, they proposed it to her. Several brilliant offers presented themselves. Many of those who sought her feared that her beauty and her wealth might give reason to suspect the disinterestedness of their attachment; but on every occasion she expressed in the strongest terms her wish to reject all proposals of the kind. Attacked by the small-pox, she was sorry it had not deprived her of those attractions which her piety caused her to regret; and yet, deeply touched with the attachment of her relations, she did not like entirely to close her doors against those they sought to introduce to her acquaintance.

Her humility made her consider herself unworthy to consecrate herself to heaven. She hesitated, and only asked for time to be allowed her to make her decision; and in the meanwhile she multiplied her acts of devotion, in the hope that God would reveal himself to her and declare his will, whilst her friends pleased themselves with the hope of obtaining her consent to an alliance with some family equally rich with their own.

Such was the person whom Bussy, without any personal acquaintance, proposed to carry off and force into wedlock, persuaded that she would consider herself honoured in belonging to him, and would be gratified in appearing at a court from which her birth and the rank of her family precluded her.

Secure in the support of the prince, he looked upon an elopement with a female, who, notwithstanding her wealth, was in his eyes only a bourgeoise, as a matter of no consequence. The elder brother of Madame de Miramion, then twenty-five years of age, was the only individual in the family to cause him any uneasiness.

His preparations were not so secret that they did not in some degree transpire. Madame had notice given her from various quarters that she was to be carried off; but as the author of the intended insult was not named, and as she was convinced that no one of those who aspired to her hand could be guilty of such an outrage, she placed no reliance in the report, and took no precautions to ward it off.

Bussy knew that she was living at Issy with her mother-in-law, and had obtained information from those in his confidence that on the 7th of August she was to go to St Valerien to perform her devotions, and he arranged his plans accordingly. He placed four relays betwixt St Cloud and Lannay, a distance of twenty-five leagues. He assembled a strong escort, composed of his brother, a friend who had served two campaigns as a volunteer under his orders, and three other gentlemen, his vassals and dependents. They were attended by servants all well mounted and armed.

Madame de Miramion, entirely engrossed with the religious duties she was about to perform, set off from Issy at seven in the morning. Her mother-in-law accompanied her, and, according to the custom with persons of a certain condition at that period, she was attended by an old equerry and two women; the one a governess, a middle-aged person, the other a young chambermaid. A man-servant was mounted behind.

Bussy's squadron was posted on the road betwixt St Cloud and Mont Valerien, opposite a bridge, which the lady's carriage had no sooner traversed than it was stopped. Two of the cavaliers attempted to let down the leather curtains which shut up the persons within from their view. Madame de Miramion endeavoured to drive them off by striking them with a bag she held in her hand, and calling loudly for help; but her cries and her efforts were unavailing. Not being able to succeed in letting down the curtains, her assailants attempted to cut the fastenings with their swords. Madame de Miramion, with a courage beyond her sex, endeavoured to wrest the weapons from them, and in doing so, had her hands severely cut. During this unequal combat, the squadron had forced the coachman to repass the bridge, and to enter the Bois de Boulogne, where a carriage was in waiting, drawn by six horses. In this Bussy would have placed the lady, but no persuasion could induce her to move; and she fixed herself so firmly in her seat, that nothing but violence could have been availing. Bussy therefore unharnessed her horses, replaced them with his own, placed Madame de Miramion's coachman and horses in the charge of two grooms, with orders to convey them to Paris and detain them there, and then set off at full gallop across the plain of St Denis into the forest of Livri. The captive lady called to all the passers by, gave her name, and intreated them to forward the alarm to her friends at Paris. But the clouds of dust caused by so large a cavalcade, the wind, the noise, and the rapid pace at which they proceeded, frustrated all her efforts. Having reached the forest, where from the nature of the road the escort could no longer surround the carriage, Madame de Miramion made an attempt to escape, by throwing herself into a thick copse, where she flattered herself she might remain concealed, heedless of the thorns and briers which covered her with blood; but she was soon discovered, and perceiving she could not avoid her pursuers, to prevent them from seizing her, with a violent effort she flew back to the carriage, and threw herself into it.

Bussy halted in the most retired part of the forest, where the escort took some refreshment; but his captive positively refused what was offered to her, declaring she would touch nothing till restored to liberty.

Still deceived with regard to her conduct, and astonished at her resistance, Bussy flattered himself that it was a feint on her part, and that she would become more tranquil if her mother-in-law and the old domestic were disposed of. He therefore turned them and the governess out of the carriage. He would only have retained the other female, but the man-servant declared he would rather die than abandon her. Whenever they stopped she made the same ineffectual efforts to obtain assistance; but those who guarded her gave out that she was insane, and her disordered appearance, her torn clothes, her bleeding face and hands, gave a colour to the assertion.

Bussy was now but too well convinced that her resistance was not feigned, and for a moment he thought of taking her back, but was dissuaded from it by his brother, who represented to him, that when her alarm had subsided, she might be prevailed upon to change her mind. Arrived at the castle, the noise of the portcullis, the dismal appearance of the structure, the number of armed men collected, all contributed to increase her alarm. She did not even know the names, or the intentions of her enemies; but from the whole of their conduct, she considered them capable of the worst crimes, and nothing could induce her to quit the carriage. At length one of the party, a knight of Malta, whom she recognised as having made part of the escort, intreated her in the most respectful manner to enter the castle.

Madame de Miramion, without moving, inquired in a firm voice whether it was by the order of the person who addressed her that she was thus treated. 'No, madame,' said he, 'it is the Comte de Bussy Rabutin, who has assured us that he was acting with your consent.'

'It is false, utterly false!' she exclaimed, raising her voice.

'Madame,' said he, 'we are here two hundred gentlemen, friends of Monsieur de Bussy; if he has deceived us, we will protect you, and restore you to liberty; only condescend to explain yourself more fully, and in the meantime do not refuse to dismount, and give yourself some repose.'

His respectful manner inspired her with confidence; she would not enter any of the furnished apartments, but remained in a low damp hall, where no preparation had been made for her reception, but where a fire was lighted in great haste, and her carriage cushions were placed for her to sit upon. On entering, she observed a pair of pistols on the table, and instantly took possession of them; and finding them loaded, placed them by her. Her attendant having attempted to leave the room, she insisted on her not quitting her: they brought her food, but she would touch nothing. Bussy, afraid of encountering her reproaches, kept aloof: he was amazed at her anger and her decision. 'I had been assured,' he said to his accomplices, 'that she was a lamb, whereas she is more like an enraged lioness.'

Still he did not despair of softening her, by employing a person who acted as governess or housekeeper in the castle, and others to speak in his behalf; assuring her of his attachment, of his regret, and throwing all the blame upon her confessor.

These explanations in some degree dissipated her alarm, but did not lessen her indignation against her captor, who had employed such means to gain his object. When they found her inaccessible to persuasion, they tried to work upon her fears. They described the comte, though naturally mild and generous, yet capable of everything if his passions were excited; and that it was her interest not to reduce him to despair. But nothing could produce the least concession on her part; and at length Bussy sent her word, that she should be restored to liberty on condition of her granting him one moment's interview.

The instant he entered she rose from her seat, and exclaimed with an uplifted hand, 'Sir, I vow in the presence of God, my Maker and yours, never to become your wife!' and then fainted away. Medical assistance was procured; she was declared to be in imminent danger; forty hours had passed without her taking nourishment, and her strength was exhausted.

In the meantime her mother-in-law had not been idle. She had made the best of her way to the nearest village, procured a horse for the old equerry, and despatched him to her family to give notice of what had occurred, whilst she secured a wagon for herself, which conveyed her to Paris. It was shortly after announced to Bussy that the town of Sens was in an uproar, and that six hundred men were coming to attack the castle. Noways alarmed at the intelligence, he made a last attempt to induce Madame de Miramion to remain at least one day at Lannay. Her only reply was a request that he would instantly give orders for her departure. The horses being harnessed, and the carriage in readiness, she ate two eggs; Bussy in secret gave fifty louis to her maid, under pretence of defraying the expenses of her journey, but in reality to make her favourable to his views. The carriage set off, escorted by the knight of Malta and two other gentlemen; the whole journey he rode by her side, endeavouring by his conversation and representations to place the comte's conduct in a favourable light; but on approaching Sens, fearful that they might be arrested by the authorities, they halted at the outskirts of the town, and having unharnessed the horses, the escort took their leave, and galloped back to Lannay. Madame de Miramion, left alone with her two attendants, dismounted from her carriage, and traversing the faubourg of Sens on foot, found the gates closed. She learned, however, that every one was under arms, by the order of the queen regent, for the rescue of a lady who had been forcibly carried off. 'Alas!' said she, 'I am that person!' The news instantly spread; her brother, her mother-in-law, and her other relations soon joined her. Great was her joy to find herself once more amongst them; but her frame had received a severe shock. She fell dangerously ill, and for a long time her recovery was doubtful. A troop of armed men in the meanwhile was sent to Lannay to seize the person of Bussy, but he had made his escape, with all his accomplices.

When the trial came on, Madame de Miramion showed the greatest leniency, and intreated her family to pardon a repentant culprit. They were the less disposed to do so, because after this event she showed herself more averse than ever to every proposal of marriage. She considered it as a warning from heaven, and determined from henceforth to dedicate herself to religion and good works. Bussy, alarmed at the scrape he had got into, intreated the Prince de Condé to interfere in his behalf, who, in consequence, wrote to her family a very urgent letter. The solicitations of a prince who, by the victory of Sens, had again saved France, were not to be resisted; the suit was dropped, but was renewed when Condé and Bussy made war against the parliament and La Fronde. Bussy acknowledges that in the course of these civil disturbances he had formed a plan of burning the castle of Rabelle, the property of Madame de Miramion; but his better feelings prevailed, and he placed a guard there to protect it, and he reaped the benefit of his good conduct.

The prosecution was dropped altogether on condition of his never appearing in her presence, and avoiding any place where she might be.

However humiliating was such a promise, he adhered faithfully to it. Thirty-six years passed, during which they never met. At the end of that period he was engaged in a lawsuit, the loss or gain of which depended on the President de Nesmond, who had married Madame de Miramion's only daughter. To do away the injury which the recollection of his past conduct might have upon the mind of her son-in-law, he determined, through the intervention of a friend of his, and a cousin of Madame de Miramion's, to obtain an interview with her. Admitted into the presence of one who had been connected with so remarkable an event in his life, he encountered no longer the young and delicate beauty clothed in silk and lace, such as she was when he carried her off from St Cloud, but a large fat woman, her head enclosed in an enormous coiffure, dressed in a gray woollen gown, with a deep cambric cape without any trimming, and her only ornament a cross, from which was suspended a lock of her daughter's hair. Her eyes still retained their brilliancy, and the charms of her features were not entirely lost under the disguise of a double chin. The expression of her countenance, her manner, her costume, were all in unison; all contributed to express the absence of tumultuous passions and the equanimity of her temper. Bussy was so struck that he remained for a time silent; but he was soon reassured by the tone of benevolence in which she addressed him, and the anxiety she expressed to learn the motive of his visit. When he had explained himself, and had proved to her satisfactorily that the right was on his side, Madame de Miramion promised to interest her son-in-law in his cause, and induce him to give it a favourable hearing: it came on shortly after, and was decided in his favour. All those acquainted with the history of the times will recognise Madame de Miramion in this generous conduct. This excellent woman, having made a vow to consecrate herself to God, preferred her duties as a parent to the idleness of a cloister: devoting herself to the care of her child, who was almost always ill, the best years of her life were given up to her education. Having introduced her to the world, and secured her happiness by a suitable marriage, discharging herself of all worldly cares, she gave herself up to the most enthusiastic charity; her strength of body and the resources of her mind seeming to increase in proportion to the amount of misery that surrounded her. She founded establishments at Paris, Amiens, and other places, bearing her name, for the instruction of schoolmistresses, and for nurses for the poor; she opened workshops for the industrious, and houses of refuge for the repentant sinner. During two years, from her own means she supported seven hundred poor persons who had been dismissed from the general hospital for want of funds. She assisted St Vincent de Paul in establishing a foundling hospital; and when the town of Melun was visited by a contagious disorder, she relieved the sick by every means in her power, and for two months—braving death in her own person—she nursed those whose relations and friends had abandoned them from fear. She contributed by her liberality to the establishment of foreign missions, and caused the name of France to be blessed to the extremities of the world. Prostrate on her knees before an irritated father, she averted the curse about to be bestowed upon an offending son, and obtained his pardon. Even princesses sought her advice in their difficulties, and implored the consolation of her presence and her prayers in their last moments. Louis XIV., with that discernment which characterised him, employed her as his almoner in the distribution of his charities, and she was consulted on all sides by those engaged in works of charity and benevolence. Madame de Sévigné in her letters designates her as 'the Mother of the Church,' and says with truth that her death, which took place in 1696, was a public loss.*

* The above has been translated from a French work by the Baron Walckener, entitled 'Memoirs Relating to the Life and Writings of Madame de Sévigné.'

USE OF OPIATES AMONG THE OPERATIVE POPULATION.

Among the numerous causes of disease and death brought to light by the publication of the report of the Health of Towns Committee, there is one to which but little attention has been paid; and yet, as appears from the statements of Dr Lyon Playfair, it is an evil of a most serious character, widely spread, and one that saps the vitals of the labouring population at their very source. The details in great part will appear incredible to those who are unacquainted with the habits of the poorer classes.

We have been accustomed to read with feelings of horror of the prevalence of infanticide in some of our Indian provinces; but what shall we think of the habitual practice of administering opiates to infants from their very birth, to lull them to quietness while their mothers are working in the factories?—in too many cases, unhappily, careless of the appalling consequences of their indiscretion, which show themselves eventually in the deformity, disease, or death of their offspring.

'The custom first originated,' says Dr Playfair, 'according to all concurrent evidence, in the frequency of disorders, having their primary seat either in the stomach or bowels, arising partly from injudicious feeding and improper nursing, but principally from the irritability produced by their continued exposure to a polluted atmosphere, and other physical causes of disease. The children thus disordered were taken to unlicensed practitioners, who prescribed opiates as a general remedy, and their mothers mistook the soothing effects produced by narcotics for proofs of improvement, and themselves continued the practice. They soon discovered that the administration of narcotic drugs prevented restlessness in the child, enabling them to pursue their ordinary avocations; and thus a practice, often originating in disease, has become habitual, even in cases where disease did not exist. Druggists who vend such narcotic preparations speak as to the extent of their use; and their evidence is perhaps the more to be depended upon, as it was their interest to diminish rather than to exaggerate the extent of the evil.' He goes on to give the evidence of 'a respectable druggist in Manchester, whose customers are, however, entirely of the poorer class, among whom it may safely be said that there is scarcely a single family in which this practice does not prevail. The way it is done is this: the mother goes out to her work in the morning, leaving her child in charge either of a woman who cannot be troubled with it, or with another child of perhaps ten years old. A dose of "quietness" is therefore given to the child to prevent it being troublesome. The child thus drugged sleeps, and may waken at dinner-time; so when the mother goes out again, the child receives another dose. Well, the mother and father come home at night quite fatigued, and as they must rise early to begin work for the day, they must sleep undisturbed by the child; so it is again drugged, and in this manner young children are often drugged three times in each day. This druggist states further that he sells, *in retail alone, about five gallons per week of "quietness," and half a gallon of "Godfrey;"* the strength of the former preparation is such as to contain one hundred drops of laudanum in an ounce; a single teaspoonful is the prescribed dose; so that, allowing one ounce weekly to each family, this one druggist supplies 700 families every week.'

A melancholy characteristic of this fatal practice is the unconcern with which it is followed. Another druggist says, there is 'no dread of laudanum now; it is often used for the same purposes as "quietness." The usual dose to produce sleep in a restless child is eight drops, and this being, like the other, gradually increased to three doses a-day, amount to twenty-four drops.' We are informed that '*three* druggists,' whose evidence is just quoted, 'all of acknowledged respectability, are selling respectively five-and-a-half, three-and-a-half, and one—in all ten gallons weekly; two of them testifying that *almost all the families* of the poor in that district habitually drug their children with opiates; and the third, after a lengthened examination of all the customers who attended a pawnbroker's shop, kept by a relative of his own, giving as a statistical result, that five out of six families in his district were in the habitual use of narcotics for children.'

In the report furnished by the Rev. J. Clay, on the sanitary condition of Preston,* there is a table illustrative of the proportions of infantile deaths in the dispensary, and in the worst streets: in the former the proportion is, in even numbers, 8 per cent.; in the latter 44 per cent.—a most striking difference, which is accounted for by the fact that, 'if the wretched inhabitants of these worst streets sought medical aid at all, they would seek it most likely where it could be obtained without charge. If the druggist is sometimes applied to for the medicine, which with greater propriety and safety would be prescribed by the medical man, he is too often asked for compounds which no medical man would prescribe; such as "Godfrey's Cordial," "Infants' Preservative," "Soothing Syrup," "Mothers' Blessing," &c. Returns have been obtained from almost all the chemists and druggists in Preston of the quantity of these mixtures sold by each; the aggregate of the whole quantity indicates that, allowing half an ounce per week to each family, upwards of 1600 families are in the habit of using "Godfrey's Cordial," or some other equally injurious compound.' Mr Robert Brown, a surgeon, states, 'A child was brought to me for a little aperient medicine; the mother suspected that the person who nursed it had been in the habit of giving it some narcotic. It had not had more than two or three motions

* See First Report, page 183.

for the space of three weeks. I advised the mother to stay at home and attend to it herself. The advice was followed, and the child recovered in a few days.'

It may be thought that the evils here pointed out being moral rather than physical, admit easily of the application of the proper remedies; but it is observed that 'the thoughtlessness and unreflecting ignorance of many parents, and the callousness towards their offspring of others, is stronger than the parental feeling, which will lead, in numerous instances, to the indiscriminate administration of opiates and spirituous liquors to sick children.'

'Similar evidence as to the prevalence of the custom is given by druggists in all the towns visited. In Wigan, four druggists examined agree in describing the practice as "very prevalent among the lower orders," and in stating that it appears to prevail with all those who have occupations in factories, workshops, and other places at a distance from home, which oblige mothers to leave their children the whole or greatest part of a day.' The same statements were made by druggists at Rochdale and Bury; and Mr Whitehead, the registrar for Ashton-under-Lyne, says, 'I conceive that the practice of administering opiates to children is very prevalent among the working-classes, and I think more particularly where there are natural children born, and left in charge of the keepers of houses where the mothers lodge, while the latter are working in the mill. In going to register deaths, I have frequently remarked children looking very ill, and on observing this to the neighbours, they have said, "It is no wonder that they are so—they are slept to death;" meaning that sleeping stuffs were given to them.'

The same fatal practice prevails also in Liverpool, accompanied, among the Irish population, by the administration of ardent spirits; equally destructive of human life. In fact, in the whole of Lancashire and the factory districts generally, the evil has been adopted with the most reckless disregard of consequences. The painful surprise which the perusal of these statements produces will, however, be diminished when we read that 'it is no uncommon thing to meet with married females at fifteen, and they are frequently mothers at seventeen; the fathers being but little older. To increase the bearing of this cause upon the mortality of children in the manufacturing districts, comes the fact, that in two, three, or four weeks after delivery, the young mother, if she have but one, two, or three children, returns to her work in the mills, leaving the charge of her children either to some old woman or young girl, or puts them out to nurse. The effects of this unnatural treatment are visible upon the infant in a very short time. A child, born apparently strong and healthy, may almost always be known two or three months after birth if it belong to a mother who goes to the factory. Instead of being plump and growing, it is almost invariably emaciated and less than at birth—commonly wasted by continued diarrhœa, brought on by the manner of its diet. The mother suckles it but at meal times and at night; the milk, having been so long secreted, is too stimulating for the child, and the succedaneous food, in quantity and kind, adds to the irritation. The greatest ignorance prevails as to the organisation and requirements of a child as regards diet. It is no uncommon thing to be consulted for emaciated children with extensive mesenteric disease; and on inquiry, to find that the food consists in great part of bacon, fried meat, and fatty potatoes, when the infant has not perhaps two teeth in each jaw to masticate it.* I am convinced of the great bearing of these facts upon the mortality of children, from the circumstance that a greater proportional number of first and second children die before they attain five years of age, than of children born after the mother has relinquished her factory employment.'† While much of this great mortality may doubtless be traced to the extremes of poverty so often met with in manufacturing districts, there is ample evidence of the waste of infant life from the causes in question; for in Wiltshire and Dorsetshire, where the wages are notoriously low, only 11 per cent. of all the children born die before they attain one year of age, while 17 per cent. are carried off in Lancashire. Dr Playfair observes that, 'in the small town of Clitheroe, the population of which, amounting to 6765, consisting partly of calico-printers, and partly of factory operatives, I found a weekly sale of four pints of Godfrey's Cordial, and an annual sale of 4000 poppy heads, for making "sleeping tea for children." One druggist describes these drugs as being sold "to an alarming extent among the factory population: not so much so among printers." Another describes the sale "as *decent* for the size of the town."'

The evil is not only serious in its actual effects, but in prospect; all the inquiries made on the subject elicited proofs of its alarming increase, with a tendency upwards to the middle classes; it has been alleged, though without any clear foundation, that the increase arises from the 'temperance movement;' the use of fermented liquors being supplied by that of opiates. But the whole weight of medical testimony is directly opposed to their exhibition. We are told that 'the administration of this class of medicines requires the greatest skill in the physician. Nothing is more uncertain than the effects of opium upon young subjects; and it ought never to be employed, even by medical men, except with the greatest caution, as it sometimes acts with much violence, and has proved deleterious even in very small doses. Half a drachm of genuine syrup of white poppy, and, in some instances, a few drops of "Dalby's Carminative" has proved fatal in the course of a few hours to very young infants.'*

In summing up the evidence, we encounter evils still more fearfully impressive. Who that has felt the endearing relation of infantile existence, can fail of being moved by the statement of a druggist who says, 'it is curious to see the children in the shop; they stretch out their little hands, for they know the bottle, and when they get it, drink it as eagerly as the drunkard does his glass. I have seen the little children in the shop put the neck of the bottle in their mouths and bite the cork, so fond are they of the preparation; for coming to the shop so often, they know the bottle.'

We read of a child who had been so much habituated to the drugs, that it 'took 100 drops of laudanum during the day;' and of parents 'who are in the habit of giving their children these drugs when the child is only three or four weeks old, and in many instances younger: this is gradually increased to a double dose, until at last some children will take six drachms a-day to produce the same effect as half a drachm did when they first began to take it.'

There is no difference of opinion among the witnesses as to the extent of the evil, which is felt not only in the loss by death, but in the deterioration and destruction of the mental and physical powers of those who survive the treatment. Dr Playfair states that 'instances have been brought before him in which idiocy and insanity have certainly followed as the result of the practice;' and further, 'I have been led by laborious inquiry to the conclusion, that the custom of administering narcotics to children originated primarily in, and is upheld by, the physical causes of disease acting upon the younger portion of the community. On the removal of these causes, the general inducement to the continuance of the system would cease, for the irritability and difficulty of management of children would diminish with their increased health. It is an evil not confined to factory districts, as some have alleged, for the recent trials in Wales have shown it to be very prevalent in rural districts; and numerous inquiries in small towns in agricultural counties have convinced me of its exist-

* See Chambers's Miscellany of Tracts, No. 6, for Management of Infants.

† Dr Strange, Ashton.

* Dr John Clarke on the Diseases of Children. London. 1815.

ence there, though to a much less extent. The diffusion of knowledge, and, above all, the removal of the physical causes of disease, will go far to check this great evil.'

We would gladly indulge the hope that our endeavour to set forth the horrible results of this practice, may be the means of directing such attention to it as will tend to diminish or remove it altogether. We agree with Dr Playfair that to education alone are we to look for the *real* remedy; 'much may be done *with* the people as well as *for* them. Health is as dear to the poor as to the rich. The most abject part of the population—creatures who belong to no class, but are the reprobates, unfortunate, fallen of all classes and several races—can understand its value, and, as we know, are capable of making sacrifices for the good of others; what may not then be expected from the great mass of the labouring English population, from the intelligent artisans of towns, who are so apt in acquiring their difficult arts, and are certainly not surpassed by other classes in the facility with which they grasp and carry out a scientific principle clearly announced? To leave many things to the people themselves will be to proceed slowly, because knowledge and new principles can only be communicated slowly, but it will be to proceed surely; and the improvement will not die away or be superficial, for it will be the act of the mind, penetrate the inmost recesses of home, and be imparted to future generations.' *

A SKETCH OF THE HOUSE OF LORDS.

A STRANGER entering the old House of Lords could hardly have failed to be struck with some degree of awe, if not from consideration of its being the meeting-place of the highest assembly in Britain, at least from the historical associations connected with it. Before him stood the gorgeous throne which Henry VII., despite his avarice, had adorned, and the bulky figure of Henry VIII. had filled. On its steps had knelt Anne Boleyn, when she sued, but sued in vain, for mercy. On it Edward VI. had reclined, when his frame was so attenuated by disease, and the medical art stood so low, that, despairing of relief from the faculty, his minister, says Hume, 'had resorted to the assistance of an old woman, or a witch.' There had sat his sister, the saturnine, bigoted, yet fond, faithful, and upright Mary Tudor: and there, in succession, the masculine and lion-hearted Elizabeth, after she had sealed the fate of the lovely, hapless, but faithless Mary Stuart. James had there been addressed by Bacon; and there had Charles whispered with Laud and Strafford. That throne had been cast aside as lumber by the astute and daring Cromwell, who cared little for either throne, or mace, or 'bauble,' or any other emblem of power, so long as he retained the substance. The tapestry which overhung the chamber walls had commemorated the defeat of the Spanish Armada and witnessed the triumph of the Reform Bill: and with many another striking scene of history that throne was identified, until the fire of 1834 consigned it to the recollections of the past.

The aspect of the present house is different, but still impressive. On entering, you perceive a long, narrow, red painted chamber, surmounted by a gallery, which in some degree obscures its light at one extremity, and terminating, in consequence of the absence of a window, in a still deeper gloom where stands the throne at the other. The appearance of the place is rather what would be called 'neat' than splendid. Its prevailing red, however, gives it an aspect of regality, though monotonous; and even the most frivolous spectator must be struck with the recollection, that here the laws of England are confirmed, and that even the Commons are obliged to stand uncovered in its precincts. It is the highest court in the kingdom, and yet the one to which access is most readily obtained. A stranger, when an absorbing case of swindling is being investigated, may have some difficulty in finding his way into a police court; and when an interesting murderer is to be tried, he will assuredly be excluded from the Old Bailey, unless—*malgré* all the orders and admonitions of judges and aldermen—he propitiates the attendant Cerberus with some shining current coin; but into the House of Lords, when in the morning they are sitting in appeal, overturning the decisions of half the judges, and disposing the interests of half the realm, he will be courteously shown by one of the attendant gentlemen doorkeepers; for all the doorkeepers of both houses are gentlemen in appearance, and most of them so in station too; the salaries of the offices being so high, and their duties so small, as to render them appointments to many exceedingly desirable. On passing the threshold, he will find the chamber much as we have described it, and in addition he will see a grave yet courteous, dignified but graceful, stern yet suave personage, in full flowing wig, before him; a bishop, in wig of less ample dimensions, and lawn sleeves—though frequently also in private dress, and distinguished only by the never-abandoned 'apron,' and primly upturned clerical hat—with some respectable-looking elderly man on one side, and on the other two of more active and business-like character. The first is the chancellor, Lord Lyndhurst, whose highly polished appearance and refined placid demeanour strangely disappoint those who, from his speeches and his reputation, would be prepared to find in him the representation of Mephistophiles or Machiavel at least; the respectable-looking man beside him, on the right or ministerial side of the house, is some member of England's hereditary nobility, whose acres or whose ancestors are better known than himself. The personages on the opposition benches are Lords Brougham and Campbell, two retired law officers, who thus do their best to make a return to the country for the pensions which they enjoy.

On another day, and at another hour, if he have interest enough—but this is a difficult matter—to procure a ticket from the lord chamberlain, let him go in, and he will there find the sovereign assembled amid England's congregated peers. Heedless of what is passing out of doors—careless of the splendour of the pageantry and the glories of the Park, the prancing of the horsemen and the acclamations of the crowd, the blaze of St James's and the crush of Whitehall—he must take his seat at least two hours before; and even then he will find the chamber beginning to be filled with the beauty and nobility of England. Nor do foreign lands fail to add lustre to the scene. In yonder box, allotted to the ambassadors, may be descried the splendour of Austria, the coarser magnificence of Russia, the dark-eyed beauties of the peninsular embassies, the graceful gaiety of the French, with the elegant frivolity of some Italian state. An Indian prince, in eastern decoration, perhaps imparts variety to the nodding plumes; and there, generally in red capote, will be found the solemn, small-poxed Turkish envoy, looking imperturbable on all around. Two o'clock approaches—the boom of the Park guns announcing the queen's arrival is heard; the trumpet, resounding through the vaulted aisles, strikes the ear so soon as she alights from her vehicle; a flourish re-echoes its notes from the martial band; the inspiring strains of 'God save the queen,' are raised; a few minutes are passed in the robing-room to don the paraphernalia of royalty; and, preceded by her chief minister in the upper house, bearing the sword of state erect in his hand, the queen of England appears amongst her peers. Led by her consort, and with her long train supported behind, she assumes her seat upon the throne: all rise on her approach; but she gracefully bids them be reseated. The usher of the black rod—an old dignified-looking man—is enjoined to summon the 'faithful Commons' to attend: another space of a few minutes elapses, during which her majesty generally chats with some royal uncle or noble attendant. By and by a pattering noise is heard at a distance, and gradually in-

* Fifth Report—Registrar-General.

creases in loudness if not distinctness. Soon it assumes a nearer sound; and, with their speaker, and scarcely less important mace at their head, in burst the representatives of the people. 'Order, order!' is perhaps heard from the lips of the chancellor, re-echoed by the voice of the speaker, if they be especially unruly; and, receiving it from her conscience-keeper on bended knee, her majesty, with marked and distinct elocution, delivers that royal speech which is generally anticipated with so much eagerness, and received with so little satisfaction. In twenty minutes the whole is over; the royal *cortège* departs as it came; the house breaks up; and the stranger is left to moralise—if moralist he be—upon the idle pageantry of the scene.

Let him return to the house about five o'clock, and if he obtain admission by a peer's order, he will find it of a character somewhat more intellectual. The lord chancellor then reads her majesty's 'most gracious speech,' as it is termed, to the surrounding senators; and some noble lord, little known to fame, who then generally makes his first appearance as a speaker, rises to propose an address in return, with the originality of which her majesty cannot fail to be eminently struck, inasmuch as it is invariably an echo of her own words. Nor, if she read the morning papers, will she often find reason to complain that the noble lord has wandered from his subject, as every sentence of his speech is generally but an amplification or paraphrase of her own, delivered in accents by no means so fluent or agreeable, but often repetitory and redundant, until they are cut down to something like form and propriety by the gentlemen of the fourth estate. When he has 'said his say'—generally a very painful process—the speaker sits down; and another noble lord, of whom the world at large usually knows about as much, gets up, goes over the same ground, hammers at the same thoughts, stammers at the same words, hopes their lordships will excuse his inexperience as a public speaker, and concludes, or begins, by declaring that his predecessor's words were so luminous, his arguments so convincing, and views so comprehensive, as to have left him little to add. If there be no opposition—as is generally the case now-a-days, when a prime minister plumes himself on his dexterity in framing a royal speech with which no fault can be found, because there is nothing decisive expressed—a leading member on the opposite benches gets up; 'just hints a fault, and hesitates dislike;' insinuates how much more satisfactory to the country would have been a royal speech from his own party; sits down; and after a few words from a principal minister, expressing how delighted he is, and how much more so her majesty must be, with their wonderful unanimity, the address is voted *nem. con.*

But if a debate take place, a different scene ensues, and the house presents a much more animated appearance. So soon as the noble mover and seconder of the address have sat down, the leader of the opposition gets up, and attacks the whole with an energy which could not be surpassed if the existence of the country, instead of his own chance of office, depended on the issue. Fast and furious the words flow: he may not speak very distinctly or grammatically, but what he wants in logic and language, he makes up in copiousness and vehemence; and you would suppose that he was to conclude by an earnest address to her majesty, craving her instantly to send the obnoxious ministry to Tower-hill. The minister on the opposite side rises with a look of unblenched boldness, and before he resumes his seat, he proves, satisfactorily to his own party at least, that the country is in a miraculous state of prosperity under his government, and that his opponents alone ought to have been impeached. Another member from the opposition benches rises; picks fresh holes, and finds new faults: an orator from the ministerial ranks succeeds him; and thus they go on abusing the wares of each other like rival blacking-makers; till, by and by, when argument and vituperation appear exhausted, the matter comes to a vote; and the bold minister, producing from his pocket the proxies of a hundred absent senators, whose intuitive wisdom enables them most unerringly to decide the merits of the debate without hearing it, settles the whole by a most satisfactory majority.

FALSE CRITICISM BY TRUE POETS.

That good poets are sometimes bad judges of excellence in their own art, may seem at first thought an untenable position, but it can easily be maintained by a reference to the history of literature. Jealousy, envy, self-conceit, an exclusive cultivation of some particular department of his art, or a strong idiosyncrasy of mind, or some early association, may as easily occasion an obliquity of judgment in the poet as in the mechanic. An author has an open or secret bias towards that branch of composition which he has most practised himself, and in which he is conscious that he best succeeds. This feeling too often influences his judgment upon the works of writers whose style and subject are essentially different from his own. To support his preferences, he invents or adopts certain theories or canons that would confine all literary merit within the narrow limits of his own sect or school. It is thus that the natural brotherhood of poets has been divided into innumerable parties, who regard each other with avowed hostility and contempt. They are blinded to all excellence that is not in some degree akin to their own.

In support of the foregoing remarks, I shall proceed to notice some of the most glaring mistakes of poetical critics.

One of the most celebrated of the poet-critics of modern times was Dr Samuel Johnson, who displayed extraordinary sagacity and acuteness in analysing the merits of the kind of poetry that was most allied to his own, but who could never pass beyond that limit with any degree of safety or success. Speaking entirely from his own feelings, he closes his review of *Paradise Lost* with the Gothic assertion, that its perusal is a duty rather than a pleasure. Of the *Lycidas*, which is so full of rich and varied melodies, he was of opinion that the diction was harsh and the numbers unpleasing. He once told Anna Seward that 'he would hang a dog that read that poem twice.' Of Collins, Johnson's unfavourable judgment is well known. With all his partiality and tenderness for the man, he had no feeling for the poet. He thought his poetry was not without some degree of merit, but confessed that he found it unattractive. 'As men,' said he, 'are often esteemed who cannot be loved, so the poetry of Collins may sometimes extort praise when it gives little pleasure;' and this is said of the finest ode-writer in the language—one of the most poetical of poets. The author of the *Ode to Evening*—a poem that floats into the reader's mind like a stream of celestial music—is pronounced harsh and prosaic in his diction. The high tone of Gray's lyric muse, and his exquisite versification, were lost upon the patron of Blackmore, Watts, Pomfret, and Yalden.* When some one spoke to him of Chatterton, he exclaimed indignantly, 'Talk not to me of the powers of a vulgar uneducated stripling.' What would he have said of Burns?

Dr Johnson was one of the best of the commentators upon Shakspeare, and yet this is saying little in his favour—'bad is the best.' His remarks and explanations are generally sensible and clear, and his preface to Shakspeare's plays is a noble piece of writing; but he never seems to enter thoroughly into the soul of that mighty poet. He could explain an obscure passage more readily than he could feel a fine one. Pope, also, was rather too much of a town wit and fashionable satirist to enjoy and appreciate the great poet of universal nature—

'Who was not for an age, but for all time.'

* The poets in Dr Johnson's collection were all selected by the booksellers, with the exception of Blackmore, Watts, Pomfret, and Yalden, who obtained admittance on the especial recommendation of the doctor, as he himself tells us in his Life of Dr Watts. Spenser and Shakspeare were excluded!

His edition of the prince of dramatic poets has fallen into deserved oblivion. He did not even understand or admire the more artificial, but yet manly and vigorous Ben Jonson. Spence tells us that Pope thought the greater part of that dramatist's productions 'poor trash.'

But 'rare Ben' himself, though a good poet, was a bad critic. He said of Spenser, that 'his stanzas pleased him not, nor his manner,' and that 'for some things, he esteemed Donne the first poet in the world.' Shakspeare, he thought, 'wanted art, and sometimes sense;' and why? because he made a blunder in geography. In the *Winter's Tale* he made Bohemia a maritime country, little dreaming that an error of locality would deduct from the miraculous truth of his delineations of the human heart.

The melodious Waller saw nothing in Milton but an old blind schoolmaster, who had written a dull poem, remarkable for nothing but its length; and Milton himself preferred the glittering conceits of Cowley to the manly energy and truth of Dryden, whom he pronounced a good rhymist, but no poet. But Dryden, also, with all his real merit as a poet, was a critic whose decisions are never to be relied on, partly because he was prejudiced, partly because he was, comparatively speaking, deficient in imagination and sensibility, and partly because he was a most unblushing adulator. He thought 'the matchless Orinda,' Catherine Philips, was a great poetess. He pronounced the versification of Spenser inferior to that of Waller. Voltaire, as every Englishman remembers, has spoken of Shakspeare's 'monstrous farces called tragedies,' and wondered that a nation which had produced *Cato* (Addison's collection of cold and stilted dialogues in the dramatic form), should tolerate such plays as *Lear*, *Hamlet*, *Macbeth*, and *Othello!* But if Voltaire has done British genius a gross injustice, he has suffered something in return. Gray declared that Voltaire (except as a writer of plays) was entirely without genius. Neither could he perceive any talent whatever in Rousseau's *Nouvelle Heloise*. He spoke in a similar strain of several British authors. He said that David Hume had continued all his days an infant, but had, unhappily, been taught to read and write. He saw no merit in Thomson's exquisite *Castle of Indolence;* and he thought Collins deficient in imagery! 'He (Collins) deserves,' said he, 'to live some years, but will not.' It would seem that the time has long gone by, when

> 'The sacred name
> Of poet and of prophet was the same.'

Gray, in his verses to the artist who embellished an edition of his poems, very oddly inverts the merits of Pope and Dryden; by speaking of the energy of the first, and the melody of the second.

To the list of bad critics, I am compelled to add the name of Collins, for he has ventured to assert, in his Epistle to Sir Thomas Hanmer, that Fletcher excelled Shakspeare in the illustration of female tenderness.

> 'His every strain the smiles and graces own,
> But stronger Shakspeare felt for man alone.'

It would be a waste of words to expose this egregious error, though I believe Collins only echoes Dryden. Gifford, in his edition of Massinger, almost repeats them both. He contends that Fletcher is at least as pathetic as Shakspeare. The pathos of *Lear* does not seem to have touched the author of the *Baviad and Mæviad*, a coarse and savage satire, in which helpless women are insulted, and 'butterflies are broken on a wheel.' But in Gifford's estimation, not only is Fletcher at least Shakspeare's equal in pathos, but Beaumont is as sublime, Ben Jonson as nervous, and Massinger superior in rhythmical modulation. The sole point of unrivalled excellence that he leaves to Shakspeare is his wit!—and yet Gifford was for many years one of our leading critics. We ought not to be surprised that he pronounced Hazlitt a dull-headed blockhead; and that he could discover neither genius nor common sense in Keats and Shelley. According to Gifford, 'the predominating character of Mr Shelley's poetry is its frequent and total want of meaning.' 'It is not too much to affirm,' he says (in speaking of the Prometheus, &c.), 'that in the whole volume there is not one original image of nature, one simple expression of human feeling, or one new association of the appearances of the moral with those of the material world.'

Anna Seward, a poetess of some note in her time, and still spoken of with respect by Southey, ranked Darwin and Hayley amongst the greatest of our bards. Of the former she thus writes:—'He knew that his verse would live to distant ages; but he also knew that it would survive by the slowly accumulating suffrages of kindred genius when contemporary jealousy had ceased to operate.' How vainly did the poet lay this flattering unction to his soul, and how completely was Anna Seward mistaken in all her sympathetic anticipations of her friend's future fame! Of the feeble and half-forgotten Hayley, she speaks with even greater warmth, and in a style of prophecy which the lapse of a very few years has rendered absolutely ludicrous. 'Hayley is indeed a true poet. He has the fire and energy of Dryden without his absurdity (!!), and he has the wit and ease of Prior (!). His beautiful *Epistles on Painting*—far even above these, his *Essay on Epic Poetry*, together with the fine *Ode to Howard*, will be considered as amongst the first Delphic ornaments of the eighteenth century.' But even Cowper thought highly of Hayley and Darwin; and Miss Seward was not a worse critic than the 'true poet,' whose productions are 'amongst the first Delphic ornaments of the eighteenth century.' In one of Hayley's letters to her, in alluding to Burns, he compares him to some obscure and humble versifier who had gained her patronage. 'I admire the Scottish peasant,' says he, 'but I do not think him superior to your poetical carpenter!'

Burns himself had a most extravagant opinion of Fergusson as a poet, whom he preferred to Allan Ramsay. Thomas Warton, though a great admirer of Milton's genius, thought nature had not blessed the divine old bard with an ear for verse. Akenside, who, observes Johnson, upon a poetical question, has a right to be heard, said that 'he would regulate his opinion of the reigning taste by the fate of Dyer's *Fleece;* for if that were ill received, he should not think it any longer reasonable to expect fame from excellence.' The prophesy of some wit, in allusion to this poem, that Dyer would be buried in his own wool, would have been fulfilled almost to the letter, if it were not for his *Grongar Hill*, on which he still breathes the vital air. Scott of Amwell, the Quaker poet, made a desperate attempt to rescue the *Fleece* from oblivion, and vainly endeavoured to persuade the public that it is much superior to the *Grongar Hill*.

Addison, who has been so much praised for his critique on Milton, was, after all, but another example of the fallibility of poetical critics. In his versified 'Account of the greatest English Poets,' he omits all allusion to Shakspeare, but praises Roscommon as 'the best of critics and of poets too!' After having taken due notice of numerous 'great' poets, he recollects that 'justice demands one labour more'—

> 'The noble Montague remains unnamed.'

That Shakspeare was unnamed, was of little consequence! But though the critic and poet was, as he elegantly expresses himself,

> 'Tired with rhyming, and would fain give o'er,'

he would have deemed himself highly blameworthy had he omitted Montague! His list of great poets would have been deplorably incomplete! Though he is so enraptured with Montague, he says little in favour of Chaucer or Spenser. Of the former he observes,

> 'In vain he jests in his unpolished strain;'

and of the latter he tells us, that though his tales

'amused a barbarous age' (the age of Shakspeare, Bacon, Jeremy Taylor, Beaumont and Fletcher, &c. &c.),

> 'An age as yet uncultivate and rude,'

that he is no longer to be tolerated—

> 'But now the mystic tale that charmed of yore
> Can charm an understanding age no more.'

Amongst the poets of the nineteenth century, we have a melancholy display of bad critics upon productions in their own art. Byron called Spenser 'a dull fellow,' and said, 'he could see nothing in him.'* He considered that Chaucer was 'contemptible,' and owed his celebrity merely to his antiquity, and that he was inferior to Pierce Plowman and Thomas of Ercildoune. He placed Rogers at the head of all his contemporaries, and looked, or pretended to look, with supreme scorn upon Southey and Wordsworth. He thus spoke of the most ambitious of the latter's undertakings:—

> 'A clumsy, frowsy poem called the *Excursion*,
> Writ in a manner that is my aversion.'

He said Cowper was 'no poet,' and intimated that Pope was at least equal if not superior to Shakspeare, for whom he had no very passionate admiration. He thought the author of the *Essay on Man* was the greatest of poets, because the science of morals is the greatest of all subjects; though he contradicted himself by an equally foolish position, that a poet ranks by his execution alone, and not by the nature of his subject or undertaking; so that the author of a good epigram must be equal in rank to the author of a good epic, which Dryden calls the greatest work of which the mind of man is capable. Young's *Revenge* was Byron's favourite play, though he had read *Othello*.

Wordsworth calls Dryden's celebrated music ode 'a drunken song,' and professes to entertain a profound contempt for some of the finest poetry of Burns. The celebrated Dr Wolcott (Peter Pindar) used to speak in the same style of Dryden's ode. 'How wofully,' he would often exclaim, 'have mankind been mistaken in their admiration of this paltry production!' Mrs Hemans, in one of her letters (published in Chorley's *Memorials* of her), records the following very remarkable conversation between herself and the great poet of the lakes:—'We were sitting on a bank (she writes) overlooking Rydal Lake, and speaking of Burns. I said, "Mr Wordsworth, do you not think his war ode, 'Scots wha hae wi' Wallace bled,' has been a good deal overrated, especially by Mr Carlyle, who calls it the noblest lyric in the language?" "I am delighted to hear you ask the question," was his reply; "overrated?—trash!—stuff!—miserable inanity! without a thought—without an image!" &c. &c. Then he recited the piece in a tone of unutterable scorn, and concluded with a *da capo* of "wretched stuff!"'

Wordsworth and Coleridge see no beauty in Gray's *Elegy*, though the latter had the most extravagantly favourable opinion of the sentimental poetry of Bowles, and praises it for its 'manliest melancholy.' Keats styled all the poets of the Frenchified English school 'a school of dolts.'

> 'Ye taught a school
> Of dolts that smooth, inlay, and clip and fit,
> Till, like the certain wands of Jacob's wit,
> Their verses tallied. Easy was the task.'

Perhaps Keats would not have found the composition of another *Rape of the Lock* quite so easy a task as he imagined. There is even in the *Essay on Man*, and the *Prologue to Cato*, something more than

> 'A puling infant's force,
> That swayed about upon a rocking-horse,
> And thought it Pegasus.'

Sir Walter Scott, though he exhibited a noble impartiality and a rare self-insight when speaking of his own poems, was not a first-rate judge of the poetry of other men. 'He often said to me,' says his friend Ballantyne, 'that neither his own nor any modern popular style of composition, was that from which he derived most pleasure. I asked him what it was; he answered'—(what does the reader suppose? Shakspeare's, Spenser's, Milton's, Dryden's, Pope's, Burns's? Oh no!)—'Dr Johnson's (!), and that he had more pleasure in reading *London*, and *The Vanity of Human Wishes*, than any other poetical composition he could mention.' Scott, however, is the only poet I have read of who judged fairly and yet unfavourably of his own poetical compositions. He always said that they could never live; and were not to be compared with the works of many of his contemporaries. In the meridian of his own poetical popularity, he felt that those comparatively neglected writers, Wordsworth, Coleridge, and Shelley, were far greater poets, and more deeply touched with the holy fire of inspiration. Nor did Scott ever prefer his worst pieces to his best. In this respect he exhibited a far clearer judgment than many other celebrated authors. Petrarch doted on his *Africa*, Milton on his *Paradise Regained*, Prior on his *Solomon*, and Byron on his *Hints from Horace*.

I have now, I think, sufficiently established my position, that good poets are not always good critics, and that we ought not to trust too implicitly to their authority on a question of poetical criticism.*

* If Byron ever read Gabriel Harvey's letter to Spenser, in which he discourages him from proceeding with the *Faery Queen*, he must have been delighted with such congeniality of taste. Harvey was a man of great learning and elegant accomplishments, and wrote verses which were well thought of by Spenser himself and other good judges of poetical merit. Spenser sent Harvey a specimen of the *Faery Queen* for his opinion, and his 'most special friend' returned it with a prayer that 'God or some good angel would put him in a better mind.' This condemnation of Spenser's noblest work is accompanied with high praises of some of his inferior productions.

* The above is presented, with the concurrence of the author, as the spirit of a paper in the 'Literary Leaves' of David Lester Richardson.

INFLUENCE OF AIR AND EXERCISE ON HEALTH.

In proof of the influence which even temporary physical education exerts upon the human frame and its stamina, may be mentioned the following example:—In the summer of 1839, we had an opportunity of witnessing one of the trial races of Oscroft, at that time one of the swiftest runners in England. On the occasion we speak of, he ran 120 yards in eleven seconds; his pulse, just before starting, beat 61 strokes per minute, and at the termination of his extraordinary feat it beat only 94! When it is further taken into account, that, whilst in the act of running, he never made a complete inspiration or expiration, the performance can be considered little short of wonderful. We were informed by the man himself, that though he was naturally remarkable for nimble-footedness, he was anything but 'good-winded.' Two months previously, he had been taken from a stocking-frame, and, by a process of merely careful training, was brought into the state of bodily condition alluded to. Had it been possible for him, before commencing to train, to have run the distance in the time stated, the effort, if it had not killed, would have nearly asphyxiated him. He would have been breathing for his life, and his pulse could not have been counted. As it was, at the completion of his task he breathed without difficulty, and his pulse was increased only 33 beats per minute! After such evidence as this, and it is only one of a multitude of examples with which the world is familiar, no man, not actually diseased, need despair of becoming active and vigorous, if he will only attend to the simple rules which are to guide his physical discipline. The man of whom we have spoken had not a good chest, for which reason he could not, under any circumstances, have run a long race; and his configuration of thorax was even opposed to an effort of speed for a short distance; but the natural obstacle was overcome for the time being by temporary training! We are, perhaps, not justified in saying *ex uno disce omnes*; but at least we can say, that if two short months of rigid living, and exercise in pure air, can do so much for a man's constitution and strength, how much more permanent service may be done by a continued observance, though in a milder degree, of the principles we have laid down. How many listless and enfeebled frames would be roused, refreshed, and made fit for the wear and tear of a protracted life! How many minds, sinking into imbecility from actual lassitude, or oppressed by the melancholy of fancied cares, would be stirred by the busy and cheerful objects of worldly enterprise! We would fain teach the man too ardently devoted to learning, to science, or to worldly business, that with all his toil, and care, and penury of time, he is not a gainer; he may appropriate to his idol object an hour that should be sacred to his own service, and in so doing he is a loser of twain; let him husband his moments as niggardly as he will, there is a certain reckoning which he must daily have with himself, a certain time for his own rest and refreshment; and if that time be not granted, it becomes no matter of idle debtorship—day after day registers a fresh account against him, and, at the end of a few years, the unsuspected fact of premature old age is announced by decrepitude, decay, and death.—*Medical Times.*

QUEEN ELIZABETH'S LAST ILLNESS.

The Archbishop of Canterbury and Cecil intreated her to receive medical aid; but she angrily told them, 'that she knew her own constitution better than they did, and that she was not in so much danger as they imagined.' The admiral came and knelt beside her, where she sat among her cushions, sullen and unresigned; he kissed her hands, and, with tears, implored her to take a little nourishment. After much ado, he prevailed so far, that she received a little broth from his hands, he feeding her with a spoon. But when he urged her to go to bed, she angrily refused, and then, in wild and wandering words, hinted of phantasms that had troubled her midnight couch. 'If he were in the habit of seeing such things in his bed,' she said, 'as she did when in hers, he would not persuade her to go there.' Secretary Cecil overhearing this speech, asked 'if her majesty had seen any spirits?' A flash of Elizabeth's mighty mind for an instant triumphed over the wreck of her bodily and mental faculties; she knew the man, and was aware he had been truckling with her successor. He was not in her confidence, and she answered majestically, 'she scorned to answer him *such* a question!' But Cecil's pertness was not subdued by the lion-like mien of dying majesty, and he told her that, 'to content the people, she *must* go to bed.' At which she smiled, wonderfully contemning to him, observing, 'the word *must* was not to be used to princes;' adding, 'Little man, little man, if your father had lived, ye durst not have said so much; but ye know I must die, and that makes ye so presumptuous.' She then commanded him and the rest to depart out of her chamber, all but Lord Admiral Howard, to whom, as her near relation and fast friend through life, she was confidential to the last, even regarding those unreal phantasms, which, when her great mind awoke for a moment, it is plain she referred to their proper causes. When Cecil and his colleagues were gone, the queen, shaking her head piteously, said to her brave kinsman, 'My lord, I am tied with a chain of iron about my neck.' The lord admiral reminded her of her wonted courage; but she replied despondingly, 'I am tied, I am tied, and the case is altered with me.' The queen understood that Secretary Cecil had given forth to the people that she was mad; therefore, in her sickness, she did many times say unto him, 'Cecil, I am not mad; you must not think to make Queen Jane of me.' She evidently alluded to the unfortunate queen-regnant of Castille, the mad Joanna, mother of Charles V., whose sad life, as a regal maniac, was fresh in the memory of her dying contemporary.—*Agnes Strickland's Lives of the Queens of England.*

PERIODICAL PUBLISHED IN A LUNATIC ASYLUM.

What a strange contrast does the following statement, by the New York Journal of Medicine, present to the state of things formerly existing in similar establishments! 'It is in the Vermont Asylum that the literary spirit has been carried even to the *cacoëthes scribendi*; for, not content with the enjoyment of being merely readers, they actually publish a small newspaper called the "Asylum Journal." As they thus receive in exchange more than two hundred newspapers, besides many other periodicals, the superintendent is enabled to furnish every patient with a newspaper from his own immediate neighbourhood, at the same time that every politician has one of his own political views, and every sectarian one adapted to his own religious sentiments.' We see it also stated by some of the medical journals of our own country, that very successful results have attended a similar undertaking in the Crichton Asylum, Dumfriesshire.

TO A BUTTERFLY IN THE CITY.

[BY S. W. PARTRIDGE.]

FEEBLE flutterer, timid thing,
Wherefore here with trembling wing?
Crowded streets can never be,
Foolish rambler, fit for thee.
Art thou tired of leafy bowers,
Sunny streams, and honied flowers;
Is the rose, thy perfumed bed,
Tempest-snapped, untimely dead;
Or, still worse, thy love unkind,
That thou leav'st the fields behind,
Here unwisely come to roam
Far from beauty, peace, and home?

Or, by travelled friend impressed,
Art thou come with curious breast?
Wouldst thou see the domes and towers
In this crowded coop of ours?
Or survey, with eager eyes,
Creatures so divinely wise?
Fly, ah! fly these swarming streets,
Seek again thy green retreats;
For, though wonders here you see,
Joy and quiet dwell with thee.

But with kinder aim, no doubt,
Thou hast come to seek us out;
Thou didst fear, so hard we moil
In the dust of care and toil,
We might be all out of tune
For the flowery joys of June,
And, with ledger-blinded eye,
Let unseen its beauties die.
Ah! thy fear was wise; we strive,
Tugging in this human hive,
Too intent on gains and losses
In life's game of 'noughts and crosses;'
While fair nature's volume lies
All unread before our eyes,
Deadened in our every sense
To her holy influence.

But return; afar from men
Seek thy sunny haunts again,
And we too, ere long, will come
To thy quiet leafy home.
There we'll seek the thyme-bank sunny
Where the flower-thief pilfers honey,
There we'll rove with dance and song
Where the carp darts swift along,
Or beneath some honied lime
Leaf-embowerèd, laugh at time.
Thus the happy hours shall be
Fraught with love and liberty;
Thus thy home and joys we'll share,
Far from toil, and noise, and care.

NOTE.

IN the article entitled Railway Literature, published on the 22d March (No. 64, New Series), an omission appears to have been made with respect to the share which the Scotsman (Edinburgh newspaper) had in promoting the trial of a high rate of speed upon railways. The same omission, it may be remarked, occurs in an article on railways in the Quarterly Review for June 1844 (p. 233). We now learn from an article in the Scotsman, that the editor of that paper, having engaged in researches into the laws of friction established by Vince and Coulomb, published the results in a series of articles in his journal in 1824, showing how twenty miles an hour was, on theoretic grounds, within the limits of possibility; and it was to his writings on this point, and not to anything that had fallen from Mr George Stephenson, that Mr Nicolas Wood alluded when he spoke of the 'ridiculous expectation' that engines would ever travel at the rate of twenty or even twelve miles an hour.

⁂ Complete sets of the *Journal*, *First Series*, in twelve volumes, and also odd numbers to complete sets, may be had from the publishers or their agents. A Stamped Edition issued for transmission, post free, price Twopence halfpenny.

Printed by William Bradbury, of No. 6, York Place, and Frederick Mullett Evans, of No. 7, Church Row, both of Stoke Newington, in the county of Middlesex, printers, at their office, Lombard Street, in the precinct of Whitefriars, and city of London; and Published (with permission of the Proprietors, W. and R. CHAMBERS,) by WILLIAM SOMERVILLE ORR, Publisher, of 8, Amen Corner, at No. 2, AMEN CORNER, both in the parish of Christchurch, and in the city of London.—Saturday, May 31, 1845.

CONDUCTED BY WILLIAM AND ROBERT CHAMBERS, EDITORS OF 'CHAMBERS'S INFORMATION FOR THE PEOPLE,' 'CHAMBERS'S EDUCATIONAL COURSE,' &c.

No. 75. New Series. SATURDAY, JUNE 7, 1845. Price 1½d.

THE ELECTRIC TELEGRAPH.

It would be difficult, amidst the numerous inventions which have of late been brought before the public for its social benefit, to select one more curious and extraordinary than the electric telegraph. The simple fact that means are now provided for the transmission of intelligence over hundreds of miles in nearly as short a time as it takes to speak to a companion with whom one is face to face, opens out a perspective view of future conveniences almost bewildering. What has already been accomplished by the electric telegraph shows the possibility of rapid communication between 'the uttermost ends of the earth.' By means of a set of electric wires, extending between London and Pekin, the privy council of St James's and the *Loo-poo* board of the Celestial emperor might without any imaginable difficulty effect an hourly exchange of official sentiments, and settle the whole details of an important treaty in the course of a forenoon!

To demonstrate this wondrous possibility, it will be only necessary to record what we ourselves witnessed at the terminus of the South Western Railway during a visit to London last month. It happened that a gentleman of our acquaintance had organised a game of chess, one of the players being stationed at the London and the other at the Gosport terminus of the railway; the moves of each to be communicated to and fro by the electric telegraph. This curious application of electricity we were politely invited to witness.

On reaching the terminus, which is situated at Vauxhall, we were ushered into the committee-room, where we observed the London player surrounded by numerous chess-advisers, with whom he was discussing the propriety of certain moves that had just been proposed. When an effective one was decided on, it was recorded on a small slip of paper, and handed to the gentleman who worked the telegraph, which stood in an ante-room. The machine was set in motion, and in the course of a very few minutes it had not only been received at Gosport, but the return or counter-move decided on by the antagonist eighty-eight miles off was indicated on the index of the telegraph on the table before us! The curiosity we had previously felt to see the wonderful machine at work was now strongly excited to learn *how* its magical powers operated. Fortunately Mr Cooke the inventor, who, with the assistance of Professor Wheatstone, has brought the instrument to its high condition of usefulness, was in the room, and readily explained to us not only the nature but the origin and progress of the invention.

Mr Cooke, by profession a military man, having served in our Indian armies several years, was, in March 1836, engaged at Heidelberg in anatomical researches, chiefly for the purpose of modelling his own dissections from nature for the embellishment of his father's museum, a professor of the Durham university. In this self-taught art he had been engaged many months, when an entirely new direction was accidentally given to his thoughts. Professor Moencke of Heidelberg had invited Mr Cooke to witness some experiments with a simple apparatus intended to illustrate the possibility of giving signals by electricity—an idea which had already occupied the scientific world for several years. So powerful was the impression produced on Mr Cooke's mind by these experiments, and so convinced was he of the possibility of applying electricity to the transmission of telegraphic intelligence along railway lines, that, abandoning his other pursuits, he devoted himself from that hour exclusively to the realisation of the present telegraph. It is no slight proof of the energy and ingenuity of this gentleman, that, within three weeks of his first conceiving the idea, he had constructed at Frankfort two galvanometer telegraphs capable of giving twenty-six signals; he had also invented the *detector*, by which injuries to the wires, whether from water, fracture, or contact, were readily traced—an instrument which Mr Cooke still retains in constant use, and without which, indeed, an electric telegraph would be impracticable. Lastly, he invented the *alarum*, by which notice is given at one end of the telegraph that something is about to be communicated from the other. He returned to London about six weeks after, and engaged himself during the succeeding year in making a variety of instruments, and in efforts to introduce the use of his telegraph on the Liverpool and Manchester Railway. In February 1837, he made the acquaintance of Professor Wheatstone, a gentleman of high scientific attainments, who had been for years employed in endeavouring to transmit signals both by sounds and by electricity. Mr Cooke immediately secured the professor's co-operation, and the two gentlemen entered into partnership as proprietors of the patent under which the telegraph is worked.

Most of our readers need scarcely be told that the readiest mode of producing a current of electricity is by means of a battery invented by Mr Smee. This consists in its simplest form of two plates of zinc separated by a diaphragm of platinised silver, and immersed in a weak solution of sulphuric acid. During the action of the acid upon the zinc, electricity is copiously evolved, and may be conducted to any distance by means of attached wires. At the termination, the electric current may be made to communicate motion to some small object, such as a bell, or the hand of an index.

Such is the merest outline of the mode in which electric telegraphing is effected. Mr Cooke's contrivance requires of course further explanation. In the ante-room before mentioned, the most striking object we beheld was a kind of cabinet having all the appearance of a handsome table clock. On a glass-covered metal plate in front, are two disks, each furnished with a needle moving on an extremely sensitive pivot, so as to point upwards and downwards. At the base of this clock-like machine are two handles by which the motion communicated to these needles by the electric current is directed. Exactly the same sort of machine stands at the Gosport terminus of the railway, and its needles move precisely in accordance with the motions of those we saw at work, so that the attendant at Gosport can read from the motion of the needles what the attendant at the London end intends to convey by the motion he gives to the Gosport needles by means of the London handles. The electricity, therefore, gives mere unmeaning motion to the needles at either end—the gentleman in charge of the instrument *directs* that motion, and by the different positions in which he puts the two needles, communicates such meaning to the motion as is perfectly intelligible to his companion at the other terminus. The code of signals thus established was partly explained to us:—The left hand needle when moved to the left gives E, to the right I; the other needle gives O and U; both pointing parallel, W or Y. The consonants most in use are given by two movements of the needle; and those very rarely required, such as J, Q, X, Z, by three movements. The word 'you,' for example, is expressed by both needles pointing parallel for Y; the right hand needle moving once to the left for O, and once to the right for U. A different set of oscillations are used for numerals. The gentlemen who direct this novel mode of communication do it so quickly, that all you see is the two needles shaking about and oscillating on their pivots with great rapidity. How the correspondent at the other end can follow such rapid signalling puzzles the uninitiated extremely; but Mr Cooke assured us that a young man, whom he pointed out, had been under instruction only three weeks, when, on going to the telegraph, he signalled so rapidly that the gentleman at the other end complained that his movements were far too electric, and that he could not follow him. Hoping to put the novice in a similar difficulty, he began signalling in return as fast as he—an experienced signaller—was able; but the tyro read off every word as fluently as from a book—so simple is the code when properly understood.

Having as yet only explained the principle of the signals, we must now follow Mr Cooke's explanation along the eighty-eight miles of wires. As before hinted, the contact of the zinc and silver with sulphuric acid produces a constant supply of electricity, and if the signal wires were always attached to the battery, a constant and unmeaning motion would be going on. When not in use, therefore, the telegraphic wire is detached. Hence there is a second wire to conduct the electricity into the earth (which it does by being simply attached to a lamp-post in the street) when the telegraph is not at work, and when consequently the working wire is permanently out of use. Some one is always in attendance before each dial, and when a signal is to be communicated, the wire is attached to the battery, and the electric fluid made to ring a small bell at the other end of the wire. This gives the proper warning. The communicant then signals the word 'Ready?' to which the reply is 'Yes.' Whatever has to be said is then proceeded with 'as quick'—to use language now no longer metaphorical—'as lightning.'

The wires, which are the conductors of the electricity, are of iron, and rather thick (being what wire-drawers number 7 or 8), coated with zinc. The earliest wires Mr Cooke laid down were enclosed in tubes, and buried in the earth, as a protection against injury from weather; but this was a most expensive plan, and he tried the experiment of exposed wires. It succeeded completely; for by a singular operation of nature, which has not yet been explained, the effect of the air and damp upon the electrified iron with its zinc coating has been to incrust it with a light-coloured pigment, which forms of itself an ample protection. Hence the wire is exposed all along the line; the mode by which it was fixed and joined being as follows:—At every 500 or 600 yards, strong posts of timber from 16 to 18 feet in height were fixed in the ground. Attached to the heads of these posts is a winding apparatus, and between every two of such posts, upright wooden standards are fixed about 60 or 70 yards apart. A ring of iron wire, which has been formed by welding the short lengths in which it is made together, is then placed upon a reel carried on a handbarrow, and one end being attached to the winder at one draw-post, the wire is extended to the adjoining draw-post, and there fixed to its corresponding winder; by turning the pin of the ratchet-wheel with a proper key, the wire is tightened to the necessary degree; thus the greatest accuracy may be attained in drawing the wires up. To sufficiently insulate the wires so suspended at the point of contact with the posts, is an object of indispensable importance, as the dampness of the wood during rainy weather would otherwise allow the electric fluid to pass off freely into the earth, without reaching the distant terminus at which the telegraphic effect is to be produced. In this, indeed, lies an important feature of Mr Cooke's invention, as the idea of merely supporting wires in the open air from poles, trees, or church steeples, is the oldest on record. To effect this object, at the draw-posts wooden boxes are employed to enclose that portion of the post to which the winders are attached, and small openings are left for the free passage of the wires, without risking any contact with the outer box. The wire, therefore, may be said to be continuous—in this instance for eighty-eight miles, or from London to Gosport. A separate wire and a separate telegraph are required for each station on the road. For six such wires the cost is about L.149, 6s. per mile. On the South Western there are only two, one for Gosport and one for Southampton.

Having received this explanation, we again directed our attention to the chess-players, to ascertain by what means the parties made each other understand the moves. This was simple enough. Each piece and each square of the board was numbered, so by simply telegraphing, 'No. 1 to No. 9' for instance, it was easy to understand that the white rook was moved one square forward. It seems that the game was commenced about eleven o'clock in the morning, and terminated a little before seven in the evening; but would have been concluded earlier, had not much delay been occasioned at Gosport in transmitting the moves to Southampton, where a third party of chess-players had congregated to 'watch' the game. Despite this extra complication in the working of the telegraphs, one hundred and seventy moves were communicated without a single error. So equal was the play, that it turned out a 'drawn' game.

In conversations with gentlemen present, we gathered some interesting conjectures regarding the future usefulness of this extraordinary invention. First, it will convey orders and messages along the line according to the instructions of the directors and managers of the railway. Next, it is to serve the important use of communicating between the Admiralty in Whitehall and the naval establishment at Portsmouth. A similar communication is in contemplation with the arsenal at Plymouth. The South Wales line may also carry the telegraph to Milford, another of our dockyards; and when all the dockyards are thus telegraphically united with the Admiralty, orders will at any instant, with the quickness of thought, be transmitted to the great naval stations of the country from headquarters, and from each to any of the others, or information be returned from them to headquarters, with greater speed than they could formerly be carried from the great room of the Admiralty to the secretary in the adjoining apartment. The energy which, in case of emergency, this would infuse into every department of the service, must be of incalculable utility to the country. It is also intended to throw the use of the telegraph open to the public for a small fee. By making an appointment with a friend, you to be at the Vauxhall and he at the Gosport terminus at a particular moment, any news which it may be important for either party to know will be instantly communicated. Nor will it serve only for distances comparatively so short, but equally well for such as that between London and Edinburgh, or even Aberdeen, when the railway lines between these places are formed, as it is now certain they soon will be. Suppose a gentleman connected with our city is on a visit to London, and one of his family suddenly takes ill. It will be possible immediately to communicate the intelligence to the station at the latter city, where a messenger or a letter by the local post will accomplish the rest of the business in a brief space of time. In such a case, we shall suppose the gentleman, on receiving the intelligence, contemplates having immediately to return to his home, though the step is grievously inconvenient to him at the moment. In former circumstances, he might deem it necessary to set out instantly, because he could not be sure but that the object of his solicitude was by this time no more. Now, however, he may well wait with patience for the bulletin of next morning, when, applying at the railway station by appointment, he will learn that the patient, we shall say, has had a good night, and is considered out of danger. He returns with an easy mind to the city to attend to his business engagements, instead of having to set out on a long journey, the whole of which would have been spent in extreme, though it might ultimately prove useless anxiety. We had an opportunity, while in the Vauxhall station committee-room, of being impressed with a sense of the perfectly practical nature of this speculation. One of our friends wished to know from his partner, who was watching the game of chess at Gosport, if he intended returning to town to dine. The needles were set to work, and made to shake for a second or so; there was a short pause, and presently they gave some dozen oscillations, when the gentleman in the magnetic secret turned to us, and said that our friend's reply was 'Yes, at five.' All this was done in about the same space of time as would be occupied by one of our readers in perusing about half a column of this journal.

LUDOVICO LANA.

AN ANECDOTE OF MODERN SICILY.

In the summer of 1811, I was travelling in Sicily, and in crossing the island from Girgenti to Palermo, paid a visit to the town of Castrogiovanni, built on the site of the ancient Enna. After a ride of some hours under a scorching sun, and in a state which fully explained the nature of the metamorphosis which sundry nymphs of the classic ages underwent in the same lovely land, when by some powerful agency they melted away into fountains, it was with infinite satisfaction that I saw before me my destined resting-place.

Not a tree had I passed for hours which afforded as much shade as a cabbage-leaf—all was desolate and uncultivated; and the flowery plains in which Proserpine was gathering nosegays when Pluto acted so very like an unconstitutional king, and, in a manner which no gentleman out of the Emerald Isle would have dreamed of, forcibly abduced the daughter of Ceres; in these self-same meads, all was as brown and burnt up as a rabbit warren in the month of August. I could however calculate at least upon shelter from the sun, if the old town afforded nothing else, which is often the case in the interior of Sicily. But I had better hopes, for a friend at Girgenti had given me letters to the Abbate Guttadouro, who would, I was assured, find me better quarters than any locanda could give; and that to the latter I could consign my servant and the mules.

Castrogiovanni stands upon a high isolated hill, and is surrounded by old walls and towers. The celebrated temple of Ceres stood, it is said, upon a similar hill, divided from that on which the town is built by the valley in which the abduction of the young lady aforesaid took place; but there are no more remains of the temple now left than there are traces of the chariot wheels by which she was borne away—the last remnants of the celebrated fane having been removed to build some of the old churches in the town. On entering the place—which seems to have retrograded in civilisation for the last two thousand years, till it has arrived at such a state as would be considered indictable by an English jury as dangerous to passengers, either biped or quadruped—I was surprised to see so little interest shown on the arrival of a stranger, as in most of these classic spots a host of mendicants assail him on one side, and guides on the other, each eager to catch fresh prey, and appropriate the spoils, whilst the idle and unemployed, who form at least nine-tenths of the population, and the hosts of the miserable locandas (the worst specimen of inn in the civilised world), swell the crowd; at Castrogiovanni affairs seemed quite in another state, and all appeared occupied in some weighty matter of general interest. The beggars forgot to hold out their hands, and the ciceroni to proffer the benefits of their local and classical erudition. We passed unnoticed through the street, and could scarcely bribe a half-naked urchin to guide us to the house of the abbate, to whom I had an introduction. When we arrived, the good priest was not to be found, but his housekeeper invited me to enter, and promised that my letter should be delivered immediately, as the abbate was readily to be found. Close at hand was the Cruce Blanco, one of the best locandas in the town, and thither I sent my servant with the mules, awaiting in patience the return of the master of the house, which was not long delayed. He was very kind, offering his house and all that he had with the accustomed Sicilian ceremonial, and it was arranged that I should become the guest of the abbate, whilst my servant remained at the inn for two or three days. I then learned the cause of the unusual excitement in the town. A brigand, belonging it was said to the band of the celebrated Ludovico Lana, had been arrested, and it was expected that he would make disclosures of great interest when condemned to death, which it was decided that he should be by the judge and other authorities before the trial took place or a question was asked. He had been arrested on the deposition of a dying man, who had been robbed and mortally wounded on the road between Catania and Castrogiovanni; but the accused stoutly maintained that at the time mentioned he had been employed as a porter at Palermo. Unfortunately, he had neither time allowed nor the means of procuring the attendance of witnesses, and the judge had fully made up his mind before-hand, as is very generally the case, and the sentence was passed just at the time of my entering the town: all the world, therefore, were assembled about the tribunal, and employed in discussing the merits of the case, which accounted for the deserted state of the streets, never at any time crowded with population. Soon after my establishment with my host, my servant returned from the locanda, and congratulated me on my good quarters, more particularly as a very great personage had arrived a short time previous, and who occupied, together with the unfortunate man just condemned, all the thoughts of the innkeeper and his family. I inquired who the great unknown might be, and was told that he was a very fine-looking young man, about twenty-eight or thirty years of age, in the uniform of an English officer of rank, and attended by two domestics. He had arrived from Palermo; and though from his dress he appeared to be in the English service, yet his accent and dialect were evidently Maltese, which circumstance strongly excited the curiosity of the worthy landlord, whose house was seldom visited by persons of such distinction. The stranger had asked the distance from Castrogiovanni to Palermo, and was told about seventeen miles. He then ordered dinner, and desired his attendants to see to the horses, as he should proceed that evening to the place of his destination. The host ventured to represent to his excellenza the danger of the route, at which the traveller laughed, and asked in what the mighty danger consisted.

'Had his excellenza never heard of Ludovico Lana?' inquired the innkeeper.

'Ludovico Lana! and who may he be?' was the reply.

'Oh signior! the most terrible brigand in the island, and who just now will be more furious than ever.'

'And why so?'

'One of his band has just been arrested and condemned to death here, in Castrogiovanni; and Ludovico is capable of setting fire to the town, and cutting all our throats.'

The stranger laughed at the alarm of his informant, and asked when the execution would take place.

'The day after to-morrow, no doubt,' replied the host.

'And at what hour?'

'Eight in the morning, excellenza, is the usual hour.'

'I have a great curiosity to see the execution,' observed the officer.

'Nothing is easier; your excellenza can return hither from Palermo to-morrow evening, and I will take care to provide a good place for you to witness the execution of this bandit. I have the honour to be acquainted with the judge, and can, I doubt not, procure you a seat by him.'

'Just the thing,' replied the stranger. 'I will return to-morrow night, and in the meantime you will take care to make the proper arrangements.'

My servant then went on to narrate the wonder of the host when about to prepare the table for his guest, at learning from the servants that they carried with them various articles of plate and linen for their master's service, who was not accustomed to the rude furniture of a Sicilian locanda, and saw with amazement the preparations made for his accommodation. His curiosity being excited to the highest degree, he contrived to learn that the stranger was a Maltese, enormously rich, who had obtained a high rank in the English service, and was called Colonel Sancta Croce.

The colonel soon after started, as he had said, for the residence of his friend Prince Paterno, leaving one of his servants with part of his baggage at the locanda, purposing to return the next night to be in readiness to witness the execution. Meanwhile the host of the White Cross had informed not only his friend the judge, but all the town, of the great personage who had become his guest, detailing his magnificence with no little exaggeration, and easily obtaining a promise of the place he sought to witness the execution. During the whole of the intervening day the only subjects of discussion in the town were the arrival of this great person at the White Cross, and the approaching event, many believing the assertions of innocence so stoutly maintained by the accused, from whom his confessor had obtained no avowal of guilt. The confessor himself seemed inclined to believe in the protestations of the condemned. At night another monk had an interview with him in the chapel where he was to pass the last hours of his existence, and remained with him till past eleven o'clock, declaring when he left him that he did not believe him to be guilty, and promising to pray for his deliverance. After this visitor had departed, the penitent seemed more tranquil and resigned than he had been at intervals during the day.

At midnight Colonel Sancta Croce arrived as he had promised at the locanda, and seemed perfectly satisfied with the arrangement he was informed his host had made for him to witness the spectacle of the next day. During the whole night the bells of all the churches and convents were tolled, to keep the good people of the town in mind of their duty to pray for the condemned; and at daybreak crowds began to assemble, and the peasantry to arrive from the neighbourhood. At seven o'clock the judge and other officials took their stations on a platform prepared for them, and were joined soon after by Colonel Sancta Croce, who was received with all the attention his wealth and rank demanded. At eight o'clock the bells again tolled forth, and announced the approach of the victim, who soon made his appearance mounted on an ass with his face towards the tail, preceded by the executioner, and surrounded by the Brothers of Mercy, whose especial duty it is to form a part on such melancholy occasions. The procession moved slowly along without any interruption, till it arrived opposite the spot where the authorities were seated, when suddenly the condemned gave a loud shout, and nodding with his head towards Colonel Sancta Croce (for his hands were tied behind his back), cried out to a monk who walked beside him, 'Father! father! there sits a gentleman who can save me if he will.'

'Where, my son?' asked the priest with no little amazement.

'There! there—by the judge, that officer in an English uniform—God has brought him here no doubt to save an innocent man—a miracle, father! a miracle!'

'A miracle! a miracle!' shouted the people who were near enough to catch the words; and 'a miracle! a miracle!' was repeated by the multitude as the word flew along their ranks. The executioner, however, seemed to have but little faith in the said miracle, and was proceeding to conduct the culprit to his fate, when the priest interfered, and advancing towards the judge, informed him that the condemned had recognised a gentleman near him whose evidence could clearly prove his innocence of the crime laid to his charge, and for which he was about to die, solemnly exhorting the magistrate to inquire into the affair.

'And who is this redoubtable witness?' asked the judge.

'The colonel!—Colonel Sancta Croce!' cried the poor culprit vehemently.

'Me!' exclaimed the colonel in amazement, 'me, my friend; you must be mistaken; and though you know my name, I have no knowledge of you whatever.'

'You have no knowledge of the man, colonel?' asked the magistrate.

'None, sir, on my word.'

'I thought so,' continued the judge; 'it is a mere excuse to delay the execution;' at the same time making a sign to the executioner to proceed.

'Oh colonel!' cried the unhappy wretch, 'do not send me thus to die when a word from you can save an innocent man; only let me ask you one question.'

'Hear him! hear him, colonel!' cried the mob; 'give him a fair hearing'

'Signior,' said the colonel to the judge, 'common humanity, I think, requires us to attend to his prayer; if he is seeking to deceive, you will easily detect him; it is only a few moments' delay'

'I will not refuse your excellenza,' said the judge; 'but I think it is scarcely worth the while to attend to him.'

'I ask the favour for my own satisfaction,' replied the officer.

The judge bowed and answered—'Be it as your excellenza pleases,' at the same time ordering the man to be brought near.

The poor fellow was as pale as death, and trembled violently.

'Now,' says the magistrate, 'ask your question; the colonel is kind enough to listen.'

'Excellenza,' said the condemned, addressing himself to the officer, 'you remember that you landed at Palermo from Malta on the 18th of last May?'

'I do not remember the precise day; but it was about that time,' replied the colonel.

'And does not your excellenza remember the porter who carried your luggage from the quay to the Hotel Inglese?'

'I certainly lodged in the Hotel Inglese, but have entirely forgotten the person of the porter who carried my luggage.'

'But you have not forgotten, signior colonel, that in passing along the Marino he was struck on the head by a bar of iron which a man was carrying on his shoulder, and very much cut?' at the same time thrusting forth his skull, and showing a wound not yet completely healed.

'You are right, perfectly right,' replied the colonel; 'I do remember the circumstance, now you recall it to my mind.'

'And your excellenza remembers,' exclaimed the culprit in a transport of joy, 'that, instead of the six carlini you promised me, you gave me two ounces?'

'All this is perfectly true,' answered the colonel in considerable surprise; and turning to the judge, he added—'if you will permit me, signior, I can verify these facts by turning to my book of memoranda?'

'Do so, colonel; do so,' replied the magistrate.

The colonel then produced a splendid pocket-book, and after turning over some of the pages, read aloud—'May the 18th—landed at Palermo at 11 A.M.; took a porter to carry my luggage, who was accidentally wounded in passing along the Marino. Lodged at the Hotel Inglese.'

'There, there!' exclaimed the prisoner in ecstacy; 'thanks be to the Holy Virgin.'

'In truth, sir,' continued the officer, turning to the magistrate, 'if the 18th of May be the day on which the crime is said to have been committed, I can bear witness that this man was in Palermo on that day, and could not have been on the road between Castrogiovanni and Catania, and must therefore be perfectly innocent.'

'Yes, yes! innocent, innocent!' cried the mob.

The judge, after some hesitation, ordered the man back to the prison.

'No, no,' exclaimed the multitude; 'set him free, set him free. He is not guilty, he is not guilty;' at the same time rushing forward, they seized him from the hands of his guards, and in an instant delivered him from the bands with which he was confined; whilst others, with a wonderful love of summary justice, began to assault the executioner with a volley of stones. The magistrate, knowing the frenzy of his countrymen, yielded without farther remonstrance; and the rescued prisoner was conveyed in triumph to the principal church to return thanks for his miraculous deliverance; after which ceremony he lost no time in taking his departure from the town, where he was seen no more. But the next day a letter was delivered to the judge by an unknown hand, and Ludovico Lana therein returned thanks to the authorities of the good town of Castrogiovanni for their great attention in giving him a place upon the platform, and listening to his evidence in favour of one of his band. The danger he had escaped, however, made such an impression upon the bandit, that he sought, and through the intercession of his priest obtained, a pardon, underwent the penance enjoined him by the church, and became as honest a man as most of his countrymen.

VISIT TO A 'RAGGED SCHOOL.'

'A RAGGED SCHOOL,' quoth the reader; 'pray, what kind of school is that?' A few words will suffice to answer this inquiry. A 'ragged school' is a Sunday school, established by private benevolence in a city district of the meanest kind, where every house is worn-out and crazy, and almost every tenant a beggar, or, perhaps, something worse. A school, moreover, in which no children are to be found who would be admitted into any other school; for, ragged, diseased, and crime-worn, their very appearance would scare away the children of well-conducted parents; and hence, if they were not educated there, they would receive no education at all.

In London there exist several 'ragged schools:' one situated in the very heart of St Giles's; another—the one we propose to sketch—established nigh that worse than St Giles's, Field-Lane, Smithfield—the headquarters of thieves, coiners, burglars, and the other outcasts of society. This Sunday school was founded in 1841, and originated in the benevolent efforts of Mr Provan, a hero in humble life. After much exertion, especially in overcoming the objections of the parents, who considered the reformation of their offspring as the loss of so much capital, forty-five young persons, varying in age from six to eighteen, were induced to attend the school. At present, the average attendance on Sundays exceeds a hundred. The school is also opened three times a-week, when instruction of an ordinary kind is imparted gratuitously by a lady. Most—we might say all—of the fathers of the scholars belong to what may be called the predacious class, and the mothers fallen characters, who bear deep traces of guilt and disease in their countenances. Many of the children have been incarcerated for felony—educated thereto by their parents, as the trade whereby they are to live; and the destiny of all, unless better principles shall be implanted at school than can be acquired at home, is the hulks or Norfolk Island. All honour, then, to the brave men and women who have consecrated the day of rest to the god-like task of rescuing their fellow-creatures from a life of shame and misery—to change the ruffian into an honest man!

The Smithfield 'ragged school' is situate at 65 West Street, a locality where vice and fever hold fearful sway. To open it in any other neighbourhood, would be to defeat the object of the projectors. The very habiliments of the boys, so patched, that the character of the original texture could scarcely be gleaned, would almost be sufficient to preclude their ingress to a more respectable neighbourhood, and make them slink back abashed into their loathsome dens. It follows, that the object of the promoters of the 'ragged school'—the in-gathering of the outcast—requires that it should be held amidst the homes of these outcasts. The house has that battered, worn aspect, which speaks of dissolute idleness; the windows are dark and dingy, and the street too narrow to admit a current of fresh air; and it needed, on the rainy day in March in which it was visited, but a slightly active imagination to call up visions of the robberies and murders which have been planned in it, and of which it has been the scene.

The entrance to the school was dark; and there being no windows to illuminate the rickety staircase, we stumbled into the school-room on the first floor before we were aware. On entering, the eye was greeted by a spectacle to which, from its mingled humour and pathos, the pencil of Hogarth could have alone done justice. We found a group of from forty to fifty girls in one room, and about sixty boys in another: the girls, although the offspring of thieves, quiet, winning, and maidenly; but the boys full of grimace and antics, and, by jest and cunning glances, evincing that they thought the idea of attending school fine fun. Foremost amongst them was a boy apparently aged seventeen, but as self-collected as a man of forty, of enormous head, and with a physiognomy in which cunning and wit were equally blended, whose mastery over the other boys was attested by their all addressing him as 'captain.' The boys had their wan, vice-worn faces as clean as could be expected, and their rags seemed furbished up for the occasion; whilst their ready repartee, and striking original remarks, and the electric light of the eye, when some peculiar practical joke was perpetrated, evinced that intellect was there, however uncultivated or misused. Unless we are greatly self-deceived, we beheld in this unpromising assemblage as good a show of heads as we have ever seen in any other Sunday school, and the remark is justified by what we learned with respect to the shrewdness generally evinced by these children. The predominant temperament was the sanguine, a constitution which usually indicates great love for animal exercise; and during the time we were present, they appeared as if they could not sit quiet one moment—hands, feet, head, nay, the very trunk itself, seemed perpetually struggling to do something, and that something generally being found in sheer mischief.

Hymns were occasionally sung to lively measures, the girls singing with a sweetness and pathos that sunk deep into the heart; but the boys were continually grimacing and joking, dovetailing into the hymns the fag-ends of popular songs, yet all the time attempting to look grave and sober, as if they were paying the most respectful attention. When the superintendent told the boys that he was about to pitch the tune, and that they must *follow* him, the boy before mentioned as the captain cried out, in a stage-whisper, 'Mr —— says we are to follow him; I wonder where he's going to?' a jest hailed with a general laugh by his confederates. During teaching, questions of an unanswerable character were submitted by the boys to their master; for example, 'If you were starving and hungry, wouldn't you steal?' 'What is the use of hanging Tapping; will that convert him?' Various other attempts were made by the captain to puzzle the teacher, and failing, he was heard to say, 'That's no go—he is too deep for us.'

Amongst these boys, however, were some to whom the word of kindness was evidently a 'word in season,' and who drank in the tender accents with which they were addressed—perchance for the first time—as if it were music to their souls. Then, again, were to be seen some poor puny lad, as gentle in mind as in body, who was obviously dying from unfitness to cope with the requirements of his circumstances—poor tender saplings, growing in an atmosphere which was too bleak for any but the forest oak to brave. Untrained, except to crime, as most of the children are, much good has already been effected. Most of the scholars can read, and books have been supplied suited to their circumstances; and that the books are read with the understanding, is proved by the questions submitted to their teachers. Due honour to their parents has been taught. Many have thus become a comfort to homes to which they hitherto had been an additional curse; and many a mother, herself regenerated through the prattle of her child, has declared, with streaming eyes, 'I thank God my girl ever went to school!' Some of the scholars have been partially clad by the Dorcas Society connected with the school; and the stress which has been laid upon personal cleanliness has served to educe proper feelings of self-esteem; no slight ingredient in civilisation. Notwithstanding their many eccentricities, the children are really attached to their teachers; the girls coming forward from natural impulse, and with true politeness giving an affectionate 'Good-by, teacher,' even to the visitor; and the boys ever striving to please, in spite of their prevailing love of fun. One outré but characteristic instance of this affection for their teachers may be noticed. A teacher, in passing through Field-Lane, was attracted by a pugilistic contest; when, on remonstrating with them on their folly, one of the most brutal came up to him in a fighting attitude. Suddenly, a boy rushed through the crowd, and cried in stentorian tones, 'You leave him alone, Bill, or I'll knock you down; don't you know that's my teacher?' If, then, to win the affections be the best prelude to the reformation of the debased, again we say, honour to those brave men and women who, despite the contempt and the slander of the Pharisee and the worldling, have not shrunk from trying to rescue from ruin the neglected youthful soul!

Our sketch ends here; but the 'ragged school' was not visited for the mere gratification of curiosity, nor is that the motive which has induced us to describe the scene. A question entered our minds as we pondered over this visit, and a practical answer to which by our readers is the chief aim of the writer—'Why is there not a "ragged school" in every large town of Great Britain?'

MEXICO AS IT IS AND AS IT WAS.

FIRST ARTICLE.

Those who have travelled first through the United States, and afterwards through Mexico, cannot fail to be struck by the different results which Anglo-Saxon and Spanish colonisation has produced. Spain in every instance, from causes which it would require more space than we can now devote to the subject to explain, has been the means of degrading rather than of advancing the countries which conquest has brought beneath her sway. In nothing is the contrast between the races more remarkable than on the point of population. In 1753 that of the United States was 1,051,000; in 1810, 7,239,814; in 1840, 17,069,453. In 1793 the population of Mexico was 5,270,029, while in 1842 it had only advanced to 7,015,509. At this rate, the Union might reach to the rank of a thickly-peopled land in a hundred years; Mexico would take 1200 to attain the same result. The two countries also differ much on the score of education. In Mexico, less than 687,000 can read and write, while amongst her neighbours there are not 500,000 who cannot do so; in the United States are 173 universities or colleges, with 16,233 students; 3242 grammar schools, with 164,159 students; 47,209 primary common schools, with 1,845,244 scholars, of whom, at public charge, are 468,264. In Mexico, while 180,000 dollars were spent for hospitals, fortresses, and prisons, and 8,000,000 for the army, only 110,000 were devoted to education. Of late, however, the prospect is brightening; and in every one of the parishes into which the city of Mexico is divided, is a school for boys and one for girls, supported by the town-council, where children are taught without charge, books and stationery being also furnished gratis. A normal school and Lancasterian company are in operation with considerable success; as also is a night school for adults, fully attended by citizens whose avocations occupy them during the day. The private schools are chiefly kept by foreigners, who find it a profitable employment. The first effect of this reformation will be, to sweep away the *evangelistas*, or letter-writers, who now, amid a population not three in a hundred of whom can write, drive a thriving trade. They may be seen, to the amount of about a dozen, on the curb stones of the eastern front of the Parian, near the Plaza. A huge jug of ink is placed before them; a board rests across their knees; a pile of different-coloured paper, cut valentine fashion, or adorned with pen and ink flourishes, is placed on it; and on a stool before them sits some disconsolate-looking damsel or heart-broken lover. As their principal customers are girls and youths, it is more than probable that love and intrigue are their most ready themes: a 'declaration can be bad for a rial, a scolding letter for a medio, and an upbraiding epistle' for a shilling. They are always bound to keep the secrets intrusted to them, and often indite epistles in relation to treason, assassination, and robbery.

There are two classes of clergy in the Mexican church—the rural clergy, who are notoriously the agents of charity and ministers of mercy, the advisers, friends, and protectors of their flocks, the defenders of the Indians, and the supporters of benevolent institutions, and consequently the poor clergy; then there are 2000 nuns, 1700 monks, and 3500 secular clergy, owning a property worth, at the lowest valuation, a hundred million of dollars, a sum capable of paying off the whole of the national debt. In a country where more than half the population is in a position beneath that of beggars, the following state of things appears out of place:—

'From the centre of the vast dome of Puebla de los Angelos depends the grand chandelier—a mass of gold and silver said to weigh *tons*. When this church was cleaned some years ago, the cost of purification alone was four thousand dollars. The altar affords the greatest display of Mexican marbles in the republic. The variety of colours is very great, among which is one of a pure and brilliant white, as transparent as alabaster. To the right of the altar is a figure of the Virgin Mary, nearly the size of life. Dressed in the richest embroidered satin, she displays strings of the largest pearls; round her brow is a crown of gold, inlaid with emeralds; her waist is bound with a zone of diamonds and enormous brilliants. The candelabras are of silver and gold, and so ponderous, that a strong man cannot move one. The Host is one mass of priceless and innumerable jewels.' In the cathedral of the city of Mexico is a rail of two hundred feet in length, four or five feet high, and of proportionable thickness, composed of gold, silver, and a small alloy of brass, and within it a figure of the virgin of Remedios, with three petticoats, one of pearls, one of emeralds, and the other of diamonds, worth three million of dollars. The church of Guadaloupe is even richer; and at Loretto the last supper is represented by figures, before whom is a pile of silver and gold plate.

Beside this splendour the Mexican people stand in rags; their diet is poor, their lodging miserable, their clothing coarse, and inadequate for the climate; and you enter Mexico city over disjointed pavements, with the water green and putrid in the stagnant gutters, festering in the middle of streets swarmed by ragged thousands, looking, says Meyer in his late work on Mexico,* more like a population of witches freshly dismounted from their broomsticks than anything else. The house of a city lepero—a term equivalent to Neapolitan lazzaroni—is a mere hovel of sun-burnt bricks, often worn by the weather to the shape of holes in the mud, and in the country are mostly built of split bamboos, set upright in the ground, with a steep roof thatched with palm leaves. The following from Meyer will give an idea of Mexican civilisation:—'Imagine a mud-hole surrounded by eight huts built of logs and reeds, stuck into the watery earth, and thatched with palm leaves. This was the stage breakfasting station on the road from Mexico to Cuernavaca. We asked for the house, and a hut a little more open than the rest was pointed out. It was in two divisions, one being closed with reeds, and the other entirely exposed, along one side of which was spread a rough board, supported on four sticks covered with a dirty cloth. It was the principal hotel.'

The miserable hovels in which the Indians are lodged are far below a dog-kennel, they being stowed away under a roof of thatch, stuck in the bare ground, with a hole left at one end to crawl in. Even the better sort are only composed of a few canes and a thatch. The inhabitants of the hovels above-described are equally wretched with their dwellings. In fact, the idea we have given us of the poor population of the city of Mexico is perfectly frightful. Blackened in the sun, their hair long and tangled, ignorant of the use of water, brush, or towel, putting on a pair of leathern breeches at twenty, and wearing them without change until forty, with, over all, a torn and blackened hat, a tattered blanket begrimed with abominations, with wild eyes, shining teeth, and features pinched by hunger, with bare breasts and arms, and, if females, two or three miniatures trotting behind, and one strapped on the back, the lepero (from *lepra*, leper), though not suffering from the malady, hang about the markets and pulque shops, quarrelling, drinking, stealing, and lying drunk, with their children crying with hunger around them. At night they slink off to the suburbs, and coil themselves up in their damp unwholesome lairs.

These of course compose the very lowest dregs of the population. The city of Mexico has also its working-class and tradesmen. First the aquador, or water-carrier, with two earthen jars, one suspended by a leathern belt thrown round his forehead, and resting on his back, and the other suspended from the back of his head in front of him, preserving the equilibrium. Meyer relates an anecdote of one of these worthies, not over-creditable to one of the actors, as the result might have been serious. 'An Englishman passing an aquador in the street, struck the jar on the fellow's back with his cane; it broke, and the weight of the other jar brought the poor carrier on his nose. He rose in a rage, but was calmed by a couple of dollars. "I only wanted to see whether you were exactly balanced, my dear fellow, and the experiment is worth the money."' Then there are pedlars, coffeehouse-keepers, old clothes, toys, and flower venders, sweetmeat makers, booksellers, and antiquity collectors; and, to return to the streets, the poor Indian may be seen with a huge coop of chickens and turkeys, or a pannier of oranges; then a woman with peas, or ducks, or fish, or potatoes; while another drives along a stunted ass. Most of the necessaries of life are supplied by hawkers. The beggars are a class too numerous to be overlooked. The city of Mexico swarms with them, and the capital usually employed is a sore leg, blindness, a decrepit father or mother, or a helpless child. One blind beggar, remarkably well dressed, was seen by Meyer to take up his place on a seat near the chief fountain of the Alameda every day at noon, attended by a couple of servants. A second had a burly porter to carry him, seated in a chair on his back. Many and many really miserable cases, however, throng the capital of the Montezumas.

The real Indian population even in the city of Mexico are superior to the leperos, especially those that ply their canoes between it and Chalco and Texcoco; and it is really a beautiful sight to behold their tiny vessels skim like floating gardens to the quays in the morning, and then in the afternoon the canals are covered with gay boat-loads of Indians passing homeward from market, dancing, singing, laughing, strumming the guitar, and crowned with wreathes of poppies. But, mixed in their races, degraded by the conquest, ground to the earth during the government of Spain, corrupted in spirit by an ignorant clergy, without education, lassoed like wild beasts when recruits are wanted for the army, their fate is sad and dreary. In fact, though slavery is abolished by law, yet are they slaves in reality. Mr Stephens describes a scene which fully substantiates this assertion. 'Looking into the corridor, we saw a poor Indian on his knees on the pavement, with his

* London: Wiley and Putnam.

arms clasped round the knees of another Indian, so as to present his back fairly to the lash. At every blow he rose on one knee, and sent forth a piercing cry; but no sense of degradation crossed his mind. Indeed so humbled is this once fierce people, that they have a proverb—the Indians only bear through their backs.' They form, in fact, a degraded caste; are subjected to the control of masters and overseers; are ignorant, intemperate; and all because they are *bonâ fide* slaves. The site of an Indian village, however, is pointed out to the traveller about three leagues from the high road near Cuernavaca, the inhabitants of which are almost in their native state. They do not permit the visits of white people; and, numbering more than three thousand, come out in delegations to work at the haciendas, being governed at home by their own magistrates, administering their own laws, and employing a Catholic priest once a-year to shrive them of their sins. The money they receive in payment of wages at the haciendas is taken home and buried; and as they produce the cotton and skins for their dress, and the corn and beans for their food, they seldom purchase at the stores. They form a good and harmless community of people, rarely committing a depredation upon the neighbouring farmers, and only occasionally lassoing a cow, which they say they do not steal, but take for food. If they are chased on such occasions, so great is their speed of foot, that they are rarely caught even by the swiftest horses; and if their settlement is ever entered by a white, he is immediately seized and conveyed beyond the limits of the settlement.

The food of the Indians in the country is simple enough—a handful of corn, a bunch of plantains, or pan of beans from the nearest bushes; and a traveller will on his journey meet with sorry fare. Eggs, beans, and bread, mutton and fish stew, mingled with onions, lard, garlic and chilé peppers, served up without knife or fork, and rarely with a plate, by a dirty waiter, Lima beans, turkey and peppers, tomales (a mixture of meal, red pepper, and meat, wrapped in husks of corn, and boiled), are luxuries which, when the wayfarer happens upon, he should appreciate highly. In the city of Mexico, however, other matters are to be found. Ducks, about fifteenpence a pair, are abundant, the lake of Mexico being covered with them. About 200,000 of these birds are annually killed by a species of infernal machine with three tiers of barrels. A very amusing narrative of duck-shooting we extract from Meyer, as quite novel:—'I was exceedingly surprised to find our guide waiting at his door, mounted on a bull! My first disposition was to laugh, but he prevented it by a smile, and a request to wait until we got among the *chichiquillotes*, and see what a sportsman his beast was. Tio is remarkable for his hunting strategy; and besides his bull (with which he hunts even in the mountains), he has invented a *pipe* that perfectly counterfeits the bleating of deer; and, by its sound, has often attracted a dozen round him while lying concealed in the forest. * * After wandering about for some time without starting game, Tio at last perceived a flock alight a hundred yards to the north of him. He dismounted immediately, waved his hand to us to remain quiet, crouched behind the bull, and, putting the animal in motion, both crept together till within gunshot. Here, by a twitch at his tail, the beast was stopped, and began munching the tasteless grass as eagerly as if gratifying a relishing appetite. Ignacio then slowly raised his head to a level with the bull's spine, and surveyed the field of battle, while the birds paddled about the fens unconscious of danger. Though within good shooting distance, Tio discovered that he had not a raking range; and, therefore, again dodging behind his rampart, put the bull in motion for the required spot. This attained, he levelled his gun and fired, honest Sancho never stirring his head from the grass! Several birds fell; while the rest of the flock, seeing nothing but an unbelligerent bull, flew about a dozen yards; and thus the conspiring beast and sportsman sneaked along, from shot to shot, until nearly the whole flock was bagged!' *

Beef in the city is about sixpence per pound, mutton a trifle more, ham five times as much, a turkey six shillings, potatoes sixpence a quart, bread threepence per pound, tea from six to nine shillings, coffee one, milk about the same as in London; but the great staple commodity is maize formed into tortillia cakes, which are made by soaking the grain in water with a little lime; when soft, the skin is peeled of, and then ground on a large block of stone. They then take some of the paste which ensues, and clap it between their hands, until they form it into light round cakes, which are afterwards toasted on a smooth plate called the comal, and ought to be eaten as hot as possible. Kendall, however, says they are tough, heavy, and unsavoury; 'and most excellent bread do the Mexicans make—white, light, and sweet—and why they spoil their corn by converting it into tortillias, is a mystery.' The sellers of these tough 'buckskin' victuals sit in lines along the curb of the side walks with their fresh cakes in baskets, covered with clean napkins to keep them warm; and as tortillias, with a little chilé boiled in lard, are indispensable twice a-day to the mass of the people, they have a ready sale. A few steps further on, another has a pan boiling over a portable furnace, and containing the required beans or chilé. The man squats down beside the seller, makes a breakfast or dinner-table of his knees, holds out his tortillia spread flat on his hand for a ladle of chilé, doubles up the edges of the cake, and so on until his appetite is satisfied. He who is better off owns a clay platter, into which he causes his frigoles, or chilé, or meat, to be thrown.

The national drink is pulque, which Meyer describes as like sour lemonade improved by the addition of cream of tartar; while Kendall, in his Santa Fé Expedition, says, 'it had the flavour of stale small beer mixed with sour milk.' The former, however, tasted some sent from Puebla, which was delicious. It is made from the *maguey aloe*, or *Agave Americana*. When the plant reaches seven years of age, it is usually ready to bloom. Upon the appearance of the first symptom of a bud, the centre stalk is cut out, and a bowl hollowed in the middle of the large leaves: into this for several days the juice of the plant exudes plentifully; and as the bowl fills at certain periods during the day, it is sucked into a long gourd by the Indian labourers, who transfer it from this to hog-skins. The outlay is calculated at about two dollars per plant, and the return from seven to ten. By distillation, a strong liquor is made from pulque, called mescal, the intoxicating influence of which tends much to the degradation of the lower classes in Mexico.

The dress of the lepero, and of the Indians, is the most scanty possible, being merely a few rags, and perhaps in the latter instance a thatch cloak of reeds; but the commonest woman of the middle classes has a fanciful petticoat and a reboso or shawl, which two articles constitute almost their whole costume. The costume and appearance, however, of some Indian girls near Jalapa must be striking. On their hair they bestow all their attention and care; two long braids fall from the back of the head, while two other braids, after circling the head twice, are fastened in front with a rose or some other flower. Their whole dress is a coarse woollen petticoat. Meyer once, however, knelt near a lady in church whose dress must have cost thousands. She wore a purple-velvet robe embroidered with white silk, white satin shoes, and silk stockings; a mantilla of the richest white blond lace fell over her head and shoulders, and her ears, neck, and fingers were one blaze of diamonds.

* A practice very similar existed, or still exists, in Scotland. Wild geese which in ordinary cases will not permit the sportsman to come within rifle reach of them, may be easily brought down by swan hail, if the individual take proper care to conceal himself between two bundles of straw on horseback, and then urge the horse in the direction in which the birds are feeding. Animals which seem to have an instinctive horror of man, have apparently little dread of any of their lowlier brothren.

A brief sketch of Mexico in the days of Cortes, and of the remaining characteristics of the people, must be reserved for another article. On both points the valuable work of Meyer gives ample details.

BIOGRAPHIC SKETCHES.

JOHN GOTTLIEB FICHTE.

EVERY one has heard of the so-called transcendental philosophy, which, from the time of its first promulgation by Immanuel Kant down to the present day, has exerted a powerful influence on the intellectual progress of Germany. In selecting for the subject of a biographical sketch one of its most distinguished teachers, we have not the slightest intention of giving any exposition of that profound metaphysical system. Fichte's career is in itself not devoid of interest, and we may perhaps gratify many of our readers by delineating the actual life of a German philosopher.

John Gottlieb Fichte was born at Rammenau, a hamlet of Saxony, on the 19th of May 1760. His family, though humble, had been long settled in his native place: its founder was a Swedish sergeant in the army with which Gustavus Adolphus invaded Germany. Having been dangerously wounded in some skirmish in the neighbourhood, this first of all the Fichtes was taken home, and carefully tended by a peasant of Rammenau. On his recovery, finding it impossible to rejoin his comrades, he remained with his benefactor, whose daughter he married, and on whose death he inherited a little copyhold, which is still in the possession of his descendants.

The father of the philosopher, besides cultivating his few roods of ground, was a weaver, and disposed of the ribbons, which were the chief produce of his loom, in Rammenau and its vicinity. Fichte was happy in his parents. Though poor, they were not uneducated, and both were of a religious, kindly, industrious disposition. Almost from his birth they learned to regard their little Gottlieb with peculiar feelings. A grand-uncle of the mother's, an aged and pious man, whose sayings were treasured up by his neighbours as of prophetic import, was present at the baptism, and when he knelt over the cradle to give his blessing, he declared that the infant would be the consolation and special joy of his parents. The death, immediately afterwards, of this venerated person, added weight to the prediction, and Fichte, as he grew up, was allowed more freedom than the other children, who had begun to follow him in quick succession. His parents hoped to see him, before they died, a clergyman, perhaps the clergyman of Rammenau itself. When the labours of the loom and the garden were at an end for the day, his father taught him to read. The child was active and earnest in doing all that was prescribed him, but of a tranquil and thoughtful nature. He loved to steal away from home, and ramble at will among the surrounding fields, and might be seen—his affectionate biographer and son assures us—for long periods 'standing and gazing steadfastly into the distance.' Sometimes, when his absence was protracted beyond sunset, one of the shepherds, who were accustomed to his strange solitary ways, would disturb his meditations, and conduct the tiny dreamer home. No man was less of a sentimentalist than the stern Fichte, yet in after-years he always looked back to those hours of early reverie as the fairest and happiest of his life.

He had reached his eighth year without having been sent to school. when a slight incident occurred which determined for ever his future career. Diendorf, the village pastor, made the boy, whose quiet ways he liked, come now and then to his house. On one occasion he happened to ask him if he remembered anything of the preceding Sunday's sermon, and was astonished to hear his own composition, fluently and pretty accurately repeated, flow from the lips of the little peasant. He mentioned the circumstance to the chief persons of the neighbourhood. Soon afterwards, a nobleman who admired Diendorf's preaching, the Baron von Miltitz, chancing in some company to express his regret at having missed the pastor's last discourse, it was said half-jokingly that there was a boy in the village who could repair the loss, and at last Fichte was sent for. He came, and, quite unabashed, began, as he was desired, to repeat what he recollected of the discourse: gradually, as he proceeded. he grew more and more vehement, and was forgetting the presence of his auditors, when the gentlemen, satisfied with the experiment, interrupted the stream of his oratory. But the good baron was touched by his warm feeling and ripe intelligence: he resolved that the boy should go home with him and receive a learned education. The parents were at first unwilling to send their child so young into the gay society of a nobleman's residence; but their scruples were overcome by the persuasions of Diendorf, and the kind promises of the baron himself, and Fichte was allowed to depart with his benefactor. He accompanied him to his estates, which were at some distance from Rammenau, and was then, after a brief stay, sent to live with the clergyman of Niederau, near Meissen. This person and his wife were without family: they received their young charge with pleasure, and treated him as if he had been a child of their own. Here Fichte lived for some years, not only happy but industrious. He became well grounded in the classical languages; and finally, at the age of thirteen, his teacher declaring that from him he had nothing more to learn, he was removed by the baron to Pforta, the best and most celebrated of the state seminaries of Saxony.

For Fichte the change from the quiet country parsonage and its kind inmates to the rigour of a public school was at first anything but pleasing. He had been accustomed all his life to live much in the open air, but at Pforta the seclusion was almost unremitting: once a-week only the pupils were allowed exercise, and then their very sports were conducted under the eye of an usher. There prevailed, too, at that seminary, the system which in this country is called 'fagging,' and Fichte fell to the share of one of those brutal tyrants whom such a system alone can form among the young. Disgusted with the place, he determined to run away; and one day, after a prudent study of the map of Saxony, he made his escape, and took the road to Naumburg. All at once he remembered a saying of his good old teacher's, that every enterprise in life should be begun by prayer. He fell upon his knees by the road-side, and then the thought of his parents' sorrow when they should hear of his flight, overpowered him with remorse. He returned immediately to school. His absence had been observed, and he was taken before the rector, who, however, on hearing his simple story, not only remitted his punishment, but gave him in charge to another and a kinder master. From this time, no longer cramped by a slavery worse than it seems, he applied himself to his studies with successful vigour. At Pforta, with all its faults, there was every encouragement for a willing learner, and Fichte became an excellent scholar. Now, too, he began to know that there were other books in the world than those of Greece and Rome. He found means to procure some odd volumes of Wieland, Goethe, and Lessing, which he read in secret with delight. The last of these writers was his chief favourite: indeed so great at this time was his enthusiasm for Lessing, that he resolved, so soon as he should arrive at the university, to wander forth and seek personal communion with that keen and genial thinker.

In his nineteenth year he repaired to the university of Jena; but soon after his arrival, the saddest cares interposed to prevent his visit to Lessing. The Baron von Miltitz died, and Fichte found that if he wished to study, he must trust to his own diligence, and not to the miserable pittance which, at irregular intervals too, was all that the kind nobleman's heirs chose to send him. For six years he managed to keep alive. During the first four he qualified himself for the degree of 'Candidate of Theology;' but the incessant exertions requisite to gain a subsistence, left him latterly no time for the studies that might have enabled him to pass his final examination before the Saxon Ecclesiastical Consistory. No details have been given us of his privations, and we cannot therefore compare them with what we know to have been those of many a scholar—our own Dr Adam, for instance, who was accustomed, when attending Edinburgh college, to live during three months upon a single guinea. Fichte's biographer declares the sufferings of those probationary years to have been intense, yet indeed considers them for him more in the light of a blessing than a curse. In the opinion of his son, the hard conflict he had to maintain with poverty and famine developed in him, as nothing else could have done, that independence of spirit and resolute unflinching perseverance by which he was afterwards to effect so much, on a far wider scale, in the highest provinces of thought. Towards the close of his twenty-eighth year, his destitution seems to have reached its height, and he abandoned the hope, that he had long cherished, of becoming one day the pastor of some quiet Saxon village. Too proud to ask for assistance, he saw nothing before him but death by starvation; and as he walked homewards on the eve of his twenty-ninth birthday, he doubted if he should live to see another. But to Fichte, as to so many others, help came when most wanted and least looked for. On arriving at his lodging he found a letter from Weisse,* with the offer of a tutorship in Zurich. He hastened to thank his friend, who perceived his emotion, and inquired the cause. Fichte's pride gave way. The good Weisse cheered him not only with words but deeds, and helped him through the three hard months which were still to elapse before he entered on his situation.

On the 1st of September 1788, Fichte found himself in Zurich. His pupils were a little boy and girl, the children of a wealthy innkeeper, who resigned them altogether to his care. But their other parent thought that Fichte wished to over-educate her children, and during the two years that he remained with them, she tried in all ways to thwart his efforts. Fichte saw that she, as well as his pupils, stood in need of reform. To effect this, he hit upon a plan which may appal our Scottish tutors: he kept a journal of her behaviour to the little ones and to himself, which he laid before her weekly, pointing out whatever in her conduct he thought required amendment. His duties occupied him the principal part of the day; the evening he spent in literary composition (as yet his philosophical talent remained latent), or in the pleasant society of the place. With the worthy and whimsical Lavater he formed an acquaintance which soon ripened into intimacy. This led, during his stay in Zurich, to a far more important connexion: Lavater introduced him to the weekly parties of a postmaster named Rahn, in a union with whose eldest daughter, Joanna Maria (the god-daughter, and, by the mother's side, niece of the poet Klopstock), Fichte was to find the highest earthly happiness of life. This gifted and affectionate lady was four years older than himself; both were past the age of youthful intoxicating passion, and the attachment which sprung up between them was grounded on a clear discernment of each other's genuine worth. Fichte became her accepted lover, and as his relations with his employers grew daily more painful, he left Zurich in the April of 1790, with letters from Lavater and Rahn to important personages at Stuttgard and Weimar, in the hope of obtaining a situation as reader at a court, or the superintendence of some young nobleman's university studies.

He met with no encouragement at Stuttgard, and proceeded to Weimar with the letters given him by Lavater for Herder and Goethe. Unhappily, Herder was seriously ill, and Goethe had gone to Italy, so that Fichte saw himself again thrown upon the world. He went to Leipsic to seek a livelihood in that great book mart as an author by profession. He endeavoured, without success, to establish a sensible journal, and to find a purchaser for a volume of essays: he began a tragedy, and, what to those who know the man will seem strangest of all, he even wrote some tales. All his efforts were fruitless, and he was forced to betake himself to his old resource of private teaching, little dreaming what a priceless boon this despised occupation was about to put within his reach. One of the Leipsic students came to engage him for a daily lesson in the transcendental philosophy. Fichte knew Kant only by name and some vague reports; but now duty itself compelled him to study his works. To his surprise, he found, after the first attempts in the obscure writings of the Königsberg philosopher, a system of metaphysics and morals of such importance, as immediately to appear to him to deserve the careful study of all thoughtful persons. Henceforth, however changeful his outward lot, he had one fixed object before his inward eye; namely, to diffuse among his fellow-men a knowledge of what he considered the only true philosophy. During the autumn and following winter, he studied and re-studied Kant's principal works, and exercised himself in committing to paper their chief doctrines in the simpler and modified form which, after laborious reflection, they gradually acquired in his mind. He passed these months not only in cheerful activity, as a teacher and a student, but with the brightest anticipations; for it was arranged that in the spring he should be united to his betrothed, take up his residence with his father-in-law, freed from the pressure of actual want, bring himself by his pen before the public, and thus strive to secure for the future an honourable existence.

The April of 1791, however, found Fichte not flying on the wings of love to Zurich, but trudging on foot to a tutorship at Warsaw. The house in which Rahn's all was invested had failed, and father and daughter were uncertain how much might be saved from the wreck of their fortune. Fichte entered Warsaw on the 8th of June, to quit it on the 25th. He had formed his engagement with a Polish nobleman, a certain Count von P——, or rather with his wife, a gay brilliant woman of the world. She had been accustomed, we suppose, to the brisk, trenchant kind of tutor so amusingly described by Mr Kohl in his Russia, and a specimen of which would make Dominie Sampson ejaculate his loudest 'prodigious.' She did not like poor Fichte's French accent, and there was not vivacity enough in his manner; so with a trifling sum, by way of compensation, the metaphysician was dismissed. That peculiar veneration for wisdom and wise men which had made him, when a schoolboy, meditate a pilgrimage to Lessing, now directed him, with higher views and deeper knowledge, to Königsberg, which was not far distant, and where Kant resided. His first interview disappointed him. He had come without a letter of introduction, and the calm old philosopher received his enthusiastic disciple rather stiffly. Fichte returned to his lodging, and in less than a month had completed a profound philosophical treatise, which he sent to Kant, from whom, on his next visit, he met with the warmest reception. But alas! his little stock of money was now drawing to an end; and the bookseller to whom Kant would have recommended his work was absent. We have now before us the letter which, in this emergency, he wrote to his master, requesting a small loan that he might return to Leipsic; and its calm dignity, far more touching than any pathos, might move, considering who was the writer, the heart of a Stoic. Kant declined: he himself, he assured Fichte, had been without funds for a fortnight.

This was the second time that Fichte had been brought to the verge of actual want; happily it was the last; and already, though he knew it not, better days were at hand. He had made some vain struggles to obtain private teaching, when suddenly a Königsberg

* A well-known German writer of children's books, &c.

acquaintance procured him a tutorship in the family of a nobleman near Dantzic. Recommended by Kant, it was with an ample salary that he accepted it; and he found himself in his new situation treated more as a friend than a dependent. Still greater happiness was in store for him. The bookseller returned to Königsberg, and consented to publish his work. Through some oversight it appeared anonymously. Coming from Königsberg, and written quite in the spirit, and with all the metaphysical acuteness of Kant, it was at once attributed to him. He, indeed, hastened to declare the real author; but meanwhile the book had obtained the sale which it deserved, and the enthusiastic criticisms already passed upon it could not be revoked. Nor was this all. The Rahns had recovered, and very advantageously invested a considerable portion of their property. There was nothing now to delay Fichte's union. Accordingly, in the summer of 1793, he bade farewell to his kind friends the Count and Countess von Krokow, and proceeded to Zurich, where, on the 23d of October, the marriage at last took place. After the vicissitudes of so agitated a life, Fichte was now to enjoy comparative repose. He was happy with the wife of his choice: at one stride he had gained the summit of philosophic fame, and the chief thinkers of Germany became his friends and correspondents. He had leisure for study and reflection. During the months which now passed at Zurich, he elaborated that modification of Kant's philosophy to which he gave the name 'Doctrine of Science;' and in improving and teaching which, his best faculties and remaining days were henceforth successfully employed. From this point onwards, Fichte's career is far better known to the British reader than the portion of it we have been describing; we shall therefore compress as much as possible the rest of our narrative.

Towards the close of 1793, Reinhold, the professor of the Kantian philosophy at the university of Jena, removed to Kiel, and his friend Fichte was at once invited to supply his place. Fichte wished to delay his acceptance of the offer for a twelvemonth, which he purposed to spend in perfecting his theory; but the Weimar authorities laughed at his scruples, and replied that the university would suffer by the long vacancy of so important a chair; and in the May of 1794 he entered on his professional duties. Jena was then the most numerously attended of the German universities, and among its professors were the most distinguished teachers of Germany. On this account, and from the popularity of his predecessor, Fichte's arrival had been looked for with anxiety. At his opening lecture the hall was crowded to excess; but both then and afterwards, the clearness which he gave to the most abstract of subjects, his lofty eloquence and impressive manner, far exceeded the expectations which his best friends had formed of his success. At Jena his situation was dignified and comfortable. In addition to other intimacies, he became the friend of Goethe and Schiller, and was enlisted by the latter among the contributors to his new periodical, 'The Hours.' Fichte was indefatigably earnest in discharging his duties as a professor. Besides sharpening in metaphysical inquiries the intellectual faculties of his scholars, he laboured to purify and exalt their moral feelings and habits. With this view he delivered, over and above his ordinary course, a series of lectures 'On the Vocation of the Scholar:' these were afterwards printed; and we can easily understand the abiding and ennobling influence which they are said to have exerted on his youthful and ingenuous hearers. One of his methods of rewarding the exertions of his class seems to us so novel and important, that we cannot refrain from mentioning it. He had established, in conjunction with Niethammer, a philosophical journal, and in that widely-circulated work he inserted from time to time a few of the most remarkable of the essays written for him by his students. Those who best know what young men are, will most appreciate the kindness and judgment displayed in this plan of Fichte's.

After five years of usefulness at Jena, some unpleasant disputes, which we have no inclination to detail here, forced him to resign his professorship, and in the July of 1799 he took up his residence at Berlin. During the next six years he lived a quiet but inwardly laborious life: he lectured occasionally to private audiences, and published several works: in both these enterprises his aim being so to expound the new philosophy that it might be understood by every person of intelligence, however unaccustomed to metaphysical inquiries. In 1805 he was appointed by the Prussian government professor of philosophy at Erlangen, where, in the summer of that year, he delivered that remarkable course of lectures 'On the Nature of the Scholar,' to which the attention of thinkers has been so strongly drawn by Mr Carlyle in the Edinburgh Review. The following year Prussia, after long wavering, determined on a war with France. Fichte saw, in the success of his adopted country, the only hope for the emancipation of the continent from the despotism of Napoleon, and he resolved that what help he could give should not be wanting in the struggle. He requested leave to accompany the army, that he might animate by words the heroism of the soldiers, since he could not, 'like Æschylus and Cervantes,' take his sword and 'fight in the ranks.' He was thanked, but his offer was declined. The campaign ended with the fatal day of Jena and Auerstadt, and a French army marched upon Berlin. Some of the officials and literary men of the Prussian capital remained, to submit to the conqueror, and take service under him; but Fichte was not among these, and he fled to Königsberg. He returned in the autumn of the ensuing year, and amid the general despondency, was almost the only one who still dared to protest aloud against foreign oppression. During the winter months of 1807-8, he delivered his celebrated 'Addresses to the Germans' in a public building of Berlin, where his voice was often overpowered by the roll of the French drums in the street beside him. In 1813, the year of the Liberation War, he renewed his former proposal, and with similar success; but as his offers had sprung less from vanity than from a lofty zeal, he was not pained by the refusal. And now when hostilities broke out, his wife too came forward to advance, in the only way permitted to a woman, the general weal. The military hospital of Berlin became crowded with sick and wounded; the authorities appealed to the inhabitants for help, and she was among the first to obey the call. 'By a courageous effort,' says her son, 'she vanquished her first repugnance to approach the stranger sick; and soon this employment appeared to her a sacred vocation, to which, at all risks, she was resolved to devote all her energies.'

Meanwhile, during these years, Fichte had been steadfastly toiling at his appointed task, the perfecting of his philosophical theories. In 1813 his system had reached its highest clearness in his mind, and he thought himself on the point of procuring for it a mode of expression so simple, that even a child, to use his own words, would be able to comprehend it. He proposed to spend the summer of 1814 in some quiet rural spot, and there, in peaceful seclusion from the world, attain the long-sought-for result. But 'the pale messenger' was at hand, and the wish had to remain unfulfilled. Towards the close of 1813, after many months of attendance on the sick, his wife caught, in the course of her laudable labours, an infectious fever, from which she recovered only to see her husband laid prostrate by it. Fichte was taken ill in the first week of January 1814, and on the 27th he was no more. His wife survived him five years, and was then laid in the grave beside him. The place of their interment is in a churchyard close to one of the gates of Berlin, and a lofty obelisk surmounts it with the inscription—'And they that be wise shall shine as the brightness of the firmament; and they that turn many to righteousness as the stars for ever and ever.'*

In person, Fichte was below the common height, but

* Daniel xii. 3.

of a strongly-knit and muscular frame. His mien and gestures, like his words, betokened earnestness and sincerity. He had only one child, a son, who is, or till very lately was, a professor of philosophy at Bonn, and from whose biography of his father the foregoing sketch has been taken.

REMINISCENCES OF MARDI-GRAS, OR SHROVE-TUESDAY, IN PARIS.

The inhabitants of the French metropolis will not allow themselves to be deterred from going through the regular routine of merry-making, even under the most unfavourable circumstances. On Shrove-Tuesday, 1831, *emeutes*, or riots, with all their frightful accompaniments, were raging in one quarter of the city. A religious edifice was ransacked, the sacristy turned into a masquerade-warehouse; and the patriot *chiffonnier*, or rag-gatherer, donned the priest's richly-embroidered vestments; whilst, at the very same time, the Boulevards were crowded with laughing groups gazing at the fooleries there enacted.

On that occasion a young sprig of fashion, who had just quitted the scene of devastation, was heard to exclaim, on entering the drawing-room of a hotel on the Boulevard des Italiens—'The church of St Germain l'Auxerrois is a prey to the mob!—they are violating the sanctuary!'

'Frightful!—abominable!' responded a beautiful and elegant lady. 'But look! look!—what a charming mask; and how lightly that little harlequin trips along; 'tis truly delightful!'

Thus, frivolity within sight is often so dazzling as to impair the moral vision, rendering us indifferent to surrounding evils.

In 1834, the expectations of the gay Parisians had been raised to the highest pitch with regard to the carnival, although certain profound reasoners declared that this diversion was progressively losing its attractions, in proportion to the improvement in the morals and tastes of the people; whilst others asserted that there was so much distress, that few had either the power or the inclination to play a part in such frolics. Nevertheless, this festive scene was not marked by any diminution of gaiety.

There was the usual assemblage of shepherds and shepherdesses, *poissardes*, clowns, and harlequins, who gesticulated, bawled, squeaked (Punch was also present), and leaped, as they were bound to do. The equipages were numerous and diversified; though, with few exceptions, not remarkable for elegance. Among those which attracted peculiar attention was an open carriage drawn by six horses, and preceded by mounted lacqueys playing upon French horns, and followed by a numerous and boisterous cavalcade. This carriage was crowded with splendidly-attired maskers, who distributed *bonbons* in profusion to the fair onlookers, and attacked their rivals with Neapolitan eggs filled with flour, which, on the light shell of sugar being broken, by coming into contact with the heads or shoulders of the recipients, powdered them profusely, to the great delight of the bystanders: the compliment was, however, returned with interest, the aggressors being still better pelted with similar projectiles.

But a more novel sight than this was a large and handsome landau, to which were harnessed four beautiful white horses decorated with green ribbons. In this vehicle were several of the young pilgrims of Prague, as they were called, from the circumstance of those youths of good family having visited the ancient capital of Bohemia, to offer their protestations of fidelity to the fallen monarch, Charles X., and the exiled royal family: the party was completed by some other dashing legitimatists.

One of the pilgrims was habited as a *Garde-Française*, with a large white cockade in his hat; another appeared in a Highland dress, similar to that worn (according to the print-shops) by the youthful Henry V. during his stay at Edinburgh; a third wore the costume of a cavalier of the time of our Charles I. The cortège passed several times up and down the Boulevards, and once stopped under the windows of the *cercle*, or club, at the corner of the Rue de Grammont, and saluted a venerable duke, father to one of the young Carlists: it was even said that cries of *Vive Henri V.!* were uttered.

This political promenade did not occasion the slightest disturbance: the people seemed determined to preserve their good humour; and they displayed as little animosity towards the Henriquinquistes (or Henry-the-fifth-ites) as they did affection for a solitary hero of July, who, mounted on a lean and miserable hack, ambled along the Boulevards. This living emblem of the three glorious days wore an old jacket turned inside out; but his shoulders were adorned with two fine epaulettes, and on his head was an officer's cocked-hat. His Rozinante was not encumbered with a saddle, and the rider's long thin legs dangled on either side of the sorry steed. The hero of July did not swagger about, but quietly moved on in the middle of the road; his subdued demeanour and turned jacket being no doubt intended as a satire on some of the actors in the memorable drama of July 1830.

Even Algiers had its representatives; for a small group, disguised as Arabs, and very well mounted, caracoled in true Bedouin style.

The procession of the *bœuf-gras*, or prize ox, took place as usual. This ceremony is curious. The prize ox—a remarkably fine one, highly fed, but not unwieldy—adorned with ribbons and garlands, was led by two journeymen butchers habited as pages: on the animal's back sat a handsome little boy in the guise of Cupid, with his bow and quiver full of arrows; his wings being of fine gauze bedecked with spangles: immediately afterwards followed an elegant car drawn by two horses richly caparisoned. In the car were three or four women, masked and attired as heathen goddesses: then came a goodly troop of horsemen, equipped as knights, and attended by squires on foot; the former were master butchers, and the latter their men: there were a few more attendants—brawny fellows, personating savages, with skins of wild beasts thrown over their shoulders, and wielding large knotty clubs.

This grotesque procession started from the premises of the butcher to whom the prize ox, or *bœuf-gras*, belonged, and traversed certain districts notified in a printed programme sold about the streets a day or two before Shrove-Tuesday. It proceeded to the Tuileries, at the windows of which palace the king and royal family were assembled to receive the homage of the *bœuf-gras*. The tractable animal had been taught to kneel down when required, by a gentle pressure from one of the men who led him: he bent his knees to the king of the French, Louis-Philippe, on the very same spot, and in precisely the same way, as his predecessors had done before the preceding monarch, Charles X. Cupid kept his seat gracefully, and bowed his little round head: the other mythological personages made their obeisances; and the butcher-knights caused their steeds to curvet as they passed in array before the royal personages, who returned all these salutes most graciously. The procession then proceeded to complete its route, visiting different public authorities and persons of note on its way back to the house of the owner of the *bœuf-gras*.

Notwithstanding the threatening appearance of the weather, the footpaths of the Boulevards were crowded with maskers and spectators. Upon the whole, it was a gay and enlivening scene—that is to say, it was so for a time, after which a painful feeling arose in one's breast; and on looking at the great number of clowns capering about in their white linen jackets and long loose sleeves, outshooting their hands by several inches, and hundreds of strange party-coloured figures, some grave, others gay, and all apparently assuming characters foreign to their natural ones; most of them laughing without gaiety, jumping, yet not seeming amused, and grinning without fun, one was tempted to exclaim—'This is bedlam broke loose; what a frenzy of forced pleasure!'

In the afternoon a cold drizzling rain came on, and a more sudden metamorphosis never followed the waving of Harlequin's wooden sword than was produced by this aqueous visitation. A noise as though a large flock of pelicans had flown up into the air out of some reedy marsh, was succeeded by the display of thousands of umbrellas, red, blue, green, and black, which eclipsed the vast body of pedestrians. Looking down from a balcony on the party-coloured mass in undulatory motion, seeking to move on in different directions, we recurred to our boyish days, when we were wont to amuse ourselves by gazing upon the ever-varying sea through the coloured glasses of a quadrant.

The usual masked balls took place; but as all sublunary things must pass away, so the carnival terminated with the night of Mardi-Gras.

DURATION OF LIFE IN THE PEERAGE AND BARONETAGE.

In a lately published number of the Journal of the Statistical Society, we observe a paper purporting to be an inquiry into the 'Duration of Life among the Families of the Peerage and Baronetage of the United Kingdom.' The facts, which are gathered from the books of the peerage and baronetage, bring out results which could not have been anticipated. The general belief is that these classes, by having at command all the means by which health may be preserved, and the best advice and assistance in case of illness, generally attain a longer life than other members of the community. This is found not to be a correct inference. A strict comparison of tables shows that the expectation of life among the families of the peerage and baronetage, from 20 years of age upwards, is really less than in the whole of England. On the other hand, the expectation of life is greater than among the inhabitants of the metropolis and Liverpool. The writer of the article confesses that it is difficult to offer any satisfactory solution of the results brought out by the comparative tables.

The inquiry has also been of use in determining 'another question of some little interest—namely, are there any particular ages marked by an excessive mortality? The ancients, it is well known, attached great importance to certain ages, attributing to them unusual danger and a high mortality. These ages, which were designated as the climacteric years, are the 49th, the 63d, and the 81st, entitled respectively the lesser climacteric, the climacteric, and the grand climacteric. Although the fanciful value attached to the number seven and its multiples is perhaps a sufficient explanation of the importance attached to the first two periods, it may possibly have happened that a rude observation of the ages at which death took place, bore its part in the establishment of the theory. It may therefore be worth while to submit this theory to the test of facts. The inquiry, indeed, derives an additional interest from the occasional revival in modern times of the superstitious importance formerly attached to certain numbers. On referring to Table I., it will be seen that the number of deaths opposite the age of 49 is somewhat in excess of the numbers in several preceding and succeeding years. It exceeds by six deaths the number at the age of 47, which is the highest number for all the earlier ages; and by eight deaths the highest number for the next five years. The precise numbers are—at 49 years 45 deaths, at 47 years 39 deaths, and at 51 years 37 deaths. The number of deaths at the age of 63, on the other hand, falls short of the number in the year preceding by two deaths, and only exceeds the number in the 61st and 65th year by three deaths. Again, the number of deaths at 81 years of age, though somewhat greater than in the year following, and higher than in every preceding year, falls greatly short of the number in the year immediately preceding. Of the three climacteric years, then, there is only one (49, or the lesser climacteric,) which displays any excess of deaths, and even in this case the excess is not so large but that it may safely be attributed to a coincidence. From all that has been now stated, it would appear that there is no sufficient reason for attaching to the climacteric years an unusual importance, though there seems to be a slight increase of deaths at or about these years.'

As a contribution to the data on which life-assurance tables are formed, we consider the paper before us of no inconsiderable value.

TRAITS OF THE NORTH TWO HUNDRED YEARS BACK.

The Inverness Courier has lately published a series of articles stringing up extracts from a manuscript history of the Family of Fraser, written about the year 1666 by Mr James Fraser, minister of Kirkhill, on the Beauly Firth. Some passages quoted from this memoir are so curious as pictures of the manners of the time, that we are tempted to bring them before a wider circle of readers. Civilisation had at that time made no great way in the north of Scotland; yet the nobles and chiefs of the country lived in a style of imposing magnificence.

'In the following account of the funeral of Simon Lord Lovat, in 1632, there seems to have been a great muster of the neighbouring clans:—

'"1632.—This great man died the 13th of April, to the incredible grief of all his clan and kindred. The Frasers of Lovat resolving to desert their burial-place in Beauly Minster, interred Lord Simon's corpse in Kirkhill, at the east end of the church, with a pale of curious timber-work above his grave, and erected that aisle and steeple there as their tomb, which now we see joined to the church. The funeral was sumptuous and splendid. Nothing was wanted to make it singularly solemn, regular, and orderly. The season was very inviting to the neighbouring clans to assemble. Mackintosh had 600 men well-appointed; the Grants 800; the Mackenzies 900; the Rosses of Balnagown 1000 pretty men; the Frasers a thousand and more; the Camerons, Macdonells, and Munroes, were not under 1000, well-ordered. Such a funeral was never seen or heard of in our country, computed to be above 5000 foot and horse. The arable ground all under braird was trod like a common foot-road all betwixt Bunchrew and the church of Wardlaw, yet it was observable that no such fertile fruitful crop was ever known upon the same lands as God's providence sent that year."

'Instances of summary justice were of frequent occurrence in the Highlands, and under the date 1633 we find a case recorded. In that year several of the younger sons of the gentry obtained commissions in the army "for the Swedish wars," among whom was Thomas Fraser, younger of Belladrum, who induced many of the Highlanders to enlist. One of his recruits, Donald M'William, deserted to the hills of Glenconvinth, and was pursued by Alexander Urquhart, "my Lord Lovat's chief gentleman." The deserter stabbed Urquhart with his dirk, and he died on the spot. The murderer was afterwards decoyed into the house of one Thomas Fraser, who promised to protect him; but, calling in two gillies, this treacherous host cut off the man's head, "which the gillies brought to Lovat." How the bloody present was received is not recorded.

'The following notice of the state of the medical art in the north of Scotland occurs in the year 1636:—"Doctors and persons of skill we had not then in the north; only a few common chirurgeons and traversing sharitans (charlatans) out of Ireland. There was one Mr John Sheils, vulgarly termed Dr Sheils, that had past some experiments in the country, and this fellow was called to Lovat by my lord and lady's desire. And at first view he confidently engaged to cure her [Lady Lovat], but quite the contrary. After his long stay in the family, and using potions and topical applications, she grew worse and worse." The dissolution of the monasteries would, in this respect, be a loss to the Highlands, for the monks were generally skilled in medicine. It is curious, however, to find Irish travelling doctors at that time wander so far in quest of practice.

'The following is what we should now call a curious coincidence. "1638.—Now is the marriage of John, Earl of Sutherland, with Mistress Anna Fraser, the Lord Lovat's daughter, going on; and it was notour [notorious] that, two years before, the earl passing this way with his first wife, Lady Jean Drummond, to pay a visit to my Lord Lovat, at the church stile of Wardlaw, riding by, the earl caught a fall with his horse, flat upon the shipping rock. His lady gave a shout, saying, 'God save you, my heart! You will be either married or buried at this church;' and so now it happened, by a good Providence, that he was married to Lady Anna Fraser, in the church of Wardlaw, and consummated a solemn wedding feast at Lovat."

'Weddings and funerals, those great landmarks in family history, are described with suitable dignity and minuteness by our local chronicler. There is a circumstantial fulness in some of his narratives of these events which presents every feature of the scene before us, though his devotion to the house of Fraser may have sometimes led him to colour his pictures too highly. We subjoin an account of the marriage of the Master of Lovat in the reign of Charles I. "1642.—The marriage betwixt Hugh Fraser, Master of Lovat, and Anna Leslie, Lord Alexander of Leven's daughter, is at length solemnised and consummated at Holyrood House, April 30, 1642. It may seem an extravagant rant to speak of the glory and expense of this sumptuous wedding feast, where eleven peers were present, besides general persons, barons, and gentlemen. All May and most of June were spent in visits and treats in city and country—those great persons being invited and regaled by all sorts of relations and acquaintances, even to the astonishment of such of their retinue as accompanied them from house to house. About the close of June, the new married couple came off from Edinburgh, accompanied with a noble train of peers and gentlemen—the Earl of Wemyss, Lords Leven, Boyne, Ruthven, Sinclair; and, coming through Moray, they were punctually attended and feasted by all the lairds and gentry. They paid a visit to old Lady Lovat, and that night to Dalcross, where they were well lodged and accommodated. The castle being the lady's own as her mansion-house, it was proper she should see it, and abide a night in it in transitu; and herself was heard to say to her friends and convoy, that they were most welcome to her habitation, and they were most cheerfully treated there at a great rate. Here the gentlemen of the name of Fraser met them, convoying their young chief in state through Inverness, where they were most sumptuously treated with all sorts of wines at the Cross, and tables covered. Provost Forbes acquitted himself to purpose. The Cuthberts now were great at Inverness; they mustered the train-bands of the town in the streets to keep off the rabble, and attended those noble persons to take a view of the castle, which was then in good order indeed. After this compliment to the Master of Lovat and his crowd of convoy at Inverness, through the streets, they went over the famous wooden bridge, where there were 400 young gentlemen in arms, well-appointed, on the Green, to conduct them forward. Some of the Lowlanders never saw such a sight of Highlanders in arms, and all present declared that the best peer in the nation might be vain and glory in such a brave guard and attendance, all of his own name. At Bunchrew, Inverallochy gave them a welcome and genteel treat. Thence to Lovat, where they arrived at their journey's end in health and safety. At the gate, my Lord Lovat, with twenty brave gentlemen of his own name, met them: and pray what could be wanting here for preparation and feasting?—liquors of all sorts, mirth, music, and good management of all things. This was a wonderful fruit year, and abundance of all kinds, field and garden fruits, berries and cherries, summer pears and pippins, such varieties and plenty, that the Lothian and Fife gentlemen declared they came not to visit the rude Highlands, but the cultivated Canaan! They admired the orchards of Lovat and Beanly, and the fishing of the river and linn was charming. They had hunting, fishing, fowling, archery—good divertisements. Nor was tilting, riding, jumping, or combating wanting; for men began now to learn the use of arms, and, alas! soon after they got sad trial of such. The Earls of Sutherland, Balnagown, and Fowlis, came here to visit the lords, and as there were good fare and cheer, so there was very jovial facetious society."

'The ravages committed by Montrose's army in 1646 are strikingly described by the annalist in a few picturesque words. "Betwixt the bridge-end of Inverness and Guisachan, sixteen miles, there was not left in my country a sheep to bleat, or a cock to crow day, nor a house unraffled, so severe were the depredations." One countryman seems to have made a firm stand, and the picture presented by his attitude of resistance is not unlike a grotesque Dutch painting. "Lieutenant William Fraser, vulgarly *William Goitach*, stopped the pass and common road above Rindowy, four men in arms with him. He takes out a strong barrel of ale from the drinking-house, and sets it on the high road, and rides straddling over it; he breathes the vessel, and calls to all going by to drink the king's good health. Not a man, horse or foot, comes near him for two days; some rode by below him, some above, and never any came near him all the while, he appeared so formidable to Montrose's people. When he drank a health it was accompanied with a shot, and there he continued, like a sentinel, for some days, until the fury was over."

'The Lovats of those days seem to have kept state to the full, even if we allow some exaggeration in the narrative of their faithful clansman. The following is a portrait of a Highland baron of the first class in the seventeenth century. There is no mention of a bard or piper, but doubtless these indispensable auxiliaries were retained at home. "1661.—My Lord Lovat and his lady came north from Edinburgh, July 27; were most sumptuously treated at Inverness by the magistrates, John Forbes of Culloden being provost; and at the bridge-end of Inverness was waited upon with sixty horse, gentlemen of his own name, and six hundred foot, well appointed, and Hugh Fraser of Struy, his lieutenant-colonel, Hugh Fraser of Foyer, major; I myself present at that pleasant parade. My lord came to Lovat in the evening with his friends and retinue; and I can say there was nothing wanting that could be necessary for a sumptuous feast and entertainment, and that which made that infer splendid was the convocation of my lord's friends and allies to welcome him home to his country. His domestic servants and attendants were John Allan, his chief gentleman, and Will White, his page; Robert Carr, master of the household, and James Fraser, steward; John Caird, groom; William Innes, groom; John M'Call, stabler; John Dawson, brewer; William Glass, cook; John Macleod, his servant; Farquhar Fraser and Alexander Peddison, chamberlains; John Maccallister, a Fraser, porter, &c. Isabel Fraser, *alias* Forbes, maid of honour; Isabel Dempster, Marion Reid, Anna Dingwall (nurse), Anna Tulloch, and Anna Hay, maids. I am the more punctual to set down the servants' names, because I had the conduct and government of this noble family for two years, until I entered minister of the church at Wardlaw. My lord spent the remainder of July and most of August in visits; went over to Brahan, Coul, Fairburn, Dochnaluag; went to see Fowlis, and Balnagown, and Tarbat; and then visited the Chisholm of Strathglass [This shows that the title *The Chisholm* is of pretty old date], at Erchless; also Struy, Culbockie, and Belladrum. And afterwards with his lady and train went to Stratherrick, visiting Foyer, and all the numerous families in that country. This I was witness to, as being his domestic (chaplain)."

'The following account of a wedding contract at Darnaway opens a scene of great festivity and splendour. It would seem to have been a very *jolly* affair. There was an old connexion between the noble families of Moray and Lovat. Hugh, the second Lord Lovat, according to our manuscript, married Janet, daughter to the Earl of Moray, in 1440. The wedding, we are told, "took place at the great hall at Tarnway; there is no such lodging in Scotland, for to this day that house hath no parallel within the kingdom. It was built by the regent, Earl Thomas Randolph; kings have been in it, and king James said that he had no such court or castle of his own." This venerable apartment, it is well known, still remains, though defaced about fifty years since by modern innovation. It is still, however, a noble and august hall. "1662.—In January, my Lord Lovat was invited by Sir Hugh Calder to witness his espousals and contract at Tarnway (Darnaway), and, though the storm was great, would not decline the call. So he gets his uncles, Alexander, the tutor of Lovat, and Thomas Beaufort, and his own train, and we were the first night at Dalcross, where we were very well treated; in the morning set forward, and came to Tarnway to dinner, where we got a generous welcome, and stayed all night. The earl waited upon Lovat to his bedchamber, telling him this was the king's apartment and bed, where he was to lodge while he stayed at Tarnway. Next morrow, the Lady Henrietta Stuart was solemnly espoused to Sir Hugh Calder of Calder, and I deemed that she loved my Lord Lovat better, and had he not been married already, this had been a meeter match by far. The gloves and contract ribbons being distributed in state, we had a most solemn feast, a wedding rather than a contract dinner. In the afternoon the wits of the house gave anagrams and acrostics in writ to the bride, and I judged Lovat gave the most apposite of all—'Henreta Stuarta, ane true sweetheart'—which, with the acrosting pertinent verse, was applauded, the bridegroom, Sir Hugh, the greatest poet in Moray, being the most competent judge in that case. After a surfeit of sincere friendship and feasting, my Lord Lovat, the fourth day, takes leave of that noble family of Moray; and at parting, the final compliment was my Lord Lovat taking horse, rides up the scale-stairs of Tarnway, and in the great hall drinks the king's health with sound of trumpet and pistol-shot; the meanest drunk bowls of wine, with snow-balls cast in for sugar. And after many a loath farewell, sounded good night and joy be with you. Taking horse at Tarnway, Mr Francis and Sir Hugh Calder, and others, convoyed my Lord Lovat off to the high road, and at parting excamb'd (exchanged) servants; my Lord Lovat leaving Thomas Fraser, Teanikill, with Calder, who sent his servant, John Campbell of Achindown, with Lovat, to attend him at his own house of Calder, where we were treated at a singular rate. The kingdom could not afford better wines than was drunk, and music of all sorts; Adam Smith (master of the musicians in Moray for virginal, violin, harp, and organ) was Calder's domestic; Mr William Cumming (an excellent learned youth), chaplain in ordinary; and varieties of divertisements. In all things the entertainment was princely, Saturday, Sunday; and on Monday Sir Hugh Calder himself came to us with an addition of what was wanting, if any at all, of good cheer and fare. We spent that day in a charming converse of sport, gaming, and singing. Next morning Calder convoyed my lord from his own house over the river to visit the baron of Kilravock and his lady; thence to Coule to see the Sheriff Rain. He at last added to our train, and rode forward to visit Culloden, and thence to Drakies to pay his respects to the Lord Macdonell; and thence to Inverness in no small state, few or none parting with my Lord Lovat that once met with him on his journey, he was so universally beloved and respected of all ranks and degrees of persons. Such a progress and parade as this of Lovat's was in the limits of ten days, through Moray, all things considered, was so singular, that such another I saw not since I came to my native soil from abroad."

'"1668.—*The Earl of Traquair's Fall.*—A remarkable death this year was that of John Stewart, the old Earl of Traquair, time, place, and manner considered. This man was king James VI.'s cousin and courtier. Charles I. sent him as high commissioner down to Scotland, and he sat as viceroy in the parliament, June 1639. He was early at court, the haven of happiness for all aspiring spirits, and this broke him at last—he became the tennis ball of fortune. What power and sway, place and preferment he had then, I need not mention; only this, keeping then with the revered bishops, and tampering under board with the Covenanters, he acknowledged to be his bane, but whether then by his own misconduct, or by paction and resignation of his interest to his son, or the immediate hand of God upon him, I search not; but he proved a true emblem of the vanity of the world—a very meteor. I saw him, anno 1661, begging in the streets of Edinburgh. He was in an antique garb, and wore a broad old hat, short cloak, and panniers breeches; and I contributed in my quarters in the Canongate towards his relief. We gave him a noble, he standing with his hat off. The Master of Lovat, Culbockie, Glenmoriston, and myself were there, and he received the piece of money from my hand as humbly and thankfully as the poorest supplicant. It is said that at a time he had not to pay for cobbling his boots, and died in a poor cobbler's house."'

THE CHOCOLATE TREE AND ITS USES.

What is generally called cocoa is merely the berries of Theobroma Cacao, pounded and drank either with water or milk, or with both. Chocolate is a compound drink, and is manufactured chiefly from the kernels of this plant, whose natural habitat would seem to be Guayaquil in South America, though it flourishes in great perfection in the West Indies. It grows also spontaneously and luxuriantly on the banks of the Magdalena. Mr Schomburg, in his recent expedition into the interior of British Guiana, found the country abounding in cocoa, 'which the Indians were most anxious to secure, as the pulpy arillus surrounding the seed has an agreeable vinous taste. Singular to say, however, they appeared perfectly ignorant of the qualities of the seed, which possesses the most delightful aroma. Mr Schomburg states, they evinced the greatest astonishment when they beheld him and Mr Goodall collecting these seeds and using them as chocolate, which was the most delicious they had ever tasted.'

The height of the cocoa shrub is generally from eighteen to twenty feet; the leaf is between four and six inches long, and its breadth three or four, very smooth, and terminating in a point like that of the orange tree, but differing from it in colour; of a dull green, without gloss, and not so thickly set upon the branches. The blossom is first white, then reddish, and contains the rudiments of the kernels or berries. When fully developed, the pericarp or seed-vessel is a pod, which grows not only from the branches, but the stem of the tree, and is from six to seven inches in length, and shaped like a cucumber. Its colour is green when growing, like that of the leaf; but when ripe, is yellow, smooth, clear, and thin. When arrived at its full growth, and before it is ripe, it is gathered and eaten like any other fruit, the taste being subacid. Chocolate, so called and so prized both in the Spanish continent and in the West Indies, never reaches Great Britain except as a contraband article, being, like nearly all colonial manufactured articles, prohibited by the customhouse laws. What is generally drank under that name is simply the cocoa boiled in milk, gruel, or even water, and is as much like the Spanish or West India chocolate as vinegar is to Burgundy.

It is, without any exception, of all domestic drinks the most alimentary; and the Spaniards esteem it so necessary to the health and support of the body, that it is considered the severest punishment to withhold it, even from criminals; nay, to be unable to procure chocolate, is deemed the greatest misfortune in life! Yet, notwithstanding this estimation in which it is held, the quantity made in the neighbourhood of Carthagena is insufficient for the demands of the population, and is so highly priced, that none is exported but as presents. The signs by which good chocolate or cocoa is known are these: it should dissolve entirely in water, and be without sediment; it should be oily, and yet melt in the mouth; and if genuine, and carefully prepared, should deposit no grits or grounds. That made in the West Indies and in some parts of Cuba is dark, but that manufactured in Jamaica is of a bright brick colour, owing to the greater quantity of arnatto which is used in the preparation, and which I think gives it a richer and more agreeable flavour. In an economical point of view, chocolate is a very important article of diet, as it may be literally termed meat and drink; and were our half-starved artisans, overwrought factory children, and rickety millinery girls, induced to drink it instead of the innutritious and unwholesome beverage called tea, its nutritive qualities would soon develop themselves in their improved looks and more robust constitution. The price, too, is in its favour, cocoa being 10d. per pound, while the cheapest black tea, such as even the Chinese beggar would despise, drank by milliners, washerwomen, and the poorer class in the metropolis, is 4s. a pound, or 310 per cent. dearer, while it is decidedly injurious to health.

The heads of the naval and military medical departments in England have been so impressed with the wholesomeness and superior nutriment of cocoa, that they have judiciously directed that it shall be served out twice or thrice a-week to regiments of the line, and to the seamen on board her majesty's ships, and this wise regulation has evinced its salutary effects in the improved health and condition of the men. Indeed, this has been most satisfactorily established in Jamaica among the troops; and a remarkable fact corroborating this statement is, that, by returns to the Horse Guards, it is shown that only one death took place at Newcastle Barracks, in that island, out of a force of 700 men, for the quarter ending September 30, 1842; and the same may be asserted of other regiments in the West Indies, and of the seamen in her majesty's ships on the coast. But the excellent qualities of chocolate were known not only to the Mexicans and Peruvians—from whom, as a matter of course, the Spaniards acquired a knowledge of its properties—but European nations also acknowledged its virtues. The Portuguese, French, Germans, and Dutch, considered it an exceedingly valuable article of diet, and Hoffman looked upon it both as a food and a medicine. In his monograph entitled 'Potus Chocolate,' he recommends it in all diseases of general weakness, macies, low spirits, and in hypochondriacal complaints, and what since his time have been termed nervous diseases. As one example of the good effects of cocoa, he adduces the case of Cardinal Richelieu, who was cured of eremacausis, or a general wasting away of the body, by drinking chocolate.

Liebig and other chemists have demonstrated beyond question that no part of an organ which possesses motion and life is destitute of nitrogen:—'All parts of the animal body which have a decided shape, which form parts of organs, contain nitrogen;' and the chief ingredients of the blood contain 17 per cent. of nitrogen, and no part of an organ less than 17 per cent. It follows, therefore, that nitrogen is that principle of the body which, being in the greatest quantity, and pervading all tissues, is that most frequently wasted, and most frequently in need of renewal. This must be admitted. It follows, then, that those substances which possess this principle in the greatest quantity in a given bulk, are those which must be best calculated to renew that which has been lost or wasted by the operations of the body. Now caffeine (the principle of coffee) and theobromine (the principle of theobroma cacao) are the most highly nitrogenised products in nature, as the following analyses will show:—Caffeine, according to Pfaff and Liebig, contains

Carbon, . .	49·77	Nitrogen, . .	28·78
Hydrogen, . .	5·33	Oxygen, . . .	16·12

Theobromine, according to Woskresensky, contains

Carbon, . .	47·21	Nitrogen, . .	35·38
Hydrogen, . .	4·53	Oxygen, . . .	12·80

—*Dr Binns in Symmonds' Colonial Magazine* (*abridged*).

DUMB DOGS.

The following curious fact in natural history occurs in a letter from the Mauritius to Professor Bell of King's College, London:—In coming from Lechelles hither we touched at Juan de Nova, where I had an opportunity of seeing for the first time an island of purely coral formation. It is of a horse-shoe shape, about twenty-one miles long, and from a half to three-quarters of a mile broad, with extensive reefs around it abounding with turtle. Dogs of different kinds have been left there from time to time, and finding abundance of food in the turtle eggs, young turtle and sea-fowl have multiplied prodigiously, so that there are now some thousands of them. I can testify from personal observation that they drink salt water, and they have *entirely lost the faculty of barking*. Some of them which have been in captivity for several months, had not yet lost their wild looks and habits; nor had they any inclination for the company of other dogs, nor did they acquire their voice. You may perhaps have heard of this before; if so, my notice will confirm your knowledge; if not, I hope the fact, as being of my own ocular demonstration, will prove interesting. On the island the dogs congregate in vast packs, and catch sea-birds with as much address as foxes could display. They dig up the turtle eggs, and frequently quarrel over their booty. The greater part of them droop their tails like wolves, but many carry them curled over their backs. They appear to consist of spaniel, terrier, Newfoundland, and hound, in various degrees of mixture, and are of all colours except pure white or brindled.

THE STOMACH.

I firmly believe that almost every malady of the human frame is, either high-ways or by-ways, connected with the stomach. The woes of every other member are founded on your belly timber; and I must own I never see a fashionable physician mysteriously consulting the pulse of his patient, but I feel a desire to exclaim—Why not tell the poor gentleman at once, 'Sir, you have eaten too much; you've drunk too much; and you have not taken exercise enough!' The human frame was not created imperfect. It is we ourselves who have made it so. There exists no donkey in creation so overloaded as our stomachs.—*Bubbles from the Brunnens.*

POWER OF MACHINERY

At Calicut, in the East Indies—whence the cotton cloth called *calico* derives its name—the price of labour is one-seventh of that in England; yet the market is supplied from British looms.—*Babbage.*

THE DEAD IN THE SEA.

[FROM THE GERMAN OF FERDINAND FREILIGRATH.]

UNDER the sea-waves bright and clear,
Deep on the pearly gravelly sands,
Sleeps many a brave his slumber drear,
Who joined the gay and gallant bands
That pushed from forth their land and home,
Companions of the wild sea-foam,
When blasts arose and tossed their bark,
Till, whelmed beneath the waters dark,
The storm-king claimed *them* for his own,
That late in life and beauty shone!

Under the sea-waves green and bright,
Deep on the pearly gravelly strands,
Sleeps many a one in slumber light,
But not by the storm-king's ruthless hands;
For there, within his narrow berth,
Lies the cold corpse of clammy earth!
Never to hail a harbour more,
Never to reach a friendly shore;
To a rude plank his form they lash;
Heave over board—waves sullen plash!

Ocean-depths yawn widely gaping,
Graves in the mirror-sea to form;
Churchyard hillocks there are shaping,
Every swell of the heaving storm!
Could we descend into the deep,
Could we but still the waves to sleep,
There might we rows of sleepers see,
Count the white bones lie glitteringly—
Things that the polypus spins so fine,
Weaving his network beneath the brine:
There might we see them pillowed fair,
On moss, and sand, and soft sea-weed;
Grinning in death, behold them there!
Fishes in shoals around them breed,
Swordfish polish their bony arms,
Mermaids mutter their mystic charms,
And deck them out to make them fair,
With many a gift of ocean rare!

One anoints, while another kneeling,
Braids the long neglected tresses,
From the soft purple shell now stealing
Bloom for the wan and bony faces.
One with a pearly necklace long,
Weaving a wild and mournful song,
Wanders among the dead in the sea,
Glittering with ornaments wondrously.

There may you see the shrivelled arm,
Gleaming in amber's golden glow;
There the bright coral's crimson charm,
Naked skull wreathing—blanched like snow.
Pearls the most precious—pure and white—
Glare in those vacant orbs of light;
And the sea-reptiles, loathsome, crawl
In and out, and around them all,
Sucking the marrow from the bones
Greedily, of those shipwrecked ones.

There might we see the stately mast
Bearing its freight of corpses lashed,
Clasped by the sea-rock, where the blast,
Shattering it fiercely, wildly dashed;
Gnawed by the worms, unconscious sleeper,
Rooted to rock-cliff all the deeper,
Dreams perchance of the granite tower
Beetling above his home's sweet bower;
For under the sea-waves bright and green,
Among pure pearls of the silvery sheen,
Many a rustic companion sleeps,
Who sank in the wave-worn ocean deeps.

Slumber they far from home and hall;
Flowers there are none to deck their bier;
Friends are not nigh to spread the pall,
O'er their pale forms to shed the tear.
Balmy rosemary there is none:
Rose-tree never shall breathe upon
Graves where, sweet, they sleep 'neath the billow,
Waving around no weeping willow.

Matters it not! Though fall no tear
Over the corpse in his briny bier,
Troubles it not the 'dead in the sea'—
Salt tears around them flow ceaselessly.

Brompton. E. L.

Printed by William Bradbury, of No. 6, York Place, and Frederick Mullett Evans, of No. 7, Church Row, both of Stoke Newington, in the county of Middlesex, printers, at their office, Lombard Street, in the precinct of Whitefriars, and city of London; and Published (with permission of the Proprietors, W. and R. CHAMBERS) by WILLIAM SOMERVILLE ORR, Publisher, of 2, Amen Corner, at No. 2, AMEN CORNER, both in the parish of Christ-church, and in the city of London.—Saturday, June 7, 1845.

CONDUCTED BY WILLIAM AND ROBERT CHAMBERS, EDITORS OF 'CHAMBERS'S INFORMATION FOR THE PEOPLE,' 'CHAMBERS'S EDUCATIONAL COURSE,' &c.

No. 76. New Series. SATURDAY, JUNE 14, 1845. Price 1½d.

VEHICULAR STATISTICS OF LONDON.

NO. I.—OMNIBUSES.

It has been calculated that the enormous concourse of houses through which the river Thames threads its long and devious way, known as London, spreads over an area not much under twenty square miles. Taking in, however, its suburbs, chiefly consisting of the towns and villages which have been gradually linked with it by long chains of bricks and mortar, the whole circumference of the metropolis may be about fifty miles. Within this fifty-mile circle there reside upwards of two millions of human beings.

It is quite clear that to keep up that intercourse with one another which is essential to men residing in the same town, the natural means of locomotion are quite inadequate. To provide, therefore, more convenient, rapid, and less fatiguing means of transport, vehicles of all sizes, shapes, and descriptions, are constantly moving about the streets of London in all directions. These conveyances form to the stranger striking objects; their use helps to reconcile him to the bewildering distances at which his acquaintance live apart, affording him cheap and ready locomotion from and to any part of the town, at any hour of the day or even of the night he may need it. The vehicles plying in the streets of the metropolis and its suburbs for hire, chiefly consist of three kinds—omnibuses, cabs, and hackney-coaches. The statistics and management of these carriages, the laws by which they are regulated, and the peculiarities of the individuals who drive and attend to them, form a curious and interesting chapter in our social history.

By far the cheapest, best regulated, and most convenient class of vehicles are what the 6th and 7th Victoria calls 'Metropolitan Stage-Carriages.' These consist of omnibuses and stage-coaches journeying within the limits of the police district; which extends over a radius of fifteen miles from Charing-Cross. The rise of the system by which these conveyances are now managed is recent, and its progress has been extremely rapid. Fifteen years ago, a few very slow and unpunctual stages were the only means of transit provided for the citizens to convey them to their suburban residences. A little earlier, only one stage plied from Paddington to the Bank, along a road over which an omnibus now passes every three minutes in the day; and this single vehicle, going in the morning and returning at night, was not always full. Its fares were two shillings inside and eighteenpence outside. The same distance is now travelled over for sixpence. Stage-coaches have been almost entirely superseded by omnibuses. Perhaps the latest 'on the road' are one or two which ply between Hampstead and the city.

The change from the quiet sober proceedings of these old-fashioned 'short' stages to the rattling activity and bustle of the new school, pictures most vividly the alteration which a few years have made in the habits and notions of the London public. Let us, for example, recall the daily routine of the vehicle which five-and-twenty years ago plied between Gracechurch Street and Peckham, a village some three miles south of London. The driver, probably an honest old broken-down guard or coachman of some 'long' stage, made his appearance in the stable-yard about an hour and a-half before the time he would be required to finish his three miles' journey. Having seen the horses 'put to,' and driven them round to the booking-office at the green grocer's to receive his orders for the day, he made his first call to take up one of those gentlemen whom he regularly drove to and fro daily. Now if, on arriving at his first patron's house, Mr Jones had not quite done breakfast, the driver made no objection to wait long enough for the leisurely imbibition of the last cup of coffee; and when, after some exercise of patience, Mr Jones was at last seated, he would drive off to Mr Smith's, who would perhaps be found waiting on his steps, having his greatcoat leisurely helped on by his maid-servant, with Mrs Smith at the parlour door wishing him good-by, and intreating him not to catch cold. The coating and shawling over, Mr Smith would get slowly into the coach, and be driven with his friend Jones to his friend Robinson's. Perhaps the last gentleman was also a little behind, and there was another delay of five minutes. At length he appears in the front garden ready to start; but lo! he has forgotten his lunch, and out rushes his wife announcing that fact, and bringing a whity-brown parcel: out also rush seven or eight children, who call papa to account for attempting to go away without kissing them. This little family scene duly enacted, Mr Robinson really *is* ready, and the stage wends its way up Camberwell Lane to make its fourth call—perhaps for a maiden lady going to spend the day with a friend in town, who makes her appearance with her dress-cap carefully screwed up in an old newspaper. Meantime a few outside passengers are picked up—people in humbler circumstances, who, however much inclined, did not dare to ride inside for fear of offending the aristocratic notions of their superiors. Had, for instance, the lady with the cap found her grocer seated inside the vehicle, in the place of either of those highly 'respectable' characters, Messrs Jones, Smith, or Robinson, she would in all probability have taken away her custom both from the coachman and the tea-man. By such class-prejudices were the suburban aristocracy of London swayed only a quarter of a century ago. But now omnibuses have changed all that. When we were last in London we rode to the Bank between a peer of the realm and a common soldier!

The Peckham stage, being at length fairly upon the

road, would arrive at its destination about the appointed time—a little before ten—its passengers separating to meet again at four, and to be set down in time for a five o'clock dinner, in exactly the same order as they were taken up in the morning. Such is a fair sample of the stage vehicles of London five-and-twenty years ago. Let us now give an insight into the state of metropolitan stage-carriages at present. The change, considering the shortness of the interval, is wondrous, and it has been mainly effected by the introduction of omnibuses.

In July 1829, a coach proprietor named Shillibeer started the first omnibus that ever successfully plied in this country. Such carriages had long been common in Paris; but when, so far back as 1800, a similar vehicle was put upon the road in London with four horses, it looked so exceedingly like a hearse, that people would not ride in it. The peculiar advantage of Shillibeer's carriage was its great capacity, which enabled him to accommodate from seventeen to twenty passengers at but little greater expenditure than what was required by the old stage-coaches to convey twelve or fourteen. This caused an important reduction in the fares. Again, at least ten of the passengers were protected from bad weather; whilst, by the old system, not more than four, or at most six, could ride 'inside,' and that at nearly double the cost of outside places. Shillibeer made no difference in the charge: his omnibus was therefore much patronised. It ran between Greenwich and Charing-Cross, and was drawn with three horses abreast; but this was found not to answer, the middle horse being always severely distressed by the irregular stepping and perspiration of its neighbours. After some of the new vehicles began to run on the Paddington road—which success between Greenwich and Westminster soon led to—only two horses were used, as now.

By this time the coaching interests of the London suburbs had risen in importance. The increase of population along the various roads 'off the stones' (as those parts of London beyond the limits of the paving-stones were designated) had called out a number of short stages, a little quicker in their motions and a degree lower in their fares than the old originals. When, therefore, Shillibeer set up his omnibuses with fares still more reduced, the proprietors of the stages violently opposed him. They lowered their prices to his standard; they sent their vehicles along side of his during each journey, to annoy his passengers and seduce them from his omnibuses. At length they fought him with his own weapons, and started omnibuses of their own. Against this powerful combination he was unable to stand, and was at length 'driven off the road,' leaving behind a very great improvement in conveyances. To Shillibeer at least belongs the merit of introducing omnibuses and cheap fares into this country, and the public owe him something for the boon. He is now, we learn, trying to make head against the extravagant charges of funeral-coach providers,* having begun an establishment of his own to furnish such vehicles at a reasonable rate.

When Shillibeer left the Paddington road, the proprietors began to quarrel amongst themselves, and to oppose each other with the fiercest acrimony. The men they employed to drive and to receive the fares were coarse fellows, who used the foulest language, and performed the most reckless feats in driving and racing. To such a degree of ruffianism was this opposition carried, and so inconvenient was it to the public, that a number of gentlemen formed themselves into a society called the 'London Conveyance Company;' thus instituting a fresh opposition, and one which was sure to succeed. They started commodious vehicles, with steady drivers, whom they forbade to race, though they exacted strict punctuality in starting and arriving. The conductors or guards were men picked out for their civil deportment and good temper. This happened in 1836, and so well did this sort of opposition answer, that the system became in a short time completely changed. The belligerent proprietors saw their error, and profited by the example of their new and orderly opponents. They shook hands, and formed *themselves* into an association with the view of framing and adhering to such regulations for the management of their vehicles as the London Conveyance Company had instituted and found of so much benefit. After a time, every trace of opposition was effaced, and the two companies joined to 'work the roads,' as they call it, for their mutual advantage. By this union a system has been formed by which an amount of coach accommodation is provided for the London public that twenty, or even ten years ago, could not have been dreamt of.

Before explaining this system, it is necessary to premise that Paddington is the terminus of two highly important arteries of transit in the metropolis. The northernmost is called the 'New Road,' which is nearly five miles long, ending at the Bank of England. On each side of this road is a concourse not only of houses, but—behind them—of whole neighbourhoods, some of which were in their time detached villages and hamlets surrounded by fields. They are now thickly inhabited, and as the omnibuses pass along, a constant supply of passengers to and from the city is furnished by these neighbourhoods. The other main line is even more densely populated, for it intersects the heart of the metropolis. Commencing with Oxford Street (or rather with Bayswater and Nottinghill), it is continued by St Giles's, Holborn, Skinner, and Newgate Streets, Cheapside, and the Poultry. By this road the distance is about four miles and a half. Though both these routes begin at Paddington and terminate at the Bank, in no district are they less than a mile apart, except near their confluence at either end. Consequently they are supplied by two separate services of omnibuses.

One of these—the most important establishment of this nature in London, and consequently in the world—is that which provides omnibuses for the Oxford Street route. It is called the 'London Conveyance Company,' which, besides the original shareholders of that society, consists of several of the old coach proprietors. The stock in trade of this company consists of eighty-two omnibuses, with a stud of not less than 1000 horses. Each of its carriages performs upon the average six journeys per day; so that it requires at the very least ten horses to work each omnibus, independent of casualties, which must be provided for. Instead of the poor worn-out animals which used to drag our Peckham friends to and fro, these horses are necessarily of great strength, are carefully attended to, and liberally fed. The work they do would have astonished a 'whip' of the old school. They occasionally draw over hill and level at a sharp trot not only the heavy omnibus, but nineteen or twenty persons, most of whom are above the ordinary weight; for it is your obese folks who have the smallest inclination to walk, and are consequently the most frequent customers to the conveyance companies. On the other hand, the animals are never taxed beyond their strength; it being an obvious policy to keep the cattle in good health. To this end the company engage an experienced veterinary surgeon, under whom is a staff of assistants and farriers, besides upwards of eighty horse-keepers or grooms. They employ also eighty-two conductors, and eighty-two drivers. The number of persons therefore belonging to the London Conveyance Company cannot be much under three hundred.

Thanks to this establishment, a person in haste who may be in any part of the line of route, and wish to be conveyed to another district, can assure himself that in three minutes at most an omnibus will approach to be at his service; and if it be at the busiest time of the day he will not have to wait longer than a minute

* See Mr Chadwick's report to the Poor-Law Commissioners on 'interment in towns' for the particulars of some of these preposterous charges.

and a-half. To insure this, the London Conveyance Company manage thus:—At their office in Paddington, at various parts of the line, and at the city terminus, they employ time-keepers to see that the driver of each omnibus starts, arrives at certain places, and at the end of his trip at particular minutes of the day, which are allotted as his instant of appearance. In this way an omnibus starts from the company's office every minute and a-half from nine o'clock till twelve; from twelve o'clock till three an omnibus starts every two minutes; from three o'clock till five the intervals are again reduced to a minute and a-half. They are increased to two minutes from five o'clock till nine at night, and then up to half-past ten o'clock the omnibuses succeed each other along the road every three minutes. Thus, from nine o'clock in the morning till half-past ten at night a constant chain of communication is kept up between Paddington and the heart of the city, the links of which may be said to vary in length from one minute and a-half to three minutes. As each vehicle performs six entire journeys, or twelve trips, the whole number of vehicles complete 492 journeys, and go over 2214 miles every day. Supposing we take as an average ten passengers for each trip, the gross receipts of the London Conveyance Company must, if that guess be an approximation to the truth, amount to L.246 per diem, or L.89,790 per year: this sum being contributed by the public for about three hundred and sixty-five thousand sixpenny rides. It must, however, be remembered that the company have to support an establishment of nearly 300 persons, and 1000 horses, besides keeping a stock of 82 omnibuses in repair, and paying a very heavy duty to government.

The other route to the city by way of the 'New Road' is provided with omnibuses by what is called the 'Conveyance Association.' This consists exclusively of the old masters with whom in this instance the gentlemen originally forming the London Conveyance Company are not immediately associated. The nature of the connexion between these two bodies is rather complicated. When the junction of the entire Paddington omnibus proprietary took place, some masters had omnibuses on both lines of road. It was agreed, therefore, that they should contribute such of their vehicles as ran 'over the stones' to the general stock of the London Conveyance Company; clubbing those which traversed the New Road under their own united management. The profits of each company are divided according to the number of 'turns out' (omnibuses, horses, and men) each shareholder originally contributed to the general stock. Thus supposing a proprietor to have contributed at the outset one 'turn out' to the London Conveyance Company, and another to the Association, no account is taken of the separate earnings of these particular vehicles, but one share of the gross respective earnings is awarded to him at the end of the day or week.

Belonging to the 'Association' there are fifty-five omnibuses, with the same number of conductors, drivers, and horse-keepers. They start without variation or interruption every three minutes from eight o'clock in the morning till half-past ten at night during the week; but at certain hours on Sunday the traffic being much greater, as many as thirty omnibuses begin their journeys within the hour. The regulations are precisely the same as those of the London Conveyance Company. Indeed, as above explained, some of its managing committee act for both companies.

One of the greatest difficulties the proprietary have to encounter arises from an inability to prevent peculation by the drivers and conductors. It is impossible for the managers at head-quarters to ascertain how many passengers may have ridden during each journey. Mechanical checks of various kinds, such as indexes, after the Parisian fashion, have utterly failed, because they gave the public some very trifling trouble; and when that is the case, such expedients never succeed. The plan adopted now partakes somewhat of the nature of a secret police. The managers of both companies employ individuals—whom they ascertain to be quite unknown to their servants—to ride occasionally in their omnibuses; and—without exciting notice—to take an account of the number of passengers. At the end of the trip the individual so employed sends a sealed memorandum to the company's office of the money which ought to be forthcoming, and if this do not agree with the account rendered by the conductor, an investigation takes place. Should a conductor be detected in one or two 'mistakes' of this kind, he is discharged. Of course the same individual cannot be long employed in this supervising office, or his or her person would be known; hence the company constantly change their spies, who are chiefly mechanics, sempstresses, or servants out of employment. Some, however, manage to retain the office, by great skill in disguising themselves. To-day one of these knowing passengers will make himself appear like a foreigner with mustaches; to-morrow he will be a carpenter, with a rule peeping out of his jacket; the next a gentleman's servant; and so on. It is gratifying to be able to add, on the authority of the secretary of the London Conveyance Company, that instances of detection very seldom occur. It is only when one conductor habitually renders a lower account than those of his colleagues who immediately precede and follow him on the road, that the secret system is employed against him. It has one good effect in his favour; providing he *be* found always correct, suspicion is removed, and his honesty better established. This kind of check is more or less adopted by all the London omnibus proprietors.

Besides these two companies, a third association of proprietors exists at Paddington, whose vehicles intersect various parts of London at right angles to those above-described. Starting from Paddington and travelling across the bridges, most of them end their trip at the Elephant and Castle at the head of the Kent road in Surrey, where coaches of all descriptions 'most do congregate.' Of these vehicles there are forty-eight, with an adequate establishment of men and horses to 'work' them. Lastly, ten omnibuses belonging to Paddington are employed in running to and from the various railway stations. Paddington, therefore, may be considered as the centre of the system, for upwards of 195 omnibuses daily ply from that suburb to various parts of London.

We now turn to the other great thoroughfares through which omnibuses ply. Besides the New Road and the line of streets beginning with Nottinghill, continued through Oxford Street, and ending with Cheapside and the Poultry—the third great east-and-west artery is that formed between the head of Sloane Street, in Knightsbridge, and Piccadilly; thence, by Charing-Cross, through the Strand, Fleet Street, Ludgate Hill, and St Paul's Churchyard, where it joins the middle route in Cheapside. This thoroughfare is crowded with omnibuses at all times of the day, not one of them limited to the length of road we have described, but all of necessity traversing it to arrive at their several destinations. For instance, at Sloane Street there is a meeting of three roads; one, commencing at the street itself, leads to Chelsea, from which at least twenty omnibuses ply; the second leads through Brompton to Fulham; the third, and by far the most frequented, intersects Kensington, Hammersmith, Turnham Green, Brentford, Isleworth, and Hounslow; whilst cross-roads over Hammersmith or Kew Bridges lead to Richmond. Each of these places has a set of omnibuses of its own, and all the vehicles pass the end of Sloane Street, and travel over the same ground till they get to the Bank, where some of them stop, whilst others continue the same line to Whitechapel turnpike, to Stepney, Bow, and other places in that direction, or branch off to the Blackwall railway-station, to Poplar, the West India Docks, and to Blackwall itself. On this road is, we believe, the longest omnibus journey in London: it extends from Brentford-end to Whitechapel gate, and is thirteen miles long, the fare for which is only one shilling, or not a penny per mile. Few persons, however, require to ride that distance, and, to use a phrase of the road, 'the short passengers pay for the long ones,' though, for small distances, only sixpence a-head is charged.

Where the journeys of most of the west going omnibuses end, that of many of the east, south, and north ones begin—namely, within a short distance of the Bank. The well-known 'Flower-pot' in Bishopsgate-Street-Within, is the nucleus of the Hackney, Hommerton, and Clapton ''buses;' whilst those whose route branches off towards the left at Shoreditch Church supply vehicular accommodation to the denizens of that road which John Gilpin has made immortal; for it leads through Kingsland, Shacklewell, Stamford Hill, Tottenham, to Edmonton. In an opposite or southerly direction a succession of omnibuses ply between Gracechurch Street over London Bridge to Newington Butts, Kennington, Brixton,Stockwell, Clapham, and Tooting; or branching off at the far-famed 'Elephant and Castle,' make their way to Walworth, Camberwell, and Peckham. Some go by a third road so far as Greenwich, though most of the vehicles that ply to that place start from Charing-Cross. Their trade has, however, been all but abolished by the steamboats and railway. The plan of proprietors clubbing together, as at Paddington, has been successfully followed out in others, especially on the western roads.

The next great omnibus station is Islington. The vehicles in this quarter convey the public between Highgate, Holloway, Hornsey, Highbury, Islington, and Balls Pond, east to the city; or else, intersecting London in an opposite direction from the well-known Angel Inn, travel between the above places south-west to Charing-Cross. Most of these belong to unassociated proprietors, among whom, it is disagreeable to add, a fierce opposition is at present raging; one of the belligerents is, too, a lady—the largest private proprietor of ''buses' in London. Another north and south route is that between Camden and Kentish towns, Charing-Cross, and Lambeth. This is intersected by the Hampstead and Bank road, upon which omnibuses regularly ply.

We have now traced, so far as we can remember, the chief routes taken by the London omnibuses. By reference to the licensing-office, we learn that the number of stage-carriages plying in and from London was, during the year ending on the 4th of last January, 1472. As 'short' stage-coaches have been, except in very rare instances, abandoned, and as the railways have driven off all the 'long' ones from the road except not quite fifty, it is believed that the number of omnibuses plying about the streets and suburbs of London in every direction all day long amounts to at least 1400. At a rough calculation, some L.2000 per day is spent in omnibus fares, making L.730,000 per annum.

Having spoken so much of the vehicles, a word or two concerning the drivers and conductors may not be amiss. It cannot be concealed that for a long time these men were looked upon by the public with aversion, sometimes with dread. 'In the heat of debate' with opposition drivers, they used the most revolting language, and even conducted themselves towards their unoffending customers with extreme rudeness. The rate at which they sometimes galloped through crowded streets caused fatal accidents, and so great was their haste in getting passengers in and out, that falls and broken limbs were of continual occurrence. They thought nothing of taking an unprotected female to Whitechapel when she wanted to go to Islington; and we were once asked in a Brentford omnibus by a stranger from the country, 'Whether the Bank of England was much further out of town?' In short, to so great an excess were the offences of these men carried, that the legislature was obliged to interfere, and by the 6th and 7th of Victoria, cap. 86, all conductors and drivers of stage and hackney-carriages are obliged to be personally licensed. That there may be no difficulty in bringing offenders to justice, each man is registered with a number against his name at an office for that special purpose, and that number is delivered to him legibly inscribed on a metal ticket, which he is bound under a penalty to display conspicuously about his person. He is also provided with a printed license. Should he misbehave himself, all that the injured party has to do, is to apply to a police-office for a summons against 'number so and so,' and the real culprit is sure to be found. In case of conviction, his printed license is endorsed by the magistrate with a statement of the penalty, and besides that, a list of stage-carriage offences is forwarded from the police-offices to the registrar every quarter. The license is renewable every year in May, and if the man be found unworthy of a fresh one, it is refused.

This plan seems to have acted in a most salutary manner. The drivers and conductors are now a different set of men; our own experience of them of late is diametrically opposed to our recollection of the class half-a-dozen years ago. As a body they may be described as civil, obliging, and well-mannered men. This reform, however, must not be wholly attributed to the act of parliament, to which the public is much less indebted than to the directors of the London Conveyance Company, who set the example of employing and encouraging the civil and well-conducted.

As may be expected, the number of conductors and of drivers in London nearly corresponds with that of the omnibuses. In May 1844 there were licensed 1854 conductors and 1740 drivers. Deduct those employed on the few short stages, and for about 300 individuals who took out licenses both as drivers and conductors, and the numbers as above stated nearly correspond.

THE SISTERS.*

BY MISS ANNA MARIA SARGEANT.

Oh what a goodly outside falsehood hath.—*Merchant of Venice.*

In one of the villages situated near the coast, in the beautiful county of Devon, stands, or rather stood, a small villa-like abode called Gothic Cottage. At the period when my narrative commences it was the residence of two sisters, the daughters of an officer in the army, who, nearly forty years previously, had retired there to spend the residue of a life, the early part of which had been engaged in active service. Captain Ramsay was yet a young man when disabled by a wound in his right arm, and consequently forced to retire on a pension. He had twice entered the marriage state, and Mary, the daughter of his first wife, was sixteen years the senior of her sister. The first Mrs Ramsay was an estimable but uneducated woman, who had been the captain's devoted nurse in a season of great bodily suffering, and to whom he offered his hand under the influence of feelings of gratitude and esteem. Unlike the general experiences of unequal marriages, he never had reason to repent of his choice. His second partner was the daughter of an old messmate who had taken up his residence in the neighbourhood. But brief was the period of his conjugal felicity with this lady: she died a few days subsequent to the birth of her first child, and so overwhelmed was the peculiarly sensitive mind of the husband by this fresh blight to his hopes of happiness, that a rapid decline soon brought him also to the grave.

The situation of the young orphans had attracted general sympathy in the neighbourhood, and Mary,

---

* The principal features of this little narrative recurred to the writer's recollection on the perusal of an article in the Journal of August 12, 1843, titled 'Credentials,' and she has woven them into a tale, thinking that they would illustrate the truthful observations there made.

being known to be expert with her needle, was offered a situation as sempstress, and advised to write to the late Mrs Ramsay's relatives, who were residing in Ireland, requesting that they would relieve her of the care of the little Eveline, or at all events provide for her support. This proposition, however, accorded not with her ideas of duty. Affection was the most striking feature in Mary's character, and now that both her parents were taken from her, its whole strength and intensity seemed centered in the motherless infant thus thrown upon her regard. She positively refused to part from the child, and, young as she was, resolved to be her future protectress. The nurse, who since Mrs Ramsay's death had taken charge of her, would, she said, still remain with them, and they should be able to live upon the remnant of her father's property, aided by her exertions with her needle, for which she would endeavour to find employment at home. This noble resolve was looked upon as utterly chimerical even by her best friends, who thought it incumbent upon them to point out the difficulties which must attend the pursuance of such a plan; but our young heroine's resolution was not to be shaken, nor was it the mere impulse of a generous nature, called forth by the circumstances of the present moment. She shrunk not from the self-denial which the fulfilment involved, but persevered with a steady undeviating constancy, which excited the admiration of all. With the dawn of morning Mary's nimble fingers might be seen plying the needle, and in the twilight she was still at her task. So much commiseration and esteem did her conduct call forth, that she was never without employment. Her only recreations were the caresses of her little charge, who fondly loved, though she was too young to comprehend how much she owed to her.

Thus the early years of Eveline Ramsay glided away, and, to the great delight of her youthful protectress, she gave promise of being gifted in mind, as well as eminently beautiful in person. This discovery, however, was to Mary a fresh source of anxiety, for she felt an eager desire that her sister's talents should be cultivated. Her own limited knowledge incapacitated her for undertaking her education, could she have found leisure for the task, and no increased effort on her part could supply the large sum which would be requisite to pay the expenses of tuition. Just at this juncture, she, to her unspeakable pleasure, received an altogether unexpected legacy from a distant relation of her mother. This sum was designed by the donor as a provision for her own unprotected youth, but she unhesitatingly appropriated the principal part of it to the education of her young charge, who now became a day pupil at a large boarding-establishment in a neighbouring town. Such a line of conduct would, she thought, insure to Eveline a genteel means of support in the event of her own removal. But unhappily this mental culture not being rightly directed, had the effect of inducing Eveline to believe that there was some superiority in herself which demanded a sacrifice on the part of Mary. There was a striking difference in the appearance of the sisters. Mary's form and features were of a homely cast, and her manners had none of that polish which education gives, yet it was impossible to behold her without admiring the placid and benevolent expression which pervaded her whole aspect. Eveline, on the contrary, possessed a face of delicate beauty, and a form of perfect symmetry; and so proud was the fond but misjudging Mary of that beauty, that she would not suffer her fingers to be soiled by any homely occupation, and was contented to wear the plainest apparel, that her sister might be arrayed in the manner she deemed suitable to her rank in life. Had the judgment of the devoted girl been as sound as her affections were strong and her spirit self-sacrificing, she would have pursued a different course.

Several eligible offers of marriage had been made to Mary by the farmers' sons in the neighbourhood, who had sufficient good sense to appreciate her character; but she resolutely refused to accept of any, though it was thought that one youth had made a serious impression upon her heart. She would never, she said, desert the charge she had undertaken; her life should be devoted to sisterly affection; and though her friends grieved to see her thus sacrifice her happiness, they could not but admire the motive from which it sprung. At the age of sixteen, Eveline discontinued her attendance at school; but her sister's labours were not in consequence lightened, her time being now principally occupied by reading and drawing. For the former amusement she selected exclusively the extravagant novels which then poured from the press, exorbitantly taxing her sister for the means of procuring them, and inflaming her own imagination by their perusal. Mary made still further sacrifices to gratify what she supposed to be an intellectual taste, not knowing that she was thereby administering a poison to the mind of her sister, which it would be impossible afterwards to counteract. Thus Eveline lived in an ideal world, and thought of the future as a golden dream which would realise all she had read of. Her peculiar position, her euphonious name, her delicate beauty, and her habits of luxurious indolence, all combined to make her believe herself to be a heroine of romance, and she confidently expected that her destiny would correspond with that of some one of the characters with whom she had of late become so conversant.

'When will you put off that everlasting brown stuff dress?' Eveline exclaimed a little pettishly, as the sisters were one Sunday morning dressing for church. 'You really are getting so prim and old maidish, no one would take you to be my sister,' she laughingly added, as she surveyed her own beautiful form, clad in rich attire, in the mirror before her.

'If I had afforded myself a new dress this season, I could not have purchased that one for you, Eveline,' was Miss Ramsay's mild reply.

'Well, but I really believe that you would *rather* wear that old dingy thing than a new one; you have such odd tastes and fancies. I declare we are as unlike as though one of us had been born at the antipodes: we have not one desire or pursuit in common.'

'Nay, I hope we in common desire to do our duty, and to love one another,' Mary smilingly interposed.

'True; but our ideas upon even those subjects are dissimilar, like everything else,' returned the volatile girl. 'Duty with you, Mary, means to attend to the domestic matters, and you have certainly a genius for the culinary art.'

'And for the dressmaking art too, I think you will allow,' her sister archly observed; 'for you are occupied in admiring the fit of that dress instead of putting on your shawl.'

'Yes, I admit that you are very clever with your needle too,' she rejoined, still keeping her position before the glass. 'Now, my duties lie in a different line. It is my part to give the refinement of taste to our little home.'

'You confess, then, that my accomplishments are the most useful, if yours are the most refined,' Miss Ramsay observed, gathering and folding as she spoke the scattered articles Eveline had thrown off.

'Why, we could not live entirely upon books and pictures, or ornamental work. Still I cannot admit that your occupations have the superiority you imagine, inasmuch as they are of a grosser nature.'

'We will decide this point another time,' said the elder sister; 'meanwhile let us each fulfil the duties which lie straight before us, be they mental or manual.'

'Dear Mary,' asked Eveline abruptly, after a short pause, during which she had completed her toilet; 'dear Mary, is it possible that you have reached the age of three-and-thirty, and never fallen in love?'

Mary's colour rose. 'Silly girl,' she said; 'why ask such a question just now? Your thoughts ought to be differently occupied.'

'Nay, but the idea just occurred to my mind, and I shall not rest till I know.'

'Then I am afraid, Eveline, that it will be a long while before you rest; for I don't think it prudent to talk on such a subject to one so young as you are.'

'Young as I am!' she repeated; 'why I am verging on seventeen, and every young woman falls in love at that age.'

'None but *foolish* young women do so,' Mary laughingly returned.

'Now that is your prudish, old-maidish idea,' said Eveline; 'but I can tell you, my sage sister, that it is useless to preach when the mischief is accomplished, for I am about to introduce to you a gallant cavalier, who has already done me the honour of laying his hand and fortune at my feet.'

Mary gazed in her sister's face as if to demand if she were in jest or earnest. Her lips moved, but her tongue could find no word of utterance, so intense were the emotions which agitated her breast.

'Why, you really look frightened,' Eveline continued. 'Is there anything so very surprising or shocking in the affair? But perhaps,' she added with mock gravity, 'I ought to have consulted my elder sister ere I suffered the urchin Cupid to aim his arrows at my vulnerable heart.'

'This is too serious a matter to be treated with levity, Eveline,' Miss Ramsay at length articulated. 'If you mean what you say, tell me, I conjure you, of whom do you speak?'

'I cannot pretend to give you the gentleman's pedigree,' the young lady replied; 'but in answer to your interrogation I can inform you that his name is Henry Woodville—that he is a man of family—that he has a large estate in prospect—and that he is the realisation of my dreams of a lover.'

'And where did you meet with him?' Mary asked in breathless agitation.

'Why, just where one would wish to meet with a lover—as I was sitting on a grassy knoll, beneath the shadow of a wide-spreading oak, whilst I was engaged in sketching our cottage at a distance.'

'You must not again walk abroad alone, Eveline; it is unfitting at your age.'

'Nay, you need not caution me on that head; I shall for the future have a companion in Mr Woodville, for he intends stopping in this neighbourhood for some months, he says. He tells me he loves retirement.'

'You must not permit him to be your companion,' cried Miss Ramsay in alarm. 'You are too young to act for yourself, and must be guided by my advice. If your suitor intend honourably, he will not shrink from being introduced to me, and visiting you here, and I shall then be better able to judge whether he is a fitting husband for you.'

'You shall see him this very day,' she gaily returned. 'He said he should meet me at church, and I bade him join us on our return, when I promised to introduce him to my sober sister. It was for that reason I wished you to put off that old brown gown, and don something smarter.'

'You treat this matter too lightly, Eveline,' cried Mary, whilst her usually placid features exhibited the agitated state of her mind; 'I shall be on the rack till I know what is likely to be the end of this affair.'

'I can tell you, then, in a sentence,' she laughingly made answer: 'the end will be a marriage, a coach and four, and, it may be, a title; for he tells me there is only a sickly cousin in the way between him and a baronetcy.'

Mary did not speak, but her heart was full of anxiety. It must be confessed that she heard little of the sermon that day, her thoughts being too much engrossed by the recent conversation.

As Eveline anticipated, they were joined on their way home by the lover. He was a tall, fashionably-attired young man of about six-and-twenty, possessing gentlemanly and even fascinating manners. A visit on the morrow succeeded, when the suitor gave to the elder lady a full explanation of his present circumstances and his future prospects. He had, he said, no proud or avaricious father to object to his union, and the estate now in litigation would, without doubt, be very shortly at his own disposal. Miss Ramsay was too little versed in the ways of the world to entertain a doubt of the truth of his statements. Her only objection arose from Eveline's extreme youth; but she was won to sanction the young man's visits, though she strongly protested against all thoughts of a union till at least three years had elapsed, at the expiration of which period the young lady would still be only twenty.

The lover was obliged to acquiesce in this decision, though it was with evident reluctance; and as the object of his visit to Devonshire was, he said, recreation, he declared his intention of remaining in the neighbourhood, instead of, as he had at first purposed, proceeding to explore the beautiful spots for which that county is celebrated. His time was now almost wholly spent in the society of the sisters, for Mary wisely put a negative to Eveline's rambles unless she were her companion. He read with the younger the impassioned works of which she was so fond, or chose subjects for her pencil, whilst the elder was engaged with her needle or pursued her domestic avocations.

Two months thus glided away, when one morning Woodville informed them that he had received a letter apprising him that his affairs required his presence in town. He hoped, he said, that he should shortly be able to return with the agreeable intelligence that the lawsuit was at an end and the estate his own. These remarks were made in the presence of Miss Ramsay; but having contrived to obtain a subsequent interview with Eveline, he, in eloquent and impassioned language, declared life to be insupportable without her, and so vehemently urged a clandestine flight and an immediate marriage, that she in a moment of weakness was induced to consent.

Woodville took his leave early in the evening, professedly to return to London alone, and the sisters parted after supper as usual, only that the younger clung around the companion she was about to desert with a closer embrace than she was wont. 'Heaven bless and prosper thee, my darling,' was Mary's affectionate benison as she stood a moment and looked after her young charge. The words rung in the ears of the conscience-stricken girl. 'Alas! *I* cannot ask the blessing of heaven upon my actions,' she exclaimed, as she threw herself into a chair; 'I am violating every tie of nature and affection; I am forsaking and giving pain to one who has been to me as a mother.' But when, after these reflections, she thought of Woodville and of the earnestness with which he had besought her to accompany him, her scruples gave way, and she was again the sport of passion. She was, she thought, but fulfilling her destiny. Her fate was to be singular, but the end, she confidently hoped, would make amends for all the trials she must undergo. With these fallacious reasonings she consoled herself, as she made preparations for her journey, and attired herself in a travelling dress. Hastily taking up a pencil, she wrote a few words of apology and farewell to her sister, when, her watch giving notice that it was within five minutes of the hour of assignation, she stepped gently down the stairs. With a palpitating heart she passed the door of Mary's chamber, and listened for a few moments to ascertain if she were yet in bed. She knew that she not unfrequently sat up even after midnight to finish some piece of needlework; but all was now still, and hoping that she was asleep, she proceeded, and was in a few minutes by her lover's side. A chaise was in readiness at a short distance, and she suffered herself to be led to it without daring to cast one more look upon her early and happy home.

The flight of Eveline was not discovered till the usual hour of breakfast, when she was missed from her accustomed seat. Fearful that the delay arose from indisposition, Miss Ramsay hastened with some anxiety to her chamber; but great was her surprise and alarm when she found it vacant, and that her bed had not been occupied that night. The scrap of paper on the dressing-table catching her eager eye, she seized it with breathless haste. 'Dearest Mary,' she read, 'my more than mother, pardon the hasty step I have taken, and think the best till you hear from me, which you soon shall do as Eveline Woodville.' Miss Ramsay stood like one who doubted the evidence of her senses. When the dreadful certainty took full possession of her mind, she threw herself into a chair, and gave vent to a flood of tears. 'Is it for this I have cherished her these seventeen years?' she exclaimed; 'is it for this I have laboured so unremittingly, to be deserted for an acquaintance of a few days? Oh, Eveline, you have almost broken the heart that loved you so dearly. He will never love you as *I* have loved you,' she passionately added, rising and pacing the room with rapidity, as if to fly from reflections which were too harrowing for endurance; 'rash, foolish girl, you will repent this step!' But this burst of anger over, the unhappy young woman began to question whether she had not herself acted an indiscreet part in suffering her sister to receive the addresses of a person of whom she knew nothing excepting from his own testimony. The most dreadful fears now assailed her lest Woodville, if correct in his statements regarding his family connexions, might not intend honourably. The fact of his enticing Eveline to quit her home clandestinely, seemed to corroborate this horrible idea. Again, if it were not true that he was the person he represented himself to be, though his motives in marrying Eveline could not be mercenary, yet he must be some worthless adventurer; and cheerless was the prospect with such a companion, more especially for one who had never yet known affliction in any of its forms. She could not help reproaching herself that she had not before taken these things into consideration; nay, she went further; she condemned herself for the injudicious training she had given her sister, which had, she feared, led to the evil she deplored.

At the expiration of three days, Miss Ramsay received a letter from Eveline, containing the information that they had arrived safely in London, and the marriage ceremony having been performed, that they had taken up their residence for the present in Westminster, at the house of a widow lady, who was an old friend of Mr Woodville's. She concluded with reiterated assurances of affection, and supplication for pardon; and Mary, whose affectionate heart could not long entertain anger against one she had loved so fondly, wrote an immediate answer expressing her forgiveness, and the most tender interest in her sister's future welfare. Feeling somewhat better satisfied, she now strove to compose her mind, and resume her accustomed avocations; but the pleasure she had before experienced while engaged in their performance was over. She was happy, however, in her ignorance, compared with what she would have been had she been acquainted with Eveline's actual situation. The home of which her sister spoke was a miserable floor in a large lodging-house, in one of the most densely populated parts of London, and the widow lady was a coarse vulgar woman, from whose manners she shrunk with disgust; yet, even amid these discouraging circumstances, she was willing to hope that a brilliant career was yet in store for her, and her letters were full of anticipations. But when month after month passed away, and the same tale was told without any advance being apparently made, Mary began to fear that the whole would prove a delusion.

A fresh source of anxiety now arose from the intelligence that Eveline was likely to have the cares of a mother added to those of a wife, and the information came accompanied by a request of a small loan, to enable her to make the necessary preparations. The next letter was from Woodville. In terms fair and smooth, he represented his deep regret that the settlement of his affairs had been so long delayed, adding, that if she could accommodate her sister with a further remittance to save her and her infant from want in their present exigency, he should shortly be able to repay her. To the generous breast of Miss Ramsay such appeals were never made in vain, though she could not help thinking that a young man of Woodville's education and address ought to make some effort to support his family, and not depend upon the precarious termination of a lawsuit. This was, however, but the commencement of a system of robbery under the garb of borrowing, which kept her in such a state of poverty that she was herself often obliged to suffer privations of the common necessaries of life; and what gave her even more pain was, she could not raise funds to pay the expenses of a visit to London, though she most ardently desired to do so. The letters of Eveline to her sister were now less frequent, the alleged cause being that her infant engrossed so much of her time; but the truth was, her confidence in her husband was shaken, and she could not bear to make known to that beloved and injured relative the dreadful apprehensions she herself entertained, that he had cruelly deceived them by false statements regarding his family and position in society. Some observations not intended to meet her ear, which were made in the adjoining sitting-room whilst she was confined to her chamber, gave her good grounds for suspecting the landlady to be her husband's mother. She heard her reproach him in the most bitter terms for adding to her cares by bringing home a wife who was too much of a lady to wait upon herself, and further tax him with curtailing her comforts for her maintenance.

The feelings of the unhappy young wife upon this discovery may be imagined better than they can be described, yet she dared not give them vent. The confession of her knowledge of the deception would, she thought, irritate the temper of Woodville, who had of late grown very petulant, and she dreaded still more the virulence of the mother's tongue. Even when she intended to treat her with civility, Eveline had shrunk from her attentions; her vulgar expressions disgusted, and her familiarity offended her. Often had she wondered that a gentleman of Mr Woodville's birth and education should ever have been on intimate terms with such a person; and that her husband, though he could not do otherwise than surmise what was passing in her mind, should offer no explanation. Now the mystery was solved, so far at least as the intimacy between the two parties was concerned. But what a prospect did it open to the unfortunate young creature who had thus cast herself upon their mercy!

This was, however, but the commencement of Eveline's trials. Hitherto the hope of a brighter future had supported her; and even under the possibility of a failure, she had consoled herself by the affiance her heart reposed in—the object of its fondest regard. Now it was otherwise. What had she to expect from a man who could act in so unprincipled a manner as her husband had done? What but wretchedness and ultimate neglect. Her forebodings of evil were but too true. The birth of her child, instead of strengthening the bond between them, served on the contrary to sever it, for it formed a plea for Woodville's continually absenting himself from his home. This unnatural conduct called forth angry feelings on Eveline's part, and the result was still further disregard for her comfort on his. She accused him of having enticed her from the peaceful and happy abode of her youth, and he recriminated with equal bitterness; and thus another six months passed away. The change from the healthful spot in which Eveline had been born and reared, to the closely pent up rooms she now occupied, added to the distress of mind she suffered, had, as might be expected, a powerful effect upon her naturally delicate frame, and symptoms of incipient consumption were the consequence. Her figure lost its beautiful proportions, the soft bloom on her cheek was superseded by a hectic flush, and the brilliancy of her deep blue eye was destroyed by constant tears. But he who had been the cause of this premature decay felt no stings of conscience for the part he had taken, nor even deemed it incumbent upon him to make a show of tenderness he evidently no longer felt. The love he had at one period so ardently professed had been called forth by the dazzling beauty for which she was once distinguished—it was not of a nature to stand the test of time.

The distresses Eveline endured were of necessity aggravated by the fact that they were self-inflicted, and bitterly did she now repent the rash step she had taken; yet she could not allow herself to make these admissions to her sister, though upon that sister's bounty it was that she still existed.

Affairs were in this unpromising state, when one cheerless evening at the latter end of autumn, after having seen her child quietly asleep, she sat down, intending to pen a few lines to Mary, in answer to a letter full of anxious inquiries which she had received in the morning. The fire, which she had not the means to replenish with fuel, was expiring in the grate, and the little candle, before which she bent her faded form, cast a faint light over the large but scantily furnished apartment; but so powerfully were the feelings of the neglected young wife wrought upon by the loneliness of her situation, that she sat and wept instead of fulfilling her task. 'Oh my sister,' she passionately exclaimed, clasping her hands together as she spoke, 'could you behold me now, how would your affectionate heart bleed at the sight; but you are spared the misery, and it is well; I have already heaped too much upon you.' A quick step upon the stairs, and the sudden opening of the door, here aroused her. She turned abruptly, dreading she knew not what, when the appearance of Woodville in an excited if not intoxicated state increased her alarm.

'Are you writing to Devonshire?' he demanded, seeing the materials for her letter lying on the table before her. 'I trust you are about to ask a further supply of money, for it is out of my power to support you any longer,' he bitterly added.

'What do you mean, Henry?' asked the young wife in breathless agitation.

'I mean,' he doggedly rejoined, 'that this day has settled my long-contested claim to the estate, and it is decided against me.'

Eveline looked at him in amazement. She had long considered the story of the lawsuit as a fabrication, but the apparent sincerity of his manner now awakened a doubt whether it were not the truth.

'You look stupified, girl,' he pursued; 'but this is no season for delay; you must pack up all we possess within a quarter of an hour, when I shall return with a vehicle to convey us from here, for we are no longer safe beneath this roof.'

'Are you in earnest, Henry?' she asked, so bewildered that she scarcely knew how to perform the task he had assigned her.

'Earnest!' he fiercely repeated. 'Is this a time for jesting, when an hour's delay may find me in prison?'

'Oh, Woodville,' exclaimed the unhappy girl, throwing her arms around him in a paroxysm of grief, 'you know that I have lived for these eighteen months upon the hope of the favourable termination of this lawsuit. You know that for love of you I left a happy home, where I knew not want or sorrow, and where, for seventeen years, I was never addressed but with words of tenderness. But I now aver, and Heaven is witness to my words, that I will follow you to beggary or to prison if you still love me and treat me with the kindness you were wont to do.'

'Foolish woman,' he muttered, putting her from him, though there was less harshness in his tones; 'this is no season for romantic scenes, those days are over; do as I bid you, as you value my safety.' And as he spoke he abruptly quitted the room.

In a state of excitement which gave her strength for the performance of the duty he had imposed upon her, Eveline collected her apparel together, and was ready by the appointed time. Mrs Jackson assisted in carrying down the luggage, whilst the unhappy wife, though totally ignorant of where she was going, caught up her still sleeping infant, and folding it within the cloak with which she was herself enveloped, followed down the stairs. A hackney-coach stood at the door, into which Woodville almost forced her, so eager did he appear to depart; then, after whispering a few words to the driver, he seated himself by her side, and the vehicle drove off with the utmost rapidity.

A few days after the above related events took place, a letter, bearing Eveline's signature, was put into the hands of Miss Ramsay, but so illegible were the characters, that she could scarcely believe them to have been penned by her. The sad information it contained was expressed in the following incoherent and passionate words—'Haste to me, my beloved Mary. Haste to me as you love me, if I have not so robbed you that you cannot raise sufficient money to pay the expenses of the journey. Nothing but your presence can comfort me or save me from self-destruction. I am deserted and alone. He for whom I forsook my only earthly friend has left me—left me penniless and without sustenance for the innocent little creature who is my companion in misery—amongst strangers, who look on me with suspicion. You will come to me, my sweet sister; I am sure you will come; *your* heart was never shut against me, and your forgiving love will pardon your erring but ever affectionate Eveline.'

Miss Ramsay, with that self-denying affection for which her character had ever been distinguished, was in less than an hour on her way to London, laden with a variety of those little comforts which she thought might be acceptable to her suffering sister. She found her occupying a miserable garret in an obscure part of the eastern suburbs, and so changed in person that she could scarcely recognise her. The meeting, on Mary's part, was characterised by tenderness and concern; on Eveline's by penitence and gratitude. 'Oh, my sister,' cried the latter, as she fondly clung around that beloved relative, 'I little thought when last I held you thus, that our next meeting would be in such a home and under such circumstances. But I deserve it all; I have brought upon myself all the misery which I suffer. But it is my greatest grief that I have involved you, dearest Mary, in my ruin.'

'Cease to reproach yourself, darling,' cried Miss Ramsay affectionately. 'You require peace of mind, and then your health will, I trust, amend. You must return with me to our once happy home, and we will try if we cannot find it such again.'

'Never, never,' Eveline energetically interposed. 'I could not endure a return. I could not meet the eyes of those who were wont to look on me with envy, humbled as I am. No; I must bury my sorrows and my shame in secret. Oh Mary,' she wept forth, as she hid her pale face upon her sister's bosom, 'it is perhaps too much for me to expect of you to give up your home for my sake, after the part I have acted towards you; but I cannot—no, I cannot return with you.'

'There is no sacrifice I would not make to save you a pang, dearest Eveline,' Mary tenderly rejoined, straining her sister's wasted form in a still closer embrace. 'I will let the cottage, and we will take up our abode in London, if it will make you more happy; and I will try to obtain some employment which will afford us a means of support. But you must promise me that you will strive to recruit your health and forget the past.'

'I will promise anything—anything but to return to Devonshire,' Eveline passionately exclaimed.

Before going further, it may be proper to state that the person styling himself Henry Woodville was in reality a mechanic's son, who, having received a tolerable education at a public school, and possessing a handsome person and good address, had formed the determination of making his fortune without giving himself the trouble of attaining it by his own exertions. An advertisement in a newspaper, purporting that a young man of that name who had left his family clandestinely when a boy, was heir to an immense estate, then lying in the hands of executors, suggested to him the idea of personating the runaway; and his previous knowledge of some particulars respecting the family of which he professed to be a member, favoured this deception so far that one of the executors espoused his cause from the conviction of its legality. The other, a shrewd man of business, suspecting the truth of his statements, delayed the decision from month to month. Meantime the real heir, who had been abroad, made his appearance. The pending litigation was then quickly terminated, leaving the hero of this story in danger of being apprehended as an impostor. He had, as we have seen, sought refuge in obscurity, but that proving insufficient to protect him, he was ultimately obliged to leave his native country for America.

Miss Ramsay removed her sister to some more comfortable apartments, where she trusted that careful nursing and the soothing tenderness of affection would re-establish her health. This done, she began to consider in what manner it would be best for her to endeavour to procure a maintenance. She suggested that they should open a little school, in which occupation Eveline could assist, whilst she added to her own duties the employment which had for so many years afforded them a livelihood. Eveline was eager to accede to any proposition made by her sister; but when the actual duties lay before her, she shrunk from the task. Never having learned perseverance, she was unable to exercise it at this juncture, when her weak state of health rendered it really difficult. The pursuit of an occupation, which would necessarily prevent her mind from dwelling upon her misfortunes, would have tended to heal her mental malady; but when Mary saw that the effort was painful to her, she, with mistaken kindness, insisted on taking the whole of the duties upon herself. Finding that the change did not effect the restoration she had hoped it would have done, Miss Ramsay now called in medical aid. Her native air was prescribed as the most effectual means of saving the invalid from an early grave; but Eveline was resolute in her refusals to return to Devonshire, protesting that instead of accelerating her recovery, it would hasten her end. The yielding mind of Mary acquiesced in her decision, but it was with many secret tears; and she too late discovered and bitterly regretted the error she had committed in the education of her youthful charge, in never having suffered her to be disciplined by that salutary contradiction which prepares for an adverse hour.

The winter passed away, and the return of spring gave some hopes to the fond sister of the invalid's recovery; but it was like the bright but evanescent light which emanates from a lamp just as it is about to expire, and before the summer brought her nineteenth birthday, Eveline was in her last resting-place. Miss Ramsay now returned with her infant niece to the cottage where her mother had been reared, there to cheat the remembrance of her griefs in commencing anew a life of self-sacrificing devotedness. But how different were her feelings as she reared her second orphan charge! Experience had taught her a lesson of wisdom—a lesson she could never forget. Many years have passed since the little Eveline first became an inhabitant of Gothic Cottage, and it has since dropped to decay. She is now a wife and mother; not as her unhappy parent had been—deserted and wretched, but the personification of health and happiness; and Miss Ramsay, or 'Aunt Mary' as she is always termed, though decidedly what the world denominates an 'old maid,' is still actively useful, shedding the beautiful halo of her undying affection around a third generation, and enjoying a rich reward in the felicity she confers.

OCCASIONAL NOTES.

THE ATMOSPHERIC RAILWAY.

We observe that the parliamentary committee have recently made their report respecting the merits of the atmospheric railway. Their verdict, contrary to the expectations of some, is decidedly favourable to the new principle, and leaves it, therefore, to a fair and unfettered competition with the locomotive now generally in use. While, however, they express a strong opinion in favour of its general merits, they distinctly state, 'that experience can alone determine under what circumstances of traffic or of country the preference to either system should be given.' This is quite as the matter ought to be; for nothing could be more hurtful to that ingenuity and skill which has raised our mechanical power to its present pitch than legislative interference. The freer the spirit of inquiry, and the more accessible the way to its application, the sooner will it correct its own blunders and arrive at precision and truth.

As is well known, the Dalkey and Kingstown line, near Dublin, is the only one yet laid down on the atmospheric principle; and this, as a matter of course, taken in connexion with the opinion of eminent engineers, forms the basis upon which the committee have founded their decision. 'This line,' say they, 'has been open for nineteen months, has worked with regularity and safety throughout all the vicissitudes of temperature, and the few interruptions which have occurred have arisen rather from the inexperience of the attendants than from any material defect of the system. Moreover, high velocities have been attained, with proportional loads, on an incline averaging 1 in 115, within a course in which the power is applied only during one mile and an eighth. These are important facts. They establish the mechanical efficiency of the atmospheric power to convey with regularity, speed, and security, the traffic upon one section of pipe between two termini; and your committee have since been satisfied, by the evidence of Messrs Brunel, Cubitt, and Vignoles, that there is no mechanical difficulty which will oppose the working of the same system upon a line of any length. They are further confirmed in this opinion by the conduct of the Dalkey and Kingstown directors, who have at this moment before parliament a proposition to extend their atmospheric line to Bray.'

In addition to the witnesses above mentioned, the committee had the advantage of hearing the objections of Messrs Nicholson, Stephenson, and Locke, against the adoption of the principle. These objections chiefly relate to the expense of keeping the atmospheric apparatus in an efficient state, and the inconvenience and irregularity attending upon a single line—there being only one exhausting tube laid down on the experimental line at Dalkey. To these objections the committee make a very unprejudiced reply. With respect to expense, 'it would scarcely be possible at the present time to institute a fair comparison between a system which has had fifteen years of growth and development, and another which is yet in its infancy;' and as to the second point, 'the majority of engineers are decidedly of opinion that any ordinary traffic might be carried on with regularity and convenience by an atmospheric line.' These matters being disposed of, the following instructive remarks are offered in comparison of the two rival systems:—'Without entering upon all the controverted points, your committee have no hesitation in stating, that a single atmospheric line is superior to a double locomotive line, both in regularity and safety; inasmuch as it makes collisions impossible except at crossing-places, and excludes all the danger and irregularity arising from casualties to engines or their tenders.

'Your committee desire also to bring to the attention of the House a peculiarity of the atmospheric system, which has been adduced by the objectors to prove how unsuited it must be profitably to carry on a small and irregular traffic—namely, that the greatest proportion of the expenses of haulage on the atmospheric principle are constant, and cannot be materially reduced, however small the amount of traffic may be. This is, no doubt, a serious objection to the economy of the atmospheric system, under the circumstances above alluded. But, on the other hand, as the expenses do not increase in proportion to the frequency of the trains, it is to the interest of companies adopting the atmospheric principle to increase the amount of their traffic by running frequent light trains, at low rates of fare, by which the convenience of the public must be greatly promoted. Upon an atmospheric railway the moving power is most economically applied by dividing the weight to be carried into a considerable number of light trains. By locomotive engines, on the contrary, the power is most conveniently applied by concentrating the traffic in a smaller number of heavier trains. The rate of speed at which trains of moderate weight can be conveyed on an atmospheric line, makes comparatively little difference in the cost of conveyance; while the cost of moving trains by locomotive engines increases rapidly with the speed.

'Now, when it is considered that we surrender to great monopolies the regulation of all the arteries of communication throughout the kingdom—that it depends in a great measure upon their view of their interest when we shall travel, at what speed we shall travel, and what we shall pay—it becomes a material consideration, in balancing the advantages insured to the public by rival systems, to estimate, not so much what they respectively can do, but what, in pursuit of their own emolument, they will do.'

Experience can alone decide this as well as other matters connected with both systems; but from all we know and have seen of the atmospheric principle, we agree with the committee that there is ample evidence to justify its adoption. Its mechanical success has been perfect. 'I consider,' says Mr Bidder in his evidence, 'the mechanical problem as solved, whether the atmosphere could be made an efficient tractive agent. There can be no question about that; and the apparatus worked, as far as I observed it, very well. The only question in my mind was as to the commercial application of it.' Even Mr Stephenson, one of the hostile evidences, admits that, under certain circumstances of gradients, and under certain circumstances of traffic without reference to gradients, the atmospheric system would be preferable. Besides this, Mr Brunel has proposed to double the line in those places where trains are intended to meet; and has further shown, that in a hilly country, with long lines of sufficient inclination to allow of the descent of trains by their own gravity, it might be possible to effect this object without the expense of a tube.

Leaving then the subject of expense to the companies interested as a matter which experience will soon decide, we see nothing in the principle, either in point of safety, regularity, or convenience, which can at all militate against its adoption, while we believe there are several points that in certain situations render it decidedly preferable. For many districts in Scotland and Wales it would be highly advantageous, and all the more so that the down train could proceed by its own gravity, and even be brought to assist the motion in the contrary direction. In point of safety, a single atmospheric line has been pronounced as decidedly preferable to a double locomotive, and this of itself is a consideration not to be overlooked, though obtainable only by a greater expenditure.

MAYNOOTH.

The little Irish town of Maynooth is situated in the county of Kildare, remote from any large or important place. It consists of one long broad street, formed by comfortless-looking habitations, few of which deserve the name of houses, being mere cabins. At one end of this humble street is the entrance to Carton, the seat of the Duke of Leinster, and at the other are the ruins of Maynooth Castle, once the stronghold of the Earls of Kildare. Near to these ruins is a building which has the appearance of a recently enlarged gentleman's mansion: this is the Royal College of Maynooth, about which there has been so much talk of late. The site, and fifty-four acres of land around the house, were originally granted by the Duke of Leinster, upon a perpetually renewable lease, at the low annual rent of seventy-two pounds a-year. It is said that the purchase of the house and the various additions which have been made to it cost in all L.40,000. The college was opened for the reception of students in October 1795.

Before that period, young Irishmen desirous of being educated for the Romish priesthood were obliged to go abroad for that purpose. Attached to various continental universities, colleges are founded for the exclusive use of Irish students, some of which are still in existence and operation. When war broke out at the end of the last century, it was of course impossible for those desirous of entering the Roman Catholic church to reach the proper colleges; hence it was found necessary to establish a place of education for divinity students in Ireland, and Maynooth was the place chosen for its site. The college is governed by a president, vice-president, dean, and procurator or cursor; and the education of the students is under the superintendence of professors of the Sacred Scriptures, of dogmatic theology, moral theology, natural and experimental philosophy, logic, belles lettres, Hebrew, Greek, and Latin, English elocution, and of the Irish and French languages. The expenses of the college are supported by various sources of revenue and by private bequests, in addition to an annual grant from the British parliament of L.8928. This sum, however, has been found inadequate to the expenses of the establishment, and it has been proposed to increase it to L.26,000.

The buildings of this college, in its present state, are fitted for the accommodation of 450 students. Of this number, 250 are free students, who are selected by the bishops of the several dioceses at yearly provincial examinations. They pay eight guineas upon their entrance into the college, and that is their only expense. The rest of the students in the establishment are either 'pensioners,' who pay twenty-one guineas per annum and four guineas entrance, or 'half pensioners,' who pay only half that amount in a year.

The discipline is somewhat strict and impartially enforced. The students usually remain at the college for their period of study for five years. Two of these are devoted to humanity, logic, and mathematics, and three to theology; the course, however, is sometimes shortened by the omission of mathematics from the list of studies. The students rise at half-past five o'clock, and retire to rest at half-past nine in the evening, eight hours being thus allowed for repose. There are two months of recess in the summer, and a short holiday at Christmas, Pentecost, and Easter. It would however appear that these recesses are nominal, for to take advantage of them special permission must be obtained from the Catholic bishop of the diocese, from which each pupil has been selected. In fact very few of the students ever leave the college for a single day, from the time they enter it to their final departure. But once a-week they are allowed to walk in the grounds belonging to the establishment, and then only under the guardianship of the dean. There is in the college an excellent and rather extensive library, chiefly formed by bequests and presents, containing the choicest works in history, belles lettres, arts and sciences. The students have not unrestrained access to them, their course of reading, even for amusement, being rigidly prescribed by their superiors.

CULTURE BY ELECTRICITY.

The stimulating effect of electricity on the growth of plants has been long suspected; a highly charged state of the atmosphere being always regarded as favourable to vegetable luxuriance, causing a healthier colour and a more rapid development of leaf and branch. Indeed every leaf and spikelet is a natural conductor, rearing its tiny lance into the atmosphere, and collecting, like the thunder-rod, the fluid that surrounds it, and this evidently to fulfil some necessary but as yet unknown purpose in its economy. Until the summer of 1844, however, we are not aware of any practical application of this principle—of any construction of apparatus by which either the free electricity of the air might be rendered more directly available, or an abundant supply generated by human means. At that time Dr Forster of Findrassie, near Elgin, bethought himself of the application, and after a few weeks' trial with the simplest apparatus, obtained evidence of its most extraordinary effects. Mr Crosse of Taunton had long since proved that the free electricity of the air might be easily collected by wire suspended on poles at many feet from the earth's surface; and Dr Forster, availing himself of this knowledge, erected poles, and laid down the necessary wires in a portion of his lawn which had been sown with Chevalier barley. The plants on the plot thus treated soon became darker in colour, grew faster and more luxuriantly, and when cut down, yielded at the rate of 13¾ quarters of grain per acre, while the surrounding land—similarly treated in other respects—produced at the rate of only about 5½ quarters! The ears of the electrified barley were not only more numerous and longer, and the grains larger and harder, but the dressed corn weighed nearly two pounds heavier per bushel than any other grown in the neighbourhood.

Such was the result of Dr Forster's experiment. The following is a detail of the plan by which the electric fluid was collected and applied to influence the crop:—

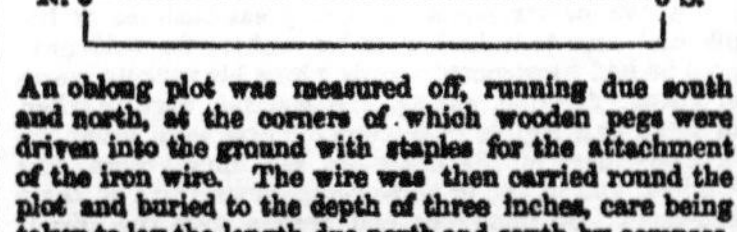

An oblong plot was measured off, running due south and north, at the corners of which wooden pegs were driven into the ground with staples for the attachment of the iron wire. The wire was then carried round the plot and buried to the depth of three inches, care being taken to lay the length due north and south by compass, and the breadth due east and west. The lines of buried wire being thus completed, poles were erected at N. and at S. for the support of the suspended wire. These poles were fourteen or fifteen feet in height, the wire being stretched from their tops and carried down on each side, so as to be in contact with the buried line. Thus the whole apparatus was completed, and the suspended wire left to collect the electricity of the atmosphere, and to convey it to the enclosed plot beneath. The cost at which the application can be made is computed at L.1 per acre, and it is reckoned to last ten or fifteen years, the wires being taken up and replaced each year.

This is certainly one of the cheapest modes in which electricity could be procured; but as the amount of free fluid in the atmosphere varies considerably, the supply might not in all cases be so powerful or so equable as to produce the desired effect. This, however, can be easily remedied in gardens and small plots by producing an artificial supply, either by plates of zinc and copper, by charcoal and zinc, or by some other of the numerous modes of eliciting an electric current. Indeed these latter methods have already been tried, though on a small scale; for we learn from the newspapers that charcoal and zinc, Leyden jars, Smee's battery, and copper and zinc, have been successfully employed to generate the electricity, and the result has been equally favourable as that recorded by Dr Forster. Thus one individual grew two boxes of mustard-seed, to one of which he applied electricity, leaving the other to its usual course; the result was, the former grew three inches and a half while the latter grew only one inch. Another person applied the charges of a Leyden jar to an open cucumber bed, and succeeded in producing cucumbers five inches in length in thirty-seven days from the time of planting the seed. Again, it is stated in the proceedings of the New York Farmers' Club, that in July 1844 a Mr Ross exhibited potatoes measuring seven inches in diameter, and growing in the following way:—He planted the seed potatoes on the 6th of May, using only leaves for manure. Across three rows, at one end he buried a sheet of copper, 5 feet long and 14 inches wide, and at the other end, 200 feet distant, a sheet of zinc of like dimensions. The sheets were placed in an upright position, and were connected by a copper wire, thus making a galvanic battery—the moisture of the earth completing the circuit. On the 2d of July other tubers were dug, which measured 2¼ inches in diameter. Some of the adjoining rows beyond the battery were also tried, but few of them had potatoes larger than marrow-fat peas, certainly none larger than a boy's marble.

All this appears very satisfactory, and if confirmed by further trial, will undoubtedly create quite a revolution in agriculture. The force is inexhaustible, can be easily and cheaply applied, and what renders it different from other appliances, is confined to no particular region. Admitting it to be as successful as we could wish, it will not supersede the necessity of tillage, draining, and manure; but it will render these much more effective, will produce a heavier crop, and what is of first importance, considerably shorten the period of production. It would be unwise and premature as yet to say more on the matter; further experiments are necessary, and we are happy to learn that these, during the present season, will neither be few nor on a limited scale.

MR METHOD.

A REMINISCENCE OF VILLAGE CHARACTER.

Mr Method had spent ten years as a general merchant in a country town, when some reverses occurring in a season of depressed trade so alarmed his prudential notions, that he resolved to retire with a small competency. Having taken this step, his irresolution prevented him, on a return of better times, from again employing his energies in business; so he retired to a country village, and there took up his abode for life, not altogether without some regrets and disappointments at his interrupted prospects of farther success in life, yet with a mind on the whole tranquil.

Mr Method was not a philosopher, nor a great politician, nor a man of fancy, nor of passion—but he had a way of his own and a will, which was law to himself and to his small household. He was one of those persons who lived by rule; he portioned out the day and the week into regular allotments, and one day and one week were to him the same during one year as during another. To say that Mr Method rose at a particular hour each morning would be a very loose statement: he got up at a particular minute; he had a razor for every day in the week, each numbered according to its day of office; and as soon would Mr Method have gone unshorn as he would have shaved with No. 3 on Monday, or used any other than No. 7 on Saturday.

Mr Method had his meals served up at particular stated times, exact to a minute. He liked a good, plain, well cooked dinner exceedingly; but he would have put up with the roast decidedly underdone, so as that it came on the table exactly at the nick of time. He delighted in having a few friends around his board; but unless they were well aware of his habits, and came in proper time, they were as well away, for any unpunctuality cast a shade over the whole entertainment: indeed, with his most trustworthy guests he was invariably seized with a nervous feverishness for at least an hour before dinner was to be served up, apprehensive lest all should not go well. His nephew well nigh totally lost his affections by twice coming in ten minutes after time. When himself asked to others' entertainments, he was more to be relied on than the dinner bell, and was generally the first guest to make his appearance. At home he had certain dishes of meat for every day of the week, varied only by the different articles of which they were composed coming in at the several seasons of the year; so that his old friends, when they were asked to dine with him on a particular day, knew to a certainty what fare they were to get. Mr Method was a great walker: indeed this was one of his chief occupations. He walked on an average ten miles a-day. Every day had its particular allotment—one day north, another south, this day east, to-morrow west. His way to church lying due north, he started on Monday in a direction north-east, choosing this because he liked to follow the sun, and by Saturday he had got pretty well round to north once more. On each road he had many houses of call, where he paid visits to his friends. A rare plant, a newspaper, ripe fruit, or other trifle often formed the purport of his visit. Everybody knew when to expect Mr Method; and if, in the country, as sometimes happened, the timepiece stopped, or was allowed to run out, his appearance was as good as a knowledge of the exact time at Greenwich. Mr Method was a cheerful being, and you would have supposed that the whole country around was his own, and everybody he met his near relative—he had something to say to every one, words of vivacity and kindness, though of little import. He seemed to delight in the open air, though I never heard him express any admiration of natural scenery: a dry day and a wet one were much the same to him, only that for the latter he took most elaborate precautions in all the particulars of his equipment. He appeared to look upon a luxuriant summer landscape and a frost-bound wintry scene with equal indifference. When walking with him along a lonely road, in a sultry summer day, about five miles from his house, he asked me if I would like a cool radish. On my assenting, he suddenly stepped aside, and from the corner of a cornfield pulled up half-a-dozen beautiful radishes. 'I sowed a handful of seeds here,' said he, 'two months ago, not doubting but that I should stand in need and reap the harvest some day.' A friend related to me that, on one occasion, passing with Mr Method across a wide furze heath, he was much in want of a piece of iron to help in striking a light. On becoming acquainted with his desire, Mr Method stepped forwards about a hundred yards, and coming to a furze bush of a peculiar round form, he poked about its centre with his stick, and at last brought out an old horse-shoe. 'It is now almost five years,' said he, 'since I found this shoe, and deposited it in this place of safety, and now you see it has come to be of use, and I make you very welcome to it, though I disapprove of your cigar-smoking as an unnecessary practice.'

Mr Method was not a great student, nor a devourer of books even of the lightest description. He had certain periods for reading, however. A good many years ago, when country posts were much less regular than they are at present, he got his daily London newspapers sometimes three or four at once. His first business was to unfold and arrange his papers according to their date; he then took the oldest, and made it form the subject of one day's reading, and next day he did the same with its successor. He thus, as he said, enjoyed all the excitement of a daily paper, and even when a very interesting debate was left unfinished in one sheet, he never allowed his curiosity to infringe upon the province of the next day's reading, although in the evening he has often expressed a longing for the arrival of the morrow that he might ascertain the result. When reading a novel, he never exceeded two chapters in a day, however intense the interest of the story; in this way he kept alive his curiosity, and prolonged his enjoyment for weeks or months.

Mr Method was of middle, or rather below the middle size, well made, and inclining to be fat. He had a full, rosy, round face, white teeth, sharp nose, a little snubbed, and soft, blue, mild-looking eyes. He was extremely neat in his dress, his linen always clean and of snowy whiteness; a small brilliant sparkled in his breast; he wore a short green coat, yellow vest, and drab trousers; in summer a white hat and in winter a black one; a walking stick, or an umbrella which folded up into a stick, was indispensable. In wet weather he was equipped in clothes curiously and artfully contrived to exclude wet, and at the same time to be light and conducive to his usual active habits of walking. On these occasions he wore India-rubber shoes of his own invention. He wore also and continually consulted a chronometer, which had been tested at Greenwich Observatory, and kept time to within a second in the year.

Mrs Method (for he was not a bachelor) was a wife worthy of such a husband. Not that she was gifted by nature with the innate habits of her spouse, but she had that better gift, and which is so beautiful a thing in woman, of a wish to accommodate herself to her destiny, and to follow the inclinations of her lord. Mrs Method had not the bump of order or regularity, and she had a very deficient memory; but she had great good nature and a love for her husband. One great business of his life had been to train her to his wishes; for this purpose he had constructed boards where his various hours of rising, dressing, eating, and walking were marked in large and legible characters. These were hung up in every part of the house—in the dining-room, the kitchen, and in two or three conspicuous parts of their bed-room. So numerous and precise were the directions, that they became a daily and perpetual study for Mrs Method; and she was to be seen at all times with her spectacles on, and one or other of the direction-boards in her hand, either reading it off for her own special use, or for the guidance of the cook, the housemaid, or the gardener. She had no children, but nevertheless her life was no sinecure, as every hour, from sunrise to sunset, had its peculiar appointments. I know not if Mrs Method had an equal enjoyment of existence as her husband; perhaps she was doomed to too much study to be perfectly happy. Yet, on the whole, they were a comfortable couple, and got through married life with not more than a fair share of snarlings, pets, and reconciliations. The last time I visited them, I found Mr Method busy with some modifications of a patent night-cap, which he expected to have an immense effect in mollifying a tendency to rheumatism in the jaw of his beloved spouse. This shows that, with all her shortcomings in punctuality, her husband never ceased to regard her with duly kind feelings. Since then, they have both passed from the stage, and taken up a position in the village churchyard, where a neat monument, exactly suitable to Mr Method's taste, and which was indeed selected at a marble-cutter's by himself, informs the passer-by of the names and ages of those who sleep below.

PERSECUTIONS IN MASSACHUSETTS.

The first settlers of the New England states, as is pretty well known, were men who fled from civil and religious persecution in England in the early part of the seventeenth century. As they had felt in their own persons and fortunes the sorrows of oppression for conscience' sake, it might naturally be expected that they would have had some sympathy for others in like circumstances. In this respect, however, the Pilgrim Fathers, as they have been termed, were no better than the men before whom they had fled. A volume might be written of their doings in the way of intolerance; but the following short chapter may suffice.

In the year 1656, when the colonists of Massachusetts were complacently congratulating themselves on having established a vigorous system of uniformity in religious matters, and expressing great thankfulness for having escaped from the troubles which had lately agitated England, they were very much surprised to learn that two women of the sect which had begun to be called Quakers were arrived in Boston from Barbadoes. There was no law in the colony against such persons; but that was considered unimportant; it was easy to make a little law for the occasion, or easier still to act without any law at all. This last alternative was adopted. The two unfortunate women, against whose character there was no reproach, were seized and put in prison; a few books found in their trunks were burnt by the hangman; and after suffering various indignities, they were turned out of the country. Persecution requires only a little spark to kindle it into a great flame. It would almost seem as if the misusage of the two women caused a flocking of Quakers from all the points of the compass to Boston, only for the sake of getting ill treated. In a short time eight made their appearance, and they in a like manner were imprisoned and banished. Thinking it now time to get a little law to regulate proceedings, a local court passed an enactment, declaring that any Quakers who should hereafter arrive in the colony should be severely whipped, and confined at hard labour in the house of correction. Immediately afterwards several came, were whipped, confined, and dismissed; and others took their place. It was evident the law was too lenient, so a fresh enactment was passed. Fines were imposed on every person who gave house-room to Quakers, or who attended their meetings, or otherwise sanctioned their pernicious opinions. Every Quaker, after the first conviction, if a man, was to lose one ear, and the second time the other; if a woman, she was each time to be severely whipped; and for the third offence, both men and women were to have their tongues bored through with a red-hot iron.

Quakers now arrived in the colony in great numbers. Glorying in their sufferings the more they were persecuted, the more they came to testify their sincerity in their belief. Whippings, confinement, hard labour, fines, cutting off the ears, and boring the tongue being thus found ineffectual, a new law was passed in 1658, declaring that in future all Quakers who intruded themselves into Massachusetts should be banished on pain of death. Three Quakers forthwith offered themselves as the first victims; they had returned from banishment. Their names were Mary Dyer, Marmaduke Stephenson, and William Robinson. From their defence at their trial, nothing is more plain than that they were persons in a state of frenzy: their general argument was, that by means of visions they had been induced to come to Massachusetts and brave the worst that could be done to them. On the 19th of October 1659, they were condemned to die as malefactors; and three days later they were led out to execution. Mary Dyer saw her two brethren die before her eyes; and she was on the point of meeting the same dreadful doom, the rope being already round her neck, 'when a faint shout was heard in the distance, which grew stronger and stronger, and was soon caught and repeated by a hundred willing hearts. "A reprieve, a reprieve!" was the cry, and the execution was stopped; but she, whose mind was intently fastened on another world, cried out, that she desired to suffer with her brethren, unless the magistrates would repeal their wicked law.

'She was saved by the intercession of her son, but on the express condition that she should be carried to the place of execution, and stand upon the gallows with a rope about her neck, and then be carried out of the colony. She was accordingly taken home to Rhode Island; but her resolution was still unshaken, and she was again moved to return to the "bloody town of Boston," where she arrived in the spring of 1660. This determination of a feeble and aged woman, to brave all the terrors of their laws, might well fill the magistrates with astonishment; but the pride of consistency had already involved them in acts of extreme cruelty, and they thought it impossible now to recede. The other executions were considered acts of stern necessity, and caused much discontent; a hope was entertained till the last moment, that the condemned would consent to depart from the jurisdiction; and when Mary Dyer was sent for by the court, after her second return, Governor Endicott said, "Are you the same Mary Dyer that was here before?" giving her an opportunity to escape by a denial of the fact, there having been another of the name returned from England. But she would make no evasion. "I am the same Mary Dyer that was here the last general court." "You will own yourself a Quaker, will you not?" "I own myself to be reproachfully called so;" and she was sentenced to be hanged on the morning of the next day. "This is no more than thou saidst before," was her intrepid reply, when the sentence of death was pronounced. "But now," said the governor, "it is to be executed; therefore prepare yourself, for to-morrow at nine o'clock you die!" "I came," was the reply, "in obedience to the will of God, the last general court, desiring you to repeal your unrighteous law of banishment on pain of death; and the same is my work now, and earnest request, although I told you if you refused to repeal them, the Lord would send others of his servants to witness against them."

'At the appointed time on the next day she was brought forth, and with a band of soldiers led through the town, about a mile to the place of execution, the drums beating before and behind her the whole way. When she was upon the gallows, it was told her that if she would return home she might come down and save her life; to which she replied, "Nay, I cannot, for in obedience to the will of the Lord I came, and in his will I abide faithful unto the death." Another said that she had been there before; she had the sentence of banishment upon pain of death, and had broken the law in coming again now, and therefore she was guilty of her own blood. "Nay," she answered, "I came to keep blood-guiltiness from you, desiring you to repeal the unrighteous and unjust law of banishment upon pain of death, made against the innocent servants of the Lord; therefore my blood will be required at your hands, who wilfully do it; but for those who do it in the simplicity of their hearts, I desire the Lord to forgive them; I came to do the will of my Father, and in obedience to his will I stand even to death." A minister who was present then said, "Mary Dyer, repent, oh repent, and be not so deluded and carried away by the deceit of the devil!" But she answered, "Nay, man, I am not now to repent." She was then asked to have the elders pray for her; but she said, "I know never an elder here." She added that she desired the prayers of all the people of God. "Perhaps," said one scoffingly, "she thinks there is none here." Then looking round she said, "I know but few here." Being again asked to have one of the elders pray for her, she said, "Nay, first a child, then a young man, then a strong man, before an elder in Christ Jesus." She spoke of the other world and of the eternal happiness into which she was about to enter; and "in this well-disposed condition was turned off, and died a martyr of Christ, being twice led to death, which the first time she expected with undaunted courage, and now suffered with Christian fortitude." "She hangs as a flag for others to take example by," said a member of the court, as the lifeless body hung suspended from the gallows.'

Instead of being a warning, her death was only an encouragement. Another Quaker, named William Leddra, soon made his appearance, and after a tedious imprisonment, during which he was chained to a log of wood, he was brought to trial on the usual charge of returning from banishment. There was a dash of the ludicrous in the proceedings. One of the charges against him was that he refused to take off his hat in court, and another was that he persevered in saying 'thee' and 'thou.' 'Will you put me to death,' he asked, 'for speaking good English, and for not putting off my clothes?' 'A man may speak treason in good English,' was the reply. 'Is it treason to say "thee" and "thou" to a single person?' No good rejoinder could here be made by the judges, and while they were trying to stop his mouth by a few more questions, to their exceeding dismay another Quaker, named Winlock Christison, who had also returned from banishment, entered the court and placed himself beside the prisoner. The case of Leddra was first despatched, by condemning him to be executed, and this atrocity was committed on the 14th of March. Christison, at a second appearance before the court, received a like sentence, but leaving him the choice of voluntary banishment, and this latter alternative he appears to have embraced. The next culprits of the same class were Judah Browne and Peter Pierson, who, for no offence that we can perceive but that of being Quakers, were condemned to be tied to a cart's tail and whipped through several towns in the colony. Immediately after, as appears from the records of the court, a day of thanksgiving was appointed to be kept in acknowledgment of the many mercies enjoyed for years past 'in this remote wilderness.'

According to Mr Chandler,* from whose interesting work we have derived these melancholy details, the persecutions in Massachusetts gave offence to Charles II., who had other reasons to be dissatisfied with the colonists. He therefore enjoined all the governors of New England to proceed no farther with corporal punishment against Quakers, but to send them to England, with their respective crimes specifically set forth, in order that they might be disposed of according to law. 'The Quakers in London immediately chartered a vessel, and the mandamus being committed to Samuel Shattock, who had been banished from Massachusetts on pain of death, he arrived in the harbour of Boston in six weeks. The king's messenger and the commander of the ship landed on the day after their arrival, and proceeded directly to the governor's house. Admitted to his presence, he ordered Shattock's hat to be removed, but after perusing the letters, restored it and took off his own. After consultation with the deputy-governor, he informed the messenger that they should obey the king's command. In the evening the passengers of the ship came on shore, and, with their friends in the town, held a meeting, "where they returned praises to God for his mercy, manifested in their wonderful deliverance."'

The colonial laws against Quakers were now abolished, and there were no more executions of this unhappy class of persons; but the magistracy were hostile to the sect, and for years afterwards they contrived to whip and otherwise maltreat any Quakers who fell into their hands; it would indeed seem doubtful whether the tortures and indignities they occasionally inflicted, particularly on the persons of females, were not worse than death. The authority to which we have referred observes with justice that the Quakers who exposed themselves to these severities were not by any means blameless. Unlike the orderly Society of Friends in the present day, they appear to have taken a delight in annoying the constituted authorities, and disturbing the public peace. Much of this, however, was produced by their sufferings in the first instance; and the more violent amongst them, from a variety of causes, were evidently wrought up to a state of religious insanity. Allowing that they were as troublesome as their worst enemies can possibly represent them, there can now be but one sentiment respecting their treatment—unqualified condemnation of their oppressors. It is true there were laws equally severe against Quakers in Virginia and elsewhere; but this does not lessen the crime of the magistracy of Massachusetts. Descendants of Pilgrim Fathers who fled to the wilderness from persecution, if not themselves refugees, they ought to have sympathised in the eccentricities or convictions of others when placed in similar circumstances. How true is the remark of our author, that 'Religious intolerance was the mistake of the age!'

* American Criminal Trials, by P. W. Chandler. 2 vols. 1840.

CURIOSITIES OF LITERATURE.

NO. I.

VARRO reckoned that, among the old philosophers, there were 800 opinions concerning the *summum bonum*. Modern philosophers do not appear to have lost the faculty of invention, for M. Reynière, in his Cours Gastronomique, affirms that they were acquainted in France with 685 different modes of dressing eggs for table, to say nothing of those which *nos savans* were discovering every day.

The earliest book in which engravings are found is a Dante, printed at Florence in 1481. Monday, the 5th of January 1665, is the date of the first number of the first review, the Journal des Sçavans, and the first book reviewed was an edition of Victor Viteusés and Vigelius Tapsensis, African bishops of the fifth century, by Father Chiflet, a Jesuit. The review was of small size, and published weekly, each number containing from twelve to sixteen pages.

Lope de Vega, the Spanish dramatist, wrote upwards of 2000 original pieces, but not more than 300 of them have been printed. He has himself stated that his average amount of work was five sheets a-day; and it has been calculated that he composed during his life 133,225 sheets, and about 21,300,000 verses.

The earliest instance of the use of linen paper is an Arabic version of the Aphorisms of Hippocrates, the manuscript of which bears date in the year 1100.

Pietro Bembo, a noble Venetian, secretary to Leo X., was noted for the fastidious revisals he bestowed upon his compositions. He had forty portfolios, through which each sheet gradually found its way; but no remove was ever made until it had undergone a fresh perusal, and further correction. Mr T. B. Macaulay states in one of his admirable essays, that he has in his possession the variations in a very fine stanza of Ariosto, which the poet had altered a hundred times. Petrarch is said to have made forty-four alterations in one verse. Gibbon wrote his memoir six times over, and after all has left it a fragment. In that work he has mentioned what a number of experiments he made in the composition of his great history, before he could hit the middle tone between a dull chronicle and a rhetorical declamation. The first chapter was written and re-written three times, and the second and third twice, before he was tolerably satisfied with their effect. Buffon wrote his *Epoques de la Nature* eighteen times before he allowed them to appear in print. Every line of Sismondi's Italian Republics was written three times, and so were almost the whole of his historical works. As he drew nearer the end of his life, composition was less laborious, and he contented himself with writing parts of the History of France twice over only. His revisal of what he had written was very careful: he corrected his proofs five or six times, and generally twice read aloud all that he penned.

A shoemaker of the free city of Nuremberg, by name Hans Sachs, composed fifty-three sacred, and seventy-eight profane dramas, sixty-four farces, fifty-nine fables, and a great quantity of other poetry. He was born in 1494.

The following whimsical will in rhyme was written by William Hunnis, a gentleman of the chapel under Edward VI, and afterwards chapel-master to Queen Elizabeth:—

'To God my soule I do bequeathe, because it is his owen,
My body to be layd in grave, where to my friends best knowen;
Executors I will none make, thereby great stryfe may grow,
Because the goods that I shall leave wyll not pay all I owe.'

The same person wrote a song commencing, 'When first mine eyes did view and mark,' printed in Campbell's Specimens, which Mr Hallam mentions with high praise.

Talk of the extensive sale which a popular work now-a-days meets with; why, in the year 1511, 1800 copies of the Encomium Moriæ (the Praise of Folly), by Erasmus, were disposed of, and in 1527, 24,000 copies of the same writer's Colloquies were printed and sold! Of the De Imitatione Christi, by old Thomas-à-Kempis, it has been calculated that 1800 editions have appeared; and sixty editions of the Orlando Furioso were published in the sixteenth century.

In 1568 there appeared a translation of Polybius, the patron of which is thus addressed in the dedication:—'Charles Watson wysheth thee Argantos' age, Polycrates' prosperity, Augustus' amitie, and after the consummation of this terrestrial tragedy, a seate amongst the celestial hyerarchie.' Mr Watson seems to have been one of those men of compliments, whose 'high-born words' Shakspeare has ridiculed in Love's Labour Lost. Sir Walter Scott has also given us a specimen of Euphuism, as this inflated phraseology was called, in one of his novels.

Dr Philemon Holland, a translator of Plutarch's Morals, having made one pen do service throughout the work, which covered more than a ream of paper, indited this distich at the close of his labours:—

'This booke I wrote with *one* poor pen, made of a gray-goose quill;
A pen I found it, used before, a pen I leave it still.'

A cousin of Jeremy Bentham's had a notion, that whatever appeared in print was a lie. This was better, perhaps, than believing every published statement to be true. The philosopher, however, intent upon rooting this crotchet out of his relation's head, proceeded logically to work, and pressed him to say whether, in his opinion, if a fact had taken place, the putting it in print would cause it not to have taken place.

One of the *bon mots* which contributed to make Talleyrand so famous as a wit, was his definition of speech as a faculty given to man for the purpose of concealing his thoughts. The prince-bishop can well afford to give up the credit of having first made this sarcastic observation to an English clergyman. Young mentions some place,

'Where nature's end of language is declined,
And men talk only to conceal their mind.'

For the sake of contrast, we may as well add Horne Tooke's proposition:—'The purpose of language is to communicate our thoughts.'

In Pratt's edition of Bishop Hall's works, there is a glossary, comprehending upwards of 1100 articles, of obsolete or unusual words employed by him.

What a pretty tale was slaughtered when Mr Grenville Piggot pointed out, in his Manual of Scandinavian Mythology, the blundering translation of the passage, in an old Scandinavian poem, relating to the occupation of the blest in the halls of Valhalla, the northern Paradise. 'Soon shall we drink out of the curved horns of the head,' are the words found in the death-song of Regner Lodbrog; meaning by this violent figure to say, that they would imbibe their liquor out of cups formed from the crooked horns of animals. The first translators, however, not seeing their way clearly, rendered the passage, 'Soon shall we drink out of the *skulls of our enemies*;' and to this strange banqueting there are allusions without end to be met with in our literature. Peter Pindar, for example, once said that the booksellers, like the heroes of Valhalla, drank their wine out of the skulls of authors.

Hooker, the friend of Jewell and Cranmer, all of them

'Unspotted names, and memorable long,
If there be force in virtue,'

made, like Socrates, an unfortunate choice of a wife. Sir Edwin Sandys, who had been his pupil, going one day to visit Hooker at his parsonage in Buckinghamshire, found him tending a flock of sheep by the order of his wife. He had a Horace in his hand, and was probably endeavouring to console himself with that pleasant picture of a country life which the poet has drawn.

In a German literary history of great merit, there is gravely enumerated, amongst the works which throw light upon the traditionary history of King Arthur, a 'Prospectus and Specimen of an intended National Work, by Robert and William Whistlecraft, proposed to comprise the most interesting particulars relating to King Arthur and his Round Table.' This of course was a burlesque.

The story of St Ursula and her eleven thousand virgins is well known. She was a Cornish princess, and set sail with her maiden train for Armorica, the modern Brittany; but by an odd conspiracy of the elements, their fleet was driven up the Rhine as far as Cologne. A tribe of savage Huns massacred the fair multitude, and their bones are shown to this day—a ghastly sight—in that city, where there is a church dedicated to their memory. It has been conjectured, and with great show of reason, that the writer who first transcribed the account mistook the name of the saint's attendant, Undecimilla, for the number *undecim millia* (11,000).

The Orlando Innamorato, a poem which preceded the more celebrated Orlando Furioso of Ariosto, was written by Count Boiardo of Scandiano, and was first published about 1495. The style is uncouth, abounding with rude Lombardisms; and consequently Berni, about half a century later, undertook the singular task of writing Boiardo's poem over again. He preserved the sense of almost every stanza, though every one was more or less altered, and he inserted a few introductory passages to each canto. The genius of Berni—playful, satirical, and flexible—was admirably fitted to perform this labour; the harsh dialect of the Lower Po was replaced by the racy idiom of Tuscany; and the Orlando Innamorato has descended to posterity as the work of two minds remarkably combined in this instance. The sole praise of invention, circumstance, description, and very frequently that of poetical figure and sentiment, belonging to Boiardo; that of style, in the limited use of the word, to Berni. Sir Walter Scott, at one period of his life, made it a practice to read through the two great poems, of which the Paladin Orlando is the hero, once every year.

The power of acquiring languages which some men possess is very extraordinary. There was an eastern monarch, named Mithridates, of whom the tradition is, that in an immense polyglot army, composed of a great variety of nations, he could talk to every soldier in his own language. The Chancellor d'Aguesseau of France made himself master of the Latin, Greek, Hebrew, Italian, Spanish, Portuguese, and English languages. So easily did he add a new language to his list, that he always spoke of its acquisition as an amusement. Niebuhr, the learned historian of Rome, and son of the celebrated traveller, was one of the greatest of modern linguists. He had actually mastered nineteen languages in addition to his own. In this showy accomplishment the Russians excel other nations. If you meet a Russ at a table d'hôte abroad, you are sure to find that he converses fluently with the miscellaneous persons about him in their own tongues. And this is the case for obvious reasons. The Slavonic languages have no literature of their own; the Russian, therefore, in order to receive any passable education at all, is made acquainted early in life with other European tongues.

THE PROBABLE APPLICATIONS OF THE ELECTRIC TELEGRAPH.

We may anticipate some most singular effects will be produced by the electric current. There is no reason why any great event might not be communicated at the same instant throughout the whole kingdom. The salutes fired on the occasion of her majesty's visit to the House of Lords might be instantaneously repeated at every station on all the railways in England; for the electric flame fires gunpowder, and the explosion of the powder is at the same instant with the crack of the discharge. The expense of Captain Warner's long range is at once spared to the country; instead of blowing up a ship at the moderate distance of six miles by one of his projectiles, we shall be enabled to do so at the distance of a thousand miles. There is, indeed, no reason why one of the lords of the Admiralty should not himself fire the guns of the batteries at Portsmouth, whilst calmly and quietly seated at the board in Whitehall. Nor is there any reason why the electric current may not be made to answer in the more peaceful or even the more elegant accomplishments of life. A galvanic arrangement might be made by which our accomplished pianista, Madame Dulcken, might, with all the taste and skill which delights her London auditory, perform at the same moment for the gratification and enjoyment of Gosport and Southampton, and wherever a few wires could be conveniently transmitted. We might also observe that the Society for the Prevention of Cruelty to Animals ought to call upon every butcher to kill the animals used for food by electric galvanism. Each of these persons should have a small galvanic battery for this purpose. Not only is all pain spared to the poor lamb 'whom thy riot dooms to bleed to-day,' but the meat is rendered more tender and more delicate. It is more than half a century since Franklin commenced those experiments which the remorseless hand of war put a stop to, and which have been the precursors of the wonders of the present day. He proposed to give a feast to electricians, when 'a turkey is to be killed for our dinner by the electric shock,' 'roasted by the electric jack, before a fire kindled by the electrified bottle; when the healths of all the famous electricians of England, Holland, France, and Germany, are to be drunk in electrified bumpers, under the discharge of guns from the electric battery.' Were we to indulge in our prognostics of what will yet be done by the powers of electro-galvanism, we should be considered as visionary enthusiasts, and the laugh of the uninitiated would doubtless be loud and long; but already are some of the wonders made known, and nothing but the expense attendant upon them prevents them from being generally brought forward. By its means ships may yet be navigated on the ocean, our cities illuminated, the weather changed, life protracted, some diseases avoided; and we may use the language of him who first by electricity drew lightning from the clouds, 'I shall never have done if I tell you all my conjectures, thoughts, and imaginations, on the nature and operations of this electric fluid.'—*Polytechnic Review for May.*

A CARGO OF WIGS.

Sometimes French ambassadors carry their powers of protection to strange lengths, and apply them to singular purposes. It is related that one La Rose, first valet-de-chambre to M. d'Argental, in 1690, was persuaded by some one in Paris to lay out his savings in wigs, as a good speculation to take to Turkey. Finding, upon reaching Constantinople, that his stock remained on hand, and that he had been duped, he fell into low spirits, and had nigh died of despondency. The ambassador, seeing this, bethought himself of applying to the grand vizir, to see if he could not devise some plan for getting rid of the cargo. 'Nothing can be more easy,' replied the sultan's *alter ego*; 'leave the affair to me.' On the following day, a firmân was issued, and read in the Jewish synagogues, commanding all Jews to wear wigs. Terrible was the confusion and running to and fro among the unfortunate Israelites of Balat and Khass Kouy. Few knew the meaning of wigs: none knew where to find them. This having quickly reached La Rose's ears, he joyously delivered his store to a broker, who disposed of the whole in a few hours, and the speculator reaped a rich harvest. He was, however, directed by his master not to renew the venture. This was not the only strange proceeding on the part of M. d'Argental: indeed he carried his vagaries so far, that he was eventually put under restraint by his own secretaries.—*Three Years in Constantinople, by C. White.*

PUGNACITY OF THE ROBIN.

A correspondent of the Magazine of Natural History relates the following extraordinary instance of the pugnacity of the robin (*Erythaca Rubecula*):—Hearing one warbling in a tree adjoining my house, I was induced to place on the window-sill a beautifully stuffed specimen of the bird, in the hope that it would attract the attention of his living brother. Nor was I disappointed. The song became louder, and in longer strains; and at last he made a flight of inspection as far as the window. Shortly after he flew up from his tree, and made so violent an attack on the stuffed specimen, as to throw it from a height of two storeys to the ground, pursuing it even while falling, and continuing its violence when down. I then perched it on an empty box in the yard—the live bird remaining within a few feet of me all the time; and, directly I had retired a few paces, the attack was renewed with double vigour, and so obstinately, that I could easily have caught the living combatant. On my withdrawing the stuffed bird from the unequal contest, its opponent resumed his place on the box, strutting about with an expanded tail and erect attitude, as if claiming and pronouncing a victory. Noticing the bird to be still hovering about the place, I replaced my stuffed specimen on the window-sill, securing the stand by a bradawl; and hardly had I done so before the robin resumed the war by settling on the head of his unconscious foe, digging and pecking at it with such ferocity and violence, that had I not interfered, the utter destruction of my poor specimen must have ensued. The experiment of course was not renewed; but the robin during the rest of the day kept watch in the immediate neighbourhood, and continued chanting his notes of defiance even in the shade of the evening.

LIGHT FOR ALL.

You cannot pay with money
  The million sons of toil—
The sailor on the ocean,
  The peasant on the soil,
The labourer in the quarry,
  The hewer of the coal;
Your money pays the hand,
  But it cannot pay the soul.

You gaze on the cathedral,
  Whose turrets meet the sky;
Remember the foundations
  That in earth and darkness lie:
For, were not those foundations
  So darkly resting there,
Yon towers could never soar up
  So proudly in the air.

The workshop must be crowded
  That the palace may be bright;
If the ploughman did not plough,
  Then the poet could not write.
Then let every toil be hallowed
  That man performs for man,
And have its share of honour
  As part of one great plan.

See, light darts down from heaven,
  And enters where it may;
The eyes of all earth's people
  Are cheered with one bright day.
And let the mind's true sunshine
  Be spread o'er earth as free,
And fill the souls of men,
  As the waters fill the sea.

The man who turns the soil
  Need not have an earthy mind;
The digger 'mid the coal
  Need not be in spirit blind:
The mind can shed a light
  On each worthy labour done,
As lowliest things are bright
  In the radiance of the sun.

The tailor, ay, the cobbler,
  May lift their heads as men—
Better far than Alexander,
  Could he wake to life again,
And think of all his bloodshed,
  (And all for nothing too!)
And ask himself—'What made I
  As useful as a shoe?'

What cheers the musing student,
  The poet, the divine?
The thought that for his followers
  A brighter day will shine.
Let every human labourer
  Enjoy the vision bright—
Let the thought that comes from heaven
  Be spread like heaven's own light!

Ye men who hold the pen,
  Rise like a band inspired,
And, poets, let your lyrics
  With hope for man be fired;
Till the earth becomes a temple,
  And every human heart
Shall join in one great service,
  Each happy in his part.

J. Gostick.

⁂ Complete sets of the Journal, *First Series*, in twelve volumes, and also odd numbers to complete sets, may be had from the publishers or their agents. A Stamped Edition issued for transmission, post free, price Twopence halfpenny.

Printed by William Bradbury, of No. 6, York Place, and Frederick Mullett Evans, of No. 7, Church Row, both of Stoke Newington, in the county of Middlesex, printers, at their office, Lombard Street, in the precinct of Whitefriars, and city of London; and Published (with permission of the Proprietors, W. and R. CHAMBERS,) by WILLIAM SOMERVILLE ORR, Publisher, of 2, Amen Corner, at No. 2, AMEN CORNER, both in the parish of Christchurch, and in the city of London.—Saturday, June 14, 1845.

CONDUCTED BY WILLIAM AND ROBERT CHAMBERS, EDITORS OF 'CHAMBERS'S INFORMATION FOR THE PEOPLE,' 'CHAMBERS'S EDUCATIONAL COURSE,' &c.

No. 77. New Series. SATURDAY, JUNE 21, 1845. Price 1½d.

PENGUINS.

On some of the shores touched at by Captain Cook in the Pacific, the sailors found long rows of the sea-birds called penguins, which, having never before seen a human being, had acquired no respect for our race, but sat still with the greatest coolness, while the men approached with sticks to knock them on the head. Doubtless, penguins of any experience are now found to have their veneration in a sufficiently active state, as far as the human figure is concerned; but the recollection of what their conduct was when they occupied uninhabited shores, leads me to apply their name to a class of men who exhibit an equal degree of indifference towards their presumable superiors. They are a strange set the penguins—very worthy, clever, sensible people perhaps—attend to their duty, owe nothing which they cannot pay, take their share in putting to rights the evils of the world—much to praise about them, nothing to say against them—only this, they have no respect to give to anybody.

A proper penguin, let it be carefully remarked, is not a person who has a sullenness at his fellows, and withholds deference because he thinks it not justly due. He is no morose malcontent, who thinks to revenge real or ideal wrongs by abjuring the forms of politeness. There is not necessarily any ill-nature in his composition. The penguin is merely a person who, average in all other respects, is strikingly deficient in veneration. All grades, natural and artificial, are alike to him. While a man of high rank, or of any other kind of distinction, finds most of his fellow-creatures treating him with deference, and addressing him with bated breath and whispering humbleness, he is met by the penguin at the second, or perhaps even the first interview, upon the footing of an old acquaintance, as if there were nothing at all particular about him. The suave delicacy and reserve with which even equals of gentlemanly condition address each other on a first acquaintance in this country, is unknown to the penguin. He is quite at his ease at the first, and never advances into intimacy with any one, simply because he is as intimate at starting as he could be at the end of twenty years.

We have, in Mr Lockhart's Life of Sir Walter Scott, a curious example of the character, where a poet, comparatively in humble circumstances, and unknown to fame, is allowed by the author of Marmion to visit him. At the first, he is, with this child of nature, 'Mr Scott,' then 'Scott' only, then 'Walter.' Mrs Scott is at the same time 'Charlotte;' and the visitor stretches himself upon the pureness of her dimity sofa with the greatest unconcern. Nothing could have been more penguin-like in all respects; for in the first place, this kind of person is as remarkable for his want of all veneration for one's upholstery, as he is for non-deference to one's self. He is fearless in his advances to reserved easy-chairs, and makes his way amongst drawing-room bijouterie-tables with the air of a rustic passing through a harvest field. Introduce him to the most elegant lady, and probably he will sit down close against her, with the back of the chair presented in front, and his arms leaning across the back. Then he is equally free and easy in his appellatives. Misters and mis'esses have no charms for him. The regular Christian name is the best which any of his friends can expect from him to their faces: while speaking *of* them, this is invariably familiarised, so that one would suppose, only hearing his conversation, that he knew nobody but persons in the humblest walks of life. There is no affectation in this; for, were he an expectant of patronage, brought for the first time into the presence of an East India director, it is ten to one he would be calling the deity of Leadenhall Street by his plain surname only, before the end of the interview. The truth appears to be, that he sees in a great man only the common human image; and this being exactly what he possesses himself, he feels no occasion for regarding it as an object to be held in any reverence. He may thus be what is called an ill-bred man; but yet, the character being perfectly natural and unaffected, he rarely is felt to be a positively offensive one. On the contrary, one cannot sometimes help being amused, if not interested, by conduct which is marked by so much simplicity, and in which we can read, that if we are little venerated, so are we as little feared.

An excellent opportunity for studying the various degrees of penguinism and ante-penguinism of mankind, is afforded by the forming of new acquaintances through letters of introduction. I presume myself to be speaking of a person who possesses some kind of worldly consequence, whether from his own qualities, or the accident of his birth and fortune. Let him watch the demeanour of individuals who come to see him, bearing letters of introduction in their hands, or who at most send them in immediately before by a servant. Some will appear to him decidedly too venerative—almost timidly so: too little manliness and self-respect: the hat will hang awkwardly in the hand, the vertebral column decline too much from the vertical. There will be a solicitude of eye and face almost painful to the beholder; and chairs will be treated with far more deference than any mortal chairs deserve. Others again will be self-possessed and easy, without either bashfulness or forwardness. But see, at length comes the penguin! A strutting or shuffling *degagé* walk ushers in a specimen of humanity, the very reverse of that above described—who, after a hasty good morning, gives you the letter, and then goes to whistle or hum at a window till you have read it. When you advance to greet him as the person whom you have ascertained him to be, he greets *you*. He wishes you to be quite at your ease in your own house, and not make any fuss on his account. He likes your prospect, hopes your wife is well, and expresses his approval of the weather, in a breath. Smith, whom you have inquired for—the common friend who has sent the letter—is an excellent fellow, or a good creature, as the whim may strike him; the fact being, that our stranger is a protegé or dependent of that gentleman, and has no notion of being anything else for some time to come. He has not read your last work yet (supposing you an author), but he hears it well spoken of, and intends to read it. He thought you rather unfortunate in the choice of subject for the one which preceded it. Then he tells you how he once gave you a favourable notice in some provincial newspaper, the very name of which you never heard of. And he has no doubt that, with one thing and another, you make a tolerable income. You may feel at first a little disconcerted by the air of easy self-confidence of the man, and his want of all those phrases of deference to which you are accustomed; but you soon see that the man means no indignity. He treats you as he would treat the shade of Milton, were it sent upon the earth, or as he would treat the queen upon the throne to-morrow. He is merely a penguin. It may be remarked that penguinism, as a characteristic, is not confined to individuals. I know penguin families, whole tribes of people, who are remarkable for their fearless indifference to all real and conventional superiority. The English, as a nation, are more penguins than the Scotch, the Americans still more so than the English. Political institutions help in bringing about this effect; and perhaps social circumstances also operate. There cannot, for instance, be more penguinism in a large dense community than in a village. A country great man is apt, when he goes to London, to regard it as a city of penguins.

Great penguinism, though many will regard it as a pardonable oddity, will not, upon the whole, serve to advance a man's fortunes. Nothing does so, perhaps, which conveys the impression, as this does, of a deficiency in the tone of society. Were I asked to set down a practical rule of life upon this point, I would say, Be not either too much or too little of the penguin. Treat real and implied superiors with a manly ease, remote alike from familiarity and servility; leaving good sense and good feeling to guide you aright in particulars. There is, in reality, a pretty wide middle field within which you may range without much danger of giving offence; but be careful not to trespass too far beyond this neutral ground in either direction.

LONDON IN 1765, BY A FRENCHMAN.

In the year above indicated a French gentleman visited England for the purpose of observing the manners of our nation, at a time when, according to the popular prejudice, his countrymen were regarded as our natural enemies. The remarks which he afterwards published occupy three volumes. They are written in a lively style, and include almost everything worthy of note in London, to which city it seems the writer confined himself. The arts and sciences, theatres, public walks, manufactures, police, jurisprudence, manners and customs, servants, poor, national melancholy, and king, lords, and commons, are all noticed; as well as the scientific societies, and Wilkes and 45. It may not be unprofitable to compare the opinions and descriptions of this foreigner with the existing state of things. The writer tells us that the only words of English he knew were *very good* and *very well*. To this circumstance we must therefore attribute many obvious errors in his descriptions.

Our traveller, who does not give his name, begins by describing his voyage across the channel from Boulogne to Dover in one of the old sailing packets, through a very rough sea, which, he tells us, operated on most of the passengers with the 'effect of the most violent emetic;' but that for his part being 'fortified by resignation to death, which ought to be the chief cargo of those who undertake voyages of curiosity,' he experienced none of the unpleasant effects which he witnessed in his fellow-passengers. Those were not the days of steam: who ever thinks of 'resignation' now-a-days in a run across the channel? On landing at Dover, where we shall leave him to speak for himself, we are informed that he took the 'two customhouse officers for beggars; they had the look of their profession, which is the lowest and vilest of any; they opened my trunk, and withdrew very humbly without having appeared to examine any of my things. It cost me afterwards a crown to release it from the customhouse. The only inhabitants at Dover are sailors, pilots, and innkeepers. There is nothing remarkable in the town but the enormous signs of the taverns. I saw several postchaises start, driven by little boys twelve or thirteen years old, who, I was told, were excellent postilions. I looked all over the town for a church, but could see nothing to lead me to suppose that such a thing was to be found. I could only obtain food at the inn by going to the kitchen, and helping myself to some of the beef-steaks that were broiling on the fire; this was the only cheer I could get.

'I left Dover for London in what they call the Flying Coach, drawn by six horses; the distance is eighty miles, and the journey consumes a whole day; for this the charge is one guinea, but your servant is carried at half price. The coachmen, who were changed with every change of horses, were jolly and good-looking, and dressed in good *plush*. The space not taken up by luggage was filled with kegs of brandy, which were distributed at the various taverns we passed on the route, so that, if we were often delayed, we had at least the pleasure of a little innocent smuggling to make up for it. The people that we saw had a sadness of physiognomy only seen in France on the faces of those who have buried their best friends.

'The roads, covered with broken flints, are well kept: there is a turnpike at every village, where you must pay according to the scale of charges; the king even is not exempted, but must pay in advance, or the gate would be shut in his face. There are footpaths for those who walk, which are well preserved: these are at the sides of the road, or, in places where it is narrow, in the field adjoining. There are several reasons for the great attention paid to foot passengers: first, life is held in particular esteem; many objects of pleasure and convenience are sacrificed to it; the laws are not exclusively made or administered by those who ride in coaches; and as people travel as fast in the country, as slow in the towns, they wish to avoid the risk of injuring the pedestrians. The farms appear everywhere in a flourishing condition: the labourers who drive the powerful teams wear convenient boots, and their garments are made of good cloth. The public authorities are content to encourage and animate rural industry, which they would fear to destroy if they attempted to direct.

'I reached London towards the close of the day: although the sun had not set, Westminster Bridge, the great road leading to it, as well as the diverging streets, were all lighted up. The sight of the bridge, the river, the streets crowded with vehicles, the throng of passengers on the wide pavements, told to the advantage of the finest quarter of London. We drove through them, and at last, quite by chance, I found myself settled in an apartment in the house of the *Cuisinier Royal*, in Leicester Fields: this neighbourhood is filled with small houses which are mostly let to foreigners.

'The next morning I went out alone, after a careful study of the map of London, and entering Oxford Street, walked down Holborn and the Strand to St Paul's, and then on to the Exchange and the Tower: I returned by crossing London Bridge, through Southwark and Lambeth to Westminster, a district full of mean houses and meaner taverns. The first view of London is favourable, and this it owes entirely to the Thames, which flows by it from south to north, turning at the bend where Whitehall stands from west to east. Whitehall seems to indicate by its position the palace of a sovereign. I have said that the Thames flows *by* London, for opposite Westminster is nothing but the open country, though the few houses which are built on that side are increasing in number. Lower down on the same side is Southwark, which the common people call *Soudrick*, an ill-built suburb, tenanted almost entirely by tanners and dyers, and connected with the city by London Bridge, which stands a specimen of the architectural boldness and skill of the days in which it was built. A little above Whitehall is Westminster Bridge, built in the last reign: it is an erection superior to any other of the kind in Europe.

'Below the old bridge the Thames forms the port of London, immense in its extent, safe, deep enough for all vessels, and unequalled in the prodigious concourse of ships which are continually arriving and departing: it is a port of which the citizens are justly proud, and justifies the reply of the alderman to James I., who threatened to remove the seat of royalty—"At least your majesty will leave us the Thames."

'The grandeur which London derives from the river is due entirely to nature; art does nothing but to destroy or conceal it. There are no quays along the whole extent of the city; and it would appear that every imaginable means is used to hide the sight of this noble stream, in the same way that the Seine was formerly imprisoned at Paris. Here there is nothing but wharfs, docks, piers, and stairs, which, while they disfigure the banks, obstruct the channel and collect all the filth of the town. Even from the bridges it is impossible to get a view of the river, as the parapets are ten feet high; so that, during my first walk, in order to gratify my curiosity I was obliged to mount to the upper storey of a building which overlooked the stream. The reason given for all this is the inclination which the English, and the Londoners especially, have for suicide. It is true that above and below the town the banks are unprotected, and offer an excellent opportunity to those who really wish to drown themselves; but the distance is great, and besides those who desire to leave the world in this manner, prefer doing so before the eyes of the public. The parapets, however, of the new bridge, which is being built between the two at present standing, will be but of an ordinary height. It would seem that the architect means to act with regard to the good citizens in the same way as children are cured of greediness, by leaving confectionary and sweetmeats at their disposal; so it is hoped that in a little time the number of deaths by drowning will diminish, and then the banks of the river will probably be thrown open, and the city derive all the advantage from purification of the air.

'The new bridge is not yet christened; the friends of England's living Demosthenes wish to name it *Pitt* Bridge; while the opposite party contend for the appellation of *Blackfriars*, from a monastery of that order which once stood in the vicinity. Whatever name may be given to it, it surpasses that of Westminster in boldness of design, magnificence of structure, and decoration. It was to have been completed in five years, in each of which the parliament voted 300 guineas to the architect; unforeseen accidents have, however, prolonged the building, which is now in the tenth year from its commencement.

'In public and private buildings, London can show nothing equal, in point of grandeur, to those of Paris and the cities of Italy. The whole list is soon enumerated: there is Somerset House, built of the remains of old churches by the uncle and protector of the last of the Edwards, in bad taste, and now partially in ruins;* the Lord Mayor's House, Temple Bar, St Paul's, the Exchange, the Monument, and some churches buried among houses. There is nothing remarkable about the Tower, except a battery of 100 cannon of large calibre, which defends it on the side towards the river: this edifice is said to have existed from the time of the conquest of the island by Julius Cæsar.

'Old London is divided in its entire length by two great streets parallel with the Thames—the Strand, which at one of its extremities takes the name of Cheapside; and Holborn, which is disagreeably intruded on by Newgate prison. These two thoroughfares are spacious, but have no direct line; St Paul's is the natural perspective object from the Strand, but in reality you only see the cathedral when close upon it. The inscription on the Monument tells us that after the fire the streets were built on new lines. This can scarcely be believed when we see houses flung down apparently at random; in fact, it would hardly be possible to build streets so narrow or so tortuous; they are paved also in such a manner that it is barely possible to ride or walk on them in safety, and they are always extremely dirty. The finest streets—the Strand, Cheapside, Holborn—would be impassable, were it not that on each side, for the convenience of the passengers, footways are made from four to five feet wide; and for communication from one to the other across the street, there are smaller footways elevated above the general surface of the roadway, and formed of large stones selected for the purpose. It is easy to imagine the inconvenience that these frequent crossings cause to the passage of wheel-carriages. In the finest part of the Strand, near St Clement's church, I noticed, during the whole of my stay in London, that the middle of the street was constantly covered with liquid stinking mud, three or four inches deep; with this, owing to the continual jolting and splashing, the walkers are bespattered from head to foot; it flies through the open windows of coaches, and covers the lower storey of the houses; every morning the apprentices may be seen washing away from their shop fronts the accumulated mud of the previous day.

'The natives, however, brave all these disagreeables, wrapped up in long blue coats like dressing-gowns, wearing brown stockings, and perukes rough, red, and frizzled. The paving consists of stones just as they are drawn from the quarry; they are nearly round, and have neither top, bottom, nor sides, and roll and rub one against the other in the foundation on which they are laid, which is nothing but an accumulation of old mud. All the art of the paviour is comprised in placing these stones as near together as possible; and bad as it is, this paving is very dear. Granite is too expensive for general use, as it is brought from the extremity of the kingdom. The great streets, however, leading from the houses of parliament to Charing-Cross and Pall Mall, are partly paved with granite, which has begun to extend itself towards the Strand. The two former of these streets were dry enough to require frequent watering in May, while all the rest of the city was deluged with mud.*

'In order to avoid as much as possible the dirt of the principal thoroughfares, the foot-passengers make use of the courts which traverse the district between the Strand and Holborn. Through these crowds are continually passing; they contain the finest shops, which, with the attractions they furnish to the fair sex, the choice arrangement and brilliance of the display of stuffs or objects of taste, with the *filles de boutique*, are quite sufficient to induce persons to choose that route, independently of their greater cleanliness. The shops of the main streets are, however, the most striking spectacle

* The building here alluded to was erected in the year 1547, a few years before the execution of the Duke of Somerset, its owner; it was given up for public use in 1775, and soon after pulled down to make way for the present structure, the principal portion of which was completed by the architect, Sir William Chambers, in 1779, and opened for the transaction of business in 1780. It occupies an area within a few feet as large as Russell Square.

* We are told in a note that, for the method of watering the streets, and for hackney-coaches and sedan-chairs, Paris was indebted to London.

which London offers to the eyes of a stranger; they are all enclosed in glass, ornamented on the outside with mouldings from the antique. Gay in the variety and arrangement of articles exposed for sale, they present an appearance to which Paris can offer nothing comparable.

'The new districts of London bear no resemblance to the old, except in their wide footways, which are every day increasing. The shops of the great thoroughfare, Oxford Street, will disappear as the houses are sought after for private dwellings by the rich: soon will the great city extend itself to *Marylebone*, which is not more than a quarter of a league distant. At present it is a village, principally of taverns, inhabited by French refugees. Up to the time of the last reign, the nobility lived on their estates, and when they visited London they occupied hired apartments; but now they have abandoned the system of their forefathers, and the mania for building in the town has seized them, which, if it continue, will double the city in extent in the course of the next century. The new streets are built uniformly of brick, of two or at the most three storeys, on the model of Bedford House, erected by Inigo Jones. There is an underground apartment, by which greater salubrity is given to the first floor, separated from the street by an area three or four feet wide, enclosed with an iron railing; underneath the pavement are cellars, which add materially to the convenience of the lower floors in the facilities they afford for cleanliness, and supplying coal to the house through an opening covered by a moveable stone. The iron railing, more or less ornamented, terminates in pilasters, forming a sort of advanced doorway, surmounted by the two little lamps which it is expected every house will furnish towards the lighting of the city during the night, thus uniting ornament with utility. The only inconvenience resulting from it is, that notwithstanding the respectful manners of the working-classes of England towards the public, it is difficult to prevent spilling the oil during the daily trimming of the lamps. I saw a person's head broken by the fall of one of them; he, however, took it in good part, and seemed well contented with the excuses of the lamplighter. These lamps, all enclosed in glass coverings, are lighted about half an hour before sunset; they illuminate the pavement, but in the middle of the wide streets there is scarcely light enough to guide the numerous vehicles. From a regard for the people, it happens that, to all the public buildings, churches, &c. a clock with a large dial is attached, so that the foot-passengers are saved the expense and inconvenience of carrying watches.

'In the new quarters of the town are situated those quadrangular openings, sometimes of great extent, here called *squares*. There is generally a fountain or a bowling green in the centre. Grosvenor Square is laid out as a garden with walks. Others have equestrian statues of some of the kings. Red Lion Square is ornamented with a truncated obelisk of great proportions, which has a very good effect. The houses round these squares are not uniform in appearance, but are decorated according to the taste of the proprietors.

'I have seen but four houses in London which will bear comparison with the great *hotels* of Paris, and these being built of brick, do not appear with the same splendour as those of the latter city. Montague House,* however, merits particular distinction, from its great extent, arrangement, the magnificence of its ornaments, and the agreeableness of its position; it is more like a royal palace than the house of a private individual. The government has purchased this building for the reception of monuments, statues, and all collections, the preservation of which may aid the cause of art or science for the present or the future. It is called the British Museum, although it is not yet complete in all its departments.

'New London is as dirty as the older parts of the town, owing to the clayey nature of the ground on which it is built: there are drains which carry off some of the excess to the river, and it is strictly forbidden to throw dirty water from any of the windows; yet the finest streets were always wet and foul during the whole time of my stay. To the inconvenience of mud must be added that of smoke, which, mingled with a perpetual fog, covers London as a pall. This smoke is occasioned in the winter, which lasts eight months, by the fires of the numerous factories, and by the coal which is universally consumed. If the city increase in extent, the inhabitants must make up their minds never to see the sun: it is but rarely that it can break through the smoky clouds, and these occasions the Londoners call their *glorious days*. The prevailing taste for walking, however, leads them to brave all weather. On the 26th of April, I saw St James's Park, covered incessantly with fogs, smoke, and rain, crowded with promenaders; a sight that excited my admiration for the remainder of the day. The rain brings down the floating particles of smoke from the atmosphere in the form of showers of ink, soiling everything exposed to the weather, and with double effect, as it is not the fashion to use umbrellas. Among the shops are great numbers of clothes-cleaners: the washing is perpetual. The same blackness is produced on the buildings: St Paul's looks as though it were built of coal; and the sombre appearance is increased by the parts most exposed retaining something of their original colour—which is that of bright Portland stone. The interior of the houses even is not exempt from the destructive effects of the smoke; the furniture, pictures, hangings, and especially books, become very soon discoloured, and wrapped in the same lugubrious covering.

'The police of London is in the hands of a few magistrates, of no more importance than the district *commissaires* at Paris: crimes are punished, but no attempt seems to be made to prevent them; there are, however, no spies kept in the pay of the authorities, nor is any secret correspondence carried on. There are no troops, or guard, or watch of any kind, except during the night by some old men, chosen from the dregs of the people; their only arms are a stick and a lantern; they walk about the streets, crying the hour every time the clocks strike, and announce the state of the weather; they also wake those persons who wish to start on a journey at any particular hour, and it appears to be a point of etiquette among hair-brained youngsters, to maul them on leaving their parties.

'London, being thus without guard or watch, inhabited by people who wear no arms, with the exception of physicians, who are always dressed in black, and wear a sword, appears to be protected by the commandment *Non occides*, and by the laws against murder. It is the only great city in Europe in which no assassinations are committed. I proved this by every means in my power; I walked at all hours of the night in the alleys and courts, which are very dimly lighted, without incurring the least danger. I have been in the middle of highly excited mobs, who were surrounded with soldiers; but the fear of shedding blood created mutual respect in both parties. In short, the people of London, though proud and hasty, are good at heart, and humane even in the lowest class. If any stoppage occurs in the streets, they are always ready to lend their assistance to remove the difficulty, instead of raising a quarrel which might end in murder, as is often the case in Paris. At public festivals and ceremonies, however great the crowd, children and persons of diminutive stature are sure to meet with attention, to open them a passage, or lift them to some elevated position where they may be able to see. There are no guards with muskets, partisans, or halberts; the only weapon employed is a hollow stick, which, when it is used—a rare occurrence—makes a great noise without inflicting pain.'

* Those who feel interested in objects of antiquity, will regret to hear that this building, spoken of in such high terms, will shortly be entirely removed, when the new building, now in progress, is completed.

Here we must take leave of our Frenchman, who, it will be seen, describes a state of things very different from those existing in our own times. Such a retrospect is fair evidence of the gradual advance of society; the evils from which great masses of the population are suffering, are light in comparison with those of the former century. What would be thought in the present day of throwing 'dirty water,' not to speak of more offensive matters, into the streets? The moral view taken by the writer of our people is favourable when compared with those of his own country; but we fear that his remarks on the 'respectful manners' of the humbler classes would hardly be borne out by the facts in modern London. It is, however, gratifying to find that, on the whole, the condition of society has improved, and this not only for the sake of the present generation, but because we may hence presume that there will be further improvement in the future.

TRICKS IN THE TRAFFIC OF OBJECTS OF ART.

The traveller who visits many of the countless churches strewed over the European continent, or the public and private picture galleries both there and in this country, cannot fail to be surprised at the number of *originals* which he meets with. There are very few collections which do not boast either of a 'real' Claude, Raffaelle, Rembrandt, Rubens, Dolce, Caracci, or Corregio; and he is forced to conclude that, if all he hears be true, the painters of bygone times must have painted night and day during their long lives to have produced such a vast number of beautiful subjects. It is, however, well understood that by far the greater number of these pictures are spurious—either copies from the undoubted works of the masters to whom they are attributed, or successful imitations of their manner by inferior and modern artists. An account of some of the ingenious methods by which such paintings are first copied and then palmed off upon purchasers, may serve various useful ends.

It is not always that artists are aware, when employed to copy pictures, that they are in the remotest degree contributing to the carrying out of a successful fraud. To show how this sometimes happens, we need only relate an anecdote which we recently heard. Our informant, who is well known in London for his fidelity in copying, was one day busy in his studio, when a carriage rolled up to his door. A stranger of aristocratic mien entered, bringing with him a beautiful female head, evidently painted by a great master. He inquired if our friend would like to copy it at his own price, and if so, when it would be done? The answer was in the affirmative, and the required time named. The new patron said he would be punctual in returning for the original and the promised copy, and without more ado, took leave and drove off. The artist regarded him as some eccentric nobleman, and when leisure permitted, commenced his task, which he completed within the required time. Sure enough, on the day agreed on, the gentleman again appeared, and professed himself so much delighted with the exactitude of the copy that he paid the painter a few pounds more than he demanded.

A week or two after, the artist was surprised by another visit from the same person, who brought a second and equally beautiful head, to be copied upon exactly the same conditions as to time and price. Our friend's suspicions were now roused, for he began to suspect that his aristocratic-looking patron was a picture-dealer in disguise; but before he could express his doubts, the gentleman vanished. After some hesitation, he set to work and completed his task within the time specified, determining, however, not to part with the pictures without some explanation. When therefore his employer again appeared, he demanded a pledge that the copies were not intended to be put to any improper use, or to be passed off as originals. The stranger was indignant, demurred to the artist's right of demanding any such pledge, and after some discussion, was allowed to take away both pictures, having first given the usual remuneration for the artist's labour.

Time passed on, and our friend had nearly forgotten the transaction, when a nobleman, from whom he had previously received many commissions, returned from abroad, and called on him to request his opinion of 'an exquisite Carlo Dolce,' which was to be sold in a collection advertised for sale in the mansion of a gentleman in the Regent's Park. 'It will,' he continued, 'form an admirable companion to a picture by the same artist I was fortunate enough to pick up in Italy for a bagatelle of three hundred guineas.' Upon this our friend posted off to the Regent's Park to examine the wonderful and undoubted Carlo Dolce. On beholding it, he was astonished to find his own work! Hastening to his noble patron's house to communicate what he had seen, he was shown into the library, when the first thing that met his eye was his other performance! His surprise was doubled; and he inquired on the entrance of his friend, 'is *that* the picture for which you gave three hundred guineas in Rome?' The answer was in the affirmative, and a detail was entered into of the circumstances of the purchase. It was bought in the palace of a decayed Italian family, 'where it had lain in a neglected apartment for more than a century.' Our painter took down the picture, turned it over, examined it minutely, saw that it had been lined with old canvas to give it an ancient look, and at last exclaimed that he had painted it himself. It was the second copy he had made for his mysterious employer!

Of course the sale of the other so-called Dolce in the Regent's Park was stopped, and the 'gentleman' who had advertised it was exposed to the world in his true character; that of a tricking picture-dealer.

It is not difficult to explain how our friend's copy got into the Italian palace, and how it was purposely placed in a neglected apartment to deceive the buyer. This kind of trick is common in Italy. It is the more easily practised, from the fact of many decayed gentlemen of that country turning picture-dealers and hanging subjects in their rooms, so as to make them pass for heirlooms or ancient family possessions; many paintings are actually imported into Italy for that purpose. This, however, is an old device, and most picture-fanciers are on their guard against it when invited to visit the gallery of an Italian gentleman, cautiously abstaining from hinting at a purchase, should a feeler to that effect be thrown out by the host. More artful contrivances are occasionally resorted to, some of which are exposed in a clever article in a recent number of the Foreign Quarterly Review. One of the most curious relates to M. K——, a Russian amateur, who was invited by some Florentine gentlemen to join a shooting excursion. Whilst they pursued their sport, he, disgusted by ill success, returned to wait for them at a cottage where their horses were put up. Having got into conversation with its occupant, the latter inquired if his guest was fond of pictures, as he had something curious that might interest him. After a long story how his father had on his deathbed confided to him the secret that a picture concealed in the house was of value sufficient to make the fortune of all his family, but that, having been feloniously obtained, it would, if ever shown or sold in that neighbourhood, certainly bring him into trouble—the rustic produced a very pleasing Madonna and Child, in an antique carved frame. The Russian cordially admired the picture, and being asked to guess the artist, named Raffaelle. 'That,' said the peasant, 'was, I do believe, the very name my father mentioned; but you can see if it was so, as he gave me this bit of paper with the name written on it.' On the dirty shred there was in fact scrawled 'Raffaelle Sanzi;' and its possessor went on to hint that, being anxious to realise what he knew to be most valuable property, and seeing no great chance of then disposing of it safely, he would accept from him, as a foreigner, a price far below its value. The negotiation thus opened, ended in the Russian offering 35,000 francs, or L.1400, which, after due hesitation, was accepted. The prize was huddled into a clothes-bag, and its new master, without waiting to take leave of his friends, started for Florence, and thence hurried on to Rome, lest it should be stopped by the Tuscan government.* There he boasted of his acquisition, and showed it to several connoisseurs, who sang its praises until Signor V——, a skilful dealer, quickly recognised the real artist. It was in fact a beautiful repetition, with slight variations, of Raffaelle's famous 'Madonna del Gran-duca;' it was painted by Micheli, an Italian painter still alive, who avows that he sold it for 150 crowns; and the shooting-party was a conspiracy by several well-born swindlers to take in their Russian friend! The latter returned to Florence to seek redress by a prosecution, which was compromised by their returning most of the price. 'Being curious to see or obtain the subject of so strange a tale, we,' continues the writer in the Foreign Quarterly, 'subsequently inquired for the picture, but were told it might probably be met with as an original in some great German collection, having been there resold by the Russian at a price almost equal to what he had himself originally paid!' Thus this picture was the subject of a double fraud. Indeed there are many 'undoubted' originals, the history of which, if faithfully recorded, would lay bare a long chain of cheateries.

Of course the regular traders in pictures, being looked upon with a sort of suspicion, require to exercise a superior degree of ingenuity to effect their sales. We learn from the above source, that among the cleverest of the Roman dealers is Signor A——, a fair-spoken fellow and facetious withal, who, conscious of his own talent, is ever ready to adduce some instance of its happy exercise. A year or two since he made a wholesale transaction, which, in a short half hour, transferred to a young Irish peer the accumulated rubbish of his magazine. At the lucky moment of *milor's* visit, there arrived a liveried servant with an official-looking missive, which A—— apologised for opening, and after glancing at it, said, 'Very good, but I have no time now to look at your pictures; come again.' The servant hesitated, and to the inquiries of the stranger, A—— said it was only the particulars of a lot of pictures which had been sent to him for sale, the heritage of an old Bolognese family, but that he had never had leisure to open the boxes, which must stand over till he could attend to the matter. On his lordship pressing to have a sight of them, A—— reluctantly opened the cases, protesting that it was of no use, as it would take much time to clean, and arrange, and value this collection; before which, of course, the pictures were not for sale. The list exhibited Guidos, Domenichinos, Caraccis, Carlo Dolces; in short, just that class of names which impose upon an Anglican amateur; and the dingy canvases were freely acknowledged to be so completely obscured by dirt and old varnish, that their merits were undistinguishable. The more the dealer seemed anxious to divert his customer to the brightly varnished ornaments of his own walls, the less willing was he to lose sight of this singular chance of procuring 'a *genuine* gallery ready made,' and ere the parties separated, a transfer was made to the peer of a mass of trash which scarcely merited the outlay of cleaning, in exchange for a thousand louis-d'or.

A still bolder *coup de main* was successfully played off by the same worthy some years before, at the expense of an experienced purchaser and acknowledged connoisseur. He persuaded the late Mr C—— to look at a picture of high pretensions and of some merit in his house. Whilst they were discussing it, the jingle of posting bells was heard in the street, and the prolonged crack of a courier's whip echoed in the doorway. A—— started, rushed out, and beheld an express, booted, spurred, and splashed, who handed him a letter. Tearing it open, he appeared struck with confusion, and exclaimed, 'Well, here is a fine scrape I have got into.'

'What is the matter?'

'Why, I am talking about selling you this picture, and here is the courier sent back from Ancona to buy it, by a Russian gentleman to whom I offered it last week, for such a sum.'

The price was a large one, and Mr C—— would not have thought of giving it for the picture, which did not interest him much; but so cleverly did A—— contrive to transfer to it the interest of this dramatic scene, that, in the excitement of the moment, a bargain was struck; and our countryman went off delighted at the idea of having 'done' the Russian; the latter being an imaginary personage, and his courier a Roman postboy, hired to gallop up in the nick of time!

It is not, however, only in pictures that this kind of fraud is carried on. In sculptures, models, cameos, and objects of virtû, the same system is extensively practised. It is well known that in the neighbourhood of the excavated cities of Herculaneum and Pompeii, regular manufactories of 'antiquities' exist for the supply of the curious who visit the neighbourhood of Mount Vesuvius. Coins, cameos, bas-reliefs, and intaglios are got up—it is true in some instances by very clever artists, and often in themselves extremely beautiful—and deposited amidst ruins, to be dug up in the presence of some gaping amateur, and sold for treble their value. An English nobleman, who was known to devote his wealth liberally to the acquisition of antiques, having some time ago arrived in Rome, set the curiosity-dealers at work to tempt him with 'antiques.' The most intelligent of them, one V——, commissioned a cameo, which he made sure would please the earl, from one of the best fabricators of antique gems. A fine stone having been selected, it was finished in the best style, and committed to a jeweller to be set as a ring. In his hands it was casually broken to bits: the plot was defeated, the dealer was furious, but the victim was *not* saved. The wily Italian fell upon a device to render the bait more than ever deadly. Having selected a principal morsel of the cameo, he carried it to the peer as a fragment just brought in by a peasant, which, though incomplete, rivalled the rarest gems in perfection of material and of art. After dwelling upon it with that mellifluous eloquence which only an Italian can employ to good purpose—for in a language whose every syllable is euphony even verbiage becomes effective—he obtained for it a sum which far more than repaid his outlay. Now, as some collectors of such relics so treasure those which time or violence has broken, as almost to give them a seeming preference, the lord and the dealer had perhaps equal reason to be satisfied with the transaction. But there were more fragments behind; so, after pocketing the price and bowing himself out, V—— returned to say, that as it would be a pity the rest of so lovely a work should be lost, he had desired the peasant to dig again for the other bits, in which he might very probably be successful. Next day he returned with another morsel, which he celebrated by another string of superlative epithets, and sold by another tissue of falsehoods for another ransom; and that in due time was succeeded by the remaining fragments—all separately produced, separately puffed, and separately paid for, until in the end the accidental fracture of the stone proved to have quadrupled its price.

The anecdote of the Carlo Dolce in the Regent's Park shows that discreditable tricks and contrivances for the sale of pictures are not confined to Italy. In England, and especially in London, this dishonesty is organised into a system. The stale devices of the auctioneer and

* In some of the Italian states the exportation of pictures is forbidden on pain of forfeiture and a heavy fine.

the saleroom have been long too well known, to deceive any but the merest tyro in picture-buying. Hence more elaborate deceptions are carried out, some of them requiring an amount of capital, time, and knowledge of art, which is in itself wonderful. Take as an example the person whom our friend exposed; he was no doubt in league with a set of Italian dealers of the same caste. He sends them copies to plant about in various residences, and they in return supply him with the deceptive produce of Italian easels, and with the refuse of sale-galleries.* He takes a large house in the Regent's Park, fits up a picture-gallery, and lives to all appearance in great style. He becomes a patron of art, employs some clever copyists, some openly, others as we have detailed, and buys a few good but cheap originals from the modern exhibitions. After a year or two thus spent, he establishes a character as a connoisseur. Presently he gives out that he is going abroad, and brings his gallery 'to the hammer.' Expensive catalogues *raisonnèes* are printed, with the (spurious) history of each picture minutely set down. Picture-fanciers flock to the mansion, and—unless an exposure supervenes—on the day of sale the gallery not only realises enough to pay all expenses, but yields a handsome profit. Upon this profit a new scheme is set on foot; and by such unworthy traffic we are assured that large fortunes have been made.

Indeed many persons who are picture-dealers, and nothing else, manage to keep up appearances for years so well, that they are seldom suspected of being anything worse than rich connoisseurs who are fickle in their tastes, and fond of changing their pictures. Instances of the style in which these persons do business are related in the May number of the Art-Union. 'A picture-dealer, living in a very showy private residence, and keeping a carriage, livery servants, &c. bought a fine picture by Decker. It was signed by his name, and purchased for L.40. A London artist, now deceased, "sharpened the foliage," and added two figures from a picture by J. Ruysdael, which was placed by his side during the alteration; the name of Decker was carefully obliterated, and that of Jacob Ruysdael inserted from the dealer's collection of imitative autographs—a store of which is possessed by all members of the trading race. The picture was soon afterwards sold for 480 guineas. The poor artist got 12 guineas for his assistance in the deception. About the same time, as Albert Cuyp was much in fashion, the same dealer obtained several copies of small works of Cuyp from France and Holland, which, after being lined and undergoing a very rapid advance into the appearance of age, were eagerly sought and purchased. They were "touched up" by a poor intemperate but clever artist, who was kept constantly at work in one of the attics, at miserable weekly wages. Their cost averaged L.18 or L.20; but they were sold at prices from L.150 to L.200 each.'

Mr Pye, in his 'Patronage of British Art,' reveals a trick by which fresh paintings are turned into 'antiques' by wholesale. 'There was in Westminster a manufactory where several persons were employed making copies, which, after having been soiled with dust and varnish, were thrown into an oven built on purpose and moderately warmed, where, in the course of an hour or two, they became cracked, and acquired the appearance of age. I will venture to assert that many of our superficial connoisseurs have been caught with this snare, and have preferred, to the best modern productions, those of what was facetiously termed "the Westminster Oven."'

Of the tricks of auctioneers and their satellites, the Art-Union makes a full exposure. Innumerable are the pleas of genuineness under which pictures are sold by auction. One is a seizure by a sheriff; another a collection upon which a London banker has advanced a large amount, and to be peremptorily sold to cover such advance; another the remainder of the collection of an Italian nobleman. 'During the two days that pictures are commonly "on view" in the sale-room, they are attended by one of the gang who is not known to the public generally as a picture-dealer. He may be a hosier, a master-carpenter, a music-seller, a corn-doctor, or of any other trade; his business in the saleroom during the view days is to endeavour to enter into conversation with any gentleman who may drop in, and to tickle him up with praises and valuations of the various specimens. The individual has an interest in the spoil, and is sometimes, or generally, the furnisher of money in these speculations.

'The day of sale arrives. The auctioneer, without the least blush of shame, assures the audience—composed principally of the owners of the pictures he is about to sell—that such an opportunity as he then offers rarely occurs; that every picture is genuine, and to be sold or sacrificed without reserve. The biddings are small and slow, if there is any show of well-dressed strangers present; great bargains appear to be knocked down—by the seller to the real owners—until some one of the well-dressed strangers is tempted to offer a bidding.

'"Gentlemen," said the auctioneer, in one very recent case, "I most particularly call your attention to this lot, which cost my employer an immense sum. He always esteemed it the gem of his collection. A finer work of this great master cannot be seen, and in such a state of purity; often and often has he refused 500 guineas for this masterpiece, which I am now submitting entirely to your hands; you will have it at your own price—there is no reserve. Gentlemen, give me a bidding; shall I begin at 400 guineas? Who says 400 guineas?" No answer—a pause. "Well, I am astonished. Gentlemen, do look again! I shall be ashamed to give an account of this to my employer. I fully expected for such a treasure of art to obtain a great sum. Say 200 guineas—100 guineas—well, anything you please: I am in your hands, there is no reserve!" Upon this the real owner of the picture, who is a dealer, left his seat, took out his eye-glass, advanced to the easel upon which the picture was placed, and went down on one knee to scrutinize his own property. The auction-room—in which this scene took place—has a low ceiling, and but indifferent light. The owner played the part of "viewing" with wondrous dramatic effect; and in a voice pregnant with affected surprise and anxiety, bid 30 guineas. The auctioneer had his cue. "Well, I am astonished! 30 guineas for such a glorious gem; you must be joking with me, gentlemen—you can't be serious." Forty guineas are now offered by a confederate, which is eagerly bid on by the owner at 45 guineas. This dalliance was carried on by the auctioneer, the owner, and the confederate, interspersed with a deal of by-play and mysterious nods and whisperings, until a stranger present was seduced into an offer of 70 guineas, when the owner of the picture shut up his eye-glass, and coolly turned his back to the auctioneer—a telegraphic signal understood by the whole party that the victim was entrapped. As the picture was of course knocked down to a *bonâ fide* purchaser, the history of it may be instructive. It was bought by the dealer some time before at a sale of imported rubbish for 25s.; was lined, the dirt cleaned off, one unsatisfactory figure obliterated, and the heads of other figures altered. A poor but cleverish artist did this for the pittance of 30s.; and the advantageous changes were made from prints. The picture was next "dirtied down," and after it had been unsuccessfully offered in sales got up at Birmingham, Manchester, and other provincial cities, it returned, after a year or two spent in wandering, to find a gulled proprietor in a dingy saleroom.'

Nothing can better illustrate, than these anecdotes, the irrational and artificial media through which pi[...]

* Of the extent to which the importation of pictures is carried on, an idea may be formed from the fact that, within the last five years, somewhere between 60,000 and 70,000 'ancient' pictures have been imported into England, paying the duty at the customhouse in London.

ures are prized and estimated. The name of the artist aises its value more than the real merit of the picture. This is not wholly unavoidable, it is true, in ordinary udgments on works of art; for it requires a high mount of intellectual taste to judge of the intrinsic beauties of a picture, while everybody can tell whether ts painter enjoys a high reputation or not; and if he lo, the inference is not unnatural that his work must be good. This mode of judging is, it appears, carried o a greater height in England than where knowledge f art is more widely diffused. In Italy good copies re looked upon with more respect and admiration han in this country; whilst bad originals are conemned as they deserve. Here, on the contrary, be he real merits of a picture ever so moderate, any rice is given for it if it only can be made to pass nder a great name. While we are disposed, therefore, o censure dealers for the frauds they practise, let us not orget the vast temptations ignorant and prejudiced purchasers hold out to them by the enormous prices hey offer for supposed 'originals.' Purchasers are in most instances parties to the frauds they themselves uffer by.

A recently deceased and witty divine had an excellent nethod of protecting himself against his own want of udgment and the frauds of dealers. One morning when we had the pleasure of breakfasting with him, we mused ourselves whilst he was temporarily occupied by looking at the pictures hung on his walls. 'Ah,' he remarked, 'you will not find anything very brilliant here! The fact is, I have closely adhered to one rule hrough life. When I take a fancy to a picture, I have never allowed myself to give more than fifty shillings or it.'

'Still you may have picked up some very valuable ones at that price?'

'I don't suppose I have,' answered our reverend friend gravely, 'for one day I had a visit from a great picturedealer, and after he had examined my collection very attentively, I asked him what he thought of them? Slowly shaking his head, he replied, "And so, sir, you gave only fifty shillings a-piece for them. Well, sir, permit me to say that you do your judgment great wrong; or allow me to tell you, sir, that there are some paintngs in your possession which are worth at least —— three pounds!"'

MILTON'S BLINDNESS.

WE do not think that any but a blind man could have written the Paradise Lost. We mean a blind man who had once enjoyed sight. Let us try to substantiate this remark, and to show what influence Milton's blindness exerted over his poetry. That it must have exerted some influence—that Milton's poetry must in some respect be different from what it would have been had he not been blind—cannot be doubted. The slightest peculiarity about an author tinges his writings; and it is only because it rarely happens that the entire character of a person's writings is decided by any one peculiarity, hat we are not more accustomed to regard this influence. But blindness is no ordinary peculiarity. Even f a person who has been in the habit of writing goes o Arabia, and comes back again, all that he writes afterwards will, to a certainty, be affected by that visit o Arabia. How much more will not a change come over the spirit of a man's writings who, after walking or forty-seven years in the light and blaze of day, passes at once and for ever into an atmosphere of darkness! That Milton's blindness should not have affected his poetry, that there should not be a marked difference between the poems he wrote before he became blind and those he wrote after, is impossible. The only queson is, whether this effect, this difference, can be ascerained. We think it can. It is no mere illusive, impalpable peculiarity, of which we are sensible, without possessing the power to lay hold of or describe it; it is easily detected. Nay, we are inclined to put the case so strongly, as to say that Milton's blindness was a *requisite* to his writing Paradise Lost.

When we affirm that Milton's blindness exerted an influence over his poetry, we do not mean merely that it enabled him to withdraw his mind from external objects, and left him at liberty to pursue his daring theme. That was a decided influence, no doubt, but it is not the one on which we lay stress. Neither do we refer to the well-known passages in which Milton deplores his loss of sight. The insertion of a few such passages, if that were all, would not amount to much. Nor, lastly, do we refer to the influence which Milton's blindness must have exerted over his verse, in respect of its having obliged him to compose at length mentally, and then dictate, although this is by no means an insignificant consideration. We propose to show that Milton's blindness affected his poetry in a way more specific and remarkable than any of these; that Milton's whole manner of conceiving and describing external objects is that of a blind man; and that this manner of conceiving and describing things was so peculiarly suitable for his great poem, that it might be made a question whether Milton's blindness did not actuate his choice of a subject.

The conception which will be most familiar to a blind man, will be that of infinitely extended blackness. The world outside will be to him like what it would be to a man with the use of his eyes standing alone on a mountain-top in a very dark night, and looking upward. Now, a blind man who has once enjoyed sight will carry with him into his own black atmosphere a memory full of images of what he has seen; and when he tries to describe things by their appearance, it will be by an effort of recollection. He will amuse himself by painting, on the dark canvas stretched before him, those objects which he has most pleasure in recollecting—the white gable of his own cottage, the faces of his wife and children. The power of love will keep the recollection of such objects as these bright and vivid, while all other images are growing dimmer and dimmer. But there is a certain class of images, the recollection of which in a state of blindness would always continue to be easy and pleasurable. It would be difficult for a person who had been blind for some time to recall the appearance of such a flower as the violet; whereas he would retain to the last a remarkably vivid conception of white or luminous objects—a lamp, the mouth of a furnace, a streak of light, the sun, the moon, a ball of glowing iron, the ground covered with snow, the winter sky studded with stars. In fact, a man who had grown blind would excel a person still retaining the use of sight in all that kind of description which consists in the contrast of white and black, of light and darkness. Now, this power of dealing with light and darkness, as it were, in masses, is exactly that which would be a qualification for writing such a poem as the Paradise Lost. Three-fourths of the description in that poem are precisely of the kind in which a blind man would be pre-eminently apt and powerful. The beings whose actions form the subject of the poem are angels, described as moving to and fro in the universe, surveying creation from some remote point beyond its limits, or descrying a silver star in the distance far away, and winging their flight towards it. This sort of description must be easier to a man to whom space and blackness are the same thing, than it could possibly be to a man to whom space is colourless, or, at the most, a sort of faint blue transparency. The most important descriptions in the Paradise Lost consist, at bottom, of contrasts of blackness with light, light in the form of masses, or particles, or streaks, or discs.

To proceed to instances. It would be quite possible to prefix to the Paradise Lost a plate or diagram of the universe as Milton conceived it mapped out. At first, according to the poet, the whole infinity of space was divided into two huge regions or hemispheres, an upper and a lower, the one all light, the other all darkness. The upper or illuminated half was heaven, the abode of the angels, then the only creatures existing. The under half was chaos or night, a thick, black, turbulent element, as of universes in a state of pulp. No beings resided in it. But after the fall of the angels, space was laid out anew, and instead of only two regions, there came to be four. The bottom of chaos was converted into hell; and at the top, where chaos pressed against heaven, a huge cavity was scooped out of the blackness, into which the light rushed down. This cavity was man's universe. The principle of gravitation being imparted to it, all the matter within the swoop of this right-royal principle left the pulpy form in which it had hitherto existed, and coagulated into balls or planets. Then the Divine impulse came, and the balls spun round each other, the planets round their suns, and the moons round their planets. So that, bounded above by heaven, and beneath by the chaos out of which it had been cut, there existed now a new azure universe powdered with stars and streaked with galaxies. It was destined to be the residence of a new race of creatures. Hell, the residence of the fallen portion of the old race, was separated from it by chaos.

This is the fundamental conception of the Paradise Lost. The infinity of space thus divided, first into two, and afterwards into four regions, is the scene in which the action of the poem is laid. Now, such a gigantic conception could not have occurred to any except a blind man; or if it had occurred to any one else, he could not have sustained it consistently throughout the poem. But how consistently has Milton sustained it! Thus, when he describes the rout of the rebel angels driven before the Messiah's thunder, the crystal wall of heaven

'Rolled inward, and a spacious gap disclosed
Into the wasteful deep; the monstrous sight
Struck them with terror backward; but far worse
Urged them behind; headlong themselves they threw
Down from the verge of heaven: eternal wrath
Burnt after them to the bottomless pit.'

It was Milton's blindness that gave him this grand figure. Reading the passage, one sees chaos, as it were, an infinite mass of solid blackness, and the descent of the angels through it like a red hissing fiery funnel. So in many other passages; that, for instance, describing the creation of man's universe; or the following one, describing Satan's glance into chaos, when, standing at the mouth of hell, he prepares to launch into it in quest of the new universe—

'Before their eyes in sudden view appear
The secrets of the hoary deep, a dark
Illimitable ocean, without bound,
Without dimension, where length, breadth, and height,
And time, and place, are lost, where endless night
And chaos, ancestors of nature, hold
Eternal anarchy, amidst the noise
Of endless wars, and by confusion stand.'

If this passage had not the tone of a narrative, it might pass for a Lamentation on Blindness. Making his way through chaos, Satan at last emerges into the light of the new universe. Directing his flight first to the sun—

'There lands the fiend; a spot like which, perhaps,
Astronomer in the sun's lucent orb,
Through his glazed optic tube, yet never saw.'

This splendid image of Satan alighting on the sun being like a spot dimming its disc, we can hardly conceive presenting itself to the mind of any but a blind man; but how readily to his!

The following is the poet's description of the creation of light—

'"Let there be light," God said; and forthwith light
Ethereal, first of things, quintessence pure
Sprung from the deep; and from her native east,
To journey through the aëry gloom began,
Sphered in a radiant cloud.'

In this passage the influence of the poet's blindness appears in two ways. In the first place, as in the former passages, the conception is that of a blind man. All at first is profound darkness, a black atmosphere; but forthwith there arises a vapour-like something in the east, which slowly creeps westward through the gloom, like a mist from the sea. This is light. In the second place, there is a sort of sentimental lingering in the description, unlike what would be natural in the case of a poet not afflicted with that calamity, which made light so dear to Milton, and all the circumstances of its appearance so delightful to his memory.

Besides the passages we have selected, fifty or sixty others might be given. The only sort of description which five-sixths of the poem required, or would tolerate, is precisely that in which the power Milton's blindness gave him of contrasting light and darkness on the great scale, and of conceiving luminous objects, enabled him to excel. No doubt, if a man having the use of his eyesight had dared to attempt the subject of the Paradise Lost, he would, as a matter of necessity, have been obliged to deal with blackness and fire, chaoses and galaxies, just as Milton has done. No doubt, also, there *are* poets, not blind, whose imagination is at home in the vast and gigantic, who figure to themselves the earth as a brown little ball wheeling through space, and whistling as it wheels. Thus Shakspeare speaks of 'striking flat the thick rotundity o' the world.' Still, none except a blind man could have been so consistent throughout in that sort of description as Milton. But not only does he, more than any other poet, contrast fire and blackness on the great scale; he employs the same contrast as a means of representing what it would never have occurred to any but a blind man to represent in that way. Thus, when Satan, seized in Paradise by Ithuriel and Zephon, is brought before Gabriel and his band of angels, he dares them to battle—

'While thus he spake, th' angelic squadron bright
Turned fiery red, sharpened in mooned horns
Their phalanx, and began to hem him round.'

Who but a blind man could have fancied the appearance of the band of angels hemming Satan in like that of a crescent moon? But luminousness with Milton served as a means of describing everything. Satan starting up when touched by Ithuriel's spear, as he was sitting in the shape of a toad at Eve's ear, is compared to the explosion of a powder magazine. Brilliancy is Milton's synonyme for beauty. The eyes of the serpent are glowing carbuncles, his neck is verdant burnished gold. The locks of the unfallen angels are inwreathed with beams of light; and their golden harps hang by their sides glittering like quivers.

But deduct those five-sixths of the Paradise Lost in which the descriptions are all grand and gigantic—of spirits warring in heaven, toiling through chaos, or winging from star to star—there remains still one-sixth of the poem in which, leaving the regions of space, the poet condescends on our dear particular planet, and outpours his imagination in rich and luscious descriptions of earth's own scenes and landscapes, the fragrant woods, the blooming gardens, the daisied banks, and green overarching bowers of Eden's Paradise. How are these passages of rich vegetable description to be accounted for? Suns and moons and chaoses were easy; but whence got he the trees, and shrubs, and flowers?—that blind old man!

If we examine Milton's earlier poems—those which he wrote before he became blind—we shall find their characteristic to be luscious and flowery description. In this respect we know none so like him as the poet Keats. Take, for instance, the following exquisite passage from Lycidas—

'Return, Sicilian muse,
And call the vales, and bid them hither cast
Their bells and flowerets of a thousand hues.
Ye valleys low, where the mild whispers use
Of shades and wanton winds, and gushing brooks,
On whose fresh lap the swart star sparely looks—
Throw hither all your quaint enamelled eyes,
That on the green turf suck the honeyed showers,
And purple all the ground with vernal flowers;
Bring the rath primrose, that forsaken dies,

The tufted crow-toe, and pale jessamine,
The white pink, and the pansy freaked with jet,
The glowing violet,
The musk rose, and the well-attired woodbine,
With cowslips wan, that hang the pensive head,
And every flower that sad embroidery wears;
Bid amaranthus all his beauty shed,
And daffodillies fill their cups with tears,
To strew the laureat hearse where Lycid lies.'

There is not a passage like this in all the Paradise Lost. If the poet, after being blind for some time, had attempted to rival it, he could have accomplished the feat only by the help of a book on botany. Here is the passage describing Eve's nuptial bower in Paradise, and we may be sure that on this occasion Milton would lavish his richest beauties—

'The roof
Of thickest covert was, inwoven shade,
Laurel and myrtle, and what higher grew
Of firm and fragrant leaf; on either side
Acanthus, and each odorous bushy shrub
Fenced up the verdant wall: each beauteous flower,
Iris all hues, roses, and jessamine,
Reared high their flourished heads between, and wrought
Mosaic; under foot the violet,
Crocus, and hyacinth, with rich inlay,
Broidered the ground, more coloured than with stone
Of costliest emblem.'

Beautiful still; brave recollections of his old loves, the flowers. But, alas, alas! the recollections are growing fainter and fewer in the mind of the blind old man. Yet, as the images of his youth are growing dimmer and dimmer, he is fast nearing that life where he shall renew them all again, and where, amid the spheres of which he sung, and thrilling to a higher music than that which his soul loved so dearly on earth, his eyes shall no more shut out the light nor the colours of the little flowers.

Milton's earlier poems, we have said, remind us of Keats. No poet is so 'lush' in description, to use his own word, as poor Keats. He knew the secrets of the flowers, as if he had been the very bee that buzzed among them, and sipped their sweets. Now, had Keats suddenly grown blind, would he not have forgotten the flowers, and would not his fine soul, then pent up and unwindowed, have employed itself building castles of sunbeams in the darkness within?

JONATHAN SHARP.

A GENTLEMAN who takes to himself the above characteristic name has recently issued to the British public a three-volume work, which professes to give an account of his personal adventures.* He is a Kentuckian, and declares in his preface a determination to be very severe on the faults of his compatriots. As the reader, however, advances into the book, he is surprised to find little that can be unpalateable to Americans. Mr Sharp began his career in Louisville, where his parents kept an inn; but the successful opposition of a rival publican, and a fire, reduced the family to poverty and the inn to ashes; but, says the author, 'my father was a man of prompt resolution. His energies did not fail him in the present emergency. He packed a scanty wardrobe in a small portmanteau, took me with him on board a steamboat going down to New Orleans, and thus got rid at once of all his difficulties.' The worthy couple at length landed at New Orleans, and the son obtained a situation as under-clerk at a cotton broker's, with a salary of 2000 dollars a-year. This employment did not suit the views of the enterprising young gentleman, and, being fond of travel, he exchanged it for a clerkship on board a steamboat. The following anecdote proves how they manage steamboats on the Mississippi. 'One day a new boat entered into competition with the Beaver. It was a light craft, recently built, and beat us by fifteen hours in the trip. This so much exasperated our captain, that he determined to race with her on her return to New Orleans. Being better acquainted with the shallows and the bars in the Red river, our skill gave us a marked superiority; but, as soon as we entered the broader and deeper waters of the Mississippi, we lost our advantage. In vain we put on more steam; our opponent shot ahead of us in no time. We now became frantic with jealousy and disappointment, and made up our mind to board and sink her, even at the price of our own lives. Unfortunately, ill-luck threw a snag* in our way. We struck, filled in ten minutes, and the Beaver sank like a bar of lead. One passenger and myself alone escaped from drowning: so sudden had been the accident, that of course nothing was saved.' After this the wrecked clerk 'having,' he adds, 'no luggage to look after, started on foot for New Orleans, which happily was only three hundred miles distant.'

The passion for travel which Mr Jonathan Sharp possessed was so strong, that he determined to see a little Spanish life in Cuba, and set sail for that island. On board ship he met with a young Irishman named O'Neil, who became the companion of his future adventures. Arrived at Havannah, he declares himself to have been transported with admiration at its beauty; and tells the following pretty story connected with its foundation. 'A short time after the discovery of the island, the Spaniards were desirous of erecting a fortified city, that might command the Gulf of Mexico. They searched a great while along the coast, till at last they entered, through a narrow rocky channel, into a deep broad bay. The engineers declared immediately that such a place, well fortified, would defy any hostile forces, and the adventurers landed on the very spot where now stands the celebrated "Moro." There was on the other side of the bay a large Indian village, built upon a beautiful green lawn, and on that spot it was determined that the new settlement should be formed. Presents were offered to the Indians, to induce them to retire to some other quarter: but no; they stoutly refused to do so. There were they born; there their fathers' bones were laid; and there they wished to live and die. The Europeans withdrew, resolving in their own minds to carry the place by force, as soon as they had collected a sufficient number of their troops; and in the meantime they erected a little village called Reglas, now employed as a quarantine ground. It was fortified as well as circumstances would allow, and Sanchez de Rebeira, a young officer of prepossessing appearance, was left in it with sixty soldiers, and a few families of Andalusian farmers. The Indians on their side distrusting the strangers, and suspecting that they would return in great force to execute their purpose, lost no time in surrounding their town with walls and palisades; yet they showed no signs of hostility, but, on the contrary, kept up a constant intercourse with Reglas, exchanging their produce, and even the precious metals—no doubt obtained from the Main—for the manufactured goods of Europe. During this friendly intercourse between the two people, Sanchez had frequent opportunities of seeing and admiring a beautiful young girl, the daughter of one of the principal chiefs. He loved her ardently, and told her of his love.' For this 'the poor girl had

* Jonathan Sharp, or the Adventures of a Kentuckian: written by himself. Henry Colburn: London.

* A tree carried down stream by the current, and fixed in the bottom in such a way as to present one end against passing vessels, which are often pierced in this manner.

to suffer all the anger and contempt of her family; and when the Spaniards attacked the town, she was compelled to perform the most menial offices of a slave. Yet was she still very beautiful, and Sanchez, who was gifted with a generous nature, resolved that, at any risk, he would free her from so wretched a fate. He found means to penetrate into the village, and pressed her once more within his arms. She had endured too much at the hands of her kindred: human nature could bear no more: her former love to them was changed into bitter hatred. She thirsted now for revenge: she told her plans to the Spaniard. A week afterwards the troops were surrounding the walls. It was a dark windy night; the soldiers were under arms. All at once yells and cries were heard, and a column of flames burst forth in the middle of the town. It was the signal. Provided with ladders, the Spaniards stormed the palisades, and the Indians, having to struggle against fire and sword, were soon overpowered; and their wish was fulfilled; they died where they were born and where they had lived.

'During the massacre, Sanchez, fearing for the safety of his love, searched for her, calling her by her name. At last he arrived at a small platform, and there beheld her. But alas! reason had forsaken her seat. The dread spirit of revenge had mastered all her faculties. There she stood, her hair flowing in the wind, the foam upon her lips—a terrible picture of passion—hideous, frantic—a bloody sword in one hand, a flaming torch in the other, and madly exulting over the ashes of her home and the corpses of her kindred. She sang some wild imprecations, and while her lover vainly endeavoured to call her to him by the most endearing expressions, she burst a blood-vessel, and died—the first that had betrayed her people. The few women who had not fallen during the slaughter mourned over her. They said that she had been "Havana"—a mad woman—one whose brain had been burned by the avenging finger of the Great Spirit.

'Faithful to his love, Sanchez raised a statue to her on the spot where she had died, representing her such as I have written above. It is to be seen even now in one of the shady walks beyond the walls of the present city, although, being entirely concealed by a luxuriant vegetation, it often escapes notice. This is what is meant by the creoles when they say to strangers, "One should not come and live in Havannah without seeing the Havana."'

The American government having at this time acquired the territory of Wisconsin in the far west—one immense bed of galena and copper ore—Mr Sharp and a friend named O'Neil 'closed for a tract of three thousand acres, one half to be paid in ready money, the other half in three years. Furnished with the necessary instructions, O'Neil started for our property, to examine into its resources, while I remained behind, in order to obtain the credit necessary to carry on our enterprise. The credit system in America has done a great deal of harm, but in principle it has been the cause of the immense progress of the country. Left to his own resources in a region where the earth, when properly managed, will yield forty or fifty per cent., the farmer, for want of a small capital, must remain for ever in mediocrity, and even in straitened circumstances. On the contrary, if he obtains a credit which the positive value of his property can cover, he may operate from the very beginning upon a large scale, and render more valuable not only his own lands, but also, through its relative vicinity, the district or even the country in which he lives.' We suppose that Mr Sharp succeeded in obtaining all the credit he required, for in three years we find him and his partner so well established on their estate, that they were looked upon 'as the two most important personages in the territory of Wisconsin. Our first establishment had become a city—Sharpville, with its fourteen hundred inhabitants, its land-office, its three taverns, and its printing-office. O'Neil had been returned for the legislature, and I elected high sheriff.' This magical progress is thus accounted for: 'In the newly-settled countries of America, three years sometimes operate a wonderful change: the phases are often striking in the extreme, either in the way of prosperity or of ruin. When we first arrived on our property, it was a wilderness for fifty miles around. Then the repose of solitude was only broken by the loud roar of the mighty Wisconsin, rolling its turbid waters across a tract of dark eternal forests. But we had scarcely erected half-a-dozen miserable shanties [temporary huts] to shelter us during night, before twenty Canadians and as many Irish had already come to us as diggers. Being among the earliest miners, we had but to tear up the earth: wealth sprang from the wild valleys, where, a few years before, the lordly buffalo had been grazing undisturbed. Immediately after our first sale in galena, we raised up a saw-mill, and built thirty houses. Two months afterwards we had a post-office, two blacksmiths' forges, three stores, and five hundred inhabitants. Twelve German families were planting and gardening; and as the final elections were at hand, we were courted for our votes. For these votes the government at Washington opened a road, which rendered easier and cheaper the transport of our ore along the banks of the Mississippi. For these votes the settlement was made a city, with all its privileges; finally, it became the capital of the county, having its court-house, its magistrates, and its recorder. Three years had, as I have said, gone by. By purchase after purchase, we had actually thirteen thousand acres of prime mineral land and nine smelting-houses. The territory was indebted to us to the amount of 160,000 dollars for roads opened and bridges thrown across the numerous streams intersecting the highway. We were immensely rich, and no longer in the wilderness. Attracted by the rumour of our success, hundreds of speculators had settled around us. Cities had sprung into existence on every point where the mineral was found; and the territory became so flourishing, that the tide of emigration from Europe poured on us its thousands, all of them considering our lead-digging as the Land of Promise—the Eldorado of the West.' From this flourishing concern Mr Jonathan retired to New York with an ample fortune. He was disgusted with Sharpville in consequence of the cowardly assassination of his friend and partner O'Neil.

To remain long in one place was quite opposed to Mr Sharp's restless disposition. He therefore turned his face towards the eastern hemisphere, choosing this island for his next visit, and Portsmouth for his landing-place. Thence he travelled to London; but a week in the great metropolis was enough for him, and he started for Ireland. At the end of a saunter all the way from Cape Clear to the Giant's Causeway—relieved by a little fishing and some pleasant intercourse with the 'finest peasantry in the world'—our truly go-a-head traveller received a letter from a Cuban friend, desiring an interview with him—in Madrid. In six days more, we find Mr Sharp landing on the shores of the far-famed Andalusia.

After this, he spent three years in travelling over the southern parts of the European continent. He returned to America. 'What an age is ours!' he exclaims; 'motion, ever motion! So rapid too: in two days I had settled my business in London; sixteen days afterwards I was on the Exchange of New York, negotiating successfully.' From Washington and Buffalo he returned to his own locality of Sharpville, to make a canal, and become a member of congress. In the former enterprise he was unable to succeed; but found it far less difficult to become a senator. Of his sayings and doings in congress Mr Sharp is silent, except that he was charged with a secret mission to Texas, which he appears to have performed with credit to himself.

In his third volume the restless Mr Sharp goes over much of the ground he has described in the two others. He revisits the Texas, Mexico, Cuba, and England, winding up by some shrewd remarks on the 'annexation' question. We conclude with a curious story which he introduces in the course of his book, from the mouth of one of its heroes.

'In the year 1828, a French frigate, cruising off the coast of Burmah, had sent several boats on shore to procure wood and water. Four of the boats' crew committed some trivial offence during the execution of their duty, and after their return on board, received so severe a punishment that they determined to desert. They watched for an opportunity, and seizing one of the boats, landed during the night. Each had provided himself with a musket and a knife; but they were totally unacquainted with the country in which they were. They cared not, however; and began to travel westward, thinking that one day or another they should meet with some town in which, they said among themselves, such hearty fellows as they were would always be sure of having something to do. In the night they slept under trees; in the day they fed upon berries, and upon the few birds which chance threw in their way; but they never diverged from the straight line until, after a march of nine days, they found themselves upon the banks of a wide and rapid river: it was the majestic Irrawaddy. They knew they could not be far from the seashore; and thinking that such a stream would most likely have a port at its mouth, they altered their course, proceeding in a southerly direction. They were not disappointed in their reckoning. As they went on, they crossed numerous tracks of beasts of burden, and reached at last a Burman village, twelve miles from the sea. There they encountered several foreigners—two Spaniards, a Dutchman, two Jews from Smyrna, and a Scotchman, who acted as English agent, and kept a coalyard for the supply of the English steamers. The four deserters soon discovered that ropemaking would be to them a source of great profit; it was a part of their profession:- they were industrious. In less than a week they had inspired the natives with so much confidence, that a house with a small portion of ground was allotted to them. They worked from morning to night, sold their ropes, learned a few words of the language, and before six weeks had elapsed, had surrounded themselves with comforts, having planted a garden with vegetables, and purchased a cow, pigs, and fowls.

'One day the French frigate anchored below the village. The Jews, jealous of the new comers, betrayed them to the officers, who endeavoured in vain to lay hands upon the fugitives. These were now much liked by the hospitable Burmans, who gave them warning, and sent them into the interior until the ship of war should leave the station, which she did three weeks afterwards. However, her captain, before sailing, left a note for the commander of an English steamer that was expected by the Scotch agent to arrive shortly. This of course the natives knew not, and as soon as they had ascertained that the frigate was fairly under weigh, they recalled their protegés, who returned in triumph, and gave a thrashing to the Jews. Some time after this event the steamboat made its appearance, and a lieutenant, with a dozen marines, presented himself before the dwelling of the runaways, summoning them to surrender. Determined, however, to do no such thing, they barricaded their door, managed to make a white flag, which they hung out of the window, and defied the marines to do their worst. The English officer charged with the capture of the sailors had accepted the task merely as an act of complaisance; but he did not like to employ force against four poor fellows resolved not to be taken alive, and who had put themselves under the protection of their national colours. Commanding his men to wheel to the right-about, he returned to his superior, to explain the matter to him. The captain, himself a man of energy, yet kind withal, went to the ropemakers to try the effect of a little gentle persuasion; but seeing that they were bent upon never re-entering the navy, he abandoned his purpose, and, touched with their gallant spirit, presented them with some arms and instruments, of which they were much in want.

'In two years' time the French sailors had rendered themselves so popular throughout the country, that the governor of the province, wishing to see them, sent an escort of fifty soldiers to bring them into his presence. He perceived at once that they would be of the greatest service to him, by helping to drill a corps of infantry, who, having no other arms than swords and pikes, could have no better instructors. Indeed, according to my new acquaintances, the troops of the province soon became renowned throughout the empire: they fought in several engagements with success against a warlike tribe of the interior, which was utterly destroyed. The news having reached the ears of the emperor, the governor of the province, his army, and the four sailors, were ordered to the capital. Our adventurers then began a career of greatness: one became privy councillor to the monarch, another commander-in-chief of the Burman armies, the third was appointed to superintend the fortifications of the town, and the last was charged with the building of large sailing-boats, to serve as a foundation for the Burman naval power. They prospered till the death of the emperor, whose son did not show so much partiality to the strangers. They were dismissed from their offices, their property was confiscated, and they were ordered to quit the empire. They had saved, however, gold and jewels to a great amount, and possessed likewise several splendid pearl necklaces, given to them by the deceased monarch. Certain that they could not suffer from want, they procured a large pirogue, and descended the Irrawaddy as far as the hospitable village in which they had first experienced the kindness of the Burmans.

'They were exceedingly surprised to see it filled with foreign soldiers and sailors, both Americans and French, who seemed to be on the best terms with the natives. To their astonishment the French flag had changed. The spotless banner of the lilies had once more yielded to the tricolour, and Europe had witnessed a great revolution. Uncertain how they should be received in France, the adventurers, fearing that the late break-out at home would not exempt them from punishment, resolved to visit America, of which, long ago, they had heard so much. It was the land of liberty, equality, and social integrity.

'It happened, however, that the new emperor, hearing of the riches which the exiles had carried away, despatched a company of soldiers to arrest them, deliver them up to the French man-of-war, and bring back to him their treasures. But the good villagers, faithful to their former friendship, warned our heroes again of the coming danger, and, giving them provisions and ammunition, conveyed them to a deserted watch-tower on the seashore. There they fortified themselves, and defended their liberty during ten days against two hundred assailants, till both food and powder failed them. Meanwhile the Scotch agent, who was a truly kind man, lost no time in exciting in their favour the sympathy of the English officers. It was in 1842. Great Britain was at war with China. The Burman station was much resorted to by the vessels of every nation navigating those seas; but the English ships were the most numerous, on account of their greater need of fuel and fresh provisions. One of them, commanded by the same officer who had befriended the fugitives twelve years before, willingly undertook to help them out of their present difficult position. A boat, well manned, was sent on shore, in the immediate vicinity of the tower, which its occupants abandoned during the night, carrying with them their baggage and treasures. The benevolent captain scarcely recognised his old acquaintances in their new garb. Their complexion, naturally swarthy, had assumed the deepest olive hue, rendered still more apparent by the stainless whiteness of their flowing robes. They had saved a part of their wardrobe, and could still present a respectable appearance. Their well-combed beards descended low upon their breasts, and from under the folds of their turbans, their black hair, slightly tinged with gray, escaped in a profusion of curls, which gave to their physiognomy a remarkable type of manly beauty. They related their history to their kind protector, who treated them more as his equals than as his inferiors, till he had seen them safe on board a New York East Indiaman homeward bound.

'The wanderers had been only two weeks in America, but they were already anxious to leave it, declaring that it was a country fit only for people who had nothing to lose, and infinitely less civilised than Burmah. They wished to go to England, whence they would petition the French king to grant them an amnesty, and to allow them the favour of dying in their native villages. As they possessed property to a considerable amount, I advised them to take their passage in the steamer, and offered to accompany them to the office, to act as their interpreter. They thanked me gratefully. Two days afterwards we were on our passage to England.

'I may as well state here, that in London I helped them to dispose of their jewels, for which they obtained a fair value of upwards of ten thousand pounds. Their petition to their king was acknowledged almost immediately by a full pardon for their past offence; and they returned home, after an absence of twenty years—somewhat better off no doubt than if they had remained all that time in their former station.'

MARRIAGE CUSTOMS IN THE PROVINCES OF FRANCE.

After all the political changes in France, the rural peasantry remain just what they were before the Revolution. Primitive in manners, few of them instructed in the elements of education, and visiting the large towns only on market or fête days, they continue to be a peculiar people, each province having its own costume, its own dialect, and its own habits and usages. Among the customs to which each district remains fixedly attached, none are so remarkable as those bearing on the all-important affair of courtship and matrimony.

In Touraine, the young peasant sometimes makes his first declaration to his mistress by affixing a bouquet to the door of the house in which she resides, and afterwards sends a friend to inform her of his intention of offering himself. Upon his first visit, he sees immediately, by the arrangement of the billets on the hearth, if his suit will be favourably received or not: if they are in the ordinary position, he will be accepted; but if, on the contrary, they are placed on end and apart, he understands that his intended offer will be refused. When his suit is favourably received, he provides the marriage gifts, which consist of the wedding-ring, generally of gold, except with the very poorest class, who provide a silver ring; but with the greater number, the usual offering consists, besides the ring, of a small gold cross, and frequently a silver cup, with a sum of money in proportion to his means. After the acceptance of these gages, the lady cannot retract without restoring all she has received. The wedding is usually fixed for a Monday or Tuesday, these being considered as the most propitious days; and the bridal party assembles at the house of the lady's father, the bride wearing on the back of her cap a wreath of myrtle, and round her waist a ribbon of the length and form of the girdle of the holy virgin preserved in the collegiate church at Loches, as mentioned in the superstitions of the province; which same ribbon she first wears on the day of her first communion, and afterwards when about to present her husband with an heir. Should the residence of the bride be at some distance from the village church, it is the custom for the miller employed by the family to convey her thither on his horse or mule, 'en troussé' behind him. During the wedding feast which follows the celebration, one of the young lads steals under the table, and endeavours to possess himself of one of the bride's garters, which is usually of rose-coloured or blue ribbon, and which, when obtained, is cut into pieces, and distributed amongst the guests, who affix it as a favour to their coat or hat. It is rare in the country for the female to bear the name of her husband without changing the termination into a feminine form; for example, if the husband's name be Robin, the wife becomes Madame Robinne; Flabeau becomes Flabelle. The husband also frequently adds the family name of his wife's family to his own. Charles Robin, for instance, marries Mademoiselle Goreau, and calls himself Robin Goreau. In the upper classes in Touraine, marriages are generally arranged by the lawyer of the family; parties who have a son or a daughter to marry employing their legal adviser to find a suitable match, principally with regard to fortune. Marriages from the mutual inclination or attachment of the young people are of very rare occurrence.

In the department of L'Orme, in Normandy, an old woman acts as general plenipotentiary in marriage affairs, and makes the first proposal; after which, if agreeable, she arranges a meeting of the parties interested. In this part of France the carrying home of the *providing* reminds us of the old fashion in Scotland. On the evening before the wedding day, the men of the family arrive with a cart to carry the trousseau of the bride, the cart with the horse or oxen being adorned with ribbons, and preceded by a violin, which continues to play till the departure of the party, who pass some time in dancing; and on their return, are still attended by the music, which never ceases its din; and led by a sister or female relative, and in some cases by the dressmaker of the fiancée, who is provided with abundance of pins, which she distributes to every one she meets, and which it would be considered as a great insult to refuse; besides which, these pins bring good luck, especially to the damsels who chance to receive them, who will consequently be married within the year—a kiss is always given and returned on receiving one of these well-omened gifts. On the wedding day, when all are assembled in their gayest attire, the sisters or nearest female relative attach a crown of flowers to the back of the bride's cap, and the party start for the church, still preceded by the violin, and accompanied by the firing of guns and shouts of the children. The family of the bride lead the procession on horseback, if they have any distance to go to the church; then follows the bride 'en troussé' behind some near relative, and followed by the family of the bridegroom. On arriving at the church gate, the party arrange themselves in two lines, up which the damsel passes, leaning on the arm of the person who has brought her to church. On the arrival of the priest, the bridegroom conducts her to the centre of the building, where the nuptial benediction is given under a crucifix which is generally suspended from the ceiling. They then follow the priest to the high altar, where the gospel is read, during which time the couple kneel, each holding a taper, whilst over their heads a white canopy is supported by two of their relatives. The husband then leads his bride to the altar of the holy virgin, where they offer their tapers, and remain a short time in prayer. The cortège then leave the church, and proceed with the wedding guests to the breakfast. Before arriving at the house of her husband, the bride has to pass the barriers erected by her young friends, and which are formed of ribbons, garlands, and wreaths of flowers. In doing this, she distributes the pins with which they are fastened, with the flowers and ornaments, to those about her; and, on arriving at the door, is received and embraced by her spouse, who also salutes his newly-acquired relatives. The cook then presents to the bride three loaves, which she distributes to the poor, who attend in a crowd, and all receive soup and bread. Whilst the bride takes possession of her new abode, it is the part of the bridegroom to betake himself to the kitchen, and aid in preparing the grand feast, towards which the guests contribute various provisions. The tables are placed in a horse-shoe form, and in the centre is a raised chair or throne covered with white linen, and ornamented with flowers, on which the bride is seated, with the principal guests on each side of her, whilst the bridegroom aids in the kitchen, and attends on the party. After dinner, dancing commences, the cook and the fiddler conducting madame round the circle, and introducing her to her new neighbours, to whom she again distributes pins; after which the newly-married couple are seated on chairs, and the guests present their various gifts of linen, flax, yarn, wine, plate, and sometimes money. The relatives of the bride then carry the bride in procession, the violin sounding, and the guests singing an old and well-known song, used from time immemorial on such occasions. Afterwards the 'momons'—mummers or maskers—present themselves, mounted on wooden horses, called bidoches, which kick and prance to the great delight of the spectators; they are attended by shepherds dressed with ribbons and flowers. About five o'clock the dancing begins again, and the cook has the privilege of dancing the first dance with the bride, the bridegroom the second; after which he confides the lady to his young friends. At nine o'clock the young lads of the neighbourhood appear, and the newly-married pair make their escape. The mirth and riot then waxes furious; they dance, eat, drink, and sing till the morning, when breakfast is served, and those who are in a state to reach their homes attempt to do so.

In Champagne, the affianced sends a piece of ribbon to all the girls in the neighbourhood above the age of seven or eight years, who present, in return, a dozen eggs, a fowl, butter, or other provisions for the wedding feast; and on leaving the church after the ceremony, a large dish of soup is presented, which is eaten in the churchyard by the wedding-party. Great importance is attached to this ceremony, which shows, it is said, the equality between the newly-married pair and the concord which ought to exist between them. In Mayenne, no such equality is allowed between the parties, and the peasants and smaller landholders keep their females in such subjection, that on the morning appointed for the nuptials the bride goes with her father to seek the bridegroom, who is always found in his working-dress, and asks the damsel why she should come for him, and she replies that perhaps he has changed his mind. He declares that such is not the case. This settles the affair; and after dressing for the ceremony, they proceed to the church, the marriage feast being always celebrated at the residence of the bridegroom. In the department of La Meurthe, in Lorraine, when the bride enters the house of her father-in-law after the ceremony, the mother of the young husband presents her with a plate of corn, eggs, and flax; the corn she scatters on the ground, preserving the flax and eggs. On the morning after the nuptials the young people of the neighbourhood carry a dish of soup to the newly-married couple before they are risen, and if not admitted, have a right to force open the chamber door. Afterwards, the two families attend a funeral service for the souls of their deceased relatives.

In some cantons of the department of the Landes, when a Landois wishes to marry, he goes to the house of the maiden's parents in the middle of the night, attended by two friends, each carrying a pitcher full of wine, knocks at the door, and requests an interview, which is never refused. The family all rise from their beds, seat themselves at the table, eat, and drink the wine, relate wonderful tales of seamen, sorcerers, ghosts, &c. without alluding in anyway to the cause of the visit. At daybreak the damsel rises from table to seek the dessert, which is the critical moment. If amongst the fruit she produces nuts, the suitor is rejected without any hope of being accepted.

A belief in the power of some disappointed rival to injure the bridegroom's happiness is very general, and various are the means to prevent any one from exerting this baneful influence. In Touraine, the brothers, cousins, or nearest male relatives, whose office it is on the marriage day to aid the bridegroom in putting on his new shoes or boots provided for the occasion, slip a piece of money into them; others carry in their pocket a small packet of salt. In the department of La Manche, a stout lad with an enormous whip precedes the newly-married man into the nuptial chamber, and makes a tremendous noise by cracking it, in order to drive away all evil spirits, enchanters, and contrivers of these deadly witch-knots, which cause the most fatal evils, instead of the love and harmony which should exist between the newly-married pair.

In some parts of Bretagne, the bride seems to adopt the old Roman custom of being carried off by violence; and towards the end of the day, endeavours to conceal herself, and sometimes does so for a day or two; at others she resists being taken from her father's house with such vigour, that her dress is torn to pieces, which is considered as a great credit to her; and the more vehemently she contends, the more respectable she is considered by her neighbours and friends. Notwithstanding all the innovations which modern civilisation has made in the habits and manners of the people, the various customs enumerated still remain in the different departments unaltered, and apparently unlikely to change for ages to come.

THE ELEPHANT IN INDIA.

[Translated from Von Orlich's *Reise in Ostindien*, 'Travels in India,' an expensive volume, published at Leipsic under the patronage of the king of Prussia.]

IN the neighbourhood of Sumalka, a town not far from Delhi, lying amongst ancient and beautiful tamarind trees, fig trees, and acacias, is the encampment of our one hundred and twenty elephants. To this place I frequently and gladly go for the purpose of watching this sagacious beast. By reason of the persecution it has endured from man, either merely for the pleasures of the chase, or that when tamed it might increase the splendour of state, or serve as a beast of burden, and render assistance in battle, the elephant has nearly disappeared from the interior of India, and is found wild only in the less elevated portion of the Himalayan chain; namely, in the forests of Dshemna, Nepaul, some parts of Ghauts Tarrai, the kingdom of Ava and Ceylon. On the upper Indus, near Attock, where Alexander the Great had his first elephant hunt, in the Punjab, and on the banks of the Jumna, not far from Kalpy, where the Emperor Baber was annually accustomed to enjoy the chase, and capture many of these animals, there is not now a trace of this noble beast to be found. Although this hand-endowed animal was used in the earliest times as an instrument of war, and it was known how to render it an obedient servant, it has never yet been possible to domesticate it so as to render it productive after being tamed. Individual instances have certainly occurred where tame elephants have produced young, and I myself saw a ten months old animal belonging to a rajah, which had been born under these circumstances. Whether they are afraid that a degenerated species would be the consequence, or whether the need of a complete domestication has never been experienced, and they are content with reclaiming each individual, I am not able to say.

I experienced a singular feeling of novelty and excitement the first time of riding upon this creature. There is first placed upon its back a cushion thickly stuffed with hair, for this is the tenderest part of the elephant, and the greatest care of the attendant is to guard against all injury at this place, the more especially as wounds are difficult to heal. Over this cushion there is thrown a long hanging cloth, red and embroidered with gold, upon which the houdah rests fastened with cords and girths. The houdah is made to contain two persons and their servant. The mahoud sits upon the neck behind the creature's ears, guiding it with an iron fork, one prong of which is curved out, whilst a man runs alongside with a large staff, and hastens its advance by blows or cries. A ladder hanging at one side completes the appointments. When it is desired to mount the elephant, the mahoud cries *beit, beit*, that is, lie down, whereupon the animal kneels down, the ladder is ascended, and the rider takes his seat. The gait of the animal of course regulates the motion of its rider; sometimes it is pleasant, sometimes fatiguing. Its pace when urged onward is so quick that a horseman must trot to keep by its side; but he soon slackens his speed, and it is not without difficulty that he accomplishes twenty-four miles a-day. To cool himself, or to remove dust, he now and then sprinkles himself with water drawn up into his trunk. An ordinary elephant costs 1000 rupees (L.100), and his keep forty rupees a-month.

In its wild state the elephant attains an age of upwards of two hundred years; but when tamed, not much more than one hundred and twenty. Its size is various; those of Ceylon and Tarra are small, and seldom have tusks. A hunter of great experience told me that in Ceylon scarcely two in a hundred have tusks. As soon as an elephant thus armed is caught, the greater portion of his tusks is sawn off, and the extremities of what remains are encased in gold or silver. The largest animals that came under my observation belonged to the governor-general, the maharajah of Lahore, the king of Oude, and the rajahs of Bhurtpoor and Alwar, and these were about eleven feet high. They were also more agile, and of greater endurance and sagacity than is usual. Such an animal would cost about 5000 rupees, whilst one of seven feet high can be bought for a thousand. The ordinary elephant, having five times the strength of a camel, is employed in the army to bear not only the chief persons and the sick, but also the tents and furniture. It can likewise be quite as serviceably employed as a draught-beast, since it can pull with the greatest ease what ten horses have scarcely power to move. The English have, in consequence, recently yoked it to their artillery-carriages with the best result. On the other hand, it is very difficult to induce the elephant to cross a river, for when he enters it is not easy to guide him in the proper direction, and he sinks so low that only the tip of his proboscis, which he lifts on such an occasion as high as possible, is visible. If he has to cross a bridge of boats, or a piece of fenny land, he ascertains the safety of his path by means of his trunk, and before he sets his foot down, he tests the strength of the support. To testify his pleasure, he lifts his trunk perpendicularly upwards; and his mahoud teaches him to raise his trunk and fall on his knees when he comes into the presence of a great man. In tiger-hunting the elephant is especially useful, not only for carriage but for defence. The chase takes place in the thick overgrown jungles, where it would be impossible for horsemen and persons on foot to penetrate through bushes and reeds sixteen feet high, and over swampy ground. The months of April and May are most favourable for hunting, because then the tiger seeks his food more daringly, approaching the abodes of men for the purpose of carrying off the cattle, and thus he is more easy to be met with. Each sportsman takes two rifles of a stronger make in his houdah, and the gunner takes the place of the servant. A large party is usually made up for a tiger-hunt, and the elephants are carefully selected with reference to previous experience and efficiency. As soon as the tiger is tracked to his lair, he endeavours to slink away, but he stands upon his defence the moment a shot touches him; and when wounded, he sends out a terrific roar, showing at the same time his teeth. Everything depends at this period of the tumult upon the elephant not turning his back on his antagonist. Most elephants show great skill in defending themselves with their trunk, so as to give the sportsman time to lodge another ball. The elephant manifests great delight when the tiger is killed, and experienced hunters have assured me that he becomes bolder and more active with his victories. When the hunter quits his elephant, and leaves him to contend with the tiger alone, it is difficult to make him useful afterwards. As soon as the elephant is freed from his burden, a stake is driven into the earth to which a forefoot is fastened by a chain. Upon occasions of festivity, the mahouds take much pains to paint his head and trunk with arabesque designs in white, red, yellow, or blue. They bestow great attention on the animal confided to their care. A mahoud never curtails an elephant of his food, or leaves him entirely without support. The tent in which he, his wife, and children are lodged, is placed near the elephant, so that the animal almost lives with them. While the mahoud cooks a cake of kascaded flour upon an iron plate, his charge stands patiently by until the cake is cool, and then he receives his sustenance out of the hands of the family. The elephant is passionately fond of the sugar cane. One of the beasts which were fed to-day upon canes, quite lost all patience when he saw his neighbours munching their favourite viand, himself apparently having been forgotten. Just as a rough boy stamps with his foot if his wishes are not complied with, this elephant angrily struck the earth with his trunk, but the moment his food was brought he was quiet. He is fond of throwing leaves and bits of earth upon his back, and in idle hours this is a never failing resource. Still more does he delight in turning himself over in the water. When his keeper cleans him, he patiently kneels down, or places himself on his side.

So full of reason are his actions, that he serves the Indians as the symbol of the highest knowledge; Ganesa, the god of art and science, being represented with an elephant's head. More especially is this animal honoured by the Hindoos, who make it the companion of the gods, the warder of the porch of the temple, the caryatide and ornament of their architecture. They believe that the souls of princes and Brahmins do penance in the bodies of elephants, and a Hindoo of low caste may hold one of them to be higher than himself. A bride, according to the law of Menu, should have the graceful gait of a flamingo, or of a young elephant; and therefore at this day the princes and princesses of the ancient Hindoo dynasties are taught the step of an elephant. When the rajah of Bickaneer came to visit Lord Ellenborough, he entered the tent with a heavy tread, conformably to the instruction he had received in this branch of Indian etiquette.

For purposes of splendour the elephant plays an important part in the immense retinues of great persons in India. When Sir Jasper Nicholls, the commander-in-chief during the late war, arrived at the camp at Ferozpoor, eighty elephants swelled his train. He had in addition three hundred camels, and one hundred and thirty-six draught-oxen. Above a thousand servants were present merely for Sir Jasper's personal service, and to attend to the animals. When the governor-general made his entry, he brought along with him one hundred and thirty elephants and seven hundred camels.

SPECULATIVE PHILANTHROPISTS.

That each man shall be free in the choice and practice of his trade or calling—that the field of competition shall be open to all—that each individual shall be permitted to make the best bargain he can, whether for the wages of his labour or the price of his commodities—all these trite but invaluable maxims are incessantly decried, and nothing is heard of but the evils of competition, and the unequal recompense of labour. In their fits of impotent benevolence, these speculative physicians assail, as the cause of the existing distress, those principles which, in fact, are the conditions of all the prosperity we have attained, or can preserve, or can hope in future to attain. This title of the individual, whether workman or capitalist, to the control and conduct of his own affairs—this 'fair field and no favour' system—is not to be described as if it were a mere theory of political economy, and disputable like some other branches of science not yet matured. It is the great conquest of modern civilisation; it is the indispensable condition to the full development of the activity and enterprise of man. The liberation of the artisan and the labourer is the signal triumph of modern over ancient times, whether we regard classic or Gothic antiquity. Viewing things on a large scale, it may be considered as a *late* triumph; and, without depreciating its value, we may easily admit that there remains much to be done in the cultivation of the artisan, to enable him to govern himself, and make the best of his position. But any scheme which, under the pretext of ameliorating his position, would place him again under tutelage, is a scheme of degradation, and a retrograde movement. He is now a freeman, an enrolled member of a civilised state, where each individual has to a great extent the responsibility thrown upon himself for his own wellbeing: he must have prospective cares, and grow acquainted with the thoughtful virtue of prudence. That release from reflection and anxiety for the future which is the compensating privilege of the slave or the barbarian, he cannot hope any longer to enjoy. Whatever its value, he must renounce it. He must become one of us, knowing good and evil, looking before and behind. In this direction—in the gradual improvement of the labourer—lies our future progress; progress slow and toilsome, little suited to the socialist who calculates on changing, as with the touch of a wand, the whole aspect of society.—*Blackwood's Magazine.*

THE SISTER OF GEORGE III.

Dinner at the duchess dowager's: great anxiety and curiosity to know whether my messenger brought me my full powers, and great disappointment at hearing he had not. I took an opportunity of mentioning to the duke that I wished to speak with him, and he appointed me at my own house the following day. Duchess very inquisitive—against his taking the command; not for his going to Holland. Said she knew his refusal had hurt the king very much. She talked of Edward Duke of York as her favourite brother; said she recollected he liked my father; praised the Duke of Gloucester; abused the queen, who, she said, was an envious and intriguing spirit; told several anecdotes to this effect on her first coming over; that she disliked her mother (the Princess of Wales) and herself, and was extremely jealous of them: took an opportunity, while the Princess of Wales was dying, to alter the rank of the ladies of her bed-chamber. King very good, but not liable to deep impressions. Talked slightingly of the Duke of York; said he behaved badly here to his duchess. I defended him. She reprobated his conduct at Hanover, and particularly that to his old flame, Madame de ——, to whom, on his return to England with the duchess, he did not speak. The Duchess of York, she said, behaved vastly well on this occasion. She then got on the marriage of her daughter—acquainted me with all the injunctions and advice she had given her, which were very excellent—declared her own intention of *never* coming to England—that she was sure she should be uncomfortable there, and give rise to all sorts of jealousy and suspicion; said she had enough of that—praised exceedingly her daughter-in-law, the hereditary princess, and admired particularly her behaviour to her son. 'Had I married such a man as Charles,' she said, 'I never could have behaved so.' Abused the Landgravine of Hesse, and her sister the Duchess of Hortemberg—told me that the Landgravine was once thought of for the king, but that her conduct was so doubtful that nobody could take upon them to recommend her. All the young German princesses, she said, had learned English in hopes of being Princess of Wales. She never would give the idea to Caroline; and she never thought it could happen, as the king had often expressed his dislike to the marriage of cousins-german. Nothing could be so open, so frank, and so unreserved as her manners, nor so perfectly good-natured and unaffected. Of the king, her brother, she said he loved her very much, as well as he could love anybody, but that twenty years' absence, and thirty years' living with the queen, had made him forget her; yet he was very kind indeed on the present occasion. She said that Queen Charlotte was very much hurt at the very fine diamond ring the king gave her (the duchess), as a *bague de mariage*, in 1764; that she wanted it back, and was quite peevish about it. This ring and a pair of bracelets were the only diamonds she brought with her from England. Declared she would never allow Caroline to have her brothers with her—that it would make her unpopular—that the queen did it to get them money—that it was shabby, &c. Said the king offered her a princess for her son, if she would first let him come over and be seen. The duchess replied, 'that Charles was a very good-humoured, harmless boy—would certainly make a good husband; but she would not send him over, as she was quite sure, if he was to show himself, none of the princesses would have him.'—*Diary of the Earl of Malmesbury.*

PUBLIC HOT-WATER BATHS IN CHINA.

In the town of Shanghae, as well as in many other large Chinese towns, there are a number of hot-water bathing establishments, which must be of great importance as regards the health and comfort of the natives. Let me describe one which I passed daily during my residence in Shanghae. There are two outer rooms used for undressing and dressing: the first and largest is for the poorer classes; the second for those who consider themselves more respectable, and who wish to be more private. As you enter the largest of these rooms, a placard which is hung near the door informs you what the charges are, and a man stands there to receive the money on entrance. Arranged in rows down the middle and round the sides of both rooms are a number of small boxes or lockers, furnished with lock and key, into which the visitors put their clothes, and where they can make sure of them when they return from the bathing-room. The bathing-room is entered by a small door at the farther end of the building, and is about thirty feet long and twenty wide; the bath occupying the whole space, except a narrow path round the sides. The water is from one foot to eighteen inches deep, and the sides are lined and covered with marble slabs, from which the bathers step into the water, and on which they sit and wash themselves: the furnace is placed on the outside of one of the ends, and the flues are carried through below the centre of the bath. The establishment in the afternoon and evening is crowded with visitors, and on entering the bath-room, the first impression is almost insupportable: the hot steam or vapour meets you at the door, filling the eyes, ears, and causing perspiration to run from every pore of the body: it almost darkens the place; and the Chinamen seen in this imperfect light, with their brown skins and long tails, sporting amongst the water, render the scene a most ludicrous one to an Englishman. Those visitors who use the common room pay only six copper cash; the other class pay eighteen; but they in addition have a cup of tea and a pipe of tobacco from the proprietors. I may mention that one hundred copper cash amount to about 4½d. of our money; so that the first class enjoy a hot-water bath for about one farthing, and the other a bath, a private room, a cup of tea, and a pipe of tobacco, for something less than one penny.—*Correspondent of Athenæum.*

WHERE WOULD I BE?

[FROM THE GERMAN OF B. WOLFF.]

WHERE would I be?
There, where the rosy wine pearls to the brim;
There, where due honours crown the poet's hymn;
There, where the foaming Rhine bounds to the sea!
There would I be.

Where would I be?
There, where success attends the good and brave;
There, where the gallant skiff light rides the wave;
Even where on rugged rocks the brave live free—
There would I be.

Where would I be?
Where slaves themselves pluck off the bond of shame,
And leap and bound in many a manly game;
Where Freedom's eagle breasts her glorious way
Through the wide ether in the blaze of day,
With god-like might where slaves themselves set free—
There would I be.

Where would I be?
Where, for a life's time, two fast friends have gone,
Through weal and wo, and lived and loved in one;
Brave, and devoted in firm unity—
There would I be.

Where would I be?
Where the one darling of my heart should rest,
Her gentle bosom to my bosom prest,
And gaze for ever with undying bliss
Within my eyes: breathe one immortal kiss
Throughout thy length and breadth, eternity—
There would I be!

E. L.

CLIMATE OF KORDOFAN.

The climate of Kordofan (in Central Africa), says Ignatius Pallme in his travels, is very unhealthy, especially during the rainy reason; no hut is then indeed to be met with in which there are not several sick. In the dry season, again, all disease disappears: at this time, however, not only man but all living creatures suffer from extreme heat. The eye then rests with melancholy on the desolate and parched plains, trophies of the victory of the heat over animated nature, where nothing is to be seen but bones of men and animals bleached by the burning sun. During the whole of this season, which endures for eight months, the sky is clear and cloudless, and the heat is insupportable, especially in the months of April and May. From 11 o'clock in the forenoon till 3 in the afternoon, when the thermometer stands in the shade at 117 or 122 degrees Fahrenheit, it is impossible for any breathing creature to remain in the open air. Every living being, both men and cattle, with equal eagerness seek the shade, to protect themselves from the scorching rays of a fierce sun. Man sits during these hours as if in a vapour bath; his cheerfulness of disposition declines, and he is almost incapable of thought; listless, and with absence of mind, he stares vacantly before him, searching in vain for a cool spot. The air breathed is hot, as if it proceeded from a heated furnace, and acts in so enervating a manner on the animal economy, that it becomes a trouble even to move a limb. All business ceases; everything is wrapped in a sleep of death, until the sun gradually sinks, and the cool air recalls men and animals again into life and activity. The nights, on the other hand, are so sharp, that it is necessary to be more careful in guarding against the effects of cold in this country than in the northern parts of Europe; for the consequences often prove fatal. During the dry season, everything in nature appears desolate and dismal; the plants are burnt up; the trees lose their leaves, and appear like brooms; no bird is heard to sing; no animal delights to disport in the gladness of its existence; every living being creeps to the forest to secrete itself, seeking shelter from the fearful heat; save that now and then an ostrich will be seen traversing the desert fields in flying pace, or a giraffe hastening from one oasis to another.

Printed by William Bradbury, of No. 6, York Place, and Frederick Mullett Evans, of No. 7, Church Row, both of Stoke Newington, in the county of Middlesex, printers, at their office, Lombard Street, in the precinct of Whitefriars, and city of London; and Published (with permission of the Proprietors, W. and R. CHAMBERS,) by WILLIAM SOMERVILLE ORR, Publisher, of 2, Amen Corner, at No. 2 AMEN CORNER, both in the parish of Christchurch, and in the city of London.—Saturday, June 21, 1845.

CONDUCTED BY WILLIAM AND ROBERT CHAMBERS, EDITORS OF 'CHAMBERS'S INFORMATION FOR THE PEOPLE,' 'CHAMBERS'S EDUCATIONAL COURSE,' &c.

No. 78. NEW SERIES. SATURDAY, JUNE 28, 1845. PRICE 1½*d*.

PRESENCE OF MIND.

THE differences of the conduct of individuals in situations of danger and sudden emergency are very striking; nor do we always find the best conduct in such circumstances from those who act best in the ordinary affairs of life. Often has it happened that a clever shrewd man of the world, such as the late Mr Huskisson, has lost all reflection and power to act when unexpectedly overtaken by danger; and not less frequently do we see prompt and vigorous conduct manifested, on like occasions, by women who have never before given token of their being in any respect endowed above their neighbours. Presence of mind thus appears as something not necessarily to be found in union with high intellect or skill. A cunning bravery of the timid, a cowardly, but laudably cowardly adroitness of the brave, it sometimes almost appears as an inspiration; and yet we know that it is but a natural endowment, capable, like all others, of being cultivated in everybody by the use of appropriate means. I have heard of a gentleman who took his son to bathe, and actually threw him into a situation of danger, in order to elicit and train his presence of mind: we also know that barbarous nations of warlike character use similar methods with their youth, by way of fitting them for every kind of peril and ambuscade. It is not, perhaps, desirable that any such plans should be resorted to in our present civilised circumstances; but certainly there is much need to prepare the minds of the young for difficulties and crises, by a full explanation of such as are still likely to occur in the course of life, and by accustoming them as far as possible to habits of prompt action and self-reliance. Much might be done in parlour existence, merely by establishing a certain cool manner for the treatment of all extraordinary matters; for we are so greatly creatures of habit, that, if we allow ourselves to be thrown into an excitement by all the little out-of-the-way occurrences of life, we are extremely likely to be thrown into a paroxysm of the same feeling by events of greater moment; nor is it less true that a steady and sober way of viewing small matters will fit us for viewing great ones without the excitement which produces confusion of mind. I verily believe that the stupid habit of getting up a clamour about trifles, has led in many instances to that wildness of alarm in cases of danger which not only forbids escape to the unhappy being exhibiting it, but tends to paralyse and endanger others. The general safety often depends on an entire suppression of excitement and outcry, and it is therefore of the greatest consequence that every person should be trained to a *quiet*, not to speak of a firm manner of acting under trivial difficulties.

The value of such conduct on occasions of peril involving many lives, was never perhaps better exemplified than in the destruction of the Kent East Indiaman by fire, when not even from the women and children was one sound of alarm heard, the consequence of which was, that the officers and sailors were enabled to do all that was possible in the circumstances for the preservation of the people on board, and the whole of the procedure connected with their transference to the saving vessel was conducted with as much regularity, and almost as much safety, as if it had taken place on an ordinary occasion. In striking contrast was the scene on board the Halsewell, where the two daughters of the captain, losing all self-command, threw themselves upon their father with such frantic cries and lamentations, as overwhelmed his naturally intrepid mind, and thus extinguished the energies upon which at the moment so much depended.

We so continually, in the journals of the day, see evil consequences from want of presence of mind, in circumstances where the proper conduct has long been generally agreed upon, that we might be tempted to believe it a quality beyond mortal reach, if we were not aware how many things, which appear notorious to all, are in reality unknown to many. Hardly a week passes without telling us of a female having caught fire and lost her life in consequence of rushing out into the open air, instead of rolling herself in a carpet, or at least prostrating herself on the floor. Panics still occasionally take place in theatres and churches, and scores of lives are lost by a crowding to the door: not one instance do I remember of an alarm in such places of resort being attended by the proper conduct—*sitting still*. Individuals are also still much given to throwing themselves out of runaway carriages, an act which may be pronounced the very opposite of the proper conduct. But the fact is, that, while some of these errors are a consequence of mere confusion of mind, many are also the result of ignorance. The right conduct in situations of difficulty is far from being generally impressed, as it ought to be, on the minds of the young. Or, if it has been taught as a lesson, there has at least been no effort to train the mind to look to it as the only course of action in which there is the least safety; so that when the critical moment arrives, we are still too prone to act upon some mere instinct for self-preservation. A young lady, a few years ago, caught fire while going to bed in a country house where she was a visitor. She had been told that the carpet and the floor were the proper expedients; but a more immediate impulse directed her to a lake in front of the house. She rushed along the passages and stairs, and was found exhausted, and almost hopelessly scorched, a few yards from the outer door. It is necessary to make the lesson a vital principle in the mind.

Presence of mind is exemplified in its simplest form,

where all that is necessary is to take a deliberate view of the circumstances, and then do that which seems most advantageous. It may be shown, for example, in a choice between the door and window in a case of fire, or in the selection of something to be saved, as that which is most important. In the year 1716, when a captain came with his troop to execute the vengeance of the government upon the house of a Jacobite gentleman in Perthshire, he humanely gave the inmates a few minutes to remove whatever they deemed most valuable. A lady, the sister of the absent landlord, flew to the store-room, thinking to save the plate; when she afterwards inspected the contents of her apron on the lawn, she found, too late, that she had only rescued a quantity of old candlesticks, butter-boats, and similar trash. A gentleman just escaped from a fire in his house, joyfully told his congratulating friends that, in the midst of the confusion, he had been able to open a drawer and save his principal papers. He emptied his pockets, and found only scraps of no use, which had chanced to lie in the same place. I have also heard of a gentleman and his wife who escaped with the greatest difficulty from their burning house, he bearing, as he thought, their infant in his arms. It proved to be but a pillow which he had snatched up in his haste! A moment devoted to a steady, thoughtful consideration of the circumstances, might in all these cases have been attended with the opposite consequences.

Presence of mind is occasionally shown in quick conception of some device or expedient, such as we usually suppose to be an emanation of superior intellect. This has been repeatedly exemplified in rencontres with the insane. A lady known to me was one evening sitting in her drawing-room alone, when the only other inmate of the house, a brother, who for a time had been betraying a tendency to unsoundness of mind, entered with a carving-knife in his hand, and shutting the door, came up to her and said, 'Margaret, an odd idea has occurred to me. I wish to paint the head of John the Baptist, and I think yours might make an excellent study for it. So, if you please, I will cut off your head.' The lady looked at her brother's eye, and seeing in it no token of a jest, concluded that he meant to do as he said. There was an open window and a balcony by her side, with a street in front; but a moment satisfied her that safety did not lie that way. So putting on a smiling countenance, she said, with the greatest apparent cordiality, 'That is a strange idea, George; but wouldn't it be a pity to spoil this pretty new lace tippet I have got? I'll just step to my room to put it off, and be with you again in half a minute.' Without waiting to give him time to consider, she stepped lightly across the floor, and passed out. In another moment she was safe in her own room, whence she easily gave an alarm, and the madman was secured.

The story of the gentleman commanded by some insane persons to jump from the top of a tower in their asylum, and who escaped by telling them he would rather jump from the bottom to the top, and ran down stairs as if to execute his intention, is well known; but the following anecdote of a similar situation will be new to most readers:—A gentleman accompanying a party to inspect an asylum, chanced to be left behind in the kitchen amongst a number of the inmates who acted as cooks and scullions to the establishment. There was a huge cauldron of boiling water on the fire, into which the madmen declared they must put him, in order to boil him for broth. They would fain have assisted him into the large pot; and as they were laying hold of him, he reflected that in a personal struggle he would have no chance with them—all he could do was to endeavour to gain time. So he said, 'Very well, gentlemen, I am sure I should make good broth, if you do not spoil it by boiling my clothes with it.' 'Take off your clothes,' they cried out; and he began to take off his things very slowly, calling out loudly the whole time. 'Now, gentlemen, my coat is off—I will soon be stripped. There goes my waistcoat—I shall soon be ready;' and so on, till nothing remained but his shirt. Fortunately, the keeper, attracted by his loud speaking, hurried in just in time to save him.

Some anecdotes of escapes from assassins and robbers, by the prompt exercise of presence of mind, are much to the same purpose. A young man, travelling in one of the public coaches, was much interested by the accounts of robberies which his fellow-passengers were detailing. An old gentleman mentioned that he always took the precaution of secreting his money in his boot, merely keeping silver for his incidental expenses in his pocket. The old gentleman appeared to be captivated with the politeness and intelligence of the young man, to whom he addressed much of his conversation, who on his part was equally pleased with the kindness and urbanity of his elder companion. Thus some hours had passed agreeably, when, just at night-fall, as they were passing a wild and lonely moor, the coach was stopped by robbers, who rifled the pockets of those nearest to them, giving the old gentleman a hearty execration for having his purse so badly furnished. They came last to the young man, who was seated in the far corner, and demanded his purse. 'I never carry any money,' said he. 'We'll not take your word for that,' said his assailants. 'Indeed I don't,' said the young man; 'my uncle always pays for us both, and there he is,' continued he, pointing to the old gentleman, 'and he has got our money in his boot.' The old gentleman was dragged from the coach, his boot pulled off, and three ten-pound notes were found. He was then suffered to resume his seat, and the coach drove on. Hot was his anger, and bitter were his upbraidings, against his betrayer, whom he did not hesitate to accuse of both treachery and pusillanimity. The young man listened in silence, as if ashamed and conscience-stricken. They passed over some miles, and at length reached an inn by the wayside. The travellers alighted, and, on going in, the young man requested the old gentleman would allow him to say a few words in private. They retired into a room by themselves. 'I have not only to ask your pardon, my dear sir,' said the young man, 'but to thank you for the fortunate expedient with which your confidence furnished me, and to hand to you the sum of thirty pounds in lieu of that which I appeared so unceremoniously to point out to the robbers. I am sure you will forgive me, when I tell you that the note-case in my pocket contained notes for L.500, the loss of which would have been utter ruin to me.' It need scarcely be added that the adopted uncle shook hands cordially with his young acquaintance, and took him into more marked favour than ever.

One of the most striking cases of presence of mind and self-possession of which I have any recollection, came to light in a trial which took place some years since in Ireland. The story looks like a fiction; but I have reason to believe it quite true. A woman travelling along a road to join her husband, who was a soldier, and quartered at Athlone, was joined by a pedlar, who was going the same way. They entered into conversation during a walk of some hours; but as the day began to wane, they agreed that they would stop for the night at a house of entertainment, and pursue their pedestrian journey the next day. They reached a humble inn, situated in a lonely spot by the road-side; and, fatigued after their long day's walk, they were glad to find themselves under the shelter of a roof. Having refreshed themselves with the substantial supper set before them, they expressed a wish to retire. They were shown into the traveller's room, and went to rest in their respective beds. The pedlar, before retiring, had called the landlord aside, and given into his keeping the pack, which he had unstrapped from his back, till the morning, telling him that it contained a considerable sum of money and much valuable property. They were not long in bed before the pedlar fell into a deep sleep; but the poor woman, perhaps from over-fatigue, or from thoughts of meeting her husband next day, lay awake. A couple of hours might have passed, when she saw the door slowly opened, and a person enter holding a light, which he screened with his hand. She instantly recognised in him one of the young men she had seen below—son to the landlord. He advanced with stealthy steps to the bedside of the pedlar, and watched by him for a few seconds. He then went out, and entered again with his brother and his father, who held in his hand a large pewter basin. They went on tiptoe to the bedside, where the pedlar lay in a deep sleep. One of the young men drew out a knife, and while the father held the basin so as to receive the blood, he cut the poor victim's throat from ear to ear. A slight half-audible groan, and all was still, save the cautious movements of the party engaged in the fatal deed. They had brought in with them a large sack, into which they quickly thrust the unresisting body. The poor woman lay silently in her bed, fearing that her turn would come next. She heard low mutterings among the men, from which she soon gathered that they were debating whether they should murder her too, as they feared she might have it in her power to betray them. One of them said he was sure that she was sound asleep, and that there was no occasion to trouble themselves more; but to make sure of this being the case, one came to her side with the candle in his hand, and the other with the knife. She kept her eyes closed as if in sleep, and had such complete command over herself, as not to betray in her countenance any sign that she was conscious of what was going on. The candle was passed close to her eyes; the knife was drawn across close to her throat; she never winced, or showed by any movement of feature or of limb that she apprehended danger. So the men whispered that she was so soundly asleep that nothing was to be feared from her; and they went out of the room, removing the sack which contained the body of the murdered man. How long must that night of horror have seemed to the poor lone woman—how frightful its stillness and its darkness! The presence of mind which had so astonishingly enabled her to act a part to which she owed her life, sustained her all through the trying scenes which she had yet to pass. She did not hurry from her room at an unseasonably early hour, but waited till she heard all the family astir for some time; she then went down, and said she believed she had overslept herself, in consequence of being greatly tired. She asked where the pedlar was, and was told that he had been in too great a hurry to wait for her, but that he had left sixpence to pay for her breakfast. She sat down composedly to that meal, and forced herself to partake with apparent appetite of the food set before her. She appeared unconscious of the eyes which, with deep scrutiny, were fixed upon her. When the meal was over, she took leave of the family, and went on her way without the least appearance of discomposure or mistrust. She had proceeded but a short way, when she was joined by two strapping-looking women: one look was sufficient to convince her that they were the two young men, and one thought to assure her that she was yet in their power, and on the very verge of destruction. They walked by her side, entered into conversation, asked her where she was going, told her that their road lay the same way: they questioned her as to where she had lodged the night before, and made most minute inquiries about the family inhabiting the house of entertainment. Her answers appeared quite unembarrassed, and she said the people of the house had appeared to be decent and civil, and had treated her very well. For two hours the young men continued by her side, conversing with her, and watching with the most scrutinising glances any change in her countenance, and asking questions which, had she not been fully self-possessed, might have put her off her guard. It was not till her dreaded companions had left her, and till she saw her husband coming along the road to meet her, that she lost the self-command which she had so successfully exercised, and throwing herself into his arms, fainted away.

But there is a still more painful test to which presence of mind may be put than even personal danger, however great. It is when, seeing a beloved object in imminent peril, one inadvertent word, one passionate exclamation, one burst of sensibility, might increase the risk tenfold. It were needless to insist on the urgent necessity of presence of mind, in the form of self-command, at such a time, and I will merely illustrate the subject by an example where the strongest sensibilities of our nature were suppressed, while some, without one particle more of affection, but many thousand degrees less of sense and self-control, would have screamed, or fainted, or acted so as to hurry on the catastrophe most dreaded. A lady with whom I am acquainted, one day returning from a drive, looked up and saw two of her children, one about five, and the other about four years old, outside the garret window, which they were busily employed in rubbing with their handkerchiefs, in imitation of a person whom they had seen a few days before cleaning the windows. They had clambered over the bars which had been intended to secure them from danger. The lady had sufficient command over herself not to appear to observe them; she did not utter one word, but hastened up to the nursery, and instead of rushing forward to snatch them in, which might have frightened them, and caused them to lose their balance, she stood a little apart, and called gently to them, and bade them come in. They saw no appearance of hurry or agitation in their mamma, so took their time, and deliberately climbed the bars, and landed safely in the room. One look of terror, one tone of impatience from her, and the little creatures might have become confused, and lost their footing, and been destroyed.

It has sometimes happened that, in hurry and confusion, a wrong medicine has been administered by the hand of one who would have sacrificed life to save a beloved object from the danger with which they were threatened by a sudden illness or accident, and who, had they preserved their presence of mind, might have been spared one of the bitterest misfortunes that can be conceived. To have self-possession in such a case may be life and health to one who is everything to us. It may happen, too, that illness or accident may overtake us while away from medical aid, or distant from any friend. The great advantages of presence of mind in such cases struck me very forcibly when I heard Captain W—— relate the following anecdote:—He was a young man when he served under General Abercromby as an ensign at the battle of Alexandria. His leg was carried off by a cannon-ball. He of course instantly fell, and remained stunned for some time. On recovering his recollection, he found his wound bleeding profusely, and no assistance near. The forces had left the field in such haste, as to be unable to attend to the wounded and the dying, who were now his only companions. He loosened his sash, and bound it as tightly as he could about the wound, and seeing a dead soldier lying near, he stretched out his hand and seized his bayonet; he then thrust it through a knot which fastened the sash, and twisted it tightly, thus forming a tourniquet, which so effectually stanched the blood, that when he was found some hours after, the great effusion had ceased. No doubt he would have been numbered with the dead, but for the extraordinary presence of mind which at once suggested the only mode by which he could be saved. He eventually recovered, and still lives.

Presence of mind may also be brought to bear with good effect in many of the trivial conjunctures of life. It is often shown in a ready answer, turning anger into good humour, or overturning a false accusation, which otherwise might have proved troublesome. There can be no question that it may be improved for serious emergencies by being cultivated in these familiar and more simple cases. But there is one caution to be observed. Let presence of mind be used only as a defence. When employed for purposes of deception, or to advance selfish objects, we may admire it as an intellectual feature, but regret must at the same time arise that the direction given to it is one in which we cannot sympathise.

THE UNJUST JUDGE.

[BY MRS S. C. HALL.]

It was an old lady who related to me the following incident. As it supplies evidence how strong a moral may be inculcated by a picture, I will endeavour to record it in her own simple words. When I knew her she was very aged; her sitting-room was adorned by paintings, generally of the higher class; but sometimes the sentiment, the conception of a subject, was so superior to its execution, that I imagined she had more feeling than knowledge with regard to works of art. She moved about her apartment, leaning on the arm of her grandniece, and pointing out her favourite pictures by a motion of the large old-fashioned fan that dangled from her arm: she was in truth a chronicle of the past—had sat to Sir Joshua when quite a child—and been the companion of West, and Opie, and Northcote, and all the great men of ancient times; seen David Garrick; and been patted on the head by Dr Johnson; laughed at and with Oliver Goldsmith; and spoke of Queen Charlotte and George III. as a handsome young couple. She was both rich and benevolent, and, despite her age and the infirmity of deafness, she was the best physician that ever entered the close atmosphere of the pale student's chamber: the ease, and grace, and gentleness with which she developed truth, added to its beauty, but did not lessen its power. She was a sound critic—yet a kindly judge. Sir Thomas Lawrence used to say of her, that her very look at ninety was inspiration!

Her general sitting-room was in admirable keeping with its mistress; old chairs, old carvings, old china, old bits of tapestry—with here and there a drapery of golden yellow—a cushion or chair covered by rich deep-toned crimson velvet—and when the sun shone through a little painted window, illumining an angle of the apartment with its fine tints, it threw a sort of halo over these silent but sure indications of pure taste, and made the artist feel at once at home. Then the delight with which, when she found an attentive listener, she would draw forth from an old cabinet some cherished and exquisite miniature—the gem of her treasure-house—and have a little tale to tell of everything she possessed. Latterly she had, as I said, become deaf; but this did not diminish the cheerfulness of her well toned mind: set her talking, and it was like a happy voice from the graves of those mighty ones who now live but in their works.

'You said, my dear madam, you would tell me the story of that picture yonder,' I observed one evening.

'Ah, yes!' she replied; 'that, my dear, was painted by a young man! Poor fellow, I shall never forget what old Northcote said to me about him; but that does not matter now. It was April—a few days before the pictures went in for exhibition to Somerset House, and I was sitting in this very chair, as I have done for the last five-and-forty years! About noon—when Nancy—(Ah, we have no such servants now-a-days!)—Nancy told me that an artist, she was sure from the country, wanted to show me a picture. I admitted him immediately. He placed his production in the best light, and apologising briefly for his intrusion, stood opposite to that very picture whose "story," as you call it, you wish to hear. Young men, my dear, in those days were more ambitious of painting than dressing, like Raffaelle; they did not wear their hair over their shirt-collars—cultivate a mustache, and scent of cigars; and yet I never saw any human being look more like a creature of glorious inventions than the poor pale boy—for he was little more—who painted "The Unjust Judge." His orb-like brow would have well become a crown of laurel; and though he was so singularly handsome, that for a few moments he was the picture upon which I looked, I felt sorry at heart for what was stamped upon his features.

'What?' I inquired.

'Death!' was the solemn reply. The old lady rose from her seat, and taking the arm of her beautiful relative, who resided with her, tottered opposite to the picture. 'Observe,' she continued, 'the hard stern countenance of the magisterial-looking man, who, seated at the head of the table, has decided that the widow—the young widow of an old and faithful tenant—has no further claim on the land, which she imagined secured to her by virtue of a letter, the fragments of which are upon the ground. Observe the look of purse-proud satisfaction the new tenant casts upon the friendless woman, whose faded mourning evinces that she has no means to apply to a higher court. Note how full is the leathern purse he has ostentatiously placed upon the table; do you not see the convulsed clutching of the widow's fingers, as she stretches forth her hands to implore mercy where she might demand justice? the veins of her small white throat are distended by suppressed emotion; her eyes are heavy with unshed tears; and observe also how indignant the boy looks; he has just ceased to grasp the crape shawl that has nearly fallen from his mother's shoulders; his little fists are clenched, as much as to say, "See how I will be revenged when I become a man!" The accessaries also are well, yet not too strongly developed. The fat and insolent cat has driven the widow's timid little dog into a corner; his eyes in utter helplessness are raised to his mistress's face, whose agony is too great to heed the distress of her puny favourite! I do not often look upon it,' she added, returning to her seat, 'though it conveys a fine moral; yet whenever I do, I turn my eyes into my own breast, lest I also may have been an unjust judge!

The old lady paused, and her last observation found an echo in my heart. Great God! how true this is: how apt are we to sit in judgment on each other—how apt to pronounce sentence on a sister's frailty, on a brother's crime—without a knowledge of the temptations which led either to the one or the other; without even inquiring whether what we have heard be true or false! How outrageous we become if we are judged—how careless in judging!

'But the story!' I said at last. 'It is not ended?'

'Hardly commenced,' she replied, and then continued.

'I expressed my approbation in a few words, for the subject touched me. There were faults in the colouring; but the moral was so true that I saw at once the youth had the elements of high art within him. It is an admirable thing to do justice to nature, to copy faithfully the immortalities amid which we live; but it is still more glorious to embody the workings of the mind, to create, to lead as it were the inventive faculties of our fellow-creatures into a higher world. The avarice of the unjust judge is stamped upon that face for ever, and the supplication of the widow seems bursting from her lips. After looking at it for some little time, I inquired what value he put upon his production. He said "he had never thought of that, he only wished it to be exhibited."

"And why, then, did you bring it here?" His pale cheek flushed, while he replied "that he resided in Northumberland; was not acquainted with any one in London; and feared that if he sent in his picture it would not be exhibited, unless some one were good enough to speak for it; so that it might obtain a place—a place where it could be seen, particularly by *one* person."

'I told him I would purchase it. He thanked me; but that, he said, was not what he wanted. He wished it to be seen at the Royal Academy. He had heard that I knew a great many of its members. Would I, if I liked the picture, say a kind word for it to those who had power? His only wish was to see it hung where one person would be sure to see it. The request was so strange, the picture and the youth both so interesting, that I desired much to unravel the mystery. I soon gained the young man's confidence, and his story was quickly told.

'His father had been one of those upright God-fearing tillers of the soil from whom our greatest men have sprung. His life was the last in the lease he held of his land, but he had received a letter from his landlord promising, in case of his death, a renewal of it on the old terms. His father died, and in less than a week after his father's death, the landlord died also. His mother had so firm a dependence upon the letter, that she never thought of the lease: indeed, as the young man said, she was too much absorbed in her own grief to think of worldly matters, until a notice to leave what had been so long her home was served upon her. It was in vain she endeavoured to see the landlord: he would not admit her: she wrote—no notice was taken of her application. "Beaten down," he said, "by circumstances, she would sit day after day looking at a small defaced water-colour drawing of my father, which had been done by some itinerant artist, and seemed her only consolation. I was too young to share her griefs, but not to observe them; and I remember the desire I felt to make a picture like the one she loved, that it might be caressed by her. One morning she had been weeping bitterly; and urged as it were by some sudden resolution, she took my hand, and we walked together in silence to the hall, regardless of the rebuffs of the servants. My usually gentle mother forced her way into the squire's library, and discovered, what I afterwards knew she expected from the information she had received, her landlord in the very act of signing the lease that was to deprive us for ever of the cherished dwelling of our ancestors. Roused by a sense of his injustice, she placed before him the letter from his father to mine; in an instant he tore it into atoms, and flung it on the floor. Stung still more deeply, she clasped her hands and uttered a prayer of few words, but deep import, that he might never die until he acknowledged his injustice. Had I known how to curse, I would—boy though I was—have cursed him from my soul; but my mother had taught me nought but blessings. We returned home: she knelt opposite to where my father's picture hung, as if it had been a shrine, and poured out her soul to God in prayers for patience. I stood by her side. 'Kneel with me,' she desired. I obeyed—but she observed the stubborn spirit that roused within me, and while tears streamed down her cheeks, she made me repeat words which for the first time found no echo in my heart. The softness of the child had altogether departed from me. I felt as if my spirit had sprung at once into manhood. We arose from our knees, I put my hand in hers, kissed her cheek, and said, 'Mother, do not weep, I will protect you.' I shall never forget the music of the sweet blessings she poured upon me then, while hot, hot tears coursed each other down her cheeks. From that time I saw her weep no more, though I knew she wept. For me, I grew hard and stern. I shunned my playmates during the few days we remained in our old dwelling; I could neither eat nor sleep; my soul swelled with indignation and revenge. We left our pleasant dwelling; the shadow of the trees fell no more upon our paths; the hum of my mother's bees, which had been as the music of the sunbeams, sounded no more in my ears; the willow, planted by my father on my birthday, which had grown to be a tree while I was yet a child, no longer waved above my head. We lodged in a small room of a small house in a neighbouring village; a small clean room, furnished out of what seemed our abundance; the window-sill crowded with plants such as my father loved—those perishable yet sweet records of affection. Our dog, our household friend, shared our exile; but even that I had little sympathy with; my mind was bent upon things above my reach, but not beyond my desires. My mother worked at her needle, and taught me all she knew, and every halfpenny I could procure, could earn—for I was no beggar—by little acts of usefulness, I laid out in purchasing paper and pencils. I did not know then what being an artist meant; but I knew that I should like to copy my father's picture, to draw the scenes of my early childhood, to depict the one particular scene that was burnt into my heart, to grow by some means to be rich and powerful, that so I might be revenged on the unjust judge. This last resolve I dared not impart to my mother, from a consciousness that it was one she would disapprove the most. And yet that man bought pictures and hung them on his walls; and people eulogised his liberality, and praised his taste; and that he had taste I cannot doubt, but he had no heart. Is it not strange," inquired the young painter, "that a man can tell what is excellent on canvas, and have no appreciation for what is excellent in life; can understand what is natural when delineated by the painter's art; be touched by painted tears, and yet be utterly incapable of feeling and combining the sensations which spring from nature? Is not this most strange and contradictory?"

'I told him he would not think so when he had seen more of the world, and understood how many contending currents meet and struggle within the heart of man. Perhaps you are already tired of the young artist's tale? I like, old as I am, to hear of struggles, of difficulties overcome, of mountains scaled by hardy enterprise, of seats upon their pinnacles; and I spoke words of hope to him, which fell like rain upon a fertile soil—for his mind was one large treasure-house of poetry. And then he related much of the past: of his own privations he evidently did not think; but his mother's sorrows, lessened as they must have been by cheerful industry, and lightened by the knowledge of his innate talent, dwelt upon his memory. Yet he confessed to moments of most keen enjoyment; the calmness of the Sabbath evening, when the music of the bell had ceased, and the voice of the preacher, or the melody of the choral hymn, chanted by infant voices, mingled with the perfumed air; when the worship was over, and playing with a pencil, which his mother kissed him "not to use on Sunday," she read within her little room the scenes from Holy Writ, which, praised be God, have taught many painters the road to immortality! And, when obliged to labour in the fields, his eye drank in the magic hues of cloud and rainbow, sunshine and shadow; in truth, he said, the more he saw of nature the weaker grew his purpose of revenge towards "the unjust judge." The beauties of the beautiful world softened his spirit; but when he looked upon his mother's hands, hardened by labour, or saw her feeble frame bending with more than woman's weakness, his purpose revived, the agonising scene stamped upon that canvas rose before him, and as he grew older, he determined, "an that he lived to be a man," to do what you see he did accomplish. Several years before (for an artist's talent is long budding before it blossoms), while his was yet in its infancy, the man who had acted so cruelly left his neighbourhood, and came to reside near London. He paid a visit to his property but once, and then offered his *patronage* to the boy artist he had so injured; by whom, I am proud to say, it was indignantly refused. The gentleman was bitterly hurt at this, for he would have greatly enjoyed the notoriety of "bringing out" such extraordinary talent. How different from the warm and noble zeal which makes and bears the torch to light the path of genius! But I grow prosy,' said my old friend, 'and will hasten onward: the desire of the young artist was, that his picture might be placed where it could be seen to advantage; *he* had grown out of the memory of his mother's persecutor, and had resolved to stand where he might watch by it, to see the effect it would produce—not upon the world, but upon him whose injustice he had depicted with so powerful a pencil. "If," he said, "I could but see him change colour; if I could perceive the least indication that he felt the reproof; that the circumstance was recalled; that the power he had crushed into the dust had risen, and stood before him to reprove his injustice; if I could only make him *feel*, I should be satisfied; it is now all the revenge I covet."'

'But his mother?' I inquired.

'She still lives,' was the reply; and then my old friend informed me, that his (the artist's) resolution on this subject almost amounted to insanity; he fancied his picture would work a miracle; soften a hard heart; change the current of a man's blood; alter his nature. Like all those who live alone, and who judge of mankind from themselves, his information, his conception of human character, seemed as contracted as his imagination was vast and vivid; and, in addition to this, he was suffering from a constitutional sensitiveness, which made him far more susceptible than rational men are supposed to be.

'His picture went at the appointed time to the appointed place. I studiously kept the secret that the persecutor—the unjust judge—was intimately known to me; and feeling as I did the utmost anxiety for the young painter, I made him consider my house his home. But his spirit had all the restlessness of genius. As a boy at school counts the days, the hours, that must elapse ere he returns to his home, so did this creature—compounded as he was from the finest essences of our nature—count the moments until the academy would open. It was almost frightful to witness his fits of anxiety as to where the picture would hang—if it would have a good place—if it (perchance) might be killed by some glaring sunset, or saffron sunrise—when the artist, "mad with glory," deepens the hues wherein Almighty God thinks best to steep His landscapes. It was positively fearful, after such ague fits of care, to see the avidity with which he drank in the inspirations poured by the old divinities upon their canvas. It was wonderful to observe how his mind, taught by nature, distinguished at a single glance the gold from the tinsel; and how he spurned whatever was counterfeit or poor. He would, after such excitements, return to his calculations touching his own picture. Sometimes depressed at its inferiority when compared with what he had just seen; at other times full of hope, calculating on the probable result—repeating the difficulties he had encountered—recalling the tears which stood trembling in his mother's eyes when some simple villager would express such natural wonder as to "how he learned it all!" Then he would picture the rich tyrant acknowledging his injustice, and confessing shame; calculate as to the probability of his picture, the first-born of his brain, being extolled by the critics; portray his mother, her thin fingers trembling, and her emaciated form bent over the column where her son's name was marked with praise; hear her read his commendation, and then fall upon her knees in gratitude to God, remembering in the hour of triumph, as well as in the hour of sorrow, that it is He who gives or takes away as seemeth best. Then, poor fellow, in the fulness of his heart he would describe such pictures as he was to paint; he did not care for poverty—not he! he knew it well! he never could be as poor as he had been. He felt his power, like the infant Hercules strangling his foes without an effort—his fortune in his hand—his patent to immortality made out! He and his mother could live in a garret—ay, and die there! But he would make a name that would defy eternity—he would! Poor—poor fellow!' repeated my old friend mournfully; 'and yet there was nothing boastful in this; it was pure enthusiasm.

'Those who had seen the picture here were delighted and astonished, and more than one assured me the placing would be cared for. I felt so convinced that the composition would stand upon its own merits, that I did not desire to lessen the dignity of my new favourite, by requesting as a favour what I felt he had reason to demand as a right. A foolish thought!' said the old lady, taking a fierce pinch of snuff—'a foolish thought for those who want to get on in the world, but a wise one for those who prefer the jewel of existence—self-respect—to aught else.

'The first Sunday in May arrived, to be followed, of course, by the first Monday. He sat with me till late, not here, but at Richmond, where I reside occasionally. He was looking out over the river, floating in the glory of the setting sun, speculating as usual about his picture, and the chance that by that time next night it would have been seen, and its merit acknowledged by its unconscious author, to whom he wished to show the moral of a picture. He was literally wild with hope and excitement, speaking of his mother, wishing for her, and then saying what glory it would be to see some of those mighty masters of his art who had lived and moved among us. Like a young eagle, he panted for the rising sun, towards which he longed to soar. Poor, poor fellow!'

There was a pause, and I longed to hear what was to follow, yet feared to inquire.

'The next morning,' she continued, 'I ordered the carriage so early as to drive under the gateway at Somerset House about a minute before the hour at which the doors were to open. There was the usual crowd—the earnest, intense-looking students, some more pale than usual, others flushed by anxiety—mixed up with critics, and poets, and persons wishful to be the first to see the national exhibition, whose quantity, quality, and arrangement indicate the nature, and progress, and power of British art. But few of the academicians were there, though one or two were recognised; and notwithstanding the density of the crowd, room was made for them, and a murmur ran, "Do you see Stothard?" or, "There is Westall;" or, "That's the young artist, Wilkie;" intimating the current of the people's thoughts. My young friend recognised me, bowed, and then the doors were opened. I saw him rush forward with the rest; and, just as he was about to enter, he turned his face towards me: it was lit with a light which disappointment would quench in death. He waved his hat, and disappeared. I waited until the crush had entered, and proceeded to obtain a catalogue. It is marvellous how quickly a crowd disperses; all had passed up stairs. Suddenly my arm was pressed: I turned round; there stood the young painter, his face shorn of its beams, his whole aspect changed from that of a living man to an almost breathless corse. He seemed rooted to the spot, while in a tone, the character of which I cannot describe, he muttered, "My name is *not* in the catalogue." There were doubtless many others that day doomed to the same disappointment—many who, perhaps, deserved the annual oblivion which overwhelmed the industry and hopes of the past year; but, unhappily, there were also many others who were condemned to the same suffering, merely because there was not space in wealthy England to display the treasures of that genius which confers honour upon the land that calls forth its existence. Many worn and anxious faces—many whose hearts were crushed—passed beneath that portal; yet I heeded but the one. I knew the boy could not survive it long. He had never anticipated its rejection, nor indeed had I. I insinuated there might be some mistake; but, easily depressed as excited, he only clenched between his hands the doom-book of so many, and shook his head. I ordered the carriage to be recalled, and taking his arm, led him towards it. As we descended the steps, I felt him start and shudder. I looked up—the unjust judge stood before me! The coincidence was strange. On the instant I invited him to dine with me the next day in town; the invitation was accepted. My footman assisted the lad into the carriage as if he had been a child; he shrunk into the corner, his noble spirit totally prostrated by his disappointment, while he turned his face away to conceal the agony he had not deserved. I think,' said the good old lady, 'I suffered almost as much. After many efforts I succeeded in turning the current of his thoughts; I assured him the picture should be seen the next day, and that he should witness the effect it produced. I insisted on his remaining entirely at my house; but he had been lessened in his own esteem, and suddenly his manners had become lofty and severe. I let them remain so for a little; but, assured that nothing would so much relieve his overcharged heart as tears, when we were quite alone on the morning of the next day, I spoke to him of his mother, of the scenes of his youth, of her piety, her tenderness, her love; the boy conquered the Stoic—I left him weeping. I had undertaken a most painful task, but it was my duty to complete it.

'As the dinner hour advanced, I placed the picture, which I had reclaimed, in the best possible light, but drew a curtain, so as to shade it from observation till the time of trial arrived; the artist was in the room, and at last my guest came. After a few minutes had elapsed I arose, as I do now, and stood here, the painter remaining in the embrazured window. Suddenly I displayed the picture, and asked him what he thought of the story? "Do you read the story clearly, sir," I said; "perhaps, as it is mine, you will help me to a name for it? A widow, sir, a poor widow believed in her landlord's honour, and intrusted to him a promissory letter for the renewal of the lease which expired with the breath of her dead husband. You see her there; beauty and sorrow are mingled in her features. He has taken the letter; and behold you how men, ay, and rich men too, value their honour; its fragments are on the carpet—the weighty purse of the rich farmer has outweighed the woman's righteous cause. Can you name my picture, sir? Her child, her boy feels though he does not understand the scene; he has dropped his mother's shawl; his hands are clenched; if God spares him to be a man, he will devise some great revenge for that injustice." I thought the gentleman turned pale, and I knew that my young friend was crouching in his lair. "Look you, sir," I continued, "out of the pictured window: is not the landscape pleasant? the tree is remarkable; a famous tree in Northumberland; the—the—something elm. And within, as you observed, the accessaries are well made out: the fierce cat pouncing on the little dog; the elk's horns stand out from the panelling; and the emblazoning of the shield and arms upon the wall—the arms are distinct——"

"Madam!" he exclaimed, in a voice hardly audible from agitation, and then paused.

"The scene took place," I continued, without heeding the interruption, "some ten or twelve years past. Is it not so, Edward Gresham?" I added, appealing to the youth.

He came forward, pale, but erect in the consciousness of his own rectitude, and satisfied that the great object of his existence was attained.

Although I was much agitated, I saw the eagle eye of the artist look down the hurried glance which the unjust judge cast towards him, and I almost pitied him, humbled as he was by the conscious shame that overwhelmed him. He was stricken suddenly by a poisoned arrow; the transcript of the unhappy story was so faithful, the presence of the youth so completely fastened the whole upon him, that there was no mode of escape; and his nature was too stolid, whatever his disposition might be, to have any of the subtle movement of the serpent about him.

"And you," he said, turning away while he spoke; "*you*, whom I have known for twenty years, have subjected me to this!"

"Do you acknowledge its truth, its justice?" demanded the young painter; "do you acknowledge the fidelity of my pencil? I have toiled, laboured, suffered, to show you your injustice in its true colours: but I see you, the proud landlord, turn from the orphan-boy whom, in open defiance of every righteous feeling, you sent houseless, homeless, fatherless, friendless, upon the world. I see you cannot meet my eye for shame. Ay, ay, proud gentleman, *that* will live when you, ay, and I too, are in our narrow graves!"

"I offered you reparation," said the landlord, overpowered by the energy of the painter and the truth of his picture; "I offered you reparation."

"You offered me *patronage!*" retorted the indignant boy; "insult with injury."

The landlord turned to me; he was greatly agitated. "Has the patronage I have extended to many, madam, even within your knowledge, been injury?" he inquired.

I could not but acknowledge that he had purchased many pictures; and replied his collection would prove that he highly appreciated art.

"I will," he added, "even now give him any sum he chooses to name for that picture."

"It is sold," replied the artist.

The old gentleman's countenance changed; he walked up and down the room; once or twice he paused and looked at the sad history, which he would then have given much to obliterate.

"I confess," he said, "the faithfulness of the portraiture; but there were palliating circumstances. Still, I confess I acted wrong—I confess it! I will make retribution; we cannot tell what our acts may produce."

"Injustice," said the youth calmly, "is the parent of misery to the injured and the injurer; it was a cruel act, setting aside its treachery; it was a cruel act, God can judge between thee and me! My mother, a delicate fragile woman, myself almost an infant; and your father's promise, sir, your own father's promise that you scorned; oh sir, how could you sleep with the consciousness of such injustice haunting your pillow?"

"You have your revenge, young man, your revenge," murmured the gentleman; "I acknowledge my injustice; I will make reparation."

"You cannot cancel the past, my mother's years of suffering, my own of labour; but enough. I see you feel I have conquered; my feeble hand has sent conviction to your heart; and I——" He staggered to a chair, and became more pale than usual. I thought he was dying, but it was not so; the heart does not often give way in the moment of triumph—for it was a triumph. I must do the landlord justice: he repeated his regret, he even entered into the young man's feelings, and commended his art; he did all this, and the next morning remitted me a large sum "as a debt due by him to those he had injured."

'How apt are the rich to think that money can heal all wounds. My poor young friend only survived sufficiently long to see his mother, though but for half an hour. It was almost in vain that, kneeling by his bedside, she implored him to think of the world to come. He believed he was too young to die.

"I triumphed, mother, I triumphed," he repeated, his eyes glittering with unnatural brightness; "I triumphed; I made his heart quail and his cheek blanch, and he begged my forgiveness; but it was altogether too much for me; first the disappointment, and then the triumph; it fermented my brain, though I found another mother who taught me that the just and the unjust are mingled together; but now that turmoil is past, you are with me—really, really with me. I will sleep on your bosom, my own mother, as I used when a little child, and to-morrow I will tell you all I mean to do."

"Then all is peace," she murmured.

"Ay, mother, all is triumph, and peace, and love," he replied. "I wonder how I could have hated him so long." He laid his head down with the tranquillity of a sleepy infant, and it was in vain she tried to repress the tears that fell upon the rich luxuriance of his hair—he felt them not.

"He has slept more than an hour," she whispered me. I saw he would never waken. I could not tell her so, but she read it in my face. It was indeed a corse she strained in her arms, and long, long was it ere she was comforted. I never saw my old acquaintance afterwards; but he requested, as I would not yield him up the picture, that I would never suffer it to pass from my possession, or mention his name in connexion with it. He died many years ago, and proved his repentance by providing, in a worldly point of view, for her who had been so long the victim of his injustice.'*

VEHICULAR STATISTICS OF LONDON.

NO II.—HACKNEY-COACHES AND CABS.

PEOPLE are often surprised at the narrowness of some of the thoroughfares in the older parts of London, so inadequate for the press of vehicles now crowding them, without knowing that they were formed before coaches came into general use. Up to the seventeenth century, street accommodation was only required for pedestrians and horsemen. Even carts were little used, the pack-saddle being generally preferred for the transit of goods and merchandise. The chief highway of the city previous to the reign of Elizabeth was the Thames, and boats were the principal vehicles. Upon its banks the most important buildings, whether of a public or private nature, were constructed, on account of the easy access to them which the river afforded. Each had its 'water-gate,' its collection of wherries and barges, with a sufficient number of watermen and rowers, for the same purpose as a modern great man keeps horses, carriages, and grooms. Theatres and other places of amusement were for the same reason built near the stream; chiefly on its southern bank. The Watermen's Company was then a rich and powerful city guild; but when carriages were introduced into England, its profits and influence were greatly diminished, and one of the body, John Taylor, commonly called the 'water-poet,' bewailed the decline of his calling in a pamphlet entitled 'The World Runs on Wheels.' He did not inveigh against coaches belonging to persons of quality, 'but only against the caterpillar swarm of hirelings. They have undone my poor trade whereof I am a member.' He maintains that the hired carriages 'have so overrun the land, that we can get no living upon the water; for I dare truly affirm, that every day in any term, especially if the court be at Whitehall, they do rob us of our livings, and carry five hundred and sixty fares daily from us.' This exact numeration of the number of passengers is probably founded on a good knowledge of the number of vehicles then let out.

The history of London hackney-carriages may be said to commence in 1634. 'Gossip' Gerard, then writing to Lord Strafford, says, 'I cannot omit to mention any new thing that comes up amongst us, though never so trivial: here is one Captain Baily, he hath been a sea-captain, but now lives on the land, about this city, where he tries experiments. He hath erected,

---

* Reprinted, with the concurrence of the author, from the Art-Union, May 1848.

according to his ability, some four hackney-coaches, put his men in livery, and appointed them to stand at the May-pole in the Strand, giving them instructions at what rates to carry men into several parts of the town, where all day they may be had. Other hackneymen seeing this way, they flocked to the same place, and perform their journeys at the same rate; so that sometimes there are twenty of them together, which disperse up and down, that they and others are to be had everywhere, as watermen are to be had by the waterside. Everybody is much pleased with it.' This sort of rivalry amongst the hackneymen of the seventeenth century was productive of similar inconvenience to that arising from the recent introduction of omnibuses, as mentioned in our former article, and in 1635 a proclamation was issued 'to prohibit all hackney-coaches to pass up and down in London streets.' Fifteen years later, another proclamation forbade hackney-coaches to course 'into the streets or to stand to be hired.' In spite of this regal mandate, Pepys records in his Diary of 1660, 'that he got a coach to carry him home on the very day the proclamation was to take effect.' The vehicle of that day was very narrow, and the driver rode on one of the horses as a postilion. As the streets widened after the great fire of London, so the dimensions of coaches were increased, and the coachman sat on a box. 'This was a thing for use,' says Mr Knight in his London, 'not for finery. Here, or in a leather pouch appended to it, the careful man carried a hammer, pincers, nails, ropes, and other appliances in case of need; and the *hammer*-cloth was devised to conceal these necessary but unsightly remedies for broken wheels and shivered panels.' The proclamation of 1660 had been found so unworkable, that, in the very next year, we find hackney-coaches, to the number of 400, allowed by law to ply in the vicinity of London, the proprietors being obliged to pay to government L.5 a-year, as a license for each vehicle. It is curious to see how the use of these conveyances increased in near proportion to the gradual increase of the London population. In the year 1694, the number of licenses was extended to 700 coaches. Twenty years later, a hundred more were added; and in the year 1768, 1000 hackney-carriages were allowed to stand for hire in the streets of London, 175 of which only were suffered to ply on Sundays. By a later act (8th George III., cap. 24), a commission was formed to manage metropolitan hackney-coaches, and to receive the duties. They also appointed coach-stands, and men to water the horses at each of them. Some of the regulations imposed on the drivers evince the aristocratic prejudices of our ancestors: one clause in the act makes a hackney-coachman liable to a penalty of L.5 for 'not giving way to persons of quality and gentlemen's coaches.'

The limitation of the number of hackney-coaches made that branch of trade a monopoly in the hands of the proprietors of the vehicles, and although the law restrained their charges to fixed rates, yet it could not prevent the incivility of the persons they employed. Secure from competition, they seemed to treat their customers as if they did them a favour by driving them.

Hackney-carriages of the old school, which kept a monopolising existence up to the year 1823, were divided into two classes—the coach, and the 'charrot' or chariot. The former was a lumbering second-hand article, in some cases half a century old, most of its services having been previously given to some nobleman's or gentleman's family. Discarded by its first master as unfit for further use, it was bought by the proprietor of a 'plate;' that is, the piece of painted tin on which was embossed the number of his hackney license. The vehicle was restrained by law to hold no more than four persons; but on a dark night, when informers might find it difficult to ply their calling successfully, it was sometimes made to hold six persons, or even a seventh on the box. The 'charrot' had no double seat, consequently it was only calculated for two sitters. Though both sorts of vehicles were drawn by two horses, vehicular motion of every sort was, while they were in fashion, much slower than at present. A hackney-coach stand presented a picture of perfect repose. The horses stood motionless, and were either fast asleep, like their master on the box, or stood quietly munching chopped hay out of nose-bags suspended from their heads. The coachman sat under the weight of a heavily-caped 'box'-coat, either in a state of profound reflection or of nodding somnolency. When, therefore, any one wanted his services, it was necessary to bawl with might and main; but as that very often proved ineffectual, the attendant 'waterman' of the stand was often obliged to use active measures to wake him. Having recovered from his reverie, or his nap, the driver slowly rolled himself off his seat, and, assisted by the waterman, removed the nose-bags, or awoke the horses, and dragged them by the headgear to the side of the pavement; the door-steps were then leisurely unfolded, and the 'fare,' or passenger, helped in. If the animals were thought to want water, a few minutes were occupied in giving it to them, and after the coachman had handed the waterman his 'rent'—a perquisite of one halfpenny, receivable every time a coach left the stand—the wheels were made to revolve at the rate of about three miles an hour. So notoriously slow were the motions of these vehicles, that when a coachman of extraordinary activity carried his enterprise so far as to solicit custom by saying to a passer-by, 'Coach, sir?' the reply frequently was, 'No, thank you—I am in a hurry.'

It is not a little singular that the London public suffered from the surliness and inactivity of the hackney-coach fraternity, well knowing that for years a light and commodious sort of vehicle had plied in the streets of Paris, to the great accommodation of its inhabitants. These were called *cabriolets de place*, of which so long ago as 1813 no fewer than 1150 existed. Efforts were, it is true, made by one or two private individuals to introduce them into London; but without effect. Their scheme was stopped at the outset, for they could not get licenses. With that reverence for 'vested rights' which is so characteristic of official operations in England, the hackney-coach commissioners thought it would be unjust that each London proprietor—who had bought his licenses with the express understanding that he should only have a certain number of rivals—should suffer by the introduction of others. At last, in the year 1823, two resolute individuals, Messrs Bradshaw and Rotch, the latter a member of parliament, caused, we believe, eight cabriolets to be built; and after some hard fighting with the commissioners in Essex Street, they procured licenses. From that day the sun of hackney-coach prosperity declined. The new vehicles were exactly suited to persons for whom the old coaches were quite unavailable—namely, those who happened to be in a hurry. They were hooded chaises, drawn by one sound, fast-trotting horse, and driven by an active man in livery, who sat beside his passenger, there being no room for a separate driving-box. They were capable of holding only one person, but him they carried at fares one-third lower than those of the original vehicles.

The old Jehus presented a slow, heavy, ill-arranged

opposition to these cabriolets; they bribed the 'watermen' not to let them have good places on the stands; and when one of them was accosted by a customer, the whole rank or row of coaches moved off the stand to entice away the 'fare;' but the 'cab' always got to the passenger first, with whom it was driven off before the hinder-wheels of some of its rivals had begun to move. The number of cabs increased, much to the detriment of the coach-proprietors' 'vested rights,' and they appealed to the commissioners, who kindly augmented the number of hackney-coach licenses to 1200, restricting those of cabs to sixty-five, and thus stood the statistics of the London hackney-trade up to the year 1832.

Meanwhile, it was found that the one-horse vehicles were capable of affording a much greater amount of accommodation than their then construction furnished, and variously-shaped carriages were invented to hold more than one person. The first improvement consisted of making a driving-seat over the right wheel, so as to leave room under the hood for two passengers; then came box-cabs, back-door cabs, four-wheel cabs, and, last of all, 'Broughams' and Hansom's patent cabs, which seem to have taken a stand as the favourites with their proprietors and the public. In 1832, every restriction as to the number of hackney-carriages being removed by a new act of parliament,* one-horse vehicles of all the shapes and descriptions we have enumerated above, besides a great many more, suddenly made their appearance in the streets of London; and most of the old drivers, with their lumbering coaches and superannuated horses, were gradually starved off the stands. What has become of them no one can tell; they were too bigoted and inactive to become cabmen; and those who were not prudent enough to save up a 'bit of money' during their days of prosperity, most likely ended them in the workhouses of their respective parishes. Their downfall was but little regretted. But they have not been wholly banished from the streets: 'not quite two hundred'—according to the information we received from the registrar of licenses—still creep about London, and earn a scanty livelihood for themselves and broken-down cattle; while, during the year which ended on the 4th of last January, there were cabs daily driving about London, in flourishing prosperity, to the number of 2400.

In viewing the moral statistics of the London hackney-coach trade, it is much to be feared that, in the aggregate, the character of the drivers was not improved by the change. The old 'Jarvies,' as they were called by their familiars, were, it is true, a tiresome, surly race; but they possessed a slow-going, rugged respectability, which cannot be overlooked when a comparison is made between them and their successors. Firstly, they never raced in the streets; and although this merit is much diminished when we remember the age of their horses and the weight of their vehicles—yet elderly people, who now walk about London at the imminent risk of being knocked down by some recklessly-driven cab, cannot but look back upon the hackney-coach times with regret. Again, we are led to believe that they were more honest; and this is partly proved by some facts which we have learnt concerning the restoration of lost property by that fraternity. It frequently happens that passengers leave articles in the vehicles they have hired, and the restoration of such waifs and strays entirely depends upon the honesty of the coachman. Since 1822, a rule has existed by which, when anything is found in a coach, the driver is bound to deposit it with the registrar of licenses, that the losers may know where to apply for it. It is then restored, upon payment of a small fee for the driver's time and trouble in bringing it. During four years and a half after this regulation was made, property was brought into the office of the estimated value of L.45,000, and not many applications for lost articles were made over and above the number of articles restored. All, or nearly all this honesty, must be put down to the credit of the old coachmen, for cabs had but just been introduced. On the other hand, the account received from the present officials of the hackney-carriage registrary wears a very different complexion. We were told that, although upon an average from fifteen to sixteen hundred 'strays' were deposited in the office during the past year, they were all of small value; that applications for at least fourteen times the number were made; and that a number of things at least ten times greater are actually lost in cabs than are brought to the office to be restored.

The pecuniary relations of cabmen and their masters are fortunately singular in this country. It appears that the masters have no chance of being honestly dealt with, if they were to pay wages to their servants. They therefore lend out the vehicles and horses at a fixed sum per day; or rather the men are expected to bring home the stipulated amount. Sometimes, in the dull season, they beg off for less, but it was remarked to us by the manager of the largest establishment of cabs in London, that, let the town be ever so full, or the season ever so prosperous, they never produce *more* than the fixed amount, so as to make up for former deficiencies. One master tried the experiment of trusting to his men's honour, and paying them in wages of a guinea per week each. During the second week circumstances came to his knowledge which induced him to reduce the stipend to ten shillings. The week after, he found he could not carry on his business profitably and pay his men more than five shillings per week. On the fourth week he paid them—like other cab-masters—nothing; for by this time experience taught him that they abstracted his profits, and pocketed the wages besides. Still, with the arrangement universally adopted, the masters seem generally satisfied.

Though gradually improving, the character of the modern hackney-carriage driver does not yet stand high. It must be owned that, before being restrained by the registration act alluded to in our previous article, the cabman was a far from pleasant person to deal with. His faults were the very reverse of those of the more patriarchal coachmen; they were active vices, such as furious driving, overcharging, and volubility in abuse, should a dispute arise. The personal licensing and badge system has had a most beneficial effect not only upon omnibus drivers and conductors, but upon hackney-carriage drivers. They have become of late infinitely more civil in their demeanour and moderate in their demands than they were before the act came into operation.

A recent official report declares, that during the past two years a decided moral reformation has taken place amongst them. Many of the cabmen are known to be regular visitors to a place of worship on Sundays, while others attend a school opened for their especial advantage. Some have given up driving cabs on Sundays, the better to observe the Sabbath. What we learnt at the registrar's office, tells very much in favour of the whole body:—In 1844, out of the 8492 drivers, conductors, &c. who applied for a renewal of their licenses, only 42 lost them from bad conduct.

The average produce of each hackney-carriage to the proprietor may be about ten shillings and sixpence a-day, to which, if about three-and-sixpence be added for cash appropriated by the drivers in lieu of wages, the amount per diem is raised to fourteen shillings. Hence we may conclude that there is spent daily by the London public for coach and cab hire L.1715, and yearly almost L.800,000. The cash annually circulated by all the metropolitan hired carriages, including omnibuses, exceeds therefore *one million five hundred thousand pounds!*

We may conclude by a recapitulation. During the year ending in May 1844, there were licensed 1854 conductors, 1740 drivers of stage-coaches, besides 4627 drivers of hackney-carriages, and 371 'watermen,' or attendants of 130 coach-stands; in all 8592 individuals.

* 1st William IV., cap. 22.

In the year ending 4th of January 1845, there plied in the streets of London 1472 stage-carriages—50 only of which travelled beyond the jurisdiction of the metropolitan police—and 2450 hackney-carriages, all of which were cabs, except not quite 200: in all 3922 vehicles.

THE GRAVE OF GRAY THE POET.

I HAD spent a day lately, by way of ovation in honour of the arrival of spring, in renewing my acquaintance with the beauties of Windsor and Eton, when I found on my return to Slough that I was just too late for the railway train. There was another train, however, at eight o'clock in the evening, and I set myself to while away the intermediate time by sauntering up and down, and pondering on the objects which had previously engaged my attention. I recalled the princely towers of Windsor, the parks, and the Long Walk with its three miles of elms. I thought of Falstaff and Herne the hunter, of the terrace and the gardens, and of the Vandyke room in the palace, where the long, oval, melancholy countenance of Charles I. is repeated by the exquisite limner till the features seem to be graven on the memory. There was also the neat little village of Datchet, with its meadows fresh and green in the spring sunshine, the cottages nestling under the protection of royalty, the Thames winding slowly in the midst, and tall Lombardy poplars shooting up here and there like spires among the massy woods and rich verdure. Certes, the land is goodly and fertile—excessive and dazzling in its exuberance—the perfection of cultivated beauty—the Eden of England. To a northern eye, it is almost

> ———— too good
> For human nature's daily food.

There is a want of rough and barren contrasts. A gray crag or a towering hill would be an advantage; but the natives, who love *comfort* and elegance, find change enough in the alternations of the seasons and the weather. Every month has its peculiar charms, and autumn must streak gloriously that wide expanse of foliage.

Brilliant as was the retrospect of this natural panorama, elevated and idealised by the imagination—aided, too, by the moral effects of ancient Eton and its groups of schoolboys—I felt somewhat baffled and dispirited at losing my conveyance, and having to wait some hours in forced and solitary contemplation. In this dilemma, I entered into conversation with one of the men engaged about the station. These liveried functionaries are generally civil and fair-spoken; for railways are certainly one of the few public things that are well managed in this busy money-hunting country. The man was intelligent, and he suggested that I had plenty of time to walk as far as Stoke Pogeis, and see the monument of 'the celebrated Mr Gray the poet.' Stoke Pogeis! Name unpoetical, yet welcome—I had entirely forgot it. There the pensive fine-spirited lyrical poet used to sojourn with his mother, 'Dorothy Gray, widow,' and his old aunts. There he wrote his humorous 'Long Story,' after visiting the antique mansion-house where 'my grave Lord Keeper,' Sir Christopher Hatton, once 'led the brawls,' and Sir Edward Coke studied law—there (at the said village of Stoke) Gray used to read Greek and study botany, noting down in his calendar the precise time when strawberries ripened, or the nightingale was first heard—there he completed his churchyard elegy, laid his mother's head in the grave—and there at length he himself, the last survivor of his race, was also buried 'in the sure and certain hope of a joyful resurrection.'

In another minute I had crossed the road, and was on my way to Stoke, a footpath by the side of the dusty highway, with relays of song-thrushes and blackbirds singing cheerily overhead. The small square fields, bounded by hedgerows, and with pollard elms at the sides, are peculiarly characteristic of the English rural landscape. Scottish fields are more extensive, and the farms generally present more ploughed land, besides being enclosed by hard dry stone fences, without the convenience of footpath, stile, or crossing. These common rights are jealously guarded in England. No 'little tyrant of the fields' dare shut out the people from their immemorial prescriptive pathways.

I thought, as I went along, of the sad, chequered destiny of poets, and of the hallowed ground in which they rest after 'life's fitful fever.' Chaucer and Spenser 'sleep well' in Westminster Abbey. They were the first to give the 'eternal blazon' of poetry to the ancient consecrated walls, and their names and memory stand out prominently amidst the mass of later occupants. Dryden lies next to Chaucer, and next to him is Cowley—the 'melancholy Cowley,' as he loved to call himself. Near Dryden is Francis Beaumont—

> Fletcher's associate, Jonson's friend beloved—

and Jonson himself, 'rare Ben,' sleeps in the silence of the north aisle. Michael Drayton, too, is in the abbey—the witty Prior, and the easy Gay—the reserved, yet gentle and cultured Addison—the rugged, warm-hearted Johnson, and, in the same grave, our own Thomas Campbell. Truly the south transept of that old minster is indeed the Poets' Corner. The name is immortal above all naming of priest, verger, or architect! Yet, high and solemn as is the repose of the abbey, enshrining some of England's most precious dust, it does seem as if, after Chaucer and Spenser—the 'gray fathers' of the temple—our poets would sleep more appropriately apart, each in his chosen ground, amidst the scenes and objects connected with his history and genius. The individuality of the bard is thus more strictly and lovingly preserved. Shakspeare's tomb in the chancel of his native church, is holier ground than if his ashes were mixed with those of even the loftiest masters of the lyre. He has the whole of that fine conventual church, the murmurs of the Avon, and the waving of its trees, for his monument and requiem—a requiem everlasting and unbroken. Milton was ever in the heart of busy London, and his grave is there, half-desecrated and hidden; but that close, low-roofed church, round which is heard the constant stir of human life, appears no unmeet sanctuary for him who with heavenly aims and inspiration, yet 'the lowliest duties on himself did lay,' and was emphatically a worker with his fellow-men 'in populous city pent.' Let the voice of praise, the anthem clear, arise in the old dim edifice, and his majestic spirit seems present with us! Pope, in the little church of Twickenham, on the margin of the Thames—brimfull, and washing the grassy borders of his ruined villa—engrosses all the interest of the spot, and is inseparably, in death as in life, identified with the scene. Thomson's grave consecrates the shades of Richmond, where he dwelt—Byron sleeps near Newstead Abbey—and Coleridge and Southey within the shadow of their 'ancient walks and daily neighbourhood.' Scott has a noble grave in Dryburgh Abbey—a Gothic temple for his sepulchre. And here, in this quiet sequestered country churchyard of Stoke—in the open air—is the grave of the recluse and contemplative Gray.

There never was a more appropriate grave for a poet than Gray's at Stoke. The spot is so completely secluded, and so still—the church old, and covered with ivy—two huge, solemn-looking yew trees in the centre of the little churchyard—two thorn trees, now in blossom—and no gaudy tombs or decorations to intrude poor human vanity amidst the thoughts of death and immortality.* We enter from the public road into a field or common, with footpaths striking across to the village; and in one corner, a few hundred yards off, separated in front by a wire-fence, on the sides by dark clumps of pine trees, are the church and churchyard. More distant to the left is Stoke Park, the magnificent residence of Mr Penn, a descendant of the founder of Pennsylvania, and which stands on the site of the manor-house that furnished the subject for the opening of the Long Story. The lawn and park stretch out till they meet and mingle with the church common, and are tenanted by a goodly herd of fallow-deer. To the south, over a large artificial sheet of water, is seen Windsor Castle, beyond which Cooper's Hill and the Forest Woods close the view. A high fluted column, surmounted by a colossal statue, commemorates the fame of the former distinguished possessor of the grounds, the great constitutional lawyer, Sir Edward Coke. But before approaching the church or mansion-house, we come upon a monument (railed in, and enclosing flowers and aromatic shrubs), being a large sarcophagus, supported on a square pedestal, with inscriptions on marble on each side. One of these tells us that the monument was erected A.D. 1799, in honour of Thomas Gray, 'among the scenery celebrated by that great lyrical and elegiac poet.' Time and the weather have effaced the remainder of this inscription, but on the other panels are verses from the Elegy, and the following lines from the Ode on Eton College:—

> Ye distant spires, ye antique towers,
> That crown the watery glade,
> Ah, happy hills! ah, pleasing shade!
> Ah, scenes beloved in vain!
> Where once my careless childhood strayed,
> A stranger yet to pain;
> I feel the gales that from ye blow
> A momentary bliss bestow!

And this calm, reflective 'bliss' seems to enter the soul of the spectator as he paces these interesting grounds. The grave of Gray is immediately in front of the chancel window. It is a plain tomb, erected by the poet to his aunt and mother, the sides built up with red bricks, and on the top a blue slab, bearing this inscription:—

'In the vault beneath are deposited, in hope of a joyful resurrection, the remains of Mary Antrobus. She died unmarried November 5, 1749, aged 66.

'In the same pious confidence, beside her friend and sister, here sleep the remains of Dorothy Gray, widow, the careful, tender mother of many children, one of whom alone had the misfortune to survive her. She died March 11, 1753, aged 67.'

There is no mention of the poet on the stone; but a former vicar of the parish (whose tomb, exactly similar, is close to the other) inserted a tablet with the subjoined inscription at the foot of the chancel window:—

'Opposite to this stone, in the same tomb upon which he has so feelingly recorded his grief at the loss of a beloved parent, are deposited the remains of Thomas Gray, the author of the "Elegy written in a Country Churchyard," &c. He was buried August 6, 1771.'

* Under one of the yew trees is a dark square tomb to the memory of a lady, Jemima, the wife of Captain Harrington of Seaforth, Cape of Good Hope, the daughter of Major Douglas of Windsor, and niece of the late Earl of Seaforth. She died in London in 1820, and was interred, as the tomb states, 'by her own particular desire, in this retired spot.' On the grave of a soldier, Captain Thomas Hay, formerly of Slough, is the following somewhat doubtful eulogy:—

> 'The aged soldier is in peace and joy;
> And heavenly notes of praise, without alloy,
> Fall soft upon his ear.
> Where creeps the deathless ivy o'er his head,
> He soft reclines upon his mossy bed,
> *A stranger now to fear.*'

In the English country churchyards, we find few tomb-stones a century old, and indeed few at all. The graves, however, are decently bound with brier, and kept free from weeds.

Honour to Mr Granville Penn for his monument, and no less to the vicar for his lowly tablet! They merit the thanks of all pilgrims to the shrine of virtue and genius. The vicar died in 1780, and most probably read the funeral service over the remains of the poet, when they were laid in the same grave with his tender parent, whose name he never mentioned without a sigh.

Gray's affection for his mother seems to have been as strong and lasting as the filial piety of Pope, which forms so fine a trait in his character. Philip Gray, the father, was harsh and inhuman, and contributed nothing to the maintenance of his family. His wife was partner with her sister in a millinery business, from the profits of which she maintained herself and children, providing everything for her distinguished son whilst he was at Eton school, and afterwards at the university of Cambridge. Gray, we are told, owed his life to a memorable instance of the love and courage of his mother, who removed a paroxysm with which he was attacked in his infancy, by opening a vein with her own hand. Her attention was unfaltering—her sacrifices great, though silent. And she lived to see her son a finished scholar and gentleman, and author of the Elegy in a Country Churchyard. The last was surely an over-payment of delight.

The people of Stoke claim the Elegy, as pertaining to *their* churchyard, while others assign it to the village of Granchester, near Cambridge. The latter seems to have the preferable right. Gray commenced the poem at Cambridge: his evening walk was often extended to Granchester, two miles from his Alma Mater, and the great bell of St Mary's would have formed the curfew of his imagination. There are no 'rugged elms' in the churchyard of Stoke, and scarcely a stone with 'uncouth rhymes and shapeless sculpture decked' of the requisite age. At Stoke, however, the poem was finished, and received the last corrections of the author. Writing to Walpole, June 10, 1750, he says, 'I have been here at Stoke a few days (where I shall continue good part of the summer), and having put an end to a thing whose beginning you have seen long ago, I immediately send it to you.' Walpole handed about the manuscript with great applause among the higher circles of society: it was printed by Dodsley, and soon circulated with a rapidity that astonished the timid and sensitive poet. But perhaps the most striking and interesting proof of the popularity of the poem is afforded by a touching and beautiful incident related in Playfair's life of Professor Robison. Robison, when employed as an engineer in the army under General Wolfe, happened to be on duty in the boat in which the general went to visit some of his posts the night before the battle which was expected to be decisive of the fate of the campaign. The evening was fine, and the scene, considering the work they were engaged in, and the morning to which they were looking forward, sufficiently impressive. As they rowed along, the general with much feeling repeated nearly the whole of Gray's Elegy to an officer who sat with him at the stern of the boat, adding, as he concluded, that 'he would prefer being the author of that poem to the glory of beating the French to-morrow.' We hope Gray heard of this incident. It would spread a momentary sunshine over his cloistered cell, superior even to the visions of his classic imagination.

I left Stoke just at the 'parting hour of day,' when the scene in some degree realised the rural imagery of the Elegy, so true to English country life. No one had been near while I pored over the tombs—there was no porteress at the gate, 'to show the place' and solicit a gratuity; I could see in the distance the 'lowing herd,' and the ploughman plodding homewards. There was a 'solemn stillness' in the air, except where the rooks cawed among the high trees at Stoke Park, or lighted on the old square tower and wooden spire of the church. The yew trees looked more dark and gloomy; but there was a mellow light and delicious coolness on the green open common. The deer were as tame and quiet as the inanimate objects around; and the whole seemed a picture of still life, over which poetry and religion had shed their softest and selectest influence.

SHORT HOURS.

For some time past the subject of early shop-shutting, and the general diminution of the hours of labour, have much engaged the attention of the well-meaning and intelligent, and the arguments in favour of such a system are alike urgent and obvious. Without at all entering upon the general merits of the question, we think there is one argument which, if not overlooked, has at least not met with that consideration which its importance deserves. It is all very well to talk of humanity and leisure for moral and intellectual improvement to men prepared to feel the force of such positions; but we need scarcely remark that views of this kind are either simply unknown to many masters, or regarded by them, from whatever cause, as visionary and extravagant. It is for this reason that we now propose to argue for short hours upon a purely economical ground. We design to show that any extension of work beyond a man's ordinary physical powers is attended with loss to his employer, and that any reduction within proper limits is followed by a corresponding gain. We mean, in other words, to establish, from facts before us, that men worked considerably within the limits of their power perform a greater amount of labour, and execute it more satisfactorily; that they are more intelligent, more apt to comprehend, more active, and more inclined to be obliging, than those who are worn-out and fagged by long and incessant toil.

It is evident, if a man be overworked to-day, that tomorrow he will be less able for his average labour; and that if a system of overworking be persisted in, the period will be hastened when he shall be totally unfitted for that species of labour, or be laid aside by disease. The same reasoning holds true in reference to time. If ten hours a-day be the average at which a man can work cheerfully and well, then twelve hours will render him dull and fatigued; and though he may continue at the work, he will not do one whit more, or, if he should do so one day, it will be at the expense of the labour of the next. This is viewing man as a mere animated machine, whose thews and sinews are capable of exerting a limited amount of force, and to which we can apply the mechanical axiom, 'that greater power cannot be gained but at the expense of time, and time cannot be saved but at the expense of power.' But this reasoning will not altogether apply to an intelligent being; and, in estimating the amount and duration of human force, we must take into account the inseparable attribute of mind. There is scarcely any species of labour—certainly none of the mechanical or mercantile—but requires care, vigilance, ingenuity, reasoning; and these are qualities so intimately depending upon a sound and vigorous bodily system, that it were folly to look for them from an overtasked and worn-out man. Reasoning in the abstract, then, we think it very palpable that any master must be a gainer, both in the amount of labour and manner of execution, by exacting from the workmen he employs rather under than above the average time during which their attention and activity can be maintained. Among the many practical illustrations of this doctrine, few could be more directly applicable than the following, which recently came under our notice. In Fifeshire, where the hours of the ploughmen are of average duration—namely, during daylight in winter, and from five to six, with a breakfast and midday interval, at other seasons—the men, as a class, are active, energetic, and well-skilled in their various duties. In activity we will back them against any similar class in the island, and the trial of skill which a few years ago came off between twenty of them and a like number from the Lothians (a pre-eminent agricultural district), places them foremost on the list at least as ploughmen. In Strathearn and the Carse of Gowrie, on the other hand, where the hours of labour are notoriously long, the farm-labourer seems to be quite the antithesis of his brother in Fife. A farmer in the latter county, a few years ago, engaged two of the first-rate Carse hands at the highest wages, and placed them at the general labour of the farm along with seven native ploughmen. In a few weeks the difference between the imports and the natives became painfully apparent; for, with every disposition to oblige, they neither performed so much labour, nor executed it so well, nor with so much alacrity, as the latter. 'I've had enough of your Carse men,' said the farmer to us one day, and his reason was as nearly as possible in the following words:—'They've got a wretched system of long hours in the north: they work the very spirit out of their men, and so it is that these have not half the smeddum (smartness) of our Fife lads. They've neither the same skill nor activity, and when a push comes, I would make my foreman work round a couple of them.' But you'll find them very willing and obliging? 'Oh yes, they are patterns in that respect, and are certainly not so independent in their way as our own blades; but they want the energy and aptitude, and really don't give their work the same finish. For one order that I have to give to my own men, I have to give two to them. They'd hang as long as I like at the plough-tail, but I want *through-put;* and so commend me to my own men and reasonable hours.' Now, these are not the preachings of any of your sentimentality men, but the plain words of a hard-driving money-making Scotch farmer, who saw from this comparison the obvious advantage to himself of keeping his men on short hours, and of never exacting from them more than they could do cheerfully and well.

The same argument applies to every species of labour, and with double force to those employments which require intelligence and care. As soon as the body begins to tire, the spirit droops, the attention flags, and if positive carelessness does not supervene, there follows at all events a dulness and lethargy which are anything but favourable either to amount of work or to manner of execution. Nor can there be any remedy for this but rest and repose. It is true you may apply artificial stimulants; but these, too, will shortly fail; and their use only renders the bodily system of their victim the less capable of being re-invigorated. These remarks apply in a special manner to in-door labour, where the long-hours abuse is more frequently seen, notwithstanding that a restrained position of body, want of fresh air and ventilation, should be potent arguments for a course quite the reverse. Nor do we argue upon mere theory, for in this case, as in the other, we have fortunately a most convincing illustration at hand. It is that of a large spinning-mill, situated beside a country village for the sake of water-power, and in which the hours of labour are from six in the morning till seven at night, deducting an hour for breakfast and another for dinner, thus reducing the hours of actual work to eleven—a space still too long, but considerably shorter than that required in any other of the neighbouring factories. In addition to this reduction, the wheel is stopped at five o'clock on Wednesdays and at three on the Saturdays; three half days a-year are allowed for fairs, two days for church fasts, two for New-Year's day and Handsel Monday, and one for the anniversary of the mill's erection—an event seemingly of great local importance. Now, however small this may seem to some, it is in reality an amount of freedom and relaxation not enjoyed, so far as we are aware, in any similar establishment. And what, according to the owner, has been the result? *Not a single spindle of yarn less, a great reduction of disease, better executed work, fewer accidents of damage to the machinery, a more orderly and more obliging set of work-people, besides the satisfaction that he is contributing in some degree to the happiness of his fellow-creatures.* It may seem contradictory at first sight, that a reduction of hours in such an establishment should not be followed by a diminution of produce; a little reflection, however, will clear away the dubiety. The last two years' wage-book shows the merest trifle of absence from ill-health; the lessening of damage has caused fewer stoppages, and even a greater degree of speed can be obtained, inasmuch as the attention of the workers is never relaxed by long and tedious confinement. The stoppage on Wednesdays permits the women to attend a little to their domestic concerns, while it allows the mill to be cleaned and the machinery to be overhauled: the advantages of the Saturday afternoons are too obvious to be adverted to.

From these examples, then, we think it sufficiently obvious that moderate hours are conducive alike to the interests of employer and employed. The latter enjoys more the life of a rational creature, and the former rather adds to, than subtracts from, his gains, inasmuch as he has the same amount of work, and has it more highly and more carefully finished. It may be urged, to be sure, that there is no tiring of the steam-engine and machinery, and that the longer these revolve, the larger the amount of produce. This would be true and just if the machine were self-acting; but in nineteen cases out of twenty, it requires the regulation and aid of human hands, and it is to these that our argument applies. We have no objection that a man work his machinery till every wheel and axle be worn to a skeleton, for its place can be readily supplied; what we condemn is the grinding of workmen to a similar condition, when it is obvious that an opposite course is in the long-run the more advantageous. The steam can be let on at pleasure to the steam-engine, but the strength of a worn-out man cannot be renewed by any similar process: he must have leisure and repose; and where this is denied him, his bodily mechanism must shortly become diseased and impotent. It forms a sorry excuse for the employer to urge that, as he has laid out some forty or fifty thousand pounds in machinery, so he must 'keep the steam up,' in order the more speedily to repay himself; nor does it better his position to put, as is sometimes done, the question—Would you have all that machinery to be employed only ten hours out of the twenty-four? What, indeed, is the use of machinery, if it be not to lessen the amount of human labour and drudgery; and what the purpose of the invention of mind, if it be not to increase the amount of our comforts and happiness? It would appear, were we to admit the arguments of some folks, that the purpose of machinery was rather to enthral than to exalt mankind; and it is curious that many manual employments, such as those of the mason, joiner, slater, labourer, and the like, should have custom sanctioning the labour hours from six to six, with breakfast and dinner intervals, while those which have been called into existence by machinery have been tasked like slaves from five to seven, or even beyond these limits. Nor is it the reasoning of a humane or enlightened mind to reply, that if the workmen feel themselves aggrieved, they can turn to some other employment. Is it right for any man, because he has power on his side, to abuse it; or can the fact of a few thousand pounds' possession dissociate him from his fellow-men, or free him of the reciprocal duties which the necessities of our condition have imposed? Every argument that militates against the great law of brotherly love must be unsound; and it is only because this law is but too little respected, that there is so much of inequality, oppression, and poverty amongst us.

Against this view of short hours of labour it is sometimes urged, that if ten hours can be proved to be more advantageous than twelve, would not eight or six be more advantageous still—and where, then, were the limit to the diminution? This species of reasoning is entirely beside the question. A certain amount of labour is to be performed, by an agent having limited powers; there must be an average at which this power can be exerted, and our argument only goes this length, 'that it is more profitable to tax these powers within than beyond this ascertained average. In dealing with human power, we cannot apply the mathematical formula by which we calculate the force of gravity, of heat, or any other purely physical agent; but we must regard it as a power imbued with mind, and as a power which nature re-invigorates by one process, and one alone. Again, it is said that any additional leisure would in all likelihood be devoted to idleness or dissipation; but, founding upon past experience, we have no ground for such a decision. It would not be idleness, surely, for the toiled mechanic to betake himself to the fields and lanes for that air which the pent-up workshop denies; nor would it be dissipation to indulge in the harmless games of the public green, or in the amusements of our halls and lecture-rooms. Or, granting that some were to dissipate, are we to withhold from eighty a just and natural boon because twenty choose to abuse it? The truth is, that where there has been little time for mental culture, we are not to wonder at some little abuse of any new privilege, and we can only hope for the rectification of such faults when men have more leisure to learn better modes. A holiday to our population at present is a boon so seldom granted, that it acts upon them like intoxication; and any extravagances they may commit should be laid to this account, rather than to any innate disposition to absurdity and folly. But be this as it may, we have taken up the reduction of the hours of labour upon other grounds—namely, its obvious advantage to the masters themselves—throwing aside altogether every consideration as to humanity, and leisure for moral and intellectual culture; and we leave it for the reader to determine whether our reasonings be in any degree corroborative of our opinion.

MEXICO AS IT IS, AND AS IT WAS.

SECOND ARTICLE.

Mexico, when Cortes conquered it, was the capital of a great and powerful nation, regulated by good laws, well and speedily administered. The relations of life were recognised and guarded; a good system of education was fostered; the arts were cultivated and encouraged; architecture had advanced to a high degree of excellence; the knowledge of astronomy, and of the calculation of time, was exact and scientific; they were powerful in war; they had built a vast empire; springing from a sparse tribe which found its first home among the reeds and marshes of the lake where they had hidden for safety from their foes; and though their religious rites were brutal and bloody, they had some faint ideas of an invisible and omnipotent God. In their capital they chiefly showed their power; and when Cortes gazed down upon it from the top of the great temple, streets, canals, shrines, presented themselves; large and beautiful houses amid groves and gardens; markets with every fruit and vegetable luxury; aqueducts bringing sweet water from the hills; streets filled with artists who wove beautifully pictured garments from plumes of birds, or fashioned the precious metals into gorgeous ornaments; palaces, houses, all crowded with a busy, active, and brave throng; and lakes covered by floating gardens. The town was entered by four causeways over the lake, made by the hand of man, as wide as two horsemen's lances; the streets were one half land and the other half water, along which the inhabitants, says Cortes in his letters, went in their canoes; all the streets at given distances were open, so that the water might pass from one to the other; and at all the openings were very wide bridges, made of massive beams joined together and well wrought. Montezuma was usually carried about in a litter, under a canopy of the richest material, ornamented with green feathers, gold, and precious stones; his buskins were of pure gold, ornamented with jewels. The clothes which he wore one day he did not put on for four days after. His cooks had upwards of thirty different ways of dressing meats, and they had earthen vessels so contrived as to keep them constantly hot. It is said that at times the flesh of young children was dressed for him; but Bernal Diaz is very doubtful on the point: his ordinary meats were domestic fowls, pheasants, geese, partridges, quails, venison, Indian hogs, pigeons, hares, and rabbits, with many other animals and birds peculiar to the country. At his meals, in cold weather, a number of torches of the bark of a wood which makes no smoke, and has an aromatic smell, were lighted, and, that they should not throw out too much heat, screens ornamented with gold, and painted with figures of idols, were placed before them. The table was covered with white cloths and napkins; and four beautiful women presented him with water for his hands, in vessels which they called *xicales*, with other vessels under them, like plates, to catch the water. Two other women brought small cakes of bread; he ate little, but drank, says Diaz, 'cocoa and chocolate' foaming hot. The following, which shows the antiquity of *tortillias*, and the similarity of the ancient with modern habits, we extract from Bernal Diaz:—'During the time that Montezuma was at dinner, two very beautiful women were busily employed making small cakes with eggs and other things mixed therein. These were delicately white, and, when made, they presented them to him on plates covered with napkins. After he had dined, they presented to him three little canes, highly ornamented, containing liquid amber, mixed with an herb called tobacco.' The accounts of Montezuma's rents in books occupied an entire house. His arsenals were well supplied, his country palaces were splendid, his menageries full and curious. All this Cortes, who at best was a great pirate, destroyed seeking for gold; and on the ruins of the magnificent empire of Montezuma stand the present wretched people.

The upper classes have still all the ancient love of splendour, and their houses are both elegant and comfortable. The streets of Vera Cruz are paved with smooth pebbles, and the side walks covered with cement. The mansion of a Mexican gentleman is built of the strongest materials, and erected round *patios*, or courtyards. On the ground-floor are the porter's lodge, offices, and carriage-house; a flight of steps then leads to a second storey, devoted to the domestics; while the upper is usually the fashionable and best one. Here the inmates are in perfect seclusion from the street and neighbours; and the arcade which fronts their doors is filled with the choicest fruit and flower trees in constant bloom. Above all this is the *azotea*, or flat-paved roof, a delightful retreat on summer nights. The front windows of the houses are all guarded by balconies covered with gaily-coloured awnings. The carriage and ever-harnessed mules stand constantly in the courtyard below, and the postilion is ready to mount at a moment's notice, until after dark, when the front gate is locked and barred. The prevalence of robbery and murder is the origin of this caution.

The unequal division of property is one fertile cause of the general poverty. Some of the estates are enormous; but as capital is scarce, an air of desolation is the sole consequence. On every side are marks of solitude and misery; ruins of houses and churches filled with weeds and creepers; neglected fields overgrown with aloes, and made still more sad by the long pensile branches of the solitary palm: nature, instead of being pruned of her luxuriance with judicious care, has been sapped and exhausted, and made old even in her youth. Traces of old cultivation are yet to be found, and also the remains of a former dense population. The sides of the hills in many places, as in Chili and Peru, are cut into terraces; but over these is spread a wild growth of mimosas, cacti, and acacias, while a thousand flowering parasite plants trail their gaudy blossoms among the aloes and shrubbery. Still there is much wealth left; and on a hacienda near Cerro Grande, a lady, according to Kendall, had 50,000 horses and mules, large herds of cattle, immense fields of corn and wheat, and several thousand peons, or labourers. A short time prior to the revolution, three hundred thousand horses were in the possession of the owner of the estate: during this period a regiment of dragoons arrived from Spain, and landed at Tampico. 'This regiment was one thousand strong, and of course the men did not bring their horses with them. The colonel of the regiment happening to be a friend of the family, and well known to the deceased husband of the wealthy proprietress, she immediately sent him a thousand white horses, as a present for the use of the regiment. There was hardly a month's difference in the ages of these horses, and every one of them had been raised upon her estate.'

The condition of the labourers on these estates is wretched. Buying their liquor, cigars, and cloth at most exorbitant prices from their employers, they are in general indebted to the proprietor, and as the law gives him a lien upon their services until such debts are paid, good care is taken that they never pay him their obligations as long as their services are in any way profitable. They are in his debt until too old to work, when the obligation is canceled, and they are cast upon the world to beg, starve, or steal, as best they may. Should any active man save enough to redeem himself, the rich proprietor is sure so to twist the law, and influence the Alcalde, that the serf is reduced once more, by means of some legal quibble, to bondage. In fact, the immense wealth of the few, and the poverty of the many, places the people of the Mexican republic in nearly the same position as were the English under the feudal system; which goes far to prove, that freedom of government is of no value to man, without the education which fits him to enjoy liberty.

The soldiers which are recruited from so tame a people are necessarily inferior; and yet their cavalry, headed by good officers (rarer in Mexico even than good soldiers), have proved far from contemptible. Nothing can be conceived more original than the mode of recruiting. A number of men are perhaps wanted to complete a new company, and a serjeant with his guard is forthwith despatched to inspect the neighbouring Indians, and Meztizoes or half castes. The subaltern finds a dozen or more working in the fields, and without even the formality of a request, immediately picks his men, and orders them into the ranks. If they attempt to escape or resist, they are at once lassoed; and at nightfall the whole gang is marched, tied in pairs, into the quartel of the village or the guard-room of the palace. Next day the volunteers are handed over to the drill serjeant; and nothing can be more comic than their first parades. About one half are always Indians, and the rest perhaps leperos or loafers. One has a pair of trousers, but no shirt; another a shirt and a pair of drawers; another hides himself as well as he can under his blanket and broad-brimmed hat; another has drawers and a military cap. 'The most ridiculous object,' says Meyer, 'I remember to have seen in Mexico, was a fat and greasy lepero, with a pair of trousers that just reached his hips, supported by a strap round his loins, with an old uniform coat a great deal too short both in sleeves and in front. Not owning a shirt, a vast continent of brown skin lay shining in the sun. He held his head, supported by a tall stock, higher than any man in the squad, and marched magnificently.' At Manantial, our American traveller examined the arms of his guard, not looking, however, at more than one carbine, which he found had lost the catch of its cock, which of course always lay against the covering of the pan, pressing it open. Meyer mentioned this to the trooper, and asked him where he put the powder. 'There, to be sure,' said he, pointing to the pan. 'And how do you fire it?' 'Pshaw,' replied the fellow, ''tis better so.'

The climate in Mexico is very varied; for between Vera Cruz and the volcanoes, where eternal snows hang over Mexico, you have every climate in the world. In the valley there is an eternal spring; for six months, the winter months, rain never falls; during the others, showers occur almost daily. It is never hot—never very cold. One side of the street is always too warm at noon. In January, the roses are already blooming in the gardens of Mexico. The flower and the leaf you admire to-day, are replaced to-morrow by fresh buds and renewed verdure. Sickness in Vera Cruz is great, and most fatal in its results, especially vomits. There are two influences at work to counteract the pestilent influence, and prevent the additional power of dirty streets in spreading malady, the zopilotes or turkey-buzzards, and the galley slaves, who both act as scavengers. To kill a zopilote is a high crime; they are under the protection of the laws, and walk the streets with the utmost nonchalance.

One relief against the pressing urgencies of poverty in the capital is the Monte Pio, or national pawnbroker establishment. It is situated in the great square, occupying the building known as the palace of Cortes, said to be erected on the ruins of the ancient palace of Montezuma. This is a most beneficent institution, and was founded in 1775 by the Conde de Regla, at a cost of 300,000 dollars. Since that time, it has been carefully administered by government, and affords succour daily to more than two hundred persons. It is ruled by a general board of directors, and receives pledges of clothes, jewels, plate, and every species of valuables. These articles are appraised at a fair valuation, the amount of which, deducting the interest, is paid to the pawner; they are then retained for six months, during which the owner can redeem them; but if the money be unrefunded at the expiration of that period, the pledges are disposed of by public sale; and should they produce anything over the valuation, the difference is handed to the owner. During the revolutionary difficulties of Mexico, this institution has saved many from disgrace and misery, 2,232,611 persons having availed themselves of it; 81,674,702 dollars* (besides 134,740 dollars given in alms) had been loaned up to 1836; and in 1837, the sum of 477,772 dollars was spent in aiding the distresses of the poor. A walk through the extensive apartments of the Monte Pio tells a tale concerning the rank and variety of persons who avail themselves of its services, which would be anything but pleasant to some even of the noble families in Mexico. You will find every species of garment, from the tattered reboso of the lepero to the lace mantilla of the high-born lady; every species of dress, from the blanket of the beggar to the military cloak and jeweled sword of the improvident or impoverished officer; and as to jewels, the choice is infinite.

In the immediate neighbourhood of this building is the Accordada, or common prison, in front of which, on an inclined plain, are laid the dead bodies found daily within the limits of the city; within are the living. 'Passing through several iron and wood-barred gates, you enter a lofty corridor, running round a quadrangular courtyard, in the centre of which is a fountain of troubled water. The whole of this area is filled with human beings—the great congress of Mexican crime, mixed and mingling like a hill of busy ants. Some are stripped and bathing in the fountain, some fighting in a corner, some making baskets. In one place, a crowd is collected round a witty story-teller relating the adventures of his rascally life; in another, a group is engaged in weaving with a hand-loom. Robbers, murderers, thieves, felons of every description, are crammed within this courtyard.' A brief glance at the statistics of crime for the year 1842 in the city of Mexico, will account for the crowded state of the prison. For bigamy, and more heinous crimes consequent on incontinence, 491, of which 179 were women; robbery, 1970, of which 470 were women; quarrelling and wounding, 3233, of which 1104 were women; quarrelling, bearing arms, 1056, of which 444 were women; homicide attempted, &c. 87, of which 17 were women; violence, &c. 86, of which 17 were women; forgery, 8, of which one was a woman; gambling, 3 men; besides for higher crimes, 1927. Further numbers were committed for throwing vitriol; 113 dead bodies were found, 894 sent to the hospital, and 17 executed by the garotte;* in all, 8861, an amount of crime, with a population of 200,000, almost unparalleled.

Smoking is the constant practice of all classes and sexes. The ladies of highest rank take their little aromatic cigaritto, and use it in a peculiarly graceful manner, if anything so unfeminine can in any way appear graceful. When on a morning visit, if you are a particular favourite, the lady of the house, who indulges in the weed, will take a delicate one from her golden *etui*, light it, touch it with her lips, and present it to you. It is, however, an almost universal custom in Spanish and Portuguese America, and Stephens relates many amusing instances of it in his several productions. The great amusement of the Mexicans is the play, the excessive indulgence in which amusement makes the women live too much abroad, and is injurious to their habits: the dull morning at home is succeeded by an evening drive, and then again by the regular visit to the opera or theatre, where they hear the same things over and over again. Were the entertainments of an intellectual character, less harm would arise; but the taste is all for comedy, or domestic tragedy of the Newgate school. The boxes are usually let by the month or year, and are filled by the families in full dress every evening, who there receive their friends. The pit seats are arm-chairs, which are also rented by the month. The music—a science in which, both in taste and execution, the Mexicans excel—is far better than the acting. Without the least knowledge of music as a science, the common people are still fond of carolling the little airs of the country in chorus, and have ears exquisitely correct in singing the different parts. Frequently, while upon the road, the Mexican prisoners or volunteers may be heard giving their native songs with pleasing effect. The different voices, from the highest falsetto to the deepest bass, were many of them of the purest and softest quality, and blended together with a harmony at once musical and soothing.

Bull-fights—the great amusement of the descendants from the Spanish conquerors—still occasionally take place in the Plaza de Icroz, an immense circus, erected when this sport was in its palmy days in Mexico, and are usually given on Sunday, when the people are quite unoccupied. This is about one of the most savage of all the amusements which have ever been devised. When the Romans had exhausted the whole round of natural excitement, they invented the circus, which tended as much as anything to brutalise and degrade that falling empire. In Mexico, the results are most demoralising; not more so, however, than the national taste for gambling, a vice in which all classes indulge. The feast of St Augustin, at San Augustin, is the signal for a great day of gambling. There are humble booths where small copper coins only are played; next for copper *medios* and *reals*; next for copper and dollars; then banks for silver alone; then for silver and gold; and lastly for gold alone. All the banks save one lost on the occasion of Meyer's visit; and the gains of the lucky corporation must have been immense, as at one time it lost 2000 doubloons, equal to about L.8000. The cockpit follows, where ladies of the highest respectability appear, their great object being to outshine each other in the splendour and variety of their garments. The rage is to have one dress for mass, one for the cockpit, one for the afternoon ball, and the other for the evening one on the occasion of the fête above alluded to. 'The cocks were placed in the centre of the pit, within the ring, the president's fowls being there generally first put on the earth. They were then thrown off for a spring at each other, and taken up again before the betting began. Brokers went round, proclaiming the amount placed in their hands to bet on any particular fowl. Whenever a bet was offered against Santa

* The Mexican dollar varies in value from 4s. to 4s. 4d.

* The culprit is seated in a chair, and his neck placed in an iron collar, which may be turned by a screw; a sudden turn drives a spike through the spinal marrow, and life is extinct.—See Meyer's Mexico. London: Wiley and Putnam.

Anna's bird, the broker was called to his box, and an *aide* covered it. Besides these bets, the general usually had some standing ones agreed on beforehand with the owners of other cocks; and in this manner five or six thousand dollars were lost or won by him in the pit daily.'

The amusements of the humbler classes in the rural districts—consisting chiefly in fandangoes or balls, where the elders look on while the young people dance, laugh, and enjoy themselves—are somewhat more rational and humanising than those which delight the heads and rulers of a nation which has very far yet to advance to lay even a primary claim to be rated among the civilised lands of the earth.

RIDING THE STANG.

About noon, when labour daily and usually refreshes itself, an uncommon stir was observable among the lower classes of the town population—something like what precedes the swarming of a bee-hive. By and by appearances took a more definite form, and a number of women and children were seen crowding together, shouting and clamouring, and rattling with sticks and pans, and, in short, raising a most intolerable din; in the midst of which, the name of one obnoxious individual was ominously heard. The characteristics of a Scotch mob are pretty generally known, before and since the fate of Captain Porteous. They are furious and formidable; and when once the passions of a generally calm and prudent race are excited, be it to lower the price of meal, or to carry any other popular purpose, it requires no small force to resist or modify the impulse. On the present occasion, rough-looking men began to mix with the screeching multitude, and soon were visible a stout *posse* of them, armed with a pitchfork. The idea that murder was about to be committed thrilled the blood of the uninformed spectators, and their terror increased when they witnessed a fierce assault made on a low tenement inhabited by the person (a shoemaker) so dreadfully denounced, who had barely time to look and barricade himself from the threatened vengeance. In vain. The windows and doors were smashed and battered in, and a violent tumult took place in the interior. Within two minutes the culprit was dragged out, pale and trembling, and supplicating for mercy. But he had shown little to his wretched partner, who, with a blackened eye, weeping bitterly, and also begging them to spare her unworthy spouse, who she was sure would never strike her again, joined her pitiful intreaties to his. The ministers of public justice were inexorable—his sentence was pronounced, his doom sealed. The portentous pitchfork was immediately laid horizontally from the shoulder of one to the shoulder of another of the ablest of the executioners, who thus stood, front and rear, with *the stang* (the shaft) between them. Upon this narrow-backed horse the offender was lifted by others, and held on by supporters on either side, so that dismounting was completely out of the question; and there he sat elevated above the rest, in his most uncomfortable and unenviable wooden saddle. The air rung with yells of triumph and vituperation. Very slight arrangements were necessary, and the procession moved on. The wife, surrounded by a party of her gossips, was compelled to accompany it; and it bent its course toward the river side. The unmanly fellow who had provoked this fate, showed by his terrors that he was just one of those cowards who could ill-treat the creature who had a right to his protection, and had not fortitude to endure an evil himself. He howled for compassion, appealed by name to his indignant escort, and prayed and promised; but they got to the brink of that clear and deep pool which mirrored the glittering sun above the mill wear (or *cauld*, Scotticè), and there the bearers marched boldly in before they tumbled their burden from his uneasy seat. Into the water he went over head and ears, and rose again, by no means 'like a giant refreshed;' and no sooner did he reappear, than a powerful grasp was laid upon him, and down again he was plunged, and replunged, with unrelenting perseverance. The screams of his distracted wife fortunately attracted the attention of a magistrate (my revered father) whose garden shelved to the edge of the stream where this scene was enacting, and he hastened to interfere. Had he not done so, life might probably have been lost; for the ruffian was execrated by his fellow-men for his continued abuse of late a pretty, sweet, and healthful maiden, now a pale-faced, bruised, and sickly matron, and one too of meek and unresisting temper, suffering cruelly without offence. As it was, the populace listened to the magistrate's voice, for he was much beloved by them; and giving the rascal one dash more, allowed him to crawl to the bank of the silver, now polluted, Tweed. From thence he was hooted the whole way to his home; and so salutary was the effect of the day's proceedings on the half-drowned rat, that he never more misbehaved in such a manner as to render himself liable to *ride the stang*.—*Archæological Album*.

THE SONG OF THE SPADE.

All honour be paid to the homely spade—
The sword and the spear are idle things—
To the king in his pride and his subjects beside,
Its tribute the spade of the husbandman brings.

A bright thought from heaven to the tiller was given,
Who first turned up to light the soil richly brown;
God told in the blast how the seed should be cast—
See the first yellow grains by the husbandman sown!

See the first harvest-morn, and the ripe yellow corn,
And the first crooked sickle thrust into the grain!
With dancing and singing the valleys are ringing,
For all that the spade has raised out of the plain.

Then all honour be paid to the conquering spade—
The sword and the shield are idle things—
To the king in his pride and his subjects beside,
Its bounties the spade of the husbandman brings.

J. G.

MAGNANIMITY.

In Germany, during the war, a captain of cavalry was ordered out upon a foraging expedition. He put himself at the head of his troop, and marched to the quarter assigned him. It was a solitary valley, in which hardly anything but wood was to be perceived. Finding in the midst of it a small cottage, he approached and knocked at the door, which was opened by an old and venerable man, with a beard silvered by age. 'Father,' said the officer, 'show me a field where I may set my troop to foraging.' The old man complied, and conducting them out of the valley, after a quarter of an hour's march came to a fine field of barley. 'Here is what we are in search of,' exclaimed the captain; 'father, you are a true and faithful guide.' 'Wait yet a few minutes,' replied the old man; 'follow me patiently a little further.' The march was accordingly resumed, and at the distance of a mile they arrived at another field of barley. The troop immediately alighted, cut down the grain, trussed it, and remounted. The officer thereupon said to his conductor, 'Father, you have given yourself and us unnecessary trouble; the first field was far better than this.' 'Very true, sir,' replied the good old man, 'but it was not mine.'—*St Pierre*.

The present number of the Journal completes the third volume (new series), for which a title-page and index have been prepared, and may be had of the publishers and their agents.

END OF THIRD VOLUME.

Printed and Published by W. and R. Chambers, Edinburgh.
Sold by W. S. Orr, Amen Corner, London.

CHAMBERS'S

EDINBURGH JOURNAL.

CHAMBERS'S

EDINBURGH JOURNAL.

NEW SERIES.

CONDUCTED BY

WILLIAM AND ROBERT CHAMBERS,

EDITORS OF 'CHAMBERS'S EDUCATIONAL COURSE,' 'INFORMATION FOR THE PEOPLE,' &c.

VOLUME IV

Nos. 79 TO 104. JULY—DECEMBER, 1845.

EDINBURGH:

PUBLISHED BY WILLIAM AND ROBERT CHAMBERS.

AND Wm. S. ORR AND CO., LONDON.

1845.

LONDON:
BRADBURY AND EVANS, PRINTERS, WHITEFRIARS.

INDEX.

FAMILIAR SKETCHES AND MORAL ESSAYS.

POETRY.

TALES.

ANECDOTES AND PARAGRAPHS.

CONDUCTED BY WILLIAM AND ROBERT CHAMBERS, EDITORS OF 'CHAMBERS'S INFORMATION FOR THE PEOPLE,' 'CHAMBERS'S EDUCATIONAL COURSE,' &c.

No. 79. New Series. SATURDAY, JULY 5, 1845. Price 1½d.

PERSISTENCY OF FAMILY FEATURES.

It is well known that personal peculiarities of all kinds, defects as well as beauties, casts of features, and traits of expression, are transmitted from parents to their children. The fact stares us in the face whenever we enter a family parlour, for there it is invariably seen that the young people bear a resemblance in one respect or another to either their father or mother, or to both. This is a subject which has never, as far as we are aware, been honoured with more than a transient notice at the hands of the learned; yet it might be worthy of philosophical investigation. We merely propose, in this place, to illustrate it by a few facts which we have picked up either from personal observation, or from books.

Sometimes the reproduction of face and figure in the child seems almost perfect. Sometimes face is borrowed from one parent, and form of head, or of body, or of some of the limbs, from the other. Occasionally, there is a remarkable blending of the two throughout the whole, or parts of the person. Even peculiarities in the carriage of the head or of the mode of walking are transmitted, and a family voice is nearly as common a marvel as a family face. A man, in a place distant from his home, and where he was totally unknown, has been distinguished as the brother of one known there by the sound of his voice heard in a neighbouring apartment. But the almost perfect reproduction of the elder Kean's voice in the younger is perhaps the most convincing illustration we could adduce upon this point. It will also be found that children resembling either parent externally, have a stronger affinity of mental character to that parent than to the other. A gentleman, very intimately known to us, is strikingly like his father, who has been deceased since his early youth: he also exhibits the same dispositions and intellectual tendencies in a remarkable degree, delights in the same studies, has the same turn for the perception of human character; nay, he often feels, in the simplest procedure of common life, so absolute an identity with what he remembers of his father in the same circumstances, and at the same period of life, as expressed by gesture and conversation, that it seems to him as if he were the same person. Nor can this, he says, be a result of imitation; it is something which takes place independently of all design, and which he only remarks, in general, after the act, or feeling, or movement which recalls his father, has passed.

But it is not parents alone who are thus reproduced in new generations. In a large family familiarly known to us, as are all its relationships, we see, in some of the young persons, resemblances at once to the father and mother, and to one or other of the two grandfathers and grandmothers, notwithstanding that, in one or two instances, the intermediate generation did not bear those features of the first which are traced in the third. It thus appears that a peculiarity will sink in one generation, and re-appear in the next. Perhaps even more generations than one are occasionally passed over. In this family, several of the children are totally different from the rest; complexion, form, gesticulations, voices, all peculiar. This seems to be owing to their 'taking after' different parents, or the families to which the different parents belonged. What makes this the more remarkable is, that one of these children, while in all respects unlike certain brothers and sisters, has one feature strikingly recalling the image of a distant cousin—a character of feature not seen in any other existing member of the family, and not remembered of any that are deceased. It would appear as if these minutiæ of family characters flitted about fitfully and vaguely, and only settled now and then upon individuals in a clan—sometimes upon not more than two, or perhaps upon one only, in the same age. From all of these facts, it may be inferred that the strong resemblances sometimes remarked between cousins are indications of their representing a common original, and of their being in reality more consanguineous than are many brothers and sisters. The unsuitableness of such relations for matrimonial alliances, must of course be affected by this consideration. Where resemblances exist, their union may be held as even more decisively condemned by nature, than is that between brothers and sisters who are not observably alike.

The limitation of portrait-painting as to time, is a bar to our knowledge with regard to instances of long transmission of family faces and features. Yet enough is ascertained to establish the law of the case. In our own royal family, a certain fulness of the lower and lateral parts of the face is conspicuous in the portraits of the whole series of sovereigns, from George I. to Victoria. It has been equally seen in other members of the family. The Duke of Cumberland, who figured at Culloden, presents generally the same visage as several of the sons of William IV. This physiognomy may be traced back to Sophia, the mother of George I.; how much farther, we cannot tell. It is equally certain that a thickness of the under lip, peculiar to the imperial family of Austria (Maria Louisa is said to be characterised by it), has been hereditary in the race since a marriage some centuries ago with the Polish house of Jagellon, whence it came.

A remarkable anecdote illustrative of this subject was told us, some years ago, by a gentleman who has since distinguished himself in the walk of fictitious literature. Born in Nova Scotia, where his family, originally Scotch, had been settled for the greater part of a century, he had not an opportunity of visiting our country till past the middle of life. Here he made it his endeavour to see as many as possible of the individuals bearing his rather uncommon name, and in this quest he often took journeys to considerable distances. Having heard of a family of the name residing at a lonely farm amongst the Lammermuir hills, he proceeded thither on foot from the nearest market town. As is not uncommon in such situations, the approach of a visitor could be observed from this house while he was yet fully a mile distant. Mr H—— was observed at that distance by some of the children, who immediately cried out with one voice, 'There is uncle George!' When the stranger arrived at the house, the seniors of the family fully acknowledged the general resemblance of the figure and carriage to the person called uncle George; and it was ascertained, after a little conversation, that the Nova Scotian was in reality their cousin at two or three removes.

When Mr William Howitt visited Stratford-on-Avon, in order to write respecting the places connected with Shakspeare, the schoolmaster informed him that a descendant of a near relation of the poet was one of his pupils. 'He marshalled his laddish troop in a row,' says Mr Howitt, 'and said to me, "There, now, sir, can you tell which is a Shakspeare?" I glanced my eye along the line, and quickly fixing it on one boy, said, "That is the Shakspeare." "You are right," said the master, "that is the Shakspeare—the Shakspeare cast of countenance is there. That is William Shakspeare Smith, a lineal descendant of the poet's sister." The lad,' continues Mr Howitt, 'was a fine lad of perhaps ten years of age; and certainly the resemblance to the bust of Shakspeare, in the church at Stratford, is wonderful, considering he is not descended from Shakspeare himself, but from his sister, and that the seventh in descent. What is odd enough, whether it be mere accident or not, the colour of the lad's eyes, a light hazel, is the very same as that given to those of the Shakspeare bust, which it is well known was originally coloured, and of which exact copies remain.'* These observations of Mr Howitt are confirmed by a portrait of the youth, which he gives in his book. We are the less disposed to entertain doubts on the subject, in consequence of circumstances which have fallen under our own notice. Some years ago, a young man in humble life came forward to claim the restoration of the forfeited titles of the Setons, Earls of Wintoun, his grandfather having been assured that he was a legitimate though obscurely born son of the noble, who lost honours and lands by joining in the insurrection of 1715. From want of evidence, the claim was a hopeless one, and it was not prosecuted; but of one fact there could be no doubt, that the young man so nearly resembled the sons of the fifth Lord Seton, as represented in a family picture painted by Antony More, that he might have passed for their brother. These persons lived in the latter half of the sixteenth century.

Such instances are perhaps less uncommon than might be supposed. We have seen an elderly lady descended from John Knox, and bearing no slight resemblance to him; and, if we are not much mistaken, a profile of Cardinal Beatoun, in Pinkerton's Scottish Gallery, might pass for a tolerably successful likeness of his brother's descendant, the present Mr Drinkwater Bethune. These instances will, we fear, serve but inadequately to prepare the reader for another, which makes a larger demand upon his faith. Walking in the country some years ago, we saw an elderly man pass in a carriage, and were instantly struck with his resemblance to the bluff majestic countenance attributed by Scottish painters to Sir William Wallace. The impression was so strong, that we spoke of it to our companion, who said, 'It is very odd, but the gentleman is General Dunlop of Ayrshire, a descendant, you are well aware, of a brother of Wallace.'* We were far from the estate of the gallant general, though in the county represented by him in parliament, and had no reason to suppose that this was General Dunlop, nor did we even remember at the moment how he stood related to the Scottish hero. There is a peculiar difficulty in the case, for no reflecting person would have previously supposed it likely that the common portrait of Wallace was a genuine likeness. It can only be said that the fact of a resemblance in General Dunlop to the portrait is a strong argument, as against merely negative evidence, for its authenticity. We may suppose it to have been painted when Wallace visited France, as he is now certainly known to have done, from documents discovered by Mr Tytler. The space of time between the death of Wallace and the birth of General Dunlop must have been upwards of four centuries and a half. The improbability of a face being kept up so long in a family is, we readily own, very great, and yet only so, perhaps, because we know of no other facts to the same purport. Such facts might be found if they were sought. It is, we are assured, a common remark amongst those who remember the last Mrs Bruce of Clackmannan, who boasted that King Robert of Scotland was of *her family*, that the features of the old lady bore a resemblance to the portraits of the heroic monarch. And even now the children of one of the gentlemen of this family, settled in Clackmannanshire, are said to have that strongly-marked form of the cheek-bones and jaws which appears in Bruce's coins, as it did in the structure of his actual face, when his bones were disinterred at Dunfermline, anno 1819.

The doubts which might rest on such cases of particular resemblance in families, ought perhaps to be in a great measure dispelled, when we reflect on the evidence that exists with respect to the persistency of external characters in sets and races of people. Not only have we such facts as a prevalent tallness in the inhabitants of Potsdam, where Frederick I. assembled his regiment of longitudinal guards, and a strong infusion of Spanish features in the people of the county of Galway, in which some centuries ago several Spanish settlements were made; but we are assured by Major Bevan that he could distinguish the several castes in India by their peculiarities of countenance; and the Jews are the same people in Egyptian entablatures of three thousand years ago, as they are in some countries at the present day. Mr Kohl, in his travels in Austria, speaks of Prague as a very garden of beauty. 'For the young ladies of 1841,' says he, 'I am ready to give my testimony most unreservedly, and many an enraptured traveller has left us his books as living witnesses to the loveliness of the grandmothers and great-grandmothers of the present generation. The old chronicler, Hammerschmidt, and his contemporaries, dwell with equal pleasure on the sweet faces that smiled upon them in their days, and the picture-gallery of many a Bohemian castle is there to testify to the truth of their statements. One witness there is to the fact, whose right few will question to decide on such a point. Titian, who studied the faces of lovely women for ninety-six years, and who, while at the court of Charles V., spent five years in Germany, tells us it was among the ladies of Prague that he found his *ideal* of a beautiful female head. If we go back beyond the times of Titian, we have the declaration of Charles IV., that Prague was a *hortus deliciarum*, and whoever has read the life of that emperor, will scarcely doubt that beautiful women must have been included in the delights of a capital so apostrophised. Nay, the time-honoured nobility of the beauty of Prague may be said to go back even to the earliest tradition, where we find it celebrated in the legends of Libussa and Vlasta, and the countless songs

* Visits to Remarkable Places. First Series. Mr Howitt adds—'Ireland, when in 1793 making collections for his *Views on the Avon*, was much struck with the likeness to this bust in Thomas Hart, one of this family, who then lived in Shakspeare's house.

* A son of Mrs Dunlop, the kind patroness of Burns.

composed in honour of the Deviy Slavanske or Tshekhian damsels.'

While there is a law of persistency, there seems also to be one modifying it, a law of variation. The continuance of national features depends much on adherence to the same region of the earth, and the same mode of living. When a people migrate to a remote and differently characterised clime, they are often seen to undergo, in the next generation, a change of features and of figure. Thus the unctuous Saxon of Kent and Suffolk, when transferred to Massachusetts, becomes metamorphosed into the lank and wiry New Englander. Descendants of British settlers in the West Indies have been remarked, after several generations, to acquire some of the peculiar features of the aboriginal Americans, particularly high cheek bones and eyes deeply set in the head. It has also been remarked in New South Wales, that the generation of English born there are changed from their progenitors—taller, and less robust, besides having a share of that nasal tone which is found in the American English. These are curious facts, conveying the impression that national forms have been determined to some extent by peculiarities of climate and other external influences.

In the main, one generation is represented in another succeeding it. We die as individuals, but the character in mind and body, 'with a difference,' is revived and continued by those who come after us, and the tissue of human races is a kind of immortality.

THE SOANE MUSEUM.

> Statues and paintings stand in meet array,
> Things of rare grace and classic age abound;
> Some hand unseen these silently display,
> Even undemanded by a sign or sound.—Thomson.

There is a public exhibition in London, at which we have from time to time spent many hours with equal pleasure and instruction, but which, from the comparatively small number of visitors, does not appear to be so highly appreciated as it deserves. We allude to the collection of pictures, antiques, articles of virtû, &c. got together by the late Sir John Soane, and deposited in the house he occupied at No. 13, Lincoln's Inn Fields. The paucity of visitors is doubtless owing in a great measure to the restrictions under which the public are admitted; Thursday and Friday in the months of April, May, and June, being the only days throughout the year on which strangers have the privilege of viewing the place. The applicant must also attend a day or two previously to procure an order from the curator. When, however, the nature of the exhibition is considered (a great number of objects in a series of rooms, none of which are very large), it is obvious that to admit the public indiscriminately would be in effect to place a slight value upon a collection, great part of which requires considerable acquaintance with art to enjoy, and would improvidently afford opportunities, in a mixed and crowded multitude, for mischief and theft. With a view of directing the attention of visitors in the metropolis to one of its treasures, we propose concisely to describe in our present paper the principal contents of the Soane Museum. 'There is no institution in London,' says Mrs Jameson * in her description of this place, 'in which a few hours may be more pleasantly whiled away, or even more profitably employed, than in this fairy object of virtû, where the infinite variety of the objects assembled together in every department of art—many indeed sufficiently trivial, some also of peculiar beauty and value—suggest to the intelligent mind and cultivated taste a thousand thoughts, remembrances, and associations, while the ingenuity shown in the arrangement amuses the fancy in a very agreeable manner.'

Some ornamental details on the exterior of the house point it out to the eye of the stranger; they are not likely, however, to detain it very long, and indeed observers of severe taste may wish them away. The door having opened and closed again, the first thing which will engage the visitor's attention is a bust in the entrance lobby of Sir Thomas Lawrence, who, though the son of an innkeeper, was, both in manners and bearing, one of the most aristocratic of men, the painter and companion of princes and nobles. A fine specimen of his workmanship may be seen in the next apartment (the dining-room and library thrown together), being nothing less than a portrait of Sir John Soane himself. It is an excellent painting, and cannot fail to charm every beholder by the clearness of its colouring; one hand seen hanging down is exquisitely painted. Exactly opposite hangs a picture by Lawrence's famous predecessor, Sir Joshua Reynolds. It represents a passage from the story of the goddess of beauty, and her 'wimpled, winning, purblind, wayward boy, Dan Cupid.' It shows the sad result of Sir Joshua's experimenting in oils and colours, being grievously disfigured with cracks, whilst a hectic flush on the countenances usurps the place of a healthy, rosy hue, a defect too common in the works of this painter. The pencil of Howard, R. A., has adorned several of the compartments in the ceiling, and a number of elegantly-bound books, principally relating to architecture, covers the walls. Passing through some lobby-like apartments—in which two small engravings by Hogarth might escape notice amongst the crowd of objects, if not specially pointed out—we arrive at the door of the room in which the most of the paintings are hung. But before entering, pray pause to admire the model of a sleeping child by Banks. The marble has been placed in Ashbourne church, Devonshire, to the memory of a daughter of Sir Brook Boothby. The helpless sleep of innocent childhood was never more perfectly represented; but as yet it has not been so fortunate as the sleeping children in Lichfield cathedral, for no one has uttered in verse the feelings it inevitably excites. By an ingenious arrangement, the space upon which paintings can be hung in the picture-room is considerably increased. Large shutters are made to move on hinges, and pictures are suspended on both sides. Thus the small space of 13 feet 8 inches by 12 feet 4 inches, is rendered capable of holding as many paintings as a gallery 45 feet long by 20 feet broad. The first objects that challenge attention are a series of four pictures by Hogarth, who may be truly said to have imitated none, and to be inimitable of any. They represent the scenes of an election. In the first an entertainment is depicted. Many figures are crowded upon the canvas, every one of which plays a part in a disgusting but 'owre true' story. The riotous license too frequently attendant upon such occasions is drawn with forcible ludicrousness. Some are seized with apoplexy, others are desperately wounded with brickbats; but still the gluttons and drunkards around continue their eating and drinking. A man who has had his face daubed with soot, talks with great animation, in entire ignorance of the cause of his neighbour's laughter. In one group a tailor, who is simple enough to keep about him that embarrassing article, a conscience, and resolutely refuses a bribe, is fiercely attacked by his termagant wife, whilst his son shows how his toes have become visible at the end of his shoe. The canvassing follows, and then the polling, where the booth is filled with freeholders, deaf, sick, maimed, and blind, as if the very hospital had been ransacked for voters. In the fourth picture, the successful candidate is seen to possess but a precarious tenure of his chair. The incidents by which this awkward result has been brought about are whimsically complicated and amusingly depicted. The member here represented was Bubb Doddington, afterwards Lord Melcombe Regis, a man of the lowest political morals, who naïvely revealed his sins in a self-complacent diary. To him

* 'Handbook to the Public Galleries of Art in and near London;' a work calculated to diffuse true and elevated ideas on the subject to which it relates, and forming a delightful and invaluable companion for the student of art to the metropolitan collection of pictures.

Thomson dedicated his Summer, and we find him there invested with those excellences with which the imagination of poets is accustomed to endow their patrons. Amongst the rest,

> Unblemished honour, and an active zeal
> For Britain's glory, liberty, and man!

These pictures were once in the possession of David Garrick, having been purchased by him from the painter. Sir John Soane bought them for 1650 guineas, when the effects of the actor's widow were sold. In another series of eight pictures, the Rake's Progress is delineated with fearful truthfulness. Repeated engravings have made these paintings well known. A course, tainted even at the beginning with depravity, then cursed with riches, is traced through darker and darker profligacy to a prison, and from that depth to a still lower—to the furthest point and most loathsome form of human degradation—madness. The moral of Hogarth's pictures it is needless to comment on. The lessons our pictorial Crabbe teaches are obvious to every eye. 'Never did I derive,' says Mr Hartley Coleridge in one of his charming essays—'never did I derive from Hogarth's paintings an unfriendly feeling towards my kind—never did they shake my faith in the true nobility of man's nature, which is ennobled not by what it is, but by what it should be. So far from it, I affirm that they bear irrefragable testimony to a principle, a moral law in man, that is above the understanding—not begotten upon sense, nor constructed by custom, self-love, or animal sensibility, but implanted by the Divinity as the key and counterpart to the law from on high.' This series was purchased from Alderman Beckford for only L.598. If now brought into the market, they would probably fetch six times that sum. Mr Beckford was also the possessor of six pictures representing the Harlot's Progress; but these were unfortunately consumed in the fire which destroyed old Fonthill in 1755. In this room may be seen the masterpiece of Canaletto. A fine work of his hangs in the National Gallery; but this is still finer. Indeed it would have been impossible for him to surpass the natural appearance here given to the surface of the water. The eye runs up the grand canal (the scene is Venetian) with astonishment at the illusive perspective, and the figures managing a boat in the foreground are brought out with wonderful distinctness. Above are two small Canalettos, one of the Bridge of the Rialto, the other of St Mark and its tall campanile. The clear precision with which Canaletto is able to place objects upon canvas, and to show them through an atmosphere of the utmost purity, make his pictures at first look almost as hard as an architect's plan; but their mannerism is soon forgotten, and their truthful representation meets with its merited applause. He may be styled the most poetical of architectural limners. His works have always been great favourites in England, where there are in consequence many vile imitations. An Italian lake is the subject of a large picture by Sir Augustus Calcott, but to us it appears unfortunate in its tone of colour. There are several other paintings by Fuseli, Danby, and others. Four designs drawn by the founder of this museum are a display, to use his own language, 'of the architectural visions of early fancy, and wild effusions of a mind glowing with an ardent and enthusiastic desire to attain professional distinction in the gay morning of youth.'

We may now descend into the cellarage, stuffed as full as the upper storeys, and divided into apartments fantastically termed 'the Monks' Parloir, Oratory,' &c. Here are to be found numerous antique objects, such as carvings in ivory, painted glass, and Peruvian vases. Passing into the adjacent corridor and anteroom, we behold numerous fragments and casts in plaster of classic statuary and architecture. But by far the most interesting object is the Egyptian sarcophagus, discovered by Belzoni in 1816 in a tomb in the valley of Beban-el-Malook, near Gournou. Its length is nine feet four inches, and its greatest width three feet eight inches, with an average depth of two feet and a half. It is cut out of a single piece of Arragonite, of such transparency, that the rays of a candle penetrate through it where it is three inches thick. 'What we found in the centre of the saloon,' says Belzoni in his narrative, 'merits the most particular attention, not having its equal in the world, and being such as we had no idea could exist. It is a sarcophagus of the finest Oriental alabaster, and is transparent when a light is placed in the inside of it. It is minutely sculptured, within and without, with several hundred figures, which do not exceed two inches in height, and represent, as I suppose, the whole of the funeral procession and ceremonies relating to the deceased, &c. I cannot give an adequate idea of this beautiful and invaluable piece of antiquity, and can only say that nothing has been brought into Europe from Egypt that can be compared with it. The cover was not there; it had been taken out and broken into several pieces, which we found in digging before the first entrance. I may call this a fortunate day—one of the best perhaps of my life. I do not mean to say that fortune has made me rich, for I do not consider all rich men fortunate; but she has given me that satisfaction, that extreme pleasure, which wealth cannot purchase—the pleasure of discovering what has been long sought in vain.' The learned scholars who have attempted to unlock the meaning of its hieroglyphic carvings, very provokingly arrive at different interpretations; therefore the laity may be allowed to suppose that their true import has not yet been fathomed. When first brought to England, the sarcophagus, or cenotaph be it, was offered to the trustees of the British Museum for L.2000, and when they declined the purchase, Sir John Soane eagerly paid the sum demanded.

Returning to the ground-floor of the museum, and entering the gallery under the dome, amongst the variety of things to attract attention, a fine cast from the Apollo Belvidere, 'the lord of the unerring bow,' and an excellent bust in white marble of Soane, by Chantrey, are conspicuous. Without pausing longer here to contemplate the tastefully-disposed vases, urns, and fragments of architectural decoration, or even the cast from Michael Angelo in the adjacent lobby, let us enter the breakfast-room, a small but beautiful apartment, lighted by a miniature dome. Here is a portrait of General Bonaparte, and another of the fallen emperor, painted at St Helena. Between them is a curiously-mounted pistol, chiefly of silver. It is said to have been taken by Peter the Great from the bey, commander of the Turkish army, at Azof, 1696, and presented by the Emperor Alexander to Napoleon at the treaty of Tilsit in 1807, who took it with him to St Helena, where he gave it to a French officer. A picture by Howard, R. A., of the contention between Oberon and Titania, in Midsummer Night's Dream, is characterised by his usual gaudy colouring. We proceed in the next place up stairs, but pause a moment at the foot to admire Flaxman's noble group of the Archangel Michael overcoming Satan—

> Him long of old
> Thou didst debel, and down from heaven cast
> With all his army.

From this model a large group was cut in marble for Lord Egremont, which is now at Petworth. A little higher in the staircase is one of the pictures 'painted for the purpose of illustrating the dramatic works of Shakspeare, by the artists of Great Britain,' at the instance of Alderman Boydell, in which laudable employment all the great artists of the day, including Reynolds, Romney, Fuseli, and Northcote, were enlisted. This picture, by Durno, is of no great merit. The scene is from the Merry Wives of Windsor, where Falstaff, in women's clothes, is ejected from Ford's house. 'I like not when a 'oman has a great peard; I spy a great peard under her muffler.' Passing a recess, in which two pictures by Howard are ensconced (the best point for viewing them is a few steps higher) we come to a small Mercury in bronze, by Giovanni de Bologna, instinct with exquisite and characteristic grace, reminding us irresistibly of that

> herald Mercury,
> New lighted on a heaven-kissing hill,

which haunted the imagination of Hamlet. Beside it is a small model by Bailey, R. A., representing, with Miltonic beauty, our first parent extended on the earth after his fall, crushed by the oppression of inexpiable guilt, and beseeching death, in his agony of grief, as the most gracious of boons—

> On the ground,
> Outstretched, he lay—on the cold ground—and oft
> Cursed his creation, death as oft accused
> Of tardy execution.

We then enter the south drawing-room, on the table in the centre of which is a series of medals, 140 in number, struck in France during the consulate and the reign of Napoleon. These medals were once in the possession of the Empress Josephine, having been selected for her by the Baron Denon. The ivory table and the four ivory chairs round it were formerly in Tippoo Saib's palace at Seringapatam. Two other curiosities in this room are worth mentioning—namely, Sir Christopher Wren's watch, the face of which is 'with centric and eccentric scribbled o'er;' and a piece of jewellery found amongst the royal baggage after the disastrous battle of Naseby. There are several of Flaxman's models in this apartment, and on the walls are drawings after Raphael's frescos in the Vatican. In the next room, connected with the last by folding-doors, are several paintings by Eastlake, Hilton, and others, but they are very inferior specimens of the handicraft of these artists. There is, however, a good picture by J. M. W. Turner—Van Tromp's barge entering the Texel in 1645, painted before he adopted the plan of obscuring his design by throwing the prismatic colours upon his canvas. There is also a beautiful little scene of greenery by Ruysdael. The glazed cases under the window contain a collection of gems, cameos, intaglios, &c. part of which were formerly the property of an Italian archbishop; many of them are very beautiful. At the foot of the next flight of stairs is a bust by Flaxman of the prime minister Pitt, in which, though merely a head, the commanding attitude of the orator is apparent. In the recess half way up is a plaster cast from Flaxman's 'Shield of Achilles,' executed for George IV. at a cost of 2000 guineas. A second was also made for the king as a present to his brother the Duke of York, a third is at Lowther castle in Westmoreland, and a fourth belongs to the Duke of Northumberland. The artist endeavoured to display in material forms Homer's famous description in the Iliad—

> Rich various artifice emblazed the field;
> Five ample plates the broad expanse compose,
> And godlike labours on the surface rose.

'Round the border of the shield,' says Allan Cunningham, in describing this magnificent work of art, 'he first wrought the sea, in breadth about three fingers; wave follows wave in quiet undulation. He knew that a boisterous ocean would disturb the harmony of the rest of his work. On the central boss he has represented Apollo, or the Sun in his chariot; the horses seem starting forward, and the god bursting out in beauty to give light to the universe around. On the twelve celebrated scenes which fill that space in the shield between the ocean border and the central representation of the universe, he exhausted all his learning, and expended all his strength. We have the labours of commerce and agriculture, hunting, war, marriage, religious rites—all, in short, that makes up the circle of social existence. The figures are generally about six inches in height, and vary in relief from the smallest perceptible swell to half an inch. There is a convexity of six inches from the plane, and the whole contains not less than a hundred figures.' On the staircase are some casts from the antique, the originals of which are in the Vatican museum, and some bas-reliefs by Flaxman. Amongst a variety of pictures and drawings in the room beyond, are Calcott's View of the Thames below Greenwich, the Smoking-Room at Chelsea Hospital by Jones, two drawings of landscape by Ruysdael, which formerly belonged to Louis XVI., and a sketch of a dog by Rubens. There is here also a cabinet, said to have been presented by Philip of Spain to Mary of England. The adjoining room contains numerous models, chiefly in cork, of the famous buildings of antiquity—such as the Temple of Venus at Baalbec, the Temple of Neptune at Palmyra, the ruins of Pompeii, and the temples at Pæstum,

> That stand between the mountains and the sea,
> Awful memorials, but of whom we know not.

There are several objects of value and rarity preserved in this museum, which are not shown to strangers without special permission. Amongst them is the manuscript of Tasso's great poem, the Jerusalem Delivered; a Latin manuscript, embellished with exquisite miniatures by Giulio Clovio, famous for his works in this line —a book containing the Psalms, illuminated by him, was sold for a large sum at the Strawberry Hill sale—a missal of the fifteenth century, containing nearly a hundred miniatures by Lucas von Leyden and his scholars, very finely finished in the Dutch style, but in other respects much inferior to the productions of Clovio; the four first folio editions of Shakspeare, which belonged to John Philip Kemble, &c. &c.

We think we have now said enough to prove that the Soane Museum is a place of great interest and attraction, and that a few hours spent amongst its accumulated wealth will neither be unpleasantly nor unprofitably occupied. In truth, there are many single objects which would be quite sufficient to attract any lover of art or archæology. It is scarcely necessary to name the Belzoni sarcophagus, the two series of Hogarths, the Canaletto, the Clovio illumination, and the Tasso manuscript, as belonging to this class.

Sir John Soane, to whom the public is indebted for assembling and preserving this collection at a great expense, was the son of a bricklayer. In his profession of an architect he acquired considerable fame, with wealth that enabled him to indulge his taste in accumulating rarities and works of art. He died in 1837, at the age of 84, having, a few years before his decease, obtained an act of parliament for settling and preserving his museum, library, and works of art for the benefit of the public, and for establishing a sufficient endowment for the maintenance of the same. Under this act the property was vested in a body of trustees, and the dividends of a sum of L.30,000 stock are applied under their direction in its support. The curator, Mr George Bailey, resides at the museum, and all who have occasion to trouble him personally must thankfully acknowledge his attentive offices.

LUCY FENNEL.

A TALE OF HUMBLE HEROISM.

In a small village near the town of Honiton, in Devonshire, there lived a widow and her son. The old woman had, till her sight failed her, not only earned a sufficient livelihood, but had saved a little money, by making that kind of lace for the manufacture of which Honiton is so widely famed. When, from the infirmities of age, she could no longer ply her vocation successfully, it happened fortunately that her son, by his labour as a farm servant, was able to make up the deficiency. He was a fine, spirited young fellow, who went through his laborious occupations with a good-will and cheerfulness which was so satisfactory to his employer, that he determined to advance, whenever opportunities offered, so assiduous a servant and good a son.

Some two years before our story opens, it happened that a young woman, the daughter of a decayed farmer in the southern part of the county, came to superintend the dairy of Luke Damerel's master. It was not unnatural that the buxom lass and the young man should form a mutual attachment. As they were both very well conducted persons, their love passages were looked upon with a favourable eye both by Dame Damerel and by the farmer's wife, Mrs Modbury, though neither openly sanctioned it, for prudence' sake. Luke and Lucy, however, loved on, as they thought, in secret, determining not to reveal their mutual affection till they should be placed in circumstances to get married. Things remained thus for more than a year and a half, when Farmer Modbury's wife died, and other circumstances occurred which induced him to promote Luke to a more lucrative and responsible situation on the farm. Shortly after the demise of his wife also, he found it expedient to give Lucy, in addition to her dairy duties, the sole charge of the housekeeping.

With the rise in his fortunes, Luke's thoughts were directed to the accomplishment of his dearest hope, and he revealed his passion to his mother, consulting her on the propriety of the step he wished to take; which was simply to marry Lucy, and bring her to live in the cottage. The old dame was not surprised at the proposal, for she expected it to be made from the day Luke's wages were increased. She had made up her mind what to advise, and did not shrink from advising it, although it would not be agreeable to her son. 'Luke,' she said, 'you must still wait. Your earnings are not sufficient to keep Lucy comfortably; and she, you know, would have to give up her place, which is now a good one. So you would not only be injuring yourself, but her also.'

Luke fired up at this, and unkindly hinted that his mother did not wish to have a companion to share their home. The old dame, though much hurt, denied that any such feeling swayed her, and advised him to consult Lucy herself. Dame Damerel had that confidence in the girl's good sense and prudence, that she was sure even Lucy would not consent to marry so soon as Luke wished.

In no very amiable mood the lover sought his mistress at the farm-house. He went into the kitchen, and not finding Lucy there, inquired of one of the maids where she was. With a sly ominous expression the girl replied 'that *Miss* Lucy was in the best parlour making tea for master.' This information gave poor Luke a sort of panic. He trembled, turned pale, and hastily retreated from the house. Discontented thoughts filled his mind. 'No doubt,' he said almost aloud, as he walked homewards—'no doubt she'll *not* consent when I propose to marry her, though I can keep her. Farmer Modbury will be a better match for her than a poor hard-working lad like me. But I'll see about that—it shall be now or never. If she wont marry me in a week, she never shall!' In truth, Luke had been feeling a pang of jealousy creep over him ever since Lucy was promoted to be Modbury's housekeeper; and that she should be admitted alone with him into the best parlour to make his tea, confirmed what were previously only suspicions. On entering the cottage, his wild looks almost frightened his mother; but he was silent as to the cause, and went sullenly to bed.

Farmer Modbury kept up the good old Devonshire custom of dining with all the people in his employment; and the day after, when Luke with the rest of his companions sat at the table, he watched the actions and countenances of Lucy and her master, to catch new causes for the tormenting feeling which possessed him. The meal concluded, he followed the girl to the dairy, as was his custom; for a short and sweet interview could always be snatched at that time. The present one was, however, the reverse. In a hard tone of voice, and with an abrupt manner, Luke inquired if she were ready to have him? The girl frankly answered, 'Of course I am, Luke; but what should make you ask the question on such a sudden?'

Luke's jealousy was a little assuaged by Lucy's open and confiding manner, and becoming more calm, he told her his plans. 'It will never do, Luke,' she replied. 'Besides, my father, whom I must send to about it, would not consent. No, no, we must wait.'

'Wait! for what, I should like to know? To give master, I suppose, a chance of—of——'

'Of what, Luke?'

'Why,' said Luke, worked up into a sort of frenzy by the very thought—'why, of asking you to take poor dead-and-gone missus's place!'

The colour mounted to Lucy Fennel's face. She cast a reproachful look on her lover, and seemed ready to cry; but woman's pride came to her aid, and she left the dairy, as if afraid to hear another of Luke's terrible words. Had the young man not gone out immediately, he might have heard ill-suppressed sobs issuing from the room into which the maiden had shut herself. 'She is afraid to face me,' said Luke to himself as he crossed the courtyard. 'No, no, she can't deceive me, though she is trying.'

The directions Damerel gave to the workmen that afternoon were so injudicious, that his master happening to overhear him tell a ditcher to fill up a drain which ought to have been opened, gave him a severe reprimand. Luke received what was said with the worst feelings, continually repeating to himself, 'Ah, he has a spite against me now. He did not make that girl his housekeeper for nothing. *I'm* not wanted here, I can see.'

When work was over, it happened that as Luke was returning to his own cottage he met young Larkin, a neighbouring farmer's son, who asked him to accompany him to Honiton, where he was going to 'see the sodgers,' a regiment being about to pass through the town on its way to form part of Plymouth garrison. To beguile the care which tormented him, he gladly consented, and having gone home to put on his Sunday clothes, was soon equipped for the evening's expedition. The two friends had to pass Modbury's parlour window, and it was tea-time. Luke cast an inquisitive glance towards it, and trembled when he saw the blind being slowly pulled up. Presently it revealed the figure of Lucy, very nicely dressed with a new and handsome cap. Something having prevented the blind from being drawn quite to the top, Lucy mounted on the window-seat to adjust it, and when about to descend, Luke plainly saw his master come forward, give her one hand, while with the other he assisted her down by the waist! Damerel grasped the tree he was resting against for support; a film came over his eyes; but a few rough jokes from Larkin recovered him, and hearing the military band in the distance, he endeavoured to forget his cares, and trudged on towards Honiton.

Meanwhile, the moment Lucy had finished her duties at the tea-table, she hastened to Damerel's cottage, in the hope, not of seeing her lover, but his mother, alone. The old dame, perceiving her pale and in low spirits, thought she divined the cause, by supposing the girl was sorrowing at the imprudence of the step Luke had proposed to her. 'Well, well,' said the kind old woman, 'things may not be so bad after all, Lucy. And since Luke has set his heart so much upon it, and you, I am sure, are nothing loath, we must try and manage it. I'll tell you what I've been thinking, girl. You see the great mischief will be your being obliged to give up your place at the farm; now, I know a plan by which that loss may be mended. You are a quick, handy maid; and suppose—suppose'—and here the good old woman took Lucy's hands in hers—'suppose I teach you lace-making?'

These words poured a light into Lucy's heart which seemed to banish all her grief. The means of rendering herself independent of her present situation was all she wished for. She loved Luke tenderly, dearly, and with a fervent, virtuous desire, wished to become his wife. This wish had grown much stronger since her painful interview with him, not only because she wished to prove she was ready to sacrifice everything for his sake, but for another and more perplexing reason. Her master had paid her attentions that evening which left no doubt on her mind that *he* desired her for his wife.

When Mrs Damerel heard the news, she was much distressed. 'Oh, it is too bad!' she exclaimed, 'to think that my Luke should be the means of preventing you from marrying so well—you who are worthy of any man.'

'Do not think of that; I could not be happy with one I do not love. So now, dear mother—for I will always call you so—let me hear what plan you propose.'

'Well, instead of talking idly, as we always do when you come to see us, you shall let me teach you the lace-making. Come every night, and in a month or two I shall be able to put you in a way to earn quite as much as you do now at Farmer Modbury's. When this is the case, we must see about getting yourself and Luke asked in church, for surely both your earnings put together will be enough to keep you comfortably.'

'But will not the farmer bear some enmity to poor Luke?'

'I will answer for him, girl. I have known him longer than he has known himself. I nursed him, and I can say with truth that a better hearted man does not live. Should he again offer you any civilities, tell him the whole truth, and I'll warrant he will not repeat them.'

That evening Lucy tripped home with a light heart. When she retired to rest, she built many an air-castle of future happiness.

The next morning, as the home-servants of Modbury's farm were going to their daily toil, they found a crowd round Damerel's cottage door. On inquiring into the cause, they were told that Luke had in a fit of despair enlisted as a soldier, and that the news had wrought so violently on the feelings of his mother, that it was thought she could never recover!

The scene inside the cottage was painfully distressing. The old dame was lying on a bed with her clothes still about her, showing that she had not gone to rest the whole night. The village doctor was by her side, having just bled her, whilst everything strewed about the room indicated that the always revolting operation had but recently been performed. The neighbours, as they crowded round the door, denounced Luke's conduct as rash and heartless. In the midst of their denunciations they were joined by another, to whom every word they uttered was as a death-wound. It was Lucy.

Whoever has had the misfortune of often seeing women placed in sudden difficulties, or overtaken by an unforeseen misfortune, must have remarked that they occasionally act with unexpected firmness. They frequently show a calmness of manner and a directness of purpose, forming quite an exception to their every-day demeanour. It is after the danger is over, or the first crisis past, that they break down, as it were, and show themselves to belong to the weaker sex. Thus it was with Lucy. When she entered the cottage, she had a full knowledge of the death-blow which had been inflicted on her hopes of future happiness. Still, she seemed calm and collected. When she took the basin from the surgeon to bathe Mrs Damerel's temples herself, her hand shook not, and she performed the kindly office as neatly as if no misfortune had befallen her. When she went to the door to intreat the neighbours to stand away from it, that sufficient air might be admitted into the room, her voice, though rather deeper in tone than usual, was calm and firm. Had she not occasionally pressed her hand tightly against her brow, as if to cool its burning agony, you would have thought that she suffered no further anxiety than that which is usually felt whilst attending the sick.

It was, however, when she was left alone with the exhausted, almost senseless mother, that the tide of grief took its full course. Lucy wept like one distraught. Through the deep, black future which lay before her, she could see no gleam of hope or sunlight. She unjustly upbraided herself for having, however innocently, given Luke cause of suspicion. The weight of blame which she took to herself was almost insupportable. 'I have been his ruin!' she exclaimed, burying her face in his mother's bosom.

When the old dame had strength to speak, she whispered Lucy not to give way, but to bear up against it. The past she wisely said was incurable; 'We must keep our senses whole for the future. While we keep heart, there is no fear of our seeing him again yet.'

The story reached Farmer Modbury as he was sitting down to breakfast. He was deeply shocked even when he knew no more than that Luke had enlisted; but when, on visiting the cottage, the whole truth was explained to him by Lucy, he felt both grief and disappointment. He was, however, determined not to abandon his suit as hopeless, and returning home, wrote to her father (he was a widower), explaining what had happened, and giving a frank exposition of his own honourable views as regarded Lucy. 'No doubt,' he concluded his epistle, 'she will soon forget this early and unhappy attachment.' Modbury was a shrewd man, and a clever farmer, but he knew very little about women's hearts.

From that day he was extremely kind and considerate to Lucy. Perceiving how much happier the girl was when she returned from visiting Mrs Damerel than at other times, Modbury diminished her labours by employing another dairymaid, so that Lucy might have more leisure, which he had no objection should be spent with the invalid.

One morning while Lucy was preparing the household dinner, a message arrived from the cottage. Her presence was desired there immediately. Lucy lost no time, and was soon in her accustomed seat at the bed-head. Mrs Damerel placed a letter in her hands. It was from her son. With beating heart Lucy opened it, and after time sufficient to master the emotions which the sight of Luke's handwriting caused her, she proceeded to read it aloud. It ran thus:—

'*Maidstone Barracks, Kent.*

MY DEAREST MOTHER—I have at last found enough courage to take up my pen, hoping this will find you in good health, as it leaves me at present. I hope you have forgiven me for what I have done. I send you two pounds, part of the bounty I received for enlisting. Do not be afraid, my dear mother, that whilst I live you shall want.

When I went to Honiton, I was persuaded to enlist, after the soldiers had passed through, by a sergeant of a horse regiment, and I took the king's money; so I am now a private in the —th dragoons. I am rough-riding every day, and expect to be passed as fit for regular duty soon, when I shall be draughted off to the Indies, where our head-quarters are. I should be very comfortable if it was not for thinking about home so much. They have found out I am a good judge of horses, and know all about their complaints, so the sergeant-major told me yesterday I shall get on very well in the Indies, if I keep a sharp look out.

Dear mother, I shall see you again when I come back —I know I shall; and we shall be happy together; for now I have nobody else to care about upon the earth. I hope she will be happy, for she deserves all this world can afford, and I have always found Mr Modbury a kind master, so I am sure he will make her a kind husband. Dear mother, there is Tom Larkin, who promised me, after I had listed, that he and his sister Sarah would look in upon you sometimes, and help you. May God bless you, my dear mother. My heart was well nigh broken; but my comrades have been very kind to me, and I want for nothing. Good-by, mother, and believe me your ever affectionate son, LUKE DAMEREL.

P.S.—I do not know when we shall sail for the Indies; but in case, please to direct to Private Damerel, —th Regiment, Light Dragoons, Maidstone, or elsewhere; and the letter will be sure to come to hand. Once more, God bless you, and may God bless *her* too, dear mother.'

To describe Lucy's feelings while she read this simply-worded epistle would be impossible. All the love and tenderness which she had felt for Luke during the time she had known him, seemed to be concentrated within her at that moment. At first she mourned the step he had taken as hopeless and irreparable; but, casting her eyes upon the lace-work she had the day before been doing, a sudden thought seized her. By means of *that*, something might be eventually accomplished. With these thoughts she quietly folded the letter, placed it on the table beside the bed, and resumed the lace-work, scarcely speaking a word.

Mrs Damerel mistook this action for indifference, and in her sincere desire for the girl's welfare, urged—not for the first time—plans and sentiments which, though well meant, were utterly revolting to Lucy. Luke had, she argued, no doubt behaved very ill, by rashly and without explanation tearing himself not only from her, but from every person to whom he was dear. On the other hand Farmer Modbury's advances were very flattering, and she could hardly blame a girl who had been so cruelly treated, even by her own son, were she to accept the good fortune that lay before her.

Still Lucy went on practising her lace-work, her heart beating, and her averted eyes swimming with tears. At length she exclaimed, 'Dame, you will break my heart if you ever talk in this way again. To you I look for comfort and strength in loving Luke, which I shall never cease to do. I, whether innocent or not, am the cause of depriving you of the comfort of his company, and I am determined to restore him to us both. You may think it impossible, but it is not. I have thought, and thought, and reckoned up everything, and am quite sure it can be done.'

'I cannot make out what you mean?' said Mrs Damerel.

'Why, that I intend, as soon as I am able to do it well enough, to take work from the town, to leave Farmer Modbury, and come and be with you. We can live on very little, and every spare shilling we will put into the savings' bank, until it amounts to a sufficient sum to buy Luke off.' She then industriously resumed her work. It was some time before Mrs Damerel could comprehend the full intent and meaning of the sacrifice the girl proposed. At first she thought it was a mere flighty resolution, that would not hold long; and even when she was made to understand that it was unshaken, she looked at the achievement as impossible; for at that time the prices for lace-work were falling, in consequence of the recent introduction of machinery.

About a week after this all her doubts vanished, for on Michaelmas day, when Lucy's term of service with Farmer Modbury expired, sure enough she brought her box, and declared she had come to stay with her adopted mother. She had previously been to a master manufacturer in Honiton with a specimen of her lace, and it was so well approved, that she obtained a commission for a large quantity on the spot. By this time the old dame had completely recovered from her illness, and was able to move about, so as to attend to the little domestic concerns of the cottage; Lucy could therefore give her undivided attention to her work.

Her proceedings were by no means agreeable to her father or to Modbury. The former wrote enjoining her by no means to leave the farmer's house; but the letter came too late, for she had already taken her departure. Modbury, however, in replying to an epistle in which Fennel had given him free consent to marry his daughter, expressed a thorough conviction of the firmness of the girl's purpose, and that at present it was impossible to shake it. Though she had left his roof, he should continue to watch over her, and hoped, by persevering kindness and attention, eventually to win her affections. Under these circumstances Lucy quietly established herself in Mrs Damerel's cottage.

At first she found it a hard matter to gain sufficient money for her labour to recompense the dame for her board and lodging, which she insisted upon doing every time she was paid by her employers. Still she wrought on, although her savings were small, and at the end of several months they bore a hopeless proportion to the large sum which was required. But time seemed a small object to her: she looked forward to the end, and in it she saw such a world of reward and happiness, that no toil would be too much to arrive at it. She had answered Luke's letter with her own hand, assuring him of her unshaken attachment, in spite of all that had happened; but unfortunately he had sailed for India, and it was sent thither after him, in obedience to the vague 'elsewhere' which had been added to the superscription according to his wish.

Slow progress was not the only trouble Lucy had to contend with. Modbury's attentions pained her as much as Luke's absence; the more so because they were so full of consideration for her welfare. She knew she never could return his kindness, and felt that she did not deserve it. She often told Dame Damerel that a show of hostility from the worthy farmer would not have pained her so much as his unremitting attentions.

Then, when the neighbours came in to gossip, they sometimes spoke against Luke. They would tell her that a man who would suspect her on such slight grounds, and act as he did, could never be true to her; that he would see some other whom he would prefer, and some day send home word that he was married; neither was it likely that he would ever come home alive from the Indies. These poisoned arrows, which were meant as comfort, glanced harmlessly from Lucy, who was invulnerably shielded by trusting love and hope. She would answer 'very likely,' or 'it may be,' or 'there is no knowing what may happen in this world of trouble,' and still rattle about her lace-pegs over the pillow on which it was made with the quickness of magic. Amongst her visitors, however, there were two who invariably offered her better consolation; these were Larkin and his sister. Tom 'stuck up,' as he expressed it, for his friend Luke, and always put the blame of the enlistment on the wiles and arts of the recruiting sergeant, who regularly entrapped him into the deed. Many a happy winter evening was spent in that humble cottage by Lucy and her friends. Luke was never forgotten in their conversations; for there was the lace which was being unweariedly made for his release to remind them of him. When Modbury made his appearance (and this was very often), the subject was of course dropped.

A year passed away. Neither Lucy nor Modbury had made much progress in their several aims; scarcely a tithe of the requisite sum for Luke's discharge had been saved; neither could Modbury perceive that his suit advanced. Lucy's conduct sorely perplexed him. She always seemed delighted when he came in, and received him with every mark of cordiality; but whenever he dropped the slightest plea in his own behalf, tears would come into her eyes, and she intreated him to desist. He began to remark also, that besides the presence of the old dame, which was surely a sufficient safeguard against any warmth of manner he might be betrayed into, Lucy always contrived to have Susan Larkin with her. Should she be absent, Lucy would be telling Modbury what a good, industrious, excellent girl she was; which, indeed, was the truth.

No letter came from Luke, and there was no proof that he had received hers. Lucy began gradually to despond; for work became slack, and at times she only got enough to employ her half the day. Not to lose ground, however, she hired herself to the neighbouring farmers' wives to sew during her spare time, leaving Dame Damerel to the occasional care of Susan Larkin. While she was sitting at work during one of these engagements, she compared her own cheerless lot with the happiness which surrounded her. The farmer was reading the newspaper, his wife and daughter assisting her in the work she was doing. As she made this comparison, and thought of Luke, banished as it were from his home, and enduring perhaps severe hardships, she could scarcely refrain from weeping.

Now and then the farmer read a paragraph from the paper, and presently exclaimed—'Ah, our young squire has got safe to his regiment in India.' At these words Lucy trembled, but went on rapidly with her work, lest her emotion should be noticed. She had previously heard that the son of a neighbouring proprietor had bought a commission in Luke's regiment, and this was almost like having news of Luke himself. Presently the reader went on with the paragraph—'We understand there has been a fatal disease which has carried off many of the——' The farmer made a pause here, and Lucy's heart sank within her. 'Oh, I see,' the old gentleman ejaculated; 'the corner is turned down'—'has carried off many'—yes—'many of the —— horses.'

This little incident produced such strong emotions in Lucy's frame, that though she felt, upon the whole, much gratified by merely hearing about Luke's regiment and its horses, yet she became too ill to proceed with her work, and found it necessary to return to the cottage.

Lucy soon altered her plan of engaging herself out; for the idea struck her, that if she were to make lace on a sort of speculation, and keep it by her till it was wanted, she would in the end make a greater profit. Having, when her father was in good circumstances, been partly educated at an Exeter boarding-school, she had acquired there some knowledge of drawing, and by exercising her pencil, she now invented some very pretty lace patterns.

Lucy wrought and hoped on for another year. Still nothing was heard from Luke. A new calamity had fallen upon Lucy. Her father, a broken and decayed man, had come to live near her, and was now nearly dependent on her for support. Both Modbury and Farmer Larkin gave him little jobs to do, for which they liberally recompensed him. The quantity of lace Lucy was employed to make was so small, that it just sufficed to keep her and her father; while her little capital, instead of increasing, was gradually absorbed by the purchase of materials for the stock her industry accumulated. Susan Larkin frequently visited her, and Modbury was seldom absent.

No ill fortune seemed to depress the persevering girl. Even though she was working almost night and day, she still kept up her spirits. Indeed, at every new misfortune, a fresh accession of firmness and resolution seemed to nerve her. About this time her father died, invoking blessings on her for having been so good a daughter. After the first shock of grief had passed, she continued her task amidst the most hopeless circumstances. The lace-trade sunk lower and lower; still Lucy wrought on, under a strong presentiment that it would improve. She did not relax one hour's labour, although she was now receiving much less for it than when she began. She accumulated so large a stock, that at last every shilling of her savings was spent for materials. In exchange, however, she possessed a large quantity of beautiful lace, that even, if it sold at the present low prices, would have yielded a small profit. At last things became so bad, that a sale seemed unavoidable, disadvantageous as it might be. Lucy, now an object of commiseration amongst the neighbours, still retained her cheerfulness. That so much patience, modesty, and firmness of purpose should not meet its reward, seemed almost impossible; and fortune smiled on Lucy when nearly every hope seemed to have left her.

It is well known by what trifles in the mercantile world fortunes are lost and won. The detention of a ship, the non-arrival of a mail, has ruined hundreds; whilst some equally unforeseen caprice of fashion or similar accident has made as many fortunes. It happened, when Lucy had the greatest cause for despondency, that within a short period two members of the royal family died. Mourning lace was then much in request, and it happened that most of Lucy's stock was of that kind. Suddenly, commissions from Honiton flowed in, and Lucy was kept constantly at work, at wages much higher than before—her own stock acquiring fresh value while the price continued to rise. Young Larkin, who was a shrewd fellow, advised her to 'hold' it till the value increased still more. She took the advice, and at the proper moment sold it at a price she never hoped to realise. At the end of a week she found herself in possession of a sum which was, within a few pounds, sufficient to procure her lover's discharge from the army!

Poor Lucy could hardly believe her eyes when the manufacturer laid down the bank-notes before her. She pinned them carefully into the bosom of her frock, and hastened to tell Dame Damerel that all their troubles were over. The old woman's eyes glistened as Lucy unpinned her treasure and laid it on the table. It was counted, re-counted, and wondered over. What was to be done with it till the rest was procured? Who would take care of it?

This delight was, however, somewhat damped when they came to consider that, putting aside all uncertainty about his fate, it would be at least six months before Luke's discharge could reach him; then an additional half year would elapse ere he could get back. It was a long time to wait. 'Never mind, dear mother,' said Lucy, 'the time that has passed since he left seems scarcely a year, although it is three. It is only because the twelvemonth is to come that it appears to be so long. Still,' she said, considering and heaving a deep sigh, 'we have not got his discharge yet, and great as this sum is, some more must be earned to make up the rest.'

'Leave that to me,' returned Mrs Damerel.

Next day, when Lucy returned from the post-office, where she had taken a letter for Luke, she found another lying on the table in Larkin's handwriting. On reading the superscription, she found it was addressed to the war-office. 'Yes,' said Mrs Damerel in answer to her inquiring glances, 'it is all done now, Lucy; and this letter is to be sent off to tell the great people that we can have the money ready to buy our dear Luke off again.'

Larkin had, in truth, gladly supplied the small sum which was deficient. The letter was sent, and in less than a week an immense despatch found its way to the village, which excited universal wonderment. It was a great oblong missive, with the words 'On his majesty's service' printed at the top. It had an enormous seal, and was directed to 'Mr Thomas Larkin.' A crowd of idlers followed the postman with this epistolary phenomenon, in the hope of getting some knowledge of its contents. Tom, however, when he read it, coolly put it into his pocket, and walked to the cottage without saying a word to anybody.

This letter seemed like a climax to Lucy's good fortune, and 'begged to inform Mr Larkin that Corporal Farrier Damerel was on his way to England to superintend the selection of troop horses, and that his discharge should be made out when he had arrived and performed that duty.'

Scarcely a month after the arrival of the official despatch, a corporal of dragoons was seen trespassing on Farmer Modbury's fields, by crossing them in great haste without any regard to the footpaths. An old ploughman roughly warned him off, threatening personal ejection. 'What, Roger Dart?' exclaimed the soldier, 'is this the way you welcome a man home after a long absence!' The ploughman stared, and said he did not know him. 'Do you know,' rejoined the corporal with a trembling voice and anxious countenance—'do you know Lucy Fennel?'

'Of course I do,' returned Roger; 'everybody knows her, and, if I may make so bold, loves her too! Why, sure enough, there she is sitting—don't you see?—there, sitting at Dame Damerel's door making lace for the life of her.'

The stranger flew across the field, and the ploughman saw him bound over the hedge, take Lucy into his arms, and drag her, bewildered and enraptured, into the cottage. 'Why, dang me if it bean't Luke Damerel!' exclaimed the rustic, slapping the thighs of his leather breeches; 'how main glad the folks will be to see 'un!—I know what I'll do.' Whereupon Roger trudged across the fields towards the church. He happened to be one of the parish ringers, and calling his mates from the fields, they all trudged off to the bell-tower, and rang out as merry a peal as ever was heard. The whole country was in a commotion; the news ran like wildfire from lip to lip and ear to ear, till the cottage was beset with visitors within and without. But Luke heard no welcome, felt no grasp, but that of Lucy and his mother. As to Lucy, an intense happiness thrilled through her, which absorbed all her faculties, except that of feeling the full extent of her bliss.

This story of patience, endurance, and faith in humble life is almost ended. Luke's furlough only extended to a week, which he spent as an inmate of the farm, at Modbury's earnest intreaty; for he now gave up all hope of Lucy, and determined to help in rewarding her patience by promoting the match with his rival. At the end of that time Luke was obliged to depart for Yorkshire, to meet the veterinary surgeon and purchase horses, in which he was found of the utmost use; but this, together with his excellent character, operated most unfavourably for his discharge. The authorities were unwilling to lose so good a soldier. The interest of the 'squire,' however, whose son was a cornet in Luke's troop, was set to work, the hard-earned money paid, and the discharge obtained. Damerel got a farm let to him on advantageous terms, close to his native village, and was married amidst more noisy demonstrations by Roger and his company of ringers. Modbury had taken to wife Lucy's friend, Susan Larkin.

The last time I was in Devonshire I called on Mr and Mrs Damerel. They are an interesting old couple, who have brought up a large family in comfort and respectability.

THE POSITION OF LITERARY MEN.

Mrs S. C. Hall, in a short paper in the *Art-Union*, on recently deceased men of genius, speaks a few poignant words respecting the condition of the literary labourer in this country. Mr Laman Blanchard perished in the most miserable manner at forty-one, for want of a kind friend to enable him to take that rest which was required for his overwrought brain. Thomas Hood, during his last illness, was obliged to 'write wit while propped by pillows,' and produced the chapters of an unfinished novel 'between the intervals and beatings of heart disease.' Well may Mrs Hall add, 'Alas, what do those endure who write for bread!' The fact of these two men—men of amiable, virtuous, and even prudent conduct—dying in the prime of life, without having been able to raise themselves above the pressure of immediate want, or make any provision for their families, is calculated to awaken a strong feeling respecting the position of literary men generally. Can it be quite right that, while commerce rewards its votaries so handsomely, the man of superior mind, if he chooses to obey its impulse to the gratification and instruction of his fellow-creatures, is almost sure of a life of mean struggles, a premature death, and the rendition of his widow and children into the mercy of the charitable? The proportion of service to the general cause surely demands some other distribution of the general wealth. Yet how is such a change to be, even in the slightest degree, effected? The arrangement established in society for the reward of all its industrious members is, that they receive a price for *what they have to sell*. The author endeavours to take advantage of the plan by throwing the productions of his brain into the form of books. But the lucrativeness of books is a matter of perfect accident, and nearly altogether irrespective of their utility to the public. There is nothing like an assurance, but rather the reverse, that a literary work of great excellence and originality shall be well rewarded in this manner. The most exquisite short poem, on which the world is to hang delighted for ever, and which is to make for its author an undying reputation, will bring only a few pounds from a magazine at the most; a meritorious history, costing years of labour, will be ten before the public without returning one penny to the writer; while novels that only serve to amuse the passing hour, or compilations of no merit but that of being adroitly addressed to a public need, will be comparatively well remunerated. There was a great noise a few years ago about extension of copyright, as favourable to the interests of authors; but if one in a thousand ever receive benefit from it, it will be a wonder. Even of successful books, except in a few brilliant instances, the profits are little, compared with the gains of successful business. The author, unlike the man of trade, can depute no share of his work. He cannot profit by those huge combinations of the labour of others which make the factory man a kind of baron among his retainers. He must work out the whole for himself; and, after all, if he can induce a bookseller to publish for him, taking the one half of the profits for the *risk attending all literary speculations*, he is considered as well off. Thus it is that the author, while in society a prominent and important being far beyond most traders and factors, cannot live on a level with even the mediocre of that class, cannot indeed emerge for a moment from a humble obscurity, without the greatest danger. He can hardly return a cup of tea for the profuse dinner to which the shopkeeper invites him, except at the hazard of degrading embarrassments. Society brings him forward for its own gratification, or from a sense that he deserves a high social place; but when it hears that he has been tempted by the common and natural wish to reciprocate civilities with it, and has fallen into pecuniary difficulties in consequence, it condemns him mercilessly, according to the prevalent rule in this country with regard to everything in the form of debt. In short, the fate of a literary man chancing to have the extraordinary prudential gifts that would be required of him, and having nothing beyond his pen to look to, is—there is no disguising the fact—a cottage or a garret. He is condemned to personal obscurity of the most profound shade, while nominally blazing in the light of day. Could there be a greater anomaly? We expect the self-denial of those rare beings—the Cincinnatuses, the Dentatuses, the Andrew Marvels—from a large class, living unavoidably in a constant exposure to the temptations of the most luxurious community on earth. It is the merest silliness to look for such fruit from such circumstances. We may deplore, we may often see special reason to condemn, but we must also be fully sensible that the arrangements made by society for the remuneration and sustenance of authors are, in the first place, blameable, and that, while human nature is what it is, we have no title to hope that these men, as a class, will ever be greatly different from what they are.

The utter falsity of the position of the literary class is shown by one painful fact, that the booksellers, the men who are most connected with them in business, have universally, in London at least, a low opinion of them. It is one of the facts never told in print, but everywhere heard in private, that the literary men residing in the metropolis are generally regarded by their publishers with the utmost degree of distrust. To show how truly this is the case, we shall relate a little anecdote. A publisher of high standing said one day to his head clerk, 'Why, there is —— [mentioning the name of a retail bookseller who had been in business for some time, but who was also a writer of books]; he seems to be doing well. I think we might subscribe with him'—[that is, let him have new books upon an open account]. 'Oh, sir,' said the official, with a hard knowing look, but in the simplest earnest, 'don't you know? He's an author.' 'Oh,' said the other; 'to be sure he is. I had quite forgot.' No more was said, because it was understood that, as a matter of course, the man's being an author was a proof of his not being entitled to credit. We cannot believe, no one having any faith in human nature can believe, that it is natural and unavoidable for the highest intellects to be deficient in *morale;* it must be mainly the effect of erroneous circumstances pressing unduly on those minds.

The unsoundness is manifest. What is to be the cure? Unfortunately, in England, all remedies for great public evils are Utopian. We therefore suggest none, but leave the evil, for the meantime, to be digested in the public mind.

DYSPEPSIA.

A DARKLY poetical notion was current amongst our forefathers, that a person of a morose, unamiable disposition was possessed of a devil. They believed that he was merely the outer casing, the sheep's clothing of a sort of supernatural wolf; that if the visible shell, in the likeness of man, could be removed, there would appear to the terrified visions of the multitude a figure with horns, hoofs, a tail, and the very sharp goad with which it was supposed to prick on its victim to say spiteful things, and to do bad actions. This idea of our forefathers has been proved by anatomy and physiology (of which they knew nothing) to be quite erroneous as far as regards the bodily presence of the evil spirit. Science has robbed us of the horns, the hoofs, and the tail; but it has, with all its poetry-spoiling discoveries, still left us the essential demon. The monster is called by nosologists 'dyspepsia,' and by the rest of the world indigestion.

Many a snappish, disagreeable man, who is feared at home as a domestic tyrant, shunned abroad as a social Tartar, and denounced everywhere as the wilful incarnation of ill-temper, is nothing more than the victim of the demon dyspepsia. Perhaps he was in his early years as good-humoured and kind a being as ever breathed. Gradually, his friends and relations perceived a change in his disposition. This began, in all probability, by snappishness to his wife, scolding his children, and occasionally kicking his dog. When expostulated with for allowing these causeless improprieties to grow upon him, he is ready enough to own his faults, but at the same time equally ready to make excuses for them. He declares business is going wrong, though you know it never prospered better; or that his children worry him, though it is evident he has terrified them into taciturnity and shrinking obedience. He makes every excuse but the right one; because, poor wretch, he is perfectly ignorant of the real cause. He really believes what he says, and thinks that he *is* on the road to the bankrupt court, and that his offspring really are disobedient. Alas! it is one of the characteristics of the insidious demon he is possessed with to hide itself from the ken of its victim. Even when the monster deranges his bodily health, and drives him to the doctor, he describes every symptom but those which are indicative of the real disease. The skilful physician, however, finds it out in spite of, or rather in consequence of, his mystifications, and proceeds to exorcise the evil spirit—not after the ancient plan with bell, book, and candle—but with pill, draught, and plenty of exercise.

When, therefore, we meet with such a man as we have described, let us be a little charitable. Don't let us denounce him without remorse or mitigation. Pity is the proper sentiment which he should awaken. Human nature is not so innately vicious as some philosophers imagine; instinctively, our good impulses predominate, and would remain dominant, were they not so often blunted, checked, and strangled by dyspepsia. Imagine *yourself* in a dyspeptic condition, and then ask whether you could be amiable to your fellow-creatures, or be able to assume that virtue when you have it not? Fancy yourself in a state which, when asked about it, you are obliged to describe as a something which makes you wretchedly uncomfortable, but you don't know what; a condition which, nevertheless, unfits you for occupation; a feeling which imparts a distressing craving for food, combined with a disgust at the very idea of eating it; a constant drowsiness, without the power of sleeping; a sensation of overwhelming fatigue and weariness, with a longing to take exercise; a weight over the brow, a weight at each joint, a weight at every extremity, and a still greater weight in the stomach. Then as to the state of your nerves: conceive yourself in the lowest of low spirits; in hourly dread of some misfortune; haunted with suspicions concerning your dearest friends; looking upon your whole household as a set of conspirators against your comfort: feeling all this, I say, with a thorough conviction that such sensations mislead you; that in reality no misfortune impends; and that your family love you dearly. Then at night, instead of enjoying the benefit of

'Nature's sweet restorer, balmy sleep,'

you are visited by your attendant demon's terrible ally, nightmare, who inflicts even greater tortures on you than his day-time colleague. 'In a half-waking or intersomnious condition,' saith the learned Dr Von Druffel of Berlin, 'you behold a monster of some kind —a goblin, a fiery horse, a wild gigantic man—glide slowly towards you. This apparition seats itself on the pit of your stomach, and presses you with such a crushing weight, that you can neither breathe nor move a limb.' You are not asleep; you are sufficiently awake to know that could you but move your little finger the charm would be broken, and the vile nightmare gallop away. But you cannot: all power is removed, and there the imaginary quadruped remains, caprioling upon your devoted breast like a heavily-shod war-horse on parade. Even when you fall asleep you are no better off. You have horrid visions. You dream yourself to be the most detestable villain in existence. In the short space of an hour's nap, you inflict tortures on some dear friend which would have frightened a Spanish inquisitor. You commit crimes of unheard-of atrocity, and only escape the gibbet by waking, the victim of remorse and despair.

After enduring all this, picture yourself seated at breakfast, and though surrounded with every comfort administered by a most affectionate household, just say whether you think it to be within the pale of human probability that you could look, speak, or behave pleasantly? If your wife were to offer you the sincerest sympathy, and the tenderest condolences, would not the internal demon 'dyspepsia' incite you to accuse her of 'teasing' you? Can you for a moment believe that, in such a state of mind and stomach, your expostulation would be mild and Christian-like, if the butter were bad, or the egg you had just broken somewhat too odoriferous? Would you, if ever so coaxingly asked, hand over a cheque for your wife's milliner's bill without grumbling? If you *could* do all these things, you are more than mortal.

Let me repeat, therefore, when you hear an individual denounced as a monster of ill-humour, do not be too harsh upon his moral character before you have inquired into his physical symptoms. Many a man who is accused of having a bad heart, ought rather to be described as having a bad stomach, for the immense influence which that organ exercises over the worldly conduct of mankind is greatly overlooked. A female patient of the celebrated French physician Pinel, who was fully possessed with the demon dyspepsia, and knew it, thus details her condition:—'The foundation of all my misfortunes is in my stomach. It is so sensitive, that pain, grief, pleasure, and, in a word, all sorts of moral affections, seem to take their origin in it. Even a frown from a friend wounds me so sensibly, that my whole system is disagreeably affected by it. I *think* by means of my stomach, if I may be allowed so to express myself.' How many apparently evil-disposed persons whom one meets with may be precisely in this lady's condition, and think and act from the dictates of the stomach, or rather from those of the demon contained in it—dyspepsia! How frequently, therefore, may not our judgment err in the matter of first causes regarding petty cruelties and small tyrannies? When, for example, a rich debtor refuses a poor creditor a long-deferred payment, may not this piece of injustice be the result, not so much of sheer dishonesty, as of deranged digestive organs? May we not attribute it less to a defect in the moral sentiments, than to evil influences diffused over his nervous system by a piece of undigested pigeon-pie? I knew a whole family whose happiness seemed to depend upon what the head of it ate for dinner. His dietary was watched, especially by the younger branches, with incessant anxiety. After mutton-chops and boiled rice, they could—providing he abstained from pudding—coax papa out of anything. Boiled beef boded evil; and in that case they cared very little to come in as usual to take their share of dessert. When lobster-salad had been partaken of, they crept about the house like mice, and kept as much as possible out of papa's way. During his paroxysms of ill-humour, reasoning was vain; neither the expostulations of his brother the rector, nor the kind intreaties of a wife whom he devotedly loved, were effectual in restraining his tetchy ebullitions of spleen. The demon within grew daily more influential, till he began to be shunned by his friends. No good effect was produced even by that. At length a medical adviser was consulted respecting his cadaverous appearance and certain pains which 'shot' across the shoulders. The doctor ordered him to Cheltenham, placed him on a strict regimen, enjoined frequent visits to the pump-room, and in three months our friend returned, to all appearance an angel of good temper. The banished roses returned to his cheeks—he felt strong and hearty, and never spoke a cross word. His meals were no longer watched, for the juveniles found him ever kind and complying, no matter what was for dinner. It was, however, observed that he ate much more sparingly than formerly, and never would allow such a thing as a round of salt beef or a lobster to enter his door.

It is not too much to affirm, that half the crimes to which human frailty is liable are concocted in the stomach. The poor are incited to mischief by the cravings of their digestive organs for something to do; whilst the rich are often impelled to wrong, because they give their digestive powers more than they *can* do. If the former could keep fuller stomachs, and the latter emptier ones, there would assuredly be fewer evil deeds in the world than are perpetrated at present.

THE FUEGIANS.

SEPARATED from the mainland of South America by the narrow Strait of Magellan, and extending southward for several hundred miles to Cape Horn, lies the Archipelago of Terra del Fuego. This name, literally signifying Land of Fire, was given to it by the early Spanish navigators, from the appearance which the whole coast presented of recent volcanic action. Subsequent voyagers, however, have been unable to detect any lava, pumice, obsidian, or other volcanic product, but have found the prevalent rock to be a trachytic trap, thus carrying us back to the geological epoch which gave birth to the Alps, Apennines, and crateriform hills of Auvergne. The group consists of one large island, four others of moderate extent, and a great number of rocky islets and reefs—the area of the whole being perhaps not less than that of Great Britain. The larger island, which forms the eastern and north-eastern portion, and occupies considerably more than half of the entire superficies, is generally known as King Charles's Southland; the four minor islands, which lie to the south and west, are Navarin, Hoste, South Desolation, and Clarence.

The physical aspect of the Archipelago is mountainous, rugged, and barren—consisting of a succession of hills and valleys, precipices and ravines. The shores are indented by deep but narrow arms of the sea, on whose sides rise the mountains to an elevation of from 2000 to 3000 feet—the highest being Sarmiento, on the west coast of Charles's Southland, and which attains the altitude of 6000 feet. During the greater part of the year the summits of the mountains are covered with snow—the snow line in that region being found so low as 3500 feet. This, together with the heavy rains which generally prevail, and the absence of sheltering forests, gives to the country a cold and inhospitable aspect. It must not be supposed, however, that the whole comes absolutely under this description, for the western district of the great island consists of a plain studded with a number of low hills, which are clothed with dwarf trees and creeping evergreens—the level grounds yielding a harsh dry grass, on which feed large flocks of the guanacoe, or wild alpaca.

The climate of Terra del Fuego is much colder than that of North Britain, though both are respectively situated at about the same distance from the antarctic and arctic circles. 'The difference,' says one authority, 'is perhaps best indicated by the different elevations at which the snow line occurs. In North Britain, it is supposed to be at an elevation of 5000 feet; but in Terra del Fuego, it occurs between 3000 and 3500 feet. The climate of Bergen, in Norway, is perhaps very similar to that of Terra del Fuego, where, as at Bergen, cloudy weather, rain, and wind, prevail throughout the year, and fine days are very rare. No season is quite free from frost: the thermometer, even in February, which corresponds to our August, descends occasionally some degrees below the freezing point; though during the winter the mean temperature is said to be 2½ degrees above that point. It seems that this peculiarity of the climate is to be attributed to the high temperature of the sea, which at its surface is never lower than 45 degrees Fahrenheit, especially in the Straits of Magellan, where the observations were made. The coasts that are exposed to the influence of the open ocean have probably a much colder climate, as during the winter they are surrounded by large fields of ice, which at that season occur as far north as 54 degrees south latitude, along the coast of King Charles's Southland. The level portion of that island suffers rather from want than from abundance of moisture, like the eastern coast of Patagonia.' This plain, indeed, is the only district that presents a habitable aspect; though, from the unsteadiness of the climate, it is very questionable if any agricultural operations could succeed.

Respecting the natural productions of the group very little is known. The United States Expedition found the lower hills covered with dense forests of beech, birch, willow, and winter-bark, but none fit for timber, the trees being not more than forty feet in extreme height. All of them had their tops bent to the north-east by the prevailing south-west winds, and looked at a distance more like heath than forest trees. Dry harsh grasses are prevalent in the lower valleys, among which occur the far-famed tussack so characteristic of the Falkland Islands; and plenty of scurvy-grass and wild celery were found close to the beach. The shores abound in fish and shell-fish; numbers of sea-fowl visit them periodically; and at certain seasons shoals of the humpback whale crowd the surrounding seas. The guanacoe is the only land animal of importance; but the natives do not seem capable either of entrapping it for food or for domestication, though it might be as serviceable to them in these respects as the llama to the Peruvians, or the rein-deer to the Esquimaux. Such are the natural features of this distant region, which, however uninviting, is not without its share of the human race, respecting whom we are enabled to glean some information from the recently published account of the United States Exploring Expedition under Captain Wilkes.

The natives belong to the Petcheree or Yacanacu tribe of Indians, a very scanty race, who are confined to the group and some of the adjacent portions of the continental coast. They lead a miserable life, only to be compared with that of some of the native Australians; they live on shell-fish, and squat themselves in places where these are found most abundantly, moving their habitations only when the supply is exhausted. 'During our stay,' says Captain Wilkes, 'we had at various times visits from the natives. They were all at first very shy, but after they found our friendly disposition towards them, they became more sociable and confiding. Before our departure from Orange Harbour, a bark canoe came alongside with an Indian, his squaw, and four children. They were entirely naked, with the exception of a small piece of seal-skin, only sufficient to cover one shoulder, and which is generally worn on the side from which the wind blows, affording them some little shelter against its piercing influence.

'The Petcherees are not more than five feet high, of a light copper colour, which is much concealed by smut and dirt, particularly on their faces, which they mark vertically with charcoal. They have short faces, narrow foreheads, and high cheek-bones. Their eyes are small, and usually black, the upper eyelids in the inner corner overlapping the under one, and bear a strong resemblance to those of the Chinese. Their nose is broad and flat, with wide-spread nostrils, mouth large, teeth white, large, and regular. The hair is long, lank, and black, hanging over the face, and is covered with white ashes, which gives them a hideous appearance. The whole face is compressed. Their bodies are remarkable, from the great development of the chest, shoulders, and vertebral column; their arms are long, and out of proportion; their legs small, and ill-made. There is, in fact, little difference between the size of the ankle and leg; and when standing, the skin at the knee hangs in a large loose fold. In some, the muscles of the leg appear almost wanting, and possess very little strength. This want of development in the muscles of the leg is owing to their constant sitting posture, both in their huts and canoes. Their skin is sensibly colder than ours. It is impossible to fancy anything in human nature more filthy. They are an ill-shapen and ugly race. They have little or no idea of the relative value of articles, even of those that one would suppose were of the utmost use to them, such as iron and glass-ware. A glass bottle broken into pieces is valued as much as a knife. Red flannel, torn into strips, pleases them more than in the piece; they wound it around their heads as a kind of turban; and it was amusing to see their satisfaction at this small acquisition.

'The children were quite small, and nestled in the bottom of the canoe on some dry grass. The woman and eldest boy paddled the canoe, the man being employed to bail out the water and attend to the fire, which is always carried in the bottom of the canoe, on a few stones and ashes, which the water surrounds.

'Their canoes are constructed of bark, are very frail, and sewed with shreds of whalebone, seal-skin, and twigs. They are sharp at both ends, and are kept in shape, as well as strengthened, by a number of stretchers lashed to the gunwale. These Indians seldom venture outside the kelp, by the aid of which they pull themselves along; and their paddles are so small, as to be of little use in propelling their canoes, unless it is calm. Some of the officers thought they recognised a party on the Hermit Islands that had been on board ship at Orange Harbour. If this was the case, they must have ventured across the Bay of Nassau, a distance of some ten or twelve miles. This, if correct, would go to prove that there is more intercourse among them than their frail barks would lead one to expect.

'Their huts are generally found built close to the shore, at the head of some small bay, in a secluded spot, and sheltered from the prevailing winds. They are built of boughs or small trees, stuck in the earth, and brought together at the top, where they are firmly bound by bark, sedge, and twigs. Smaller branches are then interlaced, forming a tolerably compact wicker-work, and on this grass, turf, and bark are laid, making the hut quite warm, and impervious to the wind and snow, though not quite so to the rain. The usual dimensions of these huts are seven or eight feet in diameter, and about four or five feet in height. They have an oval hole to creep in at. The fire is built in a small excavation in the middle of the hut. The floor is of clay, which has the appearance of having been well kneaded. The usual accompaniment of a hut is a conical pile of shells opposite the door, nearly as large as the hut itself. Their occupancy of a hut seems to be limited to the supply of shell-fish, consisting of mussels and limpits, in the neighbourhood.

'These natives are never seen but in their huts or canoes. The impediments to their communication by land are great, growing out of the mountainous and rocky character of the country, intersected with inlets deep and impassable, and in most places bounded by abrupt precipices, together with a soil which may be termed a quagmire, on which it is difficult to walk. This prevails on the hills as well as in the plains and valleys. The impenetrable nature of the forest, with the dense undergrowth of thorny bushes, renders it impossible for them to overcome or contend with these difficulties. They appear to live in families, and not in tribes, and do not seem to acknowledge any chief.

'On the 11th of March three bark canoes arrived, containing four men, four women, a girl about sixteen years old, four little boys, and four infants, one of the latter about a week old, and quite naked. The thermometer was at 46 degrees Fahrenheit. They had rude weapons; namely, slings to throw stones, three rude spears pointed at the end with bone, and notched on one side with barbed teeth. With this they catch their fish, which are in great quantities among the kelp. Two of the natives were induced to come on board, after they had been alongside for upwards of an hour, and received many presents, for which they gave their spears, a dog, and some of their rude native trinkets. They did not show or express surprise at anything on board, except when seeing one of the carpenters engaged in boring a hole with a screw-augur through a plank, which would have been a long task for them. They were very talkative, smiling when spoken to, and often bursting into loud laughter, but instantly settling into their natural serious and sober cast.

'They were found to be great mimics, both in gesture and sound, and would repeat any word of our language with great correctness of pronunciation. Their imitations of sounds were truly astonishing. One of them ascended and descended the octave perfectly, following the sounds of the violin correctly. It was then found he could sound the common chords, and follow through the semitone scale with scarcely an error. They have all musical voices, speak in the note G sharp, ending with the semitone A, when asking for presents, and were continually singing.

'Their mimicry became annoying, and precluded our getting at any of their words or ideas. It not only extended to words or sounds, but actions also, and was at times truly ridiculous. The usual manner for interrogating for names was quite unsuccessful. On pointing to the nose, for instance, they did the same. Anything they saw done they would mimic, and with an extraordinary degree of accuracy. On these canoes approaching the ship, the principal one of the family, or chief, standing up in his canoe, made a harangue. He spoke in G natural, and did not vary his voice more than a semitone. The pitch of the voice of the female is an octave higher. Although they have been heard to shout quite loud, yet they cannot endure a noise. When the drum beat, or a gun was fired, they invariably stopped their ears. They always speak to each other in a whisper. Their cautious manner and movements prove them to be a timid race. The men are exceedingly jealous of their women, and will not allow any one, if they can help it, to enter their huts, particularly boys.

'The women were never suffered to come on board. They appeared modest in the presence of strangers. They never move from a sitting posture, or rather a squat, with their knees close together, reaching to their chin, their feet in contact, and touching the lower part of the body. They are extremely ugly. Their hands and feet were small, and well-shaped, and from appearance, they are not accustomed to do any hard work. They appear very fond, and seem careful of, their young children, though on several occasions they offered them for sale for a trifle. They have their faces smutted all over, and it was thought, from the hideous appearance of the females, produced in part by their being painted and smutted, that they had been disfigured by the men previous to coming alongside. The men are employed in building the huts, obtaining food, and providing for their other wants. The women were generally seen paddling their canoes.

'When this party of natives left the ship and reached the shore, the women remained in their canoes, and the men began building their temporary huts. The little children were seen capering quite naked on the beach, although the thermometer was at 40 degrees. On the hut being finished, which occupied about an hour, the women went on shore to take possession of it. They all seemed quite happy and contented.

'Towards evening Messrs Waldron and Drayton visited their huts. Before they reached the shore, the natives were seen making a fire on the beach for their reception, evidently to avoid their entering the huts. On landing, one of the men seemed anxious to talk with them. He pointed to the ship, and tried to express many things by gestures; then pointed to the south-east, and then again to the ship, after which, clasping his hands, as in our mode of prayer, he said "Eloah, Eloah," as though he thought we had come from God.

'After a little time they gained admittance to the hut. The men creeping in first, squatted themselves directly in front of the women, all holding out the small piece of seal-skin, to allow the heat to reach their bodies. The women were squatted three deep behind the men, the oldest in front nestling the infants. After being in the hut, Mr Drayton endeavoured to call the attention of the man who had made signs to him before entering, to know whether they had any idea of a Supreme Being. The same man then put his hands together, repeating as before, "Eloah, Eloah." From his manner it was inferred that they had some idea of God or a Supreme Being.

'Their mode of expressing friendship is by jumping up and down. They made Messrs Waldron and Drayton jump with them on the beach before entering the hut, took hold of their arms, facing them, and, jumping two or three inches from the ground, making them keep time to some simple song which they chanted.

'All our endeavours to find out how they ignited their fire proved unavailing. It must be exceedingly difficult for them to accomplish, judging from the care they take of it, always carrying it with them in their canoes, and the danger they thus run of injuring themselves by it.

'Their food consists of limpets, mussels, and other shell-fish. Quantities of fish, and some seals, are now and then taken among the kelp, and, with berries of various kinds, and wild celery, they do not want. They seldom cook their food much. The shell-fish are detached from the shell by heat, and the fish are partly roasted in their skins, without being cleaned.

'When on board, one of them was induced to sit at the dinner-table: after a few lessons, he handled his knife and fork with much dexterity. He refused both spirits and wine, but was very fond of sweetened water. Salt provisions were not at all to his liking, but rice and plumpudding were agreeable to his taste, and he literally crammed them into his mouth. After his appetite had been satisfied, he was in great good humour, singing his "Hey meh leh," dancing, and laughing. His mimicry prevented any satisfactory inquiries being made of him relative to a vocabulary.

'One of these natives remained on board for upwards of a week, and being washed and combed, he became two or three shades lighter in colour. Clothes were put on him. He was about twenty-three years of age, and was unwell the whole time he was on board, from eating such quantities of rice, &c. His astonishment was very great on attending divine service. The moment the chaplain began to read from the book, his eyes were riveted upon him, where they remained as long as he continued to read. At the end of the week he became dissatisfied, and was set on shore, and soon appeared naked again. It was observed on presents being made, that those who did not receive any began a sort of whining cry, putting on the most doleful-looking countenances imaginable.

'They are much addicted to theft if any opportunity offers. The night before they left the bay, they stole and cut up one of the wind-sails, which had been scrubbed and hung up on shore to dry.

'Although we had no absolute proof of it, we are inclined to the belief that they bury their dead in caves.'

Such is the amount of our information respecting this simple and primitive people. We know nothing of their origin, of their social manners and customs, of their language, or of their religion. They are a little section of the human race removed perhaps the farthest of any from civilisation, and in whom, from that very circumstance, we take all the deeper interest. External conditions seem to detain them at the lowest verge of human existence; and yet we believe they might make progress to a better state of being, notwithstanding the apparently insuperable difficulties which now oppose it.

ARTIFICIAL DUCK-HATCHING IN CHINA.

ONE of the greatest lions in Chusan (for we have lions here as well as you in London) is an old Chinaman, who hatches duck eggs in thousands every spring by artificial heat. The first question put to a sight-seeing stranger who comes here is, whether he has seen the hatching process; and if he has not, he is immediately taken out to see the old Chinaman and his ducks. An account of the house and the process will probably interest you, and I therefore send you a leaf of my private journal, which I wrote on the morning of my first visit.

It was a beautiful morning in the end of May, just such a morning as we have in the same month in England, perhaps a little warmer; the sun was upon the grass, the breeze was cool and refreshing, and altogether the effect produced upon the system was of the most invigorating kind, and I suppose I felt it more, having just arrived from Hong-Kong, and suffering slightly from the unhealthy atmosphere of that island. The mist and vapour were rolling lazily along the sides of the hills which surround the plain on which the city of Tinghai is built; the Chinese, who are generally early risers, were already proceeding to their daily labours; and although the greater part of the labouring population are very poor, yet they seem contented and happy. Walking through the city, out at the north gate, and leaving the ramparts behind, I passed through some rice fields, the first crop of which is just planted, and a five minutes' walk brought me to the poor man's cottage. He received me with Chinese politeness; asked me to sit down; offered me tea and his pipe, two things always at hand in a Chinese house, and perfectly indispensable. Having civilly declined his offer, I asked permission to examine his hatching-house, to which he immediately led the way, and gave me the following account of the process. First, however, let me describe the house.

The Chinese cottages generally are wretched buildings of mud and stone, with damp earthen floors, scarcely fit for cattle to sleep in, and remind one of what the Scottish cottages were a few years ago; which now, however, are happily among the things that were. The present one was no exception to the general rule: bad fitting, loose, creaking doors; paper windows, dirty and torn; ducks, geese, fowls, dogs, and pigs in the house and at the doors, seemingly as important, and having equal rights with their masters; then there were children, grandchildren, and, for aught that I know, great-grandchildren, all together, forming a most motley group, which, with their shaved heads, long tails, and strange costume, would be a capital subject for the pencil of Cruikshank or H. B.

The hatching-house is built at the side of the cottage, and in a kind of long shed, with mud walls, and thickly thatched with straw. Along the ends and down one side of the building are a number of round straw baskets, well plastered with mud, to prevent them from taking fire. In the bottom of each basket there is a tile placed, or rather the tile forms the bottom of the basket; upon this the fire acts, a small fireplace being below each basket. The top is open, having of course a straw cover, which fits closely, and which covers the eggs when the process is going on, the whole having the appearance of a vase which we sometimes see placed upon a pedestal at home, or rather exactly like the Chinese manure tanks, which perhaps are less known. In the centre of the shed there are a number of large shelves placed one above another, upon which the eggs are laid at a certain stage of the process.

When the eggs are brought, they are put into the baskets described above, the fire is lighted below, and, according to some observations made with a thermometer, the heat kept up seeming to range from 95 to 102 degrees; but the Chinamen regulate the heat by their own feelings, and not by thermometer, and therefore it will of course vary considerably. In four or five days after the eggs have been subject to this temperature, they are taken carefully out, one by one, to a door in which a number of holes have been bored exactly the size of the eggs; they are then held in these holes, and the Chinamen look through to the light, and are able to tell whether they are good or not. If good, they are taken back, and replaced in their former quarters; if bad, they are of course excluded. In nine or ten days after this, that is, about fourteen days from the commencement, the eggs are taken out of the baskets, and spread out on the shelves which I have already noticed. Here no fire-heat is applied, but they are covered over with cotton and a kind of blanket, remaining in these circumstances about fourteen days more, when the young ducks burst their shells, and the poor Chinaman's shed teems with life. These shelves are large, and capable of holding many thousands of eggs; and it is really a curious sight, particularly during the two last days, when the hatching takes place. The Chinese who rear the young ducks in the surrounding country know exactly the day when they will be ready for removal, and in two days after the shell is burst, the whole of these little creatures are sold, and conveyed to their new quarters.—*Correspondent of Athenæum.*

MONASTIC LIFE IN SCOTLAND.

Their mode of living may be summed up in a sentence—an utter neglect of the duty of religious teachers, and the untrammelled gratification of every passion. Hunting was a favourite pastime of theirs, and of none of their privileges were they more jealous. Their dependents were dragged before their courts, to endure temporal punishment in this world, and to have directed against them anathemas as to the next, for the smallest infraction of their hunting or fishing privileges. With regard to nobles as powerful as themselves, complaints are made to the sovereign, and solemn obligations are taken for the security of these sacred rights. Hart and hind, boar and roe, the eyries of falcons and tersels, are to be preserved intact; and hunting with hounds or nets, or setting traps to destroy game, were sins which scarcely repentance could atone for. The monks themselves, too, appear to have been given somewhat to poaching, if we may judge from the jealousy of the neighbouring proprietors. The dull monotony of a religious life they pleasantly variegated by such exhilarating sports, and the contemporary literature is rich in the glowing descriptions of their skill. On rising at the matin bell, the monk, after his orisons were said, would, if of a placid disposition, take his rod, and on the banks of the classic Tweed, or at the Falls of Clyde, he could with great benefit pass the forenoon. But if, again, of a more energetic disposition, his hounds and his nets would do effectual execution upon the game of the monastic preserves. On the monk's return, he would shrive any unfortunate victim, who, like John de Graham, was ignorant of the law, and susceptible of flattery, and, with an appetite sharpened by his forenoon's exercise, he would sit down to the plentiful repast which his hunting or fishing skill had catered. Wheaten bread was provided by the fidelity of his flock; a flagon of wine, too, was not wanting to wash down the repast; and from a transaction with certain Florentine merchants, it would appear that the priests of Glasgow had acquired a refined taste for foreign luxuries. Good living, however, did not always thrive with the monkish constitution. Pious as they were, they still were subject to the ills of life, and not above the aid of the Materia Medica. The Glasgow fathers especially appear to have been very much troubled with peculiar affections of the stomach, and have formally preserved in their cartulary a famous pill, to prevent flatulency. The peculiar ingredients of this composition are stated in detail; but as our medical knowledge is not so extensive as to enable us to speak decidedly of its merits, we think it better not to quote the receipt, in case it may be incautiously applied. Another celebrated pill is given, with the recommendation that Pope Alexander (the Sixth?) frequently used it, and which had the great advantage of not compelling the patient to intermit his usual diet or his flagon of wine. The religious service of the day, it might be thought, would break up for a little the hilarity of the jolly brotherhood. But this opinion is founded on mistake. They threw a pleasant air even over the gloom of devotion, and in their religious duties they were unable to restrain their jokes. This having apparently scandalised the vulgar, certain rules were enacted, by which their conduct in this respect was to be regulated. The cartulary of Moray contains the *Constitutiones Lyncolnienses*, inserted as proper rules for the priests of that northern province, from which we learn that they were to enter the place of worship, not with insolent looks, but decently, and in order; and were to be guilty of no laughing, or of attempting the perpetration of any base jokes (*turpi risu aut jocu*), and at the same time were to conduct their whisperings in an under tone. Nature, however, will have its way. A full stomach is not the best provocative to lively attention, and it is therefore far from wonderful that the fathers dosed. Ingenuity provided a remedy even for this, and the curious visitor will find in the niches of the ruined walls of the ecclesiastical edifices of other days oscillating seats, which turn upon a pivot, and require the utmost care of the sitter to keep steady. The poor monk who would dare to indulge in one short nap, would, by this most cruel contrivance, be thrown forward upon the stone floor of the edifice, to the great danger of his neck, and be covered at the same time with 'the base laughter and joking' of his brethren.—*North British Review.*

SLOW PROGRESS OF IMPROVEMENTS.

The *Times*, a few months ago, had some remarks on this subject, in which there is too much truth. After alluding to the number of associations for public improvement which every day gives birth to, and which seem to imply that there is no government to take up such public matters, it proceeds to say—'The reports of commissioners published within these ten years are a perfect encyclopædia of commercial, statistical, and sanitary lore. There are blue books enough to remodel a world, if a world could be found tractable enough for the process. But there it ends. As for any good that's done, parliament might as well be a club of *savans*. It ostentatiously proclaims its knowledge. It perceives and commends improvement, but acquiesces in deterioration. Three sessions have passed away since the report from the Poor Law Commissioners on the sanitary condition of the labouring population. The volume is fast sinking down the gulf of time, and nothing is done. Other reports on the same subject have followed, and still remain, what for the present they are likely to remain, virgin reports, wedded to no legislation. Our respectable senators might as well amuse themselves with dropping straws into a stream, and watching their downward progress, as in putting out blue books, destined only for the race of oblivion. The absurdity must stare our legislators in the very face, when they find themselves announcing truisms and notorieties acknowledged and known by all the world years and years. Why do people who, in their place and legitimate post, can remedy ills, content themselves with proclaiming them to those who cannot? All the world knows, of course, that Harley Street is not only a pleasanter, but a healthier locality than Houndsditch; that streets are better than lanes, lanes than courts and alleys; that one family in a tenement is better than ten, one bed in a room better than half-a-dozen, and so on; that air, water, and fire, are as necessary to health as to comfort; that sewers under ground are better than noonday filth. Since there were cities, these truths have been matters of painful recognition. The recent reports only show, with details and circumstances, that what is true everywhere, and especially of all populous cities, is true in the most populous city of all. My lords and gentlemen, we know it—everybody knows it: what then? The answer is, that we are to have a society to further these objects. Why! what are members of parliament made for, if they are to delegate the economical functions of government to No. 17, two pair to the right, Exeter Hall? The legislature *can* effect these objects—a society *can not!* Every year only strengthens the conviction of sensible men, that governments must give a higher place to questions of social economy, and undertake them with a stronger hand, a wider aim, and more uniform system. The great object of government is the *common weal.* Whatever the state can recognise and pronounce to be hurtful to the public, ought to be considered a *crime.* Nay, it should not allow a man to hurt himself if it can prevent it, for wilful self-injury is only a degree of self-destruction. An undrained street, an uncovered sewer, a crowded garret, want of water, an atmosphere needlessly vitiated with miasma or smoke, are all so many wholesale manslaughters which kill their thousands to the ones that die less silently by the knife or the bludgeon, by careless carters or uncovered machinery. We know the jealousy which stands between sovereign power and private liberty; but we venture to predict a time when people will pronounce a liberty to foster hotbeds of moral crime and physical infection, or to poison the air breathed by myriads, as a more enormous license than the toleration of pirates or banditti.'

INFLUENCE OF ACCIDENT ON GREAT MEN.

It is a curious coincidence that the two greatest Chancery lawyers of their day should both have been forced into the profession by incidental circumstances. Romilly says, that what principally influenced his decision was the being thus enabled to leave his small fortune in his father's hands, instead of buying a sworn clerk's seat with it. 'At a later period of my life—after a success at the bar which my wildest and most sanguine dreams had never painted to me—when I was gaining an income of L.8000 or L.9000 a-year—I have often reflected how all that prosperity had arisen out of the pecuniary difficulties and confined circumstances of my father.' Wedderburn (Lord Loughborough) began as an advocate at the Scotch bar. In the course of an altercation with the Lord President, he was provoked to tell his lordship that he had said as a judge what he could not justify as a gentleman. Being ordered to make an apology, he refused, and left the Scotch for the English bar. What every one thought his ruin, turned out the best thing that could happen to him—

'There's a divinity that shapes our ends,
Rough hew them how we may.'

Lord Tenterden's early destination was changed by a disappointment. When he and Mr Justice Richards were going the home circuit, they visited the cathedral at Canterbury together. Richards commended the voice of a singing man in the choir. 'Ah,' said Lord Tenterden, 'that is the only man I ever envied! When at school in this town, we were candidates for a chorister's place, and he obtained it.' It is now well known that the Duke of Wellington, when a subaltern, was anxious to retire from the army, and actually applied to Lord Camden (then lord-lieutenant of Ireland) for a commissionership of customs! It is not always true, then, that men destined to play conspicuous parts in the world have a consciousness of their coming greatness, or patience to bide their time. Their hopes grow as their capacity expands with circumstances; honours on honours arise like Alps on Alps; in ascending one they catch a glimpse of another, till the last and highest, which was veiled in mist when they started, stands out in bold relief against the sky.—*Edinburgh Review.*

IMITATION.

Amongst the causes assigned for the continuance and diffusion of the same moral sentiments amongst mankind, may be mentioned imitation. The efficacy of this principle is most observable in children: indeed, if there be anything in them which deserves the name of an instinct, it is their propensity to imitation. Now, there is nothing which children imitate, or apply more readily, than expressions of affection and aversion, of approbation, hatred, resentment, and the like; and when these passions and expressions are once connected, which they soon will be by the same association which unites words with their ideas, the passion will follow the expression, and attach upon the object to which the child has been accustomed to apply the epithet.—*Paley.*

GOOD SEED.

Like seeds deep hid in the thankless earth,
Or buried in dead men's tombs,
'Till the spade of the labourer casts them forth,
Or the traveller's search exhumes—
Revived again in the upper air,
Not one of their powers is lost;
Plant them, they root and flourish fair,
And bring forth a goodly host
Of offspring, though centuries may have past
Since they in their darksome cells were cast.

So is the word the poet preaches:
The good seed may seem to die,
And the fruit of the holy creed he teaches
Be hidden from human eye:
If the vital germ of truth be there,
It never can perish wholly,
Rich blossom and fruit it will surely bear,
Though for long years buried lowly;
Other hands may bring it to light, and tend;
But the seed of good thoughts has a fruitful end.

D. M. M.

ROOKS BREEDING IN NOVEMBER.

In the month of November 1844, writes a correspondent of the Zoologist, my attention was attracted to a large solitary nest in the outermost branches of an old elm tree, not far from the park entrance to Broughton Castle, Oxfordshire: at first I concluded it must be a magpie's, which had become exposed by the fall of the leaf; however, on looking again, I discovered that it was inhabited by a pair of rooks; and was afterwards told by some labourers, who had watched its building, that the rooks were now sitting. By the assistance of a glass, I was soon able to confirm their statement, as well as to watch the process of incubation. I think it must have been on the 18th of November that the young were hatched, at least I judged so from seeing the old ones carry up food (grubs, &c. which seemed plentiful) for several days after that date. The frosty mornings of the following week made the young ones cry out bitterly; when the weather becoming more and more severe, put an end to their sufferings. It seemed some time before the old ones could believe it; at any rate they were very unwilling to quit the branches near their nest. The situation which they had selected was several hundred yards from the regular rookery, and, during the time of incubation, six or seven other rooks might be seen looking on in mute astonishment at their neighbours' mistake. I do not recollect ever having seen on record such an instance as the above. Was it the second brood of the year, or the brood of birds which were hatched in the early spring? [We are aware of a pair of house-sparrows having commenced building for their second brood on the 14th of September in the same year. The nest, which was among the higher branches of a plane, was completed in a day or two from an abundance of dried hay and knot-grass at hand, and the female began to sit on the 25th or 26th. A few days after, the branches were stript of their decaying leaves, and the nest thrown to the ground, showing the remains of five eggs, four of which would have been productive.]

THE REVENUES OF THE MIND.

The ear and the eye are the mind's receivers: but the tongue is only busied in expending the treasure received. If, therefore, the revenues of the mind be uttered as fast or faster than they are received, it cannot be but that the mind must needs be bare, and can never lay up for purchase. But if the receivers take in still with no utterance, the mind may soon grow a burden to itself, and unprofitable to others. I will not lay up too much, and utter nothing, lest I be covetous: nor spend much, and store up little, lest I be prodigal and poor.—*Bishop Hall.*

Published by W. and R. Chambers, High Street, Edinburgh (also 98 Miller Street, Glasgow); and, with their permission, by W. S. Orr, Amen Corner, London.—Printed by W. and R. Chambers, Edinburgh.

☞ Complete sets of the Journal, *First Series*, in twelve volumes, and also odd numbers to complete sets, may be had from the publishers or their agents.—A stamped edition of the Journal is now issued, price 2½d., to go free by post.

CONDUCTED BY WILLIAM AND ROBERT CHAMBERS, EDITORS OF 'CHAMBERS'S INFORMATION FOR THE PEOPLE,' 'CHAMBERS'S EDUCATIONAL COURSE,' &c.

No. 80. New Series. SATURDAY, JULY 12, 1845. Price 1½d.

NEW FACTS RESPECTING MARY QUEEN OF SCOTS.

A Russian noble, Prince Labanoff, has devoted fourteen years to the collection of documents respecting Mary Queen of Scots, including her own letters, and the communications of her ambassadors, and the result of his labours has just appeared in seven goodly octavos. The degree of originality pertaining to this publication may be partly estimated from the fact, that it presents four hundred of the queen's own letters, hitherto unknown to the public. The most remarkable feature of the work is its tendency to clear Mary's name of much of the reproach that has hitherto rested upon it, and to add to the likelihood which formerly an acute, and at the same time impartial person, might have apprehended, that the common view of this lady's character is in a great measure a piece of party fiction. We propose here to run over a few of the new matters which combine in Prince Labanoff's collection to this effect, not with any design to consider the question critically, which indeed in our short space would be a vain attempt, but merely to help a little towards the gratification of the public curiosity on a point which will be adverted to in many quarters where the perusal of the entire book is unattainable.

What appears most broadly and strikingly in this collection is, the zeal and firmness of Mary in her religion. From first to last—as the queen of two states, and as a hopeless captive in a foreign land—she maintains but one tone as a sincere Catholic, ready alike to use power when she has it, and when she has not, to sacrifice her life, for the restoration of that form of faith in her own country and in England. It appears that, at the close of her life, having no hope of her son siding with the Catholic party, and having been heartlessly deserted by him, she bequeathed all her interest in the English succession to Philip II. of Spain; an impotent act of course, but showing will. Seeing this determination of her mind, and remembering the atrocious acts done in those days for the objects cherished by her—and by none were more wicked deeds done than by her own uncles of the house of Guise—we are not to wonder that she should have had so little friendship from the partisans of the opposite faith, or that men of their stamp in such an age should have been governed by no nice scruples in their conduct towards her. It is not our part, however, to regard the motives or objects of parties: we are called on solely to consider their acts, to ascertain what these truly were, and to judge of them according to the abiding and universal rules of justice.

The more controverted part of Mary's life commences with her marriage to Lord Darnley in 1565. It now clearly appears that she was led to marriage at this time against her will, and as a measure of political expediency; and that she chose Darnley from no personal preference, no romantic attachment, as has been thought, but because he was a Stuart, next to herself in the English succession, and, as a Catholic, agreeable to that section of her subjects which she was most anxious to gratify. One powerful consideration in this marriage was its enabling her to bear her part against the machinations of her natural brother, the Earl of Murray, whose ambition it was to be in one shape or another the actual ruler of Scotland. The marriage was disappointing to Murray and to Elizabeth; and the former, with the secret aid of the latter, immediately raised a rebellion against his sister. Defeated by Mary and the faithful part of her subjects, he fled to the English court, where he received protection. The concern which Randolph, the English resident at Edinburgh, had in Murray's rebellion, is shown in a letter of Mary to her English ambassador, Robert Melville, now published for the first time: 'Melville,' she says, 'it is not unknown to you how, before your departing, we had granted our pardon to John Johnstown, who coming home, and this same day being before us, we inquired of him the cause of his departing. He answered, that in the middle of August last he was sent for by Master Randolph to come and speak with him at his lodging, at David Forrester's, whither he came; and after some declaration made to him by Mr Randolph, how he was my Lord of Murray's servant, and one whom he would specially trust, Master Randolph delivered to him three sacks of money sealed, wherein was contained (as was said) three thousand crowns, which he, at Randolph's desire, conveyed to St Andrews, and delivered the same to my Lady Murray, receiving her receipt for it, which he carried back to Randolph. And fearing that the matter might be discovered, he (Johnstown) durst not remain, but departed. And at the very time that we were receiving this declaration, Mr Randolph happening to be present with our council discussing matters relating to the borders, we thought it not inconvenient to report to him the report made to us, and show him plainly that in consideration the queen, our good sister, his mistress, had not only to our dearest brother, the king of France, and to his ambassador resident there, but also to Monsieur Rambouletz, his late ambassador here, and by Randolph to ourselves declared, that she had neither aided, nor was willing to aid and support our rebels with men, money, or otherwise, to our displeasure; which we take to be undoubtedly true, and will look for no other at her hands; such account do we make of her and her declaration, given in that behalf, which we can in no wise mistrust. Yet that he, her servant and minister, occupying a peaceable charge, contrary to her will and meaning, should undertake a thing so prejudicial to the peace, we could not but think very strange of it, and had right good occasion to be offended with his misbehaviour, that within our own realm had comforted them with money to our displeasure, who were our rebels, and with whom we had just cause to be offended.'* Randolph, she adds, first denied the charge, but when evidence was brought against him, he stood at bay, and announced that he held himself as only answerable for his conduct to his own mistress. The crookedness of policy thus shown in Mary's enemies contrasts strongly with her implicit, unsuspecting faith in the good feeling and conscientiousness of Elizabeth.

The documents here adduced respecting the murder of Riccio, make clear the motives of the various parties; Darnley having none besides his wish to secure the crown matrimonial, in which the poor Italian had opposed him. Randolph wrote at the time to Cecil a scandalous letter impeaching the queen's honour. His credibility as a witness against her so soon after she had convicted him of the basest duplicity, might be safely left to impartial consideration; but it is well to know that, from the various documents now brought forward, there cannot remain the slightest shade of suspicion against Mary on this score. The assassination of Riccio, over and above the personal motive of Darnley, was a Protestant move necessary to turn affairs at the Scottish court, so as to allow of Murray and his friends being pardoned for their rebellion. It was, in the sixteenth century, what a change of ministry through a vote in the House of Commons is at the present day. The religious feelings of that time, so far from forbidding, stimulated such barbarities.

The whole behaviour of Darnley from this time was such as to alienate the affections of the queen. He seems to have been an utter fool, with all the qualities of intractableness and waywardness which that term implies. Yet all the evidence that appears represents Mary as submitting to his follies with patience. In November 1566, four months after the birth of her son, her principal lords—Murray, Bothwell, Huntley, Argyle, and Maitland of Lethington—came formally to her at Craigmillar, to propose that she should divorce Darnley; but she told them that she would abide the will of Providence to be relieved from her present sufferings, and positively refused to go into the scheme. One reason for this resolution on Mary's part may have been of a political nature. In her communications at this time with Elizabeth, it is evident that her predominant aim was to secure her being declared the heir-presumptive of the English throne. It might seem to her that the English people were not the more likely to favour her hopes, if they saw her engaged in suing a divorce from her husband, not only from a consideration of the indecorum which always attends such an act, but because it lessened her prospect of heirs of her own body. Within a month of the death of Darnley, namely, on the 13th January 1567, she is found writing a complaisant letter to Elizabeth, urging her pretensions to be declared the heir of the English crown. 'Always,' she says, 'have we commended us and the equity of our cause to you, and have certainly looked for your friendship therein; whereon we have continually trusted; and now we think us fully assured of the same, having thereof so large proof by knowledge of your good mind and entire affection, declared by your said ambassador, as also by our servant Robert Melville; not doubting but in time convenient you will proceed to the perfecting and consummation of that which you have begun to utter, as well to your own people as to other nations, the opinion you have of the equity of our cause and your affection toward us; and namely, in the examining of the will supposed to be made by the king your father, which some would lay as a bar in our way; according to your own promise to us, as well contained in your letter sent by our servant Robert Melville, whereof he has made us report that you would proceed therein before your nobility (being at this present assembly) departed towards their own houses.' At the date of this letter, Darnley was sick of small-pox. Immediately after, Mary was informed of a plot which he was alleged to have formed for seizing the infant prince, and getting himself made regent in his name. Even while having such grounds of suspicion against him, she is found writing to her ambassador in France, the Archbishop of Glasgow—'Always we perceive him occupied and busy enough to have inquisition of our doings; which, God willing, shall always be such as *none shall have occasion to be offended with them, or to report of us any way but honourably*; howsoever he, his father, and their favourers speak, who we know want no good will to give us trouble, if their power equalled their inclinations.' It need hardly be asked, if a person with such reasons for standing well with the world, and who gives such incontestable evidence of her having been alive to those reasons, was at all likely to be engaged in a conspiracy for the murder of her husband? an event which, whether she had any concern in it or not, could not but be damaging to her immediate affairs, as well as her prospects.

A letter of Mary to the Archbishop of Glasgow, written the morning after the murder of Darnley, adverts to some information he had communicated to her as to designs against herself; and she expresses her belief that the explosion of the house was designed for herself likewise, as she had slept in it three out of the seven preceding days, and was only prevented from sleeping in it that night by the chance of having had to attend a masque at Holyroodhouse. Bothwell, the actual murderer, now comes prominently forward. The common supposition is, that Mary favoured his escape from the trial to which he was subjected at the instance of Darnley's father. It appears that he was in reality protected by a confederation of nobles, amongst whom were those who soon afterwards deposed the queen. These men now associated in a bond for the purpose of procuring a marriage between Mary and this atrocious member of their corps. And it is remarkable of this association that its leader, Morton, had been concerned in the murder of Darnley. That the queen had any inclination to the proposed match, there is not a particle of sound evidence; for the celebrated letters afterwards produced in a casket are manifestly a base and clumsy forgery. That it was, on religious grounds, objectionable to Mary, is indubitable, for Bothwell was a Protestant. See, then, the actual progress of events. Bothwell, armed with the bond favouring his suit of Mary's hand, seized her person as she was travelling from Stirling to Edinburgh, and immediately conducted her to his castle of Dunbar, where she was kept a prisoner for several days. Let it be remembered that, at that time, there was no standing army, not even a regiment of guards, to support the head of the government in Scotland. Mary depended, for the means of maintaining her place and function, upon the good-will of the nobility. Is it surprising that, sinking under this indignity, to which her chief nobles appeared to have conspired, she should have been induced, for the sake of her reputation as a woman, as well as for maintaining her place as a queen, to consent to the odious match which was soon after carried into effect? And can we have any doubt of the real views of Morton and his confederates in promoting the marriage, when we find them immediately after taking advantage of the infamy which it produced, to raise the standard of revolt against her, and in brief space effecting her dethronement? In the whole series of proceedings, Mary appears as the victim of force. At the marriage, she was habited in deep mourning. The state of her feelings *on the evening of the day of the nuptials*, is evinced by De Croc, the French ambassador, who visited her at her own request. 'I perceived,' says he, 'a strange formality between her and her husband, which she begged me to excuse, saying that if I saw her sad it was because she did not wish to be happy, as she said she never could be, *wishing only for death*. Yesterday,' he adds, 'being all alone in a

* For the translation of this and some of the ensuing extracts from the queen's correspondence, we are indebted to the Athenæum.

closet with the Earl of Bothwell, she called aloud for them to give her a knife to kill herself with. Those who were in the room adjoining the closet heard her.'* There is also evidence of Bothwell regarding her as a person requiring to be watched, that he might work out his ends successfully. In her own communication to the French court respecting the marriage, she speaks as follows:—'When he saw us like to reject all his suit and offers, in the end he showed us how far he had proceeded with our whole nobility and principals of our estates, and what they had promised him under their own handwriting. If we had cause, then, to be astonished, we remit us to the judgment of the king, the queen, and others our friends. Seeing ourself in his power, sequestered from the company of our servants and others of whom we might ask counsel; yea, seeing them upon whose counsel and fidelity we had before depended, whose force ought and must maintain our authority, without whom in a manner we are nothing, beforehand already won over to his wishes, and so we left alone as it were a prey unto him; many things we resolved with ourself, but could never find a way of escape. And yet gave he us little space to meditate with ourself, ever pressing us with continual and importunate suit.' It may be asked if this is the language in which she could have been expected to write to a friendly potentate respecting a husband whom she had married under the influence of an infatuated passion, as represented by her enemies. In short, while there is no worthy evidence of any love on Mary's part towards Bothwell, or of a single motive of another kind which she could have for such a marriage; while, on the contrary, it was, as the event proved, likely to be most injurious to her; there is abundant evidence of the affair having sprung from the ambition of this profligate man, and been effected by the assistance of a set of his compeers, who saw in this step a sure means of effecting an object long desired by them—the destruction of a ruler opposed to them in faith, and whose continuance in power was dangerous to the Protestant cause. In five weeks from the marriage these men had immured the queen in Lochleven, while Bothwell was an outlaw roaming through the northern seas.

The whole subsequent conduct of Mary respecting Bothwell is accordant with the supposition of the marriage having been contrary to her will. She parted with him at Carberry without a sigh. In her letters after that event, she is not found alluding to him. That she declined a proposed divorce the month after their parting, may be considered as owing to her having been pregnant of a daughter, now ascertained to have been born at Lochleven, and who died a nun in France. The trial got up between Elizabeth and the Scotch lords, during her imprisonment in England, with a view to establish her guilt, ended, as is well known, in a complete failure. But the crowning evidence on the exculpatory side is in the circumstances connected with the death of Bothwell. This wretched man perished in a Danish prison ten years after his fall. Mary then wrote as follows to the Archbishop of Glasgow:—'Information has been received here of the death of the Earl of Bothwell, and that before his decease he made an ample confession of his crime, and declared himself the guilty author of the assassination of the late king, my husband, of which he expressly acquitted me, testifying to my innocence on the peril of his soul's damnation; and since, if this be true, this testimony would be of the greatest value to me against the false calumnies of my enemies, I beg of you to investigate the truth by all the means possible. Those who were present at this declaration, which was afterwards signed and sealed by them in the form of a last will and testament, are Otto Braw, of the castle of Eloembro; Paris Braw, of the castle of Vascut; Mr Gullunstaque, of the castle of Fulkenster; the Bishop of Skonen, and four magistrates of that town. If De Menoeaulx, who has formerly trafficked in that country, would make a voyage thither to inquire more particularly, I would be glad to employ him for the purpose, and to furnish money for his travelling expenses.' Now this document, which Mary wished to be produced, was sent to Elizabeth, but *by her suppressed.* Morton, who was now regent in Scotland, is at the same time found imprisoning a man for spreading a report of the existence of such a document. Prince Labanoff has, however, obtained an original and undoubted copy of Bothwell's declaration, showing that the account which Mary had heard of it was correct. A man in Bothwell's circumstances could have no motive to clear the character of Mary, if she had actually been guilty. The publication of this important document is deferred by the prince till he shall give us an eighth and final volume, stating his own impressions from the interesting series of papers contained in the seven already published.

Such are the leading points of the evidence now brought out in favour of the innocence of Mary. It is an evidence which will not be satisfactory to the sectarian spirit still alive respecting the history of her times; but to minds independent of that influence, it will carry much weight. The wonder with candid persons will now be, that they did not long ago suspect the soundness of the prevalent views respecting Mary, seeing that she was exactly in those circumstances which make fair treatment next to impossible. All monarchs succeeded by new and hostile dynasties, all statesmen and all political ideas superseded by others of an opposite stamp, are sure to be misrepresented. Knowing these things, it appears strange that we did not long since suspect the vulgar history of Queen Mary, merely from the circumstance that the representatives of opposite religious and political systems had been in possession of power ever since her time. We might have been startled, if by nothing else, by reflecting that Mary is held infamous on a merely suspected connexion with the crime of murder, while Elizabeth, who is known for certain to have taken measures to have Mary assassinated, who called Sir A. Pawlett a precise fellow, because he would not do the deed, and who actually did murder Mary under form of law, is handed down as a paragon of excellence. The impartial public has been deficient in shrewdness, but we trust it will not be deficient in manfulness to express its sense of the new bearing of this question.

* Translation in W. Turnbull's edition of Letters of Mary Stuart. Dolman: 1845.

FARMING PAST AND PRESENT.

Nothing could be more erroneous than the attempt which is sometimes made to draw a line of distinction between the principle of raising food and the production of wares in wool, in linen, in wood, or in iron. The one is about as much a manufacture as the other; a trading with capital, an endeavour to accumulate profits, from the supply of a marketable commodity, in the shortest time, and by the cheapest process. It is true that at one time a wider difference existed between the culture of the soil and those arts which are usually termed manufactures; but that period has long since passed, and the two great branches of industry are every day more closely approximating. The farmer—we speak more particularly of Scotland—no longer builds his own sheds, makes his own harness, or fashions the implements by which he prepares the soil, but calls in the assistance of the mason, the joiner, mechanist, and chemist, himself taking only the last division of the labour by which the commodity is produced. Thus it is that farming, as a branch of industry, differs in no respect from cotton weaving: it is an art, to the perfection of which other arts must contribute their share; its demands upon their aid becoming numerous in proportion to the demands upon its produce. Nothing could be more conclusive of this view than a contrast between the realities of British farming in 1845, and those which existed sixty or eighty years ago.

Let us take, in the first place, the erections of the farm-stead, as these in every case must form the first step towards an establishment. At the period to which we refer these were little better than mud-huts, being constructed of turf, or of alternate layers of turf and stone, and covered with straw, heath, or rushes. There might be some small necessity for carpentry in the framing of the roof or door, but otherwise the whole could be accomplished by the hands on the farm. Now, a first-rate Scottish farm-stead will cost several thousand pounds, requiring the joint labour of the architect, builder, joiner, slater, plumber, and ironsmith. The walls are of well-worked stone, the woodwork usually of foreign timber, thereby calling in the assistance of the timber-merchant and ship-owner, and the slates or tiles also imply the work of another class of artisans. Indeed, a well-appointed farm-stead, with all its offices, its water-pipes, liquid manure-tanks, boiling and steaming apparatus, slicing, chopping, and thrashing machines, requires in every respect as great a variety of labour and mechanical skill as does the erection of any other factory. Or let us look at the interior of the buildings, and compare the rough rude finish of a century ago with the finely-paved, plastered, and partitioned stalls of the present day. Then, the cow-houses and stables were dark, dingy, ill-cleaned hovels; now, they are lighted and ventilated, and their inmates fed and curried with a care exceeding that—we are ashamed to own it—which some would grudge to bestow on their peasantry. In the mere erections of a farm, therefore, there is scarcely a point in common between the two periods; no comparison between the frail hovel of turf and straw, and the substantial structure calculated to endure for centuries. We never look, in fact, from the top of the passing coach at a farm-stead, with its symmetrical lines of elegant architecture and its tall chimney-stalk, but we feel we have a factory before us, as much as if a spinning-mill or iron-foundry formed the prospect.

Again, in directing our attention to the soil, either as regards the amount under culture, or the style of cultivation, nothing could be more strikingly different. Eighty years ago, only a few fields around the homestead came under the plough, the rest were left in rough pasture, heather, or furze, as laid down by the hand of nature. Nothing could be more truly primitive than the agriculture of our grandfathers. Fences were few, and these of turf or dry stones; hedges and beltings of wood were only coming into fashion round the mansions of the proprietors. Draining was unknown; the dry knolls and slopes alone were tilled; the meadows were left for hay; any spring or superabundance of water on ploughed land was led off by an open furrow, to expend itself in the next lower level; trenching was never thought of; and altogether, culture, in the literal acceptation of the term, was of the most imperfect description. Nor were the crops aimed at anything beyond what might have been expected from such a style of cultivation. Oats, peas, barley or bigg, and an attempt at wheat on some of the better lands, may be said to have constituted the whole agricultural produce of Scotland; for potatoes were merely known as a novelty, and turnips, beet-root, carrots, the artificial grasses, and other green crops, were heard of only as things peculiar to more favoured climates. At present, what is the state of matters, at least in the more available districts? Every acre that the plough and spade can reach is under culture; substantial fences of stone and lime, hedgerows and ornamental paling, are things quite common; and beltings and clumps of wood are thickly scattered over the face of the country, alike for shelter and ornament. Draining and trenching are working wonders on the soil and climate; every rough place is made smooth; the furze, heath, and broom are supplanted by crops of grain; and bogs and morasses are converted into fertile fields. Crops that our forefathers never could have dreamed of, are now reared luxuriantly under the climate of Scotland, creating a total revolution both in our style of living and in the capabilities of the country as to population. Wheat and potatoes may be said to be the staple support of the populace; turnips, beet-root, and the artificial grasses, are the basis of that enormous amount of butcher-meat which is now consumed; oats and barley are now subordinate articles of food. By this high advancement the rental of the land has in some cases been trebled; the farmer is compelled to seek from every square yard its produce; and owing to the equality to which he has brought it by modern skill, he can calculate upon its capabilities with about as much certainty as the engineer can calculate the power of his steam engine, or the printer the number of sheets which his machine will throw off in a given time.

This high state of cultivation could not, however, have been brought about except by improved implements and machinery—without, in fact, the aid of the mechanic, engineer, chemist, and naturalist. Eighty years ago, a few spades and mattocks, rude wooden ploughs and harrows, a wain or two of wicker or of boards, some pack-saddles and rope harness, a flail and a set of winnowing riddles, constituted the sum total of a farmer's mechanical outfit: now, how different is the picture! His ploughs are of iron, and fashioned upon scientific principles as to draught, width and depth of furrow; and we have at this moment upwards of a score of models before us, each laying claim to some advantage as to draught, drilling, subsoiling, trenching, or even to draining, for this process can now be executed by the plough alone. Nay, we have seen the *steam* plough at work, and have faith in the prediction that, as the surface of the country becomes more easy and regular under the present systems of culture, this gigantic machine will come into very general operation. As with the plough so with the harrow; the wooden implement has been superseded by one of iron, and by other instruments of the same family, as the grubber, the scarifier, the horse-shoe, &c. each being applicable to some special purpose. The clodpole and mallet, which were applied to the refractory glebe of former years, have generally given way to rollers of various kinds; and the hand that used to scatter the seed broadcast, has in many cases only to tend a machine that will do the work with a precision, regularity, and economy, setting the human instrument at defiance. We often wonder what would be the surprise of a departed grand-uncle, who was wont to sow his little acre of turnip by shaking a bottle of seed along the drills, the discharge being regulated by a bit of perforated paper tied over the mouth of the vessel, were he to revisit the world, and see a first-rate turnip machine taking four drills at once, and not only sowing and covering the seed, but dropping and earthing the manure at the same time. Nothing certainly could more excite his simple wonder; and yet the turnip-sowing machine is but one of a hundred similar inventions, all calculated to lessen the sum of rural labour. In former times, the mechanical skill of the country joiner and blacksmith was quite sufficient for the wants of the farmer; nay, these men were mere labourers, fashioning the material which he usually supplied. Now, the system is totally revolutionised: we have the 'agricultural implement maker,' as a distinct profession, dwelling in cities, possessing large capital, and employing draughtsmen, joiners, turners, engineers, and braziers. New inventions are rising into notice every day; patents are rife; and few of our large towns but have museums, in which the results are displayed for the study of the agriculturist.

It would be fruitless to attempt an enumeration of modern agricultural implements and inventions, and yet there are two or three which cannot be omitted in a contrast like the present. In the matter of vehicles and their outfits, nothing could be more widely dissimilar than the attainments of the two periods. For want of good roads, pack-saddles were more numerous than wains or cars; and wains were rude sledges, dragged slowly along by oxen. The harness of the cattle—whether horses or oxen—was generally made at by-hours by the ploughmen or farmer himself, and consisted of an assortment of straw or tow-ropes, wooden frames, and thongs of untanned skins. Now, the carts and wagons are of light and elegant construction, requiring the labour of a special class of artisans; and nothing could be more complete than the harness of the saddler, which calls in the skill of the tanner and currier, and the art of the brazier and silversmith. Could we recall the shaggy farm-horse of 1745, with his rude furniture, and place him alongside of the sleek stately animal of the present day, caparisoned in his elegant harness, the contrast would be as decidedly startling as that between the savage in his tattered blanket and the well-dressed gentleman. Again, if we compare the simple flail of our ancestors with the improved steam thrashing-mill of the present day, we shall find a difference even more astonishing. Sixty years ago, the ploughman prepared two rods of well-dried ash, pierced an eye in each, connected them by a free hinge of cord or dried eel-skin, and this constituted *the flail*, the only thrashing implement till a recent period which Britain could boast of. Slow, tedious, and expensive, this implement could no more have met our present requirements than could the spinning-wheel of our grandmothers. The thrashing-machine took its place, at first small and imperfect, but now on many farms a complete instrument—moved by steam, and not only thrashing out the grain, but winnowing it, dressing it, and sacking it quite ready for the market. The farmer need never unyoke his horses from their ordinary field-work, so far as thrashing is concerned; he has only to light his furnace in the morning, by breakfast the steam is up, and before dinner as much grain is thrashed, cleaned, and ready for sale, as a dozen flail-men could have prepared in a month. In fact, the thrashing-mill is one of the most obvious applications of mechanical skill to the manufacture of human food, and quite as perfect in its results as is the spinning-mill or power-loom.

It is not, however, in the mere substitution of ingenious and powerful machinery for implements simple and imperfect that agriculture is approximating more and more to the condition of a manufacture; there are inventions and appliances totally new which bear equally on this view of the matter. Take, for example, the subject of draining. The excavations are not now filled merely with stones gathered from the land or dug from the quarry, but are fitted with tiles and pipes of clay, concrete, and other substances. Nor are these tiles fashioned slowly by the hand, but are pressed and moulded into form by machines with a precision and rapidity that enables the farmer to lay down drains not by feet and yards but by miles. Or turn we to the subject of manure, the last and least thought of by our forefathers, who allowed their dung-heaps to run to waste, exposed to the sun and rain, as things of secondary importance. On this point the physiologist and chemist have created a sudden and total change of opinion, and every scrap of farm manure, and every drop of animal liquid, is now collected and preserved with as great care as is the grain that is reaped and thrashed. Not only are dung-pits and liquid manure-tanks built and carefully excluded from the causes of evaporation, but chemical substances are applied to fix the volatile principles, and an immense amount of labour bestowed in the proper preparation of the farm-yard manure. Nay, farther, bones are sought in every quarter, gathered at home, and shipped from abroad, to be crushed for manure; the droppings of sea-birds, under the name of guano, are imported from the rocky islets of Peru and South Africa at many pounds per ton, thus making the meanest of all substances the subject of the most profitable commerce. Nor does the supply of manure end here: the chemist has determined the substances entering into the composition of the various crops; he knows also the constitution of the soil, and can therefore supply to it the elements which the intended crop shall most require. Thus we have dozens of artificial manures invented, prepared, and patented by the ablest chemists of modern times—again confirming the proposition with which we set out, that in every particular agriculture is more and more approximating to our ideas of a manufacture.

As yet we have said nothing respecting the condition of the farmer as influenced by this rapid advancement; but our comparison would be partial and imperfect without some allusion to the vast change which it has effected in this particular. Formerly, the farm-house was a humble single-storeyed tenement, with two or three apartments at most, and these but very indifferently furnished; the walls were roughly plastered; there was either no ceiling, or one formed of boards and matting; and in a majority of instances, the floors were earthen. The dairy and poultry were either managed under the same roof, or in adjoining sheds; and the house being situated in the same range or square with the byres and stables, afforded anything but a facility for order and cleanliness. Now, how different is the arrangement! It is only the other day that we visited a Fifeshire farm, and found the dwelling-house rivalling the handsomest of our suburban villas in style and comfort. Embosomed in shrubbery, possessing a suite of public and private rooms, and having the kitchen, scullery, and dairy arranged behind, and screened from view with admirable taste, it was a mansion that might have accommodated a nobleman. Nor is this a solitary instance, for we could point to hundreds of such in the lowland counties, where eighty years ago there was nothing superior to a modern roadside cottage. Then, too, the farmer, dressed plainly in homespun woollen, toiled with his labourers, sat, and generally mealed with them in the kitchen, and altogether led a simple life, little exalted above that of his hinds. His sons took their regular share of out-door labour, his wife and daughters attended to the kitchen, spun, managed the poultry and dairy, and were generally the first on the harvest-field. Now, the farmer and his family dress expensively; his duty is to conduct, not to labour with his own hands; he never mingles with his servants unless to direct; his sons are beginning to be educated in those sciences necessary to the perfection of their art; his daughters are taught every accomplishment of modern education, take no share in the labour of the farm, and only attend to such household duties as devolve upon ladies in town. The farmer keeps his thorough-bred horse, or drives his own curricle; attends market as a merchant does the Exchange; transacts his business not as of old with the consumer, but with the cornfactor, thereby saving time, and avoiding expense and trouble. Nay, so perfect is his system of marketing, that, like the clothier and tea-merchant, he can send his samples, his note of weights and prices, and can thus secure every advantage of market without leaving the duties of his farm for a moment. All this speaks of high professional attainment, and betokens an improvement still greater than we can form any idea of, once the physiologist and chemist have made their deductions to bear more directly upon the science of agriculture.

We turn in conclusion to the condition of the farm labourer, the hind, the peasant, the cottager, or by whatever other name the rural section of our population is known. Here we must confess that the picture is not so cheering: this vast improvement in agriculture has told but faintly in comparison on his position, the while it has tended to separate him immeasurably from his employer. The cotton lord who lives in his suburban palace, lolls in his carriage, and dines off silver, is not farther removed from the poor girl who stands at one of his spinning frames, than are some of our modern farmers from the hind that ploughs the soil. This seems to be an inevitable effect of the accumulation of capital, and it were indeed a cheerless and staggering one, had we not faith in human progress towards a condition of less toil and greater comfort. It must not, however, be supposed that all this recent advance in agriculture has left the labourer in his position of eighty years ago. The draining and trenching of the soil have rendered it dry and smooth, and he treads over it more lightly; he has less of rheumatism, and never suffers from ague; machinery has removed in a great degree the necessity of long-continued work and heavy lifts; he is better clothed, and more regularly fed; and on well-managed estates, has a neat and comfortable cottage to dwell in. As improvements proceed, so will his condition be farther improved; every additional appropriation of machinery will lessen his manual labour; and the general advancement of the country will put in his, as in other men's possession, the little luxuries of food and clothing which are so essential to our ideas of comfort. Intellectually, too, he is a superior being; he enjoys a greater amount of freedom; and the expertness he has acquired from moving amid so much improvement and machinery, has fitted him to enter upon other pursuits with greater chance of success than he could possibly have done during the primitive ignorance of a century ago. These are great advantages certainly; and though they do not place the labourer in the proximity to the farmer that existed in former times, still they ought to be regarded as a lengthening of that lever which men, with proper attention, and care, and self-respect, may apply to their own elevation.

Altogether, therefore, it would seem that agriculture, though somewhat later in taking the start, is not in any degree behind the general advance of other industrial pursuits; and that it is every day more closely approximating to them in its modes of operation, in its requirements, and in its results.

BENONI'S MOURNING.

BY FRANCES BROWN.

In the five thousand five hundred and fifty-fifth year of the world, Rabbi Benjamin Benoni, chief doctor of the dispersed of Israel, dwelling in the Gentile city of Granada, made a vow to fast and mourn two days at every full moon for the sins and iniquities of his household.

Rabbi Benjamin Benoni was learned in all the wisdom of the Talmud. He knew to a hair's-breadth how near a Gentile might be approached without pollution, and had written three folio volumes on the proper posture for eating the passover; but the principal exploit of his life was the refutation, in public controversy, of the doctrine maintained by Rabbi Joseph Benjamin Joshua, of Malaga, that it was lawful for a Jew to lift a pin which he saw at his feet on the Sabbath day, which raised his reputation for knowledge and piety to such a height among the Jews of Spain, that they sought his advice and assistance in all difficult cases of conscience, and called him the Solomon of the dispersed. Nor was the rabbi esteemed less righteous than wise. In common with all his people since the Roman ploughshare passed over Zion, he was a man of commerce, and noted for the justice of his dealings with both Jew and Gentile. His zeal against the idolatry of the latter might have rivalled that of the ancient Jehu, had he lived in an age more conducive to its display; but as things were, Benoni had suffered much and often for the faith of his fathers. Born in Poland about the time of his people's banishment from that country by Cassimer the Great, he had early become a wanderer, and persecution had tracked the course of his after years, pursuing him from city to city over the length and breadth of Europe; till, in the sunset of his days, he found a peaceful asylum in the once Moorish, but now Christian city of Granada. Blameless in his life, and most scrupulous in his piety, Rabbi Benjamin Benoni, in the judgment of his people, was entitled to expect every promised blessing annexed to the law of Moses; and some blessings he had received. His business had prospered in every land where he had sought a temporary refuge from Gentile oppression; and his wealth was then believed to exceed that of any merchant in the city. But a strange affliction had fallen upon the rabbi in his latter days. Of the four children of his youth that grew to years of maturity, there was not one who cared for his age, or loved him as a father: all were gone from him, and he was alone; for the wife of his early choice had died in her summer, and her grave was far away among the hills of Hungary. One was a youth of promise and high hopes, who had become great and famous among the Gentiles for his knowledge of their lore. But he had forgotten his father, and, it seemed, his father's faith also; for he had long ceased to observe the ceremonies of the law, and now dwelt in the city of Salamanca, where he was renowned as a scholar, and much in favour with the Spanish nobility. The other had humbler aspirations. He wedded the maid of his heart, and dwelt in peace among his people, following their path of commerce. Love lit up his hearth, riches increased around him, and men esteemed him liberal and just; yet he never sought the house of his father, nor paused to inquire if it were well with him. The next was a daughter, deemed comeliest among the maids of Israel, fair and stately like the queens of Judah before she was made desolate. But the girl forsook her early faith and kindred for the name and the love of a noble Nazarene, and passed her father on the city streets in all her Christian splendour, as one who dreaded not his wrath, and sought not his friendship. The last was a maiden wise and gentle, but not fair. None had sought her, and she remained unwedded, but left her father in early youth to watch over the orphan children and home of an aged rabbi, and returned to his house no more.

Benoni's heart grew heavy within him as he thought of these things in his lonely chamber. Dust was on his gray locks, and sackcloth was his garment; for it was the time of the full moon, and he mourned, according to his vow, for the great and strange sin of his children. The evening of the second day was come, the hush of the dying twilight had fallen on the great city, and all was silent where the rabbi prayed, looking to the east, the place of morning, and the still promised land to which his fathers had turned through the prayers and wanderings of ages. He prayed long and wept sore; for sorrow was upon him, and he found no comfort. But when the last light was fading, there came a low knock to the chamber door, and a voice of earnest intreaty, which said, 'Benjamin Benoni, for the sake of Jerusalem arise and follow me!'

The rabbi rose astonished, for the voice was strange, and spoke in the old language of the Hebrews, that had long been silent on earth. Without, there stood a man tall and dark, and in the vigour of his years; his garb was of an ancient fashion, his beard long and flowing, and his countenance expressed majesty mixed with sweetness. He beckoned with his hand, and Benoni followed him, though he knew not whither, yet felt as if impelled to go. They left the home of his solitude behind them, and passed through the streets and gates of the city, and then along a great road leading northward, which Benoni, in all his wanderings, had never trod before. It was broad and lonely, and led far away over hill and valley, through forest and desert plain; and by the full bright moon, which shone upon their journey, the rabbi discerned with amazement the long-remembered features of many a far-distant landscape seen in his early journeys: but the ground was smooth beneath his steps, and his feet seemed swift as the wings of an eagle; for he felt no weariness, but journeyed on with that silent guide leagues after leagues, till it seemed to him they had tracked the boundaries of many a Christian realm: they paused at last, where the moon shed her silver rays on the spires of a slumbering city, and the rabbi well remembered the good old town of Presburg.

Midnight lay clear and still on the city of the Magyars; for all its thousands slept, and Benoni's guide conducted him in silence from street to street, till they reached a large but neglected house, whose doors seemed to open before them; and on entering, the rabbi recognised it as the same which he had occupied twenty years before, when his children were young, and their mother dwelt with him. Benoni would have spoken his surprise, but a spell of silence was upon his lips, and he could utter no sound. The house was still inhabited, but its dwellers saw neither the rabbi nor his guide; though days and nights seemed to pass, and they were with them from hour to hour, marking the manner of their lives at hearth, and board, and prayer. The family were Israelites, and oh how like his own as they once had been! There was a father in the noon of life, a mother fair and gentle, and four young children beautiful and fresh as the first leaves of the vine. Without they had peace, and they felt no want within; yet their home was unhappy; its chambers were solitary and cheerless, for their echoes never woke with the joy of the young, nor the sound of festal gladness: there was a shadow on the mother's beauty cast by unquiet days. The children had sad and thoughtful faces, that told of precocious care; and there were harsh words and fierce disputes that came often among them, as if the thorns of life had grown up early, and choked the flowers of childhood. But Benoni marvelled not; for he saw that the tare-sower was the high priest of the hearth. The man was one to be well spoken of in the city for grave carriage and integrity; but he sat amid his household as a reprover and a judge, who had no sympathy with their hearts, and no regard to their wishes. None among the doctors of Judah could better interpret the law, and few were more strict in its outward observance; but he made it wearisome to his household by enforcing its thousand ceremonies, and neglecting the 'weightier matters,' which his own example should have taught them by the law of love. Benoni marked the canker working its way to the hearts of the young: he saw the dew of their spring days, the keen relish of life's first enjoyments, that comes no more to those who taste the wormwood, and the blameless desires of childhood, so earnest yet so easily fulfilled, sacrificed day by day to the pride of their father's profitless wisdom, to the folly of his false devotion, and the bent of an evil nature that delighted to rebuke.

The dark seed bore its fruit: the children shunned his presence, and beheld his approach with fear: their laughter died at the sound of his step, and they learned to look upon him as an enemy, whilst round their gentle but simple-hearted mother their gathered affections were twined. She, too, felt her home unblest, and her life weary, for the manner of the husband and father was the same. The tree which she had chosen she found to be a brier. Years of hopeless discontent brought early withering, and at last disease came upon her. She heard the summons of the grave, and grieved not to go, for her wedded life had known no comfort; yet she sorrowed to leave her children, but not to part from the spouse of her youth. He saw his work, but knew it not, for his trust was still unshaken in the power of his vain wisdom and the pride of his long prayers. Benoni grew sad; for, as that fair face faded, its features grew more and more like to those of his lost Jemima, and at length it was her very self. The guide, however, again beckoned him away, and he felt constrained to follow. They left the dwelling and journeyed on; the same great road still stretched before them; but now it wound away like a long river to the west. Again the rabbi found himself passing swiftly through lands traversed before. Many a stately city, the long-desired goal of far-sailing ships and weary caravans; many a dark fortress, that guarded the boundaries of hostile nations, they passed as the wind in its unseen flight; till, fair among her vines, and crowned with the glory of centuries, rose to their view the city of the Seine. The glare of torches and the roll of chariots swept along the never-silent streets, as the gay and noble of the land returned from their long, late revels. Benoni's conductor led him on to a low but open door, far from such scenes, in the quarter inhabited by the sons of toil and Israel.

Well the rabbi knew that house and its narrow chambers, for there, in his wanderings westward, he had once dwelt with his children; but seven long winters had passed over him since then, and days and nights again seemed to glide swiftly by as he and that silent guide beheld the unconscious household. They were the same forms and faces he had seen at Presburg, though changed as if by the march of many years. The children had grown to stately youths and dark-haired maidens; but the mother's glance was wanting, for the light of her love might shine on their path no more. Grayness had come upon the father's locks, and furrows on his brow, but he had learned no lesson from the voice of time: age had only deepened the darkness of his soul, and strengthened in its shadow the love of power and gold. He barred his sons from the love of the Gentile nations, deeming it forbidden, because beyond his knowledge. One was a gifted spirit, strong to think and question, and he despised the faith of Israel because of him who taught it. The other had no gifts, but many graces, and his father esteemed him little, because he had no part in the praise of men. He denied to his daughters the ornaments of youth, and called them sinful vanities; but it was because he valued the smallest coin in his coffers more than the pleasures of his children. Yet he looked with pride on one who walked in beauty; but his glance was cold and careless on her sister, who, though less fair of face, was far more fair in soul. The tares which the old man had planted so early were ripening fast around him; his children already scorned his rebukes, and scarcely heard his counsels, for they had outgrown the fears of childhood, and he had not won the love of their youth: he had made their home solitary, and long habit had rendered them unsocial. Their sphere of society was bounded by each other; and their dwelling was indeed a world to them, but a world which contained in its narrow limits all the evils of the outer earth. The contentions of jarring opinions, the discord of opposing tempers, and the strife of conflicting, though petty interests, banished love and peace from the hearth which should have been their altar—darkened the gray of age, and withered the green of youth.

The rabbi saw, and rejoiced for the gentle mother who had escaped so much in the hush of her early grave; but once more that voiceless conductor beckoned him away from the cheerless dwelling of that joyous city. Their journey was still on the same broad and lonely path towards the place of the setting sun. Swifter still, but still unwearied, Benoni found himself speeding on, rather like one borne upon the waves of a rapid river, than the traveller of the solid earth. But now the way-marks grew more familiar; he knew the white sierras and dark-green woods of Spain, and at last entered at the very gate by which he went forth, the lost but long-beloved city of the Moors. The stranger guided him on through the hushed but well-known streets, till they reached the silence of his own forsaken dwelling. The full moon was still bright above the towers of Granada—though it seemed as if that midnight journey had tracked the course of years—and poured the full flood of her silvery splendour on a solitary chamber where an aged man sat silent and alone. Well the rabbi knew that face, though the furrows were deepened, and the eye dimmed with the shadows of life's closing twilight, since he beheld it last. It was the same he had seen among the children at Presburg and the young at Paris. But the old man's household had gone from him one by one, and left him alone in the winter of his days, like a desert to which the pilgrim desires not to look back; for the place which he filled was the dark spot of their memory. Through all its withering and changes, that form had been to Benoni as one familiar, though without a name; yet now, as he gazed on the forsaken man, the rabbi seemed to be transformed strangely and suddenly as men are in their dreams, till it was himself that stood in the moonlit chamber, with all that weight of solitude and years. 'Benjamin Benoni,' said the glorious guide, who still stood by him, 'I am the angel of wisdom who guided Solomon in his search for hidden truth. The way which thou hast trodden is the path of memory, in which the steps of the aged wax not slow, nor the eyes of the slumberer dim. By it thou hast retraced the wastes of thy many wanderings; thou hast seen the working of thy boasted wisdom, and looked on the gems of life, the trampled and cast from thee, where they lie far away in the wilderness of time. Learn from these things what sins thou shouldst lament, and tell thy tale, that others may learn from thee.' As the last words fell on the ear of the rabbi, the angel of wisdom passed from his dwelling, and we know not if he ever returned: from that hour Benjamin Benoni mourned no more for the sins of his children, but he sorely mourned for his own.

OCCASIONAL NOTES.

DISINTERESTED LEGATEES.

About forty years ago, an old man of Scottish birth, who had realised a large fortune in England, and from time to time made purchases of landed property in his native county, died after a protracted life of miserable penury, leaving only collateral relations. These persons had fully expected to be benefited by their kinsman, so that their surprise was necessarily very great when they learned that he had executed a conveyance of his whole property to a legal practitioner of Aberdeen, who had been accustomed to manage it. It appeared that the old man, under the influence of mere crotchet, or some temporary irritation, had resolved to disappoint them, at the same time that he enriched a man who had no natural claim upon his regard.

The relations had hardly recovered from the first sense of discomfiture, and the friends of Mr C—— had scarcely begun to congratulate him upon his good fortune, when he announced to the heirs that he had destroyed the deed, and that the property would consequently pass to them as if the deceased had been intestate. He had with reluctance, he said, consented to allow of the deed being drawn up, and only for the purpose of securing the property for the rightful heirs. These individuals consequently entered upon full possession of the old man's estates and effects. They pressed upon the agent's acceptance a gift of about six thousand pounds, in gratitude for his honourable conduct. It is pleasant to record that he is still living, and a considerable land proprietor in the district where he originally practised as a solicitor or agent.

More recently, a circumstance somewhat similar took place. Two aged sisters were joint-proprietors of an estate in Perthshire. The elder was married, and had a son; the other was unmarried. The elder dying first, her share of the property was inherited by her son, then an officer in the Guards. The second lady, having some groundless dislike to this gentleman, bequeathed her share to a favourite nephew, far down in the family tree, and who had no expectation of such an inheritance. Finding, after the death of the old lady, how the property was destined, this gentleman lost no time in writing to his cousin—a person, we may mention, with whom he was but slightly acquainted, for they had been living at a distance from each other, and were in totally different walks in life—informing him that he could not for a moment think of taking advantage of such a will, but begged to surrender his right, without any reserve, into the hands of the heir-at-law. What added to the merit of this action, the legatee considered the whole matter as a private family affair, and said not a word about it to any besides the party principally concerned. It only became known in consequence of legal proceedings for the transference of the property to the heir-at-law, an opinion from counsel having decided that it was best to proceed upon the will, instead of holding it as null, which was the wish of the legatee.

These examples of a high conscientiousness will be admired by all. They are felt to be the nobler, that public opinion would not have greatly resented a more selfish procedure in either instance. The agent might have appropriated the estate of his client, to the preclusion of the natural heirs, and still more might the junior cousin have sat quietly down in possession of his aunt's property, without forfeiting the esteem of society, seeing that they only did what the law allowed, and what hundreds would have done in their case. We therefore unavoidably accord high praise to their conduct, which we see to have sprung entirely from a genuine integrity and unselfishness of nature. But, it may be asked, is this approbation of such conduct a good sign of the public morality? We fear not, for absolutely the course taken by these two men was precisely what ought to have been taken, and no more. Their conduct only shines by reason of our believing that most men would have acted differently. Let us fully admit, then, the relative merit, seeing that most men feel as if they were well enough if they only act as their neighbours generally do, and any exception from common selfishness argues a superior nature. But still let us also understand that such actions ought not to be rare, nor their merit felt as calling for unusual notice or commendation.

For what are all such eccentric bequests? Are they not in almost all cases the result of mere dotage—not, perhaps, a proveable insanity, but a prave state of the natural feelings arising from age or disease, and dictating a destination of goods which the testator would himself, in an ordinary condition, view with horror? A testator, in such circumstances, is a man at issue with himself. He does now, in his seventieth year, we shall say, what, throughout the previous sixty-nine, he would have condemned in the strongest terms. He, therefore, who takes advantage of the bequest of a testator ascertained to be of this character, may be said to assist him in outraging his own normal feelings, and rendering his name a by-word and a reproach. The part which he acts is little better than that of a man who accepts some costly gift which a child in the simplicity of its heart has offered, not knowing its value, and unrecking that its parents were the true owners. Nor is this all; for all such conduct tends to lower and keep down the standard of the public morality. It gives a disgusting sanction to the maxim of every man for himself, which is the purest essence of barbarism, and tends more than anything else to retard the happiness of mankind.

PUNCTUALITY.

Punctuality to engagements is a species of conscientiousness—a conscientiousness towards our neighbours' time. The gentler sex are sadly deficient in it, probably from their being less accustomed to business arrangements than men. A whimsical friend used to recommend those having appointments with ladies always to go an hour too late. 'You thus have the moderate revenge of keeping them waiting a quarter of an hour, for the *three quarters* which they would have been sure to keep *you* waiting, if you had been punctual.'

GUNPOWDER CELEBRATIONS.

Does it never occur to any one that the firing of cannon to mark distinguished events and their anniversaries is far from being a rational practice? What is most objectionable about this folly of the grown-up world, it sanctions similar practices on a smaller scale among boys, who, on several days of every year, are a source of danger both to themselves and others. Many a quiet family are little aware of the gunpowder plot carried on in cellar, closet, or garret, by the male juveniles of their establishment for several days before the royal birthday, or that the son whom they suppose to be at school, or at least enjoying some innocent recreation, is busied in some coarse mob not far from their home firing off pigmy ordnance, squibs, crackers, and other examples of pyrotechny. Hardly a year passes without its gunpowder victims, and sometimes the spirit of the fire-worshippers leads to actual rioting and destructive violence. We must really take leave to doubt that any benefits can be derived from a sulphureous celebration of great days, comparable to the evils which it entails; and we cannot doubt that amusements of a rational and harmless kind could easily be substituted, such as the visiting of museums, zoological gardens, picture galleries, and 'show places' generally. The first step in reform is one belonging to persons in authority: the firing of cannon on such days ought to be given up.

THE GIBBET.

The gibbet has not fifteen years' life in it. If in 1860, fifteen years hence, there shall be a death punishment existing, if we shall still be in this world together, reproach me with being the falsest prophet, the veriest fool, that ever presumed to talk of the advancing spirit of the times.—*Lord Nugent.*

We cordially agree with Lord Nugent, and undertake a share of the hazards to which he here exposes himself.

RESUSCITATION.

The purpose of respiration is to expose the portion of the blood which has returned to the heart, after it has circulated through the body, and which has acquired during that circulation the properties of dark or venous blood, to the influence of atmospheric air in the lungs. The oxygenous portion of the air so received into the lungs converts this venous blood into florid or arterial blood; that is, into a state for being again circulated through all parts of the system. Any interruption to this process—by submersion in water, exposure to choke-damp, strangulation, and the like—if continued beyond a few minutes, is destructive of life. Recovery is, however, possible within certain limits; hence the resuscitative appliances to cases of 'suspended animation.'

The restoratives generally resorted to are warmth, friction, electricity, and, above all, supplying of the lungs with fresh or properly oxygenated air, either by free exposure to an external current, or by artificial injection. The cause of the latter appliance is sufficiently obvious, as the cessation of the heart's action—technically called *asphyxia*—is occasioned by the interruption of respiration, or rather by the interruption of the effect produced by that function on the blood. Any means, therefore, that can restore the process of respiration, or otherwise supply its place, till the action of the heart has been established, must be of value in resuscitation, and especially so where they can be applied with ease and rapidity. Various apparatus have been invented for the injection of common air; but as this fluid contains only about twenty parts in the hundred of pure oxygen, its effect upon the blood in the lungs cannot be so rapid as that of a mixture containing a greater proportion, and still less so than oxygen itself. This gas has accordingly been long recommended; but the difficulty of obtaining it with sufficient rapidity has hitherto proved a barrier to its application. A new mode has, however, been proposed by Dr George Wilson of Edinburgh, by which an unlimited supply can be obtained and administered in a few minutes, and it is to this that we would direct more general attention.

It has been some time known that the chlorate of potass, if mixed with a metallic oxide—such as the peroxide of iron, or the black oxide of manganese—and heated to redness, will give off oxygen in a copious stream, and without any interruption, so long as there is any of that gas in the compound. The proportion of the metallic oxide to the chlorate is a matter of difference among chemists; but Dr Wilson has found by repeated experiment that about one of the former to five of the latter is the most advantageous. We were recently invited to witness in his chemical class-room an exhibition of the apparatus by which he proposes to administer the gas, and which, in the opinion of medical men, is likely to prove efficacious. In this case the supply was on a limited scale only—some 600 or 800 cubic inches in four minutes—but from the rapidity and certainty with which the gas was produced and administered to a fictitious patient, it left the most favourable impression upon the minds of the spectators. A glass retort containing four or six ounces of the mixture was heated with a spirit-lamp, and in a few seconds the gas began to be evolved, the evolution increasing in rapidity, till at the second minute it flowed over in a continuous stream, and was conveyed into an ordinary telescope gasometer. From this reservoir it was extracted by means of injection bellows fitted with flexible tubes, and then conveyed to the lungs of the supposed patient. This contrivance was next abandoned, and the head of the patient placed in an air-tight box, into which the gas was conveyed from the gasometer. This box was fitted with a glass-slip for watching the changes produced on the countenance of the patient; and the necessary inspirations and expirations were caused by external pressure on the chest, as is done in ordinary cases of administering atmospheric air. Indeed several methods of applying the gas were suggested; but to these we need not advert, as the great merit of the proposal consists in the rapidity with which the supply can be produced and administered. On this head we think Dr Wilson deserving of the thanks of the public, and especially for the pains he has taken in laying it before the medical faculty, the directors of humane societies, and others capable of making the application. Of the individuals who are asphyxiated by submersion, exposure to choke-damp, &c. only a small per centage are resuscitated by the appliances at present in use; but there is every reason to conclude that if a supply of oxygen were obtained by the means above proposed, and kept in readiness at the offices of humane societies and otherwise, the recoveries would be trebled, or even quadrupled. It is agreed on all hands that pure oxygen is more efficacious in asphyxia than common air; and certainly no plan could be more rapid or more economical than that proposed by Dr Wilson.

THE POETRY OF ALFRED TENNYSON.*

Among the assertions most often made in the present day, is one, that the age of poetry is past, or passing. It is said that men are so engrossed with material interests and the struggle for subsistence, that they have little time or inclination to listen to the voices of the poets; and that even if the contrary were the case, they would not prefer the poets of the present day. These opinions have become an article of faith with many, and booksellers especially cling to them with a pertinacity which can only result from conviction. Whether they are right, and whether the age deserves this character, we shall not stop to inquire; we merely allude to the subject, to introduce the name of Alfred Tennyson, and to cite his popularity, either as a great exception to the charge, if it be, generally, a true one, or as a great proof of its falsehood, if it be a false one.

In the year 1830, Mr Tennyson, then a very young man, published a small volume of poems, which met with rather severe treatment from one or more of the most influential reviews. Four years later, he issued another volume, which met a reception as unfavourable. For ten years after this he ceased to publish; his name did not appear in magazines or annuals as a contributor, neither was he mentioned in any way in the catalogues of the publishers. He was not, however, forgotten. During the interval, there had been growing in many minds a sense of his merits: the number so

* This article has been written at our request, in order to convey to our readers some idea of the writings of Mr Tennyson, now rising into repute. Having ourselves had no opportunity of forming an opinion of his merits as a poet, we have to request that our readers will consider the criticism in the present paper as not ours, but that of a gentleman in whose judgment we have general reason to place confidence.—Ed.

affected was constantly increasing: and there existed, in short, a large class of well-informed men, who considered that he was a true poet. In the year 1842 appeared a reprint of the most of his pieces, some having been omitted, in consequence probably of the strictures of the reviewers, and some of them having been slightly altered, together with a series of new poems, the whole forming two small octavo volumes. Without any aid from literary cliques, without any resort to the aids of puffery now so common—arts without which even merit itself hardly appears able to obtain a hearing—these volumes found favour with the public, and in three years have run through as many editions. Suddenly, it has become the fashion to consider Alfred Tennyson as a great poet, if not as the 'poet of the age.' It must be allowed that in these days, when the multitude of competitors renders fame so much more difficult of acquirement than it was in days gone by, there must be rare merit in the writer, who, living apart from the busy world as Mr Tennyson does, and either scorning or being too indolent to employ the machinery by which reputations are partly to be made, has assumed so high a position in the eyes of his contemporaries. A careful study of Mr Tennyson's poems has numbered us in the ranks of his warm admirers; not among that unthinking portion who repeat their praise at second-hand, and who, without knowing why, exalt the object of it greatly beyond his merits, but among those who see in what he has done a very rare excellence, and the promise of still higher achievements, if he will only remain true to his vocation.

Mr Tennyson, we must admit, is inferior to no poet of the present generation; and if we were called upon to state his equal, we should have some difficulty, among the many vigorous spirits whose names are rising one after the other upon the literary horizon, to prove the immortality of the poetic spirit, in pointing out one who has written uniformly so well, and who has proved himself so capable of still greater triumphs.

Those who consider him the poet of the age, have, we think, fallen into a mistake. He may perhaps be the best the age has produced; but the poet whose genius shall reflect and be reflected by this age has yet to make himself known. With all his power and beauty, Mr Tennyson is not that man, if his claim is to rest upon what he has already done. The spirit of this age is that of hope. It is a spirit of action and of enterprise —a spirit of keen inquiry, which would have nothing hidden from its scrutiny either in the present or in the past, the more especially if any lessons can be learned from either for the improvement of the actual, or the attainment of the possible. It is a spirit of energy, of material progress, of free examination—a spirit of movement among the masses of mankind—a spirit from the operations of which we may anticipate, without being over-sanguine, that each successive generation will be wiser and happier than the generation that preceded it. The character of Mr Tennyson's muse is very different. He clings to the memories of the past, and although occasionally his aspirations for the future are elevated and ennobling, they are not so frequent as to form the pervading characteristic of his mind. His muse is one of contemplation more than of action—a muse attuned to the harmonies of nature; sweet, plaintive, and melancholy, with a classical elegance and purity, and a simplicity of loveliness that wins upon every reader the more he studies it. In an age that examines all things, questions all things, experimentalises upon all things, overthrows old systems before it has devised new ones, and whose motto is, 'On—for ever on,' Mr Tennyson anchors his poetical bark upon the traditions of yore, and allows the winds of the present or of the future to blow around him, but not to urge him to any progress. He has a deep knowledge of the human heart, great earnestness of mind, a consummate mastery of the art of versification, and sympathies that are ever on the side of the multitude; but too deeply impressed with the beauty of the classics, and with the exquisitely poetical mythology of the Greeks, he has become the poet of scholars, and not, as he might have been under a ruder and more comprehensive training, the poet of the people.

The prevailing characteristic of his style is a quaint and quiet elegance, and of his mind a gentle melancholy, with now and then touches of strong dramatic power, the whole coloured by the peculiar scenery of that part of England where he has long resided. Any attentive reader of his poetry, who may have been ignorant that he is a dweller amid the fens of Lincolnshire, would soon suspect this to be the case, when he found such constant pictures of fens and morasses, quiet meres, and sighing reeds, as he so beautifully introduces. We shall not quote as a specimen the beautiful poem of Mariana in the Moated Grange, which must be familiar to most readers, having gone the round of almost all the newspapers and periodicals of the country, although it would exemplify all the points we have stated, but shall mention a few instances from other poems less known. The exquisitely modulated poem of the Dying Swan affords a picture drawn, we think, with wonderful delicacy:—

> Some blue peaks in the distance rose,
> And white against the cold-white sky
> Shone out their crowning snows.
> One willow over the river wept,
> And shook the wave as the wind did sigh;
> Above in the wind was the swallow,
> Chasing itself at its own wild will;
> And far through the marish green and still,
> The tangled water-courses slept,
> Shot over with purple, and green, and yellow.

The ballad of New-Year's Eve introduces similar scenery:

> When the flowers come again, mother, beneath the waning light,
> You'll never see me more in the long gray fields at night,
> When from the dry dark wold the summer airs blow cool
> On the oat-grass and the sword-grass and the bulrush in the pool.

In the fragment of an epic on the death of King Arthur full of most mournful beauty, we have—

> I heard the water lapping on the crag,
> And the long ripple washing in the reeds,
> * * *
> Then quickly rose Sir Bedivere, and ran,
> And leaping down the ridges lightly, plunged
> Among the bulrush beds.
> * * *
> The barge, with oar and sail,
> Moved from the brink like some full-breasted swan,
> That fluting a wild carol ere her death
> Ruffles her pure cold plume, and takes the flood
> With swarthy webs. Long stood Sir Bedivere,
> Revolving many memories, till the hull
> Looked one black dot against the verge of dawn,
> And on the mere the wailing died away.

Many similar pictures and expressions might be cited, to show how thoroughly the poet's mind has been tinted by the scenery amid which he has studied. We find constantly throughout the volumes such expressions as 'waste fens,' 'windy fields,' 'glooming flats,' 'sullen pools,' 'sluices with blackened waters,' 'sedges dank,' water-lilies, and all the other accessories wanting to complete a Lincolnshire landscape. These expressions, constant as they are, never weary. They are never introduced inopportunely; and they impress the mind of the reader almost as vividly as the objects referred to must have impressed that of the writer, and are besides a relief to the constant sameness of English scenery, as depicted in the pages of other poets.

Another characteristic of Mr Tennyson's style is his beautiful simplicity. Let no one underrate so great a merit. The first poetry of barbarism, and the most refined poetry of advancing civilisation, have it in common. As a specimen of great power and great simplicity, we make the following extracts from his poem on the old legend of the Lady Godiva:—

> She sought her lord, and found him where he stood
> About the hall, among his dogs, alone. * *
> * * She told him of their tears,
> And prayed him, 'If they pay this tax, they starve.'

Whereat he stared, replying, half-amazed,
'*You would not let your little finger ache*
For such as these?' 'But I would die,' said she.
He laughed, and swore by Peter and by Paul,
Then fillipped at the diamond in her ear:
'Oh ay, oh ay, you talk!' 'Alas!' she said,
'But prove me what it is I would not do.'
And from a heart as rough as Esau's hand,
He answered, 'Ride you naked through the town,
And I repeal it;' and nodding, as in scorn,
He parted. * *
So, left alone, the passions of her mind—
As winds from all the compass shift and blow—
Made war upon each other for an hour,
Till pity won. She sent a herald forth,
And bade him cry, with sound of trumpet, all
The hard condition; but that she would loose
The people. Therefore, as they loved her well,
From then till noon no foot should pace the street,
No eye look down, she passing; but that all
Should keep within, door shut, and window barred.
Then fled she to her inmost bower, and there
Unclasped the wedded eagles of her belt,
The grim earl's gift; but ever at a breath
She lingered, looking like a summer moon
Half dipt in cloud: anon she shook her head,
And showered the rippled ringlets to her knee;
Unclad herself in haste; adown the stair
Stole on; and, like a creeping sunbeam, slid
From pillar unto pillar, until she reached
The gateway: there she found her palfrey trapped
In purple, blazoned with armorial gold.
Then she rode forth, clothed o'er with chastity;
The deep air listened round her as she rode,
And all the low wind hardly breathed for fear.
The little wide-mouthed heads upon the spouts
Had cunning eyes to see: the barking cur
Made her cheek flame: her palfrey's footfall shot
Light horrors through her pulses: the blind walls
Were full of chinks and holes; and overhead
Fantastic gables, crowding, stared: but she
Not less through all bore up, till, last, she saw
The white-flowered elder thicket from the field
Gleam through the Gothic archways in the wall.
Then she rode back clothed on with chastity;
And one low churl, compact of thankless earth,
The fatal byword of all years to come,
Boring a little auger hole in fear,
Peeped; but his eyes, before they had their will,
Were shrivelled into darkness in his head,
And dropped before him. So the powers, who wait
On noble deeds, cancelled a sense misused:
And she that knew not, passed; and all at once,
With twelve great shocks of sound, the shameless noon
Was clashed and hammered from a hundred towers,
One after one; but even then she gained
Her bower: whence reissuing, robed and crowned,
To meet her lord, she took the tax away,
And built herself an everlasting name.

The ballad of 'Lady Clara Vere de Vere' might also be cited as a specimen of extreme simplicity united with great force; but as it has lately gone the round of the journals, we shall make an extract from a poem less known, and the length of which has saved it from so much newspaper publicity. 'The Talking Oak' is the title of a fanciful and beautiful ballad of seventy-five stanzas, in which a lover and an oak tree converse upon the charms of a sweet maiden named Olivia. The oak tree thus describes to the lover her visit to the park in which it grew:—

'Then ran she, gamesome as the colt,
And livelier than the lark,
She sent her voice through all the holt
Before her, and the park.
* * *

And here she came and round me played,
And sang to me the whole
Of those three stanzas that you made
About my "giant bole."

And in a fit of frolic mirth,
She strove to span my waist;
Alas! I was so broad of girth,
I could not be embraced.

I wished myself the fair young beech,
That here beside me stands,
That round me, clasping each in each,
She might have locked her hands.
* * *

'Oh muffle round thy knees with fern,
And shadow Sumner chase,
Long may thy topmost branch discern
The roofs of Sumner place!

But tell me, did she read the name
I carved with many vows,
When last with throbbing heart I came
To rest beneath thy boughs?'

'Oh yes; she wandered round and round
These knotted knees of mine,
And found, and kissed the name she found,
And sweetly murmured thine.

A tear-drop trembled from its source,
And down my surface crept;
My sense of touch is something coarse,
But I believe she wept.

Then flushed her cheek with rosy light;
She glanced across the plain,
But not a creature was in sight—
She kissed me once again.

Her kisses were so close and kind,
That, trust me, on my word,
Hard wood I am, and wrinkled rind,
But yet my sap was stirred.

And even into my inmost ring
A pleasure I discerned,
Like those blind motions of the spring
That show the year is turned.
* * *

I, rooted here among the groves,
But languidly adjust
My vapid vegetable loves
With anthers and with dust;

For ah! the Dryad days were brief
Whereof the poets talk,
When that which breathes within the leaf
Could slip its bark and walk.

But could I, as in times foregone,
From spray, and branch, and stem,
Have sucked and gathered into one
The life that spreads in them,

She had not found me so remiss;
But lightly issuing through,
I would have paid her kiss for kiss,
With usury thereto.'

Oh flourish high with leafy towers,
And overlook the lea;
Pursue thy loves among the bowers,
But leave thou mine to me.

Oh flourish, hidden deep in fern:
Old oak, I love thee well;
A thousand thanks for what I learn,
And what remains to tell.
* * *

The poem of 'Saint Simeon Stylites' is of another character, and portrays the spiritual pride of an ancient fanatic, with a simple and savage grandeur of words and imagery which we have never seen surpassed. It is too long for entire quotation, but the following extracts will show its beauty:—

Although I be the basest of mankind,
From scalp to sole one slough and crust of sin;
Unfit for earth, unfit for heaven, scarce meet
For troops of devils mad with blasphemy,
I will not cease to grasp the hope I hold
Of saintdom, and to clamour, mourn, and sob,
Battering the gates of heaven with storms of prayer—
Have mercy, Lord, and take away my sin.
Let this avail, just, dreadful, mighty God:
This not be all in vain; that thrice ten years,
Thrice multiplied by superhuman pangs
In hungers and in thirsts, fevers and cold;
In coughs, aches, stitches, ulcerous throes and cramps;
A sign betwixt the meadow and the cloud,
Patient on this tall pillar I have borne
Rain, wind, frost, heat, hail, damp, and sleet, and snow;
And I had hoped that ere this period closed,
Thou wouldst have caught me up into thy rest,
Denying not these weather-beaten limbs
The meed of saints—the white robe and the palm.
Oh! take the meaning, Lord: I do not breathe,
Not whisper any murmur of complaint.
Pain heaped ten hundredfold to this were still
Less burden, by ten hundredfold, to bear
Than were those lead-like tons of sin, that crushed
My spirit flat before thee.
Oh Lord, Lord!
Thou knowest I bore this better at the first;
For I was strong and hale of body then,

And though my teeth, which now are dropt away,
Would chatter with the cold, and all my beard
Was tagged with icy fringes in the moon,
I drowned the whoopings of the owl with sound
Of pious hymns and psalms, and sometimes saw
An angel stand and watch me as I sang.

* * *

Good people, you do ill to kneel to me.
What is it I have done to merit this?
I am a sinner viler than you all.
It may be I have wrought some miracles,
And cured some halt and maimed; but what of that?
It may be no one, even among the saints,
May match his pains with mine; but what of that?
Yet do not rise; for you may look on me,
And in your looking you may kneel to God.
Speak, is there any of you halt or maimed?
I think you know I have some power with Heaven
From my long penance: let him speak his wish,
For I can heal him. Power goes forth from me.
They say that they are healed. Ah, hark! they shout
'Saint Simeon Stylites.' Why, if so,
God reaps a harvest in me. * *
It cannot be but that I shall be saved,
Yea, crowned a saint. They shout 'Behold a saint!'
And lower voices saint me from above.
Courage, Saint Simeon; this dull chrysalis
Cracks into shining wings. * *
Oh, my sons, my sons!
I, Simeon of the pillar, by surname
Stylites among men—I, Simeon
The watcher on the column till the end—
I, Simeon, whose brain the sunshine bakes—
I, whose bald brows in silent hours become
Unnaturally hoar with rime—do now,
From my high nest of penance, here proclaim
That Pontius and Iscariot by my side
Showed fair like seraphs.

* * *

While I spake then, a sting of shrewdest pain
Ran shrivelling through me, and a cloud-like change
In passing, with a grosser film made thick
These heavy, horny eyes. The end! the end!
Surely the end! What's here? a shape, a shade,
A flash of light. Is that the angel there
That holds a crown? Come, blessed brother, come!
I know thy glittering face. I've waited long!
My brows are ready! What! deny it now?
'Tis gone—'tis here again: the crown! the crown!
So, now, 'tis fitted on, and grows to me,
And from it melt the dews of Paradise.

* * *

Speak, if there be a priest, a man of God
Among you there, and let him presently
Approach, and lean a ladder on the shaft,
And climbing up into mine airy home,
Deliver me the blessed sacrament;
For by the warning of the Holy Ghost
I prophesy that I shall die to-night
A quarter before twelve.
But thou, oh Lord,
Aid all this foolish people: let them take
Example, pattern—lead them to Thy light.

One more extract from the 'Lotos Eaters' will give a specimen of our poet's exquisite modulation of rhythm. This poem represents the luxurious lazy sleepiness of mind and body supposed to be produced in those who feed upon the lotos, and contains passages not surpassed by the finest descriptions in the Castle of Indolence. It is rich in striking and appropriate imagery, and is sung to a rhythm which is music itself.

Why are we weighed upon with heaviness,
And utterly consumed with sharp distress,
While all things else have rest from weariness?
All things have rest. Why should we toil alone?
We only toil, who are the first of things,
And make perpetual moan,
Still from one sorrow to another thrown.

* * *

Lo! in the middle of the wood
The folded leaf is wooed from out the bud
With winds upon the branch, and there
Grows green and broad, and takes no care,
Sun-steeped at noon, and in the moon
Nightly dew-fed; and turning yellow
Falls and floats adown the air.
Lo! sweetened with the summer light,
The full-juiced apple, waxing over mellow,
Drops in a silent autumn night.
All its allotted length of days;
The flower ripens in its place,
Ripens, and fades, and falls, and hath no toil,
Fast-rooted in the fruitful soil.

* * *

Let us alone. Time driveth onward fast,
And in a little while our lips are dumb.
Let us alone. What is it that will last?
All things are taken from us and become
Portions and parcels of the dreadful past.
Let us alone. What pleasure can we have
To war with evil? Is there any peace
In ever climbing up the climbing wave?
All things have rest, and ripen towards the grave;
In silence ripen, fall, and cease;
Give us long rest or death, dark death, or dreamful ease.

How sweet it were, hearing the downward stream,
With half-shut eyes ever to seem
Falling asleep in a half-dream!
To hear each other's whispered speech;
Eating the lotos, day by day;
To watch the crisping ripples on the beach,
And tender curving lines of creamy spray;
To lend our hearts and spirits wholly
To the influence of mild-minded melancholy;
To muse and brood, and live again in memory
With those old faces of our infancy,
Heaped over with a mound of grass,
Two handfuls of white dust, shut in an urn of brass.

* * *

We have not space for further extracts, but the beauty of these will show that Alfred Tennyson has not acquired fame without deserving it, and that he is not to be classed among the mob of mere verse-mongers, whose pertinacious pretensions are often a sore discomfort to the critic in the present day. Among his other pieces, we must mention the names of a few, which abound in beautiful passages, and are excellent both in design and execution. Of these our principal favourites are, 'The Two Voices,' 'Locksley Hall,' 'The Vision of Sin,' and 'Œnone.' The first-named is perhaps the finest specimen of versification in the volumes: the thoughts are noble in themselves, and nobly expressed, and the argument is worthy of the high strain in which it is sung. The Two Voices are the conflicting opinions in the breast of a man who is half inclined to be weary of the load of existence, and to throw it off; and hope and despair, certainty and doubt, are pitted against each other to decide the great question of the value of existence. The victory in the argument is given at last where it ought to be given; and the man walks forth on a Sabbath morning into the fields, reconciled to himself and to his kind, and wondering, amid the beauties of nature, how he could have ever communed with a voice so barren as that of despair. Locksley Hall is a bold original ballad, constructed in a metre somewhat unusual and cumbrous at first sight, but wonderfully pliant and musical in the hands of our author; in which a lover having been jilted by a false lady, repels her memory from his heart with bitter scorn, and goes over the whole catalogue of possible excitements into which he may rush to forget her for ever, and at the same time give the world an impetus in the onward career of improvement. The poem is far too long for quotation; but any reader who may not have seen it, and who may be tempted by our praise to read and study it, will find it a masterpiece, and be convinced by every stanza that none but a poet of high and original powers could have produced it. The Vision of Sin is chiefly remarkable for the exquisite art displayed in the versification of the introductory passage, and the skilful harmonising of sound to sense, showing how thoroughly the author has studied the art of poetry; and what power is in him, if he would but wield it; whilst Œnone is full of melancholy beauty and classic dignity.

In conclusion, we must express our hope that ere long English literature will again be enriched with a new volume from the pen of this author. Though not yet the poet of the age, he may perhaps become so. To reach this eminence, however, he must not linger too much upon the memories of the past; neither must he eat of the lotos, nor stray in the gardens of the Castle of

Indolence, in which we hear he takes more delight than becomes a man so gifted as he is. Whenever he does again appear before the world, a hearty welcome will greet him in every circle where poetry is still appreciated.

CROSSING THE ATLANTIC.

SOME weeks ago we had the gratification of inspecting that wonder of modern ship-building, the Great Britain; but before we describe the interesting things we then saw, it may be advisable to give a general account of the rise and progress of steam navigation across the Atlantic.

Before the first steamer made its way over the 3000 miles of sea which divides us from New York, communication was chiefly maintained by a fleet of sailing vessels—most of them built in America—called 'liners,' from their keeping up a regular line of communication between the two countries. They are considered, for fast sailing and skilful management, amongst the best ships on the high seas, taking on the average only thirty-two days to cross the Atlantic with heavy burdens. Yet, despite their general merits, they were liable, through the same causes that worse ships suffer from, to vexatious delays. During the stormy winter of 1836-1837, west winds prevailed with such strength and constancy, that for six weeks all the liners which started from the British ports were baffled by contrary winds, and at one time no fewer than eighteen mails were due at New York. Such delays were productive of something more than commercial inconvenience. In unusually protracted voyages, the passengers suffered extremely from want of food. So late as February 1837, the British ship Diamond arrived at New York from Liverpool, having been 100 days from port to port. There were 180 passengers, of whom 17 died, not from any disorder, but from mere starvation. The principal suffering was among the steerage passengers, the crew having been put upon allowance, and supplied to the last with food, though in small quantities. The description of the appearance of these poor wretches on their arrival, given by an eye-witness, is heart-rending. One man lived nine days on potato-peelings soaked in his scanty allowance of water; although, for any ordinary voyage, the supplies were abundant. Some, who had extra quantities, sold their stock of food to their less provident fellow-passengers, first at moderate rates, but, as the scarcity more fully developed itself, at enhanced prices, until finally half a sovereign was asked for a pint of meal. Before the arrival of the vessel, a sovereign had been offered and refused for a potato, as it was roasting before the fire.

The amount of commercial disaster arising from the frequent but unforeseen delays of sailing vessels may be judged of from the fact, that during 1837 a general break-up took place among the American merchants in London, solely occasioned by the ruthless winds, which kept back their ships and remittances.

It was natural, therefore, that steam should be earnestly looked to as a means of mitigating, or, if possible, of obviating such disastrous delays. Some such effort was in reality demanded, by the rapid increase of commerce between Great Britain and America.* Steam had long been most advantageously employed in river and coast navigation, though no successful voyage had been made across the main.

When it was first proposed to send a steam-vessel across the Atlantic, scientific men, who were looked up to as authorities on the point, declared that, if attempted, it would be found impracticable. Despite this opinion, however, some spirited merchants of Bristol determined to try the experiment, and forthwith laid down the hull of a steamer, which it was their intention to send over the ocean at all hazards. While the ship was being built, it happened that the British Association for the Advancement of Science met at Bristol, and one of its members demonstrated theoretically that a steam voyage direct to New York would be quite impracticable. And here we shall take leave to relate a story quite in point to this unfulfilled prophecy:—An English nobleman, who was staying in France, proposed to run his fleetest race-horse against time. The *savants* immediately set to work to calculate whether the feat were possible or not. They reckoned the volume of air the horse should displace at each bound, multiplied the weight of this by the necessary velocity, ascertained the strength of the horse by a dynameter—and, putting w for the weight, v for the velocity, and p for the power, proved, without running far into the calculation, that the achievement was impossible ($w \times v > p$). The Englishman was puzzled, admitted the demonstration to be irrefragable, but nevertheless ran his horse—and won!

This was nearly what happened to the Great Western and her premature critics. The mathematician alluded to computed that, for each horse-power of steam, one ton of coals would be required for every 1425 miles. 'Taking this as a basis of the calculation,' said he, 'and allowing one-fourth of a ton of coals per horse-power as spare fuel, the tonnage necessary for the fuel and machinery on a voyage from England to New York would be 3·70 tons per horse-power, which, for a vessel with engines of 400 horse-power, would be 1480 tons.'* Now, as the ship referred to was only intended to be 1200 tons' burden, the voyage was demonstrably impracticable.

The owners, however, placed more confidence in the practical skill of their engineers and ship-builders, than in the theoretical calculations of the philosopher. The ship was completed, and proved to be of the following dimensions:—Length of deck 230 feet; breadth, including paddle-boxes, 58 feet 4 inches; depth of the hold 23 feet; the vessel, when laden, drawing 16 feet of water. The paddle-wheels were 28 feet in diameter, each paddle-board being 10 feet long. There were two engines, of 225 horse-power each, weighing together 200 tons; the boilers—of which there were four—100 tons additional. Instead of 1200 tons, as at first intended, the tonnage had been increased to 1340 tons. The total cost of the ship was about L.63,000. When ready for sea, she was freighted; seven adventurous persons became passengers; and on the 8th of April 1838, the Great Western started from Bristol to solve the great problem of ocean steam navigation.

A few snatches from the journal of one of the passengers were published in the Quarterly Review.† From them we learn that the new steamer had only been three days at sea when she overtook a brave old 'liner,' which had sailed from Liverpool seven days earlier, 'careering and plunging to a lively foam and a fair wind.' The Great Western dashed a-head, soon leaving the sailing-vessel astern. The new wonder of the deep continued her voyage without interruption, and arrived off New York on the afternoon of St George's day, having performed the voyage in the unprecedentedly short space of 15 days and 10 hours, without let or hindrance, and with several tons of coals to spare.

It is necessary to state here, that three days before the Great Western set out, the Sirius—a steamer which usually plied between London and Cork—was despatched, and arrived on the morning of the same day (23d of April). The wharfs and shores within view of New York harbour were crowded with thousands of spectators who had welcomed the arrival of the Sirius, and tarried anxiously for the approach of the Great Western. They had not long to wait, for a few hours after the Sirius had dropped anchor, a long trail of smoke was seen in the distance, and the hull of the expected steamer appeared. The sight afforded to those on board the Great Western was peculiarly exciting. From the time of her crossing the bar of the harbour,

* Of the total produce and manufactures exported from Great Britain and Ireland in 1836 (valued at L.53,368,572), as much as was declared to be worth L.12,425,605 sterling went to the United States—that is to say, the Americans were our customers to the extent of above 23 per cent. of our entire exports for that year!

* Report of Proceedings of British Association.—*Athenæum*, vol. ix. p. 656. See also Edinburgh Review.

† Volume lxii.

all her 'poles' were set aloft, and flags gaily streaming at each—the foreign ensign at the gaff, and at the fore a combination of the British and American. 'At 3 P.M.' continues the passenger above referred to, 'we passed the Narrows, opening the bay of New York, sails all furled, and the engines at their topmost speed. The city reposed in the distance, scarcely discernible. As we proceeded, an exciting scene awaited us. Coming abreast of Bradlow's Island, we were saluted by the fort with twenty-six guns (the number of the States): we were taking a festive glass on deck. The health of the British Queen had just been proposed, the toast drunk, and, amid the cheers that followed, the arm was just raised to consummate the naming, when the fort opened its fire. The effect was electrical—down came the colours, and a burst of exultation arose, in the midst of which the President's health was proposed. The city now grew distinct: masts, buildings, spires, trees, streets, were discerned; the wharfs appeared, black with myriads of the population hurrying down, at the signal of the telegraph, to every point of view. And then came shoals of boats—the whole harbour covered with them. And now the new-comer reaches the Sirius, lying at anchor in North River, gay with flowing streamers, and literally crammed with spectators—her decks, paddle-boxes, rigging, mast-head high. We passed round her, giving and receiving three hearty cheers, then turned towards the Battery. Here myriads again were collected: boats crowded round us in countless confusion: flags were flying, guns firing, and bells ringing. The vast multitude set up a shout—a long enthusiastic cheer—echoed from point to point, and from boat to boat, till it seemed as though they never would have done.'

So much for the first transports; and after them a little dry investigation into the wherefore of two ships crossing the broad Atlantic in defiance of mathematical calculation, will not come amiss. On examination, it turned out that, although the computations were correct enough, the scientific men were out in their data. The voyage did *not* require nearly four tons of coals per horse-power, as was proved by the consumption on board each vessel. The Sirius carried no more than 453 tons of coals; but she was also provided with 43 barrels of resin, which is said to equal 21½ tons of coals. On taking stock at New York, it was found that 22 tons of coals were still on board. Instead of the 1480 tons which it was predicted the Great Western would have to burn, she took out less than half that quantity (660 tons), of which 450 tons only were consumed! The distance she had run was 3111 nautical miles.

The Great Western having remained a fortnight in harbour, started on her homeward voyage on the 7th of May, when, at the lowest computation, one hundred thousand New Yorkers turned out to witness her departure. Sixty-six passengers had now courage to venture in her. After steaming for exactly a fortnight, and over 3218 nautical miles, she arrived at Bristol on the 22d of May. An immense multitude assembled to welcome her back into the 'king's road,' which they did with tremendous cheers. To show some of the results to be expected from this approximation in point of time of the two continents, one of the passengers, on landing, presented a splendid bouquet of American flowers to the lady of Captain Claxton, the manager of the Great Western Steam Navigation Company. They appeared as fresh as if the dew had been still on them. At a grand dinner of the Bristol citizens two days after, specimens of flax and cotton yarn were exhibited, the raw material of which had been shipped eighteen days previously, and manufactured in a recently-established mill in Bristol.

Thus the great problem of crossing the Atlantic by steam was solved, in spite of the winds, the waves, and the philosophers. 'But this is only *one* voyage,' said the sceptics; 'let us see the effect of the enormous wear and tear the Great Western will have yet to encounter.' That has been tested, and the result is as follows:—Between the 8th of April 1838, and the 23d of November 1844, she performed seventy passages, in the course of which she had run 256,000 statute miles, at an average speed of a fraction more than ten miles per hour.* She had conveyed 5774 passengers, besides an immense quantity of goods: she had not been favoured by the weather, that having been in some instances severely stormy: she has not met with any serious accident: yet we learn from the report of a surveyor appointed by government to examine her, and from the frequent reports of the Surveyor-General at Lloyd's, that she is as sound in material, and as perfect in form, as on the day she was launched.

When the practicability of this long voyage was fully established, other vessels were speedily put on the same track. The Sirius, having come back in safety, was replaced on her own station, between London and Cork; but was succeeded by the Royal William, which, however, only made a few voyages, and was likewise placed on another passage. In 1838, a British and American Steam Navigation Company was formed in London, and built a steam-ship of larger dimensions than the Great Western, at an expense of L.100,000, calling her the British Queen. Her burthen in tons was 2016. She sailed from Portsmouth on the 12th July 1839, and reached New York in 15½ days. Although she performed so well, that in the year 1840 she made five voyages to, and five from, New York, yet, from want of patronage, the company resolved, in 1841, to sell her, which they did to the Belgian government. The vessel which this company built to succeed her brings us to the most melancholy passage that occurs in the history of steam navigation. She was called the President, and registered to carry 2000 tons. In 1840 she made two complete voyages from and back to Liverpool, without any material accident.

In April 1841 the President left New York for Liverpool, with thirty passengers on board, and up to this day no satisfactory intelligence has been received regarding her fate. Her non-arrival at the usual time caused great excitement in this country; and for days and weeks, and even months, it was conjectured that she might have been driven by stress of weather to the Bermudas, or to some other islands in the Atlantic Ocean. Some thought that she might have been forced on the coast of Africa; others that she had been struck by an iceberg; but the general opinion was, after months of anxious expectancy, that she had foundered at sea during the very severe gales which then prevailed. It was remarkable that no vessel had spoken with her on such a well-frequented route as the Atlantic. The only ship that reported having seen any craft like the President was a Portuguese brig, which, on 23d April 1841, while in latitude 31 degrees north and longitude 49 degrees west, or about the middle of the Atlantic, saw a very large steamer under sails, going at the rate of three or four miles an hour. No smoke issued from the funnel, and the paddle-wheels were not in motion. The captain of the brig saw the steamer both on that and the following day, and even approached within three or four miles of her while pursuing his own homeward route. She did not hail the brig, nor did she appear to be at all in a disabled state. A British man-of-war and two Portuguese vessels were sent to cruise in search of the President, but without success; and all hope for her safety was abandoned.

The prevailing conjecture is, that she 'broke her back;' that is, had been severed in the middle in a violent storm which raged while she was at sea, and that she must have sunk bodily at a moment's warning.

A third company was formed in Liverpool, called the Transatlantic Steam Navigation Company, in whose service there are at present five vessels employed to sail between various parts of North America and Liverpool. They are named the Britannia, the Caledonia, the Hibernia, the Cambria, and the Acadia. All these ships were built in the river Clyde, and are of the same model and dimensions, carrying engines of 300 horse-power, and burdens of 1200 tons. To them the government intrusts the transmission of the mails to the United States and Canada, for which it pays the Transatlantic

* Till the year 1842, the Great Western sailed from Bristol; since then, her port of departure has been Liverpool.

Company L.80,000 per annum. Except two rather severe accidents to the Caledonia, which happened respectively in May 1842 and the 2d July 1843, nothing has occurred to these vessels to prevent their regularly fulfilling their engagements to the post-office and the public. They sail twice each month from the beginning of April to the end of November, and once during December, January, February, and March.

Meanwhile, the Great Western continues her voyages, and keeps up her fame, having her glory brightened rather than dimmed by competition with rivals. The spirited company to which she belongs have recently made another bold experiment. They have built an iron ship, which is a hundred feet longer than a first-rate man-of-war, and is propelled without side-paddles. She was named the Great Britain—a visit to her we intend to describe in a succeeding paper.

STRUGGLES OF YOUTH, IN THE CASE OF JAMES CORSON.

It has often been said that an earnest desire, steadily persevered in, is sure to bring about in time its own accomplishment, however improbable such an event may appear at first; and there has perhaps rarely occurred a more striking proof of there being some truth in this remark than in the following history.

It was the earnest wish of James Corson, when a boy of little more than seven years of age, to be a 'doctor' in England; and certainly when the wish was first uttered, there appeared very little prospect of its accomplishment. The father of the boy, who was gardener to a gentleman at Dalscairth, in Dumfriesshire, had a large family, with so small a salary, that he could scarcely spare his boys to attend the parish school; and it was with a heavy heart that 'Jamie' was often compelled to leave his books to attend to the manual labours in which his father found it necessary to employ him. When he was ten years of age, however, a heavier blow fell upon him. His father left Dalscairth, and took a situation in Yorkshire, where, as he found education much dearer than in Scotland, he was no longer able to send James to school. Still, however, the boy remained unshaken in his determination to be a doctor in England; and he spent every leisure moment in poring over his books. His perseverance and his ambition began to attract the notice of the house servants of the gentleman with whom the elder Corson was gardener. He excited a particular interest in the butler, who, being a great favourite with his master, easily obtained permission to take the boy into the family as his assistant. This step, however, at first was the occasion of pain rather than pleasure to James, as his fellow-servants, who had heard of his ambitious desires, never ceased jeering him about them; and indeed the contrast they afforded to his actual situation was sufficiently striking. He was now about fourteen, tall, and well grown for his age, but shy and awkward in his manners, and speaking with a strong Scotch accent, which the Yorkshiremen, though they perhaps speak worse English than is met with in any other county, were particularly severe upon. The jeering of his companions, however, had no other effect on James Corson than to give him another object for his ambition, for he now determined that he would conquer his Scotch accent, and learn to speak pure English, which he did do in the end.

James Corson, during the four years that he remained as assistant to the butler, contrived, with that person's assistance, to perfect himself in writing and accounts; and as he never omitted any opportunity that occurred of acquiring knowledge, he was able, when he left Yorkshire, to take the situation of usher in a school in Wigtonshire. Here he stayed two years, during which he learnt Latin and Greek, and the rudiments of French; but as his salary was very small, he took the first opportunity that occurred of removing to Whitehaven, where also he was usher in a school. In both these situations he saved all the money he could, in the hope that he might at last realise the project that had never once been absent from his thoughts.

At Christmas 1835, James Corson left his situation at Whitehaven, and returned to his father's cottage, previously to visiting London, where he had at last determined to push his fortune. He found, however, upon inquiry, that what he possessed would be nothing in London, and would but barely maintain him there while he was studying as a surgeon, without leaving him any money to pay the fees. This information depressed his spirits exceedingly, and when he returned home, after consulting with a friend at Leeds, he told his father that he began for the first time to fear his wishes never would be accomplished. The elder Corson took in the Gardeners' Magazine; and as it was lying on the table, James listlessly opened it, when his attention was caught by an advertisement for an amanuensis, which had been inserted by Mr Loudon for himself. The countenance of the young man brightened up, and he exclaimed, 'Then I'll see London at last!' His father and friends laughed at him, and argued the improbability of his succeeding in obtaining the situation. But his presentiment had been right; and though Mr Loudon had about a hundred and thirty answers to his advertisement, James Corson's letter was so well expressed, and written in such a manly, yet modest style, that he was preferred. It may easily be conceived that young Corson's delight, when he received Mr Loudon's letter, was beyond description. His father says he was wild with joy.

Mr Loudon at that time was engaged in writing his great work, the Arboretum Britannicum; and as he had also three magazines appearing monthly, a great many persons were employed in his office; but of these Mr Corson only became intimate with two; namely, Mr Rauch, a young German, who was one of the draughtsmen, and Mr W. Baxter, son to the curator of the botanic garden at Oxford, who was an amanuensis. Mr Corson's salary was a pound a-week, for which he was engaged in Mr Loudon's office from eight in the morning till six, and he had to find his own lodgings and food, with the exception of some bread and cheese and beer, which all the young men had at one o'clock. Notwithstanding his moderate salary, and the length of time he was occupied every day, young Corson now saw all his wishes on the point of being realised, and he immediately entered a class of students in surgery with a Mr Demott of Charlotte Street, Bloomsbury. He found, however, that, to enable him to pay the fees out of his small salary, it would be necessary for him to practise the most rigid economy; and he accordingly ate nothing but oatmeal porridge, which he made himself, in addition to the very moderate lunch which he ate at Bayswater. To increase his funds, he also took in writing to do at night, after he had finished his medical studies. A very strong constitution, and the most determined perseverance, enabled him to continue these exertions for two years; during the whole of which time he never took a single day's pleasure, or indulged himself with more than four hours' sleep in each night. It may also be added, that during this period, notwithstanding the severity of his medical studies, he never neglected in the slightest degree Mr Loudon's business; and that he always stayed his full time, of from eight till six, in the office at Bayswater, where his indefatigable industry, joined to his quiet and amiable disposition, rendered him a general favourite.

Few young men who have studied surgery under the most favourable circumstances have ever passed their examination with more credit than Mr Corson; and he was even praised by the examining surgeons for the very great care and attention with which he gave his answers. He had now so far attained the long desired object of his ambition, that he was a surgeon in England; but he was at a loss how to turn his newly attained honours to account, as he had no money to purchase a business, or even to fit up a surgery. In this dilemma Mr Rauch, the young German, with whom Mr Corson had formed an acquaintance at Mr Loudon's, came to his assistance, and detailed the circumstances of the case to a friend, who happened to be a ship-owner. 'I have no interest in the medical line on land,' said this gentleman; 'but if the young Scotchman does not object to the sea, I think I could get him appointed surgeon to a South-Sea whaler; and if he is careful, he may possibly save L.70 or L.100 out of his pay during the three years the ship will be on her voyage, and that will be enough to set him up as a surgeon anywhere.' It may easily be conceived that Mr Corson made no objection to the sea, and, in fact, he sailed with Captain Benson, master of the Kitty, in the autumn of 1838.

Up to this time all had gone well with Mr Corson. He had succeeded in everything he undertook; and he had so nearly attained the summit of his ambition, that even those who had laughed at his projects as wild and impracticable, were now compelled to own that all he had wished for lay almost within his grasp. The voyage out of the whaler was also highly successful; and Corson not only fulfilled all the ordinary duties of his situation most satisfactorily, but on one occasion, when a seaman had had his leg lacerated by a shark, he had performed amputation in a masterly manner. Half the voyage had been performed, and they were on their road homeward. Corson had made a collection of plants for Mr Loudon, and of shells, partly for his kind friend Mr Rauch, and partly for Mrs Loudon; and he had, besides, saved upwards of L.70 towards the L.100 he was to accumulate.

The remainder of the tale is soon told. While in the tropics, Mr Corson had occupied himself in clearing the shells he had collected from the animals they contained; and from fatigue, or perhaps from the noxious effluvia evolved by the decaying animals, he was taken ill of fever, which carried him off in fourteen days. He died on the 16th of June 1841, in the twenty-seventh year of his age, a striking illustration of what may be done by industry and perseverance.

[It will be understood that the proceedings here detailed are not held up as an example to be followed, but only as a remarkable instance of the pursuit of knowledge under difficulties. Mr Corson's application to duty and study was so far beyond what our natural powers justify, that it is surprising he did not sink under it. His not doing so may be attributed to an unusually vigorous constitution. All ordinary endowed persons must be in the greatest danger from such overtaskings; and even of those who are constituted most favourably, the greater number would fail to survive such a course as that passed through by Mr Corson while studying for his profession.—Ed.]

ORIGIN OF THE TERM 'MERRY ANDREW.'

This term, with which every child out of the nursery is so familiar, and which is inseparably associated with his ideas of grins, grimaces, and humorous sayings, has a much more exalted origin than many may suppose. The medical profession, which has given rise to more nicknames and slang phrases than almost any other, has the paternity of this one also to answer for. During the time of Henry VIII., Edward VI., and Queen Mary, there lived and practised as a physician in London one Andrew Borde, who to his vast learning and knowledge of foreign parts, added the most whimsical and facetious characteristics. This individual was originally a Carthusian monk, but the severities of the order being rather inconsistent with his irrepressible propensity to humour, he abandoned the brotherhood, and betook himself to physic. After travelling the European continent and some parts of Africa, he settled in the metropolis, where he became a physician to Henry VIII., and author of several works on medicine, poetry, and literature. 'He was a man,' says a contemporary, 'and of a whimsical head; he frequented fairs and markets, and harangued the populace in public; he made humorous speeches, couched in such language as caused mirth, and wonderfully propagated his fame.' From his use of such speeches at markets and fairs, he came to be better known as Merry Andrew than as Dr Borde; and thus those who in after times imitated the same humorous jocose language were styled 'Merry Andrews.' Though weak in these respects, he is otherwise acknowledged to have been a learned man, a good poet, and perhaps the best physician of his time. He was the author of the Merry Tales of the Wise Men of Gotham; the Introduction to Knowledge, a poem; the Miller of Abingdon; the Principles of Astronomical Prognostications; the Doctrine of Health; the Promptuary of Medicine; a book of jests; and other pamphlets. Dr Borde died a prisoner in the Fleet, April 1549; yet, it is said, not for debt, as he left considerable inheritance behind him. The conduct of Merry Andrews conveys to us certainly no very exalted notion of the medical profession three hundred years ago; though, all other progress considered, it was not then one whit more degraded by Borde and his brethren with their mountebanks, than it is now by the quacks and pill venders who batten on the credulity of the public.

AN AVIARY ON A GREAT SCALE.

It is a pleasing thing to witness, says a correspondent of the Zoologist for March, the confidence and familiarity of the nightingale when protected; as, for instance, in the promenade at Gradenfeld, in Prussia, a beautiful planted piece of ground, extending nearly a quarter of a mile along both banks of a small stream. In addition to the penalties denounced by Prussian law against those who rob the nests of the nightingale, a watchman is stationed here during the breeding season for additional security. This may perhaps appear singular in our matter-of-fact age; but I am confident that no lover of nature who had resided in Gradenfeld, and enjoyed the delicious concerts which these birds maintain both day and night, except from about two to five o'clock P.M., would refuse his aid to such a custom. Many a bird-fancier is at much greater expense, not to speak of trouble, in keeping a ghost of a nightingale caged, and why should we wonder at the inhabitants of Gradenfeld, with their open-air habits, taking care that their favourite resort shall never become songless? Seated on a broad-leaved jessamine, the shrub which generally conceals the nest, the male bird will sing although you pass within four feet of him, eyeing you as if perfectly aware that he is a privileged character. Besides the nightingales, a great variety of other birds find shelter in this privileged place, and being never molested, afford the naturalist excellent opportunities of observing their habits. Amongst others, the hoopoes generally build here; the golden oriole suspends its curious nest from the highest branches of the aspen, and breathes out its cheerful flute-notes at evening; the Bohemian wax-wing is a regular and plentiful winter visitant; whilst a variety of finches and warblers of less note complete this real 'happy family.'

THE TWO ROSES.

Being with my friend in a garden, we gathered each of us a rose. He handled his tenderly; smelt it but seldom, and sparingly. I always kept mine to my nose, or squeezed it in my hand, whereby in a very short time it lost both its colour and sweetness; but his still remained as sweet and fragrant as if it had been growing upon its own root. These roses, said I, are the true emblems of the best and sweetest creature enjoyments in the world, which, being moderately and cautiously used and enjoyed, may for a long time yield sweetness to the possessor of them: but if once the affections seize too greedily upon them, and squeeze them too hard, they quickly wither in our hands, and we lose the comfort of them; and that either through the soul surfeiting upon them, or their just removal, because of the excess of our affections to them. It is a point of excellent wisdom to keep the golden bridle of moderation upon all the affections we exercise on earthly things.—*Flavel.*

UNION.

Science, the partisan of no country, but the beneficent patroness of all, has liberally opened a temple where all may meet. Her influence on the mind, like that of the sun on the chilled earth, has long been preparing it for higher cultivation and further improvement. The philosopher of one country sees not an enemy in the philosopher of another: he takes his seat in the temple of science, and asks not who sits beside him.

Published by W. and R. Chambers, High Street, Edinburgh (also 98 Miller Street, Glasgow); and, with their permission, by W. S. Orr, Amen Corner, London.—Printed by W. and R. Chambers, Edinburgh.

CONDUCTED BY WILLIAM AND ROBERT CHAMBERS, EDITORS OF 'CHAMBERS'S INFORMATION FOR THE PEOPLE,' 'CHAMBERS'S EDUCATIONAL COURSE,' &c.

No. 81. New Series. SATURDAY, JULY 19, 1845. Price 1½d.

BARGAIN-HUNTERS.

There is a large class of persons who are so inveterately prone to bargain-hunting, that they seldom or never purchase anything of an abateable nature which they do not cheapen as much as possible. This habit is not so much attributable to any lack of means in the buyers, as to a childish love of obtaining a maximum quantity at a minimum value, which affords them the additional gratification of boasting afterwards of their bargains, and complimenting themselves on their own shrewdness. With such persons the purchase of sixpennyworth of oranges is as eagerly seized to gratify their favourite propensity as the order for a set of plate; and we have known instances of individuals, possessed of ample pecuniary resources, so confirmed in this habit, as to wander in anxious uncertainty from stall to stall before they could decide the momentous question as to which was the most eligible pennyworth of apples.

This habit of bargain-hunting, while we laugh at it for its folly, deserves to be denounced for its mischief. It holds out a premium to unfair trading, to trickery and lying: it is a cruel oppression of him who buys upon him who sells, and powerfully assists in lowering the hard-earned wages of the poor mechanic. The manufacturer is compelled, in order to gratify the morbid love of cheapness, to produce goods of the most trashy and useless description, and to reduce the wages of those whom he employs to the lowest fraction. The shopkeeper, in order to secure this description of customers, is forced to adulterate his articles; to profess them to be what he knows they are not; to exert himself, by short weight, lying puffs, inferior substitutions, and a thousand unworthy artifices, to keep on a fair equality with his neighbours. No sooner does a new shop open, the owner of which professes to sell cheaper than usual, than he is patronised by the bargain-hunters, to the great injury and often ruin of his more conscientious competitors. Whether he himself ever intend to pay for his stock is not inquired into; whether he intend to pursue an honest and honourable course is held to be no business of the customers: he sells cheapest, and this supersedes every other consideration. The consequence too often is, that the bargain-offering tradesman, after having injured many a respectable shopkeeper around him, suddenly decamps at the expiration of a few months, and the secret of his bargains is at length apparent; namely, that never having intended to pay for the goods himself, any receipt must be a clear gain to him, and he could thus afford to sell at prices which must be ruinous to the upright dealer.

This cheapening mania exercises also a most pernicious influence in producing distrust, duplicity, and unmanly feeling between seller and buyer. The seller, sharpened by past experience, is in self-defence compelled, in order to obtain a remunerating profit, to ask more than the real value of the article, in order to leave room for the abatement which he expects as a matter of course to follow. The offer by the buyer of less than is asked is really an insult, for it virtually implies that the seller is either a fool or a rogue—a fool to take so little, or a rogue to ask so much; and thus the straightforward honesty and integrity which should characterise dealings in the market or the shop, as much as anywhere else, is set aside, and seller and buyer meet together with a feeling that confidence and honour are out of place there, and that cunning and overreaching are among the recognised moralities of trade. The seller, while he introduces the article to his customer, feels a conviction that unless he adds an untruth to the specification of the price, unless an assertion is made or a warranty given which it would be absurd to believe, the article will be rejected, and the hesitating customer will not purchase it, but patronise some other less scrupulous tradesman. The bargain-hunter, on his side, turns the article over in a contemptuous manner, exerts his ingenuity to find some fault in it which shall afford a pretext for a lower offer, and having found a real or an imaginary one, bids something below what he often must know is its real value. The poor tradesman wants ready money, the article really cost him more, he knows of other shops where it may be had at that price, and, with a sickening heart and an inward condemnation of the selfishness of man, he accepts the offer, and the purchaser departs with his bargain. But, strange metamorphosis, the article so recently pronounced almost worthless, the purchaser now boasts of as excellent, worth double the money, and delights to hear his friends innocently express their surprise how it could possibly have been made for the price. Such a mode of dealing is unmanly, ungenerous, and unjust, and requires but to be candidly considered to be denounced by all who think and feel rightly.

The influence of this pernicious system upon the labouring part of the community is cruel and disastrous. Some time ago, the public were presented with accounts of the misery prevalent among a large class of women in the metropolis, whose occupation consisted in the making of shirts at the insignificant sum of three halfpence each. Indignation, as it appears to us, was on this occasion levelled at the wrong parties. The blame, we are persuaded, lay less with the immediate than the remote employers. The public, which vented its anger on the shopkeeper, was the real transgressor; for the dealer merely obeyed the popular demand. Pressed upon by the insane cry for low-priced articles, as well as by a general competition, the manufacturer and shopkeeper, if they would do business at all, must reduce their expenses to the lowest point in order to obtain any profit, and to this end are compelled to wring from their workpeople the utmost amount of work for the least possible remuneration. Unreasonably protracted hours are resorted to, toil is not allowed to cease with the day, the labour of the woman is introduced to supersede that of the man, and that of the child to supersede both, education is necessarily neglected, deformity produced, stimulants resorted to, vicious habits formed, and squalor and disease are induced; and all this too often that the purchaser may procure an article at a fractional abatement. The occasional subscription and the cold donation of charity are but a poor reparation for depriving the workman of his honest earnings, and the manly independence of pocket and of character which it is so desirable he should possess. It is true that the payment of fair prices by the buyer will not always secure fair remuneration to the operative, but the habit of cheapening must have a tendency to lower wages and inflict misery on the producers.

The pernicious practice of bargain-hunting is, we fear, by no means confined to the rougher sex. It is to be lamented that the practice is far too common among that sex whose kindness of heart and sensibility need no eulogy, and whose propensity in this respect we can attribute to no other source than thoughtlessness. It is perhaps also partly to be accounted for by the fact, that females generally have less money at command than men, and therefore when they spend it are perhaps somewhat more unreasonable in their exchanging expectations. A little thought as to the amount of misery to others which must result from the gratification of this propensity, would surely be sufficient to convince them of its unreasonableness and inhumanity. Little do ladies think, while they are cheapening the thread and the tape, or the shawls or the linens they purchase, how much poverty and misery they are assisting to entail on the sickly operative who makes them, and how much of the ignorance and destitution and vice, the bare mention of which shocks their sensibilities, is traceable to this baneful practice.

The habit we have denounced is also very fallacious in a pecuniary point of view. The most shrewd and practised cheapener is often deceived, and finds, after he has secured the bargain, that, to use the common phrase, 'it is too cheap to be good,' or that he did not really want it, and therefore it was dear at any price. He discovers too late that what he has bought was made to be looked at rather than used, to deceive rather than satisfy, and that the little he gave for it was far too much for *such* an article, as it was really worth nothing. The cheapest things may be very dear, and the dearest very cheap, and good articles cannot reasonably be expected at any other than fair prices. Independently therefore of the injury which the habit of cheapening inflicts upon the workman, it is deceptive and unprofitable even to the purchaser. The prices of shopkeepers are certainly not always to be paid without demur, for this would be to hold out a premium to imposition and extortion, but there should be considerateness on the part of the purchaser as to what ought to be the fair price of such an article. To deal as much as possible with tradesmen who are known for their integrity and uprightness, without being seduced by every unprincipled adventurer who professes to be 'selling off under prime cost,' and closing business at a 'tremendous sacrifice,' will be found in the long-run not only the truest economy, and the most satisfactory to the purchaser, but also the most advantageous to the wellbeing of society and the general interests of honesty and honour.

NOTICE OF TWO OLD PERIODICAL WORKS.

We have chanced to be lately introduced to two local predecessors of our own—that is, two Edinburgh periodicals of light literature—published upwards of a century ago; and which, to the best of our knowledge, are entirely unknown to the present generation. One is entitled *The Rêveur*,* and was commenced on Friday the 18th November 1737; the last number possessed by us —which, however, does not seem to be the last published—is dated May 19, 1738. The other paper takes the name of *Letters of the Critical Club*. To evade the duty of a halfpenny then exacted from weekly papers, it was published monthly, the various articles nevertheless being dated on particular days. We possess only the numbers of the first half of the year 1738. The Rêveur is a large quarto, each number comprising two leaves: it is stamped, and the price was 2s. 6d. per quarter. It appears to have been 'printed for A. Kincaid, and sold at his shop opposite to the Parliament Close, where subscriptions and advertisements are taken in.' The Letters of the Critical Club appear in a duodecimo form, at sixpence per monthly number: they are 'sold by A. Martin, and other booksellers in town.' At the end of our copy of the former work, there is an odd number of another Edinburgh periodical of the same character, entitled *The Conjurer*, and dated January 16, 1736. The Critical Club also speak of 'several attempts made in this place of publishing papers of this kind,' adding, 'and frequently with very indifferent success.' It thus appears that the spirit for such literary undertakings was much more active in our northern capital, about the time of the Porteous Riot, than might have been supposed. It is amusing, however, to mark the small scale on which these publications proceeded. The Rêveur states in his thirteenth number, that the demand for his paper is so great, that his bookseller 'thinks of getting another servant.' In the case of the present journal, an analogous boast would, we suppose, relate to a few more horse-power for the engine driving the printing-machines.

At the date of the Rêveur and Critical Letters, elegant literature had hardly an existence in Scotland. The Blairs, Robertsons, Humes, and Smiths, who first successfully competed with English authors, were youths barely emerged from college. Allan Ramsay is almost the only literary name of the period now remembered, and his department was that of familiar Scottish verse. We must therefore expect that any literary essays produced in Edinburgh at such a time would only show tendencies or aspirations towards those qualities which command respectful attention. The effort is certainly made in both of the papers under our notice, but with a very moderate degree of success. And in one respect, we have even to regret that such an exertion was made, for it has caused an almost total absence of such national and local allusions as would have now of themselves given the papers a value. The social features alluded to are English as much as Scotch, and there is not one vernacular expression used throughout the whole of either book. There is the appearance, however, of scholarship and reflection, especially in the Rêveur; and in both, the cause of virtue and of rational manners is zealously maintained.† Several writers

* *Fr.*—The Dreamer.

† By a strange coincidence, a friend whom we met on the day on which the above article was written, mentioned that David Ritchie, of Manor, the original of the 'Black Dwarf,' had heard of the *Letters of the Critical Club* as an excellent book, there being no 'debushery' in it. The poor dwarf, who had a strong literary taste, though of a limited kind, actually interested his neighbours, Professor Adam Ferguson and Sir James Montgomery, to write to Edinburgh and London for a copy. They were not successful; but David ultimately, our friend thinks, obtained the book.

seem to have been at work; but all conjecture as to their names is now nearly in vain. Hamilton of Bangour might have been suggested as a probable contributor, if not editor, did not the politics of both lean to the Whig side. And this reminds us to mention that the Letters bear a courteous, but not fulsome dedication to President Forbes, a generous patron of literature in those days, as the author of the Seasons well knew.

The Critical Club is described in the first number as composed of Will Portly, Dick Crotchet, Lady Courtly, her daughter Miss Jeanie, and other fictitious characters; and it is, in fact, of their letters that the subsequent papers consist. One trait of Crotchet is Scottishly characteristic, that, by his habit of humming songs, 'he has offended many good people on Sundays.' Miss Jeanie Courtly is an admirer of romances: she reads Cassandra by the parlour fire. She 'is far from having anything of the prude in her character; yet she is a very modest girl; she will allow one kiss before company, but is highly offended if he [her lover] attempts to steal it in a corner.'

In the second letter, Will Portly remarks with surprise, what is still liable to similar remark, that mirthfulness should take such possession of the public at the close of the year, when all men are so apt to complain of the shortness of life, and the rapid transit of time. 'Among the vulgar,' says our essayist, 'there is scarce a man but thinks it an incumbent duty on him to be drunk at this occasion. In these days there is no work done, no business minded, and every one gives a full swing to joy. Ask any man why he was so joyful, for instance, last occasion of this kind, he will scarce be able to give a better answer than this, "that the old year has come to a close, and the new one is begun." As if he had grounds to rejoice because so much more time has passed over his head, and because he is nearer his grave by one whole year than he was at the last occasion of this kind.'

The subjects treated in the Critical Letters are by no means *recherchés*. First we have the treatise on time; next we have an essay combating the popular ideas about apparitions and omens; afterwards one on religious intolerance; and so on. In a letter respecting theatricals, the writer expresses his regret for the loss of the Edinburgh playhouse, and proceeds to defend the stage from its calumniators. His argument as to the expense it occasioned to its votaries is characteristic of those days of false political economy. The actors are such thoughtless people, that they spend as fast as they gain; and, says he, 'I reckon nothing an expense upon a place but what carries money out of it, which this does not.' 'I think,' he says in conclusion, 'I have reason to speak thus in favour of the theatre, since I have been frequently sensible of reaping considerable instruction from attending it. I remember, some time ago, I saw the tragedy of Cato performed here; everything before the scenes seemed to be very solemn and serious, and I was taken as much with it as if I had beheld the real persons of Cato and the other Romans concerned: but taking it into my head to step behind the scenes between acts, into the dressing-room, how different was their appearance from what it had been on the stage. There I heard Lucia and the virtuous Marcia scolding like oyster-wenches; Juba, the Numidian prince, was exercising the office of barber to his general Syphax; Marcus and Portius were adjusting their full-bottomed periwigs at a glass, and making up a mixture of a Roman and a modern beau; Cato and Sempronius were very amicably drinking a mug of porter together; and Lucius was taking a chaw of tobacco. This difference in the behaviour of the actors behind and before the scenes, raised in my mind a very useful reflection, for I took this to be an emblem of the world, and of mankind in general, who appear in very different shapes, according as they act in public or in private.'

In a paper on friendship, the feeling is said to have a range of objects without limits. 'Though some may affirm that it is confined to one's family, fellow-citizens, acquaintances, or countrymen, yet I am of opinion,' says the writer, 'that the passion extends in some degree to all mankind. For instance, place a Scotsman in England, where all are strangers to him, should he meet a Scotsman there whom he never saw in his own country, he will be fond of making up a friendship with him; place him next in Germany, if he meets an Englishman, he will feel the same desire; transport him next to China, if he meets there a German, or any European, he will reckon him his countryman; translate him next, if it were possible, to Saturn, or the moon, if he sees there a Chinese, or Persian, he will know his fellow-inhabitant of the same planet, and court his acquaintance.'

Miss Courtly has a waggish description of a fop lover in the tenth letter. 'In pops Tom, our footman. "Madam," says he, "here is Mr Crotchet, and another very sprightly gentleman, come to wait upon you." I desired him to show them in. Dick advances with his gentleman following. "Miss Jeanie," says he, "here is my good friend, Mr Starchie, come to pay his respects to you." Well, after this prologue, compliments and salutation were discussed, we took seats; but had you been there, Mr Plyant, to have observed Starchie's behaviour and dress, you would have got the picture of an accomplished beau and a complete fop. With his embroideries and lace, he was the likest of anything to a man of the pastry-cook's manufacture, bedaubed with gold foliage. And in all his motions and actions, he was so stiff and affected, as he seemed to be acted upon by springs, and resembled a puppet more than anything else. I should be unsufferably prolix to describe in a letter the airs, the oaths, the nonsense of the empty thing. He talked with a great deal of familiarity, as if he and I had been for ever intimate; of my cousins, Miss Fanny and Miss Charlotte, whom you know you used to visit. He told me he had once fallen so desperately in love with Miss Fanny, that he crossed the street on foot to visit her in a rainy morning; conducted her chair home with a flambeau; gave her seven serenades; stole her garter, and wore it half a year about his waist. How Miss Charlotte had played the coquette to him, after he had been at the pains to ogle her two nights running at the playhouse; but he had half a dozen of billet-doux from her, which he could show, if he had a mind to be revenged. I could scarce suffer the puppy's pertness, especially as I knew for a truth that neither of these ladies had ever spoke three words to him. The rest of the discourse was as childish, and now and then adorned with, O lard, medem! Strike me stupid! and other such elegant phrases. And then his gestures were as apish. Had you seen how he laughed at his own jests, to show his teeth; how foppish he appeared in his conversation, with his snuff-box and his cane; what methods he took to show the diamond on his little finger in taking a cup of tea; and what wry faces he made while contemplating his own dear features in the mirror above the chimney. I soon discovered, however, that Dick was playing the rogue with him; for he asked me several oddish questions, as, How I liked Mr Starchie's toupee? If he had not the most modish way of exercising the snuff-box and cane of any man in Britain? If I did not think there was an infinity of wit and humour in the choice and fashion of the fringe on his vest? To which I answering in the affirmative, the trifle at every reply made me an affected stiff bow, with, "Lard, medem, you do me too much honour. Strike me stupid, if I be not the happiest fellow upon earth, to please the ladies so, and without studying it too,"' &c. It strikes us as hardly conceivable that such a being as this existed in Scotland in 1738. Most probably he was one of those imaginary beings who live upon the stage and in literature, and are only supposed to have prototypes in human nature.

We have looked with care over both volumes for matters characteristic of the place and time; but our collections are extremely meagre. Here and there occurs a Scotticism, as when Shakspeare is spoken of as a man of *scrimp* education. There are many references to the excessive drinking of the age, and a set of sots are described under the name of Solitary Benders; that is, topers. It is stated of one gentleman, that 'he expresses such a regard for his mistress, that he will get beastly drunk in tossing of her health; he will eat her glove as a delicious morsel; nay, he can eat hay, if it comes out of her fair hand.' The morals and good taste of gentlemen of that age are shown in a history which passes through several numbers of the Critical Letters, respecting a certain Jack Townly, who courts a beautiful young lady with a profligate design, and is only argued into matrimony by a respectable old gentleman writing from Dalkeith under the name of Scoticus. Gentlemen are represented as coming every day to the Cross to meet their friends. They spend much time in coffee-houses [the Laigh Coffee-house is cited]. They 'saunter round the meadow;' meaning Hope Park, near Edinburgh. There is also frequent allusion to the Assembly, a periodical dance which reigned at that time, and is often praised in the poems of Allan Ramsay. A young spendthrift is expected soon to secure a 'perpetual dwelling for himself in the city, either in the Abbey or the Prison, according as his fancy leads him;' the abbey implying the sanctuary of Holyrood, sacred to hopeless debtors. It is surprising, however, how successful the editors have been in suppressing those special references which mark provincialism, the terror of the Scotch literati through the whole of the last century.

One of the most successful papers of the Critical Club is one slily satirising the veneration paid to external appearances. It speaks of a new philosophy, by which the virtues and other characters of human beings are represented in material forms composed of silks, laces, clothes, linen, and other stuffs. 'For example, the philosophers of this sect tell you, that rusticity is represented by a gold or silver cord adorning a hat or a coat; wit by a broad lace and fringe; sagacity by a full-bottomed periwig; foresight by a snuff-box and a mirror in it; a plain homely taste by a Spanish Olla Podrida, or what we call hodge-podge; a polite refined taste by a French ragout; understanding by a gold-headed cane; servitude by a hat with a plain broad lace; courage by a silver-handed sword; religion by a broad-brimmed beaver; sagacity and wisdom by a scarlet cloak with large buttons; freethinking by a narrow-brimmed hat; profound humour by a pair of stockings with gold clocks; love by a gold ring; humility by a pair of high-heeled shoes; modesty by a hoop; moderation and strictness by a pair of stays straitlaced; devotion by a fan; and affability and good manners by a powdered toupee. Thus they have reduced all the moral virtues to certain substantial forms and appearances, which are more evident to the senses, and strike them in a stronger manner than when they were described in the old abstract speculative way; so that, by this new system, a man may be a judge of virtue or vice by only using his eyes; whereas the other method made it necessary for a philosopher to set his understanding, judgment, and all his reasoning faculties to work, before he could discover the nature or difference of virtue and vice. This is of singular advantage, since it points out to us the easiest way to become philosophers, and reduces the stature of the goddess philosophy to that of a little *embonpoint;* whereas before, they tell us, her head touched the stars. To know a man of virtue or merit, then, by this system, we have no more ado but to look at his outward man, without the least regard to what he has in him. For instance, should he be equipped *a-la-mode* with lace, fringe, embroidery, and brocade, well essenced and powdered, and have a genteel modish gait and air, he is company for the best; he may shine at courts or at the levees of the great; he may swear, drink, ramble, and play the fool without any questions being asked. These trifles will never diminish his character, and he will be a man of merit in spite of fate, and a pretty companion for the best man in the nation; yea, he will be courted, cringed to, respected and adored, both in ordinary discourse and in dedications, as if he were a god; yielding crowds will fall back respectfully to make way for him at the sight of his embroidery; and vulgar wretches, who come to stare, will be cudgelled, kicked, and thrown down in heaps, to cut out a lane for his passage. Now, let us view the insipid fellow, whose character is held in as much disrespect as the other is esteemed. Should we see one with a pair of shoes and hobnails in them, a plain homely dress, and a clownish gait, shabby hair, or an old periwig, be sure he is company for nobody but scoundrels, and condemned to the obscurity of alehouses and garrets.' In this passage there are truths that ever have been, and ever will be, applicable.

The Rêveur is more stiff and essay-like than the Letters, but often contains good sense, tolerably well expressed; as, for instance, in the following passage. 'Life is not to be measured by existence, but by action. Were we to apply this rule to the bulk of mankind, we should find their lives much shorter than we commonly compute them, and that many have not as yet begun to live at all. One half of our time is necessarily employed in sleeping, in eating and drinking, and in diversions and amusements, requisite for the support and for the better plight of our bodies; this is lawful and commendable. But to throw away our whole lives in the bare maintaining them, is, I may say, a sort of self-murder, or, as Seneca calls it, a breathing death, and a burying a man alive. If a man would live in a manly and becoming manner, let him exert those rational faculties which are the dignity of his nature, and which put him above the level of the beasts that perish. Let him improve every minute, and make the most of the small space which Heaven has allotted him, by rendering himself as serviceable to his fellow-creatures, and as wise and virtuous for the increase of his own happiness, as possible. He needs never sit idle for want of something to do; if the ordinary business of life be not sufficient, the search after knowledge and truth will do more than fill up all the vacancies; and if the love of fame and of happiness cannot fire his breast, the love of mankind and of his country should influence him.'

Being stamped, the Rêveur fills up its odd columns with news. We have great accounts of the wars between Turkey and Austria, and of the efforts of the Corsicans under King Theodore to maintain their independence against the Genoese. There is also a strong anxiety expressed to get the ministry brought up to a declaration of war against Spain for her aggressions upon British commerce. The excellent Queen Caroline becomes dangerously ill in consequence of a cold caught by sitting in her new library; and instantly the London tailors buy up all the black cloth. She dies, and is greatly and deservedly mourned. Soon after, we hear of the Princess of Wales being in the condition which enabled her, in June 1738, to give to the world the infant who in time became George III. At that time, as is well known, the Prince of Wales, the weak but well-meaning Frederick, kept up a party in opposition to his father, and was upon the worst terms with the king. He used to have rival levees at his house in St James's Square. The present generation will learn with surprise that the following notice, signed by the lord chamberlain, and dated February 27, 1738, appeared in the London Gazette:—'His majesty having been informed that due regard has not been paid to his order of the 11th of September 1737, has thought fit to declare that no persons whatsoever, who shall go to pay their court to their royal highnesses the Prince or Princess of Wales, shall be admitted into his majesty's presence at any of his royal palaces.' We are informed that on the Wednesday after the appearance of this notice, there was a more splendid appearance at the prince's levee than usual. Good taste, not to speak of good feeling, has certainly been improved at court since those days.

We now take leave of these two curious specimens of

the literature of a former age, hopeful that we have not very much tired the reader with what has been so interesting a treat to ourselves.

AN HOUR IN NEWGATE.

The stranger in London who may be on his way to the huge nucleus of sight-seeing, St Paul's cathedral, sometimes stops midway in his ascent of Ludgate Hill to glance down a street on the left, called the Old Bailey. He perceives that much of one side of the street is occupied by a mass of heavy blackened building; and he defers his visit to the most celebrated of churches, to take a nearer view of the most notorious of prisons—Newgate.

Passing, in his transit along the Old Bailey, two edifices, the first formerly called the New, and the further one the Old Bailey (but now the central criminal courts), he arrives before Newgate. The daily deposits of London smoke upon its walls for nearly a century, have given to the exterior a dingy aspect, quite accordant with the gloomy uses of its interior. It is a long structure, with nothing to relieve its dungeon-aspect but the governor's house standing in the middle, with glazed windows and a gaily-painted door, which offer a curious contrast to the two massive and heavily-studded entrances of the prison itself, and to the monotonous extent of blackened and windowless wall. In short, the dreary look of the outside of this celebrated prison helps to call up all those recollections of crime and misery with which its interior is associated.

The origin of Newgate dates from an ancient custom of imprisoning malefactors in the houses attached to the gates of cities. So long ago as 1218, the gate on the site of which the present prison partly stands was used as a place of confinement, and was called the Chamberlain's Gate. In 1412, it was rebuilt by the executors of the famous Sir Richard Whittington, out of the effects he had allotted for works of charity: his statue, with the traditionary cat, remained in a niche to its final demolition. The gate was destroyed in the fire of 1666, and rebuilt, whence it obtained the name of Newgate. That, again, was intentionally demolished, to make way for the present prison, which was completed in 1780.

Should the stranger wish to have a sight of the interior of the gloomy edifice, he must provide himself with an order from one of the sheriffs of London. Such an order was, some time ago, politely handed to us by one of those officials. On arriving at the proper entrance, we mounted the steps, and knocked at a high wicket, heavily spiked at the top; and on showing the signature of the sheriff, were promptly admitted into a moderately-sized hall. The porter was far from the sort of person in outward appearance which one usually pictures as a jailer. Good humour and kindliness beamed from his face, and a little circumstance which presently occurred showed that his countenance was no untrue index of his real character. It happened that a young and respectable-looking woman was seated on a bench in the hall, weeping. The moment the turnkey had asked us to wait till the proper officer came in to show us the prison, he retired to the mourner, and said something consolatory. From what we could understand, her husband had that day been committed to Newgate from one of the police-offices on some minor charge.

As the appointed cicerone was some minutes in forthcoming, we entered into conversation with the porter, who is evidently an intelligent person. It was a matter of some curiosity to us to know what the general feeling of the prison officers was regarding the moral effects of public executions, by far the greatest number of which take place within sight of where we then stood, and under their eyes. His answer to the question was, that as far as his own experience and observation went, the attracting of crowds to the place of execution had a decidedly immoral tendency upon those who attended them; and that the crowd invariably showed, from the levity of their conduct, that they assembled to seek—not a warning against crime—but amusement for the passing hour. In this opinion he believed that most of his colleagues joined, however much they may be divided in opinion as to the expediency of abolishing capital punishment altogether. No one doubted the ill effects of the present mode of its infliction. While we were conversing, the governor of Newgate entered the hall, and going up to the young woman on the bench, desired her in the kindest tones to follow him into a small anteroom, and he would speak with her. The considerate attentions shown by the Newgate authorities from one of its lowest to its highest officer, produced impressions quite at variance with the harsh and stern ideas with which prison-keepers are usually associated.

At length the person arrived who was to show us over the jail, and under his guidance we passed through several dark passages, till we emerged into a light one. The right side of the corridor is formed by a double iron grating, beyond which is one of several small yards, in which prisoners were allowed to take exercise. At the grating, such friends as are occasionally allowed to visit them, take their stand and converse, but only in the presence of an officer; each word having, moreover, to pass between the double row of iron parallels.

By the door at the end of this gallery we entered that part of the prison set aside for females, and were received by the matron. In the first apartment, there were about half-a-dozen females sitting round a table. One was mending an apron, another was reading, but the rest were idle. They rose at our approach, and all bore such an appearance of contrition and meekness, that on leaving the ward, we asked the matron what they could have done to merit imprisonment. 'Sir,' replied the lady, 'it is the rule here to classify our inmates not so much according to the enormity of the offences they are accused of, as according to their habits and reputation. Known bad characters, who have been committed here for the third, fourth, fifth, or sixth time, are never placed with the less hardened.'

We ventured to presume that the women we had just seen had but newly entered the paths of crime. 'On the contrary,' replied the matron, 'they are the worst characters in the jail! The oldest of them, who was the first to rise with such a show of respect, has been within these walls at least twenty times before.' This was startling and melancholy intelligence. The excellent matron said, with a sorrowful countenance, that she found it to be a general rule, that the more hardened the criminal, the deeper the hypocrisy.

The chief female wards are nearly all alike, and a description of that we had just left applies with but little modification to the whole. It is a long room, lighted on one side by high semicircular windows, or 'fan-lights.' Against the opposite wall are two rows of sleeping places, one under the other, and bearing some resemblance to the cabin berths of a ship. Each was provided with two rugs and a pillow. The only furniture in the room was a long deal table and a couple of forms; a comfortable fire burned in a grate at the end. On the table were some Bibles and prayer-books.

In an upper ward into which we were shown, some half-dozen accused females were confined, whose persons were less known to the officials, and consequently whose characters were deemed somewhat better than those of the prisoners below. In demeanour and appearance, they differed but little from the other prisoners. From their ward we were ushered into another set apart for a class of prisoners which must be, from their being allotted an especial apartment, from time to time numerous—namely, servants guilty of dishonesty to their employers. In most cases theirs are 'first offences;' hence they are never mixed with females who are included in what the officers call 'the promiscuous felonies.' At the time of our visit, there were thirty-eight females 'in' on suspicion of having committed various crimes and misdemeanours.

Having finished our survey of that part of Newgate

set apart for the softer sex, we retraced our steps, and entered a spacious hall cheerfully lighted, in the centre of which is a glazed enclosure. This, we were informed, was constructed for the convenience of such prisoners as wish to consult their attorneys. Closed in there, they may confer with privacy, and at the same time within sight of an attendant. The cheerful look of this hall confirmed an impression which took its rise from the general appearance of the apartments we had as yet seen. Except the iron bars before mentioned, we had seen nothing nearly so gloomy, inside Newgate, as its blackened and forbidding exterior. The wards were as unlike dungeons as the public rooms of an inn. All those ideas of severity and punishment with which a stranger enters a jail were dispelled; and so far from a penal look, an air of comfort pervaded the place. The general expression which sat on the faces of the females whom we had seen was that—not of misery, dread, or remorse—but of contentment. Many of them—especially those described as the most wicked—had all the appearance of persons who were at present placed in better circumstances than they were accustomed to. This indeed must have been true of many of them. For a scanty and precarious subsistence, they were now exchanging a sufficiency of food, comfortable lodging, and, if they need it, warm clothing. Besides this, they were allowed to be just as idle as they pleased; for any work they did was for themselves, and quite voluntary. Thus, what we had as yet seen completely overturned our previous notions of the prison, and tended to banish those terrible associations which rise in the mind on hearing or seeing the word 'Newgate,' the very dread of which one had been led to think had deterred many an unhappy person from crime. What, however, we had inspected, seemed rather tempting than deterring to the poor and wretched; to many of whom Newgate must be an enviable rather than a dreadful retreat.

To account for this apparent anomaly, it must be explained, that in fact Newgate is no longer a place of punishment. It is what has been called, since the new modelling of the English criminal courts, 'a prison of transit;' in other words, a jail set apart for the safe custody of untried prisoners, whose guilt remains to be proved; of persons, in fact, who, having been examined before the magistrates, have had circumstances of suspicion brought against them sufficiently strong to warrant their being 'committed to Newgate for trial,' either at once, or in default of bail. It would therefore be a manifest injustice to render a residence in Newgate under such circumstances so irksome as to amount to a punishment, over and above the mere confinement, which is a punishment in itself. That indeed would be unduly punishing the innocent; for, by a maxim of law, every one is considered innocent until guilt be proved. Still, when the demoralising effects of complete idleness are taken into account, it surely is desirable that there should be some routine of light employment for the unhappy inmates, were it merely from tenderness towards themselves. However, whether the change from liberty and a scanty subsistence, to Newgate and good food and lodging with nothing to do, offer a premium to crime or not, the inmates cannot enjoy the change long; the periods of trial, otherwise 'the sessions,' occur so often, that the average stay of untried prisoners is only three weeks.

Another class of prisoners *in transitu* consists of persons who have been tried and sentenced, but whom it is not convenient to remove immediately to their penal destination—such as the penitentiaries, the hulks, or the place of execution. No distinction in treatment appears to be made between them and their untried fellow-prisoners, from whom, however, they are separated. Their stay is also short.

Such were the reflections we made and the information we received in the large hall. We were now conducted to the prison chapel, which presents a very curious aspect. Ascending some dozen stairs, the stranger finds himself in what he at first imagines is a square apartment, without pews. On closer inspection, he descries that in fact the room is oblong, at least one third being cut off at each end by iron bars that reach from the floor to the ceiling; and within them a gallery or storey affords seats for two separate sets of prisoners—the tried and the untried. The opposite *grille* is covered with a thick screen, so that the occupants of that compartment—the female prisoners—may not see the males, nor be seen by them. In one corner of the square space on which we stood rises the pulpit and reading-desk, and against the opposite side wall are three parallel forms. At each end of these forms stands a common mahogany chair, with a hair-stuffed seat, and the word 'Newgate' carved on the back. In these chairs sit the wretched culprits who are to forfeit their lives, and to whom the chaplain preaches the 'condemned sermon.' The fact, that only two seats should be provided for such melancholy occasions, shows how greatly the criminal code has been modified of late years. The attendant who showed us the chapel pointed out a large quadrangular mark in the floor where we stood. 'That,' he observed, 'is the place where the condemned pew formerly stood. I have,' he continued, 'not more than five-and-thirty years ago, seen as many as sixty persons in that pew at one time, who were condemned to, and most of whom afterwards suffered, death!' With these words our conductor descended the stairs, and we followed him, occupied with no very agreeable reflections on what we had just heard.

Our inspection of the part of Newgate used for males presented nothing which we had not seen in the female wards. Each opened upon an exercise yard, in which we noticed some prisoners walking up and down; others within doors were reading or writing letters to their friends. In one ward we noticed a few respectably-dressed men, who appeared more anxious and depressed than the others; another was solely allotted to persons suspected of making and issuing base coin—a crime which appears to be more successfully practised amidst the rapid exchanges of money in London than in any other commercial city at home or abroad. Our next visit was to the apartments used for juvenile offenders. About a dozen of these were waiting to be tried; a few receiving instruction from the Newgate schoolmaster. Their ages averaged from ten to about fourteen, and more open intelligent countenances than some of them wore, it is not possible to behold. We heard them read a part of their lessons, which they did fluently. The rest, we were told, could not read, and they looked more heavy and stupid than the others. They were nearly all pickpockets, the most adroit and best known to the officers being those who were the best educated. This sort of stealing requires the utmost tact and dexterity; consequently, the cleverest of the boys were the most skilful thieves. Two of them exhibited an address and manner worthy of young noblemen, and we were told that their older confederates occasionally dressed them well, so as to pass for genteel schoolboys. In this character they push into crowds, and commit the most successful depredations. The last apartment in this section of the jail which we were shown, was one of those recently substituted for condemned cells. It is provided with a bed, a table, good fire, and indeed with accommodation superior to that found in the other places.

Our guide now bade us follow him along a short passage, when, mounting a few steps, he unlocked a door, and we presently stood in a long yard surrounded on all sides by the prison buildings. It was the 'press-yard,' which makes so prominent a figure in the newspaper accounts of public executions. The sides of the enclosure are of immense height, and as you look up at the oblong bit of sky, the thought at once strikes you how impossible escape from such a place would be; yet our companion pointed out a corner up which an escape was a few years since effected. The stones composing the wall are very much 'rusticated' or roughened, and, by the aid of the small protuberances, one William Sweet, a chimney-sweeper, climbed to the top of the perpendicular corner, got over the roofs of some adjoining houses into the street, and escaped. That part of the wall is now carefully made smooth with plaster—a striking exemplification of the adage about 'locking the stable door after the horse is stolen.' Such a precaution can hardly be necessary; for whoever sees the place, will at once be convinced that the sweep must have been a genius in climbing. Perhaps there are not ten other men in Great Britain who could perform the feat, and it is by no means likely that either of them will ever become an inmate of the press-yard.

The condemned cells were next shown to us. They are fifteen in number, and are entered by a door from the press-yard. That which we saw was a small narrow 'pen,' for it deserves no other name, scantily lighted by a high-barred window. In one corner a metal wash-basin is fixed to the wall, and there is an iron bed which all but filled the rest of the space. In each of these dismal cells as many as four capital convicts have been, before now, confined; all heavily ironed, and deprived of the use of their limbs, unless to drag their gyves along the press-yard at intervals, by way of exercise. This is now all altered, and the condemned cells are only used to punish such of the inmates of the other parts of the building as misbehave themselves. They form, in fact, a prison within a prison.

While we were inspecting these cells, a noise was heard as if some persons who had entered the press-yard were exchanging the ordinary salutations. One man exclaimed, 'How do you find yourself to-day, sir?' To which a pleasing and somewhat cheerful voice replied, 'Pretty well, thank you. How are you?' This was so completely commonplace a circumstance, that it would have passed unnoticed, but from what our companion immediately told us. Alluding to the person who so cheerfully replied to the first salutation, he said, 'That is the man who was condemned to death last Friday. Next Monday he is to be executed.' The mere words of a being thus awfully situated naturally acquired a thrilling interest, the more so that they were so glibly and cheerfully spoken.

When we entered the yard, we saw the men leisurely parading it—the condemned and two prison attendants. The former was dressed in faded black, with an oil-skin cap partly covering his head. Both hands were in his coat-tail pockets, and he sauntered along the yard exactly as if he were taking a walk—leisurely, freely, and happily—across some field. That this man should possess the full consciousness that in three days he would cease to exist, seemed almost impossible, so calm and unconcerned did he outwardly appear. He was a slim, mild, and rather genteel-looking young man; the very reverse of what is generally conjured up as the figure of a murderer.*

From the press-yard, we were shown into the bath-rooms. Crime is, in a majority of cases, associated with filth, and before the new comers can be safely allowed to mix with other prisoners, they are thoroughly cleaned. To wash their clothing is often, from its tattered condition, impossible; and next to the bath-room is an oven in which the wretched habiliments—by being thoroughly baked—are purified of the animated filth with which they too often swarm. Should the clothes remain, after this process, in a condition to be worn, the wearers are allowed to resume them; if not, they are obliged to put up with the prison-dress, to which they naturally show great reluctance.

Near to these places is the kitchen; formerly the hall in which debtors (who were confined in Newgate) were received; a door opening from it into the street. This, therefore, is the 'debtors' door,' invariably mentioned in the newspaper accounts of executions, for from its steps malefactors tread immediately upon the scaffold. The room itself is hidden from their sight; a couple of black curtains being suspended across it, from the door of entrance to that of exit, so as to form a short passage or alley.

The kitchen is completely fitted with coppers, boilers, and other utensils necessary to cooking food for so large an establishment. Here we may properly introduce the dietary which is furnished to the transitory prisoners who are confined in Newgate. Every day each male is allowed eight ounces, and every female six ounces, of bread, with one pint of gruel for breakfast and for supper. We saw and tasted the bread; it was wholesome, quite free from adulteration (an excellence not to be relied on by honest purchasers of that article outside the prison), and answered to what bakers call 'seconds.' On Sunday, Tuesday, Thursday, and Saturday, the dinner consists of the above quantities of bread, with three ounces of meat weighed after it is dressed and without bone, with a quarter of a pound of potatoes. On other days, one pint of soup is substituted, the produce of three ounces of meat. That every prisoner may be fully aware of what he is entitled to, the dietary is legibly painted on a large black board, which is nailed up in every ward, and in case he thinks himself stinted, he may complain to the governor, to whom access is always easy. A reduction of the quantity of food is sometimes purposely resorted to as a punishment to such as may misbehave themselves during their stay in the prison, but in no other cases. Thus we perceive that the sustenance provided for the inmates of Newgate is infinitely better than that which most agricultural labourers in England, or *any* husbandman in Scotland, is able to obtain by the sweat of his brow.

From the kitchen we returned to the entrance-hall, and instead of egressing as we had entered, were conducted through an anteroom, in which were ranged on shelves a grim array of casts from the heads of celebrated malefactors. Passing through an office in which sits a clerk to take note of the commitments and other official matters connected with the prison, we were politely shown into the street by the governor's private door. We must confess that on reaching the open thoroughfare we breathed more freely; for, despite the improved unprison-like appearance of Newgate, it is a melancholy place to visit even for an hour.

* There can be no indelicacy in stating that the criminal here alluded to was Hooker. He was executed on the Monday after we saw him—overpowered by fear and remorse.

SEEING THE COUNTRY BY STEAM.

'To the Lovers of the Romantic and Beautiful.—One of the speediest, most delightful, and economical trips ever offered to the public, has been opened up by the running of Mr Percy's new fast coach, "Lightning," between C. and the railway station at S. The Lightning will leave the Turf Hotel every morning at six A. M., reaching the station in time for breakfast and the second morning train for B. From B. a steamer starts for L. half an hour after the arrival of the train, so that parties can be taken there, have an hour and a half for dinner, and then proceed by the six o'clock train for D., whence an evening train will convey them by the eastern line to C.; thus allowing them to pass over upwards of 200 miles of the finest country in one day.—N. B. Tickets clearing the whole route, without any extras for guards and drivers, may be had at the Lightning office.'

Captivated by this tempting notice, I rode into C., secured a ticket, put up at the Turf, and went to bed full of hope for the morrow. What a delightful thing it is to dream! None of your airy fantastic dreamings, where you are haunted with the dread of sinking through the filmy firmament into which you are exalted; none of your scenes of bustling human enjoyment, where the suspicion of insincerity is apt to intrude upon your happiest moments; but a dream of nature, where everything is bright and veritable—the waters calm and sunlit—the turf green and soft—the flowers sweetly scented—and the music——

Rap, tap, tap!

Was ever dream so interrupted by the officious hand of a waiter? Come in.

Half-past five, sir—and here is hot water.

And what sort of weather?

Beautiful morning, sir—only the wind's a little in the east; but that will be nothing once the day's fairly up.

Rap, tap!

Well?

Boots, sir—allow me to fasten your straps, sir. This way, sir—cup of coffee in the parlour, sir.

Cream?

Yes, sir! Sorry—none till eight, sir; but here is some of last——

Coat, sir! That's the horn, sir—start in a minute, sir.

Why, it is not ten minutes since I got up yet.

Clock must be behind, sir—passengers all taken their seats—kept the box for you, sir. Back at ten, sir?—something hot, sir?—same bedroom, sir?

This side, sir—care of the wheel, sir—your umbrella, sir.

Thus had a quarter of an hour seen me knocked up, booted, coffee'd, coated, and seated on the Lightning; and away we rattled through the yet unawakened streets of C. Unless during the hasty minute that was grudgingly spent in picking up an additional passenger, I saw nothing of C. save rows of painted fronts, fastened window-boards, and gilded signs; and these reeled and danced and mingled in my eye like so many phantasmagoria, so rapidly were we wheeled along. For aught that I could discern, the gilded lamb might have been the brushmaker's boar, and the comb-manufacturer's elephant might have been safely substituted for the hatter's beaver. I do recollect, however, of a tall chimney-stalk, to the top of which two bricklayers were being hoisted—the impression being deepened by the driver's remark, that he 'shouldn't on no account like to travel in such a wehicle.' About as safe there as in the Lightning, if you go on at such a rate. 'Bless you, no, sir; this is nothing to what we do when once clear of the town.' And true it was; for, on rounding another corner, we were spinning along at the rate of twelve miles an hour, to be in time for the nine o'clock train at S., allowing half an hour for breakfast.

The route between C. and S. is described by the guide-book as one of the most picturesque in the island, 'presenting a succession of hill and valley, well-wooded estates, castellated mansions, and abounding withal in historical associations.' As to hill and valley, these I can answer for, for a more breakneck drive could not well be imagined; but as to its beauties, I had no sooner fixed my eye on a picturesque spot, than whisk went the Lightning, and a clump of wood or a shaggy knoll blotted it out from my vision. It was of no use to attempt the landscape, so I betook myself to the country seats; but here I was even worse; for before I could learn the name, the owner, and one third of the history of number one, numbers two and three stood displaying their fronts in the morning sun, and claiming their share of attention. Besides, the dread of an overturn kept my eye about as much on the road as on the country, so that all was confusion and jumble; no calm leisurely survey, that would enable a man of ordinary capacity to receive and arrange his ideas in proper order.

'What's the clock, sir?' interrupted our driver. Twenty minutes past eight. 'Three miles yet, and only ten minutes! Come, my chickies, this won't do;' and away the cattle toiled and steamed as if another ten minutes were never to be granted us.

A little past the 'pointed time we were set down at S.; but before we were fairly seated in the breakfast-room of the 'Union,' it was found there was only a quarter of an hour left for what is usually the pleasantest of all meals. As is usual upon such occasions, nothing was to be had that was wanted, and everything that we did not care for was before us in profusion. Amidst orders, counter orders, the bustling of waiters, and the struggle of every one for himself, the signal bell rang, and I had to declare myself breakfasted, though at the moment I could not for my life have told what I had ate or drank, or whether indeed I had taken anything at all. During the rush of greatcoats, carpet-bags, and umbrellas to the railway omnibus, I got a glimpse of the one street and church of S.; saw a considerable stir in the getting up of frontages; but beyond this, the little town and its trade might have as well been in the moon for anything that I could learn. In three minutes we were down at the station, and given over to the train.

Pleasant travelling by your railway train, to be sure, where one is shot along at the rate of twenty-five miles an hour, and where the fields, hedgerows, trees, and cattle, seem to the dizzy sight to be equally alive, and all equally intent on keeping up a merry dance to the music of the wheels. We had sixty or seventy miles before us; in other words, a three hours' trip; a pretty fair opportunity, thought I, for picking up a little knowledge of the surrounding country. I strained my eyes till their very nerves began to crack, for the purpose of observing the style of crop and culture on either side, but vain was the effort. Every field presented the same uniform green, which radiated, circled, and wheeled before the eye in misty indiscrimination. Nor was there any greater stability of form; for what was this minute square was next oblong or round; and before I could note the arrangement of the farmstead on the left, the mansion on the right was swimming away in the distance. In fact I felt as if placed on an island, with a current of country sweeping past me on both sides with extreme velocity. Baffled in my attempt to decipher the immediate, I betook myself to the remote, trusting, with the poet, that distance might lend 'enchantment to the view;' but in this quarter I was even more unfortunate, for the easterly breeze had brought a creeping fog, which robbed the heights in a 'more than azure hue,' and the level plain was far too flat to be interesting. Hedgerows, indistinct masses of trees, here a whitewashed front, and there such another, a cloud of smoke rising from the chimney of a coal-work, and vying in blackness with another sent forth by an iron-foundry, formed, so long as I had patience to look, the principal parts of the picture. Abandoning every idea of scenery, I threw myself back from the window, in the hope and with the intention of a conversation with one of my fellow-passengers. The first I attempted was a lady right opposite; but so convulsively did she grasp the hand-rail, and so broken were her replies, that it appeared absolute cruelty to force her to articulate. She had evidently read the last 'dreadful railway accident' in the newspapers, and sat expecting every minute to be the victim of a similar catastrophe. The next I turned to was evidently a cattle-dealer, a man of jolly dimensions, and to whom the habit of locomotion had rendered railway, steamboat, or stage-coach a matter of equal indifference. Eyeing my movement, he shrewdly intercepted me with a remark about the weather; and drawing his travelling cap over his ears, adjusted himself in a corner, evidently with the intention of sleeping out the rest of the journey. 'I always does so on a long stage; and it is the best thing one can do, 'specially if he has been over-hours the night before.' This was an extinguisher to my hopes of conversation in as far as he was concerned; and I could have no more ventured upon our only other companion, though in a public conveyance, than I would have obtruded into his counting-room. He was over head and ears among papers and calculations, evidently on some business speculation; and seemed, from the occasional glances which he stole at the surrounding country, to be grudging the time consumed in his conveyance. Three hours of travel were just to him three hours of business. He seemed, indeed, to be one of those souls who would consent to be shot from the mouth of a cannon, provided it would transport him more quickly to his destination; and had no more notion of the companionship of travel, than he would have thought of entering into conversation with every one that walked with him the same street. Luckily, our destination was near at hand, and in less than half an hour we were safely set down in the suburbs of B.

Now, thought I to myself, I shall have a survey of this fine thriving port—its docks, streets, and warehouses. It is half an hour yet from the time of embarkation, and a man with ready eye can do a vast deal in outline even in thirty minutes, provided he meet with no interruption. Out, therefore, I sallied, noticing the structure and arrangement of the new station and docks; but just as I was making the next turn, a fellow shouting and waving his hat came coursing behind me. 'Going with the steamer, sir?' 'Yes, half an hour hence.' 'She's goin' in a few minutes, sir, a-once they take in their coals, as the tide is fast falling, owin' to the easterly wind; and if you don't want to lose your passage, you'd better be waitin' on.' Most unaccountable again; just as I was in a fair way of enjoying one portion at least of my trip, to be thwarted in this way—was ever mortal so unfortunate! It was of no use, however, to soliloquise. I had engaged for my trip; and if I did not choose to move forward, I must either remain where I was, or wheel back at double expense the unenjoyed route I had passed. Abandoning my ramble round B., I stalked sulkily on board the steamer, and in fifteen minutes was out on the open sea. Now, said I, in a vaunting tone, I shall at least have thirty miles of delightful coasting; and so seating myself in a quiet nook, and unsheathing a pocket telescope, I began to reconnoitre the beautiful villas and snug villages that stud that sea-board. Out, out, however, the steamer held, every stroke diminishing the distinctness of my prospect, till at last I might have as well looked through a bit of horn as through the lenses of my telescope. 'What's all this for, captain, if you please?' 'Why, sir, the coast is shoal here, and the falling tide and easterly wind compel us to hold out as well as we can. It's our safest course, though not the best for your prospect.' Done again! and so I rushed below in despair, and in ten minutes' time got gloriously sea-sick. Ugh! groaned I, and these are the pleasures of travelling. When we steered up to the pier of L., it was fully three-quarters of an hour beyond the usual time, thus leaving those who had a stomach to dine the brief space of forty minutes for that important ceremony. As for me, dinner was out of the question; so swallowing a glass of brandy and water, I threw myself on the sofa, sick, dispirited, and discontented. The sofa, like everything else, seemed to be leagued against me, for it heaved, and rocked, and swung most tremendously; and so I sallied out to the open air to await the starting of the train by the eastern route for the little seaport I had left in the morning.

Misfortune by this time had overcome my philosophy, as well as—I am sorry to own it—my good nature; so planting myself in a first class, I drew my cloak around me, pulled down my 'templar' over ears and eyes, and drew a magic circle of sleep between me and the world of my fellow-travellers. I heard no one, saw no one, and cared not whether the train passed through barren moors or paradises of fertility. All that I wished and prayed for was to be speedily set down at the spot whence I had started. In due time we drew up at the southern suburb of C.; and now shame and confusion took hold of me. How was I to reply to the hundred queries that were sure to be made as to the way in which I had enjoyed my trip? how did the country look? what thought I of S., of B., or of L.? All these pierced me like so many daggers, till a mischievous thought shot across my brain. I shall take note of C. by gaslight, describe the magnificence of its streets, the elegance of its shops, its blaze, its beauty, and so forth, in such language that my friends at the Turf will not be able to discover their own city in the description. I shall checkmate them for once, thought I; and as I was gloating over this idea, an obsequious tap was made on my shoulder. 'Mr Brown, I suppose?' The same, if you please. 'I have been sent, sir, from the Turf with this cab, to bring you quickly up, as Mr Jones is waiting you on business. Will you step in, sir?' I instinctively obeyed the request; slam went the door; and away went the cab like fury over rough and rattling causeway. When I recovered myself, I reflected on my gaslight survey of C., and shouted to the fellow to drive slowly; but he mistook the injunction, and only plied the whip with double effect. In ten minutes I was fairly set down at the Turf, having since morning accomplished a distance exceeding 200 miles, and, as the phrase goes, 'seen the country.' After supping with my friend Jones—whose queries I parried like a fencer—I hurried to bed, and passed the night, as I had the day, amid the bustle of coaches, railway trains, and steamers, which danced, and wheeled, and circled in my brain, till the kind hand of 'boots' knocked me up to consciousness and breakfast the following morning.

Such to me at least were the delights of modern travelling—the beauties of a 'pleasure trip' taken in glowing June for the avowed purpose of seeing the country. Reader, if by your travels you wish to see and learn, and inwardly to digest, go by some decent Christian conveyance, be it even a carrier's van; but avoid as you would an enemy railway trains, steamboats, and stage-coaches that 'beat the mail.' Such whisking and shooting through space is too much for ordinary capacities; it allows no time for the mind to receive, handle, and store ideas in a proper and methodical manner. The senses must either take impressions by halves, and toss them to the memory as they come, or despairingly give up the task of receiving them at all. We who have been accustomed from our youth to a constitutional six or eight miles an hour, have no conception of thirty: our mental operations are not habituated to such haste; it is absolute cruelty to compel us to live in such a hurry. With the next generation, born and trained amid steam and bustle, it may be all very well; their perceptions will partake of the attributes that surround them, and the record of their memory may be kept in stenography, instead of, as with us, in a plain Roman hand. Train the young, say we, to as much speed as you please; but, for humanity's sake, let us who belong to a declining state of things accomplish our final stage at the pace to which we have been so long accustomed.

DISCIPLINE OF THE EYES.

Though vision be one of the most important and the most comprehensive of the senses, it is one that cannot be exercised in its full efficiency without considerable practice and self-tuition. This fact, well-known in theory, was first elucidated by experiment in the case of the boy who was cured of blindness at the age of fourteen by the celebrated Cheselden. A case of equal interest occurred lately in London, a report of which by Dr Franz is given in the Philosophical Transactions. The leading results in both cases exactly coincide.

If a person totally blind from birth were, at a mature age, and in possession of all his other faculties, at once to obtain the full use of his eyes, one would be apt to imagine that he would perceive objects around him just as other grown-up persons usually do. This, however, is by no means the case. There is none of the senses so deceptive, taken by itself, as that of vision. No just idea can be formed of any object by the eye alone; and it is only by the aid and experience of the other senses, as well as by repeated practice in vision, that an accurate notion of even the simplest object can be obtained. To the inexperienced eye all objects are flat, or seen only as surfaces. All objects too, however near or distant, appear as if in one plane; so that form, size, distance, are all indistinguishable. Even colour depends upon proximity to the eye, for the brightest objects at a remote distance appear dim, and almost colourless.

The case operated upon by Dr Franz was that of a young gentleman of seventeen years of age, the son of a physician. He had been blind from birth. His right eye was quite insensible to light, and in that state called *amaurotic*. His left eye contained an opaque lens, or cataract; with it he could distinguish a strong light, and even vivid colours, but he had no idea of the forms of objects. It was on this left eye that the operation was performed, and fortunately it proved successful. As the young man possessed an intelligent mind, and had been carefully educated as far as his condition would allow, the opportunity was a favourable one to test the accuracy of former experiments.

'On opening the eye,' says Dr Franz, 'for the first time on the third day after the operation, I asked the patient what he could see. He answered that he saw an extensive field of light, in which everything appeared dull, confused, and in motion. He could not distinguish objects, and the pain produced by the light forced him to close the eye immediately.' Two days afterwards the eye was again exposed. 'He now described what he saw as a number of opaque watery spheres, which moved with the movements of the eye; but when the eye was at rest, remained stationary, and then partially covered each other. Two days after this the eye was again opened: the same phenomena were again observed, but the spheres were less opaque, and somewhat transparent—their movements more steady, and they appeared to cover each other more than before. He was now for the first time capable, as he said, to look through the spheres, and to perceive a difference, but merely a difference, in the surrounding objects. When he directed his eye steadily towards an object, the visual impression was painful and imperfect, and the intolerance of light obliged him to desist. The appearance of spheres diminished daily; they became smaller, clearer, and more pellucid, and after two weeks disappeared. Dark brown spots (*muscæ volitantes*) floated before the eye every time it was opened; and when shut, especially towards evening, dark blue, violet, and red colours appeared in an upward and outward direction.'

As soon as the state of the patient permitted, the following experiments on his sense of vision were instituted. They were performed in succession, and on different days, so as not to fatigue the eye too much. In the first experiment, silk ribbons of different colours, fastened on a black ground, were employed to show, first the primitive, and then the complementary colours. The patient recognised the different colours, with the exception of yellow and green, which he frequently confounded, but could distinguish when both were exhibited at the same time. Gray pleased him best, because this colour, he said, produced an agreeable and grateful sensation. The effect of red, orange, and yellow was painful, but not disagreeable; that of violet and brown not painful, but very disagreeable; the latter he called ugly. Black produced subjectioned colours, and white occasioned the recurrence of *muscæ volitantes* in a most vehement degree.

In the second experiment, the patient sat with his back to the light, and kept his eye closed. A sheet of paper, on which two strong black lines had been drawn—the one horizontal, the other vertical—was placed before him at the distance of about three feet. He was now allowed to open the eye, and, after attentive examination, he called the lines by their right denominations. When he was asked to point out with his finger the horizontal line, he moved his hand slowly, as if feeling, and pointed to the vertical line; but after a short time, observing his error, he corrected himself. The outline in black, of a square six inches in diameter, within which a circle had been drawn, and within the latter a triangle, was, after careful examination, recognised and correctly described by him. When he was asked to point out either of the figures, he never moved his hand directly and decidedly, but always as if feeling, and with the greatest caution: he pointed them out, however, correctly. A line consisting of angles, or a zig-zag and a spiral line, both drawn on a sheet of paper, he observed to be different, but could not describe them otherwise than by imitating their forms with his finger in the air. He said he had no idea of these figures.

In a third experiment, light being admitted into the room at one window only, to which the patient's back was turned, a solid cube and a sphere, each four inches in diameter, were placed before and on a level with the eye at the distance of three feet. Allowing him to move the head in a lateral direction no more than was necessary to compensate the point of view of the right eye, which was visionless, he was now desired to open his eye, and say what the objects were. After attentively examining them, he said he saw a quadrangular and a circular figure, and after some consideration he pronounced the one a square and the other a disc. His eye being again closed, the cube was taken away, and a flat disc of equal size placed next to the sphere. On opening his eye, he observed no difference in these objects, but regarded them both as discs. The solid cube was now placed in a somewhat oblique position before the eye, and close beside it a figure cut out of pasteboard, representing a plain outline prospect of the cube when in this position: both objects he took to be something like flat quadrates. A pyramid placed before him with one of its sides towards his eye, he saw as a plain triangle. This object was now turned a little, so as to present two of its sides to view, but rather more of one side than of another. After considering it for a long time, he said that this was a very extraordinary figure; it was neither a triangle, nor a quadrangle, nor a circle. He had no idea of it, and could not describe it. When subsequently the three solid bodies, the sphere, the cube, and the triangle were placed in his hands, he was much surprised that he had not recognised them as such by sight, as he was well acquainted with these solid mathematical figures by touch.

There was another peculiarity in his impressions: when he first began to look at objects, they all appeared to him so near, that he was sometimes afraid of coming in contact with them, though many were in reality at a great distance. He saw everything much larger than he had supposed, from the idea obtained by his sense of touch. All moving, and especially living objects, such as men and horses, appeared to him very large. If he wished to form an estimate of the distance of objects from his own person, or of two objects from each other, without moving from his place, he examined the objects from different points of view, by turning his head to the right and to the left. Of perspective in pictures, he had of course no idea. He could distinguish the individual objects in a painting, but could not understand the meaning of the whole picture. It appeared to him unnatural, for instance, that the figure of a man represented in the front of the picture should be larger than a house or a mountain in the background. Every surface appeared to him perfectly flat. Thus, though he knew very well by his touch that the nose was prominent, and the eyes sunk deeper in the head, he saw the human face only as a plane. Though he possessed an excellent memory, this faculty was at first quite deficient as regarded vision: he was not able, for example, to recognise visitors unless he heard them speak, till he had seen them very frequently. Even when he had seen an object repeatedly, he could form no idea of its visible qualities in his imagination, without having the real objects before him. Formerly, when he had dreamt of persons—of his parents, for instance—he felt them, and heard their voices, but never saw them; but now, after having seen them frequently, he saw them also in his dreams.

The human face pleased him more than any other object presented to his view. The eyes he thought most beautiful, especially when in motion; the nose disagreeable, on account of its form and great prominence; the movement of the lower jaw in eating he considered very ugly. Although the newly-acquired sense afforded him many pleasures, the great number of strange and extraordinary sights was often disagreeable and wearisome to him. He said that he saw too much novelty, which he could not comprehend; and even though he could see both near and remote objects very well, he would nevertheless continually have recourse to the use of the sense of touch.

Such are the nature of our impressions in early infancy, before vision becomes to us a true exposition of the forms and relative positions of objects. And such is the effect of habit and association, that the actual deceptions which the sense of sight, when taken alone, is continually presenting to us, can only be appreciated or detected by the philosophic inquirer.

THE COUNTESS IDA OF HAHN-HAHN.

During the last ten years, the authoress whose name heads this article has obtained an extensive popularity in Germany. Though a woman of undoubted genius, she is somewhat eccentric—a peculiarity over which her parentage and education must have exercised much influence. Her father, Count Charles Frederick von Hahn, served in the army of the Grand Duke of Mecklenberg Schwerin in the war which was put an end to at Waterloo. Unfortunately, he had a passion for theatricals, and when peace was proclaimed, the count absented himself from his estates at Tressow, in Mecklenberg, and actually became the manager of a company of players. He so impaired his property by indulgence in his favourite pursuit, that it was found necessary to place it in the hands of trustees. Another consequence of his erratic mode of life was, that his daughter's childhood was deprived of the advantages of a settled home, and of the immediate guidance and direction of a father. She lived with her mother at Rostock, then in New Brandenburg, and, after 1821, in the Griefswald, where she was married in 1826 to the wealthy Count Frederick William Adolphus von Hahn, of the older branch of the house of Hahn, or Hahn Baselow. This union was productive of much unhappiness, and was dissolved in the year 1829. Nor were all the countess's troubles consequent on the marriage state. It was her misfortune to be afflicted with the peculiarity of vision known as a 'squint;' and, attracted by the fame of the celebrated Dr Dieffenbach, she allowed him to operate; but the result was unfavourable. After a time she lost the use of one eye entirely, and was for some time apprehensive of becoming totally blind. This incident made a great noise in Germany, for it created a furious paper war between the oculist and his impetuous patient. He maintained that she lost her sight from imprudently reading and writing by candle-light on the very evening after the operation; she, on the other side, persisting that the whole blame was attributable to the negligence of her medical attendant after the operation was performed. So perseveringly was the dispute carried on, that the countess's eye became the current topic of conversation in all the literary and medical circles of society throughout Germany.

To console herself for her misfortunes, the countess took to literature and travelling; and those who have watched her career, must admit that, if activity and industry be any consolation for trouble, she must have completely forgotten hers. Since 1835, she has visited Switzerland, Vienna twice, Italy twice, Spain, France, Sweden, Syria, and Constantinople. Since the same date she has written seven novels and five books of travel, not one of which but has met with a large share of public attention; some of them having been translated into both French and English.

The novels of this authoress, though adapted for German tastes, would find little favour with our more matter-of-fact nation. They abound in over-wrought delineations of passion and sentiment, and with events a little too melodramatic to be probable. From her books of travel, on the contrary, much that is sensible in opinion and graphic in description is to be gleaned, and it is our present purpose to afford our readers a few specimens of this eccentric but amusing lady's literary skill and humour as a descriptive tourist.

Among her most diverting descriptions, is that which occurs in 'A Traveller's Letters' (Reisebriefe) on the Spanish roads. Crossing the Pyrenees from France near the Mediterranean, she halts at Figueras to dine, and there the French vehicle in which she had been recently travelling was exchanged for a Spanish one drawn by no fewer than nine mules. 'I could hardly believe my eyes when I saw the whole herd getting into motion. In Germany, we are thankful if our coachman is able to drive four in hand; but only think of a man undertaking to manage nine steeds at once! Each mule had its particular name, such as Pajarito, Galando, Amorosa, &c. The *mayoral* (so the coachman is called) kept up a constant conversation with his cattle, calling the creatures by name, scolding the lazy, praising the diligent, and guiding the whole team apparently more by his voice than with his reins. By the side ran the *zagal*, a boy with a whip, who contributed his share to the animation of the coursers, threw himself upon the front mule when we crossed a river or passed a sharp corner, and when he was tired of running, jumped up beside the mayoral, and rested for a few minutes on the driver's seat. The roads were frightful—indescribably so. At Perpignan they told me the chaussée to Barcelona was as good as a French road. This was saying little enough; but the fact is, that after we had got clear of the Pyrenees, we found no road at all, but had to ford rivers, to drive through ditches, to cross bogs, and to climb over precipices, and all that the best way we could. Roads and bridges, and everything that should be cared for by a government, are deplorably neglected.'

In an article on a book called 'Beyond the Mountains,' which we drew up some time since,* we extracted a not dissimilar passage. It turns out that the '*Man* of Fashion,' who wrote under the name of Theophile Gautier, was no other than the Countess Ida! She certainly kept up her assumed character admirably.

The work from which the above extract is taken abounds in shrewd reflections on the fallen condition of Spain. The following is piquant and true:—'Alas! to *be* poor is no greater hardship than to be rich, for our wants increase with our power of gratifying them; but to *become* poor, that is bitter; for it carries with it an involuntary feeling of a fall! How much more, then, when it is a *nation* that has become poor. Spain is not poor, they will tell me, for it possesses inexhaustible resources within its own soil; but of what worth are those resources to people who know not how to bring them into play? In the time of the Moors, Spain contained twenty millions of inhabitants—some say thirty —now it does not contain ten. The land was then rich and flourishing, and sufficed for all the wants of a luxurious population. Of course it must then have possessed resources that became dormant in proportion as the population melted together. The land remains uncultivated, because roads and canals are wanting for the conveyance of its produce. The plains of Castile grow the finest wheat in the world, and when grown, it is given to the pigs, because the grower has no means of conveying it to a market. There is no trade except along the coast, and even there it is almost exclusively in the hands of smugglers. The land that once monopolised the trade of both the Indies—the land that could fit out the Invincible Armada for the conquest of England—possesses at present not a single man-of-war, and has no commerce but what is carried on by smugglers!'

During her subsequent journey through Sweden, the countess visited that interesting personage, Miss Frederika Bremer, whose quiet pictures of northern domestic life have rendered her so celebrated throughout the rest of Europe. 'I visited Miss Frederika Bremer at Arsta, which is her estate. It is three Swedish miles from Stock-

* A Man of Fashion in Spain; vol. 12, p. 300.

holm: she lives there with her mother and younger sister during the greater part of the year. The two last-mentioned ladies passed last winter in Nizza. She remained at home: she does not like the trouble and disturbance of travelling. She remained seven months—seven Swedish winter months—all alone at Arsta, without seeing any one but the maid-servant who attended her. I would not believe that any one could endure such seclusion, if she had not told it me herself. Arsta has its little historical recollections. In the great meadow, Gustavus Adolphus assembled and mustered the army with which he first went as king to Livonia, and he dwelt with his wife and daughter in the wooden house which still stands near the present dwelling-house. The latter is of stone, square and handsome, with large lofty rooms: it was built during the thirty years' war. The surrounding country is not cheerful—at least it did not appear so to me, perhaps because it was a dull, cloudy day. The trees looked dingy, the lawn gray, and the sea was faintly seen in the distance. A walk was proposed, but I, who am generally so fond of the fresh air, preferred not going out: without there was nothing to tempt me, and within it was so comfortable. I can understand that one must feel very much attached to home here. I begged Miss Frederika to show me her room: it is as simple as a cell. To me it would be in the highest degree uncomfortable, for it is a corner room, with a window on two sides, so that there is a thorough light, and no curtains. Three square tables stand in it, entirely covered with books, papers, and writing apparatus; and the rest of the furniture is in a style which seems simply to invite one to sit down upon sofa and chair, but not to lie down, or lean or lounge upon them, as I would willingly have done. It is the same with me on a journey as at home. I take a fancy to some particular table or chair, and the want of elegance or convenience is displeasing to me. Wherever I am travelling or living, I must have everything comfortable and soft and warm about me; not so much hard wood, or so many sharp corners. On the walls of this room there are a few pictures. "That is a genuine Teniers; but I know you will not like it," said Miss Bremer, smiling, and pointing to a picture which represents a peasant filling his tobacco pipe. I said frankly that I did not. I very often said "no" when she said "yes;" but that did not signify. * * She succeeded in conquering the difficulty of speaking in a language in which she is not accustomed to think, and said what she wished to say quite simply, naturally, and clearly, sometimes in French, sometimes in German. She has beautiful, thoughtful eyes, and a clear, broad, I might almost say a solid, forehead, with distinct, finely-marked eyebrows, which move when she speaks, especially when a sudden thought bursts into speech: this is very becoming to her. She has a small and light figure, and was dressed in black silk. In her antechamber there were two large book-cases filled with books in Swedish, German, French, and English: I think there were Italian also. In the schools, German is taught after Swedish. Goethe and Schiller have never been translated into Swedish, yet every one has read them. Our books have a much greater advantage in Sweden than Swedish books have with us. Translations are always colourless lithographs of the original, and sometimes they are wretched daubs. Miss Bremer draws portraits extremely well in miniature with water-colours, and has a very interesting album of such heads, all executed by herself, to which she has added mine.' These two authoresses present a striking contrast. The guest a dashing, fashionable countess, fond of gaiety and the world; the hostess a humble-minded, unpretending private gentlewoman, living in peace and retirement.

None of the countess's works have met with such an extended popularity as her 'Letters of a German Countess,' written from, and on her way to, the East. Several English translations have been made from them; that before us being by the clever author of 'Caleb Stukely.' In the letter to her brother dated from Pesth, there is some useful information conveyed with the countess's peculiar vivacity. 'We reached Pesth during the celebration of one of the four great fairs held annually in the city. The inns, coffee-houses, and restaurants of every grade are thronged with people, and the streets are one great sea of traffic. On the other side, at Ofen, matters are as quiet. Ofen is the older and smaller town, lying on the hill-side. High up, on the right, is the castle, the residence of the palatine; on the left is the observatory: various government buildings and a few convents are seen in different directions. From the heights you overlook not only the river and all Pesth, which, by the way, lies very low, and is on that account seriously exposed to inundations, but the country far and wide in its level uniformity. Pesth, in other respects, is a handsome, regularly built town, with large houses and straight streets; 60,000 inhabitants (whose trade and commerce are much facilitated by low position and proximity of water), a pretty theatre, a museum now building, and a chain-bridge in embryo. The completion of the last is impeded, as I hear, by the determination of the Hungarian nobles not to pay the toll which is indispensable to the defraying of the expenses. They maintain that the people hitherto have paid it, and that they shall continue so to do.

'Ofen and Pesth have so arranged matters, that they represent the capital of Hungary between them; for the former is the seat of the palatine of the empire, and of the high political and military authorities, whilst the latter is the central point of Hungarian commerce. As for curiosities, grand buildings, antiquities, museums, and churches, Pesth knows of no such things; nay, what is more astonishing, she is without a promenade, and that at Ofen is miserable in the extreme. Probably the folks prefer the Italian fashion of taking the air in a carriage, and if they do walk, to wander about the streets. And indeed the whole aspect of life here is very southerly. The people do not merely *walk* in the streets, but they actually sit, work, eat, drink, and sleep there. Every third house is a café, surrounded by a broad verandah, and supplied with sofas and blooming oleander trees; and an incredible quantity of fruit—grapes, plums, melons, and water-melons—the latter in heaps—are exposed for sale. Lazzaroni-like, the unemployed labourers lie upon the thresholds of the house-doors, or across their own barrows, enjoying the luxury of a mid-day slumber. Women sit gossiping before the houses and suckling their young. The dark eye, the loud deep voice, and here and there the piercing glance, all are southern. * * Since for the last two days I have done nothing but roam from street to street, gazing right and left, I can speak of nothing but what my eyes encountered there. Oh, would that I could draw! Is it not extraordinary that I can do nothing that I have been taught, at least for the teaching of which I have had masters, and that the only thing which I have not been taught, namely, to write a book, I can do? I am really surprised that painters of domestic life do not come here: they might procure the finest subjects. Under the doorway of a spacious house, a fruiterer had very carelessly spread his commodities, consisting of water-melons, upon the ground; he himself lay beside them, a beautiful oleander was above him, and in his mouth was the darling pipe, whose spiral cloud he watched intently as it ascended into air. The broad hat gave an additional shade to his already dark visage, and the contrast between his black, stern head, and the delicate rose-coloured blossoms which were waving above him, was splendid. The extensive trade in soap, entirely carried on in the open streets, is unpleasant to the eyes and nose, especially during the present melting weather. Hungary, with the Carpathian mountains to the north, is much warmer than the neighbourhood of Vienna, which lies north of the mountains of Styria. The exhibition of manufactures and works of industry, now open, was full of interest. The best productions are those of the cabinet-maker and leather-workers. The silks and minor articles of luxury look neither tasty nor *finished*, as the English say, and as we Germans know not how to say, simply because the point itself is one we cannot reach.'

Arrived in Constantinople, the countess visited the slave-market, on which her observations are pointed and new. 'The market 'itself is not very inviting—an irregular space, surrounded by damp galleries. In these galleries sit the salesmen with coffee and *chibouque*, the overseers, the purchasers, and the simply curious; and in the narrow, dark, low chambers, which have a door and grated window opening to the galleries, are kept the noble wares. One group is placed in the middle of the court for inspection, or rather is seated, for they are squatted upon mats as usual. Let us contemplate them. Oh, horror! dreadful, revolting sight! Summon your whole faculty of imagination—picture to yourself monsters—and you still fail to conceive such objects as yon negresses, from whom your outraged eye recoils with loathing. But the Georgians, the Circassians—the loveliest women in the world—where are they? Not here! No, dearest brother, the white slaves are kept separate in Tophana; thence they are conducted to the harem for inspection, and only by the greatest favour, and under especial escort, can you be admitted to a view of them. Here are only blacks, and with the monstrous spectacle you must fain content yourself. There they sit! A coarse gray garment envelops the figure; coloured glass rings encircle the wrists; coloured glass beads the neck; the hair is cut short. You are struck, first, with the depressed forehead, squeezed over the eyebrows, as in the Cretins; then with the large, rolling, inexpressive eye; then with the nose, innocent of a bridge, a great misshapen mass; then with the mouth, and the frightful animal formation of projecting jaw-bone, and gaping *black* lips (red lips, on the Moor, is a European fancy, which reality does not sanction); then with the long-fingered, ape-like hands, and hideous colourless nails; then with the meagre spindleshanks and projecting heel; then, and most of all, with the incredible animalism of the whole thing, form and expression combined. The colour varies: here it is bright black, there somewhat brown, and here again grayish. They give out no signs of life; they stare at us with the same unconscious gaze that they fix upon each other. A purchaser approaches, examines them; women-buyers make their remarks upon them; they are indifferent to all.' They are measured in their length and breadth like a bale of goods; scanned and tried in their hands, hips, feet, teeth, like a horse. They submit to everything without dislike, without anger, without sorrow. It is much that the exhibition proceeds with decency; that is to say, with so-called decency: the creatures do not lay aside their garments, which reach from the neck down to the calf of the leg. Now they are selected, bid for, cheapened. Do buyer and seller agree, the slave departs with her master or mistress. Do they not, she seats herself again upon the mat, unconcerned about her fate.'

When in Egypt, the countess visited the residence of the pasha, Mehemet Ali, at Schubra, near Cairo, which 'is a garden on the Nile, with a country house, of which the viceroy is very fond. You can imagine nothing more pleasant and less pretending than the entrance into this garden. The gateway has acquired an irregular form from the mass of creeping plants with blue flowers which climb about it, and which give you the notion of entering beneath two trees. The garden itself does not at all resemble that of Ibrahim Pasha upon Rouda; it is more Oriental; that is to say, it is a fruit-garden, but very differently kept and tended to the wildernesses of Damascus. Firm paths, paved with shells and little pebbles, which enclose regular squares of oranges and lemons, and are bordered with lowly-cut hedges of myrtle; shady archways, that terminate at basins for water; elevated kiosks, with a prospect of the Nile, which streams through the fields like a flowing mantle of silver; such are the constituent parts. Let me, however, not forget the Great Fountain, which is really superb. An oblong portico, borne by marble columns, surrounds a sheet of water, to which marble steps conduct, and upon which you can go about in small boats. In the four corners are fixed marble lions spouting forth water; and from the middle of the basin there rises a marble balcony upon crocodiles, who are also spitting water. Four pavilions, with chambers, are attached to the rounded edges of the portico, so that this fantastic building is really half fountain, half kiosk.' Of the pasha himself she adds, in a succeeding page: 'I wrote to you, dear Clara, how Mehemet Ali contrived to raise himself from the subordinate position of a captain of Albanian troops to be hereditary pasha of the empire of the Pharaohs. I saw the old pasha twice during my numerous promenades to Schubra, where his spring residence is situated. Everybody may visit the garden, even when he is in it; and as he always dines in the open air, amidst myrtle hedges and orange trees, close to a fountain, one can easily see him. I was once with Madame von Laurin in the beautiful marble fountain kiosk, when it was suddenly announced that he was coming. We saw no reason whatever why we should take flight, after the manner of Mahommedan women, and therefore remained as near as was permitted us. He politely greeted us. He has a small red countenance, a magnificent white beard, a somewhat stooping carriage, and the resolute but shaken gait of a robust old man. He wore the red tarbusch, and a dark-green robe, furred with sable. He receives foreigners with pipe and coffee, without any ceremony, introduced by their consuls. I asked my travelling companion what was the prevailing expression of his countenance. "Animated and friendly." "Something of the friendliness of the cat?" I inquired again. "Yes; somewhat, certainly." He was of opinion that if one could speak Turkish with him, one might hear many uncivilised but clever things: as it was, in spite of the tedious interpretation, he answered with great readiness, and well. He speaks only his bad Albanian Turkish; he cannot write at all: he learned to read at forty years of age—is not that pretty? Ibrahim Pasha (the pasha's son) speaks and writes Turkish, Persian, and Arabic. (*Apropos* of this, it occurs to me to say that the Arabs have never learnt a word of Turkish. Here, if you please, is a genuine expression of hatred on the part of a people enslaved for 300 years). Ibrahim is said to have generally a more solid judgment, more deliberation, and more consistency in his transactions, than his father, who is subject to violent fits of passion; but Ibrahim is accused of avarice. He lives very much withdrawn from affairs at his country residence, Cube, on the road to Heliopolis, and comes rarely to his palace of Casar-el-Ain.'

As Germany is by no means overstocked with lively, vivacious writers, the countess has made some welcome additions to their literature. When not abroad, she resides alternately in Berlin and Dresden, receiving the homage due as much to her literary acquirements as to her rank and lineage.

BROCK THE SWIMMER.*

Amongst the sons of labour, there are none more deserving of their hard earnings than that class of persons denominated Beachmen, on the shores of this kingdom. To those unacquainted with maritime affairs, it may be as well to observe, that these men are bred to the sea from their earliest infancy, are employed in the summer months very frequently as regular sailors or fishermen, and during the autumn, winter, and spring, when gales are most frequent on our coast, in going off in boats to vessels in distress in all weathers, at the imminent risk of their lives; fishing up lost anchors and cables, and looking out for waifs (that is, anything abandoned or wrecked) which the winds and waves

* We gather the present account of this remarkable man from a paper in the Sporting Magazine for July 1839.

may have cast in their way. In our seaports these persons are usually divided into companies, between whom the greatest rivalry exists in regard to the beauty and swiftness of their boats, and their dexterity in managing them: this too often leads to feats of the greatest daring, which the widow and the orphan have long to deplore. To one of these companies, known by the name of 'Layton's,' whose rendezvous and 'look-out' is close to Yarmouth Jetty, Brock belongs, and of him the following anecdote is recorded.

About 1 P. M., on the 6th of October 1835, a vessel was observed at sea from this station with a signal flying for a pilot, bearing east distant about twelve miles. In a space of time incredible to those who have not witnessed the launching of a large boat on a like occasion, the yawl 'Increase,' eighteen tons burden, belonging to Layton's gang, with ten men and a London branch pilot, was under weigh steering for the object of their enterprise. 'I was as near as possible being left on shore,' said Brock to me; 'for at the time the boat was getting down to the breakers, I was looking at Manby's apparatus for saving the lives of persons on a wreck then practising, and but for the "singing out" of my messmates, which caught my ear, should have been too late; but I reached in time to jump in with wet feet.' About four o'clock they came up with the vessel, which proved to be a Spanish brig, Paquette de Bilboa, laden with a general cargo, and bound from Hamburg to Cadiz, leaky, and both pumps at work. After a great deal of chaffering and haggering in regard to the amount of salvage (always the case with foreigners), and some little altercation with part of the boat's crew as to which of them should stay with the vessel, T. Layton (a Gatt pilot), J. Woolsey, and George Darling, boatmen, were finally chosen to assist in pumping and piloting her into Yarmouth harbour. The remainder of the crew of the yawl were then sent away. The brig at this time was about five miles to the eastward of the Newarp Floating Light, off Winterton on the Norfolk coast, the weather looking squally. On passing the light in their homeward course, a signal was made for them to go alongside, and they were requested to take on shore a sick man, and the poor fellow being comfortably placed upon some jackets and spare coats, they again shoved off and set all sail (three lugs): they had a fresh breeze from the W. S. W. And now again my readers shall have Brock's own words:—'There was little better than a pint of liquor in the boat, which the Spaniard had given us, and the bottle had passed once round, each man taking a mouthful, and about half of it was thus consumed. Most of us had got a bit of bread or biscuit in his hand, making a sort of light meal, and into the bargain I had hold of the main-sheet. We had passed the buoy of the Newarp a few minutes, and the light was about two miles astern: we had talked of our job (that is, our earnings), and had just calculated that by ten o'clock we should be at Yarmouth.' This hope proved fallacious. 'Without the slightest notice of its approach, a terrific squall from the northward took the yawl's sails flat aback, and the ballast, which they had trimmed to windward, being thus suddenly changed to leeward, she was upset in an instant.'

This dreadful catastrophe plunged all who were on board the yawl or boat into the sea. 'It was terrible,' said Brock, 'to listen to the cries of the poor fellows, some of whom could swim, while others could not. Mixed with the hissing of the water and the howlings of the storm, I heard shrieks for mercy, and some that had no meaning but what arose from fear. I struck out, to get clear of the crowd; and in a few minutes there was no noise, for most of the men had sunk; and on turning round, I saw the boat was still kept from going down by the wind having got under the sails. I then swam back to her, and assisted an old man to get hold of one of her spars. The boat's side was about three feet under water, and for a few minutes I stood upon her; but I found she was gradually settling down, and when up to my chest, I again left her and swam away, and now for the first time began to think of my own awful condition. My companions were all drowned, at least I supposed so. How long it was up to this period from the boat's capsizing I cannot exactly say: in such cases, sir, there is no time: but now I reflected that it was half-past six P. M. just before the accident occurred; that the nearest land at the time was six miles distant; that it was dead low water, and the flood-tide setting off the shore, making to the southward; therefore, should I ever reach the land, it would take me at least fifteen miles setting up with the flood before the ebb would assist me.'

At this moment a rush horse-collar covered with old netting, which had been used as one of the boat's fenders, floated close to him, which he laid hold of, and, getting his knife out, he stripped it of the network, and, by putting his left hand through it, was supported till he had cut the waistband of his petticoat trousers, which then fell off. His striped frock, waistcoat, and neckcloth, were also similarly got rid of; but he dared not try to free himself of his oiled trousers, drawers, or shirt, fearing that his legs might become entangled in the attempt: he therefore returned his knife into the pocket of his trousers, and put the collar over his head, which, although it assisted in keeping him above water, retarded his swimming: and after a few moments, thinking what was best to be done, he determined to abandon it. He now, to his great surprise, perceived one of his messmates swimming a-head of him, but he did not hail him. The roaring of the hurricane was past; the cries of drowning men were no longer heard; and the moonbeams were casting their silvery light over the smooth surface of the deep, calm and silent as the grave over which he floated, and into which he saw this last of his companions descend without a struggle or a cry as he approached within twenty yards of him.

Up to this time Winterton Light had served, instead of a land-mark, to direct his course; but the tide had now carried him out of sight of it, and in its stead 'a bright star stood over where' his hopes of safety rested. With his eyes steadfastly fixed upon it, he continued swimming on, calculating the time when the tide would turn. But his trials were not yet past. As if to prove the power of human fortitude, the sky became suddenly overclouded, and 'darkness was upon the face of the deep.' He no longer knew his course, and he confessed that for a moment he was afraid; yet he felt that 'fear is but the betraying of the succours which reason offereth;' and that which roused him to further exertion would have sealed the fate of almost any other human being—a sudden short cracking peal of thunder burst in stunning loudness just over his head, and the forked and flashing lightning at brief intervals threw its vivid fires around him. This, too, in its turn passed away, and left the wave once more calm and unruffled: the moon (nearly full) again threw a more brilliant light upon the bosom of the sea, which the storm had gone over without waking from its slumbers. His next effort was to free himself from his heavy-laced boots, which greatly encumbered him, and in which he succeeded by the aid of his knife. He now saw Lowestoft High Lighthouse, and could occasionally discern the tops of the cliffs beyond Gorlestone on the Suffolk coast. The swell of the sea drove him over the Cross-sand Ridge, and he then got sight of a buoy, which, although it told him his exact position, as he says, 'took him rather aback,' as he had hoped he was nearer the shore. It proved to be the chequered buoy of St Nicholas Gatt, off Yarmouth, and opposite his own door, but distant from the land four miles. And now again he held council with himself, and the energies of his mind seemed almost superhuman: he had been five hours in the water, and here was something to hold on by: he could have even got upon the buoy, and some vessel might come near to pick him up; and the question was, could he yet hold out four miles? But, as he says, 'I knew the night air would soon finish me, and had I stayed but a few minutes upon the buoy, and then altered my mind, how did I know that my limbs would again resume their office?' He found the tide (to use a sea term) was broke. It did not run so strong; so he abandoned the buoy, and steered for the land, towards which, with the wind from the eastward, he found he was now fast approaching. The last trial of his fortitude was now at hand, for which he was totally unprepared, and which he considers (sailors being not a little superstitious) the most difficult of any he had to combat. Soon after he left the buoy, he heard just above his head a sort of whizzing sound, which his imagination conjured into the prelude to the 'rushing of a mighty wind,' and close to his ear there followed a smart splash in the water, and a sudden shriek that went through him, such as is heard

'When the lone sea-bird wakes its wildest cry.'

The fact was, a large gray gull, mistaking him for a corpse, had made a dash at him, and its loud discordant scream in a moment brought a countless number of these formidable birds together, all prepared to contest for and share the spoil. These large and powerful foes he had now to scare from their intended prey, and by shouting and splashing with his hands and feet, in a few minutes they vanished from sight and hearing.

He now caught sight of a vessel at anchor, but a great way off, and to get within hail of her he must swim over Corton Sands (the grave of thousands), the breakers at this time showing their angry white crests. As he approached, the wind suddenly changed, the consequence of which was, that the swell of the sea met him. And now again for his own description:—'I got a great deal of water down my throat, which greatly weakened me, and I felt certain that, should this continue, it would soon be all over, and I prayed that the wind might change, or that God would take away my senses before I felt what it was to drown. In less time than I am telling you I had driven over the sands into smooth water, the wind and swell came again from the eastward, and my strength returned to me as fresh as in the beginning.'

He now felt assured that he could reach the shore, but he considered it would be better to get within hail of the brig, some distance to the southward of him, and the most difficult task of the two, as the ebb tide was now running, which, although it carried him towards the land, set to the northward; and to gain the object of his choice would require much greater exertion. But, said Brock, 'If I gained the shore, could I get out of the surf, which at this time was heavy on the beach? And supposing I succeeded in this point, should I be able to walk, climb the cliffs, and get to a house? If not, there was little chance of life remaining long in me; but if I could make myself heard on board the brig, then I should secure immediate assistance. I got within two hundred yards of her, the nearest possible approach, and summoning all my strength, I sung out as well as if I had been on shore.' Brock was fortunately answered from the deck, a boat was instantly lowered, and at half-past 1 A.M., having swam seven hours in an October night, he was safe on board the brig Betsy of Sunderland, coal laden, at anchor in Corton Roads, fourteen miles from the spot where the boat was capsized.

Once safe on board, 'nature cried enough;' he fainted, and continued insensible for some time. All that humanity could suggest was done for him by the captain and his crew; they had no spirits on board, but they had bottled ale, which they made warm; and by placing Brock before a good fire, rubbing him dry, and putting him in hot blankets, he was at length, with great difficulty, enabled to swallow a little of the ale; but it caused excruciating pain, as his throat was in a state of high inflammation from inhaling so long the saline particles of sea and air, and it was now swollen very much, and, as he says, he feared he should be suffocated. He, however, after a little time, fell into a sleep, which refreshed and strengthened him, but he awoke to intense bodily suffering. Round his neck and chest he was perfectly flayed: the soles of his feet, his hands, and his hamstrings, were also excoriated. In this state, at about 9 A.M., the brig getting under weigh with the tide, he was put on shore at Lowestoft in Suffolk, whence he immediately despatched a messenger to Yarmouth with the sad tidings of the fate of the yawl and the rest of her crew.

Being now safely housed under the roof of a relative, with good nursing and medical assistance, he was enabled to walk back to Yarmouth in five days from the time of the accident. The knife, which he considers as the great means of his being saved, is preserved with great care, and in all probability will be shown a century hence by his descendants. It is a common horn-handled knife, having one blade about five inches long. A piece of silver is now riveted on, and covers one side, on which is the following inscription, giving the names of the crew of the yawl when she upset:—'Brown, Emmerson, Smith, Bray, Budds, Fenn, Rushmere, Boult: Brock, aided by this knife, was saved after being seven and a half hours in the sea, 6th Oct. 1835.'

'It was a curious thing, sir,' said Brock, as I was listening to his extraordinary narrative, 'that I had been without a knife for some time, and only purchased this two days before it became so useful to me; and having to make some boat's tholes, it was as sharp as a razor.'

I know not what phrenologists might say to Brock's head, but I fancied, whilst studying his very handsome face and expression of countenance, that there I could see his heart. His bodily proportions, excepting height, are Herculean, standing only 5 feet 5 inches high; his weight, without any protuberance of body, is 14 stone; his age at the time spoken of was 31; his manners are quiet, yet communicative; he tells his tale neither tainted by bombast nor any clap-trap to awaken the sympathies of those of the 'Wrexhill school' that have flocked about him. In the honest manliness of his heart he thus addressed me just before parting—'I always considered Emmerson a better swimmer than myself; but, poor fellow, he did not hold out long. I ought to be a good-living chap, sir, for three times have I been saved by swimming.'

One trait more, which he did not tell me, and I have done. A very good subscription was made for the widows and children of Brock's unfortunate companions, and a fund being established for their relief, the surplus was offered to him. This was his answer:—'I am obliged to you, gentlemen, but, thank God, I can still get my own living as well as ever, and I could not spend the money that was given to the fatherless and the widow.'

We may add, that Brock still survives, and is by no means a stranger to the inhabitants of Yarmouth and its neighbourhood, or the numerous visitors who frequent this part of the coast.

UTILITY OF BIRDS.

Of late, says the Gardeners' Chronicle, our columns have been occupied by a discussion concerning the merits and demerits of certain small birds. It would seem that these creatures are incarnations of mischief, if the one party is to be credited; while the other maintains that they are the winged instruments of prosperity. S. declares that he would not have a gooseberry if he left a tit alive. T. as stoutly asserts that neither gooseberries nor anything else will be left if the tits are destroyed. We have thought it advisable to give this discussion full scope, because it may be truly regarded as one of the more important of the questions incidentally connected with gardening, and, moreover, one concerning which there is the most marvellous ignorance. Thousands of people imagine that birds live on nothing but corn and fruit, and are therefore supported at the personal expense of those who grow corn and fruit, without making any sort of return. 'What, say they, *is* the use of such things? We can't eat them; and there is no good in feeding a swarm of useless plunderers.' And therefore, because of this wise conclusion, the order is given to shoot, trap, and poison without mercy. Let us hope, however, that the arguments in favour of birds, to which we have lately given so much space, will have removed this error, and that the question between man and birds will have reduced itself to whether the balance of good is in favour of the latter or against them.

It would be idle to assert that birds consume nothing which, but for them, we might consume ourselves. They feed in part at our expense. They destroy the insects that infest our gardens, when they can find any; and when the insects are gone, they search for other food. The first is their labour, the second is their wages. And is not the workman worthy of his hire? The man who grudges a bird a little seed or fruit, might as well begrudge his weekly pay to the labourer. There is no doubt that a garden would be less expensive if all the work in it were done for nothing. If a master would pocket his servants' wages, he would have more to spend upon himself. But this sort of arrangement is not exactly consistent with the design of Providence; and we are sure that it would not meet with the approbation of either S. or T. We repeat it, then, let us look at birds as skilful workmen, and the fruit or seed which they eat as the coin in which they are paid their wages. Not that birds are an unmixed good. Is man himself? Is anything? There are situations, doubtless, where birds are an absolute nuisance. Imagine, for instance, a garden surrounded by a wood which swarms with blackbirds. Does any one suppose it possible to gather a ripe cherry in such a place? If he does, he is greatly mistaken. He would find the blackbird a much more dexterous gatherer than himself, and one who would relieve him from all trouble with his cherry crop. In such a case the birds must be trapped, or the crop abandoned. There would be no alternative.

But such instances are special, and form the exception, not the rule. Every day's experience tells us that birds are among the most efficient instruments of Providence for destroying the vermin that would otherwise overrun us. And people may rely upon it, that they cannot more effectually encourage the ravages of those insidious foes than by waging war upon the creatures which naturally feed upon them.

DIALOGUE ON A DRY BOOK.

B. Tragedians, if they read it, leave off their whey faces, and become dry drolls.

A. It was the author of Liston's melancholy.

B. And Charles Kemble's taking to comedy.

A. Sir, I can believe that: I know the virtues as well as the vices of the work too well to doubt it. As another instance, an enemy to unions of all kinds has for twenty years prevented the junction of two convenient canals, by obstinately keeping this book in his library, situated midway between the two water-parties.

B. Oh, that's nothing! A publican, owing to the swampiness of his ground, lost all his skittle-players. A true friend, I should call him, recommended him to try this book: he did yesterday, and to-day he has had repainted over his door, 'An undeniably *dry* ground for skittles!'

A. A man who carried the book about him for a day was afflicted with a dry cough all the days of his life.

B. The toll-tickets of a turnpike-road in Wales are printed by the same man who reprinted it. The London hackney-coachmen go down there, take a ticket, drive through the gate, return, and are dry for life.

A. A man living in a damp house kept a copy in his bedroom, and waked in the morning in a fever.

B. A gardener wrapped a water-melon in a waste sheet, and on cutting it open, it was as dusty as a dried poppy.

A. They cover warehouses for dry goods with it instead of slates, and it answers the purpose admirably.

B. A hatter makes waterproof beavers by pasting an inch of it inside.

A. A bunch of grapes bagged in it, in half an hour became raisins.

B. They dry grasses for winter fodder for cattle by reading a chapter of it through the fens of Lincolnshire.

A. If you put a page of it in a hay-rick, it never fires from damp.

B. A cow, milked by a Welshwoman who had merely said she should like to read it, never yielded a drop of milk afterwards.

A. Washerwomen recite a passage of it, and take down their clothes—dry! They have sold their drying-grounds in consequence.

B. Innkeepers keep the book in one of their bedrooms, and they want no warming-pans in the rest.

A. Dry-nurses find it the shortest method of weaning children. Two sentences out of it will make any swaddled young gentleman so thoroughly satisfied, that he will decline taking in his afternoon milk as usual.—*Webbe's Glances at Life in City and Suburb*: 1845.

PERSONAL IMPROVEMENT.

If the proper study of mankind is man, it is proper only so far as it may conduce to our own advancement in righteousness, by making us acquainted with that weakness and corruption of our nature which self-love is for ever labouring to conceal. Should we forget to apply to our own individual cases the observations which we make in the case of others, our knowledge will not only be barren of improvement, but may even serve to engender a censorious spirit, and increase that pride and presumption which we know too frequently attend the mere possession of speculative knowledge. Our own personal improvement is the centre towards which all reflections upon the nature and actions of man should converge; and whatsoever tends to unfold and bring to light any weakness lurking in the heart, should be received on our parts with all the readiness and impartiality which become creatures who are conscious of their responsible condition, and of that higher destiny which is to succeed this probationary life.—*J. S. M. Anderson.*

HUMAN LIFE.

Though we seem grieved at the shortness of life in general, we are wishing every period of it at an end. The minor longs to be of age, then to be a man of business, then to make up an estate, then to arrive at honours, then to retire.—*Spectator.*

JUDGING.

As the best writers are the most candid judges of the writings of others, so the best livers are the most charitable in the judgments they form of their neighbours' actions.—*Seed.*

THE MAN IN THE FOREST, OR THE EMIGRANT.

[FROM THE GERMAN OF FERDINAND FREILIGRATH.]

THE forest, cool and green—
The forest, wild and free—
Must shield the warworn banished man,
For not a friend has he.
All in the tomb his dear ones laid,
And he must seek the forest shade!

And he has sought his home,
And made it long ago,
There, where the wild wood winds its way
Into the vale below,
A house of houses: the gray-rock door
With swinging branches is wantoned o'er.

His bed a couch of leaves—
Leaves as yellow as gold;
While for a roof the branches weave
Their arms in flexile fold:
Oh joy! to inhabit this moss-crowned cave—
The fir and the beech trees surrounding wave.

Around the porch they weave,
And, stooping, strive to win
A glance of the stream that flows without,
And forms a bath within;
For there, in the grot so softly bright,
A fountain it flows, in liquid light!

And there a rough stone grate
Affords a warm fireside;
And there, when the snow storm whistles round,
The lonely man doth hide.
The stalactite walls that around him shine
Are his forest treasures' sacred shrine.

And there his heart is free
From discontent and care,
And lives throughout the wintry day
On hoarded flesh of bear.
But hark! at length the forest rings
With wild notes from each bird that sings!

And winking forth, each bud
Peeps from its leafy nest,
Soon as the blooming spring outpours
Sap from her dewy breast;
And the downy buds of the walnut tree
Wave through the forest all gladsomely.

High singing from the boughs,
The joyous finch and thrush
Proclaim the spring; while from his lair
Behold the exile rush!
He bounds, he flies from his cleft in the rock,
And fells the young trees with a sturdy shock;

Collects with tender care
The saplings young, and then
Rejoicing on his way he goes,
And seeks the abodes of men:
Thus to the market his store he brings,
While through the valley his wild song rings:—

'With young trees laden, all to sell,
I hie me to the city;
Let me, sweet spring, thy praises tell,
Who hast shown me wondrous pity.

These dew pearls bright, this moisture balm,
Into this heart is stealing—
The dewy oak, the alder, palm,
Each to my heart appealing,

Tell of their kindred gem—the tear
Of joy, the eye's tear-gladness!
That, silent stealing, stays each fear,
And soothes the exile's sadness.

The busy, noisy, bustling town,
Perplexed with cares the sorest,
Where charcoal fumes the kilns burn brown:
But you, my leafy forest,
Sweet spring, and all your holy train,
Will make and keep me pure again!'

The song, soft-flowing, ceased:
The dweller of the cave
Hied with his burthen gaily on;
Took what the buyer gave,
And wends him, glad of the release,
Back to his forest home in peace.

E. L.

Published by W. and R. CHAMBERS, Edinburgh; and, with their permission by W. S. ORR, Amen Corner, London.—Printed by BRADBURY and EVANS, Whitefriars, London.

CONDUCTED BY WILLIAM AND ROBERT CHAMBERS, EDITORS OF 'CHAMBERS'S INFORMATION FOR THE PEOPLE,' 'CHAMBERS'S EDUCATIONAL COURSE,' &c.

No. 82. New Series. SATURDAY, JULY 26, 1845. Price 1½d.

SIR WALTER SCOTT AND WILLIAM LAIDLAW.

FIRST ARTICLE.

The recent death of Mr William Laidlaw, a man of fine natural powers and of most estimable character, removes another of the links which connected the present generation with the daily life and personal history of Sir Walter Scott, and with the antique minstrelsy and simple manners of the Scottish Borders. The loss of Hogg, while the strong twilight from Scott's departed greatness still shone on the land, was universally regretted, and now another 'flower of the forest,' less bright, but a genuine product of the soil, is 'wede away,' and can never be replaced. As the author of one of our sweetest and most characteristic Scottish ballads—'Lucy's Flittin''—and as a collaborateur with Scott in the collection of the ancient minstrelsy, Laidlaw is entitled to honourable remembrance. Let us never forget those who have added even one wild rose to the chaplet of Scottish song and patriotism! It is chiefly, however, as the companion, factor, and private secretary of Scott, that this gentleman will be known in after-times. During all those busy and glorious years when Scott was pouring out so prodigally the treasures of his prose fictions, and building up his baronial romance of Abbotsford, Laidlaw was his confidential adviser and daily assistant. From 1817 to 1832 he was resident on the poet's estate, and emphatically one of his household friends. Not a shade of distrust or estrangement came between them; and this close connexion, notwithstanding a disparity in circumstances and opinions, in fame and worldly consequence, is too honourable to both parties to be readily forgotten. The manly kindness and consideration of one noble nature was paralleled by the affectionate devotion and admiration of another. Literary history is brightened by the rare conjunction.

Scott's early excursions to Liddesdale and Ettrick form one of the most interesting epochs in his life. He was then young, not great, but prosperous, high-spirited, and overflowing with enthusiasm. His appointment as sheriff had procured him confidence and respect. He had 'given hostages to fortune' as a husband and a father—and no one felt more strongly the force and tenderness of those ties. Friends were daily gathering round him: his German studies and ballads inspired visions of literary distinction, and he was full of hope and ambition. In his Border *raids*, he revelled among the choice and curious stores of Scottish poetry and antiquities. Almost every step in his progress was marked by some memorable deed or plaintive ballad—some martial achievement or fairy superstition. Every tragic tale and family tradition was known to him. The old *peels* or castles, the bare hills, and treeless forest, and solitary streams, were all sacred in his eyes. They told of times long past—of warlike feuds and forays—of knights and freebooters, and of primitive manners and customs, fast disappearing, yet embalmed in songs, often rude and imperfect, but always energetic or tender. Thus the Border towers, and *burns*, and rocks, were equally dear to him as memorials of feudal valour, and as the scenes of lyric poetry and pastoral tranquillity. He contrasted the strife and violence of the warlike Douglases, the Elliots and Armstrongs, with the peace and security of later times, when shepherds ranged the silent hill, or Scottish maidens sang ancient songs, and, like the Trojan dames,

> Washed their fair garments in the days of peace.

Much of this romance was in the scene, but more was in the mind of the beholder.

William Laidlaw's acquaintance with Scott commenced in the autumn of 1802, after two volumes of the Minstrelsy had been published, and the editor was making collections for a third. The eldest son of a wealthy and respectable sheep-farmer, Mr Laidlaw had received a good education. He had a strong bias for natural history and poetry, was modest and retiring, and of remarkably mild and agreeable manners.* The scheme of collecting the old ballads of the Forest was exactly suited to his taste. Burns had filled the whole land with a love of song and poetry—James Hogg was his intimate friend and companion. Hogg had been ten years a shepherd with Mr Laidlaw's father, had taught the younger members of the family their letters, and recited poetry to the old, and was engaged in every *ploy* and pursuit at Blackhouse, the name of the elder Laidlaw's farm. A solitary and interesting spot is Blackhouse—a wild extensive sheep-walk, with its complement of traditional story, and the suitable accompaniment of a ruined tower. The farm lies along the Douglas-burn, a small mountain stream which falls into the Yarrow about two miles from St Mary's Loch. Near the house, at the foot of a steep green hill, and surrounded with a belting of trees, is Blackhouse Tower, or the Tower of Douglas, so called, according to tradition, after the Black Douglas, one of whose ancestors, Sir John Douglas of Douglas-burn, as appears from Godscroft's history of the family, sat in Malcolm Canmore's first parliament. The tower has in one corner the remains of a round turret, which contained the stair, and the walls rise in

* Mr Laidlaw was born at Blackhouse, Selkirkshire, in November 1780. He was afterwards tenant of a farm at Traquair, and of another at Libberton, near Edinburgh. From 1817 to 1832, as stated in the text, he resided on the estate of Abbotsford. After Scott's death, Mr Laidlaw was successively factor on the estates of Seaforth and Balnagown, in Ross-shire. His health failing, he went to live with his brother, Mr James Laidlaw, sheep-farmer at Contin, in the county of Ross, where he died on the 18th of May 1845. He was buried in Contin churchyard, a retired spot under the shade of the lofty Tor-Achilty, and amidst the most enchanting Highland scenery.

high broken points, which altogether give the ruin a singular and picturesque appearance. It is also the scene of a popular ballad, 'The Douglas Tragedy,' in which, as in the old Elizabethan dramas, blood is shed and horrors accumulated with no sparing hand. A knightly lover, the 'Lord William' of so many ballads, carries off a daughter of Lord Douglas, and is pursued by this puissant noble and his seven sons. All these are slain by Lord William, while the fair betrothed looks on, holding his steed; and the lover himself is mortally wounded in the combat, and dies ere morn. The lady also falls a prey to her grief; and, in the true vein of antique story and legend, we are told

'Lord William was buried in St Mary's kirk,
Lady Margaret in Mary's quire;
Out o' the lady's grave grew a bonny red rose,
And out o' the knight's a brier.

The tower and legend interested Scott as they had done Laidlaw. He listened attentively to the traditionary narrative, and, like the lovers in the ballad,

He lighted down to take a drink
Of the spring that ran sae clear,

and visited the seven large stones erected upon the neighbouring heights of Blackhouse to mark the spot where the seven brethren were slain.

Mr Laidlaw was prepared for Scott's mission. He had heard from a Selkirk man in Edinburgh, Mr Andrew Mercer, that the sheriff was meditating a poetical raid into Ettrick, accompanied by John Leyden, and he had written down various ballads from the recitation of old women and the singing of the servant girls. He was constantly annoyed, he said, to find how much the affectation and false taste of Allan Ramsay had spoiled or superseded many striking and beautiful old strains of which he got traces and fragments, and how much Mr Scott was too late in beginning his researches, as many aged persons who had been the bards and depositaries of a former generation were then gone. In the course of his inquiries, Laidlaw learned that an old man, a relation of Hogg's, could repeat a grand heroic ballad of vast antiquity, which had never been published, and he procured from the Shepherd a copy of this precious relic, called 'Auld Maitland.' It was taken down from the recitation or chanting of Hogg's uncle, 'Will of Phawhope,' confirmed by his mother, both of whom had learned it from their father, an older Will of Phawbope—for the family had been herds in the Forest for many generations. These services of the olden time were marked by reciprocal kindness and attachment, not unworthy of the patriarchal age. Son succeeded father in tending the *hirsel* or herding the cows, while in the case of 'the master,' the same hereditary or family succession was very often preserved.

The person of the sheriff was not unknown to the new friend with whom he was afterwards destined to form so intimate a connexion. 'I first saw Walter Scott,' Laidlaw used to relate, 'when the Selkirk troop of yeomanry met to receive their sheriff shortly after his appointment. I was on the right of the rear-rank, and my front-rank man was *Archie Park*, a brother of the traveller. Our new sheriff was accompanied by a friend, and as they retired to the usual station of the inspecting officer previous to the charges, the wonderful *springs* and bounds which Scott made, seemingly in the excitation and gaiety of his heart, joined to the effect of his fine fair face and athletic appearance, were the cause of a general murmur of satisfaction, bordering on applause, which ran through the troop. Archie Park looked over his shoulder to me, and growled, in his deep rough voice, "Will, what a strong chield that would have been if his left leg had been like his right ane!"'

Scott and Leyden duly appeared at Blackhouse, carrying letters of introduction. They put up their horses, and experienced a homely unostentatious hospitality, which afterwards served to heighten the delightful traits of rustic character in the delineation of Dandie Dinmont's home at Charlies-Hope. If the sheriff did not 'shoot a blackcock and eat a blackcock too,' the fault was not in his entertainers. After the party had explored the scenery of the burn, and inspected Douglas Tower, Laidlaw produced his treasure of 'Auld Maitland.' Leyden seemed inclined to lay hands on the manuscript, but the sheriff said gravely that *he* would read it. Instantly both Scott and Leyden, from their knowledge of the subject, saw and felt that the ballad was undoubtedly ancient, and their eyes sparkled as they exchanged looks. Scott read with great fluency and emphasis. Leyden was like a roused lion. He paced the room from side to side, clapped his hands, and repeated such expressions as echoed the spirit of hatred to King Edward and the southrons, or as otherwise struck his fancy. 'I had never before seen anything like this,' said the quiet Laidlaw; 'and though the sheriff kept his feelings under, he, too, was excited, so that his *bur* became very perceptible.'* Laidlaw had procured a version of another ballad, 'The Demon Lover,' which he took down from the recitation of Mr Walter Grieve, then in Craik, on Borthwick water. Grieve sung it well to a singularly wild tune, and the song embodies a popular but striking superstition, such as Lewis introduced into his romance of 'The Monk.' To complete the fragment, Laidlaw added the 6th, 12th, 17th, and 18th stanzas, and those who consult the ballad in Scott's Minstrelsy will see how well our friend was qualified to excel in the imitation of these strains of the elder muse. After the party had 'quaffed their fill' of old songs and legendary story, they all took horse, and went to dine with Mr Ballantyne of Whitehope, the uncle of Laidlaw.

'There was not a minute of silence,' says Mr Laidlaw's memorandum, 'as we rode down the narrow glen, and over by the way of Dryhope, to get a view of St Mary's Loch and of the Peel or Tower. When we en-

* As they fared up o'er Lammermore,
They burned baith up and down,
Until they came to a darksome house;
Some call it Leader-Town.

'Wha hauds this house?' young Edward cried,
'Or wha gies't ower to me?'
A gray-haired knight set up his head,
And crackit right crousely:

'Of Scotland's king I haud my house;
He pays me meat and fee;
And I will keep my gude auld house
While my house will keep me.'

They laid their sowies to the wall,
Wi' mony a heavy peal;
But he threw ower to them agen
Baith pitch and tar barrel.

With springalds, stanes, and gads of airn,
Among them fast he threw;
Till mony of the Englishmen
About the wall he slew.

Full fifteen days that braid host lay,
Sieging auld Maitland keen,
Syne they hae left him, hail and fair,
Within his strength of stane.

Ballad of Auld Maitland.

Scott valued this ballad, and his other lyrical acquisitions, highly. In a letter to Mr Laidlaw, dated 21st January 1803, he remarks as follows:—'Auld Maitland, laced and embroidered with antique notes and illustrations, makes a most superb figure. I have got, through the intervention of Lady Dalkeith, a copy of Mr Beattie of Meikledale's "Tamlane." It contains some highly poetical stanzas descriptive of fairy-land, which, after some hesitation, I have adopted, though they have a very refined and modern cast. I do not suspect Mr Beattie of writing ballads himself, but pray will you inquire whether, within the memory of man, there has been any poetical clergyman or schoolmaster whom one could suppose capable of giving a coat of modern varnish to this old ballad. What say you to this, for example?—

We sleep on rose-buds soft and sweet,
We revel in the stream,
We wanton lightly on the wind,
Or glide on a sunbeam.

This seems quite modern, yet I have retained it.'

tered the Hawkshaw-doors, a pass between Blackhouse and Dryhope, where a beautiful view of the lake opens, Leyden, as I expected, was so struck with the scene, that he suddenly stopped, sprung from his horse (which he gave to Mr Scott's servant), and stood admiring the fine Alpine prospect. Mr Scott said little; but as this was the first time he had seen St Mary's Loch, doubtless more was passing in his mind than appeared. Often when returning home with my fishing-rod had I stopped at this place, and admired the effect of the setting sun and the approaching twilight; and now when I found it admired by those whom I thought likely to judge of and be affected with its beauty, I felt the same sort of pleasure that I experienced when I found that Walter Scott was delighted with Hogg. Had I at that time been gifted with a glimpse—a very slight glimpse—of the second-sight, every word that passed, and they were not few, until we reached Whitehope or Yarrow church, I should have endeavoured to record. Scott, as all the world knows, was great in conversation, and Leyden was by no means a common person. He had about him that unconquerable energy and restlessness of mind that would have raised him, had he lived, very high among the remarkable men of his native country. I cannot forget the fire with which he repeated, on the Craig-bents, a half stanza of an irrecoverable ballad—

> Oh swiftly gar speed the berry-brown steed
> That drinks o' the Teviot clear—

which his friend, when finally no brother to it could be found, adopted in the reply of William of Deloraine to the Lady of Branksome.'

The regret that Laidlaw here expresses at having omitted to note down the conversation of his friends is extremely natural, but few men could be less fitted for such a task. He had nothing of Boswell in his mind or character. He wanted both the concentration of purpose and the pliant readiness of talent and power of retention. At Abbotsford, he had ample opportunities for keeping such a record, and he was often urged to undertake it. Scott himself on one occasion, after some brilliant company had left the room, remarked half jocularly, that many a one meeting such people, and hearing such talk, would make a very lively and entertaining book of the whole, which might some day be read with interest. Laidlaw instantly felt it necessary to put in a disclaimer. He said he would consider it disreputable in him to take advantage of his position, or of the confidence of private society, and make a journal of the statements and opinions uttered in free and familiar conversation. We may respect the delicacy and sensitiveness of his feelings, but society, collectively, would lose much by the rigid observance of such a rule. The question, we think, should be determined by the nature and quality of the circumstances recorded. It is a special, not a general case. There is nothing more discreditable in noting down a brilliant thought or interesting fact, than in repeating it in conversation; while to play the part of a gossiping and malicious eavesdropper, is equally a degradation in life and in literature. It would have been detestable (if the idea could for a moment be entertained) for Mr Laidlaw to pry into the domestic details and personal feelings or failings of his illustrious friend at Abbotsford; but we may wish that his pen had been as ready as his ear when Scott ran over the story of his literary life and opinions, or discriminated the merits of his great contemporaries—when Davy expatiated on the discoveries and delights of natural philosophy—when Miss Edgeworth painted Irish scenes and character—when Moore discoursed of poetry, music, and Byron—when Irving kindled up like a poet in his recollections of American lakes, and woods, and old traditions—when Mackintosh began with the Roman law, and ended in Lochaber—when some septuagenarian related anecdotes of the past—when artists and architects talked of pictures, sculpture, and buildings—or when some accomplished traveller and *savant* opened up the interior of foreign courts and the peculiarities of national manners. Many a wise and witty saying and memorable illustration—the life-blood of the best books—might thus have been preserved, though with occasional *lacunæ* and mistakes; and all are now lost—

> Gone glittering through the dream of things that were—

and cannot be recalled. Surely society is the worse for the loss of these racy, spontaneous fruits of intellect, study, and observation.

While dinner was getting ready at Whitehope, Laidlaw and Leyden strolled into the neighbouring churchyard of Yarrow, and saw the tomb of Mr Rutherford, the first minister of that parish after the revolution, and the maternal great-grandfather of Scott. Leyden recited to his companion the ballads of 'The Eve of St John' and 'Glenfinlas,' which naturally impressed on the hearer a vivid idea of the poetical talents of the sheriff, and Laidlaw felt towards him as an old friend. This was increased by Scott's partiality for dogs. He was struck with a very beautiful and powerful greyhound which followed Laidlaw, and he begged to have a brace of pups from the same dog, saying he had now become a forester, as sheriff of Ettrick, and must have dogs of the true mountain breed. 'This request,' said the other, 'I took no little pains to fulfil. I kept the puppies till they were nearly a year old. My youngest brother, then a boy, took great delight in training them; and the way was this: he took a long pole having a string and a piece of meat fastened to it, and made the dogs run in a circular or oval course. Their eagerness to get the meat gave them, by much practice, great strength in the loins, and singular expertness in turning, besides singular alertness in *mouthing*, for which they were afterwards famous. Scott hunted with them for two years over the mountains of Tweedside and Yarrow, and never dreamt that a hare could escape them. He mentions them in the introduction to the second canto of Marmion—

> Remember'st thou my greyhounds true?
> O'er holt or hill there never flew,
> From slip or leash there never sprang
> More fleet of foot or sure of fang.'

Before the friends parted, Scott took a note of Hogg's address, and from that time never ceased to take a warm interest in his fortunes. He corresponded with him, and becoming curious to see the poetical shepherd, made another visit to Blackhouse, for the purpose of getting Laidlaw along with him as guide to Ettrick. The visit was highly agreeable. The sheriff's *bonhomie* and lively conversation had deeply interested his companion, and he rode by his side in a sort of ecstasy as they journeyed again by St Mary's Loch and the green hills of Dryhope, which rise beyond the winding-sheet of smooth water. It was a fine summer morning, and the impressions of the day and the scene have been recorded in imperishable verse.* Dryhope Tower, so intimately associated with the memory of Mary Scott, the 'Flower of Yarrow,' made the travellers stop for a brief space; and *Dhu Linn* (where Marjory, the wife of Percy de Cockburn, sat while men were hanging her husband), with Chapelhope and other scenes and ruins famous in Border tradition, deeply interested Scott. At the west end of the Loch of the Lowes, the surrounding mountains close in in the face of the traveller, apparently preventing all farther egress. At this spot, as Laidlaw was trying to find a safe place where they might cross the marsh through which the infant Yarrow finds its way to the loch, Scott's servant, an English boy, rode up, and, touching his hat, respectfully inquired with much interest 'where the people got their necessaries?' This unromantic question, and the *naïveté* of the lad's manner, was a source of great amusement to the sheriff. The day's journey was a favourite theme with Laidlaw. First, after passing the spots we have described, the horsemen crossed the ridge

* Marmion—Introduction to Canto II.

of hills that separate the Yarrow from her sister stream. These hills are high and green, but the more lofty parts of the ridge are soft and boggy, and they had often to pick their way and proceed in single file. Then they followed a foot-track on the side of a long *cleugh* or *hope*, and at last descended towards the Ettrick, where they had in view the level green valley, walled in by high hills of dark green, with here and there gray crags, the church and the old *place* of Ettrick Hall in ruins, embosomed in trees. Scott was somewhat chafed by having left in his bedroom that morning his watch—a valuable gold repeater, presented to him on the occasion of his marriage—and to Laidlaw's ejaculations of delight he sometimes replied quickly—'A savage enough place—a very savage place.' His good humour, however, was restored by the novelty of the scenes and the fine clear day, and he broke out with snatches of song, and told endless anecdotes, either new, or better told than ever they were before. The travellers went to dine at Ramsey-cleugh, where they were sure of a cordial welcome and a good farmer's dinner; and Laidlaw sent off to Blackhouse for the sheriff's watch (which he received next morning), and to Ettrick house for Hogg, that he might come and spend the evening with them. The Shepherd (who then retained all his original simplicity of character) came *to tea*, and he brought with him a bundle of manuscripts, of size enough at least to show his industry—all of course ballads, and fragments of ballads. The penmanship was executed with more care than Hogg had ever bestowed on anything before. Scott was surprised and pleased with Hogg's appearance, and with the hearty familiarity with which *Jamie*, as he was called, was received by Laidlaw and the Messrs Bryden of Ramsey-cleugh. Hogg was no less gratified. 'The sheriff of a county in those days,' said Laidlaw, 'was regarded by the class to whom Hogg belonged with much of the fear and respect that their *forbears* had looked up to the ancient hereditary sheriffs, who had the power of pit and gallows in their hands; and here Jamie found himself all at once not only the chief object of the sheriff's notice and flattering attention, but actually seated at the same table with him.' Hogg's genius was sufficient passport to the best society. His appearance was also prepossessing. His clear ruddy cheek and sparkling eye spoke of health and vivacity, and he was light and agile in his figure. When a youth, he had a remarkably fine head of long curling brown hair, which he wore coiled up under his bonnet; and on Sundays, when he entered the church and let down his locks, the *lasses* (on whom Jamie always turned an expressive *espiègle* glance) looked towards him with envy and admiration. He doubtless thought of himself as the Gaelic bard did of Allan of Muidart—

And when to old Kilphedar's church
Came troops of damsels gay,
Say, came they there for Allan's fame,
Or came they there to pray?

Mr Laidlaw thus speaks of the evening at Ramsey-cleugh:—'It required very little of that tact or address in social intercourse for which Mr Scott was afterwards so much distinguished, to put himself and those around him entirely at their ease. In truth, I never afterwards saw him at any time apparently enjoy company so much, or exert himself so greatly—or probably there was no effort at all—in rendering himself actually fascinating; nor did I ever again spend such a night of merriment. The qualities of Hogg came out every instant, and his unaffected simplicity and fearless frankness both surprised and charmed the sheriff. They were both very good mimics and story-tellers born and bred; and when Scott took to employ his dramatic talent, he soon found he had us all in his power; for every one of us possessed a quick sense of the ludicrous, and perhaps of humour of all kinds. I well recollect how the tears ran down the cheeks of my cousin George Bryden; and although his brother was more quiet, it was easy to see that he, too, was delighted. Hogg and I were unbounded laughers when the occasion was good. The best proof of Jamie's enjoyment was, that he never sung a song that blessed night, and it was between two and three o'clock before we parted.'

Next morning Scott and Laidlaw went, according to promise, to visit Hogg. The appearance of the low thatched cottage was poor enough, but the situation is fine, and the opposite mountains, from the grand simplicity of their character, may almost be termed sublime. The Shepherd and his aged mother—'Old Margaret Laidlaw'—for she generally went by her maiden name—gave the visitors a hearty welcome. James had sent for a bottle of wine, of which each had to take a glass; and as the exhilarating effects of the previous night had not quite departed, he insisted that they should help him in drinking every drop in the bottle. Had it been a few years earlier in Scott's life, and before he was sheriff of the county, the request would probably have been complied with; but on this occasion the bottle was set aside. The scene was curious and interesting. 'Hogg may be a great poet,' said Scott, 'and, like Allan Ramsay, come to be the founder of a sort of family.' Hogg's familiarity of address, mingled with fits of deference and respect towards the sheriff, was curiously characteristic. Many years after this, we recollect a gentleman asking Laidlaw about an amusing anecdote told of the Shepherd. Hogg had sagacity enough to detect the authorship of the Waverley novels long before the secret was divulged, and had the volumes as they appeared bound and lettered on the back 'SCOTT'S NOVELS.' His friend discovered this one day when visiting Hogg at Altrive, and in a dry humorous tone of voice remarked, 'Jamie, your bookbinder must be a stupid fellow to spell *Scots* with two *t's*.' Hogg is said to have rejoined, 'Ah, Watty, I am ower auld a cat to draw that strae before.' Laidlaw laughed immoderately at the story, but observed, 'Jamie never came lower down than *Walter*.' 'How do you account for it, Mr Scott,' said Laidlaw on one occasion, 'that Hogg and Allan Cunningham have such awfu' trash in the midst of very fine and splendid passages?' 'I cannot tell you, Willy,' said Scott with a laugh, 'unless it be that, like the laird of Rigg's breakfast, it comes up a' together.'

From Hogg's cottage the party proceeded up Rankleburn to see Buccleuch, and inspect the old chapel and mill. They found nothing at the kirk of Buccleuch, and saw only the foundations of the chapel. Scott, however, was in high spirits, and being a member of the Edinburgh Light Cavalry, and Laidlaw one of the Selkirkshire Yeomanry, they sometimes set off at a gallop—the sheriff leading as in a mimic charge, and shouting, 'Slaughtan! mienen kinder slaughtan!' Hogg trotted up behind, marvelling at the versatile powers of the 'wonderful *shirra*.' They all dined together with a 'lady of the glen,' Mrs Bryden, Crosslee, and next morning Scott returned to Clovenford Inn, where he resided till he took a lease of the house of Ashestiel.

These are homely details in the life of a great poet and genius, yet it was amidst these and similar scenes that Scott inhaled inspiration, and nursed those powers which afterwards astonished the world. The healthy vigour of his mind, and his clear understanding, grew up under such training, and his imagination was thence quickened and moulded. Byron studied amidst the classic scenes of Greece and Italy—Southey and Moore in their libraries, intent on varied knowledge. All the 'shadowy tribes of mind' were known to the metaphysical Coleridge. Wordsworth wandered among the lakes and mountains of Westmoreland, brooding over his poetical and philosophical theories, from which his better genius, in the hour of composition, often extricated him. Scott was in all things the simple unaffected worshipper of nature and of Scotland. His chivalrous romances sprung from his national predilections; for the warlike deeds of the Border chiefs first fired his fancy, and directed his researches. In these mountain excursions he imbibed that love and veneration of past times which coloured most of his compositions; and human sympathies and solemn reflections were forced upon him by his intercourse with the natives of the hills, and the simple and lonely majesty of the scenes that he visited. These early impressions were never forgotten. Nor could there have been a better nursery for a romantic and national poet. Scholastic and critical studies would have polished his taste and refined his verse, but we might have wanted the strong picturesque vigour—the simple direct energy of the old ballad style—the truth, nature, and observation of a stirring life—all that characterises and endears old Scotland. Scott's destiny was on the whole pre-eminently happy; and when we think of the fate of other great authors—of Spenser composing amidst the savage turbulence of Ireland—of Shakspeare following a profession which he disliked—of Milton blind, and in danger—Dante in exile—and Tasso and Cervantes in prison—we feel how immeasurably superior was the lot of this noble free-hearted Scotsman, whose genius was the proudest inheritance of his country. 'Think no man happy till he dies,' said the sage. Scott's star became dim, but there was only a short period of darkness, and he never 'bated one jot of heart or hope,' nor lost the friendly and soothing attentions of those he loved. The world's respect and admiration he always possessed.

We need not follow in further detail the various wanderings of the sheriff and his friend. They were often renewed in the course of two or three summers and autumns. One excursion was made to the wild scenery at the head of Moffat water, where there is a striking waterfall and a fine lake, Loch Skene. Scott's personal strength and agility surprised most of his associates in these country rambles. Laidlaw thus writes of the expedition to Moffat dale:—

'We proceeded with difficulty up the rocky chasm to reach the foot of the waterfall. The passage which the stream has worn by cutting the opposing rocks of greywacke, is rough and dangerous. My brother George and I, both in the prime of youth, and constantly in the habit of climbing, had difficulty in forcing our way, and we felt for Scott's lameness. This, however, was unnecessary. He said he could not perhaps climb so fast as we did, but he advised us to go on, and leave him. This we did, but halted on a projecting point before we descended to the foot of the fall, and looking back, we were struck at seeing the motions of the sheriff's dog *Camp*. The dog was attending anxiously on his master; and when the latter came to a difficult part of the rock, Camp would jump down, look up to his master's face, then spring up, lick his master's hand and cheek, jump down again, and look upwards, as if to show him the way, and encourage him. We were greatly interested with the scene. Mr Scott seemed to depend much on his hands and the great strength of his powerful arms; and he soon fought his way over all obstacles, and joined us at the foot of the Greymare's Tail, the name of the cataract.'

This excursion, like most of the others, Scott described in his introduction to Marmion. He was apt, on a journey among the hills, especially if the district was new to him, to fall at times into fits of silence, revolving in his mind, and perhaps throwing into language, the ideas that were suggested at the moment by the landscape; and hence those who had often been his companions knew the origin of many of the beautiful passages in his future works. Of this Laidlaw used to relate one instance. About a mile down Douglas-burn, a small brook falls into it from the Whitehope hills; and at the junction of the streams, at the foot of a bank celebrated in traditionary story, stood the withered remains of what had been a very large old hawthorn tree, that had often engaged the attention of the young men at Blackhouse. Laidlaw on one occasion pointed out to the sheriff its beautiful site and venerable appearance, and asked him if he did not think it might be centuries old, and once a leading object in the landscape. As the district had been famous for game and wild animals, he said there could be little doubt that the red deer had often lain under the shade of the tree, before they ascended to feed on the open hill-tops in the evening. Scott looked on the tree and the green hills, but said nothing. The enthusiastic guide repeated his admiration, and added, that Whitehope-tree was famous for miles around; but still Scott was silent. The subject was then dropt; 'but some years afterwards,' said Laidlaw, 'when the sheriff read to me his manuscript of Marmion, I found that Whitehope-tree was not forgotten, and that he had felt all the associations it was calculated to excite.' The description of the thorn is at the commencement of the second canto of Marmion, and is eminently beautiful.

We may here notice another poetical scene, the 'Bush aboon Traquair,' celebrated in the well-known popular song by Crawford. Burns says that when he saw the old 'bush' in 1787, it was composed of eight or nine ragged birches, and that the Earl of Traquair had planted a clump of trees near the place, which he called 'The New Bush.' Laidlaw maintained that the new bush was in reality the old bush of the song. One of the sons of Murray of Phillipshaugh used to come over often on foot, and meet one of the ladies of Traquair at the *Cless*, a green hollow at the foot of the hill that overhangs Traquair house. This was the scene of the song. The straggling birches that Burns saw are half a mile up the water, the remains of a wooded bog—out of sight of Traquair house, to be sure, but far out of the way between Hangingshaw, on the Yarrow, and Traquair.

One morning in autumn 1804 was vividly impressed on the recollection of Laidlaw; for Scott then recited to him nearly the whole of the Lay of the Last Minstrel, as they journeyed together in the sheriff's gig up Gala Water. The wild, irregular structure of the poem, the description of the old minstrel, the goblin machinery, the ballads interspersed throughout the tale, and the exquisite forest scenes (the Paradise of Ettrick), all entranced the listener. Now and then Scott would stop to tell an anecdote of the country they were passing through, and afterwards, in his deep *serious* voice, resume his recitation of the poem. Laidlaw had, the night before, gone to Lasswade, where the sheriff then resided, in a beautiful cottage on the banks of the Esk, and on the following morning, after breakfast, they went up the Gala, when Scott poured forth what truly seemed to be an unpremeditated lay. They returned about sunset, and found the sheriff's young and beautiful wife looking on at the few shearers engaged in cutting down their crop in a field adjoining the cottage. Mrs Scott seemed to Laidlaw a 'lovely and interesting creature,' and the sheriff met her with undisguised tenderness and affection. These were indeed golden days.

GLIMPSES OF NEW ZEALAND.

It will be remembered that in 1839 a company was formed in London for acquiring land and establishing settlements in the islands of New Zealand. An expedition was accordingly despatched in the spring of that year to treat with the natives, to select a site for a colony, and to make preparations for the reception of the emigrants. This charge was confided to Colonel William Wakefield, who sailed from Plymouth in the Tory on the 12th of May, with every necessary equipment. Such a voyage seemed to offer much novelty and adventure, and a nephew, Mr Edward Jerningham Wakefield, conceived an eager desire to be one of the party. Having obtained a passage from the patrons of the enterprise, this youth, then only nineteen years of age, set out with the intention of returning with some of the emigrant ships; but becoming interested in the progress of the infant colony, he was tempted to prolong his stay for four years. He now gives his personal narrative in two goodly volumes,* carrying us over the establishment of Wellington, New Plymouth, Nelson, and other towns, by the New Zealand Land Company in the bays of Cook Strait; the establishment of Auckland and Russell on the northern shores by the government; and the massacre of Wairau, by which he lost his uncle, Captain Arthur Wakefield, who had gone out with the Nelson settlers in 1841. The company having met with considerable opposition from the missionaries previously located in New Zealand, and with little cordial support from the resident officials of the British government, Mr Wakefield, acquiring, as he states, 'the unavoidable spirit of a partisan,' speaks of these opposing parties in terms of the severest censure, which necessarily precludes us from noticing that portion of his work which relates to the progress of the company's scheme. Moving as he did, however, with the surveyors over a great portion of the islands, his narrative abounds with interesting descriptions of the country and its natives—the capabilities of the former, and the manners and customs of the latter. It is from these that we now select what seems more especially novel and amusing, referring the reader for information of another sort to the volumes themselves, and to articles which have already appeared in this journal.

After a quick and pleasant voyage, the Tory dropped into Ship Cove, on the southern side of the strait, on the 18th of August. The first glimpse of the country was eminently encouraging. 'This morning, at daylight, we had warped farther into the cove, and anchored in 11 fathoms, muddy bottom, within 300 yards of the shore, where we fastened a hawser to a tree; thus occupying probably the same spot as Captain Cook, in his numerous visits to this harbour. There were a good many natives on board already; but, eager to touch the land, I got into a small canoe with Nayti, who paddled me ashore. The hills, which rise to the height of 1000 or 1500 feet on three sides of the cove, are covered from their tops to the water's edge with an undulating carpet of forest. How well Cook has described the harmony of the birds at this very spot! Every bough seemed to throng with feathered musicians, and the melodious chimes of the bell-bird were especially distinct. At the head of the cove is a small level space of land, formed by the alluvial deposit of three rills from the mountains, which here empty themselves into the bay. Landing here, I remained for some time absorbed in contemplating the luxurious vegetation of grass and shrubs, and the wild carrots and turnips which remain as relics of our great navigator. Rich historical recollections crowded on my mind as I tried to fix on the exact spot where Cook's forge and carpenter's shop had stood; and I was only roused from my reverie by the arrival of some more of the party, bent on the same object. We collected some shells, pebbles, and plants, and returned to breakfast on fresh potatoes and some of the fish which had been caught in abundance from the ship in the evening.'

Crossing the strait, they next entered Port Nicholson, which was subsequently chosen as the site of the company's first proceedings. This port or bay is completely land-locked, its fairway being not more than a mile in width, with a rocky reef on the north, and a high headland on the south. 'Captain Cook once anchored in the entrance of this magnificent harbour. Being anxious to rejoin the other ship in company with him, he was unable to examine it, but spoke highly of its promising appearance as a port. It was named Port Nicholson by the captain of a Sydney trading vessel some years ago, after his patron and friend, the harbour-master of Port Jackson, in New South Wales. As we advanced up the channel, which continues from two to three miles in width for four miles from a little inside the reef, we were boarded by two canoes, containing the two principal chiefs of the tribe living on shore. One of mature years, named *Epuni*, or "Greedy," advanced with much dignity of manner to greet our pilot as an old and respected friend, and was joined in this by his nephew, *Wareperi*, or "Dark House," a fine commanding man of about thirty-five.

'The harbour expanded as we advanced, two deep bays stretching to the south-west from the innermost end of the entering channel. From their western extremity the land trends round to a valley lying at the north end of the harbour, about eight miles from the reef, while the hilly shores of the eastern side continue nearly straight to the mouth of the valley, thus leaving the upper part of the great basin four or five miles in width. In this upper part lie the two islands, behind the largest and most northerly of which we anchored at the distance of half a mile from the sandy beach at the valley's mouth. Epuni eagerly inquired the motive of our visit, and expressed the most marked satisfaction on hearing that we wished to buy the place, and bring white people to it. Wareperi also expressed his willingness to sell the land, and his desire of seeing white men come to live upon it.' Upon landing, they found the bay watered by several streams, and by one considerable river, called the Hutt or Heretaonga. The valley of this river preserved an average breadth of two miles to a considerable distance, bounded on either side by wooded hills from 300 to 400 feet in height. It was covered with high forest to within a mile and a half of the beach, though swamps full of native flax, and a belt of sand-hummocks, intervened. Colonel Wakefield ascended the river until some snags prevented the further progress of the canoe. He described the banks as of the richest soil, and covered with majestic timber, except where fertile but scanty gardens had been cleared and cultivated by the natives. As agent of the company, he accordingly made purchase of this district, which subsequently became the site of Wellington, the first location of the colony.

In the meantime, a surveying vessel, together with three or four emigrant ships, had left Britain, and, without inactively waiting their arrival, the Tory proceeded to examine and purchase other tracts along both shores of the strait. On Mr Wakefield's return to Port Nicholson, in January 1840, he found that four of the expected vessels had arrived, and that several hundreds of English and Scotch had already squatted on their adopted country. The following picture of this first location is exceedingly graphic and amusing:—'The sand-hummocks at the back of the long beach were dotted over with tents of all shapes and sizes, native-built huts in various stages of construction, and heaps of goods of various kinds, which lay about anywhere between high water-mark and the houses. Thus ploughs, hundreds of bricks, millstones, tent-poles, saucepans, crockery, iron, pot-hooks, and triangles, casks of all sizes, and bales of all sorts, were distributed about the sand-hummocks. The greatest good humour prevailed among the owners of these multifarious articles: the very novelty and excitement of their employment appeared to give them high spirits and courage. They pitched their tents and piled up their goods in rude order, while the natives, equally pleased and excited, sung *Maori* songs to them from the tops of the *ware* or huts where they sat tying the rafters and thatch together with flaxen bands. As I passed along, I was greeted by many an old acquaintance among these, who would jump down from his work with a shout of joy, and inquire anxiously whether "Tiraweke" had forgotten him. Thus I advanced through a running fire of kind greetings. At the back of the hut occupied by Coghlan [a grog-shop], whither a flag-staff and New Zealand flag invited the sailors, a rough and newly-made track struck off to the settlement on the river-bank, across a miry swamp. After about a quarter of a mile of this, I reached the junction of a small creek with the Hutt, and soon found myself at the beginning of a little village of tents and huts, among the low, scrubby cop-

* Adventure in New Zealand, from 1839 to 1844; with some account of the beginning of the British colonisation of the islands. By Edward Jerningham Wakefield. 2 vols. Murray: London.

picewood which covered this part of the valley. A rough path had been cleared by the surveying men along the bank; and on either side of this the colonists had been allowed to squat on allotted portions until the survey of the town should be completed. * * I found the squatters on the Hutt no less busy and merry than their fellows on the beach. I met and welcomed two or three old friends whom I had not seen since I left England, and made several new acquaintances among the young capitalists, who were working with their retinue of labourers at putting their goods and chattels into some order and security. Three gentlemen, whom I was much pleased to see again in New Zealand, had formed themselves into a commercial firm, and had brought with them, among other things, the complete machinery of a steam-engine of twenty horse-power, adapted for sawing or flour mills. These were Mr Edward Betts Hopper of Dover, Mr Henry William Petre, and Mr Francis Alexander Molesworth. They were as busy as the rest, landing and arranging their goods. At high water, the ships' long-boats and private cargo-boats brought quantities of goods up to the owners' locations; the labourers and masters worked altogether at the casks and bales and other heavy things; the natives lent their willing aid, being very handy in the water, and then returned either to a job at hut-building, or to hawk about their pigs and potatoes, which they brought in canoes to this quick market.

'I walked some distance along the surveyor's line, and made the acquaintance of such of the new-comers as I did not already know. Each capitalist appeared to have a following of labourers from his own part of the country. Cornish miners and agricultural labourers had pitched their tents near Mr Molesworth; Kentish men dwelt near Mr George Duppa, a little higher up; and many of the Scotch emigrants were collected near a point between two reaches of the river where Mr Dudley Sinclair and Mr Barton were erecting their dwellings. At the latter place Mr Sinclair's English cow was browsing on the shrubs of her newly-adopted country.

'Small patches for gardens were already being cleared in various spots; ruddy, flaxen-haired children were playing about near the doors; and the whole thing made an impression of cheerfulness and contentment. Then the mildness of the climate, the good preparations made before leaving England, and the hearty good feeling existing among the colonists themselves, as well as between them and the natives, all tended to give the extensive bivouac the air of a pic-nic on a large scale, rather than a specimen of the first hardships of a colony. For, although all were often wet in the numerous boat-excursions and fording of streams and creeks, or occasional showers of rain, no one felt any injury to his health; master and man toiled with equal energy and good-will; and both enjoyed a good meal, often served up with all the comforts of civilised life. Thus, in a little, cramped, but weather-tight tent, you found a capitalist in shirt-sleeves taking a hasty meal of preserved meat and good vegetables (the latter grown from the seeds we had left with Smith), and drinking good beer or wine; and this from excellent glass and crockery, with plate, and clean table-cloths, and cruet-stands, and all the paraphernalia. The labourer ate an equally comfortable dinner from the *pot-au-feu*, full of ration-meat and potatoes or cabbages, which had been prepared by his wife at the gipsy fire outside.

'Each English family had got a native or two particularly attached to them. They supplied their guests with potatoes and firewood, and with an occasional pig; shared in the toils and meals of the family, delighted at the novelty of every article unpacked, and were very quick at learning the use of new tools and inventions; chattered incessantly in Maori and broken English; devoted themselves, each to his own *pakeha* [or white man], with the greatest good-breeding, patience, and kind attention; and soon accustomed themselves to observe and imitate almost every new habit, with a striking desire of emulating the superiority of their white brothers.'

Mr Wakefield, however, was not destined to be a settler, and so he left Port Nicholson for the purpose of surveying the country. On the 8th of April, we find him ascending the river Wanganui, under the guidance of a chief named E Kuru. 'A large convenient canoe was prepared; the place of honour was spread with mats for the chief and myself, and a strong crew manned the paddles. We proceeded about twenty miles up the river, which continued perfectly navigable for coasting-craft during the whole of that distance. The valley resembled that of the Waitotara on a large scale. The slopes up to the table-land were further removed, the groves of trees more extensive, and of larger timber, and the river averaged a hundred yards in width. About twelve miles above Putikiwaranui, however, the hills close in, and the river winds among scenery as majestic as that of the highlands of the Hudson. In some places, hills 800 or 1000 feet in height, clothed with every variety of forest-timber or fern, with beetling crags peeping out in places, slope down to the water's edge. Picturesque gardens and small settlements were perched on the banks, or half-way up the ascents; and many canoes, laden with food for the fishermen, glided gracefully down the river. As we met, kind greetings were addressed to the chief and his white man, and often a basket of cooked birds or other food was handed into the canoe. The weather, too, improved as we increased our distance from the sea; and at length no wind could be felt, and the fleecy scud drifting along overhead was the only sign that the gale continued. On arriving at a considerable village situate at the foot of a steep conical hill, and embowered in karaka trees, we pulled into a small tributary of the river, which gives its name, Te-kau-ara-pawa, to the pa. On the opposite bank of the creek, most of the inhabitants sat or lay basking in the sun on a raised stage, on which they had spread their mats. Muskets were fired, and loud shouts of welcome resounded through the crowd. We were handed to the *pataka* or stage, and abundance of food was set before us. A large house was prepared for our accommodation for the night, and a chief named E Taua, related to E Kuru, killed the customary pig.'

At a subsequent period, Mr Wakefield ascended the Wanganui to its source, some seventy or eighty miles inland, in the high table-land from which arise the volcanic peaks of Tonga Riro. About twenty miles from the sea his route lay through romantic dells, over craggy cliffs, everywhere covered with wood, and across swamps choked with native flax, reeds, and jungle. Amid such scenery he wandered for several days, visiting several of the lakes, bathing in the hot springs, and vainly negotiating with the chief of the mountain district for permission to ascend the snow-capped peak of Tonga Riro, for which the natives have, it seems, a religious veneration. From what he states of the inland districts, there would appear to be no great facilities for agriculture, but abundance of room for pasture, hog-rearing, felling of wood, and cultivation of the phormium tenax or native flax. Of the growth and treatment of this plant, which has been much talked of in Britain, Mr Wakefield gives the following description. 'Each plant consisted of some forty or fifty leaves resembling those of our flag, from two to four inches in breadth, and reaching to the length of eight or nine feet. The leaves diverge from the root, and two or three flower-stems also shoot from the ground. These, however, had only begun to sprout. The leaves are all folded in two longitudinally, thus giving an inner and outer side to the leaf; but when it has attained its full growth, it sometimes opens out, although never so as to lie perfectly flat. The inner side has a natural gloss, while the outer side is dull. The natives seemed to prefer the innermost leaves, cutting them at about a foot from the ground with a sharp mussel-shell, of which they had brought a large stock from the sea-side. When a quantity of leaves had been collected, they proceeded to a division of employments. Some split the leaf longitudinally along the fold above-mentioned, and a second gang cut the dull or outer side of each half-leaf nearly through transversely about midway along its length. For this operation, which is rather delicate, and requires experience, a small cockle-shell was used. The art appeared to be to cut through all but the fibres, which border closely on the glossy portion. The half-leaves, thus prepared, were handed to a third workman. He, taking a bundle of them in his left hand at the transverse cut, and spreading them out like a fan, with the glossy side upwards, took a mussel-shell between the finger and thumb of his right hand to perform the next operation. This consisted in giving each half-leaf a longitudinal scrape from the transverse cut in the middle to each end. He held the leaves extended, by seizing the ends of each in succession with his big toe. Flax-scraping is always performed in a sitting posture, and one foot works quite as hard as either of the hands. The dexterity and quickness with which this whole operation was performed, drew from us repeated exclamations of delight, of which the performers seemed not a little proud. The result of the scrape is to make about five-sixths of the leaf, beginning from the dull side, drop off on to the ground in two pieces. The fibres which compose the glossy surface remain in the hand of the operator, of the full length of the leaf, and he puts them aside, and proceeds with another bunch. The splitters and transverse-cutters worked faster than the scrapers, and when they had operated on all that was gathered, they also took up their mussel-shell and scraped in their turn. The short pieces which I have described as dropping on to the ground, were treated as refuse, and allowed to dry or rot; the full-length fibre of the glossy side alone being preserved, to undergo further processes previous to manufacture into mats. The only use that I have ever seen made of the short refuse is for the outer portion of a rough mat, much resembling the thatch of a house. These leaves being woven in close rows, hanging downwards one over the other, into the interior texture of the mat, are perfectly impenetrable to rain. I have often braved with impunity the heaviest rain, sleeping under no other shelter.'

Besides the native flax, Mr Wakefield directs attention to the fine forests of pine, black birch, and other timber, much of which seems admirably adapted for furniture purposes. The bark of many of the shrubs yields valuable dyes, and vegetable oils might be obtained in any abundance. As to the emigrant's chance of success with the ordinary vegetables of culture, we may judge from the following description of the climate:—'Nothing could be more encouraging than the mild climate, and the unceasing bounty of nature, during the winter months. In May, which answers to the chill and foggy November of England, peas were in full bloom, small salads in every stage of growth, and almost all vegetation unchecked by the season. It was likened by Scotchmen to the second month of spring in their former land. The produce of garden vegetables, as a speculation, had been long abandoned, on account of the great ease with which every one could supply himself. No matter how bare, exposed, or rough the spot of ground, excellent vegetables could be produced by the most careless cultivation. The wild pasture on the hills had improved wonderfully under the constant browsing and tread of the cattle. Grass was replacing the fern all over the barren-looking hills that were clear of timber; and, in riding after cattle, many spots could hardly be recognised, owing to the great change that had taken place. And this rich pasture, and abundant supply of choice vegetables, from comparatively neglected gardens, continued during June, the centre winter month, which rather resembled a fine English October in its pleasantness of temperature.' Even during the coldest month (September, answering to March in England), there was only a slight scurf of ice on the puddles over night. The temperature of the day rising to 60 degrees, soon dispelled every trace of frost; and towards the end of that month, spring had set in so mildly, that bats were flickering about in the twilight.

The above isolated snatches from Mr Wakefield's narrative certainly present the country, climate, and produce of New Zealand in a very favourable light; and, making allowance for a little partiality, we think the reader will agree with us, that, if wisely governed, few spots on the globe could present a finer field for an active and permanent settler.

AUTOGRAPHY.

The first thing one does on receiving a letter, is to look whether we recognise the writing as that of a hand familiar to us. Oh, this is from A, or this is from B, is a familiar exclamation. At one glance we recognise A or B, as distinctly as if either stood before us face to face, though both perhaps may be thousands of miles off. Then, again, we collect the various signatures of our friends, or of celebrated persons whom we may never have seen, or known only by their works or fame, and paste them into our albums, and take a delight in looking on them, and comparing their resemblances or differences; in short, every observation of the kind leads us to the conclusion, that almost every person's handwriting differs from another, and that there is almost as complete an individuality in their mode of writing as in their countenances, their gait and gestures, or as in their minds.

There is scarcely a collector of such signatures who is not also a diviner of the character of the person as deduced from his handwriting. How often do we hear it observed, 'This is the writing of a prim, methodical, cold, reserved mortal;' or, 'That is the signature of a gay, volatile, and careless being.' How unequivocally can we mark out the writing of a lady from that of a gentleman. How readily that of a lawyer or merchant from that of a fashionable idler, or a 'man of wit or pleasure about town.' To many, it might appear a very absurd thing to say that there exists an intimate relation between the colour of a man's hair and his handwriting, and yet it is well known that the initiated in this matter pretend infallibly to distinguish the writing of a fair-haired person from that of a dark.

A very ingenious writer in the Northern Journal of Medicine has, in a late number of that work, afforded a physiological reason for the diversities of handwriting. This diversity he attributes to temperament; that is, a certain condition of the physical and mental constitution of the individual which constitutes his peculiar character. Of these temperaments there are at least half-a-dozen kinds, pretty distinct and well-marked, and perhaps half-a-dozen more of blended or mixed temperaments, where the shades are less distinguishable. The two extremes of natural temperament or complexion are well known to every one. We shall take, for instance, a man with light auburn hair, blue sparkling eyes, a ruddy complexion, ample chest, and muscular, well-rounded, and agile frame. Such a man will rarely fail to have a smile on his countenance, or a cheerful, perhaps witty saying on his lips. You will never find him moping in a solitary corner, but flitting about in the sunshine and bustle of society, joining in everything, and dwelling on nothing long. When such a man sits down to write, he makes short work of it: he snatches the first pen that comes in the way, never looks how it is pointed, dabs it into the ink, and then dashes on from side to side of the paper in a full, free, and slip-slop style, his ideas—or at all events his words—flowing faster than his agile fingers and leaping muscles can give them a form. Such a one's handwriting can never be mistaken; it is like his own motions, hop-step-and-jump. But, on the contrary, select a man with deep black hair, black eyes, brown or sallow complexion, and thin spare form, you will generally find him alone, and silently meditating, or sitting solitary amid crowds—of few words, of slow and deliberate action. You need scarcely be told how such a man sets about writing. After weighing well his subject in his mind, he sits down deliberately, selects and mends his pen, adjusts his paper, and in close, stiff, and upright characters traces with a snail's pace his well-weighed and sententious composition. There can be no mistake in tracing the two handwritings which we have just described; and an adept in the science cannot fail in astonishing his audience with a sketch of the leading peculiarities of the mind and manners of each. But there are many intermediate shades of temperament, and many circumstances which go to modify the natural tendencies of the mode of writing, which fall to be considered. We shall, in the first place, give the following classified table of temperaments:—

1. Vigorous, light-haired, excitable temperament, what is commonly called the sanguine. The handwriting large, flowing, open, and irregular.

2. Dark-haired, excitable temperament, with brown florid complexion. The writing small, equal, and rather free and easy, with a firm and full stroke.

3. Light-haired, little excitable temperament; the complexion brown or sallow; the form spare. The writing less free and more methodical than No. 1, but less vigorous and less decided than No. 2.

4. Dark-haired, slowly excitable temperament; dark complexion, spare form, and melancholic habit. Small cramp upright writing, without ease or freedom, evidently slowly penned.

5. Feeble, light-haired, little excitable temperament; character timid and nervous. The writing small, unequal, and feebly traced, or not written with decision.

6. Mixed temperament, combining two or more of the above.

There are various combinations of these, which it would be unnecessary to particularise. Education and particular training of course make great changes on the natural tendency of the handwriting. Thus men of business acquire a mechanical style of writing, which obliterates all natural characteristics, unless in instances where the character is so strongly individual as not to be modified into the general mass. The female hand is also peculiar. Generally, it is more feeble and less individual than that of the male. In the present day, all females seem to be taught after one model. In a great proportion, the handwriting is moulded on this particular model: those only who have strong and decided character retain a decided handwriting. We often find that the style of handwriting is hereditary: sons frequently write very like their fathers; and this they do independent of all studied imitation, because the temperament happens to be hereditary also. A delicate state of health, especially if it has occurred in boyhood, has a considerable effect in modifying the natural form of the handwriting; thus sometimes connecting the free and flowing hand of the sanguine temperament into a more staid and methodical one.

A deficiency of early culture must also have a considerable influence on the form of writing. The forms, too, have varied in different historical eras. Before the introduction of printing, more pains seem to have been bestowed on penmanship. Ancient manuscripts are often found written in a beautiful, upright, and well-formed character, more in the style of print than the modern careless and flowing lines. This is easily to be accounted for: almost all that is worth preserving is now committed to that mighty engine of intelligence, both to present and future ages, the press, and therefore less care is bestowed on the original manuscript. The compositor and the pressman have now taken the place of the ancient scribe and copyist.

But even the individual handwriting varies from its character at various periods of life. In youth it is raw and unformed; in manhood it assumes its full character; and in old age it suffers somewhat of decay. Circumstances also affect its form not inconsiderably. No man is likely to dash off a note on his marriage-day in the same style that he would set about writing out his last will and testament. Our moments of joy are impressed upon the symbolical representations of them, just as are our hours of bitterest sorrow. We often approach our familiars in a scrawl, as if imprinted by birds' claws instead of quill feathers, and which we would not deliberately despatch to those that we are accustomed to look up to with respect or awe.

Ease and freedom, and an indifference to please, are the prerogatives of rank and fashion; and hence it is probable that the most wretched scrawls have become fashionable among those who ever strive to ape the manners of the great. There are also, no doubt, national peculiarities in handwriting as well as individual. The Frenchman will show a volatility and spirit in his writing very different from the sedate and thoughtful German. The Northern Russ or the Calmuk Tartar must have a different fist altogether from that of the soft and voluptuous native of Hindostan.

We throw out these few hints to collectors of autographs. Let them arrange and classify their specimens, and form of them a *catalogue raisonnée*. Thus, in the end, may some philosopher amongst their number elevate the pursuit into a science, at least not inferior to the ancient one of palmistry, astrology, and divination, or to the modern ones of mesmerism, hypnotism, homœopathy, or hydropathy.

OCCASIONAL NOTES.

STREET TRADERS.

In all crowded cities, both in these countries and on the continent, a very active retail trade is carried on in the open air. The traders being too poor to pay house-rent, their shops are portable, consisting of temporary stalls, baskets, wheelbarrows, and sometimes their own pockets. These chapmen and dealers are worthy of consideration, because, though only one degree removed from mendicancy, their callings demand both industry and honesty, whilst those virtues are exercised amidst very strong temptations to idleness and dishonesty. Having no roof to cover them, they are exposed to all the hardships of bad weather: having no legal right to carry on business in public thoroughfares, they are kept under the vigilance of the police.

One of the effects of that minute division of labour which results from an increase of population, and in the value of time, is to cause articles to be bought and sold which our predecessors made or procured quite easily at home. Take as an example the article of matches, which, though one of the earliest objects of itinerant merchandise, were not manufactured for sale till a comparatively recent period, for they were made by the persons requiring them, or by their servants. It is within our own recollection, that in an English country house one of the errands of the servant, when he went to the neighbouring town, was 'a stick of brimstone for matches,' which were invariably manufactured at home. The necessity for this household operation was soon superseded by visits of hawkers, who set up a regular manufacture and trade in the article. Perambulating match-sellers took their rise from the vagrant act which forbade begging, and the merchandise was exhibited as a sort of screen to their real employment, which was that of obtaining alms.

No branch of commerce, be it ever so unimportant, ever remains long stationary in this country, and the match-trade has made perhaps more rapid strides during the last half century than any other. The pseudo-beggars having once taken the trouble of domestic match-making off the hands of the public, it never again was willing to incur it, and ever after, the making and selling of these indispensable articles rose to the dignity of a regular employment. Small pieces of wood, each with a sharpened end, dipped in brimstone, were carried from door to door, or presented to passengers at the corner of every street. A foreigner, judging twenty years ago from the quantity displayed for sale in every part of the town and country, would naturally wonder what the English could want with such forests of matches. But closer inquiry would have convinced him that they were in many instances used as a fence to the vagrant act—as a safeguard against the stocks, and a blind to the parish constable; for, while extolling their excellence and cheapness, the vender never failed to throw in a plea of pinching poverty, shared by a wife and a large family. Far, therefore, from inferring an extensive use of the objects offered for sale, it would be discovered that a mendicant made a good living out of the mere exhibition of his stock in trade, which was not perhaps diminished or added to for weeks together. Still, a vast number of these tinder-box appliances were sold, though the demand never exceeded the supply. Of this there was not the remotest danger, for the retail trade was overwhelmingly overstocked; and though there have been instances known of match-sellers retiring upon fortunes, yet in nine cases out of ten, their capital accumulated from eleemosynary gifts from the benevolent, and not from fair trading with consumers. The match-sellers of the brimstone school were jocularly denominated 'timber-merchants.'

About the year 1826, however, chemistry created a complete revolution in this extensive trade. A new description of match was invented, which, from the ease and certainty with which it ignited, completely superseded the former ones that had been in use for so many centuries. Much suspicion was at first created concerning them, on account of the manner in which it was understood they were prepared. Fulminating powder, phosphorus, and other diabolical ingredients, were reported to be contained in them; hence they got the name of 'Lucifers.' Like all infant manufactures, they were at first sold at a high price (6d. a-box) by chemists; afterwards, the demand for them increased as improvements were made in their composition, and they got into the hands of grocers and oilmen, when further reductions took place. A London grocer, more deeply read in poetical literature than his brethren, exhibited, by way of a shop-ticket, the quotation from Milton—

'O Lucifer! how hast thou fallen!'

and to which was added the deep bathos—'Matches only twopence a-box!' From that price they soon dropped to that at which they are now sold, and consequently came within the scope of the original traders in matches—beggars and itinerant dealers. From a recent parliamentary commission, we learn that the consumption of this sort of matches is more than five *billions* a-year, and that one man in London, who makes the wooden boxes to contain them, paid a thousand a-year for timber for that purpose; thus really deserving the designation which had been applied to his predecessors in the trade in jest—that of an extensive 'timber-merchant.'

Besides the vast quantity of Lucifers manufactured in England, uncounted numbers of them are imported from the banks of the Rhine, and various other parts of Germany. The wood is floated down the river from the thick pine forests, and the small branches and waste wood made into matches at various villages on the banks, and sent over to America, and to all parts of Europe.

Another of the small trades which consumes a great quantity of wood, is that of toys, which are carried about by itinerant salesmen, not so much for the purpose of sale as of barter. A long stick, at the end of which is fastened, on a pivot, sails made of wood and paper, to imitate those of a windmill, seem to be in the greatest demand. The eagerness with which they are coveted by children is proved by the groups which are invariably seen near the distributor of these envied toys. Knowing that actual cash is seldom possessed by his little customers, he meets that unfortunate deficiency of an important element of trade by declaring he will take almost anything in exchange for his wares—phial bottles, old clothes, broken crystal, and other (to him) valuables which are within easier reach. By this means he realises a better profit than if he traded for 'ready money only,' as, on selling the produce of his traffic to old store dealers, he gets more than it is possible his young patrons would have paid for them in hard cash, even if they had it. A well-remembered toy-hawker realised a good fortune on this plan in another sort of toy: he was known all over England, and announced his presence by the couplet—

'If I had as much money as I could tell,
I never would cry *young lambs* to sell.'

He kept his word, and left off business when he *had* as much money in copper coin as he could conveniently count at a long sitting.

Perhaps the most ancient of itinerant trades was that in quack nostrums; and it is within the present century that his 'occupation' was entirely 'gone.' The quack and his merry-Andrew have now quite disappeared from the stage of existence: the only successors who remain are the venders of corn salve and cough drops, which, if not of actually curative, are mostly of a harmless character. The sellers of these articles are generally found at the corners of busy streets and markets, making eloquent orations in praise of their nostrums. They show themselves as proficient in the art of puffing as their predecessors the ancient mountebanks, though they seldom meet with such extensive success.

Not the least interesting of the small traders are the Italian image-boys. Vending, as they do, plaster casts from some of the most celebrated and beautiful sculptural works of ancient as well as modern art, they act as the pioneers of artistic taste amongst the humbler orders. The likenesses of celebrated men they exhibit and sell at a low price, are in many instances casts from marbles chiselled by artists of the highest eminence.

Itinerant dealers in eatables, particularly of vegetables, are of a less interesting, though perhaps of a more useful character. They are called indiscriminately 'costermongers,' otherwise, according to Dr Nares, traffickers in 'costards,' a species of apple of so common a sort, that it gave the name at an early period to hawkers of apples in general, and afterwards further extended as above. In poor neighbourhoods, this class of traders are of great use: they bring their wares to the doors of their customers, saving the valuable time of hard-working people, which would otherwise be wasted in going to and from shops and markets.

How much might be done to improve the popular tastes by the hawking of small tracts of a useful and entertaining class, has been already adverted to in these pages, and we are glad to know that our hints on this point have been in various places successfully adopted.

Small traders of the class we have described hold a precarious position as regards the law, by which they are tolerated rather than recognised. The truth is, law is very chary of extending protection to persons who do not pay taxes, yet is kind enough to wink at them, except when their existence is made too glaringly visible by an officious policeman bringing them before the 'bench' for some street obstruction or other nominal misdemeanour. Small traders are nevertheless a useful class of itinerants.

CHEAP TRIPS TO FOREIGN COUNTRIES.

When we pointed out, in a recent number, 'The Social Effects of Railways,' we adverted with pleasure to the opportunities they afforded to the public of making themselves acquainted with scenes and places they could never have beheld but for the well-applied powers of steam. These opportunities are rapidly increasing, and the large steamboat companies have begun to organise excursions to celebrated and interesting localities on the continent. The directors of the Dundee and London Shipping Company charter one of their commodious vessels for a pleasure trip to Hamburg; and to show the amount of accommodation they are able to afford intending tourists, they forward to any applicant a map of the places which it is practicable to visit, besides the port of entry. These, it appears, consist of the other Hans-Towns, Lubec and Bremen; also Hanover, Brunswick, Magdeburg, Leipsic, Dresden, Berlin, Potsdam, Stettin, Cologne, Dusseldorf, &c.—in other words, all the places of greatest note in Germany. The vessel remains twelve days, so as to allow sufficient time for the passengers to reach and inspect at least some of the above cities, to most of which railways are now in constant operation. This is not all: the same company having steamers which ply between London and the Rhine, passengers wishing to visit that noble river may leave the Hamburg boat to return without them, and wend their way to any part of Germany they please. So that they step on board one of the company's vessels some time during the summer, they can return by way of London by paying an extra fee of only one guinea. The cost of the trip is quite within the means of persons in the middle ranks, being L.4, exclusive of provisions.

Another company have projected a less-frequented voyage—from Aberdeen to Norway, stopping a day or two at the Shetland Islands. The places to be visited abroad are Drontheim, Bergen, and Christiana the capital, at each of which places the vessel stops three or four days, so that ample time is allowed for exploring them and other places in the interior of the country. The whole tour is expected to occupy about three weeks, and its expense will not exceed that which a journey from Edinburgh to London entailed a few years ago for mere coach-hire—namely, L.20; provisions being in this case included.

It is much to be wished that the projectors of these trips will be encouraged to repeat them. There is no surer plan for breaking down national prejudices, and for enlightening ignorance, than travel. It happens, unfortunately, that many thousands amongst the affluent in this empire stand very much in need of that sort of improvement which excursions abroad are of all means the best for effecting: we allude more particularly to those highly praiseworthy individuals who have raised fortunes from small beginnings, and whose minds have not always improved with their means. To the credit of our country be it said, that the majority of the rich mercantile class are such as we are now discussing. Convenient and cheap opportunities are now offered to them to see foreign nations—to glance at their institutions, manufactures, and exterior habits—and we trust those opportunities will not be entirely lost upon them.

THE COMFORTS OF THE CLASSICS.

The high and romantic admiration we entertain for the ancient Greeks, receives a great check when we meet with the few passages occurring in history which enable us to judge of their personal and domestic comforts. The Spartan made indulgence of any sort a crime. The law obliged him to wear the coarsest garments, and to make no difference in their warmth in summer and winter, nor to remove them during rest at night. In building his habitation, he was allowed no other tool than the axe for the timbers, and the saw to form the doors. Everything was rough and simple, with the view of making the people hardy of frame and manly in manners. But even the other Greeks, who gave way to every luxury they could invent, had scarcely any of those domestic appliances which we look upon as common necessaries. Though they had bedsteads, soft mattresses, skins, cushions, carpet-blankets, and coverlets, yet those refined ventilators—sheets—were denied them. When the model of womankind, the Greek beauty, arose from her couch to array herself in woollen, she had no stays or stockings to add to her comfort: to make her clothes air-tight, she had nothing but a buckle or a skewer, instead of pins. She painted her cheeks, lips, and eyebrows, to make herself, as she thought, outwardly fascinating; yet within, she knew not the cleanly luxury of linen. Neither had her lord a shirt, nor hose, nor buttons, nor handkerchief, nor pockets, nor lining to his cloak, nor gloves—items essential to the warmth and comfort of a modern gentleman.

The interior arrangements of a classic household were so different, that a Greek house would have been scarcely habitable by a modern. 'Their lamps,' says Mr Bernan,* 'though elegant, were offensive; and if they had wax and tallow pith and rushlights, of candles they were always entirely ignorant. Abroad, therefore, the Greek, during his sharp winter, must often have suffered much privation; and within doors, he never could enjoy artificial heat or light without smoke and risk of suffocation, for his house had not a chimney; nor, in the cold weather, could he enjoy warmth with daylight in his elegant apartment, for he made no use of glazed windows.'

POPULAR NAMES.

LA PALICE—LA RAMEE.

[From the French.]

There are certain periods in the history of most men of thought, when reason, exhausted by long and severe exercise, seems to abandon the reins, and leave to folly the control of the intellectual faculties. One instance may be found in Cowper's humorous ballad of John Gilpin; and another, which affords equally mirth-provoking amusement to our neighbours across the Channel, was the work of the grave and religious Bernard de la Monnoye, translator of the Gloss of St Theresa, who conceived the idea of personifying nonsensical truths in his *Complaint upon the Life and Death of La Palice;* careless of attaching popular ridicule to a name which should excite only recollections of heroic and military virtue.

Our little children, thanks to this strange production, know that the famous La Palice died in losing his life, and that he would not have had his equal had he been alone in the world. But, saving some other such revelations, La Monnoye has chosen to maintain a scrupulous silence upon the chief events which actually contributed to the celebrity of his hero. Doubtless it is satisfactory to know that he could never make up his mind to load his pistols when he had no powder; and that when he wrote verse he did not write prose; or that while drinking he never spoke a word. These are certainly notable details concerning the habits and character of this great man, which the poet was wise to notice; but it is also certain that La Palice had greater claims to admiration, which may be brought to light in illustrating some stanzas of the biographical ballad. We shall endeavour to fill up the gaps which occur at every step in La Monnoye's history. It is good to be merry, but it is better to be exact, especially when writing about an individual who, for three centuries, has occupied a high position among the heroes who have done most honour to France.

The song, it will be seen, is a burlesque, somewhat similar in character to that upon the valiant Malbrough. It begins thus:—

'Please you, gentlemen, to hear
The song of La Palice;
It surely will delight you all,
Provided that it please.'

Besides this proposition, so honestly and neatly enunciated, the historian would have done well to tell us that La Palice was named also Jacques II. of Chabannes. He was of noble race, for his grandfather, an earlier Jacques de Chabannes, after valiantly defending Castillon against Talbot, the English Achilles, died of his wounds at the siege of this city, which, two years afterwards (17th July 1453), cost the life of his illustrious enemy. He was of noble race this Jacques de Chabannes, and, we may add, of noble heart. Charles VIII. owed to him in part the conquest of Naples, and Louis XII. that of the duchy of Milan.

'La Palice but little wealth
To his renown could bring;
And when abundance was his lot,
He lacked no single thing.'

Abundance of glory, of honours, of treasures, of war on battle-fields; this was surely what the poet meant to say. He ought to have been rich indeed, when three sovereigns successively invested him with the titles of marshal of

* History of Warming and Ventilation, vol. i.

France, governor of Bourbonnais, of Auvergne, of Forez and the Lyonnais. He was still more rich in the esteem of his enemies, who in the battles aimed all their bullets at him; wishing, as they said, to strike down one of the bravest heads of the army. He was rich also in the love of his soldiers, whom he fed at his own expense, when the supplies failed through the carelessness or treachery of the state paymasters.

'He was versed in all the games
Played at the academy;
And never was unfortunate
When he won the victory.'

Those which he gained are faithfully chronicled in history. First stands Marignan, in 1515, that terrible struggle, in allusion to which old Marshal Trivulce said, all others were but child's play in comparison. It was a famous victory gained by Francis I. over the Swiss and the Duke of Milan, and has been ever since known as the Battle of the Giants; next Fontarabia, the key of Spain, which the same general, under the same monarch, carried at the point of the sword in 1521; then Bicocca, in Lombardy, where Lautrec lost the battle and his honour, and La Palice, being second in command, made incredible exertions to recover the fortune of the day; and last, Marseilles, which treason had given to the arms of Charles V., which went to sleep one night Spanish, and woke up French the next morning, because a great captain, Chabannes de la Palice, had scaled her walls, and effaced by dint of courage the shame with which the desertion of Bourbon had tarnished the name of French gentlemen.

'To do and dare in his career,
He readily inclined;
And when he stood before the king,
He was not, sure, behind.'

On the eve of the battle of Pavia he stood before Francis I., and, with the counsel of a brave man, addressed the monarch:—'You are eager to fight, sire; would it not be better to be certain of conquering? Our blood belongs to you, but you belong to France; and you owe to the kingdom a reckoning of your enterprises against the enemies of the state. God forbid that I should give such a lesson to the king my master, but it behoves him to take counsel when he goes to stake his crown in a single battle, which, if lost, cannot fail of being fatal. There, behind those walls, are Lannoy and Pescara, with the bravest of their troops; here, none but worn-out soldiers, few in number, and dying of fatigue. Behind those walls stands Antoine de Lève, a general of genius and resources, who has never been conquered. Were he beaten, the empire would lose but one man, but on our side we lose a king. The game is not equal, sire; sign the truce, and some day we shall find ourselves again before the place with forces enough to sustain our just rights.' La Palice was now an old man, and Francis, flattered by the opinions of his younger captains, declared for battle, and drew his sword, to give it up on the evening of the same day to the brave Lannoy, who received it on his knees from his royal prisoner.

'Fate dealt to him a cruel blow,
And stretched him on the ground;
And 'tis believed that since he died,
It was a mortal wound.

His death was sore and terrible,
Upon a stone his head;
He would have died more easily
Upon a feather bed.'

Chabannes made a sortie with a handful of brave fellows from the fort which he defended against the Spanish army, and saw all those who followed fall around him. No way of retreat remained open; and, covered with wounds, he could scarcely wield the sword with which he had opened the gates of Ravenna and Navarre. He sees a fragment of a wall, which may enable him to hold out for a time against the enemy, and plants himself against it, determined to die, as he had lived, gloriously. At each sweep of his sword an antagonist falls at his feet; they press closer upon him, and offer quarter; while a Spanish soldier climbs over the barrier of corpses piled before him, aims a tremendous blow at his head, beneath which the brave La Palice fell senseless to the earth.

'Deplored and envied by his braves,
He shut his eyes to strife;
And we are told his day of death
Was the last of his life.'

Some chroniclers have written—

'Fifteen minutes before his death,
Ah, he was yet alive;'

a space of time which he worthily employed in closing a life of glorious activity. Often, says the historian, La Palice was dragged half dead to the tent of the enemy's general, who threatened him with the ignominious death of hanging, if he did not persuade the besieged to deliver up the fort. He requested to be carried to the foot of the ramparts; two soldiers took up the captive marshal on their shoulders, and bore him to the gate of the fortress which had so long resisted the skill and courage of the besiegers. When there, in a dying voice he gave orders to summon his lieutenant Cornon. 'Brave friend,' he said to him, 'do you know the condition of the citadel?' The lieutenant, deeply affected at seeing his general in so perilous a situation, could only answer by a slight inclination of the head. 'This is not the time for tears,' continued the great man; 'say, can you hold out till the arrival of the Duke of Nemours?'

'Yes, we will hold out, be it for a month!' he replied with a firm voice.

'Good,' rejoined the chief, and turning towards the Spanish commander, said, 'Do with me as you please. I commend my soul to God; my men will do their duty.'

The ancients, sometimes unjust towards their great men, invoked the terrible law of necessity for their banishment, but preserved their memory with religious respect. It was reserved for modern times to dishonour a great name by a ridiculous abuse of humour.

We must go far back in the annals of history to arrive at the date of the birth of the famous La Ramée, popularly known as the *First Grenadier of the World*. If we are to believe the chronicles of the barracks, and the historians of the bivouac, he stood sentinel when the world was very young, and, growing tired, deserted his post, and went through numerous adventures among the nations of antiquity; until, in the progress of time, he enlisted under the banners of the emperor Napoleon. If you ask old soldiers still in the service where this ancient of ancients may be met with, they will tell you that La Ramée, together with his pipe, are supported at the expense of the state in the Royal Hospital of Invalids: the one well blackened, as a pipe ought to be which has not gone out for 5834 years; the other decorated with 1100 *chevrons*, which give him a claim to the respect of his comrades, and to the double ration of wine. If you inquire at the invalids for the number of La Ramée's room, you will be told that he sleeps upon the field of Waterloo, among the brave with whom he found himself at the memorable battle. But let war come again—an event to be desired neither for our firesides nor our frontiers—and La Ramée will revive, to be again the wonder of raw conscripts, and to add some new chapters to his already voluminous history.

If ever there was a pleasant and jocund tradition, it is this; which, passing from mouth to mouth from time immemorial, and becoming enriched at every step it has made in the world's memory, by many additions as extravagant as improbable, has at last been adopted as the immortal epic of the guard-house. But it must be remembered that there was another La Ramée, celebrated in his own day, but little known in ours.

In 1510, a little boy, clothed in the coarse rustic dress of sackcloth, a woollen cap on his head, his features sharpened by hunger, and his eyes very wide open, if not from appetite, at least from all the wonderful things which he saw around him, entered Paris. He directed his steps towards the street *de la Paille*, where the scholars of the university were playing together. He was speedily surrounded by a host of waggish boys, who were never backward in intimidating greater and stronger than he, and made to submit to a great number of mischievous questions, and a still greater number of painful blows. But when the first heat of mischief was over, the best-disposed among the young collegians gave him a portion of their bread, and made room for him on the straw with which the street was strewed. Refreshed and comfortably seated, Pierre La Ramée began the history of his life and journey with great simplicity and brevity. He was born at Cuth, in Vermandois, eight years before. When scarcely old enough to walk alone, he went from door to door begging his bread; and as the villagers could not support him in idleness, a long stick was put into his hand, with which he drove every day a flock of geese to a pond in the neighbourhood. The occupation became distasteful to him, and one day he left his intractable charge to look after themselves, threw his long stick into a thicket, and set off on the road to Paris. Begging on the way, as he had begged in the village, he arrived not richer, but wiser; for he fell into company with a learned monk, who taught him the names of all the letters of the alphabet, and the art of uniting them so as to form words. After his recital, Pierre La Ramée entered the service of some of the scholars, with the condition that they should continue his scarcely-commenced education.

During several months he went every night to sleep under one of the arches of the bridge de la cité: his days were passed in running errands for the students, and enduring the effects of their ill temper and vicious character. He, however, contrived to keep himself alive by the crusts of stale bread which fell to his lot; while the bribes of Latin, with which he was occasionally induced to undertake some errand more disagreeable than usual, furnished his mind, and rendered him more and more desirous of learning.

The vacations, however, arrived, the colleges were deserted, the servants of the university cleared the straw from the street, and Pierre La Rameé found himself without a master—deprived all at once of his hard-earned crusts and Latin lessons. To complete his misfortunes, the plague broke out in the city, and he returned in much affliction to Cuth.

Four years from that time, a youthful servant was employed at the college of Navarre, who, with broom in hand, worked all the day sweeping the various class-rooms; and who at night, when all were asleep, lit his master's lamp, and read over by himself the lessons of which he occasionally caught a few words during the hours of study. He carefully preserved the sheets of waste paper met with in the exercise of his duties, and with great labour wrote notes upon the authors he read; these sheets fell by accident into the hands of one of the professors, who summoned the boy into his presence, and after strict questioning, bade him prepare himself to support his thesis, as the time had come for conferring upon him the degree of master of arts. In those days Aristotle reigned despotically over the schools of philosophy, and no one dared to attack a system which would have brought upon him the reproach of heterodoxy. But Pierre La Ramée dared; and from that moment commenced his glory and his persecutions.

We shall not follow the youth, become man, appearing before a tribunal appointed to judge his anti-Aristotelian doctrines; nor do more than allude to the famous school of which he was the founder, and to his books condemned to the flames. Crowds flocked to hear him in wondering admiration, while the church roused herself for a severe struggle with her new opponent; but the parliament interposed itself to shield the wise and learned teacher from the blows directed against him. Being expelled from Paris, the king gave him an asylum at Fontainbleau; while his enemies, profiting by his absence, pillaged his house and devastated his college. But at last, wearied with strife, they permitted his return, and crowds of young men again listened to his lectures. Once more he was monarch of the schools, and father of his scholars; the supreme master of eloquence, appeasing the fury of the populace or military turbulence by the charm of his words. In the night of the 24th August 1572, when assassins were scouring the city of Paris, in the name of religion and the king, immolating all suspected of the odour of Protestantism, Charpentier, a doctor of the Sorbonne, profiting by the general excitement to gratify a personal hatred, roused the mob, and led them to the college of Presle, where for many years Pierre La Ramée, bestowing his science gratuitously on the poorest, reposed himself upon straw after the long fatigues of his professorship, as in the days of his youthful distress. Charpentier, after a long search through all the classes, without finding him who wished to dethrone Aristotle, and put truth and reason in the vacant place, in his thirst for vengeance descended to the cellars. There he sees an aged man, half dead with fear, who supplicates humbly for his life. 'Will you give me all your money?' demanded his persecutor. 'All,' was the reply. 'You shall teach no more,' continued the bigot. 'I will teach no more,' answered the philosopher in despair. Charpentier received his oath, and seizing upon the accumulated savings of a life of learning, called in his infuriated followers, who murdered their victim. Thus died Pierre La Ramée, or Ramus; for, according to the usage of the time, he had Latinised his name. And such was the actual person who is alluded to by the soldiers in their ridiculous legend. The change resembles that which has caused Virgil to be remembered as a sorcerer in Italy, and Michael Scott to be regarded as a wizard in Scotland. The causes which lead to such whimsical misrepresentations it were vain to inquire for.

AN HOUR BETWEEN HOLBORN AND SMITHFIELD.

Public attention is at present earnestly directed towards the health of towns, dwellings for the poor, their education, and the melioration of their moral and physical condition. New, handsome, and airy streets are now in the course of being opened in the metropolis, on sites hitherto encumbered with miserable dwellings, inhabited by the very dregs of society, and where moral and physical decadency had been in progress for many generations.

But a very natural question arises in one's breast on observing these clearings of the wilderness, as to what has become, or is to become, of the *aborigines*, if such a denomination be admissible?

There is but too much reason to believe that these 'rookeries'—a popular name for them in London—have only been transferred to other rank spots, previously over-crowded; and that the evils which, on seeing the uprooting process in action in some localities, one is inclined to think are on the eve of being remedied, are, on the contrary, hourly augmenting in consequence of a more condensed state of the contagious elements.

Reflections of this nature forced themselves irresistibly on my mind on the following occasion:—Having read in the papers that various strange discoveries had been made in the neighbourhood of Smithfield during the progress of the improvements in the way of opening new streets, I yielded to one of those sudden impulses which have carried me into a variety of curious scenes in divers portions of our habitable globe, and found myself one rainy day last autumn in a (to me) *Terra Incognita*, in the very centre of the capital of this great country—great in its commerce, its valour, its wealth, its possessions, its social ties; great in its influence in all parts of the world, mainly owing to the generally received opinion that its institutions and its moral and religious organisation are upon a scale highly superior to the general standard.

Passing down the wide space at the foot of Holborn Hill, opposite to Faringdon Street, bordered by rows of arched cellars for the houses in the course of erection, I arrived in front of a board separating the end of the new street from a lane running across and much below it, one of the miserable houses in the lane having been pulled down as far as the basement storey. Of a half-starved-looking man I purchased for a penny a little pamphlet of eight pages, printed in Seven Dials, professing to contain 'full particulars of the extraordinary houses in West Street, Smithfield, with an account'—so said the last-dying-speech-looking title-page—'of the strange discovery of human bones, &c. that was found in the residence of Jonathan Wild, formerly called the Red Lion public-house, in West Street, Smithfield, the resort of Jack Sheppard and Jerry Abershaw,' &c. &c.

With this 'hand-book' for my guide, I passed through a wicket in the boarding, and descended into the lane. Opposite the house nearly pulled down—the notorious Red Lion public-house—were several uncouth-looking people; two policemen wearing their oilskin capes were walking up and down; one of them had a switch in his hand, with which he motioned to the people to keep moving. I asked him whether the little book was to be relied upon. He answered that the facts had been much exaggerated. After contemplating the ruin for a few minutes, I moved to the right, and was again skimming the contents of the hand-book, when the same policeman passed and said to me 'They are all lies you are reading there.' Upon this official authority I closed the book, adjusted my umbrella so as to keep the rain off—for so intent had I been upon the description of the 'extraordinary houses,' that the umbrella had got awry, and my left sleeve was soaked through—and regained the upper regions through the wicket. Seeing the lean pamphlet-vender still wandering about in the rain, I gently informed him of what the policeman had said respecting his hand-books.

'It's only to keep the crowd off, sir; if you go to the back you'll know more about it.'

I immediately acted upon this opportune suggestion. It would be an infringement on literary property to enter into a description of the 'full particulars of the extraordinary houses' contained in the hand-book; suffice it to say, that from all I was able to see and learn, I believe its contents were correct.

My object is to state the 'great fact' that, up to that hour, the numerous alleys and courts, and the wretched tenements by which the Fleet-ditch was bordered, were inhabited by a population of the most revolting description; a shame and a scandal in the heart of a metropolis through whose capacious arteries — within a stone's throw of these sinks of infamy—is continually flowing the rich stream of commerce and luxury; and where floods of people sweep along without bestowing a thought on the veins, clogged with rank corruption, which branch off from those arteries.

I entered the labyrinth through Black-Boy Alley, and, proceeding down it for about a hundred yards, reached a sort of archway on the left. From the ground-floor window of a miserable one-storeyed old house at the side of it, a wretched woman—young, but blear-eyed and bloated, and with meshes of hair stiffened with dirt bristling from her uncapped head—peered out, and with a revolting leer addressed me in terms exciting not only horror and disgust in my mind, but also compassion at seeing the almost hopeless state of degradation into which this unfortunate had fallen.

Passing under the archway, which was partially choked up with matters of the most offensive description, I emerged on an open space into which the back-windows of the house just mentioned looked, out of one of which leant another woman much older than the first. Her sallow, wrinkled, unwashed face was shaded by the broad, discoloured border of a calico cap: she scowled upon me, but did not speak. The space on which I stood appeared to have been formerly occupied by a tenement, or tenements; and in front of it, about six feet below, the sides being strengthened by old brick-work, but without any parapet, flowed the Fleet-ditch, as it is called—a turbid, fetid, deep brook, or stream, rushing towards the Thames at the rate of eight or nine miles an hour; the width might be about ten feet. On the left was the lower floor of a house built over the stream. The rafters and supports were wormeaten, and I understood that the flooring was inlaid with trap-doors, through which no doubt many victims had been plunged into the rapid muddy stream below. Looking up towards the right, I saw a long line of gable ends of mean houses, many of them built of wood, and pierced with small windows, rising from the edge of the brook.

Whilst leaning over with straining eyes and offended nostrils to examine this singular scene, a knot of people had collected on the space in the rear. On raising my head, and turning round to ascertain the cause of a strange medley of sounds which assailed my ears, I perceived a group of about twenty youths and lads, and three or four slatternly girls. They were shouting, and blaspheming, and leaping up wildly into the air. But though all were young, they had the faces of old and hardened beings; their mirth was like that of half-stupified Bacchanals; their voices harsh; their eyes staring boldly, and scanning every particle of my clothing, and watching all my movements; but those eyes were entirely bereft of the brightness and animation of uncorrupted youth. These wretched beings hovered and skipped about me, cursing and swearing, and now and then making remarks one to another in (to me) an unknown tongue: anon they eyed me askance, so that as there was no policeman, nor other protection in sight, or at hand, I began to think of the means of defence or retreat.

The rushing ominous stream was before me, gathering round me was a band of most suspicious beings, and the only issue was by the dark archway, bordered and beset as already described. Presently a lad sprang from the group, and with a scream as of triumph, rushed towards the stream, and leaped over it, landing safely within a few inches of its steep bank, on the other side. This feat elicited great shouting and dispersion among his reckless companions, most of whom ran to the edge of the black rivulet, and bending over it, looked up to the right, as though something new were to be seen in that direction. My curiosity overcame the desire to profit by the favourable opportunity of effecting my retreat; so I followed their example.

What a revolting scene met my gaze! Out of the little windows in the gable-ends of the tenements were thrust heads of awful-looking men and women, and girls and lads; the men with bare brawny arms resting on the mouldering window-sills, their begrimmed shirt-sleeves rolled up above the elbows; the women either with broad-flounced night-caps almost concealing their features, or with their hair sticking out from their Medusa-like heads; as for the juveniles, they had the appearance of imps!

The cause of the tumultuous assemblage on the brink of the Fleet-ditch, of the shouts, and of the apparition of so many uncouth busts from the narrow windows, was the floundering of half-a-dozen boys in the rushing water. How they had found their way thither I could not discover; but *there* they were, disporting in the nauseous flood with as much glee as though they had been bathing in the limpid Serpentine.

I gladly took advantage of the excitement of the young reprobates about me to make good my retreat unperceived. Threading the intricate windings of the surrounding lanes and alleys, stuffed with human beings of the most revolting appearance, evidently imbedded in ignorance and vice, I came to a lofty and extensive building, to which, however, there was no perceptible entrance at that part: skirting the walls, I found it to be a large manufactory. The contrast was striking. Here, said I to myself, is an establishment belonging no doubt to wealthy people. Hard by is a capacious thoroughfare, almost in a direct line from the great docks, filled with the richest merchandise from every part of the globe, to the mansions of the great, the powerful, of this magnificent metropolis. This thoroughfare is bordered by the establishments and the residences of rich and respectable tradesmen; of that estimable middle-class which forms so essential a portion of the solid basis of English society. And yet, on the very thresholds of these persons, there is a mass of population savage as any that dwell in Afric or furthest Ind—more than that, even pests to society, active and reckless marauders, vicious to the last degree themselves, and, by their pernicious example, the ruin of all whose unhappy fate brings them under their withering influence!

It might be vain to ask, in such a case, if Christian philanthropy sanctions the fortunate and the educated in thus leaving so many fellow-creatures and neighbours in a condition so wretched in all respects. But let me limit my interrogation to something more practical, and inquire if it be good policy. These people are for the most part idle, as far as lawful occupation is concerned. They must all live, and of course their living comes out of the substance of the rest of the community. Might there not be a saving in laying out something to bring them within the pale of a decent life? They form foci of disease: would it not tend to the public health if some effort were made to place them in purer circumstances? Surely, without incurring any suspicion of extravagant views, I am justified in saying that something is wrong here, and that its redress is loudly called for. With these remarks, as perhaps a needless addition to my portraiture of what I saw, I leave the subject.

THE STUDY OF NATURE.

It is impossible that any person, however thoughtless and unaccustomed to observe the works of creation, can look around him, even during a morning's ramble through the fields, without being struck with the number of living beings that offer themselves to his notice, presenting infinite diversity of form, and obviously adapted, by their construction and habits, to occupy various and widely different situations. The careless lounger, indeed, untaught to mark the less obtrusive and minuter features of the landscape, sees, perhaps, the cattle grazing in the field; watches the swallows as they glance along, or listens with undefined emotions of pleasure to the vocal choir of unseen feathered songsters; and, content with these symptoms of life around him, passes unheeding onwards. Not so the curious and enlightened wanderer, inquisitive to understand all that he finds around him: his prying eye and mind intelligent not only can appreciate the grosser beauties of the scene, and gather full enjoyment from the survey, but perceive objects of wonder multiply at every step he takes: the grass, the trees, the flowers, the earth, the air, swarm with innumerable kinds of active living creatures: every stone upturned reveals some insect wonder; nay, the stagnant ditch he knows to be a world wherein incalculable myriads pass their lives, and every drop to swarm with animated atoms, able to proclaim the Omnipotent Designer loudly as the stars themselves. Is it upon the sea-shore that the student of nature walks? Each rippling wave lays at his feet some tribute from the deep, and tells of wonders indescribable—brings corallines and painted shells, and thousand grotesque beings, samples left to show that in the sea, through all its spacious realms, life still is found—that creatures there exist more numerously than on the earth itself, all perfect in their construction, and, although so diversified in shape and attributes, alike subservient to the general welfare. And yet how few, even at the present day, turn their attention to this wondrous scene, or strive at all to understand the animal creation—to investigate the structure and contrivance that adapt each species to perform certain important duties—to perceive the uses and relations of each group—to contemplate the habits and the instincts that direct the different tribes—and, lastly, to trace out the means whereby the mighty whole, formed of such diverse parts, is all along preserved in perfect harmony!—*Rymer Jones.*

WELSH SURNAMES.

In Sweden, hereditary surnames are said to have been unknown before the commencement of the fourteenth century. At a much later period, no surnames were used in Wales, beyond *ap*, or son, as David-ap-Howell, Evan-ap-Rhys, Griffith-ap-Roger, John-ap-Richard, now very naturally corrupted into Powell, Price, Prodyer, and Pritchard. To a like origin may be referred a considerable number of the surnames beginning with P and B now in use in England; amongst which may be mentioned Preece, Prise, Punphrey, Parry, Probert, Probyn, Pugh, Penry; Bevan, Bithal, Barry, Benyon, and Bowers. It was not unusual, a century or two back, to hear of such combinations as Evan-ap-Griffith-ap-David-ap-Jenkin, and so on to the seventh or eighth generation, so that an individual often carried his pedigree in his name. The church of Llangollen in Wales is said to be dedicated to St Collen-ap-Gwynnawg-ap-Clyndawag-ap-Cowrda-ap-Caradoc-Freichfras-ap-Llyn-Merim-ap-Einion-Yirth-ap-Cunedda-Wledig, a name that casts that of the Dutchman Inkervankodsdoaspanekinkadrachdern into the shade. To burlesque this ridiculous species of nomenclature, some wag described cheese as being

> Adam's own cousin-german by its birth,
> Ap-Curds-ap-Milk-ap-Grass-ap-Earth.

The following anecdote was related to me by a native of Wales:—'An Englishman, riding one dark night among the mountains, heard a cry of distress, proceeding apparently from a man who had fallen into a ravine near the highway, and, on listening more attentively, heard the words, "Help, master, help!" in a voice truly Cambrian. "Help what? Who are you?" inquired the traveller. "Jenkin-ap-Griffith-ap-Robin-ap-William-ap-Rees-ap-Evan," was the response. "Lazy fellows that ye be," rejoined the Englishman, setting spurs to his horse, "to lie rolling in that hole, half-a-dozen of ye; why, in the name of common sense, don't ye help one another out?"' The frequency of such names as Davies, Harris, Jones, and Evans, has often been remarked, and is to be accounted for by the use of the father's name in the genitive case, and the word son being understood; thus David's son became Davis, Harry's son Harris, John's son Jones, and Evan's son Evans. It is a well-attested fact, that about forty years since the Monmouth and Brecon militia contained no less than thirty-six John Joneses. Even the gentry of Wales bore no hereditary surnames until the time of Henry VIII. That monarch, who paid great attention to heraldic matters, strongly recommended the heads of Welsh families to conform to the usage long before adopted by the English, as more consistent with their rank and dignity. Some families accordingly made their existing *sir*names stationary, while a few adopted the surnames of English families, with whom they were allied, as the ancestors of Oliver Cromwell, who thus exchanged Williams for Cromwell, which thenceforward they uniformly used.—*Family Nomenclature.*

FROGS IN STONES.

We have several apparently well-authenticated instances on record of frogs and toads having been found enclosed in masses of rock, to the interior of which there was no perceptible means of ingress. It has been the fashion, however, with naturalists to dismiss all such cases on the assumption that there must have been some cleft or opening by which the animal was admitted while in embryo, or while in a very young state; no one, so far as we are aware, believing that the sperm or young animal may have been enclosed when the rock was in the process of formation at the bottom of shallow waters. Whatever may be the true theory regarding animals so enclosed, their history is certainly one of the highest interest; and without attempting to solve the problem, we present our readers with an instance taken from the Mining Journal of January 18, 1845:—A few days since, as a miner, named W. Ellis, was working in the Penydarran Mine Works, at forty-five feet depth, he struck his mandril into a piece of shale, and to the surprise of the workmen, a frog leaped out of the cleft. When first observed, it appeared very weak, and, though of large size, could crawl only with difficulty. On closer examination, several peculiarities were observed; its eyes were full-sized, though it could not see, and does not now see, as, upon touching the eye, it evinces no feeling. There is a line indicating where the mouth would have been, had it not been confined; but the mouth has never been opened. Several deformities were also observable; and the spine, which has been forced to develope itself in an angular form, appears a sufficient proof of its having grown in very confined space, even if the hollow in the piece of shale, by corresponding to the shape of the back, did not place the matter beyond a reasonable doubt. The frog continues to increase in size and weight, though no food can be given to it; and its vitality is preserved only by breathing through the thin skin covering the lower jaw. Mr W. Ellis, with a view of giving his prize as much publicity as possible, has deposited it at the New Inn, Merthyr, where it is exhibited as 'the greatest wonder in the world, a frog found in a stone forty-five feet from the surface of the earth, where it has been living without food for the last 5000 years!'

BOOK ERRORS.

The biographer of Francis Duke of Bridgewater, in the *Biographie Universelle*, states that the income-tax which he paid every year amounted alone to L.110,000 sterling. The fact is, that in the returns which the duke made under the property-tax he estimated his income at that amount. Lalande, the French astronomer, designates the famous philosopher Ferguson, 'Berger au roi d'Angleterre en Ecosse'—the king of England's shepherd for Scotland. The fact is, he was merely, for a few early years of his life, shepherd to a small farmer in the neighbourhood of Keith in Banffshire. Thomas Holcroft translated Madame Genlis's *Veillées du Chateau* with the incorrect title of Tales of the Castle, instead of Evenings at the Country House. Every one has heard of Shakspeare's singular mistake as to the geography of Bohemia, and his supposition that Tunis and Naples were at an immeasurable distance from each other. But his error is not greater than that of Apollonius Rhodius, who mentions the Rhone and the Po as meeting and discharging themselves into the Gulf of Venice; or that of Æschylus, who places the river Eridanus in Spain. The chorus in Buchanan's tragedy of *Jephtha* mentions, in very familiar terms, the wealth of Crœsus, who was not born till about six hundred years after Jephtha. Smollett, in his *History of England*, states that the ancient Britons 'sowed no corn, and lived in cottages thatched with straw.' If they sowed no corn, how could they get straw in an age when they were wholly cut off from the continent? In Youatt's *Treatise on the Horse*, p. 9, it is stated that 'the Barb has not the Arab's spirit or action;' yet at page 12 we are told 'the Barb *excels the Arab in noble and spirited action*.' A desire to appear very knowing as to the authorship of popular anonymous works is a frequent cause of amusing blunders. Thus in Bohn's Guinea Catalogue (1841), p. 260, we find a quotation from 'Lord Brougham's *Architecture of Birds*,' a work written by Mr Rennie; and in Nattali's Catalogue, February 1841, we read of 'Lord Brougham's *Pursuit of Knowledge*,' a work written by Mr Craik. In Thorpe's Catalogue (No. 1, 1841, p. 2), a book printed at *Mexico* is said to be an interesting specimen of 'the *South* American press.'

GURNEYISM.

This term—of whose meaning perhaps nineteen-twentieths of our readers are utterly ignorant—is applied to a new and particular kind of manuring, which has been employed with signal success by Mr Gurney, a farmer in East Cornwall. The operation consists in covering grass land with long straw, coarse hay, or other fibrous matter, about 20 lbs. to the fall; allowing this covering to lie till the grass spring through it (which it does with astonishing rapidity) to the desired length, and then raking it off to allow the bestial to reach the pasture. The covering is then applied to another portion of the field; the operation of removal and covering being repeated so long as the straw or hay remains sufficiently entire to admit of convenient application. The merits of the system, which is yet in its infancy, was thus stated by Mr Gurney at a late meeting of the East Cornwall Experimental Club:—'About seven weeks since, he had covered half a field of grass of three acres in this manner, and about a fortnight ago, when examined, the increase had been found to be at the rate of upwards of 5000 lbs. per acre over the uncovered portion of the field. At that time the straw was raked off and laid in rows 12 feet apart on the field, and 115 sheep were put on the grass, with a view to eat it down as quickly as possible. After they had been there about a week, they were succeeded by 26 bullocks, to eat off the long grass remaining, and which the sheep had left. The field was thus grazed as bare as possible. The same straw was now again thrown over the same portion of the field from which it had been raked; and on inspection that morning, he had found the action going on as powerfully as on the former occasion. He thought the sheep, on first raking off the straw, were not so fond of the grass as they were of that uncovered; but after 24 hours' exposure to the sun and air, he thought they rather preferred it. He had 40 acres now under the operation, and in consequence of it, he had had grass when his neighbours had none.' Fibrous covering, or Gurneyism, as thus described, is certainly a cheap and convenient mode of manuring; all that is wanted is only further experiment to test its general applicability.

THE LAMENT OF THE IRISH EMIGRANT.

[BY THE HON. MRS BLACKWOOD.]

I'm sitting on the stile, Mary,
  Where we sat side by side
On a bright May morning long ago,
  When first you were my bride.
The corn was springing fresh and green,
  And the lark sang loud and high,
And the red was on your lip, Mary,
  And the love-light in your eye.

The *place* is little changed, Mary,
  The day is bright as then,
The lark's loud song is in my ear,
  And the corn is green again.
But I miss the soft clasp of your hand,
  And your breath warm on my cheek,
And I still keep list'ning for the words
  You never more may speak.

'Tis but a step down yonder lane,
  And the little church stands near—
The church where we were wed, Mary;
  I see the spire from here.
But the graveyard lies between, Mary,
  And my step might break your rest;
For I've laid you, darling, down to sleep,
  With your baby on your breast.

I'm very lonely now, Mary,
  For the poor make no new friends;
But, oh! they love the better still
  The few our Father sends.
And you were all *I* had, Mary;
  My blessing and my pride;
There's nothing left to care for now,
  Since my poor Mary died.

Yours was the good brave heart, Mary,
  That still kept hoping on,
When the trust in God had left my soul,
  And my arm's young strength was gone.
There was comfort ever on your lip,
  And the kind look on your brow;
I bless you, Mary, for that same,
  Though you cannot hear me now.

I thank you for the patient smile,
  When your heart was fit to break,
When the hunger pain was gnawing there,
  And you hid it for *my* sake!
I bless you for the pleasant word,
  When your heart was sad and sore;
Oh! I'm thankful you are gone, Mary,
  Where grief can't reach you more!

I'm bidding you a long farewell,
  My Mary—kind and true!
But I'll not forget you, darling,
  In the land I'm going to.
They say there's bread and work for all,
  And the sun shines always there;
But I'll not forget old Ireland,
  Were it fifty times as fair.

And often in those grand old woods
  I'll sit, and shut my eyes,
And my heart will travel back again
  To the place where Mary lies.
And I'll think I see the little stile
  Where we sat side by side,
And the springing corn, and the bright May morn,
  When first you were my bride!

—*From an old newspaper.*

FORBEARANCE.

If the peculiarities of our feelings and faculties be the effect of variety of excitement through a diversity of organisation, it should tend to produce in us mutual forbearance and toleration. We should perceive how nearly impossible it is that persons should feel and think exactly alike upon any subject. We should not arrogantly pride ourselves upon our virtues and knowledge, nor condemn the errors and weakness of others, since they may depend upon causes which we can neither produce nor easily counteract. No one, judging from his own feelings and powers, can be aware of the kind or degree of temptation or terror, or the seeming incapacity to resist them, which may induce others to deviate.—*Abernethy.*

Published by W. and R. CHAMBERS, Edinburgh; and, with their permission, by W. S. ORR, Amen Corner, London.—Printed by BRADBURY and EVANS, Whitefriars, London.

CONDUCTED BY WILLIAM AND ROBERT CHAMBERS, EDITORS OF 'CHAMBERS'S INFORMATION FOR THE PEOPLE,' 'CHAMBERS'S EDUCATIONAL COURSE,' &c.

No. 83. New Series. SATURDAY, AUGUST 2, 1845. Price 1½d.

THE SCIENTIFIC MEETING AT CAMBRIDGE.

From the accounts given in this journal of the meetings of the British Association at Glasgow and at York, our readers are aware that we regard that body and its proceedings in a favourable light. It has always appeared to us that a good end is served when men can be brought into personal association for the promotion of common objects and the enjoyment of common pleasures, as such meetings are usually found to insure harmony where otherwise there might be hostility, or at least indifference, and much can, of course, be done by combination, where single efforts would be useless. The British Association is also serviceable in awakening and stimulating efforts in behalf of science in the special districts where it meets, and in introducing local objects of scientific and general interest to the notice of many persons who otherwise would remain ignorant of them. It affords, likewise, a brief period of pleasant excitement and recreation to multitudes of studious persons greatly in need of relief from the monotony of their ordinary toils: even on this inferior ground, it could be defended from the ridicule with which certain members of the public press are pleased to assail what assuredly does no harm to any one, whatever may be the amount of positive good which it effects.

The meeting of the present year (June 18—25) took place at Cambridge, where it had assembled for its third session (1833). It was allowed to be a good meeting in point of attendance (between a thousand and eleven hundred members), and there never had been any at which so many distinguished foreign savants were present. In one point of great importance, though of little popular interest, namely, the meteorological observations, it stands above all former meetings. Apart from this, it was not scientifically very brilliant, though it presented several salient points of considerable interest. One external circumstance added much to the enjoyment of all concerned, that the meeting was favoured throughout with the most beautiful weather.

On arriving in Cambridge on the evening of the 18th, we found, as usual, all bustle and excitement at the reception-room, which on this occasion was in the town-hall. Many members being accommodated in the colleges, we experienced little difficulty in procuring an agreeable lodging; which important preliminary being settled, we sauntered forth to enjoy an evening walk amidst the august shades of those piles of past centuries in which English learning is sheltered—a scene always striking to a Scotchman, as being so different from anything of an analogous nature in his own country. And verily, as we saw the lofty spires of King's College chapel and of Trinity piercing the blue of a June night, and tipped with its palely stars, we could have fancied ourselves transported into a scene realised out of eastern fable. We bethought us of the power of even external beauty in protecting the institutions here established. The most daring innovator might come hither full of eagerness to meddle with systems unquestionably representative rather of past centuries than the present, and we can conceive him so captivated through the agency of the mere æsthetics of the place, that, like Alaric awed by the venerableness of the Roman senate, into which he had intruded, our innovator would shrink from his task, and leave the business of reform to ruder hands.

A sunbright morning saw the members hurrying to the various sectional meetings, according to their various predilections. The first section of which we shall speak —the Geological—we found accommodated in the senate-house, a beautiful Grecian building of about the time of Queen Anne, finely decorated within with carved wood-work, and having a platform with rising seats at the upper end, surmounted by a canopy under which the existing royalty of England had recently sat. This was by far the largest and best room enjoyed by any of the sections, and it was assigned to the geological because the meetings of that body are generally the most numerously attended. It may be mentioned parenthetically, that the geological is also the section usually most frequented by the ladies; indeed it is almost the only section which enjoys any share of feminine patronage. On the present occasion, we found a brilliant assemblage of both sexes seated on benches across the room, while Professor Sedgwick, Dr Buckland, Mr Murchison, Sir Henry de la Beche, and other chiefs of geological science, were mustering on the platform. Mr Sedgwick soon after assumed the presidency of the section, and proceeded, as an appropriate commencement of business, to give an exposition of the geology of the immediate neighbourhood of Cambridge. During this and subsequent days, the geological section maintained its character, as one which mingles more pleasantries with science than any of the rest. The fact is, that its leaders are men of lively and varied talents, who, being on the most friendly footing with each other, cannot meet even before a large miscellaneous audience without indulging in their customary familiarity of discourse. There was, therefore, hardly a paper read, or an exposition made, that was not followed by a conversation in which sober and instructive remarks were relieved by facetiæ more or less generally appreciable. The quick vivacious movements of Professor Sedgwick, whose ideas flow too rapidly even for an unusually rapid discourse, contrasted delightfully with the measured oratorical tone and grave demeanour in which the jocundities of Dr Buckland were enunciated. The audience on these occasions seemed to feel that it added much to the enjoyment of the knowledge imparted, that its authors should thus be able to come down, not indecorously, to the level of the unlearned. And here we may remark, that, at one of the general evening meetings, when the beautiful electro-magnetic machine of Mr Armstrong of Newcastle was exhibited, several of the physicists, as Sir David Brewster and Mr Faraday, joined heartily in the amusement occasioned by the shocks which were circulated amongst the ladies and gentlemen present. At one time, we observed a long loop of people with joined hands, extending through the multitude in the senate-house, somewhat like a party standing up for a country dance: several philosophers were of the number. When the engine was put in motion, the whole of these persons might have been seen in a kind of dance at one moment, from the effects of the electricity. Two minutes after, Mr Faraday was on the platform, expounding the nature of the agent that had excited them all so much, in language that introduced awe and deep feeling where recently nothing but merriment had been.

Of the other sections, two were on this occasion hardly existent, namely, the Medical and Mechanical. The rest were active, and to make up in some degree for the failure of these, there was a sub-section for the new science of Ethnology (the characters of nations), which abounded in valuable papers. Hereafter, the Medical is to appear under the title of the Physiological, so as to embrace a wider range of subjects. We now propose to present notices of a few of the most generally interesting matters brought before the various sections.

MR BONOMI ON CERTAIN GIGANTIC BIRDS OF FORMER TIMES.

The existence of slabs of the new red sandstone of America marked with footsteps of large birds apparently of the stork species, is well known. As some of these animals are calculated to have been fifteen feet high, they were at first supposed to have no parallel in the present state of nature; but this was soon found to be not the case, as several specimens of the bones of a bird not less gigantic have since been sent home from New Zealand, where it is spoken of by the natives as recently existing under the name of Moa. There have also been discovered by Captain Flinders, on the south coast of New Holland, in King George's Bay, some very large nests, measuring twenty-six feet in circumference and thirty-two inches in height; resembling, in dimensions, some that are described by Captain Cook, as seen by him on the north-east coast of the same island, about 15 degrees south latitude. It would appear, by some communications made to the editor of the Athenæum, that Professor Hitchcock of Massachusetts had suggested that these colossal nests belonged to the Moa. In connection with these discoveries is another from an opposite quarter. 'Between the years 1821 and 1823, Mr James Burton discovered on the west coast, or Egyptian side of the Red Sea, opposite the peninsula of Mount Sinai, at a place called Gebel Ezzeit, where, for a considerable distance, the margin of the sea is inaccessible from the Desert, three colossal nests within the space of one mile. These nests were not in an equal state of preservation; but, from one more perfect than the others, he judged them to be about fifteen feet in height, or, as he observed, the height of a camel and its rider. These nests were composed of a mass of heterogeneous materials, piled up in the form of a cone, and sufficiently well put together to insure adequate solidity. The diameter of the cone at its base was estimated as nearly equal to its height, and the apex, which terminated in a slight concavity, measured about two feet six inches or three feet in diameter. The materials of which the great mass was composed were sticks and weeds, fragments of wreck, and the bones of fishes; but in one was found the thorax of a man, a silver watch made by George Prior, a London watchmaker of the last century, celebrated throughout the East, and in the nest or basin at the apex of the cone, some pieces of woollen cloth and an old shoe. That these nests had been but recently constructed, was sufficiently evident from the shoe and watch of the shipwrecked pilgrim, whose tattered clothes and whitened bones were found at no great distance; but of what genus or species had been the architect and occupant of the structure, Mr Burton could not, from his own observation, determine. From the accounts of the Arabs, however, it was presumed that these nests had been occupied by remarkably large birds of the stork kind, which had deserted the coast but a short time previous to Mr Burton's visit. To these facts,' said Mr Bonomi, 'I beg to add the following remarks:—Among the most ancient records of the primeval civilisation of the human race that have come down to us, there is described, in the language the most universally intelligible, a gigantic stork bearing, with respect to a man of ordinary dimensions, the proportions exhibited in the drawing before you, which is faithfully copied from the original document. It is a bird of white plumage, straight and large beak, long feathers in the tail; the male bird has a tuft at the back of the head, and another at the breast; its habits apparently gregarious. This very remarkable painted basso-relievo is sculptured on the wall, in the tomb of an officer of the household of Pharaoh Shufu (the Suphis of the Greeks), a monarch of the fourth dynasty, who reigned over Egypt while yet a great part of the Delta was intersected by lakes overgrown with the papyrus—while yet the smaller ramifications of the parent stream were inhabited by the crocodile and hippopotamus—while yet, as it would seem, that favoured land had not been visited by calamity, nor the arts of peace disturbed by war; so the sculpture in these tombs intimate, for there is neither horse nor instrument of war in any one of these tombs. At that period, the period of the building of the Great Pyramid, which, according to some writers on Egyptian matters, was in the year 2100 B.C., which, on good authority, is the 240th year of the deluge, this gigantic stork was an inhabitant of the Delta, or its immediate vicinity; for, as these very interesting documents relate, it was occasionally entrapped by the peasantry of the Delta, and brought with other wild animals, as matters of curiosity, to the great landholders or farmers of the products of the Nile—of which circumstance this painted sculpture is a representation, the catching of fish and birds, which in these days occupied a large portion of the inhabitants. The birds and fish were salted. That this document gives no exaggerated account of the bird, may be presumed from the just proportion that the quadrupeds, in the same picture, bear to the men who are leading them; and, from the absence of any representation of these birds in the less ancient monuments of Egypt, it may also be reasonably conjectured they disappeared soon after the period of the erection of these tombs. With respect to the relation these facts bear to each other, I beg to remark, that the colossal nests of Captains Cook and Flinders, and also those of Mr James Burton, were all on the sea-shore, and all of those about an equal distance from the equator. But whether the Egyptian birds, as described in those very ancient sculptures, bear any analogy to those recorded in the pages of the great stone book of nature (the new red sandstone formation), or whether they bear analogy to any of the species determined by Professor Owen from the New Zealand fossils, I am not qualified to say, nor is it indeed the object of this paper to discuss; the intention of which being rather to bring together these facts, and to associate them with that recorded at Gezah, in order to call the attention of those who have opportunity of making further research into this interesting matter.'*

DISTRIBUTION OF PLANTS.

Professor Edward Forbes, of King's College, excited great interest in the Natural History section by a curious speculative paper respecting the distribution of plants. He started with the proposition, that, admit-

* Athenæum Report.

ting or assuming the theory, that there have been several distinct centres of creation for plants (the idea now paramount amongst naturalists), the isolation or separation of assemblages of individual plants from their centres, and the existence of *endemic* or very local plants, are not satisfactorily accounted for by the agency of the sea, rivers, and winds, and carriage by animals, or through the agency of man. 'It is usual to say' (here we quote from Mr Forbes's abstract*), 'that the presence of many plants is determined by soil or climate, as the case may be; but if such plants be found in areas disconnected from their centres by considerable intervals, some other cause than the mere influence of soil or climate must be sought to account for their presence. This cause the author proposes to seek in an ancient connexion of the outposts or isolated areas with the original centres, and the subsequent isolation of the former through geological changes and events, especially those dependent on the elevation and depression of land. Selecting the flora of the British islands for a first illustration of this view, Professor Forbes calls attention to the fact, well known to botanists, of certain species of flowering plants being found indigenous in portions of that area at a great distance from the nearest assemblages of individuals of the same species in countries beyond it. Thus many plants peculiar in the British flora to the west of Ireland, have the nearest portion of their specific centres in the north-west of Spain; others confined with us to the south-west promontory of England, are, beyond our shores, found in the Channel Isles and the opposite coast of France; the vegetation of the south-east of England is that of the opposite part of the continent; and the Alpine vegetation of Wales and the Scotch Highlands is intimately related to that of the Norwegian Alps. The great mass of the British flora has its most intimate relations with that of Germany. The vegetation of the British islands may be said to be composed of five floras:—1st, A west Pyrenean, confined to the west of Ireland, and mostly to the mountains of that district; 2d, A flora related to that of the south-west of France, extending from the Channel Isles, across Devon and Cornwall, to the south-east and part of the south-west of Ireland; 3d, A flora common to the north of France and south-east of England, and especially developed in the chalk districts; 4th, An Alpine flora, developed in the mountains of Wales, north of England, and Scotland; and, 5th, A Germanic flora, extending over the greater part of Great Britain and Ireland, mingling with the other floras, and diminishing, though slightly, as we proceed westwards, indicating its easterly origin and relation to the characteristic flora of northern Germany. Interspersed among the members of the last-named flora, are very few specific centres peculiar to the British isles. The author numbers in ascending order these floras, according to their magnitude as to species, and also, in his opinion, according to their relative age and period of introduction into the area of the British islands. His conclusions on this point are the following:—

'1. The oldest of the floras now composing the vegetation of the British isles is that of the mountains of the west of Ireland. Though an Alpine flora, it is southernmost in character, and is quite distinct as a system from the floras of the Scottish and Welsh Alps. Its very southern character, its limitation, and its extreme isolation, are evidences of its antiquity, pointing to a period when a great mountain barrier extended across the Atlantic from Ireland to Spain.

'2. The distribution of the second flora, next in point of probable date, depended on the extension of a barrier, the traces of which still remain, from the west of France to the south-east of Britain, and thence to Ireland.

'3. The distribution of the third flora depended on the connexion of the coast of France and England towards the eastern part of the Channel. Of the former existence of this union no geologist doubts.

'4. The distribution of the fourth, or Alpine flora of Scotland and Wales, was effected during the glacial period, when the mountain summits of Britain were low islands, or members of chains of islands, extending to the area of Norway through a glacial sea, and clothed with an arctic vegetation, which, in the gradual upheaval of those islands, and consequent change of climate, became limited to the summits of the new-formed and still-existing mountains.

'5. The distribution of the fifth, or Germanic flora, depended on the upheaval of the bed of the glacial sea, and the consequent connexion of Ireland with England, and of England with Germany, by great plains, the fragments of which still exist, and upon which lived the great elk and other quadrupeds now extinct.

'The breaking up or submergence of the first barrier led to the destruction of the second; that of the second to that of the third; but the well-marked epoch of migration of the Germanic flora indicates the subsequent formation of the Straits of Dover and of the Irish Sea, as now existing.

'To determine the probable geological epoch of the first or west Irish flora—a fragment perhaps with that of north-western Spain, of a vegetation of the true Atlantic—we must seek among fossil plants for a furthermost starting point. This we get in the flora of the London clay, or eocene, which is tropical in character, and far anterior to the oldest of the existing floras. The geographical relations of the miocene sea, indicated by the fossils of the crag, give an after-date certainly to the second and third of the above floras, if not to the first. The epoch of the red or middle crag was probably coeval with the second flora; that of the mammaliferous crag with the third. The date of the fourth is too evident to be questioned; and the author regards the glacial region in which it flourished as a local climate, of which no true traces, as far as animal life is concerned, exist southwards of his second and third barriers. This was the newer pliocene epoch. The period of the fifth flora was that of the post-tertiary, when the present aspect of things was organised.

'Adopting such a view of the relations of these floras in time, the greatest difficulties in the way of changes of the earth's surface and destruction of barriers—deep sea being found where land (probably high land) was—are removed, when we find that those greater changes must have happened during the epoch immediately subsequent to the miocene period; for we have undoubted evidence that elsewhere, during that epoch, the miocene sea-bed was raised 6000 feet in the chain of Taurus, and the barriers forming the westward boundary of the Asiatic eocene lakes so completely annihilated, that a sea several hundred fathoms deep now takes their probable place. The changes required for the events which the author would connect with the peculiar distribution of the British flora, are not greater than these.

'Professor Forbes maintains that the peculiar distribution of endemic animals, especially that of the terrestrial mollusca, bears him out in these views. He proposes to pursue the subject in detail, with reference both to animal and vegetable life, in connexion with the researches of the geological survey.'

EXPERIMENTS OF PROFESSOR BOUTIGNY—FREEZING OF WATER IN RED-HOT VESSELS.

No subject before the Association excited more popular interest than certain experiments performed in the Chemical section by Professor Boutigny. The room of assembly being small, it was impossible that one-half of those desirous of witnessing the experiments could be admitted. They were repeated, and yet, on the second occasion, many, amongst whom were ourselves, went away ungratified. The exposition of M. Boutigny, which was in French, referred to the 'spheroidal state of bodies, and the application of this knowledge to steam-boilers.' As is well known from every-day experience, when drops of water are thrown upon red-hot

* Literary Gazette, June 28.

iron, they assume a spherical form. It is not so well known that the drops, in these circumstances, remain at a minute distance apart from the iron, and that the heat of the plate is not communicated to them. M. Boutigny showed on this occasion a red-hot platinum cup, with a small quantity of water dancing about in it like a globe of glass, without boiling. When the metal, however, cools down to a certain point, the water comes in contact with it, heat is communicated, boiling takes place, and the water quickly evaporates. The same result is observed when any substance capable of assuming a globular form is placed on a heated surface; in proof of which the professor placed in the heated cup of platinum, iodine, ammonia, and some inflammable fluid, each of which became globular, and danced about like the globule of water, but without emitting vapour or smell, or being inflamed, till the platinum was cooled. M. Boutigny also heated a silver weight, of the same shape as the weight of a clock, until it was red-hot, and then lowered it by a wire into a glass of cold water, without there being the slightest indication of action in the water, more than if the weight had been quite cold. The experimentalist advanced no theory to account for these peculiar actions, further than that a film of vapour intervenes between the heated body and the substance, which prevents the communication of heat. The facts, however, he thought were of importance in a practical point of view, both in the tempering of metals and in the explanation of the causes of steam-boiler explosions. From these experiments, it would appear that, in tempering metals, if the metal be too much heated, the effect of plunging it into water will be diminished. In steam-boilers also, if the water be introduced into a heated surface, the heat may not be communicated to the water, and the boiler may become red-hot, and without any great emission of steam; until at length, when the boiler cools, a vast quantity of steam may be generated, and the boiler burst. The last and most curious experiment performed by M. Boutigny was the freezing of water in a red-hot vessel. It has been thus described in the Literary Gazette's report:—'If any substance boils below the freezing point of water, that same substance would be below its own boiling point; and therefore water in contact would be frozen. Sulphurous acid is such a substance; and consequently, sulphurous acid in an incandescent crucible in the spheroidal shape is itself colder than ice: in addition, however, to its own coldness, it evaporates when touched by the water; therefore intense cold is produced, and the water instantly freezes.' The sight of water put into a red-hot crucible, and almost instantly turned out upon the experimenter's hand a mass of ice, elicited loud and continued applause.

MODIFICATIONS OF SHELLS IN SUCCESSIVE STRATA IN THE ISLAND OF COS.

Professor Edward Forbes made a joint communication for himself and Captain Sprat, R.N., on a remarkable phenomenon connected with certain fresh-water tertiary strata in the island of Cos. In a diagram exhibited, three such strata, marked A, B, and C, in ascending succession, lay against a mass of scaglia, and were unconformably surmounted with a marine formation. In stratum A, there were shells of well-known species of fresh-water mollusca, especially paludina and nereitina: as usual, their convolutions were devoid of ribbings or humps. But in stratum B, the same shells were found with a hump on each convolution; and in stratum C, the same shells had three humps. There were here appearances of either a transmutation of species, or a creation of new species, neither of which propositions he was willing to admit. He had therefore suppressed the surprise he felt at the phenomenon for upwards of two years, until at length a better explanation had occurred to him. It had been ascertained, that when fresh-water molluscs were put into brackish water, their shells in time experienced a distortion, provided that the species could survive and propagate in such circumstances. He was therefore of opinion that an intrusion of the sea had taken place in the fresh-water lake in which stratum B was formed, and that this had been attended by the destruction of several of the weaker-lunged species which appear in A, and the distortion of the shells of the stronger-lunged (pectenibranchiate) which remained. In stratum C, more salt water had come in, and increased the deformities, as described. There was thus a modification of forms, but not a change of species. At the conclusion of this paper, which was listened to with great interest, Mr Lyell and other gentlemen present stated other instances of a change of figure experienced by fresh-water molluscs which had been exposed to the influence of salt water. It has the effect of dwarfing and distorting them.

DR BUCKLAND ON THE AGENCY OF LAND SNAILS IN FORMING HOLES AND TRACKWAYS IN COMPACT LIMESTONE.

The learned doctor here made further observations on a subject which he had brought before the Association four years ago, and which, he complained, had then and since been treated with much scepticism. He had found limestone at various places (Tenby, Boulogne, Plymouth) presenting surfaces downwards, and in these surfaces there were holes in which land snails were sheltered. In some instances, these holes were several inches deep, and in a few, two or three met together in the interior of the stone. Dr Buckland said he had found these marked surfaces invariably in the neighbourhood of pastures where snails were numerous; and so certain was their appearance in certain circumstances, that oftener than once he had, in travelling, pointed to a rock as one that would be found marked, and it had proved to be so. He exhibited specimens of limestone from several localities, showing perforations still containing the shells of snails, or furrows leading to the perforations, and he insisted that these were unlike any that are produced by other causes. The fact of their always being on the under surfaces of ledges, and thus presented downwards, proved that they were independent of atmospheric causes. He did not mean that the snails required holes for their residence; but he maintained that the perforations were a result of their sheltering there, and acid exuding from their skin being the agent which wore down the stone. Dr Buckland had even made some approach to an ascertainment of the rate at which the stone becomes perforated. He had found the lower faces of the ledges in the wall of Richborough castle marked in this manner to the depth of about an inch and a half. Richborough was a work of the Romans, who had left it fourteen hundred years ago. Assuming that the snails commenced operations at that time, it appeared that they wrought their way into the stone at the rate of an inch in a thousand years.

The reading of this paper excited some merriment; but the view taken by Dr Buckland of the operation of the snails was generally acceded to; and its being one of no unimportant character in science, is shown by its demolishing an inference which had been drawn from certain perforated rocks, as evidence of a raised beach. It is now seen, that what a former inquirer deemed to have been effected by the wearing action of the sea, was the work of a few humble land snails.

Besides the meetings at the seven sections, there were general assemblages in the evening at the senate-house: the first, on Thursday evening, was devoted to the business of installing the president elect, Sir John Herschel. The Dean of Ely (Dr Peacock), the president of the past year, introduced his successor in terms which were almost affecting, from the allusion they contained to the two men having been competitors thirty-two years before for college honours. Sir John, on taking the chair, replied with like feeling, and read an address embracing a variety of philosophical subjects. It was painful to find that this eminent person, while possessing the usual appearances of health, has lost the power of making himself heard at any considerable distance. His address has, however, been published, and we extract from it a passage regarding that which has chiefly distinguished the meeting of this year—the congress of meteorologists. Of these, he mentioned as present M. Kupffer, the Director-General of the Russian System of Magnetic and Meteorological Observation; M. Ermann, the celebrated circumnavigator and meteorologist; Baron Von Seftenborg; M. Kreil, Director of the Imperial Observatory at Prague; M. Boguslawski, Director of the Royal Prussian Observatory at Breslau—all of whom had come on purpose to afford to the meeting the benefit of their advice and experience. 'Every member,' said Sir John, 'is aware of the great exertions which have been made during the last five years, on the part of the British, Russian, and several other foreign governments, and of our own East India Company, to furnish data on the most extensive and systematic scale, for elucidating the great problems of terrestrial magnetism and meteorology, by the establishment of a system of observatories all over the world, in which the phenomena are registered at instants strictly simultaneous, and at intervals of two hours throughout both day and night. With the particulars of these national institutions, and of the multitude of local and private ones of a similar nature both in Europe, Asia, and America, working on the same concerted plan, so far as the means at their disposal enable them, I need not detain you: neither need I enter into any detailed explanation of the system of magnetic surveys, both by sea and land, which have been executed, or are in progress, in connexion with, and based upon, the observations carried on at the fixed stations. These things form the subject of special annual reports, which the committee appointed for the purpose have laid before us at our several meetings, ever since the commencement of the undertaking; and the most recent of which will be read in the Physical section of the present meeting, in its regular course. It is sufficient for me to observe, that the result has been the accumulation of an *enormous* mass of most valuable observations, which are now, and have been for some time, in the course of publication; and when thoroughly digested and discussed, as they are sure to be, by the talent and industry of magnetists and meteorologists, both in this country and abroad, cannot fail to place those sciences very far indeed in advance of their actual state.'

The general meeting of Friday evening was distinguished by a singularly able and lucid popular exposition of the subject of the earth's magnetism by the astronomer-royal, Professor Airey. On Saturday evening there was a promenade, which excited little interest. On Monday, Mr Murchison treated the members with a discourse on the geology of Russia, which subject he has been engaged in investigating for five years, and on which he is about to publish an elaborate work. It appears that the various formations of that vast region present mainly the same records of animal life as the corresponding strata in England, thus adding to the evidence that these formations are chronicles of the advance of life from mean to exalted forms during certain definite eras of the earth's existence. The surfaces covered by single formations in Russia, are in some instances as large as the whole of England. Mr Murchison also showed that there formerly existed in Russia a huge Mediterranean sea, whose boundaries were from the Volga to the sea of Azof, the Caspian extending to an immense distance, even to Chinese Tartary.

On the evening of Tuesday there was another promenade, which was enlivened by the exhibition of Mr Armstrong's magnetico-electric machine. The last evening meeting, on Wednesday, was devoted to general business, and brought from the chiefs of the Association several eloquent speeches. It was now announced that the next meeting should take place in Southampton in the month of September 1846, under the presidency of Mr Murchison.

The Association, during the week of the meeting, had the privilege of entrée to the observatory, a little way out of town, to the college halls, chapels, libraries, and museums, and to a model-room where a few curious objects had been collected. Amongst these we were most struck by a series of preparations in the anatomy of the invertebrate animals, the work of Mr Goadby. This gentleman has devoted an ingenious and indefatigable mind for five-and-twenty years to such preparations, and he has now attained a degree of dexterity in the work, which leaves everything of the kind at an immeasurable distance. First, dismissing the cylindrical bottles, as distorting all objects placed in them, he adopts cubical glass cases, formed of soldered plates, through which each feature is seen in its exact proportions. Second, he presents animals in various appearances: one case, for instance, will give the alimentary system; another the nervous; and so on. He even studies by what colour of paper, as a background, he can best bring out the lineaments of the objects. These preparations were universally admired; and the preparer excited much amusement when he took out a brooch containing a beetle so perfectly preserved in spirits, that not a shade of colour on its wings was tarnished.

The hospitalities of the colleges on this occasion were of a moderate kind, and there was little of that mutual flattery in which such bodies are apt to indulge on social occasions. We would still remark, that, to persons like ourselves, of whom there must be many, who come for the love of science alone, and enjoy but little acquaintance with its cultivators, there sometimes appears a slight offensiveness in a certain tone of over-good fellowship which frequently bursts out amongst the leaders of the Association in public. There is something provoking in it to the uninitiated. Turning to a graver matter, we cannot but sympathise a little in the disappointment so often felt by the public with regard to the matters brought forward at the Association. There are many valuable isolated facts, but there never is such a thing as a comprehensive view of nature in any of her departments. At the beginning of the Royal Society, men were bringing forward observations on particular matters: they are doing the same at this day, though six generations have meanwhile gone to dust. Common minds see no sense in this wasting of life in the establishment of new species of moths and ascertainment of new laws presiding over the heating of bodies. They call for something either offering great practical advantages, or opening up new and better views of the relation in which we stand to the great agencies external to ourselves. It is all very well to decry rash generalisation; but while science professes to show merely a collection of bricks towards the building of a house, it will never get any credit as an architect, and the popular apprehension of the value of its researches will be dubious and obscure.

ASCENT OF MAUNA LOA.

Of the thousands whom description has rendered familiar with Ætna, Vesuvius, and Hecla, few may have even heard of the equally imposing phenomena that present themselves to the navigator of the Pacific. Among the fiery cones and simmering craters of Polynesia, those of Hawaii, one of the Sandwich islands, are by far the most gigantic—their elevation being such as to retain a perpetual cap of snow, though situated directly under the tropics. Hawaii, so memorable for the murder of Captain Cook, is of an irregular form, fully 260 miles in circumference, and from shore to shore entirely of volcanic origin. So extremely irregular is its surface, that not a square mile of level ground is to be found; in fact, it may be said to be one vast mountain, or rather congeries of mountains, having a common base, and heaving their cones to the height of thirteen, fourteen, and sixteen thousand feet above the level of the sea. The three most remarkable prominences are Mauna Kea, Mauna Loa, and Mauna Hualalai, that of Loa being still in active combustion, and vomiting forth floods of lava from various points of its surface. This mountain is described as a vast dome, sixty miles in diameter, and nearly three miles in height, having a shoulder or terrace on its eastern slope, in which is situated the active crater of Kilauea, unsurpassed for grandeur and magnitude by any similar phenomena. It is thus that Mauna Loa has been an object of the greatest interest to navigators ever since the discovery of these islands, and that we have had accounts of the partial or complete ascents by Byron, David Douglas the botanist, Dr Gardner, and by the recent Exploring Expedition of the United States. In the beginning of 1841, the officers of this expedition pitched their surveying tent on the highest scalp, gauged and fathomed the craters, cooked their food in the steam fissures—altogether accomplishing a sojourn replete with the most spirited adventure. A brief outline of the commander's narrative cannot fail to interest and inform the reader.

Having procured guides and baggage-men, and being fully equipped for a three weeks' sojourn, the party commenced their ascent on the 10th of December 1840. Having reached Olaa, 1138 feet above the level of the sea, they halted to rest and inspect their forces. From this point, they had no distinct path to follow, but scrambled over masses of lava. After considerable labour, they reached the great plain of the volcano, at an elevation of 4000 feet, where Mauna Loa burst upon them in all its grandeur. 'The day,' proceeds the narrator, 'was extremely fine, the atmosphere pure and clear, except a few flying clouds, and this immense dome rose before us from a plain some twenty miles in breadth. I had not until then formed any adequate idea of its magnitude and height. The whole dome appeared of a bronze colour, and its uninterrupted smooth outline was relieved against the deep blue of a tropical sky. Masses of clouds were floating around it, throwing their shadows distinctly on its sides, to which they gave occasional relief and variety. There was a bluish haze resting on the plain, that apparently gave it great distance, though this was partially counteracted by the distinctiveness of the dome. I now, for the first time, felt the magnitude of the task I had undertaken.

'So striking was the mountain, that I was surprised and disappointed when called upon by my friend Dr Judd to look at the crater of Kilauea; for I saw nothing before us but a huge pit, black, ill-looking, and totally different from what I had anticipated. There were no jets of fire, no eruptions of heated stones, no cones, nothing but a depression, that, in the midst of the vast plain by which it is surrounded, appeared small and insignificant. At the further end was what appeared a small cherry-red spot, whence vapour was issuing, and condensing above into a cloud of silvery brightness. This cloud, however, was more glorious than any I had ever beheld, and the sight of it alone would have repaid the trouble of coming thus far.

'We hurried to the edge of the cavity, in order to get a view of its interior, and as we approached, vapour issuing from numerous cracks showed that we were passing over ground beneath which fire was raging. The rushing of the wind past us was as if it were drawn inwards to support the combustion of some mighty conflagration. When the edge is reached, the extent of the cavity becomes apparent, and its depth became sensible by comparison with the figures of some of our party who had already descended. The vastness thus made sensible, transfixes the mind with astonishment, and every instant the impression of grandeur and magnitude increases. To give an idea of its capacity, the city of New York might be placed within it, and when at its bottom, would be hardly noticed; for it is three and a half miles long, two and a half wide, and over a thousand feet deep. A black ledge surrounds it at the depth of six hundred and sixty feet, and thence to the bottom is three hundred and eighty-four feet. The bottom looks, in the daytime, like a heap of smouldering ruins. The descent to the ledge appears to the sight a short and easy task, but it takes an hour to accomplish.

'We pitched our tents in full view of the volcano, on its western side, and the natives busied themselves in building temporary huts to shelter them from the cold blast that rushed by. All this was accomplished, and we had time to take another view of the crater before dark.

'All usual ideas of volcanic craters are dissipated upon seeing this. There is no elevated cone, no igneous matter or rocks ejected beyond the rim. The banks appear as if built of massive blocks, which are in places clothed with ferns, nourished by the issuing vapours. What is wonderful in the day, becomes ten times more so at night. The immense pool of cherry-red liquid lava, in a state of violent ebullition, illuminates the whole expanse, and flows in all directions like water, while the illuminated cloud hangs over it like a vast canopy.

'We sat on its northern bank for a long time in silence, until one of the party proposed we should endeavour to reach the bank nearest to and over the lake; and having placed ourselves under the direction of Mr Drayton, we followed him along the edge of the western bank; but although he had been over the ground the day before, he now lost his way, and we found ourselves still on the upper bank, after walking two or three miles. We then resolved to return to the first place that appeared suitable for making a descent, and at last one was found, which, however, proved steep and rugged. In the darkness we got many a fall, and received numerous bruises; but we were too near the point of our destination to turn back without fully satisfying our curiosity. We finally reached the second ledge, and soon came to the edge of it: we were then directly over the pool or lake of fire, at the distance of about five hundred feet above it; and the light was so strong, that it enabled me to read the smallest print. This pool is fifteen hundred feet long by one thousand wide, and of an oval figure.

'I was struck with the absence of any noise, except a low murmuring like that which is heard from the boiling of a thick liquid. The ebullition was (as is the case where the heat is applied to one side of a vessel) most violent near the northern side. The vapour and steam that were constantly escaping were so rarefied as not to impede the view, and only became visible in the bright cloud above us, which seemed to sink and rise alternately. We occasionally perceived stones, or masses of red-hot matter, ejected to the height of about seventy feet, and falling back into the lake again.

'The lake was apparently rising, and wanted but a few feet of overflowing its banks. When I began to reflect upon the position we were in, its insecurity, and the vast and deep fires beneath, with the high basaltic walls encompassing us on all sides, the sulphureous fumes and broad glare, throwing such enormous masses of stone in strong relief by their own fusion, I found it difficult to comprehend how such a reservoir can thus be pent up, and be viewed in such close proximity, without accident or danger. The whole party was perfectly silent, and the countenance of each individual expressed the feeling of awe and wonder which I felt in so great a degree myself, and which the scene was so well calculated to excite.'

Having determined to encamp at Kilauea for a few days, the exploration of the crater was the next subject that engaged their attention. This was done with great difficulty and no little danger. 'The pathway leads down on the north-east side over frightful chasms, sometimes on a mere edge of earth, and on rocks rent asunder to the depth of several hundred feet. Through these fissures steam issues, which, as it reaches the upper part, condenses, and gives nourishment to masses of ferns, and an abundance of small bushes (vaccinium), bearing a small berry of an agreeable flavour, called by the natives ohela. The descent, however, is not in reality difficult, except in a few places, where it requires some care in passing over the basaltic blocks, that are here piled in confused heaps. On approaching the black ledge, which from above appeared level and smooth, it is seen to be covered with large pieces of lava, rising in places into cones thirty or forty feet high, which are apparently bound down by huge tortuous masses, which surround them like cables. In other places these are stretched lengthwise on the level ledge, and look like hideous fiery serpents with black vitreous scales, that occasionally give out smoke, and in some cases fire.

'The immense space which I have described the crater as covering, is gradually filled with the fluid mass of lava to a certain point, above which the walls, or the surrounding soil, are no longer able to bear the pressure; it then finds vent by an eruption, previous to which, however, a large part that is next to the walls of the crater has in a measure become cooled, and remains fixed at the level it had attained. After the eruption, the central mass therefore alone subsides three or four hundred feet, and leaves the portion that has become solid, forming a kind of terrace or shelf: this is what constitutes the "black ledge," and is one of the most striking features of the crater. Its surface is comparatively level, though somewhat uneven, and is generally coated with a vitreous, and in some places a scoriaceous lava, from half an inch to an inch thick, very iridescent and brittle. In walking over this crust, it crumbles and cracks under the feet: it seems to be easily decomposed, and in some places had lost its lustre, having acquired a grayish colour, and become friable.

'To walk on the black ledge is not always safe, and persons who venture it are compelled for safety to carry a pole, and feel before they tread over the deceitful path, as though they were moving on doubtful ice. The crackling noise made in walking over this crisp surface (like a coating of blue and yellow glass) resembles that made by treading on frozen snow in very cold weather. Here and there are seen dark pits and vaulted caverns, with heated air rushing from them. Large and extended cracks are passed over, the air issuing from which, at a temperature of 180 degrees, is almost stifling. Masses are surmounted that it would seem as if the accumulated weight of a few persons would cause to topple over, and plunge the whole into the fiery pool beneath.

'On approaching the large lake at the southern end of the crater, the heat becomes almost too stifling to bear. I shall not soon forget my employment therein, in measuring a base to ascertain the extent and capacity of the lake, of which some account will be given hereafter. At about two-thirds of the distance from the north end are extensive sulphur banks, from the fissures in which much steam is continually escaping: in these fissures are seen many beautiful crystals adhering to their sides; while on the bank itself, some specimens of sulphate of copper, in beautiful blue crystals, were found.

'From many places on the black ledge a bluish smoke was seen issuing, smelling strongly of sulphur, and marked by an efflorescence of a white tasteless powder among the cavities: this it was difficult to detach without scalding the fingers. There were many cracks where our sticks were set on fire, and some places in the vaulted chambers beneath where the rock might be seen red-hot.

'The black ledge is of various widths, from six hundred to two thousand feet. It extends all around the cavity, but it is seldom possible to pass around that portion of it near the burning lake, not only on account of the stifling fumes, but of the intense heat. In returning from the neighbourhood of the lake to the point where we began the ascent, we were one hour and ten minutes of what we considered hard walking; and in another hour we reached the top of the bank. This will probably give the best idea of its extent, and the distance to be passed over in the ascent from the black ledge, which was found six hundred and sixty feet below the rim.

'To the bottom of the crater there was a descent at the north-west angle of the black ledge, where a portion of it had fallen in, and afforded an inclined plane to the bottom. This at first appeared smooth and easy to descend, but on trial it proved somewhat difficult, for there were many fissures crossing the path at right angles, which it was necessary to get over, and the vitreous crust was so full of sharp spiculæ, as to injure the hands and cut the shoes at every step. Messrs Waldron and Drayton, after much toil, finally reached the floor of the crater. This was afterwards ascertained to be three hundred and eighty-four feet below the black ledge, making the whole depth nine hundred and eighty-seven feet below the northern rim. Like the black ledge, it was not found to have the level and even surface it had appeared from above to possess: hillocks and ridges, from twenty to thirty feet high, ran across it, and were in some places so perpendicular, as to render it difficult to pass over them. The distance they traversed below was deceptive, and they had no means of ascertaining it but by the time it took to walk it, which was upwards of two hours, from the north extreme of the bottom to the margin of the large lake. It is extremely difficult to reach this lake, on account of its overflowing at short intervals, which does not allow the fluid mass time to cool. The nearest approach that any one of the party made to it at this time was about fifteen hundred or two thousand feet; they were then near enough to burn their shoes and light their sticks in the lava which had overflowed during the preceding night.

'The smaller lake was well viewed from a slight eminence. This lake was slightly in action; the globules (if large masses of red fluid lava, several tons in weight, can be so called) were seen heaving up at regular intervals, six or eight feet in height; and smaller ones were thrown up to a much greater elevation. At the distance of fifty feet, no gases were to be seen, nor was any steam evident, yet a thin smoke-like vapour arose from the whole fluid surface: no puffs of smoke were perceived at any time.

'At first, it seemed quite possible to pass over the congealed surface of the lake to within reach of the fluid, though the spot on which they stood was so hot as to require their sticks to be laid down to stand on. This idea was not long indulged in, for in a short time the fluid mass began to enlarge: presently a portion would crack, and exhibit a bright-red glare; then in a few moments the lava stream would issue through, and a portion would speedily split off, and suddenly disappear in the liquid mass. This kind of action went on until the lake had extended itself to its outer bank, and had approached to within fifteen feet of their position, when the guide said it was high time to make a retreat.'

The crater now described being, as already stated, on a shoulder of the hill, the summit or great dome impending over it remained to be scaled. The ascent was accordingly commenced on the 18th of December, and proved fully more fatiguing and hazardous than the previous part of the journey. As they ascended, every trace of vegetation disappeared; fierce blasts swept the mountain side; snow began to fall; and the thermometer went down successively to 25, 18, and 15 degrees. It stood at this, with a heavy fall of snow, when they reached the summit—13,760 feet above the level of the ocean. 'Nothing can exceed the devastation of the mountain: the whole area of it is one mass of lava, that has at one time been thrown out in a fluid state from its terminal crater. There is no sand or other rock; nothing but lava, on whichever side the eye is turned. To appearance, it is of different ages, some of very ancient date, though as yet not decomposed; and the alternations of heat and cold, with rain and snow, seem to have united in vain for its destruction.' Having attained the summit of the mountain, which exhibited all the traces of an extinct volcano, 'the sight was surpassingly grand. In the distance, the island of Maui emerged from and broke the line of the deep blue horizon, while its lower side was dimmed by a whitish haze, that seemed to unite it to the island of Hawaii. The same haze enveloped the hills of Kohala on our right, and the western extremity of Hawaii. Nearer to us was Hualalai, the third great mountain of Hawaii, up whose sides a compact mass of white fleecy clouds was impelled by the sea-breeze. To our right rose in bold relief Mauna Kea, covered with its snowy mantle; and at our feet was spread out, between the three great mountains, the black plain of lava, overhung by a dusky pall of clouds. All these features were so blended into each other by the mist, as to exhibit a tone of harmony that could hardly be conceived, considering the variety of the forms, characters, and distances of the objects, and which seemed to blend earth, sea, and sky into one. I can never hope again to witness so sublime a scene, to gaze on which excited such feelings, that I felt relieved when I turned from it to engage in the duties that had called me to the spot.'

Operations were now commenced for their survey. A rude enclosure of clinkers and scoriæ was built forty feet distant from the edge of the terminal crater; the tents were erected inside; and everything so disposed as to render tolerable a temperature varying in one day from 84 to 13 degrees. The attendants, most of whom had been left at various stations below, now brought the surveyors supplies of food and water, and thus they were enabled to prosecute their observations, and examine the phenomena of the terminal crater, without obstruction. This crater, or rather craters—for there are two, separated by a narrow partition of compact lava and clinkers—is an immense depression, with an elevated brim about twenty miles in circumference, which gradually narrows by successive ledges to the depth of eight or nine hundred feet. It has been dormant for many years, but is still filled with fissures and caverns, which emit steam and sulphureous vapours. 'Dr Judd, the sergeant, and Brooks, descended into the crater; they made the descent on the east bank among large blocks of lava, and reached the bottom in about an hour. There they were surrounded by huge clinkers and ridges, running generally north and south in lines across the crater; between these was the pahoihoi, or smooth lava. They passed over these obstructions to the south-west, and found in places many salts, among which were sulphate of soda and sulphate of lime. Four-fifths of the way across was a hill two hundred feet high, composed of scoria and pumice, with fissures emitting sulphurous acid gas. To the west was a plain full of cracks and fissures, all emitting more or less steam and gas. They found the west wall perpendicular; its lower strata were composed of a gray basalt. For three-fourths of the distance up it had a dingy yellow colour; above this there are a number of thin layers, apparently dipping to the south-west with the slope of the mountain. They also visited many steam cracks on the north-east side, from which fumes of sulphurous acid gas were emitted; no hydrogen was found in the gas, which extinguished flame without producing explosion.'

On the 13th of January preparations were made for the descent, and this they accomplished by the same route, but with greater difficulty, as many of the men were worn out, their shoes gone, and not a few suffering severely from the mountain sickness. On their way they again halted at Kilauea, where Dr Judd, anxious to obtain some rare specimens of lava, as well as a vesselful of the molten matter, met with a very narrow escape. He had descended into a small detached crater thirty-eight feet deep by two hundred in diameter; smoke and a little igneous matter were issuing from a small cone in its centre; but with this exception, a crust of solid lava covered the bottom. While advancing downwards, 'he saw and heard a slight movement in the lava about fifty feet from him, which was twice repeated, and curiosity led him to turn to approach the place where the motion occurred. In an instant the crust was broken asunder by a terrific heave, and a jet of molten lava, full fifteen feet in diameter, rose to the height of about forty-five feet with a most appalling noise. He instantly turned, for the purpose of escaping, but found that he was now under a projecting ledge, which opposed his ascent, and that the place where he had descended was some feet distant. The heat was already too great to permit him to turn his face towards it, and was every moment increasing; while the violence of the throes, which shook the rock beneath his feet, augmented. Although he considered his life as lost, he did not omit the means for preserving it; but offering a mental prayer for the Divine aid, he strove, although in vain, to scale the projecting rock. While thus engaged, he called in English upon his native attendants for aid; and looking upwards, saw the friendly hand of Kalumo —who on this fearful occasion had not abandoned his spiritual guide and friend—extended towards him. Ere he could grasp it, the fiery jet again rose above their heads, and Kalumo shrunk back, scorched and terrified, until, excited by a second appeal, he again stretched forth his hand, and seizing Dr Judd's with a giant's grasp, their joint efforts placed him on the ledge. Another moment, and all aid would have been unavailing to save Dr Judd from perishing in the fiery deluge.'

After much breakneck and foolhardy adventure among the craters, steam fissures, and fumiroles of Kilauea, the party made their final descent, which was accomplished after an absence of forty-two days; 'and it was delightful,' adds the narrator, 'to feel ourselves as it were at home again, after so arduous and fatiguing an expedition.'

SIR WALTER SCOTT AND WILLIAM LAIDLAW.

CONCLUDING ARTICLE.

The subsequent intercourse of Mr Laidlaw with the great minstrel may be traced with sufficient minuteness in Lockhart's Life of Scott. After some unsuccessful speculations and considerable losses, the 'gentle forester' went to reside permanently at Abbotsford. He planned, carried out, or assisted in the rural improvements—superintended the planting or thinning of the woods (an occupation equally dear to Sir Walter), looked after the tenants and labourers—or, when the day was stormy or the season severe, joined the 'genius of the place' in his antique library or study, and occasionally wrote to his dictation. Latterly, when the evil days had come to Abbotsford, he was a constant amanuensis some hours every morning—the anxious novelist looking with eager and morbid haste towards the completion of his task, and watching each successive leaf as it was written and laid on the pile of paper. When his mind was entire, he threw off his images and conceptions with careless ease and facility. 'I never saw him much elated or excited in composition,' said Laidlaw; 'but one morning when he was out of doors concocting that simple but humorous song, Donald Caird. I watched him limping along at good five miles an hour, along the ridge or sky-line opposite Kaeside, and when he came in, he recited to me the fruits of his walk.' In dictating any part of his novels, he seemed not to attend to the expression, but to the continuity of his tale or dialogue. He had obviously arranged his plot and incidents for the day ere he descended from his bedroom, and the *style* he left to chance. His memory was an inexhaustible repertory, so that Hogg, in his moments of super-exaltation and vanity, used to say that, if he had the *shirra's* memory, he would beat him as a poet!

According to Mr Laidlaw, Scott did not like to speak about his novels after they were published, but was fond of canvassing the merits and peculiarities of the characters while he was engaged in the composition of the story. 'He was peculiarly anxious,' says Mr Laidlaw, 'respecting the success of Rebecca in Ivanhoe. One morning, as we were walking in the woods after our forenoon's labour, I expressed my admiration of the character, and, after a short pause, he broke out with—"Well, I think I shall make something of my Jewess." Latterly, he seemed to indulge in a retrospect of the useful effect of his labours. In one of these serious moods, I remarked that one circumstance of the highest interest might and ought to yield him very great satisfaction; namely, that his narratives were the best of all reading for young people. I had found that even his friend Miss Edgeworth had not such power in engaging attention. His novels had the power, beyond any other writings, of arousing the better passions and finer feelings, and the moral effect of all this, I added, when one looks forward to several generations—every one acting upon another—must be immense. I well recollect the place where we were walking at this time—on the road returning from the hill towards Abbotsford. Sir Walter was silent for a minute or two, but I observed his eyes filled with tears.'

Of all his contemporaries Scott spoke kindly and warmly: he seemed to be entirely free from literary jealousy. 'I had many conversations with him,' Laidlaw remarks, 'concerning the life and poetry of Byron, particularly after the date of a visit paid to Abbotsford by Lady Byron. He seemed to regret very much that Byron and he had not been thrown more together. He felt the influence he had over his great contemporary's mind, and said there was so much in it that was very good and very elevated, that any one whom he much liked could, as he thought, have withdrawn him from many of his errors.'

The following note by Laidlaw is interesting both on account of the fact and the opinion it contains:—'I have more than once (such was his modesty) heard Sir Walter assert that, had his father left him an estate of L.500 or L.600 a-year, he would have spent his time in miscellaneous reading, not writing. This, to a certain extent, might have been the case; and had he purchased the property of Broadmeadows, in Yarrow, as he at one time was very anxious to do, and when the neighbouring land was in the possession of independent proprietors, the effect might have been the same. At Abbotsford, surrounded by little lairds, most of them ready to sell their lands as soon as he had money to advance, the impulse to exertion was incessant; for the desire to possess and to add increased with every new acquisition, until it became a passion of no small power. Then came the hope to be a large landed proprietor, and to found a family.'

The correspondence between Sir Walter Scott and Mr Laidlaw was chiefly devoted to their rural concerns. When the poet was in Edinburgh attending to his official duties as clerk of session, he sighed for Abbotsford and the country, and took the liveliest interest in all that was going on under the superintendence of his friend. Passages like the following remind us of the writings of Gilpin and Price on forest and picturesque scenery:—'George must stick in a few wild roses, honeysuckles, and sweet-briers, in suitable places, so as to produce the luxuriance we see in the woods which nature plants herself. We injure the effect of our plantings, so far as beauty is concerned, very much by neglecting underwood.' 'I want to know how you are forming your glades of hard-wood. Try to make them come handsomely in contact with each other, which you can only do by looking at a distance on the spot, then and there shutting your eyes as you have done when a child looking at the fire, and forming an idea of the same landscape with glades of woodland crossing it. Get out of your ideas about expense. It is, after all, but throwing away the price of the planting. If I were to buy a picture worth L.500, nobody would wonder much. Now, if I choose to lay out L.100 or L.200 to make a landscape of my estate hereafter, and add so much more to its value, I certainly do not do a more foolish thing. I mention this, that you may not feel limited, so much as you might in other cases, by the exact attention to pounds, shillings, and pence, but consider the whole on a liberal scale. We are too apt to consider plantations as a subject of the closest economy, whereas beauty and taste have even a marketable value after the effects come to be visible. Don't dot the plantations with small patches of hard-wood, and always consider the ultimate effect.'

In the midst of his business details, Scott's peculiar humour and felicity of illustration are perpetually breaking out. His relation of the simplest occurrence is vivid and characteristic. A high wind in Edinburgh, in January 1818, he thus notices:—'I had more than an anxious thought about you all during the gale of wind. The Gothic pinnacles were blown from the top of Bishop Sandford's Episcopal chapel at the end of Prince's Street, and broke through the roof and flooring, doing great damage. This was sticking the horns of the mitre into the belly of the church. The devil never so well deserved the title of Prince of the power of the air since he has blown down this handsome church, and left the ugly mass of new building standing on the North Bridge.'

We add a few more sentences:—'Political publications must always be caricatures. As for the mob of great cities whom you accuse me of despising too much, I think it is impossible to err on that side. They are the very *riddlings* of society, in which every useful cinder is, by various processes, withdrawn, and nothing left but dust, ashes, and filth. Mind, I mean the mob of cities, not the lowest people in the country, who often, and indeed usually, have both character and intelligence.'

'I am made president of the Royal Society [1820], so I would have you in future respect my opinion in the matter of *chuckie-stanes*, caterpillars, fulminating powder, and all such wonderful works of nature. I feel the spirit coming on me, and never pass an old quarry without the desire to rake it like a cinder-sifter.'

Scott's opinion of modern Gothic architecture is thus incidentally announced. When in London in 1821, he writes—'I have got a very good plan from Atkinson for my addition, but I do not like the outside, which is modern Gothic, a style I hold to be equally false and foolish. Blore and I have been at work to *Scottify* it, by turning battlements into bartisans, and so on. I think we have struck out a picturesque, appropriate, and entirely new line of architecture.'

Abbotsford must certainly be considered *picturesque*, but it is a somewhat incongruous pile, and without the beautiful garden-screen in front, the general effect would be heavy. Here is another scrap—

'Dear Willie—I am glad to send you the Maga [Blackwood's Magazine], which continues to be clever. I hope for two or three happy days on the brae-sides about the birthday [4th of June]. Blackwood has been assaulted by a fellow who came from Glasgow on purpose, and returned second best. The bibliopole is like the little French lawyer, who never found out he could fight till he was put to it, and was then for cudgelling all and sundry. You never saw anything so whimsical. * * I think often, of course, about my walks, and I am sickening to descend into the glen at the little waterfall by steps. We could cut excellent ones out where the quarry has been. It is the only way we shall ever make what Tom Purdie calls a *neat job*, for a deep descent will be ugly, and difficult to keep. I would plant betwixt the stair and the cascade, so as to hide the latter till you came down to the bottom.'

The employment of the people about Abbotsford seems to have engaged much of Sir Walter's attention, and on such subjects his views were patriotic and enlightened. In a letter dated December 1819, he says—'Above all, I would employ the people in draining wherever it is necessary, or may be improved. In this way many hands may be employed, and to the permanent advantage of the property. Why not drain the sheep-walk to purpose? As it is my intention to buy no books, and avoid all avoidable expenses, I hope to be able to spare L.100 or so extraordinary for my neighbours. I should be sorry that any of them thought I did this from either doubting them or fearing them. I have always consulted their interest in gratifying my own humour, and if they could find many a wiser master, they would scarce find any one more for their purpose.'

The same year (which was a period of some excitement and discontent) he writes again to Laidlaw—'I am glad you have got some provision for the poor. They are the minors of the state, and especially to be looked after; and I believe the best way to prevent discontent is to keep their minds moderately easy as to their own provision. The sensible part of them may probably have judgment enough to see that they could get nothing much better for their class in general by an appeal to force, by which, indeed, if successful, ambitious individuals might rise to distinction, but which would, after much misery, leave the body of the people just where it found them, or rather much worse.'

This considerate benevolence and liberality produced the expected reward. The labouring classes on the estate of Abbotsford and its neighbourhood were strongly attached to their illustrious master. At a later period, when the excitement of the Reform Bill penetrated even the most remote and quiet districts, Scott's popularity appeared to be partially shaded; but it was only a momentary cloud, and it occurred chiefly with the town population, not with the rural classes. In March 1831, he was present at a meeting of the freeholders of Roxburgh, held at Jedburgh, to pass resolutions against the Reform Bill. He was dragged to the meeting by the young Duke of Buccleuch and Mr Henry Scott of Harden, contrary to his prior resolution, and his promise to Miss Scott; for his health was then much shattered. 'He made a confused imaginative speech,' says Laidlaw, 'which was full of evil forebodings and mistaken views. The people who were auditors, in proportion to their love and reverence for him, felt disappointed and sore, and, like himself, were carried away by their temporary chagrin, to the great regret of the country around. The same people a few weeks afterwards, when Mr Oliver, the sheriff of Roxburgh, was foolishly swearing in constables at Melrose, said boldly, they need not bring them to fight against reform, for they would fight for it, but if any one meddled with Sir Walter Scott, they would fight for him.'

On all such subjects Scott and Laidlaw had frequent arguments, for the latter, as Lockhart says, was always a stout Whig. Sir Walter acknowledged to Hogg that he never found a mind so inexhaustible as Laidlaw's, for he had always something new to communicate, either in the way of speculation, information, or experiment.

The great crash in 1825-26, which involved the pecuniary ruin of Sir Walter, led to the breaking up of his establishment, and the derangement of all his plans. He announces the stunning event in an affecting letter to Mr Laidlaw, from which we extract a few passages:—'For you, my dear friend, we must part—that is, as laird and factor—and it rejoices me to think that your patience and endurance, which set me so good an example, are like to bring round better days. You never flattered my prosperity, and in my adversity, it is not the least painful consideration that I cannot any longer be useful to you. But Kaeside, I hope, will still be your residence, and I will have the advantage of your company and advice, and probably your services as amanuensis. Observe, I am not in indigence, though no longer in affluence, and if I am to exert myself in the common behalf, I must have honourable and easy means of life, although it will be my inclination to observe the most strict privacy, the better to save expense, and also time. Lady Scott's spirits were affected at first, but she is getting better. *For myself, I feel like the Eildon Hills—quite firm, though a little cloudy. I do not dislike the path which lies before me. I have seen all that society can show, and enjoyed all that wealth can give me, and I am satisfied much is vanity, if not vexation of spirit.* What can I say more? except that I will write to you the instant I know what is to be done. In the meantime, it is only necessary to say I am arranging my affairs, and mean to economise a good deal, and that I will pay every man his due.'

The following brief and pleasant note, without date, must be referred to 1827, as it was in June of that year that the Life of Napoleon was published:—

'My Dear Mr Laidlaw—I would be happy if you would come down at *hail-time* to-day. Napoleon (6000 copies) is sold for L.11,000!!! Yours truly, W. S.'

'*Sunday.*'

Mr Laidlaw at length removed from Kaeside, and Scott felt sorely the want of his habitual counsel and society. Under the date of August 1827, he writes in the following affectionate strain:—'Your leaving Kaeside makes a most melancholy blank to us. You, Mrs Laidlaw, and the bairns, were objects we met with so much pleasure, that it is painful to think of strangers being there. But they do not deserve good weather who cannot endure the bad, and so I would "set a stout heart to a stay [steep] brae;" yet I think the loss of our walks, plans, discussions, and debates, does not make the least privation that I experience from the loss of world's gear. But, *sursum corda*, and we shall have many happy days yet, and spend some of them together. I expect Walter and Jane, and then our long-separated family will be all together in peace and happiness. I hope Mrs Laidlaw and you will come down and spend a few days with us, and revisit your old haunts. I miss you terribly at this moment, being engaged in writing a planting article for the Quarterly, and not having patience to make some necessary calculations.'

Mr Laidlaw has written on the back of the communication—'This letter lies in the drawer in which the unfinished manuscript of Waverley was found, amongst fishing-tackle, &c. which yet remain. I got the desk as a present from Sir Walter.'

In 1830, a re-union took place. Mr Laidlaw took up his abode again at Kaeside, and remained in daily intercourse with Sir Walter till the time of his death. The record of those sad and painful days in Lockhart's Life is deeply interesting. Never was there a more affecting narrative; nor could there be a more instructive or ennobling example than Scott presented in his period of suffering and adversity. We will not attempt to lift the curtain again on this tragic scene, which saddened all Europe.

> A trouble, not of clouds, or weeping rain,
> Nor of the setting sun's pathetic light
> Engendered, hangs o'er Eildon's triple height!
> —*Wordsworth.*

Mr Laidlaw cherished with religious care all his memorials of Abbotsford, where, indeed, his heart may be said to have remained till its last pulsation. The desk in which the first manuscript of Waverley was deposited [see the introduction to the novel] stood in his room; the works inscribed and presented by the author were carefully ranged on his shelves; the letters he had received from him were treasured up; the pens with which Ivanhoe was written were laid past, and kept as a sacred thing; but, above all, he valued a brooch which was round the neck of Scott when he died. This ornament had been presented to Sir Walter Scott by his son, the present Sir Walter, and his wife (inscribed 'From Walter and Jane'), on the day of their marriage, and it contained some of the hair of each. When the grave had closed over the illustrious minstrel, his children gave the invaluable jewel to their own and their father's friend, accompanying the gift with some of the hair of Scott, which was also placed in the brooch—the white locks of age with the dark tresses of youth. Mr Laidlaw wore the brooch while a trace of sensibility remained, and it has descended to another generation—one of the most precious of the personal *reliquiæ* of a splendid but melancholy friendship.

THE LOCKSMITH OF PHILADELPHIA.

A STORY.*

Some years ago, in the city of Philadelphia, there lived an ingenious locksmith named Amos Sparks. Skilled as a maker and repairer of locks, he was particularly celebrated for his dexterity in opening them, when it was necessary to do so in cases of emergency. Like many men of talent in other departments, Amos Sparks was poor. Though a very industrious and prudent man, with a small and frugal family, he merely obtained a comfortable subsistence, but he never seemed to accumulate property. Whether it was that he was not of the race of money makers, whose instinctive desire of accumulation forces them to earn and hoard without a thought beyond the mere means of acquisition—or whether the time occupied by the prosecution of new inquiries into still undiscovered regions of his favourite pursuit, and in conversation with those who came to inspect and admire the fruits of his ingenuity, were the cause of his poverty, we cannot undertake to determine—but perhaps various causes combined to keep his finances low;

* We have abridged this story from a tale in an American newspaper, which we regret does not give the name of the writer.

and it was quite as notorious in the city that Amos Sparks was a poor man, as that he was an ingenious mechanic. But his business was sufficient for the supply of his wants and those of his family, and so he studied and worked on, and was content.

It happened that, in the autumn of 18—, a merchant in the city, whose business was extensive, and who had been bustling about the quay and on board his vessels all the morning, returned to his counting-house to lodge several thousand dollars in the Philadelphia bank, to renew some paper falling due that day; when, to his surprise, he had either lost or mislaid the key of his iron chest. After diligent search, with no success, he was led to conclude that, in drawing out his handkerchief, he had dropped the key in the street, or perhaps into the dock. What was to be done? It was one o'clock—the bank closed at three, and there was no time to advertise the key, or to muster so large a sum of money as that required. In his perplexity the merchant thought of the poor locksmith. He had often heard of Amos Sparks; the case seemed one particularly adapted to a trial of his powers—and being a desperate one, if he could not furnish a remedy, where else were there reasonable expectations of succour? A clerk was hurried off for Amos, and having explained the difficulty, speedily reappeared, followed by the locksmith with his implements in his hand.

The job proved more difficult than had been anticipated, and, fearful of losing credit by the delay, the merchant offered five dollars' reward to Amos if he would open the chest in as many minutes. Amos succeeded. The lock was picked, and the chest flew open. There the merchant's treasures lay, but they were not yet in his possession. As he enjoyed but a poor reputation for uprightness of dealing, Amos could not trust to his promise of payment. Holding the lid in his hand, he respectfully requested the sum which had been offered; and, as he had expected, it was refused. A much less sum was meanly proposed in its stead, on the plea that it was surely sufficient for a few minutes' work. Amos was indignant and inexorable. The merchant shuffled and fumed. In an instant down went the lid of the chest, and, fastening by a spring, it was again locked as securely as before.

The merchant looked aghast at Amos, and then darted a glance at the clock: the hand pointed to within twenty minutes of three, and seemed posting over the figures with the speed of light. What was to be done? At first he tried to bully, but it would not do. Amos told him, if he had sustained any injury, 'he might sue as soon as he pleased, for that his time was too precious just now to be wasted in trifling affairs;' and, with a face of unruffled composure, he turned on his heel and was leaving the office.

The merchant called him back—he had no alternative—his credit was at stake—he was humbled by the necessity of the case; and handing forth the five dollars, 'There, Sparks,' said he, 'take your money, and let us have no more words.'

'I must have ten dollars now,' replied the locksmith. 'You would have taken advantage of a poor man; and, besides opening your strong box there, I have a lesson to offer which is well worth a trifling sum. You would not only have deprived me of what had been fairly earned, but have tempted me into a lawsuit which would have ruined my family. You will never in future presume upon your wealth in your dealings with the poor, without thinking of the locksmith, and those five dollars may save you much sin and much repentance.'

This homily, besides being preached in a tone of calm determination, which left no room to hope for any abatement, had exhausted another minute or two of the time already so precious. The merchant hurriedly counted out the ten dollars, which Amos deliberately inspected, to see that they belonged to no insolvent bank, and then deposited them in his pocket. Having thus made quite sure of his reward, he dexterously opened the lock, and placed the merchant in possession of his property, in time to save his credit at the bank.

About a month after this affair, the Philadelphia bank was robbed of coin and notes to the amount of fifty thousand dollars. The bars of a window had been cut, and the vault entered so ingeniously, that it was evident the burglar had possessed, besides daring courage, a good deal of mechanical skill. The police scoured the city and country round about, but no clue to the discovery of the robbery could be traced. The public mind was powerfully excited. Everybody who had anything to lose, felt that daring and ingenious felons were abroad, who might probably pay them a visit; all were therefore interested in the discovery and the conviction of the perpetrator of so daring a deed. Suspicions at length began to settle on Sparks; but yet his poverty and known integrity seemed to give them the lie. The story of the iron chest, which the merchant had hitherto been ashamed, and Amos too forgiving, to tell—for the latter did not care to set the town laughing at the man who had wronged him—now began to be told. The merchant, influenced by a vindictive spirit, had whispered it to the directors of the bank, with sundry shrugs and inuendos; and of course it soon spread far and wide, with all sorts of exaggerated variations and additions. Amos thought for several days that some of his neighbours looked and acted rather oddly, and he missed one or two who used to drop in and chat almost every afternoon; but not suspecting for a moment that there was any cause for altered behaviour, these matters made but a slight impression on his mind. In all such cases, the person most interested is the last to hear disagreeable news; and the first hint that the locksmith got of the universal suspicion was from the officer of the police, who came with a party of constables to search his premises. Astonishment and grief were the portion of Amos and his family for that day. The first shock to a household who had derived, even amidst their humble poverty, much satisfaction from the possession of a good name—a property they had been taught to value above all earthly treasures—may be easily conceived. To have defrauded a neighbour of sixpence would have been a meanness no one of them would have been guilty of; but Fifty Thousand Dollars!!—the immensity of the sum seemed to clothe the suspicion with a weight of terror that nearly pressed them to the earth. They clung to each other, with bruised and fettered spirits, while the search was proceeding, and it was not until it was completed, and the officer declared himself satisfied that there was none of the missing property on the premises, that they began to rally, and looked calmly at the circumstances which seemed for the moment to menace the peace and security they had hitherto enjoyed.

'Cheer up, my darlings,' said Amos, who was the first to recover the sobriety of thought that usually characterised him—'cheer up—all will yet be well; it is impossible that the unjust suspicion can long hover about us. A life of honesty and fair-dealing will not be without its reward. There was perhaps something in my trade, and the skill which long practice had given me in it, that naturally enough led the credulous, the thoughtless, and perhaps the mischievous, if any such there be connected with this inquiry, to look towards us. But the real authors of this outrage will probably be discovered soon, for a fraud so extensive will make all parties vigilant; and if not, why, then, when our neighbours see us toiling at our usual occupations, with no evidences of secret wealth, or lavish expenditure, on our persons or at our board, and remember how many years we have been so occupied and so attired, without a suspicion of wrong-doing even in small matters attached to us, there will be good sense and good feeling enough in the city to do us justice.'

There was sound sense and much consolation in this reasoning: the obvious probabilities of the case were in favour of the fulfilment of the locksmith's expectations. But a scene of trial and excitement—of prolonged agony and hope deferred—lay before him, the extent of which it would have been difficult, if not impossible, for him then to have foreseen. Foiled in the search, the directors of the bank sent one of their body to negotiate with Amos—to offer him a large sum of money, and a guarantee from further molestation, if he would confess, restore the property, and give up his accomplices, if any there were. It was in vain that he protested his innocence, and avowed his abhorrence of the crime. The banker rallied him on his assumed composure, and threatened him with consequences; until the locksmith, who had been unaccustomed to dialogues founded on the presumption that he was a villain, ordered his tormentor out of his shop, with the spirit of a man who, though poor, was resolved to preserve his self-respect, and protect the sanctity of his dwelling from impertinent and insulting intrusion.

The banker retired, baffled, and threatening vengeance. A consultation was held, and it was finally determined to arrest Sparks and commit him to prison, in the hope that, by shutting him up, and separating him from his family and accomplices, he would be less upon his guard against the collection of evidence necessary to a conviction, and perhaps be frightened into terms, or induced to make a full confession. This was a severe blow to his family. They would have borne much together—for mutual counsel and sympathy can soothe many of the ills of life; but to be divided—to have the strongest mind, around which the feeble ones had been accustomed to cling, carried away captive, to brood in solitary confinement, on an unjust accusation, was almost too much, when coupled with the cloud of suspicion that seemed to gather around their home, and infect the very air they breathed. The privations forced upon them by the want of the locksmith's earnings were borne without a murmur; and out of the little that could be mustered, a portion was always reserved to buy some trifling but unexpected comfort or luxury to carry to the prisoner.

Some months having passed without Sparks having made any confession, or the discovery of any new fact whereby his guilt might be established, his prosecutors found themselves reluctantly compelled to bring him to trial. They had not a tittle of evidence, except some strange locks and implements found in the shop, and which proved the talent, but not the guilt, of the mechanic. But these were so various, and executed with such elaborate art, and such an evident expenditure of labour, that but few even of the judges, jury, or spectators, could be persuaded that a man so poor would have devoted himself so sedulously to such an employment, unless he had had some other object in view than mere instruction or amusement. His friends and neighbours gave him an excellent character; but on their cross examination, all admitted his entire devotion to his favourite pursuit. The counsel for the banker exerted himself with considerable ability. Calculating in some degree on the state of the public mind, and upon the influence which vague rumours, coupled with the evidences of the mechanic's handicraft exhibited in court, might have on the mind of the jury, he dwelt upon every ward and winding—on the story of the iron chest—on the evident poverty of the locksmith, and yet his apparent waste of time—and asked if all this work were not intended to insure success in some vast design? He believed that a verdict would be immediately followed by a confession, for he thought Amos guilty, and succeeded in making the belief pretty general among his audience. Some of the jury were half inclined to speculate on the probabilities of a confession, and, swept away by the current of suspicion, were not indisposed to convict without evidence, in order that the result might do credit to their penetration; but this was impossible, even in an American court of justice, in the good old times of which we write. Hanging persons on suspicion, and acquitting felons because the mob think murder no crime, are modern inventions. The charge of the judge was clear and decisive. He admitted that there were grounds of suspicion—that there were circumstances connected with the prisoner's peculiar mode of life that were not reconcilable with the lowness of his finances; but yet of direct testimony there was not a vestige, and of circumstantial evidence there were not only links wanting in the chain, but, in fact, there was not a single link extending beyond the locksmith's dwelling. Sparks was accordingly acquitted; but as no other clue was found to direct suspicion, it still lay upon him like a cloud. The vindictive merchant and the dissatisfied bankers did not hesitate to declare, that although the charge could not be legally brought home, they had no doubt whatever of his guilt. This opinion was taken up and reiterated, until thousands, who were too careless to investigate the story, were satisfied that Amos Sparks was a rogue. How should the character of a poor man hold out against the deliberate slanders of so many rich ones?

Amos rejoiced in his acquittal, as one who felt that the jury had performed a solemn duty faithfully, and who was glad to find that his present experience had strengthened rather than impaired his reliance on the tribunals of his country. He embraced his family as one snatched from great responsibility and peril; and his heart overflowed with thankfulness when at night they were all once more assembled round the fireside, the scene of so much happiness and amity in other days. But yet Amos felt that, though acquitted by the jury, he was not by the town: he saw that in the faces of some of the jury, and most of the audience, which he was too shrewd an observer to misunderstand. He wished it were otherwise; but he was contented to take his chance of some subsequent revelation; and if it came not, of living down the foul suspicion.

But Amos had never thought of how he was to live. The cold looks, averted faces, and rude scandal of the neighbours, could be borne, because really there was some excuse in the circumstances, and because he hoped that there would be a joyful ending of it all at some future day. But the loss of custom first opened his eyes to his real situation. No work came to his shop; he made articles, but he could not sell them; and as the little money he had saved was necessarily exhausted in the unavoidable expense of the trial, the family found it impossible, aided by the utmost exertion and economy, to meet their current outlay. One article of furniture after another was reluctantly sacrificed, or some little comfort abridged, until, at the end of months of degradation and absolute distress, their bare board was spread within bare walls, and it became necessary to beg, to starve, or to remove. The latter expedient had often been suggested in family consultations, and it is one that in America is the common remedy for all great calamities. The Sparkses would have removed, but they still clung to the hope that the real perpetrator would be discovered, and the mystery cleared up; and, besides, they thought it would be an acknowledgment of the justice of the general suspicion if they turned their backs and fled. They lived upon the expectation of the renewed confidence and companionship of old friends and neighbours, when Providence should deem it right to draw the veil aside. At length, to live longer in Philadelphia became impossible, and the whole family prepared to depart. Their effects were easily transported, and as they had had no credit since the arrest, there was nobody to prevent them from seeking a livelihood elsewhere.

Embarking in one of the river boats, they pushed up the Schuylkill, and settled at Norristown. The whole family being industrious and obliging, they soon began to gather little comforts around them; and as these were not embittered by the cold looks and insulting sneers of the neighbourhood, they were comparatively happy for a time. But even here there was for them no permanent place of rest. A traveller passing through Norristown, on his way from the capital to the Blue Mountains, recognised Sparks, and told somebody he knew that he wished the community joy of having added to the number of its inhabitants the notorious locksmith of Philadelphia. The news soon spread. The family found that they were shunned as they had formerly been by those who had known them longer than the good people of Norristown, and had a fair prospect of starvation opening before them. They removed again. This time there was no inducement to linger, for they had no local attachments to detain them. They crossed the mountains, and, descending into the vale of the Susquehanna, pitched their tent at Sunbury. Here the same temporary success excited the same hopes, only to be blighted in the bud by the breath of slander, which seemed so widely circulated as to leave them hardly any asylum within the limits of the State. We need not enumerate the different towns and villages in which they essayed to gain a livelihood, and failed. They had nearly crossed the State in its whole length, been driven from Pittsburg, and were slowly wending their way further west, and were standing on the high ground overlooking Middleton, as though doubtful if there was to be rest for the soles of their feet even there. They hesitated to try a new experiment. Sparks seated himself on a stone beneath a spreading sycamore—his family clustered around him on the grass: they had travelled far, and were weary, and, without speaking a word as their eyes met, and thinking of their prolonged sufferings and slender hopes, they burst into a flood of tears, in which Sparks, burying his face in the golden locks of the sweet girl who bowed her head upon his knee, joined audibly. At length, wiping away his tears, and checking the rising sobs that shook his manly bosom—'God's will be done, my children,' said the locksmith; 'we cannot help weeping, but let us not murmur. If we are to be wanderers and fugitives on the earth, let us never lose sight of the promise which assures us of an eternal refuge in a place where the wicked cease from troubling and the weary are at rest. I was perhaps too proud of that skill of mine—too apt to plume myself upon it, above others whose gifts had been less abundant. My error has been that of wiser and greater men, who have been made to feel that what we cherish as the means of obtaining earthly blessings, sometimes turns out a curse.'

To dissipate the gloom which hung over the whole party, and beguile the half hour they intended to rest in that sweet spot, Mrs Sparks drew out a Philadelphia newspaper which somebody had given her upon the road, and called their attention to the deaths and marriages, that they might see what changes were taking place in a city that still interested them, though they were banished for ever from its borders. She had hardly opened the paper when her eye glanced on an article which she was too much excited to read. Amos, wondering at the emotion displayed, gently disengaged the paper, and read—'Bank robber—Sparks not the man.' His own feelings were as powerfully interested as those of his wife, but his nerves were stronger; and he read out, to an audience whose ears devoured every syllable of the glad tidings, an account of the conviction and execution of a wretch in Albany, and who had confessed, among other daring and heinous crimes, the robbery of the Philadelphia bank, accounting for the disappearance of the property, and exonerating Sparks, whose face he had never seen. These were tidings of great joy to the weary wayfarers beneath the sycamore, whose hearts overflowed with thankfulness to the Father of mercy, who had given them strength to bear the burden of affliction, and had lifted it from their spirits ere they had been crushed beneath its weight. Their resolution to return to their native city was formed at once, and before a week had passed, they were slowly journeying to the capital of the State.

Meanwhile, an extraordinary revulsion of feeling had taken place at Philadelphia. Newspapers and other periodicals which had formerly been loud in condemnation of the locksmith, now blazoned abroad the robber's confession—wondered how any man could have been for a moment suspected upon such evidence as was adduced on the trial—drew pictures of the domestic felicity once enjoyed by the Sparkses, and then painted—partly from what was known of the reality, and partly from imagination—their sufferings, privations, and wrongs in the pilgrimage they had performed in fleeing from an unjust but damnatory accusation. The whole city rang with the story. Old friends and neighbours, who had been the first to shun them, now became the loud and vehement partisans of the family. The whole city was anxious to know where they were. Some reported that they had perished in the woods; others that they had been burnt in a prairie, which not a few believed; while another class averred that the locksmith, driven to desperation, had first destroyed his family, and then himself. All these stories of course created as much excitement as the robbery of the bank had done before, only that this time the tide set the other way; and when the poor locksmith and his family, who had been driven like vagabonds from the city, approached its suburbs, they were met, congratulated, and followed by thousands: in fact, theirs was almost a triumphal entry. And as the public always like to have a victim, Sparks was advised on all hands to bring an action against the directors of the bank: large damages would, they knew, be given, and the banker deserved to suffer for the causeless ruin brought on a poor but industrious family.

Sparks was reluctant to engage in any such proceeding. His character was vindicated, his business restored. He occupied his own shop, and his family were comfortable and content. But the current of public opinion was too strong for him. All Philadelphia had determined that the banker should suffer. An eminent lawyer volunteered to conduct the suit, and make no charge if a liberal verdict were not obtained. The locksmith pondered the matter well. His own wrongs he freely forgave, but he thought that there had been a readiness to secure the interests of a wealthy corporation by blasting the prospects of a humble mechanic, which, for the good of society, ought not to pass unrebuked. He felt that the moral effect of such a prosecution would be salutary, teaching the rich not to presume too far upon their affluence, and cheering the hearts of the poor while suffering unmerited persecution. The suit was commenced, and urged to trial, notwithstanding several attempts at compromise on the part of the banker. The pleadings on both sides were able and ingenious; but the counsel for the plaintiff had a theme worthy of the fine powers he possessed. At the close of a pathetic and powerful declamation, the audience, who had formerly condemned Amos in their hearts without evidence, were melted to tears by the recital of his sufferings; and when the jury returned with a verdict of ten thousand dollars damages against the banker, the locksmith was honoured by a ride home on their shoulders amidst a hurricane of cheers.

A VISIT TO THE GREAT BRITAIN.

One fine morning lately, as hinted at in a previous article, we set out to inspect the largest steam-ship which is at present afloat. She lay off Blackwall in the Thames, near London, and, by the liberality of her proprietors, the 'Great Western Steam Navigation Company,' as well as by the admirable arrangements of the managers of the Blackwall railway, the trip proved both easy of accomplishment and inexpensive. After a ten minutes' ride from Fenchurch Street, we were safely deposited on the Blackwall pier, to await the arrival of a miniature steamer which plied between the shore and the immense ship.

To those previously informed that the Great Britain is one-third larger than a first-rate ship of war, and that she carries six masts, the first view of her from a distance is generally—in reference to her magnitude—disappointing. It is not till the bows are passed, and the eye travels from one end to the other, that the vast dimensions of the Great Britain are understood. This line, though long, being very slightly bent near the head, and again at the stern, is graceful and elegant, not being interrupted by those hideous accompaniments to other steamers—paddle-boxes. Rowing beside her in a small boat, the distance from the fore to the after part of the ship may be likened to a short voyage. Under the rear part of the vessel, the chief novelty presents itself—which is the propeller. This is placed under the stern, between the stern post and the 'run' of the ship, and consists of a screw with six blades of solid iron, triangular in shape, fastened to a revolving shaft. Again the idea of smallness presents itself: the blades which appear above water seem quite diminutive, when it is considered what an immense mass they have to propel. The entire screw is only 15 feet 6 inches in diameter; yet, by its rapid revolutions, it has to drive forward a ship 322 feet long and 51 broad—a floating mass, in fact, equal to some 3450 tons, even when unencumbered with a cargo—and at the rate of 12 miles an hour. Viewed with reference to this enormous power, the screw appears like a mere toy.

Having glanced at the outside of the Great Britain, we ascended her side, and stood on her deck. The impressions of fragility and lightness were strengthened: the masts, even when close to them, appeared slender to insecurity; the rigging light; the bulwarks low and thin. As there is nothing to excite surprise so much as this general variance of the appearance of the actual ship with the preconceived ideas of its size and strength, it will be here necessary to explain whence this difference arises. The truth is, that, except the flooring and ornamental parts of the decks and cabins, the Great Britain is built of iron. After many experiments (for no previous experience existed to guide them), the Great Western Steam Company concluded that iron would afford greater strength, greater buoyancy, and more capacity, at less expense, than wood. The sides—formed of massive ribs varying from 14 to 21 inches apart—are lined within and covered without with plate iron five-eighths of an inch thick, so that the greater part of the sides is hollow. The bottom and keel are of solid iron, one inch thick, exclusive of the ribs. Even the rigging is of iron, for it is made of twisted wire. The quantity of metal used in the construction of the hull was 1400 tons. Now, it is easy to understand that the same number of tons' weight of the strongest wood would occupy infinitely more space, without affording additional strength: it is the closer disposition of materials about the ship which has given her the light, rakish appearance which first strikes the eye of an observer.

Of the length of the ship, the most complete *coup-d'œil* is to be obtained by walking to the after part of the deck, and thence looking straight a-head to the prow. The deck appears like two long narrow streets divided by the funnel, the six masts, the hatches, &c. which rise between them, to form one side; the bulwarks being the other. Along these two thoroughfares there is nothing to interrupt the smoothness of the wood-pavement; for the deck is what is called a 'flush' deck; that is to say, an even one, with no poop or other erection to alter its level, except at the forecastle, where there is a small break. The length of these two vistas bears so great a disproportion to their width, that the mind abandons calculation by means of feet and yards, and thinks of a mile. The actual length of this monster deck is, in fact, within a fraction of the sixteenth of a mile.

Having sufficiently examined and wondered at what was to be seen upon the upper deck, we descended to that below. This is divided into two parts by the space occupied by the cook-houses and machinery. It consists of two vast 'promenade saloons,' flanked by sleeping berths and state-rooms. The after-saloon was that which we first visited. It is elegantly fitted up and ornamented with coloured scrolls and flowers, to a degree which a man of severe taste would designate as finical. On each side of the promenade is a row of five doors, leading into the sleeping places; of which four are led to by every door, being divided by a short passage. The first door on each side of the saloon conducts to a 'ladies' boudoir,' whilst the fifth at either end opens into state or private rooms—of which there are eight—calculated for families. The sternmost part of the promenade is fitted up with sofas. The captain's cabin is a-midships, between the two companion stairs, which lead from the upper deck. Descending into the deck below, the counterpart of what had just been seen presented itself. This lower promenade is to be used as a dining-room; and, for the ladies' boudoirs, a steward's pantry and store-rooms are substituted. The number of sleeping berths is also greater, because there are no state-rooms. In the passage to the fore part of the vessel are, on one side, baths, lavatories, and other conveniences; and, on the other, the kitchen. This is most completely fitted with every conceivable apparatus for roasting, boiling, frying, grilling, and stewing; shadowing forth to all who can on a sea voyage enjoy them, a series of excellent and tempting dinners. At the end of the passage, the 'forward promenade saloon' is entered. Except in the shape, we saw nothing in the plan of this different from that of the after-saloon. It is of course much shorter, by reason of the sudden narrowing of the ship where the prow is formed. Where this narrowing begins, there is a partition, behind which are arranged the proper accommodations for the officers of the vessel. The saloon below is, like that 'aft' on the same level, the counterpart of the upper storey in general appearance, the partitioned part in the forecastle affording berths for the common sailors.

No one, after viewing these four saloons, but must be struck with the extent and completeness of accommodation which the Great Britain affords. Comfortable beds and berths are provided for as many as 360 passengers, without making up a single sofa.

Thus much of the passenger portion of the vessel; now for the locomotive department. Ascending to the upper deck, the spectator has to dive into the hot and black engine department by its own special entrance, composed of iron ladders. The bewildering mass of machinery which meets the view—bewildering rather from its vastness than from its complexity—is so distributed in the vessel as to form permanent ballast; and the middle of the ship has not to bear all its weight, as is the case in vessels with side paddles. It has to perform one very simple duty, which is to turn the screw we have already described, at the stern, with sufficient velocity to propel the ship. To effect this, four engines—the united power of which equals that of 1000 horses—are employed. Their action upon the machinery is readily understood. There is an enormous wheel or 'drum,' 18 feet in diameter, working on an axis or spindle. To either end of the spindle is attached an immense crank moved by one pair of engines, the other pair driving the crank at the opposite end of the axis; so that the whole four expend their force upon the gigantic drum to whirl it round. The duty of this large wheel is to cause a band composed of four iron chains to revolve with it; that, in the regions below, they may pass round and turn another and smaller wheel. Of course the chains make this little wheel revolve as much oftener as it is smaller than the *grosse caisse* or big drum; an operation they perform—a singularity in such cases—without the slightest noise. The great fault of the 'Archimedes,' in which vessel the principle adopted in the Great Britain was first tried, was the intolerable noise made by the machinery that conveyed motion to the screw. The engineers of the monster ship have obviated this objection by having each link of their chains supplied with a tooth, which juts into grooves made in both wheels, so as to 'bite' them as they pass round. Though weighing seven tons, therefore, the chains work quite silently. The little wheel below has for its axis one end of a long horizontal shaft, to the other extremity of which is attached the propeller, which we had previously seen outside at the stern, and which is made to revolve as fast as the little wheel in the water. Here is the whole secret of propulsion in the Great Britain.

The iron shaft which communicates motion to the propeller is not the least curious part of the machinery; on account of the distance of the steam power from the stern, it is 130 feet long. Each end is of solid iron—that at the smaller wheel next the engines being 28 feet in length, with a diameter of 16 inches; that to which the propeller is fastened being of the same diameter, but only 25½ feet long. The intermediate part of the shaft is hollow, 2 feet 8 inches in diameter, and 68 feet long; and this makes up the entire longitude of 130 feet. Although so much of the shaft is hollow, it weighs 38 tons.

The immense velocity with which the shaft is made to turn in order to propel the vessel, would heat it to a dangerous degree, were not means of continual cooling employed. This is effected by numerous holes in the side of the hull, through which water is constantly poured upon and within the hollow part of the shaft. It has been calculated by actual experiment that, on an average, for every three times the engine revolves in a minute, the ship will be driven through the water 2 miles in an hour. Thus 12 revolutions per minute propels her 8 miles an hour. The rate at which the vessel is intended to work her way across the Atlantic is 12 miles per hour, which will require her engines to make 18 revolutions every minute.

Having inspected as much of the machinery as we were able to see, we were preparing to ascend, when the sound of blacksmiths' hammers induced us to look through the iron grating on which we stood. A lower abyss was revealed to us by the lurid glare of a forge fire. It was the blacksmith's shop. An iron ship is of course obliged to carry blacksmiths instead of carpenters. Not having either curiosity or courage to descend, we regained the upper deck.

The leading peculiarity of the Great Britain is her great size. On this subject much has been said both *pro* and *con*. Looking at her in a nautical and scientific point of view, it is an important advantage, for reasons which are not very generally understood. It has been ascertained from past experience, that the tonnage or power of carrying cargo increases in a triple ratio with increase of size; whilst the requisite power and fuel augments only in a twofold ratio to the increase of dimension.* On this account, we find that though the ship contains nearly 800 tons' weight of machinery, with stowage for 1200 tons of coal, and 200 tons of water (in the boilers), yet she is capable of carrying 1000 tons besides of cargo, independent of passengers. On the other hand, looking at the Great Britain in a commercial point of view, much doubt exists as to whether a sufficient number of passengers, and a sufficient quantity of goods, can be collected to make her rapid voyages to New York profitable. It is well known that the British Queen failed from want of patronage in these respects. Whether the Great Britain will prove a profitable vessel to her owners, time can only determine. We sincerely hope she may.

As regards safety, every precaution has been employed in constructing the Great Britain. She is built in distinct compartments, each water-tight, and independent of the other. All steamers, whether on the score of humanity or for the preservation of property, ought to be so built; for if a vessel be divided into five or six compartments, and any one of them should from accident fill, her buoyancy would only be slightly affected. If two compartments fill, and these two were not at the extremes, the other compartments would still keep her afloat. If two consecutive compartments, either forward or aft, fill, it is certain that, were she to go down head or stern foremost, she would be some time about it; long enough, probably, to allow of all the boats being got in readiness. The Great Britain is provided, in case of such an emergency, with four large life-boats of iron, and two boats of wood, which are suspended from davits over the side of the ship, whilst one large life-boat is kept on the deck. The whole are capable of carrying 400 persons: though by far the most effectual precaution is the system of independent compartments. As a proof of its efficacy, we may instance the case of the Nemesis, which struck some time ago on the English Stones in the Bristol Channel, going nine or ten knots an hour: she slid off, after making such a slit as filled the forward compartment. She steamed several hours with the compartment full, until she obtained additional pumps in Mount's Bay, with which the space was pumped out, and the leak stopped. At Portsmouth she was examined, and drawings of the damage were made by an employé of the Great Western Company: she was repaired in a few hours, at an expense of about L.30, and then started for China. An instance of the time a complete wreck takes to go down, so as to enable the crew to escape, was afforded by the Brigand, a large iron steamer, which had been trading between Liverpool and Bristol. She struck on sunken rocks off the Scilly Islands, filled a forward compartment, and had some part of her paddle-wheel forced so far into the engine-room as to damage the plates and fill that part also. She remained afloat, in consequence of the remaining compartments, long enough to enable the crew to save themselves and their kits comfortably, and then went down in deep water.

The Great Britain was begun in 1839, and was so far finished as to be launched on the 19th of July 1843. After this, an unforeseen circumstance occurred—she was imprisoned in the Bristol docks during several months; for, when her engines were shipped, she sunk so low as to bring her greatest breadth in contact with the too narrow sides of the lock. This caused great inconvenience to her owners, and some merriment to the public. The truth is, her dimensions were well adapted for a free passage through the locks when light, but it was deemed advisable to put the engines on board before she left the works, which rendered it imperative that a certain degree of temporary accommodation, in widening the top of the locks, should be afforded. The directors of the Dock Company having at length afforded all the requisite facilities, she was on the 12th December liberated and taken down the Avon and the Bristol Channel on her first trial trip. This proved satisfactory in every respect, and the Great Britain, in the beginning of the present year, steamed round to London, beating the fastest steamer that could be found to race with her. Since then, she has gone round to Liverpool, awaiting sailing orders for America.

We left her, much gratified by our visit; and having been put on shore, ended the day very agreeably with a dinner of white-bait, which is somehow generally associated with a visit to Blackwall.

* Vide Athenæum, No. 901.

CATTLE SHOWS.

We should imagine that the descendants of Jack Sprat, who, it may be remembered by the students of our early ballad literature, 'could eat no fat,' must have vanished from the land; or else that his progeny must have wonderfully increased, and that they all take after their mother, who, according to the bard, 'could eat no lean.' We have been led into this speculative reflection by a knowledge of the fact, that sixty thousand people went to Baker Street bazaar to see the cattle show—to feast their eyes on panting porkers, asthmatic sheep, and apoplectic oxen. We should doubt whether the meat is better because the animals are stuffed out to a size hitherto unparalleled, except on the external paintings of penny shows, where the living monsters are represented about twice the height and breadth of the caravan where the public are invited to visit them. The present, however, is the age of enlargement. Shopkeepers make arrangements for the enlargement of their premises; the legislature decrees the enlargement of prisoners for debt; newspaper proprietors enlarge their sheets; and, in order to keep pace with the enlarged views which are prevalent in the present day, the agriculturists have commenced permanently enlarging their cattle. Perhaps the remains of gigantic animals that geologists have occasionally lighted on, may be traced to some antediluvian cattle show; and our ancestors may have rushed to an exhibition of prize mammoths with the same eagerness we of the present day evince in running after overgrown beeves, and alarmingly blown-out muttons. As we are informed that there is still 'room for improvement,' we must presume that more extensive bullocks, and more extravagantly exaggerated sheep, than any we have yet seen, are threatened by the Smithfield Cattle Club. To us there is something painfully pantomimic in the thought; and we look forward to the possibility of the extinction of mutton-chops, except as huge joints—a state of things that will be ruinous to the pure chop-house interest. Already does Brobdignagian beef choke up the entrance to the butchers' shops; and extensive, indeed, must be the scale upon which the business of weighing it is conducted. It has occurred to us, that the same care and expense which are lavished on the fattening of animals, might be beneficially applied to the feeding of our own species, and we would suggest that the experiment should be tried, by offering premiums for prize paupers. It is, however, to be feared that the prize pauper-show would not turn out a very satisfactory affair; for, though unlimited oatmeal has a fattening effect on beasts, the same substance, diluted into gruel, and that very sparingly administered, would hardly produce, in human beings, a degree of obesity that would fit them to enter the pens of Baker Street in competition with the annual cattle show. Perhaps the system would answer better for schoolmasters, who might form themselves into a Fat-boy Club, and exhibit annual specimens of the pinguidity attained by the scholars of their respective establishments. This would enable parents to select for their sons a school where the quality of the keep could be at once judged of by the plumpness of the boys exhibited. We merely throw out these hints as suggestions for improving the human race, by applying the principle of cattle shows, which are said to be extremely conducive to the amelioration of the breed of animals.—*Cruikshank's Table-Book.*

DESTRUCTION OF WASPS.

We observe, from the Scottish newspapers, that the Earl of Traquair has for several years past given a liberal reward to the children in the neighbourhood for the destruction of those troublesome insects during the months of April and May. At that period every wasp is in search of a location for a nest, and if unmolested, would become the parent of thousands. Owing, it may be supposed, to the limited fall of rain or snow last winter, these noxious creatures have been unusually numerous this season, as the following account will show:—The children, about fifty in number, were desired by his lordship to attend at Traquair House with their spoil every Saturday afternoon, where they were counted by the gardener, and each one paid so much per dozen. On the 26th April there were delivered 756 dozen, on the 3d May 114 dozen, on the 10th May 59½ dozen, and on the 17th May 643½ dozen—making in all the incredible number of 18,876 wasps' nests in the course of four weeks, and in one parish. It may be presumed, if each of these had been allowed to multiply, however favourable the season may prove, there would have been little fruit or honey left for miles around.

IRISH ANTIQUITIES.

'As I was passing a place called Lavey Strand, on the road from Cavan to Dublin,' says a correspondent of the Gardeners' Chronicle for June, 'I observed the bottom of an ancient canoe lying on the shore of the lake close to the road. I immediately went to examine it, and heard that it had been raised about a year ago from the bottom of the lake. When discovered, there was a gunwale above a foot in height along the sides, which, when I saw it, was almost entirely broken away. It was of very rude manufacture, hollowed out of the stem of an oak tree. The dimensions are gigantic. The bottom is four feet three inches across at one end, and about three feet at the other; the length is forty feet. The diameter of the tree could not possibly have been less than seven feet and a half at the root, and at least five and a half at the height of forty feet. This would allow only a very moderate bulge for the canoe. What could have been the use of so large a canoe, made with great toil, on so small a piece of water (not containing 200 acres), I cannot conjecture. There are two islands in the lake, which were found to be artificial when the proprietor was planting them about ten years ago. The earth is supported by a frame-work of enormous oak beams, mortised into each other, and this is supported on piles driven into the lake bottom. Some brass Celtic hatchets, ring money, and four brass swords, were found above the frame-work; and there is another canoe of smaller dimensions lying partly exposed and partly in the mud, near where the large one was found. The modern oak of this part of Ireland is not at all remarkable for its size.'

THE HAND.

[From 'Lays and Legends Illustrative of English Life,' by Camilla Toulmin.]

What is it, fashioned wondrously, that, twin-born with the brain,
Marks man from every meaner thing that bounds across the plain,
Or gambols in the mighty deep, or floats in summer air?
What is the help meet for the mind, no lesser life may share?
It is the Hand, the Human Hand, interpreter of will—
Was ever servant yet so great, and so obedient still?
Of all Creation's mysteries with which the world is rife,
It seems a marvel to my soul but second unto life!
How weak a thing of flesh it is, yet think what it has done,
And ask from poor idolaters why it no worship won.
How could the lordly forest trees first bow their heads to man,
When with their ruined limbs he delved where veins of metal ran!
Ho! ho! 'tis found, and his to know the secrets of the forge,
And henceforth earth at his behest her riches must disgorge;
And now the Hand has servants fit, it guides as it is schooled,
To keep entire the perfect chain by which the world is ruled.
For when the molten iron flowed into the first rough mould,
The heritage of cunning craft was to the right hand sold;
And it hath been a careful lord, improving every right,
Until the mind is overawed by thinking of its might.
How slender and how fair a thing is woman's soft white hand,
Yet Saragozza's maid could seize the cannon's ready brand,
And martyred Joan (but not of war or carnage would I tell,
Unless the time were ripe, and mine the deep-toned honoured shell,
Whose notes should be the requiem of the gory monarch dread—
Whose laurels still, though steeped in tears, conceal his leprous head)!
The harp is roused by fingers fair, where clinging jewels glow
With light upon the awak'ning hand, like sunbeams upon snow;
Entranced music's soul returns once more to earth again,
A vassal to the hand that wills a gay or pensive strain.
Yet think that hand which never yet knew weariness or soil,
Whose fairness neither summer's sun nor winter's cold must spoil,
Which doth not know a harsher rule than leisure's chosen toil,
Is after all but fashioned like the trembling clammy thing
With which the faded sempstress pale, in youth's yet early spring,
Digs her own grave with needle small, through nature's drowsy night—
Oh, when will fortune—justice too—unbind their eyes to light?
How is it fashion's proud array, thus wove on death's own loom,
Ne'er changes by a demon spell to trappings of the tomb?
The painter bodies forth ideas, which on the canvas live,
The sculptor bids the shapeless stone a form of beauty give;
Wise Egypt's giant Pyramids by human hands were piled,
To wrestle still with conquering time, though centuries have smiled
With gentle touch to think how they sweep man from where he stands,
Yet linger o'er the records of his wonder-working hands!
It is a thought to lift the soul beyond its prison home,
To ponder o'er such things as these beneath the fretted dome
Of Gothic fane where erst have swept the serge-clad monkish train,
Who sought to win their paradise by self-inflicted pain—
Who never knew the worship true that life's pure joys impart—
Yet what a world and history is every human heart!
Alas! material monuments too oft, like Babel's tower,
But tell of human littleness, and not of human power!
More subtle—less self-evident than marvels such as these—
Those spirit-deeds that leave behind but dream-like legacies—
Nothing that sense can see or touch, but much that thought can keep,
As when the stately ship is taught its pathway o'er the deep
By one right hand that guides the helm, beneath the watchful crowd
Of ever-silent stars that pierce through nature's nightly shroud.
But thought is lost in mazy dreams of all the wondrous band
Of things and deeds that owe their birth unto the Human Hand!

Published by W. and R. Chambers, Edinburgh; and, with their permission, by W. S. Orr, Amen Corner, London.—Printed by Bradbury and Evans, Whitefriars, London.

☞ Complete sets of the Journal, *First Series*, in twelve volumes, and also odd numbers to complete sets, may be had from the publishers or their agents.—A stamped edition of the Journal is now issued, price 2½d., to go free by post.

CONDUCTED BY WILLIAM AND ROBERT CHAMBERS, EDITORS OF 'CHAMBERS'S INFORMATION FOR THE PEOPLE,' 'CHAMBERS'S EDUCATIONAL COURSE,' &c.

No. 84. New Series. SATURDAY, AUGUST 9, 1845. Price 1½d.

JACOBINISM IN THE NURSERY.

It is fortunate for the adult, that children are dispersed in little parcels of four and a half individuals throughout private families; for, were it otherwise, they would certainly be found less manageable as a class than they are. Combined in masses—formed into unions—covenanted by charters—they might become seriously troublesome to papas and schoolmasters; and a servile might be found as nothing in comparison with an infantile war. I do not wish to see them become a rising generation in this sense; but I fully admit that we full-grown people give them all imaginable occasion for springing up in rebellion against us. The young are everywhere over the world an ill-used set of persons.

It is rather surprising, in an age when so many claims for class emancipation have been considered, that there should never have been the least attention bestowed upon the oppressed denizens of our firesides. Children are everywhere committed to an irresponsible power. Irresponsible power is acknowledged to be liable to great abuse. Yet we never think of children being in danger of suffering from this cause. There is here a selfish feeling which seems to preside in monarchists and republicans alike: all are decided for maintaining absolutism over the young. Let nations make themselves free from intruding conquerors, or sections of a people successfully assert their title to equal rights; but the young of every state, of every class, of every descent, must remain the thralls and serfs of their elders. There has never been any Tell, or Luther, or Wallace among the juveniles. And nobody dreams that there is the least occasion for such assertors of infantine liberty. Even philanthropists are silent upon this point. Nevertheless, I dare to believe that there is a vast tyranny in this department of our social economy, and that it calls for, and is capable of, remedy.

It is remarkable as, generally speaking, a well-meaning tyranny. Big man wishes well to little man. Big man is anxious to make little man as good—that is, as like himself as possible. Big man would take a great deal of trouble, and even endure a considerable sacrifice of his own feelings, for the sake of little man. Witness the sufferings which big man often undergoes in thrashing little man. Witness the distress of mind which it often costs big man to deny indulgences to little man. The misfortune is, that big man is only a kind of child himself—an unenlightened impulsive being, who either does not know what he ought to do, or, if otherwise, cannot do it; so that little man has no chance of being rightly dealt with by him. It is much worse when big man comes to have a notion of duty towards little man; for then he only pursues his wrong courses with more doggedness or fury. The lashes inflicted, and the restraints imposed by conscience, are the most cruel of all. Heaven pity little man when he falls into the hands of a papa with a conscience!

I entirely deny every pretended right of the adult to exercise any control over the young, beyond what is rigidly definable as moral influence. No control of a different kind from this is needed in the case; and no such control can be used without injury to both parties. Such control is therefore to be condemned. We have here a question taking its place beside that respecting the abolition of capital punishments, and others in which the precepts of pure Christianity, harmonising with the dictates of the highest philosophy, are proposed to be for the first time followed. The stripes, snubbings, scoldings, privations, prisonings, disgracings, with which children are visited by their protectors, form, as it were, a dispensation of the inferior feelings, which must pass away, along with all other systems having the same bad foundation. Reason and affection are the true bases of the relation of parent and child, as they are the bases of all good social relations; and I venture to propound that there is no more necessity for ever departing, with respect to the young, from the rules of courtesy and good-breeding, than there is in our intercourse with equals in the common world.

Adults who for the first time undertake the charge of a child, usually commence with a bustling, anxious feeling of responsibility, and a sad want of faith in human nature. The sense of a tremendous coming struggle with something singularly perverse and difficult, is upon them, and they rush into a fight with one who is without the power either to aggress or to defend. There is something almost ludicrous in this disproportion between the subject of treatment and the treatment itself. It is like attacking a fly in a full suit of armour. The young human being is, in reality, a simple, innocent, tractable sort of creature. He is absolutely the same as his ruler, only without the wickedness and depraved reason which often belong to that person. Why all this terror about these poor harmless little men, as worthy Mr Burchell called them? The common feeling seems to be—he is a determined liar; let us flog it out of him: whereas it is only the natural and justifiable dread of these floggings which prompts the lie. He is sure to misjudge everything, and fall into irremediable error, if left to exercise his own reason: therefore let us force him to all the conclusions at which we have ourselves arrived: the consequence of which is, that his reason, not being exercised, becomes liable to errors which it would otherwise be in no danger of. He is wild and reckless, caring little for his parents and best benefactors: therefore let us assert due authority over, and exact due honour from him; the means taken for this purpose being exactly those which unavoidably alienate regard, and either excite rebellion or produce the worse evil of an utterly broken spirit. He has no liking for his tasks, or for anything but play: therefore let us see to keep him at his books, and the more rigidly at those which he likes least; whence it results that the real aptitudes of the child for mental improvement are altogether misdirected, and he is inspired with disgust for what he might have otherwise embraced with eagerness. But, above all mistakes, is that of supposing that the better nature of a child is to be evoked and raised into the strength which we would desire to see it have in the full-grown man, by making him pass through a cold and cheerless youth. The very contrary is the case. A system of petty restraints and privations, of severe looks and incessant chidings, can only result in depraving the feelings and perverting the reason of a young person. He is, in such circumstances, entirely out of harmony with nature. He is like a flower which requires light and warmth, placed in a cold cellar, where it never can acquire its proper proportions, or colouring, or vigour. It is quite impossible that a child so treated can ever attain to the proper characteristics of a well-constituted and healthy man or woman.

Many big-man tyrants would, I verily believe, willingly adopt a different system, if they could be convinced that little man is capable of being brought to reasonable perfection otherwise. Now, I admit that the ordinary plan has usage on its side; but I would say that it is not by any means clear that the usage has been successful, seeing that many youths grow up very differently from what is expected; and that the children of the more awfully good are sometimes remarked to turn out the worst. To come more closely to the point, I would ask if there be anything in our common experiences of life to prove the efficiency of a system of terror and severity. Is it not rather found, when we use violence in act or in speech towards our fellow-creatures, or in any way treat them derogatorily, that we lose all right control over them? Do they not then usually take a stand upon their firmness and self-esteem, and set us at defiance? How, then, should it be supposed that discourtesy, harshness, painful restrictions upon personal freedom, taunts, scoldings, or any other contumelious treatment, is to succeed with children? Is it not evident, since they have the same nature as ourselves, that such treatment can only rouse their inferior feelings, as it does our own, and render them just so much the more unfit subjects of all right influence?

It is not upon the strength of theory alone that I venture to recommend the introduction into the nursery of the same principles which govern the drawing-room. My counsel is, that we should speak and act towards children upon the simple understanding that they are beings with feelings like ourselves, to be operated upon, as our own are, for good and for evil results. Seeing that we feel the force of kindness, of justice, and of reason, in our intercourse with society, I recommend that these principles alone should predominate in our relations with the young. I would never address to them a rude, harsh, or discourteous word; never exhibit before them any such passion as anger, or appeal to so mean a thing as punishment for effecting an end with them. Coming before them simply as friendly associates, possessing some advantage over them in point of experience and maturity of judgment, I would look for influence over them, as far as I desired any, simply to the love which a long course of endearing conduct must unavoidably engender in their breasts. There is, in reality, less need for what is called influence over children than is generally supposed. To give their faculties a chance of being rightly developed, they should be allowed to work out much for themselves. If the circumstances in which they are placed be pure, they will be pure also: there is no need, in such a case, for the perpetual ordering and directing which some parents deem necessary. If they be made, as they ought to be, confidential equals and friends, authority will be found an absurdity; for who seeks to have an authority over his friends? The true influence is that of love and respect, the same power which enables one man to acquire standing amongst others in the common world. With this aid, there is nothing impossible in the management of children. It is the silken tie which binds more fast than chains of iron. Thus treated, I conceive that the infantine mind would expand much more vigorously than it usually does under the rule of fear. The product must be a man instead of a slave.

It will appear to many that the impulses of a large proportion of children are not to be guided or controlled in this manner. There is sometimes seen in children, particularly of the male sex, a recklessness and waywardness which it does not appear that anything but force could duly govern. I question if such impulses are, except in a few cases, of an evil nature. Mere burstings of the spirit of enterprise and activity they mostly are, which it is only necessary to direct to good ends, in order to turn them to good account. Often what we complain of in children is the natural fruit of that system of force and fear upon which we have proceeded in our intercourse with them. With really evil dispositions, it might possibly be shown that the one system is no more efficient than the other.

Patrons of terror and severity—all ye who, from natural moroseness or mistaken dogmas, do what in ye lies to make children miserable—think for a moment what a terrible thing it is if ye be wrong in the course you take. Let the gentle innocence and helplessness of childhood plead with you for a reconsideration of your system. Reflect what it is to darken a sunshine which God himself has spread in the being of your little ones. Look forward to the day when ye shall be as children in the hands of those now young, and what it would be were they to visit your unresisting weakness with penalties such as ye now, with no better cause, inflict upon them in the morn and liquid dew of life. Oh, ponder well on these things, and so change your hand, and check your pride, that tears shall be dried, and the merry laugh introduced where it ought to be. What a rich reward will be yours in affection and true obedience, instead of the hypocritical docility which attends the system of terror! How delightful will it be to see minds thus allowed to expand to their fair proportions, instead of being cramped and withered by base cruelty! And how precious, above all estimation, will be the reflection, that, come what may of these children of your heart's hopes, at least one portion of their life has been, by your means, made a thing of beauty and a joy for ever!

THE HOME-WRECK.

FIRST PART.

A FEW years since I visited Devonshire to make the acquaintance of some distant relations, whom circumstances had prevented me from before seeing. Amongst others there was one who lived in a decayed family mansion about six miles east of the pretty town of Dartmouth. Before calling on her, I was prepared, by report, to behold a very aged and a very eccentric lady. Her age no one knew, but she seemed much older than her only servant—a hardy old dame, who, during the very month of my visit, had completed her ninety-ninth year.

The mistress never allowed any one to see her, save a young and interesting cousin of mine. She seldom went out except on Sundays, and then was carried to church in an old sedan chair by a couple of labourers, who did odd jobs of gardening about the house. She had such an insuperable objection to be seen by anybody, whether at home or abroad, that she concealed her face by a thick veil.

These, with other particulars, were narrated to me by my cousin as we rode towards Coote-down Hall, in which the old lady resided, and which, with the surrounding estate, was her own property. On approaching it, signs of past grandeur and present decay presented themselves. The avenue leading to the house had evidently been thickly planted; but now only a few stumps remained to mark where noble and spreading elms once had been. Having arrived at the house, my cousin reined up at the steps of the hall, upon which she, in a low cautious voice, desired me to alight. Having assisted her out of her saddle, I was about to utter some exclamation of surprise at the extreme dilapidation of the place, when she whispered me to be silent, adding, that I must not stir until she had returned from within, to announce whether my visit would be accepted or not.

During her absence, I had full leisure to look around and note the desolate condition of Coote-down. The lawn—thickly overspread with rank grass—could scarcely be distinguished from the fish-pond, which was completely covered with water-weeds. The shrubbery was choked and tangled, whilst a very wide rent in the wall laid open to view an enclosure which had been once a garden, but was now a wilderness. For a time the sorrowful effect which all this decay produced on my mind was increased by the extreme solitude which reigned around. This, however, was presently relieved by a cackling sign of life which issued from a brood-hen as it flew from the sill of a side-parlour window. On casting my eyes further into the landscape, I also perceived a very fat cow lazily browsing on the rich pasture of a paddock.

On turning round to view the house, new tokens of desolation were visible. Its shattered casements and worm-eaten doors, with tufts of weed growing at each corner, showed that for many years the front of the mansion had not been inhabited or its doors opened. One evidence of fallen grandeur was highly characteristic—over the porch the family arms had been carved in stone, but was now scarcely distinguishable from dilapidation: a sparrow had established a comfortable nest in the mouth of the helmet, and a griffin 'rampant' had fallen from his place beside the shield, and tamely lay overgrown with weeds.

These observations were interrupted by the light step of my cousin, who came to inform me that the lady of the house, after much persuasion, had consented to receive me. Conducting me to the back of the mansion, my fair guide took me through a dark passage into a sort of kitchen. A high and ample 'settle' stood, as is usual in farm-houses, before the hearth. In one corner of this seat reclined a figure bent with age, her face concealed by a thick veil. In the other corner was an old cheerful-looking woman busily knitting, and mumbling rather than singing a quaint old ballad.

The mistress of Coote-down made a feeble attempt to rise when my cousin presented me; but I intreated her to keep her seat. Having procured a chair for my fellow visitor (for the old domestic took not the smallest notice of us, but went on with her work as if we were not present), I established myself beside the hostess, and addressed to her a few commonplace words of greeting. She replied in a voice far less feeble than I had expected to hear from so decrepit a person; but what she said was no answer to my salutation. She went on with surprising clearness, explaining to me the degree of relationship which we bore to each other, and traced my pedigree till it joined her own; continued our mutual genealogy back to the Damnonii of Cornwall, hinting that our ancestors of that period were large mining proprietors, who sold tin to the Phœnicians! At first she spoke with doubt and hesitation, as if she feared to make some mistake; but the moment she got to where our branches joined—to the trunk, as it were, of our family tree—she went on glibly, like a child repeating a well-conned lesson. All this while the old attendant kept up the unceasing accompaniment of her ballad, which she must have sung through several times, for I heard the first line—

'A bailie's daughter, fair was she'—

at least thrice.

Though I addressed several questions to my singular relation, she made no attempt to answer them. It seemed that what she had uttered was all she was capable of: and this, I learnt afterwards, was partly true. Circumstances of her early life had given her a taste for family history, particularly that of her own, and her faculties, though otherwise impaired, still retained everything relating to what concerned her ancestry.

On our way back from this singular scene, my cousin remarked that it had saddened me. 'It would sadden you more,' she continued, 'were you to know the history of the domestic wreck we have just left behind.'

'That is precisely what I intended to inquire of you.'

'It is a deeply affecting story; but'—and here the young lady blushed and hesitated:—'I think it would not be right in me to reveal it. I believe I am the only person existing who knows the truth; and the means by which I obtained my knowledge would be deemed scarcely correct, though not perhaps exactly dishonourable.'

This avowal sharpened my curiosity, and I intreated her to say at least how she became possessed of the story.

'To that there can be no objection,' was the reply. 'In one of my rambles over the old house, I espied in a small escritoire a packet of letters bound up in tape, which was sealed at the ends. The tape had, however, been eaten by moths, and the letters liberated from it. Female curiosity prompted me to read them, and they gave me a full exposition of our great-aunt's early history.'

During the rest of my stay in that part of the country, I never failed to urge my cousin to narrate the events which had brought Coote-down to its present melancholy plight. But it was not till I called to take leave of her, perhaps for ever, that she complied. On that occasion, she placed in my hands a neatly-written manuscript in her own handwriting, which she said contained all the particulars I required. Circumstances have since occurred that render it not indelicate in me to publish the narrative, which I do with but little alteration.

In the middle of the last century the proprietor of Coote-down was Charles James Hardman, to whom the estate lineally descended from a long line of ancestors. He was from his youth a person of an easy disposition, who minded very little, so that he could follow his ordinary amusements, and could see everybody around him contented; though his habits were too indolent to improve the condition of his dependents by any efforts of his own. At the age of twenty-five, he married the heiress of a baronet belonging to the northern side of the county. She was a beauty and a belle—a lady full of determination and spirit; consequently the very opposite to himself. She was, moreover, two years his senior. As was predicted by those who knew the couple intimately, the match was not productive of happiness, and they had been married scarcely a year and a half, when they separated. It appeared that this unpleasant step was solely the fault of the wife; and her father was so incensed at her rash conduct, that he altered his will, and left the whole of his property to Hardman. Meanwhile, it was given out that the lady had brought her lord a son, and it was hoped that this event would prove a means of reconciling the differences which existed between them. Despite all intreaties, however, Mrs Hardman refused to return to her husband's roof.

Ten years passed, and she lived so completely in retirement, that she deprived herself even of the society of her child; for when the period of nursing was over, she sent him to Coote-down Hall, where he was educated. At the end of that period her father died; and, to her great disappointment, instead of finding herself uncontrolled mistress of a large fortune, she discovered it was so left, that unless she returned to her husband, she would be unable to benefit by it in the smallest degree. Mutual friends again interfered, and, after some difficulty, persuaded her to meet Hardman at her father's funeral, which she appeared to have no objection to attend. The happy result was, that a reconciliation took place, and she resumed her proper station as the lady of Coote-down Hall. It was, however, observed that, before she returned, the little son was sent away to continue his education in a foreign seminary.

Privy to all these arrangements, and in fact the chief mover in them, was Hardman's attorney. Such was the squire's indolence of disposition, that to this individual he confided everything; not only the management of his estates, the receipt and payment of all monies, but the arrangement of his most secret transactions. But, Mr Dodbury bearing the character of a highly just and honourable man, no suspicion ever existed that he abused the absolute, unbounded trust reposed in him in the slightest degree. Indeed, putting aside the native honesty of his character, his position in the district was so good, that it would have been very bad policy for him to jeopardise it by any abuse of the confidence reposed in him. Being the younger son of an ancient family, and a distant relation of Hardman, he was received in the best society. Dodbury was a widower, with an only daughter, an amiable and elegant girl. She was just budding into womanhood, when it was announced that the heir of Coote-down would shortly become of age, and that the event was to be celebrated with the utmost pomp. Many strange conjectures had for years been current to account for his being kept so long away from home; but they were partially silenced when it was known that the young man was on his way to his paternal roof.

Extensive preparations were made for his reception: all the tenantry not only of Coote-down, but those from the maternal estate near Ilfracombe, were invited to attend his debarkation at Dartmouth. The lawn, paddock, and parks, were strewed with tents for their accommodation, and refreshments of the most expensive kind were provided without limit. Several distinguished and noble friends of both families were invited to join in the festivities; and though every corner of Coote Hall, as well as the surrounding farm-houses, was made available for sleeping-room, yet there was not a bed to be had in Dartmouth a week before the day named in the invitations 'for love or money.' It appeared that the neglect which had been shown to young Hardman for so many years was to be atoned by the magnificence of the fête to celebrate his return.

Dodbury's share in managing the affairs of the family had declined every day since Mrs Hardman's resumption of her proper position as his patron's wife. She was a woman of strong intellect, and perfectly able to superintend what had been before so much neglected by her husband. She had an ambitious spirit, and Dodbury doubted not that the grand reception fête was organised for the purpose of carrying out some great project connected with her son.

The day of Herbert Hardman's arrival from France proved auspicious. It was a lovely day in the middle of June. When he landed at the village of Kingswear, opposite to Dartmouth, the fishermen saluted him with a discharge of all the firearms they could collect. His parents received him at the landing-place, his mother embracing him with every outward and public mark of affection. A long cavalcade followed the carriage in which he was conducted to Coote-down Hall, consisting of the tenantry, headed by the most distinguished of his father's guests.

At the entrance of the domain, new tokens of welcome presented themselves. The gates were plentifully adorned with flowers, and at a turn of the thickly-wooded avenue, an arch of garlands was thrown across the path. The lawn was covered with lads and lasses from the surrounding farms, who, when Herbert appeared, set up a joyous cheer, whilst the drawing-room windows of the house were filled with ladies waving handkerchiefs.

The hall of the mansion was lined with servants, who obsequiously bowed as Herbert passed them. When he made his appearance in the drawing-room, there was almost a struggle amongst the ladies for the earliest honours of salutation. One maiden, however, stood apart, drinking in deeply the attestations of favour with which the heir of the estate was received, but too timid to share in, or to add to them. This was Miss Dodbury. The gentlemen, most of whom had accompanied Herbert from the landing-place, now joined the ladies; and Mr and Mrs Hardman entered the room amidst the hearty congratulations of their guests.

The fashionable dinner hour of that period was much earlier than at present, and but little time elapsed ere the important meal was announced. Mrs Hardman led forward a tall, handsome, but somewhat haughty-looking girl, whom she introduced to her son as the Lady Elizabeth Plympton, desiring him to lead her to the dining-room. She attentively watched Herbert's countenance, to observe what effect the damsel's beauty would create on him; but to her disappointment she saw that her son received her with no more than the politeness of a young gentleman who had been educated in France.

Nothing occurred during the day worthy of remark. The usual toasts and sentiments were drunk at the dinner-table, and the usual excesses committed; for at that time it was thought a mark of low breeding for a man to remain sober all the evening. Out of doors there were bullocks roasted whole, barrels of cider and butts of ale set constantly flowing, with dancing, cricket, and Devonshire skittles, and other country games and comforts, for the amusement of the peasantry.

About a fortnight after the rejoicings had subsided, Mrs Hardman, while conversing with her son on his future plans and prospects, startled him by inquiring whether he had formed any attachment during his residence in Paris? The young man hesitated for a short time, and declared that he had not; upon which Mrs Hardman asked, somewhat abruptly, what he thought of Lady Elizabeth Plympton?

'That,' returned Herbert, 'her ladyship is an extremely tall, handsome, proud girl, who would evidently glory more in breaking half-a-dozen hearts than in winning one.'

'Take care she does not break yours!' rejoined Mrs Hardman playfully.

'There is little fear of that, mother.'

Herbert was right. He had seen one of humble pretensions, but of unbounded worth, for whom he began to feel already a more than ordinary sentiment.

Months rolled past, and Herbert began to find his position at home far from agreeable. His father had sunk into a mere nonentity through his mother's superior energy. Hence, in her hands rested the happiness or misery of all connected with the household. It soon became evident that her grand project was to effect a marriage between Lady Elizabeth Plympton and Herbert; and when she found no inducement could warm her son's heart towards that lady, her conduct altered. From being kind and indulgent, she was exacting and imperious: an old and scarcely natural dislike of her son seemed to be re-awakened, and which she now took little pains to conceal. It was therefore to be expected that Herbert should spend as little of his time at home as possible. He became a frequent and welcome visitor to the happy and well-ordered house of the Dodburys.

The sharp eyes of the mother were not slow in detecting the attraction which drew Herbert so frequently to the lawyer's house. Though grievously disappointed, she was cautious. Nothing could be done at present: for, though her son was manifestly 'entangled,' yet no overt declaration had been made, and there was nothing to act upon. She had the worldly foresight to know that opposition was food and fuel to a secret attachment, and abstained from giving grounds for the belief that so much as a suspicion lurked in her mind. In this way months rolled on, Herbert becoming more and more captivated. On the other hand, Miss Dodbury had striven against a passion with which *she* also had become inspired. Her father discouraged it, though tenderly and indirectly. It was a delicate matter for a man to interfere in, as no open disclosure had been made from either party; but this embarrassment, felt equally by the proud mother of the lover and the considerate father of the girl, was speedily but accidentally put an end to.

An equestrian party had been formed to see, from Berryhead, a large fleet which had been driven by a recent storm into Tor Bay. Mrs Hardman had purposely invited Catherine Dodbury, that she might observe her son's conduct towards that young lady, and extract from it a sufficient ground for taxing him openly with a preference for her over the belle she had chosen. It was a lovely day, and the party was all life and gaiety, as almost all such parties are; for nothing tends to raise the spirits so effectually as equestrian exercise.

Herbert laughed and chatted with the rest of the ladies, and seemed to pay no more attention to Catherine than was due to her as the belle of the party, which she was universally acknowledged to be. As, however, they passed over the drawbridge of the fort, built on the terminating point of the little promontory, they were obliged to dismount. Herbert offered Catherine his arm, and Mrs Hardman narrowly watched them. Her son said a few words in a low tone, which caused the colour to mount into the young lady's cheek; the listener overheard her reply—'Mr Hardman, it can, it must never be!' and withdrawing her arm from his, entered the fort unsupported. These words at once pleased and displeased the ambitious mother. The girl evidently did not encourage her son's suit—that favoured the Lady Elizabeth project; 'but,' thought Mrs Hardman, drawing herself up to her full height, 'does a lawyer's daughter reject the heir of the Hardmans?'

The truth is, Hardman, the night before, had declared his love; it was on the drawbridge that he pressed her to give him hopes; but her reply repressed rather than encouraged them.

The servants had brought the horses into the fort, that, mounted, the spectators might see over the ramparts the noble scene which lay before them to greater advantage. The fleet consisted of a number of merchant vessels, with a convoy of king's ships, which were just preparing to sail out of the bay. When the men-of-war had spread their canvas, and begun to move, a salute was fired, quite unexpectedly by the visitors, from the fort. Catherine's horse immediately took fright, and darted across the drawbridge with the speed of lightning. Herbert lost not a moment, but spurring his own steed, galloped away, taking a circuitous route, lest the clattering of his own horse's hoofs should impel Catherine's to run the faster. On she sped, and as long as she remained within sight, her friends trembled lest some frightful catastrophe should happen. Presently she darted out of view. Herbert, meanwhile, galloped to meet her, and at last succeeded; but, alas! when it was too late to render any assistance. On coming up, he found both the horse and its rider prostrate, the latter motionless and insensible. He lifted her from the ground, and took her into a neighbouring house. The usual restoratives were applied without effect, and it was not till a surgeon appeared and bled the patient that any signs of animation returned. It was discovered that the right arm and three of the ribs on the left side were fractured. It was necessary that the utmost quiet should be observed, lest any further and more dangerous injury might, unknown to the medical man, have taken place.

Though, therefore, the whole party assembled near the house, they were not allowed to enter it. Herbert insisted upon remaining with the father, despite Mrs Hardman's repeated strictures on the impropriety of his doing so.

TRAITS OF THE NEW ZEALANDERS.

In a former article we presented some snatches from Mr Wakefield's 'Adventures in New Zealand' relative to the scenery, produce, and capabilities of the country; we now glean some extracts illustrative of the manners and customs of the natives, and of their deportment towards the settlers. Amongst coloured races living in a state of barbarism, the New Zealanders are universally admitted to be pre-eminent both in physical development and in intellectual activity. They readily acquire the habits, modes of thinking, and arts of the white men; and consequently require to be treated with a candour and probity which would be disregarded by other savages. Bearing this characteristic in mind, the reader will be the better enabled to appreciate the observations and anecdotes of our youthful author.

The New Zealanders are very fond of joking, occasionally mingling with their wit the most pungent irony and sarcasm. In this way the early missionaries were frequently beguiled; mistaking ironical assertions for earnest intentions. It is to this characteristic also that we are to ascribe the prevalence of nicknames among the natives. The following is a pleasant instance of the propensity. 'During the time taken up in discussions, I had acquired a great many words of Maori, and began to understand a good deal, and make myself understood a little. I had become very good friends with the natives in various excursions ashore, and was designated by a nickname while here, which remained from this time my only name among them till I left the country. Some of the young people had made many attempts to pronounce "Edward Wakefield," on receiving an answer to their question as to my name. The nearest approach they could make to it was Era Weke, and some wag immediately suggested "Tiraweke," the name of a small bird which is very common in the woods, and known for its chattering propensities. As I had made it a point to chatter as much as possible with them, whether according to Maori grammar or not, they agreed that the sobriquet would do, and reported their invention at the pa. The old men and chiefs were not a bit behind their juniors in their hilarity and fondness for a joke, and never called me otherwise afterwards. They also christened Colonel Wakefield "Wide-awake," after some chief who had been so called by the flax-traders in former times; and this name also has clung to him ever since.'

The recent exhibitions of the Ojibbeway and Ioway Indians have rendered the public familiar with their war and other dances. It may not be uninteresting, by way of contrast, to learn how a war-dance and holiday is conducted by the savages on the other side of the globe. Such a fête took place on the day after the purchase of Port Nicholson. 'Canoes and parties on foot, glittering with their lately acquired red blankets and muskets, were all closing in upon the place of rendezvous; fresh smoke rose every moment on shore as a new oven was prepared for the feast; and Warepori and the other chiefs, who had slept on board, went on shore early to make the necessary preparations, accompanied by our carpenter, who was to superintend the erection of a small tree which the natives had procured for the purpose, as a flag-staff, close to the Pitone *pa* or native village. In the afternoon, on a signal from the shore, we landed in our boats with all the cabin party, and all the sailors that could be spared, to take part in the rejoicings. We were joyfully received by the assemblage, which consisted of about three hundred men, women, and children. Of these, two hundred were men, and had armed themselves with the hundred and twenty muskets they had received from us, spears, tomahawks, pointed sticks, stone and wooden clubs, &c. Even a dozen umbrellas, which had formed part of the payment, figured in the ranks as conspicuously as the emperor of Morocco's son's parasol has figured in more recent battalions. Every one was dressed in some of the new clothes; their heads were neatly arranged, and ornamented with feathers of the albatross or huia; handsome mats hung in unison with the gay petticoats of the women and the new blankets of the warriors; the latter were bedizened with waistcoats and shirts, and belted with cartouch-boxes and shot-belts. It was high holiday with everybody; and a universal spirit of hilarity prevailed among the excited multitude.

'Warepori was dressed in a large hussar cloak belonging to my uncle, to which he had taken a fancy, and brandished a handsome greenstone meri. His party having seated themselves in ranks, he suddenly rose from the ground and leaped high into the air with a tremendous yell. He was instantly imitated by his party, who sprang out of their clothes as if by magic, and left them in bundles on the ground. They then joined in a measured guttural song recited by their chief, keeping exact time by leaping high at each louder intonation, brandishing their weapons with the right hand, and slapping the thigh with the left as they came heavily upon the ground. The war-song warmed as it proceeded. Though still in perfect unison, they yelled louder and louder, leaped higher and higher, brandished their weapons more fiercely, and dropped with the smack on the thigh more heavily as they proceeded, till the final spring was accompanied by a concluding whoop which seemed to penetrate one's marrow. After this preparatory stimulant, the two parties ran down to the beach, and took up positions facing each other at about two hundred yards' distance. They then repeated the dance, and at its conclusion, the two parties passed each other at full speed, firing their guns as they ran, and took up a fresh position nearer to each other. Many of the women had joined in the wildest part of the dance, yelling and grimacing with as demoniacal a frenzy as any of the men.'

Barbarously joyous and gay as these holiday warriors undoubtedly were, we have only to turn to their dwellings to perceive the thorough abjectness of uncivilised life. In the native villages there are always two kinds of houses, the *ware puni*, or 'house of rest,' and the *ware umu*, or 'oven house.' 'The former are exceedingly low, and covered with earth, on which weeds very often grow. They resemble in shape and size a hotbed with the glass off. A small square hole at one end is the only passage for light or air. I intended to creep into one of them to examine it; but had just got my head in, and was debating within myself by what snake-like evolution I should best succeed in getting my body to follow, when I was deterred by the intense heat and intolerable odour from proceeding. Many of them no doubt are much larger and more commodious. They are all, however, built on the same principle, of keeping in the animal heat, and are therefore most repulsive to a European. Some of them have their front wall removed back three feet from the front of the roof. In this case a nice airy veranda is formed, which makes a very good sleeping-place. The ware umu, or "oven-houses," have open walls, built of upright sticks at intervals of an inch or two. They have thatched roofs to protect the cooks and the store of firewood, which is generally piled up inside in rainy weather. The open walls let out the smoke, and let in the air, and these kitchens are therefore much more adapted than the others for the bedroom of a traveller. At this time, too, the natives, although most of them professing Christianity, had by no means divested themselves of many of their ancient superstitions; one of which was a positive interdiction against the very presence of food or drink in a ware puni. To light a pipe from the fire inside was considered equally sacrilegious. In order to avoid the inconvenience of these restrictions, and yet refrain from offending against any of the customs which I found still revered by my kind hosts, I therefore found it much better to take up my abode in a ware umu or ware kauta, both which names apply to the kitchens. Here I had only to avoid one thing; namely, the hanging of food overhead; for this also is a terror, and, if done intentionally, a grievous offence to the Maori anywhere.'

Having taken this survey of the New Zealander's bedroom and kitchen, we may as well glance at his mode of cooking, upon which even English gourmands have bestowed the most unqualified eulogiums. 'The maori "umu," or cooking-hole, is a very complete steaming apparatus, and is used as follows:—In a hole scraped in the ground, about three feet in diameter and one foot deep, a wood fire is first lighted. Round stones, about the size of a man's fist, are heaped upon the fagots, and fall among the ashes as the fire consumes the wood. When they are thus nearly red-hot, the cook picks out any pieces of charcoal that may appear above the stones, turns all the stones round with two sticks, and arranges them so as to afford a pretty uniform heat and surface. She then sprinkles water on the stones from a dried gourd, of which the inside has been hollowed, and a copious steam rises. Clean grass, milk-thistle, or wild turnip leaves dipped in water, are laid on the stones; the potatoes, which have been carefully scraped of their peel with cockle-shells, and washed, are placed on the herbs, together with any birds, meat, or fish that may be included in the mess; fresh herbs are laid over the food, flax baskets follow, completely covering the heap, and the mass is then buried with the earth from the hole. No visible steam escapes from the apparatus, which looks like a large mole-hill; and when the old hags—who know how to time the cookery with great accuracy, from constant practice—open the catacomb, everything is sure to be found thoroughly and equally cooked.'

It is well known that New Zealand has no native quadrupeds of any importance—the pig, ox, and horse, all being recent imports. The first horse was landed at Port Nicholson in 1840. Mr Wakefield, in 1841, rode from Wellington to Wanganui, and mark the consternation of the natives at the sight of this novel import. 'They fled yelling in all directions, without looking behind them; and as fast as I galloped past those who were running across the sandy flat, and up the steep path leading to the pa of Tihoe, they fairly lay down on their faces, and gave themselves up for lost. Half way up the hill I dismounted, and they plucked up courage to come and look at the *kuri nui*, or "large dog." The most amusing questions were put to me as to its habits and disposition. "Can he talk?" said one; "Does he like boiled potatoes?" said another; and a third, "Mustn't he have a blanket to lie down upon at night?" This unbounded respect and admiration lasted all the time that I remained. The horse was taken into the central courtyard of the pa; a dozen hands were always offering him Indian corn, and grass, and sow-thistles, when they had learned what he really did eat; and a wooden bowl full of water was kept constantly replenished close to him; and little knots of curious observers sat round the circle of his tether-rope, remarking, and conjecturing, and disputing about the meaning and intention of every whisk of his tail or shake of his ears.'

In Mr Wakefield's narrative we find graphic accounts of tatooing, native burial, hospitality, and the like; but these we pass by for more interesting matter; namely, his account how a Scotch emigrant farmer dealt with and overcame the obstructions of the natives. Bell had located at Wanganui, built a house, stocked a garden, and was clearing his land. 'During the progress of the ploughing, E Waka used to come and watch, and keep walking by the side of the old farmer, telling him he should plough no more. But Bell pretended not to understand him, and smiled at him, and jeed the bullocks, and warned E Waka to get out of the way of them when they turned, and ploughed on. E Waka got furious; but Bell wouldn't look a bit frightened, and told him he didn't understand him: "He must go to the boys," meaning his own sons; "they'd talk Maori to him;" and he jeed the bullocks, and ploughed on. The patience of E Waka soon got exhausted, and he retired sulkily towards the house, after putting in some pegs a few yards beyond where Bell had got to, pointing to that as his ultimatum. And while the goodwife gave him a large mess of bread and milk, or a smoking dish of pork and potatoes, and the sons and daughters chatted good-humouredly to him while they built a pigsty or put up a stock-yard, old Bell was ploughing on. And E Waka ate and smoked, and basked in the sun, wondering at the industry of the pakeha, till he got sleepy, and crept back to his village for the day.

'The next morning, however, he would be a-foot pretty early, to besiege the pakeha maro, or "hard white man," as he called him. But he was never early enough; and the first sight that met his eyes was always his *bête noire*—the team of bullocks, and the old man trudging steadily along the fresh furrows. E Waka would begin by looking for his pegs, and hunt about for a long while, grumbling and puzzling, before he found out that the plough must have gone over them some hours ago, if not the evening before. And while he was hunting, the plough sped quietly on. Then came the remonstrance, and the shrug of the shoulders, and the fury, and the good-humoured indifference, and the reference to the boys, and the meal, and the sleepiness, and the return home, and the careful pegging of the ground as before. The same story over again! No patience could stand it. Old Bell and the team went on—slow, sure, and regular as the course of the sun.

'And besides, on one occasion when E Waka had brought a large troop of attendants, and threatened to commit some violence, the old man had called his stalwart sons to his side, and taking up a spade or a ploughshare, had said, in broad Scotch, while his resolute looks and prepared attitude interpreted his words into a universally-intelligible language—"Dinna ye think to touch a thing that's here noo; for if ye do, by the God that's abune us, I'll cleave ye to the grund! A bargain's a bargain; I've paid ye richt and fair, and I'll gar ye keep to it." And then E Waka would look frightened, and begin to think his good daily meal was better than a blow of old Bell's weapon, and peace was soon restored.

'And when the ploughing was done, the planting potatoes was too amusing to be interfered with, for they ridiculed the idea of expecting any crop from potatoes cut into small pieces. "Bide and see," said the old man; and they waited with anxiety for the time of crop: and the report spread far and wide that the old pakeha with the cows was very good and brave and industrious, but that he was certainly gone *porangi*, or "mad," for he had cut up his seed potatoes before he put them in. "Poor old man!" they said; "his troubles must have turned his head—such a very absurd idea!" But the crop came better than their own from whole potatoes; and they stared, and found that the foolish old man could teach them some lessons in growing food, and they soon honoured him as much for his knowledge as they had learned to stand in awe of his courage and resolution.

'And though they have not yet allowed him to use the whole of his section, he has now fifty acres under plough cultivation, sends grain and grass-seed enough to Wellington to pay for the luxuries which his family require, owns several cows and a flock of sheep, calls himself the "Laird of Wanganui," and gives harvest-home festivals. He talked of buying a horse, and caring for no man, when I last saw him.

'But, unfortunately, all settlers have not the admirable qualities of William Gordon Bell, who has indeed shown a great example of success against the numerous difficulties which staggered lesser men.'

As a counterpart to the conduct of E Waka, we may transcribe our author's picture of the chief of Horowenua:—'Watanui was perhaps one of the native chiefs who best appreciated the value of the white man's presence and brotherhood. He had adopted the Christian faith very warmly, and without in the least injuring his authority, for either he himself or his second son always read the prayers and enforced the performance of the Christian observances. He had always adopted a great degree of civilisation. His house and clothes were always kept scrupulously clean: he and all his family wore clean clothes, and washed with soap in the stream every morning. The cooking was attended to with great care, and the food was always served up on carefully-scrubbed tin plates. In short, whenever I spent an hour at this little village, I felt that it was the residence of a gentleman. There was a quiet unobtrusive dignity in the well-regulated arrangements of the whole establishment. The slaves did their work without orders and without squabbling; a harsh word was hardly ever heard. Every one vied in a tacit wish that the old gentleman should be comfortable; and it was pleasing to see him sitting in the house almost always surrounded by some of his family—the men all well shaved and combed, the women in clean frocks and blankets—busy at some sewing or other work; while his son or his daughter-in-law would be kindly teaching him to write on a slate. I remember how proud he was when he could write his name, and with what genuine kindness he pointed out his son Tommy's wife as having succeeded in teaching him. The family of Watanui, so united and homely, were indeed a notable instance of the success of Mr Hadfield's sweet and gentle teaching.'

All the New Zealanders, however, were neither E Wakas nor Watanuis. Some were jealous and troublesome, others treacherous and bloodthirsty; many idle, and inclined to loiter with the white settler; but the great majority, it must be owned, were active, intelligent, and given to trade and barter. On the whole, they are vastly superior to the other Polynesian natives, and, if properly dealt with, appear more likely to amalgamate with the white settler.

ENGLISH UNIVERSITY LIFE.

At the present time, when the subject of education is so eagerly and universally discussed, it is thought that a sketch of English university life will be acceptable to the readers of this Journal. As the writer is a member of the university of Cambridge, reference will be made principally to it in particular; but his remarks will occasionally be applicable to Oxford also.

The university of Cambridge consists of seventeen colleges, each of which is perfectly independent of the others, has its own master, fellows, tutors, and lecturers, and its yearly or half-yearly examinations of its own students, who are rewarded from the funds of the college. These rewards consist either of an annual emolument, such as scholarships, sizarships, exhibitions; or are given in the form of books, silver cups, &c. No college, however, has the power of conferring a degree. This is the office of the university as a collective body.

Each college furnishes, in proportion to its size, members of the ruling body—the senate. The examiners for public or university (as distinguished from college or private) examinations, are chosen by the senate, and are always at least of the standard of master of arts.

I will now describe the mode of admission to the university. Suppose you have fixed on what college you would wish to belong to, you write to the tutor of that college, and send a certificate signed by some master of arts; which certificate is generally to the purport that he has known you a certain time, and can testify to your moral character. With this you also send your caution money, which amounts to L.10 if you enter as a sizar, to L.15 if as pensioner, L.25 if as fellow-commoner, or to L.50 if a nobleman. Some colleges also require a certificate of baptism.* If you are poor, you will probably enter yourself at a college where there are plenty of sizarships; that is, certain emoluments. The obtaining of these is in some colleges a matter of interest, but in others requires you to pass an examination with other competitors, and the vacancies are filled up by the most meritorious. If money is no object, you enter as a pensioner (take care the name does not mislead you, for no pension will you receive). Of this class are the great majority of the students.

If you are of wealthy family, or allied to nobility, you will enter as fellow-commoner, and have the pleasure of dining with the fellows of your college, be excused, at certain colleges, lectures and other duties to a great extent, and, moreover, be entitled to wear a more gaudy gown than your fellow-students. Pensioners and sizars differ chiefly in name. It often happens that those who, from want of ability or previous training, fail to obtain sizarships, remain as pensioners—of course at greater expense. The time of entry is generally from January to June, and you get into residence in the October following. If you have entered at either of the large colleges—Trinity or St John's—you will probably be obliged to go into lodgings in the town, owing to there being no rooms vacant in college. Of these there are a very great number licensed by the university authorities; and you must not take any lodgings but such as are licensed. However, any respectable person can obtain a license, the only object of licensing being to prevent people of improper character from setting up as lodging-house-keepers. At the small colleges, and sometimes at Trinity and St John's, there are generally rooms vacant, into which you enter as soon as you arrive. The suite of apartments generally consists of three rooms—a bed-room, a sitting-room (or keeping-room, as it is called), and a gyp-room—which is a sort of pantry or closet for all sorts of purposes.

You are waited on by a woman, who goes by the name of bed-maker, although, in fact, bed-making is only a very small part of her duty. She lights your fire, brings as much bread and butter (or commons) from the college butteries as you order, lays your breakfast things, fills your kettle, dusts your keeping-room, and then goes off to perform similar offices for the rest of her masters, of whom each bed-maker has seven or eight. She comes again to clear away; and so on three or four times in the day, to set your tea things, &c. Dinner she does not prepare, as you dine in the college hall at four o'clock. In fact she has nothing at all to do with cooking: you prepare your own breakfast, make your tea yourself, and live, in short, a thorough bachelor's life. The bed-makers are generally the wives of respectable artisans in the town. Some interest is required to obtain the place; and youth is, for obvious reasons, no recommendation.

I will suppose that you have just arrived, and called on your tutor. He will take you, and send his servant with you round the college, show you the vacant rooms, of which, if you are an early comer, you will have your choice; if others have been before you, you must take what you can get. The different sets of rooms vary considerably in rent, according to size, condition, situation, &c. Those who can afford the expense, and require a great deal of waiting upon, hire a 'gyp;' that is, a man-servant.† Hardly any, however, have a gyp entirely to themselves, but are content with the services of one who, like the bed-makers, has several other masters. In the first few interviews with the tutor, you will learn what are your college duties. Every college has its chapel, in which the prayers are read morning and evening, the hours being generally seven in the morning and six in the evening. You will be obliged to keep nine 'chapels' a-week, two on Sunday counting for three. The mode of ascertaining your presence is by marking. In the large colleges, three or four men stand in the ante-chapel with lists of the men in their hands, and make a mark opposite your name as you go in. In some small colleges, the marking is done by one man, who goes into the chapel and marks as the service is going on; a much less reverent process than the other. The college gates are closed at ten o'clock, after which you cannot go out; and there is a small fine for coming in after ten. If you are after twelve o'clock, your name is sent in by the porter to the dean, and you will have to suffer a reprimand. To come in after one o'clock, and especially to stay out all night, is a very grave offence, and is punished with great severity.

The dean's office is to look after the morals of the men, and punish all kinds of irregularity. The chief items of offence are, neglecting chapel, and coming in late, or, still worse, staying out all night. Of punishments there are all grades, from simple reprimanding to expulsion from the university. For the first two or three offences, or for occasional irregularity, in men who are generally steady, he only sends a message; the marker in hall comes up to you and says, 'The dean requests you will keep nine chapels;' which is a warning that the dean is on the look-out for your delinquencies. 'Gating,' being restricted liberty, is a heavier visitation. If you are 'gated' for ten o'clock, you must be in college before ten; that is, your privilege of being out till twelve or one is taken away. If you are 'gated' for six o'clock, you must be in and not go out after six o'clock; and so on. Such restrictions are a great annoyance to the 'rowing men' (not boating men, but men fond of a row, otherwise called *fast* men), for it puts a stop to all supper parties, unless, indeed, in their own college. 'Breaking gates'—that is, coming in after the time—is a serious offence. 'Walling' is the *ne plus ultra* of 'gating;' for by it you are confined to the college walls, beyond which you must not go.

'Rustication,' or temporary exclusion, is one of the final edicts of college law. A man may be rusticated—that is, sent down into the country—for any period, according to the magnitude of his offence. The general term of rustication is for a year; sometimes, however, it extends to two or three years, or even for ever. This last, or rustication *sinè die*, is only a milder mode of expulsion, the difference between them being this—a man who is expelled from the university is rendered in some degree infamous. He cannot enter the church or any liberal profession, such as law or physic; neither can he enter at Oxford or Dublin, nor any Scotch university. Rustication *sinè die* is a milder mode of getting rid of a man. He is cut off for ever from his own university, but may enter any other, or engage in law, &c.

There are other intermediate and different modes of punishment for various offences. At some colleges, you are required to dine in hall five times a-week, and always on Sunday. During the Newmarket races you must appear in hall every day. The object of this is to prevent the sporting students from attending the races, which, as they take place only twelve miles from Cambridge, might be conveniently done, were the men not obliged to be back by four o'clock. Yet as it is, numbers of them contrive to do it; and you will see the grooms standing ready to take their horses, and others with caps and gowns (you dine in hall with your gown on), ready for them to go into hall directly they get back. What the dean is in the college, the same to a great extent is the proctor in the university. There are two proctors elected every year, and two pro-proctors to assist them. Their office is to search all houses of ill-fame; and if any university-man is found there, he is at their mercy. Drunkenness, talking with girls on the street, and such misbehaviour, as well as all breaches of university discipline, are under their cognisance. Smoking on the streets is forbidden.

The next point to be explained is the course of study.

There are two classes of students: those who are

* At Trinity college they examine previously to admission.

† For this the permission of parents is necessary.

reading for *honours*, and those who merely wish to get their degree with the least possible work. It is perfectly optional to which class you belong. A great many who begin with reading for honours get tired, or find that, from insufficient previous preparation, they are unable to compete successfully with others. They then give up their first intentions, and at last offer themselves as candidates for what is termed the 'ordinary degree of B.A.' (Bachelor of Arts). The others, or honour men, or candidates for honours, take what is called an 'extraordinary degree;' that is, not, as might be supposed, the degree of M.A., or Master of Arts, which all are entitled to take at the end of three years, but a high place in the list of mathematical or of classical honours.

Every one who is a candidate for the degree of B.A. must pass an examination. Candidates for the ordinary degree—who, on account of their being rather the larger class, are called poll-men, from a Greek word meaning 'the many'—are examined in one Greek and one Latin author, the Greek Testament, Paley's Moral Philosophy, and a little elementary mathematics. The subjects are fixed, and every one knows what he has to prepare. The selected Latin and Greek authors, however, vary every year, as also the parts of Paley; but these things are made public two years or so before the time of examination. The examination for honours is very different.

The subjects of examination here embrace nearly the whole extent of present mathematical science. From Euclid and arithmetic, the course extends up to the highest branches of physical astronomy and the theories of light and heat, and comprises algebra; trigonometry, plane and spherical; conic sections, and application of algebra to geometry; geometers of three dimensions; differential and integral calculus, including differential equations and calculus of variations; elementary mechanics; analytical statics and dynamics; hydrostatics; optics, including the undulatory theory; plane astronomy, and lunar and planetary theories. No one knows beforehand what questions will be proposed in any of these subjects.

If a man intends to be a candidate for classical honours, he is required to become previously a candidate for mathematical honours, and to obtain a place in the list. If he is rejected (as several first-rate classics almost every year are), he cannot go into the classical examination; and this, as might be expected, is a source of extreme vexation and perpetual complaint amongst the classics of the university.

Those who are sufficiently acquainted with mathematics to pass this ordeal—and many every year take high places in both—are at liberty to offer themselves for the classical examination, which consists of selections from Greek and Latin authors to be translated into English, and English prose or poetry to be turned into Greek or Latin, besides numerous critical and historical questions.

To prepare the men for these final examinations, each college has its lectures, which are of all degrees of merit, according to the ability of the lecturer and his aptitude for teaching. The lecturers are almost always selected from the fellows of the college; and accordingly those colleges whose fellows are the best mathematicians or classics have the best lectures. Trinity and St John's, on account of the high standard required to obtain a fellowship in them, are the best off in this respect. The lectures last for one hour, and are generally given from eight o'clock in the morning till nine, from nine to ten, or from ten to eleven; each college having different lectures for different sets of men, according to their proficiency. No lectures are given in the evening. Here, again, most people will be apt to make a mistake. The word *lecture* is not an appropriate one; for these so-called lectures are in fact *examinations*, interspersed certainly with an explanation now and then; but their main feature is examination. We shall suppose it is a mathematical lecture. The tutor gives out a number of questions on the particular subject he is lecturing on; these questions you write down, and spend the rest of the hour in answering them on paper. The examinations often range beyond university subjects.

The reader will naturally enough think that if the lectures are thus conducted, there is not much scope for the display of ability on the part of the lecturer. But a good man at explanation will always evince it somehow or other in his lecture; either by going over the subject before he gives out his questions, or by looking over the papers of the students carefully, and correcting any mistakes into which they may have fallen. A really good lecturer, however, is a rarity in Cambridge. Classical lectures are of course on a different plan. There each man is called upon in turn to translate a portion of the book which happens to be the subject of examination, and is asked grammatical and historical questions on it.

These lectures are the only mode in which the student receives instruction from the college. One of the most important features, however, in university education remains to be described. I allude to the private tutors.

There are very few, indeed, of the reading-men (or, in fact, of the poll-men either) who do not engage a private tutor. Some, of course, mathematical, others classical, and a few reading with both a mathematical and classical tutor. These tutors are generally men who have taken the highest honours in mathematics or classics. They are totally independent of the college, though a great number of them are fellows of their respective colleges, and reside in college. Their pupils go to them every day, or every other day, just as the pupil chooses, paying accordingly. The charge is fixed by custom at L.7 a term for a half pupil, and L.14 for a whole pupil. As I have mentioned the word 'term' here, and as there may be some who do not exactly know the meaning of it, I may as well state that it is that period during which the student is obliged to reside in Cambridge. Men are often allowed, however, to 'keep' half terms; that is, are compelled to reside for half a term. The times at which the terms commence and end may be found in any almanac. The term in which the student generally comes up for the first time is the Michaelmas, which begins October 10, and ends December 16. Then there is a vacation till the 13th of January, when he must come up again during the Lent term, which, being dependent on Easter, is of uncertain length. Then comes another vacation of about three weeks, at the end of which he must come up and reside till the middle of the Easter term, about the end of May or beginning of June. There is a peculiarity in this term which, so far as college business and residence is concerned, actually ends at the division, although in the almanacs you will find its nominal end to be in July.

Then comes the long vacation, or, as it is briefly called here, 'the long,' which lasts between four and five months; so that, on the whole, the student is not obliged to reside in Cambridge more than half the year. A great number, however, whose homes are distant, or who think they can read better or live more agreeably in Cambridge, remain up during the shorter vacations; but in the long vacation there are comparatively few, and those chiefly hard-reading men, who cannot afford to be without the assistance of their private tutor for so long a time. There are, however, reading parties formed very often, who start off for some watering-place or attractive spot, such as the Isle of Wight, Jersey, Wales, and even the Highlands of Scotland. The charge for reading as half pupil during 'the long' is L.15; L.30 if you go every day to the tutor. As may be readily supposed, the tutor, tired of the monotony of Cambridge life, is not unwilling to join four or five equally weary undergraduates in one of these pleasant excursions, or perhaps a tour on the continent, whereby recreation may be mixed with duty. Sometimes, if report speaks true, these reading parties end with less profit to the student than is anticipated.

The mode of teaching adopted by the private tutors is similar to that of the college lecturers; namely, by giving the pupils papers of questions on the subjects they have been reading, and then looking over the answers, and explaining any errors into which they may have fallen; suggesting better methods; and in mathematics, giving examples and problems illustrative of the different theories, so as to test the pupil's knowledge of the subject, and to prepare him for similar problems in the college examination papers, and also those given in the senate-house.

A great deal of a man's success depends on the character of his private tutor. If he is careless and indifferent to the progress of his pupils, or if he is not qualified for his office by the possession of thorough knowledge, united with a clear manner of explaining difficulties, his services will be of little value. One mistake seems to be especially prevalent amongst the students in their choice of a private tutor; and that is, looking out solely for one who took a high degree, without ever stopping to inquire into his qualifications as a teacher. The writer is acquainted with numberless instances in which this folly meets with its natural consequences. The senior wrangler, or second, third, fourth wrangler, as it may be, is found out to be either a careless man, or, more frequently, a man totally incapable of explaining, or at any rate a very bad hand at it. In consequence of this mania for high wranglers, there are several tutors completely blocked up with pupils: there is no possibility, by stinting the other pupils of their proper attention, of cramming in another pupil. The ill effects of one tutor having more pupils than he can manage are very evident. Many of them, too, have no idea of arranging the time to be given to each pupil, and there is, consequently, endless confusion and grumbling. Of course there are some who, to the highest attainments, unite also great perspicuity in explanation. Such are deservedly popular. There is one senior wrangler in particular, whose admirable arrangement of his pupils, and facilities of communicating his own profound acquirements, have for the last six or seven years made him the best college tutor, as well as the best private tutor, in the university.

The great object of the tutor is to prepare his men for the college or senate-house examination. As the number of subjects introduced into those examinations is very great (which may be seen from the list given above), so great, indeed, that only those who are very well prepared before entering the university are able to read them all, it is a primary object to read only those subjects, and those parts of a subject, which will 'pay' well in these examinations. It is therefore not so much the object to study fully any one department of mathematical science, as to select from each those portions in which the student is most likely to be examined. Whatever is learnt, however, must be learnt thoroughly. If there is any place in the world where rigid accuracy is required, it is in Cambridge. No superficial notions or 'half-baked' ideas will do the possessor any service. What is done must be done well. And yet the system has many serious disadvantages connected with it.

This picking and choosing necessarily involves the following evils. The student is hurried from subject to subject at such a rate, that he has no time to get interested in any one. Now, unless a man is interested in any science, it is very questionable whether he will ever attain a thorough knowledge of it; and he will certainly never make any discoveries in it. I will suppose that you come up with no preparation, or a very slender one—such as, having read your Euclid and algebra. Your private tutor marks in your book those portions which are likely 'to be set'—that is, in which you will probably be examined—and you go day after day to him for a paper of questions on the parts thus marked out. You must write out the answers to all these questions in your tutor's room, with perfect accuracy; and you must go over the ground in this way so often, that you are certain of being able to do the same in the college examination. When you have thus finished your algebra, your tutor will not allow you to delay any longer over that, but makes you begin plane trigonometry, marking out as before in the book those portions most likely to be set; and so on through the whole course, or as great a part of it as you have time to get through—the object in all this plainly being, not so much to gain a knowledge of the science, as to answer certain questions in that science. The consequence is, not one in a hundred ever gets any love of science for its own sake by this process of study. Those who have any love of it, had it before they came to college. The majority, however, even of those who rank high in the list of wranglers, give up all scientific pursuit as soon as they leave college. The hopes of a fellowship, or the necessity of gaining a living by private tutorship, or as public schoolmasters, has been their sole inducement to make the efforts they have made; and as soon as the stimulus ceases, the work stops. It has long been a matter of surprise to the public, that of scientific inventions, or literary works in general, so small a portion should belong to men educated at the universities. Oxford does not pretend to teach science; and it appears from what has been said, that Cambridge teaches it in a very unattractive way. For the correctness of my assertions, I would appeal to any reader who is acquainted with the university: the inferences of course are my own.* There are a few who come up so well prepared, that they are able to enter more fully into the respective branches of the science, and to acquire an interest in them independent of extraneous circumstances. But these are extremely rare. The generality fag away in a sort of apathetic indifference to anything but the reward. This state of things is partly occasioned by the nature of the treatises in use at Cambridge, nearly all of which are deficient in elementary instruction, and easy examples. They may be considered as synopses of the subjects of which they treat, the deficiencies being expected to be supplied by the lecturers and private tutors. Many of them are perfectly unintelligible without such assistance. The works of Dr Hymers are, upon the whole, an exception to this remark, and also those of Dr Whewell. It may occur to the reader to ask what is done by the university professors? There are professors of mathematics, natural philosophy, chemistry, geology, &c.; but their lectures are attended almost exclusively by those who have taken their degree. Most of them are, I believe, good lecturers; but they are useless, and in fact not intended for the undergraduate, who, generally speaking, has neither time nor money to spend on them.

I have dwelt longer on these points, because of their importance to the progress of knowledge, and the

---

* A Cambridge gownsman favours us (editors) with the following note upon the above paragraphs. We insert his remarks for the purpose of showing what may be said on the opposite side, though we do not coincide in his opinions:—

'The accuracy which the writer describes as required in examinations and by tutors, is surely one of the best possible methods of disciplining the mind to accuracy in reasoning and everything else—the very advantage which mathematical studies have always been supposed to possess beyond all others. It is not to be expected or desired that every one should turn out an Airey or a Herschel; but I utterly deny that such men as Lyndhurst, Alderson, Bickersteth, Jacob, Pollock, Tindall, Sedgwick, bishops without end, &c.—all men who have taken high honours, and submitted to this drudgery, as the writer describes it—have not received the greatest advantage from the training to accuracy of reasoning in their various professions, in which they have become eminent, from the course of study and mind-strengthening undergone in the universities. It is preposterous to assert that those only derive advantages in after life from university studies who have continued to make those identical studies their profession. I certainly think that much more good is done, as far as *discipline* of the mind is concerned, by a brief and general course of reading, accurately followed, than by loosely rambling over a subject which happens to take the fancy. There is some truth in these observations about picking pieces "likely to be set," as applied to the *lower* men; but all the better ones read what may be called *connected* selections, and I do not think, if these selections are well made, the plan at all stands in the way of acquiring a large extent of useful knowledge.'

misapprehensions, or rather ignorance, which prevails with regard to them. People who have not the advantage of a university education, are very apt to overrate it, and to fancy that, were they 'at the seat of learning,' they should, almost of necessity, become learned. They think, too, that if they could devote their whole time to reading, their progress would be proportionally rapid. This is a very great mistake. Experience in this, as in all other things, is the only way to convince men of their error. The mind gets tired and sick of being confined to one pursuit, especially the dry, uninteresting, and even repulsive course of Cambridge 'cramming;' and not a year passes without adding its victims to the drudgery undergone by men in the way I have described. Not one in fifty, even of the reading men at Cambridge, have any notion of science as anything but a 'bore,' a 'nuisance,' or a 'seedy thing;' such being terms in use at Cambridge. No wonder that Cambridge is taking no part in the onward movement of the age. The reason is easily given; it offers no inducements but pecuniary ones, and those very small, for the cultivation of science; and it moreover exhibits science in a form anything but amiable. The undergraduate thinks only of the situation he may obtain by his degree, and the fellow thinks only of the college-living he may become entitled to at some period of his life. While such a system lasts, the present extensive dissatisfaction with our universities must continue.

Three years and three months is the time the student has to reside before he can obtain his degree. The public examination at the end of his course has been mentioned already: there is another public—or university—examination about the middle of the three years, which is indispensable for all. It is called by the university the 'previous examination,' but passes generally by the name of the 'little go,' or 'smalls,' in contradistinction to the final one, or the 'great go.' There are no mathematics required in it. One of the gospels in Greek, one Greek and one Latin author, are annually selected—besides which there are certain portions of Paley's Evidences and the Old Testament history. These are the subjects of examination. The place of examination is the senate-house. It may as well be mentioned here, that all university (and most college) examinations are conducted by means of printed papers of questions, which have not been seen by any one but the examiners, till they are placed before the persons to be examined. Nothing is allowed but pen, ink, and paper. A certain time is allowed for answering the questions, and at the end of that time no one is permitted to write a syllable more. Part of the 'little go' examination consists, however, of vivâ voce translations and questions. In the final one, all is done in writing. The strictest impartiality is generally observed; I may say always, so far as regards the final mathematical examination; and the cases of partiality in the others are extremely rare. Complaints on this score are scarcely ever heard. I believe that, in the most important ones, the examiners have to take an oath that they will do strict and impartial justice; and very seldom, indeed, is any one found who does not acquiesce in their decision in his own case as well as in others. Of course there is a good deal of speculation beforehand as to what questions are likely to be set, and much grumbling at hard papers, or at the short time allowed for a long paper.

When a man is rejected at an examination he is said to be 'plucked.' You will often hear it said of an idle or stupid man who is going in to an examination, 'he is a dead pluck;' meaning he is sure not to pass it. Those who are plucked either at the 'little' or 'great go' must try their luck again. There are cases in which men get so disgusted at repeated failures, that they leave the university in despair.

The candidates for honours at the final examination are arranged by the examiners, after looking over their answers to the questions proposed, in three classes according to merit. Those in the first class are termed Wranglers, those in the second Senior Optimes, and those in the third Junior Optimes. There are some who have not merit enough to be classed at all, who yet are allowed their degree, and these are said to be 'in the gulf.' The last Junior Optime is called the Wooden Spoon.

OCCASIONAL NOTES.

INFLUENCE OF NEWLY-BUILT HOUSES ON HEALTH.

Dr Reidel of Berlin, in a paper of great merit and interest, has recently directed attention to the injurious influence of newly-built houses on the health and life of their occupiers. After mentioning the intimate connexion kept up between the external air and the human organisation, through the medium of the skin and lungs, he refers to experience to show the slow and dangerous diseases to which inhabitants of such houses are exposed, and considers it therefore to be the duty of the sanitary police to remove or check those evils by means of prohibitory measures. It is well known that the atmosphere is composed of nitrogen, oxygen, and carbonic acid, in certain definite proportions, and that less or more of invisible vapour is always dissolved in it. Anything which tends to derange this normal composition must be injurious to the human system; and it is Dr Reidel's object to show that newly-built apartments are a fertile source of such derangement. *First*, In new houses there is generally an increased proportion of water in the atmosphere which we breathe. This arises from the wooden materials, which may be too new and damp; from the stone-work, which only becomes dry after long exposure; or from the materials used for cementing the stones, and for colouring and varnishing the walls. The walls of those houses remain damp longest which have been plastered immediately after their completion, because the dried lime forms an external layer very difficult of penetration. As accidental causes, which may render houses damp, it is necessary to mention wet weather when building, damp situations, large cellars, and enclosure by other high edifices, which prevent the free access of sun and wind. *Second*, The proportion of carbonic acid is diminished by the mortar which attracts it from the air; it may also he attracted by certain colours, such as those containing acetate of copper. No direct injury would, however, be caused by the diminution of carbonic acid, as it belongs to the matters given off by the lungs and skin. *Third*, Certain deleterious ingredients, arising from the new materials, are mixed with the air. Thus particles of lime have been proved beyond doubt to exist in the atmosphere of new habitations, being suspended by the evaporation of the moisture; oils and metallic colours also less or more evaporate. Combinations of lead, copper, and arsenic are employed in the preparation of painters' colours; and many of these volatilise, and may be taken into the system. Besides these, there are different chemical exhalations from new wood, mould, fungi, and grasses, which arise and putrefy in damp habitations.

Attention has also been directed to the mould with which the furniture of newly-built houses is covered, and to the constant moisture of the clothes and linen, from which circumstances alone influences injurious to the inhabitants may be expected; for, on account of the increased humidity of the surrounding atmosphere, not only is the skin prevented from free transpiration, but it is even induced to attract more moisture. This is also the case with the lungs, and thus the composition of the blood is rendered unnatural, as may be seen in the pale face, wasted muscles, and sluggishness of all the functions which ensue. In other cases, protracted rheumatism, inflammation of the joints, contractions or paralysis, are produced. In addition, the sojourn in a damp atmosphere is a frequent cause of the development of scrofula, intermittent and typhoid fevers, scurvy, quinsy, croup, &c. Wounds and ulcers more quickly assume an unhealthy appearance, and have a tendency to take on gangrenous inflammation. The evaporation from organic substances favours the production of miasmata and contagions, for in no situations did the cholera occur more frequently than in new damp habitations. The inspiration of lime-particles may dispose to diseases of the chest or apoplexy; and there can be no doubt that the lead employed in painting the walls, volatilising at a high temperature, may produce in those who are constantly exposed to its injurious exhalations symptoms of chronic poisoning, disturbed digestion, cholic, and paralysis. Chronic poisoning may also be produced by being exposed to the evaporation of Scheele's green, from which arsenious compounds escape for a long time after it has been put on the walls. Lastly, the constant moisture of the clothes and beds, and the frequent effect on the food, cause certain injurious consequences on the constitutions of the inhabitants.

Since, then, the early occupation of newly-built houses and recently-plastered rooms causes so many diseases, and imparts to children the germs of prolonged sickness and misery, it becomes, argues Dr Reidel, the duty of the state to prevent these evils by all possible means. The following are the measures which he considers necessary:—1. Official examination of the materials before the commencement of the building, and the enforcement of proper arrangements as regards the structure itself. Thus, in public contracts for any building to be erected in summer, the condition ought to be made, that the materials should be procured and dried during the preceding winter, and the term of completing any edifice should always be regulated according to the weather. Lead and arsenical colours for painting the walls should be entirely forbidden. 2. A house should not be inhabited before a fixed time after its completion had elapsed. Considering the different effects of situation, a house in town should remain uninhabited for a year, and in the country, where sun and air have free access, for half a year after it has been finished. Should any house be dried before the time appointed, the proprietor might request the sanitary commission to examine it, when, if sufficiently dry, it might be inhabited. 3. A commission should be appointed for the purpose of examining every newly-built house, and testifying to its soundness before it is inhabited. Austria presents evidence of the feasibility of such an arrangement. 4. Instruction of the people as regards the injuries caused by inhabiting newly-built houses, &c. and as regards the means to be taken for the purpose of counteracting these injuries.

In absence of such a commission, people ought at least to be informed of the diseases to which they are liable by exposure to such noxious evaporation; and if compelled by circumstances to submit, they ought to use the following precautions pointed out by Dr Reidel:—Thorough drying and ventilation should not be confined to one room, but to all the adjoining rooms. Mould, fungi, &c. should be rubbed and washed off with the greatest care; fires should be frequently lighted, and the windows opened; and muriate of lime or sulphuric acid should be put in different places to attract the moisture. To purify the air from other injurious matters, chlorine, nitric acid vapours, fumes of sulphur, evaporation of vinegar, coarsely-powdered and moistened charcoal put in different places, and other fumigations, should be resorted to. For rooms already inhabited, a solution of chloride of lime is the most proper substance. Drawers and other furniture should not be placed too near the damp walls, and if the latter should be covered with mould, they ought to be touched with a solution of chloride of lime. In addition, warm and dry clothes must be provided, and the bed must not stand too near the walls. Straw or feather beds should be changed frequently, or exposed to the sun.

Such is an abstract of Dr Reidel's paper, which is replete with important but too much neglected instruction. We trust, however, that the plain and convincing manner in which he has placed his views, will be the means of directing attention to an evil to which a large section of our population is continually exposed.

SCALE OF EUROPEAN MORTALITY.

It appears by the 'Sixth Report of the Registrar-General of England,' that England is the healthiest country in this quarter of the globe; the mean annual deaths being about 1 to every 45 persons living. In France, the yearly mortality is as 1 to 42; in Prussia, as 1 to 38; in Austria, as 1 to 33; and in Russia, as 1 to 28. The average duration of life in England is 41 years—that of Russia is less than 27 years.

WATER IN THE DESERT.

Since the French obtained a footing in Algeria, engineers have been employed to procure water in the most sterile districts by means of Artesian wells. We learn from the 'Revue de Paris,'* that one of them, M. Fournel, has completed a minute survey, and he assures his government that the nature of the ground, at the foot of the Algerine mountains, near the sea coast, offers facilities for extracting large supplies of water from an inconsiderable depth below the surface. If wells can be sunk so as to produce the grand desideratum to agriculture, the face of the whole country will be materially changed: vegetation will be made to encroach on the now profitless expanse of the Sahara desert, and many spots, which are productive of nothing but sand, will afford food for man and pasturage for beasts. There is no reason to doubt that such a happy change may in time be effected; for the Artesian system, wherever it has been tried, has succeeded.

PLAGIARISMS.

Expression is said to be 'the dress of thought,' and where men feel, think, and observe alike, it follows that they will often express themselves alike; and even where this is not altogether the case, a shadow of resemblance may be traced, though the features, taken separately, afford no likeness. He who reads much will find the ideas of others imperceptibly mingle with his own, and he will often use the former with the persuasion of their being his own property. A modern writer remarks, that 'certain natural objects irresistibly suggest, to sensitive minds, the same idea, or awaken the same feeling. Who, for instance, ever listened to the hollow murmur of the sea-shell held to the ear, far away from the shore of the ocean, without being thrilled with a feeling of indescribable melancholy? Can we wonder, then, that Wordsworth, Walter Landor, and Hemans, have felt the influence, and embodied it in their verse? The lay of the lark, the glitter of the dew-drop, the thorn of the rose, with the obvious morals they suggest, are not wearisome nor contemptible because many bards have made them the subject of song, sonnet, or stanza; yet many similarities, both of thought and expression, in authors of different degrees of merit, which cannot be exactly called plagiarisms, go far to prove that, if one has not borrowed from the other, they have at least obtained information or inspiration from the same source.'

Singular resemblances are sometimes observable between the thoughts expressed by the Roman writers and those in the sacred Scriptures. Thus, in the fourth epistle of Sulpicius to Cicero, we have the following line—

'Quid horum fuit, quod non prius quam datum est, ademtum sit?'

which may be paralleled by a quotation from St Matthew, ch. xxv. 29—'For unto every one that hath shall be given; but from him that hath not, shall be taken away even that which he hath.'

If there is truth in the assertion that Shakspeare had no pretensions as a scholar, he must certainly have made use of translations of the Greek tragedians, for some of his finest passages have a close resemblance to them.

Lovers looking into each other's eyes, and seeing small reflections of themselves in the pupils, are said to see 'babies in the eyes.' In the 'History of Philocles and Doricles, Two Lancashire Lovers' (1640), Camillus, wooing his mistress, tells her, 'We will go to the dawnes, and slubber

* April 24, 1845.

up a sillibub; and I will look babies in your eyes.' Herrick, in an address to virgins, says—

'Be ye lockt up like to these,
Or the rich Hesperides;
Or those babies in your eyes,
In their crystal nunneries;
Notwithstanding, love will win,
Or else force a passage in.'

The same poet says of Susannah Southwell—

'Clear are her eyes,
Like purest skies,
Discovering from thence
A baby there,
That turns each sphere
Like an intelligence.'

Dryden filched from Shakspeare when he wrote this couplet—

'Death in itself is nothing; but *we fear*
To be we know not what, to go we know not where.'
—'Aurenz-Zebe.'

'The *dread of something after death,*
That undiscovered country, from whose bourne
No traveller returns—puzzles the will,
And makes us rather bear those ills we have,
Than fly to others that *we know not of.*'
—'Hamlet.'

'Ah; but to die!—and *go we know not where.*'
—'Measure for Measure.'

Milton took the title of his 'Comus,' as well as translated many passages, from a little Latin work entitled 'Erycl Puteani Amœnitatum Humanarum Diatribæ' (1615).

The metaphysical opinions of Hobbes remained for some time unnoticed, till Locke availed himself of them without any acknowledgment. Hazlitt has written several admirable essays, proving indisputably that the reputation acquired by Locke, as the founder of the 'new system'—the modern material philosophy of mind—is a pure imposition. Hobbes not only founded, but completed this system; for every one of its principles, even down to the latest commentators of the French school, is certainly to be found in his works. He not only took for his basis the principle, that there is no other original faculty in the mind but sensation, but he pushed this principle into all its consequences. It is probable that Locke would have been consigned to the oblivion to which Hobbes was doomed, if he had followed up the principle in question, as Hobbes had pursued it.

Tabourot's 'Bigarrures et Touches; avec les Apothegmes du Sieur Gaulard, et les Escraignes Dijonnoises,' a humorous little volume, published at Paris in 1608, has been deeply poached in by Swift, who extracted a great part of his 'Art of Punning' from it. Many of Miss Edgeworth's specimens of Irish bulls are also to be found in this old work.

Gray's 'Elegy' contains two images evidently borrowed from Thomson—

'Now fades the glimmering landscape o'er the sight.'—Gray.

'But chief when evening shades decay,
And *the faint landscape swims away.*'—Thomson.

'Full many a flower is born to blush unseen,
And waste *its sweetness on the desert air.*'—Gray.

'A myrtle rises far from human eye,
And breathes *its balmy fragrance o'er the wild;*
So flourished, *blooming and unseen* by all,
The sweet Lavinia.'—Thomson.

In the following instance, the expression copied by Gray is too highly figurative to allow our supposing that it was unconsciously stolen—

'Lo! where the *rosy-bosomed hours,*
Fair Venus' train, appear,
Disclose the long-expected flowers,
And wake the purple year.'
—'Ode to Spring.'

The most picturesque expression here, if not the whole stanza, was borrowed from Milton—

'Along the crisped shades and bowers,
Revels the spruce and jocund spring;
The graces, and the *rosy-bosomed hours,*
Thither all their bounties bring.'
—'Comus.'

The following nervous line, from Gray's 'Ode to Adversity'—

'Whose iron *scourge, and torturing hour*'—

is unquestionably taken from Milton—

'The *scourge* inexorable, and the *torturing hour.*'
—'Paradise Lost,' book ii. line 91.

Kirke White seems to have made Gray his model as much as the latter studied and imitated Thomson. From the 'Elegy' itself he has taken more than one idea—

'All dissolved,
Beneath the *ancient* elm's *fantastic* shade
I lie, exhausted with the noontide heat;
While, *rippling* o'er its deep-worn pebble bed,
The rapid *rivulet* rushes at my feet.'
—'Poetical Fragments.'

And again, in one of his juvenile poems—

'*How did he love to sit*, with upturned eye,
And listen to the stream that murmured by.'—'Clifton Grove.'

'Down at the foot of yonder nodding beech,
That wreaths its *old fantastic* roots so high,
His listless length at noontide would he stretch,
And pore upon the *brook that babbles by.*'—Gray.

To quote another example—

'Then as o'er the fields I pass,
Brushing with hasty steps the grass,
I will meet thee on the *hill,*
Where, with printless footsteps still,
The *morning,* in her buskin gray,
Springs upon her eastern way.'
—Kirke White's 'Ode to Contemplation.'

'Oft have we seen him, *at the break of dawn,*
Brushing with hasty steps the dew away,
To meet the sun upon the upland-lawn.'—Gray.

Goldsmith's poem of 'Madame Blaze' is borrowed, so far as the very peculiar style of every fourth line is concerned, from Menage's odd effusion, entitled 'Le Fameux la Galisse.' Pope's well known lines—

'That *mercy* I to *others show,*
That *mercy* show to me'—

are evidently from Spenser—

'Who will not *mercie unto others show,*
How can he *mercie* ever hope to have?'
—'Faery Queene,' book vi. c. i. st. 42.

and these again are but a paraphrase of a scriptural sentiment.

Lord Byron, after reading one of Scott's novels, was heard to remark, 'How difficult it is to say anything new! Who was that voluptuary who offered a reward for a new pleasure? Perhaps all nature and art could not supply a new idea. This page, for instance, is a brilliant one, full of wit; but let us see how much of it is original. This passage comes from Shakspeare, this bon-mot from Sheridan, and this observation from another writer, and yet the ideas are new-modelled; and perhaps Scott was not aware of their being plagiarisms. It is a bad thing to have too good a memory.' Byron acknowledged that he himself was not very scrupulous how or whence he derived his ideas, so long as they were good. When told that Japhet's soliloquy in 'Heaven and Earth,' and address to the mountains of Caucasus, strongly resembled Faust's, Byron said, 'The Germans, and, I believe, Goëthe himself, consider that I have taken great liberties with Faust. All I know of that drama is from a poor French translation, from an occasional reading or two into English of parts of it by Monk Lewis when at Diodati, and from the Hartz mountain scene that Shelley versified from the other day. I do not pretend to be immaculate, and I could lend you some volumes of shipwrecks from which my storm in Don Juan came.' Shelley's 'Queen Mab,' and Casti's 'Novelle,' were two of Byron's favourite cribbing books: the latter he could draw upon very safely, as only few Englishmen have ever read it. Indeed he is said to have taken Don Juan from Casti chiefly. To quote but one of the many proofs of this, it may be mentioned that the following lines are from the Novelle of the Italian—

'Round her she makes an atmosphere of light;
The very air seemed lighter from her eyes.'

Here, too, is a passage from Don Juan, strikingly resembling one in Dante's 'Inferno'—

industrious little fellow step by step, or to declare precisely how he dealt in cows and geese. It may be enough to say, that at the end of six years he quitted servitude a richer man than ever his father had been; on which occasion he presented the venerable goose to his mother, to whose necessities and comforts he had for some time constantly contributed. So soon as he was thoroughly established in the world, he married, but not till he had provided a neat cottage for his parent, who had the happiness to enjoy for many years the prosperity of her son, and who lived to see the poor cow-boy a man among the most respected and esteemed in his native county.

'And so, you see,' said the old apple-woman in conclusion, 'it is a foolish thing to despise small beginnings. Thrue as I am telling it ye, this is how Mr Carter got the name of Billy Egg, though, d'ye see, he never was called Billy *Goose*—no, never.'

NATURE AND ART.

I remember that, being abroad one summer day, my companion pointed out to me a broad cloud, which might extend a quarter of a mile parallel to the horizon, quite accurately in the form of a cherub as painted over churches—a round block in the centre, which it was easy to animate with eyes and mouth, supported on either side by wide-stretched symmetrical wings. What appears once in the atmosphere may appear often, and it was undoubtedly the archetype of that familiar ornament. I have seen in the sky a chain of summer lightning, which at once revealed to me that the Greeks drew from nature when they painted the thunderbolt in the hand of Jove. I have seen a snow-drift along the sides of the stone wall, which obviously gave the idea of the common architectural scroll to abut a tower. By simply throwing ourselves into new circumstances, we do continually invent anew the orders and the ornaments of architecture, as we see how each people merely decorated its primitive abodes. The Doric temple still presents the semblance of the wooden cabin in which the Dorian dwelt. The Chinese pagoda is plainly a Tartar tent. The Indian and Egyptian temples still betray the mounds and subterranean houses of their forefathers. 'The custom of making houses and tombs in the living rock,' says Heeren, in his Researches on the Ethiopians, 'determined very naturally the principal character of the Nubian Egyptian architecture to the colossal form which is assumed. In these caverns already prepared by nature, the eye was accustomed to dwell on huge shapes and masses, so that when art came to the assistance of nature, it could not move on a small scale without degrading itself. What would statues of the usual size, or neat porches and wings have been, associated with those gigantic halls before which only Colossi could sit as watchmen, or lean on the pillars of the interior?' The Gothic church plainly originated in a rude adaptation of the forest trees with all their boughs to a festal or solemn arcade, as the bands about the cleft pillars still indicate the green withes that tied them. No one can walk in a road cut through pine woods, without being struck with the architectural appearance of the grove, especially in winter, when the bareness of all other trees shows the low arch of the Saxons. In the woods in a winter afternoon, one will see as readily the origin of the stained-glass window with which the Gothic cathedrals are adorned, in the colours of the western sky seen through the bare and crossing branches of the forest. Nor can any lover of nature enter the old piles of Oxford and the English cathedrals, without feeling that the forest overpowered the mind of the builder, and that his chisel, his saw, and plane, still reproduced its ferns, its spikes of flowers, its locust, its pine, its oak, its fir, its spruce. The Gothic cathedral is a blossoming in stone, subdued by the insatiable demand of harmony in man. The mountain of granite blooms into an eternal flower, with the lightness and delicate finish, as well as the aërial proportions and perspective of vegetable beauty.—*Emerson.*

THE COTTAGES OF FACTORY OPERATIVES.

Many of the handsomest cottages in the manufacturing towns, where ground is valuable, are arranged in the most vicious forms. One of these is a parallelogram, consisting of from 16 to 40 cottages, closed on all sides by the houses, which, like a square of infantry, show a front on all sides, the backs of the cottages all meeting in the centre. In this enclosure are placed all the back-yards, pigsties, and ash-pits of the whole of the houses. In hot weather, when the wind is still, the exhalations from these concentrated nuisances are extremely offensive; and the current of air being effectually excluded, there is no chance of their being carried away except by the slow process of gaseous diffusion. The dwellers in such cottages are often astonished at their unhealthiness, when they look at their beautiful outsides. These miserable dwellings are constantly out of repair, the consequence of the badness of their materials; whilst the certainty of the rent from the superior cottages erected by the masters, enables their owners to keep them constantly in good repair, and to supply them with every requisite. Groups of cottages for factory or other operatives, who are required to live closely together, and near to their places of work, should be built in straight parallel rows, in such a manner that the wind may pass freely through the spaces between them. Regard should be had to the direction of the prevailing winds, so that their current may be more or less parallel to the rows of houses for as large a portion of the year as possible. In this country it blows either from the west or east, or from the south or north-west, or south or north-east, ten or eleven months out of the twelve; so that a more or less east and west direction of the rows of houses will insure the most perfect access of fresh air. If a gentle inclination in the ground can be made available, so much the better; but even where the ground is flat, a small inclination sufficient for good surface-drainage may be obtained by digging out in a graduated manner a few feet of soil from the lower portion of the area to be built upon, and spreading it upon the upper part.—*Strange's Address to the Middle and Working-Classes.*

CURIOUS FACT IN COMMERCE.

At the late meeting of the British Association, Mr Porter, in a paper 'on the Trade and Navigation of Norway,' stated the following curious fact in reference to the fur trade of that country:—The greater part of the skins sold by the Norwegians are obtained from the Hamburgh merchants, who buy them in London from the Hudson's Bay Company: the Norwegians convey them to Finmark, from whence they are taken to Moscow, and sold to the caravan traders for the purpose of being bartered with the Chinese for tea at Kiachta!

SUNSHINE AND SHADE.

A manufacturer of carmine, who was aware of the superiority of the French colour, went to Lyons for the purpose of improving his process, and bargained with the most celebrated manufacturer in that city for the acquisition of his secret, for which he was to pay one thousand pounds. He was shown all the process, and saw a beautiful colour produced; but he found not the least difference in the French mode of fabrication and that which had been constantly adopted by himself. He appealed to his instructor, and insisted that he must have concealed something. The man assured him that he had not, and invited him to see the process a second time. He minutely examined the water and the materials, which were in every respect similar to his own, and then, very much surprised, said, 'I have lost my labour and my money, for the air of England does not permit us to make good carmine.' 'Stay,' said the Frenchman; 'don't deceive yourself—what kind of weather is it now?' 'A bright sunny day,' replied the Englishman. 'And such are the days,' said the Frenchman, 'on which I make my colour. Were I to attempt to manufacture it on a dark or cloudy day, my results would be the same as yours. Let me advise you, my friend, always to make carmine on bright sunny days.' 'I will,' rejoined the Englishman; 'but I fear I shall make very little in London!'—*Sir H. Davy.*

CHEERFULNESS.

Cheerfulness and a festival spirit fills the soul full of harmony; it composes music for churches and hearts; it makes and publishes glorifications of God; it produces thankfulness, and serves the ends of charity; and when the oil of gladness runs over, it makes bright and tall emissions of light and holy fires, reaching up to a cloud, and making joy round about: and therefore, since it is so innocent, and may be so pious and full of advantage, whatsoever can innocently minister to this joy does set forward the work of religion and charity.—*Jeremy Taylor.*

Published by W. and R. CHAMBERS, High Street, Edinburgh (also 98, Miller Street, Glasgow); and, with their permission by W. S. ORR, Amen Corner, London.—Printed by BRADBURY and EVANS, Whitefriars, London.

CONDUCTED BY WILLIAM AND ROBERT CHAMBERS, EDITORS OF 'CHAMBERS'S INFORMATION FOR THE PEOPLE,' 'CHAMBERS'S EDUCATIONAL COURSE,' &c.

No. 85. NEW SERIES. SATURDAY, AUGUST 16, 1845. PRICE 1½d.

TWO DAYS IN WARWICKSHIRE.

I HAD never seen the land of Shakspeare. A friend going there to make some observations on the scenery for a literary purpose, asked me to accompany him, and I willingly consented. Ten of the morn, the 2d of July, saw us seated in a train upon the London and Birmingham railway, with two young men of light and cheerful spirit chatting by our sides. The characters of unknown fellow-travellers form an amusing subject of speculation, extremely alleviative of the tedium of travelling, and here were two peculiarly interesting to me, as they belonged to a department of society which does not often come in my way. One, more chatty and gay than the other, soon permitted us to know that he was in the Guards, kept horses on the turf, and frequented Crockford's. The conversation was frivolous, yet not without interest. He had lately gained five thousand pounds by racing, and invested it in a railway, which had already largely increased the sum. He had also lately been wonderfully lucky at play: for example, the *plan*, which consists in throwing fours after threes, and which does not in general occur above once a month with the men who play most, had been thrown by him several times in succession! The usual odds against its being thrown once is a hundred to one, though in reality the chances are much more adverse. Admitting the fact to be as stated, and it is consonant with some others known to me, one might almost believe that there was something in the affairs of chance above mere chance—an influence causing runs of fortune and of misfortune—a deceitful devil luring on gamblers, independently of the operation of their own rash hopes.

A Quaker soon after came in at a station, and assumed a quiet seat in the corner of the carriage. The conversation took a turn towards duelling, and it was distressing to find these youths fully of opinion that it was a justifiable mode of redressing grievances. I reasoned strongly on the other side, but had no chance against minds so imbued with the common world's feelings on this subject. At my worst, however, the Quaker came to the rescue, and argued out the question admirably. It was put to him if he would in no way resent a slap on the face, and he manfully answered, No. He would calmly remonstrate, or he would leave time to bring his injurer to penitence; but he would take no revenge. And he expressed his decided conviction, that no Christian could rightly act otherwise; as also that such conduct was the best even as a matter of policy. 'I believe,' said he, 'that a man going into a barbarous country, is safer without arms than with them. Having arms, shows the power, if not the disposition, to act on the offensive, and is apt to excite combative feelings in the natives; whereas the unarmed man, being beyond all suspicion of bad designs, cannot be attacked except under the most wanton spirit of aggression.' Our plain friend then adverted to the remarkable fact, that the settlers of Pennsylvania had acted upon this policy for seventy years, during which only three persons were killed by the Indians; and in one of these instances the principle had been departed from, as the unfortunate individual carried weapons. I am afraid that our young friends were not converted by our arguments; but let us not therefore presume that the conversation was in vain. Sometimes truths which we battle off at the time they are told us, gradually impress the mind afterwards, and lead to permanent changes of opinion. It is, meanwhile, agreeable to consider that society is now beginning to discountenance duelling, the contingency above all others necessary for its cessation.

In a wonderfully short space of time we were at Coventry. Soon after we were conducted by a branch railway to Leamington, where an artistic friend, well acquainted with the country, joined us. Early in the afternoon, after a slight lunch, we were proceeding in a light vehicle through Warwick, on our way to the neighbourhood of Stratford-upon-Avon. When Shakspeare used to visit his native town, he probably spent the greater part of a week upon the way, resting at the house of Will Davenant's father in Oxford. Now, we are transferred from London to the same place in a few hours. The country of Shakspeare, as the district may well be called, is generally flat, but extremely rich, the Avon winding gently through a slight hollow, marked here and there by slight undulations. Our first object was Charlcote, the residence of the Lucy family, which Shakspeare is supposed to have satirised. Probably, to avoid the constant intrusion of Shakspearian enthusiasts, perhaps in some degree from a lingering resentment for the imputed satire, or for the imputation, the Lucies usually deny access to their house to strangers; but in our case there was to be an exception. It had been arranged that we were to be admitted next day. We therefore had resolved to spend the night at Wellsbourne, a village near Charlcote, and to employ the evening in seeing whatever else in the neighbourhood was worth seeing.

Having bespoken accommodation in the little inn at Wellsbourne, we walked out at five o'clock of a fine summer evening into the lanes surrounding the stately mansion of the Lucies. It struck us curiously, as we moved along, to see a light cart passing, with the name GEORGE LUCY, ESQ. CHARLCOTE, inscribed upon it; indicating as this did the persistency of the name in one spot of ground from Elizabeth's time to the present. 'But, after all,' remarked our Leamington friend, 'you have but an imperfect idea of the antiquity of the Lucies. When Shakspeare stole deer from the park before us, the Lucies had been in their estate for nearly four centuries.' Our friend added, that the eldest son of the existing proprietor was to come of age next month, and that preparations were now making to celebrate the event; 'so that you see the name of Lucy is not likely to become soon extinct.' Chatting about the family and its connexion with Shakspeare's history, we advanced to the borders of the park, and beheld the brick-red towers of the building closing the vista formed by an avenue of ancient limes. Then proceeding a little farther, we found the ancient parish church on the skirt of the park, with its little hamlet close by. 'Everything, then, is as it was in Shakspeare's time. There is the house and its park, with the deer strolling about, the very objects which must have met the eyes of our great bard when he rambled here in his reckless youth. Here is a village where he probably had acquaintances—simple, quaint, and old, as it was then. And here is a little church, where he might have heard service on a Sunday's ramble, and where his prosecutor, Sir Thomas Lucy, is buried.' The deer wander to within ten yards of this humble mansion of prayer. Entering it by favour of the sexton's daughter, we found it old fashioned beyond our hopes; rude old benches and pews; one or two brass inscriptions on the floor, and several monuments with recumbent figures in the chancel; the only object out of keeping being a coarse modern painted east window. The very books in the pews seemed dilapidated with age. I had the curiosity to take up a much relaxed Bible, which I found to be dated 1634.

The Lucy monuments are of course the principal objects. We have those of three successive Sir Thomas's, the first being Shakspeare's Sir Thomas Lucy, a grave substantial-looking personage in plate armour, with his wife by his side, and two children kneeling in front. The third, whose age extended down to the days of Cromwell, is stated to have been killed by a fall from his horse: his figure, and that of his wife, are beautifully executed in white marble. We were standing amongst these memorials of a race which starts with Doom's-day-book, when the girl said, in subdued accents, 'Mr Lucy died last night, sir.' It was most striking, and for a few seconds none of the party could speak a word. To hear at such a moment, and in such a place, of the death of a Lucy, had an effect which I would vainly attempt to describe. It was the least remarkable consequence of the intelligence, that we had to abandon the hope of seeing the interior of the house. Mr Lucy, it appeared, had been for a short time ailing; but, being still in the prime of life, no apprehension of an early removal had been felt.

It was with saddened feelings that we walked to a point in the park where the chief external features of the house could be surveyed. It had been built by Sir Thomas Lucy in 1558, and is a very perfect specimen of what, from its predominance at that time, has been called the Elizabethan style, the chief features being 'projections, peaked gables, bays, and square-headed windows, and stacks of chimneys of twisted and other quaint shapes.'* On one side its walls are almost laved by the waters of the Avon. There has been an anxiety shown of late years to discredit the story of Shakspeare having been concerned in deer-stealing at Charlcote, and of his having been 'had up' before the knight in the hall. His admirers are too dainty, it seems, to like this story, and therefore we are to lose it. A fico for such scepticism and the pedantry it springs from. Handed to us by a man who had at least been a child before Shakspeare's death, it is in reality one of the best facts we have regarding him. And as to discredit, what mind of any manliness would think of imputing it? For my part, as I wandered through these fine glades, amidst whole droves of deer, I felt that not a jot of the tale was to be given up. I was in the midst of Shakspeare's moonlight adventure; these were the descendants of his deer; this was the paling which he broke. And talking, by the way, of the paling, it is a curiosity worthy of some notice, for its simple and antique appearance. It is composed of rude unhewn slabs of timber, fastened with wooden pins upon single length pieces, with a strong earth-fast post at every two yards, to give solidity to the structure. Not an iron nail in it all the way round. It would tell capitally in young ladies' sketch-books, being singularly picturesque in form. We afterwards sauntered round to Hampton Lucy, a beautiful village on the Avon, provided with an elegant modern parish church, which forms a fine feature in the landscape. The house of Charlcote came well out at various points in this perambulation, and there were also some highly sketchable mills. The whole stretch of the river from Charlcote to Stratford abounds in scenes which a poet would delight in; and it is not without reason that some local speculators trace some of Shakspeare's descriptions of natural scenery to this spot.

At an early hour in the morning, we started from our unsophisticated little inn at Wellsbourne, and came in less than an hour's drive to Stratford. It is a clean neat town of about 6000 inhabitants, accessible on the east by a bridge across the Avon, erected in the reign of Henry VII. by Sir —— Clopton, a man of territorial importance in the neighbourhood. We stopped at the Red Horse Inn, because it was that at which Mr Washington Irving had tarried during his sojourn in Stratford; and there, accordingly, we were duly introduced to Mr Irving's room, the scene of the pleasant meditations described in his Sketch-Book—'the arm-chair his throne, the poker his sceptre, and the little parlour, of some twelve feet square, his undisputed empire.' We were soon abroad upon the streets in quest of the objects associated with the name of Shakspeare.

The house in which the poet was born has been so often described, that I dread to be tiresome in adverting to it. It has a remarkable appearance, as being the only one of an antique form in the street. The ground-floor is merely a disused butcher's booth, open in front, and stone-paved. Passing backward, we enter a dark confined place, in which there is a roomy chimney of the old construction—the family fireside, doubtless, of Shakspeare's father. Small rooms open towards the rear of the house, and by a narrow timber stair we reach a front room over the booth, the accredited birth-place of the poet. The sight of such places is necessarily disappointing, for the mind is always in a pre-disposition which the real object can by no means gratify. We think of the glory of a great literary name, and we see a mean chamber, such as poor people now live in. The walls are scribbled over with the names of mortals seeking thus to attach themselves to the car of immortality, and, to relieve such aspirations more legitimately, there is a dingy album upon a deal table, wherein the aged crone who occupies the mansion exhibits the names of various eminent persons. Shakspeare's father paid forty pounds for this and a neighbouring house. This is now rented at as much, on account of the revenue drawn from the exhibition. Unluckily, owing to a dispute about rent, the old furniture of the house, including several curious articles, and some little relics of the Shakspeare family, were removed about forty years ago to another house, where they are now shown under circumstances of greatly diminished interest. Inspired by more than the usual curiosity, I poked into almost every nook of the ancient tenement—even into the garret. It was worth while to see the 'roof-tree' of the house of Shakspeare.

The Shakspeare Hotel now stands upon the site of the handsome house of New Place, which the poet bought out of his earliest savings, and where he spent the latter years of his life in gentlemanlike retirement. So also is perished the mulberry tree planted by him in the garden. There is, however, on the plot behind

* Thorne's Rambles by Rivers.

the house, a very interesting object connected with the poet, namely, the old baptismal font of the parish church—the font in which doubtless he was christened. Passing but a little way along the street from this place, we pass over, as it were, the remainder of the poet's life, and accompany his remains to their last resting-place in the chancel of the parish church. This structure—a fine example of its class, containing specimens of the Gothic of various ages—occupies a beautiful site close to the Avon, at the southern extremity of the town. A solemn alcove of limes across the churchyard, awes the mind down to a proper tone for visiting the grave of Shakspeare. We enter the church, and are agreeably surprised by its internal elegance and neatness. All, however, becomes insignificant in comparison with the well-known space within the remote chancel, where we are aware that we are to see the sepulchre of one greater than kings. How readily the eye recognises that mural monument and bust on the left side! There steadfastly looks forth the mighty bard, over the spot containing his dust and that of his children. The bust is directly above the communion rail, and the communicants kneel along a line of graves containing Shakspeare, his daughter Susanna (Mrs Hall), her husband Dr Hall, and their daughter Lady Barnard, besides perhaps others of the family. The arresting object is of course the effigy of the poet. My impression was, that full justice has never been done to this figure as a memorial of Shakspeare. To my mind, it is a highly important supplement to his meagre biography. It is by far the most human-like representation of his features. First, as to mere details, the upper lip is deeper, and the nose and forehead shorter, than in the portraits. We find it necessary to go to a considerable distance, so as to bring into view the towering central region (the organs of firmness and conscientiousness, according to the phrenologists), before we realise the height usually given to the head of Shakspeare. And it is not till we climb upon an adjoining tomb, and view the profile closely, behind the side pillar of the monument, that we catch the actual character of the face. The result of the whole is, to make Shakspeare less ideal and intellectual, but to improve the sense of what I believe to have been his actual character—a worthy, upright, good-natured man, who was incapable of assuming any of the airs of authorship, and who, being content to pass through life with common enjoyments, and in cheerful communion with common fellow-beings, had nearly escaped being regarded by his contemporaries as an author at all. The face expresses very sensibly the age of the poet at his death—fifty-three—particularly in the lower part of the cheeks, and in the baldness. It is intensely English, and hundreds of such soft-featured, well-skinned, bald, middle-aged men, may be seen every day in London. There is, it may be remarked, good reason to put faith in the bust as a likeness, for it was erected a very few years after his death by his near relations, and Sir Francis Chantrey was of opinion that it must have been copied from a cast of the real visage. Hereafter, the image of Shakspeare in my mind is the recollection of the bust.

The slab covering Shakspeare's grave contains only the quaint lines, supposed to have been dictated by himself:—

> Good frend, for Jesus' sake forbeare
> To digg the dust encloased heare;
> Bleste be ye man y^t spares thes stones,
> And curst be he y^t moves my bones.

A reason is surmised for his having been so anxious to secure the repose of his bones. Immediately below his bust is a door which formerly gave access to a charnel-house, now demolished. Such places were formerly common appendages to churches, being used for keeping the bones removed from re-opened graves. Fearful of his contiguity to such a filthy receptacle—his sense of which he expresses pithily in Romeo and Juliet—it is supposed that the gentle bard caused these lines to be inscribed on his tomb; and they have been effectual for the purpose, notwithstanding that about thirty years ago the opening of a grave near by enabled several persons to see into the space once occupied by his coffin, which they found perfectly empty. There is also an impressive inscription upon the slab covering Susanna Shakspeare; and her husband does not pass without epitaph honours. The usurer John Combe, upon whom Shakspeare is said to have written some verses, rests in a handsome sarcophagus close to the communion-table. The whole place forms no inappropriate final mansion for a poet who, in all his productions, never rose for a moment above the nature of which he partook, and as a man, was ever kindly amongst men. The sexton—grandson of him whom Washington Irving celebrates—is an intelligent guide to the spot. He says the Americans are the most enthusiastic of all his visitors; the Germans next; then the English. I inquired about my own countrymen, and learned that they were even cooler than the English. The Scotsman's feelings, however, are constantly misjudged in the south. He is thought to be unimpassioned, when he is only secretive. He does not choose to wear his best feelings upon his sleeve, 'for daws to peck at.'

Having been favoured with an introduction to Mr Wheeler, we were shown by that gentleman, at his house near the church, a number of relics of Shakspeare. Amongst others are the chief papers connected with the lands which the poet purchased near his native town. But by far the most important is a gold signet-ring, which was found a few years ago in a field beside the churchyard. It presents the initials W. S., enclosed in a looped cord with tassels. Some circumstances point to this being the ring of Shakspeare. First, its being of that age, is shown by the impression of a perfectly similar ring which belonged to Arthur Quiney, a Stratford contemporary of the great dramatist. Second, that the initials probably refer to Shakspeare, is shown by there having been no other man of consequence in Stratford at that time with these initials, besides one William Smith, whose signet-ring is known to have been different. Finally, in Shakspeare's will, dated 25th March 1616, less than a month before his death, the words, 'with my hand and seal,' have been written; but the words, 'and seal' are erased, and no seal is applied; as if in the meantime the seal had been lost. All these circumstances considered, we can entertain little doubt that we have here one of the most interesting possible relics of the bard of Avon.

One duty still remained; to visit the cottage-home of Shakspeare's wife, Anne Hathaway. It lies a mile off along the fields, at a place called Shottery. Passing by stiles across a series of grassy meadows, we reach the humble hamlet, and find Anne's residence at one of its extremities, embowered amongst old orchards and massive hedgerows. The house is a long one, of two storeys, built, in the old English manner, of timber and brick, having a gable to the road and a little patch of garden in front. Shakspeare, as is well known, married at eighteen a woman of five-and-twenty, who in too short space thereafter bore him two children. Judging from her paternal dome, she must have been of a class inferior to her husband in grade, probably a very ordinary village maiden. But the scene of a Shakspeare's courtship has charms notwithstanding. We greet with pleasure the labourer's wife (Mrs Baker) who introduces us into the interior, and tells us that her great-grand-mother was the last Hathaway in possession of the property. We muse over an ancient oaken bedstead, which has been from old time in the house. We pause beside the roomy chimney, in whose nook sweet Will may have sat. And passing again to the outside, we hail, as a little discovery, the letters 'J. H., 1695,' inscribed on a slab at the top, probably for one of these past-away Hathaways. I then close my observations on the land of Shakspeare, but not without feeling that, in seeing it, I have wonderfully extended my knowledge of the man, if not also of the poet. And it is therefore with perfect confidence that I recommend, to all whom it may concern, TWO DAYS IN WARWICKSHIRE.

SHOOTING STARS AND AËROLITES.

THE Baron Alexander Von Humboldt, so distinguished by his scientific travels in America, has employed his advanced years in writing, under the title of *Cosmos* [the World], a general physical history of the universe; and of this work two *parts* of an English translation have appeared.* The means of composing an entire view of nature do not exist: science has not as yet made the requisite advances. Much, however, has been ascertained by the wit of busy man, and the effect of a survey of this so far imperfect kind may be likened, Von Humboldt thinks, to that of a landscape viewed from a mountain, where a stranger will, praise what he sees, although large tracts of the country lie hidden in mist; there being a certain mysterious charm even in the concealment. The Baron does not hide from himself the difficulty of his mighty task, but he nevertheless enters upon it with hopefulness. His general plan may be presumed from one sentence: 'We begin,' he says, 'with the depths of space, and the region of the farthest nebulæ; we descend step by step through the stratum of stars to which our solar system belongs, and at length set foot on the air-and-sea-surrounded spheroid we inhabit, discussing its form, its temperature, and its magnetical tension, till we reach the LIFE, that, under the stimulus of light, is evolved upon the surface.'

In the parts already published, we find the first steps only, but they are the grandest. The masses suspended in space, from astral systems and nebulæ down to our solar system, are vividly though briefly described. The hypothesis of the formation of spheres from nebulous matter is touched upon. Comets, aërolites, the zodiacal light, are accurately described. The author then descends to the terrestrial sphere, and discusses its various physical phenomena—the internal temperature, magnetism, and volcanic forces—on all of which subjects we find the latest and amplest intelligence. Perhaps the manner is less exact than the British scientific mind demands: it is, nevertheless, a striking picture of nature as far as it goes.

The subject of shooting-stars is almost a new one. It had attracted little attention till a few years ago, when it was at length observed that the chief displays of this phenomenon take place on particular nights of the year. They are now connected with fire-balls and meteoric stones or aërolites, and a curious theory pends with regard to these associated phenomena. They are 'regarded as small masses moving with planetary velocity in conic sections round the sun, in harmony with the laws of universal gravitation. When these masses,' says Von Humboldt, 'encounter the earth in their course, and, attracted by it, become luminous on the verge of our atmosphere, they frequently let fall stony fragments, heated in a greater or less degree, and covered on their surface with a black and shining crust.' The appearances are beheld on a much grander scale in elevated tropical climes, where the sky excels in clearness.

According to our author, 'the connexion of meteoric stones with the grander and more brilliant phenomena of fire-balls—that stones actually fall from these fire-balls, and penetrate ten or fifteen feet into the ground—has been shown, among many other instances of the kind, by the well-known fall of aërolites at Barbotan, in the department Des Landes, on the 24th July 1790, at Lima on the 16th of June 1794, at Weston, in Connecticut, on the 14th of December 1807, and at Juvenas, in the department of Ardèche, on the 15th of June 1821. Other phenomena connected with the fall of aërolites are those where the masses have descended, shaken, as it were, from the bosom of a small dark cloud, which had formed suddenly in the midst of a clear sky, accompanied with a noise that has been compared to the report of a single piece of artillery. Whole districts of country have occasionally been covered with thousands of fragments of stones, of very dissimilar magnitudes, but like constitution, which had been rained down from a progressive cloud of the kind described. In rarer instances, as in that which occurred at Kleinwenden, not far from Mühlhausen, on the 16th of September 1843, large aërolites have fallen amidst a noise like thunder, when the sky was clear, and without the formation of any cloud. The close affinity between fire-balls and shooting stars is also shown by the fact of instances having occurred of the former throwing down stones, though they had scarcely the diameter of the balls that are projected from our fireworks called Roman candles. This happened notably at Angers on the 9th of June 1822.'

We have still but an imperfect conception of the physical and chemical processes concerned in these phenomena; but their uniformity shows general causes operating in reference to them. 'If meteoric stones revolve already consolidated into dense masses (less dense, however, than the mean density of the earth), then must they form very insignificant nuclei to the fire-balls, surrounded by inflammable vapours or gases, from the interior of which they shoot, and which, judging from their height and apparent diameters, must have actual diameters of from 500 to 2600 feet. The largest meteoric masses of which we have information, those, to wit, of Bahia and Otumpa in Chaco, which Rubi de Celis has described, are from 7 to 7½ feet in length. The meteoric stone of Aegos Potamos, so celebrated through the whole of antiquity, and which is even mentioned in the Marble-chronicle of Paris, is described as having been of the magnitude of two millstones, and of the weight of a wagon-load. Despite the vain attempts of the African traveller Browne, I have not yet abandoned the hope that this great Thracian meteoric stone, which must be so difficult of destruction, though it fell more than 2300 years ago, will again be discovered by one or other of the numerous Europeans who now perambulate the East in safety. The enormous aërolite which fell in the beginning of the tenth century in the river at Narni, projected a whole ell above the surface of the water, as we are assured by a document lately discovered by Pertz. It is to be observed, however, that none of these aërolites, whether of ancient or modern times, can be regarded as more than principal fragments of the mass which was scattered by the explosion of the fire-ball or murky cloud whence they descended.

'When we duly consider the mathematically-determined enormous velocities with which meteoric stones fall from the outer confines of our atmosphere to the earth, or with which, as fire-balls, they speed for long distances through even the denser fields of air, it seems to me more than improbable that the metalliferous mass, with its internally-disseminated and very perfect crystals of olivine, labrador, and pyroxene, could have run together in so short an interval into a solid nucleus from any state of gas or vapour. The mass that falls, besides, even in cases where the chemical constitution varies, has always the particular characters of a fragment: it is commonly of a prismatoidal or irregular pyramidal form, with somewhat arched surfaces and rounded edges. But whence this figure, first observed by Schreibers, of a mass detached from a rotating planetary body?' The ingenious Chladni was the first (1794) to recognise 'the connexion between fire-balls and the stones that fall from the atmosphere, as well as the correspondence between the motions of these bodies and those of the planetary masses at large. A brilliant confirmation of this view of the cosmic origin of such phenomena has been supplied by Denison Olmsted, of Newhaven, Massachusetts, in his observations on the showers of shooting stars and fire-balls, which made their appearance in the night from the 12th to the 13th of November 1833. On this occasion all these bodies

* Baillière, Regent Street, London. The translation is to fill two volumes 8vo.

proceeded from the same quarter of the heavens—from a point, namely, near the star γ Leonis, from which they did not deviate, although the star, in the course of the lengthened observation, changed both its apparent elevation and its azimuth. Such an independence of the rotation of the earth proclaimed that the luminous bodies came *from without*—from outer space into our atmosphere. According to Encke's calculations of the entire series of observations that were made in the United States of North America, between the parallels of 35° and 42°, the whole of the shooting stars came from the point in space towards which the earth was moving at the same epoch. In the subsequent American observations on the shooting stars of November 1834 and 1837, and the Bremen ones of 1838, the general parallelism of their courses, and the direction of the meteors from the constellation Leo, were perceived. As in the November periodical recurrence of shooting stars, a more decided parallel and particular direction has been noted than in the case of those that appear sporadically at other seasons, so in the August phenomenon it has also been believed that the bodies came for the major part from a point between Perseus and Taurus, the point towards which the earth is tending about the middle of the month of August. This was particularly remarked in the summer of 1839. This peculiarity in the phenomenon of falling stars, the direction of retrograde orbits in the months of November and August, is especially worthy of being either better confirmed or refuted by the most careful observations upon future occasions.

'The altitudes at which shooting stars make their appearance, by which must be understood the periods between their becoming visible and their ceasing to be so, are extremely various; in a general way, they may be stated as varying between four and thirty-five geographical miles. * * The relative velocity of the motion is from four and a quarter to nine miles per second; it is therefore equal to that of the planets. Such a velocity of movement, as well as the frequently observed course of shooting stars and fire-balls in a direction the opposite of that of the earth, has been used as a principal element in combating that view of the origin of aërolites, in which they were presumed to be projected from still active volcanoes in the moon.' * *

'It is highly probable,' continues the Baron, 'that a great proportion of these cosmic bodies pass undestroyed in the vicinity of our atmosphere, and only suffer a certain deflection in the eccentricity of their orbits by the attraction of the earth. We may conceive that the same bodies only become visible to us again after the lapse of several years, and when they have made many revolutions round their orbit.' * *

'Shooting stars fall either singly and rarely, and at all seasons indifferently, or in crowds of many thousands (Arabian writers compare them to swarms of locusts), in which case they are periodical, and move in streams generally parallel in direction. Among the periodic showers, the most remarkable are those that occur from the 12th to the 14th of November, and on the 10th of August; the "fiery tears" which then descend are noticed in an ancient English church-calendar, and are traditionally indicated as 'a recurring meteorological incident. Independently of this, however, precisely in the night from the 12th to the 13th of November 1823, according to Klöden, there was seen at Potsdam, and in 1832, over the whole of Europe from Portsmouth to Orenburg on the river Ural, and even in the southern hemisphere, in the Isle of France, a great mixture of shooting stars and fire-balls of the most different magnitudes; but it appears to have been more especially the enormous fall of shooting stars which Olmsted and Palmer observed in North America between the 12th and 13th of November 1833—when they appeared in one place as thick as flakes of snow, and 240,000 at least were calculated to have fallen in the course of nine hours—that led to the idea of the periodic nature of the phenomenon of great flights of shooting stars being connected with particular days. Palmer of Newhaven recollected the fall of meteors in 1799, which Ellicot and I first described, and from which, by the juxtaposition of observations which I had given, it was discovered that the phenomenon had occurred simultaneously over the New-continent from the equator to New Herrnhut, in Greenland (N. lat. 64 degrees fourteen minutes), betwixt 46 degrees and 82 degrees of longitude. The identity in point of time was perceived with amazement. The stream, which was seen over the whole vault of heaven between the 12th and 13th of November 1833, from Jamaica to Boston (N. lat. 40 degrees, 21 minutes), recurred in 1834, in the night between the 13th and 14th of November, in the United States of North America, but with something less of intensity. In Europe, its periodicity since this epoch has been confirmed with great regularity.

'A second even as regularly recurring shower of shooting stars as the November phenomenon, is the one of the month of August—the feast of St Lawrence phenomenon—between the 9th and the 14th of the month. Muschenbroeck had already called attention, in the middle of the preceding century, to the frequency of meteors in the month of August; but their periodic and certain return about the time of the feast of St Lawrence was first pointed out by Quetelet, Olbers, and Benzenberg. In the course of time other periodically-recurring showers of shooting stars will very certainly be discovered—perhaps from the 22d to the 25th of April; from the 6th to the 12th of December; and, in consequence of the actual fall of aërolites described by Capocci, from the 27th to the 29th of November, or about the 17th of July.

'However independent all the phenomena of falling stars yet witnessed may have been of polar elevation, temperature of the air, and other climatic relations, there is still one, although perhaps only accidental, accompanying phenomenon which must not be passed by unnoticed. The NORTHERN LIGHTS showed themselves of great intensity during the most brilliant of all these natural incidents; that, namely, which Olmsted has described (Nov. 12–13, 1833). The same thing was also observed in Bremen in 1838, where, however, the periodic fall of meteors was less remarkable than at Richmond, in the neighbourhood of London. I have also referred in another work to the remarkable observation of Admiral Wrangel, which he has confirmed to me verbally oftener than once, that during the appearance of the Northern Lights, on the Siberian shores of the Icy Sea, certain regions of the heavens which were not illuminated became inflamed, and continued to glow, whilst a shooting star passed through them.

'The different meteor-streams, each of them made up of myriads of little planets, probably intersect the orbit of our earth in the same way as Biela's comet does. Upon this view we may imagine these shoot-star asteroids as forming a closed ring, and pursuing their course in the same particular orbit. The smaller telescopic planets between Mars and Jupiter, with the exception of Pallas, present us, in their closely-connected orbits, with a similar relationship. It is impossible as yet to decide whether alterations in the epochs at which the stream becomes visible to us, whether retardations of the phenomenon, to which I long ago directed attention, indicate a regular recession or change of the nodes (the points of intersection of the earth's orbit and the ring), or whether, from unequal clustering, or very dissimilar distances of the little bodies from each other, the zone is of such considerable breadth, that the earth only passes through it in the course of several days. The lunar system of Saturn likewise shows us a group of most intimately-associated planetary bodies of amazing breadth. In this group, the orbit of the seventh or outermost satellite is of so considerable a diameter, that the earth, in her orbit round the sun, would take three days to pass over a space of like extent. Now, if we suppose that the asteroids are unequally distributed in the course of one of the closed rings which picture to ourselves as forming the orbits of the riodic currents, that there are but a few thickly-congated groups, such as would give the idea of conuous streams, we can understand wherefore such lliant phenomena as those of November 1799 and 1833 extremely rare. The acute Olbers was inclined to nounce the return of the grand spectacle, in which oting stars, mixed with fire-balls, should fall like a ower of snow, for the 12th-14th of November 1867.

'The solid, heated, although not red-hot, masses ich are seen to fall to the earth from fire-balls by ght, from small dark clouds by day, accompanied with id noises, the sky being generally clear at the time, ow, on the whole, a very obvious similarity, in point external form, in the character of their crust and the emical composition of their principal ingredients. is they have maintained through centuries, and in ery region of the earth in which they have been colted. But so remarkable and early-asserted a phygnomical equality in these dense meteoric masses, is bject to many individual exceptions. How different the readily-forged masses of iron of Hradschina, in district of Agram, or that of the banks of the Sisim, the government of Jeniseisk, which have become ebrated through Pallas, or those which I brought with from Mexico, all of which contain 96 per cent. of n, from the aërolites of Siena, which scarcely contain er cent. of this metal, from the earthy meteoric stone Alais (Dép. du Gard), which crumbles when put into ter, and from those of Jonzac and Juvenas, which, thout metallic iron, contain a mixture of oryctognosally distinguishable, crystalline, and distinct constients! These diversities have led to the division of the mical masses into two classes—nickeliferous meteoric n, and fine or coarse grained meteoric stones. Highly aracteristic is the crust, though it be but a few tenths a line in thickness, often shining like pitch, and occanally veined. So far as I know, it has only been nd wanting in the meteoric stone of Chantonnay, in Vendée, which, on the other hand—and this is equally e — exhibits pores and vesicular cavities like the teoric stone of Juvenas. In every instance, the black st is as sharply separated from the clear gray mass, is the dark-coloured crust or varnish of the white anite blocks which I brought from the cataracts of the inoco, and which are also met with by the side of er cataracts in different quarters of the globe—those the Nile, the Congo, &c. It is impossible to produce ything in the strongest heat of the porcelain furnace ich shall be so distinct from the unaltered matter neath, as is the crust of aërolites from their general ss. Some, indeed, will have it that here and there lications of penetration of fragments, as if by kneadg, appear; but in general the condition of the mass, absence of flattening from the fall, and the not very narkable heat of the meteoric stone, when touched mediately after its fall, indicate nothing like a state fusion of the interior during the rapid passage from limits of the atmosphere to the earth.

'The chemical elements of which meteoric masses nsist, upon which Berzelius has thrown so much light, the same as those which we encounter scattered rough the crust of the earth. They consist of eight tals—iron, nickel, cobalt, manganese, chrome, copper, senic, and tin; five earths—potash and soda, sulphur, osphorus, and carbon; in all, one-third of the entire mber of simple substances at present known. Despite is similarity to the ultimate elements into which inganic bodies are chemically decomposable, the appearce of meteoric masses has still something that is genely strange to us: the kind of combination of the ments is unlike all that our terrestrial mountain and ky masses exhibit. The native iron, which is met th in almost the whole of them, gives them a peculiar, t not therefore a lunar character; for, in other regions space, in other planetary bodies besides the moon, ter may be entirely wanting, and processes of oxidan may be rare.'

Von Humboldt, after some further discussion of this point, says—'Wherefore should not—and here I might refer to a remarkable conversation between Newton and Conduit at Kensington—wherefore should not the matter belonging to a particular cluster of celestial bodies, to the same planetary system, be for the major part the same? Why should it not be so, when we feel at liberty to surmise that these planets, like all larger and smaller conglobated masses which revolve about the sun, have separated from particular and formerly much more widely-expanded sun-atmospheres, as from vaporous rings, and which originally held their courses round the central body? We are not, I believe, more authorised to regard nickel and iron, olivine and pyroxene (augite), which we find in meteoric stones, as exclusively terrestrial, than I should have been had I indicated the German plants which I found beyond the Obi as European species of the flora of northern Asia. If the elementary matters in a group of planetary bodies of various magnitudes be identical, why should they not also, in harmony with their several affinities, run into determinate combinations—in the polar circle of Mars, into white and brilliant snow and ice; in other smaller cosmic masses, into mineral species that contain crystalline, augite, olivine, and labrador? Even in the region of the merely conjectural, the unbridled caprice that despises all induction must not be suffered to control opinion.'

He then proceeds to advert to the 'extraordinary obscurations of the sun which have occasionally taken place, during which the stars became visible at mid-day (as in the three days' darkness of the year 1547, about the time of the fateful battle near Mühlberg), and which are not explicable on the supposition of a cloud of volcanic ashes, or of a dense dry fog—were ascribed by Kepler at one time to a materia cometica, at another to a black cloud, the product of sooty exhalations from the sun's body. The observations of shorter periods of darkness—of three and six hours, in the years 1090 and 1203—Chladni and Schnurrer have explained by the passage of meteoric masses. Since,' he says, 'the stream of shooting stars from the direction of its orbit has been regarded as forming a closed ring, the epochs of these mysterious celestial phenomena have been brought into a remarkable connexion with the regularly-recurring showers of shooting stars. Adolph Erman has, with great acuteness, and after a careful analysis of all the data collected up to the present time, directed the attention of philosophers to the coincidence of the conjunction with the sun, as well of the August asteroids (7th of February) as of the November asteroids (12th of May), at the epoch which coincides with the popular belief in the celebrated *cold days* of Mamertius, Pancratius, and Servatius.'

He thus finely winds up: 'The presumptuous scepticism which rejects facts without caring to examine them, is, in many respects, even more destructive than uncritical credulity. Both interfere with rigour of investigation. Although, for fifteen hundred years, the annals of various nations have told of the fall of stones from the sky—although several instances of the circumstance are placed beyond all question by the unimpeachable testimony of eye-witnesses—although the Bætylia formed an important part of the meteor worship of the ancients, and the companions of Cortes saw the aërolites in Cholula, which had fallen upon the neighbouring pyramid—although caliphs and Mongolian princes have had sword-blades forged from meteoric masses that had but lately fallen, and men have even been killed by stones from heaven (a certain monk at Crema, on the 4th September 1511; another monk in Milan, 1650, and two Swedish sailors on ship-board, 1674), so remarkable a cosmical phenomenon remained almost unnoticed, and, in its intimate relationship with the rest of the planetary system, unappreciated, until Chladni, who had already gained immortal honour in physics by his discovery of phonic figures, directed attention to the subject. But he who is penetrated with the belief of this connexion, if he be susceptible of emotions of awe through natural impressions, will be filled with solemn thoughts in presence, not of the brilliant spectacles of the November and August phenomena only, but even on the appearance of a solitary shooting star. Here is a sudden exhibition of movement in the midst of the realm of nocturnal peace. Life and motion occur at intervals in the quiet lustre of the firmament. The track of the falling star, gleaming with a palely lustre, gives us a sensible representation of a path long miles in length across the vault of heaven; the burning asteroid reminds us of the existence of universal space everywhere filled with matter. When we compare the volume of the innermost satellite of Saturn, or that of Ceres, with the enormous volume of the Sun, all relation of great and small vanishes from the imagination. The extinction of the stars that have suddenly blazed up in several parts of the heavens, in Cassiopea, in Cygnus, and in Ophiucus, leads us to admit the existence of dark or non-luminous celestial bodies. Conglobed into minor masses, the shooting-star asteroids circulate about the sun, intersect the paths of the great luminous planets, after the manner of comets, and become ignited when they approach or actually enter the outermost strata of our atmosphere.

'With all other planetary bodies, with the whole of nature beyond the limits of our atmosphere, we are only brought into relationship by means of light, of radiant heat, which is scarcely to be separated from light, and the mysterious force of attraction which distant masses exert upon our earth, our ocean, and our atmosphere, according to the quantity of their material parts. We recognise a totally different kind of cosmic, and most peculiarly material relationship, in the fall of shooting stars and meteoric stones, when we regard them as planetary asteroids. These are no longer bodies which, through the mere excitement of pulses, influence us from a distance by their light or their heat, or which move and are moved by attraction: they are material bodies, which have come from the realms of space into our atmosphere, and remain with our earth. Through the fall of a meteoric stone, we experience the only possible contact of aught that does not belong to our planet. Accustomed to know all that is non-telluric solely through measurement, through calculation, through intellectual induction, we are amazed when we touch, weigh, and subject to analysis a mass that has belonged to the world beyond us. Thus does the reflecting, spiritualised excitement of the feelings work upon the imagination, in circumstances where vulgar sense sees nothing but dying sparks in the clear vault of heaven, and in the black stone that falls from the crackling cloud the crude product of some wild force of nature.'

Judging of Cosmos from the two parts which we have read, we earnestly recommend it to public attention. From its popular construction and style, we should suppose it a highly eligible work for mechanics' and parish libraries.

THE HOME-WRECK.

SECOND PART.

SCARCELY a week had elapsed, after the accident recorded in the first part of this tale, ere it became a matter of gossiping notoriety that the young squire of Coote-down had fallen in love with the lawyer's daughter. In truth, he had not stirred from the vicinity of the cottage in which Catherine lay, that he might get the earliest information from the medical attendants concerning her condition. From day to day, and sometimes from hour to hour, he watched with intense anxiety. The symptoms improved daily; the anguish caused by the fractures having subsided, the patient was in progress of slow, but, to all appearance, certain recovery.

Mrs Hardman now had sufficient cause to ground a strong opposition to the match her son was endeavouring to make. She spoke to her husband; but he, good, easy man, could not, he said, see any objection to the alliance. She was of their kindred, and although poor, would doubtless make an excellent wife. The imperious and disappointed lady next applied to Dodbury. She placed before him the inequality in the position of Herbert and his daughter, and was very vehement in her arguments against the marriage.

'Your fears, madam,' said Dodbury calmly, 'are at least premature. However passionately your son may express himself in reference to my daughter, she, I know, feels what is due to herself, as well as to Mr and Mrs Hardman. She would never consent to become a member of a family in which she would not be cordially received. Besides, I have yet to learn that she reciprocates the attachment which you say Mr Herbert evinces for her.'

The correct light in which Dodbury thus considered the matter, induced Mrs Hardman to change her policy. After complimenting the lawyer and Catherine for their honourable forbearance, she went on to say that she unhappily had but little influence over her son. 'Would *you*, therefore, endeavour to point out to him the folly of his persistence in following a young lady whom he can never marry?' Dodbury promised to do so, and the lady departed so well pleased with the interview, that she wrote to Lady Elizabeth Plympton, inviting her to spend the ensuing month at Coote-down.

That day, after hearing the most favourable report of Catherine's recovery which had yet been made, Dodbury invited Herbert to dine with him. After the cloth was removed, the subject of the morning's conversation with Mrs Hardman was introduced. Herbert stammered, and blushed: he was not prepared to talk about it just then, and endeavoured to change the topic more than once; but Dodbury kept to the point, till Herbert owned, in fervent and glowing words, that Catherine had completely won his heart, and that he would rather die than be forced into a match with another woman.

'All which,' replied the matter-of-fact man of parchment, 'is very spirited and romantic no doubt. But let us look at the affair with calm and clear eyes. You profess to love my child with strong and unquenchable passion?'

'Profess! Do you doubt me?'

'I do not doubt that you are perfectly in earnest *now*; but my knowledge of mankind forbids my putting much faith in the endurance of the sort of feeling with which you profess (I cannot give up the word, you see) to be inspired. My child, so says the world, is beautiful—very beautiful. Yours may be a mere passion for her beauty.'

'You wrong me,' replied the young man; 'I have known and admired her long enough to appreciate her intrinsic worth. Her image is as dear to me as my own life!'

Dodbury bent on his young friend a long and earnest look of inquiry. He was a good reader of human nature. He saw, that as the lover spoke, his eye lightened with enthusiasm, his lips quivered with emotion, his cheeks glowed with blushes. 'I have little faith in these violent emotions,' thought the wary man of the world, as he leant back in his easy-chair for a moment's reflection. 'Fierce flames burn out quickly. This affair surrounds me with difficulties.'

About a month after Miss Dodbury's complete recovery, her father opened the same topic gradually and delicately to her. Catherine had scarcely nurtured a thought which she had not confided to her father; being her only parent, she looked up to him as the directing source of all her actions. He was 'the king of her narrow world.' In discussing this matter, therefore, though overwhelmed with a maiden shame, she was not reserved. From what she said, the sorrowing father gathered that her maiden affections *were* twined around a man whom her own innate propriety and pride, not to include other obstacles, should prevent her from marrying. This disclosure gave Dodbury great pain. He determined to use more vigilance, caution, and prudence, than ever. His obvious course was to bring about, if possible, a reconciliation to the match with Mrs Hardman; but he refrained. The purity of the young lover's sentiments had yet to be tried. Time he determined should put that to the test.

Meanwhile, Lady Elizabeth had accepted Mrs Hardman's invitation. She and Herbert Hardman were constantly thrown together; and it was manifest, after a time, that, despite the almost studied neglect with which he treated her ladyship, she entertained a strong feeling in his favour. This Mrs Hardman endeavoured by every means in her power to induce Herbert to reciprocate; but in vain; the attraction of Catherine Dodbury was too powerful. It must be owned, however, that his vanity *was* a little flattered by the haughty beauty condescending to feel a sentiment for him.

This state of things was too equivocal and uncertain to last. Catherine strove, as long and as firmly as maiden could strive, against her love; whilst Herbert fed his by every sort of attention it was possible to evince. At length Dodbury felt the necessity of some strong measure. He perceived that consent to the match was less likely than ever, since the tender regard which Lady Plympton had evinced. He, therefore, after a long interview with Mrs Hardman, penned a kind note to Herbert, in which he, with every expression of regret for the step he felt bound to take, forbade him his house, or any further communication with his daughter.

Though long anticipated, this was a bitter blow. Catherine strove not to check the master-feeling which had now taken possession of her whole thought and being; for she knew that was impossible; but, in the purity of her heart, she felt she could love on—more tranquilly, more calmly, now that all hope was abandoned, than when it was nursed in suspense. Deprived of Herbert's presence, she would love him as an imagined, ever-remembered being—an abstraction, of which the embodiment was dead to her for ever. With this new and consolatory sensation she determined, without a tear, never to encounter his real presence again. She wrote him a note to that effect, and, accompanied by her father, went immediately to London.

Herbert was frantic. He upbraided his mother with unfilial earnestness. He appealed to his father, who consoled him by saying he was sorry that, as he always left these matters to his mother's management, he could not interfere; adding, that, so far as he was a judge, the Lady Elizabeth Plympton was an uncommonly fine young woman.

After calm consideration, Herbert made up his mind as to what he should do. The estate was entailed; that made him comparatively independent; and he would endeavour, as well as his impetuous passion would allow, to live on in the hope that at length his mother would give her consent, and that Catherine would retract her determination. In pursuance of this plan, he apologised to his mother for his previous wrath, and treated Lady Elizabeth, during the remainder of her visit, with politeness; but it was a studied, constrained, and ironical sort of courtesy, which pained the unoffending but humbled beauty much more than overt rudeness. When the young lady was about to depart, he surprised his mother by the gallant offer of accompanying her and their visitor to her father's, near Plymouth.

These favourable symptoms Mrs Hardman reported to Dodbury, who, seeing his daughter's perfect resignation, thought it might be not imprudent to return home, especially as young Hardman was to remain at the Earl of Plympton's for a few weeks. He, however, carefully concealed the apparent attachment of Lady Elizabeth from his daughter. Accordingly they returned to their home, Catherine appearing but a slight degree saddened and changed in spirit. A feverish languor, however, of which she neglected to complain or to ask medical advice for, was making inroads on her health.

Mrs Hardman, after staying a week at the earl's, returned, congratulating herself on the seeming change which was gradually creeping over her son's sentiments. She allowed him to remain a month unquestioned; but after that time family matters required Herbert's presence at Coote-down, and she wrote, desiring him to come home. To her surprise, her letter was returned unopened, franked by the earl. Herbert must have left Plympton Court then, and would doubtless be home in the course of the day.

But that day passed, and another, and another, yet no tidings of Herbert. Mr Hardman now became alarmed, and wrote. The answer was, that his son had started for Coote-down that day week! Inquiries were set on foot in all directions. Every house was sent to at which the young man was known to visit. Advertisements were circulated throughout the country, and afterwards published in the London newspapers, for tidings of Herbert Hardman, but without effect. The most distressing fears were apprehended respecting his fate. His parents were distracted; and the only conjecture which could be formed was, that as war had just broken out with America, he had been kidnapped by a pressgang for the sea-service.

This was a last hope, and Hardman hung upon it as upon life. He wrote to the admiralty, and, starting for Plymouth, made every inquiry likely to settle the doubt. Alas! though pressgangs had been busy at their oppressive work, no such name as Hardman had been returned as having been one of their victims. The conviction slowly stole over him, that some fatal accident or rash determination had ended Herbert's term of life. The dislike of her son, of which Mrs Hardman had been suspected, now melted completely away into the fondest affection for his memory. She, however, did not entirely abandon the hope of seeing him again.

What, however, of Catherine all this while? Alas! a misfortune had overtaken her, in the midst of which the mysterious disappearance of Herbert had not reached her. While in London, she, by some unknown means, had contracted that fatal disease, then violently raging in the metropolis—the small-pox. For months her life was despaired of, and of course all knowledge of the absence of Herbert was kept from her.

Mr Hardman grieved to that excess, that he gradually sunk into the grave. His funeral was a melancholy spectacle, for all knew the cause of his demise. His good easy disposition made him extensively regretted. Mrs Hardman's native strength of mind, however, kept her up amidst her double loss. She found a great consolation in assiduously attending Catherine's sick-bed. Misfortune had schooled every particle of pride from her breast, and she was a prey to remorse. She accused herself—not indeed entirely without justice—of having caused the miseries, the effects of which she was now suffering. 'Would,' she exclaimed to Dodbury one day, 'I could recall the past!'

Catherine's recovery was protracted; and, alas! when she appeared in public, it was perceived that the disease had robbed her of her brightest charms. Her face was covered with unsightly marks. Still, the graceful figure, the winning smile, the fascinating manner, remained; and few, after the first shock of the change had passed away, missed the former loveliness of the once beautiful Catherine. A year passed. By slow and cautious hints and foreshadowings, the truth was revealed; but Miss Dodbury bore all with resignation. 'It is perhaps better for me,' she one day said to Mrs Hardman, 'that it is so. Had he loved and wedded another, I dared no longer to have cherished his image as I do. But now it is my blessed privilege to love him in spirit as dearly as ever.'

The hitherto proud, tearless woman of the world wept a flood when unconsciously, innocently, Catherine spoke of the lost Herbert. On one such occasion she threw herself on the girl's neck, exclaiming, 'Oh, what have I done! what have I done!'

Mrs Hardman never spent a day apart from Catherine. What a change of feeling one short year had wrought! Formerly, she looked on the girl as a bar to her ambitious projects; now, she could not lavish love and kindness enough to satisfy her sentiment of atonement towards the same being. One evening they were walking in that part of the park which overlooks the sea, when a sail appeared in the horizon, then another, and another. The sight of ships never failed to remind the mother of her son; for the presentiment regarding his disappearance never forsook her. 'Dearest Catherine,' she exclaimed, 'would that one of those sails were wafting him back to us.' The girl trembled, and Mrs Hardman begged forgiveness for an involuntary allusion which deeply affected her companion. 'But I *must* be forgiven for telling you that I cannot, will not, abandon every hope of seeing him again. If you knew the pictures of happiness I sometimes draw, in which you and he are the chief actors, I am sure they would please instead of paining you. I sometimes fancy him returned; I go through in imagination your marriage; I feel a real delight in fancying myself placing your hand in his at the altar; I——' Here the speaker was interrupted. Her companion, clasping her suddenly for support, had, overcome with emotion, fainted in her arms!

From that day Mrs Hardman forebore all allusion to her lost son.

That summer went by, and grief had made such inroads on Mrs Hardman's mind, that her health gradually declined. Catherine also was weaker than she had ever been for a continuance previous to her last illness. Besides the disfigurement the disease had made in her countenance, grief had paled her complexion and hollowed her cheek. Yet she kept up her spirits, and was a source of unfailing consolation to Mrs Hardman, who gradually weaned her from her father's house to live entirely at Coote-down, where Dodbury also spent every hour he could spare from business. He had recovered all his lost influence in the family affairs, and was able, by his good management, to avert from the estate the embarrassments with which his fair client's former extravagances had threatened it. Mrs Hardman was now gradually becoming a rich woman.

Ere the winter arrived, she expressed a wish to pay a visit to her late father's attorney, who lived at Barnstable. Dodbury offered to accompany her; but she declined this civility. She wished to go alone. There was something mysterious in this journey. 'What could its object be?' asked the lawyer of his daughter. 'Surely, if Mrs Hardman require any legal business to be transacted, I am the proper person to accomplish it.' Catherine was equally ignorant, and the mistress of Coote-down was evidently not inclined to enlighten her.

The journey was commenced. 'I shall return in a fortnight,' said Mrs Hardman. 'Should anything occur requiring my presence earlier, pray ride or send off for me.' These were her parting words. They did not surprise Catherine, for well she knew that an irrepressible presentiment kept possession of the mother's mind that the lost son would one day return. There was not a morning that she rose from her pillow, but the expectation of seeing her son before sunset existed in her mind.

Mrs Hardman had been away a week. Catherine had removed to her father's house, and was preparing to sit down to sew, as was her custom, when her father, returning from the office adjoining, brought her a letter. 'It is very odd,' he remarked, 'but amidst my business communications I find this epistle addressed to you. See, it is marked "sailor's letter." I imagine it must be intended for one of the servants.'

Catherine made no reply; a presentiment darted into her mind. Usually a quiet, calm girl, her nature seemed suddenly to have changed. She snatched the letter from her father's hand, tore it open, looked at the signature, and fell into his arms in an agony of emotion. Absorbed by her painful struggles, Dodbury overlooked the cause of them; and Catherine, with one intense overwhelming thought burning within her, placed the letter before him. She tried to speak, but the agony of joy which she felt choked her. The father read the signature; it was 'Herbert Hardman!'

The reaction came, and Catherine for a time was calm. She said she could listen to the contents of the letter; and Dodbury began to peruse it. Hardman was alive and well; and a new tide of emotion gushed forth from the panting listener. With the ardent impulse of a pious heart, she sunk upon her knees and uttered a fervent thanksgiving to the universal Protector. It was long ere she could hear more. There might be something behind—some dreadful qualification to all the rapture with which her soul was flooded. This thought was insupportable, and as Dodbury saw that his child *must* hear the whole, he read the epistle word for word. It was a strange narrative.

When Herbert left Plympton Court, he determined to stay a night at Plymouth. Walking on a place called Britain Side, near the quay, he was unexpectedly seized by a pressgang. They hurried him on board the Tender, lying off Cat-down; and immediately draughted him to a small frigate, which was to sail the next morning, as part of a convoy to some Indian ships. Accordingly, they sailed. The frigate was commissioned to drop despatches at Gibraltar, and arriving off that place she was obliged to lag some miles behind, to fulfil her orders. After having done so, and made all sail to rejoin the convoy, she was attacked by a Barbary rover of superior strength, was beaten, most of the crew captured, and conveyed into port. They were taken to the market-place, and sold as slaves. Herbert described these extraordinary events as occurring so rapidly, that it was not till he was established with his purchaser—a man of some property, who lived on an estate at the edge of the Sahara desert—that he had time to reflect on them. Hoping that some of the officers or crew had escaped, and would take means to ransom him, he worked on from day to day for a whole year. At last an Egyptian merchant came to visit his master, to whose servant Herbert intrusted a letter, addressed to the British consul at Alexandria. This letter was fortunately delivered, and after a time, his liberty was procured. The moment he got on board ship he wrote the epistle which was now being so eagerly devoured.

Dodbury sent instantly to Mrs Hardman such a letter as was calculated to break the news not too abruptly to her. No time was mentioned for Herbert's arrival, so that suspense and some degree of uncertainty tempered the joy both father and daughter felt in making this communication.

Dodbury busied himself in corresponding with the navy office to obtain Herbert's release from the service; but to his mortification, a reply arrived, stating, as was announced before, that no such name was in the books. It was, however, added, that a person entered as 'H. Hard' was pressed on the identical day that Herbert was, and it was suggested that his name may have been misspelt. That, however, remained to be seen.

By the time Mrs Hardman arrived at Coote-down, a second letter addressed to her had come from her son. It was dated 'off Havre,' and mentioned the probable time of his reappearance in England. The mother's joy was intense; yet the news had not fallen like a shock upon her, as upon Catherine. Holding fast by the daily hope that her son *would* some day reappear, the event was vaguely expected. Hence she was filled with unalloyed delight. All the old gaiety and pride of her disposition returned, and her first thoughts were expended on plans for once more receiving her son—now, by right of inheritance, the possessor of Coote-down—with a splendour to exceed that which welcomed him from France on attaining his majority. Nor was Catherine for a moment forgotten. Every particular of the nuptials was sketched out, and every preliminary prepared. Never were two minds so filled with happiness.

Dodbury started off a little before the time Herbert

was to arrive at Portsmouth. On arriving in London, he endeavoured to pave the way for Herbert's discharge, by clearing up the mistake about the name. Luckily, Lord Plympton held office, and a note from him to the proper authorities was of great service. How eagerly were the lawyer's letters to Coote-down looked for by its inmates! The first announced that, thanks to Lord Plympton's influence, everything had been arranged, and that, on producing Herbert, and proving him to be the representative of the name 'Hard' found in the list of seamen, his discharge would be granted. The second letter was dated Portsmouth. Herbert had arrived! He was much browner than heretofore, but more robust and manly. His manners had altered most: from bordering on the polite and finical, adversity and rough usage had made them more direct and blunt. The third communication was from London, and stated that the Earl of Plympton had insisted on Herbert making his lordship's house his home. Nothing could exceed the friendly warmth with which he had been received by the whole family, especially by the Lady Elizabeth. After some difficulty, the discharge was obtained, and the letter concluded by actually fixing a day for Herbert's appearance in the hall of his fathers.

The vastitude of Mrs Hardman's preparations were equal to the greatness of her joy. The scene of the former reception was to be enacted over again, but with additional splendour.

The time came, and with it the long-lost son. Mrs Hardman met him on the hall steps, and clasped him in her arms with a fondness she had never evinced before. But he was impatient. There was another being whom he longed to fold in his arms. Mrs Hardman conducted him, impelled by impatience, into her dressing-room, where Catherine waited trembling and expectant. Herbert rushed forward and clasped her in an embrace which seemed to pour forth an age of long-suppressed and passionate affection. The mother looked on in silent delight. She seemed to share in the lovers' slightest emotion.

The first raptures having subsided, Herbert gazed upon the face of his mistress. At the first glance he would have started back, had not the firm affection of Catherine's embrace detained him. From the vividest signs of love and hope fulfilled, his countenance altered to an expression of doubt and disappointment. 'Catherine?' he said in a tone of inquiry—'*my* Catherine?'

'Yes,' replied the mother sorrowfully.

'But how changed,' replied Herbert somewhat abruptly; 'how very much changed!'

A mass of thought and recollection, a revulsion of feeling, passed through Catherine's brain; but tears burst forth to relieve her. Herbert gradually released her from his embrace, and his mother stepped forward to support her. She gazed steadfastly at her son, and read in his countenance a presage which she dreaded to interpret. After a time Hardman withdrew to receive the congratulations of the guests, amongst the foremost of whom were Lord and Lady Elizabeth Plympton. He had scarcely closed the door, ere Mrs Hardman placed her weeping charge gently in a chair, and sat beside Catherine, holding her hands to her bosom.

At this moment Dodbury entered to share his daughter's joy. But what a reverse was here! Tears, silence, despondency. He was amazed, disappointed; and anxiously inquired the cause. 'My son,' said Mrs Hardman calmly, 'was a little shocked at Catherine's altered appearance. Doubtless, when his first emotions of surprise are over, all the happiness we anticipated will be realised.' But she mistrusted her own thoughts: a dark presentiment had cast its shadow over her mind.

That night was spent in festivity, in which Catherine was too ill to join. She retired to her chamber, not to give way to unavailing grief, but to fortify her mind against the worst. Mrs Hardman's duties as hostess could not be neglected, and she mixed with her guests with the dignified affability of former years. In watching her son's proceedings, she had frequent occasion to bewail a coarseness and impetuosity of manner, which had doubtless been imbibed from his recent adventures. His attentions to Lady Elizabeth were as incessant and warm as on a similar occasion they were cold and distant. When the guests were retiring, he asked in a careless tone, 'By the by, mother, what has become of Catherine?'

The answer to this question implied an accusation of cruelty in the interview with Catherine. This brought a retort from Herbert, that time was when Mrs Hardman pleaded another's cause. 'True,' replied the mother, 'but since I have known Catherine's unmatched excellence, I have grievously repented that I ever contemplated *that* alliance. Tell me, Herbert, at once, and honestly, have your feelings changed towards Catherine?'

'When I left her she was beautiful,' was the reply; 'now she is——'

'You need not finish the sentence,' rejoined Mrs Hardman. 'I see it all, and will urge you no further: our household's happiness is wrecked.'

The sorrowing lady sought Catherine's chamber. She took her in her arms, exclaiming, 'Catherine, we are women, but we must act like men.' A flood of mingled tears relieved the dreadful emotions which agitated the wretched pair. One moment's consideration showed them the worst—a future of hopeless despair. Hardman's love *was*, then, a mere fitful passion, lit up by Catherine's former surpassing beauty.

Upon her face and form, with their matchless loveliness, his fancy had fed since his banishment; his imagination, rather than his heart, had kept her image constantly before him. But when he beheld her in reality so different from the being his memory-dreams had lingered over, his passion received a sudden check. When he beheld her pallid cheek, there was no heart-love to tell him it was grief for him which had hollowed and blanched her beauteous face. His lightly-based passion all but extinguished, instead of soothing the misfortune which the ravages of disease had brought upon her, gradually became colder and colder. In two months after his return the final blow was struck, and Herbert Hardman became the husband of the Lady Elizabeth Plympton!

From the day of the nuptials, Catherine Dodbury covered her face with a thick black veil, and no mortal had ever seen her face, except her faithful domestic, to the day of her death. She and Mrs Hardman retired to a distant part of the country, to leave the bride and bridegroom in undisturbed possession of the estate. Mrs Hardman did not long survive her son's marriage. On her death, it was discovered that all the property at her disposal she had left to her son—to be enjoyed after his death by Catherine—who, the testatrix never doubted, when she executed the will (for which purpose she made her solitary journey to Barnstable), would, if ever he reappeared, become Herbert's wife.

But how fared the married pair?

At first they lived happily enough; but, when the enthusiasm of love was over, other excitements were sought. They removed to London. Herbert became wildly dissipated, and his wife habitually expensive. The estate was soon impoverished, trees cut down, and the whole steeped in mortgages. Crime succeeded. By a legal juggle, Catherine was deprived of her reversionary rights; and when every penny was gone, the wretched Hardman ended his days in a debtor's prison. His wife followed him, leaving no child to inherit the estates.

Catherine had, during all this while, lived with her father till his decease, which took place just before that of Herbert. She then removed to Coote-down, which had come into her possession, failing nearer heirs—her father having been a cousin two degrees removed from the late Mr Hardman, senior. There she had lived on for years, without any attempt to improve the ruined property, and in the seclusion in which I saw her at my visit.

Such is the history of the 'Home-wreck,' whose effects I witnessed in my visit to Coote-down. Since then, however, things have materially changed. A very short time ago I received notice that the heroine of the above events had sunk into the grave, leaving most of her property to my cousin and fascinating cicerone, who is now happily married. By this time the estate has resumed its former fertility, and the house some of its past grandeur. Singular to say, the hardy old servant still survives, and pursues her song and her knitting at her own corner of the settle to this day.

HE'S A KIND-HEARTED FELLOW!

Ay, so he is; and the world intuitively ratifies the decision. A more generous, frank, and guileless heart never beat within human bosom; nor is he all feeling to act without sense; nor all impulse to proceed without discrimination. He is not to be melted into sympathy by every idle story; and yet Hudson could no more resist the call of genuine distress, than could a snow-flake the heat of a furnace. He is a right-hearted man, who finds his own happiness in the happiness of others, and on whom nothing could inflict more positive misery than the knowledge that he was the cause of wrong to the meanest fellow-creature.

This kindness of disposition is in truth an enviable gift: it is to society what sunshine is to cloudy weather, or what a green spot is to a barren desert. It knows no partiality, and has no object to serve. It flows as lavishly for the beggar's 'God bless you,' as for the rich man's friendship; and is as much at home amid childish prattle, as in the counsels of wisdom. Indeed, if we are to judge by their conduct, the young come in for a notable share of it, and seem to be peculiarly alive to its influences. They know at first sight your kind-hearted fellow, and will pitch upon him with an aptitude more unerring than could have a Gall or a Lavater. They are shrewd physiognomists these embryo humanities, or it may be that their little guileless souls are drawn by some natural affinity towards that which is pure and generous. Only let Hudson make an evening call, and half-a-dozen of these tiny hosts are absolutely boisterous in their welcome. Here a couple pinion his hands, a pair still more diminutive do their best to fetter his limbs, while the elder two have each a seat ready for his reception. There is no mistaking of this heart-kindness among children; the man who owns it is sure to be the load-star round which they gather, even though they should never have seen him before. There is something in his looks, and tones, and little acts of attention which they can keenly appreciate; nor are they to be deceived by the assumption of these by any other. They know their man too well ever to be found in fault; and while they will gradually slink out of the room to be freed from the presence of his cousin, it is absolutely imperative to issue an order of ejectment to make them quit the chair-side of Hudson. They have always so many questions to put, so many wonders to show, that one is almost inclined to pity poor Hudson; and yet no man could be happier, answering, wondering, and amusing with an equanimity that would baffle patience herself to surpass. Nor must his kindness be shown to themselves alone. It is only the other day that a young hopeful, scarcely four years old, came dragging into the parlour a large Newfoundland dog, shaggy and wet, against the dress of our friend; nor could he be persuaded to desist, but urged as his plea that 'Blucher wanted *to know* Mr Hudson.' And know him certainly Blucher did, for animals as well as children have an instinctive knowledge of kindness, and read our looks and interpret our tones with a precision still more unerring.

Hudson, kind-hearted fellow, is also an amazing favourite with the other sex. The girl that opens the door would not do it half so readily for any other person. She knows his knock; the very sound of his footfall tells her 'that's Mr Hudson.' His coat and hat are laid aside with unusual care; he is ushered in with a graceful confidence, and a tone of modest familiarity, that seems to say, 'I know master is always so happy to see you.' Or if we are not at home, he is told that 'Mistress and the children are just in the parlour;' or is greeted with, 'Would you not wait a little, sir?' or with some such expression of humble regard, that never meets the ear of any save your kind-hearted gentleman. The ladies also are all in raptures with him. When their health is proposed, he is invariably selected to reply: indeed, not a party or pic-nic could take place without him, any more than it could be summer without sunshine. He is an active assistant in all their schemes of charity and benevolence, as he is an abettor of their frolic and amusement. They associate a certain good luck with his name, and if the word Hudson only stand at the head of their subscription list, be it in behoof of a fancy fair or blanket society, then they are assured all will go well. It has often puzzled us to understand how Hudson contrives to answer the thousand demands that are made upon his time; and yet in business he has never had a reverse, but prospers more than those who make twenty times more bustle. The fact is, that kindness of heart is a centre of attraction in business as it is in social life; and his readiness ever to oblige is the very reason why people of sense refrain from exacting too much, and why even the worthless feel ashamed to impose upon it.

As amid the amenities of private life, so amid the struggles and severities of public duty, your kind-hearted fellow is pre-eminently conspicuous. He is a leading man on 'Change, if not for the depth of his opinion, at least for the honest cordiality with which it is given. You know him there among his compeers by his open countenance, the frankness with which he salutes them, and by a certain portliness of figure which well assorts with our ideas of the mental dispositions within. The angularities and wrinkles which settle on the face of the surly and peevish have no business with him; the unsettled lurking eye of the man bent on deception, or the driving of a hard bargain, never disfigured that divine index to his kindly heart. A poor but well-meaning creditor finds relief from his friendly tones, and is thereby nerved for renewed endeavours; and we firmly believe that this kindness has saved from ruin, and reclaimed to honesty of purpose, tenfold the number that ever were deterred by dread of exposure and punishment. The demands made upon the time of our friend in public life are quite as numerous as those made upon his attention in private. If there is a bankrupt affair to wind up, he is sure to be nominated trustee; a dispute to settle, 'Oh, we'll refer it to Hudson;' a subscription to be raised for an orphan family, undoubtedly let him be treasurer. Indeed one would almost imagine that he had the gift of multiplying himself, in order to discharge the duties which this innate goodness of heart insensibly gathers around it. And yet our friend, though ever busy, is never bustled: 'can't attend'—'call again'—'not my business,' are phrases that never escape his lips.

It is astonishing to see the happy complacency with which your kind-hearted fellow passes through the world. He has his joke with one, a bit of banter with another, and a kind word for everybody; and everybody has as friendly a disposition towards him. If he err, his errors are soon forgot; few indeed are to be found who could harbour a malignant feeling against him. His superiors meet with him readily, as with one whom it is an honour to know. He is the adored of his equals, and is as indispensable to their dinner-tables and public meetings, as he was to the drawing-rooms of their ladies. With the poor he must ever be in especial respect; for it is the conduct of your kind-hearted men that sweetens their cup of life, and renders more tolerable the unequal distributions of fortune in the present artificial state of society. The beggar has an intuitive knowledge of your kind-hearted fellow, and while he will step out of the way of the churl, will meet the former with the conviction that he beseeches a brother; nor is he ever disappointed. If Hudson has not a penny to give, he has at least a kind word and a friendly tone; and we verily believe, judging from the lighted-up countenance of the pauper, that he would twenty times rather have had that refusal than the coin of the churlish and unfeeling.

This kind-heartedness is eminently the development of a high civilisation and refinement. It may exist inherently in human nature; but it is with its manifestations, and not with its dubious existence, that we have now to do. Savage life is too intent upon mere selfish necessaries to admit of much of this quality; and feudalism has too little of equality to admit of it as a genuine feeling and cause of conduct. It is only in a free and rational state of society that this heart-kindness can attain its full development: and the freer and more enlightened we become, the more will it diffuse its happy influences amongst us. To think otherwise, would be to take but a mean estimate of the religious and educational efforts of the present century: there would be little fulfilling the high expectations man has formed, were they not to infuse into society more truth, more forbearance, and more brotherly affection. There may not be associated with this disposition much of what the world calls superior talent and brilliant genius, but it is ever accompanied by what is more useful to the everyday business of life—a fund of good common sense, and quick appreciation of what is necessary for the exigencies of the moment. And, after all, what were the value of the most exalted genius, the brightest gifts of the head, if the heart was cold, and selfish, and scornful? It is but dubious wisdom that does not make men better and happier—very questionable talent that tells only of the intellect, while the affections are left barren and desolate.

PUBLIC HEALTH—SCHOOLS.

The further our inquiries are pursued into the condition of the humbler classes, the more are we convinced of the necessity for diffusing even the simplest knowledge of scientific principles in their relation with every-day life. It is somewhat surprising, that while so much has been done to regulate the opinions of society by civil law, so little has been done for the explanation and application of physical laws. Pernicious principles, unwholesome and fatal customs, have been immemorially transmitted from generation to generation as matters of hereditary necessity. While science has traced with unerring exactitude the path of the distant comet—we speak not disparagingly—it has forgotten things which lie nearer to us—health and life. Dr Channing, in his lectures on the Elevation of the Labouring-Classes, observes—'Health is the working-man's fortune, and he ought to watch over it more than the capitalist over his large investments. Health lightens the efforts of body and mind; it enables a man to crowd much work into a narrow compass. Were the mass of the community more enlightened on these points, they would apply their knowledge not only to their private habits, but would insist on municipal regulations favouring general health, and for prohibiting the erection or the letting of such buildings as must generate disease. With what face can the great cities of Europe and America boast of their civilisation, when within their limits thousands and tens of thousands perish for want of God's freest, most lavish gifts? We forbid by law the selling of putrid meat in the market: why do we not forbid the renting of rooms in which putrid, damp, and noisome vapours are working as sure destruction as the worst food? If people understand that they are as truly poisoned in such dens as by tainted meat and decaying vegetables, would they not appoint commissioners for houses as truly as commissioners for markets?'

These remarks apply themselves forcibly to certain facts brought to light by the publication of the Report of the Health of Towns Commission. We make in the present case, especial reference to the ventilation of schools. We learn from the evidence that these establishments are, in too many instances, nothing more than large receptacles for impure air. The evil, we learn, is rather owing to defective structural arrangement, than to carelessness on the part of the superintendents, most of whom displayed the greatest solicitude with regard to ventilation. Dr Fleming states, 'I have gone to a school-room where I was told they had abundant ventilation by their many windows. I have visited that school-room at three o'clock on the Sunday afternoon, when crowded. I have then found its atmosphere insufferable, and all the glass in the windows covered with condensed vapour; and on asking the teachers "Why they did not open the windows?" they have properly replied, "Because it would give the children their death of cold."' Christchurch school, in Bow Lane, Preston, is thus described by the visitors:—'It is situated in the lowest part of the street, which slopes from both extremities to the position of the building. It is erected over one of the principal sewers of the town; to the east there is a factory, to the west a number of mud-traps, where all the solid part of the drainage is preserved; and a little beyond there are several meadows flooded from the drain. The room in which the boys are taught is considerably below the level of the adjoining street, and appears to be very damp. The children look pale and unhealthy, and ten on an average are said to be absent from sickness. The late master ascribed his death to the unhealthiness of the room. Many of the other schools are equally badly situated; some are in the vicinity of pigsties, and some in courts. Even in those schools in which provision is made for ventilation independent of the doors and windows, the most gross ignorance is frequently manifested as to its first principles. In St Mary's school, while there is a good arrangement for ventilation around the stove pipe, the ventilator from the boys' school passes into that occupied by the girls, so that they are obliged to breathe the air already vitiated by the school beneath.'

No greater mistake can be made than to suppose that the proper mode of ventilating a room is by opening the windows, or by any openings above the level of the floor. In such cases, the cold air on entering strikes downwards, causing much discomfort to those seated underneath: the vitiated air, which had risen upwards, is lowered in temperature, and being heavier than common air, descends again to be breathed a second time by the occupants of the room. A very slight acquaintance with the laws that govern the motions of fluids would enable a builder to obviate the fatal consequences here noticed, by making the openings for the admission of fresh air invariably on a level with the floor. The condition of some of the Manchester schools, included in Dr Fleming's evidence, clearly demonstrates 'the injurious effects of bad ventilation.' 'The infant school in Lower Mosley Street was insufferably close the day I visited it. The only mode of ventilation is by throwing open the windows above the backs of the heads of the children, the forms being ranged round the room. It did not surprise me when I was told, in the language of my informant, that the children suffer very much from toothache, and in sharp winds from bad coughs. They suffer from these two causes more than any other. On inspecting the Blue-Coat boys, I observed a cutaneous eruption on the hands and arms, and I have seen it since on the bodies of some of the boys. Three whom I examined look delicate, and appear to have suffered from indigestion. On inquiry, I found that this disease (I should call it scurvy) had prevailed some time ago to a more alarming extent, and that it was comparatively subdued. The first relief they obtained was from a change in diet, giving a portion of meat every day, with beer, and more potatoes and less bread. I desired to be shown into the dormitories, where I saw that large apertures had been recently made in the side walls near the ceiling. I was informed that the object had been to improve the ventilation, and that they had to a great extent answered the purpose. Upon comparing dates, it seemed clear that the disease to which I have alluded, though relieved by a change in diet, assumed a much milder form from the time of the alterations in the dormitories, and is now almost overcome.'

We next find some tables bearing on the physical condition of the children when at home. Out of 222 selected for examination, 176 recollected having 'always lived in houses,' 18 formerly 'in cellars,' 21 'now in cellars,' and 7 in houses 'where shops are attached.' With regard to cleanliness, 6 washed their hands and face six times a-day, 10 three times a-day, 48 twice, 143 once, 9 alternate days, 2 twice a-week, and 1 once a-week. The washing of feet seems to be more neglected: 18 who were shoeless washed them 'every night,' 9 'twice a-week,' 103 'once a-week,' 30 'once a-month,' 15 'every fortnight,' 6 wearing shoes 'every night,' and 39 'seldom or never, being forbidden by their mothers.' Tables are also given as to the frequency of changing the clothing or bed linen of the children, and although they are not 'of the lowest or improvident poor,' we are not very favourably impressed as to the practice of cleanliness by the parents. It appears also that there is great difficulty in persuading the very lowest classes to send their children to the schools: they are running about the streets by hundreds, and are rarely found 'sprinkled' among the other scholars. In concluding his evidence, Dr Fleming recommends, 'with the most unqualified conviction, that a competent officer of public health should be appointed by government, one of whose duties it would be to inspect, free of expense to the schools, all our schoolrooms, and to point out the most effectual and economical mode of healthy ventilation.'

In Dr Reid's report on the northern coal-mining districts, we read of schools erected of more than one storey, where the vitiated air from the lower apartment formed the only supply to the room above it; and 'that under a large free school in the Low-Row, Bishop-Wearmouth (and in which a very great number of children are daily educated), there are a series of vaults in which already upwards of sixty or seventy bodies are deposited, and where it is intended to deposit more;' while 'on these vaults being opened, the effluvium which escapes is most offensive and dangerous.' At the Blue-Coat school in Durham, 'out of 387 boys, about 60 were on the sick list; and in the girls' school, immediately above it, there were more than 20 unwell among 234. In an infant school in the same town, 30 children out of 90 were absent from illness (scarlet fever). There were no means of systematic ventilation; a slaughter-house and a piggery were noticed opposite the principal window. But in no public buildings did systematic ventilation appear to be so desirable as in schools, where the long period spent in them, as well as the age of the pupils, and the numbers so often crowded in a given space, render them peculiarly prone to suffer from a stagnant atmosphere. Great errors are often made in schools, where rooms intended at first only for a few individuals are crowded subsequently to an extent altogether incompatible with the original provisions made for ventilation. Cases have come under my notice in other districts, where three and four times the number of pupils for whom ventilation was originally provided have been introduced into the schoolroom. If any buildings should be subjected to inspection, in reference to their arrangements for ventilation, schoolrooms pre-eminently present themselves for consideration, not only from the powerful effect which ventilation must have upon the health of the pupils, but also from the influence which the maintenance of a pure atmosphere, and the example of the simple manner in which it may be sustained, must exert in disseminating widely throughout the whole community a practical knowledge of means that are equally applicable to the habitations of the higher classes and the dwellings of the poor.'

The evils of imperfect ventilation would be very much lessened were all schools situated near a playground; but we are informed that public as well as private schools are often deficient in this requisite. We have said enough to show the amount and extent of the evil, and the necessity for the application of a remedy. In that portion of the report furnished by Dr Reid, the subject of ventilation is treated of with all the attention it deserves, and numerous plates are given illustrative of the injurious effects resulting from defective construction, with the means to be employed for their removal. These plates would be of the greatest use to local committees desirous of introducing the improvements they represent, which it is scarcely possible to convey by mere description.

'Vitiated air from lamps and candles, as well as from respiration, tends to ascend, though, as projected from the nostrils and the mouth, it moves at first more or less downwards, or in a horizontal direction.' As in natural temperatures there is a continually ascending current, 'it is obvious that if the natural movements of vitiated air in ordinary apartments be facilitated by one opening at the lower part, and another above, every room will ventilate itself sufficiently to prevent the more extreme effects that are so often observed at present. If the lower opening be diffused, by extending it along the skirting, the current becomes more mild and equal, and less liable to strike upon the person, so as to produce an offensive draught, than when distinct apertures are made for the purpose; and if the upper aperture be led into a chimney flue, or into an independent flue, warmed by its near position to a hot chimney, its action is more powerful and more uniform than a mere aperture in the wall near the ceiling, and not so subject to modification in windy weather.'

Even a pure atmosphere, unless the air be kept in motion, cannot be perfectly wholesome, for the human body is continually emitting various exhalations, which form around it a species of atmosphere of its own, requiring force to drive it off: this force will be found to exist in the warmth which the body induces in the air it vitiates. When it is remembered that the perspiration from the body will saturate four and a half cubic feet per minute, and that the vapour from the lungs amounts to three grains in the same short space, it will be found that a great natural power exists, which requires merely a little simple artificial action for its entire removal.

It is a gratifying sign to find the health and wellbeing of the people the object of legislative attention. 'A large and comprehensive system of prevention will be found to answer better, and be less costly, than isolated attempts at relief and cure. Schools and churches are cheaper than prisons; pure air than physic; wholesome houses and workshops than hospitals and dispensaries; a population comprising a due proportion of adults and old men—of strength and wisdom—than one of which so large a part consists of widows and young children.'

TORRINGTON HALL.

The work recently advertised under this name, or rather with the extended one quoted below,* is different from what the name would lead us to expect. Instead of a silly puff of some real lunatic asylum, as we surmised from the advertisement, it proves to be a quaint *jeu d'esprit*, satirising the present arrangements of society. Torrington Hall is, in fact, a clever little volume of innovatory ideas with regard to the definition of madness and the principle of competition.

'There is nothing,' says the author at the outset, 'which puzzles the intelligent public more, in these days of discussion and trial of old notions, than the subject of madness. What is madness? is a question which is beginning to be asked, with an unpleasant feeling of doubt, by various persons whose fathers never

* Torrington Hall; being an Account of Two Days, in the Autumn of the Year 1844, passed at that Magnificent and Philosophically-Conducted Establishment for the Insane. By Arthur Wallbridge, author of 'Jest and Earnest.' London: Jeremiah How. 1845.

doubted about the matter. What is madness? and what distinguishes madness from crime? What sort of action entitles a man to comfortable lodgings in a lunatic asylum? and what sort should send him trembling, a miserable offender, to Botany Bay? How are we to know when we must pity, and when abhor? What constitutes misfortune, and what wickedness? What is the social meaning of responsibility?

'These momentous questions have been answered with great readiness, as soon as proposed, by gentlemen learned in the law, who have proved, from venerable authorities, that a line can be boldly and surely drawn between madness and crime—between cases deserving tenderness, and others deserving toughness; that we can sort out accurately human beings who must be nursed until they are well, from others who must be hanged until they are dead; and that the art of performing these ingenious operations depends upon a mental faculty called "judgment."

'The gentlemen learned in the law have sometimes, as a graceful form, called in the testimony of gentlemen learned in physic, who have usually given evidence with great discreetness, and have shown themselves far too gentlemanly to shock the oldest prejudice of the oldest lady living.

'Yet, though a respectable appearance of agreement on the debated point has been presented officially and publicly on due occasion, still the comparatively few dissenters from established metaphysical principles have managed to keep up such a coil, and have somehow made their doctrines so plausible, that the orthodox systems of mental philosophy and criminal jurisprudence seem ready to tumble down in ruins. People who would formerly have been thought madmen, are now suspected to be geniuses; and heroes are beginning to be degraded into madmen. Inspired prophets are made to go through a course of cooling medicine; and blisters instead of ropes are put behind the ears of murderers. The lunatic asylum is replacing altogether the prison; and the gallows may soon be chopped up for firewood.

'How different is this "confusion worse confounded" from the practice of the good old times, when men, women, and children, were sent to Tyburn or Bedlam, as the case might be, according to set rules, which nobody was impertinent enough to bring into question! The well-to-do citizen was then frequently struck by the sight of a dozen or so of scapegraces dangling in the air, and of wild-looking faces peering from behind iron-barred windows. He knew immediately that the first were the wicked and the last the mad; and breathing forth his satisfaction that *he* was neither, he passed on, with a sense of moral and intellectual dignity, to the duties of that station unto which Providence had been pleased to call him.

'All now is changed. Innovators and philanthropists have unsettled everything; and a decent plain man is absolutely at a loss what to think, say, or do. There will by and by be no opportunity whatever for displaying a little virtuous indignation at vice; and any observation about insanity is, even at present, very likely to provoke some pragmatical fellow or other to catechise you on human physiology.

'As a natural result of this new philosophy, the best lunatic asylums of the existing era are no more like the madhouses of past days than light is like darkness. There is such opportunity here for easily reducing to practice theories which seem hopelessly inapplicable to general society, that these asylums for the afflicted portions of our race are actually becoming models of social arrangements, which may be studied with advantage by the sane world outside their boundaries. No "Mad Tom" is confined any longer in a "dark and dismal cell;" and the old appurtenances of whips and chains are dispensed with. The ignorant and ferocious "keeper" is transformed into an educated and kind companion; and the physician has been appointed the all-powerful director. Insanity now is not only a less affliction in itself, but there is a much greater chance of its being cured.'

So much being premised, the author proceeds to give an account of his two days' visit to Torrington Hall, which he describes as a large new establishment, near Bath, under the care of a gentleman named Dr Elstree, a disciple of Gall and Spurzheim, and a believer in the indefinite power of external influences in modifying human nature. This gentleman regarded the notions of general society as if combined for the purpose of debasing all who came within their operation: falsehood honoured; truth sneered at and persecuted; wealth acquired at the sacrifice of every wise and good consideration; the upper classes looking with contempt upon the lower; these returning the contempt with the bitterest hatred; such appeared to him the way of the world. Considering it as a state of things only proper to an early and rude condition of humanity, he wished to contribute to its translation into a finer form of civilisation, and this he did by founding an improved institution for the insane. With the aid of a body of shareholders, he secured a lease of eight hundred acres in Somersetshire, and erected thereon not only a large mansion, comprising, besides domestic rooms, a theatre, chapel, and lecture-rooms, but factories of different descriptions, large workshops, barns, a flour-mill, wash-houses, &c. all furnished with the most labour-saving machinery. While the space nearest the house was laid out as a pleasure-garden, all beyond was devoted to the raising of various agricultural produce, the great object kept in view being to render the establishment as much as possible independent with regard to the necessaries of life. Seven hundred persons were admitted to Torrington Hall; each of whom, after being recovered from the worst influences of the sane world in the infirmary, was allowed to take his or her part in the duties of the establishment, and thus contribute to render it self-supporting, at the same time that they completed their cure.

The author paid his visit in company with a good-natured London friend, Jack Bryant, and they arrived a sufficiently long time before dinner to see over the house, the arrangements of which they found perfect. At half past three, a large bell rang to summon the inmates from their various employments in the fields and workshops, and at four, the whole had assembled in the drawing-room, ready to proceed to dinner. The company, comprising persons of both sexes and of all ages above youth, was of various appearance and manner; 'but all had a certain *trained* air, and absence of vulgarity. They were dressed neatly and plainly in garments of different make and colour, according to individual taste; for, as I afterwards learned from Dr Elstree, their regular daily work for the establishment was now over, and the interim, from dinner-time till bed-time, was at their own disposal. The doctor announced the names of Bryant and myself, and introduced us to the assembly generally. He then introduced us specially to the Rev. William Delany, chaplain of the institution. I was favourably disposed towards this gentleman at first sight: his pale, massive forehead, and noble features, both to the phrenologist and less scientific physiognomist, indicated the presence of pure and elevated tendencies. We had not opportunity for much conversation; for in five or six minutes the sound of a gong was heard, and we moved towards the refectory. A very pretty girl intrusted herself to my care; Bryant selected another; all the men offered their arms to all the women; and we walked off to dinner in very much the same style that would be practised in Belgrave Square.

'The entire length of the apartment which we now entered was occupied by three tables, running parallel with each other. That in the centre was rather larger than the other two, and had a great arm-chair at the upper end. Dr Elstree took this chair, Bryant and myself were placed on either hand of him, and the inmates, and the assistants of Dr Elstree, to the number of nearly three hundred and forty, seated themselves in commodious chairs, either at our central table, or a side one, as they preferred, or found it convenient.

'Whilst we thus carried on operations in *our* refectory under the superintendence of Dr Elstree, another refectory of equal size was in possession of an equal number of inmates under the superintendence of the chaplain.

'The viands with which we were served were plentiful, and capitally cooked. But no very rich dishes were present, and no wine was on the table—nor was any offered. It is a rule of the institution that all fermented liquors are forbidden to the inmates; and visitors have no indulgence shown to their hankering after alcohol. We had sparkling cold water, instead of sparkling champagne; and this rational beverage, standing in elegantly-formed cut-glass jugs all down the table, looked so tempting, and tasted so fresh and pure, that we could have wished for nothing better. A cheerful feeling seemed to prevail, with an inclination to please and be pleased, and a loud hum of conversation sounded over the hall, intermixed with frequent light laughter.'

At a later period of the day, the visitors found all sorts of amusements in progress, the rule being, that labour concluded at dinner-time. 'A drama was in course of performance in the theatre—a concert was going on in one part of the institution, and a ball in another—classes in various studies were formed in the class-rooms—the rattle of billiard-balls was heard as we passed the billiard-room—the reading-room was well filled—and little social parties were held in many private sitting-rooms: *ennui* seemed banished by universal consent.'

After an early breakfast next morning, Dr Elstree proposed to his two visitors that they should view the agricultural operations, the factories, workshops, and exterior arrangements generally. He was not, however, to accompany them all the way, for he had, like others, to take his share of rustic labour; for which purpose he now assumed an appropriate dress.

'"You have probably heard a great deal," said he, "about the subsoil plough, as tending to increase the productiveness of land. We tried it here at first; but, in consequence of the substrata being stiff and difficult to break, we replaced it by a combined system of ploughing and digging with the spade. Lately, however, we have exchanged the spade for a strong three-pronged fork, which we find answers much better. It is about fourteen inches deep, and seven inches and a half wide, and is very manageable and efficacious."

"But is not the labour severe?" asked Bryant.

"It is so to a novice," replied the doctor. "If it were not, I should have invited you and our friend Wallbridge to take a turn—but I had some care for your comfort: to-morrow, you would not have been able to lift your hand, or move one foot before the other. Digging with the fork, however, is easier work than with the spade. The three prongs enter the ground much more readily than a continuous edge; and though they do not bring up so much earth, yet they mix it better, and that compensates. The fork is superior to the spade too, from its rendering the soil uneven and broken. Into these cavities the air can penetrate, and the superfluous water of the soil escape, and the roots of the plants are permitted to extend in search of sustenance."

"I have often heard of spade-husbandry," said I; "but never before of fork-husbandry."

"Which shows that you may live and learn," said the doctor; "but perhaps you take little interest in agricultural matters?"

"As much as most confirmed metropolitans," replied I. "Occasionally, I read of cultivating the land; but my practical researches are principally confined to the shops in Covent-Garden market."

'We had now arrived at the field where Dr Elstree was to remain. He immediately commenced digging in union with several others—the whole being under the control of a superintendent. Bryant and I looked on for some time; and then leaving, went to inspect various agricultural, horticultural, and floricultural operations which were in progress. In three hours the doctor joined us, as we had agreed.

"Well, gentlemen," said he; "I hope you have contrived to get through the morning agreeably? *My* hard work for the day is over; and we will go and see the factories and workshops, if you feel inclined to do so."

"But don't you work in them as well?" said Bryant. "This is such an unaccountable place altogether, that nothing here would astonish me now."

"No," replied the doctor; "my practice in medicine is a set-off against the ingenuity and industry in manufactures of the other inmates. Besides, I am their master. Like Alexander Selkirk, 'I am monarch of all I survey;' and have to keep my social island in order. I work in the fields and gardens, because muscular exertion in the open air is necessary to health; and I see no reason why I should neglect my own benefit whilst I attend to that of others. If I were living in the sane world without, I should perhaps seek the same end by riding furiously after a fox, or by pulling a boat eight or nine miles on a river, and then pulling it back again. Here, we content ourselves with useful labour, performed pleasantly and sociably in groups of different numbers."

'Conversing thus, we reached the door of a flax-mill; and on entering, Bryant and I were astonished by the world of mechanical aids which was disclosed. On all sides machinery was in motion, and it appeared to be principally attended by women. The process of "heckling," or straitening and cleansing the fibres of the flax, interested us greatly.

'From the flax-mill we went to a linen factory; and there again we were lost in wonder at the machinery, which was of the newest and most perfect description. More men were employed than in the flax-mill.

'We next visited a paper-mill, a soap-factory, a gas-factory, a washing, bleaching, and dyeing establishment, carpenters', shoemakers', and other workshops, and returned to the central buildings just as the bell rang out the half hour before dinner.

'Bryant and I were now getting quite used to the Torrington way of life. We refreshed ourselves after our excursion, and repaired to our accustomed refectory with as matter-of-course an air as any other inmates of the establishment. We took our usual seats; Dr Elstree presided as usual; and the dinner was as cheerful a *réunion* as on the preceding day.'

Mixed with these descriptions are conversations on the present arrangements of society, and the means of improving them—all pointing to a plan which shall realise fully the dictates of Christianity, and make the world a scene of pleasant affection, instead of one of fretful contention. There are also biographies of inmates, illustrating the views of the author. Here, as is found in other works of the same kind, he is much more successful in showing the evils essential to a system of competition, than in convincing us of the practicability of any other. The love of gain and aggrandisement we see to be powerful stimulants to exertion, and to the consequent realisation of the means of supporting a large population. It is not easy, without the proof of experience, to be assured that such large results could be attained by a system of co-operation, where each would be incited to exertion only 'by his individual conviction of its necessity to the welfare of the community—by the pleasure of the employment itself—and by the influence of public opinion'—even although 'these indispensable exertions would amount to little, because the citizens of such a social system would avail themselves to the utmost of the enormous, and day-by-day increasing, powers of machinery, which would do all the hard and disagreeable work, and need human beings only as superintendents.' Perhaps, in the revolution of ages, as Johnson somewhere says, when the rule of secondary sentiments shall have run its course, we shall see some large portions of the earth transferred to the superior bond of love, and whole nations living in mutual helpfulness, like the fancied inmates of Torrington Hall.

THE VISITORS OF KEW GARDENS.

In a report by Sir William Hooker on the Royal Botanic Gardens at Kew, dated December 1844, the following passage occurs:—'With the fact before me that the vast stores of the British Museum are freely opened to the public, and visited by thousands of persons in a day with impunity, or comparative impunity to the collections, I did not hesitate, on my arrival here, to have it announced that the grounds should be thrown open from one to six o'clock, with free admission to the hothouses and greenhouses, without the ceremony of conductors; and the public have taken ample advantage of this privilege, and prize it highly; the number of visitors annually increasing, till so many as 15,000 persons have frequented the garden during the past twelve-months. The experiment was considered by many a dangerous one; but it has been pursued now for nearly four years, and, thanks to the diligence and attention of those employed in the garden, *with little or no damage to the plants*, nothing worth recording; and this being the case it becomes easy to show the benefit accruing to the establishment itself, and to the public, by such an act of liberality. The institution gains friends and numerous contributors to its already unrivalled stores; and it is impossible to see so many visitors of all classes frequenting this noble garden, without a conviction that, while educated and scientific individuals cannot fail to derive instruction from such an assemblage of well-arranged and skilfully-cultivated productions, including the useful and the ornamental, the minds of the middle and lower ranks are enlarged and enlightened by a display of all that is most beautiful and lovely in the vegetable creation; and thus *a gradual improvement must ensue in the habits and morals of the people.*' The philanthropic reader will duly appreciate such an additional testimony to the general harmlessness of crowds admitted freely to public places.

INDIA.

Queen Victoria now governs India as much as she does England; and this is a great fact by no means adequately impressed on the public mind. Steam navigation, perhaps, will be the most efficacious means for bringing it home to our bosoms and consciences. Bombay is now distant about as many weeks as it was months in times gone by. The voyage and journey thither seem about to become a holiday trip to the enterprising tourists who are resolved to make the most of a long vacation. They rush to Marseilles, embark for Malta, glance at Alexandria and the needle of Cleopatra, visit Cairo, and mount the pyramids, cross the desert, call at Aden, steam through the far-famed Straits of Babel Mandel, splash along for a delicious fortnight over the Indian Ocean, and inscribe their names in an album at the caves of Elephanta, literally within less than fifty days! Such expeditions, growing into general fashion, may serve to remind us of our perils and responsibilities with respect to the glorious Orient.—*Eclectic Review for July.*

EARLY ASSOCIATIONS.

It is said that at that period of his life when the consequences of his infatuated conduct had fully developed themselves in unforeseen reverses, Napoleon, driven to the necessity of defending himself within his own kingdom, with the shattered remnant of his army, had taken up a position at Brienne, the very spot where he had received the rudiments of his early education, when, unexpectedly, and while he was anxiously employed in a practical application of those military principles which first exercised the energies of his young mind in the college of Brienne, his attention was arrested by the sound of the church clock. The pomp of his imperial court, and even the glories of Marengo and of Austerlitz, faded for a moment from his regard, and almost from his recollection. Fixed for a while to the spot on which he stood, in motionless attention to the well-known sound, he at length gave utterance to his feelings, and condemned the tenor of all his subsequent life, by confessing that the hours then brought back to his recollection were happier than any he had experienced throughout the whole course of his tempestuous career.—*Kidd.*

THE STRUGGLE FOR FAME.

ADVICE TO AN ASPIRANT.

[From 'Legends of the Isles and other Poems,' by CHARLES MACKAY, author of 'The Salamandrine,' &c. Blackwood and Sons. 1845.]

IF thou wouldst win a lasting fame;
If thou th' immortal wreath wouldst claim,
And make the future bless thy name;

Begin thy perilous career;
Keep high thy heart, thy conscience clear;
And walk thy way without a fear.

And if thou hast a voice within,
That ever whispers, 'Work and win,'
And keeps thy soul from sloth and sin;

If thou canst plan a noble deed,
And never flag till it succeed,
Though in the strife thy heart should bleed:

If thou canst struggle day and night,
And, in the envious world's despite,
Still keep thy cynosure in sight:

If thou canst bear the rich man's scorn;
Nor curse the day that thou wert born
To feed on husks, and he on corn:

If thou canst dine upon a crust,
And still hold on with patient trust,
Nor pine that fortune is unjust:

If thou canst see, with tranquil breast,
The knave or fool in purple dressed,
Whilst thou must walk in tattered vest.

If thou canst rise ere break of day,
And toil and moil till evening gray,
At thankless work, for scanty pay:

If in thy progress to renown,
Thou canst endure the scoff and frown
Of those who strive to pull thee down:

If thou canst bear th' averted face,
The gibe, or treacherous embrace,
Of those who run the self-same race:

If thou in darkest days canst find
An inner brightness in thy mind,
To reconcile thee to thy kind:—

Whatever obstacles control,
Thine hour will come—go on—true soul!
Thou'lt win the prize, thou'lt reach the goal.

If not—what matters? tried by fire,
And purified from low desire,
Thy spirit shall but soar the higher.

Content and hope thy heart shall buoy,
And men's neglect shall ne'er destroy
Thy secret peace, thy inward joy.

But if so bent on worldly fame,
That thou must gild thy living name,
And snatch the honours of the game,

And hast not strength to watch and pray,
To seize thy time, and force thy way,
By some new combat every day:

If failure might thy soul oppress,
And fill thy veins with heaviness,
And make thee love thy kind the less;

Thy fame might rivalry forestall,
And thou let tears or curses fall,
Or turn thy wholesome blood to gall;—

Pause ere thou tempt the hard career—
Thou'lt find the conflict too severe,
And heart will break, and brain will sear.

Content thee with a meaner lot;
Go plough thy field, go build thy cot,
Nor sigh that thou must be forgot.

Published by W. and R. CHAMBERS, High Street, Edinburgh (also 98, Miller Street, Glasgow); and, with their permission, by W. S. ORR, Amen Corner, London.—Printed by BRADBURY and EVANS, Whitefriars, London.

☞ Complete sets of the Journal, *First Series*, in twelve volumes, and also odd numbers to complete sets, may be had from the publishers or their agents.—A stamped edition of the Journal is now issued, price 2½d., to go free by post.

CONDUCTED BY WILLIAM AND ROBERT CHAMBERS, EDITORS OF 'CHAMBERS'S INFORMATION FOR THE PEOPLE,' 'CHAMBERS'S EDUCATIONAL COURSE,' &c.

No. 86. New Series. SATURDAY, AUGUST 23, 1845. Price 1½d.

EIGHTEEN-FORTY-FIVE IN RETROSPECT.

One day, having pondered much on several of the great questions of the age, I fell asleep. In my sleep, the vision of a year of the twenty-second century was presented to me, and I dreamed that, living then, I was engaged to write a history of the present reign. On awaking, the following chapter was so thoroughly photographed upon my mind, that I was enabled to write it down without hesitation:—

It is difficult, in the present state of society, to form any idea of its condition in the reign of Victoria I. Yet it was an age of promise—there were hints, as it were, of the good things that have since come, and, while the bulk of the community was marked by barbarism, there were a few spirits which soared towards a genuine civilisation. Many others there were who had become sensible of public and social evils, but could not agree about the best means of remedying them. Each man would be found going about with his nostrum for making all as it ought to be, but all different from each other; so that, amidst the contending claims of various dogmas, it was impossible for a rational person to say what should be done.

War was at that time too recent to be altogether despised as it deserved. The populace liked the roll of the drum, and the measured tread of a regular force as it moved along in its glaring livery and with glancing arms. Surviving commanders were looked on with pride; monuments were raised to the deceased. Accordingly, young men at school were extremely apt to pine for commissions in the army and navy, although there was scarcely any life more devoid of all that can interest an intelligent and generous mind. Young ladies, too, were apt to regard soldiers as far more interesting than the members of more useful professions. There was a disinclination to go to war, on the ground that it was expensive, and interfered with commerce; but few were ever heard to condemn it because it tended to cutting of throats and brutalising of minds, or because it was inconsistent with Christian brotherly love. Indeed, the clergy themselves would still be occasionally seen affecting to confer heavenly benedictions on the colours under which men were to rush against their fellow-creatures in ruthless conflict, as if the God of peace could have been expected to smile on what were only the emblems of deadly rage and hatred between man and man. War was spoken of at the worst as a resource which in some circumstances might be unavoidable; and thus men might have been heard in that age gravely counselling to go to war at an expense of forty millions a-year, in order to save a nook of waste territory not worth as many pence in fee simple. Such ideas were then extremely plausible with a large portion of the people; and two nations would be seen maintaining great armies and navies against each other; each fearing that, if he were unarmed, the other might fall upon him. France and England might have each saved at least fifteen millions a-year, if they could have been mutually sure that they neither inclined to go to war, which in reality proved to have been the case with both many years afterwards.

While public war was generally regarded as right and proper, it is not surprising that private persons who happened to quarrel should have thought themselves entitled to settle their disputes by fighting. A man who had been insulted by another, was expected by society to go out to a retired place and fight that person with pistols, although he might be quite unskilled in the use of the weapon, while the other was the reverse. He was to seek for satisfaction by exposing himself to a chance of being shot through the heart, while the aggressor was exposed to no worse fate. And it did accordingly happen, in many instances, that a poor gentleman who had been assailed with bad words, or wounded by calumny, was slain in an attempt to bring his injurer to account, the said injurer escaping quite free, except that he had to submit to have his innocence pronounced by a jury of his countrymen. There might now be some doubt that any custom so unreasonable had existed even in that age, if it were not substantiated by incontestable evidence in the national archives. It further appears that, when any man was so poor-spirited as to decline fighting, however trifling might be the cause of dispute, he was made miserable by the contempt of society. The people acknowledged 'Thou shalt not kill' as a divine command; but they practically told their neighbour, 'If you do not take your chance of killing or being killed, we will hunt you out from amongst us.'

A strange custom of that age was to use artificial liquors of an intoxicating quality. It had come down from antiquity, and was much modified by the progress of reason, but still held great sway over mankind. Gentlemen would continue at table after dinner, in order to drink more or less of these liquors, and poor people were wont to resort to houses called taverns and beer shops in order to indulge in the same manner. The professed object was to exhilarate their spirits and promote social feeling; but it was merely a bad old custom, which the people at length found it better entirely to abandon. While it lasted, men were accustomed to drink to each other's healths, although every particle they took tended to derange their stomachs, and consequently to injure their own health. It was also customary to select a particular person distinguished for some merit, and pronounce an oration over him, full of such flatteries as no man could then address to another in private without being thought guilty of the grossest rudeness; and after this speech was concluded, the company would toss off a glass of liquor, by way of expressing their wishes for his welfare. It was then expected that he would stand up and disclaim all the merits attributed to him, for modesty demanded no less at his hands; and the whole company would sit with apparent delight, listening to a contradiction of everything they had said or approved of formerly. But indeed liquor so affected the brains of men, that nothing but absurdity could be expected from it. Its effects were worst amongst the humbler class of people. They sometimes spent so much of their earnings upon liquor, that they and their families could hardly obtain the common necessaries of life. And what is strange, the poorer any man was, the more disposed was he to resort to drink, notwithstanding its being a costly article. Some pictures of that age, and certain portions of its poetical literature, convey a striking idea of the extent to which the madness of drinking was carried. Men, under the influence of liquor, would reel to and fro, and fall into gutters and ditches, and beat their wives and tender little ones. In short, it depraved all who were addicted to it. It was the ruin of hundreds of thousands every year; and murders, and almost every inferior crime, continually flowed from it. At length a few bold philanthropists determined to attempt a reform. They lectured, wrote, and argued for the disuse of liquor with the greatest zeal, and, what was best of all, they abjured it themselves. Though much ridiculed at first, they were in time successful, and in the course of a single age, the world was corrected out of an error which appeared to have been in vogue from the dawn of history. Specimens of liquor-measuring vessels, and of drinking cups and glasses, are to be seen in our principal museums.

The ideas of that age with respect to education were extremely curious, so unsuitable do they appear to have been to the purpose. Men had then a very indistinct idea of what they themselves were. Their notions about the constitution of the human mind were of the most childish and fantastic nature. Not knowing the real character of the subject to be treated, they could not be expected to treat it well. One very prevalent notion was, that to learn to read one's own tongue was education. The English language was then written in a manner which now could only excite ridicule, there being no sort of systematic relation between the pronunciation and the spelling. Consequently, there were great and unnecessary difficulties in the way of learning it, and he who could spell well—that is, who had overcome this unnecessary difficulty—was considered as possessing one of the strongest marks of a good education. It was just beginning in that age to be perceived that merely to read English, or even to possess the art of writing it, was not education. To understand it also was now seen to be essential. Still, in many schools, to possess the art of reading English was thought all in all. For the higher classes, who required a better education to distinguish them from the mass, it was thought sufficient to learn one or two dead languages. Thus youths were turned out into the world without the least preparation for its actual duties, much less any knowledge of nature, or of the relations in which Providence had placed them; so that it was a mere matter of chance that they should become tolerable members of society, or acquire any fair share of knowledge. Nor were the plans adopted for conducting schools more rational. The means chiefly trusted for inducing the children to apply to their tasks was the rod or scourge, which never failed to be applied to the backs of all dunces. There is still preserved in the British Museum a board said to have then been fixed up in Winchester school, on which is represented a lash of three thongs, being the instrument employed in compelling the boys to learn their unsuitable lessons. It is justly regarded as a curious illustration of the barbarism of that age. Another custom was that of place-taking. The children were all ranged in a row, and encouraged to contend with each other for the uppermost places, at the same time that they were expected to be loving and kind with each other, and punished for any exhibition of envy and uncharitableness. Thus the seeds were sown, at the tenderest age, for an after-growth of that selfishness which rendered the society of the nineteenth century a scene of continual mutual grinding, sharping, and strife.

In the present age, there is no feature of those remote times more difficult to realise than what appertained to criminal jurisprudence. The very idea of crime is now happily unknown. In our improved social relations, any analogous demonstration of a selfish or unregulated mind is easily repressed by a little treatment in the asylums for mental disease. But in those days, when selfishness was the predominant rule of life, there were frequent instances of what were called offences; that is, demonstrations of selfishness which society had come to consider as inconvenient, and which it therefore wished to repress. To effect this end, a frightful system of terror was kept up. Offenders were subjected to severe punishments, such as imprisonment, banishment, and death, it being thought that, when bad men were seen thus suffering, others would be prevented from becoming bad. The government of that day had immense prisons for the reception of culprits—also colonies, to which they were consigned as slaves; and it was no uncommon thing to see a man or woman put to death in a public place, with legal officers and clergymen standing by their sides all the time, while vast multitudes of the humbler classes gloated over the butchery, as if it had been a spectacle designed for their especial gratification. At this very time, the greater part of the community would have shrunk from any cruelty deemed wholly unnecessary, such as trampling on a worm or killing a fly; yet hardly any one but sanctioned the killing of human beings in this manner, believing that it was unavoidably necessary for preserving life and property. We thus see what strange things custom and the tyrant's plea, necessity, will induce tender hearts to consent to. It would be painful to dwell longer on such a subject. With the conclusion of the dark ages in the twentieth century, vanished the last vestige of a system which had only reacted for evil throughout thousands of years.

A perusal of the newspapers of that age, copies of which have been carefully preserved, would serve better than anything else to convey a due sense of the character of the time, 'its form and pressure.' We see strong traces of the zeal and success with which mechanical, labour-saving, and money-making improvements were followed out. The wits of men appear to have been sharpened to an extraordinary degree, in devising all sorts of plans for making sensual life more agreeable. Some men realised enormous sums of wealth, the most of which was employed in establishing means of accumulating still more. Luxury and refinement were carried to an extreme in some quarters. On the other hand, vast numbers of persons, chiefly resident in large towns, had sunk into a degree of misery which was unknown in earlier and more barbarous times. Society seemed as if polarised, the rich being unprecedentedly rich, and the poor unprecedentedly poor. A few strides would have conducted the philanthropic inquirer from the portals of the superb millionaire, to the stifling dens 'where hopeless want retired to die.' While the higher circles also displayed a delicacy, and in many cases a purity, such as had not previously been known, the lower exhibited a savagery exceeding even that of the most primitive ages. Elegance learned through the newspapers that hordes of the humbler classes lived in places worse in all respects than those in which the domestic animals are usually lodged. Piety heard from her luxurious oratory that hundreds of thousands grew up in a state of exemption from almost every kind of moral influence. Wealth, which could have succoured and restored to righteous feelings the want that growled with rage and despair, was expended in frantic attempts at its own increase, and in frivolities which could not be enjoyed. The finest natures, which could have operated to the most beneficial results upon those less fortunately endowed, whom Providence designs to be their care, sickened with ennui in the pursuit of idle pleasures. In that uneasy system of things, men turned round upon human nature itself, and attributed half the evils they suffered to the increase of the population. And yet this age, which was full of ignorance and error, and animated by but one ruling spirit—the spirit of self—was accustomed to speak of itself as a civilised age, and to look back with pity upon such simple times as those of the Plantagenets and Tudors. It was, indeed, an improvement upon those times; but to us who live under circumstances so different that we can hardly perceive any distinction, the pretensions which it sets forth to be an age of true civilisation must appear supremely ridiculous, and we only can set them down amongst those delusive notions which mankind have in all ages conceived for their own glorification.

THE STORY OF ROSA GOVONA.

A LITTLE before the middle of the last century, there resided at Mondovi, a city in Italy, a young girl called Rosa Govona. Left an orphan at an early age, she had no other apparent means of earning a livelihood than the use of her needle, in which she showed great skill, combined with the most remarkable industry. Being of a reflecting mind, she took no delight in those pleasures and frivolous amusements which too often engage the female heart. Confiding in the resources of an active and benevolent nature, she wished for no companions save those of misfortune, and for no recompense save the blessing of Heaven.

Whilst Rosa was thus living and labouring by herself, she happened to meet with a young girl who had lost both her parents, and who had no means of supporting herself in an honest manner. No sooner did the good Rosa become acquainted with the sad story of the distressed girl, than she generously stretched forth her hand to help her. 'Come and live with me,' she said; 'you shall share my bed, and drink out of my cup, and, above all, you shall live honestly by the work of your hands.' When she had thus made a commencement, others joined her, and she soon congregated round her a society of young girls, all equally poor, and, by the most assiduous application, procured the necessaries of life for them all.

But the little house in which the young girls dwelt soon attracted the attention of all the dissolute young men of the place, who were for ever seeking after adventures of some kind or other. They began by following them whenever they left the house; but the young women silently repulsed all their impertinences, and even forced them, after some time, to blush at their conduct. The house incurred, also, the displeasure of those old people, who, considering all innovations (whether of a beneficial character or not) as dangerous, wish for ever to abide by the old forms and regulations which governed the actions of their ancestors. They could not divest themselves of a mean suspicion that all was not right, and many of the citizens observed Rosa with much curiosity, and began to whisper all manner of things to her prejudice. Thus this retreat of industry and virtue became the object of the most malignant calumnies, and the good Rosa saw herself the subject of impertinent inquiries, of rumours the most vexatious, of suspicions the most unjust. But the wise and courageous girl, fully assured in the purity of her actions and intentions, opposed perseverance to indiscretion, and sense to calumny. The truth could not remain long doubtful; Rosa soon gained the applause of the virtuous, and the commune granted her a larger house, in the plain of Carrasone, as the number of her companions increased daily. This augmented the jealousy of her enemies, who had been hitherto unsuccessful in their endeavours to injure her character; but these new obstacles served only to redouble the ardour of Rosa, and to raise her courage. There were now about seventy young women in the house, all of whom worked in common with herself to procure an honest livelihood. As the house they inhabited was scarcely large enough to accommodate the number of workwomen, she solicited the commune to grant her another still larger habitation. The municipal body, to show their sense of her exertions in the cause of virtue, voluntarily made her a gift of a very large and commodious dwelling in the valley of Brao: here she established a workshop for the manufacture of woollen articles.

The excellent Rosa, who was now about thirty-nine years of age, had at this period, by her indomitable perseverance, triumphed over all obstacles; and by her exertions in extending the association, and her wisdom in superintending the affairs of the community, created an asylum for poor and indigent females. The more she considered the utility of her institution, the greater became her desire to extend the benefits which such an asylum presented. 'How many poor and destitute beings,' thought she, 'must there be in a large and populous city, who are deprived of all means of procuring an honest livelihood.' Filled with this idea, and relying entirely on the sanctity of her mission, she proceeded to Turin in the year 1755. Arrived in the capital of Sardinia, she asked the use of a building suitable for the carrying out of her intentions, and obtained from the priests of the Oratory of St Philip several capacious rooms. Some chairs, tables, and different articles of furniture, were also provided for her use by the good priests. She received the little they gave her with the greatest delight; and thus established, with some of her companions, in the capital city of the kingdom, she resolutely set about prosecuting the objects of her mission.

The novelty of the idea soon engaged the attention of the citizens: they saw, and, what is more astonishing still, they applauded her design; and her shop, or rather factory, soon became the talk of the whole city. At this period, Charles Emanuel III., having established on a firm footing the independence of his people, gave himself up entirely to the paternal administration of the country. As a protector of labour, he accorded to the pious Rosa some houses which had formerly belonged to a religious establishment. Rosa installed herself here, increased the number of her companions, and greatly extended the branches of labour to which they applied themselves.

Two years after this, by order of the same prince, the manufactures carried on by Rosa were properly organised, and registered by the magistrates of commerce; and regulations were drawn up for the government of the institution, which now received the name of Rosines (from that of the foundress), and above the principal entrance was inscribed the following words, addressed by Rosa to her first companions—'You shall live honestly by the work of your hands.'

The prosperous condition of her institution filled the heart of the pious foundress with joy, but she could not divest herself of a desire to extend its blessings still further. She had left an establishment at Mondovi, and she wished now to form similar ones at other populous places. With this end in view, she visited several provinces of the kingdom, called around her all the young women who were desirous of finding a decent means of subsistence, and founded asylums at Novare, Fossano, Savigliano, Saluces, Chieri, and St Damiano d'Asti, all of them towns of considerable note and population. These were provided with the necessary materials for work, and every other want was generously supplied by the excellent Rosa.

She lived twenty-two years after quitting her native city, during all of which period she was engaged in work, labouring unceasingly for the establishment of her eight institutions, and providing asylums for the sustenance both of the bodies and souls of the unfortunate of her sex. On the 28th February 1776, this excellent woman expired, in the midst of her sorrowing pupils, being quite worn out, not with age, but fatigues. Her memory was held in the greatest veneration, as well by those, many of whom she had rescued from misery and idleness, if not from the depths of sin and shame, and rendered good and useful members of society, as by all classes of the Sardinian subjects who had experienced the benefits arising from her exertions, and who knew how to applaud, and take example from the virtue of a simple maiden, who, from the lowest condition of poverty, had raised, by her wisdom and virtue, a monument in the hearts of all well-disposed and charitable persons.

In the establishment of Rosines are received all indigent young girls, of from thirteen to twenty years of age, who have no means of subsistence, but who are qualified for manual labour. 'You shall live honestly by the work of your hands'—such is the fundamental rule and the base of the establishments of Rosines, which rule is never perverted. All the means of subsistence are derived from the labour of the young girls; and the resources for the support of the aged and infirm members are procured from the work of their more youthful companions. The establishment at Turin is a centre of manufactures, and so are the other affiliated houses, all of which flourish at the present time, with the exception of that at Novare, which was closed when that city became part of the kingdom of Italy, and which has never been re-opened since. To avoid all interference with the manufacturers elsewhere, Rosa ordained that all connected with the different establishments should be at the charge of each, and that all should correspond with the principal institution at Turin, which should exercise a surveillance over the others, and be considered as the centre of their operations.

The arts and manufactures carried on by the Rosines are as varied as the taste of woman can make them. After receiving the raw material, the whole operations from first to last are carried on by them. Take, for example, all silken articles. The cocoons of the silk-worm are purchased at the proper season; these are divided by the hands of the Rosines, and the silk is then spun, and undergoes every other preparation necessary, before it is delivered into the hands of the weavers. The most beautiful stuffs, gros de Naples, levantines, satins, &c. are thus fabricated, and more particularly ribbons, for the manufacture of which there are more than twenty looms. These ribbons are of excellent quality, and really beautiful. Those silken stuffs, the fabrication of which requires a frequent change of machine, are never made by the Rosines, as in other manufactories, because in that case, and in every change of fashion, they would be obliged to introduce people from without into the house. But all that is really convenient and useful may be found in their warehouses at almost any time. Linen is also fabricated in these institutions, particularly table-cloths; but this species of work is very laborious to young women, and consequently there are not many employed in it. A large number are likewise occupied in the manufacture of cotton articles: the raw material being purchased by the Rosines, it is then transformed into all kinds of goods. The woollen factory is at Chieri, because at Turin it would interfere greatly with the silk trade. This establishment is complete in all its arrangements, the wool being here scoured, carded, spun, and woven entirely by the Rosines, who fabricate cloths of every quality from it.

As may be supposed, there are many industrious Rosines employed in the article of embroidery. In fact, in this particular branch the Rosines have acquired as much perfection as can possibly be obtained by the industry of women. A new species of manufacture has lately been introduced into the establishments, namely, that of gold thread for the fabrication of lace: this is a most beautiful article, and particularly adapted for church ornaments. All the habiliments of the clergy are made in these institutions.

Our readers will no doubt be curious to know by what means the young women contrive to dispose of their various goods, in order to cover the outlay, and to gain a profit on the raw material. This is managed in the following simple manner:—Each establishment acts, as we have said, as a centre of manufacture—as a great commercial depôt; and each of them has a magazine or shop attached to it, in which the handiwork of the Rosines is sold by persons in the employment of the institution.

All the cloths necessary for the army are purchased by the government from the warehouses of the Rosines. They not only fabricate the cloth itself, but also every other article of ornamental attire, and skilful tailors are employed by them to cut out the different coat pieces, which are then perfected by the Rosines, and delivered to the government all ready to be put on by the soldiers. Besides this, the inhabitants of Turin, and even the tradesmen themselves, are glad to make their purchases at the institution, because here they are sure to get everything good and cheap.

In this manner, then, the institutions are never in want of employment, and a considerable profit is generally left after deducting all the expenses of the different establishments. That at Turin alone brings in a sum of L.3,333, 6s. 8d. per annum; it contains three hundred females, amongst whom there are about fifty aged or infirm inmates, who in consequence are chargeable to the community. 'I visited this remarkable institution,' says Signior Sacchi, 'thanks to the kindness of a worthy ecclesiastic who presided over its administration. He accompanied me round the different apartments, which contained many young females animated by the holy ardour of labour. With an air of quiet content, the girls were engaged in their several tasks, all apparently animated with an anxiety like that which a mother displays when labouring with her children for their common subsistence. Six mistresses and a matron preside over the different workrooms, and the institution is frequently visited by one of the ladies of honour to the queen (of Sardinia), bearing the commands of her majesty, who gives her special protection to the industrious girls.

'Such is this asylum, truly admirable in all its details, founded by the exertions of a poor woman; so true is it that Providence frequently, from the smallest origin, produces the greatest results. The story of Rosa Govona serves to prove in what way, without saddling any expense upon the citizens, and without donations or legacies, so vast a scheme of labour may be brought to a successful termination. In a little chapel adjoining the work-rooms, I read the following monumental inscription:—"Here repose the remains of Rosa Govona de Mondovi, who from her youth consecrated herself to God, for whose glory she founded in her country, in this city, and divers others, retreats for unfortunate young females, in order to lead them to serve God, and gave them excellent rules, to attach them to piety and labour. During her administration of more than thirty years, she gave constant proofs of an admirable charity and an indomitable perseverance. She passed to the life eternal the 28th day of February, in the year 1776, and of her age the 60th. The children recognise in her their mother and benefactress, and consecrate this monument to her memory."

'Humble words these, when one considers the good which has been done, and the benefits which these institutions still continue to confer upon the country, and for which Rosa merits the highest possible eulogium. I was deeply affected, especially when I considered that the good Rosa Govona had as yet received no place amongst the list of the benefactors of the human race.' May this little paper make her known as she deserves to be.

THE LADY HESTER STANHOPE.

SCARCELY a book of eastern travel has been issued for the last twenty years, but has contained some notice of the singular character whose name appears at the head of this article. Her career was at once brilliant, eccentric, and sad. Born of parentage as illustrious for extraordinary talent as for high rank, she appears to have inherited a degree of natural ability which falls to the lot of few women. As the niece and associate of the great statesman William Pitt, she possessed, in the early part of her career, an indirect influence over the destinies of the British empire; yet she ended her days immured in an almost deserted habitation on Mount Lebanon. The course of events, and the imperiously-unbending disposition, which gradually transferred her from the dazzling halls of a splendid court, and the political intrigues of Downing Street, to voluntary exile and solitude in Palestine, deserve, from their unusual nature, to be called a romance.

Materials for a complete biography of the Lady Hester Stanhope do not exist; but from the scattered notices of travellers, and from a work recently published by her medical attendant,* such an outline may be drawn up as will prove interesting and instructive.

Hester Lucy—eldest daughter of Charles, third Earl Stanhope, and of Hester, daughter of William Pitt, first Earl of Chatham†—was born on the 12th March 1776. Her father rendered himself famous by his mechanical inventions; amongst which are the 'Stanhope' printing-press, a monochord for tuning musical instruments, a calculating machine, a method of securing buildings against fire, besides many minor contrivances. By the extreme republicanism of his political opinions, he gained another sort of celebrity. All the trappings and conveniences of rank he at one time summarily abolished: he put down his carriages, and caused his armorial bearings to be erased from his furniture and plate.

Some of his talents, with much of his eccentricity, descended to his daughter; but her opinions, when she was of an age to form them, were directly opposed to her father's: so far from leaning towards democracy, she was a slave to aristocratic notions. At an early age she showed great ingenuity. When two years old, she states, during one of her conversations with her physician—'I made a little hat. You know there was a kind of straw hat with the crown taken out, and in its stead a piece of satin was put in, all puffed up. Well, I made myself a hat like that; and it was thought such a thing for a child of two years old to do, that my grandpapa had a little paper box made for it, and had it ticketed with the day of the month and my age.' The solicitude of Earl Chatham, the most eminent politician the country ever saw, about a child and its toy-hat, deserves notice, as one of the amiable little doings of great men. The anecdote makes a pleasing pendant to the story of another remarkable politician—Henry Quatre, who was not ashamed to be caught playing at leap-frog with his little children.

Lady Hester was scarcely eight years of age when that love of enterprise which afterwards so much distinguished her was first evinced. Just before the Revolution, the French ambassador, Comte d'Adhémar, was a guest at her father's mansion at Chevening, near Seven Oaks, in Kent. 'There was such a fuss with the fine footmen with feathers in their hats, and the count's bows and French manners, and I know not what, that, a short time afterwards, when I was sent to Hastings with the governess and my sisters, nothing would satisfy me but I must go and see what sort of a place France was. So I got into a boat one day unobserved, that was floating close to the beach, let loose the rope myself, and off I went. Yes, doctor, I literally pushed a boat off, and meant to go, as I thought, to France. Did you ever hear of such a mad scheme?' Her juvenile ladyship failed in getting much nearer to France than the Hastings beach; but how she got ashore again is not stated; though we suppose in safety. Her masculine tastes may be judged of from her confession that she 'played at horses' at Chevening, performing the part of driver, whilst once, at least, Mr Abercrombie, late Speaker of the House of Commons, was the 'wheeler.' Who completed the team, we cannot ascertain: men, perhaps, who have risen to equal eminence. That she was an imperious little personage, there can be no doubt; for from her early girlhood she obtained and exercised a vast degree of command over her sisters. 'They never came to me when I was in my room, without sending first to know whether I would see them.'

These traits of Lady Hester's childhood—cleverness, enterprise, and love of power and rule—grew with her growth, and strengthened with her strength. To put a well-known proverb into the feminine gender—'the girl was mother to the woman;' for it will be seen that there occurred no single incident in her after life, the first cause of which is not to be traced to one or other of these characteristics, or to a romantic rather than a useful degree of benevolence, which formed a prominent feature in her disposition.

Her education, with that of her sisters, was solely conducted by governesses. Her mother died when Lady Hester was only four years old, and Lord Stanhope married again some ten months afterwards. So little share did the earl and countess take in the management of the girls, or in their progress in the schoolroom, 'that,' remarked Lady Hester, 'if Lucy met her stepmother in the streets, she should not have known her. Why, my father once followed to our own door in London a woman who happened to drop her glove, which he picked up. It was our governess; but, as he had never seen her in the house, he did not know her in the street.' In those days the intellectual accomplishments taught to young ladies were much more limited than at present, whilst their physical culture was carried on by means not very dissimilar to some of the milder modes of torture employed by the Spanish Inquisition. Back-stays, spine-boards, and foot-stocks, were then the implements in use to force the natural graces of the female form into what were supposed to be 'good figures.' From these punishments, Lady Hester had her share of suffering; but, notwithstanding, she grew up to be one of the finest women of her time. She was tall, well-proportioned, and possessed so exquisite a complexion, that at five paces' distance the sharpest eye could not distinguish her pearl necklace from her skin. Her head, seen in front, was a perfect oval; her cheeks presented a fine contour, rounding off towards the neck: her eyes were large, and of a grayish blue. The effect of her *tout ensemble* was commanding and striking. 'When you first came out,' said Sir Sydney Smith to her, 'you entered the room in your pale shirt, exciting our admiration by your magnificent and majestic figure. The roses and lilies were blended in your face, and the

* Memoirs of the Lady Hester Stanhope, as related by herself in conversations with her physician. In 3 vols. Colburn: London. 1845.

† The Earl Stanhope was twice married: Hester Lucy, Griselda, and Lucy Rachel, were the produce of his first marriage. His second wife, Louisa, niece of the Marquis of Buckingham, brought him Philip Henry, the present Earl Stanhope, Charles Banks, a major in the army, who was killed at Corunna with the unfortunate Sir John Moore, and James Hamilton, who died in 1825.

ineffable smiles of your countenance diffused happiness around you.' Lady Hester's own criticism on herself is perhaps more characteristic of the describer than the described. Lord Hertford had been praising her attractions, 'but,' she answered, 'he is deceived if he thinks I am handsome, for I know I am not. If you were to take every feature in my face, and put them, one by one, on the table, there is not a single one would bear examination. The only thing is, that, put together, and lighted up, they look well enough. It is homogeneous ugliness, and nothing more.' This self-judgment was scarcely correct; for, from the time she made her appearance in society, to the death of her uncle, William Pitt, Lady Hester was the reigning beauty and wit of the court of George III. 'Her mien,' says her biographer, 'was majestic; her address eminently graceful; in her conversation, when she pleased, she was enchanting; when she meant it, dignified; at all times eloquent. She was excellent at mimicry, and upon all ranks of life. She had more wit and repartee, perhaps, than falls to the lot of most women. She was courageous, morally and physically so; undaunted, and proud as Lucifer.'

Lady Hester took the earliest opportunity of leaving her father's roof. She went to live with her maternal uncle, William Pitt, then prime minister; and her residence with him forms the most brilliant part of her career. To show how highly her talents were estimated by Pitt, he allowed her unreserved liberty of action in state matters: the consequence was, that people who had favours to ask, or intrigues to forward, managed, if possible, to gain over Lady Hester first. But in this they were generally foiled; for soon acquiring a vast insight into human nature, she could turn that knowledge to account to its utmost extent, and in the minutest trifles. Pitt would say to her in the troublesome times of his power, 'I have plenty of good diplomatists, but they are none of them military men; and I have plenty of good officers, but not one of them is worth sixpence in the cabinet. If you were a man, Hester, I would send you on the continent with 60,000 men, and give you *carte blanche;* and I am sure that not one of my plans would fail, and not one soldier would go with his shoes unblacked; meaning,' added her ladyship, 'that my attention would embrace every duty that belongs to a general and a corporal—and so it would, doctor.' This, indeed, was most true of her; for, to an almost inordinate love of rule, Lady Hester added an invincible propensity to teach people what they ought to do. She would have been one of the most inveterate givers of advice ever heard of, had not her counsels been usually delivered more in the spirit of commands.

Her domiciliation with Pitt afforded her opportunities of observing the excess of occupation to which a premier is doomed. 'People little knew what he had to do. Up at eight in the morning, with people enough to see for a week, obliged to talk all the time he was at breakfast, and receiving first one, then another, until four o'clock; then eating a mutton-chop, hurrying off to the house, and there badgered and compelled to speak and waste his lungs until two or three in the morning!—who could stand it? After this, heated as he was, and having eaten nothing, in a manner of speaking, all day, he would sup with Dundas, Huskisson, Rose, Mr Long (all these gentlemen were officials of the government), and such persons, and then go to bed to get three or four hours' sleep, and to renew the same thing the next day, and the next, and the next.' Even when the unfortunate prime minister got to rest, it was often broken. Frequently he was 'roused from his sleep (for he was a good sleeper) with a despatch from Lord Melville; then down to Windsor; then, if he had half an hour to spare, trying to swallow something. Scarcely up next morning, when tat-tat-tat—twenty or thirty people one after another, and the horses walking before the door from two till sunset, waiting for him. It was enough to kill a man—it was murder!' In this hard work his servants necessarily shared. 'He had four grooms who died of consumption, from being obliged to ride so hard after him; for they drank, and caught cold, and so ruined their constitutions.' Connected with one of these servants, Lady Hester told a very interesting anecdote, showing the solicitude both her uncle and herself showed towards their domestics. The groom she spoke of fell, like his fellows, a victim to a pulmonary complaint, and 'was placed at Knightsbridge, and then sent to the seaside. One day Mr Pitt, speaking of him, said to me, "The poor fellow, I am afraid, is very bad; I have been thinking of a way to give him a little consolation. I suspect he is in love with Mary, the housemaid; for, one morning early, I found them talking closely together, and she was covered with blushes. Couldn't you contrive, without hurting his feelings, to get her to attend on him in his illness?" Accordingly, soon after, when he was about to set off for Hastings, I went to see him. "Have you nobody," I asked him, "whom you would like to go to the seaside with you?—your sister or your mother?" "No, thank you, my lady." "There is the still-room maid, would you like her?" "Ah, my lady, she has a great deal to do, and is always wanted." From one to another I at last mentioned Mary, and I saw I had hit on the right person; but, however, he only observed he should like to see her before he went. Mary was therefore sent to him; and the result of their conversation was, that he told her he would marry her if he recovered, or leave her all he had if he died; which he did.'

According to Lady Hester, the duties of prime ministers are frequently less grave than they are vulgarly supposed. 'Most simple persons,' writes Dr M., 'imagine that prime ministers of such a country as England, when promoted to so elevated a station, are only moved by the noble ambition of their country's good; and, from the first moment to the last, are ever pondering on the important measures that may best promote it.' He then relates an anecdote to correct such erroneous notions. There was, it seems, a Mr Rice, who had been a *maître d'hôtel* in Mr Pitt's family, and who, having been employed by the Duchess of Rutland to arrange a grand *fête* on her son's coming of age, attracted her grace's admiration by his 'pretty eyes,' which she voted to be 'too good for a kitchen.' This was the man whose interests took precedence of all other questions in the newly-appointed premier's mind.

'The very first thing Mr Pitt did,' said Lady Hester, 'after coming into office the second time, was to provide for Mr Rice. We were just got to Downing Street, and everything was in disorder. I was in the drawing-room; Mr Pitt, I believe, had dined out. When he came home, "Hester," said he, "we must think of our dear, good friend Rice. I have desired the list to be brought to me to-morrow morning, and we will see what suits him." "I think we bad better see now," I replied. "Oh no; it is too late now." "Not at all," I rejoined; and I rang the bell, and desired the servant to go to the Treasury and bring me the list.

'On examining it, I found three places for which he was eligible. I then sent for Rice. "Rice," said I, "here are three places to be filled up. One is a place in the Treasury, where you may fag on, and, by the time you are forty-five or fifty, you may be master of twenty or twenty-five thousand pounds. There is another will bring you into contact with poor younger sons of nobility: you will be invited out, get tickets for the opera, and may make yourself a fine gentleman. The third is in the customs: there you must fag a great deal; but you will make a great deal of money. It is a searcher's place."

'Rice, after considering a while, said, "As for the Treasury, that will not suit me, my lady; for I must go on plodding to the end of my life. The second place your ladyship mentioned will throw me out of my sphere: I am not fit for fine folks; and, if you please, I had rather take the third." So the very next morning I got all his papers signed.'

Such is the anecdote, which, after all, has a benevolent aspect; and there are many things in these volumes which give an amiable impression of Mr Pitt's character; indeed Lady Hester affirmed that nobody ever knew or estimated it rightly. 'His views,' she asserted, 'were abused and confounded with the narrow projects of men who never could comprehend them; his fidelity to his master was never understood. Never was there such a disinterested man; he invariably refused every bribe, and declined every present that was offered to him. Those which came to him from abroad he left to rot in the customhouse; and some of his servants, after quitting his service, knowing he never inquired about them any more, went and claimed things of this sort: for Mr Pitt would read the letter, and think no more about it. I could name those who have pictures hanging in their rooms—pictures by Flemish masters of great value—procured in this way.

'Mr Pitt used to say of Lord Carrington, when he saw him unable to eat his dinner in comfort, because he had a letter to write to his steward about some estate or another—"*Voilà l'embarras de richesses*:" but when he heard of some generous action done by a wealthy man—"There's the pleasure of being rich," he would cry. He did not pretend to despise wealth, but he was not a slave to it, as will be seen by the following anecdotes:—

'At one time a person was empowered by his city friends to settle on him L.10,000 a-year, in order to render him independent of the favour of the king, and of everybody, upon condition (as they expressed it) that he would stand forth to save his country. The offer was made through me, and I said I would deliver the message, but was afraid the answer would not be such as they wished. Mr Pitt in fact refused it, saying he was much flattered by their approval of his conduct, but that he could accept nothing of the sort.

'Yet these people,' added Lady Hester, 'were not, as you might at first suppose, disinterested in their offer: I judged them to be otherwise. For if it had been to the man, and not to some hopes of gain they had by him, would they not, after his death, have searched out those he esteemed as angels, and have honoured his memory by enriching those he loved so much? [alluding to herself and brothers.] But no—they thought if Mr Pitt retired from public affairs, the country and its commerce would go to ruin, and they, as great city men, would be the losers; whereas, by a few thousand pounds given away handsomely, if they got him to take an active part in the government, they would in turn put vast riches into their own purses, and make a handsome profit out of their patriotism.' She added, 'There are no public philanthropists in the city.

'I recollect once a hackney-coach drawing up to the door, out of which got four men: doctor, they had a gold box with them as big as that' (and she held her hands nearly a foot apart to show the size of it), 'containing L.100,000 in bank-notes. They had found out the time when he was alone, and made him an offer of it. It was all interest that guided them, but they pretended it was patriotism—rich merchants, who were to get a pretty penny by the job. He very politely thanked them, and returned the present.

'I was once in the city at an Irish linen warehouse—very rich people, but such a nasty place—so dark! You know those narrow streets. They offered to buy Hollwood for him, pay his debts, and make him independent of the king, if he would contrive to take office; for he was out at the time. I mentioned it to him, as I thought it my duty to do so; but he would not listen to any such proposal.

'When I think of the ingratitude of the English nation to Mr Pitt, for all his personal sacrifices and disinterestedness, for his life wasted in the service of his country!'—Here Lady Hester's emotions got the better of her, and she burst into tears. After alluding to the work he had to perform, she condescended to minute particulars; such, for instance, as the following:—

'Latterly, Mr Pitt used to suffer a great deal from the cold in the House of Commons; for he complained that the wind cut through his silk stockings. I remember one day I had on a large tippet and muff of very fine fur: the tippet covered my shoulders, and came down in a point behind. "What is this, Hester?" said Mr Pitt; "something Siberian? Can't you command some of your slaves—for you must recollect, Griselda, Hester has slaves without number, who implicitly obey her orders" (this was addressed to Griselda and Mr Tickell, who were present)—"can't you command some of your slaves to introduce the fashion of wearing muffs and tippets into the House of Commons? I could then put my feet on the muff, and throw the tippet over my knees and round my legs."'

It appears that Mr Pitt was far from being so insensible as was supposed to the fascinations of female society. He was even anxious to have married, and we have here a curious story of an attachment he had formed with that view to the daughter of a peer; but, if we are to believe what Lady Hester reports of his feelings, he abstained from marriage that he might have nothing to interfere with the duty he owed to his king and country. Lady Hester Stanhope's personal sympathy for her own sex does not seem to have been equal to that of her great patron and relative. Dr M. soon found reason to repent of bringing his wife within her influence, and most married travellers found it impossible to get access at Syria to her with theirs. Lady Hester Stanhope seems, however, to have felt deeply for the wrongs of women, particularly those done to the humbler class of females by aristocratic seducers, whose conduct she indignantly exposed, but into which delicacy prevents us from entering; and, as illustrations of her argument, she adduced the case of Lady Hamilton and Mrs Jordan. But she felt little sympathy with the cause of Queen Caroline, notwithstanding her decided expression of dislike to George IV. himself. It must not be supposed that we concur in all her decisions and estimates of character; for obvious reasons, this would be absurd. To Mr Canning her ladyship is especially unjust; and we are told by her biographer, that such was her antipathy, she never could speak calmly of him, and that his name once introduced, was sure to lead to an angry diatribe. She confessed, however, that his literary talents were useful to Mr Pitt. 'He was clever,' said she, 'and wrote well, whilst Mr Pitt could never trust Lord C. to draw up an official paper, without having to cross and correct half of it.'

Some anecdotes relating to her relative Lord Camelford, the noted duellist, are of an unexpected character: —'People were very much mistaken about him. His generosity and the good he did in secret, passes all belief. He used to give L.5000 a-year to his lawyer to distribute among distressed persons. "The only condition I enjoin," he used to say, "is not to let them know who it comes from." He would sometimes dress himself in a jacket and trousers, like a sailor, and go to some tavern or alehouse; and if he fell in with a poor-looking person, who had an air of trouble or poverty, he would contrive to enter into conversation with him, and find out all about him. "Come," he would say, "tell me your story, and I will tell you mine." He was endowed with great penetration, and if he saw that the man's story was true, he would slip fifty or a hundred pounds into his hand, with this admonitory warning—"Recollect, you are not to speak of this; if you do, you will have to answer for it in a way you don't like."

'I recollect once he was driving me out in his curricle, when, at a turnpike-gate, I saw him pay the man himself, and take some halfpence in exchange. He turned them over two or three times in his hand without his glove. Well, thought I, if you like to handle dirty copper, it is a strange taste. "Take the reins a moment," said he, giving them to me, and out he jumped; and before I could form the least suspicion of what he was going to do, he rushed upon the turnpike-man, and seized him by the throat. Of course there was a mob collected in a moment, and the high-spirited horses grew so restive, that I expected nothing less than that they would start off with me. In the midst of it all, a coach and four came to the gate. "Ask what's the matter," said a simpering sort of gentleman, putting his head with an air out of the coach-window, to the footman behind. "It's my Lord Camelford," replied the footman. "You may drive on," was the instant ejaculation of the master, frightened out of his senses at the bare apprehension lest his lordship should turn to him.

'The row was soon over, and Lord Camelford resumed his seat. "I daresay you thought," he said very quietly, "that I was going to put myself in a passion. But the fact is, these rascals have barrels of bad halfpence, and they pass them in change to the people who go through the gate. Some poor carter, perhaps, has nothing but this change to pay for his supper; and when he gets to his journey's end, finds he can't get his bread and cheese. The law, 'tis true, will fine them; but how is a poor devil to go to law?—where can he find time? To you and me it would not signify, but to the poor it does; and I merely wanted to teach these blackguards a lesson, by way of showing them that they cannot always play such tricks with impunity."

'Doctor, you should have seen, when we came back again, how humble and cringing the turnpike-man was. Lord Camelford was a true Pitt, and, like me, his blood fired at a fraud or a bad action.'

But the god of her idolatry is, after all, Mr Pitt. Of him she never wearied of discoursing; things great and little concerning him were to her of equal importance; made so by the strength of her undying regard. The following correction of the current description of Mr Pitt's death is curious. Dr M. happened to observe that he had 'read an account of Mr Pitt's last moments in Gifford's life of him, and that his dying words, praying for forgiveness through the merits of his Redeemer, or words to that effect, together with the whole scene of his deathbed, appeared, as I thought, too much made up, and too formal to be true; leaving the impression that the author, and those from whom he gathered his information, had considered it a duty to make the close of a great man's life conformable to their religious feelings rather than to facts and reality.'* 'Who is it that says it of him?' asked Lady Hester. 'Dr Prettyman and Sir Walter Farquhar.' 'Oh, it's all a lie!' she replied, rather indignantly. 'Dr Prettyman was fast asleep when Mr Pitt died; Sir Walter Farquhar was not there; and nobody was present but James. I was the last person who saw him except James, and I left him about eight o'clock, for I saw him struggling as if he wanted to speak, and I did not like to make him worse.' After a short pause, she resumed: 'What should Mr Pitt make such a speech for, who never went to church in his life? Nothing prevented his going to church when he was at Walmer; but he never even talked about religion, and never brought it upon the carpet.'

Nor are the reflections that succeed the narrative unsuggestive:—

'When I think of poor Mr Pitt, I am the more and more persuaded that the greater part of mankind are not worth the kindness we bestow on them. Never did so pure an angel enter upon life as he; but, when he died, had he had to begin the world again, he would have acted in a very different manner. The baseness and ingratitude that he found in mankind were inconceivable. All the peers that he had made deserted him, and half those he had served returned his kindness by going over to his enemies.

'Then see, doctor, what fortune and luck are! Mr Pitt, during his life spent in his country's service, could seldom get a gleam of success to cheer him, whilst Liverpool and a Castlereagh have triumphs fall upon them in showers. Oh! it makes me sick to think that Mr Pitt should have died through hard labour for his country; that Lord Melville, so hearty as he was, should almost have sunk under it, and should have had nothing but difficulties and disappointments; whilst such fellows as H. and C., who do not care if the country were ruined, provided they kept their places, should have nothing but good fortune attend them, as if it were the effect of their stupid measures. But, not contented with that, they must even bring discredit on his memory, by attributing to him a line of conduct he never pursued. To think of Canning's going about and saying "This is the glorious system of Pitt!" and the papers echoing his words—"This is the glorious system of Pitt!" Why, when Louis XVIII. came to England, Mr Pitt would not receive him as king, but only as count somebody. (I declare I forget what, it made so slight an impression on me.) And when I used to say to Mr Pitt, "What does it signify?—do let him be king if he wants it"—"No," replied Mr Pitt, "I am not fighting to re-establish the Bourbons on the throne: only let the French have some stable government that we can make peace with, that's all; I am not going to sacrifice the interests of my country to the Bourbons, Hester."'

We cannot quit this part of the subject without another extract or so:—

'After Mr Pitt's death, I could not cry for a whole month and more. I never shed a tear, until one day Lord Melville came to see me; and the sight of his eyebrows turned gray, and his changed face, made me burst into tears. I felt much better for it after it was over.

'Mr Pitt's bust was taken after his death by an Italian, named, I think, Tomino—an obscure artist, whom I had rummaged out. This man had offered me at one time a bust worth a hundred guineas, and prayed me to accept it, in order, as he said, to make his name known; I refused it, but recollected him afterwards. The bust turned out a very indifferent resemblance; so, with my own hand, I corrected the defects, and it eventually proved a strong likeness. The D. of C. happening to call when the artist was at work in my room, was so pleased, that he ordered one of a hundred guineas for himself, and another to be sent to Windsor. There was one by this Tomino put into the exhibition.

'A fine picture in Mr Pitt's possession represented Diogenes with a lantern searching by day for an honest man. A person cut out a part of the blank canvas, and put in Mr Pitt's portrait.'

The influence which Lady Hester exercised in affairs of the highest moment to the interests of this nation, at a time when it was placed in most unfavourable circumstances by foreign wars and commercial depression, proved her to have been a woman of extraordinary genius; though it also showed that her genius was only suitable for the circumstances in which it happened to be then exercised. This the event proved. When Pitt died, and his political opponents came into office, her ladyship's reign in Downing Street was of course over; and she was obliged to retire into private life—a sphere for which her energetic mind was found to be totally unfitted.

Scattered over these interesting memoirs, are a few passages which, portraying the manners of bygone times, show, by comparison with those of the present day, what great changes a half century has worked. To begin with the education of young ladies. 'How well I recollect what I was made to suffer when I was young!' exclaimed her ladyship to her physician, 'and that's the reason why I have sworn eternal warfare against Swiss and French governesses. Nature forms us in a certain manner, both inwardly and outwardly, and it is in vain to attempt to alter it.

* Lord Malmesbury cites Lady M.'s account of Mr Pitt's last words as follows:—'Lady M., who saw Sir Walter Farquhar three days after Pitt's death, and received from him an account of his last hours, said, that almost the last words he spoke intelligibly were these to himself, and more than once repeated—"Oh! what times! oh! my country!"'

One governess at Chevening had our backs pinched in by boards, that were drawn tight with all the force the maid could use; and as for me, they would have squeezed me to the size of a puny miss—a thing impossible! My instep, by nature so high that a little kitten could walk under the sole of my foot, they used to bend down in order to flatten it, although that is one of the things that shows my high-breeding.

'Nature, doctor, makes us one way, and man is always trying to fashion us another. * * But nature was entirely out of the question with us: we were left to the governesses. Lady Stanhope got up at ten o'clock, went out, and then returned to be dressed, if in London, by the hairdresser; and there were only two in London, both of them Frenchmen, who could dress her. Then she went out to dinner, and from dinner to the opera, and from the opera to parties, seldom returning until just before daylight.'

Tutors, physicians, and men of science, were not allowed to mix so familiarly with the nobility as they do in these more enlightened times. 'As for tutors, and doctors, and such people, if, now-a-days, my lords and my ladies walk arm-in-arm with them, they did not do so in my time. I recollect an old dowager, to whom I used sometimes to be taken to spend the morning. She was left with a large jointure and a fine house for the time being, and used to invite the boys and girls of my age—I mean the age I was then—with their tutors and governesses, to come and see her. "How do you do, Dr Mackenzie? Lord John, I see, is all the better for his medicine. The duchess is happy in having found a man of such excellent talents, which are almost too great to be confined to the sphere of one family."—"Such is the nature of our compact, my lady; nor could I on any account violate the regulations which so good a family has imposed upon me." "It's very cold, Dr Mackenzie; I think I increased my rheumatic pains at the opera on Saturday night." "Did you ever try Dover's powders, my lady?" He does not, you see, tell her to use Dover's powders; he only says, did you ever try them? "Lord John, Lord John, you must take care and not eat too much of that strawberry preserve." "How do you do, Mr K.?—How do you do, Lord Henry? I hope the marchioness is well? She looked divinely last night. Did you see her when she was dressed, Mr K.?" "You will pardon me, my lady," answers the tutor; "I did indeed see her; but it would be presumptuous in me to speak of such matters. I happened to take her a map" (mind, doctor, he does not say a map of what), "and certainly I did cast my eyes on her dress, which was no doubt in the best taste, as everything the marchioness does is." Observe, here is no mention of her looks or person. Doctors and tutors never presumed formerly to talk about the complexion, and skin, and beauty of those in whose families they lived or found practice. Why, haven't I told you over and over again how Dr W—— lost his practice from having said that a patient of his, who died, was one of the most beautiful corpses he had ever seen, and that he had stood contemplating her for a quarter of an hour? She was a person of rank, and it ruined him. Even his son, who was a doctor too, and had nothing to do with it, never could get on afterwards.'

Servants were also kept in much better order, according to the ideas of our seniors, than they are at present. 'There was the groom of the chamber at Mr Pitt's,' continued Lady Hester; 'I don't think I ever held half an hour's conversation with him the whole time he was there: he was, however, a man with quite a distinguished look, and ten times more of a gentleman than half those who call themselves so. He came in, delivered a note or a message with a proper air; and, if I had one to send anywhere, I threw it along the table to the end, so' (and here Lady Hester put on one of those—what shall I call them?—queen-like airs which she was fond of assuming), 'or else gave it into his hand, telling him, or not telling him—for he could see by looking at it—where it was to go. He afterwards married one of the maids, and took Thomas's, or some such named hotel, where he was well patronised by the great.'

The management of a nobleman's household is graphically described. Speaking of the last day of each year, Lady Hester remarked, in reference to the mansion of Chevening, at Seven Oaks, in Kent, 'To-night in my father's house there used to be a hundred tenants and servants sitting down to a good dinner, and dancing and making merry. I see their happy faces now before my eyes; and when I think of that, and how I am surrounded here, it is too much for me. * * Lady Hester reverted again to Chevening, and spoke at great length of her grandmother Stanhope's excellent management of the house, when she (Lady Hester) was a child. At all the accustomed festivals, plumpuddings, that required two men to carry them, with large barons of beef, were dressed, &c. &c. All the footmen were like gentlemen ushers, all the masters and mistresses like so many ambassadors and ambassadresses, such form and etiquette were preserved in all the routine of visits and parties. Every person kept his station, and precise rules were laid down for each inmate of the family. Thus, the lady's-maid was not allowed to wear white, nor curls, nor heels to her shoes beyond a certain height; and Lady Stanhope had in her room a set of instruments and implements of punishment to enforce her orders on all occasions. There were scissors to cut off fine curls, a rod to whip with, &c. &c. No poor woman lay-in in the neighbourhood, but two guineas in money, baby-linen, a blanket, some posset, two bottles of wine, and other necessaries, were sent to her. If any one among the servants was sick, the housekeeper, with the still-room maid behind her, was seen carrying the barley-water, the gruel, the medicine, &c. to administer to the patient, according to the doctor's orders. In the hopping time, all the vagrants and Irish hoppers were locked up every night in a barn by themselves, and suffered to have no communication with the household. A thousand pieces of dirty linen were washed every week, and the wash-house had four different stone troughs, from which the linen was handed, piece by piece, by the washerwomen from the scalder down to the rinser. In the laundry a false ceiling, let down and raised by pulleys, served to air the linen after it was ironed. There was a mangle to get up the table linen, towels, &c. and three stoves for drying on wet days. The table-cloths were of the finest damask, covered with patterns of exquisite workmanship. At set periods of the year, pedlars and merchants from Glasgow, from Dunstable, and other places, passed with their goods. The housekeeper's room was surrounded with presses and closets, where were arranged stores and linen in the nicest order. An ox was killed every week, and a sheep every day.

'Servants work twice as hard in England as they do here. Why, there was the boy of twelve or thirteen years old, that used to go to Seven Oaks to fetch papa's letters. Every day but one in the week did that boy ride backward and forward; and sometimes I have seen him lifted off his horse with his fingers so benumbed, that he could not even ring the bell; and his face and hands were rubbed with snow, and he was walked about for a quarter of an hour before he was allowed to go into the servants' hall. There was the shepherd's daughter, who would take up a sheep over her shoulders, and carry it like a nothing; ay, and whilst it was struggling too pretty stoutly, I can tell you. Then the washerwomen, who used to begin every Monday morning half an hour after midnight, and work all through the day and the next night until eleven or twelve, without ever sitting down, except to their meals. There was hard work!'

When the late George IV. was Prince of Wales, and the leader of fashion, he was very fond of inviting himself out to dinner. Such entertainments were of course obliged to be prepared in a style commensurate with the high rank of the guest. Many of the poorer friends of his royal highness were therefore often put to greater expenses than they could afford. At some brilliant assembly 'there you would see him' [the prince], remarked her ladyship to her medical adviser, 'at the doorway of two rooms, speaking loudly to some one:—"Well, then, it's all fixed; on Wednesday next I dine with you, and shall bring about a dozen friends." "Why does your royal highness say a dozen? let it be fifteen." "Well, a dozen—fifteen; but we shall dine precisely at four." And there was the man's wife, standing breathless, with scarce strength to keep down a suppressed sigh, thinking with herself, "What shall we do, and how shall we provide for all this?" Then the husband, with a forced smile, would endeavour to relieve her with, "My dear, did you hear? his royal highness intends us the honour of dining with us on Wednesday—you forget to thank him:" and the poor wife strains at a compliment, ill-worded from her uneasiness. Oh! doctor, it has made my heart ache.'

MORE WORDS FROM THE COUNTER.

Since noticing, two years ago, the efforts made in London to bring about an earlier shutting of places of business, and thus relieve many thousands of young persons from an irksome and unnecessary protraction of daily labour, we are glad to know that a number of shopkeepers of respectability have consented to the very reasonable claims made on their humanity, that the public have been roused on a subject of such vital interest, and that in time we may expect to see realised nearly all those reforms which the more intelligent of the shop-assistants have pointed out as desirable.

In the course of the agitation which has taken place on the present shop-system, a variety of curious particulars have been made known respecting the number of assistants, their duties, and the physical and moral evils which beset their course of life. There can be no doubt that there are many most respectable establishments in London and elsewhere conducted on a humane and honourable plan; but it is equally true that there are yet more houses where the assistants are systematically taught the most unwarrantable tricks, for the sake of inducing customers to purchase their goods. Common sense tells us that those who conduct their affairs in this manner must belong to that unscrupulous class who are determined at all hazards to drive a quick business. Thus, when we find an establishment in which the assistants are harshly and unfairly treated—for instance, condemned to remain in the heated atmosphere of a draper's shop fifteen or sixteen hours out of the twenty-four, forbidden, even if there be nothing to do, to rest themselves by being seated for five minutes—(it is a by-law in such establishments to seem busy at all times, and to roll and unroll goods if there be no better occupation)—and debarred all fresh air, and the necessary portion of time for bodily and mental recreation—we may fairly conclude, that the absence of high principle, remarkable in this portion of the management, will also prevail in that affecting the public at large.

The very praiseworthy exertions of the Metropolitan Drapers' Association have brought so many traits of harsh rule and mean trickery to light—not to mention the incidents which the newspapers now and then reveal—that there can be no breach of confidence in our referring to the subject. In inferior establishments, it is a custom to recommend old goods, declaring them to be of the newest fashion, and citing imaginary customers and titled personages as admirers and wearers of the same. This kind of falsehood, however, can only succeed with the very credulous, and is adopted with caution. It is a more common trick, when ladies complain of an article being not so good as they desire, to bring out something for their inspection which is represented as very superior, and of course higher in price, but which in reality is no better than the first which had been offered. Instances have even been known of the same piece of goods being only removed out of sight, there divided in two, so as to alter its outward appearance of form and bulk, and then offered as a superior fabric, with an increase of price. It may be argued that this evil would bring its own remedy, that purchasers would soon discover such deceptions, or, at any rate, that they must be deficient in the powers of observation to be so easily deceived. But, on the other hand, it is affectation to suppose that a lady, whose experience has been limited to the purchase of clothing for herself and family, can be so competent a judge of the real worth of articles offered to her, as the tradesman whose life has been spent in acquiring that kind of knowledge, and with whom it is an engrossing thought and occupation: and the confidence which she places in a tradesman, when she relies on his word and recommendation, seems to us only to make his falsehood the more detestable. Besides, many persons possessing limited incomes apportion certain sums for certain purposes, and such individuals not unfrequently mention the price they are inclined to give, thus offering a guide to the shopkeeper as to the articles most likely to suit them—worthy of a better return than it often receives.

Those ladies who are in the habit of giving much inconsiderate trouble to drapers' assistants, turning over a variety of goods, having ribbons unrolled and silks unfolded, without effecting a purchase after all, are perhaps not aware that there is always a person in the shop deputed to keep an account of those assistants who are unsuccessful; that is to say, who fail to persuade the ladies to make purchases. A harsh word or discouraging look may be the only punishment for a first offence of this kind; if repeated, a reprimand is sure to follow; afterwards the penalty of a fine is resorted to; and if, after all, the young man does not become such an adept in insinuation, or the tricks of his trade, as to persuade ladies that black is white, that though they require coarse cotton, fine linen will answer their purpose better; and, in fact, run through the whole jargon of insidious deceit, he is turned adrift as unfit for his profession. Why so much talk and blandishment should have been lavished on the attempt to dispose of such a trifle as a yard of ribbon, may often have surprised our lady readers; but let all surprise on the subject vanish. What seems a trifle on one side of the counter, may be a matter of life and death on the other. 'If I fail to charm her into a purchase, though never so small, I am a done man; in six hours hence I may be an outcast!' Thinking, if he does not say this to himself, the young assistant desperately increases his eloquence, adds lie to lie, and happy does he consider himself if his manifold efforts finally succeed: if unsuccessful, what mortification, what an agony of discomfiture! This, then, is one of the prevalent causes of that vexatious importunity which most persons must have encountered at one time or another in their shopping excursions; and who can doubt the demoralising results of a system based on such falsehood, trickery, and deception?

As already mentioned, these revelations from the counter are not by any means of universal application. Oppression and deceit are not English vices, and are only found in alliance with what may be called flash or struggling concerns, of which, however, there are more than could be suspected from external appearances. In the shopkeeping, as in the factory system, the establishments best conducted—we mean as respects justice, mercy, and kindness—are uniformly those in which the proprietors are the most opulent and most prosperous. There are thus many shopkeepers in London distinguished not less for their integrity than their considerate liberality towards their assistants. What we would wish to see is an exaltation in tone of mind both in masters and men. Trade, not united with a keen sense of justice, becomes sordid and mean, and will pull down to a base level the highest aspirations. But to cultivate those moral and intellectual amenities which exalt the character, a certain portion of daily existence must be devoted; and assuredly not less by masters than servants is this time required. Leaving the proprietors of shops to look about for such means of relaxation as fall within their reach, we would in an especial manner plead the cause of the large body of youth whose fate it is to consume so much time—almost their whole waking existence—in the toils of an irksome profession. There are, it is alleged, twenty thousand drapers' assistants in London, performing an unvarying dull round of duty; and it is no small matter that this large body of young men, not to speak of many others, should be habitually, and by a pernicious custom, shut out from the means of that moral improvement which would lift them above the trickery to which too many of them are at present condemned. We cannot attempt to deny that in many instances additional leisure might be abused; but this we suspect would most likely be the case among those the most corrupted. It is hard that the well-intentioned should suffer for their faults.

One subject of complaint among those who are striving for the early closing of shops—and we think a very just one—is, that when released from the counter, at ten or eleven o'clock at night, assistants have no alternative but to roam the streets, or enter those places of public entertainment where temptations to many kinds of dissipation exist. At this hour lectures are over, and these opportunities of mental recreation and improvement are lost. At this hour the doors of their friends are virtually closed against them, for they cannot pay visits at nearly midnight; and so in a little time the healthful pleasures and cordial sympathies of the domestic circle become forgotten things.

After all, it rests with the public to amend this state of things. The members of the association—acting, be it always remembered, under the sanction of the most respectable employers—can only promote investigation, and draw attention to the evils of the late-hour system—evils which press most heavily on the youth of the country; that body, or rather the survivors among it, who in a very few years will fill the responsible offices of parents and masters, and who even in the present are not unfrequently the chief hope and stay of aged or infant relatives. It remains with the public to achieve the victory by abstaining from late shopping. Tradesmen will soon close their shops when they find that no customers enter them after six or seven o'clock. We are aware that it will be argued that servants and others are so much tied by their own duties during the day, that only in the evening can they find the opportunity of making purchases. But our gorgeous shops are not supported by this class; and when the time arrives that they are the only late shoppers, let us be sure some plan—such, for instance, as setting apart one evening in the week for their accommodation—will be resorted to, and meet their wishes. It is highly satisfactory to learn—and this we have heard from the lips of employers themselves—that, in adopting the humane system of closing at an early hour, those who have done so have already found their reward. They are unanimous in declaring that the increased activity of their assistants during business hours, and the general elevation of their character, have done much more than compensate for the grace awarded to them. Such employers have, in numerous instances, established libraries and reading-rooms under their own roof, and have in no case found reason to lament their generous indulgence. We believe that the public would find it a safe plan to rely on the general integrity of those establishments in which they perceive the more enlightened system adopted. In these an elevation of character prevails, which is their best protection from the meannesses and trickeries of the trade.

NEWSPAPERS FROM 'FOREIGN PARTS.'

Several newspapers—each a curiosity in its way—have been sent to us from the most distant parts of the globe. One file is dated from the Sandwich Islands, another from Hong Kong in China, a third from Boston, and a fourth from Philadelphia in North America. A selection from their contents, with a passing word on the places in which they are printed, will be amusing and useful to many of our readers.

The Sandwich Islands file was sent by some unknown friend residing in Honolulu—the capital—where the newspapers were printed. Honolulu stands on the island of Oahu, one of the ten situated in the midst of the Pacific Ocean, known as the Sandwich Islands. It is not the largest, that being Hawaii, commonly called Owhyhee, which contains 11,000 inhabitants, whilst Oahu numbers only about 7000. Since the time of Captain Cook, who was murdered at Owhyhee in 1779, civilisation has been gradually spreading its blessings over the Sandwich Islands. The metropolis, Honolulu, is inhabited partly by settlers from America and Europe, and partly by natives. The houses of the former are built of stone, but the aborigines still prefer wigwams or huts, so that the town presents a grotesquely irregular appearance. As Christianity and civilisation have made more way in the Sandwich Islands than in any of the neighbouring groups, there is a well-attended English school, which is the chief building in the place, two churches, and a chapel expressly devoted to the use of the sailors who may touch at the island. That European tastes and modes of life have been extensively adopted in these islands, is attested by the articles exhibited for sale in the shops of Honolulu, which include every sort of food, clothing, and luxury, even (as the advertisements in the Sandwich Islands Gazette prove) to ladies' shoes from Paris, and *eau-de-Cologne!* It would seem that the baneful indulgence which has nearly everywhere accompanied white men amongst their uncivilised brethren, had for many years a most demoralising effect on the natives of the Sandwich Islands. Ardent spirits were largely imported, and did infinite mischief. Happily, however, the temperance movement has extended itself into the very midst of the Pacific, and with the most signal success. The publications which have reached us from the Sandwich Islands are almost entirely occupied in the inculcation and furtherance of temperance. One is entitled 'The Friend—a semimonthly journal devoted to temperance, marine, and general intelligence.' It is neatly printed on good paper, and contains eight pages. The numbers before us were published at the end of the last, and the beginning of the present year. The other journal, though printed at Honolulu, appears from its title to be intended for circulation amongst the inhabitants of Owhyhee. It is called the Hawaiian Cascade and Miscellany, and contains a lighter and more amusing sort of information than 'The Friend.'

From the latter publication we learn that many useful works have been translated and printed in the Hawaiian or native tongue, on several branches of science, art, and religion; and that an almanac, and four newspapers, are regularly published in the same tongue. No fewer than 22,652 individuals were in 1844 in full communion with the Protestant churches planted by the American missionaries; the entire population has been estimated at 150,000. The commercial prosperity of these islands chiefly arises from the visits of whalers, particularly of those from America. During the past year 224 whale-fishing vessels, navigated by 4600 American and 1662 foreign seamen, visited the various ports of the Sandwich Islands. A series of very interesting articles, entitled Notes on the Shipping-Trade, &c. of the Sandwich Islands, has been continued in 'The Friend' from week to week by an intelligent English merchant, and contains a host of minute and interesting particulars.

Turning to the 'Hawaiian Cascade' for matters of less import, we find amidst some earnest warnings against intemperance one or two amusing pieces, which we shall take leave to extract. The first may be, for aught we know, a specimen of the Honolulu muse. Beneath a veil of jocularity, it gives a strong practical exemplification of the effects of drunkenness. It is an address to a brandy bottle.

You old brandy bottle, I've loved you too long,
You have been a bad messmate to me;
When I met with you first I was healthy and strong,
And handsome as handsome could be.
I had plenty of cash in my pocket and purse,
And my cheeks were as red as a rose,
And the day when I took you for better for worse,
I'd a beautiful aquiline nose.

But now, only look! I'm a fright to behold,
The beauty I boasted has fled,
You would think I was nearly a hundred years old,
When I'm raising my hand to my head;
For it trembles and shakes like the earth when it quakes,
And I'm constantly spilling my tea;
And whenever I speak I make awful mistakes,
Till every one's laughing at me.

The ladies don't love me, and this I can trace
To the loss of my aquiline nose,
Like an overgrown strawberry stuck on my face,
Still larger and larger it grows.
And I hav'n't a cent in my pocket or purse,
And my clothes are all dirty and torn;
Oh, you old brandy bottle, you've been a sad curse,
And I wish I had never been born!

You old brandy bottle, I'll love you no more,
You have ruined me, body and soul,
I'll dash you to pieces, and swear from this hour,
To give up both you and the bowl.
And I'll now go and 'sign'—I could surely do worse—
On that pledge all my hopes I repose,
And I'll get back my money in pocket and purse,
And perhaps, too, my beautiful nose!

With the following extraordinary but well attested anecdote, we conclude our extracts from these interesting specimens of the Sandwich Islands press:—

What a Bill-Fish can do.—Under what genus and species the ichthyologist will class the specimen of the finny tribe called *bill-fish*, we know not; but according to Captain Lincoln of the William Penn, this fish possesses great physical power, sufficient to thrust its bill through the solid oak sides of a ship. Shortly after the William Penn sailed from the Sandwich Islands, in the spring of 1842, she was obliged to put in at the Society Islands on account of a leak. On heaving out, about six feet from the keel was found the *bill* of the above-mentioned fish. It had been thrust several inches through the following materials:—1st, copper; 2d, sheathing, 1-inch pine; 3d, plank, 3-inch oak; 4th, timber, 4-inch oak; 5th, ceiling, 2½-inch oak. In all, 9½ inches solid oak and 1 inch pine—total 10½ inches. Captain Lincoln has preserved the identical bill, being about 1½ inch in diameter, so that he is able to convince the incredulous by ocular demonstration. We recollect some years since to have seen the blade of a sword-fish thrust through a piece of solid oak timber: it was cut from the side of a whale-ship, and is now preserved as a curiosity in the Marine Museum, Nantucket, Massachusetts.

In point of typography and paper, these journals do great credit to the Sandwich Islanders. They must be a vast improvement on the first newspaper essay made at Honolulu, which was—we learn from the United States Exploring Expedition—effected by means of a common mangle.

Turning from these Sandwich Islands sheets, our ideas are rapidly transferred to the opposite corner of the map of the world, by a perusal of the 'China Mail'—the first number of a newspaper edited, printed, and published at our new colony of Hong Kong. This little island is situated in the Chinese sea, at the mouth of the Canton river, and not far from the mainland of the province of Quang-tung. At the conclusion of the recent war, it was ceded to this country, and has already become a flourishing entrepôt of trade between Hindostan, Europe, and the rest of China, *via* the old port of Canton. A town called Victoria has already sprung up, besides detached residences, which are dotted all over it. There is a regular staff of government officers, headed by Mr J. F. Davis, whose work on the Chinese affords us nearly all that is known concerning that singular and mysterious people. His viceroyalty, though small—being only fifteen miles in circumference—is flourishing, as the newspaper before us testifies.

It is a goodly sheet of four well-printed pages. The number of advertisements it contains is one proof that the new colony can boast of a busy trade, whilst a government return shows that a lively communication is kept up between the snug little island and the interior of China, by the fact, that during the year ending 31st December 1844, no fewer than ninety-six native boats (lorchas), having an aggregate of 3774 tons burthen, were employed in conveying merchandise between Hong Kong and Canton.

A list of prices informs us that on the 27th February of the present year (the date of the paper before us), beef at Victoria was 12 cents per catty; pork, when 'fat,' 10, but when not fat, fifty per cent. dearer; mutton, 40; eggs were 1 dollar per 160, whilst their parents were from 15 to 18 cents each; the latter being also the price of capons, which were dearer than geese at 12 cents. Pigeons, partridges, and quails, were 1 dollar each. The Chinese never use milk in any form, hence we are well prepared to find it scarce and dear: 25 cents was the price of a quart bottle, whilst fresh butter was 1 dollar per pound.

The editor apologises in his first number for whatever errors it may contain, declaring that he had to educate his own compositors before he could get the types properly set. Some were natives, others soldiers—the only persons, in short, whom he found willing to undertake a share of the task. It is the more creditable to his own skill and energy, therefore, that very few mistakes appear; indeed, the second number of the China Mail would do credit to any provincial press in Great Britain. We wish the editor, Mr Shortrede, every success in his novel undertaking—the more so as he is a worthy and widely-esteemed fellow-townsman, whose social qualities have caused his absence to be much felt in Edinburgh.

The third periodical is a sign of the times in the United States, which we hail with pleasure; it being evidently the result of a struggle amongst a humble class of citizens to do good, by advocating sound moral principles. It is entitled the 'Mechanic Apprentice,' and published on the 15th of every month, at a small price. The conductors are members of an association called 'The Mechanic Apprentices' Library Association;' and although the compositions are not always very clearly or forcibly worded, yet they evince a propriety and earnestness of intention, which is all that can be expected from youth. The gross personalities and exciting political tirades with which too much of the North American press is occupied, are much in need of counteracting influences directed to better aims; and although the little work we are now discussing contributes in itself but a drop to the ocean of good which remains to be done, yet it shows the existence of a spirit amongst the younger community, of at least one important city in the states, from which much may be expected hereafter.

Another equally gratifying attestation of an improving spirit in the states, is the increase of periodicals devoted to the working out of some defined and special object of social improvement. Temperance, for instance, is inculcated by numerous publications. There is scarcely a native state or a colony in which America holds influence (of which the Sandwich Islands is an instance), where at least one such print is not widely supported, and eagerly read. If, therefore, the mere subject of temperance be interesting to the vast population of North America, the inference follows, that the virtue itself is fast gaining ground. In like manner, the iniquity of slavery in a nation whose reiterated boast it is to be the freest in the world, is happily lessening through the influence of newspapers, and other works set on foot expressly to advocate abolition. We hold all such circumstances as cheering indications of social progress.

COLONISATION OF PALESTINE BY THE JEWS.

The recent persecutions of the Jews by some of the bigotted people of the East, and the opposite efforts which are now making in this and neighbouring countries to abolish their civic and legislative disabilities, have of late attracted much public attention. It would appear that nearly seven millions of this persecuted race are now scattered over the face of the globe,* in various degrees of prosperity; and to better the condition of the poorest, a plan has been proposed, which appears to have in it the elements of success. This is simply the colonisation of Palestine.

The Jews, in whatever country residing, have always exhibited an aversion to engage in agricultural pursuits, or to invest their capital in land. Relying on the Scripture promise of being eventually restored to their country and united again as one nation, they hold themselves in readiness to depart from the place of their present sojourn at the shortest notice. Most of the property they accumulate is either readily transportable, or is convertible into articles which are current coin everywhere—such as gold, silver, and jewels. They are seldom handicraftsmen or artisans, especially of arts peculiar to their abiding places; from which it has always been their policy to be able to sever themselves as speedily as possible, when the wished-for day of union in Palestine shall arrive. Most of the attempts, therefore, to amalgamate the people of Israel with those they may reside amongst, have signally failed. Recently, in Poland and Russia—where the largest section of the nation resides—the emperor ceded a portion of the crown lands to be allotted amongst certain Jews deported from the frontiers; but many of them showed reluctance to take advantage of the cession. Wishing to abolish distinctions, he also issued a ukase or proclamation for the abandonment of the peculiar garb worn by his Jewish subjects; but they considered it as an intolerant hardship, and so few obeyed the injunction, that the emperor, visiting the Jewish hospital at Warsaw, found one only of the patients not dressed in the Jewish garb. The czar noticed this one particularly, and commended his example to the others; observing, that in five years he should command them to adopt the general costume; meanwhile, he would ask it of them as a favour. How many have complied with this polite wish, we have not ascertained.

The rooted aversion of the bulk of the Hebrew nation to regard any country as their permanent home, is of course a bar to their civilisation and advancement. Several benevolent persons, with Sir Moses Montifiore at their head, have however found a way out of the difficulty, by proposing a colonisation of Palestine by the Jews. This proposition seems to reconcile all difficulties, and to remove all prejudices. 'The Voice of Jacob,' a periodical supported by the most influential London Jews, and previously noticed in this Journal, approves of such a plan; whilst the organ of the French Jews, the *Archives Israelites* for February last, proposes 'a European committee for Jewish colonisation.' Every Jew, looking towards Palestine with a pious love as his true home, would no longer object to 'put his hand to the plough,' and to possess a property in the soil. That the land is capable of supporting a vast body of emigrants, is proved by the Parliamentary Report on Syria, published in 1840. Mr Consul Moore states, that the population of the whole country is at present reduced to a tithe of what the soil could abundantly support. Lands, therefore, with the permission of the sultan, could easily be found; and, as to another great necessary in every undertaking—money—who, according to the proverb, are so rich as the Jews?

An important advantage which would result from such a colonisation to the region itself and its neighbourhood, is pointed out in a pamphlet recently issued by Colonel Gawler.* The Jews, who, wherever located, are acknowledged to be an orderly and industrious people, would form the nucleus of a well-doing and peaceful population amidst whole tribes who are now the reverse. The Turkish provinces have become, since the declension of Ottoman power, nothing better than diplomatic nuisances. They give more trouble to European governments than all the rest of Asia, and, indeed, of the entire globe. The pashas, each struggling for independence, are constantly squabbling with their neighbours; while in many of these squabbles the already independent ruler of Egypt thinks it necessary to interfere on one side, and his late master, the sultan, finds it his duty to interfere on the other. Hence a constant fermentation is kept up, and the simplest advance towards civilisation cannot be effected. But if the very generally expressed desire of the Jews were acceded to—that is, the colonisation of Palestine under European protection—most of these evils would vanish. The belligerent pashas would not dare disrespect such powerful protection, even in prosecuting their own quarrels, whilst the industrious colonists would be showing them the advantages of peace and industry.

A number of Jews have already established themselves in Jerusalem; but, from various causes, are not at present in a very flourishing condition. Efforts are making, however, to introduce manufactures into the city, and three intelligent inhabitants have recently made a tour in the English manufacturing districts, for the purpose of learning power-loom weaving, with the view of exporting spinning-mills, and setting them up in Jerusalem. Cotton, silk, and wool, are abundantly produced in and near the city, the first being now spun and woven after the most primitive methods.

The known enterprise, energy, and prudence of the Jews turned into a new, and to them most exciting channel, will, should the scheme be carried out, be productive, there can be little doubt, of the most important results. If, after eighteen centuries of wandering and persecution, they should at last return to the home of their fathers, they will surely excite the interest and good wishes of the whole civilised world.

CURIOSITIES OF LITERATURE.

NO. II.

All letters, even those of a private nature, were composed in Latin until the commencement of Edward I.'s reign, when the French language was suddenly made use of for that purpose. French had been spoken by the higher classes from the entrance of the Conqueror, and continued to be orally employed to the reign of Edward III. That period was distinguished by Chaucer, whose works are oftener praised than read. His writings ennobled the vulgar speech; and it is no wonder that it should be then declared by act of parliament to be the language of legislation. The oldest private letter in English that we are aware of is one written by the lady of Sir John Pelham to her husband in 1399.

One of the most wonderful things about Sir Walter Scott's mental constitution was the strength of his me-

* The Jewish population of Russia and Russian Poland is 1,700,000; that of Great Britain and Ireland is 30,000; France, 80,000; Austria, 453,524; Prussia, 194,558; Germany, 145,000; Holland and Belgium, 80,000; Denmark, 6000; Sweden, 1250; Switzerland, 2000; Turkey in Europe, 325,000; Italy, 200,000; Gibraltar, 2000; Portugal, 1000; Ionian Islands, 8000. Making in the whole of Europe about three millions and a quarter. America is said to contain 75,000; Asia, 3,000,000; Africa, 500,000. The total number of Jews scattered over the face of the globe may be above 6,800,000.

* Observations and Practical Suggestions in Furtherance of Jewish Colonies in Palestine. London.

mory. By some extraordinary process, it seemed able, amidst the bustle of active employment, to fix upon everything presented to it which could by possibility be afterwards required. No little fact, trivial incident, old threadbare story, or ragged song, once heard, was forgotten. It was laid by with little effort, to be brought out when an opportunity occurred for using it. The ancient mythology called the Muses the daughters of Memory, and we may perceive a good deal of truth in the fiction. It would not be difficult to give several instances of the wonderful power of memory displayed by some people, either of original strength, or perfected by discipline. Porson, the Greek professor, used to say that, originally, he had a good memory, but what he obtained in this respect was the effect of discipline only. He could not remember anything but what he transcribed three times, or read six times over. His power of retention was thus rendered extremely great. He has been known to challenge any one to repeat a line or phrase from any of the Greek dramatic writers, and would instantly go on with the context. The Letters of Junius, the Mayor of Garratt, and other favourite compositions, he would repeat until his hearers were fairly tired out. Mrs Hemans, by way of testing her memory, once learned by heart a poem of Heber's, containing 424 lines, in an hour and twenty minutes.

Gibbon the historian, being then resident abroad, but on a visit to friends in London, was present at the august spectacle of Mr Hastings's trial in Westminster Hall. Sheridan, in the course of his speech, declared that the facts which made up the volume of narrative were unparalleled in atrociousness, and that nothing equal in criminality was to be traced either in ancient or modern history, in the correct periods of Tacitus, or the luminous page of Gibbon. 'It is not my province,' says Gibbon in his autobiography, 'to absolve or condemn the governor of India; but Mr Sheridan's eloquence commanded my applause, nor could I hear without emotion the personal compliment he paid me in the presence of the British nation.' Nor would the historian have heard without emotion the malicious turn which the wit afterwards gave to his 'compliment.' 'I meant to say voluminous.' By the way, there has been much difference of opinion expressed with regard to the History of the Decline and Fall, and its style has been highly praised and as deeply condemned. A late writer (Professor Smyth), whose learning is unquestioned, and whose simplicity of style is in striking contrast with the ornament and swell of Gibbon's, says that it must be confessed the chapters of that work are replete 'with paragraphs of such melody and grandeur, as would be the fittest to convey to a youth of genius the full charm of literary composition, and such as, when once heard, however unattainable to the immaturity of his own mind, he would alone consent to admire, and sigh to emulate.' The words in which Gibbon has described the conception and completion of his great work are so solemnly fine, and so soon brought together, that we cannot refrain from transcribing them here:—'It was at Rome, on the 15th of October 1764, as I sat musing amidst the ruins of the Capitol, while the barefooted friars were singing vespers in the temple of Jupiter, that the idea of writing the decline and fall of the city first started to my mind. * * I have presumed to mark the moment of conception; I shall now commemorate the hour of my final deliverance. It was on the day, or rather the night, of the 27th June 1787, between the hours of eleven and twelve, that I wrote the last lines of the last page in a summer-house in my garden. After laying down my pen, I took several turns in a *berceau*, or covered walk of acacias, which commands a prospect of the country, the lake, and the mountains. The air was temperate, the sky was serene, the silver orb of the moon was reflected from the waters, and all nature was silent. I will not dissemble the first emotions of joy on recovery of my freedom, and perhaps the establishment of my fame. But my pride was soon humbled, and a sober melancholy was spread over my mind, by the idea that I had taken an everlasting farewell of an old and agreeable companion, and that whatsoever might be the future date of my History, the life of the historian must be short and precarious.'

In that very interesting work of D'Israeli's, 'The Literary Character,' there is an allusion to the vivid dreams which sometimes disturb the sleep of poets, and he mentions that Tasso frequently awoke himself by repeating a verse aloud. There is a most extraordinary instance of the mental activity during sleep related by Coleridge, respecting the composition of a poetical fragment called 'Kubla Khan.' Being in a state of ill health, he had taken an anodyne, from the effects of which he fell asleep in his chair, just as he finished reading this passage from Purchas's Pilgrimage—'Here the Khan Kubla commanded a palace to be built, and a stately garden thereunto, and thus ten miles of fertile ground were enclosed with a wall.' He continued about three hours in a profound sleep, at least of the external senses, during which time he had a vivid confidence that he could not have composed less than from two to three hundred lines. All the images rose up before him as things, with a parallel production of the correspondent expressions, without any sensation or consciousness of effort. On awaking, he appeared to himself to have a distinct recollection of the whole; and taking his pen, he eagerly wrote down the lines preserved in his poems. At that moment he was unfortunately called out by a person on business, and detained by him above an hour. On his return he found, to his great surprise and vexation, that though he still retained a vague recollection of the vision, yet, with the exception of a few scattered lines, all the rest had vanished. Other instances of the assiduity of the intellectual powers whilst the corporeal faculties are entranced, can be furnished, to show that *if le fait n'est pas vraisemblable il est vrai*. Lord Byron once became delirious when attacked by a tertian fever. The Countess Guiccioli states that in his delirium he one night composed several verses, which he directed his servant to put into writing at his dictation. The metre was perfectly correct, and no one could have guessed from the matter under what circumstances they had been written. The poet kept the lines some time after he recovered, and then burned them.

How pleasant is it to turn from the heyday and the bustle of modern literature, to the twilight stillness of some quaint old writer! It is like quitting the full stream of human life, pouring through Fleet Street (pardon the illustration of a Londoner) for the quiet verdure of the Temple Gardens, or the 'sacred calm' of the Temple church. Burton's Anatomy of Melancholy, Sir Thomas Browne's Religio Medici, Lord Bacon's Essays, and Jeremy Taylor's Discourses, are such books as we allude to. As to the first, a prime favourite of Charles Lamb, Byron said it was the most amusing and instructive medley of quotations and classical anecdotes he ever perused. Half your modern books, said Beckford, are decanted out of it. We may add, that it contains a poem which suggested to Milton his L'Allegro and Il Penseroso. Talking about old books, it is curious to observe, when looking over an old library, into what utter oblivion many works, to which contemporaries confidently promised an immunity from literary death, or whose intrinsic merit bade fair to secure that privilege, have fallen past all revivication. Swift, in his Tale of a Tub, says 'the Earl of Orrery's Remarks will be read with delight, when the Dissertation he exposes will neither be sought nor found.' The dissertation here meant is Bentley's, on the Epistles of Phalaris, a book still in repute, whilst Boyle's Remarks have been long unread. '*L'Immortel auteur de la Barvigliana*,' so writes M. Beyle the author; perhaps in some one's estimation the '*immortel auteur*' of a History of Painting in Italy. But who now-a-days knows anything about M. Beyle or his apotheosised friend? Have any of our readers ever met with Barclay's Argenis, a Latin romance published about 1620, which once enjoyed such reputation, that translations were made into French, English, German, Italian, Spanish, Swedish, Polish, and Islandic? Cowper declared that it was the best romance ever written; and Coleridge bestows great praise upon it. It absolutely distresses me, says the latter, when I reflect that this work, admired as it has been by great men of all ages, should be only not unknown to general readers.

The term 'classic' is of Latin origin, and derived from the social economy of Rome. One man was said to be of the second class, another man was in the third, but he who was in the highest was said emphatically to be *of the class*—*classicus*—as we say, 'men of rank,' meaning those who are of the highest ranks in the state. Hence, by an obvious analogy, the best authors were termed classic; that is, of the highest class.

Greek wills were executed in the presence of the magistrates. In the time of Nero, a special method of sealing was adopted with respect to Roman wills, in order the more effectually to prevent the forgeries which had become shamefully common. When signed, they were sealed up, after they had been pierced, and a linen envelope passed three times through the holes. The names of those who had affixed the seals were then indorsed. Upon the first page, or left-hand tablet, were written the names of the principal heirs; upon the second, or right-hand tablet, the names of the legatees. The Germans and Gauls copied these Roman ceremonies. Anglo-Saxon wills were transcribed three times upon the same sheet, or parchment. They were then read over in the presence of witnesses, cut off from each other with a waving or indented line, so as to match like a tally, and the copies transferred to different persons for safe custody. This custom continued down to a late period. Du Cange mentions a will written on bark about 690, and also wills written on wood.

Those manuscripts are called Palimpsest which have been written on a second time, after the original writing was erased or expunged. The expense of parchment, and the demand for books of devotion, and copies of the Fathers, induced the monks of the middle ages to perform this barbarous process. In this way many very valuable manuscripts have been irrecoverably lost; but in some instances, where the original writing had not been entirely destroyed, works of great interest have been found overlaid by a later manuscript, and, after a laborious investigation, recovered. A palimpsest manuscript was discovered in 1816, which some German literati undertook to decipher. The original writing turned out to be a famous treatise on Roman law, which it was imagined had been lost. The manuscript consisted of 127 sheets of parchment, and the patient labour required to disinter the buried text may be estimated from the fact, that it had as far as possible been washed out or erased, and nearly the whole re-written with the epistles of St Jerome. The lines of the first and second writings ran in the same direction, and were frequently similar. Moreover, sixty-three pages had been covered with writing *three times*. At length the Institutions of Gaius were entirely retrieved, to the delight of continental jurists.

Parchment was at one period so valuable, that when Gui, Count of Nevers, presented the monks of the Chartreux, near Paris, with some plate, they sent it back, begging him to let them have parchment instead.

In 1765 there appeared a translation of the Old and New Testaments, with notes, critical and explanatory, in two volumes, by Anthony Purver. This translator was a poor shoemaker, who was seized with the notion that he was called to render the Scriptures into English. In pursuance of this divine command, as he imagined it was, he diligently began the study of Hebrew, and then acquired a knowledge of Chaldee, Syriac, Greek, and Latin. Thus armed, he commenced his translation, which he was enabled to publish by the pecuniary assistance of some of his friends.

Our authorised version of the Holy Scriptures was begun in 1607, and finished in 1611. Forty-seven divines, in six companies, distributed the labour amongst them, twenty-five being assigned to the Old Testament, fifteen to the New, and seven to the Apocrypha. Three copies of the whole Bible, one from each university, and one from Westminster, were then sent to London, where a committee of six persons, two being deputed by the companies at each place, reviewed and polished the whole work. The pure Saxon of the translation has been much commended, and some have ventured to style it the perfection of English.

THE OLD MAN OF THE AGE OF LOUIS XIV.

[From Silliman's Tour between Hartford and Quebec, in 1819.]

Two miles from Whitehall, on the Salem road to Albany, lives Henry Francisco, a native of France. Having a few hours to spare before the departure of the steamboat for St John's in Canada, we rode out to see (probably) the oldest man in America. He believes himself to be 134 years old, and the people around believe him to be of this great age. When we arrived at his residence, a plain farmer's house, rather out of repair, and much exposed to the wind, he was up stairs at his daily work of spooling and winding yarn. This occupation is auxiliary to that of his wife, who is a weaver, and although more than 80 years of age, weaves six yards a-day. Supposing he must be very feeble, we offered to go up stairs to him; but he soon came down, supported by a staff, but with less apparent inconvenience than most persons exhibit at 85 or 90. His stature is of the middle size; and although his person is rather delicate and slender, he stoops but little even when unsupported. His complexion is very fair and delicate, and his expression bright, cheerful, and intelligent: his features are handsome, and, considering that they have endured through one-third part of a second century, they are regular, comely, and wonderfully undisfigured by the hand of time: his eyes are of a lively blue: his profile is Grecian, and very fine: his head is completely covered with the most beautiful and delicate white locks imaginable; they are so long and abundant, as to fall gracefully from the crown of his head, parting regularly from a central point, and reaching down from his shoulders: his hair is perfectly snow-white, except where it is thick in his neck; when parted there, it shows some few dark shades, the remnants of a former century. He still retains the front teeth of his upper jaw: his mouth is not fallen in, as in old people generally, and his lips, particularly, are like those of middle life: his voice is strong and sweet-toned, although a little tremulous: his hearing very little impaired, so that a voice of ordinary strength, with distinct articulation, enables him to understand: his eye-sight is sufficient for his work, and he distinguishes large print, such as the title-page of his Bible, without glasses: his health is good, and has always been so, except that he has now a cough and expectoration. He informed me that his father, driven out of France by religious persecution, fled to Amsterdam: by his account, it must have been in consequence of the persecutions of the French Protestants or Huguenots, in the latter part of the reign of Louis XIV. At Amsterdam his father married his mother, a Dutch woman, five years before he was born, and before that event, returned with her into France. When he was five years old, his father again fled on account of 'de religion,' as he expressed it; for his language, although very intelligible English, is marked by French peculiarities. He says he remembers their flight, and that it was in winter; for he recollects that they were descending a hill which was covered with snow, and he cried out to his father, 'Oh, fader, do go back, and get my little carrole'—(a little boy's sledge or sleigh).

From these dates, we are enabled to fix the time of his birth, provided he is correct in the main fact; for he says he was present at Queen Anne's coronation, and was then 16 years old, the 31st of May, old style. His father, as he asserts, after his return from Holland, had again been driven from France by persecution, and the second time took refuge in Holland, and afterwards in England, where he resided with his family at the time of the coronation of Queen Anne in 1702. This makes Francisco to have been born in 1686; to have been expelled from France in 1691; and therefore to have completed his 133d year on the 11th of last June: of course he is now more than three months advanced in his 134th year. It is notorious that about this time multitudes of French Protestants fled, on account of the persecutions of Louis XIV., resulting from the revocation of the edict of Nantes, which occurred October 12, 1685; and notwithstanding the guards upon the frontiers, and other measures of precaution or rigour to prevent emigration, it is well known that for years multitudes continued to make their escape, and that Louis lost 600,000 of his best and most useful subjects. I asked Francisco if he *saw* Queen Anne crowned; he replied, with great animation, and with an elevated voice, 'Ah, dat I did, and a fine-looking woman she was too, as any dat you see now-a-days.' He said he fought in all Queen Anne's wars, and was at many battles, and under many commanders, but his memory fails, and he cannot remember their names, except the Duke of Marlborough, who was one of them. He has been much cut up with wounds, which he showed us, but cannot always give a very distinct account of his warfare. He came out with his father from England to New York probably early in the last century, but cannot remember the date. He said pathetically, when pressed for accounts of his military experience, 'Oh, I was in all Queen Anne's wars; I was at Niagara, at Oswego, on the Ohio (in Braddock's defeat, in 1755, where he was wounded). I was carried prisoner to Quebec (in the revolutionary war, when he must have been at least ninety years old). I fight in all sorts of wars all my life; I see dreadful trouble; and den to have dem we toughi our friends, turn Tories; and the British too, and fight against ourselves; O, dat was worst of all.' He here seemed much affected, and almost too full for utterance. It seems that during the revolutionary war he kept a tavern at Fort Edward, and he lamented, in a very animated manner, that the Tories burnt his house and barn and 400 bushels of grain. This, his wife said, was the same year that Miss M'Crea was barbarously murdered. He has had two wives, and twenty-one children. The youngest child is the daughter in whose house he now lives, and she is now fifty-two years old; of course he was eighty-two when she was born. They suppose several of the older children are still living, at a very advanced age, beyond the Ohio; but they have not heard of them for several years.

The family were neighbours to the family of Miss M'Crea, and were acquainted with the circumstances of her tragical death. They said that the lover, Mr Jones, at first vowed vengeance against the Indians; but, on counting the cost, wisely gave it up.

Henry Francisco has been all his life a very active and energetic, although not a stout-framed man. He was formerly fond of spirits; but that habit appears to have been long abandoned. In other respects he has been remarkably abstemious, eating but little, and particularly abstaining, almost entirely, from animal food; his favourite articles being tea, bread and butter, and baked apples. His wife said that after such a breakfast he would go out and work till noon; then dine upon the same, if he could get it; and then take the same at night; and particularly he always drank tea, whenever he could obtain it, three cups at a time, three times a-day. The old man manifested a great deal of feeling, and even of tenderness, which increased as we treated him with respect and kindness. He often shed tears, and particularly when, on coming away, we gave him money: he looked up to heaven and fervently *thanked* God, but did not thank us; he, however, pressed our hands very warmly, wept, and wished us every blessing, and expressed something serious with respect to our meeting in another world. The oldest people in the vicinity remember Francisco as being always, from their oldest recollection, much older than themselves; and a Mr Fuller, who recently died there, between eighty and ninety years of age, thought Francisco was one hundred and forty. On the whole, although the evidence rests in a degree on its own credibility, still, as many things corroborate it, and as his character appears remarkably sincere, guileless, and affectionate, I am inclined to believe he is as old as he is stated to be. He is really a most remarkable and interesting old man. There is nothing either in his person or dress of the negligence and squalidness of extreme age, especially when not in elevated circumstances; on the contrary, he is agreeable and attractive, and were he dressed in a superior manner, and placed in a handsome and well-furnished apartment, he would be a most beautiful old man. Little could I have expected to converse and shake hands with a man who has been a soldier in most of the wars of this country for 100 years; who, more than a century ago, fought under Marlborough, in Queen Anne's wars, and who (already grown up to manhood) saw her crowned 117 years since; who, 128 years ago, and in the century before last, was driven from France by the proud, magnificent, and intolerant Louis XIV.; and who has lived a 44th part of all the time that the human race have occupied this globe! What an interview! It is like seeing one come back from the dead to relate the events of centuries, now swallowed up in the abyss of time! Except his cough, which they told us had not been of long standing, we saw nothing in Francisco's appearance that might indicate a speedy dissolution, and he seemed to have sufficient mental and bodily powers to endure for many years to come. [He died the year after of fever and ague.]

IDLE WISHES.

He that waits for an opportunity to do much at once, may breathe out his life in idle wishes; and regret, in the last hour, his useless intentions and barren zeal.—*Idler*.

THE GLOW-WORM.

BY S. W. PARTRIDGE.

Hail, little joyful, glimmering spark,
So gaily shining in the dark,
I love to see thy emerald light,
Thus gladdening the gloomy night;
And more because thy lamp, in sooth,
Doth light my mind to many a truth,
And many a lesson doth impart
To teach the head and mend the heart.

Say, dost thou trim thy lamp to guide
Thy insect lover to thy side,
Like fair enamoured Sestos' daughter,
Who lit her love o'er Helle's water?
Love is the life of life, no doubt—
A secret thou hast long found out,
And, therefore, to divide thy cares,
Liv'st not in units, but in pairs,
And seal'st the truth by heaven made known—
It is not good to live alone.

Thou doest well to hide by day,
Nor in the glare of noon display
A form with little grace endued,
But fit for night and solitude.
Ah, modest worm, thou'rt wiser far
Than many empty upstarts are,
Who, leaving their appointed sphere,
Would needs be shining everywhere,
And who, with justice most undoubted,
Are only noticed to be scouted;
Yet who, in an obscurer place,
Might some small circle please and grace;
And, would they but the day resign,
By night perhaps the worms might shine;
And, to their proper station thrust,
Might dazzle whom they now disgust.

And ah! methinks, poor worm, thy light
Is like to genius, dazzling bright,
Whose glare but lures the heartless eye
Of every clownish passer-by,
And, pelted by each brainless knave,
Its very glory digs its grave;
While Ignorance soundly slumbers on,
Secure, because unseen, unknown.

And then, to moralise again,
Another truth thou teachest plain—
That though the brightest, 'tis confessed,
Are but, like thee, poor worms at best,
Yet each has some small talent given
To adorn the earth and honour Heaven;
And wise is he who well doth know
Both what he can and cannot do;
The one, ambitious, never tries,
The other may not dare despise,
And knows (oh, knowledge half divine!)
Both when to hide and when to shine;
Nor once presumes, a child of night,
To obtrude upon the glaring light,
Nor yet at eve withholds his ray,
Because he cannot shine by day.

FLATTERERS.

Take care thou be not made a fool by flatterers, for even the wisest men are abused by these. Know, therefore, that flatterers are the worst kind of traitors; for they will strengthen thy imperfections, encourage thee in all evils, correct thee in nothing, but so shadow and paint all thy vices and follies, as thou shalt never, by their will, discern evil from good, or vice from virtue: and because all men are apt to flatter themselves, to entertain the additions of other men's praises is most perilous. A flatterer is said to be a beast that biteth smiling, and has been compared to an ape, who, because she cannot defend the house like a dog, labour as an ox, or bear burdens as a horse, doth therefore yet play tricks, and provoke laughter. Thou mayest be sure that he that will in private tell thee thy faults is thy friend, for he adventures thy dislike, and doth hazard thy hatred; for there are few men that can endure it, every man for the most part delighting in self-praise, which is one of the most universal follies that bewitcheth mankind. —*Sir Walter Raleigh*.

Published by W. and R. Chambers, High Street, Edinburgh (also 98, Miller Street, Glasgow); and with their permission, by W. S. Orr, Amen Corner, London.—Printed by Bradbury and Evans, Whitefriars, London.

CONDUCTED BY WILLIAM AND ROBERT CHAMBERS, EDITORS OF 'CHAMBERS'S INFORMATION FOR THE PEOPLE,' 'CHAMBERS'S EDUCATIONAL COURSE,' &c.

No. 87. New Series. SATURDAY, AUGUST 30, 1845. Price 1½d.

A VISIT TO THE GARDEN PAVILION IN THE GROUNDS OF BUCKINGHAM PALACE.

Amongst the subjects of public attention in London last month, was the newly-finished summer-house or pavilion erected by her majesty and Prince Albert in the grounds connected with Buckingham Palace. Tickets having been issued to enable a limited portion of the public to see this novel object, and one of these having fallen into the hands of a friend, I was enabled to pay the place a visit. For the information of those who are not familiarly acquainted with London, I may begin by mentioning that Buckingham Palace—built in the reign of George IV.—occupies a somewhat disadvantageous situation on the west side of St James's Park, contiguous to the suburban district of Pimlico. In the rear of the palace is a piece of pleasure ground, comprising wood and lake, and really a beautiful retired scene, notwithstanding that the roar of Piccadilly speaks, in a way that cannot be mistaken, of the near neighbourhood of an active city. Between the grounds and the adjacent suburb, an artificial mound, covered with shrubbery, helps to shut in the place; and on the summit of this mound is perched a small Chinese-looking building with a little platform in front. This is the Pavilion.

The external appearance is by no means impressive. Many a lodge at a gentleman's gate is finer. It is on entering that we become aware that something extraordinary is intended. The fact is, that the queen and her consort have here made an experiment in that combination of Decorative Painting with Architecture, for which Italy is remarkable, but which has as yet been scarcely exemplified in our own country. The great and affluent in England have recently been made comparatively familiar with this style, by the publication of a superb work by Mr L. Gruner, embodying the decorations contributed by Raphael to the Vatican, and the similar productions of other Italian masters. When her majesty, therefore, determined on having this summer-house decorated in such a manner, she very appropriately employed Gruner to direct the general arrangements, and engage the various artists and others required for the purpose. So much being premised, let us step across the threshold, and inspect what it requires no great stretch of imagination to conceive as a fairy palace. We enter at once a small octagonal room (15 feet 8 inches in diameter, and 15 feet in height), being, little as it is, the chief room of the building. From the gray marble floor to the centre of the vaulted ceiling, it is one blaze of the most gay and brilliant colouring. Before, however, going into the particulars of the decoration, let us see the remainder of the house, in order to have a general idea of its character and proposed uses. Opposite, then, to the entrance of this room are two doors, occupying compartments in the octagonal arrangement, but having one compartment containing a fireplace and mirror between: these lead into two smaller rooms (8 feet 10 inches by 9 feet 7 inches, and 12 feet in height), betwixt which is interposed a small kitchen, provided with every suitable convenience. Such are the whole accommodations.

The principal or octagon room is an illustration of Milton's youthful production, the Masque of Comus, 'in itself, like an exquisite many-sided gem, presenting within a small compass the most faultless proportion and the richest variety.'* The suitableness of this poem for being illustrated in such a room, where more heroic and solemn subjects would have been altogether inappropriate, must strike every one. 'Comus,' says Mrs Jameson, 'at once classical, romantic, and pastoral, with all its charming associations of grouping, sentiment, and scenery, was just the thing fitted to inspire English artists, to elevate their fancy to the height of their argument, to render their task at once a light and a proud one; while nothing could be more beautifully adapted to the shades of a trim garden devoted to the recreation of our Sovereign Lady, than the chaste, polished, yet picturesque elegance of the poem, considered as a creation of art.'

From the eight angles of the room rise as many 'ribs,' which, meeting in the centre, form a dome-shaped roof, divided into eight compartments. In these are painted circular openings, with a sky background, for the purpose of indicating the *time* of the scenes depicted below: those on the west side present midnight, with its star, and those on the east the approaching dawn. At the point where the walls and dome meet, there is a rich cornice, below which are eight lunettes or semicircular spaces, filling the upper portion of the eight sides of the room; and in these lunettes are as many frescoes, or paintings upon plaster, containing scenes from the poem. Each lunette is six feet by three, and over each is a tablet, on which is inscribed in gilt letters, on a brownish-red ground, the particular passage of the poem which has suggested the subject of the picture. All of these paintings are by English artists of the highest reputation. Such are the chief objects which meet the eye in this room: there is, besides, a great quantity of minute ornament. The spandrils, or angular spaces left by the curves of the lunettes, are occupied by figures relating to the subjects of the respective pictures. Beneath the lunettes are panels adorned with arabesques, in harmony with the main subjects. Over each door are winged panthers, in stucco, with a head of Comus, ivy-crowned, between them. Beneath each window is the cipher of her majesty and Prince Albert, encircled

* Mrs Jameson's introduction to a volume entitled 'The Decorations of the Garden Pavilion of Buckingham Palace, engraved under the superintendence of L. Gruner.' 1845.

with flowers. The pilasters running up the angles of the room present, in medallions, figures and groups from a variety of Milton's poems—as Eve relating her dream to Adam, Adam consoling Eve, 'the bright morning star, day's harbinger,' Samson Agonistes, &c. Red, blue, and white mingle beautifully in this profusion of ornament, by which the eye is for some time too much dazzled to apprehend the details.

The Masque of Comus was a compliment paid by Milton to the Earl of Bridgewater, then residing in Ludlow Castle as president or viceroy of Wales. It was acted at Ludlow before the earl's family in 1634. The story is of the simplest kind, relating only how a lady lost her way in a wood, and, falling under the enchantments of Comus, a son of Bacchus and Circe, was with some difficulty rescued and restored to her friends. Besides Comus and the lady, the characters presented are her two brothers, an attendant spirit who puts on the guise of a shepherd, and Sabrina, the goddess of the Severn river. In the age following that in which Spenser spun his fine allegories, and Drayton personified every wood and stream in the country, this union of ancient mythology with British scenery, and the calling in of a river spirit for the protection of a benighted young lady, would appear sufficiently rational. The first lunette (by Mr Stanfield) is designed to realise the passage near the commencement of the poem, in which the attendant spirit speaks of his errand being to those exceptions from the common run of human beings who

> by due steps aspire
> To lay their just hands on the golden key
> That opes the palace of eternity.

The scene is a landscape—a river flowing through forest scenery; the spirit, in shepherd weeds, is seen leaning meditatively upon his crook, while in the background, through the glade, we see the rabble rout of Comus holding their nocturnal orgies by torchlight. In the spandrils are a cherub weeping and a fiend exulting. In the poem, the spirit describes Comus's birth and character, and his haunting 'this tract that fronts the falling sun,' for the purpose of tempting weary travellers to drink of his glass, when,

> Soon as the potion works, their human countenance,
> The express resemblance of the gods, is changed
> Into some brutish form of wolf or bear,
> Or ounce or tiger, hog, or bearded goat,
> All other parts remaining as they were;
> And they, so perfect is their misery,
> Not once perceive their foul disfigurement;
> But boast themselves more comely than before.

The spirit announces his own function to be the preservation of 'any favoured of high Jove' from the spells of this dangerous deity. Comus then enters; and proposes to commence his usual revels for the night; but presently an interruption takes place, from the entrance of the lady, who, having been left for a while by her brothers, had wandered on through the forest till thick night overtook her, and she had become exhausted with fatigue. The second lunette (by Mr Uwins) represents her standing under an oak, saying,

> This is the place, as well as I may guess,
> Whence even now the tumult of rude mirth
> Was rife, and perfect in my listening ear;
> Yet nought but single darkness do I find.
> What might this be? A thousand fantasies
> Begin to throng into my memory,
> Of calling shapes and beckoning shadows dire,
> And airy tongues that syllable men's names
> On sands, and shores, and desert wildernesses. * *
> Was I deceived, or did a sable cloud
> Turn out her silver lining to the night? * *

Comus is seen amidst the neighbouring foliage listening to her soliloquy. In the spandrils, a seraph looks down with anguish, and a satyr with triumph.

Comus appearing before the lady as an honest homely swain, the lady agrees to accept his hospitality; and when they have left the stage, the two brothers enter, to express their distress at the loss of their sister. Some parts of their conversation betoken, in the Milton of six-and-twenty, what he was to become in his riper days.

> Wisdom's self
> Oft seeks to sweet retired solitude,
> Where with her best nurse contemplation
> She plumes her feathers, and lets grow her wings,
> That in the various bustle of resort
> Were all too ruffled, and sometimes impaired.
> He that has light within his own clear breast,
> May sit i' the centre, and enjoy bright day:
> But he that hides a dark soul, and foul thoughts,
> Benighted walks under the mid-day sun;
> Himself is his own dungeon. * *
>
> So dear to Heaven is saintly chastity,
> That when a soul is found sincerely so,
> A thousand liveried angels lackey her,
> Driving far off each thing of sin and guilt,
> And in clear dream, and solemn vision,
> Tell her of things that no gross ear can hear,
> Till oft converse with heavenly habitants
> Begin to cast a beam on th' outward shape,
> The unpolluted temple of the mind,
> And turns it by degrees to the soul's essence,
> Till all be made immortal.

The attendant spirit, in his shepherd dress, joins them with intelligence of their sister, of whom the three then proceed in quest.

The next scene presents the lady sitting in a palace, 'full of all manner of deliciousness,' while Comus tempts her; the brutish rabble standing by. This is the subject of the third fresco (by Mr C. Leslie), the precise point being that when the lady exclaims,

> Hence with thy brewed enchantments, foul deceiver!
> Hast thou betrayed my credulous innocence
> With visored falsehood and base forgery?
> Were it a draft for Juno when she banquets,
> I would not taste thy treasonous offer.

After a colloquy between the two, in which Comus confesses himself foiled by her words, the brothers rush in with drawn swords, wrest his glass out of his hand and break it against the ground: his rout make sign of resistance, but are all driven off. The attendant spirit then enters, and says,

> What! have you let the false enchanter 'scape?
> Oh, ye mistook; ye should have snatched his wand
> And bound him fast.

This incident is the subject of two of the lunettes; an unlucky consequence of the artists having been left to choose the subjects from the poem at their own discretion. Fortunately, however, they present the subject in styles so dissimilar, that no one at first sight could detect the identity. In Sir William Ross's picture, the lady in her chair forms the central figure, while the enchanter is seen flying off at the side from before an armed figure. In Mr Landseer's painting, we have Comus's rabble presented most conspicuously, their animal heads affording a most appropriate subject for the peculiar genius of that artist. Comus, alarmed at the appearance of the armed brothers, receives a Bacchante with a greyhound's head, who has thrown herself upon his arm. The mixture of grotesque and imaginative in this picture, and the union of tipsy stupidity and terror in the separate figures, render it by far the most remarkable picture in the series, though it certainly is far from being the most pleasing.

To return to the poem: the lady being fixed by enchantment to her chair, it is necessary to call in the aid of the river goddess, Sabrina, who, having been duly invoked, rises from her cave, and says

> Brightest lady, look on me;
> Thus I sprinkle on thy breast
> Drops that from my fountain pure
> I have kept of precious cure.

This is the subject of Mr Maclise's fresco, which is marked by his usual liveliness and brilliancy, profusion of figures, and painstaking in their execution. The lady sits in her chair, 'in stony fetters fixed and motionless.' Sabrina and her attendant spirits hover around her. One nymph presents in a shell the water of precious cure, which Sabrina is about to sprinkle over the victim of enchantment. The brothers and the star-browed spirit stand by. In the spandrils are two of the rabble rout looking down in affright.

The lady, being now disenchanted, returns with her friendly guardians to her father's mansion, where she and her brothers are presented to their parents by the spirit.

> Noble lord and lady bright,
> I have brought ye new delight;
> There behold, so goodly grown,
> Three fair branches of your own;
> Heaven hath timely tried their youth,
> Their faith, their patience, and their truth.

Mr Dyce gives us this scene in a very pleasing picture, 'graceful, simple, full of intelligence, and the colouring rich without trickery,' according to a critical contemporary. In the connected spandrils are two guardian angels presenting crowns of white roses and myrtle. In conclusion, the spirit flies to

> Happy climes, that lie
> Where day never shuts his eye,

but first calling on mortals to follow virtue. She, he says,

> can teach you how to climb
> Higher than the sphery chime;
> Or if Virtue feeble were,
> Heaven itself would stoop to her.

The two last lines, with which the poem terminates, are the subject of the last fresco of the series (by Mr Eastlake), where Virtue is represented fainting upon the high and rugged path, and succoured there by a seraph; while Vice, represented by a serpent, is seen gliding away; a choir of angels leaning from the clouds above, to receive the coming visitant.

Having thus at some length given a description of the chief room, I proceed to the next, which may be called the *Scott Room*, since its decorations wholly bear reference to the productions of that illustrious person. The four sides of this apartment are painted in imitation of gray veined marble, so exquisitely, that I only became aware of their not being real marble after I returned home. Round the upper portion of the walls runs a rich frieze, presenting three compartments on each side, the central one a bas-relief in white stucco on a blue ground, the side ones paintings of small size, representing views of places celebrated by Scott. Here we have Melrose, Abbotsford, Loch Etive, Dryburgh Abbey, Craig Nethan, Loch Awe, Aros Castle, and Windermere Lake, painted by Mr E. W. Dallas from Mr Gruner's sketches. In the bas-reliefs we have groups from the poems—Clara recognising Wilton on the field of battle, Bruce raising his page from amidst the slain (these two by Mr Timbrell), William of Deloraine taking the book from the magician's tomb, and Roderick Dhu overcome by the Knight of Snowdown (these last by Mr J. Bell). In eight lunettes are as many scenes from the Waverley novels, the production of different artists, two of whom are, I understand, sons of the celebrated caricaturist (Doyle), who usually passes by the name of H. B. Eight heads in white stucco, surrounded by arabesques in relief, represent as many of Scott's heroines. This completes the list of figures, but not the whole ornaments of the room, for the flooring—not yet laid down—is chequered, and surrounded by a border of thistles, along with festoons of the various tartans of the Highland clans. Only one specimen of the tiles forming this pavement was shown when we visited the pavilion; it contained the tartan of the Camerons, with the name of that clan inscribed upon it. In 1745, this kind of cloth was looked upon at court as a spell to raise fiends: in 1845, it is cherished in the most private domestic retreats of royalty as a memorial of a romantic period of our national history. In a late visit to Hampton Court, I observed a picture equally indicative of change of times and of feelings; namely, a portrait of the poor old Chevalier taking his place among the other royal personages who figure in such profusion in that palace.

The remaining small room is designed as an imitation of the style which prevails in the ancient city of Pompeii; all the ornaments, friezes, and panels being suggested by, or accurately copied from, existing remains, except the coved ceiling, which is the invention of Mr Augustine Aglio. 'This room,' says Mrs Jameson, 'may be considered as a very perfect and genuine example of classical domestic decoration, such as we find in the buildings of Pompeii—a style totally distinct from that of the baths of Titus, which suggested to Raphael and his school the rich arabesque ornaments in painting and relief which prevailed in the sixteenth century, and which have been chiefly followed in the other two rooms.'

I spent fully two hours in *perusing* the pavilion in all its various parts, and yet left it without having got above half way through its bewildering minutiæ. The work as a whole, and in its parts, has been keenly criticised by those who assume the duty of warning the public against being too much pleased with books, pictures, and other productions of the finer intellect of our species. It has, doubtless, some faults and infelicities, the want of harmony being, I think, the chief. Yet, taken as the first English attempt at such a style of decoration, and considering the merely nascent condition of art in our country, I cannot help regarding the whole as creditable, and calculated to afford pleasure to the exalted personages for whose use the little mansion is designed.

THE LADY HESTER STANHOPE.

SECOND ARTICLE.

The government were not unmindful of the services of our extraordinary heroine, and Mr Fox, Pitt's successor in the premiership, sent to offer her a princely reward. 'It was,' according to her ladyship's account, 'as good as ten thousand pounds a-year to me. He was to make me ranger of some park, with a house; and then I was to have a house in town; and the rest was to be done in the way they shuffle those things through the public offices.' This splendid income Lady Hester had the magnanimity to refuse. Mr Ward was sent to endeavour to make her ladyship alter her determination. 'I told him that it was not from a personal disregard for Mr Fox that I refused; because, when I asked Mr Pitt upon one occasion who was the cleverest man in England, he answered, "Mr Fox;" but as the world only knew Mr Pitt and Mr Fox as opposed to each other, I should be considered as receiving benefits from Mr Pitt's enemy. "You will live to repent your refusal," said Mr Ward. I answered him that might be, but that if he talked for a year, he never would alter my resolution.' On his deathbed, however, Mr Pitt had written a request to the king that she should be allowed a pension; and her name was eventually placed on the pension-list for L.1200 per annum.

With this and some small family property, another woman would have retired, and become the ornament, or perhaps the oracle, of a smaller sphere than that in which she had hitherto moved; but Lady Hester, though she made an attempt of the kind, could not persevere in it. She took a house in Montague Square. 'But,' she would say, 'a poor gentlewoman, doctor, is the worst thing in the world. Not being able to keep a carriage, how was I to go out? If I used a hackney-coach, some spiteful person would be sure to mention it:—"Who do you think I saw yesterday in a hackney-coach? I wonder where she could be driving alone, down those narrow streets?"'

She remained almost shut up in Montague Square (for she gave many reasons for not going otherwise than as formerly in a carriage), till the death of her brother Charles at Corunna disgusted her with London; and, breaking up her little establishment, she went down into Wales, residing in a small cottage at Builth, somewhere near Brecon, in a room not more than a dozen feet square. Here she amused herself in curing the poor, in her dairy, and in other rustic occupations; until, not finding herself so far removed from her English acquaintances but what they were always coming across her, and breaking in upon her solitude, she resolved on going to the Mediterranean. Accordingly she left England, accompanied by a faithful female companion, the medical gentleman to whom we are indebted for the memoirs so often quoted, and a suite of servants.

After remaining some time at Gibraltar and Malta, she departed for Zante about July 1810; from whence she passed over to Patrass, visited Constantinople, and sailed for Egypt. At Rhodes she was shipwrecked, where Dr M., who then accompanied her on her travels, lost his journals, and the public consequently much information.

After many wanderings in the East, the doctor saw her, as he states, finally settled on Mount Lebanon, when, after seven years' uninterrupted service, he took a temporary leave of her. At the end of a year or two he revisited Syria; but finding 'that her ladyship had in the meanwhile completely familiarised herself with the usages of the East, conducting her establishment entirely in the Turkish manner, and adopting even much of their medical empiricism,' he again left her. Circumstances, however, at length restored them to each other; and in December 1829, Dr M. returned to Lady Hester's service, in which he continued till her death.

The scene is now changed. Having once left England, Lady Hester Stanhope had left it for ever. Reduced from power and greatness to dependence and relative poverty, she, like Coriolanus, banished her country, and in so doing banished herself. Her old habits and feelings, however, never forsook her; she was the same woman in the wilderness that she had been in the court, thirsting for dominion, and exercising influence, by the force of rooted habit. Her master passion was the love of absolute power, which, whether in Britain or Syria, she seemed resolved to gratify. She had, however, a difficulty in doing this at first in her new position; for, though taking up her residence two miles distant from the city—the ancient city of Sidon—she was still too much in the midst of society to suit her purpose. A lonely and insulated residence was necessary for her, if she would prevent her servants from absconding when wearied of her tyranny, or desirous of change. She accordingly removed to Jôon, to a house situated 'on the summit of a conical hill, whence comers and goers might be seen on every side.' From hence, also, 'a poor slave could rarely muster courage enough to venture by night across lonely mountains, when jackals and wolves were abroad; or, if he did, by the time he reached Sayda, or Beyrout, or Dair-el-kamar, the only three towns within reach, his resolves had cooled, the consequences of the step he had taken presented themselves forcibly to his mind, or there was time to soothe him by promises and presents.' On one occasion, however, we are told that, notwithstanding these precautions, all her free women decamped in a body; and, on another, her slaves attempted to scale the walls, and some actually effected their escape. But this was a solitary instance: in general, her arrangements were sufficient security. Besides, 'she was known to have great influence with Abdallah Pasha, to whom she had rendered many services, pecuniary and personal; for to him, as well as to his harem, she was constantly sending presents; and he, as a Turk, fostered despotism rather than opposed it. The Emir Beshyr, or prince of the Druzes, her nearest neighbour, she had so completely intimidated by the unparalleled boldness of her tongue and pen, that he felt no inclination to commit himself by any act which might be likely to draw either of them on him again. In what direction, therefore, was a poor unprotected slave or peasant to fly? Over others, who, like her doctor, her secretary, or her dragoman, were free to act as they liked, and towards whom she had mere *ménagemens* to preserve, there hung a spell of a different kind, by which this modern Circe entangled people almost inextricably in her nets. A series of benefits conferred on them, an indescribable art in becoming the depositary of their secrets, an unerring perception of their failings, brought home in moments of confidence to their bosoms, soon left them no alternative but that of securing her protection by unqualified submission to her will.'

Such power belongs to force of character. It is but justice, however, to Lady Hester Stanhope to add, that hers had its root in piety; which, too, was of a kind to procure her favour in the East. A passage in one of her letters places this trait of her character in a beautiful light.

'A young seyd, a friend of mine,' she wrote to Dr M., 'when riding one day in a solitary part of the mountain, heard the echo of a strange noise in the rocks. He listened, and, hearing it again, got off his horse to see what it was. To his surprise, in a hollow in the rock, he saw an old eagle quite blind and unfledged by age. Perched by the eagle, he saw a carrion crow feeding him. If the Almighty thus provides for the blind eagle, he will not forsake me; and the carrion-crow may look down with contempt on your countrymen.

'I say this, because I have seen two doctors—they were English—and they tell me that, though my eyes are good, my nerves are destroyed, and that causes my blindness. Writing these few lines will be some days' illness to me; but I make an effort, in order to assure you of the grief I have felt at being, I fear, the cause of your affairs being worse than if you had not known me. All I can say is, if God helps me, I shall not forget you. You can do nothing for me now; trust in God, and think of the eagle. Remember! all is written: we can change nothing of our fate by lamenting and grumbling. Therefore, it is better to be like a true Turk, and do our duty to the last, and then beg of the believers in one God a bit of daily bread, and, if it comes not, die of want, which perhaps is as good a death as any other, and less painful. But never act contrary to the dictates of conscience, of honour, of nature, or of humanity.'

A person with such a turn of mind is half an Asiatic already; the costume which she afterwards adopted was not more so than her creed. Of the latter Dr M., however, finds it difficult to give a distinct account—the former he thus describes:—

'Her turban, a coarse, woollen, cream-coloured Barbary shawl, was wound loosely round, over the red fez or *tarbôosh*, which covered her shaved head; a silk handkerchief, commonly worn by the Bedouin Arabs, known by the Arabic name of *keffeyah*, striped pale yellow and red, came between the fez and the turban, being tied under the chin, or let fall at its ends on each side of her face. A long sort of white merino cloak (*meshlah*, or abah in Arabic) covered her person from the neck to the ankles, looped in white silk brandenburghs over the chest; and, by its ample and majestic drapery and loose folds, gave to her figure the appearance of that fulness which it once really possessed. When her cloak happened accidentally to be thrown open in front, it disclosed beneath a crimson robe (*jooby*) reaching also to her feet, and, if in winter, a pelisse under it, and under that a cream-coloured or flowered gown (*koombaz*), folding over in front, and girded with a shawl or scarf round the waist. Beneath the whole she wore scarlet pantaloons of cloth, with yellow low boots, called *mest*, having pump soles, or, in other words, a yellow leather stocking, which slipped into yellow slippers or papouches. This completed her costume; and although it was, in fact, that of a Turkish gentleman, the most fastidious prude could not have found anything in it unbecoming a woman, except its association, as a matter of habit, with the male sex.'

In the land of her adoption, Lady Hester became much mixed up with the affairs of pashas and princes: among these, as already mentioned, her nearest neighbour was Emir Beshýr, prince of the Druzes, and with him she had most to do. At a remote period, the ancestors of this treacherous man had migrated from the neighbourhood of Mecca. Their origin was noble, and the family reached to great consideration in Mount Lebanon, and stamped him who sprung from it as an emir, or prince. Though a Mahommedan born, he occasionally professed Christianity; but never was a man guilty of more barbarities. He became Lady Hester's determined enemy; but she was not a woman to be frightened; and openly cultivated, notwithstanding, the friendship of his rival, the Sheikh Beshýr; nay, she even sent to him insolent messages, calling him 'dog and monster.' On one occasion 'one of the Emir Beshýr's people came on some message to her, but, before he entered her room, laid by his pistols and his sabre, which, in Turkey, these myrmidons always wear on their persons. Lady Hester's maid whispered to her what the man was doing, when her ladyship, calling him in, bade him gird on his arms again. "Don't think I'm afraid of you or your master," she said; "you may tell him I don't care a fig for his poisons—I know not what fear is. It is for him, and those who serve him, to tremble. And tell the Emir Khalyl (the Emir Beshýr's son), that if he enters my doors, I'll stab him—my people shall not shoot him, but *I* will stab him—I, with my own hand."

'Lady Hester, after relating this to me, thus proceeded:—"The beast, as I spoke to him, was so terrified, doctor, that he trembled like an aspen leaf, and I could have knocked him down with a feather. The man told the Emir Beshýr my answer; for there was a tailor at work in the next room, who saw and heard him, and spoke of it afterwards. The emir puffed such a puff of smoke out of his pipe when my message was delivered, and then got up and walked out."'

Emir Beshýr, it appears, is now more than eighty-four years old, and has been compelled to fly more than three or four times from his principality to Egypt, having, on many occasions, with difficulty escaped the vengeance of three successive pashas of Acre, who, for his treasonable practices, sought his head. In his last flight, it is suspected that he laid the plan with Mahomet Ali for the invasion of Syria, which Ibrahim Pasha subsequently undertook. The Druzes, of whom he is the emir, are a warlike people, hardy, accustomed to fatigue and to the use of arms, living in villages difficult of access and easily capable of defence, the houses being of stone. Besides the Druzes, there is a race of Christians, known as the Maronite population, whose villages cover that part of the chain of Mount Lebanon which runs behind Tripoli as far as Caläit el Medýk, and the plain of Accár, where a narrow defile occurs, through which there is a communication between the plains of Accár and the Bkáa, which is the plain that divides Lebanon and Ante-Lebanon. Beyond this defile the mountain rises into a lofty chain, running towards Latakia, and there dwell the Ansaréas, the Ishmaelites, and some other races. In connexion with these localities we have the following important narrative, explanatory of events which are even now acting there, and with which the columns of the daily papers frequently teem.

'By arrangements, supposed to have been previously made between the emir and Ibrahim Pasha, and in order that it might look as if the emir was taken totally by surprise, one fine night in the summer several regiments of Ibrahim Pasha's troops were marched from Acre, Sayda, and Tripoli on one side; and from Damascus and Báalbec on the other, so as to arrive at *Btedýn* (the emir's palace), at Dair-el-kamar (the chief town), and at all the other important points of Mount Lebanon precisely on the same day, and, as nearly as possible, precisely at the same hour. Either that the time had been well chosen, inasmuch as the Druzes were then employed in harvesting and other agricultural labours, or else the plan had been so laid as to insure success and to preclude resistance; the result was, that the mountain was taken possession of without firing a gun. The Emir Beshýr, acknowledged to be the most consummate and perfidious hypocrite of modern times, played his part so well, and feigned such great trepidation and alarm when two regiments marched into the courtyard of his palace, that he persuaded his household, his minister, and the Druze people in succession, that he was the victim of the stratagem as much as they were themselves.'

The Druzes thus betrayed were of course treated with indignity: the whole of Syria also was thereby defenceless. Nothing was more likely than such conduct to excite Lady Hester's spleen and activity. Meantime, the spirit of the Druzes was not broken; though they fled from Mount Lebanon to the Horàn, where they were joined by Bedouin Arabs, who hover round that quarter. The part that Lady Hester took was characteristic.

'When Ibrahim Pasha made so easy a conquest of the mountain, a word fell from his mouth which, if ever the Druzes succeed in expelling him, may be said to have been the cause of his reverses. He is reported to have exclaimed from his divan, when the news of the entire occupation of Mount Lebanon, without firing a single shot, was brought to him, "What! those dogs of Druzes had not a single bullet for us!" This little sentence was repeated to Lady Hester, and not long afterwards a Druze of some note came to pay her a visit. As he entered the room, she abruptly addressed him in the same words. "Dog of a Druze! what! hadn't you one single bullet for Ibrahim Pasha?"—and then, with a sort of sarcastic pity, dilated on Ibrahim Pasha's exultation over them. She made it a byword among her servants; and not a Druze came near the house but he was saluted with, "Dog of a Druze! what! had not you a single bullet for the pasha?" To people connected with Ibrahim Pasha's government she told the same story, seemingly as if in praise of the pasha's bravery, who loved war so much that he could not bear an easy and bloodless conquest, even though to his own advantage. In every quarter, through every channel, the pasha's saying was echoed in the Druzes' ears; and his followers, thinking it an anecdote that told well for their master, never considered that it rankled in the bosoms of the Druzes, who, stung to the core by these cutting words, swore never to sleep until the hour of vengeance came.'

The hour of vengeance did come; nor has it, as we may see from the daily papers, yet passed. Lady Hester foresaw and promoted the Druze insurrection. On the first outburst, she exclaimed, 'I don't fear; I would throw all my doors open if the Druzes were on the outside, and should not be afraid that anybody would touch me!' She was, no doubt, moved also by fanatical feelings: this is indicated by a dream in which she believed, and in which the dreamer had seen a hand waving over her head, and several crowned heads humbled before her—interpreted, of course, to mean the greatness that, at this juncture, she thought awaited her. It was thus she expected that she should be relieved of all her debts and disappointments. Most of these events, too, she connected with the Second Advent, in which doctrine she was a believer, and looked upon herself as the Woman desiderated by the St Simonians and the Freemasons. Many of them, she said, had been sent as spies on her actions. It was therefore with 'feverish greediness' that 'she received all reports of insurrections, revolts, and political changes. Even her servants knew her weakness on these points,' and constantly took advantage of it. She looked then for the coming of the Mahedi,* and in expectation of it kept two favourite mares, which she never suffered any person to mount. 'They were called Läila and Lulu. Läila was exceedingly hollow-backed, being born saddled, as Lady Hester used to say, and with a double backbone: she was a chestnut, and Lulu a gray. They were both thoroughbred: they had each a groom, and were taken the greatest care of. The green plat of ground on the east side of the house-wall was set apart entirely for exercising them twice a-day; and round this the grooms, with *longes*, were made to run them until they were well warmed. This spot was sacred; and, whilst they were at exercise, nobody, neither servant nor villager, was allowed to cross it, or to stand still to look at them, under the penalty of being dismissed her service. Such an order, from its nature, would necessarily be violated very often, but unknown to Lady Hester; for, as she never went out of her house, and could not overlook that side of it, a tacit understanding among the people made them true to their own secrets: but, from time to time, accident, or the unguarded disclosures of some of the maids, made her aware that her orders had been slighted, and then her anger exceeded all bounds. Few were the travellers who were admitted to see these mares in their stable; and never was the permission granted, until it had been ascertained that their star would not be baneful to them.

'Horses in Syria, for about seven months in the year, are tethered out of doors, where they are fed and littered down. It was under a shed, covered with thatch, shut in at the two sides by a treillage, with three parterres of flowers and shrubs behind them, that these two beautiful animals stood. Every morning, in the summer, the grooms washed their tails, legs, and manes in soap and water, and watered the ground beneath their feet, to keep them cool; but during the winter months, they were stalled in their stables, and warm felts covered their delicate limbs. Apis, in his most glorious days, and surrounded by his priesthood, could not have been better attended to.

'Lady Hester Stanhope one day assured me that, when her pecuniary difficulties pressed hardest upon her, had it not been for the sake of those two creatures, she should have given up her house and everything to her creditors, sold her pension to pay them, and have quitted the country: but she resolved to wait for the consummation of events on their account. "Ah, doctor," added she, "I recollect, when I was at Rome, seeing, in a beautiful bas-relief, that very mare, with her hollow back made like a saddle. Two Englishmen were standing by, and were criticising the very same thing that caught my attention. 'How very beautiful,' said one, 'is that basso-relievo! but the ancients, somehow, never could set about a good thing without spoiling it. There is that hollow-backed horse—did you ever see such a thing?' I heard it all, but I made my own observations; and now, you see, I have got a mare of the very same breed."'

What we have just related shows plainly enough that Lady Hester Stanhope had compounded her religion of the Bible and the Koran. It seems, indeed, that she professed no specific creed, and defined religion to be simply 'the adoration of the Almighty.' She had also a faith in spirits, astral influence, magic, and demonology. Early in life, too, the notorious Brothers had prophesied her seclusion in the desert; and truly some strong stimulus was needed to fortify her mind against the annoyances to which she was hourly liable. All her attempts to introduce European order into her Syrian establishment failed, and her temper, always ungovernable, was constantly irritated in consequence. Still, she was better off than she would have been with European servants, for these could never have reconciled themselves to the seclusion, the unceasing activity, and long vigils required. As Turkish servants (to use a nautical phrase) *turn in* almost universally in their clothes, only drawing a counterpane over themselves when they lie down, they are enabled thus to steal a short sleep at any hour they can get it, 'and are ready to rise at a moment's call. This is a great advantage, especially to sick people: indeed, in Lady Hester's case, it almost compensated for all their faults. In the twinkling of an eye, upon an emergency, the whole household, only a moment before buried in profound sleep, would start up on their feet; and, their duty once over, would suddenly drop again into a deep slumber.' To compensate, on the wrong side, for this virtue—if it deserve so grand a name—they had no other which could be relied on, being neither honest nor chaste, and, least of all, diligent, save when under *surveillance*, and scarcely then.

If Lady Hester left England with the expectation of living more cheaply, she wofully deceived herself. Her generosity was so frequently in request, first, by the injured Jews of the pashalik, next by Abdallah Pasha himself, when outlawed by the Porte, that she soon found herself left without a farthing, and deeply burdened with debt, being compelled to borrow money at twenty-five per cent. Great were the anxiety and persecution she consequently suffered. But, nevertheless, her beneficence was not impaired in the least by her want of means. She was, says her biographer, 'indeed generous and charitable, giving with a large hand, as eastern kings are represented to have given. She would send whole suits of clothes, furnish rooms, or ... camels and mules to convey two or three quarters of wheat at a time to a necessitous family, and pay carpenters and masons to build a poor man's house; she had a munificence about her that would have required the revenue of a kingdom to gratify. Hence ... sprung that insatiable disposition to hoard—not money, but what money could buy: she seemed to wish to have stores of whatever articles were necessary for the apparel, food, and convenience of man. Beds, counterpanes, cushions, carpets, and such-like furniture, lay rotting in her storerooms. Utensils grew rusty, wine spoiled; reams of paper were eaten by the mice, or mildewed by the damp; carpenters' work lay unserviceable, from an over-supply; mats rotted; candles, almonds, raisins, dried figs, cocoa, honey, cheese—no matter what—all was laid by in destructive profusion; and every year half was consumed by rats, ants, and other vermin, or otherwise spoiled. One storeroom, which was filled with clothes, linen, bedding, cushions, books, carpets, and counterpanes, together with locked-up trunks, full of what was most valuable, had not been entered for three years; and oh, what ruin and waste did I not discover!

'When I told her of all this, and suggested that it would be better to give them to her poor pensioners, she said—"Such things do not ever cause me a moment's thought: I would rather they should have been used to some good purpose; but if I have got such rascals about me, why, let the things all rot, sooner than that they should profit by them. Money can replace all that; and if God sends me money, I will do so. If he does not, he knows best what should be; and it would not give me a moment's sorrow to lie down in a cottage with only rags enough to keep me warm. I would not even then change places with Lord Grosvenor, the Duke of Devonshire, the Duke of Buckingham, or any of them: they can't do what I can; so of what use are all their riches? I have seen some of them make such a fuss about the loss of a ten-guinea ring, or some small bauble; not that they cared for it, but they could not bear to lose it. But if I want to know what is passing at Constantinople, or London, or anywhere, I have ...

* The title of Mahedi was given to Abulcassem Mohammed, the last of the imams of the race of Ali, born in the year 255 of the hegira. At nine years of age, he was shut up in a cavern by his mother, who is supposed, by the superstitious followers of Mahomet, still to keep watch over him, until he shall reappear at the end of the world, when he will unite himself with Jesus Christ; and the two religions, Mussulman and Christian, being merged into one, he will, in conjunction with our Saviour, finally overcome the machinations of the antichrist.—HERBELOT.

thing to do but to turn my thoughts that way, and in a quarter of an hour I have it all before me, just as it is; so true, doctor, that if it is not actually passing, it will be in a month, in three months—so true: isn't it extraordinary?"

'Upon some occasions her munificence wore the appearance of ostentation. She would bestow on strangers, like dervises, sheikhs, and fakirs, large sums of money, and yet drive hard bargains with those about her neighbourhood: and would sometimes make presents, not so much to comfort those who received them, as to display her own superiority and greatness over others.'

In the midst of this penury and extravagance came a sudden and unexpected blow from England. An application had been made to the English government by one Mäalem Homsy, a creditor of Lady Hester Stanhope, in consequence of which an order was sent from Lord Palmerston to stop her pension unless the debt was paid. The letter conveying this intelligence reached Lady Hester at a time when she was expecting one from Sir Francis Burdett, with news of good fortune in an accession of property. What with the disappointment on the one hand, and the insult, as she esteemed the official announcement to be, on the other, her indignation knew no bounds. It is painful to go into the particulars; but her well-known letter to the queen was the result of the disease of mind, driven almost to insanity, which she experienced on the occasion. To the Duke of Wellington and other official persons she also wrote on the same subject; but every new step she took was only an additional imprudence, and, in fine, she was, by her own conduct, thrown into a condition of irretrievable bankruptcy. But in the proportion that her affairs became desperate, her spirit rose, her pride augmented, and, as her frenzy increased, she triumphed in her ruin.

She had long suffered under a pulmonary complaint, her health was further affected by her afflictions, and her irritability became intolerable both to herself and others. The picture drawn by Dr M. of Lady Hester's mental sufferings is ghastly; and it is with reference to them that he defends her from the censures of travellers, for declining their visits. It appears that she sometimes declined visits, merely because she had not the means of entertaining guests.

We must now draw our imperfect notices to a conclusion. Lady Hester at length resolved to reduce her establishment, and to dismiss Dr M. and his family. She hastened his departure, employing him a few days before it in paying off the servants. She had determined to keep none but two boys, a man to fetch water, the gardener, and some girls. These arrangements completed, she turned her attention to the accomplishment of her strange project—that of building up every avenue to her premises, and waiting there with patience, immured within the walls, until it should please God to send help. The gateway was completely masked by a screen, which left a side opening just large enough for a cow or an ass laden with water to enter. She was suffering at the time under 'the most formidable attack of pulmonary catarrh which Dr M. had ever seen a human being withstand.' But she thought, nevertheless, her constitution invulnerable; 'she thought she should yet live to see her enemies confounded, the sultan triumphant, her debts paid, and an ample income at her disposal. She dwelt with the same apparent confidence as ever on the approaching advent of the Mahedi, and still looked on her mare, Läila, as destined to bear him, with herself on Lulu by his side. "I shall not die in my bed," she would say, "and I had rather not; my brothers did not; and I have always had a feeling that my end would be in blood: that does not frighten me in the least."'

In all this she was, however, mistaken. In June 1839 she died; 'slowly wasting away, everybody being in ignorance of her approaching end, except Logmagi and the servants immediately about her. She had no Frank or European near her, and Lunardi, who was coming out to her from Leghorn, reached Beyrout unfortunately too late. Her emaciated corpse was interred in the same grave where the body of Captain Loustaunau had been placed, some years before, in her own garden.'

Such was the termination of a life which Dr M. justly terms 'extraordinary'—full of vicissitudes—'beginning in pomp and power, and closing in pecuniary difficulties and neglect.' An aristocrat by birth, Lady Hester Stanhope was eminently one in her feelings, her principles, and her conduct. Every thing she did was, as a Dr Canova said of her, '*en grand*—there was nothing little about her.' Whatever we may think of her extravagances, whether in action or opinion, we must confess that she was a great woman. There was certainly a want of balance in her mind, owing to her intellectual not having been so well cultivated as her moral powers; but there was a wonderful energy of faith in the good and true. That she always meant to act and speak in accordance therewith, there is no doubt; that frequently she did neither, there is as little. Much of her conversation, there is reason to suspect, is misrepresentation; but she thought it quite accurate. In fact, it was rendered merely *mythical* by her blending with the stern fact the unsuspected impression of her own fancies and feelings. Lady Hester Stanhope trusted also too much to unassisted memory; and though hers evidently was strong, yet the most tenacious will, in the course of time, become indistinct and confused in its relative bearings, and places, periods, and persons, will shift about with extraordinary mutation. Dr M. attempts to draw a moral from the evident unhappiness of her latter life. 'Although her buoyant spirits usually bore her up against the weight by which she was oppressed, still there were moments of poignant grief, when all efforts at resistance were vain, and her very soul groaned within her. She was ambitious, and her ambition had been foiled; she loved irresponsible command, but the time had come when those over whom she had ruled defied her; she was dictatorial and exacting, but she had lost the talisman of that influence which alone makes people tolerate control when it interferes with the freedom of thought and action. She had neglected to secure wealth while she had it in her power; but the feelings which prompted her princely munificence were as warm as ever, now that the means were gone which enabled her to gratify them. Her mind was in a perpetual struggle between delusive schemes and incompetent resources. She incurred debts, and she was doomed to feel the degradation consequent on them. She entertained visionary projects of aggrandisement, and was met by the derision of the world. She spurned the conventional rules of that society in which she had been bred, and perhaps violated propriety in the realisation of a singularity in which she gloried. *There* was the rock on which she was finally wrecked; for, as Madame de Staël somewhere says, a man may brave the censures of society, but a woman must accommodate herself to them. She was thought to defy her own nation, and they hurled the defiance back upon her. She held in contempt the gentler qualities of her own sex, who, in return, were not slow to resent the masculine characteristics on which she presumed to maintain her assumed position. She carried with her from England the disposition to conciliate, by kindness and forbearance, the fidelity and obedience of her domestics; but she was eventually led into undue harshness towards them, which became more and more exaggerated in her by the idleness, the ignorance, and irritating vices of her eastern household.'

There is much truth in these remarks; but we must recollect that the mark by which we generally distinguish original genius, is its freedom from conventional restraints. In a worldly point of view, the exercise of this liberty is too often imprudent; but the inconvenience thence resulting is the penalty which great minds pay for fame. In asserting superior privileges, we take on ourselves increased responsibilities. If Lady Hester

Stanhope had been more conventional in her habits and habits, she would never have become the subject of Dr M.'s memoirs—she would have died without celebrity, as she might have lived without reproach.

AFFABILITY.

It was a happy saying of the half-civilised New Zealander, when apologising for the rather vehement eloquence of his untutored brother, 'that his mouth was great because his heart was warm.' In other words, the savage was of a frank, generous, and open nature. Had he been a sulky, morose barbarian, he would have drawn his cloak up to his chin, and met the white man with frowns instead of words, or slunk away to the forest; a cunning, selfish barbarian, only intent on presents of muskets and tobacco, and he would have cringed and touched noses till he had melted the expected donor into liberality; or a treacherous savage, and he would have brought pigs and potatoes, spread the mat, and lighted the fire for the stranger against whom, during sleep, he had determined to raise the tomahawk. But he had a warm heart, and therefore he shook hands, talked, whooped, and danced—shook hands, talked, and whooped again. 'His mouth was great because his heart was warm.' The same attribute obtains among every class of people — enlightened as well as barbarian; only amongst the former it is known by the more familiar and less figurative term—Affability.

Though literally signifying the disposition to talk to, or converse with, affability is totally distinct from garrulity. A garrulous person is ever chattering either from vanity of some fancied acquirement, or for the mere gratification of a gossiping propensity. There is no generosity or nobleness of sentiment in his talk; no reflection or feeling which you can associate with any amiable quality either of head or of heart. In fact, he speaks more the less he thinks, and, like a shallow brook, makes all the greater noise that there is no breadth or volume in the source whence his chattering proceeds. He is an annoyance and hindrance to every one, inundating them with talk, without respect to time, situation, or occasion. He would much rather that he was listened to only by great people; but, failing these, he will stick like a limpet to any one forbearing, or weak enough to grant him an audience. The 'indeed,' 'very good,' and 'ah, really,' which the listener meant as conclusive interjections, the chatterer mistakes for incentives, and so proceeds with increased volubility. Nay, the direct 'so I have heard,' or 'I don't care for that,' has no power to obstruct the current of his words: he rather glories in a little interference, that he may have the pleasure of placing the matter in what he conceives to be an entirely new light. Be the listeners gay or sad; exulting over success or sorrowing under some severe privation, it is all one to the chatterer; he has no more appreciation of their feelings than if he had been a speaking automaton. Not so with the affable man: he addresses this or that one, because he acts from the impulses of a frank, generous, and brotherly nature. There is an unmistakeable import in his words, however few; nay, his very air and manner would amply interpret his feelings, though his words were altogether wanting. This gift of affability has no special hankerings after the titled or great. Its morning salute or weather remark comes in tones as frank and kindly to the pauper as to the peer, perhaps more so, as considerations arise in connexion with the former to which the feelings of the affable are peculiarly alive. Open and generous as is this disposition of affability, it knows that the tones of hilarity are as bitterness to the mourner, and that condolence is not for the individual boisterous with joy. The affable man has a head to perceive as well as a heart to feel, and thus he knows when, where, and to whom to address his conversation. No one ever wished that he should say one word less, or felt for a moment as if he could have bowed him from his presence.

As affability has nothing in common with garrulity, so it is far removed from officiousness. The officious man elbows himself forward where his presence is often the least desired; and tenders his questionable services in cases where such offers are a positive rudeness and annoyance. In company, conversation is absolutely drugged with his opinions; and he questions with such pertinacity, that one would imagine he had received the commission of confessor-general to society. He is ever obtruding on other people's business, on the plea of tendering assistance; and his advice follows so rapidly, that it would seem all other men were dolts, and he the only one capable of directing them. To be sure officiousness often manifests itself where it cannot possibly have any personal object to serve, and where it is evidently the result of vanity, or of a want of power to discriminate between what is strictly private, and what is the legitimate object of a friendly interest. The affable man is never at fault in this respect. He has a delicate perception of where he shall or shall not present himself; and his generous courtesy often renders him a welcome visitor, under circumstances which would be absolutely exclusive of other individuals. He is frank, because it is his nature to be so, but his generosity teaches him what is due to others; hence he is never found obtruding. Officiousness is an offence, a characteristic of mind, which impinges on others; affability a virtue, which appears chiefly as flowing from its possessor. In the one case we look upon society as the sufferers, in the other we admire the amiable gifts of the individual. The affable man converses freely on subjects which he may approach, maintaining all the while a proper deference for the opinions of others. His sentiments are expressed without any semblance of opinionativeness; and though approaching and approachable in every respect, there is none of that interference and counsel-tendering which renders the officious so insufferable.

Again, affability, though implying a frank, courteous, and kindly demeanour, has nothing to do with impertinent familiarity. Proceeding upon the idea, that it is only from members of the same family, and from the most intimate acquaintances, that we are to permit familiarity, there can be nothing so objectionable in ordinary behaviour as this characteristic. Your familiar man is quite as intimate with you on the occasion of your second meeting, as though he had been your brother or bosom companion. He thrusts his arm into yours with an air of easy assurance, takes you by the button, or slaps your shoulder, calls you by your Christian name, which, if John, he is sure in a few seconds to familiarise into Jack; congratulates, condoles, or questions you on matters so strictly personal, that you are really at a loss whether to pity him for his stupidity, or kick him for his impudence. Affability never offends on this score. It is the emanation of a manly sensibility, discharging itself in society freely and generously, yet without overstepping the bounds of the strictest politeness. The affable man can converse, or can be conversed with, on the occasion of his first meeting, with the most perfect freedom, can render the stage-coach or steamboat agreeable by his obliging and intelligent demeanour; and this too without appearing at the end of the journey in any other light than that of a pleasant stranger. You may meet him five times or fifty times, he will be the same respectful acquaintance—the same frank and buoyant conversationist, who feels that he owes the duty of cheerful words to his fellow-men—a debt which he can perfectly well discharge, without transgressing the limits of a merely general relation. Nay, it is this very generality of feeling, this truly cosmopolite spirit of social frankness, that carries him beyond officiousness and familiarity. In the light of kindness, every man stands in the same relation to him; and it is a littleness of which he has no conception, to drop from the broad principle of brotherly recognition to that of personal intermeddling.

It is sometimes objected by a certain narrow-minded set, that the practice of affability tends to lessen the respect of their subordinates; in other words, interferes with what they imagine to be their personal dignity. 'Dignity' must have a very questionable foundation indeed if its stability even runs the risk of being affected by a frank and courteous demeanour. There may be such a thing as servility engendered by fear and hypocrisy, but there can be nothing like true respect when it is not acquired by kindness and consideration. It is familiarity on the part of a superior, not affability, that induces subordinates to indulge in improper liberties. The nobleman may have a kind and pleasant word for the meanest man on his estate without losing one tittle of real dignity: and so may the master have for his employé, without compromising either his authority or right to direct. It often happens, because there is too little attention bestowed upon the culture of this characteristic, that the employed conceives a dislike for the employer, and acts as if his interests were at variance. A few kindly words, a little considerate attention, on the part of masters, always supposing it to be in union with substantial justice, would prevent, we are confident, much of that unpleasant feeling of class which so frequently prevails, and would be the most effectual extinguisher to those strikes and feuds which form one of the most unamiable features of the present age.

Such is affability, taken in contradistinction to garrulity, officiousness, or familiarity. As a quality by itself, it is one of the most amiable that can adorn the human character. Proceeding from a generous feeling of brotherly love—from a broad principle of philanthropy, which knows no personal or sectarian antipathies—it breathes kindness and encouragement to all. It carries an atmosphere of cheerfulness around it, makes the desponding think that the world is not quite so bad after all, lightens the burden of the oppressed, smooths the wrinkles of the fretful and sulky, and reconciles to each other the offending and offended. The public street would be but a vista of moving automatons, were it not for the friendly recognition, the hearty shake of the hand, or the affectionate inquiries of your affable men. Without them the business of life would be a sullen huckstering, interrupted only by the impertinences of the officious and familiar. Be it in public or in private, affability is ever a welcome attendant, soothing down asperities, and thawing that reserve which is apt to degenerate into heartless coldness or positive ill-breeding. As it is pleasant and agreeable and useful to others, so it is indicative of a manly and generous sensibility. It is incompatible with a morose, selfish, or deceitful nature; and we may rest assured, with the New Zealander, that he who owns it, 'has his mouth great because his heart is warm.'

THE HARTSDALE VINDICATOR, OR MODERN INNOVATIONS.

BY CAMILLA TOULMIN.

'Well, my dear sir, have you heard the news?' said Major Stakely, a retired officer in an English country town, to a friend who had only just returned home after an absence of some weeks.

'Not a word have I heard that deserves to be called news,' replied he; 'what is going on, pray?'

'Why, a railway is to pass through the town; that is all.'

'A railway! nonsense,' cried the other; 'we are very well as we are. Everything goes on very nicely at present. The stage-coach that comes to the town daily, is sufficient for all the traffic; and to break in upon this quiet rural scene with one of their horrid snorting locomotives, would be a downright sin.'

'Gentlemen, you will all come to my way of thinking at last,' interposed Mr Elliot, the medical practitioner of the place, as he joined the group. 'We must have a paper to protect our interests. What with the new poor-laws, and fifty other newfangled things, we shall go completely to the wall if we do not assert our opinions, and have our say against such innovations. Ah, if old Sir George had been living, he would have taken care to preserve such a fine hunting county as this from these abominable changes. For my own part, I should not wonder if, in twenty years, there is not a fox to be found. As for our member, the present Sir George, he is not a bit of a sportsman; in fact, I look upon him as a traitor, and think, when we do establish a paper, he ought to be shown up. Why, he has actually given permission for the railway to pass right through his park.'

'But he stipulated for a bridge over it, and really some persons think his property is in no way injured,' interrupted one who, though speaking in a gentle voice, ventured to have an opinion of her own on two or three subjects. 'And as for the foxes,' she continued, 'if the end and aim of hunting be their extirpation, as we must suppose, the result of all these changes which you anticipate will be a very happy one.'

'Ah, Miss Somers,' said Mr Elliot, 'you have not led a country life, or you would not speak in that way.'

'Nay, ever since I left school, for seven years Hartsdale has been my home,' she replied; 'yet I think now, as I thought long ago, that the chase is an occupation only fit for savages, and that the lover of it must of necessity be devoid of humanity and intellectual cultivation. To be sure I feel so great a disgust towards sportsmen, that I have as little compassion for them as they bestow on the brutes, and never can grieve when the loss of life or limb brings them their just deserts. However, as you say, had I lived all my life in the country, and been taken when a little girl to see the hounds throw off, and been taught by my brothers that it was a fine thing to maim poor birds, and to torture a timid hare, perhaps I might have thought differently. But I am thankful to Providence that, as it is, I know how to call some things by their right names.'

Louisa Somers warmed as she spoke, for she felt keenly on the subjects then under discussion. And it is a happy thing for the improvement of the world, that young minds are for ever springing up, untrammelled by old habits or deep-rooted prejudices, but with strong energies and fresh hearts, ready to open out new and better paths.

'I was saying,' proceeded Mr Elliot, who was an excellent man, though a little wrong-headed on some points—'I was saying that, since Sir George has declared himself on the side of these ridiculous and mischievous innovators, I have no hope for Hartsdale but in the firmness and consistency of its inhabitants; and I think the idea of a monthly newspaper an admirable one. Every considerable body requires its organ. We have been too long without one, and have consequently become the prey of interlopers and speculators of all sorts.'

The somewhat pompous major, who had carried into private life some of the prejudices of his military career, and was a hater of all new plans and projects, perfectly agreed with the doctor, and favoured him with many suggestions thought by both to be very admirable.

The conversation to which I have alluded took place on the occasion of a tea-party at the house of the Misses Gunning, two ancient ladies, who, though they bore the traces of having been dowered in their youth with beauty not inferior to that of their famous namesakes, had passed their lives in a calm seclusion the very opposite to the career of the celebrated dames. Miss Elizabeth, the younger, had been betrothed forty years ago to a handsome soldier cousin, who fell in the peninsular war. The shock to her mind, and the grief that followed his death, brought on a tedious illness, and during many years her sister Susan devoted herself to the sufferer with that self-devotion, patience, and affection, which belong to the heroism of private life. Tenderly attached to each other, the minds of both were sobered down from youth's giddiness by that which had been a mutual grief; and even when Time, the healer, had worked its cure, they looked on the world with different eyes, different wishes, different expectations, from those of their untroubled days. They determined to live for each other only, and, several years before this little story opens, they chose Laurel Cottage for their residence.

If I am too minute in sketching the incidents which had moulded such simple characters as theirs, the reader will bear with it, because it is only by remembering the quiet course of their latter years, and the tone of feeling—so averse to change—which prevailed in the little town, that he can understand the perplexities which came upon its inhabitants. A word must be said about Hartsdale itself. Tradition attributes the name to some romantic incident of a hart escaping thither from the hunters, one of whom lost his life in attempting to follow it down a ravine. The spot is shown by the learned to the curious to this day. Situated in a beautiful valley of one of the midland counties of England, and distant about twelve miles from a cathedral city, Hartsdale, though it boasts a market once a-week, and enumerates other privileges which help to constitute a town instead of a village, is a place to which change and improvements for some time travelled but slowly; and this, although in the 'old times' of fiery red, bright blue, and blinding yellow stage-coaches, no fewer than ten of these machines passed down the High Street in the course of the day. But alas! they passed, or seldom indeed stopped to cast upon the barrenness one particle of news. Yet stay! The 'Telegraph,' moving with a four-horse power at the rate of eight miles an hour, did in those golden days change horses at the White Hart Inn, and consequently and naturally the Telegraph was voted by the Hartsdalians to be the safest, quickest, finest, and everyway most desirable vehicle on the road. From the driver or passengers of the Telegraph a morsel of news sometimes fell, like a crumb to the hungry; but the mail even dropped the letter-bag without stopping! Nevertheless I have a firm conviction that the circumstance of the town lying in a road through which ten coaches per day, to different parts of the kingdom, must pass, had been a pride, a pleasure, and an attraction, not to be estimated by those who, from their proximity to populous places, have rather an aversion than otherwise to the sound of wheels.

But a new era was at hand; within the last two years the railways had intruded on Hartsdale: those moral arteries which, traversing the kingdom from end to end, carrying intelligence of all sorts to and from its mighty heart, and so removing prejudices, jealousies, and enmities, are destined to prove among those triumphs of science which bless and regenerate mankind. But the little community, not clear-sighted or long-sighted enough to perceive all these advantages, and full of local pride and present interests, saw nothing but the petty inconveniences and personal injuries attendant on the changes of the time. One by one the stage-coaches dropped away, just in proportion as the new lines in the neighbouring counties were thrown open. No longer could the schoolmistress dismiss her little flock without reference to clock or sun-dial, knowing full well that when the horn of the 'Defiance' fast coach was sounded, it must be one o'clock. No longer could the grocer's wife regulate her spouse's dinner-hour by the appearance of 'Lightning' on the brow of the hill. The proud Defiance lay humbled to the dust, wheelless and degraded, in a coachmaker's yard, preparatory to being chopped up for firewood; and Lightning was extinct, or departed no one knew whither. At last a pert new-stuccoed station was erected within three miles of the town, and the encroaching iron enemy thus brought as it were to their very door. Even the Telegraph—their own dear Telegraph—that had been true to them through all, showed symptoms of desertion. Yet what could IT do, poor thing? It died very hard. Day after day it drove through the town without a single passenger; then the four horses were reduced to two; and, finally, so convinced were the Hartsdalians that it had 'done all which it became a coach to do' in the maintenance of its existence and its dignity—so clearly did they perceive that it was vanquished only by the stern power of a resistless foe—that though tears were shed at the announcement that IT too had found its 'occupation gone,' pity was bestowed upon the proprietor and coachman, instead of the torrent of reproach which had been showered on the heads of the earlier deserters.

And now the blow had fallen—Hartsdale was without a coach! And it must be acknowledged that several inconveniences were the result. Not only did the Misses Gunning feel lonely and desolate, now that they could no longer start to their window half-a-dozen times a-day to behold a coach-load of dusty or mud-bespattered travellers, but whenever they themselves made an excursion of a few miles—it scarcely mattered in which direction—a calamity fell on them, to which custom brought no reconciling feelings. Their elderly man-servant Peter, in addition to his care of the garden, was groom to, and driver of, a stout horse, to which was ordinarily attached a low phaeton. The body of the carriage only held the two ladies conveniently—though there were many persons who thought there was abundant room for a third—but the seat beside the driver was one surely open for lawful competition. Now that there were no coaches to take them short stages, what could people possessing neither carriages nor horses do but—beg the use of them from their more fortunate neighbours? Sometimes—if the weather were doubtful there was the readier plea—there came a courteous message at breakfast-time to ask, 'if the Misses Gunning were going into C—— that day, would they be so very kind as to give Mr So-and-so a seat beside Peter? or if they were not going to use the phaeton any day that week, he would consider it a particular obligation if they would lend it to him. Mrs So-and-so had heard that their darling Eleanor, at school seven miles off, had fallen down and hurt her wrist, and she was so anxious to see her—cross roads—no conveyance—a thousand apologies,' &c. &c.

Now, the dear old ladies had the kindest hearts in the world—hearts so kind that their humanity extended to the brutes; and they plainly perceived that the position of their horse Tartar was ceasing to be the enviable one it had long been considered. A council was held, to which Peter was called; and he, judging, as he said, by the manner in which Tartar threw back his ears, either when he started with an unusual load or took up a stray pedestrian on the way, was of opinion that the horse could not stand it. Alas! alas! many a time the ladies deprived themselves of their accustomed ride to oblige an acquaintance, stipulating always, however, that Peter should drive, on which occasions he took care that Tartar should neither go too far nor too fast.

And now another disturbance was coming, like an avalanche, upon Hartsdale. The railway had brought so many strangers to the spot, that its 'capability' and 'resources' were perceived and acknowledged. It was thought a pity that the clear and rapid stream, which flowed like a girdle half round its sheltering hills, should sink into the navigable river, which nearer to the ocean it fed, without fulfilling some useful destiny—something more important, if less poetical, than laving the graceful willows which overhung its waters. In fact, rumour said that a great capitalist was in treaty for some land, and that a paper mill would be erected in the valley. The idea of a newspaper to support what seemed the tottering interests of Hartsdale was certainly a bold one, and its establishment was a proof what great things determined perseverance may accomplish. Mr Elliot was the apothecary of the place, but fortunately for him he possessed some private property, for really the Hartsdalians were so remarkably healthy that it is very probable his gentle wife and rosy children would have fared something worse than they did. Fortunate, too, was it in another sense; for his labours were so light, that they afforded him abundant leisure for the cultivation of a literary taste, which it was said had descended to him thus:—His grandfather had, in the brilliant days of his contemporary Hayley, contributed verses to the Gentleman's Magazine, which same effusions, though published anonymously, were registered in the family archives as his; albeit certain critics of the time had attributed them to the immortal bard before mentioned. His immediate progenitor had once had the honour of dining in company with Byron—had even spoken to and shaken hands with him. Whereon it was supposed he took the infection of poesy; for immediately on his return home, he, being very much in love with the lady who ultimately became Mr Elliot's honoured mamma, did indite to her sundry verses or stanzas, which were deemed in themselves so admirable, and every way worthy of preservation, that they were, on the occasion of the marriage, which took place soon afterwards, placed beside the celebrated printed extracts from the Gentleman's Magazine. In the present Mr Elliot the propensity had been more strongly and decidedly developed: he had been a poet from his youth; was quite accustomed to see himself in print; had thrice sent verses to the very editors who now treated his prose communications with so much neglect, which verses had been by them promoted to a place in the Poets' Corner of their respective journals; and had absolutely published a pamphlet on some political topic—I forget what—in which he took great interest.

It was now discovered that Mr Elliot must have been intended by nature for a newspaper editor, an opinion in which, it must be confessed, he was not slow to join. And yet what a mighty weight of business fell on his shoulders! What consultations, what meetings, what tea-parties were there, before even a name could be decided on! At last, and by almost universal consent, 'The Hartsdale Vindicator' was adopted as a title that would express the championship, which was undertaken most completely. But when it was known to all the active spirits of the place, and to at least two-thirds of the Hartsdalians in general, that Mr Elliot was self-appointed to the cares and difficulties of editing 'their paper,' it all at once occurred to him that an air of mystery was customary in these important literary offices. The majestic editorial WE ought to be a concealing visor, as well as an Achilles' shield, from behind which the champion should hurl the arrows of honest indignation. Mr Elliot knew himself to be but mortal: how could he be sure to resist the beseechings of friends, or the workings of party interests, if his privacy were to be invaded by open petitions? How could he anathematise a railway, when his dearest friend confided to him that he held many shares therein? How could he utterly extinguish the spreading light of a new book, on the title-page of which appeared his name, 'with the author's kindest regards?' It was not to be thought of. No; the strictest incognito must be preserved; and forthwith the editor of the Vindicator was spoken of as a mysterious shade: indeed hints were thrown out (the Hartsdalians would not have told a downright fib for the world) of two or three of these incorporeal personages being rolled into one. It was almost, if not altogether impossible, they said, that one person could manage such an affair. A variety of style was indispensable. Departments of politics, literature, science, and art, were spoken about as things requiring each an Atlas shoulder for its support; and any confirmation of another's opinion beyond the nod or the shake of a head, was looked upon as an act of high treason. Of course there was a little knot, including the Misses Gunning, Major Stukely, and Louisa Somers, who owned to each other that they knew all about it.

The directing mental influence being thus decided on, and contributions of various sorts having been received, and accepted or rejected with due forms and proper courtesy, some duller and more matter-of-fact details came under discussion. As the little knot included the chief 'proprietors' of the work, they were consulted on the size of the projected paper, and the manner of printing it. One timid spirit suggested that it should be printed at the cathedral city, which was the capital of the county; but his single voice was drowned in the exclamations of disapprobation which escaped from the others, at a suggestion so derogatory to the proper dignity of all. The circumstance of Hartsdale not possessing a printing-press within the circle of its entire domain, was one of no importance; or rather, such a fact brought to light was only a reason they should more quickly rid themselves of a reproach so suggestive of barbaric darkness. And I do not think the community will easily forget the day on which the carrier's cart brought in the dingy apparatus—a second-hand press, which had seen considerable service—whose destiny it was to usher forth the first number of the glorious Vindicator. Old and young, rich and poor, rushed forth to get a peep at it; and although the bells were not set ringing, I know many persons thought the omission very culpable.

The first number at length appeared, in all the importance of eight pages, three columns each. The title was printed on a flourishing scroll, and beneath it was seen a Shakspeare motto. The leading article treated temperately but firmly on the injuries the Hartsdalians had endured, were suffering, and were likely to receive, from divers daring intruders on their rights and privileges. The local intelligence, on which considerable pains had been bestowed, was of a fair average quality, and that was all that could be expected. Louisa Somers—who would not write one line in opposition to what she felt were coming improvements, but who dared not yet become their defender, knowing well that to attack prejudices violently is the way to strengthen them—had contributed an amusing column of gossip about a recent visit to the metropolis, and which everybody, who was not in the secret, attributed to a London correspondent; and somebody else had written a punning poem on the Ruin of the County, taking for his text certain fragments of brick and stone, said to be the remains of an ancient castle, but turning the word with punsterial dexterity to the miseries which threatened their hearths and homes. Altogether, the Hartsdale Vindicator was pronounced a neat and interesting paper. A copy was sent to Sir George, the member, who instantly subscribed for a twelvemonth's supply; and the early numbers went off capitally, for most of the Hartsdalians took several to send to distant friends. If the truth must be owned, however, the sale was not such as to promise an increase of revenue to the proprietors; and though friends flattered, strangers often applauded, and foes at any rate were silent, there were drawbacks on the dignity of proprietorship and the joys of editorial authority. The interval of a month between the numbers was a long one, and mischief of a grave kind was often done before the Vindicator had an opportunity of raising its voice in defence of good old customs. Excavations were made, and lines laid down, with alarming rapidity; a tall red chimney was already showing itself, seeming, at a little distance, to grow up foot by foot from the rich foliage which skirted the river; till it was soon evident that, before the end of the next summer, the paper-mills would be in full operation.

All looked on with terror and dismay, except Louisa Somers, the curate's sister, who ventured sometimes to own she thought it possible much good might arise from the seeming evil. But then Louisa was not a Hartsdalian born or bred, and so her eccentric notions were looked upon with some leniency. And yet she must have loved Hartsdale very much I think; and certainly the poor of the place loved her most dearly, notwithstanding her heterodox opinions. Possessed of a small fortune, just enough for lady-like independence, and no more, she preferred the useful life she fashioned for herself, as mistress of her brother's quiet home, to all the vanities and vexations she might have found amid the gaieties of the metropolis, where the remainder of the family resided. But she was one of those young women, to whose lists I would fondly hope each year adds many, who believe that, whether high or low their station, they have duties to perform in the world apart from mere selfish gratifications, and who would blush to declare what I have twice heard gravely said, 'I have only to get up in the morning and amuse myself all day!' Louisa found something sweeter than amusement in the performance of the active duties she had marked out for herself, or perhaps, more properly speaking, had fallen into. She had made the great discovery, that it is truer benevolence to assist the poor to help themselves, than to bestow on them gold and silver; and though some people thought it a great inconsistency, the fact remains, that she would often give out dresses of her own to be made by the chief dressmaker of Hartsdale, at the very time that she was devoting morning after morning to patiently instructing the children of the poor in the mysteries of the needle and the thimble, in which she was a great adept. Not that she neglected to perform the Christian duties of visiting the sick and feeding the hungry, but her chief aim in all her exertions was to instruct the young, and urge them to habits of self-dependence. And, alas! to own the truth, the poor of Hartsdale were very numerous and very wretched; they were of that low class with whom beggary is held to be no shame.

'And, Martha,' said Miss Somers one morning to her servant, as, with only a garden bonnet to shade her from the sun, and wearing a simple morning dress, which nevertheless was anything but unbecoming, she stood in the garden opposite the open laundry window—'Martha, I have promised the widow Forster's girls that they shall have the benefit of seeing you iron to-day. You know you are the best clear-starcher in the town, and I daresay they will be here directly. I had to bribe them, it is true, by offering to pay them for their assistance; but take care you let them touch only such things as they cannot spoil. Poor things, they are sadly——'

But at this moment Louisa stopped, for, happening to turn round, she perceived a gentleman, a stranger, just at her elbow.

'Your pardon, madam, for this intrusion,' he exclaimed, removing his hat with an air of perfect good-breeding; 'but as neither my groom nor I could discover the bell, I have left my horse with him, and ventured to enter at a side gate which I found open. I have the honour of bearing a letter of introduction to Mr Somers,' he added, 'and feel almost sure that I have the pleasure of addressing his sister.'

Miss Somers led the way to the drawing-room, which in the curate's cottage was not very distant from the laundry, but where books, drawings, and musical instruments, proclaimed that the young mistress found time to cultivate the refinements of life, as well as discharge its useful active offices. The stranger was Mr Percival, who had recently purchased the land by the water's edge, and was erecting paper-mills thereon. Louisa was not at all alarmed at her visiter, not even surprised to find him a handsome and very agreeable person; though it is pretty certain the Hartsdalians in general entertained much such a notion of him as children deeply read in fairy tales may be supposed to do of an ogre.

'From the few words I accidentally overheard,' said Mr Percival, after chatting for a while on several more general topics, 'I feel sure that in Miss Somers I shall find no opponent to my views and wishes. You have discovered that the mere donation of money and food to the poor is but one way to increase pauperism, by destroying all feelings of self-respect and self-reliance. I foresee that you, madam,' he added with a smile, 'will not think it harder for a strong girl to fold or smooth paper for ten or twelve hours a-day, than for her to walk half a dozen miles to some great house and back again in search of the refuse of the larder; and it may even occur to you that the meal honestly earned will in a very little time seem much the sweeter of the two.'

'I do think so,' replied Louisa; 'but I believe we must act by the poor of Hartsdale in the same manner as it is prudent to do with the higher classes of its inhabitants—we must let them perceive the advantages of these coming changes themselves; rather than reiterate them from day to day. A prejudice is like a porcupine, which only bristles up the more it is attacked.'

Mr Percival smiled at the simile, but heartily agreed with Louisa.

In short, after a somewhat lengthened morning visit, they parted, mutually pleased with each other; he rejoicing that he had found one Hartsdalian—and that the one of all others the most popular among the poor—with liberal and enlightened views, and she perceiving that, though a Revolution was at hand, it must, from its nature, prove an entire Reformation.

The ensuing summer passed rapidly away, during which time the paper-works were completed, and operations commenced therein; although the poor of the place, so newly startled from the sort of lethargy which had fallen on them, had not yet decided whether work was good for them or not. During this summer the monthly numbers of the Vindicator had duly appeared; yet it was remarkable that its violent party spirit was somewhat tamed—at any rate the editor had doubts if, after all, the mill might not prove a most opportune relief to the working-classes. Advertisements connected with the railway crept in, affording a curious illustration of expanding usefulness. But among all the doings of that summer, perhaps not the least important to the Hartsdale community was the fact, that Mr Percival had become a frequent and most intimate visitor at the curate's cottage; and although it is quite certain he had the highest esteem and respect for Louisa's brother, it is equally true what the Hartsdalians had sometimes suspected, that he entertained yet warmer feelings for Louisa herself. To own the truth, the time appointed for their marriage was drawing near—a circumstance which will account most satisfactorily for the unrestrained confidence now existing between them.

They were in the drawing-room of the cottage, the scene of their first interesting conversation. Louisa was seated near the window, with the last number of the Hartsdale Vindicator in her hand, and Mr Percival was leaning over her chair, reading some paragraph with her. Both smiled as their eyes met a moment afterwards.

'You know I have discovered you are quite a literary lady,' exclaimed Mr Percival; 'so tell me, Louisa dear, did you send that paragraph yourself?'

'Vanity! Do you suppose I should praise you so much?' she replied archly; but added in a moment, 'Really and truly I have had nothing to do with it; but I told you long ago the worthy editor was coming round to our opinion of things in general; and here he shows himself a wise and brave man, by owning he has been in the wrong. I only hope this evident change in the Hartsdale politics may increase the sale of the paper, and so make up for past losses.'

'Have they really lost so much by it?' asked Mr Percival with evident interest.

'Much is such a comparative word, I hardly know how to answer the question; especially to you who, in all your concerns, have to speak of tens of thousands rather than tens of pounds.'

'Ay, but tens of pounds are often as important in small undertakings as tens of thousands are in great ones. Do you know, I have sometimes thought of buying the Hartsdale Vindicator, employing a first-rate editor to conduct it, and make it what we really want, an important literary organ. Do you think this could be done? Do you believe the proprietors would sell it, or sell the right of conducting it? And, above all, do you think this generous amateur editor could be persuaded to lay down his wand of office?'

'I am certain he would be but too delighted to do it,' exclaimed Louisa; 'for he owned to me the other day that it cost him much time and labour, and interfered sadly with his professional duties, which are very much on the increase since all the new villas are inhabited, and the railway enables him to visit several old patients who have removed. Dear Walter,' she added with pride and animation, 'you are really the good angel of the place!'

'My angelic doings are of a very matter-of-fact mundane description,' he replied laughing; 'but you know I have some deep obligations to the Hartsdalians, since I take their best and wisest all to myself.'

'Her who has been a traitor in the camp all along, you mean,' she said, smiling; 'did I not encourage the Vindicator at first, only because I knew that the more affairs were investigated, the more would the true interests of the place be discovered? If it could have been shown that the old state of things was the better one, I would have owned myself in error—as now some of our old friends have been brave enough to do.'

'And it is for this very prudence that you are the wisest,' repeated Mr Percival.

Gladly did the proprietors of the Vindicator dispose of their shares to the great capitalist, especially as his offer was so liberal that it much more than remunerated them for their temporary loss. Behold, too, their pride in the first number brought out by the new potentate. It had grown to double its former size, and was to be published weekly: in fact, in outward appearance and absolute literary importance it now competed with the County Herald itself—that insolent rival, that had not even deigned to notice its former existence! No one, however, spoke of the early, modest Vindicator with contempt; on the contrary, its double-sheeted offspring alluded in the most respectful terms to the services it had rendered the entire county, and the skill and taste with which it had been conducted; and this was no more than truth, for its unpretending columns, devoted to subjects of local interest, had made the history, the beauties, and the advantages of the valley more extensively known than would have been likely to be the case from any other means. The consequence was, that capital was brought into the neighbourhood, which, distributed in wages amongst the poor, was exactly, in its results, like a fertilising stream to some arid desert. The temporary inconveniences inevitable from a state of transition are already nearly forgotten, or remembered only to provoke a smile. As an omnibus runs six times a-day to the railway station, people have ceased to miss the stages. It is true the White Hart Inn is shut up, but very much more in consequence of a temperance movement among the poor, than because the glories of the Telegraph have departed; an event most significant of the happy moral elevation of the humbler classes.

The Misses Gunning are restored to the undisputed possession of their carriage; and, as if to make amends for the trials to which poor Peter was subjected, he is now relieved from all floricultural duties, since his mistresses, having been tempted to invest some property in railway shares, find an increase in their income, which permits them to add a gardener to their establishment. Major Stukely was the last to hold out for good old customs; but having been twice detected in walking to the station for the mere pleasure of seeing the train come up, he owned there was something very exciting and interesting in the contemplation of such stupendous undertakings—a confession which was taken on all hands as acknowledgment of a defeat. In fact, Hartsdale bids fair to become a considerable and important place, and to be as much distinguished for its intelligence, activity, wealth, and general prosperity, as it was in the 'olden time' for the wretchedness and ignorance of its poor, and the primitive condition of its general inhabitants. [illegible] tures of a really beautiful country; and emotions arise in contemplating the advancement of mankind, it may be of a loftier kind than those which kindle at the sight even of the most exquisite scenery.

THE RAUHE HAUS OF HAMBURGH.

The following account of the Rauhe Haus or Redemption Institute of Hamburgh reads like something from a different sphere; but, in reality, it is part of a very sober document—a Report on Education in Europe, prepared from personal observation by the Hon. Horace Mann of Massachusetts, and presented last year to the secretary of the Board of Education for that state. As very few copies of Mr Mann's report have found their way to this country, the extract may be regarded as equal to so much original matter; not to speak of its absolute interest, which, it seems to us, could hardly be over-estimated:—

The school of Mr J. H. Wichern is called the 'Rauhe Haus,' and is situated four or five miles out of the city of Hamburgh. It was opened for the reception of abandoned children of the very lowest class—children brought up in the abodes of infamy, and taught, not only by example but by precept, the vices of sensuality, thieving, and vagabondry—children who had never known the family tie, or who had known it only to see it violated. Hamburgh having been for many years a commercial and free city, and of course open to adventurers and renegades from all parts of the world, has many more of this class of population than its own institutions and manners would have bred. The thoughts of Mr Wichern were strongly turned towards this subject while yet a student at the university; but want of means deterred him from engaging in it, until a legacy, left by a Mr Gercken, enabled him to make a beginning in 1833. He has since devoted his life and all his worldly goods to the work. It is his first aim that the abandoned children whom he seeks out on the highway, and in the haunts of vice, shall know and feel the blessings of domestic life; that they shall be introduced into the bosom of a family; for this he regards as a divine institution, and therefore the birthright of every human being, and the only atmosphere in which the human affections can be adequately cultivated. His house, then, must not be a prison or a place of punishment or confinement. The site he had chosen for his experiment was one enclosed within high strong walls and fences. His first act was to break down these barriers, and to take all bolts and bars from the doors and windows. He began with three boys of the worst description; and within three months, the number increased to twelve. They were taken into the bosom of Mr Wichern's family; his mother was their mother, and his sister their sister. They were not punished for any past offences, but were told that all should be forgiven them, if they tried to do well in future. The defenceless condition of the premises was referred to, and they were assured that no walls or bolts were to detain them; that one cord only should bind them, and that the cord of Love. The effect attested the all but omnipotent power of generosity and affection. Children from seven or eight to fifteen or sixteen years of age, in many of whom early and loathsome vices had nearly obliterated the stamp of humanity, were transformed not only into useful members of society, but into characters that endeared themselves to all within their sphere of acquaintance. The education given by Mr Wichern has not been an æsthetic or literary one. The children were told at the beginning that labour was the price of living, and that they must earn their own bread, if they would secure a comfortable home. He did not point them to ease and affluence, but to an honourable poverty, which, they were taught, was not in itself an evil. Here were means and materials for learning to support themselves; but there was no rich fund or other resources for their maintenance. Charity had supplied the home to which they were invited; their own industry must supply the rest

Mr Wichern placed great reliance upon religious training; but this did not consist in giving them dry and unintelligible dogmas. He spoke to them of Christ as the benefactor of mankind—who proved by deeds of love his interest in the race, who sought out the worst and most benighted of men to give them instruction and relief, and who left it in charge to those who came after him, and wished to be called his disciples, to do likewise. Is it strange that, enforced by such a practical exemplification of Christian love as their fatherly benefactor gave them in his every-day life, the story of Christ's words and deeds should have sunk deeply into their hearts, and melted them into tenderness and docility? Such was the effect. The most rapid improvement ensued in the great majority of the children; and even those whom long habits of idleness and vagabondry made it difficult to keep in the straight path, had long seasons of obedience and gratitude, to which any aberration from duty was only an exception.

As the number of pupils increased, Mr Wichern saw that the size of the family would seriously impair its domestic character. To obviate this, he divided his company into families of twelve, and he has erected nine separate buildings, situated in a semicircle around his own, and near to it, in each of which dwells a family of twelve boys or of twelve girls, under the care of a house-father or house-mother, as the assistants are respectively called. Each of these families is, to some extent, an independent community, having an individuality of its own. They eat and sleep in their own dwelling, and the children belonging to each look up to their own particular father or mother, as home-bred children to a parent. The general meeting every morning—at first in the chamber of Mr Wichern's mother, but afterwards, when the numbers increased, in the little chapel—and their frequent meetings at work, or in the play-ground, form a sufficient, and, in fact, a very close bond of union for the whole community. Much was done by the children themselves in the erection of their little colony of buildings; and in doing this, they were animated by a feeling of hope and a principle of independence in providing a dwelling for themselves, while they experienced the pleasures of benevolence in rendering assistance to each other. Mr Wichern mentions, with great satisfaction, the good spirit of the architect who came upon the premises to direct in putting up the first house. This man would not retain a journeyman for a day or an hour who did not conduct himself with the utmost decorum and propriety before the children who were assisting in the work.

Instruction is given in reading, writing, arithmetic, singing, and drawing—and in some instances, in higher branches. Music is used as one of the most efficient instruments for softening stubborn wills and calling forth tender feelings; and its deprivation is one of the punishments for delinquency. The songs and hymns have been specially adapted to the circumstances and wants of the community, and it has often happened that the singing of an appropriate hymn, both at the gatherings in the mother's chamber, which were always more or less kept up, and in the little chapel, has awakened the first-born sacred feeling in obdurate and brutified hearts. Sometimes a voice would drop from the choir, and then weeping and sobbing would be heard instead. The children would say they could not sing—they must think of their past lives, of their brothers and sisters, or of their parents living in vice and misery at home. On several occasions the singing exercises had to be given up. Frequently the children were sent out to the garden to recover themselves. An affecting narrative is recorded of a boy who ran away, but whom Mr Wichern pursued, found, and persuaded to return. He was brought back on Christmas eve, which was always celebrated in the mother's chamber. The children were engaged in singing the Christmas hymns when he entered the room. At first they manifested strong disapprobation of his conduct, for he was a boy to whose faults special forbearance had been previously shown. They were then told to decide among themselves how he should be punished. This brought them all to perfect silence, and after some whispering and consulting together, one, who had formerly been guilty of the same fault of ingratitude under still less excusable circumstances, burst out in a petition for his forgiveness. All united in it, reached out to him a friendly hand, and the festival of the Christmas eve was turned into a rejoicing over the brother that had been lost but was found. The pardon was not in words merely, but in deeds. No reference to the fact was afterwards made. A day or two after, he was sent away on an errand to the distance of half a mile. He was surprised and affected by this mark of confidence; and from that time never abused his freedom, though intrusted to execute commissions at great distances. But he could never after hear certain Christmas hymns without shedding tears; and long subsequently, in a confidential communication to Mr Wichern respecting some act of his former life (an unburdening of the overladen conscience, which was very common with the inmates, and always voluntary; for they were told on their arrival that their past life should never be spoken of unless between them and himself), he referred to the decisive effect of that scene of loving-kindness upon his feelings and character.

One peculiar feature of this institution is, that the children are not stimulated by the worldly motives of fame, wealth, or personal aggrandisement. The superintendent does not inflame them with the ambition that if they surpass each other at recitation, and make splendid displays at public examinations, they shall, in the end, become high military officers, or congress men, or excite the envy of all by their wealth or fame. On the other hand, so far as this world's goods are concerned, he commends and habituates them to the idea of an honourable poverty; and the only riches with which he dazzles their imaginations are the riches of good works. He looks to them as his hope for redeeming others from the sphere whence they themselves were taken; and there have been many touching instances of the reformation of parents and families, for whom the natural affection first sprang up in these children's hearts, after they had learned the blessings of home and what the ties of nature really are.

One of the most interesting effects of this charity is the charity which it reproduces in its objects; and thus it is shown that, in the order of nature, the actions of good men—provided they are also wise—not less than good seed, will produce thirty, or sixty, or a hundred fold of beneficent fruit. Mr Wichern makes a great point of celebrating Christmas, and the friends of the school are in the habit of sending small sums of money, and articles of various kinds to adorn the festival. This money has often been voluntarily appropriated by the children to charitable purposes. They frequently give away their pennies; and instances have happened where they have literally emptied their little purses into the hands of poverty and distress, and taken off their own clothes to cover the naked. On one occasion, six poor children had been found by some of the scholars, and invited to the Christmas festival. There they were clothed, and many useful and pleasing articles, made by the givers, were presented to them. One of the boys read a passage from the history of Christ, and the Christmas songs and other songs of thanksgiving and praise were sung. To the sound of the organ, which a friend had presented to the little chapel, some verses welcoming the strangers succeeded. The guests then departed, blessing the house and its kind inhabitants; but who can doubt that a voice of gladness, more precious than all worldly applauses, sprang up unbidden and exulting in the hearts of the little benefactors?

But among numerous less conspicuous instances of the change wrought by wise and appropriate moral means in the character of these so lately abandoned children, the most remarkable occurred at the time of the great Hamburgh fire, in May 1842. In July 1843 I saw the vast chasm which the conflagration had made in the centre of that great city. The second day of the fire, when people were driven from the city in crowds, and houseless and half frantic sufferers came to the Rauhe Haus for shelter, the children—some of whom had friends and relatives in the city—became intensely excited, and besought Mr Wichern for leave to go in and make themselves useful to the sufferers. Not without great anxiety as to the force of the temptations for escape or for plunder, that might assail them in such an exposed and tumultuous scene, he gave permission to a band of twenty-two to accompany him, on condition that they would keep together as much as possible, and return with him at an appointed time. This they readily promised; nor did they disappoint him. Their conduct was physically as well as morally heroic. They rushed into the greatest dangers to save life and property, and though sometimes pressed to receive rewards, they steadily refused them. At stated intervals they returned to the appointed place to reassure the confidence of their superior. On one occasion, a lad remained absent long beyond the time agreed upon, but at last he appeared, quite exhausted by the labour of saving some valuable property. Mr Wichern afterwards learned from the owner—not from the lad—that he had steadily refused the compensation offered to, and even urged upon him. When the company returned home at the appointed time, he sent forth another band under the care of a house-father, and these exerted themselves in the same faithful and efficient manner. This was done as long as the necessity of the case required. From this time the Rauhe Haus was the resort of the poor and homeless—and not for days only, but for weeks. The pupils shared with them their food, and even slept upon the ground to give their beds to the destitute, sick, and injured. I can hardly refrain from narrating many other facts of a similar character connected with this institution; for if the angels rejoice over a rescued sinner, why should not we partake of that joy when it is our brother who is ransomed?

In his last report, Mr Wichern says the institution was actually so impoverished by the demand made upon it at that time, and the demands upon public charity have since been so great in that unfortunate city, that the inmates have been almost reduced to suffering for the necessaries of life, particularly as he was induced to receive several children rendered homeless by that calamity. To this object, however, even the children of the house were ready and willing to contribute portions of their wardrobe, and they submitted cheerfully to other privations. Mr Wichern regretted above all other things the necessity of refusing many applications—and it is but doing justice to the citizens of Hamburgh to state, that on an appeal made by him for funds to erect a new building, they were generously and promptly raised by those who had such unusual claims upon their charity.

A single remark I must be allowed to make. When an individual effects so much good, it seems to be often thought that he accomplishes it by virtue of some charm or magic, or preternatural influence, of which the rest of the world cannot partake. The superintendent of the Rauhe Haus is a refutation of this idea. Laboriously, perseveringly, unintermittingly, he uses MEANS for the accomplishment of his desired ends. When I put to him the question, in what manner he produced these transforming effects upon his charge, his answer was, 'By active occupations, music, and Christian love.' Two or three things should be stated in explanation of this compendious reply. When a new subject comes to the Rauhe Haus, he is first received into Mr Wichern's own family. Here, under the wise and watchful guardianship of the master, he is initiated into the new life of action, thought, feeling, which he is expected to lead. His dispositions are watched, his character is studied; and as soon as prudence allows, he is transferred to that one of the little colonies whose house-father is best qualified to manage his peculiarities of temperament and disposition. Soon after the opening of the establishment, and the increase of its numbers, Mr Wichern found that it would be impossible for him to bestow the requisite care and oversight upon each one of his pupils which his necessities demanded. He cast about for assistance, and though he was able to find those in the community who had enough of the spirit of benevolence and self-sacrifice to undertake the difficult labour to which his own life was devoted, yet he soon found that they had not the other requisite qualifications to make their benevolent purposes available. He could find enough of well-intentioned persons to superintend the workshops, gardens, &c. but they had not intellectual competency. So he could find schoolmasters who could give good lessons, but they were not masters of any handicraft. He was therefore driven, as he says, to the expedient of preparing a class of teachers, to become his auxiliaries in the work. For this end he has superadded to his original plan a school for the preparation of teachers; first to supply himself; then to send abroad to open other institutions similar to his own, and thirdly to become superintendents of prisons. This last object he deems very important. Questions about prison-architecture, he says, have given a new literature to the world; but as yet nothing, or but little, is done to improve the character or increase the qualifications of prison-keepers. I have often felt the force of this remark in the numerous continental prisons which I have visited. Though the masters of the prisons have generally appeared to be very respectable men, yet the assistants or deputy-turnkeys have very often seemed to belong to a low order of society, from whose manners, conversation, or treatment of the prisoners, no good influence could be expected.

This second institution of Mr Wichern is in reality a normal school, which the necessities of his situation suggested and forced him to establish.

During the ten years of the existence of this institution, there have been 132 children received into it. Of these about 80 were there on the 1st of July 1843. Only two had run away, who had not either voluntarily returned, or, being brought back, had not voluntarily remained. The two unreclaimed fugitives committed offences, fell into the hands of the civil magistrate, and were imprisoned.

Who can reflect upon this history, where we see a self-sacrificing man, by the aids of wisdom and Christian love, exorcising as it were the evil spirits from more than a hundred of the worst children whom a corrupted state of society has engendered; who can see this without being reminded of some case, perhaps within his own personal knowledge, where a passionate, ignorant, and perverse teacher, who, for the sake of saving a few dollars of money, or from some other low motive, has been put in possession of an equal number of fine-spirited children, and has, even in a shorter space of time, put an evil spirit into the bosom of them all? When visiting this institution, I was reminded of an answer given to me by the head master of a school of a thousand children in London. I inquired of him what moral education or training he gave to his scholars—what he did, for instance, when he detected a child in a lie? His answer was literally this—'I consider,' said he, 'all moral education to be a humbug. Nature teaches children to lie. If one of my boys lies, I set him to write some such copy as this—"Lying is a base and infamous offence." I make him write a quire of paper over with this copy; and he knows very well that if he does not bring it to me in a good condition, he will get a flogging.' On hearing this reply, I felt as if the number of things in the condition of London society, which needed explanation, was considerably reduced.

What is most remarkable in reference to the class of institutions now under consideration, is the high character of the men—for capacity, for attainments, for social rank—who preside over them. At the head of a private orphan house in Potsdam is the venerable Von Türk. According to the laws of his country Von Türk is a nobleman. His talents and acquisitions were such that at a very early age he was elevated to the bench. This was probably an office for life, and was attended with honours and emoluments. He officiated as judge for fourteen years; but in the course of this time, so many criminal cases were brought before him for adjudication, whose only cause and origin were so plainly referable to early neglect in the culprit's education, that the noble heart of the judge could no longer bear to pronounce sentence of condemnation against the prisoners; for he looked upon them as men who, almost without a paradox, might be called guiltless offenders. While holding the office of judge he was appointed school inspector. The paramount importance of the latter office grew upon his mind as he executed its duties, until at last he came to the full conception of the grand and sacred truth—how much more intrinsically honourable is the vocation of the teacher, who saves from crime and from wrong, than the magistrate who waits till they are committed, and then avenges them! He immediately resigned his office of judge, with its life-tenure and its salary; travelled to Switzerland, where he placed himself under the care of Pestalozzi; and, after availing himself for three years of the instructions of that celebrated teacher, he returned to take charge of an orphan asylum. Since that time he has devoted his whole life to the case of the neglected and destitute. He lives in as plain and inexpensive a style as our well-off farmers and mechanics, and devotes his income to the welfare of the needy. I was told by his personal friends that he not only deprived himself of the luxuries of life, but submitted to many privations in order to appropriate his small income to others whom he considered more needy; and that his wife and family cordially and cheerfully shared such privations with him for the same object. To what extent would our own community sympathise with, or appreciate the act, if one of the judges of our higher courts, or any other official dignitary, should resign an office of honour and of profit to become the instructor of children!

Even now, when the once active and vigorous frame of this patriarchal man is bending beneath the weight of years, he employs himself in teaching agriculture, together with the branches commonly taught in the Prussian schools, to a class of orphan boys. What warrior, who rests at last from the labours of the tented field after a life of victories; what statesman, whose name is familiar in all the courts of the civilised world; what orator, who attracts towards himself tides of men wherever he may move in his splendid course; what one of all these would not, at the sunset of life, exchange his fame and his clustering honours for that precious and abounding treasury of holy and beneficent deeds, the remembrance of which this good old man is about to carry into another world! Do we not need a new spirit in our community, and especially in our schools, which shall display only objects of virtuous ambition before the eyes of our emulous youth; and teach them that no height of official station, nor splendour of professional renown, can equal in the eye of Heaven, and of all good men, the true glory of a life consecrated to the welfare of mankind?

WOMAN'S POWER.

Those disasters which break down the spirit of a man, and prostrate him in the dust, seem to call forth all the energies of the softer sex, and give such intrepidity and elevation to their character, that at times it approaches to sublimity. Nothing can be more touching than to behold a soft and tender female, who had been all weakness and dependence, and alive to every trivial roughness, while treading the prosperous paths of life, suddenly rising in mental force to be the comforter and supporter of her husband under misfortune, and abiding, with unshrinking firmness, the bitterest blasts of adversity. As the vine which has long twined its graceful foliage about the oak, and been lifted by it in sunshine, will, when the hardy plant is rifted by the thunderbolt, cling round it with its caressing tendrils, and bind up its shattered boughs, so is it beautifully ordered by Providence that woman, who is the mere dependent and ornament of man in his happier hours, should be his stay and solace when smitten with sudden calamity; winding herself into the rugged recesses of his nature, tenderly supporting the drooping head, and binding up the broken heart. I was once congratulating a friend, who had around him a blooming family, knit together in the strongest affection. 'I can wish you no better lot,' said he with enthusiasm, 'than to have a wife and children; if you are prosperous, there they are to share your prosperity; if otherwise, there they are to comfort you.'—*W. Irving.*

VALUE OF USEFUL KNOWLEDGE.

The value of useful knowledge is well illustrated by the following anecdote, which occurs in a recently-issued memoir of the late Mr Reid of Bellary, by Dr Wardlaw. Mr Reid, in returning from London to Leith by smack in October 1825, encountered a severe storm, in which, with the rest of the passengers and crew, he was exposed to imminent danger. 'They struck, in the darkness of the night, on the Goodwin Sands. The captain seemed to lose his presence of mind, and to be at his wits' end. Mr Joseph Hume, M.P. was on board. To his self-command, and such knowledge of navigation and seamanship as he had acquired on repeated voyages across the Atlantic—a knowledge which now became of use—Mr Reid ascribed their preservation. He took the helm himself, and worked the vessel out of danger. And since I have thus mentioned Mr Hume, and shown how the acquisition of knowledge, much as it may be out of a man's own line, may one day come to be of service, and the propriety therefore of never slighting any opportunity of attaining it—it is no more than justice to that gentleman to add, that to Mr Reid and several fellow-students who were returning to college along with him, he was exceedingly attentive and kind, turning his superior acquaintance with the little mysteries of travelling to good account for their direction and accommodation. He was conversible and communicative; and my young friend, having some little portion of a kindred inquisitiveness after general information, availed himself of this, and was indebted to him for various items to his stock of knowledge. In a letter to his mother, after speaking gratefully of his opportune kindness and aid, he adds—"The way we got familiar was this: the captain's chart was all in tatters. On Monday, Mr Hume wanted to look at it, to show us our situation at different times; and finding it in this state, he told the steward to make some paste and he would mend it. I immediately went and offered my assistance, and was with him, I suppose, three hours repairing it. During this time he kept talking to me on many subjects; and finding me inquisitive, he took an interest in giving me information." The member for Montrose and the young logician appear to have mutually fancied each other; the former inviting the latter to breakfast with him in his hotel in Edinburgh, and by the same frankness and familiarity in conversation, increasing not a little his stock of information.'

REASON AND KINDNESS.

The language of reason, unaccompanied by kindness, will often fail of making an impression; it has no effect on the understanding, because it touches not the heart. The language of kindness, unassociated with reason, will frequently be unable to persuade; because, though it may gain upon the affections, it wants that which is necessary to convince the judgment. But let reason and kindness be united in a discourse, and seldom will even pride or prejudice find it easy to resist.—*Gisborne.*

FLAX-GUM.

It is not generally known, says the editor of the New Zealand Journal, that the gum of the phormium tenax, or New Zealand flax, is admirably adapted for sealing letters; and, when remittances are enclosed, is frequently made use of by the colonists for that purpose. It is insoluble either in water or spirit, and so thoroughly penetrates the envelope as to become part and parcel of it; nor is it possible to get at the contents of a letter so sealed.

Published by W. and R. Chambers, High Street, Edinburgh (also 98, Miller Street, Glasgow); and, with their permission by W. S. Orr, Amen Corner, London.—Printed by Bradbury and Evans, Whitefriars, London.

☞ Complete sets of the Journal, *First Series*, in twelve volumes, and also odd numbers to complete sets, may be had from the publishers or their agents.—A stamped edition of the Journal is now issued, price 2½d., to go free by post.

CONDUCTED BY WILLIAM AND ROBERT CHAMBERS, EDITORS OF 'CHAMBERS'S INFORMATION FOR THE PEOPLE,' 'CHAMBERS'S EDUCATIONAL COURSE,' &c.

No. 88. New Series. SATURDAY, SEPTEMBER 6, 1845. Price 1½d.

'THROUGH.'

There are seasons when we dream over a 'book' as we would over a 'running brook'—when the mind indulges in a reverie at the sight of words, similar to that which, during its listless moods, the murmur of waters sometimes induces. Music, also, will excite the like effects; when the mere time will lead to suggestions far other than the composer designed. We once knew a man who could thus dream over a 'dismal treatise' in a language which he did not understand, and put a meaning into every line of it—such a meaning as to prove the best mirror of his own intelligence that he ever looked into. Lexicons, collections of proverbs, and mottoes, are books naturally calculated to possess this influence. No one thinks of reading these in the usual way, on and on; but we pause, and dwell on words and phrases, until the mind becomes fixed, as it were, on one idea, and the eye remains gazing on one sentence or syllable: the brain at length slightly but pleasantly reels, and the object seems to vanish, and perception, introverted, wanders amid a world of associations, each following the other with the wildest rapidity, and connected by the slightest affinities. We have been led into this speculation by a little fact of this kind in our mental history. We were indolently amusing ourselves by turning over a book of heraldry, reading here and there, as it happened, this and that family motto, and examining this and that family crest, until at length our attention got arrested by the word which gives the title to our present paper. It is the motto of the Hamiltons; but, somehow, we thought immediately of Puck and his companion fairy in the 'Midsummer Night's Dream'—identifying the word with its older synonyme 'thorough.'

> *Puck.* How now, spirit? Whither wander you?
> *Fairy.* Over hill, over dale,
> Thorough bush, thorough brier,
> Over park, over pale,
> Thorough flood, thorough fire;
> I do wander everywhere,
> Swifter than the moones sphere.

And we have heard now and then of a man, though generally spoken of as a miracle, who would go 'thorough flood, thorough fire,' to serve a friend, ay, or even an enemy. We are disposed to believe, too, that existing instances of the character are less occasional than the ungenerous of mankind would wish us to expect. The 'common earth' is as fruitful of examples, we hope, as the land of Faërie. All the inhabitants of either, it were not likely, should reach the desired standard. We know not whether the prankish knaveries of Puck himself, though benamed also Robin Goodfellow, were consistent with the possibility of his fulfilling all the conditions required by the rule; but we are certain that in this 'work day world' of ours there is many a plain human Mr Goodfellow, who would think himself a very bad man, though he might make a tolerable fairy, if he were not habitually willing and ready to go all lengths for a deserving neighbour. Yes, there is many a plain human Mr Goodfellow who would *think* so; but are there many who would *do* so? Ay, that is the question.

Now, here it is that the subject becomes practically important. Mr Goodfellow may have good intentions; but to be Mr True Goodfellow, Mr Thoroughgoing Goodfellow, these intentions must be realised in actions. It is not enough to be 'pure in the last recesses of the mind;' the moral sense will not be satisfied unless this purity be shown in the daily deeds and conversation of a person; the ordinary habits must testify to its existence; it must shape our manners, and regulate our intercourse with society. Neither business nor leisure must be exempt from its operation. In love, in friendship, in trifles as well as in serious occupations, the principle of Thorough-going-ness must be manifested; for whatever is worth doing at all, is worth doing well; and the friend or lover who is suspected of being either, 'only so far'—'to such an extent'—is sure to be despised. It is an instinct of our better nature to visit such a delinquent with sovereign contempt.

Too many of us, however, stop far short of this. One man is in love perhaps, and his mistress has expectations; marriage under the circumstances would be a comfortable thing; but the lady's reasonable hopes are blighted, and he suddenly finds that he was mistaken in the state of his affections. He never proposes that they shall wait until he, by personal exertions, shall make 'the odds even;' but cuts short the affair at once, that he may not be deprived of the chance of a better matrimonial alliance. Another had a friend whom he loved dearly; but then that friend was prosperous; a day came when his friend would borrow a guinea, and, alas! he was out of cash. He was indeed fain to take up with the hypocritical lamentation of Lucius—'What a wicked beast was I to disfurnish myself against such a good time, when I might have shown myself honourable! How unluckily it happened, that I should purchase the day before for a little part, and undo a great deal of honour.' Yes, and a deal of honour is lost when thus 'policy sits above conscience.' In these few words, Shakspeare has condensed the entire truth of the argument. Only the thoroughgoing man can be truly honourable, truly religious.

For a while, however, Mr Worldly Policy and Mr Heavenly Conscience may seem to get on pretty smoothly together. They make excellent partners in business for a time; but this is while Mr Policy acts in subordination: so soon, however, as he claims to be the head of the firm, it is ten to one but it becomes bankrupt.

To commercial success, perhaps, there is no principle

so essential as the thoroughgoing one. We have known many a good speculation fail because the parties had not spirit enough to go 'through' with it. There will be 'rubs and botches' in the best calculated processes. We should make up our minds from the beginning to allow for friction; we should not expect that matters of business will proceed with strictly mathematical precision, though we should endeavour to make them as exact as possible. Having once formed a project, being duly satisfied of its propriety, and having taken the most eligible means of succeeding in it, we should suffer no accident that may arise in its progress so to affect our resolution as to preclude its ultimate attainment. Before the goal is reached, we readily concede that there is a weary and 'phantasmal interim' which puts the most manly courage to the test. But life is a battle, and time the battle-field; worthily occupy the latter, and bravely prosecute the former, and no fear need arise of the final, though perhaps remote result. It is a debt that you owe equally to yourself and your neighbours, to carry the project 'through.' Whatever your original means, you cannot prosecute it to a successful, or even to a partial issue, without their aid; and they must suffer as well as yourself by your want of perseverance. Both your honour and your honesty you will find involved, sooner or later, in the transaction; therefore, we say, let not impediments stop you, but 'through' them, like the ploughshare 'through' the soil, and heap them up on each side of you like ridges, leaving a midway channel before you in which progress is easy. Difficulties in such speculations generally arise from unforeseen circumstances, when you have got some little way in them; they are unexpected from inexperience; but to meet with them is to understand them, and once to understand is to vanquish them. A little decision here will do much, and once exerted, will most probably not again be wanted, at any rate not frequently. These dangers passed, all then is for the most part plain sailing; and the true man of business will come out of the affair with credit and profit.

The accomplishment of a meritorious design is a triumph; to fail in it, a shame. The world will laugh at you if, from weakness or terror, you stop short; it may laugh at you even while you are struggling. It sometimes does so spitefully, to induce the enterprising to pause. But you must not suffer yourself to be betrayed by this artifice. Laugh in your turn, and proceed in your work rejoicingly. The time will come when the scorners will 'laugh on the wrong side of the mouth.' It is generally the idle who thus seek to depress the energies of the diligent: let them then *waste* their time while you *use* yours. The end will justify your conduct. The time will come when you can afford to pity and forgive them for their want of sympathy and encouragement, and when they will wish that they had imitated instead of having disparaged your example.

DR WOLFF'S MISSION TO BOKHARA.

WHATEVER may be thought of the policy of Dr Wolff's mission to Bokhara, or of Captain Grover's motives in promoting the inquiry, it may be readily apprehended that the information obtained by it could not prove otherwise than interesting both to the general and studious reader. The narrative of Dr Wolff's journey* has been therefore received by us with special welcome, and, though unwilling to enter into the political question involved, we have thought it but right to glean from the record before us such items of knowledge as promised to be useful. In the character of Dr Wolff himself there are also extraordinary traits, rendering a portrait of him desirable; and we are happy to state that the reverend gentleman has not neglected to gratify the reasonable curiosity of his readers, but has introduced his 'Narrative' with a sketch of his life previous to the period of his undertaking the perilous adventure of ascertaining the fate of Colonel Stoddart and Captain Conolly

Dr Wolff was born a Jew; but 'at an early period' he received what he calls 'pure Christianity in the schools of the enlightened Friedrich Leopold, Count of Stolberg, the well-known poet, celebrated Greek scholar, and statesman; next from the distinguished Roman Catholic bishop, Johannes Michael Sailer, Frint at Vienna, Bolzano at Prague, and the writings of Fenelon, Pascal, and Bossuet.' Afterwards introduced to Pope Pius VII., to Cardinal Litta, and the present Cardinal Ostini, he entered the Collegio Romano, and then the Propaganda at Rome. At length, for protesting against the abuses of the church, he was banished from Rome, and took refuge in the convent of Val-Saint, in Switzerland, amongst the monks of the order of the Congregatio Sanctissimi Redemptoris, or the so-called Ligorians. Growing conviction having compelled him to quit this community, he came to England and settled in Cambridge, in the year 1819—acquiring there the knowledge of theology under the Rev. Charles Simeon, of King's College, and studying Persian and Arabic under the direction of Professor Lee. In 1821 he commenced a series of missionary labours among the dispersed Jews in Palestine, Egypt, Mesopotamia, Persia, Krimea, Georgia, and the Ottoman empire, which lasted five years. From 1826 to 1830, he employed himself among his brethren in England, Scotland, Ireland, Holland, and the Mediterranean. 'I then,' he writes, 'proceeded to Turkey, Persia, Türkistaun, Bokhara, Affghanistaun, Cashmeer, Hindüstaun, and the Red Sea, from 1831 to 1834. Bokhara and Balkh—when, in 1829, at Jerusalem—occupied especially my attention, on the ground that I expected to find in them the traces of the lost ten tribes of the dispersion. This led to my first visit to Bokhara.'

It is much to Dr Wolff's credit that he applied himself to the literary as well as to the theological objects of his different missions. Accordingly, he omitted no opportunity of examining both Armenian, Persian, Hebrew, Arabic, and Greek manuscripts. In the Armenian Bible he found 'an important variation. In Daniel viii. 14, they read 2068, whereas in our version it is 2300. In this passage, a manuscript in the possession of the Jews of Bokhara reads 2400 instead of 2300.'

Some of his personal adventures we will relate in his own words:—

'Amid the khans of Khorassaun, Muhammed Ishak Kerabe of Torbad Hydarēa, the rustam of the East, was the most remarkable for ferocity. At Sangerd the caravan was attacked by robbers; one of them seized my horse, crying out, "Pool!" (money): I gave him all I had. I was soon surrounded by others, stripped even of the shirt on my back, and had a rag covered with vermin thrown over me, and was brought out into the highway, where all my fellow-travellers of the caravan were assembled, weeping and crying, and bound to the tails of horses. The robbers were twenty-four in number. We were driven along by them in continual gallop, on account of the approach of the Türkomauns; for if the Türkomauns had found them out, our robbers would have been made slaves by them, they being sheahs themselves. During the night three prisoners escaped. At two in the morning we slept in a forest. They had pity on me, and gave me a cup of tea made of my own; they then put a price on me and my servant, valuing him at ten, and myself at five tomauns. They took his money from him, by which I found that he had previously robbed me of sixteen tomauns. After this we were put in irons. They consulted about killing me, but did not do so, from fear of Abbas Mirza. The promise of a good ransom at Torbad Hydarēa saved my life. The first question put by the robbers openly before the people of Torbad was, "How is the tyrant Muhammed Ishak Khan going on? Is he not yet dead?"

* Narrative of a Mission to Bokhara, in the Years 1843-1845, to ascertain the fate of Colonel Stoddart and Captain Conolly. By the Rev. Joseph Wolff, D.D., LL.D. London: John W. Parker, West Strand.

They replied, "No; but one of his sons is dead." *Robbers.* "A pity that he died not himself; then we should be free from that tyrant, and not be obliged to plunder people in the path, and eat the bread of blood." * *

'Though naked, they examined us narrowly as we entered Torbad, thinking we might have money concealed about us. I exclaimed, "Hear, Israel" (a common exclamation of my countrymen throughout the world), and was soon surrounded by Jews. They pledged themselves that I should not run away, and received me to their homes. * * The next day I was desired to go back to the robbers, when I was suddenly put into irons, and chained with the rest of the slaves. One of the slave sellers, a malicious kurd, squeezed the irons over my legs crossways, to pain me still further. My fellow slaves, though bound in one common chain, cursed me incessantly. The director of the police said, "To this infidel you must give neither water to drink nor a galyoon to smoke, for he is nedshas (unclean). If he is thirsty, he may go to the well and drink like any other dog." Suddenly, in the midst of my persecutions, a man appeared, who exclaimed, "Is any Englishman here?" "Yes, yes," was my exclamation. The chains were removed, a soldier of Abbas Mirza had arrived with a letter for Muhammed Izhak Khan, ordering him to release me. He gave instant orders to that effect, and bastinadoed the robbers, wishing the whole matter to appear as done without his consent. I was brought before him. He is a tall stout man, with very large eyes, of black complexion, never looking into your face but with a down glance, a deep thundering voice. His sword, they say, is continually girt about him, and he does not lay it aside even in the bath. No one knows where he sleeps. He was seated upon a high throne, all others standing at a distance, terror in every look. He demanded what sum had been taken from me. I replied, Eighty tomauns. He got it from the robbers, but kept it himself. He then said, "You came here with books in order to show us the right way; well, go on."'

It was during this journey, it would appear, that Dr Wolff confirmed that affection for Captain Conolly which he has since so singularly manifested. The Jews of Meshed having spoken to him of an exoteric and an esoteric religion, and been reproved by him for not yielding to the influence of Christianity, they observed that he 'was the second Englishman they had seen who was attached to the Book; THE FIRST WAS LIEUTENANT ARTHUR CONOLLY.' He had been in Meshed in 1829, and Dr Wolff had previously known him for 'an excellent, intrepid, and well-principled traveller;' and regretted that, from his want of patronage, he had not been remunerated for his journeys to Meshed, Heraut, and Candahar. Meshed, the doctor tells us, is, despite its holy character, 'a grossly immoral place;' adding, that 'the number of pilgrims that arrive at the tomb of Imam Resa amounts to 20,000.' Shortly afterwards, Dr Wolff reached Bokhara: this was his first visit. Then Behadur Khan was king, twenty-eight years of age, who spent 'his mornings in reading the Arabic writings of Jelaal and Bydawee with the mullahs, visited the grave of Baba Deen, a sanctified derveesh of Bokhara, and heard causes of dispute, during the remainder of the day, among his subjects.' After an interesting sojourn, Dr Wolff procured a passport, and, crossing the Oxus, proceeded to Balkh, Muzsur, Cabool, Peshawr, the Punjaub, Belaspoor, Cashmeer, Delhi, Agra, and Cawnpore; at which last place he met with Lieutenant Conolly. But here we must quote Dr Wolff's own words:—

'When I travelled first in Khorassaun, in the year 1831, I heard at Meshed, by the Jews, that an English traveller had preceded me there, by the name of Arthur Conolly, as I have already mentioned. They described him as a man who lived in the fear of God and of religion. The moment I arrived, he took me to his house, and not only showed me the greatest hospitality, but, as I was at that time short of money, he gave me every assistance in his power; and not only so, he revised my journal for me with the most unaffected kindness. He also collected the Muhammedan mullahs to his house, and permitted me not only to discuss with them the subject of religion, but gave me most substantial assistance in combating their arguments. Conolly was a man possessed of a deep Scriptural knowledge; a capital textuary; and I bless God that he enjoyed that comfort in his captivity, that inward light, when the iron of tyranny—in his case as in that of holy Joseph—entered into his soul. Various enemies are always found to attack the lone missionary. Nobly and well did this gallant soldier acquit himself in the church militant, both in deeds of arms and deep devotion to the cause of Christ. In 1838, I again met with him in England. Here our friendship was renewed. At Constantinople I learnt that he expressed his deep affection for me to Count Stürmer. I often wished to repay him my debt of gratitude; and the instant the news reached me of his captivity in Bokhara, I offered my aid to release him, in letters to his family.'

We find Dr Wolff afterwards at Lucknow, Benares, Calcutta, Masulipatam, Hyderabad, Madras, Trichinopoly, Cochin, Goa, Poonah, Bombay, Mocha, Jiddah, Suez, Cairo, and Alexandria. He returned to England in 1835, but quitted it again in the autumn of that year, and revisited Alexandria and Cairo, and other places. On the 30th May 1836 he arrived at Massawah, on the African coast, from whence he proceeded to Eylet, Zansaga, and other localities in Abyssinia and Arabia, particularly visiting the Rechabites around Sanaa. While at the latter place, a fever seized him—and again at Hodeydah. Next year, however, we find him in America, at New York, where he was received into the Episcopal church, and preached at Philadelphia, Washington, and Baltimore. He quitted New York on January 2, 1838, and arrived in England on the 28th; and shortly afterwards received his degree of LL.D. from the university of Dublin, and that of D.D. from America. In June following, he underwent priest's orders in Ireland from the lord bishop of Dromore; and immediately afterwards was made honorary chaplain to Lord Viscount Lorton.

'After eighteen years' peregrination in the world,' he continues, 'tired out and enfeebled in constitution, I contemplated now seriously settling in England as one of the clergy of its national church, when the Rev. Hugh Stowell, of Manchester, was kind enough to procure me the situation of incumbent at Linthwaite, near Huddersfield, Yorkshire, where I had the princely income of twenty-four pounds per annum, collected by pew rents, and no augmentation from Queen Anne's bounty. Previous to my arrival, the Pastoral Aid Society had given eighty pounds to my predecessor; but as I did not apply for it previous to my accepting the living, and as they said Lady Georgiana had a sufficient income, they refused to give it to me.'

After a stay of two years at Linthwaite, Dr Wolff exchanged it for the curacy of High Hoyland, near Wakefield; which, however, he left in 1843, having, the previous year, offered to travel to Bokhara to save Stoddart and Conolly.

There can be no doubt that, from his habits and experience, Dr Wolff was precisely the man to send on such a mission. Without repeating particulars with which our readers may be presumed to be already well acquainted, it may suffice to state that all preliminary arrangements were settled, and that Dr Wolff departed from England for Gibraltar on October 14, 1843. General anxiety was felt for his safety and welfare while engaged on the heroic adventure to which he had piously devoted himself. Extracts from his correspondence, reporting his progress, were regularly inserted in the papers; and on his arrival at Bokhara, public interest was excited in an almost unexampled degree. His safe deliverance thence was hailed as an event in which no less than the honour of England itself was greatly implicated. An authenticated and consecutive narrative of the whole transaction was therefore eagerly expected, and is given to us in the two bulky volumes on our table.

There is no utility in retracing ground already travelled over. We will therefore proceed at once with Dr Wolff to Constantinople, where he had an interview with Sir Stratford Canning, who from first to last rendered him every possible assistance and protection; and he was introduced to the Sheikh Islam, the first mullah of the Muhammedan religion, who received him kindly, and told him that he had already corresponded on the subject with the mullahs of Khiva, Bokhara, Khokand, and Daghestaun. The Reis Effendi also delivered to Dr Wolff eight letters of introduction:—

'I. From the sultan: 1, to the king of Khiva; 2, to the king of Bokhara, which his majesty wrote with his own hand at night.

'II. From the Sheikh Islam: 1, to the mullahs of Bokhara; 2, to the mullahs of Khiva; 3, to the mullahs of Khokand.

'III. From the Reis Effendi: 1, to the pasha of Trebizond; 2, to the pasha of Erzroom; 3, to the general-in-chief of the army at Erzroom.'

At Trebizond, Dr Wolff was received with similar civilities—and, in addition, a sum equivalent to forty-four pounds was subscribed towards defraying his expenses. At Erzroom, he likewise met with great sympathy; there were there many English and Russians, besides Persians and Turks. The pasha showed him great respect, and promised to defray the whole expense of his journey to the Persian frontier. The next village of any importance at which Dr Wolff stopped was Tabreez, where he was introduced to the prince of Tabreez and the chief mullah. Here he came to the conclusion, not only that Conolly and Stoddart were yet alive, but that the power of Muhammedan fanaticism is declining. On his arrival at Teheraun, Dr Wolff had an interview with Colonel Shiel, the British envoy in Persia, who then seemed to be of opinion, on the evidence of the eljee or ambassador from Bokhara, that Colonel Stoddart and Captain Conolly were not killed, but kept in prison. But this evidence was, after all, doubtful; for the same eljee had told the ambassador of Russia that they were dead; and that the ameer of Bokhara had proceeded against Stoddart for having, contrary to his warning, continued his correspondence with his countrymen in India, and against Conolly for having gone to Khokand. But whether they were dead or not, Dr Wolff resolved on entering Bokhara; and, in case of the worst proving true, there demanding their bodies, to put them in camphor, and convey them to Constantinople, and thence to London. To that city, accordingly, armed with a letter from the shah of Persia to the ameer of Bokhara, he proceeded without delay.

We pass over the occurrences at Meshed and Mowr, as not containing matter of general interest, and hasten at once to Karakol, where rooms were assigned to Dr Wolff 'by the governor, by order of the ameer of Bokhara, and proper provision sent for him.' Here his mind soon felt misgivings—nor without reason, for his servants deserted him, and he learned besides that the ameer persisted in looking upon all Europeans as spies, and would execute them accordingly: the governor himself, indeed, expressed his opinion, that the instant Dr Wolff reached Bokhara he would be beheaded. Perceiving that his only safety depended on his maintaining his character as a mullah, Dr Wolff dressed himself in full canonicals, and kept the Bible open in his hand. 'The uncommon character of these proceedings,' he says, 'attracted crowds from Shar Islam to Bokhara.' Thus armed with his sacred vestments and book, he had courage to resist the temptation of his escort, Dil Assa Khan, who counselled him to enter Bokhara as a poor man. The rest of the description must be given in Dr Wolff's own words:—

'Shouts of "Selaam Aleikoom" from thousands rang upon my ear. It was a most astonishing sight: people from the roofs of the houses, the Nogay Tatars of Russia, the Cassacks and Girghese from the deserts, the Tatar from Yarkand or Chinese Tartary, the merchant of Cashmeer, the serkerdehs or grandees of the king on horseback, the Affghauns, the numerous water-carriers, stopped still and looked at me; Jews with their little caps, the distinguishing badge of the Jews of Bokhara; the inhabitants of Khokand, politely smiling at me; and the mullahs from Chekarpoor and Sinde looking at me and saying, "Inglees Saheb;" veiled women screaming to each other, "Englees eljee, English ambassador;" others coming by them and saying, "He is not an eljee, but the grand derveesh, derveesh kelaun of Englistaun."

'My addresses had been circulated throughout all the parts of Persia, Türkistaun, and Bokhara; my object had become widely understood, and I doubtless reaped the fruit of making the object of my mission thus clear and intelligible to all the Mussulman world. Amid the continued shouts of "Selaam Aleikoom," I looked closely among the populace, in the hope that I might recognise Stoddart or Conolly. It was vain.

'Before we were carried to our assigned quarters, we were brought what they emphatically call it bala, up to the palace of the king. This is situated on a lofty eminence. When we reached it, the serkerdehs, that is the grandees of the empire, were just leaving it, riding upon horseback. The people crowded in masses on me demanding, "What book have you in your hand?" I replied, "the *Tooraut-e-Moosa* (Laws of Moses), the *Suboor-e-Dawood* (Psalms of David), and the *Anjeel-e-Esau* (Gospel of Christ), and the Prophecies of Daniel, Isaiah, Ezekiel, Jeremiah, &c." Devoutly did these poor unenlightened souls touch the book. At the entrance of the palace gate we were ordered to dismount from our horses. Only the grandees of the empire, and ambassadors of the sultan of Constantinople, or the shah of Persia, should they come to Bokhara, are permitted to enter the palace gates on horseback. No Christian, heathen, or any other ambassador, is allowed this privilege. Singular to say, however, I was allowed this privilege at my audience of leave, prior to my departure from Bokhara.

'Previous to our entrance, one of his majesty's mahrams appeared before me, and said, "His majesty condescends to ask whether you would be ready to submit to the mode of salaam," (for Stoddart Saheb refused, and drew his sword). I asked, "In what does the salaam consist?" He replied, "You are placed before his majesty, who will sit upon the bala hanah (from whence balkan is derived), and the shekhawl (minister of foreign affairs) will take hold of your shoulders, and you must stroke your beard three times, and three times bow, saying at each time, "Allah akbar, Allah akbar, Allah akbar"—"God is the greatest, God is the greatest, God is the greatest;" "Salaamat padishah!"—"Peace to the king." On being asked if I would do so three times, I said, "Thirty times, if necessary." Entering the gate, we were desired to sit down upon a stone seat, and after a few minutes' delay, were ordered to send up our letters.

'After the letters were sent up, we were brought before the king—Dil Assa Khan and myself. His majesty was seated in the balcony of his palace, looking down upon us; thousands of people in the distance: all eyes were bent on me, to see if I would submit to the etiquette. When the shekhawl took hold of my shoulders, I not only submitted to his doing so to me three times, but I bowed repeatedly, and exclaimed unceasingly, "Peace to the king," until his majesty burst into a fit of laughter, and of course all the rest standing around us. His majesty said, "Enough, enough, enough!" We were then ordered to retire. The shekhawl, an officer who answers to our Secretary of State for Foreign Affairs, then assured me that his majesty had smiled upon me, and exclaimed, "What an extraordinary man this Englishman is, in his eyes, and his dress, and the book in his hand."'

From Dr Wolff's account, this monarch must be a sad barbarian; his ascent to the throne, effected by the killing of his father, was attended by the murder of se-

-veral of his brothers. Notwithstanding that Dr Wolff was at first graciously accepted, the clouds of danger soon gathered around him. The house formerly belonging to Turah Zadeh, brother to the present king, who was killed by order of the latter, being assigned to him as his dwelling, all liberty of going out as he pleased was from that moment taken from him: he was watched day and night by the makhrams of the king; and was continually subject to official examinations. At one of these, the Nayeb Abdul Samut Khan certified Dr Wolff of the deaths of Conolly and Stoddart in the following manner:—

"When Colonel Stoddart arrived at Bokhara, his majesty sent a whole troop of soldiers to receive him; he came to Bokhara, and to the Ark, just when Hazrat returned from a pilgrimage to Baba Deen Nakshbande (a holy man buried outside the town). Colonel Stoddart was on horseback. The shekhawl and several other serkerdehs (grandees) went up to him and said, "This is his majesty; you must dismount;" but he replied, "I have no orders for doing so." The ameer smiled, and said he is a mehmoun (guest). When you, Joseph Wolff, made your salaam before the ameer, the shekhawl took slightly hold of your shoulders to make you bow down; you submitted with your book in the hand; but when the shekhawl only touched Colonel Stoddart, he laid his hand on his sword and drew it. Nothing was said to this. The house of Turah, the same house in which you live, was assigned to him as his quarters. When, a few days after, the reis (one of the mullahs who watch over the people, and have power to flog any one who does not observe strictly the Mohammedan religion) sent one of his friends to Stoddart, and asked him whether he was an eljee (ambassador) or a sodagur (merchant), Stoddart replied, "*Eat dung!*"

His imprisonment upon this occasion the nayeb passed over in silence, and continued, "At last, from fear, Stoddart said he would become a Mussulman; and according to the Mohammedan religion, if a person says he will turn Mussulman, he must either do so or die. He became a Mussulman, and a short time after openly avowed again the Christian religion. At last it was agreed that he should write to England to be acknowledged as the accredited agent of Great Britain at the court of Bokhara, and that the king of Bokhara should be the acknowledged sovereign of Turkistaun, &c.; and Colonel Stoddart promised that in four months an answer should arrive from the government of England. Though at his (Stoddart's) request, japar khanas (post houses) were established from Bokhara to Serakhs, which did not exist either at Bokhara or in the land of Turkistaun from the time of Afrasiab, *fourteen months* elapsed, and no answer arrived. During the time that Colonel Stoddart was at Bokhara, Captain Conolly went from Orgunjah (Khiva) to Khokand, where he stopped a considerable time, exciting both countries to wage war against the ameer of Bokhara. He at last arrived at Bokhara, announcing himself as a British agent, without having any letters from the British government; and whatever Colonel Stoddart had agreed to, he upset, announcing to the king of Bokhara that the British government would never interfere with the affairs of Turkistaun, and all that Colonel Stoddart had agreed to went for nothing. Thus it was clear that Colonel Stoddart was a liar. During the stay of Conolly and Stoddart, they took every opportunity of despatching, in the most stealthy manner, letters to Cabul; and on this account his majesty became displeased, and both Captain Conolly and Colonel Stoddart were brought, with their hands tied, behind the Ark (palace of the king), in presence of Makhram Saadat, when Colonel Stoddart and Captain Conolly kissed each other, and Colonel Stoddart said to Saadat, "Tell the ameer that I die a disbeliever in Mohammed, but a believer in Jesus—that I am a Christian, and a Christian I die." And Conolly said, "Stoddart, we shall see each other in paradise (beheesht), near Jesus." Then Saadat gave the order to cut off, first the head of Stoddart, which was done; and in the same manner the head of Conolly was cut off."

By the order of the ameer, Dr Wolff also addressed a letter to Captain Grover, containing the official details of their execution, stating that it took place in the month of Sarratan 1259. Relatively to this date, considerable difficulty exists; as given in the letter referred to, it corresponds with July 1843. To Colonel Shiel, however, Dr Wolff gave the date as being July 1842. This difference becomes important from the circumstance, that, if the latter be the correct time, the event happened too early for the English government to have prevented it; if the former, its interference would have been possible. We perceive that Dr Wolff, for more reasons than one, adheres, in the volumes before us, to the date he first gave. He regrets, he says, the paper which he gave to Colonel Shiel, which, he adds, 'should not have been demanded from me when I was in a state of the greatest excitement, ill and miserable, and attended by Dr Kade, the physician of the Russian embassy.' At the same time, we cannot refrain from saying that the subject is, even on the most favourable showing, involved in so much doubt, that no argument can be maintained on it either on one side or the other. So far as the settlement of this question is concerned, the mission to Bokhara has been fruitless.

For this inadvertence Dr Wolff, however, should be pardoned; since it is quite clear that he was in such peril at Bokhara, as would have daunted the bravest man, and involved the most cautious in a thousand perplexities. From time to time he was detained on frivolous pretences, long after his immediate mission was finished, and exposed to every kind of annoyance, extortion, insult, and tribulation, either for the purpose of involving him in some transactions that should justify his punishment, inducing him to apostatise, or augmenting the terms of his ransom. He was, in fact, a state prisoner, under a tyrant used to passive submission; and in the hands of barbarians, who took no pains to conceal from him that they were thieves and robbers. 'On one occasion a mullah came, and asked me, in his majesty's name, whether I would turn Mussulman. I replied, "Tell the king, never—never—never!" He asked me, "Have you not a more polite answer for the king?" I said, "I beg you to tell his majesty that you asked me whether I had not a more polite answer for his majesty; and I said, 'Decidedly not.'" A few hours after, the executioner came—the same who had put to death Stoddart and Conolly—and said, "Joseph Wolff, to thee it shall happen as it did to Stoddart and Conolly," and made a sign at my throat with his hand. I prepared for death.' By, however, the interference of the Persian ambassador, Wolff was released: and, with a suddenness of caprice for which tyrants are famous, was even taken into favour at court. He was then dismissed with presents, and in great state; the infamous nayeb, Abdul Samut Khan, having, however, made provision that certain assassins should be in the train, who were pledged to murder him on the road. All these difficulties, however, he was destined to escape, greatly owing to his own prudence in never separating from his Persian friends. Dr Wolff arrived in the Persian capital on the 3d November 1844, and left it three days later. He returned to London by way of Tabreez, Erzroom, Trebizond, and Constantinople.

Before we close this subject, we are desirous of extracting some account of Bokhara. 'Bokhara is situated in 39 degrees 27 minutes north latitude, 80 degrees 19 minutes east longitude. It is surrounded by deserts, and watered by the little river Wafkan, which flows between forests of fruit trees and gardens. It has eleven gates, and a circumference of fifteen English miles; three hundred and sixty mosques, twenty-two caravanseries, many baths and bazaars; and the old palace called Ark, built by Arslan Khan one thousand years ago; and has about one hundred splendid colleges. The houses have neither roofs nor windows. The population amounts to one hundred and eighty thousand, composed of Tatshicks, Nogays, Affghauns, Mervee, Usbecks, and ten thousand Jews, who are dyers and silk traders, and must wear a small cap, and girdle around their waist, to be distinguished from the Mahommedans. There are several thousand slaves. There are about three hundred merchants from Scinde, and many derveeshes. Whole streets contain nothing but shops and magazines for merchants from all the parts of Türkistaun, Cashgar, Hindustaun, and Russia. There are great numbers of country houses, with gardens called Jehaar-Bagh, all around Bokhara. Most delightful villages are to be found eight miles around Bokhara. A sickness prevails, chiefly in the city, called Rishta—an immense worm comes out of the knees, and makes people frequently lame for life: it is ascribed to the water. Ophthalmia is also prevalent. There is only one Jewish physician of some skill, who prides himself on knowing the sense of the word "antimonial," and perpetually uses it, as Abdul Samut Khan prides himself on knowing how to say, "Halt! front!"'

The principles of absolutism are dominant in Bokhara. 'Whatever crime or cruelty the king of Bokhara commits, the people simply observe, "This was an act of the king"—"Who can fathom the heart of a king?"' The colleges of Bokhara are, it appears, 'splendid and beautiful buildings.' In them the writings of the learned Sunnées, as well as of the Sheahs, are read and discussed. Oratory, rhetoric, poetry, and logic, are studied besides the Koran; disputations are carried on in a scholastic manner; Jelaal, Beydawee, are read. They take as their guide the schools established in Yemen. There is also an ancient Jewish synagogue in Bokhara, though it is out of repair; indeed the ameer has some predilection for the religion of the Hebrew, since he witnesses the celebration of the Feast of Tabernacles, and partakes of the banquet. Besides, he has never seized on a Jewish woman, as he has done on the wives of his great ministers. Both he and his nayeb are connected with the Ismaelee, whom the former 'sends for some great purposes always to murder people whom he suspects, like the old man of the mountain, the chief of the assassins. Thus, for instance, one of his serkerdehs, whom he suspected, and who had fled to Shahr-Sabz, was murdered in the palace of the khan of Shahr-Sabz, and the head was brought in triumph to Bokhara.' Dr Wolff, therefore, did not feel himself safe even when so far from Bokhara as Trebizond, and was thrown into considerable trepidation by being assigned there an apartment close to the ambassador of Bokhara.

'He did not,' says the doctor, 'himself come near me, but, what is extraordinary, a makhram, sent after us by the ameer, called on me, and he told me that he believed that the nayeb, Abdul Samut Khan, had met with his deserts already, or would certainly meet with punishment shortly. I confess that I was not easy in his company; though I know that people will think that my fear was imaginary, I am not ashamed to confess it.' 'I have already,' says Dr Wolff in another place, 'adverted to the circumstance that one of the ameer's brothers was murdered at Khokand, and another at Orenbourg, and besides this, that makhram, whose name was Shereef Sultaun, whenever he came to me, desired me to send away my servants. It may be objected that the ameer would not do such a thing, for he would put in jeopardy his own ambassador; but to this I answer, such an argument is quite ridiculous, for a savage like the ameer does not care a straw for the life of his ambassador. It may be objected also that the nayeb would not do such a thing, for he is in the power of the ameer; but to this I answer, that it remains still to be seen whether the ameer will put to death the nayeb or the nayeb the ameer. Both are bent upon each other's destruction, and the self-interests of both cause each to delay the execution of the deed.'

Such facts as these are sufficient to show the savage state in which Bokhara is lying; for the distinct conception which we have now obtained of this, we are greatly indebted to the perseverance of Dr Wolff. The charges made against the two victims of its barbarity by the nayeb are probably false, and Captain Grover, we fear, has too rashly assumed their truth; but the question, whether the Foreign Office is or is not censurable for neglecting its officers in peril, depends on the date of their execution; and this is a matter now involved in such doubt, that no solution of the difficulty is possible. Dr Wolff's conduct, however, cannot fail of having considerable influence both at home and abroad.

THE TREE AND THE FOREST.

A STORY WRITTEN FOR THE YOUNG, BUT WHICH MAY BE READ BY THE OLD.

[From the French of Madame Guizot.]

'WHAT splendid trees!' said Monsieur D'Ambly, as he was passing by a fine forest of oaks.

'What a splendid fire they would make!' replied his son Eugene. Eugene had read a few days before in a book of travels the description of a wood on fire, and he could think of nothing else. He was an admirer of everything that was uncommon; everything that produced an effect or a commotion, and, like most children, he seldom carried his ideas beyond what he saw.

'If it would not injure any person,' said he, 'I would be very glad this forest would take fire; it would be a glorious sight. I am sure, papa, that its light would extend as far as the chateau.'

'Would it then be such a pleasant thing to see a tree burning?'

'Oh, a tree,' said Eugene, 'that would be hardly worth the trouble; but a forest would be magnificent.'

'Since we are on the subject of burning,' said Monsieur D'Ambly, 'I think it would be well to cut down that young lime tree on the lawn opposite the chateau. it grows too fast; and if it should spread much more, it would quite intercept our view; I will therefore cut it down for fuel.'

'Oh, papa,' exclaimed Eugene, 'that lime tree that has grown so beautiful since last year! I was looking at it the other day, and I saw shoots of this year as long as my arm.'

At this moment they came to a young poplar which had been blown down by a storm the preceding day. Its leaves were not yet withered, but its young shoots, though still green, began to lose their vigour; they were soft and weak, as if drooping from want of water, but in that case a refreshing shower would have restored it to health and freshness, whereas now it was beyond recovery. Eugene stopped before the poplar, and lamented it.

'Such,' said Monsieur D'Ambly, 'will in two days more be the state of our lime tree.'

'Ah!' cried Eugene, 'can you have the heart to say so?'

'Why not? A lime is not more valuable than a poplar, or an oak; and you would like to see this whole forest in a blaze.'

'Indeed, papa, that is a very different thing.'

'Yes, there is certainly a vast difference between a person cutting down a tree that incommodes him, and that he would then make use of for fuel, and fourteen or fifteen thousand that you would burn for your pleasure.'

'But I do not know those trees.'

'Neither do you know this poplar that you have just been lamenting.'

'But at least I see it.'

'You can as easily see all those that surround it. Look at this one, how strong and how straight it is!'

'Oh, what a fine oak! I do not think my arms could reach round it. See, papa, how high it is, and those three great branches which grow from it look like large trees.'

'It must be sixty or seventy years old: it will grow at least twenty more.'

'How enormous it will be then! I hope I shall see it.'

'But if it should be burned in the meantime?'

'I should be very sorry, now that I know it.'

'You would, then, only spare those trees from the fire which have come under your own particular notice: this is too common a case. Would it give you more pleasure to see this one burning?' said Monsieur D'Ambly, as he showed him another, divided into four enormous trunks, which shot from the same root.

'No, indeed. Look, it makes quite an arbour. Papa, some day when we have more time we will come and sit here, shall we not?'

'So, then, here are two that you would spare from the conflagration of the forest.'

'Oh, if I could but see it on fire, what a fine effect it would have from the windows of the chateau; I should think only of my two favourite oaks that I should be so sorry to see burning.'

'But all those you see equally deserve to become favourites, and those you cannot see are quite as fine; they have each in their different forms something that would interest you as much as your two favourite oaks, the poplar, or our lime tree.'

'I do believe that if I were to think of every particular tree that composed a forest, it would take away all wish to see it burned.'

'That shows the necessity of consideration, my son, to avoid the risk of forming unreasonable wishes, to put them in practice, perhaps, when you grow up. You will probably never have a forest to burn, but you may have men to conduct: just think what might be the consequence of your forgetting that a district, a town, a community, is composed of individuals, as you just now forgot that a forest is composed of trees.'

'Ah, papa, in such a case I could not forget myself.'

'I knew some years ago,' said Monsieur D'Ambly, 'a very good, but rather obstinate man, of the name of De Marne. He had a quarrel with the director of an hospital established in a small town on one of his estates. The greater part of the property of the hospital was situated on this estate, and dependent on it, as was then the custom; that is to say, the hospital only held these lands on condition of paying certain rents to Monsieur de Marne, and of receiving two patients at his option. This right he held in consequence of his ancestors having given these lands to the hospital, and it descended to all the proprietors of the estate. The director began to dispute with Monsieur de Marne about the payment of the rent, and maintained that he had no right to send more than one patient to the hospital. Monsieur de Marne was exceedingly angry, and a lawsuit was the consequence; and it so happened that the person employed by Monsieur de Marne, in searching the papers which had been sent to him, to prove his right, discovered, or thought he had discovered, that the ground which had occasioned the lawsuit belonged to Monsieur de Marne, and not to the hospital, because, said he, the ancestors of Monsieur de Marne only gave it for a certain time, and on certain conditions which had not been fulfilled; so that Monsieur de Marne ought to take possession of it. This would be the ruin of the hospital. The day Monsieur de Marne received this intelligence he was delighted; and the more so, as he had just learned that one of the patients whom he had sent to the hospital had died, in consequence of a relapse from having been discharged too soon. His widow, who was left destitute, travelled on foot to Paris, with her youngest child on her back, to implore the assistance of Monsieur de Marne. She cried bitterly as she related the last words of her husband, who said, when he was dying, "If Monsieur de Marne had been here, he would have had me kept in the hospital, and I should have recovered."

'As Monsieur de Marne listened, with tears in his eyes, to this recital, he exclaimed, "That villain of a director, I will be the ruin of him!" He forgot that it was the hospital he would ruin, and that he would thus put out perhaps a hundred patients, all as poor and as sick as poor Jacques, and whose condition, had he recollected it, would be equally grievous.

'The lawsuit was carried on with great vigour, not by Monsieur de Marne, who was detained by business in Paris, but by his law agent, who, being interested in supporting what he had advanced, pursued it warmly; and fearing that Monsieur de Marne would relinquish his right, took care to keep back what was said in the country, of his folly and madness in trying to ruin an hospital which was such a public benefit, and the daily melancholy accounts of the state to which the patients were reduced, because the director, being obliged to give up a great deal of time and money to the lawsuit, had not enough for the necessary expenses of the hospital. Had Monsieur de Marne known all these particulars, his kindly feelings would have returned; he could not have endured the idea of causing so much evil; but instead of that, his agent only entertained him with accounts of the ill doings of the director, and of the designs he had against him. Every letter he received made him more and more angry; and his hatred of one man made him forget the claims of a hundred others, on whom he should have had compassion.

'At length he gained his lawsuit. He had for some days been endeavouring to procure admission for a poor woman into the hospital of incurables at Paris. "Here are two pieces of good news," said he, as he read the letters which announced the success of each of his undertakings; and he wrote immediately to his law agent, expressing his satisfaction at the manner in which he had conducted his suit, and to the person who had procured admission for the poor woman into the hospital of incurables, thanking him for his kindness.

'For some time he thought no more of the matter; however, he one day received a letter from his agent, telling him that the director had become a bankrupt, and had fled; that no one knew where he was; and to increase his dislike to the man, he added, that during three days that his flight was unknown, because he said he was only going into the country, the patients had neither bread nor broth, and that only for some charitable individuals in the neighbourhood who had sent them relief, most of them must have died; and that it was probable some of them would die from the effects of their sufferings, and from their dismay at hearing that the hospital was likely to fall to the ground. He said it had obtained some respite, as the gentry in the town and neighbourhood had given great assistance; but it was all insufficient, and they were obliged to discharge the least suffering; that they left the hospital in tears; and that several who lived in distant villages had fallen on the road from weakness and disappointment. All these details began to make Monsieur de Marne very uneasy. The agent added at the end of his letter, "Every one observed that the director had neither order nor economy: for a long time the affairs of the hospital have been in a bad state, and the loss of the suit has completed it." Then Monsieur de Marne felt his conscience reproach him for what he had done: he pictured to himself those unfortunate people leaving the hospital in tears, sinking with weakness and grief, and perhaps calling for curses upon him. He thought of the three days that they had been without either bread or broth, and he fancied he saw their pale and emaciated countenances, and began to consider each of them individually, as you just now began to consider the trees of the forest. There was not one of them that he would not have shed his blood to save. He could not endure the idea of all the evil which he had caused them, and endeavoured to throw all the blame upon the director. He wrote to his agent, desiring him to send relief to a considerable amount, and as soon as it was possible, he set off himself to this estate, where he had not been for a long time. On his arrival, he repaired to the town where the hospital had been: it was closed: the last patient had left it, and the house was to be sold to satisfy the creditors. Monsieur de Marne perceived that a great many people avoided him; the lawsuit had given them a very bad opinion of him, and the friends and relations of the director had contributed to increase it; indeed the misery which had been caused to so many poor people had thrown an odium over the whole affair, and turned every person against him. The report spread that he was come to purchase the house and the rest of the hospital lands; and one day, as he was passing through the streets, the children threw stones at him. He began to feel all the injury he had done, and a thousand circumstances perpetually reminded him of it. The son of Jacques, the poor man whose widow he had assisted, had broken his leg, and it remained quite distorted. Monsieur de Marne told his mother that she ought to have had it set. "That would have been easy," she replied, "when there was an hospital here; but now——" and she stopped.

'He saw that the country people were neglecting to cultivate their gardens, which he knew had been profitable to them, and inquired the reason. "Oh," said they, "we used to sell our vegetables to the hospital; but now——" and they stopped; and Monsieur de Marne saw that every one's mind was filled with a subject which it would be impossible for him ever to forget. He was about to quit the country, and even to sell his estate, when an epidemical disease broke out in the next village. It was prevalent there almost every year; and it was for that reason especially that the hospital had been originally founded by a man of wealth, who, having been attacked by the disease, made a vow that, if he recovered, he would found an hospital, into which all the poor of the village, and of a certain distance round it, should be received and taken care of. When his benevolent object was completed, all the poor, on the first symptom of disease, repaired to the hospital, where, from the care and attention they received, they in most cases soon recovered; and it was also a great means of preventing contagion. This year the disorder was particularly severe, and the ill feeling towards Monsieur de Marne rose to a great height. He sent large assistance to the village, and endeavoured to mitigate the sufferings of the poor people; but he still heard it said as he passed along, "There goes Monsieur de Marne, who has come to restore some small part of the hospital land." If he visited a sick person, and inquired after his health, he would say, "I thank you, sir; it is tolerable; but I should have recovered much sooner at the hospital." Overwhelmed with remorse, uneasiness, and fatigue, he took the disorder and died, chiefly of grief, for having at any time forgotten that an hospital is filled with individuals, as you just now forget that a forest is composed of separate trees.'

'Ah, papa! how melancholy that was,' said Eugene, who had listened with the greatest attention.

'My son,' said Monsieur D'Ambly, 'when you grow up, you will see even worse consequences arise from that want of reflection which makes us regardless of everything that does not come under our own observation, so that when objects are too great for us to see their details, we think nothing about them.'

At that moment Eugene, in a musing mood, took up a stone, as was his custom, to throw among a flight of sparrows which had alighted near him: he paused. 'Papa,' said he, 'I will not throw a stone at those sparrows; for I remember how sorry I feel when any person torments my sister's canary bird, and when I see the poor little thing trying to save itself in every corner of the cage: it seems to me as if each of those sparrows, were I to frighten them, would feel just as my sister's bird does.'

'That is precisely, my son, what you ought to do if ever you are intrusted with the interests of a number of persons at once; and that you may be tempted to forget that the regiment you command, or the department you have to manage, is composed of men like yourself; and you should always put yourself, or those you love, in the place of each of them.'

They now reached home, and passed close by the lime tree.

'Ah!' said Eugene, 'I must take my leave of you.'

'No,' said Monsieur D'Ambly, smiling, 'it shall remain, provided you promise to remember, every time you look at it, that each tree in a forest is entitled to as much respect as your lime, and that in an assemblage of persons, whatever may be their denomination, each person's interest is of as much importance as your own.'

WANT OF READING-ROOMS IN LONDON.

Denizens of the provinces are sometimes told by their London friends, that in that city there is every imaginable luxury and convenience. The assertion is liable to exception. We have never visited the metropolis without experiencing a difficulty in seeing the newspapers. Did we belong to a club, or to a literary institution, this difficulty would not be experienced. Were we willing to frequent taverns or coffee-houses, we might see at least a morning, if not also an evening or weekly paper. But if the contrary be the case, an ordinary stranger has no chance of procuring these gratifications without a considerable expense. The cause of this is the want of reading-rooms, where one may see the journals at a small charge, free from all other responsibilities. There is not in London any institution corresponding to the Exchange Rooms of Manchester, Glasgow, and many other cities, where a stranger is allowed to attend free for some time, and where he sees the principal newspapers of the empire. Neither, as far as we could hear, is there any private newspaper reading-room, such as are seen in many smaller cities, where, for a small charge per visit, he can indulge to the utmost possible extent in journal-devouring, having spread before him the Heralds, Gazettes, and Chronicles of not only London, but the principal towns in the country. One may, indeed, have a London paper left at his lodgings for an hour by a newsman at a small charge; but this is very far short of what is needed. A gentleman from the country would like, while in London, to see the whole of the newspapers of the district to which he belongs, as well as a variety of the metropolitan and other provincial journals. Thousands of such persons must every day feel this want, and suffer inconvenience from its not being supplied.

There are, we believe, in London a few reading-rooms apart from houses of entertainment; but they are conducted on a very slender scale, and are thinly scattered. There are also a few houses of entertainment, in which a great number of journals are to be found, which strangers are allowed to consult by paying a small fee, should they not require refreshment. This we believe to be the case at the Messrs Deacon's of Walbrook. These individuals, besides keeping a coffee or tea house, are the London agents for a vast number of provincial newspapers: consequently, in their establishment at least one journal from each town in Great Britain, besides all the metropolitan newspapers, may be seen. The same may be said of the older established house known as 'Peels' in Fleet Street. There is, besides, a large coffee-house in High Holborn called 'The Crown,' where a great many newspapers, magazines, &c. are taken in. But these places exist almost in vain for the stranger, as he may visit London a score of times (as we have done) without once hearing of them; or, should he know of their existence, they may be so far from his ordinary resorts as to be useless to him. In short, the practical state of the case, we know, is such, that to most visitors of London, the time spent there is a time of defective intelligence. A gentleman feels himself cut off from all but one or two of the sources of information which he enjoys in the country. Instead of the scores of papers, as well as other journals, which he may see at any hour of the day in his own town, he is probably condemned to a single brief visit of the one sole and eternal *Times*, containing, over and above the public news, only such minor matters as are interesting to a Londoner. And even the ordinary inhabitants of London, unless those who frequent the Hall of Commerce in the centre of the city, and the other places above specified, have nothing like the same advantages in this respect as the inhabitants of the secondary cities of the empire. They may have their one or two London journals at a coffee-house, and such as belong to the 'clubs' may command a somewhat more liberal share of intelligence; but they have no opportunity of consulting anything like that variety of home, foreign, and colonial journals which the gentlemen of most of the lesser cities of Britain obtain for their annual guinea, and to which, in most cases, strangers are admitted for a month without any charge whatever.

Amongst the many schemes continually under trial in London, why is there not one for supplying this want? To give some idea of what is required, let us advert to the character of the provincial news-rooms. They are mostly of one class, namely, Subscription Reading-rooms; that is to say, the principal men of business in the town subscribe one or at most two guineas each for a room, usually called the Exchange Room, where they may meet at any hour, and where all the principal newspapers and shipping and commercial lists of the empire are taken in. Manchester, Liverpool, Newcastle, Glasgow, Dundee, and many other large towns, are thus provided. In other instances, the room is a matter of private enterprise: for example, in Edinburgh there is a room of this kind, instead of one upon the subscription plan. The proprietors (Messrs Harthill and Son) charge a pound a year, or five shillings a quarter, for the privilege of access; but a stranger, or any other person, may visit it if he puts a penny into a box at the door. What is rather surprising, there is no one of the Subscription Rooms so liberally furnished with papers as this. We find, on inquiry, that it takes in eight London daily papers (several copies of each), forty-five London weekly, forty-four English provincial, thirteen Irish, fifteen Edinburgh (of some ten copies of each), forty-eight Scottish provincial, being all that are published, and nineteen foreign and colonial. There are, besides, five-and-twenty of the principal periodicals, monthly and quarterly, and all the share-lists published throughout the country; in all, 706 papers per week, or above 100 for each working day. So liberal an entertainment laid before the stranger in our northern capital, at the charge of a penny, contrasts strangely with the single *Times* which the same money obtains from a newsman in London. But it is not here alone that this conveniency is upon a better footing than in the metropolis. There is now hardly a small burgh or thriving village in Scotland, where it is not possible to command more sources of public intelligence at a small charge, than in that city which boasts of supplying every imaginable want with unprecedented nicety.

It has sometimes been remarked that there is less interest in public affairs in London than in the provinces. It is still more certain that such interest as the Londoners have to bestow upon public matters is extremely limited in its scope. The view of an intelligent person in the country comprehends London as well as the provinces; but persons of intelligence in London are very apt to look little beyond their own city. Hence there is often a greater provinciality in the London mind than in that of the provinces. May not this be owing, in some measure, to the habits of the people of London with regard to the reading of newspapers? The everlasting diet upon the one morning paper, must tend greatly to narrow the mind and concentrate the sympathies; a wider range of intellectual pasturage might be expected to have the opposite effect. For this reason, as well as with regard to our own interests as occasional visitors of that all but paperless metropolis, we desire most earnestly that right and fitting reading-rooms were established in it.

THE HISTORY OF HOUSE LIGHTS.

A GREAT deal of discussion has been kept up concerning the respective merits of various inventions for lighting apartments. The question of lamps or candles has for the last dozen years been argued and experimented upon, and, except in localities where pure gas is to be obtained, it is not yet finally settled. To give fresh interest to the discussion, we propose producing some facts concerning the contrivances our predecessors adopted for lighting the darkness of their habitations.

To begin at the very beginning, we may readily conceive that aboriginal man, having provided himself with a hut to cover him, and with fire to make a comfortable temperature, naturally sought to enliven his rude abode, and to lengthen the short days of winter, by a more steady and enduring light than that given forth by the flickering and smoking fuel on the hearth. He therefore procured strips of dry wood, and setting one end on fire, stuck the other into the sides of his hut. The light thus afforded enabled him to perform his labours or enjoy his amusements during the night. The quantity of smoke and the resinous stench emitted by that sort of torch, soon drove him to some better expedient; hence we find that, at an early period of history, oil placed in some sort of vessel, and burned by means of a fibrous wick, was substituted. Still, for out-door purposes, and in large apartments, flambeaux or torches have never fallen entirely into disuetude. In the baronial times they were much employed; but instead of being fastened to the wall, were held by human candlesticks—serfs whose whole business it was to give light to their master and his guests. Sir John Froissart states, in his minute description of the Count de Foix's mode of life at 'Orthes' (Ortes), that when 'he quitted his chamber at midnight for supper, twelve servants bore each a large lighted torch before him, which were placed near his table, and gave a brilliant light to the apartment.' Even so late as the seventeenth century, a similar practice existed in the Scottish Highlands. During great entertainments, a torch-bearer stood behind the chair of each guest; and long stripes of dry fir are still called 'cannel' or candle fir.

In tracing the origin of the lamp, we naturally turn to the records of the earliest civilised people; but it is singular that the paintings and sculptures of Egypt, which afford such ample and curious information on other subjects of ancient domestic comfort, leave us in the dark on the subject of artificial light. 'The paintings,' says Sir Gardner Wilkinson, 'offer no representation which can be proved to indicate a lamp, a torch, or any other kind of light.' A close inspection, however, of some of the funeral processions, reveals, in the hand of one of the figures, something which looks like a torch. The sculptures of Alabastron, again, represent a guard of soldiers, one of whom holds before him an object which resembles a lantern; but the forms of both torch and lantern are so uncertain as to be insufficient to decide the question. At a later period, lamps were commonly used in Egypt as in other parts of the world. The earliest notice of them is by Herodotus,* who mentions 'a feast of burning lamps' which took place at Sais, and indeed throughout Egypt, at a certain period of the year. The lamps were 'small vases filled with salt and olive oil, on which the wick floated and burnt during the whole night.' The modern lamp-maker, therefore, who flattered himself that he made a discovery when he put forth his 'floating lights,' only reproduced what was in common use more than two thousand years ago. Doubtless the lamps employed for domestic purposes were similar to those described by

* Book ii. sec. 62.

Herodotus. Those commonly used by the Jews, after their establishment in Judea, were probably of the same kind. By them lamps formed—as at present in many other creeds and forms of worship—an important feature in their religious ceremonies. The golden lamp-stand, or, as it is rendered, 'candlestick,' was one of the sacred utensils made by Moses to be placed in the Jewish tabernacle. It was made of hammered gold, a talent in weight. It consisted of seven branches supported by a base or foot. These branches were adorned at equal distances with six flowers like lilies, and with as many bowls and knobs placed alternately. Upon the stock and branches of the candlestick were the golden lamps, which were immeveable, wherein were put oil and cotton. These seven lamps were lighted every evening, and extinguished every morning. They had their tongs or snuffers to draw the cotton in or out, and dishes under them to receive the sparks or droppings of the oil. This candlestick was placed in the antechamber of the sanctuary, on the south side, and served to illuminate the altar of perfume and the tabernacle of the show-bread. When Solomon had built the temple of the Lord, he placed in it ten golden candlesticks of the same form as that described by Moses—five on the north, and five on the south side of the holy place; but after the Babylonish captivity, the golden candlestick was again placed in the temple as it had been before in the tabernacle by Moses. This sacred utensil, upon the destruction of the Jewish temple by the Romans, was lodged in the temple of peace built by Vespasian; and the representation of it is still to be seen on the triumphal arch at the foot of Mount Palatine, on which Vespasian's triumph is delineated.

Except in the shape and fashion of lamps, no improvement of any importance was made in their construction. Up to a recent period, the principle of the lamp was the same, consisting of an oil vessel—generally open—with a sort of spout along which a wick of rush, pith, or cotton was laid, to conduct the oil to the flame. A vast number of these lamps have been found amongst the remains of Pompeii, Herculaneum, and other places, some having elegant, and others grotesque shapes; according, of course, to the places they were designed to illuminate. They were applied to three principal uses:—First, for religious rites in temples, or for festivals, for both the Egyptians and the Athenians celebrated certain festivals by means of public illuminations. Secondly, lamps were deposited in sepulchres; but their chief use was, thirdly, in domestic life. These, among the Romans, were mostly of *terra cotta*, and bronze; but golden, silver, glass, and even marble lamps, are mentioned by various authors. Those of terra cotta were usually of a long, round form, flat, and without feet; but when expensive materials were used, more elaborate forms were adopted. At the orifice for pouring in the oil, a mythological figure was designed in relief. Sometimes the whole lamp consisted of an elegant or a grotesque figure. In the Gentleman's Magazine for 1751, there are several plates of very curious Roman lamps. The stand of one is formed by a representation of a fowl's leg and claws supporting the bust of a man with his mouth open, out of which protrudes the wick of the lamp. Another is a sandaled foot, with a hole in the nail of the great toe for the burner. The heads of all sorts of animals were fashioned for lamps, and indeed every object which presented an orifice out of which a flame might naturally or unnaturally be made to issue. One of the prettiest of these designs is that of a Mercury crouching behind the stump of a hollow tree; from the hollow proceeds the light, and the figure is represented as kindling the flame by blowing with his breath.

Roman domestic lamps (*lucernæ*) were either suspended by chains from the ceiling, or stood on candelabra. These are perhaps amongst the most elegant objects which have been spared to us by antiquity. They were very tall, and consisted of three and sometimes four pieces—the foot, the shaft, and the *discus* or plate. The slender shaft was usually fluted, and rested on three feet of animals, above which was some leaf ornament; it terminated in a capital, on which was a kind of vase, covered by the plate bearing the lamp. Sometimes a head or figure was above the capital, and supported the plate. The candelabra produced at Ægina and Tarentum were especially remarkable for the beauty of their workmanship, and each place signalised itself in the construction of certain parts. Some have a second plate immediately above the foot, and are beautifully ornamented. There were also Corinthian ones, as they were called, which sold at high prices; but Pliny denies that they are genuine. There were also candelabra so constructed that the lamps could be raised or lowered; in these the shaft was hollow, and into it a staff was fitted; this bore the plate, and had several holes, into which a pin could be inserted. In some, the animal's feet could be laid together by a hinge attached, and it seems to have been thus made for use on a journey: it was only three palms five inches high, but could be lengthened if necessary. There were also four other sorts of candelabra, in which the simple shaft became either a statue holding a torch, from which the lamp burned, or above which two arms were raised, holding the plate; or the shaft was changed into a column, whereon a Moor's head served as a lamp. But still more numerous are those called *lampadaria*; they are stems of trees, or pillars standing on a base, from the capital of which the lamps were suspended. But these must not be confounded with the *lychnuchi* mentioned by Pliny, as he was describing something unusual; and the *lychnuchi pensiles* may perhaps be compared to our chandeliers.*

The lamp, either hung from the ceiling of the apartment, or placed on one of these superb stands, was filled with vegetable oil by means of vessels very like modern butter-boats, and called *infrondibula*. The wick was either of hemp, flax, or the leaves of a kind of verbascum or lungwort, whence this plant is sometimes called torch-weed. A lamp is said to have been found at Stabiæ, with the wick still preserved. Instruments for snuffing were fastened by a chain to the lamp, together with small pincers for raising the wick; though, when the lamp was in the form of a human figure, these instruments were held in its hand.

When lighted, nothing but constant wont and habit could have made the smoke and smell of the lamp tolerable to the ancients. Their faces and clothes—especially at a feast where an unusual number of lights were employed—became blackened; and a Roman beauty could hardly retain her charms long after the commencement of a night festival. The gorgeous ornaments of the rooms were also damaged from the same cause; and Vitruvius directs, in his work on architecture, that, to hide the unsightly stains of smoke, the panels should be black, with red and yellow margins, and polished, so that the smut may be readily removed by servants. Various efforts were made from time to time to do away with the inconvenience, but they never thought of having glass chimneys. Candles were resorted to; and, indeed, the candelabra were originally made to hold them, though, from the imperfect manner in which the *candelæ* were manufactured, they were replaced by lamps. Rushes and papyrus fibres, smeared over with wax or tallow, were in use for temporary purposes—for lighting lamps, or for going from one chamber to another. Becker, in his admirable classical novel of 'Gallus,' makes his hero return home late at night, and is received by his freed-man, Chresimus, who 'proceeded to light a wax candle at one of the lamps, and led the way through the saloons and colonnades to the sleeping apartment of his lord.' According to Pliny, wax and tallow candles were employed in religious offices, and they have continued to be so used ever since. In the twelfth century, wax candles, some of them of great length and thickness, were generally seen in Roman Catholic churches, smaller ones being upheld in chandeliers; the lighting, trimming, and putting out of

* See Becker's 'Gallus,' translated by Frederick Metcalfe, B. A.

which, being occasionally performed as a religious rite. Thus, there was the process of excommunicating by inch of candle: the sinner was summoned to appear at the lighting of a small piece of candle, and was allowed to come to repentance while it continued burning; but should he neglect to present himself before the candle went out, he remained finally excommunicated. To this practice is traced the custom of auction sales 'by the candle,' which is still in vogue, especially in seaports. When the merchandise is put up for sale, the bystanders are allowed to bid while a small piece of candle remains ignited, but when it goes out, the 'lot' is adjudged to the last bidder.

As refinement increased, candles were gradually introduced from sacred to private edifices, and used for domestic purposes, almost to the exclusion of lamps. They have remained pretty much the same for centuries; consisting chiefly of cotton wicks surrounded by tallow or wax. Even those made with all the improvements of modern science are expensive, and give very little light; but those still used in countries into which such improvements have not penetrated, are only calculated to make darkness visible. The following picture of a room in Cairo at night, presents as cheerless an aspect as an apartment must have done in Europe during what we call 'the dark ages:'—Mr Lane, in his 'Modern Egyptians,' informs us that the light of one or two candles, placed on the floor, or on a stool, and sometimes surrounded by a large glass shade, or enclosed in a glass lantern, on account of the windows being merely of lattice-work, is generally thought sufficient for a large and lofty saloon. In the winter, the saloon is quite as sombre, for, as there is no fireplace, it is warmed by a brasier, or chafing-dish (called *mankal*), made of tinned copper, full of burning charcoal, placed on the floor, into which perfume is occasionally thrown. The Egyptians take great delight in perfumes, and often fumigate their apartments, most commonly with frankincense, benzoin or cascarilla bark, and aloes wood; ambergris is rarely used on account of its costliness. The wood is moistened before being placed on the charcoal.

We must now describe the manner in which artificial light is produced. So little commonplace will this information be, that we believe there are comparatively few persons who know upon what principle illumination from the lamps or candles which they are so constantly using is effected.

'Every light is a gas-light; with this simple difference, that coal gas is made at a distance from the burner, whilst candles and lamps manufacture their gas *at* the burner. Oil or tallow cannot take fire, unless previously volatilised by heat, which is effected by means of the wick, through the fibres of which the melted tallow or wax rises, in consequence of capillary attraction. The wick, itself easily inflamed by another ignited body, when lighted, heats the oil to a degree which brings it to the condition of vapour or gas, and that igniting as it rises, supplies the flame. The oil first raised and volatilised is in this manner dissipated by combustion; more succeeds to fill its place, and thus a constant combustion is kept up. A candle, however, differs from a lamp in a very essential circumstance. The oil of the lamp is always fluid, and only requires to be boiled into vapour by the heat of the wick; but the tallow, being at first solid, has first to be liquefied and brought into the state of oil. That which is in the vicinity of the wick is first melted, and the external rim of the candle not being rendered fluid, a cup is thus formed which contains the melted portion. The melted tallow or oil being boiled by the flame into the state of vapour, ascends in a column, and, being heated to a high temperature, it combines rapidly with the oxygen of the surrounding atmosphere, the heat evolved being so great as to cause the vapour to be white hot, and very luminous, thus constituting visible flame. But the combustion that occasions this can only take place in that part of the column of hot vapour which is in contact with the atmosphere, namely, the exterior surface. The flame of a candle or lamp, then, is not solid throughout, but is only a thin film of white hot vapour, enclosing a quantity of heated vapour, which, for want of oxygen, is incapable of attaining the greatest degree of heat in burning. In other words, it is only the vapour which rises from the outside of the wick, which, coming in contact with the atmosphere, takes up from it sufficient oxygen to cause ignition. That in the inside of the flame not being immediately supplied with oxygen, rises unburnt from the centre of the wick in the form of smoke. By a pretty experiment, it is possible to extract the unburnt vapour from the centre of the flame, and to inflame it. Procure a piece of a small glass tube, having a bore of an eighth of an inch; insert the end of it dexterously into the dark part of the flame where the hollow is supposed to be, and the unburnt vapour will ascend through the tube, and may be set fire to at the top by a piece of lighted paper, forming a smaller flame of the same kind as the first.'* Exactly upon this principle coal gas is manufactured and conducted through pipes.

Candles no sooner came into general domestic use, than their superiority over the oil lamps of old was found so great, that up to a recent period no other light was so much used. Still, they have their faults, and though these are trifling, they are felt to be extremely inconvenient in this age of luxurious comfort. Tallow candles, especially, constantly require to be snuffed; their light, therefore, is uncertain. Wax candles, which require no snuffing, are too expensive for general use; hence numerous compositions have been made, meant to combine the conveniences of wax with the cheapness of tallow; such as spermaceti, stearine, &c. Comparatively, *all* candles are expensive, considering the small quantity of light each gives, and there always has been a desire to readopt lamps, so improved as to make house-lighting a cheaper process. For this reason an immense aggregate of mechanical ingenuity has been from time to time expended upon the construction of lamps, so as to render them fit for domestic purposes.

Yet from the earliest times to 1780, no serviceable improvement was made; but in that year M. Argand, a native of Geneva, promulgated an invention of great advantage. It has been before explained, that the interior of an ordinary flame consists of gas which is not inflamed, because it is debarred from mixing with the oxygen of the atmosphere. Argand, therefore, caused a circular wick to be constructed, so burnt in a hollow burner, that the air not only came to the outside, but also to the inside of the flame; a draught of air being produced by a glass chimney, which, protecting the flame from draughts, caused little or no smoke. So excellent was this principle proved to be, that every succeeding inventor made it a basis of improvement, few attempting to adopt any other sort of burner; their ingenuity being chiefly expended on other parts of the lamp. The most elegant improvement was the annular table lamp, the oil reservoir of which consisting of a circular tube placed below the light, casts comparatively no shadow,† which all lamps upon the old construction did. The rays of light were the more equally diffused by the intervention of a large ground-glass shade.

The chief objections to the best lamps are the difficulty of keeping them in order, from a constant clogging of the burner and ducts, and the expense of oil, the very best of which can only be used in them with success. A late inventor has introduced a lamp in which cheap oil may be burnt, by causing it to be heated before rising to the flame. The cistern in this case is contained in a tube which immediately surrounds the upper part of the flame, so that while it is burning, the oil is kept hot, and the more readily volatilised when

* Cyclopædia of Domestic Economy, p. 123.

† This sort of lamp, much improved, is called the sinumbra (*sine umbra*, no shade) lamp.

taken up by the wick. Another very clever, because simple invention, is that called the solar lamp. A cap is placed upon the burner, so as to cause a great draught of air to discharge itself at the bottom of the flame, keeping up a constant supply of oxygen. Common oil in this lamp burns with little smoke, and if the best oil be used, the smoke is hardly perceptible.

To enumerate a tithe of the light-giving inventions which have been made during the last fifty years, would occupy a vast amount of space and patience. We can only add, therefore, that bituminous substances have been used to manufacture inflammable fluids as substitutes for oil, such as naphtha. An essential oil called camphine has been lately introduced, and employed, in a lamp made expressly to burn it, with success.

A singular fate has attended most of these inventions. When they first appear, their patrons and purchasers are in a sort of rapture at their apparent perfection. They are employed for a certain time with gratification to the customer and profit to the inventor; but in a little while, some little fault not evinced at first makes its appearance, the charm of the invention gradually disappears, and the disappointed housekeeper returns to candles. One or two of the lamps we have enumerated have, however, maintained a very good reputation.

Good coal gas, conducted from the manufactory by means of metal pipes to the place of burning, appears to supply every desideratum; but the difficulty of procuring it pure, combined with a strong prejudice against it, has retarded its introduction into English private houses. In the large towns of Scotland, however, gas is all but universally in use for domestic illumination. The coal from which it is made being better adapted for its manufacture than that used in English gasometers, renders it of a better quality; though the great improvements which have been made of late in the purifying process have so greatly bettered the quality of English gas, that private families are gradually adopting it. The advantages of gas light are thus summed up in the Cyclopædia of Domestic Economy:—'Its cheapness, compared with any other, when much light is required; the vast saving of the time and labour that would be necessary for cleaning and trimming lamps, or in cleaning candlesticks and snuffing candles, together with the constant attendance required for these operations. Gas lights are perfectly cleanly, and are not accompanied with the dropping of grease and spilling of oil which accompany the other modes of lighting. They may likewise be easily conveyed by pipes to situations where it would be difficult to fix any other lights. When the gas is managed in the best way, the light is extremely agreeable, and the smoke which always proceeds from candles is avoided. No sparks fly off to set houses on fire, and when artificial light is not required, by stopping off the gas from the main pipe, no escape and after-explosion need be dreaded. The chief objection to gas is its want of portability.'

In reference to economy, Dr Ure's experiments have determined the following facts:—If a certain quantity of light from tallow candles cost 1s., an equal quantity from an Argand lamp will cost $6\frac{1}{2}$d., and from gas $2\frac{3}{4}$d.

N. P. WILLIS'S DASHES AT LIFE.

The Pencillings by the Way of our American friend Mr Willis made some noise in England. Many exclaimed against the liberties taken with private life, but all felt the charm of the lively description. Perhaps there never was a better thing of its kind than the account of the morning at Gordon Castle. Since then, the American attaché has been pursuing a literary career in his native country, and occasionally making himself heard of on this side of the water. He is a magazine-writer of the first mark—sharp, rattling, superficial, and all this with the twang of his country's peculiarities.

On the present occasion, he gives the British public three volumes of his magazine papers, and three amusing volumes they are.* Here and there we find ourselves at fault with some New York or Massachusetts refinement of humour; now and then there is a dash of—we must say it—vulgarity; but the book is nevertheless a capital afternoon one, for one thing Mr Willis has covenanted never to be—dull. In 'Passages from a Correspondence Written at New York,' we find him describing a plan for a novel kind of hotel, of the kind which grow out to such luxuriance in America:—'I understand it has lately occurred to some gentlemen with open eyes, that anchorage is cheaper than ground-rent—that a ship of war is but a spacious hotel upside down, and that the most desirable site for a summer residence, as to pure air, neighbourhood, novelty, and economy, is now occupied by the Independence and North Carolina, the men-of-war just off the battery. The latter ship being unseaworthy, it is proposed to purchase her of the government for the experiment. It is estimated that she can accommodate comfortably three hundred persons. The immense upper-deck is to be covered with a weather-proof awning, blue and white, in the style of the Alhambra, and given up entirely to dining, dancing, lounging, and the other uses of hotel drawing-rooms. A more magnificent promenade than this immense deck, cleared of guns and lumber fore and aft, and surrounded entirely by luxurious sofas, could scarcely be imagined. The kitchens and offices are to occupy the forward part of the second deck, or, if the vessel is crowded, to be transferred to a small tender alongside. The port-holes are to be enlarged to spacious windows, and the two decks below, which are above the water-line, will be entirely occupied by splendid rooms, open to the entire breadth of the bay, and furnished in the Oriental and cushioned style, suitable to the luxurious wants of hot weather. Minute barges will ply to and from the shore, connected with the Waverley line of omnibuses; bath-houses will be anchored just astern; a café and ice-cream shop will be established in the main and mizen-tops (to be reached by a covered staircase); and sofas, for the accommodation of smokers, will be put under a pent-house roof, outside the vessel, in the main-chains. The cockpit and hold will of course take the uses of a hotel garret and cellar. It will have the advantage of other hotels, in swinging round with the tide, so that the lodgers on both sides of the ship will see, by turns, from the windows the entire panorama of the bay. When lightened of her guns, and her upper spars and rigging, it is thought she will float so much higher as to bear piercing for another line of port-hole windows, affording some bachelors' rooms at the water-line, corresponding in price and convenience with the sky-chambers of the Astor. An eccentric individual, I am told, has bargained for a private parlour, to be suspended under the bowsprit, in imitation of the nest of the hanging-bird. Altogether, the scheme seems charming and feasible. The name of the hotel, by the way, is to be "Saratoga Afloat;" the waiters are to be dressed in the becoming toggery of tars; and the keeper of the house is to wear a folded napkin, epaulette fashion, on either shoulder, and to be called invariably "commodore."'

The light tales in this book we can only speak of as sparkling and clever; passages from them would be of no avail. The manner in which Mr Willis tells a story may, however, be conceived from a passage in a sketch called 'Mr Goggins.' This person is an American tradesman, who, suddenly enriched, goes to Paris with his family, and commences a brilliant style of life, in which he secures general admiration purely by the efficacy of 'plain business tact.' 'Perhaps we should,' says the author, 'give more credit to this faculty in Goggins. It is possibly not far removed from the genius of a great financier or eminent state treasurer. It is the power of coming directly at values, and ridding them of their

* Dashes at Life with a Free Pencil. By N. P. Willis. 3 vols. London: Longman and Co. 1845.

"riders"—of getting for less what others from want of penetration get for more. I am inclined to think Goggins would have been quite as successful in any other field of calculation, and one instance of a very different application of his reasoning powers would go to favour the belief.

'While in Italy, he employed a celebrated but improvident artist to paint a picture, the subject of which was a certain event, of rather a humble character, in which he had been an actor. The picture was to be finished at a certain time, and at the urgent plea of the artist the money was advanced. The time expired, and the picture was not sent home, and the forfeited bond of the artist was accordingly put in suit. The delinquent, who had not thought twice of the subject, addressed one or two notes of remonstrance to his summary employer, and receiving no reply, and the law crowding very closely upon his heels, he called upon Goggins and appealed, among other arguments, to the difference in their circumstances, and the indulgent pity due from rich to poor.

'"Where do you dine to-day?" asked Goggins. "To-day—let me see—Monday—I dine with Lady ——." (The artist, as Goggins knew, was a favourite in the best society in Florence.) "And where did you dine yesterday?" "Yesterday—hum—yesterday I dined with Sir George ——. No! I breakfasted with Sir George, and dined with the grand chamberlain. Excuse me! I have so many engagements ——." "Ah!—and you are never at a loss for a dinner or a breakfast?" The artist smiled. "No!" "Are you well lodged?" "Yes—on the Arno." "And well clad, I see." (The painter was rather a dandy withal.)

'"Well, sir!" said Goggins, folding up his arms, and looking sterner than before, "you have, as far as I can understand it, every luxury and comfort which a fortune could procure you, and none of the care and trouble of a fortune, and you enjoy these advantages by a claim which is not liable to bankruptcy, nor to be squandered, nor burnt—without the slightest anxiety, in short."

'The artist assented.

'"So far, there is no important difference in our worldly condition, except that I have this anxiety and trouble, and am liable to these very casualties." Goggins paused, and the painter nodded again. "And now, sir, over and above this, what would you take to exchange with me the esteem in which we are severally held—you to become the rich, uneducated, and plain Simon Goggins, and I to possess your genius, your elevated tastes, and the praise and fame which these procure you?" The artist turned uneasily on his heels. "No, sir!" continued Goggins; "you are not a man to be pitied, and least of all by me. And I don't pity you, sir. And what's more, you shall paint that picture, sir, or go to prison. Good morning, sir."

'And the result was a painting, finished in three days, and one of the masterpieces of that accomplished painter; for he embodied, in the figure and face of Goggins, the character which he had struck out so unexpectedly—retaining the millionaire's friendship and patronage, though never again venturing to trifle with his engagements.'

We conclude with another very brief extract, where some of Mr Willis's English recollections are drawn upon. 'The covered promenade of the Burlington Arcade is, on rainy days, a great allure for a small chop-house hard by, called "The Blue Posts." This is a snug little tavern, with the rear of its two storeys cut into a single dining-room, where chops, steaks, ale, and punch may be had in unusual perfection. It is frequented ordinarily by a class of men peculiar, I should think, to England—taciturn, methodical in their habits, and highly respectable in their appearance—men who seem to have no amusements and no circle of friends, but who come in at six, and sit over their punch and the newspapers till bed-time, without speaking a syllable, except to the waiter, and apparently turning a cold shoulder of discouragement to any one in the room who may be disposed to offer a passing remark. They hang their hats daily on the same peg, daily sit at the same table (where the chair is turned down for them by "Villiam," the short waiter), daily drink a small pitcher of punch after their half-pint of sherry, and daily read, from beginning to end, the Herald, Post, and Times, with the variation of the Athenæum and Spectator on Saturdays and Sundays. I at first hazarded various conjectures as to their condition in life. They were evidently unmarried, and men of easy though limited means—men of no great care, and no high hopes, and in a fixed station; yet of that degree of intelligence and firm self-respect which, in other countries (the United States, certainly, at least), would have made them sought for in some more social and higher sphere than that with which they seemed content. I afterward obtained something of a clue to the mystery of the "Blue Posts" society, by discovering two of the most respectable-looking of its customers in the exercise of their daily vocations. One—a man of fine phrenological development, rather bald, and altogether very intellectual in his "*os sublime*"—I met at the rooms of a fashionable friend, taking his measure for pantaloons. He was the foreman of a celebrated Bond Street tailor. The other was the head shopman of a famous haberdasher in Regent Street; and either might have passed for Godwin the novelist, or Babbage the calculator—with those who had seen those great intellects only in their imaginations. It is only in England that men who, like these, have read or educated themselves far above their situations in life, would quietly submit to the arbitrary disqualifications of their pursuits, and agree unresistingly to the sentence of exile from the society suited to their mental grade.' The truth of this remark must be recognised by all who have looked below the surface of that mass of artificial life which constitutes London.

MESSRS CHAMBERS'S SOIRÉE.

(From the Glasgow Citizen—with additions.)

On the evening of Wednesday last (6th August), the annual soirée or entertainment given by Messrs W. and R. Chambers to the numerous persons in their employment, took place in the large Waterloo Room, Edinburgh, which was appropriately fitted up for the occasion. The manner in which the tables were disposed was somewhat peculiar, and deserves to be mentioned. Instead of a platform for the speakers being placed at one end, there was a platform ranged along one side, in the centre of which was the seat for the chairman, while in front of it tables were radiated like a fan, so that all could see and hear, and be at the same time in the eye of the speakers. On the opposite side of the room was a similar platform and seat for the vice-chairman. When we entered, shortly after six o'clock, we were struck with the elegant appearance of the company, albeit the greater number belonged to the operative class, as well as with the neatness of the arrangements and decorations. On a raised stage opposite the door, Spindler's band was booming forth a favourite national air; but our attention was soon distracted by the entrance of the givers of the entertainment, Mr William Chambers, who took his seat as chairman, and Mr Robert Chambers, who acted as vice-chairman. Both sat down amidst loud bursts of applause, and the congratulations of the numerous friends who supported them on either side.

After tea and coffee being served, Mr William Chambers rose and spoke as follows:—Ladies and Gentlemen—It is my duty to open the business of the present meeting by mentioning its objects and character. This is the eighth annual soirée or entertainment given by my brother and myself to the persons in our employment, now about 150 in number; besides whom, on the present occasion, there are a number of their and our friends, altogether forming a party of upwards of 300. Our object is now, as in former years, to unite the two classes of employers and employed in a friendly social meeting, with a view to the cultivation of a good spirit between the parties. This spirit it has always been our desire to promote, and that our efforts have not been thrown away is evidenced in the harmony which has prevailed for years, and still prevails, in our establishment. In addition to the ordinary payment for labour, my brother and I feel that we do no more than our duty in now tendering our best thanks for the diligence and good conduct displayed by all in our employment during the past twelve months—and not only so, but for the uniform courtesy and respect shown towards us, as well as those to whom more immediately belongs the superintendence of our affairs. And in doing so, I entertain a lively hope that nothing shall ever occur to mar the happy feeling that now subsists between us. Hitherto, it has been customary to give this entertainment in one of the halls of our printing-office; but that is no longer possible or convenient, in consequence of the growth of our numbers and the extension of our business. We regret the change, for there was something extremely interesting in finding ourselves seated at the social board amidst the very scenes of our daily industry. It has, however, been unavoidable, and I can only express my hope that the meeting in this public room will be marked as much by the spirit of peace and good-will as our former assemblages. It has been customary for me, in opening proceedings, to bring forward a sort of budget of the operations of the year. I do not know whether this be quite right, seeing that it is somewhat egotistical; yet I daresay it may, after all, not be the worst way of entertaining you for one or two minutes, to present to you a statement of our recent operations. You are of course aware that we print and otherwise prepare nothing but our own works, and such has latterly been the increased demand for these productions, that we have, during the last six months, doubled the extent of our premises. We now accommodate ten printing-machines, driven by a steam-engine of from ten to twelve horse-power, and calculate on being able to print and send forth 50,000 sheets daily. During the past year, for a part of which we had only five machines, we have printed altogether twelve millions of sheets, and thus used about twenty-five thousand reams of paper. Among the works absorbing this mass of paper, the leading one has been the *Miscellany of Useful and Entertaining Tracts*, the average circulation of which has been 159,000 weekly, while of some particular numbers not fewer than 240,000 have been sold. The next place is taken by the *Journal*, the oldest of our publications, which averages 88,000 weekly. The remainder of the account is made up by reprints of our *Information for the People*, *Cyclopædia of English Literature*, and *Educational Course*. Such a vast diffusion of literary matter is of course a novelty in the world, and may be pointed to as an undeniable proof of the activity of mind in our time among the middle and humbler classes. I cannot but feel pleasure in the reflection that, as far as our abilities permit, the whole of this literary mass is fraught with beneficial objects. We seek, while entertaining mankind, also to instruct and moralise them—to elevate each reader a step higher in the moral and intellectual scale. Every new idea that appears likely to lessen the sufferings or promote the happiness of our race, is sure of encouragement from us. It must be known to you that our *Journal* and other publications are carried on without the aid of sect, party, or association of any kind. Trusting to our own pens and our own purposes, with such literary assistance as could be obtained, we have addressed the human heart, and have there found a response which enables us to pursue our course. Convinced that in literature, as in everything else, integrity and independence of principle are the soundest policy, it is our resolution to continue to avoid all sectarian or controversial topics, and to address ourselves to all sects, all parties, all races, on one common ground of enlarged humanity, leaving to others what they may further believe to be necessary.' Mr Chambers concluded by referring to various arrangements connected with their establishment designed to render the men comfortable, in particular a library for their free and daily use. He then in a feeling manner called up several boys to receive prizes for good conduct, which were distributed amidst much applause.

Among the other proceedings of the evening was a reply from the working-men of the establishment, delivered by Mr Daniel Anderson, one of the compositors.

'Mr Chairman—The recurrence of the present festal occasion brings me before you as representing the various individuals composing the establishment of Messrs Chambers, to respond to those sentiments of affectionate kindness which have just fallen from our respected chairman; and to express our ardent desire, that such declarations of reciprocal regard may not merely be exchanged between us on such occasions as the present, but that each individual in this large and increasing establishment—from its more important functionaries to the most humble and obscure of its members—individually imbibing the spirit which has pervaded the address of Mr Chambers, may henceforth resolve to conduct himself towards those with whom he is associated in the business of this establishment, as to impress more thoroughly upon our hearts, by seeing it run through all our actions, the interesting and humanising truth of the 'brotherhood of man.' This truth it is the object of such meetings as the present, if not to *create*, at least to cherish and perpetuate. And by making it thus to appear as a principle tinging our external behaviour, we will learn that, in the prosecution of what is sometimes called the 'every-day business of life,' there is a possibility of doing it in such a manner as to manifest it is not mere *duty* in which we are engaged, but as affording scope for the exercise of a principle by which we not only impart, but also simultaneously receive, good of a very salutary nature; that good which you, our employers, have sought in years past, and do still seek to find existing among the various individuals in your establishment, as also among the various classes into which society is divided; we mean, the principle which leads men to respect and esteem each other, so as to live peaceably together. Need we say, in accordance with this remark, that we congratulate you upon the success which has attended your literary exertions during so many past years, but especially during the one just drawing to a close; insomuch as to compel you greatly to extend your premises, and to increase the number of your servants.

'That the success of your various undertakings in periodical literature is to be ascribed at once to their cheapness, and, generally speaking, their adaptation to that class of the community for whose benefit they are intended, we do not doubt; indeed the voice of our country has removed all grounds for such doubt, in the liberal patronage it has bestowed upon your efforts. In this respect, our present meeting has a very important and interesting aspect over all former ones; for we thought the name of the Messrs Chambers had already been rendered sufficiently familiar and honourable to every man in the country, as standing associated with the Journal, the Information for the People, and the Cyclopædia of English Literature; but to-night we have listened to their doings for another year, and the result is such as to excite in us feelings of surprise and delight.

That these periodicals, to which we have referred, in connexion with the Miscellany of Useful and Entertaining Tracts, have been the means of informing the minds and improving the hearts of our fellow-workmen, and so preventing numbers of them from resorting to more vicious indulgences, is a fact which few will be disposed to call in question; and we could heartily wish that thousands more of them would become convinced of the superior, refined, and innocent pleasure derivable from association with a book in any one of the favourite departments of literature, as also of the immense advantage which would thereby accrue to themselves, to their families, and to society itself. Gentlemen, to be employed in dislodging from this stronghold of the mind those barriers to its expansion and profitable development—ignorance and superstition—is unquestionably a noble and patriotic vocation, worthy of the greatest efforts. So, by presenting to your readers select treatises upon the various branches of scientific knowledge, you serve to awaken feelings calculated to rouse them from that moral lethargy which too often envelopes the masses of mankind, and to afford the momentum which may afterwards induce them to a steady progression in the attainment of useful knowledge.

We have given expression to these simple thoughts, as being generally indicative of the benefits of such knowledge to the humble mechanic; as tending to raise him on the platform of intelligent existence; and as forming a useful recreation for his leisure hours. But education has also an extensive and powerful effect upon the civilisation of mankind. Enlighten the mind of the barbarian as to the true position he is intended to occupy in creation, and his capability of doing so after a little training; explain to him the true nature of the universe in which he is [illegible], of the nature of those laws by which it is governed, and the true principle of Theism, together with his relation to his brethren, and you have at least pioneered the way to [illegible] one of the most glorious revolutions of which we can conceive. Let in, for example, any of the truths of science upon the darkened mind, and you behold the soul of an intelligent being becoming sensible of its own inherent powers—struggling to burst those trammels which, when annihilated, usher him, delighted and astonished, into a new world, because you furnish him with a new optical medium through which to view it.

Finally, those privileges which we under your superintendence have now enjoyed for a number of years, and which have been already on former occasions duly acknowledged, we cannot refrain from noticing yet again, as their importance we continue to appreciate and value. We refer to our library, the seasonable time at which we receive our wages, the regularity of hours which most of us enjoy—a regularity which has only been interrupted by the extraordinary demand for the Miscellany and some other works, thus compelling you to extend our hours of labour to an *otherwise* inconvenient length; but which, we hope, the recent extension of your premises, and the increase you have found it necessary to make in your machinery and servants, will tend in a great measure, if not wholly, to supersede; the Saturday afternoons also, which, although the hours of freedom we then enjoy are made up during the other days of the week, we still reckon a great privilege, and long to see all the other establishments in the country put in possession of the same blessing. The encouragement you have also given to those two individuals in your employment who, in the spirit of true philanthropy, have devoted a portion of their time on the Sabbath evenings to the religious instruction of the junior members of the establishment, is worthy of present mention. For all these benefits we tender to you our sincere thanks, and conclude with expressing our hope that you may be still spared to continue your efforts in the dissemination of that information whose tendency is to remove ignorance and superstition from the human mind, and to aid in the progression of that enlightenment which, in co-operation with Christianity, is to effect the moral conquest and regeneration of the world, when the now somewhat trite, but beautiful sentence, shall have a complete embodiment in the actual affairs of life, 'Men shall beat their swords into ploughshares, and their spears into pruning-hooks; they shall hang their trumpets in their halls, and study war no more.'].

An address, or essay, on the condition of the working-classes was next delivered by Mr Robert Chambers.

[My friends—I would take this opportunity of making a few remarks on the condition and prospects of the working-classes. I mean to be very short, for this is not an occasion when patience is to be expected for long speeches or dissertations.

That discontent with their position and share of the profits of industry prevails very generally among the working-classes, is too obvious a fact to require being here insisted on. It is less heard of at present than it was two or three years ago, because at present almost every man fit for work is in good employment, and there is accordingly little immediate sense of hardship. But the existence of a deep and settled feeling of discontent is nevertheless true, and it is to this that I am to address myself on the present occasion. Now, I not only admit the fact of the discontent, but I believe that it is not without cause. But I think, at the same time, that there is a right as well as a wrong way of expounding and arguing upon the case of the working-classes, as against the rest of society, and the employing class in particular. I also believe that much of what the working-classes complain of is essentially connected with the present state of society, and only can be remedied by favour of certain social improvements which it will require time to effect. The arrangements between masters and their people partake of that imperfection which may be said to characterise all existing institutions, through the ignorance and prejudices of man, and which it is the grand object of the wise and good of this age to remove.

The position of the working-classes is now, like many other things, in a transition state. They were once slaves, afterwards retainers; now they are free workmen. This is the highest point which they have as yet been able to reach in any country; but we may fairly expect that this is not to be their ultimatum. It cannot be—if they improve, and society improve with them. It is common to express doubts if the last move of the workers, namely, that from the retainer to the free operative, has been an improvement. I would class this notion with that which asserts the beatitude of our quondam West India slaves, and deplores their being brought to the miseries attendant upon emancipation. It seems sad for the working-man to lack that kindly protection which he enjoyed from his feudal master. Such protection, I grant, was well in its own time, when there could be nothing better. But does it never occur to the scions of Young England that there is a very alarming resemblance between the protection which a baron extended to his servants, and that which he extended to the animals which equally served him, his horses, and his dogs? Do they not see that, when one man assumes even the position of a protector over another, he degrades that other person? For my part, I am totally unable to see what right any human being has to act the protector towards another. No—upon all such relations as this, I cannot but think the present position of the independent labourer a great improvement. Ten times rather let me have my stipulated wages and no more—even though I never once interchange a word with my master—than have him pretending to a right to take care of me, as if, forsooth, I were such a child as to be unable to take care of myself. In the one condition, the manly virtues must shrink and die; the other tends to elicit self-reliance, and is the needful step to something better. There may, however, be much kindly feeling between employers and the most independent of labourers. My brother and I, for example, while we respect the independence of our co-operators, are not on that account the less friendly with them. I believe, on the contrary, that there is a purer kind of good-will between us, from the very fact that each party is independent of the other. Our mutual good feelings are the more nearly those which exist between equals in the common world. Any interchange of civility stands the more clear of all imagination of an inferior motive.

I regard, then, the position of the independent working-man as a point in progress. It is something better than anything which has been before, wanting, no doubt, some of those pleasant-looking features which marked the condition of the retainer, but more than making up for this by peculiarities of its own; anyhow, it is a point in progress. Now, the first question is, in what light are we to regard this position? It seems to me that the great error of those who write upon the subject, is in treating it as a final position, as if the system of HIRE were a thing so perfect, that it could never be changed for anything else, and as if we had nothing to do but consider by what means the relation of hirer and hired could be made as agreeable to both parties, and as fruitful of good results, as possible. To me, the fact that workers have gone through various phases, already denotes that they are only now going through another phase, and that there are still other phases through which to pass. The world is altogether a system of flux and change. Nothing stands still: new combinations and developments are constantly taking place. With fresh generations come fresh ideas, and dogmas in political and moral philosophy, which are the worship of one age, become the scoff of another. I therefore expect that amongst the improvements of the future, there is to be one regarding the relations of the directors and the executors of labour. To obtain some notion of what this is to be, the readiest course is to consider what are the leading defects and evils of the present arrangements, for it will be in the removal of these that the chief change will take place.

What I think is mainly to be complained of in the present system is, that it tends to send off the hirers and hired in two different directions—the one towards a high intellectual tension and an elevated moral state, along with the possession of great wealth and the consequent enjoyment of great luxury, and the other towards a condition the reverse in all respects. The master, exposed to so many risks, obliged to watch every opportunity of obtaining any advantage in the mercantile world, his mind kept ever on the stretch to devise the most economical means of conducting his operations, necessarily has his faculties called into high exercise. The opportunities he has for the profitable employment of additional capital, prompt him to be self-denying and prudent, even for the better gratification of his acquisitiveness; and thus he advances as a moral being, and as a man of wealth at the same time. How stands it, on the other hand, with the working-man? He has a limited and monotonous range of duties. His intellectual resources are accordingly not brought into full use. Or he is condemned to severe physical exertion, which leaves the mind languid and inert, and thus equally he remains in a low intellectual state. To state the matter in perhaps its least unpleasant shape, the master is often oppressed with his intellectual duties, while the mind of the workman is starved for want of anything beyond routine to occupy it. Workmen, again, having in general a fixed position and income, and hardly any expectation of ever rising out of it, are not under the same temptations which the masters are, to pursue a frugal and self-denying course, and to cultivate character. Human nature has not such fair-play in their case. It wants the moral land-marks, beacons, and paradises of reward which are planted around the course of the master. Generally speaking, the working-men of a country will be of the average intellect. Here, then, we have the ordinary grade of intellects placed by a mere social arrangement—an institution of man's making—in the circumstances least favourable to moral development and edification. And does not the actual state of matters tally only too well with these assumed causes? There surely can be no offence in saying that, while there is one class of workmen, such as our own here assembled, who conduct themselves respectably, and actually are at this moment tending upwards, there is a still larger class who give themselves little trouble about decent appearances, or anything beyond the gratification of immediate sensual wants. I see the condition of this class, and also such causes for it, that blame on the general point is out of the question; we must feel that we are called upon, not to rebuke or condemn, but, by subtracting the cause, to abolish the effects. We may preach for ever about the want of foresight and prudence in this class, but till we place them in favourable instead of unfavourable circumstances, we shall make no great progress in their reformation.

My idea is, that, through the general progress of the nation in moral conditions, and the particular progress of the working-classes themselves, not even excepting the least promising section of them, we shall in time reach a point when the Independent Worker will advance into something more dignified still. He will pass into a new phase, as much in advance from the present as the present is an advance from the retainer, or the retainer from the slave. I foretell this change, because I have such a faith in the reason and benevolence comprised in our nature, that I believe every error in social polity, and every obstacle to the perfect harmony of man with man, must in time be removed. In the new state, the workers would need to have a more particular interest in the success of the concerns with which they are connected. Their application, their skill, their good behaviour, would need to depend, not on the present inducements, which I think inadequate for the generality, but on their sense of their own particular interests. Their fate should be, like that of masters, expressly dependent, and that to the minutest degree, on the way they acted. Thus we might expect their moral and intellectual being to be fully developed. The condition of masters or directors of labour would also be improved; for though there might be less of mere command, there would be more of mutual kindness, and all harassment about the duty of the worker would be spared, as each man would be a master's eye to himself.

As, in order to attain this means of a large advance, there must in the first place be a certain lesser advance through the operation of weaker causes, we are not to look for any change as to be immediately realised, except, perhaps, in partial experiments under unusually favourable circumstances. Men are naturally prepossessed for what *is*, in preference to what only *might be*. Nor can they be instantly forced by any arguments out of such prejudices. We must wait for time to imbue them with better views, or to replace the old and impracticable with new and better men. We must wait till the workmen themselves have, through external moral means, been fitted for entering upon improved arrangements with their masters. Patience is necessary; for the life of the individual is in no relation whatever to the chronology of great moral revolutions. But is there not much in the meantime to make this lingering endurable? Everywhere throughout Britain, the attention of the best intellects is arrested by the condition of the masses. Evils are seen and acknowledged. Men, without regard to party or sect, express themselves with kindly sympathy regarding the sons of toil. The use of any ungracious language towards them, such as statesmen and wits indulged in fifty years ago, would now be resented by all. Measures are in contemplation for practical improvements both in the physical and moral state of the working-classes. It may indeed be said that the condition of these classes is the great question of this age: it is one which seems likely in a little while to absorb all others. Can we then doubt that the present system of things will, in the course of a few years, be visited with at least great ameliorations? There is here, surely, some consolation for the complaining parties; some reason why they should sit not altogether without trust and hope under the evils which they feel to be besetting their state. Even in that general moral advance which distinguishes the present age, they may read the promise of better things for themselves; for it is impossible that society at large could be much more humanised than it is, and yet admit of the present unsatisfactory relations between the industrious orders and the rest of the community.

I have now delivered myself of the thoughts which have for some time been in my mind with regard to the condition and prospects of the working-classes. To some they will appear visionary; to myself they might have done so a few years ago; but men are forced, by circumstances emerging in the course of time, to modify their views. I have thought it best to come frankly out with these ideas, such as they are; for, so presented, they at least convey to you a true sense of what one person, and he one to whom such matters are not new, has concluded upon with respect to a great question. I finish, therefore, by asking for my speculations that toleration which I am myself willing to allow to all those who think with sincere good intentions, and pronounce with candour and courtesy.]

Speeches of a fervid and cheering nature from Mr Simpson, the indefatigable friend of the working-classes, and by Mr Vincent on temperance, were given with the best effect; each address being followed by songs and instrumental music. A short but emphatic address from Mr W. Chambers, directed to the junior members of the establishment, concluded this very happy evening.

WILD FLOWERS.

'Tis fair to see our cultured buds their shining tints unfold,
In leaves that wear the sapphire's hue, or mock the sunset's gold;
The lily's grace, the rose's blush, have drawn the admiring gaze,
And won from many a minstrel harp the meed of song and praise;
Oh! they are meet for festal hall, or beauty's courtly bowers,
For those I love the wreath shall be, of wild and woodland flowers!

Bright clustering in the forest shades, or springing from the sod,
As flung from Eden, forth they come, fresh from the hand of God!
No human care hath nurtured them; the wild wind passeth by;
They flourish in the sunshine gleam and tempest-clouded sky;
And oh! like every gift that He, the bountiful, hath given,
Their treasures fall, alike to all, type of his promised heaven!

They bear to us sweet memories of childhood's happy years,
Ere grief had wrung the heart with pain, or dimmed the eye with tears;
They have been twined with playfulness round many a sunny brow,
Where costly pearls and Indian gems are proudly flashing now!
But hiding many a line of care beneath their gorgeous blaze,
That lurked not 'neath the wild flower wreath of youth's untroubled days!

Oh! chide not at the simple theme that wakes the minstrel's lay,
Earth were less bright without the flowers that blossom by the way:
He at whose word the universe her ancient might did yield,
Hath taught proud man a lesson from the lilies of the field.
I thank thee, God! for every boon thy hand in mercy showers,
And oh, not least among thy gifts, the beautiful wild flowers!

—*From an old newspaper.*

COMPASSION.

Compassion is an emotion of which we ought never to be ashamed. Graceful, particularly in youth, is the tear of sympathy, and the heart that melts at the tale of wo. We should not permit ease and indulgence to contract our affections, and wrap us up in a selfish enjoyment; but we should accustom ourselves to think of the distresses of human life, of the solitary cottage, the dying parent, and the weeping orphan. Nor ought we ever to sport with pain and distress in any of our amusements, or treat even the meanest insect with wanton cruelty.—*Dr Blair.*

Published by W. and R. Chambers, High Street, Edinburgh (also 98, Miller Street, Glasgow); and, with their permission, by W. S. Orr, Amen Corner, London.—Printed by Bradbury and Evans, Whitefriars, London.

CONDUCTED BY WILLIAM AND ROBERT CHAMBERS, EDITORS OF 'CHAMBERS'S INFORMATION FOR THE PEOPLE,' 'CHAMBERS'S EDUCATIONAL COURSE,' &c.

No. 89. NEW SERIES. SATURDAY, SEPTEMBER 13, 1845. PRICE 1½d.

THE URBANOS OF CENICERO.

THAT most dreadful of all national scourges, civil war, whilst it sets in turbulent motion the worst passions of human nature, and leaves society so saturated with its demoralising virus, that the paralysing effects are usually visible for a long period after the cessation of the armed struggle, has also frequently brought to light many noble qualities, and has produced deeds of heroism in resisting lawless attacks on domestic peace, or in defending institutions which the people feel to be essential to the honour, welfare, and security of their country.

The late fierce struggle in Spain—which was not merely a contest for the possession of a throne, but a hot dispute between antagonist political principles—afforded numerous examples of the bright as well as of the dark side of the picture.

It was in the autumn of 1834, when the Carlist rebellion had lasted more than a year, that the pretender's army began to assume an imposing attitude under the command of the celebrated chief Zumalacarreguy. The system of warfare adopted by that remarkable man was well calculated to strengthen the position of Don Carlos in a military point of view. At that early period of the civil war, the sturdy inhabitants of the Basque provinces and Navarre believed that their *fuéros*, or privileges, as well as their religious institutions, were in imminent peril, and that Don Carlos was the only means of salvation from such dreaded evils: they accordingly took up arms without hesitation against the queen's forces, and in every way aided and seconded the operations of Zumalacarreguy; supplying his troops with provisions and resources of every description, and adopting those efficacious means of harassing and attacking the enemy, which their mountainous country enabled them to put in practice, with comparatively little danger to themselves, but with deadly effect upon the Christinos, whenever they ventured to penetrate into the Carlist territory. After six years or more of sacrifices of every kind, they discovered their grievous error: but to our narrative.

In the autumn of 1834, when the rebellion was in its full force, although Zumalacarreguy wisely confined his operations, in a general way, to Navarre and the Basque provinces, his troops occasionally crossed the Ebro at places where it is fordable at certain periods, and made incursions into Castile, carrying off whatever booty they could seize, inflicting the severest calamities on the unprotected inhabitants, and wreaking dire vengeance upon those who might unsuccessfully oppose them.

One of his most active and intelligent agents was in Castile disguised as a *por-dioséro*, or beggar for God's sake. His seemingly decrepit frame was scantily covered with patched and tattered garments, his face was overgrown with stubby matted hair, whilst an old dirty brown cloth cap, of uncouth form, encased his head and overshadowed his eyes. In this miserable guise, and with a wallet slung across his shoulders, the spy went from place to place soliciting alms and broken victuals from the unsuspecting and charitable inhabitants, from whom he frequently contrived to gather much valuable intelligence.

Having ascertained that eight wagons laden with military clothing were on their way from Miranda de Ebro to Logronno, under a comparatively feeble escort, and that there was not any considerable body of the queen's forces in the vicinity, or within several days' march, the por-dioséro took his leave of the worthy labrador or small farmer under whose humble roof, near the Venta de la Estrella, in the rich and fertile district of La Rioja, in Old Castile, he had received shelter and sustenance, and leaning on his staff, with body bent apparently with infirmity, he crept along the road from Miranda de Ebro to Cenicéro, a small town on the right bank of the Ebro, on the high road to Logrohno, and two leagues from that city.

The day was drawing towards its close; the vineyards were glowing with clusters of ripe grapes; the ancient olive trees cast the shadows of their picturesque trunks on the rich soil; thick stubble showed that the harvest had been abundant, and the fruit trees were still adorned with their luscious burdens; on the brown hills, variegated and perfumed with wild thyme, rosemary, and other aromatic herbs, large flocks of sheep were feeding; and all told of a state of society still consistent with the pursuit of the ordinary occupations of peaceful life, though the consciousness that the focus of war was so nigh at hand grievously interfered with its enjoyment.

'*Una limosnita por Dios, senor!*—' A trifling alms for God's sake, senor!' drawled the pseudo-beggar, as he was overtaken by a hardy-looking man, wearing a rough brown jacket, a military cap with a tarnished gold band, and having a heavy sabre pendent at his side from a broad black leathern belt, and mounted on a powerful, though not a handsome horse.

The traveller gave him a few *quartos*.

'Heaven will repay you,' said the por-dioséro; and kissing the small copper coin, put it into his wallet.

The horseman was followed by a good-looking man in a peasant's garb, who bestrode a fine mule lightly laden with personal baggage, including the *alforjas*, well stuffed with stomach comforts.

'Antonio, give that poor creature a piece of bread and a draught of wine,' said the horseman as he rode forward.

'Si, senor,' replied Antonio; and halting his mule, he sprang lightly from his back, lifted up the flap of the alforjas or woollen saddle-bags, took out a good-sized loaf, opened a long knife which he carried in a side-pocket, cut the loaf in halves, and gave one of them to the por-dioséro, who accepted it with humble demeanour, breaking a piece off directly, and eating it with apparent eagerness and appetite. Meantime the muleteer lifted out from the other side of the alforjas a bota or wine-skin, and having untied the muzzle, poured some of its contents into a horn cup, and presented it to the por-dioséro.

'How good it is!' cried the latter, after having with trembling hand lifted the cup to his lips, and quaffed a portion of the generous liquid. 'What a good man your master is!'

'Indeed he is,' replied the muleteer, 'and though only a *factor* (a commissariat storekeeper), he does much good in these trying times. But he is far in advance. Make haste, my good man, and finish the wine. We must travel as far as Logronno to-night, to announce the arrival of the *comboy*, which will start early in the morning from Briones.'

The por-dioséro emptied the cup, and returned it, with renewed thanks, to the active and kind-hearted *paysano*, who mounted his mule, and trotted off briskly to rejoin his master.

It was now nearly dark: the spy hobbled along the road, until he reached a spot where there was a path to the left, leading to some sloping vineyards. Turning down it, he continued his seemingly feeble pace for about fifty yards; then, after looking cautiously round, he suddenly stood erect, grasped his staff in the centre, and plunged down the slope—still directing his course to the left—with the speed of a vigorous man bent on an urgent mission. In about an hour he descried the Ebro, and having reached its bank, paused for a few moments to take breath; then grasping his long staff at the upper end, and feeling his way with it, he advanced into the stream. At first the water only reached his knees, then his waist. Still he waded on, the river deepening more and more every step he took, until, at about the centre, he reached a little island covered with reeds. Here he rested for a few minutes, looking anxiously towards the Alavese shore. He soon perceived a glimmering light, and again entering the stream, made direct for it.

For a little distance the water reached his armpits, but it gradually shallowed, and he landed in the Carlist country without accident. Before quitting the water, however, he washed his matted hair and beard, his face, eyes, and hands; and the decrepit-looking por-dioséro of the Rioja emerged from the Ebro a well-formed man of about thirty, a little above the middle height, full of vigour and spirit, though still covered with tattered garments dripping wet. He stopped for a minute to squeeze the water from those garments, and then, taking long leaps by the aid of his staff, and, anon, running swiftly with it balanced in his hand, he soon reached a cottage, through whose only window gleamed a bright light—his beacon when fording the river.

'*Hola!* Francisco,' he cried, knocking sharply at the door with the end of his staff; 'open the door; here am I.'

On hearing the well-known voice, a man leaped from the bench on which he had been reposing, and unbarred the door. 'Welcome,' said the cottager, as his friend crossed the threshold: 'go into the *alcoba*, and doff those wet shreds; you'll find your own garments all ready; meantime, I will cast some wood on the fire, and Ramona will get the supper ready; it only requires warming.'

'Thank you, good Francisco; but let your task be to saddle Moro without a moment's delay.'

The blaze crackled, and Ramona, the cottager's wife, bustled about, and took two *ollas* or earthen pipkins from a cupboard, and placed them before the fire: she then spread a coarse but clean cloth on a little table, and just as the contents of the pipkins began to bubble, the alcove curtain was drawn aside, and Astuto—that was the name of the newly-arrived guest—stepped forth clad in the uniform of a Carlist officer.

'Do you bring good news, captain?' inquired Ramona.

'Excellent—but not a moment must be lost. Where is Zumalacarreguy?'

'At La Guardia,' replied Ramona, and removing one of the pipkins from the hearth, she took out a portion of its savoury contents with a wooden spoon, and transferred it to a homely but perfectly clean deep earthen plate. 'Come, Captain Astuto,' she said, 'take some of this nice *puchero*—you must be quite exhausted.'

'*Muchas gracias*, kind Ramona: pray go and hasten Francisco; tell him to bring the horse to the door instantly.'

Ramona vanished, and Astuto discussed his meal with the avidity and tact of a man accustomed to snatch his food on all opportune occasions.

The moment the horse appeared, Astuto mounted, and rode off at a sharp pace in the direction of La Guardia, a town in Alava, about two leagues off, and whither it had been preconcerted that Zumalacarreguy should repair with his forces, and station them in the town or its vicinity, in order to be at hand in case the fruits of Astuto's spying mission should render it expedient to make a dash on the enemy's territory. The captain rapidly traversed the five or six miles between Francisco's cottage and La Guardia; and proceeding direct to Zumalacarreguy's quarters, he in a very few words imparted to his chief the valuable intelligence he had collected. Military clothing was much wanted in the Carlist army; here, then, was an unforeseen opportunity of obtaining a supply from the Christinos themselves. Orders were instantly issued for the troops to be got under arms, quietly, not only in La Guardia, but in the villages and hamlets, where several battalions were lodged; the whole force being about five thousand active, willing, and brave men, whom nothing would so much delight as to make a successful foray in the enemy's country. By daybreak the whole five thousand men were within a mile of the Alavese bank of the Ebro, in the direction of a place where it was at that period fordable, and nearly opposite to the town of Cenicéro, in that part of Old Castile called La Rioja, already mentioned. The ford is called El Vado de Tronconegro. The troops were carefully concealed behind some hillocks, and among the brushwood, where they were ordered to lie down.

Early on the same morning the Christino comboy, protected only by a company of caçadores, or light infantry, and about a hundred cavalry, left Briones, a small town on the high road from Miranda, in conformity with the statement of the muleteer to the Carlist spy the evening before. The escort was commanded by a brave and active officer, Colonel Amor, who, although he was aware that El Vado de Tronconegro was passable at that time, in consequence of the low state of the Ebro, had not the slightest idea that Zumalacarreguy was lying in wait for him, with so overwhelming a force, on the opposite side of the river. All went on well during the march from Briones to Cenicéro; but soon after the comboy had passed through that town, the Carlist commander-in-chief arrived on the opposite bank of the Ebro, and immediately led the way to the ford of Tronconegro. It was a strange scene when the bold and crafty Zumalacarreguy, clad in a black sheep-skin zamarra, with a scarlet boyna, or Basque bonnet on his head, a long sabre pendent from his loins, and mounted on a noble charger, full of fire and spirit, but perfectly under command, advanced into the waters of the Ebro, followed by his staff, all in similar costume, their boynas only being of varied colours—blue, red, and white. The troops, wading up to their waists, and holding their muskets over their heads, soon formed a living chain across the Ebro, emerging in succession on the Castilian shore with the utmost alacrity, and forming rapidly close to Cenicéro.

The inhabitants beheld this sudden and unlooked-for invasion with dire alarm. They knew how hateful they had rendered themselves to the Carlists by the numerous proofs they had given of their warm attachment to the constitutional cause: about fifty of the most respectable men in the place had enrolled themselves as Urbanos, or national guards; and the church had been fortified: in short, Cenicéro was one of the most compromised of the towns in La Rioja. Large bodies of the queen's troops were frequently stationed there; but at this critical moment it was protected only by the fifty Urbanos, against an army of facciosos amounting to five thousand resolute men. Before the Carlist column entered Cenicéro, the fifty

Urbanos threw themselves into the fortified church, firmly resolved to defend that important post to the last.

Zumalacarreguy, having thus entered Cenicéro without opposition, passed rapidly through the town with his main force, leaving a battalion, with peremptory orders to take the church, no matter at what sacrifice. Relying upon the accomplishment of this object by a strong battalion against fifty armed civilians, thus securing a strongly fortified point to fall back upon in case of need, Zumalacarreguy hastened forward on the high road to Logronno, in pursuit of the convoy.

The church of Cenicéro is a strong stone edifice of considerable extent, with a lofty tower. It stands near the extremity of the town, overlooking the Logronno road, and is approached thence by a rather steep ascent, after passing a few small houses at its foot. It has two gates, one on the north, the other on the south. The former had been walled up with strong masonry, and the other was protected by a tambor, or stone redoubt, in a semicircular form, masking the gate, and affording room inside the semicircle for a party of men, who could fire through twelve or fourteen loopholes in the wall of the tambor, which was about seven feet in height, but not roofed, as there was no fear of attack from those who might occupy the church and its tower. These were the outward defences of the church, into which there was a retreat from the tambor by the gate which it protected. The principal internal fortification was the tower, the entrance thereto being through a small door, opening on a winding stone staircase. Six of the stone steps had been removed, and their place supplied by a ladder, which could be drawn up, in case a hostile force should gain possession of the church.

The Carlist battalion attacked the church vigorously. *Tiradores*, or sharp-shooters, were planted in all directions, firing at the belfry, with a view of preventing the Urbanos from annoying the besiegers from that commanding post. Forcible possession was taken of the houses in front of the southern gate; the mattresses were dragged off the beds, and, being stuffed into the open windows, formed parapets from behind which volleys of musketry were poured upon the roofless tambor; but the bullets generally struck against the wall of the church, became flattened, and fell harmless at the feet of the brave Urbanos, who, watching through the loopholes, picked off every faccioso who might venture to raise his head above the mattress barricades opposite.

Eight facciosos were killed, and only one Urbano wounded (in the finger), during this attack and defence, which lasted until two in the afternoon; at which hour Zumalacarreguy returned with the bulk of his force, after capturing six of the eight wagons at about a league from Logronno. The two others, being considerably in advance, escaped, and succeeded in entering the city, whose walls Zumalacarreguy did not venture to approach.

There was a skirmish between the slender escort of the tomboy and the advance of the overwhelming Carlist force. Colonel Amor defended his charge to the uttermost, killing a Carlist officer and two soldiers with his own hand; but he was at last forced to retire to Logronno.

When Zumalacarreguy found that the gallant little civic garrison of the fortified church of Cenicéro still held out, and that several of his men had been killed and wounded, his fury exceeded all bounds.

He sent for the cura, and ordered him to go instantly to the church, and summon the Urbanos to a parley.

'Tell them,' cried Zumalacarreguy, with that vehemence of voice and gesture which all knew were unequivocal signs of his determination to fulfil his threats—'tell them that I demand immediate surrender, and that, in case of refusal, they shall all be shot upon being made prisoners, which they will inevitably be in a few hours.'

The cura wended his way to the church with an anxious heart. He was a pious and exemplary clergyman, and was beloved by his parishioners, in whose constitutional sentiments he fully participated.

Orders were given to the Carlists to cease firing during the conference; and the Urbanos drew back their musket-barrels from the loopholes, of their own accord, the moment they perceived their venerable cura.

He advanced to the redoubt, and delivered his message. His benevolent heart dictated to counsel submission, seeing that Zumalacarreguy had so large a force, and being anxious to save the lives of this meritorious fraction of his flock, now in such imminent peril; and yet his tongue refused to give utterance to words of persuasion to surrender a post of such vital importance to the national cause.

'Tell Zumalacarreguy,' answered the gallant Urbanos, 'that we will resist until the death; that we would prefer being crushed under the ruins of our church, to making terms with a rebel.'

Zumalacarreguy was seated on a stone bench outside the gateway of a house at the other extremity of the town whilst the cura was parleying with the Urbanos. His troops were so stationed as to guard against a surprise, and his advanced posts were pushed as far as Montalvo, a picturesque village a league off, on the Miranda road; scouts being despatched both in that direction and towards Logronno, to ascertain if any large body of the queen's forces was on its way to attack him.

On the cura's approach, Zumalacarreguy started up, crying—'Have they surrendered?'

'No, senor.' And the cura stated the noble reply of the Urbanos in their own emphatic words.

Zumalacarreguy's rage was terrific. Stamping his feet, he threatened the cura with death; and, infuriated at being thus foiled by a handful of civilians, he ordered his officers to proceed with parties of soldiers and seize all the female relatives of the brave men who were defending the church. His mandate was speedily carried into effect, and the trembling women were brought before him.

Zumalacarreguy fixed his piercing eyes on them for a few moments, without speaking a word; then turning to a man who stood by his side—one of the few inhabitants of Carlist principles—he communed with him in an under tone.

Amongst the women was the mother of two of the Urbanos. She stood watching, with anxious glances, the gestures of her neighbour, who, whilst conferring with Zumalacarreguy, had more than once furtively directed his attention towards her. At length the Carlist chief bade the mother approach.

'Senora,' he said with a ghastly sneer, 'I presume that your sons, who are firing upon my men from the church yonder, would be sorry to hear that their mother had been shot?'

The poor woman cowered beneath the flash of deadly light which fell upon her wan countenance, as Zumalacarreguy uttered these cruelly sarcastic words; but almost immediately recovering her serenity, she replied, with a calm dignity worthy of a Roman matron—'Senor, my sons love their mother!'

'Very well, I doubt it not,' said Zumalacarreguy, still leaning on his sword, his boyna-covered head bent slightly towards the mother, and regarding her with eyes whose dark balls had a deadly expression—'very well; we will put their affection to the proof. Go with that officer, and tell your sons and their companions that, unless they yield instantly, you shall be shot: not only so, but all the female relatives of the other fellows who call themselves Urbanos shall also have their anxieties put an end to by *cuatro tiros*.* Go and fulfil your mission.'

The stern Carlist chief resumed his seat on the stone bench, and the mother accompanied the officer, a rough-looking man, wearing a very shaggy black zamarra, and a white boyna ornamented with a gold tassel. They were escorted by a file of Carlist soldiers, not two of whose half-military half-peasant costumes were alike. There was also a trumpeter, a lad of about sixteen, dressed in a blue velveteen jacket with bell buttons, loose coarse linen trousers, a flaming red boyna covering his bushy head, and his hair hanging in thick meshes on each side of his sunburnt face.

When arrived within a short distance of the church, the little trumpeter sounded a parley, by order of the officer. The firing on both sides ceased, and the mother advanced, followed by the officer and the Carlist guard.

'Go forward and deliver your message,' said the officer roughly.

The space between one edge of the semicircular loop-holed tambor, or redoubt, and the church wall, was barely sufficient for a full-grown man to pass sideways; and that space was now blocked up so as to completely enclose and barricade the gallant Urbanos, who nevertheless called through the loopholes in front, and told the mother to go round to the side. She did so.

'Madre,' said one of the sons, whose head appeared above the wall of the tambor, his lips all black with gunpowder from biting his cartridges when loading his

* That is, four shots, the mode of military execution in Spain being, that four soldiers fire together on the victims.

musket over and over again—'madre, what brings you hither?'

She delivered her appalling message.

'Wait a moment, madre,' said the son, and disappeared.

Presently the anxious mother heard stifled sounds within the tambor, as though heavy stones were being removed with caution; then the upper part of the narrow barricade just described was removed, and she saw her other son's bust in the space it had filled. She stretched forth her arms to greet him, but he said in a low voice, 'Come close to the wall, madre mia,' and he disappeared, but only for an instant. Another layer of large stones was rapidly removed, and she saw the figures of her two sons as low as their waists, and the crescent-like interior of the tambor crowded with her armed neighbours and friends, with blackened lips and flushed faces. Whilst they were greeting her, and inquiring, all together, about their families, the two brothers pulled down two more layers of stones. Their mother imagined that they were about to sally forth, and, with the rest of the little band, lay down their arms, rather than allow their nearest and dearest connexions to be sacrificed.

'Mother,' said the eldest son, 'give me your hand.'

She held it out, and her son drawing her gently towards him, took her up in his arms, lifted her over the remaining part of the narrow barricade, and carried her across the inner space of the tambor into the church; his comrades replacing the stones, and again completely blocking up the entrance to the tambor with surprising rapidity. All was performed in much less time than has been occupied in thus briefly describing this singular scene.

A voice was now heard through one of the *tronéras* or loopholes calling on the Carlist officer—'Tell the rebel Zumalacarreguy to come himself for the answer, and he shall receive it *á balazos* (in a volley of bullets). His messenger is with her children and her friends; and wo betide all Carlist prisoners now in the power of the Christinos if a hair of the head of one of our female relatives, or of any Christino prisoners, be touched!'

The astounded Carlist officer, filled with alarm lest Zumalacarreguy should wreak condign vengeance on him for having allowed the mother of the two Urbanos to be snatched from him, departed with his escort, after having been warned by the voices from the tronéras, and the apparition of the musket-barrels thrust through them, and pointed at him, that, should he tarry longer, his mortal career would probably be suddenly terminated.

The firing on both sides immediately recommenced, and was continued until nightfall.

After dark, the Urbanos held a consultation upon the course to be adopted during the night. They felt that it was more than probable that the Carlists would take advantage of the darkness to endeavour to take the tambor by assault, and that against so large a force it would be impossible for them to defend so comparatively fragile a work, the reduction or abandonment of which would enable the Carlists to batter down the gate and occupy the church. They therefore wisely decided that the only way to enable them to act efficiently, would be to retire to the tower, and, after accumulating all available offensive and defensive resources within it, to block up the entrance, and to fortify themselves for withstanding the brunt of an attack, however furious it might be.

With the promptitude and energy inspired by the impulse of self-preservation, and of indomitable fidelity to their cause, the gallant Urbanos commenced their willing labours immediately. First, they loosened the large ancient grave-stones or slabs with which the church was paved; for in the olden time the dead were interred in the sacred edifice. With these thick slabs they formed a strong wall, by placing them inside the door of the tower, so as to completely block it up; leaving, however, a few small spaces or loopholes to fire through, and a very narrow opening for the Urbanos to pass through, one at a time.

At about half-past nine at night—it was a very dark night—a stout party of facciosos silently crept close up to the wall of the tambor, placing themselves below the loopholes, in order that the bullets from the muskets of the Urbanos might pass over their heads. With pick-axes, which they had collected in the town, they began to loosen the stones in the lower part; whilst the brave Urbanos fired through the loopholes, but with little effect, until they perceived that the wall was giving way. They then retired into the church, as preconcerted, and closing the gates, placed against them the props and supports which had been accumulated beforehand for strengthening them. The wall of the tambor soon fell, and the Carlists rushed over the ruins to pounce upon the Urbanos; all they found, however, was stones and rubbish, and the church gate closed! But this did not damp their exertions. A quantity of wood was speedily collected, piled up against the strong gate, and set fire to. The gate, which was studded with large iron bolts with massive heads, soon ignited, and whilst it was burning, a ponderous beam was brought from a neighbouring timber-yard, and being lifted up horizontally by a number of facciosos, was used as a battering-ram, with tremendous force, against the half-consumed gate.

But they were not permitted to pursue their work of destruction unmolested. The brave Urbanos pelted their assailants with tiles from the roof of the church, and wounded a great number of them, some very severely; but they were promptly replaced by others from the battalions, which were drawn up close at hand.

At length the gate gave way; its shattered remnants falling inwards with a loud crash, carrying the internal barricade along with them. The Carlists rushed impetuously over the ruins, thinking to make an easy prey of the Urbanos. The church was, however, deserted; but two large wax flambeaux were burning on the altar.

The Urbanos had retired to their last stronghold, the tower; but before doing so, the mother of the two young men had called upon all who were in the church to prostrate themselves before the altar, and implore Divine support in their great strait. They obeyed, and, on rising, swore, one and all, to perish rather than surrender. Whilst making this solemn vow, they heard the gate yielding to the repeated assaults of the Carlists, and had barely time to reach the stair and close up the narrow entrance, before the crash took place.

Zumalacarreguy directed this desperate attack in person. A volley from the lofty roof, which stretched several of his men dead on the church floor, announced that the Urbanos had availed themselves of the apertures caused by the removal of the tiles, which had wounded so many of his men, as a passage to the inner roof, in which they had made holes, and from that novel, elevated, and impregnable battery, they fired upon the facciosos; whilst a discharge from the tronéras or loopholes of the fortified entrance to the stairs leading to the tower, imperatively called Zumalacarreguy's attention to the place whence they had mounted to the roof. 'Pensions for life,' cried Zumalacarreguy, 'for those who force the door of the tower!'

A company composed of daring fellows stepped forward, and rushed to the barricade. They were welcomed by a discharge of musketry from the loopholes. Sixteen were killed, and their panic-stricken comrades fled in different directions, running to and fro about the church in the utmost confusion. An officer hastened to Zumalacarreguy, who had left the church, and reported what had occurred; adding, that the tower-door could not be stormed and taken without immense loss, and that it was even doubtful whether it could be obtained possession of at all. But the Carlist chief would not give ear to these representations. 'Cowards!' he cried, and called for more volunteers, promising instant pecuniary rewards and pensions for life to the successful storming party.

Another vain attempt, followed by the loss of many lives, convinced Zumalacarreguy that it was not by assault that this well-contrived and admirably-defended barricade could be taken. He therefore adopted another plan. He ordered a large quantity of wood, and whatever other combustibles could be procured, to be heaped up in front of the parapeted door. The townspeople, whom he held as prisoners, were forced, at the point of the bayonet, to assist in collecting these materials. The terrified inhabitants, buffeted and maltreated by the ruffianly facciosos, were forced to deliver up their chairs, bedsteads, and arcas or trunks, which serve the purpose of chests of drawers; all of which were added to the pile.

Those who first advanced to cast down the combustibles in front of the barricade met their death from a volley from behind it. But more and more was heaped up, until it formed a huge mass. Several sacks of red pepper had been found in a shop, and in another warehouse the Carlists discovered some casks of spirits of turpentine. The pepper was thrown upon the wood and furniture, and the whole drenched with the spirits of turpentine, and immediately set on fire. But in the confusion, the spirits of turpentine had been spilt in considerable quantity on the floor of the church. It ignited; the strong fire ran along the ground with the rapidity of lightning, catching the old woodwork of the church, which blazed furiously, and all was confusion and dismay. The Carlists, in their trepidation and haste to escape from the flames, fell over each other; the smoke blinded and nearly suffocated them; and many were burnt to death, after suffering the most excruciating torments, from their clothing having become saturated with the spirits of turpentine. A poor man, whom they had forced to carry wood into the church, was also burnt to death.

And what was passing in the tower during this frightful scene? The gallant Urbanos, though they beheld the church on fire, and were half-choked by the pungent smoke from such a medley of turpentine-anointed combustibles, rendered doubly fierce by the red pepper heaped up in front of their loopholed barricade, far from contemplating a surrender under such fearfully trying circumstances, called out to their comrades above them to cast down the mattresses and bedclothes; for the last guard of Urbanos in charge of the church had removed their bedding to the tower when the building was invested. This was done in an instant, and the bedding was compactly placed against the interior of the barricade, so as to fill up every aperture. Thus the smoke was kept out of the tower, to the summit whereof all the Urbanos who had been defending the barricade now hastened. The interior of the church was burning throughout the night, and the Carlists could do nothing against the Urbanos in the tower.

At daybreak, when the flames had subsided, though the heat was still intense, the Carlists made fresh attempts to gain an entrance into the tower; but they found the brave citizens still at their post. They had removed the mattresses, and though confined to the heated region of the half-calcined stone staircase, they still kept their ground, firing through the loopholes, and killing several Carlists, whilst their comrades were flinging tiles, with fatal aim and force, from the perforated ceiling, on those who had again ventured into the church; until at last—at noon—the surviving facciosos fled precipitately from the spot where so many of their companions lay dead in the frightful postures into which their agony had cast them, and where the ashes of others were mingled with those of the combustibles which they had collected and ignited for the purpose of forcing the gallant Urbanos to surrender.

News now arrived that a division of the queen's army was on its way, by forced marches, to Cenicéro. Zumalacarreguy, therefore, lost no time in collecting his troops together, and they recrossed the Ebro by the same ford of Tronconegro which they had waded over so gaily thirty-six hours before. They found time, however, to plunder the houses of all the Urbanos, and of others known to be attached to the constitutional cause, and what they could not carry away they destroyed.

The loss of the Carlists was about forty killed by musket-balls, besides those who were burnt to death in the church, and upwards of a hundred and twenty wounded, who were placed on mules, with the exception of some who were in so pitiable a state as to be obliged to be carried on mattresses, borne by four men each. Several died before they reached La Guardia.

The fifty Urbanos who had so nobly defended their post, and had thereby rendered such invaluable service to their country, were received with enthusiasm by their relatives and friends; and it is worthy of remark, that though they had sent so many of their foes to their long homes, and had wounded between one and two hundred more, the only casualty in their gallant little band, was the wound in the finger of one of them at the commencement of the attack on the tambor.

* *

The writer passed through Cenicéro repeatedly in the course of the late civil war, and often visited the church in company with some of the Urbanos who defended it with such determined bravery. The stone staircase of the tower—bereft of its lower steps—the ladder, the half-calcined walls, all these palpable mementos remained unchanged until the end of the war. The tambor was rebuilt, and the fortified church was always confided, as a post of honour, to the Urbanos, even when the town was occupied by the regular troops.

Cenicéro was never revisited by the Carlists, who had too painful a recollection of the tremendous lesson they had there received, to run the risk of encountering a repetition of it.

To the honour of the Urbanos be it added, that though some of their neighbours aided the Carlists during the attack, and otherwise conducted themselves obnoxiously, they were not molested in the slightest degree afterwards. 'Thus,' said the exemplary cura, to whom the writer was, on various occasions, indebted for the most frank hospitality, and to whom he never failed to pay his respects when passing through Cenicéro—'thus affording a practical proof of the sincerity of the principles which they professed.'

THE VALLEY OF THE MEUSE.

The Meuse river, flowing northward from France into Holland, takes a sweep completely through Belgium, and has formed along its sides, by its never-ceasing current, some of the most picturesque scenery in Western Europe. It has excavated a valley through an elevated platform of transition slate and limestone, to a depth, in some places, of eight hundred feet, and a mile or two in width.* No stream in this part of Europe—except, perhaps, the Moselle—presents such varied and extensive windings. After a circuit of fifteen or seventeen miles, it in some places returns to within a few hundred yards of the point it passed before; thus making juttings and headlands to contrast with the flatness and fertility which are the general characteristics of the Netherlands.

But the beauty of the scenery is not the only attraction to this valley; it awakens historical associations of the most stirring events, from the days of chivalry downwards. In or near it are situated Dinant, Charlemont, Namur, Liege, Maestricht, and other places much renowned in history. Near the sources of the Meuse is spread out the forest of Ardennes, the scene of Shakspeare's comedy of 'As You Like It;' and many of the incidents of Sir Walter Scott's 'Quentin Durward' are supposed to have been enacted beside its waters. Yet although, or perhaps because, the Meuse may be reached from our own coasts in some four-and-twenty hours, it has been comparatively neglected by tourists. It is too near home to be thought worth attention. A very pretty book, however, which now displays its gay frontispiece on our table, is perhaps destined to rescue the district from the neglect of fashionable tourists—in other words, to bring the 'Valley of the Meuse' into vogue.†

Mr Dudley Costello, its author, determining to visit the neglected valley, proceeded by way of Calais, Dunquerque, Bergues, and Ypres, to Liege. Thence ascending the Meuse, he passed through Namur, where the junction of the Sambre swells the stream; and, continuing along the banks of the Meuse, reached Dinant, and made an excursion to the Ardennes. His observations were not confined to scenery—his research penetrated the mist of many local histories and antique curiosities; so that he has brought several interesting legends to light, which have never before been 'done into English.'

'Liege,' says the tourist, 'is a city of striking appearance, whether it be approached by land or water. Seated in a broad and fertile valley, at the base of lofty hills which shelter it on the north and west, and open to the south in the direction of the noble river whose rapid waters divide it from the populous faubourg of Outre-Meuse, it occupies a space on which the eye rests with pleasure as it embraces the general mass or examines its details.' Its general aspect, however, 'contrasted with the quaint old cities of Flanders, is comparatively modern; but on the quays that extend below the Pont des Arches, ranges of buildings appear, carved and decorated with all the fantastic ornament that used to mark the dwellings of the citizens during the fifteenth and sixteenth centuries: the streets which

* Lyell's Principles of Geology.

† 'A Tour through the Valley of the Meuse, with the Legends of the Walloon Country and the Ardennes. By Dudley Costello.' London: Chapman and Hall, 186 Strand.

intersect these masses are so extremely narrow, as to be almost impassable for carriages, and many that are used for thoroughfares are accessible only to the foot-passengers. It is in this quarter chiefly that vestiges remain of the old town, which, more perhaps than any other in Europe, has experienced the horrors and desolation of internal and foreign warfare. But the necessities of a large population, and the restored commerce of a great city, such as Liege, have led to a great deal of improvement within the last few years; and new streets and buildings have risen in every part, replacing what was old and dilapidated, and giving an air of life and health to the whole. So great has been the change wrought within the last fifteen years, that any former recollection of the town was of little service in enabling us to find our way from the point where we were set down, the principal hotels in the neighbourhood of the theatre not being at that time in existence.'

The truth is, Liege is a manufacturing town, and nothing widens old streets so effectually, or builds new houses so fast, as busy constant traffic. A manufacturing town is a hive, where every working bee must find for itself a cell, and convenient transit for its produce. Liege—such is the bathos of history—which few can think of without recurring to Charlemagne, Bishop Notger, Henry of Guelders, and other heroes of the past, has now become the Birmingham of Belgium. In its neighbourhood iron, with other metals, and coal abound. Concerning the discovery of the latter, Mr Costello has dug out of the local annals the following legend:—'Under the reign,' says Gilles d'Orval, an old chronicler, 'of Albert de Cuyck (at the commencement of the thirteenth century), a certain old man, of venerable appearance, with long white hair and a flowing beard, and wearing a white robe, passed one day through a street of Liege called Coché, and observing a blacksmith at work, who was complaining bitterly that with all his toil he could scarcely earn a livelihood, owing to the great expense of firewood, stopped and addressed him. "Cease your lamentations," he said, "and go to the neighbouring mountain where the monastery stands; you will there find certain veins of black earth, which you must dig out and burn: it will heat your iron far better than wood." Having uttered these words, the old man disappeared. At a later period, it was found out that the lucky blacksmith's name was Hulloz, and etymologists have hence derived the word "Houille," the generic name for coal throughout the Pays de Liege and the north of France. The old man of course passed for an angel; for the historian Fisen observes—"Angelus fuisse creditus est." The Père Bouille, in his Histoire de Liege, accounts for Fisen's opinion in an ingenious manner. "It is at least probable," he observes, "that this old man was an English traveller, since coal had, according to the testimony of Matthew Paris, been used in England as far back as the year 1145."'

Ascending the river, our traveller reached Huy, than which few towns are more picturesquely placed. 'The Meuse here makes a sudden curve, retreating from the hills which have for some miles confined it on the right bank, and sweeping now beneath the ridge that protects the left. Like Soracte's height, which on "the curl hangs pausing," the citadel of Huy seems suspended above the cathedral, as if to threaten it with instant ruin; and until one has fairly crossed the bridge, it is difficult to imagine where the road runs that is to let one out of the town again. Then, indeed, it becomes apparent; but there is not much space to boast of between the perpendicular rock and the river.' After threading the banks of the branching Mehaigne, Mr Costello proceeded to Namur, where the Sambre pours its waters into the Meuse. The city, according to our author, does not contain much that is attractive. Connected with its ancient customs are, however, some curious facts; amongst them the use of stilts, which is usually supposed to be confined to the people of the marshy and sandy plains of the Landes, which lie between the Garronne and the Adour in southern France. Stilts have for centuries, it seems, enjoyed a far greater celebrity at Namur. 'The frequent inundations of the Meuse and Sambre, which formerly used to flood the whole city, led doubtless in the first instance to their employment; but that which was originally a necessity, became in the course of time an amusement, and one that developed singular features. As far back as the eleventh century may be traced the existence of games on stilts; these games gradually assumed a party character, and the players finally resolved themselves into distinct bodies, ready at all times to do battle against each other, even to the peril of life and limb. These combats were conducted with great formality whenever a sovereign or other great personage honoured the city with his presence. The market-place of St Remy was usually selected as the *champ-clos*, and there the opposing brigades assembled to the number of from fifty to a hundred each, besides those who were called *souteneurs*, who came into the field to aid their comrades in case of accident, and when disabled, to supply their places. These bodies were regularly marshalled under proper officers, and there being frequently as many as twelve brigades on each side, the number of combatants amounted sometimes to nearly two thousand. Few spectacles could have been more animated than those which were presented in Namur when these conflicts took place: the whole of the population were present—every window, roof, and "coign of vantage" was filled with eager spectators; and amidst the ranks of the stilted warriors might be seen the wives and daughters of the combatants stimulating their husbands, sons, and lovers, by their reproaches and exhortations, and giving effect to the stimulus by administering the refreshment of strong waters. It was, in short, a scene of universal excitement, and its influence over the minds of those who shared in it was so great, that, as an instance, a story is yet remembered in Namur of a certain canon of St Aubain, who, leaving the field of battle for the cathedral, was so impressed with all he had heard and seen, that for every *amen* and *oremus* which he should have uttered, he substituted the war-cries of *Mélans* and *Avresses*.'

When the Archduke Maximilian visited Namur, one of these stilt-fights was got up for his express amusement. 'The place St Aubain, in front of the cathedral, was once more selected for the exhibition, and some hundreds of cart-loads of sand were strewed upon the pavement, to soften the violence of a fall. A large semicircular enclosure was formed with posts and ropes, and two companies guarded the entrance. The archduke, travelling under the title of the Count of Burgaw, had arrived in Namur the evening before the combat, and had been met at the extremity of the faubourg by the magistracy of Namur, accompanied by the brigades of stilters. On the following day, the 31st of May 1774, after having visited the fortifications, and dined at the palace of the governor, the Prince de Gavre, he proceeded with his suite to the palace of the bishop, where, from the broad balcony that overlooked the square, a perfect view of the mimic field of battle was obtained.

'The Mélans, who had assembled their forces in the Place St Remy, were the first to arrive, and entered the arena by the lower part of the Place St Aubain; the Avresses, whose muster had been made in the Place Lillon, soon made their appearance at the opposite side of the square. Both bodies marched in regular order, preceded by drums and fifes, and every man proudly carried his stilts over his shoulder, while on the flanks capered a number of hobby-horses, whose business it was to keep off the crowd. At five o'clock in the afternoon of a splendid day the ceremony began. As soon as the contending parties had entered the camp, the order was given for mounting, and after having defiled before the archduke, each side prepared to do its *devoir*. The Mélans were drawn up on the left hand in two lines; the first was composed of the brigades of the captain, the volunteers of Gavre, the brewers and the boatmen; the second of those of the porters, the men of the pen, advocates, notaries, &c. the butchers, and the guards. The brigades of the hussars, placed on the left flank of the two lines, formed the reserve. The Avresses, more numerous, were disposed in three lines: the brigades of the captain, of the hussars of Wepion, and La Plante, were in the first line; those of St Croix, of Astalle, and the stone-hewers, formed the second; and the third consisted of the mountaineers, the tanners, the cuirassiers, and the commune of Jambes, on the other side of the Meuse. The porters and tanners, who constituted the *élite* of each force, were posted in the last line. On a signal being made by the governor, the battle began, the foremost lines advancing with slow and steady pace to the attack; and soon the arena resounded with the rattling weapons of the combatants, and many a "tall fellow" measured his length on the sandy plain. The fortune of the day was various: sometimes the party of the Mélans, headed by their valorous chief, Castaigne, seemed to be carrying all before them; anon the Avresses would rally, and, led to the charge by their captain, Godinne, drove back their impetuous assailants. It was not long before the sustaining lines joined in the affray; and the reserve, disdaining to be idle, made the fight general. The struggle was long and fierce; and, in the moment of excitement, many a voice was raised for the *Boute-à-tot;* but the leaders, fearing the consequence in the presence of the archduke, refused to give the word, and the fight was therefore marked by no more fatal consequences than distinguished those "gentle passages of arms" where fractured collar-bones and broken legs and arms rewarded the exertions of the adventurous knights of old. The battle lasted for two hours, and then the Mélans, whose lines were completely broken, whose reserve had been put to flight, and whose best champions had fallen before the "clanging blows" of their adversaries, were compelled to yield to the superior numbers of the Avresses. The stilt was raised, the drums and fifes joined in a martial strain, and the colours of Catherine of Savoy waved triumphantly over the field.'

These encounters were very properly abolished by the civic authorities. The use of stilts is not, however, forgotten by the Namurois; at fairs and village festivals, groups of half-a-dozen may still occasionally be seen amusing the crowd with their antics, and sometimes, though rarely, engaging in single combat.

From Dinant, a long narrow town, which almost seems to be pressed into the stream by the heights behind it, Mr Costello left the Meuse, traversing the country to Rochefort, to reach the far-famed forest of Ardennes. Having rested at St Hubert, our tourist plunged into the forest. As he set out across a desolate moor, in the direction of Champion, a large kite that kept circling over his head was the only companion of the journey. 'After a time, he too left us, having no doubt scented his quarry, and for some miles we pursued our silent, lonely route. As we advanced deeper into the forest, an occasional woodcutter might be seen; in some of the more open spaces large coveys of partridges were feeding; and in one sylvan spot we were agreeably surprised by the apparition of a superb fox, leisurely cantering across the road, as if on his way—which was probably the case—to breakfast at somebody's expense. We stopped for ours at Champion, a large inn standing alone at a point where four roads meet, on the skirts of the most picturesque part of the forest. It is here truly the scene as Shakspeare has painted it—a perfect picture of sylvan beauty. Except the "green and gilded snake," and the "lioness, with udders all drawn dry," that lay in wait for Orlando's elder brother, all the features of "the forest of Arden," in "As You Like It," are drawn to the life. The truth of the description arises of course from the poet's quick sense of the beauties of nature, and his ready apprehension of all that unites to render forest scenery delightful, whether in England or beyond the Meuse. Nurtured in tradition, and steeped in the recollection of the days when he

"did lay him down within the shade
Of waving trees, and dreamed uncounted hours,"

the forest of Ardennes was to him as real an object as the woods that bordered the Avon; and thus the scenery of his unrivalled comedy is as true as the personages with whom he has filled these wilds are instinct with life. At every step we meet with

"Oaks whose antique roots peep out
Upon the brooks that brawl along the wood:"

we cannot penetrate beyond the glades without disturbing some "careless herd, full of the pasture," the "dappled fools" that formed the subject of the moralising reverie of the "melancholy Jacques:" we linger in many a spot where still seems to echo the song of the forester lord; nor can we refrain from chanting with him—

"Who doth ambition shun,
And loves to lie i' the sun,
Seeking the food he eats,
And pleased with what he gets,
Come hither, come hither, come hither;
Here he shall see
No enemy,
But winter and rough weather."'

This was the last place of note, except Treves (famous for its relic of the holy coat which has of late been causing so much discussion on the continent), which Mr Costello visited.

His work is tastefully adorned with wood engravings, which are executed in a style of unusual excellence.

LONDON AT DAYBREAK.

Those whose observation of London has been confined to its sombre appearance in the fogs of November, or its comfortless aspect in the rains or snows of January or February, can form little conception of its brightness and cleanliness as seen in the vivid light of an early summer morning. Many who take up the common cry of 'smoky, dirty London,' would be agreeably surprised could they behold it at such a time; though thousands have probably spent more than half of their threescore years and ten within its boundary, or in its vicinity, without having once seen this city of cities under these favourable circumstances.

The solitary appearance of the streets of London at the hour of daybreak is singular and striking. With a mighty city we naturally associate crowd and bustle, and to be surrounded on all sides with the myriad habitations of man, and yet scarcely to behold a single human being in the whole length of a street, to hear one's own footsteps echoing in the silence, and that in broad daylight, and in so crowded a thoroughfare as Cheapside, excites strange emotions. The contrast, too, with the appearance of the same streets when, in the noonday, the anxious noisy tide of life pours through their too narrow pathways, is striking. No lumbering wagons, no unwieldy brewers' drays, no rumbling omnibuses or dashing cabriolets, disturb the silence; a slow market cart or a country wagon is the only vehicle to be seen, except the costermonger's barrow, who is wending his way to Billingsgate for a supply of fish, or a butcher's cart rattling along to the wholesale markets. A solitary newsman is already on the alert to secure the first copies of the morning papers, and the yawning printer is wearily bending his steps homewards from the scene of his nocturnal labours. At the corner of the street the nomadic tea-vender invites to his temporary tent the early labourer, the mechanic of higher grade has taken his place in the snug box of the already opened coffee-house, while the half-open door of the 'night-house' offers to the depraved taste of the less temperate the pernicious gratification of an early dram.

The general effect and the minor details of the public buildings, of which London boasts so many notable specimens, are now seen to the best advantage. In the light of the yet untainted atmosphere, the mouldings and cornices are seen with an effect of unusual sharpness and distinctness, and the yet vacant street affords room to move with facility from one point of view to another. The picturesque towers and spires of Sir

Christopher Wren stand out in bold relief against the sky, and the harmonious proportions of his numerous works are now seen to the greatest advantage; and many beauties in the more elevated parts of the buildings, scarcely noticeable in the thickened atmosphere of noonday, are now apparent. In the more ancient parts of the city, where some of the houses are still of wood, with quaint overhanging upper storeys, many an antiquated piece of wood-carving, and many a picturesque 'bit,' will strike the eye at such an hour, which in the bustle and crowd of noon would escape observation; and even the most frequented and well-known haunts will, in the 'smokeless air' of this silent hour, present many new points of interest and beauty, which the early lounger will wonder he never observed before. Not a little interesting is it also at such an hour, while sauntering along some quiet street, or exploring some untrodden nook, to call to mind the men who, by their virtues or genius, have hallowed the spot, or the stirring events which in bygone days gave a celebrity to the locality. Here was the 'whereabout' of a celebrated divine; here the school where the talents of a great genius first began to dawn; beneath the shadow of that spire sleeps a poet; in that old grotesque house, with its strange and uncouth carved work and elaborate monstrosities, died a celebrated author; here formerly stood a gate of the city; and there, again, is the site of its ancient wall. Connecting thus great men and events with the localities explored, every step introduces us to something interesting, and the most commonplace house and dull street become objects of absorbing interest, and still more so when visited in the favourable quietness and bright light of early morning.

Of the suburban views of London, perhaps that from the archway at Highgate is one of the best. The rural appearance of the road beneath, with the overhanging trees in the shrubbery on the side, and the glad chirp of birds, contrast pleasingly with the world of brick and mortar that stretches forward before the eye, evidently fast encroaching upon the few remaining fields in the foreground, and apparently determined to exterminate all that is green and rural. The spires of several modern churches relieve the monotony of the mass of houses, which at this end of London are destitute even of the charm of antiquity to render them interesting; and right before the eye, in the distance, St Paul's cathedral rears its well-known colossal form: a misty line beyond denotes the course of the river, and the Surrey hills form the background.

London is seen to advantage from some of the bridges, among which we might especially mention Blackfriars Bridge, as observed from which St Paul's cathedral has a very imposing effect, and the more ancient parts of the city lie in immediate proximity. But the finest point of observation is Waterloo Bridge, whence the view on a clear morning is magnificent. Little do many, who have lived perhaps all their lives only a short distance from this spot, imagine—while scouring the continent in search of the beautiful and picturesque—how fine a view is unnoticed at their doors; a view which, had it been met with in Germany or Switzerland, would have been chronicled in every guide-book, and have attracted thousands of admiring tourists. Nothing of its kind can be finer than the prospect from this spot on an early summer morning. Let the reader imagine himself standing on a seat in one of the recesses in the centre of the bridge, itself one of the finest in Europe; not a cloud in the sky, the sun gilding and gladdening with his beams everything around, and the fresh breeze blowing upon his cheek. Beneath, 'the river windeth at his own sweet will' (as Wordsworth expresses himself in his fine sonnet written on the contemplation of this view at such an hour), sauntering, as it were, along its sinuous course, and ruffled only by the tiny waves that seem to rejoice in the returning light and warmth of morning. The thickly clustered houses on every side proclaim the vast population of the city, and the numerous towers and steeples, more than fifty of which, together with five bridges, are visible from this spot, testify to its enormous wealth.

The features of the south shore on the right hand are comparatively flat and uninteresting, there being on this side of the river few other buildings besides coal and timber wharfs, and tall chimneys, which pour out their volumes of smoke by night and by day. The ancient church of St Mary Overie, however, which forms on this side a prominent feature in the distance, must not be overlooked. On the north shore, the features are grand and impressive in the extreme. In the foreground, with its noble terrace overlooking the water, Somerset House stretches magnificently along the side of the river. Further on, the Temple Gardens, with their trees and verdure down to the water's edge, contrast refreshingly with the masses of brick and stone around. Glancing over the elegant steeple of St Bride's church, St Paul's cathedral towers above every object, as it were with paternal dignity, its huge cupola forming the principal feature in the scene. Behind these, among a cluster of spires and towers, rises the Monument; and further on, the Tower, so pregnant with associations of the romantic and the fearful; and the extreme distance presents a bristling forest of masts, belonging to vessels of all nations, unmistakeably proving the vast extent of the commerce and wealth of the country.

Turning westward, looking up the river, several objects of interest meet the eye. The Lambeth shore is marked by little except a lion-surmounted brewery, which somewhat relieves its flatness and monotony; the sombre dome of Bethlehem Hospital is seen behind, fraught with the most gloomy associations, and the tall chimney of a shot manufactory, not forgetting Lambeth palace in the distance. On the opposite shore is the interesting locality of the Savoy, the beautiful chapel of which still remains; and also the Adelphi, conjuring up a thousand recollections of Queen Elizabeth, one of whose palaces formerly stood here. Further on stands Hungerford market, with its graceful suspension bridge, its venders of fish, &c. bustling about even at this early hour; while behind rise the column of Nelson, and the towers of the venerable abbey of Westminster, the shrine of so much valour, genius, and piety. At the back of Whitehall, the gardens belonging to the mansions of some of the aristocracy, reaching down to the river's brink, form a pleasing feature; and the yet unfinished erection of the new houses of parliament, in all its elaborate majesty, stretches its vast length along the water-side with a dignity befitting its high destination.

As the eye glances around from spot to spot and from spire to spire, what numberless recollections of the past crowd upon the mind! How different must have been the scene when the only communication between the two shores was by means of the ancient ferry where London Bridge now stands! How different a feature must the north shore have presented, ere the fire of London had cleared a space for the genius of a Christopher Wren, and the wooden erections of ancient London had given place to the more durable materials—brick and stone! The Tower, too, which forms so prominent a feature in the distance, how much of history and romance does it suggest to the mind! There the lustful Harry immured and decapitated the beauteous Anne Boleyn; and there the upright and amiable Sir Thomas More cheerfully laid down his head on the block at the command of his tyrannous master. In the church of St Mary Overie, at one end of London Bridge, rests the lawyer poet Gower; and in the church of St Magnus the Martyr, at the other end of the bridge, lie the bones of the memorable Coverdale. How many associations also are suggested by the sight of the Temple Gardens! There, in former times, proudly lived in splendour the Knights Templars; and the admirer of the 'Essays of Elia' will not forget that close by was the lodging of the amiable and interesting Charles Lamb. A little further on, near the waterside, stands the little church where the immortal Milton was baptised; and nearly opposite, on the other side of the river, is the site of the celebrated Globe theatre, so intimately connected with the names of Shakspeare and Ben Jonson. The sight of those venerable towers of Westminster carries us back in imagination to the remote period when Sebert, the pious Saxon king, built a church on Thorny Island, which was the foundation of the present proud structure; and that picturesque palace of Lambeth, scarcely seen in the distance, revives in the mind fearful recollections of persecution and oppression, as we think of the sufferings of the Lollards, who were imprisoned there for daring to think for themselves in religious matters. Those houses of parliament, too, how often have those roofs echoed the eloquence of a Pitt, a Sheridan, and a Burke! how often has the pathetic appeal of a Wilberforce, and the tasteful oratory of a Canning, moved the hearts and influenced the minds of spell-bound listeners! But the new houses of parliament attract the eye: the mind throws itself forward into the future, as well as lingers on the past, and the wonder as to who will be the distinguished ornaments and leaders within these walls, and what the character of their measures, unites itself to the prayer that the men may be philanthropic and their measures patriotic.

OCCASIONAL NOTES.

WATER-TIGHT COMPARTMENTS IN SHIPS.

A correspondent, referring to our account of a 'Visit to the Great Britain,' and the advantages of water-tight compartments, claims the merit of their introduction into the British navy for the late Sir Samuel Bentham. This officer, in obedience to an order from the Admiralty, dated in 1795, built seven vessels with water-tight compartments, and in his report to his employers, he describes the improvement so as to leave no doubt that in principle it is the same as that adopted in the Great Britain. In consideration of his various services, Sir Samuel was appointed inspector-general of naval works.

The principle was, however, by no means a new one; nor does Sir Samuel Bentham in his evidence* claim to be the inventor. An ancient galley was, it has been ascertained, built with compartments independent of each other; and the Chinese have always constructed their clumsy vessels upon the same plan. It may therefore seem surprising that modern British ships should not have more generally been built with water-tight compartments or bulk heads since Bentham's improvements. The solution may be, that the additions of that not very compact material—wood—necessary for extra partitions, would render ships too cumbersome; whilst iron, of which the Great Britain is built, being lighter in proportion to its strength, allows of the full adoption of water-tight compartments without any of the former disadvantages.

As it may be interesting to many to know who first directed the attention of the naval public to, and carried out the principle, we cheerfully accede to our correspondent's wish, and give all due credit to his gallant ancestor Sir Samuel Bentham.

COUNCILS OF HONEST MEN.

The French journals inform us that about four months ago a sort of tribunal was formed, which would, we sincerely believe, prove of the utmost benefit if imitated in this country. It consists of a mixture of masters and workmen, and is called the *Conseil des Prud'hommes*, which may be rendered the 'Council of Honest Men.' The design is, that each trade should delegate a certain number of employers and employed, so as to form a board or council, whose function consists of hearing and deciding any disputes which may arise between the two classes belonging to each branch of industry. The Conseil is not a legal tribunal, but merely a court of arbitration, leaving appellants the choice of submitting or not to its judgments, which it has of course no means of enforcing. So far, however, as the experiment has been tried in Paris, it has succeeded so well, that of 400 cases which were decided during the first three months of the tribunal's existence, in only *three* were the decisions not final or satisfactory.

If such an institution be found of benefit in France, of how much greater utility would it prove in this infinitely more manufacturing and commercial country? We are confident that much of the misunderstanding which exists between representatives of capital and of labour, arises from the few opportunities there exist for their meeting together, and being made to feel how inseparable their interests really are. Apart, therefore, from the special object of such a tribunal—the settling of disputes—'Councils of Honest Men' would have the effect of lessening the gulf which now unhappily exists between masters and men. Intelligent individuals, selected from the operatives, would meet their superiors to perform the *same function*, which in itself would tend to bring about a much more cordial community of sentiment than now exists. The great body of workmen, again, would feel greater independence, and work with greater zest, when they found their employers uniting with the chosen of their body to set whatever little grievances they may labour under to rights. It may perhaps be argued that the working-classes, as a body, are not yet fully prepared to take a part in proceedings demanding great consideration, or requiring logical skill in reasoning. We are aware that many certainly are not; those, for example, who habitually yield to intemperance; but it is equally true that a great number are morally and intellectually able for the due performance of duties of this nature; and we know of nothing which could so powerfully promote habits of order and propriety, as the expectation of being placed on the councils of honest men we speak of.

Aside from these general considerations, the particular advantages of such a tribunal would be even greater. It may, without danger, be asserted, that common or equity law, as an impartial mediator between employers and employed, is totally inefficient. In the first place, it is an expensive arbitrator to call in; and to the poor man is, in mere commercial or manufacturing disputes, a dead letter. It is an instrument he cannot afford to employ in righting himself, whilst his rich master can, on the other hand, readily call in its aid. Secondly, if the law of the land were ever so accessible, it is generally inefficient in adjusting the nice differences which are liable to arise in the various trades. There is no special law for one manufacture more than another. It makes no distinction between printers, weavers, tailors, miners, or any other artisans, and is consequently unable to reach the cases of minute injustice which may arise in each profession, and be quite peculiar to itself. A council, therefore, of 'honest men,' selected from the respective trades, would be much better judges of the cases brought before them than the best lawyers breathing. This is daily exemplified in our common law or jury courts. Causes of the utmost complication occasionally arise, involving technicalities of which the attorneys or writers, and advocates, are totally ignorant, until they glean a superficial knowledge of them from the cases themselves. These technicalities, which it takes, be it remembered, years of experience in the people actually engaged in the trade or manufacture to learn, and which form the gist of the case, are then argued before jurymen who are in *total* ignorance of them, not having had the lawyer's opportunity of previously 'getting up' one spark of the technical information so essential. Yet, in their ignorance, they are bound to decide. Hence it is that jury decisions concerning patents, 'hot-blast,' and similar cases, demanding much mechanical, engineering, or manufacturing knowledge, seldom satisfy the litigants, and are more frequently carried into higher courts than any other class of causes. This is an evil which has been long

* Published by Longman and Co. 1828.

felt, and loudly exclaimed against, especially in Scotland, where juries for civil causes are of comparatively recent introduction. Were, however, technical misunderstandings submitted to a council of individuals—masters and operatives—fully conversant with the technicalities out of which the disagreements arise, justice would be better done. A tribunal of iron-founders, for instance, would assuredly be better able to understand and decide upon the merits of a hot-blast case, than the best legal functionaries and most generally intelligent jurymen in Great Britain. There is little fear that their arbitrations would not be abided by; for experience has already proved the inutility of going to law, which is only now done because it is the only means of settlement at present existing. It would be safe to predict, that the proportion of appellants would be about the same as that in Paris—three in 400.

Upon these various considerations, we would strenuously advocate the institution of Conseils des Prud'hommes in Great Britain.

WHAT TO DO WITH TRANSPORTED CRIMINALS.

There are at present nearly fifty thousand culprits in the Australian colonies and other dependencies of Great Britain (almost wholly in the former), and about five thousand are transported every year. The present arrangements for the management of this unhappy class of our fellow subjects are extremely defective; at least they are attended with very unsatisfactory results; and it has become an important question—By what means can they be improved? The present system has two leading distinctive features—the predominance of physical coercion, and the comparative absence of persuasive motive; being precisely those which mark the everywhere detestable form of slavery. The system is condemned even by the instances in which comparatively good effects have been realised, for these have always occurred where the system was most departed from: thus, good masters—men who treat the convicts granted to them as servants with most persuasive, and fewest directly coercive stimulants—have always 'turned out the best men;' bad masters—severe-natured men, keeping more strictly to rules—have always had the worst men; 'and the worst of all have been found in the service of the government, where the strictest rules have been the most strictly carried out.' The general tendency of the present plans is to harden and further deprave the convicts. What is desirable, is a treatment which would unite punishment—the due condemnation of error—with the reform and restoration of the unfortunate men. We must avoid being too lenient, for there a very definite evil lies; but we ought equally to avoid any plan of treatment which only can make the bad worse. It is a terrible thing for man to do—to put his brother into circumstances which unavoidably sink his soul deeper in the mire of sin, punishing him for a little error by forcing him into the predisposition to commit a greater. Yet this is what our nation is doing every day with fifty thousand of its members.

A proposal for a new plan has been laid before the government, and partially before the public also, by Captain Maconochie, R.N., who for some years conducted the establishment at Norfolk Island. Captain Maconochie is a philanthropist; but views founded in humanity are not necessarily visionary. On the contrary, we sometimes think that those who persist for years in plans found to be bad in result, but which they nevertheless persist in believing to be the best, have more of the theorist in their constitution than those who, in such circumstances, would try something new. The mode suggested by Captain Maconochie is of business-like aspect, although directed to a Christian-like end. He proposes that criminals should be condemned, first, to a comparatively brief term of banishment; second, to a certain amount of duty and self-denial, which they must regard as a debt, and expunge before they can be restored to liberty. Such duties and efforts of self-denial would, according to Captain Maconochie's plan, be expressed in marks; and men would be condemned to 6, 8, or 10,000 marks, in proportion to the gravity of their offences. Starting with whatever debt against him, the culprit would have before him the opportunity of reducing it daily by his well-directed labour or by the frugality of his living, all above bread and water being left to his own option. A persuasive motive would thus be substituted for direct coercion, although the latter might still be reserved for extreme cases, if any such arise. 'With the alteration thus made in it,' says Captain Maconochie, 'this punishment [transportation], from being, as now, the worst, would speedily become the best secondary infliction at our command. It would more certainly wean convicted offenders from their vicious habits—more powerfully deter the hesitating from committing crime—and prove in the end also, as I think, more economical than any other punishment that has yet been devised. The originally worst purposed men, when placed in a painful situation, from which only steady exertion and self-command could rescue them, with the strongest and highest motives to please, instead of low and deteriorating motives merely to avoid offending, would be unable to resist the infectious example of a whole community steadily pursuing the same object on the same principles; and trained thus to good habits by impulses proceeding from within themselves, and the class to which they belong, these habits would much more certainly become in time natural to them, than any created through mere restraint. Again, the example of their submission, and the recognised necessity for all similarly submitting before they can hope to recover their liberty when once forfeited, would be far more deterring to others than the example of vague suffering; for the pride of evil-minded men would recoil from the one picture, and it is only challenged by the other.'

All, however, is not left to the power of this appeal to the convict's hopes. 'On first arriving at a penal settlement—for a period not under three months, but beyond that depending entirely on his own regularity and proficiency, and the acquisition of marks exhibiting them—his treatment should consist of moral, religious, and other intellectual instruction in a penitentiary. The great object in this is to wean from vicious recollections, cast the views forward, penetrate with a sense of benevolent purpose in all the other regulations, and, by enlarging the intelligence, increase the power of deliberate reason over blind impulse. I speak from experience in attaching great importance to it, and the voyage out should be also made systematically subservient to it. After this he should, for a time not under eighteen months, but this period also depending on the acquisition of marks, serve in a mutually responsible party, labouring for government, and disqualified for any situation of trust, authority, or indulgence under it, or for any private service. The object of this, apart from the punishment it will inflict, is to create a common interest in a whole party, and in all parties, to behave well—thus to produce an esprit de corps towards good in all—to subdue selfish feeling—to assist the weak by giving them the aid of the strong, and to fetter the ill-disposed by combining the interests of the better men with theirs. Experimentally, I also attach much importance to it. After this he should hold, for not less than fifteen months (making three years in all), and beyond this till he has fully redeemed his marks and earned his entire discharge, a ticket of leave in the settlement. In this last stage, every reasonable facility should be afforded him to accumulate a little money against his return to society. * * On discharge, every reasonable assistance should be given to the men to disperse; and their final liberation, as well as every intermediate step towards it, should in every case depend solely on having served the minimum time, and accumulated the corresponding number of marks.'

In the brochure from which we make these extracts, there are some traits of the convict population of Australia and Norfolk Island which can scarcely be read without interest. It appears that, in the obstinate state of mental rebellion in which the present system retains the men, they have come to alter entirely their ideas of good and evil. A bad man with them is one who shows an inclination to behave unusually well, by way of making favour with his superiors. A good man is one disposed to every outrage against rule: he would rob and murder, but not give evidence. The attention of convicts in church exceeds that of most ordinary congregations: many show great religious excitability; but these are generally not the best men. Captain Maconochie says—'In administering justice, I was always most particular in my way of receiving an oath. On important occasions, I would question the man tendering it about his early religious education, his father's and mother's care of it, and his recollection and still abiding sense of the sacred nature of its obligations. He would very frequently be moved, and sometimes even to tears, under this cross-examination: yet almost the best of them would perjure themselves immediately afterwards, rather than lose caste among their companions by divulging what they were under a general, by no means necessarily a particular, pledge to conceal.

'The attention of prisoners,' he says, 'to their sick companions is usually very striking; and their emotion on occasion of a death far exceeds any that I have usually seen in either army or navy. It is difficult also to say how this should be: it is not through fear; for though, as a body, timid when opposed to regular authority, this arises from their habitual submission, their want of confidence in each other, and of the habit also of acting in numbers together; and individually, they expose their lives even recklessly. The feeling exhibited is not either the expression of fear, but rather of sympathy, as it were, with one who has passed from among them, and from their trials, to another audit. I have often observed this thought in the minds of otherwise rather hardened men, and in no case did I ever see a trace of that disgusting levity with which death is sometimes adverted to in military and even high civil society. Before I went to Norfolk Island, only a limited number, I think twelve, were allowed to attend any funeral, and no headstones were permitted to be erected at a prisoner's grave; but agreeing entirely with the Mettray directors as to the moral benefit to be derived from an opposite conduct, I abrogated both regulations. Two or three hundred men would thus frequently accompany an interment, all dressed in their best, and walking most respectably in files together; and a decorum, modesty, and even taste, were occasionally exhibited in their headstones really wonderful. I recollect one now, having been struck with it at the time. It was a low humble stone over an old man, with the words, "THE WEARY ARE AT REST" above, and name and date beneath. It seemed to me very touching, and at the same time highly characteristic. It expressed the *tædium vitæ* which elderly prisoners, who especially feel the discomforts of their position, and have outlived their relish for its palliations, almost always testify; and the omission of the first clause of the sentence exhibited also the absence of remorse which in most cases singularly characterises their dying moments. Their crimes have been so long their only sources of support and enjoyment, that they cease to regard them in this light; and their punishment is also universally considered by them to have exceeded the measure due to their offences. One of the worst men I ever knew, a fellow without a single manly principle, except that of courageous endurance of punishment when incurred, died when I was at Norfolk Island, and I went to see him at the last, to endeavour to get him to retract a false and scandalous charge he had recently brought against one of the free overseers. With some difficulty he consented, and I then asked him if he was prepared for the change awaiting him? He answered "Quite." "Have you no fears in relation to it?" "None in life." "And yet severe punishments have been denounced against a life such as yours has been." "I can never be worse off than I have been here, where I have been used worse than a dog." I held out my hand to him on leaving, and his first movement was to reject, though he afterwards took it, and seemed a little softened. He died within a few hours. His conduct had been so bad, and on several occasions even gratuitously treacherous (a great offence in prisoners' estimation), that scarcely any volunteered to bury him; and a party was ordered for the purpose, of which I recollect scarcely any other instance. One rather respectable man did, however, accompany him voluntarily; and on my asking afterwards how this had happened, the answer was also characteristic, "I was long in jail with him up the country." By such associations are those social feelings now guided, which man cannot shake off, which, if debarred their legitimate exercise, take to taming mice and spiders, of which so much might be made in recovering even the worst, were they properly recognised and respected, but which at present only bind good, bad, and indifferent together by the tie of a common crime or punishment.'

The following anecdote is striking. 'When I landed on the island, three very desperate men were working in irons in a quarry by themselves, and it was thought utterly unsafe to let them go at large. I proposed to them, as I did to all others, much to extend their indulgences, provided they would become "mutually responsible" for each other, so that if any transgressed, I should have the right to replace them all under the original duress. They objected strongly, and I was struck even with the form of objection. It was not, "if so and so behaves ill, why should I suffer?" but, "if I behave ill, why should so and so suffer?" I replied, that my object was to get all to behave well for the sake of each other, as I could not hope they would do so as yet for mine; and at all events these were the only conditions on which I would grant them any indulgence whatever. Two days passed before they consented; but after they did, though not immaculate, they behaved generally very well. One of them at length showed strong indications of approaching insanity. He became moody, and twice attempted to destroy himself. I thought that possibly change of occupation and diet might benefit him, and I brought him to my own garden in consequence, and sought to feed him up; but he rather got worse. I remonstrated with him, and his answer was a striking one—"When I used to be this way before, I would get into trouble (commit an offence, and incur a severe punishment), and that took it out of me; but now that I try to behave myself, I think I am going mad altogether." (There is a strong tendency in irritable tempers, under coercive discipline, from time to time to "run a muck;" and after a time, this becomes almost a necessity to them.) At length it became unsafe to trust him at large, yet still the surgeon wished him to have air and exercise; on which one of his old "quarry" comrades volunteered to be handcuffed to him, his left hand to the patient's right, and thus walked about with him many days, till he was sent to Sydney a confirmed lunatic.'

What is here added is scarcely less interesting: the preliminary remark strikes us as particularly just. 'Instances of individual attachment to myself I could multiply without number, but these, for obvious reasons, I forbear to quote; and in truth they as often pained as pleased me, by being too deferential. It is a great and very common mistake, in managing prisoners, to be too much gratified by mere obedience and servility; duplicity is much encouraged by this; and of two opposite errors, it is better rather to overlook a little occasional insubordination. I cannot, however, refuse to cite two traits, whose character cannot be mistaken. I had a large garden within a few hundred yards of the ticket-of-leave village at Cascade, where from 300 to 400 men lived, four to six in a hut, never locked up, nor under other guard through the night than that of a police sentry, one of their own number. The garden was by the roadside, very imperfectly fenced with open paling, and fully stocked with choice fruit and vegetables, bananas, pine apples, grapes, melons, and others, which to men on a salt ration must have offered a great temptation; and a well of particularly good water being within it, almost public, these were constantly under view; yet I scarcely ever lost any. And by a letter received a few weeks ago, I learn that five men, having picked up an old black silk handkerchief that had belonged to me, have had their prayer-books bound with it. The only one named to me was once a notorious bushranger in New South Wales, and is on the island under the heaviest of all sentences, "Life, never to return." He was thus at one time rather ill-conducted—boat-building, or otherwise scheming to recover his liberty—and often in trouble in consequence. And it gives me the greatest pleasure now to hear so different a report of him, at once for his own sake, as the anecdote illustrates what I have elsewhere said of the acquiescence of prisoners in just, if not vindictive or extreme severity or restraint; and as it further shows me the gratifying direction which remembrance of old times and lessons still gives to these poor fellows' minds. Their present value for these prayer-books may be in a degree false and factitious; yet who knows what they may yet do for them? or how far, under the varied impulses to which humanity is subject, their influence may not be deepened, in the most critical circumstances of temptation or of suffering, by the associations thus connected with them?'

We cannot leave this subject without expressing our cordial approbation of the leading features of Captain Maconochie's plan, and our earnest wish that a fair trial were given to it.

THE PARTITION OF AN ISLAND BETWEEN TWO GREAT NATIONS.

[The following humorous account of a territorial division between contending nations, is translated from a French periodical, and perhaps our readers may not think it *mal-a-propos* to see it in an English dress.]

In the year 1648, whilst Europe, torn for a century and a half by wars carried on from one end of the old world to the other, at length sought repose, and sent plenipotentiaries from all parts to the village of Munster to negotiate a peace, at the same moment, but at a distance of two thousand leagues from that village and its excited population, the representatives of two great nations met, in the midst of a world of waters, with scarcely less solemnity, for the purpose also of arriving at a mutual understanding. The place of meeting was a hill beaten by the sea waves, and commanding a horizon of prodigious extent. The attention of the ambassadors, who came upon the ground about sunrise, was at first wholly taken up with the sublime spectacle spread before their eyes. Both on the right and left there was the glittering ocean, upon whose surface of fire many islands of the Archipelago, wrapped in the blue haze of distance, were scattered. One by one, from east to west, were they touched by the solar rays, and awakened like a troop of nymphs from their slumbers.

The ambassadors approached, the conference began—a grave and delicate negotiation. In fact, it was no less than the apportionment between France and Holland of the island of St Martin, a plot of *terra firma* four leagues by three. France was represented on this elevation (since called Concord Height) by four of her sons; namely, a captain who had lost his regiment in these remote latitudes, a Gascon turned planter, and two friends who were independent gentlemen. Holland was represented by four Dutchmen, of whom one had made a considerable fortune by selling beer to the others.

After some formal preliminaries, the discussion became lively enough.

'Talk of concessions made by Holland, forsooth!' cried the French captain: 'concessions, indeed! it is France who, in her generosity, has been inclined to grant them to you; for were we not in this island before you?'

'Certainly not,' said the Dutchman stiffly.

'What! have you forgotten our astonishment when we first discovered you here?'

'Our surprise was quite as great as yours.'

'We believed ourselves to be the sole occupants of the island. We settled on the northern part, built houses, planted the flag of France on a height: we were contented and happy; when, behold! one morning, urged by the ardour of the chase, we crossed for the first time a mountain that separated us from the southern part of the island. Imagine our surprise when we found you settled just as comfortably as ourselves.'

'Very true,' said the Dutch leader; 'and you can readily believe that our astonishment was not a whit less than yours, when all of a sudden we saw you descend the mountain with that easy air that people wear who think themselves at home.'

'Well, well; but what passed at our first interview?'

'You demanded what we did here. We replied it was our colony.'

'Your colony!' you exclaimed; 'just climb to that mountain-ridge and you will see another colony, and, what is more, with our flag.'

'We climbed the mountain,' said the Dutchman, 'and we found in truth on the other side three vessels and a flag.'

'Exactly.'

'Exactly; you had seen as much on our side.'

'Yes; but which of the two nations arrived here first; that is the point. There can be no doubt that we did; for who expressed the greatest surprise at seeing the other? Surely we did.'

'So, gentlemen,' retorted the Dutchman, 'it pleases you to say. But we can assure you that our amazement was just as great as yours, only we are not in the habit of expressing our feelings so noisily as you are. That was all the difference.'

'Truly you are a phlegmatic people!'

'Phlegm, let me tell you, sir, is indicative of a landed proprietor.'

'What have you to say, then, to the fort? Ours is already constructed, beside the flag.'

'Just what we ourselves have done.'

'This state of things, however, France cannot put up with; and it is to have an end of these disputes that we have here assembled. We must now settle the matter once for all.'

'We must settle the matter by all means. Holland cannot consent to occupy an equivocal position. In everything we like to know whether we stand on our head or our heels.'

'There seems to be only one method of arriving at that piece of knowledge,' replied the captain; 'you are four, so are we. Let us fight, and the victors shall be masters of the island.'

'And this you style the generous concessions of France?'

'Well, have *you* any better plan? If so, let us hear it.'

'It seems to us that there are simpler plans than the one you have proposed—an equal partition, for instance. You occupy the north of the island, we the south. Good; let each remain at home, and, instead of fighting, as if we were hostile armies, instead of ruining ourselves by building useless forts, let us live in peace, and establish between ourselves a great system of commerce. Will not that be better, gentlemen, than cutting one another's throats? We happen to have just now some capital beer to sell. What do you say to that?'

'How do you sell it?'

'Oh, we are content with a moderate profit.'

'Well, well, we will talk the matter over hereafter. If, however, we found two neighbouring empires, there remains an important question to settle—what shall be our frontier lines? It will of course be absolutely necessary to determine this point; else how shall we know where to erect our customhouses?'

'True, true,' replied the Dutchman; 'we must certainly fix upon a boundary.'

'Well, then, we will tell you a very simple mode of doing that. You see we are standing on the north coast. Do you turn to the left, and, keeping along the shore, march right onwards. We will start in the other direction. In this way we shall pass round the island, and meet again on the other side. We will then draw a line from the hill where we now are to the place of meeting. This will divide the island into two parts: you shall have one, and we will take the other.'

'A very ingenious scheme,' said the Dutchman. 'We agree to your proposal. Your course is to the right, ours to the left. As the sun has attained no great height, we will, if you please, begin the perambulation at once.'

'Very well; so here we are off.'

The two parties then separated, and with mighty solemnity they set out on their respective ways. They were scarcely at the foot of the mount where the conference had taken place, before the Frenchmen set up a shout of laughter. 'Now I will wager,' said the Gascon planter, 'that those fat Dutchmen are at this moment bearing themselves with all the gravity of a priest carrying the host. I should like to have a peep at them. What do you say to our climbing the hill once more? We shall have a jovial ten minutes in looking at them from the top.'

'But don't you see that they will be gaining ground all the time?' retorted the captain.

'Bah!' said the Gascon; 'cannot we have a run afterwards, and so make ourselves even with them? Come, let us go back.'

'Faith no,' said the captain; 'the hill is somewhat steep. I have not the slightest inclination to climb it again.'

Well, I confess I should like to see them. You wont have anything to say to the hill; now suppose we run forward as fast as we can? We shall then surprise them in the midst of their ceremonious airs. How we shall enjoy the sight!'

'No, no, we must not play them a trick. If they walk, we have no right to run.'

'Pooh! what matters it? In the first place, no pace was stipulated on. In the second, if we obtain a territory twice the size of theirs, where is the harm? Do not the French move about twice as fast as the Dutch, and ought they not therefore to have twice as much space? In strict justice we ought to have two-thirds of the island.'

'Very well then, let us run.'

Bursting with laughter, the four Frenchmen immediately set forward at a rapid speed, and after moving at this accelerated pace about half an hour, all of a sudden, in doubling a promontory, they came face to face with the four Dutchmen, who were no little astonished at the meeting.

'How is this?' cried the Batavians, coming to a full stop.

'Parblieu! here we are, the sons of France. And now, gentlemen, we must erect a cross, and then some of these days we can draw the boundary line.'

'Well, this is a little surprising,' said Meinherr; 'we have scarcely come a mile.'

'That,' said the Gascon in a grave tone, 'was your fault. If you choose to walk so majestically——'

'Most surprising!' Holland repeated. 'Have you not been running, messieurs, a little?'

'Sir,' rejoined the Gascon, 'we used the pace of France.'

The next day a line was solemnly drawn from the point of parting to the place of meeting; and hence it is that Holland is owner of only one-third of the island of St Martin.

CLASS REPROBATION—TWO HONEST LAWYERS.

We still occasionally meet with individuals who entertain prejudices against whole professions, declaring, for instance, that all engaged in the law must needs be tainted with roguery. That there may be something unfavourable to general morality in the maxim which sanctions a legal man in taking up causes which he fully believes to be bad, we are not prepared to deny; that there are many despicable pettifoggers continually engaged in dirty and roguish work, cannot be doubted; but it is at the same time evident to all who can take a comprehensive view of the profession, that the great mass are men of the purest honour, while many exhibit even an unusual exactness in their dealings with their fellow-creatures. The effect of the following *true story* will be, we think, to show that honour and shame are not necessarily connected with any of the walks of life in which common prejudice expects to find them.

In a certain mercantile town, which need not be named, there existed, thirty years ago, a house transacting business under the firm of B. M. H. and Co. Their trusty clerk, J. S., having been one day sent to the bank for a large sum, which was paid to him in hundred-pound notes, was returning with it, when, having gone into a shop for some unimportant purpose, he unluckily dropped one of the notes, which he did not miss till he had reached the counting-house of his employers. The junior partner of a thriving manufacturing house happened to observe it immediately after the loser had departed, and, having picked it up unobserved, he showed it to his partners as a windfall, and they agreed to regard it as a common good, and enter it as such in their books. The loss of the note was duly advertised in the newspapers and by placard: the fact became universally known, and was as universally regretted; but no trace of it was ever discovered. The very men who had appropriated it, joined heartily in deploring the misfortune of the poor clerk, upon whom it was known that the loss would fall. When all efforts had failed, J. S. was obliged to make up the sum to his employers, out of a little fund which he had accumulated as a provision for a lunatic daughter. Worse still; the misfortune preyed upon his spirits. He fell into ill health, and soon after died, leaving a destitute family.

For twenty years, the trio who had divided the hundred pounds pitilessly beheld the struggles of the poor widow and her children. At length their copartnery was dissolved, and the junior partner, in consulting his legal agent, Mr W., as to some details of that transaction, incidentally stated that he had hardly got his fair share of that hundred-pound note which he had picked up twenty years ago. Little more passed at that time; but, about three months after, Widow B., the surviving child of poor S., who had lost the note, having occasion to consult the same legal gentleman, made allusion to that circumstance as what had produced the ruin of her father's family. Struck with the coincidence of time, place, and the sum lost, Mr W. made further inquiries, and the result was, that he recommended Mrs B. to call upon the principal partner of the dissolved concern, and ask pointedly if a member of his house had ever found a hundred-pound bank note, and if the sum had been credited to cash in their books.

The poor woman acted according to direction, and by the person to whom she applied, was ordered to quit his house, and never trouble him again on such a subject. Not daunted by this repulse, Mr W. caused his poor protegée to apply to Mr B., the principal partner of the house by which her father had been employed, requesting that he would kindly exert himself to see justice done to her. Mr B. was a benevolent, as well as conscientious man; he had ever regretted the fate of poor S., and he now felt the deepest indignation at the trio whom, from the report of Mr W., he believed to have appropriated the note. He applied by letter, and personally, for the restoration of the money; but met only shuffling denials and refusals. A rupture then took place between the parties, and, with Mr B.'s concurrence, a summons was served by W. upon the three partners of the dissolved firm, narrating all the circumstances of the case, and concluding for the value of the missing note, with interest and expenses. An agent was employed in defence; but, happily, like Mr W., he was an honest man. Mr M. observing something suspicious in the case, assembled the three partners in his chamber, where a conversation somewhat like the following took place:

Mr M. Well, gentlemen, your defence in this case, what is it?

Trio. Oh, there is no *proof* that the pursuer's father lost *any* note, or that we found the *one* he lost.

M. Did any of you find a Royal Bank L.100 note at the time and place stated in the summons?

Trio. Ay; but what *proof* is there that it is the one he lost, if indeed he lost *any* note?

M. Did you at the time know of the advertisements and reward narrated in the summons?

Trio. Oh, we cannot remember these far-back stories.

M. Yes; but I see you do not deny them, and I wish to know if you yourselves advertised the finding of the note, as was clearly your duty as honest men?

Trio. No; and surely there was no law of the land which obliged us to do so.

M. Well, gentlemen, I tell you frankly that this seems to me an ugly affair, and you had better settle it, for certainly I shall not defend you.

Struck with the straightforward honesty of their own agent, the partners could not resist his advice. The opposite agent, Mr W., was sent for, and asked what rate of interest he demanded. He answered to Mr M., 'Whatever you, sir, as agent for the defenders, think fair.' 'Then,' said M., 'I fix it at bank interest;' and the matter was immediately settled.

Thus was a monstrous wrong, which had been inflicted by individuals of a class held generally in respect, redressed by the honesty and zeal of two members of a profession often spoken of as wholly predatory and vile. Could anything show us in a more expressive light the necessity of caution in applying general characters to large bodies of men?

COMPENSATION.

[From Essays by R. W. Emerson, an American writer.]

POLARITY, or action and reaction, we meet in every part of nature; in darkness and light, in heat and cold, in the ebb and flow of waters, in male and female, in the inspiration and expiration of plants and animals, in the systole and diastole of the heart, in the undulations of fluids and of sound, in the centrifugal and centripetal gravity, in electricity, galvanism, and chemical affinity. Superinduce magnetism at one end of a needle, the opposite magnetism takes place at the other end. If the south attracts, the north repels. To empty here, you must condense there. An inevitable dualism bisects nature, so that each thing is a half, and suggests another thing to make it whole; as spirit, matter; man, woman; subjective, objective; in, out; upper, under; motion, rest; yea, nay.

Whilst the world is thus dual, so is every one of its parts. The entire system of things gets represented in every particle. There is somewhat that resembles the ebb and flow of the sea, day and night, man and woman, in a single needle of the pine, in a kernel of corn, in each individual of every animal tribe. The reaction so grand in the elements, is repeated within these small boundaries. For example, in the animal kingdom, the physiologist has observed that no creatures are favourites, but a certain compensation balances every gift and every defect. A surplusage given to one part is paid out of a reduction from another part of the same creature. If the head and neck are enlarged, the trunk and extremities are cut short.

The theory of the mechanic forces is another example. What we gain in power, is lost in time, and the converse. The periodic or compensating errors of the planets are another instance. The influences of climate and soil in political history are another. The cold climate invigorates; the barren soil does not breed fevers, crocodiles, tigers, or scorpions.

The same dualism underlies the nature and condition of man. Every excess causes a defect; every defect an excess. Every sweet hath its sour; every evil its good. Every faculty which is a receiver of pleasure, has an equal penalty put on its abuse. It is to answer for its moderation with its life. For every grain of wit, there is a grain of folly. For everything you have missed, you have gained something else; and for everything you gain, you lose something. If riches increase, they are increased that use them. If the gatherer gathers too much, nature takes out of the man what she puts into his chest; swells the estate, but kills the owner. Nature hates monopolies and exceptions. The waves of the sea do not more speedily seek a level from their loftiest tossing, than the varieties of condition tend to equalise themselves. There is always some levelling circumstance that puts down the overbearing, the strong, the rich, the fortunate, substantially on the same ground with all others.

Every act rewards itself, or, in other words, integrates itself in a twofold manner; first, in the thing, or in real nature; and secondly, in the circumstance, or in apparent nature. Men call the circumstance the retribution. The casual retribution is in the thing, and is seen by the soul. The retribution in the circumstance is seen by the understanding; it is inseparable from the thing, but is often spread over a long time, and so does not become distinct until after many years. The specific stripes may follow late after the offence, but they follow because they accompany it. Crime and punishment grow out of one stem. Punishment is a fruit that, unsuspected, ripens within the flower of the pleasure which concealed it. Cause and effect, means and ends, seed and fruit, cannot be severed; for the effect already blooms in the cause, the end pre-exists in the means, the fruit in the seed.

Life invests itself with inevitable conditions, which the unwise seek to doge, which one and another brags that he does not know; brags that they do not touch him; but the brag is on his lips, the conditions are in his soul. If he escapes them in one part, they attack him in another more vital part. If he has escaped them in form, and in the appearance, it is that he has resisted his life, and fled from himself, and the retribution is so much death. So signal is the failure of all attempts to make this separation of the good from the tax, that the experiment would not be tried—since to try it is to be mad; but for the circumstance, that when the disease began in the will, of rebellion and separation, the intellect is at once infected, so that the man ceases to see God whole in each object, but is able to see the sensual allurement of an object, and not see the sensual hurt: he sees the mermaid's head, but not the dragon's tail; and thinks he can cut off that which he would have from that which he would not have.

All things are double, one against another. Tit for tat, an eye for an eye, a tooth for a tooth, blood for blood, measure for measure, love for love. Give, and it shall be given you. He that watereth shall be watered himself. Who doth not work shall not eat. Harm watch, harm catch. Curses always recoil on the head of him who imprecates them. If you put a chain around the neck of a slave, the other end fastens itself around your own. Bad counsel confounds the adviser.

It is thus written, because it is thus in life. Our action is overmastered and characterised above our will by the law of nature. We aim at a petty end quite aside from the public good, but our act arranges itself by irresistible magnetism in a line with the poles of the world.

A man cannot speak but he judges himself. With his will, or against his will, he draws his portrait to the eye of his companions by every word. Every opinion reacts on him who utters it. It is a thread-ball thrown at a mark, but the other end remains in the thrower's bag; or, rather, it is a harpoon thrown at the whale, unwinding, as it flies, a coil of cord in the boat, and if the harpoon is not good, or not well thrown, it will go nigh to cut the steersman in twain, or to sink the boat.

You cannot do wrong without suffering wrong. 'No

man had ever a point of pride that was not injurious to him,' said Burke. The exclusive in fashionable life does not see that he excludes himself from enjoyment, in the attempt to appropriate it. The exclusionist in religion does not see that he shuts the door of heaven on himself, in striving to shut out others. Treat men as pawns and nine-pins, and you shall suffer as well as they. If you leave out their heart, you shall lose your own.

All infractions of love and equity in our social relations are speedily punished. They are punished by Fear. Whilst I stand in simple relations to my fellow-man, I have no displeasure in meeting him. We meet as water meets water, or a current of air meets another, with perfect diffusion and interpenetration of nature. But as soon as there is any departure from simplicity, and attempt at halfness, or good for me that is not good for him, my neighbour feels the wrong; he shrinks from me as far as I have shrunk from him; his eyes no longer seek mine; there is war between us; there is hate in him and fear in me.

All the old abuses in society, the great and universal, and the petty and particular, all unjust accumulations of property and power, are avenged in the same manner. Fear is an instructor of great sagacity, and the herald of all revolutions. One thing he always teaches, that there is rottenness where he appears. He is a carrion crow, and though you see not well what he hovers for, there is death somewhere. Our property is timid, our laws are timid, our cultivated classes are timid. Fear for ages has boded, and mowed, and gibbered over government and property. That obscene bird is not there for nothing. He indicates great wrongs which must be revised.

Experienced men of the world know very well that it is always best to pay scot and lot as they go along, and that a man often pays dear for a small frugality. The borrower runs in his own debt. Has a man gained anything who has received a hundred favours and rendered none? Has he gained by borrowing, through indolence or cunning, his neighbour's wares, or horses, or money? There arises on the deed the instant acknowledgment of benefit on the one part, and of debt on the other; that is, of superiority and inferiority. The transaction remains in the memory of himself and his neighbour; and every new transaction alters, according to its nature, their relation to each other. He may soon come to see that he had better have broken his own bones than to have ridden in his neighbour's coach, and that 'the highest price he can pay for a thing is to ask for it.'

A wise man will extend this lesson to all parts of life, and know that it is always the part of prudence to face every claimant, and pay every just demand on your time, your talents, or your heart. Always pay; for, first or last, you must pay your entire debt. Persons and events may stand for a time between you and justice, but it is only a postponement. You must pay at last your own debt. If you are wise, you will dread a prosperity which only loads you with more. Benefit is the end of nature. But for every benefit which you receive, a tax is levied. He is great who confers the most benefits. He is base—and that is the one base thing in the universe—to receive favours and render none. In the order of nature, we cannot render benefits to those from whom we receive them, or only seldom. But the benefit we receive must be rendered again, line for line, deed for deed, cent for cent, to somebody. Beware of too much good staying in your hand. It will fast corrupt and worm worms. Pay it away quickly in some sort.

The cheat, the defaulter, the gambler, cannot extort the benefit, cannot extort the knowledge of material and moral nature, which his honest care and pains yield to the operative. The law of nature is, Do the thing, and you shall have the power; but they who do not the thing have not the power. Human labour, through all its forms, from the sharpening of a stake to the construction of a city or an epic, is one immense illustration of the perfect compensation of the universe. Everywhere and always this law is sublime. The absolute balance of Give and Take, the doctrine that everything has its price—and if that price is not paid, not that thing but something else is obtained, and that it is impossible to get anything without its price—this doctrine is not less sublime in the columns of a ledger than in the budgets of states, in the laws of light and darkness, in all the action and reaction of nature. I cannot doubt that the high laws which each man sees ever implicated in those processes with which he is conversant—the stern ethics which sparkle on his chisel-edge, which are measured out by his plumb and foot-rule, which stand as manifest in the footing of the shop-bill as in the history of a state—do recommend to him his trade, and, though seldom named, exalt his business to his imagination.

The league between virtue and nature engages all things to assume a hostile front to vice. The beautiful laws and substances of the world persecute and whip the traitor. He finds that things are arranged for truth and benefit; but there is no den in the wide world to hide a rogue. There is no such thing as concealment. Commit a crime, and the earth is made of glass. Commit a crime, and it seems as if a coat of snow fell on the ground, such as reveals in the woods the track of every partridge, and fox, and squirrel, and mole. You cannot recall the spoken word, you cannot wipe out the foot-track, you cannot draw up the ladder, so as to leave no inlet or clew: always some condemning circumstance transpires. The laws and substances of nature—water, snow, wind, gravitation—become penalties to the thief.

On the other hand, the law holds with equal sureness for all right action. Love, and you shall be loved. All love is mathematically just, as much as the two sides of an algebraic equation. Bolts and bars are not the best of our institutions, nor is shrewdness in trade a mark of wisdom. Men suffer all their life long, under the foolish superstition that they can be cheated. But it is as impossible for a man to be cheated by any one but himself, as for a thing to be, and not to be, at the same time. There is a third silent party to all our bargains. The nature and soul of things takes on itself the guaranty of the fulfilment of every contract, so that honest service cannot come to loss. If you serve an ungrateful master, serve him the more. Put God in your debt. Every stroke shall be repaid. The longer the payment is withholden, the better for you; for compound interest on compound interest is the rate and usage of this exchequer.

ROBBERS IN INDIA.

Various classes of robbers, under the designations of Thugs, Dakoits, Choars, Kuzzaks, and Budhukes, infest the entire country. The first and the last would appear to be identical, being sets of villains distinguished by their practice of strangling unsuspecting travellers with whom they may contrive to fall in upon a journey; they are sometimes formed into secret societies, not dissimilar from some of those in the middle ages: and it was vainly hoped that Lord William Bentinck had utterly extirpated them. The Kuzzaks are mounted robbers, who singly beset the highroads, or, being collected into parties, attack and plunder entire villages: in other words, they are Turpins, or Robin Hoods, or Rob Roys, as occasion may require. The Dakoits and Choars are more like the early companions of Gil Blas—thieves who naturally and constitutionally assemble in gangs, and who usually limit their depredations to the houses or persons of those reputed to possess valuables or money in concealed hoards. These were once the most formidable, being thoroughly organised under sirdars, or leaders: they commonly meet for their lawless procedures under cover of the night; being, by day, to all appearance, among the most peaceable and quiet members of the community. Their grand characteristic, wherever they subsist, still continues to be that of Dan—'an adder in the path.' They have watchwords and secret signals. Companies, variously armed with swords, clubs, pikes, and matchlocks, will grow, as it were, out of the ground, coming together nobody knows how, and gathered from no one knows where, in numbers from fifteen to fifty. The spot will be some tope or grove adjacent to the desired spoil. The following is a midnight picture of what these worthies were some thirty years ago, as also of what they too often are now:—'When collected, their marauding excursion was usually preluded by a religious ceremony—the worship of the goddess Durga—the patroness of thieves, typified by a water-pot, or a few blades of grass. The ceremony was conducted by a Brahmin of degraded condition and dissolute life. Having propitiated the goddess by the promise of a portion of their spoil, they marched, with lighted torches, and little attempt at concealment, beyond disguising their faces by pigment, or covering them with masks, to the object of their expedition, usually the dwelling of some shopkeeper, or money-changer, in which it was expected to discover treasure. Occasionally, the motive of the attack was vengeance; and information given by the householder, or any member of his family, against some member of the gang, brought upon him the resentment of the whole fraternity. Upon entering the village, it was customary to fire a gun as a signal to the inhabitants to keep within their dwellings: the house against which the operation was designed was then surrounded; and whilst some of the gang forced an entrance, others remained as a guard without. Unless exasperated by resistance, or stimulated by revenge, the Dakoits did not commonly proceed to murder; but they perpetrated atrocious cruelties upon such persons as refused to give them, or were unable to give them, information regarding property which they suspected of having been concealed; burning them with lighted torches or blazing straw, or wrapping cloth or flax steeped in oil around their limbs, and setting it on fire; or inflicting various tortures which caused immediate or speedy death. The object being accomplished, and the booty secured, the gang retired before daylight, and the guilty individuals resumed their daily occupations.' In Bengal alone, six hundred and ninety such atrocities disgraced a single year. —*Eclectic Review for July.*

REMARKABLE NATURAL PHENOMENON.

In the Mining Journal of August 2, we find the following details of a most singular but instructive phenomenon:—The river Wear, immediately above and below Framwellgate Bridge, Durham, now presents a singular appearance, as, when unruffled by the wind, it appears to be in a state of ebullition, occasioned by numerous streams of air-bubbles issuing from below. The circumstance, however, had not been regarded with much attention, until Mr Wharton of Dryburn, having accidentally observed an unusual agitation of the water, was induced to take particular notice of one of the principal jets of air, and finding its position the same on three successive days, was led to the conclusion, that it must flow from some fissure under the bed of the river, and would prove to be an escape of the light carburetted hydrogen gas generated in such fearful abundance in the coal and other strata of the district. A boat having been moored alongside the jet of air, and its inflammable nature fully ascertained by the application of a lighted taper, a large inverted funnel, furnished with a pipe of the requisite length, was fixed over the supposed fissure, and all the gas issuing from it thus collected and conveyed into a small open-bottomed tin reservoir, or gasometer, floating on the surface, and provided with a burner and glass chimney. The gas could now be ignited at pleasure, and the supply was found to be sufficiently abundant to produce a large and brilliant jet of flame, arising, as it were, from the bosom of the old 'river of Wear'—a strange and extraordinary spectacle, which has already collected many hundreds of spectators curious to see the river on fire. The stream of gas appropriated to the above experiment is one only of a great many others which occupy an area of from fifty to a hundred square yards of water, and which must together discharge very many gallons of gas per minute. When the air is perfectly calm, large bubbles, formed by the ascent of the gas to the surface, and readily taking fire on contact with a lighted candle, mark the limits of the principal cluster of gas jets above the bridge; two others of smaller dimensions are observable below, and a still smaller one at some distance above the bridge, each of them being marked by the presence of numerous air-bubbles whenever the surface of the water is smooth. They are all situated nearly in a straight line, crossing the river diagonally under the bridge in a north-north-east and south-south-west direction. The distance of the extreme clusters being upwards of a hundred yards, furnishes a strong presumption that the source of this extraordinary discharge of gas is situated at a great depth below the bed of the river, and that it finds its way up the fissures of some 'trouble,' fault, or dislocation of the strata from some of the lowest beds of coal or shale reposing below. No coal workings are known to exist within several hundred yards of the bridge, nor are there any within the distance of two miles which are sufficiently deep to have become instrumental to the appearance of this curious phenomenon. It must therefore in all probability be traced to one of those extensive natural accumulations of gas lurking in the fissures and pores of the strata far below the surface of the ground, which, when tapped by the operations and fired by the candles of the miner, have been the frequent causes of those dreadful explosions, of one of which the workings of Haswell colliery bore such awful testimony last year. It has been proposed to light the bridge from this source, and other parts of the town, if there appears a probability of its continuance. Many persons assert that they have noticed bubbles rising from the water for eighteen months or two years past, and as the remarkable emission of hydrogen from one of the old shafts of Wall's End colliery has been burning for many years, and giving a clear light, which is visible at night for miles, it is probable this natural supply on the Wear may last for years.

THE QUESTIONER—A CHANT.

I ask not for his lineage,
I ask not for his name—
If manliness be in his heart,
He noble birth may claim.
I care not though of this world's wealth
But slender be his part,
If Yes you answer, when I ask—
Hath he a true man's heart?

I ask not from what land he came,
Nor where his youth was nursed—
If pure the stream, it matters not
The spot from whence it burst.
The palace or the hovel,
Where first his life began,
I seek not of; but answer this—
Is he an honest man?

Nay, blush not now—what matters it
Where first he drew his breath?
A manger was the cradle-bed
Of Him of Nazareth!
Be nought, be any, everything—
I care not what you be—
If Yes you answer, when I ask—
Art thou pure, true, and free?

—*Robert Nicoll's Poems.*

PERFUME OF PLANTS.

It is not sufficiently observed by all the admirers of flowers, that the agreeable perfume of plants in full bloom, when diffused through close apartments, becomes decidedly deleterious, by producing headache, giddiness, and other affections of the brain. But it is in confinement alone that such effects become evident. In the garden, when mingled with a wholesome and exhilarating atmosphere, amidst objects that awaken the most delightful sensations of our nature, these sweets are a part of our gratifications, and health is promoted as a consequence of enjoyment so pure. Who has not felt the excitement of spring? of nature, in that delightful season, rising from lethargy into beauty and vivacity, and spreading the sweets of the thorn and the violet, auxiliary to our gratifications? Amidst the beauties of the flower-garden, these pleasures are condensed and refined; and the fragrance there, hovering on the wings of the breeze, cannot be imagined less wholesome than pleasant. Whatever increases our gratifications, so peculiarly unmixed with the bad passions of human nature, must surely tend to the improvement of mankind, and to the excitement of grateful feelings towards that beneficent Creator who has so bountifully supplied those luxuries, which none are denied.—*Maund.*

GOOD CONSCIENCE.

A good conscience is more to be desired than all the riches of the East. How sweet are the slumbers of him who can lie down on his pillow and review the transactions of every day without condemning himself! A good conscience is the finest opiate.—*Knox.*

LOVE AND FRIENDSHIP.

Love is the shadow of the morning, which decreases as the day advances. Friendship is the shadow of the evening, which strengthens with the setting sun of life.—*La Fontaine.*

Published by W. and R. Chambers, High Street, Edinburgh (also 98, Miller Street, Glasgow); and, with their permission by W. S. Orr, Amen Corner, London.—Printed by Bradbury and Evans, Whitefriars, London.

☞ Complete sets of the Journal, *First Series*, in twelve volumes, and also odd numbers to complete sets, may be had from the publishers or their agents.—A stamped edition of the Journal is now issued, price 2½d., to go free by post.

CONDUCTED BY WILLIAM AND ROBERT CHAMBERS, EDITORS OF 'CHAMBERS'S INFORMATION FOR THE PEOPLE,' 'CHAMBERS'S EDUCATIONAL COURSE,' &c.

No. 90. New Series. SATURDAY, SEPTEMBER 20, 1845. Price 1½d.

THE USE AND ABUSE OF GREAT NAMES.

Every one must have noticed the fact, that some of the greatest names among the ancients have been strangely degraded and misapplied by the moderns. Demosthenes, Themistocles, Anaxagoras, and other names of many syllables, have escaped in consequence of their length; but shorter ones have fared badly. In England, in the days when it was fashionable to keep black footmen, and in the United States of America at the present time, the illustrious names of Cæsar, Pompey, Gracchus, Scipio, and Cato, were and are constantly given in derisive dignity to slaves and menials, and as frequently bestowed upon dogs of all breeds and sizes. Nero has been another favourite name, but, being suggestive of ferocity, has been reserved for the exclusive use of the brute creation—most commonly for lions or bull-dogs. Brutus, although the name might provoke a pun, has not been considered good enough even for the brutes, and has been applied in modern parlance to the peculiar cut of a man's hair. Cupid has been the tender name for an ape or a monkey; and Neptune, Hebe, Juno, Juba, and other names of mortals and immortals, have been lavished upon pet dogs, and all the brute favourites of the ladies.

While the moderns have taken these liberties with the names of the ancients, they have not exempted the names of their contemporaries from the same kind of popularity. The hero of Waterloo has given almost as much renown to the fashion of our boots as to the field on which he fought; and his name is nearly as closely identified with them as with the remembrance of his great victory. 'Brougham—a kind of carriage,' may hereafter stand in the dictionaries of our vernacular tongue as long as the name of Brougham the lawyer, philosopher, and statesman, stands in the page of English history; and the name of the husband of our present sovereign may be as well remembered by future ages in connexion with the shape of a military hat and the tie of a cravat, as with the crown of Great Britain.

But while this abuse of names, slight as it is, has been noticed by most people, there is another and greater abuse connected with names which has excited but little attention, and which might be remedied with advantage; or, more properly speaking, there is a use for great names to which they have never yet been sufficiently applied. We allude more particularly to the names of places. In primitive periods of society such names have been singularly appropriate, and often highly poetical, being derived either from the physical conformation or peculiarities of the spot to be designated, or from some remarkable event of its history. It has not been possible in a later stage of civilisation to carry out this principle to its full extent, and names have been necessarily given in a more arbitrary manner. The reader will remember Wordsworth's poem on the 'Naming of Places,' in which, with much gracefulness and fancy, he has given names to such of the hills and dales of his own neighbourhood as have received none from the shepherds or country people, but are associated with family incidents or recollections of his own life. Upon a similar principle, though with less dignity of result, the builders of most of our new streets seem to choose designations for them. The name of a member of their own or a friend's family generally supplies the readiest hint, and Charles Streets, or John Streets, or Anne Streets, or Catharine Streets, as the case may be, abound all over the country. Failing these, loyalty, often very absurdly manifested amongst us, supplies the next hint, and the names of the sovereign and the royal family are brought into requisition. Thus we see in the neighbourhood of London and of other large cities, Victoria Streets, Victoria Places, and Victoria Terraces, with Albert Rows, Albert Crescents, and Albert Squares innumerable. So little invention and taste are displayed, that the only varieties that seem at all popular are such names as Belvidere, Bellevue, or Prospect Places or Terraces; and these, as far as London and its views are concerned, are generally as inappropriate as names can well be. In the metropolis alone, besides these countless Prospect Places, it has been observed that there are upwards of forty King Streets, with as many Queen Streets, Princes Streets, Duke Streets, Charlotte Streets, and George Streets. The most beautiful portions of Edinburgh are named in this way, chiefly after members of the family of George III. Very frequently, too, some great event of modern history, which has taken a firm hold upon the popular imagination, supplies another hint for names for our thoroughfares. The battle of Waterloo is the most remarkable example that we can think of, and it would be interesting to know to what precise number of streets and buildings, from Waterloo Road and Bridge downwards, it has given the name, not in London alone, but throughout England, Scotland, and Ireland. The linen-drapers' shops in London that are called 'Waterloo Houses,' would of themselves fill a long list. Wellington has been almost as popular a name as Waterloo for this purpose; but, strange to say, considering that we are a naval people, Nelson and Trafalgar have not been favourites to anything like the same extent. We are not sure whether Nelson Square in the Blackfriars Road was named after the hero, or after some obscure individual (the builder or proprietor perhaps) with the same patronymic; but Trafalgar Square, Charing Cross, is the only public place that has been named after his greatest victory. This was done at the especial request of his late majesty William IV., who, with a characteristic love of his own profession, did not think it quite fair to consecrate the military victory to so enormous an extent, and to leave the great naval one altogether unassociated with any public thoroughfare in the country. Small as our own inventive powers are in this respect, even less are employed in the new towns and cities that rise so rapidly in the United States of America. We must, however, admit that they display considerably more of method and regularity. Thus we hear of long lines of streets crossing each other at right angles, with such names as First North Street, Second North Street, Third North Street, Fourth North Street, and so on to ten or a dozen; while South Streets, East Streets, and West Streets, are numbered in the same manner. They have also in New York, First Street, Second Street, Third Street, and so on up to Thirty-seventh Street; with room enough, extending in the same direction on Manhattan Island, to realise at no very distant day a Thousand-and-oneth Street—to use an expressive Yankeeism. In Philadelphia, they have A Street, B Street, and C Street, and South A Street, South B Street, &c. This, if not poetical or graceful, is at all events convenient, and far better than the eternal John Streets and King Streets of Great Britain.

In this matter, unimportant as it may seem at the first glance, there is surely great room for improvement. We throw out the hint for a better system to all proprietors and projectors of new streets, and more especially to the enterprising and intelligent men under whose auspices the town of Birkenhead is rising so fast into beauty and greatness. They have an opportunity of making it an example to be copied in due time by the whole country, and of raising a series of cheap and enduring monuments to the distinguished men who have conferred honour upon the British race and name either in past or in present times. We would urge them to name their streets upon a more enlightened and philosophic plan than has ever yet been attempted; and by so doing, they will give the crowning grace to a city (for city it will become) which has better arrangements for draining, lighting, and the supply of water, than any old or new town that has yet arisen, and which is constructed in every other respect as a town of the new generation ought to be constructed. Let them by all means make out a list of the most eminent men in art, science, literature, philosophy, or statesmanship, or who have conferred renown upon their country, and benefit on the human race, by their intellectual or moral greatness, and name their streets after them. In the United States of America they have not only squares, terraces, and streets, but whole counties named after their illustrious men—Madison, Jefferson, Clinton, Monro, Adams, Jackson, Everett, Lafayette, Washington, Franklin, and others of less note to Europeans. In France, too, similar honour is paid to Frenchmen and to Englishmen, of which there is a remarkable instance in the Avenue de Lord Byron at Paris. London has no Shakspeare Street (Edinburgh has a square unworthy of so great a name), neither has it an Isaac Newton Street, a Herschel Street, a Harvey Street, a Jenner Street, a John Locke Street, an Arkwright Street, a Watt Street, a Byron Street, a Napier Street, a Tillotson Street, a Latimer Street, or, unless by accident, a street named after any man whose intellectual achievements were the glory of his age. An exception must be made in favour of Milton Street, which is the name the moderns have very properly given to the new street that has arisen on the site of the ancient Grub Street. The Addison Road, near Holland House, Kensington, may also be called an exception, as having been named after the celebrated essayist of the Spectator. It is true that the name was not given entirely for his literary renown, but partly because, by his marriage with the Countess of Warwick, he was connected with the ancestry of the present proprietors. Still, a good example was set by it, and, as such, it is right that it should be recorded. Birkenhead has now a fine opportunity of being superior to London in this respect, and we shall be most happy if this slight notice of the subject shall lead its projectors to even a partial adoption of the reformation we have suggested.

One word in conclusion upon the naming of ships. If we look over a list of the British navy, or at the shipping list of any port, we find a similar disregard of all the truly great names of the country. Thunderers, Spitfires, Gorgons, Medusas, Furies, Harpies, Victories, Defiances, Growlers, Bucentaurs, Dreadnoughts, Terrors, Erebuses, Invincibles, Beelzebubs, and other names of equal fierceness, abound in our navy, whilst our commercial marine is mainly composed of Elizabeths, Lucys, Janes, Kates, Mary Annes, and Carolines, varied occasionally by names of flowers, or by the titles of the local aristocracy of the ports to which they trade. As has been said a thousand times before, with reference to other subjects—'they order these matters better in France.' A glance at the list of the vessels composing the steam navy of our neighbours, supplies us with the names not only of eminent Frenchmen, but of Englishmen, Spaniards, Portuguese, &c. and of the ancients as well as the moderns. Amongst others, we find the Vauban, the Descartes, the Magellan, the Christopher Columbus, the Cuvier, the Colbert, the Newton, the Plato, the Socrates, the Roland, the Gassendi, the Lavoisier, the Coligni, and the Fulton. Trifling as these matters may appear to some, they do not appear so to us. They show the disposition of the people to appreciate intellectual greatness, and to give honour where honour is due: and from such honour to the departed grows the emulation and the glory of the living.

LOVE AT FIRST SIGHT.

A TALE OF THE SIOUX INDIANS.

BY PERCY B. ST JOHN.

In the very centre of one of the thickest and heaviest woods of the American continent, where now stands a busy manufacturing town, there was, some twenty years ago, an Indian camp occupied by a small band of the wild and warlike Sioux. They were not more than fifty in number, having visited the spot merely for the purpose of hunting, and laying in a store of provisions for the winter. It chanced, however, that, coming unexpectedly upon certain Assineboins, who also were out lying in the woods, following the exciting duty of the chase, a quarrel ensued, ending in a bloody contest, in which the Sioux were victorious. With rude tents pitched, without order or method, in an open glade of the forest, with horses tethered around, and little dusky imps fighting with the lean dogs that lay lolling their tongues lazily about, there was yet a picturesque air about the place and its extraneous features, which would have captivated the eye of one in search of nature's sunshiny spots. Deeply embosomed within the autumnal tinted wood, a purling spring that burst from the green slope of a little mound was the feature which had attracted the Indians to the locality. Rank grass had once covered the whole surface of this forest meadow, but this the cattle had closely cropped, leaving a sward that would have rivalled any European lawn in its velvety beauty, and that, falling away before the eye, became inexpressibly soft as it sunk away in the distance.

The setting sun, gilding and crowning the tree tops in wreathed glory, was gradually paling behind the heavy belt of forest that enclosed the Sioux camp, the animals, both plumed and four-footed, that filled the woods, were seeking their accustomed rest, the squaws were busily engaged in preparing for their expected husbands their evening meal, just as a long line of grim and painted warriors issued from the shelter of the trees. A loud cry from the urchins that squatted round the purlieus of the camp, with a growl of friendly recognition from the ragged dogs, brought the women to the entrance of the camp.

The Indians came in in that silent and solemn manner which they are wont more particularly to assume after the occurrence of important events. To the no little surprise of the squaws, a prisoner accompanied the returning party, and all thoughts were effaced but those in connexion with the promised scene of torture and amusement. It was a young man, faultless in form, with features which in any land would have been remarkable for their intellectuality and engaging expression. His round limbs, and his erect figure, well displayed as he trod unshackled and nearly naked, were the admiration even of his enemies. His eye was keen and piercing, his lips curled in an expression of scorn and defiance, while his inflated nostrils no less marked the inward struggle of his mind, as he scowled fiercely on his captors.

In the centre of the camp was a strong but rudely erected log-house, that served the purpose of a council-chamber, and in this the prisoner, having been so bound as to render escape, unaided, a matter of impossibility, was left, while the warriors dispersed to their wigwams in search of refreshment and repose. A large fire burned in front of the council hall, which gave forth so bright a glare, that any one leaving or entering its precincts could scarcely avoid being seen by those around. Several maidens, too, having no hungry husbands requiring their ministering hands, were congregated in front conversing upon the probable fate of the Assineboin, and even in some measure expressing pity for his expected death, so far had his good looks and youth gone to create sympathy in the hearts of the fair Sioux.

'Let us see if the warrior weeps,' at length said one of the girls with a laugh; 'perhaps he will ask for a petticoat, and become a squaw.'

Curiosity induced the whole bevy to agree, and next moment they were all within the walls of the council-chamber, the warriors smiling grimly in their wigwams at this evidence of the universal feminine failing. A dim and fitful glare from the fire served to reveal the form of the luckless Indian youth seated upon a log, his eye fixed upon vacancy. For a moment curiosity kept the whole party silent, and then, education and habit exerting their influence, the group began to put in practice those arts which might be expected to awaken in the prisoner an exhibition of feeling derogatory to his dignity.

'An Assineboin has no eyes; he is a burrowing mole,' said one tauntingly; 'he creeps about the woods like a serpent, and falls into the trap of the hunters: a beaver is wiser than he. He is very cunning, but he cannot deceive a Sioux: he is very brave, but he is a prisoner, and not a wound shows that he struggled. Go; it is a squaw whom my people have brought in by mistake.'

A general laugh was the reward of the speaker's wit, while the Indian moved neither eye, limb, nor muscle. The girl, irritated, opened upon him with all that volubility of tongue which so strongly characterises their race. It was, however, in vain. The sun in the heavens was not more unmoved—a marble statue would have been life behind him—not a look or sound, not a glance, testified that he even heard what was passing. Wearied at length with their vain efforts, the bevy rushed forth into the open air, and, joining hands, commenced, with loud cries and laughter, a dance round the fire.

A deep and heavy respiration was the only sign the Indian gave of consciousness—his quick and practised senses told him he was not alone.

'Son of the Evening Light,' said a low and gentle voice, addressing him by a name which was well known in her tribe as that of their most dreaded enemy, 'the morning will come, and it will find my brothers thirsting for blood.'

'The veins of Ah-kre-nay are very full,' replied the warrior calmly; 'they can all drink.'

'The Son of the Evening Light is very brave,' said the other hurriedly, and in tones which exhibited strong feeling; 'but life is very sweet. Would he hunt again in the forest?—would his hand once more strike the grizzly bear?'

Suspecting some deep and cunning artifice of his enemies beneath this unmistakeable offer of escape on the part of the fair Peritana, the Indian was sternly silent; though the tones which truth assumes are so powerful and expressive, that he felt almost convinced at heart she was sincere. The young maiden probably understood his doubts, and therefore spoke no more, but with quick and ready hands placed a knife before him, and, cutting the bonds, left him free.

'My sister is very kind,' said the young warrior warmly, after giving vent to the guttural ugh! the jocund laugh and the romping of the dancers permitting conversation—'and Ah-kre-nay will remember her in his dreams.' With this the Assineboin turned towards the entrance of the wigwam.

The Sioux girl replied not, but, pointing to the throng without, and then passing her hand significantly round her head, folded her arms, and stood resignedly before the youth.

'Would the Sioux maiden leave her tribe and tread the woods with an Assineboin?' said the warrior curiously.

'Peritana will die if the Assineboin warrior be found to have escaped, and Peritana would rather live in the woods than in the happy hunting-ground.'

The Assineboin now felt sure that his youth, his appearance, or, at all events, his probable fate, had excited the sympathies of his visitor, and gratitude at once created in him a desire to know more of his fair friend.

'Ah-kre-nay will not depart without his sister; her voice is very sweet in his ears, sweeter than the cluck of the wild turkey to the hungry hunter. She is very little; let her hide in the corner of the wigwam.'

'Peritana has a father, tall and straight—an aged hemlock—and two brothers, bounding like the wild deer—Ah-kre-nay will not raise his hand against them?'

'They are safe, when Peritana has folded her white arms round them.'

This point settled, the Indian girl handed the youth his tomahawk and knife, and then obeyed his commands with as much alacrity as if she had been his legal squaw. The warrior then resumed his former position, placing the willow withes which had bound him in such a manner as readily to appear, by the light of the fire, as if they were still holding him firm.

This arrangement had scarcely been made, when a couple of grim warriors appeared in the doorway, after listening to the report of the girls. Peritana, closing her eyes, held her very breath, lest it should betray her presence to her people, and thus render all her bold efforts for him whose fame, beauty, and unfortunate position had won her heart, of no avail. The young warrior, too, sat motionless as a statue, his keen ear listening for the sound of the girl's breath. To his admiration and infinite surprise, her respiration had apparently ceased. The Sioux at this moment entered, and, glaring curiously at their enemy, as if satisfied with the survey they had taken, turned away and moved towards their wigwams. Silence now gradually took the place of the activity and bustle which had previously reigned. A sense of security lulled the Indians to rest. Every one of their enemies, save the prisoner, had perished in the fight, or rather surprise, by which the victors had mastered their unarmed foes. No thought was given to treachery within the camp.

Still, the young Assineboin knew that each moment he might be missed. He therefore listened with deep attention for the slightest sound; and some quarter of an hour having passed, he rose from his half-recumbent posture, and stood perfectly erect in the very centre of the wigwam. Peritana at the same instant stood at his side, coming from without: she had left the wigwam with so noiseless a step, that even the exquisite organs of the Indian had been eluded. Neither spoke, but the girl placed in the warrior's hands a short rifle, a powder-horn, and a short pouch, which he clutched with a delight which a sense of the danger of his position alone prevented him from manifesting openly.

Slinging them in their proper places, Ah-kre-nay moved with caution to the door of the wigwam, and next moment was stalking firmly but noiselessly along the camp, followed by Peritana, gazing mournfully at the habitations of her tribe. Suddenly, as they reached the outskirts of the wigwams, and were passing one of the largest and most conspicuous of the whole, a voice from within growled forth a hoarse demand of who was there?

'Peritana,' said the girl, in a voice which was choked with emotion, 'is not well; she seeks the woods, to drive away the bad spirit.'

During this brief colloquy the young brave had stepped within the deep shadow of the tent, his rifle ready cocked. As the girl ceased speaking, the head of an old warrior was protruded from the wigwam door.

'Thy sisters have been asleep since the dance was over,' said the aged Indian; 'why is Peritana awake?'

The girl saw her companion level his rifle—her agitation was intense. Her feelings were deeply moved on both sides.

'Father,' said she, and the rifle was raised instantly, 'Peritana goes to the woods; she will not tarry long. Her head is hot; she cannot sleep now.'

Satisfied with this explanation, the old Sioux retired once more within the tent, leaving the young warrior and his sad companion to reach the forest unmolested. Peritana was deeply moved at parting from her parents, and, but that she knew that death would be her portion on the discovery of her aiding the escape of Ah-kre-nay, would gladly have returned to where, as her father had told her, her sisters slept soundly. The die, however, was cast, and she was now in the woods, the companion of the runaway.

We must pass over a year of time, and take up our narrative at some distance from the spot above described. It was a deep dell on the banks of the upper waters of one of those streams that serve to swell the Ontario. Perhaps a lovelier spot was never discovered by man. At a place where the river made a bend, there rose from its bank, at some distance from the water, a steep but not perpendicular cliff, thickly grown with bushes, and spotted with flowers, while tall trees crowned the crest of the eminence. Of a horse-shoe form, the two ends approached the edge of the stream, leaving, however, to the east a narrow ledge, by which the vale could be approached. The space between the water and the bottom of the cliff was occupied by a sward of velvety smoothness, while beneath the rock was a dark and gloomy natural cavern. The most prominent feature of the scene, however, was of human formation. It was an Indian hut, which doubtless rose in this spot for the purpose of concealment. No better place could have been found within many miles, as the portion of the river which flowed in sight, from its proximity to a fall, was navigable only to the smallest canoe, and was therefore never made use of by travelling parties. The wigwam was of the usual dome-like shape, roofed with skins tastefully and elegantly adjusted, while a mass of creeping and flowering shrubs that entwined themselves around it, showed it to be no erection of a day. It was a model of cleanliness and neatness, while a fireplace at some distance out of doors, within the cavern, showed that, at least during the summer months, the inconvenience of smoke was dispensed with within its walls. The whole was wrapped in deep silence, looking as if utterly abandoned by every trace of humanity.

The sun was at its fullest height, proclaiming midday to the tenants of the woods and fields, when a rustling was heard at the entrance of the little dell, and an Indian bounded headlong within its shelter. The wild gleaming of his eye, the fresh wounds which covered his body, the convulsive thick breathing, the fierce clutching of his tomahawk and rifle, showed that he fled for his life, while the sound of many voices below the crag betokened how near his pursuers were to him. Shaking his empty powder-horn with a look of deep grief, the Indian warrior threw aside his rifle, now more useless than a pole of equal length, and, a fire of energy beaming from his eye, raised his tomahawk. It was, however, but for a moment—his wounds were too severe to allow any hope of a successful struggle, and next moment the brave stood unarmed, leaning against the entrance of his wigwam. On came the pursuers, with an eagerness which hatred and the desire of revenge rendered blind, and, as they leaped headlong down through the narrow gap between the water and the cliff, the wounded Indian felt that, with a firm arm and a good supply of powder and lead, he might have driven back his enemies in confusion.

No sooner did the Sioux behold their former prisoner, Ah-kre-nay, standing with dignified calmness at the door of his own wigwam, than their self-possession at once returned, and the whole party surrounded him in silence, casting, meanwhile, envious but stealthy looks round his romantic retreat. An aged warrior, after a due period of silence, advanced and addressed the captive.

'Ah-kre-nay is very nimble; twelve moons ago he ran like a woman from the Sioux; to-day he ran again, but his feet forsook him.'

'Twelve moons ago,' replied the captive with exultation flashing in his eyes, 'Ah-kre-nay was in the midst of a nest of vultures—fifty warriors surrounded him; but the manitou blinded all their eyes, and the Assineboin cheated their revenge.'

'But Ah-kre-nay was not alone?' said the old warrior, deeply moved at his own question.

'The flower of the hills fled to the woods with him—her tongue was the tongue of a lying Sioux, but her heart was that of a brave Assineboin.'

'Where is my child?' said the old warrior, in vain endeavouring to penetrate the mystery of the hut's contents, and dropping his figurative language under the influence of excitement—'say, Son of the Evening Light, where is my child?'

The warrior gazed curiously at the old man; but folding his arms, made no reply.

The Sioux warrior paused a moment, and then turning to his young men, ordered them to bind the prisoner, and commence that long list of atrocious cruelties which ever precede the death of a victim among the Indians. The hut was scattered to the winds in a moment, and its wood served to commence the pile which was to play the principal part in the scene of torture. Ah-kre-nay looked on in silence, his lip curling scornfully, until the preparations were all made; he then took his place at the post with sullen composure, and prepared to suffer in silence all the horrors meditated by the Sioux. A grim warrior now stood forward with a keen and glittering tomahawk in his hand, which he began waving and flourishing before the eyes of his victim, in the hope of making him show some sign of apprehension. In vain, however, did the old Sioux try every feint; now he would aim a blow at his feet, and as suddenly change to his face; now he would graze his very ear; and at length, enraged at the stoicism of his victim, he raised the gleaming hatchet, as if about to strike in earnest. The smart crack of a rifle was simultaneous with the attempt, and the tormentor's arm fell useless by his side. With habitual fear of the fatal weapon, the Sioux sought cover, and gazing upward, saw on the summit of the cliff Peritana—a babe slung in a cradle at her back—in the act of loading her rifle.

'Father,' cried she somewhat wildly, and pointing out how completely she commanded the pass of the dell, 'in the green days when Peritana walked not alone, you fed and sheltered me; warm was my wigwam, and sweet the venison with which my platter was ever filled. Peritana is very grateful, but'—and she pointed to her child—'Peritana is a mother, and she sees her husband, the father of the Little Wolf, in the hands of his enemies. Her eyes grow dim, and her memory departs. She cannot see her father, but she sees the enemy of her husband; she forgets she was ever a Sioux, and remembers only she is now an Assineboin. If his enemies kill her husband, Peritana will use her rifle as long as her powder lasts, and then will leap into the water, and join Ah-kre-nay in the happy hunting-ground of his people. But a Sioux warrior will not forget he has a daughter,' continued she more tenderly: 'give her back the father of her child, and Peritana will bring a great warrior into the Sioux camp.'

The Sioux saw at once the force of her proposition. Certain death awaited many, if not the whole band, should they strive to ascend the pass in the face of an infuriated widow; while, should she prevail upon Ah-kre-nay to forget, for her sake, his hereditary antipathies, and join the Sioux band, a mighty advantage would accrue. When free, and acting with perfect freedom, it was probable that the young Assineboin would show but little resistance to this offer. In ten minutes after the appearance of Peritana on the cliff, her husband, who had been an attentive listener, stood fully armed at the mouth of the pass, free. He was just about to commence the ascent, when, determined to win the admiration of the Sioux at once, he turned towards them once more, and, standing in their midst, laid his arm affectionately on the shoulder of the chief, and cried, 'Come, Peritana; Ah-kre-nay is with his friends; let not his squaw be afraid to join him.'

Placing himself and wife thus completely in the power of the Sioux, without any agreement as to treatment, was a tacit reliance on their honour, which won upon them at once, and a loud shout of applause proclaimed that enmity was at an end; and in a few moments more the old Sioux warrior was gazing, with all the pride of a grandfather, upon the offspring of his favourite daughter. A few hours of rest ensued, during which Ah-kre-nay's wounds were bound up, after which the whole party went on their way rejoicing, and the Sioux numbered one great warrior more within their bosom. Thus, by the exertion of remarkable presence of mind, Peritana preserved herself a husband, saved the babe from orphanship, restored a daughter to her father, and added a brave soldier to the forces of her tribe. Weeping and wailing would have availed her nothing; undaunted courage gave her the victory. The facts of this tale are current still among the wandering Sioux, who often relate to their wives and young men the famous deeds of the lovely Peritana.

SKETCHES IN NATURAL HISTORY.

SEA-WEEDS.

To most minds, the word 'sea-weed' may suggest no idea of importance, and yet few vegetable orders are more interesting either as regards their history or uses. Sea-weeds, or *algæ*, as they are botanically termed, are strictly submerged plants, growing either in fresh or in salt water, but by far more abundantly in the latter medium; hence their common appellation. Compared with perfect land plants, they may be said to be destitute of stems and leaves, their substance consisting of mere leaf-like expansions which assume a thousand forms; being either laminar, tubular, thread-like, globular, or capillary; and these again either branched, continuous for many yards, or jointed. They have no root, in the ordinary sense of that term, but attach themselves indiscriminately to any surface, be it the solid rock, a rounded pebble, a decaying shell, or the bottom of a sailing vessel. Many, indeed, are always met with in a floating state, and seem to grow without being fixed to any object whatever. They do not extract nutriment from the substances to which they are attached, as land plants do from the soil in which they grow, nor do their fronds inspire or expire the gases of the atmosphere, for most of them are sunk beneath its influence. Theirs is altogether a peculiar economy, and yet they grow as varied in kind as the vegetation which clothes the dry land: they appropriate different elements from the waters of the ocean, possess different properties, and propagate their kind by sporules, or little embryo plants, which are produced upon or within the substance of their leaf-like expansions. Let us glance at some of their peculiarities.

Respecting their reproduction, it is evident that the modes of flowering and fruiting which we perceive in land plants would have been wholly inappropriate. Not exposed to sunshine, there was no use of reflecting petals; continually submersed in water, a sheltering calyx would have been superfluous; and seeds, in the ordinary structure of that organ, could not have endured. Nature, however, is never in lack of means to an end; and the vegetation of the ocean is propagated with as unerring certainty and as great rapidity as the most prolific family on land. For this purpose, certain species have their surface studded with blistery expansions, or part of their substance is fitted with little cells, which expansions and cells contain many minute germs floating in mucilaginous matter. As these germs arrive at maturity, the enclosing pustules burst open, and the germs are consigned to the ocean, where they float about, coated with their glutinous mucilage, and are sure to adhere to the first surface upon which they impinge. In a few weeks they spring up into new plants, and in their turn give birth to thousands. Thus we have seen half a dozen different weeds attached to the same oyster-shell, and have seen a pebble of twenty pounds' weight buoyed up by one plant of bladder-wrack, the primary germ of which had glued itself to the surface. Once established, they expand with amazing rapidity. Mr Stephenson, the Scottish engineer, found that a rock, uncovered only at spring-tides, which had been chiselled smooth in November, was thickly clothed on the following May with fucoids from two to six feet in length, notwithstanding the winter had been unusually severe. Many species, as the disjointed algæ, have a fissiparous reproduction; that is, separate into numerous fragments, each of which, though having a common origin, has an individual life, and is capable in turn of increasing its kind.

Though possessing no floral attractions, the algæ are often very beautiful in their forms and colours, as may be seen by studying any preserved collection. They branch, radiate, and interlace like the most delicate network, float in long silken tresses, or spread along the rocky bottom in forms that surpass the most intricate tracery of human invention. Nor are their colours often less attractive; for though the prevailing hue be a sober chocolate, there are patches of the brightest green, yellow, and vermilion, not surpassed by the gaudiest shells that lurk below. It is true that

'The rainbow hues of the sea-trees' bloom'

is a mere fanciful absurdity, only fit to be classed with the 'coral bowers' and 'sparkling caves' of the versifier; yet the reader has only to pick up a few of the masses drifted by the latest tide, and to float them in pure water, to be convinced that both in form and colour many of the algæ would lose nothing by a comparison with the gayest products of the flower garden. As in form, so in size they vary exceedingly; presenting fibres the delicacy of which requires the aid of the microscope to examine, floating leaves to which those of the fan-palm are mere pigmies, or tangling cables extending from three to four hundred feet in length. Captain Cook, in his second voyage, found at Kerguelen land the *Macrocystis pyrifera*, a species of kelp springing from a depth of twenty-five fathoms; and other navigators have since corroborated his statements.

'This plant,' says Darwin, in speaking of Terra del Fuego, 'grows on every rock from low-water mark to a great depth, both on the outer coast and within the channels. I believe that, during the voyages of the Adventure and Beagle, not one rock near the surface was discovered which was not buoyed up by this floating weed. The good service it thus affords to vessels navigating near this stormy land is evident; and it has certainly saved many from being wrecked. I know few things more surprising than to see this plant growing and flourishing amidst those great breakers of the western ocean, which no mass of rock, let it be ever so hard, can long resist. The stem is round, slimy, and smooth, and seldom has a diameter of so much as an inch. A few taken together are sufficiently strong to support the weight of the large loose stones; and yet some of these stones were so heavy, that when drawn to the surface, they could scarcely be lifted into a boat by one person. I do not suppose the stem of any other plant attains so great a length as 360 feet, as stated by Captain Cook. Captain Fitzroy, moreover, found it growing up from the greater depth of forty-five fathoms. The beds of this sea-weed, even when not of great breadth, make excellent natural floating break-waters. It is quite curious to see, in an exposed harbour, how soon the waves from the open sea, as they travel through the straggling stems, sink in height, and pass into smooth water.'

In their distribution, the algæ obey laws equally imperative as those which regulate the habitats of land vegetation. The nature of the bottom, the depth, temperature of the water, and the like, are all regulating causes; and we not only find different regions clothed with a peculiar marine vegetation, but the same shore bearing different kinds, according to belts of depth and tidal influence. Thus, the bladder-wrack luxuriates most where alternately exposed and covered by the tide, the dulse on the very confines of the lowest ebb, and the tangle and sea cat-gut in a zone where the lowest ebb never reaches. Again, a sandy or muddy bottom is as barren of vegetation as the drifting sands of the desert, while one of rough and irregular rocks is as luxuriant as the tropical jungle. We know little of the bottom of the ocean over extensive spaces; but this we are warranted in affirming, that sea-weeds flourish most abundantly on rocky patches of moderate depth, that they never spring from sandy or muddy silts, and that they are altogether unknown in the greater depths of the sea. Many of them seem to float about quite unattached, and though these may have been torn from some rocky shore, yet, continually in water, they absorb their proper nutriment, and increase in size almost as much as their fixed congeners. Being less subjected to fluctuations of temperature, the algæ are more regular in their growth than land plants; and, with the exception of a few within the tidal influence, the majority seem to experience no cessation of growth or propagation. It must be borne in mind also that the algæ are inhabitants of fresh as well as salt water, and that some of the most curious and beautiful genera are found in our streams and pools, or spread in the form of the most delicate slime on stones and gravel. Nay, what is more wonderful still, some, like the *Ulva thermalis*, flourish even in hot springs at a temperature not less than 117 degrees of Fahrenheit!

It will naturally be asked, what purposes in the economy of nature are fulfilled by plants so numerous, so luxuriant, and universal? Although it is always dangerous to decide on the designs and intentions of creative wisdom, it must be apparent to every one the least accustomed to observation, that numerous fishes, molluscs, and other creatures, find food and shelter among the tangling sea-weeds of the ocean. Many sea animals are strictly herbivorous, others are so fragile, that they would be perpetually exposed to fatal injuries without the shelter of these submarine groves, while the spawn and young of a thousand species find amid their leaves and branches a safe and fitting nursery. They are useful, moreover, in many districts in protecting the shores from rapid disintegration, by diminishing the grinding power of the waves, just as green turf resists more effectually than bare soil the scour of a swollen river. We have seen it stated by Mr Darwin how much the long tangles of the macrocystis aided in allaying the fierce breakers of the western ocean, and in a proportionate degree, there is no doubt but every sea-weed tends to the same effect. It has also been surmised by chemists, from the quantity of alkaline matters found in the algæ, that they probably exercise a purifying influence on the waters of the ocean, and assist in maintaining that equilibrium which evaporation and the discharge of rivers continually tend to disturb. They are, moreover, as we shall see from the following slightly simplified extracts from Dr Greville's *Algæ Britannicæ*, of no mean importance in human economy.

'*Rhodomenia palmata*, the dulse of the Scots, the dillesk of the Irish, and the saccharine fucus of the Icelanders, is consumed in considerable quantities throughout the maritime countries of the north of Europe, and in the Grecian Archipelago. *Iridæa edulis* is still occasionally used both in Scotland and the south-west of England. Several species of *Porphyra* are stewed, and brought to our tables as a luxury, under the name of Laver; and *Enteromorpha*, a common genus on our shores, is regarded as an esculent by the Sandwich islanders. *Laurentia*, the pepper-dulse, distinguished for its pungency, and the young stalks and fronds of the common tangle, were often eaten in Scotland; and even now, though rarely, the old cry, "buy dulse and tangle," may be heard in the streets of Edinburgh. When stripped of the thin part, the beautiful *Alaria* forms a portion of the simple fare of the poorer classes of Ireland, Scotland, Iceland, Denmark, and the Faroe islands. To go farther from home, we find a large species of tangle peculiar to Australia, furnishing the aborigines with a portion of their instruments, vessels, and food; and on the authority of Bory St Vincent, the *Durvillea* and other tangles constitute an equally important resource to the poor on the west coast of South America. In Asia, several species of *Gelidium* are made use of to render more palatable the hot and biting condiments of the East. Some undetermined species of this genus also furnish the materials of which the edible swallows' nests are composed. It is remarked by Lamaroux, that three species of swallow construct edible nests, two of which build at a distance from the sea-coast, and use the sea-weed only as a cement for other matters. The nests of the third are consequently most esteemed, and are sold in China for nearly their weight in gold. And here we cannot pass over our own *Chondrus crispus*, the Irish moss or carageen of the shops, now so frequently used as a culinary article, especially in desserts, or as a light nutritious food for invalids. It is not, however, to mankind alone that the marine algæ have furnished luxuries or resources in time of scarcity: several species are greedily sought after by cattle in the north of Europe. The dulse is so great a favourite with sheep and goats, that Bishop Gunner named it *Fucus ovinus*. In some of the Scottish islands, as well as in Norway, horses, cattle, and sheep feed chiefly upon the bladder-wrack during the winter months; and in Gothland it is commonly given to pigs. In medicine, also, we are not unindebted to the algæ: as, for example, the Corsican moss of the Mediterranean, which was once held in high repute as a vermifuge. The most important medical use, however, derived from sea-weeds, is through the medium of iodine, which may be obtained either from the plants themselves or from kelp. Iodine is known to be a powerful remedy in cases of goitre and other scrofulous diseases; and when not derived from sea-weeds, is procured from the ashes of sponge.

'But were the algæ not really serviceable either in supplying the wants or administering to the comforts of mankind in any other respect, their character would be redeemed by their usefulness in the arts; and it is highly probable that we shall find ourselves eventually infinitely more indebted to them. One species—the *Gracillaria tenax*—is invaluable to the Chinese as a glue and varnish. Though a small plant, the quantity annually imported at Canton from the provinces of Tokien and Tchekiang is stated by Mr Turner to be about 27,000 pounds. It is sold at Canton for sixpence or eightpence a pound, and is used for the purposes to which we apply glue and gum-arabic. The Chinese employ it chiefly in the manufacture of lanterns, to strengthen or varnish the paper, and sometimes to thicken or give gloss to silks or gauze. They also employ it as a substitute for glass, smearing with it the interstices of bamboo work, which, when dry, presents lozenge-shaped spaces of transparent gluten. It is in the manufacture of kelp, however, for the use of the glass-maker and soap-boiler, that the algæ take their place among the most useful vegetables; and for this purpose the various species of *fuci* or wrack, tangle, sea cat-gut, and the like, are the most abundant and useful.'

Kelp is an impure carbonate of soda, procured from the ashes of sea-weed, the manufacture of which was introduced into the Scottish islands about the beginning of last century. At first the innovation was resisted by the inhabitants; but it soon became a profitable article of export, and has contributed not a little to enrich the proprietors, as well as to benefit the population, who in many instances were almost supported by its means. Latterly, Spanish barilla, obtained from the ashes of the salsola kali and other maritime plants, has been found superior to kelp in the formation of glass and soap; and from the removal of duty off salt (muriate of soda), the impure alkali can be procured at such a cheap rate by chemical means, that the demand for kelp has almost ceased. Besides their utility in the manufacture of kelp, sea-weeds are extensively used as manure, and at certain seasons are assiduously collected for that purpose.

Such are the sea-weeds, an order of vegetation at first sight apparently valueless and unimportant. But thus it always is; we know nothing intuitively, and require long ages of observation and experience before we can discover the uses either in creation or in human economy of the most familiar products.

VISIT TO A PRIVATE ASYLUM FOR THE INSANE OF THE HIGHER CLASSES.

When lately in London, we received an invitation to dine at Wykehouse, near Brentford, with Dr and Mrs Costello and their *patients*. What would the 'Man of Feeling,' who wrote a *sentimental* description of the horrors of Bedlam sixty years ago, with its ferocious maniacs, and more ferocious keepers—its cells, and straw, and chains, and scourges—have said to such an invitation! In one of the richest and most beautiful vicinages of London, about a mile up the hill from Sion House, shaded and dignified by oaks, ancient elms, and blooming horse-chestnuts, and adorned by shrubbery, flower-beds, and general vernal verdure, we found Wykehouse, a seat of the Earl of Jersey, and rented by Dr Costello, as an establishment for the safety and cure of the richer insane. The bell at the gate was answered by a servant, who conducted us to the house through a perfect flush of lilacs, laburnums, rhododendrons, and flowering shrubs of all descriptions; and, as one symptom of the *safety* of the place, we met a nurse carrying an infant, a child of the doctor's.

As the *family* had begun dinner, we were introduced at once to the dining-room, in which sat at table the master and mistress of the house, with eight gentlemen, all patients. We were cordially received by our host and his lady, and introduced to the rest of the company, who rose to welcome us. During the meal, we were the objects of much polite attention. Each individual seemed to wish to take his share of the duty of dispensing the hospitalities; offering the condiments, recommending the dish near him, remarking on the topics of the season and the day, and showing much curiosity to hear our news and ascertain our sentiments. During the time we were at table, not a word, look, or gesture occurred which could have raised the slightest suspicion that we were not in the company of the perfectly sane. One of the patients, a clergyman, who performs the religious exercises of the house, including a sermon on Sunday, was asked to return thanks, which he did with becoming reverence, when the eight gentlemen rose and retired from table, leaving us with our host and hostess.

We were in a spacious and elegant dining-room, built by the celebrated 'Jack Robinson,' who, before Joseph Hume's time, feathered his nest from the consolidated fund to so audacious an extent, that Sheridan called the attention of parliament to his practices; and when challenged to name the delinquent, declined, though he added he could as easily have named him as say 'Jack Robinson.' The dining-room was built for the visits of George III., of whom Robinson was a favourite. He built extensive ranges of bedrooms in barrack fashion for numerous guests of rank, of whom his lavish house was always full; which apartments have been found conveniently convertible to the present purposes of the mansion. Before leaving the table for a walk in the grounds and gardens, we were favoured by our host with a brief exposition of his mode of dealing with his patients, powerfully suggesting the advance which has been made in the treatment of the insane during the last fifty years. The inmates of this establishment are under no personal restraint whatever. There is not a strait-waistcoat, a belt, or pair of hand-mufflers under the roof. Taking advantage of the fact, that there is much more sanity than insanity in the great majority of the insane, and of the improved knowledge now acquired on the nature of insanity itself, the paroxysms of which alone require watching, Dr and Mrs Costello (for the lady does a large and most important part of the duty) direct all their moral energies upon the balance of sanity remaining in the patient's favour, and always with the most satisfactory results. Confidence is reposed; the patient's word of honour is trusted to, and seldom if ever broken. The beautiful grounds and gardens are freely ranged; even the neighbourhood is free to some. An elegant drawing-room, where the lady presides, is open—the place secures decorum. The lady's power is an interesting phenomenon: it seems to be, and really is, greater than her husband's. None but *gentlemen* can come into her mild and gentle presence; and we were assured that a look from her, still more, a quiet caution, will check a strong man who may for the moment be in danger of forgetting himself. It is remarkable how seldom the hallucinations of the patients come out in the dining-room or drawing-room. These are voted 'parish business,' and a bore; and although one of the party might just have discovered the longitude or the perpetual motion, another received the thanks of parliament for a victory, or a third a judgment in chancery, declaring him master of millions, not a word would be heard on those tempting topics in the drawing-room or at the dinner-table of Wykehouse. A breach of these mild yet rigid laws would be followed by the temporary exclusion of the individual, with the full approbation of the rest. Abuse of liberty is punished by narrowing by degrees its limits, till it is at last circumscribed by the wall of a paved court. No one needs to stay long there; but enlargement has its conditions, perfectly intelligible to every patient in the establishment.

When we walked out, we saw some of the gentlemen playing with the child, others reading in the beautiful groves, and three or four assisting Mrs Costello to cull and pack an enormous bouquet of lilacs and hawthorn blossom for a jar in the drawing-room. We joined the party, and assisted, and were much struck with the gallantry, politeness, and respect with which the lady was treated. This direction of female influence is a new element in its various applications in society. It reforms the imprisoned criminal; it purifies and humanises the educators of the young of the rougher sex; it exercises a power over the insane themselves that renders them as pliant as children. Yet Mrs Costello is a slight, little woman, whom any one of the subjects over whom she rules could annihilate in an instant. Indeed, we should say that the insane are peculiarly amenable to just such an influence; for their malady in most cases produces a simplicity of general character, often almost child-like.

We assembled at tea in the drawing-room, and enjoyed an hour of general conversation, when the party again dispersed through the grounds; and as we drove off in the twilight of a beautiful June evening, we had hands held out to us by the near, and hats lifted by the distant, till the gate shut behind us, and we were on our road to London. On our way, Dr Costello, who accompanied us, showed us a villa or cottage a mile or two from Wykehouse, which, on account of its romantic groves and large lake teeming with fish, he has taken on lease, as a sort of occasional holiday and pic-nic resort for his well-behaved patients.

Dr Costello had just then published a letter to Lord Ashley, on the reform of private asylums for the insane. A copy of that pamphlet is now before us. It is an appeal in behalf of the *rich* insane for legislative protection. The bill lately introduced by Lord Ashley contemplates chiefly the insane poor; not observing the fallacy, that, because the sane rich are well able to take care of themselves, the insane rich must be so too. There is, unfortunately, a prejudice which leads the friends of the insane to seek extreme privacy for them, and thus they become exposed not merely to inadequate accommodation and treatment, but all the imaginable evils attending their becoming objects of speculation. Dr Costello exposes the deficiencies of the generality of private houses for the insane, and recommends the ample and interesting scenery which is found in his own establishment. Private asylums should never be in cities; they should be in cheerful rural situations, where the inmates may avail themselves of the composing and health-restoring effects of husbandry and gardening. Within doors, the patient should find no deprivation of his accustomed conveniences, comforts, luxuries, and even elegances; but rather an improvement in them all. While deprecating the idea of surrounding the patient of condition with unnecessary deprivations in externals, the author says—'While delirium runs high, it is true, external objects will be too little noticed to suggest unfavourable comparisons; but this stage is often evanescent, often only periodical, and the bitter pang is felt in full force when the mist begins to clear away. The poor derive benefit from the better food and better care of the public asylum, and can we doubt the influence of causes relatively the same in regard to the rich? The internal arrangements, therefore, of a private asylum, should be in accordance with the tastes and occupations of the inmates; and the tedium of uniformity must be prevented by such aids as are employed for the same purpose in every-day life. Billiards, books, and music, are not enough. There must be social re-unions, and even dancing, with a view to affording opportunities of mixing in the society of persons of sound mind. This is a point in the moral treatment of great importance. To have the world and its recreations brought, from time to time, into contact with the insane, is less valuable even as an amusement or a pastime, than as a means of satisfying them, especially when allowed to meet their friends or relatives, not only that they are not forgotten, but that their return to that world, its business and its duties, is still looked for with anxiety and delight. How much of happiness, how much of sanity, do they secure by this oft-presented idea!

'If one could forget early impressions, and instances of proved delinquency in some ill-conducted establishments, we should modify our feelings in a great degree as regards private asylums. Proofs of the most interesting description abound, to show that these are anything but places to inspire horror.

'When well-conducted, and there are many such, mirth and cheerfulness—not forced or feigned—appear to be pervading influences. Lasting friendships are often formed; and many whom restored mental health recalls to the world, experience lively and sincere regrets in parting with those whose care or companionship had solaced them under so heavy a dispensation; and many, too, would remain, preferring to any other abode that which friends had consigned them to in the hour of affliction.

'The family group in an asylum is, or ought to be, associated in conversation, light reading, and all the diversified occupations that embellish refined society, with no other restraint than what individual circumstances may require, and the enlightened kindness of the head of the house may dictate.

'In this ideal of an establishment, the patients are the guests and associates of the physician and his family, and without such directorship and association, it cannot be realised. In his own person are combined the characters of parent, friend, guide, and physician, and this amounts to saying that he is indispensable. To him is assigned the task of moderating the impressions from without—of regulating, through the medium of his own family, the desirable degree of intercourse with the world; his table and his family circle are the sole, safe channels for such intercourse. Here the first public efforts of a returning healthy mental activity meets its needed encouragements, and here, too, the poor sufferer, doomed never to know the delights of recovery, experiences protection, and even pleasure, to the full measure of his blighted faculties. Advantages so obviously desirable are placed completely, and perhaps voluntarily, out of the reach of patients kept at home or in private families, and the case is even worse where they are confided to keepers or servants, with the occasional attendance of a medical man. Under such circumstances, cure is not only likely to be marred, but it may be wilfully and maliciously prevented. The continued employment of these attendants depends on the continuation of the malady; the resources available for moral treatment from uninterrupted intercourse with persons of their own station, are wasted, from their inferiority of social position, want of education, or irritability of disposition, which, in the circumstances we are contemplating, is uncontrolled, and therefore the more likely to arise. Fretfulness and bickering, as permanent conditions of the patient's mind, induced by the small excesses of an unreasoning domestic authority, which he is ever ready to dispute, either in fear or in anger, can have none other than unfavourable consequences. He distrusts and dreads his attendant, and the latter, goaded by what he considers injustice and ingratitude in the patient, gives way to peevishness, and, by way of beguiling the monotony of the occupation, repays him with sour looks, coarse and contemptuous language, neglect, or something worse. The effect of treatment in which caprice and recrimination, waywardness and spite, hold such unhappy sway, may be easily foreseen. The patient has none of the repose so essential to comfort, and indispensable for recovery. His views of things, already prismatised by a disordered brain, are still more bewildered by the false position in which he is placed, and the unfavourable circumstances by which he is surrounded. The time when cure was possible passes quickly away; the excitement subsides into a calm; the disease changes its character; the acute is followed by the chronic stage, and the brightness of the mind is dimmed for ever.'

The author states the argument for the *early* treatment of insanity as concisely as powerfully:—'The protection of the brain from the effects of the high irritation and congestion that prevail in the acute stage of mania, can only be secured by vigorous and prompt medical treatment at the very outset. The penalty of neglect or delay on this point, when not promptly fatal, will be to reduce the brain, the organ of the mind, to a ruin, which no effort of skill or kindness can repair. The proper use, therefore, of the time for medical treatment is all-important. The period for the moral treatment begins only when the first violence of the storm has spent itself. The best authorities on the statistics of this form of cerebral disease assert that it is curable, in the vast majority of cases, when the proper means are employed at the proper time.

'But where shall we look for such a well-organised system of moral management for the rich and the elevated, as will meet the wants and habits of this class? This is, in fact, the grand desideratum, the difficulty to be provided for. Where are we to find the ever-watchful kindness—the considerate forbearance in the discharge of duties often irksome, harassing, and even dangerous—the ready inventiveness to suggest new thoughts to cheer and amuse? We shall look for them in vain in the crippled resources for such objects, in the private lodging or the private family, where the rich man is doomed to solitary confinement in a modified form, and in the dreariness of his isolation, to expiate an infirmity as if it had been a crime. This is a blotch on our civilisation from which our continental neighbours are in progress of being freed. With us, alas! it will continue to prevail until the apathy, ignorance, and selfish pride that so extensively provide such a doom for fellow-creatures, who might still enjoy the benefit of superior arrangements, shall have disappeared, and given place to sounder views and feelings on this subject.'

The author advances a new idea, the *voluntary* resort of the 'nervous'—those (and they are many) who dread the coming disease—to the care and treatment of a private asylum. This the law, as it stands, renders impossible; for it requires the certificate of two medical men that the patient is of unsound mind. This might be altered. To prevent abuse, the free and voluntary resort might have its own conditions, and such patients might be made subject to the inquiries and inspection of visiting commissioners, in the same manner as the others. 'But these benefits, important as they are, would not be the sole ones resulting from a change of the law. The very character of the asylum would be changed. From a prison, which it is now so universally regarded, it would become an hospital, and those prejudices which now operate so extensively against the recovery of persons attacked with insanity, would disappear. Every enlightened physician acknowledges and laments the extent of this evil. Persons so attacked, and for whom recovery might be calculated on, almost with certainty, had they been promptly transferred to such a place, are, from a notion that kindness and attention will be all that is required, restrained from sending their relatives from home. This mistaken kindness is fatal. In the experiment of love and duty, the time is consumed between alternating hopes and fears; and when the asylum is resorted to at last, it receives a poor fellow-creature, for whom, at the beginning, cure was possible, but who is henceforward an irreparable wreck, doomed to live on, exhibiting the gradual extinction of the noblest faculties. It is with the brain as with the other organs of the body; the congestion or irritation that can be moderated and subdued at first, if allowed to persist and make progress unchecked, will at last produce such morbid changes in the organ itself, that it becomes incurably incapable of performing healthy functions. And why, then, make an exception as regards the affections of the brain, which experience and common sense condemn in regard to other organs? In pneumonia or bronchitis, who would be absurd enough to confine the treatment to kindness, quiet, and water-gruel? And shall our conduct be less wise or less energetic in the case of the brain than in that of the lungs, involving, as the perversion of the cerebral action does, a double death? It is quite time that the views and practice of society should be changed on this point; it is one of startling urgency and importance, now that a closer view of this awful scourge (rendered so much more destructive by unreflecting kindness) and its statistical bearings, have all but proved that out of every 500 of the population, we have one case of insanity. The pernicious practice that inflicts so much evil on the community, calls aloud for animadversion: it scatters desolation and mourning amongst families—blasting happiness and hope: it cannot be palliated—it must be abandoned.'

After some judicious observations on the importance of numbers and classification in the arrangements for the care of the insane, the letter concludes as follows:—'None of our private asylums come up, in all respects, to the ideal we have been tracing. "I am not acquainted," says the late Sir William Ellis, "with any asylum at all coming up to my notions of what an asylum for the rich ought to be; but I still think that it is perfectly practicable to provide for them in an institution possessing every means for cure, and every requisite for their comfort and happiness, combined with but little risk of their being improperly detained."

'But it will perhaps be said that a comprehensive plan, embracing the means of treatment and liberal accommodation for the rich, will be above the reach of the well-educated middle classes. It should not be so. The question of accommodation should decide that of the terms of payment. A patient requiring several rooms, special attendance, and a separate table, should contribute to the funds of the establishment a larger sum in proportion than those who are contented with the accommodation provided for all. This is, in fact, the principle on which a family hotel, as well as many other forms of public enterprise, are carried on. Upon a graduation of this kind, in the working of which there is no practical difficulty, persons paying from L.60 or L.70 a-year, to L.200 and L.300, might be provided for on a scale of comfort totally unknown either in private lodgings or in our private asylums, as they are at present conducted.

'The superior administration of such an establishment should be aided by a committee of philanthropic persons, whose duty it should be to see that every improved method of treatment recommended by experience should be adopted. There should be no private arrangements for the treatment of lunatics, and *no private* asylums in the present sense of the word.'

THE AUTOBIOGRAPHY OF DR ZSCHOKKE.

FIRST ARTICLE—YOUTHFUL DAYS.

A few snatches which have been published in this Journal from time to time, together with an abridgment of the diary of a poor Wiltshire vicar, issued in our 'Miscellany of Useful and Entertaining Tracts,' have rendered the name of Zschokke not unfamiliar to our readers. No one who has fallen in with any of his writings, but must desire to know something of the man; and fortunately, the spirited proprietors of the Foreign Library place means at our disposal to present an outline of the life of one of the most interesting characters of the present age.*

A variety of circumstances renders this, with scarcely any exception, one of the best autobiographies ever published. The author kept a diary regularly from twelve years of age, noting down events at the time they occurred to him with all the vigorous earnestness of youth. The work was not, however, prepared for the press until he had reached the advanced age of seventy. Thus the exuberance of immatured enthusiasm is toned down by the sober experience of age. From a neglected orphan, Zschokke had meanwhile been a teacher, lecturer, dramatist, poet, historian, traveller, diplomatist, stadtholder, newspaper editor, popular instructor, and, added to all these characters, always a reformer and philosopher.

Heinrich Zschokke was born in the year 1770 at Magdeburg, in Lower Saxony. His father—a cloth-maker and *oberältester*, or deacon of his guild—was his only guardian, for his mother died seven weeks after his birth. 'I, his youngest child,' says the writer, 'became, like most Benjamins, the darling of my father's heart;' whilst the young favourite looked up to his father as 'the chief and king of his childish world.' The rule he was subjected to was extremely indulgent, and the young adventurer soon made himself an adept in all manner of gymnastic exercises and boyish games, before he acquired any useful accomplishments. At the age of nine, however, his play-days were interrupted

* Autobiography of Heinrich Zschokke, forming the 33d part of the Foreign Library. London: Chapman and Hall.

by the death of his father, and he was intrusted to the care of an elder brother. This new protector tried to turn the young harum-scarum into a gentleman. Tailor and hairdresser were set to work upon him; but the fine clothes and his brother's regulations deprived him of his ragged street companions and their rough pastimes; and being much confined at home, he took a great dislike to the well-polished floors and gilded panels of his fine brother's fine house. When sent to school, the wayward pupil neglected accidence and grammar for the more fascinating study of the Arabian Nights and the Adventures of Robinson Crusoe. The latter took such a firm hold on his imagination, that he resolutely determined to shipwreck himself some day on a beautiful desert island, but to prepare himself better beforehand than did the unfortunate Robinson Crusoe.

Such was young Zschokke's waywardness, that his friends considered him a wrong-headed fellow, who would never come to any good; as an untaught, idle, untidy little vagabond, given to laughing and crying at improper times and places; now credulous even to silliness, now mistrustful to his own detriment; sometimes obstinate, sometimes foolishly docile. Beneath all these failings, however, there ran a copious stream of repressed affection. He was coldly and carelessly treated, thrust about from one member of his family to another as a useless incumbrance, and forced into a kind of antagonism with them, or thrown back upon his own impulses. 'I was obliged to accustom myself to my solitary condition, and to seek my best enjoyment in the delusions of imagination. Thus forsaken by all, I first began clearly to understand that I was an orphan, supported indeed by the interest of my paternal inheritance, but the most useless and superfluous being upon earth. This estranged mankind from me, and me from mankind: I was alone in the world. The consciousness of my separation from others only increased and embittered my intense longing for sympathy and affection. Without jealousy, yet not without a certain secret bitterness of feeling, have I often stood by when one of my companions enjoyed the praises and smiles of a father, or the embraces and kisses of a mother. Me no one pressed to his bosom; my tears were dried by no loving hand; and every reproach, which to other children is sweetened by the consciousness of their parents' affection, fell upon me with unmingled bitterness. Now first the death of my father became to me a quite infinite loss. I eagerly endeavoured to recall to my memory his slightest actions, his most insignificant words and looks. I longed to die, and be with him once more. Often I left my bed at night, and lay weeping on my knees, imploring my father to appear to me at least once again. Then I waited with breathless awe, and gazed around to see his spirit; and when no spirit came, I returned sobbing inconsolably to my bed, while I murmured reproachfully, "Thou, too, best darling father, dost not care about me any longer!"'

No one can peruse the account given of the sorrows of orphanhood without being affected by it, and at the same time acknowledging it to be a faithful record of the sorrows of an abused and parentless child.

Amidst all his eccentricities, he possessed an unusual aptitude for learning, as the way in which he acquired the rudiments of Latin will show. At a school to which he was sent, the only pupil who studied that language was the pedagogue's favourite. 'Whenever there was anything to be seen in the streets—rope-dancers, soldiers, puppet-shows, dancing bears or monkeys—this favourite alone was invariably allowed to leave the school-room, on asking permission in Latin. I, who had not yet got beyond the catechism, could not resist this powerful attraction, and resolved to become master of the magic spell. Its little possessor in vain represented to me the length and difficulty of the way, through an endless wilderness of declensions, adjectives, pronouns, and conjugations. Undaunted, I traversed the hard and thorny path from *Mensa* to *Audio*, and, at the first opportunity, not without fear and trembling, I stammered out my conjuring formula. The schoolmaster, amazed at my sudden learning, examined me incredulously in various ways; at length, satisfied of my acquisition, he praised my perseverance, prophesying that something might be made of me, and formally declared me his second *Lateiner*, with all rights and privileges thereunto appertaining.'

Like the greater number of youths of his temperament, Zschokke was passionately fond of reading, and of acquiring knowledge; but as he chose to arrive at it by more erratic paths than are beaten out for the schools, he went to live with an old rector, who was, moreover, a hack-author. This prolific writer gave him, besides plenty of employment in transcribing and translating, unrestrained access to his large and varied library. Into the sweets of this treasure Zschokke dipped during several years, till, at the age of seventeen, he panted to 'see the world.' But where to go? He conned over a map to fix his choice; and after a little consideration, determined to choose Schwerin, in Mecklenburg, for no other reason than because a former schoolfellow had settled there as a court-actor. He suddenly conceived a passion for the stage, packed up his little property, and without more ado set off. It was on a cold, foggy, but snowless morning, the 22d of January 1788, that the young adventurer gaily approached the frontiers of the old Obotritenland, and with a light free heart, like a bird escaped from its cage, followed the impulses of youthful activity, and wandered freely over hill and dale. His native city, with its heavy girdle of walls and moats, and its towering spires and gables, grew smaller and smaller, and vanished in gray mist far behind him. Unknown landscapes, unknown villages, trees, and cottages, all silvered over with morning rime, rose one after another out of the misty air before him. He sang, he danced, he shouted with joy; he longed to embrace every peasant that he met. Voices of sweet prophecy made the air ring wildly around him. He was not superstitious; but there are times when wiser men than he have dreamt of intercourse with future events and unseen powers.

'The pleasantest of my omens,' says he, 'occurred on the second day of my Hegira. As night drew on, I stopped at an inn in the village of Grabow. As I entered the parlour, darkened by the evening twilight, I was suddenly wrapt in an unexpected embrace, and pressed to a warm female heart; while, amid showers of kisses and tears, I heard these words—"Oh, my child, my dear child!" Although I knew, of course, that this greeting was not for me, yet the motherly embrace seemed to me the herald of better days, the beautiful welcome to a newer, warmer world. Let my reader put himself in my place, and imagine the feelings of a poor young orphan, who had never been folded to one loving heart since his father's death, and to whom, for ten long melancholy years, caresses and tender words had been utterly unknown! A sweet trembling passed over me, as I felt myself folded in that warm embrace. The illusion vanished when lighted candles were brought into the room. The modest hostess started from me in some consternation; then, looking at me with smiling embarrassment, she told me that my age and height exactly corresponded to those of her son, whom she expected home that night from a distant school. As her son did not arrive that night, she tended and served me with a loving cordiality, as if to make amends to herself for the disappointment of her son's absence. The dainties which she had prepared for him with her own hands she now bestowed upon me, and my healthy boyish appetite did ample justice to their merits. Nor did her kindness end here. She packed up a supply of dainty provisions for me the next day, procured me a place in a diligence to Schwerin, wrapt me up carefully against frost and rain, and dismissed me with tender admonitions and motherly farewells. She refused to impoverish my scanty purse by taking any payment for my night's lodging, but she did *not* refuse a grateful kiss, which at parting I pressed upon her cheek. Yet all this kindness was bestowed not on me, but on the image of her absent son. Such is a mother's heart!'

His friend at Schwerin received him coldly, and laughed at his projects; but a third person who was present at the interview followed him out of the house as he left it disappointed and hopeless, and did him the kindness to introduce him to a printer, partly as tutor, and partly as literary assistant. With this person he was extremely happy; but the restless spirit of change, after a time, overcame him.

Zschokke left all his happiness at Schwerin, to carry out his still existing dramatic predilections; for, becoming acquainted with the manager of a theatre—a decayed nobleman—he joined his corps, which was bound for Prenzlau, on the Uckermark. Here his duties were sufficiently varied. He 'curtailed the trains of heroic tragedies; altered old-fashioned comedies to suit modern taste; mutilated and patched all sorts of pieces to suit the wants of the company; wrote, on my own account, a few *raw-head and bloody-bone* pieces; rhymed prologues and epilogues, and corresponded with the most worshipful magistrates and grandees of various small towns, exhorting them to ennoble the taste of their respective small publics, by liberal encouragement of our legitimate drama.' When tired of the vagrant life and miscellaneous employments of a dramatic author, Zschokke determined to enter a university, for which he had never ceased to qualify himself. That which he chose was at Frankfort-on-the-Oder. He wrote home for some of his patrimonial funds, much to the surprise of his guardians at Magdeburg, who had heard nothing of him for ten years, and it was supposed that he had perished somehow or other during his vagabondising. The requisite cash was, however, remitted. The biographer's description of his matriculation is highly characteristic. 'As the "Rector Magnificus" of the high-school at Frankfort, the venerable Professor Hausen, was about to inscribe my name in the list of academical citizens, he asked, "What do you wish to study?" I could not tell, and replied, "Allow me to keep for a while my freedom of choice among the nine muses." He looked at me in amazement, and said, "You must belong to one of the faculties, and can take only one of the nine sisters for your lawful spouse. That does not hinder you from flirting a little with each as you go by." I stood irresolute for a few moments; for I only desired to gather together at this public market-place of the sciences a miscellaneous treasure of learning, for use or ornament, and still more to rid myself, once for all, of my religious doubts. I at length threw the handkerchief to theology, and thought with satisfaction of the approval this choice would meet with from my pious relatives at Magdeburg.'

Here Zschokke made up for lost time, and, abstracting himself from the companionship and vagaries of the *Burschen*, employed his whole time in reading. He had scarcely studied a year, when he was called on to make a funeral oration over a deceased class-fellow. This he did with so much effect, that he suddenly became the pet of the professors, and the friend and confidant of all the Frankfort sons of the muses.

Soon after, he wrote a melodrama called Abellino, 'which soon flew on the wings of the press into almost all the theatres of Germany. It procured for the beardless author, among other honours, a formal invitation from a company of merchants near Stettin, to witness, as their guest, the triumphant representation of the piece. My modesty could hardly have resisted so tempting a harvest of laurels, had not a most untimely deficit in my finances—deficits are apt to be untimely—compelled me to shun the trifling but unavoidable expenses of the journey.' This was no affectation of modest self-denial. Zschokke expresses, a few pages further on, but little respect for the taste of a public which could so highly applaud his 'schoolboy melodrama. And although,' he adds, 'the love of fame had always appeared to me scarcely less contemptible than the love of money, literary celebrity had never appeared so thoroughly despicable in my eyes as now, when I learnt *who* could obtain it, and for *what*.' Surely this is a rare instance of an author criticising himself and his muse so severely. But he wished, and determined, to rest his fame upon higher things.

After a visit home—where he was received with enthusiasm by the very relations who had previously driven him away by their unsympathising coldness towards him—he was, on his return to Frankfort, dubbed doctor, and became a tutor and extra-academical lecturer. His classes were always full, and his fame was much increased during the three and a half years he was thus employed, when he aspired to become a 'professor extraordinary;' but his political principles stood in his way, and the government refused him the office. Disgusted with this, his old travelling desires returned, and one morning in May 1795, he mounted the stage on his way to Switzerland.

At Zurich, Zschokke made the acquaintance of the patriot Paul Usteri, Henry Pestalozzi the celebrated and pure-minded educational reformer, and Nägeli, the inventor of the system of national singing which has been so successfully followed by Wilhelm and Mainzer. Paris was his next destination, and he entered France while the effects of the terrible Revolution were still visible. 'Is this *la belle France?*' I involuntarily exclaimed. Oelsner [his companion] smiled, and replied, '*La belle France* means Paris; that is, the mansion, of which the whole country, from the Rhine to the Pyrenees, is but the courtyard, with the barns and outhouses;' and this is true of France to this day.

Paris had few charms for the practical philosopher, and he soon left it to see Rome, proceeding on his journey by way of Switzerland, a country with which he was already in some degree acquainted. We leave the young and ardent-minded German on this pilgrimage, and will take up the continuation of his narrative in a succeeding number.

AN UNEXPECTED VISIT TO FLINDERS' ISLAND IN BASS'S STRAITS.

It was my misfortune to be wrecked in the ship Isabella, of Leith, on the coast of Flinders, or Great Island, in Bass's Straits, in the month of June 1844, while on my passage from Port Phillip to England.

This ill-fated vessel was driven on a reef of sunken rocks a few miles from the island, and was in a few hours dashed to pieces. The passengers and crew were, however, all preserved, having succeeded by various methods, and at different intervals and places, in getting ashore among the neighbouring islands. I landed in the long-boat with twelve others, including three ladies and two children; but so critical was our situation when the Isabella struck, and so absorbing the feeling of self-preservation, that no one on board saved a single article of clothing or value belonging to them, except what they had on their persons at the moment of their leaving the ship. For three days and nights we lay in our wet clothes on the beach. On the fourth day, the gale having abated, we were able to communicate with our fellow-sufferers, and visit the adjoining islands. On Woody Isle, about four or five miles distant, we fell in with a party of sealers, who took us to their settlement, and treated us with the greatest hospitality and kindness. Their settlement was situated in a small crescent-shaped bay, about half a mile wide at the entrance, with here and there little patches of sandy beach and rocky inlets, just sufficiently large to enable the sealers to shelter their boats from stormy weather. While we were there, the bay was smooth and placid as a summer lake; on one side huge rocks of the most fantastic shapes were piled upon each other, and poised in such a manner by nature's unerring hand, as to appear as if the slightest pressure or breeze would hurl the giant pillars into the waters beneath. The sealers' huts were about five or six in number, and although of the most rude and primitive kind, yet by no means of a comfortless description. Our guide to this romantic retreat was an old white-headed man, upwards of eighty years of age, and who had lived for more than thirty years amongst these islands. When I first saw his venerable form and pate, he reminded me of the description of old Adams, one of the mutineers of the Bounty, when he was discovered in Pitcairn's Island by the crew of the Pandora. He was as hale, active, and strong, as most Europeans of fifty, and carried, with a light step, across the rugged isle, a little girl of six years of age, one of the Isabella's passengers. When we came in sight of the huts, several noisy dogs seemed disposed to give us rather an unfriendly welcome; but their barking was soon reduced to a smothered growl by our octogenarian guide. In front of the huts stood with wondering gaze the wives and families of the sealers, and a more barbarous-looking group seldom meet the eyes of the distant voyager. They were literally half-savage and half-civilised; half-black and half-white. The wives or gins, three in number, were aboriginal natives of Van Diemen's Land. A life of ease and plenty had expanded them to more than double their usual bulk.

We remained for three days on Woody Isle, and received the most hospitable treatment from the sealers. When all collected, we mustered, including passengers and crew, forty individuals—no inconsiderable addition to the population of the island. We had full permission to help ourselves to a goat or pig as inclination prompted us, these animals being pretty numerous, and roaming over the island in all the delights of abundance and liberty. Damper, milk, and potatoes, were given us by the gins, and after our four days' fasting on Flinders' Island, we enjoyed our plentiful meals with a relish which a gourmand would have envied. The number of persons living on Woody Isle when I was there might be about fifteen or sixteen, five or six of whom were male adults, the others women and children. If contentment and plenty are amongst the greatest blessings we can possess in this world, these sealers must live a happy life. They seem to have three prominent means of earning a livelihood: 1st, Sealing, which occupies that portion of the year when these animals are most abundant and accessible—until lately, they were very plentiful about all the islands in Bass's Straits, but owing now to the number and perseverance of their assailants, their haunts are confined to the most solitary isles and rocks, and their capture is attended with both difficulty and danger. 2d, The hunting of the kangaroo, opossum, and walleby, which are still pretty numerous about Flinders' (or rather Furneaux's) group of islands. Like the seals, the value of those animals consists of their skins, which find a ready sale in Van Diemen's Land. 3d, The catching and curing of the mutton bird, a dark-coloured, web-footed bird, about the size of a large pigeon, and which at certain seasons visits these islands in such countless numbers, as literally to darken the air in their progress. After being plucked and cleaned, they are hung up in the large chimneys of the sealers' huts, until smoked and dried, similar to a red herring in Scotland. They are very fat, and the flesh is thought, in its prepared state, to resemble mutton in taste; whence their name. I decidedly, however, give the preference to legitimate mutton. They are taken, when cured, to Launceston, and are readily disposed of there among the inhabitants. This town is visited two or three times a-year by the sealers, when they dispose of the produce of their industry, and purchase stores and necessaries for themselves and families. These sealers are generally runaway convicts, or sailors, or restless and discontented individuals from the various Australian colonies.

The storm having completely abated, we made arrangements to communicate with a schooner which we learnt was anchored about fifteen miles from us, and engaged in landing sheep on a small grassy island, for the use of the settlement of the Van Diemen's Land aborigines on Flinders' Island. This vessel calls twice a-year at the same island for the above purpose, and, fortunately for the Isabella's passengers and crew, was now on one of her half-yearly visits. I was deputed by my fellow-passengers to communicate with this schooner, and arrange with the captain to convey us back to Port Phillip or Van Diemen's Land. Accordingly, with a stout boat's crew, and the venerable sealer for our pilot, I proceeded to Green Island, where the vessel was said to be anchored; and after about four hours' rowing we reached the schooner, which belonged to Hobart Town. When I got on deck, the sails were unfurled, and the captain in the act of getting her under weigh for Port Phillip. My story was soon told, and the captain at once agreed to receive us all on board, and wait another day or two for that purpose. He, however, stated that an addition of forty souls to his crew was rather more than his larder was prepared for, and therefore recommended me to proceed with my boat's crew to the aboriginal settlement, about sixteen or seventeen miles farther along the coast, and there state to the superintendent the particulars of the loss of the Isabella, and also receive from him what additional supply of stores would be required for the schooner.

Our approach to the settlement must have been observed by some of the inhabitants, for before our boat touched the beach, three or four individuals were waiting as if ready to receive us, the most important of whom was the sergeant of the military guard, if three soldiers may be designated by such a title. He insisted on immediately taking me to the superintendent of the establishment. As yet, I observed no appearance of dwellings; and the coast, though not presenting so bleak and cheerless an aspect as the other parts of the island, appeared wild and uncivilised. After walking about a quarter of a mile, on a well-defined track through the brushwood, we came upon the settlement. It consisted of a substantial and comfortable group of buildings, partly of timber, but more generally of stone and brick. I was received by the superintendent and his wife with all the consideration and hospitality due to my unlucky situation: an abundance of stores was immediately ordered to be got ready for the schooner; and an ample supply of female apparel for the lady passengers and children of the Isabella, some of whom had been barefooted and bonnetless for the last two or three days.

I had now leisure to make my observations of the island. Flinders' Island is the largest of Furneaux's group of islands, stretching from north to south, and is situated at the east end of Bass's Straits, and designated in charts by the name of Great Island. It is visible in clear weather from the northern shores of Van Diemen's Land, and is from thirty-five to forty miles in length, and averages about fifteen in breadth. It is very mountainous, rather thickly wooded, and many parts of it are covered with a strong wiry grass and coarse fern. I went with a small party of the Isabella's passengers and crew about twelve miles in a northerly direction from where I landed, along the coast and into the interior; but beyond one or two streams of excellent spring water running through an almost impenetrable tea-tree scrub, we saw or found nothing to recommend it to particular attention. I understand, however, that two small rivers and some open grassy plains have recently been discovered; but, comparatively speaking, very little is known of this island beyond the immediate vicinity of the settlement. This says but little in favour of the scientific minds, energies, or enterprise of those gentlemen who have resided here. It has now been more than ten years inhabited.

On this island Governor Arthur, in 1834, formed an establishment for the reception of the expatriated aboriginal natives of Van Diemen's Land. It was, previous to this time, rarely visited, little known, and altogether uninhabited. At the period of my visit, June 1844, the settlement numbered eighty-five souls, fifty-seven of whom were the remaining survivors of the last of the Vandiemonians. Those acquainted with the colonisation of Van Diemen's Land, are aware that for many years previous to 1834—indeed almost from its first colonisation in 1804—the settlers in that island suffered great annoyances and loss of stock from the continued aggressions of its aboriginal inhabitants. A petty and harassing warfare was in constant existence between the natural and the self-constituted possessors of the island, which was attended on both sides by acts of great oppression and inhumanity. Government was at length compelled to interfere; and, after a protracted struggle, and the expenditure of many thousand pounds, the natives were, by a large party of volunteers and military systematically closing upon them, driven into a corner, and captured. The result was the settlement in Flinders' Island; and the conquered savages were taken from the almost boundless hills and forests of their native land, to linger out an indolent and miserable existence on a few circumscribed and cheerless acres on a desert island. The site chosen for the settlement is on the west side of the island, towards its northern extremity. Beyond being rather romantically situated in a valley formed by the surrounding high hills, it did not appear to me to possess any qualification to recommend it, and must have been hurriedly selected, without due deliberation or care. It is destitute of any running stream or spring of fresh-water, and they have consequently to carefully preserve the water in tanks. It is situated amidst a thickly-wooded but otherwise unproductive soil, and the landing-place, or rather open beach, is only available for boats, and is much exposed to the prevailing west and south-west winds. The dwellings for the natives form two sides of a square, and, with the area in front, are remarkably clean and neat. They reminded me of the little whitewashed cottages that are now occasionally to be seen in Scotland appropriated to the workmen of some well-regulated colliery or manufactory. At its formation, there were nearly two hundred blacks, but the ravages of disease and death, which were very prevalent prior to the appointment of the present superintendent, have reduced that number to fifty-seven. Since his residence in the island, there has not been a single death. I conversed with several of these remnants of a bygone race, and found them generally cheerful and communicative. They were by this time aware of the wreck of the Isabella, and inquired by words and gestures if any one had been drowned. When I told them there was plenty flour and sugar, plenty tobacco, and plenty rum on board, but all gone, they seemed then to comprehend, by their solemn looks to each other, that the loss must have been very great. These articles now constitute the dictionary of their wants and luxuries; the latter is of course never given to them but on particular days; and for good conduct they are allowed a small portion of tobacco. Their habits since their arrival on Flinders' Island are indolent in the extreme, and it is rare indeed that any of them can be induced to work. One or two may be occasionally prevailed upon, by flattery or extra indulgence, to weed the garden or some vegetable plot, but such an employment of their time is by no means of frequent occurrence. Although under very little control, they almost never roam beyond the boundaries of their circumscribed settlement: all idea of liberation or escape seems to be entirely dormant in their dispositions; and they are generally to be seen lying in groups on the ground before their cottages, or basking on some green and sunned spot within a few yards of the establishment. The furniture of their huts is of the most limited description, and may be said to consist of a fixed bed-place, with a blanket and coverlet, a bench and table, and one or two of the simplest utensils for cooking and containing their food. It is seldom, however, that any of these articles are used; the bed-place almost never, for they prefer sleeping on the floor or in the open air. Their provisions are generally consumed immediately on their being served out. At one time their allowance of bread and sugar, &c. was distributed to them only twice a-week, but it was so frequently all consumed within a few hours after they received it, that a daily delivery had to be resorted to. This takes place in the morning, when the storekeeper carefully weighs out every ration; and it is amusing to hear him crying out such names as Hannibal, Pompey, Bonaparte, Cleopatra, Venus, Desdemona, &c. when the sable representatives of these *great folks* come running forward with their little wooden platters, and receive their allowance for the day. They are all decently clothed, the women in blue serge gowns, and the men in coarse gray jackets and trousers. Strange to say, although the proportion of the sexes is about equal, and many of them young and robust, and united in matrimony, not a single birth has taken place among these exiled aborigines for several years. There were only two children when I was there, the youngest four years old. From these facts, and their gradually decreasing numbers, a few years must witness the extinction of this last of their race—a race who but lately roamed in freedom and joy, the lordly savages of the hills and dales of Van Diemen's Land.

Although comfort and contentment appeared to reign throughout this obscure and isolated settlement, and the poor exiles were respectably clothed and healthy-looking, yet there seemed to be an air of melancholy depression hanging around everything I saw.

After receiving much attention and kindness from the superintendent and his lady, and visiting everything worthy of inspection, I departed to return to the schooner. I was, on the whole, more interested than pleased with the condition of these unfortunate aborigines; if there was much to admire in the treatment they received, there was also much to pity, and something to condemn. It must be confessed that cruel necessity required that these rude and ignorant savages should be placed under some control; but their lot is now so degraded and humiliating, so totally opposed to, and destructive of, all their natural feelings and habits, that I am sure no reflecting mind that considers their past and present state, but must admit that the oppressor's yoke has fallen heavily upon them, and that they are a doomed and unhappy race, and fated soon to be numbered with those tribes who have lived and passed away.

On arriving on board the vessel destined to take us back, I found all the Isabella's passengers and crew assembled on the deck. The anchor was immediately weighed, and on the third day afterwards we entered Port Phillip bay. On the fourteenth day after my departure for England, I again landed in Melbourne, and surprised my many kind friends there by my unexpected return amongst them. J. B.

CURIOSITIES OF LITERATURE.

NO. III.

The number of portraits of King Charles I. by Vandyke is very great, and the sternest republican must admit that, in a pictorial point of view, the artist could not have had a finer subject. Though eminently handsome, the king's destiny seemed written on his forehead: his face was a 'title-leaf' that clearly foretold the nature of the 'tragic volume' which Time was to open. So palpable was this, even in Charles's lifetime, that when Bernini the sculptor received the picture now hanging in one of the apartments at Windsor, in which two profiles and the full face of the monarch are represented, for the purpose of making a bust, he was so impressed with the mournful countenance, that he prophesied the unhappy end of the original. These portraits are now the ornaments of all the great galleries in Europe. There is a full-length in armour at St Petersburg, that was formerly in Sir Robert Walpole's collection at Houghton, and had previously belonged to the notorious Lord Wharton, whom Swift lashed under the name of Verres. By mistake, both gauntlets are drawn for the right hand. When this picture was in Lord Wharton's possession, old Jacob Tonson, the bibliopole, who had remarkably ill-made legs, found fault with it on this account. Lady Wharton with witty rudeness replied, that one man might have two right hands as well as another two left legs. 'The amiable

Mr Tonson,' as Dr Johnson styles him, used to speak of the authors whose books he published as 'eminent hands,' a phrase that tickled Lord Byron exceedingly. Pope mentions him in his 'Farewell to London;' and he is the subject of a triplet that dropped from the pen of Dryden in a moment of irritation, where he is not so favourably alluded to. Tonson declined to give the poet what the latter required for his translation of Virgil; Dryden scribbled the following lines on a slip of paper, which he sent the publisher, with an insinuation that he who wrote them could write more. The threat had the desired effect, and the money was paid.

With leering look, bull-faced, and freckled fair,
With two left legs, and Judas-coloured hair,
And frowsy pores that taint the ambient air——

Edward Fairfax, the translator of Tasso's Jerusalem Delivered, was the brother of the celebrated parliamentarian general, Thomas Lord Fairfax. A new edition of this translation has recently been printed, and although unfaithful in many passages, where Fairfax has taken the unjustifiable liberty of expanding the original, under the pretence of improving, it is the best version of the Italian epic we have. The versification is rich and melodious; King James read it with admiration; and it solaced the prison hours of his unfortunate son. Waller acknowledged that the smoothness of his own verse was copied from Fairfax, whilst Dryden ranks him along with Spenser. Fairfax was so powerfully influenced by the superstitions of his age, that he prosecuted some old women for the crime of witchcraft, believing that his own children had fallen under their malign spells. They were acquitted, however, little to the satisfaction of the prosecutor, since he left behind him a manuscript, never yet printed, entitled 'Dæmonologia: a discourse touching witchcraft, as it was acted in the family of Mr Edward Fairfax of Fuyistone, in the county of York, in the year 1621.' He also wrote some eclogues, which his son declared were so learned, that no one but himself could explain the allusions in them. They have not been printed; and indeed that would be a useless proceeding, unless we had the interpretation, which he alone could furnish. This reminds us of a passage in Gibbon's Decline and Fall, where, after mentioning three Roman emperors in periphrastic terms, he places their names in a note for the edification of the reader. A French nobleman, whose handwriting had not the gift of legibility to a remarkable extent, in writing to another man of rank, forwarded also a copy of his letter, and explained the reason thus—'Out of respect, my lord, I have written to you with my own hand, but to facilitate your perusal, I send a transcript of my letter.'

It was counted unlucky, and with superstitious people the notion still survives, to give to another anything with a point or an edge. Milton, in his 'Astrologaster,' observes that 'it is naught for any man to give a pair of knives to his sweetheart, for feare that it cuts away all love between them.' Thus Gay, in one of his pastorals—

But wo is me! such presents luckless prove,
For knives, they tell me, always sever love.

There are some pleasing verses addressed by Samuel Taylor, master of Merchant Tailors' school, to his wife, on presenting her with a knife fourteen years after their marriage, which begins thus—

A knife, my dear, cuts love, they say;
Mere modish love perhaps it may.

Grose also says that it is of unfortunate omen to give a knife, scissors, razor, or any sharp or cutting instrument to one's mistress or friend, as they are apt to cut love and friendship. To avoid the ill effects of this, it was necessary to give in return a pin, a farthing, or some trifling recompense. Lord Byron gave Lady Blessington a gold pin which he usually wore in his breast for a keepsake, and we afterwards find him requesting her ladyship by letter to return it, and he would present her with a chain instead, 'as memorials with a point are of less fortunate augury.'

When Voltaire visited Congreve, the Frenchman, whose ambition was supremacy, and whose laurels had been won in the field of literature, was surprised and shocked to find the play-writer turn a deaf ear to praise of his works. He looked on them as trifles beneath his notice, and desired to be visited as a gentleman living in easy retirement. This was not only contemptible affectation, but sheer ingratitude towards the means by which he had raised himself. Voltaire sarcastically remarked, 'Had you been so unfortunate as to be only a gentleman, I should not have visited you at all.' Gibbon seems to have had a similar weakness, but it was early in life. He records in his journal that the Duc de Nivernois treated him more as a man of letters than as a man of fashion.

Turning over some manuscripts at the British Museum, we met with a letter, of which we give some extracts. It is dated December 1, 1589, and an endorsement states that the nameless unfortunate was Sir George Peckham. The letter is addressed to Cecil, Lord Burghley. Looking at the request contained in the postscript, it seems strange that the lines should not only still exist, but be now perpetuated by printing—lines, to quote the words of Shakspeare,

Picked from the worm-holes of long-vanished days,
And from the dust of old oblivion raked.

'I have so worn myself out of apparel, as I have no more to my back than I do wear every day, which are more like unto the rags of some rogue than the garments of a gentleman; and my poor wife is likewise such-like unto myself. Nevertheless, for anything that I do know as yet, they are like to be our Christmas apparel. And further, unless I can make some shift for to pay for my half-year's board at Candlemas, the simple bedding, and such other trifles as I have, shall be distrained and taken away; then may my wife and I both go seek the wide world with a bag and a wallet. And therefore I do not make any moan before such time, as I am driven by extreme necessity.' The writer then states that he had expected, but was unable to obtain, assistance from Lord Southampton, 'for I am the nearest kinsman, both by father and mother, that his lordship hath in England, the only issue of my lord, his grandfather's body excepted, and his lordship beareth my poor goose in his escutcheon. * * Thus referring myself and my present miserable estate unto your lordship's accustomed goodness towards me with these few Latin words, Bis dat qui tempestive donat [He who gives in good time gives twice], I do humbly take my leave—

Your Lordship's poorest Orator, and so bounden.

I do most humbly beseech your lordship to burn this letter so soon as you have perused the same, for I am very loath that any other person beside your lordship should see the same, craving pardon for not subscribing my name.' Was this humble petition complied with?

The audacious manner in which Milton's Paradise Lost was treated by Dr Bentley, is pretty generally known from a paper in D'Israeli's Curiosities of Literature. Giving the reins to his critical sagacity, he conjectured that the blind poet's amanuensis had not only ignorantly blundered as to words dictated by Milton, but had wilfully interpolated lines of his own. Proceeding upon this gratuitous assumption, Bentley did not hesitate to alter the poem to suit his own ideas. His emendations of Horace are not founded on such an absurd notion as this, and there was more reason to believe the text corrupt. But even there it has been said that many of his alterations go to crop the most delicate flowers of Horatian fancy, and shear away the love-locks on which the world has doted. Pope, whose friends opposed Bentley in the memorable controversy as to the epistles of Phalaris, frequently lets fly the arrows of his wit against the presumptuous critic. For instance, in the Dunciad,

The mighty scholiast, whose unwearied pains
Made Horace dull, and humbled Milton's strains.

Observe what different ideas the same fact will excite in different minds. Every one knows the lines of Burns, in which he says pleasure is

——like the snowfall in the river,
A moment white, then melts for ever.

William Cartwright (born 1611, died 1643), in a poem entitled Love's Darts, asks and answers the question—

Where is the learned wretch that knows
What are those darts the veiled god throws?
Fond that I am to ask! Whoe'er
Did yet see thought? or silence hear?
Safe from the search of human eye
These arrows (as their ways are) fly.
The flight of angels part
Hot air with so much art,
And *snows in streams*, we may
Say, *louder fall than they*.

How different is the application of the same incident by

the two poets. In one it is used to point a moral, in the other to adorn a tale.

If the honour of authorship be denied Charles I., there is good reason to believe that he once at least dipped his pen in a critic's inkstand; and as the circumstance showed a favourable trait in his character, it is worth repeating. A play of Massenger, called the King and the Subject, was submitted to his majesty before it went to the licenser. Sir Henry Herbert, who then held that office, records this anecdote:—'At Greenwich this 4th day of June (1638), Mr W. Murray gave me power from the king to allow of the King and the Subject, and tould mee he would warrant it.

"Monies! We'll raise supplies what way we please,
And force you to subscribe to blanks, in which
We'll mulct you as we think fit. The Cæsars
In Rome were wise, acknowledging no laws
But what their swords did ratify," &c.

'This is a piece taken out of Philip Massenger's play, and entered here for ever to be remembered by my son, and those that cast their eyes on it, in honour of King Charles my master, who, readinge over the play at Newmarket, set his marke upon the place with his owne hande, and in these words, "This is too insolent, and to be changed." Note that the poet makes it the speech of a king—Don Pedro of Spayne—and spoken to his subjects.' The play is now lost.

It seems that cwene or quen (the original of our queen) was used as a term of equality, applied indifferently to either sex. In the Norman chronicle, the historian speaks of the duke and his quens, meaning peers. A collection of verses written by Charles of Anjou and his courtiers is mentioned in a book of the thirteenth century as the songs of the quens of Anjou. A poem of the twelfth century, in detailing the war-cries of the French provinces, says,

And the quens of Thibaut
'Champagne and passavant' cry.

One of the victims of the sanguinary Robespierre was Roucher the poet. The day previous to his death he sat for his portrait, which he sent to his family with the following beautiful lines in French:—

Loved objects! cease to wonder when you trace
The melancholy air that clouds my face;
Ah! while the painter's skill this image drew,
They reared the scaffold, and I thought of you.

John Heywood, the playwright and epigrammatist, was patronised by Henry VIII. and Elizabeth. What the Fairy Queen, says Warton, could not procure for Spenser from the penurious Elizabeth and her precise ministers, Heywood gained by puns and conceits. The object of one of his books, as disclosed by the title-page, is singular—'A Dialogue, containing in effect the number of all the Proverbs in the English tongue compact in a matter concerning two marriages.' When the Marquis of Winchester, lord high treasurer, was presented with a copy of this book by the author, he inquired what it contained, and being answered, all the proverbs in English, replied, 'What! all? No, no: *Bate me an ace, quoth Bolton*'—a form of speech once in vogue. By my faith, said Heywood, that is not in. It happened that the Marquis casually uttered the only proverb not in the book. Camden mentions an interview of Heywood with Queen Mary, at which her majesty inquired what wind blew him to court. He answered 'Two, specially; the one to see your majesty.' 'We thank you for that,' said the queen; 'but I pray you what is the other?' 'That your grace,' said he, 'might see me.' The curious work on proverbs is in rhyme, and contains many sayings that are now forgotten, as well as allusions to superstitions still remaining. Thus he says—

I suppose that day her ears might well glow,
For all the town talked of her, high and low.

This alludes to the notion still common in many places, that a man's ears burn when others are talking of him. 'What fire is in my ears!' exclaims Beatrice in Much Ado about Nothing. And Sir Thomas Browne, in his Vulgar Errors, says, 'When our cheek burns, or ear tingles, we usually say somebody is talking of us—a conceit of great antiquity, and ranked among superstitious opinions by Pliny. He supposes it to have proceeded from the notion of a signifying genius, or universal Mercury, that conducted sounds to their distant subjects, and taught to hear by touch.'

WASTING POWER OF RIVERS.

The rivers which flow in the valleys of the Cordilleras ought rather to be called mountain torrents. Their inclination is very great, and their water the colour of mud. The roar which the Maypu made as it rushed over the great rounded fragments, was like that of the sea. Amidst the din of rushing waters, the noise from the stones as they rattled one over another was most distinctly audible even from a distance. This rattling noise, night and day, may be heard along the whole course of the torrent. The sound spoke eloquently to the geologist: the thousands and thousands of stones which, striking against each other, made the one dull uniform sound, were all hurrying in one direction. It was like thinking on time, where the minute that now glides past is irrecoverable. So was it with these stones: the ocean is their eternity; and each note of that wild music told of one more step towards their destiny. It is not possible for the mind to comprehend, except by a slow process, any effect which is produced by a cause which is repeated so often, that the multiplier itself conveys an idea not more definite than the savage implies when he points to the hairs of his head. As often as I have seen beds of mud, sand, and shingle accumulated to the thickness of many thousand feet, I have felt inclined to exclaim that causes, such as the present rivers and the present beaches, could never have ground down and produced such an effect. But, on the other hand, when listening to the rattling noise of these torrents, and calling to mind that whole races of animals have passed away from the face of the earth, and that during this whole period, night and day, these stones have gone rattling onwards in their course, I have thought to myself, can any mountains, any continent, withstand such waste?—*Darwin's Journal.*

STRENGTH OF THE HUMAN FRAME.

One of the most remarkable and inexplicable experiments relative to the strength of the human frame is, that in which a heavy man is raised with the greatest facility when he is lifted up the instant that his own lungs and those of the persons who raise him are inflated with air. The heaviest person in the party lies down upon two chairs, his legs being supported by the one and his back by the other. Four persons, one at each leg and one at each shoulder, then try to raise him, and find his dead weight to be very great, from the difficulty they experience in supporting him. When he is replaced in the chair, each of the four persons takes hold of his body as before, and the person to be lifted gives two signals by clapping his hands. At the first signal, he himself and his four lifters begin to draw a long full breath, and when the inhalation is completed, or the lungs filled, the second signal is given for raising the person from the chair. To his own surprise and that of his bearers, he rises with the greatest facility, as if he were no heavier than a feather. Sometimes, when one of the bearers performs his part ill, by making the inhaling out of time, the part of the body which he tries to raise is left behind. The experiment was performed at Venice by sustaining the heaviest man of the party on the points of the forefingers of six persons. It is asserted that the experiment will not succeed if the person to be lifted is placed upon a board, and the strength of the individuals applied to the board.—*Abridged from Sir D. Brewster's Natural Magic.*

PALM SUGAR.

This sugar—a considerable quantity of which has been recently imported—belongs to the class of white or refined sugars. It is yellowish-white, and has the texture and flavour of refined cane sugar. Subjoined is a notice of its origin and manufacture, furnished by the surgeon of the importing vessel to Dr Pereira, by whom specimens were laid before a late meeting of the London Pharmaceutical Society. Palm sugar is manufactured principally at Cuddalore, on the Coromandel coast, by some French merchants of Pondicherry. It is obtained by refining the *jagory* or crude sugar used by the poorer classes in India. Jagary is darker coloured than the coarsest Muscovado; is granular or moist; and is packed in mats or bags made of palm leaves. It is chiefly brought from the island of Ceylon by native vessels, and is made by thickening the juice of various kinds of palm—principally the Palmyra palm, the cocoa palm, the lesser fan palm, and the wild date palm. The juice is collected during the night, by making incisions in the upper part of the stems of the trees, and afterwards boiling it down before fermentation takes place. The thick syrup thus obtained is mixed with sand and stone to the amount of ten or fifteen per cent., to make it more solid, portable, and heavier. This jagary is refined by dissolving it in water over a fire, at the same time mixing chunam (lime from sea shells) with it to check fermentation; after this it is strained through a filter of animal charcoal, again boiled, and strained through cotton bags. For the purpose of clarifying, eggs and chunam are used. When the syrup is of a proper consistence, it is put into wooden or earthen coolers, and the molasses allowed to drain off. To whiten it as much as possible, rum, or sometimes a fine syrup, is poured over the sugar whilst in the coolers; it is then exposed to the sun to dry, and lastly packed in bags for exportation. It is never mixed with cane sugar. The sugar thus produced, the writer thinks, will eventually supersede that obtained from the cane. It can be manufactured at a less cost, and the palms affording it grow in abundance in all parts of the tropics, in a dry sandy soil, which could yield nothing else of value. They require very little cultivation, merely enough to keep the luxuriant vegetation from springing up into a jungle around them, and to remove the numerous parasitical plants from their stems. Of course the sugar will improve in quality when more experience has been gained in the way of manufacturing it. The quantity produced last year was upwards of six thousand tons.

THE MANAGEMENT OF THE FINGER-NAILS.

According to European fashion, they should be of an oval figure, transparent, without specks or ridges of any kind; the semilunar fold, or white half-circle, should be fully developed, and the pellicle, or cuticle which forms the configuration around the root of the nail, thin and well-defined, and, when properly arranged, should represent as nearly as possible the shape of a half-filbert. The proper arrangement of the nails is to cut them of an oval shape, corresponding with the form of the fingers; they should not be allowed to grow too long, as it is difficult to keep them clean; nor too short, as it allows the ends of the fingers to become flattened and enlarged, by being pressed upwards against the nails, and gives them a clumsy appearance. The epidermis which forms the semicircle around, and adheres to the nail, requires particular attention, as it is frequently dragged on with its growth, drawing the skin below the nail so tense as to cause it to crack and separate into what are called agnails. This is easily remedied by carefully separating the skin from the nail by a blunt, half-round instrument. Many persons are in the habit of continually cutting this pellicle, in consequence of which it becomes exceedingly irregular, and often injurious to the growth of the nail. They also frequently pick under the nails with a pin, penknife, or the point of sharp scissors, with the intention of keeping them clean, by doing which they often loosen them, and occasion considerable injury. The nails should be cleansed with a brush not too hard, and the semicircular skin should not be cut away, but only loosened, without touching the quick, the fingers being afterwards dipped in tepid water, and the skin pushed back with a towel. This method, which should be practised daily, will keep the nails of a proper shape, prevent agnails, and the pellicle from thickening or becoming rugged. When the nails are naturally rugged, or ill-formed, the longitudinal ridges or fibres should be scraped and rubbed with lemon, afterwards rinsed in water, and well dried with the towel; but if the nails are very thin, no benefit will be derived by scraping; on the contrary, it might cause them to split. If the nails grow more to one side than the other, they should be cut in such a manner as to make the point come as near as possible in the centre of the end of the finger. —*Durlacher.*

JUVENILE SAGACITY.

He who is wise enough in youth to take the advice of his seniors, unites the vivacity and enterprise of early, with the wisdom and gravity of latter life; and what can you lose by at least asking their opinion, who can have no abstract pleasure in misleading you; and who can, if they please, furnish you with a chart of that ocean, to many unexplored, but over which they have passed, while thousands have perished there for want of that wisdom they are willing to communicate to you? The ancients fabled part of this lesson in the history of Phaëton, who vainly attempted to guide the chariot of Apollo. The world is too much for juvenile sagacity, and he must have become gray-headed who is wise enough to walk in and out amidst the machinery of nature and the subtleties of human life, without being either crushed by the one or duped by the other.—*Andrews.*

THE GARDEN IN THE CHURCHYARD.

Would you know where is my garden?—Where the church-tower gray and lone
Casts a shade o'er nameless hillock and white monumental stone—
Where the yet fresh mould is lying over one, young, good, and fair,
Bring I flowers of waning summer, and I make my garden there.
Not to mourn above the sleeper, for in life I knew her not—
Yet a strange and mingled feeling makes this grave a hallowed spot.
There I bring my worldly sorrows—in that stillness does it seem,
That the burthen of them falleth from my spirit like a dream.
And my vain heart's restless beating, with its earthly hope and fear,
Ceases, hushed by the remembrance of the heart that moulders here.
Blue and quiet shines the heaven where is now the spirit's rest;
Here is laid the cast-off garment that encumbered and oppress't.

In this place all worldly feelings slumber, but the mental eye
Strives to pierce the veil tha. hideth from us immortality;
While the soul its pinions trieth, and, sustained by earnest faith,
Soars unto the land of glory, whose dark entrance-gate is Death.
There the spirit's ardent longings for the beautiful and good,
That on earth ne'er meet fulfilment, are enjoyed in plenitude;
There the world-wide love that worketh good for ill to all around,
Is unchecked by cold repulses, and its fulness knows no bound;
There are gained those aspirations which at times upon us gleam,
'Till that inner life seems real, and our outward life a dream.

So I mused beside my garden—thoughts not mournful, and not dull;
On each unknown grave beside me stands an angel beautiful,
Pointing up from earth to heaven. As we journey to our home,
It is good to have such glimpses—shadows of the life to come.

D. M. M.

BEAUTY.

There is something in beauty, whether it dwells in the human face, in the pencilled leaves of flowers, the sparkling surface of a fountain, or that aspect which genius breathes over its statue, that makes us mourn its ruin. I should not envy that man his feelings who could see a leaf wither or a flower fall without some sentiment of regret. This tender interest in the beauty and frailty of things around us, is only a slight tribute of becoming grief and affection; for nature in our adversities never deserts us. She even comes more nearly to us in our sorrows, and, leading us away from the paths of disappointment and pain into her soothing recesses, allays the anguish of our bleeding hearts, binds up the wounds that have been inflicted, whispers the meek pledges of a better hope, and, in harmony with a spirit of still holier birth, points to that home where decay and death can never come.—*Constantinople.*

SELF-GOVERNMENT.

Let not any one say he cannot govern his passions, nor hinder them from breaking out and carrying him into action; for what he can do before a prince or a great man, he can do alone, or in the presence of God if he will.—*Locke.*

DIFFICULTIES.

Whatever difficulties you have to encounter, be not perplexed, but think only what is right to do in the sight of Him who seeth all things, and bear without repining the result.—*The Original.*

NOTHING LOST.

It is well said that nothing is lost. The drop of water which is spilt, the fragment of paper which is burnt, the plant that rots on the ground, all that perishes and is forgotten, equally seeks the atmosphere, and all is there preserved, and thence daily returned for use.—*Macculloch.*

Published by W. and R. Chambers, High Street, Edinburgh (also 98, Miller Street, Glasgow); and, with their permission, by W. S. Orr, Amen Corner, London.—Printed by Bradbury and Evans, Whitefriars, London.

CONDUCTED BY WILLIAM AND ROBERT CHAMBERS, EDITORS OF 'CHAMBERS'S INFORMATION FOR THE PEOPLE,' 'CHAMBERS'S EDUCATIONAL COURSE,' &c.

No. 91. New Series. SATURDAY, SEPTEMBER 27, 1845. Price 1½d.

M. LECLAIRE OF PARIS.

At the present time, when the 'claims of labour' are occupying so much of public attention, and when all sorts of schemes for ameliorating the condition of the working-classes are so eagerly received and discussed, it gives one pleasure to find the enthusiasm beginning to concentrate itself in plans promising practical benefit. One of these plans contemplates the extension of a partnership principle into fields of labour where it has not hitherto been known. 'In some form of this policy,' says the writer of a recent article in one of our most influential periodicals, 'we see the only, or the most practicable means of harmonising the rights of industry and those of property, of making the employers the real chiefs of the people, leading and guiding them in a work in which they also are interested—a work of co-operation, not of mere hiring or service.'

As hinted, this plan, or at least the idea of it, is not new. It is acted on in some mercantile houses, where it has been found advisable to remunerate subordinates occupying situations of peculiar trust, not by a fixed salary, but by a per centage on the returns. A trace of the same system is visible in the custom, which has prevailed from time immemorial in the sheep-districts of Scotland, of allowing the shepherd to feed a few sheep of his own in the same pasture with those of his master. It is also not unusual in our country for contractors engaged in the making of drains and building of field walls to allow the workmen a share of the profits, in order to induce them to complete the work in the shortest possible time. Reaping is often conducted on a similar principle. The good agriculture observable in the small farms of Lombardy and Tuscany is attributed by some to the circumstance, that there landlords and tenants are connected by a bond of partnership as masters and men; the landlord supplying the stock, and receiving in return half the produce, while the tenant gets the other half as the wages of his labour.

The application of the system, however, amongst men engaged in arts and manufactures, must be considered as a novelty. So far as we are aware, the individual to whom the honour is due of having been the first to make the experiment in a workshop, is M. Leclaire, a master house-painter in Paris. M. Leclaire employs on an average two hundred workmen. These he pays in the usual manner by fixed salaries or weekly wages; he assigns also to himself a fixed allowance, proportionate to his rank and duty as the head of the concern. At the end of the year, when the accounts are made up, the surplus profits of the establishment are divided among all connected with it—master, foremen, journeymen, and apprentices—in the ratio of their fixed allowances. The details of the experiment for the year 1842 have been made public by M. Leclaire in a pamphlet,* the substance of which we propose to lay before our readers.

'On commencing business as a master-painter,' says M. Leclaire, 'I at first adopted the same system which I saw others practising—a system which consists in paying the workman as little as possible, and in dismissing him frequently for the smallest fault.' Finding that this system of low wages and harsh treatment produced a result directly contrary to what he wished, he speedily changed it; and with a view to introduce stability into his establishment, he began to pay his workmen at a more liberal rate. The good effects of this plan soon became evident; a body of excellent workmen attached themselves to his service, and would not quit it for any other; the work was more diligently done, and the profits of the establishment were increased. Having thus succeeded in producing some sort of stability in the arrangements of his establishment, M. Leclaire expected, he says, to enjoy greater peace of mind. In this, however, he was disappointed. So long as he was able to superintend everything himself, from the general concerns of his business down to its minutest details, he did enjoy a certain satisfaction; but from the moment that, owing to the increase of his business, he found that he could be nothing more than the centre from which orders were issued, and to which reports were brought in, then, he says, notwithstanding the stability which he had introduced into his establishment, and notwithstanding the attachment and zeal of many of his workmen, his former anxiety and discomfort returned upon him. Being, however, as is evident from the pamphlet before us, a person of strong determination of purpose, as well as of a keen feeling for order and regularity, he set himself resolutely to the task of devising some mode of management which might prove more satisfactory. In the course of his inquiries for this end, he was led to overhaul the whole house-painting trade, in which he discovered much that he disapproved of; and in 1841, he published a pamphlet advocating certain reforms. This, however, was merely preliminary to the more important change in his own arrangements with his men.

'Under the present system,' says he, in his pamphlet of 1842, 'a master tradesman has to endure not only the disquiet arising from bad debts and the failure of persons he may be connected with in business—losses from these causes, especially from the latter, are always trifling when the tradesman is possessed of

* Of the Ameliorations which may be Effected in the Condition of Journeymen House-painters, followed by Rules for Management, and for the Division of the Profits of Labour, by M. Leclaire; as put in practice in 1842 in his establishment, 11 Rue Saint Georges, formerly 8 Rue Cassette, Paris.

prudence—but what is to him an incessant cause of torment, is the losses which arise from the misconduct of the workmen in his service. We have no fear of being accused of exaggeration when we say that he will find workmen whose indifference to his interests is such that they do not perform two-thirds of the amount of work which they are able for; hence the continual fretting of masters, who, seeing their interests neglected, believe themselves entitled to suppose that workmen are constantly conspiring to ruin those from whom they derive their livelihood.' . . . The remedy he proposes is introduced with some explanations. In painting, as in other trades, the price of labour is determined by the expenses incurred. These expenses are of various kinds, such as the rent of premises, the patent, the equipment of tools, the materials in the warehouse, the circulating capital necessary for the payment of wages, the idle expenses, the hiring and maintenance of vehicles and horses, the time lost even involuntarily, and, finally, the profit which the master conceives he ought to have. But this profit, which in painting depends in general upon the workmanship, is so variable, that it often happens that the master, in spite of all his pains, reaches at the end of the year nothing more than an even balance, if indeed he does not find himself sometimes a loser, in consequence of miscellaneous wastages which he could not guard against himself, and which no workman has any interest in preventing. Accordingly, if the journeyman were sure of constant employment, his position would in some respects be more enviable than that of the master, because he is assured of a certain amount of day's wages, which he will get whether he works much or little. He runs no risk, and has no other motive to stimulate him to do his best than his own sense of duty. The master, on the other hand, depends greatly on chance for his returns: his position is one of continual irritation and anxiety.

This would no longer be the case to the same extent if the interests of the master and those of the workmen were bound up with each other, connected by some bond of mutual security, such as that which would be obtained by the plan of a yearly division of profits. It is not difficult to fix an equitable basis for such a division. The workmen, the clerks, and the other employés of an establishment, receiving, as at present, a fixed allowance, varying in amount with their skill, their intelligence, and the nature of their employment, let the master also allow himself a fixed salary proportioned to his importance as the head and director of the establishment; then, at the end of the year, let the surplus profits be shared among all the members of the establishment in the ratio of the fixed allowances which they respectively enjoy. Thus, supposing the business of an establishment to amount to the sum of L.4200 a-year; supposing, also, that the expenses of the establishment for rent, taxes, materials, interest of money in circulation, losses, and small expenses of all kinds, amount to L.2000; and further, that the pay of all the employés of the establishment, master included, amounts to the same sum of L.2000, then the total expenses of the year will be L.4000, and the surplus profits will be L.200. Now, of this sum of L.200, each member of the establishment ought to receive as his share exactly the same proportion as he received of the larger sum of L.2000, which constituted the gross amount of the wages-expenses of the establishment. Thus, if a workman receives L.40 of wages in the year, making a fiftieth part of the total wages-expenses of the establishment, his share of the profits will be L.4, or a fiftieth part of the gross profit. A clerk, again, who receives L.60 of yearly wages, or something more than a thirty-third part of the total wages-expenses, will receive as his share of the profits L.6; that is, something more than the thirty-third part of the whole profits. An apprentice who receives L.4 of yearly wages, will in like manner receive 8 shillings as his share of the profits. Or should any workman have wrought so short a time as only to have earned 8 shillings of wages, still he will receive his proportionate share of the profits, which will amount to something less than tenpence. Lastly, the master, supposing the fixed salary which he has allowed himself to be L.240, will, as his share of the profits, receive L.24. In short, each member of the establishment will receive the same proportion of the profits as he receives of the total wages-expenses; so that, if the wages received by the different employés be equitably proportioned, as they in most cases are, the division of the profits must also be equitable.*

'If such a plan were adopted,' says M. Leclaire, 'the losses of time would vanish almost to nothing, for the indolent and lazy workman would be ashamed to stand with his arms crossed in the presence of an active and laborious companion. The general emulation which must result from such a division of profits would permit labour to be brought to a better market, and cause work to be better done. By removing many subjects of vexation, it would prevent much disorder; it would put it in the power of an economical man to lay up some little thing for the wants of his old age; it would act as a check, on the other hand, upon the adventurous tradesman of too ardent and flighty an imagination, preventing him from rashly undertaking all kinds of jobs without calculating what might be the consequence; it would enable meritorious individuals to rise to the more profitable situations within their reach;† and finally, by compelling masters to be orderly and systematic in their business, it would render them more prudent, and reduce the number of failures.'

Such, described for the most part in his own words, is the plan which M. Leclaire has put in practice. The 'word to our workmen,' which he addressed to the two hundred persons in his employment on the occasion of commencing the scheme, and which is also printed in the pamphlet before us, is really worthy of a 'chief of industry.' After alluding to his recent isolation from them, which he accounts for by the number of preparations he had to make before he could fairly put his scheme in practice, he thus concludes—'Now, however, that all the preparations are terminated, I come to place myself at your head with the same ardour as you have seen me display in other circumstances; nay, my ardour and my diligence will henceforth be so much the greater, that I shall represent the interests of a greater number, and be disembarrassed of that heavy burden which constitutes the functions of what is called a *master*—a position so envied, but which in general does not procure to its occupier passing enjoyment any more than real happiness.'

In connexion with his scheme, M. Leclaire laid down a series of regulations for his establishment, in addition to those of a general nature which had been in force before. The following are the most important particulars in these regulations, as observed during 1842, and slightly modified in the following year. The number of persons to be admitted to the benefits of the plan was to be left undetermined; it was to depend entirely on the opinion of the master. On first reading this regulation, we did not understand it to mean that M. Leclaire was to be at liberty to admit part of his workmen to the benefits of the plan and exclude the rest, but simply that he alone was to decide what number of hands the establishment required, and to have the power of engaging and dismissing, like masters under the present system; we find, however, that he did retain the right of deciding which and what number of his workmen should be

* M. Leclaire suggests the propriety of deducting something from the share of each employé, so as to constitute a kind of sick-fund sufficient to cover the little casualties arising from accidents, illnesses of workmen, &c.

† If in the house-painting trade, says M. Leclaire, the foremen were to be chosen by the votes of their companions, the selection would in general be better than it is at present, and access to the more advantageous situations would be open to workmen whose superiority and intelligence often remain long unknown to the master.

admitted to the benefits of copartnership—a precaution which perhaps was more necessary in a first experiment than it would be if the plan were generally adopted. Still, it appears that the great majority of M. Leclaire's workmen, if not eventually the whole of them, enjoyed the benefits of the plan; and that the purpose of an order of merit among his workmen was served rather by another device, which consisted in the selection of about sixty of his best workmen, whom he constituted into the *noyau*, or kernel of his establishment, retained even when work was scarce, and enjoying other advantages. Besides the liberty of nominating the workmen who should belong to the *noyau*, M. Leclaire retained all the other rights of a master. He was to have the sole charge of the business, the sole right of concluding bargains, of purchasing materials, of fixing the rate of wages, of contributing, as occasion required, to public charities, &c.

When a workman was admitted to the benefits of the plan of partition, he was to be furnished with a check-book, in which was to be entered every pay day the amount of wages he received: the general rate of pay of journeymen in M. Leclaire's establishment being four francs a-day (about a pound a-week) in summer, and three francs a-day (about fifteen shillings a-week) in winter. These sums were also to be entered under each workman's name in a general ledger, and, as already described, they were to constitute the basis of the division of profits at the end of the year.

At that period, the books were to be made up in the following manner:—First, all the general expenses of the establishment were to be added together, consisting of the following items: the expenses incurred in making the necessary arrangements for the execution of the new scheme; the rent of premises, taxes, insurance, &c.; the purchase of materials; the interest at the rate of five per cent. of the capital employed, whether consisting of the materials in the warehouse or of the money spent in the payment of wages, &c.; the losses arising from failures, bad debts, and such like. All these were to be added together under the head of general expenses. Then, distinct from these, were to be added up all the wages-expenses of the establishment, consisting of all the sums marked in the check-books of the workmen and other employés, and in the house ledger, and including also the sum of 6000 francs (L.240), being the amount of salary which M. Leclaire allowed himself as head of the concern. After deducting these two sums—the general expenses and the wages-expenses—whatever remained in the treasury was to be accounted the surplus profits, and, as such, was to be distributed among the various members of the establishment, each being entitled to the same proportion of these surplus profits as he had received of the total wages-expenses. The division for the first year was not to be made all at once, but in two instalments; the first to take place on January 1843, the second not till July following. Should it turn out, contrary to expectation, that at the end of the year there should be no surplus profit, M. Leclaire engaged on his own responsibility to award to his workmen the following sums by way of compensation for their disappointment:—for six months' labour from the date of admission, 25 francs (one pound); for nine months, 40 francs (thirty-two shillings); for a whole year, 50 francs (two pounds). Workmen also whom M. Leclaire should see fit to discharge in the course of the year, for misconduct or for bad workmanship, were to be entitled to compensation at the same rate for the loss of their share of the possible profits at the end of the year; that is, to 25 francs if they had wrought six months, 40 francs if they had wrought nine months, and 50 francs if they had wrought a whole year. Or if, during the year, M. Leclaire should find it necessary, owing to the misconduct of his workmen, to break with one or more of them, or even with the whole number, he was to be at liberty to do so, on condition always that he indemnified them as above for their disappointment. Finally, knowing, to use his own language, 'how difficult it is to make men comprehend their true interests, especially when new means are adopted to further them,' he did not bind himself to continue his plan for longer than one year.

Having adopted all these precautions, and laid down at the same time a code of judicious regulations for the conduct of his workmen, both in town and country, and for the guidance of his foremen in their dealings with the men of whom they had the oversight, M. Leclaire commenced putting his plan into execution, and persevered vigorously in it throughout the year 1842. The result was most satisfactory to all concerned. The pamphlet does not furnish us with a list of the sums realised by each member of the establishment on the occasion of the first division of profits, but we learn from another source, that 'not one of his journeymen who worked as much as three hundred days obtained in the year 1842 less than 1500 francs (L.60), and some considerably more.' Supposing the regular wages of each of the workmen who obtained as much as L.60 to have been four francs a-day, then only 1200 francs out of the 1500, or L.48 out of the L.60, consisted of regular wages, and the share of profits alone which remained to each at the end of the year amounted to 300 francs, or L.12—a surprisingly large sum, but not more than we can imagine to have been the result of the increased zeal and industry of the workmen, conscious of what they had at stake. To this zeal and industry M. Leclaire bears ample testimony in the pamphlet before us. 'We avail ourselves of the present opportunity,' he says, in reprinting his rules for the year 1843, 'to express publicly to our workmen the satisfaction which we have experienced in observing their zeal to conform with our regulations. The position in which we have placed ourselves is such as to enable us to have nothing to do with any except intelligent and diligent workmen. Ours, therefore, are workmen who understand that order, activity, and steadiness are the sources of the happiness enjoyed in labour. Ours are workmen who understand that their time is their only marketable commodity, and who would blush to receive a salary which they had not earned.'

M. Leclaire also bears testimony to the great improvement of manners among his workmen which his new system of management had directly or indirectly effected. 'The master has remarked with pleasure,' he says in a note to his workmen, 'that not only has the pipe disappeared in the workshops, but also that the *quid* is becoming rarer and rarer: he has also observed with satisfaction that noisy and indecent songs are no longer to be heard in the workshops: moreover, that at diet hours, if the workmen gather in the street, it is not to amuse themselves with malicious jokes on the passers-by, nor with annoying the weak and feeble. He has remarked, also, that his workmen have come to know that *friends* are not so common as the name is; that the disgusting talk which results from too great familiarity with each other is banished from his workshops; and that it is more customary for his workmen to converse about serious and instructive subjects, than to be making jests at each other's expense. He has observed, too, that the presence of parties who sometimes visit the workshops imposes respect, and that the workmen conduct themselves on such occasions like well-bred persons.' 'No one,' he says in another part of the pamphlet, 'except such as have had intimate dealings with us, would believe that two hundred workmen can move about alone, and without almost any superintendence, through the different parts of Paris, as well as through the country, and that yet no disorderly action has ever been committed, nor any complaint addressed to us; but that, on the contrary, every one in his own department has done the work he was sent upon in such a way as to win us esteem and flattering testimonies. Such, however, is the fact.'

Having thus described the interesting experiment made by M. Leclaire, we need add little by way of comment. Whether the application of the plan of copartnership between master and men would be as easy in other trades and professions as he found it in house-painting; whether, for instance, it could be applied to agricultural labour, can only be ascertained decisively by further trials; but certainly, at first sight, no insurmountable difficulty seems to lie in the way of the application of the plan to any kind of employment in this country, provided the way were cleared by certain necessary changes in the present laws affecting partnership. Of course, the only motive that can induce employers to adopt the plan, is a conviction or a hope that it will lead to a greater personal advantage: as a class, they cannot be expected to adopt it merely for the sake of their men, unless they find also that it will result in a positive increase of gain, or of satisfaction to themselves. In M. Leclaire's case, as we have seen, the success of the experiment, both in a pecuniary and a moral point of view, was decided; and there is no reason to conclude that, in other cases, with similar energy and prudence on the part of the employer, the result would be different. At all events, it is hardly questionable that, if any amelioration of an effective kind is to be made in the condition of the working-classes, it must be grounded on *some modification or other* of the principle of M. Leclaire's experiment. There is a universal complaint that the distance between the upper and the lower classes of society is widening. The relation between employer and employed, it is said, is now little else than the meagre one between two parties, one of whom contracts to do so much work, the other to pay so much wages; or, as it has been strikingly expressed, 'cash payment is now become the universal nexus between man and man.' 'I give you my work, and nothing more,' says the labourer to his master, 'and you give me my wages, and nothing more.' It was not so formerly. The servant in the feudal times not only did his master's work, but he reverenced and obeyed his master as a social superior; the master, on the other hand, not only paid his servant his wages, but he cherished and protected him as his dependent and social inferior. Now, however, the servant in many cases gives his labour without any accompaniment of reverence; and the master, on the other hand, gives the wages without any accompaniment of protection or kindly interest in his servant's general welfare.

This is the complaint universally made by benevolent persons who take an interest in the condition of the working-classes, and there is no doubt that it is but too well founded. It is absurd, however, to expect the relation between landlord and tenant, between master and workman, to be the same in the present age—when the labourer for a few shillings can be carried by railway fifty or eighty miles in search of work—as it was three hundred years ago, when the bit of sky under which a man was born was the bit under which, as a matter of course, he remained all his life. Taking it for granted that 'cash payment' is becoming universally 'the nexus' between employer and employed, and that it is impossible to prevent its becoming such, our study ought to be to organise labour in such a way that this 'nexus' of cash payment may no longer be a sordid one, but that even under a system in which work and wages are the sole equivalents of each other, we may secure all that is generous and desirable in the intercourse between the upper and the lower classes of society. Instead of trying to resist and thwart the tendency complained of, we ought to try to manage it, or, as it were, to put it in harness. To teach labourers to touch their hats to their employers, to advocate short hours of labour, to send jellies to one's dependents when they are sick, to join in a game of cricket with the working-men of a village—all these are right and praiseworthy in their way; but the only really effective method of restoring good feeling between the upper and the lower classes—not the old feudal feeling, but a feeling compatible with the general spirit of the nineteenth century—is by adopting if possible a better organisation of labour, *by improving the system according to which the employer's wages are exchanged for the labourer's work.*

What the true principle of such an organisation may be in its exact form, we could not undertake at present to say; but M. Leclaire's plan seems to be a movement towards it, and, as such, we desire to see it receive due attention.

A JOURNEY TO CAMBRIDGE A HUNDRED AND FIFTY YEARS AGO.

We learn, by newspapers of a recent date, that the railway between London and Cambridge having been completed, the whole distance (57 miles) is accomplished in a little more than two hours. It happened that, while receiving this information, we were perusing some extracts from a newspaper of an old date, called 'The London Spy,' which was published towards the end of the seventeenth century, and written by one 'Ned Ward,' of witty celebrity. One paper is descriptive of a journey to Cambridge in a stage-coach and six, which forced upon us a contrast to the present state of things at once curious and striking.

Instead of two hours, a journey to Cambridge was, a hundred and fifty years ago, a business of *two days!* for the travellers per stage slept on the road. 'I resolved,' says the facetious narrator, 'since the season of the year proved dry and pleasant, to make a short visit to Cambridge. In pursuance of this my design, I gave earnest for a place in the stage-coach; and the next morning, having lined my pockets, and bundled up a sufficient quantity of linen to refresh me for the fortnight, I took a hackney wheelabout (coach) for expedition sake to the Green Dragon within Bishopsgate, where our travelling conveniency stood ready to receive me. But by the time I got thither, the country tub-driver began to be impatient; all the company but myself being already come, and had taken up their stations in the dirty, lumbering, wooden hovel, being more in shape like a tobacco hogshead than a coach, bellying out like the stern of a Dutch fly-boat, and was built more for burthen, and the horses' ease, than to commode travellers. The rest of the company being most of them pretty burly, had made a shift to leave me a nook in the back part of the coach, not much wider than a chair for a jointed baby. I nestled and I squeezed, and drew in my sides like a fat man going through a narrow stile, till with much ado I had wedged myself in between the side of the coach and that of a bouncing Blowzabella who sat next me. When I had thus by storm, and a great deal of fatigue, taken my place, which, notwithstanding the troublesome coming at it, I had before paid for, I sat with patience upon force, crowded up like a great plum in the corner of a minced-pie. But before many minutes were spent, our brawny and storm-beaten carrion-flogger, whose empty noddle was armed against the weather with a leather cap as thick as a church bucket, gave a cherrup or two, and, with an enlivening slash, away scoured the half-dozen bony hacks in a body.' The travellers stopped at the inn at Ware, celebrated in 'John Gilpin,' as well as for its great bed, 'talked of as much among the citizens (who seldom travel beyond the bounds of the home circuit), as the gigantic greatness of the Herodian colossus and the magnitude of the Trojan horse are amongst the sober inquirers into lost antiquities. The extravagant largeness of this bed is very much wondered at by all that see it, being wide enough to lodge a troop of soldiers, with the assistance of a trundle-bed.' The enormous sleeping accommodation is as much wondered at by travelled and untravelled citizens of this day as when Ned Ward saw it. Ware, being twenty-one miles from London, was the resting and dining place; and for an indifferent fish dinner (chiefly of eels), the company had to pay half-a-crown a-head, besides 'twelvepence for the cook.' This, considering the value of money at that time, must have been a very dear meal, and the guests did not fail to take, to a full extent, the travellers' privilege; but the landlord 'very politically presented us with a dram a-piece of right French brandy, to wash away the grumbling in our gizzards, that we might not report, to his prejudice, the hardness of our usage.' At Puckeridge the coachman stopped, 'to wash the dust out of his mouth. All that was remarkable here was an axe, which they showed us, kept as sharp and as bright as if it were whetted as often as their knives, or scoured as often as their andirons. This antiquated weapon, as they tell you, had the honour of cutting off some great man's head, but who, or upon what account, they are at a great loss to inform you. From thence we jogged on, till we came to our evening's stage, a town called Barley; where we put into an inn distinguished by the name of Old Pharaoh, which title it acquired from a stout elevating malt liquor under the same name, for which it hath long been famous. Here our entertainment was very good, though not so cheap as to be attended without fault; here we heartily enjoyed the true English pleasure of good substantial eating, and supplied that emptiness the slippery eels had left in our stomachs with well-fed mutton and fat fowls, which we washed down with Old Pharaoh, till we made ourselves as merry as bumpkins at a harvest-home.' The company having travelled what was then considered a fair day's distance, namely, thirty-seven miles, went, after this good supper, leisurely to bed, and next morning, after a famous breakfast, 'to keep the fogs from offending our stomachs, we set forward on our journey, and proceeded without anything remarkable till we came to Saffron Walden, so called from the great quantities of that most excellent flower that grows there, so valued by physicians for its admirable virtues in abundance of distempers, being held to be one of the greatest cordials the whole universe produces. It is said the yellow jaundice is never incident to the inhabitants of this place, against which lazy distemper this true English medicine is so infallibly efficacious, that, let a person but ride through the town who is under this disorder, and the effluvia that arise from their saffron gardens shall fill the air with such a salubrious quality, that the odoriferous breath you suck into your nostrils shall prove an effectual cure for not only the afore-mentioned, but many other distempers. As for my own part, I found myself quite enlivened, which I may justly ascribe to the great influence of this golden-coloured product, which is of a nature so good, that physicians themselves allow it can scarce be used amiss.'

From Saffron Walden they jogged on at an 'ass's gallop' to within four miles of Cambridge, 'at which distance the top of King's College chapel was discernible, appearing in a figure resembling a cradle, and by travellers is so called; which happened to draw into my noddle this following scrap of poetry—

> Old Cambridge brings forth men of learning and parts,
> Dame nature's dark law to unriddle;
> And since she's the midwife of science and arts,
> 'Tis fit she be known by a cradle.

When from thence we had travelled about three miles further, we came to a small village called Trumpington, a mile on this side Cambridge;' and the last place 'we arrived at was our journey's end, Cambridge, where black and purple gowns were strolling about town, like parsons in a country metropolis, during the bishop's visitation; some looking with as meagre countenances, as if, in search of the philosopher's stone, they had studied themselves into a hypochondriac melancholy; others seeming so profoundly thoughtful, as if, in pursuance of Agrippa's notions, they were studying how to raise sparagrass (asparagus) out of rams' horns, or to produce a homunculus (ranunculus) as gardeners do pumpkins, by burying the sermon in a dunghill; some looking as plump and as jolly as a painted Bacchus bestriding a canary butt, smiling, as he passed by, at his own soliloquies, as if he was muttering over to himself some Bacchanalian ode he had conceived in praise of good claret; others seeming as sottishly sorrowful as if they were maudlin fuddled, and lamenting the misfortune of poor Anacreon, who choked himself with a grape-stone; some strutting along, about eighteen years of age, in new gown and cassock, as if they had received orders about two hours before. After the coach had set me down, and I had taken a fair leave of my fellow-travellers, I walked about to take a more complete survey of the town and university.' Our author found the town 'so abominably dirty, that Old Street, in the middle of a winter's thaw, or Bartholomew Fair after a shower of rain, could not have more occasion for a scavenger than the Miery Street of this famous corporation; and most of them so very narrow, that should two wheelbarrows meet in the largest of their thoroughfares, they are enough to make a stop for half an hour before they can clear themselves of one another, to make room for passengers.'

Such was Cambridge, and such a journey to it a century and a half ago, presenting a striking contrast to things as they are. We are now whisked down to the seat of learning in less time than Ward and his fellow-travellers occupied in eating their dinners at Ware. Since his visit, the streets of Cambridge have become patterns of cleanliness, and though one or two narrow thoroughfares still remain, yet we question whether there be one in which that ancient vehicle, the wheelbarrow, does not find ample 'room and verge enough.'

EXTINCT RACES OF SOUTH AMERICA.

Without speculating on the changes which South America may have undergone previous to assuming its present configuration, we have certain evidence that the great river plains or *Pampas*, lying between the Cordilleras and the Atlantic, are of comparatively recent origin. The nature of the deposits, and the character of the remains imbedded in them, indicate a period subsequent to the European tertiaries, and demonstrate, beyond doubt, that while the Paris and London basins were emerging into dry land, the Pampas were submerged estuaries, receiving the detritus of the western elevations, and the mingled spoils of terrestrial and marine animals. Mr Darwin's discoveries* are conclusive on this point, and prove that the great plains of South America are but recent elevations from the ocean, in a continent still gradually rising above the waters.

Knowing, as we do, that animal and vegetable life are intimately dependent upon conditions of climate, altitude, and the like, we need only expect to find these vast physical changes accompanied by the extinction and appearance of certain races—each perfectly adapted to the conditions then existing. Compared with the old world, South America is but scantily peopled with native quadrupeds; but a time did exist, and that not very remote, when its animals were more numerous and gigantic than anything that the most favoured region of Asia can boast of. Mr Darwin is the first who has successfully broken ground in this new field of research, his earliest discovery of gigantic remains being made on the plains bordering the present estuary of the river La Plata. In this district, as in most of the Pampas, the formation consists of reddish clay and a soft marly rock, overlaid in many places by more recent alluvium and beds of gravel. Nearer the coast, there are minor plains, formed of the wreck of the upper plain, and from mud, gravel, and sand, thrown up by the sea during the slow elevation of the land, of which elevation there is evidence in upraised beds of recent shells, and in rounded pebbles of pumice scattered all over the country. It was in an exposed section of one of these minor plains, near Punta

* Journal of Researches into the Natural History and Geology of the Countries Visited during the Voyage of H. M. S. Beagle round the world. By Charles Darwin, F.R.S. London: Murray. 1845.

Alta, that the relics of gigantic land animals were first disinterred by our author.

Within the space of two hundred yards, there were found the remains of nine great quadrupeds, varying from the size of a camel to that of the largest elephant, besides a number of detached bones belonging to other species—the whole proving how numerous in kind the ancient inhabitants of this continent must have been. The recentness of their existence was demonstrated by the facts, that shells still found in the surrounding seas were mingled with the debris in which they were imbedded. Of these quadrupeds, one was the megatherium, or 'great wild beast,' described in every geological work; another, the megalonyx, a nearly allied animal; and a third, the scelidotherium, an animal as large as a rhinoceros, but partaking of the structure of the Cape ant-eaters and armadillos. The others were large edental quadrupeds; a great armadillo-like animal with a bony covering; the macrauchenia, a huge beast with a long neck like a camel; and the toxodon, perhaps the strangest animal ever discovered. The macrauchenia is described as belonging to the same division of the pachydermata as the rhinoceros and tapir; but showing, in the structure of its long neck, a clear relation to the camel, or rather to the alpaca and llama. As to the toxodon, it equalled in size the elephant or megatherium; but the structure of its teeth proves indisputably that it was intimately related to the gnawers, the order which, at the present day, includes most of the smallest quadrupeds. In many details it is allied to the pachydermata; and judging from the position of its eyes, ears, and nostrils, it was probably aquatic, like the dugong and manatee, to which it is also allied. 'How wonderfully,' remarks the discoverer, 'are the different orders, at the present time so well separated, blended together in different points of the structure of the toxodon!'

Respecting the habits and life of these wonderful quadrupeds, Mr Darwin, adopting the views of Professor Owen, makes the following remarks:—'The teeth indicate, by their simple structure, that these megatheroid animals lived on vegetable food, and probably on the leaves and small twigs of trees; their ponderous forms and great strong curved claws seem so little adapted for locomotion, that some eminent naturalists have actually believed that, like the sloths, to which they are intimately related, they subsisted by climbing back downwards on trees, and feeding on the leaves. It was a bold, not to say preposterous idea, to conceive even antediluvian trees with branches strong enough to bear animals as large as elephants. Professor Owen, with far more probability, believes that, instead of climbing on the trees, they pulled the branches down to them, and tore up the smaller ones by the roots, and so fed on the leaves. The colossal breadth and weight of their hinder quarters, which can hardly be imagined without having been seen, become, on this view, of obvious service, instead of being an incumbrance: their apparent clumsiness disappears. With their great tails and their huge heels firmly fixed like a tripod on the ground, they could freely exert the full force of their most powerful arms and great claws. Strongly rooted, indeed, must that tree have been which could have resisted such force! The mylodon, moreover, was furnished with a long extensile tongue like that of the giraffe, which, by one of those beautiful provisions of nature, thus reached with the aid of its long neck its leafy food.

'The beds including the above fossil remains stand only from fifteen to twenty feet above the level of high-water; hence the elevation of the land has been small since the great quadrupeds wandered over the surrounding plains; and the external features of the country must then have been very nearly the same as now. What, it may naturally be asked, was the character of the vegetation at that period?—was the country as wretchedly sterile as it now is? For my own part, I do not believe that the simple fact of many gigantic quadrupeds having lived on the plains round Bahia Blanca, is any sure guide that they formerly were clothed with a luxuriant vegetation: I have no doubt that the sterile country a little southward, near the Rio Negro, with its scattered thorny trees, would support many and large quadrupeds. That large animals require a luxuriant vegetation, has been a general assumption which has passed from one work to another; but I do not hesitate to say that it is completely false, and that it has vitiated the reasoning of geologists on some points of great interest in the ancient history of the world. The prejudice has probably been derived from India and the Indian islands, where troops of elephants, noble forests, and impenetrable jungles, are associated together in every one's mind. If, however, we refer to any work of travels through the southern parts of Africa, we shall find allusions in almost every page either to the desert character of the country, or to the numbers of large animals inhabiting it.' This is a most important suggestion, and one which should at all times enter into our estimate of the past conditions of our globe. Pringle, Moffat, Backhouse, and other travellers, describe large tracts of South Africa as comparatively barren, and subject to severe droughts, and yet we know that immense herds of elephants, hippopotami, rhinoceroses, buffaloes, gnus, and deer, inhabit that region.

At a subsequent period, when Mr Darwin ascended the Parana, he discovered the osseous armour of a gigantic armadillo-like animal, the inside of which, when the earth was removed, was like a great caldron; he also found the greater part of the skeleton of a macrauchenia, the teeth of the toxodon and mastodon, and of the horse. 'This latter tooth greatly interested me, and I took scrupulous care in ascertaining that it had been imbedded contemporaneously with the other remains; for I was not then aware that, amongst the fossils from Bahia Blanca, there was a horse's tooth hidden in the matrix: nor was it then known with certainty that the remains of horses are common in North America. Mr Lyell has lately brought from the United States a tooth of a horse; and it is an interesting fact, that Professor Owen could find in no species, either fossil or recent, a slight but peculiar curvature characterising it, until he thought of comparing it with my specimen found here: he has named this American horse, *Equus curvidens*. Certainly it is a marvellous fact in the history of the mammalia, that in South America a native horse should have lived and disappeared, to be succeeded in after ages by the countless herds descended from the few introduced with the Spanish colonists!'

Such is an outline of our author's important discoveries—important as regards the light they throw upon the past conditions of our globe, and specially important as confirming that immutable law of external conditions by which every living being is governed. We see a relationship between the past and present races inhabiting South America—between the macrauchenia and alpaca, the toxodon and capybara, the extinct edentata and the living sloths, ant-eaters and armadillos, now so characteristic of the zoology of that continent. But this relationship is all. The extinct races were huge and numerous—the living are diminutive and comparatively few. The geological changes which South America has undergone are no doubt great; but not, according to our conceptions, such as to have wrought such a startling revolution in the character of its fauna; and yet on this head science is not warranted to decide, for we know almost nothing of those nice conditions, relations, and balances, which are necessary to the existence or extinction of a single species. Mr Darwin's reflections on this topic are replete with sound reasoning, and apply with equal effect to similar changes which have taken place in other regions of the world:—

'It is impossible to reflect on the changed state of the American continent without the deepest astonishment. Formerly, it must have swarmed with great monsters: now we find mere pigmies, compared with the antecedent allied races. If Buffon had known of the gigantic sloth and armadillo-like animals, and of the lost pachydermata, he might have said, with a greater semblance of truth, that the creative force in America had lost its power, rather than that it had never possessed great vigour. The greater number, if not all, of these extinct quadrupeds lived at a late period, and were the contemporaries of most of the existing sea-shells. Since they lived, no very great change in the form of the land can have taken place. What, then, has exterminated so many species and whole genera? The mind at first is irresistibly hurried into the belief of some great catastrophe; but thus to destroy animals, both large and small, in Southern Patagonia, in Brazil, on the Cordillera of Peru, in North America up to Behring's Straits, we must shake the entire framework of the globe. An examination, moreover, of the geology of La Plata and Patagonia, leads to the belief that all the features of the land result from slow and gradual changes. It appears, from the character of the fossils in Europe, Asia, Australia, and in North and South America, that those conditions which favour the life of the *larger* quadrupeds were lately co-extensive with the world: what those conditions were, no one has yet even conjectured. It could hardly have been a change of temperature, which at about the same time destroyed the inhabitants of tropical, temperate, and arctic latitudes on both sides of the globe. In North America, we positively know from Mr Lyell, that the large quadrupeds lived subsequently to that period, when boulders were brought into latitudes at which icebergs now never arrive: from conclusive but indirect reasons, we may feel sure that in the southern hemisphere the macrauchenia also lived long subsequently to the ice-transporting boulder period. Did man, after his first inroad into South America, destroy, as has been suggested, the unwieldy megatherium and the other edentata? We must at least look to some other cause for the destruction of the little tucutuco at Bahia Blanca, and of the many fossil mice and other small quadrupeds in Brazil. No one will imagine that a drought, even far severer than those which cause such losses in the provinces of La Plata, could destroy every individual of every species from Southern Patagonia to Behring's Straits. What shall we say of the extinction of the horse? Did those plains fail of pasture, which have since been overrun by thousands and hundreds of thousands of the descendants of the stock introduced by the Spaniards? Have the subsequently-introduced species consumed the food of the great antecedent races? Can we believe that the capybara has taken the food of the toxodon, the alpaca of the macrauchenia, the existing small edentata of their numerous gigantic prototypes? Certainly no fact in the long history of the world is so startling as the wide and repeated exterminations of its inhabitants.

'Nevertheless, if we consider the subject under another point of view, it will appear less perplexing. We do not steadily bear in mind how profoundly ignorant we are of the conditions of existence of every animal; nor do we always remember that some check is constantly preventing the too rapid increase of every organised being left in a state of nature. The supply of food, on an average, remains constant; yet the tendency in every animal to increase by propagation is geometrical; and its surprising effects have nowhere been more astonishingly shown than in the case of the European animals run wild during the last few centuries in America. Every animal in a state of nature regularly breeds; yet in a species long established, any *great* increase in numbers is obviously impossible, and must be checked by some means. We are, nevertheless, seldom able, with certainty, to tell, in any given species, at what period of life, or at what period of the year, or whether only at long intervals, the check falls; or, again, what is the precise nature of the check. Hence, probably, it is that we feel so little surprise at one of two species closely allied in habits being rare, and the other abundant in the same district; or, again, that one should be abundant in one district, and another, filling the same place in the economy of nature, should be abundant in a neighbouring district differing very little in its conditions. If asked how this is, one immediately replies, that it is determined by some slight difference in climate, food, or the number of enemies: yet how rarely, if ever, we can point out the precise cause and manner of action of the check! We are therefore driven to the conclusion, that causes generally quite inappreciable by us determine whether a given species shall be abundant or scanty in numbers.

'In the cases where we can trace the extinction of a species through man, either wholly or in one limited district, we know that it becomes rarer and rarer, and is then lost: it would be difficult to point out any just distinction between a species destroyed by man, or by the increase of its natural enemies. The evidence of rarity preceding extinction, is more striking in the successive tertiary strata, as remarked by several able observers: it has often been found that a shell very common in a tertiary stratum is now most rare, and has even long been thought to be extinct. If, then, as appears probable, species first become rare and then extinct—if the too rapid increase of every species, even the most favoured, is steadily checked, as we must admit, though how, and when, it is hard to say—and if we see, without the smallest surprise, though unable to assign the precise reason, one species abundant, and another closely allied species rare, in the same district—why should we feel such great astonishment at the rarity being carried a step further, to extinction? An action going on, on every side of us, and yet barely appreciable, might surely be carried a little further, without exciting our observation. Who would feel any great surprise at hearing that the megalonyx was formerly rare compared with the megatherium, or that one of the fossil monkeys was few in number compared with one of the now living monkeys? And yet in this comparative rarity we should have the plainest evidence of less favourable conditions for their existence. To admit that species generally become rare before they become extinct—to feel no surprise at the comparative rarity of one species with another, and yet to call in some extraordinary agent, and to marvel greatly when a species ceases to exist, appears to me much the same as to admit that sickness in the individual is the prelude to death—to feel no surprise at sickness—but when the sick man dies, to wonder, and to believe that he died through violence.'

These remarks put the matter in a clear and satisfactory light. No great geological changes have taken place in Britain during the last two thousand years, beyond the cutting down of some forests, the draining of morasses, the silting up of a few estuaries, and the like; and yet these changes have been the proximate cause of the disappearance of portions of its former fauna. The elk, bear, wild hog, wolf, and beaver, which once plentifully inhabited our island, have passed away; and if we go back a little further, the same could be proved of the rhinoceros, elephant, and mastodon. From their era till now, our island has experienced no overwhelming cataclysm, no eruptive fires; and why should we seek for violent causes to produce similar results in other regions? A small elevation of the land above the sea might drain innumerable lakes; a further elevation would exalt extensive forests to an altitude in which they could not flourish; and, with the disappearance of the luxuriant swamps and the verdant foliage, numerous races fitted for such localities would as inevitably perish. All existence is mutually dependent, and not a loop of the linked web can be let down without affecting many others, according to their proximity or remoteness. It is only because we are ignorant that we marvel, and because we fail to comprehend that we are prone not to believe. But if we could comprehend the whole plan of creation, in its progress from past to present, and from present to what shall inevitably follow, we would be no more surprised at the extinction of old, and the appearance of new races, than at the familiar alternation of day and night, with their attendant phenomena.

LADIES' LOGIC.

There is a sort of reasoning very prevalent in domestic circles, and especially amongst the female members of them, that may be called the non-sequential. It is a style of argument which, although perfectly satisfactory to the propounder, and to most of the household, is found, on being analysed, to be quite inconclusive. It consists either of a simple assertion, destitute of all support from evidence; or—in its more complicated form—of an argument, the first and last parts of which have not the faintest connexion. My fair friends must not imagine me too severe on this little peculiarity; which is, after all, an amiable weakness, often arising from a fervent impulse towards truth, and what they believe to be justice, which men—generally of colder, more calculating temperaments—do not possess. I only desire to extract a little amusement, or perhaps edification, out of a peculiarity which themselves will hardly deny forms a prominent characteristic of their sex.

Ladies' logic is, as above stated, of two kinds. The *first* is an asseverative substitute for argument, so frequently employed by the fair sex, that a proverb has truly designated it 'a woman's reason.' Your wife, for instance, presents you with the draper's quarterly account for payment. You glance at it, and though you take a pride in seeing the chosen of your heart well dressed, yet the amount is startling. The lady sees a play of dissatisfaction hovering over your countenance, and divining the cause, thinks that it *is* hard to be thought extravagant, when she had, during the past three months, been unusually economical. She therefore determines, should there be a demur, to question your right of objection and investigation by resorting to the unanswerable woman's reason. 'How happens it, my love,' you ask, 'that the draper's bill is so much greater this quarter than it was last?'

'How happens it?' she repeats, '*because it is!*'

'Because it is!' The assertion is unanswerable: it summarily cuts off discussion, and blows up the best-laid train of argument. However eloquent and convincing the rejoinder you had arranged in your mind, you feel it impossible to tail it on to 'because it is.' Before 'because it is' was uttered, 'it was a very pretty quarrel as it stood;' but now it is no quarrel at all: the elements of disagreement are withdrawn. Your beloved opponent admits that the bill 'is' large. You cannot contradict *that*, because it forms the ground of your complaint; unless, indeed, you change sides, and contradict yourself. In short, you are as effectually disarmed as if you had—however 'cunning of fence'—taken up a finely-tempered rapier to defend yourself against a bludgeon. One blow from the formidable club shivers your fragile foil to pieces, and leaves you at the mercy of your opponent.

To understand the full efficiency of 'because it is,' let us for a moment cast a glance back to the days of ancient schoolmen, and suppose some of them to have changed their sex. Imagine such lady logicians sticking their theses against college gates, and daring all comers to disprove them, in the manner of the admirable Crichton and the inimitable Gil Blas. Picture a whole class of capped and gowned reasoners coming forth from the cells of learning, and assailing the aforesaid with catalogues of pithy 'whys?' and hosts of pungent 'wherefores?' Fancy—to bring the illustration more home to you—your wife 'gating' her linen-draper's bill at Trin. Coll. Cam., as a mathematical thesis, and, in answer to all the whys and wherefores, exclaiming, 'Because it is.' Why, the most the senior wrangler himself could do, would be to sneer at it as an 'identical proposition,' and slink away to his rooms. Then what chance of *you*, my good friend? Believe me, only one available kind of rejoinder exists, and that is—Pay, and have done with it.

That, however, you may not take my dictum unsupported, or act upon the expensive advice without reason, let me calmly conduct you a few turns into the maze of dispute in which you will assuredly be involved should you make any other rejoinder. If you are so presumptuous as to reply in words, the lady will resort to the *second* sort of logic for which her sex is famous. She will cite a multitude of so-called reasons, which have no relevancy whatever, except in her own mind. Finding the links of a good argumentative sequence *there*, she will not condescend to take you along with her, but merely raps out the results of her rapid reasonings, as if she had never heard of such a thing as a non-sequitur. Some day, about dinner-time, for instance, you will innocently ask, 'My dear, what o'clock is it?' and perhaps your wife's reply will be, 'Why, dinner was not ordered till six.' To your unsophisticated ears this is no reply at all; yet, if you follow the process of reasoning by which it was dictated, you will find it more or less in point. The truth may have been, that when you put the query, it was a little after six, and your anxious wife mistook your inquiry for a piece of delicate satire on the unpunctuality of her domestic arrangements—as a hint that dinner ought to be then on table. With this little dive into her plan of ratiocination, the reply must be deemed more or less apt. But the case in hand—the draper's bill—will illustrate this branch of ladies' logic much more forcibly.

Having been signally beaten from your first position, you must needs take up a new one. Suppose you run over the items of the bill till you come to 'twelve yards of satin velvet, at 30s. per yard ... L.18,' and upon this frame a *viva voce* indictment, putting the first count into the mildest possible form—'Do you not think, dearest, that L.18 is an extravagant price for a single article of dress?'—the defence is immediately entered upon. 'What! do you consider L.18 for a Genoa silk-velvet extravagant? Impossible! Why, did not you give seventy-five guineas for a park-hack only last Thursday? And I should like to know what you paid for that Italian picture: I heard it was L.200, though you were ashamed to tell me. Then there was the diamond clasp you gave to your sister on her birthday; I am convinced you did not get it under L.25.'

It instantly strikes you that, according to logic of the other gender, your laying out a few hundreds on horses, pictures, and diamonds, does not prove that L.18 is cheap for your wife's velvet. You tell her this: she denies the conclusion, and demands that you shall make it good. Nothing can be easier, and, intreating the lady's attention, you pull out your pocket-book, and put down the terms of the argument in logical order on a clean leaf of asses'-skin.

Proposition.—L.18 for twelve yards of velvet is an extravagant price.

'But I say it is *not*,' urges the lady.

'Well, we shall see! Be patient, my dear, and let us proceed.'

Opposition.—But to spend L.300 on a horse, a picture, and a clasp, is also an extravagance.

'Ah, you own *that!*' is the next interruption. 'Very well, then, with all your cleverness, see if I do not convict you out of your own mouth.'

'But the demonstration comes next, love.'

'*I'll* demonstrate for you. Just tell me'—and here the partner of your life assumes a look of triumph—'is not L.300 more than L.18? You can't deny it. Well, if it be extravagant to throw away L.300, how can it be otherwise than economical to spend only L.18?'

It is in vain that you endeavour to show the fallacy: useless are your efforts to impress upon her that velvet and horses, pictures and trinkets, have nothing whatever in common; consequently, what might be dear in the one case, might be cheap in the other. Futile is all your trouble. Not Whately, nor Mill, not the senior wrangler of Cambridge, could reduce her triumph. The lady declares her logic to be unassailable, and you are obliged to take her word for it. You enjoy the joke, and—pay for it.

The rapid process of inexpressed thought, in which many of the fair sex indulge, occasionally betrays them into the oddest specimens of inconclusiveness. When asked whether she could speak French, a lady once answered in my hearing, 'That she could not; which was rather remarkable, for her mother was born in the Mauritius.' This sounds ludicrous enough; but if the links in her broken chain of reasoning, which the speaker left out, be supplied, the answer is not irrational. The island of Mauritius was formerly a French colony, and that language is still generally spoken there; consequently, it may have been the vernacular of the lady's mother; hence it *was* a little singular that the daughter should not have learned to speak French.

Ladies are little skilled in the mysteries of analysis. I complained one day of the leg of lamb being—what it ought not to be; when my wife instantly put in the caveat, 'It cannot be—I bought it myself in the market only the day before yesterday.' Analysis would have here enabled her to see that the date of putrefaction does not necessarily commence from the time of buying, but from the time of the killing of the animal. On another occasion, the evening being very cold, I vainly endeavoured to coax a glow from the fire. 'These are very bad coals,' I remarked. 'Bad coals!' repeated Mrs Peppercorn; 'that cannot be. Why, we have dealt with the same man ever since we were married. Besides, is not he coal-merchant to the Queen? and you may be sure she would not employ him if he supplied a bad article. Then, again, most of our friends deal with the same man, and I have never heard a single complaint before. No, no; it is not the coals, my dear: perhaps the chimney requires sweeping, or the draught is stopped up.' Finding it useless to contend against this sort of argument, I took a half-heated slate out of the grate, and went shivering to bed. The truth is, Mrs Peppercorn having in reality been well served by the coal-merchant, had conceived a very good opinion of him, which she would not on any account—in spite of ocular demonstration and shivering experience—have disturbed.

A stronger exercise of this sort of logic was some time ago employed in a worse cause. There lived in our neighbourhood a solicitor of—as it is usual to describe persons like him—the utmost respectability. He was a most agreeable man in society. He told excellent stories excellently well. He gave parties; and was so uncommonly charitable to the neighbouring poor, that his name appeared at the top of the list of every *public* charity. The gossips never pronounced his name but they had something to say in praise of his conduct as a husband and a father. He went to church as regularly as the parish clerk. The confidence all the old ladies and gentlemen of his acquaintance had in him was so unbounded, that they intrusted him with their savings to invest, and people used to wonder how successfully he placed their capital, for he made it yield regularly five per cent. per annum. However, the morning after one of his most brilliant entertainments, his name appeared in the Gazette; and when he came to be examined before the commissioners, a career of hypocrisy and dishonesty so consummate was laid bare, that it made *me* shudder. Not so my wife, who, by the logic peculiar to her sex, strove to make out her friend the attorney a man more sinned against than sinning. 'Why, when the old shoemaker's house was burnt down, did not he buy him a new set of tools?—the fact was so notorious, that it got into the papers;—then, do you think it likely he would have ruined those two poor orphan girls to whom he was guardian? As to his dishonesty, why, it was only last month he lost five games of sixpenny whist to me, and as he had no change at the time—did not he send round the half-crown before we were up the next morning? No, no; I am sure there is some mystery—something behind the curtain that we do not know.' It was not till the betrayed orphans had got situations as nursery-maids, and three of our esteemed old neighbours had been driven by starvation into almshouses, through his deceitful peculations, that Mrs Peppercorn's convictions in favour of her friend the hypocrite were removed; and even then she seldom spoke of the man without adding, 'Ah, I daresay he was led into it somehow.'

This is the sort of ladies' logic which gives rise to endless inferences from one datum. If there be a single prominent good quality in an individual that is supposed to colour and influence his whole character, I have only to tell my wife that such a man is a disagreeable companion, and she will immediately contradict me by asking, 'How can I say that, when he is so kind to his nephews?' How often do we hear the fair sex praise the sound doctrines and eloquence of an orator merely because he has a fine voice! *Something* pleases them, but they are not sufficiently analytical to trace whether it is the music of the voice or sound reasoning. I shall never forget being present at a discussion on one, perhaps, of the most eloquent preachers who ever stood in a pulpit. A lady remarked that she thought some of his doctrines were a little wild, and that his language was occasionally overstrained. 'Dear me,' said another, 'I am surprised you think so, for finer hair, eyes, and teeth I never beheld!' This lady was perhaps but a poor judge of divinity or rhetoric, but on hair, eyes, and teeth, she was an authority. The effect of the preacher's discourses was extremely pleasing to her; and whether that pleasure arose from the handsome person and elegant delivery, or from the—in her estimation—subordinate qualifications of eloquence and sound doctrine, she could not determine.

In nothing is ladies' logic so strenuously employed as in persuasion, and in nothing does it show itself so characteristically. Some years ago my wife wanted to persuade me to dine at the supper, instead of the dinner time of day. Her reasons for the change were of the most feminine character. Convenience, health, and comfort were quite out of the question, but—'Sir Charles Grander never thinks of dining till eight, and, in fact, there is hardly a family whom we visit that thinks of sitting down before seven.'

The ladies will, I am sure, agree with me that that which we call logic is not their forte. Their powers of conquest over us are derived from other more potent sources—the convincing eloquence of their eyes, the irresistible persuasion of their smiles, to say nothing of their lips. But about them we dare not enter into farther particulars, except to observe, that nature never intended them for chopping logic.

AUTOBIOGRAPHY OF DR ZSCHOKKE.

SECOND ARTICLE—MIDDLE LIFE.

We left Zschokke journeying from France to Rome, by way of Switzerland, in which country he arrived in the latter part of the year 1796. While at Berne, he was unexpectedly attacked by fever, which confined him three months, and left him in a feeble state of bodily health. On his recovery, he made a pedestrian journey to Chur, a pretty town, the capital of the Grisons. Before setting out, he sent on his baggage from Berne, but on getting to Chur, found he had arrived before it, and was consequently obliged to wait its appearance. This trifling event proved to be the turning-point of his history. To pass away the time, he called on the only two men of eminence belonging to Chur whose names he knew. These were the poet Salis-Seewis and Director Nesemann, conductor of an educational institution, which had once attained great celebrity, but appeared to be now verging towards its decline. It was situated at the castle of Reichenau, and contained now only fifteen scholars. Nesemann was the head master, but the owner of the whole was the head of the republic of the Grisons, the President Baptista von Tscharner. This was not the first time that Reichenau had received and given shelter to a wandering gentleman and scholar. It was here that, towards the end of October 1793, a certain young Monsieur Chabas of Languedoc arrived, weary and penniless, with all his worldly goods upon his back, and presently threw himself for refuge on Tscharner and Nesemann, by imploring their protection —a boon instantly conceded. This humble stranger, who resided for some time as a teacher in the establishment, is now, as we all know, Louis-Philippe, king of the French.

Zschokke was, after a few days, asked to take the sole management and direction of the declining school; and he accepted it. 'Thus were my wanderings, by a very agreeable and unexpected occurrence, brought to a sudden termination. The delay of a lazy courier had changed the course of my life. Farewell now, Florence and Rome, palette and brush! A schoolmaster's vocation was now to be my sphere of action, and no fairer or wider had I ever desired; mine was a home in the rock fortress of the Alps, a more delightful one than I had ever dreamt of in the gardens of the Tuileries. The spacious castle, with its adjacent buildings, only two miles from Chur, was flanked by an extensive garden, against whose rocky terraces foamed the impetuous waters of the Rhine. On the opposite shores, bordered by green meadows and clumps of larches, the landscape opened into a beautiful wilderness, beyond which the mighty Alps rose range after range, peak into peak melting away in blue distance, round the snow-capped summit of St Gothard.' The establishment revived and flourished. 'Yet,' says Zschokke, lamenting the deficiency of a *merely* classical education, 'with secret shame I soon discovered my ignorance of much which it most behoved me to know; of matters which all children inquire after, and concerning which, when a boy, I had myself vainly endeavoured to obtain information. I understood neither the stones under my feet, nor the stars over my head, nor the commonest flower that blossomed in forest or meadow. In this I was probably in the same predicament with most of our pedagoguish hirelings, who, in spite of all their Greek, Latin, Hebrew, and Sanscrit, are unable even to name the objects that lie around them in daily life. They study everything except the realities which lie at their feet. In these branches of learning, I and my adopted children became, therefore, fellow pupils; and the innumerable universe was our schoolroom. It was now that I first discovered how much more a teacher may learn of children, than children can of a teacher.' The English reader will remember Wordsworth's lines—

'Dear little boy, my heart
For other lore would seldom yearn,
Could I but teach a hundredth part
Of what from thee I learn.'

Zschokke set about conquering his deficiencies by studying natural history where it ought to be studied—in the fields and forests. On one occasion, his ardent pursuit of this sort of knowledge saved his life.

The French army having overran Switzerland, revolutionary troubles followed, and Zschokke, taking part with the patriots, was obliged to dismiss his school, and keep himself closely confined to his castle. One day he had the imprudence to visit a friend, Professor Bartels, who lived opposite the city of Chur, at the foot of Mount Calanda. 'I spent a delightful afternoon with him, in company with the beautiful Baroness Salis-Haldenstein, and some young friends of hers. We sang, played, conversed, and told stories, until the evening began to close in. They then all accompanied me back as far as a hill, commanding a glorious prospect of the valley and the river, where we sat down and ate some fruit together before parting. The last glimmer of day had departed when I reached Reichenau; for, on my return, I had wandered far out of my way, into various sequestered byways and forest nooks, in search of the summer offspring of the woodland Flora. In the courtyard of my own house, I found the whole population of Reichenau assembled together. They rushed towards me with shouts of joy, and, surrounding me, besieged me with a hundred questions as to "how I had escaped the murderers?" A messenger from Haldenstein had brought to Reichenau the most alarming intelligence. A letter from Bartels was now handed to me, which contained a few hasty and tremulous lines, as follows:—"If this messenger finds you safe and uninjured, send word directly, for God's sake. We are all in the greatest anxiety on your account. When, after leaving you, we were walking down the hill, a party of armed peasants met us, and asked with threatening gestures after you. It is said that you are outlawed, and a price is set upon your head. In vain we adjured the rascals to give it up for to-day, and go back. They went off, on the way you had gone, cursing and swearing at you. The ladies screamed and implored, and the baroness nearly fainted. If you are still alive, fly the country, and save yourself." My little favourites of the forest had, by drawing me far out of my direct way, saved me from my pursuers.' It was now quite time that Dr Zschokke should speedily retire from his adopted country, which he lost no time in doing. He flew across the Rhine, and was informed that a price was set on his head; a portrait of which, together with his name, was affixed to the public gallows of Chur. His offences seem to have been, publishing a liberal history of the Grisons, and penning a patriotic address, previous to a small and unsuccessful revolutionary outbreak.

Dr Zschokke now threw himself wholly and ardently into the political strifes of the time. His talents always aided the cause he espoused; and on the union of the Grisons with the Swiss republic, he was taken into official favour, and appointed proconsul of the Unterwalden districts. Amidst the struggles and vicissitudes which befell Switzerland, Zschokke's prudence, benevolence, and energy, were of the utmost service: and other important offices were intrusted to him in succession. At the age of thirty-one he was appointed governor of Basle.

The political part of his career we purposely pass over, as being uninteresting to our readers. All, however, find some interest in tracing the history of a great man's courtship. It began thus:—'One day, whilst I was riding through the streets of Basle with my chasseurs (citizens' sons from the best families in the town), I noticed a group of ladies at a window, who were pressing forward, curious perhaps to see the new young governor. He, on his part, was no less curious to see them; and looking up, while returning their salutation, beheld a lovely youthful face, worthy to belong to those winged forms which hover round the Madonnas of Raffaelle. Willingly, had etiquette permitted it, would I have made a halt under the window—a proceeding which doubtless would have been just as agreeable to my warlike escort as to myself. As we rode on, the fair one was mentioned among us: it was said she must be a stranger in Basle, and the pleasure of the moment, like many others, was forgotten.'

Not long after this trifling event the governor resigned and retired into private life; and it happened that, at Aarau, he went to a concert, and there, as his eye ran over the parterre of assembled beauties, his attention was arrested by one half-opened rose—a flower of Eden. 'Who is she?' he inquired of a neighbour. 'The daughter of the pastor of Kirchberg,' was the answer; and a faint recollection came across his mind of a clergyman who had once visited him in Basle, and that the damsel was the same whose smiles had gone straight to his heart when they beamed from the window at Basle. Of course it immediately occurred to him as a most urgent duty to return her father's visit as soon as possible. The doctor did so, and repeated his calls; but merely as a good neighbour, once or twice a-week, and resolved, when there, to keep a strict watch on his behaviour. He adhered to his resolution, and did not betray himself by word or look, more especially when he perceived, even before the innocent creature herself, that Anna's inclinations corresponded with his own.

After a few more struggles, he determined that Anna, or no one, should be the companion of his life. The doctor was saved the trouble of asking the important question, by the intervention of no less an agency than that of—a thunderbolt! 'One evening, after a hot summer's day, I was sitting at a table in my bedroom with a book before me, when suddenly the light of the candle was extinguished, and in its place appeared a ball of fire, which darted down from the iron of the window-shutter, and remained visible for some seconds. It soon became evident that the lightning, attracted by the high metallic ornaments of the roof, had struck the building, rending not only the wainscot, but even the thick wall of the castle, and shattering the two windows, so that the floor and furniture were covered by splinters of glass. As for me, although the fiery visitant had left its marks on my neck and on my side, I neither felt any shock nor heard any very loud report, and, in fact, was so little disturbed, that I had leisure to observe with curiosity and admiration the splendour of the fire-ball. Cautiously feeling my way through the darkness that succeeded, I left the chamber; but I believe my composure was rather to be ascribed to the rapidity of the phenomenon, than to any particular presence of mind. Fortunately, the house was not set on fire, but several persons were struck down in the hall. In the course of two hours, however, before the arrival of the surgeon whom I sent for from Aarau, I succeeded in restoring them by the use of the means customary in such cases. It was neither the first nor the last time in my life that the lightning did me the honour of a visit. This occurrence threw the family at the parsonage into far greater consternation than it had occasioned me, and in her agitation, Anna betrayed the secret that her life hung upon mine.' In a short while Anna became Mrs Dr Zschokke. 'From this time forward,' says the autobiographer, 'the stream of my life, which, near its source, had to force its way, foaming and struggling, over a rocky bed, flowed on in a calm and tranquil course. There are no more striking adventures or wonderful vicissitudes, and I may therefore comprise the history of a long series of years in a very brief space. I was no longer a young man; and with the deep experience of life, through which I had attained to manhood, I had gained also a nobler and more extensive sphere of action.' He revived a publication, which he had started at the suggestion of Pestalozzi, soon after his exile from Chur, and which he quaintly called 'The honest, truth-telling, and well-experienced Swiss Messenger, who relates, in his own plain-spoken way, all that goes on in our dear native country, and what the wise folks and the fools are doing all over the world.' This weekly messenger, once more set on foot, had a vast circulation, being read wherever German was spoken, and even in Italy, France, and America. It was revived in 1804, and went on prospering for thirty years. He also organised a 'Social Instruction Society' at Aarau, where he still resided, and assisted in forming other such institutions in various parts of Switzerland and Germany. Several sums of money which he had given up for lost since the Revolution, including arrears of his income as stadtholder of Basle, were fortunately paid to him; and in 1814 he built a beautiful villa on the left bank of the Aar, on a sunny elevation at the foot of Mount Jura, and opposite to the town. In this residence, which he called Blumenhalde, Zschokke has resided ever since in happy retirement, surrounded by an estimable family.

We must not conclude our notice of this most interesting of autobiographies without affording an account of a remarkable faculty Zschokke possesses, and which he calls his 'inward sight.' 'I am,' he remarks, 'almost afraid to speak of this, not because I am afraid to be thought superstitious, but that I may thereby strengthen such feelings in others. And yet it may be an addition to our stock of soul-experiences, and therefore I will confess! It has happened to me sometimes on my first meeting with strangers, as I listened silently to their discourse, that their former life, with many trifling circumstances therewith connected, or frequently some particular scene in that life, has passed quite involuntarily, and as it were dream-like, yet perfectly distinct, before me. During this time I usually feel so entirely absorbed in the contemplation of the stranger life, that at last I no longer see clearly the face of the unknown, wherein I undesignedly read, nor distinctly hear the voices of the speakers, which before served in some measure as a commentary to the text of their features. For a long time I held such visions as delusions of the fancy, and the more so as they showed me even the dress and motions of the actors, rooms, furniture, and other accessories. By way of jest, I once, in a familiar family circle at Kirchberg, related the secret history of a sempstress who had just left the room and the house. I had never seen her before in my life; people were astonished, and laughed, but were not to be persuaded that I did not previously know the relations of which I spoke; for what I had uttered was the *literal* truth: I on my part was no less astonished that my dream-pictures were confirmed by the reality. I became more attentive to the subject, and, when propriety admitted it, I would relate to those whose life thus passed before me the subject of my vision, that I might thereby obtain confirmation or refutation of it. It was invariably ratified, not without consternation on their part.* I myself had less confidence than any one in this mental jugglery. So often as I revealed my visionary gifts to any new person, I regularly expected to hear the answer—"It was not so." I felt a secret shudder when my auditors replied that it was true, or when their astonishment betrayed my accuracy before they spoke. Instead of many, I will mention one example, which pre-eminently astounded me. One fair day, in the city of Waldshut, I entered an inn (the Vine) in company with two young student-foresters; we were tired with rambling through the woods. We supped with a numerous society at the *table-d'hôte*, where the guests were making very merry with the peculiarities and eccentricities of the Swiss, with Mesmer's magnetism, Lavater's physiognomy, &c. &c. One of my companions, whose national pride was wounded by their mockery, begged me to make some reply, particularly to a handsome young man who sat opposite us, and who had allowed himself extraordinary license. This man's former life was at that moment presented to my mind. I turned to him, and asked whether he would answer me candidly, if I related to him some of the most secret passages of his life, I knowing as little of him personally as he did of me? That would be going a little further, I thought, than Lavater did with his physiognomy. He promised, if I were correct in my information, to admit it frankly. I then related what my vision had shown me, and the whole company were made acquainted with the private history of the young merchant: his school years, his youthful errors, and lastly, with a fault committed in reference to the strong-box of his principal. I described to him the uninhabited room with whitened walls, where, to the right of the brown door, on a table, stood a black money box, &c. &c. A dead silence prevailed during the whole narration, which I alone occasionally interrupted, by inquiring whether I spoke the truth. The startled young man confirmed every particular, and even, what I had scarcely expected, the last mentioned. Touched by his candour, I shook hands with him over the table, and said no more. He asked my name, which

* 'What demon inspires you? Must I again believe in possession?' exclaimed the *spiritual* Johann von Riga, when, in the first hour of our acquaintance, I related his past life to him, with the avowed object of learning whether or no I deceived myself. We speculated long on the enigma, but even his penetration could not solve it.

I gave him, and we remained together talking till past midnight. He is probably still living!'

Any explanation of this phenomenon, by means of the known laws of the human mind, would, in the present confined state of our knowledge, assuredly fail. We therefore simply give the extraordinary fact as we find it, in the words of the narrator, leaving the puzzle to be speculated on by our readers. Zschokke adds, that he had met with others who possessed a similar power.

In gentle alternation of light and shade, years rolled over the head of the good philosopher. He wrote copiously, and his works have enjoyed a degree of popularity few authors can boast of. He was, moreover, intrusted with many civil offices by the Swiss government, only one of which he consented to be paid for, and that yielded scarcely L.50 per annum.

Heinrich Zschokke still lives amidst the beautiful lawns and groves of Blumenhalde, the living representative of a sound, benevolent, practical philosopher. No one can read his autobiography without being a wiser, perhaps a better man. The lessons of wisdom which he inculcates win their way to the mind, because they are not formally or dictatorially conveyed, but are put forth with a playful kindness, and a graceful ease, which are more impressive than the haughty solemnity of less sympathising moralists.

THE GOOD CONSCIENCE.

TRANSLATED FROM THE FRENCH OF MADAME GUIZOT.

A band of robbers had secretly entered a provincial town in France, several houses had been plundered, sideboards of plate emptied, and desks forced open. The robbers had played their part with so much skill and success, that they had in every case escaped detection. They directed their attacks to the houses of the most wealthy, and chose the most favourable hours for the execution of their plans, first entering those houses whose inhabitants retired early to rest, and afterwards those in which later hours were kept. It was evident that they were well informed, well directed, and that facility was given them to enter and to leave the town by the windows or roofs of some houses on the ramparts, where traces of them had been discovered. One of those houses was inhabited by a carpenter named Benoit, on whom suspicion strongly fell; for he had but lately come to live in the town, and was very little known. Besides this, he had a gloomy expression of countenance, which repelled people; his brows were dark and closely knit, and he had a long scar across his face. He scarcely ever spoke, even to his wife, to whom he was otherwise a kind husband; though it must be confessed that his taciturnity, and his dislike of repeating the same thing twice, inspired her with a little awe, so that the gossips of the neighbourhood greatly pitied Madame Benoit. He never beat his son Silvester, but he did not allow him to be disobedient or to argue; and though he was but seven years old, he made him work; and the little boys who saw Silvester run off to his work when he observed his father coming, were afraid of him, and called him 'the wicked Benoit.' Finally, it was known that Benoit had followed various callings; that he had been a soldier, that he had seen a great deal of the world, and must consequently have met with many adventures; but as he never related any stories, it was concluded that he could have nothing good to relate. From the time that suspicion fell on him, every little incident was collected that could tend to confirm it. He had never been in the habit of frequenting public-houses, and it was remarked that he had been at one the day preceding the robbery; that he was drinking and conversing familiarly with two ill-looking men, who did not belong to the town, and who had not been seen there since. A neighbour declared that, having gone to the window at eleven o'clock on the night of the robbery, Benoit's door, which was usually shut at nine o'clock, was half open, though there was no light in the shop. At length they proceeded to examine the place by which it was suspected the robbers had entered, and where a silver spoon, supposed to have been stolen by them, had been picked up. It was exactly opposite a garret window in Benoit's house: they perceived also a bit of cord hanging from the window, which had probably served to fasten a ladder; they even discovered the marks of the ladder, and the print of men's feet under the window. From all these circumstances, Benoit was apprehended and put in prison. He suffered himself to be conducted there with the greatest composure, for he felt that he was innocent. The occurrences which led to his apprehension were as follows:—An old soldier named Trappe, a comrade of Benoit's, had lately come and established himself as a hairdresser in the town. He had on one occasion saved the life of Benoit when sorely pressed by the enemy, so that Benoit received him kindly, though he disliked his character, and considered him a boasting liar, if not a rogue.

The day before the robbery, Trappe came to visit Benoit, and told him that two of their old comrades, who had served in the same regiment, were passing through the town, and that he must come and drink a bottle with them. He reminded him that it was the anniversary of the battle in which he had saved his life. Benoit scarcely knew how he could refuse the invitation, and wished even to pay his share, but they would not allow him. They endeavoured to make him drink, and to make him talk, in hopes of getting information from him; for Trappe and his companions formed part of the gang who were to enter the town that night. They wished to make him drunk that he might not hear what would happen in his house, or be in a less fit state to resist them: however, Benoit spoke but little, and only drank enough to make his head rather more heavy, and his sleep rather more sound, than usual. The next morning he perceived that his shop door had been opened, which astonished him a good deal, as he was certain that he had fastened it on the previous evening. He went up stairs, and found that his garret window, which he had also secured, was open, and that a bag of beans which he had left there had been carried off. He did not say a word about all this, for it was not his custom to speak of things before he well understood them; but he thought a good deal of the matter. On going out to his work, he found the whole town in a tumult; every one was talking of the robbery which had been committed during the night. It was reported that two suspicious-looking men were seen the day before in some of the public-houses, and the one in which he had been with Trappe and his companions was particularly mentioned. Ere long, he perceived that people avoided speaking before him, and that they looked at him with suspicion. He recollected that when he left the public-house on the previous evening, Trappe had followed him with a bottle in his hand, and went up stairs to the room in which his wife and son were, and that he made them drink two glasses of wine—most probably to intoxicate them; he also remembered, that having looked out of the window, just after Trappe went down stairs, he did not see him go out. From all these circumstances, he concluded that he must have concealed himself in the house, and that it was he who had opened the window and door for the robbers. He went in search of him, and taxed him with the fact. Trappe at first pretended not to understand him, and then grew angry; but he was evidently agitated. 'You saved my life,' said Benoit, 'and I do not wish to injure you; but if you have done this deed, be off, and never let me see you more, or I may bring you into trouble.' The next morning Trappe disappeared, and it was on that day that Benoit was arrested. He was asked whether it was he who had opened his window and door; to which he answered no. He was then asked if he knew by whom they were opened. He replied that he did not: in fact, he had no certainty that it was Trappe. He was next asked whether there was any person he suspected; to which he replied that, as he was himself arrested on suspicion, his suspicions might cause another to be arrested who might be equally innocent, and that therefore, if he had any, he would not divulge them. In fine, he gave true answers to every question, but without any addition, or saying a word that could inculpate Trappe. When the examination was over, as there was no proof against Benoit, they were obliged to set him at liberty, though every one felt fully persuaded that it was he who had given admission to the robbers. He saw this by the manner in which they announced to him that he was free, and also by the conversation he heard in crossing the court; but it did not seem to affect him in the least. When he reached home, after having embraced his wife, who was overjoyed at his return, he embraced his son, and said calmly, 'Silvester, you will hear it said everywhere, that though I have been acquitted, I am not the less a rogue, and that it was I who opened the way for the robbers; but do not let that trouble you, for it will not last long.' His wife was frightened by what he said, but would not believe it till she went out to receive the congratulations of her friends. Some turned their backs on her, others looked at her with compassion, and shrugged their shoulders, as much as to say, Poor woman! it is not her fault. Others again told her what they thought about it. After having been insulted by three or four, she returned crying and sobbing, and declared that she could not live any longer in that place, and that they must absolutely quit it.

'If I leave this,' said Benoit, 'I shall leave nothing after me but a bad name.'

'What good will it do you to remain here?' asked his wife.

'I will recover a good one.'

'You will lose all your customers.'

'No; for I will be the best workman in the town.'

'There are good workmen besides you. What will make you superior to them?'

'When things are most difficult, it is only to take more trouble about them.'

Benoit had some work in hand at the time he was apprehended: he completed it with so much promptitude and perfection, and at such a moderate charge, that those for whom he was working continued to employ him, although they had not a very good opinion of his character. He now determined to rise two hours earlier, and go to bed later, than he had been in the habit of doing, and also to work with greater assiduity, so that, by seldom being obliged to hire workmen, he could make moderate charges, although he gave the very best timber and workmanship. By these means he not only retained his old customers, but gained new ones.

He plainly perceived that he was still a suspected person, and that precaution was taken not to leave him by himself in a room; but this he took no further notice of than by a quiet smile. But if, in passing through the streets, any one proposed to him to join in some wicked design, he gave him a look that prevented all desire to repeat it.

He saw that his accounts were examined with peculiar care; but he made them out so clearly, so detailed, and so minute, that people ended by saying he was too particular. 'No,' he would say; 'I know very well that you have a bad opinion of me, and it is necessary that you should be thoroughly convinced that I am not cheating you.'

A fire broke out in a house in the neighbourhood, and threatened to reach the adjoining one; several workmen had endeavoured to cut off the communication; but all had abandoned it as being too hazardous. When Benoit arrived at the door of the threatened house, he saw that the servants were afraid of admitting him without their master's orders; but he pushed past them, and forced his way, saying, 'The first thing is to save your house; you can afterwards see whether any thing is lost.' He went up alone to the top of the house, which had been deserted by every one. As he was crossing one of the rooms, he saw a watch upon a mantelpiece, which he put in his pocket, lest any one else should take it; but recollecting that he might perish in the enterprise, and that if the watch was found on him, it would be supposed that he had stolen it, he hid it in a hole in the wall. He then climbed to the place which had begun to take fire, cut through it with a hatchet, and stopped all communication. As he was returning down stairs he met the master of the house, and showed him where he had concealed the watch. 'I put it there,' said he, 'because any person could have taken it, and you would have believed that it was I.'

So many proofs of honesty and sincerity in the regular conduct of Benoit, in which all the espionage of his neighbours could not detect a flaw, began to make an impression in his favour.

A man of great wealth came to settle in the neighbourhood, for the purpose of building a large manufactory. He inquired for the best carpenter, and it was impossible not to point out Benoit. He employed him, and was so much pleased with his intelligence, his zeal, and his integrity, that he declared it to be his conviction that Benoit could not be anything but an upright, honest man. As he was a person of influence, this produced a great effect, and his reputation as a workman extended through the province, and brought him a considerable increase of business; it also made him acquainted with a great many influential persons, and every one by whom he was employed formed a good opinion of his character. He was no longer watched, though he was still asked how it was that his window and door were found open for the passage of the robbers, many believing that he knew. The gentleman who had employed him in the building of the manufactory and who took a great interest in him, told him that he ought to try to explain that circumstance. 'I will leave it to the character I shall establish as an honest man, to make such an explanation needless,' said Benoit. At length people began to think no more of the matter, and felt sure that he could have had no part in it.

One of the robbers was taken some time afterwards, and related the whole circumstance.

People came to congratulate Benoit. 'Whatever I may have suffered from unjust suspicion,' said he, 'a good conscience enabled me to bear it, as I felt sure that one day all would be cleared up. I well knew that a just Providence would not long suffer that an honest man should pass for a rogue.'

TEACHING OF GEOGRAPHY.

The Rev. Mr Hume, of the Collegiate Institution, Liverpool, has printed a small tract,* containing some very useful hints on the teaching of geography. He condemns, with truth, the too frequently-adopted plan of giving a dry catalogue of names and localities, totally unconnected, in most instances, with anything else which the mind can grasp, and suggests modes by which not only the study might become more pleasant, but more profitable. The first principle he lays down is, that the judgment should be called in to aid the memory, and this may be done in various ways. 'We may lead the mind of the pupil, for instance, into the way of cause and effect, so that many important results may be reached independently *a priori;* we may introduce rational comparisons, so that the circumstances of one country will always suggest those of another, and thus give rise to important general ideas; or we may diminish the intellectual labour of the very youngest, by pointing out obvious inferences, which render several of the statements of the book unnecessary. For example, what

* Suggestions on the Teaching of Geography, by the Rev. A. Hume. Privately printed for distribution among teachers. John Henderson, Castle-Place, Belfast.

is more natural than to infer that the English language is spoken in the United States, that French is common in the Mauritius, or Dutch at the Cape of Good Hope, when the most meagre outline of these colonies is known? By simple inferences, I mean such as the climate, and natural productions, animal or vegetable; of which every one can form some idea from the latitude and general situation. And to take an example of comparison, let us place side by side the two facts, that England proper contains 15,000,000 of population, and that Spain, which is twice as large as the whole island of Great Britain, contains only 15,000,000. The most indolent and stupid boy is roused to ask, either of himself or his teacher, or his book, "*why* is this?" And he then begins to think, for the first time, of the effects of peace, intelligence, and varied industry in the one country, or of bloodshed, ignorance, and national habits in the other, though he may have heard the separate facts stated twenty times before.'

The application of this principle in impressing the physical features of a country must be obvious. For example, the rivers are a general guidance to the form of the country which they drain. Association may also be called in with good effect. 'This,' says Mr Hume, 'is easily done in the case of battle-fields, towns that have been besieged, places noted for convulsions of nature, or for being the birth-place or the burial-place of some distinguished individual. Thus, Gibraltar will never be forgotten, if once its famous siege be alluded to; every schoolboy knows about the burning of Moscow; and an obscure speck on the map of Africa, Cape Coast Castle, is sought for with eagerness, from its melancholy association with her who was once Miss Landon. A similar association might be formed with a thousand other places, in which the great historical facts would present themselves at once. But even in minor matters, what an interesting thing does a map of the world become, when a boy can show where Byron died, where Falconer was wrecked, where Captain Cook was killed, where Lander terminated his labours, where Stoddart and Connoly were put to death, or Wolff imprisoned, where Howard became a martyr to his benevolence, where Park was encouraged by a flower in the desert, or where Napoleon was an exile. It is no longer a couple of circles, with printing and scratches, or with blotches of colouring, but a living, speaking picture, which he bears in his mind as long as memory exists. Nor is this all: the spirit of inquiry has been stirred within him, and "the intellectual appetite," curiosity, must be supplied. He searches for a copy of Park's travels, to ascertain more on a subject of which he knows something already; he is led by reference and association to Lander, Bruce, Salt, and others; he reads Falconer's poem, which he would never have thought of opening; he refers to a biographical dictionary for particulars concerning Howard or Byron; and some friend is obliged to yield to his importunity, and get him Cook's voyages to read. And if it be true, as it undoubtedly is, that "all knowledge is money laid out at compound interest"—since every fact enables us to understand others that, without it, would remain unknown—these suggestions, however trite they may appear, rise in magnitude and importance.'

Tracing the routes of distinguished travellers is one of the plans recommended. 'There are other means of producing the same effects, apparently unimportant, but really not so. Such, for instance, is the simple quotation of a line of poetry bearing upon any particular place, which, as it is more easily retained than any other description, gives more marked and vivid ideas. Thus, if the first line of Heber's missionary hymn were explained to a boy, he could never lose sight of the local characteristics—

"From Greenland's icy mountains,
From India's coral strand,
Where Afric's sunny fountains
Roll down their golden sands."

Or, again—

"From Lapland's woods, and hills, and frost,
By the rapid reindeer crossed."

Or Macaulay's line—

"Thou, Rochelle, our own Rochelle, proud city of the waters!"

Or that of Watts—

"I would not change my native land
For rich Peru and all her gold."

In some "modern instances," as in Murray's Continental Hand-Books, poetical quotations are often given with great appropriateness. The writings of Byron, Scott, Rogers, &c. abound with allusions to localities, of the kind suggested here; so that a reading teacher could have no difficulty in finding enough. The peculiar turning of an expression has often a most marked effect upon our associations, as "sunny Italy," "the pleasant land of France," "the beautiful Rhine;" and there is an entire class which are all particularly useful in particular countries, like "from Dan to Beersheba," "from Eddystone to Berwick bounds, from Lynn to Milford Bay," "frae Maidenkirk to John-o'-Groats." The reason why any imaginative association of this kind is seized with such avidity is, that it gives a more tangible existence to the place. The recollection is no longer a mere idea, an abstraction; but its use is apparent, as means to an end; it is connected with literature, and associated with genius.'

'It is evident,' adds Mr Hume, 'that the subject of geography is not taught when all the facts contained in a meagre text-book are elicited by cross-examination. But what must be taught to a pupil besides? The use of his own intellect, we reply, to retain what he has got, and to acquire more; the inclination to do so; the pleasure connected with knowledge; the classification and connexion of various kinds of it; and last, and not least important, an additional number of facts. It is evident that no two teachers would go over the same ground in the same way; but each, in the independent exercise of his own mind, might do it well, and answer the end fully. So far as my own experience goes, I find that by far the most convenient plan is to give the association—whether fact, allusion, or anything else—when we are actually treating of the place. On a separate day the interest is gone, and the prolixity of a tale, or narrative of travels, with many useless digressions—when at best it is not so pointed as one requires—fails to fix the attention, if indeed it does not occasionally dissipate it. When once these pictures are placed in the mind, they are indelible, or may be revived in their full colouring in an instant. For example, the single application of the term "New France" to Canada, awakens the recollection of its early inhabitants, of their language and manners, of General Wolfe, of M. Papineau, of the recent rebellion. And with what unmixed delight does the intelligent student of geography look upon the map of such a country as Spain. He forgets for the moment its size, and form, and colouring. He thinks of Hannibal and of Carthage, of Scipio and the Celtiberian prince, of the Goths, of the victorious Moors, of their gorgeous palaces, of their dances and their songs. He glows with the chivalry of Rodrigo the Cid, or he thinks of the petty jealousies of Gallegan, Catalan, Andalusian, and Castilian, in a country which nature has made one; he recollects Ferdinand and the Inquisition, Charles V. and America; or fancies he sees an *auto da fé*, a bull-fight, or a castanet dance. There is not a country of Europe, and there is scarcely a country of the world, that would not afford the materials for a most interesting essay, in which all these suggestions could be appropriately applied, and beautifully blended with every important town, province, mountain, and river.'

Other modes of impressing geographical and statistical facts are pointed out in this excellent little tract; the wider circulation of which could not, we think, fail to awake many from the errors of their ordinary procedure in this department of instruction.

ITINERANT VOCALISTS.

[From 'Musings of a Musician,' by H. C. Lunn, in the Musical World.]

The Foreign-looking Man with the cap.—In criticising the style of this candidate for our favours, we freely confess that his sentiment is overpowering, and the selection of his songs a pattern to the youth of the day. He usually accompanies himself upon a *seraphine*, and invariably composes his own symphonies, which recommend themselves to your notice on account of their extreme brevity. By his method of singing and gentlemanly bearing, he evidently wishes to impress you with an idea that he has travelled much on the continent in early life, and has, in fact, seen more of the world than most men: he only patronises English songs in order that his audience may understand him; but he usually sings Italian to his private friends, and rather prefers them too. If threepence is thrown towards him, carefully wrapt in white paper, he motions with dignity to a boy to pick it up; and as soon as he has opened it, he pockets it with a smile, as if he were doing the whole thing for a wager, and rather enjoyed the joke. In the summer season he usually goes down to a watering-place for a little sea-bathing, and is quite a favourite with the sentimental young ladies who stroll out in the evening to enjoy the refreshing air.

The Old Man with the stick.—This vocalist is remarkable for his unflinching patronage of the English school of music; Dibdin and Shield are his stock favourites: and the hearty manner in which he delivers their compositions, is only to be equalled by the stern manner in which he swears at his boy when he does not look sharply enough after the halfpence. He has lately got rather husky, and occasionally mars the effect of his songs by vain endeavours to clear his voice, which always fails him in the most sentimental part of the poetry. When this occurs in the middle of Dibdin's patriotic songs, he generally strikes his stick against the ground, thereby indicating his total want of power to express by any other means the way in which he would, most unhesitatingly, sink an opposing fleet, and blow all our enemies into thin air. By thus continually hurling defiance at all the nations of the earth, he has managed to acquire the name of the 'old sailor;' but whether he is entitled to this appellation, I know not; certain it is that he is a most desperate character in his vocal moments; and if he would only act as energetically with his guns as he does with his stick, he would be a most invaluable person on board a man-of-war.

The Glee Singers.—These peripatetic vocal bands are remarkable for the dignified manner in which they arrange themselves before your door, with the evident idea of carrying you away by a mass of scientific harmony. They have generally a female amongst them, who appears to have been selected from the fact of her possessing no voice. The consequence of this is, that although you hear the vocal powers of the two males strained to the utmost, you are left quite in the dark as to the melody, which, being intrusted to the soprano, is totally imaginary. . . . I believe that it has never been correctly ascertained what particular compositions they aim at, but I have no doubt that they imagine they are singing glees; and as the pence usually come in tolerably briskly, there is no reason why this delusion should not go down with them to the grave.

The Sentimental Man with the white apron.—Every person must have observed this individual, who, having somewhat the appearance of a journeyman carpenter, seems, either by misfortune or inclination, to have expressly devoted himself to the service of our most popular English composers. . . . It is a curious fact, that he invariably selects the most sentimental airs, which he generally delivers thus:—having sung the first four bars at the top of his voice, he takes three or four steps forward, and mutters the next four bars to himself; he then takes off his hat and looks upward, as if invoking a blessing upon the composer of such delightful music; you then hear nothing of him for a minute or two, and you almost imagine that he has thought better of it, and left off—when suddenly a few notes strike upon your ear, which, being very near the conclusion of the melody, convince you that the greatest portion of his performance has been private and confidential; and that, although you may not have heard it, he has gone through the entire composition without missing a note. In this manner he proceeds from street to street, singing with melancholy voice the hopeful songs of youthful love, and exciting laughter where he looks for sympathy.

The Serious Man with the violoncello.—Other vocal miseries to which all residents in a metropolis are subject, may be borne with tolerable temper, but this man is really too much for human endurance. He commences at the top of the street by reciting a verse, apparently from a psalm—then comes the violoncello—and such a voice! If anything can convey to the mind a perfect idea of the intense wretchedness to which a fellow-mortal can be brought, and the dreadful purposes for which catgut can be used, it is fully shown by this individual and his violoncello. If they could only agree in their misery, it would not be so bad; but here we have the voice and the instrument eternally fighting against each other, and each declaring that it has got hold of the right note, and intends to keep it. This person leads a solitary, wretched life: the man with the clarinet eyes him with pity, and Punch lowers his voice as he passes him; the girl on stilts looks down upon him with reverence; and the man with the pandean pipes and guitar hugs himself in the idea, that if he cannot play in tune, he can at least play lively music out of tune. Various conjectures are afloat as to his origin: many persons assert that he has escaped from some prison, and is thus pursuing a deadly revenge upon society for having sent him there; others say that he has been thwarted in love, and has resolved to commit suicide by slow music instead of slow poison. Whoever he may be, I am convinced that the inhabitants of London would willingly enter into a subscription to pension him off for life; and I can only say that, should such an idea be really entertained, my guinea is ready.

AUTHORS ON AUTHORS.

Authors have frequently too much self-interest and jealousy to permit them to see, or rather to acknowledge, the full merits of their rivals and predecessors. A partiality for their own theories, and their own style of writing, renders all others next to intolerable. On the other hand, their admiration is often elicited by insignificant trifles. We have read of a lawyer who threw away a celebrated novel because the first chapter contained a bad will; and of a geometrician, whose sole pleasure in the Æneid consisted in tracing the voyage of Æneas. Milton was disparaged by more than one eminent author. Isaac Newton is related to have said, 'Paradise Lost is a fine poem, but what does it prove?' Winstanley, crowing too soon, said, 'Milton's fame is gone out, like a candle in a stink.' The learned Bishop Hacket called him 'a petty schoolboy scribbler;' and the celebrated Barrow, who regarded poetry as ingenious nonsense, in a letter to Skinner presumed to speak of him as 'one Milton.' In a similar paltry spirit of contemptuousness, Burnet drew upon himself more popular censure by an unlucky sentence in which he spoke of 'one Prior,' than by all the inaccuracies of his statements and his style. Although Shenstone's reputation as a poet almost entirely depends upon his imitation of Spenser, he does not speak of him with much regard. 'The plan of the Faery Queen,' he says, 'appears to me to be very imperfect. Spenser's imagination is very extensive, though somewhat less so, perhaps, than is generally allowed, if one considers the facility of realising and equipping forth the virtues and vices. His metre has some advantages, though in many respects objectionable. His good nature is visible through every part of the poem. His conjunction of the pagan and Christian scheme (as he introduces both acting simultaneously) is wholly inexcusable. Much art and judgment are discovered in parts, and but little in the whole. One may entertain some doubt whether the perusal of his monstrous descriptions be not as prejudicial to true taste as it is advantageous to the extent of imagination. Spenser to be sure expands the latter, but then he expands it beyond its true limits. After all, there are many favourite passages in his Faery Queen which will be instances of a great and cultivated genius misapplied.' Some of these remarks are accurate; but the tone is cold and disagreeable. He, of whose pictures we may say, as Reynolds remarked of Rubens, that one is sufficient to illuminate a room, demands a different style of criticism. Addison himself has expressed a contemptuous criticism of Spenser's Faery Queen, which he did not read until fifteen years afterwards. It must have been in a similar spirit of adventurous ignorance that he found fault with Chaucer for want of humour. Cowley, too, has expressed a dislike of Chaucer, whom he 'read over' at the Earl of

Leicester's request. Dryden suggests that he was perhaps too much shocked at the poet's rough and antique style to search into his good sense. He had not the curiosity to force his way into a garden through a few brambles. It was not till nearly thirty years after the death of Collins that Cowper had ever heard his name. He saw it first in Johnson's Lives of the Poets, and was so little impressed by what he saw there, that he called him a poet of no great fame, and appears not to have formed the slightest conception of his powers. Dr Johnson's Dictionary abounds with the most absurd definitions of natural objects, yet he ventured to say, in reference to Goldsmith's Animated Nature, that 'you must not infer from this compilation that Goldsmith possessed any knowledge of the subject; for if he knows that a cow has horns, it is as much as he does know.' The Edinburgh Review spoke of 'a stupid Journal of Montaigne's Travels;' a work in fact so interesting that a recent English translation of it has met with very great success and applause. It is far from improbable that the reviewer had never so much as seen the journal which he so rashly stigmatised. With respect to the ordinary criticism in reviews, it may be said that scarcely in any single case has a reviewer either brought a great author to light or prevented him from becoming popular. It is, after all, the public, not reviewers who settle the merits of books.

LONDON POLICE IN 1768.

A dispute having arisen between the coalworkers and the coalheavers, the latter of whom were chiefly Irish, nay, some of them whiteboys, an act of parliament had passed the last year, subjecting the coalheavers to the jurisdiction of the alderman of the ward; an office had been erected, and one Green who kept an alehouse had been constituted their agent. Houston, a man who wanted to supplant Green, had incensed the coalheavers against him, and they threatened his destruction. Apprised of their design, he every night removed his wife and children out of his house. One evening he received notice that the coalheavers were coming to attack him. He had nobody with him but a maid-servant and a sailor, who by accident was drinking in the house. Green asked the sailor if he would assist him. 'Yes,' answered the generous tar, 'I will defend any man in distress.' At eight the rioters appeared, and fired on the house, lodging in one room above two hundred bullets; and when their ammunition was spent, they bought pewter pots, cut them to pieces, and fired them as ball. At length with an axe they broke out the bottom of the door; but that breach the sailor defended singly, while Green and his maid kept up a constant fire, and killed eighteen of the besiegers. Their powder and ball being at last wasted, Green said he must make his escape; 'for you,' said he to the friendly sailor, 'they will not hurt you.' Green, retiring from the back-room of his house, got into a carpenter's yard, and was concealed in a sawpit, over which the mob passed in their pursuit of him, being told he was gone forwards. I should scarce have ventured this narrative, had not all the circumstances been proved in a court of justice. Yet how many reflections must the whole story create in minds not conversant in a vast capital—free, ungoverned, unpoliced, and indifferent to everything but its pleasures and factions! Who will believe that such a scene of outrage could happen in the residence of government? that the siege lasted nine hours, and that no guards were sent to the relief of the besieged till five in the morning? Who will believe that while such anarchy reigned at one end of the metropolis, it made so little impression at the court end that it was scarce mentioned? Though in London myself, all I heard was, that a man had been attacked in his house, and had killed three of the rioters. Nor were the circumstances attended to till the trial of Green for murder, of which he was honourably acquitted, divulged his, his maid's, and the sailor's heroism. Yet did not the fury of the colliers cease, though seven of them were taken and executed. Green was forced to conceal himself from their rage, but his sister giving a supper to her friends for joy of her brother's safety, her house was attacked by those assassins, their faces covered with black crape, who tore her into the street, and murdered her. Yet perhaps of all the circumstances of this tragedy, not one was so singular, from the display of so great a mind, as the indifference of the sailor, who never owned himself, never claimed honour or recompense for his generous gallantry. As brave as the Cocles of fabulous Rome, his virtue was satisfied with defending a man oppressed; and he knew not that an Alexander deserved less fame than he, who seemed not to think that he deserved any.—*Walpole's Memoirs of the Reign of George III.*

SONG.

[BY S. W. PARTRIDGE.]

SUMMER is flying,
Flowerets are dying,
Brown leaves are lying
Under the tree;
Reapers are singing,
Golden sheaves bringing,
Birds their flight winging
Over the sea.

Soon Winter scowling,
With his winds howling,
Like demons prowling,
Hither will roam;
Round blazing piled wood,
Borne from the wild wood,
Manhood with childhood
Nestle at home.

While beauty lingers,
Ere Frost's cold fingers
Hush the glad singers
On the green spray,
Far from life's madness,
Tumult and sadness,
To nature's gladness
Hasten away.

CARTER, THE LION KING.

Carter, the celebrated lion king, possessed perhaps as much daring and self-possession as has ever been known. A full-grown and powerful Bengal tiger was landed out of an Indiaman for him, and was to be trained for his theatrical exhibitions. Carter expressed no concern at the task, nor anticipated any difficulty; and when he judged the fitting moment to have arrived, he caused the door of the cage to be opened, and suddenly stood in the presence of the astonished beast, armed merely with a slight horsewhip. Cowed by the effrontery and stern glance of the man, the tiger crouched into the most distant corner of its cage, terror-stricken. A blow with the whip, and an indication of the finger, sent the now submissive beast to another corner; and thus it was kept on the move from spot to spot, till Carter, retiring from the cage, declared its entire subjugation. The feats of this extraordinary man on the stage are well known, but he would often amuse himself in private by matching his strength against that of his animals. I have seen him, for instance, release a puma from its cage, and, seizing the beast by its tail, attempt to drag it along: indeed I do not believe he knew what fear was. Frequently on the stage he has been severely bitten and mauled, without exhibiting the slightest uneasiness, or even fear of the beast, which had converted its feigned ferocity into an actual attack. Altogether, his command over his animals was an astonishing exhibition, and proved forcibly how completely the majesty and dauntless daring of man can effect dominion.—*E. P. Thompson.*

RIDICULE.

Ridicule, which chiefly arises from pride, a selfish passion, is at best but a gross pleasure, too rough an entertainment for those who are highly polished and refined.—*Lord Kaimes.*

REWARDS OF VIRTUE.

When a man chooses the rewards of virtue, he should remember that to resign the pleasures of vice is part of his bargain.—*Wilberforce.*

Published by W. and R. CHAMBERS, High Street, Edinburgh (also 98, Miller Street, Glasgow); and with their permission, by W. S. ORR, Amen Corner, London.—Printed by BRADBURY and EVANS, Whitefriars, London.

☞ Complete sets of the Journal, *First Series*, in twelve volumes, and also odd numbers to complete sets, may be had from the publishers or their agents.—A stamped edition of the Journal is now issued, price 2½d., to go free by post.

CONDUCTED BY WILLIAM AND ROBERT CHAMBERS, EDITORS OF 'CHAMBERS'S INFORMATION FOR THE PEOPLE,' 'CHAMBERS'S EDUCATIONAL COURSE,' &c.

No. 92. New Series. SATURDAY, OCTOBER 4, 1845. Price 1½d.

SELF-ESTIMATES.

Humility is universally allowed to be a beautiful thing; but there is also a lurking, if not avowed notion amongst mankind, that, without some degree of what is called modest assurance, men speed but little in the world. There is a great deal of truth in this doctrine, unpleasant as it may be to make such an admission. We admire the modest man, and our good opinion is to a certain extent serviceable to him. But the man who entertains a stout, good opinion of himself, forces and cheats us out of much more that is favourable to his interests, even although we may have an unpleasant sense of his self-esteem and presumption. This is because of our being more ready to concede to what is actively, than to what is passively claimed from us. There is always an indifference amongst mankind to the interests of individuals: we do not naturally go about seeking to discover modest worth; we have not time; our own affairs will not allow of it; the social feeling does not carry us to such a length. But if a man of some degree of respectability makes his merits tolerably conspicuous; if he duns, and even pesters us for an admission of his worth, talent, or any other good quality, we are obliged to give attention, and, unless we be very greatly displeased with the breadth of the application, so as to be forced to break with him altogether, it is almost unavoidable that we make a greater concession in his favour than we do in the case of the unassuming possessor of much higher attributes.

Is this disputed by any one? Let him candidly investigate the matter in his own heart, and see if it is not one of the principles governing his ordinary actions. He will find that he is in the constant habit of treating his friends very much according to their estimates of themselves. Mrs Vapour, who, without any personal merit worth speaking of, is known to stickle much on the score of family dignity, and to look down on all kinds of new people—will he not be self-compelled to give her a high place at board, and to pay her more than her fair share of attentions there, in order to meet in some measure her own ideas of her importance? Will he not, at the same time, leave the charming, clever, but unpretending Mrs Simple to find that level to which her more modest self-estimate consigns her, notwithstanding that, in point of personal qualities, the former lady could never stand for a moment abreast of her, not to speak of above? Will he not, in like manner, put the magnificent Sir John Empty, who has published a pompous book of travels, which he is constantly referring to, far before the humble-looking Mr Downcast, who, in the midst of obscure and depressing circumstances, wrote one of the most delightful books of imagination that have appeared in our age, but is never heard to say a word about his literary productions, so that a stranger might pass a whole evening in his company, without surmising that he ever wrote a line? It is impossible entirely to resist the tendencies to such conduct. It is not that, in the depths of our hearts, we think little of Mrs Simple or Mr Downcast, and proportionately much of Mrs Vapour and Sir John Empty. Take us fairly to task on the bare question of merits, and we are found just as a balance. But we require to be roused into this justice. We are constantly apt to forget the true merits from their unobtrusiveness. We can take our friend, in that case, into our own hands, and treat him as may suit our convenience, because we know he will never resent it. But the claims of the self-esteeming are always kept before us. They come with an impressiveness derived from the strong convictions of the party. We are awed by them, and concede them. It is like the difference between a well-sized man who stoops and does not look straight forward, and one of short stature who walks with erectness and dignity. In such a case we always consider the short figure the best, and even the tallest.

It is easy to see how this rule should affect the worldly interests of both men and women. The unpretending might thrive best, or attain the highest places, if the pretending would leave the dispensers of patronage and the promoters of prosperity alone. But, unluckily, the pretending are constantly on the alert in pushing their interests wherever they think they can obtain any advantage. They worry the influential out of that which cool and undisturbed election would assign to the modest. Besides, it is not always easy to form a decided conviction of the deservings of a man who chooses to take rearward seats on all occasions, and never is heard to profess a power to do anything. Such a man may have proved his powers by acts; but it is difficult to connect the idea of such acts with a person who appears so indifferent to their results, and takes no trouble, in his common demeanour and conversation, to identify himself with them. They therefore do not tell in his favour nearly so much as would a bold, though really ill-grounded pretension. We may every day see families determining their social position, and the fortunes of their rising members, entirely by their self-estimates. I could point to many who, in very disadvantageous circumstances, have attained a good place in society almost entirely through their setting a high value upon themselves, and never encouraging intimacies except in advantageous quarters. It is equally common to see families which have the power of rising in the social scale, remaining in an inferior position, in consequence of their being modestly content with any friends who choose to make advances to them—these being sure, in such a case, to be of a kind not calculated to promote an advance in the social scale. The matrimonial locations of ladies are in a very great measure determined by the value they put upon themselves. We constantly see them, through modesty of this kind, accept men strikingly unworthy of them, but who have had the assurance to believe themselves entitled to such brides. So do literary men take their places in the temple of fame. For a respectable niche, it is not only necessary to possess some reasonable degree of ability and accomplishment, but also that sufficiency of self-esteem which will forbid the undertaking of inferior tasks, and prompt to the setting forward of proper claims to notice. Powers would almost appear to be of less consequence than the mode of their employment. There are even some qualities, good in themselves, which do not promote the ascent to the house which shines afar. For example, if an author be industrious, he will never be acknowledged to possess talent, for the world cannot entertain two ideas of a man at once:—thus, let two men start in a literary career, the one with talent as 1, but no industry, and the other with talent as 2, but great industry, and it will be found that mankind look upon the first man as a clever dog, who only wont work, and the second as a dull respectable fellow, who does wonders by application. Industry, in fact, expresses a humble self-estimate, and the self-estimate, in its direct and indirect working, almost wholly decides the place in the house of the babbling deity. Turning one's abilities to a useful purpose is, upon the whole, condemnatory. The artisan is useful, but nobody heeds him. The ass is useful, and gets thistles and thwacks for its pains. To be useful, expresses a lowly turn of mind, and it is therefore always more or less despised; for, though men generally profess to hold it in esteem, they only do so under a cold intellectual sense of what the useful leads to, and against the heart's sentiment of contempt for what it springs from. If a literary man, therefore, wishes for true fame, let him write some single brilliant thing, and rest under the shade of his laurels for ever after. If he once condescends to make himself useful, he sinks into the base crowd at once, and mankind despise him for that which they daily profit by and enjoy.

The only consolation for the modest is, that there is something more precious than either world's wealth or world's praise. Neither is the hope of reward the source of the highest endeavour, nor is reward of any kind the source of the highest satisfaction. It is quite possible to pass happily through life without a single merit duly acknowledged, or even the consciousness of any such possession.

THE BRIDAL WREATH.

FROM THE ITALIAN OF URSIGLIO.

'This wreath must be finished before the evening. Down with those tiresome hands; you jumble together all my leaves; you give me one colour instead of the other: you are spoiling all I have done. Be it known to you, however, that I am determined you shall not leave Padua until I have put the last leaf to our garland.'

These pettish words, qualified by the sweetest of smiles, were addressed by a beautiful girl of sixteen to a young man who was sitting beside her, and taking a mischievous pleasure in disturbing her work; now catching hold of her hands; now removing out of her reach something that she wanted; now playing with her long and luxuriant hair, which floated negligently on her shoulders: affectionate interruptions, which left a doubt whether the name of brother or lover better suited them. But the light which flashed from the eyes of the youth, and seemed to irradiate the countenance of the maiden, showed that his emotions were more rapid and ardent than those inspired by fraternal love. They were seated at a table strewed with shreds of cloth, gummed cotton, green taffeta, little palettes of colours, small pencils, and all the necessary apparatus of artificial flower-making.

'Well, then,' replied the youth 'I will do as you wish; but what haste with a wreath that is not to be used till Heaven knows when? Ah! if you were to wear it to-morrow, I would then assist you with hands, eyes, heart, mind—with my whole being.'

'What matters it? What harm will it do these flowers to wait for us? I promise you to keep this garland so carefully, that it shall look quite new on the day when it shall encircle my head; and then it will seem to all others but an ordinary wreath; but to us—to me—oh, what charms it will have! It will have been born, as it were, and have grown with our love; it will have remained to me in memory of you when you were obliged to leave me for a time; it will have spoken to me of you when absent; will have a thousand times sworn love to me for you. I shall have consulted, and kissed it a thousand times, till that day in which I shall be yours. Do you hear that word, Edoardo? Yours! yours for ever! never more to leave you!—to be divided from you only by death.'

'That will indeed be a blessed day, the loveliest day of our life. The desire of devoting all the powers of my mind to your happiness will then become a right. Poor Sophia, you know not yet what happiness is: so young, so good, you have hitherto met with thorns only in your path. Poor Sophia, I desire no other glory in this world than that of being able to make you feel the sweet that Providence in pity mingles with the bitter of human existence. There is no sweetness in the life of mortals that is not the offspring of love.'

'Yes,' added Sophia, 'when love is united with constancy. But what are you daubing at, Edoardo? You are actually putting red on orange leaves. Where have you learned botany? And what does that rose signify? Is not this a bride's wreath, and are not bridal wreaths always made of orange flowers? Do you know what I mean to do with those roses? Ah, you would never guess. I shall make of them a funeral crown. Here, take these leaves, and reach me the palette. You have positively learned nothing all the time you have been seeing me make flowers.'

A servant entered the room, saying, 'There is no post to Venice either to-day or to-morrow: the Signor Edoardo cannot set out before Friday.'

'Friday!' exclaimed Sophia; 'vile day!' and with a clouded countenance she silently resumed her self-imposed task. Edoardo, on the contrary, seemed glad of the delay.

'No matter; but,' he added, 'is not this a trick of yours?—a plot concocted by you and Luigia to prevent me from leaving Padua?'

'You mistake, Edoardo; I would wish rather to hasten your departure.'

'I am very much obliged to you,' replied Edoardo, half vexed. 'What do you mean? If you do not explain your words, I shall be very angry.'

'The explanation—the explanation, Edoardo, is here in my head, but not in my heart. The explanation, Edoardo, is, that I love you too much, and I am not pleased with myself. Yes, but there are sorrows, Edoardo, which sadly wear away our life; but these sorrows are a need, a duty, and to forget them is a crime. My poor sister, the only friend I have ever had, that poor saint, the victim of love, dead through the treachery of a man hardly two years since: on memory of her I have lived for eighteen months; but I even forget her when I see you, when I speak to you. Perhaps I do not bestow on my mother as much attention as her unhappy state requires. Alas! there is no reproach more bitter than this—"You are a bad daughter!" And this my conscience reproaches me with being a thousand times. Thus, Edoardo, I am wanting in my duties. I am a weak creature: a powerful, and too sweet sentiment threatens to take entire possession of me, to the detriment of the other sentiments that nature has implanted in our heart. Go, then, Edoardo; I have need of calm—I have need of not seeing you. Suffer me to fulfil my duties, that I may be more worthy of you. When you are far away,

I shall have full faith in you. But if your father should refuse his consent to our union?'

'Leave those sad thoughts. My father wishes only to please me, and it will be sufficient for me to ask his consent, to obtain it. Even should he refuse it, in two years the law will permit me to dispose of myself as I choose.'

'May Heaven remove this sad presentiment from my mind; but it makes me tremble. Oh! if you return with the desired consent of your father!—oh! if my mother, as the physicians gave me reason to hope, should then be well! we shall be the happiest of mortals.'

The sound of a silver bell, heard from a chamber close by, took away Sophia from her occupation. She rose hastily, saying, 'My mother! oh, my poor mother! Adieu for a while, Edoardo.'

Edoardo Valperghi was the son of a wealthy Venetian merchant. He had received a grave but unprofitable education, it being that which is wholly directed to the intellect and nothing to the heart. He was studying in one of those colleges in which the system of education is as old as the walls of the edifice. He had been told that he had a heart, but no one had spoken of how it was to be directed to good. He had been told that he must resist his own passions, but no one had shown him what arms to make use of in this moral warfare. He had been told to love virtue and to hate vice, but no one had furnished him with a criterion for distinguishing true virtue from its counterfeit. The temper of Edoardo was ardent and hasty, but flexible and weak. Nature had made him good, but society could make him very bad. He was like a ship without a good pilot—one to become good or bad according to circumstances. Enthusiastic, easily impressed by example, he would be most virtuous if his first steps had moved among the virtuous; if among the wicked, he would rush to perdition.

A letter of recommendation to the father of Sophia, who had formerly had some commercial dealings with the Valperghi, introduced him into the house. His timidity made him prefer that family to richer ones with which he was also acquainted, and amongst whom he could have found youths, amusements, and habits similar to those he had left behind in Venice. But Sophia, lovely, amiable, and frank, had shown him the affection of a sister. He had soon conceived a passion for her; declarations of love, promises, oaths, everything had thus been impetuous and sudden with him, as his disposition prompted. The inexperienced girl believed that a sentiment so strong, so ardent, must be equally profound and constant, and yielded to the enchantment of a first love. Edoardo had terminated the first year of his legal studies, and was now preparing to return to Venice.

Alberto Cadori, the father of Sophia, was also a merchant. He had begun business in a small sphere; but having guided his industry prudently, from being poor he had gradually become rich, and at length retired from commerce with a considerable fortune. Cadori was avaricious, harsh, exacting: he wished rather to be feared than loved: he was not the father, but the tyrant of his family. There was seemingly some secret cause of disagreement between him and his wife: it was perhaps for this reason that he did not love his children; but what it was no one could tell. His family was now limited to Sophia and his wife. He had had another daughter, fair and amiable as Sophia; but the sad school of the world, and the all-powerful empire of love, had untimely laid her low. The Signora Cadori, though still young, was already on the brink of the grave. The grief that preyed on her life, and especially the lamentable end of her first-born, had brought on paralysis. She could no longer move without assistance.

One other person formed part of the family, without being connected with it by relationship—a woman who seemed at first sight to have reached her seventieth year, so slow and difficult were her movements. Her words savoured a little of obscurity, and her countenance was rather repulsive. She was a Milanese. Having come to the baths in Padua, she had taken lodgings in Cadori's house. She seldom spoke, and paid no attention to what was passing around her. She always seemed unconscious of the loud and angry language of Cadori, which was proving fatal to the neglected wife and the oppressed daughter. She appeared to love no one; no one loved her. However, as she paid largely for her apartments, Cadori did everything to keep her in his house.

Though Sophia led a melancholy life, it was much relieved by the exercise of her accomplishments, which were numerous. No female in Padua, for instance, could compare with her in the art of flower-making. Her friends contended among them for the pleasure of adorning themselves with one of these flowers; courteous and kind to all, she distributed some to each. Even the mercers of the city, when they had need of flowers of superior beauty, applied to Sophia, who willingly acceded to their requests.

The two days of delay to Edoardo's departure were past, and in those two days the Signora Cadori had had a new and very violent attack, which placed her life in danger. Edoardo came to take leave of the family. When alone, the conversation, the adieus of the lovers, were not long; they both wept, looked at each other, and were silent. Yet how many things had they to say to each other, how many promises to renew, how many hopes and fears to exchange!

They parted; Edoardo pleased with himself, and Sophia dissatisfied with him and herself, without knowing why.

The heart is a true prophet: the fears of Sophia were about being realised; the days of her mother were drawing to a close. Sophia, sad and terrified, was never absent from her bedside. Her heart, her heart alone, sometimes wandered after the footsteps of another beloved, but less unhappy being. Forgive that thought of love to the maiden; call it not a sin. Sixteen!—a soul so tender!—the first love! The maternal eye saw into the inmost heart of the daughter, and felt no jealousy at those thoughts flying to her distant love. In those moments she silenced her own wants, lest she should disturb her in her reveries, and humbly prayed for the happiness of her child. Sophia, on recollecting herself, would testify the greatest sorrow, ask pardon of her dear invalid, and redouble her attention. Neither day nor night was she away from the pillow of her dying mother. Her strength supported her, as if by a miracle. No one divided with her this pious office, except the Countess Galeazzi, the mysterious guest of that house, and she came but seldom to the chamber of suffering.

But the last hour had struck for the Signora Cadori. With her dying breath she spoke of Edoardo. 'You love,' she said, 'and your love may be the source of good to you. Take this cross, which I have worn on my heart since the day of your birth; it was the gift of your father; take it, and wear it in memory of your poor mother. You will find in my chest a sum of money, and some bills on the imperial bank of Vienna. It is no great riches, but it is sufficient for the unforeseen wants that may press upon a woman. I would never consent to give up these sums to your father, and that was one source of our disagreement; but it was impossible for the heart of a mother to deprive herself of what she could one day share with her children. And I am glad that I have not done so; for, without such aid, your poor sister would have died of misery, as she did of grief and despair.'

She said more, and seemed to make other confidences to her daughter, but her words were uttered so feebly that they were lost. She then leant her head on the shoulder of Sophia, never to raise it more.

Four months after this event, the time of study returned, and Edoardo came again to Padua. He did not bring the consent of his father to their marriage, but only some distant hopes. Cadori, who was aware of Sophia's inclinations, forbade Edoardo to frequent his house, until the formal permission of his father could be procured. Thus was Sophia deprived of the pleasure of being often near her lover, of enjoying his society, his conversation. She could see him but seldom, and that unknown to her father.

But Edoardo was changed. He was no longer the frank, the loving Edoardo of former times. A residence of five months in Venice, without being subjected to restraint, or having means to elude it; the company of other young men, familiar with vice and dissipation; above all, a fatal inclination, had depraved and ruined him! He had suffered himself to be fascinated by the fierce delight which is found in gaming; play had become his occupation, his chief need. Play and its effects, the orgies that precede, the excesses that follow, were the life of Edoardo. Waste and debt were the consequences; and when he had, under a thousand pretences, extorted from his father all the money he could, he began, on arriving in Padua, to apply to Sophia, whom he neglected, at least did not see as often as he might, though he still loved her. Sophia was as indulgent as he was indiscreet. At every fatal request for money, she offered him double the sum he had asked. When Edoardo began to tell her some feigned story, to conceal the shameful source of his wants, and to give her an account of how he had employed those sums, she would not listen to him.

'Why,' said she, 'should I demand an account of your actions? Why should I think over and debate what you have already considered? Will not all you have be one day mine? Shall we not be one day man and wife?' And these words took away from Edoardo every sense of remorse: conscience ceased to reproach him for the baseness of despoiling that poor girl of the little she possessed. The thought that he was one day to make her his wife, justified him in his own eyes; for by this he thought he should have recompensed her for all her sacrifices.

Edoardo's demands increased with his exigencies. He was making rapid advances into the most terrible phases of the gamester's vice; and the mania in Sophia of giving, of sacrificing all her means for Edoardo, did not stop. All the money left her by her mother had already disappeared; most of her valuable ornaments had been sold; some of the bank bills had been parted with: but as this could not be done without her father's knowledge, he had made the laws interpose, and sequestrated the remainder. Sophia did not dare to speak or complain. She felt in her heart that her father was probably in the right, that her own conduct was at least unreflecting, and that Edoardo's expenses were too great; but still she found a thousand arguments to excuse both herself and him. She spent all the day making flowers, and stole a great part of the night from repose to devote it to this labour; but she, formerly so ready to make presents of her flowers, and adorn with them the young girls of her acquaintance, now exacted payment for them; so that every one wondered at this new and sudden avarice. But what did she care what was said of her? What did she care for appearing without those ornaments which women so love, and which add so much to their charms? What mattered it to her that she was ruining her own health by depriving herself of rest, toiling, and weeping? One look, one smile of Edoardo, the having satisfied one of his desires, compensated for all. What afflicted and troubled her was, that her labour should be so insufficient to meet his wants. Often did it occur to her mind that he gambled, that he was ruining himself, and she thought of reproving him for it, but had not courage to do so. Sometimes she accused herself of aiding him to destroy himself. Then she thought that she was mistaken; her doubts seemed to her as injuries to his love, and she grieved for having for a moment admitted them.

One treasure alone remained, the cross which her mother had given her on her deathbed. It was of brilliants, and might bring a large sum. She thought over this, and wept for a whole week. Many times she went out with the intention of selling it, but her heart could not resolve to do so, and she returned penitent and sorrowful.

Meanwhile, Edoardo was involving himself more and more in debt. Assailed by creditors on one side, and drawn to the gaming-table by desire and necessity on the other; menaced with a prison, threatened to be denounced to his father, stupid from want of rest, midnight revelling, and anxiety, he one day presented himself before Sophia in a state so different from usual, that the poor girl was terrified at him. Whither, Edoardo, has departed the beauty, the freshness of your youthful years?—whither your simplicity of heart? Buried, buried amid dice and cards. Sophia no longer doubted that Edoardo gambled, that he had given himself up to a life worthy of reprehension; but she was disposed to pardon him, to hope that he would repent and turn to better counsels. But what made her tremble was the hoarse and desperate accent in which he told her that he had need of money, that he was hard pressed by necessity, obliged to pay ten thousand *lire*. The glance that he directed to every corner of the apartment, perhaps because he did not dare to look her in the face, was dark and unsteady: some broken words, uttered in a low voice, pierced her heart like a dagger. And without any available means, she promised Edoardo to procure him the required sum by next day.

When he left the house, therefore, she threw herself at her father's feet, and begged him for a sum of money that belonged to her, but of which she could not dispose without his signature; but Cadori refused it. I shall not repeat their dialogue. I shall only say, that she came out from that conference in a state of distraction. Her mind was fraught with desolation. Hideous thoughts passed through her brain. It was night: she found she was alone. She felt desperate. A terrible temptation passed through her mind. Her father, she knew, had heaps of gold lying useless in his coffers; but locks and bolts placed their contents out of reach. She then bethought herself of the countess's bureau, in which her own cross had been deposited, secure from the old man's covetousness. There, too, the countess kept her treasures. She took a light, observed whether any one saw her, or could follow her, and repaired to the apartment of the Countess Galeazzi, who was from home, spending the evening with an old acquaintance. Hardly breathing, and walking on tiptoe, Sophia took a key from under a bell-glass, and opened the bureau. Oh, how she felt her heart throb! She was terrified; she trembled in every movement! The noise she made in opening the money drawer seemed to be the footsteps of some person following to lay hands on her. The light of the lamp, reflected in the mirrors and in the furniture, seemed to her so many eyes that looked on and reproached her. She opened the drawer, and took out her cross. Under it were several notes of the bank of Vienna. The temptation was strong; she laid her hands on the papers; but a thrill of terror seemed communicated through her frame by the touch, and, overcome by intense excitement, she fell senseless on the floor.

Some time afterwards the Countess Galeazzi returned home. On entering her apartment, she beheld the wretched girl stretched on the floor with the diamond cross in her hand. The bureau was still open. She ran to succour Sophia, and by the application of essences recalled her to life. The moment the latter awoke to consciousness, she threw herself on her knees, wept desperately, tried to speak, but could not; the only words she was at length able to articulate were—'Forgive me! forgive me!'

The countess used every means to pacify her, by the compassionate expression of her countenance, by her maternal gestures, caressing and pressing her to her bosom, with words of comfort and tenderness.

'Calm yourself, calm yourself,' she said; 'go and take some repose; you have need of it.'

'Countess,' replied Sophia, then wept anew. 'Shame,

shame and desperation! Oh, wretch that I am! Oh, my poor heart!'

'Go, go to bed, Sophia; to-morrow we will talk. Here is the light.' Saying this, she reached her the lamp with one hand and led her by the other, using a little affectionate violence to conduct her out of the room, and prevent her from speaking another word.

The next day, Sophia was so overwhelmed with grief and shame, that she took to her bed, struck down by a violent fever, which was the commencement of a dangerous illness. The countess was her nurse.

Edoardo, having lost the source whence he derived all his supplies, through the illness of Sophia, could no longer prevent his father from coming to the knowledge of his irregularities. He was immediately recalled to Venice, and shut up in a house of correction. Disgraced in the eyes of the companions of his debaucheries, and forced in his solitary confinement to make painful reflections on the consequences of his conduct, he seemed to be cured of his fatal passion, and when released, he returned no more to Padua; but, giving up the study of the law, he devoted himself to commerce, to which the contagious mania of making money, of becoming rich, made him steadily apply himself. His old inclination had changed its name; it was 'mercantile speculation;' but the substance remained the same. He had written to Sophia that his father would not consent to his marriage, unless it were with a lady of large fortune: unfortunately, she was not rich enough; however, that he would wed none but her, and that they must be resigned, and trust to time; and Sophia, living on the few letters that Edoardo continued to write her, and grieving that she was not as rich as Valperghi would have wished, waited and hoped. Her illness had been long and dangerous; her youth, and the care bestowed on her, had alone been able to save her life. She had long been oppressed by remorse: it was long ere she dared to lift her eyes to the countess, or address one word to her.

The latter had sought to evade every allusion to the past; and the poor girl, beginning to overcome her fears, ended at length in making her her friend, her confidante. She told her everything, and was fully forgiven everything.

After a time, Sophia recovered. They had lived together for four years, during which Sophia had opened her whole heart to that lady, made her the repository of all her everyday thoughts, her hopes; but the countess had always answered her with vague, uncertain words, or with silence. Alas! Sophia was fated to lose every object on which she had set her affection. After having closed the eyes of her mother and sister, adverse fortune obliged her to witness the death of the Countess Galeazzi.

When her affairs were looked into, it was found that she left her large fortune to Sophia Cadori; so that that which deprived her of so tender, so generous a friend, should also have made her happiness complete. Every obstacle that divided from her Edoardo, which separated her from him she loved so ardently, had vanished. In a few days a boundless love, a love of six years, a love she had cherished through so many sorrows, would be crowned! In a few days she would be Sophia Valperghi!

She wrote a letter full of the joys and hopes soon to be realised to her dear Edoardo; she was happy, as happy as she had desired, as happy as she had so long dreamt of being; she made all preparations for her marriage. Being now quite independent of him, she spoke of it to her father—to every one; she sought garments of the colour and taste that she knew Edoardo liked; she imagined and planned a thousand surprises. How many times did she put the cherished wreath on her head, consult her mirror, study every position in which those flowers might appear to better advantage and increase her beauty! How often did she open the box that contained it to kiss it, to look at it, scarcely daring to touch it for fear of spoiling a leaf, of disarranging a fibre!

At length came the answer to her letter; an answer that to any other person might have seemed constrained, cold, terrible; but it was, on the contrary, to Sophia the seal of her felicity. She was only afflicted that Edoardo should have made illness an apology, which he said prevented him from coming immediately to Padua. To Sophia it was as clear as the sun that expressions of affection did not abound, because they had now at command what she and Edoardo had so long hoped and looked for; that the letter did not dwell on particulars, precisely because great joy is not talkative, and because the illness of Edoardo prevented it. She made ready to set out to Venice without delay, expecting that her father would join her there, and that the nuptials would be celebrated in that city when the health of Edoardo would permit.

Arrived at Venice, she was set down at the house of the Valperghi, and ordered the trunk which contained the few robes she had brought with her to be brought into a room, into which she had been introduced while the servants went to announce her arrival to Edoardo.

After a few minutes, he entered the apartment, to discover who wanted to see him; and, on recognising Sophia, was disconcerted and abased. She was surprised at seeing him splendidly dressed, as if for some extraordinary occasion. Then he was *not* ill! She read confusion and terror in his countenance.

'My own Edoardo,' said she, after some moments of silence; 'are you quite recovered?'

'It was but a slight indisposition, as I have written to you,' replied he; 'nor was there any reason for your hasty presence in Venice.'

'Edoardo, Edoardo!—there was no reason!—I have written to you! Edoardo, why do you speak so to me? Why are you disturbed? Are you no longer my own Edoardo? Tell me, tell me what is the matter with you?'

'Nothing. But what do you think will be said of you? A young girl alone in the house of a family she does not know!'

'Oh, Edoardo, you kill me! Explain yourself more clearly. This a house I do not know? Am I not to be mistress in this house? Am I not to be your wife?'

'But without any previous announcement of your coming, it would not be well if my father were to find you here so unexpectedly. I think it would be better if you were to lodge, at least for a very short while, in an inn.'

'Your father! But am I not rich enough for him? This is a fearful mystery. Explain it, if you do not wish me to die.'

This conversation was interrupted by the entrance of a servant saying, 'Signor Edoardo, your bride requests you to pass into her apartment for a moment.'

Sophia had strength to command herself until the man was gone away. She then threw, or rather let herself fall into a chair, covering her face with her hands, crying, 'His bride! his bride! Is it true?—is it not a dream? For mercy's sake, if you have the heart of a man, tell me that it is false, that I have not heard rightly. For pity's sake answer me—answer me or kill me.'

'It is too true, Sophia; it was my father's will. In a little time I am to give my hand to another woman.'

'Oh, merciful Heaven! I have heard these words, and live. Oh, my poor life! But it cannot be: it is not true: you are not yet married: there is still time. Go—fly to the feet of your father, tell him you do not love that woman, that you love me, me only; that you have loved me for six years!'

'Impossible, Sophia; things have already gone too far. She is a princess—one of the first families of Florence. It breaks my heart, but it is impossible.'

'What matters her rank, her relatives, if you do not love her?'

'And if I did love her?' said Edoardo, wavering, rather to see whether it would be a means of ridding him of Sophia than expressing the sincere feeling of his heart.

'If you did love her? oh, then, you would be the most infamous of men—you would be a monster. But no; you cannot have forgotten your vows; you cannot have forgotten all your words, our life of six years.' Then rising, and throwing herself on her knees, 'Oh! forgive me, Edoardo; forgive my words. I rave; I know not what I say! Tell me that you have only wished to put my affection to the proof—that you love no other woman—none but me alone! Oh, do not drive me from this house, Edoardo; do not give yourself to another woman!'

'Sophia, if I could help it, do you think I would make you weep thus?'

'If you could help it? What prevents you? Nothing—nothing.'

'Honour, Sophia.'

'Honour! Where was your honour if you have forgotten all your sacred promises—if you have perjured yourself?'

'Sophia, Sophia, pity me. Do not make me the talk of all Venice. I am the most infamous of men; but I can do nothing for you. Now I will confess to you the whole truth—a truth I had not the heart to tell you before. That woman is already my wife; I have married her by civil contract; and the ceremony that is about to be performed presently is a mere formality. Sophia, forgive me if you can—forgive me, and depart.'

'Oh, no, no, I cannot go from this house. I will die here before your eyes.'

A sound of footsteps was heard. It was easy to guess that those light steps were a woman's. Edoardo turned towards a table, as if to look for some papers, saying to himself, 'I am lost.' And Sophia knelt down by the trunk that contained her clothes, pretending to rummage for something in it, while she wiped away her tears and suppressed her sighs.

Edoardo's bride entered. She stood for a moment perplexed, seeing a woman with him; then said, 'Edoardo, I sent for you that you might yourself choose one of these wreaths. Which of them do you think will become me best?' showing him at the same time two bridal wreaths which she held in her hand.

'Neither,' said Sophia, rising and presenting a third wreath to the bride. 'The Signor Edoardo ordered me to make this some time ago for his bride, and I trust I have not laboured in vain.'

'In truth it is much handsomer than either of these others,' said the bride; 'but you told me nothing of this, Edoardo?'

'It was a surprise,' added Sophia.

'My own Edoardo,' said the bride again; 'another kindness; a new expression of your love. Oh, how dear this wreath will be to me!' and she retired, taking it with her.

Sophia looked at the door through which the lady had disappeared, and bursting into tears, exclaimed, 'Oh my poor wreath!'

'Sophia, Sophia, you are an angel,' said Edoardo. 'Once more I owe you my life.'

'Since she is yours,' replied Sophia mournfully, and sitting down faint and exhausted on her trunk—'since she is yours, ought I to bring death to her mind, the death that I feel already in my poor heart? No one knows, no one can know what is suffering but those who suffer; oh, no woman ever endured what I endure at this moment! Go—go, Edoardo; prepare yourself for the ceremony: they are waiting for you. I have no more reproaches to make you—no more right to make them. All was in that wreath, and in renouncing that, I have renounced this. Go—I have need of not seeing you. I promise you that when you return I will be no longer here to trouble you with my presence.'

Edoardo, pale, confused, penitent, bent a long last gaze on Sophia; then left the room, saying, 'I am a villain—I am a villain.'

Two hours after, the marriage ceremony was performed. The gondolas that bore the bridal cortège, on their return from the church of St Moisè, were met by some fishing-boats that had drawn up a drowned female. The gondolas had to stop, in order to let them pass. 'A sad omen for the bride and bridegroom,' said an old woman of the company.

Edoardo, who had recognised that pale corpse, had thrown himself at the bottom of his gondola, in order to conceal his emotion, and with a convulsive motion pressed the hand of his bride, which he held between his own. The simple girl, interpreting that squeeze as an expression of love, said, 'Oh, my Edoardo, you will ever love me?'

'Ever, ever,' replied Edoardo, wiping away a tear. He then muttered to himself, 'Poor, poor Sophia!—she was an angel, and I am a villain.'

LUMINOSITY IN PLANTS AND ANIMALS.

There are few subjects more curious, and none, perhaps, less understood, than the occasional luminosity of certain plants and animals. We do not allude to that phosphorescence which arises from decomposing substances, and which every one must have observed on putrid fish, decaying fungi, and the like; but to those luminous appearances exhibited under peculiar conditions by living structures; as, for example, by the flowers of the marigold, and by the female fire-fly. The former phenomena are owing to an actual combustion of phosphoric matter in the atmosphere, precisely similar to that which takes place when we rub a stick of phosphorus on the walls of a dark chamber; the latter belong to peculiar states of growth and excitement, and seem at times to be ascribable to electricity, at others to phosphorescence, and not unfrequently to plain optical principles. It must be admitted, however, that not only are the causes but little understood, but that even the appearances themselves are questioned by many, who would resolve the majority of instances on record into mere visual delusions. It is, therefore, to little more than a recital of the better authenticated facts that we can as yet direct attention.

Flowers of an orange colour, as the marigold and nasturtium, occasionally present a luminous appearance on still, warm evenings; this light being either in the form of faint electric sparks, or steadier, like the phosphorescence of the glow-worm. The tube-rose has also been observed in sultry evenings, after thunder, when the air was highly charged with electric fluid, to emit small scintillations, in great abundance, from such of its flowers as were fading. It is not always the flowers which produce the light, as appears from the following record:—'In the garden of the Duke of Buckingham at Stowe, on the evening of Friday, September 4, 1835, during a storm of thunder and lightning, accompanied by heavy rain, the *leaves* of the flower called *Œnothera macrocarpa*, a bed of which was in the garden immediately opposite the windows of the Manuscript Library, were observed to be brilliantly illuminated by phosphoric light. During the intervals of the flashes of lightning, the night was exceedingly dark, and nothing else could be distinguished in the gloom except the bright light upon the leaves of these flowers. The luminous appearance continued uninterruptedly for a considerable length of time, but did not appear to resemble any electric affect.'

Several of the fungi which grow in warm and damp places manifest a similar luminosity, and that when in their most healthy and vigorous state. Delile found it in the agaric of the olive-grounds near Montpelier, and, what was curious, observed that it would not manifest itself in darkness during the day. The fungi of the coal-mines near Dresden have been long celebrated for their luminosity, and are said to emit a light similar to that of bright moonshine. The spawn of the truffle, the most esteemed of the fungus family, is also accounted luminous; and, from this circumstance, may be collected at night in the truffle-grounds. When in Brazil, Gardner discovered a highly shining fungal, which grows only on the leaves of the Pindoba palm. He was led to this discovery by observing one night a group of boys in the town of Natividade playing football with a luminous object, which happened to be the agaric in question. Some varieties of the lichens are occasionally phosphorescent, and are more or less luminous in the dark. The *subcorticalis*, *subterranea*, and *phosphorea*, often spread themselves luxuriantly in caverns and mines, where they create an extraordinary degree of splendour.

Another example, and perhaps the most wonderful of any, has been recently added to the list. The plant in question is an East India tree, the true family of which has not yet been ascertained, but which appears to be abundant enough in the jungle. A dead fragment was laid before a late meeting of the Asiatic Society in London, with an accompanying notice by General Cullen. The plant was stated to have been discovered by a native who had accompanied Captain Bean on a journey, and who, having been compelled by rain to take shelter at night under a mass of rock in the jungle, had been astonished at seeing a blaze of phosphoric light over all the grass in the vicinity. The plant, though said to be only now discovered, has been long known to the Brahmins, who celebrate its luminous properties in several of their mythological and poetical works. The fragment exhibited to the society was dead, and perfectly dry; but on being wrapped in a wet cloth, and allowed to remain for some time, its luminosity was revived, and it shone in the dark like a piece of phosphorus, or perhaps somewhat paler, more like dead fish or rotten wood. This unnamed plant abounds in the jungles near the foot of the hills in the Madura district, and was found by Dr Wallich in Burmah. Commenting on this novelty, Dr Lindley remarks—'It is not at all improbable that it, or something having similar qualities, may exist in our English collections; and it is for that reason that we now mention it. We therefore advise gardeners to be on the outlook for this curious phenomenon, and to examine all such rhizomes as they may have in their possession, in the hope of finding it; for assuredly they would hardly hit upon a thing of more interest. Plants habitually luminous, and constantly so at night, and retaining their properties years after they are dead, and capable of being cultivated, as this Madras plant most certainly is, would form quite a new feature in our gardens, and are well worth any degree of trouble that may attend their discovery.'

It must be observed, that the above instances of luminosity refer only to the living and healthy organism, and are independent of that phosphorescence which is often exhibited during the decomposition of vegetable matter. That this light may sometimes depend upon phosphoric excretion, is very likely, as it has been found that the parts emitting it are most luminous when immersed in pure oxygen, and cease to emit when excluded from that element. This is precisely what would take place with a stick of phosphorus; and it may be, that at certain seasons phosphoric substances are taken up from the soil by the growing vegetable, and excreted under those conditions of warmth, moisture, and atmospheric influence above alluded to. It is equally evident, if observers are not mistaken as to the scintillating nature of the light occasionally emitted, that there must be some other cause than phosphorescence, and to no agency can it with more likelihood be ascribed than to electricity. The earth and atmosphere are often in different electric states, and when so, the leaves and spikelets of vegetables would afford the most prominent points for the elimination of the passing fluid. Besides the luminosity arising from phosphorescent or electric matter, there is sometimes light occasioned by actual combustion of the volatile oils which are continually flying off from certain plants. Thus the atmosphere surrounding the *dictamnus* or *fraxinella*, a shrub inhabiting the Levant, will inflame upon the application of fire, and yet the plant not be consumed.

Turn we next to luminosity in animals—a phenomenon which has been observed and commented on from the earliest times of natural history. And here, again, we throw out of view those instances of phosphorescence which arise from decomposition, and which have been observed over the spots where animals are buried, or on their bodies even before death, as in cases of human consumption. As in the vegetable, so in the animal kingdom, luminosity is a rare and somewhat irregular phenomenon, appearing not in the higher and more perfect races, but chiefly in the obscure and least important. The most vivid, perhaps, of all luminous creatures is the lantern-fly of the tropics—the *Fulgora lanternaria* of Linnæus—which attains a length of three or four inches. It affords a light so great, that travellers walking by night are said to be enabled to pursue their journey with sufficient certainty if they tie one or two of them to a stick, and carry this before them in the manner of a torch. It is common in some parts of South America, and is described by Madame Merian in her work on the insects of Surinam. 'The Indians once brought me (says she), before I knew that they shone by night, a number of these lantern-flies, which I shut up in a large wooden box. In the night they made such a noise, that I awoke in a fright, and ordered a light to be brought, not being able to guess from whence the noise proceeded. As soon as I found that it came from the box, I opened it, but was still more alarmed, and let it fall to the ground in my fright, at seeing a flame of fire come out of it; and as many animals came out, so many different flames appeared. When I found this to be the case, I recovered from my alarm, and again collected the insects, much admiring their splendid appearance.' The light, she adds, of one of these insects is so bright, that a person may see to read a newspaper by it. The phosphorescence proceeds entirely from the hollow part, or lantern, of the head, no other part of the animal being luminous. It is but proper to add that, notwithstanding this positive statement of Madame Merian, certain naturalists not only question, but altogether deny the possession of luminosity by any of the *Fulgoridæ*; a denial which, in our opinion, rests at best upon a very slender foundation. The luminosity of the insect differs at different times, and under different circumstances; and it by no means proves its non-luminous properties, because it gave forth no light when examined by the naturalists in question.

Next in order comes the less luminous, but more familiar fire-fly or glow-worm—*Lampyris noctiluca*. In this genus the male insect has expansive wings and horny wing-covers, and makes his flight through the air; the female is wingless, and crawls on the ground; hence the English appellation glow-*worm*. The light of the former is comparatively feeble, that of the latter beautiful and brilliant. These insects are frequently met with in June and July in woods and meadows, and on banks beneath hedges. The utility of the light of the females is supposed to consist in attracting the attention of the males during the dark, when alone they are able to render themselves conspicuous—a circumstance to which Moore beautifully alludes:—

'For well I knew the lustre shed
From my rich wings, when proudliest spread,
Was in its nature lambent, pure
And innocent as is the light
The glow-worm hangs out to allure
Her mate to her green bower at night.'

This theory, though probably not correct, is not altogether fanciful, as was proved by Olivier and Robert who frequently caught males by holding the females in their hand. Besides, without some such apparatus, it is difficult to conceive how a crawling insect could attract the attention of its mate, whose principal medium of motion is the atmosphere. Be this as it may, the light undoubtedly serves some important purpose in the economy of the glow-worm, and manifests itself even when the insect is in its larvous state. Dieckhoff suggests, in addition to the nuptial theory, that it may serve the insect as a protection against animals of prey. The part which emits the luminosity is the lower region of the abdomen, and near the tip, the light varying in intensity according as the animal moves or is disturbed.

Mr Templer, whose observations on these insects are recorded in the Philosophical Transactions, says that he never saw a glow-worm exhibit its light at all without some sensible motion either in its body or legs. He also fancied the light emitted a sensible heat when it was most brilliant. Latreille found the insects most luminous when immersed in oxygen, and that they sometimes detonated when placed in hydrogen. If the luminous portion of the abdomen be removed, it retains its luminous property for some time; and, when apparently extinct, it may be reproduced by softening the matter with water—a circumstance which the reader cannot fail to associate with what took place when the root of the recently-discovered Indian plant was wrapped in a piece of moistened rag. Robert, in his experiments, could only reproduce it within thirty-six hours after the death of the animal, and that only once, and by the direct application of heat. Darwin, who examined the *Lampyridæ* of South America, found also that the light was most brilliant when the insects were irritated. 'The shining matter,' he says, 'was fluid, and very adhesive: little spots, where the skin had been torn, continued bright, with a slight scintillation, whilst the uninjured parts were obscured. When the insect was decapitated, the rings remained uninterruptedly bright, but not so brilliant as before: local irritation with a needle always increased the vividness of the light. From these facts, it would appear probable that the animal has only the power of concealing or extinguishing the light for short intervals, and that at other times the light is involuntary. The larvæ possessed but feeble luminous powers: very differently from their parents, on the slightest touch they feigned death, and ceased to shine, nor did irritation excite any fresh display.' The brilliancy of the light is increased by plunging the insect in warm water; but cold water extinguishes it. If the insect is crushed, and the face or hands rubbed with it, they contract a luminous appearance, similar to that produced from phosphorus. Such is all that is known of the nature and uses of the glow-worm's luminosity. We are not aware that any chemist has subjected the matter to analysis; and it were almost a pity that sober fact should destroy the charm with which poetical fancy has arrayed the subject.

Passing over several land insects—such as certain beetles, scolopendræ, &c.—which exhibit less or more of luminosity, some of the marine animals presenting similar phenomena may next be adverted to. One of the most common is the night-shining nereis—*Nereis noctiluca*. The body of this little creature is a mere oblong speck, so minute as to elude examination by the naked eye. It inhabits every sea, and is one of the causes of the shining of the water in the night, which is sometimes so great as to make that element appear as if on fire. Myriads of these creatures are found on all kinds of sea-weeds; but they often leave them and swim on the surface of the water. They are common at all seasons, but particularly in summer before stormy weather, when they are more agitated and more luminous than at other times. Their numbers and wonderful agility, added to their luminous property, must contribute not a little to that phosphorescence so often observed on the ocean; for myriads are contained in a single glass of water. The iridescence or lustre of various fishes may be also caused by these animalcules attaching themselves to their scales. 'I have observed with great attention,' says Barbut in his *Genera Vermium*, 'a fish just caught out of the sea, whose body was almost covered with them, and have examined them in the dark: they twist and curl themselves with amazing agility, but soon retire out of our contracted sight, probably on account of their glittering numbers dazzling the eye, and their extreme minuteness eluding our researches. It is to be observed that, when the unctuous moisture which covers the scales of fishes is exhausted by the air, these animals are not to be seen; nor are the fishes then noctilucous, that matter being perhaps their nourishment when living, as they themselves afford food to many marine animals. They do not shine in the day-time, because the solar rays are too powerful for their light, however aggregate, or however immense their number.' If water containing these animalcules be kept warm, they will retain their luminosity for some days after they are dead, but in cold water they lose it in a few hours. Motion and warmth, which increase their vivacity and strength, increase also their light.

Besides the nereidæ, there are many other sea-animalcules, as the minute crustacea, the medusæ, infusoria, and certain corallines, possessing luminous properties, and which, when congregated in shoals, give to the agitated waters that phosphorescent brilliancy observed by almost every navigator. It is difficult, however, in many of these instances, to say whether the luminosity is the result of decay, or of a vital and peculiar principle; and therefore we shall not found any conclusion upon them. It may be remarked, however, that, when the waves scintillate with bright green sparks, the light is owing to the presence of minute living creatures; and that, when the phosphorescence is steadier, and of a paler hue, the proximate cause is the decay of gelatinous particles with which the ocean abounds. Ehrenberg no doubt ascribes a certain degree of irritability to these particles; but in this he is not borne out by other observers. The phenomenon happens most frequently in warm countries, and most brilliantly immediately after a few days of still weather. Now, though such would certainly be most favourable to the rapid increase of minute animals, it would at the same time be equally active in hastening the process of decay; so that, in the majority of instances, the phosphorescence of the ocean may be safely attributed to the decomposition of organic particles.

From all the experiments which have been made, it would seem that animal luminosity is a true phosphorescence, increased by warmth, and made most obvious when the animal is disturbed or put in motion. In plants, it was surmised, upon pretty good grounds, that electricity was sometimes the illuminating agency; but in animals we have no such reason. In all the experiments of Dr Williamson upon the electric eel, he never obtained so much as the trace of a spark; and if the fluid is not perceptible when thus concentrated, as in the gymnotus, we are not to expect it when manifesting itself in the common operations of vitality, even if certain that it was concerned in producing that phenomenon. Altogether, then, the luminosity in living plants and animals may, in the present state of our knowledge, be thus resolved:—The light occasionally yielded by plants seems to be in most cases the result of phosphoric emissions; in some it appears to arise from the presence of electricity. In the former case, the phosphorus must be taken up from the soil, which is known to contain many phosphates; in the latter, the plants seem to act as the mere conductors of electricity from one medium to another. On the other hand, luminosity in animals seems in all cases to be owing to the presence of phosphoric matter; nor is there any difficulty in accounting for its presence. In the dead organism of plants and animals, phosphorescence is no rare phenomenon; nor are we to seek for any supernatural cause or presentiment when it manifests itself on the countenances of those whose frames are melting away under consumption, or otherwise labouring under peculiar diseases. Its appearance in plants prepares us for its occurrence in the humbler animals, and its presence there ought to do away with any surprise at its occasional manifestation in the higher forms of animation.

NAMES OF PLACES IN THE UNITED STATES.

There is perhaps nothing in which the Americans have displayed so little of their usual ingenuity and originality, as in the choice of names for the various places in their territories. The names of the principal towns and counties in Britain—particularly those of England—have been repeatedly applied to counties and towns on the other side of the Atlantic. The names of the most famous cities of ancient and modern times in the old world have been selected for the districts and cities of the new; and the Americans have practised with great zeal that species of hero-worship that assigns to places the names of distinguished men. It may not be uninteresting to give, on the authority of a gazetteer recently published by Messrs Sherman and Smith of New York, some account of the extent to which this method of nomenclature has been adopted in the United States.

Commencing with the great names of antiquity, we find that there are eighteen counties, townships, towns, villages, and other minor places bearing the name of Athens. Of this number there are two which appear to be well worthy of the name. One is situated in the state of Ohio, on a peninsula formed by a bend in the river Hockhocking: its whole appearance is stated to be picturesque and imposing. It contains only 710 inhabitants, but is the seat of the Ohio university, which has a president, five professors, and 165 students, with 2500 volumes in its libraries. The college edifice is built on an eminence in the south part of the town, with a beautiful green of several acres in front. The other Athens is in the county of Georgia, with 3000 inhabitants. It also contains a university, with a president and six professors. The state of New York contains a township named Sparta, with a population of nearly 6000; while other twelve Spartas are found in other states. In 1777, a township named Corinth was settled in the state of Vermont; it now contains 1970 inhabitants. The name of a village on the Hudson river has lately been changed from 'Jesup's Landing' to Corinth; and the state of Georgia contains another Corinth, which has about thirty houses. The representative of Babylon is a village in New York state, with a population of 250; and on the river Susquehanna is found a Nineveh, with a population of 125. Rome has in modern, as she did in ancient times, taken the lead of Carthage; for we find that the places bearing the former name are fourteen in number, while of the latter there are only twelve. It happens also curiously enough that the capital of Athens county, in Ohio, is named Athens, while two of its towns are termed Rome and Carthage. There are, in various states, four Delphis, which no doubt will contain many village oracles; and though Leonidas fell at Thermopylæ, yet there is a Leonidas in the state of Michigan, whose population outnumbers the glorious 300 by 110. The ancients had one Arcadia, the Americans have three; and of four Atticas, one is described as a village in the township of Venice, Seneca county, state of Ohio. Ithaca is the name of a township with a population of 5650, in New York state; and of a village in Ohio. The ruins of the great Memphis have long been buried in silent obscurity under the mud of the Nile, but another Memphis now rears its head on an elevated bluff of the Mississippi river, contains 3300 inhabitants, and possesses, what the ancient Memphis in all its glory never had, three printing-offices and three weekly newspapers. The Asiatic Troy, though it caused noise enough in the eastern world 3000 years ago, is scarcely heard of now, except in the pages of Homer and Virgil, but a new Troy has arisen on the banks of the Hudson, which already contains 20,000 inhabitants. The other American Troys are twenty in number. Nor are the names of ancient poets, philosophers, and warriors, found in less profusion. Seven places in ancient times claimed the honour of having given birth to Homer, but six places in the United States have taken his name. There are a Horace and a Virgil in the state of New York; and the name of Ovid, besides being applied to a township in the same state, is also found in Michigan, Ohio, and Indiana. The proportion which Senecas bear to Morals is as ten to one; and there is one Plato, with one Republic, and three Republicans. The application of the name of Brutus to two townships, while that of Cæsar is only given to one, is a literal commentary upon the speech which Shakspeare makes Cassius speak to Brutus. The great Hannibal of antiquity crossed the European Alps 2000 years ago, but his name has now crossed the Alleghany Mountains of the new world, and is found on the banks of the Mississippi. The name of his great rival, Scipio, is found north in Michigan, west in Indiana, and east in New York. The states of Maine, Ohio, and New York, contain each a Solon; and on the banks of Lake Erie there is a Euclid. New York likewise possesses a Cato and a Cicero; while the former is again found in Illinois, and the latter in Indiana. The greatest deities of Greece and Rome have likewise their representatives; for we find Jupiter far west in Arkansas, Mars in Indiana and Alabama, Ceres and Apollo in Pennsylvania, and Flora in Illinois. Diana, the mighty huntress, has given her name to a township in New York; and the great Minerva is found in Ohio and Kentucky, as well as on the banks of the Hudson.

The names of places mentioned in Scripture have also been extensively made use of. There is a Jerusalem in the state of New York, where it is reported that Jemima Wilkinson, the founder of the strange religious sect called Shakers, resided, and died in 1819. Virginia contains another Jerusalem; and seven states possess each a Bethlehem. The name of Goshen is used nineteen, and that of Lebanon twenty-one times. Of Canaans there are thirteen, and of Palestines eleven. There are seven places named Mount Carmel, and seven named Mount Sion. There is a Mount Pisgah in North Carolina, and a Mount Sinai in New York. There are also twelve Edens, four Jerichos, eight Hebrons, and one Emaus. Names have also been brought from the far east of the old world, and given to places in the far west of the new. There is a Pekin in Illinois, with a weekly newspaper and 900 inhabitants; and the other Pekins are four in number. Michigan contains a China, a Nankin, and a Canton; Ohio a Canton and a Nankin; New York and Maine both a China and a Canton; and other eleven Cantons are found in the other states. There are a Bombay and a Delhi in New York, and a Calcutta and a Delhi in Ohio. There is a Persia in Missouri, and another in New York. At the junction of the Ohio and Mississippi rivers there is a Cairo; and the state of Michigan contains the township of Bengal. In Maine there is a township named Levant; and two rocky ridges frowning on each other from opposite sides of the Arkansas river are called the Dardanelles.

The names of the capital cities of Europe are found in great profusion. There are two Londons, and ten New Londons. One of the latter is situated on the river Thames in Connecticut, and contains a population of 5519. There are nine Edinburghs, the largest of which is in the state of New York, and contains a population of 1485. There is one Edina, which, appropriately enough, is the capital of a county named Scotland. Of Dublins there are ten, besides an Upper and a Lower Dublin. There are nine Lisbons, two Madrids, and five Bernes; and though there are two Switzerlands, yet there is neither a Spain nor a Portugal. The capital of Bourbon county, in Kentucky, is named Paris; and though the name of the capital of France is applied to other twelve places, France itself is nowhere to be found.

Orleans, Lyons, Brest, Versailles, Bordeaux, Alsace, and other French names, have, however, been extensively used. Of Copenhagens there are three, one of which is situated in Denmark county. There are five Amsterdams, four Hollands, a Dutchman's-Point, a Dutch-Settlement, and a Dutchville. There is only one Christiana, but there are two Norways; while there are three Swedens, and two Stockholms. Though the name of Berlin is such a favourite that it is used twenty times, yet there is not a single Prussia. The largest of the twelve Viennas is situated in Oneida county, New York, and contains 2530 inhabitants. There are ten Warsaws, one of which is the capital of a county named Kosciusko; and of four Polands, one is situated in the township of Russia, New York. The names of Geneva, Genoa, Venice, Milan, Turin, Verona, Mantua, Naples, and Palermo, are found in various states. There is neither a Constantinople nor a Stamboul; but the Petersburgs are eleven, and the Moscows nine in number.

The ancient names borne by the divisions of the United Kingdom, have sprung from their long sleep into new life in the United States. Perhaps some French journalist may carry his hatred to the Albion, which he styles 'la perfide,' so far as to quarrel with the Americans for giving its name to *Orleans* county, in the state of New York, and for using it seven times besides. Of Caledonias there are ten, of Cambrias five, and of Hibernias two. Many names have likewise been derived from Scotch and Irish towns. There is a Glasgow situated on the river Missouri; another, for some unstated reason, is made the capital of Barren county, in the state of Kentucky; while a third is found in Ohio, and a fourth in Delaware. On the Ohio river there is an Aberdeen, which contains sixty dwelling-houses, six stores, and various mechanics' shops; while a village of the same name is found still further west in the state of Mississippi. New York state contains a township named Perth, of which it is recorded that the surface is rolling, the soil clay loam, and the population 737. Dundee is represented by a township in Michigan, near the Raisin river, and contains a population of 773, and a capital of 8000 dollars, invested in manufactures. On a branch of the Potomac river, in the state of Virginia, is situated the village of Dumfries. In Maine there is a Kilmarnock, with a population of 319; and in Virginia another, containing 140 inhabitants. New York state has one Elgin, and Illinois another. Dunbar is the name of a township in Pennsylvania, containing a population of 2070, and with a capital of 90,208 dollars, invested in manufactures. 'A fine farming town' in New Hampshire, with 950 inhabitants, is named Dumbarton. The village of Montrose, in Iowa, is described as 'situated on elevated ground, on a beautiful prairie, and commanding a view of the Mississippi river, and of the surrounding country for twenty miles.' It is opposite to the notorious city of Nauvoo, the head-quarters of the Mormons. Another Montrose, with three printing-offices, one weekly newspaper, and 632 inhabitants, is the capital of Susquehanna county, in the state of Pennsylvania. There are three counties named Lauderdale among the southern states, the aggregate population of which is 23,278, of whom 7332 are slaves. In the county of Wayne, New York, there is a river Clyde; there is no Greenock at *its* mouth, but there is a Greenock on the west bank of the Mississippi, in the state of Arkansas. Beautifully situated at the head of Belfast Bay, on the west side of Penobscot river, in the state of Maine, is the town of Belfast, with a printing-office, a weekly newspaper, and a population of 4186. There are two Belfasts in Pennsylvania, and one in each of the states of New York, Ohio, and Tennessee. The Antrims are six in number, and the Waterfords thirteen. There is a Galway in New York: of Coleraine there are eight; and there is a Cork in Ohio. In the state of Pennsylvania alone there are three Donegals, and the same state contains a couple of Armaghs.

The above names are selected almost at random, and the summary could be considerably increased. Nomenclature derived from places in England, however, is by far the most common; and indeed it may be said that there is scarcely a county or a town of any consequence between the Tweed and the English channel, that has not stood godfather a dozen times for some infant location on the other side of the Atlantic. These and other specimens, however, we must reserve for another occasion.

HERIOT AND HIS HOSPITAL.

Among the more conspicuous public edifices which decorate Edinburgh, is one in the southern district of the city, known as Heriot's hospital, an institution, in object and munificence of management, not unlike that of the far-famed Christ's hospital in London. For the establishment and endowment of this foundation, Edinburgh was indebted to the benevolence of George Heriot, who, as goldsmith and jeweller, and, we may add, humble acquaintance and money-lender to James VI., has been immortalised in the pages of the 'Fortunes of Nigel.' The publication for the first time of a veracious and minute memoir of 'Gingling Geordie,' as Scott has been pleased to call him,* affords us an opportunity of saying something of Heriot and his institution.

Of George Heriot's early history, it is acknowledged that little is known. It is only ascertained that he was the son of a goldsmith in Edinburgh, was born in the year 1563, and in due time brought up to his father's profession, then one of the most lucrative trades in the country. While a young man, he entered into business on his own account, and almost at the same time formed a respectable matrimonial connexion. His wife was an heiress in a small way, and brought her husband, what was then esteemed a little fortune, property yielding L.6, 2s. 7d. annually. With some cash contributed by Heriot's father, as 'ane beginning and pak,' the newly-married pair commenced the business of life. Their capital, amounting exactly to L.214, 11s. 8d. in reality commanded as much consideration in the Scottish metropolis in the early part of the reign of James VI., as would some thousands of pounds in the present day.

It was in the year 1586 that young Heriot thus adventured in the career in which he afterwards attained not a little celebrity and wealth. His first shop was by no means of an aspiring character, but consisted of a booth or krame, adjoining St Giles's cathedral, forming one of a row of such places of business which till recent times hung parasitically about that building. In this humble erection, and afterwards in one at the west end of the cathedral, Heriot acquired an extensive connexion in trade as a goldsmith, to which, there being as yet no banks, he added the profession of money-lender. He soon recommended himself to the notice of his sovereign, by whom, on the 17th July 1597, he was declared goldsmith to Anne of Denmark, the gay consort of James VI. Ten days afterwards, Heriot's appointment was publicly proclaimed at the cross of Edinburgh by sound of trumpet. This, it must be confessed, was a most fortunate appointment, for never, truly, did tradesman get a better customer. Anne was addicted to extravagances little in harmony with the slenderness of the royal resources. She was fond of purchasing costly jewellery for presentation to favourites, as well as for her own personal decoration; and when desirous of procuring articles of this kind, or an advance of money, it was no unusual thing for her to pledge with Heriot the most precious of her jewels. Thus divested of some of her most valuable ornaments, she was sometimes in great straits to make a decent appearance at court, and poor James, her husband, appears to have been driven to his wits' end to procure the cash necessary to redeem the

* Memoir of George Heriot, &c. By W. Steven, D.D. Edinburgh: 1845.

impledged articles. A less rigid tradesman would have permitted himself to be coaxed out of the deposit by a few fair words; but Heriot was too firm and cautious to surrender his charge on such terms, and yet possessed the rare merit of pleasing his royal customers by his independence. The *suaviter in modo* appears to have been never more happily blended with the *fortiter in re*, than in the case of George Heriot. On the 4th April 1601, Heriot was appointed jeweller to the king, by which he gained a considerable accession to his business. So entirely did the royal household seem to require the services of Heriot, in his double capacity of goldsmith and cashier, that an apartment in the palace of Holyrood was actually prepared, in which he might regularly transact affairs. 'It has been computed,' observes our authority, 'that during the ten years which immediately preceded the accession of King James to the throne of Great Britain, Heriot's bills for the queen's jewels alone could not amount to less than L.50,000 sterling,' a sum which will appear incredible in amount to those who are not acquainted with the silly rage for personal decoration which prevailed in these half-barbarous times. Imitating the extravagance of the court, the principal nobility and gentry in Scotland vied with one another in their adornment with jewellery, and, like royalty, found their way, in times of emergency, as suitors for pecuniary accommodation to the young goldsmith. In ransacking the charters and papers now treasured up in Heriot's hospital, Dr Steven has alighted on a number of documents illustrative of the difficulties to which both king and queen, from want of prudent foresight, were put occasionally for a little ready cash. The queen having on one occasion found it necessary to pay a hurried visit to Stirling to see her son, Prince Henry, despatched the following note to Heriot, requesting a supply of money.

'GORDO HERIOTT, I ernestlie dissyr youe present to send me twa hundrethe pundis vith all expidition, becaus I man hest me away presentlie.—ANNA R.'

To think of a queen sending to one of her tradesmen for a loan of L.17, 13s. 4d. sterling, the sum expressed by 'twa hundrethe pundis' in the old Scots money!

On the accession of James to the English throne, and his removal to London, Heriot participated in the change, being too intimately connected with his sovereign's arrangements to be allowed a long absence from his wonted post. Accordingly, we soon find our goldsmith and money-lender in London, his place of business being somewhere in Cornhill, opposite the Exchange. Here he was concerned in numerous and large transactions on behalf of the royal family: and, on one occasion, so great was his press of business, that government issued a proclamation requiring all mayors and justices of peace to aid and assist him in procuring workmen at the current rate of wages. While thus prosperous in his affairs, he was bereaved of his wife. Five years afterwards, he entered into a matrimonial alliance with Alison Primrose, eldest daughter of James Primrose, first Earl of Rosebury. Mr Primrose filled the office of clerk to the Scots privy council; and being burdened with a family of nineteen children, it may be supposed that the marriage of one of his daughters to a wealthy London jeweller must have been considered a particularly advantageous arrangement. The connexion, however, was of no long duration. Alison Primrose was cut off in the flower of her days, and Heriot was again a childless widower. The event appears, from private papers, to have been a source of sincere grief. Two months afterwards, we find him tracing, on a slip of paper, the short but significant sentence—'She cannot be too mutch lamented who culd not be too mutch loved;' a declaration doubtless sincere, as it does not seem to have been intended for the public eye. Heriot ever afterwards remained a widower, devoting himself to the prosecution of his now greatly extended business, and devising plans for the investment of his large property at his decease. Having no relations for whom he entertained any affection, his mind became occupied with the idea of establishing an institution at Edinburgh, to resemble in character Christ's hospital in London; and accordingly such was finally resolved upon, his designs being assisted by his cousin, Adam Lawtie, a lawyer in the Scottish capital, who long acted as his confidant in the purchasing of property and disposal of his means. With his house thus set in order, the venerable Heriot died in London, at the age of sixty years, on the 12th of February 1624. The whole of his large property, after payment of various legacies, was ordered by his will to go to the civic authorities and ministers of Edinburgh, for erecting and maintaining an hospital in that city 'for the educatione, nursing, and upbringing of youth, being puir orphans and fatherless childrene of decayet burgesses and freemen of the said burgh, destitut and left without meanes.' It would be needless to detail the steps taken to carry the pious design of the founder into execution; suffice it to say, that in due time a large and handsome structure was erected as the desired hospital, which remains, as we have said, till the present time, as one of the most conspicuous public edifices in Edinburgh. The funds realised for the use of the institution seem to have been under L.24,000; the hospital was opened on the 11th April 1659, by the admission of thirty boys.

For now nearly two hundred years, Heriot's hospital has continued to flourish and enjoy a deserved local fame. With an annual revenue, we believe, of nearly L.15,000, it affords maintenance, clothing, and education, also some pecuniary presents, to a hundred and eighty boys, such being all that the house, large as it is, is able conveniently to accommodate. Instead of increasing the establishment in correspondence with the extent of the funds, it was suggested a few years ago by Mr Duncan M'Laren, one of the governors, to devote an annual overplus of about L.3000 to the erection and maintenance of free schools throughout the city, for the education of poor children, those of poor burgesses being preferred; and this judicious proposal being forthwith adopted, and sanctioned by an act of parliament, there have since been erected, and are now in operation, five juvenile and two infant schools, unitedly giving an elementary education to 2131 children; and when other two schools, now in progress, are finished, the advantages of this well-designed arrangement will be materially extended.

In these seminaries, apart from the head establishment, the children, as in ordinary schools, are received and dismissed daily at stated hours; and it is not uninteresting to observe, that the sense of the community has begun to set in in favour of a similar arrangement with the hospital itself. The arguments pursued by the objectors to a strictly hospital education carry with them some degree of weight, and may in brief be stated as follows:—'Family relationship is a primary ordination of Nature. It is a fundamental design in Providence that children should be reared under the control and direction of parents. The school in which character and habits are to be correctly formed, is *the fireside circle*. The school of schoolmasters can do little more than impart technical knowledge, and enforce discipline. The parents, therefore, who neglect their proper duty, and shuffle on the back of the schoolmaster or hired assistant, in a public hospital, the burden which they are in reason bound to carry, commit a grievous error; which, like all errors, carries with it its own punishment. There are, unquestionably, as in orphanage, cases in which the parental relation is deranged or destroyed; but a public asylum, conducted on the principle of a monastery, is far from being the proper means for its restoration. In cases of this lamentable nature, society is bound to supply an artificial relationship—to hand over the orphans to persons who, for a reasonable hire, will act the part of parents. Improved as hospitals are in some of their arrangements, it is matter of observation that children reared in them, however well their bodily wants may be attended to, or however much they are crammed with technical instruction, are lamentably behind in a thousand particulars in which children reared at home are proficient; while the cultivation of their affections, an important element in education, is altogether neglected.' Startling from their novelty, yet not without truth, such are the sentiments now beginning to be entertained respecting hospital nurture in Edinburgh, where it is in the course of being carried, by the erection of new hospitals, to what may become a dangerous excess. As the subject is one of great importance to society, we shall endeavour to treat it with all the deliberation it merits on a more suitable occasion.

LONDON IN 1765, BY A FRENCHMAN.

SECOND ARTICLE.

We continue, in the present article, the extracts from the author already noticed under the above title in a recent number of the Journal. As we advance, we find still the same favourable opinion of London and its inhabitants generally; but the writer, when he enters more fully into the discussion of metropolitan habits and customs, is often betrayed into error, connecting effects with causes to which they bear no adequate relation. We are led to infer, from the perusal of his remarks, that although his nation may have excelled ours in the courtesies and amenities of social life, yet in all that is of sterling value, all that constitutes character, he conceded the superiority, with some few exceptions, to England:—

'In no particular does London less resemble Paris than in its police arrangements. The English themselves say that London is full of thieves, as bold as they are cunning. And yet, although always in the streets, in the crowd, and amid the mobs which I sometimes encountered, and without paying the least attention to my pockets, I never had cause to complain of their subtlety, which I solicited even by the absence of precaution. I was walking one afternoon in the avenue of Chelsea hospital, and having sat down on one of the benches, fell asleep with a book in my hand. When I awoke, I found myself surrounded by old soldiers, one of whom, speaking French, said that I had run great risk by sleeping in that manner. "I knew," was my answer, "that I was among soldiers and honest people, and what was there to fear in such company?" and gave him a shilling for his caution.

'If the inhabitants of London believe themselves to be surrounded by thieves, at all events they do not so act with regard to the pots of beautiful Cornwall pewter, in which the dealers in beer distribute their beverage through every district at all hours in the day. For when the pots are empty, in order that the pot-boys may have but little trouble in collecting them, they are placed in the open passages of the houses, and sometimes on the door-step in the street. I saw them thus exposed in all my walks, and felt quite assured against all the cunning of thieves.

'The police leave theatrical exhibitions to take care of themselves, considering it a duty to respect the pleasures and temporary gaieties of a nation which has only these in which to relieve itself of its melancholy and seriousness of character. Thus absolutely without supervision, the theatres of London are more free than were those of Paris before M. D'Argenson gave them up to the French guards; a liberty the more astonishing, as footmen and lackeys are admitted without payment to a large gallery that surrounds and overlooks the pit. All the newspapers of Europe sometimes resound with the brawls, riots, and combats, the consequence of this liberty. The last riot which they noticed had for its object a troop of French dancers exhibiting at Covent Garden, and against which the pretended patriotism had got up a cabal. The struggle was a sharp one, as the rioters returned to the charge, during several successive days, with blows of fists and cudgels; and the victory having at last declared for the patriotic party, the French abandoned the field of battle to the victors. During this struggle, the police and other public functionaries maintained a strict neutrality.

'Such are, at London, the effects of the absence of the police from the theatres; but it constitutes a part of the national liberties, and it is easy to imagine what a free course it leaves to insult, which reaches at times to the highest authority. When the new tax on beer was imposed, the reigning sovereign was made to feel what the sourness of discontent can suggest to a haughty people. His majesty was compelled to relinquish his visits to the theatre, in consequence of an atrocious witticism boldly and distinctly addressed to him.

'The affair of Wilkes with his 45th number of the North Briton, has taught all Europe to what point the liberty of the press is carried in London. The powers of Europe and their ministers have long claimed to be treated with greater respect and reverence by writers in London, than is shown to the British monarch and his cabinet. Of how many satirical and virulent attacks was not Louis XIV. the object, even long after the entire defeat of the Jacobite party. Lord Molesworth, on his return from his embassy to Copenhagen, at the commencement of the present century, wrote a work on Denmark, filled with caustic observations on the court and condition of that kingdom. The king of Denmark was at that time on terms of great intimacy with the court of England, and he gave orders to his ambassador to demand from the king, William III., a marked apology on the writer's part, or that he might be given up to the justice of the laws of Denmark. "Have a care," replied the king to the ambassador—"have a care of making this order public; it would only tend to enrich a second edition, and to insure its sale."

'Caricatures engage the attention of the police still less than books. An infinity of little shops, especially in the district of Westminster, are covered over daily with sheets on which the principal personages of the ministry, or of the parliament, are pitilessly torn to pieces, in emblems as grossly imagined as pitiably executed. The engraver gains his object, if he can preserve some features by which the persons whom he wishes to expose to ridicule may be recognised. I saw one of these, which represented the principal judges piled in a heap, with their great wigs, profoundly asleep in a contrast of grotesque attitudes, while their physiognomies were easily recognisable.

'The police pay no attention to anything that does not directly affect the life or liberty of the citizen, and, in consequence, an open field is left to the individual fights, so frequent in London among the common people, and sometimes even among the better class, who, for recreation, wish to maul or be mauled. The mob is the born umpire of these fights, which are governed by traditional rules; of which the first is, that the fight shall continue until one of the combatants acknowledges himself beaten, either by crying for quarter, by remaining on the ground without an attempt to rise, or by refusing the assistance of the spectators, who are always ready to put the defeated on his legs. The fights take place with blows of fists and heads; and it is a rule to strip even to the skin, to show that the fighters neither fear the blows, nor have anything on their bodies to deaden their effect.

'So much is this taste diffused in the English blood, that in the great schools of Westminster and Eton, the sons of the first nobility fight in the same way, and consider themselves disgraced for life if they are beaten. It extends even to the women: I saw in Holborn a woman at blows with a man, who struck her with all the fury and force of which he was capable, while he animated his courage by a torrent of abuse. The woman, not less furious, attacked him vigorously over the face and eyes. I saw five or six rounds of this brawl, which astonished me the more, as the woman held on her left arm a child of two years old, who, instead of howling, as is natural to children in less serious circumstances, did not even wink an eye, and seemed to be quietly taking a lesson in that which he would one day practise. In Parliament Street, I saw one of the scoundrels who line the pavement in that quarter attack a respectable individual, who passed near him, with insult and abuse, shaking his fist at the same time under the other's nose. The person insulted raised the large cane which he carried and struck the aggressor, who fell senseless, while the striker continued his walk. I was informed that the insult being gratuitous, he had nothing to fear, even if the insulter should die of the blow.

'One of the principal reasons why the police are so inoperative in all the cases of which I have treated, is, that there are no poor in London—a consequence of its rich and numerous charitable establishments, and the immense sum raised by the poor-rates. Every parish collects and makes the division. This is one of the first and heaviest charges to which houses are liable; and its pressure may be judged of by the total amount raised by this means, twenty-two millions [francs?]* This impost is, however, one which the little householders pay most cheerfully, as they consider it a fund from which, in the event of their death, their wives and children will be supported.

'Notwithstanding the abuses inseparable from pecuniary affairs, and its enormous amount, this tax is the best means by which an opulent nation can honour itself by its riches. In banishing mendicity from London, it has relieved the police from the care of the principal object of their solicitude in other places.

'If we judge of the condition of the people of London by the daily wages of the workmen, we should regard them as rich in comparison with those of Paris, their gains being double that of the artisans of the latter city. At the same time, they might be considered, relatively, as in much better circumstances, being as steady and uniform in manners and conduct, as the Parisians, generally speaking, are the reverse. But the Londoners live well and dress well;† they multiply rapidly; and everything is of such an excessive dearness, that, with great earnings, and expending only for absolute necessaries, they live, as elsewhere, from hand to mouth. An opinion may be formed of the dearness of provisions from the prices during my stay, of which I noted the particulars: bread is sold at from 5 to 6 sous the pound; common meat, 9 sous; best beef, 16 to 18 sous; bacon, 20 sous; butter, 25 sous; candles, 14 sous: the price of a milch cow is from 12 to 15 guineas; and an acre of land near the city lets for the same sum annually; a load of manure is ten shillings. The high prices excited the clamours of the populace, who, however, were not suffering from famine; and when parliament met, their first business was with the energetic petition of the rioters. The only measures taken were to forbid the export of wheat from England, and to open the ports for three months to that of foreign countries.

'English bread is good and delicate, but with a great deal of crumb; and as the Londoners live on this, with butter and tea, from the morning until three or four o'clock in the afternoon, a great quantity is consumed—cut in transverse slices, whose thinness does as much honour to the skill of the cutter as to the edge of the knife. Three or four of these slices suffice for a breakfast: so economical are the people in their repasts, that what would be necessary for a Frenchman of ordinary appetite, is sufficient for three hearty Englishmen. They seem to use bread only from the fear of eating one meal without it; and yet the physicians consider bread as the heaviest and most indigestible of aliments. It is this taste, and the consequent usage, which enables the English to export a prodigious quantity of grain from their islands—an exportation which proves less the abundance than the smallness of the consumption. The dearness of grain, also, causes but little sensation even among the people, who would readily do without bread if circumstances required it.

'I had often heard of the excellence of the meat eaten in England; but having eaten of it in every way in which it is served, either roast or boiled, I have not found it either so firm, juicy, or tender as that of France. The poultry is soft and watery; veal has all the imperfection of an unformed meat; mutton has no other merit than its fat, so much the more striking, as the butchers remove none of the suet from any part; and the beef, although less compact and more divisible than that of France, and consequently more easy of mastication and digestion, can only have imposed on the French who have praised it by its enormous fat, which is never seen in France.

'The English have no knowledge of soup, or of *bouilli*. If they sometimes make soup for invalids, or foreigners who cannot live without it, the beef used in its preparation is never seen again, at least upon good tables.

'The price of vegetables is in proportion to the dearness of other articles of food, while they are not of very good quality. All those which grow in the neighbourhood of London are impregnated with the flavour of the smoke with which the atmosphere of this city is loaded, and have a very disagreeable taste, which they impart to the meat cooked with them.

'Owing to the humid, and nearly always foggy air in which London is enveloped, the greatest cleanliness is required on the part of the inhabitants, who in this respect may be compared with the Hollanders. The apartments, furniture, hearths, earthenware, staircases, and even the street doors, with their locks and great brass knockers, are washed, rubbed, and scoured every day. In the houses where rooms are let as lodgings, the middle of the stairs is covered with a carpet, which protects the wood from the dirt brought in from without. All the apartments have similar carpets, which have for some years gone out of use in France.

'But that which is a necessity in England, would only be an extravagance in France. The houses in London are all built with pine; staircases and floors are all of this material, which will not bear the continual friction of the feet without peeling and splintering; hence the use of carpets. Otherwise, floors of good pine, washed and rubbed, have an appearance of whiteness and cleanliness not always found in the most highly-finished inlaid floor. This love of cleanliness has banished from London the little dogs kept by all classes in Paris, where they fill the streets, houses, and churches.

'The servants of the middle classes, and the ladies'-maids of the nobility, salute their mistresses when they meet them in the streets and public places, dressed in such a manner that, if one does not know the lady, it is very difficult to distinguish her from her servant. The assiduity, attention, cleanliness, work, and punctuality which the English require of their domestics, regulate the amount of their wages; in other words, their wages are very high. This may be judged of by the sum paid in the house where I lived to a great Welsh servant just arrived from her country, speaking scarcely a word of English, who knew only to wash, sweep, and scrub, and would learn nothing else. The wages of this girl were six guineas a-year, besides one guinea for tea, which all the domestics take twice a-day, either in money or in kind. The wages of a cook who roasts and boils meat are twenty guineas. The perquisites of servants double their wages: these are not derived exclusively from the established exactions on foreigners, as has been commonly supposed; all the natives pay them, even at the houses of their nearest friends and relations. My landlady's sister paid every time she came to take tea in her company. The Scottish lords have been the first to exert themselves to relieve strangers from these charges, and they formed an association whose primary object was the augmen-

* In 1843, the amount collected in England and Wales for poor-rates was less than L.5,000,000, of which the city of London contributed L.460,000.

† In crossing the Thames, I have frequently observed that my

tation of servants' wages. Lord Morton himself informed me of this, as I was about to take my leave after dining with him, adding that he was one of the heads of the association. In other houses of the same rank which I visited, the same order was probably given; for, not seeing the servants place themselves in an attitude for receiving, I walked out *à la Française*. The newspapers have been filled with accounts of the riots of the domestics, occasioned by the suppression of the ancient usage. It is to be presumed that victory will declare itself for the masters, unless the spirit of English liberty take part in the quarrel.

'The melancholy of the English is no doubt owing to the fogs and humidity which continually cover London and the three kingdoms. The people, too, live principally on meat. The quantity of bread consumed in a day by one Frenchman would suffice for four Englishmen: beef is their ordinary diet; and this meat, which they relish in proportion to the quantity of fat, mixed in their stomachs with the beer which they drink, must habitually produce a chyle whose viscous heaviness conveys only bilious and melancholic vapours to the brain.

'The coal smoke which fills the atmosphere of London may also be reckoned among the physical causes of the melancholy of its inhabitants. The earthy and mineral particles contained in it pass into the blood of those who breathe it continually, imparting heaviness and other melancholic principles. The moral causes, resulting in part from the physical, aggravate and perpetuate what the latter have begun; while education, religion, theatricals, and the press, seem to have no other object than to maintain the national lugubriosity.

'Rents are a cause of considerable expense. Except some few in the centre of the city, all the houses in London belong to speculators, who build on land taken by lease for forty, sixty, or ninety-nine years; and upon the length of the lease depends the solidity of the structure. Those which are near the end of their terms are but shells. It is true that the outer facing is of brick, but only of one in thickness; and these bricks are made of the first earth that comes to hand—just shown to the fire, not burnt. In the new quarters of London, the bricks are made upon the ground itself, with the earth dug from the foundations and drains, mixed with cinders. The interior of the houses is of the same lightness as the exterior; strips of pine are used instead of beams; while all the joiner work is of the thinnest possible material. The rooms are wainscoted to two-thirds of their height; and the hollow wainscot at the sides of the windows contains the weights by means of which the sash is raised or lowered, with the slightest force. In houses thus constructed, it is easy to imagine what must be the progress and ravages of the almost inevitable conflagration.*

'All the houses in London are insured against fire—a precaution originating probably in the deep impression left by the great fire of 1666. These establishments, which assure the perpetuity of the city, have not yet reached Paris.

'The rent of the house in which I lodged was thirty-eight guineas a-year; it had, however, only three storeys; and there were, besides, payments of one guinea for water, two for poor-tax, and three for the charges on windows, scavengers, and *ouach-men* (watchmen).

'The water supplied to the houses three times a-week is not good. It is raised from the Thames by *fire*-pumps, invented and placed in the river by a German gentleman in the reign of Elizabeth. A French refugee, named Savary, has since improved this machine, whose moving power is the vapour of water raised and rarefied by ebullition—a power whose force would be incomprehensible, were it not there actually before our eyes.'

Here we have an incidental notice of the steam-engine in its infancy, before Watt had brought out its stupendous powers. The inaccuracies and exaggerations in the traveller's statements will be readily detected by most of our readers; we have indicated only some of the more important.

* These observations apply equally well to the present day.

GOOD-WILL AND WORKS TO ALL MEN.

I REMEMBER a poor patriot in Renfrewshire, whose anxiety as to the national debt made him neglect his own debts, until he found himself within the walls of a jail. Now, weak and improvident though that man was, he seemed to me a more respectable and even amiable member of society than

'The wretch concentred all in self,'

whose sympathies, oyster-like, never extend beyond the limits of his own shell. The former character excites pity, the latter contempt; for he whose affections are *wholly* those of his own fireside, is unworthy of society, and should have Spitzbergen for his abode. There are few men, however obscure, who have not had opportunities of rendering signal service to some of their fellow-creatures, even at little cost of time or money, provided the service was prompt, prudent, and hearty. Almost every man's life will be found, on a review, to afford proofs more or less striking of that consolatory fact, and the following veritable anecdote, communicated to the writer by a friend, confirms it in no ordinary degree:—

Upon the 4th of April 1823, I was pacing as usual the Glasgow Exchange rooms, when my eyes got a glimpse of some Jamaica gazettes on a side-table, and remembering that piracies were then prevalent in the West Indies, I glanced over them, till I met with a case which arrested my attention. One Henrique Buche had been recently tried in Jamaica for piracy, on the testimony of a person who swore that he was mariner in the ship Malcolm, belonging to James Strang and Company, merchants in Leith; that they sailed from that harbour on the 9th of November 1819, and upon the 30th of December following, whilst in the Bay of Honduras, they were boarded by pirates; that these plundered the ship of a great variety of stores, of which the witness specified the weights, quantities, and qualities with a minuteness which seemed to me quite incredible, as he *confessedly* took no notes of them at the time; was a mere forecastle man; was stationed at the helm all the time; and that *several years* had elapsed since the alleged piracy took place. The witness added, that the pirates departed with their booty, and he did not see any of them till *three years* afterwards, when he pointed out to a police officer the prisoner at the bar as one of them, whilst he was entering the harbour of Kingston in a boat.

The only other witness was the police officer who had seized poor Buche on the allegation of the sailor, so that the latter was the sole witness to the crime charged—a charge which Mr Buche indignantly denied on his trial, stating that, if an extension of time had been allowed him, he could have proved that he was of respectable connexions in the island of Guadaloupe, where he possessed a competency which placed him far beyond the necessity of following the infamous and perilous profession of a pirate; adding that it would be seen from Lloyd's lists that no ship of the name stated by the crown witness had left Leith at the time alleged.

In reply, the prosecutor stated that the prisoner had been already allowed time sufficient to produce evidence of his alleged *status* in Guadaloupe, and that, as to the inference drawn from the silence of Lloyd's lists, it was well known to the jury that these lists, though correct as to the port of London, were far from being so as to distant ports like Leith. He therefore demanded a verdict of guilty: and my surprise was inexpressible when I found that twelve men had consigned a helpless stranger to an ignominious death, on the single unsupported and incredible testimony of an obscure seaman and common informer, of whom no one seemed to know anything, and who probably had been stimulated by the hope of *blood money*, then given freely for such disclosures.

Animated by these feelings and fears, I instantly stepped to the side bar of the Exchange rooms, and soon discovered incontestable evidence that poor Buche had been convicted, condemned, and, I feared, hanged, on the testimony of a perjured man. The Leith shipping lists proved that no vessel of the name stated by the crown witness had left Leith on the day in question, or during the whole of the month. I also found from the directory that there was no company of shipowners, or of *any* profession, of the firm sworn to in Leith or Edinburgh during the whole of the year in question. These facts I instantly communicated to Lord Bathurst, as minister for the colonies, with a view to the rescue of Buche, if, happily, his *execution* had not taken place, or, at all events, for the seizure and punishment of his perjured enemy. And great was my delight when, in the course of post, his lordship's chief secretary wrote me thus:—

'*Colonial Office, Downing Street, 9th April* 1823.

'SIR—I am directed by Lord Bathurst to acknowledge the receipt of your letter of the 4th instant, and to express his thanks for the information which you have so *properly* conveyed to him respecting Henrique Buche, who had been convicted at Jamaica as concerned with others in acts of piracy.

'It will, I am persuaded, be satisfactory to you to be informed that the governor of Jamaica, in officially reporting the trial and conviction of these unfortunate persons, has stated the circumstances which induced him to grant a *respite* to Henrique Buche, in order that the necessary inquiries might be made to establish the truth of the particulars which he stated in his defences. I have therefore to acquaint you that *your letter will be transmitted to the governor*, with the other documents which apply to this case. I am, sir, your most obedient humble servant, (Signed) R. WILMOT.'

'To G—— B——, Esq. Glasgow.'

Sixteen years afterwards, in the course of my travels, I visited Jamaica, and was introduced to the gentleman who had been foreman on the *grand* jury in the case of Buche. He remembered it, and frankly owned that he thought the evidence was not sufficient to *convict*, though it seemed to him *prima facie* enough to entitle the *grand* jury to send the case to a *petty* jury. Perhaps he was not singular in that opinion; but I saw with regret that he still felt a lurking suspicion of Buche. I found also that, such had been the power of prejudice against the innocent and much injured Buche, that, soon after his liberation, he found it necessary to quit Jamaica, and return to his native island; otherwise I should probably have had the pleasure of seeing the man whom, though unknown to me, and distant some thousands of miles, I had aided in saving from an ignominious death, by a very small expenditure of time and trouble.

It now only remains for me to close my friend's anecdote with what seems its proper moral—'*That each of us should be prompt to help the other, and all of us to help humanity at large;*' in the spirit of a certain Italian aphorism, which is both poetic and benevolent—

'Le mani l'avano l'un l'altra,
Ed ambidue l'avano la faccia.'

Which may be rendered thus—

Kindly the *hands* each other rinse,
And both unite the *face* to cleanse.

WEARING OF THE SUFFOLK COAST.

A lady of our acquaintance, who has lately visited the coast of Suffolk, writes as follows respecting the rapid wearing away of the cliffs:—

'The rapid disappearance of this coast is its most interesting feature. One reads of it without realising it. When one stands on the site of Dunwich, once a great city of twenty-five churches, and sees the heaps of ruin, and a little miserable fishing village, and the quiet blue sea washing smoothly over all the rest, it is a very strange feeling which is induced. The common rate of destruction is about twenty or thirty feet a-year, but in some places much more. The inhabitants see field after field, house after house, swept away. At Cromer, as you walk on the sands, looking up, you see the floors and rafters of houses which have been undermined and washed away, sticking in crevices of the cliff, with a most desolate aspect, and good houses standing empty, abandoned to their fate, because the sea has now encroached too near to admit of a further residence being safe. A good deal of this town (Cromer) is gone, and the rest, as well as a noble old church, must inevitably follow ere long. It is curious that people should go on building on a cliff which they see crumbling before their eyes. A gentleman in this neighbourhood has built a house in one of these places, and spent L.1000 in trying to wall out the sea. His defences were soon swept away. He has now repaired them at nearly the same expense. They are like huge fortifications faced with flint. How long they will last is a wonder.'

OUT-DOOR TUITION.

'I THINK it of the utmost importance,' says Mrs Loudon, 'to cultivate habits of observation in childhood, as a great deal of the happiness of life depends upon having our attention excited by what passes around us. I remember, when I was a child, reading a tale called "Eyes and No Eyes," which made a deep impression on my mind, and which has been the means of procuring me many sources of enjoyment during my passage through life. That little tale related to two boys, both of whom had been allowed half a day's holiday. The first boy went out to take a walk, and he saw a variety of objects that interested him, and from which he afterwards derived considerable instruction when he talked about them with his tutor. The second, a little later, took the same walk; but when his tutor questioned him as to how he liked it, he said he had thought it very dull, for he had seen nothing; though the same objects were still there that had delighted his companion. I was so much struck with the contrast between the two boys, that I determined to imitate the first; and I have found so much advantage from this determination, that I can earnestly recommend my young readers to follow my example.' To encourage and assist in such habits of observation, Mrs Loudon has published the very pretty little book whose title is quoted below.*

There can be no doubt that the knowledge of things derived from observations of the things themselves is not only deeper than that acquired from books, but is more durably impressed on the mind. In the one case knowledge comes in the form of actual experience, in the other it is imbibed by rote. Abstract subjects can of course only be acquired in the study; but whatever can be taught to the young out of doors, should be so imparted. Stores of information can be furnished to them in the shortest walk, for there is something interesting to tell and to know about the most commonplace object.

To show how readily and instructively this may be done, Mrs Loudon repeats in her book the information she imparted to her little girl during a tour in the Isle of Wight in the autumn of 1843. At every step something pleasing was communicated, coming as it did in a less repulsive form than didactic tasks. In the transit from London to Southampton by railway, Mrs Merton (the name assumed by the authoress), in pointing out to her daughter (Agnes) the windings of the river Mole, told her that it 'received its strange name from the manner in which it creeps along, and occasionally appears to bury itself under ground, as its waters are absorbed by the spongy and porous soil through which it flows. Agnes was very anxious to hear more of this curious river. "It is remarkable," said Mrs Merton, "that it is not navigable in any part of its long course of forty-two miles. With regard to the phenomenon of its disappearance at the foot of Box-Hill, near Dorking, in Surrey, it is supposed that there are cavities, or hollow

* Glimpses of Nature, and Objects of Interest, described during a Visit to the Isle of Wight. By Mrs Loudon. London: Grant and Griffith. 1845.

places, under ground, which communicate with the bed of the river, and which are filled with water in ordinary seasons, but in times of drought become empty, and absorb the water from the river to re-fill them. When this is the case, the bed of the river becomes dry; and Burford bridge often presents the odd appearance of a bridge over land dry enough to be walked on. The river, however, always rises again about Letherhead, and suffers no further interruption in its course."'

Arrived at the Isle of Wight, the little pupil is told that in shape it 'has been compared to that of a turbot, of which the point called the Needles forms the tail. From this point, which is the extreme west, to Foreland Farm, near Bembridge, which is the extreme east, the whole island measures only twenty-four miles in length; and its greatest breadth, which is from Cowes Castle to Rock End, near Black Gang Chine, is only twelve miles. It is therefore extremely creditable to this little island to have made such a noise in the world as it has done; and its celebrity shows that, small as it is, it contains a great many things worth looking at.'

At Carisbrook Castle the tourists repaired to the well-house, 'to visit the celebrated donkey. When they first entered, Agnes was a little disappointed to see the donkey, without any bridle or other harness on, standing close to the wall, behind a great wooden wheel. "Oh, mamma," cried she, "I suppose the donkey will not work to-day, as he has no harness on?" "I beg your pardon, miss," said the man; "this poor little fellow does not require to be chained like your London donkeys; he does his work voluntarily. Come, sir," continued he, addressing the donkey, "show the ladies what you can do." The donkey shook his head in a very sagacious manner, as much as to say, "you may depend upon me," and sprang directly into the interior of the wheel, which was broad and hollow, and furnished in the inside with steps, formed of projecting pieces of wood nailed on, the hollow part of the wheel being broad enough to admit of the donkey between its two sets of spokes. The donkey then began walking up the steps of the wheel, in the same manner as the prisoners do on the wheel at the treadmill; and Agnes noticed that he kept looking at them frequently, and then at the well, as he went along. The man had no whip, and said nothing to the donkey while he pursued his course; but as it took some time to wind up the water, the man informed Mrs Merton and her daughter, while they were waiting, that the well was above three hundred feet deep, and that the water could only be drawn up by the exertion of the donkeys that had been kept there; he added, that three of these patient labourers had been known to have laboured at Carisbrook, the first for fifty years, the second for forty, and the last for thirty. The present donkey, he said, was only a novice in the business, as he had not been employed much above thirteen years; and he pointed to some writing inside the door, in which the date was marked down. While they were speaking, the donkey still continued his labour, and looked so anxiously towards the well, that at last Agnes asked what he was looking at. "He is looking for the bucket," said the man; and in fact, as soon as the bucket made its appearance, the donkey stopped, and very deliberately walked out of the wheel to the place where he had been standing when they entered.'

Various lessons in natural history were conveyed when suitable objects presented themselves; and the young pupil, though only absent from home six days, received a greater amount of useful information than if she had studied from books during a much longer period. It is in the power of every parent to communicate instruction on the same plan, and we have noticed this little work chiefly for the purpose of recommending the 'out-door' system of instruction.

SUPERSTITIONS.

It is singular that superstitious ideas of the same character should be prevalent in different countries—that the same inference and deduction should be drawn from the same false data, and the same sayings become current: it is a subject for the consideration of a physiologist. It is a common remark, as regards some birds, that they bring good luck to the houses on which they build. Swallows and storks belong to this category, and they build, especially the latter, on such houses as seem to offer the greatest security to the nest, from the state in which they are kept; and because industrious and provident people take care of their houses and property, and generally prosper in their worldly affairs, it is easy to establish a paralogism, and to argue from the effect rather than the cause. The luck is to the nest, not to the house.—*Note-Book of a Naturalist.*

TO THE UNSATISFIED.

[BY E. W. OF PORTLAND, MAINE.]

Why thus longing, why for ever sighing,
For the far-off, unattained and dim;
While the beautiful, all around thee lying,
Offers up its low perpetual hymn?

Wouldst thou listen to its gentle teaching,
All thy restless yearning it would still;
Leaf, and flower, and laden bee are preaching,
Thine own sphere, though humble, first to fill.

Poor, indeed, thou must be, if around thee
Thou no ray of light and joy canst throw,
If no silken cord of love hath bound thee
To some little world, through weal and wo;

If no dear eyes thy fond love can brighten—
No fond voices answer to thine own;
If no brother's sorrow thou canst lighten,
By daily sympathy and gentle tone.

Not by deeds that win the world's applauses,
Not by works that give thee world-renown,
Nor by martyrdom, or vaunted crosses,
Canst thou win and wear the immortal crown.

Daily struggling, though unloved and lonely,
Every day a rich reward will give;
Thou wilt find, by hearty striving only,
And truly loving, thou canst truly live.

Dost thou revel in the rosy morning,
When all nature hails the lord of light,
And his smile, the mountain-tops adorning,
Robes yon fragrant fields in radiance bright?

Other hands may grasp the field and forest,
Proud proprietors in pomp may shine;
But with fervent love if thou adorest,
Thou art wealthier—all the world is thine!

Yet if through earth's wide domains thou rovest,
Sighing that they are not thine alone,
Not those fair fields, but thyself thou lovest,
And their beauty and thy wealth are gone.

Nature wears the colour of the spirit;
Sweetly to her worshipper she sings;
All the glow, the grace she doth inherit,
Round her trusting child she fondly flings.

—*From a newspaper.*

GUILT.

Guilt, though it may attain temporal splendour, can never confer real happiness. The evil consequences of our crimes long survive their commission, and, like the ghosts of the murdered, for ever haunt the steps of the malefactor. The paths of virtue, though seldom those of worldly greatness, are always those of pleasantness and peace.—*Sir Walter Scott.*

MODERATION.

Let your desires and aversions to the common objects and occurrences in this life be but few and feeble. Make it your daily business to moderate your aversions and desires, and to govern them by reason. This will guard you against many a ruffle of spirit, both of anger and sorrow.—*Watts.*

FUTURE STATE.

We are led to the belief of a future state not only by the weaknesses, by the hopes and fears of human nature, but by the noblest and best principles which belong to it, by the love of virtue, and by the abhorrence of vice and injustice.—*Adam Smith.*

Published by W. and R. Chambers, High Street, Edinburgh (also 98, Miller Street, Glasgow); and with their permission, by W. S. Orr, Amen Corner, London.—Printed by Bradbury and Evans, Whitefriars, London.

CONDUCTED BY WILLIAM AND ROBERT CHAMBERS, EDITORS OF 'CHAMBERS'S INFORMATION FOR THE PEOPLE,' 'CHAMBERS'S EDUCATIONAL COURSE,' &c.

No. 93. NEW SERIES. SATURDAY, OCTOBER 11, 1845. PRICE 1½d.

'SENTIMENT OF PRE-EXISTENCE.'

THIS is an expression of Sir Walter Scott for a peculiar feeling which he is supposed to have been the first to describe. The description is thrown into the mouth of Henry Bertram on his return to Ellangowan Castle: 'How often,' he says, 'do we find ourselves in society which we have never before met, and yet feel impressed with a mysterious and ill-defined consciousness that neither the scene, the speakers, nor the subject are entirely new; nay, feel as if we could anticipate that part of the conversation which has not yet taken place!' It appears, from a passage in the 'Wool-gatherer,' a tale by James Hogg, that that extraordinary son of genius was occasionally conscious of the same feeling. Wordsworth, too, hints at it, with an intimation that it is the recollection of a former existence—

> Our birth is but a sleep and a forgetting:
> The soul that rises in us, our life's star,
> Has had elsewhere its setting,
> And cometh from afar

In a curious and original book, entitled 'The Duality of the Mind,' written by Dr Wigan, and published last year, this strange sentiment is adduced as an evidence in favour of the conclusion aimed at, that the mind is double in its whole structure, correspondently with the duplicity of the structure of the brain. 'It is a sudden feeling, as if the scene we have just witnessed (although from the very nature of things it could never have been seen before) had been present to our eyes on a former occasion, when the very same speakers, seated in the very same positions, uttered the same sentiments in the same words—the postures, the expression of countenance, the gestures, the tone of voice, all seem to be *remembered*, and to be now attracting attention for the second time: *never* is it supposed to be the third time. This delusion,' pursues the writer, 'occurs only when the mind has been exhausted by excitement, or is, from indisposition or any other cause, languid, and only slightly attentive to the conversation. The persuasion of the scene being a repetition, comes on when the attention has been roused by some accidental circumstance, and we become, as the phrase is, wide awake. I believe the explanation to be this: only one brain has been used in the immediately preceding part of the scene; the other brain has been asleep, or in an analogous state nearly approaching it. When the attention of both brains is roused to the topic, there is the same vague consciousness that the ideas have passed through the mind before, which takes place on re-perusing the page we had read while thinking on some other subject. The ideas *have* passed through the mind before; and as there was not sufficient consciousness to fix them in the memory without a renewal, we have no means of knowing the length of time that had elapsed between the *faint* impression received by the single brain, and the *distinct* impression received by the double brain. It may seem to have been many years. I have often noticed this in children, and believe they have sometimes been punished for the involuntary error, in the belief that they have been guilty of deliberate falsehood.

'The strongest example of this delusion I ever recollect in my own person was on the occasion of the funeral of the Princess Charlotte. The circumstances connected with that event formed in every respect a most extraordinary psychological curiosity, and afforded an instructive view of the moral feelings pervading a whole nation, and showing themselves without restraint or disguise. There is, perhaps, no example in history of so intense and so universal a sympathy, for almost every conceivable misfortune to one party is a source of joy, satisfaction, or advantage to another. The event was attended by the strange peculiarity, that it could be a subject of joy or satisfaction to no one. It is difficult to imagine another instance of a calamity by which none could derive any possible benefit; for in the then state of succession to the throne no one was apparently even brought a step nearer to it. One mighty all-absorbing grief possessed the whole nation, and was aggravated in each individual by the sympathy of his neighbour, till the whole people became infected with an amiable insanity, and incapable of estimating the real extent of their loss. No one under five-and-thirty or forty years of age can form a conception of the universal paroxysm of grief which then superseded every other feeling.

'I had obtained permission to be present on the occasion of the funeral, as one of the lord chamberlain's staff. Several disturbed nights previous to that ceremony, and the almost total privation of rest on the night immediately preceding it, had put my mind into a state of hysterical irritability, which was still further increased by grief, and by exhaustion from want of food; for between breakfast and the hour of interment at midnight, such was the confusion in the town of Windsor, that no expenditure of money could procure refreshment.

'I had been standing four hours, and on taking my place by the side of the coffin, in St George's chapel, was only prevented from fainting by the interest of the scene. All that our truncated ceremonies could bestow of pomp was there, and the exquisite music produced a sort of hallucination. Suddenly after the pathetic Miserere of Mozart, the music ceased, and there was an absolute silence. The coffin, placed on a kind of altar covered with black cloth (united to the black cloth which covered the pavement), sank down so slowly through the floor, that it was only in measuring its progress by some brilliant object beyond it that any motion could be perceived. I had fallen into a sort of torpid reverie, when I was recalled to consciousness by a paroxysm of violent grief on the part of the bereaved husband, as his eye suddenly caught the coffin sinking into its black grave, formed by the inverted covering of the altar. In an instant I felt not merely an *impression*, but a *conviction* that I had seen the whole scene before on some former occasion, and had heard even the very words addressed to myself by Sir George Naylor.'

The author thus concludes—'Often did I discuss this matter with my talented friend, the late Dr Gooch, who always took great interest in subjects occupying the debateable region between physics and metaphysics; but we could never devise an explanation satisfactory to either of us. I cannot but think that the theory of two brains affords a sufficient solution of the otherwise inexplicable phenomenon. It is probable that some of the examples of religious mysticism, which we generally set down as imposture, may have their origin in similar hallucinations, and that in the uneducated mind these apparent recollections of past scenes, similar to the present, may give to an enthusiast the idea of inspiration, especially where one brain has a decided tendency to insanity, as is so often the case with such persons.'

In the more recently published 'Dashes at Life' of Mr N. P. Willis, there is an article entitled 'A Revelation of a Previous Life,' in which the actuality of such a life is assumed as the veritable cause of the phenomenon. The whole paper has the air of fiction; yet, as it relates to a subject on which our materials are meagre, we shall make some reference to it. The writer first makes the following statement of (apparently) a serious nature:—'Walking in a crowded street, in perfect health, with every faculty gaily alive, I suddenly lose the sense of neighbourhood. I see—I hear—but I feel as if I had become invisible where I stand, and was, at the same time, present and visible elsewhere. I know everything that passes around me, but I seem disconnected and (magnetically speaking) unlinked from the human beings near. If spoken to at such a moment, I answer with difficulty. The person who speaks seems addressing me from a world to which I no longer belong. At the same time, I have an irresistible inner consciousness of being present in another scene of every-day life—where there are streets, and houses, and people—where I am looked on without surprise as a familiar object—where I have cares, fears, objects to attain—a different scene altogether, and a different life from the scene and life of which I was a moment before conscious. I have a dull ache at the back of my eyes for the minute or two that this trance lasts, and then slowly and reluctantly my absent soul seems creeping back; the magnetic links of conscious neighbourhood, one by one, re-attach, and I resume my ordinary life, but with an irrepressible feeling of sadness.'

The author then relates an adventure which occurred to him a few years ago at Gratz, in Styria, on the occasion of his being taken by a friend to an evening party, at the house of a noblewoman of that country. 'It was a lovely summer's night when we strolled through the principal street toward our gay destination; and as I drew upon my friend's arm to stop him while the military band of the fortress finished a delicious waltz (they were playing in the public square), he pointed out to me the spacious balconies of the countess's palace, whither we were going, crowded with the well-dressed company, listening silently to the same enchanting music. We entered, and after an interchange of compliments with the hostess, I availed myself of my friend's second introduction to take a stand in one of the balconies beside the person I was presented to, and, under cover of her favour, to hear out the unfinished music of the band.

'As the evening darkened, the lights gleamed out from the illuminated rooms more brightly, and most of the guests deserted the balconies, and joined the gayer circles within. The music ceased at the beat of the drum. My companion in the balcony was a very quiet young lady, and, like myself, she seemed subdued by the sweet harmonies we had listened to, and willing to remain without the shadow of the curtain. We were not alone there, however. A tall lady, of very stately presence, and with the remains of remarkable beauty, stood on the opposite side of the balcony, and she too seemed to shrink from the glare within, and cling to the dewy darkness of the summer night.

'After the cessation of the music, there was no longer an excuse for intermittent conversation, and starting a subject which afforded rather freer scope, I did my best to credit my friend's flattering introduction. I had discoursed away for half an hour very unreservedly, before I discovered that, with her hand upon her side, in an attitude of repressed emotion, the tall lady was earnestly listening to me. A third person embarrasses even the most indifferent dialogue. The conversation languished, and my companion rose and took my arm for a promenade through the rooms.

'Later in the evening, my friend came in search of me to the supper room.

"*Mon ami!*" he said, "a great honour has fallen out of the sky for you. I am sent to bring you to the *beau reste* of the handsomest woman of Styria—Margaret, Baroness R——, whose chateau I pointed out to you in the gold light of yesterday's sunset. She wishes to know you—*why*, I cannot wholly divine—for it is the first sign of ordinary feeling that she has given in twenty years. But she seems agitated, and sits alone in the countess's boudoir. *Allons-y!*"

'As we made our way through the crowd, he hastily sketched me an outline of the lady's history: "At seventeen, taken from a convent for a forced marriage with the baron whose name she bears; at eighteen, a widow, and, for the first time, in love—the subject of her passion a young artist of Vienna on his way to Italy. The artist died at her chateau—they were to have been married—she has ever since worn weeds for him. And the remainder you must imagine—for here we are!"

'The baroness leaned with her elbow upon a small table of *or-moulu*, and her position was so taken that I seated myself necessarily in a strong light, while her features were in shadow. Still the light was sufficient to show me the expression of her countenance. She was a woman apparently about forty-five, of noble physiognomy, and a peculiar fulness of the eyelid—something like to which I thought I remembered to have seen in a portrait of a young girl many years before. The resemblance troubled me somewhat.

"You will pardon me this freedom," said the baroness, with forced composure, "when I tell you that—a friend—whom I have mourned twenty-five years—seems present to me when you speak."

'I was silent, for I knew not what to say. The baroness shaded her eyes with her hand, and sat silent for a few moments, gazing at me.

"You are not like him in a single feature," she resumed, "yet the expression of your face strangely, very strangely, is the same. He was darker—slighter."

"Of my age?" I inquired, to break my own silence; for there was something in her voice which gave me the sensation of a voice heard in a dream.

"Oh, that voice! that voice!" she exclaimed wildly, burying her face in her hands, and giving way to a passionate burst of tears.

"Rodolph," she resumed, recovering herself with a strong effort—"Rodolph died with the promise on his lips that death should not divide us. And I have seen him! Not in dreams—not in reverie—not at times when my fancy could delude me. I have seen him suddenly before me in the street—in Vienna—here—at home at noonday—for minutes together, gazing on me. It is more in latter years that I have been visited by him; and a hope has latterly sprung into being in my heart, I know not how, that in person, palpable and breathing, I should again hold converse with him—fold him living to my bosom. Pardon me! You will think me mad!"

'I might well pardon her; for as she talked, a vague sense of familiarity with her voice, a memory powerful, though indistinct, of having before dwelt on those majestic features, an impulse of tearful passionateness to rush to her embrace, well-nigh overpowered me. She turned to me again.

"You are an artist?" she said inquiringly.

"No; though intended for one, I believe, by nature."

"And you were born in the year ——?"

"I was."

'With a scream she added the day of my birth, and, waiting an instant for my assent, dropped to the floor, and clung convulsively and weeping to my knees.

"Rodolph! Rodolph!" she murmured faintly, as her long gray tresses fell over her shoulders, and her head dropped insensible upon her breast.

'Her cry had been heard, and several persons entered the room. I rushed out of doors. I had need to be in darkness and alone.'

The hero of the tale then receives a letter from the baroness, professing to consider him as her lost Rodolph Isenberg, and offering him her undying affections. 'Your soul comes back,' she says, 'youthfully and newly clad, while mine, though of unfading freshness and youthfulness within, shows to your eye the same outer garment, grown dull with mourning, and faded with the wear of time. Am I grown distasteful? Is it with the sight only of this new body that you look upon me? Rodolph!—spirit that was my devoted and passionate admirer! soul that was sworn to me for ever!—am I—the same Margaret, re-found and recognised—grown repulsive? O Heaven! what a bitter answer would this be to my prayers for your return to me! I will trust in Him whose benign goodness smiles upon fidelity in love. I will prepare a fitter meeting for two who parted as lovers. You shall not see me again in the house of a stranger, and in a mourning attire. When this letter is written, I will depart at once for the scene of our love. I hear my horses already in the court-yard, and while you read this I am speeding swiftly home. The bridal dress you were secretly shown the day before death came between us, is still freshly kept. The room where we sat, the bowers by the stream, the walks where we projected our sweet promise of a future, they shall all be made ready. They shall be as they were! And I, oh Rodolph! I shall be the same. My heart is not grown old, Rodolph! Believe me, I am unchanged in soul! And I will strive to be—I will strive to look—Heaven help me to look and be—as of yore!'

The revived Rodolph was unfortunately engaged to a youthful mistress, and he was therefore obliged to leave the baroness to the tragic consequences of her too deep feelings.

We would now remark, that the so-called sentiment of pre-existence may often be produced by a simpler cause than that suggested by Dr Wigan; namely, the recollection of some actual circumstances in our life, of which the present are a repetition. In the routine of ordinary existence, there is much that is the same from day to day. We must often stand in exactly the same relations to certain persons and scenes that we stood in many years ago; those of the past are, in their particulars, forgotten, but still the shade of their general memory lasts, and this may be what revives on the new occasion. With regard to such apparent revivals of a whole being, as Mr Willis's story describes—and to us it is the same at least as if founded on fact, for we have undoubted knowledge of a case precisely similar in the main features—we can explain it to our own satisfaction by the fact that individuals are occasionally met with who very nearly resemble, in person, features, voice, and even moral characteristics, certain other persons living far apart, and in no degree related; nature having, as it were, a certain set of moulds for the various peculiarities of her children, and of course now and then associating the whole in more instances than one.

MR LYELL AND THE AMERICANS.

In 1841-2 Mr Lyell, the well-known geologist, took a run through a great portion of the United States, Canada, and Nova Scotia. His primary object was the geology of the North American continent, but the manners and customs of the people did not altogether escape his attention. Dismissing his scientific observations for the present, it may be interesting to learn the opinions of such a traveller*—as distinguished from the mere literary or fashionable tourist—respecting the social characteristics of the young republic. Accustomed to reflection and accuracy of statement, his remarks are of more than ordinary value; at least they are not likely to be biassed by the desire of producing an attractive book, in which sober truth is subordinated to satirical brilliancy.

Mr Lyell sailed from Liverpool in the steam-ship Acadia, on the 20th July 1841, and after a voyage of twelve days dropped quietly into the harbour of Boston. Here he found everything bearing a close resemblance to what he had left in the mother country. 'Recollecting the contrast of everything French when I first crossed the straits of Dover, I am astonished, after having traversed the wide ocean, at the resemblance of everything I see and hear to things familiar at home. It has so often happened to me in our own island, without travelling into those parts of Wales, Scotland, or Ireland, where they talk a perfectly distinct language, to encounter provincial dialects which it is difficult to comprehend, that I wonder at finding the people here so very English. If the metropolis of New England be a type of a large part of the United States, the industry of Sam Slick, and other writers, in collecting together so many diverting Americanisms, and so much original slang, is truly great, or their inventive powers still greater.' After some pleasant excursions in the neighbourhood of Boston, our traveller started for Newhaven in Connecticut, going the first hundred miles on an excellent railway in three and a half hours, for three dollars. At Newhaven, which is a town with a population of 21,000, and having a university, Mr Lyell attended divine worship according to the Presbyterian form, and found things differing so little from what he had been accustomed to, that he could scarcely believe that he was not in Scotland.

Completing his investigations in the neighbourhood of Newhaven, Mr Lyell steamed for New York—a distance of ninety miles, in six hours; and from thence up the Hudson to Albany. Having the best of all introductions, an established fame, the American geologists were ever willing guides and companions, and thus he was enabled to pass on directly to the objects of special interest. From Albany he proceeded to Niagara, to examine the falls, and the deposits along the lakes Erie and Ontario. In this route he passed through many new and flourishing towns, the nomenclature of which is grotesque and incongruous in the extreme. In one short month 'we had been at Syracuse, Utica, Rome, and Parma, had gone from Buffalo to Batavia, and on the same day breakfasted at St Helena and dined at Elba. We collected fossils at Moscow, and travelled by Painted Post

* Travels in North America; with Geological Observations on the United States, Canada, and Nova Scotia. By Charles Lyell, Esq. F.R.S. 2 vols. 8vo. London: Murray. 1845.

and Big Flats to Havanna. After returning by Auburn to Albany, I was taken to Troy, a city of 20,000 inhabitants, that I might see a curious landslip, which had just happened on Mount Olympus, the western side of that hill, together with a contiguous portion of Mount Ida, having slid down into the Hudson. Fortunately some few of the Indian names, such as Mohawk, Ontario, Oneida, Canandaigua, and Niagara, are retained. Although legislative interference in behalf of good taste would not be justifiable, congress might interpose for the sake of the post-office, and prevent the future multiplication of the same name for villages, cities, counties, and townships. That more than a hundred places should be called Washington is an intolerable nuisance.'

Notwithstanding the absurdity of their names, the fact of towns with 20,000 inhabitants flourishing in the wilderness where, twenty-five years ago, the first settler built his log-cabin, gives rise to pleasing and hopeful reflections. 'The vast stride made by one generation in a brief moment of time, naturally disposes us to magnify and exaggerate the rapid rate of future improvement. The contemplation of so much prosperity, such entire absence of want and poverty, so many school-houses and churches rising everywhere in the woods, and such a general desire of education, with the consciousness that a great continent lies beyond, which has still to be appropriated, fills the traveller with cheering thoughts and sanguine hopes. He may be reminded that there is another side to the picture; that where the success has been so brilliant, and where large fortunes have been hastily realised, there will be rash speculations and bitter disappointments; but these ideas do not force themselves into the reveries of the passing stranger. He sees around him the solid fruits of victory, and forgets that many a soldier in the foremost ranks has fallen in the breach; and cold indeed would be his temperament if he did not sympathise with the freshness and hopefulness of a new country, and feel as men past the prime of life are accustomed to feel when in company with the young, who are full of health and buoyant spirits, of faith and confidence in the future.'

Having inspected the falls and the lake district, Mr Lyell returned to New York; from which, after a short stay, he departed for Philadelphia. In this journey he met with all sorts of people, and had excellent opportunities for studying the national peculiarities. The following anecdotes, dismissed in a dozen lines, would have supplied Mrs Trollope with comment for a chapter:—'I asked the landlord of the inn at Corning, who was very attentive to his guests, to find my coachman. He immediately called out in his bar-room, "Where is the gentleman who brought this man here?" A few days before, a farmer in New York had styled my wife "the woman," though he called his own daughters *ladies*, and would, I believe, have freely extended that title to their maid-servant. I was told of a witness in a late trial at Boston, who stated in evidence, that "while he and another gentleman were shovelling up mud," &c.; from which it appears that the spirit of social equality has left no other signification to the terms "gentleman" and "lady," but that of "male and female individual."' Though thus confounding the terms which with us bear so important a distinction, the Americans are everywhere most polite and attentive to the fair sex. 'One of the first peculiarities,' says Mr Lyell, 'that must strike a foreigner in the United States, is the deference paid universally to the sex with regard to station. Women may travel alone here in stage-coaches, steamboats, and railways, with less risk of encountering disagreeable behaviour, and of hearing coarse and unpleasant conversation, than in any country I have ever visited. The contrast in this respect between the Americans and the French is quite remarkable. There is a spirit of true gallantry in all this; but the publicity of the railway car, where all are in one long room, and of the large ordinaries, whether on land or water, is a great protection, the want of which has been felt by many a female traveller without escort in England. As the Americans address no conversation to strangers, we soon became tolerably reconciled to living so much in public. Our fellow-passengers consisted, for the most part, of shopkeepers, artisans, and mechanics, with their families, all well dressed, and, so far as we had intercourse with them, polite and desirous to please. A large part of them were on pleasure excursions, in which they delight to spend their spare cash. On one or two occasions, in the newly-settled districts of New York, it was intimated to us that we were expected to sit down to dinner with our driver, usually the son or brother of the farmer who owned the vehicle. We were invariably struck with the propriety of their manners, in which there was self-respect without forwardness. The only disagreeable adventure, in the way of coming into close contact with low and coarse companions, arose from my taking places in a cheap canal-boat, near Lockport, partly filled with emigrants, and corresponding somewhat, in the rank of its passengers, with a third-class railway carriage in England.

'Travellers must make up their minds, in this as in other countries, to fall in now and then with free and easy people. I am bound, however, to say that, in the two most glaring instances of vulgar familiarity which we have experienced here, we found out that both the offenders had crossed the Atlantic only ten years before, and had risen rapidly from a humble station. Whatever good breeding exists here in the middle classes, is certainly not of foreign importation; and John Bull in particular, when out of humour with the manners of the Americans, is often unconsciously beholding his own image in the mirror, or comparing one class of society in the United States with another in his own country, which ought, from superior affluence and leisure, to exhibit a higher standard of refinement and intelligence.' In addition to this good breeding, which makes travelling in America so pleasant, Mr Lyell met with no beggars—witnessed no signs of want, but saw everywhere unequivocal proofs of prosperity and rapid progress in agriculture, commerce, and great public works. This prosperity he ascribes neither to a republican institution, nor to an absolute equality of religious sects, and still less to universal suffrage; it is, he believes, owing to the abundance of unoccupied land, and a ready outlet to a redundant labouring population.

From Philadelphia our traveller proceeded to the chalk district of New Jersey, and thence westward to the anthracite coal-measures of Pennsylvania. By the time he had reached the summit of the Alleghanies, symptoms of approaching winter were around him, and so he retraced his route to Philadelphia, which he found (October 12) in the bustle of a general election. Processions, music, banners, and other paraphernalia suiting the occasion, thronged the streets, and the great bell of the State House tolled all day to remind the electors of their duties. This leads Mr Lyell into some reflections on politics and repudiation, both of which we gladly eschew; trusting that a country with such resources and enterprise will not be guilty of any breach of faith which would be to it a disgrace that ages could not obliterate. From Philadelphia our tourist passed on to Boston, where he delivered a course of lectures on geology, and spent part of the winter. His audience, he informs us, usually consisted of 3000 persons, of every station in society, from the most affluent and eminent in the various learned professions to the humblest mechanics, all well-dressed and observing the utmost decorum. Attendance on public lectures seems, indeed, to be a common feature in the habits of the New Englanders. 'At a small town,' says our author, 'I was getting some travelling instructions at the bar of an inn, when a carpenter entered who had just finished his day's work, and asked what lecture would be given that evening. The reply was, Mr M. on the astronomy of the middle ages. He then inquired if it was gratis, and was answered in the negative, the price being 25 cents (one shilling), upon which he said he would go, and accordingly returned home to dress. It reflects no small credit on the national system of education, that crowds of the labouring classes, of both sexes, should seek recreation, after the toils of the day, in listening to discourses of this kind.' There are, it seems, many munificent bequests for this purpose, for we are told that in the state of Massachusetts alone, there has, during the last thirty years, been bequeathed for religious, charitable, and literary institutions, not less than six millions of dollars, or more than a million sterling.

With Boston, which seems one of the most enlightened and wealthy cities in the union, our author was perfectly delighted. Its institutions and society were quite to his liking, and he and Mrs Lyell 'often reflected with surprise in how many parts of England they should have felt less at home.' It is somewhat common for Englishmen travelling in the United States to complain of the Americans as a disagreeable people, but on this point Mr Lyell wisely remarks—'It would certainly be strange if persons of refined habits, even without being fastidious, who travel to see life, and think it their duty, with a view of studying character, to associate indiscriminately with all kinds of people, visiting the first strangers who ask them to their houses, and choosing their companions without reference to congeniality of taste, pursuits, manners, or opinions, did not find society in their own or any other country in the world intolerable.' This is putting the matter in its true light: no one need leave his own country, nay, his own city, to find disagreeable people, if he throw aside considerations of tastes, habits, and feelings.

In December Mr Lyell set out for the southern states, and there enjoyed the most delightful weather for geologising, while the inhabitants of Boston, Lowell, with its genteel factory girls, and other northern cities, were careering, in their gaily-caparisoned sledges, over the frozen snow. The most southerly point visited was Savannah, in Georgia; and thus he had an opportunity of passing through the densely-populated slave districts, to the condition of which he directed no small share of his attention. Though not inclined to advocate slavery, his impression of the condition of the slaves was rather favourable than otherwise. 'After the accounts I had read of the sufferings of slaves, I was agreeably surprised to find them, in general, so remarkably cheerful and light-hearted. It is true that I saw no gangs working under overseers on sugar-plantations, but out of two millions and a half of slaves in the United States, the larger proportion are engaged in such farming occupations and domestic services as I witnessed in Georgia and South Carolina. I was often for days together with negroes who served me as guides, and found them as talkative and chatty as children, usually boasting of their master's wealth, and their own peculiar merits. At an inn in Virginia, a female slave asked us to guess for how many dollars a-year she was let out by her owner. We named a small sum, but she told us exultingly, that we were much under the mark, for the landlord paid fifty dollars, or ten guineas a-year for her hire. A good-humoured butler, at another inn in the same state, took care to tell me that his owner got L.30 a-year for him. The coloured stewardess of a steam-ship was at great pains to tell us her value, and how she came by the name of Queen Victoria. When we recollect that the dollars are not their own, we can hardly refrain from smiling at the childlike simplicity with which they express their satisfaction at the high price set on them. That price, however, is a fair test of their intelligence and moral worth, of which they have just reason to feel proud, and their pride is at least free from all sordid and mercenary considerations. We might even say that they labour with higher motives than the whites—a disinterested love of doing their duty. I am aware that we may reflect and philosophise on this peculiar and amusing form of vanity, until we perceive in it the evidence of extreme social degradation; but the first impression which it made upon my mind was very consolatory, as I found it impossible to feel a painful degree of commiseration for persons so exceedingly well satisfied with themselves.'

Mr Lyell, however, is not the advocate of slavery; but, while admitting the iniquity of the system as regards the negroes, its dangers as regards the numerically weaker whites, the dearth of labour and other inconveniences it occasions, he is perplexed, like other philanthropists, to devise a remedy. Immediate abolition would not only be dangerous to the white population, but disastrous to the unprovided-for and improvident blacks, who could never successfully compete with the acute and enterprising American. The way in which the planters would best consult their own interests, and that of the negroes, appears to him to be something like the following. 'They should exhibit more patience and courage towards the abolitionists, whose influence and numbers they greatly over-rate, and lose no time in educating the slaves and encouraging private manumission to prepare the way for general emancipation. All seem agreed that the states most ripe for this great reform are Maryland, Virginia, North Carolina, Tennessee, Kentucky, and Missouri. Experience has proved in the northern states that emancipation immediately checks the increase of the coloured population, and causes the relative number of the whites to augment very rapidly. Every year, in proportion as the north-western states fill up, and as the boundary of the new settlers in the west is removed farther and farther beyond the Mississippi and Missouri, the cheaper and more accessible lands south of the Potomac will offer a more tempting field for colonisation to the swarms of New Englanders, who are averse to migrating into slave states. Before this influx of white labourers, the coloured race will give way, and it will require the watchful care of the philanthropist, whether in the north or south, to prevent them from being thrown out of employment, and reduced to destitution. If due exertions be made to cultivate the minds and protect the rights and privileges of the negroes, and it nevertheless be found that they cannot contend, when free, with white competitors, but are superseded by them, still the cause of humanity will have gained. The coloured people, though their numbers remain stationary, or even diminish, may in the meantime be happier than now, and attain to a higher moral rank. They would, moreover, escape the cruelty and injustice which are the invariable consequences of the exercise of irresponsible power, especially where authority must be sometimes delegated by the planter to agents of inferior education and coarser feelings. And last, not least, emancipation would effectually put a stop to the breeding, selling, and exporting of slaves to the sugar-growing states of the south, where, unless the accounts we usually read of slavery be exaggerated and distorted, the life of the negro is shortened by severe toil and suffering.'

Leaving the perplexing subject of slavery, we find Mr Lyell retracing his steps northward, and spending the spring of 1842 in the great coal districts of the Ohio. From Ohio his investigations led him again to Niagara, Ontario, Queenston, Montreal, and Quebec, and latterly to Nova Scotia, from which he embarked for England in August 1842. The attention which he met with in our colonies was highly flattering, and speaks volumes for the good-sense of our brethren on the other side the Atlantic. 'I never travelled in any country where my scientific pursuits seemed to be better understood, or were more zealously forwarded, than in Nova Scotia, although I went there almost without letters of introduction. At Truro, having occasion to go over a great deal of ground in different directions, on two successive days, I had employed two pair of horses, one in the morning and the other in the afternoon. The postmaster, an entire stranger to me, declined to receive payment for them, although I pressed him to do so, saying that he heard I was exploring the country at my own expense, and he wished to contribute his share towards scientific investigations undertaken for the public good.'

On the whole, Mr Lyell's opinions of the Americans are eminently favourable; and, as he can have no reason for stating matters otherwise than they appeared to him, we are inclined to be swayed more by his remarks than by those of the mere fashionable or literary tourist, who, with the slenderest qualifications, often indulges in the most absurd prejudices and silliest satire.

A FEW FACTS IN THE HISTORY OF TERRESTRIAL MAGNETISM.

The magnetism of the earth has for a long time engaged the attention of philosophers, who have seen the necessity of obtaining a correct knowledge of the elements of this phenomenon; but it is only of late years that the high importance of applying these elements, as the basis of a science, has been fully recognised.

Those who have read the works of travellers, such as Erman, Hansteen, and Humboldt, will have seen that many of them made this subject the object of especial research, with a view to establish its physical laws in different geographical positions. Isolated exertions were, however, found too insignificant in comparison with the magnitude of the subject, whose phenomena are continually changing; a diligent and long-continued course of observation was therefore determined on, as the only possible means of arriving at accurate results.

The re-discovery of the fact, that magnetic disturbances occur simultaneously at places widely separated from each other, in the year 1825, by Arago at Paris and Kupffer at Kasan, led to the establishment of magnetic stations in many parts of the continent, and subsequently, on the representations of Baron Von Humboldt, in Great Britain, where the observatories for this branch of science were established at Greenwich and Dublin in 1837.*

In the year 1834, a magnetic survey of the British islands was commenced and completed in the course of the two following years; the results were published by the British Association in the report of 1838, and on the presentation of their memorial to government, in conjunction with the Royal Society, the South Polar Expedition, under Captain Ross, was determined on and equipped in the following year.

At the same time, the necessity for fixed points of observation having been fully recognised, observatories were established, at the charge of government, in various parts of the globe, where all the fluctuations could be duly watched and noted. Canada and Van Diemen's Land were chosen as points conveniently near to the positions of greatest magnetic intensity; St Helena, where it would be lowest; and the Cape of Good Hope, as presenting a favourable station for the observation of extraordinary phenomena. These establishments are generally under the direction of an officer of artillery, with a staff of three non-commissioned officers and two gunners, and are conducted at an expense of nearly L.400 annually. The East India Company also consented to co-operate in the great work, and established observatories at various stations in the eastern continent, extending from the sea-coast to the Himalaya.

Towards the end of 1839, the persons selected for the service sailed for their respective destinations: those for St Helena and Van Diemen's Land, in the ships of the Antarctic Expedition. The period of observation was fixed for two terms of three years, in which time it was believed a sufficient number of facts would be collected to enable scientific men to found correct data for the exposition of the laws of magnetic and meteorological science. The registered observations have been regularly forwarded to London, where they are reduced and published as rapidly as is consistent with their complex nature. Such was the importance attached to these observations by the Magnetic Conference at the late meeting of the British Association, that they recommended their continuance, with some exceptions, for a further term of three years, which will expire at the end of 1848.

For the institution of correct comparison between the observations at the various stations, the mean time at some fixed point is taken, by which the operations of all the others are regulated. The point chosen is Göttingen, the residence of Gauss, one of the most celebrated magneticians; and some idea of the labour incurred may be conceived from the fact, that results of all the instruments, which are very numerous, are read off and recorded in some cases every hour, or every two hours, night and day, excepting Sundays. On one specified day in each month, known as a 'term day,' the observations are made hourly and simultaneously at all the stations, which continue to follow the instructions prescribed at their first establishment.

It may now be asked what are the phenomena, or what facts have been elicited as a return for all this trouble and expense? Every person has some general acquaintance with the existence of magnetism, which, however, does not go far beyond the popular knowledge, that the needle points to the north. Very few, however, are aware of the universal influence of this mysterious agency, the seat of which was for a long time matter of dispute. Some placed it in a small star, forming part of the constellation the Great Bear; others at the zodiacal pole; and others, still more daring, imagined a centre of attraction existing far beyond the remotest stars. It was only at the end of the sixteenth century that the magnetism of the earth itself was proved, and its action ascertained to be the cause of movement in the magnetic needles.

If we regard the earth as one vast magnet, we shall find its power lowest in the equatorial regions, and increasing in intensity as we approach either pole: the active medium which excites the phenomena in the northern hemisphere is known as the *boreal* fluid, while the *austral* fluid is that which prevails in the opposite hemisphere; and as the fluids of contrary names attract each other, it follows that it is the south pole of a needle which points towards the north, and the north pole towards the south.

When two needles rest in the same place, their direction is parallel; but this parallelism disappears in proportion as one of the needles is removed from the other in any direction. The magnetic intensity of the earth is indicated by needles suspended vertically; and in sailing from England towards the north pole, it is seen that the needle dips or inclines more and more with the increase of latitude, until at a certain point it remains exactly perpendicular, with its south pole downwards; this point is thus known to be the magnetic pole of the earth. In sailing towards the equator, on the contrary, the inclination or dip gradually decreases, until the needle rests in a perfectly horizontal position.

The diurnal action of the magnetic fluid is shown by horizontal needles delicately suspended, as in a ship's compass; and these frequently exhibit the presence of extraordinary phenomena. Sometimes they are seen to move suddenly and accidentally, but in general regularly and periodically; the former movements are classed as perturbations or disturbances, the latter as diurnal variations. In this country, on days unmarked by any perturbation, the needle is seen to be almost stationary during the night; but at sunrise, its south pole, or northern extremity, moves towards the west, as though it fled from the influence of the great luminary: at noon, or more generally between twelve and three o'clock, it reaches the maximum of western deviation, when, by a contrary movement, it returns to the east until ten or eleven o'clock at night, and then remains nearly or exactly in its original position until the morning, when it recommences a similar oscillation. It might be supposed that solar light or heat influenced the movement, but the same phenomena have been observed in the cellars of the observatory at Paris, thirty feet below the surface of the earth, where daylight does

* To these may be added that more recently established and supported by the private expense of Sir Thomas M. Brisbane at Makerstoun, near Kelso.

not enter. In more northerly countries, the variations are greater; the needle does not reach its maximum until the evening, neither does it remain at perfect rest during the night. In the southern hemisphere, the needle moves in an inverse direction, or towards the east, in the same degree, and precisely at the same time, as when on our side of the world it moves towards the west. There are several natural causes which act upon and produce perturbations in the magnetic needle; some of these are known, while others are involved in doubt and obscurity. Among the known causes, the aurora borealis appears to be the most efficacious and infallible. During the appearances of this light in the heavens of the northern regions, the needle undergoes a continual agitation and unusual deviation. It is generally observed that the summit of the glittering boreal arch is in the magnetic meridian: and it is not only in places where the aurora is visible that the agitations are seen, for the same disturbances are remarked in places where no trace of the light is perceptible; these are, however, greatest in proportion to their nearness to the cause which produces them. Sometimes, either in the night or day, the observer sees a sudden deviation of the needle, amounting often to more than a degree, without being able to trace it to any apparent cause. He, however, afterwards learns that at Paris and St Petersburg the needle experienced similar movements at the same moment, and that in the remote regions of the north a brilliant aurora was visible. Thus the patient watcher in the observatory at Greenwich is informed by his needle of all that passes in the polar regions, as he is informed by his barometer of the changes in the higher regions of the atmosphere.

Earthquakes and volcanic eruptions appear also as causes of disturbance, with at times a permanent effect. In 1767, Bernouilli observed a diminution of half a degree of inclination during an earthquake; and La Torre remarked changes of declination during an eruption of Vesuvius. More recently, in 1839, Signor Capocci, director of the observatory at Naples, noticed a sudden decrease of more than half a degree of declination, also at the time of an eruption.

The simultaneity of disturbances in places remote from each other has been incidentally noticed; and it appears, on a comparison of the observations made at Prague, at Toronto, at Van Diemen's Land, and St Helena, places very widely separated, that nearly the whole of the perturbations manifested themselves at each of the stations at the same time, though modified by various local circumstances. Not the least important advantage that may be expected to result from the establishment of these observatories, will be the preservation of the record of such phenomena whose effects appear to be universal. During Cook's voyages, whenever he observed an aurora australis, the auroræ boreales were seen in Europe. In January 1769, an aurora was visible at the same time in Pennsylvania and in France; and later, in January 1831, the same phenomenon was simultaneously observed in central and northern Europe, and on the borders of Lake Erie in North America; and it is now believed that local manifestations are connected with magnetic effects prevailing at the same time all over the globe.

The science of magnetism is intimately connected with that of meteorology: a knowledge of both is necessary to enable us to define with certainty the action of the unseen physical agencies. Something has already been done towards a determination of the laws of storms and atmospheric changes, and still further knowledge may be expected from the number of observatories—nearly one hundred—now at work; as, by means of the recorded facts, the extent of disturbance is ascertained. It was thus known, on the morning of February 3, 1842, that 'rain was falling throughout nearly every portion of the United States, from an unknown distance in the Atlantic to far beyond the Mississippi, and from the Gulf of Mexico northward to an unknown distance beyond Lake Superior. The area on which rain is ascertained to have been simultaneously falling was more than 1400 miles in a north and south direction.'

One of the great objects of the present Arctic Expedition is the prosecution of magnetic and meteorological observations, that shall render our knowledge of the magnetism of the northern hemisphere as complete as that obtained by Sir James Ross of the Antarctic regions.

If, by the concurrence of so many observers, and by persevering investigations of magnetic phenomena, we at last discover their laws, as we have discovered the laws by which a Divine Hand has regulated the motion of the planets—if we find the cause of those singular perturbations which agitate the magnetic needle at indeterminate epochs, and which seem to reveal to us mysterious evolutions in the liquefied masses surrounding our globe—if, by prolonged study, we succeed in dissipating the obscurity in which popular belief has enveloped this branch of natural science, not only will a new object of investigation be opened, and a new career given to ideas, but a new element will be added to the intellectual well-being of society. 'Whatever difficulties may have hitherto opposed the development of this science, it has yet made very notable progress since the end of the last century, and it now advances with a rapid and certain pace. Future ages will erect the edifice of which we have laid the foundations; and we may already say, with certainty, that the general plan is simple, and that its apparent complexity only arises from the close connexion of the parts with each other—a connexion so intimate, that it is difficult to circumscribe the limits of the phenomena.' 'Should the government observatories at Toronto and Van Diemen's Land ultimately come to be handed over to their respective colonies as part of their domestic institutions, not only would a permanent contribution of data be secured to science, but incalculable benefit would arise to the colonies themselves, in the possession of establishments in which the art of observing has been wrought up to elaborate perfection, and in which practice, going hand-in-hand with theory, would act as a powerful engine of public instruction.'

THE GO-ALONGS.

It is a common saying among military men that there are in the army two kinds of officers—the Come-alongs and the Go-alongs; or, in other words, if the saying can need any explanation, the skulkers, who are content with merely urging others onward in the path of duty and danger, and the brave fellows who stimulate by their example, and are as ready to share the peril as the glory.

In looking round upon the busy walks of life, we find that not a few consist of this Go-along kind of people. They will listen attentively to your benevolent projects; they will express their approbation of your principles of action; they will profess unqualified admiration of your mode of proceeding, and their cordial sympathy with the end you have in view; but immediately you solicit their countenance and aid, they shrink from your appeal, and endeavour to shuffle you off by protests of inability, or by plausibly insisting that they shall require time to consider of it; and endeavour to hide their indolence or parsimony under the plea of waiting to see 'how it will work.' They are convinced that the end is desirable, and the means unexceptionable, but any one may do the work, so that you will not trouble them; and, sinking back in their easy-chairs, these well-meaning Go-alongs sigh over the ignorance and wickedness of the world, bidding you good speed in your enterprise, but do not dream of putting a finger to the work.

Now, it is evident that if every one acted in this manner, no plan or project, however excellent, could by possibility be carried out. If every one thus shrunk from taking a part in the initiative, no benevolent enterprise would have a practical beginning, and its cradle would be also its grave. The thought and wish must be mere abortions, which would never have strength to come to the birth, much less attain to manly stature and robustness. The great and noble institutions on which, as a nation, we justly pride ourselves, would never have seen the light, or have only dragged on a miserable and useless existence as bad as nonentity, and the mighty machinery for good which they have contributed to form, with all their vast and glorious results, must have been lost to the world. What an incalculable loss would it have been to society had some of the great men whose names adorn the page of history been mere Go-alongs! But our Hampdens, Newtons, Howards, and Wilberforces, were not such. Their hands moved with their hearts: they stamped their image upon the age in which they lived, and originated a circle of light and love which has extended to the ends of the civilised earth, and will continue to exert its influence to the end of time. If all, in fact, were mere Go-alongs, abuses could never be remedied, society could not improve, and all things must remain, as far as man is concerned, in an irremediably stagnant and corrupt state.

Far more injurious is the promised assistance of these Go-alongs to the success of a good project, than decided antagonism. A little opposition, indeed, often engenders a corresponding strength on the contrary side, and infuses an energy into the infant Hercules which fits it for giant struggles, and secures it an ultimate victory. But to be 'damned with faint praise'—to meet with a cold Go-along where we hoped to find a Come-along, is the deadliest of all opposition. Decided enemies, louring prospects, anything, in fact, is better than the meaningless promises of cold friends—the assurances of assistance of the mere Go-alongs.

The class of Go-alongs have not a little to answer for. They may hug themselves as being very well-meaning people, they may lament sincerely the ignorance, degradation, poverty, and the various ills under which many of their fellows are labouring, but they are chargeable with much that they little think of. The buds of a thousand blighted benevolent projects lie at their door; the unaided exertions of the brave Come-alongs, that march in the van of all that is useful and praiseworthy, beckoning onward the lagging rear, reproach them; and however unwilling they may be to bear the stigma, they must nevertheless be reckoned among the opponents of those benevolent projects which they only charge themselves at most with neglecting to countenance and assist. Many a social evil which inflicts misery and ruin, many a practice which is disgraceful and degrading, many a giant abuse, would be scouted and heard of no more, but for the apathy of these Go-alongs.

The other day I had occasion to call on one of these people, a friend of mine, a gentleman of property, on a benevolent errand. I knew him to be a kind-hearted man, and every way well able to afford the assistance which I, from the most disinterested motives, wished him to render to an embryo institution, in the prosperity of which I felt deeply concerned, and which I introduced to his notice. He listened to me in the most attentive manner while I put before him the necessities and claims of the project. In conclusion, he expressed himself in strong terms of admiration, and declared that in his opinion it was worthy of the most cordial support. Of course I expected after this eulogy he would offer us some assistance, or at least the use of his name; but as he made no such offer, I plainly asked him if he could in any manner advance our objects. 'Well,' said he, 'as to assisting your institution'—and here he began to play with his watch seals—'as to assisting you—why, I should be very happy, very, to lend you my name, but your society is at present hardly formed. I think I would rather wait a little while, and see how you get on, and if it come to anything, I will do something for you.' I had not the remotest personal interest in the prosperity of the institution for which I was pleading; but thinking remonstrance useless, I departed, sorely vexed at the strange apathy of this anomalous, warm-hearted, cold-handed man, this freezing negative specimen of humanity, and wishing that I could convert this useless Go-along, hanging like a dead weight upon the rear of philanthropy, into a Come-along in the van, for which his position in society and ample means so well qualified him.

But the Go-alongs do not altogether escape punishment. Independently of the superior respect always felt for those who act manfully and uncalculatingly upon the good impulses of their nature, compared with those who shrink from the call of duty, and are the slaves of some cowardly expediency, posterity treats their memory with indifference and forgetfulness. History—both the history of nations and the more circumscribed history of smaller communities—deals impartially with the memory both of the Come-alongs and the Go-alongs. The memory of the Go-alongs dies, for the most part, with them; none have much reason to hold their name in esteem or reverence. History deals with what men do, not what they think or intend; and they leave little behind them for their fellows to love or imitate. But the Come-alongs still live in their deeds; their name, if history inscribe it not in her pages, is enshrined in the heart of the family, the village, the city; and the footprints of departed philanthropy are looked on with love and veneration by their successors.

THE BRIDE'S JOURNEY.

BY MRS CROWE.

In the year 1809, when the French were in Prussia, M. Louison, an officer in the commissariat department of the imperial army, contracted an attachment for the beautiful Adelaide Hext, the daughter of a respectable but not wealthy merchant. The young Frenchman having contrived to make his attachment known, it was imprudently reciprocated by its object; we say imprudently, for the French were detested by her father, who declared that no daughter of his should ever be allied to one of the invaders and occupants of his beloved country. Thus repulsed, M. Louison had the good sense not to press his suit, and proceeded to Vienna, where he was installed in a lucrative office suitable to his wishes and abilities. Here, however, he could not altogether relinquish the expectation of being one day married to the fair Adelaide Hext, with whom he continued to correspond.

After the lapse of a few months, the aspect of affairs underwent a material change. Hext lay, as he supposed, and as the doctors told him, on his deathbed, and, pondering on the probable destitution of his family, he repented his rash vow, and stated to Adelaide that he should no longer oppose her wishes. M. Louison, procuring leave of absence for a few days, was speedily on the spot, and, with as little loss of time as possible, was united to the daughter of the seemingly dying merchant. As, in such circumstances, it would have been cruel for Madame Louison to leave the bedside of her aged parent, it was arranged that she should remain till the period of his decease, and then join her husband, who, in the meanwhile, was compelled to return to Vienna. The old man, however, recovered as soon as his son-in-law departed, and he now almost wished the marriage were undone; but as that was impracticable, he, with as good a grace as possible, saw his daughter set out on her journey to Dresden, whence she was to be escorted to Vienna by M. de Monge, a friend of her husband.

Nothing occurred to interrupt the journey of Madame Louison, for the intermediate country was tranquil, and she had the happiness of arriving safely under the roof of her husband's friend. This person was one of those who will act conscientiously in all situations of life, until they encounter an irresistible temptation to error. Such was the present occasion. Overcome with the beauty of his unsuspicious guest, he basely attempted to divert her affections from her husband—an attempt which the noble Friedlander repelled with becoming scorn. To cut short a long tale, this mortification filled De Monge with vengeful sentiment, at the same time that his fears were awakened, as he could hardly doubt that the lady would acquaint her husband with his treachery. He affected to pass off his overtures as nothing more than a jocular trial of her resolutions, but secretly suffered from the torments of fear and resentment, insomuch that he was at length driven to the contemplation of a dreadful crime. The story is almost too incredible for belief, yet our authority assures us that the facts occurred as we propose to state them.

Having detained the lady in Dresden considerably beyond the day when she expected to set out, De Monge was at length compelled to allow her departure. Her escort through the partially-disturbed country in which she was to travel, was to consist of an individual who was well acquainted with the roads, and had frequently acted as a courier on the Italian frontier. Mazzuolo, as this man was called, was an Italian by birth, and gladly undertook a commission which promised him a rich harvest of booty. His bargain with the treacherous De Monge was, that if he made away with the life of Madame Louison while on the journey, and before she could communicate with her husband, he was to be at liberty to carry off all her baggage, which contained valuable articles to a large amount. The Italian only stipulated that his wife, dressed in male attire, and a lad on whom he could depend, should accompany him. Every thing being settled, the morning of departure arrived.

Adelaide had not seen her travelling companions till they arrived with the carriage, into which she was handed by Mazzuolo, with all the deference that her beauty and elegant attire might naturally command. She wore a black velvet bonnet and Chantilly veil, a crimson silk pelisse trimmed with rich furs, a boa of Russian sable; and, over all, a loose velvet pelisse, lined with fur. Mazzuolo and his wife thought that this augured well for the contents of her trunks.

The length of the journey, the dangers of the road, and the goodness or badness of the inns they should have to rest at, formed the subjects of conversation for the first hour or two. The stage was very long, and it was eleven o'clock before they reached their first relay of horses, by which time the young traveller had decided that she had great reason to be satisfied with her companions. The Italian was polite and entertaining; he had travelled a great deal, and was full of anecdote; and being naturally lively and garrulous, the design he entertained of taking away the life of his charge did not prevent his making himself agreeable to her in the meantime. With his well-seared conscience, he neither felt nervous nor saturnine at the prospect of what was before him—why should he indeed?—for the only part of the prospect he fixed his eye upon was the gain; the little operation by means of which it was to be acquired, he did not think very seriously of; besides, he did not intend to perform it himself.

When they stopped to change horses, a lad of about seventeen years of age, named Karl, nephew of Mazzuolo's wife, came to the carriage door: he seemed to have been waiting for them. Mazzuolo spoke to him aside for some minutes, and when they started again, the youth mounted in front of the carriage. The Italian said he was a lad they had engaged to look after the luggage, and be useful on the journey. He was, in fact, one who was hired to do any piece of work, good or bad. He possessed no moral strength, could be easily led by the will of his employers; in short, was a very useful ally. He had a broad, fair, stolid, German face; and from the glimpse she had of him, Adelaide thought she had seldom seen a more unprepossessing-looking person. His home had been a rude and unhappy one; his manners were coarse and unpolished, and his dress shabby.

The first day's journey passed agreeably enough. When they arrived at their night's station, Mazzuolo having handed out the ladies, bade them go up stairs and order supper, whilst he and Karl looked to the putting up of the carriage. Agostina, or Tina, as her husband commonly called her, insisted very much on having a room for Adelaide adjoining her own, alleging as her reason that they were answerable for her safety. The bride thanked her for her caution, but added, laughingly, that she did not think she had much to fear. It was some time before the two men joined them; and then they sat down to supper, the lad Karl acting as waiter. As he stood behind his aunt's chair, and exactly opposite Adelaide, he appeared much affected by her beauty; but of this, of course, the lady took no notice. When supper was over, being fatigued, she retired to her room; and then the party that remained closed the door, and bidding Karl sit down and eat his supper, they held a council on her fate.

Mazzuolo opened the conference by mentioning that he had already given the lad a hint of what was expected of him, and Tina asked him if he thought he was equal to the undertaking. Karl said he did not know; whereupon they encouraged him with promises of a handsome share of the booty, telling him also that they would stand by him, and help him if necessary. But the question was, how was the thing to be done, and where? Whether on the road by day, or in the night where they stopt? In either case there were difficulties; many parts of the road they had to pass were extremely lonely, and fit for the purpose, but then how were they to get rid of the postilion? And as they had a fresh one at every stage, there was no time to win him to their purpose. Then, at the inns, the obstacles were also considerable, especially as the houses were generally small. Tina suggested that whenever the bride dropt out of the party, she had only to resume her female attire, and the people would never miss her. 'Karl can take my place in the carriage,' she said, 'and I Madame Louison's. Thus we shall appear to be as many as we were; and there will be no discrepancy with the passport.' The hint was approved; but after an hour's discussion, they found it impossible to conclude upon any plan; the execution of their projects must be left to chance and opportunity—all they had to do was, to be prepared to seize upon the first that offered.

During the progress of this conversation, Karl made no observation whatever. He listened in silence; not without attention, but without objection, even although, in the different plans that were proposed, he heard himself always designated as the active agent in the murder. When the council broke up, the parties retired to bed—their present station being too near Dresden for their purpose. Next day they resumed their journey; and as their way lay through a gloomy forest, nothing but the presence of the postilion saved the young bride's life. The night was passed at a post-house, where there were so few rooms, that Adelaide had to sleep in the same apartment with the daughter of the owner: so here was nothing to be done either. The Italians began to grow impatient at these difficulties, and Mazzuolo proposed a change in their tactics. On the previous evening, the weather being very cold, Madame Louison had ordered a fire in her chamber. She would doubtless do the same on the ensuing night; and all they had to do was to fill the stove with charcoal, and her death would follow in the most natural way in the world. They were to pass the night at Nuremburg; and, as soon as they arrived, Karl was sent out to procure the charcoal; but, after remaining away a long time, he came back saying the shops were all shut, and he could not get any; and as the inn at Nuremburg was not a fit place for any other kind of attack, Adelaide was respited for another four-and-twenty hours.

On the following day, in order to avoid such another *contretemps*, the charcoal was secured in the morning whilst they were changing horses, and placed in a sack under the seat of the carriage.

It happened on this day that the road was very hilly, and as the horses slowly dragged the carriage up the ascents, Madame Louison proposed walking to warm themselves. They all descended; but Tina, being stout, and heavy on her feet, was soon tired, and got in again; whilst Mazzuolo, with a view to his design against Adelaide, fell into conversation with the driver about the different stations they would have to stop at. He wanted to extract all the information he could—so he walked beside the carriage, whilst Madame Louison and Karl, who were very cold, walked on as fast as they could.

'You look quite chilled, Karl,' said she; 'let us see who will be at the top of the hill first—a race will warm us.'

The youth strode on without saying anything; but as she was the more active, she got before him; and when she reached the top, she turned round, and playfully clapping her hands, said, 'Karl, I've beaten you!' Karl said he had had an illness lately, and was not so strong as he used to be; he had gone into the water when he was very warm, and had nearly died of the consequences. This led her to observe how thinly he was clad; and when the carriage overtook them, she proposed that, as there was plenty of room, he should go inside; to which the others, as they did not want him to fall ill upon their hands, consented. With the glasses up, and the furs that the party were wrapt in, the inside of the carriage was very different to the out; and Karl's nose and cheeks, which had before been blue, resumed their original hues.

It was late when they reached their night station, and, whilst the ladies went up stairs to look at their rooms, Karl received his orders, which were, that he should fill the stove with charcoal, and set fire to it, whilst the others were at table. The lad answered composedly that he would. 'And when you have done it,' said Mazzuolo, 'give me a wink, and I will step out and see that all is right before she goes to her room.'

Karl obeyed his directions to a tittle, and when all was ready, he gave the signal, and Mazzuolo, making a pretext, quitted the table. He found the arrangements quite satisfactory, and having taken care to see that the window was well closed, he returned to the supper-room. He was no sooner gone than the boy took the charcoal from the stove and threw it into the street; and when Adelaide came to undress, there was no fire. Cold as it was, however, she had no alternative but to go to bed without one, for there was not a bell in the apartment; and Mazzuolo, who had lighted her to the door, had locked her in, under pretence of caring for her safety. Karl, having watched this proceeding, accompanied him back to the supper-table, where they discussed the plans for the following day. Whether would it be better to start in the morning without inquiring for her at all, and leave the people of the house to find her dead, when they were far on the road, or whether make the discovery themselves? Karl ventured to advocate the first plan; but Tina decided for the second. It would be easy to say that the lad had put charcoal in the stove, not being aware of its effects, and there would be an end of the matter. If they left her behind, it would be avowing the murder. This settled, they went to bed.

What to do, Karl did not know. He was naturally a stupid sort of lad, and what little sense nature had given him, had been nearly beaten out of him by harsh treatment. He had had a miserable life of it, and had never found himself so comfortable as he was now with his aunt and her husband. They were kind to him, because they wanted to make use of him. He did not want to offend them, nor to leave them; for if he did, he must return home again, which he dreaded above all things. Yet there was something in him that recoiled against killing the lady. Grossly ignorant as he was, scarcely knowing right from wrong, it was not morality or religion that deterred him from the crime; he had a very imperfect idea of the amount of the wickedness he would be committing in taking away the life of a fellow-creature. Obedience was the only virtue he had been taught; and what those in authority over him had ordered him to do, he would have done without much question. To kill his beauteous travelling companion, who had shown him such kindness, was, however, repugnant to feelings he could not explain even to himself. Yet he had not sufficient grasp of intellect to know how he was to elude the performance of the task. The only thing he could think of in the meanwhile was to take the charcoal out of the stove; and he did it; after which he went to sleep, and left the results to be developed by the morning.

He had been desired to rise early; and when he quitted his room, he found Mazzuolo and his wife already stirring. They bade him go below and send up breakfast, and to be careful that it was brought by the people of the house. This was done; and when the waiter and the host were present, Tina took the opportunity of knocking at Madame Louison's door, and bidding her rise. To the great amazement of the two Italians, she answered with alacrity that she was nearly dressed, and should be with them immediately. They stared at each other; but presently she opened the door, and appeared as fresh as ever; observing, however, that she had been very cold, for that the fire had gone out before she went to bed. This accounted for the whole thing, and Karl escaped all blame.

During the ensuing day nothing remarkable occurred: fresh charcoal was provided: but at night it was found there were no stoves in the bedchambers; and as the houses on the road they were travelling were poor and ill furnished, all the good inns having been dismantled by the troops, the same thing happened at several successive stations.

This delay began to render the affair critical, for they were daily drawing near Augsburg, where M. Louison was to meet his wife; and Mazzuolo resolved to conclude the business by a *coup de main*. He had learnt from the postilion that the little post-house which was to form their next night's lodging was admirably fitted for a deed of mischief. It lay at the foot of a precipice, in a gorge of the mountains: the district was lonely, and the people rude, not likely to be very much disturbed, even if they did suspect the lady had come unfairly to her end. It was not, however, probable that the charcoal would be of any use on this occasion; the place was too poor to be well furnished with stoves; so Karl was instructed in what he would have to do. 'When she is asleep,' said Mazzuolo, 'you must give her a blow on the head that will be sufficient to stun her. Then we will complete the job; and as we shall start early in the morning with Tina in female attire, they will never miss her.' Karl, as usual, made no objection; and when they arrived at night at the inn, which fully answered the description given, and was as lonely as the worst assassins could desire, the two men sallied forth to seek a convenient place for disposing of the body. Neither had they much difficulty in finding what they wanted: there was not only a mountain torrent hard by, but there was also a deep mysterious hole in a neighbouring field, that looked very much as if the body of the young traveller would not be the first that had found a grave there.

Every circumstance seemed to favour the enterprise; and all arrangements made, the two men returned to the house. Karl thought it was all over with him now. He was too timid to oppose Mazzuolo, and he had nobody to consult. Tina had found a weapon apt for the purpose, which she had already secured; and when they sat down to supper, considering the completeness of the preparations, nobody would have thought Adelaide's life worth six hours' purchase. However, she was not destined to die that night. Just as they had finished their supper, the sound of wheels was heard; then there was a great noise and bustle below; and Karl being sent down to inquire what was the matter, was informed that a large party of travellers had arrived; and as there was a scarcity of apartments, it was hoped the lady and gentlemen would accommodate the strangers by allowing them to share theirs. Consent was inevitable; so, like the sultan's wife in the Arabian tale, the victim was allowed to live another day.

'Now,' said Mazzuolo, 'we have only two nights more before we reach Augsburg, so there must be no more shilly-shallying about the matter. If there is a stove in the room to-night, we may try that; though, if the house be in a pretty safe situation, I should prefer more decisive measures. The charcoal has failed once already.'

'That was from bad management,' said Tina; 'we could be secure against such an accident on another occasion. At the same time, if the situation be favourable, I should prefer a *coup de main*.'

When they arrived at their night's station, the absence of a stove decided the question. It was merely a post-house, a place where horses were furnished; the accommodation was poor, and the people disposed to pay little attention to them. Close by ran a river, which obviated all difficulty as to the disposal of the body.

'The thing must be done to-night,' said Mazzuolo; and Karl said nothing to the contrary. He also feared that it must; for he did not see how he could avoid it. His aunt said everything necessary to inspire him with courage and determination, and made many promises of future benefits; whilst Mazzuolo neither doubted his obedience nor his resolution, and spoke of the thing as so entirely within the range of ordinary proceedings, that the boy, stupid and ignorant, and accustomed, from the state of the country, to hear of bloodshed and murders little less atrocious committed by the soldiery, and neither punished nor severely condemned, felt ashamed of his own pusillanimity—for such his instinctive pity appeared to himself.

But as he stood opposite Madame Louison at supper, with his eyes, as usual, fixed upon her face, his heart involuntarily quailed when he thought that within a few hours he was to raise his hand against that beautiful head; yet he still felt within himself no courage to refuse, nor any fertility of expedient to elude the dilemma.

When supper was over, Tina desired Karl to bring up two or three pails of warm water, and several cloths, 'for,' said she, 'it will do us all good to bathe our feet;' whereupon Adelaide requested one might be carried to her room, which was done by Karl. He was now alone with her, and it was almost the first time he had been so, except when they ran up the hill together, since the day they met. When he had set down the pail by her bedside, he stood looking at her with a strange expression of countenance. He knew that the water he had fetched up was designed for the purpose of washing away the blood that he was about to spill, and he longed to tell her so, and set her on her guard; but he was afraid. He looked at her, looked at the water, and looked at the bed.

'Well, Karl,' she said laughing, 'good night. When we part the day after to-morrow, I shan't forget your services I assure you.' The lad's eyes still wandered from her to the water and the bed, but he said nothing, nor stirred till she repeated her 'good night,' and then he quitted the room in silence.

'Poor stupid creature!' thought Adelaide; 'he has scarcely as much intelligence as the horses that draw us.'

'Now we must have no bungling to-night, Karl,' said Mazzuolo; 'we will keep quiet till two o'clock, and then, when everybody is asleep, we'll to business.'

'But what is it to be done with?' inquired Tina.

'There's something in the carriage under the seat; I brought it away the night we slept at Baireuth,' replied Mazzuolo; 'I'll step and fetch it;' and he left the room; but presently returned, saying that there were people about the carriage, and he was afraid they might wonder what he was going to do with so suspicious-looking an instrument. 'Karl can fetch it when they are gone to bed.'

As it was yet only midnight, Tina proposed that they should all lie down and take a little rest; and the suggestion being agreed to, she and her husband stretched themselves on their bed, whilst Karl made the floor his couch, and, favoured by his unexcitable temperament, was soon asleep, in spite of what was before him.

It was past two o'clock when he felt himself shaken by the shoulder. 'Come, be stirring,' said Mazzuolo; 'we must about it without delay—the house has been quiet for some time.'

Karl was a heavy sleeper, and as he sat up rubbing his eyes, he could not at first remember what he was awakened for, nor how he came to be upon the floor. 'Come,' said Mazzuolo, 'come; she's fast asleep; I have just been to her room to look at her. You must step down now to the carriage and bring up the axe I left under the seat.'

Karl began to recollect himself, and, awkwardly rising from his hard couch, shaking and stretching himself like a dog, he prepared to obey, indifferent to everything at the moment but the annoyance of being disturbed in his slumbers. 'If you should meet anybody,' said Mazzuolo, 'say that your mistress is ill, and that you are going to fetch the medicine-chest.'

By the time he got below, the motion and the cool air had aroused the lad, and, with his recollection, revived his repugnance to the work before him; but he saw no means of avoiding it, and with an unwilling step he proceeded to the yard where the carriage stood, and having found the axe, he was returning with it, when he observed hanging against the wall a large horn or trumpet. Now, he had seen such a thing at several of the post-houses on the road, and he remembered to have heard one sounded on the night they slept in the mountains, when the travellers arrived late, and prevented the projected assassination. Instinctively, and without pausing to reflect how he should excuse himself—for if he had, he could not have done it—he placed the instrument to his mouth, and lustily blew it; and then, terrified at his temerity, and its probable consequences, rushed into the house, and up the stairs again to his master.

'The travellers' horn!' said Mazzuolo frantically. The lad was too frightened to speak, but stood still, pale and trembling. 'Wait,' continued the Italian; 'perhaps it may only be for horses, and they may go on again. I hear the people stirring.'

Feet were indeed heard upon the stairs, and presently a lantern gleamed beneath the window. 'I hear no carriage,' observed Mazzuolo. And for some time they sat listening; but there being no appearance of any travellers, he said he would go below and see how matters stood.

'Nobody is yet arrived,' said the master of the post-house in answer to his inquiries; 'but doubtless the signal was given by the avant courier, who has rode on to the next station; and the carriage will be here presently. We must be ready with the horses.'

As the travellers, however, did not arrive, but continued to be expected, the postmaster and the postilions remained up to watch for them; and when four o'clock came, Karl was bidden go to bed, as nothing could be attempted under such circumstances.

'Now,' said Mazzuolo on the following day, 'we sleep to-night at Meitingen, which is our last station. I know the place; it is too busy a house for a *coup de main*; we must try the charcoal again; but this time we must be sure of our game.'

Karl hoped there might be no stoves in the bed-chamber; but it was a well-furnished house, and there were. Adelaide said how glad she should be to have a fire again, she had suffered so much by the want of one, and desired Karl to light hers early. It appeared, however, that the servant of the house had already done it. Mazzuolo said 'So much the better. The stove will get well heated, and when you put in the charcoal, there will be no danger of its not burning.' And Tina suggested that that should not be done till just before Adelaide went to bed, lest she should perceive the effects of the vapour whilst she was undressing.

The young traveller had never, on her journey, been in such high spirits as to-night. Well she might; it had been so prosperously performed, and to-morrow she was to meet her husband. She prattled and laughed during supper with a light heart; expressed her gratitude to the Italians for their escort; and said that, if Monsieur Louison could be of any use to them, she knew how happy he would be to acknowledge their kindness to her. 'Really,' she said, 'travelling at such a period, with so many valuables, and such a large sum of money as I have with me, was a bold undertaking!'

Mazzuolo, during the first part of her speech, was beginning to weigh the advantages of the commissary's favour against the dangers and difficulties of the assassination—difficulties which had far exceeded his expectations, and dangers which were of course augmented by the proximity to Augsburg—but the latter part of it decided the question; the money and valuables preponderated in the scale, and the good opinion of the commissary kicked the beam.

Partly from the exaltation of her spirits, and partly because the day's journey had been a short one—for the stoppage at Meitingen was quite unnecessary—they were within four hours of Augsburg, and might very well have reached it—Adelaide was less fatigued and less willing to go to bed than usual. She sat late; and it was past twelve when, having asked for her candle, Karl received the signal to go and prepare the stove. Mazzuolo followed him out, to see that the work was well done, and the charcoal ignited before she went to her room. When all was ready, her candle was put into her hand, and Mazzuolo having conducted her to the door, took the precaution of turning the key, which he afterwards put in his pocket. She rallied him on the strictness of his guardianship; but he alleged gravely that the house was a busy one, and she might perchance be disturbed if her door were not secured.

They listened till she was in bed, and then Mazzuolo said that they could not do better than go to bed too; 'for,' said he, 'the earlier we are off in the morning the better. There will be the fewer people up, and the less chance of her being missed.'

When Karl reached his room, he sat down on the side of his bed and reflected. He had observed that the last thing Mazzuolo had done before leaving Adelaide's chamber, was to see that the window was well closed. 'If I could open it,' thought he, 'to-morrow we shall be at Augsburg, and then I should not be told any more to kill her. I wish I could. They'll go away in the morning before she is awake, and so I should never be found out.' With this idea in his head, he went down stairs, and letting himself out, he crept round to the end of the house where her window was.

She slept on the first floor, and the difficulty was how to reach it; but this was soon overcome. In the stable-yard stood some high steps, used for the convenience of passengers when they mounted the wagons and diligences. These he carried to the spot, and having reached the window, he was about to break some of the panes, since, as it fastened on the inside, he could not open it, when it occurred to him that the noise might wake her, and cause an alarm that would betray him. The window, however, was in the lattice fashion, and he saw that, by a little contrivance, he could lift it off the hinges. He did so, and drew aside the curtain; there lay the intended victim in a sound sleep; so sound, that Karl thought he might safely step in without disturbing her. There she lay in her beauty.

He could not tell why, but, as he stood and looked at her, he felt that he *must* save her at all risks. The air he had let in might not be enough; he would take the charcoal from the stove and throw it out of the window; but what if she awoke with the noise, and screamed? He hesitated a moment; but he remembered that this would be a safer plan than leaving the window open, as that might be observed in the morning from below, and he would thus be betrayed. So, as quietly as possible, he emptied the stove, and then, having sufficiently aired the room, he hung on the window again, and retired.

During the whole of these operations Adelaide had remained quite still, and appeared to be sound asleep. But was she? No. The opening of the window had awakened her: surprise and terror had at first kept her silent—a surprise and terror that were by no means diminished by discovering who the intruder was. Although she had always spoken kindly to Karl, and even endeavoured, by the amenity of her manner, to soften his rude nature, she had from the first moment disliked him exceedingly, and felt his countenance most repulsive; so that when she saw him entering her room through the window, she did not doubt that he was come for some very bad purpose, probably to rob her, although the booty he was likely to get was small, since her trunks, with all her valuable property, were nightly placed under Mazzuolo's care for safety. Still, the little money she carried in her purse, together with her rings and watch, would be a great deal to so poor a creature; and expecting to see him possess himself of these, she thought it more prudent to lie still, and feign sleep, than to disturb him. But when she saw that all he came for was to take the fire out of the stove, she was beyond measure puzzled to conceive his motive. Could it be a jest? But what a strange jest! However, he did nothing else; he touched neither her money nor her watch, though both were lying on the table, but went away as empty-handed as he came.

The amazement and alarm that so extraordinary a visit necessarily inspired, drove sleep from her eyes, and it was not till the day dawned that she so far recovered her composure and sense of safety, as to close them in slumber. Then, however, fatigue got the better of her watchfulness, and she gradually sunk into a sound sleep.

In the meantime Karl, whose unexcitable temperament insured him his night's rest even under the most agitating circumstances, was in a happy state of oblivion of the whole affair, when he felt himself shaken by the shoulder, and heard his uncle say, 'Come, come, rise, and make haste! The sun is up, and we must get the horses out and be off.'

Karl was as anxious to be off as anybody: the sooner the better for him; for if Adelaide should awake before they started, he, on the one hand, dreaded that he might incur his uncle's suspicion, and, on the other, that some new plot might be formed, which it would be impossible for him to evade; so, between the exertions of one and the other, the horses were out, the bill paid, and the carriage at the door, very soon after the sun had shown his broad disc above the horizon. Tina, in female attire and a veil, was handed down stairs by Mazzuolo; the waiter stood on the steps and bowed, for the landlord was not yet up; they all three stepped into the carriage; the postillion cracked his whip, and away they drove, rejoicing.

In the meantime, Monsieur Louison had become very uneasy about his wife. He had received no intelligence since she quitted Dresden; for although she had in fact written more than once, Mazzuolo had not forwarded the letters. Day after day he had waited in impatient expectation; till at length, unable to bear his suspense any longer, he resolved to start on the road she was to come, in the hope of meeting her. When he reached the gate called the Gözzinger, his carriage was stopped by a berlin containing two men and a woman. It was loaded with luggage; and thinking that this might be the party he expected, he jumped down, and put his head into the window of the berlin, to ascertain if his wife were there. She was not: so, with a bow and an apology, he proceeded on his way. At Meitingen he stopped to change horses; and the first question that was asked him was, if he had seen a heavily-laden berlin, containing two men and a woman. On answering in the affirmative, he was informed that they had gone off with the property of a lady, whom they had left behind, and who was then in the inn; and in a moment more the young husband pressed his bride to his heart. But, eager to chase the thieves, they wasted no time in embraces, but started instantly in pursuit of them. On reaching the same gate where the berlin had been seen, the officers described in what direction the party had driven; and the police being immediately on the alert, the criminals were discovered and arrested just as they were on the point of starting for Vienna.

The ample confession of Karl disclosed the villany of the Italians, and made known how narrowly the commissary had escaped the loss of his fair young bride; whilst, as he told his rude and simple tale, without claiming any merit, or appearing to be conscious of any, Adelaide learnt that to this repulsive stupid clown she had three times owed her life.

The Italians were condemned to the galleys; whilst Monsieur Louison and his wife discharged their debt of gratitude to Karl, by first educating him, and then furnishing him with the means of earning his living with respectability and comfort.

De Monge was degraded from his situation, and the universal execration that pursued him drove him ultimately to America, where, under a feigned name, he ended his days in obscurity.

LEGENDS OF THE ISLES, &c.*

This is the third volume of poetry which Mr Charles Mackay has given to the world within the last five years. He evidently writes from fulness of heart, happy in his high and pure vocation; and he is, moreover, convinced, as he tells his readers, 'that poetry, and the love of poetry, are not necessarily extinguished by the progress of railroads, as all the smatterers have taken delight in affirming.' The true spirit of poetry can never become extinct among a people, though poetry, as an art, has its seasons of exaltation and depression. Nature rarely produces genius of a high order, and the direction which genius takes must also, to a considerable extent, be regulated by the prevailing national taste. This is the case both in literature and in art. The drama, for example, which, in the reigns of Elizabeth and James, attracted the brightest and most imaginative spirits of the age, would scarcely now be selected by a youthful aspirant; and the poetry of manners or artificial life, blended with personal satire, would not at present be relished so keenly, or so eagerly pursued, as in the days of Dryden, Swift, and Pope, and their immediate successors. The fact is, we have *advanced* since those times. We have thrown off some stiff conventional rules, and have gained in the appreciation, if not in the production, of great and original works of genius. Thomson, Cowper, and Burns, elevated the public taste and feeling by drawing them nearer to nature, and to the genuine fountains of inspiration—the ever-living passions of mankind, and the beauties or sublimities of creation; and hence the great masters—Chaucer, Shakspeare, Milton, and others—have attained to a new and a wider empire over the public mind. The works of Scott and Byron kindled a passion for animated and romantic poetry, which still survives, especially among the young; but the very extent of their popularity, and of the excitement which their works produced, led to a reaction after their death, which for a time seemed to throw poetry into the shade. Then we had the succeeding marvels and occurrences of actual life—the triumphs of steam on sea and land—inventions of all kinds—travellers into every country—and the increased study of the exact and physical sciences. Men were animated with high and lofty aims. The love of truth led to philosophical and historical inquiries far deeper and more profound than were deemed necessary a century ago—criticism became more searching and universal in its sympathies and judgments—the depths of humanity were sounded—and the pursuit of moral and political amelioration vastly extended. The vocation of the poet was thus in some measure subordinated to other studies and designs; but the spirit of the 'divine art' was still undiminished. Poetry had retired into her strongholds, but had not lost an inch of her territories, nor an iota of her power. Countless editions of the old poets were called for by the poor as well as the rich; and in spite of adverse criticism from high places, the writings of Wordsworth, Coleridge, Keats, &c. worked their way into popular favour. If we have had few poets since the death of Byron, we have had more readers of poetry than ever were before. All booksellers' and publishers' catalogues show this result: all experience tells us that the progress of mechanics has certainly not extinguished the love of song.

Among the few who have cultivated poetry of late years with perseverance and success, is the author before us. His first volume, 'The Hope of the World,' &c. contained some excellent didactic verse, in that 'simple, natural, and enduring school of poetry which has produced such writers as Pope, Goldsmith, Rogers, and Campbell.' In his second volume, entitled 'The Salamandrine, or Love and Immortality,' Mr Mackay departed in some degree from the models of his early taste, and copied rather the style of Shelley and Coleridge. His poem is founded upon a passage in the Rosicrucian romance of the Count de Gabalis, by the Abbe de Villars, to which we are partly indebted for the Rape of the Lock and the story of Undine—the primary idea being the efforts made by a lovely elemental spirit to gain an immortal soul by means of love. The Salamandrine is a very charming poem, written with great sweetness of versification, and a fine flow of fancy and imagery. Even the want of human interest, which such a subject would seem to imply, is scarcely felt by the reader, owing to the variety of incidents and situations through which the author conducts his heroine, and the number of fine sentiments and descriptions with which the poem abounds. The diction is also pure and simple, without descending to the prosaic, or swelling into extravagance.

This third publication of Mr Mackay's is of a miscellaneous character. His 'Legends of the Isles' occupy rather more than a third of the volume, and embrace some of those striking superstitions and wild beliefs which still linger among the rocky shores and caves of the Hebrides. The first of these, 'The Sea-King's Burial,' is the most powerful. It is founded on the fact, or tradition, mentioned by Carlyle in his Hero Worship, that the old Norse kings, when about to die, had their body laid in a ship; the ship sent forth with sails set, and slow fire burning in it; that, once out at sea, it might blaze up in flame, 'and in such manner bury worthily the old hero, at once in the sky and in the ocean.' Mr Mackay has treated this poetical and romantic subject with great felicity. His versification, and some of his lines, remind us of Campbell's Battle of the Baltic; but there is an original force and freedom in his style, and a power of picturesque painting in his sketch of the old sea-king, the fatal vessel, and the solitary conflagration, that have rarely been surpassed. He has heightened the effect of his strange and appalling death-scene by representing the ship as overtaken by a heavy storm, in the midst of which the fire bursts out from below, flinging a lurid radiance on the sky and waters, but without depressing the courage or resolution of the stern old savage Vikinger.

'Once alone a cry arose,
Half of anguish, half of pride,
As he sprang upon his feet
With the flames on every side.
"I am coming," said the king,
"Where the swords and bucklers ring—
Where the warrior lives again
With the souls of mighty men—
Where the weary find repose,
And the red wine ever flows;
I am coming, great All-father,
Unto thee!
Unto Odin, unto Thor,
And the strong true hearts of yore—
I am coming to Valhalla,
O'er the sea."

* Legends of the Isles and other Poems, by Charles Mackay, author of the 'Salamandrine,' the 'Hope of the World,' &c. Edinburgh: Blackwood and Sons.

Red and fierce upon the sky
Until midnight shone the glare,
And the burning ship drove on
Like a meteor of the air.
She was driven and hurried past,
'Mid the roaring of the blast;
And of Balder, warrior born,
Nought remained at break of morn,
On the charred and blackened hull,
But some ashes and a skull;
And still the vessel drifted
Heavily,
With a pale and hazy light,
Until far into the night,
When the storm had spent its rage
On the sea.'

Another of these poetical legends embodies the tradition (consecrated by some beautiful lines in the 'Pleasures of Hope') that St Columba once, or oftener, every year is seen on the top of Iona cathedral counting the surrounding islands, to see that they have not been sunk by witchcraft. Mr Mackay invests the Celtic tradition with some poetical accessaries. He describes the tutelar saint of the holy island as sailing to Iona in a boat, without sail or oar, and, on his landing, being met on the beach by a 'pale and shadowy band,' uncovered, and each holding a taper. They proceed in silence to the church, which is lighted up as for a festival, and, after solemn music, the saint ascends the altar, while the ghostly company of kings and thanes, monks and jarls, kneel around—

'He craved a blessing on the Isles,
And named them, one by one—
Fair western isles that love the glow
Of the departing sun.
From Arran looming in the south,
To northern Orcades,
Then to Iona back again,
Through all those perilous seas,
Three nights and days the saint had sailed
To count the Hebrides.'

We are not certain that this group of ghastly personages, assembled in the church, like the uncoffined spectres in Alloway Kirk, is so striking as the common conception of the saint standing alone, a giant form, on the ruined walls of the towering cathedral, 'conversing with the storm,' and numbering the islands of the ocean. Our author, however, has thrown a veil of romance and superstitious awe over the solitary voyage of Columbus, and has depicted the saint in a strain of great tenderness and solemnity. Our limits will not permit us to describe all these legends in detail. 'The Witch of Skerrievore' is a rapid and animated sketch; 'The Dance of Ballochroy,' a more luxurious and impassioned strain; and 'The Invasion of the Norsemen' is imbued with the rough energetic spirit and picturesqueness of the old ballad style. Independently of the poetry in these pieces, there is a charm in the scenery and objects with which they are connected. They recall the exquisite and sublime aspects of nature in our western islands, which may well challenge comparison with the rock scenery of Switzerland or the Rhine; while they are consecrated in the minds of our countrymen by many national and patriotic associations. The rude towers of Ordtornish, and the ruined walls of Dunstaffnage, beetling over the stormy sea, impart to the grand and solitary landscape a far deeper interest than can ever attach to the mere rock, sky, and water. Nor is the magic halo of genius awanting. Scott and Wordsworth sailed among these scenes, and pictured them in verse, while Campbell spent several of his early and happy years amidst the wild cliffs and ocean music of the Hebrides.

The second part of Mr Mackay's volume consists of 'Songs and Poems.' Some of these have already appeared in print; and two of the songs—'The Founding of the Bell,' and 'Tubal Cain'—have been set to music, and enjoy considerable popularity. Indeed we do not know that finer specimens of elevated lyrical poetry have appeared since Campbell produced his inimitable war odes. They are highly original in conception, and have an easy strength and felicity of expression and sentiment, that are seldom seen in modern poetry. Of the same elevated cast, but totally different in subject and versification, is a classical poem, 'The Death of Pan,' which we are tempted to subjoin entire. It is not unworthy of being ranked with the magnificent Hyperion of Keats.

THE DEATH OF PAN.

[In the reign of Tiberius, an extraordinary voice was heard near the Echinades, in the Ægean Sea, which exclaimed, 'Great Pan is dead!'—PLUTARCH.]

Behold the vision of the death of Pan.
I saw a shadow on the mountain side,
As of a Titan wandering on the cliffs;
Godlike his stature, but his head was bent
Upon his breast, in agony of wo;
And a voice rose upon the wintry wind,
Wailing and moaning—'Weep, ye nations, weep!
Great Pan is dying:—mourn me, and lament!
My steps shall echo on the hills no more;
Dumb are mine oracles—my fires are quenched,
My doom is spoken, and I die—I die!'

The full moon shone upon the heaving sea,
And in the light, with tresses all unbound,
Their loose robes dripping, and with eyes downcast,
The nymphs arose, a pallid multitude;
Lovely but most forlorn, and thus they sang,
With voice of sorrow—'Never, never more,
In these cool waters shall we lave our limbs;
Never, oh never more! in sportive dance
Upon these crested billows shall we play;
Nor at the call of prayer-o'erburdened men
Appear in answer; for our hour is come;
Great Pan has fallen, and we die! we die!'

Emerging slowly from the trackless woods,
And from the umbrageous caverns of the hills,
Their long hair floating on the rough cold winds;
Their faces pale; their eyes suffused with tears;
The Dryads and the Oreads made their moan:
'Never, oh never more!' distraught they cried,
'Upon the mossy banks of these green woods,
Shall we make music all the summer's day;
Never again at morn, or noon, or night,
Upon the flowery sward, by fount or stream,
Shall our light footsteps mingle in the dance;
Never again, discoursing from the leaves
And twisted branches of these sacred oaks,
Shall we make answer at a mortal's call!
Our hour is come, our fire of life is quenched;
Our voices fade; our oracles are mute;
Behold our agony; we die! we die!'
And as they sang, their unsubstantial forms
Grew pale and lineless, and dispersed in air;
While from the innermost and darkest nooks,
Deepest embowered amid those woods antique,
A voice most mournful echoed back their plaint,
And cried—'Oh, misery! they die! they die!'

Then passed a shadow on the moon's pale disc;
And to the dust, in ecstacy of awe,
I bent adoring. On the mountain-tops
Thick darkness crept, and silence deep as death's
Pervaded Nature. The wind sank—the leaves
Forbore to flutter on the bending boughs,
And breathing things were motionless as stones,
As earth, revolving on her mighty wheel,
Eclipsed in utter dark the lamp of Heaven;
And a loud voice, amid that gloom sublime,
Was heard from shore to sea, from sea to shore,
Startling the nations at the unwonted sound,
And swelling on the ear of mariners
Far tossing on their solitary barks,
A month's long voyage from the nearest land—
'Great Pan has fallen, for ever, evermore!'

The shadow passed, light broke upon the world;
And Nature smiled rejoicing in the beam
Of a new morning blushing from the east;
And sounds of music seemed to fill the air,
And angel voices to exclaim on high,
'Great Pan has fallen! and never more his creed
Shall chain the free intelligence of man.
The Christ is born, to purify the earth,
To raise the lowly, to make rich the poor,
To teach a faith of charity and love.
Rejoice! rejoice! an error has expired;
And the new Truth shall reign for evermore!'

There are two apologues, and several lines and allusions in Mr Mackay's volume, designed to encourage poets who sing in solitude, and to inculcate on them a love and reverence of their art, 'heedless of the world's applause.' One of these fabulous songsters tries in vain to be heard amidst the smoke and noise of a great city, where all are too much absorbed in business or pleasure to listen to his melodies.

'The other nightingale, more wise than he,
With fuller voice and music more divine,
Stayed in the woods, and sang but when inspired
By the sweet breathing of the midnight wind—
By the mysterious twinkling of the stars—
By adoration of the Great Supreme—
By beauty in all hues and forms around—
By Love and Hope, and Gratitude and Joy:
And thus inspired, the atmosphere was rife
With the prolonged sweet music that he made.
He sought no listeners—heedless of applause—
But sang, as the stars shone from inward light,
A blessing to himself, and all who heard.
The cotter, wending weary to his home,
Lingered full oft to listen to his song,
And felt 'twas beautiful, and blessed the strain:
And lonely students, wandering in the woods,
Loved nature more because this bird had sung.'

This intellectual purity of thought and purpose, and calm self-reliance, must ever characterise high genius. At the same time, it matters not where the 'full voice' and 'divine music' be uttered. Most of our great poets have lived in cities, and partaken largely of the stir and business of the world. We would interpret our author as seeking only to inspire a pure and independent love of poetry, without sordid aims or servile devotion to public taste or criticism—as Scott threw off his tales of chivalry, or Byron his Oriental romances, or Wordsworth his philosophic and contemplative prelections, without any immediate prototype or copy. All are different, yet each is original. Scott, amidst law and society, was as devoted to literature as Wordsworth amidst his lakes and mountains; nor was Milton less a poet because he was Latin secretary to the commonwealth, and lived in London. The 'power and faculty divine' may subsist, and be felt equally in the populous city and the desert solitude; for poetry, like religion, has its shrine in the human heart, and like it also, it is its own exceeding great reward. Among the worshippers at this shrine, free from all alloy of selfishness, and animated by a true and hopeful spirit, we may well include Mr Charles Mackay. He has done much, and promises more. We should wish to see him exercise a more rigid scrutiny over his lines—to aim more at condensation and severe correctness of measure; and to lop off relentlessly every prosaic and halting couplet. With this subordinate labour, there is scarcely any degree of power or fame that he may not anticipate. He has great fluency and fancy, warm and strong affections, and that fine delicacy and depth of moral feeling which, like sunshine on a landscape, lightens up and sheds beauty on all around.

CURIOSITIES OF LITERATURE.

NO. IV.

OLDYS states that two hundred authors had written in praise of Sir Philip Sidney, who trod, says an eloquent writer, 'from his cradle to his grave, amid incense and flowers, and died in a dream of glory.' The Stella of his poetry, the Philocles of his Arcadia, was the Lady Penelope Devereux, sister of the Earl of Essex, whose rash conduct was tyrannically punished. She was his destined bride from childhood, but for some unknown reason their parents broke off the match, and it was never renewed. She is described as being a woman of surpassing beauty and of commanding figure. She was twice married, but her after-life was full of wretchedness. As for him who, if events had taken their natural course, would have been her husband—

Immortal Sidney, glory of the field,
And glory of the muses—

he, it is well known, perished in his thirty-third year at the battle of Zutphen, 1586. His sonnets formed the favourite reading of Charles Lamb; and it is delightful to hear that writer, whose works have the true smack of originality about them, resound their praises. 'The general beauty of them is, that they are so perfectly characteristical. The spirit of learning and chivalry, of which union Spenser has entitled Sidney to have been the president, shines through them. They are not rich in words only—in vague and unlocalised feelings—the failing too much of the poetry of the present day; they are full, material, and circumstantiated. Time and place appropriate every one of them. It is not a fever of passion wasting itself upon a thin diet of dainty words, but a transcendent passion, pervading and illuminating action, pursuits, studies, feats of arms, the opinions of contemporaries, and his judgment of them.' We believe it was Campbell who said that Sidney's life was poetry put into action.

Dr Donne is one of that race of writers whom Johnson styles metaphysical. Conceits, a forced combination of dissimilar things, a profusion of unsuitable allusions and comparisons, disfigure their pages to an intolerable degree. Donne's versification is extremely rugged, exhibiting an unusual defect of ear; which arose, it is said, from the sound of his own name, John Donne, injuring its sense of euphony from his earliest days. Pope gave a new version of his satires, and called it a translation. Donne's character was not less eccentric than his verses. When secretary to Lord Elsinore, he privately married that nobleman's niece. His father-in-law was so much enraged, that he threw Donne into prison, and took his wife from him. Towards the close of his life, as he was recovering from a severe attack of illness, he caused himself to be enveloped in a winding-sheet like a corpse. He then sent for a painter, and shutting his eyes, ordered his portrait to be taken. The picture hung by his bedside until the close of his life. His biography is given by Isaac Walton in a volume which Wordsworth enthusiastically says was written by a pen made from a feather that dropped from an angel's wing.

The name of the author of 'Peter Wilkins,' a well-known fiction, was not discovered until very lately. By some persons the work was attributed to Bishop Berkeley, the metaphysician who, according to Pope, was possessed of every virtue under heaven. At a recent sale of manuscripts, the assignment of the copyright from R. Paltock to Dodsley, for ten guineas, was disposed of. 'It is a work of great genius,' says the late poet-laureate; 'and I know that both Sir Walter Scott and Mr Coleridge thought as highly of it as I do. His winged creatures are the most beautiful creatures of imagination ever devised.'

In consequence of some remarks in a periodical publication, we were induced to look once more at the poems of the courtly Waller, who has the reputation of being a great improver of the language, and one of our most polished versifiers. Undoubtedly the harmony of his numbers was a considerable advance before the majority of his predecessors, but his verse, upon the whole, is far inferior to the strength of Dryden and the brilliancy of Pope. Like all the writers of that age, with one illustrious exception, he is full of conceits. His fancy was less fantastic and agile than Cowley's, but he excelled that poet in the diffusion of colouring through his verses, and in rhythmical melody. The best of his smaller pieces, in our opinion, are the lines addressed to Lady Lucy Sidney, and the epitaph on the only son of Lord Andover. So tender a feeling pervades them, that we cannot but wish he had written more in the same style; and yet Campbell has neither given these in his Specimens, nor others which rank amongst Waller's most successful efforts. There are some lines in his poem on Divine Poesy, suggested by a copy of verses written by Mrs Wharton, wife of the notorious marquis, which are of admirable rhythm, and quite equal to anything in Pope—

'The church triumphant, and the church below,
In songs of praise their present union show.
Their joys are full; *our* expectation long;
In life we differ, but we join in song.
Angels and we, assisted by this art,
May sing together, though we dwell apart.'

Waller's verse dealt too much in mere prettinesses to earn an enduring reputation; and 'compositions merely pretty,' says Dr Johnson, 'have the fate of other pretty things, and are quitted in time for something useful; they are flowers, fragrant and fair, but of short duration; or they are blossoms, to be valued only as they foretell fruits.' He was too much of the fine gentleman to be sincere; and indeed lived so much with the great, that telling truth would have been something more than a foible. He joined the crowd of adulators who tendered their congratulations in rhyme to Charles II. upon his majesty's 'happy return.' Upon that occasion Waller said—

'We have you now, with ruling wisdom fraught—
Not such as books, but such as practice taught.'

Nothing could be more untrue than this couplet, for neither the monarch nor the man had profited by the bitter lessons of the past. He exhibited an example of a class of persons to whom the schoolmistress Experience cruelly administers chastisement without teaching. 'One has little merit,' says Gray to his friend West, 'in learning the lessons of experience, for one cannot well help it; but they are more useful than others, and imprint themselves in the very heart.' Even this little merit did not belong to Charles. In glancing over Waller's pages, two coincidences with a greater poet were obvious. The passages in Paradise Lost and Il Penseroso, to which the following lines bear a strong resemblance, are too well known to be more particularly indicated:—

'As a church window thick with paint,
Lets in a light but dim and faint,
So we the Arabian coast do know
At distance, when the spices blow;
By the rich odours taught to steer,
Though neither day nor stars appear.'

It is always an interesting employment to track the reading of great writers through the fields of literature, and to discover the places where they met with a thought which they took the trouble to carry home. Few poets were so entirely original as Burns; he sung for the most part from the impulses of his own spirit, and struck out a path too peculiarly his own to derive much light from others. But with respect to the passages we are about to place before the reader, there seems reason to believe that, if the thoughts were not deliberately copied by the Scottish bard, their sound was yet lingering in his ear when he wrote the lines we subjoin:—

'The rank is but the guinea's stamp,
The man's the gowd for a' that.'

'Honour, like impressions upon coin, may give an ideal and local value to a bit of base metal; but gold and silver will pass all the world over without any other recommendation than their own weight.'—*Tristram Shandy.*

'All hail, ye tender feelings dear;
The smile of love, the friendly tear,
The sympathetic glow:
Long since, this world's thorny ways
Had numbered out my weary days,
Had it not been for you!'

'Sweet pliability of man's spirit, that can at once surrender itself to illusions which cheat expectation and sorrow of their weary moments. Long, long since had I numbered out my days, had I not trod so great a part of them on this enchanted ground: when my way is too rough for my feet, or too steep for my strength, I get off it to some velvet path, which fancy has scattered over with rosebuds of delight, and having taken a few turns on it, come back strengthened and refreshed.'—*Sentimental Journey.*

'Auld Nature swears, the lovely dears,
Her noblest work she classes, O!
Her prentice han' she tried on man,
And then she made the lasses, O!'

'Oh women, since we were made before ye, should we not admire ye as the last and perfectest work of nature? Man was made when nature was but an apprentice, but woman when she was a skilful mistress of her art.'—*Cupid's Whirligig, an old drama.*

'But pleasures are like poppies spread,
You seize the flower, its bloom is shed;
Or like the snowfall in the river,
A moment white—then melts for ever.'

'Joy graven in sense, like snow in water, wastes;
Without preserve in virtue nothing lasts.'
—*Marlowe's Hero and Leander.*

What an interesting chapter might be written upon the relics of great men, but here we can only mention a few in a paragraph as they occur to us at the moment. The houses where Ariosto, Rubens, Beethoven, and Goethe were born, are pointed out with pride at Reggio, Cologne, Bonn, and Frankfort. The chair in which Petrarch died is shown, with other memorials of the poet, at Arquà. The house where Boccaccio lived is preserved at Certaldo; and the houses of Voltaire, Madame de Staël, and Gibbon, are visited by every tourist to the Lake of Geneva. Dr Johnson's watch, teapot, and punch-bowl, are reverently preserved by their owners from crack or flaw. Rubens' chair is kept in a glass case in the Antwerp Gallery. Sir David Wilkie's palette may be seen under a glass by the side of his statue in the National Gallery. The mast of Nelson's ship, the Victory, penetrated by a cannon ball, is at Windsor. Sir Walter Scott's body-clothes are shown at that 'romance in stone and lime,' Abbotsford. The ink-stands of Ariosto and Gray are in safe keeping. The bedstead of George Fox, the proto-Quaker, carved with his initials, may be seen by the inquisitive traveller at Swart Moor, in Lancashire. The cradle of Henri Quatre is in the castle of Pau, at the foot of the Pyrenees. Cups carved out of the mulberry tree planted by Shakspeare are treasured by admirers of the bard. Some autograph letters of Petrarch are in the possession of Lord Holland. Of the five known autographs of Shakspeare, the three which have come into the market of late years have commanded astonishingly high prices. One is in the British Museum, one in the City of London Library, and the others, excepting the will at Doctors Commons, are in the hands of private individuals.

There are instances of authors who have distrusted their native language as a means of expressing their thoughts, either because they fancied it intrinsically mean, or because they apprehended its longevity would not equal that of their fame. Petrarch thought slightingly of his sonnets and amatory pieces—for which alone 'the bones of Laura's lover' have been canonised—and rested his hopes of being transmitted to posterity upon a Latin epic that celebrated the exploits of Scipio in the second Punic war. Walter Savage Landor, the author of Gebir, almost avows that he has adopted the Latin tongue on several occasions, 'in order to secure,' says a critic, 'an imperishable name when the English shall be forgotten, so that when the planks of the British vessel fail him, he may step on the terra firma of the imperial literature of Rome.' Byron used to say that his greatest poem should be written in Italian, but that ten years' previous study would be required. It is not often that modern languages have been acquired with sufficient accuracy to justify a foreigner in the use of them for compositions meant to live. Gibbon, through an early residence abroad, wrote French with as much ease as English, and several of his writings preceding the History were composed in the former tongue; his English works are deeply tinctured with Gallic idioms in consequence. That wild fever-dream, Vathek, was originally written in French, at one sitting; and Mr Hope wrote Anastasius in the same language before it appeared in English. Mr Townley translated Hudibras into French.

PLOUGHING NEAR SOLERNO.

The fields being without fences, have an open look; and the mingling of men and women together in their cultivation, gives them a chequered appearance, and renders them very picturesque. In the middle of a large green wheat field would be a group of men and women weeding the grain; the red petticoats and the blue spencers of the latter contrasting beautifully with the colour of the fields. In one plot of ground I saw a team and a mode of ploughing quite unique, yet withal very simple. The earth was soft, as if already broken up, and needed only a little mellowing; to effect this, a man had harnessed his wife to a plough, which she dragged to and fro with all the patience of an ox, he in the meantime holding it behind, as if he had been accustomed to drive, and she to go. She, with a strap around her breast, leaning gently forward, and he bowed over the plough behind, presented a most curious picture in the middle of a field. The plough here is a very simple instrument, having but one handle, and no share, but in its place a pointed piece of wood, sometimes shod with iron, projecting forward like a spear; and merely passes through the ground like a sharp-pointed stick, without turning a smooth furrow like our own.—*Headly's Letters from Italy.*

SOCIAL FEELINGS.

The social feelings have not been unaptly compared to a heap of embers, which, when separated, soon languish, darken, and expire; but, placed together, they glow with a ruddy and intense heat.—*Private Life.*

Published by W. and R. Chambers, High Street, Edinburgh (also 98, Miller Street, Glasgow); and, with their permission, by W. S. Orr, Amen Corner, London.—Printed by Bradbury and Evans, Whitefriars, London.

CONDUCTED BY WILLIAM AND ROBERT CHAMBERS, EDITORS OF 'CHAMBERS'S INFORMATION FOR THE PEOPLE,' 'CHAMBERS'S EDUCATIONAL COURSE,' &c.

No. 94. New Series. SATURDAY, OCTOBER 18, 1845. Price 1½d.

CLUB-LIFE.

The least observant stranger, whose track lies in the western portion of London, cannot choose but stop to admire the cluster of mansions which have been reared in and near Pall-Mall. Whatever his taste, he must indeed be fastidious if he do not find it gratified in one or other of these edifices; for they exhibit every order of architecture, from the severest Doric to the most florid Composite. Until informed what they really are, he would be pardoned for mistaking one for a restored Grecian temple, another for a modern Italian palace. Inquiry, however, would convince him that nothing classical belongs to them, except their exteriors, and, in one or two instances, their names. On the contrary, they are devoted to the unclassical and every-day purposes of eating, drinking, lounging, and reading newspapers. They are simply domestic club-houses; numbering twenty-two. Nor are these economical and convenient institutions monopolised by the metropolis; for there is now a club-house in every principal town in the three kingdoms. In Manchester there are two, in Dublin four, in Edinburgh three.

Clubs may be generally described as houses combining the characters of restaurants and reading-rooms, for the use of a select number of associated persons, who agree to make an annual payment for their support, whether they resort to them little or much, and pay besides for whatever refreshment they may require, at a cost free of profit. Originating within the present century, and concentrating a large proportion of the men of fortune, station, and political note in the metropolis, clubs may be divided into three classes: first, those consisting of members following similar pursuits, such as the United Service and the literary clubs; secondly, those whose members hold a particular set of political opinions; thirdly, those claiming no speciality, and known as miscellaneous clubs. These establishments have had a striking effect upon the manners, not only, we would say, of the departments of society from which their members are drawn, but upon society in general; and the change has been decidedly for the better. In the first place, they have brought economy into fashion. In the old time, associations were formed for the purpose of spending money, in a manner which did but little good either to the receiver or disburser. Drinking clubs, for wasting money and health; four-in-hand clubs, which cost each member some five or six hundred a-year to adopt the habits and manners of a stage-coachman, together with similarly senseless associations, had the effect of encouraging reckless extravagance, accompanied with certain collateral irregularities, which caused the picture of English society, as presented towards the end of the last and beginning of the present century, to be the reverse of a bright one.

The main object of modern clubs is directly the reverse. They were set on foot for the purpose of supplying to their members the necessaries of life at the lowest possible rate. They are, it is admitted, furnished and conducted on a scale which may be called luxurious; but, be it remembered, we are all creatures of habit, and luxuries are necessities to those who have been used to them. Considering, therefore, the high amount of convenience and comfort they afford, clubs are extremely economical. An excellent dinner at a modern club costs no more than a very bad one at an old tavern. Thus clubs have tended to establish wholesome economy amongst the rich as a principle and a duty, whilst formerly it was considered an evidence of contracted notions and meanness for a man of a few thousands a-year to practise it. It is recorded of one of the highest and richest officers of state, that fifteenpence instead of a shilling having been charged at his club for an item in his dinner bill, he bestirred himself till the odd threepence was struck off. Now, as this individual's income ranges somewhere between fifty and a hundred thousand a-year, the actual saving must have been the last thing in his thoughts. His motive was obvious: he took the trouble of objecting, to promote the principles of economy. A poor member would not perhaps have dared to object; although threepence overcharged for each of *his* dinners would have been an inconvenient diminution of his income at the end of the year. The duke in all likelihood felt this, and for the sake of his poorer brethren, put a stop to the abuse.

Clubs, again, have helped to abolish the once fashionable vice of drunkenness. Formerly, one drunkard made many, because, for the sake of conviviality, all were compelled to drink alike. Now, the individual is independent of his neighbours in this respect, and so thoroughly has the scale been thus turned in favour of sobriety, that no intemperate man is allowed to remain a member of a club. A careful examination of the statistics of several of these establishments brings out the fact, that the average quantity of wine drunk by each member has not exceeded of late years half a pint per diem. The moral bearing of the upper classes has been vastly amended by this improvement, not to mention health. It is said of one of the old school—an early member of the 'Union'—that he regarded with envy the daily half-pint, and no more, which was served to a certain witty and temperate author. One day he took up the small decanter and exclaimed with a sigh, 'Ah! I wish I could make up my mind to stick to your infallible *life-preservers*.'

Against the advantages of clubs, certain disadvantages have been urged; the gravest of which is the notion that they tend to withdraw men from female society—the best of social influences. This objection is disposed of by the fact, that the modern establishments present no inducements for social pleasures. As an instance of this, we learn that, in the month of June 1843, the number of dinners served at the Athenæum was 1457, of which all but thirty-six were single. Of the latter, thirty were served to two persons, five to three, and one to four. Again, in all modern clubs, the only convenient place for sociality is the drawing-room. Now, precisely because ladies—the crowning charm of the drawing-room—are absent, this apartment is always the most deserted in the house; for the majority of the members, if not officially employed, are where they ought to be—with their families. A graphic writer gives the following as a true picture of the evening aspect of the drawing-room of a certain club:—'One elderly gentleman, with a shining cocoa-nut head, asleep at the fireplace at one end of the room, matches with another elderly gentleman, with a cocoa-nut head, slumbering at the fireplace at the other end of the room.' In further proof of the non-attendance of members at the time when ladies' society is most accessible, we happen to know that, at a committee meeting of the largest house in Pall-Mall, a whist player complained that he could not get a 'healthy rubber' in the whole house. In commiseration for his sufferings, the committee ceded to him one end of the drawing-room; that being the most deserted, and consequently the quietest corner in the building.

It may be supposed, on the other hand, that all sociality is suppressed by the club system. But this is not wholly the case; for although it enables a man to dine alone if he choose, and have his thoughts as much his own as if he were shut up in his own study, yet if he wish company, there it is for him. The first rule, however, does not hold good with a man who happens to be popular and agreeable. *He* is apt to be 'bored' with companions when he may not want them. The late Theodore Hook was a martyr in this way; for it is well known that many members dined at the Athenæum when they otherwise would have stayed away, for the chance of enjoying some of his pleasantries. It is stated by a Quarterly Reviewer, that, since the renowned humorist disappeared from his favourite table near the door (nicknamed 'Temperance Corner'), the number of dinners has fallen off by upwards of 300 per annum.

The most visible of all influences which clubs have exercised, is that which they have wrought on the aristocracy in their intercourse with those of a lower grade. Constant association with individuals of humbler rank has thawed that exclusiveness, and broken down the not very estimable pride, in which the higher classes of the old school shrouded themselves. Groups are now constantly seen which are composed of elements that were formerly as immiscible as oil and water. A high-church dignitary, a humble curate, an author, and a peer, may be seen partaking of the same meal. In Lady Hester Stanhope's younger days,* the very idea of such an incongruous party would have been regarded as the commencement of a disastrous revolution in society!

Having pretty nearly characterised the changes in high life which clubs have produced, an account of their rise may not be uninteresting. For the origin of these establishments the public are indebted to the military. The officers of the army, whether in camp or in quarters, have always experienced the advantage and economy of clubbing for their provisions. They have found that the pay of each individual, spent separately, would scarcely procure him ordinary necessaries; whilst, by adding it to a general fund—to be judiciously disbursed by a clever provider or 'caterer'—he obtains for his subscription not only requisites, but luxuries. This goes on very successfully during active service; but when retirement on half-pay takes place, the plan was, till lately, impracticable. At the peace of 1815, a reduction of the army withdrew a number of officers from the 'messes' to which they had belonged. Thus a great many gentlemen of comparatively limited means were thrown into private life, a prey to the by no means moderate exactions of hotel, tavern, and boarding and lodging-house keepers. In many instances long and continued absence from home had severed these brave men from domestic ties; yet having always lived amongst a congenial brotherhood, society was essential to their happiness. The chief refuge for such comparatively desolate warriors in London was at that period 'Slaughter's Coffee-house,' St Martin's Lane; a very excellent abode when full pay and prize-money were rife, but far too expensive for 'half-pay.' In these circumstances the mess-system was naturally thought of; and the late General Lord Lynedoch, with five brother-officers, met for the purpose of devising a plan by which it could be applied to non-professional life. So effectual were their deliberations, and so well-grounded their preliminary measures, that a club was formed during the same year (1815). The military founders, knowing that many of their naval brethren were, like themselves, placed upon reduced allowances, afterwards brought them within the scope of their design; and an association was enrolled, entitled the 'United Service Club.' A building fund was formed; a neat edifice—the design of Sir Robert Smirke—was raised at the corner of Charles Street, St James's, and in the year 1819 it was opened for the reception of the members. A society of sailor officers also established a snug home of their own in Bond Street, called the 'Naval,' which now consists of about 350 members.

Meanwhile candidates for admission to the United Service Club increased so rapidly, that a larger habitation was rendered necessary. A new and magnificent edifice, from plans and designs by Mr Nash, the architect of Buckingham Palace, was erected at the east corner of the grand entrance to St James's Park from Pall-Mall, and taken possession of in 1828. At present there are about 1490 members.

By the second rule of this club, no officer is eligible below the rank of major in the army, and commander in the navy; but to provide for officers below those grades, a new association was formed, for the reception of all ranks, from general and admiral, down to subalterns, either in the Queen's or in the East India Company's service. Having purchased the house in Charles Street vacated by the senior club, the new one was opened in 1827, under the title of the 'Junior United Service Club.' It is now the most numerous in London, being composed of 1500 'effective' members, with 400 'supernumeraries,' who, being abroad, are not called on to pay their subscriptions.

Besides these three establishments, the officers belonging to her majesty's household troops had an exclusive club of their own, commenced so far back as 1809, though not for domestic purposes. But latterly they imitated the other clubs, and built a tall, thin, but withal pretty edifice, squeezed in, as it were, between Crockford's gaming-house and their own bootmaker's shop—that of the well-known Hoby—at the head of St James's Street, and nearly opposite to White's celebrated bow window. This, called the 'Guards,' made the fourth club composed of military men: but candidates for admission to all of these had, by 1837, so far exceeded the limits set to each, that a fifth, called the 'Army and Navy Club,' was instituted in St James's Square, to which about a thousand members already belong. We may now fairly conclude that the officers in the British service are at last adequately provided with cheap accommodation during their residence in London: and not only there, but in provincial quarters also; for United Service Clubs exist in all the important garrison towns of Great Britain.

* See our extracts from her book at page 191 of present volume.

The original United Service Club had been scarcely founded, when news of the comfort and economy it afforded was spread throughout all classes amongst whom similar associations were practicable. As may be expected, those most gregarious in their pursuits and habits first copied the plan. Many members of the universities, who, when at college, daily met to dine 'in hall,' or, for instruction, in lecture-rooms, found themselves inconveniently alone when in London. They therefore instituted and built a club called the 'United University'—a very grave and reverend-looking edifice, which occupies the corner of Suffolk Street and Pall-Mall east. This association consisted, in 1841 (to which year most of our returns refer), of 1116 members.—Another club for the same class of men was afterwards called into existence in Pall-Mall, and named the 'Oxford and Cambridge,' whose average number of members is 1177.

Next to the army and the church, it is usual to take the law into consideration. Gentlemen of this profession having formed, in Chancery Lane, an institution for purely professional purposes, attached to it a domestic club, which, in 1841, numbered about 350. The higher branches of the profession appear to require no especial establishment of the kind. Consisting mostly of members of the universities, or of literary men, they belong to the United University, to the Oxford and Cambridge, or to the Athenæum. Of the last, a large proportion of the judges are members. To complete our review of the club-life of the learned professions, we must make a single allusion to the medical faculty. Their lives are too incessantly passed in alleviating the maladies of society, to partake very largely in its comforts and pleasures. Hence, of medical domestic clubs, 'there are'—to borrow a terse chapter on 'the antidotes to corrosive sublimate' from an ancient toxicological work—'none!' The names of a few physicians may, however, be found amongst the lists of the miscellaneous and literary clubs, but they are almost honorary members. Of all the professional clubs, none received so much support, or has risen to so much distinction, as that established for literary scientific men and artists—the 'Athenæum,' whose gorgeous mansion stands at the west corner of the Pall-Mall entrance to St James's Park, and forms a fine contrast to the more severely tasteful 'United Service' on the opposite side. The history of this institution is more than usually interesting, from including the names of the brightest ornaments of each department of the arts. We learn that on the 12th of March 1823, Mr Croker, then secretary to the Admiralty, addressed a letter to Sir Humphrey Davy, in which he represented that 'the fashionable and military clubs had not only absorbed a great portion of society,* but have spoiled all the coffee-rooms and taverns;' and urged the formation of a club for the classes referred to. In the year following, a committee was formed, consisting of Sir H. Davy, president of the Royal Society, the Earl of Aberdeen, president of the Society of Antiquaries, Sir Thomas Lawrence, president of the Royal Academy of Painting and Sculpture, Sir James Mackintosh, Sir Walter Scott, Samuel Rogers, John Wilson Croker, and other noblemen and gentlemen connected with literature and art, to the number of twenty-nine. At first they were housed in temporary apartments in Waterloo Place, but in 1830, the new mansion was finished from the designs of Mr Decimus Burton, at a cost of L.45,000, including furniture. The nominal limit of members is 1200, but certain honorary elections of eminent persons swell the actual roll to 1250 names. In such high estimation is this club held, that belonging to it is deemed a guarantee for the greatest respectability.

The lesser stars of the literary firmament formed themselves, like the 'Junior United Service,' into a minor club, and took possession of the house vacated by the Athenæum. This was for some years called the 'Literary Union;' but having gradually admitted individuals unconnected with letters, it changed its title to the 'Clarence.' Since then it gradually languished, and died in 1843.—Gentlemen connected with the theatrical profession, either as authors, performers, or scene-painters, enjoy each other's society at the 'Garrick,' which is conveniently situated near the best theatres in Covent Garden. They form the smallest body of London clubbists, only amounting to 197.—Our list of professional clubs is completed by the mention of those set aside for the mercantile community near the Bank of England and the Royal Exchange. One, called the 'City,' stands in Old Broad Street, and is made up of 600 members; and the other, known as the 'Gresham,' is scarcely yet settled in its new house in King William Street. Another commercial club is now in progress of formation, with the high-sounding title of the 'St George.' It is to be composed of gentlemen interested in railways.

Thus the most numerous London clubs are those made up of individuals attracted to social and domestic companionship by pursuing similar professional careers. In a few others, the basis is community of politics. The 'Carlton Club' consists of members of parliament and others professing Tory principles, to the number of 1200. The 'Conservative Club' sufficiently indicates, by its name, the party to which its members (of whom there are upwards of 1000) belong; as does the 'Reform Club,' to which 1421 reformers are attached. It must, however, be understood that these associations do not exist for political purposes—do not profess, as bodies, to take any share in public events whatever. It is the mere congeniality of political sentiment which attracts the members, to share the same accommodations for the ordinary requirements of existence. They must not, therefore, be confounded with what are called the 'St James's Street Clubs,' such as White's and Brookes's, which are of a more decidedly political character, and are conducted on a different principle. As in the days of Dryden and his companions—when the original White and Brookes flourished—they remain the property of tavern-keepers, who are licensed by the magistrates in the same manner as the proprietors of public hotels and taverns. But they only admit their subscribers. These select a committee to manage the internal affairs of the house; such as deciding who shall be admitted, and fixing the charges for refreshments to be made by the proprietors. As before explained, they are of much older date than domestic clubs. Recently, they have lost much of their political character, and are now considered principally as lounges for people of little occupation.

To be eligible for admission to the 'Travellers' Club,' a gentleman must either be a foreigner, or have travelled at least five hundred miles in a straight line from London. It numbers 700 members, amongst whom are several authors; for in these days there are few persons who, having 'done' their five hundred miles or more, refrain from favouring the world with their journals, or notes of travel, in the form of one or more octavo volumes.—There is another and much larger class of travellers to whom the convenience of a club is a great boon; namely, such gentlemen as are connected, either in a civil or military capacity, with our vast Indian possessions. Those on the retired or on the sick list, who either reside permanently, or are visiting London for a year or two, are provided for by the 'Oriental.' Their elegant establishment stands on the sunny side of Hanover Square, and, in 1841, accommodated 523 members.

It must be obvious that numerous individuals—besides those who have been able to class themselves into separate bodies from the similar nature of their pursuits—remain ineligible for admission to any of the establishments we have enumerated. They therefore find

* Besides the United Service, the Alfred, the United University, the Union, and the Travellers' clubs, had been established. The Athenæum was the sixth club which was formed in London.

refuge in what go by the designation of Miscellaneous Clubs. Many of these started as class clubs; but—by the gradual admission of very agreeable companions unconnected with the profession or class of which the society was composed, or from an inability to keep their funds by a too rigid selection of candidates—they have become generalised. The 'Alfred' (23 Albemarle Street) was originally a whist club; but, like the Guards, adopted the domestic system, added a coffee-room, and became miscellaneous. The 'Windham'—which borrowed the name of William Windham, an eminent senator, who was secretary-at-war till 1801—started as a political, but is now a miscellaneous club of 613 members. The 'Parthenon' (732 strong), and the 'Erectheum' (250), are both miscellaneous. Into the latter opulent tradesmen are admitted. But of all the non-professional clubs, none stands so high as the 'Union,' which accommodates its 1025 members in Cockspur Street. It was formed soon after the United Service, and boasted at one time of no fewer than 400 members of both houses of Parliament.

We have now completed the list of London clubs. It should be understood, that the aggregate of the members set down to each far exceeds the number of individuals. Many men belong to more than one; and the vanity of some who can afford it, induces them to get admission into four, five, or even six, should they be eligible. For instance, a soldier—one of a military club—may be also a scientific man, and get into the Athenæum: he may have travelled, and be on the roll of the Travellers. Should he have been in the East, he may join the Oriental; and *all* the miscellaneous clubs are open to him. Some imagine that, having passed the ordeal of so many scrutinising ballots, they obtain great eclât and importance in society. Characters of this stamp form a new generation; they are essentially, and to all intents and purposes, club-men. Having been created by clubs, in clubs they have their being. They are perfectly conversant with the domestic arrangements of each establishment. They know to a nicety at which house the most perfect soups are served; from which of the kitchens the best soufflées are wafted; and can tell to a day when the best bin of the United University's claret was bottled. They are also oracles in higher things. Constantly 'looking in' at the morning rooms of the political clubs, they are able to prognosticate the precise number of a majority on any important parliamentary question. Their frequent visits to libraries, and intercourse with authors, give them an extensive acquaintance with literary matters, and they will name the writer of an anonymous work on the day of publication. They have a vast number and variety of acquaintances, and speak familiarly of my friend the duke, because 'he is a member of our club.'

Their extensive connoisseurship in small details of management, makes them valuable 'house' committee-men, and in that character they look uncommonly sharp after the goings on of the servants and the quality of the edibles. Some, again, are not so fortunate as to 'obtain office,' especially those who endeavour to get into it by dint of grumbling. Like Hector Boreall in one of Poole's clever though exaggerated sketches, these troublesome members write furious complaints on the backs of their dinner bills, because, perhaps, the cook sends up two sprigs of fennel instead of three, with a mackerel, and 'cracks the skin near the tail.'* This sort of clubbist is the horror of committees, the dread of servants, and the terror of members, whom he is constantly canvassing for support for his frivolous complaints at the general meetings; enforcing his arguments by the incessant question, 'What do we pay our six guineas a-year for?' Men of this sort are appropriately called 'bores,' and happily form a very small minority in club-life. Apart from such exceptions, a more agreeable person than your regular club-man does not exist. The variety of information he possesses, the freedom and ease with which he imparts it, and the excellence of his manners, make him a most popular character in general society; from which his clubs do not withdraw him, as we have before argued.

* Advantages of belonging to a Club, published in the New Monthly Magazine.

SKETCHES IN NATURAL HISTORY.

THE FUNGUS FAMILY.

The common edible mushroom is usually taken as the type of this order, which includes the puff-ball, truffle, morel, the mould on cheese and stale bread, the mildew on trees, the rust on corn, the substance called dry-rot, and many other minute and yet unexamined appearances of a similar nature. The fungi are amongst the lowest forms of vegetation, are entirely composed of cellular tissue, and have no organs corresponding to the roots, branches, or leaves of higher plants. It may be difficult to persuade some who have never given attention to botany, that such substances as the reddish dust often found on the ears of corn, and the white silky mould on decaying fruit, are really vegetable forms; but he has only to place them under the lens of a good microscope, to discover that they are as perfect as the mushroom that springs on the lawn, and to observe, moreover, their reproductive organs studded with minute grains, each granule destined to become a fungal like its parent. Though low in their organisation, the fungi are extremely diversified in their size, shape, colour, and consistence: so much so, that the naturalist will find in them as wide a field for his inquiry—as curious adaptations for his wonder—as are presented by any other order in nature.

Like all non-flowering and lowly-organised plants, the fungals are either propagated by spores or granules (seed), or by filamentous processes called spawn. The spores are generally produced within or under the conical cap or ball which springs above ground; the spawn in membranes attached to the part underground, or not unfrequently in the whole substance of the fungus. In point of reproduction, indeed, the family may be said to be infinite. The millions of spawn particles which Lewenhoek counted in the roe of the cod are as nothing in comparison; for there reproductive power is confined to one portion of the animal, and that at a certain period only, whereas in the fungi every cell of tissue may contain its germs, and every germ spring up into new forms equally fitted for propagation in the space of a few hours. Nay, some pass through the course of their existence in a few minutes, and have given birth to thousands, even while under the field of the microscope. So minute are the spores of many species, that they float unseen in the atmosphere around us, may be in every drop of water we drink, or even circulate through our system unobserved. Individually, a fungus developes itself circularly; that is, the original germ increases by additions of tissue, which produce a spherical form; and this form, when mature, disperses its spores after the same concentric manner. A succession of such developments—proceeding from a common centre, and enlarging in space year after year—produces in many instances those deep green circles on lawns known as *fairy rings*; the decay of the latest crop of fungi serving as manure to the ring on which they grew.

Though some genera are rare, and rather local, it may be said of the family generally that they are scattered everywhere, without reference to those conditions which limit other vegetation, that they flourish on every substance, whether organic or inorganic, and that many luxuriate only on the structures of living plants or animals. Let any vegetable or animal substance begin to show symptoms of decay, and one night will suffice to establish myriads of these tiny moulds and mildews on its surface; let fruit, bread, cheese, flesh, milk, or the like, be laid aside in any damp unventilated place, and countless colonies of these parasites will succeed each other, till they have utterly consumed the source from which they sprang. 'They usually prefer,' says a recent writer, 'damp, dark, unventilated places, such as cellars, vaults, the parts beneath decaying bark, the hollows of trees, the denser parts of woods and forests, or any decaying matter placed in a damp and shaded situation; and are most especially averse to dryness and bright light. Even when they appear upon the live leaves of trees, the stems of corn, or in similar situations, it is either at the damp and wet season of the year, late in the autumn, or in moist, airless places; and M. Andouin has shown experimentally, that when live insects are attacked by them, it is only when they are confined in damp, unventilated places.' Such facts are of practical utility; for often in storehouses, silk-worm nurseries, orchards, and corn-fields, there are not more destructive agencies than the parasitic fungi. Passing over such as the mushroom and truffle, which spring directly from the soil, and those which attach to the boles of trees and the like, we may notice the nature and habitat of some of the more curious genera.

Among the most familiar and universal are the *mucors*—moulds which abound on bruised fruit and other substances containing fecula and sugar. These moulds are of all shapes—simple, branched, spherical, radiating—presenting a surface like velvet, or a network of the most delicate texture; and of all hues—blue, yellow, and vermilion, but seldom or ever green. One of the most common, the *Mucor mucedo*, consists of a single filament, headed by a very minute ball-shaped receptacle. In the young state, this little ball is covered by a thin membrane, which bursts as the spores arrive at maturity, and which then present themselves like so many dusty particles congregated round a central nucleus. Being so minute, the slightest touch, or the gentlest breath of air, is sufficient to scatter them in thousands, and thus the mucors increase like wildfire. As they require abundant nutriment, it is only on succulent parts they luxuriate; and for this reason they are principally injurious to fruits—the slightest injury from an insect affording them a basis for propagation. Though individually small, the moulds, in the aggregate, are capable of effecting immense damage, and sometimes collect in masses truly astonishing, as is well illustrated by the instance recorded by Sir Joseph Banks. Having a cask of wine rather too sweet for immediate use, he directed that it should be placed in a cellar, that the saccharine matter it contained might be more decomposed by age. At the end of three years, he directed his butler to ascertain the state of the wine, when, on attempting to open the cellar door, he could not effect it, in consequence of some powerful obstacle. The door was consequently cut down, when the cellar was found to be completely filled with a fungous production, so firm, that it was necessary to use an axe for its removal! This appeared to have grown from, or to have been nourished by, the decomposing particles of the wine—the cask being empty, and carried up to the ceiling, where it was supported by the surface of the fungus. The expansive force of growing fungi is often curiously exemplified under stones and other moveable objects: we have seen a slab of pavement of considerable size raised several inches from its level by the growing power of a bed of puff-balls beneath.

The disease called *dry-rot* in timber, is owing to the presence of minute fungi, which insert their filaments into the pores and tubes of the wood, and there luxuriate and multiply at the expense of those substances which give to the timber its cohesion. If once established in a damp and unventilated situation, dry-rot increases with such amazing rapidity, that the largest beams in a few years become soft and tender as tinder. We have seen, for example, the beams and flooring of a building erected in 1830 so thoroughly destroyed by this disease in the course of eight years, that a child would have been in danger by placing his weight upon them. When taken up, the moulds were found adhering to them in masses of nearly two feet thick—a fact which will convey some idea of their infinite numbers, when it is remembered that, individually, each plant can only be examined with the aid of a microscope. The genera chiefly instrumental in producing this disease are *merulius*, *polyporus*, and *sporotrichum*—the latter being perhaps the most rapidly-spreading and destructive. Damp, want of ventilation, and a slightly subacid state of the wood, are conditions most favourable to the development of dry-rot; free exposure to air and sunshine are thorough preventives; and where these cannot be secured, the wood should be steeped in some solution destructive of fungi. It is not merely dead timber, but living vegetables also that suffer from its ravages—as is often exemplified, to the cost of the farmer and gardener, in cases of mildew, smut, rust, ergot, &c. And if found on living plants, we need not be surprised at their appearance in animals. Many insects are attacked by them in such a manner, that the whole juices of the body are speedily consumed, and their space filled with the filaments of the fungi. One of the most common instances of animal dry-rot is the disease in silkworms called *La Muscadine*. These insects are liable at all ages to become sickly, and to die, soon after death becoming stiff, and acquiring such a degree of rigidity as to be readily broken. There is then thrown out from their surface a white efflorescence, which is the fructification of the fungus, *Botrytis basiana*—the inside being filled with the thalli or filaments of the same plant. If some healthy caterpillars are placed beneath a bell-glass, along with a small portion of worm killed by the botrytis, they soon catch the disease, exhibit the same symptoms as those already mentioned, and eventually perish; having no doubt been infected either by rubbing themselves against the dead worm, or, what is more probable, having received upon their skins the infinitely minute seeds dispersed by the botrytis.

It is often a matter of wonder and inquiry how the minute fungi are generated so abundantly on substances and in situations where one cannot well conceive how their germs can gain admission. That their generation is not owing to any mere chemical action, but to the presence of their seeds or germs, is the common belief among naturalists; and yet it is sometimes impossible to account for their growth in this manner. It is true that the most impalpable dust is not finer than their spores, that these may be borne about by every current in the atmosphere, may be in every drop of exposed liquid, and may insert themselves in the finest organic tissues. It is also to be borne in mind that these spores may be present without their being developed; for, like higher forms, they will not germinate unless under fitting conditions. Thus Dutrochet found that distilled water holding a small quantity of white of egg in solution, did not generate fungi in a twelvemonth; but upon the addition of the minutest quantity of an acid, it generated them in eight days' time in abundance. Alkalescent infusions were found to possess the same property; and the only poisons which prevented the growth of these minute fungi, were the oxides or salts of mercury. Upon this principle Mr Kyan and others have obtained patents for solutions of corrosive sublimate, &c. which render timber, cordage, sail-cloth, and other vegetable substances indestructible, so far as the attacks of fungi are concerned.

Though possessing no apparent beauty either of colour or of structure, the fungi are not without their interest in this respect, as any one can readily convince himself by placing a patch of mould under the lens of a good magnifier. The colours are generally tawny-brown, yellow, or pure white, often red and blue, but never green. The forms are for the most part stalked, with a conical or mitre-like head; some are globular; others are produced in irregular masses; and many are simple filamentary processes, with a productive speck at the apex. Many genera appear to be mere blotches of jelly, others froth-like masses, as unlike anything in vegetation as could well be imagined. Yeast, for example, according to Mülder and others, is a spherical fungus; so that fermentation is a fungus development, the plants propagating ıd increasing so long as they find the elements of nutri- on in the fermenting liquid. A spherule of yeast, a vege- ble capable of multiplying itself by myriads—what a onderful microcosm of vitality! In their consistence the ugi are fleshy, spongy, leathery, gelatinous, or corky, ıt never herbaceous. They are of all sizes, from the herule, which the naked eye can scarcely detect, to e monster fungus four and five feet in circumference. hough possessing no floral attractions, many species ssess the more wonderful attraction of being lumi- ous. The coal-mines near Dresden have long been lebrated for their fungi, which emit a light similar to at of pale moonlight. Gardner found some agarics owing on leaves of palms in Brazil, and illuminating e forests like so many stars—the light being visible r several hundred yards; and Delile found others in e olive-grounds of Montpelier. The spawn of the uffle is also accounted luminous, and can thus be de- cted when all other means would have been fruitless.

The purposes which the fungi fulfil in the economy nature are as yet but little understood. Useless and ıimportant as they may seem, destructive as they ten are to the products of human labour, their num- ers and universality demonstrate that they must sub- rve some great design in creation. Unlike other ants, they do not purify the air by robbing it of its rbonic acid, and exhaling oxygen, but rather tend to vitiation, by exhaling carbonic acid, and absorbing ygen. This has been proved by the experiments of arcet; and yet, as a function, it seems as necessary as at to which it is opposed. According to a popular riter, 'fungi and insects may not inaptly be called the avengers of nature; for both labour, and with asto- shing effect, in the removal of refuse matters, which, ere they left on the surface of the earth, would be und not only useless incumbrances, but injurious nants. These they help to disintegrate and dissolve, ıd speedily remove, converting the exuviæ of one gene- ıtion into manure and vegetable mould, for the support ıd maintenance of the next. For these duties, their inute seeds and wandering habits particularly fit them.' lany of them also furnish food for innumerable insects, ıeir soft pulpy substance being readily available for ıch a purpose, at the same time that their carrion-like lour adds a zest to the feast.

Though the minuter genera are often noxious to man, et many of the larger are not without their uses. Some these are wholesome and palatable, as the mushroom, orel, truffle, and champignon; others are deadly poisons, every summer demonstrates, by some unlucky indi- dual mistaking the noxious for the wholesome species. lany of the minuter fungi, as moulds, smuts, rusts, and on, are injurious when taken into the human system; ıd there is not a more powerful drug in the whole ma- ria medica than the ergot found on the ears of rye. erman tinder, so much used by gentlemen for lighting ıeir cigars, is prepared from a species of puff-ball or *Boletus*, which, after being dried, is impregnated with itre. Some species were at one time used like the chens by country people in dyeing yellow; but the lvancement of the arts has long since banished such ıgredients. As showing the value of the order in uman economy, some of the edible genera may be ıortly described. First and most familiar among these the common field mushroom, *Agaricus campestris*, ound abundantly in every country of Europe, and sed either in a fresh state, employed in cookery, or ıanufactured into ketchup. As the produce of the ıushroom in a cultivated country like Britain is very ncertain, many noblemen have it reared in their own ardens, where proper beds are prepared and sown ith its spawn. The morel is a more delicate fungus, paringly found in the south of England, but abundantly France and Italy. It is highly prized by gourmands, ut has not, so far as we are aware, been brought into ıltivation.

The truffle is the most valuable of the family, and ommands a good price in the markets of Italy and France. It grows beneath the surface, and has no appearance of a root; its form is that of an irregular globe, covered with small rounded tubercles, and its colour varies from that of white to a grayish or marbled brown. In general, it attains a diameter of two or three inches, and when full grown, emits a powerful but rather pleasant odour. Unlike other fungi, the truffle, when ripe, does not become a powdery mass, but dissolves into a gelatinous pulp. Truffles are found in most of the temperate climates of the old world, especially in the oak and chestnut forests of France and Italy, and in the chalk districts of southern England. Being strictly underground growers, it would be difficult to discover them, were it not that the pigs which feed in the woods are extremely fond of them, and commence to grub wherever they are abundant. Dogs can also be trained to recognise them by the smell; and a practised gatherer knows where to dig, by the appearance as well as by the hollow sound of the soil. The season of collecting them continues from October to January, after which they begin to split in all directions, and to fall to pieces. Many gardeners have endeavoured to cultivate the truffle, and at the present moment are making vigorous attempts; but they have as yet made but indifferent progress. The tuber is cooked in several ways, being either simply broiled, cut up into salad, or used like the mushroom as seasoning; but it must at all times be sparingly used. It may be kept in ice or covered with lard; and in some countries it is dried. The truffle was early known, and has been in repute among gourmands since the time of the Greeks and Romans. Other species of mushroom have been used for food from time immemorial in China, in India, and in Africa.

Besides these edible fungi, well known in the old world, there are others found in North and South America. The most remarkable of these is the genus *Cyttaria*, important from its forming an article of food to the inhabitants of Terra del Fuego. 'It is,' says Mr Darwin, 'a globular, bright yellow fungus, which grows in vast numbers on the beech trees. When young, it is elastic and turgid, with a smooth surface deeply pitted or honeycombed; in its tough and mature state, it is collected in large quantities by the women and children, and is eaten uncooked. It has a mucilaginous, slightly sweet taste, with a faint smell like that of a mushroom. With the exception of a few berries, the natives eat no vegetable food besides this fungus. In New Zealand, before the introduction of the potato, the roots of the fern were largely consumed; but at the present time, I believe Terra del Fuego is the only country in the world where a cryptogamic plant affords a staple article of food.'

THE CONDITION OF SPAIN.

THAT part of the European peninsula which is occupied by Spain, contains some of the most fertile territory in the world. In the delicious climate of the south, the progress of vegetation is never suspended, except during the short period of excessive heat in summer. Yet Spain, from being at one time the queen of empires, is now the poorest and most unsettled country in the civilised world. Her lands demanding but little labour to yield abundance of food, do not call forth that energy which is characteristic of less favoured nations; hence her natural advantages have been but little improved, and in manners, and in the practice of the useful arts, her people remain so stationary, that the Spaniard of to-day is the counterpart of the Englishman four or five centuries ago. A recent writer, who appears to be well acquainted with his subject, declares that, 'upon landing in the peninsula, and making a short excursion for a few miles in any direction, you see reproduced the manners of England five centuries back, and find yourself thrown into the midst of a society which is a close counterpart of that extinct semi-civilisation, of which no trace is to be found in our history later than the close of the fourteenth century and the reign of Richard II. You behold the scant and ill-tended roads, frequented by no vehicles but the rude and springless agricultural cart, now laden with manure, and now with village beauties; and the resort of no other passenger than the weary plodder upon foot, and the rudely accoutred equestrian of the Canterbury Tales; and if you extend your journey a little further, you will probably light upon a party of skirmishers, a besieged town, a hurried detachment of marching troops, as in our own days of civil strife and our wars of the rival Roses. The face of the country is as little changed since the time of Cervantes, as the popularity of his inimitable Don Quixote; and, bating a little dissimilarity in the strictly professional costumes, the panorama is as dirty and as picturesque as ever. The greater preponderance of mules and donkeys, round hats, red belts, and jackets, forms the only striking difference from the cortège of Chaucer's pilgrims, the high-peaked saddle and heavy iron stirrups being pretty much the same as in England of old (for the iron-work here, from the stirrup to the plough, is unchanged from the earliest times). The very horses are branded, as a protection from thieves, as they were in Chaucer's time by statute. Romerias, or pilgrimages in Spain, are still commonly resorted to by the votaries of piety and pleasure; and there are more highwaymen than ever met at Gad's-hill, to strip them on their journey.'*

To idleness, which has its root in the ease with which the necessaries of life are procured from the soil, must the stationary condition of the Spanish nation be traced. But all people deficient in regular systematic and profitable employment, substitute for it a bad activity; and that activity in Spain has for ages, with few intervals, taken the form of intestine strife, occasioning a great uncertainty in the tenure of life and property. This is the surest bar to improvement and progress; hence it is that the Spaniards are even worse, both intellectually and socially, than the ancestors of whom they are proverbially so proud.

Recently, the Spanish people have been unusually active in discord. To their ordinary internal quarrels was lately added a war of succession, vigorously prosecuted by Don Carlos, uncle of the present queen. This, however, having subsided, has, it would seem from the work before us, given place to intrigues at court, originating frequent and sanguinary, though short outbreaks amongst the people. Spain is the classic ground of intrigues; and one of the most entertaining parts of Mr Hughes's work is the account he gives of the court, the composition of which presents a curious picture to the English reader.

The present ruler of Spain is Isabella II., daughter of Ferdinand VII. and Christina of Naples. When she ascended the throne in 1833, she was only three years old, and the affairs of the state were carried on by a regency, of which her mother was for a time at the head. She has also a younger sister, and our author presents them in a group. 'During the enormously protracted ceremonies of Holy Week, every one had an opportunity of seeing the royal family at their devotions. It was an interesting spectacle; three female personages of regal rank ranged by the side of the altar, isolated and exalted over the rest of the community both by power and by the accidents of social position; no husband, nor father, nor brother, at hand, to afford the support of masculine protection, and their nearest male relative a hostile usurper.' At the early age of thirteen Isabella was pronounced of age, and now governs on her own responsibility. The following is a picture of the maiden-queen, as drawn by Mr Hughes. 'The appearance of Queen Isabel Maria to the eye of a stranger is that of a precocious but somewhat careworn and sickly girl—exceedingly pale, and with nothing either expressive or interesting in her countenance. But that her brow is circled with a crown, at a period of unparalleled youth to emerge from legal nonage, there is little there to arrest your attention; you are neither forbidden nor attracted; you deem her more advanced than her age; but this precocity, as compared with England, is universal in the peninsula.' Though imperfectly educated, her majesty is blessed with an extraordinary memory, and was able to repeat by rote the whole constitution of 1837, which she had sworn to observe, but which her ministers have in great part repealed. She possesses the most perfect museum of confectionary in Europe. It extends over every apartment of the palace, and contains some most interesting specimens; and the most striking characteristic of the youthful majesty of Spain, is her relish and constant use of these *bonbons* and sweetmeats. 'Her papers of comfits strew the palace, her bags of sugar-plums visit the council-chamber, her *dulces* line the throne. The books of heraldry are not in her case vain, which, as females have nothing to do with shields, inscribe their armorial bearings in a *lozenge*. When she is in a good humour, the most remarkable evidence of amiability which she affords is distributing these bonbons freely amongst her ministers and palace grandees. She does not ask whether these gentlemen have a sweet tooth, but very naturally infers that what she likes herself must be pleasing to all the world. The degrees of ministerial favour may be estimated by the number of presents of confectionary; and the minister of the interior is first fiddle by right of four bags of sugar-plums, till the minister of grace and justice produces five sticks of barley-sugar. When she despatches business with her ministers (which she does twice a week), she despatches a prodigious quantity of sweets at the same time; and the confection of decrees and discussion of dainties proceed *pari passu*.' In the important office of governing, her majesty is assisted by a cabinet; but to such vicissitudes are Spanish state affairs subject, that her ministry has been changed exactly thirty-six times in ten years. This may be chiefly accounted for by a peculiarity which has attached itself to the Spanish throne for so many ages, that it may now be considered a governmental institution, and known as the camarilla.* This consists of a few persons, who associate for the purpose of forming 'a power behind the throne,' and may be designated as a board of intrigue. It is a small body, consisting of the favourites of the ruler, male and female, and acts as a purveyor of scandal, news, and too often of calumny, to the royal ear. In this capacity the camarilla, without having any official connexion with the state, rules its destinies.

Mr Hughes devotes one chapter to the history of camarillas, from which it appears that they first began to be formed so early as the fourteenth century. The sort of persons who have since composed them, have of course varied with the tastes and leading characteristics of the sovereign they surrounded. A warlike prince selected, like Juan II., a camarilla of generals; a fanatical prince was led by a camarilla of monks and priests, like Philip II. and Ferdinand, the father of the present queen. It was a camarilla which influenced the otherwise illustrious Ferdinand and Isabella against Columbus and his projects of geographical discovery. Finally, the camarillas of the present young and inexperienced queen, have occasioned many of those disastrous changes of ministry and consequent unsettlement in state affairs, of which the Spanish nation is so much the victim. The present camarilla consists of a rough and unbending soldier, a bustling diplomatist, and two marchionesses. Our author characterises these combinations of intrigue with a rough hand. 'The formation of camarillas is a mystery, as their deeds are deeds of darkness. An impenetrable cloud is over their origin, and all their after-movements are occult. Their intercourse with the crown is illicit, their action on the nation's destinies is a crime; they are compelled to work

* Revelations of Spain in 1845. By T. M. Hughes. Second Edition. 2 vols. London: Colburn.

* The literal meaning of this word is a small chamber.

in secret by the force of an involuntary shame. Creeping, grovelling, and insidious, inured to baseness, and accomplished only in the arts of cunning, the camarilla burrows into the palace like a rat, to emerge a thundering charger. It does not enter boldly by the door, but wriggles through the narrowest hole it can find. It crawls in upon all-fours like a dwarf, and comes forth an armed giant.'

Such being the state of affairs at head-quarters, the unsettled condition of the rest of the nation can easily be accounted for. As a specimen of how readily political excitement is engendered, and to what fatal results it leads, the following coffee-house scene may be taken: —'The Spanish café is a club; for men of simple wants and social habits, a very convenient one; and, as if in contempt of London exclusiveness, it is open to all the world. Here the political effervescence of Spain often leads to the most violent scenes. At the beginning of 1844, in the principal café of Zaragoza (after Barcelona, the most turbulent city of Spain), an officer of the garrison was assailed and insulted for the despotic acts of Narvaez and the Moderados. From language of increasing asperity, and of that vehemently energetic character which belongs to Spain, they passed to hustling, and the officer's epaulettes were brushed and ruffled in the mêlée. He instantly drew his sword, wounded some of his antagonists, had missiles flung at him, and was driven with his back to the wall. Other officers and soldiers repaired to the scene, and blood was shed; nor were the combatants separated until the political chief and municipal guard arrived to make them prisoners. So great was the violence used on this occasion, that firearms were produced, and numerous shots discharged within the café; and after the other officers and military interposed, an alferez (ensign) of the regiment of America was hit by a pistol bullet—the carrying of pocket pistols being too common in Spanish cities during periods of excitement. Thereupon the officers fell with their swords upon the civilians, but the latter were well provided with sword-sticks to meet them; and while these fenced and dealt each other some severe blows, the two or three soldiers who took part in the fray deliberately fired on the body of civilians, and the latter discharged all the pistols they carried. The café subsequently bore tokens of the skirmish, several bullets being lodged in the woodwork, and divers chairs and tables shattered to pieces. Fortunately, though several of the combatants were wounded, none died; and, as a bystander remarked with peculiar *nonchalance*, "There was good practice for the surgeons of Zaragoza." So strong, unfortunately, became the animosity between the townspeople and the troops of the line, that on the same night an attempt was made to poniard Captain Don Bernardo Taulet, by three men muffled in cloaks, who dogged him to his door.' This led to further outbreaks, and the café was closed for a week.

Despite, however, of all this anarchy, such is the excellence of the soil, that the picture drawn of the condition of the lower classes is surprisingly favourable. 'Let this astonish you, sagacious statesmen—let this fact confound the more polished world's wisdom: there is no poor-law here, no compulsory relief; the rural society is very barbarous; agriculture is no more advanced than it was a century after the flood; industry there is little, occupation trifling, energy none; the soil is but scratched, manures little used, irrigation, which is in truth indispensable, but slightly resorted to; and yet distress there is almost none. * * You may sojourn long enough in a Spanish town before you will meet any of those evidences of downright misery which so soon strike the eye at home, and which abound even in London, in the vicinity of its most splendid squares. There may be rags and filth enough, but there is not the squalor of suffering, or the gaunt aspect of famine. No one starves in this country; few are in positive distress. Those who seek alms are for the most part of the class of jolly beggars, and how thriving is the trade, may be inferred from the independence of its practitioners, from the impudence of their unimploring demands, and the obstinate sturdiness of their persistence. The beggar, having no property of his own, is king and lord of all the properties in the country. The Spanish beggar is more of a visitor and a familiar acquaintance than a suer for alms. He has his own set and circle, like those who move in the best society, and pays his regular round of visits upon fixed days. He does not sow cards to reap dinners, nor does he deal in drawing-room scandal, small-talk, or pointless tattle. No; he conjures you by the love of God and of the Virgin to give him a *quart*, and having kissed the same, and crossed and blest himself with it, he passes to your next-door neighbour. If you are deaf to this appeal, he does not hesitate to tap at your windows and knock at your door with the authority of a postman; if you conceal yourself in your inmost recess, his voice is sure to reach you with its impressive and imperious:—"*De alguna cosa por el amor de Dios y de la Virgen!*"—[Give something for the love of God and of the Virgin!]'

Learning, which once held her chief seat in Spain, has now nearly deserted her. The walls of the universities remain, but they enclose but few students; though professors remain for the sake, it would seem, not so much of teaching, as of granting diplomas. The arts and sciences are therefore at a low ebb. Medicine is chiefly practised by the quack. He is known as the Curandero, and is of various kinds. 'There is the vender of Orviétan, or counter-poison, who has an antidote for everything; the barber-surgeon, who, like Sangrado, bleeds for everything; the Curandero Maravilloso, or Spanish Morison, who has a pill or a powder to cure everything (I don't suppose Englishmen have any right to inveigh against Spanish quacks); the Nevero, or snow-vender, who makes up an imitation of snow, and vends it in phials at fairs as a remedy for aches and pains; and the Caracol-Curandero, or snail-doctor, who with snails and frogs professes to cure every inward complaint. Finally, there is the Gusano-Curandero, or worm-quack, who attacks the thousand diseases which flesh is heir to with decoctions or plasters of powdered reptiles; and the Saludador, who kisses the most dangerous sores, and undertakes to cure them with his breath.

'A Curandero in the district of Cuenca had perhaps the most extraordinary pharmacopœia that has ever been heard of. His name was Campillo, and his renown spread far and wide—into Castile on the one hand, and into La Mancha on the other. He was endowed with extraordinary eloquence, and his influence over his patients was immense. He wrought upon their imagination and enthusiasm, and was thus probably indebted to a species of natural magnetism for many of his triumphs. He was the Napoleon of quacks; and some of his cures, though nearly incredible, are well attested. A dropsical patient, thirty years of age, applied to him. He had passed through the hands of the most expert members of the faculty, and had vainly tried every recognised remedy. He was so weak as to require to be carried about. Campillo resolved, in this man's case, to try a most extraordinary species of allopathy. He carried him to the hospital, where a number of children then were lying, and purposely infected him with small-pox! The disease was completely developed in him, his sufferings were excessive, and his face and body were pitted for life; but his dropsy disappeared for ever. One would suppose that the remedy here was almost worse than the disease. Not so, however, thought the good Cuencans. Scores of dropsical and other patients flocked to him, requesting to be cured by small-pox. And Campillo records I know not how many cases, but does not say a word of those he killed. This genius had a great contempt for all ordinary sorts of plasters, whether designed for cuts, contusions, or ulcers, and accordingly he invented lotions and plasters of his own. A rich proprietor wounded his leg against a tree in hunting: his ordinary surgeon applied cataplasms composed of bread-crumb, milk, and saffron, to allay the inflammation. A large ulcer unfortunately ensued, the limb became swollen, and acute pains were felt. He tried another surgeon—worse and worse. He lost his appetite and his sleep. Such was the fruit of sundry decoctions, ptisans, and medicines, prescribed (said the doctors) to make his blood fluid, and correct its acrid humours. He next applied to the Cirujano-mayor of the royal armies, who left nothing untried, applied the most powerful alteratives, and salivated him most effectually. The ulcer, notwithstanding, became so large, that there was soon a talk of amputating the limb. Before this last resort, Campillo was applied to, and told him to pour three times a day on the limb the contents of a pint bottle with which he supplied him, rigidly enjoining him not to taste the contents of the bottle. The leg was speedily cured; and Campillo afterwards confessed that the cure was effected with common water!'

Many a pleasant story of Spanish life is scattered over Mr Hughes's graphic pages; and his pictures possess that sort of vividness and vraisemblance which guarantee their likeness to the originals. They impress the reader with a conviction that the manners, actions, habits of thought, and even the condition of the people of Spain, are precisely the same now as described in the life-like history of the renowned Gil Blas de Santillaine. But the picture, however amusing when seen in detail, is when viewed as a whole, much to be deplored. It is lamentable to reflect that, with every natural advantage, Spain should stand at zero in the scale of European civilisation.

THE DUKE OF NORMANDY.

A ROMANCE OF REAL LIFE.

The continental journals announce that, on the 10th of last August, there died at Delft, in Holland, Charles Louis, known as the 'Duke of Normandy.' This individual presented one of those extraordinary instances of doubtful identity which we find scattered over ancient and modern biography. The mystery of his birth has not been cleared up by his death, and continues as impenetrable as that of the celebrated Man with the Iron Mask.

It is well known that, in 1791, Louis XVI. of France was overtaken during his attempted flight from France at Varennes, and afterwards dragged to the prison of the Temple. He was accompanied by his family, which consisted of his wife, Marie Antoinette, his sister, daughter, and his only son, the dauphin of France. On the 21st January 1793, the unfortunate monarch was beheaded; and his son, still a prisoner, was partially acknowledged as Louis XVII., though only in the ninth year of his age. This was but a mockery, for his captivity only became the more close and cruel. He was separated from his mother, and handed over to the custody of one Simon, a ferocious cobbler, and his wife, who, besides practising all sorts of external cruelties on him, tried every means to demoralise his mind. When this ruffian was promoted to a seat in the 'Commune' (a kind of common council), the royal prisoner's hardships increased. He was shut up in a room, rendered totally dark both night and day. In this he was kept for a whole year, without once being allowed to leave it; neither was his body or bed linen changed during that time. The filth, stench, and vermin amidst which the child dragged on his existence, at length, it is said, terminated it.* On the eve of death, his persecutors sent the physician Dessault to see if his life could be prolonged by better treatment; but the doctor's reply was that it was too late: nothing could save him; and his demise was announced to have taken place on the 8th of June 1795, at the age of ten years and two months. The National Convention, which then managed the public affairs, appointed a commission to verify the event, and the body was opened by two surgeons, named Pelletan and Dumangin. In speaking of the remains, they describe them as a corpse 'represented to us as that of Charles-Louis.' The doctor Pelletan took out the heart, and preserved it in spirits of wine; which he gave to the deceased's sister when she had married the Duke D'Angoulême. The rest of the body was huddled with other corpses into a common grave in the cemetery of the parish of St Margaret; so that, at the restoration of the Bourbons in 1815, when Louis XVIII. desired that the remains of his predecessor should be disentombed, they could not be distinguished.

The equivocal wording of the medical report, aided by other suspicions, caused an idea to gain extensive currency that a dead child had been substituted for the royal infant; and that he had escaped from his jailers by a well-laid plan, carried out by his partisans. This notion was so prevalent, that we find, amongst the records of the Convention, a decree dated June 14, 1795—only six days after the date fixed as that of the young king's death—ordering him to be sought for along all the roads of the kingdom. However, the better-informed part of the community were firmly convinced that Louis XVII. was dead and buried; and from that time till very lately, the belief was never effectually disturbed. Taking advantage of the doubt, several impostors made their appearance, claiming to be the prince. The first of these was one Hervagaut, who, when discovered to be a tailor's son, was condemned in 1802 to four years' imprisonment. In 1818 Mathurin Bruneau, a shoemaker, tried the same trick; but failing, was sentenced to seven years' imprisonment. In short, no fewer than fifteen impostors have been enumerated; all of whom pretended to be the wretched young prince, returned from exile after escaping from the Temple. The latest claimant is the subject of the present notice; and so startlingly do some of the circumstances of his career coincide with the short history of the son of Louis XVI., that many well-informed persons really believe he was the person he represented himself to be.

Between the termination of Charles-Louis's imprisonment by death or otherwise, and the appearance of this individual on the scene, it may be necessary to remind the reader that several revolutions and counter-revolutions had swept over France. Napoleon's career had begun and ended; the allies had seated the Bourbons on the throne in the person of Louis XVIII., brother to Louis XVI., and uncle to his latest predecessor; Charles X. had succeeded, and was driven from the throne by the revolution of 1830, which seated Louis-Philippe on it in his stead. All these events had taken place when the story of the so-called Duke of Normandy commences.

On an unusually hot evening for the season—an early day in the May of 1832—a man covered with dust, and who appeared to be borne down with fatigue, entered Paris through the barrier d'Italie. Still, he traversed the Boulevard de l'Hôpital with a firm step, being a fine well-made man, apparently about forty-eight years old. On arriving at the bridge of Austerlitz, he crossed to the toll-bar at the farther extremity, and was accosted by the keeper, an invalid soldier, who demanded the toll. Upon this he made a sign that he did not understand French; but, on the other pulling out a sous piece, to intimate the nature of his demand, the stranger shook his head, heaved a deep sigh, and, after some hesitation, drew forth a fine handkerchief, which he threw towards the toll-keeper, and hastened away in the direction of the Boulevard Bourbon, to Père la Chaise. He got within the gates just before they were closed for the night, and concealing himself amongst

* For a minute account of this interesting and much-abused child, we refer to our tract entitled 'The Little Captive King.'

the tombs and bushes, escaped the notice of the watchmen. It was thus that the stranger passed his first night in Paris.

The day was far advanced when he was found, too much overcome by hunger and fatigue to rise. A gentleman accidentally passing, observed and pitied his condition. After supplying him with some food, he recommended him to solicit the assistance of a benevolent lady whom he named, as she was known far and near for her readiness to help foreigners in distress; besides, she spoke the German language fluently, the only one the worn-out traveller understood. Acting upon this advice, he repaired to the generous Comtesse de R.'s residence, at No. 16, Rue Richer. She was a lady well stricken in years, and preserved an enthusiastic veneration for the Bourbon branch of the royal family, having been femme de chambre to the son of Louis XVI. When the wretched wayfarer presented himself to her, she naturally inquired who he was. To which he replied in German, 'I am Charles-Louis, Duke of Normandy, son of Louis XVI. and Marie Antoinette.' Upon hearing this unexpected reply, the good old comtess fainted. On recovering her senses, she exclaimed, 'Good Heavens! he is the very image of his unfortunate mother!' On calmer reflection, however, she was but half convinced, and determined to put the stranger's identity to another test. She had kept as a relic a little blue robe with metal buttons, which was worn by the royal infant when she nursed him. This she brought forth; and the stranger no sooner saw it, than he exclaimed, 'Ah, my little coat!' After this, Comtesse de R. declared her belief that he was her prince to be so firm that she would have died on the scaffold rather than recant. Without hesitation, she gave up the best apartments of her house for his use and occupation; she even offered for his acceptance the remains of her fortune. This, however, he at once refused, asking no more from her than that she would send for a tailor to equip him with habiliments more in accordance with his pretensions, than the tatters he then wore. This the comtess did, and was not slow in imparting to her royalist friends of whom she was the honoured hostess. All acknowledged the extraordinary similarity both in person and manner which the stranger bore to the royal family. Some were enthusiastic believers; others, with all their *legitimist* enthusiasm, were sceptical. Amongst the former was a certain Monsieur S. de L., who thought the appearance of the 'prince' a miracle in reference to that particular time. Louis-Philippe, when he accepted the crown nearly two years before, had done so with great apparent reluctance. 'How happy therefore will he be,' said this visionary politician, 'to remove the burthen of the state from his own shoulders to those of the rightful heir to the throne!' But before so curious a proposition was made to the king of the French, the other royalists consulted M. de Talleyrand. He replied, with his usual epigrammatic irony, 'There are some people who are born with two left hands. This is poor S.'s case: added to which, he seems to have been brought into the world without brains.' Upon this the party wisely determined to keep the 'prince's' presence in Paris as quiet as possible. Another of his adherents, M. de Forbin Janson, the fiery bishop of Nancy, suggested that, as the illustrious stranger's chance of the throne was somewhat remote, he should enter the church, in which the highest dignities awaited him. This was also found to be impracticable when Neündorf (the name by which the 'prince' now declared he had hitherto been known) revealed that he was a married man, and the father of six children.

The more sceptical part of his adherents very naturally wished to know—supposing his story to be true—how in his early years he escaped from the Temple; and when the stranger had sufficiently mastered the French language—which he took but a short time to acquire—he gave a most circumstantial and plausible account of his early adventures. His narrative was carefully noted down at the time, and, translated, consists in substance as follows:—'I cannot be said to have *escaped* from my jailers,' he began, 'for I left the prison in the most natural manner possible. Some time before the day of my supposed death, a royalist committee was formed for the purpose of saving me. One of these was M. Frotté, who, as the pupil of my physician Dessault, was allowed free ingress and egress to the Temple. One day he entered my cell, motioned me to be silent, seized me, and dragged me to a cabinet under the spire of the tower. A sick child who had been given over by the faculty was substituted in my place, and he, dying two days after (9th June 1795), was buried as Louis XVII. At my supposed death, there being no more prisoners in the Temple, all the keepers and guards were withdrawn, and I was conducted outside the walls without meeting a single official. The ruse, however, got wind, and the decree of the 14th of June was the consequence. To frustrate this, the royalist committee caused several children to personate me, imparting to the impostors several circumstances connected with my family. One they sent to Bordeaux, another to La Vendée, a third to Germany, and so on. These are the children who, when they became men, tried to keep up the character which they had been previously taught to play. This explains the incredible number of false *dauphins* who have appeared.' He ended by declaring, that when, in 1814, the congress of Vienna ceded the crown of France to Louis XVIII., they knew perfectly well of his existence; but the obligations the allies were under to 'his uncle,' overwhelmed the scruples they felt at investing that prince with a sovereignty to which he had no title.

One thing appeared improbable—how the assumed prince should have forgotten his native language. He was ten years of age at the period of his leaving France, and spoke French as cleverly as any other boy, if not more so. How, then, did he lose this faculty? A residence in Germany, even for so great a length of time as thirty-seven years, could hardly have obliterated the French language from his mind. This does not appear to have been explained, and, with some other circumstances, it served to check the credulity of parties half inclined to believe the representations of M. Neündorf.

Further proofs were therefore required; and several were afterwards afforded. The details of the first are somewhat singular. At this time (July 1832) there lived in the village of Gallardon, at the extremity of Beauce, a peasant named Martin, who had the reputation of receiving revelations from above, which he acquired so far back as 1818, when Mathew Bruneau and other spurious princes made their appearance. One Sunday in that year, during mass, Martin saw a vision in which he said an angel commanded him to get an interview with Louis XVIII., the purport of which should be afterwards revealed to him. Immediately after his return from church, Martin having taken leave of his wife and family, commenced his journey on foot to Paris. On the fifth day he arrived there, went straight to the palace of the Tuileries, and demanded to be admitted to the king. In the simplicity of his heart, he told the guards that his mission was of a celestial nature; but they, not finding messengers from above among the list of visitors set down in the orders of the day, handed poor Martin over to the municipal authorities, who transferred him to the Bicêtre lunatic asylum. Here he remained for some time, during which his exemplary piety and touching resignation attracted the attention and respect of the principal physician, who often made him the subject of general conversation. At the end of two months Louis heard of the circumstance, and actually consented to see the harmless man. At the interview, he imparted to the king the substance of a second revelation; which was, that his majesty's nephew, Louis XVII., was still alive, and would return at no distant period; and that if the king he addressed attempted to undergo the ceremony of coronation, the direst calamities would follow; amongst others the dome of the cathedral (of Rheims) would fall in, and crush every soul taking part in the rites. Whether the majesty of France took any serious heed of this enthusiast's warning, it is impossible to say; but one thing is certain—Louis XVIII. never *was* formally crowned. When Martin returned to his village, he found that the king had bought the house which he rented, and presented it to him to live in for the rest of his days. This, together with his interview with royalty—of which he of course made no secret—elevated the poor visionary to the character of a prophet amongst the population of that part of the country; many of whom indeed formed themselves into a sect called Martinists, and devoutly expected the re-appearance of the son of Louis XVI.

As these facts were notorious in 1818, they had not been forgotten in 1832, and it was not at all unnatural that the least credulous of the Comtesse de R.'s friends should suggest that Neündorf should be shewn to the Beauce prophet. Accordingly, in September, a journey to St Arnould, near Dourdan, was undertaken; and without saying who he was, or pretended to be, Neündorf was there confronted with Martin. In an instant, it is said, the prophet recognised him as the person he had seen in his second vision as Louis XVII. His enthusiasm knew no bounds; he embraced the 'prince' with tears of joy, and in the evening the whole party heard mass at the modest little church of St Arnould.

Whatever effect this scene may have had upon Neündorf's more educated companions, it created a prodigious sensation in that part of the country, and one which was extremely beneficial to the 'prince.' The honest people could not do enough to testify their delight. After his return to Paris, they organised subscriptions, in collecting which the village priests took the lead. Under their influence the farmers and peasantry subscribed not only cash, but produce, a regular supply of which was sent every Saturday to Paris, under the charge of a farmer of St Arnould, named Noël Pequet. It was ascertained that, during the four months succeeding his appearance at St Arnould, the value of upwards of L.16,000 sterling was remitted to him from various parts of France!

With these supplies, and the contributions of the Comtesse de R. and her friends, Neündorf was able to take a house, and set up an establishment, which he did as Duc de Normandie, the title which had been given by Louis XVI. to his son. He began housekeeping on a scale of regal magnificence. He bought a carriage, and collected a handsome stud of horses. His servants' liveries were splendid, and adorned with gilt buttons, on which was embossed a broken crown. He even went so far as to form a court and appoint a ministry; and, that nothing should be wanting, he actually started a newspaper to advocate his cause. The gentleman who undertook the responsible editorship of this journal having, however, neglected to deposit the securities required by law with the proper authorities, was arrested, and condemned to a long imprisonment; which he duly suffered. The unfortunate victim to loyal sentiments was one M. Widerkeer. This was the only evidence vouchsafed by the higher powers of their knowledge of the duke's proceedings. That the government of Louis-Philippe did not apprehend any very serious extent of belief in Neündorf's pretensions, must be inferred from the immunity with which they allowed him to carry on his proceedings, and to accept the contributions of the royalists. On the other hand, it must be noticed that Louis-Philippe's seat on the throne was not so firm as it is now; and he may have been afraid to disturb Neündorf, lest he should have excited the enmity of a very powerful party.

It must be owned that the evidence which the pretender had hitherto produced, was only calculated to gain over persons of limited experience and strong legitimatist prejudices. A circumstance, however, which afterwards took place, was of a nature to stagger more obstinate sceptics: it had indeed that effect. We translate it from the words of an individual who was present when it happened. The Duc de Normandie was at dinner, surrounded by several friends. 'Among the company was an old lady who, having recently arrived from the provinces, had never heard of the "prince," and, on being presented to him, was extremely astonished to find herself in the presence of so illustrious a person. After dinner, the conversation turned upon the duke's younger days, and the lady referred to addressed him in these words—"I, monsiegneur, never saw the dauphin; but an old friend who was constantly near his person in his infancy, has described to me that from the midst of his lower jaw there sprung out two teeth. They were incisors, and as straight and pointed as the teeth of a rabbit." Without speaking a word, he pulled open his lower lip, and exhibited to the company such a pair of rabbits' teeth as were described.'

This occurrence confirmed the duke's adherents in their belief of his identity with the victim of the first revolution, and the presence of the rightful heir to the throne of France created some stir in Paris. Perhaps the aspirant to royalty and his friends felt disappointed that the government did not evince its dread by some little persecution, over and above the imprisonment of Widerkeer. To account for this forbearance, dark suspicions were whispered regarding the *secret* intentions of the ruling powers; and these were not long in being corroborated. One day in November, the duke expressed a desire to imitate certain other royalties by examining the streets of the capital, and mixing with its humble citizens *incog.* To this end he sallied forth alone, and even condescended to take his dinner at Véfour's celebrated restaurant. The evening was unusually dark, and while returning to his house across the open space at the back of the Tuilaries (La Place de Carousel), he felt his shoulder suddenly grasped by a strong hand, and in another instant a poniard was plunged more than once into his breast, with the words, 'Die, Capet!'* Fortunately, the intended victim wore inside his coat a medal of the Virgin, which had belonged, it was understood, to Marie Antoinette, his mother; this, receiving the point of the dagger, preserved his life, though several flesh wounds were inflicted. The assassin fled; nor did the duke make any alarm, for fear of being obliged to appear at the municipal guardhouse, and thus get into the power of the government. When he reached home, he was faint from loss of blood, and kept his bed for a fortnight.

The suspicions of foul play entertained by his 'court' were confirmed; they regarded the bravo as an emissary of the government, and the '*Meurs, Capet!*' as an acknowledgment of the duke's right to the crown! There were, however, ill-natured people who went about hinting that, as the victim was quite alone, and became the teller of his own story, the diabolical deed *might* have been done by himself, to strengthen the faith of his followers. Nor were these sceptics silenced when the gashes in the coat, the dents in the medal, and the blood of the royal sufferer, were pointed out. But, upon the whole, whether true or false, the circumstance materially strengthened the duke's position; and, on recovery, he began to play the prince in earnest.

He wrote to the Duchess of Berri, and to 'his sister' the Duchess of Angoulême. To the latter he offered to prove his identity in the following manner:—'When in the Temple,' he said, 'our royal mother and our aunt wrote several lines on a paper, which paper was cut in halves. One piece was given to you, and when we meet I will produce its fellow, which has never been out of my possession since our fatal separation.' The truth of this was never put to the test, for no answer was deigned to his letter.

At length the state in which the Duke of Normandy

---

* *Meurs, Capet!*—Capet is the family name of the Bourbons, as Guelph is that of the house of Brunswick.

lived, the constant visits of his increasing partisans, and his general proceedings, attracted the attention of the police; and the heir to the French throne was made to understand that he stood a likely chance of being thrown into prison, and brought up to answer for his conduct before the court of assize. Upon this he determined to live less ostentatiously, and withdrew to a hotel in the Rue St Guillaume (No. 34), with which address none but a chosen few of his devoted partisans were made acquainted. Though formerly disappointed at having been passed so contemptuously over by the authorities, he now seemed in great dread of them. He never dared to appear abroad, and instituted particular signs and modes of knocking at his door when those in the secret wished admittance. The proprietor of the house entertained from these proceedings very disagreeable suspicions, and, lest he should get into trouble himself, gave his illustrious lodger notice to quit. Some weeks after, the claimant of the crown was really arrested; but exile, and not imprisonment, was his doom. He was placed in the coupè of a diligence between two policemen, and conducted beyond the frontiers of France. In 1838 we find him in England, still calling himself the Duke of Normandy.

He took up his quarters in Camberwell Green, near London, and in November of the above year, suffered a second attempt upon his life. He was, it seems, returning from an outhouse in the garden, when a man confronted him, and fired two pistols at his breast. He pushed aside the weapons with the candlestick he happened to be carrying; but two bullets entered his left arm. The assassin escaped over a drain into a back street; but having been recognised, was subsequently captured. A surgeon was sent for, and the bullets extracted, after having done no serious injury. The criminal turned out to be one of his late adherents, by name Desirè Rousselle; who, on examination before the magistrates of the police-office at Union Hall, could assign no motive for the deed; and after two more examinations he was discharged, the duke declining to prosecute. The next appearance of his grace of Normandy at a police-office was in character of defendant. It seems that he had turned his attention to the art of pyrotechnics, and his explosive experiments were so alarming to the quiet neighbourhood of Camberwell, that he was summoned to answer for his conduct; but on promising not to repeat it, the complaint was dismissed. It would appear that his experiments were not altogether useless; for at a trial of newly-invented shells before the Board of Ordnance at Woolwich, the duke's missiles were declared either second or third, we forget which, in point of efficiency. Indeed he seems to have occupied himself almost exclusively with scientific pursuits whilst in England. At Chelsea, whither he removed, the duke constructed a set of workshops and laboratories, in which he, with his assistants and pupils, diligently wrought. In what his scientific labours and experiments would have resulted, it is impossible to say, for they were interrupted by a third attempt on his life. While alone in one of his workshops, late at night, a bullet was fired at him from a hidden and still undiscovered enemy. The shot missed him; but, afraid to remain in this country any longer, he retired to Delft, in Holland, where it seems he died a natural death on the 10th of August last.

Whatever opinions may be formed of the truth of this individual's story of his birth, it is certain that a great many persons in France, whose opinions are entitled to respect, believe him to have been Louis XVII. Amongst the notices in the French papers to which his decease has given rise, we find a note written by M. Herbert, once director of the military posts in Italy. It appears that when in that office, the man Neündorf was, in 1810, arrested at Rome, and interrogated by M. Radet, chief of police in that city: the latter pronounced him to be in reality the son of Louis XVI. Than M. Radet, there could not be a better judge of the matter, for he happened to be one of the five persons who arrested Louis and his family when they tried to quit France, and were intercepted at Varennes. Our own impression is, notwithstanding this and all other circumstances to the contrary, that the man was an impostor, and such we believe will also be the impression generally among our readers.

A FASHION OF 1745.

We have lately formed acquaintance with a rare pamphlet of the year 1745, which may perchance amuse our readers. The title at full length is as follows:—'The Enormous Abomination of the Hoop Petticoat, as the Fashion now is, and has been, for about these two years, fully displayed in some Reflections upon it, humbly offered to the Consideration of both Sexes, especially the Female. By A. W., Esq. London: printed for William Russell, at the Golden Ball, near St Dunstan's Church, Fleet Street, 1745. (Price Sixpence.)' It starts with a disclaimer of all preciseness and moroseness, professing rather an unusual regard for the fair sex: neither is the author an old man clamouring against things new. This, indeed, he says, could not well be the case; for fashions have undergone little change in his remembrance: 'among men scarce any, except a broader or narrower hat, and some little variation in the sleeves, skirts, and pockets of their coats.' He enters the field on public grounds alone.

The chief invention of his time is, he says, the hoop petticoat. In its original institution about the year 1709, it was sufficiently bad, inasmuch that most people thought it could not long survive, especially after Isaac Bickerstaff, in the *Tatler*, opened his batteries against it. Having, in spite of ridicule, stood its ground since then, it has within the last two years 'spread into such an enormous circumference, that there is no enduring it any longer. It is now,' the writer declares, 'past a jest: the whole sex, in a manner, especially the younger sort, the misses, are by this prodigious garment become a perfect nuisance.' 'I pass over,' he adds, 'the foolish expense of so much silk and other costly materials, to cover such a huge extent of canvas, or striped linen and whalebone, though that is beyond measure ridiculous.'

Determined, if possible, to write it down, our pamphleteer proposes to 'treat the wearer of this rotunda in a fivefold view or aspect; 1, as merely hooped; 2, as hooped, and coming into a room; 3, as hooped, and actually in a room; 4, as hooped, and in a coach or chair; and, 5, as hooped, and in any public assembly, particularly at church.'

First, with a mere regard to proportion, the hoop puts the lower section of the female figure out of all harmony with the upper. 'Can anything be a greater jest than to see a girl of seventeen taking up the whole side of a street with her hollow strutting petticoats? Behold one of them at church walking down the wide empty middle aisle, one corner of her petticoat touching the pews on the right, the other those on the left. . . . But be it where it will, what a figure does a creature make with two cumbrous unwieldy baskets or hampers rising orbicularly from either side, then spreading to an exorbitant size as they descend, swagging from side to side, one up and t'other down, like a pair of scales, pretty near, but not quite at an equilibrium! I say, what a figure does such a creature make!'

'Thus in general: now for the particulars. Suppose the fine lady coming into a room, the graceful manner of doing which was formerly reckoned no small part of female education and good-breeding. First enters wriggling, and sideling, and edging in by degrees, two yards and a half of hoop; for as yet you see nothing else. Some time after appears the inhabitant of the garment herself, not with a full face, but in profile; the face being turned to or from the company, according as they happen to be situated. Next, in due time, again follows two yards and a-half of hoop more. And now her whole person, with all its appurtenances, is actually arrived, fully and completely, in the room, where we are in the next place to consider her.

'She sits down: if it be upon a couch or squab, though the couch or squab be five yards long, her hoop takes up every inch of it from one end to the other. If upon a chair, it is the same thing in effect; only the hoop is suspended in the air, without anything else to rest upon. But now enter two, or three, or four more, with hoopage of equal dimensions. Upon their sitting down, too, *insequitur stridorque, strepitusque*. The ladies need not check at the Latin; they shall have it in English: the ruffling and crush of silk and silver, and the crash and cracking of whalebone, immediately ensue. The hoops and petticoats, when contracted and huddled up into a heap, make, if possible, a more awkward and ungainly show than when they were free and unconfined. They rise, and sink into such hideous wrinkles, into such mountains and valleys, into such a variety of uncouth, irregular shapes, as exceed all the descriptions of painting or poetry. For myself, I will not pretend to enter into the detail of them; but appeal to the eyes and judgment of all who see them. It is nevertheless to be observed, that whoever, of any three, happens to sit in the middle, has her hoop on each side tossed up at least a foot higher than before, in which attitude she looks like a higgler-woman that sells apples or cabbages sitting on horseback between two panniers; only the higgler's panniers are well enough shaped, these the ugliest that can possibly be contrived or imagined. Such is the exquisite taste and fancy of the fair sex in this refined age, so famed for elegance and politeness.

'Consider next two, or three, or four of them crammed into a coach. If I guess right at what they endure, I would almost as soon ride the wooden horse, be tied neck and heels, sit in the stocks, or stand in the pillory, as suffer what they suffer, by being so cramped, squeezed, bruised, and crushed, only to gratify this unnatural piece of foppery; for which, too, everybody laughs at them. But be that as it may, though they are the best judges of their own feeling, we, I am sure, can best judge of what we see. And what do we see here? Why, a woman's petticoats half within doors and half without, such a quantity of stuffage turned out into the street at each window, it being impossible for the coach to contain all. And was ever sight more odious and ridiculous? Thus for the coach or chariot. As to the chair, though it can receive but one at a time, yet in that both the confinement and uneasiness, and the amazingly absurd figure, are as bad, if not worse, than in the other. The hoop is hoisted to the very roof of the chair, whether the glasses are up or down; you see nothing on each side but petticoat inverted; the woman is totally hidden. And in front you see but little of the face; the two wings of the hoop covering all but the nose, and a small part of the forehead.

'But now for public assemblies. Is there any equity, that one woman should take up as much room as two or three men? At the playhouses, indeed, at ridottos, oratorios, &c. it is no great matter how much both sexes are incommoded; the more, perhaps, the better. But ought it to be so at church too? We (whatever they may do) come thither to serve God, but are hindered from performing our duty as we should, and as we desire, by the crowd and embarrassment of these ungodly hoops. We can neither kneel, sit, nor stand with any tolerable convenience, for a parcel of worthless flirts, the most considerable of whom, perhaps, exceeds not the quality of a tailor's daughter. One with the stiff ribs of her petticoat dashes against me, and almost breaks my shins; two or three more attack me in the rear, banging my hams and the calves of my legs. A man of more devotion than I pretend to, may be somewhat disturbed in it while he is thus buffeted; and that by those who, in all appearance, have no devotion, but come to church for one only purpose, to show their hoops and themselves.

'But besides their being thus grievous to those within the pews, how many do they keep out of them? Suppose all, both men and women, as willing to come to church as they ought to be, many cannot come, unless they will stand in the aisles, being excluded from the pews by these heathenish hoops. I call them heathenish, not that they were ever worn in any heathenish nation, but because they tend to heathenism by the mischief they do to Christianity. For my part, I wonder how the wearers of them have the confidence to look us, or even one another, in the face. But modesty, which used to be the most amiable and most distinguishing character of that sex, seems now to be as much out of fashion as the hoop is in fashion. To ask a question in passing: Did you never see a hoop hedged in by other hoops, thrown up into the air half a yard above the wearer's head, and that at church too? I am sure I have, and so, I suppose, have others. How decent is this, especially in the house of God, and in the time of divine service! Having thus said something to all the particulars, I now resume the hoop in general. It certainly takes up much less time, and pains, and expense to hoop a cask completely, than to hoop a woman. And since I have made this comparison, which, I hope, is natural enough, I would by all means have the tall and big females called hogsheads, the middle-sized barrels, and the dwarfish kilderkins. Of which last sort, by the way, there are not a few who would be pretty, were it not for their hoopage; but as they, too, must needs be surrounded with that fashionable incumbrance, they strut and waddle, like a crow in a gutter, to the great diversion of the ill-natured, and no less concern of the compassionate spectators.

'The tall, in this habit, are the most tolerable; yet some even of them you shall see, who, having little round faces, being short to the waist, long downwards, and wearing a wide-extended hoop, look like a pair of kitchen-tongs set a-straddle, and provoke laughter to a high degree.

'To say the truth (I am aware it is an unmannerly truth, but I cannot help that; let those bear the blame who make it necessary to be spoken), in this debauched profligate age, with regard to luxury, dissoluteness, extravagance, ruinous gaming, irreligion, immoderate love of pleasure, diversions, and recreations, the men are very bad, and perhaps the women worse. What excess of riot do these she rakes run into at their masquerades, ridottos, oratorios, Vauxhall, Ranelagh gardens; and at races, balls, assemblies, in almost every large town, sitting up all night, acknowledging that it is grievous, fatiguing, and destructive of their health, yet still indulging themselves in these scandalous practices! And all this at a time when the hand of God lies heavy upon us, when his judgments are visibly poured out upon the nation; when abroad we are involved in a most deplorable, expensive, bloody, and everywhere unsuccessful war; at home harassed to death with insupportable taxes, the decay of trade, the empty houses in the city, and the untenanted farms in the country, being evident proofs that the whole kingdom, in a manner, is beggared and undone.

'What then? Ought the hoop to be wholly discarded? I heartily wish it were, for it is bad enough at best. However, my invective has all along been levelled not against any, but against so much hoop; against the insufferable bulk of it, as the fashion now is, and has been for about these two years. Some few ladies even now (I speak it to their honour) carry a circumference of a moderate compass; let the rest of the hoops at present be conformed to these, and who knows but in time we may get rid of them all?'

So much for this extravagance of our great-grandmothers. Of course the preaching must have been in vain, as such preachings ever are. The following of fashions is a moral phenomenon, which has not yet been thought worthy of notice by the philosopher. In reality, it is an extremely curious illustration of the power of one of our sentiments—love of approbation. No style of form so extravagant, no material so absurdly expensive, but it will be adopted by the multitude, if supposed to be what everybody wears. The individual is helpless, however sensible of the folly. And the strange consideration is, that everybody may be disgusted with the mode, and yet it will keep its ground, just as a tyrant who has not one friend, may continue to rule through the terror exercised over individuals. Let those who think public opinion never wrong, ponder on this curious fact.

NAMES OF PLACES IN THE UNITED STATES.

SECOND ARTICLE.

The number of counties, townships, &c. in the United States, bearing the same names as the counties of England, are—we had almost said—innumerable. Of Cumberland, for example, there are six counties and eight townships; of York, four of the former and nineteen of the latter; while there are three Chester counties, and twenty-five Chester townships. Indeed the only English counties whose names have not been adopted some six or eight times, are Shropshire, Wiltshire, and Devon; but, as if to make up for the omission, the name of Shrewsbury, the capital of Shropshire, is used five times; that of Salisbury, the capital of Wiltshire, eleven times; and that of Exeter, the capital of Devon, eight times.

A flourishing manufacturing village, named Manchester, is rising up at the falls of Amoskeag, in the state of New Hampshire; in a township of the same name in Vermont, white marble is found in inexhaustible quantities, which would be a treasure indeed to the Manchester on this side the Atlantic; in another township of the same name in Massachusetts, the inhabitants, 1355 in number, are extensively engaged in the fisheries; while another Manchester, in Connecticut, possesses a capital of 220,000 dollars invested in manufactures. There are nineteen other Manchesters scattered among the various states. There is a township in Maine named Leeds, which contains a population of 1736, twelve schools with 604 scholars, and a capital of nearly 7000 dollars invested in manufactures; and there is a small village of the same name in the state of New York. Besides these, there are three Leedsvilles, and one North Leeds. In the state of Ohio there is a 'growing village,' which contains 'one flouring-mill, one saw-mill, one forge, several stores, and various mechanics' shops.' This village is named Birmingham. There is another of the same name in Michigan, which contains four stores, a flouring-mill, and a furnace, and is reputed to be flourishing. There are other four Birminghams in the states. There is a county named Preston in Virginia, with a population of 6866; a township of the same name in Connecticut; another in New York; and other four variously distributed. Of Sheffields there are seven, whose aggregate capital, invested in manufactures, is 35,200 dollars; and it is stated of one of them, that it is the oldest township in the county of Berkshire, Massachusetts, containing five distilleries, three tan-works, two fulling, one grist, and eight saw-mills. The population is 2322. Halifax seems to be a favourite name, for two counties and seven townships, &c. bear it; while Bradford is equally popular in one county and eight townships, &c. There are several townships in New York and Pennsylvania named Stockport; and if the phrase, 'sending to Coventry,' is ever adopted in the states, it will be necessary to tell to which of the seven places known by that name the offender is to be despatched. The names of the minor manufacturing towns of England, such as Huddersfield, Rochdale, Bury, &c. have not yet come into use. The English town of Liverpool is the great town of export for salt; and in the township of Liverpool, in the state of New York, there were produced from saline springs, in 1840, upwards of 800,000 bushels of this commodity. There are two Liverpools in the state of Ohio, one in Pennsylvania, and one in Indiana. There is a large maritime county named Bristol, with a population of 60,000, in the state of Massachusetts, which possesses a capital in manufactures of upwards of four millions of dollars, and which excels the Bristol on this side of the water so far as the number of newspapers is concerned, for it has two daily and eight weekly papers! There is another Bristol in the state of Maine, with a population of about 3000, which is said to have 'good harbours, and considerable shipping engaged chiefly in the coasting trade and the fisheries.' In it a settlement was commenced as early as 1625. In Rhode Island there is a flourishing town named Bristol, which has now a population of 3500, and possesses a weekly newspaper; and it is reported that on its site 'the celebrated King Philip, chief of the Pequods, and the terror of the early colonists, held his court.' There is also a Bristol in Connecticut, in which clocks and buttons are extensively manufactured; another in New Hampshire, which was first settled in 1770; and, in addition to all these, there are eleven other places of the same name in the United States. It is curious to find so many Bristols, most of them with large populations, and in a flourishing condition, in the eastern part of the states near the sea-coast. It is, however, sufficiently accounted for by the fact, that at the time America was discovered, Bristol was perhaps the greatest port in the west of England; and in the charter given by James I. to the colonists in 1606, it was agreed that the adventurers from Bristol, Exeter, and Plymouth, should settle in the lands lying between the 38th and 45th degrees of north latitude. Within these parallels we find all the *eastern* Bristols situated. In those days Liverpool was scarcely known except as an insignificant port at the mouth of the Mersey, and the Bristol settlers would have very little idea that the field of commerce which they were opening up would be the means of causing this fishing village of Lancashire to become a formidable and successful rival of their own native city.

Among the eastern states, the name of Plymouth very frequently occurs. The Plymouth in Massachusetts, where, in 1620, the 'pilgrim fathers' landed, contains a population of 5281; it has two weekly newspapers, two academies with 123 students, and forty-one schools with 1378 scholars. In the same state there is a county named Plymouth, with a population of 47,373, and a capital invested in manufactures of 1,657,265 dollars. The same name is given to a township in Pennsylvania, which is inhabited chiefly by Friends. The name given by the pilgrim fathers to the spot on which they first landed has travelled to the far west, and is found in the states of Missouri, Indiana, and Illinois. The Southamptons are ten in number, and, consistently enough, one of them is situated in the county of Hampshire. The fashionable English Brighton has given its name to a township distinguished as being the most extensive cattle market in the county of Middlesex, state of Massachusetts. The only Brighton which would appear to be worthy of its name, is a beautiful flourishing place situated on the west side of the Big Beaver river, in the state of Pennsylvania. On the east bank of the same river is *New* Brighton, and the two places are connected by a bridge 500 feet long. The other Brightons are eight in number. Hastings, the seaport in England, proved, in the year 1066, a convenient landing-place for William the Conqueror; and a Hastings situated on the east side of the Hudson, in New York, is reported to 'possess a convenient landing.' In the state of Delaware there is a Kent county, whose capital is Dover; and scattered among the states are twenty-one other Dovers. Not one of these places, however, is situated opposite to a Calais; but there is a Calais in the state of Maine, opposite to the British town of St Andrews in New Brunswick. The description of Yarmouth in Massachusetts—that it has a number of vessels employed in the fisheries and the coasting-trade—would apply equally to the Yarmouth on the German Ocean. Hull, a township in Massachusetts, incorporated in 1644, has a beach four miles long, but a population only of 231. The names of seaports on the east coast of England, north from Hull, have also been adopted, for we find three Sunderlands, two Stocktons, and two Scarboroughs. In England there are two Newcastles, and it is thought necessary to distinguish them by the names of 'upon Tyne' in the one case, and 'under Lyne' in the other; but no distinguishing mark is attached to the twelve Newcastles of the United States. There is a Bath on the east side of the Hudson river, which contains a sulphur spring of some celebrity; and another Bath in Virginia, which contains a medicinal spring with a temperature of 96°, reputed to be 'useful in rheumatic and other complaints.' Of a third Bath, in Georgia, which contains about fifteen houses, it is stated that 'the situation is elevated and healthy, and it is resorted to in the sickly season.' The other twelve Baths that exist do not seem to possess anything like the characteristics of the English Bath. One Bath county, in Kentucky, contains a population of 9763, of whom 1951 are slaves; and another, in Virginia, contains a population of 4300, 347 of whom are slaves. There is one Cheltenham and one Buxton; but neither a Matlock nor a Harrowgate. Cambridge in Massachusetts possesses a university, founded in 1638. This university is named Harvard, and has a president and twenty-seven professors, 246 classical students, and upwards of 50,000 volumes in its libraries. Oxford in Ohio possesses a university named Miami, which has a president and five professors, 139 students, and 4352 volumes in its libraries. The land with which it is endowed yields a yearly income of 4500 dollars.

We might go on multiplying instances of the use of the names of English towns in the states, but the above will serve to give an idea of the extent to which the practice is carried. If the facilities for communication between one place and another go on increasing as much in future as they have done in past years, it will become necessary to exercise the utmost precision in speaking or writing of any town. Blunders enough have already arisen from the confusion of such names of persons as Smith, Thomson, Jones; and it would appear as if the United States were about to enter on the experience of similar blunders, but of a more serious kind, regarding the names of their places. Story-tellers on this side of the water have hitherto found such names as Smith very convenient as disguises for the real names of their heroes, but the names of places they have often been forced to conceal under an initial letter, or to disguise altogether under a fictitious one. The American story-tellers need never have recourse to such a shift.

The 'far west' is a term which has been very often used with a very general meaning. No specific place was indicated by the name, and in the course of years it was found that the 'far west,' like the poor Indians, was moving every day *farther* west. Its 'local habitation' has now, however, been fixed to be in the state of Missouri, 1072 miles from the city of Washington. There the post village of Far West, with a population of 500 souls, is to be found. *One* Far West is, however, insufficient for the Americans, as another is found in the state of Indiana, about 500 miles nearer to Washington. Other points of the compass have been fixed in a similar manner. East and West townships are found in the state of Ohio; and in the state of Pennsylvania, where it would be least expected, is found another township named West. The same state has a township named North East; New York another; and Maryland contains a village of the same name. In eleven of the states we find that each contains a Bridgewater; in one state there is a North Bridgewater; in another a North-west Bridgewater; in a third a West Bridgewater; and in a fourth an East Bridgewater. The places to whose names the prefix *New* is attached, occupy forty of the 750 pages of Sherman and Smith's Gazetteer. Many of the American names seem to have become old already, for we find New Echota, New Hackensack, New Ohio, New Philadelphia, New Columbia, &c. &c.; while there are six Old Towns, one Old Jefferson, and two Old Hickories.

The names of abstract virtues are found in great abundance, and if the character of the inhabitants corresponds to the names of their towns, they must have reached a point in social bliss which would leave little more to be desired. Concord is applied to twenty-seven places; Harmony to thirteen; Amity to six; Unity to eight; and Friendship to half a dozen. Of New Concords there are three, and of New Harmonies two. There are four Fair-Plays, and one Fair-Dealing; one Philanthropy; and a settlement named Economy, consisting of Germans from Swabia, on the banks of the river Ohio. There is a Home in India, and another in Pennsylvania; but Sweet Homes are to be found only in North Carolina and Arkansas. As if to make up for this scarcity, there is a Paradise in Illinois, and two in Pennsylvania; while, at the same time, the Promised Land is in Maryland; and the visionary may find an Eldorado far west in Missouri. Success is found both in New Hampshire and New York; but there is only one Patriot in Indiana, and one in Ohio. Of Unions there are eighty-six, besides a number of Union-towns and Union-villes.

Honour has likewise been paid to Napoleon and some of his generals. There are five Napoleons and one Bonaparte. The name of his great rival Moreau, the victor of Hohenlinden, has been given to one township in New York and to two in Missouri. The name of Bernadotte is found in Illinois; while there is a township in New York named Massena. Nor have the famous victories of France's great emperor been forgotten; for there are two Arcolas, nine Lodis, four Marengos, and one Jena; and, to commemorate his final overthrow, there are a dozen Waterloos. The famous French republican tune of Ca Ira has given its name to a village in Virginia; and the name of the republican general Lafayette is applied to three counties and fifteen townships. The great objects for which men have in all ages struggled, and to gain which states have been both raised and overthrown, have supplied their names very freely to places in the United States. The appellation of Liberty has, with a strange inconsistency, been given to a county in Georgia which contains a population of 7241, of which 5561 are slaves. In addition to this Liberty, there are other forty-seven in the various states. Freedom is the name of a borough situated on the east bank of the Ohio; and other twelve Freedoms exist in the states. Equality exists in North and South Carolina, Illinois, and Missouri; and thirteen states contain Independence. Arkansas has a county named Independence, of whose population 514 are slaves!

For the names of their presidents the Americans appear to entertain much respect, for we find them broad-cast among the states in the most plenteous manner. The capital city is named after Washington. There are only two or three of the states that have not counties bearing his name; and the townships, &c. named Washington are 165 in number, of which thirty-six are found in the state of Ohio alone! The name of Adams, who succeeded Washington as president, is applied to five counties and sixteen townships, &c. besides which there are nine Adamsvilles. Jefferson, who was third president, has his name given to sixteen counties and fifty-two townships, &c. His successor was Monro, whose name is used for fifteen counties and forty-eight townships, &c. There are fourteen counties and thirty-five townships, &c. named Madison; while the name of Jackson has been given to thirteen counties and eighty-one townships, &c. Among the western states there are five counties named Van Buren, and ten townships and six villages bear the same name. Harrisons and Tylers are also very common; while the states of Tennessee and Missouri possess each a county named Polk.

Other names are found quite peculiar to the United States. There is a Sunset in Georgia; and on the north bank of the Ohio there is a Rising Sun. A Morning Sun rises in Tennessee, and another in Ohio; while the states of Pennsylvania and Ohio possess each a Moon. The United States have three Dead, three

Mad, seven Little, one Big, one Muddy, four Deep, four New, three Vermilion, three Red, one Green, and seven Black rivers; besides a river Styx in Ohio, a Dismal Swamp, thirty miles long and ten wide, in Virginia and North Carolina; and to bring this strange summary to a conclusion, an Ultima Thule situated on a branch of Little River, in the state of Arkansas.

SLAVERY.

On the 19th of August 1836, says Darwin in his journal of a voyage round the world, we finally left the shores of Brazil. I thank God I shall never again visit a slave country. To this day, if I hear a distant scream, it recalls with painful vividness my feelings when, passing a house near Pernambuco, I heard the most pitiable moans, and could not but suspect that some poor slave was being tortured, yet knew that I was as powerless as a child even to remonstrate. I suspected that these moans were from a tortured slave, for I was told that this was the case in another instance. Near Rio de Janeiro I lived opposite to an old lady, who kept screws to crush the fingers of her female slaves. I have stayed in a house where a young household mulatto daily and hourly was reviled, beaten, and persecuted enough to break the spirit of the lowest animal. I have seen a little boy, six or seven years old, struck thrice with a horse-whip (before I could interfere) on the head; I saw his father tremble at a mere glance from his master's eye. These latter cruelties were witnessed by me in a Spanish colony, in which it has always been said that slaves are better treated than by the Portuguese, English, or other European nations. I have seen at Rio de Janeiro a powerful negro afraid to ward off a blow directed, as he thought, at his face. I was present when a kind-hearted man was on the point of separating for ever the men, women, and little children of a large number of families who had long lived together. I will not even allude to the many heart-sickening atrocities which I authentically heard of; nor would I have mentioned the above revolting details, had I not met with several people, so blinded by the constitutional gaiety of the negro, as to speak of slavery as a tolerable evil. Such people have generally visited at the houses of the upper classes where the domestic slaves are commonly well treated; and they have not, like myself, lived amongst the lower classes. Such inquirers will ask slaves about their condition; they forget that the slave must indeed be dull who does not calculate on the chance of his answer reaching his master's ears. It is argued that self-interest will prevent excessive cruelty; as if self-interest protected our domestic animals, which are far less likely than degraded slaves to stir up the rage of their savage masters. It is an argument long since protested against with noble feeling, and strikingly exemplified by the ever illustrious Humboldt. It is often attempted to palliate slavery by comparing the state of slaves with our poorer countrymen: if the misery of our poor be caused not by the laws of nature, but by our institutions, great is our sin; but how this bears on slavery I cannot see. As well might the use of the thumb-screw be defended in one land, by showing that men in another land suffered from some dreadful disease. Those who look tenderly at the slave owner, and with a cold heart at the slave, never seem to put themselves into the position of the latter—what a cheerless prospect, with not even a hope of change! Picture to yourself the chance, ever hanging over you, of your wife and your little children—those objects which nature urges even the slave to call his own—being torn from you, and being sold like beasts to the highest bidder! And these deeds are done and palliated by men who profess to love their neighbours as themselves, who believe in God, and pray that his will be done on earth! It makes one's blood boil, yet tremble, to think that we Englishmen and our American descendants, with their boastful cry of liberty, have been and are so guilty; but it is a consolation to reflect that we at least have made a greater sacrifice than was ever made by any nation to expiate our sin.

PETER BELL.

We observe from the newspapers that the great 'Peter Bell' in York Minster is now safely suspended in its own tower. The weight of the bell and its appendages, together with the frame, is calculated to be 29 tons; but the strength of the tower is equal to triple that weight. The bell is the largest in the kingdom, being 5 tons heavier than 'Old Tom' of Oxford, and 7 tons heavier than the celebrated 'Tom' of Lincoln. The cost of it is above L.2000; its height 7 feet 4 inches, and its diameter 8 feet 4 inches. It is placed (at a height of nearly 200 feet) diagonally in the tower, for the greater security to the building, and above 300 cubic feet of timber have been used for its support. It may be rung with two wheels, and will revolve entirely, if necessary.

THE MOTHERLESS CHILDREN.

ADDRESSED TO THE INFANTS LEFT BY MADAME LEONTINE GENOUDE.

[FROM THE FRENCH OF DE LAMARTINE.]

Poor sable-clad children, who ceaseless, forlorn,
Ask your sire, saying, 'What is this death that you weep?
And why from our couch do we waken each morn
Uncaressed, and how long lasts this sad gloomy sleep?'

Hush little ones! Only in dreams you will feel
The kiss on your brow, fingers twined in your hair,
The nest on her knees where your head loved to steal,
The heart pressed to yours—the eyes meeting yours there.

Love will wean you from grief: now, 'tis bitter for you;
Your milk is dried up; like the lamb that is born
From its dam by the shepherd, and cast forth all new,
To teach it to browse on the herb and the thorn.

You will have but a memory—a vague distant dream,
Of what is the sweetest in life's early years;
A mother's fond love but a history will seem,
By a sad lonely father told, mingled with tears.

And when in your souls you would bring back to light
Those memories under the cold marble sealed,
Those sweet whispered words, and that smile fond and bright,
When the mother's heart-love to the child is revealed.

And when, in your day-dreams, tears, causeless, unbidden,
Burst forth, and your souls up to Heaven arise,
When you see the young babe in its mother's breast hidden,
Or the desolate father absorbed in his sighs—

Come, come to this grave, where the green turf upswells,
Sit down at the feet of your mother, and pray;
Look up, full of hope, to the heaven where she dwells,
Imploring her smile like a light on your way.

From that blest home eternal, her soul evermore,
Like an unsetting star, o'er her babes loves to rest;
So the eagle, when soaring to heaven's high floor,
Still watchful looks down on her own beloved nest.

D. M. M.

AN AWKWARD CLERICAL ERROR.

Soon after Dr Trench's consecration, he accompanied his father one Sunday to the Magdalen Asylum, in Leeson Street, Dublin; where his person being unknown, but his dress indicating his ministerial character, the sexton approached him respectfully, and requested that he would, in compliance with the general rule observed there when any strange clergyman was present, give his assistance to the chaplain. He instantly complied with the request; read the service of the day; and, after the sermon was concluded, he was told by the unceremonious chaplain that his duties were not yet over, and that he expected him to administer the Lord's Supper to the congregation. 'In fact,' said his grace, in repeating the anecdote, 'the humblest curate in Dublin could not have more of the burden of the day laid upon him. However, I did everything he desired; and, after service, followed him into the vestry and disrobed, whilst he scarcely condescended to notice me. When I made my bow to depart, he said, "Sir, I am greatly obliged; may I ask to whom I am indebted?" "The Bishop of Waterford," said I; and I shall never forget the poor man's countenance. He seemed thunderstruck; and I was glad to escape from the apologies he was forcing upon me.'—*Sirr's Memoir of Archbishop Trench.*

LITERARY OVERSIGHTS.

Sabbathier, a compiler of the last century, published a work entitled 'Manners, Customs, and Usages of the Ancients,' in which he forgot to say one word about the Romans!—*Curiosities Bibliographiques.* Paris. 1845.

Published by W. and R. Chambers, High Street, Edinburgh (also 98, Miller Street, Glasgow); and with their permission, by W. S. Orr, Amen Corner, London.—Printed by Bradbury and Evans, Whitefriars, London.

CONDUCTED BY WILLIAM AND ROBERT CHAMBERS, EDITORS OF 'CHAMBERS'S INFORMATION FOR THE PEOPLE,' 'CHAMBERS'S EDUCATIONAL COURSE,' &c.

No. 95. New Series. SATURDAY, OCTOBER 25, 1845. Price 1½d.

SHY MEN.

Individuals are often judged of very erroneously from their external and ordinary demeanour. Of a particular class of misjudgments I am peculiarly assured, namely, those relating to men who have the reputation of being reserved through pride. In a large proportion of such cases, it is not any form of pride which produces the reservedness, but the opposite quality of shyness. It is the defect of self-esteem, rather than an undue endowment of it, that causes the conduct complained of.

Among the persons known to me as friends and associates, I could point to a number who are usually considered as proud men, and to whom it is customary to attach the—of late much misused—epithet aristocratic; while I know, with all possible certainty, that the real cause of the conduct and demeanour which obtains them this character, is nothing else than mere timidity of face. You may meet one of these men in company, and after a little time get into easy and familiar converse with him; yet, next day, encountering him in the street, and expecting a frank recognition, will be frozen by the most distant bow. You set him down as a cold proud man, too much absorbed in self to have any sympathies with you; but the fact is, that he has a boy-like shyness, which makes the usual courtesies of life a burden to him, and he only passes you in this reserved manner because he could not address you without an embarrassment painful in itself, and which would leave him in a state of self-humiliation, doubling that pain twice over. Thus, what you deem an assumption of superiority on his part, is in reality a silent confession of the most distressing weakness.

A Scottish peer, who died a few years ago in the prime of life, was unpopular from this cause. Alike to equals and inferiors, to country neighbours and to tenants, he appeared a freezing aristocrat. But there was no absolute want of a kindly nature in this gentleman. He was only oppressed with constitutional shyness. One of our late sovereigns, spending a morning at his father's house during his youth, the children of the family were ordered to be prepared to be formally introduced to the king. When the time came, all were found duly ready for the introduction, excepting the eldest son. He—the hope of the house—had been missing all morning, and could nowhere be found. The venerable earl had the mortification of bringing his young flock under the eye of royalty without its chief ornament: the awkwardness of his apology for the absence of Lord ——, may be imagined. In reality, the young nobleman had secretly left home at an early hour, for the express purpose of avoiding the dreaded ceremony; nor did he reappear till some time after the royal guest had departed. On acceding, a few years after, to his titles, and large estates and influence, his natural shyness experienced no abatement; and it had the effect of, in a great measure, neutralising his high social and political rank. To convey an idea of the extremity of the case—he was one day driving with a friend over the estates of a neighbour, when his curricle broke down. An honest farmer, seeing the distress of the party, came up to offer the horse he was riding upon, and another from a neighbouring field, for their use. The earl's companion accepted the offer with thanks; but the noble himself stalked aside, and took up a position at a little distance. There he waited till the horse was brought to him; there he mounted it; and then he rode off, without having said a single word to the worthy man who was putting himself to inconvenience on his account. The farmer, it may be believed, was astonished; but there cannot be the shade of a doubt that this strange conduct was the consequence of mere shamefacedness, or an inability to enter upon a few graceful commonplaces, which to another man would not have cost one moment's thought or pain.

The character of a late English noble was felt to be a great puzzle, in as far as, professing the extreme of liberalism in politics, he was observed to be practically 'aristocratic' far beyond the most conservative of his compeers. It was said of him that, in his own house, the servants had instructions to avoid, as far as possible, meeting him in staircases and passages; whence it was inferred that he disliked the very sight of his humbler fellow-creatures. I know not how the case might actually be; but from others which have come under my immediate observation, I think it by no means unlikely that Lord —— was only shy, not proud. He was perhaps one of those to whom greetings are intolerable, and from whom a 'Good morning' is wrung like gold from a miser. The great mass of the humble can hardly form an idea of the difficulties experienced, through this cause, by some of those whom they consider as men of consequence. A gentleman occupying one of the highest offices in the country, and in the enjoyment of great public respect, on account of the manner in which he discharges his important functions —a man equally sound in judgment and kindly in the affairs of private life—this gentleman, to the knowledge of the present writer, often uses efforts to pass his friends in the street without being seen by them. A colleague in office, who for half the year sits several hours every day in the same room with him, states that he had often found himself on the point of encountering —— —— in the course of a country walk, when he had observed him deliberately quit the footpath, and cross to the opposite side of the road, where he would stand looking over a hedge, affecting to take an interest in the landscape, or some object near or remote, until he thought his friend would be past, when he would quietly return to the footpath and resume his walk, thus accomplishing what?—nothing but the avoidance of a kindly greeting with his colleague and friend! Such a fact will to many appear incredible; but its value consists in its strict truth, and its serving to illustrate a disposition of mind which, though hitherto little noticed, is only a too painful reality.

Shy men are generally persons of a diffident and amiable character—often possessed of a fine taste and nice moral feelings. They shrink from society and from individual rencontres, very much because of a certain over-delicacy of nature, which makes the common bustle of life unpleasant to them. Another element of their case, is a deficiency of mere animal spirits. In their ordinary moments, they lack the backing of excitement to force their minds into active and healthy play. Laxly screwed, the strings refuse to twang, and the men start back, not from the sound themselves have made, but from the absence of all sound. A sense of the dull unvital state of their minds reacts upon them in producing greater embarrassment, and the more they keep out of society, the more unfitted for it do they become. Sometimes a chance plunge into life, or an impulse from the contiguity of a bustling friend, will waken up a little energy in them, and for a while they will feel the comfort of a healthy normal state of mind. But when the external stimulus has spent its force, or been removed, they sink back into their unmanly timidity, and cheat the gleam of hope which their friends had begun to entertain. Usually, these men are altogether misunderstood by the world, being thought haughty when they are in reality modest, and cold and repelling when they may perhaps be glowing with benevolence to all mankind. At the best, they are regarded as odd and incalculable persons, and find their best and noblest qualities insufficient to protect them from the neglect which must ever be the fate of men of unpopular manners, however deserving of esteem.

Wherever the persons thus characterised are liable to any kind of external influence, it were well that their case should be properly understood and treated. The tendency of the patient himself—for a patient he should be considered—is to retreat from the society which is painful to him, into still deeper obscurities, and there foster the disease which preys upon him. He should, on the contrary, be tempted by all fair means into the bustle of the world, and induced, if possible, to take an interest in its affairs. Even a liking for its frivolities might, in such a case, be redemption from worse evil. When friends have any influence in proposed matrimonial arrangements, they should seek to unite the victim of shyness to a person of cheerful social nature, instead of to one who, while deemed perhaps more solid, might be apt, by less gay and active disposition, to lead to further restraints being imposed. In children, the incipient manifestations of the malady might be met by the encouragement of active sports and social habits. Above all, it is important that the victim be not left to himself, or thrown into the hands of persons of sombre tempers. Disheartening views of individual merits, and of human nature generally, must also be deeply injurious.

The facts here brought forward ought to warn us against rash-judging from external appearances. The heart of man is a thing of infinite contrarieties; and often where we think ourselves surest of the ground on which we are forming an estimate, we are at the remotest point from the truth. Let us make a rule of pausing when we are asked to condemn a man for his pride, whether as an incidental demonstration or a habitual characteristic. Where we think there is disdain, there is perhaps only a pitiable embarrassment, arising from natural and irresistible awkwardness. Nor may we even be sure, where we see a somewhat forward or over-confident manner, that we are not contemplating the effects of this same foible, for it is natural to assume one vicious manner in order to escape the tendency to another, and a decisiveness, however constrained, may seem to the victim a blessed exchange from the pain of a habitual vacillation.

MR LYELL ON THE GEOLOGY OF NORTH AMERICA.

The reader must not expect from this title any lengthened disquisition on the geology of the American continent, but merely a passing notice of some of the more interesting facts adverted to by Mr Lyell, in his recent travels through the United States, Canada, and Nova Scotia.

1. *Falls of Niagara.*—These celebrated falls were first seen by the tourist when about three miles distant. It was a lovely morning in August, the sun was shining full upon them—no building in view—nothing but the green wood, the falling water, and the white foam. 'At that moment they appeared to me more beautiful and less grand; but after several days, when I had enjoyed a nearer view of the two cataracts, had listened to their thundering sound, and gazed on them for hours from above and below, and had watched the river foaming over the rapids, then plunging headlong into the dark pool, and when I had explored the delightful island which divides the falls, where the solitude of the ancient forest is still unbroken, I at last learned by degrees to comprehend the wonders of the scene, and to feel its full magnificence.' This is ever the case with the magnificent and sublime; the mind, habituated to ordinary things, fails at first to form a proper estimate of the object it contemplates, but gradually enlarges with the contemplation, partaking of the attributes by which it is surrounded. Leaving this matter, however, to the metaphysician, let us follow the geologist in his description and estimate of the stupendous cataract.

As is known to every reader, the falls of Niagara are situated between Lakes Erie and Ontario—the last of those great fresh-water seas so characteristic of Upper Canada. The distance between the two lakes is about twenty-nine miles, and the difference of level 330 feet. As the river issues from Lake Erie, 'it resembles a prolongation of the tranquil lake, being interspersed with low wooded islands. This lake-like scenery continues for about fifteen miles, during which the fall of the river scarcely exceeds as many feet; but on reaching the rapids, it descends over a limestone bed about fifty feet in less than a mile, and is then thrown down about 165 feet perpendicularly at the falls. The largest of these, called the Horse-shoe fall, is 1800 feet, or more than a third of a mile broad, the island in the midst being somewhat less in width, and the American fall about 600 feet wide. The deep narrow chasm below the great cataract is from 200 to 400 yards wide, and 300 feet deep; and here in seven miles the river descends 100 feet, at the end of which it emerges from the gorge into the open and flat country, so nearly on a level with Lake Ontario that there is only a fall of about four feet in the seven additional miles which intervene between Queenston and the lake. The great ravine is winding, and at some points the boundary cliffs are undermined on one side by the impetuous stream; but there is usually a talus at the base of the precipice, supporting a very ornamental fringe of trees. It has long been the popular belief, from a mere cursory inspection of this district, that the Niagara once flowed in a shallow valley across the whole platform, from the present site of the falls to the Queenston heights, where it is supposed the cataract was first situated, and that the river has been slowly eating its way backwards through the rocks for a distance of seven miles. According to this hypothesis, the falls must have had originally nearly twice their present height, and must have been always diminishing in grandeur from age to age, as they will continue to do in future so long as the retrograde movement is prolonged. It becomes, therefore, a matter of no small curiosity and interest to inquire at what rate the work of excavation is now going on, and thus to obtain a measure for calculating how many thousands of years or centuries have been required to hollow out the chasm already excavated.'

Unfortunately for such an estimate, our data are very incomplete, the earliest authentic notice of the falls being that of Father Hennepin in 1678. 'As to the waters of Italy and Swedeland,' says the worthy missionary, 'they are but sorry patterns of it: this wonderful downfall is compounded of two great falls, with an isle in the middle, and there is another cascade less than the other two, which falls from east to west.' By 1751, when Kalm, the Swedish botanist, visited the district, the lesser cascade had vanished in consequence of the demolition of the projecting ledge by which it was occasioned. In 1818 and 1828 there were extensive falls of the undermined limestone, which are said to have shaken the adjacent country like an earthquake. Since 1815 the settlers have noticed an indentation of the American fall to the extent of forty feet, at the same time that the Horse-shoe fall has been altered, so as less to deserve that name. Goat Island, which divides the falls, has also suffered degradation to the extent of several acres within the last four or five years. All this, though scanty information, evinces a gradual recession of the falls, and points to a time when they shall approach the shores of Lake Erie, and convert its expanse into a dry and fertile plain. When this may happen is altogether matter of conjecture. Mr Bakewell estimates the recession during the present century at three feet per year, while Mr Lyell thinks one foot a more probable estimate. At the latter rate, it would have required 35,000 years to excavate the gorge between Queenston and the falls, and will take more than double that period to recede to Lake Erie. It must be borne in mind, however, that the recession depends upon the nature of the rocks to be worn down, on the height of the fall, and other contingencies. At present the ledge over which it passes is limestone resting on soft shales, and as the latter are washed away by the water the former is undermined and falls down; a new undermining soon takes place, a fresh fall occurs, and thus the process of decay, though slow, is perpetual. By and by the rocks to be cut through will be sandstones of a softer texture; and though the fall will be diminished in height, the wasting effects of the cataract may be equally or even more rapid.

Be this as it may, it must have required a long series of ages to hollow out the chasm between the falls and Queenston; and if we knew the rate of erosion, Niagara would form, as it were, a great natural chronometer. And though it proved to us the lapse of many thousand years, yet is its action altogether recent compared with the events exhibited by the geology of the district. The surface is covered with shells and gravel more modern than the clays of the London basin, and which were deposited ere yet Niagara poured its waters over the escarpment at Queenston; these, again, are but of yesterday compared with the underlying strata through which the river now cuts its way. 'Many,' says Mr Lyell, 'have been the successive revolutions in organic life, and many the vicissitudes in the physical geography of the globe, and often has sea been converted into land and land into sea since that rock was formed. The Alps, the Pyrenees, the Himalaya, have not only begun to exist as lofty mountain chains, but the solid materials of which they are composed have been slowly elaborated beneath the sea within the stupendous interval of ages here alluded to.'

2. *Coal-fields of the United States.*—Like everything else in the American continent, the coal-fields are on an unusual and gigantic scale. That of Pennsylvania, Virginia, and Ohio, extends continuously from north-east to south-west for a distance of 720 miles, its greatest breadth being about 180 miles! Its area thus amounts to 63,000 square miles, a superficies considerably greater than the whole of England and Wales. That situated in Illinois, Indiana, and Kentucky, embraces an area of 14,000 square miles; while others, many times much larger than the largest coal-field in Britain, are found in Michigan and other parts of the union. The coal is of two kinds—bituminous, such as that found in Britain; and anthracite, or debituminised coal, which is a natural coke deprived of its gaseous matters by subterranean processes. This anthracite burns without smoke or flame does not soil the fingers, is not easily broken, and has a metallic or ringing sound when struck. It is found in various degrees of purity, containing from 3 to 16, or even to 25 per cent. of inflammable matter. The most thoroughly debituminised portions of the field are those most intimately associated with the Alleghany mountains, thus pointing to the subterranean fires by which the bituminous materials were expelled; and it is curious to learn that as the field recedes from the mountains, it gradually becomes more and more bituminous, till it cannot be distinguished from ordinary coal. For a long time this anthracite was rejected; but science has taught its use to the Americans, to whom, for countless ages, it will be an indispensable source of wealth and comfort. In speaking of its use at Potsville, Mr Lyell says, 'Here I was agreeably surprised to see a flourishing manufacturing town with the tall chimneys of a hundred furnaces, burning night and day, yet quite free from smoke. Leaving this clear atmosphere, and going down into one of the mines, it was a no less pleasing novelty to find we could handle the coal without soiling our fingers. The slow combustion of anthracite can be overcome by a strong current of air, not only in large furnaces, but by aid of a blower in the fireplaces of private dwellings; and its drying effect on the air of a room may be counteracted by the evaporation of water. As managed by the Americans, I have no hesitation in preferring its use, in spite of the occasional stove-like heat produced by it, to that of bituminous coal in London, coupled with the penalty of living constantly in a dark atmosphere of smoke which destroys our furniture, dress, and gardens, blackens our public buildings, and renders cleanliness impossible.'

Again, the coal-fields of America are as remarkable for the ease with which they can be worked, as for their vast extent and excellent qualities. There are no deep shafts requiring eight or ten years of expensive labour, no gigantic engines for drainage, no complicated machinery for ventilation, no precautions necessary against explosions, for such disasters are totally unknown. 'I was truly surprised,' says our authority, 'now that I had entered the hydrographical basin of the Ohio, at beholding the richness of the seams of coal which appear everywhere on the flanks of the hills and at the bottoms of the valleys, and which are accessible in a degree I never witnessed elsewhere. The time has not yet arrived, the soil being still densely covered with the primeval forest, and manufacturing industry in its infancy, when the full value of this inexhaustible supply of cheap fuel can be appreciated; but the resources which it will one day afford to a region capable, by its agricultural produce alone, of supporting a large population, are truly magnificent. In order to estimate the natural advantages of such a region, we must reflect how three great navigable rivers—the Monongahela, Alleghany, and Ohio—intersect it and lay open on their banks the level seams of coal. ... found at Brownsville a bed ten feet thick of good bituminous coal, commonly called the Pittsburg seam breaking out in the river cliffs near the water's edge. Horizontal galleries may be driven everywhere at very slight expense, and so worked as to drain themselves while the cars, laden with coal and attached to each other, glide down on a railway, so as to deliver their burden into barges moored to the river's bank. The same seam is seen on the right bank, and may be followed the whole way to Pittsburg, fifty miles distant. As it is nearly horizontal, while the river descends it crops out, at a continually increasing but never at an inconvenient height above the Monongahela. Both above and below the seam are others of workable dimensions, and almost every proprietor can open a coal-pit on his own land. The stratification being very regular, they may calculate with precision the depth at which the coal may be won. So great, indeed, are the facilities of procuring this excellent fuel, that already it is found profitable to convey it in flat-bottomed boats for the use of steam-ships at New Orleans, 1100 miles distant, in spite of the dense forests bordering the intermediate river plains, where timber may be obtained at the cost of felling it.' On cannot read this account of these coal-fields without speculating on the future condition of North America, and associating therewith all that is great, and powerful, and enlightened. Without her mineral resources, Britain never could have been what she now is; and America has started as it were full-grown into life with resources to which those of our island can hardly be compared. The mineral wealth of Britain has already accomplished wonders, and will bring about still more stupendous results; but America, when Britain's last pound of coal shall have been consumed, will only be emerging into meridian glory.

3. *Natural gas-light.*—Many of our readers may be aware that the carburetted hydrogen which issues from some of the north of England mines, as, for example, that of Wallsend, has been collected in gasometers, and used for the purposes of illumination. In no case, however, has it been of much importance, beyond the mere illustration of the fact, that such an illumination could be effected. Not so, however, on the other side the Atlantic, as we hear from the following extracts from Mr Lyell's journal:—'Sailed in a steamboat to Fredonia [on Lake Erie], a town of 1200 inhabitants, with neat white houses, and six churches. The streets are lighted up with natural gas, which bubbles out of the ground, and is received into a gasometer, which I visited. This gas consists of carburetted hydrogen, and issues from a black bituminous slate. The lighthouse-keeper at Fredonia told me, that, near the shore, at a considerable distance from the gasometer, he bored a hole through this black slate, and the gas soon collected in sufficient quantity to explode when ignited.'

4. *Great Dismal Swamp.*—Among the recent and superficial formations of America, there is none more interesting than those swamps or morasses which occur in the low flat regions of the Carolinas and Florida. The largest of these lies between the towns of Norfolk and Weldon, in North Carolina, and is traversed in part by a railway, supported on piles. 'It bears,' says Mr Lyell, 'the appropriate and very expressive name of the "Great Dismal," and is no less than forty miles in length from north to south, and twenty-five miles in its greatest width from east to west, the northern half being situated in Virginia, the southern in North Carolina. I observed that the water was obviously in motion in several places, and the morass has somewhat the appearance of a broad inundated river-plain, covered with all kinds of aquatic trees and shrubs, the soil being as black as in a peat-bog. The accumulation of vegetable matter going on here in a hot climate, over so vast an area, is a subject of such high geological interest, that I shall relate what I learnt of this singular morass.

'It is one enormous quagmire, soft and muddy, except where the surface is rendered partially firm by a covering of vegetables and their matted roots; yet, strange to say, instead of being lower than the level of the surrounding country, it is actually higher than nearly all the firm and dry land which encompasses it, and, to make the anomaly complete, in spite of its semi-fluid character it is higher in the interior than towards its margin. The soil of the swamp is formed of vegetable matter, usually without any admixture of earthy particles. We have here, in fact, a deposit of peat from ten to fifteen feet in thickness, in a latitude where, owing to the heat of the sun and length of the summer, no peat-mosses like those of Europe would be looked for under ordinary circumstances.' In northern latitudes, where the climate is damp and the summer short and cool, the growth of one season does not rot away before the growth of the next has risen above it; and the more so that the situation is wet and boggy. The vegetation in fact is protected from decay by the comparative absence of heat and the presence of water, but in Carolina the former of these causes does not operate. Mr Lyell, therefore, accounts for the formation of the 'Great Dismal' in the following manner:—'There are many trees like the willow which there flourish in water. The white cedars stand firmly in the softest part of the quagmire, supported by their long tap-roots, and afford, with many other evergreens, a dark shade, under which a multitude of ferns, reeds, and shrubs, from nine to eighteen feet high, and a thick carpet of mosses, four or five inches high, spring up and are protected from the rays of the sun. When these are most powerful, the large cedar (*Cupressus disticha*) and many other deciduous trees are in full leaf. The black soil formed beneath this shade, to which the mosses and the leaves make annual additions, does not perfectly resemble the peat of Europe, most of the plants being so decayed as to leave little more than soft black mud, without any traces of organisation. The evaporation continually going on in the wet spongy soil during summer cools the air, and generates a temperature resembling that of a more northern climate, or a region more elevated above the level of the sea.'

Though the swamp has been described as highest towards the middle, there is a lake seven miles long and five broad in its centre, but of no great depth. Much timber has been cut down and carried out from the morass by means of canals, which are perfectly straight for long distances, with the trees on each side arching over and almost joining their branches. There are also numerous trunks of large and tall trees buried in the mire, which, being kept wet, do not decompose, but yield the finest and most durable planks. The animals chiefly found inhabiting the 'Dismal' are bears, wild cats, and occasionally a solitary wolf; but otherwise the region is as lifeless and gloomy as can be imagined. Mr Lyell regards this swamp as a fine illustration of the mode in which coal has been formed, and argues that if the district were submerged beneath the ocean so as to receive a covering of sand or mud, that the whole vegetable mass would be converted into a modern coal-seam.

Such are a few random gleanings from a work whose pages, whether they relate to the geology, statistics, or people of the districts through which the author travelled, are replete with sound and attractive information.

POSITION AND APPEARANCE.

BY CAMILLA TOULMIN.

It is certainly one of the peculiarities of the present day, that people are more inclined to think for themselves, to examine time-established customs and opinions, and, if they find them mischievous or false, to break from their trammels, than they were even twenty years ago. Indeed there are few who walk through the world, endeavouring to keep their eyes open, and notice what is going on around them, who have not an 'experience' of one sort or another to oppose to some erroneous but current opinion. *Apropos* of one such conviction is the following sketch from life.

'Sweet are the uses of adversity.' *That*, courteous reader, is not a proverb against which I would break a lance or wear down a goose-quill. No; so wrote one of old, whose pearls of wisdom Time cannot corrode; nor in them can the world's accumulated knowledge and developed reason find speck or flaw. The adversity to which Shakspeare alluded, was the change from a high and proud position to one of humble obscurity; from a life of ease and luxury to a precarious existence, dependent on toil and daily exertion, and not without dangers and difficulties. Such changes must have been frequent at all times, yet are they most so in an age like the present. In a country whose crowded population are striving and wrestling for place and precedence, some must be continually losing ground. Now, the opinion with which I *do* quarrel, is that which shapes itself into the words I have often heard—'Bad enough to be poor, but still worse to seem poor.' Think of the contrariety of human nature; this is the very thing the miser, stooping beneath the weight of his money-bags, strives to *seem*. 'Ah,' exclaims some struggling stickler for the value of appearances—'ah, *he* can afford to seem poor!'

Excuse me, my dear friend; no man is so rich in virtues as to be able to afford a falsehood; and none can be made happy or respectable by holding a false position. And for the rich to feign poverty, is as false a thing as for the poor to cheat the world by hollow appearances. The fable of the dog and the shadow has a meaning the most profound. I believe that more than one-half of the amount of human miseries arises from the struggle to maintain the appearance of things, instead of to acquire the realities. And, after all, how shallow they are! The people who keep but one eye open can see through them. Folks who struggle to maintain a position higher in a worldly sense than that to which they are entitled, seem to have chosen a footing slippery and insecure as thin ice. What foundation can they trust on which to build? What purchase have they from which to spring or climb higher? I think I could illustrate this truth by many facts which I have observed. I will try to do so by recalling two or three odd chapters of biography.

A few years ago—so few, that the youthful actors of that day are only now entering on the summer of life—I chanced to be intimately acquainted with two families, the heads of which were connected by the close band of commercial partnership. They had been brought up in ease and luxury, or, as the world afterwards said, extravagantly; for the day of reverses came, and either from unfortunate speculations, or some of the thousand causes by which we are told the intricate wheels of business may be clogged, the firm of Freeman and Sanders, which had stood for two generations in proud security and unblemished repute, bent its head to the dust in acknowledged bankruptcy. The senior partner, Mr Freeman, died, it was said, of grief and shame, within three months from the period of this catastrophe; and thus were his children and their mother deprived of a stay and protector in the very hour of their extremest need. The scene and circumstances were those, alas! but too common in real life, but over which pride drops so thick a veil, that strangers seldom penetrate behind it—a scene and circumstances so gloomy of aspect, that the writer of fiction shrinks from making the world familiar with their details, while the moralist sighs and doubts how it were wisest to deal with them.

No one seemed to have observed that there was anything remarkable about the eldest daughter, Mary Freeman, who was then about nineteen years of age. Neither tall nor short, nor handsome nor plain; neither particularly gay, nor, on the other hand, given to melancholy, the slanderers of women who believe in Pope would have been likely enough to pronounce her one with 'no character at all.' If anything had been noticed of her, it was, that she was quiet and lady-like, and a great reader. We shall see what had been the moulding of quiet reflection and judicious reading, added to the early impressions made by a truthful and high-minded mother. I was in the house in those sad hours when the dead lay unburied, and the distressing details consequent on death pressed heavily on the living, and seemed, as they always do, to clash rudely and profanely on their aching hearts. Here, too, and at this hour, cowered Poverty in one of its darkest forms. The widow, blinded with heart-wrung tears, lay exhausted in a room apart. On Mary devolved all cares, all responsibility. She knew that the very furniture of the house belonged to her father's creditors; and she knew that the means in her mother's hands would not suffice a month for the family's support. She was very pale, and a dark circle round the eyes showed that she had wept bitterly; but she was calm now, and gave her orders with distinctness and composure. The draper had brought mourning habiliments for her selection.

'This is too good,' said Mary quietly, putting on one side some articles he had displayed before her. The tradesman looked surprised, and said something about seldom supplying ladies with goods inferior to those. 'We *cannot afford* so high a price,' continued Mary in a manner unmistakeably different from the affectation with which the wealthy sometimes talk of their means; and she chose the very cheapest articles which would combine durability with economy. A peculiar expression passed over the draper's face. If I read it aright, it half arose from pity for the fallen family, and half from a sudden conviction that at any rate he should be paid immediately or certainly for his goods, having doubtless remarked that dangerous customers always endeavour—to keep up appearances. Mary Freeman had acted from her own instinctive love of truth and justice: she knew not then that she had already made her first stand against the despot Poverty—combated with him hand to hand. Boldly to say, 'I cannot afford,' is the true way to keep him at bay.

Mary Freeman appeared to possess nothing of what is called worldly wisdom; and yet her position was one which worldly people would have said required a great deal of worldly policy to guide her; and she really had only great simplicity of character, the power of distinguishing between right and wrong, and the habit of always and promptly deciding on the former line of conduct. So completely had the mother been spirit-crushed by adverse fortune, that the management of affairs was silently, yet as a matter of course, ceded to Mary. She was well educated and accomplished, and every way competent to be an instructress; her sister, two years her junior, was a fine musician, and she calculated that if both could obtain pupils, they should be able to support their mother, certainly to maintain her above want, though not to procure her the luxuries to which she had been accustomed. A cheap lodging was taken, and the creditors, admiring the energy and right-mindedness the young girl was displaying, permitted her to remove, before the sale, sufficient necessaries to furnish their new abode. A situation of a very humble class offered for her young brother. 'Take it, Harry,' she advised; 'you *cannot afford* to remain idle; anything is better than that. If they find you attentive, and superior to this occupation, your employers will perhaps promote you to something better—at any rate take it, until something more advantageous appears.' And while these young people are buffeting the world bravely and wisely, let us turn to the Sanders family, who, seeking to retrieve their fortunes, were pursuing a very opposite course.

'We must keep up appearances,' was the text from which a silly woman was perpetually preaching; and when her husband had the weakness to yield to her persuasions, it was not to be expected that her sons and daughters should see the error and folly of their course. Soon after the failure, Mr Sanders had obtained a situation of from two to three hundred a-year, as superior clerk in a mercantile house. Properly managed, such an income, however inferior to that which they had formerly spent, might have supported his wife and the two young children in real respectability and independence; and had the elder son and daughter, who were about the ages of Mary and Fanny Freeman, been taught to contribute to the general stock, the inconveniences of which, to their intimate friends, they so bitterly complained, would surely have been removed. But no: a really excellent situation might have been procured for George Sanders; but, alas! it was in a retail establishment, and his mother would not listen to such a falling off from the dignity of the family. 'It would be the ruin of him,' she exclaimed: 'how could he show himself in genteel society when it was known that he might be seen serving behind a counter? He could not escort his sister to evening parties if he were chained to business three nights a-week; and if Clara did not "go into society," what, poor girl, would become of her? It was not giving her a chance.' The chance was, of course, that of 'making a good match,' as the phrase goes. Poor Mrs Sanders! her castle-building was about as unreal as that of the girl in the old story with her basket of eggs. 'Appearances' were, with her, the brittle commodity on which fortune was to be founded.

No matter that at home there were heart-burnings and discontent; tradesmen calling for bills which there was not the money to discharge; or that, for the providing of showy luxuries, the necessaries of life were curtailed; and so, in the family the petty selfishnesses of humanity were painfully brought out, as, except in the very highest natures, they always are when individual comfort is tryingly trespassed on. Even the bonds of affection, which alone could have held together such discordant elements, wore weaker and weaker. Instead of instructing her children to exert themselves, she taught them that, by cultivating appearances, fortune would call at their door; and certainly they waited with a patience which would have been admirable if practised in a better cause.

In the days of their equal prosperity the two families had been intimate, but their unequal adversity had brought out in such strong relief the lights and shades of their character, and their paths seemed so opposite, that, without any disagreement, calls became less frequent, till sometimes they did not meet for months together.

Five years glided away. At the end of that time Clara Sanders was still unmarried; and though at last, wearied and worn out with waiting for some unexceptionable and lucrative employment to present itself, her brother had accepted a situation, it was one infinitely inferior in point of remunerative advantages to several he had rejected; but then it was perfectly 'genteel;' and he was released from business in time to join in the fashionable promenades, and had no veto put upon evening parties. Bred up in a bad school, he did not perceive that his 'position' was one that to a high and upright mind would have appeared positively degrading. His paltry salary scarcely found him in pocket-money and cigars, while for his real maintenance the strong able-bodied man of twenty-two was indebted to an impoverished and hard-working father; nay, worse, to a parent involved in debt, and surrounded with difficulties. To my thinking, the world in this nineteenth century knows no such martyrs as those who are struggling to uphold themselves in a false position.

It was a warm evening, just at that season of the year when spring is melting into summer, when London is full of the 'fashionable world,' and when, consequently, the descending grades of society, following their example, revel also in gaiety and visiting. A party was projected to take place in the showy but really wretched home of the Sanderses; and little could the invited guests suspect the crooked plans—laughable, if they were not most melancholy—to which their hosts must have recourse ere they could receive them; the curious stratagems, born of the inventive mother, Necessity, by which they must keep the bubble 'appearances' from bursting. At the present moment, how to obtain five pounds to purchase articles for which they could not obtain credit, was the question in agitation between mother and daughter. There was a loud rat-tat at the door—surely street-door knockers are nowhere so noisy as in London—and presently Mr George entered the room, drawing off a pair of lemon-coloured gloves, the cost of which might have given them all a better dinner than they had tasted that day.

'Just met Harry Freeman,' he exclaimed, throwing himself into the nearest chair; and finding that he received no answer to this important piece of information, he continued, 'What luck some people have to be sure!'

'Has he been in luck's way, then?' inquired Mrs Sanders.

'Only that he has been pushed up over the heads of clerks of a dozen years' standing, and made foreign correspondent in ——'s house.'

'I should think his sisters would give up teaching *now*,' said Clara, with an emphasis on the last word.

'I don't believe it—they are such screws,' replied her brother. 'I declare I would not have worn the coat he had on.'

'What!—shabby?'

'No, not shabby; but such a cut! East of Temple Bar all over.'

There was a slight whispering between mother and daughter.

'If you do that,' said Mrs Sanders, 'you must invite them.'

'He will be too busy to come,' replied Clara; 'and they will be sure to wear white muslin; girls always look nice in that.'

'George and you might walk there this evening: it would be better than writing.'

'I'll leave you at the door, and call for you in half an hour,' said he, as they walked along; for he had learned that her mission was not solely to invite their old friends to join the evening party, and his cowardly vanity shrunk from being present when the other solicitation was made.

Clara found Mary and her brother studiously engaged with a German master, and Fanny and Mrs Freeman busily plying the needle. She must seek a private audience for her more important request; but she felt that 'she was giving her friends a little consequence,' by inviting them to the party before the stranger.

'We are particularly engaged on Wednesday,' said Mary; '*very* particularly,' she added, with a smile, which somehow or other brought a blush to the cheeks of her sister Fanny.

Clara expressed in courteous phrase all due regrets that they should not have the pleasure of seeing them, with all the et ceteras usual on such occasions; and on the first opportunity, asked to speak to her in private for five minutes. It was not an agreeable thing to ask the loan of five pounds, and she put it off yet another moment, by dwelling once more on the disappointment Mrs Sanders would feel at not seeing her young friends.

'When I tell you,' said Mary Freeman, now released from all restraint, 'that our dear Fanny is going to be married on Thursday morning, you will see that it is not likely we should go to a party the night before. Though indeed we seldom go into anything like gaiety; you know we cannot afford finery and coach-hire.'

In her astonishment Clara could not help ejaculating, 'That chit Fanny!'

'Nay, though younger than we are,' said Mary, 'she is two-and-twenty.'

'Is it a good match?' asked Clara.

'Excellent, I think,' replied Mary, again smiling, and now at her friend's use of that vulgar hackneyed phrase, 'inasmuch as her intended is a gentleman of the highest character. Their attachment I believe to be a most warm and sincere one; and though not absolutely rich, he can surround her with all the comforts of life. I assure you I rejoice that she did not accept either of the other offers she received, although they were what the world calls better ones.'

'Other offers!—and yet you never go out!' exclaimed Clara with undisguised astonishment.

'I sometimes think they must have been because we never put ourselves in the way of seeking admirers.'

Clara was not inclined to ask what Mary meant by using the plural 'we,' and so she proceeded to seek the loan.

'I will lend it you with pleasure,' replied the kind-hearted girl, 'if you will promise to return it to me by the first of next month. It is part of what I have put away to pay for our lessons in German and Spanish, and the quarter will be due then. I do not think Harry will need to go on any longer, for he has a talent for acquiring languages, and he has fagged very hard for the last three years. I am not so quick, and shall take lessons till Christmas, if I can possibly *afford it*.'

The promise was given; ay, and I am afraid without even the positive intention of fulfilling it. For those who are slaves to 'appearances' live only in the present, and regard the future but little.

The first of the month arrived—the second—the third—and no communication from the Sanderses. On the fourth came a letter full of excuses and apologies.

Mary had discrimination enough to read through such phrases the simple truth—that they had not the money. She was too sorry for them to feel angry, though the disappointment to herself was a serious one. She determined to break off her lessons for a few weeks, until she could replace the sum she had generously lent and —lost. Those who know what it is to study ardently, and with a specific object in view, will believe how vexatious such an interruption was. How the party 'went off,' or what further stratagems the Sanders family resorted to during the ensuing months, there is no record to show. Ashamed of seeing the friend she had wronged, Clara took no further notice of the broken promise, putting off perhaps from time to time the fulfilment of some vague intention she might have formed of calling or writing again. But the crisis was coming; the bubble was bursting; appearances could be kept up no longer. One of the many penalties attending those who struggle to maintain a false position is, that they seldom or never draw round them friends able or willing to assist them in the dark hour of adversity. The really high-minded and generous, who would respect honest poverty, and hold out a helping hand to it in the time of need, recoil from the mockeries of life and all false people; instinctively they shun them, and so know them not. Of all their butterfly associates, the Sanderses had not one of whom to seek counsel or aid in the hour of their second and deeper fall. Deeper, indeed; for now was disgrace. The world saw that the ruin came from personal extravagance; and creditors cheated, as they believed themselves to have been, intentionally, were different to deal with from the sufferers by mercantile failure. When Clara next called on Mary Freeman, it was with humbled mien and tearful eyes, not to pay the borrowed pounds, but to seek the further loan of—a few shillings. Fortune had smiled upon the orphans. With Harry's increased salary, he had insisted that Mary should confine her earnings to the defraying her own personal expenses—thus she had already saved money.

'Say no more about the old debt, my dear Clara,' she exclaimed: 'I long ago looked upon it as a gift; that is, if you would accept it from an old friend. I should have written to tell you so, but I feared to hurt your feelings.' And she slipped another five-pound note into her hand, to be returned 'whenever she grew rich.'

And this was the friend whom for years she had slighted!—whom her mother had hesitated to invite to the house, lest she should appear ill dressed! The good that was in her nature seemed to rise above the evil-teaching by which it had been crushed, and, throwing herself on her knees, she buried her face in Mary's lap, and burst into a passionate flood of tears.

'My poor girl,' said Mary, herself somewhat overcome by the interview, 'I do feel for you. I know what poverty is—bitter and hard to bear. Yet it is a foe that, to be conquered, must be bravely met. You are still young——'

'Five-and-twenty!' murmured Clara.

'Well, so am I.'

'But you have overcome your troubles; mine are just beginning.'

'I have worked very hard for six years, it is true, and I have had my reward.'

'I—I,' exclaimed the wretched Clara, wringing her hands, 'feel older—much older than I am. I have seen so much misery, so much falsity; all the energy of my youth seems gone.'

'Some of it will come back when you set yourself resolutely to some suitable occupation. Independence is so delightful a feeling, and the money one earns so very sweet, so much more *one's own* than any other can be. No one ever forgets his or her *first* earnings, and you have this pleasant emotion still to know!'

Mary Freeman tried to cheer her suffering friend; and in part she succeeded. She persuaded her to seek independence resolutely and perseveringly, and, after a while, she did find a sweet return for her exertions. But it was quite true that the rich strong energies of youth had been frittered away in folly and the pursuit of mockeries and unreal vanities.

Most melancholy is it to witness the misfortunes of those who suffer for the faults of their parents; yet rarely is this denunciation of Scripture avoided. In few things, indeed, are cause and effect so easily traced. And surely, of all injuries inflicted on the young, none is so fatal as evil training. Clara's young brother and sister, mere children still, have, to my thinking, a better chance of prosperity than she had. Plunged as they are into absolute and acknowledged poverty, at least they escape the misery of a 'false position:' they have a firm footing, from which let us hope that, by some honest means, they may rise to comfort and independence. As for George, selfish and idle habits, it is true, had taken deep root in his nature; yet he was young, and in those few words lies a world of hope. The thin ice of false appearances had broken beneath him, and for that, were he already wise, he would have been most thankful, yea, though for the time he were plunged into very troubled waters. They could not have stranded him on a more insecure resting-place. I know not his present lot.

Another four years passed away, bringing myriads of changes—some sudden, some gradual—to many a hearth and home. During this period Mrs Freeman, who had been for many years in delicate health, was taken from her children; but, saving this bereavement, her family had prospered beyond the brightest paintings of hope. The affection between Mary and her brother was something beautiful to contemplate. His life had been too busy to afford him much time to cultivate acquaintances; thus his warm affections were concentrated on a few very dear friends, and his sisters, especially Mary, to whom he looked up with no small degree of reverence as well as love. The most perfect confidence had always subsisted between them; yet now, for the first time, Mary suspected that Harry hid some secret from her. The mystery, whatever it might be, seemed not of a disagreeable kind; yet that there was a mystery, she felt certain, else why so many letters—some of them, too, looking like tradesmen's bills—about which he said not a word, though he generally looked rather pleased than otherwise when he opened them? True, he had told her an acquaintance of his was furnishing a house, and had consulted him a good deal about it; and he, appealing to Mary's taste, as superior to that of two gentlemen, insisted on her deciding on several matters—choosing paper for a drawing-room, and many such et ceteras. It was rather odd, she thought; but Mary retained the simplicity of character inseparable from a truthful nature, and nothing doubted.

One day Harry Freeman proposed an excursion some half-dozen miles from town, to visit the residence of this mysterious friend. It was a beautiful day in spring, when everything in nature seems to gladden the heart; and, exhilarated by the ride, Mary was in high spirits when they drove up to the gates of a substantial villa, beautifully situated on the rise of a hill which commanded a fine view — the house being surrounded with extensive and highly-cultivated pleasure-grounds. When they entered the dwelling, Mary found that everything corresponded with the outward appearance of elegance. One room, especially, seemed to charm her—a sort of breakfast-parlour or morning-room, in which books and musical instruments were arranged, and which, leading into a conservatory, seemed to hint that the intended occupier had a feminine passion for flowers.

'I suppose this beautiful house, this exquisite room, are intended for some young and interesting bride?' exclaimed Mary.

'No, my dear sister, not so,' replied Harry. 'Sit down on this sofa beside me, and I will give you a brief history of the owner of this dwelling. There was a poor boy thrown adrift on the world without friends, without money. He remembers to this day that he felt himself as if cast on an ocean without anchor, or compass, or rudder. There was no settled purpose in his young heart, which was filled with bitter recollections of indulgences no more to be tasted, and overgrown with wrong notions and false pride of all sorts. To the beautiful example of one dear relative, and to words which, on a day of most intense agony, he heard from her young lips as a message from on high, he feels that, under Heaven, he owes a degree of worldly prosperity almost unparalleled. It is for this sweet relative and himself,' he added smiling, 'if she will let him share her home, that he has prepared this abode. Do you not think he does right to devote his income to her comfort, her enjoyment?'

'Quite right,' replied the unsuspecting Mary: 'but, Harry, who are they? I am sure I should like to know them.'

'Mary, murmured he, with much tenderness, and drawing her yet nearer to him, 'I was the poor boy, and you the sweet sister, whose wise example and brave words have made me what I am. Nay, do not start and look so wildly; indeed I *can afford* this home; ay, and the saddle-horse in the stable, and half a hundred things I have yet to show you. I am partner in the house where I served—I hope faithfully. That I should become so, was almost the last wish expressed by Mr——, the head of the firm, on his deathbed.'

'I do not think it can be real,' said Mary, when at last she could speak, after gushing tears of joy had relieved her heart: 'but, Harry,' she continued, as if a new idea had just occurred to her, 'you may marry?'

'And so may you,' replied her brother: 'indeed I am almost selfish enough to *fear* you will. But,' he added, as again he held her in his arms and kissed her cheek, 'if I should marry you will but have another sister. *I* could not love a wife who did not love and reverence *you!*'

OCCASIONAL NOTES.

'THE WEATHER AND CROPS.'

About harvest-time in each year, the newspapers throughout this empire teem with paragraphs headed as above. The people of Great Britain, proverbial as they are for incessantly talking about the state of the atmosphere, are more anxious and loquacious about it in August and September than at other seasons. The smallest change creates a great excitement. A dull or wet day produces long faces and fearful forebodings: the farmer expresses terrible apprehensions, and the stock-jobber 'speculates for a fall;' nor does he speculate in vain; for a succession of hazy or sunless days is certain to depreciate government securities. Politicians look grave; wonder, if there should happen to be a short crop, how the country is to get on till next year; and tremble lest a rise of a halfpenny in the loaf should cause a rising of the disaffected in what used to be called the 'disturbed districts.' Such are the gloomy perspectives conjured up in this country by one or two wet autumn days. That these exaggerated fears are engendered by these very small causes, only shows our immunity from great calamities. The worst which is ever apprehended in Great Britain, is a crop below the average; a total failure, such as takes place in other countries, is unheard of; and we would just remind the apprehensive of what frequently takes place abroad, that they may derive consolation from the contrast.

Perhaps the most destructive of all calamities which foreign agriculture suffers, and from which that of England is exempt, are inundations. In territories intersected by rivers which, from having their sources in extensive mountain ranges, are liable to sudden and immense accessions, the waters overflow and sweep away the next year's food of an entire province. A few seasons ago, a calamity of this nature occurred no farther away than the south of France, when the Soane burst its banks, and submerged a vast expanse of standing corn. As we write, the French papers inform us that the harvests both of Upper and Lower Hungary have been destroyed by the violence of inundations, which lasted for eight days. Not only is all the corn swept, but whole villages have been carried away, and old and valuable woods much injured. More than a million of individuals are threatened with actual famine, in consequence of this widely-spread calamity.

If we turn to the East, we shall see that the destruction of grain about harvest-time is much more frequent. Besides drought and blighting winds, swarms of locusts frequently darken the air, and descend to eat up whole acres of grain in a night. In the more prolific districts, again, such as Egypt and some parts of Turkey, the cultivator is oppressed by a plague surer in its operations than the worst elemental disasters; namely, an oppressive system of taxation, which exacts dues great in proportion to the goodness of the crop, so as to leave the *fellah*, or agriculturist, but scarcely enough to support existence. From all these plagues the climate, situation, and political constitution of Great Britain exempt us. Yet, instead of being thankful for the superior blessings which we enjoy, we tremble at the smallest likelihood of a less than average abundance of corn, and fill our newspapers and our conversation with doleful prognostications concerning 'the weather and crops.'

AN EXTENSIVE RAILWAY.

The longest line ever yet contemplated is one proposed to extend between St Petersburg and Odessa, a distance of 1600 miles. It will connect the Baltic with the Black Sea; but, by taking an eastward sweep, might also bring direct communication with the Caspian within its track. Commencing at St Petersburg, it will be cut southward to Novgorod and Moscow, and thence to Odessa, taking in the most important of the intervening cities. Besides the vast uninterrupted distance, the traveller will pass through a variety of climates, and will be able to accomplish the hitherto unheard-of feat of travelling from winter into summer. Supposing he get into the train at St Petersburg amidst frost and snow late in the winter, he will find himself, before he leaves the terminus at Odessa, suffering from the heats of summer!

It is not easy to foresee all the difficulties by which the formation of such a rail will be opposed. These will principally arise from the snow-storms which occur in the northern regions, and we have not heard that any scheme has been projected for clearing away such an obstruction, by means of the locomotive or otherwise, during its progress. Of mere engineering difficulties one has ceased to hear; for, after the wonders in levelling and tunnelling which have been performed in Great Britain, a railway in any part of the globe does not appear at all impracticable. The paragraph from which we copy the above information adds, that it is intended to continue the line from Odessa into Persia, through its capital Tehran to Ispahan; but whether the Caucasian range is to be tunnelled, is not stated. Should the gigantic scheme be carried out, a branch from Odessa to Constantinople may be fully expected to the west, whilst another eastward through Tartary to Pekin must be regarded as a no very distant probability. But the speculator who projects his railway anticipations thus far into futurity, be he ever so sanguine, cannot regard the possibility of a break-down in the Kobi desert—with no station nearer than Sou-tchou close under the great Chinese wall—without a shudder. Altogether, the Russian undertaking, with the vast branches which may be imagined in connexion with it, presents materials for a sublime prospectus; and it is almost to be regretted that the Emperor of Russia did not send his scheme into 'the market.' It would have been curious to observe how far the force of prospectus-writing would have gone.

There seems little doubt, however, that the Russians

are quite in earnest about connecting Odessa with St Petersburg.

INDICES—A HINT TO PUBLISHERS.

In the last number of the Quarterly Review, we find the following judicious note appended to an article on the collective edition of Lord Chesterfield's letters:—'We have a serious complaint to make of this "Collective Edition of Chesterfield's Letters"—it has no index. It was the same with the "Collective Edition of Walpole's Letters," lately issued from the same establishment, and, like this, in other respects satisfactorily arranged. The publisher ought to know that, though such omissions may not be regarded by the keepers of circulating libraries, they are most annoying to people who have libraries of their own, and buy books to be bound, preserved, and consulted—not merely to be read or glanced over, like a "standard novel," or some sentimental spinster's *mince* or jocular captain's *hash* of history or memoirs. In every considerable printing-office there may be found some intelligent man willing and able to compile a sufficient index for such a book as this now before us, for a very moderate remuneration, at his leisure hours.'

Scarcely a day passes but we suffer great inconvenience and loss of time, either from imperfectly drawn-up indices, or from the total want of them, in standard works. Every book worth reading through (except perhaps a novel), and which is deposited in a library, is virtually a book of reference; for if it did not contain passages worthy being read over again, it would hardly have been preserved; and to wade through several pages of context to find a particular piece of information, is a trial of patience which an index obviates.

The learned French bibliophile, Magré de Marolles, states that not till the middle of the sixteenth century were alphabetical indices added to printed books. 'They have ever since,' he says, 'been considered indispensable. Since the invention of printing learning has spread, and the utility of this plan is universally acknowledged. It gives to authors the means of quoting with precision, and to readers a facility of verifying their quotations at once.' A century or two ago, indices appear to have been more general accompaniments to books than at present; the Delphin Classics, for example, having a copious and complete index. Amongst modern works, we may mention D'Israeli's Curiosities of Literature, neither series of which has an index; yet the matter in these learned volumes is more useful for reference than for continuous reading; being, though highly valuable, detached and memoranda-like. We could cite a hundred similar instances, were we disposed to be tedious.

Besides the want of indices, there is another defect in many books of biography and history—the paucity of dates. The author contents himself with recording the year once, and thinks that is sufficient for a great many succeeding pages. He refers to 'this year' after perhaps a long episode or series of reflections, expecting that the reader has carried the date in his head through perhaps a couple of chapters, and gives him the trouble of referring back, to find out the place where the figures of the date are set down. Nay, he sometimes goes further in confusion, and ingrafts upon 'this year' a heap of perplexities, the unravelling of which demands some proficiency in mental arithmetic. In reference to the dateless period, he will say that so and so happened 'the year before;' or he begins an important paragraph with, 'In the year after ——,' which, without careful collation with the date set down a dozen pages back, gives you no clue to the chronology of the subject whatever. As, however, it may be inelegant, and create tautology, to be continually repeating the numerals in the text, we would recommend that all historical and biographical books should have the year to which the matter relates printed at the top of each page—a good old fashion, the reason for abandoning which we could never comprehend: and this brings us to a third objection presented by a great many modern books—the utter uselessness of their running titles. Not to select real instances invidiously, we will imagine a work on 'the history of the world:' if it contain a thousand pages, 'the history of the world' will appear at the head of each, and consequently be repeated some thousand and one times, for the sake, the printer will tell you, of uniformity. Were utility, however, made the more rational aim, he would substitute a word or two at the top of each page to denote the nature of its contents.

We throw out these hints to publishers and printers, assured that their adoption, simple as they are, would be highly gratifying to the patrons of literature.

ECONOMY OF A CLUB-HOUSE.

Whoever has read the article in our last number on 'Club-Life,' will be prepared to admit that the system which has engendered it is an important novelty in social economics. The interior of a modern club-house presents a set of apartments, and a plan of domestic arrangement, not to be found associated in any other sort of domicile abroad or at home. The best analogy we can think of, is that presented by the union of a nobleman's mansion with a first-rate tavern; for clubbists have at command all the elegances and luxuries of the one, with the promptitude in getting served of the other. To give our readers a correct idea of the internal arrangements of a modern club-house, it is our intention in this sketch to describe them in detail.*

The visitor, on entering one of these palace-like edifices, finds himself in a lobby tenanted by two servants—the hall-porter, who is seated at a desk, and his assistant. It is their duty to ascertain that none have access to the club but members, whose names are inserted in a book as they enter; to receive letters, and to keep an account of the postage. For the despatch of letters, there is a letter-box, which is opened when the official carrier calls in making his collections from the regular receiving-houses. The porters are often attended by one or two lads, in pages' livery, to convey messages from inquiring strangers to such members within the club as may be required. Close to the hall is a reception-room, for the convenience of individuals wishing to see members, and this passed, a hall or vestibule presents itself. Some of these have called forth the highest skill of the architect and decorative artist. The hall of the Reform Club is, we believe, the largest. It is a quadrangle, with a piazza projecting from each wall, and supporting a gallery by massive marble pillars, the whole forming a fine specimen of the Italian style of interior architecture. The vestibule of the 'Conservative' is an example of the opposite school. On entering it from the lobby, it presents to the eye one blaze of colour and prettiness. It is a circle (broken only by the staircase and gallery) surmounted by a cupola. It is covered with designs—chiefly floral—in the most dazzling hues, but so harmoniously blended, that they have a gorgeous rather than a flaring effect. The floor is tesselated with different-coloured marbles.

Doors from the hall or vestibule open upon the various apartments on the ground-floor. First, there is a 'morning-room,' which is used for reading newspapers and writing letters. At the largest clubs, nearly all the best periodicals are taken in. Some idea of their profusion may be formed from the fact, that the Athenæum club expended, in 1844, for English and foreign newspapers

* A description of the 'Reform' club-house will be found in the twelfth volume of our old series, page 234.

and periodicals, the sum of L.471, 2s. 6d. Stationery is supplied to an unlimited extent, not only for writing letters, but even for literary members to feed the press with 'copy,' should their inspirations visit them at the club. The morning-room is comfortably rather than elegantly furnished.

The 'coffee-room' is put to the same use as in a tavern; namely, to that very necessary one of eating and drinking. It is furnished with rows of small tables projecting from each side, with an avenue up the middle. These tables are laid for breakfasts and luncheons till four o'clock in the day, after which they are arranged for dinners. A *carte de jour* (daily bill of fare) is brought to any one wishing to dine, and from it he selects what he prefers. That he may be promptly and correctly served, the following attendants remain in the coffee-room:—a butler to furnish the wine, a head-waiter and many assistants to supply the dishes (which are wound up from the kitchen by a machine called a 'lift'), and a clerk to make out the bills and keep the accounts. The process of getting and paying for a dinner at the Junior United Service Club is thus described,* and we have reason to know it is the same in nearly every other establishment. 'Members, when intending to dine at the club, fill up a form of dinner-bill with the dishes which they may require; this bill is sent by the head-waiter in attendance to the clerk of the kitchen, who attaches the price of each dish as established by the carte, and adds a charge of sixpence (in some clubs a shilling), commonly known as "table money," and intended to cover the expense of bread, cheese, butter, table ale, potatoes, &c. and copies the bill into the kitchen-book. The bill is then returned to the coffee-room, where the charge for such wine as may be taken is added by the butler; and it is finally delivered to the coffee-room clerk, who adds it up, and receives the amount from the member.' An answer to the question—'What does a member pay for his dinner?' shows us the prandial economy of the club plan. From the fiscal reports of the Athenæum, it appears that the average cost of each dinner has been for many years only 2s. 9d., exclusive of wine. To people in humbler life this may seem quite enough to pay for a single meal; but it must be remembered that the two-and-ninepenny dinner is not only excellent in itself, but is served with luxurious accompaniments, which are not to be surpassed at the table of the richest nobleman. Whereas, if we compare it with the price of tavern-dinners, we shall find that the same sum would be charged for a tough beefsteak, served in a second-rate inn, by a slovenly waiter on a dirty table-cloth. Besides, a man *can* dine at his club for eighteenpence if he choose; and well too. Moreover, he is thought no worse of for making a habit of dining economically. The frequenter of a fashionable tavern, on the contrary, is given to understand by the inattention of the waiters and the freezing politeness of the proprietor, that his custom is not much coveted, unless he launches out into a few extravagances 'for the good of the house;' and many a poor gentleman has been made to feel his poverty bitterly, by the vulgar notion which, in former years, construed economy into meanness. Clubs have happily altered all that. In them a member is in his own house, and can be lavish or inexpensive just as he pleases, without exciting remark. He is quite independent; he dreads not the discontented looks of waiters at the smallness of his *douceurs;* and he feels no apprehension lest he should be 'expected' to take more wine than he actually wants.† This appears to have had an extensive effect in abolishing over indulgence at table. From the accounts of three of the largest of the clubs, we ascertain that the average quantity of wine taken at and after each dinner, supplied during some six years past, was only a half-pint. In 1844, there was expended by the 1250 members of the Athenæum only L.722, 6s. 6d. in wine and spirits. Even supposing only half the club habitually ate and drank in the house during that year, this would give but the small sum of twenty-three shillings as the club expenditure of each member throughout the year for stimulants. What a happy change in manners since the old convivial times, when our own forefathers thought nothing of drinking wine to double the above value at a single sitting!

The detached, rather than solitary mode of dining in clubs, bespeaks a tendency to destroy the sociality which is essential to maintain a genial tone in every society. To obviate this in some degree, a snug and handsomely-furnished dining-room is provided on the ground-floor. In it from six to a dozen members may dine together exactly as they would in a private family. To facilitate the arrangement of these parties, printed forms are left in the coffeeroom, and as many as wish to join the 'house dinner' (as it is called) subscribe their name. The lowest number that such a meal can be provided for is six, in some clubs eight; and members having signed the list, must pay whether they dine or not. The charge for these dinners is about seven-and-sixpence per head.—On looking over a table of statistics of the various clubs,* we find that houses most in request for dinners are, first, the Parthenon, where, in 1841, the number supplied to its 732 members was 24,581, being at the rate of nearly thirty-four dinners each;† and, secondly, the 'City,' in which 600 members ate during the same year 18,515 dinners, or thirty-one and three-quarters each. The greatest number of dinners ever taken in a club during one year was served in the Junior United Service in 1839, when 29,527 were eaten. Their average cost was 2s. 3d. each, exclusive of wine.

We have seen that the ground-storey of a club-house consists of a morning, a coffee, and a dining-room, with their accessories. We will now mount the stairs to the upper apartments. Some architects attempt to make the staircase a grand and attractive object, as in the Athenæum; others try to hide it as much as possible, supposing that art is incapable of making such an object a pleasing one. The architect of the Reform Club was of this opinion; and, by keeping it out of sight, has succeeded in producing one of the grandest halls perhaps in London.

The chief apartment above-stairs is the drawing-room, in which members take their evening coffee and tea. Here the decorator and upholsterer's finest taste is generally called into requisition. In some clubs, the display of luxury and expensiveness is carried to a point which may be characterised as absurd; particularly as the drawing-room of every club is less used than any other in the house. Near to it is the library, which is fitted up with every convenience for reading, consulting maps, &c. and is attended by a resident librarian. The books are accumulated by donation, and by a sum set aside from the general funds for their purchase. The number of volumes of course varies with the age and affluence of the club. The most extensive library is, we believe, that of the Athenæum, which, in March 1844, contained 20,300 volumes. Five hundred pounds is annually expended by this club for increasing its library, exclusive of the cost of periodicals.—Near to the library is, in some houses, a card-room, in which, however, no game of pure chance is allowed; and at whist, half-guinea points are the highest stake to be played for. Breaking either of these rules is attended, on proof, with summary expul-

* In 'The System of Management of the Junior United Service Club,' &c. drawn up by Mr Thomas Hatch, the secretary, and printed for the information of the members.

† The proprietors of some taverns formerly caused it to be understood that their charges for eatables were not remunerative, and that gentlemen were 'expected' to take a certain quantity of wine.

* In a manuscript on the subject kindly lent for our use by the secretary of one of the principal clubs.

† This proportion is, it will be obvious, no index to the number of *diners*. Some five-and-twenty per cent. of each club never dine in the house at all, but merely go occasionally to read the papers or write their letters—the family-men, for example.

sion. In the Reform Club, there is no place exclusively set apart for whist; a small supplementary drawing-room, called the 'house-dinner drawing-room,' being used. Indeed gaming, even of the most moderate kind, is discouraged as much as possible.

The third storey contains at least one billiard-room, which is attended by a marker. For cards and billiards a charge is made; as it would be very unfair to make members who do not indulge in those games participate in the extra expenses they entail.—In only twelve of the twenty-two clubs is there a smoking-room, which, we have usually remarked, is the worst-looking place in the house. This completes the description of such of the public apartments as tend to give an idea of club-life. The highest storey consists of dormitories for the resident servants. The rooms in the basement of the building, such as kitchens, larders, pantries, still-room, dressing-rooms, lavatories and baths, need merely be mentioned, to show what other conveniences are provided for the members.

Thus much of the apartments in a modern club, and their uses. We will now take a glance at the management and governance of the complicated domestic establishment:—The direction of the affairs of every club is confided to a general committee selected from the members, which numbers from thirty to forty. From three to eight of these form a quorum, and meet once a-week to regulate the financial concerns of the institution, to superintend the election of new members, to appoint tradespeople, to engage or dismiss servants, and to inquire into and redress any complaints which may be made by members. The general committee also prepares annual reports and statements of account, which are printed for the information and satisfaction of the rest of the club. As, however, all these duties could not be efficiently performed by one board, it divides itself into sub-committees for special objects. These are the 'house committee,' which has the superintendence of the household affairs; the 'wine committee,' always composed of acknowledged connoisseurs of that article, to whom its choice, and all matters respecting its cellarage and distribution at table, are confided; and the 'book committee,' for the management of the library, to which all works are submitted for approval before they can be admitted, and from which all orders for their purchase issue. Where there are billiard-rooms, amateurs of that game are selected to form a 'billiard committee.' As organ and agent of all these boards, a secretary is appointed, who also conducts the official correspondence of the club. This enumeration includes the managing direction: the minor details are carried on by servants.

The chief of these is the house-steward, to whom is intrusted the management of the domestics; the purchasing, storing, and superintending of the daily supplies of viands. He is in some clubs aided by a 'superintendent,' who has the charge of the drawing-room floor, and sees that proper supplies of stationery and newspapers are furnished to the writing and reading rooms. The butler and his assistant supply and keep accounts of the wines and spirits. The duties of the coffee-room clerk are sufficiently obvious: he sits at the top of the 'lift,' whilst the kitchen clerk's post is at the bottom. This arrangement justifies the definition of a 'lift,' given by an Irish friend, who declared it to consist of a 'wooden spout with a moveable bottom, having a clerk at each end.' The head coffee-room waiter is the lowest servant in rank who does not wear livery, which all the other male servants do. The cook of most club-houses is generally a foreigner, so accomplished in his profession, that he almost deserves the name of an artist. He has a male assistant and a number of kitchen-maids under his orders. The female servants—who never appear in the public part of the house—are superintended by a housekeeper, who has under her charge a needle-woman, a still-room maid (to make tea and coffee), and several housemaids. The number of domestics in each club varies from 56 (in the Reform Club) to 11, the number employed in the Garrick and Naval Clubs. Most clubs subscribe, either in money or in kind (such as waste linen, &c.), to an hospital, that their servants may be received into them, in the case of accidents or prolonged ailments; but for temporary maladies, a surgeon is engaged to attend and supply medicines. The broken victuals are given to the poor, under the direction of the parish authorities.* One feature connected with the servants' hall of the Athenæum is deserving of notice and imitation. It contains a library collected by the servants by means of small quarterly contributions out of their wages. 'The beneficial effects are,' remarks the secretary to that institution, 'that the servants will frequently stay at home and read when off duty in bad weather; and in fine weather in summer, they may be often seen reading under the trees in St James's Park.' They are very proud of their books, and several who could formerly read but imperfectly, have been stimulated to exertion by the example of the pleasure derived by others. None have an excuse for being unable to read and write, because a person in the house is employed to instruct gratuitously such as desire it.

This completes our description of the internal arrangements of a club-house; but we must not omit to show how, and at what expense, all its advantages are attainable. To be a member of a club, unimpeachable respectability, not only of station but of conduct, is essential. When an individual becomes a candidate for admission, his name and profession are legibly exhibited, and on a stated day a ballot by every member who chooses to vote, takes place. In some establishments one negative in ten, in others a single negative of the whole votes, excludes. Exclusion (called 'blackballing') is not always, however, a proof that a man is not worthy of admission; for the candidates of some clubs are very numerous. There are at present on the list of candidates for admission to the Junior United Service Club no fewer than 2000 names. In such cases there is of course a strong competition for suffrages; and as many voters have their bias in favour of friends, they will often blackball a stranger to secure the election of the candidate in whom their personal interest is strongest. Still, there *is* an unpleasant feeling attached to rejection, and we cannot applaud the practice of some clubs, of keeping their list of candidates and members in the coffee-room for general reference. The rejected are easily known by the date of the unfortunate event being placed against their names. We do not see the justice of thus indirectly publishing this sort of disgrace. When elected, a candidate has to pay an entrance-fee, which, in most clubs, is about twenty guineas. The Union is the highest, being L.32, 11s.; and the Law the lowest, being only L.5, 5s. The annual subscription is, in a majority of clubs, six guineas; in only two as low as five; and in none higher than ten guineas.

We would point out, in conclusion, that for this moderate subscription, the member may occupy a palace from nine in the morning till after midnight. He may partake of the choicest cookery and the finest wines at cost price, which are served with scrupulous cleanliness by civil servants, whom he has neither to pay nor to manage. He has access to an extensive and well-selected library, and to every paper and periodical that is worth reading. He can come when he pleases, and stay away when he pleases, without anything going wrong: he is perfectly independent, and has nobody to please but himself. 'Clubs,' remarks the experienced author of The Original, 'are favourable to economy of time. There is a fixed place to go to, everything

* To check carelessness, an excellent rule is adopted in some establishments: a sum is annually allowed to cover losses by breakage (the Junior United Service set aside L.90 yearly); and if articles greater in value have been destroyed during the year, the deficiency is supplied out of the wages of each servant; if, however, the contrary, the surplus is divided amongst them. We note these minute facts as hints to private housekeepers.

is served with comparative expedition, and it is not customary in general to remain long at table.'

The system having been found so beneficial amongst the higher circles of society, it might safely be recommended for imitation amongst the lower grades, in which economy—the chief advantage of the club-principle—is so much needed. We see no reason why the middle and operative classes could not have their domestic clubs, as well as the nobility and gentry.

NEW ZEALAND AS A COLONY.

The number of conflicting statements which continue to be published respecting our colonies, renders it almost impossible for any one to form a satisfactory conclusion on the subject. One, a hard-working, enterprising, and prosperous settler, views everything from the sunny side of success; another, whose education and habits are utterly at variance with the sturdy duties of a backwoodsman, emigrates, loses his money, returns and denounces the country as the most wretched in creation; a third travels to visit some relations, or for amusements' sake, and then publishes his reminiscences of a month with all the confidence of a twenty years' resident; while a fourth, who has never been beyond the environs of the metropolis, indites his 'personal experiences' for the benefit of intending emigrants. Be it Canada, Australia, or New Zealand, it is all the same; book contradicts book so directly, that it would be better for a person to set out without having perused a single line, than to be perplexed and bewildered among such heterogeneous materials. Fortunately, however, there are in this, as in other cases, a few exceptions: a book does occasionally make its appearance by an honest and impartial author, whose opportunities are known to have been such as enable him to arrive at an accurate judgment. In this class we feel inclined to include a recent work on New Zealand,* as knowing the author, and as believing him capable of estimating, with tolerable accuracy, the facts and appearances which came under his notice.

Mr Brown entertains a high opinion of the physical and mental qualities of the aborigines, considering them intelligent and manly, acute in their perceptions, and keenly given to trading and barter. He admits, no doubt, their superstitious observances, which are often repugnant to Christian morality, and their deficiency in gratitude and conscientiousness; but, on the whole, regards them as more likely to amalgamate with Europeans than any other known race of coloured people. Of their country, as a field for British emigration, he forms an equally flattering estimate. Its climate is mild and equable, its soil capable of bearing the usually cultivated crops in abundance, and though possessing no river-plains to be compared with those of America, has still a fair proportion of surface fitted for the plough. When cleared of the original copse and fern, the finest pasture springs up spontaneously; and we are told that pigs, sheep, and oxen fatten with much greater rapidity than in the most fertile counties of England. Not subjected to destructive droughts, and having no continuously wet season, it presents an open pasturage the whole year round, and thus sheep become not only heavier animals, but yield finer fleeces than they do in Australia. Though wheat, rice, maize, and potatoes flourish luxuriantly, it should be borne in mind that as yet New Zealand is better adapted for pastoral than for agricultural purposes. All kinds of stock introduced by the settlers have prospered amazingly; and bees, unknown till 1840, have thriven so well, that an export trade in honey is shortly expected. Though possessing some fine timber, both for building and ornamental uses, it is not a forest country like North America; and though copper, manganese, tin, lead, sulphur, rock-salt, coal, and other minerals have been found in several places, yet we know too little of the country in this respect to speak with certainty on the abundance or extent of the supply. As is well known, New Zealand has many fine harbours, and would form the most eligible station for the South-Sea whale fishing, which could be prosecuted at all seasons. From its position also, it is eminently fitted to be the great mercantile emporium of the Southern Pacific. Exporting minerals, timber, its native flax, gum, bark, hides, wool, oil, &c. and taking in return our manufactures and machinery, the while that it would afford a permanent and comfortable home for our redundant population, this infant colony certainly deserves all the praise which its friends bestow, and all the attention from the British government which they so anxiously crave.

Admitting the superiority of the aborigines to other savage races, and also the eligibility of the country as a field for emigration, the first question which naturally arises is—Why have our efforts up to this period proved so unfortunate? Mr Brown answers—The infatuated procedure of the government officials. 'In the beginning of 1840, when Captain Hobson arrived in New Zealand to establish British authority, he found an extensive trade carried on between the immigrants, under the New Zealand Land Company, and the natives. The settlers, flushed with past prosperity, and enjoying still brighter hopes of the future, had pushed their enterprising spirit into every part of the country where vessels could go, or where produce of any kind could be obtained. The natives were actuated by similar feelings. To satisfy their increasing wants, they made every effort to raise additional supplies, and effected sales of land, now so eagerly sought after by the Europeans, but not less valued by the natives, not only on account of the large quantities of goods to be obtained for it, but also from their anxiety to get Europeans to settle among them for the purposes of trade—a sale of land being, in their estimation, sure to effect this object. Like the settlers, therefore, the natives were, at the period of Captain Hobson's arrival, hoping much from the future. Not merely did they anticipate increased trading advantages from the additional number of settlers to which they looked forward, but we were regarded by them as beings of a higher order. In physical power we were acknowledged to be vastly superior; they were impressed with this truth by the sight of our ships of war, and the feeling was continually kept alive by individual exhibitions of that superiority; as a single settler, by his courage and determination alone, would frequently withstand and frighten off numbers of natives bent on robbing or otherwise molesting him. However manifested, or on whatever grounds it rested, it cannot be disputed that, at the period referred to, our moral and physical power were regarded by them with the utmost respect; and it is mortifying to make the admission, that ever since that period the respect of the natives, both for our moral qualities and physical power, has been gradually weakened by our own conduct, and to such a degree as to have entirely changed the nature and objects of the very government, and even to have endangered our personal safety in the country.' Such is Mr Brown's opinion, and he proceeds to confirm it by adducing several reasons, the principal of which was the treaty of Waitangi, which he styles 'a farce,' and to which he affirms that the signatures of many of the chiefs were obtained by improper influences.

This treaty stipulates on the part of Britain for the sovereignty of the islands, and the exclusive right of buying all the land; and in effect, though not in words, at whatever price the government choose to give, and at whatever time they find it convenient to purchase. In return for this, the New Zealanders were to be admitted to all the rights and privileges of British subjects; 'in other, and in more intelligible words,' adds our author, 'the privilege of being taxed, and of living under our civil and criminal laws.' When this treaty came to be acted

* New Zealand and its Aborigines; being an account of the aborigines, trade, and resources of the colony. By William Brown, lately a member of the legislative council of New Zealand. Smith, Elder, and Co. London. 1845.

upon, it operated against the settlers of the New Zealand Company, and others who had directly purchased land from the natives, raising questions as to the validity of their titles, and otherwise creating confusion and discontent. The natives were perfectly aware that they had in many instances parted with certain lands; but when government thus started the question of validity, the savage, intent only upon additional quantities of goods, was also but too ready not only to raise the same objections, but to deny the sales altogether. Besides this confusion, new purchases could only be made when and where the government chose, and thus sales went on slowly; fewer goods came to the natives, who began to show symptoms of dislike to the terms of the treaty—a dislike which many of the company's settlers did everything in their power to foment—representing government as the common enemy both of immigrant and native. The government and settlers being thus pitted against each other, the natives were by far too shrewd not to perceive 'the house divided against itself,' and so committed aggressions upon the colonists, without being punished as they deserved: obedience they rendered to government only in as far as presents and new purchases made it their interest to do so. Under the plea of 'protecting' the aborigines, the public functionaries exercised a rigid severity towards the settlers for aggressions against the natives, and thus impressed them with an idea of their importance; while their offences, on the other hand, were either treated with lenity or altogether overlooked. For example, 'on the frivolous pretence of a tapu having been broken, they robbed a Mr Forsaith, a settler at Kiapara, to a very large extent. The authorities on this occasion made no attempt to punish them; but, after sundry interviews with the protector, the matter was hushed up, by the natives making over to the government a tract of land (12,000 acres) by way of compensation! Considering themselves on the whole successful, the natives, within a few months afterwards (March 1842), made a predatory excursion to Wangari, and, without any pretext of injury received, robbed the settlers of a large amount of property. Government never made the slightest attempt to punish the offenders, and the settlers to this day are without any compensation for their losses.'

Such conduct produced results the very opposite of those intended; for, instead of gratitude and consideration, the New Zealanders began to treat the government and its orders with contempt, as well as to become more insulting and annoying to the immigrants. In addition to these infatuations, Mr Shortland (acting as the representative of government after Captain Hobson's decease) began to put the treaty of Waitangi into effect, not only as regarded the settlers, but as affecting the titles of the respective chiefs, who claimed certain tracts by right of conquest. This of course was indignantly resented; and when he found that he could not carry the treaty into effect with the natives, the settlers on these tracts (and who had purchased them from the chiefs) were informed that they would be allowed to sit still 'on payment of a small fee by way of acknowledgment.' This, like other measures, was scouted: the settlers had no fear of an armed force to compel them to immediate subjection, and so appealed to the Land Commission, knowing well that British justice would not despoil them of lands which they had already honestly paid for. 'The infatuated government,' says Mr Brown, 'proceeded, and gave deeper and deeper offence to the colonists, each measure being more destructive than another, until it arrived at the climax of unpopularity; having excited the derision and hatred of every individual in the country, north, south, east, and west. Even the missionaries could not conceal their displeasure, as their countenance to the measures of government had at first been purchased by promises which were never fulfilled. In addition to these indirect and perhaps unintentional causes of injury to the natives, the government is chargeable with practising deception in many ways towards them. For instance, from the importunity of the natives, promises to purchase land were freely made—but to be broken; and, worse than all, payments for land actually purchased were not duly made; while the repeated but fruitless applications for it, produced in many cases the greatest exasperation.' Over and above all these causes of dissatisfaction, customs' regulations were enforced at the ports, and taxes imposed on tobacco and other articles. To a people who had never been accustomed to imposts of this nature, and into whose harbours vessels of every nation had hitherto entered without any restriction, these exactions were especially offensive, and led, as will be seen, to open resistance. These remarks apply more particularly to the northern parts of the island, where government had planted Auckland and other townships; but the same spirit of discontent was rapidly spreading along Cook's Strait, where the New Zealand Company had already established Wellington, Nelson, and New Plymouth.

The ultimate results of the government procedure were frequent quarrels between the settlers and natives, a diminution of trade and enterprise, the massacre of Wairau, the insurrection headed by Heki at the Bay of Islands—and so on through a series of defiances and obstructions, till Mr Shortland was superseded by Captain Fitzroy, who arrived in December 1843. The hopes excited by this change caused a temporary cessation of hostilities; for both natives and settlers looked forward to some speedy and effective remedy. After a few weeks, however, their patience became completely exhausted, and the new governor was compelled to waive the right of pre-emption, and to allow the natives to dispose of their land as they thought proper, the purchaser merely paying a fee of ten shillings per acre to government. This tended for a short time to allay the hostility of those whose lands lay in the vicinity of the townships, as such met with ready purchasers even at that rate; but to the inland chiefs it was no advantage. The consequence was, that the old spirit of hostility returned, burning all the fiercer that many of the settlers made common cause with the aborigines. This alliance was effective; for on the 10th of October 1844, all restrictions on the sale of lands were removed—the government retaining its superiority and right to grant titles, by exacting payment of only one penny per acre. Lands, therefore, can now be purchased for whatever sum the natives will agree to take, in any district, and at whatever time parties choose to agree. In addition to this, all the ports in the islands were declared free, customs in every shape were abolished, the distillation prohibition removed, and instead of indirect taxation for the purposes of the local government, a property rate of L.1 per cent. was imposed. All these measures were popular in the highest degree, and infused new life and vigour into the infant colony. 'In the course of a few weeks, the feelings of both native and European were completely changed, and the bustle and activity of business took the place of languor and despair: the foundation of the prosperity of the colony of New Zealand may be said to have been then laid.' Reverting to the aborigines, it is gratifying to learn that, notwithstanding the continued mismanagement of affairs, they were fast acquiring the manners and habits of the Europeans; were generally adopting their dress, their style of living, their system of trade and modes of agriculture; and everywhere showed the greatest anxiety to possess sheep, cows, bullocks, horses, and ploughs. The women, too, were imitating those little domestic arts peculiar to the British housewife; and even shops and hotels in English fashion had been opened by natives. Another important index to their advancement was the desire they manifested to be near the townships; some of the chiefs actually taking up their residence within the capital.

Such is the substance of Mr Brown's statements respecting New Zealand, as derived from his personal experiences, from the commencement of the colony in 1840, till the beginning of the present year, at which time he sailed for England. Since then, accounts have arrived of the destruction of the township of Kororarika by the natives, the loss of many lives, and damage to the amount of sixty or seventy thousand pounds. This calamity also our author places to the account of the Hobson-Shortland infatuation, considering it as the off-spring of that discontent which was first engendered by the land questions and commercial restrictions. He seems to entertain no fear for future aggressions, if the authorities observe a mild but firm procedure; for the character of the natives is altogether opposed to the supposition of large combinations against the whites, with a view to their expulsion from the country. On the contrary, they rather court the settler's presence, and are ever ready to trade with him, knowing well that their own comforts are bound up with those of the colonists. 'It is now sufficiently obvious, however, that a large body of troops are indispensably necessary for the defence of the settlers, and to preserve order; and if the power of the troops shall be confined exclusively to these objects, there can be little doubt of this being easily attained. But if, on the contrary, that power shall be employed to uphold injustice, or to coerce the natives out of their rights, there will be no peace or personal security, and the natives will combine together, and if unable to expel their oppressors, they will at least effectually prevent the colonisation of the country. In particular, this result will inevitably happen if any interference with, or restrictions upon, the free sale of their lands be again attempted, whether in the form of an open prohibition or hindrance of sale, or by the equally unjust but more deceitful scheme of taxing their lands. *Absolute free trade in land has now become indispensable to preserve peace with the natives; and New Zealand upon other terms is not worth having.*'

Supposing such a course were followed as is here shadowed out, Mr Brown entertains no doubts of the co-operation and amalgamation of the aborigines—an amalgamation which, in his estimation, would be greatly facilitated by the adoption of such measures as the following:—1. An efficient protector's establishment, including sub-protectors, at every important station; for though there is at present an establishment under this name, its sole use, previous to Captain Fitzroy's arrival, was 'to make land purchases for the smallest sums for government, varying, it is believed, from threepence to sixpence per acre, and to cajole the natives into a belief of our good intentions towards them, without making any effort towards their real improvement.' 2. The establishment of a gazette, to be published both in English and Maori, for the purpose of affording information to the natives of the intentions of government, and also to elicit from them information respecting land, their titles, disputes, and other matters of public interest. 3. The making of roads by native labour, under the inspection of government. 4. Stimulating the aborigines, by means of public awards, to industrial pursuits, such as agriculture after the European mode, stock-rearing, flax-growing, and the like. 5. The encouragement, by similar means, of the adoption of our dress, houses, style of living, &c. 6. The establishment of schools, and the adoption in these, as well as in churches, of the English language exclusively. 7. No favour by government to any particular religious sect, but equal protection to all. These and other steps Mr Brown believes would essentially contribute to the improvement of the natives, and would assist in amalgamating them more speedily with the settlers. Though not attaching the same value to some of these suggestions which the author apparently does, we may yet believe that their adoption could not fail to affect materially the character and conduct of the susceptible New Zealander.

Looking upon New Zealand, therefore, as one of our colonies, almost everything has yet to be done by the British government. The natives require to be dealt with honestly and firmly—honestly as regards the disposal of their lands, and firmly as concerns the fulfilment of their bargains. To 'protect' them, as was done between 1840 and 1844, would be to retain them as savages; to befriend them in deed, is to instruct them in the arts and accomplishments of civilised life. Respecting the immigrants, immunity from farther aggressions must be afforded them: numerous land-disputes have to be decided, and compensation made for losses already sustained. They do not wish large grants of money from the Home Treasury; all that they demand is, 'the assurance that the funds raised within the colony be expended judiciously and economically, for the purposes of the colony.' Such a course, coupled with free trade in all its purity, would, according to Mr Brown, render New Zealand one of the most eligible fields for British emigration, inasmuch as the country is neither exclusively agricultural, pastoral, nor commercial, but preserves a desirable relation to each of these resources; thus allowing of that variety of interests which is the foundation of all permanent prosperity

THE PRISON OF OPORTO.

The Portuguese seem to be at present in much the same state of advancement, as respects prison discipline, that we were about a century ago. A coarse principle of vengeance is that which rules in the management of criminals; and whether the unhappy sufferers survive the pains of incarceration, or die under them, would appear to be a matter of indifference.

While on a visit to Oporto in 1844, I had an opportunity of witnessing the manner in which prisoners are treated in the common jail of that city. Not being in the habit of visiting such places, I should not now have entered this one, but for a circumstance which attracted my attention. In daily passing the prison, a large building of handsome architecture, I could not help noticing a very curious appearance. From the unglazed windows there were projected numerous long poles, to each of which was attached a string and bag, the whole being kept in pretty constant motion, accompanied with screams and wailing lamentations from the inmates. On looking up, wretched faces, sallow, and matted with long beards, were seen crowding against the gratings, and the urgent appeals made by them to the passengers for food or money were among the most dismal sounds which had ever fallen upon my ear.

Interested as well as shocked, I resolved to visit this abode of misery. On consulting with some friends as to the best manner of gaining admission, all endeavoured to dissuade me from the attempt, assuring me that no one ever entered the place willingly, as the scenes I should there witness were dreadful, and the danger from infectious diseases great. A feeling, however, of something higher than curiosity induced me to persevere, and I succeeded in procuring an order from one of the magistrates. This was attended with some difficulty, as, at the period of my visit, one of those insurrections or revolutions with which the peninsula is almost annually visited, had just broken out, in consequence of which the town was under martial law, and many arrests were taking place. On proceeding to the prison, at each corner of which is placed a sentry, who challenges all who pass after sunset, I was admitted into a large hall, in which there was a strong guard of soldiers, and thence ascended a long flight of steps, at the top of which is an iron gate.

On showing the order the gate was opened, and I was requested to inscribe my name in a book, after which the jailer desired me to follow him, informing me it was the prisoners' dinner hour. I accordingly accompanied him and four assistants, and, after passing through a long vaulted passage, came to a hall about forty feet square, in the centre of which was an immense tin case containing the soup, and close to it a pile of loaves for the prisoners. I tasted the soup, which was made of beans and other vegetables, and a large proportion of oil, which I did not find unpalatable. In a little I followed my guide through another passage, and my attention was directed to a trap-door, on which the jailer gave three loud knocks with a heavy stick; and, being almost instantly responded to from below, the bolts were withdrawn, the door lifted up, and immediately first one and then another of the most miserable-looking creatures issued forth, each holding a ration can. Both were tall men, very thin, of sallow unhealthy complexion, long hair over their faces, and most repulsive melancholy expressions. Casting their eyes upward on mounting from below, they walked quickly to the soup can, held out their ration tin, and received from another under-jailer a piece of bread, and without a syllable having been uttered, returned to the trap-door and descended. The door was closed over them, the iron bars padlocked, and there they were to remain until rations were again distributed. I thought I had never seen such wretched-looking fellow-creatures; but I confess my sympathy in their fate was not increased, on being told that these two men were the executioners of the prison: having been condemned to death for murder, they had availed themselves of the option offered, either to suffer themselves, or to put others to death. One of them had been confined for thirteen, and the other for seven years, during which time they had lived in the same apartment.

We then proceeded to a trap-door in another passage, and, being desirous of seeing the room in which the prisoners were kept, I accompanied one of the jailers. After descending a long narrow winding staircase, nearly blocked up by prisoners anxious to get up for their rations, I found myself in a large high-vaulted apartment with windows without glass, and up the bars of which the jailers mounted, sounding each with a short piece of iron, to discover if any of them had been filed. There were eighty-one prisoners in the room, several of whom were deserters, young fellows in military costume; others were murderers and robbers. Some were still untried; others had long been sentenced to the galleys or death; all were huddled together, whether their crimes were great or small.

I could not help feeling I had got into strange company; but although a very melancholy, it was a very interesting scene, to be in the midst of so many human beings whose features betrayed the violent passions that had caused the perpetration of the bloody deeds which had brought them there. Among them were some handsome men, and the variety of dress had a singular and picturesque effect. Many of them were well clothed, others were in straw cloaks or sheepskins, and others had nothing but a shawl wherewith to cover themselves. Some had provided themselves with mattresses; but most of them had the bare floor for their couch. A very few were working as carpenters and weavers. All were very polite; and, on the whole, I found their quarters greatly superior to what I had been led to imagine. Owing to there being no glass in the windows, it must be extremely cold during the winter; but there is, consequently, a current of fresh air, which counteracts the close atmosphere and pestilential diseases which would otherwise inevitably arise.

I was greatly struck by the proof which even these lawless men exhibit of the necessity for a distinction of rank and power; for they invariably elect from among themselves a judge or chief, whom all must implicitly obey, and the one whom they had selected while I was there was a very tall gentlemanlike man, who had committed some half-dozen murders. On receiving permission, the whole, provided with ration cans, mounted the steps, ranged themselves in the hall, and one by one marched past the man dealing out the soup and the bread, and again immediately descended.

Some had complaints to make, and one man became violently excited, and gesticulated with an elegance and energy which would have called down rounds of applause had it been on the stage. I afterwards descended into another room, where there were about fifty men, and into another with the same number of women, many of whom had children with them, and to whom the rations were served out in the same way as to the men. We then proceeded up another staircase, and entered various rooms occupied by those who could afford to pay for superior accommodation, many of them being gentlemen and tradesmen, who had been arrested in consequence of the existing insurrection. I had reason to believe that some of the prisoners were kept concealed from visitors, and on a small door being opened by the jailer, I entered (though at first held back by one of the assistants) a cell so dark, that at first I could see nothing; but shortly observed an object covered with a white cloth moving in one corner. This was no doubt a political prisoner; and, without a syllable being uttered, his rations were left with him, and the door closed. While waiting in the hall, a man, apparently a farmer, was brought in upon suspicion of being connected with the rebels, and underwent a most minute examination, in order to discover if he was the bearer of any treasonable papers; and so searching was this scrutiny, that his shoes were actually taken off, and the soles ripped open. Nothing suspicious was found; yet the jailer ordered one of the trap-doors to be raised and closed over this unfortunate man, who, unless he had some friend with influence or with money to bribe the officers or judges, would probably remain in prison for years; but even if condemned to death, he may have the execution deferred as long as money is 'judiciously' applied.

Within the last two or three years, the town and country police has been rendered so efficient, that murders or robberies are comparatively rare in the neighbourhood; and the prison is not nearly so full as formerly, when not unfrequently, owing to its crowded state, the wretched creatures became so excited and violent, that it was thought necessary to order the sentries to fire through the windows indiscriminately among them.

During the time of Don Miguel's usurpation, a time still spoken of with horror by the inhabitants of Oporto, the prison was crammed so full that it was represented to the governor of the town (the notorious Jelles Jourdao) that there was not space for more. 'Is it full to the ceiling?' he demanded. 'No.' 'Then,' added he, 'don't tell me that it is full.' At that dreadful period there was scarcely a respectable family in the town who had not relatives in this prison, and many of them were beheaded in the adjoining square. When Don Pedro entered Oporto, the doors of the jail were broken open, and all were liberated, with the exception of the jailer, whose skull was fractured by the mob as he tried to escape.

Since the period of my visit to this horrible place of confinement, the Portuguese legislature has had under consideration the state of the national prisons, and the establishment of penitentiaries; but I have not heard that any improvement has yet resulted from their deliberations.

FURNISHING A HOUSE.

All things are according to the ideas and feelings with which they are connected; and if, as old George Herbert says, dusting a room is an act of religious grace when it is done from a sense of religious duty, furnishing a house is a process of high enjoyment when it is the preparation for a home of happy love. The dwelling is hung all round with bright anticipations, and crowded with blissful thoughts, spoken by none, perhaps, but present to all. On this table, and by this snug fireside, will the cheerful winter breakfast go forward, when each is about to enter on the gladsome business of the day; and that sofa will be drawn out, and those curtains will be closed, when the intellectual pleasures of the evening, the rewards of the laborious day, begin. Those ground windows will stand open all the summer noon, and the flower-stands will be gay and fragrant; and the shaded parlour will be the cool retreat of the wearied husband when he comes in to rest from his professional toils. There will stand the books, destined to refresh and refine his higher tastes; and there the music with which the wife will indulge him. Here will they first feel what it is to have a *home of their own*, where they will first enjoy the privacy of it, the security, the freedom, the consequence in the eyes of others, the sacredness in their own. Here they will first exercise the graces of hospitality, and the responsibility of control. Here will they feel that they have attained the great resting-place of their life—the resting-place of their individual lot, but only the starting-point of their activity. Such is the work of furnishing a house once in a lifetime. It may be a welcome task to the fine lady decking her drawing-room anew, to gratify her ambition, or divert her *ennui*; it may be a satisfactory labour to the elderly couple, settling themselves afresh, when their children are dispersed abroad, and it becomes necessary to discard the furniture that the boys have battered and spoiled; it may be a refined amusement to the selfish man of taste, wishing to prolong or recall the scenes of foreign travel; but to none is it the conscious delight that it is to young lovers and their sympathising friends, whether the scene be the two rooms of the hopeful young artisan, about to bring his bride home from service, or the palace of a nobleman, enriched with intellectual luxuries for the lady of his adoration, or the quiet abode of an unambitious professional man, whose aim is privacy and comfort.—*Deerbrook, by Miss Martineau.*

THE PAMPEROS.

Amongst the most remarkable phenomena connected with the Pampas of South America, are those hurricane-like storms known by the name of *pamperos*. They occur in summer after a continuance of northern wind and of sultry weather. Before the setting in of the storm, clouds gather in the south-west, which soon assume a singularly hard and rolled or tufted appearance, like great bales of black cotton, and are continually altering their forms. They are followed by gusts of hot wind, blowing at intervals of about a minute. Then suddenly the storm, which apparently proceeds from the snow-capped summits of the Andes, rushes down with an indescribable violence, sweeps over the Pampas, and, ere it reaches the town of Buenos Ayres, often becomes a hurricane. The pampero is frequently accompanied by clouds of dust, collected from the parched-up soil, so dense as to change the brightest light in an instant, as it were, to the most intense darkness, so that people are unable to find their way. Instances have occurred at Buenos Ayres of persons bathing in the river being drowned ere they could find their way to the shore. These clouds are often attended by a heavy fall of rain, which, mingling with the dust as it pours down, forms literally a shower of mud. Sometimes the pampero is accompanied by the most terrific thunder and lightning, doing great damage, and frequently attended with loss of life. The shipping in the La Plata river always suffers greatly from a pampero, and the loss of property is considerable. The force of these storms must be immense, as it is able to remove heavy bodies to a great distance. Captain Fitzroy mentions that a small boat, before the setting in of the storm, had been hauled ashore just above water-mark, and fastened by a strong rope to a large stone; but after the storm it was found far from the beach, shattered to pieces, but still fast to the stone, which it had dragged along.—*Curiosities of Physical Geography.*

THE ELECTRIC EEL.

In no part of the world is the electric eel, or *gymnotus*, found in such numbers as in the numerous rivers which join the Orinoco in its middle course, and in that river itself. These animals resemble a common eel, except that they are rather thicker in proportion to their length. They are of a yellowish and livid colour, with a row of yellow spots on each side from head to tail. They are difficult to catch, on account of the great agility with which they hide themselves in the mud. The Indians take them in the following way. They force a herd of horses to go into shallow water, which they know to be frequented by these eels. The noise which the horses make with their feet, brings the eels out of their muddy retreat, and they immediately attack the horses, by pressing themselves beneath their bellies, and discharging on them their electric shocks. The frightened horses make efforts to get out of the water, but the Indians prevent them, and the eels repeat their discharges. Some of the horses, being stunned by these repeated strokes, fall down and are drowned; others evince all the signs of horror, and endeavour to escape, but are prevented by the Indians. At last the eels become exhausted, in consequence of the repeated electric discharges, and are easily taken. The shock which these animals communicate is so severe, that it is impossible to hold them in the hand, or to tread on them. They can give a shock exactly similar to that of an electric battery, stunning fish through the medium of water, and, if they are small, killing them. This shock is evidently given by a voluntary act of the fish, for it is not always felt instantaneously on handling them; and the moment of the effort being made, can be distinguished by the corrugation of the skin and the changing of the colour.—*Wittich.*

SUPERSTITION RESPECTING THE BAY.

It was a superstition entertained both in ancient and modern times, that the lightning paid respect to the bay tree, and consequently its leaves were used as a charm against the electric stroke. Thus in an old English poem we find these lines—

> As thunder nor fierce lightning harmes the bay,
> So no extremitie hath power on fame.

In a copy of complimentary verses to the memory of Ben Jonson, there is this allusion to the supposed protection which the bay conferred on its wearer—

> I see that wreathe which doth the wearer arme,
> 'Gainst the quick strokes of thunder, is no charme
> To keep off death's pale dart: for, Jonson, then
> Thou hadst been numbered still with living men;
> Time's scythe had feared thy lawrell to invade,
> Nor thee this subject of our sorrow made.

It is related of Tiberius the Roman emperor, that whenever the sky portended a storm, he placed a chaplet of laurel round his neck. A Dutch writer of the seventeenth century takes upon him to combat the notion; and in order to show its falsity, states that, only a few years previously, a laurel tree had been shattered by lightning in the neighbourhood of Rome. The iron crown of laurels upon the bust of Ariosto in the Benedictine church at Ferrara was melted by lightning, an incident which Childe Harold notices and comments on—

> Nor was the ominous element unjust;
> For the true laurel wreath which glory weaves,
> Is of the tree no bolt of thunder cleaves.

NATURAL HISTORY.

The consequences of this pursuit, when not even carried to the length of a study, are self-evident, and the day has happily passed away in which the votaries of nature were taunted with ridicule, and as addicted to childish fancies. There is a kind of freemasonry in the study or pursuit of natural history; it operates on our kindly affections, and in many instances opens the communication to the most pleasing acquaintances, which, from congeniality of disposition, ripen into the warmest friendships. Our walks cease to be solitary; something there is always to observe, something to note down, to verify or compare. The effect on the mind, too, is not one of its least advantages: we look round on the creation, and exclaim with Stillingfleet—

> How wondrous is this scene! where all is formed
> With number, weight, and measure! all designed
> For some great end.

We admire with astonishment the Providence which has assigned to each thing its place, forming a harmonious whole, through such innumerable and inseparable links; and feel, with deep humility, how richly we are endowed, and how great is our debt of gratitude and praise to nature's God. From casual observance, in the first instance, we are led on to serious contemplation, and higher feelings are awakened, which operate most influentially on the mind and conduct. I have ever noticed as a sequence, that kindness of disposition, consideration for others, and a greater calmness of mind, become the portion of the admirer and observer of the works of Providence: he rises from the perusal of the book of nature a better man.—*E. P. Thompson.*

PASSION.

He submits to be seen through a microscope, who suffers himself to be caught in a fit of passion.—*Lavater.*

Published by W. and R. CHAMBERS, High Street, Edinburgh (also 98, Miller Street, Glasgow); and, with their permission, by W. S. ORR, Amen Corner, London.—Printed by BRADBURY and EVANS, Whitefriars, London.

CONDUCTED BY WILLIAM AND ROBERT CHAMBERS, EDITORS OF 'CHAMBERS'S INFORMATION FOR THE PEOPLE,' 'CHAMBERS'S EDUCATIONAL COURSE,' &c.

No. 96. New Series. SATURDAY, NOVEMBER 1, 1845. Price 1½d.

THE WEALTH OF PATIENCE.

'How poor are they that have not patience!' This is one of those sayings given by Shakspeare to Iago, which shows that the poet thought better of the character than many of his readers. How vast are the intellectual resources, how great is the intellectual strength, which the dramatist attributes to this jealous and revengeful, but originally 'honest' man! It is a vulgar stage error to suppose that Iago's honesty was merely assumed. He had won his reputation fairly; Othello had had full experience of him; and it was this which justified that extreme confidence which the noble and unsuspecting Moor so fatally manifested. Here, however, lay the misfortune: Iago's honesty was of a worldly nature, and expected reward. Cassio had stepped in between the lieutenancy and his hopes; and his expectations being disappointed, the motives of his conduct suffered mutation. Nevertheless, Iago could not part with all that was meritorious in him: much, indeed, survived. The 'learned spirit' which he brought to bear on 'all qualities of human dealings' yet was paramount, and ever and anon would break forth in such aphorisms as that which we have quoted. Some of them were strongly condemnatory of his own new plans of proceeding; yet (perverse infatuation!) while he remained true to them in the letter, he contrived to evade their legitimate application by force of that 'divinity of hell' which, for the nonce, he had invented, whereby truth itself might be perverted to evil uses. This very maxim we have quoted condemned him. The identical poverty which he spoke of was specifically that under which he was suffering—the want of patience. He could not tarry for his guerdon, but would snatch at once at the crown. Another competitor had gained it, and, instead of awaiting patiently a second chance, he chafed at delay. To hasten on the day of recompense, he sacrificed the labours of a life of service, its well-earned reputation, and the future fruits of its continuance. Had 'the ancient' not been naturally jealous, perhaps he had not been so easily soured; but this only serves to suggest that impatience has a cause more bitter than itself—that the poison-flower has a root, in which was concentrated the gall as an elementary particle, ultimately developed in pernicious fructification.

Why are we impatient? This, then, is an important inquiry. Impatience is but a superficial symptom of a more deeply-seated disease; it indicates a rebellious nature. Iago demands,

> 'What wound did ever heal but by degrees?'

The impatient man requires that it should heal at once. He insists on a miracle, as a special interference in his personal case; and thinks it only reasonable that, on his account, the laws of nature should be suspended. If Providence will not so work for him, he forthwith undertakes to usurp its office, and so work for himself; setting aside the order of circumstance and duty, that he may constitute and begin a series of events that shall conduce speedily to his own private behoof. He never stays to question whether the good he proposes to himself be one probably in the estimation of Supreme Wisdom. He has been disappointed in his lieutenancy; that is enough. To repair this loss, 'both the worlds he would give to negligence,' that he may have the satisfaction of trying, once for all, a desperate throw with fortune, even though he perish in the attempt. Better not to be at all, than to deserve, and not to possess, even for an instant. Have not, however, others suffered like delay? Let them, if they will, be contented fools; he will, at any rate, show more spirit, and estimate himself at his true worth.

> 'By the faith of man,
> I know my price; I am worth no worse a place;'

and will not cease contriving until I get it; and let them who would oppose me look to the issues!

Iago, as we have said, could read this lesson to Roderigo, but failed to apply it to himself. Such judicial blindness has only too frequent illustration. Would that each man might make the other a mirror to himself; or

> 'That some Power the gift would gie us,
> To see oursélves as others see us!'

To return. Among the chief arguments to patience, we reckon this one—that each man born into, has virtually sworn allegiance unto, nature and society. There may be much in both to displease and irk an ardent and sanguine temperament; but in this we should recognise the destiny of the race, or of a people, rather than of an individual. The laws and principles which regulate both are, in themselves, unalterable—they are the primary land-marks which no created intelligence or power can remove. We cannot, therefore, too soon declare our submission to these inevitable limitations, and learn therewith to be content. Content!—therein lies all true wealth.

> 'Poor and content, is rich, and rich enough;
> But riches, fineless, is as poor as winter,
> To him that ever fears he shall be poor.'

Thus also, to him who rebels against the barriers, as it were, of his being, wishing for more liberty than belongs to the human condition, this entire world of time itself is, as it was to Hamlet, 'a prison;' 'this goodly frame, the earth, a sterile promontory; this most excellent canopy, the air, this brave o'erhanging firmament, this majestical roof fretted with golden fire, no other thing than a foul and pestilent congregation of vapours.' Nor is the speculation on which we now venture too refined in character for the popular mind in these days. The tribe of Hamlets is on the increase. The general diffusion of literature has made even the crowd theoretical; and the thinking mind may be detected even in the lowest places of society. Well accordingly is it to guard right early against the diseases to which they are liable—such as were manifested in the mental constitution of a Byron and a Rousseau, so that much of the misery they suffered may be avoided by others. It is a mistake to suppose that any rank or station is free from it: hard work even will not take it out of a man; often, indeed, it embitters the melancholy impression. There are Werters in humble as well as in high life; sentimentalists, in fact, in all classes, just as there are suicides among the rich and poor; and to both, the world is either a prison or a kingdom, according to the sanity or elevation of the mind that contemplates the creation, of which it is a part.

Such an idealist as we have described is indeed an irretrievable pauper: his case is hopeless, since there are no possible means of appeasing his discontent. Moreover, while his mind is perhaps dictating to the Author of the universe how it might have been better made, he is neglecting his own sublunary duties, and suffering ruin in his daily affairs.

> 'Not to know at large of things remote
> From use, obscure and subtle, but to know
> That which before us lies in daily life,
> Is the prime wisdom.'

In rendering in our allegiance, however, to the primary laws and principles which regulate, and perhaps constitute, nature and society, we must not be understood to mean that the truly patient man will be idly submissive to corrupt customs and bad governments. To reform these, indeed, may require all the patience that any man can possess, and circumstances of time and place may compel him to undertake the task as the continuous duty of his life. No other single virtue is so effective an instrument of reform as that of patience. Sudden outbreaks, strikes, and insurrections, only too often retard the improvements which they would injudiciously advocate. Physical force is a bad argument; it knocks a man down, but leaves social evils erect; nay, frequently aggravates the mischief. Moral power, on the other hand, works gradually, and gains an impetus from persecution itself; it has all the right on its side, and wisely surrenders all the wrong to the enemy; conditions these which try the patience for a while, but insure a triumph in the end. Not only are the paths of wisdom those of peace, but the paths of peace are those of wisdom. Only in this way, for instance, will the ameliorations of labour in this country, so happily begun, proceed: it is not by violence, but by the gentle law of progress, that the labourer will win an independent station. Link by link, the chain of destiny is weaving which will necessitate the results of freedom, if impatience interfere not with the mysterious process. All the greatest works of nature and art are conceived and engendered in silence and in secret; and even thus the crises of society are prepared in the womb of time, during long intervals of apparent rest, by that Divine Wisdom which disposes of events both to individuals and to nations. But let us not, we repeat, by these remarks, be supposed to intend a tame and blind acquiescence in oppression and injury; no, we mean rather to show the superiority of moral over physical force in procuring the remedy—the former as requiring patience, and the latter as unwisely indicating the contrary. 'Haste,' says Dante, 'mars all dignity of act;' and nature, though her method, as Emerson tells us, be one of 'ecstasy,' is, properly speaking, never in a hurry. Thus also it should be with social revolutions; let the necessary changes be gradually introduced, that the least possible wrong may be done to existing interests, as well as the greatest possible benefit accrue to the rising order. God, who might have created his universe in one day, preferred to occupy many cycles of time in the accomplishment of his work; nor is the philosopher ignorant that uniform progression is essentially much more miraculous than sudden intervention, though the constancy of the wonder abates our sense of it, except when we pause to reflect, and then we are thrown into amazement by the detection of a law which previously we had neglected to study.

If, however, patience should be discriminated from mere passive obedience, so, likewise, it is not to be confounded with positive stoicism. This seems to have been the great error of the ancients, who, for the sublime doctrine of suffering, hastily substituted that of insensibility. Suppose that the desirable stoical state were acquired or inherited, it wants virtue to commend it; for, if rendered unsusceptible of pain, we can deserve no credit for not resisting the attempted infliction. There are natural differences between individuals which help to illustrate this truth. One man is more irritable than another both in mind and body, by reason of his native temperament; the event, which is no exercise of patience to another, is a great one to him. Patience, then, is in proportion to sensibility, and is mensurable by the degree of pain endured. It springs, too, from humility, and not from pride, as with the stoics. Neither is it a careless indolence, nor a mechanical bravery, nor a constitutional fortitude, nor a daring stoutness of spirit, nor a form of fatalism—too frequently ranked among the more humble and obscure virtues: rightly considered, it is nothing less than a divine habit of mind, accompanying every circumstance of life, and essential both to duty and to happiness. The man who possesses his soul in patience, is either placed beyond vexatious interruption, or surrounded with defences which mediate between him and evil accident.

ADVENTURE OF AN ENGLISH CARLIST.

During the summer of 183–, Don Carlos took up his quarters in an old ruined Carlist castle in the valley of the Bastan, in Navarre. The king occupied a room which had escaped the general wreck, while his ministers, generals, and agents, lodged as they best might. The soldiery, such as they were at that time, were scattered over the country, sleeping under hedges, in groves, or, in some few instances, occupying the huts and farm-houses of the Navarrese. I slept in the remnant of a stone kitchen, near the ruined gate of the castle. A pile of straw, with my cloak, formed my bed, with my saddle-bags for a pillow, and there was I disposed, ruminating over the events of the day, and endeavouring to snatch a portion of rest, which I much required. My position in Don Carlos's establishment will explain itself in the course of my narrative; I need only here mention that I had been, at the date I now write, about three years in his service, and a great portion of the time in constant and confidential communication with the claimant to the throne of Spain, Charles V.

I lay on my bed, I have said, and had gradually dropped off into a happy state of oblivion, when I heard the heavy tramp of a spurred and booted foot approaching along the stone passage that led to the kitchen. The sound of footsteps ringing in the deserted halls of the castle, woke me at once to consciousness; my slumbers being soon further dissipated by the sound of a rough voice calling for Don G——. Springing on my feet, and clutching sword and pistol, I answered the call, and next moment one of the lancers composing the regal body-guard stood before me. 'His majesty, signor,' said the soldier, uncovering himself, 'commands your presence immediately.' I signified my readiness to obey, though displeased at the whim that robbed me of my sleep, and followed the messenger, who bore in his hand a wretched oil lamp, which scarcely sufficed to illumine the long dark passage sufficiently to save me from tumbling against the scattered stones and rubbish which encumbered them.

At length a sentry at a door in the only clear passage of the castle proclaimed the king's apartment. I knocked, and received an instant summons to enter.

The room was of the usual bare description, but vast in its dimensions. A bed stood in one corner, very little better than that which I have above described. At a table sat the king, writing by the light of two oil lamps. I advanced, and, according to custom, knelt and kissed his hand. He rose and spoke, with one hand resting on the table, and the other hanging by his side. 'Don G——, when will you be ready to proceed to Paris?' 'At once, sire,' I replied. The king smiled, and said, 'Many thanks; to-morrow morning will be time enough. Be ready then. There are your instructions. You will have an escort to the frontier. Once there, you will act on your own responsibility. Somehow or other you must reach Paris without exciting suspicion: thence you will proceed to the Hague, and return to Spain with despatches. I know your ability in these matters: I trust all the details to you.' After a few more verbal instructions, Don Carlos gave me his hand to kiss, smiled most graciously, promised never to forget my zeal in his service, and dismissed me to his minister's room, where the despatches lay. I received these important papers, and once more retired to my old stone kitchen, rest having become now still more necessary to me. The task was no easy one. As an agent of Don Carlos, the French government would certainly stop me, if I should fall into their hands. My despatches I was sure to lose in the event of discovery, and their contents would be instantly made known to the Christino party. With this conviction, I felt the necessity of using every available precaution to avoid being arrested in France.

At dawn I was on foot, and equipped for the journey, while a party of twenty lancers, in their gallant and picturesque costume, awaited my orders. We started immediately, and halted only when, having crossed the Pyrenees, we reached the banks of the Bidassoa. While yet on Spanish ground, I dismounted from my mule, and assuming the costume of a Basque peasant, dismissed my escort. I was now alone, with France before me: I was unarmed; while a purse and my despatches were as carefully concealed as possible. While awaiting the disappearance of my Spanish lancers, I sat down and endeavoured to mature my plan of operations. I had no passport. Three documents of that nature, made out in three several names, were at my lodgings at Bayonne. I knew that, were I made a prisoner, my passport would be at once taken from me; whereas, if found without that necessary protection, I should have leisure to decide upon which of my three characters I should assume. It will be seen at once what a precarious and anxious life is that of a secret diplomatic agent.

The bridge near Zugaramurdi lay about a mile below; but my policy was to swim the Bidassoa. Accordingly, no sooner was my escort out of sight, than I approached the water's edge, looked carelessly up and down the opposite banks, and seeing no sign of any living being, plunged in, and made for a spot fringed with thick bushes. A brief space of time brought me within twenty feet of the French shores, when, quick as thought, two gun barrels were protruded from amid the bushes, and I was summoned to surrender. In two minutes more I was in the safe keeping of a couple of douaniers—armed customhouse officers. 'Ha! ha! Carlist,' said one of these whiskered gentlemen; 'we've caught you, have we?' I at once threw aside all idea of disguise, and played the Englishman. 'Gentlemen,' said I, quietly eyeing my two antagonists, 'take care what you are about. I am an English gentleman rambling about for my amusement; beware how you offer me any insult.' 'If monsieur is an Englishman, he has of course a passport?' 'Unfortunately I have left it at Bayonne.' This of course led them to suppose that my residence was at Bayonne, the very object for which I had lodgings there. 'Well, sir,' said they, 'Englishman or not, we find you crossing the Bidassoa in a suspicious manner. You have no passport, and it is our imperative duty to take you before the maire.' I made no opposition to this command; and away they started with me, walking one on each side, to their quarters. The beginning of my journey, though unpropitious, was, however, exactly as I expected.

On reaching the mairie, we found the maire not at home, and I was unceremoniously walked into the public room of an auberge, the solitary window of which overlooked a paved yard, with very high walls, composed of loose stones. I seated myself at a table, and at once, on the plea of my walk and the consequent hunger, ordered dinner, inviting the douaniers to join me. The invitation was immediately accepted; and from that instant the worthy satellites of the customhouse treated me with the utmost deference. After dinner, I ordered brandy and cigars; but feigning not to smoke myself, demanded permission, while they were inhaling the weed, to walk up and down the yard. To this my now merry guardians made not the slightest objection, and into the yard I went. To escape was impossible; besides, the very fact of my doing so would have been betraying my secret. My object in entering the yard was far otherwise. After talking some time through the window with the douaniers, and when I saw clearly that the wine and brandy had somewhat confused their intellects, I seized a favourable opportunity, removed a stone from the wall, thrust my despatches therein, and returned the stone to its place. My heart was now as light as a feather—my despatches were safe.

Shortly after dinner I was taken before the maire, and questioned. With him I assumed a higher tone than with the douaniers; said I was an Englishman, as he could well see; complained bitterly of having been arrested while pursuing my pleasure; and demanded imperatively to be taken to Bayonne, where my passport was, and where *my friend* the maire would satisfy them as to my innocence. The words, '*my friend*, the maire of Bayonne,' startled the worthy magistrate, who became excessively polite; and in a few minutes more I was on my road to that town. The maire of Bayonne was my friend, but under circumstances which I cannot here explain. I little knew, however, that the government suspected him of being a Carlist.

On arriving at my destination, I went with the douanier to the street in which my lodgings were situated—induced him to wait outside—and in a very few minutes again stood before him in the costume of an English gentleman, and with my passport in my pocket. The maire was at home—immediately satisfied the douanier—vised my passport for Paris; and I was at once placed, without any difficulty, in the very best position possible, not being supposed to have come from Spain at all. Under this comfortable impression I returned with the douanier, secretly obtained my despatches, and booked myself in the diligence for Paris direct. But the little maire had his suspicions still, and next day the telegraph was at work; and long before I reached Paris, the fact of my being on my road there was known, and a plan of operations decided on. The little maire was too cunning for me.

Unconscious of this circumstance, I left the diligence at the messageries of Lafite and Gaillard, with my little valise under my arm, and immediately retired to a bed-room, there to wash off the dust and other marks incident to a long journey, preparatory to dining. I had been in the room five minutes, and had, luckily, not opened my valise, when I heard a polite knock at the door. Perfectly unprepared, I opened the door, and one glance told me the intruder was a commissary of police. I knew my fate hung on a word—a look; and, young diplomatist as I was, I acted with a presence of mind which since has many times astonished me. 'Mr ——?' said he, politely mentioning my name. 'Mr —— is up stairs at No. —,' said I, without flinching, at the same time smiling most benignly. 'Oh, ten thousand pardons, monsieur, for the mistake: what number did you say, sir?' I repeated the number; the commissary of police thanked me, re-entered the passage, and began quietly to ascend the stairs. Before he had reached the summit of the flight, I was in the street with my valise in my hand. With such a police as Paris can boast of, to have taken a *fiacre* or cab would have been to betray my hiding-place at once. I therefore hurried along on foot, plunged into the *cité*, reached as low a neighbourhood as I could find, and entered a house of very suspicious character, where, however, I was quite safe until dark. Here I dined; and as soon as night came on, sallied forth in search of a more safe place of concealment.

In a street in the Quartier Latin, some months before, I had often spent an evening with a very clever, but very poor young artist. We had been great cronies, and to him I determined to apply for shelter for the night. With some difficulty I found the house, and being admitted to the porter's lodge, inquired for Monsieur Jules Victor. '*Au quatrième*'—[On the fourth floor,] said the laconic Cerberus, and up the stair I at once sallied. After a journey up a narrow and dark flight of stairs, I reached the desired door, and knocked: 'Entrez,' said a soft female voice. I started, but still obeyed the summons, and found myself in the presence of a very pretty and neatly-dressed young Frenchwoman. 'This is Monsieur Victor's apartment, I believe?' said I with some hesitation. 'It is; he will be here directly. Will monsieur be seated?' said she with a most engaging smile. I seated myself, and Victor instantly came out of the adjoining chamber. 'Delighted to see you, my dear fellow; what earthquake has cast you up? But excuse me; allow me to introduce you to Madame Victor—Madame Victor, Monsieur ——!' This announcement rather disarranged my plans; but determined to make a trial, I sat down, and at once told my story, concluding by casting a sly look at madame, and saying, 'Had you been a bachelor, I meant to beg half your bed?' 'And of course now you will stay?' said madame kindly; 'we will do the best we can for you.'

This point settled, I rose from my chair, and drawing my passport from my pocket, burned it quietly before them. Very much surprised, they inquired the reason, which, however, was obvious—that I could no longer travel under my own name, and another had become absolutely necessary. I spent a most pleasant evening with this worthy and kind couple; amused them with my multifarious adventures; and next morning sallied forth to call on an intimate English friend. With him I could not be explicit; but, after the ordinary topics which occur to men meeting after an absence of some duration, I said, 'I have lost my passport. Will you go to the English embassy with me, and vouch for my respectability?' 'Certainly.' 'But will you be quite silent with regard to my real appellation? My name is Henry Seymour!' He started. 'I do not ask you to say my name is Henry Seymour, but simply to say you know me.' Though very much surprised, he agreed; and away we went to the English embassy. We saw the usual official—the usual questions were asked—my friend vouched for my respectability. I mentioned that I had lost my passport. A new one was made out at once; and after the usual particulars, the official said, 'What name?' 'Henry Seymour.' 'Where last from?' 'Calais.'

That night, after transacting my business in Paris, and perfectly satisfied with the neat manner in which I had eluded the vigilance of the police, I was on my road to Brussels. But the eternal telegraph was at work. Ere I was half-way on my road, the deceit I had practised was suspected, and intelligence transmitted, with orders to watch me closely. On arriving at Brussels I gave up my passport, and in an hour afterwards called for it at the police-office. The commissary eyed me in a hesitating manner, quite sufficient to awaken alarm, and told me to call next morning. This was enough for me: I knew at once that I was suspected.

I must here mention that Belgium and Holland were at war—the former being, with France, opposed to the Carlist dynasty, and the latter in secret league with Don Carlos. My plan of operations was at once decided on. I left the hotel (*the Grand Laboreur*) at which I had taken up my quarters, and fixed myself in a cabaret. As soon as night came, I sent for one of the common carts of the country, and offered the driver a handsome sum to get me across the frontier. 'But you will be taken prisoner, sir,' said he. The very thing I want, I thought to myself. I contented myself, however, with saying that I would risk the danger. Tempted by the somewhat brilliant offer I made him, he agreed, and I mounted the cart, lay down on a pile of straw, threw my cloak over me, and in a very short time was fast asleep. Having scarcely had a proper night's rest since I left Spain, my slumber was heavy and unbroken, and I only woke when challenged by the Dutch sentinels. I at once knew that I was within the lines of the Hollanders, and demanded to be taken before the distinguished general in command. His name, and what passed between us, I cannot now reveal; suffice that I instantly received a pass, and reached the Hague without farther molestation.

My despatches presented, and my mission fulfilled, I sailed for England, and thence took ship again for Spain. Such was my adventure—one of many which I underwent when in the secret diplomatic service of Don Carlos. What the exact object of my journey was, it is not for me to reveal; suffice it, however, that my return was hailed with delight, as I brought with me that from the want of which monarch and peasant equally suffer—GOLD.

CLUB-LIFE OF THE PAST.

HAVING in two preceding articles endeavoured to give our readers some idea of club-life as it at present exists, they will perhaps feel interested to know what kind of life was led by such of our forefathers as belonged to the clubs of their day. The contrast of the old with the new state of things will appear immeasurably in favour of the moderns, especially in respect of morals. We may now be without the flashes of wit that were wont

'To set the table in a roar;'

but we are also without the intemperance, coarseness, and improvidence which the old club system fostered and kept alive.

Abstractly, clubs are necessary to man, for he is a social animal. From his earliest history, he has associated for the purpose of increasing his comforts and his pleasures. Clubbing, therefore, is as old as the oldest community, for nations may be regarded as extensive clubs; of which the king may be considered the president; the vizier, or prime minister, vice-president; the rest of the government office-bearers, and the populace simply members.

The success of the principle having been fully established by past experience on a large scale, certain members of our own nation have found it convenient from time to time to form themselves into small sectional associations, denominated *par excellence* clubs.* The chief reason which appears to have moved them thereto, was a community of sentiments or opinions; for amongst 'congenial souls' are social pleasures best cultivated. This tendency shows itself in every nation, although it is only in England that it is fully developed. In the East, there is no occasion for them; coffee-houses for men, and public baths for women, answer the purpose. Though, in the continental states of Europe, they have occasionally existed for political purposes, they were always short-lived; for in monarchies less limited than our own, it has been considered dangerous to allow a number of persons to meet together frequently, for

* This word is a recently-employed adaptation of the Anglo-Saxon *cleafan*, to divide; 'because,' says Skinner, 'the expenses are divided into shares or portions.' Though Shakspeare, as will presently be seen, belonged to a club or clubs, we do not find the word used in his writings, nor indeed in that of his contemporaries, in the above sense. The essayists of Queen Anne's reign were amongst the earliest writers who applied the term to convivial meetings.

fear of disaffection. For this reason, even our nearest continental neighbours cannot form social associations like our clubs. The geography of the subject, therefore, is soon disposed of, and we proceed at once to its history.

We hear little about convivial societies till the reign of Elizabeth. We then find men of taste fond of meeting at places of public entertainment to enjoy each other's society. 'Domestic entertainments were at that time rare. The accommodations of a private house were ill calculated for the purposes of a social meeting, and taverns and ordinaries were almost the only places in which we hear of such assemblies.'* The best remembered of such meetings, is that known to posterity as the Mermaid Club, having been held at a tavern of that name. It was established by Sir Walter Raleigh. Besides its founder, Shakspeare, Beaumont, Fletcher, Selden, Ben Jonson, and Donne, were amongst its members; who, to mental intercommunion, added the less refined pleasures of eating, drinking, and smoking. But intellectual recreation was in the ascendant, for which we have Beaumont's unimpeachable testimony. In a poetical and cordial letter to Ben Jonson, he exclaims—

'What things have we seen
Done at the Mermaid! heard words that have been
So nimble and so full of subtle flame,
As if that every one from whence they came
Had meant to put his whole wit in a jest,
And had resolved to live a fool the rest
Of his dull life; then, where there hath been thrown
Wit able enough to justify the town
For three days past; wit that might warrant be
For the whole city to talk foolishly.'

The boon companions of those merry days often met at other places, and Ben Jonson drew up, for another club which he originated, a set of rules entitled *Leges Conviviales*, in which he advocated, amongst other excellent things, temperance. If we may credit the elegant apostrophe of Herrick, 'rare old Ben' and his companions practised what he preached.

'Ah, Ben!
Say how, or when
Shall we thy guests
Meet at those lyric feasts,
Made at the Sun,
The Dog, the Triple Tun?†
Where we such clusters had,
As made us nobly wild, not mad;
And yet each verse of thine
Outdid the meat, outdid the frolic wine.'

We hear little of clubs throughout the reign of the first James, and during that of his son Charles nothing; for in his unhappy time, to borrow a Hudibrasian jest, cudgelling was more rife than clubbing. The puritanical manners adopted during the commonwealth scarcely admitted of any sort of recreation; and the resuscitation of clubs arose appropriately enough out of the Restoration. For many years monarchical principles had been so very unpopular, that the name of 'king' was banished from the vocabulary of Cromwell's adherents; and when the reaction took place, and sovereigns came into fashion with the reappearance of the second Charles, the royalists testified their exuberant satisfaction by the wildest or most eccentric tokens. Amongst the latter was a club held at the sign of the King's Head, called the King's Club, the only qualification for which was, that the candidate's surname should be 'King.'

In and more immediately after the days of the 'merry monarch,' there were a greater number and variety of clubs than ever existed before or since; and although they were principally established for convivial purposes, leading to excesses, and engendering habits and manners much to be deplored, yet we, who live in better times, should not be too harsh in denouncing them. At the Restoration, society—taking that expression in its general sense—had ceased to exist. Throughout the previous half century, public discord, private dissension, and all the several ills that civil war is heir to, had shivered the social compact. The Restoration was not only that of the single prince, but the beginning of peace and good-will amongst his subjects; except that the process in the latter case was slower, and more cautiously carried out than the reseating of Charles on the throne. Men, in choosing their companions—especially those of their least guarded moments—were obliged to be extremely careful; yet, after so much turmoil and estrangement, they naturally yearned for fellowship. It is not, then, to be wondered at, that when a few individuals found themselves to possess sentiments of a congenial cast, political or otherwise, they should have made arrangements for meeting as frequently as possible, to enjoy each other's company. The tavern was the most convenient place of assembly, and the bottle was considered in those half-dark days the best promoter of reconciliation and good cheer. Clubs, therefore, however much their use has been since abused, had their use then: they formed points of union, and gradually operated to promote the general harmony which had long been broken.

Independent of this, at the end of the seventeenth, and even to the middle of the succeeding century, the very smallness of the population was a bar to much spontaneous sociality. If neighbours wanted to meet, they could only do so by special and previous arrangement; which arrangement generally took the form of a club. It was even customary, so late as the year 1710, for the inhabitants of the same street to form themselves into a club. The Spectator of that date records, that there were, in several parts of the city, street-clubs, in which the chief inhabitants of the street converse together every night. 'I remember, upon my inquiring after lodgings in Ormond Street, the landlord, to recommend that quarter of the town, told me there was at that time a very good club in it; he also told me, upon farther discourse with him, that two or three noisy country squires, who were settled there the year before, had considerably sunk the price of house-rent; and that the club (to prevent the like inconveniences for the future) had thoughts of taking every house that became vacant into their own hands, till they had found a tenant for it of a sociable nature and good conversation.' The story of the rackety squires actually lowering the rental by damaging the local society, and the curious qualification demanded of a tenant, that, besides being quiet, and able to pay his rent, he should be of 'good conversation,' show the vast influence of small clubs at that time.

The chief bond of union amongst persons who meet for relaxation and entertainment, is congeniality of some sort or other; which, as we have seen above, the mere accident of living in the same street did not always insure. But, of all sorts of congeniality, none is so universal as that arising out of eating and drinking; 'in which,' says Addison, 'most men agree, and in which the learned and the illiterate, the dull and the airy, the philosopher and the buffoon, can all bear a part.' Clubs for dining and supping were plentifully established both in town and country, and amateurs of particular dishes met together to discuss them. The most celebrated club that ever existed took its rise from a congenial fondness for mutton pies. Just before the Revolution of 1688, there lived in Shire Lane, close to Temple-Bar, one Christopher, a pastry-cook, whose peculiar mutton pies had rendered his shop famous. On the pretence of eating these delicacies, Lords Montague and Dorset, the poets Prior and Garth, Jacob Tonson the bookseller, and others, met under Christopher's sign; which bore the elegant effigies of a cat and a fiddle. They periodically took possession of the shop-parlour, and gave themselves the name of the 'Kit-Cat Club;' but, as Arbuthnot sung—

'Whence deathless Kit-Cat took its name,
Few critics can unriddle;
Some say from pastry-cook it came,
And some from Cat and Fiddle.'

* Gifford. Life of Ben Jonson.

† The Three Tuns, still existing at the Fleet Street end of Fetter Lane.

Ward, in his 'Complete and Humorous Account of the Remarkable Clubs and Societies,' gives the derivation which has been generally received. 'The cook's name,' he writes, 'being Christopher, for brevity called Kit, and his sign being the Cat and Fiddle, they very merrily derived a quaint denomination from puss and her master, and from thence called themselves the Kit-Cat Club.' At the time it was formed by the above-named individuals, the country was in a very critical position. The efforts of King James II. in favour of popery was so strenuous, that the seven principal protestant bishops were prisoners in the Tower. Members of the club increased, and were ostensibly attracted to Shire Lane by the mutton pies; but really met to concert measures for the bloodless rebellion which very soon followed. 'The Kit-Cat Club,' remarks Horace Walpole, 'though generally mentioned as a set of wits, were in fact the patriots who saved Britain.' The club long outlived its original purpose, and Christopher grew rich enough to remove to the Fountain Tavern in the Strand. In Queen Anne's reign, it comprehended above forty noblemen and gentlemen of the first rank, talent, and merit. Sir Godfrey Kneller painted their portraits, of that peculiar dimension which is now denominated 'Kit-Cat.'

The Beefsteak Club is, if we mistake not, still in existence. It was instituted in 1735,* in consequence of the Earl of Peterborough's visit to the work-room of a celebrated theatrical mechanist, named Rich. The artist began to cook his beefsteak on a gridiron, over the fire used for melting his size. The earl was asked to partake, which he did with so much relish, that he determined to dine with his host once a-week. He brought on the next visit a few friends, who formed themselves into a club; amongst them were Hogarth and Sir John Thornhill. From time to time the club has numbered some of the most celebrated men of genius this country has produced.—These are the most famous of what may be classed as the special-dish clubs. Hosts of others were, however, established, such as the Calves'-head Club, held in Charing-Cross; the Tripe Club of Dublin; Oyster, Eel-pie, and Goose clubs.

Not only a concurrent taste for the good things of this life, but similarity in the most ridiculous particulars, served as an excuse to form a club. The Spectator satirises this, by describing a market-town 'in which there was a club of fat men, that did not come together (as you may well suppose) to entertain one another with sprightliness and wit, but to keep one another in countenance.' A club of tall men was established in Edinburgh, which went by the name of the Six-feet Club. An 'Ugly Club,' instituted at Cambridge, is also mentioned; but as few could be found to put in a voluntary claim to unenviable ugliness, it was but a limited and transient affair. The 'Hum-drum Club' consisted of a set of very honest gentlemen of peaceable dispositions, that used to sit together, smoke their pipes, and say nothing till midnight. The Mum Club was an institution of the same nature, and as great an enemy to noise. The Spectator also tells of a Lovers' Club established at Oxford, into which 'a mistress and a poem in her praise' were the only passports.

Meanwhile, the wits of Dryden's day continued to assemble and exchange smart sayings at places of public entertainment, like their predecessors the companions of Ben Jonson. Taverns, such as 'The Mermaid,' had by this time changed their name to coffee-houses, and in some measure their nature; for they were not, at particular times of the day, open to all comers; and although, on the other hand, no subscription was exacted for the privilege of entering them, yet we find, by the account which Colley Cibber gives of his first visit to Will's in Covent Garden, that it required an introduction to this society, not to be considered as an impertinent intruder. There the veteran Dryden had long presided over all the acknowledged wits and poets of the day, and those who had the pretension to be reckoned among them. The politicians assembled at the St James's coffee-house, whence all the articles of political news in the first Tatlers are dated. The learned frequented the Grecian coffee-house in Devereux Court. Locket's, in Gerard Street, Soho, and Pontac's, were the fashionable taverns where the young and gay met to dine: and White's, and other chocolate houses, seem to have been the resort of the same company in the morning. The bay window of this house was then, as now, its great attraction as a morning lounge. Generations of 'company' have continued to frequent the establishment down to the present moment, a committee of the predecessors of the present frequenters having taken the management of the concern into their own hands, and formed it into a political club for gentlemen professing Tory principles. The history of Brookes's, also in St James's Street, is the same, except that it is composed of Whig partisans. Its proprietor appears to have been extremely popular in his day; and no wonder, if any faith is to be placed in the following couplet, penned by a grateful debtor:—

> 'The generous Brookes, whose honest, liberal trade,
> Delights to trust, and blushes to be paid.'

Boodle's, not far from Brookes's, was first set up by a man of that name, and is now also supported by subscription. It has always been a lounge for country gentlemen visiting London. These three establishments bear the closest resemblance to modern clubs to be found amongst the social relics of a bygone age.

The effects of coffee-house meetings upon the habits of our forefathers are thus described by Miss Berry:—'Three o'clock, or at latest four, was the dining hour of the most fashionable persons in London, for in the country no such late hours had been adopted. In London, therefore, soon after six, the men began to assemble at the coffee-house they frequented, if they were not setting in for hard drinking, which seems to have been less indulged in private houses than in taverns. The ladies made visits to one another, which, it must be owned, was a much less waste of time when considered as an amusement for the evening, than now as being a morning occupation.'*

Such nightly meetings—which were clubs without a regular organisation, and bore the name of the keeper of the house they were held at—were kept up by Pope, Swift, and Arbuthnot, and afterwards by Dr Johnson, Burke, Reynolds, Goldsmith, Topham Beauclerc, Gibbon, Boswell, and Garrick. For a long time these celebrated men met at the 'Mitre,' in Fleet Street, as a club, but one without a name. At the funeral of Garrick, they agreed to call their meetings the 'Literary Club,' which afterwards included Sheridan and other choice and intellectual spirits.

Dr Johnson, it is well known, was a great lover of clubs, and belonged to several. Of the Pandemonium, held in Clarges Street, Mayfair, we are enabled to give some notion from the Memoirs of the late Sir James Campbell of Ardkinglas, who was a member. He narrates that, on being introduced into the club, he first addressed himself to Oliver Goldsmith, whose absence of mind prevented him taking any heed of the new member. Dr Johnson was next bowed to, and, in return, 'he gruffly nodded to me, and continued some observations of a ludicrous nature which he was making, in a tone of mock solemnity, to the little man by his side, who proved to be no other than David Garrick. The Roscius received me with an air of cordiality and politeness which was quite delightful to me. At length Mr Foote, and a number of other members having arrived, we adjourned to dinner. The conversation, to my great relief, became general before even the cloth was removed. It seemed to be a favourite object with several

* A former club, under the same title, had by this time expired.

* Comparative View of the Social Life of England and France. By the editor of Madame du Deffand's Letters.

of the members to bring out the peculiar vein of Dr Goldsmith. About this period he had produced the Good-Natured Man and other successful comedies. Mr Foote observed to him, that he wondered to see Goldsmith writing such stuff as these, after immortalising his name by pieces so inimitable as the Traveller and the Deserted Village. "Why, Master Foote," said Goldsmith, with his rich Irish brogue, in reply, "my fine verses you talk of would never produce me a beefsteak and a can of porter; but since I have written nonsense, as you call it, for your bare boards, I can afford to live like a gentleman." Dr Johnson, who had taken his seat at the head of the table, then began, in a monotonous tone of affected gravity and grandiloquence, to pronounce a eulogium on folly, and to prove that it was more pleasing, and therefore more useful than good sense. In the course of the evening, every conceivable variety of topic was introduced; but, in general, the subjects under discussion had some reference, more or less remote, to the current literature of the day. They thus acquired an interest which to me was peculiarly striking, from the connexion which subsisted between the topics of conversation and the speakers themselves, without much regard, probably, to the undoubted talent with which the discussion was handled: for I may declare with unaffected sincerity, that the whole scene was perfectly new to me, the actors in it, not less than the topics on which they declaimed. At the same time, I had *nous* enough to perceive the prudence and propriety of exercising the peculiar talent which had recommended me as a candidate for admission into the club—(silence). It called for no extraordinary sagacity to discover that I had got into a most pugnacious society, who, like others of their class, had acquired an undoubted right to be regarded as of the *genus irritabile*.'

Clubs of a convivial nature, though much on the decline, are even now common to all classes of society in England. Whigs, Tories, squires, travellers, lawyers, engineers, doctors, scholars, soldiers, sailors, merchants, and others, have each their exclusive institutions. The multiplicity of tradesmen's clubs is both notorious and proverbial; and besides convivial associations, there are many ostensibly for charity and useful purposes. Yet under whatever name and pretence they are frequented, drinking and smoking are the real purposes for which their members meet. The design of the benefit and benevolent clubs is excellent; but as they are held at public-houses, the manner in which it is carried out is highly prejudicial. Many clubs are set a-foot for economical ends. The manufacturing districts, for example, abound with societies into which each member pays a small weekly sum, and, after a time, he becomes entitled to some article of dress. Upon this plan there are hat, coat, and boot clubs. The economy of such associations is, however, a pure fallacy. At each meeting there must be 'something to drink,' and conversation about the business in hand cannot be enjoyed without a pipe. By the time, therefore, that each member becomes entitled to his coat, he has in all probability spent as much money on beer and tobacco as would have bought a whole suit of clothes.

Having pretty nearly characterised the convivial clubs of the past, we may be permitted to say a word on the effect they have had on manners; and in this point of view we cannot find a single good word to say in their favour. Though there were, as we have before hinted, some excuses for their first formation amongst our disunited forefathers, they have since had the most baneful effects upon the public. Much of that excessive drinking which characterised the past age, must be charged to the universal habit of frequenting convivial clubs. They have, we venture to affirm, kept back most hurtfully the progress of civilisation. They withdrew men from their families, and interfered with studies which would have been more beneficial than ribald conversation suggested by intellects fuddled with drink.

A distinct sort of clubs, belonging to the past, have not yet been alluded to—gaming clubs. That irrational vice was practised at nearly every coffee-house, and to such a degree, that the legislature interfered to prevent it. Gamblers, therefore, to evade the law which forbade play in public-houses, clubbed to take private ones. Such houses as White's, Brookes's, and Boodle's, the law did not touch, and the propensity was indulged in them; whilst others were started on the same plan for the special purpose of gaming. It is pleasing to record that they have gradually faded away; Crockford's, the most splendid and extensive, having been broken up last year. Indeed, what were known as 'fashionable vices' are fast vanishing, or are deemed decidedly vulgar. A person who games deeply, or gets often intoxicated, no longer finds ready admission into the higher circles: he is a tainted man; his exclusion from the best modern clubs is equally rigid. This example, so worthily set by the aristocracy, will not be lost upon the operative classes, and the time is not far distant when a confirmed card-player, or habitual drunkard, will lose the countenance of his companions, in however humble a walk of life he may exist.

OCCASIONAL NOTES.

EFFECTS OF COLOURED LIGHT ON PLANTS.

Most persons are familiar with the fact, that solar light is indispensable to the growth, health, and perfection of every vegetable. Without exposure to sunshine, plants could not acquire their colours, could not elaborate their various secretions, or properly mature their seeds. This sunshine, or 'white light,' as it is called, consists of several coloured rays which are known to possess very different illuminating, heating, and chemical properties; hence it has become a subject of interest among men of science to examine whether all the rays assist alike in the progress of vegetation. One of the most recent inquirers is Mr R. Hunt—well known for his researches on light—whose experiments are detailed in the Gardeners' Chronicle for August.

The solar beam of white light, when subjected to prismatic analysis, is found to consist of seven or more distinct colours; namely, red, orange, yellow, green, blue, indigo, and violet. Mr Hunt, however, adopting the views of Sir David Brewster, is inclined to admit only three primitive colours—red, yellow, and blue—all the others being made up of mixtures of these. By experiment, the red rays yield the greatest amount of heat, the yellow the largest quantity of light, while the blue produce the strongest chemical effect. It is evident from this, that by the use of red, blue, and yellow glasses, the natural conditions of a plant may be materially altered; thus, heating rays may be admitted while light and chemical effect are partially excluded; or light may be admitted while heat and chemical effect are excluded; or, lastly, the maximum chemical power may be exerted without exposure to either illuminating or heating rays. Subjecting seeds or plants to light which has passed through these variously-coloured media, Mr Hunt has found the following general results:—

1. Under *yellow* glass, it was found that in nearly all cases the germination of seeds was prevented; and even in the few cases where germination commenced, the young plant soon perished. Mr Hunt is inclined to ascribe these instances of germination to the action of heat-rays which had passed through the glass, rather than to light. Agarics, and several of the fungus tribe, flourished luxuriantly under the influence of the yellow medium. Although the luminous rays may be regarded as injurious to the early stages of vegetation, there is reason to believe that, in the more advanced periods of growth, they become essential to the formation of woody fibre.

2. Under *red* glass, germination took place, when the seeds were carefully watched, and a sufficient quantity of water added to supply the deficiency of the increased evaporation. The plant, however, was not of a healthy

character, and, generally speaking, the leaves were partially blanched, showing that the production of chlorophyl (green colouring matter) had been prevented. Most vegetables, instead of bending towards red light, in the same manner as they do towards white light, bent from it in a very remarkable manner. Mr Hunt found that plants in a flowering condition could be preserved for a much longer time under the influence of red light than under any other, and is inclined to think that red media are highly beneficial during the fruiting processes of plants.

3. Glass of a deep *blue*—such as is used for finger-glasses—has the property of allowing the free passage of all chemical rays, whilst it obstructs both the heat and light radiations. The rays thus separated from the heat and light rays, Mr Hunt regards as a distinct principle, for which he proposes the name of *actinism*.* They have the power of accelerating in a remarkable manner the germination of seeds and the growth of the young plant. After a certain period, varying nearly with every plant upon which experiments were made, these rays became too stimulating, and growth proceeded rapidly without the necessary strength. When this was perceived, the removal of the plant into the yellow rays, or, which was better, into light which had passed through an emerald green glass, accelerated the deposition of carbon, and the consequent formation of woody fibre proceeded in a regular and perfect way.

'Such,' adds Mr Hunt, 'are the conditions and the results of my experiments. They seem to point to a very great practical application, in enabling us in this climate to meet the necessities of plants, natives of the tropical regions. We have evidence, at least so it appears to me, from these and other results, that the germination of seeds in spring, the flowering of plants in summer, and the ripening of fruits in autumn, are dependent upon the variations in the amounts of actinism or chemical influence—of light and of heat—at those seasons in the solar beam. Many results obtained by the photographic processes appear to prove this to be the case.' Altogether, independent of their practical advantages, these experiments point to principles in nature, the further explication of which may lead to the solution of some of the most interesting problems in organic development.

A NOVELTY IN LOOKING-GLASSES.

Amongst the productions of human industry, there are some, the common and daily use of which effaces the marvels connected with them. Among such things mirrors may be classed. That the exact image of every object should be reproduced with the most perfect fidelity, is surely an extraordinary fact, and one which can only be appreciated to the full by savages who see a reflector for the first time. Clear water is the only means which nature, unaided by art, has provided for mirroring the features of the human face or other objects; and the belles of the earliest ages arranged their costume, and practised their little coquettish arts, over a sheet of pellucid water. But a more efficient and portable substitute was found in polished metal, and mirrors of such material were adopted. To whom the invention must be attributed, it is impossible to say: 'probably,' remarks a French writer, 'the inventor was a woman.' That brass mirrors are of high antiquity, there can be no doubt. They were in use among the Jewish women, as we learn from the Pentateuch; for Moses made the laver of the tabernacle of that metal, much of which was contributed by the women, who voluntarily gave up their mirrors for the purpose. It is, however, conjectured that the use of such reflectors was borrowed from the Egyptians, who were the earliest people to bring them into use. As refinement increased, brass, ever so well polished, was found not so reflective as silver—a discovery for which a certain Praxiteles (not the sculptor, but a contemporary of Pompey) has the credit, and mirrors of that metal were adopted; but their expensiveness precluded their use by any but the most affluent. The common people of Rome employed a great variety of polished materials; amongst them, straw carefully plaited, which, it is not generally known, acts as a reflector of the sun's rays sufficiently powerful to burn; in consequence of the natural glass produced by the silex with which all reeds are coated.

The most acute historians have been unable to discover when glass was first used as mirrors, but they were first supplied to the ancient fashionable world from Sidon; and, when history emerges from the dark ages, we find those lustrous articles made almost wholly at Venice, which remained the seat of the manufacture up to a comparatively recent period. To this we may probably trace the fact, that the makers and hawkers of looking-glasses in England, France, and other parts of Europe, are nearly always Italians. The Venetian trade was much damaged by Colbert,* who, by the force of capital, seduced many workmen from Italy, and deprived the Venetians of the profits of an art which had been for some ages looked upon as their patrimony. Colbert set up a large establishment in his native country, in which he introduced several improvements in the manufacture of looking-glasses. The most important was the substitution of cast for blown glass, by which not only a smoother and more faultless surface was produced, but also larger plates. This was the latest improvement; for the mode of silvering the backs is done precisely in the same manner now as it ever was. The term 'silvering' is scarcely correct: it is derived from the fact of the chief ingredient used being mercury, vulgarly called quicksilver. The French, with more propriety, designate the process 'tinning' (étamage), that being the metal which is employed along with mercury. This explanation is necessary to render the more intelligible an improvement in this process which has been recently patented, and in which silver, properly so called, is substituted for tin. But we must first describe the not uninteresting, but extremely insalubrious process by which the manufacture of looking-glasses is now carried on. The so-called silvering consists in applying a layer of tin-foil alloyed with mercury to the posterior surface of the glass. The workshop for executing this operation is provided with a number of smooth tables of fine freestone or marble, truly levelled, having round their contour a rising ledge, within which there is a gutter or groove which terminates by a slight slope in a spout at one of the corners. The glass-tinner, standing towards one angle of his table, sweeps and wipes its surface with the greatest care, along the whole breadth to be occupied by the mirror-plate; then taking a sheet of tin-foil adapted to his purpose, he spreads it on the table, and applies it closely with a brush, which removes any folds or wrinkles. The table being horizontal, he pours over the tin a small quantity of quicksilver, and spreads it with a roll of woollen stuff; so that the tin-foil is penetrated, and apparently dissolved by the mercury. Then taking the plate of glass, he lays it carefully on the smooth bed of tin and mercury, which adheres to the glass in obedience to the law, that bodies contract a close adhesion when they touch at all points. The glass is then removed from the table, and placed under heavy weights for twenty-four hours, so as to make the adhesion more perfect and durable. Even after this, a portion of the superfluous [illegible] remains on the glass, and has to be gradually drained off by placing the plate on a frame sloped like a writing-desk. This is a very nice and difficult operation, and requires the most minute care to prevent the glass from contracting during the operation, in which case the whole process must be recommenced. Moreover, the bed of tin is easily cracked; and every one knows with

* See paper on Actino-Chemistry, in No. 59, New Series, of this Journal.

* The interesting story of Colbert will be found in the first volume of Chambers's Miscellany of Useful and Entertaining Tracts.

what rapidity the action of the sun, or the least humidity, spoils the best looking-glasses.

It is fortunate, therefore, that, nearly coincident with the reduction of the glass-duties, a new process for manufacturing reflectors by chemical instead of mechanical means has been discovered. Everything which tends to cheapen so ornamental and harmlessly useful an article as mirrors, may be looked upon as a not unimportant advance in social economy. We do not hold with those utilitarians who would banish inexpensive luxuries from the humblest abodes; and we would therefore do all in our power to promote the adoption of any improvement in such articles, with a view to their general accessibility. To this end we gladly give publicity to the new invention for silvering looking-glasses.

Towards the end of 1843, Mr Thomas Drayton, of Brighton, sealed a patent, the subject of which was a mode of silvering looking-glasses without the employment of quicksilver. The material used is composed of coarsely-pulverised nitrate of silver, spirits of hartshorn, and water. This, after standing for twenty-four hours, is filtered, and an addition is then made of spirit of wine and a few drops of oil of cassia. The glass to be silvered with this solution must have a clean and polished surface; it is to be placed in a horizontal position, and a wall of putty or other suitable material formed around it, so that the solution may cover the surface of the glass to the depth of from an eighth to a quarter of an inch. A deposition of the silver then takes place in two hours or less, and when the required deposit has been obtained, the solution is poured off; and as soon as the silver on the glass is perfectly dry, it is varnished with a composition formed by melting together equal quantities of bees' wax and tallow. This serves as a protection to the residuum which adheres closely to the glass, and affords a more clear and brilliant reflection than the old process; besides being done in infinitely less time, and with no risk of failure. The term 'silvering' looking-glasses is rendered by the new plan quite correct, for it is silver, and nothing but silver, which converts the glass into a mirror.

It may be asked why so useful an invention should have as yet remained unknown to the public, and unacted on? The answer is, that although the inventor proved fully that the principles of his invention were correct, there were some difficulties of a purely technical nature connected with the manufacture, which he was not very readily able to overcome. In this emergency M. Tourasse, to whose working Mr Drayton had committed the patent he had taken out for France, has succeeded, after a year spent in experiments, in perfecting the process. M. Tourasse submitted the invention to the Académie de Sciences, who appointed a commission to inquire into its merits, which it fully confirmed. On the 20th of August last, Mr Drayton's agent experimented before a committee of the Society for the Encouragement of the Useful Arts, and succeeded in silvering a double glass in half an hour.

'Whoever,' it is remarked in the report from which we copy this information, 'has compared looking-glasses prepared after the old and the new processes, must be struck with the superior reflective powers of the latter. The adhesion of the metallic coating to the glass is firmer, and the protection afforded by the outer varnish more complete.' One great advantage is, that, by the patent, glass tubes and other globular surfaces can be silvered by it. This was impossible by the old method; for, except the concave and convex mirrors used in dining-rooms, nothing of the sort could be accomplished, from the purely mechanical nature of the process. This advantage will be most apparent to those who have occasion for optical instruments, in which many improvements will doubtless follow. In a salubrious point of view, it will be a great boon to workmen who are now engaged in one of the most unhealthy employments existing. They at present exist amidst the fumes of mercury, which, despite all the elaborate precautions employed to preserve the skin and lungs from injury, prove fatally injurious. Although the material used be silver, the public are promised looking-glasses at prices very little differing from those at present charged.

In conclusion, we may remark generally on the gratifying march which chemical processes are making upon mechanical ones in all kinds of manufacture. There is no body of men who have from time to time proved such benefactors to mankind as operative chemists.

DESECRATION OF MELROSE ABBEY BY TOURISTS.

It is with pain we perceive, by advertisements in the Edinburgh newspapers, that, in consequence of the wanton and malicious damage done to the abbey of Melrose by persons calling themselves tourists, and other visitors, by chipping and defacing the beautiful carvings and stone-work, and carrying off the fragments as memorials or relics, its noble owner, the Duke of Buccleuch, has felt it his duty to close it to the public for the future. Thus, in consequence of the covetous depredations of a few well-dressed petty larcenists, the honest and moral part of the community is shut out from one of the finest ruins in Great Britain. The venerators of antiquity will naturally feel this as a sort of injustice to themselves, for it is difficult to conceive a private right sufficiently strong to exclude them from a ruin which historic and national associations have in one sense made public property. But the duke is not only the owner, but the conservator of the structure. He feels himself responsible to posterity for the proper care-taking of a building which to our successors will be even more valuable as a memorial of the past than it is to ourselves. At least we can conceive his grace feeling in this way, and, if he acts accordingly, who can blame him? We can only hope that, when the public have received a sufficient lesson on the subject, some relaxation of the rule may take place. Meanwhile, let every effort be used to aid in the detection of the offenders, for whose discovery the duke's agents in Edinburgh further offer a (we hope needless) reward of ten pounds.

There are some petty offences to which their perpetrators appear to attach neither importance nor blame; they are glozed over with the varnish of custom, or the shortcomings of the law. A man who would not wrong you of a penny in money, thinks nothing of borrowing a book or an umbrella, and never returning either. Peccadilloes of this nature have become so familiarised from frequency, that conscience seems to take no trouble about them. The evil more particularly under discussion is freely committed, because the law does not take much notice of it. Chipping monuments, and pocketing the leaf of a folious capital, or the wing of a cherubim, are amongst the unpunishable offences, because the crime is so wanton, that the statutes never contemplated it; hence, when the silly fellow smashed the Portland vase in the British Museum, the law could be no more severe with him than if he had wilfully broken a Delft teapot. What the law cannot effect, however, public opinion can; and we are severe enough to hope that, should any of the Melrose Abbey depredators be discovered, their names, addresses, and professions will be published in the newspapers as fully as if they had to appear upon an indictment in the Court of Justiciary, or the Old Bailey.

Whoever has visited Melrose Abbey, and examined its details with attention, will not deem this hope too vindictive. Its beauty chiefly lies in the exquisite finish of its ornaments, and the high state of preservation in which a sheltered position has kept the friezes and capitals. The forms are as clear, and their outlines as sharp, as if they had been cut in the eighteenth, instead of the fourteenth century. It is therefore obvious that the smallest morsel chipped from one of these beautifully-executed stone carvings destroys the whole figure, whether it be that of a human being or of a leaf. A lump from the shaft of a column, or the corner of an entablature, could better be spared. But these do not satisfy our relic-hunting tourists: whilst they are robbing the house, they like to take away something worth carrying.

It is a sad blow to national pride to reflect, that the untameable propensity for defacing objects exposed in public places is almost peculiar to Great Britain. On the very first day that the ornamented walks of Windsor castle were thrown open to the public, the statues and shrubs were so defaced and damaged, that the privilege was instantly withdrawn. In the British Museum, the attendants of the sculpture saloons are obliged to be constantly on the watch, lest some 'John Smith' should have the impudence to pencil his name on the statue of Memnon, or deface the instep of Minerva with a coarse epigram. In Scotland, several articles of value have been stolen from Abbotsford by visitors. The tombstone of Burns's father in Alloway kirkyard was gradually nibbled away, and a new one substituted by subscription. In short, wherever we go, evidences of the propensity present themselves. Be it, however, remembered, that the humbler orders do not stand alone in this petty turpitude. As truly remarked by Sir Robert Peel in the debate on the question of throwing open certain royal palaces and public monuments for general inspection, the poorer classes offend less in this way than the 'vulgar rich.' Abroad, either in France or Germany, the wanton destruction of public property is seldom met with. To be sure, a much sharper supervision is maintained, and one does not move a step in any public place without being confronted by a policeman. But whatever the cause of the superior moral conduct of our continental neighbours, the fact is creditable to them.

In conclusion, let us hope that the Melrose Abbey depredators may be discovered and exposed. We express the hope, less from a desire to see the failings of tourists, or those of any other class of persons blasoned forth, than from a belief that such a punishment would operate in checking the practice. It is the custom of farmers to nail the skins of rats to their barn doors, from a supposition that the spectacle terrifies other rats, and prevents them from stealing the corn. In imitation of this practice, it may be found expedient, should the duke relent and once more open the abbey, to expose a list of those who have been convicted of the crime peculiar to tourists, as a warning to entrants not to do the same.

TWO DAYS ON LAGO MAGGIORE.

Early on the morning of the 5th of August 1848, a friend and myself found ourselves seated on the outside of a *velocifera* in the Corte della Posta at Milan, and indulging a vain regret that the city, its Duomo of white marble, its pictures and arches, would soon for us change from a reality to a remembrance. We were not long in discovering that our vehicle had as much right to the name it bore as it had to be called 'The Comfortable.' In movement, it was unequalled by the tardiest German schnell-post; and the necessity our seats imposed, of placing knees in neighbourly acquaintance with chins, was suggestive, upon sitting down, of aches and pains, which very soon were fearfully realised. I know not how many tedious hours were occupied by the journey, through a country, fertile and luxuriant to the last degree, which spreads itself on a dead level between Milan and the Lago Maggiore. There was little to attract attention by the way, and yet the road crosses the field of a great battle between those two renowned captains of elder time, Hannibal and Scipio. But battle plains, how much soever of interest they possess for historians and their students, lie inordinately flat before the eye of an actual visitor. I had much rather read of them than traverse them; unless, as in the present instance, they are directly in the route, and not to be avoided except by additional trouble; or unless there may have been some recent conflict, in which a personal, or at all events a national interest is involved, as at Waterloo. Battle fields, moreover, invariably disappoint a present spectator. Some chronicle tells you of them afar off, and the inner eye instantly peoples them with crowding troops, whilst the ear catches, as it were from a great distance, the din of glorious war. But when you are upon them, what do you see and hear? Nothing more than a plain, devoted, like any other plain, to the common uses of agriculture, where the most you shall hear is the sighing of breezes amongst the grass. The poetry of the place has evaporated, and a dull reality is the residuum. You look at the particular spot where armies have met and contested for victory through the optic glass of fancy. By the shedding of blood, it has become separated with an imaginary line from the rest of the earth's surface, and has risen into an importance to which, locally, it is not entitled. To the mental eye, the air above is lurid—the ground torn and trampled. But when the eye of flesh alights upon the scene, how changed, how different! The two hosts have drawn off, ages ago, from that mighty strife which is carried on in books to this hour; the place is in nowise distinguishable from the surrounding country, and daylight quietly illuminates everything within the compass of the horizon with one common lustre.

In passing along, we noticed a few upright stones by the wayside, each marked with its forlorn P. R.; and a little further, our thoughts on this grave subject ran appropriately enough against a tall cypress tree which stands at a turn of the road. It is pleasing to be informed that Napoleon caused the Simplon, which pushes forward elsewhere regardless of much more serious obstacles, to deviate a little, that this tree might be spared. Tradition declares that this identical cypress existed in the time of Julius Cæsar; but its appearance does not confirm the tale. At Sesto Calende, where an end was put to the Velocifera, our passports were inspected by Austrian officers, and shortly afterwards we embarked on a small steamer with her prow towards the head of the Lago Maggiore. A 'blue breeze' from the mountains ruffled its surface, and gave animation to the scene, whilst the waters, stretching away before us, seemed to penetrate into the recesses of the snowy Alps. As we proceeded, the ruined castle of Angera crowned a rocky ridge on our right, and added the element of masculine grandeur to the effeminate softness of Italian scenery. At Arona, the vessel stopped to land and take in passengers. It is just behind Arona that the brazen statue of San Carlo Borromeo takes its colossal stand—an image sixty-six feet high, erected by subscription in 1697 in honour of a saint, once a famous personage in these parts, who was born in the town, to which he is here made to extend his hand, as if in the act of pronouncing a benediction. Ladders are placed in the interior, by means of which tourists well affected to hagiology and climbing, may ascend into the nose of the statue, provided they do not labour under the affliction of gout or corpulency. St Charles was archbishop of Milan, and his breviary is represented under his left arm.

On, on the steamer paddled; village after village spotted the shores, which grew more and more undulating as we advanced. Then the bay of Baveno opened out on the left, its surface diversified with the Borromean islets of European celebrity. The steamer stopped once more, whilst a boat hove to, into which we and our baggage were injected, and which then made towards one of those towns which we had seen glittering white on shore. Here our knapsacks were examined (for we had quitted the Austrian for the Sardinian territory); and that operation concluded, we launched in the direction of Baveno, a hamlet lying at the head of that broad indentation which makes one considerable compartment of the lake. Our course lay amongst the islands: the appearance of the Isola Madre attracted us in preference to the artificial and more celebrated Isola Bella. Having been without food since morning, we began to be conscious of an abstract quality which wise and simple agree in terming hunger; and if the Isola Bella had really been what one traveller compared it with, namely, a Perigord pie, it would have been impossible to resist landing and cutting a huge slice thereout for the immediate satisfaction of our appetites. The island, however, appeared provokingly inedible, and in our haste we could only afford to cast a glance upon the exterior of the house standing upon it, which Gibbon, in 1747, called 'an enchanted palace, a work of fairies in the midst of a lake encompassed with mountains, and far removed from the haunts of men.' At an inn standing prettily on the edge of the water, we procured rest and refreshment, and then I sallied out alone. It was just the hour, and precisely one of the places at which we most wish to be unaccompanied, that the full stream of reverie, along which we are irresistibly borne, may flow on in undisturbed peace; that the flowers which fancy is then pleased to scatter around our path, may be gathered 'untalked of and unseen;' that the storied designs on the arras-work she loves to weave, may be gazed at and spelled over without reproof or fear of check. The hour was evening; the place Italy. The loveliness of the sky, tinted with colours such as are alone in the power of evening to let drop from her magic brush, was answered and contrasted by the loveliness of earth. The hills, terminating with a happy characteristic abruptness, broke out into rocks that were mossed over, adorned with flowers, and scattered with trees, exactly in the way that an artist would have desired. That was on one side; on the other, the lake extended like another sky, with islands here and there interrupting the blank level, like spots of cloud. The outline of the second tier of hills on the further side of the bay, was the most strangely jagged I ever beheld. If they should ever, in any repetition of the physical disturbances which have befallen our globe, be used as a saw, wo to the substance they come in contact with.

Wandering along in this idle mood for a mile or two, I came to some houses, where I engaged a boat to the Isola Bella. A few minutes sufficed to land me at the marble steps leading to the Count Borromeo's palace, a large pile, which, in spite of Gibbon, I will venture to say possesses no beauty but that of situation. Close upon its rear is a number of miserable huts, where some hundreds of poor people house themselves. The palazzo, though incomplete, contains several lofty, well-proportioned rooms, with floors of marble and painted ceilings. There are several pictures on the walls; but they are of little excellence, being of that stupid class styled *family*, representing red-draped cardinals, ruffled courtiers, and rough warriors. There is a story of the dark Italian cast told of a painter, some of whose works are shown here. He was fitly named Tempesta; for the story goes that he was passion-tossed, and killed one wife for the purpose of taking another to his conjugal bosom. When pursued for the crime, he fled to this island, where he was protected by the then count. Beneath the grand apartments on the ground-floor there is a suite of rooms, decorated with Mosaic pavement, shell-work, and statuary, where the luxurious owner is accustomed to ice himself during the heat of summer. The present nobleman makes Milan his principal residence; though still wealthy, he has no longer a little empire in his hands. The twelve castles and the entire lake, which once belonged to his line, have passed in great part to other persons.

The gardens occupy the rest of the islet, and consist of no less than ten hollow terraces raised one above another. The fact is, that the island was formerly nothing but a bare rock. One of the Borromeos, having a taste for gardening, caused the spot to be doubled in size, by conveying an immense quantity of the richest earth from shore. A profusion of trees and plants were then procured, including a quantity of rare exotics. The effect of the whole, artificial as it strikes a stranger at first sight, is, as one wanders from terrace to terrace embellished with marble balustrades and sculpture, eminently beautiful. Instead of the culinary thought which Simond indulged in, I confess that when I saw the mingling of aloes and orange trees, myrtles, cactuses, and magnolias, and revelled in the perfumes which these and other odoriferous shrubs diffused through the air, the words of Mignon's song came to my memory, and I caught myself involuntarily muttering—

> Kennst du das Land wo die Citronen blühn?
> Vom dunkeln Laub die Gold-orangen glühn.
> Ein sanfter Wind vom blauen Himmel weht,
> Die Myrte still und hoch der Lorbeer steht.

> [Knowst thou the land where the lemon trees bloom—
> Where the gold orange glows in the deep thicket's gloom—
> Where a wind ever soft from the blue heaven blows,
> And the groves are of laurel, and myrtle, and rose?]

The whole is, in truth, a hanging garden of plants from the tropics, interspersed amongst those of northern climes, and a fine mist of delightful scents droops over all—a realisation of the fables of eastern magnificence. The vaults beneath the terraces are accessible, and, if you choose, you may walk into their cold dark recesses, whose only inhabitants are troops of bats. If you cast your eyes from this 'summer isle of Eden' into the world without, a glorious prospect is ready to greet them. In one direction the pellucid waters of the lake stretch towards Milan; in all the others the sinuosities of its margin are wildly romantic with bay and promontory; whilst, lifting your eyes, you perceive that mighty chain of snowy summits which severs the skies of Italy from the mists of the rest of Europe. Before quitting the place, a tall cedar is pointed out whereon Napoleon, in one of those 'whittling' moods especially patronised by schoolboys and Yankees, carved the word 'Battaglia,' just before Marengo was fought. Only a scar in the bark is visible, so that the tradition may have no greater amount of truth in it than the majority of *show* tales. There is a room in the palace where it is said Bonaparte slept. By the time I again stepped into the boat, the moon was shining from a speckless sky upon the lake and mountains, not with the chilly coldness of our English luminary, but with the glowing gaiety that became the Italian clime. I thought of that 'blessed moon' which once at Verona 'tipped with silver all the fruit tree tops,' and of twenty other pieces of romance that would look very silly if put down here. 'Last night,' said I, 'just at this hour, I was in Milan cathedral, and saw the moonlight streaming through the windows upon the marble floor; and now, beneath as bright a moon, I am upon Lago Maggiore!'

Next day my companion and I, instigated by the recommendation of the inn album, undertook to ascend Monteronte, a hill lying behind Baveno, but invisible from that place. The day was warm, and, by not taking the shortest cut, we found the ascent toilsome. Soon after quitting the inn, we struck into a belt of chestnut trees, that girdles the base of all the eminences, and obtained amongst the branches, as we ascended, many glimpses of the lake glittering in the morning sun. The side of the hill, almost all the way to the top, was bescattered at wide intervals with farm-houses and cottages, many of whose inhabitants were busy making their second crop of hay or tending cattle. The careful industry of the people, notwithstanding their reputation for do-nothing habits, was very observable. In the belt of wood through which we passed at an early period in our ascent, we saw streams carefully conducted down the declivities by channels of gentle curve, so as at once to prevent the ground being converted into a swamp, and to feed the grass with a suitable supply of moisture. This must have been a work of no slight labour, when the extent of ground, and the number of rivulets gushing out by hundreds, are taken into consideration. The result was, that the soil underneath the trees, instead of being arid and useless, as it is in every English forest, produced a fine crop of nutritious grass. Again, higher up, not only had care been taken to convey the water in courses best adapted to effect these purposes, but the drainings of each farm-yard were carried abroad by channels, so as to give the land an excellent manuring.

The views of the Mere below were inconceivably beautiful. As we approached the summit, island after island came out of its lurking-place into the lake, and the adjacent cliffs were perpetually undergoing changes of form and attitude. But what could rival in united grandeur and beauty the prospect from the highest point? A series of snowy peaks bounded more than half the horizon. To the south, the eye ran over a vast plain, until stopped by a faint blue bar that indicated the Apennines, and in the midst of that plain the dome of Milan cathedral was just discernible. Here and there a distant glitter betrayed the errant propensity of two rivers, and one or two sheets of water that contributed to feed them, shone from far like plates of burnished metal. Turning westward, we beheld Monte Rosa, 'so named from roseate hues,' towering boldly upwards from amongst his radiant brethren, whilst between that lofty pinnacle and the verdant point on which we stood, the eye sunk into a vale which contained a lake about as large as our Windermere. This was the Lago d'Orta; its one little island tufted with trees, that half concealed a chapel. In the north, the Galgenstock, its broad bosom occupied by the snow and glacier which feed the Rhone, was conspicuous. A score of notches in the ridge-line indicated the principal passes. But the finest prospect of all was that towards the east, where almost the whole length of the Lago Maggiore lay beneath our feet with all its towns, villages, and towers; and amongst them the castle of Angera and town of Arona were not to be mistaken. That view was splendid beyond description, and I shall not ruffle the calm image of its beauty, that my memory in quiet moments loves to bend over, by wasting more words upon it.

The descent from the top was excessively fatiguing. Before reaching the bottom, we called at one of the farmhouses and procured a cup of rich milk from a large reservoir secreted from the sun's influence, and hence possessing a delicious coolness. We proceeded the same day by diligence up the Toccia valley to Vogogno. It was late when we reached that place, and yet there was ample time to make two discoveries; namely, that the village had the remains of what had once been a strong castle, and that the Simplon road, in pursuing its course of independence, had neglected the crooked, narrow, stony street, and struck out a new route for itself. Thus it happens that the casual traveller sees nothing of Vogogno; a loss he will not fret over, when he is told there is nothing to see.

WIENHOLT ON SOMNAMBULISM.

FIRST ARTICLE.

Among the numerous works which have recently appeared in this country on mesmerism and kindred subjects, there is none perhaps more deserving of attention than the translation of Wienholt's Lectures on Somnambulism, by Mr Colquhoun, the well-known advocate of animal magnetism. Dr Arnold Wienholt was a German physician, eminent in his profession, and of studious, scientific habits. He was born at Bremen in 1740, and died there in 1804. His Lectures on Somnambulism form only a portion, but the most important, of what he published on medico-magnetic subjects during his life. We shall endeavour to present our readers with an abstract of their contents.

Dr Wienholt thus describes the phenomenon which he is about to investigate. 'The sleep-walker, when otherwise healthy, falls at a particular period into a common sleep, which cannot be distinguished from the natural state of repose. After a longer or shorter time, he rises from his couch, and walks about the room, sometimes about the house. He frequently goes out into the open air, walks upon known or unknown paths, as quickly, and with as much activity and confidence, as in his waking state; avoids all obstacles which may stand, or have been designedly placed in his route, and makes his way along rugged paths, and climbs dangerous heights, which he would never have thought of attempting when awake. He reads printed and written papers, writes as well and as correctly as in his waking state, and performs many other operations requiring light and the natural use of the eyes. All these actions, however, are performed by the somnambulist in complete darkness, and generally with his eyes firmly closed. When the period of his somnambulism has elapsed, he returns to bed, falls back again into his natural sleep, awakes at his usual time, and in most instances knows nothing of what he had done in the *sleep-waking* state.' Few somnambulists, he adds, exhibit *all* the above phenomena, most of them only walking about in their sleep, without speaking or performing any such delicate manual operations as writing and such-like. Still, the annals of medicine contain many well-authenticated instances of somnambulism of a very remarkable character. Of these a few are narrated by Wienholt, in order to form the groundwork of his inquiry.

One very striking case is that of a 'rope-maker who was frequently overtaken by sleep even in the daytime, and in the midst of his usual occupations. While in this state, he sometimes recommenced doing all that he had been engaged in during the previous part of the day. At other times he would continue the work in which he happened to be engaged at the commencement of the paroxysm, and finish his business with as great ease and success as when awake. When the fit overtook him in travelling, he proceeded on his journey with the same facility, and almost faster than when awake, without missing the road, or stumbling over anything. In this manner he repeatedly went from Naumburg to Weimar. Upon one of these occasions he came into a narrow lane, where there lay some timber. He passed over it regularly, without injury; and with equal caution and dexterity he avoided the horses and carriages which came in his way. At another time he was overtaken by sleep just as he was about to set out for Weimar on horseback. He rode through the river Ilme, allowed his horse to drink, and drew up his legs, to prevent them from getting wet; then passed through several streets, crossed the market-place, which was at that time full of people, carts, and booths; and arrived in safety at the house of an acquaintance, where he awoke. These, and many similar acts requiring the use of eyes, he performed in darkness as well as by daylight. His eyes, however, were firmly closed, and he could not see when they were forced open and stimulated by light brought near them. His other senses appeared to be equally dormant. He could not smell even the most volatile spirit. He felt nothing when pinched, pricked, or struck. He heard nothing when called by his name, nor even when a pistol was discharged close beside him.' A second case is that of a young girl between twelve and thirteen years of age, belonging to a family of distinction, who was afflicted with a violent nervous complaint, and, during her paroxysms, while her eyes were firmly closed, 'distinguished, without difficulty, all colours that were presented to her, recognised the numbers of cards, and the stripes upon those which were variegated, wrote in the same manner as usual, and cut figures in paper as she was accustomed to do in her waking state.' Another is that of a young man, a gardener, who used to rise from bed, go out of the house, clamber over walls, and even upon the roof of the house, uninjured, and who once, that a table was likely to fall upon him, contrived dexterously to evade it —all in a state of sleep.

A fourth case, mentioned by Wienholt, is that of a student who, 'during a severe nervous complaint, experienced several attacks of somnambulism. Upon these occasions he would go from his bed-room to his parlour, and back, open and shut the doors, as well as his closet, and take out of the latter whatever he wanted—pieces of music, pen, ink, and paper—and all with his eyes shut. From among his music he selected a march from the opera of Medea, laid the sheet in a proper situation before him, and having found the appropriate key, he played the whole piece with his usual skill upon the harpsichord. In the same manner he also played one of Bach's sonatas, and gave the most expressive passages with surprising effect. One of the persons present turned the notes upside down: this he immediately perceived, and when he recommenced playing, he replaced the sheet in its proper position. While playing, he remarked a string out of tune, upon which he stopped, put it in order, and again proceeded. He wrote a letter to his brother, and what he wrote was not only perfectly rational, but straight and legible. While Professor Feder was on a visit to him one afternoon, the somnambulist observed that it was snowing, which was actually the case. On the same occasion, notwithstanding that his eyes were still completely closed, he remarked that the landlord of the opposite house was standing at the window, which was true; and that hats were hanging at the window of another room, which was also the fact. He opened Professor Feder's "Compendium of Logic and Metaphysics," and pointed out to him several passages which he thought interesting, as also some of his own written notes of the professor's lectures, in a volume which had been recently bound. He pointed out to another of his teachers the exact place where he had left off in his last theological lecture. It is a remarkable circumstance, however, that there were many things which he did not perceive. Thus, while writing to his brother, he did not observe that there was no more ink in the pen, and continued to write on.'

Another of the cases referred to by Wienholt is one observed by the archbishop of Bordeaux, and reported first in the French Encyclopædia. A young ecclesiastic in the same seminary with the archbishop 'was in the habit of getting up during the night in a state of somnambulism, of going to his room, taking pen, ink, and paper, and composing and writing sermons. When he had finished one page of the paper on which he was writing, he would read over what he had written, and correct it. On one occasion he made use of the expression *ce divin enfant*. In reading over the passage, he changed the adjective *divin* into *adorable*. Perceiving, however, that the pronoun *ce* could not stand before the word *adorable*, he added to the former the letter *t*. In order to ascertain whether the somnambulist made any use of his eyes, the archbishop held a piece of pasteboard under his chin, to prevent him from seeing the paper on which he was writing; but he continued to write on, without appearing to be incommoded in the slightest degree. The paper on which he was writing was taken away, and other paper laid before him; but he immediately perceived the change. He wrote pieces of music while in this state, and in the same manner with his eyes closed. The words were placed under the musical notes. It happened upon one occasion that the words were written in too large a character, and did not stand precisely under the corresponding notes. He soon perceived the error, blotted out the part, and wrote it over again with great exactness.'

Having thus given a few of the best authenticated examples of somnambulism then known, Dr Wienholt proceeds, in his subsequent lectures, to examine the various theories most commonly offered in explanation of such striking facts, long familiar to medical men and physiologists.

The first hypothesis which he examines is that supported by Hoffmann, Haen, and Haller, and prevalent in the first half of the eighteenth century; namely, that in somnambulism no use at all is made of the organ of vision, but that all the phenomena are to be attributed to the operation of the imagination of the somnambulist, assisted by the sense of touch. According to this hypothesis, the somnambulist 'has in his mind a perfect picture, comprehending even the most minute details of his previous experience, of the way he has to traverse, of the known locality of certain apartments, streets, roofs of houses, &c.;' and as he proceeds through these images of his own mind, the sense of touch steers him clear of every obstacle. But, argues Dr Wienholt very justly, supposing the possibility of such a perfect picture or recollection of the whole scene he was to traverse in the mind of the somnambulist, and supposing, also, that the sense of touch may be awake, how happens it that the actions of the somnambulist always correspond so exactly in point of time with external objects? If a man with his eyes bandaged enter the same room, let the picture of it, and the arrangement of the furniture in it, be never so familiar to him, two or three paces forward will confuse him; the picture of the room may still remain distinct in his mind, but he will not know *whereabouts in the picture* he is. None of this helplessness or hesitation, however, is observed in the somnambulist. He proceeds as confidently and boldly as he does in his waking state; nor, in doing so, does he commit mistakes. It will not do to suppose an increase of susceptibility in the sense of touch or in the other senses, for this increase never takes place except in consequence of long practice; whereas somnambulists conduct themselves as perfectly in their first sleep as in their tenth or twentieth. But supposing the sense of touch sufficient to pilot the somnambulist past obstacles which he had distinctly conceived beforehand, how would it pilot him past obstacles purposely placed in his way at the moment, or how would it pilot him in places perfectly strange to him?

The next hypothesis which Dr Wienholt examines, resembles the one just discussed. It is, that somnambulism is a middle state between sleeping and waking, in which the somnambulist is dreaming, while at the same time his senses and his will are completely, or to a great extent, active. The somnambulist, intermingling the phantasms of his dream with the perceptions of his senses, conducts himself strangely, but yet accurately, so far as external objects are concerned. All his senses, sight, hearing, touch, taste, smell, are as active as when he is awake, or nearly so; and the only difference between him and a man completely awake is, that he is absorbed in a dreamy train of thought. In opposition to this theory, Wienholt argues that, so far from somnambulism being a half-sleep, all the symptoms of the most profound sleep are exhibited by the somnambulist, even in an exaggerated degree; as if somnambulism were something farther removed from the ordinary waking state than sleep is. The most intense light produces no impression upon the eyes of somnambulists, pistol-shots no impression upon their ears; nay, they do not feel pain when they are struck or pricked. Yet, while all their organs of sense are thus dormant, they conduct themselves as if they saw, heard, felt, smelt, and tasted perfectly well. If, as is natural, people should still insist that the somnambulist sees by his eye in the ordinary way, it must be supposed either that his eye is not completely closed, or that he opens it imperceptibly at intervals. But allowing, for the moment, either of these suppositions to be true, neither would be found sufficient. 'When the eyelids are nearly closed, we see only the small circle which more immediately surrounds us, and even this, in consequence of the small quantity of light which can enter the eye, only faintly illuminated; and this circle vanishes when the eyelids become united. But the somnambulist requires visual perceptions of distant as well as of near objects; he requires, in those perilous operations which he performs with such ease and rapidity—in his running, leaping, dancing, climbing, &c.—rather stronger and more lively perceptions than usual; which the supposition of a small part of the pupil only being uncovered would not afford him. Add to this, that these perambulations are undertaken chiefly during the night, not only in moonlight, but in complete darkness,' when, to be of any service at all, the eye would require to be opened more widely than usual. Suppose, then, that the somnambulist has his eyes shut, but opens them now and then, so as to receive as much information as he requires; in this case the opening must be the result either of pure chance, or of some impression from without; if the former, the opening of his eyes would be of no use to the somnambulist, because he might receive visual impressions when he had no need for them, and be deprived of them at the very instant when they were most necessary; and if the latter, some hesitation would be observed on the part of the somnambulist, as he felt the influence of the impediment which obliged him to open his eyes. But the somnambulist 'is never observed to hesitate in his progress, to meet with difficulties, or to rectify his proceedings. He conducts himself, and continually acts, just as he would do if he possessed the complete use of his eyes.'

The supposition that the somnambulist sees with his eyes as in the ordinary waking state, is set at rest by an examination of the eyes of somnambulists. The eyes of persons in this state are either completely closed or very wide open; there is no medium. 'If we examine the eyes of somnambulists whose eyelids are closed, the following circumstances appear. If we attempt to draw their eyelids asunder, we meet with resistance. The antagonist muscles of those which usually keep the eyes open, act strongly in opposition to our efforts, and the latter are at rest. The eye can be opened only to the extent of one-half. When this takes place, the apple of the eye is perceived to be turned upwards towards the internal angle, and we see only the margin of the iris peeping from under the upper eyelid, and remaining immoveable in the same place. The approach of light to the eye does not occasion the slightest change. There is no winking of the eyelids, no expression of feeling, when the light is brought ever so near to the half-opened eye. One somnambulist exhibited no sign of sensibility when a candle was brought so close to his eye that his eyebrows were singed by it.' This insensibility of the eyes, however, is best exhibited by those somnambulists whose eyes are open. 'A young lady, during a severe nervous complaint, fell into paroxysms, during which she walked about the sick-room. Her eyes were wide open, and appeared to be quite insensible. Sauvages, who suspected deception, made use of several means of ascertaining the truth. In vain did he unexpectedly aim a blow at her with his hand; she made no effort to evade it, nor did she interrupt her discourse, and the eyelids did not move in the slightest degree. He held spirit of hartshorn before her eye, moistened a feather with it, and applied it to the cornea; suddenly touched one of the eyeballs with his finger; nay, at last he held a lighted candle so close to her open eye, that her eyelashes were burnt. During this insensibility of her eyes she rose from her bed, walked about the room, kept the middle way between the bedsteads as well as she could have done when awake, turned round at the proper time, did not once stumble against anything, although several things were placed in her way; and all this she did without touching the objects.'

There is only one plausible argument, says Dr Wienholt, which can still be had recourse to in support of the idea that it is through the ordinary medium of the senses that the somnambulist receives his knowledge of external things. This argument is embodied in the ingenious theory of somnambulism started by Dr Darwin in his Zoonomia. It supposes that the somnambulist's sensual organs are open to impressions as in the waking state; but that his mind is so absorbed by a dreamy train of ideas, that only such impressions are conveyed to it by the senses, as harmonise and fit in with that train of ideas. Thus, a very loud noise may excite not the least attention on his part, because he cannot incorporate it with what is passing in his mind; whereas, on the other hand, a very slight sound may throw him into a state of agitation, because it instantly and naturally falls in with the course of his dream. This hypothesis is not without some plausibility. It is observed, for instance, that extremely absent persons, like Newton or Adam Smith, pursuing some train of thought, are insensible to all impressions foreign from the subject they are occupied with; but that the moment any remark is made, or any incident occurs, bearing on the subject of their thoughts, they instantly clutch at it, as it were, thankfully, and incorporate it with the current of their ideas.

To this hypothesis of Darwin, Wienholt objects that it is totally gratuitous, and at variance with all ascertained facts respecting somnambulism, particularly with the fact of the immobility of the pupil of the eye in somnambulists whose eyelids are open. 'There is no doubt,' he says, 'that an individual may occupy himself so profoundly and so constantly with one particular train of ideas, that other objects falling within the sphere of his senses are not perceived. But what a difference between this state and that of which we are now speaking! In the case of a person in a reverie, there is manifestly no organic change in the eye; in the case of a somnambulist, there is a very remarkable and permanent change. Again, the sensations which are not remarked by persons in a reverie, are sensible impressions of the usual kind. But let unexpected sensations of a particular kind, affecting the nerves in an unusual degree, be produced, as, for instance, by a sudden flash of lightning, a violent clap of thunder, a musket discharged in the neighbourhood, shaking the body, powerful excitement of the skin, &c. they would certainly, however deep the abstraction, occasion an immediate awakening.' Not so, however, in the case of somnambulists. Many other objections are urged by Wienholt to the same effect, the last of which is the most decisive. Whatever value the Darwinian hypothesis might be supposed to have, he says, in explaining cases of somnambulism with the eyes open, it is totally inapplicable to all those cases in which the eyes are shut; and these are probably the most numerous.

Having thus discussed and exploded the various theories entertained by the physiologists of his time respecting somnambulism, Dr Wienholt proceeds to state his own belief on the subject; but this we must reserve for another article.

BOOKBINDING.

Bookbinding may be said to have been coeval with the art of writing books, though at first the covers were cases of wood, stone, and earthenware. Catullus has described the general style of binding in his time, and we have the testimony of Aquila and Lambert Bos, that the titles were written or worked on the outside. There was often some degree of splendour about the bindings of Greece and Rome. Phillatius, an Athenian, was the inventor of glue for bookbinding.

In England, the art was first practised by the monks. There was a room in religious houses called the *scriptorium*, for the purpose of writing and binding books, and grants were made to provide skins for covers, &c. Many missals and other books exist, which exhibit the splendour of the bindings fabricated in these establishments. It was the sacrist's duty to put bindings and clasps to the holy manuscripts. The British Museum library contains the *Textus Sancti Cuthberti*, bound by Bilfrid, a monk of Durham, about A. D. 720. Herman, Bishop of Salisbury in 1080, was a writer, illuminator, and binder of books. Henry, a monk of Hyde Abbey in 1178, used not only to bind books, but to form the brazen bosses of them. The bindings were frequently adorned with elegant devices. In the British Museum is a manuscript gospel in its original wooden binding, with ivory-carved ornaments. Other specimens are embellished with rubies, diamonds, sapphires, and silver. Eleanor, Duchess of Gloucester, Sir John Fastolfe, and other persons of rank, had their arms engraved on the clasps of their books. Numbers of the books of the church constructed in early times were protected with brass corners, bosses, and bands. The usual materials for common works were wood covers and deer-skin. A line in Pope's Dunciad conveys a good idea of the substantial bindings of antiquity—

> There Caxton sleeps, and Wynkyn at his side,
> One *clasped in wood*, and one *in strong cow-hide*.

Long before the invention of printing, books were bound also in calf-skin, coloured cloth, velvet, &c. After the invention of printing, they were chiefly bound in parchment, or forrel, velvet, vellum, calf, and morocco. The old English poet Skelton has left us a description of the splendid bookbinding in his time; and the German traveller Hentzner has described the bindings which he saw in the royal library of England in 1598. Queen Elizabeth loved to have her books splendidly bound, and there are rich specimens which belonged to her and James I. in the British Museum. Her Golden Manual of Prayers was bound in solid gold, and she had other books bound in silver, enriched with precious stones. Queen Mary, Lady Jane Grey, Queen Elizabeth, and many other ladies, were in the habit of working embroidered ornaments on the silk and damask covers of their books.

Some whimsicality is occasionally displayed in the choice of the material in which a book is bound. In a bookseller's catalogue, we read of a Latin copy of Apuleius's Golden Ass (1501) bound in ass's-skin. The Duke of Roxburghe's library contained a collection of pamphlets respecting Mary Toft, the rabbit-woman of Godalming, Surrey, bound in rabbit-skin; and the Hon. George Napier had a work relating to the celebrated dwarf Jeffrey Hudson bound in a piece of Charles I.'s silk waistcoat. Mordaunt Cracherode, the father of the celebrated book-collector of that name, wore one pair of buckskin breeches exclusively during a voyage round the world; and a volume in his son's collection, now added to the library of the British Museum, is bound in a part of these circumnavigating and memorable mentionables. As a binding for sporting books, nothing can be more appropriately pretty than the fallow-deer skin; while for young ladies' albums, nothing can surpass the superfine *noli-me-tangere* skin of the hedgehog. Often have hog-skin and fox-skin been used for bindings; human skin only rarely.

London bookbinders are unrivalled for their elegant leather bindings. The cheap, neat, and substantial cloth-binding, now so common, was first commenced on a large scale by Mr Pickering.

Authors' notions of neatness may be partly conceived, according to the taste they display in their bindings. Thus Gibbon, a dandy in dress, was a dandy in bindings; while Dr Johnson, somewhat of a sloven, had a ragged regiment of rough calf-skin books, which he could toss about with savage carelessness, and complained, when he borrowed a book from Stephens, that it was too well bound. On the other hand, Adam Smith, who was plain and unpretending in his own exterior, indulged in an elegant library. 'I am only a beau,' he used to say, 'in my books.' From two passages in Shakspeare, we may infer that he held that fine works should have fine bindings, and that bad works should be bound only in the commonest style—

> How would he look to see his work, so noble,
> Vilely bound up.—*Winter's Tale*, iv. 3.
>
> Was ever book, containing such vile matter,
> So fairly bound.—*Romeo and Juliet*, iii. 2.

Dibdin says, in his Literary Reminiscences, that 'the binding of the Harleian Library (chiefly in red morocco) cost Lord Oxford L.18,000.'

When a deputation from the university of Cambridge announced to Lord Burghley, their chancellor, an intention of presenting a book to Queen Elizabeth on her visit to Audley End, he cautioned them that 'the book must have no savour of spyke, which commonly bookbinders do seek to make their books savour well; for that her majesty could not abide such a strong scent.' Bookbinders probably had recourse to scents to preserve their books; for it is a known fact, that a few drops of any perfumed oil will secure libraries from the consuming effects of mouldiness and damp. Russian leather, which is perfumed with the tar of the birch tree, never moulds; and merchants suffer large bales of this article to lie in the London docks in the most careless manner, knowing that it cannot sustain any injury from damp.

COAL.

What so important in the actual condition of the world as this extraordinary mineral, coal?—the staff and support of present civilisation, the great instrument and means of future progress! The very familiarity and multiplicity of its uses disguise from observation the important part it bears in the life of man and the economy of nations. We have often thought, with something of fearful interest, what would be the condition of the world, and of England in particular, were this subterranean treasure exhausted, or even much abridged in quantity. Yet such is the term to which, if the globe itself should last, our posterity must eventually come; and as respects our own country, the period, at the present rate of consumption, can be defined with some exactness. The immense coal-basins of the Ohio and Mississippi will yet be yielding their richness to the then innumerable people of the western world, when our stores are worked out and gone. Yet here also time will fix its limit. Geology gives no indication whatsoever of natural processes going on by which what is once consumed may be recreated or repaired. The original materials of the formation may be said to be no longer present; the agencies and conditions necessary to the work are either wanting, or partial and deficient in force. Whether human science, grasping at this time what seem almost as new elements of power committed to man, may hereafter discover a substitute for this great mineral, is a problem which it belongs to future generations to solve.—*Quarterly Review.*

JEROME'S CLOCK FACTORY.

The following account of a visit to the clock manufactory of Mr Jerome at Newhaven, in one of the New England states, is given by a correspondent in an American paper:—'Curiosity to examine his works, and the process of making a clock, led us to pay a visit to this establishment. Mr Jerome, on being informed of the nature of the call, very politely showed us through the whole of his extensive works. On entering, our ears were greeted with the mingled hum and buzz of saws, the thunder of two powerful steam-engines, and the clatter of machinery. Our attention was first drawn to the sawing works, by which the cases are cut out and fitted as if by magic. Boards in the rough state are cut in proper lengths for the front, sides, top, and bottoms of cases. These are again subject to the action of finer saws, and cut in perfect order for being matched and put together; and this alone, of all the woodwork about a clock, is smoothed, or in anyway remodelled, after being cut from the unplaned timber. The veneering, which is principally of mahogany, rosewood, and black walnut, is taken, after being glued to the different parts composing the case, to a room set apart for the purpose, in which are employed at this branch some eight or ten hands, and there receives an even surface, and six coats of varnish, which, when finished, will compare in elegance with the finest articles of furniture in the cabinet warerooms of our city. The movements are all cut in proper forms and sizes by dies, with great precision and rapidity, even to the pivot-holes in the plates, which have before been drilled. The cogs in the wheels, the second, minute, and hour stops, are grooved out by the same rapid and skilful process. The post, pins, and smaller pieces of the inside work are turned from the more rough material, polished, and finished at the same time, while the plate and wheels are cleansed and polished by rinsing first in a strong solution of aquafortis, and then in pure water. We cannot describe minutely the whole process of making a clock, or the life-like movement of the machinery; it would take more time and space than we can at present devote to this purpose. In short, the case, movements, plates, face, &c. which, when put together, form one of Jerome's celebrated "brass clocks," go through some fifty different hands before being completed. One man can put together about seventy-five movements per day; while every part, from the first process to the finishing, goes on with equal rapidity. Mr Jerome informed us that he anticipates making this year fifty thousand clocks, and these are to be turned out by some seventy-five hands. This may seem a large number of clocks to be made in a year by so small a number of workmen; but, after witnessing the perfection of the machinery, the systematic equalisation of each department of labour, the almost incredible despatch and precision of the whole arrangement, it is easily accounted for. Machinery, in this instance, is made to take the place of physical and mental labour, and to do what has hitherto been considered as capable of execution only by the genius of man, assisted by numerous and skilfully-used tools. He yearly consumes of the various articles used in the manufacture of clocks the following enormous quantities:—500,000 feet pine timber; 200,000 feet mahogany and rosewood veneers; 200 tons of iron for weights; 100,000 lbs. of brass; 300 casks of nails; 1500 boxes glass, 50 feet per box; 1500 gallons varnish; 15,000 lbs. wire; 10,000 lbs. glue; 80,000 looking-glass plates. 2400 dollars are paid yearly for printing labels, and for screws, saws, coal, and oil: workmen employed, 75; paid wages yearly, 30,000 dollars; clocks made per day, 200; per year, 50,000. Little, doubtless, did Mr Terry, the inventor and first maker of a Yankee wooden clock, dream, when he whittled out the movements of his first production in the clock-line with a penknife, and afterwards served his customers with a clock, uncased, from his saddle-bags, that in a few years an article constructed on the same plan, though of different material, would be manufactured at one establishment to the extent of fifty thousand in the year. But Yankee ingenuity and enterprise stop at no point where a penny can be turned to advantage, or so long as the offspring of his genius finds a demand in the market at a living profit.'

THE FARMERS OF BELGIUM.

The farmers of Belgium are a hard-working class of men—in the habit of labouring their farms, and generally ignorant of every other subject but their profession. But in it truly they show rare sagacity and experience; and though unaided by, and almost despising the light of science, they discover in some parts of their system of agriculture a perfection to which science has never yet guided the farmers of this or any other country. When we look back to the ancient grandeur of Belgium, when its cities were the marts and factories of Europe, and consider the consequent increase of population in a country naturally unproductive, we will discover a sufficient stimulus to excite the energies of a people gifted by nature with an indomitable perseverance and unwearied industry. This disposition, as well as its effects—their agriculture—has been handed down to the present generation of farmers, and still manifests itself in many operations which the negligent farmer would consider unprofitable, or at least superfluous; and it is from this praiseworthy industry that Belgium, comparatively a poor country, is considered by strangers as unrivalled in the salubrity of its climate and the fertility of its soil, and that the great part of the kingdom is prevented from returning to its original barrenness.—*Journal of Agriculture.*

FABLED MELODY OF THE DYING SWAN.

The melody ascribed to the dying swan has long been well known to exist only in the graceful mythology of the ancients; but as few opportunities occur of witnessing the bird's last moments, some interest attaches to Mr Waterton's personal observations on this point, which we can ourselves corroborate, having not long since been present at the death of a pet swan, which, like Mr Waterton's favourite, had been fed principally by hand; and, instead of seeking to conceal itself at the approach of death, quitted the water, and lay down to die on the lawn before its owner's door. 'He then left the water for good and all, and sat down on the margin of the pond. He soon became too weak to support his long neck in an upright position. He nodded, and then tried to recover himself; he nodded again, and again held up his head; till at last, quite enfeebled and worn out, his head fell gently on the grass, his wings became expanded a trifle or so, and he died while I was looking on. * * Although I gave no credence to the extravagant notion which antiquity had entertained of melody from the mouth of the dying swan, still I felt anxious to hear some plaintive sound or other, some soft inflection of the voice, which might tend to justify that notion in a small degree. But I was disappointed. * * He never even uttered his wonted cry, nor so much as a sound to indicate what he felt within.'—*Blackwood's Magazine.*

TRUTH'S PROGRESS.

When a great truth is to be revealed, it does not flash at once on the race, but dawns and brightens on a superior understanding, from which it is to emanate and to illuminate future ages. On the faithfulness of great minds to this awful function, the progress and happiness of men chiefly depend. The most illustrious benefactors of the race have been men who, having risen to great truths, have held them as a sacred trust for their kind, and have borne witness to them amidst general darkness, under scorn and persecution, perhaps in the face of death. Such men, indeed, have not always made contributions to literature, for their condition has not allowed them to be authors; but we owe the transmission, perpetuity, and immortal power of their new and high thoughts to kindred spirits, who have concentrated and fixed them in books.—*Channing.*

MY GRAVE.

[The following verses are given by the *Dublin Nation* as one of the earliest pieces which came from the pen of its late editor, Thomas Davis, Esq., whose sudden and unexpected decease has lately taken place.]

SHALL they bury me in the deep,
Where wind-forgetting waters sleep?
Shall they dig a grave for me
Under the greenwood tree?
Or on the wild heath,
Where the wilder breath
Of the storm doth blow?
Oh, no! oh, no!

Shall they bury me in the palace tombs,
Or under the shade of cathedral domes?
Sweet 'twere to lie on Italy's shore;
Yet not there—nor in Greece, though I love it more.
In the wolf or the vulture my grave shall I find?
Shall my ashes career on the world-seeing wind?
Shall they fling my corpse in the battle mound,
Where coffinless thousands lie under the ground—
Just as they fall they are buried so?
Oh, no! oh, no!

No! on an Irish green hill-side,
On an opening lawn—but not too wide;
For I love the drip of the wetted trees—
I love not the gales, but a gentle breeze,
To freshen the turf; put no tomb-stone there,
But green sods decked with daisies fair;
Nor sods too deep; but so that the dew
The matted grass-roots may trickle through.
Be my epitaph writ on my country's mind,
'He served his country, and loved his kind.'

Oh! 'twere sweet unto the grave to go,
If one were sure to be buried so.

CURIOUS GOLD CARRIERS.

Sir James Campbell (of Ardkinglas) relates in his memoirs that while at Zante, one of the Ionian Islands, he observed a curious fact relative to the small Barbary pigeons. At a certain period of the summer they arrive in incredible numbers from, it is supposed, the African coast. 'If so, their flight must be amazingly rapid, as they arrive in excellent condition, and very fat. It is certain at least that they come from a country where gold is produced, as I had an opportunity of proving by personal observation. I remarked that numbers of them had particles of sand sticking to their feet, which were sometimes pellucid, and generally glittering. I had some of this sand collected, spread upon paper, and carefully analysed, when I ascertained that the result produced a considerable proportion of gold. Birds of passage probably drink immediately before setting out on their migration, and the aureous particles were probably brought down by some stream which must have passed through a country impregnated with the metal which is the object of such universal pursuit.'

ROADSIDE FENCES.

Let any one take a ride about the outskirts of London, the seat of so much wealth and refinement, and he will presently observe fences on the roadside, half dead, half alive, patched in many places with brushwood, full of weeds and rubbish, and resting upon a foundation at least four times wider than a rightly-constructed fence requires. Around provincial towns it is the same; close to the outlets, where in general the finest buildings are erected, stands many an old irregular fence full of nettles, docks, and other herbage, presenting anything but an appearance in keeping with the trimly-kept grounds of a suburban villa. Our roads are, in general, well kept; and if they were bounded with fences at all in character with them, the suburbs of our cities and towns would assume something of the air and neatness observable in a pleasure-ground. More of a garden-like character would be diffused, and though the appearance thus introduced would be perhaps less picturesque, it would at any rate bespeak a more refined and careful taste.—*Grigor's Prize Essay.*

Published by W. and R. CHAMBERS, High Street, Edinburgh (also 98, Miller Street, Glasgow); and with their permission, by W. S. ORR, Amen Corner, London.—Printed by Bradbury and Evans, Whitefriars, London.

CONDUCTED BY WILLIAM AND ROBERT CHAMBERS, EDITORS OF 'CHAMBERS'S INFORMATION FOR THE PEOPLE,' 'CHAMBERS'S EDUCATIONAL COURSE,' &c.

No. 97. NEW SERIES. SATURDAY, NOVEMBER 8, 1845. PRICE 1½d.

LED BY IDEAS.

A MAN is properly and ordinarily the king of his ideas; but it sometimes happens, as in other empires, that one of the subjects, rising into too much favour at court, becomes practically the real monarch. We have then presented to us the singular phenomenon of a Man led by an Idea. Let any one dip for a month into the more intellectual circles of London, and he will be astonished at the number of such revolutionised monarchies which meet his observation. Talk of spoiled children ruling their weak parents; of easy-natured people governed by their servants; of kings in the hands of too powerful ministers; all these are nothing to the spectacle of a man—probably a clever and well-informed one—led by an idea.

Men led by ideas are usually of benevolent character, and their master-thoughts are generally of the nature of plans for putting the whole faults of the social machine at once to rights. It is a curious feature in the condition of the greatest country the world has yet known, that it ever believes itself in the most dreadful state imaginable, and expects nothing but ruin in a very short time. Tenderly concerned for themselves and countrymen, a few worthy persons are continually going about with nostrums for averting the calamity. One holds that over-population is the cause of the whole mischief, and proposes to bleed off the disease by a system of emigration, which, it becomes quite clear, would carry away units for the tens added in the ordinary course of things each year. Another has a faith in pauper colonies, or allotments of inferior lands. With a third, more schools is the cry. Some, again, are ostentatiously material in their views. What, they say, can be done with the minds of men until they have got plenty of four-pound loaves? They hold it to be necessary to give the people a more ample store of good things in their larders and cupboards. Unfortunately, no one pretends to show how this is to be accomplished otherwise than by the usual means of a prosperous industry. Some have dilettanti ideas. They are all for honeysuckled cottages and schools of industry. A few think a more universal diffusion of cricket, with gentlefolks bowling to labourers, and spiced ale sent down from the manor-house, the true plan for setting Britain on its legs. Mr Owen stands smiling by, fully assured that no good is to be expected till the plan of competition has been exchanged for that of co-operation. But, meanwhile, somehow the commerce of the country takes a start; new fields of capital are found, and hardly an idle person is to be seen: all the difficulties which we lately contemplated then vanish, and John Bull is found to be a safe enough person after all; so that only he has work to do, and money and grub to get by it.

Such a denouement is rather awkward for the leading-idea men; but the fact is, the ideas are good enough ideas nevertheless, taken simply by themselves, and not as panaceas. Scarcely any doubt exists that colonisation, and cottage gardens, and cricket, and schools, are all capital things: the error lies in thinking any one of them sufficient to patch up a diseased commonwealth, and going about seeking to pin down mankind to that narrow conclusion. It seems, however, to be essential to enthusiasts of this class to have but one idea—at least at a time. Engrossed by it, they can see no value in any other. An emigration man, for instance, despises allotments, and an allotment man looks with contempt, if not indignation, at the idea of sending the people out of the country. It is hardly possible, indeed, for one person to listen for a moment to another who lives under the regime of a different idea. The four-pound-loaf system is a perfect weariness of the flesh to a man of schools, and *vice versa*. Such appears to be the nature of the case, and we have never yet had an Admirable Crichton who could argue for and prosecute all the various objects at once. It would be the most amusing thing in the world to bring a few such persons together, and listen while they each struggled to advance his own monarch fancy, and debar all the rest.

A. B. It has been fully proved in practice that allotments satisfy the poor labourer, at the same time that they return an equal, if not greater rent to the landlord. The whole of our surplus population might be provided for in this way, if gentlemen would only set their shoulder to the wheel. [The shoulder in connexion with the wheel is constantly in requisition among the idea men.]

C. D. But why not bring the people into little local co-operative communities, where they might have a range of the various trades, keep up a church and school of their own, and live at one table? Here is an engraved plan that makes my whole idea intelligible at a glance.

E. F. All these schemes are absurd in political economy, for that must always be the best mode of employing men in which they use their powers to the effect of the utmost possible production. Fix a man down in a piece of ground, whether by himself or with others, where he only can labour in one limited way, and he subserves an inferior end to what he does when he takes a part as high as his faculties will permit in some great combination of labour. The real curse of the country is, the number of people being too great in proportion to the demand for their work. Hence low wages, and hence misery. There will be no good till a few millions are sent to clear ground in the colonies. Then wages would rise, and it would be good times for the reduced number remaining.

G. H. What stuff! you do not see that the labours of men, if rightly directed, and not restricted by any external pressure, must be sufficient to maintain them wherever they are. Free trade is my remedy.

I. J. I never trouble myself with the science of anything. I only know that England was once merry England, and that the Book of Sports and Brand's Popular Antiquities show us how it may be restored to that condition. Let us always take care to set the peasantry in motion at Christmas with their carols, and at Easter with their egg-songs; let us revive archery and metheglin, and all will be well.

K. L. For any sake instruct them, and make them rational beings. An ignorant man is a volcano or a piece of pyrotechny, ready to explode at any time. Educate him, and he becomes a harmonious part of the social enginery. We must have a national system of education, giving the needful nurture free to all, like the air they breathe. How is it to be wondered at that we have strikes, riots, heavy calendars, and thousands of evils, when one half the community are reared without any tincture of learning?

M. N. Away with your march-of-intellect nonsense! When did a book ever fill a belly? I want to see the people have plenty of eggs and bacon. They ought always to have large wages, and everything comfortable about them, whether they choose or not. Unions are bastiles where the poor are starved. There should be an act of parliament to let everybody have at least a pound a-week, even when they cannot or choose not to work for it.

O. P. Well, it is my opinion that intemperance is the cause of most of our sufferings. If you would only embrace and agree to support the system of total abstinence, you would soon see this a very different country from what it is. The water cure is the cure, you may depend on it. Only see how drinking absorbs the earnings of the working-man, how it renders him idle and sensual, and reduces his household to starvation! Everything we complain of is traceable to alcohol. And you may plant schools, form allotments, promote emigration, and try whatever else you please, but till you take away the fatal cup, you will make no true improvement.

Q. R. Well, I think you may promote the advancement of our species by different means, namely, by establishing galleries of pictures and statues. What was the glory of ancient Greece?—Her works of art. The great Hellenic democracies were refined by continually regarding beautiful forms in their temples and theatres. There is nothing wanting to make us as great a people, but a proper annual grant for national and provincial galleries. About a million a-year would serve, and I am sure we spend many millions in a worse way. I lately published a letter to the prime minister upon the subject; but he was then struggling to get a majority on the sugar duties, and I suppose never had time to take my suggestions into consideration.

S. T. Galleries for works of art! More need to build new sewers! The effects of defective draining upon the health of the inhabitants of large towns has been fully proved, and it is time that measures were taken to remedy so great an evil. I have given my thoughts to sewers night and day for twenty years. It is a great, but neglected subject. The world might be lighted by the profits made from cleaning it, and health promoted at the same time. I could send you ten folio blue books to illuminate you upon drainage; or, should you prefer it, come to me some day, and I will tell you all about it by word of mouth. Only come early, that we may have a long day to discuss it.

U. V. That is not a subject to my liking. Have you ever considered the solitary system of prison discipline? I like a prison. When I come to a town where I never was before, I inquire for the jail, and generally go to visit it. Crime is, in fact, my favourite study. There is at present a striking want of settled principle with regard to the management of malefactors. When you treat them severely, with a view to their punishment, the public gets squeamish, and a daily newspaper makes you its useful grievance for the time: when you are lenient and kind, with a view to their reformation, the same newspaper proclaims that culprits are treated more kindly, and enjoy more of the good things of this life, than honest hard-working labourers. All this perplexity would give way if my plan were adopted. You may find an account of it, commencing at the fifteen-hundredth page of the tenth report of the committee on Prison Discipline.

W. X. I am sorry to dissent from a great number of you gentlemen. I consider war, and the employment of force in general, as the grand means of depraving human society; and till we can make all men converts to peace principles, I believe there is no good to be done with them. See the evils of war, in the misexpenditure of public money, the setting up of false objects to love of approbation, the making of widows and orphans, the brutalisation of the public mind, and a continual inflammation of the minds of young ladies in garrison towns. A few worthy people have joined me in setting up a peace society, and we have already made great way in different quarters. We take care every year to send a set of our tracts to the members of her Majesty's government, about the time when they bring forward the army and navy estimates in parliament. I have no doubt we shall succeed in bringing the public at large to our way of thinking, and thus put an end to war—in time.

Y. Z. Well now, I don't care much about anything so unpractical as inculcating what you call peace principles. Neither am I zealous about temperance, or cottage gardens, or the establishment of picture galleries. I wish to wash the people. Only let me once get them into a way of cleaning their skins regularly, and all will be well. And the way I argue is this: cleanliness is the mother of all the virtues. Therefore, let the people be clean, and they will be everything else that could be wished. Hence I look to baths as the universal regenerators. Men once called for the sponge to wipe out the national debt; they will do far more good by now applying it to their own persons. Revolutionists used to call on the nation to take the plunge; let them now take the plunge-bath. Trust me, till we can set all the world a-washing, there will be no real improvement effected. You might preach for ages on other subjects: but nothing will avail while men remain uncleansed. Of all the conservative powers, dirt is decidedly the greatest.

This alphabet of favourite ideas is no fancy. The men led by them may be met with every day in the highways and byways of the world; some as conversation-men at dinner parties, some as button-holders in the porticoes of clubs, some as listener-seekers in general and wherever they are to be had. Secretaries of state, and Messrs Ridgway the publishers, know such men well by their handwriting. They are the Vanderdeckens of the social Cape, continually looking for the means of getting their letter conveyed to the public, but rarely or never finding it. There is something distressing in the idea of so much good intention, and so much excellent suggestion, not only running to waste, but subjecting its authors to a disesteem which never befalls the quiet selfish men of the world. It suggests, however, a remark which may possibly be of service to such men. The main cause of their failure is their becoming so much and so exclusively absorbed in their plans, as to lose the practical tone of common life. For the want of this, nothing will atone. It would excite distrust respecting the most admirable discovery or moral scheme which the wit of man ever devised. The world likes safe, realisable measures; it will only, in ordinary circumstances, move a short way at a time; it distrusts theory—that is, suggestion unproved by experiment. Hence it is necessary to use some caution in bringing any proposed improvement or change before the public. However clear it may be in its entire scope, it may, in that form, be too much for the common run of minds.

and it will therefore fail; but possibly, if some practicable, common-world-looking step be proposed, leading towards the entire scheme, that may be sanctioned and put in practice, and a way may thus be formed for the realisation of the whole.

THE BLIND SQUATTER.

BY PERCY B. ST JOHN.

NEARLY four hundred miles up the Trinity river, Texas, at the extreme point to which the flat-bottom steamboats run up in search of cotton and other productions, is Robins' Ferry. Below, the river is narrow, with high steep banks, within the deep shadow of which the waters roll noiselessly and swiftly towards the ocean, while groves of somewhat stunted trees run down to the very edge of the cliffs: here, however, the stream expands into a broad and shallow lake, the shores of which are low, and even unsightly, as is generally the case in Texas.

We arrived at a landing-place three miles below the junction of the lake and river late one night, and early the following morning I was paddling up against the stream in a light bark canoe, which, having but a slight hold in the water, served better to stem the current than one of larger dimensions. For some time I continued within the shadows of the cliffs in comparative gloom; but, after a somewhat fatiguing hour, my eye first caught a glimpse of the shallow lake, where I hoped to find sufficient abundance of wild-fowl to glut my most murderous appetite as a sportsman. The dawn had long since passed, but nature appeared yet asleep, so calm, so still was that almost untrodden spot. Gliding swiftly out of the influence of the current, I allowed my canoe to stand motionless, while I gazed around. Far as the eye could reach, spread a perfect wilderness of waters, forward, to the right and to the left, perfectly unruffled, for not so much as a blade of grass or a leaf was stirring on the shore. Here and there rose huge trunks of trees, borne from above by the almost periodical inundations, and which, reaching some shallow part, became stationary, until time and decay removed them by degrees from their resting-place. Snags were visible all around, while a low bushy island lay about a quarter of a mile to the southward. The waters sparkled in the sun, revealing at some distance the presence of hundreds of ducks, geese, and swans floating upon the surface. For some time they remained unheeded, so charmed was I by the quiet beauty of the landscape; but at length the prospect of a late breakfast awoke my killing propensities, and, raising my paddle, I gave a true Indian sweep, and glided noiselessly towards the little island above alluded to.

My progress was rapid, but not a sound could have been detected by any save an aboriginal. The bevy of ducks which had drawn me in that direction were sailing towards the island, and I was within gun-shot long before I was perceived, as, the better to deceive them, I lay almost on my face at last, and paddled with my hands. At length I allowed the canoe to drift with whatever impulse it had previously received, and cautiously clutching my double-barrelled apology for a Joe Manton, rose in the boat. Ere, however, I could gain my feet, crack! crack! went the two barrels of a fowling-piece, a whistling was heard close to my ears, and the ducks, save and except a few victims, flew away with a loud rustling of wings. I was astounded. My first impulse was to return the fire at random, as the idea of Indians crossed my brain. I could, however, plainly detect the presence of a fowling-piece by the peculiar report, while it was clear the ducks had been the object aimed at. Still, the proximity of the lead to my ears was far from pleasant, and I hastened to prevent a recurrence of so dangerous an experiment. 'Hollo! friend,' cried I, in a loud and somewhat angry voice, 'are you duck-shooting or man-shooting, because I should like to know?' A man rose instantly above the bushes. 'Merciful Heaven,' cried he, 'have I wounded you, sir? Come in, and I will explain this accident.'

I readily complied, and a few minutes placed me beside the sportsman. I at once saw that he was blind. Nearly six feet high, thin, even gaunt, he presented a most remarkable appearance. Clothed in the ordinary garb of a backwoodsman, there was yet an intellectuality, and even nobility of character in his features, which struck me forcibly, while the sightless orbs at once revealed the cause what had nearly proved a fatal accident. 'You are not alone?' said I, glancing curiously around the bushes. 'I am,' he said with a smile, 'quite alone. But let me most sincerely beg your pardon for having endangered your life.' 'No excuses,' said I, depositing the victims of his volley at his feet; 'but if you would explain to me how you are here alone, and how, being here, you are thus employed, you will assuage a very strong feeling of curiosity.' 'With pleasure,' he replied, 'I owe you an explanation; and besides,' he continued, 'I believe we are countrymen, and this meeting gives me true delight.' 'I am an Englishman,' I said. 'And I a Scotchman. In Britain it makes us countrymen; in a strange land it makes us brothers.'

Struck by the blind man's manner, I loaded, prairie fashion, a couple of corn cob pipes with some excellent leaf tobacco, and handing him one, seated myself quietly by his side. Closing his eyes, from habit, as if to read the past, he was silent for a few moments. 'My name is Campbell,' he said at length, without further preface, 'and by trade I am a cabinetmaker. To begin at the beginning. When I was twenty, and that is not so long ago as you may think, I received an offer to go to New York. I was engaged to be married to a sweet cousin of mine. Poor Ellen! I could not go without her, and yet it was, they said, owre young to marry. Still the offer was good, and rather than I should lose the opportunity of advancing myself, they all consented it should be a wedding. The day after our happy union we sailed for the far west.

'We reached New York in safety; I entered upon my employment with a firm and settled determination to secure, if not fortune, at least competence. Wages were in these days very high; I was a good workman; my master had confidence in me, and besides my wages as journeyman, paid me a salary as his foreman and clerk. As determined to lose no opportunity of advancement, I kept all his books after my regular day's work was done. I saved more than half my earnings, and was as happy, I believe, as an industrious honest man can be; and if he, sir, cannot be happy, I know not who can.' 'You are right,' said I; 'an honest, sober, industrious working-man, with ample employment, respected by his masters, with a little family around him, should be the happiest of created beings. His wants are all supplied, without the cares and troubles of wealth.' 'So it was with me; I was very happy. At the end of ten years I had saved a large sum, and then, and only then, my wife presented me with my first and only child.

'With the consent, and by the advice even of my employers, who had my true interests at heart, I determined to start in business for myself; but not in New York. New Orleans was a money-making, busy place, and thither I removed. My success was unexpectedly great; my own workmanship was eagerly bought up, and I employed many men at the enormous wages of the south. Two misfortunes, however, now clouded my felicity; both attributable, I fear, to my desire for independence. The south did not agree with my wife, and ere I could restore her to a genial climate, she died. Sir, my sorrow was the sorrow, I hope, of a man and a Christian; but I felt it sorely. He only who has seen wife or child removed from him by death, can estimate my feelings. Existence for a time was a blank. I worked mechanically, but no more did her cheerful voice encourage my labours. I ate, I drank; ah, sir! it was then I missed her; at the morning meal, at dinner, over the tea board. As my eye rested on the empty chair on the opposite side of my little table, I could see in it the accustomed form; and then my heart seemed to turn cold, and the very blood to cease to flow. He who has not lost a wife or child, knows not real sorrow in this world. It is the severest trial man ever is put to. Well, sir, she died, and I was left alone with a little image of herself, my Ellen. A gayer, happier being never lived—always smiling, always singing. In time, she brought back some glimpse of joy to my soul.

'One morning I awoke with a peculiar sensation at my heart—I had caught the yellow-fever. I will not detail the history of this illness. Suffice, that it was three months ere I was restored to health; and then, by some extraordinary accident, it proved that I was blind; while my business was gone from me. I knew not what to do. You know, sir, the usual course of ruined men in New Orleans; they sell off secretly, shut their shutters, write G. T. T. (Gone to Texas) on the door, and are no more heard of. But I, sir, could not do this. I was, however, no longer fit for business: a quiet retreat in the woods was my best course of proceeding. Besides, my health was shattered, and I should not have lived in New Orleans. Accordingly, I contrived to raise a thousand dollars when I wound up my accounts, and with this and a negro slave, I and my child started for Texas. Blind, I was not fit to cope with men, and my object, therefore, was to retire, as far as was consistent with safety, into the woods.

'Eight years ago I journeyed up this river, and reached this very spot. Francisco, my negro, was a devoted and faithful fellow, and worked hard, because I was a good master to him. We erected a hut upon yonder shore: it was a laborious operation; but it was at length completed. I have said I was a cabinetmaker; so was my negro; we therefore furnished the place elegantly for a backwoods dwelling.

'Now to speak of my daughter. When we left New Orleans she was eight years old, and up to that age had been educated most carefully, her existence being, of course, that of a town girl. You know, sir, the lazy, luxurious habits of the pestilential city, and how little they fit one for roughing life in the woods. Well, Nelly was transplanted hither, preserving and increasing her accomplishments, and yet has she become a perfect prairie bird. Her fingers ply the rude needle required to make these coarse garments; she and Francisco prepare them for use. We have a female slave, Francisco's wife, but hers is out-door work; and Nelly makes butter, cooks, ay, sir, and even cleans. And she is quite happy, singing all day long; and if an hour can be found for a book, she is in paradise.

'Singular as it may seem, I do most of the hunting; at all events, all the wild-fowl shooting. With the dawn I am up; and in my dug-out, which I pull, while Nelly steers, I land here, and conceal myself in the bushes, while she returns to prepare breakfast. With my loss of sight I have gained an additional strength of hearing. I can detect immediately the approach of the ducks and geese on the water, and if once they come near enough, am sure not to waste my powder and shot. After about a couple of hours she returns for me. Her time is now nearly up: you shall see her, and breakfast at New Edinburgh.'

At this instant a diminutive sail caught my eye at the distance of a hundred yards. Rising, I perceived a small canoe gliding before a slight breeze which had arisen, and rapidly approaching. The foresail and mainsail concealed its occupant; but presently a melodious voice was heard carolling a merry ditty.

'There is my child,' said Campbell, his voice hushed to a whisper; 'there is my child. I never hear her sing but I see her mother before me.'

'Well, father,' cried Nelly, taking in her little sail; 'no ducks for me to pick up? not one. You are unlucky this morning.'

At this moment she caught sight of my naval uniform, and stopped short. 'This gentleman was kind enough to pick them up for me, and you must give him a seat in the boat.'

Nelly approached. Though tanned by the sun, one could still see the blue-eyed Scotch girl in her. Light curls fell from beneath a vast straw-hat over her shoulders, while a simple fur pelisse, and buckskin mocassins, with red worsted stockings, was all her visible attire. But never had I seen anything more graceful or more elegant. A woman, and yet a girl, she had evidently the feelings of the first, with the joyous artlessness of the second. We were friends directly, while I mentally compared her with my interesting Irish friends Mary Rock and her sister.*

In a few minutes more we were sailing for the shore, and in a quarter of an hour were in sight of New Edinburgh. To my surprise I discovered a substantial log-hut, several outhouses, Indian corn-fields, while pumpkins, &c. flourished around in abundance. Two cows were grazing in the neighbourhood; as many horses were near them; while pigs and fowls were scattered in all directions. I was amazed, the blind Scotchman's industry was so novel in Texas. I expressed my surprise. 'Eight years of perseverance can do much,' said Campbell quietly: 'thank Heaven I am very happy, and my Nelly will not be left a beggar.' 'But you must find her a steady, hard-working young fellow for a husband,' replied I, 'to preserve all this.' 'I think,' said he, smiling, 'if you were to ask Nelly, she would tell you that that was done already.' The slightly heightened colour of the maiden was her only answer, and at that moment we reached the landing, where the negro couple and their pickaninnies were standing. The slaves were sleek and hearty, and showed their white teeth merrily.

Campbell led the way to the house, which was, for Texas, superabundantly furnished. Comfort was everywhere, and abundance. The breakfast was, to a hunter, delicious, consisting of coffee, hot corn cakes, venison steaks, and wild honey, while a cold turkey graced the centre of the board. What I enjoyed, however, better even than the breakfast, was the attention of the daughter to her blind father. He seated himself at the board, and Nelly having first helped me, supplied all his wants with a care and watchfulness which was delightful to behold. She anticipated all his desires, her whole soul being seemingly bent to give him pleasure. She was, in fact, more like a mother with a child than a daughter with a father in the prime of life. Breakfast concluded, we talked again of his history, particularly since his arrival in Texas.

The routine of the day was simple enough, as they explained to me. The negroes, overlooked by the father and daughter, worked in the fields from dawn until six in the evening, the father fashioning some rural implement, an axe or plough handle, while the daughter plied her needle. They breakfasted at half-past six, dined at half-past eleven, and supped at six: after this last meal, Nelly generally read to her father for two hours. Their library was good, including several standard works, and the four first volumes of 'Chambers's Edinburgh Journal.'

Campbell went out into the air after a while to talk to the negroes, and I was left alone with Nelly. I took advantage of his absence to learn more of her character. Never was I more delighted. Not a regret, not a wish for the busy world of which she read so much; while it was quite clear to me that her lover, whoever he was, had only succeeded by promising to reside with the father. To leave her blind parent seemed to her one of those impossibilities which scarcely even suggested itself to her mind. Yes! Nelly Campbell was a sweet creature, perhaps the only truly romantic recollection I bore with me from Texas.

I remained with them all day; I visited their whole farm; I examined Nelly's favourite retreat, in a grove at the rear of the house, and then I left them. We

* See Journal, new series, Nos. 13 and 56.

parted with a regret which was mutual; a regret which, strange to say, was quite painful on my side, and I never saw them again. Still I did not lose sight of them. I always wrote by the steamer to Nelly; and many a long letter did I obtain in reply. More and more did I discover that she was a daughter only, and that even a husband must for a time hold a second place in her heart. At length she wrote—'And now, sir, I am married, and I am very happy, though I almost sometimes regret the step, as I can no longer give my whole time to my dear blind father. He is, however, so happy himself, that I must resign myself to be less his nurse, especially as the only quarrel John and I ever have, is as to who shall wait on him. If he has lost part of his daughter, he has found a son.' This picture of happiness made me thoughtful, and I owned that, great as is the blessing of civilisation, and vast and grand as are the benefits of communion with your fellows, a scene of felicity might yet be found in the woods. Though I am a strong lover of mankind, and wish to be among them, and to enjoy the advantages of civilisation, yet do I think, if I were an old blind man, I would be a backwood squatter, with a daughter such as Nelly.

I heard no more from them, as I soon after returned to England, and the busy life of the world and other avocations have always prevented me writing. Should I, however, ever revisit Texas, my first care will be to run up the Trinity, and once more enjoy hospitality at the table of the BLIND SQUATTER.

WIENHOLT ON SOMNAMBULISM.

SECOND ARTICLE.

ACCORDING to Dr Wienholt, somnambulism is an abnormal state, in which visual impressions, or impressions tantamount to visual ones, are conveyed to the mind of the somnambulist through some other medium than the eyes. This idea, he acknowledges, is unusual, inharmonious, apparently unnatural; but he thinks there is evidence tending to prove that the function of sight has in many cases been carried on independently of the eyes. Proceeding in his inquiry with a view to exhibit this evidence, he first calls attention to the fact, that our most intimate knowledge of the physical construction of the eye gives us no information whatever as to how sight is carried on. Let the eye and the optic nerve do their utmost, it is the mind, and the mind only, that sees. In the operation which we call seeing, how much, for instance, is purely the work of judgment and long training, the idea of the size of the object looked at, its distance, &c. Again, what modifications of the organ of vision do we not observe in the animal creation, yet all apparently serving the end of simple vision. 'Most insects possess eyes; but in regard to their number, as well as their form and condition, these organs differ not only among themselves, but also from those of other animals. The eyes of the common fly, for instance, are sexangular; the spider has no less than six of these organs; and yet, judging from their operations, they appear to receive only a single perception from these various images. The chameleon moves only the one eye without the other, and can thus see before and behind, towards the sides, upwards and downwards. In birds, the eyes are placed on the sides of the head; they do not, therefore, like us, see only one object with their two eyes, but several. In the polypi, we perceive nothing analogous to our finer senses, and yet, without eyes, they manifest the most delicate sensibility to light; they are visibly affected by light and darkness; and when any nourishment comes near them, they immediately perceive it.'

All this should tend, Wienholt argues, to shake our conceit, that sight and eyes stand together in any relation closer than that of an arrangement suitable to a special condition of being. Seeing with eyes is no doubt the arrangement which we see prevailing in the present animal system; but we have no reason to believe that this arrangement is the only one which might have been adopted. Seeing in some other way than by eyes is at least not inconceivable.

Whether, however, the act of seeing without eyes has ever been performed, can be decided only by reference to authentic cases. Putting aside the cases previously cited, of difference of structure in the organ of vision, of insects, &c. the doctor refers to experiments made upon the *bat*. 'A series of recent and decisive experiments,' he says, 'has demonstrated that, in the bat, the faculty of vision continues even after the organ has been completely destroyed. Eminent philosophical naturalists, with Spallanzani at their head, instituted these experiments, and verified the fact in different parts of Italy—in Pavia, Pisa, and Turin; and in Genoa, also, they have been repeated with the same success by Spadone, Rossi, Casalli, and Turine; and no objection has been made to their accuracy. These naturalists discovered that the bat, even when blinded, regulates its motions in the same manner as when possessing the complete use of the eyes. Completely blinded bats were not in the slightest degree obstructed in their motions. They flew about by night or by day with their wonted ease and rapidity, avoiding all obstacles which lay, or were intentionally placed in their way, as dexterously as if in full possession of their sight. They turned round at the right time when they approached a wall, rested in a convenient situation when fatigued, and struck against nothing. The experiments were multiplied in the most varied and ingenious manner. A room was filled with thin twigs, in another silken threads were suspended from the roof, and preserved in the same position, and at the same distance from each other, by means of small weights attached to them. The bat, though deprived of its eyes, flew through the intervals of these threads, as well as of the twigs, without touching them; and when the intervals were too small, it drew its wings more closely together. In another room a net was placed, having occasional irregular spaces for the bat to fly through, the net being so arranged as to form a small labyrinth. But the blind bat was not to be deceived; in proportion as the difficulties were increased, the dexterity of the animal was augmented. When it flew over the upper extremity of the net, and seemed imprisoned between it and the wall, it was frequently observed to make its escape most dexterously. When fatigued by its high flights, it still flew rapidly along the ground, among tables, chairs, and sofas; yet avoided touching anything with its wings. Even in the open air its flight was as prompt, easy, and secure, as in close rooms; and in both situations, altogether similar to that of its associates who had the use of their eyes.'

Can any evidence be adduced in proof of the position, that beings of the human species, when deprived of the use of their eyes, have still continued to receive visual impressions, as these blind bats appear to have done? As a means of deciding this question, our author refers to the following well-authenticated examples of extraordinary accuracy of perception in blind persons. Diderot mentions a man who was born blind, and who was a chemist and a musician. 'He judged correctly as to beauty and symmetry; knew very well when another object came in his way; and made no mistake, in passing a street, whether it was a *cul-de-sac* or an ordinary thoroughfare. He wrought at the turning-lathe, and with the needle; took machinery to pieces, and reconstructed it, &c.

'All have heard of the famous Saunderson, the great, although blind mathematician. When only in the twelfth month of his life, he lost his sight by small-pox. He had, therefore, no more idea of light than a person born blind, and he did not recollect to have ever seen. Yet he made very rapid progress in the acquisition of languages and sciences, and, in his thirtieth year, had attained such eminence in the mathematics, that, upon Newton's recommendation, he was appointed to succeed Whiston in the mathematical chair, and became an excellent teacher. He wrote a work upon algebra, which was much esteemed by the learned; and what was the most remarkable, the blind man gave instruction regarding the laws of light, and taught optics. Every change in the state of the atmosphere, when calculated to excite visual perceptions, affected him; and he became aware, especially in calm weather, when objects approached him. One day, in a large garden, while he was assisting some astronomers in making their observations, he always knew when clouds passed over the sun. He went out with his pupils at night into the open air, and pointed out to them the situation of each star. He married his wife from love of her bright eyes. The perception he had of these could have been derived only from the touch, and this could hardly have been sufficient to inspire him with love.'

Dr Wienholt then gives a detailed account of three other cases—one, that of a Swiss peasant who went through a number of minute mechanical processes; another, that of a lady who wrote, sewed, and corrected her own manuscript; and the third, the well known case of Metcalf, the celebrated blind surveyor of roads. To these he adds that of 'Mademoiselle Paradies, the great musician. This lady, when only in the second or third year of her life, was seized with amaurosis, which entirely deprived her of sight. She never recovered; and became so blind, that she could neither perceive the lightning in a stormy night, nor the light of the sun at noon. Mademoiselle Paradies sews well, and in her early years made lace. She plays all games of cards, and is very fond of the game of skittles. Dancing is one of her favourite amusements, and she takes a part in all German and foreign dances. She is passionately fond of the theatre. In her youth, she frequently performed important characters in private companies. She is also sensible of the approach of other bodies, and judges correctly of their distance and magnitude. She clearly perceives when any larger body stands in her way. She goes about the whole house like a person possessed of sight. When chairs or tables are displaced, and stand in her way, it sometimes happens that she comes against them; but this never occurs in the case of a person. When she enters a strange room, in which she had never previously been, she perceives whether it is large, moderate, or small. When near the centre of the room, she can determine whether it is long, broad, or round. When taken to the street, she easily perceives when she passes a cross street; and this even when the air is perfectly calm. When led past a house or garden in the open air, nothing escapes her attention: she inquires to whom this house or this garden belongs. The most remarkable thing is, that she can distinguish whether a garden is surrounded by boards, walls, or stakes. Of her perception of near objects, she convinced one of her sceptical friends in a remarkable manner. He led her along a narrow path through an alley of trees, and, with a stick given her by this friend, she struck every tree in passing, drawing back her hand each time, and she did not miss a single tree out of twenty.

'Her ideas of beauty are derived from the perception of proportion in examining statues. She has much æsthetic pleasure in feeling them. This pleasure is in proportion to the beauty and correctness of the work. In the Müllerian cabinet and collection of antiques, therefore, she experiences great delight; and the observations she makes upon the objects are quite wonderful. Laughing, angry, weeping, calm and quiet countenances she recognises in a moment. She herself selects all the stuffs and colours for her clothes, and never could she be persuaded to choose a dress of green and yellow, black and green, or green and blue. Her head-dress, also, is of her own choosing; and she has her own little vanities in regard to her dress as well as any other lady. Her relations and friends, who are accustomed to her ways, often forget that they are conversing with a blind person, and it happens not unfrequently that they consult her upon objects of sight—for example, in purchasing cloth, ribbons, and flowers. They show her everything, and are not satisfied if anything displeases her. Although her eye can give her no perception of the objects around her, yet she exhibits a preference for one situation over another. The Augarten pleases her more than the Prater. She prefers Dornbach to the Augarten. There she finds purer air, waterfalls, green fields, and hills. She likes those situations best where nature presents most variety of scenery, and where the activity of the senses and the imagination is equally excited.'

The explanation usually given of cases such as these, with which the world has been long familiar, is, that in blind persons there takes place a remarkable intensifying of the remaining senses, so that the co-operation of an intenser touch, an intenser hearing, an intenser taste, and an intenser smell, frequently compensates for the loss of the eyesight. Dr Wienholt admitting the fact of an increase of the sensibility of touch, &c. in blind persons, denies that this affords a sufficient explanation of the phenomena in question. Entering into a minute examination of the various operations attributed to the blind persons above mentioned, such as distinguishing a *cul-de-sac* from a thoroughfare, discovering an error in a manuscript, going through a series of intricate mechanical processes, he argues that the supposition of an intensification of the sense of touch, or of the other senses, is totally inadequate, according to every mode of reasoning, to account for the facts; and that impressions analogous to visual ones must in some way or other reach the minds of the individuals, to enable them to act in the manner related. 'Let us only dwell a little,' he says, 'on the operations of the blind surveyor of roads. When any one, like him, traverses pathless mountains, climbs steep hills, and proceeds through deep valleys, he must have before him the respective situations of the different objects, the way he proposes to go, and that which he has already passed, and continually compare them with those notions which exist in his imagination. And in all this his sense of touch, however constantly exercised, could not be of the slightest use to him. For here he requires, at every step, a consciousness of the particular spot upon which he happens to stand, and the direction of the way by which he is to proceed farther. Without eyes, or something that can supply their place in a more perfect manner than the other senses, he would be like a mariner on an extensive open sea without a compass. Give the latter all the other means for prosecuting his voyage—let him use his sounding-line as assiduously as possible—let him observe the distance he has traversed, the nature and depth of the bottom, &c. all this will not enable him to discover his latitude, or assist him in his farther progress. For this he requires the constant use of the compass, just as the blind man, in order to keep the right direction on such paths, would require the use of his eyes. Farther, this blind traveller, in order to proceed with safety, must possess a knowledge of all the obstacles which lie in his way, by which he may avoid or surmount them. These must be present to his mind, as well as to his body; the picture of the landscape, with all its minute parts, must be constantly before his soul, and always continue in harmony with that which lies before his imagination; both must change in the same way: and here, how could his touch or any other sense assist him? Consider also his business as a guide over the snow in a dark night, when the road becomes quite different from what it was, and therefore he could derive no assistance from his previous knowledge of the localities acquired through the touch; and when it is not easy to comprehend how he, without the use of his eyes, or something that might supply their place, could find his own way, far less act as a guide for others. For this last purpose, we should not be disposed to select a man who was himself obliged to grope in the dark, and has to seek his way by feeling. Lastly, throw a glance into the soul of this man who was about to construct a road through a wild pathless district, taking the best possible direction, avoiding everything that could make a road inconvenient, difficult, or expensive, and choosing the shortest and most suitable line. What a detailed plan of the country must he not have had in his contemplation! how correct and definite must it not have existed in his mind, in order to enable him, amidst such various difficulties, to effectuate his object!'

After a great many ingenious remarks to the same purpose, Dr Wienholt concludes by saying, that 'he is entitled to hold it as demonstrated, that our soul, if it has once acquired perceptions through the medium of the eye, may afterwards, in an incomprehensible manner, and without the use of this organ, receive similar impressions, and continue to remain in the same connexion with the external world in which it had previously stood by means of light and natural vision.' And if so, he argues farther, he is entitled to suppose that 'man may also be deprived of other organs, and yet be capable of performing the same functions as he previously did only by their instrumentality.'

Now, Dr Wienholt holds that somnambulists are persons in this abnormal state, in which vision and other operations of the senses are performed in some other way than by the instrumentality of the usual organs. Natural somnambulists are those who fall naturally into this abnormal state; artificial somnambulists are those who are thrown into it by the passes, &c. of the animal magnetist.

Here the doctor leaves us; but Mr Colquhoun, in his appendix, carries us on to the consideration of the phenomena of clairvoyance, which he accounts the highest known degree of this abnormal state. The adoption of Wienholt's conclusion he regards as leading necessarily to a belief in the possibility of clairvoyance; and legitimately so; for if the somnambulist sees through his own closed eyelids, he may also see through the walls of the room he is in. The idea of opaqueness belongs only to our present arrangement for vision; and in the somnambulic arrangement for vision, in which the eyes perform no part, this idea may vanish. In the somnambulic state, also, many other of our dogmatic conceptions of nature may turn out to be mere illusions connected with our present state of being. Such is the drift of Mr Colquhoun's appendix to the lectures before us. We will not, however, attempt to follow him into this mysterious subject.

POOLE'S TALES, SKETCHES, AND CHARACTERS.

We missed this volume at the time of its publication; but it is not now too late to do justice to one who is far less known than he deserves to be. John Poole is the author of the successful play of Paul Pry. He is also a magazine writer of high acceptability. The book now under our notice* seems to have been designed as a combination of some of his most happy miscellaneous writings. It exhibits its author as a man of lively wit and playfulness, without any tincture of malice, and as a shrewd observer and clever describer of human character, with just that degree of exaggeration which is necessary for telling effect. Of all former English writers, Sterne is the one whom Mr Poole most resembles.

The first and longest paper in the volume describes a Christmas visit to Dribble Hall, the residence of a highly peculiar specimen of the English country gentleman. The author and his two friends arrive too late for dinner on Christmas eve, and the following is their reception:—

'With folded arms and outstretched legs, in a large, easy, red morocco chair, in the warm corner of the fireplace, reclined the squire. He did not rise to receive us, but welcomed us with—"Well, how d'ye do? Come, sit down without ceremony. A miserable night, eh? Sitting here in my snug corner, I didn't envy you your ride, that I can tell you. Come, sit down. Just the party I told you you'd meet. Mrs Dribble, my dear, Mr Heartall and his friend; my cousin, Mr Ebenezer Dribble; and my wife's brother and sister, Mr John Flanks and Miss Susan Flanks. Worthington, I needn't introduce you: you know everybody, and everybody knows you. Well, I'm glad you're come at last, for it is more than half-past six, and I was beginning to want my tea."

"Tea!" exclaimed Heartall; "why, sir, we have not dined!"

"Whose fault is that, then?" said the squire; "I'm sure it is not mine. I told you most particularly in my letter that I should dine at four precisely—I'm certain I did. Here, Ebenezer, take this key and open the middle door of the under part of the little bookcase in my private room, and in the right-hand corner of the left-hand top drawer you'll find a book in a parchment cover, lettered on the outside 'Copy of Letter Book.' Bring it to me, and lock the door again. I'll show you copies of my letters to you all, and you'll see I'm right."

"My dear Dribble," said Worthington, "you may spare Mr Ebenezer that trouble. The fault is neither yours nor ours; but some impediments in the city, together with the fog——"

"Well," said Dribble, "all I desire is, that you should be satisfied it is no fault of mine that you have lost your dinner. But did you take nothing by the way?"

"Oh yes," said Worthington, "we took a sandwich."

"Well, then," rejoined the squire, "you wont starve." This he uttered with a chuckle of delight, as if at the consequent escape of his larder. "However," he continued, "we'll do the best for you, under the circumstances; instead of supping at ten, we'll order supper to be served at a quarter before."

"To speak the truth, Mr Dribble," said Heartall, "I am exceedingly hungry, and I believe so are my travelling companions: we have had a very uncomfortable ride, and——"

"Oh, in that case," replied Dribble, "perhaps you'd like something to eat. Well, I'll order tea, for I can't wait any longer for my tea; and Sam shall bring up a slice or two of something cold for you to take with your tea. Or, if you would prefer a glass of ale with it, say so. Here, Sam; here is the key of the ale barrel: draw about—let me see—one, two, three of them—ay, draw about two pints, and bring me the key of the barrel again."

"I never drink ale, sir," said Heartall.

"Nor do I, sir," said I.

"Oh, don't you?" said the squire. "Why, then, if you prefer wine you can have it; only I think you had better not spoil your supper. It is fair to tell you we have a hot roast turkey for supper. I'm very fond of a hot roast turkey for my supper—in fact I always have one for my supper on Christmas eve."

"Hadn't we better order tea in the drawing-room," said Mrs Dribble, "and leave the gentlemen to take their dinner quietly in this?"

"Nonsense, Mrs Dribble!" angrily exclaimed the squire: "it is no dinner, but a mere snack. Besides, where is the use of lighting a fire in the drawing-room at this time o' night? Pray, madam, don't interfere with my orders." Then, addressing himself to us, he continued—"Perhaps you would like a little hot water up stairs whilst they are putting your snack on a tray?"

'The "snack on the tray" was particularly emphasised: no doubt, with the humane intention of saving us from

* Christmas Festivities: Tales, Sketches, and Characters. With Beauties of the Modern Drama, in Four Specimens. By John Poole, Esq. London: Smith, Elder, & Co. 1845.

the mortification of any disappointment which our own wild expectations of a more profuse collation might otherwise have occasioned.

'We readily accepted the offer of the hot water, and Sam was ordered to conduct us to our room.

"Stop!" cried our host, as Sam was preparing to marshal us the way; "stop—there is no fire in any of your rooms; but as I always like to have a fire in my own dressing-room in such horrid weather as this, perhaps you might find it more comfortable to go there."

'Admiring this delicate attention on the part of our "considerate" host, we accepted the offer "as amended." As we were about to move forward, Sam nodded and winked at his master, at the same time twitching the sleeve of his fustian jacket. The squire put a key into his hand, accompanying it with an injunction that he would carefully lock the door, and bring him the key again. On entering the dressing-room, this mystery was explained by Sam's unlocking one of his master's wardrobes, and taking from it his own dress livery coat, which the former always kept under lock and key, and which, upon this occasion, he had forgotten to leave out.

'After as comfortable a toilet as the time would admit of, we re-descended to the dining-room—our expectations of a merry Christmas not much enlarged by the manner and circumstances of our reception.

'The family were taking their tea; and, on a table in a corner of the room, we found a very inefficient substitute for what ought to have been our dinner; for the squire's directions had been rigidly followed. The repast consisted of nothing more than a few slices of cold boiled veal served on a tray, and (as we had declined his ale) the remains—somewhat less than half—of a bottle of sherry. Worthington's "I hope so," which struck me at the time as being of a very suspicious character, was now shown to deserve the worst we might have thought of it. To despatch such a provision, where the duty of so doing was to be divided amongst three hungry travellers, did not require a very long time; and the moment Squire Dribble saw that the last drop was drained from the decanter, he did not ask whether it would be agreeable to us to take any more, but desired Sam to "take all these things away, and bring a card-table."'

Rigid regulations, all formed with a view to his own comfort, and from which no hospitable feeling will admit of the slightest departure, painfully remind the reader that Mr Dribble is not entirely a fancy sketch. It is, in fact, that pure selfishness, under the mask of regularity, which is often met with in unaccommodating persons. In the morning, after a sleepless night in a chilling bed-room, the author is roused by his host.

'"Not stirring yet, sir?" cried the squire. "Why, sir, it is almost nine; I have been up this hour, and want my breakfast; I always breakfast at nine."

"Then pray, sir," said I, with an unaffected yawn, "pray get your breakfast, and don't wait for me. This is much earlier than my usual hour of rising. Besides, I have not slept well, and there is nothing peculiarly inviting in the weather. I will take some breakfast an hour or two hence."

"Pray get up, my dear sir, and come down stairs, or the rolls will be cold; and I can't bear cold rolls. Now do get up: I hate—that's to say, Mrs Dribble hates to see breakfast about all day long; and" (continued my kind-hearted, considerate host) "you would find it very uncomfortable to take breakfast in your own room 'without a fire'—for it is a bitter cold morning. I'll tell Sam to bring you some hot water."

'Away he went; and not long after came Sam with hot water—Sam informing me that his master (polite creature!) had instructed him to say that he could not be so rude as to sit down to breakfast till I came—nor could the ladies. This hint was of course decisive: so, greatly to my dissatisfaction, I arose; and (having dressed with as much speed as the discomforts of my position would allow) with a blue nose, shrivelled cheek, and shivering from head to foot, I descended to the breakfast-parlour.

'Scarcely had I time to salute the assembled party, when I was thus addressed by the squire:—

"A late riser, eh, sir? We have nearly finished breakfast, but no fault of mine. You know I called you in time, and I told you I wanted my breakfast. You must be earlier to-morrow though, as you'll start at eleven. But come, my dear sir; what do you take? I'm afraid I can't recommend the tea, but I'll put a little fresh into the pot if you wish it? However, here is plenty of coffee, and" (putting his fingers to the coffee-biggin) "it's nice and warm still. The eggs are all gone, but you can have one boiled on purpose for you, if you like—or what say you to a slice of the cold veal? I believe you found it excellent yesterday? I should have made my breakfast of it, if I had not had my broiled leg of the turkey. I had just finished eating it as Mr Worthington and Mr Heartall came down: for they were rather late-ish like yourself."

'Freezing as I was, this was no time for the exercise of an overstrained delicacy, which would have inflicted upon me cold veal and cold coffee; so I requested to have some hot tea and an egg.

"Then bring me the tea-caddy again, Sam," said Squire Dribble somewhat peevishly; "and here, take the key and get an egg out of the cupboard—or two—and let them be boiled. Be sure you lock the cupboard again, and bring me the key. And, Sam—come back. Put a ticket into the basket for the two eggs you take out, or I may make a mistake in my egg account."

'The squire made some fresh tea, and in due time poured it out for me; for Squire Dribble gallantly relieved his lady from the performance of all the onerous and unfeminine duties of the breakfast table—such as making and pouring out the tea, serving the coffee and cream, distributing the eggs, and doling out the portions of whatever else there might happen to be—by taking them upon himself.

'When Sam returned with the eggs, he brought along with him the newspaper, which had just arrived.

"Give that to me," said Dribble, who had not quite finished his breakfast. So, taking it from the hands of the servant, he, without offering it to any one else, put it beneath him, and sat hatching it till he himself had leisure to read it.

"It is an odd fancy of mine," said the squire; "but I would not give a farthing for my newspaper unless I see the first of it." This was a reason sufficient to reconcile the most fastidious to the proceeding.'

The entire two days at Dribble Hall form an inimitable unique picture, for which we would commend our readers to a perusal of the book, as sufficient in itself to remunerate them for their trouble. In the hope of their following our advice, we may point out Sir Harry Skurry and Pompenius Ego as sketches particularly worthy of their attention; nor may they be the worse of knowing that the clap-trap nautical drama of Dibdin, the intense ruffian-labourer style of Morton, and other favourites of the playgoing public, are most successfully burlesqued in the concluding part of the volume. Perhaps, however, the most mirth-provoking part of the book is an anecdote which has a remarkably real appearance, under the title of *Secrets in all Trades*. The author, meeting a stranger in a country churchyard, recognises Burley, the late landlord of an inn he used to frequent near Cambridge, but now, it appears, retired to enjoy the fruits of his industry. Falling into a confidential discourse about the way in which this worthy conducted his business, the author receives from him a most luminous and satisfactory account of his wines.

'"You can't deny it, Burley; your wines, of all kinds, were detestable—port, Madeira, claret, champagne—"

"There now, sir! to prove how much gentlemen may be mistaken, I assure you, sir, as I'm an honest man, I never had but two sorts of wine in my cellar—port and sherry."

"How! when I myself have tried your claret, your——"

"Yes, sir—*my* claret, sir. One is obliged to give gentlemen everything they ask for, sir: gentlemen who pay their money, sir, have a right to be served with whatever they may please to order, sir—especially the young gentlemen from Cambridge, sir. I'll tell you how it was, sir. I never would have any wines in my house, sir, but port and sherry, because *I knew them* to be wholesome wines, sir; and this I will say, sir, my port and sherry were *the very best* I could procure in all England——"

"How! the *best?*"

"Yes, sir—*at the price I paid for them.* But to explain the thing at once, sir. You must know, sir, that I hadn't been long in business when I discovered that gentlemen know very little about wine; but that if they didn't find some fault or other, they would appear to know much less—always excepting the young gentlemen from Cambridge, sir; *and they are excellent judges!*" [And here again Burley's little eyes twinkled a humorous commentary on the concluding words of his sentence.] "Well, sir; with respect to my dinner wines I was always tolerably safe: gentlemen seldom find fault at dinner; so whether it might happen to be Madeira, or pale sherry, or brown, or——"

"Why, just now you told me you had but two sorts of wine in your cellar!"

"Very true, sir; port *and* sherry. But this was my plan, sir. If any one ordered Madeira:—From one bottle of sherry take *two* glasses of wine, which replace by two glasses of brandy, and add thereto a slight squeeze of lemon; and this I found to give general satisfaction—especially to the young gentlemen from Cambridge, sir. But, upon the word of an honest man, I could scarcely get a living profit by my Madeira, sir, for I always used the best brandy. As to the pale and brown sherry, sir—a couple of glasses of nice pure water, in place of the same quantity of wine, made what I used to call *my delicate pale* (by the by, a squeeze of lemon added to *that* made a very fair Bucellas, sir—a wine not much called for now, sir); and for my old *brown* sherry, a *little* burnt sugar was the thing. It looked very much like sherry that had been twice to the East Indies, sir; and, indeed, to my customers who were *very* particular about their wines, I used to serve it as such."

"But, Mr Burley, wasn't such a proceeding of a character rather——?"

"I guess what you would say, sir; but I knew it to be a wholesome wine at bottom, sir. But my port was the wine which gave me the most trouble. Gentlemen seldom agree about port, sir. One gentleman would say, 'Burley, I don't like this wine—it is too heavy!' 'Is it, sir? I think I can find you a lighter.' *Out* went a glass of wine, and *in* went a glass of water. 'Well, sir,' I'd say, 'how do you approve of *that?*' 'Why—um—no; I can't say——' 'I understand, sir, you like an *older* wine—*softer;* I think I can please you, sir.'—Pump again, sir.—'Now, sir,' says I (wiping the decanter with a napkin, and triumphantly holding it up to the light), 'try this, if you please.' 'That's it, Burley—that's the very wine; bring another bottle of the same.' But one can't please everybody the same way, sir. Some gentlemen would complain of my port as being poor—without body. In went *one* glass of brandy. If that didn't answer. 'Ay, gentlemen,' says I, 'I know what will please you—you like a fuller bodied, rougher wine. Out went *two* glasses of wine, and in went *two* or *three* glasses of brandy. This used to be a *very* favourite wine—but *only* with the young gentlemen from Cambridge, sir.

"And your claret?"

"My good wholesome port again, sir. Three wines out, three waters in, one pinch of tartaric acid, two ditto orris-powder. For a fuller claret, a little brandy; for a lighter claret, more water."

"But how did you contrive about Burgundy?"

"That was *my claret*, sir, with from three to six drops of bergamot, according as gentlemen liked a full flavour or a delicate flavour. As for champagne, sir, that *of course* I made myself."

"How do you mean 'of course,' Burley?"

"Oh, sir," said he, with an innocent yet waggish look; "surely everybody makes his own champagne—*else what* CAN *become of all the gooseberries?*"

IMPROVEMENTS IN LONDON.

There is scarcely a city in Europe in which improvements are more required, or so reluctantly undertaken, as in London—a city to which history will point as the metropolis of the world, and marvel that she tolerated within herself so many evils, originating in selfishness and short-sightedness, and perpetuated by the operation of the same causes down to our own time. The evils here complained of are those of imperfect or insufficient channels of communication between one part of the great city and another; the existence of densely-crowded districts, untraversed by direct or available thoroughfares; and the pertinacity with which the 'rights of property' are allowed to militate against the 'rights of society.' While we cannot refuse to acquiesce in the statement of the Committee of Metropolitan Improvements, that 'the alteration of an ancient city, with a view to adapt all its streets and buildings to the increased wants and improved habits of modern times, is a work of much greater difficulty and expense than the construction of a new town,' we are at a loss to account for the improvements, in too many instances, being planned as the readiest means of overcoming a difficulty, rather than what they really *ought* to be, as the great commercial channels of a mighty city.

On reference to a map of London, it will be seen that the general direction of the principal thoroughfares has been influenced by the course of the river on which it is built, from the seat of government and fashion on the west, to the seat of commerce, the Royal Exchange, and Port, on the east. These thoroughfares are, however, not more numerous, and but little more convenient, than they were two hundred years ago, while the population has increased sevenfold, and the traffic augmented to a degree that almost defies calculation. The consequence is the continual obstruction of the streets, confounding the already existing confusion, and creating dangers where before there were only difficulties. Let any one walk from Temple-Bar to the Exchange, at any time of the day, but particularly between the hours of two and four, and he may verify the truth of these observations. On arriving at a crossing, the chances are ninety-nine to one against his finding the smallest opportunity of passing over under a delay of a quarter of an hour; while the noise, the jostling, cursing, and shouting around him, are absolutely deafening. Suppose him at length arrived in safety at the west end of Cheapside, he finds not only the traffic of the line along which he has come, but that also of the parallel or Holborn line, pouring into this *one* channel, while the resistless tide advancing from the opposite direction, here diverges to the two main lines in its progress westwards, creating a scene which, for confusion and effect, cannot be paralleled by any other city in Europe. He fights his way along Cheapside to its east end, the Poultry, contracted suddenly to some twenty-five feet in width, through which the four conflicting streams struggle in intense embarrassment; and having reached the open space fronting the Mansion-House, may rest for a few minutes to afford time for the evaporation of the surprise which he must inevitably feel on seeing that a narrow street of the Plantagenet era is expected to suffice for the rushing tide of life, pleasure, and commerce of the age of Victoria. It is possible that the capacity of the Poultry Market may have been sufficient for the times when Edward III. rode through it with his court to the 'joustings in Chepe,' or led the procession from the Tower, with his fair Mistress Alice, the Lady of the Sun, to witness the 'passage of arms' in Smithfield. Wheel carriages were then not used, nor to any extent in immediately subsequent periods. We read, however, that in 1631 complaints were made that the streets were 'encumbered;' and yet the same thoroughfare remains, apparently for no other purpose than that of exasperating 'drivers,' endangering passengers, and perpetuating absurdity.

We must not, however, forget that something has been done towards diminishing or removing the evils we have attempted to describe; and we regard the recent opening of new streets as indicative of a movement which will not stop short of effectual amelioration. The line from Piccadilly through Coventry Street into Long Acre opens a new channel midway between the two great thoroughfares referred to above, which it will beneficially relieve of a portion of their traffic, and prove of the highest public utility, if farther extended to one of the leading lines, instead of terminating, where it does at present, in Drury Lane. But when we consider that the plans for this improvement were first submitted to the committee in 1837, we cannot help thinking that some very powerful antagonistic influence must have been at work to prevent its completion, or rather commencement, for a period of nearly ten years. It is, however, gratifying to observe that the new streets are not to be left to the convenience or the caprice of individual builders, for the display of architectural abominations or abortions, but are to be built on a regular plan, which will contribute materially to the effect of the new lines. Although the committee tell us that they regarded mere 'embellishment as a matter of subordinate importance,' we find that the houses already completed in New Coventry Street are in a light and pleasing style, with just enough of ornament to relieve what would otherwise be a dull mass of brick and mortar. The same observation will apply to the junction of the new portion of Oxford Street with Holborn, where the houses have red brick fronts with white stone 'dressings,' and form altogether an architectural improvement that will be a real 'embellishment' to that quarter of the metropolis. But we regret that the facts prevent our speaking favourably of the new opening from the Strand by Bow Street to Holborn, originally contemplated as an important thoroughfare in an almost direct line from Waterloo Bridge to the British Museum, which a culpable spirit of parsimony has diverted from the proposed direction. It is, however, possible that we are indebted for the break in the route to the evidence given before the committee in favour of *diagonal* crossings, which, it was asserted—with a blindness that could only be equalled by that of the old woman who put a big stone into the empty pannier on one side of her donkey, to make it balance the full one on the other—were preferable to *direct* crossings, especially when the convenience and safety of foot passengers were taken into the account. Will it be believed that a parliamentary committee, sitting in the nineteenth century, would listen to or tolerate such nonsense, or to that which denies that the presence of an ungainly block of buildings, such as that standing in Holborn, near Gray's Inn, and by which a broad thoroughfare is suddenly contracted from a width of one hundred feet to that of forty feet, is any inconvenience? And yet it would appear that, by a blind fatality, it is precisely on such evidence as this that the plans for some improvements which would be real public benefits, whether as regards business, health, or convenience, are converted into lasting monuments of stinginess and error. There would be some excuse for all this, were it inevitable: but will any one believe for a moment that a saving of a few thousand pounds should be weighed against the improvement of a city like London, whose local revenue is L.3,000,000 sterling? 'There are some things which can only be well done when done on a large scale. They not only require large means, but unity of purpose.'

If we compare what has been done in London with what might have been done, or with what really has been done in other places, we shall find that the metropolis is the 'slowest,' as well as one of the most antiquated cities, and might learn a useful lesson from many comparatively humble examples. The writer of the present article, during a residence in New York, once had occasion to leave that city for the country, just at the time that an important improvement had been determined on; and on his return at the end of *six months*, found that an unsightly and loathsome mass of buildings had been cleared away, and replaced by a broad and handsome street half a mile in length, which opened a serviceable line of communication between the northern and southern portions of the city. In this case the money was raised by assessment on the wards most benefited by the improvement, and although complaints were made of the unequal pressure of the tax, yet the work was carried on with all the spirit of a people who know what utility means, and are wise enough to act upon that knowledge. Other instances might be brought forward, were further proof required, to show that, if so much can be done with restricted means, the inhabitants of London have not the shadow of an excuse for tolerating her monster evils.

Here, however, measures are dreamed over for many years before those who have the power wake to the necessity of action; and then how much delay must be incurred in the adjustment of conflicting claims, and the settlement of preliminaries. Sometimes the refractoriness of one individual is allowed to derange a well-arranged plan, or supersede it altogether. We willingly concede all that can be reasonably urged in favour of the rights of property; but common sense is sometimes to be preferred to prescription; and does the simple position of houses on certain portions of land constitute a sufficient reason for the eternal toleration of a nuisance or formidable inconvenience? It is matter of notoriety how summarily railway companies possess themselves of the property of belligerent country gentlemen, when it is necessary for their purposes. Could not some such process as this be applied to city improvements? Or is there a sacredness in outrageous evils, which inspires a dread of laying violent hands upon them?

In the report of the parliamentary committee on this subject, there are many other new streets contemplated, which, if completed, would make London architecturally what she is now commercially. Among these are a new line from the Bank to the Post-office, a little to the north of Cheapside; one from St Paul's to Blackfriars Bridge; from Southwark Bridge to the Mansion-House; from King William Street to the Tower and the Docks, which are now connected solely by narrow, crooked, and inconvenient thoroughfares; from Oxford Street, through Clerkenwell, to Shoreditch Church; and from Westminster Abbey to Belgrave Square. The line from the London Docks to Spitalfields Church, as well as the further extension of Farringdon Street northwards, are now in actual progress, and these, with the others, are not to be regarded solely with reference to the facilities of intercourse which they will afford; for they will intersect, in the words of the report, 'some districts in this vast city through which no great thoroughfares at present pass, and which, being wholly occupied by a dense population, composed of the lowest class of labourers, entirely secluded from the observation and influence of wealthier and better educated neighbours, exhibit a state of moral and physical degradation deeply to be deplored;' but, 'whenever the great streams of public intercourse can be made to pass through districts such as these, the cure of this lamentable evil will speedily be effected. The moral condition of these poorer occupants must necessarily be improved by immediate communication with a more respectable inhabitancy; and the introduction, at the same time, of improved habits and a freer circulation of air, will tend materially to extirpate those prevalent diseases which are now not only so destructive among themselves, but so dangerous to the neighbourhood around them.'

We have thus every variety of argument—moral, physical, and pecuniary—brought to bear upon the question; we trust that all will not be swamped in the purely selfish. We are pleased to see that the Victoria Park, in the neighbourhood of Spitalfields and Bethnal Green, is approaching completion, as, from its extent—nearly 300 acres—it will afford scope for health, exercise, and recreation, to the inhabitants of a district notorious for its squalor, and remoteness from any similar strolling ground. On a board at one end of the enclosure is written the words Victoria Park; some wag has, however, erased the name of royalty, and substituted 'Weavers'.' We hope this is an indication that those who toil at the loom through dreary days and weary nights, value the advantage offered to them, and will be prepared, with their wives and children, to do their best to enjoy it.

We have said nothing of the new Royal Exchange, of Trafalgar Square, or fountains and statues, as they do not properly belong to the object of the present paper; although we may look upon them as an earnest that more will be done some day, as their existence proves that the difficulties which lay in their way were not insurmountable. But we repeat, that what is to be done must be done on a great and comprehensive scale; a bit by bit reform by various unconnected and irresponsible bodies will not do: we want the resources and authority of legislative supervision. And here we may call attention to the improvement which has, within the last few years, taken place in Paris (where the evils arising from want of space are greater than in the most crowded parts of London), which is so striking, and the method pursued leads to so few complaints, as to hold out the promise of a rapid advance in the same direction. A comprehensive plan of the city, accessible to the public, and approved and sanctioned by the municipal authorities, indicates the improved and widened lines of streets, to which houses, when rebuilt, must conform; and in their tortuous and narrow thoroughfares are to be seen, from distance to distance, new houses built, or being built, from five to ten or fifteen feet back from the old frontage, and in such directions as (when all the old houses shall have been rebuilt) ultimately to present regular instead of the existing tortuous lines, which, by the irregular projection and retreating of the houses, interrupt the traffic, and impede the free sweep of the winds.

If some such far-seeing measure as this were adopted in London, we should not hear of the ruinous delays in the purchase of vacant lots along the contemplated lines. Notice has frequently been given to the commissioners that certain pieces of ground are for sale; but no attention was paid to the fact until the lot was let and a house built upon it, and then they bought it. A case of this kind occurred on the Coventry Street line, where a lot which, in the first instance, was offered for L.1400, was afterwards purchased for L.5000. It strikes us also that if the new lines were planned to *cross* instead of to *follow* existing streets, an economical advantage would be gained, as the expense of removing a few houses on each side to form the opening, would be much less than that of removing one whole side; while the general utility of the line would not be at all affected by this arrangement.

We are fully aware of the difficulty of moving an immense population like that of the metropolis, where two millions of human beings are shut up in a 'province' of 251,000 houses. But the prospective advantages are so great, that they may fairly be allowed to weigh against a present sacrifice. 'London, in its most fashionable localities west of Regent Street, gives but a faint indication of what the whole metropolis might become, and with it every town in England, if the duty of promoting public health, and of checking all abuses of local administration, were made cabinet questions, in lieu of many others which absorb the time and energy of party leaders.'*

THE ARCHÆOLOGICAL MEETING AT WINCHESTER.

[The following letter, from a lady in London to a friend in the country, giving an account of the late meeting of archæologists at Winchester, has been handed us for publication.]

* * * I must tell you that of late there has been a revival in London of a taste for antiquities of all kinds—old furniture, old carvings, old coins, old houses, old castles, old churches; in short, every object of art which happens to be of a considerably past date. It is now a kind of fashion to show a love of antiquities, and as the taste is taking a practical turn, and introducing a finer order of architecture, with domestic furniture and ornaments to match, the reign of Victoria I. in England bids fair to rival that of the illustrious François Premier in France, and be remembered as the age of the *renaissance*. As it would never do for Uncle Philip and his family to be behind their neighbours in this universal rage, we have all become great antiquaries, and look with much interest on the proceedings of the two associations by which the taste is cultivated. Do not suppose from this that we leave evening parties to go to dull meetings, where long prosy papers are read; for nobody in their senses would think of doing anything half so absurd. The meetings we attend are very nice affairs. They take place annually at the dull time of the year, when not a soul is in London, and always at some delightful old-fashioned town, where there are plenty of ancient churches, old halls, and such curiosities to be overhauled. Last year we went to the meeting of the association at Canterbury, and had some very pleasant jaunting about its neighbourhood; this year we attended the meeting of the seceding association (now to be called the British Archæological Institute) at Winchester, where there were likewise some agreeable out-of-door proceedings, as well as in-door assemblies. I need hardly tell you that such meetings help greatly to rub up the gentry in these towns, and tend to establish acquaintances, of a lasting and pleasant kind, between strangers and natives.

Having thus opened the subject, I may try to entertain you with a short account of the meeting which took place at Winchester, from the 9th to the 14th of September last, to which we proceeded from the Isle of Wight, where we had been rusticating for a few weeks. On settling ourselves in lodgings, and making a few inquiries, we found the means of admittance to all the daily meetings, for every two persons, to be simply the purchase of a ticket, price one pound: so this was soon arranged. Early on the morning of Tuesday the 9th, the usually dull aspect of the streets and lanes of Winchester was considerably changed. On walking out, we observed numerous important-looking gentlemen bearing rolls of paper in their hands, and hurrying to the St John's Rooms in St John's House, where the meeting was appointed to be held. We soon followed, and on admission, found ourselves in a spacious apartment, now used as the assembly-room, which, however, in days of yore, had been the refectory of the hospital dedicated to St John the Baptist. The walls on the present occasion were hung with a fine collection of articles, collected from various old churches in the country. At twelve o'clock the Marquis of Northamp-

* Westminster Review, June 1845.

ton, president of the association, took the chair, in the midst of a goodly number of men eminent in church, state, and science.

The first thing done was the delivery of an address on the pleasures and advantages of cultivating a taste for antiquities, by Dr Wilberforce, the dean of Westminster; and I need hardly say that he was throughout listened to with both attention and delight—the effect being heightened by a sweet deep-toned voice, which the dean inherits from his father. He concluded by observing that, while casting aside all fanatical love of what was absurd in past times, it was our duty to reverence what had in its day been great and noble. 'Let us,' said he, 'love to look into the old past; let us visit the scenes of its departed greatness, not to array ourselves in its worn-out customs, but that, having ears to gather up the whispers of their oracular advices, we may, by our own skill in art, fashion for ourselves the outward circumstances we need.' Dr Whewell, master of Trinity College, Cambridge, having seconded the vote of thanks to the eloquent dean, launched forth on the merits of the study of architecture, related how much be himself owed to the labours of Rickman, who, he said, had done for Gothic architecture what Linnæus had done for plants. While still a schoolboy, 'Rickman's Gothic Architecture' had fallen into his hands—it became to him a grammar and dictionary of a new language, and this language he endeavoured to impart to his fellow-collegians. He looked back with extreme pleasure to this incident in his life, and its consequences; and he looked forward with delight, in the hope that this meeting might be attended with the same agreeable and valuable consequences; for the study of architecture was not a mere mental amusement, but a most profound and valuable mental culture—a branch of culture which would soon dissipate all prejudices respecting it, and clothe the dry bones with hue and colour.

Dr Williams (the warden of New College, Oxford) remarked, that as holding a high appointment in William of Wykeham's college, he might be allowed to express how much gratified he felt in seeing so brilliant a company assembled to aid the study of that science in which that great man excelled. He hoped that, instructed by the information which he might derive, he might hereafter look with more intelligent eyes on scenes so familiar to him, and with gratitude towards those who had aided him in better estimating the character of that great man. At three o'clock, parties were formed to visit the ruins of Wolvesey Castle, the museum in the deanery, and the church and hospital of St Cross. We first went to Wolvesey Castle, so called from King Edgar's obliging Ludwell, a refractory Welsh prince, to deposit here annually three hundred wolves' heads. It was built by Henry de Blois, bishop of Winchester, and brother to King Stephen, in 1138. The ruins now remaining are supposed to have belonged to the keep; they are built of large flints, faced with a thick coating of hard mortar, giving it the appearance of freestone. Until Oliver Cromwell's time, it continued to be the abode of the bishops of Winchester; it was then demolished, and, some years after, the present Episcopal palace was raised close to the former site. The museum of archæological curiosities, arranged for the present occasion in the library at the deanery, was contributed by different members of the association, and included many rare antiquities: a series of enamels of exquisite workmanship, fine impressions of seals, also a variety of embroidered ecclesiastical vestments—one we particularly noticed, upon the hood and orfrais of which the twelve apostles were represented. The crowd here was so great, that we soon left it for St Cross, one mile distant from Winchester. We walked by the clear silvery stream of the river Itchen, and we all agreed that if the pilgrimages of ancient days were even one-half so delightful, those engaged in them were more to be envied than pitied. The day was superb; and on our entering the quadrangle, one side of which is formed by the church, quite a gay scene greeted our eyes—knots of ladies and gentlemen standing upon the very green grass, and small groups of the quiet happy-looking old men, the brethren of the hospital, dressed in their Sunday gear. This hospital was built in 1136 by Henry de Blois for thirteen resident brethren, a master and steward; and 100 poor honest men were to have a plentiful dinner every day. Owing to the rapacity of the master, the original intention of the founder became perverted in process of time, until William of Wykeham restored the charity, and repaired the buildings. A certain portion of good wheaten bread and beer (rather small) is given every morning to the porter, for the refreshment of such poor travellers as may apply at the gate. Most of the archæologists claimed it, but for myself, not being curious in that respect, I was content to take the testimony of others regarding the quality of the dole. The church was erected at the time when Gothic architecture was beginning to be ingrafted on the Romanesque; therefore it gives a valuable lesson in the transition of style from Roman to Gothic. It is a cruciform building, and, although small, possesses all the features of a collegiate or conventual establishment. The intersecting arches in the trifanum are very curious. The refectory is entered by a flight of steps from the large quadrangle: it has a tower on one side, and the master's residence on the other. It is adorned with rich Gothic windows, and at the east end a raised floor for the table of the officers, the brethren being placed at the side. There is also a raised hearth in the middle of the floor, and a gallery at the west end, from whence the chaplain pronounced the benediction at dinner time. After a full inspection of this curious establishment, we returned to Winchester.

At the eight o'clock general meeting, the Rev. John Bathurst Deane read a most interesting paper on Avebury, Carnac, Stonehenge, and other primeval temples. He entered at length into the spirit, rites, and ceremonies of Druidical worship: he thinks the circle and semicircle indicate the joint dedication to the sun and moon, and showed good reason why the large artificial hill at Avebury, known as Silbury Hill, should not be regarded as having been a barrow, but as a place for burning the sacred fire during the performance of the service within the sacred circles of stones. The architecture of the hospital of St Cross and Romsey Abbey church formed the subjects of two other papers. Wednesday morning, long before the appointed hour (half-past eleven), St John's large room was crowded; every one being anxious to get a good place, in order to hear the very popular and pleasing lecturer, Professor Willis, descant upon the architectural history of the cathedral. He repudiated the idea of any of the Saxon foundation of Ethèlwold remaining, and attributes the earliest portion to the time of Walkelyn, the Norman bishop appointed by William the Conqueror. Now, continued he, we know for certain that the centre tower of the building fell not long after the interment of William Rufus in the choir of the cathedral, in consequence, as it was then believed, of this king's wickedness, and his having died without receiving the last rites of the church. Walkelyn died before William, so he could not have rebuilt the tower, but as he left money for repairing the church, it was most likely done out of his funds. The tower-piers of the present edifice are the largest in England—a great deal too much so for architectural elegance, and for the weight they were required to carry; therefore I think they were erected by a people labouring under a panic: a people determined to erect an edifice not likely to fall for a long time. These piers are as much too large as the others had been too small; and it was from the faults thus committed on both sides that the mediæval architects learned those true and beautiful proportions which were now so admired by all who viewed them with any interest. The plan of the crypt showed that Walkelyn's choir was the same size as the present. From examinations that had been made under the auspices of members of the association, a bed of concrete had been found, which proved that it had been originally intended to have towers at the west front, making the nave fifty feet longer than at present. In 1262, according to a manuscript in Queen's College, Oxford, Bishop Luez built the aisles and vaulting outside the Lady Chapel. In 1370, Bishop Edington left a sum of money for the completion of the nave. In 1357, William of Wykeham was appointed architect by that bishop. The professor then read a long extract from William of Wykeham's will, showing what he had done, and what he wished to be done with the money he left for beautifying the church. When this admirable lecture was concluded, the professor said he would be happy to explain, to as many as would honour him with their company in the cathedral at four o'clock, the various peculiarities and parts of that splendid building. Mr C. R. Cockerell read an elaborate paper on St Mary's College, Winchester, and New College, Oxford, wherein he highly eulogised the great talent displayed by William of Wykeham in the architectural beauty of these two colleges, of which he was at once the founder and architect. Early in the afternoon, almost all the members (and our party amongst the number) visited St Mary's College. This was very appropriate, as all its beauties had just been pointed out by the able lecturer, who accompanied us here also. It is a noble pile, and the chapel a perfect bijou in architecture: its groined ceiling in wood is considered the most elegant specimen of its day. The east window is very curious; in its gorgeous stained glass is portrayed the genealogy of our Saviour. Jesse is laid across the very centre of the bottom, 'the root;' three small kneeling figures near his head are known to be the likenesses of the surveyor, carpenter, and glazier of this noble edifice. The library of the college is situated in the area of the cloister; until 1629, it was a chantry or chapel for the dead. It now contains some very curious books. One I was much entertained with, entitled, 'A Briefe and True Report of the New-Found Land of Virginia; of the Commodities, and of the Nature and Manners of the Natural Inhabitants, discovered by the English Colony there seated by Sir Richarde Greinuile, Knight, in the yeare 1583.' The engravings are very strange. This book was printed at poor Sir Walter Raleigh's expense. On the principal desk lay a large book, wherein were inscribed the names of all the benefactors of the college, and a list of their gifts: some were not very costly. The school-room is modern in comparison with the rest of the college, only dating from 1687. It is a noble apartment: at the east end the laws to be observed by the students are inscribed in Latin on a tablet, and upon a corresponding one at the west end are the following devices and inscriptions:—

Aut Disce.	A mitre and crosier.	The expected reward of learning.
Aut Discede.	An inkhorn, a case of mathematical instruments, and a sword.	The emblems of those who depart and choose a civil or military life.
Manet sors Tertia, cædi.	A scourge.	The lot of those who will qualify themselves for neither.

The Latin implies, 'Either learn or depart; a third chance remains, to be beaten.' The moveable desks, which shut up, called *scobs*, form, when raised, a sort of screen from the noise of the adjoining student. William of Wykeham endowed this college for a warden, ten fellows, three chaplains, three clerks, a master, an usher, seventy poor scholars, and sixteen choristers. After more than four centuries, it still flourishes in all its original importance. I must not forget the refectory and buttery hatch: in the centre of the former is a large hearth, the roof immediately over it being higher than the rest: the sides are perforated, to discharge the smoke. A large mahogany box with a ponderous padlock daily receives the fragments of the dinner, which are immediately doled out to a certain number of poor women, with the addition of some good beer. This beverage, the bread, butter, and cheese, are dispensed from the buttery hatch, which is separated by a screen from the dining-room: the allowance is most liberal.

At the time of our visit, the boys happened to be cricketing in their playground, from which the spot on a neighbouring hill was pointed out to us where the celebrated song of *Dulce Domum* was composed. The boy author who thus tried to solace his grief at being refused permission to go home at Christmas, died of the disappointment. At the commencement of every vacation, his song still reverberates through the schoolroom, as all the boys sing it, accompanied by a full band. From William of Wykeham's college we adjourned to the cathedral to hear Professor Willis's peripatetic lecture. He moved from the lady chapel to the transept, and from thence to the choir, aisle, and nave, explaining as he went the different alterations. In the evening we attended a brilliant soirée, kindly given by the dean to all the members of the association, as well as to the nobility and gentry of the neighbourhood. The noble apartments of the deanery were well lighted, and the refreshments most *recherché*. Amongst the company, which amounted to four hundred, were such a host of distinguished men as could rarely be seen collected together. The drawing-rooms were once the great hall of the priory which was attached to the cathedral. There is a floor now placed between them and the roof, which forms a commodious suite of bedrooms. We went up stairs to see the fine arches, which doubtless were originally filled with stained glass. Thursday morning, at ten o'clock, owing to the accumulation of papers, two supplementary meetings were held in the county courts, formerly the hall of the castle of Winchester. The historical and mediæval section took place under the presidency of Mr Hallam, who, in his brief opening address, remarked, that although there are some defects belonging to the English historical school, yet its distinctive character is remarkable accuracy, arising from the patient and business habits of the people, which produce a more just appreciation of evidence than is usual among our continental neighbours. Mr Smirke read a most interesting paper on the building in which the meetings were then convened, and upon its noble ornament, King Arthur's Round Table, which is placed on the wall of the Nisi Prius Court, just over the judge's seat.

Mr Kemble read a paper on Saxon surnames, and showed, from an extensive and interesting series of examples, how the names of our Anglo-Saxon forefathers were derived from their rank, pursuits, and occupations, and their qualities of mind or body. Next, Mr Hudson Turner read a paper on the ancient customs and usages of St Giles Fair, near Winchester, and then the meeting dispersed, in order to visit the abbey church of Romsey. The section of Early and Mediæval Antiquities, held at the same time as the preceding, was presided over by the well-known Egyptian traveller, Mr Hamilton. The dean of Hereford gave a detailed account of researches made under his superintendence at the ancient Roman station at Kenchester, near Hereford. He described the numerous traces of buildings, mosaic and other pavements, of which he exhibited drawings. He connected the introduction of Christianity into this kingdom with Caractacus, who, he said, was a prisoner in Rome at the same time with St Paul, and whose daughter Claudia is mentioned by that apostle in his second epistle to Timothy, chap. iv. 21. She was the wife of Pudens, also spoken of there. Short papers were then read by Mr Bloxam on Roman burial-places, and by Lord Alwyn Compton (son to the noble president) on encaustic tiles. Mr W. H. Thoms read a most curious essay on coronals of roses as badges of honour, and on the golden rose annually blessed by the pope. Mr Thoms thought that kings bestowing coronals of roses on those whom they delighted to honour, was only a regal copy of the custom which prevailed at Rome. He gave a long list of those upon whom the pope was pleased to bestow this mark of consideration; amongst the number, Henry VIII. received it from Julius II. in 1510; Philip and Mary from Pope Julius III.; and the king of the Belgians this year from the present pope. As soon as the sections were over, we drove to Romsey abbey church, eleven miles from Winchester. *En route* we passed through several pretty villages, the cottages of the labourers being everywhere decked in flowers.

Of the abbey founded at Romsey in the reign of Edward the elder, not a trace remains. The church is of the same class as that at St Cross, and displays an instructive mixture of the peculiarities and style of various successive periods. The Rev. J. L. Petit and Mr Cockerell explained the plan of the edifice. In all the excursions two or three gentlemen, learned in architectural lore, invariably acted as cicerones to as many different parties. In the external wall of the south transept is a curious sculptured figure of Christ on the cross, about five and a half feet high, with a hand from the clouds above pointing to it; and near it is evidence, that to one of the masons who repaired the wall, 'reading and writing did not come by nature,' the word *who* being built into it, turned upside down, evidently part of a tombstone. I felt a peculiar interest in this church, as our Princess Matilda, daughter to Malcolm III., was educated here by the Benedictine nuns, who were then in possession of the abbey. The Hon. Gerard Noel, the vicar, is now restoring it to its ancient splendour, and has contributed himself nearly two thousand pounds. Mr Albert Way collected seventy pounds by begging from every one on this occasion for the same purpose. Lord Northampton took drawings of the most curious arches, and asked questions which elicited much information: his lordship always looked as if he were engaged just upon a matter or subject chosen by himself. This evening a public dinner took place at the St John's Rooms, which was attended by 170 members of the association.

Friday morning, at half-past nine, we all left Winchester by railway, some for Porchester Castle, others for Southampton, Netley Abbey, or Beaulieu Abbey. Our party went to Southampton, and from thence crossed over the river to Netley Abbey. Little now remains but the east window and southern transept to tell of the glories of its once magnificent church. The kitchen, chapter, and refectory, may still be distinctly traced, but in complete ruin. It was once beautifully mantled o'er with ivy; but although the removal of this covering has detracted from the beauty of the ruin, yet one must rejoice, as it induces decay. Several trees have sprung up amongst these mouldering walls, adding much to the beauty of the place. After satisfying our curiosity, we set off for Porchester Castle, distant about thirteen miles. On the way, we passed some fine old seats and pretty village churches. Porchester Castle is one of the most interesting ruins in England; it was the Portus Magnus of the Romans, under whose walls their galleys lay for 400 years. It was also the chief fort of Britain, and the origin of the dockyard at Portsmouth. The walls of the *enceinte* are perfect, and built on Roman foundations; the Norman keep is likewise nearly so; and there are considerable remains of buildings of the fifteenth century. French prisoners, to the number of about 8000, were confined here during the revolutionary war. After the fall of the French West India possessions, the garrisons of St Vincent and other islands, chiefly emancipated negroes, were imprisoned here, and, sorrowful to relate, many hundreds died from cold during the ensuing severe winter. The floors which were temporarily laid for the prisoners are now pulled up; but the large holes into which they were fastened remain open, and the spots are well marked where the chimneys once smoked. Awful scenes took place here during the residence of the French, as they took advantage of the slightest remissness to attack the sentinels, in the hope of escaping. The church in the quadrangle is a fine Norman structure, originally cruciform, but the south transept is destroyed. The west front is very rich, and has undergone less alteration than any similar structure in England of the same date. It was the church of the priory founded by King Henry I. within the walls of the castle, and removed twenty years after to Southwick, distant three miles. We all enjoyed our trip very much, and returned by railway from Foreham to Winchester, where it was necessary to despatch dinner quickly, in order to get to the St John's Rooms in time to hear the Rev. C. H. Hartshorne's paper 'On the Architecture and Peculiarities of the Fortress and Church at Porchester,' which he illustrated by elaborate drawings of all the Roman stations round the coast. John Gough Nichols, editor and proprietor of the Gentleman's Magazine, read a curious paper, developing the secret history of a passage in the lives of Margaret, Duchess-dowager of Savoy, regent of the Netherlands, daughter to the Emperor Maximilian, and Charles Brandon, Duke of Suffolk. Two of the lady's letters proved they had been contracted whilst he was under promise to marry another: and the sequel of the story is still more extraordinary; for notwithstanding this double nuptial engagement, the duke actually married a third lady, Mary, sister to Henry VIII., and dowager-queen of France.

Saturday morning, again at the County Courts. Sir Thomas Philips, Bart. read a manuscript account of the magnificence and various pageants which took place at the marriage of the Duke of Burgundy with the Princess Margaret, sister to Edward IV., king of England. Mr Hawkins (British Museum) delivered an instructive address upon the 'Ancient Mint and Exchange of Winchester.' All our mints are taken from the Greek, particularly from Macedon; during the sway of the Romans in Britain, their money circulated here; after their departure, it became very spurious. King Athelstan was the first sovereign who cared to have a pure or good coinage. The Saxons had the name of their king on one side of their money, and that of the moneyer on the other. Winchester was of so much importance formerly, that, whilst there were eight moneyers appointed for London, there were six for that city. The coinage became so much adulterated in Henry II.'s time, that he issued a command that all the moneyers should assemble in Winchester, and be there tried for their evil-doings; three men alone were found to have acted honestly, and, to the honour of Winchester, they were her sons. They attained great esteem, whilst all the rest were condemned either to lose an eye or an ear as a punishment for their malpractices: 1248 appears to be the latest date of the money coined at Winchester. After leaving the court-house, we visited the subterranean passage which has been recently opened: it appears to have commenced near the north-west end of the County Hall; and, descending into the earth in an eastern direction, branches off into two distinct passages, one running into the town, the other most probably terminating without the outer wall. It was the private entrance into the castle either from the town or country, when siege or other circumstances rendered necessary a secure and secret admission into this stronghold of arbitrary power. It is a lofty and ample passage, built solidly of stone, with the remains of flights of stone steps, affording easy egress and ingress. The gentleman to whom it belongs kindly had it illuminated.

At two o'clock we again assembled, having had only one hour's respite, when several papers on churches were read, one particularly good, by A. J. Beresford Hope, Esq. M.P., on the priory church at Christchurch, Hants. The last paper I shall notice at this sitting was one which brought out a great number of curious customs which obtained formerly in England. It was entitled 'The Ancient Parliament at Acton Burnell,' in Shropshire, and was by Mr Hartshorne. 'This little village, picturesquely placed near the Stretton Hills in Shropshire, and contiguous to a Roman road, is remarkable in its history, as possessing buildings that illustrate the ecclesiastical and domestic architecture of the time of Edward I., and for having been the spot where a parliament had been assembled in the thirteenth year of his reign, that has given rise to a discussion on the constitutional formation of our early national conventions that still admits of consideration.' Henry III. gave it to Robert Burnell, the clerk of Edward, his eldest son, in 1265. Nicholas Burnell, the descendant of this Robert, was the cause of a very curious heraldic dispute in the Court of Chivalry with Robert de Morley, on account of the arms that Nicholas bore in right of certain lands of the barony of Burnell, bestowed on him by his mother. De Morley and Burnell being both arrayed in the same arms at the siege of Calais in 1346, the latter challenged the arms as belonging to the Burnells only, having at the time under his command a hundred men, on whose banners they were displayed. The dispute was referred to the Court of Chivalry, held on the sands before Bohun, Earl of Northampton, high constable of England. It lasted several days, finally terminating by the king himself requesting Lord Burnell to permit Robert de Morley to bear the arms in dispute for his life only, which Nicholas assented to. The judgment on this question was given in the church, and immediately proclaimed by a herald throughout the whole army.

The dean gave us all much pleasure this evening, by permitting the cathedral to be opened for one hour, from eight until nine o'clock, and a few lights to be placed in it. The effect was truly beautiful; the lofty arches, with the 'long drawn aisles' dimly seen through the obscure light, with the pealing tones of the organ, reminded me so strongly of the great days of the Roman church, that I almost fancied I heard the deep voices of the monks chanting their midnight mass. From the cathedral we adjourned to St John's Rooms, and were much edified by Dr Whewell's paper on the distinction of styles in architecture in general, and their names. It was read by Mr Petit, as the writer had taken his departure. Several other interesting matters were brought before the meeting; and at nearly twelve o'clock, we all separated rather tired.

Sunday morning, at ten o'clock, the gorgeous cathedral was filled to overflowing, and the service was, as is usual here, admirably performed. The voices of the choristers in chanting were very fine, and, with the reading of the dean, the whole was a treat which I shall not soon forget.

Monday, at noon, the indefatigable marquis again took the chair. The room was crowded; the chief business being to pass votes of thanks to different societies and individuals who had aided the association, and to fix the next place of meeting. The number of subscribing members was mentioned by Mr Albert Way as amounting to 700. Lord Northampton then drew attention to the causes of the division in the association, read part of his correspondence with Lord Albert Conyngham, and descanted on the terms proposed to the other party. Then came a discussion on the next place of assemblage; when York was finally fixed on; after which, various complimentings took place. The dean of Winchester was most happy, both in his address to the president and members of the body. The Marquis of Northampton, having agreed to take the chair for the ensuing year until the general meeting, when he hoped they would have some person connected with the locality to take the office, and under whom he should be proud to act as vice-president, dissolved the meeting amidst general cheers.

Thus ended this pleasant meeting, and with it the most delightful week I have passed for a long time; and although, my dear * * *, I must have sorely tried your patience, yet, as it has afforded me so much pleasure, I could not refrain from imparting a share of it to you. By four o'clock, Winchester was again left to its former dulness, and we set off for Salisbury, the cathedral of which town has been frequently paired with that of Winchester. The former being airy, light, and graceful, has been compared to the lady; while the latter, ponderous, majestic, and massive, has been called the gentleman. I must now bid you farewell, hoping that, although you may not be entertained by this long epistle, yet that you may have learned something by it. And remain yours, &c.

PHYSIOLOGY OF GENIUS.

It is noticed by a writer who was present at a meeting of the British Association, that one feature was nearly universal among the philosophers there assembled; namely, a certain expansion of the head, which habit teaches us to connect on all occasions with superior intellect. This is an observation which we have often made at the meetings of learned societies; and we have further remarked, that the fact is *more* frequently to be noticed among men of science—as naturalists, experimental chemists, &c.—than among purely literary men. Whatever may be said of the internal capacity, thickness of skull is, we apprehend, no mark of mind either way. That of Buchanan is said to have been as thin as paper. On the other hand, the brain-case of Porson, the first Greek scholar of modern times, was discovered to be exceedingly thick. Gall, on being required to reconcile Porson's tenacious memory with so thick a receptacle for it, is said to have replied—'I have nothing to do with how the ideas got into such a skull; but once in, I will defy them ever to get out again.'

If there be any feature in which genius always shows itself, it is the eye, which has been aptly called the index of the soul. 'We have seen,' says Mr Jerdan, 'every other part of the human face divine without indications of the spirit within—the mouth which spoke not of the talent possessed, and the brow that indicated no powers of the capacious mind—but we never knew a superior nature which the eye did not proclaim.' The Greeks and all the Oriental nations regarded the brightness of the eye as a supernatural sign. The emerald eyes of their gods shone with mysterious splendour through the gloom of the Adytum. Availing themselves of this prevalent belief, impostors have sought to deceive men by an assumed lustre of countenance. Dr Leyden tells us that Ibn Makna, the founder of the Maknayah sect, hid himself from the public gaze, and covered his features with a veil; asserting that no eye could endure the glory of his countenance. To support this deception, he prepared some burning mirrors, placing them in such a situation that the rays fell upon the faces of those who approached him. Having taken these precautions, he uncovered his face, and directing his votaries to draw nigh, the foremost were struck by the burning rays, and retired exclaiming, 'We cannot look upon him, but he gazes upon us.' Many tender and beautiful things have been said of eyes; yet how inferior to the sweet things uttered by themselves! A full eye seems to have been esteemed the most expressive. Such was the eye that enchained the soul of Pericles. The American writer Haliburton declares he would not give a piece of tobacco for the nose, except to tell when a dinner is good; nor a farthing for the mouth, except as a kennel for the tongue; but the eye—'study that,' says he, 'and you will read any man's heart as plain as a book.'

Galileo's eyes were remarkably penetrating; so were those of Linnæus, which were hazel, and possessed that exquisite power of vision which naturalists are generally noted for. Alexander Wilson's eyes were quick, sharp, and intelligent, especially when he was engaged in conversation. This ornithologist visited, when in New York, the celebrated Thomas Paine, author of the 'Rights of Man,' and describes him as possessing a Bardolph kind of face; 'but the penetration and intelligence of his eye bespoke the man of genius and of the world.' Shelley's eyes were noted for their beauty. Otway had a thoughtful, speaking eye. Sir Humphrey Davy had 'a glowing eye, the finest and brightest,' says Lockhart, 'that ever I saw.' Colley Cibber's eyes were small, but all vivacity and sparkle. When reciting any great deed, Sir Walter Scott's eye, and his whole countenance, would kindle with a congenial expression. A native of Weimar, describing Goethe, says, 'his eyes were like two lights.' Hazlitt had an expressive eye. Coleridge's greenish-gray eyes were very quick, yet steady and penetrating. Audubon, speaking of Bewick, says he had 'a large head, with fine sparkling eyes, placed farther apart than those of any other man that I have ever seen.' To draw a phrenological inference from this observation, it may be concluded that Bewick possessed, in a most wonderful degree, the organ of form, which is indicated by the breadth between the eyes, or, which is the same thing, by the breadth of the bridge of the nose. The same peculiarity is observable in a celebrated living author, Mr Thomas Carlyle, whose eyes are placed at an unusual distance apart, and their spiritual intensity of expression is extraordinary, being only equalled in this respect by those of Leigh Hunt, which are singularly fine and expressive, tinged with a watchfulness and melancholy which persecution has put into them, but without dimming the cheerfulness with which the heart and mind ever light them up.

Many authors have been remarkable for excessive mildness of countenance. This was the case with Milton. In some very touching and affectionate verses, Spenser has recorded the gentle benignity of Sir Philip Sidney's countenance, which formed the correct index of his temper. His voice was so sweet and agreeable, that by one of his contemporaries he is styled nectar-tongued Sidney. The countenance of Kirke White was rendered particularly interesting by an air of great humility and patience.

Byron says nothing is so characteristic of good birth as the smallness of the hands. We believe, however, that small hands are not nearly so common among noblemen, especially those who are addicted to active field-sports, as among authors, whose fists are rarely employed in any other work but holding the pen, and therefore do not attain to a large and muscular development. Miss Costello, describing Jasmin, the poetical barber, not only notices his 'black sparkling eyes, of intense expression,' but 'his handsome hands.' Mozart, though not vain of having written the 'Requiem,' was rather conceited about the proportion of his hands and feet.

Ugo Foscolo has left us a circumstantial and rather flattering description of himself, written in Italian, from which the following is translated :—

A furrowed brow, intent and deep sunk eyes,
  Fair hair, lean cheeks, are mine, and aspect bold;
The proud quick lip, where seldom smiles arise;
  Bent head and fine-formed neck; breast rough and cold,
Limbs well composed; simple in dress, yet choice:
  Swift or to move, act, think, or thoughts unfold;
Temperate, firm, kind, unused to flattering lies;
  Adverse to the world, adverse to me of old.
Ofttimes alone and mournful. Evermore
  Most pensive—all unmoved by hope or fear:
By shame made timid, and by anger brave—
  My subtle reason speaks; but ah ! I rave;
'Twixt vice and virtue, hardly know to steer;
  Death may for me have fame and rest in store.

RETENTIVE MEMORIES.

Magliabecchi, the founder of the great library at Florence (himself no author, but the collector of many), had so wonderful a memory, that Gibbon styled him 'la memoire personnalisée'—memory personified. At one period of his life, Seneca could repeat two thousand words precisely as they had been pronounced. Gassendi had acquired by heart six thousand Latin verses, and the whole of Lucretius's poem, De Rerum Naturâ. In order to give his memory sufficient exercise, he was in the habit of daily reciting six hundred verses from different languages. Saunderson, another mathematician, was able to repeat all Horace's odes, and a great part of other Latin authors. La Croze, after listening to twelve verses in as many languages, could not only repeat them in the order in which he had heard them, but could also transpose them. Pope had an excellent memory, and many persons have amused themselves by looking through his writings, and pointing out how often he had brought it into play. He was able to turn with great readiness to the precise place in a book where he had seen any passage that had struck him. John Leyden had a very peculiar faculty for getting things by rote, and he could repeat correctly any long dry document, such as a deed or act of parliament, after having heard it read; but if he wanted any single paragraph, he was obliged to begin at the commencement, and proceed with his recital until he came to what he required. There was a French novelist who, being, like our Richardson, a printer, composed a volume in types, and thus the book was printed without having been written. Bishop Warburton had a prodigious memory, which he taxed to an extraordinary degree. His 'Divine Legation' would lead one to suppose that he had indefatigably collected and noted down the innumerable facts and quotations there introduced ; but the fact is, that his only note-book was an old almanac, in which he occasionally jotted down a thought. Scaliger obtained so perfect an acquaintance with one Latin book, that he offered to repeat any passage with a dagger at his breast, to be used against him in case of a failure of memory.

THE ADVENT OF TRUTH.

A TIME there is, though far its dawn may be,
  And shadows thick are brooding on the main,
When, like the sun upspringing from the sea,
  Truth shall arise, with Freedom in its train ;

And Light upon its forehead, as a star
  Upon the brow of heaven, to shed its rays
Among all people, wheresoe'er they are,
  And shower upon them calm and happy days.

As sunshine comes with healing on its wing,
  After long nights of sorrow and unrest,
Solace and peace, and sympathy to bring
  To the grieved spirit and unquiet breast.

No more shall then be heard the slave's deep groan,
  Nor man man's inhumanity deplore ;
All strife shall cease, and war shall be unknown,
  And the world's golden age return once more.

And nations now that, with Oppression's hand,
  Are to the dust of earth with sorrow bowed,
Shall then erect, in fearless vigour, stand,
  And with recovered freedom shout aloud.

Along with Truth, Wisdom, her sister-twin,
  Shall come—they two are never far apart—
At their approach, to some lone cavern Sin
  Shall cowering flee, as stricken to the heart.

Right shall then temper Justice, as 'tis meet
  It should, and Justice give to Right its own :
Might shall its sword throw underneath its feet,
  And Tyranny, unkinged, fall off its throne.

Then let us live in hope, and still prepare
  Us and our children for the end, that they
Instruct may those who after them shall heir,
  To watch and wait the coming of that day.

—*Poems by William Anderson.* 1845.

THE SOUTH AMERICAN BAMBOO.

The *guadua*, or South American bamboo, abounds in many of the tropical parts of that continent, forming rather large groves along the banks of the rivers. This is a gigantic species of cane, growing to the height of ninety feet, and frequently even more, with a beautiful feathery appearance. The upper part bends gracefully downward, and is covered with long slender branches, which spring from the joints, and bear very small light leaves. This cane is extremely useful for the purpose of building houses and bridges, as well as for fencing plantations, and surrounding the *corrals* or cattle pens, as it resists the weather for many years. The thickest parts serve for beams, posts, and rafters. They are also formed into broad planks, by being split open longitudinally with an axe, and spread out, by cutting through the alternate joints at sufficient distances to allow of their hanging together. In this state they answer very well for roofing and for flooring the upper storey, which is that which is generally inhabited in the marshy districts. The guadua also serves for making bedsteads, tables, and benches, which are both light and neat. The walls of the houses are made of the small branches, tied closely together, fastened with thin thongs of raw hide, and plastered over with clay. The thickest canes, being frequently eight or nine inches in diameter, are made into buckets, by cutting off joints for that purpose. Small barrels are also made in the same way. The guadua is also in great demand for building bridges across the narrow rivers in the plains.—*W. Wittich.*

Published by W. and R. CHAMBERS, High Street, Edinburgh (also 98, Miller Street, Glasgow); and, with their permission, by W. S. ORR, Amen Corner, London.—Printed by BRADBURY and EVANS, Whitefriars, London.

☞ Complete sets of the Journal, *First Series*, in twelve volumes, and also odd numbers to complete sets, may be had from the publishers or their agents.—A stamped edition of the Journal is now issued, price 2½d., to go free by post.

CONDUCTED BY WILLIAM AND ROBERT CHAMBERS, EDITORS OF 'CHAMBERS'S INFORMATION FOR THE PEOPLE,' 'CHAMBERS'S EDUCATIONAL COURSE,' &c.

No. 98. New Series. SATURDAY, NOVEMBER 15, 1845. Price 1½d.

VISIT TO THE ABERDEEN SCHOOLS OF INDUSTRY.

One morning lately I found myself crossing the Firth of Forth on a journey northwards, which had for some time hung on my mind as a thing which must be sooner or later accomplished. It was a self-imposed mission to Aberdeen, for the purpose of making myself acquainted with a class of humble institutions possessed by that city. To undertake a journey of a hundred miles, in the raw weather of October, merely to see two or three charity schools, may appear somewhat Quixotic. But nothing which is really useful is altogether ridiculous. The schools to be examined, though obscurely nestling in the heart of a distant northern town, had been more than once spoken of in the interesting reports of the Inspector of Scottish Prisons, as not only meritorious in themselves, but likely to prove extensively useful, if made as generally known as they deserved to be. Behold me, then, on this expedition. Crossing the Firths of Forth and Tay, I had afterwards a long and not very agreeable ride; but the pleasure of a couple of days' loitering amidst the hospitalities of old Bon-Accord, were more than a compensation for all deficiencies in the journey—a couple of rainy days included.

Before saying a single word on the objects of my inquiry, I may allude to what is doubtless a very observable and lamentable feature in all our large towns—the number of poor ragged children, apparently homeless and parentless wanderers, who, like troops of wild animals, roam about our streets, begging for morsels of food, or whining for the more acceptable donation of a halfpenny from the better-dressed passengers. Against these urchins the police wage a constant but ineffectual war. Committing no precise statutory offence, the law has a difficulty in dealing with them very severely. When brought before a magistrate accused of begging, the ready reply is, 'that they did it because they had nothing to eat.' Pursuing the inquiry, it is probably discovered that their parents are in the most abject state of poverty, or perhaps so lost to all sense of decency, that, whatever be their means, they think it no disgrace to send out their children daily to pick up a precarious subsistence in the streets. Perplexed, and in some degree distressed with these revelations, the magistrate dismisses the complaint. The police, aware of what is next to ensue, still watch the progress of the culprits. It requires little foresight on their part to discover that children of eight or nine years of age, sent out day after day to beg their bread, will acquire habits of restless idleness, which will unfit them for steady industry; and that by nothing short of a miracle can they avoid becoming habitual and reputed thieves. Reaching this stage in their miserable career, they fall within the legitimate scope of the statutes made and provided for the punishment of crime, and now the magistracy are able to see their line of duty more clearly before them. Hitherto, the culprits may be said to have been below the law: now, they have grown up to it. The law has been waiting patiently for the event, and it has at length arrived. Appearing on a charge of theft, they are sent to prison, where, so far as relates to personal comfort, they are infinitely better off than in their own miserable dwellings. Although for a time they have lost their liberty, they are not exposed to the pangs of hunger. The term of imprisonment expires before they have thoroughly imbibed the lessons of industry, morality, and religion inculcated; and when dismissed, they very naturally resort to their former practices, with the knowledge that the jail is not the terrible place it has been represented to be. Undeterred from crime by confinement, they are often found inmates of the same prison two or three times in the course of a year. All is of no use. They are, according to police notions, incorrigible. Admonitions from judges on the bench, admonitions from teachers and preachers in prison, threats of transportation, and, it may be, the gallows, go pretty much for nothing. Advancing from smaller to greater crimes, they usually finish as shop or housebreakers; and, coming before the higher tribunals, they are sent to close their miserable existence in the hulks or penal colonies.

That such is the ordinary rise, progress, and termination of the career of these numerous juvenile vagrants whose presence afflicts society, is too notorious to require any verification. Where the poor-law chances to be administered in a benign and comprehensive spirit, the spectacle of infant mendicants and thieves is less flagrant than in those places where its efficacy is little better than a sham; but as a general fact, the thing is incontestable. I know of no town, at least in the northern part of the United Kingdom, in which the condition of the poor and their offspring has not, up till the present moment, been a scandal to a Christian community.

This great and growing evil has not been unnoticed by the more philanthropic portion of society. Private benevolence, stepping forward where public duty had been remiss, has done much to lessen the amount of juvenile pauperism, as is testified by the variety of hospitals, houses of refuge, and such-like institutions. Nevertheless, all helps put together, leave not a little to be done. Beggar children are still seen in the streets, and until that social malady disappears, crime, as a matter of course, must continue to flourish. The reader will now be prepared for understanding the full value of the institutions which fell under my observation in Aberdeen. They are schools got up for the express purpose of extinguishing juvenile mendicancy; *and they have done it.*

Towards the end of the year 1841, it became a matter of painful remark in Aberdeen, that, notwithstanding all that was done by the ordinary means for suppressing mendicancy, there were still two hundred and eighty children under fourteen years of age known to maintain themselves by begging, having no other visible means of subsistence; and that seventy-seven children, of whom only about one-half could either read or write, were, within the preceding twelve months, inmates of the prisons. In other words, there were, out of the mass, seventy-seven children already advanced to the criminal stage, the others making a daily progress towards it. The announcement of these startling facts roused inquiry, and led to a subscription for the purpose of establishing a school of industry, in which pauper boys, from eight to fourteen years of age, might receive daily shelter, food, work, and education. The school was opened on the 1st of October 1841, the pupils consisting partly of homeless boys from the house of refuge, and partly of boys who were gathered from the lowest haunts in the town. From the amount of funds subscribed at the time not exceeding L.100, the committee felt it necessary to limit the number of admissions to sixty. The primary claim to admission was destitution, and that claim, once established, entitled the boy to attend the school, and to receive food and education in return for the profits of his labour. During the first six months, 106 boys were admitted, and the average daily attendance was 37. Afterwards, the average increased to from 40 to 50. The removal of so many boys from the streets not only occasioned a perceptible diminution in the swarms of street beggars, but the superintendent of police reported that, subsequent to the opening of the school, a considerable decrease in juvenile delinquencies had taken place. This was corroborated by the Inspector of Prisons, who, in his seventh report to parliament, observes that 'during the half year ending 20th May 1841, 30 boys under fourteen years of age were committed to prison in Aberdeen; but that during the half year ending 20th May 1842, the number was only six.' This marked success led to the establishment, in 1843, of a similar school for girls; which proved equally efficacious. The apparatus for extirpating juvenile mendicancy and crime, however, was not yet complete. Children who, from bad character, or some other cause, could not be received into either of the schools, remained unprovided for; while many parents, who made profits by their children begging, withdrew them, and the streets continued to be infested by the worst description of juvenile mendicants, almost all of them being known to the police as common thieves. It was evident that an additional institution was desirable, and that it should be conducted on the broadest principle of admission. A school of industry on a new plan, supplementary to the others, was accordingly resolved on.

This school, quite novel, I believe, in Britain, was opened on the 19th of May in the present year. On that day the authorities, taking advantage of powers in the local police act, issued instructions to seize and bring to this new school of industry every boy and girl found begging. Upwards of seventy children were brought in. Instead of being treated as criminals, they were washed, fed, given some little instruction, and when dismissed in the evening, were informed that they might or might not return next day, but that it was resolved that street-begging should no longer be tolerated. Nearly all came back voluntarily; and so on from day to day has the school ever since been in operation, the average attendance being about fifty. The expectations of the benevolent founders of the institution were to the utmost extent realised. Not a begging or vagrandising child was to be seen in the streets, nor, as far as general observation goes, has there been till the present day. I was sorry to learn that great financial difficulties were experienced in establishing this interesting school. Sceptical of its success or utility, the public did not readily contribute funds for its support, and the whole money in hand when it was begun amounted to no more than L.4. Some aid, however, was obtained from the police authorities: they pay a male and female police officer, who act as teachers; and the institution was fortunate in obtaining the gratuitous use of a vacant soup kitchen and its appendages, which answer as cooking and school-rooms. From this localisation, it is known as the soup-kitchen school.

On the day after my arrival, I made a round of visits to these different schools, commencing with the school of industry for boys, to which I have first alluded. Occupying a species of garret in an old building near the house of refuge, it owes nothing to exterior or internal decoration; but with that I was the better pleased. The too common practice of lodging abject pauper children in fine houses, is in my opinion fraught with the worst consequences. In this garret, which was large, clean, and airy, I found nearly fifty little boys, of the ordinary ragged class whom one is accustomed to see roaming about the streets. They were seated around the place, at a proper distance from each other, in perfect silence, under the eye of a superintendent; and were occupied, some in teasing hair for mattresses, some in picking oakum, and others in making nets. To relieve the irksomeness of the employment, they occasionally sing in full chorus; and to give me a specimen of their powers in this respect, they all struck up a hymn, in a style at least equal to what is usually heard in country parish churches. Next, a bundle of copy-books was laid before me; and a few, who seemed to be a kind of novices, not yet fully trained, gave me a specimen of their reading powers. Beneath, was a room fitted up with benches, which answers as school and eating-room; and here, on my second visit, I saw the whole at dinner, each with a hunch of bread and tin of barley broth before him—the food being supplied from the adjoining house of refuge.

The discipline of the school is a happy blending of instruction with exercise and industrial training. The pupils meet at seven o'clock in the morning; first, they receive religious instruction suited to their capacities, after which their attention is directed to the elements of geography, and the more striking facts of natural history, till nine o'clock. On two mornings of each week, an hour is devoted to instruction in vocal music. From nine to ten they get breakfast, which consists of porridge and milk. At ten they return to school, and are employed at different kinds of work till two in the afternoon. From two to three they dine, usually on broth, beef, and bread; occasionally on potatoes, soup, &c. From three to four they either work within doors, or, if the weather permit, are employed in the gardens partly in recreation. From four to seven they are instructed in reading, writing, and arithmetic. At seven they get supper, same as breakfast; and are dismissed to their homes for the night at eight o'clock. A half holiday is allowed on Saturday after dinner, and on other days the half of each meal hour is allowed for recreation; and occasionally, when other arrangements allow, and the conduct of the scholars appears to deserve it, an hour or two is devoted to out-of-door exercise. On Sunday morning, the scholars assemble at half-past eight o'clock, get breakfast at nine, attend public worship in the house of refuge during the forenoon, and after dinner return home, to enable them, if so disposed, to attend church with their relations. At five o'clock they meet again in school, and are catechised; get supper at seven; and are dismissed as on other days.

The labour to which the scholars are put, such as teasing hair and net-making, is of a light nature, requiring no great exertion, and does not seem by any means irksome. At net-making several boys have acquired great expertness, and can easily earn a penny an hour. If a sufficiency of this kind of employment could be procured, the school would soon be self-supporting. Unfortunately, this is not the case; and, as a general average, the amount of each boy's earnings is at present about 28s. per annum; such, however, being exclusive of the profits of a garden, which, if taken into account, would make the yearly earnings nearly 30s. This sum is inadequate for the support of the institution, which, therefore, on its present footing, requires public assistance. During the past year the expenditure was L.309, and the earnings L.95; the sum actually required for the maintenance of the establishment being thus L.214.

On the whole, the spectacle of this little colony of workers was satisfactory. A peculiar feature, remarked by every visitor of the school, is the order and quiet contentment manifested by the boys, and the interest with which they seem to pursue their several occupations. Acquiring habits of industry, they are gradually prepared for employment in the factories, to which, when the proper time arrives, they have little difficulty in gaining admission. And such we might naturally expect to be a result of the training here acquired. There is evidently a virtue in labour, which cannot be secured by mere theoretic teaching; and I only lamented, on leaving the institution, that means are not formed for considerably extending the field of its operations.

The next school to which I was introduced was the female school of industry, situated in a more open part of the town, and in a house of more extensive accommodations. This institution, which I visited several times, is conducted under the auspices of a body of ladies, and superintended by a resident female teacher and assistant. The pupils, about fifty in number, are gathered from the humblest homes in the city. The routine of labour is more various, and perhaps more practically useful, than that of the boys. Besides being taught to sew, they assist in cooking and other household operations, and therefore may be said to be in a course of preparation for entering domestic service. Neat, clean, and orderly in appearance, and under moral and religious instruction, I should expect that the aim of the foundresses of the institution would be fully realised. The produce of the sewing done in the school helps to meet the current expenditure. After the instructions and labours of the day, the pupils are dismissed to their respective residences for the night. On Sunday they attend church in a body, dressed in garments which remain with, and belong to the institution. At this, as well as the other schools which I visited, the principal reading-books appeared to be favourite numbers of the work edited and published by my brother and myself under the title of 'Chambers's Miscellany of Useful and Entertaining Tracts.' Stitched in strong brown paper, they were described as forming an exceedingly acceptable species of class-books, and I was satisfied, by cross-questioning the pupils, that they really comprehended and took an interest in what they read.

The last of my visits to the female school of industry was in the evening on the occasion of the inmates being treated to tea and some musical entertainments by the lady patronesses, as a reward for good conduct; and it was gladdening to see the pleasure which universally beamed in their rosy countenances. It has been on divers occasions observed of this institution, that the plan of dismissing the children every evening, and sending them home to the wretched, if not polluting homes of their parents, must be calculated to root out any beneficial impressions made on their minds during the day; but while there may be some truth in remarks of this kind, it admits of the most conclusive evidence that, as a general principle, home lodgment is attended with the best effects. Domestic affections continue in activity; the child is delighted to return home at night, and to repeat the lessons and rules of conduct learned at school; and frequent instances have been known of a decided improvement in the character of the parent through the humble efficacy of the child. Each little girl may be considered a species of missionary of civilisation, reaching and influencing the most miserable hovels. I was informed that it is a matter for observation, that the houses of the parents of these children were in general much more cleanly than others of a similar class. Such are some of the practical benefits of this well-directed institution.

The school next in order to which my attention was directed, was that under the charge of the police in the soup kitchen. Here, as I said before, compulsion was the primary agent of attendance; the streets being daily swept of every begging child, each of whom, on being caught, was forthwith marched off to school. Such, it appears, were the attractions of warmth and daily food, that in a short space of time attendance became not only voluntary, but as regular as at any of the other schools in town. I found forty-six children, of an age varying from seven or eight to twelve or thirteen years, divided into two separate classes—the boys under a male, and the girls under a female instructor. Seated in an orderly manner on benches, the boys were picking oakum, and the girls were in the course of receiving lessons in sewing. The plainest elements of reading and writing, with religious knowledge and singing, are the sum of the general education. They are received at eight o'clock in the morning, and dismissed at half-past seven in the evening; having, during the day, in the intervals of labour, instruction, and exercise, received breakfast, dinner, and supper—the food, which is cooked in the premises, being of the same plain kind as is dispensed at the house of refuge. The children in this school had a much less tidy appearance than those in either of the other schools I visited; yet there seemed nothing like discontent. All were cheerful at their allotted tasks, and on the teacher raising the note, they set off in a hymn with becoming spirit. One could not contemplate the scene presented by the well-filled apartment without emotion. Nearly fifty human beings rescued from a life of mendicancy and crime—the town rid of a perplexing nuisance—private and public property spared—and the duties of courts of justice reduced almost to a sinecure!*

Considering the manifest advantages of this very interesting school, it is a subject of regret that it continues to experience financial difficulties which threaten to bring it to a close. The loan of the soup kitchen being only during pleasure, and likely to be withdrawn in the course of the approaching winter, and there being no funds wherewith to hire any other apartments, the school is not expected to maintain its footing many weeks longer. This is a result, however, which, it is to be trusted, the Aberdonians will not suffer to come to pass. Yet on private benevolence neither this nor the other schools ought to be thrown. If it be the duty of the state to pay for the *punishment* of crime, should it not with equal reason pay for its *prevention?* To my mind, there would be nothing more absurd in leaving courts of justice and prisons to be supported by voluntary contributions of shillings and half-crowns, than is the present practice, here and elsewhere, of leaving the prevention of crime to private caprice and benevolence. It is only, indeed, a public board, drawing its revenue alike from all, and armed with legal powers, that can conduct these crime-preventive institutions without risk of social injury. It must not be forgotten,

* In a note which I have since received from Mr Robert Barclay, superintendent of police in Aberdeen, after alluding to the diminution of begging and stealing by the establishment of the boys' and girls' school of industry, he observes that, in consequence of the opening and continuance of the soup-kitchen school, 'there are now no begging children in the town, though there may be in the outskirts, and when any are found, they are taken to the school. Complaints of thefts by children are now seldom made, while at one time the complaints were numerous. Formerly, numbers of children (as many as ten at a time) were brought to the police-office; now, few are ever brought. I think the schools have tended greatly to diminish juvenile vagrancy and delinquency. Several of the children from the soup-kitchen school—and these of the worst character—have got into employment, and are working steadily.'

that, productive as these schools are of good, unless great caution be exercised, they may silently weaken the motives to industry and providence among the working-classes, and thereby impair the general framework of society. Parents who have brought children into existence, whom, from their own idleness, drunkenness, or improvidence, they are unable to maintain, and whom they cast as a burden on others, ought themselves, in law and reason, to be placed in a state of discipline and restraint, so that the evil may at least be stopped. By means of the recently-established poor-law, the double object of training neglected and destitute children aright, and of putting their parents under control, I should hope will be satisfactorily attained.

Before quitting Aberdeen I visited some other schools—one an evening school for girls employed in the different factories, and doing, I was told, much good; but these do not come within the scope of the present paper. My object has been to spread the knowledge of a class of humble industrial schools, which, within the sphere of their operation, have been of incalculable service. They have in a great measure, at an insignificant cost, rid a large town of the elements out of which its prisons have hitherto been filled, transforming a wicked and miserable horde of beings into useful members of society. W. C.

ZOOLOGY OF THE ENGLISH POETS.

It is common to make claims for poetry beyond its more obvious qualities of fancy and eloquence; but when was there ever an error or a delusion corrected by a poet? Even Shakspeare only puts into more engaging terms the common notions of mankind in his own and preceding ages. Not one new philosophical idea proceeds from him; nor does he correct any prevailing form of belief which reigned in his time. It is the object of a little volume which has been lately published, to show how much of error runs through the works of our chief poets, even with regard to the familiar animals.* The fact is, they take popular views of such subjects, and never seek to be more correct than the simple swains whom they praise so much. Much more apt are they to stamp a superstition about animals with classical authority, than to attempt either to inculcate humane views respecting them, or to impart fresh and more valuable knowledge.

The popular, and consequently poetical ideas about animals, are usually of a very capricious nature. One animal is a favourite without any real merit; another is an object of dislike, although no charge can be brought against it. For example, the Robin-redbreast enjoys universal regard, apparently for no other reason but that he approaches our houses when pinched by cold and hunger. Thus esteemed, he has become the subject of superstitious legends. One is expressed in Webster's wild play of the *White Devil*:—

> 'Call for the redbreast and the wren,
> Since o'er shady groves they hover,
> And with leaves and flowers do cover
> The friendless bodies of unburied men!'

And in the ballad of the *Children in the Wood*—

> 'No burial these pretty babes
> From any man receives,
> Till Robin Redbreast piously
> Did cover them with leaves:'

which stanza, Addison thinks, must have saved thousands of redbreasts from destruction. The Irish, again, tell that the Robin acquired his scarlet gorget from hovering near our Saviour at the time of his crucifixion, the few drops of blood which fell upon him being allowed to remain as a record of his fidelity. The actual character of the redbreast is certainly very opposite to the popular ideas; for he is a solitary and selfish bird, who fights with, and never rests till he destroys or beats off any one of his own species who dares to intrude upon what he considers as his own domain. On the other hand, the toad, which modern naturalists affirm to be a harmless animal, is an object of disgust and horror, merely on account of its ugly exterior, and is persecuted and killed wherever it appears.

The little volume before us will help to introduce more just feelings respecting animals, and for that reason we should rejoice to see it extensively circulated. The author has been extremely industrious, both in collecting allusions to animals from the poets, and corrections upon these from the writings of the naturalists. The whole is presented in a simple and unpretending style. We shall briefly run over a few of the more conspicuous articles.

The ant is no longer to be reputed as the pattern of industry, which it has been rendered by popular error. It neither stores grain pickles, nor bites off their ends to prevent them from germinating. It is a carnivorous animal, living upon small insects and the juices of aphides, which it extracts at pleasure; and, in reality, putting over the winter-time by falling then into a state of torpidity. The stories about its carrying grain, have arisen entirely from its being often seen bearing about its larvæ, which require to be removed to greater or less elevations, according to the state of the atmosphere. See what a goodly pile of verse is thus at once overthrown like a castle of cards—

> 'The *sage industrious ant*, the *wisest insect*,
> And *best economist* of all the field:
> For when as yet the favourable sun
> Gives to the genial earth the enlivening ray,
> ——— All her subterraneous avenues,
> And storm-proof cells, with management most meet,
> And unexampled housewif'ry, she frames;
> Then to the field she hies, and *on her back*,
> *Burden immense! brings home the cumbrous corn*:
> Then, many a weary step, and many a strain,
> And many a grievous groan subdued, at length
> Up the huge hill she hardly heaves it home:
> Nor rests she here her providence, but *nips*,
> *With subtle tooth, the grain*, lest from *her garner*
> In mischievous fertility it steal,
> And back to daylight vegetate its way.'
>
> SMART. *On the Omniscience of God.*

Milton speaks of the *honied*, and Shakspeare of the *waxen* thigh of the bee; but the fact is, that the bee only packs up the pollen of flowers upon its thighs, and from this makes neither honey nor wax, but what is called bee-bread, with which to feed the community of the hive. It is another prevalent error among the poets and the common people, that the working-bee is a female—

> 'The *female bee* that feeds her husband drone
> Deliciously, and builds her waxen cells
> With honey stored.'
>
> *Par. Lost*, b. vii. [illegible]

In reality, the working-bees are neuters in sex, and the queen is the only true female, wife, or mother of the hive.

'Mr Rogers, in his elegant poem, supposes the bee to be conducted to the hive by retracing the scents of the various flowers which it had visited—

> "Hark! the bee winds her small but mellow horn,
> Blithe to salute the sunny smile of morn.
> O'er thymy downs she bends her busy course,
> And many a stream allures her to its source.
> 'Tis morn, 'tis night; that eye, so finely wrought,
> Beyond the reach of sense, the soar of thought,
> Now vainly asks the scenes she left behind,
> Its orb so full, its vision so confined!
> Who guides the patient pilgrim to her cell?
> Who bids her soul with conscious triumph swell?
> *With conscious truth retrace the mazy clue*
> *Of varied scents, that charmed her as she flew?*
> Hail, memory, hail! thy universal reign
> Guards the least link of beings' glorious chain."
>
> *Pleasures of Memory*, Part I.

'This idea, however, is more poetical than accurate, bees *flying straight* to their hives from great distances. The poet might have employed, with as much effect, the

* Zoology of the English Poets, corrected by the writings of Modern Naturalists. By R. H. Newell, B.D., Rector of Little Hormead, Herts. London: Longman and Co. 1845.

real fact of bees distinguishing their own hive out of numbers near them, when conducted to the spot by instinct. This recognition of home seems clearly the result of memory.'*

We may pass over the death-watch, as the public has been made generally aware of the simple and harmless character of that insect. Of the gad-fly, we are only tempted to remark that Thomson, who had good opportunities of observing nature, describes it as coming in swarms, which it never does, but in single examples. Shakspeare calls on the fairies to light their tapers at the fiery glowworm's eyes. The light of the glowworm, in reality, resides at the tail of the insect. The same writer says—

> 'The glowworm shows the matin to be near,
> And 'gins to pale his ineffectual fire.'

Wrong again. It is the female, not the male, which displays this light. The substance called gossamer, which usually spreads over the fields in October, has been for ages the subject of popular and poetical error, being supposed to be dew condensed.

> 'More subtle web Arachne cannot spin;
> Nor the fine nets, which oft we woven see,
> Of *scorched dew*, do not in the ayre more lightly flee.'
>
> SPENSER.

The gossamer is, in reality, composed of the inconceivably minute threads of a field spider, not above the size of a small pin's head. According to M. Bechstein, a German naturalist, 'These spiders first appear in the beginning of October, in woods, gardens, and meadows, where their eggs are hatched in safety; thence they spread themselves over whole districts, and during the rest of October, and till the middle of November, may be found in dry fields throughout Europe. In the beginning of October, when but few are hatched, some single threads of their webs, extending from twig to twig, are seen only in the sunshine. About the middle of the month their threads are more perceptible; and toward the end, if a person stand in such a position as to see the sunbeams play on the slender threads, hedges, meadows, corn-fields, stubble land, and even whole districts, appear covered with a sort of fine white gauze. The gossamer spider does not weave a web, but only extends its threads from one place to another: these are so delicate, that a single thread cannot be seen unless the sun shines upon it. One of them, to be visible at other times, must be composed of at least six common threads twisted together. In serene, calm days, these spiders work with great diligence, especially after the disappearance of the morning fogs: between twelve and two, however, their industry excites the greatest admiration. A person with a pretty quick eye, or by the help of a glass, may sometimes perceive among the barley stubble such a multitude of these insects extending their threads, that the fields appear as if covered with a swarm of gnats.'

Many will be surprised, as we have been, to learn that the splendours of the peacock do not reside in his tail, but in feathers extending along the back. The real tail is a range of short, brown, stiff feathers, which serves as a fulcrum to prop up the train. 'When the train is up, nothing appears of the bird before but its head and neck; but this would not be the case were those long feathers fixed only in the rump, as may be seen by the turkey-cock when he is in a strutting attitude.'

The pelican, as is well known, has long enjoyed pre-eminence as an image of parental tenderness, being supposed to bleed herself for the support of her nurslings.

> 'To his good friends thus wide I'll ope my arms,
> And, like the kind life-rendering pelican,
> Repast them with my blood.'
>
> SHAKSPEARE. *Hamlet.*

The animal would probably be astonished to learn that it had acquired such a repute amongst mankind, as the idea has no other foundation than this, that she fills a neck-pouch which she has with fish, and thence supplies the cravings of her young ones.

Two fallacies are in vogue respecting the chameleon—that it lives upon air, and changes colour according to that of the surrounding objects. Both of these notions have made extensive settlements in our literature. The chameleon, in fact, lives upon flies, which it catches by means of a quick darting tongue; and its colour is habitually green, but subject to changes, through the action of temperature and the state of the animal's feelings—the skin being so thin, that, on any quickening of the circulation under the influence of passion, the blood shines through it.

Mr Newell, we think, does not give us a complete view of the errors regarding the salamander. He speaks merely of its being supposed capable of resisting fire: according to the lines of Cowley—

> 'I would not, salamander-like,
> In scorching heat always desire to live;
> But, like a martyr, pass to heaven through fire.'

And suggests, as a cause for this, that the cold glutinous fluid secreted on the skin of the animal, may have been found to cause the fire to destroy it less instantaneously than other animals of the same size. The popular delusion goes further, and supposes that, when any fire is kept alive for seven years, a salamander is produced in it. A curious memorial of the notion is presented in the seaport of Leith, near Edinburgh, where a street skirting certain glass-works bears the name of Salamander Street, with obvious reference to the perennial fires sustained in those works. The salamander is only a simple reptile, allied to the newt kind, and prevalent in Germany, Italy, and France.

We conclude with Mr Newell's notice of the lion. 'The disposition attributed to this animal, of making nothing its prey which appears dead, is entirely imaginary, or arises from accidental circumstances.

> "And I no less her anger dread
> Than the poor wretch *that feigns him dead*,
> While *some fierce lion doth embrace*
> *His breathless corpse, and licks his face*;
> Wrapt up in silent fear he lies,
> Torn all in pieces if he cries."—WALLER. *Song.*

> "Under which bush's shade,
> A lioness, with udders all drawn dry,
> Lay couching, head on ground, with cat-like watch,
> When that the sleeping man should stir; for 'tis
> *The royal disposition of that beast*
> To prey on nothing that doth seem as dead."*
>
> SHAKSPEARE. *As You Like It*, Act iv. sc. 3.

> "So when the generous lion has in sight
> His equal match, he rouses for the fight;
> But *when his foe lies prostrate on the plain*,
> He sheaths his paws, uncurls his angry mane;
> Pleased with the bloodless honour of the day,
> Walks over, and disdains the inglorious prey."
>
> DRYDEN. *Hind and Panther*, Part 3.

'Unlike some carnivorous animals, which appear to derive a gratification from the destruction of animal life, beyond the mere administering to the cravings of appetite, the lion, when once satiated, ceases to be an enemy. Hence, very different accounts are given by travellers of the generosity or cruelty of its nature, which result, in all probability, from the difference in time and circumstances, or degree of hunger, which the individual experienced when the observations were made upon it. There are certainly many instances of a traveller having met with a lion in the forest during the day—

> "Who glared upon him, and went surly by,
> Without annoying him."

But when urged by want, this tremendous animal is as fearless as he is powerful; though, in a state of confinement, or when not exposed to the extremity of hunger, he generally exhibits tokens of a more tender

* Kirby and Spence, Entomol. vol. ii. p. 181-185.

* Shakspeare has boldly availed himself of poetical license, by transporting the lion from his native Africa to the Forest of Arden.

feeling than is usually to be met with in the tiger, and most of the felinæ.*

'The supposed generosity of the lion has been sometimes explained as resulting from its treachery and indolence. It seldom makes an open attack, but, like the rest of the feline genus, lies in ambush till it can conveniently spring upon its prey. Happy for those animals which are objects of its destruction were its noble and generous nature, that has so often fired the imagination of poets, realised; and that its royal paw disdained to stain itself in the blood of any sleeping creature. The lion is, in fact, one of the most indolent of all beasts of prey, and never gives himself the trouble of pursuit, unless hard pressed with hunger.'†

Again let us express our favouring wishes for the circulation of this pleasantly instructive little book. We cordially recommend it to our readers.

* Cuvier, vol. ii. p. 432. † Wood, Zoography, p. 203.

DUTCH ANNA.

It was shortly after the outbreak of the French Revolution that the humble heroine of this story made her appearance in my native village. Dutch Anna (for so she was called by the country people) was, as the name implies, a native of Holland; and at that time she might be about twenty-five years of age. She was of the middle size, stoutly and firmly built, with a round, good-humoured face, dark hair, clear, honest-looking hazel eyes, and a mouth which, though wide, was expressive of decision and firmness. Her dress, which never varied in style, consisted of a coloured petticoat of a thick woollen material, a short bed-gown of striped cotton, confined round the waist by the strings of a snow-white apron, a close-fitting, modest cap, underneath the plaited border of which appeared her glossy hair, neatly braided over her low, broad forehead; add to this a pair of well-knit stockings, which the shortness of her petticoats afforded ample opportunity of admiring, with heavy wooden shoes, and you have a complete picture of Dutch Anna's costume. At the time I speak of, the prejudice entertained by the mass of the people against foreigners was much greater than in the present day, when the means of communication between different countries are so much improved, and the general diffusion of knowledge has shown the unreasonableness of regarding with distrust and contempt those of our fellow-creatures who have been born in a different climate, and trained in different customs to our own. It may therefore be readily imagined that Anna was for a time regarded with suspicion and jealousy, for the very reason which ought to have commanded the sympathy and good-will of her neighbours—'that she was a stranger in the land.' Her mode of life perhaps increased the prejudice against her. Respecting the reason of her voluntary exile, she preserved a studied silence; though I afterwards learned that the persecution she endured from her own family on the subject of religion was the principal cause. Our village adjoined a populous manufacturing district, and Anna, having been accustomed to such occupation, soon obtained employment. Being a person of a peculiarly reserved and serious turn of mind, she could not endure the thought of living in lodgings; and as she was not able to furnish or pay the rent of a cottage, she hired for a trifling sum an old lonely barn belonging to my father, who was a small farmer, and, with the labour of her own hands, managed to put it into a habitable condition. The furniture of this rude dwelling was simple enough, consisting of a bed of clean straw, a round deal table, and two three-legged stools. The whitewashed walls were ornamented with coloured prints on Scripture subjects, framed and glazed; and a small looking-glass, placed in a position to secure the best light afforded by the little window, completed the decorations. Various were the conjectures formed by the villagers respecting this inoffensive though singular woman; and many were the stories circulated, all tending to keep alive the prejudice her eccentricities were calculated to excite.

A casual circumstance, which led to my becoming obliged to Anna, at length enabled me to overcome the suspicion and dislike with which our neighbour was regarded. Our acquaintance speedily ripened into friendship; for with the reaction natural to the generous, I felt as though I could never sufficiently compensate for my former injustice towards her. Often in an evening I would put on my bonnet, and, taking my work with me, go to spend a leisure hour with Dutch Anna; and on these occasions she generally entertained me with descriptions of her own country, and of the customs and manners of its inhabitants; or with striking anecdotes and incidents which had come under her own personal observation; never failing to draw some useful moral or illustrate some important truth from what she related. She could read well, and write a little—rare accomplishments in those days for one in her situation in life. Her powers of observation were extremely acute, and her memory retentive; but what struck me as her most remarkable characteristics, were her sincere and unaffected piety, her undeviating truthfulness, and her extraordinary decision and fearlessness. When I have said, on bidding her good-night, 'Anna, are you not afraid to be left alone here during the night, with no one within call?' she has replied, 'Afraid, Miss Mary! no; how can I feel afraid, knowing myself under the protection of One so great and powerful as He is wise and good? I am never alone, for God is ever present with me.' After Anna had resided some years in this country, during which time she had, by her constant good conduct, gained the esteem of all who knew her, and, by her good nature and willingness to oblige, won the kindly feeling of even the most prejudiced, she became anxious to pay a visit to her native land; and as the accommodations for travelling at that period, besides being few, were costly, she obtained letters of recommendation from her employers and other gentlemen in the place to friends residing in different towns on her route, and set out, intending to perform the greater part of her land journey on foot. At the end of several months she returned, and quietly resumed her former mode of life. Not till fully a year after this period did she relate to me an adventure which had occurred to her on her journey homewards, and which I shall now transcribe:—

It was at the close of an autumn day that Anna, who had been walking since early morning with scarcely an interval of rest, found herself, in spite of her great capability of enduring fatigue, somewhat foot-sore and weary on arriving at the town of ——. As she passed along the streets, she observed an unusual degree of bustle and excitement; and, on inquiring the cause, found that a large detachment of soldiers, on their way to the continent, had arrived in the town that afternoon, and that some difficulty was experienced in finding them accommodation. This was not very agreeable news for Anna, tired as she was; however, she pursued her way to the house of the clergyman, where she had, in passing that way before, been hospitably entertained, hoping that there she might be able to procure a lodging, however humble. But in this she was disappointed; for though the good clergyman and his wife received her kindly, they could not offer her shelter for the night, as they had already more guests than they could conveniently accommodate. Anna would have been contented and thankful for a bed of straw by the kitchen fire; but even this they could not give, as the lower apartments were wanted by those who had been obliged to give up their beds.

At length, after some hesitation, the clergyman said, 'I know but of one place where you could at this time find a lodging. You appear to be a woman of good courage, and if you dare venture, you may occupy a room in that house you see from this window. It is uninhabited, and has been so for some years, as it has the reputation of being haunted.' Anna looked in the direction indicated, and saw through the deepening twilight a large two-storied house, built of a dull red brick, with stone copings, standing at some distance from the high road. The house itself occupied a considerable extent of ground, being beautifully situated, with fronts to the south and west. The principal entrance was by folding-doors, half of which were glass; and the house was sheltered on the north and east by a grove of trees, whose branches, now but thinly covered with leaves, waved mournfully to and fro in the night wind. 'The last proprietor of that place,' continued the clergyman, 'was a vicious and depraved man, whose very existence was a curse to the neighbourhood in which he dwelt. At an early age he came into possession of a large property, which he spent in the gratification of every base and lawless passion. His life, as far as I can learn, was one unmixed course of cruelty, lust, and impiety, unredeemed by one noble aspiration, one generous, unselfish action. He died suddenly, in the prime of life, in the midst of one of his riotous midnight orgies, and the house has ever since been deserted. It is said, and believed by our good townsfolks, that there he still holds his revels, with fiends for his companions; and many affirm that they have heard the sound of their unearthly merriment, mingled with shrieks and wailings, borne upon the night breeze; whilst the few who have ventured within its walls, tell of shapes seen, and sounds heard, which would cause the stoutest heart to quail. For myself, I am no great believer in the supernatural, and have no doubt that imagination, united to the loneliness of the spot, and the strange freaks the wind plays through a large uninhabited house, have originated reports which we are sure would lose nothing in the recital; so if you are inclined to make the trial, I will see that what is necessary is provided, and I think I may venture to promise you an undisturbed night's rest.'

Anna, as I have before said, was remarkable for her fearlessness; so she thanked the gentleman for his proposal, saying 'that she had not the least fear of spirits, good or bad; that the former, if indeed they were ever visible to mortal eyes, could be but messengers of mercy; and for the latter, she could not conceive that a Being infinite in goodness would ever permit them to revisit this earth for the sole purpose of terrifying and tormenting innocent individuals like herself; that she far more dreaded evil men than evil spirits; and that as, from the estimation in which the place was held, she should feel herself secure from them, she would thankfully accept his offer.' As soon, therefore, as the necessary preparations were made, and Anna had partaken of the good substantial fare set before her, she begged to be allowed to retire to rest, as she was fatigued with her day's journey, and wished to set out again early the next morning. Her request was immediately complied with; the good clergyman himself insisting upon seeing her safely to her destination; when, having ascertained that proper provision had been made for her comfort, and told her that refreshment should be provided for her early next morning at his house, he bade her good night, and left her to repose. As soon as he was gone, Anna proceeded to take a more particular survey of her apartment. It was a large, but not very lofty room, panelled with oak, and having two windows looking across a wide lawn to the main road. The bright fire in the ample fireplace illuminated the richly-carved cornice, with its grotesque heads and fanciful scroll-work. It had evidently been a dining-room, for some of the heavy furniture, in the fashion of the period in which it had been last inhabited, still remained. There were the massive table and the old-fashioned high-backed chairs, with covers of what had once been bright embroidery, doubtless the work of many a fair hand; but what attracted her attention most, was a picture over the chimneypiece. It was painted on the wooden panel; perhaps the reason it had never been removed, though evidently the work of no mean artist. It represented a scene of wild revelry. At the head of a table, covered with a profusion of fruits, with glasses and decanters of various elegant forms, stood a young man; high above his head he held a goblet filled to the brim with wine; excitement flashed from his bright blue eyes, and flushed the rounded cheek; light-brown hair, untouched by powder, curled round the low narrow forehead; whilst the small sensual mouth expressed all the worst passions of our nature. Around the table sat his admiring parasites; young beauty and hoary age, the strength of manhood and the earliest youth, were there, alike debased by the evidences of lawless passion. With what a master-hand had the painter seized upon the individual expression of each! There the glutton, and here the sot; now the eye fell on the mean pander or the roystering boon companion; now on the wit, looking with a roguish leer upon his fair neighbour, or the miserable wretch maudlin in his cups; and again on the knave profiting by the recklessness of those around him. The bright blaze of the fire lit up the different countenances with a vivid and life-like expression; and as Anna gazed, fascinated and spellbound, her thoughts naturally reverted to what she had heard of the life and character of the last owner of the place. Was that youthful figure, so evidently the master of the revel, a portrait of the unhappy man himself who had thus unconsciously left behind him not only a memorial, but a warning. How often had the now silent halls echoed to the brawl of the drunkard, the song of the wanton, the jest of the profane, the laugh of the scorner! It was here, perhaps in this very room, that the dread hand of death had struck him; here he had been suddenly called to account for property misused, a life misspent. Saddened by these reflections, she turned from the picture, and taking her Bible from her bundle, she drew aside the tarnished curtains, and seated herself at one of the windows. The moon had by this time risen, and was shedding her soft light on the peaceful landscape without. The beauty of the scene soothed her excited feelings; and as she read, her mind resumed its accustomed serenity. Closing her book, she prepared to retire to rest, first examining the doors, of which there were two: the one by which she had entered, opening into the front hall, she found to be without a lock, or indeed any fastening at all; the other, leading in an opposite direction, she was unable to open. As, however, she was quite free from apprehension, she felt no uneasiness from this circumstance; and, commending herself to the care of her heavenly Father, she composed herself to rest, and soon fell soundly asleep.

How long she had slept she could not tell, when she was awoke by what seemed to her the confused sounds of song and merriment. So deep had been her sleep, that it was some time before she could rouse herself to a recollection of her situation. When, however, she had done so, she raised herself in bed, and listened; all was silent, save that the night, having become rather gusty, the wind at intervals swept moaningly round the deserted mansion. The fire was almost out, but the candle in the lantern which stood by her bedside shed a feeble light upon the oaken floor; and the moon, though occasionally overcast, was still high in the heavens. Readily concluding the disturbance to have been wholly imaginary, the result of the impression made by her waking thoughts upon her sleeping fancies, Anna composed herself again to sleep; but scarcely had she lain down, when the same sounds, low at first, but gradually becoming louder and more distinct, broke in upon the silence. The noise appeared to her to proceed from a distant part of the house, and came with a kind of muffled sound, as though doors of some thickness intervened. Peals of laughter, bursts of applause, snatches of song, crashing of glass, mingled in wild confusion. Higher and higher grew the mirth, louder and louder swelled the tumult, until, when the uproar appeared to have reached its height, there was a pause—a silence as profound as it was sudden and appalling. Then there rang through the wide deserted halls and chambers a shrill, despairing shriek, whilst far and near, above, below, around, rose mocking and insulting laughter. Dauntless as Anna was, and firm as was her reliance on the protection of Heaven, it would perhaps be too much to say that she felt no quickening of the pulse, no flutterings and throbbings of the heart as she listened. But surprise, and a strong desire to penetrate the mystery, greatly preponderated over any feelings of alarm, and her first impulse was immediately to endeavour to find her way to the scene of the disturbance. But a moment's consideration showed her how foolish and imprudent this would be, totally unacquainted as she was with the house, and with no better light than the feeble glimmer of her lantern. If it was the work of designing persons, such a step would be but to expose herself to danger, whilst, if the effect of supernatural agency, she could neither learn what they wished to conceal, nor shun what they chose to reveal. She therefore decided upon passively awaiting the result of her adventure. As these thoughts passed rapidly through her mind, the noise subsided, the laughter became fainter and fainter; until at length it died away, seemingly lost in the distance, and silence once more reigned around. After the lapse of a short interval, this was again broken by a noise resembling the rattling and clanking of a chain dragged heavily along, which seemed to approach by slow degrees towards her apartment, and as gradually receded; then again approached, and again receded; and so on several times, but each time coming nearer than before; until at length it paused beside that door of her room which Anna had been unable to open. Cautiously raising her head from the pillow, Anna endeavoured, with fixed and strained look, to pierce the darkness in which that part of the room was enveloped; but though she could not distinguish anything, and though no sound was made, she became, with a thrill more nearly approaching terror than she had before experienced, instinctively conscious that she was no longer alone. Resolutely determined, however, not to yield to feelings of alarm, Anna said, in a firm, unfaltering voice, 'Whoever or whatever you are that thus disturb my repose and intrude upon my privacy, show yourself, and name your errand, if you want anything from me; if not, begone, for your attempts to terrify me are vain. I fear you not.' The only answer returned was a low laugh; and where the moonlight streamed in through the partly-drawn window-curtain, there stood a frightfully grotesque figure. Its body, as well as Anna could distinguish, resembled that of a beast, but the head, face, and shoulders, were those of a human being; the former being decorated with a horn over each shaggy eyebrow. It stood upon all fours, but the front legs were longer than those behind, and terminated in claws like a bird. Round its neck an iron chain was hung, which, as it now slowly advanced, sometimes in the light, and sometimes in the shade, it rattled menacingly. The sight of this creature, far from increasing Anna's alarm, considerably diminished it, and she lay perfectly quiet, steadily watching its movements, until it came within arm's length of her, when, suddenly springing forward, she seized hold of it with a firm grasp, exclaiming, 'This is no spirit, for here is flesh and bone like myself.' Apparently, the ghost being composed of too solid materials to melt in air, had no other resource than to oppose strength to strength, for it struggled vigorously, and with some difficulty succeeded in freeing itself from Anna's hold. No sooner was it at liberty, than it made for the door with as much speed as its various encumbrances would allow; and Anna, now completely roused, and forgetting all prudential considerations in the excitement of the moment, hastily put on a few articles of clothing, and, throwing her cloak around her, seized her lantern and followed. The ghost had, however, gained so much in advance of her, that it was with some difficulty she could decide which way to turn, but, guided by the clanking of the chain, she went boldly along a wide stone passage, and through several rooms, opening one out of another, until just as she was again within sight, and almost within reach of the object of her pursuit, it suddenly disappeared; and Anna, in her eagerness, springing quickly forward, was herself the next moment precipitated through an opening in the floor, in her fall breaking her lantern. Fortunately she alighted on a heap of straw, or the consequences might have been fatal. As it was, though bruised and stunned by her sudden descent, she did not entirely lose consciousness, but was sensible of a confused murmur of voices near her; and as her perceptions became clearer, she was aware that the tones, though low, were earnest and angry, and that she herself was the subject of conversation. 'I tell you it is the only thing to be done; so what's the use of talking about it, you fool;' were the first words she distinguished. 'But,' interrupted another voice, evidently a woman's, 'would it not be better to wait and see?' 'Death and fury, wait and see what?' fiercely exclaimed the first speaker. 'If she's dead, it'll do her no harm; and if she isn't, the sooner a stopper's put in her mouth the better.' Completely roused from her stupor by the danger with which she was threatened, Anna opened her eyes, and perceived that she was in a large vaulted cellar, at one end of which was a small heated furnace. Scattered about the floor, and on rudely-constructed work-benches, as though the persons using them had hastily abandoned their employment, were many curious-looking tools and machines, together with heaps of metal of different sizes, and in different stages of manufacture, from the merely moulded shape to the finished shilling or guinea. Some half-dozen or eight men and women were grouped together, amongst whom she recognised the *ghost*, not quite divested of his masquerade dress. In a single glance Anna perceived all this, and it needed no conjuror to tell her that she had fallen into the hands of a gang of coiners.

Fully sensible of the peril of her situation, her extraordinary courage did not forsake her; for Anna, though somewhat peculiar in her religious opinions, was perfectly sincere, and even at this awful moment felt unshaken confidence in the protecting care of Providence. Though a foreigner, she possessed great command of the English language, and her style, notwithstanding its singularity and quaintness, was well calculated to overawe the rude and lawless band into whose hands she had fallen. With a calm and steady gaze she met the eye of the ruffian, who brandished his weapon before her, and said—'I pray you, do not commit this great wickedness, nor shed the blood of a helpless woman, who has never injured you.' 'Oh, come,' interrupted the man in a surly tone, 'let's have none of that gammon, for it'll be of no use. If folks will meddle in other folks concerns, they must take the consequences; we're not such fools as to put the rope round our own necks, I can tell you.' 'Nay, but hear what I have to say,' repeated Anna, eluding the man's grasp as he endeavoured to seize hold of her; 'my coming here was no fault of my own, and I promise not to betray you.' 'Oh ay, a likely tale,' said the man with a brutal laugh.

'We're all for ourselves in this world, and no mistake; so we shall just put you where you can tell no tales, old girl.' 'Stop; hear what she has to say: you shall; you must,' cried a young woman who started up from a table at the farther end of the cellar, at which she had been seated, with her face buried in her hands, during the foregoing colloquy. 'I tell you, Jack,' she continued, advancing into the midst of the group, and laying her hand on the man's arm, 'you shan't touch that woman: you wont; I know you wont. Bad enough you are—we all are, God knows—but there's no blood upon our hands yet; and,' added she, lowering her voice, 'blood will speak, you know—*remember*.' The man's countenance fell as the girl uttered the last words; he relaxed his hold of the knife; and Anna, taking advantage of his indecision, and the relenting expression she thought she read in the dark faces round her, related her simple story, dwelling particularly upon the danger the coiners would incur were she missing, and their security in case she was allowed to proceed on her journey, after seeing her friend the clergyman. Taking courage from the attention of her hearers, she even ventured to remonstrate with them upon their dangerous mode of life, and intreated them to abandon it, and seek their subsistence honestly.

There was a pause of some minutes after Anna ceased speaking, during which the coiners exchanged with each other looks of mingled admiration and astonishment. At length one of them, who appeared to take the lead, addressing his companions, said, 'The woman has spoken well, and there is reason in what she says. It is true enough that murder will out; and though she is a stranger, she was known to come here. Her disappearance might excite suspicion, suspicion would lead to inquiries, inquiries to search, and then all would be up with us; besides, a few weeks will see us clear of this place, if we have luck, and I think we may trust her so long.' Then turning to Anna, he continued, 'You have a spirit of your own, and I like you the better, and would trust you the sooner for it; none but fools rely on the word of a coward, but one who dare speak the honest truth, without fear or favour, when in peril of life, is not likely to break faith, I think; so you shall go free, on condition that you take a solemn oath not to reveal to any one the events of this night until six months have passed; by that time we shall have quitted not only this neighbourhood, but the country, and,' he added with a laugh, 'the ghost that has kept all the men in —— quaking after dark, like a pack of frightened children, will be laid for ever. Have I said well, my comrades?' There was a general murmur of assent, and the man continued, 'Recollect, then, that if you break your oath, your life will be the forfeit: we have means to ascertain and punish treachery; and should you attempt foul play, you can no more escape our vengeance than here in this lonely place you can resist our power. Will you swear, by all you hold most dear and sacred, to keep our secret inviolable for the time agreed?' To this proposition Anna, as will be readily believed, joyfully assented, and being conducted by her strange acquaintances back to her sleeping apartment, she most gladly, when morning dawned, bade adieu to the scene of her singular and alarming adventure. On arriving at the clergyman's house, she was not sorry to find but few of the family stirring, as she naturally wished to avoid much questioning. In answer to the inquiries which were made as to how she had passed the night, she said that she had been much annoyed and disturbed; and though she avoided entering into particulars, she strongly advised that no one should be permitted to try a similar experiment, assuring them that she believed few could pass through what she had done without sustaining severe, if not permanent injury from it. Having thus, as far as lay in her power, acquitted her conscience, she pursued her journey. In a few days she arrived at home; but it was not until several months over the time specified had elapsed, that she related the adventure to me, in order to show how little dependence is to be placed on the stories told of ghosts and haunted houses. As Dutch Anna said, 'Evil men have generally more to do with such stories than evil spirits, and, after all, it is possible to give a certain gentleman and his agents more than their due.

THE ENGLISH HOUSEWIFE IN 1645.

Two hundred years ago, Mr Gervace Markham was the leading authority to the stock-rearers, farmers, and housewives of England. He was the Liebig, the Stephens, and Meg Dods of his time, instructing in every matter appertaining to country life, from the management of a farm to the baking of a pudding-pie. He was the author of at least a dozen treatises, each of which ran through several editions; but from the enumeration of these we are sure the reader will gladly excuse us when he learns that the following quotation is merely the title of a single publication:—'The English Housewife, containing the inward and outward vertues which ought to be in a compleat woman; as her skill in physick, surgery, cookery, extraction of oyles, banqueting stuffe, ordering of great feasts, preserving of all sorts of wines, conceited secrets, distillations, perfumes, ordering of wooll, hemp, flax, making cloth, and dyeing, the knowledge of dayries, office of malting, of oates, their excellent uses in a family, and of all other things belonging to a household. A work generally approved, and made most profitable and necessary for all men, and the generall good of this nation.' Notwithstanding his elaborate titles, and the prefatory assurance that his path was 'both more easie, more certaine, and more safe than any, nay, by much lesse difficulte and dangerous to walke in,' Mr Markham is now all but unknown, his quaint and homely directions having long since been rendered obsolete by the progress of the arts, which require a very different sort of guide for their practical development. It may, however, afford our fair readers some amusement, as well as points for comparison, to transcribe a few of these maxims and recipes, which were as 'golden rules' to their great-great-grandmothers.

Perhaps the standard of excellence with which Mr Markham sets out is rather too high, and may make the housewife of the present day despair of the possibility of ever attaining to such perfection. There is nothing, however, without an endeavour; an honest, cordial determination to do the best one can; and with this preliminary, we have little doubt of her becoming such a paragon as is delineated in the following quotation:*—'Next unto sanctity and holiness of life, it is meet that our English housewife be a woman of great modesty and temperance, as well inwardly as outwardly; inwardly, as in her behaviour and carriage towards her husband, wherein she shall shun all violence of rage, passion, and humour, coveting less to direct than to be directed, appearing ever unto him pleasant, amiable, and delightful; and, though occasion of mishaps, or the misgovernment of his will, may induce her to contrary thoughts, yet virtuously to suppress them, and with a mild sufferance rather to call him home from his error, than with the strength of anger to abate the least spark of his evil, calling into her mind that evil and uncomely language is deformed, though uttered even to servants; but most monstrous and ugly, when it appears before the presence of a husband. Outwardly, as in her apparel and diet, both which she shall proportion according to the competency of her husband's estate and calling, making her circle rather strait than large; for it is a rule, if we extend to the uttermost, we take away increase; if we go a hair's-breadth beyond, we enter into consumption; but if we preserve any part, we build strong forts against the adversaries of fortune, provided that such preservation be honest and conscionable; for as lavish prodigality is brutish, so miserable covetousness is vile. Let, therefore, the housewife's garments be comely and

* We give the text entire, but modernise the orthography.

strong, made as well to preserve the health as adorn the person, altogether without toyish garnishes, or the gloss of light colours, and as far from the vanity of new and fantastic fashions, as near to the comely imitation of modest matrons. Let her diet be wholesome and cleanly, prepared at due hours, and cooked with care and diligence; let it be rather to satisfy nature than our affections, and apter to kill hunger than revive new appetites; let it proceed more from the provision of her own yard, than the furniture of the markets; and let it be rather esteemed for the familiar acquaintance she hath with it, than for the strangeness and rarity it bringeth from other countries.'

Above all this, she is to be of 'chaste thought, stout courage, patient, untired, watchful, diligent, witty, pleasant, constant in friendship, full of good neighbourhood, wise in discourse, but not frequent therein; sharp and quick of speech, but not bitter or talkative; secret in her affairs, comfortable in her counsels, and generally skilful in the worthy knowledges which do belong to her vocation.' These 'knowledges,' according to Mr Markham, are skill in household physic, in cookery, in the arrangement of feasts, in distillations and wines, in dressing of wool, in dyeing, spinning, dairy-work, malting, brewing, and baking; and having so decided, he proceeds to indite for her behoof the necessary information. Of his medicinal receipts, we can say little by way of recommendation. They bear the unmistakeable impress of the ignorance and empiricism of the time, as one or two examples will amply testify; and yet it must be remembered that, until a very recent period, a country family, in cases of emergence, had no better guide to follow. To remove deafness, we are directed 'to take a gray eel with a white belly, and put her into a sweet earthen pot quick, and stop the pot very close with an earthen cover, or some such hard substance; then dig a deep hole in a horse dunghill, and set it therein, and cover it with the dung; and so let it remain a fortnight, and then take it out, and clear out the oil which will come of it, and drop it into the imperfect ear, or both, if both be imperfect.' To promote a luxuriant growth of hair, as the puffing quacks of the present day would say, Mr Markham orders his patient to 'take southernwood, and burn it to ashes, and mix it with common oil, then anoint the bald place therewith morning and evening, and it will breed hair exceedingly.' For the quinsy, 'give the party to drink the herb *mouseare*, steeped in ale or beer, and look where you see a swine rub himself, and there, upon the same place, rub a sleight stone, and then with it sleight all the swelling, and it will cure it.' One recipe more, as, if effectual, we lay our toothached readers under a world of obligation for promulgating so humane and simple a remedy. If teeth give pain, draw them; the thing can be done as gently as you could pick a pin out of a pincushion. 'Take some of the green of the elder tree, or the apples of oak trees, and with either of these rub the teeth and gums, and it will loosen them so as you may take them out.' Enough, however, of honest Gervace's physic, and now for his cuisine.

Of the outward and active 'knowledges' which belong to the English housewife, Mr Markham holds 'the first and most principal to be a perfect knowledge and skill in cookery;' and further, plainly tells the ladies of his time, and we believe the ladies of all future times, that if ignorant in this respect, they can only perform one-half of their marriage vow, 'for though they may love and obey, yet they cannot cherish, serve, and keep their husbands with that true duty which is ever expected.' We shall not follow our author over the hundreds of curious receipts which he gives for the kitchen; nevertheless thus much may be noticed, that he orders everything in true old English abundance, and so sauced and garnished, that the stomachs of our ancestors must have been of 'sterner stuff' than ours, if they could endure under such an amount of duty as he chalks out for their performance. However, as to the getter-up of the feast, 'she must be cleanly both in body and garments, she must have a quick eye, a curious nose, a perfect taste, and ready ear; she must not be butter-fingered, sweet-toothed, nor faint-hearted, for the first will let everything fall, the second will consume what it should increase, and the last will lose time with too much niceness.' With such qualifications, she is to enter upon the business of the kitchen, which, being accomplished according to the satisfaction of Mr Markham, she will find her course of instruction only half gone through; 'for what avails it our good housewife to be never so skilful in the parts of cookery, if she want skill to marshal the dishes, and set every one in his due place, giving precedency according to fashion and custom? It is like to a fencer leading a band of men in a rout, who knows the use of the weapon, but not how to put men in order.'

So much for the *modus operandi*, now for the result; and here we must observe, that if the following list constitute only a 'humble feast,' then we should have been quite willing any day to put up with the crumbs which fell from the great man's table. 'Now for a more humble feast, or an ordinary proportion which any good man may keep in his family for the entertainment of his true and worthy friends, it must hold limitation with his provision, and the season of the year; for summer affords what winter wants, and winter is master of that which summer can but with difficulty have. It is good, then, for him that intends to feast, to set down the full number of his full dishes, that is, dishes of meat that are of substance, and not empty, or for show; and of these, sixteen is a good proportion for one course unto one mess; as thus, for example: first, a shield of brawn, with mustard; secondly, a boiled capon; thirdly, a boiled piece of beef; fourthly, a chine of beef roasted; fifthly, a neat's tongue roasted; sixthly, a pig roasted; seventhly, chewets baked; eighthly, a goose roasted; ninthly, a swan roasted; tenthly, a turkey roasted; the eleventh, a haunch of venison roasted; the twelfth, a pasty of venison; the thirteenth, a kid with a pudding in the belly; the fourteenth, an olive pie; the fifteenth, a couple of capons; the sixteenth, a custard or doucets. Now, to these full dishes may be added in salads, fricassees, *quelque choses*, and devised paste, as many dishes more, which make the full service no less than two-and-thirty dishes, which is as much as can conveniently stand on one table, and in one mess; and after this manner you may proportion both your second and third course, holding fulness in one-half of the dishes, and show in the other, which will be both frugal in the spender, contentment to the guest, and much pleasure and delight to the beholders.'

Passing over the chapters on distillation, perfumes, wines, the dressing and dyeing of wool, &c. we come to that on the preparation of flax, spinning, and bleaching. Spinning, which occupied so much of the time of our great-grandmothers, is thus ordered; the quotation giving insight into customs of which not a vestige, we believe, is to be found in England:—'After your teare is thus dressed, you shall spin it either upon wheel or rock; but the wheel is the swifter way, and the rock maketh the finer thread: you shall draw your thread according to the nature of the teare, and as long as it is even, it cannot be too small; but if it be uneven, it will never make a durable cloth. Now, forasmuch as every housewife is not able to spin her own teare in her own house, you shall make choice of the best spinners you can hear of, and to them put forth your teare to spin, weighing it before it go, and weighing it after it is spun and dry, allowing weight for weight, or an ounce and a half for waste at the most: as for the prices for spinning, they are according to the natures of the country, the fineness of the teare, and the dearness of provisions; some spinning by the pound, some by the lay, and some by the day, as the bargain shall be made.' Equally amusing is much matter which might be extracted in reference to dairy work, malting, brewing, baking, but these our space compels us to avoid. There is one subject, however, which we cannot pass over, as at once curious and instructive; it is a panegyric on oatmeal and haggis, and that, be it observed, by a thorough Englishman.

It is too much the custom for Southerns of a certain stamp to turn up their noses at oatmeal, and for ladies of the same class even to drop hints respecting 'pigs' meat' when the very name is mentioned. These 'double-distilled humanities,' as Carlyle would call them, somehow or other always associate oatmeal with Scotland and the Scotch, as if, forsooth, the 'fine old English gentry,' from whom they boast to be descended, had not been as much in love with 'the wale of food'* as the veriest Scotchman. If they doubt us, let them listen to good old Saxon Markham. 'First, for the small dust, or meal oatmeal, it is that with which all pottage is made and thickened, whether they be meat-pottage, milk-pottage, or any thick or else thin gruel whatsoever, of whose goodness and wholesomeness it is needless to speak, in that it is frequent with every experience; also with this small meal oatmeal is made in divers countries six several kinds of very good and wholesome bread, every one finer than other, as your anacks, ianacks, and such-like. Also there is made of it both thick and thin oaten cakes, which are very pleasant in taste, and much esteemed; but if it be mixed with fine wheat meal, then it maketh a most delicate and dainty oat-cake, either thick or thin, such as no prince in the world but may have them served to his table; also this small oatmeal, mixed with blood, and the liver of either sheep, calf, or swine, maketh that pudding which is called the *haggas*, or *haggus*, of whose goodness it is in vain to boast, because there is hardly to be found a man that doth not affect them. And lastly, from this small oatmeal, by oft steeping it in water and cleansing it, and then boiling it to a thick and stiff jelly, is made that excellent dish of meat which is so esteemed of in the west parts of this kingdom, which they call wash-brew, and in Cheshire and Lancashire they call it flammery or flummery, the wholesomeness and rare goodness, nay, the very physic helps thereof, being such and so many, that I myself have heard a very reverend and worthily renowned physician speak more in the commendations of that meat than of any other food whatsoever; and certain it is that you shall not hear of any that ever did surfeit of this wash-brew or flummery; and yet I have seen them of very dainty and sickly stomachs which have eaten great quantities thereof, beyond the proportion of ordinary meats. Now for the manner of eating this meat, it is of diverse diversely used; for some eat it with honey, which is reputed the best sauce; some with wine, either sack, claret, or white; some with strong beer or strong ale; and some with milk, as your ability or the accommodations of the place will administer. Now there is derived from this wash-brew another coarser meat, which is, as it were, the dregs or grosser substance of the wash-brew, which is called gird-brew, which is a well-filling and sufficient meat, fit for servants and men of labour; of the commendations whereof I will not much stand, in that it is a meat of harder digestion, and fit indeed but for strong able stomachs, and such whose toil and much sweat both liberally spendeth evil humours, and also preserveth men from the offence of fulness and surfeits.

'Now for the bigger kind of oatmeal, which is called grits, or corn oatmeal, it is of no less use than the former, nor are there fewer meats compounded thereof; for first, of these grits are made all sorts of puddings, or pots (as the west country terms them), whether they be black, as those which are made of the blood of beasts, swine, sheep, geese, red or fallow deer, or the like, mixed with whole grits, suet, and wholesome herbs; or else white, as when the grits are mixed with good cream, eggs, bread-crumbs, suet, currants, and other wholesome spices. Also of these grits are made the Good-Friday pudding, which is mixed with eggs, milk, suet, pennyroyal, and boiled first in a linen bag, and then stripped and buttered with sweet butter. Again, if you roast a goose, and stop her belly with whole grits beaten together with eggs, and after mixed with the gravy, there cannot be a more better or pleasanter sauce; nay, if a man be at sea in any long travel, he cannot eat a more wholesome and pleasant meat than these whole grits boiled in water till they burst, and then mixed with butter, and so eaten with spoons, which, although seamen call simply by the name of loblolly, yet there is not any meat, how significant soever the name be, that is more toothsome or wholesome. And to conclude, there is no way or purpose whatsoever to which a man can use or employ rice, but with the same seasoning and order you may employ the whole grits of oatmeal, and have full as good and wholesome meat, and as well tasted; so that I may well knit up this chapter with this approbation of oatmeal, that, the little charge and great benefit considered, it is the very crown of the housewife's garland, and doth more grace her table and her knowledge than all grains whatsoever! Neither, indeed, can any family or household be well and thriftily maintained where this is either scant or wanting. And thus much touching the nature, worth, virtues, and great necessity of oats and oatmeal.'

So much for our first dip into old Markham, whose quaint but sensible treatise on 'husbandrie' may some day furnish us with matter for another article.

* 'Parritch, thou wale of Scotia's food.'—BURNS.

CIVILISATION IN MADAGASCAR.

THERE is no event more interesting in the history of a nation, than that of its first acquaintance with, and progress in, civilisation—from the dawn of moral perception to the full comprehension of moral dignity. In some instances, as at Hawaii, the progression is silent but sure, until the new customs are perfectly domiciliated among the people; while in others, after a favourable movement, retrogression takes place, and the good is lost in original darkness. The events which have transpired in Madagascar within the past twenty years, present themselves in painful illustration of the latter position.

This island, situated, as is generally known, off the south-east coast of Africa, is nearly as large as France, but contains not more than five millions of inhabitants. It was discovered in 1506, twenty years after their first view of the Cape of Good Hope, by the Portuguese, who attempted to establish a mission among the people; but after some time, judging them to be inconvertible, it was abandoned. Towards the year 1640, the minister Richelieu planted a colony on the island, which subsisted, with varying fortune, for more than a century, during which time the Dominicans, after various unfruitful missions, also abandoned the attempt to convert the natives. From this period it was held impossible to civilise the Madegasses, and when, in later years, some Englishmen endeavoured to gain a footing in the country, with a view to the instruction of the natives, they were met everywhere by the outcry of, 'Useless trouble—they are brute beasts, with whom nothing can be done.' A little acquaintance, however, with this nation, will show how far the appellation and caution were applicable.

Until the commencement of the present century, numerous tribes, as diverse in origin as in colour—from the olive to the black—divided the inland among them. One of these, the most important of the inland tribes, the Ovahs, governed by an able and daring chief, obtained a marked superiority over the others; and under Radama, son of this chief, became a powerful government, to whose domination nearly the whole of the island submitted. It was in Tananarivo,* a city of about 30,000 souls, and capital of the kingdom, that the labours of the first English visitors were principally carried on.

* Tanane-arrivou, or thousand cities.

Radama, the first who took the title of king, mounted the throne at the age of eighteen: he was endowed with rare intelligence, wit, and sensibility, and possessed an insatiable desire for instruction. A favourable trait of his childhood has been recorded. His mother, whom he tenderly loved, was one day driven from the palace by her husband in a fit of ill-humour, greatly to the grief of her little son. The next morning, profiting by the temporary absence of his father, he caught a young chicken and tied it by the leg to some portion of the furniture of the apartment. 'What is that?' asked the chief, hearing the cries of the captive bird on his entrance. 'Nothing,' answered Radama, 'but a little chicken crying after its mother.' His father understood his meaning, and said nothing; but the same day the discarded wife was restored to her former position. In the midst of one of the most licentious people in the world, the young prince exhibited a remarkable purity of morals and self-command, characterised by lofty views. His father, however, could not comprehend how a young man devoid of passions could be capable of reigning: his old age was fast approaching; and not knowing to whom he should leave the reins of the government he had founded, he offered great rewards to those of his officers who might succeed in leading the prince into libertinism. Radama's better feeling resisted for some time; but once having yielded, his errors became terrible, and his premature end but too well proved the fatal success of his perfidious counsellors.

One of his first acts on mounting the throne after the death of his father, was to place himself in communication with the English governor of the island of Mauritius, where he sent his two younger brothers to be educated. From the correspondence which ensued, Sir Robert Farquhar, then governor, took advantage of the generous disposition of the youthful monarch to urge the abolition of the slave trade, which was not only a part of the domestic policy of the country, but formed a great export trade, carried on with European and American merchants, creating everywhere mistrust and terror, with their attendant evils. Mr James Hastie, the deputy employed to represent the question to Radama, found in him a remarkable union of the infantile simplicity observed among savages, with an extraordinary intelligence and desire for civilisation. He would burst into fits of laughter while standing before a clock sent to him as a present, dance round it every time it struck, and at the same time enter with sagacity and generous philanthropy into the views of the English governor. A great *khabar* or assembly was convoked, to explain the object to the people; and after a stormy discussion, the recommendation was adopted, and a convention signed, by which the king agreed on his part to abolish entirely the slave trade throughout his dominions, while, on the other hand, Sir Robert Farquhar advanced a sum of money and various munitions of war. A proclamation was then issued, which, leaving domestic bondage untouched, interdicted the export of slaves, under penalty of slavery, and threatening with death whoever should speak ill of the measure.

This treaty was unfortunately broken, during the temporary absence of the governor, by the French and English merchants, who deluded Radama, though with great difficulty, into a compliance with their representations. On Sir Robert's return some time afterwards, he was deeply grieved at the breach of faith countenanced by the vice-governor, and set himself immediately to remedy the evil. 'Do you not know,' replied Radama to the request for a renewal of the treaty, 'that my subjects will not comprehend the reason for a second change? *False as an Englishman* is become a proverb among us!' The deputy on this occasion was accompanied by a missionary, who had been invited by the king to take up his residence at the capital; and on their declaration that no persons would settle there as teachers during the continuance of the slave trade, the traffic was again abolished; the king stipulating that twenty young Madegasses should be educated by the English, one-half of the number in Mauritius, and the other in England.

The first school was opened at Tananarivo in 1820, under the sanction of the king, but at first met with great opposition: and as the natives could not comprehend how thoughts could be expressed by writing, they accused the teacher of sorcery. The school, however, prospered under the protection of the monarch; a few children attended; and at the end of the first year a public examination was announced. This was attended by several old men, among whom was a judge who had been extremely violent in his opposition. He beckoned one of the youngest scholars with slate and pencil to approach, and whispered a few words into his ear—'It is not true that writing can supply the place of speech.' The child immediately wrote the phrase, while the old man shook his head incredulously over the strange characters. Another scholar was then called from the end of the room; and on the slate being placed in his hands, he read the words without hesitation. 'Oh! *solombava tokoa*,' exclaimed the opponents with one voice—['Oh! substitute for the tongue']—by which appellation writing has ever since been known in the country. The next trial was in arithmetic, a science in which the natives had been accustomed to reckon by the aid of stones of various sizes; a process that rendered the simplest calculation extremely laborious. The same old judge had prepared a question. 'Now,' said he to the children, 'if I send a hundred sheep to Tamatave, and sell sixty at four dollars each, twenty at three dollars, and twenty at two dollars, how much ought my slave to bring back to me?' Scarcely had he finished, than an intelligent little girl answered, '340 dollars.' 'Yes, yes, 340, 340,' cried out all the little voices. The aged examiners agreed that the case was astonishing, and the cause of the schools was gained.

Still, it was not without a struggle that popular favour was secured. The natives' distrust of Europeans made them suspicious; parents could not divest themselves of the belief that secret mischief was intended by the schools, and that some day all the children would be bound and led away into slavery. Two other teachers, however, arrived; and on their application for permission to build another school, the king answered, 'Radama says—My friends, live long, and in peace. If my subjects can build such a house, it shall be built. Thus says your good friend.—(Signed) Radama.' Soon after this the prejudices of the people gave way, and in three years from the commencement, there were more than a thousand scholars in fourteen schools, directed by the English teachers and the most intelligent of the pupils. The king became more and more interested in them, and issued frequent proclamations respecting them to his subjects, some sentences from which will exemplify his feelings. 'In future, those only who know how to read and write shall be advanced to any place;' or, 'The young people who have left school ought carefully to occupy themselves with what they have learned; for if they neglect and forget, the king will cause them to return to school;' and again, 'The king again invites his people to send their children to the schools, where they will acquire only good principles. There they learn to read and write, and may then confide their affairs to paper; so that in future all cheating will be impossible, and there will be neither quarrels nor disputes in families.' While smiling at this innocent illusion of the king of the Madegasses, it may be remembered that he is not the only one whose expectations of the benefits of education have been equally illusory; the quotations, however, show a decided tendency in the right direction. By his orders all the schools of Tananarivo were united in one central establishment, where the masters, who were afterwards sent to found schools in the villages, were instructed. So rapidly did education make its way, that in 1828 there were in the kingdom ninety schools, attended by not less than four thousand children. The examinations took place annually in March, and were presided over by the king in person, who on these occasions showed great favour to the teachers, and enlarged the facilities for the advancement of education. On the publication of the Bible in the Madegasses language, he took every opportunity of exposing the false pretensions of the native priests, who complained that the spread of education diverted their revenues. On one occasion, when a man was running frantically about the streets with an image in his hand, declaring to the superstitious bystanders that he was under the influence of the god, and could not stand still, Radama went up to him, and taking the little statue into his own hand, overwhelmed the pretender with ridicule, by showing that it did not affect his movements. His wishes for improvement extended to the mechanical arts as well as to letters; and when some artisans were sent out to him from England, he received them with the greatest joy.

The Madegasses are in general very hospitable, kind, and obliging, and seem to regard selfishness with great aversion: the little tales related by the parents to their children generally contain some ugly feature of selfishness as a moral. They have also a great love for their country, and if about to leave it for any length of time, they take away with them, like the Poles, a small quantity of the soil on which they were born in their bosoms, and frequently look at it with melancholy. The sound of the *valiha*, a species of monotonous guitar, their favourite instrument, produces at such times the same effect upon them as the *ranz des vaches* upon the Swiss soldiers when at a distance from their native country. On the other hand, they are as vindictive, deceitful, and apathetic as the most savage nations. The crime of infanticide, which was common among them, was abolished, though not without great opposition, by a royal edict, which also established new regulations respecting baptism and marriage; and it was found that there was less difficulty in deciding on these points, than on the orthography to be adopted in Madegasses writing. This was at last regulated by a law which enacted that every one should make use of the English consonants, but that the vowels should be French, in order, said the king, 'that an *a* may be always *a*, and not sometimes an *o* or an *e*.'

It must not be supposed that all these changes were equally well received: in barbarous, as in civilised communities, it is not always safe to brave the popular prejudices. Radama, however, did not content himself with making laws; he watched over their execution. Often, like the Caliph Haroun al Raschid, he left his palace disguised, and walked about the city in the evenings to hear what his people said of him. He particularly insisted that hospitality should be exercised with liberality and cheerfulness, and frequently visited families incognito to test their conduct in this respect, and the next day rewarded or reproved them according to the manner in which he had been entertained. Commerce received from him due encouragement.

This monarch, possessed of such remarkable endowments, superior to all his people, who had so nobly invited and cherished the civilisation of Europe, died, in 1828, at the early age of thirty-six, a victim to the excesses into which he had been tempted. What Madagascar lost in him, may be best judged of by the lamentable occurrences which followed his decease. One of his queens, Ranavalona, having assumed the reins of government, gradually revoked all the laws of her predecessor. The slave trade was again legalised; infanticide permitted; the schools were shut up, and the teachers banished; the possessors of books were required to give them up, under penalty of death; hundreds of families were reduced to slavery for their adherence to the new opinions; while many were publicly executed, victims of the queen's hatred of civilisation.

Some few escaped to the mountains, where they lead a harassed and wandering life. In them, however, may possibly be preserved the germ of the future regeneration of the island. Ranavalona, however, is still on the throne, firm in her determination to exclude foreigners, of whatever nation, from every part of her kingdom. It is therefore impossible to predict the time when the improvements, so happily commenced, may again take root, and permanently flourish among this interesting people.

THE PAINTER'S GRAVE.

BY MRS S. C. HALL.

[From the Art-Union.]

The island of Bute is at the 'opening out' of the Firth of Clyde; and although neither so wild nor so grand in character as Arran or others of its majestic neighbours, it is still abundantly rich in the picturesque. The northern portions are as barren and rocky as those whose delight is in 'rough scenery' can desire; but the southern sides are fertile—have been cultivated with care and considerable taste—and in any other locality 'Mount Blair' would be elevated from its rank as a 'hill' to the dignity of a 'mountain.' The air is deliciously soft and mild, differing essentially from the sharp atmosphere which pierces 'the Sassanach' with cruel keenness—no matter how well shielded he may be—while wandering along beautiful glens, or by the sides of cloud-wreathed mountains 'farther north.'

Rothesay, the capital of this charming island, lies in a lovely bay. On one side are the Kyles of Bute, on the other the dark and rugged peaks of Arran are seen towering over the green and fertile hills. Roads diverge in various directions, vying with each other in interest; but our favourite walk winds by the water's edge towards Ascog—a place of silent and quiet beauty, somewhat more than two miles from Rothesay. The road is overhung by a line of rock, in some parts bare and rugged, and in others thickly covered with trees, shrubs, and wild flowers, here tangled together in the wildest luxuriance, and a few yards beyond formed into natural parterres. At intervals the scenery is tamed by elegant and well-built villas and cottages, of greater or less pretension—some exceedingly *ornée*, others of a more retiring character, nestling against the rich and sheltering hill; while on the opposite side the waters of the all-beautiful Clyde rush boldly around the masses of rock, which Time, the disturber, has hurled from the heights above. The climate is so genial, that shrubs and plants grow in Bute that are quite unknown in any other part of Scotland, except in greenhouses: here they flourish in full health and vigour along the winding paths that lead to the hill-top.

But there is at Ascog one object, of simple yet deep interest, which it will be well to visit, to learn a lesson and to offer a tribute—a lesson on the uncertainty of all earthly hopes, and a tribute to the memory of one whose career, uncertain and varied as it was, deserves to be recorded with sympathy and respect.

On a point of rock jutting out into the water, a kirk has been erected in connexion with the Free Church of Scotland. The spot is exceedingly picturesque; and the church, destitute of everything like ornament, or even design, is rendered interesting to the stranger from the dignified solitude of its situation. The Scottish churches present such unpromising exteriors, that it is well continually to call to mind the holy purposes which 'beautify within;' but, plain as the little church of Ascog is, there are few who would not look at it twice, so as to be able to recall to memory a place hallowed by deep and earnest prayer, standing like a sentinel on the firmest rock. It is intended that a burial-ground shall surround this place of worship: at present the graveyard has but one occupant: on the western side, against the outer wall, and looking seaward, a stone tablet has been erected, bearing the words, 'Montague Stanley:' this is enclosed within an iron railing, marking off the lonely grave.

'And *who* was Montague Stanley?' He is well remembered in Edinburgh—*well* remembered in the best meaning of the word. There are many who, when they hear the name, will remember a fine young man, distinguished, but a very few years ago, as an actor of the most gentlemanly and prepossessing appearance, valuable to the manager of the Edinburgh theatre in various ways, for he possessed much dramatic taste, and his conduct and character were alike respected. He was the personification of enjoyment, standing well with the world, and the world with him; united to a worthy love—worthy of all the affection he bestowed. Let no one sneer at this, from an idea that the wear and tear of theatrical life leave no quiet spot wherein the best and purest affections of our natures may be cherished; let no one believe there are human creatures set apart, by profession, from high and holy feelings; let them rather seek to discover the golden links which, however concealed by circumstances, bind us firmly—in the midst of needed labour to which we are called—to what is right and true.

Mr and Mrs Stanley found that constant exertion not only in, but out of their profession, was necessary to meet the claims of a young family. Mr Stanley never suffered his wife to appear in public after her marriage; but she was considered a successful teacher of the graceful art in which she excelled, and had dancing classes at her own house; while her husband occupied the hours between rehearsal and performance by teaching elocution and drawing. Drawing had long been the delight of his leisure moments. The handsome Montague Stanley rapidly gained a local celebrity, and his landscapes became annually exhibited in Edinburgh. His fame was at its zenith, when, urged by conscientious scruples which for some time had disturbed his tranquillity, he withdrew from the stage, and applied himself altogether to teaching and painting. His family increased rapidly, and his labours were redoubled; his friends told him, as friends generally do, that he 'worked too hard;' that he must 'take care of himself,' and 'abridge his hours of toil;' that it was a pity he left the stage; that he could return to it, and labour less; that it was a certain income, while teaching and the sale of pictures depended upon the taste or caprice of others. But he was not one to do what he considered wrong, because it militated against his interests. He had learned to believe that his former profession was at war with his duties as a Christian, and he turned from it, not when his fame was diminishing, or his manly beauty was on the wane, but when both were in their zenith. Thus he proved the strength and truth of his moral character: and the Scotch are a people ever ready to appreciate both. He had abundance of occupation; but his health rapidly declined, and those who loved him best began to fear that his days were numbered.* Early in the past year he went to the Isle of Bute, where the mild and genial air is highly recommended in cases of pulmonary disease; but the complaint, the pestilence of the British isles, had seized upon him with its most tenacious grasp; and, after much suffering, he found a grave in the place where he had hoped to have been restored to health and strength. The love and tenderness of his wife and children were with him through all his exertions; but it needs strong faith to look from a dying bed into the faces of tender children, and know that they are left to struggle through the waters of life with slender help; it needs strong faith to do this, and yet say, 'All is peace.' After her husband's death, Mrs Stanley collected and sent on to Edinburgh the pictures and sketches that were the memorials of his genius, hoping to realise something by their disposal; but, most unfortunately, the carriage by which they were to be conveyed from Glasgow to Edinburgh took fire, and the paintings were either destroyed, or so injured as to be unfit for sale.

Those who know the painter's widow speak in terms of admiration and respect of her amiable qualities and numerous accomplishments: and she is now anxious to establish a school in the island, where she continues to reside. Nothing can be more thrilling than the contrast between the early and the latter days of Montague Stanley: the glittering lights, the loud applause, the admiration that never fails to attend upon personal grace and beauty, either in man or woman—all that excites the passions or fevers the imagination—were present with him in his youth; and these, as he grew older, were exchanged for the intense and lonely labour of the studio. Instead of the stirring sounds of clapping hands, he had the smiles of his children and the quiet affection of his wife: his fine taste and tender nature appreciated these blessings; but they were to give way in their turn to the certainty that he should never aid them to battle with the strife of life, and that his *future* must very soon deepen into *eternity*. On his deathbed, we have heard, he desired to be buried in the churchyard of Ascog—within sound of the waters of the Clyde. And a fitting spot it is for a painter's grave—so solitary and sublime in its simplicity. You can hear the preacher's voice and the deep chant of the sacred psalm from within, while the waves ripple beneath, and the shadow of the sea-bird's wing passes as transiently as the sigh of childhood over the raised sod. And as you gaze thereon, the fever of life's anxieties becomes subdued; the deceptive veil is lifted, even as the mist rises from yonder mountain; and the reality of revealed truth becomes more and more distinct. The imagination takes a higher and a loftier range: in proportion as it is elevated, it is purified, and the beauty of the material becomes blended with that of the eternal world.

Feelings such as these crowded upon us as we contemplated the simple tablet which bore only the painter's name; and so softly did their footsteps fall, that we fancied we were alone, until some little children, dressed in the deepest mourning, arrested our attention by a few words whispered to each other, while they looked earnestly at us. Another glance, and we saw they were accompanied by their mother—one little creature, not able to walk without the assistance of its parent's hand, looked lovingly and smilingly into her sad face: *her* gaze was fixed upon the *tablet*.

There is something sad beyond all description in seeing children dressed in deep mourning: it contrasts wofully with their young fair faces; it tells far too plainly of their early acquaintance with the most bitter trial incidental to humanity, and that they have already learnt a bitter lesson as to the uncertainty of life; but to see so many, little more than infants, accompanied by one parent, crowding round the grave of the other, was yet more full of sorrow. We could no longer remain, or intrude upon a scene so sacred in its nature. We quitted it, with the conviction that the grave could not be called 'solitary,' while those the painter dearly loved bedewed it with their tears!

PARAGRAPHS WITH TAIL-PIECES.

ESQUIRES.

Real Esquires are of seven sorts.—1. Esquires of the king's body, whose number is limited to four. 2. The eldest sons of knights and their eldest sons born during their lifetime. It would seem that, in the days of ancient warfare, the knight often took his eldest son into the wars, for the purpose of giving him a practical military education, employing him meanwhile to be his Esquire. 3. The eldest sons of the younger sons of peers of the realm. 4. Such as the king invests with the collar of SS., including the kings of arms, heralds, &c. The dignity of Esquire was conferred by Henry IV. and his successors, the investiture of the collar, and the gift of a silver pair of spurs. Gower the poet was such an Esquire by creation. 5. Esquires to the Knights of the Bath for life, and their eldest sons. 6. Sheriffs for counties for life. Coroners and justices of the peace,

* Mrs Hall has not mentioned, probably from not being aware of the fact, that Mr Montague Stanley, while residing in Edinburgh, on several occasions, and at the risk of his own life, saved persons from drowning—services in the cause of humanity which more than once were alluded to in becoming terms in the papers of the day. It is not improbable that these efforts had an injurious effect on a frame never robust.—Ed.

and gentlemen of the royal household, while they continue in their offices. 7. Barristers-at- w, doctors of divinity, law, and medicine, mayors of towns, and some others, are said to be of scutarial dignity, but not actual Esquires. Supposing this enumeration to comprise all who are entitled to Esquireship, it will be evident that thousands of persons styled Esquires are not so in reality. It is a prevailing error that persons possessed of L.300 a-year in land are Esquires; but an estate of L.50,000 would not confer the dignity. Nothing but one or other of the conditions above-mentioned is sufficient.—*Curiosities of Heraldry.* [If such be the limited number of real Esquires, how many mock ones there now are! Almost everybody above the grade of the mechanic and inferior tradesman is now styled *Esquire*. It is not uncommon, for instance, to see such an announcement as James Paterson, Esq., grocer; which, upon the above showing, is nothing less than a contradiction in terms. The prevalent custom is the more indefensible, in as far as the deserted term 'Mr' is one of high respect, implying as it does Magister or Master, the possessor of command and dignity. And it is a term, moreover, by which some of the greatest of modern Britons have been familiarly recognised, as *Mr* Pitt, *Mr* Canning, &c. Why should there not be an *Anti-use-of-the-term-esquire* Association, by way of putting down this wide-spread and still spreading absurdity?]

FIRST RAILWAYS IN GREAT BRITAIN.

Everything about the growth, development, and administration of our modern railroads is on so gigantic a scale, that one contemplates, almost with incredulity, the principal points or stages of their advance, from their rude prototype, the tramways, which appear to have first been laid down in the collieries about the middle of the 17th century, to the perfect construction of iron ways on our greatest lines in 1845. From the 'Life of the Lord Keeper North,' Haydn gives the following notice of these trams, under the date of 1676, by the learned narrator (Charles II.'s chancellor):—'The manner of the carriage is by laying rails of timber from the colliery to the river, exactly straight and parallel, and bulky carts are made with four rollers fitting those rails, whereby the carriage is so easy, that one horse will draw down four or five chaldrons of coal, and is an immense benefit to the coal merchants.' The colliery trams were made of iron, at Whitehaven, in 1738; but the first considerable iron railroad was laid down at Colebrook Dale in 1787. Canal and mining companies occasionally laid down metal trams to connect their smaller branches with their larger works. The first iron railroad to which the formal sanction of parliament was given, by an act passed in 1801, was the Surrey iron railway (by horses), from the Thames at Wandsworth to Croydon. This part of the recapitulation should probably close with the Liverpool and Manchester railway (by engines), as the first of those larger and more costly enterprises which are at present the admiration not only of this country, but of Europe.—*Newspaper paragraph.* [Scotland possesses a railway of old date, which is connected with history in an unexpected way. It was laid down by the York Buildings Company in 1738, after they had purchased the forfeited estates of the Winton family in East Lothian; being designed to connect the coal-pits near Tranent with the seaport of Cockenzie. When a romantically-inclined stranger goes to visit the field of Preston, where, just about a century ago, the Highland army of Prince Charles Edward overthrew the royal troops under General Cope, he is apt to be much grieved at seeing the ground crossed by a thing so mechanical as a railroad, which he of course thinks a base intrusion upon a spot which should be consecrated to historical recollection. But the fact is, that this mechanical object was established on the spot before romance had anything to do with it; and Cope's half-dozen cannon actually stood upon this railway when the wild Camerons of the brave Lochiel sprung upon and took them, immediately after the first fire. While this railway may be regarded as having a right to be where it is, and even as an interesting memorial of one of the principal events of the battle, it must be owned that within the last few months the scene has been considerably changed by the laying down of a new line, namely, the North British, which forms a deep trench skirting the whole field of action. Amongst other violences done by this railway to the original character of the ground, is the cutting through of the avenue of Bankton House, the now dismantled mansion of Colonel Gardiner. Verily, it must be admitted, railways are no respecters of the sentimental.]

A GOOD EXAMPLE FOR SMALL PROVINCIAL TOWNS.

The inhabitants of Taunton are displaying no little spirit and judgment in carrying out their determination to improve their town, and thereby render it more attractive to strangers, as well as more pleasant and healthy to themselves. A public meeting is about to be convened for the purpose of electing a committee of taste, and of devising means to carry into execution those improvements which may be considered desirable. Many excellent suggestions have already been made; among them we may mention the removal of the alms-houses in Magdalene Lane, and building in their stead a number of elegant and uniform cottages—the purchasing ground for public walks—the erection of a suitable building for public concerts, lectures, &c. A prospectus for the erection of public baths has also just been issued. It is proposed to raise a capital of L.800, in shares of L.10 each; L.500 to be appropriated to the building, and the remainder to furniture and incidentals. These and other improvements will not only raise Taunton in the scale of places of resort, especially during the winter months, but will confer a permanent benefit upon her denizens.—*The Builder.* [It is curious to observe the dozy indifferent state into which country towns allow themselves to fall, when there is no external impulse to keep them awake. We do not know Taunton, but we have no doubt that, till lately, it resembled many small towns which we do know, and which have not yet plucked up any similar spirit. A town is, in fact, very much like the human individual, liable to be languid and careless, or active and smart, just as it may be affected by fortune. Long chilled by the breath of poverty, it at length gets into that state of inaction in which we sometimes feel ourselves when, being under-clothed, we dread to move, lest we expose ourselves to fresh inroads of the cold. We then see it becoming negligent as to the state of its highways and byways, and extremely contemptuous of everything that may be said by strangers with respect to the improvements of other towns; the real fact being, that it has no objection to improvement, but only dreads the expense. At length rises some stirring citizen—perhaps a retired stranger with some superfluous time and waste energy, or possibly a native of an abnormal degree of public spirit—who goes bustling about with a subscription paper to get the streets newly paved, and a few decorations effected; and, to the surprise of all, contrives to make everything neat as a new pin in a couple of years; so that strangers could hardly know it to be the same place. Such has been the history of a series of improvements formerly noticed by us (Journal, No. 3, new series) as taking place at St Andrews, where the prime agent was an energetic gentleman (Major Playfair) filling the office of provost. And such improvements, by the force of the St Andrews example, are now being effected in the less wealthy and populous town of Peebles. Having lately an opportunity of reviewing the proceedings at the former town, we were delighted, as well as surprised, at the change which had taken place. From being a dull, dispirited-looking town, full of deformities, and with a pavement which it was a penance to walk upon, it has become smart, cheerful, well-paved, and, apparently, half renewed; for, it must be observed, the bustle attendant on public renovations has acted as a stimulus to private enterprise, and a vast number of persons have rebuilt, repaired, or freshened up their houses, in order to fulfil and support the general design. Considering that little more than a thousand pounds were required for the public portion of these improvements, and that *one person* was the sole primary agent by which the money was collected and the end attained, we would say that nothing but ignorance of such an example can excuse similar country towns from similar transformations. There is not, we seriously believe, any such town, however defective in public funds, wo-begone in general, sunk and lost in mud and disrepair, but might have itself scrubbed and brushed up, so as to look almost spick-and-span new, if there were in it but so much as one active and judicious citizen—and where was there ever any town so small but had its clever fellow, as well as its parson and its crier? Only let the said genius have some magnanimity to bear the sneers and cavils of the mean and invidious, with a determination, *coûte qui coûte*, that the object shall be effected, and ten to one the thing is done even in less time, and with less difficulty, than he himself could have expected.]

THE DYING FLOWER;

BEING A DIALOGUE BETWEEN A PASSENGER AND A FADING VIOLET.

[The following is extracted from 'German Anthology; a series of Translations from the most popular of the German Poets, by James Clarence Mangan. 2 vols. Dublin: Curry and Co. 1845.' We have perused this collection with much pleasure and advantage. The pieces are so various, and from such a variety of sources, as to leave hardly any author or style of verse of our German neighbours unrepresented; and the style of translation is free, bold, and energetic, at the same time that special character is well preserved. In short, it is such a collection as could only be expected from a man of original genius, deeply imbued with the spirit of the literature which he endeavours to make his own.]

PASSENGER.

Droop not, poor flower!—there's hope for thee:
  The spring again will breathe and burn,
And glory robe the kingly tree,
  Whose life is in the sun's return;
And once again its buds will chime
  Their peal of joy from viewless bells,
Though all the long dark winter-time
  They mourned within their dreary cells.

FLOWER.

Alas! no kingly tree am I,
  No marvel of a thousand years:
I cannot dream a winter by,
  And wake with song when spring appears.
At best my life is kin to death;
  My little all of being flows
From summer's kiss, from summer's breath,
  And sleeps in summer's grave of snows.

PASSENGER.

Yet grieve not! summer may depart,
  And beauty seek a brighter home,
But thou, thou bearest in thy heart
  The germ of many a life to come.
Mayest lightly reck of autumn-storms;
  Whate'er thine individual doom,
Thine essence, blent with other forms,
  Will still shine out in radiant bloom!

FLOWER.

Yes!—moons will wane, and bluer skies
  Breathe blessing forth for flower and tree;
I know that while the unit dies,
  The myriad live immortally:
But shall my soul survive in them?
  Shall I be all I was before?
Vain dream! I wither, soul and stem;
  I die, and know my place no more!

The sun may lavish life on them;
  His light, in summer morns and eves,
May colour every dewy gem
  That sparkles on their tender leaves;
But this will not avail the dead:
  The glory of his wondrous face
Who now rains lustre on my head,
  Can only mock my burial-place!

And wo to me, fond foolish one,
  To tempt an all-consuming ray!
To think a flower could love a sun,
  Nor feel her soul dissolve away!
Oh, could I be what once I was,
  How should I shun his fatal beam!
Wrapt in myself, my life should pass
  But as a still, dark, painless dream!

But, vainly in my bitterness
  I speak the language of despair:
In life, in death, I still must bless
  The sun, the light, the cradling air!
Mine early love to them I gave,
  And, now that yon bright orb on high
Illumines but a wider grave,
  For them I breathe my final sigh!

How often soared my soul aloft
  In balmy bliss too deep to speak,
When zephyr came and kissed with soft,
  Sweet incense-breath my blushing cheek!
When beauteous bees and butterflies
  Flew round me in the summer-beam,
Or when some virgin's glorious eyes
  Bent o'er me like a dazzling dream!

Ah, yes! I know myself a birth
  Of that All-wise, All-mighty Love,
Which made the flower to bloom on earth,
  And sun and stars to burn above;
And if, like them, I fade and fail,
  If I but share the common doom,
Let no lament of mine bewail
  My dark descent to Hades' gloom!

Farewell, thou lamp of this green globe!
  Thy light is on—my dying face;
Thy glory tints—my faded robe,
  And clasps me in—a death-embrace!
Farewell, thou balsam-dropping spring!
  Farewell, ye skies that beam and weep!
Unhoping and unmurmuring,
  I bow my head and sink to sleep!

GREAT EVENTS FROM TRIFLING CAUSES.

We hear sometimes of great events being produced by trifling, and, one would think, inadequate causes. Within these few years, in this country, the inadvertence of slightly misplacing a single figure on a scrap of paper occasioned to one person, who was ill able to afford it, the loss of a thousand pounds, and to another the punishment of seven years' transportation. Two builders in Glasgow, carrying on business in company, discounted a bill for L.120 with a bank of that city. The slip on which the discount was marked, attached to the bill, was handed by the accountant's clerk to the teller. This charge, deducted from the bill, showed a balance of L.117, 14s. 4d. to be paid to the person who presented the bill acting for the company. On the slip, however, it was ascertained afterwards by concurring circumstances, though the slip itself was lost, that the 1 of the shillings being rather near the 7 of the pounds, the teller had mistaken the sum for L.1171, 4s. 4d., and gave away above L.1000 more than he should have done; though, what is strange, the proper sum was entered in his own cash-book. The deficiency was of course immediately discovered, but neither the teller himself, nor any others in the bank, could at that time trace out how the error had been committed. The teller had, indeed, to give up his place, and his cautioners to make up the deficiency. He was still retained, however, in another department of the same bank; but he removed afterwards to an Edinburgh bank connected with that in Glasgow. Three years had now elapsed since this transaction had taken place, when the secretary of the bank discovered the real cause by comparing the amount of the deficiency with the supposition of the above error; but this did not enable the bank to bring home the charge to the person who received the money. The builders at length becoming bankrupt, and their books getting into the hands of the trustee for their creditors, the sum was found marked with pencil at the end of their cash-book. But the thing was made still more clear by the partner who managed their money matters having told the story to another person, who it appears did not keep it a secret. This partner, therefore, being apprehended, and tried before the circuit Court of Justiciary at Glasgow, the above evidence, both direct and circumstantial, sufficed to convict him, and he was sentenced to seven years' transportation.

CREATING A WANT.

The Rev. Dr Trench, the last archbishop of Tuam, though a wealthy man, was extremely simple and temperate in his mode of living—a plain joint of meat supplied his dinner. Whenever he saw one of his children about to try a new dish, not tasted perhaps at any time before, he always said, with a smile, 'Now, you are going to create a want.'

Published by W. and R. Chambers, High Street, Edinburgh (also 98, Miller Street, Glasgow); and with their permission, by W. S. Orr, Amen Corner, London.—Printed by Bradbury and Evans, Whitefriars, London.

CONDUCTED BY WILLIAM AND ROBERT CHAMBERS, EDITORS OF 'CHAMBERS'S INFORMATION FOR THE PEOPLE,' 'CHAMBERS'S EDUCATIONAL COURSE,' &c.

No. 99. New Series. SATURDAY, NOVEMBER 22, 1845. Price 1½d.

TO WANT AND TO HAVE.

In a late lecture to the farmers on scientific agriculture, it was pointed out that, when a hill-side is left undrained, its dampness forms an attraction to clouds to come and discharge themselves on that hill; so that what least needs moisture, and is most apt to be injured by it, is the most apt to have it; while land where care has been taken to do away with humidity, is likely to remain exempt from all such additions of that evil. This natural fact serves to recall certain reflections which we often have occasion to make upon human affairs.

Things somehow seem so constituted, as to be always unfavourable to the person who *wants*, whether it be in natural endowment or in worldly wealth.

When a boy is put to school, if he be of ordinary, or say below ordinary talent, it might be presumed that he had the greater need of assistance from the teacher. But does he get such extra assistance? Assuredly not. The master proceeds as well as he can with the bright and the tolerably bright, who would do passing well without him. The dull he leaves to form a residuum of repose at the bottom of the class, to the mortification of anxious parents and the dismay of hopeful grandfathers. Thus, because the poor fellows have been treated ungenerously by nature, they must be treated ungenerously by man too. Because they want, they remain unsatisfied. Requiring a push, for that very reason they do not get it. Being helpless, they must remain without help. It seems the very contrary of what is called for in the case, by common sense; for better, one would say, leave the clever and inherently active to their own energies, and bring on the laggards, so as to induce a kind of equality between the two sets. But the ways of the world are different, and it would be more than is to be expected of mortal pedagogue, to suppose that he was to give up the feeding of those who take their meat kindly, and appear to thrive upon it, and devote himself to a struggle with the intellectual languor of the dunces.

Who, again, is the favourite at the bar for employment before railway committees? It is not any of the great horde of young men who go about endeavouring to look smart, knowing, and *engaged*, but who in reality have nearly the whole of their time upon their hands. No; it is the man who is known to be utterly oppressed with the amount of his business, so as to have hardly the least chance of being able to spare five minutes for the case when it comes on. Agents have more hope from the moments of this man than from the days and weeks of those who have no business. The disqualification of the young man is, that he is without that which he desires to have. It is an insuperable ground of suspicion against him, that he has time to execute what he undertakes. For why has he time? Were he highly fitted for his employment, he would get employment; he would then have no time. Thus things seem to go with him in a vicious circle. Because he wants business, he does not get it. Because he does not get it, he wants it. The wonder is, how any one in such circumstances ever gets business. Perhaps it happens thus. If he be a clever person, little casual matters in the course of time come his way, and break the spell. By using these advantages well, he ultimately surmounts the difficulty.

It has ever been observed, that the destruction of the poor is their poverty. Because they are penniless, they get no pennies, or only pennies. Because, from their narrow means, they would require to obtain everything cheap, they are just for that reason obliged to buy everything dear. If they require a loan, probably they have to pay three times the interest upon it which is demanded from persons in better circumstances. Fortune, perhaps, makes them an offer once in a lifetime; but often, from their want of funds, they have to forego it, and it is snapped up by their wealthy neighbour, who so little needs it, that he is hardly sensible of its making any increase to his means. The man who *has* thrives, indeed, just because he has. He has money—men become his creditors without fear. He has money—the customer is sure he can afford to keep the largest stock and the best article, and sell at the smallest profit. It is not only that himself works; the money works too. It is like having so many more hands. Here, as in the case of the barrister, the first steps are the great difficulty. It generally requires excessive self-denial and dexterity to make the first accumulations; and it is usually long before they are made. But with the smallest advantage of this kind in one's favour, the next steps are always easier, until at length the money seems to make itself.

If increase of means be the more difficult in proportion to the smallness of means, it is easy to see how inequality in this respect must always tend to exaggerate itself. In a country where fortunes, from whatever cause, are unusually various, and men are all free to advance their individual interests, the house of Have must enjoy an uncommon degree of advantage over the rest of the community. The members of that family, having the disposition of all things in their favour, will continually tend to become richer in proportion to their neighbours. It will show itself in the contrast between the master and his thousands of workers, in the power of the wholesale trader over retailers, in the voracity of the blood-sucking private-bill discounter, and of banks generally, over men of little capital. Even in literature it will make its appearance; and the man of intellect will be the working slave of the brute-force Capital, personified in the bookseller. It may not make any man absolutely worse off than he would have been otherwise; but the multitude will feel relatively worse; because they have a more painful subject of invidiousness and ealousy set up before them, and are less able, by any ersonal merits or exertions of their own, to escape rom the *Want* to the *Have* party. There will always, ndeed, be a possibility of passing into the domains f Have; because there is no amount of self-denial hich men will not be found capable of exemplify- ig, and natural and acquired talents, with a little ood fortune, will always be performing wonders. But he difficulty will be great for the mass to make any ach transitions. Nor does it appear that there is any atural check to this progress, besides the limitation nposed upon the power of obtaining suitable hired ssistance in the higher departments of business, and ie conclusion which death and the failure of natural ower put to all great mercantile, as well as heroic con- uests. In a system of independent individual exertion, ach a progress must go on—as long as human nature an endure it. But it were a libel on Providence to appose that such a plan is that designed to form the erfection of human society. It will have its era, and ien pass away.

We have, meanwhile, this consolation under a system hich obviously produces vast evils, that it is an active ystem. It evokes human powers, and strains them to ie uttermost. There is no dallying or languor in this orm of the human problem. Work is done—physical ifficulties are smoothed down—the field is prepared or whatever better system is in store. Let us, then, iake the best, as individuals, of a plan which we evi- ently cannot, as individuals, control. Wealth is power -let the power be used for good ends. Social influence ivolves a responsibility towards moral objects; let it e so used accordingly. Let due encouragement be iven to the civilising influences which, notwithstanding ll drawbacks, real and apparent, are constantly at work mongst us. Thus we may hope that, as the spirit of iivalry brightens the memory of the age of rude aronial power, so shall there be a glory on the page hich commemorates even this mechanical and money- iaking era—the glory of an enlarged humanity working owards noble issues, even in the midst of what we ight sometimes think a more sordid kind of selfishness ian any which has ever before become conspicuous pon earth.

HE OLD BACHELOR IN THE OLD SCOTTISH VILLAGE.*

'HIS is the title of a little volume, half descriptive, half ctitious, by a gentleman who is known in literary rcles in our northern land as a successful writer of erses. The tales, by which a large portion of the olume is filled, are, in general, not characteristic; but ie chapters devoted to simple village scenes, life, and iaracter, must strike every one qualified to judge, as i many parts faithfully reflective of the subject. And at Mr Aird is not the best qualified kind of person r such homely painting. He is too fine and poetical, o much given to effusions of pathetic sentiment. ften we find his villagers expressing feelings of deep fection in the various relations of life: an entire iistake, as we apprehend it; for in all our experience ' Scottish life, we never yet knew an instance of such elings being expressed in words. The Scotsman never lls his child or his parents, or his brothers or sisters, iat he has any regard for them—not even in the most rigent circumstances: he leaves his acts to speak for im.

The book appears as written by one who returns from rtune-seeking, in middle life, unmarried, to spend the maindar of his days in his native village. The pic- ture of his home and little library, and the sketches of his simple neighbours, are interesting, and often a strain of beautiful moralising is indulged in. It appears to us that the following bit of painting is perfect:—'The most uncomfortable weather on earth is the breaking up of a snow-storm at a lonely farm-house in the country, on a cold and clayey bottom. The sickly feel- ing of reading a book by the fire in the forenoon could still be endured, were there a book to read; but there is not a fresh page in the house. Out, then, you must sally; but what to do? The hills are cheerlessly spotted; the unmelted snow is still lying up the furrows with indentations, like the backbone of a red herring; a cold blashy rain is driven from the spongy west by a wind that would certainly blow you away, did not your feet stick fast in the mud, as you wade along the sludgy road. Determined to have some exercise, you set your face winkingly against the storm, and make for the black Scotch firs on the hill-side. Finding no shelter, you return to the farm soaked to the skin, and the leather of your shoes like boiled tripe. Hearing the fanners at work in the barn, you make for the stir; and winking against the stour as you bolt in, step up to the ankles in chaff, which sticks to you like a bur. The dusty atmosphere clings lovingly to you, and in a trice you are cased in drab. The luxury of clean dry clothes is now fairly earned: the change is truly an enjoyment, and doubly so in helping you to loiter away an hour. But would, would the evening were come! Such were the leading features of a late visit I paid to a farming acquaintance some three miles off from our village. I don't like such visits at all now. I confess myself afraid of unused bed-rooms, glazed curtains, and cold sheets. Ah! I fear I am getting old.'

Equally perfect in description and in feeling is an account of the wild fruit put by October in the attain- ment of a Caledonian youth. 'In quantity and in quality there is always a natural correspondence be- tween the wild and home fruit of the season: so the wild, like the home, is very abundant this year upon the whole. Haws, however, are rather scanty. Indeed the hawthorn is a capricious and delicate plant in this re- spect, and seldom yields a very good crop. Even in seasons when the flower (chivalrously called "Ladies' Meat") covers the long line of hedges as with a snowy sheet, and delights every nose of sensibility in the parish, we are by no means sure of a harvest of haws entirely correspondent; as the blossom, with the first set of the fruit, is exceedingly tender. Well do the boys know the fat ones. Hips (called in some parts of Scotland jupes) are a fair yield this harvest, whether smooth or hairy, hard or buttery. That all-devouring gourmand, the school-boy, who crams every crudity into his maw, from the sour mouth-screwing crab up (though down in literal position) to the Swedish turnip, sweetened by the frost, riots in the luxury of the hip, caring not how much the downy seeds may canker and chap the wicks of his mouth, and render his nails an annoyance in scratching his neck. See the little urchin slily watching the exit of the "lang" cart from the stackyard; then jumping in from behind, he takes his seat on the cross- bench, or ventures to stand erect by the help of the pitchfork, his black, dirt-barkened little feet overcrept by earwigs, beetles, and long-legged spinners, the living and hither-and-thither-running residuum of the last cartload of peas; till, when the half-cleared field is reached, Flibbertigibbet, who ought all the while to be "gathering," bolts through a slap in the hedge, and is down upon the buttery hips in the Whitelea braes. Our hedgerows, sandy banks, and wild stony places, are quite black with brambles this autumn. Clean them from the worms of the thousand-and-one flies that feed on them, and they are capital for jelly and jam; and for painting children's faces, as we see every day in the by- lanes around our village. The bramble is called in Rox- burghshire (*honi soit qui mal y pense*) "Ladies' Garters." There, however, the land being mostly a stiff clay, it thrives poorly. It loves a sharp sandy soil, and espe-

* By Thomas Aird. Small octavo. Edinburgh: Myles Mac- iail. London: Simpkin and Marshall.

cially those rough stony knowes in the middle of fields, where also in the warm still sunny days of harvest you startle the whirring partridge, and see her feathers where she has been fluttering in the stour, and where you hear the whins, with their opening capsules, crackling on the sun-dried braes. Blaeberries were abundant this year, and ripe in the beginning of July. The barberry bears a fair crop. In my boyish days this bush was called gule-tree; and we made yellow ink of it, to give a variety of flourish to our valentines to the little lasses—from whom we got pins in return to be played for at tee-totum. Ill fares the poor gean-tree by the road-side, torn down and dismantled in all its branches by the village urchins, bent at once on provender and "papes." Scarcely ever does its fruit see the first blush of red. A guinea for a ripe black gean within three miles of a country school! The juniper is a scarce bush; but it has plenty of fruit this year—green, red, and black—on the different exposures of its close-matted evergreen branches. In my days of childhood, I had a sort of religious regard for the juniper, from the "coals of juniper" mentioned in Scripture along with "sharp arrows of the mighty;" and also from the circumstance that I had never seen the berries till they were brought me by my granny, who plucked them on a remote hill-side, as she came from a Cameronian sacrament. So far as eating was concerned, their resinous tang of fir helped my veneration, and I never got beyond chewing one or two. I am compelled to add, however, that my reverence for the holy berries was considerably abated when I found out that the sly old wife had popped a dozen or two of them into her own whisky bottle, to give it the flavour of gin. Crabs are not so plentiful as might have been expected; and (as Johnson said of Churchill) their spontaneous abundance being their only virtue, they are below notice this season. But look at the seed of the ash—how thick! The light green bunches of it, relieved against the somewhat darker verdure of the leaf, make it well seen, and the whole thing has a very rich effect. The pods of the pea-tree (*laburnum*) hang from every branch in clusters. When ripe, the peas are glossy black as jet, and are much sought after by bits of country lasses for making necklaces of beads—for the little monkeys have early notions of finery. They are unsafe to be meddled with, however, as they are very poisonous. It is worthy of remark that, come good year or bad year, the pea-tree never fails to have loads of depending flowers as thick as swarms of bees a-skepping; and the fruit is always equally abundant. Of all plants, and shrubs, and trees in garden and field, and on the mountain sides, none is to be compared in this respect with the prolific pea-tree. It is one of nature's richest gifts to adorn our hedgerows. The wood, I may add, is extremely beautiful, and that the turner knows right well.

'The rowan-tree, the beauty of the hills and the terror of witches, is red all over with berries this autumn. May she ever see her fair blushing face in the sleeping crystal of the mountain pool! Her berries are also for beads. The boor-tree, famous for bullet-guns, bored with a red-hot old spindle, and tow-charged, in the days of boyhood, is also very rich this autumn with her small black-purple berries. "Miss Jeanie" would not take the "Laird o' Cockpen" when she was making the "elder-flower wine;" let him try her again in this the time of the elder-berry vintage: she is herself *elder* now, and has had time to think better of his offer; not to say that a sip of the richer berry may have softened her heart. Never had the "bummie" such a "summer high in bliss" as this year among the honied flowers of the lime. The autumn of its fruit is not less exuberant. The ground where it grows is quite littered with the small round seed. The broom is all over black with its thin pods. Plantagenet, more swain-like than king-like, has coined his glory of summer bullion into a bushel of peas. Mushrooms, in their fairy rings in the rich old unploughed pastures, are a fair crop this season. By the way, when does the mushroom come first? Tom Campbell, in his "Rainbow," says—

> "The earth to thee its incense yields,
> The lark thy welcome sings,
> When, glittering in the freshened fields,
> The snowy mushroom springs."

Now, the lark ceases to sing early in July; and I rather think, Thomas, the mushroom is rarely seen till August; what say you? But I refer the matter to William Wordsworth, that master martinet of poetical accuracy. Meanwhile, having thrown Thomas this metaphorical nut to crack, I go on to the literal nuts; and I beg to say that their white young clusters are almost the loveliest fruit that grows in glen or shaw. Now, however, they are glossy brown, and lots of them. So mask yourself, gentle swain, in the most tattered gear you can muster (buckskin breeches, if you have them), as recommended in the said William Wordsworth's poem of "Nutting," and, bag and crook in hand, sally forth with your lady-love, bedizened like Otway's witch in the "Orphan," and Pan speed you! And if any lurker, on the spy system, among the bushes, hear you drawing a simile from the hazels among which you are in praise of your sweetheart's eyes, why, he can only take you at worst for King Cophetua and the Beggar Maid. So still speed you! Sloes, being harsh and salivating in their sourness, are almost always plentiful; for Dame Nature is a queer old economist, giving us fine things sparingly, but lots of the coarse. But ah! Flibbertigibbet aforesaid delights in the sloe. No matter how deceptively that blue-purple down, or rather film, of seeming ripeness veils the sullen green of harsh immaturity; it's all one to "Ill Tam." Away he goes with his pocketful, whooping through the dry stubble fields to the village cow-herd boy on the common, who, smitten with the eager hope of company in his cheerless waiting on, perks up his head out of his dirty-brown maud from beyond the beilding heap of divots; starts up with an answering holla; and comes running over the bent to meet his welcome crony, the rush cap on his head nodding like a mandarin's, and his doggie, with its ears laid back in the wind, gambolling on before. Straightway the fire of whins and dry barren thistles is set a-going, and sends up what Æschylus calls "its beard of flame," better seen by its wavering smoke-topped flicker than by its gleams of colour, deadened in the daylight; and the roast of sputtering sloes, with an eke of beans and potatoes, which provident little Patie has in store, is more to our genial worthies, sitting on their hunkers, and nuzzling and fingering among the ashes, than Ossian's Feast of Shells. And thus they feast till the day begins to decline. And then they run to the distant road to ask the passing traveller what o'clock it is; and, in the fearless necessities of rude nature, the question is popped whether the passer-by be a charioted buck of seven seals, or a trudging hind who hangs out a crooked sixpence, a simple spotted shell, or a bit of polished parrot-coal, by an affectionate twine of his grandmother's hair.

'Then come the hoar mornings of November frost, and the sloes begin to crack, and are really not so bad; and "Ill Tam" has another day at Eildon hills. He finishes the ploy by tearing and wearing his corduroys, up trees and down "slidders," to very reasonable tatters; and thus the light of knowledge is let in by many and wide holes upon his mother at night, that her son "has been out;" and her patience being worn out as well as his breeks, a good sound thrashing winds up the day to Thomas. Anything like a full crop of acorns is a very rare harvest indeed. This year, however, they are "plenty as blackberries;" and now that the air is beginning to smell of winter, they are popping down upon your head wherever you go; clean, glossy, and slightly ribbed in their brown and white. They must have been better to eat in the Golden Age than now, or the stomachs of our simple sires must have been more easily pleased than those of their degenerate and luxurious sons; for hang me from an oak branch if I could eat an acorn, so harsh and stringently tasteful of the tannin, even to see the lion lie down with the lamb. So my age of gold is not likely to get beyond pinchbeck. But swine can eat acorns, though old bachelors are not so innocent; and therefore I advise all my country friends, after the wants of the nurseryman are served, to turn the snouts of their pigs among the mast, or have it gathered by the bairnies and flung into the trough. The porkers grunt almost graciously over it, and it helps to give that fine flavour to the flesh which touches the tongue so racily in the wild-boar ham.'

We must not part with Mr Aird till we have remonstrated against a certain leaning to the past, which appears to us to be not the true feeling of its kind, for it is needlessly insulting to the present. He sees only mischief threatened by the efforts now making to educate the masses, and seriously expresses his willingness to give up all modern popular literature for the filth which filled the pedlar's basket thirty years ago. This is only maudlin sentimentalism, not manly feeling. It is putting rational choice between good and evil at scorn, and playing into the hands of those who hate the public good for reasons which they think important to their own interests. We believe that men, in writing in this manner, do not exercise judgment at all; they are only indulging in caprices and fancies. We greatly prefer to see a man writing with his head clear, and his heart open, and as if he felt every word he put down to be upon oath. It is by such earnest men that the world is to be made better, not by sickly indulgers in whimsy and paradox.

THE ARTIST'S DAUGHTER—A TALE.

BY MISS ANNA MARIA SARGEANT.

Act well thy part—there the true honour lies.—POPE.

'I WISH, papa, you would teach me to be a painter,' was the exclamation of a fair-haired child, over whose brow eleven summers had scarcely passed, as she sat earnestly watching a stern middle-aged man, who was giving the last touches to the head of a Madona. 'Pshaw,' pettishly returned the artist; 'go play with your doll, and don't talk about things you can't understand.' 'But I should like to learn, papa,' the child resumed: 'I think it would be so pretty to paint, and, besides, it would get us some more money, and then we could have a large house and servants, such as we used to have, and that would make you happy again, would it not, papa?' 'You are a good girl, Amy, to wish to see me happy,' the father rejoined, somewhat softened by the artless affection of his little daughter; 'but women are never painters, that is, they are never great painters.' The child made no further comment, but still retained her seat, until her father's task was accomplished.

The chamber in which this brief dialogue took place was a meanly-furnished apartment in a small house situated in the suburbs of Manchester. The appearance of the artist was that of a disappointed man, who contends doggedly with adversity rather than stems the torrent with fortitude. Habitual discontent was stamped on his countenance, but ever and anon a glance of fierceness shot from his full dark eyes, as the thought of the position to which his talents ought to have raised him would flit across his brain. A greater contrast could scarcely be conceived than existed between the father and child: the latter added to the charms of that early period of life a face and form of exquisite beauty. Her dazzling complexion, rich auburn hair, and graceful attitudes, accorded ill with the rusty black frock which was the mourning habiliment for her maternal parent, and the expression of her features was that of natural joyousness, tempered, but not wholly suppressed, by thoughtfulness beyond her years.

Leonard Beaufort had once been, as was implied by his daughter, in a different station to that he now occupied. He was by birth and education a gentleman; but partly owing to his own mismanagement and extravagance, and partly from misfortunes altogether unavoidable (though he chose to attribute his reverses wholly to the latter cause), he found himself suddenly plunged from competence into utter destitution. He had hitherto practised painting as an amateur, but now he was forced to embrace it as the only means afforded him of supporting his family, which at that time consisted of a wife and two children. He was not without some share of talent; but unhappily for those who depended on his exertions, he was too indolent to make much progress in an art which requires the exercise of perseverance, no less than the possession of genius; and after struggling for more than three years with the bitterest poverty, his wife and youngest child fell victims to their change of circumstances. Little Amy was thus left motherless, and would have been friendless, but for the care of a neighbour, who, pitying her forlorn condition, watched over her with almost maternal regard. Mrs Lyddiard was the widow of a merchant's clerk, who had no other provision than that which was afforded her by her own labours in a little school; but from these humble means she was enabled, by prudent management, to give her only child Herbert (a boy about three years the senior of Amy) a tolerable education, which would fit him to undertake a similar situation to that which his father had filled.

Towards this amiable woman and her son, the warm affections which had been pent up in the young heart of our little heroine, since the death of her mother and infant brother, now gushed forth in copious streams; for, though she loved her father with a tenderness scarcely to be expected, and certainly unmerited by one who manifested such indifference in return, she dared not express her feelings in words or caresses. Beaufort would usually devote a few of the morning hours to his profession, and then, growing weary, throw aside his pencil in disgust, and either wander about the neighbourhood in moody silence, or spend the rest of the day in the society of a few dissolute persons of education, with whom he had become acquainted since his residence in Manchester. The indolence of the parent had, however, the effect of awakening the latent energies of the daughter's mind; and young as she was at the time we introduce her to our readers, her thoughts were engaged upon a scheme which, if successful, would, she deemed, reinstate them in competence. This was for her to become possessed of a knowledge of her father's art (secretly, since he had given a check to her plan), and she believed she could accomplish it by watching his progress, and practising during his long absences from home. As Mrs Lyddiard warmly approved of the proposition, it was immediately put into execution; and Herbert, who was also made a confidant, volunteered to purchase her colours and brushes; for she dared not make use of her father's, for fear of discovery.

The performances of the young artist for the first twelve months, as might be expected, did not rise above mediocrity; but by increased perseverance and a determination to excel, she rapidly improved. The disposal of a few of her pictures furnished her with the means to procure materials for others; but she still studiously concealed her knowledge from her father, intending to do so till her skill approximated in some degree to his.

Eight years thus glided away, and the beautiful and artless child had now become an elegant and lovely young woman. Her nineteenth birthday was approaching, and she determined to prepare a specimen of her abilities to be displayed on that occasion. She selected Lear and Cordelia for her subject, thinking it would tacitly express the affection which had instigated her desire to acquire a knowledge of her father's profession. She completed her task, and the Lyddiards were lavish in their praises of the performance. Herbert declared it to be quite equal to any her father had done, and his approbation, it must be acknowledged, was highly valued by the fair artist. On the evening before the eagerly-anticipated day, Beaufort came home at an unusually early hour, and, what was of rare occurrence, in excellent spirits.

'I've sold that piece from Shakspeare I finished last week to a gentleman who is going abroad,' he said, addressing his daughter with unwonted confidence and kindness; for it was not often that he deigned to make her acquainted with anything connected with his profession.

'What, the Prospero and Miranda I admired so much, papa?' Amy asked.

'Yes; and he wants another to pair it done within a fortnight, so I must rise early and labour hard, for the days are short; but I was better remunerated than commonly, which makes it worth my while to put myself to a little inconvenience.'

'You will like to have your coffee at six to-morrow morning then? Amy observed.

'Yes, child, not a moment later.'

The coffee was prepared to the minute, and, contrary to the expectation of the daughter, her father was up to partake of it; for it was not an uncommon case for him to talk of executing a painting in a hurry, and then be more than usually dilatory in its performance. In this instance, however, he seemed in earnest, for, after having hastily swallowed his breakfast, he sat down to sketch out the piece. Amy silently withdrew from the room, not daring at present to broach the subject which was uppermost in her thoughts, and employed herself with her domestic duties till the time when she deemed he would require her assistance in mixing his colours, which was her usual task.

'It won't do; the design is bad,' the artist petulantly exclaimed as his daughter re-entered the apartment, and he angrily dashed his pencil to the ground.

'What won't do, dear papa?' Amy gently inquired.

'I've spent the whole night deciding on a subject, and now that I have sketched it, see that it's not suitable,' he pettishly made answer.

'What is it, papa?'

'Coriolanus and his mother.'

'Well, in my opinion, that would be very appropriate. As the other was a father and daughter, here is a mother and son; but if you don't like it, what think you of Lear and Cordelia?' Amy's voice faltered, and she dared not raise her eyes from the sketch which she affected to be examining.

'I'm not in a mood for painting to-day. I'll try to-morrow.'

'But your time, you said, was short?' Amy ventured to interpose.

'Well, if I can't get it done, he must go without it,' was his irritable reply. 'I'm not going to be tied down to the easel, whether disposed or not, for such a paltry sum.'

'I thought you told me that this gentleman would remunerate you handsomely?'

'Handsomely!' the artist scornfully repeated; 'it is better than I am usually paid, but not a fiftieth part of what I ought to receive. See, how some men, not possessed of half my talent, succeed! but they have the patronage of the great to aid them.'

'And perhaps brighter days may yet dawn on you, dear father!' pleaded the daughter.

'Never!' and Beaufort rose in haste to attire himself for departure.

'Papa,' cried Amy, gently catching his arm, 'will you just stay for a few minutes; I have something to say to you;' and a deep flush of crimson suffused her cheek as she spoke. Beaufort turned hesitatingly. 'It is my birthday,' she pursued—'I am this day nineteen.'

'That is no subject for rejoicing, girl,' he doggedly observed.

'I have been looking forward to this period with intense anxiety, meaning then to make you acquainted with a subject which has long engrossed my thoughts,' she timidly said.

'No foolish love affair, I hope?' Beaufort almost fiercely demanded, looking sternly in his daughter's agitated and flushed countenance as he uttered the words. 'Perhaps,' he sarcastically continued, without giving her time to reply—'perhaps you deem yourself marriageable at the matron-like age of nineteen, and have selected some country boor for my son-in-law?'

This speech was directed at Herbert Lyddiard, and Amy felt it; but her thoughts were at this moment occupied by another subject of absorbing interest. 'No,' she returned with modest dignity; 'I have at present no desire to alter *my* condition, but I have for years been intent upon bettering *yours*. I may be presumptuous in supposing it possible that any effort of mine could do so; but I was resolved to make the trial, and this shall speak for me.' As she concluded, she drew from a closet the picture she had so anxiously prepared, and displayed it to her parent's astonished gaze. Beaufort could not speak, but stood for some minutes immoveable, with his eyes fixed on the piece, as if doubting the reality of what he beheld.

'Amy,' he exclaimed, 'is it possible that this is your performance?'

'It is, father.'

'And you have had no teacher?'

'Yes, you have been my teacher. For eight long years I have been your pupil—a silent but a most attentive pupil. I owe all my knowledge to you.'

'It is admirable,' he murmured, 'and the very thing I want; as like my execution as if I myself had done it.'

'Do you say so, my father?' Amy exultingly exclaimed. 'Do you say so? That is praise beyond what I had ever dared to hope for;' and, for the first time in her life, she threw herself into her parent's embrace.

Beaufort re-examined the work. 'Did you intend it to pair my Prospero and Miranda?' he asked.

'I did, though not with the idea of its ever being sold as such. I greatly admired your father and daughter, and thought I would attempt a similar piece. I thought, too'—she stopped for a moment, then blushingly added—'I thought it an appropriate offering from one who desires to be a Cordelia to you.'

The sale of his daughter's picture was a fresh era in the life of the artist, as it was the means of introducing him to several persons of rank and influence, who were at the time visitors at the house of the purchaser. Though Amy's picture was more highly finished than her father's, no one guessed that the Lear and Cordelia, and the Prospero and Miranda, were not done by the same hand. Amy had caught her father's bold style, but added to it a delicate softness which he, from impatience, not want of ability, usually omitted. The calls upon her time were now incessant; for Beaufort grew more indolent than ever when he found that she cheerfully took so large a portion of his labour off his hands. He would frequently sketch an outline, and then leave it for her to finish, without regarding the inroads he was by these means making on his daughter's health. Meanwhile he spent the profits of her toil in luxuries, in which she shared not; still allowing her the miserable pittance which barely kept want from their dwelling, and would not permit of her making, either in her home or her person, an appearance above the humbler class of mechanics.

'We will bid a joyful adieu to this hateful town, and settle again in London,' the artist exclaimed, as, late one evening, he entered his house in an excited state, after a visit to one of his new patrons.

'Are you in earnest, papa?' Amy asked, whilst the colour forsook her cheek.

'In earnest, girl?' he repeated, 'to be sure I am. I think I have droned here long enough, and it is time that some change took place for the better. The purchaser of my last picture is a young baronet who has just come into possession of a princely fortune, and, by a little flattery, I have so far got myself into his good graces, that he has promised to provide money, to enable me to make a suitable appearance in town: he says, too, that amongst his acquaintances alone he can procure me sufficient employment, which shall be liberally remunerated. 'Tis true,' Beaufort laughingly added, 'he has no more taste for paintings than his valet, and perhaps not so much; but that matters not: he thinks that he has, and it is not my place to undeceive him; for, as he is rich and influential, he may be a valuable friend to us."

Amy listened without making any reply.

'You are silent, girl?' her father resumed. 'I thought you would be delighted with the intelligence. Will you not be glad to exchange this miserable hovel for a handsomely-furnished house? And you shall have masters to instruct you in dancing, singing, and music; for I expect that you will now have an opportunity of getting settled in the rank of life in which you were born.'

Still Amy replied not.

'Well, you are the strangest girl I ever met with,' Beaufort pursued, in tones indicative of rising wrath. 'But I see how it is. I have suspected as much for some time. You would rather marry a beggarly clerk. I can tell you, however, that Herbert Lyddiard is no husband for you, and I positively forbid you to hold any further intercourse with him or his mother.'

'Oh, father,' cried Amy in the agony of her feelings, now finding utterance, 'can you require me to be so base as thus to treat a friend who has been to me like a mother?'

'I have no personal objection to the woman, nor to her son either, had I not reason to believe that he aspires to an alliance with you,' he rejoined; adding—'Now hear what I say, girl; I start for London tomorrow, and shall send for you in a few days, during which time I shall get a house prepared for your reception. Here are the means to provide suitable apparel for the position we shall resume in society; and I expect that you hold yourself in readiness to depart at an hour's warning.'

Amy dared not oppose her father's commands, and took the offered purse in silence.

As might be expected, the knowledge of Miss Beaufort's intended departure drew from Herbert Lyddiard a full confession of his long-cherished love; and Amy could not deny that it was reciprocal, though she thought it right to make known to him the cruel prohibition her father had enjoined. The mother strove to console the young couple, by representing that it was probable that some change might take place which would induce Mr Beaufort to withdraw his opposition to their union, and counselled Amy for the present to yield implicit obedience to her father's commands. 'You are yet very young, my dear children,' she said, 'and that directing Providence which has hitherto smiled upon your early attachment, will not, I trust, see fit to sever you.'

The dreaded summons came within a week, Beaufort not thinking it safe for her to remain longer than necessity obliged in the neighbourhood of her humble lover's residence. He received her in an elegant house in the vicinity of Portman Square, which in this brief time he had handsomely furnished and provided with servants. Amy entered it with a sickening heart; and, as he led her from room to room, demanding her approbation, she felt more disposed to weep than to rejoice.

'Amy,' he said, when they were quite alone in the room designed for his studio, 'you are to reign mistress here; but be careful never to drop a hint regarding the humble manner in which you have lived for so many years: no one must surmise that we have been in poverty, or our ruin is certain. I intend giving an entertainment to my friends a few nights hence, and then I shall introduce you to society; meantime I expect that you will provide yourself with elegant and appropriate attire for the occasion; for on you much of my success may depend.'

'On me!' Amy exclaimed in astonishment; then recollecting herself, she added, 'If you mean on my exertions, father, you may still depend upon them.'

'No, I do not mean your exertions, though at present I must avail myself of your assistance; but I mean by the manner in which you receive my friends. Amy,' he continued, looking steadily in his daughter's face, 'you are possessed of uncommon beauty; you are doubtless aware of it. Herbert Lyddiard has not failed, I daresay, to tell you so. A beautiful young woman is at all times a powerful attraction, and to me it is everything, to extend the circle of my acquaintances.'

Amy's cheek, which had been flushed by the former part of this speech, turned deadly pale at its conclusion. How could she, who had all her life been shut out from society, entertain her father's male guests—she, a retiring and almost ignorant girl, without one female friend or adviser! She did not speak; but Beaufort saw that powerful feelings were agitating her breast, and strove to laugh away what he termed her foolish fears.

'A few evenings will dispel all your *mauvaise honte*,' he gaily said. 'I will hear of no silly objections;' and, thrusting a purse of gold into her hand, he left the room.

Amy could scarcely realise the truth of the position in which she stood. The events of the last few days seemed like a dream; but if so, it was a dream from which she would have been glad to have awakened, and to have found herself in her former humble home. She could not but fear that all her father possessed was held upon a very uncertain tenure, and, what was worse, that it was obtained by dishonourable means. This idea was strengthened when the gala evening arrived, and our heroine was introduced to her father's principal patron, a vain and weak-minded man, who listened to his host's extravagant adulation with evident complacency, though to every one else it was palpably insincere. Beaufort insisted on his visiting his studio, to give his opinion of the grouping of a historical piece he had sketched out for Amy to fill up. The baronet, thus flattered, suggested some alterations which would have made it absolutely ridiculous; and the artist would actually have complied, had not his daughter, who had been requested to be present, interposed; and her guest gallantly acquiesced in her judgment.

From this period a new trial awaited the unhappy girl, for Sir Philip Rushwood now became her professed admirer. Beaufort had planned this affair from the moment of his first introduction to the young man, though he had warily concealed his wishes from Amy. He had contrived to display, as if by accident, a miniature portrait he had once taken of his daughter; and as he pretended unwillingness to make known the name of the original, the curiosity of the baronet was naturally excited. On finding that the beautiful young woman he so much admired was the artist's daughter, he became anxious to see her; but her father was determined that a meeting should not take place until Amy was in a situation to set off her natural charms, and was removed from her humble lover. Little suspecting the scheme which had been laid, she met Sir Philip with feelings of gratitude; but they were exchanged for sentiments bordering on disgust when he became a suitor for her hand. There was nothing vicious about the young man: he was the dupe, not the deceiver; but to a mind like Amy's, filled too as it was with the image of Herbert Lyddiard, his attentions were intolerable. The open encouragement he now received from the father, however, emboldened him to persevere, and he professed to look upon her marked disapproval as nothing but maidenly diffidence, and proceeded to address her as though a positive engagement existed between them.

Amy now spent her days either at the easel, or in receiving instructions from the masters her father hired, and her evenings in entertaining his guests. He appeared not to have an idea that prudence required that some matronly lady should become the chaperon of his isolated child, much less that her heart could yearn for feminine society. To one who was naturally so sensitive and timid, the task was exquisitely painful; yet she dared not murmur, or a volley of abuse would have been the result. Nine months thus passed away in splendid misery, during which period Beaufort had often indirectly expressed his wishes that his daughter would accept the overtures of the baronet; but on the morning of her twentieth birthday, he called her into his studio, saying that he had a matter of importance to consult with her upon. Poor Amy guessed too well the subject he was about to introduce; but she was appalled when, in a few hurried words, and with a voice almost choked by agitation, he told her that it depended on her decision, respecting the acceptance of Sir Philip Rushwood's suit, whether he was to give her away at the altar as a bride, or be himself dragged to a prison.

'But why, father, should there be so dreadful an alternative?' she eagerly asked.

'Because I have nothing but what I owe to him. On his credit this house has been furnished, and his tradespeople have supplied our table. Your very apparel has been purchased from sums of money I have from time to time borrowed from him—for I have not yet met with the increased sale and handsome remuneration for my pictures I was led to expect. Indeed many of those you supposed to be ordered, were pledged for a tenth part of their value. If, however, you become his wife,' he proceeded, 'we shall never want; for his fortune is immense, and he is easily persuaded to part with it; but if you refuse, his vanity, which is his ruling passion, will be so deeply wounded, that he will withdraw his assistance from me, and our ruin is inevitable. I have amused him with hopes of success and assurances that you will smile on him at last, in spite of your girlish coquetry, till he is incensed at the delay; and he last night told me that he would be put off no longer, but have a positive answer *from your own lips* this very evening.' Amy pressed her hands upon her burning brow in unutterable anguish. 'Yes,' her father resumed, 'this very evening you must set your seal to our destiny. It remains for you either to open a brilliant career before me, or to shut me up in a prison in disgrace. I ask you not to give *me* an answer. Your bane and antidote are both before you; but remember that on the decision of your lips to-night our mutual welfare depends.'

As Beaufort concluded, he rose from his seat and hurriedly left the room, whilst poor Amy remained panic-struck, and scarcely comprehending the extent of her wretchedness. Her energies were, however, aroused, and directed into a fresh channel; when, a few minutes after her father's departure, a servant placed a note in her hand, bearing the well-known characters of Herbert Lyddiard, which she said had been delivered at the door by a meanly-dressed young man. She almost flew to her chamber to peruse the contents, which, though written by Herbert, were dictated by his mother. She stated that her son, having lost his situation in Manchester by the death of his employer, had been induced to remove to London, with the hope of obtaining a more lucrative one in that city; but, being disappointed in his expectations, that they were consequently reduced to the greatest distress. Her health, she concluded, had suffered so severely from intense anxiety and privations, that, believing herself to be dying, she solicited, as a last request, one brief visit from her beloved young friend.

Amy Beaufort possessed a mind which never sunk under difficulties whilst there was any active duties to perform, and in less than half an hour she was in a hackney-coach on her way to Mrs Lyddiard's residence, bearing with her, besides a few articles of nourishment for the invalid, a large packet containing some of the early efforts of her pencil, which she, with prompt thoughtfulness, imagined might be disposed of, if only for a trifle, to aid her unfortunate friends in their present exigence. She had a few guineas left from her father's last gift; but she now shrunk from using them even for so sacred a purpose. The coach stopped at the door of a large but mean-looking house in a narrow crowded street, and her inquiry if Mrs Lyddiard lived there, was answered in the affirmative by a ragged boy, who asked if he should carry her parcel. Amy followed him, not without some apprehension, up three flights of dark steep stairs; but her fears were relieved when her gentle tap at the door to which her guide pointed, was answered by the well-known voice of her early friend.

The meeting was affecting in the extreme; but Amy did not find the invalid reduced quite so low as her imagination had pictured. Though a few months only had elapsed since they parted, each had a long tale of trials to tell, and that Amy had to relate was rendered doubly distressing by the confession she was forced to make of a parent's delinquency. At length she spoke of the decision which was expected from her that night.

'And how do you intend to act?' asked her companion in breathless anxiety. 'I feel that I dare not offer you counsel. I am too deeply interested; for it would be draining the last drop of earthly bliss from my cup to see you wedded to any other than to my son.'

'I never will, Mrs Lyddiard,' cried Amy energetically, rising at the same time from her kneeling position beside the bed of the invalid. 'I feel myself justified in making this resolution. I have been an unwilling, nay, I may say an unconscious agent in a scheme of dishonour; but I should be culpable if, by any act of mine, I furthered it, even though the motive should be to save a parent from disgrace and a prison. Still, my father claims my duteous regard, and so long as my personal exertions and self-denial can afford him aid, I will never desert him.'

'You have spoken nobly, my dear Amy,' Mrs Lyddiard exclaimed, her eyes brightening, and her pale cheek flushing with pleasure. 'Your own upright heart is your best adviser, and Heaven will aid your filial piety.'

As our heroine prudently wished to avoid a meeting with her lover, she left the house earlier than she otherwise would have done, and returned home to prepare her mind for the trial which awaited her. She resolved to decline the baronet's suit respectfully, yet firmly, alluding with gratitude to the services he had rendered her father; and she hoped much, notwithstanding the anger he had evinced, from the natural mildness of his character. She had not, however, been long in her chamber, when she, to her surprise, received another summons from her father, who she had imagined to be from home. The dark frown which clouded his brow too surely indicated the state of his feelings. 'You may spare yourself the trouble of refusing Sir Philip Rushwood, Miss Beaufort,' he sneeringly remarked, as she tremblingly took a seat by his side; 'you will not have the opportunity of displaying your triumph.'

'What do you mean, papa?' Amy interrogated, wholly at a loss to understand the import of his words.

'Oh, you are in utter ignorance that your vagabond suitor, Lyddiard, left a billet for you this morning,' he resumed in the same sarcastic strain; 'and you are quite unconscious that you were carried in a coach to his residence; but the lynx-eye of jealousy watched you.

and you have converted a friend into a foe. It is I, however,' he fiercely added, 'who must suffer the penalty of your disobedience and duplicity, and either die in a prison, or become an exile from my country. I prefer the latter, and must leave you to reap the fruits of your own self-will.'

'Oh, my father!' Amy almost wildly exclaimed, throwing herself at his feet, 'had you given me time I should have explained everything to you connected with my visit to Mrs Lyddiard; but I intreat you not to add to the dishonour you are already involved in by flight. Surely the debts you have contracted are not to so large an amount but they may be liquidated in time by our mutual exertions. Let us descend to the sphere from which we have so lately risen, if by that means we can honourably overcome our difficulties.'

'Talk not to me in this manner,' Beaufort angrily interposed; 'I will not brook the disgrace your obstinacy has brought upon me; and you have yourself alone to blame that you are not the mistress of a princely fortune. Go to your beggarly lover, if he will receive you when penniless and homeless—the tie between *us* is broken.' And with these words he rose to quit the room.

'Do not leave me, father!' Amy shrieked forth, clinging around him to prevent his departure. 'I will share a prison with you, if such be the dreadful alternative. I will labour for your support; but do not—do not leave me.'

Beaufort shook her from him with a violence which threw her to the ground. 'Go, wretched girl!' he vociferated as he descended the stairs, 'you have been *my* ruin.' It was the last words he addressed to her—they met no more.

Scarcely allowing herself to believe that her father would not repent of his determination to leave the country, Amy awaited with intense anxiety the event of the evening. The shades of twilight fell, but he appeared not. The guests he had invited arrived; still he did not return. She was obliged to send an apology for her absence; for she was really ill, and felt unequal to the trial of meeting the baronet in her present agitated state of mind.

The morning brought a confirmation of her worst fears. A rumour of Beaufort's sudden flight had gone abroad, owing to his absence from his guests; and the consequence was, that creditors poured in from all quarters. Amy met the emergency with a presence of mind she was herself surprised at. Her first care was to have all the effects sold, that the debts might be liquidated as far as possible; but now, to her unspeakable concern, she discovered that her father had carried off the principal part of the plate and small valuables. She next met her late suitor, Sir Philip Rushwood, and after soliciting an account of the sums due to him by her parent, declared her intention of refunding them from the labours of her own hands. 'I may perhaps make trial of your patience by some delay, Sir Philip,' she said; 'but so far as my receipts will allow, no one shall be the loser from having placed confidence in my unhappy father. Had I accepted your addresses, you would have had reason to despise me; but I am not so base as to form a union in which my heart has no share.'

The baronet was astonished. He had hitherto formed a mean opinion of the female character, having been incessantly beset by manœuvring mammas with marriageable daughters ever since he became possessed of his fortune. His desire to win the beautiful young artist, who never appeared so lovely as at this moment, increased; but he felt that he dared not urge his suit after this declaration.

Amy now sought the home of her early friend; and, deserted by her only natural protector, thought herself justified in consenting to become the wife of Herbert Lyddiard when circumstances would admit of the union taking place. She employed herself indefatigably at the easel; and Sir Philip Rushwood having with some difficulty discovered the mart at which her pictures were exposed for sale, bought them up (though with the strictest secrecy) as fast as she produced them, paying considerably more than the price she hoped to obtain for them. Herbert was at this period so fortunate as to obtain a situation, which, though not very lucrative, yet afforded him the means of providing the family with a more comfortable home; and as Mrs Lyddiard's health rapidly amended with her improved circumstances, no further obstacle opposed the marriage of the young couple. Amy's only anxiety now arose from the uncertainty of her father's fate; for she could gain no further intelligence of him than that he had fled the kingdom, having obtained a passport under a feigned name.

The ready and profitable sale of her paintings enabled our heroine to set aside sums for the liquidation of her father's debts earlier than she expected. Herbert volunteered to become the bearer of her first payment to Sir Philip Rushwood; and as his manners and appearance were those of a gentleman, he was shown by the footman into the dining-parlour, to wait a few minutes till his master was at liberty. The young man started on entering the apartment, for he, to his astonishment, perceived it to be hung around with the pictures Amy had executed since her residence with them. He was examining them more minutely, that he might be certain he was not mistaken, when the baronet appeared.

'You are admiring those paintings, sir,' the latter observed. Herbert bowed assent. 'They were executed by a lady who is no less distinguished for her virtues than for her beauty and talent,' he added, his features glowing with animation. 'And should you become a purchaser, you will confer an obligation on me.'

'Happily for me, sir, *I* possess the fair artist herself,' his visitor smilingly interposed.

Sir Philip drew back in amazement, and Herbert proceeded to explain the object of his mission.

'I cannot take the money, Mr Lyddiard,' the baronet returned with evident emotion. 'The loss of a few hundreds is of no real importance to me; and do you think that I could suffer that noble young woman to toil incessantly to pay the debt of an unprincipled parent? No, I am not so mercenary. Miss Beaufort refused me as a husband, but she must allow me the pleasure of becoming her friend. You need not be jealous, sir, of the title I am solicitous to assume, for it was for your sake that she rejected me; but whether as a maiden or wife, I shall deem myself happy in being permitted to serve her.'

'I am most grateful for your kindness, Sir Philip,' Herbert returned; 'but I cannot avail myself of it with respect to the money. Mrs Lyddiard is, I know, too desirous to rescue, as far as possible, her unhappy father's character from disgrace, to suffer a debt of his to remain uncancelled.

Thus urged, the baronet reluctantly took the sum; determining, however, to return it through some medium which would not compromise the independence, or hurt the feelings, of the person he was so anxious to serve; and he had soon an opportunity of proving the sincerity of his professions, by using his interest in procuring Herbert an appointment far superior to that he at present filled.

It was nearly three years subsequent to the period at which Beaufort quitted England, that his daughter received the sad intelligence of his death. He had been a miserable wanderer on the continent for that space of time, and he breathed his last in a lazaretto at Naples. It was not till he lay upon his dying bed that he could summon courage to address his deserted child. When all earthly hope was over, and the awful realities of a future state presented themselves to his appalled vision, he thought of the misery he had caused one who had ever been an affectionate and devoted daughter to him; and as this epistle expressed the deepest penitence for the errors of his misspent life, Amy clung to the hope that it was sincere.

Thus Leonard Beaufort, with genius which would have done honour to his profession, died a miserable outcast, through its misuse; whilst his noble-minded daughter, by industry, integrity, and perseverance, rose by slow but sure degrees to competence, and enjoys that peace known only to those who pursue a virtuous course.

SNATCHINGS IN A LIBRARY.

It is with a glad feeling of escape that day after day we close the door on the din of the streets, and, mounting the broad stairs which lead to the upper floors, find ourselves in grateful silence, surrounded by the now familiar array of books; more familiar than when, erewhile, we discoursed concerning them,* yet not less welcome, less venerated. In our first acquaintance there was a sense of mysterious awe—a dim anticipation of the unknown. We were like Columbus standing on the island shore, gazing with earnest hopes towards the uncertain west: but now we have crossed the intervening ocean, planted our foot on the mighty continent beyond, coasted some of its islets, and, with glimpses of lofty mountains and tall promontories, have returned, if not deeply laden with solid treasures, at least with the certainty that treasures exist, that our freight may always equal our courage and diligence.

Sometimes there is nothing but the title to commemorate; at others, a quaint paragraph, an incidental opinion, a bygone superstition, may be pleasurably transcribed, and set up to twinkle again for a brief space before the eyes of men. One who has recorded the titles of manuscripts, gives us the concluding words of a 'Cronycle,' whose date is 1460:—'And after that ther bred a raven at Charyng Crosse at Louden. And neuer was seen noon brede there before. And after that came a gret dethe of pestilence, that lasted iij yer. And peple dyed myhtely in every place, man, woman, and chylde. On whos soulys God have mercy. Amen.' An instance of the popular method of educing cause from effect, not confined to those times. Latimer observed, in one of his sermons, that the people of Kent attributed the appearance of the Godwin Sands to the building of Tenterden steeple. When the new style was introduced in this country in the last century, 'the mob pursued the minister in his carriage, clamouring for the ten days by which, as they supposed, their lives had been shortened; and the illness and death of the astronomer Bradley, who had assisted the government with his advice, were attributed to a judgment from Heaven.'—The fear of change, and the inclination to regard it as of evil tendency, is not a modern feeling; for in another of these old manuscripts, we read a poem entitled 'Now-a-dayes,' in which the writer, though earlier than the great accelerator of innovation—printing—laments,

'We Englisshemen beholde
our auncient customs holde
more precious than golde
be clene cast away:
And other new be fownd,
the which ye may vnderstand
that causethe all your land
so gretly to decay.'

Endless were the task to search through the authors reposing there in legions, and yet it is one we could commence without wearying anticipations of the completion. Might we not hope to reap a rich harvest of motives—to discover the causes of the writers' patient labour—the secret spring that urged them on? Yet fear we that human passion and weakness would hold a prominent place in the catalogue. Some have written for vain-glory; some from prejudice; some from envy, hatred, and malice; many from integrity of heart, earnest for the truth. What a mountain of smouldering opinion must have been developed with the invention of printing! 'Along with the great change which called upon men to read and judge for themselves, came the great discovery which made it possible that they should do as was enjoined. The age in which religious principle declared the Bible to be every man's book, was the age in which natural invention placed it within every man's reach.'* How truly the new power was appreciated, may be seen in the countless host of works that started into existence during the controversies of the early reformers. But leaving these for a future notice, we may dwell on the sincerity and zeal characteristic of the primeval printers. The issuing of a book was an event not to be regarded merely in the prospect of profit; they seemed reluctant to part with their editions, and wrote phrases so full of hope and thankfulness on the introductory leaves, that we admire them as much for their earnestness as their quaintness. One of them tells us on his title-page, that

'He who reads a booke rashly, at random doth runne;
He goes on his errande, yet leaues it undone.'

And we may judge of Caxton's reverence for the art to which he consecrated his life, from the language of his prefaces or commentaries. In the 'Prohemye' to the edition of Chaucer in 1475, he says, 'Grete thankes, lawde, and honour ought to be gyven and unto the clerkes, poetes, and historiographs that have wreton many noble bokes of wysedom;' and goes on to tell that he accomplished his labour 'by thayde of Almighty God, whom I humbly beseche to gyue me grace and ayde to achyeue and accomplysshe, to his lawde, honour, and glorye; and that alle ye that shal in thys book rede, or here, will of your charyte, emong your dedes of mercy, remembre the sowle of the sayde Gefferey Chaucer, first auctour and maker of thys book; and also that alle we that shal see and rede therein, may so take and understonde the good and vertuous tales, that it may so prouffyte unto the helthe of our sowles, that after thys short and transitorye lyf, we may come to euerlastyng lyf in heuen. Amen.' What would be thought of such a preface now-a-days, when so many books are issued merely 'at the request of friends?' That this was not a solitary instance of old Caxton's reverent earnestness, is shown in all his works: his 'Book for Travellers' begins—

FRENSSHE.	ENGLISSHE.
'Ou nom du pere,	'In the name of the fadre,
Et du filz,	And of the soone,
Et du saint esperite,	And of the holy ghoost,
Veul commencier,	I wyll begynne
Et ordonner vng livre.'	And ordeyne this book.'

One of the books printed by him was the 'Mirrour of the Worlde,' in looking over which we are struck by the curious titles of some of the chapters; among them are, 'Wherefor God made the world round'—'For to know how the wyndes growe'—'Wherefore men see no starres by daylight'—'Why men see not the sonne by night.' These quotations show the unsettled form of spelling of that day, for in some cases the spelling of the same word is seen to vary.

We may trace this same pious tone of feeling in the works of Wynkyn de Worde, Caxton's assistant and successor. At the end of 'The Chastysing of Goddes Children,' printed by him in 1493, are the lines—

'Infynyte laud, with thankynges many folde,
I yielde to God, me socouryng wyth his grace,
This boke to fynyshe which that ye beholde,
Scale of perfection calde in euery place:
Whereof thauctour Walter Hilton was,
And Wynkyn de Worde this hath sett in print,
In William Caxston's hows so fyll the case,
God rest his soule.'

* Alluding to a former paper nearly similar to the present, and by the same writer—entitled 'A Library—Old Books'—which appeared in No. 49, new series (Dec. 7, 1844).

* Vaughan. Age of Great Cities.

And again we read at the end of a translation of *Bartholomeus de proprietatibus rerum*—

'And also of your charyte call to remembraunce
The soule of William Caxton, first printer of this book'—

which lines conclude with a notice of early paper-making, thus:—

'And John Tate the yonger, joy mote he broke,
which late hathe in England make this paper thynne,
That now in our Englisshe this boke is printed inn.'

In 1521, Wynkyn printed a collection of Christmas carols, one of which relates to the preparation of a feast; and 'a caroll' enters 'bringyng in the bores heed,' singing—

'The bores heed in hande bringe I,
With garlans gay and rosemary,
I pray you all synge merely.'

Was this jingle ringing in Scott's memory when he wrote, in the introduction to the sixth canto of Marmion,

'Then the grim boar's head frowned on high,
Crested with bays and rosemary?'

The almost universal credulity of that day was taken advantage of by the retailers of prophecies and predictions, who flattered the popular prejudices to their own profit; but we find occasionally that the seers could be humorous as well as mysterious. Another of Wynkyn's books begins—

'A merry prognosticacyon,
For the yere of Chryste's incarnacyon,
A thousand fyue hundreth forty and foure.

This to prognostycate I may be bolde,
That whan the newe yere is come, gone is the olde.'

The early printers did not content themselves with the simple insertion of 'errata' for the correction of errors; they generally prefaced it with a humble apology to the reader; but in some instances the apology alone appeared, and the reader was left to detect the faults for himself. To a metrical version of some of the books of Scripture, printed in 1560, is appended—

'Such faltes as you herein shall find,
I pray you be content;
And do the same with will and mynd,
That was then our intent.
The printers were outlandish men,
The faltes they be the more,
Which are escapyd now and then,
But hereof are no store.'

The vision of Pierce or Peter Plowman has been so frequently alluded to, that but few persons can be unacquainted with the existence of this ancient poem. It was 'fyrst imprinted by Robert Crowley, dwellyng in Ely, rentes in Holburne, anno Domini 1550.' The printer appears to have devoted much pains to his work, as he tells his readers. 'Being desyerous to know the name of the authure of this most worthy worke (gentle reader), and the tyme of the writynge of the same, I did not onely gather together such aunciente copies as I could come by, but also consult such men as I knew to be more exercised in the studie of antiquities, then I myself have ben. And by some of them I have learned that the autour was named Roberte Langelande, a Shropshere man, born in Cleybirie,* about viii myles from Maluerne hilles..... We may justly conject, therefore, that it was first written about two hundred yeres paste, in the tyme of kynge Edwarde the thyrde. In whose tyme it pleased God to open the eyes of many to se hys truth, geuing them boldnes of herte to open their mouthes and cry oute againste the worckes of darcknes, as did John Wicklefe, who also in those dayes translated the holye bible into the Englishe tonge; and this writer who, in reportynge certaine visions and dreames, that he fayned himself to have dreamed, doeth most christianlye enstructe the weake, and sharply rebuke the obstinate blynde. There is no maner of vice, that reigneth in any estate of men, which this wryter hath not godly, learnedlye, and wittilye rebuked. He wrote altogether in miter (metre), but not after the maner of our rimers that write nowe adayes (for his verses ende not alike), but the nature of his miter is to have thre wordes at the leaste in euery verse, which beginne with some one letter. As for ensample, the first two verses of the boke renne upon S, as thus:—

In a somer season whan sette was the sunne,
I shope me into shrobbes, as I a shepe were.

The next runneth upon H, as thus:—

In habite as an hermite unholy of werckes, &c.

This thing noted, the miter shal be very pleasaunt to read; the English is according to the time it was written in, and the sence somewhat darcke, but not so harde but that it may be understande of suche as will not sticke to breake the shell of the nutte for the kernelles sake.'—Owen Rogers, who lived 'near unto great Saint Bartholomew's gate, at the sign of the Spread Eagle,' printed a prose edition of this work about 1561, which ends with the lines—

'God saue the king, and speede the plough,
And send the prelats care inough,
Inough, inough, inough.'

* Cleobury.

It would be curious to search for the methods adopted to inform the community of the publication of new editions before the introduction of newspapers: we see, indeed, advertisements stitched in at the end of books; these, however, would be rarely seen except by the actual purchaser. At the end of a work called the 'Philosopher's Game,' printed in 1563, we find the publisher anticipating the rhyming advertiser of later days in the lines—

'All things belonging to this game,
for reason you may bye,
At the booke shop vnder Bochurch,
in Chepesyde redilye.'

And in looking through some of those old catalogues, we meet with many quaint and characteristic titles. 'The cristen state of matrymonye, wherein housebandes and wyues maye lerne to kepe house together wyth loue'—1552; 'A detection of heresie, or why heretickes bee brent'—1565; and 'The storie of the parson of Kalenbbrowe, who,' a commentator informs us, 'pretended to fly, to get off his bad wine in a hot day.'

A book printed in Latin and English, at Oxford, in 1589, contains a quis on the unfortunate result of the attempted invasion of England by Spain—

'A Skeltonical salutation,
Or condigne gratulation,
And just vexation,
Of the Spanish nation,
That in a bravado,
Spent many a crusado,
In setting forth the Armado,
England to envado.'

A grave character pervades most of the early works on divinity; and the writers appear to have felt extremely zealous in their labours, and desirous that they should not fail of due effect. One who wrote in 1483, finishes his volume by saying—

'In heuen shall dwelle alle cristen men,
That knowe and kepe Goddes byddynges ten.'

Others tell us that their books were written 'to the praise of God and profite of all good christien readers. Sometimes we have 'A most fruitefull and necessary boke, therwyth to enarme all symple and ignorant folkes agaynst the raveninge wolues and false prophetes;' or, 'Very necessary and profitable for yonge gentilmen and gentilwomen abiding in court, palaice, or place.'

The Abbé Barthélemy, in his *Voyage du Jeune Anacharsis*, makes a Greek philosopher say, in speaking of the prevalent desire for praising everything, that he had a book entitled *l'Eloge du Sel*, or 'Praise of Salt,' in which all the riches of imagination are exhausted to exaggerate the services which it renders to mortals: but without resorting to imaginary titles, we may find such works in the reality. Valerianus wrote in praise of beards; the celebrated Heinsius found a theme in donkeys; and Erasmus wrote a panegyric on folly while travelling in a post-chaise. Bishop Wilkins observes, in his 'Philosophical Language,' published in 1668, that many persons may consider his inquiries concerning the letters of the alphabet as 'too minute and trivial for any prudent man to bestow his serious thoughts and time about,' and cites names of 'most eminent persons, in several ages, who were men of business,' and 'have not disdained to bestow their pains about the first elements of speech.

'Julius Cæsar is said to have written a book *De Analogia;* and the emperor, Charles the Great, to have made a grammar of his vulgar tongue. So did St Basil for the Greek, and St Austin for the Latin; both being extant in their works.'

'Besides divers of great reputation, both ancient and modern, who have written whole books on purpose concerning the just number of the letters in the alphabet, others have applied their disquisitions to some particular letters. Messala Corvinus, a great man, and a famous orator amongst the Romans, writ a book concerning the letter S. Adamantius Martyr was the author of another book concerning the letters V and B. Our learned Gataker has published a book concerning diphthongs. And Jovianus Pontanus, esteemed a learned man, hath two books *De Adspirationa*, or the letter H. M'Franklyn hath published a particular discourse concerning accents; and Erycius Puteanus hath written a book purposely—*De Inter Punctione*—Of the True Way of Pointing Clauses and Sentences.'

The quotation of these instances, Wilkins thinks, 'may be a sufficient vindication against any prejudices' to which he had referred; and speaking of the difference between the 'writing and pronouncing of words,' he remarks, that 'it should seem very reasonable that men should either speak as they write, or write as they speak. What is said of our English tongue is proportionably true of most other languages, that if ten scribes (not acquainted with the particular speech) should set themselves to write according to pronunciation, not any two of them would agree in the same way of spelling.'

''Tis related of Chilperick, king of France, that he did, for the compendiousness of writing, add to the French alphabet five letters, enjoining, by a strict and solemn edict, the reception and use of them through his dominions; and that in all schools youths should be instituted in the use of them: and yet, notwithstanding his authority in imposing of them, they were presently after his death laid aside and disused.' And ''tis said that the Arabic hath above a thousand several names for a sword, and 500 for a lion, and 200 for a serpent, and fourscore for honey.'

'Though the Hebrew tongue be the most ancient, yet Rabbi Judah Chiug of Fez, in Afric, who lived A.D. 1040, was the first that reduced it to the art of grammar. And though there were both Greek and Latin grammarians much more ancient, yet there were none in either till a long time after those languages flourished; which is the true reason of all those anomalisms in grammar—because the art was suited to language, and not language to the art. Plato is said to be the first that considered grammar; Aristotle the first that, by writing, did reduce it into an art; and Epicurus the first that publicly taught it among the Grecians.'

'And for the Latin, Crates Mallotes, ambassador to the Roman senate from King Attalus, betwixt the second and third Punic war, presently after the death of Ennius, U.C. 583, was the first that brought in the art of grammar amongst the Romans, saith Suetonius.'

We could go on thus, collecting facts and illustrations between floor and ceiling, through many pleasant and unheeded hours; but narrow limits check too wide a range. One secret, however, have we learned in our slender researches—that much of that which daily makes its appearance trumpet-mouthed as *new*, lies snugly ensconced in the pages of some author whose brain conceived and fingers moved long centuries ago—

> 'For ought of old feldis, as clarkis saith,
> Commyth new corne, from yere to yere,
> And out of old bokis, in good faith,
> Commeth all the new science that men lere.'

OCCASIONAL NOTES.

MEANINGLESS TITLES TO RAILWAYS.

The names given to many of the railways, either in progress or completed, are so utterly devoid of meaning, that the public, and especially foreigners, will require a sort of education before they shall be able to understand with what places they communicate. An individual wishing to travel from London to Edinburgh, can get no information as to his route from the indices of the railway guides. It is in vain to look under the head of 'London' or of 'Edinburgh;' for anything the index tells, there might be no line between the two capitals; not till he has stated his case to some more knowing friend, does he discover that he will have to go first by the 'Great North of England' to Newcastle, and be steamed by the 'North British,' or the 'Caledonian,' *via* Berwick or Carlisle. The mere points of the compass mentioned in so many of the titles, convey but scanty information; for although most people know the position of Bristol, of Dover, and of Southampton, yet it is only by undergoing a sort of training that a passenger understands that he must place himself on the 'Great Western,' the 'South Eastern,' or on the 'South Western,' to get to those respective places. To render this sort of perplexity worse, there are two 'Eastern Counties,' one of which leads to Colchester, and the other to Cambridge and Ely; and who can tell, from its title, where the 'Direct Northern' is to end? How far short of John o' Groats, it is impossible to say.

Then there are the various 'junctions,' between which few can distinguish except commercial travellers, and even they by dint of much practice only. Besides the 'Grand Junction' (Lancaster, Liverpool, and London), there are some having the name of one place attached, and yet none but a good topographical scholar can know what other places they unite; such as the 'Brandling Junction' (Gateshead, Shields, and London), the 'Clydesdale Junction,' and 'Trent Valley Junction.' That confusion may be a little more complete, the same vague signification is conveyed by a different word, and the result is, the 'Grand Union'—the grandeur of which appears to arise from uniting the two not very important places of Nottingham and Lynn; and the 'North Union,' from Preston to Liverpool, Manchester, or to Wigan. But the most inextricable botheration is that caused by the number of railways whose uninventive sponsors have borrowed the term 'Midland.' In a share list before us, we find no fewer than eight lines, in the titles of which this word occurs; namely—The Midland Counties; Great Western Midland, (Irish); Extension Midland, (to Sligo); Scottish Midland; Somersetshire Midland; South Midland; North Midland; and Welsh Midland.

Some of these schemes are only in progress, and it would be well if the projectors would ease the public of the mental labour they are imposing, by changing some of the titles. The first railways had plain and understandable names, and it is a sad pity that their successors have not followed their good example. The 'Manchester and Liverpool,' the 'London and Brighton,' the 'Edinburgh and Glasgow,' tell at once what they are for, and where their termini are situated. There surely can be no insuperable objections to this excellent mode of naming railways being still followed.

'PUBLISHED THIS DAY.

An ancient fiction is maintained at the head of the literary advertisements with remarkable pertinacity. Six months, or perhaps more, after a book has first seen the light, we still find the bookseller announcing it as 'published *this* day.' The book published this day is probably recommended in a pithy sentence from the Edinburgh Review, which has perhaps issued no number for nearly three months. Or it is represented as published this day, in the midst of the period during which every one is aware that no books are ever ventured into the market. It does not seem ever to occur to the persons concerned in preparing these advertisements, that they are uttering a deliberate and misleading falsehood, in announcing as a new publication one which has been in the world for several months. Yet such is really the case. We would wish to see the trade of literature superior to all such despicable tricks, which we verily believe must do more harm, by degrading an honourable calling, and introducing a doubt about the honesty of all literary announcements, than they ever could do good, even supposing them in any tolerable degree successful, which we believe they cannot be, as all roguery is only met by additional vigilance on the part of those against whom it is aimed.

PASSAGE OF THE FIRTH OF FORTH FIFTY YEARS AGO.

In a recent more than usually complete edition of the works of Alexander Wilson, the author of 'Watty and Meg,'* is a journal of the poet's wanderings as a pedlar throughout Scotland in the year 1789. The notices which he gives of the ferries across the Firth of Forth are curious, as a contrast with present arrangements. 'At Bruntisland,' he says, 'there is a passage-boat every day, save Sunday, and even then, if encouragement offers.' The passenger pays sixpence. Kinghorn was, however, the most frequented passage on the Firth. 'In a large boat, the passenger pays sixpence; in a pinnace, which is most convenient in a smooth sea, tenpence. The inhabitants are almost all boatmen, and their whole commerce being with strangers, whom perhaps they may never see again, makes them avaricious, and always on the catch. If a stranger come to town at night, intending to go over next morning, he is taken into a lodging. One boatman comes in, sits down, promises to call you in the morning, assists you to circulate the liquor, and, after a great deal of loquacity, departs. In a little while another enters, and informs you that the fellow who has just now left you goes not over at all; but that *he* goes, and for a glass of gin he will awake you, and take you along with him. Willing to be up in time, you generously treat him. According to promise, you are awakened in the morning, and assured that you have time enough to take breakfast, in the middle of which, hoarse roarings alarm you that the boat is just going off. You start up, call for your bill—the landlord appears, charges you like a nobleman—there is no time for scrupling—you are hurried away by the boatmen on the one hand, and genteelly plundered by the landlord on the other, who pockets his money and bids you haste, lest you lose your passage. Perhaps, after all, when you get on board, you are detained an hour or more by the sailors waiting for more passengers.' In comparing this system of things with the frequent passage of elegant steamers at certain hours, and in definite times, now established—with, moreover, low-water piers for embarking and debarking—we are hardly able to believe that we live in the same country described by the Paisley poet.

* Henderson, Belfast.

ACTION OF SUGAR UPON THE TEETH.

It has long been a matter of common belief that sugar, comfits, and other sweetmeats are injurious to the teeth, causing their premature decay, and its infallible attendant, toothache. We were not aware, however, that the subject had been taken up by the chemist—to whose province it more immediately belongs—till glancing over the proceedings of the French societies, when we found that M. Larrey, from certain researches, had arrived at the following conclusions:—1. Refined cane, or beet-root sugar, is prejudicial to the teeth more from its direct contact, than from the evolution of gaseous matter during digestion. 2. If a tooth be allowed to macerate in a saturated solution of sugar, it is so decomposed as to acquire almost a gelatinous character, whilst the enamel becomes opaque and spongy, and crumbles down under the slightest pressure. Sugar ought not, therefore, to enter into the composition of tooth-powder. 3. The erosion of the teeth by this substance does not depend on an acid, for none is present in sugar, but on the tendency which this organic principle has to enter into combination with the calcareous base of the tooth. 4. If the enamel be less attacked than the osseous part of the tooth, the reason is, that it contains fluoride of calcium, a body which resists chemical agency even more than the sulphate of lime.

Commenting on these conclusions, the editor of the Medical Gazette remarks, that the greater resistance of the enamel is probably owing to its hardness and close texture, and not to the presence of fluoride of calcium, of which it contains only the slightest trace. He farther adds, that it would be interesting to know 'whether these chemical results are borne out by observations made among those who are in the habit of taking large quantities of molasses and saccharine substances.' Independent of the popular opinion to which we have alluded—and which, by the way, like all other current opinions, is likely to have some foundation in reality—we believe that the experiments of M. Larrey are corroborated not only by what is observed in Europe, but by what takes place more notoriously among the coloured population of the West India islands.

EUSTACE THE NEGRO.

The following is the simple and true history* of an old negro slave, whose self-devotion, intelligence, and noble spirit are worthy of a higher commemoration. Toussaint L'Ouverture, by his stern heroism, excited the interest and warm sympathy of thousands of Europeans, despite his colour. Eustace, whose whole life was passed in doing good, is surely a noble instance that the spirit of patience, gratitude, and benevolence, may exist and bear fruit in the bosom of a poor black slave, as in that of his nobler and more refined master.

Eustace was born in 1773, on the estate of M. Belin de Villeneuve, one of the proprietors in the northern part of St Domingo. From his very infancy he sought the company of the whites as much as lay in the poor negro's power: not through servility, but in the hope of improving his mind. This disposition won his master's notice, and induced him to place Eustace immediately under the white overseers attached to his sugar plantation. He there conducted himself in a manner so irreproachable, that he never incurred the slightest punishment even from these hard taskmasters; and, while his gentleness appeased his white masters, he acquired over his negro brethren the influence of a superior mind, though he never showed it by haughtiness.

It was during a voyage made by M. Belin to Europe, that the first symptoms of the revolution broke out at St Domingo. Eustace was then about twenty. Then commenced his life of self-devotion, the characteristics of which are summed up in these words of a phrenologist, who, without knowing him, thus defined the disposition of Eustace, after examining his head: 'Wisdom and courage devoted to the service of goodness and benevolence.' This is an undoubted fact, however the disputers of the science of phrenology may esteem it.

The revolted negroes did not conceal from Eustace their projects; and, by timely information, he contrived

* Translated from 'Le Caméléon,' a French periodical.

to save the lives of more than four hundred whites. But he did no more; he felt for the injuries of his brethren, and never betrayed them, confining himself to the preservation of those whose lives would otherwise have been sacrificed. Soon after, the tumults in the north of the island were almost entirely calmed, and M. Belin returned to St Domingo. His faithful slave, who in the interim had served as many masters as there were unfortunate whites to succour, returned gladly to his service. But the proclamation of Santhonax and Polverel, the emissaries of the French Convention, soon kindled the revolt afresh, and the memorable burning of Cass took place. Seeing that his master was no longer safe in the plantation, Eustace concealed him in the depth of a thick wood, and daily brought him subsistence for some time. M. Belin was chief magistrate of Limbé; as such, he was required by the commissaries of the Convention to furnish General Lasalle, who had reached Cass with his wife, with a carriage and horses for his journey. For M. Belin to quit his retreat was certain death; but the acuteness of his faithful slave preserved him. Eustace sought Polverel and Santhonax, told them his master had fled he knew not whither, but he himself was ready to fulfil the duty required. By this means he turned away the attention of the commissaries from his master, and he then conducted General Lasalle and his wife on their hazardous journey. Returning to Limbé, he met an entire family flying from the burning of Cass—father, mother, and three young children. Eustace received them in the carriage, and saved all.

At last an opportunity offered for his master's safe retreat from the dangers which surrounded him. An American vessel anchored at Limbé: Eustace went to the captain, made arrangements for the passage of M. Belin, and agreed that he should be conveyed on board by night. But this was not all. M. Belin was in a state of the most complete destitution. Eustace went to the negroes of the sugar plantation, and, by his eloquence, induced them to supply their former master with sufficient to preserve him from absolute want. When M. Belin earnestly expressed his gratitude, Eustace only requested, as a return, that he might be permitted to follow and serve him. Two days had scarcely passed before the American ship was taken by three English privateers. Eustace and his master were now prisoners; but the negro did not lose courage. He was an excellent cook, and by his culinary talents won the good graces of the captors, who were not insensible to the good things of this life. Eustace, who ministered so successfully to their gastronomic appetites, was allowed to go at liberty over the ship. He used his freedom to work the deliverance of his master. One day, when the captors had indulged in wine more than usual, Eustace, armed with a sabre, the American captain and M. Belin equally protected, came down upon them. One of the Englishmen rose, but Eustace bound his arms, and the others, struck with terror, begged their lives. Meanwhile the other prisoners fell upon the English sailors, and disarmed them after a short contest. The American captain conducted in safety to Baltimore his own recovered vessel and the three prizes.

At Baltimore, M. Belin and his preserver found numbers of the unfortunate inhabitants of St Domingo, who, formerly opulent, had taken refuge there in the deepest poverty, and were preserved from starvation only by the generosity of the inhabitants. Their necessities furnished the industrious activity of Eustace with an idea which he, with great exertions, carried out. He established a sort of commercial store, the profits of which he devoted to the succour of the most needy of these unfortunate planters, whose former habits of wealthy idleness but ill fitted them for industrious exertion. The poor negro slave was now become their chief comfort and dependence.

Towards the commencement of 1794, St Domingo again became apparently tranquil. The Spaniards occupied Fort Dauphin: the English established themselves at St Nicholas, Port-au-Prince, and elsewhere in the west of the island. Nearly a hundred of the old inhabitants quitted their place of exile, and freighted a vessel to convey them to Fort Dauphin. M. Belin and Eustace were among the number. Scarcely had the exiles disembarked, when they heard that an army of 20,000 men, led by the negro Jean François, had encamped not far from the town. Fort Dauphin then contained a population of about 600 whites, who might have resisted; but the Spanish commander of the garrison refused them arms. An assault took place. M. Belin, separated by chance from his slave, owed his safety to the protection of a Spanish captain whom he knew. Eustace sought him in vain for a long time; but still, not giving up all hope, he saved from pillage everything belonging to his master. To insure their preservation, he went to the wife of Jean François, to whom he was known, and put under her protection money and jewellery belonging to M. Belin, saying they had been left to himself as a legacy. At Fort Espagnol he at last learned the safety of his master, who was about to embark for the English settlement at St Nicholas. Eustace at once resolved to join him; but he had first to obtain from the wife of Jean François the property of M. Belin. This he did, though not without considerable suspicion and difficulty.

The arrival of Eustace at St Nicholas was celebrated like a festival. M. Belin had spread the report of all he owed to his devoted slave, and Eustace was welcomed with a generous homage due to his character, and escorted through the town. M. Belin remained but a short time at St Nicholas: he went to Port-au-Prince, and was there appointed by the governor-general president of the privy council. Eustace now exerted himself to obtain for his master an establishment equal to his new dignity. M. Belin, accustomed to opulence, never imagined that the honourable competence which he enjoyed was the fruit of the daily labour of Eustace. The rich are easily pardoned by the world for the coldness of their gratitude; and when M. Belin, some time after, gave Eustace his freedom, he was considered, in the ideas of the colonists, to have acquitted himself towards his slave. But this liberty was to Eustace a mere formality, which changed neither his conduct nor his devotion. One day, when M. Belin, whose sight failed him, regretted having not taught Eustace to read in his childhood, as in that case he might have become a source of amusement as reader, without saying anything to his master, the faithful negro applied to a school teacher; and, that his daily work might not suffer through his new studies, he used to take his lessons at daybreak. Three or four months after, he came to M. Belin—his countenance radiant with pleasure—with a newspaper in his hand, which he read aloud exceedingly well. From that time he became secretary to his master.

When Toussaint L'Ouverture, now supreme governor of St Domingo, recalled the ancient proprietors to their estates, and guaranteed their safety, M. Belin was among those who confided in these promises. He was put in possession of his sugar plantation, and lived there in peace until the expedition of General Leclerc destroyed all the good work of Toussaint L'Ouverture, and consummated the ruin of the colony. Eustace once more, and for the last time, saved the life of his beloved master; but M. Belin, who had become quite blind, died soon after in his arms. Eustace found his sole consolation in doing at Cass as he had done at Baltimore. M. Belin had left him all his property which was preserved from this last wreck of fortune, and Eustace devoted it to the succour of the unfortunate. After this last revolution, inconceivable misery was felt in the island; and there was Eustace found, always doing good. Some he supplied with money from the small store left him by M. Belin, to others he distributed clothes, linen, and furniture; he put orphan children out to nurse at his own expense; he assisted poor soldiers whose pay was in arrear from the disastrous state of the country; and, when there was no more left for him to do, he offered himself as attendant on General Rochambeau, accompanied him to England, and from thence to France.

The useful and benevolent career of Eustace the negro terminated but with his death. He arrived at Paris in 1812, and from that time he suffered not a day to pass without exercising his charitable disposition, as far as lay in his humble power. For example, he heard that a poor widow, with four young children, was reduced to cut grass for cattle to procure a subsistence. Eustace sought her out, clothed herself and children, apprenticed the eldest of them, supplying him with necessary tools, so that the boy soon became the prop and support of the family. Another time, knowing that his master was unable to assist a poor relation whom he had long lost sight of, Eustace secretly devoted all his gains to the support of the sick and feeble man for more than a year, leaving him to suppose that these benefits flowed from the general. The secret was not discovered until the sick man, now cured, came to thank his relative for his supposed generous assistance.

The French Academy granted to this benevolent man, in 1832, the prize of virtue founded by Monthyon. This little history shows how well it was merited. Eustace died on the 15th March 1833, aged sixty-two. If virtue were honoured equally with fame and genius, this poor negro would have been considered worthy of a noble monument.

THE LEECH.

THIS animal has had a reputation from the earliest periods of medical science. Even from the time of Homer, the appellation of leech was given to the practitioners of the art of surgery. It is amongst the lowest classes of the animal chain of being; is literally a worm; and yet it has been sought after and valued in all ages. There are about thirteen or fourteen species of the leech, some of which are found in most parts of the world; but the medicinal species is the best known, and abounds in various parts of Europe—as Russia, Hungary, Spain, Portugal—in the marshy plains of Egypt, and in various parts of Asia. It belongs to the class *annelides*, or ringed worms, its body being composed of a series of rings or circular muscles, by the successive contractions of which it moves along, either in the water or upon the surface of leaves, reeds, or other solid bodies. The tail extremity is in the form of a cup or sucker, by which it adheres firmly to flat substances, on the same principle as a boy's leather sucker adheres to and lifts up a stone. The mouth is also in the form of a sucker, and is, moreover, furnished with three cartilaginous teeth, placed so as to form with each other a triangle. These teeth are very curious bodies. When examined, and felt with the point of the finger, they seem soft and blunt; but the animal, when about to pierce the skin, seems to have the power of erecting them into firm, sharp-edged lancets, which saw through the integuments in a single instant, and almost without inflicting any pain. Having made the puncture, the blood is extracted by a process of suction, and is passed through the œsophagus into the stomach, or rather stomachs, of the animal, which consist of a series of communicating cells, that occupy the greater part of the interior of its body. The leech having thus gorged itself to the utmost, if undisturbed, remains in a half-torpid condition till it has digested its gory meal, and not unfrequently dies of the surfeit. If it survives, it will have increased very greatly in size. Considering the myriads of these animals that exist congregated together in their native pools, it must only be on rare occasions that each individual of the group can get an opportunity of fastening on any of the larger animals, and thus obtaining a meal; in fact, such an occurrence may not happen in months, or even in a lifetime. It is said that they attack smaller animals, such as frogs and other reptiles, grubs, worms; and that they will even prey on each other; though they suck the blood of living animals only. But even supposing that they have no access to blood, nature has endowed them with other resources. They can live for months and years on what appears pure water alone. This forms the singular circumstance in the diet of these animals. They delight to gorge themselves with a full meal of blood, even to a surfeit, and yet with plain water they live, grow, and seem to have the greatest enjoyment of existence. It would appear as if their three lancet-formed teeth, and their carnivorous appetites, were bestowed more for the benefit of man than for themselves, and that in their system of dietetics water is the rule, and blood the exception.

In a domestic state, leeches are frequently kept for years in a glass jar, without other food than clear river water; a change of which is necessary every few days. On this they thrive, and gradually increase in bulk. Occasionally, too, they change their skins, which come off in successive rings from their body. Now, as water is an inorganic substance, and, besides, does not contain all the elements of the animal tissues, we must suppose that, mingled with the clearest river water, there is always a sufficient quantity of vegetable infusion and minute animalcules, or other animal juices, to afford them a sufficiency of nourishment.

The medicinal leech is a native of many parts of Britain, but is now become very rare. It still is seen among the lakes of Westmoreland; but even, on the authority of Wordsworth's Leech-Gatherer, they are fast disappearing—

> 'Once I could meet with them on every side,
> But they have dwindled long by slow decay;
> Yet still I persevere, and find them where I may.'

During the continental war, the British supply was completely exhausted, and a single leech not unfrequently sold for two shillings and sixpence, and even five shillings. Since the peace, the supply has been abundant from France and Spain. France is supplied chiefly from Strasburg, whence they are imported from Hungary, Turkey, Wallachia, and Russia, and kept in ponds. They are carried into France on spring wagons, and are contained in moistened bags, each bag containing one hundred and twenty leeches. Previous to 1834, upwards of forty-six millions of leeches were imported into France annually; at present, the numbers have decreased to seventeen millions. They are imported into London and Leith by sea, packed in little bags, which are occasionally moistened with water during the short voyage. In general, they arrive fresh and healthy; but they are not unfrequently liable to disease, which destroys great numbers. There are three sorts or sizes; the largest and middle sorts being reckoned the best. A large leech is calculated to abstract half an ounce of blood, besides the quantity which flows from the wound afterwards. The smaller sizes are comparatively inefficacious.

The test of a good leech is, that it should, when squeezed in the palm of the hand, contract into a firm ball, and not remain elongated and flabby. After having been used once, and gorged with blood, they are never so lively as before: for the most part they are dull, and will not readily bite. A leech suspected to contain blood may also be tested by applying to its mouth a little salt, when the contained blood will in a few seconds be ejected. This is one plan of making leeches disgorge their full of blood. If, when taken off, their mouth be placed in a little salt, they immediately sicken, and discharge the contents of their stomach. Another plan is to seize them by the obtuse end, and strip them firmly but slowly through the fingers. Others, again, place them in tepid water, and allow them to make the best of their luxurious meal; but in such cases the usual fate of gluttons and epicures sooner or later cuts them off.

A common animal in the pools of this country is the horse-leech. It nearly resembles the other, but is of a more uniform black colour, and not so decidedly marked with greenish streaks on the back as the medicinal species. The horse-leech has no great inclination to fasten on the human skin; but when it does so, it takes its fill, just like the other, and no more. There is a popular, but unfounded belief that, if a leech of this description do fasten on the skin, it will continue to suck and discharge the blood till every drop in the body is exhausted. Hence they are the dread of every schoolboy who happens to wade with naked legs into their domains.

The leech, like many other animals, appears to have a very nice sensibility in regard to atmospheric changes, and especially in what regards the electric modifications of the air. Before storms, or any sudden change in the atmosphere, the leech is seen in great activity, and darting up to the surface of the water in its jar. These animals too, at certain times, are found to move out of the water, and to remain for considerable periods clustered on the dry upper sides of their jar; while on other occasions they will remain for days immersed in the water near the bottom. They produce small eggs, which form into cocoons from which in due time the living young make their appearance.

The art of cupping, now generally practised, has greatly superseded the use of leeches. This art is an imitation of the natural process of the leech. It gives little pain, and is more speedily accomplished, but is not in all respects equally efficacious.

SHARK ADVENTURE.

Sailors, as is well known, bear a most deadly enmity towards the race of sharks. Hannibal's hostility to the Romans can give but a faint idea of the hostile feelings of sailors towards this monster of the deep. They will do almost anything towards capturing one; at any hour of the day or night, even when it is their watch below, they would willingly mount on deck to assist in the capture, or to witness its sufferings when on board. This feeling may arise from the frequent instances of sailors being deprived of their limbs, and often their lives, by sharks, and the superstitious feelings which exist among them that, if any one of their number dies on board, a shark is sure to know it, and will follow the ship until the body is thrown overboard, when it will immediately devour it. They regard, therefore, the capturing of a shark as an act of retributive justice; for though, as they are ready to admit, the poor victim that falls into their hands may have done nothing worthy of death, yet they look upon him as the representative of his race, and bestow their revenge accordingly.

The shark is very stealthy in his movements; he may be close about the ship without being perceived, though more frequently his approach is seen by the dorsal fin appearing a few inches above the water, but seldom any other part of the body is seen. My gentleman is no sooner seen, than the news fly fore and aft the ship that John is in the neighbourhood (John being a name generally applied to a shark). The fishing gear is immediately got ready, and which consists of a hook about eighteen inches long, made of bar iron the thickness of one's little finger; to the hook is attached a chain, and to the chain one of the stoutest spare ropes on board. The bait generally used is a piece of salt pork, four or five pounds in weight: this apparatus is thrown over the stern, and the bait kept about fifty yards from the ship. Now, though the shark is such an acknowledged gourmand, yet he does not always allow his voracity to get the better of his judgment; for when he first espies the alluring bait, he does not rashly snap at it, but swims around and beneath, and examines it attentively. Very frequently he makes off without attempting a bite; at other times he succeeds in nibbling the bait by degrees entirely away; and as frequently tears the whole piece off the hook; so that it is no easy matter to capture a shark. I have been for days in a ship followed by them, and every effort made to catch one, but in vain.

On one occasion we were followed by a shark to whom we had thrown an invitation, and which he was not long in accepting; for in the course of a few minutes he darted towards it, turned upon his back, and the next instant was seen plunging and lashing his tail in a most furious manner. We saw he had taken the hook, and was so far secured; but still he was but half caught, as the sequel will prove. All the spare hands were called to lay on the shark line, in order to haul him on deck. We soon got him alongside; but on account of his violent plunging, found it impossible to get him on board, unless he was allowed to exhaust some of his immense strength. To assist this, our mate proposed harpooning him; and in the absence of a proper instrument, took the boat-hook, to which he attached a line, and after a few attempts, succeeded in fastening it in the fore part of the back, when, singular to relate, my gentleman, by a violent tug, snapped the rope, and made himself off with the boat-hook sticking like a flag-staff erect in his back. He remained in sight for some time, evidently very uneasy; but whether he succeeded in disengaging himself from this disagreeable appendage, I know not.—*Incidents of a Voyage from Liverpool to the Brazils, by One before the Mast.*

MINERAL WATERS IN FRANCE.

By a statistical return, which has been published by the Mining Department at Paris, it appears there are 864 mineral springs throughout the kingdom that are open to visitors, besides many other private ones. In the vicinity of the Pyrenees, the mountains in the centre of France, the Vosges, the north-western districts, the Alps, Jura, and Corsica, the Ardennes, Hainault, and different other parts, there are 474 warm mineral springs; 218 cold, but ferruginous properties; 172 ditto, strongly impregnated with iron—making a total of 864. In the vicinity of the Pyrenees, the mineral springs are the richest, particularly the warm. The department of the Upper Pyrenees has some of the finest establishments; two at Barèges, seven at Couterets, fourteen at Bagnes de Bigorre, and three others in the vicinity. These, the same as nearly all the others, were first opened by the Romans. The waters of St Christan, in the department of the Lower Pyrenees, are so abundant that they work not only the wheels of the different iron factories, but are employed in the irrigation of the country, in consequence of their high temperature, and the saline qualities they possess, so much so, that, if there were not the restrictions imposed by government, an immense quantity of salt might be extracted annually. The springs of the department of Allier, of which there are twenty, run through granite rock and porphyry, and are strongly impregnated with mineral. In the department of the Puy-de-Dome, there are about ninety mineral springs. In the Cantal, the Vosges, the Bouches-du-Rhone, Aix, Lyons, &c. the springs are warm, passing through extensive coal beds, strongly impregnated with iron, copper, and lead, and also a saline quality. The generality of the mineral waters in France are of a ferruginous nature; some, however, are strongly saline. The government has appointed a commission of the most scientific men to analyse the different springs throughout the kingdom, so as to see if they cannot be made useful to the commercial industry of the country. The profits arising from these mineral waters, and bathing, are annually upwards of L.500,000, and likely to increase.

THE DRESS OF AUTHORS.

Anthony Magliabecchi, who passed all his time among his books, had an old cloak, which served him for a gown in the day, and for bed-clothes at night; he had one straw chair for his table, and another for his bed, on which he generally remained fixed, in the midst of a heap of volumes and papers, until he was overpowered with sleep. Emerson the mathematician made one hat last him the greater part of his lifetime, the rim gradually lessening bit by bit, till little remained except the crown. Another 'shocking bad hat,' which belonged to a celebrated geologist of the present day, is honoured with a place among the curious relics of costume in the Ashmolean Museum at Oxford, to which valuable collection it was presented by some waggish university youths. In the 'History of Holy Ghost Chapel, Basingstoke' (1819), p. 51, it is stated that the Rev. Samuel Loggon, a great student of antiquities, 'used to wear two old shirts at once, saying that they were warmer than new ones.' Dr Paris, in his 'Life of Sir Humphry Davy,' tells us that this great philosopher was, in the busiest period of his career, so sparing of time, that he would not afford a moment to divesting himself of his dirty linen, but would slip clean linen over it. This practice he would continue, until as many as even six shirts were on his back at a time. When at length he had found leisure to extricate himself from all except the one that was clean, his bulk was so visibly and suddenly reduced, that his friends, not knowing the cause, would remark that he was getting thinner with alarming rapidity. But their fears of his being in a consumption would shortly be removed, when shirt over shirt began to accumulate again. He was then like a plump caterpillar, existing under several skins. In later days, Davy became more attentive to the toilet; in fact, the thinking and busy philosopher merged into a frivolous fop, cultivating curls, and wearing piebald waistcoats of patchwork pattern. Shenstone was somewhat of an exquisite. He loved showy colours in dress, delighted in trinkets and perfumes, designed patterns for snuff-boxes, played music, sung, and painted flowers. He had, however, a great antipathy to card-playing and dancing; yet he says that ecstatic, rough, unsophisticated dancing, is one of the most natural expressions of delight, for it coincides with jumping for joy; but when it is done according to rule, it is, in his opinion, merely *cum ratione insanire.* Benjamin Stillingfleet generally wore a full dress suit of cloth of the same uniform colour, with blue worsted stockings. In this dress he used frequently to attend Mrs Montague's literary evening parties, and as his conversation was very interesting, the ladies used to say, 'We can do nothing without the blue stockings;' hence arose the appellation of *bas bleu*, or blue stocking, to literary ladies. Mezerai, the French historian, was so extremely susceptible of cold, that immediately on the setting in of winter, he provided himself with twelve pairs of stockings, all of which he sometimes wore at once. In the morning he always consulted his barometer, and, according to the greater or less degree of cold, put on so many more or fewer pairs of stockings.—In reference to the general seediness of literary costume, a recent writer has justly remarked, that to laugh—as has been the custom since the days of Juvenal—at the loutish manners, threadbare cloak, and clouted shoe of the mere man of letters, is a stale and heartless joke, for the poorest, threadbare, ungainly scholar (if he be indeed a scholar), is a gentleman in his feelings.

INFLUENCE OF AN ECLIPSE ON INSECTS.

Signor Villa of Milan thus describes the influence of the solar eclipse of July 1842 upon the manners of different insects, which he observed during its continuance:—The insects in general were very restless, moved their feelers strongly here and there, and hid themselves. Some genera disappeared before the darkness came on, others flew about till its commencement. Most of them again appeared about half an hour after the obscuration had passed away. It is curious that though the day-insects thus sought to conceal themselves as they do on the approach of night, yet none of the nocturnal species made their appearance.

MINING UNDER THE OCEAN.

The most extraordinary of the Cornish tin mines—says Mr Watson in his 'Glance at Cornish Mining'—was the 'Wherry,' established upon a shoal near Penzance, about 720 feet from the beach at high water. The rock was covered about ten months in the twelve, and the depth of water on it at spring-tides nineteen feet; and in winter the sea burst over the rock in such a manner as to render useless all attempts to carry on mining operations. In the early part of the last century, attempts were made to work it, but abandoned as hopeless. Notwithstanding all the difficulties, however, a poor miner named Thomas Curtis, in 1788, had the boldness to renew the attempt, and, after innumerable difficulties, succeeded in forming a water-tight case, as an upper part of the shaft, against which the sea broke, while a communication with the shore was established by means of a wooden-frame bridge, as the work could only be prosecuted when the rock appeared above water. Three summers were consumed in sinking the pump shaft; and the use of machinery becoming practicable, the water-tight case was carried up a sufficient height above the reach of the highest spring-tides. To support this boarded turret from the violence of the surge, eight stout bars of iron were applied in an inclined direction to the sides. A platform of boards was then lashed round the top of the turret, supported by four poles, which were firmly connected with the iron rods. Upon this platform was fixed a winch for four men. The water, notwithstanding, forced its way through the shaft during the winter months, and it was not till April that work could be resumed. In the autumn of 1791, the depth of the pump shaft and of the workings was twenty-nine feet, the breadth eighteen feet. Twelve men were employed in pumping out the water for two hours, and then working on the rock six more. Thirty sacks of tin stuff were taken on an average every tide; and ten men, in the space of six months, working about a tenth of that time, broke L.600 worth. After a time, a steam-engine was erected on the green on shore, and hanging rods from it carried along the wooden bridge to the mine, and in this manner tin to the value of L.70,000 was raised from it. While the work was in full operation, an American vessel broke from its anchorage in Gwavas Lakes, and striking against the stage, demolished the machinery; thus putting an end to this ingenious and extraordinary undertaking.

THE SNOW-STORM.

[From *Scenes in My Native Land*, by Mrs L. H. Sigourney. Boston. 1845.]

How quietly the snow comes down,
When all are fast asleep,
And plays a thousand fairy pranks
O'er vale and mountain steep.
How cunningly it finds its way
To every cranny small,
And creeps through even the slightest chink
In window or in wall.

To every motionless hill it brings
A fairer, purer crest,
Than the rich ermine robe that decks
The haughtiest monarch's breast.
To every reaching spray it gives
Whate'er its hand can hold—
A beauteous thing the snow is
To all, both young and old.

The waking day, through curtaining haze,
Looks forth with new surprise,
To view what changes have been wrought
Since last she shut her eyes;
And a pleasant thing it is to see
The cottage children peep
From out the drift, that to their eaves
Prolongs its rampart deep.

The patient farmer searches
His buried lambs to find,
And digs his silly poultry out,
Who clamour in the winds;
How sturdily he cuts his way,
Though wild blasts beat him back,
And caters for his waiting herd
Who shiver round the stack.

Right welcome are these feathery flakes
To the ruddy urchins' eye,
As down the long smooth hill they coast,
With shout and revelry;
Or when the moonlight, clear and cold,
Calls out their throng to play;
Oh! a merry gift the snow is
For a Christmas holiday.

The city miss, who, wrapt in fur,
Is lifted to the sleigh,
And borne so daintily to school
Along the crowded way,
Feels not within her pallid cheek
The rich blood mantling warm,
Like her who, laughing, shakes the snow
From powdered tress and form.

A tasteful hand the snow hath—
For on the storied page
I saw its Alpine landscapes traced
With arch and sculptured fane,
Where high o'er hoary-headed cliffs
The dizzy Simplon wound,
And old cathedrals reared their towers
With Gothic tracery bound.

I think it hath a tender heart,
For I marked it while it crept
To spread a sheltering mantle where
The infant blossom slept.
It doth to Earth a deed of love
Though in a wintry way,
And her turf-gown will be greener
For the snow that's fallen to-day.

Published by W. and R. CHAMBERS, High Street, Edinburgh (also 98, Miller Street, Glasgow); and, with their permission by W. S. ORR, Amen Corner, London.—Printed by BRADBURY and EVANS, Whitefriars, London.

CONDUCTED BY WILLIAM AND ROBERT CHAMBERS, EDITORS OF 'CHAMBERS'S INFORMATION FOR THE PEOPLE,' 'CHAMBERS'S EDUCATIONAL COURSE,' &c.

No. 100. New Series. SATURDAY, NOVEMBER 29, 1845. Price 1½d.

LIFE IN A SCOTTISH COUNTRY MANSION.

There is perhaps no portion of the British islands more favoured in all the most agreeable attributes than Perthshire. Connecting towards the south with the low country, in whose fertility it there participates, it extends towards the north and west into the bosom of the Grampian range, where it presents such an assemblage of hill and vale, lake and river, as is rarely paralleled. The county is rich in a resident proprietary, including several of our wealthiest nobles and a vast number of gentlemen, and the effect which these produce upon the interests of the district is very manifest. It is not so much that the expenditure of income on the ground where it is realised does service, as that the constant presence of a set of landlords completes the range of requisites for conducting rural business, and keeps the country *in heart*.

I had, a few months ago, the pleasure of paying a brief visit to a gentleman in the upper part of this county; on which occasion it struck me that, what with the natural beauty of the place, the character of the people, and the mode of life of my entertainers, I saw so much that was peculiar, that it might be worth while to jot down a few particulars on the subject. Is it possible, I have since asked, that the multitudes who never saw Perthshire, and the still larger multitudes who know nothing by personal observation of the life of a country gentleman, might have any gratification in perusing these jottings? By no means impossible, I have decided: so let me try. Enough may be said to convey an individual picture to the mind, without necessarily giving offence to delicacy.

The mansion of my host is a castellated building, for the most part of old date, placed at once beautifully and comfortably on a south-looking slope, whence it commands an extensive vale, bounded by lofty mountains. Woods clothe the cliffy hill-sides on each hand; a mountain stream hops and skips shiningly through a chasm on the left. Nothing meets the view but natural objects, interspersed with pleasant mansions and granges. Towns, ports, manufactories, are all remote. And here I cannot but remark the superiority of such a situation over one of the ordinary English mansions placed in a flat, with its artificial, unvarying lake, its canal-like river, and its woods, which, though beautiful, can only be seen by little at a time. There is not only genuine natural beauty in all the adjuncts of this Perthshire mansion, with a liability to continual variation from season and from weather, but, though the elevation is only a hundred and fifty feet above the level of the sea, a range of thirty miles is commanded. An Englishman who has only seen the level portions of his own country, can have no idea of what it is to reside in one of highly varied surface like Perthshire.

My host presents, in this mansion, a style of life suitable to his fortune, which is handsome, but still moderate. Attached to country life, he resides chiefly at his seat, and only now and then visits the capital for a short time. There is, however, no such thing as solitude in such a rural life, for a country mansion is a kind of town rather than a single house; comprising, as it does, wings for servants, stables and their adjuncts, residences for a gardener, a gamekeeper, and so forth, not to speak of a village near by. There is, in such a place, a population of not much under sixty persons, even when no company is present; but when there are visitors, this number will sometimes be nearer to a hundred.

Having arrived at my friend's house after dark, I saw nothing of it beyond a handsome entrance-hall, hung with stags' horns, old arms, and other curiosities, and a comfortable parlour, where the family was assembled—until next morning, when, awaking early, and looking out, my eyes were saluted by a magnificent range of semi-Highland scenery, seen under the favourable auspices of a delicious June morning. The hour for breakfast being half-past nine, I walked out to enjoy the beauties of the scene and of the hour. An old man—a member of a corps of superannuated adherents, which I heard the family afterwards speak of as the Veteran Battalion—was quietly, and in a most leisurely way obliterating the marks made in the gravel-walk by my vehicle the preceding evening, as if it had been a work of a very solemn and important kind. An image of gentle duty it was, most refreshing to my hurry-skurry city mind, and preparative of all that I afterwards found in connexion with this scene of rural comfort. Taking a survey of the house, I now found it to be an irregular but picturesque structure, comprising a tall tower of the sixteenth century, with grated windows near the bottom; an addition in the taste of the seventeenth century, with pepper-box turrets at the angles; and, finally, certain modern additions, comprising a dining-room, a conservatory entering from the same, and divers other *asiamenta*,—to quote a term of old Scotch title-deeds. On the lowest corbel-stone in the first building, my eye readily detected the date 1591—a time when fortification was still necessary for the security of a Scottish household. The second building spoke its time by presenting, triangle-wise, on the pediments of the windows, the letters S. P. T. and D. E. C., which I knew to be the initials (including S. for Sir, and D. for Dame) of the first baronet of the family and his lady, who had flourished in the reign of Charles II. My superficial glance discovered nothing further remarkable about the building, besides its abundance of tall chimneys and lead-covered minarets, the latter of which bore each its weathercock, so that there was a superabundance of the means of meteorological observation, sufficient to have served a colony of retired admirals. On one side, the mansion was approached by a winding avenue of pines and other evergreens, mixed with tall old sycamores, thickly covered with comfortable ivy. On the other was a beautiful little domain devoted to floriculture, where circular patches of dahlias, and lozenge-shaped clusters of heart's-ease and calceolarias, and numberless other favourites of the modern garden, showed that the elegant tastes of the day had made their way to this northern solitude. Passing through this lovely area by a slight wire gate, I found my way to a terrace walk which passes through the wood along the side of the hill, and there regaled myself with the many variations of view which the occasional openings amongst the trees afforded, seeing on one hand hills from which I knew Edinburgh was visible, and on the other mountain peaks which probably looked far into Lochaber and Morven. Tufts of primroses bursting forth from the bank, a hen turkey peeping out from her wild nest among the bushes, fantastic fungi springing from old tree roots, a strangled shrew mouse on the walk, bees humming along from one wild-flower to another, pigeons to-whooing from the tree tops, lesser birds twittering on every spray, the smoke of the village curling up through the calm sunny air at a little distance—such were the objects and sounds presented to me. From the close murky atmosphere of a city, with all the vexing duties of such a scene, what a change was here! Oh Nature, thought I, thou art, after all, the true physician for thy children! Thy breath, thy voice, thy placid face, how truly medicative they are to those worn out with the artificialities of the social world! And, viewing this beauteous scene as the property of my friend, I could not but see some natural basis for that prejudice which exists in favour of land as property. Thus to possess a portion of the geographical surface, with all its ordinary accompaniments, was, I could well see, something more calculated to attract the regard and respect of mankind, than merely to have a certain number of figures attached to one's' name in the stock-book of a joint-stock bank, or be one of a firm understood to realise large returns in a dingy counting-room in a dingy alley in 'the city.' The common feelings of man's bosom are at the bottom of the earth-hunger which Scott spoke of as his predominant passion, and of which every man is more or less sensible. No wonder, as the laird of Abbotsford used to say, that Scotsmen, in particular, no sooner get their heads above water, than they make for land!

Returning at the breakfast hour, I found the family just taking their seats, little ceremony being used at the morning meal. To persons quite unacquainted with country-mansion life, it may be worth while to mention, that besides the usual breakfast apparatus, was a small heap of letters just disengaged from the post-bag. A copy of the Morning Herald and Edinburgh Courant, with two or three periodical works, had been drawn from the same receptacle, and were lying at the command of the party in general. When my host had cast one glance along the leading articles of the London journal, and seen that there was no news, and each person had just peeped into their several letters, breakfast was applied to with cordial appetite, and, servants not being retained at this meal, all presently was gaiety and *abandon*. Startled out of the languor of an overworked system, I was surprised to find myself devour a turkey's egg and a slice of broiled salmon, without the slightest symptom of difficulty, though a slice or two of dry toast would have been excess two days before. When the meal drew towards a close, we began to discuss plans for the day, and it was soon settled that I should join a walking party at two o'clock. Till then, however, there was an interval of a few hours, and it was agreed that these should be spent by me in looking over the various objects within doors, under the care of the eldest young lady, who happened, for her sins, to have been found the best cicerone in the family.

The in-door ramble was an interesting one. It is now proper to mention that, from the giving of the family baronetcy by king James II., during his brief and clouded reign, the family had been zealous and unswerving friends of the house of Stuart, down to the comparatively recent period when such feelings had ceased to have any distinctly recognisable object. Concerned they had been in both the 'risings,' and once they had lost their lands; but by purchase, and the relenting mercy of later sovereigns, both these and the forfeited title had been regained. The house, therefore, contains many objects interestingly connected with those events and characters that form almost the only relief from the commonplace of our last-century history. In the best bed-room of the middle-aged part of the house, had the elder chevalier spent a night during his residence in Scotland in 1715; his mild and gentlemanly, but feeble countenance, shone from the walls, with his pale gentle wife, Clementina, for *vis a vis*. The furniture of that time had been lost in the evil days of the family; but they had since happened to become possessed of the little camp-bed used by Prince Charles in his campaign, and this was now erected in the room once graced as the lodging of his father. In the same apartment they now keep a collection of vestiary curiosities—high-heeled spangle-decked shoes of the beauties of a century ago, a coat in which the late knight had paid his court to Louis XVI. at Versailles, just before the Revolution, a pair of beautiful green silk stockings, danced with by a grand-aunt of the present baronet at the wedding of her younger sister, by way of carrying off the joke which lay against her for being left unwedded on that occasion—and many other trifles with a history.

From hence I passed to the drawing-room, which contains the principal family portraits, besides other objects of an interesting kind. Here I saw the poor gentleman of the '45, dressed in a Highland dress, as he had appeared at Culloden, but now under hiding and in fear of being taken prisoner by the red-coats. It is understood that the picture was designed to represent a particular event in his skulking days, when, a party of the royal troops being near, he was induced, by some unaccountable impulse of his mind, to go off in a different route, by which he had escaped being captured. A party of soldiers is represented as passing off in the back-ground, and the unfortunate cavalier is obeying the guidance of an angel who is addressing him. Reader, laugh not at such things—they show, though in a quaint way, the deep feelings which have resided in honourable bosoms. Near this portrait is one of Hamilton of Bangour, the gay poet of the Jacobite cause, writing at a table, the sheet below his hand containing the following inscription:—

'Hail, Wallace! generous chief! who, singly brave,
When all were trembling round, aspired to save:
Hail, Bruce! intrepid king! beset with foes,
Who, from defeat, to fame and empire rose:
Hail, Stuart! much suffering youth!—Yes, I foresee
Imperial crowns and certain palms for thee;
The land thy fathers ruled has oft been vigored,
Enthralled unbroke, and vanquished unsubdued;
Scotia, for genius famed and gallant deed,
Has yet her bards to sing, her chiefs to bleed—
Yes, freedom shall be hers, her kings shall reign,
For; know, Culloden was not lost in vain.

Written at Rouen, in France, in the third year of our exile, 1748.'

Besides a couple of pictures representing the prince and his brother Henry (afterwards Cardinal York), painted when they were youths, and sent as a present to the great-grandfather of my host, there was seen, over a deeply-moulded doorway, a bust of the former personage, done also in early life, but probably after the rebellion. The countenance is one of extraordinary elegance and vivacity, set upon a beautiful neck, and adorned with the graceful flowing hair of the period. In looking at it, one is not at a loss to account for the singular fascination which Charles Edward exercised over his adherents.

and particularly those of the fair sex. There is one melancholy legend of the family connected with Charles's expedition. A younger son of the then baronet, being in the prince's army at Preston, mounted on an uncommonly spirited black horse, outrode all his associates in pursuit of the craven dragoons. At length, two miles from the field of battle, a party of them, observing that only one cavalier pursued, turned and fired at him. He fell dead on the spot, and was buried beneath an elm tree near the mansion of St Clement's Wells. The family tell, as a curious anecdote, that one of the servants, being in Perth some months after at a fair, saw and recognised the horse which poor Mr David had ridden—bought and brought it home, where it was kept ever after in honourable ease in a park. When nearly forty years had passed, the boy who in time became Sir Walter Scott, spent some weeks with a relative at St Clement's Wells, and heard the story from the old people living thereabouts. The child used to wander down to the still distinguishable grave, and pull the wild-flowers growing upon it. He also obtained, and took care of, till mature years, a clasp which had formed part of the young Jacobite's dress. The conclusion is, that, thirty years after, he introduced the incident of the young man's death in his novel of Waverley, though substituting for the real person one of a totally different character. More than this—and it was something from a nick-nack collector—he gave up to the family the little clasp which he had got fifty years before at St Clement's Wells; and this clasp, now doubly curious, they continue to possess.

I had the curiosity to inquire how the family now regards the struggles of their ancestors in behalf of the elder branch of the royal family, and found that, though loyal subjects to the reigning monarch, they all feel a pride in their name having been ranked with the enemies of the first Georges. They know that their grandfather, who was out with Charles Edward, was as honourable a man as ever breathed; and they had always been taught to believe that he was but a fair specimen of many. Braving so much for their opinions, however mistaken these opinions might be—suffering so much for the cause of their best affections, such men could not but be worthy of honour.

At the appointed hour, after a slight lunch, I joined a party, chiefly composed of ladies, who had agreed to take a walk. Brought up in the country in a manner partaking much of old fashions, these ladies had acquired a power of locomotion which would have caused others of their own rank in different circumstances to stare. It was nothing unusual for them, between breakfast and dinner, to cross the mountains into the neighbouring vale, and return—a journey involving some considerable 'gradients,' and not less than eight miles in extent. On the present occasion we took a shorter perambulation. Passing up a little glen behind the house, we kept for some time close to the banks of a 'burn,' or rivulet, which there descends from the mountains—one of those tumbling, sparkling, brawling streams which remind one of a roistering witty fellow, who never can be quiet three minutes at a time, and are general favourites, although no one can say that they ever do any good. In a more southern domain, this rill would have been arranged into a series of waterfalls, and embowered in plantations, with nice gravel-walks. Far dearer to me the natural pebbled channel, and the green sod banks, pranked with wild-flowers of every hue. At the head of this glen we climbed the hill, and soon began to descend along a vale of similar character, but wider, and full of little farms, most of them nearly altogether pastoral. It was interesting to observe, wherever we went, the peasantry making their simple obeisances to the ladies—an old fashion much in decay in some districts, but here kept up in all its pristine vigour, very much in consequence of the popular, obliging manners of my host and his family. Not a cow-boy but tugged his cap, or the front of his sun-bleached hair; not a girl but dropped her timid curtsey. I became convinced that it is a mistake to suppose the ancient manners much changed in rural Scotland; at least, the fact is only true under great limitations. There was as much homely kindliness between these ladies and the tenantry, as ever there could have been between the two classes. Whatever house we entered, the inquiries were mutual and affectionate. Here and there a rheumatism of the goodwife, or a late visit of measles to the children, was fully entered upon and discussed. At one place there was no end to the joking about a headache the goodman had complained of for two days, after the last rent-day entertainment at the castle. Sheer good social feeling seemed to have obliterated all the usual repelling effects of diverse rank and condition; and the perfect ease on both sides admitted of no suspicion of insincerity on either. After a delightful ramble of five or six miles, we arrived at the castle, just in time for dinner.

Two or three neighbours graced this meal with their presence, but only added to the hilarity of the party, without altering its character. In due time we adjourned to the drawing-room, where the chill of the evening had made a fire acceptable even at that season. Gathering round a circular table, we enjoyed tea in a manner which puts to shame the tame and comfortless fashion of bringing it in upon salvers. The conversation, which was general from the first, turned very appropriately, considering the old-world character of the house, upon the superstitious notions which yet linger in such retired parts of the country. And when we, by and by, turned to form a semicircle in front of the fire, I was surprised to find how fresh these still are in the minds of the people. I doubt, indeed, if our company did not comprise two or three persons who adhered to ultra-natural views of our world, although no one decidedly made the admission. The fact is, almost every family of any distinction in that part of the country is understood to have some ghostly circumstance connected with it. It is almost as necessary for aristocratic distinction as to have a coat armorial. In one, for instance, a peculiar-looking sparrow always makes its appearance on the window-soles of the family mansion when any one is about to die. I apprehend it is a passerine new to naturalists, for it is said to appear as if it wore a coat of black velvet. One of the ladies present had been living at the mansion when this odd bird one day made its appearance; and, certainly, news immediately came of the death of the head of the house at Edinburgh. Over one family in the neighbourhood there hung an ancient prophecy, that no third generation in lineal succession should ever inherit the estates: another, whose ancestor had been concerned in the massacre of Glencoe, was doomed, in consequence of the curse of a bereaved Highland widow, never to see a generation pass without a bloody deed falling in the hands of some member of the house. There is a dreary fascination in some of these curious tales. I could not help feeling interested in one relative to a mansion in a distant part of the country, round which a white lady was said to go moping and moaning on Christmas night, when any important member of the family was to die during the ensuing year. The enlightened part of mankind have long condemned all notions of this kind as gross superstition; but no one can deny that there is something romantic in them, forming a not unpleasing offset to the rigid scientific accuracies and mechanical commonplaces of our age. I thought proper, nevertheless, to show the great liability to fallacy about all such stories, by narrating one which I had heard related when attending a recent meeting of the British Association. In the town of Lancaster, not above fifteen years ago, a quiet tradesman's family were sitting at tea one evening, when their parlour-door was suddenly burst open, and a black human head rolled along the floor up to their very feet! In an instant they had all burst away from the room, frenzied with fear and horror. On venturing back half an hour after, they found everything as they had left it, and no appearance of anything unusual. Next day, however, it was published throughout the town that this family had been visited by a ghastly supernatural spectacle, which had given them a dreadful fright; and from that day to the present, no explanation of the occurrence has ever reached the honest Lancastrians. But is it, therefore, to be considered as inexplicable? By no means. The present Professor —— perfectly knows how it was that the frightful spectacle was presented. He was then a student of surgery, residing in the house of the tradesman in question. Having attended a poor negro servant on his deathbed in the town hospital, he had cut off the head of the deceased, in order to make some investigations of the nature of the fatal disease. Carrying the dismal object home in a handkerchief, he happened to make a slip in going down the steep descent which led to the door of his lodging. Before he could recover himself, the head escaped from the handkerchief, and rolled down the slope. The outer door being open, and the parlour-door directly opposite, the head burst through the latter, and rolling along the floor, only stopped at the feet of the astonished tea-party. When the young anatomist reached the place, he found the room empty, and lost no time in removing the head; the reality of which he did not afterwards think himself bound to affirm, as it might have led to an unpleasant responsibility. And thus has a capital accredited apparition story taken root in the good town of Lancaster! At the conclusion of my anecdote, several expressed their belief that the majority of such tales would be found to have a similar foundation, if any foundation for them there were; but I could see that two or three of the ladies did not at all approve of that pestilent way which some people have of explaining away all wonderful things by a reference to familiar causes.

The two or three subsequent days gave me an opportunity of forming a kind of general estimate of the pleasures and advantages of country-gentlefolks' life. It boasts of much greater social conveniences than could be expected in such a remote situation, and of course has its drawbacks. First, the post brings every day the news of the busy world, and that excellent and infallible person, 'the carrier,' supplies from the county town all desirable luxuries, as well as necessaries, not omitting a selection of the publications of the day from a book-club. Then, as to society, the neighbourhood—by which is meant a district extending ten miles in each direction—supplies an abundance of families of equal rank and harmonious manners, who both pay morning and afternoon visits, and occasionally spend a few days with each other in an easy and familiar way. The latter autumn and early winter are the seasons when these visits chiefly take place. In latter winter, or spring, a visit of a few weeks to the capital keeps up a connexion with the gay world, and with friends who usually reside there. The summer, spent of course at home, never fails to bring dropping tourists and other visitors from a distance, to vary the circle of familiar faces and the ordinary routine of conversation. Thus there is no want of society, in the moderate extent in which it is proper to indulge in it. Some country families, however, require much more of this gratification than others, feeling quite miserable when they have not a house full of company. It becomes with such persons a chief consideration how to provide for having a new set of visitors as another takes its departure. But all such cases must be understood as exceptions from the common strain of country life. In general, much of the time of a resident country family of moderate fortune, where neither fox-hounds nor racers absorb (as they always do) exclusive attention, is employed in a routine of duties almost as fixed as those of any member of the community. The gentleman himself has what is called county business to attend to. He takes a share in the management of the roads, and in the business of the justice-of-peace court. Improvements in agriculture, and in the management of farming business, demand his encouragement and patronage. The ladies are equally concerned in protecting schools, and keeping up various little schemes of a benevolent nature for the benefit of the poor. Never wanting some interesting occupation, the country gentleman and his family appear to realise as much happiness as we see anywhere falling to the lot of humanity. Of drawbacks, the chief, I would say, is the want of that stimulating, mind-advancing excitement which is to be obtained only amidst great numbers of our fellow-creatures, and which, accordingly, renders cities everywhere the great centres of civilisation. Hence truly arises that particular strain of opinion and sentiment which marks country gentlemen generally, and causes them too often to appear as the drag upon the social engine. This, however, is a matter which does not so much concern them, as it does the rest of the community.

Having duly exhausted the period which I had assigned as the utmost to which my visit should extend, namely, the Rest day, the Dressed day, and the Pressed day, I took my leave of this hospitable mansion, full of the frank but graceful kindness of its inmates, and plunged back again into the smoke, clangor, and toil, of lofty Edinburgh.

TRANSCRIBERS.

The copiers of manuscripts, who hold now the humblest rank in literature, were, before the invention of printing, of the utmost importance. Amongst the Hebrews, transcribing the holy Scriptures was deemed a profession of the highest honour, and the responsible office of commenting on difficult passages was sometimes joined with it. This of course required a great amount of learning, and it is inferred, from a passage in the Septuagint, that a residence separate from the rest of the people was allotted to the ancient scribes. According to Dr South, a Jewish scribe was a church officer, skilful to copy, and conversant with the law, to interpret or explain it. The civil scribes were lawyers or notaries.

Wherever literature existed, copyists of course abounded; and even at the dawn of Grecian letters, three sorts of transcribers plied their pens. Some who had distinguished skill in writing, were called Chirographoi, or Caligraphers; others made it their business to take down discourses and addresses by means of abbreviated characters, similar to what is now called short-hand. Such persons were much in request, as almost all instruction was delivered orally, and to them we are indebted for many valuable passages from ancient authors, which would otherwise have been lost to posterity. They were known as Semeiographoi and Tachygraphoi. A third sort of transcribers cultivated the fine arts, for their business was to figure ornamental letters in blanks left for that purpose by the Caligraphers. Among the later Greeks, transcribers received the Roman appellation of notarii. Alexandria was the principal resort of the copyists in the later periods of Grecian literature. In the same edifice with the celebrated library, were extensive offices completely fitted up for the business of transcribing books. Here the Caligraphers were very numerous, even until the irruption of the Arabs in 640. Indeed so proficient were the Greeks always considered in this art, that wherever it was practised, they would be found plying their profession; and amongst the Romans, most of the copyists' names which have been preserved are Greek. These, it seems, kept in Rome regular establishments of journeymen, who were chiefly slaves; and when a number of copies from one work were required, one sat in the middle of the room and dictated to the rest. When a book was specially ordered, the rate of remuneration was so much per hundred lines; but the librarii (as the proprietors of these offices were called) also copied good works on speculation, and were in fact amongst the earliest regular booksellers.* The art of forming books, that is, of collecting and fastening the leaves into a volume, was, according to Photius, invented by a certain Phillatius, to whom the Athenians erected a statue in consequence of his invention. To perform this operation, the master copyists employed apprentices, or those as yet but little skilled in penmanship, and called them 'glutinatores.'

The manuscripts sold by the librarii were, as might be expected, often incorrect. Cicero knew not to whom to apply to purchase correct copies of certain works which his brother Quintus had commissioned him to procure; and his own compositions were, he complained, generally ill copied. In Strabo's time, the manuscripts sold at Rome and Alexandria were full of mistakes.

Instead of trusting to the librarii, every wealthy and enlightened Roman gentleman educated his most intelligent slaves for transcribers; and these, in consequence, became of infinitely greater value to their owners than their fellows. Persons who wished to acquire a character for science, kept them in their establishments, however little there may have been for them to do. It was found an excellent speculation to instruct slaves in writing; for some masters condescended to allow their slaves to copy for others, and pocketed their earnings. In any case, the condition of the transcribers was infinitely better than that of other bondsmen, on account of their extreme value; and sometimes they were enfranchised. We learn from Cicero's letters to Pliny the younger, that when a valued copyist fell ill, nothing was spared to restore him to health. He even travelled at his master's expense; and Pliny sent one of his freed men, who was subject to repeated attacks of indigestion, first into Egypt, and then to the south of Europe.

After the fall of Rome, nearly all the copying, not only of ancient classical works, but of the holy Scriptures, which was done at all, was performed in monasteries. In every monastery there was a room built and specially set apart for writing, which was called the Scriptorium. Ducange tells us, in his glossary, that it was consecrated by certain Latin words, the meaning of which was—'Lord! wilt thou deign to bless this *scriptorium* of thy servants, and all that dwell therein, that whatever of the divine Scriptures will have been by them read or written, they may receive with understanding, and bring the same to good effect.'

The rules regarding the Scriptorium were very strict. That perfect silence might be secured, no person besides the copyists was allowed to enter the apartment on any pretence whatever, except the abbot, the prior, the sub-prior, and the librarian. It was the duty of the last to point out what was to be transcribed, and to furnish the necessary stationery; and the monks were strictly forbidden to copy anything but what was prescribed. Few employments were considered so pious as to copy the Scriptures. 'The books which we copy,' say the statutes of Guy, the second prior of the Chartreux, 'are so many heralds of the truth. We hope that Heaven will recompense us, by causing them to banish error from the minds of men, and confirm them in the Catholic faith.' This employment was even deemed an instrument of salvation, as may be gleaned from a monkish legend, related by Theodoric, abbot of Ouche. 'A certain friar lived in a monastery, and was guilty of many infractions of the rules of the order: but he was a clever and industrious scribe, and voluntarily copied a large volume of the divine law. One night he dreamt he was dead, and that his soul was at the judgment-seat. The accusing angels brought a vast number of evil deeds against him; but his good angel, taking the book he had copied, counted its contents letter by letter, and it was decreed that each letter should atone for one sin. A balance was struck, and there was exactly one letter in his favour. The judgment was, that his soul should return to his body, and that time should be given him to repent of his former transgressions. On awakening, he determined to reform, and to lead an exemplary life. From that time his labours in the Scriptorium were more persevering than ever.' The monks so employed were specially called 'clerks,' whence is derived the modern use of the word in that sense. The division of labour was carried to a high point in the Scriptorium. The preparation of ink, of pens, the ruling of guiding lines and of columns in red ink, were each performed by a separate person, who did nothing else. When the stationery was thus prepared, one corrected what another had copied; a third inserted ornaments above, below, and in the midst of the columns; a fourth drew the initial letters and more elaborate ornaments; another collated the pages; and a sixth boarded them; for they were placed between small wooden planks.

Not only in monasteries, but in nunneries, was copying carried on. At the end of the fifth century, St Cesarius having established a nunnery at Arles, certain regular hours for copying holy books were prescribed to certain of the nuns. But even then women copyists were no novelties, for it appears, by a Latin inscription published by Gruter, that in 231, when Origen undertook to revise the Old Testament, St Ambrose sent him certain deacons and virgins skilled in caligraphy as amanuenses.

That the Scriptorium should be of a comfortable temperature in winter, it was placed near the *calefactory* or furnace for communicating warmth to the rest of the edifice. This we learn from an anecdote of the ninth century, which is worth transcribing, for the purpose of exhibiting a little monastic life in a more familiar aspect than that in which it is usually regarded. The story is told by Ekkehard, the historian of the monastery of St Gall. According to his narrative, there were in the house, sometime towards the latter end of the ninth century, three monks—Notker, a mild, amiable, and patient brother; Tutilo, a person the very opposite, robust and strong, with such limbs 'as Fabius teaches us to choose for a wrestler;' and the third, Ratpert, a schoolmaster in the schools attached to the monastery. These were fast friends, and all members of the chapter, or senate of the monastery: as such, they were liable to misrepresentation to the superior by the other monks; amongst whom the most active in detraction was Sindolf, who, from the office of refectorarius (caterer or house-steward), had been promoted to be clerk of the works (*decanus operariorum*). 'It was the custom of Notker, Tutilo, and Ratpert, says the historian, to meet, by permission of the prior, in the Scriptorium, 'at the night in the interval before lauds, and to discourse together on such Scriptural subjects as were most suited to such an hour. Sindolf, knowing the time and the fact of these conversations, went out one night, and came privily to the glass window against which Tutilo was sitting, and, applying his ear to it, listened to catch something which he might carry in a perverted form to the bishop. Tutilo, who had become aware of it, and who was a sturdy man, with full confidence in the strength of his arms, spoke to his companions in Latin, that Sindolf, who did not understand that language, might not know what he said. "There he is," said he, "and he has put his ear to the window; but do you, Notker, who are timorous, go out into the church; and you, my Ratpert, catch up the whip of the brethren which hangs in the calefactory, and run out; for when I know that you have got near to him, I will open the window as suddenly as possible, catch him by the hair, drag in his head, and hold it tight; but do you, my friend, be strong and of a good courage, and lay the whip on him with all your might, and take vengeance on him."

'Ratpert, who was always most alert in matters of discipline, went softly, and catching up the whip, ran quickly out, and came down with all his might like a hail-storm on the back of Sindolf, whose head was dragged in at the window. He, however, struggling with his arms and legs, contrived to get and keep hold of the whip; on which Ratpert, catching up a stick which he saw at hand, laid on him most lustily. When he found it vain

* See our article on 'The Trade,' Vol. iii. (new series), p. 141.

to beg for mercy, "I must," said he, "cry out;" and he roared vociferously. Part of the monks, astounded at hearing such a voice at such an unwonted time, came running with lights, and asking what was the matter. Tutilo kept crying out that he had caught the devil, and begging them to bring a light, that he might more clearly see whose shape he had assumed; and turning the head of his reluctant prisoner to and fro, that the spectators might the better judge, he asked with affected ignorance whether it could be Sindolf? All declaring that it certainly was, and begging that he would let him go, he released him, saying, "Wretch that I am, that I should have laid hands on the intimate and confidant of the bishop!" Ratpert, however, having stepped aside on the coming up of the monks, privately withdrew, and the sufferer could not find out who had beaten him.'* We perceive, from this amusing passage, that the rules prescribed for the conduct of the scribes in the Scriptorium were either broken during 'play hours,' or much relaxed.

Before quitting the monkish transcribers, it may be useful to mention that ornaments and illuminations in manuscripts were but little used till the sixth century. Ornamental letters employed for the titles, the principal divisions, and initial letters of chapters, were of the most fantastic and grotesque forms. Sometimes they occupied the entire page. They represented not only men with the most monstrous deformities, but animals, plants, and fruits. To such an excess had this arrived in the fifteenth century, that, in the words of a contemporary, 'writers are no longer writers, but painters.' These ornaments increased the price of books immensely, without enhancing their intrinsic worth.

The commencement of the university system drew transcribers forth from the monastic Scriptoria, and attracted an immense number of clerks (most of them literally 'in orders') to Paris. When Faust took his printed Bibles to that city in 1463, there were 6000 persons who subsisted by copying and illuminating manuscripts;† but they were notorious for the clerical errors they allowed to escape. The condition in which manuscripts were turned out of their hands, is quaintly described by Petrarch, the immortal sonnetteer (1304-1374). 'How will it be possible,' he asks, 'to remedy the evils brought upon us by copyists whose ignorance and indolence destroy all our race? They prevent many a work of genius from seeing the day, which would perhaps gain immortality. This is a just punishment of the present age of idleness, when people are less curious about books than expensive dishes, and prefer having good cooks to clever copyists. Any one who can paint on parchment, and hold a pen, passes for a good transcriber, though he may have neither skill nor knowledge. I do not complain of their orthography: it would be useless; for that has been past amendment for a long while. We must be thankful, I suppose, that they will copy, however badly, whatever is given them. Such of their patrons even as are sensible of their misdeeds, still will have books, because a book is a book, whether correct or not. Do you think that if Cicero, Livy, and other ancient authors—above all, Pliny—were to rise from the dead and read their own works, that they would understand them? Would they not, think you, at each page, at each word, declare that these were no composition of theirs, but the writing of some barbarian? The evil is, that there are no laws to govern copyists; they are submitted to no examination. Locksmiths, farmers, weavers, and other labourers, are obliged to conform to certain rules; but none exist for copyists. Wanton destroyers are obliged to pay damages; and surely copyists ought to be made to pay handsomely for all the books they have spoiled.'

* From 'The Dark Ages,' a most interesting work, by the Rev. S. R. Maitland, librarian to his grace the Archbishop of Canterbury.

† See further on this subject, Journal, new series, vol. iii., p. 149.

So cautious was Petrarch to whom he trusted his writings, that, referring to his treatise on Solitude, he writes to Boccaccio—'It appears incredible that a book which took only a few months to compose, I cannot get satisfactorily copied in the space of many years.' In corroboration of Petrarch's complaint, a French writer remarks, 'The mistakes of copyists are like the posterity of Abraham, numberless. To count them, would be as difficult as to numerate the stars or the sands of the sea.' This is readily comprehended when we consider the number of transcribers through whose hands the classics passed before they even reached the Italian poet's time. First there were the Greek penmen, of whom Cicero complained, then came the monks, and lastly the Parisian professional and public copyists, who excited Petrarch's ire. Each transcriber of each age copied the errors of his predecessor, besides making mistakes of his own; and when we add to these the more recent ignorance of commentators, as displayed in their so-called 'restorations' of texts, alterations, and additions, it is so far from surprising that we occasionally meet with passages in ancient authors which are totally incomprehensible, that the only wonder is, how we get at the sense so well as we do.

Errors of transcription, sometimes trivial, sometimes gross, have produced amusing results. It was, for example, hotly argued by the learned at one time that Aristotle was a Jew, from the misplacing of a comma in George of Trebisond's version of the works of Josephus. The vitiated passage stood thus: *Atque, ille inquit, Aristoteles Judæus erat*—[And, he says, Aristotle was a Jew]: the correct version being, *Atque ille, inquit Aristoteles, Judæus erat*—[And he, says Aristotle, was Judæus.] The ancient Martyrology of St Jerome sets down, for the 16th February, A.D. 309, eleven martyrs who perished with St Pamphylius. After the words, *Juliani cum Ægyptiis V.*, he added *mil.*, an abbreviation of *militibus*; the whole signifying—'Julian, with five Ægyptian soldiers.' The copyists, supposing *mil.* to mean *millibus*, wrote, *Juliani cum aliis quinque millibus*; that is, 'Julian, with five thousand others!' and this was copied into all the martyrologies as subject for additional execration of the great Christian persecutors Diocletian and Maximian. Instances like these may be multiplied to infinity.

On the other hand, the correctness of religious works was regarded as of the utmost importance, and transcribers were in the habit of placing a note at the commencement or end of their manuscripts, in which they recommended future copyists to collate their work carefully with the original. Such advertisements occasionally took the form of imprecations against those who falsified the text. Such an imprecation will be found in the 18th and 19th verses of the last chapter of the Revelation of St John.

Still, errors occurred even in copies of holy writ; but a summary remedy for them astonished the Parisians in 1463. John Faust made his appearance with *printed* Bibles, and the copyists were gradually, as a body, superseded. With the invention of printing, indeed, the history of the scribes almost ceases in Europe. In the East, however, the profession is still much employed and followed.

At Grand Cairo, which is the metropolis of Arabic literature, copyists abound, because printing is discountenanced by the singular religious scruples of all strict Mussulmen. The respect they feel not only towards the Koran, but to the names of the Deity and of the prophet, wherever they are inscribed, carries them to the length of guarding the words from coming in contact with anything unclean. Mr Lane once asked a Cairean tobacco-pipe maker why he did not stamp the bowls with his name like other manufacturers; his answer was, 'God forbid! My name is Ahhmad (one of the names of the prophet): would you have me put it in the fire?' This strange veneration is the chief reason why the Moslims object to printing. They have scarcely a book that does not contain the name of God;

it being a rule among them to commence every work with the words, 'In the name of God, the compassionate, the merciful,' and to begin the preface or introduction by praising the Deity, and blessing the prophet; and they fear some impurity might be contracted by the ink that is applied to the names, in the process of printing, or by the paper to be impressed. They fear also that their books, becoming very cheap by being printed, would fall into the hands of infidels, and are much shocked at the idea of using a brush composed of the unclean hogs' hair (which was at first done in Cairo) to apply the ink to the word of God. Hence books have hitherto been printed in Egypt only by order of the government; but two or three persons have lately applied for and received permission to make use of the government press. Mr Lane was acquainted with a bookseller who has long been desirous of printing some books which he feels sure would bring him considerable profit, but cannot overcome his scruples as to the lawfulness of doing so. All Arabic books, therefore, are the work of copyists; most of whom are Copts, descended from the ancient inhabitants of Egypt. Books are not bound, but about twenty leaves are doubled in half, and placed one within the other, like our parcels of writing paper. These *livraisons*, called *karras*, are kept in regular order in a case, instead of being bound. The charge for copying a karras of twenty pages, quarto size, with about twenty-five lines to a page, in an ordinary hand, is about three piasters (or a little more than sevenpence of our money), but more if in an elegant hand, and about double the sum if with the vowel points.* What is said of Arabic applies to the literature of all the countries which lie between Egypt, Arabia, &c. and China. None of it is printed, the whole being executed by transcribers.

On the other hand, in China, the birthplace of printing, all books are printed; but copying is a part of the process. The author's manuscript is first transcribed by a professional copyist whose work is printed, or, to use a printer's term, 'set off,' upon a block of wood, and all his lines are exactly preserved and cut in relief by a wood-engraver. From the block the printing is effected in a way which has already been described in this Journal.† But copyists are not wholly employed in this manner. The Chinese attach a high importance to caligraphy, and large ornamental inscriptions or labels are frequently exchanged as remembrances amongst friends, or are used, as pictures are with us, for the purposes of taste and decoration. In producing such pieces of penmanship, professional copyists find profitable employment, as well as in the notes and letters which this ceremonious people exchange with each other. They are generally copied on beautifully illuminated coloured paper, known as 'flowered leaves.' Those who, to neatness of writing, add a fertility of invention in contriving grotesque or elegant ornaments, are very handsomely paid. Indeed there is no country on earth where copyists are so liberally remunerated as in China. Compared with the profits of the same class in our own quarter of the globe, their condition is princelike.

The printing-press has indeed left us, in this quarter of the globe, but little occasion for their assistance. Except in the law, copyists are very seldom employed. In England, deeds are engrossed, and briefs are copied, by persons who, retaining the name given to the ancient Roman copyists, are designated law-*stationers*. Their mode of charging is so much per seventy-two words, which is called a folio. But in Scotland, even these, the latest representatives of an old and important profession, are generally dispensed with; for nearly all law proceedings are printed.

Scarcely any class of authors—except dramatists—require their manuscripts to be re-written before they reach the compositors; who possess such great facilities of deciphering the irregular hieroglyphics which some *littérateurs* are pleased to call their 'handwriting,' that they manage to print correctly from 'copy' of which few else could make out a line.

Plays are generally acted before they are printed, and are consequently copied;—first entire for the prompter, and next in 'parts' for the various actors. That each may know when he has to speak, the last few words of the speeches spoken with and to him are also written out for him to learn. These catch-sentences are called 'cues,' and give a strangely incoherent reading of the play. For instance, that portion of Macduff's part in the tragedy of Macbeth, which occurs in the celebrated scene between him, Malcolm, and Rosse, is written by the copyist thus—

Enter Rosse.

Macduff. See, who comes here?
——————— Yet I know him not.
M. My ever gentle cousin, welcome hither.
——————— Sir, amen.
M. Stands Scotland where it did?
——————— Dying, ere they sicken.
M. O! relation
Too nice, and yet too true:

and so forth. Dramatic copyists are chiefly supernumerary actors, and get about five shillings per act for their labour.

A few persons are occasionally occupied in copying petitions to parliament and to the different boards of revenue; but there is not enough of such work to employ any single person wholly, and it is usually performed by lawyers or law-stationers' clerks during their over-hours. In fact, copying may be looked upon like distaff spinning and hand-loom weaving—as amongst the almost extinct professions.

THE CHEAP SHOP.

A few miles from London, sufficiently removed to escape from its smoke and din, yet affording many characteristic tokens of its vicinity to the modern Babylon, is situated what was, some twenty years ago, a little hamlet, by no means one of the least pleasant that clustered round the mammoth city.

The restless genius of improvement, ever so busy in London, had here exerted but little influence: a stranger would scarcely have believed that the city, the towers and steeples of which were visible in the distance, was so near. The small casements, the prominent beams, the red bricks, and the quaint overhanging style and general irregularity of most of the houses, proclaimed their antiquity; and though these features added to the picturesqueness and interest of the locality, yet they excited some surprise, as existing in the vicinity of so much grandeur and opulence. More especially was this contrast apparent in the appearance of the shops, and the manners and habits of the shopkeepers. Unlike their flaunting fellows of the metropolis, the shops were small, and but ill fitted up—the wares in the windows were displayed to anything but the best advantage—the tinkling shop-bell, in the most primitive simplicity, announced the entrance of a customer—and many of them boasted no better illumination at night than that afforded by a flickering and inefficient candle. The shopkeepers, a contented and plodding race, knew little about the tricks and allurements which competition had taught their fellows of the city; and, if they were not realising fortunes, they were doing still better, namely, obtaining an honourable and honest living, without being compelled to sacrifice either bodily health, by undue exertion and anxiety, or principle and honour, by descending to petty and doubtful expedients to push business.

Such was the state of things in the hamlet, when the hasty alteration of two old adjoining houses, and the

* Lane's Modern Egyptians.

† See vol. ii. (new series), p. 391.

union of the two into a something which was evidently intended for business, in the centre of the hamlet, set all the inhabitants on the tiptoe of expectation, and excited no little curiosity and alarm among the shopkeeping fraternity as to its meaning and destination. Some imagined that the new premises were, from the costliness of their decorations, intended for a gin palace, for the situation was indeed excellent; others contended it was some capitalist linendraper from town; but the secrecy observed by all parties concerned was so great, that nothing could be ascertained.

The premises, however, were soon completed, and the mystery was at length unfolded by the name and business painted in gay colours on a large board in front; and 'Driver and Co.,' it appeared, was the important firm which had settled down its giant limbs among the pigmies. Their line of business—'general dealers'—was somewhat vague; but it was unmistakeably interpreted by the universal character of the articles exhibited in the shop, to which certainly no less comprehensive term could have been adequate. Grocery and hardware, butter and blacking, slops and drugs, anything and everything, were to be obtained at the new shop, and, the premises being extensive, each was arranged according to its peculiar department; and one-half the neighbouring tradesmen beheld with dismay, in the new establishment, a gigantic opponent.

The new shop immediately became, as may well be supposed, quite a feature in the quiet little hamlet; and its splendid glass front and new fittings-up certainly appeared to great advantage, at night especially, when the profusion of gas-lights formed a perfect blaze of light, which threw every other shop in the place far into the shade. The young urchins could scarcely believe that those immeasurable panes of glass were in one piece, and the simple rustics lifted up their eyes in amazement at the 'power of money' it must have cost. Everything was arranged in the windows in the most tempting manner, with price-tickets appended, the figures on which astonished and delighted the marketing folks of the neighbourhood, so much so, that the establishment soon became known by the name of 'the Cheap Shop.'

Besides these temptations, other demonstrations were made by the new firm, which added not a little to its popularity. The neighbourhood was deluged with cards and handbills; the walls were placarded for miles round; and no expedient of puffing was left unresorted to. The shopmen, who were young and active, seemed always in a bustle; empty casks and boxes, and unopened bales, were always about the door; and a gay light cart was continually to be seen on the roads in the neighbourhood; though there were some in the hamlet ill-natured enough to assert that it was kept for show rather than for use, and was merely a kind of locomotive advertisement. All these things, however, had their use, and served to attract the attention of even the least regardful; and many, who were astonished at the show of business made, were curious to deal at a shop apparently so universally patronised by the neighbourhood.

Many other expedients, and some not a little ingenious and singular, were adopted by the new shop for attaining publicity. Besides the hackneyed pretences of 'selling off,' 'alteration of premises,' 'damaged stock,' &c. which kept the hamlet in a state of continual excitement, one of their manœuvres was pre-eminently successful, and was so plausible as to conciliate many who had formed an ill opinion of the honesty and honourable intentions of Driver and Co. Bills were posted on all the walls in the neighbourhood, stating that a bank-note had been picked up in the shop, presumed to have been dropped by one of their customers, and that the owner, by making good his claim, might have it upon application. This was a capital advertisement; the tongues of the simple and unsuspicious were full of the praise of the honest and honourable firm, and many who had hitherto continued their patronage to the old-established shopkeepers, determined they would henceforth support a firm of such integrity and principle. There were certainly some far-seeing people in the hamlet who laughed at the affair with an air of suspicion and incredulity, but the majority scouted such uncharitableness; and the popularity and custom of Driver and Co. visibly increased from week to week. Some were attracted by the extreme civility of the young men, who were so attentive, so anxious to please, and invariably wrapt up the change in paper. Some of the labourers' wives declared they could save a shilling a-week by dealing there, so cheap were the articles. Some were attracted by the splendid appearance of the shop; but perhaps the greater part went at first from curiosity to see the place, and to try the articles that were sold at such marvellously low prices. Certain it is that the new shop was abundantly patronised, and on Saturdays was always crowded till long past midnight.

Things went on in this way for several months, and Driver and Co. were gradually absorbing the custom of the district. Notwithstanding this apparent prosperity, rumours were spread abroad that wholesale dealers were pressing in vain for their money; that the most trivial and unsatisfactory reasons were continually urged for deferring payment, and that the concern must soon come to a stand-still. It was asserted also that the head of the firm (some said that he constituted in himself the entire company) had a large country-house, kept his cab and footman, rejoiced in a large establishment and expensive table; and that his lady showed, by her style of dress, she was determined to be not a whit behind her husband in the liberality of her expenditure. The surrounding tradesmen also declared it was impossible to purchase many of the articles at the price for which they were sold at the new shop; and that either they were never paid for, or else the proprietor would soon be ruined. However this might have been, certain it was that, within a twelvemonth from its opening, a knot of early customers was seen one fine morning vainly striving for admittance: the shop was closed, and for ever. Driver and Co. were in the Gazette, and the stock was shortly afterwards advertised to be sold off for the benefit of the creditors.

Great was the consternation in the hamlet and neighbourhood at this sudden *dénouement*; and the elongated faces of the many commercial-looking men who inquired anxiously in the neighbourhood, indicated how extensively the mischief had operated. Many houses of respectability, it was rumoured, had been deluded by the specious representations of the firm, and had credited them so extensively, that they were unable in turn to meet their engagements; and more than one promising young tradesman, who had liberally advanced goods on the faith of their respectability and good intentions, saw themselves involved in ruin. Disastrous also were the results to the little tradesmen in the hamlet. Most of the shopkeepers in the same line of business had been more or less affected, and many, seeing their custom forsaking them, and no other mode of escape from the crushing evil, left the neighbourhood to try their fortunes elsewhere. One poor grocer, who had previously struggled hard to maintain his family of six children in respectability, after some time manfully endeavouring to brave the impending storm, had no other alternative than to tear his heart from all his long-cherished associations, and emigrate to a distant land; and an industrious cheesemonger, who had previously to the settling down of 'the Cheap Shop,' contrived for many years to support an aged relative, was compelled, owing to the decline of his business, to send her down to her own parish in the country. Independent of the injury done to the morality of trade in the district and neighbourhood, many a year passed away before the evil was neutralised which was bred and fostered by the Cheap Shop.'

SCHOOLS OF INDUSTRY.

Our article, 'Visit to the Aberdeen Schools of Industry,' in the number for November 15, appears to have excited some attention, and we trust may be a means of promoting the establishment of schools of industry for poor children in all large towns, or at least of raising public attention to the subject. Among the communications which have reached us, is the following:—

'About two years ago I was summoned to appear as a juror in the sheriff's criminal court at ——. On attending at an early hour in the morning, I found that I was one of forty-five persons brought together on the same errand; many from distant parts of the county, and the whole, from the cast on their countenances, appeared to feel that the sacrifice they were making to the injunctions of the law was by no means a light one. At length the court met, and was constituted by the chair being taken by a grave-looking judge in a formidable wig. The culprit was brought in and arraigned. He was a little boy of twelve or thirteen years of age, dressed in a pair of tattered corduroy trousers; and his tangled hair, dirty face, and bare feet, told pretty plainly to what class of the population he belonged—one of those poor, wretched, vagrant urchins who haunt area doors in quest of a mouthful of food, and whose whinings for halfpence, as you have observed, are the annoyance of all well-dressed passengers. Well, here was the little fellow caught up at last. When addressed by the judge, he seemed puzzled in making a reply before such an awful assembly, the terrible white wig of the sheriff doubtless contributing materially to his mystification. It was at length gathered from him that he pled "not guilty," and so the case "passed to the knowledge of an assize." With my usual luck I was drawn from the five-and-forty to sit on this important trial by jury, and to it we went. There was something exceedingly droll in the whole affair. The apparatus evoked to try the little vagrant seemed like erecting a steam-engine of five hundred horse power to kill a mouse. On the one side were the judge, prosecutor, solicitors pro. and con., sundry subordinate officials, and the jury—a selection of fifteen from five-and-forty men dragged from their daily avocations over a compass of at least thirty miles. On the other was a poor little dirty urchin, so short in stature that his face barely reached the top of the table behind which he was placed; and to have a proper look of him, he was caused to stand upon a chair in front of the court. Crime charged—stealing an old brass candlestick worth sixpence. The theft was proved, as a matter of course; and in a very cool commonplace sort of way the culprit was condemned to six months' imprisonment, the hint being added, that as this was his third offence of the kind, he should on the next occasion be brought before a higher tribunal. The warning was well meant; but as the poor creature could neither read nor write, and had been a neglected child since infancy, it may be doubted if he understood a single word that was addressed to him. After another case of a similar kind, the entire members of the jury were informed they might depart, and the court broke up. The expense to the country and to the individuals employed in these miserable trials, could not, I am told, be estimated at less than one hundred pounds.

'Nine months later, I was summoned as a juror in the supreme criminal court, and there, amidst a much more imposing apparatus of law and lawyers—for one thing, three learned judges on the bench—appeared to undergo his trial the same unfortunate little boy whom I had formerly seen before the sheriff. Working his way up, as it is called, he had passed through all the inferior tribunals, and improving as he proceeded, had committed a crime which inferred one of the highest statutory penalties. The hint of the sheriff had been made good. He was now before a higher court—the highest he could reach. Again there were all the minutiæ of evidence, with harangues from lawyers; and again was the culprit found guilty, and condemned. Again was there an admonition from the presiding judge; again did the court break up; and again did every member of the jury wend his way home, in a state of moody discontent and indignation at having lost so much valuable time, and been put to so much trouble, on so pitiful a business. On this occasion the country could not have incurred a pecuniary obligation of less than three hundred pounds; reckoning all things, perhaps five hundred pounds would be nearer the mark. Five hundred pounds to punish a crime: five pounds rightly laid out at first would most likely have prevented its commission. The probable ruin of a boy, body and soul, is a different question.

'It is of no use mincing the matter. The cumbrous, expensive, and imposing methods adopted for clearing the country of crime in the manner here pointed out, surely fall very far short of what common sense assures us is desirable. Our courts of justice are, of course, well enough in their way; their administration is perhaps all that can be desired; but it is equally evident that they do not reach the seat of the disease which they are designed to remedy. Nor can they, from their constitution, do so. An entirely different machinery requires to be erected for this important end.

'According to all recent experience, there is in every town a certain known number of persons, juvenile and adult, who prey on the public. The superintendents of police, and their assistants, can usually tell, within two or three, how many men, women, and boys, in each large town live by the habitual commission of depredations. They likewise know their haunts, and all their ways. Criminals may be said to form a kind of corporation. They have sprung from the people, but their course of life produces a distinct interest. It is the begging, thieving, and plundering interest. And to watch this interest, and keep it in check, is the business of the police. By the universal vigilance now exercised, the interest has been greatly lowered in tone and in numbers. To appearance, indeed, there is more crime now than formerly; the activity of the constabulary bringing hundreds of cases forward to swell returns which at one time would have been neglected. Crime, though magnified in amount, is really degenerated. Criminals of real consequence belong to the past.

'Leaving all the ordinary means in operation for quelling the thieving confederacies of large towns, and also for reclamation during imprisonment, we would offer a substantial obstacle to any recruitment in the number of depredators. The corps is kept up from beneath. It is like a growing plant. Let us then attack the root, which consists of the half or almost wholly destitute children who are seen roaming like creatures of the wilderness through the busy streets of our towns and cities. In your article on Aberdeen, you have shown how this vagrancy has been humanely considered and treated; why may not the same thing be done elsewhere? Is it creditable, or decent, or safe, or economical, to allow this perpetual growth out of the vagrancy and destitution of children, into the moral disorder and crime of youth and manhood? Nay more—is it just—just to leave a child in a state of constant necessity and temptation, and in nearly as great a degree of ignorance as a brute, and then inflict on him a punishment for an offence of which he cannot be morally conscious?

'Whatever be the degree of blame imputable to society at large for this species of neglect, a still greater blame rests on the heads of the magistrates and judges before whom these juvenile criminals are in the habit of being brought. They have seen the whole thing going on for years, and taken no active means to quell it. They know quite well that, by a very little outlay and attention at first, not a tenth of the cases which now come before them would ever exist. Were I judge, I should be in some degree ashamed of being constantly occupied in trying and condemning dirty ragged children. When I found myself, year after year, obliged to sit in judgment, along with other aged and grave men, on young creatures utterly abject and ignorant, and found it my duty to put questions on all sorts of mean details, such as, for example, how a tattered shirt worth sevenpence was stolen from a broker's door (shirt held up by an officer of court amidst the suppressed titter of the unprofessional audience), I should feel that I was altogether in a false position; that surely there was something wrong in a function by which I was obliged to drudge through such dirty work. It is at all events certain that no mercantile man has ever to put his hands to such an offensive occupation; nor would he. Every man of the least feeling loathes the idea of sitting as a juror on the heart-sickening scenes of which I speak; and never does a court break up, in which the strangers present do not express their wonder at seeing judges take the matter so coolly. No doubt judges must undertake any kind of trial that comes before them. But, although judges, they do not cease to be men; and I should think that, for their own feelings, if not for the sake of humanity and public decency, they would try to avert the appearance of these shoals of children at their bar.

'That the establishment of schools of industry, partly on a compulsory principle, would sweep nearly every juvenile vagrant and thief from the streets, may be now pretty safely admitted; and in the getting up of these valuable institutions, every judge and magistrate is, in my opinion, deeply concerned. Let every man amongst them, then, put himself in possession of the facts necessary for this purpose. Money is less wanted than personal services. We want no fine buildings, fine uniforms, and fine food. A garret for a school, with ragged children for pupils, will answer every reasonable expectation. Again, I say, let the magistracy take a lead in this good work, and I shall have no fears for the result.'

Our correspondent, it will be noticed, has spoken somewhat warmly in behalf of the ragged urchins of the streets; but his good intentions will be an apology for any undue fervour. The subject is one of the most important of the day.

BIOGRAPHIC SKETCHES.

ADMIRAL LORD EXMOUTH.

EDWARD PELLEW, Viscount Exmouth, the second son of a commander of a post-office packet on the *Dover* station, was born on the 19th of April 1757. His father died in 1765, leaving six children to the care of a second wife, slenderly provided for. They were, however, educated by their grandfather, and Edward was sent to various grammar-schools, where he learnt to 'construe Virgil,' which was considered at that time an achievement that bespoke a good education. At fourteen he evinced a passion for the sea, and through the interest of Lady Spencer (grandmother to the present lord), was received into the naval service in the year 1770. He entered on board the Juno, Captain Stott, which was commissioned for the Falkland Islands. On the homeward voyage he exhibited a degree of firmness and generosity which always in after-life honourably distinguished him. He had formed a strong friendship for a fellow-midshipman named Cole. This young gentleman had displeased his captain, who had the cruelty to put him ashore at Marseilles; and Pellew, feeling very strongly the injustice of this act, insisted upon bearing his friend company. They were accordingly both turned out of the ship, and left penniless on a foreign shore. Lord Hugh Seymour and the late Captain Keppel, who were then lieutenants under Stott, befriended them, and the former furnished them with enough of cash to pay their way back to England. On their return, the harsh captain so far repented of his conduct as to give both the lads certificates of good behaviour and abilities; and Pellew was received into the Blonde.

Captain Pownoll, who commanded the Blonde, soon estimated Pellew's worth above that of his other midshipmen. Active beyond his companions, Mr Pellew did the ship's duty with a smartness which none of them could equal; and as every one takes pleasure where he excels, he had soon become a thorough seaman. At the same time the buoyancy of youth, and a naturally playful disposition, led him continually into feats of more than common daring. In the spring of 1775, General Burgoyne took his passage to America in the Blonde, and when he came alongside, the yards were manned to receive him. Looking up, he was surprised to see a midshipman on the yard-arm standing on his head. Captain Pownoll, who was at his side, quieted his apprehensions, by assuring him that it was only one of the usual frolics of young Pellew, and that the general might make himself quite at ease for his safety, for that, if he should fall, he would, only go under the ship's bottom and come up on the other side. What on this occasion was probably spoken but in jest, was afterwards more than realised; for he actually sprang from the fore-yard of the Blonde while she was going fast through the water, and saved a man who had fallen overboard. Pownoll reproached him for his rashness; but the captain shed tears when he spoke of it to the officers, and declared that Pellew was a noble fellow. These two feats foreshadowed, as it were, the future adventures of young Pellew; but as he grew older, a greater degree of prudence and foresight tempered that ardent and impulsive activity which originated some of his most extraordinary achievements.

The Blonde formed part of the force against the Americans during their war of independence, and her destination was Canada. To forward the operations of the land forces, it was found necessary to have a flotilla on Lake Champlain; but of course it had to be built. A lieutenant, a senior midshipman, and sixty sailors, were detached from the Blonde. Pellew also volunteered for this service; and fortunately, as the event proved, was added to the party. The first thing to be done on the borders of the lake was simply to—build a little fleet; and this was actually accomplished under the superintendence of Lieutenant (afterwards Admiral) Schanck, an officer of great mechanical ingenuity. The timbers or skeletons of the largest of these impromptu vessels were 'laid down' in Quebec. They were then taken to pieces, and conveyed in parts to the lake, where the ships were completely equipped. The progress of the work was like magic. Trees growing in the forest in the morning, would form part of a ship before night. In this manner a ship of 300 tons, called the Inflexible, with two schooners, and twenty-six other vessels and boats, were, in an incredibly short time, launched on the lake. The Blonde party manned one of the schooners, called the Carleton. In the first action with the enemy, both Pellew's superior officers were killed, and he took the command, and performed two of his most daring feats. In attempting to go *about*, being close to the shore covered with the enemy's marksmen, the Carleton hung in stays, and Pellew, not regarding the danger of making himself so conspicuous a mark, sprang out on the bowsprit to push the jib over. Some of the gun-boats now took her in tow; but so thick and heavy was the enemy's fire, that the tow-rope was cut with a shot. Pellew ordered some one to go and secure it; but seeing all hesitate—for indeed it looked like a death-service—he ran forward and did it himself. His conduct was so highly approved, that when it was detailed at head-quarters, Lord Sandwich, first lord of the Admiralty, sent him a voluntary letter, promising him a lieutenant's commission.

Pellew and his little party were afterwards selected to accompany the army overland to the Hudson river. Here the enemy was completely successful, and, amongst other things, captured a boat filled with provisions upon which the forces were mainly to depend. The loss was most disastrous, and appeared irreparable; but Pellew, at the head of his little band, made a successful attack, and recaptured the vessel. She was carried by boarding, and taken in tow by our sailors; the tow-rope was twice shot away, and twice replaced by Pellew swimming with it on board under the enemy's fire. The commander-in-chief of the land forces (General Burgoyne) wrote to him, returning his own sincere thanks and that of the whole army 'for the important service rendered them.' So high an opinion had the general of his young auxiliary's judgment, that when it was deemed necessary to capitulate, he admitted him into his council of war. Finally, he was selected to return to England with despatches—about as high a compliment as it was possible to pay an officer at that time only twenty. He came home in a transport, which was attacked by a hostile privateer. Pellew, though only a passenger, insisted on taking the command and fighting the ship. This he did with such success, that he beat off the privateer.

Immediately after Pellew's arrival home, he received a lieutenant's commission, and was appointed to a guard-ship. In 1780, we find him first lieutenant of the Apollo, under his old friend Captain Pownoll. In an action with the French frigate Stanislaus, on the 15th June, this officer was killed, and the command of the Apollo having devolved on Pellew, he drove the enemy, dismasted and beaten, on shore. For this exploit he obtained a step of rank, and was made commander of the Hazard war-sloop. In the Pelican, his next ship, he defeated several French privateers in so gallant a style, that he was made a post-captain.*

In 1783, soon after this promotion, peace was proclaimed, and Captain Pellew married Susanna, second daughter of J. Frowd, Esq. of Knoyle, Wiltshire, with whom he appears to have enjoyed three successive years of uninterrupted domestic happiness. In 1786 he was called from his wife and his home to commission the Winchelsea for the Newfoundland station, and on board this ship performed several acts of daring intrepidity. It was his boast that he would never order a common seaman to do what he was not ready to set about himself. Some of his orders were indeed so perilous of execution, that his smartest hands hesitated to obey them. When he saw this, he invariably did what was required himself. Some of these exploits were of too technical a nature to be understood by the general

* As this term is not very generally understood, some explanation of it may be useful. The term 'captain' means chief or head, and is thus applied to an officer commanding a ship, even though in actual rank he be only a lieutenant or 'commander.' In that case it is merely temporary, or local rank. A post-captain, on the contrary, is permanent rank, for his name is recorded in its proper place on the list of captains, and thus he takes his *post* or place according to seniority, and will in course of time become an admiral, if he outlive those above him; so that when an officer is placed on the roll of captains, his promotion no longer depends upon favour, but upon death vacancies. He is therefore said to be *posted*.

reader; but one anecdote, related by an officer of the Winchelsea, everybody will understand. 'We had light winds and fine weather after making the coast of Portugal. One remarkably fine day, when the ship was stealing through the water under the influence of a gentle breeze, the people were all below at their dinners, and scarcely a person left on deck but officers, of whom the captain was one. Two little ship-boys had been induced, by the fineness of the weather, to run up from below the moment they had dined, and were at play on the spare anchor to leeward, which overhangs the side of the ship. One of them fell overboard, which was seen from the quarter-deck, and the order was given to luff the ship into the wind. In an instant the officers were over the side; but it was the captain who, grasping a rope firmly with one hand, let himself down to the water's edge, and, catching hold of the poor boy's jacket as he floated past, saved his life in as little time as I have taken to mention it. There was not a rope touched or a sail altered in doing this, and the people below knew not of the accident until they came on deck when their dinner was over.'*

Having served three years in the northern seas, Pellew returned; but his visit ashore was cut short by the breaking out of the French war. He was appointed to the Nymphe, which had been previously captured from the French; and with her he deprived them of another vessel. Having fallen in with the Cleopatra, a ship of equal force, he took her after a well-fought action, in which the French showed good training and courage. For this Pellew was, on his return home, knighted.

In 1794 we find Captain Sir Edward Pellew commanding the 'Saucy Arethusa' (as Dibdin calls her in one of his most popular songs), as part of a frigate squadron under Sir John Warren. This fleet was so successful, that the Admiralty was induced to increase it, and to divide the command between Warren and Pellew. One of the ships taken, 'La Revolutionnaire,' was commissioned in the British service by Sir Edward's early associate, the oppressed midshipman Cole. In the Indefatigable, into which Pellew removed from the Arethusa, he performed one of his diving feats, which astonished the whole ship's crew. In May 1795, while chasing a vessel near the shores of Cape Finisterre, the Indefatigable struck on a rock. The mischief was serious, and it was with great difficulty that the ship was kept afloat. In order to ascertain whether both sides of the ship had been injured, Sir Edward resolved to examine the bottom himself; and to the astonishment and admiration of every witness, he plunged into the water, thoroughly examined both sides, and satisfied himself that the starboard side only had been damaged. This saved much time and expense; for had not Sir Edward hazarded the experiment, the apparatus for heaving down must have been shifted over, at so great a loss of time, that serious damage might have ensued. In this ship, indeed, he performed several heroic acts in the cause of humanity. Once in Portsmouth harbour, where he was instrumental in saving two poor fellows; and again at Spithead, where one of the coxswains of his own ship fell overboard, the captain was instantly in the water, and caught the man just as he was sinking quite exhausted; life was apparently extinct, but, by the usual means, was happily restored. On the third occasion, the attempt had nearly proved fatal to himself. Two men had been dashed overboard in a very heavy sea; Pellew jumped into a boat, and ordered it to be lowered—in the attempt, the ship happened to make a deep plunge—the boat was stove to pieces, and the captain thrown out much bruised, his nostril slit by one of the tackles, and bleeding profusely; but his coolness and self-possession did not forsake him, and calling for a rope, he slung himself with one of the many which were

* The Life of Admiral Viscount Exmouth. By Edward Osler, Esq. Pp. 67, 68.

thrown to him, and was hauled on board. Another boat was then lowered with better success, and the men, who seem to have supported themselves by the wreck of the first boat, were eventually saved.

But Sir Edward's most extraordinary and celebrated achievement remains to be told. On the 26th January 1796, while the Indefatigable was being refitted in Plymouth harbour, he was proceeding in his carriage with Lady Pellew to dine with the Rev. Dr Hawker.* It was blowing a hurricane, and crowds were running towards the sea-shore. Sir Edward soon learnt that the Dutton, a large transport, was driven ashore under the citadel, and was beating against the rocks in a tremendous and impassable surf, at a rate which threatened her destruction every minute. She had part of the 2d regiment on board, who had given themselves up for lost. Sir Edward sprang from his carriage, and, 'arrived at the beach,' writes his biographer, 'he saw at once, that the loss of nearly all on board, between five and six hundred, was inevitable, without some one to direct them. The principal officers of the ship had abandoned their charge, and got on shore, just as he arrived on the beach. Having urged them, but without success, to return to their duty, and vainly offered rewards to pilots and others belonging to the port to board the wreck—for all thought it too hazardous to be attempted—he exclaimed, "Then I will go myself!" A single rope, by which the officers and a few others had landed, formed the only communication with the ship, and by this he was hauled on board through the surf. The danger was greatly increased by the wreck of the masts, which had fallen towards the shore; and he received an injury in the back, which confined him to his bed for a week, in consequence of being dragged under the mainmast. But disregarding this at the time, he reached the deck, declared himself, and assumed the command. He assured the people that every one would be saved if they quietly obeyed his orders; that he would himself be the last to quit the wreck; but that he would run any one through who disobeyed him. His well-known name, with the calmness and energy he displayed, gave confidence to the despairing multitude. He was received with three hearty cheers, which were echoed by the multitude on shore; and his promptitude at resource soon enabled him to find and apply the means by which all might be safely landed. His officers, in the meantime, though not knowing that he was on board, were exerting themselves to bring assistance from the Indefatigable. Mr Pellowe, first lieutenant, left the ship in the barge, and Mr Thomson, acting master, in the launch; but the boats could not be brought alongside the wreck, and were obliged to run for the Barbican. A small boat belonging to a merchant vessel was more fortunate. Mr Edsell, signal midshipman to the port-admiral, and Mr Coghlan, mate of the merchant vessel, succeeded, at the risk of their lives, in bringing her alongside. The ends of two additional hawsers were got on shore, and Sir Edward contrived cradles to be slung upon them, with travelling ropes to pass forward and backward between the ship and the beach. Each hawser was held on shore by a number of men, who watched the rolling of the wreck, and kept the ropes tight and steady. Meantime a cutter had with great difficulty worked out of Plymouth Pool, and two large boats arrived from the dock-yard, under the directions of Mr Hemmings, the master-attendant, by whose caution and judgment they were enabled to approach the wreck, and receive the more helpless of the passengers, who were carried to the cutter. Sir Edward, with his sword drawn, directed the proceedings, and preserved order; a task the more difficult, as the soldiers had got at the spirits before he came on board, and many were drunk. The children, the women, and the sick were the first landed. One of them was only three weeks old; and nothing in the whole transaction impressed Sir Edward more strongly than the struggle of the mother's feelings before she would intrust her infant to his care, or afforded him more pleasure than the success of his attempt to save it. Next the soldiers were got on shore, then the ship's company, and finally, Sir Edward himself, who was one of the last to leave her. Every one was saved, and presently after the wreck went to pieces.' Pellew's principal assistant in this heroic act met his reward. Coghlan was taken, through his influence, into the royal service, and became a post-captain by 1810. Nor was the chief actor in this courageous enterprise forgotten. Praise was lavished on him from every quarter. The corporation of Plymouth voted him the freedom of the town. The merchants of Liverpool presented him with a valuable service of plate. On the 5th of March following he was created a baronet, as Sir Edward Pellew of Treverry, and received for an honourable augmentation of his arms a civic wreath, a stranded ship for a crest, and the motto, 'Deo adjuvante, Fortuna sequatur'—(God assisting, success must follow). In writing to a friend on the subject, Pellew said, 'I was laid in bed for a week by getting under the mainmast (which had fallen towards the shore); and my back was cured by Lord Spencer's having conveyed to me by letter his majesty's intention to dub me baronet. No more have I to say, except that I felt more pleasure in giving to a mother's arms a dear little infant only three weeks old, than I ever felt in my life; and both were saved. The struggle she had to intrust me with the bantling, was a scene I cannot describe.'

In 1796 the French made their attempt on Ireland, and Sir Edward having been sent in the Indefatigable as part of a fleet to oppose them, suffered severely from the gale which nearly destroyed the enemy's ships. On returning home, however, the vessel got severely handled by a French two-decker, the Droits de l'Homme; and the storm continuing, she was nearly lost. The years 1797 and 1798 were passed in the blockade of Brest and other Channel services, with great perseverance and so much success, that in the course of 1798 alone Sir Edward's squadron took no fewer than fifteen of the enemy's cruisers. One of the captures was of more than common interest. It was La Vaillante, a national corvette, taken by the Indefatigable after a chase of twenty-four hours. She was bound to Cayenne with prisoners, amongst whom were twenty-five priests; and, as passengers, the wife and family of an exiled deputy, M. Rovère, who were proceeding to join him, with all they possessed—about £3000. Sir Edward and his officers vied in attention to the poor ecclesiastics, and, on landing them in England, he gave them a supply for their immediate wants; to Madame Rovère he restored the whole of her property, paying out of his own pocket the proportion which was the prize of the crew. Sir Edward was now removed into a larger ship, the 'Impétueux,' which bore the singular distinction of carrying 78 guns. He was in this ship when the widespread naval mutiny took place, and a part of his crew rose against their officers. On investigation, however, it turned out that not one of the men who had followed him from the Indefatigable joined in the mutiny. No better proof could be adduced of the attachment to his person of those who knew him best.

The peace of Amiens placed Pellew on half-pay. He was solicited to become a member of parliament, and at the general election of 1802 he was returned for Barnstaple in Devonshire. The senate soon proved not to his taste, and he took the earliest opportunity to escape from it. The very day that fresh hostilities against France were declared, he solicited employment, and was appointed to the Tonnant, an 80-gun ship, in which he cruised with the Channel Fleet. At the general promotion of 1804, Pellew was advanced to the rank of rear-admiral, and intrusted with the post of commander-in-chief of the East Indian seas; whither he proceeded, and remained till 1809. In the spring of 1811, he suc-

* Author of a commentary on the Bible, sermons, and several religious works. He was, for half a century, vicar of the parish of Charles the Martyr, Plymouth.

ceeded to the Mediterranean command, and acquitted himself so well, that at the downfall of Napoleon, occasioned by the Russian campaign, Sir Edward was created, even before his return home, Baron Exmouth of Canonteign, a mansion and estate in South Devon he had previously purchased. This was no empty honour; for a pension was added to it.

The return of Napoleon from Elba soon required a British force in the Mediterranean, and Lord Exmouth having been selected for this service, again performed, with his usual prudence and energy, all the duties which the position of affairs required or admitted. Marseilles had shown some disposition to favour the Bourbons, and Marshal Brune was marching from Toulon upon that city, avowedly to destroy it. Lord Exmouth, on this emergency, took upon himself to embark about 3000 men, part of the garrison of Genoa, with whom he sailed to Marseilles. Forty years before, he had landed at this port a poor penniless boy turned out of his ship—he now entered it a British admiral and peer, and, what was still more gratifying to him, a conqueror and deliverer! The inhabitants, grateful for their preservation, were unceasing in their attentions to the fleet and army, and, as a mark of their sense of his important services to their city, they presented him with a large and beautiful piece of plate executed in Paris, bearing a medallion of the noble admiral, and a view of the port of Marseilles, and the Boyne, his flag-ship, entering it full sail, with this simple and expressive inscription:—"*A l'Amiral Lord Exmouth—La Ville de Marseilles reconnoissante.*"—[To the Admiral Lord Exmouth; the town of Marseilles, grateful.]

The final overthrow of Napoleon at the battle of Waterloo secured that peace which has not even yet been broken in Europe; and we now approach Lord Exmouth's most splendid naval achievement on the coast of Africa.

While the fleet was still assembled in the Mediterranean, the British government thought its presence there would be a good opportunity of putting down the abominable system of piracy carried on by the Barbary states. Lord Exmouth, amongst other duties, went on shore at Algiers to endeavour to extract a pledge from the Dey that slavery should be abolished—a promise which he had already drawn from the Beys of Tunis and Tripoli. But at Algiers both himself and his officers were insulted. This, with several other aggressions, and an obstinate refusal of the demands of the British government, induced the issue of orders for the bombardment of Algiers; the execution of which was confided to Lord Exmouth.

On the 27th August 1816, he led his fleet under the fortifications of Algiers, placing his own ship, the Queen Charlotte, within twenty yards of the mole-head, the most formidable of the enemy's batteries, and when the immense ship had only two feet of water to spare, being within that short distance from the bottom. M. Salamé, his lordship's Arabic interpreter, was sent on shore with certain written demands, and with a message that, unless a satisfactory answer were returned in two hours, that would be deemed a signal for the commencement of hostilities. Salamé waited three, and then put off to the admiral's ship. 'On getting on board,' he remarks,* 'I was quite surprised to see how his lordship was altered from what I left him in the morning, for I knew his manner was in general very mild; but now he seemed to me all-fightful, as a fierce lion which had been chained in a cage and was set at liberty. With all that, his lordship's answer to me was—"Never mind—we shall see!" and at the same time he turned towards the officers, saying, "Be ready!" whereupon I saw every one standing with the match or the string of the lock in his hand, anxiously waiting for the word "Fire." During this time the Queen Charlotte, in a most gallant and astonishing manner, took up a position opposite the head of the mole; and at a few minutes before three, the Algerines, from the eastern battery, fired the first shot at the Impregnable, which was astern, when Lord Exmouth, having seen only the smoke of the gun, and, before the sound reached him, said with great alacrity, "That will do!—fire, my fine fellows." I am sure that before his lordship had finished these words, our broadside was given with great cheering, which was fired three times within five or six minutes; and at the same instant the other ships did the same.' Of the action, Lord Exmouth gave an account in a letter to one of his brothers. Amongst other things, he relates, 'It was a glorious sight to see the Charlotte take her anchorage, and to see her flag towering on high, when she appeared to be in the flames of the mole itself; and never was a ship nearer burnt; it almost scorched me off the poop. We were obliged to haul in the ensign, or it would have caught fire. Everybody behaved nobly. I was but slightly touched in thigh, face, and fingers—my glass cut in my hand, and the skirts of my coat torn off by a large shot; but as I bled a good deal, it looked as if I was badly hurt, and it was gratifying to see and hear how it was received even in the cockpit, which was then pretty full. I never saw such enthusiasm in all my service.' After the bombardment, which was completely successful, Salamé, on meeting his lordship on the poop of the Queen Charlotte, observed, that 'his voice was quite hoarse; and he had two slight wounds, one on the cheek, and the other on his leg. It was indeed astonishing to see the coat of his lordship, how it was all cut up by the musket-balls and by grape. It was as if a person had taken a pair of scissors and cut it all to pieces.'

The effect of this engagement was, that piracy and slavery were put an end to in that quarter of the world for ever—a result of no small importance. On his return to England, he was created a viscount, with an honourable augmentation to his already so honoured escutcheon, and the word *Algiers* as an additional motto. He received from his own sovereign a gold medal struck for the occasion, and from the kings of Holland, Spain, and Sardinia, the stars of their orders—a sword from the city of London; and, finally—what was likely to please such a man most of all—an unusually large proportion of distinction and promotion acknowledged the merits of the brave men who had served under him. On the death of Admiral Duckworth in 1817, he was appointed to the chief command at Plymouth, where he continued till the 21st February 1821, when he struck his flag, terminated his active service, and retired to the pleasant neighbourhood of Teignmouth. Viscount Exmouth had served his country during the long space of fifty years and three months, and with such indefatigable activity, that out of that time his periods of inactivity only amounted to eight years altogether. In 1822 he obtained the high station of Vice-admiral of England.

His lordship lived on in placid retirement—which was only occasionally broken by attendance on his place in the House of Lords—enjoying to the full the affection of his beloved partner, and the comforts of rest. Bodily infirmities crept upon him, and on the 23d of January 1833 he expired, surrounded by his family, and in full and grateful possession of his faculties. His viscountess and five of his six children survived him.

Lord Exmouth's life adds another to the many instances we have already adduced, of what may be achieved by a steady and unflinching discharge of professional duties. He began his naval career a poor and almost friendless boy, and ended it holding the highest station but one it is possible for a sailor to fill. His contemporaries spoke of him as the *beau ideal* of a British sailor. He knew and could perform all the duties of a ship, from the furling of a sail in a storm to the manœuvring of a fleet in a battle; and there was nothing he ever attempted that he did not do well. Amidst all the violent and demoralising tendencies of warfare, he never forgot his religious duties. 'Every hour of his life is a sermon,' said an officer who was often with him; 'I have seen him great in battle, but

* Salamé's Expedition to Algiers, p. 39.

never so great as on his deathbed. Full of hope and peace, he advanced with the confidence of a Christian to his last conflict; and when nature was at length exhausted, he closed a life of brilliant and important service with a death more happy, and not less glorious, than if he had fallen in the hour of victory.'

THREE ROMANCES OF REAL LIFE.

The French newspapers have recently reported, amongst their accounts of law proceedings, three traits of struggling poverty, so affecting and instructive, that we reproduce them for the edification of our readers.

The first came before the authorities in the shape of a fraud on the revenue, but one attended by circumstances which have softened the hearts of the otherwise rigid and exact functionaries on whom it was perpetrated. It had been remarked at one of the post-offices that a letter, coming from the frontiers of Siberia, and of course entailing heavy postage expenses, arrived regularly every three months in Paris, addressed to a Polish count. A few days after each letter reached its destination, a tall man, with thick black mustaches, and a military bearing, came to claim it. Little difficulty was of course made in giving the missive into his hands, the clerk at the same time informing him of the price of the postage. The Pole, attentively examining the superscription, after shaking his head with emotion, would return it, saying that the letter bore his name, but was not intended for him. The same circumstance, repeated at stated intervals for several years running, awakened curiosity. The opening of the letters after the time appointed by the rules of the post-office, afforded no elucidation to this mystery, for the contents were in blank paper. Some indiscretion at length revealed the secret; and it turned out that the Polish count was one of a family who took an active part in the revolution of Poland, and, after the events of 1831, was, together with his father, his three brothers, and two uncles, condemned to banishment in Siberia. He alone escaped, and found an asylum in France; but, reduced to the utmost straits, unable to pay postage from so great a distance, and longing to receive tidings of his relations, they agreed upon the following plan, which they carried on with success for several years:—On the cover of the letter, each word in the address was written by the different members of his family; thus the unfortunate Pole, from his exact knowledge of the handwriting of each, obtained, by mere examination of the outside, certitude of the existence of his captive relations, and of their continuing together on the same spot. On hearing this pitiable statement, the functionaries overlooked the fraud on the revenue in the affection which prompted, and the ingenuity which contrived, the scheme.

The second incident is of a more tragic cast, and resembles one of those strange coincidences which are met with in fictions. A young workman of good character supported a sorrowing mother, whose husband had many years previously basely abandoned her to great pecuniary distress. Though generally a sober and industrious person, he was, one Saturday night, enticed by several fellow-artisans to visit a public-house near the Barrier d'Enfer. The wine circulated freely; but after a little indulgence, the young man stopped short, saying that he could not afford to spend any more money away from his mother and his home. Accordingly he left the house, and walked towards his residence, a little confused, it is true, by the quantity of wine he had swallowed. Presently one of the boon companions, an elderly stranger, overtook him, and after commending his forbearance, and expressing much admiration of the sentiments he had uttered, offered to 'treat' him at the first house of entertainment they passed. The youth assented. They entered a wine shop, drank, and in a short time the guest felt his senses gradually overcome. Still, he retained sufficient sense to understand what was going on, and to feel the hand of his entertainer gliding stealthily into his pocket. Rendered desperate by the dread of losing his week's earnings, he aroused himself, called in the police, had the robber arrested, and taken before a commissary or magistrate. The deceitful old man defended himself by saying he merely wished to play a trick upon his young companion, and in proof of his respectability, produced his passport. The magistrate examined it, and reading it aloud, pronounced the name of 'Jaques Antoine ——.' The accuser, rubbing his eyes, and looking at the defendant attentively, called out, after a pause, in a tone of agony, 'Mon Dieu! c'est mon pere!' and, overcome by emotion, fell back in a swoon. At first, dissipation, altered attire, and the time which had elapsed since they had met, had effectually disguised the father from the son; but when the name was mentioned, recognition ensued. By the law of France, the accusation of a child cannot be taken against a parent, and the defendant was about to be dismissed, when he was confronted by other accusers whom he had defrauded, and was committed for trial upon bygone charges of felony. The son returned, and told the sad tale to his mother; and has, it is hoped, been taught a lesson of the necessity for temperance which he will profit by. The father will, it is to be feared, end his days an outcast from society.

The third little romance, perhaps the most affecting of all, is derived from the *Gazette de Tribunaux*. One day in October, a widow, who keeps a book-stall near the bridge of St Michael, was accosted by an old man, who seemed borne down with hunger and wretchedness. From under a worn and tattered coat he drew forth a thick volume, which was torn, and bore other marks of long use. He offered it for sale, owning that its intrinsic worth was little, 'though,' he continued, 'it is and always has been valuable to me, and I shall part with it most unwillingly; but I have not the courage to allow myself to die of hunger while I have even this treasured relic to sell. Give me for it anything you please.' The stall-keeper examined the book, and found it to be the first edition of the 'History of Astronomy amongst all Nations,' by Bailly, but in so bad a condition, that it was scarcely worth buying at all: but, out of compassion, the benevolent woman bought it for a franc. The old man immediately entered a baker's shop, brought out a loaf, and, sitting down beside the river, ate it greedily, and in solitude. It happened that a canon of Notre Dame, who is an indefatigable collector of old books, had witnessed the whole proceeding; and when the old man had left the stall, he took up the book. On examining the back of the title-page, he found the following lines traced with a firm hand with ink, which had now faded to the colour of rust:—'My young friend, I am condemned to die: at this hour to-morrow I shall be no more. I leave you friendless in the world—in a time of dreadful trouble; and that is one of my bitterest griefs. I had promised to be a father to you; God wills that my promise shall not be performed. Take this volume as the pledge of my earnest love, and keep it in memory of me.—Bailly.'* This, then, was a presentation copy sent fifty years ago from the unfortunate author, on the eve of his execution—to the distressed individual who had but now sold it to keep himself from starving. The canon, throwing down two francs to the good stall-keeper for her bargain, hastened to the old man, who still sat eating his cheerless crust. From him he learned that he was the natural son of a person of high rank, and had, after the death of his parents, been committed to Bailly's care, whose adopted child and

* John Sylvanus Bailly was born in 1736; and, besides being an astronomer, was a poet of considerable fame. On presenting the above work to the French Academy in 1784, he was admitted one of its members, and at the Revolution was made president of the first National Assembly. Afterwards he became mayor of Paris; but his humane conduct in suppressing tumults, and the honest sympathy he evinced towards the royal family, made him so unpopular, that he was obliged to resign his office. In 1793 he was denounced by the anarchists of the day, and guillotined.

pupil he became up to the day before his execution, when the above inscription was written, and the book sent. The worn old man has since laboured in the capacity of instructor of children; but having been attacked by illness, and compelled to resign his duties, he gradually sank to such a state of destitution, that he was driven to turn the last gift of his friend and benefactor into bread. The priest took the old man to his home, fed and comforted him, till he was enabled to procure him admission into an asylum specially instituted for receiving respectable persons fallen into decay—the hospital of Larochefoucauld. There he now remains, to end his days in peace.

Column for Young People.

THE LAKE AND ITS INHABITANTS.

A gentle shower had moderated the heat of a glowing summer day, and had cooled and refreshed the green face of nature, without throwing a damp on its beauties: it was near sunset when our evening walk brought us to the margin of a little lake. Some of our party had gone on before; and when I arrived, Elizabeth was seated on the trunk of an old fallen tree, busily occupied sketching the scene before us. It was a landscape worthy of Cuyp. The water of the lake was as still and transparent as the blue sky above. On its margin were scattered numerous birches, with their drooping branchlets and hoary trunks; the latter reflected like silvery pillars in the deep blue waters. Two cows were standing knee-deep near the rushy shore, and a little ragged herd-boy was leaning over a few paling-bars, eagerly watching the fate of his baited hook suspended from a rude fishing-rod. A gleam of the full red sky coming through the distant break between the surrounding hills, lighted up the whole with a glow and softness which mellowed every object into beauty. We paused over the scene for a full quarter of an hour, 'till fancy had her fill,' and then proceeded to find out what could occupy the judgment as well as the imagination. We had not proceeded far, till Henry called our attention to a beautiful wild drake gliding among the rushes, and which at intervals darted out its green neck, and with quick bill picked up some bodies from the surface of the water. Its quick eye discovered our nearer approach, and, darting under water, in a few minutes we saw him rise up far on the other side.

'I should like to know what Mr Wilddrake has been supping on,' said Henry; and we walked up to the place to make a minute examination. We saw some minnows in the water; but they were too deep to be taken in the manner we observed. We searched among the rushes, and could see nothing. At last Anna called our attention to some creatures floating on the surface of the water. We recognised them at once to be several species of shell snails—the *physa*, *planorbis*, and *lymnea*. These little animals were floating on the water, their shells reversed, and their soft bodies buoyed up by a little globule of air which they retained within the orifice of their breathing apparatus. On touching and alarming any one of them, it was seen instantly to throw off the air globule, and by this means being rendered heavier than the surrounding water, at once sunk to the bottom. We saw dozens of these animals thus floating about, and had no doubt but such had formed the prey of the wild drake.

'Look here,' cries Henry, 'at this large fresh-water mussel among the pebbles, with his shell widely expanded; he no doubt is enjoying the evening sunset too; but let him beware, else he may form a supper to some wild drake also.'

'Is not that the pearl mussel?' observed Elizabeth.

'It is,' I replied; 'and sometimes pearls of a very good size and lustre have been found here, and in several of the rivers of Scotland.'

'What is this?' cries Mary, with her bright eyes ever on the watch; 'I see a mass of little shells as if glued together, all of them apparently empty; and yet the whole is moving along briskly. Here is another, and another: they chase each other, and run about as if they had one common life.'

'I know these,' replied Henry; 'they are caddice-worms, the larvæ of the May-fly. The living animal is in the centre: observe his head peeping out; and those empty shells form his house. He glues around his body shells, pieces of wood, and small pebbles, and thus forms a defence against his enemies.'

'Oh, I see myriads of those empty shells on the beach,' cries Elizabeth—'shells of various kinds. I have picked up at least half-a-dozen different ones; and, let me remember, where was it that you showed us shells of this kind under a very different form?'

'I suppose you allude,' said I, 'to those marl beds which the workmen dug up in the field the other day? You now have an example from what sources it is that such beds of marl are derived. The whole bed of this lake is probably one mass of such shells, which have been accumulating for ages; and were it drained and dug into, it would present the same appearance as the marl beds which we lately inspected. There, you recollect, there were various layers on layers of a soft crumbling limestone, to the depth of eight and ten feet, intermixed with mud, fragments of reeds, wood, and shells of various animals; thus affording, on a small scale, an example of the way in which many of the deepest strata of the earth's surface have been accumulated.'

We now came to a little stream which poured its crystal current into the lake. Farther up the sloping hill-side, from whence it derived its source, it chafed and dashed over and among the rocky fragments opposing its course; but here, like other more noted rivers, it swelled out near its termination into a calm diffused estuary, with many a flower and aquatic plant peeping up amid its shallow waters. We rested here, at the request of Henry, to examine some objects which had arrested his attention. He pointed out to us, on the leaves of some of the aquatic plants, a number of brown, jelly-looking substances, about the size of a pin-head or small pea. On watching them attentively, we clearly perceived motion and life. These little points would in an instant suddenly expand to the size of half an inch, and thrust out little arms on all sides, by which they entangled and caught substances floating by. I at once recognised them to be the *Hydra*, or fresh-water polype; those singular animals which, when first discovered by Trembly, a naturalist of France, made so much noise in the scientific world. 'I am quite pleased that you have made this discovery for us, Henry. These are perhaps the simplest of all organised beings, and their habits and properties afford us a singular insight into the humblest manifestations of life. They are, as you see, composed of a pulpy, grayish jelly. They have few parts: only a body, with a hollow in the centre, corresponding to the stomach of other animals; a mouth leading to this stomach; and, surrounding this opening or mouth, eight filaments or arms, which they spread out all around, and with which they seize hold of their food, which consists of small worms, or pieces of any animal matter. They have no organs of sense, and no sensations but that of touch. They are very retentive of life, and may be cut into various pieces, and every separate piece will in a short time become a perfect polype. Their young are produced by a gem or bud which grows out from the body of the parent, and when it has arrived at a mature state, it drops off to enjoy a separate existence. Not unfrequently before this scion drops off from its parent, another bud is seen to spring out of its own body, and thus two or three generations are seen in progress at one time. They are very voracious and very lively, moving about from leaf to leaf by first pushing forward and attaching the mouth to any object; and then drawing forward the other end, attaching it in the same way, and again pushing forward the head. They will thus travel over a whole plant in the course of an hour or two. You may now take this magnifying lens, make your observations cautiously, and tell us what farther you can discover.'

'I see them distinctly and beautifully now,' whispers Henry. 'Three of them are within view, attached to the mid-rib of this leaf. They appear now somewhat like a clove, or a very little nail or tack standing on its point. How they ply their thin slender arms all around, now lengthening them out into a small hair or thread, and now again contracting them into a thick knob or point! These are in miniature somewhat like the horns of a snail, and as soft and pliant. I declare one has seized upon a small worm—he surrounds its end with the whole of his arms—the worm struggles and wriggles out of his grasp—it is instantly seized in the middle by another polype, doubled up, and a piece of it swallowed—the two ends of the worm dangle out on each side—the first polype seizes one of the ends—they now both tug and fight hard.'

There was here a considerable pause. We were all anxious to have a look, and each got the glass in turn. Henry after this resumed his observations and remarks. The worm had nearly disappeared between them. It was originally half an inch in length. They still struggle, and approach nearer and nearer to each other. The doubled-up portion of worm is pulled out of the mouth of the second polype: but it appears macerated—it breaks into two. A third polype now comes in for a fragment—another portion falls into the water—the worm at last disappears, and peace is restored with the satiated appetites of the combatants. We counted hundreds of these polypes. Could they all get worms? And what became of those which did not? We watched long for another worm feast; but saw none. No doubt many other more minute animals are found to feed these hungry creatures. They appear all lively; and assuredly they are all cared for by some means or other.

The sun had now fairly disappeared; light failed us for minute observations; but as we took our way homeward, the greater objects of nature were beautifully and softly depicted before us. The bright green birches now stood before us black masses—the surface of the lake alone sent up a lively gleam—the dusky bat flitted silently overhead, roused to his evening meal of the moths and night-flies that now peopled the air. The cows had strolled homewards, and their distant lowings reached our ears. 'How such a night as this,' says Elizabeth, 'raises our thoughts to the Author of nature! the whole earth, and air, and even waters, teem with life and with enjoyment.'

TASTE FOR SCIENCE.

A mind which has once imbibed a taste for scientific inquiry, and has learned the habit of applying its principles readily to the cases which occur, has within itself an inexhaustible source of pure and exciting contemplations: one would think that Shakspeare had such a mind in view, when he describes a contemplative man as finding

> Tongues in trees, books in the running brooks,
> Sermons in stones, and good in everything.

Accustomed to trace the operation of general causes, and the exemplification of general laws, in circumstances where the uninformed and uninquiring eye perceives neither novelty nor beauty, he walks in the midst of wonders; every object which falls in his way elucidates some principle, affords some instruction, and impresses him with a sense of harmony and order. Nor is it a mere passive pleasure which is thus communicated. A thousand subjects of inquiry are continually arising in his mind, which keeps his faculties in constant exercise, and his thoughts perpetually on the wing, so that lassitude is excluded from his life; and that craving after artificial excitement and dissipation of mind, which leads so many into frivolous, unworthy, and destructive pursuits, is altogether eradicated from his bosom. It is not one of the least advantages of these pursuits, which, however, they possess in common with every class of intellectual pleasures, that they are altogether independent of external circumstances, and are to be enjoyed in every situation in which a man can be placed in life. The highest degrees of worldly prosperity are so far from being incompatible with them, that they supply additional advantages for their pursuit, and that sort of fresh and renewed relish which arises partly from the sense of contrast, partly from experience of the peculiar pre-eminence which they possess over the pleasures of sense, in their capability of unlimited increase and continual repetition, without satiety and distaste. They may be enjoyed, too, in the intervals of the most active business; and the calm and dispassionate interest with which they fill the mind, renders them a most delightful retreat from the agitations and dissensions of the world, and from the conflict of passions, prejudices, and interests, in which the man of business finds himself continually involved.—*Sir John Herschel.*

THE SECRET OF GREAT WORKERS.

Great workers are always frequent and orderly, and being possessed of incessant activity, they never lose a moment. They apply their whole mind to what they are about, and, like the hand of a watch, they never stop, although their equal movements in the same day almost escape observation.

THOUGHT.

Though patrons shun my house and name,
  Who tells me I am poor?
Though fashion trumpets not my fame,
  And rank goes by my door;
Though ignorance my fortunes mar,
  My mind shall never sink,
For nature made me greater far—
  She bade me live and think.

The gold that drops from wealthy hands,
  Feeds those on whom it falls;
And oft, as hire for base commands,
  It feeds while it enthrals:
But thought is like the sun and air,
  Twin blessings with the shower;
It nurtures millions far and near,
  And millions sing its power.

The fool who stalks in titles clad,
  By chance or knavery bought,
Who rates a nod of his weak head
  As worth an age of thought;
Could he but see the brain in me,
  And taste its common drink,
The burthen of his prayer would be
  For liberty to think.

Oh! poor are they who spend their power
  In sensual joys and strife,
I'll *think* more rapture in an hour
  Than they *feel* through a life.
Sweet Thought's the she whom I adore,
  Entwined by many a link;
God! what can I of thee crave more?
  Do I not live and think?

—*Poems by Alexander Hume.* Second Edition: 1845.

PIGEON EXPRESSES.

The system of communication, by means of carrier-pigeons, between London and Paris, is carried on to a very considerable extent, and at a great cost. There are several perfect establishments kept up by parties interested in the quick transmission of intelligence at the ports of Dover and Calais, and at regular distances on the roads of the two countries, whence the birds are exchanged in regular order as they return with their little billet. The interruption occasioned by the hours of night is made up by a man on horseback; who again at daylight, on arriving at a pigeon station, transfers his despatch to the keeper, who has his bird in readiness. The distance by day is accomplished in less than eight hours. It has been found that hawks have proved themselves dangerous enemies even to these quick-flighted birds, and a premium of half-a-crown is paid for every hawk's head produced. The pay of a keeper is L.50 a-year; and when this is added to the cost of food and the expense of sending the pigeons on from station to station, to be ready for their flight home, it will appear that the service is attended with considerable outlay. The duty of training young birds, and the management of the old ones, in feeding them at proper times, and in keeping them in the dark till they are thrown up, is very responsible, and almost unceasing. A good bird is not supposed to last more than two years.—*Note-Book of a Naturalist.*

REASON.

Without reason, as on a tempestuous sea, we are the sport of every wind and wave, and know not, till the event hath determined it, how the next billow will dispose of us; whether it will dash us against a rock, or drive us into a quiet harbour.—*Lucas.*

THOUGHTS OF THE MOMENT.

A man would do well to carry a pencil in his pocket and write down the thoughts of the moment. Those that come unsought for are commonly the most valuable, and should be secured, because they seldom return.—*Bacon.*

Published by W. and R. Chambers, High Street, Edinburgh (also 98, Miller Street, Glasgow); and, with their permission by W. S. Orr, Amen Corner, London.—Printed by Bradbury and Evans, Whitefriars, London.

☞ Complete sets of the Journal, *First Series*, in twelve volumes, and also odd numbers to complete sets, may be had from the publishers or their agents.—A stamped edition of the Journal is now issued, price 2½d., to go free by post.

CONDUCTED BY WILLIAM AND ROBERT CHAMBERS, EDITORS OF 'CHAMBERS'S INFORMATION FOR THE PEOPLE,' 'CHAMBERS'S EDUCATIONAL COURSE,' &c.

No. 101. New Series. SATURDAY, DECEMBER 6, 1845. Price 1½d.

A BALL AT A LUNATIC ASYLUM.

About two miles south of Edinburgh is situated the picturesque little village of Morningside, under the shadow of Blackford hill, where

> 'Lord Marmion stayed;
> For fairer scene he ne'er surveyed.'

The known salubrity of this locality, which attracts many invalids to reside in it, induced the projectors of the asylum for lunatics, assisted by government, to erect it on the favoured spot. This institution consists of two edifices; one built some thirty years since, for the reception of invalids of the higher classes, and the other, a more extensive structure, for the reception of pauper patients. Within the asylum, these two establishments are denominated, from their situation, the East and the West departments. The system pursued in both is that of kindness and personal freedom, as far as is consistent with the safety of the inmate; the old method, which included strict discipline and restraint, being entirely abolished. Occupation and amusements take the place of listless and irksome personal bondage, and the results have been extremely beneficial. Among the most extraordinary, is that which allows of as many of the patients as may choose, to assemble every Thursday evening, and indulge in the exhilarating exercise of dancing. Favoured by an invitation, we attended one of these soirées; certainly the most interesting, instructive, but, moreover, saddening, we ever assisted at.

The night was somewhat dark, and as the gates of the asylum closed on us, and we drove along the thickly-hedged avenue which leads to the older mansion, a feeling of sadness and of dread could not be suppressed. The heavy pressure of ideas which are awakened by the sight of an abode of the insane, was not even lessened by the cheering lights which gleamed from the windows, or by the smiling faces which welcomed us on the threshold. Still, at every step, something occurred to dispel sombre thoughts. Habit and past experience induce us to associate with persons who have charge of the insane a certain degree of sternness, or, at the least, decision of manner and character. Indeed these *were* requisites for carrying out the old system of practice. But the first introduction to the officers of the Morningside establishment, by no means bore out this preconception. The suavity and placid politeness of the chief physician struck us at once as a guarantee of the mode in which the unhappy people under his care are treated. The immense responsibility which rests with him and his equally humane associates, appears to be worn with the lightness of a thorough confidence in the system, and in the orderly and proper behaviour of the inmates. Indeed, so far as we could observe and hear, the house had the appearance of a well-ordered gentleman's residence. Yet we afterwards learnt that much of it was managed by patients: for instance, the horse which brought, and the man who drove us, were handed over to the care and companionship of an insane groom.

As the soirées are held in the building devoted to the poor classes, we were conducted through the grounds to the more humbly appointed, but much larger structure. The careful unlocking and locking of the doors of each gallery, as we entered and left it, was the only indication of restraint which we met with. This is necessary, to keep the various classes of patients within those parts of the building which are assigned for their residence; 'though,' said our guide, 'we would do without locks if we could.' Ascending a flight of stairs, we saw, by the bustle apparent at the end of a long gallery, that we were approaching the scene of festivity, and presently the opening of folding-doors revealed the strange scene.

Around a large square apartment were ranged two rows of seats. On one side females sat; on the other males. The end seats were occupied by the inmates of the 'East Department,' the musicians occupying benches in the midst. The instruments were a violin, played by a demented dancing-master, and a violoncello, the performer on which was also a patient. After taking the places allotted to us, a survey of the scene imparted a feeling of awe; and now, for the first time, one could appreciate the sentiment which is felt in the East for idiots and madmen.* It was, indeed, an awful sight to look round upon the staring or vacant faces by which we were surrounded. In fact it cost some effort to suppress a rising fear; for, to be enclosed within four walls with from a hundred and fifty to two hundred lunatics, seemed a situation not altogether devoid of peril. Nor was a detailed investigation of the company calculated to lessen the feeling. Though sitting quite close to each other, we could see but few conversing together; each appeared too much occupied with his or her own cogitations, to bestow time or attention on a neighbour. This was explained to us as more or less characteristic of all kinds of derangement. The insane are less communicative than the sane. Monomaniacs, in particular, have, as might be expected, a tendency to dwell upon the one subject on which they have gone wrong, until moved by some external cause. This was exemplified at the ball; for whenever a dance was announced, abstraction ceased in all capable of partaking of the amusement, and they rose on the instant to choose partners. Some, alas! were incapable

* Mahomedans believe insanity to be rather an inspiration from above, than a misfortune; hence, persons afflicted with it are treated by the poorer classes with a respect almost amounting to reverence.

of being roused; and the most painful contrast to the festivities, was that presented by the few patients who suffered under dementia or melancholia: they either gazed on vacancy, heeding nothing, and apparently seeing nothing, or sat with their faces buried in their hands, the pictures of despair.

Shortly after we were seated, a programme was placed in our hands, which, as it was printed within the establishment, and by the inmates, may be regarded as a curiosity:—

'PROGRAMME OF THE CONCERT AND BALL.

'REEL. Song—"Yellow-haired laddie." Song. COUNTRY DANCE—"The Triumph." Song—"Life is like a summer flower." REEL. Comic Song—"Sandy M'Nab." Song—"M'Gregor's Gathering." COUNTRY DANCE—"Petronella." FINALE—"Auld Langsyne."'

Presently an attendant announced the reel; and where all had been hitherto quiet, all was now bustle. The men got up with alacrity, and crossing the floor to the women's side, selected their partners. It is remarkable that, although the same persons meet every Thursday throughout the year, few preferences are shown in the selection of partners. It is evidently a matter of indifference to himself with whom each individual dances. The choice is directed to whoever may be disengaged. Thus the rule of non-sympathy and non-communicativeness, which exists in all sorts of insanity, applies not only to those of the same sex, but to individuals of opposite sexes.

The order and precision with which the couples—perhaps to the amount of fifty—arranged themselves, could not have been exceeded in the most fashionable ball-room. In scrutinising their faces, while waiting to commence the dance, we could not detect much that differed from what is seen in ordinary assemblies. On some there sat an expression of pleasurable expectation; others, again, appeared as much abstracted as when seated; and it became a matter of speculation whether they would be roused out of their reverie, so as to begin when the signal for starting was given; but the 'band' struck up an inspiriting reel, and at the end of the first eight bars, the whole of the dancers put themselves in motion with the promptitude and regularity of a regiment of soldiers.

Spectators who, like ourselves, derive their knowledge of insanity from the old and scarcely exploded theories and systems of treatment, would have pronounced this exhibition as fraught with the most mischievous tendencies. Here were at least one hundred unfortunates, of both sexes, dancing with might and main, and undergoing all the unrestrained excitement which the most active of exercises is capable of creating. One would think that such an occupation, instead of having beneficial, would produce the worst effects; but experience has proved the reverse. Most of the dancers are monomaniacs, and to excite to frenzy an individual suffering under that malady, it is necessary to present to him the special object or idea on which he is mad; dancing, not being one of these, proves not only harmless, but, by diverting their thoughts and senses from the exciting cause of their malady, is a relief and a benefit. This in some measure accounts for the curious fact, that the same patients who are often noisy and obstreperous in their ordinary abodes in the asylum, behave with the utmost decorum at the soirées.

When the music ceased, the women retired to their seats alone; they were not, as is usual elsewhere, handed to them by their partners. The men also walked at once to the places they had before occupied. All was now silent. There was a sudden reaction, and the lull which followed appeared more fraught with danger than the previous excitement: the vulgar notion of violence associated with insanity, is not easily effaced from the spectator's thoughts, and at this sudden change—during the stillness which reigned throughout the apartment—one could scarcely help dreading that some of the maniacs would start up to do something eccentric or desperate. But no approach to an attempt of this kind took place. The excitement they had undergone showed no lasting effect upon them: the stimulant appeared to have acted, as it were, mechanically; for the moment it was withdrawn the patients returned to their ordinary condition. Still, it seems, the meetings are looked forward to with pleasure during the rest of the week. One unhappy inmate is so nearly in a state of dementia, that only two ideas exist within him—the ball on Thursdays, and the chapel on Sundays. Nor are the other patients so inattentive to the proceedings between the dances as they seem. Later in the evening, one of the attendants happened to announce a country dance by mistake. In a minute there was a rustling of programmes, and more than a dozen voices, both male and female, exclaimed, 'No, no; it's a reel—a reel!'

Partners were chosen for the country dance, and the 'Triumph' was struck up with vigour by the violinist. The 'figure' of this dance requires a little more attention than a reel, and the ex-dancing-master eyed the proceedings with critical attention. When a top couple failed to lead off at the proper moment, he gave them the hint, and when everything was going on swimmingly, he seemed to enjoy the pastime as much as if he were capering himself. Of the dancers, it may be said that they performed the figures with, if not so much grace, quite as much correctness, as is seen in more fashionable assemblies. This, in some cases, was evidently the result of habit, for these balls have been continued for more than three years. One or two of the parties, whilst they were not actually dancing, appeared totally unconscious of all that was going on around till the evolutions demanded their assistance, when, at the right moment, they began to dance as if some instinct, apart from the necessary attention, prompted them to do what was required. When a sign of hesitation was shown by one of the dancers, a neighbour, who, until that instant, may have appeared as if plunged in the depths of abstraction, gave him a monitory nudge, and, starting up from his dream, the lagger began to join correctly in the evolution. It is evident, therefore, that the abstractions of insanity are more apparent than real; for, in the above instances, the patients, though seemingly so rapt, were manifestly attending not only to their own affairs, but to those of their neighbours. At the prescribed time the music ceased, the dancers resumed their seats, and the almost painful silence recurred.

This was broken by a new subject of attention. One of the attendants prepared to sing the comic song of Sandy M'Nab. Many of the patients laughed at the broader parts of the ditty, many apparently listened without laughing, whilst others laughed without either listening or looking at the singer. When he had finished he was much applauded, as he deserved to be. The songs of a serious cast were very pleasingly sung by another of the attendants, who is gifted with a voice of unusual sweetness. Some expressions of praise were emitted, even in the midst of one of the airs; and from a female patient near us, who had hitherto appeared pleased and cheerful, several deep sighs escaped. Perhaps the melody brought back broken recollections of happier days. Indeed the most saddening thing of all was, the involuntary but unsatisfied inquiry which arose in the spectators' thoughts on hearing an indication of that kind, as to what was likely to be passing in that diseased and troubled mind.

The figure of 'Petronella' commences with a little waltzing, and in that, more than in any other department of the Terpsichorean art, the eccentricities of the patients were developed. One elderly person, in particular, displayed his agility by the most elaborate contortions and whirls; but what is remarkable, despite their complexity, he managed to bring them in to the time of the music. A tall and handsome young man, on the contrary, performed the figure with a condescending formality which formed a strong contrast to the proceedings of his elder companion. He, we understood, imagines himself to be an injured young nobleman. There are many striking examples of this sort of delusion amongst the inmates of the asylum. One declares herself to be Empress of the World, whilst another is content with the humbler supposition that she is Queen of England. With Petronella the ball closed, for Auld Langsyne was not sung.

In making—before leaving the room—a hasty retrospect of what we had seen, the first reflection which presented itself was, the extraordinary propriety and decorum of the whole proceedings. To say that the assembly was conducted as well as similar parties in ordinary life, would hardly be doing it justice; for, comparing this with other balls—especially those which are prolonged till after supper—we are justified in saying that we perceived fewer and less glaring inconsistencies committed by these unfortunate beings, than we have occasionally witnessed in the sane world. This must be attributed mainly to the system of general treatment to which they are subject. They are daily in a state of comparative freedom, consequently the personal liberty enjoyed amidst an assemblage at a soirée is no novelty to them, and they do not abuse it. Yet it is a surprising spectacle. Nearly two hundred human beings, in an unfortunate condition of diseased reason and hardly accountable will, congregated; many of them joining in the dance, without one—even of the most insane—committing one glaring eccentricity! It does not appear that the invited guests are very exclusively selected for their peaceable demeanour; for, on a subsequent visit to the institution, we met with the energetic waltzer in an apartment set aside for the noisy patients. He was on this occasion singing a bass song amidst some half-dozen scarcely less quiet companions.

When the soirée was concluded, most of the assembly moved towards the door quietly. It is true they 'stood not upon the order of going,' but went without regularity. At the door there was for a minute a little crowding. In such a situation elsewhere, an accidental push, or the merest jostle, is apt to rouse in the party inconvenienced a transient anger; but here nothing of the kind occurred. The patients walked to their several galleries and apartments of their own accord; each group guided by an attendant. The poor creatures labouring under dementia and melancholia were obliged to be roused ere they attempted to move: they had not altered their attitudes of wretchedness during the entire evening, and were partially lifted from the seat before they could fully understand what was required of them. Each was led out by an attendant. They were brought upon the festive scene with a hope that it might distract them from their malady. But in the two cases we saw, no such effect was produced.

In a few minutes the room was untenanted, and we left it with feelings far less sad than those with which we entered it; for we had seen how much can be done under judicious management, if not always to cure, to alleviate the sufferings of the insane.

THE BLIND MAN OF ARGENTEUIL.

A NORMAN TRADITION OF THE SIXTEENTH CENTURY.

At Rouen, in the antique-looking library of a vast and gloomy hotel, sat a venerable old man, seemingly engrossed in meditation and study. He was Laurence Bigot of Thibermeanil, king's counsel to the parliament of Normandy, a wise magistrate, and a learned and virtuous man. At five in the morning he was wont to commence his daily employment, and after giving sage and just advice to the parliament, the indefatigable old man would devote himself, as now, to other toils, which seemed to him like amusement, namely, laying the foundation of a rich collection of books and manuscripts, which afterwards became celebrated, and, though now dispersed, is not forgotten. Bigot was employed in examining an ancient manuscript which he had lately obtained. His son, Emerie Bigot, and a young companion, Etienne Pasquier, were reading Horace at another part of the library.

The studies of all three were interrupted by the sudden entrance of a magistrate—at least his costume bespoke him so; but at this moment his extreme paleness, changed features, and humiliated manner, made the lieutenant of Rouen appear like one of the criminals that daily trembled before him; for he was a severe and upright judge.

'I have been foiled, I confess it,' cried he to Laurence Bigot. 'I am guilty, but do not condemn me unheard.'

The king's advocate listened calmly, while the young men, with the curiosity of their age, paid eager attention to the lieutenant's recital, which was as follows:—

'A citizen of Lucca, named Zambelli, went on business to England, where he settled. His affairs prospered greatly. At fifty years old having made his fortune, he felt a desire to end his days at Lucca, near a brother whom he tenderly loved. He wrote to his family, who were delighted at the news. Soon another letter, dated Rouen, announced his arrival there from England, and that he should reach Lucca in about two months. This space of time was requisite for the transaction of his business at Paris, and his journey onward. He was daily expected at Lucca; but two, three, six months passed by, and he arrived not; nor, what was stranger still, did any other letter from him reach his family, whose anxiety was extreme. Cornelius, his brother, went to Paris in search of him. He visited all the houses whither Zambelli's commerce was likely to lead him. Many persons had seen, or believed they had seen Zambelli. An individual bearing that name had claimed the payment due to bonds of a considerable amount: the merchants showed the signature "Zambelli" at the bottom of the receipts. "All these signatures are forged," cried Cornelius. "Describe the person of the forger, so that I may bring him to justice." But it was in vain; for no one could recollect precisely the appearance of a man who had been seen so short a time.

'It was plain that an audacious robbery had been committed—perhaps a murder. Cornelius went from Paris to Rouen, where he visited successively all the hotels in the place. At one of them Zambelli had been seen. He had left it for Paris, accompanied by a valet. This valet had been little noticed: besides, six or eight months had passed since the departure of Zambelli; and how could one domestic excite attention among the numbers who had inhabited this hotel, the most frequented in Rouen?

'It was at this time,' continued the lieutenant of police, 'that Cornelius brought his complaint before me. Like him, I felt assured that a great crime had been committed between Rouen and Paris; but how could it be proved? How could the criminal be discovered? At last a sudden thought struck me. Six or seven months since, a goldsmith, named Martel, had opened a shop at Rouen, where he was entirely unknown. There was something strange in his manner, and the expression of his face: he said nothing of his parents or family; and those who hazarded questions on the subject, received from him evasive answers, given with ill-disguised embarrassment. Struck with his business being the same as Zambelli's, and acting under an involuntary presentiment, I sent a person, who, under pretence of making purchases, entered into conversation with Martel, in which, as if by chance, he introduced the name of Zambelli. At this name Martel grew pale, and showed signs of inquietude, looking anxiously at his questioner. This strengthened my suspicions: I resolved to satisfy myself; but here, I confess, the excess of my zeal led me into error.

'By my orders a sergeant went to Martel to demand payment of a bond for four hundred crowns, which I had fabricated under a false name. Martel, when he saw the bond, cried out that it was feigned, and refused to pay it. When taken to prison by the sergeant, Martel, following his first impulse, accompanied him with the security of a man who is certain he owes nothing; but soon, stopping suddenly in great agitation, he said, "I am quite easy as to the bond; it is entirely false, and I can prove it. But is there nothing else against me? Have you heard of anything?" The sergeant having feigned astonishment, and protested that he knew nothing, Martel became calm, and followed him with a firmer step to the jail, where his name was registered among the list of prisoners. An hour afterwards, he was brought before me. "It is now no time for pretence," said I in an imperative tone. "Yes, the bond is false; but as you have betrayed fear, I must tell you that there are other things against you. A citizen of Lucca, named Zambelli, is dead, and you are his murderer. Deny it not. I have proofs—certain proofs. But calm your fears: Zambelli was a stranger; no one here cares to avenge his death. With some sacrifices on your part, we can hush up this sad affair; only you must confess all with sincerity—your life is the price of it."

'Petrified by the assurance with which I spoke, and glad to purchase with gold the life which hung on a thread, Martel cried out, "I see—I see it is Heaven's doing, since that which no eye witnessed, save my own, is revealed. I will confess all: let my fortune save my life!" He was about to begin, when the appearance of the notary, whom I had sent for to take down his confession, roused him as out of a dream. He perceived the snare, and when I commanded him to begin, he said firmly, "No, I have nothing to tell; I am innocent."

'All my efforts to induce him to confess were vain. I sent him to prison. But now he protests against his incarceration, declares the falseness of the bond, and accuses publicly the sergeant and myself.

'This is my error. You, my lord, cannot doubt the purity of my motives; but what will the parliament say?—always so severe towards inferior officers. Must the services of thirty years be blotted out, because I was carried away by excess of zeal? My lord advocate, you know all; now judge me as you will.'

'Be encouraged!' said Laurence Bigot. 'The parliament is acquainted with all, and pardons you. The Chamber assembled to-day to judge this matter. I have spoken for you with the warmth of a man who esteems and respects you; but your thirty years of service and integrity have pleaded more eloquently than I could do. The proceedings which Martel dared to commence against you have been stayed for three months: the suit relative to the murder of Zambelli is brought before parliament, and Martel is transferred to the conciergerie. Every search shall be made to discover the body of the murdered man; for though I firmly believe that you have discovered the assassin, yet there are no proofs. For you, lieutenant, though pardoned, you are not guiltless. Listen!' said the old man, turning to his son and to Etienne Pasquier, 'you are both destined to wear the toga of justice—you, Emerie, perhaps to succeed me; and you, Etienne Pasquier, probably to distinguish yourself in the judgment-seat at Paris, or some foreign court. Remember that none may do evil that good may come! Above all, a judge should not seek to discover the truth by means of a lie, and do himself what he punishes in others. Such means are unworthy of a magistrate.'

Three weeks from that time there was great excitement in the village of Argenteuil. The inhabitants had suspended their labours, quitted their houses, and gathered together about the door of the Hôtel du Heaume. By their earnest conversation among themselves, and their eager questioning of those who came out of the hotel, it was clear that something unwonted was going forward there. In short, the large room of the hotel was for this day transformed into a justice-chamber, where Laurence Bigot, assisted by the magistrate of Argenteuil, questioned numerous witnesses about the murder of Zambelli.

How many efforts had this zealous judge made since he quitted Rouen on his search for the traces of the crime! He visited many villages, questioned numerous officers of police; but all in vain. When he was about to return, in despair of accomplishing his object, he was informed that, some months before, a corpse had been discovered hid in a vineyard near Argenteuil. Bigot hastened thither, and the state of preservation of the remains enabled him, on viewing the body, to decide clearly that it was that of Zambelli, according as he had been described by Cornelius his brother.

The magistrate began to read the evidence aloud, when he was interrupted by a piercing cry; and a blind man, whom no one had as yet perceived, presented himself before the assembly. It was old Gervais, a wandering beggar, born in the neighbourhood, well known, and much liked. When his way led through Argenteuil, he was always admitted to the hotel, and having arrived that day, he had seated himself, unnoticed, in his usual place in the chimney corner. He had sprung forward with a loud cry when, in listening as the magistrate read, he heard of a corpse being discovered among the vines. But what could a blind man, and one so long absent from Argenteuil, have to communicate? Laurence Bigot regarded with a kind of respect the serene and venerable countenance of the old beggar.

'Unfortunate man,' said he, 'what can *you* have to tell us?'

But after his first involuntary movement, the blind man appeared embarrassed and undecided. 'Ah, my lord,' said he, 'may I speak without danger of my life?' and he turned his white head on every side with a terrified air.

'Speak freely,' said Bigot; 'fear nothing.' Then the old man related how, many months since, he was leaving Argenteuil on his usual pilgrimage, and had gained the high ground beyond the village, when the violent barking of his dog caused him to listen attentively. A man's voice, feeble and suppliant, was distinctly heard. 'Monster!' it said; 'thy master, thy benefactor—mercy! Must I die so far from my country and my brother! Mercy, mercy!'

Then the blind man heard a fearful cry, like that of a dying man in his last agony, and all was silence. After a time he distinguished the steps of one who seemed staggering under a heavy burden. 'Influenced by a sudden impulse,' said Gervais, 'I went forward, asking what was the matter, and who had been moaning so?'

'"Nothing, nothing," said a voice in an agitated tone; "only a sick man who is being carried home, and has fainted on the way." And the voice added, in a lower and menacing tone, "You may thank God that you are blind, or I would have done the same to you." I knew then that a horrible crime had been committed, and was seized with terror. All things conspired to overwhelm me with fear; for immediately a dreadful storm arose, and the loud thunder seemed to pursue the murderer. I thought the world was at an end. Trembling, I continued my journey, resolving never to reveal what I had heard; for the criminal may belong to these parts, and the life of a poor old blind man is at the mercy of every one. But when the judge spoke of a corpse being found so near to the place where I heard the voice, I could not avoid a sudden exclamation. I have now told all; God grant that no evil comes to me from it!'

During this relation Laurence Bigot appeared absorbed in a deep reverie, which lasted long after the blind man ceased to speak. Then addressing Gervais, 'Old man,' said he, 'I wish to ask you a question; reflect well before answering it. Do you remember exactly the voice that you heard that day on the hill, which replied to your questions and threatened you? Do you think that you could recognise it again—recognise it so as not to confound it with any other?'

'Yes, my lord advocate,' cried Gervais immediately: 'yes! even as I should recognise the voice of my mother, if she were living still, poor woman!'

'But,' said the judge, 'have you considered that eight or nine months have passed since then?'

'It seems but a few hours ago,' answered the blind man. 'My terror was so great, that even now I seem always to hear the voice that cried for mercy, and that which spoke to me, and the awful thunder.' And when Bigot still doubted, Gervais, lifting his hands to heaven, said, 'God is good, and forsakes not the poor blind. Since I lost my sight, I can hear wonderfully. Call the people of Argenteuil; they will tell you how they amuse themselves with embarrassing me, and saying, in counterfeited tones, "Who speaks to thee?" Ask them if they have ever succeeded in deceiving me!' The people cried out that all that the blind man said was true; his knowledge of voices was wonderful. Some hours after, Laurence Bigot departed for Rouen, and everything went on as usual in the village of Argenteuil. Bigot conveyed Gervais with him to Rouen.

In the sixteenth century, the great hall of audience of the Norman parliament was renowned for its beauty. The ceiling was of ebony, studded with graceful arabesques in gold, azure, and vermilion The tapestry worked in fleurs-de-lis, the immense fireplace, the gilded wainscot, the violet-coloured *dais*, and, above all, the immense picture in which were represented Louis XII., the father of his people, and his virtuous minister and friend, the good Cardinal d'Amboise—all united to give the great hall an aspect at once beautiful and imposing. The effect was increased when, on days of judicial solemnity, a hundred and twenty magistrates were seated in judgment there, with their long white beards and scarlet robes, having at their head the presidents, attired in ermine mantles, above whom was a painting depicting the legislator Moses and the four evangelists.

It was in this magnificent hall that the parliament assembled, by a special convocation, on Christmas eve, in the year 16—. But this time they were attired in black robes, and their serious countenances showed they had a rigorous office to perform. This secret meeting of parliament excited great curiosity throughout the whole town. The murder of the merchant of Lucca, the arrest of the presumed criminal, the discovery of the body of his supposed victim, the unhoped-for testimony given by a blind man at Argenteuil, furnished an inexhaustible subject of discussion for the crowd that thronged the avenues of the palace. Every one agreed that the day was come which would liberate an innocent man, or dismiss a murderer to the scaffold.

The parliament, after many long debates, had decided that the blind man of Argenteuil should be heard. Gervais appeared before them. His frank and circumstantial deposition made a deep impression; but some doubt still remained. It was a fearful thing to place a man's life at the mercy of the fugitive reminiscences of a blind man, who could only trust to his hearing. It seemed almost impossible that Gervais should recognise faithfully a voice which he had heard but once only. The parliament determined to prove him, and to bring before him successively all the prisoners of the conciergerie, Martel among the rest. If, after having heard them speak, the blind man spontaneously, and without once hesitating, should recognise the voice which had struck him so powerfully, this evidence, united to others, should be held conclusive. It was not without design that Christmas eve was chosen for this strange trial, unheard of in the annals of justice. To have brought up the prisoners together on an ordinary day, would have awakened their suspicions, perhaps suggested to them various stratagems, and thus left the success of this novel experiment to chance. On Christmas eve the order excited no surprise, as it was customary on the eve of high festivals to bring all the prisoners of the conciergerie before the parliament, who sometimes, out of respect to the day, liberated those criminals who had been imprisoned for trifling offences.

Above all, as it was necessary to make the blind man understand the almost sacred importance of the judgment with which Heaven had invested him, a solemn oath was administered by the president of the assembly. The old man took the oath in a truthful, earnest manner, which left no doubt of his sincerity, and the trial commenced. Eighteen prisoners were brought up, and answered the questions proposed to them, but the old man never moved; and they, on their part, on perceiving the unknown man, evinced no sign of alarm. At last the nineteenth prisoner was introduced. Who shall paint his horror and stupefaction at the sight of Gervais! His features grew contracted, his hair rose up, and a sudden faintness overpowered him, so that the turnkeys were obliged to lead him to a seat. When he recovered a little, his involuntary and convulsive movements seemed to show the poignant remorse of a guilty and tortured soul, or perhaps the horrible regret of not having committed a second crime, and finished his work.

The presidents and judges anxiously awaited the result. At the first words that Martel uttered, in reply to the president's questions, the blind man, who, ignorant of his presence, had hitherto remained quiet and immoveable, suddenly bent forward, listening intently; then shrinking back with horror and fear, cried out, 'It is he!—it is the voice that I heard on the heights of Argenteuil!'

The jailer led away Martel more dead than alive, obeying in this the president's order, who in a loud tone had desired him to bring out another prisoner. But this command was accompanied by a sign which the jailer understood, and some minutes after, he again introduced Martel, who was interrogated under a false name. Fresh questions elicited fresh replies; but the blind man, shaking his head with an air of incredulity, immediately cried out, 'No, no; it is all a feint; that is the voice which conversed with me on the heights of Argenteuil.'

At last the horrible mystery was cleared up. The wretched criminal, trembling, despairing, stammered out a confession, which was now almost needless, since the magistrates were fully convinced of the truth which had been wonderfully elicited by the sole witness who could declare the crime.

But a few hours passed, and Martel lay in a gloomy dungeon of the conciergerie, whilst in a public place, not far from the prison, were made the preparations for execution; for at this period the scaffold followed the sentence so rapidly, that a condemned man never beheld the morrow's sun. Ere nightfall all was over. The wretched man died penitent, confessing his crime, and denouncing the cupidity and thirst of gold which had led him on to murder.

In fifty years from this period, Laurence Bigot had been long dead. Emerie his son had succeeded him in his office. Etienne Pasquier had become a learned and reverend old man, with silver hair. He was then composing his curious and interesting '*Recherches sur la France*,' and there related the almost miraculous discovery of a murder long since committed—of which discovery he had in his youth been an eye-witness. It is from his statement that this history is taken.

TRAVELS IN LURISTÁN AND ARABISTÁN.*

LURISTÁN, or the country of the Lurs, embraces the greater portion of the mountainous district of Persia, situated between the Turkish frontier on the west, and Ispahan and Fars on the south and east. Arabistán, or, as it is sometimes called, Khuzistán, is the low-lying country to the south of this mountainous chain. These extensive districts, which are now in many parts little better than a wilderness, are the ancient Elam mentioned in Scripture, and the Elymais of the Greeks. They are covered with the remnants of their former greatness, and the traveller, as he journeys over their desolate plains, comes ever and anon upon the vestiges of cities that were once powerful, now crumbling into the dust. Ahvaz, at one time the capital of the Parthian kings, is nothing more than a confused heap of ruins. Susa, once the rival of Babylon itself in power and splendour, 'hides,' says the Baron de Bode, 'its ancient ruins under thick grass and waving reeds.' The plough is levelling with the soil the only remaining mounds which mark the place of the ancient city of Jondi-Shapur; and the relics of other towns are scattered over the waste, without having left any record behind to bequeath even their names to posterity, or tell the nations to which they belonged, or the time at which they flourished. To this interesting region the attention of the Baron de Bode was accidentally directed in the year 1840, and the following particulars of his journey are selected from the two volumes which he has just published.

At the close of the year above mentioned, the baron set out from Teheran, with the intention of proceeding to the far-famed ruins of Persepolis, which he had long desired to see. On his arrival at Ispahan, circumstances occurred which induced him to extend his journey still further. The governor of that city, with whom he had some previous acquaintance, was, on his arrival, engaged in preparations for a military tour into Luristán and Arabistán, and proposed to the baron, 'being acquainted with his roving propensities,' that he should accompany him. Our author, who had often entertained a wish to penetrate into this country—so little known, and yet so full of interest for its associations with the early history of the world—agreed without difficulty to the proposal. The savage and unruly nature of the tribes which peopled the mountainous portion of the district, had been the means of preventing the access not only of European travellers, but of the native Persians themselves; and it was rare indeed that there was so favourable an opportunity for exploring it as that afforded by the incursion of the governor, with an armed force and all appliances. The baron therefore determined to proceed to Persepolis, and to join the governor afterwards at Shushtier, travelling alone through the country of the Bahktiyari, so celebrated for its memorials of the expedition of Alexander the Great and his successors, and for its many interesting remnants of antiquity.

At noon, on the 1st of January 1841, he left Ispahan with his attendants, riding post, and directed his course to the south, by the road leading to Shiraz; but as his route has been sufficiently described by many previous travellers, it will not be necessary to dwell upon the incidents narrated by the baron, or upon his descriptions of the scenery. For the same reason it will be needless to accompany him to Persepolis. The ground has been often described, and the ruins of that city have been the theme of many a traveller, English, French, and German, whose works are so well known as to have familiarised Europe with every conspicuous object of art and antiquity in that remarkable region.

On the 20th of January, the baron arrived at Kazerùn—the commencement of the country of Arabistán—and from this point his adventures and descriptions have more novelty. His route lay over a wild district, inhabited by the Mamaseni, Khogilù, and Bahktiyar mountain tribes. At Kazerùn he procured guides, who undertook to deliver him safe and sound into the hands of Jehangir Khan, the chief of the Mamaseni. He adopted this plan, of causing himself to be passed like a bale of goods from hand to hand, during the whole of his journey through this rude tract of country, and had every reason to be satisfied with the effect of the precaution, which made the last person who had given a certificate of his being alive responsible for his safety. The residence of the chief to whom he was first consigned, consisted of a square tower constructed of clay, whitewashed externally, furnished with loopholes, and surrounded by the huts of the Mamaseni, made of reeds, and by black tents covered with mats. On entering this country, he cautioned his servants to keep a sharp look-out after the baggage, as the natives were known to be notorious thieves. Our traveller was fortunate enough, during his whole sojourn among them, not to lose a single article; but he learned afterwards, from a friend who visited the encampment a few months later, that the Mamaseni contrived to steal from under his pillow, when he was asleep, his sword, which they drew cautiously out of its scabbard, leaving the latter behind. Suspecting Jehangir Khan himself of the theft, yet admiring the clever way in which it had been committed, the European next morning handed over the scabbard to his host, observing that his newly-acquired sword probably required one. The khan took it and thanked him; and no more was said of the matter.

Between this station and Fahliyan, the next, the road lay through the plain of Behram, and by the ruins of the town of Nobendjan, to the valley of Shàb-bevan. While descending into this valley, the traveller's sense of smell was agreeably affected by the perfume of the narcissus, which was spread like a white carpet over the plain for the space of many miles. All the party pushed into this rich parterre up to their horses' girths, to enjoy the fragrance as much as possible. The valley is celebrated by the Persian and Arabian poets as one of the four terrestrial paradises, and is interspersed with cultivated fields, producing cotton, rice, barley, and wheat. The narcissus, however, seems indigenous, and wherever the soil is left fallow, it springs up in rich profusion. Fahliyan is a small town, or rather village, in this valley, consisting of sixty or seventy houses at the utmost; but is enclosed by very extensive walls, now in ruins, which show that formerly it was a place of more importance. It is surrounded by fine palm trees, and has a fort, in ruins, on the summit of a small hill. As a lofty and precipitous mountain rises close behind it, the inhabitants receive only the rays of the morning sun, and are the rest of the day in shade. The baron did not make any stay in this town, but proceeding along the banks of the river Abshur, arrived at another valley, that of Ser-Abi-Siyal, or Black-Water-Head, lying between two parallel chains of hills. Here he was met by, and handed over to the protection of, Khan Ali Khan, the chief of the Rustemi, with whom he alighted to partake of luncheon. This chief handed him over to another, named Allah Kherim Khan, chief of the Bovi, a tribe of the Khogilù, whose head-quarters were at a town or fort called Basht. This place very much resembled the castles of the old feudal barons in Europe. It consisted of the chief's fort, enclosed by high walls, and flanked with turrets. Around this were grouped the habitations of his vassals, who lived under the shadow of his protection, aided him in his predatory incursions (for, like the other chiefs, he was a robber on a large scale), and furnished him with the means of defence or offence, whenever either might be necessary.

---

* Travels in Luristán and Arabistán, by the Baron C. A. de Bode. 2 vols. London: Madden and Co. 1845.

He found this personage very hospitable and communicative, and was entertained by him with a long account of the implacable feuds by which the mountaineers were divided, and of the intestine wars to which they gave rise. On quitting Basht, where he only stayed one night, he met a migratory horde of Iliyats, another of the numerous tribes who had broken up their encampment in one place, and were travelling with their flocks and herds to other pastures. The sheep and goats went first, led by young shepherds, the flower and strength of the tribe, with their faithful companions, the shaggy dogs, of a breed said to be peculiar to Persia. Next followed the asses, and oxen of a small species, laden with the black canvas and poles of the Iliyat tents, with bags thrown over their backs, filled with various articles for consumption; while some were bestrode by the weaker and more aged portion of the community. The poultry were likewise placed on the backs of the loaded cattle, with a leg or a wing tied to the pack-saddle, spending their time in trying to keep their balance in this awkward position as well as they could. Men, women, and children, followed the caravan on foot, some in groups, and some walking separately, each bearing some kitchen utensil or piece of household furniture. The young lambs and kids that were brought forth on the way were placed in baskets, and carried by some of the men, or stowed away in hampers, with their heads peeping out, and thrown, along with the poultry, across the pack-saddles. Such of the sheep or goats as were lame, or with young, had their separate conductors, who gently encouraged them forward, or stopped and fed them when they appeared fatigued—a trait of the Iliyat life and character which reminded the baron of the passage in Isaiah xl. 11, 'He shall feed his flock like a shepherd: he shall gather the lambs with his arm, and carry them in his bosom, and shall gently lead those that are with young.' The women had their spinning utensils on their shoulders. Some were twisting woollen yarn; others were bent forward in a stooping position, with their children astride on their backs, or toiling with their infants (cradles and all) upon their heads or shoulders.

After passing this group, the Baron de Bode continued his course for twenty-seven miles to the next station of Daghúmbezún. Throughout the whole tract there were no habitations, and at that season of the year (January) no water; though it appears that formerly this was not the case. Along the side of the road he observed the remains of *kanats*, or underground channels; and about seven miles from Daghúmbezún were the ruins of a caravanserai, and, a little further on, of a village. At this place he passed the night in an old dilapidated caravanserai; his servants barricading it as well as they could, to keep out the predatory mountaineers, who might have paid them an unwelcome visit for the sake of plunder. He escaped, however, from all molestation, the mountaineers having apparently become, if not less addicted to plunder, more cautious as to the manner in which they carried on their depredations since the imprisonment of their great chief, one Veli Khan. This person had once great authority over the tribe of the Mamasseni—amounting in all to about 4000 families. He was originally valet to the viceroy of the district of Fars, and organised a band of robbers, at whose head he placed himself, for the purpose of robbing the caravans. 'Each successful attack,' says the Baron de Bode, 'by spreading abroad his reputation, increased the number of his adherents; and the feeble authorities of Fars, unable to restrain his predatory inclinations, endeavoured to give another direction to his pursuits, by ministering food to his vanity. A union was concerted between his daughter and one of the sons of the viceroy, Prince Timur Mirza (afterwards well known in the fashionable circles of London). This match did not effect the object intended. Veli Khan remained as unruly as before; erected a fort called Núrabád, and continued to exercise his trade of plundering with greater impunity than ever, especially during the period of misrule and disorder which in the southern provinces of Persia followed the death of the old king. A new governor or viceroy being appointed to the district of Fars, Veli Khan, on the faith of promises held out to him, was induced to go to Shiraz, and aid the governor in the collection of taxes, as tribute from the tribe. Whilst out on an expedition of this kind, the governor, whose name was Muhamed Taghi Khan, when heated one day with wine, made some irreverent observations with respect to the great freebooter's daughter, which so offended her brother (Saghir Khan), who appears to have been next in authority to Veli Khan himself, that he rose suddenly and called upon his followers to avenge the honour of their clan. His call was obeyed: the greater part of the governor's force was put to the sword, and he himself hurried, handcuffed, to Khisht, amid the mountains. On the arrival of this news at Fars, a great force was sent against Veli Khan and his son, who both fled—one to a small village on the Persian Gulf, and the other to the fortresses of Gúl-i-Ghúlat, built one above the other on a steep rock, with a communication between. Veli Khan, who was fond of the bottle, was making free with some Shiraz wine, the property of an English officer in the shah's service. In the hurry of his escape, and in the state of intoxication he was then in, he made too great an effort to vault into the saddle, and fell over to the other side, when he was immediately picked up and secured by his pursuers.* These two robbers, father and son, have ever since been imprisoned in the citadel of Tabriz; 'but their popularity in Fars,' says the baron, 'is so great, that their names, deeds, and exploits are perpetuated in songs, and pass from mouth to mouth among the Iliyats.'

These tribes outwardly profess Mahomedanism; but, like the generality of the nomade people of this region, they have a very faint idea of religion, their whole faith consisting in some superstitious rites, and a traditional veneration for their piri, or holy men, to whose shrines they make pilgrimages. Among the offerings which they bring with them on these occasions, are little tin lamps, which they string on ropes over the tombs; or coloured rags, which the women attach to their consecrated trees. The Baron de Bode saw trees of this description, with more rags upon them than leaves. Their chief occupation, when not plundering, consists in tending their flocks of sheep and goats. Their most common food is the acorn, which is first bruised between two stones, and made into flour by being dried in the sun. The women bake cakes of this flour. The paste is likewise eaten raw, and is considered very nourishing.

The principal town of this district is Behbehan, the inhabitants of which are very expert in the preparation and dyeing of woollen cloth. The soil around it is very productive, being watered by several noble streams, such as the Shemai-arab, the Kheirabad, and the Kurdistán, together with the lesser rivers flowing from the Ardehan mountains. It would become a rich agricultural district if more densely peopled, and, above all, if there were more security and stability in the administration. On the spacious plain surrounding the town, the inhabitants grow corn. Among the fruit trees, the palm takes the precedence; and orange, lemon,

* The reader will see, in the incident connected with the saddle, a newly-discovered beauty in Shakspeare, and a happy piece of justice recently done him by one of his commentators. The passage in which the bard speaks

'Of vaulting ambition that o'erleaps itself,
And falls on the other,'

has again and again been alluded to, and quoted with admiration; until the commentator showed that it was without meaning, and should be read 'vaulting ambition that o'erleaps its *sell*, and falls on the other *side*.' Sell is the old word for *saddle*, derived from the French *selle*. Read with this amendment, the passage, instead of being obscure, becomes instinct with life and meaning, and affords a beautiful simile, complete in all its parts.

and pomegranates are cultivated with success. The whole plain, as well as the valleys in the mountains, present traces of considerable towns. Half way towards the Khurdistán river are ruins, scattered over a large extent of ground, consisting of kiln-burnt bricks, white mortar, and elevated mounds of earth. Sir John Macdonald Kinneir found among them a stone slab with an arrow-headed inscription—a sure sign of remote antiquity. Nearer the water, on both sides of the river, are buildings in a better state of preservation, which appear to be of a more recent date, though still of Sasanian origin, and probably coeval with the stupendous remains of two bridges of which the Arab writers speak in terms of high praise. On the left bank, but further inland, are some Mahomedan tombs, with arched domes over them, and open on every side. This place is considered the true site of the ancient city of Arreján. Besides the tombs, the ruins consist of stone and brick buildings, scattered over the lofty banks of the river, mostly on the left shore. With the exception of the bridges, there are no remains of large edifices. The houses seem to have possessed but one storey, with vaulted roofs. The river intersecting the town was spanned by two bridges, a short distance from each other; they were of stone and brick, and, to judge from what remains, must have been constructed on a grand scale. Some of the platforms of the piers on which the arches rested are still visible on the right and left banks; but nearly all the rest have been carried away by the force of the current, which is excessively rapid. They are now known by the names of the *Puli Begum* and the *Puli Dokhter*—the bridges of the Lady and of the Damsel.

During the few days that the baron remained in this neighbourhood, he was made acquainted with the existence of some curious sculptures and inscriptions about twenty-six miles to the north-west of Behbehan, among the Behmeï mountains. As no European traveller had ever, to his knowledge, advanced so far in that direction, nor even alluded to these sculptures, he became the more anxious to see them. Having been furnished with a guide, and an attendant train mounted on fine Arab mares, he proceeded thither, across a fertile plain, remarking the same luxuriant fields of the narcissus, which has been already noticed, scenting the air for miles around. The first place of any note he reached was Táshún, where, according to the native tradition, the patriarch Abraham was thrown into a burning furnace by Nimrod, 'the mighty hunter before the Lord.' In the same neighbourhood, within a few miles, is a village called Ur, which, according to the Scripture, was the name of the birthplace of Abraham, in Chaldea. On his arrival at the valley of Tengi-Saulek, where the remains were, the baron halted for a time, and sent out scouts to examine whether the coast was clear, and also placed videttes, to give warning in case of a surprise. Having ascertained that all was right, he entered the narrow defile, hemmed in between lofty rocks, which overhung the path. As he and his party toiled on by a very steep ascent, among loose stones, they came at times upon an old pavement, the polished stones of which were so slippery, that the horses could with difficulty advance. The path soon widened, and they found themselves in a grove of oak, cypress, and kúhnar trees, surrounded on every side by the ancient monuments, to see which was the object of their visit. The most conspicuous of these was a huge black rock, streaked with yellow veins, between thirty and forty feet in height, and eighty or ninety in circumference, and which stood detached from the rest. It had bas-reliefs and inscriptions on two of its sides. The first represented an altar, surmounted by a conical pile somewhat in the shape of a sugar loaf, round which a fillet was tied in a knot, with the two ends streaming downwards. Close to this altar stood the *mobed*, or high priest, his right arm extended towards the altar, and his left concealed in his bosom. On the right of this principal figure was a group of nine others, which, with the exception of one nearest the priest, seated on a low stool, were in an erect posture, but so dilapidated, that none of their faces could be distinguished. On the extreme right was a figure on horseback, with a bow and arrow, in the act of attacking a wild beast, which was standing on its hind legs, but which, being much defaced, could not be distinguished sufficiently to determine whether it were a lion, a bear, or a wild boar. Close to this was an inscription of five lines, in a character totally unknown to the baron; and under the altar was another inscription in the same character, and also of five lines. On the second face of the rock were the sculptures of four persons in a row, the principal of the group reclining on a couch, with the left arm on a cushion, and holding a circlet in the right hand. The head was ornamented with two clusters of thick hair; but no feature of the face was distinguishable. Two figures were seated at the foot of the couch, each with an arrow-headed spear in the right hand. One of them had a sort of diadem on the head, consisting of six spreading rays, with little globules at the extremity of each ray. There were various other stones, which the baron has minutely described. He does not give any decided opinion on their probable antiquity, but merely observes that their style is totally different from all that he had seen at Persepolis and elsewhere. As he was now in the ancient Elymaïs of the Greeks, he could not divest himself of the impression that he was standing on the ground once sacred to the goddess Anaïtis or Myletta, where the Elamites of old had performed their religious rites and mysteries. On their way out of the valley, they found more of these old sculptures on a stone close to the road, but owing to long exposure to the air and rain, the figures were nearly all effaced.—(*To be concluded in a second article.*)

THE PERSECUTIONS OF HOSPITALITY.

'The knife of the surgeon,' says Boswell in his Life of Johnson, 'hurts as much as the sword of an enemy;' and, upon the same principle, the mistaken attentions sometimes showered upon guests by too-hospitable hosts and hostesses, are as inconvenient as intentional hostilities.

An antiquated politeness still lingers amongst many of the more venerable part of the community, which urges them to persecute their guests to eat or drink what they do not choose, or more of what they do choose than is agreeable. Happily the present generation is gradually adopting a new code of etiquette, which rules that true politeness consists in allowing people to act as is most agreeable to themselves. But the daily experience of this common-sense practice only makes the occasional suffering from its opposite the more intense. What is chiefly felt under the pressing system is the impossibility of escaping from, or remonstrating against it; for who could say or do anything in direct rebuke of what so evidently springs, in most instances, from amiable feelings? There is a tradition in Edinburgh of a lady, the wife of a distinguished naval victor of the last war, and a genuine specimen of the old school, who pressed a gentleman one day to such a degree, and thus encroached so far upon his politeness and good nature, that he finally tumbled off his chair in a fit, the consequence of overeating. Things are not generally carried to such an extravagance as this; but they often are bad enough in the case of old-fashioned kindly people, and especially such as have any fears about their style of manners and entertainment. Giving abundantly and urging its acceptance seems to these persons a sufficient offset against all defects, when, in reality, it is only adding another to those traits of inferior breeding which they are concerned about.

Want of consideration respecting variety of tastes is

another great source of this evil. There are some persons so full of a heady egotism, though often of a good-natured kind, that they never imagine but that their own feelings and tastes are a just criterion for those of their fellow-creatures. The things which they prefer they cannot doubt to be those which all other persons most affect. Where they go, and what they do, they think all other people would like to go and to do. This peculiarity is most strongly exhibited in the robustuous hospitality of the English country squire. A gentleman who passes his days in a great city is invited to some country house, the owner of which has most of his thoughts absorbed in agricultural improvements. Anxious to do everything possible to amuse his guest, and fancying that rural enthusiasm is common to all men, the host drags his unfortunate visitor into every part of his grounds—up hill and down dale, over fields savouring strongly of guano, and through preserves thickly bristling with brambles and furze. At the same time he volunteers explanations which are unheeded, either because they do not interest, or are quite incomprehensible to the hearer. Although the sufferer heartily wishes himself back in town beside his own fire, yet the enthusiastic amateur of tillage mistakes his commonplace replies and occasional questions—made out of politeness—for manifestations of interest. He presses him, till refusal is impossible, 'to try his hunter,' and sets the poor Cockney off after the hounds like a second Mazeppa; peradventure to be torn to pieces by bushes; certainly to be put in imminent jeopardy. After dinner he insists upon t'other tumbler, although the town-bred man has no stomach for grog, or no head to carry it; and the inflexible country squire—whose general character shows that his heart overflows with human kindness, and that he would not hurt a fly, or see a tenant want a meal if he could help it—imagines that the rites of hospitality have not been duly performed till he has persecuted his friend into a condition from which recovery cannot be expected for a week. This was true of the great majority of country squires who entertained our fathers: now, however, the picture is only a likeness of such of the English squirearchy as are grandfathers. Still a few of these killing-with-kindness hosts are in existence, in spite of the change which good sense has worked in the social mass.

As, however, the dispensation of hospitality chiefly devolves upon the mistress of the house, it is the ladies of the old school whose excess of benevolent intentions leads them most frequently into the error of persecuting whilst attempting to please their guests. I think I see the late much respected Mrs Peppercorn at the head of her table, her own person partly hidden by a huge cod's head and shoulders. The board, like that at the marriage feast of the fair Imogine, 'groans with the weight of the feast.' As a matter of course, the most honoured guest sits at her right hand, and, as a matter of course, he is the most persecuted man at table. The hospitable lady surveys his proceedings out of the corners of her eyes with the most unmitigated perseverance. Alas for him when his plate happens to be empty! 'A little more cod, Sir James?' Sir James bows a negative. 'Oh, don't say no—try a slice of the thick, with a little of the sounds.—No?—What *can* I tempt you with? My dear (to Mr Peppercorn), send Sir James a fillet of sole.' Sir James would rather not. 'Then some stewed prawns.—Not any?—Oh, just one.—I am sure you can manage one. John (to the servant), bring Sir James a stewed prawn—the largest, John.' Further opposition is useless; and although Sir James never ate a prawn in his life without becoming afflicted with indigestion, yet he thinks the prospect of dyspepsia a far preferable evil to his hostess's persecutions, and partakes of the gigantic shrimp with all the relish of a man eating henbane.

But even this sacrifice only purchases immunity for that particular course. A second attack comes on with the second course: the persecuted guest offers to carve for his hostess, to escape her importunities; but she will not 'hear of such a thing,' and hands the task over to a poor cousin, who has been seated on her left for the express purpose of assisting her. During this part of the entertainment, a number and variety of dishes are brought under Sir James's notice, which, mixed together even in name, are enough to give him a distaste for all sorts of food; and vain is his attempt to escape in the middle of the meal by declaring that he has dined. This is thought a good reason why the attack should be strengthened, so that no persuasion shall be wanting to induce him to 'enjoy himself;' and in the end he is obliged to appear capricious, and to alter his mind for a minute's peace. Nor is he the only sufferer, for a persecution of the other guests fills up Mrs Peppercorn's leisure moments.

In my boyhood, tea-parties were far more fashionable than the lateness of modern dinner hours renders practicable now. Well do I recollect the formulary by which each guest was persecuted before the operation of the 'second cup,' as Mercutio says. When the empty vessels were handed in, the hostess bent over the tea-board, and earnestly intreated her friend to 'take another cup.' Then came, after the refusal—'Now do—let me intreat you, just one more: I fear the tea is not agreeable to you?' 'Quite, thank you.' 'Indeed? then I am sure you can venture on another cup.' Still a refusal. 'Now *do*:' and then, as a compromise, which it was impossible to reject, came the pressing offer—'half a cup;' the non-acceptance of which was thought to be a piece of great rudeness. Though tea-parties are nearly abolished, the persecutions with which they were accompanied are now, alas, transferred too often to other meals.

It must be owned that this good-hearted vice does not extend to the higher classes, and only lingers amongst the middle and humbler orders of society. Indeed our aristocratic friends have run into an opposite extreme, and inflict a different kind of persecution by deputy. They leave their guests a little too much at the mercy of their domestics. The servant must be asked for what may be desired—and one does not always get it; he either brings something else, or has his attention distracted so as to forget the want altogether. The instant you lay down your knife and fork upon the plate, a dexterous and rapid hand whips it away, as if by magic. This is an abominable sort of persecution to an epicure. Perhaps he is protracting, by a pleasing rest, the pleasure derived from some favourite *bonne bouche*, and whispering to his neighbour how delicious it is, when, on turning his head to resume his gratification, he finds that the tit-bit has vanished, and recovery is impossible.

But these, it must be owned, are petty annoyances compared with the vast reforms which modern usages are slowly—perhaps too slowly—effecting. The abolition of late sittings is one of them. A dinner commencing at six o'clock, will seldom be found protracted till after nine; whereas, by the old rule of hospitality, the host thought it his duty to detain his friends as far into the following morning as possible. To effect this object, he set certain persecutions at work, the most serious of which amounted—if judged of by the statutes at large—to a misdemeanour. He locked the door, put the key into his pocket, and inflicted upon them a false imprisonment; or, if there were heavy rains abroad, he preferred hiding their hats.

Though such abominations are seldom thought of now, yet a few of the well-meant persecutions I have commented on are occasionally practised even by persons from whom more rational views of hospitality might be expected. Every one should remember, in giving an entertainment, to provide such things as appear, according to his judgment, best calculated to please his friends. There let them be, placed within procurable distance, leaving each guest to ask for what he wishes, and to partake of it in peace. To make a friend happy, it is only necessary to allow him, so far as means are at your command, to follow the bent of his peculiar inclinations. To attempt to constrain him into partaking of your own methods of enjoying yourself, is the way to render him extremely uncomfortable, and yourself—with every desire to be kind and hospitable—far from agreeable.

OCCASIONAL NOTES.

A NEW 'READING MADE EASY.'

It has been for some time a theory with us, that, from the present progress of things, the world (to some at least) threatens to be made too comfortable. It is becoming dangerously full of nice appliances, tending to make us too much in love with it. Among the last we have seen is a contrivance called the *Patent Reading Easel*, the invention of a Mr Howell, and the object of which is to save us, while reading, the trouble of holding the book, as well as to enable us to have the book in a position which will be more convenient generally. A jointed stalk, fastened at the bottom by a screw to the side of a chair or sofa, sustains a book-desk, furnished in the usual manner, and which, by various arrangements, can be shifted in position to suit convenience; the whole being capable of folding up into the space of about half a cubic foot. It is altogether a curious specimen of that mechanical ingenuity which we only see exemplified in England; and the utility for persons who read much, and more particularly for those in delicate health, seems indubitable.

IMPENDING DESTRUCTION OF A VILLAGE.

The calamities glanced at in a former Occasional Note* from which Great Britain is exempt, occur nowhere so frequently as in Switzerland. This, without doubt, the most picturesque country in Europe, pays dearly for her beauty in the destructive catastrophes to which she is subject; thus bearing out a favourite line by a French poet, signifying that 'the loveliest things have the vilest destinies.' In this beautiful but unfortunate land avalanches of snow, torrents of ice (which glaciers truly are), inundations of rivers, and the fall of huge rocks, sweep away not only the produce, but the inhabitants of valleys, and convert villages and towns into ruins. Not long ago the little town of Pleurs, comprising 2430 inhabitants, was buried under rocky masses suddenly detached from Mount Conto; and Goldau still lies hidden under a portion of Mount Rufiberg. At present, Felsberg, another village, is daily expected to be swallowed up; and its destiny is so certain, that its inhabitants remain in it at the risk of their lives. An appeal in their behalf is going the round of the continental papers, to which we are anxious to give farther currency.

The traveller, whilst ascending the Rhine, and whose destination is Coire, the capital of the Grisons, having passed Reichenau (in the castle of which the present king of the French was once an assistant schoolmaster, and where Dr Zschokke presided in the early years of his career†), perceives, opposite to Ems, the church steeple of a village, surrounded by meadows, and half-concealed by orchards. This is Felsberg, or the 'Mountain of Rock.' It is situated between the left bank of the river and the southern base of Mount Calanda. The rock, which supplies Felsberg with its name, is about 800 feet in height, and forms the base only of the mountain; for above it the well-wooded brow of the Calanda rises to a further elevation of 6000 feet. At a distance, the situation of this village appears everything that human imagination could desire; but a nearer approach reveals the awful fact, that the place, with all it contains, is in hourly danger of destruction. Already huge blocks of stone, which have rolled violently down from the steep sides of the mountain, are seen close to the houses, under the trees, and in the midst of the fields. Looking upward, an enormous mass, sufficient to entomb a large city, topples over the village, and is so nearly disengaged from the rest of the mountain, that it is by no means improbable that before these pages meet the public eye, Felsberg will have been crushed under its overwhelming fall!

Various efforts have from time to time been made to postpone the catastrophe; but now competent engineers have decided that farther efforts are of no avail. The most threatening part of the mountain has separated itself from the rest, and inclines fearfully forward over Felsberg. The chasm thus formed has been intersected with horizontal props and girders, so that the one side may be made to support the other. But other chasms are constantly opening, in consequence of the incessant disintegration that is going on. The largest of these is already almost a thousand feet deep and ten feet broad. The inhabitants, who for ten years have resisted all sense of fear from the dangers with which they have been threatened, are now at length, by the persuasions of their minister, disposed to remove from the doomed village.

But, alas! now that they are brought to this point, it is found that they have nowhere to go to. The district immediately adjacent offered an asylum; but one spot had no water, whilst another was constantly subject to the inundations of the Rhine. In this dilemma, the people of Felsberg supplicated the neighbouring communities to grant them shelter. Ems was willing to receive them, but on a condition which could not be complied with. Ems is a Catholic city, the people of Felsberg are Protestants, and the former would only shelter them on condition of their becoming Roman Catholics. Coire, where they afterwards applied, was more tolerant; but social and political difficulties, of too complicated a nature to be explained here, prevented that negotiation from succeeding. Finally, however, after numerous discussions, a suitable locality has been found; but the obstacle which prevents the unfortunate people from taking possession of it, is no less formidable than those they were unable to surmount. To obtain the desired spot, and to construct upon it a new village, the Felsbergians require money. They are poor; and if public sympathy does not step in with sufficient force and promptitude to provide the necessary funds, they will be constrained to remain where they are till the rock sink them out of the reach of further help. Should this happen, the affluent throughout all Europe will be for ever disgraced. Although in every nation cases of home-distress demand our *first* attention, yet after those are relieved, surely there will be some to spare to rescue a whole community in a foreign land from destruction. The people of the Grisons have already made noble sacrifices to aid their endangered neighbours, but out of their poverty enough could not be expected to effect the desired object. The government of the district has addressed circular letters to the authorities of the twenty-one cantons, in the hope of moving their pity and obtaining their aid. In Germany, concerts have been given, the proceeds of which have been forwarded to the Felsberg fund; and in Paris a subscription has been opened at the office of the Swiss legation.* Should any of our readers be inclined to swell the subscriptions, we have no doubt that the Swiss agent and consul-general in London will not object to receive them.

THE RAILWAY MANIA.

The history of railways, with steam as a locomotive, supplies some interesting views respecting human nature. The reduction of friction attainable by such a mechanically-arranged ground for carriages, was proved upwards of two centuries ago. Men had it as clearly presented to their eyes, in common wagon railroads, throughout the whole of the last century, and during the first thirty years of this, as it is at the present moment. Here was one great element of the case which ought, one would think, to have been held as settled. Then, as to the possibility of driving a carriage by steam power, which is the other element, it was equally

* 'The Weather and Crops,' p. 264. † See his life, p. 201.

* Rue de Tivoli, No. 8.

settled at least fifty-six years ago; for Symington was then driving a steam-carriage every day for a whole summer or more along the roads in the high country forming the upper parts of the counties of Lanark and Dumfries. Trevithick and Vivian exhibited a similar carriage in 1802; and the idea was kept awake by other experimenters down to a recent period. Steam locomotion on this plan—that is, on common roads—was a failure; but this is nothing to the purpose; for the possibility of impelling a carriage by steam was proved, which is all we are concerned about. Here, then, were the two elements of the present railway system set before mankind, in a manner which did not admit of a single well-grounded doubt, many years ago; and yet, as we all know, the knowledge was not taken advantage of. The idea had not entered the public mind, and any one who had expressed a belief that steam locomotion upon railways was practicable, and contained the germ of vast improvements for the world, would have been regarded as a dreamer. Even when the practicability had at length been subjected to full and satisfactory experiment upon the Liverpool and Manchester railway in 1830, the bulk of the public remained in a state of mind which was the same as non-conviction. Three years elapsed before a bill for any longer railway was introduced into parliament. The acts for the Birmingham and Manchester, and the Grand Junction, were only then obtained. So late as 1840, the Great Western and the South-Eastern were only in progress. Great landproprietors at that time resisted them with the most determined hostility, as a thing half-nuisance half-convenience, designed only for the benefit of the manufacturing interest. All this, we hold, shows that the mind does not instantaneously receive proof as preclusive of further doubt. If the subject be new and startling, and still more so, if any interest or prejudice be disturbed by it, the clearest demonstration on earth is of no avail. At the best, a few persons of unusual liberality will, if strongly pressed, make a few slight admissions. If the evidence show, for instance, a speed of thirty miles an hour, they will admit fifteen—but no more. Another set, more cautious, but still unable altogether to resist the pressure of evidence, will—after taking great care to distinguish themselves from the crazy men who admit fifteen miles—yield a strongly qualified assent to ten. Truth is continually and everywhere made the subject of chaffering admissions of this kind; and the good name of her advocates is often, on a like principle, defended, or their assumed faults extenuated, where only honour ought to be rendered. Finally, what do we see?—an excitement arise on the subject of railways, and hundreds of millions ventured without thought or consideration, where formerly, with equal evidence on the general question before them, the public would not have laid out ten! Reason dead, in the first place, to clear, incontestable proof—afterwards, passion or frenzy doing ten times the work that reason could justify! After all this, is man a rational animal? Is he not rather passion's slave, and, to this day, a child?

FOOD OF THE IRISH POOR.

'I asked one man—a cobbler—who spoke English, to show me into one or two of the cottages near. I entered that of Nelly Gallagher; she pays 30s. rent for one "cow's grass." She was preparing her dinner of potatoes, and—what think you?—*sea-weed*. They gather, I was told by some twenty of them (and saw them using it), a kind of sea-weed called "dillisk," which they dry, and boil as "kitchen" with their potatoes. It boils down to a kind of gluten with the potatoes, and the salt in it, they say, makes the potatoes more palatable. In winter they gather the common sea-weed which grows on the rocks, and which they call "dhoolaman" in Irish; and cutting off the thin leaves at the extremities of the weed, boil these, when they cannot get "dillisk," which is a better kind of sea-weed.'—*The Times 'Commissioner.'*

[Sea-weed has vulgarly a bad reputation. Horace speaks of it as if there could be nothing viler. But that many of the numberless *algæ* are esculent, there cannot be the slightest doubt. This very dillisk or *dulse* has been sold by women in the streets of Edinburgh, as a popular delicacy, 'since beyond the memory of the oldest inhabitant;' carigeen, or Irish moss, is a delicacy even among the rich; and, as may be seen by referring to an article on the *Algæ* in the present volume, p. 181, many of them are held in equal repute in other countries. Our mentioning these circumstances is not designed to check the feeling of commiseration due to the depressed condition of the unfortunate Irish, but to moderate the assumed importance of dillisk-eating as a proof of it. The 'well-off' have no conception of the ways of the poor, and often that appears an evil to the one party which the other regards as a comfort.]

GILFILLAN'S GALLERY OF LITERARY PORTRAITS.*

THIS is a book which will be extensively reviewed, but little read. It wants applicability to the common mind. The author—a preacher, we understand, amongst the old dissenters of Scotland—has sought to convey his impressions respecting a limited set—his own favourites—of the modern literary men of England. The principal are Godwin, Hazlitt, Hall, Chalmers, Carlyle, Coleridge, De Quincey, Professor Wilson, Landor, Wordsworth, Shelley. The manner of the work is bold, ardent, and diffuse, like the style of a high-flown pulpit orator: often it enshrines beautiful and generous thoughts; but the judgment of the sober mind at the close is unfavourable, from a lingering sense that such is not the way in which Truth speaks, except when she is sore stung indeed, or, like Brutus, has to veil her dicta under a seeming madness. We shall enable the reader to judge from a few specimens.

Here is one from the article on Ebenezer Elliott. 'We have sometimes wondered that the forge has not sooner sent forth its poetical representative. It is undoubtedly one of the most imaginative of the objects of artificial life, especially when standing solitary, and on the edge of a dark wood. Hear how a man of genius describes it:—"As I rode through the Schwarzald, I said to myself, That little fire, which glows across the dark-growing moor, where the sooty smith bends over the anvil, and thou hopest to replace thy lost horse-shoe, is it a detached separated speck, cut off from the whole universe, or indissolubly united to the whole? Thou fool! that smithy fire was primarily kindled at the sun; is fed by air that circulates from before Noah's Deluge—from beyond the dog-star—therein, with iron force, and coal force, and the far stronger force of man, are battles and victories of force brought about. It is a little ganglion or nervous centre in the great system of immensity. Call it, if thou wilt, an unconscious altar, kindled on the bosom of the All, whose iron smoke and influence reach quite through the All—whose dingy priest, not by word, but by brain and sinew, preaches forth the mystery of Force." A smith, surrounded by an atmosphere of sparkles—sending out that thick thunder which Schiller seems to have loved above all other music—presiding at the wild wedlock of iron and flame, and baptising the progeny of the terrible Hymen in the hissing trough—so independent in his lonely stithy—lord of his hammer and his strong right arm—carrying back your imagination to the days when the hammer of Tubal-Cain awoke the virgin echoes of the antediluvian world, and made him a mythic one, by first bending the stiff neck of the iron and the brass—or to the bowels of Ætna and Vulcan—or to the groves and lucid streams of Damascus—or to Spain, and the Ebro, and Andrew Ferrara—while, perhaps, sweeps before the mind's eye a procession of the instruments of death, from the first shapeless mass of iron, fitted to the giant-hand of a son of Cain, down through the Grecian javelin, the Roman spear, the Persian scimitar, the

---

* A Gallery of Literary Portraits, by George Gilfillan. Tait, Edinburgh. 1845.

Saracen blade, bright and sharp as the crescent-moon, the great two-handed sword of the middle ages, the bayonet, which bored a passage for the armies of Turenne, the pike, the battle-axe, the claymore of Caledonia: thus does imagination pile up a pedestal, on which the smith, and his dusky visage, and his uplifted hammer, and his patient anvil, look absolutely ideal; and the wonder is excited why till of late no "message *from* the forge" has been conveyed to the ears of men beyond its own incessant and victorious sound. And yet the forge had wrought and raved for ages, and amid all its fiery products, reared no poet till it was said, "Let Ebenezer Elliott be."' In answer to all this, it is irresistible to say that the simple reason why the forge has sent forth no great poetical voice to justify this account of its poetical character, is, that the character is wrong—wrong from beginning to end, a mere effusion of conceits; and, there being no cause in operation, there is of course no effect. The very confession of the non-effect is presumption overpowering against the truth of the supposed cause; and the writer should have seen this, and stayed his hand. The fact, in its unpretending simplicity, is, that a man of genius, called Ebenezer Elliott, has happened to be reared as an ironmonger, and wrote poetry because it was in the natural constitution of his mind to do so; or, if external causes operated upon him in stimulating in any degree the native inspiration, they were not of a professional character at all, but rather arose from the political circumstances of his country. There may be nothing here that is striking or exciting; let, then, nothing be said upon the subject. What good is to be got by anything untrue?

The exclusive regard of the author for what is merely impressive in style, and his possession of no true standard whereby to judge of the real merits of the great writers, is shown in numberless places. Of Foster, for example, he says, 'He had as distinct a faculty for seeing everything through his own medium, as any writer of his day. Were the medium dim, or party-coloured, as it sometimes was, or were it vivid and lustrous, it was always his own. Authors, characters, books, the face of nature, were all seen and shown by him in a new, strange, and striking light. "He read the universe, not by sunlight, nor starlight, nor moonlight, but just by the fairy lustre round his own head." His thought had a stamp about it altogether his own. With no air of affected singularity, with no desperate efforts at solving the inscrutable and sounding the fathomless, with little metaphysical verbiage, and with few carefully-wrapt-up commonplaces, his train of thinking ever sought the profound as its natural element. A necessity was laid upon his mind not to think shallowly, or like other men. And even when he did bring up half truths, or whole errors, like sea-weed instead of coral, there was something in its very worthlessness which spoke of the depths, and betrayed the vigour and wind of the diver.' Here the mere peculiarity of Foster, as a medium of thought and expression, is appreciated; not a word of anxiety about the justness or the truth of thought, or the moral result, as apart from that medium. And this preference and this indifference are habitual. Mr Gilfillan is indeed about the most pure worshipper of intellect and intellectual impulse that we have any recollection of.

The book will nevertheless be a favourite with many, though not the many. It is full of rich poetical expression, and presents many masses of magnificent imagery. One description, standing almost solitary in the critical musings, strikes us as eminently fine: it refers to a glen in Perthshire, where Hogg lays the scene of his 'Kilmeny.' 'This ballad,' says Mr Gilfillan, 'we love, like all the world, for its sweetness and spirituality; a sweetness more unearthly, a spirituality more intense, than are to be found anywhere else in the language of men, save (at a vast distance of superiority) in the songs of Ariel in the "Tempest." We love it, too, because we know well, and from infancy have known, the glen up which went alone the maid in the "pride of her purity." It lies along a deep green valley, sunk in between two high chains of hills—those of Abruchill and Dundurn—lifting their "giant-snouted" crags on the south, and on the north the hills of Crappich and Cluan, piled up like leaning Titans. This valley has evidently been once a part of Loch Earn. It is level, but sprinkled with little wooded eminences, once no doubt islets, and toward its western end rises a remarkable hill, called the hill of St Fillans, strangely contrasting with the black and heathery mountains which tower above it. It is green, round-headed, grassy, like a young Ochil which had been flung down among the gloomy Grampians. At the foot of the northern bulwark of the valley lies Dunira, alluded to in the poem ("It was na to meet wi' Dunira's men"), a place where the utmost refinement of art, in the form of a whitewashed mansion, rich lawns, "shaven by the scythe, and smoothed by the roller," fine shrubbery and elegant garden, is brought into contact, contrast, yet harmony, with the utmost wildness and grandeur of nature—a bare knotted hill before, and behind it a mountain, wooded almost to the summit, like some awful countenance veiled, but speaking in the tongues of a hundred waterfalls, which you hear, but see not, dashing, leaping, and murmuring down their downright and headlong course till reaching the plain; and, as if in deference to the inmates of the dwelling, they hush their voices, and become "stillest streams watering fairest meadows." To the west of this lovely place lies the blue sheet of Loch Earn, back from which retires Benvoirlich, like a monarch, almost unseen by the lake, yet owns its sway.

'We have seen this scene from the summit of Dunmore and the side of Melville's monument, which stands upon it: seen it at all hours, in all circumstances, and in all seasons—in the clear morning, while the smoke of a thousand cottages was seen rising through the dewy air, and when the mountains seemed not thoroughly awakened from their night's repose—in the garish noonday, when the feeling of mystery was removed by the open clearness, but that of majesty in form and outline remained—in the afternoon, with its sunbeams streaking huge shadows, and writing characters of fire upon all the hills—in the golden evening, when the sun was going down over Benmore in blood—in the dim evening, to us dearer still, when a faint rich mist was steeping all the landscape in religious hues—in the waste night, while the moon was rising red in the north-east, like a beacon, or a torch uplifted by some giant hand—under the breezes and bashful green of spring—in the laughing luxuriance of summer—under the yellow shade of autumn—at the close of autumn, when the woods were red and the stubble sovereign of the fields—and again, when hill, valley, and wood were spotted with snow, have seen it in a hush so profound, that you might have imagined nature listening for some mysterious tidings, and hardly dared to breathe—and in the cloudy and dark day, while the thunder was shaking the column, and the lightning painting the landscape. And gazing at it, whether in glimmer or in gloom, have we sometimes fancied that we saw that fearless form "gaeing" up through the plains of Dalwhinnie and the fairy plantations of Dunira,

"To pu' the cress-flower round the spring,
The scarlet hyp and the hyndberrye,
And the nut that hang frae the hasel tree;
For Kilmeny was pure as pure could be."

And when gloaming especially had poured her dim divine lustre over the dark hills and white castle of Abruchill, and allowed the last lingering ray of sunshine to rest on the crest of Benvoirlich, and hushed the streams of Glenlednick behind, and drawn a dewy veil over the plain of Dalginross before, and softened the call of the Cauldron in the glen below, and suffused over all the landscape of earth and heaven a sense unutterable of peace; and introduced into the scene, as a last glorious touch, the moon, to enhance the sense of solemnity, and to deepen the feeling of repose, have we, reclining on the hill, and seeing the stars coming out above the silent column, thought of the "eve in a sinless world," when,

> "In ecstasy of sweet devotion;
> Oh then the glen was all in motion;"

and owned the power of the "consecration," and felt the might of the "poet's dream."'

There are also many passages of rich and just criticism; as the following on Campbell (written while the poet was yet among the living), which seems to us unsurpassably correct:—'Campbell's great power is enthusiasm—subdued. His tempest moves on gracefully, and as to the sound of music. His muse keeps the step at the same time that she shakes the wilderness. You see him arranging the dishevelled and streaming hair, smoothing the furrowed forehead, compressing the full and thrilling lips of inspiration. He can arrest the fury of his turbulent vein by stretching forth the calm hand of taste, as an escaped lunatic is abated in a moment by the whisper of his keeper, or by his more terrible tap of quiet imperious command. There is a perpetual alternation going on in his mind. He is this moment possessed by his imagination; the next, he masters and tames it, to walk meekly in the harness of his purpose; or, to use his own fine image, while his genius is flaming above, his taste below, "like the dial's silent power,"

> Measures inspiration's hour,
> And tells its height in heaven.

He is inferior thus to the very first class of poets, whose taste and art are unconscious. His are at once conscious to himself, and visible to others. Their works, like nature's, arrange themselves into elegance and order, amid their impetuous and ecstatic motion; their apparent extravagances obey a law of their own, and create a taste for their appreciation; their hair, shed on the whirlwind, falls abroad, through its own divine instinct, in lines of waving beauty; their flashing eye enriches the day; their wild, uncontrollable step, "brings from the dust the sound of liberty." But if Campbell be too measured, and timid, and self-watchful, to appertain to those demi-urgi of poetry, he is far less to be classed with the imitative and the cold—the schools of Boileau and Pope. He not only belongs to no school, but in short deep gushes of genuine genius—in single thoughts, where you do not know whether more to admire the felicity of the conception, or the delicate and tremulous finish of the expression—in drops of spirit-stirring or melting song—and in a general manliness and chastity of manner, Campbell is perhaps the finest ARTIST living. His mind has the refinement of the female intellect, added to the energy of the classic man. His taste is not of the Gothic order, neither is it of the Roman; it is that of a Greek, neither grotesque nor finically fastidious. His imagery is select, not abundant: out of a multitude of figures which throng on his mind, he has the resolution to choose only the one which, by pre-established harmony, seems destined to enshrine the idea. His sentiment is sweet, without being mawkish, and *recherché*, without being affected. Here, indeed, is Campbell's fine distinction. He never becomes metaphysical in discriminating the various shades, nor morbid in painting the darker moods of sentiment. He preserves continually the line of demarcation between sentiment and passion. With the latter, in its turbulence, its selfish engrossment, the unvaried but gorgeous colouring which it flings across all objects—the flames of speech which break out from its white lips, he rarely meddles. But of that quieter and nobler feeling which may be called, from its stillness, its subdued tone, its whispered accents, its shade of pensiveness, the moonshine of the mind, he is pre-eminently the poet. His lines on "Revisiting a Scene in Argyleshire," and those on "Leaving a Scene in Bavaria," are the perfection of this species of poetry. They are meditations, imbued at once with all the tenderness of moonshine, and all the strength of sunshine. Manly is his melancholy, and even his sigh proclaims the breadth and depth of the chest from which it is upheaved.'

Mr Gilfillan delights in quaint views of things, but there is often sense in what he pens in that strain; for example, the following from the paper on Charles Lamb:—'It is a singular circumstance, in the present day, that the commercial and the literary character have, in certain instances, been blended, without destroying each other. Literature, in our strange era, has entered the counting-room. Wit, of the rarest grain, has assisted in unpacking bales of goods. Genius, of the true and sovereign seed, has seated itself upon the tall three-legged stool, and worn a quill, instead of laurel, behind its "trembling ears." The genius, thus enthroned, has not, to be sure, been of the most romantic or ethereal order. The idea is ridiculous of a clerk now with fire and fury enditing a mystery, and now taking in a consignment of muslin; dropping the pen, which had been dashing down the terrible syllables of a Walpurgis night, to make out an invoice of yarns. With all reverence for trade, in its various departments, we cannot believe it possible for a Goëthe or a Schiller, a Byron or a Shelley, a Coleridge or a Wilson, to have been bred in a warehouse. Had they not been "wild and woodland rovers," known, through broad lands, to "every star and every wind that blows," with foot free to tread, as it listed, the deck or the heather, the soft sod or the incrusted lava, the sand or the snow; and, with faces imbrowned by the sunbeams which had smote them by day, and spiritualised by the starry eyes which had shot down influence upon them by night, they could not have been what, to the honour of their species and the glory of the universe, they have become. Only conceive Goëthe, with that lofty forehead and stately form, bending over a ledger; or the wizard Coleridge, with those dreamy eyes, deep in calculation of the price of stocks. And yet Charles Lamb, Coleridge's dear friend, thus spent the greater portion of his life. But then Charles Lamb, though as true a genius as any of those we have named, was a genius of quite a different and inferior order. And we know not how much greater he might have become, had he received a diverse training, and instead of being the slave of a counting-room, had been free of that city, the builder and maker of which is God.' There cannot, we think, be a doubt that commonplace duties may be compatible with much devotion to literary pursuits, and to a literary power calculated to be of some importance to mankind, but not with the highest powers and their highest exercise.

We have spoken of Mr Gilfillan with freedom, and feel sure that he will like us the better for it. There is enough of him, after many parings, to make a good writer; but it will be infinite pity if such a mind continues a mere votary of intellectual excitement, and, from want of inner or outer light, fails to get upon some of the great tracks of truth and goodness which lead to the palpable benefit of humanity

A PLEA FOR VEGETABLE DIET.

MANY speculations have been made regarding the original and natural food of man, and of late a pretty large octavo volume has been published on the subject.* The ingenious author of this volume, himself a vegetable feeder, argues for an exclusive vegetable diet. The structure of the teeth in all the vertebrated animals affords a sure index of their kind of diet. Thus all the flesh-feeders have sharp-pointed teeth, both before and in the back part of the jaw; while the herbivorous orders have the grinders flattened and rounded. In man, the teeth form an uninterrupted series: they are all nearly of equal length, and placed close to each other, and occupy the whole jaw—a character by which man is distinguished from all existing animals. His canine teeth, which have been said to indicate his carnivorous tendency, are less prominent

* Fruits and Farinacea the Proper Food of Man. By John Smith. London.

than in animals admitted to be exclusively graminivorous—as the horse, camel, or stag. His bicuspids, or first grinders, have two prominences instead of one, as in the carnivora. His grinders bear a close resemblance to those of the monkey tribe, but differ from the rest of the herbivora in the arrangement of the enamel. In the flesh-feeding animals, the inferior molars fall inside the upper, so as to tear the flesh; and the jaws have but one motion upwards and downwards. In man and the herbivora, the upper and lower teeth meet exactly; and the jaw has a rotatory motion, so as to grind the food. On the whole, the digestive organs of man bear a closer similarity to those of the monkey tribe than to any other family; though the teeth of the orang-outang, which lives on fruits and farinaceous nuts, have a more carnivorous character than those of the human species. We must also bear in mind that man, even in his rudest state, is a cooking animal, and has various means of preparing his food before he comes to masticate it; and thus the true carnivorous teeth, even supposing that flesh were his natural food, would be to him unnecessary. If we appeal to long experience, however, it appears evident that man may be either a flesh-feeding animal, a vegetable-feeding, or both, as circumstances may happen. There can be no doubt that the great mass of mankind on the earth's surface are, in reality, very nearly exclusively vegetable eaters. Yet there are some tribes, as the Esquimaux, that live entirely on animal food; and many nations of hunters that partake of little else than the flesh of animals killed in the chase. The American travellers, Lewis and Clarke, spent upwards of two years among the natives of the far west; and during the greater part of this period, lived exclusively on animal food, without even salt. They enjoyed excellent health; and on returning to civilised life, they gave up their hunter's fare with some degree of reluctance. Certain carnivorous animals may also, in time, be brought to live on grain; and herbivorous quadrupeds have no objections to eat fish, or even flesh, when they can obtain such fare. Such is the effect of habit on the animal system.

As recent discoveries in chemistry have shown that vegetables contain the same elements as flesh, we need not be surprised that man may live and thrive on a diet almost or altogether vegetable. The same gluten, albumen, fibrin, and oily matters that exist in a beefsteak or mutton-chop, are also found in our esculent vegetables; the difference only amounting to a peculiarity of taste, or a slight diversity in the arrangement of particles. The starch and sugar of the farinacea are soon manufactured by the digestive apparatus into oil, and the albumen into animal muscle. Experience proves that a vegetable diet is lighter, and less liable to bring on diseases, than one in which animal food largely prevails. It is affirmed to be equally nutritious, and equally capable of sustaining the strength even of the hardest labouring men. We have undoubted evidences of this in the robust Irishman, fed on potatoes; and the hardy Scottish peasant, who rarely indulges in a flesh diet. From a very early period, the philosophers of Greece advocated, and even practised, an exclusively vegetable diet, as being more conducive to clearness of intellect and mental activity. The Pythagorean sages inculcated the same; hence the prevalence of the rice diet over the vast and densely-peopled regions of Asia. It is related that Newton, while writing his great work on optics, lived entirely without animal food; while Descartes, Haller, Hufeland, Howard the philanthropist, Byron, Shelley, and a host of other men of genius, were the advocates of a vegetable diet. The tendency of a full diet of animal food to bring on various complaints—such as gout, scurvy, liver disease, and calculous disorders—is not more clearly ascertained than that a contrary regimen of vegetable food is decidedly efficacious in their cure. To children too, a farinaceous, combined with a milk diet, is found by universal experience to be that which is least exciting, and most conducive to their health and full development. It is also affirmed that a vegetable diet is favourable to longevity. Among the Norwegian, Russian, and Scottish peasantry, who lead a simple life, and live on simple fare, there are more instances of extreme old age than among many other more luxurious nations.

It is worth while to show upon how moderate an allowance of food human life may be comfortably supported. In the year 1840, some experiments were instituted in the Glasgow prison on the diet of a selected number of the inmates. Ten persons were fed for two months on the following fare: to breakfast, each had eight ounces of oatmeal made into porridge, with a pint of butter-milk; to dinner, three pounds boiled potatoes, with salt; to supper, five ounces of oatmeal porridge, with one half-pint of butter-milk. At the end of two months they were all in good health; each person had gained four pounds in weight; and they liked the diet, the cost of which, including cookery, was twopence three farthings per day. Other ten young men were fed for the same period solely on boiled potatoes and salt; each had two pounds for breakfast, three pounds to dinner, and one pound to supper. They gained three and a-half pounds each; and they declared that they preferred this fare to the ordinary diet of the prison. Twenty others were fed on the same allowance of porridge and milk for breakfast and supper as the first ten; but to dinner they had soup, containing two pounds of potatoes to each, and a quarter of a pound of meat. At the end of two months they had lost each in weight one and a quarter pounds; and they all disliked this dinner: the expense of each daily was threepence seven-eighths. Twenty others had the same breakfast and supper, with one pound of potatoes to dinner, and half a pound of meat. They preserved good health, but rather decreased in weight, and preferred the ordinary diet of the prison. The expense was fourpence seven-eighths each. In these cases, perhaps the previous habits and tastes of the prisoners had some influence; yet it appears evident that the six pounds of potatoes daily was a more nutritious diet than the smaller quantities of soup or animal food. If variety of dishes be desired, there is certainly a wider range in the vegetable department even than in the animal. Rice, sago, peas, beans, carrot, turnip, are all at hand to ring the changes upon. An excellent and nourishing soup may be made of a pound of pease-meal, a carrot or two, and a turnip; and jellies and blancmanges, of as beautiful an aspect, and of a much easier digestion, are as procurable for the dessert as those from animal products.

We have known persons who, from a peculiarity of constitution, or perhaps rather from a vagary of taste, have lived entirely without the use of animal food; and these were certainly not deficient either in physical or mental powers. A writer in the Dublin Journal of Medicine thus gives his own case:—When about four years of age, having been much bantered by some friends for petting lambs and rabbits, and afterwards eating the flesh of such animals, in a fit of childish indignation he declared he would never again eat flesh. This resolution was adhered to; and his parents, who were not very much impressed with the necessity of animal food, and who believed that the whim would soon wear off, did not interfere. For the last twenty-one years he has entirely abstained from eating anything that ever had life, as well as from eggs and cheese; whilst he never partook of even one glass of wine, spirits, or any intoxicating liquor; nor does he make use of tea or coffee. His health has been invariably good; and at school and college he was possessed of more activity and strength than any of his associates of the same age, whilst he exceeded all in endurance. Though sedentary habits must have prevented the full development of his muscular powers, he has on more than one occasion walked sixty English miles in one day, without any other inconvenience than blistered feet. His average weight has continued much the same for the last seven years; but increases half a stone during summer, and diminishes in the same ratio in winter. To abridge the number of our wants, is to increase our happiness and independence; and the writer affirms that he derives as high gratification, or at least as high as he would wish to derive, from satisfying his appetite with fruits and farinacea, as can be afforded by the 'gory banquets' of others; whilst he is at least free from those after-consequences which he hears so often complained of by his friends. Several other similar cases are mentioned by this writer, and among others that of a cousin of his own, who came to reside with him when seven years of age, and who was led, from motives of attachment, to adopt his Pythagorean habits, in which he persevered for above fifteen years, and was at last induced to become carnivorous only by the painful sense of peculiarity which he experienced on mingling with society.

[We would be understood as only sanctioning the principles advocated in this paper to a certain extent. We are of opinion that a larger proportion of vegetable food might advantageously be introduced into the diet of the middle and higher classes in this country; but we have no faith in an exclusively vegetable aliment, which, we understand, often has a detrimental effect on the excretions, rendering them unusually offensive, and also on the intellectual operations, which it tends to weaken. One fact seems to tell strongly against all attempts to make out man naturally a vegetable feeder, that for the first few months of his existence, while nursing, he is exclusively supported by animal food.—ED.]

CRIME IN NORTH LANCASHIRE.

A REPORT, just published, of the Preston House of Correction for the past year, discloses the pleasing fact, that in North Lancashire, as well as elsewhere, there has latterly been a sensible diminution of crime. There has likewise been a change, to a certain extent, in a chief cause of commitment. Some time ago it was poverty; now it is intemperance. It is made apparent that in hard times *destitution*, with its accompanying idleness, is a prevailing cause of criminality; whereas in good times, when employment is abundant, and wages high, a principal cause is *drunkenness*. Idleness among the working-classes generally seems to produce wide-spread demoralisation; for, having few amusements of a harmless kind, and little inclination to pass the time in mental improvement, they easily lapse into vices which bring them within the scope of the criminal law. Regular employment, on the other hand, is the safeguard of virtue, and but for the mean temptations of the public-house, the working-classes, when occupied in their ordinary labours, would present a model of good behaviour.

Mr Clay, the writer of the report before us, speaks most emphatically on this melancholy subject. 'Persons,' says he, 'who in hard times could resist every temptation arising from poverty, give way before the temptations which return with high wages; and liquor, which the labourer has been trained to regard as his greatest source of enjoyment, leads him into acts which nothing could have driven him to when sober. It will be remembered that the country had suffered more and more from a depression in trade for some years, until, in the winter of 1842-3, that depression was at its lowest point. The following summer, however, brought a beneficial change; and since then, commercial life has been restored to unusual activity. But as some disorders of the body are aggravated by a full habit, so the moral malady of drunkenness has been encouraged by the commercial plethora. The following extracts from my journal illustrate what I am so anxious to impress:—

'1. I. W., aged thirty, committed for one month as drunken and disorderly. His appearance and manner bespeak the comparatively respectable and intelligent mechanic, who, for the first time in his life, has been led by intoxication into further offence. He is one of the numerous class who maintain themselves easily and honestly without devoting any time or thought to religion.

'2. R. R., sentenced to transportation at the last sessions, said, "It's all drink from one end to the other. Just before I came here I was earning 40s. a-week (I have got as much as L.4). I have three fine boys of ten, fourteen, and sixteen years old; and a few weeks ago I was as happy a man as there was in England. I was secretary to the Temperance Society at ——. I went to buy a book to teach my boys arithmetic; but I never gave them a single lesson; for I met an acquaintance who persuaded me to have some ginger-beer. They put rum in it, unknown to me, and I became intoxicated. I recovered from this, however; but in a short time afterwards I was waylaid by —— and ——. They persuaded me to drink with them; and I never stopped until I committed the offence for which I am to be transported."

'3. An old man of sixty-nine, with silvery hair, says, "I have had both my legs broken through intoxication: I once rented a farm with twenty head of cattle and a team of horses. My wife died sixteen years ago, and then I got into low company, and began to drink. I have four good children, who have all turned their backs upon me; but they would very gladly take to me again if I would give up drink."

'4. J. P., aged twenty-four, under sentence for felony; a shoemaker—"I have been ruined by drink: I have been twice imprisoned through it. I was teetotal for twelve months; and after maintaining myself comfortably, I had L.15 in my pocket; but I was tempted to break out, and in less than a month I spent everything—my watch and all my clothes. I have to confess to you—and it stares me in the face so that I can't be easy till I have told you—that I have often worked on Sunday, and then drunk from Monday until Thursday."

'5. J. W., aged twenty-six, convicted of felony—"If I can only do without drink—and I am sure I can—I shall be a different man. I did try once for thirty-two weeks, and was never so well nor so happy in my life. . . . It is through drink I came here; but if anybody had told me six weeks ago that it was possible I could be sent to prison, nothing could have made me believe it."

'6. A young man, aged twenty-five, committed on a charge of felony arising from intoxication, had been earning 8s. per day for some weeks in Liverpool—"I left that place to come home to be married; but I got on the spree, and lighted on this misfortune. I was once teetotal for three months, and saved L.15 in that time; but before now I have spent as much in one week's drinking."

'7. J. H., committed for felony. One of his children having died, he received L.2, 10s. from the Burial Club. He expended 18s. in clothing for himself and his wife, and the funeral dues and expenses were 14s. 2d. The balance, 17s. 10d., was squandered in liquor, under the influence of which he committed the felony with which he stands charged. His earnings are 18s. per week; he had never been before a magistrate on any former occasion, and bore as good a character as the working-men around him.

'8. J. H., a convict, aged sixty-nine, who has for many years tenanted a small farm of twenty acres, and whose family are only weavers, has been reckoning, while in his cell, that, since his twenty-first year, he has spent in liquor about L.650.

'9. J. M'C., a tailor, thirty-two years old, just able to read—"belongs to no religion," and (happily) is unmarried. When he chooses to work, he can earn 30s. weekly; yet was committed for begging, after having been "on the spree" for three or four days. He admits that, when in work, he spends in drink 12s. or 15s. a-week, and had not saved a sixpence: the "trade" is bound to support him when out of work, &c.

'10. J. P., "Before I married I was an overlooker of power-looms, and earned 30s. a-week regularly for five years together. All that time I never spent less than 20s. a-week in drinking, and treating others to drink. When I married I had not saved a sixpence."

'These extracts,' continues the reporter, 'give mere examples of the various circumstances connected with the ruinous vice under consideration. Already inclined to it, an otherwise industrious artisan or labourer has additional temptation set before him by the ease with which he can earn the means for his demoralising enjoyment. Another gives way before the wicked determination of his associates to overcome his resolution to refrain. A third is encouraged in his excess by the (to him) highly satisfactory conviction that he may spend the whole of his wages in drink, and then fall back for support upon the funds of his *trade*. A fourth, coming into possession of what to him is a large sum, intended for a very different purpose, spends great part of it in drink, and turns a season of sorrow into an occasion for vicious dissipation. And—most to be wondered at and lamented—a fifth, as the reward of his activity and exertion in his honest calling, has the cup of poison held out to him by—his employer! by one who, although bound to promote the moral welfare of those who labour for him—and with abundant means of doing so—nevertheless panders to their besetting sin, and puts them on the path to shame and punishment. Our social and religious progress will be much quickened when employers become more alive to their responsibilities in relation to the morals of those whose skill and labour they hire. That the practice of excessive drinking diminishes or increases with the fall and rise of employment and wages is, I think, almost demonstrated by the 18th table, which clearly shows that when (in 1842-3) the operative was suffering most severely from want of employment, intoxication, as a cause of crime, was, compared to other causes, less than 17 per cent.; while now that labour and skill are in the greatest demand, and wages are unusually high, the criminality attributable to this debasing propensity has swollen to 41 *per cent.!'*

With regard to the loss entailed on the community from causes of this nature, the reporter enters into the following calculations:—'Four hundred and fifty drunkards were committed to the Preston House of Correction in the last year; each of these, at a low estimate, spends 5s. weekly in liquor. To this add the loss of wages during imprisonment (average of the former 15s., and of the latter six weeks), and the cost of prosecuting 125 felons at L.8 each, and of hearing 325 minor offences at L.1 each. Twenty-five drunkards were transported last year at an expense of between L.70 and L.80 each. Six weeks' maintenance in prison for 450 prisoners (excluding interest of money sunk in buildings, &c.) may be taken at L.1650. The proportion of the annual charge for county and borough police appertaining to these 450 prisoners, may be considered L.2500; and the cost to the Union for destitute families about L.300 or L.400. When all these items are taken into account (and there are more which might be included), the aggregate cost to the community, for *one year only*, and of those drunkards only who have been brought into prison, will be found to exceed *sixteen thousand pounds*—a sum four times as great as the last year's cost of maintaining this house of correction. But though we may calculate the money-charge entailed by drinking, we cannot reckon up the whole moral cost of it; the idleness and blasphemy, the fraud and violence, the ruin of family peace, the neglect and corruption and brutalising of children. We are astonished at the apathy with which the people of the East regard the visitations of the plague, while we look with composure on the ravages of this ever-present pestilence at home.'

THE WANT OF SKILFUL AND EARNEST OPERATIVES.

Every architect in practice has cause to complain of the want of skilful and earnest operatives—men who understand the trade they profess to practise, find pleasure in the exercise of it, and are anxious to produce good work. We have before this commented on the decline apparent in many of the constructive arts, and showed that it proceeds from excessive competition, which induces the master to require a certain quantity of work from a man, without reference to its quality. He cannot afford to develop a man's ability, but demands the greatest amount of work in the smallest space of time. 'Superior work wont do; work that will pass is all that he can hope to give;' and the natural result is, that our workmen, as a body, have gradually 'lost their cunning,' and that the majority of operatives now employed are incapable of executing work which is at all out of the common way. Our bricklayers and smiths afford the most striking examples of this decline; the old enthusiasm which still lingers, though feebly, amongst other trades, especially with the masons, seems to have departed from them: they do their work as mere labourers, and have no pride in the result. There are of course many clever exceptions, but we speak of the mass.—*The Builder.*

AIR CHURN.

The bishop of Derry has invented an atmospheric churn. Instead of the present unscientific mode of making butter by churning, his lordship accomplishes this measure by the simpler manner of forcing a full current of atmospheric air through the cream, by means of an exceedingly well-devised forcing-pump. The air passes through a glass tube connected with the air-pump, descending nearly to the bottom of the churn. The churn is of tin, and it fits into another tin cylinder provided with a funnel and stopcock, so as to heat the cream to the necessary temperature. The pump is worked by means of a wince, which is not so laborious as the usual churn. Independently of the happy application of science to this important department of domestic economy, in a practical point of view it is extremely valuable. The milk is not moved by a dasher, as in the common churn; but the oxygen of the atmosphere is brought into close contact with the cream, so as to effect a full combination of the butyraceous part, and to convert it all into butter. On one occasion the churning was carried on for the space of one hour and forty-five minutes, and eleven gallons of cream produced twenty-six pounds of butter.—*Newspaper paragraph.*

A PSALM OF LIFE.

WHAT THE HEART OF THE YOUNG MAN SAID TO THE PSALMIST.

TELL me not, in mournful numbers,
'Life is but an empty dream!'
For the soul is dead that slumbers,
And things are not what they seem.

Life is real! life is earnest!
And the grave is not its goal;
'Dust thou art, to dust returnest,'
Was not spoken of the soul.

Not enjoyment, and not sorrow,
Is our destined end or way;
But to act, that each to-morrow
Find us farther than to-day.

Art is long, and Time is fleeting,
And our hearts, though stout and brave,
Still, like muffled drums, are beating
Funeral marches to the grave.

In the world's broad field of battle,
In the bivouac of life,
Be not like dumb driven cattle;
Be a hero in the strife!

Trust no future, howe'er pleasant
Let the dead Past bury its dead;
Act—act in the living present;
Heart within, and God o'erhead.

Lives of great men all remind us
We can make our lives sublime,
And, departing, leave behind us
Footsteps on the sands of time.

Footprints that perhaps another,
Sailing o'er life's solemn main,
A forlorn and shipwrecked brother,
Seeing, shall take heart again.

Let us, then, be up and doing,
With a heart for any fate;
Still achieving, still pursuing,
Learn to labour and to wait.

—*Longfellow's Poems.*

THE FUNERAL SERVICE IN THE DIN OF LONDON.

The ceremony went on, the solemn sentences tuned with the music of eternal hopes, fitfully heard through cries of 'chairs to mend' and 'live mackerel.' The awful voice of Death seemed scoffed, derided by the reckless bully Life. The prayer that embalmed poor human dust for the judgment, seemed as measured gibberish that could never have a meaning for those who hurried to and fro, as though immortality dwelt in their sinews. And that staid and serious-looking man, with upturned eyes and sonorous voice, clad in a robe of white, and holding an open book, why, what was he? Surely he was playing some strange part in a piece of business in which business-men could have no interest. The ceremony is not concluded; and now comes an adventurous trader with a dromedary and a monkey on its back, the well-taught pug, with doffed feathered cap, sagaciously soliciting halfpence. And there, opposite the church-yard, the prayer of the priest coming brokenly to his ears, is a tradesman smiling at his counter, ringing the coin, and hardly snuffing the Golgotha at his door, asking what article he next shall have the happiness to show. And thus in London highways do Death and Life shoulder each other. And Life heeds not the foul impertinent warning; but, at the worst, thinks Death, when so very near, a nuisance: it is made, by familiarity, a nasty, vulgar, unhealthy thing; it is too close a neighbour to become a solemnity.—*Douglas Jerrold's Magazine.*

Published by W. and R. CHAMBERS, High Street, Edinburgh (also 98, Miller Street, Glasgow); and, with their permission, by W. S. ORR, Amen Corner, London.—Printed by BRADBURY and EVANS, Whitefriars, London.

CONDUCTED BY WILLIAM AND ROBERT CHAMBERS, EDITORS OF 'CHAMBERS'S INFORMATION FOR THE PEOPLE,' 'CHAMBERS'S EDUCATIONAL COURSE,' &c.

No. 102. NEW SERIES. SATURDAY, DECEMBER 13, 1845. PRICE 1½d

DOES TALENT GO IN THE MALE LINE?

THERE are some notions which, having perhaps been sanctioned by a favourite author, and never afterwards rigidly examined, acquire a popular currency, and may almost be said to rank as axioms. One of these is, that men of talent are always indebted for what gives them distinction to their mothers, either in the way of an inheritance of natural ability, or through the means of unusually good nurture and education. Men, it is supposed, can only be the parents of the ordinary, unless there be a mother of talent, and then it does not matter how stupid the father may be. It is a gallant and courteous idea; and one could almost wish it to be true, seeing that it appears to adjust the balance of power between the sexes. Women are excluded from political and professional situations, although often fitter for them than most men. Here, it might be thought, is a compensation for them. They may not be Gracchi; but they may be the mothers of Gracchi. They may not be Alexanders, or Napoleons, or Wellingtons; but they may be Olympiases, or Letitia Ramolinis, or Countesses of Mornington, to rejoice in the thickening laurels of their sons, as they go conquering over the earth. Alas, gentle dames, as Burns waggishly says, 'it gars me greet' to think that you have no such peculiar privilege—for this really seems to be the fact. There are noted instances, it is most true, of great men springing from clever mothers, while their fathers were of ordinary attainments; but this is not decisive of the question. If it be a rule, it should have only such a few exceptions as are expected from all rules—not as many contrary as supporting instances. I fear that it is only the result of a prepossession springing from amiable feelings, and supported by the natural love of paradox. Early dependence upon the mother makes us partial to her in judging as in feeling. Poets, who are only children in breeches, keep up the tendency by their continual ravings to the same purport. Then, when cases do occur, the unexpectedness of great and vigorous qualities from this source—as if it were too much to be looked for from the weaker vessel—completes the delusion, leading us, without more inquiry, to affirm that as invariable which is only occasional.

There is at least ample and ready evidence of men of note having had able fathers, while either nothing has been remembered of their mothers, or it is known that they were not above ordinary. Let us first look at the immediately past age: have we not, in the very highest walk of English political life, the remarkable instance of the two Pitts—so alike in commanding genius, in eloquence, and even in moral qualities, that we cannot doubt the younger to have been a reproduction of the elder. Hester Grenville, the mother of the heaven-born minister, is described as a woman of merit. A good mother, we doubt not, she was; but Pitt was 'yon gude blood o' auld Boconnock's.' Even his faults tell this. Walpole, too, we may remember, had a son whose talents, if of an essentially different order, were still such as to place him far above the common run of men. Fox also had a minister for his sire, though one who was not a favourite with the public. The passing of an identical talent from Sir William to Sir John Herschel, is another 'modern instance' on which we might expatiate, if the second of the parties were not yet, to the gratification of his countrymen, in the land of the living.

Looking across the Channel, our attention is quickly arrested by the instance of the Mirabeaus, father and son; the first an esteemed writer on financial and political subjects, the second the hero of the Revolution. Necker, too, gives us De Staël. A different and inferior talent is in the paternal position in both these instances; but still it is talent—superior intellect—descending from father to child; while the mother, as far as we know, had nothing to do with the matter. With facts of so decided a character in the opposite counsel's hands, the case for the ladies seems to have a poor chance. On the other hand, Catherine of Russia, a woman of masculine ability, if ever there was one, gives birth to—the wretched Paul! And Lady Mary Wortley Montague is the mother of an eccentric gentleman, only remarkable for whimsical conversation and wearing a beard!

Instances of poets and philosophers who have had fathers, either of decided and often kindred talent, or showing some kind of tendency to intellectual distinction, are plentifully sown over the biographical dictionaries. We see, in Pascal, the son of a father who was esteemed for his scientific and literary attainments. Tasso's father, Bernardo, had attained universal fame in Italy as a poet, before his son had begun to write; and it is only owing to there having been a second and superior Tasso, that the first is now little heard of. In our own land, the poetical gift passed from the Earl of Dorset, the first of the Elizabethan geniuses in point of time, to a great-grandson, well known as the friend of Dryden. Sacchi, the Italian painter, was the son of an artist, who taught him. The fathers of Mozart and Beethoven were both musicians: men no doubt inferior to their sons, but from whom, nevertheless, we can conceive their talents to have been derived, only experiencing a great improvement in the transmission. And this is no uncommon case among the cultivators of the fine arts. Lot fixes the man of moderate abilities in an obscure situation, perhaps below his deservings; the son, more fortunately placed, more ardent, and having some benefit from early tuition, springs forward and makes a figure before the world. The father of the celebrated Sebastian Bach was a musician, in good esteem, though not famous. Sebastian, in his turn, gave birth to two sons, both of whom were eminent in their art.

In 'the north countrie' there have been several remarkable instances of a transmission of talent through paternal channels, and that for more than one remove. An Aberdeenshire clergyman, who lived early in the seventeenth century, was the progenitor of a family of Gregories, who have ever since kept their name before the public as professional and learned men. First, there was James Gregory, inventor of the reflecting telescope, and an eminent mathematician; next, three nephews of the preceding, David, James, and Charles, all of them professors of mathematics. Then we have another member of the family, though the precise relationship is not stated—Dr John Gregory, professor of medicine in the university of Edinburgh, but best known to the world by a small book called 'A Father's Legacy to his Children.' Dr James, the son of the above, was of unapproached eminence as professor of medicine in the same university, and as a physician in our city. His son, Dr William Gregory, now flourishes in the chair of chemistry. This is a surprising series of learned men, all of one line, and there is of course no need to suppose that the talent has gone otherwise than from father to son, or at least passed in the paternal line. We have, however, a curious admission to make as to the Gregories—that the talent of the first or geometrical batch came in through the honest minister's wife, a lady named Anderson, whose paternal ancestors had been noted for mechanical ingenuity and a taste for mathematics. The anatomy-teaching Monroes are hardly less remarkable than the Gregories. Three generations of this family, bearing the same Christian name, have now possessed this chair in the Edinburgh university for a hundred and twenty-five years; and with the word Monro is associated no small portion of the distinction of our city as a medical school. Passing to literature—we see, in Mr P. F. Tytler, author of the History of Scotland, a third generation of penmen; his father having been the accomplished Lord Woodhouselee, and his grandfather the 'revered defender of beauteous Stuart.' *Vires acquirit eundo.* Allan Ramsay too, the writer of the one unapproached pastoral of the world; to him was born a son of the same name, who perhaps showed his abilities less as a painter than in the private effusions of his pen and his lively conversation, which made him the favourite of the highest literary and political circles in his time. Only two months ago did the line of the author of the Gentle Shepherd become extinct in his grandson, General John Ramsay, who was also a man of social qualities, removing him far above the mass of his fellow-creatures. In him, however, there had been an infusion from a different fountain, the clever Stormont family, his mother having been a niece of the Chief Justice Earl of Mansfield. If any feel surprised at the blood of a Scottish bard ascending to mingle with that of the Scottish nobility, he must be referred to ancient gossip for an account of a certain young painter being employed not long after the middle of the last century in teaching drawing to the children of a Sir Alexander Lindsay of Evelick, when it chanced that one of the young ladies formed a violent attachment to him, and took him, against her parents' wishes, for a husband. This, however, is a digression: to return. We may only further advert, under this head, to a singular fact which rests upon the authority of sundry sepulchral inscriptions—that the duties of master mason, or architect to the king, were performed in Scotland by eight generations of a family of Mylnes, the last of whom seems to have lived early in the eighteenth century.

'What Phidias or Apelles could have done
In brass or marble, that could he in stone,'

says the epitaph of one of them who rebuilt Holyrood Palace in the reign of Charles II. A scion of the family was the architect of Blackfriars Bridge. There might not be a high talent at work in all of these generations; but still the duties must have called for a degree of ability and taste which it is surprising to think of as persisting, without failure, throughout eight generations.

Against a host of instances so large, which yet, being only drawn from the memory of a single person, might easily be extended, it will be impossible for the theory any longer to stand.* We do not, indeed, know in all these cases that the mother was not a woman of unusual ability; but it is a good rule to be content with what explains the point which may be in question, without passing beyond that into needless surmises of other causes. The father in these cases being notedly a man of talent, ought to go far to satisfy us. We only, however, come to conclude, that abilities are derived from the father in a certain class of instances. There are doubtless many in which they come from the other parent. Thus we find the mother of Scott to have been superior to her husband. But, on the other hand, of the couple who dwelt in the clay cottage at Alloway, and there gave birth to a wonderful genius, who seems yet to have gathered but half his fame, any intellect that exceeded the ordinary, lay unquestionably with that shrewd, hard-headed old gardener, who argued so stiffly on doctrinal points; while the simple mother only tended household work. Gilbert was the mother's son; Robert belonged to his father, as far as he belonged to anybody besides Nature. Since such is the case, may it not be safest to suppose that, as children bear an external resemblance, some to one parent, and some to another, so, in cases where there is a superior intellect, it may be from either parent as it happens? To put the idea in different terms: there may be supposed to be an equal chance for its being derived from either, unless, indeed, it may have passed over an intermediate generation, and be derivable from some grandfather or grandmother.

If we admit this view, we can be at no loss to account for both men and women of ability having commonplace children. In these cases the other parent is most probably the source of the dulness. How little is this reflected on by great men! Chesterfield seems to have never doubted that his son, who was a lump of commonplace, could be made a brilliant character; and even Burke, whose lamentations for the youthful heir of his name are so touching, is understood to have greatly over-estimated the youth's abilities, and his likelihood of distinguishing himself. A Cromwell sees his name betrayed, as it were, into the possession of a spiritless changeling, who is truly the mother's child, not his, and therefore utterly disqualified for holding the reins of government after him. The ardent hero of Agincourt is nominally, and but nominally, represented by the innocent Henry VI. It were well if great men would open their eyes to the possibility of disappointments from this quarter, or only select wives who were sure not to produce simpletons. One of the last Hackstons of Rathillet became sensible of this when he found his wife's imbecility represented in an odd Tony-Lumpkinish son, at whose sallies he would sometimes observe, 'Ah, Helenus (for such was his name), ye ha'e o'er mickle mother wit.'

This is a sad attack which we are committing upon the fairer part of creation, but let them be quite at their ease. The general conviction of their being exclusively possessed of all the finer qualities of human nature, and able to transmit them to their offspring, is so rooted, that we have little hope of gaining even a fair hearing for

* The reader will find some speculations favouring the opposite view in an article entitled 'Clever Women,' which appeared in the Journal thirteen years ago (No. 36). We have since then reflected more deeply on the subject, and the present paper is the result of our deliberations.

these ideas. It will therefore remain as prevalent a notion as ever, that eminent men owe all to their mothers. As usual with pertinacious theory-mongers, who can get nobody to listen to them in their own age, we enter an appeal to Prince Posterity.

TRAVELS IN LURISTÁN AND ARABISTÁN.

CONCLUDING ARTICLE.

FROM Behbehan the Baron de Bode proceeded by slow stages to the great plain of Màl Amir, and thence over several steep shoulders of the Bakhtyari mountains by a stone pavement or causeway. This, he says, although much impaired by time, and in several places scarcely passable, on account of the huge stones which have been cast down by the rushing of torrents from the heights, produces, even in its dilapidated state, a grand idea of him, whoever he was, who conceived and executed the vast project of carrying a stone road, worked in mosaic, across stupendous mountains, which seem as if they had been formed by nature as insurmountable barriers to the traveller. This road is now, and has been for ages, the high road for caravans; but history, which in general is so prolix in commemorating events that carry devastation and destruction in their train, has set apart no page whereon to inscribe the name of the man who deserved so well of posterity. The causeway is known by the name of the *Jaddehi-Atabeg*, or the high road of the Atabegs; but the Baron de Bode doubts whether the petty chiefs of Luristán, who bore that appellation from the twelfth to the fourteenth century, had the skill or the enterprise to form or carry out a design like this, which would have done honour to imperial Rome in the days of her greatest grandeur. He is more inclined to the opinion that it was the work of some of the Susanian monarchs, or even of an earlier date, although there is no historical evidence in support of his views. We learn from the Greek and Latin writers, that the followers of Alexander the Great, in their frequent marches and countermarches through the hilly country between Susa and Persepolis, met with stone pavements in the mountains, to which they applied the name of the Climax Megale, or Great Ladder. Had Alexander himself been the constructor of these roads, his historians, who have enumerated all the cities of which he laid the foundations, would not have passed over a work of such vast dimensions, and it is therefore to be inferred that it is older than the time of that renowned conqueror; though we can scarcely agree with the Baron de Bode, unless he gives us some better reasons for our belief than he has afforded, that it was originally constructed by Chedorlaomer, king of Elam, who is mentioned in the 14th chapter of the book of Genesis.

On stopping at a ruined caravanserai in the midst of the mountains, he found great preparations going on for the reception of his friend the governor of Ispahan, who, it will be recollected, had agreed to meet him at Shushter. Here a small tent was prepared for him, and another for his attendants, on his expressing his desire to await the governor's arrival. The latter was greatly surprised to find him amongst the mountains, and especially in the company of the Bakhtyari tribes. He recollected the rendezvous he had given the baron when they parted at Ispahan, to meet again at Shushter, but imagined that, on arriving at Shiraz, the European would have been dissuaded from undertaking a further journey, on account of the uncertainty of the road. Undeceived on this point, he gave the baron some valuable information as to the route he should now pursue, and invited him to go back with him as far as the plain of Màl Amir, where he intended to make some stay, and where the chiefs of the mountains were to make some parade of their forces, both in honour of his arrival, and to show how formidable they might become if offended. To this proposal our traveller agreed, and retraced his steps accordingly.

On his return to the plain of Màl Amir, he visited several natural caves in the sides of the hills, in which he found some curious remains of antiquity. In one, he noticed two colossal figures sculptured on the wall, but nearly obliterated by the water which constantly oozes through the fissures of the rock. One of the figures was in profile, and looked towards a smaller cave, with his hands clasped, and in an attitude of adoration, and round the base of his garment was an inscription in arrow-headed characters. The other figure had a long beard ending in two curls, and a lock of hair falling down the right shoulder. Between the two figures was an inscription in the same arrow-headed characters, extending to no less than thirty-three lines, each from eight to ten feet in length, and which, it is much to be regretted, the baron had no means of deciphering. He afterwards visited several other caves, abounding in similar antiquities; and finally taking leave of his friend the governor, and the Bakhtyari chiefs, proceeded towards the ancient city of Shushter, where he arrived after an uninteresting journey of three days.

Having a letter of introduction, he proceeded to the house of the civil-governor, Aga Mahomed Ali Basha, the head of one of the principal native families of Shushter. By this personage he was received with great cordiality, and in him he recognised one whom he had known three years previously in another part of Persia. Shushter was formerly a very populous city, but suffered so greatly from the plague in 1831, and the cholera in 1832, that its population does not now exceed 5000. Another cause of its downfall has been the preference given to the neighbouring city of Dhizful as the seat of the government of the province. Its aspect, says our author, is original. The dwellings are generally two storeys high, with spacious terraces surrounded by parapets. In the interior of the courts, lofty covered passages run along the walls of the buildings. The vaulted cells of the houses are deep and capacious, and to these in the summer-time the inhabitants resort during the heat of the day. The *ark*, as the fortress of the city is called, stands apart on a rising ground, facing the river Kuren, which lower down passes under a stone bridge of forty-four arches. Shushter had in former years large cotton plantations, and furnished the raw material for numerous native looms; but since the introduction of English cotton stuffs, the cotton looms have been brought to a stand-still. The sugar-cane was also cultivated here with much success at one time, but is now entirely abandoned.

The inhabitants of Shushter have the reputation in Persia of being very quick and witty in their repartees; and as the people are of a gay, lively character, the town swarms with buffoons, dancers, musicians, and jugglers of all descriptions. It is added, that the place is not more remarkable for the wit than for the profligacy of its inhabitants; and that even in Persia, where morality is at a low ebb, Shushter is notorious for the want of it.

The baron only stayed one day in Shushter, and departed at midnight, in company with a very intelligent young Persian nobleman, who tried to keep him awake by his jokes and vivacity, but whose name he very ungratefully 'forgot to remember.' He was in the shah's military service, and had been a pupil of Colonel Stoddart; and, when he learned that the baron kept a journal of his travels, was exceedingly anxious that not only his name, but his good sayings should be recorded in it—an anxiety which makes the baron's forgetfulness the more unpardonable. The next place of any note where he stayed was Dhizful, about four hours' hard riding from which are the ruins of Shush, the ancient Susa, and, next to Persepolis, one of the most interesting spots in that interesting country. Shush is situated south-south-west from Dhizful, on the right bank of the river of the same name, and thither our traveller proceeded early on the morning after his arrival, accompanied by a guide and several attendants, all on horseback. 'Although,' says the baron, 'we went at a pretty brisk trot, we were outstripped by a turbaned old Arab, riding on a donkey at a swift amble, with a thick iron nail in his hand, with which he urged the animal forward by pricking it under the mane.' This turned out to be the mutaveli, or guardian of the tomb of the prophet Daniel, who was thus hurrying on before them to do the honours of the place, and reap the benefit. On approaching the ruins, they overtook several groups of Arab families, who were hastening in the same direction to the shrine of the prophet, to whose memory equal honour is paid by Christians, Jews, and Mahomedans. His supposed tomb, surmounted by a white conical roof, similar to the section of a honeycomb, was discernible amid a grove of palm trees as they approached. On arriving at the gate, they found the platform swarming with men, women, and children, from some neighbouring black tents, all pressing forward to enter the inner court, which was likewise full of people. The scene was highly picturesque. The white turbans, negligently twisted round the heads of the men, contrasted with their dark complexions and jet-black hair; while their broad striped *abbas* or cloaks hung loosely over their shoulders in graceful plaits. The women and girls, who appeared with their faces uncovered, wore black turbans, and were dressed in the gaudiest colours—red, yellow, and dark-blue predominating. The children ran about in red shifts, without any other apparel. The baron's appearance excited some curiosity among them, and they made no opposition to his entering the chapel where the coffin of Daniel is said to be deposited, on learning that the Christians acknowledge the holiness of his name, and admit his pretensions to the sacred character of a prophet. The tomb is of modern architecture, and bears no traces of its antiquity, with the exception of the fragments of some marble pillars, with the leaves of the lotus carved upon them. In the interior of a four-cornered cell stands the coffin, a high box of a dark sort of wood, surrounded by a grating, on which are hung several boards, inscribed with quotations from the Koran. It is stated that the natives, although ignorant of the value of, and otherwise indifferent to, the ancient monuments of their country, hold it as sacrilegious to allow them to be carried away; and the traveller noticed that they narrowly watched his movements while in the tomb of the prophet, whenever he touched any of the marble fragments which lay scattered about on the ground.

Beneath the apartment containing the coffin is a vault, the entrance into which is from the outside of the court, and is said to represent the den of lions into which Daniel was cast by the order of Darius, king of the Medes and Persians. Into this, however, the Baron de Bode did not enter.

The western wall of the edifice is close to the left shore of the Shapúr or Shôver river—the same with the Eulœus of ancient writers, and the Ulai of Scripture. It is a narrow but deep stream, with high banks, and is navigable to its junction with the Kuren river near Ahvaz. Close to the water's edge are three white marble fragments. The first is the capital of a column, with chiselled ornaments in the form of the lotus leaf; the second is a slab, with arrow-headed inscriptions; and the third is a bas-relief, representing a human figure and two lions, very roughly sculptured, and evidently intended, at some subsequent period, to commemorate the events mentioned in the book of the prophet.

The ground about Shush (which, it is to be regretted, the baron has so imperfectly described) is very uneven, and numerous mounds, called *tepehs* by the natives, are scattered in different directions to a considerable distance; some of them being partially covered with brushwood. The highest among them is supposed to be the place where the palace stood in which the prophet Daniel had his vision (Dan. viii. 2). 'And I saw in a vision, And it came to pass when I saw that I was at *Shushan* in the palace, which is in the province of *Elam*, by the river of *Ulai*.' From the top of this mound are seen the ruins of Ivani Kherk, beyond the river of Kherkeh, about five miles to the west. A column, with the ruins of Shapúr, is likewise discernible in a north-westerly direction. An oblong white slab, with inscriptions in arrow-headed characters, of thirty-three lines, like those at Mâl Amir, lies on the slope of the mound; and a few more marble fragments are found at the foot of it, nearly overgrown with grass and brushwood. Our author learned from the Arabs who accompanied him, that old coins, tombs, and blocks of marble, were often found in the adjacent country, but they could give him no particulars concerning them.

Dhizful, where the baron stayed one day on his return from Shush, is on the left bank of the river, and bears, in the general features of its architecture, a great resemblance to Shushter. A number of water-mills project far into the stream, and are built on rocks which jut across the river, and produce rapids. These little islets are united by narrow bridges; and at the approach of night, when they are all lighted up by the millers, there is a complete and very pleasing illumination. The great bridge across the river consists of twenty-two arches; and its construction is attributed by the Persians to Husheng, one of the ancient kings of the Pishdadian race, and their first legislator before Zoroaster.

For four days after leaving this town, the baron traversed a portion of country which has been described by Major Rawlinson and other travellers; but on arriving at the ruins of the ancient town of Joider, he congratulated himself on reaching a 'terra incognita'—or at least a country of which, to his knowledge, with the exception of the one town of Khorremabâd, no particular account had previously appeared. In half an hour after leaving this point, he reached, with some Ilyat guides whom he had hired to accompany him, the banks of the large river Kashgan. Ten athletic men from a neighbouring hamlet came to tender their services and show him a ford. The river at this spot presented two channels, having, nearly in the middle, a long strip of land, or narrow island. His new guides stripped off their clothes, and with loud cries of *Ya Allah!* (God help us!) soon cleared the first channel; the traveller and his train following on horseback. When they came to the second channel, they declared it impossible to cross, but after a time some of them ventured in. They soon, however, lost their footing, and were carried down the stream. The remainder of the party, by dint of perseverance, afterwards found a ford; but it was so deep, and the river was rising so rapidly—as is generally the case after noonday with streams that are fed by the melting snow in the mountains—that the whole of them prepared to swim. They disengaged themselves of the greater part of their apparel, which they tied in a bundle on their heads or backs, and with some difficulty gained the opposite shore. The baron, when the time came to remunerate these guides for their trouble, offered them some gold coin, but to his great wonder, found them totally ignorant of the value of that metal, and they preferred to take a few silver *sahib-corans*, each of less value than a shilling, which he had about him, although the recompense was greatly inferior to his first offer.

During the next three days he crossed and recrossed several times the river Kashgan, and various of its tributaries, and arrived, late in the evening of the third, at the town of Khorremabâd. This, according to Major Rawlinson, is a singular place. A range of rocky hills stretches across the plain in the usual direction of north-west and south-east, and appears to have been suddenly broken through to admit the passage of the river (of the same name as the town) for the space of about three quarters of a mile, leaving in the centre of this open space a solitary rock of about 1000 yards in circumference. This rock is very steep, and near its summit is a most copious spring. This forms the fort of Khorremabâd. It is surrounded by a double wall at the base, and the summit where the palace is built is also very strongly defended. The modern town, which is small, containing not more than a thousand houses, is built below the fort, upon its south-western face. The river, a broad shallow stream, passes to the south-east of the fort and town. The banks are covered with gardens, amongst which are to be seen the ruins of the old town, once the capital of the Atabegs of Luri-Kuchuk. The town contains four mosques, eight public baths, and has a separate quarter assigned for the Jews, the number of whose houses averages from forty to fifty. It carries on a trade in *chubuks* for pipes; in the skin of the otter, which animal abounds in the rivers of Luristán; and also a considerable traffic in the juice of the pomegranate, the produce of its gardens. On the left side of the river is a spacious garden, remarkable for its rows of splendid cypress trees, to which a superstitious belief is attached. The inhabitants imagine that every year, on a certain day (the 10th of Moharem, when the Imaum Hassan, the son of Ali, was slain), these trees are supernaturally agitated, and shake as if a violent wind were blowing, although there may not be a breath of air at the time.

From this town to Búrújird, the next place of importance, is a distance of twelve or thirteen farsangs, or from forty to forty-three miles, in a north-east direction, which it took the baron two days to accomplish. On the second day (February 22) they were in sight of the lofty chain of the Alverd mountains; and as the rain of the previous day had been followed by a heavy fall of snow, it was doubtful whether they could succeed in crossing the mountains. However, eight stout peasants were at last procured to lead the way, and, there being no road, to tread the snow under foot, and open a path for the horses. Fortunately, the weather cleared up as they were ascending; but the difficulties and fatigues they had to encounter during their progress appear to have been most severe. Notwithstanding the efforts of the men to form a beaten track, the snow was not sufficiently solid, and it was so deep, that the horses were continually sinking up to their girths. There being no possibility of riding, the party dismounted, each leading his horse. Man and beast stumbled every moment, falling, sinking, and plunging, to extricate themselves from the snow. Mountain seemed to overhang mountain as they passed, and far away the loftiest summits looked over all, clad in the white mantle of eternal winter. Though it was a chilling sight to look around, the party was far from feeling cold. The perspiration ran down their faces in consequence of their violent exertion, while columns of steam rose from the bodies of their panting horses. They arrived at last at a summit, where the guide, to their great relief, told them that the greatest difficulties had been overcome; then gradually descending into a valley, they stopped to refresh themselves at a small village called Búzihúl, in which a colony of Lurs is settled. From this place they continued their road across a secondary range of mountains, of a clayey and chalky nature, and at last descended into the plain of Búrújird, studded with villages, and having plenty of pasture-ground.

Búrújird lies out of the line of the high road, between the capital and the principal cities of Persia, and is seldom visited by European travellers. It is governed, together with the province of the same name, and the adjoining provinces of Meloir and Hamadan, by Behmen Mirza, the second brother of the reigning shah. The province contains, besides its capital, 386 villages, great and small, and pays a yearly tax of 50,304 *tomans* in cash (about L.25,000), and 3832 harvars of grain, amounting in value to 5748 tomans, or about L.2600 additional. The town is renowned for its manufactories for printed chintzes, which, although inferior in quality to those of Ispahan, are much in request all over Persia. The dyes used are chiefly the produce of the country. A red dye, for which there is a great demand, is made from the root of a plant which grows wild in the fields, called by the natives *rengi runas*, and which is sold at the rate of twopence-halfpenny a-pound, English money. Indigo is brought from Shushter, and sometimes imported from India. The yellow dye is obtained from the rind of the pomegranate, and the green from the same, mixed with indigo. Cochineal is imported by means of the Russian trade. There are fifty establishments altogether in the town for printing cotton stuffs. The greater part of the cotton is grown in the ninety-four villages of the neighbouring and rich district of Túsúrkán. The manufactories are all in the hands of private individuals, forming a powerful corporation. The yearly revenue of the crown from these, amounts to 2000 tomans, which sum is paid by a person who farms it of the government; he himself being satisfied by the manufacturers, who pay him in kind, at the rate of one piece of cloth out of every sixty they manufacture. It is a flourishing place, though out of the beaten track, and maintains an industrious and happy population.

From Búrújird the baron proceeded by easy stages to Kum, and thence to Teheran; but his travels after this point possess no feature of interest. He arrived at the latter city on the 28th of February, after an absence of sixty-seven days, of which forty-six had been spent in actual travelling, and the remaining twenty-one either in resting at Ispahan, Persepolis, and Shiraz, and examining the antiquities of those cities and their neighbourhoods, or in visiting the country around Behbehan, Màl Amìr, Shush, and Dhizful.

WORDS BORROWED FROM THE FRENCH.

FIRST ARTICLE.

The English language is a curious compound of tongues blended together with more or less harmony. We point to the Norman conquest for the infusion of many French words into the Anglo-Saxon vernacular; but this infusion did not take place at once; it was the work of centuries. So has it been with every new element in the composition. The change from rude to polished styles of speech and writing, has been exceedingly gradual, and no one can say that the language is yet by any means perfect, or that it ever will be complete. This is a fact quite in accordance with the national character, which is one of advancement and improvement. Unlike some of the continental nations, the English do not set themselves to prevent the intrusion of new or foreign words into their ordinary speech. They pick up, naturalise, and make good use of any form of expression, as they would of any fact in science, which suits their taste or necessities. Liberal and compromising, their language increases in richness and variety of terms, in the same manner as the nation and individuals increase their general resources. And thus has the English language continually extended its boundaries, and still is beneficially extending them.

It is interesting to observe how a word makes its way into our language. The people are too conservative to receive the new expression till it has run through a preliminary course, and been, we might say, rendered respectable by familiar use. Many words commence as a kind of slang, and are not for half a century perhaps found in any dictionary. Of this class *mob* and *bore* are fair examples. Mob (an abbreviation of *mobile vulgus*, 'the easily-moved vulgar'—a phrase which took its rise in Charles II.'s time) has gained a lodgment, and is now an accepted expression, which it once was not; while bore is only in the way of gaining a footing, and may not get into dictionaries for a quarter of a century. That it will gain admission into them, nobody can doubt, for it expresses an idea, and it is the genius of the people to abandon no idea that is really natural. On the same grounds many French phrases cannot escape naturalisation, especially those which express ideas for which we happen to possess no English word of an old date. A few of these it is our purpose to instance and explain.

Aide-de-camp.—The French being, historically, a great military nation, who have carried the science of war to a high point, it is natural that many of the words used by other soldiers should be borrowed from them;

just as most of our nautical terms are taken from the Dutch, at one time the greatest naval nation of Europe. The above is in most frequent use, and signifies literally a 'camp-assistant.' In the English service, a field-marshal is entitled to four aides, a lieutenant-general to two, and a major-general to one. Each general officer, with these assistants, is called a staff. The duty of an aide-de-camp is chiefly to act as a sort of messenger in conveying the orders of his principal to inferior officers, and to report what is going on in the various parts of the field to which his duties may have sent him. In the French army an adjutant is sometimes called an *aide-major*, because he assists the major in his duties. Nor in its native language is the word aide confined to military affairs; it is used in many trades and professions: thus, in the art of cookery—which the French excel in quite as much as in that of war—a *chef-de-cuisine*, or head cook, being commander-in-chief of the kitchen, has his *aides-de-cuisine* as well as the field-marshal. In like manner, the bricklayer's labourer is called an *aide-de-maçon;* and so on.

Attaché.—This is a diplomatic term, borrowed from the French from sheer necessity; for there is no English word which would so well express the office of a man who has comparatively nothing to do. An attaché is a part of the train of an ambassador; but his official duties are not very clearly defined. In the morning he occasionally does a little translation of state documents—that is, if he happen to understand sufficiently the language of the court to which he is accredited—and issues the invitations for the ambassador's balls and parties. In the evening, he goes out to diplomatic dinner-parties, to pick up floating political news. When company is received at the embassy, he waltzes with ladies whose papas or husbands are in the cabinet; or makes the fourth for a rubber of whist (which is now played in every civilised court), to oblige a minister of foreign affairs or a princess-dowager. In short, the designation of his office sufficiently expresses the lightness of his employments: he is neither a secretary to write despatches, a clerk to copy them, nor a courier to convey them. He is simply *attached* to the embassy—an ornamental appendage rather than a useful adjunct.

The word is not, however, wholly monopolised by diplomacy. It is gradually creeping into more general use. Thus, the especial admirers of a reigning beauty are called her attachés: the members of what is vulgarly termed the 'tail' of a popular member of parliament, are also occasionally designated by the more refined word attachés. These, with many other applications of French words, were ingrafted upon our language during the fashionable novel mania which raged so fiercely about twenty years since. In those books, some of the characters were made to converse in a sort of slip-slop polyglot, consisting chiefly of slovenly English, bad French, and worse Italian. Some of the French words, however, managed to retain their hold.

Au-fait.—'Quite acquainted with the subject in hand.' The vulgar idiom, being 'up to' the facts connected with various matters, is the best equivalent to *au-fait* we could instance.

Badinage is a delicate modification of our word 'raillery,' and means a sort of half-earnest jesting. As established in that sense, it is a good word, for it expresses a meaning, for which we have no exact equivalent. Badinage is of early adoption, for we find it in Cole's dictionary, published two centuries ago; but at first it was employed to express mere 'foolery.' Lord Chesterfield, however, gave it its true application in one of his letters—'When you find your antagonist beginning to grow warm,' he says, 'put an end to the dispute by some genteel *badinage.*' The French employ the term in many senses collateral to the above. We can think of no better illustration of the sportive way in which they use it, than the proverb, *Le marriage n'est pas un badinage;* which is a truth conveyed in a pleasing bit of irony; namely, 'Marriage is no joke.'

Bagatelle has been naturalised in England for at least a couple of centuries and a half, and means a trifle. Howell, in his 'Instructions for Foreign Travel' (1610), remarks, that 'the nuns will entertain discourse till one be weary, if he bestow on them some small *bagatels;* as English gloves, or knives, or ribbons.' Jeremy Taylor uses the word in 'Artificial Handsomeness,' but spells it *bagatelloes*, and makes it mean toys. Since the time of these writers, the term has gained popularity, and is made so completely English, that Dr Johnson gives it a place in his dictionary, with the definition—'A thing of no importance.' Besides this general signification, the word 'bagatelle' is specifically applied to an effectual mode of trifling away time, by thrusting, with a mace or wand, a few ivory balls into holes indented in a small table lined with green baize. The game is, in fact, a puerile modification of billiards. The French use of the word is in all respects the same as ours, with this addition, that they sometimes utter 'bagatelle!' interjectionally upon such occasions as when an elderly English gentleman would say, 'Poo, poo! nonsense!' or a more impatient one—'Pshaw!'

Beau.—'Handsome, graceful,' says Boyer; from which signification we derive '*beau*tiful;' but to the borrowed monosyllable we give a slightly derisive tinge. A beau, writes Dr Johnson, 'is a man of dress—a man whose great care is to deck his person.' He is, in fact, an elegant dandy. What, however, is unworthy of a man's too exclusive attention—such as adorning his person—is quite proper and necessary for a woman to cultivate; hence *belle*, the feminine of beau, does not carry with it the smallest implication of dispraise. It is indeed rather a complimentary term, signifying a gracefully-fashionable young lady. *Beau* is frequently compounded with other French words for various purposes. *Beau-monde* is applied to the fashionable world. *Beau-idéal*, 'the standard of the ideal,' expresses the height of conceivable perfection. The French compound it to designate marriage relationships—as *beau-fils*, 'son-in-law;' *beau-frère*, 'brother-in-law;' *beau-père*, 'father-in-law;' in which respect they are imitated by the Scotch, who say 'good-son,' 'good-mother,' &c.

Billets-doux are those tender effusions of which so many are penned during courtship. The words, literally rendered, mean a 'sweet letter' or note, and has been in fashionable use since the reign of Charles II., whose court—so famous for such missives—probably imported it. Pope was the first to make it classical, by introducing it in his 'Rape of the Lock.' The heroine is awoke by her lap-dog, after Ariel's warning of the impending evil—

> 'Twas then Belinda, if report speak true,
> Thy eyes first opened on a *billet-doux.*'

Valentines come under the denomination of billets-doux; and on the 14th of every February, some hundred-thousand sheets of soft nonsense pass through the post-office of Great Britain. That courtship as well as more tangible things should contribute its quota to the revenue by means of billets-doux, may seem unromantic, but it is nevertheless true.

Blasé is the preterite of the verb *blaser* (to surfeit), and is said of a shattered beau, who has, from excessive indulgence, lost all relish for pleasure, or even for existence. It is a modern introduction, having gained additional currency from a clever and popular farce, which points a good moral. The hero, whose every sense of enjoyment is worn out, meets with an adventure which, to save his life, demands the utmost activity. He is obliged to fly his home, and take shelter in the country. For the sake of disguise, he hires himself as a farm-labourer—he ploughs, thrashes, and drives carts; and, though the work is hard, finds it far more agreeable than his former indolence. When the danger he apprehended is over, he continues an active life, as the more preferable to that of *blasé* inanity.

Bon-gré.—'With a good grace; willingly'—of which *mal-gré* is the antithesis. We often borrow both expressions, and say that so-and-so has been obliged to do something *bon-gré, mal-gré*—'whether he would or not.'

Bon-mot is literally a 'good word;' but the adjective being used in the sense of 'clever,' the expression is applied to a 'smart saying,' with a dash of satire in it. At least this is the idea the French have of their own word. The author of the volume of '*Ana*,' belonging to the 'Encyclopédie Française,' defines it, we must think, a little harshly, when he says that 'a *bon-mot*—(good word) ought perhaps to be designated (*mot-malin*—(bad word); for it sometimes consists in giving a ridiculous aspect to a praiseworthy motive.' The same hostility to professed jokers must have suggested the proverb, '*Diseur de bons-mots, mauvais caractère*'—(Utterer of bon-mots—bad character); and also the notion, that '*Ils aiment mieux perdre un ami qu'un bon-mot*'—Such people 'would rather lose their friend than their joke.'

The word *bon-mot* has been received into the English language for at least two centuries, as Lord Chesterfield's use of it implies. He tells his son, with his usual good sense, that 'the jokes, *bons-mots*, and little adventures which may do very well in one company, will seem flat and tedious when related in another.' The signification we give to it would scarcely justify any of the severities with which it is visited in the above examples from the French. Bon-mot is used in English to imply simply a saying sufficiently apt and ready to be humorous without being witty; and which may or may not be satirical. We should place it, in the scale of meaning, between the puerility of a pun, and the brightness of a piece of wit. Other expressions have been borrowed from the French to express nicer shades of the same meaning: a *jeu-de-mot* partakes more of the character of a pun: a *jeu-d'esprit* is something vivacious and lively merely. *A double entendre* is an expression to which two meanings may be attached.

Bonne-bouche.—Something 'good' for the 'mouth'—a tit-bit.

Brochure.—'A stitched book;' from the verb *brocher* (to stitch). *All* books, it must be admitted, are stitched; but some are bound also; hence *brochure*, designating those which are stitched only, is the borrowed appellative for a pamphlet.

Brusque is one of those words which has been adopted into our language to take the place of its exact equivalent, for the purpose of conveying a more softened meaning. The French employ it when we should say of a man that he is 'blunt,' or of a woman that she is 'pert;' but we soften the harshness of our censure by using a foreign word, and applying the term '*brusque*.' Our forefathers Anglicised it, as appears from Sir H. Wotton's Letters, wherein he says, 'We are sorry to hear that the Scottish gentleman who has been lately sent to the king found, as they say, but a *brusk* welcome.'

Chef-d'œuvre.—The chief work, a master-piece.

Ci-devant.—'Formerly.' We apply this word very nearly in the same manner as the prefix *ex* is used. Of a minister who has resigned, or an army captain who has sold out, we say the one is an ex-minister, and the other a *ci-devant* captain.

Chaperon.—New customs require new words to designate them, and as the duties of a 'chaperon' were never so systematically defined or performed as they have been during the present century, the above very expressive word was adopted. The history of this adoption is somewhat curious. Literally, a chaperon is a hood, and was confined for a long time to the head-dress worn by the knights of the Garter, and to the masks of headsmen, as described in Howell's Letters, thus:—'The executioner stands by, his head covered with a *chaperon*, out of which there are but two holes, to look through.' Some years later, we find the term cited with a similar meaning to that we now attach to it. 'Chaperon,' says Todd, 'denotes a gentleman attending a lady in a public assembly;' whilst Boyer affords us, in very plain terms, its present signification. According to him, a chaperon is 'an elderly person who accompanies a young female, for decency's sake.' Thus, then, arises the word;—*Chaperon* is a hood; *chaperonner* (see Boyer) is to 'hoodwink;' hence we derive the name of a fashionable female character whose business or pleasure it is to take timid young ladies under her wing, and introduce them into society; to act, in short, as a hood; to hide their blushes, and to conceal their little defects from admirers by a species of clever hoodwinking. The old-fashioned term for these useful ladies was 'match-makers.'

In giving the etymological history of this expression, we are of course bound unswervingly to the truth; but we must hasten to add, that the uncomplimentary impression it conveys is not quite correct as to chaperons of the present day. They are important members of society, as a short explanation of their utility will prove. The natural chaperon of every young lady is of course her own mamma; but it may occur that, when the time comes for the damsel to make her *debut* in the world, her lady-mother may be indisposed, or have withdrawn herself from society altogether. In that case, a friend (generally one who has been successful in forming good alliances for her own daughters) is selected to take charge of the young belle. The chaperon's first step is to have the debutante's name engraved under her own on her visiting cards, and to take her on all her visits. She also introduces her at court, at Almacks, and at all the fashionable parties. Should, in process of time, an approach to a preference be shown by any gentleman, the chaperon inquires into his character and pretensions, and advises the young lady how to act. If everything prove favourable, the chaperon negotiates the preliminaries, provides the wedding breakfast, and performs the last duty of her office by supporting and comforting the bride during the interesting and trying ceremony; laying down her office on the steps of the hymeneal altar.

Congé.—'Leave,' permission to retire, a polite loan from the French, always applied to leave-taking; which, however, has been so long in use, that custom has made it almost English. Indeed some of our old writers, especially Burton (Anatomy of Melancholy), has Anglicised it by spelling the word *congie*. Spenser writes it (Faery Queen) in its Gallic form—

> 'So courteous, *congé*, both did give and take,
> With right hands plighted, pledges of good will.'

Shakspeare turns it into a verb in 'As You Like It.' Among the 'sixteen businesses' which Bertram boasts of having despatched in one evening, he says, 'I have *congeed* with the duke, and done my adieux with his nearest.'

Besides its literary use, the word occurs in ecclesiastical law, with many others introduced into our jurisprudence by the Normans. *Congé d'elire* (leave to elect), is the permission of the crown forwarded to a dean and chapter to choose a bishop. The king was formerly patron of all bishoprics, and chose whomsoever he pleased; but in process of time the election was made over to others, under certain forms and conditions, one of which was, that they should ask the king's leave or *congé* to elect the prelate they had selected. The whole ceremony is at present a mere form; for the real patrons are the ministry for the time being in power. Addison, in the 475th Spectator, makes a playful application of the phrase in the case of people asking leave to do a thing which they have already resolved upon doing at all events. 'A woman,' he says, 'when she has made her own choice, for form's sake sends a *congé d'elire* to her friends.'

In common conversation, the word *congé* has never been wholly out of use. It is employed in the passive voice in the case of a treasury clerk or a lover when they are dismissed. They are said to have had their *congé*. In the active voice, a person, on going away, is said to have made his *congé*. In paying visits, the leave-taker inscribes in the corner of his address-card the letters P. P. C.; an abbreviation of the words *pour prendre congé*, signifying that he has called 'to take leave.'

Cortège.—A train of attendants either on foot or in

coaches (for if on horseback, the term 'cavalcade' is substituted). It is much used by the court-newsman in his descriptions of the movements of royalty.

Coup.—There is scarcely a word in the French language which does such severe duty as *coup*. In the dictionary of the Academie, two closely-printed columns give its meanings, and examples of its varied use. The primary signification is a 'blow;' but this is so extended, as to make it mean any sort of sudden action, especially when compounded with other words. So many of these compound expressions have we borrowed from our neighbours, that on the present occasion only a list of the more popular can be given. *Coup-d'eclat*, a stroke of cleverness; *coup-d'essai*, a trial stroke, a first attempt; *coup-d'état*, a piece of state policy; *coup-de-grace*, the finishing stroke; *coup-de-main*, a stroke of the hand, applied mostly to military exploits of a desperate character, but otherwise to anything done with promptitude and vigour; *coup-de-maître*, a master-stroke; *coup-d'œil*, a stroke of the eye, a rapid glance; *coup-de-plume*, a dash of the pen; *coup-de-soleil*, a stroke of the sun; *coup-de-théâtre*, a clap-trap. One of the most successful *coups-de-théâtre* on record was performed by Mr Burke during the debate on the Alien bill in 1792. He declared that three thousand daggers were being, at the moment he was speaking, manufactured for certain aliens, who were connected with the French Revolution, then fiercely raging. In the midst of his fiery peroration he suddenly plucked one of the daggers from under his coat, and threw it on the floor of the house. 'These,' he exclaimed, 'are the presents designed for you! By these are freedom and fraternity to be propagated! But may Heaven avert such principles from our minds, and such daggers from our hearts!' The effect thus produced on the minds of the auditors was seldom surpassed; yet the orator must have previously obtained the dagger and secreted it about his person, for the purpose of giving an extrinsic effect to his arguments. It was indeed a genuine clap-trap, or, in more polite parlance, a *coup-de-théâtre*.

Crochet.—The diminutive of *croc*, a hook. This word has recently come much into use, in consequence of the universal knitting, knotting, and embroidery practised by the fair sex as an amusing occupation. Some kinds of this pastime are performed by means of a small hook, by which the loops of network are pulled through each other; hence called *crochet*, pronounced in the French style. From this term we derive crotchet, a crooked fancy or whim, and one of the characters of musical notation which formerly terminated in a small hook.

DOMESTIC ERAS.

A CERTAIN cashier in a London merchant's office was for forty years so punctual in the discharge of his daily duties, that the monotony of his life was only relieved by a single circumstance:—When the principal became lord mayor, the cashier was appointed his lordship's private secretary. From that wonderful year the formal clerk reckoned all the other events of his existence. He did not, for example, date his marriage, and the birth of his children, from certificates and parish registers, but according as those little circumstances took place before or after the great era. It was the same with public events. Inquire of him when the capture of Seringapatam took place, and he would tell you that it occurred so many years before he had the honour of being intrusted with the confidence of the great civic functionary. Ask him about the battle of Waterloo, and he would give you its date as so many years after it was his privilege to act as private secretary to the lord mayor. If, therefore, his biography were to be written, it would contain exactly one remarkable event.

The majority of families have their monotony broken by the occurrence of little out-of-the-way events of a like nature. Accidents or unforeseen haps, in themselves trifling, are, by the force of mere contrast, magnified into great epochs in the smooth current of parlour existence, and serve to fix the chronology of lesser events, just as effectually as the Olympic games regulated the Greek calendar, and the Hejira that of the Mahommedans. These waves in the straight line of domestic routine, are to a quiet household what the battle of Bunker's Hill is to the annals of the United States, or the last earthquake to the history of Lisbon. My late revered aunt, for instance, sole keeper of a christening bowl which had remained in our family for ages, and which it was my childish misfortune to shiver, made that catastrophe her register to the day of her death: it was her Hejira—her earthquake. When at a loss for a date, the fracture of the china fixed it. If you asked her when I was born, she would answer, so many years before the porcelain went to pieces: inquire when my brother went to India, and she replied, so many years after. When young, and living a life of excitement, I used to smile at my aunt's china calendar; but now that I am old, and exist in a scarcely varying round of domestic sameness, I feel the use of such insignificant resting-places for the memory. My chronology, therefore, is chiefly confined to the glorious call-dinner I gave when donning my wig and gown (the only professional event of my life, for I never had a brief); the publication of my first book; my marriage; and lastly, the birth of my eldest boy—for, since his advent, births have become ordinary instead of remarkable events.

Of late years things have gone on with little variation. The dismissal of a cook, the hiring of a new nursery governess, my son's launch into the world as an articled clerk, and my eldest daughter's departure to finish her education in Paris, have been the chief events in the history of Clover Hall for the last dozen years; but a small circumstance which has recently happened has worked a great change. The last remarkable event was the return of my daughter Clotilda from France. When Clotilda departed she was a girl; she has returned a woman. From a theoretical education, she has entered upon a practical one. This is our last remarkable event; for by it the whole of our domestic arrangements have been more or less unsettled.

Mrs Johnson, having retired from active service, has resigned the commissariat and *ménage* of our household to Clotilda. I regret to mention that the young lady's arithmetic has been found sadly deficient. The tradesmen's accounts sometimes show that twice two sovereigns make fifty shillings, and that tea is five guineas a pound. Punctuality has also fled our roof. The dinner-bell, which has so regularly drowned the sound of the clock whilst striking five, never rings now two days running within the same half-hour. The truth is, that (may I say?), unfortunately, Miss Johnson is an accomplished young lady. She is a very average pianoforte player, and sings Italian scenas whenever people are patient enough to listen. She is comely too. Mrs Johnson's expression for her is, 'a lovely girl;' and I must so far agree with her as to say, that when the child departed for Paris, she was a decided improvement on her mother at her age. Her return, alas! threatens to be our great era: when at a loss for a date, every one in the house, from the errand-boy upwards, refreshes his memory by saying such and such a thing happened so many days, or so many months, before or after Miss Clotilda came back from Paris. I have ceased to buy almanacs; for my family takes no note of time, except as it bears reference to my daughter's French expedition.

But it is not families and lord mayors' secretaries only who date by remarkable events. Professional people have also their time-marks. The lawyer dates by the great causes which have happened in his time. When Mr Latitat of Lincoln's Inn is at fault for a date, he gets at it by referring to the various stages of the great Small and Attwood cause. As the action of Peebles against Plainstanes was the almanac of the plaintiff, so the celebrated Douglas case serves as a whet to the memory of the Scottish writer.—The medical man dates by the bad celebrity of a great pestilence, and helps out his recollection by references to the 'cholera year,' or the 'fever season.'—The amateur of the turf keeps a regular racing calendar in his head, and gauges the minor events of his life—such as the breaking of his arm, his marriage, or succession to his property—by the winners of the Derby stakes at Epsom. Of the lesser occurrences he will say, they happened in the 'Bloomsbury' year, or the 'Little-Wonder' year, or the 'Mazeppa' year.—Collegians also have a similar sort of chronology. They date by their examinations—by their 'little goes' or their 'great goes,' or by their matriculation. Thus, if asked when Mr Little or Mr Scamper took his degree, they will reply, 'Oh, he went up in my year.' Or if asked when a gentleman first entered the university, they reverse it, and say, 'He came down in my year.'

An amusing instance of this kind of help to memory existed in a certain opulent knight of the city of London, who took a pride in having risen from low estate by unaided industry and perseverance, and who occasionally shocked his less unassuming wife and daughters by dating his little stories by the four remarkable events of his life. Reminiscences of juvenile pranks he would commence thus: 'When I went as an errand-boy in Clerkenwell,' so and so happened; or, 'When I was put apprentice in Bowling-green Lane,' I did such a thing. Anecdotes of his middle life often had this beginning —'A year or two after I set up for myself in Jerusalem Passage;' while his stories of more mature years commenced with, 'A month after I was knighted at St James's Palace.' Besides these four occurrences, no other markings of time does he appear to have heeded. A similar instance is recorded of Napoleon. When he was dining with the many crowned heads who were brought under his thrall at Leipsic, he had the bad taste to humble them (it is said purposely), by fixing the chronology of an anecdote with, 'When I was a sous-lieutenant of artillery.' Many events so truly remarkable had occurred since he held that humble rank, that it has been urged he might have selected one of a more noble and elevated character instead. But it is a nice question whether he did not, in looking back and recalling the feelings with which he received his lieutenant's commission, estimate it at the moment as one of the most impressive, and therefore remarkable events of his brilliant career.

LIEUTENANT WAGHORN AND THE NEW LAND ROUTE FROM INDIA.

When a mere man of letters of the present day bethinks him of arraying the spirits of the age before the public eye, he selects a number of poets and tale-writers, some of whom, perhaps, have hardly been heard of beyond the set amongst which they are worshipped. The true spirits of the age are not writers at all, or at least are not spirits of the age, by reason of their being writers. They are the men who take a lead in operations calculated to bring about great social changes—such men as Stephenson, Hudson, Cobden, or the subject of this sketch. We learn from an interesting article in the *Pictorial Times*, that Mr Waghorn passed his earlier years of manhood as an officer in the service of the East India Company, in which capacity he took part in many desperate battles, and got some severe wounds, but only with the effect of hardening him to the ardent enterprises in which he has since been engaged. Having several times had to pass from India to England, and back, when it was a four-months' voyage, his impetuous nature felt keenly this loss of time, and he resolved to effect the means of a quicker transit. It cost him seven years to bring this to bear, and a full recital of his difficulties would form a most interesting narrative.

'At the outset,' says our authority, 'his attention was directed to an extraordinary man—whose natural talents are such, that in other circumstances they might have made him the Napoleon of his age—who had accumulated a large amount of wealth and power, who had built up an army and a fleet at a vast expense, and who might, had he pleased, have interposed stupendous obstacles to the accomplishment of Lieutenant Waghorn's design. This man was Mohammed Ali, the pasha of Egypt, whose character and position would have extinguished all hope of success in a mind less determined than that which was now absorbed in contemplating a mighty work, and inflexibly determined on its achievement. He entered the service of the pasha, conciliated his esteem, secured his confidence, and then—knowing that none could cross the desert from Suez to Alexandria, a distance of between seventy and eighty miles of sandy waste, without being friendly with the Arab tribes—he proposed to Mohammed Ali the hitherto impracticable task of establishing commercial relations with the freebooters of the wilderness, the wild descendants of Ishmael.

'The appeal was successful. Lieutenant Waghorn was appointed by the sagacious ruler of Egypt his secret emissary to the Arabs, and to that people he went, without a single attendant. Among them he lived three years, and in the course of that time exerted so much influence upon them, as to induce them to exercise forbearance, and to treat that mysterious thing, a letter, with due respect.

'His next step was to prevail upon Mohammed Ali to open a house of agency in Suez, which, being situated at the northern extremity of the gulf of its own name, which is also at the north-west angle of the Red Sea, would be of great importance as an outpost on the proposed route. Caravanseras were then to be established at different spots in the desert; and in this project also he was successful. Lieutenant Waghorn subsequently built a house at Cairo, to be employed as an outpost. This town is the modern capital of Egypt, and the second city of the Mahommedan world; and being near the eastern bank of the Nile, and containing a large population, it was of great moment to have a station here. Alexandria also being a town of great importance, it was necessary that another should be constructed there; which was accordingly done. Most complete were all these arrangements; and, after a while, Lieutenant Waghorn had the high gratification of conducting the late Earl of Munster and a party of officers by the new route across the desert, by way of the Red Sea, and through France, direct from Bombay. Various improvements in the means thus employed were gradually effected; and so permanent were the advantages secured to the parties immediately concerned, that it became a matter of interest with them to secure their continuance. Mohammed Ali learned so much from what had been accomplished, that every existing facility was continued even during the war between Great Britain and the pasha. A slight notice of his generosity at that time must not be omitted. During the attack on the castle of Gebail, on the night of the 12th of September 1840, and in the midst of the firing, a white flag being seen hoisted in the town, hostile proceedings were instantly suspended; but on the boat's reaching the shore, the Indian mail, which had arrived by way of Bagdad, was handed to the officer, with "Suleiman Pasha's compliments to Admiral Stopford." The latter, on his part, immediately forwarded a warm letter of thanks to the pasha, and accompanied it with a package of foreign wine, which had been seized in an Egyptian vessel directed to Suleiman. This interchange of courtesies being ended, firing was at once resumed, and the result is well known. For the feeling thus displayed during this arduous war, Mohammed Ali afterwards received an honourable tribute from the merchants of Britain, who justly felt that conduct so unexampled deserved its prompt and hearty approbation.'

The result, in short, of Mr Waghorn's exertions was the establishment of a communication from India, by Egypt and Marseilles, to England, occupying about thirty-five days. Such at least was the route used for letters, and available for travellers also, unless they preferred, for cheapness, to take the steamer by Gibraltar. It was unlucky, in this arrangement, that the route passed through France, for the French, animated by hostile feelings towards England, clogged that passage with as many difficulties and humiliations as possible. Indignant at the vexations thus experienced, Lieutenant Waghorn lately determined to try if it was possible to find another and equally convenient line of transit across the continent. Convinced that such a course was practicable, he communicated his ideas to many, but received no assistance in carrying them out. The British government was unable to entertain it, from the diplomatic difficulties which invariably occur in moving the complicated political machine for such an object. Many persons, indeed, denounced the project as wild and absolutely impracticable.

To pursue the intelligent narrative in the *Pictorial Times*—'Nothing was more clear to the eagle eye of Lieutenant Waghorn, than that it was very desirable to effect the transit without touching on the French territory, and that there would be an actual saving of 240 miles by way of Trieste over that of Marseilles. The former is the principal seaport town of the Austrian empire, and is situated near the north-eastern extremity of the Adriatic Sea. The depth of water is such, that ships of 300 tons burden can lie close to the quays, those of greater size being moored in front of the city. Lieutenant Waghorn considered, too, that the saving of a mile, or the gaining of a minute, in so great an enterprise, was of the utmost importance; and on the accomplishment of it in the shortest possible time he set his heart. That great and petty governments might thwart or retard his movements, he did not forget; but, with fixedness of purpose, he communicated with them, and, as the result, succeeded in allaying their prejudices, dispelling their fears, and stimulating their hopes of great and ultimate advantage. Two years have been spent in these arrangements, and he has just been permitted to reap their first and most gratifying fruits.'

The requisite preparations having been made, Mr Waghorn sailed for Alexandria to receive the mail, which started from Bombay on the first of October. This was brought, as usual, by steamer to Suez, by Arab couriers across the desert to Cairo, and thence up the Nile and canal by steamers to Alexandria. Off this place Mr Waghorn awaited the mail in the Austrian steamer 'Imperatore;' and it was placed in his hands on the twentieth day of its transit from Bombay. The steamer instantly made off across the Mediterranean, where it encountered extremely rough weather and head winds: nevertheless, in six days and thirteen hours it reached the head of the Adriatic, and ran into Dwino, fifteen miles nearer to London than Trieste, which had been his first destination. The whole European continent was now before the lieutenant, and he hastened to begin his journey across it. We learn from the *London Illustrated News*, in which an accurate sketch of his route is published, that, making his way from Dwino through Inspruck, Ulm, and Burchall by post-chaise, thence to Manheim by railway, and from the latter place to Bergen by steamer down the Rhine—where an accident prevented him from continuing his voyage—he landed and posted to Cologne, and went on to Ostend by railway. Here the 'Herne' steamer waited to convey him to Dover; and he arrived in London by railway, after one of the most rapid journeys ever made across Europe. It occupied, despite delays and accidents, only ninety-nine hours and forty-five minutes.

On the 1st of October another mail was despatched from Bombay, with extra speed, by the route *via* Marseilles, to see which would arrive in London first. That was anticipated by Mr Waghorn by *two days*, thus proving the superiority of the German over the French route. He is of opinion that he shall be able, in his next attempt, to complete the same journey in twenty-five days; and, with less than two years' experience, despatches will be in London on the twenty-first day from Bombay.

This new route will be an extremely useful variation from the French one. It secures an overland transit to India in the event of anything occurring to interrupt that by way of Marseilles; besides giving travellers their choice as to scenery, and the countries they would wish to get a glimpse of. As it will be much to the interests of the various states which the road passes, they will doubtless alter their passport system, so as to do away with the necessity of a separate document for each frontier, and will in all probability combine their ambassadors' and agents' signatures on one passport, for the special accommodation of each traveller intending to go to India. Still, the new route could never wholly supersede the Indian traffic through France. The truth is, there are some natural difficulties of an important kind attending the German route. The experiment tried by Mr Waghorn during the fine season, will be far more difficult during mid-winter. The storms so frequent in the Adriatic, and the snows which cover the roads of Germany, will present impediments to the progress of the mails which they do not encounter in their passage through France; besides, at no very remote period, the railway between Marseilles and Calais will greatly shorten the distance. For these reasons, no very speedy change in the bulk of the communication with India is to be anticipated, since the new road opened by Mr Waghorn is only available when the state of the sea and the fine season combine to insure success.

The new triumph of rapidity in travel is entirely accomplished by private enterprise. The proprietors of the Times newspaper supplied the pecuniary means, and Lieutenant Waghorn did the rest. It may seem anomalous at first sight that an undertaking so purely national should be left to individuals to carry out, and not be prosecuted by government; but it is one of the blessings of this nation that an adequate elasticity is given to individual enterprise; for without it, the greatest undertakings could not be accomplished. Had, for instance, the cumbrous machinery of state been set to work some dozen years ago—when Mr Waghorn commenced his negotiations with Mohammed Ali—it is probable the route would not have been opened yet. To preserve peaceful diplomatic relations with foreign powers, the utmost caution is required in state negotiations: there must be preliminaries, protocols, and stipulations out of number, before the wished-for 'ratification' is effected; whilst to have brought the mail through France, a separate treaty would have been required. Whereas the English private gentleman, in the person of Mr Waghorn, was enabled to make his own bargains and his own stipulations, without involving his native government any further than if he were a person travelling, and hiring post horses or dromedaries for his own pleasure. Again, in the present instance, had government taken the new route in hand, complicated negotiations demanded by state policy would have been opened with Austria, Switzerland, Bavaria, Wirtemberg, Nassau, and Prussia, and the Foreign Office would have occupied several years in accomplishing what the irresponsible Mr Waghorn managed in two. In this case, therefore, the advantage of the *laisser-faire* principle, so extensively adopted by the British government, is fully illustrated.

We are happy to see that a testimonial is in progress to Mr Waghorn, to enable the public to mark their grateful sense of the eminent services of, without doubt, the most rapid and *useful* traveller of modern times.

THE GOVERNMENT SCHOOLS OF DESIGN.

Among the educational measures which have from time to time received the sanction and support of the government, may be instanced, as not the least important, the Schools of Design, which have been for some years in active operation, imparting 'the best instruction at the smallest amount of payment.' From the central school at Somerset House, an annual report of the managing council is issued, giving a general account of the proceedings of each school, the progress of the pupils, financial statements, and other matters worthy consideration. We shall avail ourselves of the third and fourth reports, embracing a period of time from May 1843 to June of the present year, to bring the position and prospects of these useful institutions before the readers of the Journal.

The school at Somerset House was 'originally established as a school of design in ornamental art, for the special purpose of teaching its application to manufactures;' and a systematic plan of instruction was adopted, by which the students were divided into elementary drawing, and other classes, having reference to the particular objects of their studies. A certain position in the school is assigned to them on entrance, from which they work gradually onwards, commencing with elementary drawing in outline, which they are not permitted to leave until they can draw with correctness; the next step is to the class for shading, at first from the flat, so as to educe skill in the use of the chalk; after which they pass to drawing from casts, modelling, the study of colour, chiaro oscuro, water colours, and painting from nature; to this succeeds drawing the figure, perspective; and the highest class, in which is acquired a knowledge of 'the history, principles, and practice of ornamental design, and its application to the various processes of manufacture, including the study of oil, tempera, fresco, encaustic, or wax painting; and the practice of the various branches of decorative art.'

This, it will be acknowledged, opens a valuable course of study, which, it is gratifying to observe, is not confined exclusively to the male sex; for female schools, conducted by ladies, under the general supervision of the director appointed by the council, exist as parts of the central and provincial establishments; thus offering to the gentler sex an advantage which, in their present want of profitable occupation, promises to be important and elevating.

The fees of admission to the central school are four shillings per month for the morning classes, and two shillings per month for the evening; the hours of attendance being, for five days in the week, from ten till three in the one case, and from half past six until nine P.M. in the other; thus giving those whose occupations prevent their attendance in the day, an opportunity of doing so after working hours. The fees at the branch school in Spitalfields are just half of those paid respectively at the central establishment for the same period of study; and the subscription to the female school is not more than two shillings monthly, for which their course of instruction includes, in connexion with that already detailed, 'the practice of pattern drawing and designing, for those branches of industry which are most suited to the pursuits of females—such as lace, embroidery, &c.; and instruction in drawing on wood, for the purpose of engraving, cross-hatched lithography; porcelain painting, and other kinds of ornamental work, in the execution of which they may be advantageously employed.'

In order to secure as far as possible the legitimate ends for which the schools were established, 'candidates for admission are required to be recommended by two respectable individuals, and are expected to leave with their application one or more drawings, as specimens of their ability.' Blank forms of certificate may always be had if applied for, which, when filled up, and properly signed, must distinctly state 'the present and proposed occupation of the applicant.' No pupil under the age of twelve is admitted; and we find from the table in the third report, that the whole number of students in the central school in 1843-4, comprehended, from 12 to 15 years, 40; 15 to 20 years, 189; and 46 above the latter age; while the attendance showed an average monthly increase of 48 over the preceding year, with a proportionate increase in the amount received for fees. The report for the present year proves 'that schools of design, as the means of attaining improvement in the productions of ornamental art in this country, are very highly estimated throughout our commercial communities; and that there appears to exist in the minds of all who are most competent to judge, and most interested in the prosperity of our national manufactures, a decided conviction of the practical importance of continuing and extending the instruction which it is the object of schools of design to impart'—there being an average monthly increase of 33 in the attendance throughout the year, with a corresponding augmentation of the total amount of subscriptions. Of these students, 31 are from the age of 12 to 15; 159 from 15 to 20; 104 from 20 to 25; 24 from 25 to 30; 12 from 30 to 35. It will thus be seen that the largest attendance is among the young, from whom, their habits being yet unformed, the most is to be hoped.

The occupations of the pupils are given in a tabular statement, from which we learn that twenty-three are arabesque painters and decorators, nine cabinetmakers, twenty-three ornamental wood-carvers, twenty-two architects, eight joiners, four carpenters, three upholsterers, fifteen copperplate engravers, seven builders, nine clerks, five wood engravers, eighteen designers for manufactures; of weavers, watchmakers, smiths, surveyors, and engineers, one each. These are but a few of the whole number, of which forty-four come under the head of 'occupation undetermined.' It is expressed in the fourth of the printed rules, that 'no student be admitted who is studying fine art solely for the purpose of being a painter or sculptor;' and we are further informed that, 'in opening national schools of design for the almost gratuitous instruction of the industrial classes, it was by no means intended to afford accommodation to such as seek only to acquire a little knowledge of fine art as a mere educational accomplishment.' These regulations, though open to evasion, must have the effect of confining the instructions more particularly to the large class for whom they are specially intended, and lead to the creation of a numerous body of ornamentists, who may be able to place British art in a position of high excellence.

The pupils are expected to provide themselves with the requisite drawing materials at their own expense; but this is compensated for by the free use of a library connected with the schools being afforded to them; of which we read, that 'the utility of small lending libraries, in educating ornamentists, is found to be highly appreciated in all the schools established by the council; and this appreciation appears to proceed from considering that such education implies considerable development, cultivation, and training of the mental powers, as well as mechanical exercise of the hand and eye; for, although the ornamentist is to be educated not to write, but to work, he is required to work intelligently; the degree of excellence of that which his hand executes being dependent on a correspondent superiority of his suggestive and thinking faculties.' This object is further effected by access to the works of arts contained in the schools: among them are 'casts of the most important Greek sculptures; busts, masks, and portions of statues; examples of alto and basso-relievo from Greek, Roman, and middle-age monuments; architectural ornament of every style and era; specimens of Byzantine decoration; Gothic enrichments; and a very extensive collection of engraved and lithographed drawings.' 'But examples of ornament in casts and prints are not all that is necessary for the purposes of schools of design. Real specimens of various kinds of ornamental manufactures and decorative work, are found to be indispensably requisite, both for teachers and learners, in the education of practical ornamentists. With this conviction, the council have already procured, as the commencement of a more important collection, some very useful and valuable specimens of this nature, chiefly from Germany, France, and Italy, consisting of patterns of stained paper-hangings, rich embroidered silks, and tissues of silk and glass, printed calicoes, wood-carving, ornaments of lacquered embossed metal, models in papier maché, imitations of antique stained glass from Nuremberg, iron castings in panel-work, fancy earthenware, enameled tiles, and several examples of decorative painting in tempera, enamel, fresco, encaustic, &c. including some valuable coloured tracings from fresco ornaments in Mantua.'

'The school is open to the inspection of the public every Monday, between the hours of one and three; and at all times is visited, not only by those who take a zealous interest in the improvement of ornamental art in this country, but by a numerous class of persons whose practical pursuits and employments as manufacturers of articles of ornament, or decorative artists, induce them to apply to the director for information and useful suggestions. To all such applicants the examples of designs possessed by the school are freely shown, and the permission to examine and copy them is accompanied by every endeavour on the part of the director to render them practically serviceable, by explanatory observations.'

Under certain restrictions, and 'with the view of developing talent and exciting emulation, and as a means of indicating to what extent the students have advanced in improvement, the council have always deemed it beneficial to the school to appropriate a small portion of the funds at their disposal to the distribution of prizes.' In the year 1843, twelve prizes, amounting to L.31, 10s., were awarded; the value of the list advertised in 1844 was L.94; and for the present year, L.165: the latter were distributed at the annual meeting in July, on which occasion it was stated that the specimens showed an improvement in taste and execution far exceeding that of any former year. Among the names of the successful competitors were those of *nine* females; thus satisfactorily proving that women are fitted for other pursuits than those of the needle.

At the time of the late 'Exposition' at Paris, the council, being desirous of keeping pace with the progress of improvement, deputed the director to visit the French capital for the purpose of providing 'more efficient collections of appropriate examples of ornamental art for the metropolitan and provincial schools, most of which are yet very inadequately supplied with normal examples and specimens;' of which purchases were made to the amount of L.1300, in all the departments and varieties above enumerated. As some difficulty was experienced in properly apportioning this supply among the whole of the schools, a selection from it, with other examples, was formed into a collection, 'to be sent successively to each of the provincial schools for exhibition during a limited period; and the council has reason to conclude, from expressions of satisfaction conveyed in various communications from the masters of the schools, and from eminent manufacturers interested in the progress of ornamental art, that this mode of affording to the designers and workmen of the provincial towns opportunity to examine and compare specimens of superior merit, is calculated to be very serviceable in suggesting points and means of improvement.

'The advantage and desirableness of good designs are shown in the very high appreciation of them by the principal manufacturers, many of whom find it expedient to devote very large sums to the purchase of foreign designs, and the payment of professional designers. The sum expended by the manufacturers of Manchester alone in French designs, is stated to amount to at least L.20,000 per annum; and instances may be adduced of single firms whose annual expenditure for English and foreign designs, and for the services of designers and draughtsmen, amounts to thousands of pounds. French, and especially German painters, are employed by the principal house decorators in London, and foreign draughtsmen are found in the warehouses of Manchester.

'During the past year, various applications have been made by manufacturers and others for draughtsmen; and from time to time students in the school have been recommended, and engaged as apprentices, to practical designers and other parties employed in ornamental work, to whom it is found to be a great advantage to obtain youths as apprentices whose usefulness, with regard both to artistical qualifications and propriety of conduct, can be at once ascertained by inquiry in the school, and by inspection of their productions *previous* to engagement, instead of depending, as appears to have been the usual mode of proceeding, upon the chance of finding by experience, *after* engagement, that the youth possesses the requisite disposition and talent. Several instances can be adduced in which the services of apprentices selected from the school have been highly satisfactory; and here it may be remarked, as relating generally to all the schools, that instances continually occur of students who possess superior natural endowments, with competent knowledge of art, and power of execution, but who, from deficiency of that technical information respecting manufacturing processes which can be effectually learned only by actual experience in the factory and workshop, cannot procure from manufacturers the employment they seek, as ornamental draughtsmen and designers. Those who, to the general knowledge they have acquired in the school of design, have found means to add the requisite information as to the practical application of it to particular manufactures, readily obtain engagements; but with regard to many others, who possess in general the prerequisite qualifications of good designers, it is to be regretted that manufacturers are not more generally disposed to meet the views of such candidates for their service, and to afford them such facilities and liberal encouragement as would serve to secure, for the purposes of ornamental manufactures, much available talent, which, in default of such encouragement, is often withdrawn from the further study of ornament, and directed exclusively to the pursuit of fine art.

'The very munificent remuneration which designers receive from manufacturers in France, is commonly, and no doubt correctly, assigned as one of the principal causes of the comparative superiority which is displayed in French designs; and it is to be hoped that, in England, the development of talent for ornamental art will be promoted by a higher estimate of its commercial value.'

The certain promise of valuable employment here held out, should have the effect of awakening the attention of artisans in every part of the country, but more especially in the manufacturing districts, to the existence and advantages of these schools, of which there are already nine in the provinces, namely, at Manchester, Birmingham, Coventry, Sheffield, Nottingham, York, Newcastle-upon-Tyne, Glasgow, and Norwich.* It is also in contemplation to form a central institution for Ireland, in the building of the Royal Society of Dublin, from which beneficial improvements may be expected to result to the manufactures of that part of the kingdom.

* Applications have been received by the council praying for an additional branch school for London, to be established in Southwark; and from Hanley, in Staffordshire, signed by upwards of 600 artisans and artists in the Potteries.

The greatest proportion of those who attend either the male or female provincial schools, is of course found amongst those occupied in the prevalent manufactures of the place. At Manchester, we find 'designers to calico-printers, 23; youths intended for ditto, 18;' while those engaged in cotton, woollen, and silk manufactures, comprehend two-fifths of the whole number of students. At Birmingham, the greatest proportion lies among die-sinkers, japanners, and architects; at Coventry, intending designers and draughtsmen; at Nottingham, lace-makers; at Glasgow, pattern-drawers, warehousemen, clerks, and schoolboys. Should it become generally known that the schools already in progress, or those which may hereafter be established, are supported by annual parliamentary grants,* we may fairly expect that every town which can boast of a mechanics' institute, will also have its government school of design, especially as the council express themselves ready to give any information towards the laudable object.

'To numerous classes of artisans and operatives employed in ornamental manufactures, a practical knowledge of drawing is, in fact, of the greatest value and importance; it being evident that, however excellent may be the pattern supplied by the professional designer, its effective and successful execution in the required material must greatly depend upon the educated eye and hand of the workman. The excellence displayed in many of the ornamental productions of France, is evidently attributable to the superior competence of *the workmen*; while among our manufacturers, especially of metal, it is a common source of complaint that, in the reproduction of the best designs, the peculiar delicacy and sentiment exhibited by the designer are not only unappreciated, but destroyed, by the workman.

'As we manufacture for every part of the world, commercial speculation has led to much enterprise in imitating foreign manufactures. In Glasgow may be seen printed cotton dresses for Ceylon, and other Indian possessions, exhibiting in some instances very beautiful designs, to suit the peculiar tastes of the people of those countries. This species of enterprise is so extended, that even religious idols have been manufactured and exported to some of our foreign possessions; and the ornamental buttons which distinguish the costume of the Chinese mandarins, have been supplied from the workshops of England. But, as the agents employed by commercial parties to procure patterns for imitation and reproduction are not always persons of correct taste, the best specimens of foreign manufactures are rarely introduced.

'In England, the more highly educated classes have acquired a refined taste, which in many instances cannot be satisfied by the present knowledge, taste, and skill of our own manufacturers and artisans, who are merely beginning to receive some of the advantages which have long been possessed by many of their foreign competitors in ornamental work; and the costly and extensive public museums, and excellent schools of art, to which all classes in the more advanced nations of the continent have gratuitous and ready access, are doubtless the primary means by which our neighbours have been enabled to excel us in the various ornamental departments of industry which demand superior knowledge, taste, intelligence, and training. In the Louvre are galleries not only of pictures and statues, but of choice specimens of ancient manufactures, carved work, brass, steel, and iron-work, and numerous examples of the productions of industrial art in general.'

We have not hesitated to quote largely from the report, whose circulation being limited, necessarily operates against the just appreciation of a subject, only to be found in a wide diffusion. We are willing to believe that a numerous class of our artisans need only to have their deficiencies pointed out, to induce them to take effectual measures for their instruction and improvement; and in no case can the fostering aid of government be more legitimately applied, than in the support of educational institutions whose influence may rouse the toiling millions to a perception of the beautiful in art and the pure in morality.

* At the close of the late session of parliament, the sum of L.4911 was voted for the schools of design.

THE PLEDGE REDEEMED.

Towards the close of the reign of Louis XIV., a plant of Mocha coffee was brought to the king's garden, which very soon increased; and the genius of the government of that day thought that, by transplanting into their West India colonies this shrub, an immense source of riches might be opened to the country. The carrying out of this idea was intrusted to Chevalier Desclieux, who, provided with a young coffee-plant, set out from Nantes, thence to convey it to Martinique. Imbedded in its native mould, the precious exile was placed in an oak-wood box, impenetrable to cold, and covered with a glass frame so formed as to catch the least ray of the sun and double its heat; and in case the sun did not shine, a small aperture, hermetically sealed, could admit heated air when it was thought proper to do so. We can imagine all the charges Desclieux received when he entered the ship in which he was to embark: but he did not need them; he saw at a glance all the distinction he would gain by this expedition, which would secure to his country an inexhaustible source of riches. It was then, with a really patriotic feeling, that he took the plant under his care, promising to devote himself to it as he would to his country, and to all the duties of his profession. And when the skiff, after having quitted the vessel, returned again to renew the charge, and to remind Desclieux once more that the plant must be watered every day, and that copiously, he pledged his honour that, rather than fail in this, he would himself die of thirst.

The ship sailed: the crew was composed of about one hundred men, and of some passengers about to settle in the Antilles, amongst whom was an amiable family, consisting of father, mother, and their only daughter Louisa, a beautiful and accomplished girl of eighteen. In a vessel where people are so much thrown together, meeting constantly for a length of time, destined perhaps to share the same death, but little time is required to form an intimacy which often ripens into lasting friendship; and thus it proved in the case of the parents of Louisa and Desclieux. Scarcely had they passed the lighthouse of Cordouan, glittering in the twilight of a lovely evening, when they were already friends. Already this fresh and delicate plant, interesting as an exile, as a flower transplanted from its own soil, as a child torn from its mother, became a mutual object of attraction. It was thus that Louisa pointed it out to her parents as it lay on the deck in its glass-case, exposed to the midday sun. She charmed the tedium of the voyage in hourly watching the progress which she believed visible in the feeble offset. She had felt interested in it from the moment Desclieux had shown her all the glory he was to gain by it for France, and then she had become attached to it; for it is a beautiful proof of the magnanimity of women—their love for all that is glorious. Even during the five days they had been at sea, the little coffee-plant had evidently increased; two small leaves of a most delicate green had appeared; and every morning Louisa's first thought after prayer was the cherished plant; but she could not see it till Desclieux had left his room, for he always kept the sacred deposit with him. Every evening he watered it abundantly, and then let hot air into the frame by means of the tube, as he had been directed: he kept it as close as possible to him at night, that even during sleep he might administer heat to it. Never did bird brood over its young more fondly, never did nurse cherish more tenderly the new-born babe.

As soon as Desclieux appeared on deck in the morning to lay his precious charge in the sun, Louisa immediately ran thither. She delighted to point out to her mother its growth during the night, a growth imperceptible to indifferent eyes; but she had become attached to it; and as the slightest emotions are visible to us in the features of those we love, though unperceived by strangers, so she discovered the least change even in the thickness of the stalk or the length of the leaves; and Desclieux, seeing the young girl thus attaching herself to what had been confided to him, and what he so cherished, felt touched and grateful.

They met with a terrible assault when close to Madeira. It was about the middle of a dark night, though not stormy; the vessel was gliding along noiselessly; and all on board were asleep except the officer on watch—and indeed he too perhaps slept, or he would have heard the noise of the keel cutting the waves as a bird's wing cuts the air, and he would have cried 'Ship ahoy!' A ship was indeed quite close to Desclieux's vessel, and the token it gave of its vicinity was a cannonade which awoke up every one in a moment, both crew and passengers. It was a pirate vessel of Tunis, a poor chebeck, but formidable in the night—a time that magnifies every fear—and formidable, too, from the desperate bravery of the banditti who manned her. Believing themselves assailed by superior forces, the ship's crew prepared for a resistance as vigorous, as desperate as the attack. Better far to die than to be carried slaves to Africa! All the passengers were at prayer, distracted, trembling, or half dead. Louisa alone remained calm, for she was sustained by the thought that to her Desclieux had intrusted his precious charge. The fight commenced; the ship fired eight cannon on the chebeck; and it was time, for already the captain had boarded the French ship, but was immediately cut down by Desclieux's axe. A last discharge of guns on each side, and the firing ceased. The pirate felt its inferiority, and retreated, while the conquerors continued their course.

Two hours of torturing suspense had passed since the terrible awakening, which but served to make the feeling of restored security the more delightful, and the remainder of the night was spent in relating the events of the rencontre. Louisa's was not the least interesting: she had been regardless of danger during the combat, while watching over her charge; then she took it to Desclieux, who admired her the more—loved her the more; for courage, always beautiful, has a still greater charm when displayed by a woman.

It was a lovely morning; the sun was unusually bright and warm, and Desclieux left the plant on deck, the glass frame half raised to admit the fresh air and reviving heat, while he, with Louisa and her parents, sat near and enjoyed seeing it expand its pretty leaves, and, as it were, smilingly greet the sun's rays which infused into it such genial warmth, and seeming to thank them for their care. But Desclieux's brow now kindled with higher thoughts. In this feeble offset he saw the pretty little starry flowers, then the perfumed berries, and the negroes gathering it abundantly, and then the ocean bearing vessels to France laden with its produce. All this he could see in the few small leaves scarcely above ground. Enthusiastically did he tell these bright visions to Louisa, and as she kindled in her turn, the coffee-plant became dearer and dearer to her, and she lavished as tender care upon it as she would upon a new-born brother. She seemed to have common sympathies with it, and if she felt that the heat might be too much for its slender stem, she drew over it little curtains of green silk which she had made expressly for it, just as a tender mother curtains the cradle of her infant. And then she read to Desclieux and her parents a long account of the coffee of Mocha, and pictured vividly to their imagination the tree to grow out of the nursling whose infancy they watched over. Sometimes the conversation took a different turn, and the parents of Louisa spoke, as if to an old familiar friend, of their fortune, of their family interests, of their views for the establishment of their only daughter; and Desclieux in return imparted to them his plans. By degrees these communications led to projects of marriage between him and Louisa. It was no unpleasing thought to either, and the very day they crossed the line, a declaration was made, and an engagement formed, and it was agreed that their union should take place immediately on their return to France.

We may well think that Louisa became more attached than ever to the plant, now become a source of distinction in which she would one day share: imagine, then, her consternation when, one morning, she beheld it languishing. She said nothing, hoping it might revive; but the next morning found its leaves still more withered. She did not trust herself to speak of it to Desclieux, who also had but too plainly seen it. At last the thought occurred to him that, whilst in the intense heat of the tropics, the plant would require more water; he therefore poured on it almost his whole allowance. The effect was immediate in restoring it to life and verdure, and Louisa was again happy. The ship was still some hundreds of leagues from Martinique, when a violent tempest arose, apparently the last of a fearful hurricane which had raged through the Antilles. It was found that the ship had sprung a leak; the pumps were not sufficient: they were in imminent danger, and the necessity of lightening the vessel was so urgent, that they were forced to throw overboard almost all the merchandise, a part of the ballast, and even several barrels of water. This last sacrifice was an appalling one: it was with a solemn feeling they made it, similar to that with which one hears the earth fall upon a coffin, or gives to the departed over the ocean for its tomb. Indeed these casks of water carried with them the lives of many individuals, who had now no escape from a cruel death by thirst. Desclieux, impressed, like the others, with this idea, only thought of his precious coffee-plant. However, they were not very far from port, and, with a favourable wind, might get in in a few days; and in effect the tempest being over, and the leak closed with great difficulty, a fresh breeze sprang up, and for a day and a night they sailed fast, and the stormy state of the atmosphere had produced on the coffee-plant the usual effect. It might almost have been said to have flourished the more for the tempest. Louisa and Desclieux contemplated it with a sweet joy, as at once the emblem and the omen of domestic happiness amid the storms of life. But, alas! the wind suddenly lulled—not the least breath to fill the sails, not a wave broke against the motionless vessel: an awful calm succeeded; and what is more terrible upon this scene of continual agitation than a calm unwonted and too often fatal? The dead heat of the tropics was felt in all its power by the helpless voyagers; they languished and fainted with a continual thirst; and, horrible to relate, the water was failing; for they had thrown so much overboard, that they were limited to a very small allowance—a cupful at most.

If men, notwithstanding their energies, sunk under the sufferings caused by the intense heat and burning thirst, what must have been the state of the poor little plant which faded away before the eye! It had its allowance also, but it was not enough; and every morning and evening Desclieux gave it his, only for which it would have died. Louisa was astonished to see the feeble plant yet bearing up; but Desclieux carefully concealed from her the means he was using, lest she also would deprive herself of water for it, and that he did not wish; he preferred suffering alone; and a long sojourn in the hottest parts of Arabia had in a great measure inured him to the climate, so that he did not feel it so much as others. The calm was uninterrupted; the remainder of the water was nearly exhausted, their situation was become dreadful, and there was no hope in their case, of any relief from another vessel, for they were alike becalmed; and it was sad to see the ocean without a sail in the horizon, or, if there was one, it too was motionless. Their ration of water was now reduced to one small liqueur glass. One drop only, just to moisten his lips, and Desclieux poured the rest on the plant. now apparently dying.

'Alas! how you are changed!' said Louisa to him one day: 'how pale you have become. You are suffering: this heat is killing you.'

He knew it; but he had promised to water the plant, even though he himself was to die of thirst; and he was faithful to his word. One evening, when Louisa and her parents were questioning him, he thus answered in a feeble voice, 'You are right; I die of thirst, that my charge may live. It is my duty;' and saying these words, he laid his parched lips upon its withered leaves, as one would kiss the hand of an expiring friend, and continued, 'You have all promised to love me: if I do not live, be careful of this coffee-plant, which held out to us such brilliant prospects. I ask it of you as a favour, and bequeath to you the distinction I hoped to have gained by it.' At the moment they were distributing the scanty portion of water, and though he was perishing, he threw the whole of it upon the shrub—Louisa did the same. It was, as it were, a sacred bond between them—an indissoluble tie. I am convinced that many of my readers have frequently felt a lively and almost inexplicable pleasure in watering a flower dried up by the scorching sun, and, in seeing it revive, have felt as if benefited themselves. What pleasure, then, it must have given to Desclieux and Louisa to see their plant raise its sickly leaves once more!

At length the wind began to rise lightly, and the vessel moved, though slowly. Desclieux was ill—in a burning fever; but he continued to share with the plant his allowance of water; and Louisa added hers. It increased their happiness that it owed its recovery to their mutual self-denial; and it seemed as if their household life had begun in a common endurance of suffering.

The breeze still freshened; and when the vessel anchored in the port of St Pierre, there was not a single drop of water on board. But the coffee-plant was saved; the colony enriched by it; Desclieux's pledge redeemed; and, three months after, Louisa was his wife.

FESTIVAL OF AGRICULTURAL LABOURERS.

The following pleasing account of a festival lately given by C. B. Wall, Esq., M.P. for the borough of Guildford, to his tenants, agricultural labourers, and others, at his mansion of Norman Court, Hampshire, occurs in the letter of a lively correspondent to the League newspaper, and will doubtless interest all who feel concerned in the interchanges of kindly sentiments between different classes of the community:—

'Mr Wall's festival occurred on Tuesday the 17th of September. Having breakfasted at the Greyhound, or the Hare and Hound, or the Dogs—I am not sure which it is; but the traveller who likes a good breakfast, the freshest of water-cresses, and eggs, and bread and butter, and coffee and cream, will not make any mistake, as it is "the house of the village," [Broughton]—having breakfasted, and read, while at breakfast, the printed rules of that day's vegetable, fruit, and flower-show, the competitors in which were all to be labourers living in cottages rented from Mr Wall, in Broughton, the two Tytherleys (east and west); for which show a liberal and comprehensive scale of premiums were awarded—having breakfasted, and also read at breakfast the catalogue of the Norman Court Lending Library, which library consists of 500 or more volumes, provided at Mr Wall's expense, the only qualifications to obtain which is a desire to read, and a request to be allowed to borrow a book—the books consisting of the best periodical and serial works of the day, and of the standard works in religious, moral, and scientific biographies, poetry, instructive tales, and so forth; having also, when at breakfast, listened, as I have often done since, not only in Broughton, but in all the villages and districts around Norman Court, to the respectful, grateful, almost reverential remarks on Mr Wall, as a kind landlord and liberal helper of all who need a rich man's help—as an employer of many men, and a payer of good wages—as the protector not only of the living, but of the dead—the restorer of gravé-stones, of churchyards, and of churches—having breakfasted, read, and listened to all these things, I, with some other friends, drove off in a "trap" for Norman Court.

'Up Broughton-hill, westward, we toiled, one or two getting out, that the horse might have less toil. Having surmounted it, and left the wide expanse of woodless farm-fields behind, turning only round to look down upon Broughton in its nest of trees for a minute, and upon the three Wallops, in their bourne farther north, and upon "Lennard's Grove" (the cross roads which so named tell their own tale), between us and the villages of the Wallops, we looked westward and southward into a country all different from that east and north of us. A succession of woodlands, now in hollows and now in heights; now with open fields and elsewhere with winding glades; now humble and copse-like, and again lofty and majestic, lay before us and below us, over a distance of six miles, bounded by another bold range of chalky hills, resembling that which we had just come over. By turns we went down, and again up; to the left and to the right, and on forward, turning again and again. Elderly men and women were standing aside to let us pass in the narrow woodland roads, or sitting down to rest themselves with their baskets of vegetables which they were carrying to the show. Boys with clean "smocks" on, or new jackets, were pushing on as fast as they had breath to Norman Court, and shouting as we passed; old and young, male and female, rich and poor—most of the rich, who had horses at home, walking as well as the poor, lest there might be no stabling for all the horses expected there; all these peopled the roads; and each gave the other joy of the fine day as they journeyed onward.

'We arrived near the front of the mansion, commanding a magnificent view southward over woods and meadows and fields, dells, eminences, openings, thickets, and through noble park trees, amid which the carriage-roads led off, and lost themselves. On the side of the mansion next us, extending over a dozen acres or so backward, and now on our right hand, was a green smooth sward embosomed in lofty lines of trees, these lines being but the front-rank men of deep thickets. Into this we turned, and drove to the tent of Mr Lane, from Broughton, which stood fronting downward and towards us.

'On our right hand, at entering under the trees, was the sign of the Lion (Mr Beauchamp, from West Dean); and half-way up, in front of the trees, was the Black Horse (Mr Fowkes, from West Tytherley). Varieties of other smaller tents with confectionary, and exhibitions of natural curiosities and such-like, were in the intermediate spaces. But the grand attraction were two tents of Mr Wall's, on the left-hand side, near the centre: one was for the show of vegetables, fruits, and flowers; and the other was a kind of store, at which Mr Wall himself presided, furnished with a variety of fancy and useful articles, to be given as prizes to those who might win them at such games as archery, for which there were six targets, with bows and arrows in abundance; such games also as cricket; and nearly all kinds of ball-playing, puff and dart, quoits, hurdle-racing, leaping, and so on. There were generally such chances as twelve shots for a penny; the men attending to the targets, &c. receiving the pennies, and giving a ticket to the winners, who carried it to Mr Wall, and received prizes according to its amount. If it was a 2s. 6d. or 3s. ticket, there would be a silk handkerchief, and a knife perhaps, or a hat, or a waistcoat. For the children there were swings and roundabouts; and ropes with seats on them were suspended between the venerable trees, that young people who wished to swing might swing there.

'The vegetable and fruit show was exceedingly good, and would have done credit to many professional gardeners. It certainly did credit to Mr Wall's cottagers, of whom about 100 were competitors. The judges were Mr White, the gardener at Norman Court, and two other gentlemen, whose names I now forget. The beautiful fuchsias, and other flowering plants from the cottage-windows, showed favourably for the domestic neatness and taste. So did the garden products tell for cottar industry. But if all dwellers in humble houses had as good dwellings and gardens, with as good a squire, and as good a steward between them and the squire as they have, there would be more comfort, and more industry exercised to obtain it, throughout England than there now is.

'As visitors arrived, some in carriages, some in vans, and some in holiday wagons, others in gigs and trap-carts, from distances varying from one to ten miles, those who were known had tickets given them by Mr Sergeant, the land steward, to the dinner. A yeoman cavalry band, in their uniform, played music, which the woods re-echoed, or would have re-echoed, had there been less din of human voices, and a lower breeze of wind. There were several policemen of the county constabulary on the ground, but, as it was observed at the time, every man was his own constable; no mischief was done.

'The chief dinner was spread in the courtyard of the mansion twice, from 250 to 300 dining each time. The great body of the people, however, dined in the tents on the green, having tickets which paid for their admission and their fare. Each party dining in the court passed into the mansion, and went through the splendid suite of rooms on the ground-floor by way of exit. On a former occasion, the house was left open to every person indiscriminately. They did no wilful damage, but there being many thousands of them going in and out for a whole day, they did damage to elegant furniture, whether intending it or not. On that occasion, a gentleman staying on a visit with Mr Wall had left his bed-room door open, not expecting that any of the strangers would penetrate there; also he left his money, in sovereigns, and his jewellery, lying open on his table. The staring wonderers, who had never before been in such a house, went, hundred after hundred, into that room, as well as into others; but there was not there, nor in the house, a single act of theft committed. Yet these people had the full complement of poachers, petty thieves, and loose reputations among them; persons who were honest against their inclination, because they saw and felt they were trusted.

'On the present occasion, Mr Wall sat down at one of the tables, but did not preside; the presidency and several other offices of honour devolved on some of the principal tenants and the farm-steward. The domestic servants, from the house-steward downward, waited on and served the visitors with alacrity and kindness; as much so, indeed, as if the kind spirit of their master was thoroughly infused into them.

'On Mr Wall's health being given, he delivered a short address, "thanking the people for coming to see him and dine with him," and hoping to see them again and again, and to see a closer bond of friendship established between persons of all ranks than there ever yet had been.

'The sports upon the green went on. Every minute some prize was won at one or other of the games. The floor of the tent in which the vegetable show had been was boarded for dancing, with a platform for the band. Accordingly, there was dancing. And when night closed in, there were fireworks; and these were on a scale of grandeur rarely excelled, if ever excelled at all. Artists of first-rate ability were brought from London to conduct their exhibition. Fire-balloons went off and away; and rockets went up and shot off, and showered down brilliancies that illumined the wondering country. While the multitudes gazed and admired, devices in fire of all shapes and colours, and of many meanings, succeeded each other, rockets firing all the time with a magnificence that would have made Vauxhall clap hands and shout. But there was little shouting here, and not a hand was clapped. The excessive wonder at such prodigies done in fire constrained to silence.

'The fireworks at Norman Court were sublime; and the people who looked upon them, upwards of 2000 in number, seemed at a loss whether to have most gratitude to Mr Wall for his kindness, or most admiration for his unrivalled liberality. They gave him the best return they could give: they went all to their homes without mishap or disturbance, all pleased with the day's entertainment, and pleased with one another.'

PECULIARITIES OF LANGUAGES.

In all hot countries men use, in speaking, a multitude of vowels, which are all pronounced by greater or lesser apertions of the mouth, in breathing and in speaking, and use very few consonants, all of which are produced by more or less complete interruption of the breath, and contact, or even closure of parts, among the organs of speech. Any one who examines the Italian language, will find, therefore, about sixty vowels in every hundred letters; and in the Otaheitean (Tahitian) language, which sounds very like Italian, there are even more; it is said about seventy-five or eighty vowels in every hundred letters. The proportion is very different in English, in which consonants preponderate; and if we examine the language of Lapland or Greenland, or of the Arctic-American Esquimaux, we shall find that there are an enormous number of consonants in their more than sesquipedalian words, and that most of these are guttural, as they do not like to open their mouths to the cold air sufficiently to pronounce the labial, dental, or lingual consonants, much less the vowels, and least of all the more open of the vowels. This is a universal law; though immigration or colonisation, or the ancient transplantation of a whole nation by a tyrant conqueror, may sometimes present an apparent exception or anomaly, by our finding a language or a people originally temperate or torrid, in a frigid zone, or *vice versa*.—*Medical Times.*

SONNET.

[BY S. W. PARTRIDGE.]

We toil unduly: labour's ponderous wheels
Even on the blessed Sabbath grudging rest;
The twilight o'er the weary earth that steals,
And woos the songster to his welcome nest,
Scarcely can man allure from toil unblest:
Mercy in vain against the wrong appeals;
Against repose his gainful heart he steels,
His own worst foe, self-burdened and oppress'd.
We get to live; ah no, we live to get:
Ambition, Avarice, Ostentation goad
Our panting feet along life's flinty road,
Self-yoked, at Mammon's car to tug and sweat.
To buy and sell—is this earth's best employ?
To calculate and gain, its chiefest joy?

EFFECTS OF CROSSING ON THE CONSTITUTION.

Those classes of the human race which preserve their blood free from mixture with strangers, while they have less variety in external appearance, and perhaps less variety in the scope of mental capacity, than those who cross and recross at pleasure, have more endurance in action, firmer attachments to purposes, and less desultory impetuosity. This is a physical truth. The explanation of it is difficult; but it may be illustrated and comprehended in some degree by those who study the animal fabric, and who are acquainted with the laws of animal economy. In brute animals (horses, sheep, and cattle), the mixture of different races is observed to change the qualities, to improve the beauty, and to enlarge the size; it diminishes the hardiness and the security of the physical health. In man, the mixture of different races improves beauty, augments the volume of the bodily organs, and even perhaps expands the sphere of intellect. It diminishes the power of enduring toil, and renders the habit more susceptible to the causes of disease.—*Jackson's Economy of Animals.*

SINGULAR MODE OF INCUBATION.

Mr E. J. Eyre, in his journals of several expeditions he undertook into Central Australia, proceeding with a guide and several other natives, he came in one place to a large circular mound of sand, about two feet high and several yards in circumference: this his companions immediately began to explore, carefully throwing away the sand with their hands from the centre, until they had worked down to a deep narrow hole, round the sides of which, and imbedded in the sand, were four fine large eggs of a delicate pink colour, and fully the size of a goose-egg. I had often seen these hills before, but did not know that they were nests, and that they contained so valuable a prize to a traveller in the desert. The eggs were presented to me by the natives; and, when cooked, were of a very rich and delicate flavour. The nest was that of a wild pheasant (Leipoa), a bird of the size of a hen-pheasant of England, and greatly resembling it in appearance and plumage. These birds are very cautious and shy, and run rapidly through the underwood, rarely flying unless when closely pursued. The shell of the egg is thin and fragile; and the young are hatched entirely by the heat of the sun, scratching their way out as soon as they are born; at which time they are able to shift for themselves.

Published by W. and R. Chambers, High Street, Edinburgh (also 98 Miller Street, Glasgow); and with their permission, by W. S. Orr, Amen Corner, London.—Printed by Bradbury and Evans, Whitefriars, London.

☞ Complete sets of the Journal, First Series, in twelve volumes, and also odd numbers to complete sets, may be had from the publishers or their agents.—A stamped edition of the Journal is now issued, price 2½d., to go free by post.

CONDUCTED BY WILLIAM AND ROBERT CHAMBERS, EDITORS OF 'CHAMBERS'S INFORMATION FOR THE PEOPLE,' 'CHAMBERS'S EDUCATIONAL COURSE,' &c.

No. 103. New Series. SATURDAY, DECEMBER 20, 1845. Price 1½d.

A VISIT TO THE SLAVE MARKET OF CONSTANTINOPLE.

Nothing could be more beautiful than the rising of the sun over Constantinople on the morning of the 5th of May 1845. From the hotel in which we had already passed some days, I could watch to the greatest advantage the effect of his rays, as they stole down from the deep blue sky, and gradually lightened up the varied scene of enchantment that lay at my feet; gliding over the clear waters of the Bosphorus, glittering on every tree and flower of its innumerable gardens, and rendering visible the graceful caïques that were shooting to and fro beneath their shade.

Soon the soft light had caught on every slender minaret and golden dome. St Sophia's, towering above the rest, stood out in strong relief against the clear sky. The exquisite effects of light and shade, produced on the Seraglio Point by the contrast of the dark cypresses with the fresher green of the luxuriant shrubberies, became beautifully striking; and the palace itself, with its admirable Oriental architecture, added not a little to the singular loveliness of the scene. On leaving the sea of Marmora to enter the Bosphorus, I own I had been thoroughly disappointed with the first view of the city. This was partly caused by the weather being dull and gloomy; for the Bosphorus, without sunshine, is like a fair face without a smile: but it is also certain that no one should judge of this queen of eastern cities from the first view of her position; it is not till the Seraglio Point is fairly passed, and Europe and Asia lie on either side, like a vast garden divided by a mighty river, that her unquestionable beauty bursts on the mind, and Venice and Naples sink into utter insignificance in comparison. I had already had ample time to become convinced of this, and yet, on the morning of which I speak, as I looked down on the bright Oriental city, I could not help applying to it the words of the poet—'The fairest things have still the worst fate.' This reflection was caused by my having that day made arrangements to visit what has been aptly termed the plague-spot of this fair land—the slave market. Surely it is a bitter thing to think that the most beautiful city of which Europe can boast, should also be the scene of her most degrading and revolting commerce; that the spot where nature has lavished her most luxuriant loveliness, should be defaced by the foulest stain on humanity. I had little or no idea of what the slave-trade in European Turkey really was, notwithstanding my long residence in the East, until this day, when I visited the seat of it. I own it seems strange to me that the many travellers who pour every day into Constantinople should, in their published accounts of that city, show themselves so singularly indifferent, or perhaps so politic, as to touch very slightly on what, at least to those who profess the name of Christian, must be a most painful sight. I believe the simple recital of what I saw will justify me in speaking strongly on the subject.

On the morning, then, of the 5th of May, I set out to visit the slave market, in company with a fellow-traveller who, by his great talent and extensive information, has already attained an elevated position in his own country, and who, if he lives to follow up his brilliant career, will undoubtedly give to France a name that all Europe will delight to honour. I had already visited most of the lions of Constantinople in his company, a pleasure greatly enhanced by his sound and original observations. All that the city possessed of splendour had been displayed before us—the Seraglio, St Sophia's, and the singular and somewhat repulsive magnificence of the tombs of the sultans, who have been laid down to rot and decay in their gorgeous sarcophagi, in what is neither more nor less than an elegant lady's drawing-room. All this formed the subject of our conversation as we toiled along the villanous streets of Pera, mutually agreeing that there was very little real comfort in all this Oriental magnificence. We passed through several of the bazaars, long covered passages, with stalls on either side, and crowded at that early hour with half the population of the 'quartier.' We had some difficulty in pushing our way through the very phlegmatic Turkish crowd; but our guide, who was a Frenchman long established in the East, walked stoically on, armed with a long stick, with which he vigorously attacked the stupid wolfish-looking dogs which lay literally in masses on the streets. At length we reached the place of our destination. It was a long low building, forming a square of considerable size. We mounted a few unsteady dirty steps, and found ourselves on a large wooden platform, running the whole length of the building. It was divided into pens, shut in by wooden railings, in which were confined the black slaves; whilst through the open doors leading into the house itself we could distinguish the veiled forms of the white women grouped behind the wooden screens. On benches, so placed as to command a view of both, were seated the buyers, for the most part heavy, ill-looking Turks, dressed in the hideous costume introduced by the late sultan, and occupied as usual in smoking, though the quick glance of their calm, piercing eyes, seemed to take in everything around in complete detail. The sellers stood before them, vociferating and gesticulating in the true Oriental manner. The court below, which we were to visit afterwards, was filled with all the less valuable part of this human merchandise, consisting of those afflicted with any infirmity, very aged persons, and young children. It was some time before we comprehended the scene in all its details: it is not to be wondered at that we were stupified in witnessing such a sight on European ground. At length we approached one of the pens, determined to examine, to the fullest extent, into all that was revolting and horrible in this market of human life. It was filled with young Circassian women, some of whom were remarkably handsome. They were seated close together on the ground, seemingly in an attitude of listless despondency, with their long white garments flowing round them. As we came up, they fixed their large dark eyes upon us, and I certainly never met a gaze of more unutterable sadness. The conviction thrilled through me, as my eyes met theirs, that these unfortunate beings *are not*, as modern philanthropists would have us believe, utterly unconscious of, and incapable of feeling the dishonour and wretchedness of their fate. I felt, as I stood before them, and encountered their soft melancholy glance, that they looked on me as the free and happy stranger come to gaze on them in their infamy and their misery. Presently the slave-trader, to whom the poor creatures belonged, came up, followed by a tall phlegmatic-looking Turk, with the unmeaning features and coarse corpulency which are so characteristic of his nation. The merchant advanced, and seizing one of the slaves by the arm, forced her to stand up before this personage, who, it appeared, wished to buy her. He looked at her for a few minutes from head to foot, whilst her master descanted on her merits; then he placed one hand on the back of her neck, whilst he jerked her head rudely with the other, so as to force her to open her mouth, that he might examine her teeth; he roughly handled her neck and arms, to ascertain if the flesh were firm; and, in short, the examination was such, that I do not hesitate to declare I have seen a horse or a dog more tenderly treated under similar circumstances. After all, the decision was unfavourable, for the Turk turned away with a contemptuous movement of the head, and the slave-dealer, in a rage, thrust back the unfortunate creature, who sunk down trembling amongst her companions in misery.

Neither my friend nor I had uttered a word during this scene; we stood silent side by side, and mechanically followed our guide, who led us into the adjoining enclosure. Here we became witnesses to a sale that was just about to be completed. A most interesting group presented itself before us: two young female slaves, both with most pleasing countenances, stood together closely embraced, the arm of the one round the neck of the other; their attitude, as well as the strong likeness between them, pointing them out at once as sisters. By their side was an African slave-dealer, in whose ferocious countenance it seemed impossible to discern a trace of human feeling: he was armed with a large heavy stick, with which he drove them to and fro, literally like a herd of animals. Three or four Turks were discussing, with considerable animation, the price of one of the women; but the bargain had been struck just before we came in, and one of the party, a stout good-looking man, was paying down the money. When this was completed, with an imperious movement of the hand he motioned to his newly-purchased slave to follow him. It was the youngest and the most timid of the two sisters whom he had selected: nothing could have been more painful than to watch the intense, the terrified anxiety, with which both had followed the progress of sale; and now it was concluded, and they knew that the moment of separation was arrived. She whose fate had been sealed, disengaged herself, and, turning round, placed her two hands on her sister's shoulders with a firm grasp, and gazed into her eyes. Not words, not tears, could have expressed one-half of the mute, unutterable despair that dwelt in that long heart-rending gaze. It were hard to say which face was most eloquent of misery: but the Turk was impatient: he clapped his hands together. This was a well-known signal. A slight tremor shook the frame of the young slave; her arms fell powerless at her side, and she turned to follow her master. The voiceless but agonised farewell was over. In another moment we could just distinguish her slender figure threading its way through the crowd, in company with the other slaves belonging to the Turk. Her sister had hid herself behind her companions, and now sat on the ground, her head sunk upon her folded arms. Our guide would have led us into another pen; but we had seen enough: we hurried through the various groups till we reached the open court; then for the first time we addressed each other, and the same words burst simultaneously from the lips of both—'C'est infame!'

'But I have heard,' I said, willing to relieve myself from the painful oppression this sight had caused, 'that these poor slaves are brought up to this situation [illegible] their infancy, and, knowing nothing else, do [illegible] their degradation or their misery.'

'Let us ask Joseph,' said my friend, shaking his head incredulously; 'he is an intelligent person, and can doubtless initiate us into the mysteries of the slave-trade. Are these wretched creatures born in captivity?' he asked, addressing the guide; 'or, if not, how are they procured?'

'Very easily, monsieur,' said Joseph composedly. 'None of these are born slaves, and they are all procured in the same manner. Any pacha who wishes an addition to his establishment, mans a vessel with a well-armed crew, and sends it over to Circassia. They go on shore, penetrate some little distance into the country, attack the first quiet village they come to, burn it to the ground if they meet with any resistance, and carry off all the women and children. They throw them in a heap into the hold of the ship, and bring them to Constantinople. The pacha chooses what he thinks fit for himself, and then sends the rest to the slave market. Some of the more extensive slave-dealers often undertake such expeditions on their own account.'

'But after they are bought, they are well treated, are they not?' I asked.

'In many cases they are. It depends entirely on the temper of the master; he has the power of life and death over them; and at all events the bastinado is always more or less in use.'

'And what is the fate of the children who are brought in such numbers into the world in consequence of this most infamous system?' asked my friend.

'They are sold as slaves,' said Joseph.

'Do you mean to say that they sell their own flesh and blood?' I exclaimed.

'Certainly they do. They can acknowledge them, and give them their freedom if they choose; but they never do. They have the children of their wives to provide for, and that is enough.'

We asked no more questions, for we had heard quite sufficient, and willingly turned our attention to the inhabitants of the court in which we now stood. The sight which presented itself here was even more revolting than what we had already seen. Huddled together on dirty mats, and exposed to the full power of the burning noon-day sun, lay a number of miserable-looking beings—blind, lame, and deformed; some crawling about on crutches, others unable to use their distorted limbs; and, in short, afflicted with every imaginable infirmity. Nothing can be conceived more wretched than their fate. They are considered as almost quite worthless by their masters, and are starved and beaten in proportion as their misfortunes render them unprofitable. This lasts till they are bought in lots for a mere trifle by some one who takes them as a sort of speculation, trusting that, amongst several, one or two may be found of use: the treatment of the remainder may be imagined! We distributed a few piastres amongst them which they begged from us in tones of the most piteous intreaty, and then left the slave market, to embark in the caique which was to convey us to visit the vast burial-grounds of Scutari; and we had ample time, whilst traversing the quiet waters which separate Europe from Asia, to reflect on all we had seen and heard.

The inhuman system of the slave-trade had been fully displayed before us, and imagination pictured to us the brutal servants of yet more brutal masters coming down like a pestilence on the happy repose of some quiet Circassian village—disturbing the peace of innocent and harmless lives—trampling under their rude steps the dear home which had been perhaps for years the sanctuary of domestic and natural affection—rifling these rustic dwellings of their brightest treasures, and tearing, with the ruthless power of armed force, the wife from her husband, the bride from her lover, and the child from her parents. And when every tie which makes life dear is broken, and the chains of a hopeless captivity are securely riveted on the limbs of the broken-hearted slaves—when they have been subdued by blows, and have ate the food thrown to them as to a dog—when they have been displayed for sale, and the living, palpitating flesh and blood has been bought and sold like the vilest merchandise—then what is the fate reserved for them? The facts I witnessed were too deplorable and too palpable to admit of temporising or hiding a bitter truth under the colourless refinement of modern 'convenance.' These beings, formed in the image of God, go forth to make a trade of their very wretchedness, to gain their bread by a life of infamy, and to bring into the world a miserable offspring, stigmatised from their very birth, and destined to the same unnatural existence. And where is it that this commerce of human life is carried on, day after day, in all its unconcealed details of refined brutality? In Europe! in civilised Europe! within fifteen days of Paris and London, under the very eyes of thousands of travellers, who openly go to witness this 'curious sight,' and as openly return to free England and liberal France to publish the 'interesting account!' Surely these nominally Christian countries are strangely apathetic on this subject? But the reason is most obvious: the abolition of the slave-trade in European Turkey would necessarily involve a great political question. 'La Question d'Orient' is of too much importance to the three Great Powers—who have chosen it as the field of their diplomatic manœuvres—to admit of mere humanity weighing in the scale. Yet I think, were there a few more honest revelations of some of the secret doings of the Sublime Porte, no one could visit Turkey without at least earnestly wishing that this beautiful and valuable country might pass into other hands than those of the Turks.

Much has been said in favour of this people, and until I had sufficient opportunity of judging them without prejudice, I was decidedly prepossessed in their favour. The feelings with which I now regard them may therefore fairly be admitted to result solely from the actual facts witnessed. With some few redeeming qualities—honesty, cleanliness, and real respect for their religion, such as it is—it appears to me that the Turks are an essentially cruel, sensual, and unfeeling race. What I have mentioned on the subject of slavery, is but one of the many inhuman and cold-blooded systems which demonstrate this only too plainly. To give another instance, I may mention an atrocity currently in practice, though perhaps not generally known. In order to prevent the inconvenience or the danger of there being too many members of the royal family in the direct line of succession to the throne, all the children of the sultan's numerous brothers and sisters are systematically strangled a few hours after their birth, and the infant forms, still warm with the life which is torn from them ere well received, are thrown into the Bosphorus.

Oh, could they speak, those beautiful, serene, and voiceless waters, how many an awful tale of blood and infamy they would reveal! Could they but open and display to the stoical gaze of the travellers who glide in such delicious ease over their glassy bosom, the putrifying mass which loads their hidden depths, formed by the mangled bodies of those innumerable victims! It seemed to me, as the light caique which bore me shot over the scarce rippling waves, that I beheld the venerable form of the good old patriarch (who, twenty years before, was flung there, warm and bleeding, from the hands of his executioners) floating by with his white hair dabbled in blood, and his hands still uplifted in the last vain prayer for mercy. I know not if this appalling history is generally known, but the blood of that holy old man alone would suffice to leave an indelible stain on the Turkish nation.

It was at the period of the first outbreak of the war of independence, whereby Greece attained her nominal liberty; the news had reached Constantinople of the revolt of some of the more distant provinces; it was, I think, on Easter Sunday, or some other high festival of the church; thousands of the Greeks inhabiting the city were assembled at the cathedral where the venerable patriarch was administering the communion. The Turks, infuriated on finding that the slaves they had so long crushed beneath their haughty feet had still retained in their degradation some spark of the unextinguishable love of liberty, now rushed to the church, crying out for vengeance. The Greeks, whose necks were still too completely under the Moslem yoke to attempt resistance, even had their numbers been adequate, fell back before the irritated crowd. The patriarch, bending beneath the weight of eighty years, stood on the steps of the altar, his withered hands uplifted to bless the people; the Turks rushed towards him, they seized him, and tore him down to the ground; they twined their sacrilegious hands in the flowing white hair that fell round his venerated head, they dragged him over the stone pavement of the church, through the open street, to the foot of the nearest tree—and there, still in his pontifical robes, with the last accents of the half-uttered blessing trembling on his withered lips, they passed a common rope round his neck, and hung him, along with three of his cardinals! It did not take long to extinguish the feeble spark of life in that aged frame. As soon as he was dead, they cut him down and flung him into the Bosphorus. By some strange accident the body did not sink. That same evening a Russian vessel was sailing towards the entrance of the Black Sea, on its way to Odessa; suddenly a sight presented itself which caused the superstitious crew to fall on their knees, seized with a reverential awe. Gently borne along by the current, the body of the murdered patriarch came floating by. The holy old man lay on the bosom of the waters, still and serene as a child in dreamless sleep. His pontifical robes were folded decently around him; his hands were yet in the posture of prayer; his hoary head moved slowly with its undulating pillow; and the distinctive mark of his priesthood, the long snowy hair, flowed over the wave. With a respect amounting to worship, the Russian sailors drew the corpse from the water, and carried it to Odessa, where he was buried. He has since been canonised, and is now considered one of their most powerful saints.

But it were indeed useless to multiply instances of Turkish barbarity; any one at all acquainted with the modern history of the Ottoman empire cannot be ignorant of them. Would it were rather possible to suggest some means by which the most fertile and beautiful country in Europe might be rescued from the hands of a race whose social systems, whose religion of crimes permitted and sensuality authorised, whose government of open despotism and concealed intrigue, have succeeded in rendering it the abode of the most deep-seated and corroding evils. In fact, the Turks, deists in theory, are materialists in practice. But such was the policy of the wily founder of their creed: it is evident that he well understood the bent of the human mind, and felt that he could not fail to render his own name immortal by giving them a religion essentially formed to administer to every selfish passion.

But alas! though slight the tenor by which the indolent Mussulmans keep possession of their promising and fertile country, at a time like the present, when expediency, and expediency alone, is the mainspring of every government, we may not look to see it wrested from their loose and easy grasp. So carelessly, indeed, do they sit in possession, so perfectly sure that no nation will ever be audacious enough to attack them, that their empire is in fact already crumbling into dust beneath their feet; and assuredly it would require but a very slight movement on the part of any one of the great European powers to conquer and subdue it entirely, if the resistance were only from the internal force of the country. How many a brave old Palikar in Greece makes it his dream by night and his thought by day, that he may yet behold his countrymen march triumphant into the land to which they claim a prior right! Doubtless this is of all dreams the most futile; yet had Greece, which may well be compared to a frail and tempest-driven bark, been provided with a wiser pilot at her helm, she might perhaps have deemed the vision not altogether vain. As it is, I think the wishes of every unprejudiced visiter in Turkey will limit themselves, for the present, to the earnest desire that those travellers who so assiduously publish their observations, would at least frankly and openly relate what they see; and when the flimsy veil which diplomacy has thrown over the actual state of the Ottoman empire is raised for them, as to a certain extent it must be for every intelligent observer, let them not, complying with the culpable policy of the present day, conceal or extenuate the actual and most painful truths which must present themselves before them.

THE THREE FRIENDS—AN OSAGE LEGEND.

BY PERCY B. ST JOHN,

AUTHOR OF 'THE TRAPPER'S BRIDE.'

The tribe known as the Osages, or Wa-saw-sees, as they denominate themselves, wander perennially round the head waters of the Arkansas and Neosho, or Grand Rivers, hunting, fishing, and trading with the Americans at Fort Gibson, the outermost south-western fort on the frontier of the United States. Tall, even gigantic in stature, they have many qualities which excite the admiration and applause of their white brethren. Like most Indians, they are brave and warlike; but their peculiarity consists in rejecting the customs of the whites, particularly the use of whisky. Wearing their wild and primitive costume, they stalk amid the hunters, squatters, trappers, and trampers that frequent the neighbourhood of Fort Gibson, overtopping them in general by a head, but still more surpassing them in the essential virtue of sobriety and temperance—a failure in the exercise of which would doubtless soon remove them from the pre-eminence they now enjoy.

In a secluded valley, through which a stream that fell into the Neosho wound its way, lay some time back one of the villages of this nomadic tribe. The wigwams were about a hundred in number, scattered over the narrow plain near the mouth of the valley, and surrounded by a rude picket. Built of bark and reeds, they were evidently constructed simply for the necessities of the summer season, during which the warriors chased the deer and buffalo for immediate consumption, and to lay up in store for winter. Overlooking the village was a grassy mound, that narrowed the mouth of the valley, and caused the rippling stream that flowed at its feet to turn abruptly from its course. From the summit of this hillock, the lodges wore the appearance of a huge congregation of bee-hives, while the eye rested pleasantly on many adjuncts to the scene, which rendered it agreeable and picturesque. The village was alive with a busy throng of women, few if any men being discovered; while children were seen at every point, adding still greater animation to the picture. The first were all actively employed. Some stood at the entrance of their wigwams, busily engaged in cooking; others were drying and packing the results of the hunting of the warriors; while others, again, were laboriously occupied in cleaning fresh buffalo skins, preparatory to their being cured for use as robes. Not a married woman was idle. Not so, however, the maidens. They were yet enjoying the sweets of a liberty which, however, despite the hardships incident to the married state in the wilds, they were no less anxious to sacrifice than are many bright-eyed beauties nearer home. The Osage girls—and many of them were exceedingly pretty—were congregated near the edge of the stream, in which dozens of little urchins were bathing. Dancing was usually their chief amusement; but on the present occasion they were spectators of a scene which possessed more immediate interest.

Somewhat apart from the maidens was a group, on which the Osage girls gazed curiously and enviously. Three Indian youths, all under twenty, nowise related by blood, but connected only by the bonds of friendship, stood on a rising bank in deep abstraction. Nah-con-e-shee, Koha-tunka, and Mun-ne-pushee—for such were the names of the young men—had at an early age contracted for one another one of those peculiar affections which inexplicably arise sometimes between persons of the same sex, and which often are more sincere and durable even than love. So wedded were they to this feeling, as to have publicly declared their intention of never marrying, in order that their amity might suffer no division. Their hearts, they said, were so occupied by friendship, that love could not find the remotest corner to creep into. How many smiling faces were clouded by this strange announcement, we cannot say; but sure we are, if any had before suffered them to occupy their thoughts, this resolution increased the number of their admirers manifold. Indian girls have ways and means of setting their caps at young men, as the phrase is, as well as more civilised damsels, and the Osage maidens were not idle on this occasion. Besides that many really loved the youths, the honour of the sex was concerned. It was not to be borne that friendship should triumph over love, and it may therefore be readily conceived what an artillery of bright eyes was reproachfully opened upon the three friends. They, however, remained insensible to all the attractions of female society; they joined not in the dance, nor told nor listened to the tale of love or war by the evening fire; but rode together, hunted together, trapped together, and earned the highest renown as indefatigable and bold huntsmen.

The ambition of the three friends, however, reached to higher flights than emulating the first hunters of their tribe. They wished to equal in renown the greatest warriors of the Osage nation; and it was in knowledge of the fact that they were about to start on a marauding expedition, which created so great a sensation in the throng of maidens. The three youths had been deeply engaged in discussing their plans, and were, at the moment we speak of, uttering a silent prayer to the great Manitou for success in their undertaking. Tall, erect, and admirably proportioned, they presented an excellent group for a statuary. While their shaven heads were adorned with the boldest crest and eagle plume, they bore round their necks ornaments of the gayest kind. A magnificent cloak of buffalo skin adorned their shoulders, while a spear, shield, [illegible] hawk, bow and quiver, formed their arms. Leggings, mocassins, with wampum garters tied below the knee, completed, with the waist-cloth, their attire. Three fine horses were tied to an adjoining tree, showing that they were in every way ready for the expedition. It was still morning, and many miles of ground were to be crossed before night, the youths having signified their intention of making an excursion into the Pawnee Pict territory.

As soon as their silent invocation was ended, the Osage braves stalked gravely towards their richly-caparisoned steeds, and mounting them, rode slowly from the camp. For some miles, their course was along a wide-spread rolling prairie; but soon the presence of trees gave sign of their approaching a river. It was not, however, until nightfall that they gained the banks of the Arkansas. Hitherto, their progress had been open and bold, being within the hunting-grounds of their own people; but now the frontier line of the Pawnee Picts lay before them, in the shape of the dark rolling waters of the Arkansas, and it was time to use caution and artifice. It was determined, as their horses were somewhat fatigued, and as they depended on them for escape in case of need, that they should seek repose upon the friendly side of the river, and cross the Arkansas in the morning. Their horses were accordingly tethered, a diminutive fire lighted in a deep dell or hole, and every other needful preparation made to pass the night. A frugal repast was consumed, and then each warrior leant against a tree, and, smoking his pipe, gravely conversed upon the best mode of acquiring distinction and renown. Many opinions were given; but nothing less than surprising a whole Pawnee village, slaughtering the inhabitants, and returning to their homes loaded with scalps, appeared to the heated imaginations of the youths a sufficiently glorious enterprise to satisfy their ambition. At length the fatigues of the day overpowered them, and the three friends fell into a deep sleep.

The sun had just tipped with gold the summits of the trees, the wild cock was crowing in the woods, the thousand choristers of the forest were pealing in rich harmony, when the Osage warriors awoke. They smiled grimly on one another, and then started, each man mechanically placing his hand upon the back and crown of his head. Their scalp locks, helmet crests, and eagles' plumes had all disappeared. Petrified with astonishment, they started to their feet. 'Who could have done so daring a deed?' Not an enemy surely, or they would have taken the lives thus placed within their power. The friends wasted their thoughts in vain conjecture, and then, burning with indignation, turned to seek their horses. The long sweeping tails of these animals had also been cut off. That it was the Pawnee Picts, they no longer doubted; and fearful was the ire of the Osages at the contempt with which they had been treated. The trail of their night visitors was plainly marked, and led towards a copse, where they had evidently left their horses. It then turned to the river bank, and was lost. Nah-com-e-shee, however, glancing his eye over the opposite plain, gave a cry of delight, and pointed out to his companions the flashing of spears in the morning sun.

To plunge into the river, to reach the other shore, and to ride madly over the plain in chase of their audacious foes was the work of an instant. In vain, however, they strained their eyes to catch another glimpse of the retreating party, until again the flashing of the spear-heads was seen near at hand, and plunging over the next hillock, the friends found themselves in presence of—three lances stuck in the ground. If the Indians boiled with passion before, their rage now knew no bounds; they vowed, with little consideration for the possibility or probability of the matter, to exterminate every Pawnee Pict from the face of the earth. This resolution being unanimous, a halt was made, and a council of war held. Some ten minutes were passed in discussion, and then away went the Osages on the trail of their foes, just as they caught sight, in the rear, of a perfect cloud of horsemen pouring over the plain in the distance. It was a war-party of the Pawnee Picts, about twenty of whom came riding fast in pursuit of the three friends. A thickly-wooded ravine lay about a mile distant. Towards this the Osages hastened for refuge, their souls bounding with delight at the prospect of a contest which now opened before them.

The ravine was soon reached. It was narrow, and on both sides thickly wooded, while several clumps of timber lay near its mouth. The Osages saw that the only hope of coping with a superior force was by defending the entrance, and, accordingly, dismounting from their steeds, turned them loose, and strung their bows. On came the Pawnee Picts, riding furiously over the prairie. The intentions of the Osages were too plain to be mistaken, and none of their pursuers ventured to brave the discharge of arrows which was ready for their reception; but, imitating the example set them, cast loose their horses, and sought the shelter of a copse. The unequal struggle now commenced, and loud war-whoops rung through the valley. Arrows flew constantly from foe to foe. The Pawnees, having a great superiority in numbers, succeeded oftenest in wounding their adversaries. Still they gained not upon them; the Osages, though soon severely hurt, preserving the same undaunted front, and returning their missiles with unabated vigour.

At length, however, their arrows were spent, and clutching their tomahawks, the friends, casting a glance of stern but undying affection on each other, prepared to die like men. On came the Pawnees, yelling the fearful war-whoop, and waving their hatchets on high. Already were a dozen of them within a few yards of the devoted trio, when their yell was echoed from the forest, and three of their foremost warriors lay low, slain by a flight of arrows from the top of the ravine. Back turned the Pawnees to their shelter, while the Osages, taking advantage of the confusion, snatched the usual trophy of victory from their fallen foes, and then, catching their steeds, mounted and fled. Guided by the trampling of horses, they rushed in pursuit of those to whose timely assistance they owed their lives. In vain, however, did they urge their steeds; their unknown assistants were not to be overtaken. For about an hour the three friends continued their ride, and then halted to bind up their wounds, and conceal themselves for the rest of the day.

The spot selected was admirably adapted for the purpose, being an open glade in the forest, surrounded on all sides by trees. Here they turned their horses loose once more, and lay down upon the grass, weary and faint. To find herbs, and with them to form a kind of poultice, fastened on with bark by means of ligatures of grass, was their first duty, and then the inner man was considered. None of them had tasted food since the previous night, and there was none in their possession. Nah-com-e-shee, being the warrior who was least severely wounded, and having picked up several Pawnee arrows, started into the forest in search of game. With the keen perception of an Indian, he selected that side which appeared a little inclined to descend, as it naturally excited his suspicion that a stream lay in that direction. This was the more probable, that a little purling spring that bubbled up in the green open glade tended thither. Nor was the warrior's sagacity at fault, for a smart walk brought him to the banks of a narrow and slowly-running river. Within sight of this Nah-com-e-shee concealed himself, and prepared to wait even for hours the passage of a deer or elk. His patience was not, however, put to so severe a test, as, ere long, a rustling in the bushes opposite attracted his attention. Raising his eyes from their fixed position, he saw the antlers of a buck rearing themselves over a thicket of brush, and next moment a noble deer bounded to the bank to drink. An arrow pierced its heart from the Indian's unerring bow ere its lips had touched the water, and Nah-com-e-shee rushed eagerly towards the spot. Three mounted warriors were before him, and while he sought cover, captured and bore away the prize.

The Osage knew that it was useless to remain on the watch any longer, and, pursuit being madness, turned back and sought his companions, who were more indignant than ever at this new outrage. Repose was, however, absolutely necessary, and was now sought, all trusting to the keenness of their senses to awake ere they could be surprised. It was dark night ere they awoke, and then the three friends groaned with rage that was absolutely frightful. Each felt himself ornamented by a squaw's petticoat, thrown loosely over him. Burning with passion, they grasped one another's hands, and vowed terrible vengeance.

At this instant a dim light was seen through the trees, blazing up at a considerable distance in the forest. It was the fire of a camp, and the hearts of the Osage warriors were at last glad. They had been so often outwitted, that the utmost caution was used. Each divested himself of every unnecessary article of clothing, while their tomahawks were the only arms they preserved. Clutching these, they crept stealthily, and with a serpent's tread, into the forest. As they advanced, the glare of the fire grew brighter; and at length, when within a couple of hundred yards, they could plainly hear the green wood crackling in the full stillness of evening. A faint odour of broiled venison came pleasingly to their nostrils, and then three figures were plainly discerned round the fire.

Between the spot occupied by the Osages and the hostile camp lay a rough piece of ground, full of holes and natural ditches. Across this the three friends began to crawl, holding their breath, and clutching their deadly weapons, while their hearts beat with anxiety lest their victims should escape. Half the distance was passed over, and still more strongly was the cooking made evident to the hungry senses of the creeping Osages. Still the unconscious warriors moved not, but kept their backs turned to the approaching foe. They were evidently eating, and holding converse at intervals. At length, as the friends came still nearer, they appeared to finish their meal, and sunk gradually on the leafy ground to rest. The Osages breathed more freely, and advanced with less caution, until at length, when within half-a-dozen yards, they rose, gave the terrific war-whoop, and leaped madly upon the camp. It was vacant—their victims had escaped. The friends, amazed, were about to fly from their dangerous proximity to the light, when three distinct laughs were heard.

The Osages stood immoveable, gazing at one another with a grim, half-angry, half-comic expression, and ere they could speak, three maidens disguised as warriors stood meekly one before each brave, a horse's tail in one hand, and the other trophies in the other. The friends tried their utmost to look angry; but the countenances of the girls were so meek, and yet so malicious, that the gravity of the braves was overcome, and they laughed heartily at the conclusion of their expected deadly struggle.

The girls then explained that, for reasons of their own, disapproving of the celibacy of the three friends, they had resolved to excite their admiration and interest, that they had followed them immediately after their departure, had crept on them in the night, and divested them of their crests, &c. and played them every other trick which has been recorded in this legend. The warriors listened, and when they narrated how they had saved their lives in the ravine, seemed each struck with the same sudden conviction; namely, that the lives thus preserved belonged to the preservers, and at once made public their opinion. The damsels laughed gaily, and promised to entertain the notion, but recalled their lovers to a remembrance of their hungry state. Merrily and blithely supped the three maidens and the three friends that night beneath the greenwood tree; and when in after years they met at eventide, all happy husbands and wives, with dusky boys and girls crowding round them, that it was the brightest moment of their existence, was the oft-repeated saying of the THREE FRIENDS.

SUPPLY OF WATER TO THE METROPOLIS.

THE inhabitants of London occasionally come to a pause in the midst of their hurrying pursuit of wealth, commerce, or pleasure, and look round, apparently in a state of uncertainty as to their real position, morally or physically. At such times they generally become aware of the existence of some inconvenience or crying abuse, which they apply themselves to remove or remedy; public meetings are called, long speeches made, strings of resolutions moved and adopted—and there the matter ends; they settle down to their usual routine, to wake up again at the end of twenty years, and go through a precisely similar state of ebullition.

This phenomenon, however, shows itself, in some instances, connected with really important objects, as in the meetings which have been held from time to time on the question of the supplies of water for the daily consumption of the metropolitan population—a thoroughly legitimate subject of inquiry. They who know anything of the water drunk in London, must remember how vapid and unrefreshing it is, when compared with that obtained in the country, or in other towns where the supply is less polluted. But this is not the worst; insipidity and unsavouriness are but a small portion of the evil, which resolves itself into positive unwholesomeness and deleteriousness; and so loud have, at times, been the manifestations of complaint, that many practical measures have been suggested which would tend to the purification of an element so essential to healthful existence.

Water for the use of the inhabitants was first drawn from the Thames in 1568, by machinery erected at Dowgate Hill. From this date the evils complained of went on accumulating, up to the time of the first authorised inquiry in 1819, subsequently continued by a Royal Commission, and Committees of the House of Commons, down to 1834; but without leading to any beneficial result, for the water of the Thames was more polluted at the termination of their proceedings than at the commencement, owing to the greater number of drains that discharged themselves into the river; which, in the words of the report published in 1836, 'receives the excrementitious matter from nearly a million and a half of human beings; the washings of their foul linen; the filth and refuse of many hundred manufactories; the offal and decomposing vegetable substances from the markets; the foul and gory liquid from slaughter-houses; and the purulent abominations from hospitals and dissecting-rooms, too disgusting to detail.'

The plans which had been suggested for the supply of water of a less objectionable quality were, purification by filtration or subsidence; pumping from a part of the river above the contaminated districts; or to 'draw the supply from other sources than the Thames, and convey it, by means of extensive aqueducts, to London.' These propositions were objected to as imperfect, ineffective, and too expensive; and a meeting was called to discuss a plan devised by Mr J. Martin, which, it was said, completely realised all that the public required, and, to quote again from the report, 'consists in diverting altogether from the river every possible source of pollution within the London district; so that the water supplied from it to the inhabitants by the existing water companies, shall become as unobjectionable as a noble river in its natural state ever offered to man.' This was to be effected 'by the construction of a close sewer, twenty feet wide, and of adequate depth, along both banks of the river,' from a point near Vauxhall Bridge, and terminating respectively in large receptacles to be situated in Limehouse and Rotherhithe, after running by the side of the stream for a distance of five miles and a quarter, completely preventing the discharge of offensive matter into the tideway, by depositing all the drainage in the two grand receptacles, in which provision was to be made for the destruction of noxious effluvia, and the ventilation of the sewers, by large fires burning over grated openings.

To show the necessity for so great a work, a large amount of evidence was published as to the actual state of the water derived from the Thames; which will apply equally well at the present day, as the best portions of the metropolis, or four-fifths, are exclusively supplied from that source. It was shown that one company drew their supply from the river immediately opposite the mouth of the 'great Ranelagh sewer,' and another at a short distance below it; and although it was urged that the companies allowed time for the 'depuration of the water by subsidence,' yet proofs were adduced that complete purification from the deleterious particles held in suspension did not take place. Calculations were made, which, going beyond the ordinary generalities, showed that upwards of three millions of pounds of impure matter, solid and fluid, were poured into the Thames every day; to which must be added, 'the impure water resulting from the body ablutions of at least half a million of people who wash daily, and of the rest of the inhabitants who do so less often—no mean source of pollution, charged, as the water must be, with the excrementitious matter from the surface of the body.'

The evidence goes to show that this sickening mass of filth was not removed by the tide, as had been asserted. A witness, Mr Evans, in speaking of the sewers, observed, 'that these discharge their horrid contents into the river Thames; and that the progress of the tide defies any complete clearance, no one can attempt to deny. The filth, in fact, is carried as far down the river as the tide will carry it, and again, by the next tide, brought the same way back; so that the river Thames, as far up as the tide flows, can be considered neither more nor less than the great common sewer of London, and consequently unfit to be the source from whence the supply of water ought to be taken for the use of the metropolis.' Dr Bostock, another witness, stated, 'that he had understood, by the engineers conversant with the subject, that the tide, near London, produces rather an oscillation than a change of water; that, in fact, the water remains very nearly stationary near the metropolis, being, as I said, backed up when the tide rises; and when the tide falls, a certain portion is suffered to escape; but there is only a *very gradual transmission or interchange of water*.'

With regard to the purification of the water by subsidence, Dr Granville testified—'Within the last few weeks, I had occasion to clean the upper cistern at the top of the house, on account of some fracture in the bottom lead, when I found two inches of thick, filthy, and foul-smelling deposit in it; although the operation of cleaning the same cistern had been performed only twelve months before. Indeed the water in the said cistern, placed at an altitude of ninety feet from the street, does never look otherwise than like dirty pea-soup, owing to the frequent stirring up of it by the coming in of the fresh supply three times a-week.' 'Supposing that the companies were to establish reservoirs of such magnitude as to allow the water to be lodged undisturbed therein, during a period of time sufficiently long for the depurative process by spontaneous fermentation to take place, which is to destroy all animal impurities in it, they would still supply the public with what, although clear and inodorous, would contain enough of chalk and plaster of Paris to multiply, and render more severe, the various and innumerable degrees of derangements of the stomach and bowels which so generally prevail in, and are almost peculiar to, this metropolis. Would any one knowingly, and with cheerfulness, drink a tumbler of water from a river-spring which should have previously run through a succession of cess-pools, and afterwards been filtered through sand and gravel, because it may then appear clear and transparent? Yet such is the case with us collectively, who drink, in some way or other, the Thames water of the London district!'

Other advantages comprehended in the proposed plan were of equal importance with the purification of the water, and would have supplied a great want under which London labours to the present day—open embankments, and public thoroughfares along each bank of the river. The report states that one of the improvements would have been, 'the erection, over the two sewers, of a line of colonnaded wharfs, which will afford, in front of the present wharfs, additional room; increase the convenience of the merchant and the labourer; facilitate the operations of trade; give greater security to property landed from vessels and barges; improve the navigation of the river by the assistance of the subjacent sewers, which will constitute uniform embankments.' It was further contemplated to convert the roofs of the colonnaded wharfs just described into parapetted thoroughfares, serving the purpose 'of a magnificent and extensive public walk along both banks of the Thames, unequalled in any part of Europe; to which the public will be admitted gratuitously on Sundays, and at the smallest rate of charge on every other day in the week.' In this way it was hoped to realise the often-expressed wishes of 'parliamentary committees, of affording to the mass of the population the luxury, salubriousness, and recreation of great public walks in the very heart of London,' together with 'the formation of collateral public baths, which shall induce persons to abstain from bathing in the Thames;' all to arise from 'the saving of a vast quantity of the most fructifying manure, which, employed on cultivated soil, will nearly double its produce.'

It cannot be doubted that this scheme, if carried out, would have made London the most magnificent capital in Europe, while the advantages offered to the health and recreation of the inhabitants would have been without a parallel. This latter consideration was urged in the report—'It cannot be necessary to point out how requisite some public walks or open spaces in the neighbourhood of large towns must be, to those who consider the occupations of the working-classes who dwell in them. Confined as they are during week days, as mechanics and manufacturers, and often shut up in heated factories, it must be evident that it is of the first importance to their health, on their day of rest, to enjoy the fresh air, and be able to walk out in decent comfort with their families. Deprived of any such resource, it is probable that their only escape from the narrow courts or alleys (in which so many of the humbler classes reside) will be to those drinking-shops where, in short-lived excitement, they may forget their toil, but where they waste the means of their families, and too often destroy their health.' Dr Granville's evidence shows that 'want of the means of taking exercise produces, moreover, in the same classes of people a melancholy and morose disposition, and a spirit of dissatisfaction, increased by the want of domestic attraction and impaired health. . . The remedy lies in the establishment of public walks and public recreations, by means of which the classes of people alluded to are enticed into the open air. At present, the banks of the Thames, and the various narrow streets which run parallel or at right angles with them, are justly considered as unhealthy situations to live in. Medical officers of dispensaries, and amongst them myself, who during the last twenty years have acted in the capacity of physician to three medical institutions, can testify to the inferior degree of health generally found among the inhabitants of these districts; where aguish and low fevers, scrofula, and all such complaints as depend on the action of foul effluvia on the human constitution, are much more common than in the more elevated sections of the metropolis.'

It will be remembered that the subject of supplies of water received a large share of attention from the Health of Towns Commission, to whose labours we have frequently adverted; and from the foregoing statements, we find that it has, at various times, been made to involve many highly important considerations. It will long be matter of regret that a scheme offering so good an opportunity for the embellishment of the capital, and increase of its commercial resources, while contributing to the wellbeing of the population, should not have received efficient support from the legislature. From the financial tables accompanying the report, we learn that the whole expense of the works was calculated at a little more than L.1,300,000, for which there would have been an annual return of nearly L.400,000; half of the amount being produced by the sale of the manure prevented from running to waste in the river. Valuable statements were published of the great value of this species of manure in agricultural operations; among others, reference was made to the manufactories of the French, who 'prefer, for the sake of easy and convenient transport, to dry the substances in question down to a powder, which bears the name of "*poudrette*," and which is forwarded to different parts from the neighbourhood of the capital, and sold at a high price. The success of the establishment for the manufacture of the *poudrette* alluded to, first formed near Paris forty years ago or thereabouts, has been such, that in almost every part of the kingdom similar undertakings have been entered into, and nothing is now wasted.' The committee, in referring to these facts, explained that 'the drainage received into the great receptacles before mentioned will be converted into manure, according to the method and practice very extensively adopted in China, on the continent of Europe, and, of late years, also in some parts of Scotland. This will be conveyed, by well-devised arrangements, and under the influence of scientific measures, to different parts of the country in covered barges or properly-constructed land-carriages. The value of this species of manure is almost incalculable. The best authorities place it far above every other, as containing, in much greater abundance, the very elements of which vegetable substances are composed, and on which their existence and growth depend. By saving, therefore, the vast quantity of it which has hitherto been wasted in the metropolis, a most important benefit—that of fertilising and rendering the land considerably more productive—will be conferred on the public, through the identical plan which alone can secure to us the luxury of drinking wholesome and unpolluted water.'

THE OFFENDED.

Every one is ready to admit the duty of not giving offence to others. It is one of the universally acknowledged laws of the society in which we are units, to live peaceably and harmoniously with all around us, and to avoid anything which may cause estrangement, and produce angry and bitter feeling; and he who wantonly violates this law, and needlessly irritates and provokes, proves himself unworthy of the blessings which civilisation and society were intended to secure. If every one acted in an offensive manner, the component parts of society must be broken up, and man must again retrograde into solitariness and barbarism; for it is only by mutual respect and good-will that society can cohere and exist.

But though every one is ready to admit the duty of not giving offence, few consider the obligation of a duty which is of little less importance, namely, that of not *taking* offence. Offenders are numerous enough, but the offended are innumerable, and the same consequences ensue in the one case as in the other, namely, estrangement and ill-will, and a tendency to sap the harmony, and even the existence of society.

The mischief resulting from a proneness to take offence, is the more to be regretted, from the character of the agents who produce it. The offended are not, for the most part, the vulgar-minded and the unscrupulous, as is too often the case with the offenders, but estimable, refined, and conscientious people, who would be deeply pained at the idea of offending any one, but who, through an excess of proper feeling, a morbid sensitiveness, and an undue self-respect, are continually finding something at which to take offence. Persons of such temperament not only make their fellows offenders for a word, but construe an imaginary look, a peculiarity of accent, into insults; thus reserve and estrangement ensue, and often cause more lasting ill consequences than a violent quarrel, inasmuch as there is nothing to reconcile, and the offender is wholly unconscious of having committed any offence.

Were it not for the sad effects resulting from such an unfortunate temperament, it would be not a little amusing to observe its manifestations, and the absurdly frivolous grounds on which the imaginary insult is often based. One good lady, on returning from a casual visit, declares she will never darken her friends' doors again; they offered her nothing to eat and drink; they were as cool as if they had not known her; they asked her if she had dined certainly; but it is easy to tell by people's manner what they mean, and she could see in a moment that she was not wanted. Another sensitive gentleman thinks every one is insulting his poverty. If any of his friends well to do in the world do not notice him, they are proud upstart creatures—not that he cares for them, or wants their attention, but he hates such pride. If, on the other hand, they are polite and affable, he wants not their patronising airs; their lordly civility is little better than an insult; and for his part, he has no wish of accepting invitations to dinner which can only make himself appear contemptible, and serve to contrast with their ostentatious greatness. An easily offended young lady vows she will visit her gay young friends no more, for their dress is so fine, it is quite disagreeable to sit in their company, and be quizzed after she is gone, as no doubt she is. Although perhaps their own dress may be only what is perfectly according to their station and prospects, and they neither think of quizzing her while present, nor making remarks on her when absent, and any idea of giving offence is the farthest from their thoughts or intentions.

Thus too often do these in many respects estimable people strenuously fight with phantoms which they themselves have conjured up, and complain of insults which only exist in their own imaginations. The world soon becomes with such a burying-place for friendships, the habit gains strength, and the morbid feeling of offence and insult grows into a habitual activity, inimical to peace of mind, cheerfulness, and good-will. For want of a kind interpretation of actions and conduct that were never intended to give the slightest offence, how often the friend of youth ceases to be the friend of age; the once familiar companion is passed without recognition; families that once were closely allied withdraw to cold distance from each other; and those who once shook each other by the hand as warm-hearted friends, now meet one another with averted eyes.

'It is the glory of a man,' says the sacred proverb, 'to pass over a transgression;' and it is the truest wisdom and the best philosophy sometimes to shut our eyes to an insult, even when there may be some reason to fear it was not entirely unpremeditated. At all events, we shall meet in the world with quite enough of offences, unless we are more than ordinarily fortunate, without seeking out imaginary insults, and wasting our strength and destroying our peace by fighting with the wind. Our severest scrutiny is best turned to ourselves, that we may not be offenders, and our most favourable judgment formed respecting the conduct and actions of others, that we may not be offended. While we may be sure that, in the crowded path of life, we ourselves do not intend to run wilfully against others, though we may sometimes stumble against them, so we must hope and believe that they in turn have no intention of offending us, though they may sometimes accidentally jostle us in their turn. The duty of endurance has undoubtedly its proper limits, but it is a wise determination not only not to offend, but also not to be easily offended. Every one desires that others should interpret his actions kindly, and where any may be of doubtful import, to hope the best; and such is the way in which their actions should be regarded by us. Were the duty of not taking offense more thought of and better understood, the peace of individuals, of families, of communities, of nations, would rest on a firmer foundation, and something would be added to the general amount of human harmony and happiness.

WORDS BORROWED FROM THE FRENCH.

SECOND ARTICLE.

Débris is an expression which geologists and civil engineers have borrowed from the French, to express the remains of rock and other matter which have been broken up either by the sudden agency of bygone catastrophes, by gradual decay, or by mechanical violence. It means strictly the remains of anything which has been destroyed. If a lodger in French apartments break anything, he is called upon to pay for the *débris*; because, having given the full value of the article in its perfect state, he is made quite welcome to the fractured remains.

Debut signifies an entrance, or a first appearance. A young lady who is allowed to appear for the first time in a grown-up party, is said to have made her *debut* in society; and her first presentation to royalty is called making her *debut* at court. An actor who appears for the first time on any stage, is called a *debutant*. Though this is a comparatively new word in our language, we find it in Todd's Johnson, which is, we believe, its *debut* in an English dictionary.

Dégagé.—A gentleman whose manners are of the free-and-easy school—a penguin,* who has but little diffidence to prevent him from addressing a duke or an archbishop with familiarity; one who will take the place of honour at table, and help himself to wine without waiting for the butler—a person of that class is said to have an air *dégagé*. We have no English word which expresses that kind of man so well: it means 'disengaged;' that is to say, free, unbound; having no compact with modesty, timidity, or with the nicer conventionalities of society. As the character it describes is of modern creation, so the word is of new introduction. Fifty years ago, the formalities of 'etiquette' would not have allowed of the sort of penguinism which the removal of cold and irrational restrictions has admitted into society.

Déjeûner, or *Déjeûné.*—This—the French word for the morning-meal—is applied, in fashionable life, to breakfasts which take place in the middle of the day, or, breakfast-parties. The more substantial sort, which are two meals in one, and answer for luncheon as well, are called *déjeûners à la fourchette*—because meats requiring *forks*, and by consequence knives, to eat them, are there introduced. *Déjeûner* is commonly thought to be a modern Gallicism; but this is a mistake, for it occurs in Ben Jonson's 'New Inn,' wherein one of the characters is recommended to 'take a *déjeûné* of Muskadel eggs.' Old-fashioned Scotch people also to this day talk of their *disjune*. In the 'Wife of Auchtermuchty,' a droll poem of the sixteenth century, it is said of the heroine—

> 'Then in the morning up she gat,
> And on her heart laid her *disjune*.'

Devoirs.—'Duties,' used in a sense nearly equivalent to our old English term 'respects.' A dependent is said to pay devoirs or court to a patron: thus Pope—

> 'Awkward and supple each *devoir* to pay,
> She flatters her good lady twice a day.'

The word is most frequently used in reference to the complimentary attentions paid to the fair sex. Addison says, 'Gentlemen who do not design to marry, yet pay their *devoirs* to one particular fair.' Hood's inimitable 'Young Ben,' on returning from sea, and visiting Sally Brown, is described as going

> ——— 'to pay her his *devoirs*,
> When he devoured his pay.'

When first adopted into the English language, the term appears to have been taken to mean service. In the 'Knight of the Burning Pestle,' by Beaumont and Fletcher, we find the following passage:—

> 'Madam, if any service or *devoir*
> Of a poor errant-knight may right your wrongs,
> Command it.'

Distingué.—'Distinguished.' A person is said in France to have *un air distingué*, in whom a natural nobleness or intellectual superiority shines through the accidents of dress and circumstances. We speak of a man or woman as *distingué*, who has from outward or inward qualities an appearance strikingly removed above vulgarity. And it would appear as if the French also partly admitted this more general sense, if we can trust to an anecdote of the congress of Vienna. On that occasion, most of the plenipotentiaries were attired in gorgeous uniforms, covered with orders and costly ornaments. The English legate, on the contrary, was dressed in plain black, with the ribbon of the Bath lying across his chest. On one of the officials ridiculing this as commonplace, Talleyrand said—'You are quite wrong. His lordship's tasteful simplicity makes him the most *distingué* amongst us.'

Douceur.—The literal signification of this word is 'sweetness,' in which sense it has been employed by some English authors. Chesterfield advises that we should 'blame with indulgence, and correct with *douceur*.' But the secondary meaning attached to the expression in its native language, is that in which it is best understood with us; namely, 'lure,' or 'inducement.' A person in want of a situation very often advertises for one, and, heading the announcement '*Douceur*,' offers the inducement of a sum of money to any one who will procure the desired appointment. Indeed the term is scarcely ever used now, except on such occasions.

Eclat.—Two meanings are attached to this word by the French—'a sudden noise,' and 'lustre.' They apply it to human conduct in the sense of a high approbation. Thus, if a gentleman has been involved in unpleasant charges, and stood the test of a searching legal investigation, he is said to come off with *éclat*. Amongst us, the word is applied on various occasions, often with reference to very small matters: for example, we say a gentleman has come off with *éclat*, if he has given a witty or pleasant turn to any half-serious accusation brought against him. We do not find *éclat* used by English authors earlier than Pope, who praises Homer for 'the *éclat* of his battles.'

Elite.—That which has been chosen or taken by preference, was originally the sense conveyed by this word; but in modern French it signifies the highest or best, as *l'élite d'une armée*—(The flower of an army). Its earliest appearance on this side of the Channel is in the old Scottish chronicles, as applicable to an elected bishop. Wyntoun, recording the death of Bishop Arnold, says that—

> 'Rychard Byschape in his stede
> Chosyn, he was concorditer,
> And *élite* twa yhere had eftyr.'

The term has descended to the service of the chroniclers of fashionable movements in the English newspapers; who speak of an assemblage of great folks as the *élite* of fashion.

Empressement—amongst the French expresses a rapid or eager movement. A Parisian, learning that a dear friend had come to town, would go to him with *empressement*. With us, the word implies merely a more than usually earnest or affectionate manner. We would say of two friends who met after a long absence, they shook

* See our article on this genus, vol. iii., p. 385, new series.

hands with *empressement*. A lady, told that a female friend of hers was about to be married, and at the same time informed of the gentleman's name, remarked—'Oh, I now remember, when I was present with her at Mr ——'s visits, I used to think he came into the room with a great *empressement*.'

Ennui—Weariness, the sense of tedium; sometimes implying also a mixture of vexation or care. In England, the word is applied solely to weariness. Gray defines it in his letters, when he says of something, 'The only fault of it is insipidity, which is apt now and then to give a sort of *ennui*, which makes one form certain little wishes that signify nothing.' Ennui is an inconvenience only felt by the leisure classes, as Mrs Austin designates people in easy circumstances. It arises from a want of some sufficiently attractive occupation, or of energy to set about what is not immediately attractive. When novelists or painters wish to depict the feeling, they portray a person lying on a sofa with a book, which, tired of reading, he has thrown on the floor, indulging at the same time in an extensive yawn. The Countess of Hahn Hahn, in her amusing travels, 'Tra los Montes,' makes a powerful use of this expression. Describing the skulls in the catacombs of Bordeaux, she declares 'that their mouths yawn as if they were shrunk back by the incommensurable *ennui* of eternity.'

Ensemble.—'The result of a union of parts;' 'the totality as distinguished from the details.' Of a good musical band we would say, 'the *ensemble* was perfect;' that is, the various parts required in a good band were all present in just proportion, and thoroughly in accord with each other, so as to produce a correct and satisfactory whole. A famed beauty may be allowed to have one or two unfortunate features, and certain faults of figure; but yet the *tout ensemble* may deserve to be admired. That is, take her all in all, she is a fine woman.

Façade—Borrowed from the French by architects, and applied to the chief frontage of a building.

Feu-de-joie—Literally 'a bon-fire,' but amongst us applied to a mode of musketry-firing practised by the military on occasions of rejoicing. When well executed, the firing goes in an uninterrupted succession along the line.

Gauche—'The *left*'—the designation of the opposition in the French chamber of deputies. The *extrême gauche*, the appellation of the most 'liberal' of that party, which takes its position farthest from the tribune and seat of the ministers. These words have obtained a certain currency amongst us, to express the corresponding political sects of our own country. *Gauche* had, however, an acceptance with us from a time antecedent to the existence of these parties, being employed to describe those who, from want of handiness and tact in small matters, are always meeting with little misfortunes, as they are pleased to call them. When filling a lady's glass, for instance, they spill the wine; in sealing a letter, they burn their own or somebody else's fingers; they knock over vases, overturn inkstands; in the ball-room tread on cherished flounces; when asked to hold a bouquet, let it fall, and then most likely tread it to destruction. All these little accidents are called *gaucheries*; because, as Talleyrand observed of one of the class, 'this sort of people seems to be born with two left hands.' We have borrowed another expression for these unfortunates—*mal-adroites*.

Gourmand—A mild substitute for 'glutton.' Milton uses the word in one of his political pamphlets; and Bishop Hall declares of a contemporary that 'this *gourmand* sacrifices whole hecatombs to his paunch.' In some of the flimsy productions of the fashionable-novel school, we have seen this word used indifferently with

Gourmet, which means a connoisseur of wine.

Goût—Literally 'taste;' but borrowed by us to mean 'relish' also. Todd indignantly calls it 'an affected cant word;' and certainly its use does occasionally betray affectation, as when Woodward, in his work on Fossils, speaks of 'catalogues for a direction to any one that has a *goût* for the like studies;' in which passage our own word 'taste' would have been more expressive than the French term. It is, however, useful in the sense in which we find it most frequently employed; for example, 'He follows the sport of angling with *goût*.' In this sentence there is no English word which would express the required meaning. The English equivalent certainly would not; for it could never be said of an angler that he catches fish—though he may eat them—with 'a relish.' It is remarkable that the Scotch use the word to imply merely a taste or savour.

Hauteur—Literally 'height.' In morals, the French sometimes use the word to express a good quality—Voltaire, for instance, speaks of a spirit full of justice and *hauteur*, meaning elevated thoughts—and sometimes to convey the idea of a haughty insolence. Used in the plural, the word expresses acts of insufferable superciliousness. The English have introduced *hauteur* as a convenient term for a proud manner not uncommon in the higher classes. They are also beginning to make considerable use of the phrase *De haut en bas*, by which the French graphically depict a contemptuous manner, as if that of a man always looking down from a height on persons below him.

Haut-ton—'High tone' or 'style;' applied to the upper circles of society.

Hors—A prefix, meaning 'out of,' and except. We say of a soldier when wounded, and removed from the field of battle, that he is *hors-de-combat*. In fortification, a work removed from the main body of defences is called *hors-d'œuvre*; an expression which is also analogously employed by cooks to comprehend 'side-dishes;' little enticements supplementary to the more solid parts of the feast.

Mauvaise-honte—'False shame;' especially indicative of that sort of shamefacedness which arises less from real modesty than from a want of honest confidence. Hence mauvaise-honte is substituted for the less complimentary term 'sheepishness.' *Mauvais-ton* (a bad manner or style) is applied to persons who are ill-bred, as *bon-ton* is employed to designate good-breeding. *Mauvais-goût* means 'in bad taste;' *Mauvais-sujet*, literally a 'bad subject,' is one of those expressions which enable ladies, and persons of delicate nerves, to say what they mean without seeming harsh or vulgar; its English signification is simply—'a scamp.' The term, however, which a British lady would resort to by way of delicacy would be avoided by a French lady, because, across the Channel, it awakens as unpleasant associations as its English equivalents do with us.

Messieurs—The plural of 'monsieur,' which has been taken as a prologue to the names of persons associated together in business. The prefix *Misters* Brown, Jones, and Robinson, wants euphony; hence the French word, Monsieur, its singular form, has no exact counterpart in English; for its literal rendering is, 'My Sir,' which we never say in conversation, and only make use of at the beginning of a letter, with the intervention of the word 'dear.' The history of Sire, Sieur, or Sir, is one of gradual decline. From having been the style of addressing a king only, it is now indiscriminately used to all classes who are *not* noble.

Naïveté, says a contributor to the 'Ana' of the Encyclopédie Française, 'is the expression of frankness, simplicity, or of ignorance, and often of all three at once.' Anecdotes will illustrate a part at least of this complete definition. The French jest-books relate that a gentleman not overburthened with sense awoke one night, and told his servant to look out and see if it were daylight. The man did as he was told, and, stepping in from the balcony, declared that he could not see any signs of approaching day. 'Poo! poo!' exclaimed his master, 'I know it must be dawn. Light the candle, and you will be able to see it better.' This sort of naïveté arises from stolidity. Another anecdote supplies an instance of it when taken to shadow forth simplicity. A certain class of persons and children are said always to tell the truth, and that peculiarity is precisely expressed by the word *naïveté*. We were once dining with a gentleman who talked much of the extent and choiceness of his stock of wines, and whose interesting little daughter was our next neighbour. When the champagne was opened, one of the guests refused it, upon which the *naïve* little lady exclaimed, 'Pray, take some champagne, Mrs ——. There is *another bottle* in the cellar!' This simple disclosure prevented the host from saying another word about wine for the rest of the evening. There is no English word by which such interesting simplicity could be expressed; hence *naïveté* is a most useful addition to our vocabulary.

Nonchalance is a French term for indolence, an indifference as to taking trouble about anything. We have come to use it with reference to a cool carelessness of manner, and a want of sensibility to danger. At the battle of Toulon, a lieutenant was selected by Napoleon (then chief of artillery) to write a despatch. The young soldier knelt, and was penning it from dictation on one knee, when a cannon ball passed close before him, scattering a cloud of sand over the paper. Instead of starting back, the amanuensis turned over the leaf, exclaiming, 'Bravo! What capital pounce this sand makes!' This nonchalance, as we would call it, though the French would rather perhaps say *insouciance*, made the fortune of young Junot, for Napoleon kept his eye upon him, and he became finally Duke of Abrantes.

Outré, exclaims Todd, 'is a most affected and needless introduction to the English language.' The words 'exaggerated' and 'overstrained' seem to bear out this opinion, for they convey, when used in their proper places, all that *outré* is capable of expressing. This, it may be remarked, is another of the French words which found their way to Scotland in old times, and are now familiar to the humblest classes in that kingdom. An uncouthly eccentric man is said by the Scotch to be very *outray*; accenting the last syllable.

Par excellence—'By excellence;' the French translation of an old scholastic term, *per excellentiam*, meaning with regard to a special quality or attendant circumstance. We have adopted the French term, because the literal translation of *per excellentiam* does not convey that peculiar idea. A gentleman acquired the odd nickname of Uncle throughout the circle of his acquaintance. He had so many nephews and nieces who were frequently speaking of him in society, that he came to be considered as Uncle *par excellence*; hence his name.

Passé—The preterite participle of the verb 'to pass'—a word terrible to single ladies of a certain age. When cruelly applied to such of the fair sex as can be by no stretch of polite exaggeration termed 'girls,' it implies that their charms have gone by—'passed.' To say that a lady is *passé*, is to describe faded beauty and beginning decay, and to pronounce a judgment of old maidenhood—to ban her, as it were, from the hymeneal altar. We have no equivalent for this ungallant word in English. Another inflection of the verb *passer* has also been in frequent use for at least two centuries and a half, namely, *en passant*—'in passing.' It is used to denote anything that is said parenthetically, or by the by.

Patois—With the French, the peculiar language spoken in any of the provinces, usually something very different from the classic French of Paris; with us, the mere variety of intonation which marks men reared in Scotland or Ireland. The term is useful. We could not, for instance, say of an Irish lady that she spoke with a brogue: we therefore adumbrate her mode of pronunciation under the phrase, 'an interesting *patois*.' An Irish author of aspiring character, who figured some years ago in London gay life, allied himself with another fashionable writer, for the purpose of conducting a periodical work. The English gentleman was slightly deaf. The Irishman, who wished to sink all association with his country, and believed that he had wholly expunged the brogue from his speech, was one evening launching out before a brilliant party on the unfavourable effect which the least trace of national peculiarity of tongue was calculated to have upon an Irishman or Scotchman, with regard to his advances in society; when his friend broke in with—'Oh, my dear ——, don't speak so strongly of your *patois*, for no one ever thinks the worse of you for it.' The mortification of the wouldn't-be Hibernian may be imagined.

Penchant—'An inclination'—a word not without its use. The nearest approach to one of the senses in which we employ it, is the inelegant phrase, 'a sneaking kindness.' It also stands for a weak propensity, and we hear in common conversation of a man who has a *penchant* for the pleasures of the table, the turf, &c.

Précis—A summary or abridgment, very much in use by Scotch lawyers.

Prestige.—The original signification of prestige is a piece of jugglery or imposture; and the word was borrowed by some good English writers of the old school for exactly the same sense. Thus Warburton speaks in his sermons of 'the sophisms of infidelity, and the *prestiges* of imposture.' But of late, the word has been received in a new acceptation in both languages—that of a prejudiced and presentimental faith. The military successes of Napoleon were said to have invested him and his soldiers with a *prestige*: it was thought they had been destined never to be beaten. When the disastrous reverses in Russia took place, he exclaimed, 'Alas! the *prestige* of the army is gone.' We speak of an author's name bearing a *prestige* in favour of any new works to which it may be attached.

Programme.—This word—borrowed from the Greeks by the Romans, taken from the latter by the French, and lastly from the French by the English—properly denotes 'a preface' (*gramma*, a word, *pro*, before); but is now exclusively adopted for the printed synopses of the performances at concerts, or the proceedings of public meetings.

Protegé—One who is protected or taken by the hand by a superior. The *clients* of ancient Rome were protegés. This is a good adoption from the French; for we have no word which comes in such complete apposition to the term patron: hence it is much wanted.

Qui-vive—The cry of the French sentinel, equivalent to our 'Who goes there?' As it is his duty to be constantly on the alert, to prevent surprise, his interrogatory has been borrowed by us to express extreme watchfulness. A person whose vigilance never relaxes, or a weasel which we are told never sleeps with its eyes shut, is said to be on the *qui-vive*.

Rapport.—To be placed *en rapport* with another, is an expression which owes its English currency to the mesmerists. It implies a sympathy of sensation which is supposed to exist between the operator and his patient, when the latter has been placed in what is designated the mesmeric state. 'Affinity' or 'similarity' of thought, are the only expressions which in our language convey the same idea; and as they are not nearly so apt, *en rapport* may be regarded as a useful addition.

Recherché—The past passive participle of *rechercher* (to search), meaning to be much sought after, and to be out of the common. This word is not of an old date in our tongue. To the fashionable novelists must, we believe, be conceded the merit of introducing it.

Renaissance—'Regeneration,' or 'new birth;' the revival of anything which has long been in decay or extinct. The term is specially applied in France to the time of the revival of letters and arts, and still more particularly to the style of building and decoration which came into vogue in the early part of the sixteenth century.

Rendezvous.—'I know not,' says Bishop Hurd, 'how this word came to make its fortune in our language. It is of an awkward and ill construction, even in the French.' It seems to be a substantive form of the imperative mood of the verb *rendre* (to render), and means a place of appointment, as if men there rendered themselves into a general account. The word is most in use amongst naval and military men, who sometimes make a verb of it, by saying that "the fleet is ordered to *rendezvous* (or to assemble) at such a place." Clarendon gives to it a military application. "The king appointed his whole army to be drawn together to a *rendezvous* at Marlborough." Sprat, in his history of the Royal Society, by adding to it a plural termination (which no other author has ventured to do), gives it a ludicrous sound. He talks of the fellows having their *rendezvouses* after the Wednesday lectures of the astronomy professor. So completely has this word been incorporated into English, that it is found in Johnson's and every succeeding dictionary.

Séance.—A sitting, of which it is the exact synonyme. The word, which is of recent introduction, is usually applied to a meeting or sitting for some kind of scientific or artistic purpose. In Scotland, the Latin word *sederunt* has a similar meaning, but is applied to the sitting of the chief court of law, whose private acts for their own regulation are called acts of sederunt.

Soirée.—Literally, "an entire evening," but used in England to describe an evening passed in social enjoyment. The want of such a word was proved by the eagerness with which it was adopted into our vocabulary when once introduced. First, the fashionable world took it into service; now it is used by all classes. Its congener, *matinée*, is used by the upper circles alone, morning entertainments not being practicable amongst the humbler orders.

Tableau.—A "picture;" but when pressed into our service, it is made to designate a group. Thus we observe of the groups of a procession, that they formed "interesting *tableaux*." A pleasing amusement was lately in vogue amongst the higher classes, which consisted of representing the finest and best known pictures of the great masters by means of living figures, attired in the proper costume, and arranged precisely in imitation of the painted original. These displays were called *tableaux-vivants*, or living pictures.

THE SHOE-MENDER OF PORTSMOUTH.

ONE day, in passing along the streets of London, I was arrested by a crowd at a print-shop window. It is perhaps not altogether 'respectable' to be seen forming one of such assemblages; but every man has his failings, and one of mine is, to take a peep at any very nice-looking prints which the sellers of these articles considerately put in their windows for the public amusement. On the present occasion, in taking a survey of the printseller's wares, I was much interested in observing a print which differed considerably from anything else in the window. Hanging between an opera dancer and a general—both pets of the public—was the representation of an old cobbler sitting professionally in his booth, with a shoe in one hand and his knife in the other, while, with spectacles turned up over his brow, and head averted, he was apparently addressing a ragged urchin who stood beside him with a book. In the background was a miscellaneous collection of books, lasts, old shoes, and bird-cages, interspersed with the heads and faces of a crowd of children—the whole forming a unique combination of a school and cobblery. Beneath was the inscription, "John Pounds and his school." I was, as I have said, interested, and I resolved to know something, if possible, of John Pounds and his seminary. On making inquiries accordingly, I discovered, through the agency of a little pamphlet (sold by Green, 50 Newgate Street), who John Pounds was, and what kind of a school he conducted.

John Pounds was born of parents in a humble rank of life, in Portsmouth, in the year 1766. In early life, while working with a shipwright in the dockyard, he had the misfortune to have one of his thighs broken, and so put out of joint as to render him a cripple for life. Compelled, from this calamity, to choose a new means of subsistence, he betook himself to the shoe-making craft. The instructions he received in this profession, however, did not enable him to make shoes, and in that branch of the art he was diffident in trying his hand. Contenting himself with the more humble department of mending, he became the tenant of a weather-boarded tenement in St Mary Street in his native town.

John was a good-natured fellow, and his mind was always running on some scheme of benevolence, and, like all other benevolent self-helpful people, he got enough to do. While still a young man, he was favoured with the charge of one of the numerous children of his brother; and, to enhance the value of the gift, the child was a feeble little boy, with his feet overlapping each other, and turned inwards. This poor child soon became an object of so much affection with John, as thoroughly to divide his attention with a variety of tame birds which he kept in his stall. Ingenious as well as kind-hearted, he did not rest till he had made an apparatus of old shoes and leather, which untwisted the child's feet, and set him fairly on his legs. The next thing was to teach his nephew to read, and this he undertook also as a labour of love. After a time, he thought the boy would learn much better if he had a companion—in which, no doubt, he was right, for solitary education is not a good thing—and he invited a poor neighbour to send him his children to be taught. This invitation was followed by others; John acquired a passion for gratuitous teaching, which nothing but the limits of his booth could restrain. His humble workshop, to follow the language of his memoir, 'was about six feet wide, and about eighteen feet in length; in the midst of which he would sit on his stool, with his last or lapstone on his knee, and other implements by his side, going on with his work, and attending at the same time to the pursuits of the whole assemblage, some of whom were reading by his side, writing from his dictation, or showing up their sums; others seated around on forms or boxes on the floor, or on the steps of a small staircase in the rear. Although the master seemed to know where to look for each, and to maintain a due command over all, yet so small was the room, and so deficient in the usual accommodations of a school, that the scene appeared, to the observer from without, to be a mere crowd of children's heads and faces. Owing to the limited extent of his room, he often found it necessary to make a selection, from among several subjects or candidates, for his gratuitous instruction; and in such cases always preferred, and prided himself on taking in hand, what he called "the little blackguards," and taming them. He has been seen to follow such to the town-quay, and hold out in his hand to them the bribe of a roasted potato, to induce them to come to school. When the weather permitted, he caused them to take turns in sitting on the threshold of his front-door, and on a little form, on the outside, for the benefit of the fresh air. His modes of tuition were chiefly of his own devising. Without having ever heard of Pestalozzi, necessity led him into the interrogatory system. He taught the children to read from hand-bills, and such remains of old school-books as he could procure. Slates and pencils were the only implements for writing, yet a creditable degree of skill was acquired; and in ciphering, the Rule of Three and Practice were performed with accuracy. With the very young especially, his manner was particularly pleasant and facetious. He would ask them the names of different parts of their body, make them spell the words, and tell their uses. Taking a child's hand, he would say, "What is this? Spell it." Then slapping it, he would say, "What do I do? Spell that." So with the ear, and the act of pulling it; and in like manner with other things. He found it necessary to adopt a more strict discipline with them as they grew bigger, and might have become turbulent; but he invariably preserved the attachment of all. In this way some hundreds of persons have been indebted to him for all the schooling they have ever had, and which has enabled many of them to fill useful and creditable stations in life, who might otherwise, owing to the temptations attendant on poverty and ignorance, have become burdens on society, or swelled the calendar of crime.'

Will the reader credit the fact, that this excellent individual never sought any compensation for these labours, nor did he ever receive any? Of no note or account, his weather-boarded establishment was like a star radiating light around; but of the good he was doing, John scarcely appeared conscious. The chief gratification he felt was the occasional visit of some manly soldier or sailor, grown up out of all remembrance, who would call to shake hands and return thanks for what he had done for him in his infancy. At times, also, he was encouragingly noticed by the local authorities; but we do not hear of any marked testimony of their approbation! Had he been a general, and conquered a province, he would doubtless have been considered a public benefactor, and honoured accordingly; being only an amateur schoolmaster, and a reclaimer from vice, John was allowed to find the full weight of the proverb, that virtue is its own reward. And thus obscurely, known principally to his humble neighbours, did this hero—for was he not a hero of the purest order?—spend a long and useful existence; every selfish gratification being denied, that he might do the more good to others. On the morning of the 1st of January 1839, at the age of seventy-two years, when looking at the picture of his school, which had been lately executed by Mr Sheaf, he suddenly fell down and expired. His death was felt severely. 'The abode of contented and peaceful frugality became at once a scene of desolation. He and his nephew had made provision on that day for what was to them a luxurious repast. On the little mantelpiece remained uncooked a mugful of fresh sprats, on which they were to have regaled themselves in honour of the new year. The children were overwhelmed with consternation and sorrow; some of them came to the door next day, and cried because they could not be admitted; and for several succeeding days the younger ones came, two or three together, looked about the room, and not finding their friend, went away disconsolate.' John Pounds was, as he had wished, called away, without bodily suffering, from his useful labours. He is gone to await the award of Him who has said, 'Inasmuch as ye did it unto one of the least of these, ye did it unto me.'

A WORD ON EMIGRATION.

We frequently receive letters from individuals making inquiries respecting emigration,—whether it would be advisable, in their circumstances, to emigrate; what countries we should recommend them to go to; and so forth. For everything like details, we usually refer our correspondents to the sheets on emigration in our Information for the People; but we are less able to offer any distinct advice as to the countries most eligible for the intending emigrant. At one time, we were favourable to schemes of emigration to Australia, Van Diemen's Land, and New Zealand; but the financial disorders in the two former, and the ruin from other causes of the latter, now dispose us to entertain different views. New Zealand, in particular, we recommend no one to proceed to. That that naturally fine country might, at this time, have been one of the most prosperous English settlements, we had, like everybody else, reason to expect; but the conflicting and disastrous policy pursued in regard to it, has unfortunately ruined its prospects, at least for a time; and until its affairs are rectified, and placed on a satisfactory footing, we imagine no man, who values his life or property, will select it as a field of enterprise.

Shut out in a great measure from these remote Australasian countries, the only choice, we presume, is between the United States and Canada. In either, the emigrant will find lands to suit his fancy, and we should have some difficulty in recommending him to select one country in preference to the other. It is, however, fair to confess, that were we to emigrate, we should, for reasons of nationality, &c. wend our way to Canada; or, to speak more precisely, that part of western Canada bounded by Lake Huron on the north, and Lakes Erie and Ontario on the south—a district fertile, and perhaps more agreeable in point of climate than others open for settlement. The comparative advantages of situation are, in general circumstances, less important than the means of selection and settlement. There are thousands of admirable spots, if emigrants could only find them out, and get them readily under culture when they reached them. *There*, in our opinion, lie the chief difficulties in the way of emigration. The cause of this unfortunate state of affairs is the want of a comprehensive and rational plan of operations. At present, no one knows what another is doing, and the best energies of men are spent in individual and often useless efforts. A number of individuals, who are known or unknown to each other, as the case may be, take a passage on board a vessel for Montreal. Having escaped from the fangs of the skipper and his associates—almost every one of whom aims at preying on passengers—the emigrants fall for the most part into the hands of land jobbers and false advisers, who waylay them on landing. Many are stripped of the principal part of their money while inquiring and bargaining for land, and either sink into poverty in the large towns, or return home dispirited. Others, more acute, and impressed with the necessity for pushing off into the country, proceed westward, and drop away in different directions; till finally, after a world of trouble, they respectively secure lots of uncleared ground, on which they propose to settle. Each man, however, is separated by many miles from those who have been his companions in his journey, and perhaps he is pitched in a spot far from any village or civilised neighbours.

Let us for a moment picture the condition of a man placed in these circumstances. Freshly arrived in a strange country, he is in the midst of a forest, surrounded by his wife and children, and the few moveables which he has been able to drag along with him. He looks about him in a kind of stupor approaching to despair. The land he knows is his. He is the owner of a small estate; but the soil is encumbered with trees standing pretty closely together, each of great thickness, and almost as tall as a church steeple. To his dismay, he cannot see more than twenty or thirty yards before him; and if he climb to the top of the tallest pine, he will most likely see nothing but one unbroken black mass of tree-tops to the very verge of the horizon. The stillness, the solitariness of the scene, is awful. There is something grand and poetical in the situation of such a man. He possesses some share of heroic enterprise, otherwise he would not have been here; and that in itself renders him respectable. Disconsolate though he be, and poor as are his immediate prospects, he is independent. Having thrown himself loose from his moorings in society, he is now his own master, and altogether untrammelled as to his proceedings. Seated in the midst of the little group of beings who claim his aid, he is prospectively a patriarch, the first of his line—the man of the wilderness, from whom a race is to spring. Other things, however, now occupy the poor fellow's mind; the great question is, what is to be done? This is already solved on looking at his wife, who, worn out with fatigue, is in the act of hushing baby to sleep under the lee of the largest trunk. A house of some sort must be erected. To it he goes, hacking away at trees with his axe, and lopping off branches; and after several hours' toil, he is able to look with a degree of complacency on a hovel which rears its verdant roof over his family and chattels. This structure, called a shanty in backwoods phraseology, would be considered much too bad for a pigsty in England; but John's ideas of what a person may be brought to put up with, have been a good deal altered since he left home; and the shanty, all things considered, is pronounced passable. It must at least serve till something better can be achieved. Carrying forward our imagination to the second day, we see John emerge from his den on all-fours, and commence operations on that terrible black forest which surrounds him. Observe him, after eyeing a tree, making the woods ring with the sharp stroke of his glittering axe; look how manfully he lays on, making the splinters fly about him; and what a gash he has already made! That tree is doomed. You may take your last look of it. But what dreadfully-fatiguing work it is to lay it in the dust. Wiping his brow, and fetching a long breath, John gives an inquiring look around; but it is useless, nothing of the kind is to be had. He was thinking how satisfactory it would be to have a pull at a pint of porter. He could drink a gallon, let alone a pint; and how he is to cut down some hundreds of trees, all equally productive of thirst, is more than he can possibly comprehend. Thus the poor man goes on, tugging with his lot, toiling worse than a slave, living in a condition little superior to that of one of the lower animals, and prevented only by a small gleam of hope, from throwing up the whole affair and returning to Old England.

The early sufferings of settlers in the backwoods are often appalling, and they serve to discourage hundreds ere they have made a fair trial of the country. Laying the more laborious toils aside, there is much to dishearten before land is got into crop. Frequently, the settler has to purchase every mouthful of food for his family for twelve or fourteen months after his arrival. This of course robs him of his means, or, what is worse, he gets into debt, and then he is fairly done for. Any way, he is placed at a great disadvantage. He cannot afford to hire labour; and, by not having had a fair start, he toils on for fifteen or twenty years, before he can make headway against the circumstances which come streaming on, one after the other, against him.

We do not think it creditable to the age, that the settlement of new countries should be conducted in so hap-hazard and disheartening a way. *Here*, we have a country overflowing with people and with capital; *there* lies a fertile country, wanting only people and capital to render it productive and valuable. Why are not the three things—the land, the people, and the capital—brought together? Passing over several schemes designed for this purpose, which have been found too refined to be workable, we feel justified in bringing the following practical-looking hints before our readers; they appear in a recent Kingston newspaper:—

'The emigrants to Canada this year appear to be more respectable than in former years. Many of them have, apparently, considerable means, and it is to be deeply regretted that proper steps have not been taken, in many cases, for the proper application of their little capital. The Canadian summer is now far advanced, and ere these persons can be settled on land, the season will have gone by for planting and sowing, and, consequently, they will be obliged to purchase all their food for at least a twelvemonth, which will prove a serious drain upon their funds. To obviate this, and a host of minor evils, we should like to see something like the following plan adopted, which, in a great many instances, would be quite practicable. We will suppose that there are a number of families intending to emigrate from some particular locality in Great Britain or Ireland; that each family will have at least L.100 at their command when they arrive in Canada. We would recommend such persons to depute one of their number, in whom they can place confidence, to come out to this country one year in advance of the main body, and purchase a block of land, say 150 acres for each family; employ hands to clear and sow five acres on each lot with fall wheat, which will cost about L.15; during the winter clear up five acres more, and erect a good shanty on each lot; the land to be planted with potatoes, and sown with oats in the spring, which would probably cost L.20, making in all, for the ten acres under crop, and the shanty, L.35. When the emigrants arrive in midsummer for whom these locations have been made (say six to twelve families), they proceed direct to their farms, under the guidance of their deputy, who will probably meet them at Quebec for the purpose, and, to save them from imposition, there they will find a roof to shelter them, their crops growing around them, their fall grain nearly ready for the sickle, and their roots requiring the immediate use of the hoe or plough. They go to work immediately; they are at hand to cheer and assist each other in cases of sickness or distress; old associations are continued; and everything goes merrily on. They have no more than two months' food to purchase, and that, where a quantity is required, can always be bought on more favourable terms than in moieties. This little settlement will in the next year be able to employ the heads of at least a dozen poor families to assist in enlarging their clearings, and in a short time they will be able to support a clergyman amongst them, a well-qualified teacher to instruct their children, and a physician to cure their bodily ills: they will possess all the elements of a thriving settlement, improve their own condition by emigrating to the province, and at the same time contribute to its wealth, intelligence, and consequent prosperity.

'This is by no means a highly-coloured picture of what might be the almost immediate condition of thousands who emigrate to Canada, did they only pursue the course we have pointed out. It is thus that the Germans, and the Swiss, and the New England Americans emigrate to the western states, and hence their success. There are thousands of acres of the best land in the province to be obtained in the way referred to, and on the most reasonable terms; indeed proprietors generally would be willing to accept 20 per cent. less, than to sell their lands by piecemeal.'

There is much good sense in this proposal, and we can see no other obstacle to the plan being executed on a wide scale, than the difficulty which families may have in finding sufficiently trustworthy and intelligent agents among their number. It would, we think, materially lessen any such practical difficulty, if the Canada Land Company were to relieve families of all trouble in making the preparatory arrangements. Let this company enter into engagements with clusters of families to furnish them with farms on which there are cleared and cultivated spots, and log-huts ready for occupation; undertaking at the same time to carry the families at an appointed season to their locality, free of all expense. Such an arrangement might be in the form of an assurance, a certain payment being taken in advance from the parties. If the payments commenced three years previous to embarkation, and were made in small sums monthly or quarterly, under the usual forfeiture in the event of death or demission of payment, there cannot be a doubt that many thousands of persons would embrace the offer. Either, then, by the plan proposed by the Canadian editor, or by that we have indicated, emigrants would be conducted with tranquillity and satisfaction of mind to their respective new homes, and spared the ruinous loss of time and money, not to speak of the dreadful bodily toils, to which they are now exposed.

The present month of December seems a favourable opportunity for intending emigrants forming associations, and preparing to take active steps in spring. Should they decide on intrusting the execution of their scheme, whatever it be, to the Canada Land Company,*

* The address of this company is 13 St Helen's Place, London; or 22 Hill Street, Edinburgh.

they may, according to all testimony, rely on the integrity of that association for receiving the most courteous and honourable treatment.

GREGARIOUS AVARICE.

Avarice and the other selfish passions do not, like those which are more social in their workings, become ennobled when they move great masses at once. On the contrary, their repulsive features become exaggerated when they take possession of crowds. Of all the passions, avarice is the one which to first thoughts appears most exclusively the source of solitary enjoyment; yet, in fact, more than any other of the unamiable emotions, it is found to derive augmented power from companionship and example. It is not to sympathy, but to emulation, that this is owing. The avaricious herd together and goad each other on by the stimulus of rivalry alone: they are jealous of each other, waspish even in their co-operation. Avarice must have been the devil that entered into the herd of swine, and urged them down the steep into the sea where they were drowned. The avaricious epidemic is of frequent recurrence, and has many exciting causes. It was gregarious avarice that drew shoal after shoal of Cortezes, Pizarros, and Almagros, to rob and murder in America. It was gregarious avarice that urged men into the bubble mining companies, and frenzied projects of founding new states among the swamps of Poyais in 1825. Gregarious avarice goaded Portuguese, Dutch, and English, to pillage the natives of the Indian Archipelago, and murder each other for the booty, from the time that Cape Horn was first doubled, down to the crowning massacre of Amboyna. The disease does not always appear in a simple form; its feverishness is mixed up with, and concealed by, more generous excitements. The leaders of the crusades were animated by a great and generous, though mistaken idea; but the love of booty among men of the sword, and the cool callous calculations of the traders of Venice and Genoa, brought them as many recruits as religious enthusiasm. It is when least mixed and qualified with more generous emotions, that gregarious avarice appears most hateful and contemptible. The Mississippi mania in France, the South-Sea mania in England, the present railway mania throughout Europe and America, have scarcely any redeeming features about them. City satirists harp upon the 'stags' and their shifts; they are the least numerous class among those who are sick of avarice even to the death; their small game is little more than the chronic avarice always lurking in the social frame. If you would see the real ugliness of railway speculation, go to a meeting of some respectable company. The scene is the largest hall in some crack London tavern. The body of the apartment, the spacious music-gallery, is crammed with proprietors. They are substantial men. Three mustaches may be detected on a close scrutiny—one coat, with suspicious-looking lapels of sumptuous velvet, ostentatiously folded back—one huge double breast-pin, of paltry stones, on a frayed and faded neckcloth: but the mass consists of seemly burgesses, with shrewd, healthy, pleasant countenances, well arrayed in broad cloth. They are in outward appearance the *élite* of the trading and manufacturing class. They are obviously in a state of high excitement. Groups start up in different parts of the hall, and look eagerly towards the outskirts of the crowd whenever a rustle is heard. At last the whole mass rises with a simultaneous cheer. A shrewd hard-featured man, preceded and followed by a dozen well-dressed attendants, proud as peacocks of their proximity, enters and takes the chair. Amid rapturous applause, he proceeds to develop the course of action recommended by himself or his brother directors. It evinces no comprehensive views of general utility, not even a high degree of mechanical skill. It is merely a sample of skilful jobbing on a grand scale—dexterous reconciliation of discordant selfish interests, in order to bring a numerous body to work together. And its great recommendation is, that it will raise the price of shares. The imitative herd, who speculate without knowledge, merely through greed, because they see others gain, could place their necks beneath the tread of their instructor, or carry him on their shoulders. They gloat upon him with admiring glances; they subscribe thousands to his testimonial. And yet he is not even an inventor or improver of the system by which they hope to profit. His talent is simply the cleverness or luck to hit on profitable schemes, or to associate himself with those most likely to win. In the age of Elizabeth, Spenser and Jonson unconsciously breathed a spirit of poetry into their conceptions of Mammon; but the incarnation of Mammon in our age, the last avatar of the Brahma of Avarice, is merely grasping, greedy, imitative; there is nothing of intellect or imagination about it. A scene such as we have been describing, and have lately witnessed, does not excite indignation, but a melancholy contempt.—*The Spectator.*

COACH TRAVELLING.

A retrospect on coach travelling will not be unwelcome in these days, when all the empire is thinking about it. Bourne's history of the Birmingham Railway furnishes us with the following:—The reign of Elizabeth is usually assigned as the period when coaches were introduced into England; but vehicles with wheels, under the denomination of chares, cars, chariots, coaches, and whirlicotes, had been long previously employed. The term chariot seems formerly to have denoted a sort of wagon; and in the will of Bartholomew Lord Burghersh (1369), the bier or other conveyance on which his corpse was to be carried is spoken of as a chariot. Henry, the fifth Earl of Northumberland, was accompanied in his journeys by no less than thirty-six horsemen and seventeen carriages, conveying the household furniture and other necessaries. Queen Catherine, the first, and Anne Boleyn, the second wife of Henry VIII., were each conveyed to Westminster in litters; that of the latter being 'of white cloth of gold, led by two palfreys,' and on each of these occasions, 'chariots covered, with ladies therein, accompanied the litters.' When Cardinal Wolsey visited France in 1527, we find that the king's mother, the dame regent, entered Amiens 'riding in a very riche chariot, and with her therein was the queen of Navarre, her daughter.' A train of ladies on horseback followed, besides 'many ladies—some in riche horse litters, and some in chariots.' Vehicles called chares were prevalent at the same time; but Mr Markland observes, that the 'litter appears to have been the more dignified carriage, and was generally used on state occasions only as a conveyance for a single personage of high distinction. The last notice of the litter met with by Mr Markland is by Evelyn, under the date of 1640. Stow informs us that the first coach built in England was in the year 1564. In 1572, Queen Elizabeth visited Warwick in a '*coche* or *chariot*;' and in the following year, we find a member of the Kytson family, of Hengrave in Suffolk, paying L.34, 14s. for what is called in the account 'my Mres Coche, with all the furniture thereto belonging, except the horses.' In 1619, the Duke of Buckingham first drove a coach with six horses, whereupon his rival, the Duke of Northumberland, set up another with eight. Although the use of coaches was at first deemed effeminate, they increased rapidly in number, as shown in a curious pamphlet published in 1636, called 'Coach and Sedan Pleasantly Disputing,' wherein the number of them then used in London and its immediate vicinity is computed at more than 6000. Dekker and others satirise the citizens' wives for riding in coaches; and Taylor the water poet appears to consider their introduction as a national calamity. Speaking of the breaking up of large households, he says, 'The witchcraft of the coach has transformed, in some places, ten, twenty, thirty, forty, fifty, sixty, or one hundred proper serving men into two or three animals.' Wagons conveying both goods and passengers are known to have been in use so early as 1564. The first notice of coaches for public accommodation adduced by Mr Markland is from Sir W. Dugdale's Diary, under the date of 1659, where the *Coventry coach* is mentioned; but that gentleman thinks they were employed some years earlier. Dugdale's Diary mentions the St Alban's, Chester, Bedford, and other stage-coaches between 1662 and 1680 (*ut supra*). In a letter from Edward Parker of Browsholme, in Lancashire, to his father (dated 1663), the writer complains of severe indisposition, caused by his being compelled to travel in the *boot* of the stage-coach. In the Harleian Miscellany (vol. viii.), a writer urges the propriety of suppressing the multitudes of stage-coaches and caravans which were travelling in 1673.

MAGNETIC ATTRACTION OF MUD.

The smaller lakes of America, whose wild and solitary shores attract the tourist, have some singular physical peculiarities. One of the early explorers of its northern regions, Sir Alexander Mackenzie, was the first to notice the attractive power of the mud at the bottom, which is sometimes so great, that boats can with difficulty proceed along the surface. This extraordinary fact is thus stated:—'A the portage or carrying place of Martres, on Rose Lake, the water is only three or four feet deep, and the bottom is muddy. 'I have often plunged into it a pole twelve feet long, with as much ease as if I merely plunged it into the water. Nevertheless, this mud has a sort of magical effect upon the boats, which is such that the paddles can with difficulty urge them on. This effect is not perceptible on the south side of the lake, where the water is deep, but is more and more sensible as you approach the opposite shore. I have been assured that loaded boats have often been in danger of sinking, and could only be extricated by being towed by lighter boats. As for myself, I have never been in danger of foundering, but I have several times had great difficulty in passing this spot with six stout rowers, whose utmost efforts could scarcely overcome the attraction of the mud. A similar phenomenon is observed on the Lake Saginaga, whose bottom attracts the boats with such force, that it is only with the greatest difficulty that a loaded boat can be made to advance; fortunately the spot is only about 400 yards over.' This statement has received confirmation from the experience of Captain Back during the recent Arctic land expeditions. A part of Lake Huron likewise, in the same district, appears to be the centre of a remarkable electrical attraction. There is a bay in the lake, over which the atmosphere is constantly highly charged with electricity, and it has been affirmed that no person has ever traversed it without hearing peals of thunder.—*The Gallery of Nature.*

THE TEST BY BUTCHER MEAT.

If we take the market of the metropolis, we shall find that the number of cattle and sheep annually sold at Smithfield has doubled within the last century, whilst the weight of the carcase has also more than doubled in that interval. In the early part of last century (1710), according to an estimate made by Dr Davenant, the nett weight of the cattle sold at Smithfield averaged not more than 370 pounds, whilst calves averaged about 50 pounds, and sheep 28 pounds. In 1830, the nett weight of the cattle was estimated at 800 pounds, of the calves at 140 pounds, of the sheep at 80 pounds. Again, in 1742, we find 79,601 head of cattle, 503,260 sheep, to be the numbers sold at Smithfield; in 1842, the numbers had increased to 175,347 cattle, 1,438,960 sheep. According to the calculation which Mr M'Culloch adopted for the amount in 1830, when he sets down 154,434,850 pounds for the supply of butcher meat required in London, if we assume the population to have then amounted to 1,450,000, exclusively of some suburban districts, we should find the average annual consumption of each individual to be very nearly 107 pounds. The returns obtained by the Statistical Society of Manchester as to the cattle sold in the markets of that town, furnish an annual consumption of not less than 105 pounds of butcher meat for each inhabitant. In Paris, on the other hand, the quantity has been estimated by M. Chabrol at from 85 to 86 pounds per head; and in Brussels, it is supposed to average 89 pounds. We thus find that the consumption of animal food in the towns of England far exceeds that of foreign cities; and as this consumption has gone on steadily increasing, we are warranted in concluding that the labour of the English people is not only more efficient as compared with that of other nations, but is daily acquiring greater efficiency, if the present be contrasted with previous results.—*Tests of a Thriving Population.*

THE RATIONALE OF THE AMERICAN FEDERATION.

So many Americans migrate from north to south for the sake of mild winters, or attendance on congress, or the supreme courts of law at Washington, or congregate in large watering-places during the summer, or have children or brothers settled in the Far West; everywhere there is so much intercourse, personal or epistolary, between scientific and literary men in remote states, who have often received their university education far from home, that in each new city where we sojourn, our American friends and acquaintances seem to know something of each other, and to belong to the same set in society. The territorial extent and political independence of the different states of the union, remind the traveller rather of the distinct nations of Europe, than of the different counties of a single kingdom like England; but the population has spread so fast from certain centres, especially from New England, and the facilities of communication by railway and steamboat are so great, and are always improving so rapidly, that the *twenty-six* republics of 1842, having a population of seventeen millions, are more united, and belong more thoroughly to one nation, than did the *thirteen* states in 1776, when their numbers were only three millions. In spite of the continued decline of the federal authority, and the occasional conflict of commercial interests between the north and south, and the violent passions excited by the anti-slavery movement, the old colonial prejudices have been softening down from year to year; the English language, laws, and literature, have pervaded more and more the Dutch, German, and French settlers; and the danger of the dismemberment of the confederacy appears to all reflecting politicians less imminent now than formerly.—*Lyell's Travels in America.*

THE TEETOTALLER'S RHAPSODY AT THE PUMP.

Oh spring of pure delight, and fount of bliss,
In spite of bottle-imps and all their scandal,
While thus I quaff thy liquid happiness,
Fain would I sing thy praise—thy poor pump-Handel!

Spirit of water, aid my feeble lay,
And condescend to speed my sober mission;
Nymphs of the fountain, teach me what to say—
A humble member of the T division.

The chubby children come with ugly mugs,
To thee, great pump, and all thy noble pump-kin;
With open mouths, wide throats, and ready jugs,
Thou welcom'st all alike, both squire and bumpkin.

To ye, great Tees and Tay, I drink to ye,
And all the glorious family of rivers;
And thou, Drinkwater, mayst thou live to see
Gin-ocracy all shattered into shivers.

Beer—the worth naught but as a butt for fun,
And brandy suits but hog's-heads, as we've taught her;
Rum shall a puncheon have, and that alone,
And—sotting rascal!—Half-and-half no quarter!

Ah, when shall every chest a tea-chest be,
And Gin no more in his pale corps enlist 'em?
All to our simple game of draughts agree,
The sober converts to the cupping system?

Oh for the loan of that famed Wapping Tunnel,
To light a fire in, and to heat the Thames!
'Twould suit tea-parties to a T, good Brunel—
Just stand our friend, and place it 'mong your gems.

For friends, alas! we need, the truth to say,
So numerous are our foes, and such hard hitters;
They quote Val. Max. to sneer our Milky Way,
Because we will not share their gin and bitters.

Because we scruple not their drams to curse
(And, differing on these pints, we can't refrain),
They call us fish, Aquarii, and worse,
And tell us we have water on the brain.

But with our pot and kettle soon we'll speed us
Far hence to Assam—pure and temperate spot,
Where no gin-bibulator shall impede us,
Nor pour contempt on our gunpowder plot.

R. W. W.

TRUTH.

The study of truth is perpetually joined with the love of virtue; for there is no virtue which derives not its original from truth; as, on the contrary, there is no vice which has not its beginning in a lie. Truth is the foundation of all knowledge, and the cement of all societies.—*Casaubon.*

Published by W. and R. Chambers, High Street, Edinburgh (also 98, Miller Street, Glasgow); and, with their permission by W. S. Orr, Amen Corner, London.—Printed by Bradbury and Evans, Whitefriars, London.

CHAMBERS'S EDINBURGH JOURNAL.

CONDUCTED BY WILLIAM AND ROBERT CHAMBERS, EDITORS OF 'CHAMBERS'S INFORMATION FOR THE PEOPLE,' 'CHAMBERS'S EDUCATIONAL COURSE,' &c.

No. 104. New Series. SATURDAY, DECEMBER 27, 1845. Price 1½d.

THE POPULAR MAN.

It is often said that no successful ambition of any kind produces entire satisfaction. I had lately an amusing illustration of the maxim presented to my attention. Not to tire the reader with a long story, I may tell him that, returning a few months ago to the city where I had studied for my profession, I renewed acquaintance with a gentleman who had been the bosom friend of my student days. We were then both poor, as I, speaking comparatively, am still; but my old friend had, in the twenty intermediate years, blossomed and thriven wonderfully, and was now not only a wealthy, but a highly respected citizen. It was gratifying to find him standing high in half the lists where the leading men of his community were enrolled. He had also published a work which, though of local celebrity, was sufficient to make him a great man in his own circle. One day, after dining at his family board, and when we had been left by ourselves to discuss old recollections, I ventured to remind him of the days when he was an obscure and friendless youth, whose merits were known only to one or two associates like myself; and I added, 'Surely success like yours must have for once made a happy man—you—you on whom fortune and the world smile, and whose domestic circumstances are all of so agreeable a kind—you surely are happy?'

'Well,' said he, laughing, 'I am afraid I am not. Even with me, whom you think so fortunate in many respects, there is no want of vexations.'

'Strange that it should be so,' said I; 'but what, may I ask, is the drawback in your case?'

'You will think it very odd,' replied he, 'but I believe my case may be described in two comprehensive words—I have an over-good character.'

'An over-good character! Pray, how in the world should that affect you?'

'Why, it affects me in many ways. It harasses me almost every hour of my life.'

'Enlighten me with particulars, if you please.'

'You will laugh at me, and I daresay, justly; but it is a serious matter for all that. First, then, you can readily understand what it is to be reputed as a person of an obliging disposition. Don't suppose that I take any credit to myself for being of this character; it is only a part of my unfortunate case, which I must explain to you, if I would enable you to understand why my lot is not one of entire happiness. I am, then, one who is, for his sins, or those of his forefathers, afflicted with a desire to make himself of service when any other body's benefit is to be promoted, or evil avoided, or when anything can be done to advance a philanthropic object. The consequence is, that not a day passes when I have not my patience taxed, and my time occupied, with such duties. You would be amused at the offices I have to undertake for persons who unluckily cannot help themselves. Sometimes they involve an anxious correspondence—sometimes a journey over half the town—often I must beg, or at the least *bore*. Occasionally the business I have thus to undertake is almost of a servile kind—yet it must be done. The compulsion of a habitual feeling, nay, a kind of regard for consistency, admits of no shying. I do it, half blaming, half laughing at myself the while—so mixed may our feelings be. It would equally surprise you to be informed of the public business which falls, in like manner, to be attended to and executed by persons who have any goodness of heart about them. There are some modern persons, I believe, of an Arcadian degree of acquaintance with the world, who represent the possessors of means and influence as systematically unbending towards the poor and unfortunate. Happy delusion! I wish I knew that blessed spot below, where one could live four-and-twenty hours without either having to do duty in this way, or to pine for being unable to accomplish what one would wish to do. It is not in this portion of the earth at least that the middle or upper classes can manifest a sublime indifference on these points.'

'Well, but there must be great satisfaction to repay all these labours—the sense of having mitigated the woes of your fellow-creatures—their gratitude—the public approbation even, though that is of course not the object.'

'That the object! My dear friend, don't speak of it. If it were possible to do any good in this world, and have no fame from it, I should have an easy life. The great misfortune of the obliging and philanthropic men is, that their good deeds, spite of their teeth, get wind, and so bring fresh loads of duty upon their backs. The new applicant always comes encouraged by hearing of your kindness in other cases. It is only because you last week spoke and subscribed at a meeting for the relief of the sufferers by a conflagration, that you are this week pressed to do the same at one in favour of those who have lost their all by a flood. Case begets case—there is no end to it once you begin. My own wish, I assure you, is for obscurity. I wish I could do what I choose to do in a mask, and thus escape that which oppresses me in the doing. Would that I *could* "do good by stealth"—trust me, I do not "blush," but "groan to find it fame."'

'And how is it, then, as to expenditure of money? for of course this must be an element in your unfortunate position.'

'It is so. And here it is equally unnecessary to be delicate in explanation. The fact is, that the mishaps and miseries of mankind lay an indefinite tax on the comparatively limited class who have anything to spare, joined to an inclination to spare it. There is no use for mincing the matter: it is what every such person experiences; it is a recognised feature of our social economy. And so, as hardly a day passes without its duty in behalf of some unfortunate, or bringing some public object of benevolence above board, so does hardly one elapse which does not see me compelled to give away money, and that often in not inconsiderable sums, either in a public or private manner. It is amazing how one's resources are thus drained. For my part, I sometimes think of declaring myself a rebel against society for the errors which I cannot help thinking must be involved in it, before such severe amerciaments could become necessary with all those who are what is called well off. Either this money should not be got by them at all, or there should not be a need for giving it back to the less fortunate in a way that impairs their self-respect. But to speak more particularly of my own case—here also behold the effect of over-good character. One benefaction leads irresistibly to scores. It is hopeless to attempt to conceal such things. There is a system of secret information among the unfortunate which makes knowledge of one the knowledge of the whole, and with a celerity like that of wildfire. What should be a pleading for mercy towards you, that you have given to one, or given before, only serves as an encouragement for an application calling upon you to give to another, or to give again; for, unluckily, necessity admits of no discretion. All this time, the men who have a bad or indifferent character as givers, are very snug. No one thinks of pestering them. And it is the same when any benevolent effort is to be made by a combination of citizens. The whole duty and expense come upon the soft-hearted few, while the men so lucky as to be able to bear the misfortunes of their fellow-creatures with tranquillity, are never even applied to. Oh, my friend, for the luxury of a stingy character for a single quarter of a year! Not so much for the money, as for the cessation of this continual dunning, the relief were inexpressible.'

'You quite amuse me with your earnestness on this point. But tell me, is your over-good character productive of any other inconvenience?'

'Ay, plenty of it. Have you any idea, from your own experience, of being too much liked?'

'Why, no. I think I have been rather moderately in favour with my fellow-creatures all my life.'

'Lucky for you. I am so unfortunate as to be that unhappy being, a general favourite. And this, joined to my being a little famed as a writer, lecturer, speech-maker, and so forth, makes my case truly dreadful.'

Why, one would think such popularity rather enviable than otherwise?'

'Ah! you can have no idea of the inconveniences it creates. In the first place, by way of a small evil to begin with, one who acquires any note on such grounds becomes a kind of lion, and is, as it is called, run after by all sorts of people except the sensible and the charming, whom he would like alone to meet with. He has to keep up a constant struggle with these followers, in order to get clear of their worship: that is to say, his good nature has to be put to violence twenty times a-day to maintain even a decent privacy. If he lectures in a place where he is a stranger, six or seven always wait after the dispersion of the audience, and surround him on the platform, congratulating him, telling him of the good he is doing, and beseeching him to do something for the local auxiliary association of so-and-so. Then the whole class of the Unconfined are let loose upon him. Some come to interest him in hopeless lawsuits; some to consult him about the publication of epics excelling Homer, or philosophical speculations putting down Newton, which they expect him to read carefully before he can give an opinion worth having. Others wish to enter upon some great new trade, which they only require a little money to commence, and this, as you are a man with a reputation for benevolence and liberality, they expect you to furnish. But these I regard, after all, as trifling annoyances, compared with what I feel at the various meshes of restraint which gradually invest a man who is a favourite with the world. Such a man, being appreciated for a particular presumed character, cannot act in any other, however slightly divergent, without incurring odium. He has no freedom of speech or act. He is the victim of character: and this is because it is ten times more disagreeable to forfeit approbation once gained, than to live without gaining any. I think, then, that I could have lived far more happily in obscurity, than now as a favourite public man; for I should have been comparatively free, and never have known what it was to dread falling in the esteem of the world. The effect of this tyranny of reputation, this committal to past appearances, and the light in which the public has accepted a man, must be productive of extreme vexation to many who appear as floating gaily on the tide of popularity. No such man but must have misgivings about past views, and tendings towards greater and better conceptions of what is good for the common weal; assuredly, then, must his spirit often quail with self-contemning bitterness under the promptings of the stern monitor which tells him he must keep the course, if he would not be driven ignominiously from its boundaries. Alas, my friend, you who pursue your private career in perfect independence of mood, can have but a slight idea of what is sometimes felt by men, whose horror of encountering a change from universal smiles to universal frowns, condemns to that worst of slaveries, a slavery where one's self is master!'

'Truly,' said I, 'it seems to be no joke to have such popularity as yours. You present the matter in quite a new light to me. But tell me now, are you not, after all, happier in doing what you can for the good of individuals and masses, than if you were to lead a close and sordid life, as do many who have means equal to yours?'

'I don't know. They follow their nature, and are content; and were I of their temper, I might be content with their mode of life also. What I say is, that even the life which makes benevolence one of its ruling principles, is not unattended with vexations.'

'But it is delightful to have to give, and to give it.'

'I allow that the pleasure of doing good is great; but, then, is one sure that he is really doing good? He may be doing harm, notwithstanding all appearances to the contrary. My nature, for example, impels me to be continually lending a hand in benevolent projects, but I am often conscious that the best-looking scheme is only a futile attempt to improve the condition of those whom, from natural imbecility, there is no preventing from going down. Others, more selfish, or with less susceptible feelings, are seen standing by, with the sneer on their lips, and considering you little better than a fool for all your pains. Ever and anon they ask you for results, and perhaps you can only show a series of feeble, though well-meant efforts. All these things are vexing. Even the applause that is obtained distresses; for you know painfully well how imperfectly it is deserved.'

'Every one, however, will allow that it is well to stand high in the general esteem. Since it is what all men may be said to aim at, success in this line must surely be a source of gratification?'

'Well, you have heard my experiences on that point. They lead to a contrary conclusion; and such, I fear, must ever be the consequence of what is called popularity. The fact is, one cannot rightly in this world be generally liked. From the great diversity of men's minds on what is worthy of regard, it is not to be expected that a consistent decisive character will stand favourably with any large portion of mankind. One only can do so by modifying himself to suit the many, and thus sacrificing much that is necessary for inward satisfaction. Show me, then, the popular man, and I will show you a man who must needs be ill at ease, if he have any respect for himself. I fear, my friend, we are thought to be great men when we are only weak, as I am sure we are full of pain when men think us supremely happy.'

I went home from my friend's house with somewhat different notions about his position in life from what I had entertained. 'Well, thank my stars,' said I, as I broke the smouldering coal in my little parlour fire—'thank my stars I am totally unknown, and only a favourite with poor Snap.' Next morning, however, I reflected maturely on the conversation of my friend, and became convinced that, while there was much truth in what he said, it was not the whole truth. The obliging and popular have no doubt their troubles, and what my friend said might be considered as an exposition of them, given with a certain pungency from the feelings of the moment; but the life of active serviceableness towards good objects, public and private, must be, after all, the happiest, seeing that it speaks of a wide range of sympathies in the course of continual gratification. Every good thing has its seamy side: this was the seamy side of a life upon the whole enviable.

PRISON ADVENTURES OF LAFAYETTE.

The Marquis de Lafayette entered upon the scenes of the French Revolution with the idea fixed in his mind, that republican institutions were reconcileable with a monarchy. He was, therefore, a friend to the royal family, at the same time that he promoted the reforms which were successively conducted by the States-General and Legislative Assembly. His chivalric fidelity to Louis and Marie Antoinette was powerfully tried on the 5th and 6th of October 1789, when, as commander of the National Guards, he protected them from the populace who had assailed them in their palace of Versailles. Subsequently, when the king was deposed and imprisoned (August 1792), Lafayette, then with the army on the frontiers, endeavoured to incite the soldiers to march upon Paris, in order to restore the throne, and put down Pétion, Danton, and their associates. But the revolutionary tide, impelled as it was by the fears of the people for the foreign armies pressing on the country, was too strong to be thus resisted; and a few days thereafter, Lafayette was obliged to seek his own safety by flying from the kingdom.

He and the officers of kindred sentiments by whom he was accompanied, had scarcely passed the frontier, when their further progress was arrested by a body of the Limburg volunteers; and the national cockade, which, unthinkingly, they had retained, betraying them to the leader, they were, by his command, arrested and conveyed to the prison of Luxemburg, from thence removed to Wesel, then to Magdeburg, and lastly to Olmütz.

On the plea of Lafayette having been seized on neutral ground, and that, having ceased to be a soldier, he could not properly be considered a prisoner of war, strenuous efforts from all quarters were made to obtain his release; but the emperor of Germany, who regarded him as a principal instigator of the Revolution, as well as one of the chief instruments of the insulting degradation and subsequent death of the royal family of France, was not to be moved. The vengeance of Robespierre for the loss of his victim was, meanwhile, wreaked with savage inveteracy against the unfortunate wife of Lafayette; for no sooner was the escape of her husband known, than that unhappy lady was arrested and thrown into prison. She escaped death by something like a miracle; different members of her family perished on the scaffold; and she herself, for the space of fifteen months, endured all the horrors of a loathsome confinement. On the death of the tyrant she was released from prison, and so soon as her health was sufficiently reinstated to allow of her undertaking so long a journey, without servants, or the means of procuring the most necessary comforts, she, accompanied by her children, set out for Vienna, and, throwing herself at the feet of the emperor, implored his influence for the liberation of her husband.

What Francis III. had denied to the various authorities interested in the fate of Lafayette, he yielded to pity; and, raising the suppliant, he granted her request, allowed of her repairing immediately to Olmütz, and held out the prospect of the speedy deliverance of the prisoner. Whether the emperor afterwards regretted the clemency he had shown, or that other powers were interested in prolonging the captivity of Lafayette, does not appear; but so far from obtaining his hoped-for release, Madame de Lafayette found herself and her daughters immured in the same dungeons that contained her husband. I have, however, anticipated this event, for it was not until within two years of the release of Lafayette, that his wife and family were thus unexpectedly made the partners of his imprisonment.

Two years of solitary confinement had, from the period of his capture, been dragged on by Lafayette, when the romantic scheme of procuring his liberation was formed by one, an utter stranger to the prisoner, and a foreigner. From motives of pure compassion, and an earnest desire to free from so galling a thraldom the great promoter of liberty, M. Balman, a Hanoverian by birth—young, active, intrepid, and intelligent—repaired, alone and on foot, to Olmütz, there to gain such information as might enable him to judge of the best means of executing the purpose he had in view, and releasing Lafayette from the power of Austria. He soon found that, without an able coadjutor, the difficulties that presented themselves were insurmountable, and repaired, therefore, to Vienna, where he devoted himself exclusively to the society of young Americans; for among them, from their veneration of the character of Lafayette, he hoped to find one who, with enthusiasm like his own, would dare the great undertaking.

What followed is interesting as a proof that the spirit of nationality may engender a principle of gratitude. Lafayette, as is well known, had in his early youth proceeded to America, and served in her armies. Shipwrecked at his first arrival, he had been kindly received into the house of a gentleman named Huger, residing in Charlestown. And by him was the youthful votary of liberty introduced to the American army. By chance, a son of this gentleman was now in Vienna, and to him did M. Balman apply. Although a mere child when the shipwrecked party visited his father's house, the young American retained a vivid recollection of, and the highest admiration for, M. de Lafayette; and he entered, therefore, with all the zealous ardour of youth, and the enthusiasm of a generous nature, into Balman's scheme for the release of his favourite hero.

From the vigilance of the Austrian police, and their jealous watchfulness of strangers, it was necessary that the greatest caution and secrecy should be maintained; and the scheme proposed promised well for the completion of their design. Huger assumed the pretence of ill health, and M. Balman, who had already adopted the character of a physician, was upon this account to travel with him. In company with only one servant, who was not intrusted with the secret, and mounted upon the best horses money could procure, the friends set out on their tour; and visiting different places, the better to conceal their real purpose, and confirm the idea that curiosity was the motive of their journey, they lingered so long at each, that a considerable time had elapsed before their reaching Olmütz.

As they had desired, a rumour of their insatiable curiosity had preceded them thither; and, acting up to their assumed character, after viewing everything worthy of notice in the town, they repaired to the castle, examined the fortifications, and, having made acquaintance with the keeper, obtained permission to visit the interior of the prison on the following day.

Thus their first step being happily achieved, they continued, by frequent visits, to improve their acquaintance with the jailer; and now trusting that any suspicion of their intentions, had it ever existed, must be lulled to sleep, they ventured carelessly to inquire what prisoners were under his care. Among other names, that of Lafayette was mentioned, and they expressed curiosity to know how he contrived to occupy himself, how he bore his imprisonment, and whether greater indulgences were granted to him than to captives of lesser note. He was, they were informed, strictly confined, but, on the plea of bad health, had obtained permission, under charge of an armed guard, to take daily exercise without the walls. Besides this, he was allowed the use of books, pen, ink, and paper. M. Balman then remarked, that some new publications he had with him might afford amusement to the prisoner, and inquired whether he might be allowed to make the offer.

The jailer agreed, upon condition that they were sent open, so as to assure himself, he said, that no conspiracy was to be carried on against the state. This caution was complied with, and the same evening a book and open note, addressed to Lafayette, were sent to his care. As afterwards appeared, he was unacquainted with French, the language in which the note was written; but, suspecting no treachery where all was so openly carried on, he conveyed it to Lafayette. It contained apologies for the liberty thus taken by strangers, but as they were anxious, they said, to contribute to his happiness, they hoped he would attentively read the book they had sent, and if any passages in it particularly engaged his notice, they begged he would let them know his opinion.

This unusual mode of expression attracted, as was intended, the attention of Lafayette, and carefully perusing the book, he found in certain places words written with a pencil, which, being put together, acquainted him with the names, qualities, and designs of the writers, and requiring his sentiments before they should proceed further. He returned the book, and with it an open note, thanking them for their civility, and adding that he highly approved of, and was charmed with the contents.

Having thus commenced a correspondence, no day passed in which open notes were not written and received. Some of these were brought for the inspection of persons acquainted with the French language; but so carefully were they worded, that no cause of suspicion appeared, and the correspondence was allowed to continue. A greater difficulty, however, now appeared, for the plan of escape being at length arranged, they were at a loss how to acquaint Lafayette with particulars that could not be hazarded in an open note. A happy expedient presented itself; the whole was written in lemon juice, and on the other side of the paper, a note of inquiry after Lafayette's health concluded with these words, '*Quand vous aurez lu ce billet mettez-le au feu.*' The experiment was a hazardous one, but it succeeded. The note was conveyed to Lafayette, and, obeying the injunctions given, on holding the paper to the fire, the writing that appeared made him acquainted with the well-digested scheme of his unknown benefactors.

The day following was that fixed for the attempted escape, and all the caution used by M. Balman and his friend was in truth required, to hold out any chance of success. The city of Olmütz, about thirty miles from Silesia, is situated in the midst of a plain extending three miles on either side, and bounded by dark woods, so that the smallest object on any part of the level ground is distinctly visible from the walls. Sentinels, too, hold a continual guard, for the purpose of giving the alarm should any attempt at escape be made, and the whole people are bound to assist in the pursuit, while the successful individual is liberally rewarded for the recapture of a prisoner.

These obstacles to the success of their scheme were well known to the adventurous friends of Lafayette; but they were not intimidated, and the hour of exercise allowed to the prisoner was that selected for its completion.

In company of an officer, and attended by an armed guard mounted behind the carriage, Lafayette was in the habit of daily driving in an open cabriolet on the plain, and had so far won upon the confidence of the officer, that when at a distance from the walls, they used to quit the carriage and walk together.

The plan determined upon was as follows:—Balman and Huger were to ride out on the plain, the latter leading a third horse, while Lafayette was to gain as great a distance as possible from the town, and, as usual, quitting the carriage with the officer, draw him imperceptibly as near the boundaries as might be without awakening his suspicion. The two friends were then to approach, and, if necessary, to overpower the officer, mount Lafayette on the led horse, and ride at full speed to Bautsapp, a town at the distance of fifteen miles, where a chaise had been prepared to convey the party to the nearest town on the Prussian dominions. In the morning Huger had attempted to ascertain the precise time at which Lafayette would leave the castle, and then, with beating hearts, they set forward on their expedition; but having almost reached the wooded country, and still no carriage appearing, they believed some unforeseen accident had led to their discovery, and hesitated how to proceed, till, recollecting that their movements were in all probability watched from the walls, they slowly retraced their steps, and, on nearing the town, beheld, to their great satisfaction, the wished-for cabriolet pass through the gates. It contained two persons. One was in the Austrian uniform, and a musketeer as usual was mounted behind. Neither of the friends being personally acquainted with M. de Lafayette, a signal had been agreed upon between them. In passing, it was made, returned, and the carriage moved on, they continuing for a time their ride towards the town, and then slowly following the cabriolet at such a distance as to allow of Lafayette's executing his part of the agreement. Upon the two gentlemen quitting the carriage, and continuing their exercise on foot, the friends gradually approached, and perceiving M. de Lafayette and the officer engaged in earnest conversation about the sword of the latter, which Lafayette held in his hand, they seized the favourable moment, and putting spurs to their horses, galloped forward. Their rapid approach alarmed the officer; he attempted to draw Lafayette towards the carriage, and, finding that he resisted, struggled to repossess himself of his sword. At that moment Huger reached the spot. 'You are free,' said he; 'mount this horse, and fortune be our guide;' but the words were scarcely uttered, when the sun, glancing on the naked blade of the sword, startled the horse he led; he reared, broke his bridle, and galloped across the plain. M. Balman, in the vain hope of overtaking the frightened animal, rode after him, while Huger generously insisted on Lafayette mounting his horse, and making all speed to the place of rendezvous. 'Lose no time,' he exclaimed; 'the alarm is given; the peasants are assembling; save yourself.' Lafayette obeyed, and mounting Huger's horse, he left him on foot, and was soon out of sight. M. Balman had, meantime, pursued the flying animal, but perceiving it had taken the road to the town, he gave up the chase as hopeless, and returning to Huger, he sprang on the saddle behind him, and they galloped off together. But the double burden proved too much for the already wearied horse. He stumbled and fell, and M. Balman, thrown to some distance by the shock, was so injured as with difficulty to be raised from the ground. Once more the gallant Huger, with the same forgetfulness of self that had characterised him through the whole undertaking, sacrificed the chance of his own safety to secure that of his friend, and, assisting Balman to remount, he insisted that he should follow Lafayette, and leave him to make his escape on foot; for, as he was a good runner, he said he could easily reach the woody country, and then find a safe place of concealment. His friend consented with reluctance; but there was no time for argument: the whole occurrence had been seen from the walls, the cannon had been fired, the country was raised, and the plain covered with men, women, and children, all eager to join in the pursuit. By pretending to follow in the chase, Balman contrived to escape unsuspected. Huger was less fortunate. Noticed from the very first by a party who never lost sight of him, his fleetness of foot was of no avail; for his pursuers being constantly joined by new comers, fresh for the chase, they soon gained upon him, and at last, breathless and exhausted, he sank upon the ground. He was instantly seized; and further resistance being now hopeless, he was conveyed back to Olmütz in triumph; and while secretly consoling himself with the idea that, whatever might be his own fate, he had rescued from tyranny and oppression the man who, in his eyes, was one of the first characters upon earth, was consigned to one of the dungeons of the castle as a state prisoner.

M. de Lafayette had, meanwhile, followed the directions given by his gallant deliverers, and, without any obstacle, had reached a small town about ten miles off; but here the road dividing, he unfortunately took the wrong turn, and suspecting he had mistaken the way, inquired of a person whom he met the road to Hautrapp. The appearance of Lafayette, his foreign accent, the inquiries he made, and his horse covered as it was with foam, led the man to suspect the truth, and directing him to a narrow lane which, by a long circuit, led back to the town he had just left, he himself hurried there by a shorter cut; and thus, when about to regain, as he thought, the road which would secure his retreat, Lafayette found himself surrounded by a guard of armed men, who, regardless of his protestations, conveyed him to the magistrate. His collected manner, the plausible answers returned to the interrogations put to him, and the apparent truth of his story—that, belonging to the excise at Trappau, he had visited some friends at Olmütz, and having exceeded his leave of absence, was now hurrying back under the fear of losing his office—all so won upon the faith of the magistrate, that he was about to dismiss his prisoner, when the good fortune of Lafayette again forsook him. As he was about to retire, a young man entered the room to have some papers signed, and after fixing his eyes for a moment on Lafayette, he whispered to the magistrate that, having been present when the French general was delivered up prisoner to the Austrians, he could not be mistaken, and that the person now before him was he.

Lafayette intreated to be heard; but in vain. The indignant magistrate directed that he forthwith should be conveyed to Olmütz, where his identity would be ascertained; and, disheartened and hopeless, the unfortunate prisoner was thrust again into those miserable dungeons which but that morning he had left with so fair a prospect of liberty. M. Balman, the first instigator of the whole scheme, was now the only one who had successfully avoided the search of his pursuers. He reached in safety the place where the chaise had been ordered to wait their coming, and finding it still there, yet no appearance of Lafayette, he foreboded evil. For some time he lingered, in the hope of their coming, and then dismissing the chaise, trusted that his friends, having made their escape by a different route, might still meet, as had been agreed upon, on the frontiers of Prussia. Three days from that time a rumour reached him that Lafayette had been retaken, and, eager to learn the truth, he took the road to Olmütz. He was not long left in suspense; the whole story of the attempted escape and the recapture of the prisoner, was well known; and in addition to this he learned the fact of his generous and disinterested friend, the young and gallant Huger, having shared the same fate.

This last seems to have been too much for the sensitive mind of M. Balman, and, in despair at having been the primary cause of misfortune to the young American, he resolved, since he could not rescue his friend from captivity, to share it with him, and voluntarily surrendering himself, he was committed a prisoner to the castle. Such was the unfortunate issue of a plan which, for skilful projection and generous self-devotion, merited a happier close. But even now, the friends little apprehended what was to follow. Being directed to prepare for examination, they believed that, having told their story, and declared the real motives of their attempt, they might be subjected to perhaps a short imprisonment, but no more; and great, therefore, was their amazement on finding themselves accused of having entered into a conspiracy against the Austrian government, and that they were consequently to stand a trial for life or death.

Huger was first placed at the bar. As he was unacquainted with the Austrian language, the examination was carried on by means of an interpreter—a young man who, by his looks and voice, seemed to compassionate the situation of the prisoner, and who, when repeating his answers to the court, omitted such expressions as he thought might tend to his disadvantage. Huger quickly caught at the good intentions of his new friend, and resolving to rely on his judgment, he took the kindly hints as they were intended. One examination followed another, and the repeated exhortation of the magistrate to prepare for the worst, for that there was little likelihood of a pardon being obtained, forced upon the unfortunate Huger the unwelcome conviction, that he had laid down his own life for the visionary project of rescuing a stranger from imprisonment. The severity of his treatment also exceeded that even of Lafayette; the dungeon in which he had been placed was without light, he was fed upon the coarsest food, during the night was chained to the floor of the vault, and his own clothes, which had been taken from him, were replaced with those worn by many an unfortunate predecessor.

For three months he dragged on this miserable existence; but at the end of that time there was some amendment in his condition; he was removed to a better room, into which was admitted a small but welcome light; better clothes, and more wholesome food, were allowed him; and altogether, his circumstances were improved; but he still continued in total ignorance as to what his future fate was to be; for the jailer, the only human being he ever saw, was unable or unwilling to answer any questions on the subject. At length one day, much to his surprise and joy, his young friend the interpreter entered his cell, and nothing could exceed the delight of the poor prisoner at once again meeting with a kindly face. Huger now learned for the first time the total failure of their scheme—that Lafayette had been retaken, and that Balman, a fellow-prisoner, was under the same roof with himself. Shortly afterwards, he discovered him to be in the room immediately above his own; and, after various efforts, he succeeded in holding communication with him, in a manner as venturous and ingenious as that adopted with M. de Lafayette. The window, which threw a borrowed light into his own cell, served likewise to light that of Balman, and, with a piece of lime taken from the wall, Huger contrived to scratch a few words upon a black silk handkerchief, which, by fastening to a stick, and climbing up the side of the room, he raised as near the common window as he could. It attracted the attention of M. Balman, and, after many efforts, making himself master of it, he returned an answer by the same method. From this time no day passed without their holding communication with each other; while to the exertions of the friendly interpreter they were indebted for the means of making their situation still more comfortable. By small presents and occasional bribes of money, he had secured the good offices of the wife of the jailer, so that, secretly, she provided them with books, food, wine, and warmer clothes. Through her interest also the two friends procured a long-wished-for meeting. At first the visit was short, but by degrees becoming less timorous, they were permitted to pass some part of every day together.

The government being at length satisfied that the attempt to liberate Lafayette had been planned independently by these two adventurers, and was not, as was supposed, a plot laid by the secret agents of France, they were remitted to receive sentence from the supreme magistrate of Olmütz. In this condition they were permitted every indulgence but that of liberty; and, in the enjoyment of each other's society, and the hope of a speedy release, were already beginning to forget past suffering, when, by a visit from their newly-found friend, the kindly interpreter, they learned with dismay that the intended punishment was to be heavy indeed, seeing it was no less than imprisonment for life. A hint was at the same time conveyed that, if by any means they could procure money, that sentence might be changed for one much less severe, as it was in the power of the magistrate to make it what he chose, and even to release them entirely.

This information seemed to bode the unfortunate prisoners little, at least of immediate good; for Balman had no fortune, and Huger being without credit in Austria, could not, within a short time, receive a remittance from England. Their friend, however, did not desert them; he withdrew, promising to use all his influence for their release; and it is probable he had already formed that design, which the generosity of another, equally a stranger to the prisoners, whose name, instead of being unknown, should be published aloud, enabled him afterwards so happily to carry through. A Russian nobleman of large fortune, residing near Olmütz, was perhaps, from a resemblance in character, the most intimate friend of the young interpreter, and from him had learned the whole story of the projected release of Lafayette, of its failure, and of the generous conduct of the two friends. To him W——, for the initial only has been given for the name of the good Samaritan, flew for assistance in this new difficulty; and having stated the case as it then stood, he was about to intreat, in his own name, a loan for the use of the prisoners, when he was interrupted by an offer of whatever sum might be required to secure their release.

Judging the heart of his noble friend by his own, he hesitated not for a moment to accept the offer, and scarcely affording himself time to speak the gratitude he felt, he hurried off to sound the sentiments of the magistrate. His situation as interpreter afforded him the desired opportunity, and he soon discovered that the hints thrown out of the chance of a large reward, led the upright judge to listen favourably to any proposal for mitigating the severe punishment of the prisoners. The show even of delicacy was then laid aside; an exorbitant demand was made; and, after some further discussion, W—— withdrew to arrange preliminaries, first with their generous benefactor, and lastly with the prisoners themselves. Matters now were soon settled; the term of their imprisonment was first fixed at fourteen years, then shortened to seven, soon after to one, then to a month, and lastly to a week, at the end of which time they were released from prison. The first use they made of restored liberty was, as may be supposed, to seek an interview with the Russian nobleman, and pour out their grateful acknowledgments for his unlooked-for and welcome munificence; while from the noble-minded and generous W——, to whose kindness they owed all the comforts they had experienced in prison, and to whose friendly and humane exertions they were ultimately indebted for their liberation, they parted with those feelings of esteem, admiration, and gratitude, which never afterwards faded from their recollection.

The principal hero of the tale did not, however, meet with so speedy a conclusion to his misfortunes. It was not till the year 1797, when, a peace taking place between Austria and France, that Lafayette was released from confinement at the request of the then General Bonaparte.

THE POTATO.

It is singular to think that, not more than two hundred and fifty years ago, an insignificant plant, in size not larger than our common weeds, of no external beauty, with a nauseous odour, and a juice of a poisonous quality, should have grown among the crevices of the rocks which bound the shores of Chili, unknown to the world at large, and all but neglected by the rude natives; and that this same plant, transferred to the soil of Europe, should have become one of the most important articles of human food, so much so, as to have greatly influenced the population of half the globe.

There can be no doubt that the potato is a native of America. It is found in its wild state in several parts of that continent, especially in Chili and Peru. Don José Pavon says that it grows in the environs of Lima, and fourteen leagues along the coast; he also found it in the kingdom of Chili. A late traveller in that region, Mr Darwin, also mentions that he saw this plant in such situations, and under such circumstances, as seemed to leave little doubt of its being in a state of nature.

The potato belongs to a natural family of plants (the *solanaceæ*), most of which, as the deadly nightshade, possess poisonous qualities. Indeed the juice of the leaves, stem, and even skins of the tubers of the potato, are of a highly poisonous nature. In its native state the plant is small, and the tubers seldom exceed the size of a walnut or common chestnut. They are also of a moist waxy consistence, and have a slight bitterish taste. The colour of the blossom is generally white, and rarely of the red and purple hues of the cultivated sorts. These tubers are not the roots of the plant, but are true underground stems; and their use in nature appears to be to afford another means of propagating the plants besides that of the seeds, which are contained in the fruit or apple. The tubers contain germinating points or eyes, just as aerial stems have leaf-buds, from which young shoots spring forth. These tubers, after their maturity, are washed out of the soil by rains, and carried by the torrents along the crevices of the rocks, and into the intervening valleys, where they take root, and give rise to new plants. Such is their primary use; but, like many other productions of nature, they have no doubt been destined by the beneficent Contriver of Nature to serve also in a secondary capacity. By the careful cultivation of man, these small waxy and bitter tubers have been swelled out into large farinaceous palatable potatoes—one single stem producing many pounds weight of a sort of food nearly resembling, and little inferior to, that of wheat, or oats, or barley. There never was such a gift bestowed on man since Ceres is fabled first to have brought the grains from heaven. But although three centuries have not yet elapsed since the introduction of the potato into Europe, strange to say, the name of him who first introduced the root rests upon nearly as doubtful authority as that of the planters of the cerealia more than three thousand years ago. It seems to be generally believed that the expedition sent by Sir Walter Raleigh to explore America in 1584 first brought the potato to Britain; but then it would appear that it had been introduced into the south of Europe before this period. In the Chronicle of Peter Cieca, printed in 1553, it is stated that the inhabitants of Quito cultivated a tuberous root called *papas*, which they used as food, and that this root was then cultivated in Italy, where, in common with the truffle, it was called *taratouffli*. Gerard, an English botanist, mentions in his Herbal, which was published in 1597, that he cultivated in his garden the potato, of which he gives a drawing, and calls it the Virginian potato, to distinguish it from the sweet potato or *batata*, which was common to Europe. Another curious circumstance in the history of this root is, that for more than a century after its introduction into Britain, it was little known, and less prized. For some time it was confined to the gardens of botanists and the curious, and when used at all as food, only at the tables of the rich, as a rare vegetable rather than as a standing dish. The potatoes furnished to the table of the queen of James I., bore the high price of two shillings per pound. Afterwards, though patronised by the Royal Society, and recommended by some of the leading men of the day, the culture of the potato was long of being generally adopted. In 1687 Woolridge thus writes of the tubers:—'I do not hear that it has been yet essayed whether they may not be propagated in great quantities for the use of swine and other cattle.' In Mortimer's Gardeners' Kalendar for 1708, the potato is directed to be planted in February; and it is added, 'the root is very near the nature of the Jerusalem artichoke, although not so good and wholesome; but it may prove good for swine.' Several reasons besides mere prejudice may be given for this neglect. Cultivation had not yet perhaps improved the wild stock to its present perfection; the proper mode of cooking, though simple enough, had not perhaps yet been hit upon; and vegetable food of any kind, except bread, was less sought after, or rather less within the reach of the mass of the people than now. In time, however, the grand discovery began to be made, that this esculent was pre-eminently the poor man's food and comfort. In Ireland, in Lancaster, and the western districts of England, and in Scotland, where land was portioned out in small parts on the cotter system, the potato culture, once begun, rapidly advanced, and spread over the whole country. A cottager in Stirlingshire, of the name of Prentice, about the year 1728, was the first to introduce the profitable culture of the potato among his fellow-labourers; and in 1734 the first field-crop was grown in the same county. This man made a little competency by the sale of seed potatoes to his neighbours, and thus was the means of spreading their culture among his countrymen. Within the last fifty years, such has been the rapid extension of this culture, that now there is not perhaps a table spread on any one day throughout the year among the many millions of Great Britain, from the prince to the peasant, where this root is not to be found.

Of the potato there seems to have been originally but one species; but by culture, an endless number of varieties have sprung up. These varieties are produced by planting the seeds of the apple, and when once obtained, are preserved by propagating by the tubers only. The potato grows in every kind of soil, and in all varieties of climate. It is now to be found in every corner of Europe; its culture is rapidly extending in India; it is abundant in North America, in Australia, and wherever an English colony settles. It thrives in low grounds, in elevated situations, in dry soil, or even in mossy lands with a superabundance of moisture. If it has a choice, however, the uplands and light arenaceous soils are much better adapted for the perfection of its tubers than strong rich lands or adhesive clay soils. In sharp, light, pulverisable soils, it seems to meet with its natural nourishment, and the potato is generally of a dry rich flavour, though small. In rich soils, with abundance of manure, it attains a large size, but is apt to be moist and waxy. A newly-improved soil produces better potatoes than land that has been long cultivated, even though in high condition. It is not, like the grain crops, so apt to be injured by autumnal rains or cold summers, and hence it is a surer produce for the cottager or small farmer. For seed, good middle-sized potatoes should be selected, and these are cut into pieces of not less than two ounces weight, each containing a single eye, which, according to Mr George Lindley, will produce a stronger stem than when two eyes are selected. The tail end of the potato should be rejected; indeed, in Lancashire, where much attention is paid to this root, both ends are cut off, and only the middle portion used for seed. A good large cutting is always found to produce the strongest and healthiest plant. Some recommend planting potatoes whole. This may succeed well in a very rich soil, but in inferior soils, several stems proceeding from the same root are found to injure the ultimate growth of the whole. It is, besides, an expensive plan.

The potato, like all other cultivated plants, is liable to disease. The most common is that termed the *curl*, which consists in the leaves, after the plant has grown up, curling inwards and decaying, followed by a decay of the stems, and of course the failure of the crop of tubers. This curl ensues most frequently from imperfect seed, giving rise to a feeble and diseased plant. The seed may be too small cut, or it may have been kept too long in a heap after cutting, by which fermentation may have been caused; or, lastly, the quality of the potato may have been such as to prevent a proper germination. It has been found that, when seed is allowed to be too ripe, it will not readily germinate; and that the best seed potatoes are those that are taken up out of the ground before they are fully matured. A frequent change of seed also is much recommended, and particularly a selection of seed from high-lying mossy or mountain soil, for a crop to be planted in low-lying fertile grounds. An occasional recourse to seedling plants is also recommended; although it is consistent with long experience, that if sufficient care be taken in the selection of good and not over-ripe tubers, a healthy plant will, under other favourable circumstances, be almost invariably insured. But it sometimes happens that, notwithstanding all due care in the selection of seed, and after the plants have shown a healthy appearance, the *curl* will seize them. This appears to be owing to peculiar states of the atmosphere; and on such occasions wheat and other grain crops are also affected with disease. In the highly luxuriant, we may truly say forced and unnatural, condition which vegetables are brought to by the art of culture, where every pore and cell is full to overflowing of nutritive juices, it is not surprising that certain extremes of temperature, or of moisture and dryness, and perhaps, more than all, of electric conditions of the atmosphere, should exert a deleterious influence. From atmospheric influences of this kind the juices, instead of obeying the vital actions of the plant, commence a fermentive or chemical process. This deranges their structure; the leaves become feeble and inactive; myriads of minute fungi and animalcules take up their abode in them; the disease passes to the stem, and at last to the roots. Such is the nature of the rust and smut in wheat, and such, there are strong reasons to believe, is the nature and origin of the disease which has this season so extensively seized on the potato crops.

It cannot be peculiarities of soil, manure, or seed; for the disease is too universal over Britain and the continent to lead to the supposition of such partial causes. The only general apparent cause, then, is atmospheric influence; and there has certainly been sufficient peculiarities in the changeable nature of the past season to warrant such a supposition. There have been great excess of moisture, sudden variations of temperature, and great electric vicissitudes, indicated by the almost daily changes of wind from east to west, and the prevalence of two conflicting currents in the atmosphere. This disease of the potato has appeared first in the leaf, which shrinks and withers, then in the stem, and lastly in the farina of the tuber. The affected potato evidently appears to have lost its vitality; the starch proceeds to the saccharine fermentation; and after this destruction of vitality, a minute fungus takes up its abode in the plant. These minute vegetables multiply by millions; and thus the rapid spread of the disease.

It is remarkable that those potatoes raised on dry light soils, where of course the juices of the plant were not superabundant, have escaped.

The chemical analyses of the potato hitherto made, show that rather more than one-half of the solid substance is a pure starch, the rest being fibrous matter and mucilage. It is probable, however, that more minute researches will indicate a considerable proportion of azotised matter in its composition, for otherwise, the well-ascertained facts of its very nutritious qualities could not be well accounted for. The potato also contains a small portion of a peculiar essential oil, which no doubt gives it that slight odour or flavour which it possesses, more especially in its uncooked state.

CITY TIME.

Among the many peculiar features which distinguish city from country life, not the least striking is the different estimation in which time is regarded. In the country, the rustic plods along the road, or leans over a stile, unknowing and uncaring for the hour, much less the minute. The deep tones of the church bell tell their tale to very careless and inattentive hearers; and the countryman thinks his watch correct enough if it be within a quarter of an hour of the village clock, in whose accuracy he places as much confidence as if old Time himself had the winding-up of it every day.

Very different, however, is the manner in which time is estimated in a large city. There, where thousands of persons congregate, and where business of great magnitude is hourly transacted, it is of importance that strict punctuality be observed—that the standard of time be correct—and that time, even in its most fractional parts, be not despised. Of course, without this arrangement, no plans or purposes could be satisfactorily carried out, and all would be disorder, uncertainty, and disappointment.

It is, however, in a colossal city like London that we see to perfection Time exercising his uncontrolled dominion; and perhaps no city in the world could furnish such striking illustrations of its paramount importance. Here it is not enough that your watch is right by the parish clock; the question is, is it in accordance with St Paul's or the Horse Guards? No genuine Londoner would think of passing either of those chronological standards without setting his watch right by it; which, having done, he talks of the time with authority, and 'right by St Paul's' is an assertion which cuts short the dispute. In passing along the streets too, what anxious pulling out of watches by evidently-belated pedestrians is observable on every hand; what rating of omnibus-conductors for having stopped for 'full five minutes.' Here a traveller, with his greatcoat and carpet-bag, and his face glowing like a red coal, urges his way along the crowded street, fearful of being too late for the train; and there a cab is stuck fast in a crowded thoroughfare, the inmate of which raves that the steamer will have started in another three minutes. Here a tradesman from the west end is hurrying to get his cheque cashed at the banking-house, the appointed hour for closing which is even now ready to strike; and there a country gentleman has arrived, just in time to see the door of the public-office whither he was bustling closed against him. Appointments are made to the minute; and a delay of five or ten minutes in keeping one, is at the hazard of disarranging the next. Clocks are conspicuous in most of the better description of shops: watches are ticking in every business-man's pocket. 'How goes the enemy?' is one of the commonest inquiries; and everything testifies to the immense importance of time in the social arrangements of a great city.

As in the immense establishments with which London abounds, and especially in the government offices, punctuality is of the first importance, some amusing illustrations of the value of time, even in its vulgar fractions, are there exhibited, which, to the eye of a stranger, are very striking, and are probably, from the national superiority of our business-habits, unique.

In the morning, as the clock is about to strike nine, omnibuses and stages draw up in the vicinity of the bank, filled with well-dressed, gentlemanlike men. The 'thousand and one' clerks are arriving, all of whom are required to be at their post by the precise time, under pain of a fine. The old stager who has filled his situation there for the last quarter of a century, and fears lest, peradventure, something on the road might detain him, and who prides himself not a little on his punctuality, always contrives to leave his house in the suburbs, where most of the clerks reside, a few minutes before the necessary time; but some of the younger ones, who are not so wary, show by their flushed faces the quick step they have been obliged to adopt in order to arrive in time. Another and another omnibus unburdens itself of its load; quick as thought the 'thirteen inside and five out' are hurrying to the bank gate; gouty old gentlemen hobble up to the entrance with all the quickness they can muster; and at ten minutes past nine, the twice five hundred men are at their desks ready for action.

Still more animated and striking is the scene at the General Post-office in St Martin's-le-Grand a few minutes before six o'clock in the evening. At a quarter before six, the fray has scarcely commenced; there is ample time, and few care to hurry themselves, except it be some unaccustomed dame, who eagerly inquires whether she is too late to post her letter. But the minute-hand silently moves onwards, and boys arrive with bags of newspapers and packets of letters, which are poured in at the all-receiving window. Onwards, onwards moves the minute hand; only five minutes to the hour—and boys and men come hurrying in from all parts with letters and papers, the young urchins glorying in just 'nicking the time.' Bag after bag is thrown in at the window, at the peril of the official who stands there to receive them, packet after packet of letters being aimed at him by their respective and irrespective bearers. St Paul's clock strikes—*one*; still more and more come running up the steps—*two*, a cab draws up, and a sack of newspapers is hastily hauled out and thrown in at the window—*three*, a porter puffs up at his very quickest speed with a bag of letters—*four*, a panting, meagre horse arrives, and another sack of papers is safely lodged—*five*, a young bare-armed paper-capped urchin pours in his armful of Suns and Globes—*six*,—the window-keeper unceremoniously slams to the shutter, and the score of surrounding urchins, having safely deposited their burdens, salute with a shout of derision the disconsolate lad who rushes up to the place with his packet one minute too late.

A MORNING AT MORNINGSIDE.

One of the strongest impressions which remained after leaving the ball at the Morningside Lunatic Asylum, described in a late number, was curiosity to see more of the institution; and having been invited, we inspected it more at leisure on the Monday morning after the soirée.

As our first visit was on a moonless night, we had little opportunity of noticing the general aspect of the place; but now we took means to supply that deficiency. The visitor is admitted through a pair [illegible] into a gravel walk of moderate length, bordered by two primly-trimmed hedges. At the end of the hedge to the right stands a neat cottage, similar in every respect to a suburban villa. This is occupied by a single patient, who has a regular establishment of servants, a carriage, and indeed everything in the same state and order as if he were not an inmate of the establishment. Continuing along the avenue, the visitor finds, facing him, a handsome and extensive building, designed for such persons as have the ability to pay for their accommodation. This edifice, from its situation, is called the 'East Department,' and its inhabitants pay L.56 per annum, as an ordinary charge; though separate sitting-rooms entail an additional expense. On the other hand, which patients are in straitened circumstances, a yearly deduction of ten, or even of twenty pounds, is made from the ordinary rate. The newer and larger building, situated at some distance westward from this (hence called the 'West Department'), is filled with patients of the humbler orders, whose friends or parishes pay for them from L.15 to L.20 per annum. The Morningside Asylum, therefore, is available to all classes except the very rich. The total of inmates at present residing within its precincts is 406.

Having been received by one of the principal officers in his study, we proceeded under his guidance to inspect the arrangements of the mansion designated the East Department. A short flight of stairs conducted us to a small vestibule of semicircular form, the flat side being occupied by the stairs. Opening a door, and then closing it carefully after him, our conductor ushered us into a gallery. 'This suite of apartments,' he remarked in a low tone, while pointing to the doors which lined the passage, 'is occupied by females. Each has a bed-room to herself, besides access to a common sitting-room.' We were then admitted into one of the chambers. Nothing could exceed the neatness of the furniture, or the cheerful aspect of the scenery from the window. Its inhabitant joined us, and with the most unreserved politeness directed our attention to the prospect, praising it very highly. As this sleeping-room is the counterpart of all the others, we went immediately to the sitting-room; which is well furnished, and has a pianoforte for the amusement of the patients. Except by two unhappy women afflicted with dementia, who sat one on each side of the instrument in a state of unconsciousness, the parlour was unoccupied, as most of the ladies were taking their morning exercise in the grounds.

From this gallery we followed our guide to one opposite, occupied by males; and observed that its plan and general arrangements are precisely like the one we had just quitted. In the sitting-room were several patients, amongst whom little sociality seemed to exist; according fully with our experiences at the ball. No conversation was going on. One lay on a sofa, apparently in deep thought; another, seated on a chair with his hands thrust into his pockets and his legs protruded on the carpet at full length, was intently contemplating the toes of his boots. A third was engaged at the bagatelle-board; but as he had no antagonist, the game seemed not to be interesting him much. Others were reading; nor did our presence disturb their studies. In this room we recognised two as having been at the ball. There, their countenances occasionally exhibited gleams of animation; but here, a settled listlessness was apparent: they looked like the victims of a want of something to do; though, in reality, they are not; for every plan it is possible to put in practice is adopted to entice them to employment; in some instances successfully; in others—like the present—not. Want of energy, and not want of occupation, therefore, prevents them from shaking off the tiresome ennui they were labouring under. In the way of amusement there is, for fine weather, a bowling-green; whilst at the top of the house a billiard-room is at the service of all who may choose to play. For more active exercise, and for those who are fond of horticulture, a botanical garden has been formed. Every inch of it was dug by the voluntary labour of some of the patients of the East Department, under the direction of a practical gardener; and by them it is kept up. As, however, it happens with the rest of the world, so it is with the insane: to be industrious from choice is the exception—to be idle from inclination the rule.

Once more in the vestibule, we were introduced into a small apartment, possessing an interest of a more abstract character than that awakened by the objects of insanity we had hitherto seen. This was the museum; the contents of which are extremely curious. The first thing the eye lights upon is a row of casts; some taken post-mortem, others from the heads of living patients. They are sixty in number, and are continually being added to. In viewing them one after another, one is struck with their characteristic physiognomies. No person could behold these lifeless effigies without saying that the originals had been afflicted with a disease of the mind; for even the cold, white, motionless plaster appears expressive of insanity. Some of the heads are by no means abnormal in appearance, either in shape or feature; many, again, are remarkably small; whilst others are as remarkably large; one in particular—taken from an idiot—bearing a not flattering resemblance to the head of Sir Walter Scott. A few are very deficient in symmetry; whilst several would be considered good heads. 'In some,' says the physician in his last report, 'the character of the insanity has corresponded remarkably with the phrenological development; in others, such connexion cannot be remarked.'* These casts, when sufficiently accumulated, and carefully observed upon, to justify a sound generalisation, will form a valuable addition to our stock of knowledge on psychology and cerebral physiology. It is to be hoped that similar collections are in progress in other institutions, so that the experience and deductions of each physician may be eventually compared and generalised. Besides the casts, the striking physiognomical manifestations of insanity make graphic portraits of patients not without their value, and many are deposited in this little museum, together with drawings of diseased organs taken after dissection. A library is also in course of formation of all the works which have as yet appeared on the subject of insanity, for the benefit of the medical students who are admitted to assist the regular medical staff of the establishment. Plans of other asylums have also been collected, in case of additions or alterations in the building we are describing. To these some degree of importance is attached, for much depends, in regard to the care, comfort, and recovery of the inmates of a lunatic asylum, on its construction.

The two galleries we had visited being precisely the same as the apartments of the other inmates, there was no necessity for a farther inspection of the East Department. We were therefore conducted through the grounds to the larger and more modern structure set apart for the insane poor. In this department the new system of things is much more strikingly exemplified than in the one we are now quitting; it having been erected since 1840. In the older building, various traces of the restrictive plan are observable. Within, the door of each gallery is perforated with a glazed peep-hole, through which the keepers of the old school were wont to watch the actions of the patients in a manner that rendered them objects of suspicion, and consequently of dislike; without, it is surrounded with high walls: but the moment the Eastern boundary is passed, the aspect of the premises is totally changed. Everything is open and unconfined. A low wooden

* The phrenological doctrine is, that comparative size of brain, *other circumstances being equal*, indicates comparative capacity. From lack of attention to the specialty in italics, many are led to misapprehend the value of form and size as a demonstration of character. In reality, large size is often of no avail, in consequence of inferior quality of brain, lymphatic temperament, or disease. Vaticination upon the heads of insane persons is therefore disclaimed by phrenologists.—ED.

paling, which a child might overleap, is all that separates the grounds from the open country; and as we were passing along, the doctor pointed to a field beyond the enclosures of the institution in which a group of persons were digging: they were all patients except a gardener, who directed their operations, and an attendant.

The new edifice is calculated to accommodate 400 inmates, in equal numbers of both sexes; and, owing to its being subdivided into apartments of a large size, the number may be diminished or increased according to circumstances, without materially affecting the general arrangements of the institution. Another and still more important advantage of this plan is, that the inmates are enabled to enjoy greater comfort, and the attendants to exercise more efficient control, than is attainable under the cell system of construction hitherto adopted.

Passing to a side entrance, our cicerone opened a door, and introduced us to some eight or ten shoemakers, all busily plying their trade. When we entered, they gave the doctor a sign of friendly recognition, and appeared pleased to see him. This happened in nearly every room which we afterwards visited, showing the new relations which have been established between the officers of lunatic asylums and their unfortunate charges. Formerly, their presence produced a shudder, or some equally significant token of dread. On the present occasion, one of the patients, addressing us in a pleasing tone, handed a shoe for our inspection: it was well and strongly made; and on some remark of that sort being uttered, a neater and lighter article was produced; 'for,' said our informant, 'we can do light as well as heavy work.' Indeed he seemed quite proud of his own and his companions' productions. He then resumed his seat, and lustily plied at his lapstone. All the others were equally busy, and were so much absorbed in their occupation, that our departure was scarcely noticed.

The tailors' shop was occupied by about a dozen patients busily stitching. Another sat by the fire with his hat on, and seemed to have installed himself into the office of director-general of the whole proceedings. He was the first loquacious patient we had seen; but his remarks and admonitions were not in the least heeded by his hearers, whilst we noticed that a single word uttered by the regular attendant of the room, was paid the utmost attention to. This is invariably the case; and it has always been found impracticable to appoint ever so comparatively sane a patient to any office of supervision. The others know well enough that he is, like themselves, mentally diseased, and pay him no respect whatever. The volunteer director of the tailors, finding his instructions thrown away, turned his attention to us, and after a short chat on 'things in general,' in which the doctor joined, we retired.

On certain days of the week the patients are allowed visits from their friends, and the next apartment we inspected was that used for receiving them. It is well furnished; and in a neat glass-case are displayed several fancy articles, such as silk purses, worsted reticules, d'oyleys, embroidery, toys, &c. made by the female patients. These are for sale to such visitors as may wish to become purchasers; the proceeds being allowed to accumulate till enough is collected to purchase some article of luxury, perhaps a pianoforte, for the use of the West Department. From the visitors' receiving-room we were conducted to the kitchen, in which all the victuals for the establishment are prepared.

Respecting the food of the insane, the practice at Morningside is wholly subversive of the old system. Depletion by means of low diet was formerly employed, to keep down the muscular strength of those from whom the least violence was expected. Here, on the contrary, the rule is—good and sufficient food. Experience has proved that low diet tends to increase insanity: in hot climates, indeed, it produces it. We learn that a number of the Milanese peasantry are, at a particular season, brought into the Milan Lunatic Asylum in a state of raging mania; which is invariably cured by the administration of a sufficiency of wholesome nutriment. This fact fully bears out the theory and practice of the Morningside physician, who strongly advocates that pauper lunatics should have a more genial diet than that to which they were accustomed when sane. In his last annual report he says—'All observation shows that, in a large proportion of the insane, the constitution has been originally weak; and that where it has been otherwise, the disease has the effect of weakening and depressing it. This remark applies particularly to the insane poor, for whom remedies of a tonic nature are most frequently attended with beneficial effects; and the exhibition of wine itself is often found to allay, rather than to increase excitement.' So completely subversive is this of old theories, that had the worthy physician advocated an abundant dietary for the insane twenty years ago, it would have been thought very good evidence of his own insanity.

We found the kitchen and its appurtenances in admirable order, and the distraught domestics attending to their business with the same attention and propriety as exist in every well-regulated cuisine. This part of the institution is never without a supply of assistants; for of all classes of the community, none appear to be so liable to insanity as domestic servants—a fact exhibited in the statistics of almost every lunatic asylum for the poorer classes. In the year 1844, there were admitted into the Morningside establishment 162 persons, of whom 55, or almost one-third, were servants; namely, 26 females and 29 males.—The washing-house adjoining was also in full use—about twenty women being employed at their tubs. They seemed more cheerful than the rest; and we found it to be a rule, that the more active and constant the occupation of the patients at work, the happier they seemed. One extremely communicative old female gave us a glowing account of a visit she had been allowed to pay the day before to her relations at Newhaven; and was particularly anxious to impress upon the doctor that she had reported to all her friends how comfortable she was, and how kindly she was treated. A kind word to some of the other washers from the doctor (of which they seemed both proud and pleased), and we adjourned into the laundry. Here an inmate was pacing up and down with a stately tread: she scarcely deigned to notice us; and, as she was at that time the only person present, we left this section of the building to ascend to the galleries, in which the other female inmates resided.

The social, as opposed to the cell system of treating the insane, was fully developed in the galleries into which we were now shown. Besides eating and sitting rooms, common to all the inmates of each gallery, they have only two dormitories. These consist of large rooms, along the sides of which are ranged about twenty beds, in which the patients take their nightly rest, with no more than two attendants. In no other institution has the dormitory system been carried so far; and here it has been signally successful. Amongst other good effects, it tends to establish a kindly feeling between the patients and attendants; the latter, be it remarked, being in no dread of personal injury; for it is a peculiarity of the insane, that they seldom combine to do mischief. On the contrary, when one is inclined to become troublesome, his companions take part against him, and support the attendants. There are few inmates who, whilst they believe themselves to be hardly dealt with by being secluded from the rest of the world, do not possess a thorough conviction of the lunacy of their fellows; hence they, fancying themselves the sane, do all they can to keep the insane in order. For these reasons it is that the dormitory system has succeeded. On the other hand, a certain number of single apartments is absolutely necessary for the violently maniacal; but in this institution it is always esteemed a step towards improvement or recovery when a patient is transferred from the cell to the dormitory.

In the sitting-rooms of the first gallery we visited several females, who were busily employed in various sorts of needlework. Some were making articles of dress, others knitting, and constructing such tasteful articles as we had seen for sale in the visitors' room. A few were reading, and fewer still were altogether idle; but were to all appearance incapable of employment. All seemed pleased at the appearance of the doctor. In a gallery for men, we found several parading in a state of complete idleness. Amongst them was the inmate whose performances on the violin contributed so much to the success of the Thursday night's ball. In a modest tone he announced to our companion that he had a favour to ask. 'The fact is,' he said, 'I have very important business to transact with Dr ——; and as his residence is so near this, I trust you will allow me to call on him.' The physician received the request with the earnest consideration he would have shown to a sane person, and replied that he would have had much pleasure in granting it, only Dr ——, having retired from public life, does not receive visitors now. 'But, sir,' continued the applicant earnestly, 'he will see *me*, I know.' To this the doctor replied soothingly, 'Very well, very well; we will see about it,' and we walked away. It is a part of the system of treatment neither to contradict a patient, to treat his delusions with levity, nor 'to laugh him' out of his fancies. One clause of the printed instructions to attendants runs thus:—'The delusions of a patient are on no account to be made the subject of merriment or amusement; they are, as a general rule, not to be contradicted, but when introduced by the patient, his attention is, if possible, to be directed to some other subject.'

When we stepped in from the verandah in which the above little colloquy occurred, our guide was greeted with great hilarity by a patient, who inquired 'what he had done to be kept there?' 'Done?' echoed the doctor with affected surprise, 'nothing: but the truth is, Mr ——, your health is not very good, and——' Here he was interrupted by a hearty laugh from the merry patient. 'Ha, ha! I know what you mean, doctor; but as to *health*, as you are pleased to call it, I'll be bound I am quite as well as you are!' and with another laugh he turned away. He seemed perfectly happy and contented; yet his jocularity produced a more painfully affecting sensation than the profoundest melancholia. The quickness with which he took up the doctor's delicate allusion to the state of his mind, showed that he must have known where he was, and that he was deemed by the world a lunatic. With these convictions, it is difficult to believe that his hilarity could have been anything but forced. Still, it is consolatory to observe, that the wretchedness and depression which it is usual to associate with insanity, was by no means observable on the countenances of the majority of the patients. Most of them appeared contented and happy, even amidst their abstraction.

Connected with the next apartment which we visited, is one of the most interesting features of the institution. It was the printing-office, whence is issued 'The Morningside Mirror,' a monthly sheet, whose literary contents are supplied wholly by the inmates. Our readers are already aware of the possibility of the insane producing sane and sensible lucubrations, from the extracts we made from a similar work issued from the Crichton lunatic press.* A quotation from the sheets before us will strengthen this conviction. The second number of the Morningside Mirror is chiefly occupied with an account of a trip to Habbie's Howe, which a select number of the inmates were allowed to take in the summer, under proper guidance.† The scenery is described with minute accuracy, and there are a few playful hits and puns which would not disgrace the habitual writers of facetious 'articles.' From the poets' corner of the sheet we extract the following lines;—

SUNSET.

The sun, the blazing sun is setting,
Fading in the west away,
The clouds, the thronging clouds are getting
Glory from his bright decay.

Thick and wide o'er all the heaven
Spread the clouds in dull array,
Save the brilliant space that's given
For the sun to close the day.

He disappears; but still he sendeth
Glory far above, around;
Hues to every vapour lendeth
Brighter than on earth are found.

* * *

Far away the sun is wheeling
To begin another day,
And I gaze with sadd'ning feeling
On the latest lingering ray.

Gone—the azure vault is darkling,
Night enshrouds yon mountain dome,
Bright a silvery star is sparkling;
I must hie me to my home.

Our inspection closed with a peep at the carpenters' shop, where we had the pleasure of being introduced to one of the poetical contributors to the 'Mirror,' who was busily employed with two companions amongst the shavings. A timid physician of the old school would hardly have been persuaded to trust himself with lunatics surrounded by, and handling instruments capable of the deadliest uses. Axes, chisels, and saws, were in busy requisition, in defiance of the ancient prejudices against allowing edge tools to be within the reach of fools. On leaving this place, we saw an amusing specimen of exclusiveness: on a board was painted, 'No attendants admitted here on any pretence whatever.' The carpenters were not to be disturbed at their work by the merely sane.

From all we had seen of this establishment, it was manifest that the main object of those to whom its management is intrusted, is to maintain the inmates in a condition as nearly similar to that in which they existed when at large as possible. Not only is the general rule of personal non-restraint unreservedly followed out, but each patient is allowed to follow the bent of his inclination, as far as is consistent with the wellbeing of the whole establishment. Though opportunities are provided for such employment as they have been used to, they are not *obliged* to work; persuasion, and the example of others, being the only incentives resorted to. Even from the most refractory and noisy patients, every symbol of restraint was removed when the present chief physician commenced his duties. Besides the blessings conferred on the patients by the change, its good effects have proved of no less importance on the attendants. Formerly, when the lunatic became troublesome, the easiest way of rendering him quiet was to pinion and gag him, and by these horrible expedients the attendant was relieved of a vast amount of vexation; but now he has no such resource to fly to. He knows that moral means only are at his command; hence in the worst cases his vigilance must be unceasing to soothe and divert the mind of his charge, at the earliest stages of its appearance, from the irritating cause. At length, in consequence of incessant attention and perseverance, the predispositions to excesses become of unfrequent recurrence.

At Morningside, in short, nothing is left undone to banish from the patient's mind that he is in confinement. High walls do not bound his view of the surrounding country; no harsh words are employed towards him; his delusions are treated with respect; and no promises are made, or enticements held forth, which are not to be rigidly fulfilled: the very name of 'keeper' is abolished, and that of 'attendant' substituted: occupation is supplied for his mind, and exercise for his body.

From the list of the professions of patients appended to

* See No. 61, p. 43, new series.

† Many such trips were taken by different parties of the inmates during the summer.

the report, we perceive that there are some of nearly all the useful trades, which are industriously followed; so that the Morningside asylum supplies most of its own wants. It is a little world, almost complete in itself; which, instead of being some two hundred millions of square miles, is only about fifty-six acres in extent.

FINDEN'S BEAUTIES OF MOORE.

THE most superb Christmas book of the year which we have seen is *The Beauties of Moore*, a series of imaginary portraits for the heroines of the author of Lalla Rookh, engraved chiefly by, and wholly under the direction of, Mr Edward Finden, from paintings by Frith, Elmore, Egg, Middleton, &c.; each portrait being accompanied by a slight piece of pleasant letterpress, half critical, half descriptive. The impression which this volume gives of the state of the arts in England is really cheering; the portraits themselves are exquisite things—twenty-four variations of feminine loveliness and feminine character—and even the decorations surrounding the pictures are strikingly beautiful. On opening such a book, one wonders at the vast amount of artistic talent of high character which modern invention and enterprise now bring into the service of what may be called the Many, as compared with the few for whom artists once plied their pencils. The very binding of this volume is a work of grace, beauty, and originality.

The literary sketches accompanying the portraits present here and there remarks worth listening to. For example, under the portrait referring to the verse,

'The brilliant black eye
May in triumph let fly
All its darts, without caring who feels 'em;
But the soft eye of blue,
Though it scatter wounds too,
Is much better pleased when it heals 'em'—

we have an exception pointed out. 'We confess our reluctance,' says the writer, 'to differ from such an authority, but we must testify to having found a blue eye mischievous beyond all telling—lurking in ambush beneath the silken tresses, natural *jalousies* given in Nature's merriest mood, for the express purpose of facilitating such trickery—sparkle forth with a laughing indifference, a needless mockery—an utter recklessness of intense suffering; and then, with a downcast lid, and a lip trained to smiles, look as unconscious as though never embarked in a single love-chase. We protest that we have found blue eyes cruel to the very extent of cruelty; and, taught by experience, we never now venture on a soft whisper, or even a simple quotation, without having first ascertained to a nicety the colour of the orb; and though

'The black eye may say,
"Come and worship my ray;
By adoring, perhaps you may move me!"'—

we have found the black eye, *when moved*, steadfast as brilliant; while the blue eye was, to us, as uncertain as the meteor dancing through the sky, whose hue it borrowed.' We add our testimony to the truth of these observations. The associations of the poet with the various colours of female eyes are not, we believe, associations of recollected experience, but of other ideas in his mind with respect to the colours in question.

Having occasion to allude to the Irish air of the *Little Harvest Rose*, the writer relates the legend connected with it in the following charming style, reminding us of an Irish female writer well known to fame. The heroine, 'having wearied herself by gathering flowers, fell asleep; and, behold! the month was changed from sunny June to weeping April; and a mysterious hand held forth to her a tender rose-bud, and a voice whispered in her ear, "It is love!" and the half-blown flower looked so charming, with little globules of dew looking from each fragment of moss, that she longed to take it and place it in her bosom; and so she was about to do, when the fairy who had presided at her birth sprang between her and the proffered gift, exclaiming, "Touch it not, darling of my heart! it is too weak to enjoy a long life; and if you watch, and have patience for a minute, you will see it fade and wither; young love is never lasting." And she took the advice of her fairy god-mother; and truly the rose faded and died before her eyes. And again she slept—and it seemed to her that the same hand presented to her another rose—a full-blown flower, of splendid dye, but small fragrance; and the same voice whispered, "It is love!" and her fancy inclined her to take it, but again the fairy (and, be it remembered, that as an Irish fairy may be supposed to do, she spoke warmly, and mingled English and Irish together) interposed and said, "Jewel, avourneen, deelish! touch it not—it's forced by the sun into unnatural life, without a morsel of true love in its heart for anything but itself; so let it alone—a false love would wither up your young pulse, and no blossom, jewel, is fragrant that hasn't been steeped in showers." The maiden turned from the rose, though she began to apprehend that the fairy was singularly difficult to please; fearing that her youth would fade, and she should have no true love of her own wherewith to pass her life, and end her days, she thought she would sleep as often as she could on the seat of dreams; and she repaired thither frequently; but sleep did not come at her desire for many weary hours; yet at last, as the evening sun was setting, she fell into *a deep sweet slumber, that pressed upon her eyelids as softly as the leaves that shade, without crushing the blossoms of the purple violet.* And again the hand came forth, and presented to her a rose; and again the voice whispered, "It is love!" and though the rose was not delicate, like the first, nor large blossomed, like the second, its petals were full of the richest perfume, and bowed beneath a weight of dew; and the fairy appeared as before, and said, "You've waited through wisdom, and your wisdom is crowned. The rose did not come forth until strength was given it for long life; nor was it forced into blossom by the art of man; but has been perfected by nature. Take it, avourneen!—let it be your love; it has gone through the rain of spring and the heat of summer—take it, and keep it; the clouds and mists that others cannot endure, increase the beauty and fragrance of the Little Harvest Rose."'

The superstitions connected with Irish brides are drolly sketched off. 'She (young Kitty) should have been told that on her bridal morning it was dangerous to rise before the sun; such an act indicating, strange as it may seem, that she would become a shrewish wife. She should have been taught the old rhymer's instructions to the Bride of May—

"When the sun shall rise,
Unclose your eyes."

She should have waited until the warm sunshine had driven away the "murky spirits" that work mischief to young maids, and then the poor butterfly would not have been sacrificed, nor would the heart's-ease have escaped from its sweet confinement beneath her shoe. Yet omens, far more prophetic of evil than the two which made young Kitty thoughtful—and, for a moment, sad—might have crossed her mirror and her path. Being Irish, she *might* have heard the croaking of a raven in her dreams, and seen the shadow of his wing flit through the twilight of a summer morning; she *might* have heard the death-watch, or the knock of the invisible hand three times, nightly, at the same hour; or have seen the elaborately-notched, winding-sheet curling down her candle as the clock struck twelve. The ruby in the ring that circled the *engaged* finger of her hand, *might* have faded into the pallor of a pearl whenever he who bestowed the gift drew near; or she *might* have encountered a red-haired woman on the first of May; or crushed a *dar-dael* on St Martin's eve—the loathsome beetle that, according to Irish tradition, stole the Virgin Mary's apples, and whose death bodes fire and pestilence; or the ringlet, when tied into a true lover's knot, and pressed beneath her pillow, might have been found there in the morning in the [illegible] of a serpent; or her prayer-book might have opened at the burial instead of the bridal service; or—but it is to be hoped she learnt the art of overcoming ill omens by creating good ones—a mystery well worth the study of maid or wife.'

In this princely volume, it is surprising to find, after all, so little of Moore; in general, a couple of lines, and in some extraordinary instances a stanza, from the poem or passage referred to by the pictured 'beauty,' is all that is given, where, as a matter of course, one would expect to see the poet's entire description. This is strangely disappointing; and the effect is not palliated, but rather enhanced, when we find some awkward prose paraphrase of the original presented instead. Let this, however, be cited as no disparagement of the book, but merely as an illustration of the footing on which men of letters and publishers now stand with relation to each other. To have given extracts from Mr Moore's poems in connexion with these splendid engravings, so complimentary to his standing as a poet, would have been held as an invasion of literary rights. A question of pounds, shillings, and pence, comes to forbid the banns between picture and poem. A modern author cannot afford to write a single line for nothing, and never must word of his be put into type without a 'consideration.' Hence it sometimes happens in these prosperous times of literature, that where one author thinks to do a courtesy to another, by quoting a passage from his writings, the second man cries, 'Halt, my good friend—much obliged to you, but you will first settle with me for leave to reprint that said passage.' Or, what comes to the same thing, a publisher, who has possessed himself of the author's copyrights, interposes the same demand. The representation of everything by money, which marks our age, is shown as strikingly in such matters as in any other. How different from the days when Robert Burns, living in Dumfries on an income of seventy pounds a-year, positively refused a farthing of remuneration for some hundred songs which he poured out in the course of three or four years, and which to this day remain unapproached as specimens of verse for music.

Column for Young People.

THE PARTICULAR DUTY.

FROM THE FRENCH OF MADAME GUIZOT.

MONSIEUR DE FLANMONT said one day to his children, I am going to tell you a story I have just been reading, and I want you to give me your opinion of it.

Henry, Clementina, and Gustavus, immediately came and seated themselves around him, when he related as follows:—

A tradesman named Paul, the father of three children, whom he supported by his industry, was walking on the banks of a rapid river, swollen by the rain. A whirlpool was under one of the arches of a bridge close by, which was drawing into its vortex the wreck of a boat laden with planks, which had been broken to pieces. Paul beheld the torrent, and said within himself, 'If I were to fall in there, I should find it hard to get out again;' yet Paul was a good swimmer, and had more than once saved the lives of persons who were in danger of being drowned in the same river; but at that moment, in spite of his courage, he felt that there was really cause for fear. Then he thought of his children, who depended upon him for their support, of his eldest son, twelve years old, who promised to become a good workman; but if he lost his father, would have no one either to instruct or to protect him. He thought of his daughter, whom he hoped soon to be able to apprentice, and of his youngest child not long weaned, and whom his sister took care of, as they had lost their mother. He reflected with pleasure that they were all well and comfortably supported, and in good health, and could not help thinking how different their situation would be were they to lose him. He instinctively withdrew from the water's edge, as if afraid of trusting his footsteps. As he walked along, he saw a man on the bridge carrying a parcel of old iron on his shoulder; he was looking at the river, and watching a plank that was approaching the bridge; he leaned over the parapet to see if it threaded the arch, but, leaning too low, the iron on his shoulder impelled him forward, and he fell into the water, uttering a piercing shriek.

Paul also cried out in despair, for he felt himself retained upon the bank by the consideration of his children, while at the same time he would willingly have endeavoured to save the unfortunate man, whom he saw in such danger of perishing. He looked about in inexpressible anguish, and seeing a long pole, he seized it, and taking it into the water as far as he could without going beyond his depth, he tried to push a plank over towards the man. But all his efforts were in vain; the river was furious, and, after a few ineffectual struggles, the poor man sunk, rose again, and then sunk to rise no more in life.

Paul stood immoveable upon the shore, with his eyes fixed on the spot where he had seen him disappear; he remained there until night, and then returned home, deeply grieved, but saying that he did not think he could have acted otherwise. He was for several days without being able either to eat or sleep, and scarcely answered those who spoke to him. His neighbours, who saw him in this state, inquired the cause. He told them what had occurred, when the greater number said he had done right; others said that he had done wrong, while he still maintained that he did not think he had. What is your opinion?

Clementina.—He certainly did right to take care of himself for his children.

Henry.—Oh yes; it is always easy to find excuses when people do not act as they ought.

Gustavus.—But he owed nothing to that man, who fell into the water by his own awkwardness; he did not even know him.

Henry.—Papa has often told us that we ought to do all the good in our power to others, and Paul might very well have tried to save the man; he was not sure that he would perish with him.

Clementina.—Ah! but then it was very probable.

Henry.—There would be no great merit in performing brave actions, if we were sure that there was no danger in them.

M. de Flanmont.—But consider, my son, that in exposing himself to this danger, which was undoubtedly very great, and in which he would probably have perished, he likewise exposed his children to the danger of dying from want, or of becoming bad characters, in consequence of having no honest means of earning their bread. Do you not think that this consideration was sufficiently important to counterbalance the desire he might have had to save the drowning man?

Henry.—That is very possible, papa; but still I am sure that a person who risked his life to save another, would be thought much more worthy of regard than he who would so well consider all the reasons for not doing so.

M. de Flanmont.—That is easily accounted for: we have an unquestionable proof of the courage of him who performs a brave action, while we cannot be sure of the motives by which another may be prevented. But suppose it was satisfactorily proved to you that Paul had every desire to jump into the water to save this man, and that he was only withheld by the consideration of his children, do you not think he would be more deserving of esteem than of reproach?

Henry.—I only know that I should be sorry to find myself in a similar situation.

Clementina.—I think one would hardly know how to get out of it.

Gustavus.—Well; and while you would be deliberating, the man would be left in the water, and so it would be all the same to him.

M. de Flanmont.—Indecision is surely in such a case what is most to be avoided, and it is therefore necessary that we should accustom ourselves to reflect upon the order of our duties, that we may have no doubt as to which is the most important.

Henry.—But when we meet at the same time with two, which are equally important?

M. de Flanmont.—That is what there cannot be, for we are never obliged to do more than is possible. For instance, do you think that Paul could at the same time have thrown himself into the river, and not have done so?

Gustavus (*laughing*).—Ah, that would be quite impossible.

M. de Flanmont.—Do you think, then, that we can at the same time be obliged to perform an action, and do what would make that action impracticable?

Henry.—Certainly not.

M. de Flanmont.—It is then quite clear, that if we were necessarily obliged to perform one of those actions, our duty would be to discard everything that could prevent it, even what might appear to be a duty in another case.

Clementina.—And you think, papa, do you not, that the duty of maintaining one's children ought to precede every other?

M. de Flanmont.—No, not every other, assuredly. The first duty is to be an honest man—never to injure any one, or to betray the trust committed to our charge.

Clementina.—But people are intrusted with the interests of their children.

M. de Flanmont.—Their own integrity is their first concern, for no other person can be intrusted with that. We are commanded to be just to others; but not doing all that they require from us, is not doing them injustice; therefore Paul was not unjust to the man who wanted his assistance, because he took care of himself for the sake of his children.

Henry.—Because his children also wanted his assistance? But, papa, according to what you say, neither would it have been injustice to his children not to have done all in his power for them; and they were not in greater need of him than the man who was drowning, and had no other person to help him.

M. de Flanmont.—Certainly not. But do you think you can do good to every one?

Gustavus.—To do that, we should have to spend our days running about the streets, giving to all the poor people.

Clementina.—Yes, or even travel abroad, and spend all your fortune in giving to all who most want your assistance.

Henry.—I am sure that is a subject which has very often puzzled me.

M. de Flanmont.—That is because you have not considered that each man, being but a very small part of the community, can only be specially charged with the very small portion of good that he can do in the world. It is even the only way that he can do any good, for if every person were to undertake to do everything, they would not know which to attend to; every person, therefore, should examine what is the particular portion of good with which he is naturally intrusted. Thus, if it were not our imperative duty to attend first to the interests and welfare of our own family, it would be a duty of common sense; for it would be ridiculous to neglect the good we can do at home, for the sake of doing good abroad; we must first fulfil our duty there, and then see what means are left for accomplishing those which are to be considered afterwards as benevolence and kindness towards those who have no claim upon us, except that they require our assistance.

Henry.—After all, papa, I cannot understand that because a man has children who require his care, he must give up assisting others whenever it exposes him to the least risk.

M. de Flanmont.—You are right not to understand that, for it is not the case; a man even so circumstanced may, and certainly ought to be willing to expose himself to some degree of danger in order to confer a great benefit. For instance, had the river been calm, or had he seen a good prospect of being able to save the man, Paul would have acted wrong in not having swam to his assistance.

Clementina.—But since he might have been drowned, he would have run the risk of neglecting his duty to his children.

M. de Flanmont.—Undoubtedly, but he would also have risked the loss of an opportunity of saving a man, when it was probable he could have done so without injury to his children.

Clementina.—Ay, that is where the case again becomes difficult.

M. de Flanmont.—It is then that duties may be compared and balanced one against the other. But suppose you were told that, by subjecting your children to a trifling loss, such as being not so well dressed or well fed, you could save a man's life, do you not think you ought to do so?

Clementina.—Certainly.

M. de Flanmont.—As it is impossible for us to know how matters may turn out that are liable to danger, I think we should do that which offers the most probable chance of being the greatest benefit, and look upon a trifling danger as we would upon a trifling loss, to which we would subject our children, for the sake of conferring a great benefit upon another. Are you satisfied, Henry?

Henry.—I think not, papa; I must only try to become very clever and very courageous, that all dangers may appear trifling to me.

M. de Flanmont.—That will be well done; but I must finish the history of Paul.

Clementina.—What, is it not finished?

Gustavus.—Ah, tell it then, papa.

M. de Flanmont.—Paul, as I told you, was almost inconsolable; he would sometimes say to himself, 'the river was not so high; I was too easily frightened; we might both have been saved;' and he never could bring himself to walk by the river-side again, and would often go a long round to avoid it. He sometimes heard of persons being drowned while bathing in that river; a thing which too frequently happened, as those who were not well acquainted with it, by approaching imprudently too near the whirlpool, were drawn into it and ingulfed. Then Paul would feel as if his heart would break; but the most singular thing was, that his late adventure had given him quite a dread of the water, and he was continually thinking that if, after having done so much for his children, he should then be lost to them, it would all go for nothing, and he would avoid every danger with the most scrupulous care. People scarcely knew him to be the same man, he had become so cautious and timid. His neighbours all said, 'It is very extraordinary, but Paul has become quite a coward;' and they thought it was from cowardice that he had not saved the man. He was, besides, more assiduous than ever at his work, never losing a moment in trying to put his children in a way of providing for themselves, as if he felt afraid that he should die before he accomplished it.

He succeeded very well in bringing them up, and establishing them; his son became a good tradesman, and married and settled in another town; his daughter married a shopkeeper in good business, and of excellent character; and the youngest son, being a good scholar, the schoolmaster of the town, who was very fond of him, took him when he was fifteen as an assistant, and promised that, if he conducted himself well, he would give him up the school in a few years. The day that Paul established his son with the schoolmaster, and that he could consequently say that all his children were provided for, and would no longer be exposed to want, were they to lose him, he felt himself relieved of a great weight, and in the joy of his heart, the courage seemed to return to him which for twelve years had appeared lost; for it was twelve years since the event occurred which had made him so unhappy. He left off work earlier than had been his custom, and went out to walk alone. For the first time he turned his steps towards the river, and thought of the different persons he had drawn out of it before the fatal day which had robbed him of his peace. It was an autumn evening; the weather was gloomy and cold, the rains had swelled the river, and it was agitated by a violent wind; it was nearly in the same state as when he had last seen it. He approached, and considered it attentively. 'The river is much swelled,' said he; 'well, if I were to fall in to-day, I am sure I could get out of it;' and he said this because, not having the fear of leaving his children destitute, he did not think of danger, but only of the means of getting out of it. On raising his eyes mechanically to the bridge, he saw a young lad approaching the parapet. The youth looked at the water for some time, and Paul could not take his eyes off him. At length he mounted upon the parapet, and his legs seemed to totter under him. Paul cried out to him, 'You will fall;' but at the same moment the youth made a sudden spring, and jumped into the river. Paul, as if he had felt a presentiment, already had his hand upon his coat; he threw it off, and was in the water almost as soon as the youth himself, and swimming over to the spot where he had fallen, he tried to reach him before he should be caught in the whirlpool, where he well knew that they would both perish. He reached him just in time, and, supporting him with one arm, he swam with the other. The wind was at the time extremely high, accompanied by violent rain, which impeded his view; the wind and the current were both drawing him towards the vortex. Paul redoubled his efforts: he felt himself animated with extraordinary vigour; and at length succeeded in reaching the bank, and landing in safety. The youth appeared to be quite dead; but Paul, from the experience he had had in similar cases, knew how to restore animation. He laid him under a thick tree, to shelter him from the rain, and then gave him all the assistance which such a situation would allow. His efforts [illegible]; and as soon as he was in some degree restored, he took him on his shoulder, and carried him as quickly as he could to his own house, where, by dint of care, he soon quite recovered. He was about seventeen, and appeared emaciated from poverty and sickness. When he was able to speak, Paul asked him what had induced him to throw himself into the river. The lad, whose name was Andrew, replied that it was misery and despair. He told him that, twelve years previously, his father, who had been a travelling tinker, was drowned, it was supposed by accident, in the same river, where his body had been found a few days afterwards. Paul shuddered when he heard that, but he said nothing. Andrew continued to narrate that he had lived with his mother, who supported him as well as she could by her industry, until he was ten years old, when she died, and left him friendless and destitute. He then endeavoured to gain a subsistence by working here and there, sometimes at the harvest, and sometimes attending masons; that he had suffered a great deal, had often been in want, and at last fell sick, and was taken into an hospital. When, upon his recovery, he was discharged, he had neither food, money, nor shelter, and had been obliged to lie in the fields, and pass two days without food, which had reduced him to the extremity of weakness. It was on the evening of the second day that, finding himself on the bridge from which his father had fallen, and feeling scarcely able to go any further, he was seized with despair, and determined to end his existence. While listening to this melancholy recital, Paul thought that, as he had saved the son, he might also have been able to have saved the father; but then he recollected that if he had perished, his children would have been in the same condition as Andrew. He rejoiced greatly in having saved him, and hoped that, after this new trial of his strength, he should never again feel afraid of the river, especially as his children no longer depended on him.

He was not able, however, to put his resolution into practice, for the day after he had saved Andrew, he was seized with a violent fever, and acute pains all over his body. On coming out of the river, being solely occupied in attending to Andrew, he had remained so long in his wet clothes, that it brought on a rheumatic fever, which for three days increased in violence, so that his life was despaired of. Occasionally he was delirious, when he would express great uneasiness about his children; but when he came to himself, and recollected that they were all provided for, he appeared, notwithstanding his pain, to be quite happy. Andrew, who began to recover his strength, nursed him attentively, and would often weep at his bedside when he witnessed his sufferings. Paul at length recovered, but remained subject to rheumatic pains, which sometimes entirely deprived him of the use of his limbs. 'How thankful I ought to be,' he would say, when unable to use his arms, 'that my children are all settled in life!' Andrew, whom he kept in his house, and who possessed both good feeling and intelligence, soon learned his trade well enough to assist him when he was able to work, and to work under his directions when he was ill; and the shop prospered more than ever, as the people became much interested for Paul and Andrew. Here M. de Flanmont stopped, and the children waited a minute or two in silence, to know whether the story was finished.

'Ah,' said Henry, after a deep sigh, 'I am very glad of the end of that story.'

Clementina.—Yes; but then poor Paul remains crippled with the rheumatism.

Gustavus.—His good action has, I am sure, not been very well rewarded.

M. de Flanmont.—It has been, in the only way we should expect our good actions to be rewarded—by the consciousness of having done right. This is the reward that must result, and is quite independent of any consequences that may afterwards arise.

Clementina.—It is, however, melancholy to see a good man suffering for having acted well.

M. de Flanmont.—It would be more melancholy to see him suffer for having acted badly. Would you rather that he had not saved Andrew?

Clementina.—Oh no!

M. de Flanmont.—It was also possible that Paul might have died. Even in that case, could we have regretted that he had saved Andrew?

Henry (*eagerly*).—No, certainly, we could not have regretted it.

M. de Flanmont.—That proves to you that the reward is, as I told you, quite independent of the action. Were a tradesman to work for a person who did not pay him, you would regret that he had done the work, because his wages are the natural reward of his labour, whereas you could never regret that a man had performed a good action, even when it turned out badly for himself, because you would always feel that the action brought its own reward.

However, my children, added Monsieur de Flanmont, you must not think that virtue is always so difficult. Our real duties are generally placed around us, so that we can fulfil them without any very great efforts. But as it is possible that circumstances may arise to render efforts necessary, we ought to be prepared to meet them. We should accustom our minds to look upon duty as equally indispensable when it is difficult as when it is easy; we should at the same time be careful not to augment the difficulties, so as to render it impossible we should ever exaggerate one duty at the expense of others; but, once convinced that there cannot exist at the same time two duties opposed to each other, we must, in cases of difficulty, apply ourselves to the most important point, and however we may regret that we cannot yield to impulse, and gratify our feelings, we must beware how we regard that as a duty which another duty forbids our performing.

MANUFACTURE OF GUNPOWDER.

The saltpetre is taken to the mill, placed on the bed of the trough, and broken to pieces by a hammer; the millstones being then set in motion, it is reduced to the state of coarse powder, in which condition it is removed to another mill, very much like that used for grinding corn, and reduced to impalpable powder. The charcoal and sulphur being pulverised in a similar manner, all these ingredients are taken to the mixing-house, and weighed out in proper quantities. Then the charcoal is spread in a trough, and the sulphur and nitre being sifted upon it, all these ingredients are incorporated by the hand. The ingredients being thus imperfectly mixed, are taken to the powder-mill, which is a brick building with a light boarded roof. In the midst of this apartment is a circular trough, provided with a cast-iron or stone bed, on which revolve two millstones attached to a horizontal axis, and each weighing from three to four tons. Manufacturers are forbidden by law to employ in these operations more than forty-two pounds of composition, on account of the frequent accidents which take place. The danger varies according to the degree of trituration to which the materials have been exposed; usually, however, it is mixed, or if mixed not grained, and in all cases damp, a little water being purposely added during the operation, not enough, however, to form a paste. The time during which the operation must be continued differs according to the goodness of the powder required, the nature of the atmosphere, and some other circumstances. At the government mills the time is usually three hours, and in general terms we may say from one to six hours. Time, however, is never made a criterion, but great attention is paid to a plasticity which the mass ultimately acquires, when, in the workmen's language, it is said to be *alive*. It then glides from beneath the stones without attaching itself to them, and, under the name of mill-cake, is broken up and conveyed to the press-room. The next operation consists in spreading this mill-cake on alternate copper plates, in layers of three inches thick, until the press is full, when a compressing force is applied, either by the screw and capstan, or by Bramah's hydrostatic engine. The latter was first employed for this purpose by Sir W. Congreve, and of course is much more powerful than any other; but it is found that the extremity of compressing force capable of being exerted by this machine must not be applied, for in that case the mass is rendered so compact as materially to interfere with the rapidity of combustion: in other words the resulting power is deteriorated. The next operation is that of corning or graining—a very ingenious contrivance, without which gunpowder would burn so slowly as to be inapplicable to most purposes. The graining is accomplished in the following manner. In the graining-house are sieves, the bottoms of which are made of thick parchment prepared expressly for this purpose from bullocks' hides and perforated with small holes. These sieves are so arranged that they can be put in rapid circular motion by the aid of machinery, and each sieve contains two discs of lignum vitæ. Into the sieves is placed the mill-cake just described, which, by the circular motion to which it is subjected, and the friction of the discs of lignum vitæ, is forced through the minute holes of the parchment in the state of grains. These, however, are not all of the same size, but require to be separated into various lots by the agency of different sieves. The next operations are drying and glazing, without the latter of which gunpowder would look dull. Glazing is accomplished by placing the grains in a barrel fixed on a horizontal axis, and made to revolve with great velocity. It will be seen from this that the glazing is due to friction, consequently some powder-dust must result. This is separated from the grains by means of a gauze cylinder, into which the whole material is put, and subjected to violent rotation, during which the dust flies off, and the polished grain remains in the cylinder. The operation is now finished.—*Polytechnic Magazine.*

A NICE POINT.

It is asserted, but with what truth I cannot pretend to state, that the inhabitants of Inniskea [a small island on the west coast of Ireland] are exceedingly prone to litigation, and a curious legend of a lawsuit is told upon the mainland, illustrative of this their quarrelsome disposition. A century ago, two persons were remarkable for their superior opulence, and had become the envy and wonder of their poorer neighbours. Their wealth consisted of a flock of sheep, when, unfortunately, some trifling dispute occurring between them, a dissolution of partnership was resolved upon. To divide the flock, one would suppose, would not be difficult, and they proceeded to partition the property accordingly. They possessed one hundred and one sheep; fifty fell to each proprietor; but the odd one—how was it to be disposed of? Neither would part with his moiety to the other; and, after a long and angry negotiation, the animal was left in common property between them. Although the season had not come round when sheep are usually shorn, one of the proprietors, requiring wool for a pair of stockings, proposed that the fleece should be taken off. This was resisted by his co-partner; and the point was finally settled by shearing one side of the animal. Only a few days after, the sheep was found dead in a ditch. One party ascribed the accident to the sufferings of the animal from cold having urged him to seek shelter in the fatal trench; while the other contended that the wool remaining upon one side had caused the creature to lose its equilibrium, and thus the melancholy catastrophe was occasioned. The parties went to law directly, and the expenses of the suit actually devoured the produce of the entire flock, and reduced both to a state of utter beggary. Their descendants are pointed out to this day as being the poorest of the community, and litigants are frequently warned to avoid the fate of 'Malley and Malone.'—*Wild Sports of the West.*

WHIRLPOOLS.

Whirlpools appear to be occasioned by currents meeting with submarine obstacles, which throw them into gyration. When the movement is rapid, the centre is the most depressed portion of the rotating circle, and objects drawn within it are submerged in that point. Several small whirlpools, capable of whirling round a boat, are seen among the Orkney islands. That of *Corriverckin*, in the narrow channel between Scarba and Jura, in the Hebrides, is caused by a rock of a conical form rising abruptly from the bottom, where the depth is 600 feet, and reaching to within ninety feet of the surface. This obstruction, in a tortuous rocky channel, causes a succession of eddies; and when the flood-tide sets in, with a fresh breeze in the opposite direction, the eddying waters rise in short heavy waves, which are highly dangerous to boats, and even to decked vessels. The *Malstrom*, on the coast of Norway, near the island of Moskoe, is a whirlpool of a similiar kind, the perils of which are probably much exaggerated. The flood-tide setting from the south-west among the Lofoden islands, especially when it meets with a strong gale from the north-west, produces a great agitation of the waves, and a whirlpool is formed, the roaring of which is heard at the distance of many miles. Its agitated vortices are dangerous to vessels, and it is said that seals and whales, when caught within its eddies, are unable to extricate themselves from destruction. It is now well ascertained that *Charybdis*, in the straits of Messina, owes its terrors to the imagination of seamen in the infancy of navigation, and all its celebrity to poetic fancy.—*Trail's Physical Geography.*

PRUDENCE AND GENIUS.

That a genius inferior only to a Shakspeare or a Milton, should not be able to keep a coat on his back to save himself from starving amid his poetic fire, at the same time that an honest citizen, whose utmost reach of thought only enables him to fix a reasonable profit upon a piece of linen or silk, according to its first cost and charges, should, from nothing, raise himself to a coach and six; to account for what in theory seems so strange, it is to be considered of what consequence it is towards a proper behaviour, that a person apply a due attention to all the minute circumstances, and seemingly inconsiderable particulars, in the conduct of life. Let a man have what sublime abilities he will, if he is above applying his understanding to find out, and his attention to pursue, any scheme of life, it is as little to be expected that he should acquire the fortune of the thriving citizen, as that the plain shopkeeper, who never applied his mind to learning, should equal him in science. There is no natural incompatibility between art or learning, and prudence. Nor is the man of learning or genius, who is void of common prudence, to be considered in any other character than that of a wrong-headed pedant, or of a man of narrow and defective abilities.—*Dignity of Human Nature.*

INGENIOUS APPLICATION OF SNOW.

During the severe and protracted snow-storm of 1838, Mr Robert Miller, market-gardener at Gorgie, near Edinburgh, was completely successful in preserving his cauliflower plants in the open border, by the simple expedient of heaping snow over them to the depth of eighteen inches or two feet. Occasional slight thawings were followed by intense frosts, when the cold was from 20 even to 10 degrees Fahrenheit; but the only effect was the glazing of the surface of the snow with a thin coat of ice. The plants remained imbedded below at an invariable temperature of 32 degrees, which they could well enough sustain; and ran no risk from the expanding effects of freezing.—*Neill's Horticulture.*

PRIDE *versus* TRUTH.

There is no single obstacle which stands in the way of more people in the search of truth than pride. They have once declared themselves of a particular opinion, and they cannot bring themselves to think they could possibly be in the wrong; consequently they cannot persuade themselves of the necessity of re-examining the foundations of their opinions. To acknowledge and give up their error, would be a still severer trial. But the truth is, there is more greatness of mind in candidly giving up a mistake, than would have appeared in escaping it at first, if not a very shameful one. The surest way of avoiding error is, careful examination. The best way of leaving room for a change of opinion, which should always be provided for, is to be modest in delivering one's sentiments. A man may, without confusion, give up an opinion which he declared without arrogance.—*Burgh.*

The present number of the Journal completes the fourth volume (new series), for which a title-page and index have been prepared, and may be had of the publishers and their agents.

END OF FOURTH VOLUME.

Printed and Published by W. and R. CHAMBERS, Edinburgh.
Sold by W. S. ORR, Amen Corner, London.

Lightning Source UK Ltd.
Milton Keynes UK
UKHW020625221218
334411UK00006B/874/P